lonely planet

W9-BNT-304

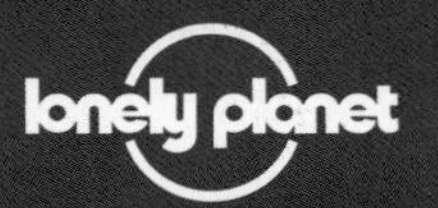

Western Europe

Ryan Ver Berkmoes
Aaron Anderson, Alex Leviton, Andrew Stone, Becca Blond, Craig McLachlan, Duncan Garwood, Geert Cole & Leanne Logan, John Lee, Josephine Quintero, Miles Roddis, Oliver Berry, Sarah Andrews, Sarah Johnstone, Simon Sellars, Stuart Schuffman, Terry Carter & Lara Dunston, Virginia Maxwell

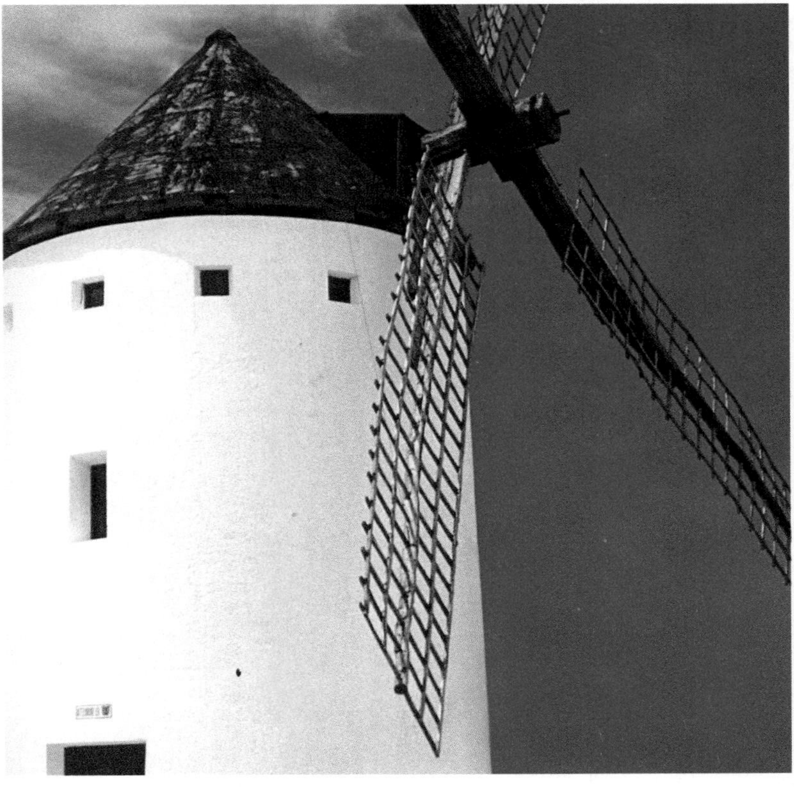

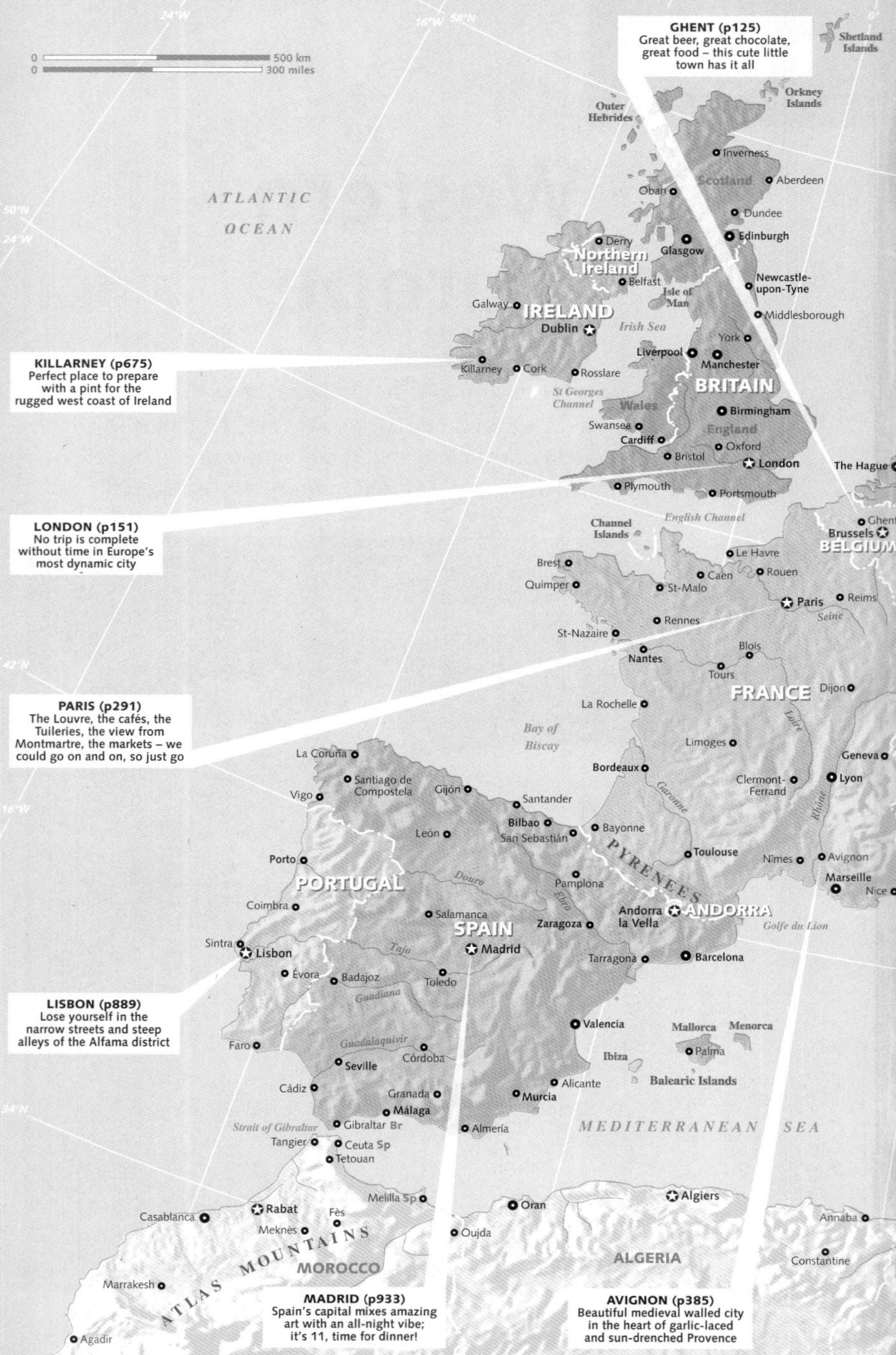

GHENT (p125)
Great beer, great chocolate, great food – this cute little town has it all
KILLARNEY (p675)
Perfect place to prepare with a pint for the rugged west coast of Ireland
LONDON (p151)
No trip is complete without time in Europe's most dynamic city
PARIS (p291)
The Louvre, the cafés, the Tuileries, the view from Montmartre, the markets – we could go on and on, so just go
LISBON (p889)
Lose yourself in the narrow streets and steep alleys of the Alfama district
MADRID (p933)
Spain's capital mixes amazing art with an all-night vibe; it's 11, time for dinner!
AVIGNON (p385)
Beautiful medieval walled city in the heart of garlic-laced and sun-drenched Provence
0 500 km
0 300 miles
ATLANTIC OCEAN
Shetland Islands
Orkney Islands
Outer Hebrides
Inverness
Scotland
Aberdeen
Oban
Dundee
Edinburgh
Glasgow
Derry
Northern Ireland
Belfast
Newcastle-upon-Tyne
Isle of Man
Galway
IRELAND
Dublin
Irish Sea
Middlesborough
York
Liverpool
Manchester
Killarney
Cork
Rosslare
BRITAIN
St Georges Channel
Wales
Birmingham
Swansea
England
Cardiff
Oxford
Bristol
London
The Hague
Plymouth
Portsmouth
English Channel
Channel Islands
Ghent
Brussels
BELGIUM
Le Havre
Brest
Caen
Rouen
Quimper
St-Malo
Paris
Reims
Seine
Rennes
St-Nazaire
Blois
Nantes
Tours
FRANCE
Dijon
La Rochelle
Loire
Bay of Biscay
Limoges
Geneva
La Coruña
Bordeaux
Lyon
Santiago de Compostela
Clermont-Ferrand
Vigo
Gijón
Santander
Garonne
Rhône
Bilbao
León
San Sebastián
Bayonne
PYRENEES
Porto
Toulouse
Nîmes
Avignon
Douro
Marseille
PORTUGAL
Pamplona
Ebro
Nice
Coimbra
Salamanca
Andorra la Vella
ANDORRA
Zaragoza
Golfe du Lion
SPAIN
Sintra
Lisbon
Madrid
Tajo
Tarragona
Barcelona
Évora
Badajoz
Toledo
Guadiana
Valencia
Mallorca
Menorca
Faro
Guadalquivir
Palma
Córdoba
Ibiza
Seville
Alicante
Balearic Islands
Cádiz
Granada
Murcia
Málaga
Strait of Gibraltar
Gibraltar Br
Almería
MEDITERRANEAN SEA
Tangier
Ceuta Sp
Tetouan
Melilla Sp
Algiers
Oran
Casablanca
Rabat
Fès
Annaba
Meknès
Oujda
ATLAS MOUNTAINS
MOROCCO
ALGERIA
Constantine
Marrakesh
Agadir

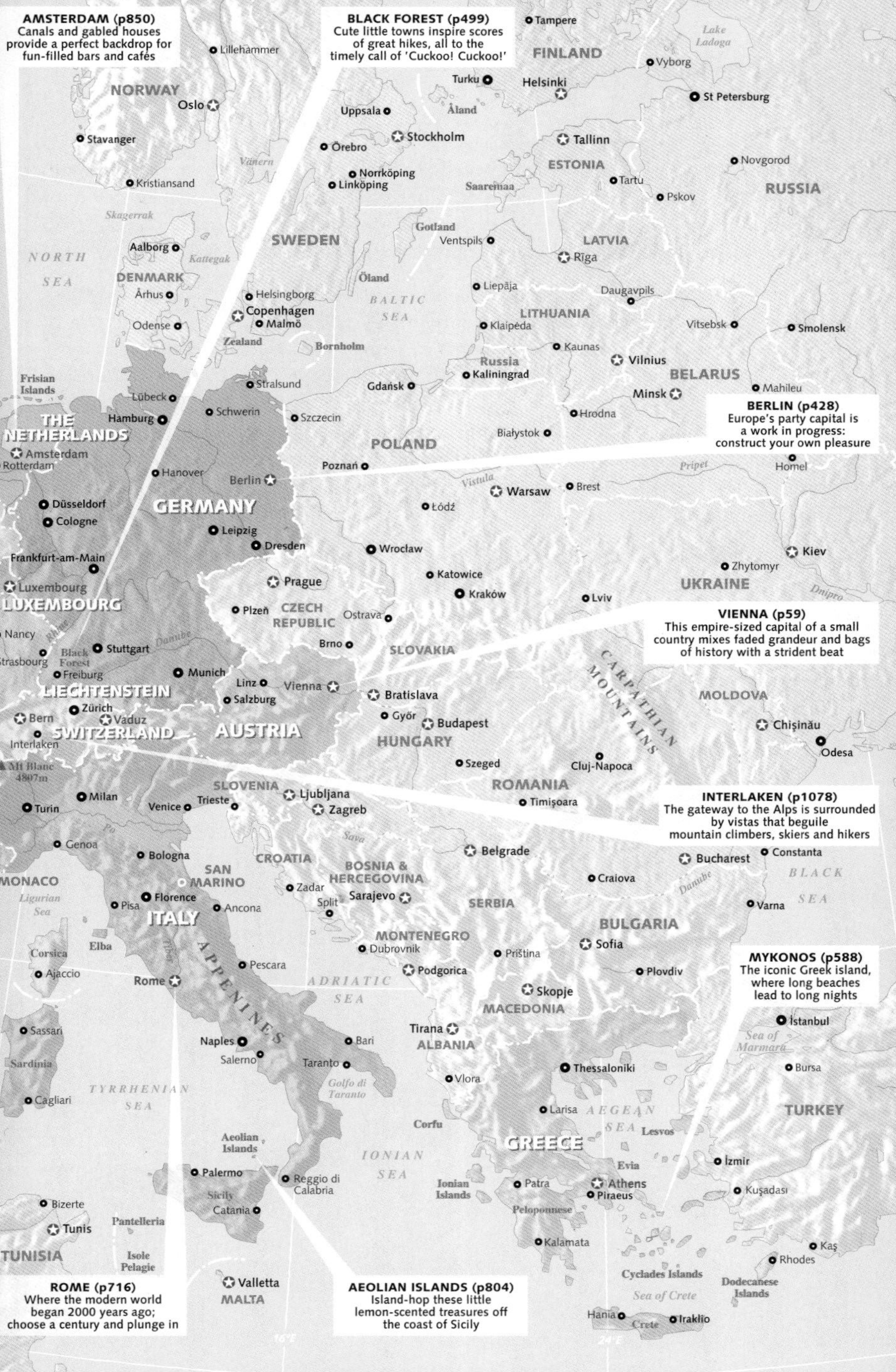

AMSTERDAM (p850)
Canals and gabled houses provide a perfect backdrop for fun-filled bars and cafés
BLACK FOREST (p499)
Cute little towns inspire scores of great hikes, all to the timely call of 'Cuckoo! Cuckoo!'
BERLIN (p428)
Europe's party capital is a work in progress: construct your own pleasure
VIENNA (p59)
This empire-sized capital of a small country mixes faded grandeur and bags of history with a strident beat
INTERLAKEN (p1078)
The gateway to the Alps is surrounded by vistas that beguile mountain climbers, skiers and hikers
MYKONOS (p588)
The iconic Greek island, where long beaches lead to long nights
ROME (p716)
Where the modern world began 2000 years ago; choose a century and plunge in
AEOLIAN ISLANDS (p804)
Island-hop these little lemon-scented treasures off the coast of Sicily
NORWAY
SWEDEN
FINLAND
ESTONIA
LATVIA
LITHUANIA
RUSSIA
DENMARK
THE NETHERLANDS
GERMANY
POLAND
BELARUS
UKRAINE
LUXEMBOURG
CZECH REPUBLIC
SLOVAKIA
LIECHTENSTEIN
SWITZERLAND
AUSTRIA
HUNGARY
MOLDOVA
ROMANIA
SLOVENIA
CROATIA
BOSNIA & HERCEGOVINA
SERBIA
MONTENEGRO
BULGARIA
MACEDONIA
ALBANIA
GREECE
TURKEY
ITALY
SAN MARINO
MONACO
TUNISIA
MALTA
NORTH SEA
BALTIC SEA
ADRIATIC SEA
TYRRHENIAN SEA
IONIAN SEA
AEGEAN SEA
BLACK SEA
Sea of Crete
Sea of Marmara
Ligurian Sea
Golfo di Taranto
Skagerrak
Kattegak
CARPATHIAN MOUNTAINS
APPENINES
Oslo
Stockholm
Helsinki
Tallinn
Rīga
Vilnius
Minsk
Copenhagen
Berlin
Warsaw
Prague
Vienna
Bratislava
Budapest
Amsterdam
Luxembourg
Bern
Vaduz
Ljubljana
Zagreb
Belgrade
Sarajevo
Podgorica
Skopje
Tirana
Sofia
Bucharest
Chişinău
Kiev
Rome
Athens
Valletta
Tunis

Western Europe

You haven't been anywhere until you've been to Europe and for many this means the countries at the core: Western Europe. There is no other place on earth where so many cultures and so much history are jammed together so close. It's a patchwork quilt of tiny dots and connecting them all is a delight that has enthralled generations.

Just think about the contrasts and accomplishments found here: Plato and the Olympics in Greece, the Roman Empire and Christianity in Italy, the Magna Carta and the rule of law in England, humanism and war in Germany, empire-building and the Impressionists in France. The list goes on and on – explore it all and revel in delight after delight. The craggy coasts and cheery pubs of Ireland, the vibrant mix of old and new in Britain, the food, wine and beauty of France, the warmth and allure of Spain and Portugal, the beer and 17th-century wonders of Belgium and the Netherlands, the future tempered by the past in Germany and Austria, the smug character and glacial beauty of Switzerland, and of course all those centuries of wonders in Italy and Greece spiced up by today's pleasures.

Travelling around these countries you can see the art you've always dreamed of, see the places you've always heard of and have the kinds of adventures you'll always speak of. So pack a bag with lots of extra room to fill with memories and head out on everyone's trip of a lifetime.

NEIL SETCHFIELD

Iconic Sights

BARBARA VAN ZANTEN

Nab a bird's-eye view on the London Eye (p163)

Get snap happy at the Eiffel Tower (p294), Paris

ANN CECIL

CHRISTOPHER GROENHOUT

Be gobsmacked at La Sagrada Familia (p968), Barcelona

Must-do Sights

NEIL SETCHFIELD

Celebrate contemporary architecture at the Reichstag (p434), Berlin

Opposite:
Feign nonchalance at the Duomo (p772), Florence
MARTIN MOOS

RICHARD NEBES

Soak up seven centuries of power at the Hofburg (p63), Vienna

Meander along the canels in Amsterdam (p850), the Netherlands

THOMAS WI

SCOTT BARBOUR

Uncover the wonders of ancient Greece at the Parthenon (p565), Athens

Lose yourself in the Musée du Louvre (p299), Paris

JEAN-BERNARD CARILLET

Art History Culture

BETHUNE CARMICHAEL

Let your fancies take flight at Palácio Nacional de Sintra (p901), Portugal

LEANNE LOGA

Reflect in WWI cemeteries (p133), Belgium

Rediscover fairy tales in Vianden (p837), Luxembourg

WAYNE WALTON

MICHAEL TAYLOR

Try your luck in Alicante (p995), Spain

NEIL SETCHFIELD

See and be seen in Soho, London (p151)

Take it down a notch and relax in Innsbruck (p93), Austria

GLENN BEANLAND

Entertainment & Nightlife

RICHARD NEBESKY

Mix it up with the locals in Berlin (p428)

JULIET COOMBE

Have fun, go mad at the Notting Hill Carnival (p165), London

You know what you're here for – get messy at Oktoberfest (p477), Munich

KRZYSZTOF DYDYNSKI

Great Outdoors

RUSSELL MOUNTFORD

Soak up the sun in Nice (p389), France

CHRISTIAN ASLUND

Carve it up in Tirol (p93), Austria

Let your jaw drop again and again in Grindelwald (p1081), Switzerland

DAVID TOMLINSON

Contents

The Authors 21

Getting Started 27

Itineraries 32

Snapshots 36

Andorra 45

Highlights 46
History 46
People 46
ANDORRA LA VELLA 46
Orientation 46
Sights & Activities 46
Sleeping 48
Eating & Drinking 49
Shopping 50
Getting There & Around 50
AROUND ANDORRA LA VELLA 50
Sant Julià De Lòria 50
Canillo & Soldeu 50
Ordino & Around 51
Arinsal & Pal 51
ANDORRA DIRECTORY 52
Accommodation 52
Activities 52
Business Hours 52
Embassies & Consulates 52
Internet Resources 52
Post 52
Telephone 53
TRANSPORT IN ANDORRA 53
Getting There & Away 53
Getting Around 53

Austria 55

Highlights 56
Itineraries 56
Climate & When To Go 56
History 56
People 58
Religion 58
Arts 58
Environment 59
Food & Drink 59
VIENNA 59
Orientation 61
Information 61
Sights 62
Activities 67
Tours 67
Festivals & Events 67
Sleeping 67
Eating 69
Drinking 70
Entertainment 72
Shopping 73
Getting There & Away 73
Getting Around 74
THE DANUBE VALLEY 75
Krems An Der Donau 75
Dürnstein 75
Melk 76
Linz 76
THE SOUTH 78
Graz 78
Klagenfurt 81
SALZBURG 82
Orientation 83
Information 83
Sights & Activities 83
Tours 85
Festivals & Events 85
Sleeping 85
Eating 86
Drinking 87
Getting There & Away 87
Getting Around 88
Around Salzburg 88
SALZKAMMERGUT 89
Bad Ischl 89
Hallstatt 91
Wolfgangsee 92
Northern Salzkammergut 93
TIROL 93
Innsbruck 93
Mayrhofen 97
Kitzbühel 98
Lienz 98
Hohe Tauern National Park 99
VORARLBERG 100
Bregenz 100
Arlberg Region 101
AUSTRIA DIRECTORY 101
Accommodation 101
Activities 102
Books 103
Business Hours 103
Embassies & Consulates 103
Festivals & Events 103
Gay & Lesbian Travellers 104
Holidays 104
Internet Resources 104
Language 104
Money 104

Post 105
Telephone 105
Time 105
Tourist Information 105
Visas 105
TRANSPORT IN AUSTRIA 106
Getting There & Away 106
Getting Around 107

Belgium 109

Highlights 110
Itineraries 110
Climate & When To Go 110
History 111
People 112
Religion 112
Arts 112
Sport 113
Environment 113
Food & Drink 113
BRUSSELS 114
Orientation 114
Information 114
Sights 115
Tours 115
Sleeping 115
Eating 118
Drinking 118
Entertainment 119
Shopping 119
Getting There & Away 120
Getting Around 120
Around Brussels 120
FLANDERS 121
Antwerp 121
Ghent 125
Bruges 129
Ypres 132
WALLONIA 133
Liège 133
Around Liège 134
Charleroi 135
Tournai 135
Namur 135
Dinant 136
Rochefort & Han-Sur-Lesse 136
La Roche-En-Ardenne 137
Bastogne 138
BELGIUM DIRECTORY 138
Accommodation 138
Activities 139
Business Hours 139
Embassies & Consulates 139
Festivals & Events 139
Holidays 140
Money 140
Post 140
Telephone 140
Time 140
Visas 140
TRANSPORT IN BELGIUM 140
Getting There & Away 140
Getting Around 142

Britain 143

Itineraries 144
Climate & When To Go 144
History 144
People 144
Religion 144
Arts 146
Environment 147
Food & Drink 148
ENGLAND 148
History 148
People 151
LONDON 151
History 154
Orientation 155
Information 158
Dangers & Annoyances 158
Sights 158
Tours 165
Festivals & Events 165
Sleeping 165
Eating 168
Drinking 172
Entertainment 173
Shopping 175
Getting There & Away 176
Getting Around 177
Around London 179
SOUTHEAST ENGLAND 179
Canterbury 180
Dover 182
Hever Castle 183
Leeds Castle 183
Brighton & Hove 183
Portsmouth 186
Winchester 188
Channel Islands 189
SOUTHWEST ENGLAND 190
Salisbury 190
Stonehenge 191
Avebury 192
Exeter 192
Plymouth 193
Dartmoor National Park 194
Exmoor National Park 195
Cornwall 196
Bath 199
Wells 202
Glastonbury 202
Bristol 203
CENTRAL ENGLAND 205
Oxford 205
Blenheim Palace 209
Stratford-Upon-Avon 210
The Cotswolds 212
Birmingham 213
Shrewsbury & Around 213
Peak District National Park 215
EAST ENGLAND 216
Cambridge 216
Ely 219
Lincolnshire 220
Norfolk 220
NORTHEAST ENGLAND 220
York 221
Around York 224
Yorkshire Dales & Around 224
North York Moors National Park 225
Durham 227
Newcastle-Upon-Tyne 228
Northumberland 230
NORTHWEST ENGLAND 232
Manchester 232
Chester 234
Liverpool 235
Lake District 237
Carlisle 240
SCOTLAND 240
History 240
Environment 243
People 244
Language 244
Edinburgh 244
Glasgow 250
Southwest Scotland 255
Southeast Scotland 255
Central Scotland 256
Eastern Highlands 257
Western Highlands 259
Northern Highlands & Islands 260
WALES (CYMRU) 264
History 266
Environment 267
People 267
Language 267
Getting There & Away 267
Getting Around 267
South Wales 268
Cardiff (Caerdydd) 268
Southwest Wales 270
Mid Wales 270
North Wales 271
BRITAIN DIRECTORY 272
Accommodation 272
Activities 273
Books 274
Business Hours 274
Embassies & Consulates 274
Festivals & Events 274
Gay & Lesbian Travellers 275
Holidays 275
Media 275

Money 276
Post 276
Studying 276
Telephone 276
Tourist Information 277
Travelling With Disabilities 277
Visas 277
Work 277
TRANSPORT IN BRITAIN 277
Getting There & Away 277
Getting Around 279

France 283

Itineraries 284
Climate & When To Go 284
History 284
People 287
Religion 287
Arts 288
Environment 289
Food & Drink 290
PARIS 291
History 291
Orientation 291
Information 291
Dangers & Annoyances 294
Sights 294
Tours 301
Sleeping 301
Eating 305
Drinking 307
Entertainment 307
Shopping 308
Getting There & Away 309
Getting Around 309
AROUND PARIS 312
Disneyland Paris 312
Versailles 312
Chartres 313
CHAMPAGNE 314
Reims 314
Épernay 315
Troyes 316
ALSACE & LORRAINE 317
Strasbourg 317
Massif Des Vosges 322
Nancy 322
NORTHERN FRANCE 323
Lille 323
Calais 325
Dunkirk 326
Battle of the Somme Memorials 327
NORMANDY 327
Rouen 327
Bayeux 329
D-Day Beaches 331
Mont St-Michel 332
BRITTANY 333
Quimper 333
Carnac 334
St-Malo 335
Around St-Malo 337
THE LOIRE 338
Blois 338
Around Blois 340
Tours 341
Around Tours 343
Amboise 344
SOUTHWESTERN FRANCE 345
Nantes 345
Poitiers 347
Around Poitiers 348
La Rochelle 348
Bordeaux 350
Arcachon 353
Bayonne 354
Biarritz 355
Lourdes 356
THE DORDOGNE 357
Sarlat-La-Canéda 358
Les Eyzies De Tayac 358
Montignac 358
QUERCY 359
Cahors 359
BURGUNDY & THE RHÔNE 360
Dijon 360
Côte D'or Vineyards 363
Beaune 364
Lyon 365
THE FRENCH ALPS 369
Chamonix 369
Annecy 372
Grenoble 375
THE JURA 378
Besançon 378
Around Besançon 380
Parc Naturel Régional DuHaut-Jura 380
PROVENCE 380
Marseille 380
Aix-En-Provence 384
Avignon 385
Around Avignon 388
CÔTE D'AZUR 388
Nice 389
Cannes 394
St-Tropez 397
Menton 398
MONACO 398
Orientation 399
Information 400
Sights & Activities 400
Festivals & Events 400
Sleeping 400
Eating 400
Getting There & Away 401
LANGUEDOC-ROUSSILLON 401
Carcassonne 401
Nîmes 402
Around Nîmes 403
CORSICA 403
Bastia 403
Calvi 405
Les Calanques 406
Ajaccio 406
Bonifacio 408
FRANCE DIRECTORY 409
Accommodation 409
Activities 410
Business Hours 411
Embassies & Consulates 411
Festivals & Events 412
Gay & Lesbian Travellers 412
Holidays 412
Legal Matters 412
Money 412
Post 413
Telephone 413
Visas 413
TRANSPORT IN FRANCE 414
Getting There & Away 414
Getting Around 416

Germany 419

Itineraries 420
Climate & When To Go 420
History 420
People 423
Religion 424
Arts 424
Sport 426
Environment 427
Food & Drink 427
BERLIN 428
History 429
Orientation 430
Information 430
Dangers & Annoyances 431
Sights 431
Festivals & Events 438
Sleeping 438
Eating 441
Drinking 442
Entertainment 443
Shopping 444
Getting There & Away 444
Getting Around 445
BRANDENBURG 446
Potsdam 446
Sachsenhausen Concentration Camp 448
SAXONY 448
Dresden 448
Around Dresden 452

Leipzig 453
THURINGIA 456
Erfurt 457
Around Erfurt 459
Weimar 459
Around Weimar 462
SAXONY-ANHALT 462
Magdeburg 462
Dessau 463
MECKLENBURG-WESTERN POMERANIA 466
Schwerin 466
Wismar 467
Stralsund 470
Rügen Island 472
BAVARIA 472
Munich 473
Dachau 481
Romantic Road 482
Würzburg 483
Bamberg 484
Rothenburg Ob Der Tauber 485
Nuremberg 485
Regensburg 487
Augsburg 488
Füssen 488
BAVARIAN ALPS 489
Berchtesgaden 489
Garmisch-Partenkirchen 490
Oberstdorf 491
BADEN-WÜRTTEMBERG 492
Stuttgart 492
Around Stuttgart 494
Heidelberg 495
Baden-Baden 498
BLACK FOREST 499
Freudenstadt 499
Schiltach 499
Triberg 501
Titisee 501
Freiburg 502
LAKE CONSTANCE 504
Constance 505
Meersburg 506
Lindau 506
RHINELAND-PALATINATE 507
Moselle Valley 507
Trier 508
Rhine Valley – Koblenz To Mainz 510
HESSE 511
Frankfurt-Am-Main 511
NORTH RHINE-WESTPHALIA 517
Cologne 517
Around Cologne 522
Düsseldorf 522
Aachen 525
LOWER SAXONY 527
Hanover 527
Around Hanover 528
Wolfsburg 529
BREMEN 531
Orientation 531
Information 531
Sights & Activities 531
Sleeping 531
Eating 533
Getting There & Away 533
Getting Around 533
HAMBURG 533
Orientation 533
Information 533
Dangers & Annoyances 536
Sights & Activities 536
Sleeping 537
Eating 538
Drinking & Entertainment 539
Getting There & Away 540
Getting Around 540
SCHLESWIG-HOLSTEIN 540
Lübeck 540
NORTH FRISIAN ISLANDS 542
Sylt 542
Amrum & Föhr 543
GERMANY DIRECTORY 544
Accommodation 544
Activities 544
Books 545
Business Hours 545
Dangers & Annoyances 545
Discount Cards 545
Embassies & Consulates 545
Festivals & Events 546
Gay & Lesbian Travellers 546
Holidays 546
Media 546
Money 547
Post 547
Telephone 547
Time 547
Travellers With Disabilities 548
Visas 548
Work 548
TRANSPORT INGERMANY 548
Getting There & Away 548
Getting Around 549

Greece 553

Highlights 554
Itineraries 554
History 554
People 558
Sport 558
Religion 558
Arts 558
Environment 559
Food & Drink 560
ATHENS 561
Orientation 561
Information 563
Dangers & Annoyances 564
Sights 564
Festivals & Events 566
Sleeping 566
Eating 567
Drinking 568
Entertainment 569
Shopping 570
Getting There & Away 571
Getting Around 572
Around Athens 572
THE PELOPONNESE 574
Patra 574
Diakofto–Kalavryta Railway 575
Corinth 575
Ancient Corinth & Acrocorinth 576
Nafplio 576
Epidavros 577
Mycenae 577
Sparta 577
Mystras 578
Gefyra & Monemvasia 578
Gythio 578
The Mani 579
Olympia 580
CENTRAL GREECE 580
Delphi 580
Meteora 581
NORTHERN GREECE 582
Igoumenitsa 582
Ioannina 582
Zagoria Villages & Vikos Gorge 583
Thessaloniki 583
Mt Olympus 585
Halkidiki 586
Alexandroupolis 586
SARONIC GULF ISLANDS 586
Aegina 587
Hydra 587
Spetses 587
CYCLADES 588
Mykonos 588
Delos 598
Paros 598
Naxos 600
Ios 602
Santorini (Thira) 604
CRETE 606
Iraklio 607
Knossos 609
Phaestos & Other Minoan Sites 609
Rethymno 609
Hania 610

Samaria Gorge 612
Paleohora & The Southwest Coast 612
Lasithi Plateau 613
Agios Nikolaos 614
Sitia 614
DODECANESE 615
Rhodes 615
Karpathos 618
Symi 619
Kos 619
Patmos 620
NORTHEASTERN AEGEAN ISLANDS 621
Samos 621
Chios 623
Lesvos (Mytilini) 624
SPORADES 626
Skiathos 627
Skopelos 628
Alonnisos 628
IONIAN ISLANDS 629
Corfu 629
Lefkada 631
Ithaki 632
Kefallonia 632
Zakynthos 633
GREECE DIRECTORY 634
Accommodation 634
Activities 634
Business Hours 635
Children 635
Customs 635
Dangers & Annoyances 635
Embassies & Consulates 635
Festivals & Events 636
Gay & Lesbian Travellers 637
Holidays 637
Internet Access 637
Internet Resources 637
Language 637
Money 637
Post 638
Solo Travellers 638
Telephone 638
Tourist Information 638
Travellers With Disabilities 639
Visas 639
TRANSPORT IN GREECE 639
Getting There & Away 639
Getting Around 641

Ireland 645

Itineraries 646
Climate & When To Go 646
People 650
Religion 650
Arts 650
Environment 651
Food & Drink 651
DUBLIN 652
Orientation 652
Information 652
Sights 653
Tours 658
Sleeping 658
Eating 659
Drinking 660
Entertainment 661
Getting There & Away 662
Getting Around 662
Around Dublin 663
THE SOUTHEAST 663
County Wicklow 664
Wexford 665
Waterford 666
Kilkenny 667
THE SOUTHWEST 668
Cork 668
Around Cork 673
West Cork 674
Killarney 675
The Ring Of Kerry 678
The Dingle Peninsula 679
Limerick 681
THE WEST COAST 682
The Burren 682
Galway 683
Aran Islands 686
Connemara 687
Westport 688
THE NORTHWEST 688
Sligo 689
Donegal 689
NORTHERN IRELAND 690
Belfast 691
The Belfast–Derry Coastal Road 697
Derry 698
Enniskillen & Lough Erne 701
IRELAND DIRECTORY 701
Accommodation 701
Activities 702
Books 702
Business Hours 702
Embassies & Consulates 702
Festivals & Events 703
Gay & Lesbian Travellers 703
Holidays 703
Internet Resources 703
Maps 703
Money 703
Post 704
Telephone 704
Tourist Information 704
Travellers With Disabilities 705
Visas 705
TRANSPORT IN IRELAND 705
Getting There & Away 705
Getting Around 706

Italy 709

Itineraries 710
Climate & When To Go 710
History 710
People 712
Religion 712
Arts 712
Environment 714
Food & Drink 715
ROME 716
History 716
Orientation 716
Information 716
Sights & Activities 717
Eating 732
Drinking 734
Entertainment 735
Shopping 736
Getting There & Away 736
Getting Around 737
Around Rome 738
NORTHERN ITALY 740
Genoa 740
Riviera Di Levante 742
Turin 743
Milan 745
Mantua 749
Verona 750
Padua 751
Venice 752
Ferrara 762
Bologna 763
Ravenna 766
THE DOLOMITES 767
Cortina D'ampezzo 768
Canazei 768
Val Gardena 768
San Martino Di Castrozza 769
TUSCANY 769
Florence 769
Pisa 777
Siena 778
San Gimignano 781
UMBRIA & LE MARCHE 781
Perugia 781
Assisi 784
Ancona 784
Urbino 785
SOUTHERN ITALY 785
Naples 786
Around Naples 792
Capri 792
Sorrento 794
Amalfi Coast 795

Matera 797
Brindisi 798
Lecce 799
SICILY 800
Palermo 801
Aeolian Islands 804
Taormina 806
Mt Etna 806
Syracuse 807
Agrigento 808
SARDINIA 809
Cagliari 810
Cala Gonone 812
Alghero 813
ITALY DIRECTORY 814
Accommodation 814
Activities 815
Books 816
Business Hours 816
Dangers & Annoyances 816
Embassies & Consulates 816
Festivals & Events 817
Holidays 817
Internet Resources 817
Money 818
Post 818
Telephone 818
Travellers With Disabilities 819
Visas 819
TRANSPORT IN ITALY 819
Getting There & Away 819
Getting Around 821

Liechtenstein 823

Climate & When To Go 824
History 824
Food & Drink 825
VADUZ 825
Information 825
Sights & Activities 825
Sleeping 826
Eating & Drinking 826
AROUND VADUZ 827
Malbun 827
LIECHTENSTEIN DIRECTORY 827
TRANSPORT IN LIECHTENSTEIN 828
Getting There & Away 828
Getting Around 828

Luxembourg 829

Itineraries 830
Climate & When To Go 830
History 830
People 831
Religion 831
Arts 832
Environment 832
Food & Drink 832
LUXEMBOURG CITY 832
Orientation 832
Information 832
Sights 833
Sleeping 833
Eating 835
Drinking 836
Entertainment 836
Getting There & Away 836
Getting Around 836
AROUND LUXEMBOURG 837
Vianden 837
Clervaux 837
Esch-Sur-Sûre 838
Wiltz 838
Echternach 838
Diekirch 839
Moselle Valley 839
LUXEMBOURG DIRECTORY 840
Accommodation 840
Activities 840
Business Hours 840
Embassies & Consulates 840
Festivals & Events 841
Holidays 841
Money 841
Post 841
Telephone 841
Visas 841
TRANSPORT IN LUXEMBOURG 841
Getting There & Away 841
Getting Around 842
Highlights 843

The Netherlands 843

Itineraries 844
Climate & When To Go 844
History 844
People 846
Religion 846
Arts 846
Environment 848
Food & Drink 849
AMSTERDAM 850
Orientation 850
Information 850
Sights & Activities 851
Sleeping 853
Eating 855
Drinking 856
Entertainment 856
Shopping 858
Getting There & Away 858
Getting Around 858
Around Amsterdam 859
THE RANDSTAD 860
Haarlem 860
Keukenhof Gardens 861
Leiden 861
Den Haag 863
Delft 866
Rotterdam 867
Utrecht City 871
THE DELTA REGION 872
Middelburg 872
THE NORTH & EAST 873
Groningen City 873
Texel 875
Ameland 875
Hoge Veluwe National Park 876
THE SOUTHEAST 876
Den Bosch 876
Maastricht 877
THE NETHERLANDS DIRECTORY 879
Accommodation 879
Activities 879
Business Hours 880
Dangers & Annoyances 880
Discount Cards 880
Embassies & Consulates 880
Festivals & Events 880
Holidays 881
Legal Matters 881
Money 881
Post 882
Telephone 882
Visas 882
TRANSPORT IN THE NETHERLANDS 882
Getting There & Away 882
Getting Around 883

Portugal 885

Highlights 886
Itineraries 886
History 886
People 888
Religion 888
Arts 888
Environment 888
Food & Drink 889
LISBON 889
Orientation 892
Information 892
Sights 893
Tours 895
Festivals & Events 895
Sleeping 895
Eating 896
Drinking 898
Entertainment 898

Shopping 899
Getting There & Away 899
Getting Around 900
Around Lisbon 900
THE ALGARVE 903
Faro 903
Tavira 904
Lagos 905
Monchique 906
Silves 906
Sagres 906
CENTRAL PORTUGAL 907
Évora 907
Monsaraz 909
Estremoz 909
Castelo De Vide & Marvão 909
Óbidos 910
Nazaré 910
Tomar 911
Coimbra 911
Luso & The Buçaco Forest 913
Serra Da Estrela 913
THE NORTH 914
Porto 914
Along The Douro 919
Viana Do Castelo 919
Braga 919
Parque Nacional Da Peneda-Gerês 920
PORTUGAL DIRECTORY 921
Accommodation 921
Activities 922
Business Hours 922
Embassies & Consulates 922
Festivals & Events 923
Holidays 923
Money 923
Post 923
Telephone 923
Visas 923
TRANSPORT IN PORTUGAL 923
Getting There & Away 923
Getting Around 925

Spain 927

Highlights 928
Itineraries 928
Climate & When To Go 928
History 928
People 931
Religion 931
Arts 931
Environment 932
Food & Drink 932
MADRID 933
History 934
Orientation 934
Information 934
Dangers & Annoyances 935
Sights & Activities 935
Courses 941
Tours 941
Festivals & Events 941
Sleeping 942
Eating 943
Drinking 945
Entertainment 947
Shopping 949
Getting There & Away 949
Getting Around 950
Around Madrid 951
CASTILLA Y LEÓN 951
Ávila 951
Salamanca 952
Segovia 954
León 956
Burgos 958
CASTILLA-LA MANCHA 959
Toledo 959
Cuenca 962
CATALONIA 963
Barcelona 963
Monestir De Montserrat 975
Girona 976
The Costa Brava 977
Tarragona 978
ARAGÓN, BASQUE COUNTRY & NAVARRA 980
Zaragoza 980
Aragón 982
San Sebastián 982
Bilbao 986
Pamplona 987
CANTABRIA, ASTURIAS & GALICIA 988
Santander 988
Around Santander 989
La Coruña 989
Santiago De Compostela 990
VALENCIA & MURCIA 992
Valencia 992
Alicante 995
Costa Blanca 998
Murcia & The Costa Calída 998
BALEARIC ISLANDS 999
Mallorca 1000
Ibiza 1003
Menorca 1006
ANDALUCÍA 1007
Seville 1008
Córdoba 1013
Granada 1016
Costa De Almería 1019
Málaga 1020
Ronda 1023
Algeciras 1024
Cádiz 1024
Tarifa 1025
GIBRALTAR 1026
EXTREMADURA 1027
Trujillo 1027
Cáceres 1028
Mérida 1029
SPAIN DIRECTORY 1030
Accommodation 1030
Activities 1030
Business Hours 1031
Courses 1031
Dangers & Annoyances 1031
Embassies & Consulates 1032
Festivals & Events 1032
Holidays 1032
Language 1033
Legal Matters 1033
Maps 1033
Media 1033
Money 1033
Post 1034
Telephone 1034
Time 1034
Tourist Information 1034
Visas 1035
Work 1035
TRANSPORT IN SPAIN 1035
Getting There & Away 1035
Getting Around 1036

Switzerland 1039

Highlights 1040
Itineraries 1040
Climate & When To Go 1040
History 1040
People 1043
Religion 1044
Arts 1044
Environment 1044
Food & Drink 1045
BERN 1045
Orientation 1045
Information 1045
Sights 1046
Activities 1048
Sleeping 1048
Eating 1049
Drinking 1050
Entertainment 1050
Shopping 1050
Getting There & Away 1050
Getting Around 1051
FRIBOURG, NEUCHÂTEL & THE JURA 1051
Neuchâtel 1051
Val De Travers 1052
Fribourg 1052
Gruyères 1053
Jura Canton 1053
GENEVA 1054

Orientation 1054
Information 1054
Sights & Activities 1054
Festivals & Events 1056
Sleeping 1056
Eating 1057
Drinking & Entertainment 1058
Getting There & Away 1058
Getting Around 1058
LAKE GENEVA REGION 1059
Lausanne 1059
Vevey 1061
Montreux 1061
Gryon & Leysin 1062
VALAIS 1062
Zermatt 1062
Leukerbad 1064
TICINO 1064
Bellinzona 1064
Locarno 1065
Lugano 1066
GRAUBÜNDEN 1067
Chur 1067
Flims-Laax 1067
St Moritz 1068
Swiss National Park 1069
ZÜRICH 1070
Orientation 1070
Information 1070
Sights 1070
Activities 1072
Festivals & Events 1072
Sleeping 1072
Eating 1073
Drinking 1074
Entertainment 1074
Getting There & Away 1075
Getting Around 1075
CENTRAL SWITZERLAND & BERNER OBERLAND 1075
Lucerne 1076
Interlaken 1078
Jungfrau Region 1081
NORTHERN SWITZERLAND 1084
Basel 1084
Schaffhausen 1087
Appenzellerland 1087
SWITZERLAND DIRECTORY 1088
Accommodation 1088
Activities 1088
Business Hours 1088
Embassies & Consulates 1088
Festivals & Events 1089
Gay & Lesbian Travellers 1089
Holidays 1090
Internet Resources 1090
Language 1090
Money 1090
Post 1090
Telephone 1090
Tourist Information 1091
Visas 1091
TRANSPORT IN SWITZERLAND 1091
Getting There & Away 1091
Getting Around 1092

Regional Directory 1095

Transport in Western Europe 1112

Health 1123

Language 1125

Behind the Scenes 1137

Index 1142

World Time Zones 1154

Map Legend 1156

Regional Map Contents

The Authors

RYAN VER BERKMOES

Coordinating Author, Destination, Getting Started, Itineraries, Snapshot, Directory, Transport & Germany

Ryan Ver Berkmoes once lived in Germany. He spent three years in Frankfurt, during which time he edited a magazine until he got a chance for a new career with Lonely Planet. One of his first jobs was working on the Germany chapter of the 4th edition of this very book. Since then he's travelled the world as a writer for LP and others, but was more than happy to return to Germany for this book. Fortunately he won't have to worry about withdrawal from German beer as he lives in Portland, Oregon – one of the world's great beer cities.

The Coordinating Author's Favourite Trip

Tough call this one, as I love almost every part of Western Europe. Here are a few places that have captured my heart: Wales (p264), for its little villages and lonely hikes; London (p151), lived there and loved it; Paris (p291), for annual café time; Amsterdam (p850), because there's so much more than the hash joints beloved by amateurs; Maastricht (p877), a beautiful, fun town in the country of my ancestors; Bamberg (p484), another picturesque, lively place; the Alps in the Jungfrau Region (p1081), where you can kick back and watch avalanches; most places in Italy, especially Rome (p716), the pesto of Genoa (p740); and finally, the magnificent south of Spain with Granada (p1016) and Córdoba (p1013).

AARON ANDERSON

Austria

Aaron was first drawn to Austria when his Western Europe travels were temporarily suspended by an extended stopover in Mayrhofen, Tirol. He became so happy with the alpine lifestyle and serenity that he took on a part-time job wrenching on bikes to help make the experience last longer. A month quickly turned into a year of living it up and garnering an appreciation for everything Austrian. He is based in Boulder, Colorado, and enjoys Saturdays at home with his girlfriend (also a Lonely Planet author), and dog (not an LP author…yet), loves anything outdoors, wears a mohawk in the summertime, and isn't afraid to sport a handlebar moustache. When not travelling the world, he works part-time in a friend's microbrewery as a professional brewer.

LONELY PLANET AUTHORS

Why is our travel information the best in the world? It's simple: our authors are independent, dedicated travellers. They don't research using just the Internet or phone, and they don't take freebies in exchange for positive coverage. They travel widely, to all the popular spots and off the beaten track. They personally visit thousands of hotels, restaurants, cafés, bars, galleries, palaces, museums and more – and they take pride in getting all the details right, and telling it how it is. For more, see the authors section on www.lonelyplanet.com.

SARAH ANDREWS

Spain

An American now based in Barcelona, Sarah has been using travel writing as an excuse to get to know her adopted country since 2000. For this guide, she got to revisit some of her favourite spots in Spain, including the Ganbara tapas bar in San Sebastián, the Reina Sofía temple of art in Madrid, and Calella, the prettiest town on the Costa Brava. Sarah has written about Spain for several Lonely Planet guides.

OLIVER BERRY

France

Oliver graduated from University College London with a degree in English and now works as a writer and photographer in Cornwall and London. His first trip to France was at the tender age of two, and subsequent travels have carried him from the streets of Paris to the Alpine mountains and from the vineyards of southern France to the chestnut forests of Corsica. For this book he had the enviable job of updating the France chapter. He is a regular contributor to various film, music and travel publications and has won several awards for his writing, including the *Guardian* Young Travel Writer of the Year.

BECCA BLOND

Switzerland & Liechtenstein

Becca and Switzerland became acquainted at an early age – she was born in Geneva. Although she moved to the States when she was a toddler, her American parents didn't let her forget the country. She has slightly embarrassing childhood memories of wearing traditional Swiss alpine dresses to holiday functions and fonder ones of trying to feed local goats during family vacations in the Swiss Alps. These early holidays inspired Becca's desire to travel. When she realised the monotony of a nine-to-five job was not something she could live with, she swapped newspaper reporting on rock stars and homicides for wandering the world for Lonely Planet. When not on the road she calls Boulder, Colorado home.

TERRY CARTER

Greece

Terry's first visit to Greece was with a Greek-Australian friend returning to his local village in Rhodes for their annual festival. He quickly learnt that even the coolest Greek guys only need a couple of ouzos for the inner *zeïmbekiko* dancer to surface. While still preferring to play the Turkish *saz* to the bouzouki, he now has a clear understanding on how making Greek coffee differs from brewing Turkish coffee. When not dreaming of hiding away in Monemvasia with a few good books, Terry is a freelance writer and photographer based nowhere in particular.

GEERT COLE

Belgium & Luxembourg

Geert's one of those few Belgians who was born without a brick in his stomach, as the local saying goes. An avid traveller since his late teens, he combed continents for years before discovering that only one nation on earth is founded on beer, chocolate and chips. It's good to be home! Back in Antwerp one time, Geert met partner, Leanne, whom he enticed with all the great things in life that Belgians accept as everyday. In return, Leanne offered Geert life amongst the wallabies in Australia. The pair now enjoys the best of both worlds with their two little daughters in tow.

LARA DUNSTON

Greece

Lara has degrees in cinema, communications, international studies and screenwriting, and a career that's embraced writing, filmmaking, media education and now travel writing – motivated by journeys to 55 countries. Lara first visited Greece eight years ago and has made countless trips since – one with her frappé-loving mother in tow! While her idea of fun in Greece was basking on a beach in Symi or leaning over the edge of an infinity pool in Santorini, after this research trip she's fallen in love with the wildlife and wildflowers of northern and central Greece, and is now mad about the Mani.

DUNCAN GARWOOD

Italy

After years of watching Italian football on TV, Duncan moved to the Adriatic port town of Bari in 1997. Two years later he moved to Rome, where he's been ever since. An Italian speaker and enthusiastic follower of the nation's convoluted politics, he's spent much of the past six years travelling up and down the peninsula for Lonely Planet. He's contributed to various LP Italy guides, including a guide to Piedmont, whose capital, Turin, he rates as one of Italy's great unsung destinations.

SARAH JOHNSTONE

Germany

Sarah Johnstone is a freelance journalist based in London. She hates author bios and wishes the editors would stop asking for them. Having studied German (and journalism) at university, worked for employers from news agency Reuters to business travel magazines, and done an MSc at the London School of Economics, she's spent the last few years dutifully traipsing back and forth across Europe for Lonely Planet.

JOHN LEE

Britain

Born in leafy St Albans, a swift train ride from London, John came to Canada's west coast to study in 1993 and never left. After taking a long-dreamed-of trip on the Trans-Siberian Railway, he became a full-time freelance travel writer. Now specialising in stories about Canada and the UK, his work has appeared in dozens of major newspapers and magazines around the world. He returns 'home' to Britain several times a year to feast on Marmite, Yorkie bars and cheese-and-onion crisps.

ALEX LEVITON

Italy

This is Alex's fourth time in Italy for Lonely Planet, leaving her usual haunt of Umbria to explore Rome and the south. She's now a big fan. Alex has returned almost annually to Italy since accidentally discovering it in 1998, and has been known to take seven-hour Italian train journeys to nowhere in particular for fun. After graduating UC Berkeley with a master's degree in journalism in 2002, she has split her time between Durham, North Carolina and San Francisco, California, with as much time as possible in Perugia, Italy.

LEANNE LOGAN

Belgium

Leanne's first taste of Belgium was a cone of mayonnaise-smothered *frites* (chips) which, at the grand age of 12, she was instructed to eat using a tiny wooden fork without getting her fingers dirty. Some ask. Many years later she left her job as a journalist in Australia to try that again. En route around Belgium and Luxembourg for Lonely Planet, she not only mastered the dextrous art of devouring chips but also developed an appetite for both beer and chocolate and love for a Flemish man. Fifteen years later and a dozen times around both countries, Leanne is introducing her half-Flemish daughters to all the fine things Belgium offers – including finger-licking *frites*.

VIRGINA MAXWELL

Spain

Before taking to the road to write a host of guidebooks to the Middle East, Virginia worked as a publishing manager at Lonely Planet's head office in Melbourne, Australia. She travels with her partner Peter and young son Max, and is usually found somewhere between Istanbul and Cairo, only occasionally veering off course to investigate rewarding destinations such as Spain.

CRAIG MCLACHLAN

Greece

A Kiwi with a bad case of wanderlust, Craig enjoys nothing more than visiting the Greek Isles to down Mythos beer, *retsina* and to consume countless gyros. Describing himself as a 'freelance anything', Craig runs an outdoor activity company in Queenstown, New Zealand in the southern hemisphere summer, then heads north for the winter, working for Lonely Planet and leading tours to Greece and Switzerland. Other jobs have included pilot, hiking guide, interpreter and karate instructor. A self-confessed 'island-lover', Craig once walked the length of Japan (3200km) and says that the islands of Greece and Okinawa are his top spots for a holiday.

JOSEPHINE QUINTERO

Portugal

Josephine started travelling with a backpack and guitar in the late '60s. Further travels took her to Kuwait where she was held hostage during the Iraq invasion. Josephine moved to the relaxed shores of Andalucía, Spain shortly thereafter, from where she has enjoyed exploring neighbouring Portugal, delighting in the differences between the two countries and enjoying her daily quota of *vinho verde* and custard tarts.

MILES RODDIS

Andorra

Living in Valencia, on Spain's Mediterranean coast, Miles loses count of the times he's nipped up to Andorra for a ski holiday or walking break – though never, ever to shop. Andorra marks the starting point for the 23-day Pyrenean Traverse described in Lonely Planet's *Walking in Spain*, a route he's twice trekked with enormous satisfaction. Miles has contributed to over 25 Lonely Planet titles, including guides, both general and walking, about Spain and France, Andorra's immediate neighbours.

STUART SCHUFFMAN

Ireland

Stuart's writing career began when he self-published *Broke-Ass Stuart's Guide to Living Cheaply in San Francisco*, which somehow snowballed into him writing about Ireland for Lonely Planet (something his doctor has subsequently called 'a two month bender'). Luckily for him, he has a penchant for Guinness, good whiskey and fried food, so he managed to fit in perfectly. He currently lives in beautiful San Francisco, and occasionally wakes up craving real Irish black-and-white pudding.

SIMON SELLARS

The Netherlands

Simon Sellars has been fascinated by the Netherlands ever since he was old enough to fashion his own Dutch oven. He wishes Dutch film director Paul Verhoeven would stop mucking about and make another dystopian sci-fi blockbuster – preferably starring Rutger Hauer.

ANDREW STONE

Britain

Brought up in southern England, and educated in part in Wales (where he attended journalism college), Andrew has tramped over much of the rest of the UK in his 30-something years. His favourite area remains Scotland, where he has been holidaying on student backpacking jaunts, boating and fishing trips, city breaks and walking holidays since the 1980s. His big hope is that one day someone comes up with a deterrent for the bloodthirsty Scottish midge that actually works. Andrew, who updated the Northern England, Wales and Scotland sections of the Britain chapter for this edition, has contributed to several Lonely Planet guides, including the previous two editions of Western Europe.

Getting Started

One of the great joys of travel in Western Europe is that you can plan as much or as little as you want. Some people will have a must-see list of sights they will feel cheated if they miss. Others will go with the flow and let their moods and experiences shape their journey. Neither is the better way to go and many people will combine aspects of both. They'll have a realistic idea of what they can accomplish while still having the freedom to take a detour on a whim.

Planning also helps you figure out how much you'll spend and when is the best time to travel for the sort of trip you want.

WHEN TO GO

Any time can be the best time to visit Western Europe, depending on what you want to see and do. Summer lasts roughly from June to September and offers the best weather for outdoor pursuits in the northern half of Europe. In the southern half (Mediterranean coast, Iberian Peninsula, southern Italy and Greece), where the summers tend to be hotter, you can extend that period by one or even two months either way, when temperatures may also be more agreeable.

You won't be the only tourist in Western Europe during the summer months – all of France and Italy, for instance, go on holiday in August. Prices can be high, accommodation fully booked and the sights packed. You'll find much better deals – and far fewer crowds – in the shoulder seasons on either side of summer; in April and May, for instance, flowers are in bloom and the weather can be surprisingly mild, and nice weather can stretch past September into October.

'Some people will have a must-see list... others will go with the flow...'

On the other hand, if you're keen on winter sports, resorts in the Alps and the Pyrenees begin operating in late November and move into full swing after the New Year, closing down when the snow begins to melt in March or even April.

The Climate and When to Go sections in individual country chapters explain what to expect and when to expect it, and the climate charts (p1100) will help you compare the weather in different destinations. As a rule, spring and autumn tend to be wetter and windier than summer and winter. The temperate maritime climate along the Atlantic is relatively wet all year, with moderate extremes in temperature. The Mediterranean coast is hotter and drier, with most rainfall occurring during the mild winter. The continental climate in eastern Germany and the Alps tends to have much stronger extremes in weather between summer and winter.

When summer and winter are mentioned throughout this book we generally mean high (May to September) and low (October to April) tourist seasons.

You might want to time your trip to coincide with a major local festival or celebration – see the list in this chapter and those in the individual country chapters for details. Or if it's your first trip to Europe, you might want to list the European icons that have inspired your trip and make certain you see them.

COSTS & MONEY

One of the big questions when travelling is 'how much money will I need?' Luckily, in this day of the euro (€), travellers won't have to fiddle with changing money at every border crossing. However, this doesn't necessarily mean prices are comparable throughout Western Europe. Expect your money to be stretched in noneuro countries like Switzerland and the UK, and in capital cities. Backpackers eating street meals and sleeping in hostels can expect to pay from about €40 per day. Midrange travellers eating in cafés and sleeping in hotels should allow a daily budget starting from €100. Travellers opting for full-course restaurant meals and resort-style accommodation, expect to pay from €200 and right on up. Day passes on public transport average €4 in cities. Renting a car costs €25 to €70 per day. See the Transport in Western Europe chapter for more details.

Tips on stretching your money include picking up local magazines and newspapers and looking for coupons and discounts on attractions and dining out (most museums have a 'free' day once a week/month; many restaurants have 'fixed-price menus' that are half the usual price). Search the web for packages; these can be especially good for families, as can family admission rates. Look for discount cards sold by tourist offices.

A combination of credit or cash card and travellers cheques is recommended so you have something to fall back on if an ATM swallows your card or the banks are closed. Credit cards are widely accepted throughout Western Europe, and you'll find ATMs in all but the tiniest of villages. Travellers cheques (see p1107) are exchangeable in major cities at banks and *bureaux de change*. It's a good idea to travel with some local currency in cash; the equivalent of, say, US$100 should usually be enough.

READING UP

Half the fun of going on a trip can be in the preparation. Certainly you should read a few books to both get you in the mood and get a grounding in what life is like in the places you're visiting. You'll also find no end of experiences and resources on the web.

Books

European travelogue classics include the *Provence* series by Peter Mayle and Frances Mayes' *Under the Tuscan Sun*, but you may well find that

DON'T LEAVE HOME WITHOUT...

Pack less than you want as you'll buy more along the way. Besides it's Western Europe and you can buy anything you forget there. Also make darn sure that your bag is easy and comfortable to haul about, whether it's a backpack or has a shoulder strap. If you're under 30 and use something with wheels, you've just defined 'daggy' and/or 'dork'. Otherwise, consider the following:

- sandals or thongs (flip-flops) for when the weather is great
- raincoat, waterproof jacket or umbrella – it will rain
- sewing kit – all that beer and chocolate lead to burst seams
- padlock – for hostel lockers
- good pair of earplugs
- alarm clock– so you don't miss the morning train
- menu phrasebook – so you don't just order boring stuff or get an offal surprise
- favourite brand of sunscreen
- favourite brand of mosquito repellent
- map – so you can show new friends where you come from
- extra duffel bag to deploy when you buy more than you planned

half the other people you meet have read these as well. There are plenty of classics that intrepid travellers feel compelled to buy. James Joyce's *Ulysses* comes to mind, although you can have many a fun conversation in Dublin pubs asking people if they have ever finished it. And *The Da Vinci Code* by Dan Brown is part travelogue, part fantasy and part exercise in bad writing.

You can do better. The country chapters in this book all have excellent recommendations. Additionally, here are some titles that can't help but get you starting a countdown for your trip. These titles are recommended by the authors of this book and will make great companions on any trip.

- *Bollocks to Alton Towers* (Jason Hazeley et al) A celebration of eccentric Britain and places like Eden Ostrich World and the Cumberland Pencil Museum.
- *The Great Beers of Belgium* (Michael Jackson) One of the world's best beer writers details all that Belgium has to offer.
- *Stasiland* (Anna Funder) A fascinating investigation into the secret police of East Germany with chilling accounts of their victims.
- *The World from Italy: Football, Food & Politics* (George Negus) Noted Aussie journalist spends a year on sabbatical in Italy.
- *A Moveable Feast* (Ernest Hemingway) A deeply personal and affectionate account of life as an expat in Paris in the 1920s.
- *Neither Here Nor There: Travels in Europe* (Bill Bryson) The best-selling author retraces his journey as a backpacker 20 years before. Things have changed, his back aches.
- *McCarthy's Bar* (Peter McCarthy) A truly funny and original writer ventures to the west of Ireland and drinks in every bar bearing his surname.
- *A Time of Gifts* (Patrick Leigh Fermor) This gifted writer paints a picture of 1933 Europe in words as he travels across it on foot.

Websites

The Internet is a rich resource for travellers. You can research your trip, hunt down bargain air fares, book hotels, check weather conditions or chat with locals and other travellers about the best places to visit. For a list of country-specific websites, see Tourist Information in each country chapter.

Airline Information (www.skyscanner.net) What budget airlines in Europe fly where, when and for how much.

Currency Conversions (www.xe.net/ucc) Exchange rates for hundreds of currencies worldwide.

Lonely Planet (www.lonelyplanet.com) Here you'll find succinct summaries on travelling to most places on earth, postcards from other travellers, and the Thorn Tree bulletin board, where you can ask questions before you go or dispense advice when you get back.

Train Information (www.seat61.com) Tons of information about getting around Europe by train. Great descriptions of various journeys.

Travel Planning (www.travelpete.com) Big and fun site with travel information for Europe.

Check out the website www.americangirlsareeasy.com. Written by two American women, the motto says it all: 'How to find a man in Europe and leave him there.'

MUST-SEE MOVIES

- *A Lisbon Story* Directed by Wim Wenders, this fascinating quasi documentary is about a day in the life of a movie soundman wandering the streets, trying to salvage a film that's been abandoned by the director.
- *All About My Mother* (p931) Pedào Almodovar's heart-warming film about life, love and transvestites, in which a woman searches for the secret to her past in Barcelona.
- *Amélie* (p288) An utterly charming Parisian fairytale.

- *The Icicle Thief* This farce sends up classic film *The Bicycle Thief* as it skewers modern Italian life in Rome and elsewhere.
- *Good Bye Lenin!* (p424) Sweet comedy where Berliners pretend the wall never fell.
- *On Her Majesty's Secret Service* Excellent but forgotten James Bond caper with Blofeld hiding out in the Alps above Interlaken.
- *Roman Holiday* Director William Wyler sends Gregory Peck and Audrey Hepburn on a fun-filled romp.
- *The Third Man* (p67) Just try to get the theme song from this Orson Welles classic, shot and set in post-war Vienna, out of your head.
- *Trainspotting* (p146) Scrappy Scottish heroin junkie eventually chooses life. Great soundtrack and gritty London scenes.
- *Turks Fruit* (p846) Directed by Paul Verhoeven, this is one of the Netherlands' most famous flicks. A Bohemian sculptor learns about life in Amsterdam and elsewhere.

TOP FIVE FESTIVALS

Europe has no shortage of festivals that are worth a trip. Many are outlined in the country chapters. Here's five that you won't want to miss.

Cannes Film Festival (p394) The famous, not-so-famous and the merely topless converge on the Mediterranean for a year's worth of movies in only a week.

Edinburgh International Festival (p247) Three weeks of innovative and fantastic drama, comedy, dance, music and more from around the globe.

Notting Hill Carnival (p165) Over 100 languages are spoken in London's schools and at this massive multicultural street fair you'll see why.

Oktoberfest (p477) Germany's biggest beerfest takes over Munich.

San Fermine (aka 'Running of the Bulls'; p987) Huge male bovines and the people who want to be close to them invade Pamplona.

RESPONSIBLE TRAVEL

As a visitor, you have a responsibility to the local people and to the environment. When it comes to the environment, the key rules are to preserve

CONDUCT IN EUROPE

Although dress standards are fairly informal in northern Europe, your clothes may well have some bearing on how you're treated in southern Europe.

Dress casually, but keep your clothes clean, and ensure sufficient body cover (eg shoulders covered and wear trousers or a knee-length dress) if your sightseeing includes churches, monasteries, synagogues or mosques.

Some nightclubs and fancy restaurants may refuse entry to people wearing jeans or sneakers (trainers).

While nude bathing is usually restricted to certain beaches, topless bathing is very common in many parts of Europe. Nevertheless, women shouldn't immediately drop top. The basic rule is that if nobody else seems to be doing it, then you shouldn't either.

You'll soon notice that Europeans are heavily into shaking hands and even kissing when they greet one another. Don't worry about the latter with those you don't know well, but get into the habit of shaking hands with virtually everyone you meet. In many parts of Europe it's also customary to greet the proprietor when entering a shop, café or a quiet bar, and also to say goodbye when you leave.

Use common courtesy. It's very easy to be another 'ugly _____' (insert your nationality here) by talking louder than everyone else, taking flash photos where not allowed, yakking on a mobile phone in quiet places, putting your dirty shoes on train seats, proclaiming you're a Philistine with comments like 'we got a bigger one of those at home' etc.

natural resources and to leave the countryside as you find it. Those Alpine flowers look much better on the mountainside than squashed in your pocket (and many species are protected anyway).

- Wherever you are, littering is irresponsible and offensive. Mountain areas have fragile ecosystems, so stick to prepared paths whenever possible, and always carry your rubbish away with you.
- Do not use detergents or toothpaste (even if they are listed as biodegradable) in or close to any watercourses.
- If you just gotta go when you're out in the wilderness somewhere, bury human waste in holes at least 15cm deep and at least 100m from any watercourse.
- It's always good to know a few handy phrases, such as 'please', 'thank you' and 'where is…?' in the local language – you'll be addressed more cordially and the locals really do appreciate your efforts.
- Recycling is an important issue, especially in Austria, Germany and Switzerland, and you will be encouraged to follow suit. Look for bins with multiple receptacles.
- Traffic congestion on the roads is a major problem, so visitors will do themselves and residents a favour if they forgo driving and use public transport.

Itineraries

CLASSIC ROUTES

THE ULTIMATE EUROPEAN VACATION

One to Two Months

This 8000km-plus trek hits all the hot spots, providing a technicolour postcard selection to write home about. You could do it in one month – barely – but if you want to fully experience what Western Europe has to offer, take two.

Have limited time but want to see a bit of everything? Start in **Dublin** (p652) and sample the vibrant pubs and traditional Irish craic. From Ireland, either take a ferry to **Liverpool** (p235) or a flight to **London** (p151) for some great theatre. From London, take the Eurostar train to **Paris** (p291).

From Paris, head north to **Antwerp** (p121) for some amazing beer, and then further north to **Amsterdam** (p850), not forgetting to ride a canal boat. Head east, stopping for a Rhine cruise, and spend a few days exploring (and surviving) the amazing nightlife of **Berlin** (p428). Next, **Vienna** (p59) beckons with its classical music riches. From here, head west to **Zürich** (p1070) and the Alps for awe-inspiring ski slopes and vistas.

Head south to the canals of **Venice** (p752) and through **Florence** (p769) in Tuscany to historic **Rome** (p716). Take a ferry to **Athens** (p561), and then explore an island with beaches such as **Rhodes** (p615). Head back to the south of France and Mediterranean towns like **Nice** (p389). Continue on to **Barcelona** (p963), before heading to the Moorish towns of the south like **Granada** (p1016). End your trip in laid-back **Lisbon** (p889), and enjoy a glass of local port wine to celebrate completing your grand journey!

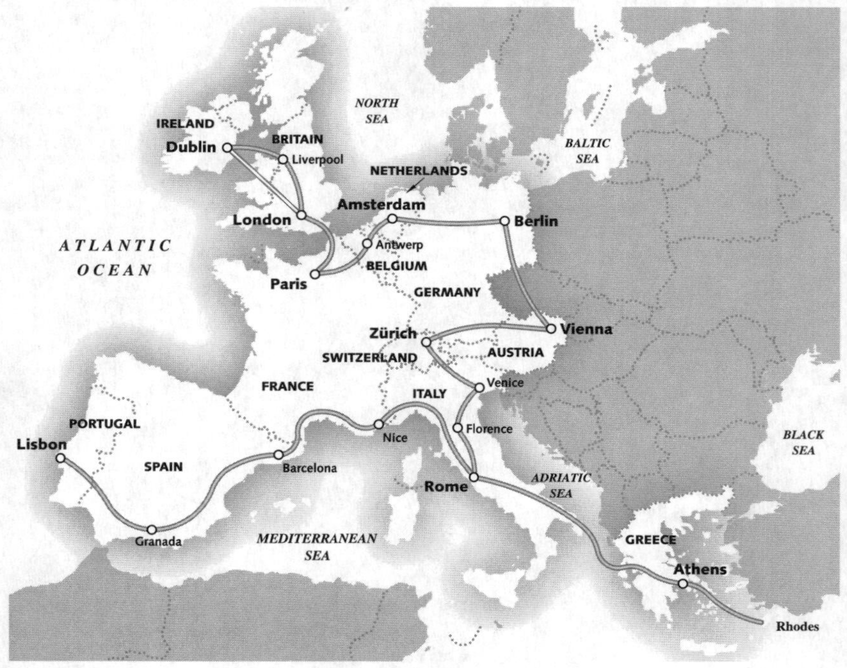

MEDITERRANEAN JOURNEY

Two Months

Start in southern Spain with a hint of British flavour in **Gibraltar** (p1026), where you can view the only wild primates in Europe. Make your way up the eastern coast past the Moorish town of **Málaga** (p1020) and on to **Valencia** (p992), where you can take a ferry to the **Balearic Islands** (p999).

Back on the mainland, **Barcelona** (p963) is a beautiful Basque town, filled with the architecture of Gaudí. From here, head into France's **Provence region** (p380) and the town of **Marseille** (p380), where you can see the fortress that was the inspiration for the novel *The Count of Monte Cristo*. On to the **Côte d'Azur** (p388), and the playground for the rich and famous, **St Tropez** (p397). A quick stop in the capital of the French Riviera, **Nice** (p389), makes a good jumping-off point for other Riviera hot spots like **Cannes** (p394).

Take a ferry to **Corsica** (p403), where you'll experience the traditional lifestyle of quiet fishing villages. Hit the snowy peaks at **Calvi** (p405) and the groves of **Les Calanques** (p406), before hopping down to **Sardinia** (p809). From Sardinia, take a long ferry ride or a quick flight to **Sicily** (p800) to visit its colossal Greek temples and the famous volcano, **Mt Etna** (p806).

Catch a ferry to **Naples** (p786) on Italian mainland and take a trip to **Pompeii** (p792). Move east to **Brindisi** (p798) for a ferry to Greece, landing in **Patra** (p574). Head to **Athens** (p561) to wonder at its ancient treasures before getting a plane or ferry to islands such as **Crete** (p606) and **Mykonos** (p588). Retrace your steps back to Italy. Head north to **Rome** (p716), allowing time to wander amid its ruins and piazzas. Continue through Tuscany, stopping at **Pisa** (p777) to see the famous 'leaning tower'. Finish up along the Ligurian coast in the port city of **Genoa** (p740) via the coastal towns that make up the **Cinque Terre** (p742), where you can stroll along the Via dell'Amore.

Blue skies, azure waters and white beaches are among the colours you'll see on this approximately 4000km-long sun-drenched journey around the Mediterranean. Ancient ruins, grape-covered hillsides, foam-filled clubs and lots of tan lines are among the sights you'll see.

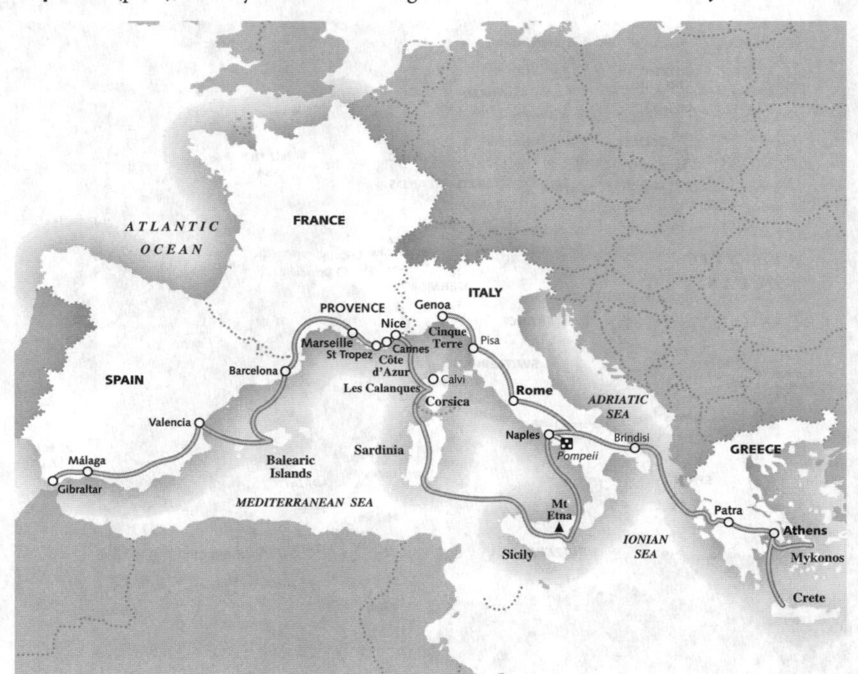

ROADS LESS TRAVELLED

Everyone goes to London, Paris and Rome, but take a detour off the beaten path and you'll experience places that really embody the character of their countries. Don't expect them to be tourist-free – nowhere worthwhile truly is – but do expect to be surprised and charmed on this 6000km trip.

EUROPE'S OTHER PLACES One to Two Months

The far north of Ireland is rugged and uncrowded; base yourself in **Donegal** (p690). Head over to the often misunderstood yet very welcoming Northern Ireland – **Belfast** (p691) in particular. Traverse the single-track roads of the far north of Scotland around **Durness** (p263) with its bogs and brogue. Next head south to the gritty yet charming town of **Newcastle-upon-Tyne** (p228) in England and catch the ferry to the Netherlands. **Rotterdam** (p867) combines splendid modern architecture with convivial charm. Go east to the old East Germany where the cities of **Dresden** (p448) and **Leipzig** (p453) are creating a new future from their historic pasts. Linger in the hikeable **Harz Mountains** (p464) before you go far south to the temperate Swiss town of **Lugano** (p1066). Traverse Italy and the hidden gem of **Mantua** (p749) followed by beautiful Umbria and towns such as **Perugia** (p781). In the south, take time to wander frenetic **Naples** (p786) and the ruin-filled **Amalfi Coast** (p795) before pressing on to **Sicily** (p800) and its rich culture.

Fly or ferry to Greece and enjoy some of the less-visited islands such as **Naxos** (p600) or **Lesvos** (p624). Return to Italy and the spiffed-up town of **Turin** (p743). Crossing to France, **Carcassonne** (p401) has a rich medieval past and great food. Head across the Iberian Peninsula to the Basque city of **Bilbao** (p986) and the pilgrimage shrine of **Santiago de Compostela** (p990). Finally, return to France and the rural beauty of **Brittany** (p333).

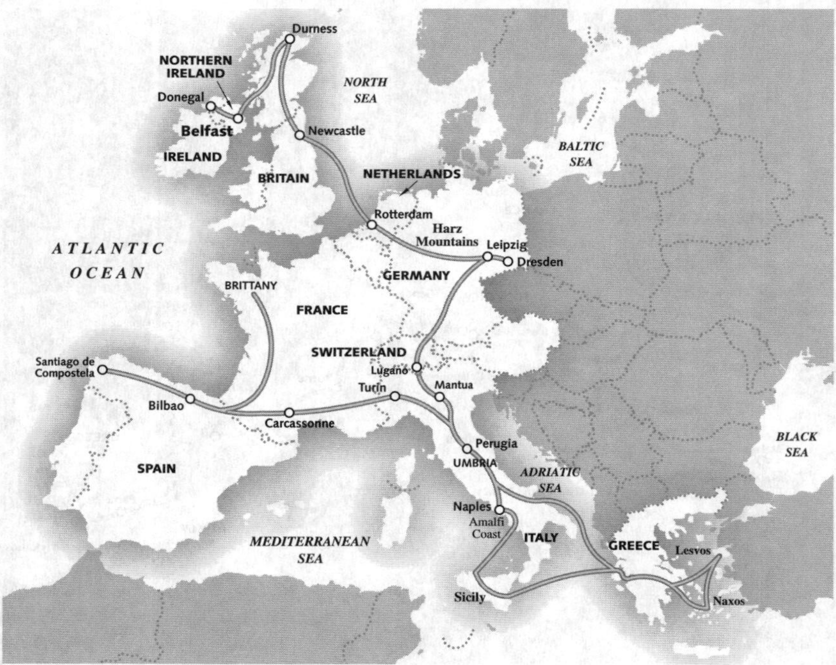

TAILORED TRIPS

EUROPE ON A JAG

Cheap flights and fast trains mean that you can have a maximum adrenaline trip in a minimum amount of time – say two weeks or less. Start at party-central **Mallorca** (p1000) in Spain's Balearic Islands, then fly cheap to Spain's late night and early morning capital of **Madrid** (p933). From here hop a plane to **London** (p151), where you can save money on a room by never sleeping – there's that much to do (and the new drinking laws let you do it). Ride the new fast tracks through the tunnel to **Paris** (p291), where the pace may be a tad slower than London but both the food and drink are better. Take the TGV train to **Marseille** (p380) for its gritty nightlife and then over to Europe's capital of style, **Milan** (p745). Take a cheap flight to the buzzing avenues of **Vienna** (p59) and then get back in the air to **Munich** (p473) with its beer gardens and clubs. Zip on an ICE train to **Berlin** (p428), which is easily the apex of the adrenaline lifestyle. More ICEs will zap you over to **Amsterdam** (p850), where though the pace is slower, the vibe is even wilder, and you can settle in and decide where to zip off to next.

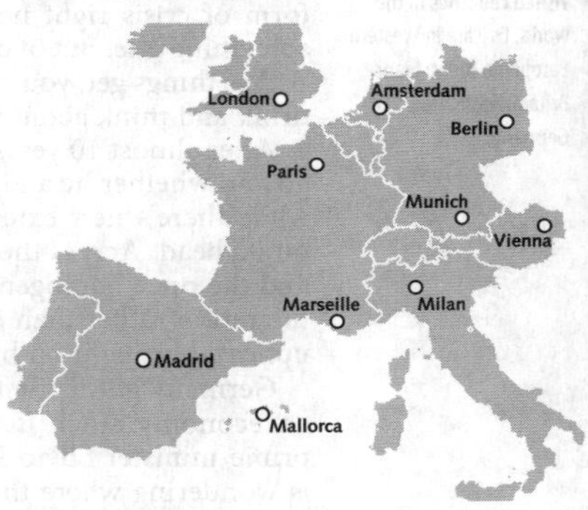

WORLD HERITAGE WONDERS

Western Europe's World Heritage (Unesco) sites, both manmade and natural, often evoke an audible gasp from awestruck travellers. In Ireland, marvel at **Brú na Bóinne** (p663), neolithic tombs that predate Egypt's pyramids by more than six centuries. Step lightly over the geometric patterns of the **Giant's Causeway** (p697) in Northern Ireland. See how far the Roman Empire stretched in Britain at **Hadrian's Wall** (p231). Spend a day at the magnificent 13th-century **Cathédrale Notre Dame de Chartres** (p313) in France and admire one of the world's largest ensembles of medieval stained glass. Climb 366 steps for the breathtaking view from Bruges' famous **belfry** (p129) or check out the Netherlands' Kinderdijk region in summer to see all 19 **windmills** (p870) twirl simultaneously. Roam the ramparts in Switzerland's beautiful castle city, **Bellinzona** (p1064), or spend an afternoon wandering through the Old Town's **fortifications** (p833) in Luxembourg City. In Germany explore the **Roman ruins** (p508) in Trier. In Italy don't miss **Pompeii** (p792) and its eternally stoned partiers. Stroll through lavish gardens and the 1440-room Habsburg palace, **Schloss Schönbrunn** (p66), near Vienna. In Greece the ancient city of **Delphi** (p580) is a must-see. Finally, gape at the towering aqueducts in **Segovia** (p954) and **Tomar** (p911).

Snapshots

CURRENT EVENTS

Western Europe long thought of itself as the heart of Europe and in a way it was. This is where the hard political decisions were made after two world wars in one century to form the genesis of today's European Union. But as that Union has come to embrace much of the rest of Europe, what about the original core?

Of the top 10 most visited countries in the world, five are in Western Europe (in order: France, Britain, Spain, Italy and Germany).

It's safe to say that almost every country in Western Europe is in some form of crisis right now, whether it is political, cultural, economic or something else. But of course this being Europe, crisis is merely a concept. Bad as things get, you can still have a good meal washed down with a fine drink and think about your next weekend jaunt to a beautiful place.

After almost 10 years of Tony Blair, Britain is wondering when he will go and whether he and George Bush really are the best of friends. Meanwhile there's new extended drinking hours, which could turn pub life on its head. Across the sea, Ireland has become a magnet for foreigners and the once homogeneous culture is for the first time confronting immigration rather than emigration issues. France is grappling with social upheaval brought on by disenfranchised youth of all races.

Germany got its first woman chancellor in 2005 and is obsessed with an economy stuck in neutral. Italy couldn't shake its wacky former prime minister Silvio Berlusconi even after he lost an election. Greece is wondering where the gloss went after the 2004 Olympics, and Spain is wondering if the cease-fire announced by Basque terrorist groups will really put an end to this deadly chapter.

Together, the Western Europe countries are casting a seemingly welcoming yet wary eye on the many new members of the EU in the east. How many people will seize the chance to move west, where scores are already out of work? And the European Constitution seems dead in the water after it couldn't pass in France and other countries.

Meanwhile there's even greater concerns: what will all those new antismoking laws do to a night out, and just who will win the Euro Cup football championship in 2008, held in Austria and Switzerland?

And amidst it all, travel to Western Europe has never been more popular. For a place so often overrun with outsiders snapping pics and talking too loud, it's amazingly welcoming and accommodating. Perhaps this is because Western Europeans are such good travellers themselves. Everybody is talking about their weekend trip on a bargain airline and the new high-speed train lines that open every year. Further – literally – if there's one thing Europeans are sacrosanct about right now, it's their long annual holidays.

HISTORY

'In the beginning, there was no Europe,' writes Professor Norman Davies in *Europe: A History*. In the beginning, all that existed was an unpopulated peninsula attached to the western edge of the world's largest landmass (Asia). But after humanoid settlers arrived between 850,000 and 700,000 BC, Europe's temperate climate and unthreatening environment would make it the cradle of agriculture and the birthplace of great civilisations such as Greece and Rome.

Greece (first emerging around 2000 BC) was renowned for its philosophers (Aristotle, Plato, Socrates) and democratic principles. Rome –

boasting brilliant politicians, and writers like Cicero, Ovid and Virgil – spread its influence by military might. At its peak, the Roman Empire stretched from England to the Sahara and from Spain to Persia.

By the 4th century AD, both empires were in terminal decline. Greece had been swallowed by Macedonia's Alexander the Great, then by Rome itself in AD 146. Although Roman emperors in Constantinople hung on for another 1000 years, the empire's western half was toppled by Germanic tribes in 476.

This marked the start of the Middle Ages in Western Europe. In 768 conquering king Charlemagne grandly named his lands the 'Holy Roman Empire'. After this territory passed into the hands of Austrian Habsburgs in the 13th century, it became the continent's dominant political power. Elsewhere, an alliance of Christian nations repeatedly sent troops to reclaim the Holy Land from Islamic control. These unsuccessful 'Crusades' (1096–1291) unfortunately set the stage for centuries of skirmishes with the neighbouring Ottoman Empire as it took control of Asia Minor and parts of the Balkans from 1453 onwards.

During the infamous Spanish Inquisition (1478–1834) King Ferdinand and Queen Isabella tried to unite their country politically behind a Catholic national identity. Jews, Muslims and Protestants were systemically exiled or persecuted or both.

Europe's grand reawakening also began in the mid-15th century, and the subsequent Renaissance, Reformation and French Revolution ushered in enormous social upheaval.

The Renaissance fomented mainly artistic expression and ideas (see p38). The Reformation was a question of religion. Challenging Catholic 'corruption' in 1517, German theologian Martin Luther established a breakaway branch of Christianity, Protestantism. Struggles between Catholics and Protestants flared during the Thirty Years' War (1618–48).

The French Revolution in 1789 was about political power, specifically the populace's attempt to wrest it from the monarchy. But in the ensuing vacuum, plucky general Napoleon Bonaparte (1769–1821) crowned himself emperor. Napoleon's efforts to colonise all of Europe ended in defeat by the British at Waterloo in 1815, but the civil laws he introduced in France in 1804 would spread the revolutionary ideas of liberty and equality across the globe.

Having vanquished Napoleon, Britain became a major world player itself. With the invention of the steam engine, railways and factories, it unleashed the Industrial Revolution. Needing markets for goods, it and other European powers accelerated their colonisation of countries around the world, a process that had begun in the 16th century.

Meanwhile, the death throes of the Habsburg Empire (now called the Austro-Hungarian Empire) were about to rock the entire continent. Serbia was accused of backing the assassination of the heir to the Austro-Hungarian throne in 1914 and the battle between the two states developed into WWI. Crippled by a huge bill for reparations imposed at the war's end in 1918, Austria's humbled ally, Germany, proved susceptible to politician Adolf Hitler's nationalist rhetoric during the 1930s. Other nations watched as Nazi Germany annexed Austria and parts of Czechoslovakia, but its invasion of Poland in 1939 sparked WWII. During the final liberation of Europe in 1945, Allied troops from Britain, France, the USA and the USSR uncovered the full extent of the genocide that had occurred in Hitler's concentration camps for Jews, Roma (gypsies) and other 'degenerates'.

Thomas Crapper is widely credited with inventing the flush toilet, however many plumbing historians would eliminate his honour and instead make Englishman Sir John Harrington flush with pride for his efforts in 1596.

The Allies carved out spheres of influence on the continent, and Germany was divided to avoid its rising up again militarily. Differences in ideology between the Western powers and the communist USSR soon led to a stand-off. The USSR closed off its assigned sectors – East Germany, East Berlin and much of Eastern Europe – behind the figurative Iron Curtain.

This 'Cold War' lasted until 1989, when the Berlin Wall finally fell. Germany was unified in 1990 and one year later the USSR was dissolved. Czechoslovakia, Hungary, Poland and Bulgaria grasped multiparty democracy.

The Dutch on average are Europe's tallest people, the Greeks the shortest.

The end of the Cold War brought a sense of peace to Europe and allowed for great expansion of the European Union. Formed in 1951 as a trade alliance in Western Europe, the EU now has 25 members, including newcomers in the east. The west however still sets the course: this is where the common currency, the euro, was launched in 2002.

PEOPLE

The population of the 15 countries covered in this book is about 370 million. That figure is not expected to increase greatly in the coming years as collectively, the population of Western Europe is not growing. This is primarily due to low birth rates in places like Italy where it is common for married couples to only have one – very spoilt – child. Germany and France also have low birth rates and governments have responded with various tax incentives to inspire procreation – a romantic notion for sure. Only Ireland shows signs of significant population growth over the next few decades.

A favourite toast among Catalans is 'Eat well and shit hard'. Conversely there's a whole school of comedy in Germany based on breaking wind.

In fact Western Europe could well lose 20% of its population by 2050 if present trends continue. This adds yet another twist to the debate over immigration. Central and Eastern Europe, Africa and nearby parts of Asia are all growing rapidly and there are millions who would move to Western Europe given the chance.

RELIGION

Ironically, although they weren't particularly fond of them at the outset and fed early believers to the lions, the Romans did much to spread Christianity. Not only did this minority religion go with the Roman Empire as it spread across Europe, eventually Rome performed an about face; in AD 313 Emperor Constantine converted to Christianity and made it Rome's official religion.

When the Roman Empire fell in the west, the church's existing independent hierarchy of popes often assumed state power. In 1054 the church split over a theological debate on the Roman Catholic Church, which spread through most of Western Europe, as well as the Eastern Orthodox, in Asia Minor. The Roman Catholic Church dominated political, artistic and cultural life in Europe for nearly 500 years until the Protestant Reformation in the 1520s. Inspired by the teachings of Martin Luther, parts of Germany, Switzerland, Scotland, Hungary and England broke away from Rome, adopting Protestant tenets that assumed a variety of subsects (Lutherans, Evangelicals, Episcopalians).

The Irish refer to strangers and friends alike as 'your man', as in 'Ask your man over there.' The English refer to someone as 'mate' for any manner of reasons, from kinship to threats.

Today traditionally Catholic countries like France have a large Muslim minority thanks to immigration from former African colonies. However, Islam (emerging in Saudi Arabia in the 7th century) has had a permanent presence in Europe and North Africa since the 12th century. That is due largely to military conquest, particularly of Spain and the Balkans.

ARTS

Western Europe and art are synonymous. All forms of creative work have a rich heritage here and, with the help of state support not found elsewhere (even after budget cuts), thrive today. For details about the vast array of trends and styles see the relevant country chapters.

Visual Arts

Today it's considered slightly politically incorrect to promote Europe as 'the cradle of Western civilisation', but the continent's legacy to the world unquestionably includes some renowned paintings, as well as a fascinating array of philosophies.

After the prolific creativity of ancient Greek and Roman culture, the continent went through a fallow period – a kind of communal artistic block – during the early Middle Ages. Times were hard, mere survival was difficult enough and the church, the leading patron of the arts, wanted religious icons not realism.

But then in the 15th century a sea change occurred and European art came storming back with the Renaissance. The movement began slowly in the Italian city-states of Florence and Venice, with the rediscovery of Greco-Roman culture. Then it spread further afield over the next several centuries.

Leonardo da Vinci and Michelangelo Buonarroti led the Italian Renaissance, spurred on by Jan Van Eyck and other Flemish masters who led the Northern Renaissance in art.

The baroque period that followed in the 17th century, defined by Rembrandt and Peter Paul Rubens' ornate portraits, was also influenced by classic ideals. During the 18th century, Romantic painters (such as Eugène Delacroix and Francisco de Goya) chose exultant political themes of liberty and great battles that eclipsed in reverence the old Christian allegories.

The late-19th-century impressionists (including Edgar Degas, Édouard Manet, Claude Monet and Pierre Auguste Renoir) progressively moved away from realism, depicting ordinary people (instead of royalty) pursuing ordinary pursuits and using small disjointed brushstrokes to create an 'impression' of subject and light. Their work segued into that of their successors, like Vincent Van Gogh and Paul Gauguin.

Then in the 20th century came the Fauvists and the cubists. The Fauvists used colour to suggest figures and motion and are probably best represented by Henri Matisse. Among the cubists was one Pablo Picasso, who went on to become almost a one-man art movement, abandoning perspective and drawing heavily on African and other native art to forge a style of wholly modernist painting. Following generations stripped away more elements of reality. In the 1930s René Magritte, Joan Miró, Max Ernst, Salvador Dali and Alberto Giacometti visually explored dream themes and the subconscious. Sculpture was escorted into modernity by Auguste Rodin and later by Constantin Brancusi.

Contemporary European art often rebels against the barriers of 'good taste', using shock and wit as tools for making statements on politics, sexuality and social issues. Artists such as Germany's Katharina Fritsch,

Ode to Joy, the choral finale to Beethoven's Ninth Symphony, uses words by poet Friedrich Schiller to espouse universal brotherhood and has been adopted as the official EU anthem.

Over 50 years old, the Eurovision Song Contest is watched by at least 300 million TV viewers annually. ABBA is still its best-known winner (in 1974).

TEN CLASSIC EUROPEAN NOVELS

- *Anna Karenina* by Leo Tolstoy (1877)
- *Crime and Punishment* by Fyodor Dostoevsky (1866)
- *Death in Venice* by Thomas Mann (1912)
- *Don Quixote* by Miguel de Cervantes (1605)
- *Madame Bovary* by Gustave Flaubert (1857)
- *Oliver Twist* by Charles Dickens (1838)
- *Remembrance of Things Past* by Marcel Proust (1913)
- *The Outsider* by Albert Camus (1942)
- *The Trial* by Franz Kafka (1925)
- *Ulysses* by James Joyce (1904)

with her sculpture *(Rat-King)* of 13m-tall black rats, Britain's Jenny Saville with her immense nude portraits, and Mark Quinn, known for his self-portrait sculpture made of his own refrigerated blood, are just a few examples.

Literature

In the pantheon of European storytellers, the Greek epic poets (including Homer), dramatists (Aeschylus, Sophocles, Euripides) and philosophers (Plato, Aristotle) occupy revered positions. Rome's dominance of the continent impressed Latin as the voice of learning and literature (namely Virgil's *Aenid* and Plutarch's histories) until Geoffrey Chaucer *(The Canterbury Tales),* Miguel de Cervantes *(Don Quixote)* and Dante Alighieri *(La Divina Commedia),* among others, fashioned their native tongues into epics.

Johann Gutenberg invented the printing press in 1450, which was to contribute to the spread of ideas during the Renaissance and the following Enlightenment (1650–1789), the so-called 'Age of Reason'. During this period, science and human logic for the first time took supremacy over religious belief as big-hitters like Voltaire (prorationalism)and Jean Jacques Rousseau (somewhat anti-) traded ideas across the divide.

The period building up to the Enlightenment was also a period of unbridled creativity in mathematics (Francis Bacon, René Descartes, Blaise Pascal), political theory (Niccolò Machiavelli) and theatre and poetry (William Shakespeare, Molière, John Milton).

Europudding: Underwhelming pan-European film or TV show, often financed by state grants

Eurotrash: Kitschy, sex-obsessed, trailer-trash TV show of deliberately doubtful taste

Eurosceptic: Opponent, often rabid, of the EU and further integration

With the advent of the machine age, the Romantics (Johann Wolfgang von Goethe, Aleksander Pushkin, Lord George Gordon Byron, John Keats, Percy Bysshe Shelley) bemoaned the severed ties with nature and looked to ancient Greece for guidance. Henrik Ibsen and Charles Baudelaire were also eminent literary figures in the 19th century. Here too, at the front door of modernity, philosophers including Friedrich Nietzsche dismantled the absolutes of morality and reality, and Sigmund Freud's theories opened a lid on the subconscious.

The modern age saw the rise of the novel, from the character-driven stories of George Eliot, Jane Austen, the Brontë sisters, Charles Dickens, Thomas Hardy, Fyodor Dostoevsky, Leo Tolstoy and Thomas Mann to the literary experiments of James Joyce. In 1960s France, Jean-Paul Sartre and Albert Camus were the two leading lights of the existentialist movement. Many contemporary writers (like VS Naipul, Salman Rushdie, Milan Kundera, Zadie Smith, Monica Ali, Hanif Kureishi) wrestle with such modern problems as straddling two cultures, escaping political persecution, and balancing love and desire.

Meanwhile, as always, the British have a thriving publishing industry, with profits led by JK Rowling's *Harry Potter* juggernaut.

SPORT

The running joke is that the English now regularly lose in sports they invented. This phenomenon is not just confined to cricket, where no other European country fields a national side, but extends to the continent's most popular pastime, football (soccer). England claims, perhaps tenuously, to be the birthplace of the 'beautiful game', because the rules were standardised here in the 19th century. However, England hasn't won a major tournament with a round football since 1966.

If 'football's coming home' is the fan's perennial catch cry, in 2006 it did, at least in the sense that the World Cup was held across Germany. There are major teams across Western Europe such as Manchester United and Arsenal in Britain, and AC Milan and Real Madrid in Spain. National

TOP SPORTS WEBSITES

For more information on Euro sports, check out the following:

- Union of European Football Associations (UEFA; www.uefa.com)
- Wimbledon (www.wimbledon.org)
- French Tennis Open (www.rolandgarros.org)
- Tour de France (www.letour.fr)
- Skiing & Snowboarding World Cups (www.fis-ski.com)

leagues play the same season from October to May. In 2008 the UEFA Cup, known as the Euro Cup, will be held in Austria and Switzerland. To the surprise of many, Greece is the defending champ from 2004.

Although the English also devised tennis, their players continually struggle – even on home turf at Wimbledon in London every June. Here, Swiss, Russians, Belgians and Americans dominate. The French Open, Roland Garros, is held in Paris at the end of May. At least the English have fared better in rugby in recent years, where other heavyweight European teams are France, Ireland and Wales.

In 2004 the Olympics returned to its historic home, Athens (where they were first held in 776 BC). In 2012 they will be held in London, which beat out Paris and New York for the honour.

Another huge draw is the annual Tour de France cycling race every July, newly competitive with the retirement of American Lance Armstrong.

ENVIRONMENT

The Land

In between the Baltic Sea and the spine of the Alps lies the European Plain, one of the greatest uninterrupted expanses on earth, stretching from the Pyrenees and the Atlantic coast to the Ural Mountains in Russia. This arable region of grassland and dense forests drains into the Rhine, Danube and Main.

Belting the centre of Europe, the Alps were carved by the retreating glaciers as ice ages passed and stretch from France to the Carpathian Mountains in Eastern Europe. Mont Blanc is Europe's tallest mountain at 4807m, followed by the Matterhorn at 4478m.

In the southern range is the Mediterranean area, with ready access to the sea and running along a volcanic range that was most active between 1628 BC (Thera) and AD 79 (Vesuvio), although Europe's largest live volcano, Mt Etna in Sicily, erupted most recently in 2001. The land is rocky and exhausted from mismanagement, although olive trees, cypresses and grape vines thrive.

Lisbon's 1755 earthquake is about the largest ever recorded. It is thought that it would have registered 8.9 on today's Richter scale. Italy is also prone to earthquakes, especially in the volcanically active south.

Wildlife & Plants

With its dense populations and centuries of development, Western Europe is not a place to expect to find an abundance of unusual wildlife or undisturbed natural vistas.

The Mediterranean forests are a range of cultivated corks (providing three-quarters of the world's cork supply) and holm oaks, cedars and pines, as well as olive trees. The Mediterranean Sea has the world's second-highest percentage of native species, including the endangered monk seal. The Adriatic Sea shelters underwater pastures of the *Posidonia* seagrass, which is abundant with commercial fish.

Europe has experienced 17 ice ages through its geologic history.

The Carpathians are considered one of the last refuges of wilderness with healthy populations of brown bear, wolf and lynx, Imperial eagle and Ural owl, species that have all but disappeared elsewhere. The last population of Iberian lynx lives in the southwestern corner of Spain and Portugal.

The northern Atlantic Ocean and North Sea provide unique habitats for sharks, seals and migratory birds. Rich blankets of kelp, seagrass and cold-water coral reefs also inhabit the chilly waters.

Environmental Issues

Name all the big environmental problems related to heavily populated areas and Western Europe suffers from them. Air and water pollution from industry are high in many regions, and approximately over half of Europe has been deforested. Rivers have been dammed or straightened, resulting in destruction of wetlands, floodplains and forests, and in more loss of wildlife habitat. The once-abundant Mediterranean Sea has been overfished and its role as a popular tourist destination puts additional stress on limited resources, like fresh water and open space. Homes and hotels crowd more than half the Mediterranean coast, clawing over each other for a water view.

Germany's favourite fast food is the *Doner,* spiced meat served in pita bread. It came to Germany with the scores of Turkish immigrants in the 1970s. The Dutch like raw herring on a stick.

Global warming is taking a toll and is responsible for heatwaves that have caused a dramatic increase in wildfires along the Mediterranean. According to the Swiss Academy of Natural Sciences, Switzerland's glaciers have retreated by up to 200m already this century, causing landslides and the creation of new lake accumulations in the valleys.

This said, most of Western Europe has embraced an environmental agenda. Recycling is found in almost every country – especially in Germany where it is taken to great and carefully sorted lengths. Water treatment plants are being built and have done much to improve the quality of rivers such as the Rhine. There's societal pressure as well, particularly in Britain where initiatives such as carbon replacement have become popular.

FOOD & DRINK

Europeans take great pride in their different regional cuisines and it's no exaggeration to call the best of them exemplary. When modern nutritionists want to encourage us to adopt a healthy diet, the word we hear is 'Mediterranean'. After all, the fresh vegetables, seafood, olive oil, garlic and red wine ritually consumed on the Med supposedly reduce heart-disease risk, help keep depression at bay and generally prolong life.

Even if you don't give a damn about your health, it's no sacrifice to eat like this, tucking into grilled sardines in Portugal, enjoying a fresh paella dish of seafood and rice in Spain, or snacking on vegetable, meat and seafood tapas. Surely sharing in the Spanish love of ham can't hurt too much either?

In much of Spain if you show up at a restaurant before 11pm you'll find it almost empty. The real rush is near midnight. Meanwhile in the colder parts of Western Europe, you'd best be seated and ordering by 8pm.

Pasta generally tastes better in Italy, its country of origin, where home-made noodles are dished up with deliciously creamy sauces or cooked with oodles of garlic and tomatoes that have frequently just been picked. Each region has its own distinctive pasta (from *ziti* in Naples to *orecchiette* in Apulia). They know the right way to make pizza and polenta here too, and rustic Italian cooking also boasts healthy and tasty ingredients like truffles and white beans.

When the subject moves on to French cuisine our nutritionists get confused. How can all the elaborate recipes, meat and rich cream sauces that define classic *haute cuisine* be good for the arteries? Yet the French have long dined on steak tartare, *coq au vin*, duck confit and goose-liver pâté without apparent harm. Indeed, they relish a mind-boggling array of cheeses – from the Normandy region's famous Camembert to the Dordogne's blue-veined Roquefort – and have a penchant for sweet crepes. Yet still they manage to have a low rate of heart disease.

In many Belgian bars you can choose from hundreds of beers, each served in its own unique glass with a little snack such as cheese. Spanish wine bars often serve dozens of snacks.

The answer to this 'French paradox' lies not in the occasional foray into ratatouille (vegetable stew) or bouillabaisse (a seafood stew from Marseille), but in the national habit of enjoying a glass of red wine nightly. Quite right, too, with such excellent choices at their doorstep – from the busty Bordeaux and cocky Côte du Rhône reds to a bouquet of Loire Valley varietals.

Modern Germans might have learnt to cut back just a little on the wurst (sausages) and smoked pork of their traditional cuisine, but both dishes are still prominent. Just try to have only a couple of the addictive Nuremberg sausages.

Other European regions have their own specialities: the Swiss are known for fondue, *rösti,* chocolate and cheese. The Belgians are renowned for their cuisine in general, including mussels and chips, chocolate and hundreds of varieties of beer. Greece has a penchant for lamb (such as in the *gyros* skewer), tangy cheeses like feta or *haloumi,* yogurt, hummus, eggplant (aubergine) and olives, all followed by honey-sweet baklava for dessert.

Over 350 cheeses are made in France (the three biggies are Camembert, Brie and Roquefort). Germany has almost as many varieties of sausages.

British food probably has the worst 'meat and three veg' reputation, and in parts of the country it's still unfortunately deserved. However, the larger cities boast just about every ethnic cuisine, and London, in particular, is awash with world-class chefs. Here even old comfort food like bangers and mash or fish and chips are often given new twists (say, merguez sausages with mustard mash). If in doubt, order a curry. Its links to the Indian subcontinent mean this is something at which Britain excels.

Finally, of course, Europe is a brilliant spot for an alcoholic tipple, from the French wines and Belgian beers already mentioned to German *Weissbier* ('white' wheat beer), Italian reds and Greece's aniseed liquor ouzo. We'll leave you to explore that subject yourself.

pate without apparent harm. Indeed, they relish a mind-boggling array of cheeses – from the Normandy region's famous Camembert to the Dordogne's blue-veined Roquefort – and have a penchant for sweet crepes. Yet still they manage to have a low rate of heart disease.

The answer to this 'French paradox' lies not in the occasional foray into ratatouille (vegetable stew) or bouillabaisse (a seafood stew from Marseille), but in the national habit of enjoying a glass of red wine nightly. Quite right, too, with such excellent choices at their doorstep – from the musty Bordeaux and cocky Côte du Rhône reds to a bouquet of Loire Valley varietals.

Modern Germans might have learnt to cut back just a little on the wurst (sausages) and smoked pork of their traditional cuisine, but both dishes are still prominent. Just try to have only a couple of the addictive Nuremberg sausages.

Other European regions have their own specialities: the Swiss are known for fondue, rösti, chocolate and cheese. The Belgians are renowned for their cuisine in general, including mussels and chips, chocolate and hundreds of varieties of beer. Greece has a penchant for lamb (such as in the gyros skewer), tangy cheeses like feta or haloumi, yogurt, hummus, eggplant (aubergine) and olives, all followed by honey-sweet baklava for dessert.

British food probably has the worst 'meat and three veg' reputation, and in parts of the country it's still unfortunately deserved. However, the larger cities boast just about every ethnic cuisine and London, in particular, is awash with world-class chefs. Here even old comfort food like bangers and mash or fish and chips are often given new twists (say, merguez sausages with mustard mash). If in doubt, order a curry; its links to the Indian subcontinent mean this is something at which Britain excels.

Finally, of course, Europe is a brilliant spot for an alcoholic tipple – from the French wines and Belgian beers already mentioned to German Weissbier (white 'wheat-beer'), Italian reds and Greece's aniseed liquor ouzo. We'll leave you to explore that subject yourself.

In many Belgian bars, you can choose from hundreds of beers, each served in its own unique glass with a little snack such as cheese. Spanish wine bars often serve dozens of snacks.

Over 350 cheeses are made in France (the three biggest are Camembert, Brie and Roquefort); Germany has almost as many varieties of sausages.

Andorra

People may tell you Andorra's nothing but skiing and shopping. They might add that Andorra la Vella, its capital and only town, is a fuming traffic jam bordered by palaces of consumerism. (Fact: Andorra has over 2000 shops – more than one for every 40 inhabitants.)

They're right to a point, but also way off course. Shake yourself from Andorra la Vella's tawdry embrace, take one of only three secondary roads in the state and discover some of the most dramatic scenery in all of the Pyrenees.

A warning though: this may not be the case a few years from now. Greed and uncontrolled development risk spoiling those side valleys. Already the pounding of jackhammers drowns out the winter thrum of ski lifts and threatens the silence of summer.

This minicountry wedged between France and Spain offers by far the best skiing in the Pyrenees. In the last five years, its resorts have invested over €50 million in mountain cafés and restaurants, chairlifts and gondolas, car parks and snow-making machines. And once the snows have melted, there's great walking in abundance, ranging from easy strolls to demanding day hikes in the higher, more remote reaches of the principality.

FAST FACTS

- **Area** 468 sq km
- **Capital** Andorra la Vella
- **Currency** euro (€); A$1 = €0.60; ¥100 = €0.67; NZ$1 = €0.50; UK£1 = €1.48; US$1 = €0.78
- **Famous for** skiing, shopping, smuggling
- **Phrases** *hola* (hello); *adéu* (goodbye); *si us plau* (please); *gràcies* (thanks)
- **Official Language** Catalan
- **Population** 76,900
- **Telephone Codes** country code ☎ 376; international access code ☎ 00

HIGHLIGHTS

- Shush your way over the snowfields of **Grandvalira** (p50).
- Tramp a sample of the walking trails that thread through the principality, especially those above **Ordino** (p51) and **Soldeu** (p50).
- Steep yourself in the warm mineral waters of the space-age **Caldea** (right).

HISTORY

From the Middle Ages until 1993, Andorra's sovereignty was vested in two 'princes': the bishop of the Spanish border town of La Seu d'Urgell and the French president (who got the job from France's pre-Revolutionary kings). Nowadays, democratic Andorra is a 'parliamentary coprincedom', the bishop and president remaining joint but nominal heads of state. Andorra is a member of the UN and the Council of Europe, but not a full member of the EU.

PEOPLE

A mere 36% of Andorra's inhabitants are Andorran nationals, a percentage equalled by the number of Spanish residents. The official language is Catalan, which is related to both Spanish and French. Most inhabitants speak a couple of these languages and most younger people, especially those in the capital and in ski resorts, can manage more than a smattering of English as well.

HOW MUCH?

- **Midrange hotel** €30-50
- **Restaurant meal** €15-35
- **Loaf of bread** €0.50
- **One-day ski-lift pass** €27-37
- **Cup of coffee** €1.25

LONELY PLANET INDEX

- **1L petrol** €0.90
- **1L water** €0.60
- **Small beer** €1
- **Souvenir T-shirt** €10-15
- **Medium pizza** €6-8

ANDORRA LA VELLA

pop 22,900 / elevation 1030m

Squeezed within the Riu Gran Valira Valley, Andorra la Vella (Vey-*yah*; literally 'old') is both the capital and sole town of this tiny principality. A small historic quarter remains but the place's main preoccupation is retailing electronic and luxury goods.

ORIENTATION

Andorra la Vella is strung out along the main drag, whose name changes confusingly from Avinguda del Príncep Benlloch to Avinguda de Meritxell to Avinguda de Carlemany along its length.

The town merges with the once-separate villages of Escaldes and Engordany to the east and Santa Coloma to the southwest.

INFORMATION

Internet Access

E-Café (Carrer l'Alziranet 5; per hr €2.40; 🕑 7.30am-11pm Mon-Sat, 10am-11pm Sun)

Future@point (Carrer de la Sardana 6; per hr €2.80; 🕑 10am-11pm Mon-Sat, 10am-10pm Sun)

Medical Services

Hospital Nostra Senyora de Meritxell (☎ 871 000; Avinguda Fiter i Rossell)

Post

Correus (Correos) i Telègrafs (Carrer Joan Maragall 10; 🕑 8.30am-2.30pm Mon-Fri, 9.30am-1pm Sat) Spanish post office.

La Poste (Carrer de Pere d'Urg 1; 🕑 8.30am-2.30pm Mon-Fri, 9am-noon Sat) French post office.

Tourist Information

Municipal tourist office (☎ 827 117; turisme@comuandorra.ad; Plaça de la Rotonda; 🕑 9am-1pm & 3.30-7pm Mon-Sat, 9am-1pm Sun Sep-Jun, 9am-9pm daily Jul & Aug) Also carries pan-Andorra information.

National tourist office (☎ 820 214; sindicatdiniciativa@andorra.ad; Edificio Davi, Local C, Carrer Doctor Vilanova 13; 🕑 9am-1pm & 3-7pm Mon-Sat, 10am-1pm Sun Jul-Sep, 10am-1pm & 3-7pm Mon-Sat Oct-Jun)

SIGHTS & ACTIVITIES

Pamper yourself at **Caldea** (☎ 800 999; www.caldea.ad; Parc de la Mola 10; adult/child €29.50/22; 🕑 10am-11pm, last entry 9pm) in Escaldes, just a 10-minute walk upstream from Plaça de la Rotonda. Looking like some futuristic cathedral, Caldea is Europe's largest spa

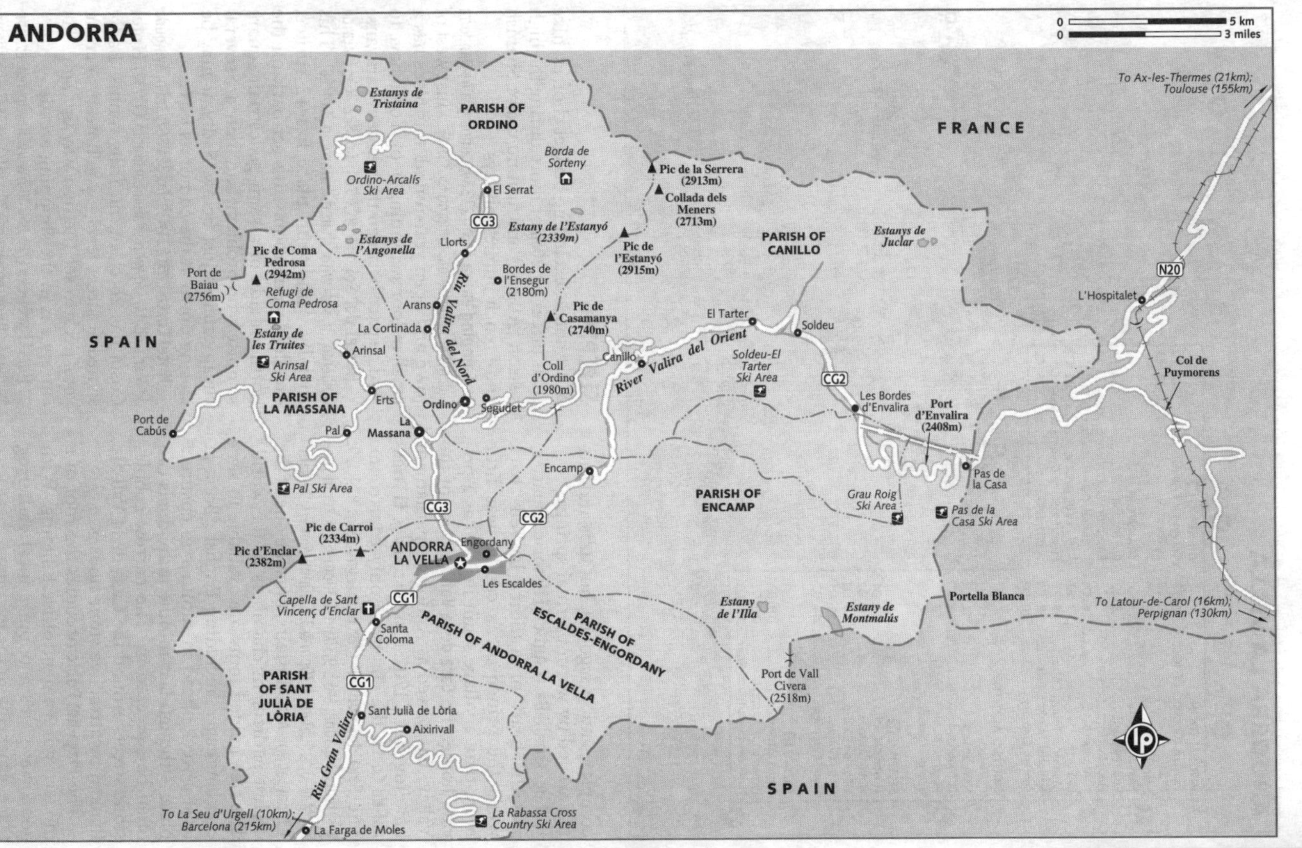
ANDORRA
0 5 km
0 3 miles
Estanys de Tristaina
PARISH OF ORDINO
Borda de Sorteny
FRANCE
To Ax-les-Thermes (21km); Toulouse (155km)
Pic de la Serrera (2913m)
Collada dels Meners (2713m)
Ordino-Arcalís Ski Area
El Serrat
CG3
Estany de l'Estanyó (2339m)
Pic de l'Estanyó (2915m)
PARISH OF CANILLO
Estanys de Juclar
Estanys de l'Angonella
Llorts
Pic de Coma Pedrosa (2942m)
Port de Baiau (2756m)
Refugi de Coma Pedrosa
Bordes de l'Ensegur (2180m)
Riu Valira del Nord
N20
L'Hospitalet
Arans
Pic de Casamanya (2740m)
El Tarter
Soldeu
Estany de les Truites
La Cortinada
SPAIN
Arinsal
Arinsal Ski Area
Coll d'Ordino (1980m)
Canillo
River Valira del Orient
Soldeu-El Tarter Ski Area
CG2
Col de Puymorens
PARISH OF LA MASSANA
Erts
Ordino
Segudet
Les Bordes d'Envalira
Port d'Envalira (2408m)
Port de Cabús
Pal
La Massana
Encamp
Pas de la Casa
PARISH OF ENCAMP
Grau Roig Ski Area
Pas de la Casa Ski Area
Pal Ski Area
CG3
CG2
Pic de Carroi (2334m)
Pic d'Enclar (2382m)
ANDORRA LA VELLA
Engordany
Les Escaldes
Capella de Sant Vicenç d'Enclar
CG1
Santa Coloma
PARISH OF ANDORRA LA VELLA
PARISH OF ESCALDES-ENGORDANY
Estany de l'Illa
Estany de Montmalús
Portella Blanca
To Latour-de-Carol (16km); Perpignan (130km)
Port de Vall Civera (2518m)
PARISH OF SANT JULIÀ DE LÒRIA
CG1
Sant Julià de Lòria
Aixirivall
Riu Gran Valira
SPAIN
To La Seu d'Urgell (10km); Barcelona (215km)
La Farga de Moles
La Rabassa Cross Country Ski Area

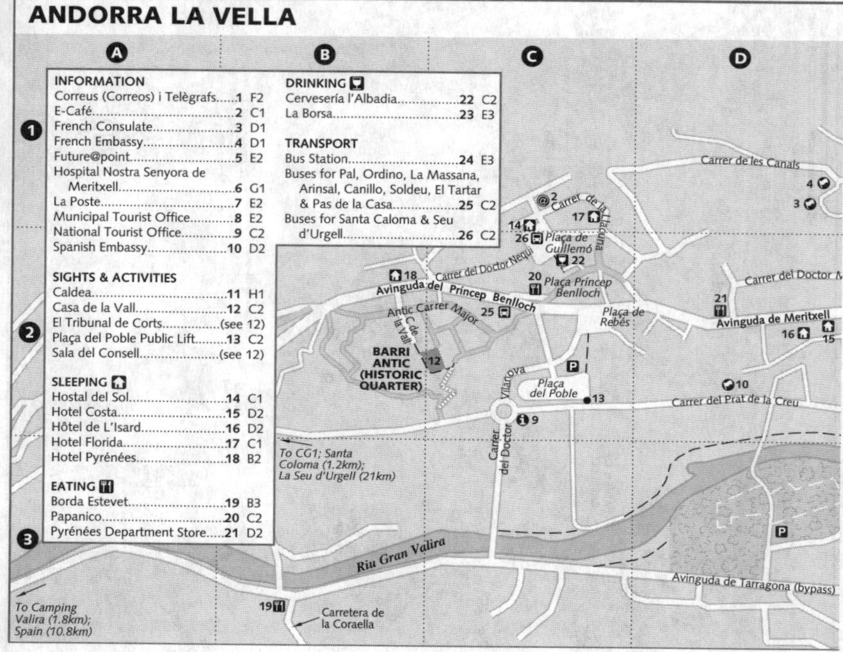

complex, and its lagoons, hot tubs and saunas are fed by warm thermal springs.

The small **Barri Antic** (Historic Quarter) was the heart of Andorra la Vella back when the principality's capital was little more than a village. Built in 1580 as a private home, the **Casa de la Vall** (House of the Valley) has served as Andorra's parliament building since 1702. Downstairs is **El Tribunal de Corts**, the country's only courtroom. The **Sala del Consell** (☎ tour reservations 829 129; tours 3-6.30pm Mon, 9.30am-1.30pm & 3-6.30pm Tue-Sat May-Oct, 9.30am-1.30pm & 3-6.30pm Mon-Fri, 9.30am-1.30pm Sat Nov-Apr), upstairs, must be one of the cosiest parliament chambers in the world. The free guided tours are available in several languages, including English. Book at least a week ahead in summer to ensure a place – though last-minute individuals can often be squeezed in. The narrow cobblestone streets around the Casa de la Vall are flanked by attractive stone houses.

The **Plaça del Poble** occupies the roof of a modern government office building. With good views, it's a popular local gathering place, especially in the evening.

SLEEPING

Most hotels, excluding budget choices, hike their prices by 20% or more during the high season (August) and around major Spanish and French public holidays.

Camping Valira (☎ 722 384; campingvalira@andorra.ad; Avinguda de Salou; camping €5.35;) Just west of town and open year-round, this place has a small indoor swimming pool. You'll have to find a space between the resident caravans.

Hostal del Sol (☎ 823 701; fax 822 363; Plaça de Guillemó 3; s/d with shared bathroom €14/28) This friendly, family-run place has 12 spruce, excellent-value rooms. It's set back on the northern side of a semi-pedestrian square so noise is no problem, and there are several cheap eateries just below. Sadly, it may be closing down at the end of its lease.

Hotel Costa (☎ 821 439; fax 824 867; 3rd fl, Avinguda de Meritxell 44; s/d with shared bathroom €17/32) Hotel Costa has 26 clean, no-frills rooms. Badly signed at street level – you'll need to crane your neck to see the sign way up high – its entrance is in the shopping arcade.

Hotel Pyrénées (☎ 860 006; www.hotelpyrenees.com; Avinguda del Príncep Benlloch 20; s/d from €35/56, half board

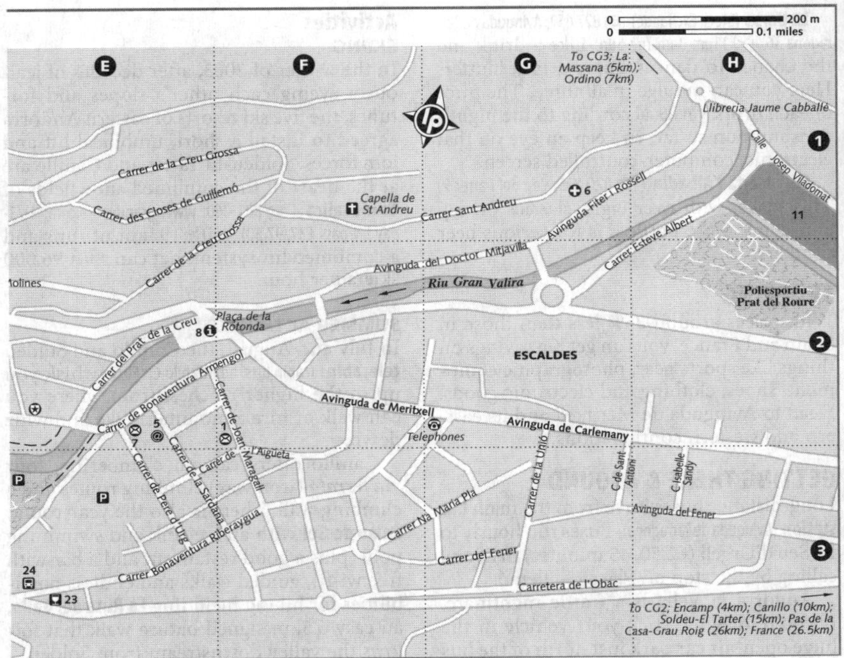

per person €69; (P)) Constructed in 1940 and speaking style, Hotel Pyrénées ranks among Andorra's few venerable buildings. Its 70 attractively furnished rooms have plenty of appealing dark woodwork. During the high season, half board is compulsory. Its restaurant (menu €15, mains €9 to €14) serves French and Spanish cuisine amid sparkling chandeliers and two-tone tablecloths. Parking costs €12.

Hotel Florida (☎ 820 105; www.hotelflorida.ad; Carrer de la Llacuna 15; s/d incl breakfast from €37/45) This welcoming modern hotel sits on a quiet side street. Relax in the sauna and *hammam* (Turkish bath), free for guests, or tone yourself up in the minigym. Rooms vary considerably in size – ask for one of the larger ones.

Hôtel de L'Isard (☎ 876 800; www.hotelisard.com, in French & Spanish; Avinguda Meritxell 36; incl breakfast s €56-80, d €71-110; (P)) Behind the attractive stone façade is a comfortable, family-run hotel. Ask for a room at the rear, overlooking the valley and mountain beyond. It also runs a good restaurant (menu €15, mains €10 to €14.50). Parking is €15.

EATING & DRINKING

In the heart of Barri Antic you'll find a few good restaurants specialising in local cuisine. Keep an eye out for the menu, a value-for-money option that usually comprises a three-course meal and (sometimes) drinks.

Pyrénées department store (Avinguda de Meritxell 21; salad/mains/platos combinados €4.95/4.65/7.25) The top-floor cafeteria and restaurant of this megastore offers great fare at reasonable prices. Pile your salad plate high at the self-service buffet and follow it with the dish of the day, or select from one of the *platos combinados* (mixed plate). One floor down is a well-stocked supermarket.

Papanico (☎ 867 333; Avinguda del Príncep Benlloch 4; mains €9.50-13) This cheery place does tasty tapas from €2.95 and a range of sandwiches and mains.

Borda Estevet (☎ 864 026; Carretera de la Comella 2; mains €14.60-18.50, menu €35.50) Here's a place for meaty mountain fare. Try its *graellada de muntanya*, a selection of meats and sausages sizzled on hot slates. Among the chef's many accolades and commendations is the intriguing Golden Cock Award.

La Borsa (Stock Exchange; ☎ 827 657; Avinguda de Tarragona 36; 11pm-3am Tue-Sun) Like a drink and the chance to dance? Enjoy a little flutter? Here you can indulge in all three. The price of each drink varies according to the night's consumption so far, so keep an eye on that electronic, computer-controlled screen.

Cervesería l'Albadia (☎ 820 825; Cap del Carrer 2) This place, with over eight classics on tap and many more bottled, is for serious beer drinkers.

SHOPPING

With prices around 25% less than those in Spain and France, you can get big savings on things like sports gear, photographic equipment, shoes, clothing and electronic goods. Head to Avinguda de Meritxell and its eastern and western continuations.

GETTING THERE & AROUND

Long-distance buses leave from the main **bus station** (Avinguda de Tarragona). Buses run hourly to La Seu d'Urgell (€2.50, 45 minutes) in Spain, calling by the stop on Plaça Guillemó.

Andorra la Vella is a traffic nightmare. If you're driving, stick your vehicle in the huge open-air car park just north of the bus station. To order a taxi call ☎ 863 000.

AROUND ANDORRA LA VELLA

SANT JULIÀ DE LÒRIA

Here, 6km south of Andorra la Vella, is the splendid **Museu del Tabac** (☎ 741 545; Carrer Doctor Palau 17; admission €5; 10am-8pm Tue-Sat, 10am-2.30pm Sun). Occupying a one-time tobacco factory, it recalls the pleasurable sins of tobacco and smuggling. Three rooms are furnished with the trappings of tobacco cultivation, and cigarette and cigar making; there's an optional English audio accompaniment and a 15-minute film. Allow at least an hour.

CANILLO & SOLDEU

Canillo (1500m), 11km northeast of Andorra la Vella, and Soldeu, a further 7km up the valley along the CG2, share a helpful **tourist office** (☎ 751 090; www.vdc.ad; 9am-1pm & 3-7pm Mon-Sat, 8am-4pm Sun), on the main road at the eastern end of Canillo.

Activities

SKIING

In the winter of 2003, after decades of jealously eyeing each other's slopes and fortunes, the five ski resorts of eastern Andorra agreed to install a short, umbilical lift and join forces. Soldeu-El Tarter and Canillo are at the heart of the combined snowfields of **Grandvalira** (☎ 801 060; www.grandvalira.com; 1-/3-day lift pass €37/97.50), with 193km of runs and a combined lift system that can shift 96,000 skiers per hour.

SUMMER ACTIVITIES

In July and August, the Canillo and Soldeu **telecabins** (cabin lifts; adult/child €8.50/7) whisk you up to the higher reaches, from where you can walk or hire a mountain bike and whiz down.

Canillo offers canyon clambering, four *via ferrata* (iron way) climbing routes and a climbing wall. There is also the year-round **Palau de Gel** with an ice rink and swimming pool (plus a good restaurant and a bar with free wi-fi), guided walks and endless possibilities for hiking including **La Ruta del Gallo**, an easy 6.5km signed nature walk that follows the valley downstream from Soldeu.

You'll find a week's worth of walks around Canillo and Soldeu in Lonely Planet's *Walking in Spain*.

Sleeping & Eating

Camping Santa Creu (☎ 851 462; camping_santacreu@yahoo.com; camping €3.50; mid-Jun–Sep) The greenest and quietest of Canillo's five camping grounds.

Hotel Roc de Sant Miquel (☎ 851 079; www.hotel-roc.com; half board per person winter €30-68, summer €27-45; Nov-Apr & Jun-Sep) This relaxed, laid-back Soldeu hotel – the owner also plays lead guitar in a local band – hires out mountain bikes to guests and can arrange nature walks and hikes.

Hotel Bonavida (☎ 851 300; hotel.bonavida@andorra.ad; Plaça Major; per person incl breakfast Dec-Apr €40-59, Jun-Oct €34-40; P) Most of the rooms at the Bonavida, right beside Canillo's *telecabin*, have balconies overlooking the river and mountain beyond. The copious buffet breakfast includes real espresso coffee.

Cal Lulu (☎ 851 427; Canillo; pizzas €7.50-10.35, menu €13.60, mains €16-18; daily high season, Wed-Sun low season) Divided into small booths, intimate and often packed to the gills Cal Lulu serves large portions of excellent Catalan and French dishes.

Hotel Bruxelles (menus €11.10-20.30) A cheerful hotel restaurant on Soldeu's main drag with a small terrace, well-filled sandwiches, whopping burgers and tasty menus.

Getting There & Around

Hourly buses run from Andorra la Vella to Soldeu (€2.50) via Canillo till 8pm. In winter hourly ski buses (free if you flash your ski pass) also cover the same route.

ORDINO & AROUND

Despite ongoing development Ordino, 8km north of Andorra la Vella on highway CG3, is a charming village with most buildings constructed of local stone. At 1300m, it's a good starting point for summer-activity holidays. The **tourist office** (☎ 737 080; www.ordino.ad; 8am-7pm Mon-Sat, 9am-5pm Sun Jul-Sep, 8.30am-1.30pm & 3-6pm Mon-Sat, 9am-1pm Sun Oct-Jun) is within the Centre Esportiu d'Ordino sports complex beside the CG3.

Sights & Activities

Museu d'Areny i Plandolit (☎ 836 908; adult/student €2.40/1.20; 9am-9pm Tue-Sat, 10am-2pm Sun Jul & Aug, 9.30am-1.30pm & 3-6.30pm Tue-Sat, 10am-2pm Sun Sep-Jun), in a 17th-century manor house, offers half-hour guided tours, in Spanish or Catalan, of its richly furnished interior.

In the same grounds the **Museo Postal de Andorra** (adult/student €2.40/1.20; 9am-9pm Tue-Sat, 10am-2pm Sun Jul & Aug, 9.30am-1.30pm & 3-6.30pm Tue-Sat, 10am-2pm Sun Sep-Jun) is fun, even for non-philatelists. It has a 15-minute audiovisual presentation (available in English) and set upon set of stamps issued by France and Spain specifically for Andorra.

There are several excellent walking trails around Ordino. Pick up *Thirtysix Interesting Itineraries on the Paths of the Vall d'Ordino & the Parish of La Massana* (€2) from the tourist office. Walk descriptions are altogether more taut than the title.

Sleeping & Eating

Camping Borda d'Ansalonga (☎ 850 374; www.campingansalonga.com; person/tent/car €4.80/4/4; mid-Jun–mid-Sep;) This large, grassy option enjoys an attractive valley site just outside the village.

Hotel Santa Bàrbara de la Vall d'Ordino (☎ 738 100; www.santabarbara-hotel.com; Plaça d'Ordino; s/d €45/60; P) Above the main square and facing the church, this 21-room, family-run hotel with a small, attractive bar is excellent value. Its two large split-level rooms (€96) are ideal for a family or two couples.

Casa León (☎ 835 977; menu €12.50-18.50; Tue-Sun) This restaurant offers a wide range of tapas and plentiful à la carte meat and fish dishes (€9.50 to €15).

Bar Restaurant Quim (menu €10) Next door to Casa León, this place is friendly and more snacky than its neighbour, with plenty of tapas and a filling midday menu.

Getting There & Away

Buses to/from Andorra la Vella (€1) run every half hour from 7am to 9pm.

ARINSAL & PAL

In winter Arinsal, 10km northwest of Andorra la Vella, has good skiing and snowboarding and a lively après-ski scene. It's linked with the smaller ski station of Pal, in turn part of the **Vallnord complex** (www.vallnord.com; 1-day lift pass low season/high season €27/32). They have 63km of pistes with a vertical drop of 1010m.

In summer Pal has a wealth of activities including mountain biking, horse riding, go-karting and archery. From Arinsal, a good departure point for many a mountain walk, a trail leads northwest then west to **Estany de les Truites** (2260m), a natural lake with a staffed mountain hut that has beds, refreshments and meals.

Sleeping & Eating

Camping Xixerella (☎ 836 613; www.campingxixerella.com; camping €4.95; Nov-Sep;) Between Pal and Arinsal, this large, well-equipped site has plenty of shade and greenness.

Hotel Coma Pedrosa (☎ 737 950; hotelcomapedrosa@hotmail.com; d €40, half board per person €30; Apr-Nov) The new owners of this welcoming place have brightened the rooms up. Most have a bathtub, there's free public parking and you can relax in the cosy bar. In winter, it's fully occupied by ski tour operators.

Refugi de la Fondue (☎ 839 599; dishes €14) As a change from the plentiful snack and sandwich joints, dip a fork into cheese or meat fondue dishes. In summer it puts on outdoor barbecues.

Restaurant el Moli (☎ 835 281; pasta & pizzas €7.50-9.75) Billing itself as Italian, Restaurant

AUTHOR'S CHOICE

Hostal Pobladó (☎ 835 122; sti@andorra.ad; B&B per person €30, with shared bathroom €22.50; Dec-Oct;) Hostal Pobladó sits right beside the *telecabin*, handy for skiing in winter and for taking off on summer day walks. It's friendliness itself and a great place to make contact with other skiers or walkers. There's a lively bar with an Internet point (€3 per hour) and you couldn't be more at the heart of the action.

el Moli indeed offers the usual staple pastas and pizzas. However, the chefs are Argentinean and also offer more exotic fare such as Thai green coconut chicken curry (€12). Both restaurants are located on the main drag.

Getting There & Away

Nine daily buses leave Andorra la Vella for Arinsal (€1.50) via La Massana. There are also at least nine local buses daily between La Massana and Arinsal (€0.90) and four buses between La Massana and Pal (€0.90).

ANDORRA DIRECTORY

ACCOMMODATION

Tourist offices stock a free booklet, *Guia d'Allotjaments Turístics,* but it's not comprehensive and, while the rest of the information is reliable, the prices it quotes are merely indicative.

Outside Andorra la Vella there are few budget options for independent travellers. To compensate there are plenty of camping grounds, many beautifully situated. During the high season (December to March, July and August) some hotels raise prices substantially, won't take independent travellers and may insist upon half board.

For trekkers, Andorra has 26 off-the-beaten-track *refugis* (mountain refuges), all except one are unstaffed and free; ask at tourist offices for the free *Mapa de Refugis i Grans Recorreguts,* which pinpoints and describes them all.

Unless otherwise noted, prices quoted for accommodation in this chapter include private bathroom.

ACTIVITIES

Above the main valleys you'll find attractive lake-dotted mountain country, good for skiing in winter and walking in summer. The largest and best ski stations are those of the Grandvalira complex (p50). Those within Vallnord (p51) in northwestern Andorra are cheaper but can be colder and windier. Downhill ski-gear hire costs around €10 per day, while snowboards go for €17.50 to €20 per day.

La Rabassa, nudged up against the frontier with Spain, is a great little cross-country skiing centre with 15km of marked forest trails.

In summer, you can rent mountain bikes from some resorts for €15 to €18 a day.

BUSINESS HOURS

Banks are open from 9am to 1pm and 3pm to 5pm Monday through Friday, and from 9am to noon Saturday. Restaurants open their doors from 1pm to 3.30pm and 8pm to 10.30pm. Shops are generally open from 9.30am to 1pm and 3.30pm to 8pm Monday to Saturday then from 9.30am to 1pm on Sunday.

EMBASSIES & CONSULATES

Andorran Embassies & Consulates

Andorra has embassies in both France and Spain.

France (☎ 01 40 06 03 30; place d'Andorre 1, 75016 Paris)

Spain (☎ 91 431 74 53; Calle Alcalá 73, 28009 Madrid)

Embassies & Consulates in Andorra

France and Spain maintain reciprocal missions in Andorra la Vella.

France (Map pp48-9; ☎ 736 730; Carrer de la Sobrevia 7, Andorra la Vella)

Spain (Map pp48-9; ☎ 820 013; Carrer del Prat de la Creu 34, Andorra la Vella)

INTERNET RESOURCES

Two useful websites are www.andorra.ad, the official site of the Ministry of Tourism & Environment, and www.turismeandorra.com, run by the local hotel association.

POST

Andorra has no postal system of its own; France and Spain each operate separate systems with their own stamps for Andorra (you can't use regular French or Spanish stamps).

It's swifter to route international mail (except letters to Spain) through the French postal system. Tourist offices sell stamps.

TELEPHONE

The cheapest way to make an international call is to buy a *teletarja* (phonecard), sold at tourist offices and kiosks for €3 to €6; ring during off-peak hours (9pm to 8am Monday to Saturday and all day Sunday).

EMERGENCY NUMBERS

Police, fire, ambulance ☎ 112

TRANSPORT IN ANDORRA

GETTING THERE & AWAY

Unless you trek across the mountains the only way to reach Andorra is by road from neighbouring Spain or France. If you're driving, top up your tank when you get there; fuel in Andorra is about 20% cheaper than in Spain and a good 30% cheaper than in France.

Spain

Alsina Graells (☎ 826 567; www.alsinagraells.com) Four buses daily to/from Barcelona's Estació del Nord (€20, 3½ hours).

Autocars Nadal (☎ 805 151; www.autocarsnadal.com, in Spanish & French) Six buses daily to/from Barcelona's airport (€26, 3¾ hours), calling by the city's Sants train station (€21, 3¼ hours).

Autocars Novatel (☎ 803 789; www.andorrabybus.com) Five buses daily to/from Barcelona's airport (€26, 3½ hours).

La Hispano Andorrana (☎ 821 372; www.hispanoandorrana.com) Hourly buses between Andorra la Vella and La Seu d'Urgell (€2.50, 40 minutes).

Viatges Montmantell (☎ 807 444) Four buses daily to/from Lleida (€17, 2½hours) to connect with the Madrid-bound high-speed AVE train. Services stop outside La Caldea.

France

Autocars Nadal Twice each Friday and Sunday to/from Toulouse's bus station (€21, 3½ hours).

Autocars Novatel Two minibuses daily to/from Toulouse's airport and train station (€29, 3½ hours).

GETTING AROUND

Six bus routes run by **Cooperativa Interurbana** (☎ 806 555) radiate out from Andorra la Vella along the three main roads. Tourist offices carry a free leaflet with timetables.

The speed limit is 40km/h in populated areas and 90km/h elsewhere. Two irritations while at the wheel in Andorra are the recklessness of local drivers and Andorra la Vella's horrendous traffic jams – bypass the latter by taking the ring road around the south side of town.

Austria

It sounds clichéd to say, but this country really is alive with the sound of music. Mozart's symphonies waft through the cobbled streets of Salzburg like Julie Andrews floating around the picturesque Austrian countryside. The story of Austria is surely an opera, a concerto, a work in progress, complete with elaborate sets and a plot that's as bloody as it is beautiful. Monarchs, political instability, assassinations and the Great War narrate just one side of the story, however. Juxtaposed against them is incredible natural beauty blanketed in an edifying patchwork of depth and character like no other. Gorgeous enough to make you gasp in awe, its snow-capped peaks stare back at you with jagged smiles. Its verdant valleys, strewn with summer wildflowers, make the perfect outdoor playground. Graceful old cities exude genteel airs of times long past and even the smallest rural villages are cultural reservoirs rich in history. In Austria the past is as pertinent as the present and the country surprises with its ability to change without sacrificing its time-honoured heritage and traditions.

FAST FACTS

- **Area** 83,855 sq km
- **Capital** Vienna
- **Currency** euro (€); A$1 = €0.60; ¥100 = €0.67; NZ$1 = €0.50; UK£1 = €1.48; US$1 = €0.78
- **Famous for** apple strudel, Wiener schnitzel, Adolf Hitler, Arnold Schwarzenegger, Freudian psychoanalysis
- **Official Language** German (Slovene, Croat and Hungarian are also official languages in some southern states)
- **Phrases** *Grüss Gott* (hello); *Servus!* (hello and goodbye); *Ba Ba* (bye bye)
- **Population** 8.2 million
- **Telephone Codes** country code ☎ 43; international access code ☎ 00

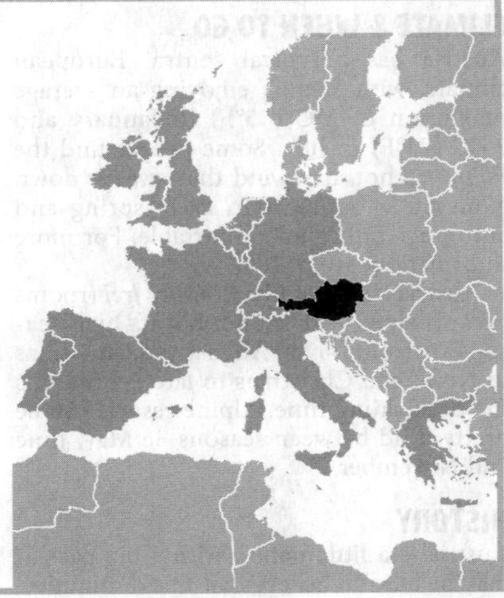

HIGHLIGHTS

- Take in art from a completely different standing (literally) at the popular **Kunst HausWien** (p65) by Friedensreich Hundertwasser in Vienna.
- Relive scenes from *The Sound of Music* while singing along on a fabulously kitsch tour in the picture-postcard city of **Salzburg** (p82).
- Experience Tyrolean culture with plenty of recreation opportunities and nightlife on the side in **Innsbruck** (p93) or **Mayrhofen** (p97).
- Road-trip through the Hohe Tauern National Park along one of the world's most scenic highways, the **Grossglockner Hochalpenstrasse** (p99).
- Gaze at what locals have dubbed 'the friendly alien', the spaceship-shaped **Kunsthaus Graz** (arts centre; p79) in Graz.

ITINERARIES

- **Two days** Spend this entire time in Vienna, making sure to visit the Habsburg palaces and the Riesenrad before cosying up in a *Kaffeehaus* (coffee house). At night check out the pumping bar scene or catch a Vienna Boys' Choir concert.
- **One week** Spend three days in Vienna, plus one day on a wine tour in the Wachau, a day each in Salzburg and Innsbruck, and one day visiting the Salzkammergut lakes district to hike or ski (depending on the season).

HOW MUCH?

- **1L milk** €0.95
- **Loaf of bread** from €1.20
- **Bottle of house white wine market/restaurant** from €3/10
- **Newspaper** €0.80 to €1.45
- **Short taxi ride** €5

LONELY PLANET INDEX

- **1L petrol** €1
- **1L bottled water** €0.40 to €2.50
- **Bottle of beer** from €2.50
- **Souvenir T-shirt** €15
- **Street snack (wurst)** €3

CLIMATE & WHEN TO GO

Austria has a typical central European climate, with Vienna enjoying an average maximum of 2°C (35°F) in January and 25°C (77°F) in July. Some people find the *Föhn* – a hot, dry wind that sweeps down from the mountains in early spring and autumn – rather uncomfortable. For more information, see p1100.

Austria hangs out its *Zimmer frei* (rooms vacant) signs year-round, but its high seasons are from July to August and Christmas to New Year. Christmas to late February is the peak skiing time. Alpine resorts can be pretty dead between seasons, ie May, June and November.

HISTORY

Austria is a little nation with a big past. It may be hard to believe that this diminutive, landlocked Alpine country, bordering eight other states (Germany, Switzerland, Liechtenstein, Italy, Slovenia, Hungary, Slovakia and the Czech Republic) was once the epicentre of the mighty Habsburg empire and, in the 20th century, a pivotal player in the outbreak of WWI. For centuries the Habsburgs used strategic marriages to maintain their hold over a territory now encompassing parts of today's Bosnia-Hercogovina, Croatia, Poland, Romania, the majority of the aforementioned proximate nations and, for a period, even Germany. But defeat in WWI brought that to an end, when the small republic of Austria was formed in 1918.

There had been military and political struggles before. Twice the neighbouring Ottoman Empire reached Vienna, in 1529 and 1683. In 1805 Napoleon defeated Austria at Austerlitz. Austrian Chancellor Metternich cleverly reconsolidated Austria's power in 1815 after Waterloo, but in the 1866 Austro-Prussian War the country (hampered by an internal workers' revolution in 1848) lost control of the German Confederation. At this point the empire's Hungarian politicians asserted themselves and forced the formation of Austria-Hungary.

However, these setbacks pale beside Archduke Franz Ferdinand's assassination by Slavic separatists in Sarajevo on 28 June 1914. When his uncle, the Austro-Hungarian emperor Franz Josef, declared war on Serbia

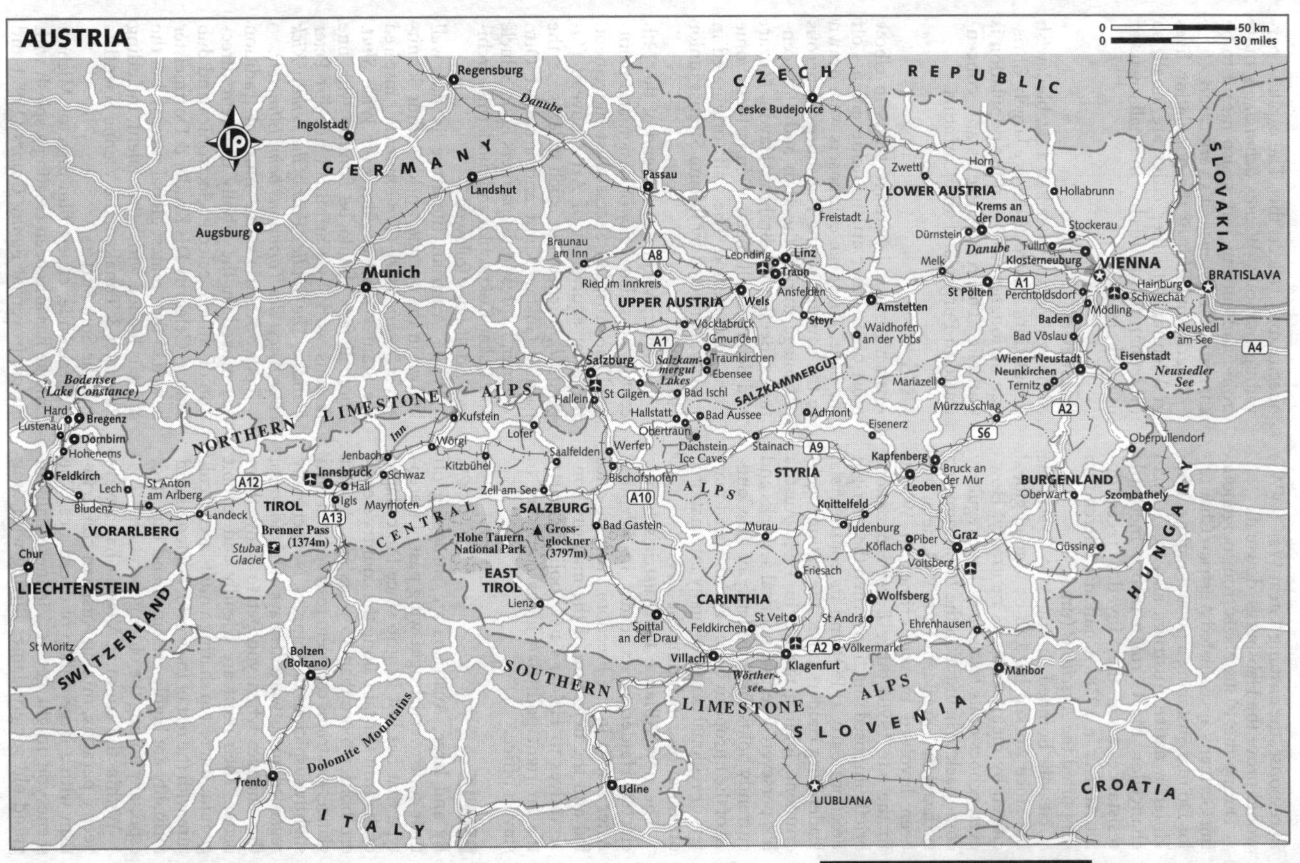
AUSTRIA
0 50 km
0 30 miles
CZECH REPUBLIC
SLOVAKIA
BRATISLAVA
HUNGARY
CROATIA
SLOVENIA
LJUBLJANA
ITALY
SWITZERLAND
LIECHTENSTEIN
GERMANY
Munich
Regensburg
Danube
Ingolstadt
Landshut
Augsburg
Passau
Ceske Budejovice
Bodensee (Lake Constance)
Hard
Lustenau
Bregenz
Dornbirn
Hohenems
Feldkirch
Lech
St Anton am Arlberg
Bludenz
VORARLBERG
Chur
St Moritz
NORTHERN LIMESTONE ALPS
Inn
Kufstein
Wörgl
Jenbach
Innsbruck
Schwaz
Hall
Igls
Kitzbühel
Mayrhofen
A12
A13
TIROL
Landeck
Brenner Pass (1374m)
Stubai Glacier
CENTRAL ALPS
Lofer
Saalfelden
Zell am See
SALZBURG
Hohe Tauern National Park
Grossglockner (3797m)
EAST TIROL
Lienz
Braunau am Inn
A8
Ried im Innkreis
UPPER AUSTRIA
Salzburg
St Gilgen
Hallein
A1
Vöcklabruck
Gmunden
Salzkammergut Lakes
Traunkirchen
Ebensee
Bad Ischl
SALZKAMMERGUT
Hallstatt
Bad Aussee
Obertraun
Dachstein Ice Caves
Werfen
Bischofshofen
A10
Bad Gastein
Leonding
Linz
Traun
Ansfelden
Wels
Steyr
Freistadt
Admont
Stainach
A9
STYRIA
Murau
Spittal an der Drau
CARINTHIA
Feldkirchen
St Veit
Villach
Wörthersee
Klagenfurt
A2
Völkermarkt
SOUTHERN LIMESTONE ALPS
Bolzen (Bolzano)
Dolomite Mountains
Trento
Udine
Zwettl
Horn
LOWER AUSTRIA
Krems an der Donau
Dürnstein
Danube
Melk
St Pölten
Amstetten
Waidhofen an der Ybbs
Mariazell
Eisenerz
Kapfenberg
Bruck an der Mur
Leoben
Knittelfeld
Judenburg
Friesach
Piber
Köflach
Voitsberg
Graz
Wolfsberg
St Andrä
Ehrenhausen
Maribor
Mürzzuschlag
S6
Hollabrunn
Stockerau
Tulln
Klosterneuburg
VIENNA
Perchtoldsdorf
Hainburg
Schwechat
Mödling
Baden
Bad Vöslau
Neusiedl am See
A4
Wiener Neustadt
Neunkirchen
Ternitz
Eisenstadt
Neusiedler See
Oberpullendorf
BURGENLAND
Oberwart
Szombathely
Güssing

AUSTRIA

in response, the ensuing 'Great War' (WWI) would prove the Habsburgs' downfall.

During the 1930s Nazis from neighbouring Germany assassinated Austrian Chancellor Dolfuss, installing a puppet regime. With Hitler, a native Austrian, also as German chancellor, the German troops met little resistance when they invaded recession-hit Austria in 1938. A national referendum supported the *Anschluss* (union).

Heavily bombed during WWII, Austria has since worked hard to be a good global citizen by maintaining its neutrality. However, echoes of its fascist past have regularly come back to haunt it. In the 1980s rumours surfaced that President Kurt Waldheim had been involved in war crimes in WWII. In the late 1990s other European nations briefly imposed sanctions when the far-right Freedom Party (FPÖ) and its controversial leader, Jörg Haider, joined the national government. Joining the EU in 1995, Austria has persevered despite political setbacks and currently holds the Presidency of the Council of the European Union and the headquarters or regional centre of many international organisations, including the UN.

The new Alliance for Austria's Future elected Haider as its leader in Salzburg. After a split in the Freedom Party he once led and the defection of the majority conservatives to Haider's new political party, the far-right politician looks confident to stay in office.

PEOPLE

By and large, Austrians are shrugging off their controversial right-wing past, a stereotype that has lost its grip since the collapse of the Iron Curtain along the country's eastern border more than 15 years ago. At first glance, Austrians can seem reserved and even slightly suspicious of strangers. Not generally regarded for outward displays of friendliness, this changes when you get to know them better. Then most are friendly and exhibit genuine interest in sharing a multifaceted culture with the rest of the world. Politeness and formality are highly esteemed and expected, especially among the older generation.

Within the country, Vienna has always been a paradox, mixing Austrian conservatism with a large dollop of decadence. The scene you might get at Viennese balls of grand old society dames flirting with drag queens aptly reflects this. The capital's pervading humour, *Wiener Schmäh,* is quite ironic and cutting, but is also meant to be charming. In essence, it's very camp.

Nearly one-fifth of the population lives in Vienna, but other cities are small, so more than two-thirds live in small towns or in rural areas.

RELIGION

Although Vienna once had a sizable Jewish population, Austria today is a largely Christian nation. Some 80% of the population is Catholic. The rest is Protestant, concentrated in Burgenland and Carinthia.

ARTS

Austria's musical heritage tends to elbow most of its other artistic achievements off the page. European composers were drawn to the country by the Habsburgs' generous patronage during the 18th and 19th centuries: Beethoven, Brahms, Haydn, Mozart and Schubert all made Vienna their home during this period. The waltz originated in the city, perfected by Johann Strauss junior (1825–99).

However, Vienna at the end of the 19th century was also a city of design and painting. The Austrian Secessionist movement, the local equivalent of Art Nouveau *(Jugendstil),* turned out such talents as the painter Gustav Klimt and architect Otto Wagner. Expressionist painters Egon Schiele and Oskar Kokoschka and modernist architect Adolf Loos followed.

While Austrian literature is not well known in the outside world, Arthur Schnitzler's *Dream Story (Traumnovelle)* inspired the Stanley Kubrick film *Eyes Wide Shut.* Football fans should be familiar with one famous work by Carinthian novelist Peter Handke, *The Goalie's Fear of the Penalty Kick (Der Angst des Tormanns beim Elfmeter).*

Today Austria's fine musical tradition has moved in the wholly different direction of chilled, eclectic electronica and dub lounge. Celebrity DJs Kruder & Dorfmeister have had the greatest global success, but the scene is loaded with other talent, including Pulsinger & Tunakan, the Vienna Scientists and the Sofa Surfers.

Meanwhile, expert film director Michael Haneke has also been creating a splash with his controversial *Funny Games* (1997) and the twisted romance of the much-lauded *The Piano Teacher* (2001). The country's most famous TV export is the detective series *Inspector Rex (Kommisar Rex)*. As well as being big in Germany and Australia, Rex, a German shepherd dog who regularly proves invaluable to his police owners, apparently has a cult following in some 93 countries. In recent times perhaps the most noteworthy Austrian imprint to be stamped on the world (and particularly the USA) is former professional bodybuilder/actor turned politician, and current governor of the state of California, Arnold Schwarzenegger, who was born near Graz.

ENVIRONMENT

More than half of Austria's 83,855 sq km is mountainous. Three chains run west to east: the Northern Limestone Alps, the Central (or High) Alps, which have the tallest peaks in Austria, including the 3797m Grossglockner, and the Southern Limestone Alps. They are banded around the middle and the south of the country, occupying most of its western half, and leaving flats around the Danube Valley and Vienna in the northeast and Graz to the southeast.

Meadows and forests cover much of the country. Although Austria is home to Europe's largest national park, Hohe Tauern, only 3% of its landmass is national park. These protected wilderness areas are good places to spot wildlife, such as marmots. Hohe Tauern itself has many species of alpine wildflower, and the bearded vulture and lyre-horned ibex were reintroduced in recent years.

Austria is highly environmentally conscious and no one wants to spoil the pristine landscape by littering. Recycling and biocompost bins are ubiquitous throughout the country.

FOOD & DRINK

Staples & Specialities

There's more to Austrian cuisine than *Wiener schnitzel* (a veal or pork cutlet coated in breadcrumbs). Traces of the country's wider historical reach endure in the Hungarian paprika used to flavour several dishes, including *Gulasch* (beef stew), and in the Styrian polenta and pumpkinseed oil popular in Italian and Slovenian cuisine respectively. Some staples like wurst (sausage) and regional dishes, such as *Tiroler Bauernschmaus* – a selection of meats served with sauerkraut, potatoes and dumplings – can be very fatty and stodgy. However, hearty soups often include *Knödel* (dumplings) or pasta.

Besides *Strudel* (filo pastry filled with a variety of fruits, poppy seeds or cheese), *Salzburger Nockerl* (a fluffy soufflé) is a popular Austrian dessert.

Known for its lager beer – from brands like Gösser, Schwechater, Stiegl and Zipfer to *Weizenbier* (wheat beer) – Austria also produces some white wines in its east. *Heuriger* wine is the latest vintage, and is avidly consumed, even in autumn while still semi-fermented (called *Sturm*).

Where to Eat & Drink

A traditional Austrian inn is called a *Beissl* or *Stüberl*. A *Beissl* (from the Hebrew word for 'house') tends to be more about meeting friends and having a drink, with food a necessary but ancillary pastime, whereas the emphasis is usually more on the food itself in a *Stüberl* (from the word *Stube*, meaning 'cosy living room'). Not all *Beissl* or *Stüberl* will be 100% traditional; however, only a few of them in the middle of Vienna are touristy enough to be wary of.

Of course, lots of Asian restaurants and pizzerias dot the countryside. These, in addition to the dumplings in local cuisine, mean that vegetarians shouldn't have any trouble finding satisfying meals.

For cheap food, try *Mensens* (university canteens). The main meal is at noon, when many restaurants provide a good-value *Tagesteller* or *Tagesmenu* (set meal).

VIENNA

☎ 01 / pop 1.6 million

The Ottomans referred to Vienna (Wien) as the city of the 'golden apple', but this crossroads of Eastern and Western Europe is more akin to a big wedding cake; a vivacious, multilayered concoction, stuffed full with galleries, museums and exhibitions, and a sensation of resuscitated times past. The demarcation between antiquity and contemporary is hazily represented here. Take the time to absorb the copious vestiges of grandiose marzipan-like buildings filling the streets, and the many ornate

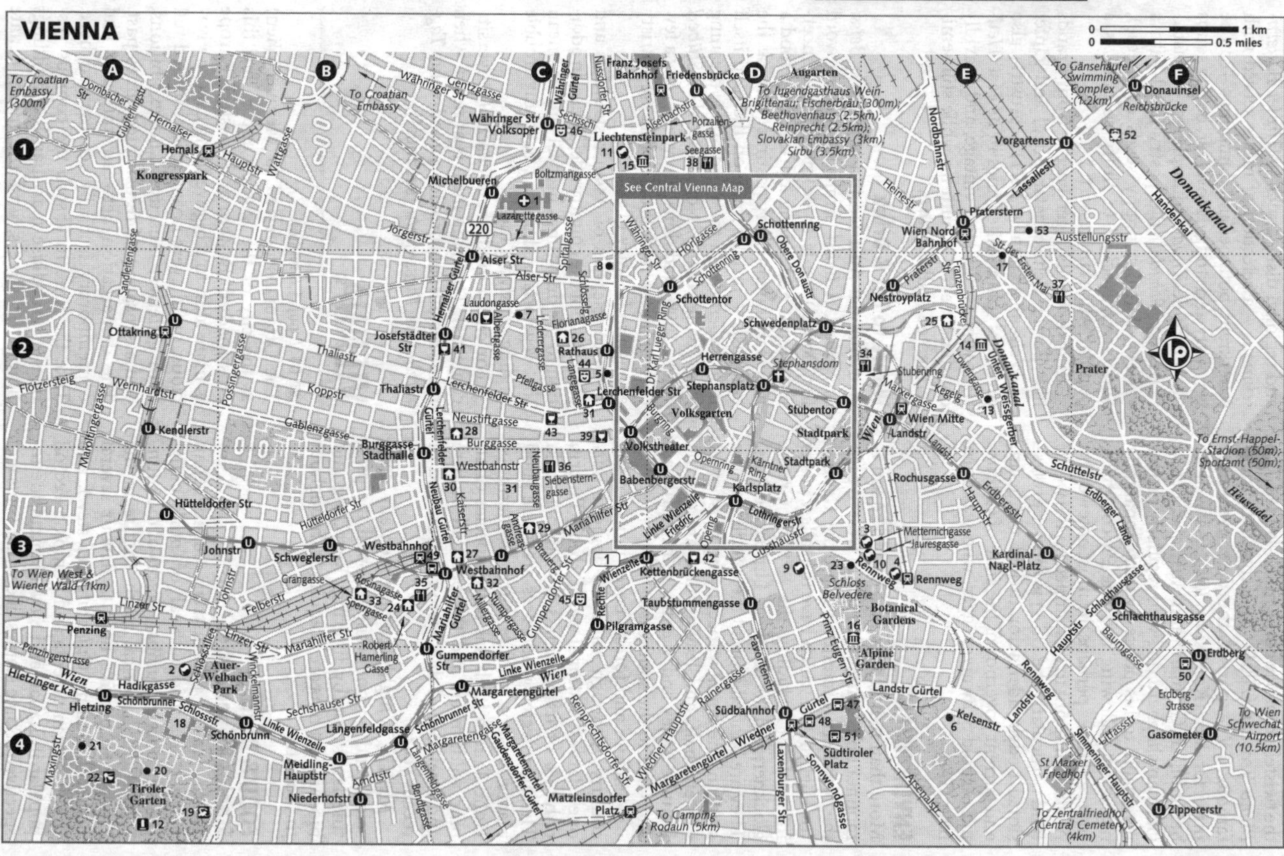
VIENNA
0 1 km
0 0.5 miles
See Central Vienna Map
To Croatian Embassy (300m)
To Croatian Embassy
To Gänsehäufel Swimming Complex (1.2km)
To Jugendgasthaus Wien-Brigittenau; Fischerbräu (300m); Beethovenhaus (2.5km); Reinprecht (2.5km); Slovakian Embassy (3km); Sirbu (3.5km)
To Ernst-Happel-Stadion (50m); Sportamt (50m);
To Wien Schwechat Airport (10.5km)
To Zentralfriedhof (Central Cemetery) (4km)
To Camping Rodaun (5km)
To Wien West & Wiener Wald (1km)
Donaukanal
Donauinsel
Reichsbrücke
Handelskai
Prater
Praterstern
Lassallestr
Vorgartenstr
Ausstellungsstr
Nordbahnstr
Wien Nord Bahnhof
Franzenbrücke Str
Nestroyplatz
Untere Weissgerber
Wien Mitte
Landstr
Rochusgasse
Erdbergstr
Kardinal-Nagl-Platz
Schlachthausgasse
Erdberg
Gasometer
Zippererstr
Simmeringer Hauptstr
St Marxer Friedhof
Rennweg
Botanical Gardens
Alpine Garden
Schloss Belvedere
Landstr Gürtel
Arsenalstr
Südtiroler Platz
Südbahnhof
Laxenburger Str
Sonnwendgasse
Prinz Eugen Str
Favoritenstr
Taubstummengasse
Kettenbrückengasse
Pilgramgasse
Karlsplatz
Stadtpark
Stubentor
Schwedenplatz
Stephansdom
Herrengasse
Stephansplatz
Schottentor
Schottenring
Augarten
Friedensbrücke
Franz Josefs Bahnhof
Liechtensteinpark
Währinger Str Volksoper
Michelbeuern
Alser Str
Rathaus
Lerchenfelder Str
Volkstheater
Volksgarten
Babenbergerstr
Neubaugasse
Westbahnhof
Mariahilfer Str
Gumpendorfer Str
Margaretengürtel
Matzleinsdorfer Platz
Längenfeldgasse
Meidling-Hauptstr
Niederhofstr
Schönbrunn
Hietzing
Hadikgasse
Tiroler Garten
Schweglerstr
Johnstr
Hütteldorfer Str
Kendlerstr
Burggasse Stadthalle
Thaliastr
Josefstädter Str
Ottakring
Hernals
Kongresspark
Penzing
Auer-Welbach Park
Wien

INFORMATION		
Allgemeines Krankenhaus	1	C1
Czech Embassy	2	A4
German Embassy	3	E3
Italian Embassy	4	E3
KlangBoden	5	C2
Max Mobil	6	E4
Seniorenbüro der Stadt Wien	7	C2
STA Travel	8	C2
Swiss Embassy	9	D3
UK Embassy	10	E3
US Embassy	11	C1
SIGHTS & ACTIVITIES		
Gloriette Monument	12	A4
Hundertwassershaus	13	E2
KunstHausWien	14	E2
Liechtenstein Museum	15	C1
Oberes Belvedere & Österreichische Galerie	16	D3
Reisenrad	17	E2
Schloss Schönbrunn	18	A4
Schönbrunn Baths	19	A4
Schönbrunn Maze	20	A4
Schönbrunn Palmenhaus	21	A4
Schönbrunn Zoo	22	A4
Unteres Belvedere	23	D3
SLEEPING		
Hostel Ruthensteiner	24	B3
Hotel Urania	25	E2
Hotel-Pension Zipser	26	C2
Intercity Hotel	27	C3
Lauria	28	C2
Pension Hargita	29	C3
Pension Kaffeemühle	30	C3
Pension Wild	31	C2
Westend City Hostel	32	C3
Wombat's	33	B3
EATING		
Indochine 21	34	E2
Sato Turkish Café-Restaurant	35	B3
Schnitzelwirt Schmidt	36	C3
Schweizerhaus	37	E2
Stomach	38	D1
Vegetasia	(see 30)	
DRINKING		
Das Möbel	39	C2
Die Wäscherei	40	C2
Rhiz	41	C2
Schikanader	42	D3
Shebeen	43	C2
ENTERTAINMENT		
English Theatre	44	C2
Rosa Lila Villa	45	C3
Volksoper	46	C1
TRANSPORT		
Bus to Airport	47	D4
Bus to Airport	48	D4
Bus to Airport	49	C3
Eurolines Office	50	F4
Eurolines Office	51	D4
G Glaser	(see 52)	
Hydrofoil & Boat Wien Landing Stage	52	F1
Pedal Power	53	E1

baroque edifices decorating the city's inner circular road, the Ringstrasse. But these are only the proverbial icing on this beguiling marvel. The flavour of this city is as elaborate as its heritage and is many centuries in the making. The colourful narrative of the Habsburg dynasty can be traced through the rooms of the Hofburg palace or Schloss Schönbrunn, while the legacy of Art Nouveau artists Gustav Klimt and Egon Schiele is on show at the Secession Building, Schloss Belvedere and at the Leopold Museum.

This busy intersection of ethnicities, beliefs and cultural facets has always percolated with creative energy. It was here that Johann Strauss invented the waltz and where Sigmund Freud developed his psychoanalytic theories. And it was not too long ago that Vienna's artisans, musicians and academia flocked to coffee houses (chiefly as a respite from their drafty, more often than not, unheated flats) to embrace and disseminate ideas. So, if this city's rich diet of music, art and philosophy starts to feel a bit stodgy, ease up and relax in one of the many cafés, or take to the top of the *Riesenrad* (the Ferris wheel featured in the film *The Third Man*) for a panorama 65m aloft.

ORIENTATION

Many of the historic sights are in the old city, the Innere Stadt. The Danube Canal (Donaukanal) is located to the northeast and a series of broad boulevards called the Ring or Ringstrasse encircle it.

Most of the attractions in the city centre are within walking distance of each other. Stephansdom (St Stephen's Cathedral), in the heart of the city, is the principal landmark.

In addresses, the number of a building within a street *follows* the street name. Any number *before* the street name denotes the district, of which there are 23. District 1 (the Innere Stadt) is the central region, mostly within the Ring. Generally, the higher the district number, the further it is from the city centre. The middle two digits of postcodes refer to the district, hence places with a postcode 1010 are in district 1, and 1230 means district 23.

The main train stations are Franz Josefs Bahnhof to the north, Westbahnhof to the west and Südbahnhof to the south; transferring between them is easy. Most hotels and *pensions* (B&Bs) are in the city centre and to the west.

INFORMATION

Bookshops

British Bookshop (Map p64; ☎ 512 19 45; 01, Weihburggasse 24-6) Stocks English-language titles.

Freytag & Berndt (Map p64; ☎ 533 86 85; 01, Kohlmarkt 9) Sells maps and guidebooks.

Reisebuchladen (Map p64; ☎ 317 33 84; 09, Kolingasse 6) Specialises in guidebooks.

Shakespeare & Co Booksellers (Map p64; ☎ 535 50 53; 01, Sterngasse 2) Sells new and second-hand books.

WHAT'S ON A COFFEE DRINKER'S MIND?

From the way customers linger over their cappuccino, *Grosser Brauner* or *Melange* in a Viennese *Kaffeehaus* (coffee house), it's easy to believe Austrians have always been born with a coffee spoon in their mouths. But those great tea drinkers, the English, opened their first coffee house before the Austrians ever did, so how did the tradition take such a hold here?

Local schoolchildren are taught that the beverage entered their country after the Ottoman Empire's siege of Vienna in 1683. Polish merchant Georg Kolschitzky smuggled a message out of his adopted city to the Polish king, who eventually came to Vienna's rescue; and Kolschitzky asked to be rewarded with the sacks of coffee beans abandoned by Kara Mustafa's retreating army. As historian Simon Schama put it, Austria managed to 'resist the Turkish siege but (was) defenceless against the coffee bean'.

Only much later, from the 18th century, did the tradition of spending long hours in coffee houses really became entrenched. To escape Vienna's mostly unheated apartments, impoverished artists and intellectuals would set up shop at their coffee-house tables, writing and holding meetings and debates. Sigmund Freud and Leon Trotsky spent hours at Café Central (p71), plotting, playing chess and running up a tab for hot drinks. When the Russian revolution started, Trotsky left Vienna (much to the chagrin of the head waiter) without paying his bill.

Today coffee drinking remains a central part of Viennese, and to a lesser extent Austrian, life. It goes beyond a simple Starbucks culture (but surprisingly that chain now exists here, too). The true coffee house is still a place for music, exhibitions and cultural events; see what's on at the **Viennese Coffee House** (www.wiener-kaffeehaus.at). Above all, in the birthplace of psychoanalysis, it's somewhere to offset the stresses of the everyday. As the owner of a Viennese coffee shop once theorised to the *Guardian* newspaper, 'The coffee is the medicine, the waiters, the therapists'.

AUSTRIA

Internet Access

Bignet (Map p64; ☎ 503 98 44; Kärntner Strasse 61; per 30 min €3.90)

Speednet Café (Map p60; ☎ 892 56 66; 15 Europlatz 1, Westbahnhof; per 30 min €3.30) Conveniently located inside the train station.

Surfland Internetcafé (Map p64; ☎ 512 77 01; Krugerstrasse 10; initial charge €1.50, per extra min €0.08)

Medical Services

Allgemeines Krankenhaus (general hospital; Map p60; ☎ 40 400; 09, Währinger Gürtel 18-20; 24hr)

Dental Treatment (☎ 512 20 78; 24hr) German-speaking only.

Post

Main Post Office (Map p64; 01, Fleischmarkt 19; 24hr) Other post offices open long hours are at Südbahnhof, Franz Josefs Bahnhof and Westbahnhof.

Tourist Information

Tourist offices and hotels sell the Vienna Card (€16.90), which provides admission discounts and a free 72-hour travel pass.

Information & Hotel Reservation Counters Westbahnhof (8.30am-9pm); Airport arrivals hall (7am-10pm) Opposite the baggage-claim areas.

Jugend-Info Wien (Vienna Youth Information; Map p64; ☎ 17 99; 01, Babenbergerstrasse 1; noon-7pm Mon-Sat) Offers various reduced-price tickets for 14- to 26-year-olds.

Tourist-Info Zentrum (Map p64; ☎ 24 555; www.wien.info; 01, cnr Am Albertinaplatz & Maysedergasse; 9am-7pm) Near the state opera house, with loads of regional information.

Travel Agencies

Amex (Map p64; ☎ 5124 0040; Kärntner Strasse 21-23; 9am-5.30pm Mon-Fri, 9am-noon Sat)

STA Travel Vienna (Map p60; ☎ 40 148-0; 09, Garnisongasse 7; 9am-5.30pm); Central Vienna (Map p64; ☎ 40 148-7000; 09, Türkenstrasse 6B; 9am-6pm); Central Vienna (Map p64; ☎ 50 243-0; 04, Karlsgasse 3; 9am-6pm)

SIGHTS

Vienna's ostentatious buildings and beautifully tended parks make it a lovely city just to stroll through. If you catch tram 1 or 2 around the Ringstrasse (the road circling the city centre) you'll acquire a taste of the city, passing the neo-Gothic **Rathaus** (city hall; Map p64), the Greek Revival-style **Parliament** (Map p64) and the 19th-century **Burgtheater** (Map p64), among others. You can even glimpse the baroque **Karlskirche** (St Charles' Church; Map p64) from the tram.

Strolling along the pedestrian-only tree-lined **Kärntner Strasse** (Map p64) will take you past plush shops, cafés and street entertainers. The main point of interest in Graben is the knobbly **Petsäule** (Plague Column; Map p64), designed by Fischer von Erlach and built to commemorate the end of the Plague. There's also a concrete **Holocaust memorial** (Map p64) by Rachel Whiteread in Judenplatz, Austria's first monument of its kind. Look closely and you'll notice that the sides are constructed of cement books facing open-end out, perhaps to convey a lack of closure coupled with an enduring remembrance for the victims of the holocaust.

Interesting buildings in the city centre include **Loos House** (Map p64), now a Raiffeisen bank, across from the Hofburg. The Art Nouveau **Postsparkasse** (Savings Bank; Map p64; Georg Coch Platz) and **Stadtbahn Pavilions** (train station pavilions; Map p64; Karlsplatz) are both by archi tect Otto Wagner.

Stephansdom

The prominent latticework spire of **St Stephen's Cathedral** (Map p64) makes this 13th-century Gothic masterpiece one of the city's key points of orientation, and the geometric pattern of its roof tiles is also striking. Bearing in mind the significance of the church in daily medieval commerce, run your fingers across over-200-year-old rudimentary circular grooves on the cathedral's face (right side of front), once used for standardising and regulating exact measurements of bread loaves, and over two horizontally fastened iron bars at one time utilised for gauging proper lengths of cloth.

Inside, you can take the lift up the north tower (€4) or the stairs up the higher south tower (€3) – but travellers are sometimes disappointed by the fairly mediocre views. Some of the internal organs of the Habsburgs reside in urns in the church's **Katakomben** (catacombs; admission €3).

Hofburg

The **Hofburg** (Imperial Palace; Map p64) was the Habsburgs' city-centre base. Added to many times since the 13th century, resulting in a mix of architectural styles, the palace continues to be a seat of power, housing the office of the president of Austria and a major congress centre. Wander around a bit and admire the exterior before venturing inside. While not as ornate as Schönbrunn's rooms, the **Kaiserappartements & 'Sissi' Museum** (Map p64; ☎ 535 75 75; Hofburg; admission €7.50; 🕑 9am-5pm; Ⓤ U-Bahn Herrengasse) are worth seeing because they relate the unusual life story of Empress Elisabeth (Sissi). You don't particularly have to be a fan to enjoy the experience: the empress' 19th-century gym and her obsession with her looks are attention-grabbing enough. Plus, the museum helps explain why Sissi's face still adorns shop windows in Vienna today. A ticket to the Kaiserappartements includes entry to the **Silberkammer** (silver chamber).

Among several other points of interest within the Hofburg you'll find the Burgkapelle (Royal Chapel), where the Vienna Boys' Choir performs (see p73), and the Spanish Riding School (p73).

Kaisergruft

Also known as the Kapuzinergruft, the **Imperial Vault** (Map p64; 01, Tegetthofstrasse/Neuer Markt; admission €4; 🕑 9am-5pm; Ⓤ U-Bahn Stephansplatz) offers another weirdly compelling take on the cult of 'Sissi'. Stabbed by an Italian anarchist on the waterfront in Geneva in 1898, Empress Elisabeth was brought back here as her final resting place. Her coffin, still strewn with flowers by fans, lies alongside that of her husband, the penultimate emperor Franz Josef, and other Habsburgs. It's as bizarre as anything on TV's *Six Feet Under*.

VIENNA IN TWO DAYS

Starting at the **Stephansdom** (above), head via Graben and the Kohlmarkt to the **Hofburg** (above). Drop by the **Kaisergruft** (above), before finding a coffee house and settling into a long break. After lunch, hop on tram 1 around the Ringstrasse. Do one circuit and a half, just taking in the sights, before alighting near the **Museums Quartier** (p65). Try to get tickets to the **opera** (p72) for the evening or head to a club like **Flex** (p72).

Choose a few galleries or a museum and explore them in-depth on your second morning. If it's a warm afternoon, laze in the gardens at **Schloss Schönnbrunn** (p66). At night venture into the suburbs for delicious wine in Vienna's *Heurigen* (wine taverns; p71).

AUSTRIA

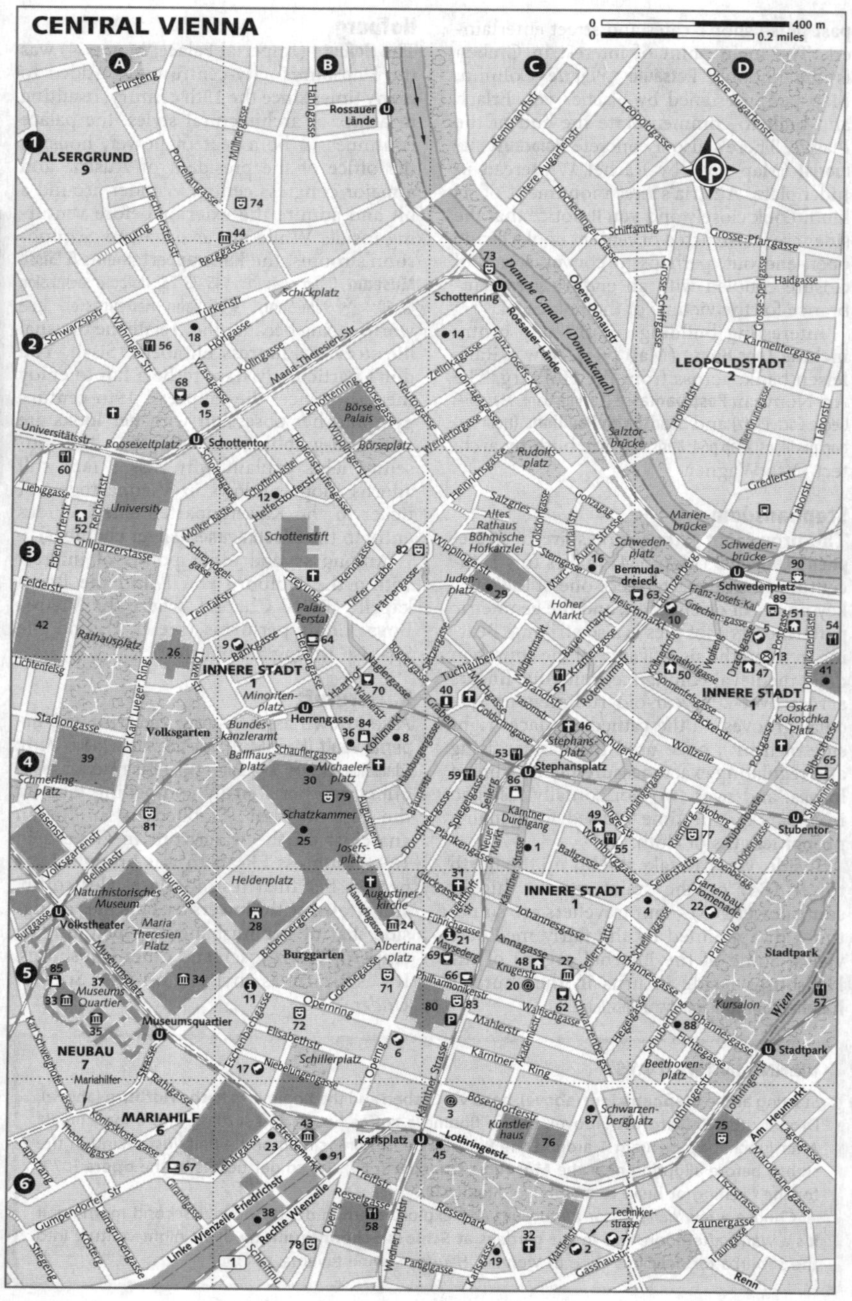
CENTRAL VIENNA
0 400 m
0 0.2 miles
ALSERGRUND
9
LEOPOLDSTADT
2
INNERE STADT
1
NEUBAU
7
MARIAHILF
6
Danube Canal (Donaukanal)
Schottenring
Schottentor
Rossauer Lände
Schwedenplatz
Stephansplatz
Herrengasse
Stubentor
Stadtpark
Karlsplatz
Museumsquartier
Volkstheater
University
Volksgarten
Heldenplatz
Burggarten
Schatzkammer
Naturhistorisches Museum
Maria Theresien Platz
Museums Quartier
Rathausplatz
Börse Palais
Schottenstift
Palais Ferstal
Altes Rathaus Böhmische Hofkanzlei
Bermuda-dreieck
Hoher Markt
Judenplatz
Stephansplatz
Michaelerplatz
Josefsplatz
Augustinerkirche
Albertinaplatz
Künstlerhaus
Kursalon
Schwarzenbergplatz
Beethovenplatz
Oskar Kokoschka Platz
Schwedenbrücke
Marienbrücke
Salztorbrücke
Ringstrasse
Kärntner Ring
Opernring
Burgring
Wien
Lothringerstr
Am Heumarkt
Mariahilfer

INFORMATION
Amex....1 C4
Australian Embassy....2 C6
Bignet....3 C6
British Bookshop....4 D5
Canadian Embassy....5 D3
Dutch Embassy....6 B5
French Embassy....7 C6
Freytag & Berndt....8 B4
Hungarian Embassy....9 B3
Irish Embassy....10 D3
Jugend-Info Wien....11 B5
Junge Hotels Austria....12 B3
Main Post Office....13 D3
Österreichischer Jugendherbergsverband....14 C2
Reisebuchladen....15 A2
Shakespeare & Co Booksellers....16 C3
Slovenian Embassy....17 B5
STA Travel....18 A2
STA Travel....19 C6
Surfland Internetcafé....20 C5
Tourist-info Zentrum....21 C5
US Consulate....22 D5
Wiener Festwochen....23 B6

SIGHTS & ACTIVITIES
Albertina....24 B5
Austrian Camping Club....(see 88)
Burgkapelle....25 B4
Burgtheater....26 A3
Haus der Musik....27 C5
Hofburg....28 B5
Holocaust Memorial....29 C3
Kaiserappartements....30 B4
Kaisergruft....31 C5
Karlskirche....32 C6
Kunsthalle....33 A5
Kunsthistorisches Museum....34 A5
Leopold Museum....35 A5
Loos House....36 B4
Museums Quartier....37 A5
Naschmarkt....38 B6
Parliament....39 A4
Pestsäule....40 C4
Postsparkasse....41 D4
Rathaus....42 A3
Secession Building....43 B6
Sigmund Freud Museum....44 B1
Silberkammer....(see 30)
'Sissi' Museum....(see 30)
Stadtbahn Pavilions....45 C6
Stephansdom....46 C4

SLEEPING
Hotel Post....47 D4
Hotel zur Wiener Staatsoper....48 C5
Kaiserin Elisabeth....49 C4
Kärtnerhof....50 D4
Pension Dr Geissler....51 D3
Pension Residenz....52 A3

EATING
DO & CO....53 C4
Expedit....54 D3
Immervoll....55 C4
OH Pot, OH Pot....56 A2
Ra'an....(see 68)
Steiereck....57 D5
Technical University Mensa....58 B6
Trzesniewski....59 C4
University Mensa & Café....60 A3
Wrenkh....61 C4

DRINKING
1516 Brewing Company....62 C5
Bermudadreieck (Bermuda Triangle)....63 D3
Café Central....64 B3
Café Prückel....65 D4
Café Sacher....66 C5
Café Sperl....67 A6
Café Stein....68 A2
Crossfield's Aussie Pub....69 C5
Esterházykeller....70 B4

ENTERTAINMENT
Bundestheaterkassen....71 B5
Burgkino....72 B5
Club U....(see 45)
Flex....73 C2
International Theatre....74 B1
Konzerthaus....75 D6
Musikverein....76 C6
Porgy n Bess....77 D4
Roxy....78 B6
Spanish Riding School....79 B4
Staatsoper (State Opera)....80 C5
Volksgarten....81 A4
Why Not?....82 B3
Wien Ticket....83 C5

SHOPPING
Café Demel....84 B4
Lomo Shop....85 A5
Österreichische Werkstätten....86 C4

TRANSPORT
Austrian Airlines....87 C6
Austrian Automobile Club....88 D5
Buses to Airport....89 D3
Danube Canal Tour Landing Stage....90 D3
DDSG Blue Danube....91 B6

AUSTRIA

Museums Quartier

Small guidebooks have been written on the popular **Museums Quartier** (Map p64; ☎ 523 04 31; 07, Museumsplatz 1; U-Bahn Museumsquartier), so only a taster can be given here. The highpoint is undoubtedly the **Leopold Museum** (Map p64; ☎ 525 700; adult/senior/student €9/7/5.50; 10am-7pm Wed-Mon, 10am-9pm Fri; U-Bahn Museumsquartier), which houses the world's largest collection of Egon Schiele paintings, with some minor Klimts and Kokoschkas thrown in.

Schloss Belvedere

This **palace** (Map p60; ☎ 79 557-134; www.belvedere.at; combined admission €7.50; 10am-6pm Tue-Sun Apr-Oct, 10am-5pm Nov-Mar; tram D to Schloss Belvedere) consists of two main buildings. One is the **Oberes Belvedere & Österreichische Galerie** (Upper Belvedere & Austrian Gallery; Map p60; 03, Prinz Eugen Strasse 37; adult/student €6/3; 10am-6pm Tue-Sun Apr-Oct, 10am-5pm Nov-Mar), where you'll find instantly recognisable works, such as Gustav Klimt's *The Kiss*, accompanied by other late-19th to early-20th-century Austrian works. The other is the **Unteres Belvedere** (Lower Belvedere; Map p60; 03, Rennweg 6A; admission €6; 10am-6pm Tue-Sun Apr-Oct, 10am-5pm Nov-Mar), which contains a baroque museum. The buildings sit at opposite ends of a manicured garden.

Secession Building

This popular Art Nouveau 'temple of art' **building** (Map p64; ☎ 587 53 07; 01, Friedrichstrasse 12; adult/student €5.50/3; 10am-6pm Tue-Sun, 10am-8pm Thu; U-Bahn Karlsplatz) was built in 1898 and bears an intricately woven gilt dome that the Viennese say looks like a 'golden cabbage' – and it definately does. The highlight inside is the 34m-long *Beethoven Frieze* by Klimt.

KunstHausWien

This formerly inconspicuous factory building, now fairy-tale **art gallery** (Map p60; ☎ 712

04 91; 03, Untere Weissgerberstrasse 13; admission €9, half-price Mon; 10am-7pm; tram N or O to Radetzkyplatz) designed and transformed by Friedensreich Hundertwasser into a repository for his art, is redolent of Antonio Gaudi's buildings in Barcelona. Irregular elements, like uneven floors, misshapen windows, amalgamations of glass, metal, brick and ceramic tile, almost literally sweep you off your feet. Down the road there's a block of residential flats by Hundertwasser, the **Hundertwassershaus** (Map p60; cnr Löwengasse & Kegelgasse). To the west, heading towards the town of Dürnstein, another spectacle arises that would make Willy Wonka proud. Visible by its towering, golden-tiled smoke stack, this is Vienna's architecturally unique rubbish incinerator that also heats water for homes in the surrounding area.

AUSTRIA

Albertina

Simply reading the highlights among its enormous rotating collection – several Michelangelos, some Raphaels and Albrecht Dürer's *Hare* – might give a misleading impression of this reopened **gallery** (Map p64; 53 483-540; www.albertina.at; 01, Albertinaplatz 1A; adult/senior/student €9/7.50/6.50; 10am-6pm Thu-Tue, 10am-9pm Wed; U-Bahn Karlsplatz or Stephansplatz). When we visited, the exhibitions ranged from pop art to Rembrandt and included two fascinating photography displays, making it feel quite modern. The curators do a superb job, so keep an eye out for what's on here.

In addition to the mostly temporary exhibitions, a series of Habsburg staterooms are always open.

Schloss Schönbrunn

The single attraction most readily associated with Vienna is the Habsburgs' **summer palace** (Map p60; 81 113-0; 13, Schönbrunner Schlossstrasse 47; self-guided 22-/40-room tour €8/10.50; 8.30am-5pm Apr-Oct, 8.30am-4.30pm Nov-Mar; U-Bahn Schönbrunn). However, the sumptuous 1440-room palace is so vast, crowded and out of the way that you'll need to put aside at least half a day to see it, and it won't be to everyone's taste. Students get a slight discount.

Inside this mini-Versailles you'll traipse through progressively more luxurious apartments. The most impressive, the **Audience Rooms**, are only included in the 40-room grand tour.

The grounds are more enjoyable and are home to the world's oldest zoo, the **Tiergarten** (adult/senior/student/child €12/10/5/4), founded in 1752. Highlights include the formal gardens and fountains, the **maze** (admission €2.10), the **Palmenhaus** (greenhouse; admission €3.30) and the **Gloriette Monument** (admission €2.10), whose roof offers a wonderful view over the palace grounds and beyond.

Liechtenstein Museum

The collection of Duke Hans-Adam II of Liechtenstein is now on show at Vienna's new **museum** (Map p60; 319 57 67-0; 09, Fürstengasse 1; adult/senior/student €10/8/5; 9am-8pm Wed-Mon; U-Bahn Friedensbrücke or Franz Josefs Bahnhof), located in a refurbished, frescoed, baroque palace. There are classical paintings, including some by Rubens.

Kunsthistorisches Museum

A huge range of art amassed by the Habsburgs is showcased at the **Museum of Fine Arts** (Map p64; 52 524-0; www.khm.at; 01, Maria Theresien Platz; admission €10; 10am-6pm Tue-Sun, 10am-10pm Thu; U-Bahn Volkstheater or Museumsquartier). Included are works by Rubens, van Dyck, Holbein and Caravaggio. Paintings by Peter Brueghel the Elder, including *Hunters in the Snow*, also feature. There is an entire wing of ornaments, clocks and glassware, and Greek, Roman and Egyptian antiquities.

Other Museums

Vienna has so many museums you might overlook the superlative **Haus der Musik** (House of Music; Map p64; 51 648-51; www.haus-der-musik-wien.at; Seilerstätte 30; admission €10; 10am-10pm; U-Bahn Karlsplatz or Stephansplatz). Try not to. Interactive electronic displays allow you to create different forms of music through movement and touch, and to connect with something a lot deeper than just your inner child.

Some former homes of the great composers, including one of Mozart's, are open to the public; ask at the tourist office. There is also the fairly low-key **Sigmund Freud Museum** (Map p64; 319 15 96; 09, Bergasse 19; admission €5; 9am-6pm Jul-Sep, 9am-5pm Oct-Jun; U-Bahn Rossauer or Schottentor).

Cemeteries

Beethoven, Schubert, Brahms and Schönberg have memorial tombs in the **Zentralfriedhof** (Central Cemetery; 11, Simmeringer Hauptstrasse

232-244), about 4km southeast of the city centre. Mozart also has a monument here, but he is actually buried in the **St Marxer Friedhof** (Cemetery of St Mark; 03, Leberstrasse 6-8).

Naschmarkt

Saturday is the best day to visit this **market** (Map p64; 06, Linke Wienzeile; 6am-6pm Mon-Sat; U-Bahn Karlsplatz or Kettenbrückengasse) when the usual food stalls and occasional tatty clothes stall are joined by a proper flea market. Curios and trinkets sit beside produce from Austrian farms, plus there are cafés for an alfresco breakfast, lunch or refuelling stop.

ACTIVITIES

Riesenrad

In theory, riding the **Riesenrad** (giant wheel; Map p60; admission €7.50; U-Bahn Praterstern) in the Prater amusement park allows you to relive a classic film moment: when Orson Welles ad-libbed his immortal speech about peace, Switzerland and cuckoo clocks in *The Third Man*. In practice, you'll be too distracted by other passengers and by the views as the Ferris wheel languidly takes you 65m aloft. It's fun, but not quite the London Eye.

Water Sports

You can swim, sailboard, boat and windsurf in the stretches of water known as the Old Danube, northeast of the Donaustadt island and the New Donau, which runs parallel to and just north of the Donaukanal (Danube Canal). There are stretches of river bank with unrestricted access. Alternatively, visit the **Schönbrunn baths** (Map p60; Schönbrunner Schlossstrasse 47; full day/afternoon incl locker €9.50/6.50; 8.30am-5pm May-Sep; U-Bahn Schönbrunn), within the Schloss Schönbrunn grounds.

TOURS

The tourist office publishes a monthly list of guided walks, called *Wiener Spaziergänge*. **Vienna Walks** (774 89 01; www.viennawalks.tix.at) organises **Third Man tours** (tour €16; 4pm Mon & Fri), including through the city's sewers, and a tour of **Jewish Vienna** (tour €11; 1.30pm Mon).

FESTIVALS & EVENTS

The **Vienna Festival**, from mid-May to mid-June, has a wide-ranging arts programme. Contact the **Wiener Festwochen** (Map p64; 58 922-22; www.festwochen.or.at; Lehárgasse 11; Jan–mid-Jun; U-Bahn Karlsplatz) for details.

The extremely popular **Vienna Spring Marathon** is held in April/May and Vienna's **Summer of Music** runs from mid-July to mid-September; contact **KlangBoden** (Map p60; 40 00-8410; 01, Stadiongasse 9; U-Bahn Rathaus).

Look out for free rock, jazz and folk concerts during the **Donauinselfest**, held at the end of June. The free open-air **Opera Film Festival** on Rathausplatz runs throughout July and August.

Each year Vienna's traditional **Christmas market** *(Christkindlmarkt)* takes place in front of the Rathaus between mid-November and 24 December.

SLEEPING

Budget

Vienna has lots of budget choices, although rooms fill quickly in summer, so try to book ahead when possible.

Wien West (914 23 14; www.wiencamping.at; Hüttelbergstrasse 80; camp site per adult/tent Sep-Jun €5/3.50, Jul-Aug €6/3.50, 2-/4-person cabin Apr-Oct €27/37; closed Feb) On the edges of the Wiener Wald (Vienna Woods), but just 20 minutes from the city centre, this well-equipped

GRAPE GRAZING

Cycle, sit, swirl, sip, cycle, slurp, savour, then cycle again, your way from winery to winery and let your taste buds reap the rewards of one of Austria's best wine regions. Expert guides and a lovely path along the Danube river make **Mitch's Tours Grape Grazing Tour** (699-1882 0155; www.mitchstours.com; Grangasse 4, 1150 Vienna; adult/student €55/45) a great choice for the authentic Vienna countryside excursion.

You'll spend a day touring the breathtakingly beautiful scenery and old medieval villages of the Wachau by bike. Wander through the fortress ruins in Durnstein, where England's King Richard the Lion-Heart was imprisoned, perhaps the most historically infamous stop on the route. Learn how Austrian schnapps is made. You can also go swimming, play beach volleyball or relax while enjoying a barbecue. Tours depart 9.30am daily (except Monday and Wednesday) and hotel pick-up is available.

camping ground has modern facilities, and even a wi-fi hotspot. Take U4 or the S-Bahn to Hütteldorf, then bus 148 or 152.

Jugendgästhaus Wien Brigittenau (☎ 332 82 94; jgh1200wien@chello.at; 20, Friedrich Engels Platz 24; dm from €15) This large Hostelling International (HI) hostel is popular with school groups. Take the U6 to Handelskai and then bus 11A one stop to Friedrich Engels Platz.

Wombat's (Map p60; ☎ 897 23 36; www.wombats.at; 15, Grangasse 6; dm/d €18/24; 🖳) Top-flight cleanliness and comfort fuse with a gregarious party bar to make Wombat's immensely popular. The mixed-gender dorms have secured entry, wooden bunk beds and modern bathrooms. It's where the hip kids stay – if they remember to do something as terminally un-hip as book ahead. Rates include breakfast.

Westend City Hostel (Map p60; ☎ 597 67 29; www.westendhostel.at; 6, Fügergasse 3; dm €18, s/d €41/49; ☒ 🖳) The weirdest thing behind the pale purple façade isn't the knowledge that this was once a *bordello*. It's the particle board–encased en suite bathrooms in some of the mixed dorms; these bathrooms have extra mattresses on their mezzanine roof. Still, the place is well located and friendly.

Pension Kaffeemühle (Map p60; ☎ 523 86 88; www.kaffeemuhle.at; 07, Kaiserstrasse 45; s/d from €48/60; Ⓟ ⚄) Family-run *pension* offering comfortable clean rooms and a central location not far from the Westbahnhof. It's a good place to rest up before another day in the city.

Pension Hargita (Map p60; ☎ 526 19 28; www.hargita.at; 07, Andreasgasse 1; s/d €55/66, with shared bathroom from €38/53) One of the cleanest and most charming budget *pensions* in Vienna. Rooms have aqua blue or sunny yellow features, the friendly Hungarian owner keeps things spotless and breakfast is included in the rates.

Midrange

There are lots of charming guesthouses and small hotels in this price bracket.

Hotel Urania (Map p60; ☎ 713 17 11; www.hotel-urania.at; 03, Obere Weissgerberstrasse 7; s/d/tr/q from €55/70/95/115) This hotel is tacky, but fun. Episodes of various Austrian TV series (eg *Inspector Rex*) have been filmed here, and as a guest you'll feel you're in one, too. Not all of the eclectic rooms will be to everyone's taste (a knight's boudoir with animal skins on the floor, anyone?). Others, as in the Hundertwasser and Japanese rooms, are actually quite chic. The hotel is quiet, but central.

Pension Residenz (Map p64; ☎ 406 47 86-0; www.pension-residenz.co.at; 01, Ebendorferstrasse 10; s/d €60/90; Ⓟ) This *pension* is a model of restraint. Traditionally decorated, with white, light-coloured fittings, it has a pleasant, if not overly personal, feel. Its location near the university is also handy.

Lauria (Map p60; ☎ 522 25 55; www.lauria-vienna.at; 3rd fl, 07, Kaiserstrasse 77-8; d/tr/q from €62/78/96, with shared bathroom €48/66/84) A good place for young couples or small groups of travellers staying a couple of nights – you get your own homy quarters, your own keys and access to a fully equipped kitchen. There is a €7 surcharge for single-night stays.

Pension Dr Geissler (Map p64; ☎ 533 28 03; www.hotelpension.at; 01, Postgasse 14; s/d from €65/88, with shared bathroom from €39/50; Ⓟ) Don't let the slow lift deter you: when you do make it to your floor, you'll find rooms are an eclectic mix of faux baroque and 1950s retro. The airport bus to Schwedenplatz almost brings you to the door, making it handy for jet-lag rehab.

Pension Wild (Map p60; ☎ 406 51 74; www.penions-wild.com; 08, Langegasse 10; s/d €65/90, with shared bathroom from €37/45) Most of the rooms at this gay-friendly *pension* have been recently renovated, but some cheaper accommodation remains, with showers and toilets outside the rooms. All guests can prepare snacks in the small kitchenette on each floor.

Hotel-Pension Zipser (Map p60; ☎ 40 454-0; www.zipser.at; 08, Langegasse 49; s/d from €69/109; Ⓟ) This

AUTHOR'S CHOICE

Hostel Ruthensteiner (Map p60; ☎ 893 42 02; www.hostelruthensteiner.com; 15, Robert Hamerling Gasse 24; dm/d from €12.50/25; ☒ 🖳) If stars were given out for hostels, this place would be a 5. The first truly independent backpackers in central Europe, the über-friendly owners, Erin and Walter, have been catering to travellers for 34 years strong. Start with a quirky low-key vibe then add an immaculate, modern facility with more renovations in progress, mix in a strong dose of personality and options galore, and you'll have a feel for this place. A beautifully handmade wooden bar, music/lounge room and a lovely garden area also enhance the surroundings.

place has elegant contemporary furnishings and some rooms have balconies facing a garden.

Hotel Post (Map p64; ☎ 51 583-0; www.hotel-post-wien.at; 01, Fleischmarkt 24; s/d €75/115, with shared bathroom €44/70; P) The strongest feature of this hotel is its location, right in the heart of things. With its parquet flooring in the rooms, long, carpeted hallways and decorative cast-iron lift, it feels like a grand, if somewhat faded, 19th-century boarding house.

Kärtnerhof (Map p64; ☎ 519 19 23; www.kartnerhof.com; 01, Grashofgasse 4; s/d from €80/105; P) Tucked away in a cul-de-sac in the city centre, Kärtnerhof is a terrific find with quietly elegant rooms, many of them with bathtubs. It has a policy of not accepting tour groups.

Hotel zur Wiener Staatsoper (Map p64; ☎ 513 12 74; www.zurwienerstaatsoper.at; 01, Krugerstrasse 11; s/d from €85/126; P) Famous for its appealing façade, this hotel's rooms are small, but its prices are great value for the central location.

Top End

Vienna has a glut of four- and five-star hotels. Every major chain is represented and even the city's most recognisable names now belong to one of these groups.

InterCity Hotel (Map p60; ☎ 52 585-0; www.intercityhotel.de; 07 Mariahilfer Strasse 122; s/d €121/205; P ⊠ ⌘) Located on a major shopping thoroughfare, with soundproof modern rooms and tasteful décor, this place is a fine choice for convenience and comfort. Use of local transport included in the rate means you won't fret about getting around the city.

Kaiserin Elisabeth (Map p64; ☎ 51 526-0; www.kaiserinelisabeth.at; 01, Weihburggasse 13; s/d from €175/200; P ⊠ ⌘) The central Kaiserin, with its mix of chandeliers, red velvet, wooden floors and rugs, is a plush option.

EATING

The city's signature dish, *Wiener schnitzel*, is widely available and Vienna is renowned for its excellent pastries. You can buy groceries outside normal shopping hours at Franz Josefs Bahnhof and Westbahnhof.

Restaurants

Schnitzelwirt Schmidt (Map p60; 07, Neubaugasse 52; schnitzel from €5.50; ⏲ Mon-Sat) With fabulously grumpy waiters – who'll shout at you if you get in their way – and huge *Wiener schnitzels*, this buzzing place lets you experience the authentic Vienna of today.

OH Pot, OH Pot (Map p64; ☎ 319 42 59; 09, Währinger Strasse 22; hotpots lunch/dinner €6.50/8.50) Painted in warm Mediterranean colours, this sweet boho restaurant has decent ethnic stews (or hotpots) on the menu. Whether African, Asian, central European or South American, they all come with either soup or salad. The best deal is from 3pm to 6pm, when prices drop to €5.

Ra'an (Map p64; ☎ 319 35 63; 09, Währinger Strasse 6-8; lunch €6, dinner €6.50-13) Ra'an is a cool noodle bar and has what listings magazine *Falter* has decreed the 'cutest cardboard lunch boxes in town'. The menu ranges from sushi and rice dishes at lunch to more elaborate Thai and Vietnamese in the evening.

Vegetasia (Map p60; ☎ 523 10 91; 07, Kaiserstrasse 45; mains €6.50-22) Flavourful and eclectic combinations of fresh vegetables, Asian spices and pure vegetable-based home-made dishes will bring gastric delight to anyone wanting to avoid *Fleisch* (meat) in their diet. Every item on the menu is vegetarian.

Immervoll (Map p64; ☎ 5135 2288; 01 Weihburggasse 17; mains €9-14.50) Run by a famous Austrian actor, Immervoll (literally, 'always full') attracts an arty crowd to its uncluttered small room. The menu changes daily, but the delicious food often has Hungarian and Italian influences.

Stomach (Map p60; ☎ 310 20 99; 09, Seegasse 26; mains €9-15; ⏲ dinner Wed-Sat, lunch & dinner Sun) Many vegetarian dishes have dropped off

AUTHOR'S CHOICE

Expedit (Map p64; ☎ 512 33 13-0; 01, cnr Wiesingerstrasse & Biberstrasse; mains €11; ⏲ lunch & dinner Mon-Fri, dinner Sat) In this old warehouse on the edge of district 1, patrons enjoy a cross between an upmarket Italian bistro and a minimalist pub. In its room filled with imported pasta, pesto and panini around an open-plan, bare-floored dining space, the food is 'Ligurian' (ie Italian – mainly pasta and salads). There are a few long communal tables to squeeze around and it can be quite crowded at times, but an extensive list of imported wines and a *boccia* (Italian bowling) alley in the basement enhance the experience.

AUSTRIA

AUTHOR'S CHOICE

1516 Brewing Company (Map p64; ☎ 961 15 16; 01, Schwarzenbergstrasse 2) Flaunting exposed copper and stainless-steel piping, wine-barrel tables and a long bar extending along the front room, this hip brewpub is an awesome place to go for a drink while you're in the city centre. Unfiltered ales and lagers, an unpretentious ambience and friendly staff are all on tap here. Specifically named after the year of one of the oldest 'consumer protection' laws (the *Reinheitsgebot*), beer enthusiasts will imbibe with glee knowing that their pint is made exactly the same as it was in the year 1516, using only water, malt, hops and yeast.

the menu at Styrian-style Stomach, but some remain, and the quaint, ramshackle rooms and the courtyard create a rustic outpost in the big city.

Schweizerhaus (Map p60; ☎ 319 35 63; 02, Strasse des Ersten Mai 116; mains €10-20; ⌚ Mon-Sat Mar-Oct) In the Prater park, this place serves *Hintere Schweinsstelze* (roasted pork hocks) and the like to a rowdy crowd of international travellers who wash it all down with huge mugs of beer.

Wrenkh (Map p64; ☎ 533 15 26; 01, Bauernmarkt 10; mains €11) Quiche, mung beans and nut roast are *not* on the menu at this vegetarian restaurant. Instead, this is an upmarket affair, with sleek customers and lip-smacking Mediterranean, Austrian and Asian fare – from risotto to tofu.

Indochine 21 (Map p60; ☎ 513 76 60; 01, Stubenring 18; mains €12.50-38; ⌚ lunch & dinner) This is one of Vienna's hotter, newer eateries, having been named the best Asian restaurant in the city a few years back. The food is trendy French/Vietnamese, while red-lacquered umbrellas hang on the walls and exotic potted plants evoke a vaguely colonial ambience.

DO & CO (Map p64; ☎ 535 39 69; 01, Haas Haus, Stephansplatz 12; mains €15-24) The food and the views from seven floors above Stephansplatz keep this elegant restaurant in business. Contemporary Viennese dishes are highlighted, but it also serves Austrian classics, Uruguayan beef and Asian specialities. The service is flawless. Booking ahead is advised.

Steirereck (Map p64; ☎ 713 31 68; 03, Heumarkt 2a-Stadtpark; mains €22.50-30; ⌚ lunch & dinner) This long-standing gourmet temple's name means 'corner of Styria' and is famous for traditional Viennese fare and new Austrian selections. Try the Styrian roast beef with red-pepper risotto. Patrons can examine the vast wine cellar, which holds some 35,000 bottles, or choose from 150 different types of cheese. Reservations are required.

Cafés

Trzesniewski (Map p64; ☎ 512 32 91; 01, Dorotheergasse 1; sandwiches €1) You can really feel like one of the Austrian emperor's minions on the way home from the factory at this stand-up café. It sells tiny open sandwiches, usually featuring egg or fish of some description, which you wash down with a tiny *Pfiff* (125mL) beer.

Sato Turkish Café-Restaurant (Map p60; ☎ 897 58 54; 15, Mariahilferstrasse 151; mains €3-13; ⌚ 8am-midnight) This restaurant entices clientele with generous portions of bona fide Turkish cuisine, an easy atmosphere, and inexpensive *Tagesmenus* sure to satisfy every taste and budget. Live traditional music on the weekends is also worth checking out.

Quick Eats & Self-Catering

Cheap student cafeterias include **Technical University Mensa** (Map p64; 04, Resselgasse 7-9; mains €3.50-5; ⌚ 11am-2pm Mon-Fri) and **University Mensa** (Map p64; 7th fl, 01, Universitätsstrasse 7; mains €4.50-5; ⌚ 11am-2pm Mon-Fri). Though the latter is closed in July and August, its adjoining **café** (⌚ 8am-3pm Mon-Fri) remains open year-round.

DRINKING

Bars

The area around Ruprechtsplatz, Seitenstettengasse and Rabensteig near Schwedenplatz is dubbed the Bermudadreieck (Bermuda Triangle; Map p64) for the way drinkers disappear into its numerous pubs and clubs, but you'd have to seriously overindulge to become lost here. Venues are lively and inexpensive, and draw a mix of crowds.

Crossfield's Aussie Pub (Map p64; ☎ 241 000; 01, Maysedergasse 5) There's a saying on some of the touristy T-shirts – 'there's no kangaroos in Austria'. Well, this pub proves the contrary, with upstairs and downstairs bar areas serving Australian, import and local beers, plus enough outback charm to make you forget what country you're in. Grub like crocodile, ostrich fillet, grilled grasshoppers and plenty of roo any way you like it, makes this place one of our favourites.

Shebeen (Map p60; ☎ 524 79 00; 07, Lerchenfelder Strasse 45-47) This African-inspired pub remains a popular evening spot for English-speaking travellers, expats and internationals alike. Major football matches, decent music and activities, like nightly quizzes of the Trivial Pursuit variety, all create a lively atmosphere.

Das Möbel (Map p60; ☎ 524 94 97; 07, Burggasse 10) The interior is never dull at this bar near the Museums Quartier. It's remarkable for its funky décor and furniture – cube stools, assorted moulded lamps, plus a round ping-pong table.

Café Stein (Map p64; ☎ 3197 2419; 09, Währinger Strasse 6-8; 💻) This trendy, student café/bar-cum-diner offers a smoke-free environment in which to curl up with a good book or surf the Net. It also hosts poetry slams and modern art exhibitions.

Also recommended:

Die Wäscherei (Map p60; ☎ 409 23 75-11; 08, Albertgasse 49) Lots of draught beers.

Rhiz (Map p60; ☎ 409 25 05; Lechenfelder Gürtel 37-38) A mecca for Vienna's electronic music scene; it's near the U-Bahn arches.

Schikanader (Map p60; ☎ 585 58 88; 04, Margaretenstrasse 22-4) In the foyer of a cinema.

Coffee Houses

Vienna's famous *Kaffeehäuser* (coffee houses) are like economic forecasts; ask two people for a recommendation and you'll get four answers. Following are a few local favourites – a full-sized coffee will cost roughly €3 to €3.50, but you can take as long as you like to drink it without being moved on.

Café Sacher (Map p64; ☎ 151 45 69; 01, Philharmoniker strasse 4; ⏲ 8am-noon) Arguably home to the world's most famous chocolate cake – the Sacher Torte, fastidiously baked in-house. Savour a slice of this exquisite speciality that has been a well-kept secret since 1832. Wash it all down with an Original Sacher Café coffee and enjoy the conservatory, which faces the Staatsoper (State Opera) and in summer is transformed into a huge terrace.

Café Central (Map p64; ☎ 533 37 63; 01, Herrengasse 14; ⏲ Mon-Sat) A lot more commercialised than when Herrs Trotsky, Freud and Beethoven drank here, we dare say, but still appealing with vaulted ceilings, palms and baroque architecture.

AUTHOR'S CHOICE

Café Sperl (Map p64; ☎ 586 41 58; 06, Gumpendorfer Strasse 11; ⏲ 7am-11pm Mon-Sat year-round, 11am-8pm Sun Sep-Jun) With its scuffed but original 19th-century fittings and cast of slacker patrons playing chess and reading newspapers, this is exactly how you expect an Austrian coffee house to be. Under the high ceiling and old-fashioned lights, wooden panelling reaches up to meet mustard-coloured wallpaper, while battered wooden legs hold up red-patterned chairs and a few billiard tables add a modern twist.

Café Prückel (Map p64; ☎ 512 61 15; 01, Stubenring 24) This 1950s-style café is the epitome of shabby chic. A traditional Viennese coffee house, it's been around some 100 years.

Heurigen (Wine Taverns)

Vienna's *Heurigen* are a good way to see another side of the city. Selling 'new' wine produced on the premises, they have a lively atmosphere, especially as the evening progresses. Outside tables and picnic benches are common. There's usually buffet food, and often strolling piano-accordion musicians entertaining with folk songs.

Because *Heurigen* tend to be clustered together, it's best just to head for the wine-growing suburbs to the north, south and west of the city and look for the green wreath or branch hanging over the door that identifies a *Heuriger*. Opening times are approximately 4pm to 11pm, and wine costs less than €2.50 a *Viertel* (250mL).

The *Heurigen* areas of Nussdorf and Heiligenstadt are near each other at the terminus of tram D, north of the city centre. In 1817 Beethoven lived in at 19, Pfarrplatz 3, Heiligenstadt in what is now know as Beethovenhaus. Down the road (bus 38A from Heiligenstadt or tram 38 from the Ring) is Grinzing, an area favoured by tour groups.

Reinprecht (☎ 320 14 71; 19, Cobenzlgasse 22) This is the best option in the row of *Heurigen* where Cobenzlgasse and Sandgasse meet. It's in a former monastery and boasts a large paved courtyard and a lively, if somewhat touristy, atmosphere.

Sirbu (☎ 320 59 28; 19, Kahlenberger Strasse 210; ⏲ Mon-Sat Apr-Oct) This spot has great views

AUSTRIA

of the Danube. Catch bus 38A east to the final stop at Kahlenberg, from where it is a 15-minute walk.

Esterházykeller (Map p64; ☎ 533 34 82; Haarhof 1; ⏲ 11am-11pm Mon-Fri, 4-11pm Sat & Sun) If you don't have time to venture out into the suburbs, you can get a genuine taste of the *Heurigen* experience here. After descending sharply down a steep stairwell, aromas of dank air, hints of pipe and cigar smoke combined with mugs of wine and food befall olfactory senses in this truly 'underground' *Heurigen* that's as authentic as it gets. Dating from 1683, it was also allegedly used as a way for Viennese to gather provisions during the unsuccessful Turkish siege by tunnelling under the wall that enclosed the city.

AUSTRIA

ENTERTAINMENT

Check listings magazine *Falter* (€2.05) for weekly updates. The tourist office has copies of *Vienna Scene* and produces monthly events listings.

Cinemas & Theatre

Burgkino (Map p64; ☎ 587 84 06; 01, Opernring 19; admission €6-8) Screens *The Third Man* every Friday evening and Sunday afternoon, if you want to revisit this classic movie while in Vienna. Otherwise, check local papers for listings. Seats are cheapest on Monday.

There are performances in English at the **English Theatre** (Map p60; ☎ 402 82 84; www.englishtheatre.at; 08, Josefsgasse 12) and the **International Theatre** (Map p64; ☎ 319 62 72; 09, Porzellangasse 8).

Classical Music

The state ticket office, **Bundestheaterkassen** (Map p64; ☎ 51 444-7880; www.bundestheater.at; 01, Goethegasse 1), sells tickets without commission for both the Staatsoper and Volksoper. In the hut by the Staatsoper, **Wien Ticket** (Map p64; ☎ 58 885; Linke Wienzeile 6, 1060 Wien) also charges little or no commission for cash sales.

The cheapest deals are the standing-room tickets that go on sale at each venue an hour before performances. However, you may need to queue three hours before that for major productions. An hour before the curtain goes up, unsold tickets also go on sale at cheap prices to students under 27 years (from €3.70; home university ID plus international student card necessary).

Staatsoper (State Opera; Map p64; ☎ 51 444-2960; 01, Opernring 2; standing room €4, seats €5.50-220) Performances are lavish, formal affairs, where people dress up.

Volksoper (People's Opera; Map p60; ☎ 51 444-3670; 09, Währinger Strasse 78; standing room €1.50-24, seats €17-75) Productions are more modern here and the atmosphere is a little more relaxed.

Musikverein (Map p64; ☎ 505 18 90; www.musikverein.at; 01, Bösendorferstrasse 12; standing room €5-7, seats €16-110) The opulent and acoustically perfect (unofficial) home of the Vienna Philharmonic Orchestra. You can buy standing tickets three weeks in advance at the box office to hear this world-class orchestra.

There are no performances in July and August. Ask at the tourist office for details of free concerts at the Rathaus or in churches.

Nightclubs

Flex (Map p64; ☎ 533 75 25; Donaukanal/Augartenbrücke) The stairwell leading from the U-Bahn stop to its doors constantly reeks of urine and the circling dealers are an annoyance, but Flex is still the finest club in the city. Time after time this uninhibited shrine to music (it has one of the best sound systems in Europe) puts on great live shows and features the top DJs from Vienna and abroad. Each night is a different theme, with dub club on Monday and London Calling on Wednesday among the most popular.

Porgy n Bess (Map p64; ☎ 512 88 11; 01, Riemergasse 11; ⏲ 8am-4am Mon-Sat, 7pm-4am Sun) Vienna's best spot to catch modern, local and international jazz acts. It has a relaxed and sophisticated atmosphere that attracts a professional crowd. DJs are a ruling feature on weekends and Wednesday night sees impromptu jam sessions.

Volksgarten (Map p64; ☎ 533 05 18; 01, Burgring 1) In the middle of the park of the same name, this place is very popular. There's modern dance and an atmospheric 1950s-style salon that was once a former *Walzer Dancing* venue. Friday and Saturday are the big nights, although it's open other evenings, too.

Roxy (Map p64; ☎ 961 88 00; 04, Operngasse 24; ⏲ Tue-Sat) Often leading the way, or at least keeping pace, with Vienna's progressive clubbing scene. Its tiny dance floor is therefore regularly bursting at the seams. The sounds range from jazz to world music.

Club U (Map p64; ☎ 505 99 04; 04, Karlsplatz; ⏲ Tue-Sun) In the ornate Otto Wagner Stadtbahn

Pavilions café, Club U is a bit like a squat party and plays indie/alternative music.

Why Not? (Map p64; ☎ 535 11 58; 01, Tiefer Graben 22; ⌚ Wed-Sun) A popular gay and lesbian bar/disco; on Wednesday night it's men only.

Rosa Lila Villa (Map p60; ☎ 586 81 50; 06, Linke Wienziele 102) This pink-and-purple building is another favourite spot with alternative lifestyles types. Along with the on-site bar, it also has an information centre. It's a good place to link up with like-minded locals.

Spanish Riding School

The famous Lipizzaner stallions strut their stuff at the **Spanish Riding School** (Map p64; tickets@srs.at; Michaelerplatz 11010; standing room €24-25, seats €45-145) behind the Hofburg. Performances are sold out months in advance, so write to the Spanische Reitschule, Michaelerplatz 1, A-1010 Wien, or ask in the office about cancellations (unclaimed tickets are sold 45 minutes before performances); there's no phone. Travel agents usually charge commission on top of the listed prices.

You need to be pretty keen on horses to pay the high admission price, although a few tricks, such as a stallion bounding along on its hind legs like a demented kangaroo, do tend to stick in the mind. Same-day **tickets** (€11.50, or with entry to the Lipizzaner Museum €15; ⌚ 10am-noon Tue-Sat Feb-Jun & Sep-Dec) can be bought to watch the horses train. The best riders go first and queues disappear by 11am. Watching the weekly final **rehearsal** (tickets €20; 7pm Fri & Sat) is also an option.

Vienna Boys' Choir

Never mind bands like Take That and Nsync; the Vienna Boys' Choir *(Wiener Sängerknaben)* is *the* original boy band. The first troupe was put together back in 1498 and the latest bunch of cherubic angels in sailor suits still holds a fond place in Austrian hearts.

The choir performs weekly at the **Burgkapelle** (Music Chapel; Map p64; ☎ 533 99 27; hofmusikkapelle@asn-wien.ac.at; Hofburg, Rennweg 1; standing free, seats €5.50-30, tickets Fri & 8.15am Sun) at 9.15am on Sunday, except from July to mid-September. Concerts are routinely sold out and there's often a crush of fans to meet the choir afterwards. The group also performs regularly in the **Konzerthaus** (Map p64; ☎ 242 002; 03, Lotheringerstrasse 20) at 3.30pm on Friday in May, June, September and October.

SHOPPING

Stephansplatz (Map p64; ☎ 514 130; Kärntner Strabe 19; ⌚ 9.30am-7pm Mon-Fri, 9.30am-5pm Sat) Set along the famous plaza by the same name, the Stephansplatz is filled with all the stores a good mall needs.

Österreiche Werkstätten (Map p64; Kärntner Strasse 6) Good for Art Deco–type jewellery and household objects in the Viennese tradition; other local specialities include lamps, handmade dolls, and wrought-iron and leather goods.

Café Demel (Map p64; ☎ 535 17 17-0; 01, Kohlmarkt 14) Lavish Café Demel has the old-world atmosphere that makes for the perfect landmark coffee house, but it's usually too crowded. Instead, pop in to buy some fantastic cakes, pastries or sandwiches here.

GETTING THERE & AWAY

Air

Regular scheduled flights link Vienna to Linz, Salzburg, Innsbruck, Klagenfurt and Graz. Check with **Austrian Airlines** (code OS; Map p64; ☎ 051 789; www.aua.com; 01, Kärntner Strasse 11, Vienna). There are also daily nonstop flights to all major European destinations. For further details, see p106.

Boat

Between April and November, fast hydrofoils travel eastwards to Bratislava (one-way/return €23/35, bike extra €7, 1½ hours, Wednesday to Sunday June to September) and Budapest (one-way/return €76/100, bike extra €19, 5½ hours, daily). Bookings can be made through **DDSG Blue Danube** (Map p64; ☎ 58 880-0; www.ddsg-blue-danube.at; 01, Friedrichstrasse 7) or **G Glaser** (Map p60; ☎ 726 08 20; www.members.aon.at/danube; 02, Handelskai 265).

Heading west, a series of boats plies the Danube between Krems and Passau (in Germany), with a handful of services originating in Vienna. Two respectable operators include DDSG Blue Danube and **Brandner** (☎ 07433-25 90; www.brandner.at; Ufer 50, Wallsee). Both run trips from April through October that start at around €17 one-way.

Bus

Bus company Eurolines operates from two locations. At least daily, buses leave from its terminal at **Südbahnhof** (Map p60; ☎ 796 85 52; 03, Arsenal strasse; ⌚ 7am-7pm) heading to Belgrade (one-way/return €40/60, nine hours), to Budapest

AUSTRIA

(one-way/return €26/40, 3½ hours), to Ljubljana (one-way/return €36/60, 15 hours 20 minutes), to Warsaw (one-way/return €34/62, 13½ hours) and to Zagreb (one-way/return €26/42, 4¾ hours).

Services to Bratislava (one-way/return €4/8, 1½ hours) leave from outside Euroline's **city office** (Map p60; ☎ 798 29 00; 03, Erdbergstrasse 202; 🕒 7am-7pm).

Euroline's services to Prague depart from 01, Rathausplatz 5 (Map p64; one-way/return €22/36, five hours). Call ☎ 93 000-34305 for details.

Car & Motorcycle

The Gürtel is an outer ring road that joins up with the A22 on the north bank of the Danube and the A23 southeast of town. All the main road routes intersect with this system, including the A1 from Linz and Salzburg, and the A2 from Graz.

Train

International trains leave from Westbahnhof (Map p60) or Südbahnhof (Map p60). Westbahnhof has trains to northern and Western Europe, and western Austria. Services to Salzburg leave roughly hourly; some go on to Munich and terminate in Paris (14½ hours total). To Zürich there are two trains during the day (€80, nine hours) and one night train (€80, plus charge for fold-down seat/couchette). Eight trains daily go to Budapest (€39, 3½ hours).

Südbahnhof has trains to Italy (inlcuding to Rome, via Venice and Florence), Slovakia, the Czech Republic, Hungary and Poland, and southern Austria. Five trains daily go to Bratislava (€17, 1½ hours) and four to Prague (€41, five hours), with two of those continuing to Berlin (10 hours in total).

Wien-Mitte Bahnhof handles local trains only, and Franz Josefs Bahnhof has local and regional trains.

For train information, call ☎ 05-17 17.

GETTING AROUND

To/From the Airport

It is 19km from the city centre to **Wien Schwechat airport** (VIE; ☎ 70 07-0; www.viennaairport.com). The **City Airport Train** (☎ 25 250; www.cityairporttrain.com) takes 15 minutes between Schwechat and Wien Mitte (one-way €9). The S-Bahn (S7) does the same journey (single €2.90, 25 minutes).

Buses run every 20 or 30 minutes, 24 hourly, from the airport (single €6). Services include to Südtiroler Platz, Südbahnhof and Westbahnhof, and another direct to Schwedenplatz in the city centre.

Taxis cost about €32. **C&K Airport Service** (☎ 44 444) charges €22 one-way for shared vans.

Bicycle

There's a system of **Vienna city bikes** (☎ 0810-500 500; www.citybikewein.at/; deposit €2, 1st hr free, 2nd hr €2, 3rd hr €3, per hr thereafter €2). You'll need a Maestro debit card, Austrian visa or city bike card to be able to use the payment machines. Check its website for locations.

The rather steeply priced **Pedal Power** (Map p60; ☎ 729 72 34; 02, Ausstellungsstrasse 3; hire per half-/full day €18/28) is the city's dominant operator, but the tourist office should be able to point to others near your hostel or hotel. *Tips für Radfahrer*, available from the tourist office, shows circular bike tours.

Car & Motorcycle

Parking is difficult in the city centre and the Viennese are impatient drivers. Blue parking zones allow a maximum stop of 1½ or two

HAPPY SNAPS

Want to give your holiday photos extra pizzazz? Want to be able to put on a slide show back home that won't send friends and family to sleep? Well, as Vienna is the home of Lomo – inventor of the ActionSampler – it's the perfect place to rediscover your love of photography.

Of course, Lomo cameras – plastic compacts that, for example, put nine identical images in one frame or that capture a sequence of four actions in one picture – are a worldwide cult. Although originally a Russian brand, they are now designed in Vienna, which also hosts the Lomographic World Archive at **Lomography Society International** (www.lomography.com). The **Lomo Shop** (Map p64; ☎ 521 890; Museums Quartier; 🕒 10am-7pm; U-Bahn Volkstheater), next to the Kunsthalle, is eminently browsable, as you can just admire the artistic photos on its walls.

hours from 9am to 8pm (to 7pm in the Innere Stadt) on weekdays.

Parking vouchers (€0.40 per 30 minutes) for these times can be purchased in *Tabak* (tobacconist) shops and banks. The cheapest parking garage in the city centre is at Museumsplatz.

Fiakers
Before hiring a *Fiaker* (horse-drawn carriage) by the Stephansdom for a ride around the city, it's worth asking yourself whether these are pony traps or tourist traps. Sure, they're kind of cute, but at around €65/95 for a 30-/60-minute ride…well, you do the maths.

Public Transport
Vienna has a unified public transport network that encompasses trains, trams, buses, and underground (U-Bahn) and suburban (S-Bahn) trains. Routes are outlined on the free tourist office map.

Before use, all advance-purchase tickets must be validated at the entrance to U-Bahn stations or on trams and buses. Tickets are cheaper to buy from ticket machines in U-Bahn stations or from *Tabak* shops, where single tickets cost €1.50. On board, they cost €2. Singles are valid for an hour, and you may change lines on the same trip.

Daily passes *(Stunden-Netzkarte)* cost €17 (valid 24 hours from first use); a three-day pass costs €12 (valid 72 hours); and an eight-day multiple-user pass *(8-Tage-Karte)* costs €24 (validate the ticket once per day per person). Weekly tickets (valid Monday to Sunday) cost €12.50.

Children under six years travel free; those under 16 travel free on Sunday, public holidays and during Vienna school holidays (photo ID necessary). Senior citizens should ask about discounts.

Ticket inspections are not very frequent, but fare dodgers pay an on-the-spot fine of €62. Austrian and European rail passes (see p1121) are valid on the S-Bahn only. Public transport finishes around midnight, but there's also a comprehensive night bus service, for which all train tickets are valid.

Taxi
Taxis are metered for city journeys and cost €2 or €2.10 flag fall, plus from €1.09 per kilometre. There is at least another €2 surcharge for phoning a radio taxi.

THE DANUBE VALLEY

Cruise along the country's most picturesque stretch of the Danube River between Krems an der Donau and Melk. The beautiful valley is filled with terraced vineyards, ruined castles and medieval towns.

KREMS AN DER DONAU
☎ 02732 / pop 23,000

Quaint as it is, Krems is unlikely to be more than a stopover on a boat or bike trip through the Danube Valley. There's riverside camping at **ÖAMTC Camping Krems** (☎ 84 455; Wiedengasse 7; camp site per person/car/tent €5/4/4; ⌚ Apr-Oct) and an HI **Jugendherberge** (☎ 83 452; Ringstrasse 77; dm from €15; ⌚ Apr-Oct) with basic facilities. Otherwise try the atmospheric **Gästehaus Einzinger** (☎ 82 316; fax 82 316-6; Steiner Landstrasse 82, Krems-Stein; s/d €36/52), which has individually designed rooms around a leafy sunken courtyard (watch out for the rather precarious stairs).

The **tourist office** (☎ 82 676; www.tiscover.com/krems; Kloster Und, Undstrasse 6; ⌚ 9am-6pm Mon-Fri, 10am-noon & 1-5pm Sat, 10am-noon & 1-4pm Sun Apr-Oct) can offer more accommodation details.

The *Schiffsstation* (boat station) is a 20-minute walk west from the train station along Donaulände. Between three and five buses leave daily from outside the train station to Melk (€8.50, one hour and five minutes). Trains to Vienna (€10.50, one hour, multiple daily) arrive at Franz Josefs Bahnhof.

DÜRNSTEIN
☎ 02711 / pop 1000

This pretty town, on a curve in the Danube, is not only noted for its beautiful buildings but also for the castle above the town, which at one time imprisoned English king Richard I (the Lion-Heart) in 1192. His unscheduled stopover on the way home from the Crusades came courtesy of Austrian archduke Leopold V, whom he had insulted.

There's not much left of **Küniringerburg castle** today. It's basically just a pile of rubble. Still, it's worth snapping a picture and the views from the top are rather breathtaking.

For more about Dürnstein, contact the **Rathaus** (town hall; ☎ 219; www.duernstein.at; Hauptstrasse 25; ⌚ 9am-5pm Mon-Fri).

AUSTRIA

MELK

☎ 02752 / pop 6500

The sheer size and majesty of Melk's imposing abbey-fortress, rising above the Danube and the small town, is stunning. Featured in the epic medieval German poem *Nibelungenlied* and Umberto Eco's best-selling novel *The Name of the Rose,* the impressive Benedictine monastery endures as a major Wachau landmark. It's an essential stop along the Danube Valley route, however, so be prepared to fight through loads of tourists to explore the place.

Orientation & Information

The train station is 300m from the town centre. Walk straight ahead from the train station along Bahnhofstrasse, turning right into Abt Karl Strasse if you're going to the hostel or continuing ahead for the town. The quickest way to the central Rathausplatz is through the small Bahngasse path (to the right of the cow's-head mural at the bottom of the hill), rather than veering left into Hauptplatz.

Turn right from Bahngasse into Rathausplatz and right again at the end, following the signs to the **tourist office** (☎ 52 307-410; www.tiscover.com/melk; Babenbergerstrasse 1; 9am-noon & 2-6pm Mon-Fri, 10am-2pm Sat Apr-Jun & Sep-Oct, 9am-7pm Mon-Sat, 10am-2pm Sun Jul & Aug, closed Nov-Mar).

Sights & Activities

On a hill overlooking the town is the ornate golden abbey **Stift Melk** (☎ 555 232; www.stiftmelk.at; adult/student €7/4.10, guided tours extra €1.80; 9am-6pm May-Sep, 9am-5pm Oct-Apr, guided tours only Nov-Mar). Home to monks since the 11th century, the current building was erected in the 18th century after a devastating fire. Consequently, it's an elaborate example of baroque architecture, most often lauded for its imposing marble hall and beautiful library, but just as unforgettable for the curved terrace connecting these two rooms. The **Abbey Museum** on the grounds outlines the history of the building and the church with its exhibition topic entitled 'The Path from Yesterday to Today – Melk in its Past and Present'. Various rooms using computer animation, sound and multimedia accurately narrate the 910-year-plus Benedictine monastic history of Melk.

Useful explanatory booklets (€4) for the whole building are available in various languages, or phone ahead if you want a tour in English, which works out cheaper.

Sleeping & Eating

Camping Melk (☎ 53 291; Kolomaniau 3; camp site per person/tent/car €4/3/2; Mar-Oct) Located on the west bank of the canal that joins the Danube, this camping ground is a tranquil spot. If you get hungry, there is an attached restaurant, where you'll also find reception.

Jugendherberge (☎ 52 681; Karl Strasse 42; dm €17; Mar-Oct, check-in 5-9pm) This HI hostel is modern and comfy, although it often plays host to large groups. Call ahead to see if it's full.

Gasthof Goldener Stern (☎ 52 214; Sterngasse 17; s/d from €22/44; P) When the friendly owners renovated recently, they decided to keep some cheaper 'student' rooms for budget travellers – they share bathrooms but are clean and excellent value. At the other end are the so-called 'romantic' rooms, all individually decorated. The place has a welcoming feel and a secluded location above the main square. It also has a fine restaurant.

Pasta e Pizza (☎ 53 686; Jakob Prandtauerstrasse 4; pizza €6-8) Tucked away from the main tourist trail, this eatery offers heaps of pizza and pasta dishes in cheerful environs.

Self-caterers should stock up at the **Spar supermarket** (Rathausplatz 9).

Getting There & Away

Boats leave from the canal by Pionierstrasse, 400m behind the monastery. Multiple daily trains to Vienna's Westbahnhof (€12, 75 to 90 minutes) are direct or via St Pölten.

LINZ

☎ 070 / pop 218,000

Austria's second-largest city is essentially industrial by nature and largely overlooked by tourists. It was discovered years ago that its small, old-town centre couldn't compete with Vienna or Salzburg. Linz's biggest claims to 'fame' were being Adolf Hitler's favourite town and having a type of cake – the Linzer torte – named after it. So the city carved a niche for itself by becoming technologically industrial as well. Its world-leading cybercentre, stunning first-rate contemporary art gallery and appealing attractions for kids prove that Linz certainly has the ability to please and interest.

Orientation

Most of the city is on the south bank of the Danube. The main square, Hauptplatz, is reached from the train station on tram 3. To walk here, turn right (northeast) out of the station forecourt, Bahnhofplatz, and continue straight ahead until you come to a park on the left. Turn left here into Landstrasse and continue for 10 minutes to get to Hauptplatz.

Information

Ars Electronica Center (☎ 72 720; www.aec.at; Hauptstrasse 2; 9am-5pm Wed & Thu, 9am-9pm Fri, 10am-6pm Sat & Sun) Offers free Internet access.
Main Post Office (Bahnhofplatz 11-13; 7am-9pm Mon-Fri, 7am-6pm Sat, 7am-1pm Sun)
Tourist Office (☎ 707 017-77; www.linz.at; Hauptplatz 1; 8am-7pm Mon-Fri, 10am-7pm Sat & Sun May-Oct, 10am-6pm Nov-Apr) Has the Linz City Ticket (€20), which offers free public transport, sightseeing discounts and a free €10 meal.

Sights & Activities

Architecturally eye-catching and artistically impressive, the riverside **Lentos Kunstmuseum Linz** (☎ 7070 3600; www.lentos.at; Ernst Koref Promenade 1; admission €7; 10am-6pm Wed-Mon, 10am-8pm Thu) is an important new addition to the Linz scene. It's built a little like an asymmetric tray table, with legs on either side. Behind its partially reflective glass façade lie works by artists such as Klimt, Schiele, Picasso, Kokoschka, Matisse, Haring and Warhol. Lit up at night, the building looks spectacular.

Across the Danube lies an older art and technology centre that will help you indulge your childhood superhero fantasies, without having to jump off the garage roof and graze your knee. At the **Ars Electronica Center** (☎ 72 72-0; www.aec.at; Hauptstrasse 2; adult/student €6/3; 9am-5pm Wed & Thu, 9am-9pm Fri, 10am-6pm Sat & Sun) you'll be given a virtual-reality headset, then strapped to the ceiling and sent 'flying' over Linz and into the future. If you like this, you'll also love the world's only public 'cave', a virtual environment where you can travel through space and time.

A ride on the **Pöstlingbergbahn** (funicular railway; ☎ 7801 7002; one-way/return €2/3.20, children half-price; 5.20am-8pm Mon-Sat, 11.40am-8pm Sun) offers great views and is bound to keep kids of all ages happy. It looks like a quaint street trolley from a movie and climbs slowly to the ornate twin-spired church and **children's grotto railway** (☎ 3400 7506; www.linzag.at; adult/child €4/2; 10am-5pm Oct-Apr, 10am-6pm May-Sep) atop the Pöst-lingberg hill. To reach the Pöstlingbergbahn take tram 3 to Bergbahnof Urfahr.

Festivals & Events

The **Ars Electronica Festival** (☎ 72 72-0; www.aec.at) in early September showcases cyber-art, computer music, and other marriages of technology and art. This leads into the **Brucknerfest** (Bruckner Festival; ☎ 775 230; www.brucknerhaus.at; Brucknerhaus Kasse, Untere Donaulände, A-4010 Linz), which pays homage to native son Anton Bruckner with a month of classical music between mid-September and mid-October. For this, you should book early.

In July there's the **Pflasterspektakel street performers' festival**.

Sleeping

The tourist office offers a free accommodation booking service for visitors, but only face-to-face and not over the phone.

Jugendgästehaus (☎ 664 434; www.oejhv.or.at; Stanglhofweg 3; dm/s/d €18.50/28.50/41) Modern and comfortable, even if it's a little way from the centre of town; take bus 17, 19 or 27. Half- and full-board options are available.

Wilder Mann (☎ 656 078; wilder-mann@aon.at; Goethestrasse 14; s/d/tr from €36/60/77, with shared bathroom from €26/44/53) Despite first impressions at this boarding house–style place, the rooms are reasonably comfy and the bathrooms clean. Try to avoid the top floor, where frosted-glass door panels let in hall light.

Goldener Anker (☎ 771 088; Hofgasse 5; s/d from €42/70) A tastefully decorated family-run *Gasthof* (guesthouse) inside Linz's oldest pub, rooms are comfortable and conveniently located.

Novotel Linz (☎ 347 28 10; www.accorhotels.com/novotel_linz.htm; Wankmüllerhofstrasse 37; s/d €69/84; P) Packed with all sorts of amenities, including a sauna and tennis courts, this place is popular with business travellers as well families on weekends or holidays. Rooms are modern and efficient, and there's a playground for the kids.

Hotel Wolfinger (☎ 773 291-0; www.austria-classic-hotels.at/wolfinger; Hauptplatz 19; s/d €83/115, with shared bathroom from €44/65) A central option, this hotel is in a wonderful former cloister renovated in baroque style and with unique flair. It has a very limited number of cheaper rooms.

AUSTRIA

Eating & Drinking

Café Traximayr (☎ 773 353; Promenadestrasse 16; snacks from €5; ⏰ Mon-Sat) An elegant coffee house, with only a few snooker tables breaking up the formal environment of white walls, marble, mirrors and chandeliers. Try the Linzer torte – this heavy, nutty-tasting sponge filled with strawberry jam isn't on the menu but it is on the cake trolley, so just ask.

p'aa (☎ 776 461; Altstadt 28; mains €8-12; ⏰ 11am-midnight Mon-Sat) Serving mainly vegan cuisine in an elegant interior, the menu is an eclectic mix of Tibetan, Indian and Mexican. Sit on the cobblestones outside or inside under low arched ceilings.

Stiegelbräu zum Klosterhof (Landstrasse 30; mains €11-17.50) A huge beer garden and a fine gastronomic reputation, it's as popular for business lunches as it is for tourist outings.

Sky Loft Media Bar (Ars Electronica Center, Hauptstrasse 2; ⏰ 9am-5pm Wed & Thu, 9am-2am Fri & Sat) This glassed-in bar is a great place for a beer or cocktail overlooking the Danube and the Lentos museum.

Getting There & Around

Low-cost Ryanair flies in daily from London Stansted to **Linz airport** (LNZ; ☎ 600-0; www.flughafen-linz.at), which provides a shuttle bus (€2.20, 20 minutes) to the main train station.

Linz is halfway between Salzburg and Vienna on the main road and rail routes. Trains to Salzburg (€17.70) and Vienna (€23.50) take between 1¼ and two hours. Trains leave approximately hourly.

City transport tickets are bought before you board: €0.70 per journey or €3 for a day card. Some of the bus services stop early in the evening. The suburban **Lilo train station** (☎ 654 376; Coulinstrasse 30) offers bike hire for €7 per day.

THE SOUTH

Austria's two main southern states, Styria (Steiermark) and Carinthia (Kärnten), often feel worlds apart from the rest of the country, both in climate and attitude. Elements of Italian, Slovenian and Hungarian culture are present here, and residents have historical connections with each of those countries. Styria is a blissful amalgamation of genteel architecture, rolling green hills, vine-covered slopes and soaring mountains. Its capital, Graz, is one of Austria's most attractive cities (with some of the highest standards of living in Europe).

A jet-setting, fashion-conscious crowd heads to sun-drenched Carinthia for summer holidays. The region (right on the border with Italy) exudes an atmosphere that's as close to Mediterranean as this staunch country gets.

GRAZ

☎ **0316 / pop 250,000**

European Capital of Culture in 2003 and recently included in the list of world cultural heritage sites, this provincial capital of Styria offers a little something for everyone. Funky and laid-back at the same time, the futuristic, bluish-bloblike Kunsthaus Graz will make you think that aliens have landed nearby. There's so much to see and do in Graz that it's fair to say your hotel room will not enjoy much use. Experience the unique blend of Mediterranean and medieval atmosphere of the Old Town and see why it leaves such an indelible impression on other travellers.

Orientation

Austria's second-largest city is dominated by its *Schlossberg* (castle hill) looming above the city centre. The River Mur runs in a north–south path in front (west) of the hill, separating the city centre from the main train station (Hauptbahnhof). Trams 3, 6 and 14 all run from the train station to the central Hauptplatz. Several streets radiate from this square, including café-lined Sporgasse and the primary pedestrian thoroughfare, Herrengasse. This thoroughfare leads to Jakominiplatz, which is a major transport hub.

Information

Graz Tourismus (☎ 80 75-0; www.graztourismus.at; Herrengasse 16; ⏰ 9am-6pm Mon-Sat, 10am-6pm Sun)

Main Post Office (Neutorgasse 46; ⏰ 7.30am-8pm Mon-Fri, 8am-noon Sat)

Medien.kunstbar (Kunsthaus Graz, Lendkai 1; ⏰ 10am-6pm Tue-Sun, 10am-8pm Thu) Offers free Internet access.

Speednet-café (Hauptbahnhof Europaplatz 4; per hr around €6; ⏰ 8am-10pm Mon-Sat, 9am-9pm Sun) Offers Internet access.

Tourist Information Counter (☎ 80 75-21; Hauptbahnhof; ⏰ 8.30am-1pm & 2-5.30pm Mon-Wed & Fri, to 6.30pm Thu)

AUSTRIA

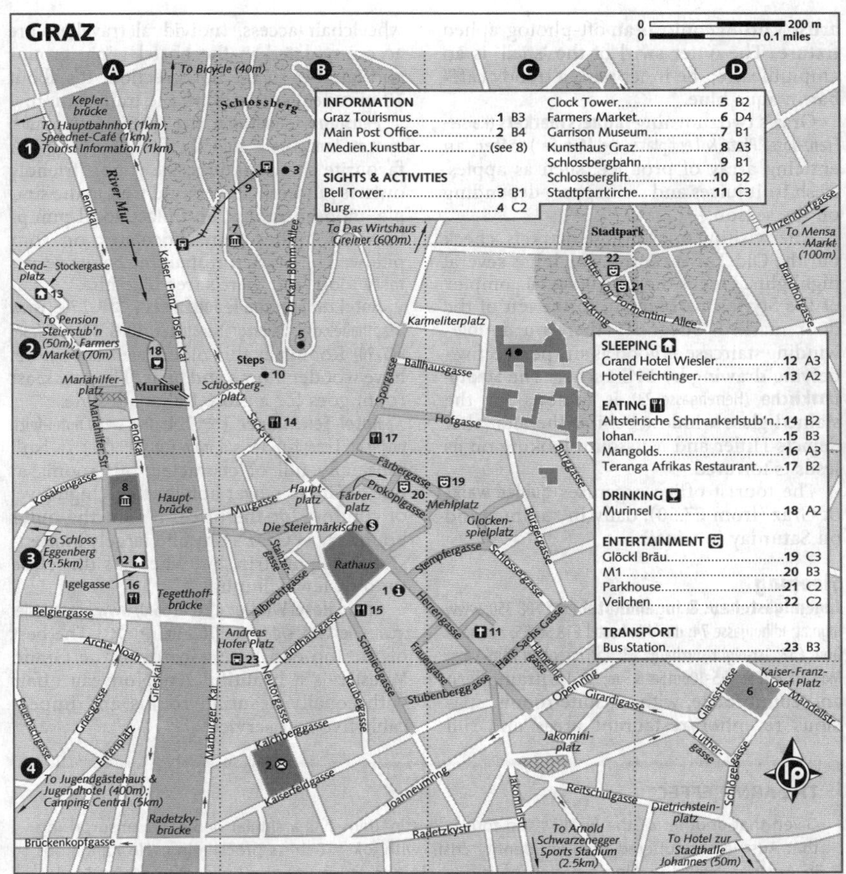

Sights & Activities

Here you'll find a plethora of museums, galleries, grandiose architecture, churches and unusual surprises. Most visitors head first for the **Schlossberg** to get an overview of the city and explore what remains of its fortress. This includes the medieval **clock tower**, plus a **bell tower**, **bastion** and **garrison museum** (☎ 827 348; adult/concession €1.50/0.85; 🕑 10am-5pm Tue-Sun Apr-Oct). There are three main ways to ascend: the glass **Schlossberglift**, hewn through the hill; the **Schlossbergbahn** funicular railway (both requiring a Zone 1 transport ticket, €1.70); and the 260 steps near the lift (free).

From this vantage point, you can't help but notice the bubble-shaped **Kunsthaus Graz** (☎ 8017 9200; www.kunsthausgraz.at; Lendkai 1; adult/senior/student €6/4.50/2.50; 🕑 10am-6pm Tue, Wed & Fri-Sun, 10am-8pm Thu). Notice anything extraterrestrial? This creation by UK architects Colin Fournier and Peter Cook is referred to as the 'friendly alien'. It has also been compared to a mutant bladder and a spaceship, but there's general agreement that it's one of Europe's leading modern buildings. Whatever the temporary exhibitions – and these are often very good – it's the structure that's the star.

Likewise, the **Murinsel** (🕑 24hr), an artificial island in the River Mur that's connected to both banks, north of the Kunsthaus and Hauptbrücke (main bridge). Designed in the form of an open seashell, the glass, concrete and steel construction, by New York artist Vito Acconic, is an oft-photographed fixture. The outer swirl of the 'shell' is an amphitheatre; the inner part, a trendy café/bar in aqua blue.

Graz's two morning **farmers markets** (Kaiser-Franz-Josef Platz & Lendplatz; ⌚ Mon-Sat) offer an enticing array of produce, such as apples, fresh fruit juices and schnapps – depending on the season.

After visiting one of these markets, check out the Old Town centre, which has several highlights. One is the **Burg** (Hofgasse) complex of the Styrian parliament; to the left of the door marked 'Stiege III' there's a double-winding staircase as good as any perspective-defying drawing by MC Escher. The **Stadtpfarrkirche** (Herrengasse 23) is famous for the stained-glass window behind the altar that depicts Hitler and Mussolini looking on as Jesus is tortured.

The tourist office organises **guided walks** of Graz (from €7.50), daily in summer and on Saturday in winter.

Sleeping

Jugendgästehaus & Jugendhotel (☎ 708 350; www.jfgh.at; Idlhofgasse 74; dm/d in hostel €18.50/55, r in hotel from €47, 1st-night surcharge €3; ⌚ reception 7am-10pm Mon-Fri, 7-10am & 5-10pm Sat & Sun; P) Ultramodern and comfortable, with en suite rooms, spacious reception/restaurant areas and full wheelchair access. Individual travellers are accommodated in the hostel wing, groups and families in the hotel section. It's about 10 minutes on foot from the train station.

Pension Steierstub'n (☎ 716 855; www.pension-graz.at; Lendplatz 8; s/d/tr from €39/70/100; P) A favourite choice of ours, the young, friendly owners put fresh flowers and fruit in the simple, modern rooms, and place local pumpkinseeds, rather than chocolates, on your pillow. The Styrian restaurant below serves tasty food, and there's free bike hire.

Hotel zur Stadthalle Johannes (☎ 837 766; www.stadthalle.co.at; Münzgrabenstrasse 48 & 87; s/d from €47/70) Rooms at this older, well-kept hotel have wooden floors and beds. The breakfast room goes for a more Italianate style.

Hotel Feichtinger (☎ 724 100; www.hotel-feichtinger.at; Lendplatz 1A; s/d from €50/94; ⊠) It isn't especially full of character, but rooms at one of Graz's newer hotels offer a high level of comfort for the price. It's on the outer boundary of Graz's tiny and largely inoffensive red-light strip, but when it's this close to town few will mind.

Grand Hotel Wiesler (☎ 70 66-0; www.hotelwiesler.com; Grieskai 4; s/d from €170/230; P ⊠) The best of the top-end hotels in town, the Grand Wiesler is a beautiful Art Nouveau affair with equally beautiful rooms and impeccable five-star service.

THE ARNIE EFFECT

Given that another of the world's top tourist destinations has a similar name, it's unsurprising that Austria has suffered from an identity crisis, with jokey T-shirts proclaiming, 'No Kangaroos in Austria'. Now the Alpine nation believes help has arrived in the bulky shape of a Styrian bodybuilder-turned-movie-star-turned-politician.

Arnold Schwarzenegger, locals hope optimistically, will help even the most geographically ignorant American schoolchild locate their tiny country on a map.

When the Terminator became the Californian 'Gubernator' in late 2003, even left-wing Austrians put aside their reservations for the evening. Bar-goers in Graz, just a few miles from Schwarzenegger's boyhood home of Thal, erupted in cheers.

'Mozart is no longer the world's most famous Austrian', Dieter Hardt-Stremayr of the Graz tourist office told AFP.

While Californians have since been welcomed in Austria like long-lost members of the family, there's little Arnie memorabilia for them, or anyone else, to see. Two Russian artists have been trying to erect a huge Terminator statue in Graz's Stadtpark. However, they've met with resistance because, ultimately, Arnie is a controversial figure in Austria.

In fact, in 2005 it appeared the Governator was actually trying to sever ties with his hometown. A museum exhibiting training equipment used by the former bodybuilder closed in 2005 due to money woes. Museum officials say they reached out to Schwarzenegger for financial help to save it but were ignored. Now all that marks his presence in Graz is the Arnold Schwarzenegger Sports Stadium. The stadium is to the southwest of the city centre; take tram 4.

AUTHOR'S CHOICE

Teranga Afrikas Restaurant (☎ 818 306 56; Sporgasse 16; mains around €1) Find that Styrian cuisine isn't far enough from the sometimes bland Austrian fare and don't mind adventurous arrangements? Then head into a sometimes-marked alleyway where it looks like you are going nowhere at all and enter the last door on the left. Inside you'll find a simple dining room with five tables, two bar stools, sparse African décor and one of the most surprising things – no written menu. The cuisine is from West Africa. There are usually two choices, one meat, one vegetarian, which vary nightly, but always include soup. Ask if it has the spicy mango soup with yams – it's excellent. Credit cards are not accepted.

Eating

With green, leafy salads dressed in delicious pumpkinseed oil, lots of polenta, fish specialities and *Pfand'l* (pan-grilled) dishes, Styrian cuisine feels lighter and healthier than most regional Austrian cooking.

Mangolds (Griesgasse 11; salad per 100g from €1.05; 🕑 11am-8pm Mon-Fri, 11am-4pm Sat) An ultra-healthy and reasonably cheap vegetarian buffet, with loads of salads to choose from.

Mensa Markt (Schubertstrasse 2-4; menus €4-4.50) This spot by the university has a range of inexpensive takeaway.

Altsteirische Schmankerlstub'n (☎ 823 211; Sackstrasse 10; mains €7.50-16.50) Hidden in a passageway off Sackstrasse, this rustic restaurant serves Styrian staples, such as *Bauernschmaus* (roast pork with blood sausage, sauerkraut and dumplings), *Ochsenfetzen* (beef strips with sour cream and roast potatoes) and *Vogerlsalat* (green salad) with roast potatoes, egg, tomatoes and pumpkinseed oil.

Iohan (☎ 821 312; Landhausgasse 1; mains from €18; 🕑 dinner Tue-Sat) Locals come here for a treat. In the former cold-storage room of the city hall, it has formal white tablecloths, draped white canvas chairs and a cool, somewhat more relaxed, bar. The select menu might include saddle of lamb with black lentils or veal with polenta and mushrooms.

Drinking & Entertainment

Graz, like Vienna, has a 'bar zone' known as the Bermudadreieck. It's located between Sporgasse, Färbergasse and Stempfergasse, where you will find venues ranging from the humble **Glöckl Bräu** (☎ 814 781; Glockenspielplatz 2-3) to the 3rd-floor **M1** (☎ 811 233; Färbergasse 1), favoured by the beautiful people. There are other clusters of hip bars at the top of Sporgasse and behind the Kunsthaus Graz.

Murinsel (☎ 818 669; 🕑 café/bar 9am-11pm Sun-Wed, 9am-2am Thu-Sat) You'll never again drink anywhere quite like the Murinsel, so at least start the evening in this shimmering, fluorescent-lit platform in the middle of the river. There are DJs on some evenings.

Parkhouse (☎ 827 434; Stadtpark 2) Join the crowd at this atmospheric and friendly place in the city park if you're looking to party minus any type of pretentious vibe.

Veilchen (☎ 8277 3416; Stadtpark 1) Near the Parkhouse, this can be an interesting venue. It's an art gallery and community centre that usually has DJs on Saturday.

Getting There & Away

Ryanair has flights daily from London Stansted to **Graz airport** (GRZ; ☎ 29 02-0; www.flughafen-graz.at, in German). Direct Intercity (IC) trains to Vienna's Südbahnhof depart every two hours (€30, 2¾ hours). Trains depart every two hours to Salzburg (€40, 4¼ hours), either direct or changing at Bischofshofen. Two daily, direct trains depart for Ljubljana (€38, four hours), and every hour or two to Budapest (€63, 6½ hours) via Szentgotthard and Szombathely. Trains to Klagenfurt (€30, three hours) go via Bruck an der Mur. The A2 autobahn from Vienna to Klagenfurt passes a few kilometres from the city.

Getting Around

Public transport tickets cover trams, buses, the Schlossbergbahn and the Schlossberglift. Tickets cost €1.60 each. The 24-hour/weekly passes cost €3.20/7.50. Buses 600, 630 and 631 connect the airport with the train station, Hauptplatz or Jakominiplatz (€1.60); the same journey by taxi costs about €15.

You can hire a bike from **Bicycle** (☎ 821 357-0; Körösistrasse 5) from €7.50/42 per day/week.

KLAGENFURT

☎ 0463 / pop 87,000

In a salacious location on the water, this sunny provincial capital makes a handy base for exploring the Wörthersee's lakeside villages and elegant medieval towns to the north. The town is not hugely interesting, but gets buzzing in summer when Austrians on weekend holiday flock here.

Orientation

The heart of the city is Neuer Platz, which is 1km north of the main train station. Walk straight down Bahnhofstrasse and turn left into Paradiesergasse to get there, or take bus 40, 41 or 42 to Heiligengeistplatz, just around the corner from Neuer Platz.

Information

Gates Cafebar (Waagplatz 7; per 10 min €1; 9am-1am Mon-Fri, 7pm-1am Sat & Sun) Offers Internet access.
Main Post Office (Dr Hermann Gasse 4; 7.30am-6pm Mon-Fri, 8-11am Sat)
Tourist Office (537 22 23; www.info.klagenfurt.at; Rathaus, Neuer Platz; 8am-8pm Mon-Fri, 10am-5pm Sat & Sun May-Sep, 8am-6.30pm Mon-Fri, 10am-3pm Sat & Sun Oct-Apr)

Sights & Activities

The **Wörthersee**, 4km west of the city centre, is one of the region's warmer lakes, thanks to subterranean thermal springs: the average water temperature between June and September is 21°C (69°F). Events from go-kart rallies to avant-garde festivals of tattoo and body painting ensure you'll never be left without something to see. The 50km **cycle path** around the lake is one of the 'Top 10' in Austria. There is a *Fahrad Verleih* (Hire a Bike) scheme in summer; hire a standard bicycle at one of several outlets around the lake and return it at any other outlet (five hours/24 hours/one week €5/9/35). Mountain and road bikes are available, and you can also arrange to return the bike to the same location, although it costs a few euros more.

Also near the lake, Europa Park has various attractions, including the theme park **Minimundus** (21 194-0; Villacher Strasse 241; adult/student €10/4.50; Apr-Oct), which displays more than 150 models of famous international buildings on a 1:25 scale.

Sleeping & Eating

When you check into your accommodation in Klagenfurt, ask for a copy of your *Gästekarte* (guest card), which entitles you to a range of discounts on local attractions and public transport.

Jugendherberge (230 020; jgh.klagenfurt@oejhv.or.at; Neckheimgasse 6; dm €17.50, dm as d €42; reception 7-11am & 5-10pm; P) Modern and clean, this HI hostel is near the university and Europa Park. Take bus 12 to get there. Book ahead, as it's often full with school groups.

Hotel Liebetegger (56 935; www.liebetegger.com, in German; Völkermarkterstrasse 8; s/d from €28/60) The décor is modern, with interesting touches like cast-iron door handles and Gustav Klimt prints on the walls, making this three-star hotel quite a good deal. There's an inviting café/bar (mains €7 to €10) attached, and breakfast is available for an extra €7.50.

Hotel Geyer (57 886; www.hotelgeyer.com; Priesterhausgasse; s/d €55/95; P) Everyone's favourite Klagenfurt hotel, the public areas are quite funky with loads of modern art on the walls. Rooms were recently renovated, and although they're compact, they're still comfortable. A generous breakfast buffet is included.

Zum Augustin (513 992; Pfarrhofgasse 2; mains €7-16) A smoky brewery that makes its own beer – it has eight different ales on tap. It is popular with the after-work crowd, serves a decent range of regional food and has a pleasant cobblestone patio.

Getting There & Around

Flights are available with Ryanair from London daily, with a bus running to the city centre. Trains to Graz (€28, five hours) go via Bruck an der Mur and depart every two hours. Trains to western Austria, Italy and Germany go via Villach, 40 minutes away.

Bus drivers sell single tickets (€1.50), while a strip of 10 costs €12 from ticket machines. Daily/weekly passes cost €3.30/13. For the Europa Park vicinity, take bus 10, 11, 12, 20, 21 or 22 from Heiligengeistplatz in the city centre. To the airport, take bus 42 or a taxi (about €16). Bikes can be hired from **Zweirad Impulse** (516 310; 24hr hire adult/child €10/7).

SALZBURG

0662 / pop 145,000

The joke 'if it's baroque, don't fix it' would make a perfect maxim for Salzburg; the tranquil Old Town burrowed in below steep hills looks as much as it did when Mozart lived here 250 years ago. Second only to Vienna in numbers of visitors, ornate 17th-century buildings still shadow the narrow, cobbled streets, while gorgeous manicured grounds surround the baroque Schloss Mirabell.

By night, the medieval Hohensalzburg fortress hovers in an arc of lights above the city. By day, the warren of courtyards, fountains and churches below is fully revealed. And visitors still tour film locations used for *The Sound of Music* in and around Salzburg, Austria's charming capital of kitsch.

ORIENTATION

The pedestrianised Old Town is on the south bank of the River Salzach, wedged between the river and Mönchsberg behind it. Many attractions and the shopping street of Getreidegasse are here. On the north bank is Mozart's Wohnhaus and Schloss Mirabell, as well as the new city centre, with most of the cheaper hotels. Buses 1, 6, 51 and 55 will take you from the main train station (Hauptbahnhof) to the city centre. To walk, turn left out of the train station into Rainerstrasse and follow it (taking the second, not the first tunnel under the railway) to Mirabellplatz.

INFORMATION

Tourist offices and hotels sell the Salzburg Card (€21/28/34 for 24/48/72 hours), which provides free museum entry and public transport, and offers various reductions. Students get a 10% discount. The tourist office's commission for hotel reservations is €2.20 or €4 for three or more people.

Amex (☎ 80 80; Mozartplatz 5; 🕑 9am-5.30pm Mon-Fri, 9am-noon Sat) For travel agency information.

Cybar (☎ 844 822; Mozartplatz 5; per 10 min €1.50-1.80; 🕑 9am-10pm) Offers Internet access.

Main Post Office (Residenzplatz 9; 🕑 7am-7pm Mon-Fri, 8-10am Sat)

Main Tourist Office (☎ information 88-987 330, hotel reservations 88-987 314; www.salzburg.info; Mozartplatz 5; 🕑 9am-6pm May-Jun & Sep-Oct, 9am-7pm Dec, Jul & Aug, 9am-6pm Mon-Sat Nov & Jan-Apr)

Piterfun (Ferdinand-Porsche-Strasse 7; per 10 min €1.50-1.80; 🕑 10am-10pm) Offers Internet access.

St Johanns-Spital (☎ 44 82-0; Müllner Hauptstrasse 48) For medical treatment.

STA Travel (☎ 458 733; Fanny-von-Lehnert Strasse 1; 🕑 Mon-Fri)

Tourist Information Counter (Platform 2A, Hauptbahnhof; 🕑 9.15am-8pm) Opening hours vary.

Train Station Post Office (Hauptbahnhof; 🕑 7am-8.30pm Mon-Fri, 8am-2pm Sat, 1-6pm Sun)

SIGHTS & ACTIVITIES

A Unesco World Heritage site, Salzburg's Old Town centre is equally entrancing whether viewed from ground level or from the hills above.

Residenzplatz is a good starting point for a wander. The **Dom** (cathedral), just to the south, is worth checking out for the three bronze doors symbolising faith, hope and charity. From here, head west along Franziskanergasse and turn left into a courtyard for **St Peterskirche**, an abbey dating from AD 847. Among lovingly tended graves in the abbey's grounds you'll find the entrance to the **Katakomben** (catacombs; adult/student €1/0.70; 🕑 10.30am-5pm summer, 10.30am-3.30pm winter). The western end of Franziskanergasse opens out into Max Reinhardt Platz, where you'll see the back of Fisher von Erlach's **Universitätskirche** (Universitätsplatz), an outstanding example of baroque architecture. The **Stift Nonnberg** (Nonnberg Abbey), where *The Sound of Music* first encounters Maria, is back in the other direction, to the east of the Festung Hohensalzburg.

Festung Hohensalzburg

This **castle fortress** (☎ 842 430-11; www.salzburgburgen.at; Mönchsberg 34; admission €4, for interior & audioguide €7.50; 🕑 9am-6pm 15 Mar-14 Jun, 9am-7pm 15 Jun-14 Sep, 9am-5pm 15 Sep-14 Mar), built in 1077, was home to many archbishop-princes (who ruled Salzburg from 798). Inside are the impressively ornate staterooms, torture chambers and two museums.

It takes 15 minutes to walk up the hill to the fortress, or you can catch the funicular **Festungsbahn** (☎ 849 750; Festungsgasse 4; adult/concession one-way incl admission to fortress grounds €5.60/5; 🕑 9am-9pm May-Sep, 9am-5pm Oct-Apr).

Schloss Mirabell

The formal gardens of **Schloss Mirabell** (🕑 dawn-dusk), with their tulips, crocuses and Greek statues, are the main attraction at this palace built by the archbishop-prince Wolf Dietrich for his mistress in 1606. The view from the western end (looking east towards the fortress) is one of Salzburg's most attractive. The gardens were featured in *The Sound of Music*, and are now popular with wedding parties. Concerts are often held in the palace, and there are sometimes open-air performances in the garden. Parts of the garden are off limits in winter.

Museums

Although Mozart is now a major tourist drawcard, the man himself found Salzburg

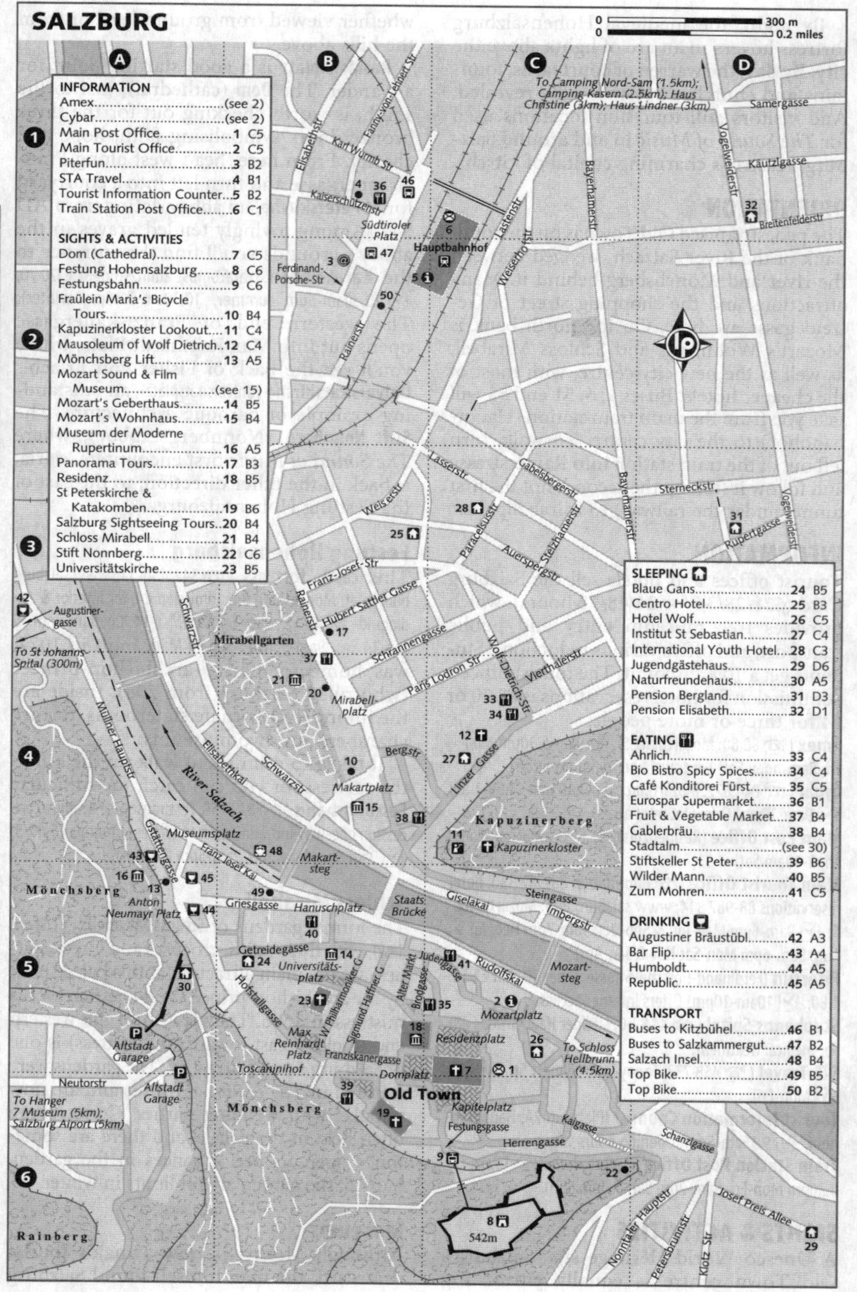
SALZBURG
0 300 m
0 0.2 miles
A
B
C
D
1
2
3
4
5
6
INFORMATION
Amex.....(see 2)
Cybar.....(see 2)
Main Post Office.....1 C5
Main Tourist Office.....2 C5
Piterfun.....3 B2
STA Travel.....4 B1
Tourist Information Counter.....5 B2
Train Station Post Office.....6 C1
SIGHTS & ACTIVITIES
Dom (Cathedral).....7 C5
Festung Hohensalzburg.....8 C6
Festungsbahn.....9 C6
Fräulein Maria's Bicycle Tours.....10 B4
Kapuzinerkloster Lookout.....11 C4
Mausoleum of Wolf Dietrich.....12 C4
Mönchsberg Lift.....13 A5
Mozart Sound & Film Museum.....(see 15)
Mozart's Geberthaus.....14 B5
Mozart's Wohnhaus.....15 B4
Museum der Moderne Rupertinum.....16 A5
Panorama Tours.....17 B3
Residenz.....18 B5
St Peterskirche & Katakomben.....19 B6
Salzburg Sightseeing Tours.....20 B4
Schloss Mirabell.....21 B4
Stift Nonnberg.....22 C6
Universitätskirche.....23 B5
SLEEPING
Blaue Gans.....24 B5
Centro Hotel.....25 B3
Hotel Wolf.....26 C5
Institut St Sebastian.....27 C4
International Youth Hotel.....28 C3
Jugendgästehaus.....29 D6
Naturfreundehaus.....30 A5
Pension Bergland.....31 D3
Pension Elisabeth.....32 D1
EATING
Ahrlich.....33 C4
Bio Bistro Spicy Spices.....34 C4
Café Konditorei Fürst.....35 C5
Eurospar Supermarket.....36 B1
Fruit & Vegetable Market.....37 B4
Gablerbräu.....38 B4
Stadtalm.....(see 30)
Stiftskeller St Peter.....39 B6
Wilder Mann.....40 B5
Zum Mohren.....41 C5
DRINKING
Augustiner Bräustübl.....42 A3
Bar Flip.....43 A4
Humboldt.....44 A5
Republic.....45 A5
TRANSPORT
Buses to Kitzbühel.....46 B1
Buses to Salzkammergut.....47 B2
Salzach Insel.....48 B4
Top Bike.....49 B5
Top Bike.....50 B2
To Camping Nord-Sam (1.5km); Camping Kasern (2.5km); Haus Christine (3km); Haus Lindner (3km)
Samergasse
Kautzlgasse
Breitenfelderstr
Vogelweiderstr
Bayerhamerstr
Lastenstr
Weiserhofstr
Hauptbahnhof
Südtiroler Platz
Kaiserschützenstr
Karl Wurmb Str
Fanny-von-Lehnert Str
Elisabethstr
Ferdinand-Porsche-Str
Rainerstr
Lasserstr
Gabelsbergerstr
Sterneckstr
Rupertgasse
Paracelsusstr
Stelzhamerstr
Auerspergstr
Weiserstr
Franz-Josef-Str
Hubert Sattler Gasse
Schrannengasse
Paris Lodron Str
Wolf-Dietrich-Str
Vierthalerstr
Linzer Gasse
Bergstr
Mirabellgarten
Mirabellplatz
Makartplatz
Schwarzstr
Elisabethkai
River Salzach
Augustinergasse
To St Johanns Spital (300m)
Müllner Hauptstr
Gstättengasse
Museumsplatz
Franz Josef Kai
Makartsteg
Staatsbrücke
Giselakai
Steingasse
Imbergstr
Kapuzinerberg
Kapuzinerkloster
Mönchsberg
Anton Neumayr Platz
Griesgasse
Hanuschplatz
Getreidegasse
Universitätsplatz
W Philharmoniker G
Sigmund Haffner G
Alter Markt
Judengasse
Brodgasse
Rudolfskai
Mozartsteg
Mozartplatz
Hofstallgasse
Max Reinhardt Platz
Franziskanergasse
Residenzplatz
To Schloss Hellbrunn (4.5km)
Toscaninihof
Domplatz
Old Town
Kapitelplatz
Festungsgasse
Herrengasse
Kaigasse
Schanzlgasse
Altstadt Garage
Neutorstr
To Hanger 7 Museum (5km); Salzburg Airport (5km)
Rainberg
542m
Josef Preis Allee
Nonntaler Hauptstr
Petersbrunnstr
Klotz Str

stifling and couldn't wait to leave. Consequently, Mozart's **Geburtshaus** (birthplace; ☎ 844 313; Getreidegasse 9; adult €5.50; 🕑 9am-6pm Sep-Jun, 9am-7pm Jul & Aug, last entry 30 min before closing) and his **Wohnhaus** (residence; ☎ 874 227-40; Makartplatz 8; adult €5.50; 🕑 9am-6pm Sep-Jun, 9am-7pm Jul & Aug, last entry 30 min before closing) cover only his early years as a prodigy and young adult, until he left town in 1780 at 24 years of age. A combined ticket to both houses is €9 (students and seniors €7). The Wohnhaus is more extensive, and houses the **Mozart Sound and Film Museum** (admission free).

In the **Residenz** (☎ 80 42-2690; www.salzburg-burgen.at; Residenzplatz 1; adult/student €7.30/5.50; 🕑 10am-5pm, gallery closed Wed Oct-Mar) you can visit the archbishops' baroque staterooms and a gallery housing fine 16th- and 17th-century Dutch and Flemish paintings.

The **Museum der Moderne Rupertinum** (☎ 8042 2541; www.museumdermoderne.at; Mönchsberg; prices vary; 🕑 10am-6pm Tue-Sun, 10am-9pm Wed) adds a contemporary touch to historic Salzburg. Ask at the tourist office about other museums.

Mausoleum of Wolf Dietrich

In the **graveyard** (Linzer Gasse; 🕑 9am-7pm Apr-Oct, 9am-4pm Nov-Mar) of the 16th-century St Sebastian's Church sits Wolf Dietrich's not-so-humble **memorial** to himself. Both Mozart's father and his widow are also buried in the graveyard.

TOURS

Sound of Music Tours

Although these are the tours that interest the greatest number of visitors, how much fun you have depends on whether your fellow passengers enter into the necessary kitsch, tongue-in-cheek attitude. If you can, try to get together your own little posse. Otherwise, hope to find yourself among manic Julie Andrews impersonators flouncing in the fields, screeching 'the hills are alive' or some such thing.

Tours take three to four hours and usually spend most time in neighbouring Salzkammergut, rather than Salzburg itself. Following are some recommended operators:

Fraülein Maria's Bicycle Tours (☎ 0646-342 62 97; Makartplatz; adult €16; 🕑 9.30am mid-May–Sep) At the entrance to Mirabellgarten, behind Hotel Bristol.

Panorama Tours (☎ 874 029; Mirabellplatz; adult €33; 🕑 9.30am & 2pm)

Salzburg Sightseeing Tours (☎ 881 616; Mirabellplatz; adult €33; 🕑 9.30am & 2pm)

River Tours

Boats operated by **Salzburg Schiffahrt** (☎ 825 769-12) cruise along the Salzach (adult/child €11/7, 40 to 50 minutes) leaving half-hourly to hourly from 10am to 6pm May to September. Others go to Schloss Hellbrunn (adult/child €14/10), departing at 12.45pm from September to June, and 9.30am and 12.45pm from July to August. The company also has atmospheric tours by night in late July and August.

Boats leave from the Salzach Insel, on the city side of the Makart bridge.

FESTIVALS & EVENTS

Austria's most renowned classical music festival, the **Salzburg Festival** (www.salzburgfestival.at), attracts international stars from late July to the end of August. Book on its website before January, or ask the **Festspielhäuser ticket office** (☎ 80 45; Herbert von Karajan Platz 11; 🕑 9.30am-6.30pm during the festival, 9.30am-3pm during the few weeks before) about cancellations during the festival.

SLEEPING

Ask for the tourist office's hotel brochure, which gives prices for hotels, *pensions*, hostels and camping grounds. Accommodation is at a premium during festivals.

Budget

Naturfreundehaus (☎ 841 729; Mönchsberg 19; dm €13.50; 🕑 mid-Apr–mid-Oct) The rooms are little more than glorified shoeboxes, but the hostel is atop the Mönchsberg hill and you soon forget the cramped conditions when you wake up to such amazing views. There is a 1am curfew. To get here, take the Mönchsberg lift (€2.60 return) from Anton Neumayr Platz or the stairs from Toscaninihof, behind the Festival Halls.

International Youth Hotel (YoHo; ☎ 879 649; www.yoho.at; Paracelsusstrasse 9; dm with shared bathroom from €16, s/d/tr €28/21/19; Ⓟ) If you're hankering after a lively bar scene with cheap beer, friendly staff and regular events, including daily screenings of *The Sound of Music*, this hostel is for you. Book ahead on its website – phone reservations are accepted only one day in advance for its spartan, but spotless, rooms. Reception doesn't close during the day.

Jugendgästehaus (☎ 842 670-0; jgh.salzburg@jgh.at; Josef Preis Allee 18; dm from €18, d €36, with shared bathroom from €14, 1st-night surcharge €2.50; check-in from 11am, access to rooms from 1pm; P) Lots of Austrians and families stay at this comfy HI hostel that is also popular with backpackers. The eight-bed dorms feel a bit like boarding school, but the en suite four-bed dorms and doubles on the floors above could belong to a nice budget hotel.

Institut St Sebastian (☎ 871 386; www.st-sebastian-salzburg.at; Linzer Gasse 41; dm €18, s/d €36/57, with shared bathroom €31/51) Just a few minutes walk from the bridge, through the gate marked 'Feuerwache Bruderhof', on Linzer Gasse, Institut St Sebastian is closer to the action than any other Salzburg hostel-style accommodation. In fact, when the church bells ring next door, you might find this student abode is almost too close to the action. Don't expect much of a social atmosphere, as there is no bar or comfortable lounge; however, there is a roof terrace and kitchen.

Haus Lindner (☎ 456 681; info@haus-lindner.at; Panoramaweg 5; d/tr €30/45) The largest and one of the most popular private-room options in the city, with comfortable rooms and a homy atmosphere. Breakfast is provided, but there are kitchen facilities, too.

Try the following camping recommendations:

Camping Kasern (☎ /fax 450 576; campingkasern@aon.at; Carl Zuckmayer Strasse 4; camp site per adult/car/tent €4.50/3/3; Apr-Oct) Just north of the A1 Nord exit.

Camping Nord-Sam (☎ 660 494; www.camping-nord-sam.com; Samstrasse 22A; camp site per adult/car & tent €5.50/8; Easter & May-Sep) Slightly closer to the city.

Midrange & Top End

Salzburg has a fair number of options in these price brackets.

Pension Elisabeth (☎ 871 664; Vogelweiderstrasse 52; s/d from €44/66, with shared bathroom from €35/42; P) A small, friendly budget hotel; bright rooms come with white duvets, coloured upholstered chairs and wooden floors. It's near the Breitenfelderstrasse stop of bus 15, which heads into the city every 15 minutes. Beware there can be price increases during the high season for single-night stays.

Pension Bergland (☎ 872 318; www.berglandhotel.at; Rupertgasse 15; s/d/tr/f €56/86/102/120; P ⊠) Austrian rustic collides with '70s retro in the folksy rooms at this friendly, family-run *pension*. It's about a 15-minute walk from the Old Town.

Centro Hotel (☎ 882 221; www.centro-hotel.com; Auerspergstrasse 24; s/d €68/104; P ⊠) Slightly minimalist décor, the well-proportioned rooms have wooden furniture offset with touches of green. Ask for one with a private balcony.

Hotel Wolf (☎ 843 453-0; www.hotelwolf.com; Kaigasse 7; s/d from €70/100) With its neat living room set off from the main entrance hall, this family-owned hotel immediately feels like a real home. Austrian country-style bedrooms have been reconstructed in this 500-year-old abode, which has none of the mustiness of most buildings its age.

Blaue Gans (☎ 842 491-0; www.blauegans.at; Getreidegasse 41-43; s/d from €120/170) One of Salzburg's oldest inns converted into a trendy 'art hotel', it combines modern luxury with its historic setting.

EATING

Restaurants

If you wish to eat cheaply in Salzburg, it's worth following the Austrian tradition of making lunch your main meal, because some cheaper restaurants open only during daylight hours on weekdays.

Bio Bistro (☎ 870 712; Wolf-Dietrich-Strasse 1; mains €5.50) Vegetarian and vegan food is prepared

HANG(AR)TIME AT THE SALZBURG AIRPORT

Whether you have time to kill and want to get out of the airport or Salzburg is your final stop, it's worth a trip to check out the **Hangar-7** (☎ 662 2197; www.hangar-7.com; Wilhelm-Spazier-strasse 7A, Salzburg airport; admission free). This huge, clear plexi-enclosed airplane hangar is large enough to house a Douglas DC6 jumbo jet, a B-52 bomber, a plethora of assorted Red Bull Team Formula One racing cars, motorcycles and other cool historical aircraft. There's also a café where you can recharge your engine with a snack and, of course, a can of the silver and blue elixir that 'Gives you Wiiings'. Red Bull's founder and motorsports/aviation enthusiast, Dietrich Mateschitz, came up with the idea for his energy drink in 1984, after drinking a locally brewed tonic in Thailand. He is now one of the most successful businessmen in Austria.

fresh daily, along with Eastern 'holistic' specialities and salads.

Wilder Mann (☎ 841 787; Getreidegasse 20; mains €5.50-12; ⏰ Mon-Fri) Traditional Austrian food in a friendly, bustling environment, located in the passageway off Getreidegasse. Tables, both inside and out, are often so packed it's almost impossible not to get chatting with fellow diners.

Zum Mohren (☎ 484 23 87; Judengasse 9; mains €9-16) This cellar restaurant offers traditional food in a cosy environment. Dishes include roast pork, Hungarian goulash and Tirolean calf's liver with bacon.

Ährlich (☎ 871 275-60; Wolf-Dietrich-Strasse 7; mains €11-17; ⏰ dinner Tue-Sat, lunch Jul & Aug, closed Feb & Mar) If you've had enough of wurst and *Tafelspitz* (boiled beef with apple and horseradish sauce), this organic restaurant provides relief, with a brief, seasonal menu of international veggie and meat mains. It does sometimes have a bit of a weird health-farm vibe, but the food is tasty.

Gablerbräu (☎ 88 965; Linzer Gasse 9; mains €12) Low-key and pleasant, choose from homemade pasta and lip-smacking Styrian specialities served in four atmospheric rooms with a stained-glass arch, tiled oven and other rustic features.

Stiftskeller St Peter (☎ 841 268-34; St Peter Bezirk 1/4; mains €12.50-20) Be prepared to play the tourist when you visit the much advertised Austrian specialist. Environs are in a huge dining complex. The baroque main salon is worth a peek even if you don't stay for the food.

Cafés

Café Konditorei Fürst (☎ 843 759; Brodgasse 13 in Alter Markt; confections from €3) Café Konditorei Fürst boasts that its *Mozartkugeln* chocolates – wrapped in blue and silver paper instead of the usual red and gold – are the original 'Mozart's Balls'. They're still made here from the same recipe.

Stadtalm (☎ 841 729; Mönchsberg 19C; mains €6-10; ⏰ 10am-5pm Tue-Sun Apr-Oct) The meals are standard Germanic fare – wurst, *Wiener schnitzel* and *Züricher Geschnetzeltes* (veal in cream sauce). You won't care, though, with such fantastic views.

Quick Eats & Self-Catering

Salzburg has no shortage of markets, with a **fruit and vegetable market** (Mirabellplatz) on Thursday morning, and market stalls and fast-food stands on Universitätsplatz and Kapitelplatz. There's a **Eurospar supermarket** (⏰ Mon-Sat) opposite the train station.

DRINKING

Salzburg's most famous stretch of bars, clubs and discos remains Rudolfskai, but it's largely patronised by teenagers. Those who've already hit their 20s (or beyond) will probably prefer the scene around Anton Neumayr Platz, where things keep going until 4am on weekends.

Augustiner Bräustübl (☎ 431 246; Augustinergasse 4-6; ⏰ 3-11pm Mon-Fri, 2.30-11pm Sat & Sun) It's Oktoberfest year-round here. Well, perhaps it's not *quite* so boisterous, but this hillside complex of beer halls and gardens is not to be missed. The local monks' brew keeps the huge crowd of up to 2800 humming.

Bar Flip (☎ 843 643; Gstättengasse 17) This is a dark, low-ceilinged student bar serving cocktails and cheap beer.

Humboldt (☎ 843 171; Gstättengasse 4-6) Slightly more upmarket, with jellybean dispensers, a video projection of the Mirabellgarten on one wall and a pair of traditional antelope's horns…painted purple.

Republic (☎ 841 613; Anton Neumayr Platz 2) A hip, American bar/brasserie, it is liable to have MTV DJs in for its regular club nights.

GETTING THERE & AWAY

Air

The **airport** (SZG; ☎ 85 80-100; www.salzburg-airport.at) handles regular scheduled flights to Amsterdam, Brussels, Frankfurt, London, Paris and Zürich, and charter flights to the Mediterranean. Contact **Austrian Airlines** (☎ 854 511-0) or no-frills Ryanair, which has two flights daily (three on Saturday) from London.

Bus

Services to the Salzkammergut region leave from just to the left of the main train-station exit. Destinations include Bad Ischl (€7.60, 1¾ hours), Mondsee (€5, 50 minutes) and St Wolfgang (€7, 1½ hours).

Buses to Kitzbühel (€13, 2¼ hours, at least three daily) go via Lofer; they depart from Südtiroler Platz, across from the train station post office.

There are timetable boards at each departure point and a bus information office in the train station. Alternatively, call ☎ 46 60-333 for information.

Car & Motorcycle

Three autobahns converge on Salzburg and form a loop around the city: the A1 from Linz, Vienna and the east – the A8/E52 from Munich and the west; and the A10/E55 from Villach and the south. Heading south to Carinthia on the A10, there are two tunnels through the mountains; the combined toll is €10 (€7 for motorcycles).

Train

Fast trains leave for Vienna (€37, 3¼ hours) via Linz hourly. The express service to Klagenfurt (€28, three hours) goes via Villach. The quickest way to Innsbruck (€30, two hours) is by the 'corridor' train through Germany via Kufstein; trains depart at least every two hours. There are trains every hour or so to Munich (€26, two hours), and hourly trains to Salzburg (€7.40) via St Gilgen.

GETTING AROUND

Salzburg airport is 4km west of the city centre. Bus 2 goes there from the main train station (€1.70). A taxi costs about €12.50.

Bus drivers sell single bus tickets for €1.70. Other tickets must be bought from the automatic machines at major stops, *Tabak* shops or tourist offices. Day passes cost €3.20 and weeklies €10. Children aged six to 15 years travel half-price; those under six travel free.

Most of the Old Town is pedestrianised. The nearest central parking area is the Altstadt Garage under the Mönchsberg. Attended car parks cost €1.40 to €2.40 per hour. On streets with automatic ticket machines (blue zones), a three-hour maximum applies (€0.50 for 30 minutes) during specified times – usually shopping hours.

Bicycle hire is available from **Top Bike** (☎ 0676-476 72 59; www.topbike.at; 2hr/4hr/day €6/10/15), which has two locations: just outside the train station and on the bridge.

For a taxi, call ☎ 81 11, or go to the ranks at Hanuschplatz, Residenzplatz or the train station.

AROUND SALZBURG

Four kilometres south of Salzburg's Old Town centre is the popular **Schloss Hellbrunn** (☎ 820 372-0; www.hellbrunn.at; Fürstenweg 37; adult/student €7.50/5.50; ⏲ 9am-10pm Jul & Aug, 9am-5.30pm May, Jun & Sep, 9am-4.30pm Apr & Oct). Built by bishop Markus Sittikus, this 17th-century castle is known for its ingenious trick fountains and water-powered figures. When the tour guides set them off, expect to get wet! Admission includes a tour of the **baroque palace**. Other parts of the garden (without fountains) are open year-round and free to visit.

City bus 55 runs to the palace every 30 minutes from Salzburg's main train station, via Rudolfskai in the Old Town. Salzburg tickets are valid.

Werfen

☎ 06468 / pop 3000

The world's largest accessible ice caves are in the mountains near Salzburg. These **Eisriesenwelt Höhle** (Giant Ice Caves; ☎ 56 46; www.eisriesenwelt.at; adult/student with cable car up €17/15, without cable car €8/7; ⏲ 1 May-26 Oct) house elaborate and beautiful ice formations; take warm clothes because it gets cold inside and the tour lasts 1¼ hours – you also need to be reasonably fit.

The **Hohenwerfen Fortress** (adult/student €9/7.50; ⏲ Apr-Nov) stands on the hill above the village. It was originally built in 1077, although the present building dates from the 16th century. Admission includes an exhibition, a guided tour of the interior and a dramatic falconry show, in which birds of prey swoop low over the heads of the crowd. The walk up from the village takes 20 minutes.

Both attractions can be visited in one day if you start early (tour the caves first and be at the castle by 3pm for the falconry show). The **tourist office** (☎ 53 88; www.werfen.at; Markt 24; ⏲ 9am-7pm Mon-Fri, 5-7pm Sat mid-Jul–mid-Aug, 9am-5pm Mon-Fri mid-Aug–mid-Jul) is in the village's main street.

Werfen can be reached from Salzburg along the A10. By train it takes 50 minutes and costs €8. The village is a five-minute walk from Werfen train station. Getting to the caves is a bit more complicated, though scenic. A minibus service (€6.50 return) from the train station operates along the steep, 6km road to the car park, which is as far as cars can go. A 15-minute walk then brings you to the cable car (admission €9 return), from where it is a further 15-minute walk to the caves. Allow four hours return from the train station, or three hours from the car park (keep in mind that peak-season queues may add an hour). The whole route can be hiked, but it is a very hard four-hour ascent, rising 1100m above the village.

SALZKAMMERGUT

A picture-perfect wonderland of glassy blue lakes and tall craggy peaks, Austria's Lake District is a longtime favourite holiday destination attracting visitors in droves from Salzburg and beyond – including Habsburg emperors and their hangers-on. The waters in this salt-mining region (mining has taken place in the area since Celtic times) are rich in minerals, and believed to have medicinal value. In fact, Emperor Franz Josef once declared the region to be 'an earthly paradise' and spent a large part of every summer at Bad Ischl, whose healing waters were credited with his conception.

Whether you're looking for a way to entertain the kids or hoping to just commune with nature, the area is big on variety. The peaceful lakes offer limitless opportunities for boating, fishing, swimming, or just sitting on the shore and chucking stones into the water. Favourite waterside beauty spots include the picturesque villages of Hallstatt and St Wolfgang, and the Riviera-style port of Gmunden. You can also tour the salt mines that made the region wealthy or plunge into the depths of the fantastic Dachstein caves, where glittering towers of ice are masterfully illuminated in the depths of a mountain.

Getting There & Around

The major rail routes bypass the heart of Salzkammergut, but regional trains cross the area north to south. You get on this route from Attnang-Puchheim on the Salzburg–Linz line. The track from here connects to Bad Ischl, Hallstatt and Obertraun in one direction, as well as to Gmunden in another. When you're travelling from a small, unstaffed station *(unbesetzter Bahnhof)*, you buy your ticket on the train; no surcharge applies.

After Obertraun, the railway continues eastwards via Bad Aussee before connecting with the main Bischofshofen–Graz line at Stainach-Irdning.

Attersee can also be reached via Vócklamarkt, the next stop on the Salzburg–Linz line before Attnang-Puchheim.

Regular buses connect the region's towns and villages, though less frequently on weekends. Timetables are displayed at stops, and tickets can be bought from the driver.

Passenger boats ply the waters of the Attersee, Traunsee, Mondsee, Hallstätter See and Wolfgangsee.

To reach Salzkammergut from Salzburg by car or motorcycle, take the A1 or Hwy 158.

BAD ISCHL

☎ 06132 / pop 13,000

A longtime favourite of the imperial family, Bad Ischl also has the dubious distinction of being the birthplace of WWI, or at least the concept of it (Emperor Franz Josef was enjoying his annual holiday here in 1914 when troubles with Serbia arose). It's hard to picture the Bad Ischl of today as the conception point for such brutality, given it's a spa resort devoted to rather more holistic pursuits.

Many of Bad Ischl's dignified buildings still wear an imperial aura. It's a handsome-looking place and makes a good base for visiting the region's five main lakes.

Orientation

The town centre rests within a bend of the Traun River. To head into town, turn left into the main road as you come out of the train station; you'll pass the tourist office and post office.

Information

Post Office (Aübockplatz 4; 🕒 8am-6pm Mon-Fri, 9am-noon Sat)

Salzkammergut Touristik (☎ 24 000-0; www.salzkammergut.co.at; Götzstrasse 12; 🕒 9am-8pm) Has Internet access.

Tourist Office (Kurdirektion; ☎ 27 757-0; www.badischl.at, in German; Bahnhofstrasse 6; 🕒 8am-6pm Mon-Fri, 9am-3pm Sat, 10am-1pm Sun Jul-Sep, 8am-5pm Mon-Fri, 8am-noon Sat Oct-Jun)

Sights & Activities

The **Kaiservilla** (☎ 23 241; www.kaiservilla.at; Kaiserpark; 🕒 May–mid-Oct) was Franz Josef's summer residence and shows he loved huntin', shootin' and fishin' – it's decorated with an obscene number of animal trophies. It can be visited only by guided tour (€12; in German but with written English translations), during which you'll pick up little gems, like the fact that Franz Josef was conceived in Bad Ischl after his mother, Princess Sophie, took a treatment to cure her infertility in 1828. There are several 40-minute tours daily (main season) and only three on Wednesday (noon, 2pm and 3pm) from January to April.

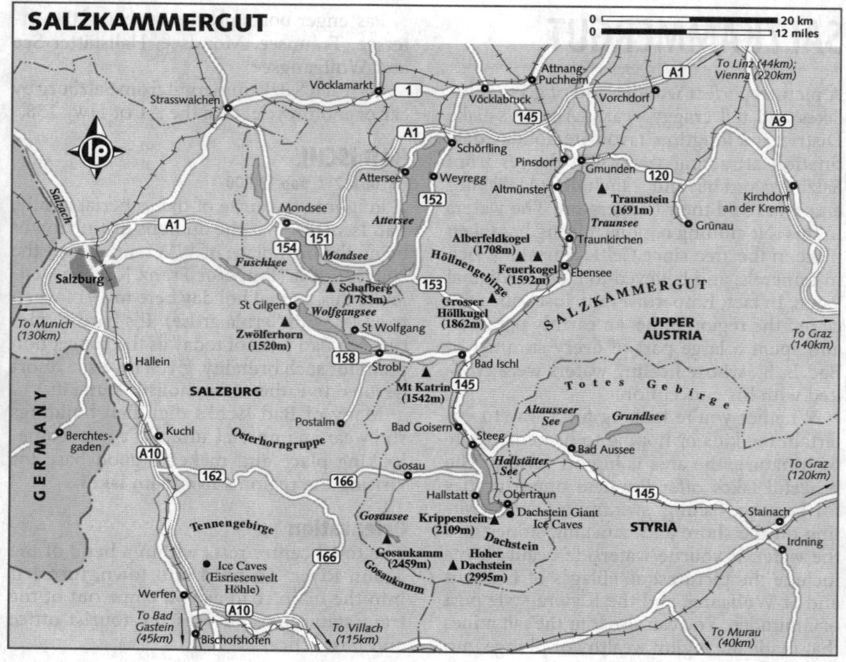

The teahouse of Franz Josef's wife, Elisabeth, is now a **photo museum** (admission €3). Admission to the grounds alone costs €4.20/3.50 per adult/child.

Free *Kurkonzerte* (spa concerts) are held regularly during summer; the tourist office has venues and times. An **operetta festival** takes place in July and August; for details and advance reservations call ☎ 23 839.

Bad Ischl has downhill skiing from **Mt Katrin** (winter day pass €21); however, there are only three trails. It also has various cross-country skiing routes. In summer the Mt Katrin cable car costs €12.50 return.

The tourist office has information on **health treatments** in Bad Ischl.

Sleeping & Eating

Jugendgästehaus (☎ 26 577; www.oejhv.or.at; Am Rechensteg 5; dm €13, s/d €27/38; ⏲ reception 8am-1pm & 5-7pm) Rooms are standard hostel fare, but comfortable enough for a night or two. The exterior is rather nondescript. Look for it in the town centre behind Kreuzplatz.

Haus Rothauer (☎ 23 628; Kaltenbachstrasse 12; s/d €25/55) You'll feel as if you're staying with longtime family friends when spending a few days at this immaculately clean, super-friendly guesthouse. Do phone ahead, however, to make sure there's space and someone is around to let you in.

Hotel Garni Sonnhof (☎ 23 078; www.sonnhof.at; Bahnhofstrasse 4; s/d €45/90; P) Nestled into a leafy glade of maple trees next to the train station, this is an excellent option – it has cosy, traditional décor, a lovely garden (complete with a pond), a sunny conservatory, and large bedrooms with interesting old furniture and wooden floors. There's a billiard room, sauna and a steam bath on-site.

Café Zauner (☎ 23 013; Pfarrgasse 7; snacks from €5) This café has changed little since imperial times, retaining its glittering chandeliers, marble floors and fantastical displays of confectionary. Founded in 1832, it was Franz Josef's bakery of choice – his mistress ordered their morning pastries here when he was in residence. Its summer pavilion on the Esplanade by the river is equally atmospheric.

Blue Enzian (☎ 28 992; Wirerstrasse 2; mains €7-14; ⏲ Mon-Sat) The laid-back Enzian does a variety of pastas, salads, and regional and seasonal dishes with solid results. It's an informal place set back from the main street. When you've finished eating, check out the popular Hofbeisl (open 9am to 4pm), almost next door. It's an atmospheric spot with baroque décor.

Weinhaus Attwenger (☎ 23 327; Lehárkai 12; mains €7-20) High-quality Austrian food is served at this quaint chalet with a relaxing garden next to the river. The menu changes seasonally, with wines to match. Ask about set-course meals.

Getting There & Around

Trains from Salzburg (€17, two hours) arrive via Attnang-Puchheim. Trains on to Hallstatt depart roughly hourly between 6am and 6pm (€4, 50 minutes); however, be aware that you need to catch a ferry from this train station to the actual village (see p92).

Buses arrive and depart from in front of the train station. They run hourly to Salzburg (€7.40, 1¾ hours) via St Gilgen between 5am and 8pm. To St Wolfgang (€3.10), you generally need to change at Strobl (although you can buy one ticket straight through). Buses depart for Hallstatt every couple of hours (€3.60, 50 minutes), arriving in the village itself.

Salzkammergut Touristik (☎ 24 000-0; www.salzkammergut.co.at; Götzstrasse 12; 9am-8pm) has bikes for hire. Call ahead for reservations and rates as they change periodically.

HALLSTATT

☎ **06134 / pop 1150**

With pastel-hued homes, swans and towering mountains on either side of a glassy green lake, breathtakingly beautiful Hallstatt looks like some kind of greeting card for tranquillity. Boats chug lazily across the water from the train station to the village itself, which clings precariously to a tiny bit of land between mountain and shore. So small is the patch of land occupied by the village that its annual Corpus Christi procession takes place largely in small boats on the lake.

There's evidence of human settlement at Hallstatt as long as 4500 years ago, and the village has been classified as a Unesco World Heritage site. Mining salt in the peak above the village was the main activity for thousands of years. Today tourism is the major money-spinner. Fortunately, the crowds of summer day-trippers only stay a few hours, then calm returns.

> **TIP!**
>
> Throughout the year resorts have a holiday/guest card *(Gästekarte)* offering region-wide discounts; ask at your hotel, hostel or camping ground. Alternatively, buy the Salzkammergut Card (€4.90; available May to October), which provides a 25% discount on sights, ferries, cable cars and some buses.

Orientation & Information

Seestrasse is the main street. Turn left from the ferry to reach the **tourist office** (☎ 82 08; hallstatt@inneres-salzkammergut.at; Seestrasse 169; 9am-noon & 1-5pm Mon-Fri year-round, 10am-5pm Sat May-Oct, 10am-2pm Sun Jul-Aug). The **post office** (Seestrasse 160) is around a bend in the road.

Sights & Activities

Hallstatt is rich with archaeological interest. Near the mine, 2000 graves were discovered, dating from 1000 to 500 BC. Don't miss the macabre **Beinhaus** (Bone House; ☎ 82 79; Kirchenweg 40; admission €1; 10am-6pm 1 May-27 Oct) near the village parish church; it contains rows of stacked skulls painted with flowery designs and the names of their former owners. These human remains have been exhumed from the too-small graveyard since 1600 in a practice that recalls the old Celtic pagan custom of mass burial. The last skull in the collection was added in 1995. Gross.

Around the lake at Obertraun are the intriguing **Dachstein Rieseneishöhle** (Giant Ice Caves; ☎ 8400 1830; www.dachstein.at; tours adult/child €9/5; early May-late Oct, tours 9.20am-4pm).

The caves are millions of years old and extend into the mountain for nearly 80km in places. The ice itself is no more than 500 years old, but is increasing in thickness each year – the 'ice mountain' is 8m high, twice as high now as it was when the caves were first explored in 1910. Ask at the ticket office about tours in English – if none are available you can take a sheet of printed information around the caves with you.

Above the village are the **Salzbergwerk** (Saltworks; ☎ 84 00; admission €20; 9am-4pm late Apr-26 Oct, 9am-3.30pm from mid-Oct). Riding the funicular up adds €5 to the salt mine ticket, or costs €7.50 return if you just want to get up the mountain. Ask the tourist office about the two scenic hiking trails you could take to get there.

Sleeping

Some private rooms are available during the busiest months of July and August only; others require a minimum three-night stay. The tourist office will telephone around for you without charge.

Campingplatz Krausner-Höll (☎ 83 22; Lahnstrasse 7; per adult €8; ⏲ 15 Apr-15 Oct) This camping ground is conveniently located south of the town centre.

Gasthaus zur Muhle (☎ 83 18; www.toeroe.f@magnet.at; Kirchenweg 36; dm €13) On the Hallstatt hillside and overlooking the lake, this place is popular with independent travellers. Dorms are rather basic, however.

Jugendherberge (☎ 82 12; Salzbergstrasse 50; dm €15; ⏲ May-Oct, check-in 5-6pm) Some dorms in this hostel have lots of beds and can be cramped. Phone ahead as reception hours are irregular. It is usually full with groups in July and August.

Gasthof Hallberg (☎ 82 86; www.pension-hallberg.at.tf; Seestrasse 113; s/d from €45/60; Ⓟ) An excellent-value guesthouse, the best rooms are light and airy, furnished with pale wood and boasting superb lake views on both sides. Even the more ordinary rooms are still great quality, with many featuring quaintly sloping ceilings and mountain views.

Eating

Hallstatt's steep footpaths certainly help you work up an appetite. The following eateries are open for lunch and dinner.

Pferdestall (☎ 20 00; Seestrasse 156; mains €7.50-20) A one-time stable, tables are built into the old horse stalls complete with wooden partitions and iron bars. This small bar and trattoria turns out cheap pizza and pasta, along with some pricier meat dishes.

Bräu Gasthof (☎ 20 012; Seestrasse 120; mains €8-20; ⏲ May-Nov) Served in vaulted rooms or on tables by the lake, the menu promises hearty local fare and turns out dishes like sirloin steak with onions (€13) or game goulash (€12), as well as a few salads.

Getting There & Away

There are six buses daily to/from Bad Ischl. You alight at 'Lahn', just south of the road tunnel. Beware, as services finish very early and the last guaranteed departure from Bad Ischl is 4.10pm. There are at least nine train services daily from Bad Ischl (€4, 50 minutes). The train station is across the lake from the village, but the ferry captain waits for trains to arrive before making the short crossing (€2). Though trains run later, the last ferry departs from the train station at 6.30pm (leaving Hallstatt just after 6pm). Parking in the village is free if you're staying the night and therefore have a guest card.

WOLFGANGSEE

You can swim or go boating on this lake, climb the mountain above it, or just sit on the shore, gazing at the scenery. The only downside is that its proximity to Salzburg means it can become crowded in summer.

The Schafberg peak on the northern shore dominates the lake. Next to it is the resort of St Wolfgang. St Gilgen, on the western shore, provides easy access to Salzburg, 29km away. The **St Wolfgang tourist office** (☎ 06138-22 39-0; info@stwolfgang.at; ⏲ 8am-8pm Mon-Sat, noon-6pm Sun Jul & Aug, 9am-noon Mon-Sat & 2-5pm Mon, Tue, Thu & Fri Sep-Jun) has regional tourist information.

Some people like to climb mountains because they're there; others prefer the less-strenuous train ride to the top. The former will love the four-hour hike to the peak of the **Schafberg** (1783m). The rest need to get there between early May and the end of October, when the Schafberg cog-wheel railway operates. It runs approximately hourly during the day and costs €13 to the top or €22 return. There is also a stop halfway up.

The village of St Wolfgang's 14th-century **Pilgrimage Church** (⏲ 9am-6pm) still attracts pilgrims interested in viewing this highly ornate church.

On the lakefront, **Camping Appesbach** (☎ 06138-22 06; Au 99; adult/tent & car €5/6; ⏲ Easter-Oct), 1km from St Wolfgang heading south towards Strobl, is a favourite with Austrians on holiday.

The **Jugendgästehaus Schafbergblick** (☎ 236 575; www.oejhv.or.at; Mondseestrasse 7; dm/d from €13/16; ⏲ reception 8am-1pm & 5-7pm Mon- Fri, 8-9am & 5-7pm Sat & Sun) is in nearby St Gilgen. It's an upmarket hostel with a great position near the town's swimming beach. Some of the rooms have lake views. There's no lock-out.

Both St Wolfgang and St Gilgen have numerous *pensions*, starting from about €20. Ask at the local tourist office for details and bookings.

A ferry operates from Strobl to St Gilgen, stopping at various points en route, including St Wolfgang. Services are from late April to 26 October, but are more frequent from early July to early September. The ferry journey from St Wolfgang to St Gilgen takes 45 to 50 minutes (€4.50), with boats sailing during the high season approximately twice hourly between 8am and 8pm.

Buses from St Wolfgang to St Gilgen and Salzburg go via Strobl on the east side of the lake. From St Gilgen the bus to Salzburg (€4.80, 50 minutes) departs hourly until at least 8.30pm.

NORTHERN SALZKAMMERGUT

West of Attersee is **Mondsee**, a lake whose warm water makes it a favourite swimming spot. Mondsee village has an attractive church that was used in the wedding scenes of *The Sound of Music*.

East of Attersee is another lake, **Traunsee**, and its three main resorts: Gmunden, Traunkirchen and Ebensee. **Gmunden** is famous for its twin castles, linked by a causeway on the lake, and its ceramic manufacturing.

TIROL

With converging mountain ranges behind lofty pastures and tranquil meadows, Tirol (also Tyrol) captures a quintessential Alpine panoramic view. In the northeast and southwest are superb ski resorts. In the southeast, separated somewhat from the main state since part of South Tirol was ceded to Italy at the end of WWI, lies the protected natural landscape of the Hohe Tauern National Park, and the country's highest peak, the Grossglockner (3797m). Back further west, in the middle of the main state, Innsbruck is the region's jewel.

INNSBRUCK

☎ 0512 / pop 140,000

Sandwiched between majestic snow-capped mountains dominating your periphery, it's hard to resist the urge to get up high when in Innsbruck. Whether you're visiting the reopened winter Olympics stadium and the Bergisel ski-jump tower or partaking in an all-day hiking adventure, the region around this gorgeous Alpine town embodies just about everything a good skiing mecca should. In fact, on the Stubai Glacier (Austria's largest), 40km to the south, you can ski or snowboard at any time of the year.

Orientation

Innsbruck, in the valley of the River Inn, is scenically squeezed between the northern chain of the Alps and the Tuxer mountains to the south. The city centre is compact, with the main train station (Hauptbahnhof) only a 10-minute walk from the pedestrian-only Old Town centre (Altstadt). The main street in the Old Town is Herzog Friedrich Strasse.

Information

Bubble Point Waschsalon (☎ 565 007; www.bubblepoint.com; Brixner Strasse 1; per 30 min €1.50) Internet café and laundrette combined.

Internetcafé Moderne (☎ 584 848; Maria Theresien Strasse 16; per min €2) Offers Internet access.

Landeskrankenhaus (University Clinic; ☎ 504-0; Anichstrasse 35) For medical treatment.

Main Post Office (Maximilianstrasse 2; 🕒 7am-9pm Mon-Fri, 7am-3pm Sat, 8am-7.30pm Sun) There is another branch in the main train station.

Main Tourist Office (☎ general information 59 850, tickets & packages 53 56, hotel reservations 562 000-0; www.innsbruck.info; Burggraben 3; 🕒 9am-6pm) There is a €3 booking fee for hotel reservations. Check out the tourist office's free newspaper *Innsbruck Hallo!* for a map and lots of useful information.

Tourist Counter (main train station, lower concourse; 🕒 7am-7pm)

Sights

OLD TOWN

Innsbruck's atmospheric, medieval Old Town is ideal for a lazy stroll. The famous **Goldenes Dachl** (Golden Roof; Friedrich Herzog Strasse), built by Emperor Maximilian I in the 16th century as a display of wealth, is a good starting point. Comprised from 2657 gilded copper tiles, Maximilian used it to observe street performers from the balcony beneath.

The **Hofkirche** (Imperial Church; ☎ 584 302; Universitätsstrasse 2; adult/student under 27yr €2.20/1.45, admission free Sun & holidays; 🕒 9am-5pm Mon-Sat, before 8am, noon-3pm & after 5pm Sun) is another favourite (and worthwhile) attraction. It contains a memorial to Maximilian, and although his 'sarcophagus' has been restored, it's actually empty. Perhaps more memorable are the 28 giant statues of Habsburgs lining either side of the cask. You're now forbidden to touch the statues, but numerous inquisitive hands have already polished parts of the dull bronze, including Kaiser Rudolf's codpiece!

AUSTRIA

BERGISEL TOWER

If you've ever wondered what it feels like to stand on top of an Olympic-sized ski jump, you'll leave the **Bergisel tower** (☎ 589 259; adult/child €7.90/3.90; ⏰ 9am-6pm Jun-Nov, 9am-5pm Dec-May) with a better idea. And if you've never been curious about such death-defying feats, you'll still be rewarded with truly fantastic views; the tower sits 3km south of the city centre on the crest of the refurbished Winter Olympics ski-jump stadium, overlooking Innsbruck. (Some wag has built a cemetery over the lip of the hill, directly in line with the end of the ski jump.)

The tower evinces the curving design typical of its designer – Iraqi-born, British-based celebrity architect Zaha Hadid. For the full experience, stop for coffee in the Café im Turm (meals €8.50 to €16.60), whose panorama windows give a whole new meaning to the term 'caffeine high'.

To get here, take tram/bus 1 (direction Bergisel) or tram 6 (direction Igls) from Museumstrasse. At the stop, follow the signs to Bergisel, up a fairly steep path for 15 minutes. The stadium is still used for ski-jumping in June and January, so ring ahead to check that it's OK to visit.

SWAROVSKI KRISTALLWELTEN

To get to the heart of Swarovski you must visit the mind-blowing **Crystal Worlds** (☎ 05224-51 080; www.swarovski.com/kristallwelten; Kristallweltenstrasse 1; adult/child €8/free; ⏰ 9am-6pm). Enter behind sparkling crystalline eyes and the waterfall-spewing mouth (frozen in winter) of a giant cranium, and an interactive exhibition awaits further inside. It features the works of Eno, Warhol and Dali. Navigate your way through numerous black curtains and into ambient sound rooms, trippy interactive exhibits, and one-of-a-kind fusions of crystals, lights, sounds and mirrors. The centre is in Wattens and best reached by bus (€8.50 return, 30 minutes).

ALPENZOO

The **Alpine Zoo** (☎ 292 323; www.alpenzoo.at, in German; Weiherburggasse 37; adult/student/child €7/5/3.50; ⏰ 9am-6pm) houses a comprehensive collection of alpine animals, including ibexes, bears, an eagle and a bearded vulture. Walk up the hill to get there or take the Hungerburgbahn, which is free if you buy your zoo ticket at the Hungerburgbahn station.

OTHER SIGHTS

The **Landesmuseum Ferdinandeum** (☎ 59 489; Museumstrasse 15) has a massive collection of Gothic statues and altarpieces. The **Alpenverein Museum** (Alpine Club Museum; ☎ 59 547-19; Wilhelm Greil Strasse 15; adult/child €2.20/1.10; ⏰ 10am-5pm Mon, Tue, Thu & Fri, noon-7pm Wed, 10am-1pm Sat May-Oct) has a collection of Alpine art and relief maps.

A new 'hop on, hop off' **Sightseer bus** (adult/concession day ticket €8/5.60; ⏰ services every half-hour btwn 9am-5.30pm May-Oct, 10am-5pm Nov-Apr) does make getting to some of the more remote sights a little easier. Pick up a brochure at the tourist office.

Activities

HIKING

Those staying in Innsbruck are entitled to the Club Innsbruck card, available at your hostel or hotel, which includes free guided mountain hikes. This is a fantastic deal, offering remarkable views for nothing more than the cost of your own food and water. The hiking programme runs from June to September, with most of the 40-odd diverse hikes leaving at 9am from the **Congress Centre** (Rennweg 3). The popular sunrise hikes leave at 4.45am Friday and you'll need to book by 4.30pm the previous day. Night-time lantern walks depart at 7.45pm Tuesday.

SKIING

The ski region around Innsbruck is constantly improving with new runs added each year. A one-day ski pass is around €26. Downhill equipment hire starts at €15.

You can ski or snowboard year-round at **Stubai Glacier**. A one-day pass costs €36 (€25 in summer). Catch the white IVB Stubaltalbahn bus, departing hourly from near the main train station. The journey takes 80 minutes and the last bus back is at 5.30pm. Several places offer complete packages to the glacier, which compare favourably with going it alone. The **tourist office** (☎ 53 56) has a package for €49, including transport, passes and equipment hire. This works out to be a good deal in summer. In winter, however, there's a free ski bus leaving from various hotels, so compare going it alone with taking a tourist office package first.

Sleeping

The tourist office has lists of private rooms in Innsbruck from €20 per person. If you're

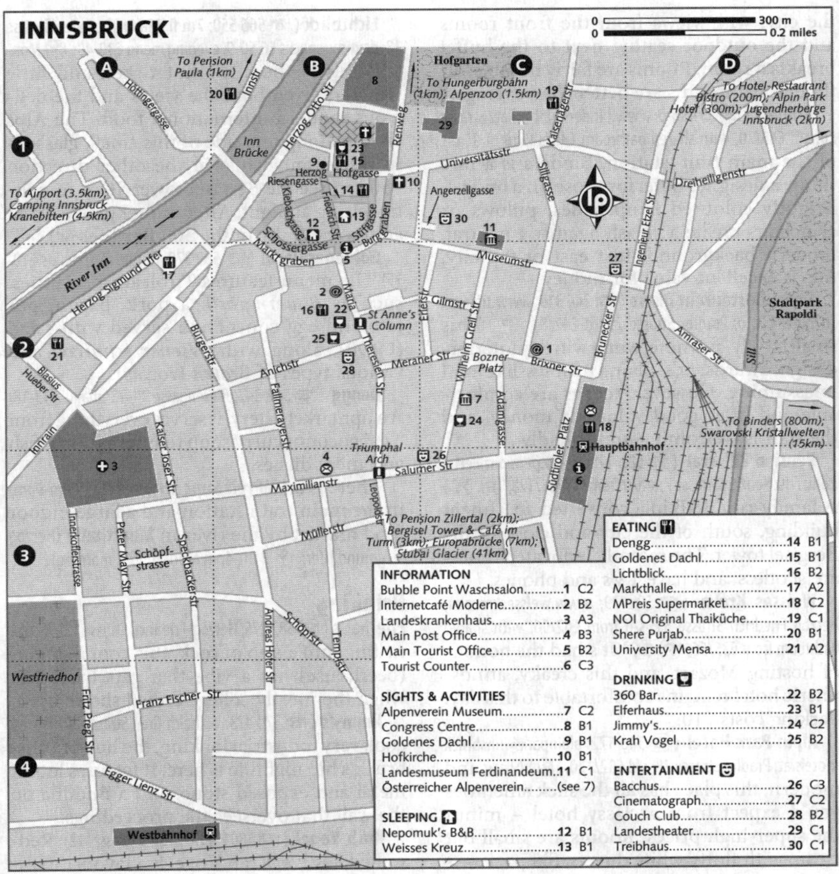

staying at a hostel or hotel, ask for the complimentary Club Innsbruck card. It provides various discounts and benefits.

Camping Innsbruck Kranebitten (☎ 284 180; www.campinginnsbruck.com; Kranebitter Allee 214; adult/tent/car €5/3/5) In an idyllic location 5km from the Old Town centre, under the mountains, this camping ground is open year-round. It has a restaurant and bike hire, and offers a shuttle service into the city.

Jugendherberge Innsbruck (☎ 346 179; www.jugendherberge-innsbruck.at; Reichenauerstrasse 147; dm from €15.60, d with shared bathroom €46; closed 10am-3pm summer, 10am-5pm rest of year, curfew 11pm;) Seen from afar, this hostel resembles a building from the former USSR – a huge, concrete monstrosity. Up close the picture is a bit prettier – its dorms are actually quite modestly sized. Prices include breakfast. To get here, take bus O (direction Olympisches Dorf/Josef Kerschbaumer Strasse) from Museumstrasse.

Nepomuk's Bed & Breakfast (☎ 584 118; Kiebachgasse 16; dm/d with shared bathroom €25/30) At the time of research this was the newest kid in one of the oldest buildings on the block. The staircase has been around since the year 1800, but the charming rooms are newly remodelled (only 10), and the breakfast in the wonderful attached patisserie downstairs will get your day going.

Pension Paula (☎ 292 262; www.pensionpaula.at; Weiherburggasse 15; s/d €36/58, with shared bathroom €29/49; P) This hilltop *pension* looks out over

AUSTRIA

the city, with views from the front rooms and the outdoor seating next to the buffet breakfast room. Rooms are fairly humble, although bathrooms are better than average.

Binders (☎ 33 436-0; www.binders.at; Dr Glatz Strasse 20; s/d €45/70, with shared bathroom €40/54; P) East of the main train station, Binders is a rare thing: a designer hotel for those on a budget. Brightly coloured lampshades, pillows or armchairs create a splash against a neutral, modern background. Just east of the city, this is excellent value for money.

Hotel-Restaurant Bistro (☎ 346 319; www.tiscover.at/hotel-bistro; Pradler Strasse 2; s/d €42/84; P) This small family-run hotel won't win any interior-design awards; it's plain, businesslike and unassuming. However, rooms are comfortable and offer good value for money, and the staff is welcoming and friendly.

Pension Zillertal (☎ 582 129; www.pensionzillertal.com; Fritz Konzert Strasse 7; s/d/tr from €54/85/128; P ☒) A family-run B&B in a converted apartment building, south of the city and close to the Bergisel tower. The recently renovated rooms are spotless, and have TVs and phones.

Weisses Kreuz (☎ 59 479; www.weisseskreuz.at; Herzog Friedrich Strasse 31; s/d from €62/96, with shared bathroom from €35/66; P ☒) It's had the honour of hosting Mozart, and this creaky, atmospheric hotel remains comfortable to this day. Parking costs €10.

Alpin Park Hotel (☎ 346 172; alpinpark@innsbruck-hotels.at; Pradler Strasse 28; s/d €82/120; P) New and modern, this place has all the slick amenities you'd expect from a classy hotel – minus the super-high prices. Rooms are small but clean, with fluffy white duvets. Ski packages can be arranged. Parking costs €8.

Eating

University Mensa (Herzog Siegmund Ufer 15; mains €4-5; ⏲ 11am-2pm Mon-Thu, 11am-1.30pm Fri) Enjoy great views of the Alps while lunching here. The food is cheap, but just OK.

NOI Original Thaiküche (☎ 589 777; Kaiserjägerstrasse 1; mains €4-11; ⏲ lunch & dinner Mon-Fri, dinner Sat) Serves delicious Thai staples, such as soups, noodle dishes and curries. It's small, but in summer there are lots of outdoor tables with brightly coloured chairs.

Shere Purjab (☎ 282 755; Innstrasse 19; mains €6-10) Innstrasse is lined with cheap eats, including this cut-price Indian restaurant, which has a daily menu and, naturally, lots of veggie food.

Lichtblick (☎ 566 550; 7th fl, Maria Theresien Strasse 18; daytime snacks €6.50-9, evening menu €30-40; ⏲ Mon-Sat) This is the city's hot ticket, and little wonder, given both the views and the delicious modern international food. The Alps rise up along one side of this small, glassed-in restaurant, while in the other direction you can see the Bergisel tower. It's a romantic setting at night. After dinner grab a drink across the foyer in the 360 Bar (below).

Goldenes Dachl (☎ 589 370; Hofgasse 1; mains €10-15) The menu features Tirolean specialities, such as *Bauerngröstl*, a pork, bacon, potato and egg concoction served with salad (€9.90), along with *Wiener schnitzel* and various types of *Braten* (roasts).

Dengg (☎ 582 347; Riesengasse 11-13; mains €13-18) An upmarket eatery, it serves everything from Thai coconut curry soup to international fish and meat dishes.

There is an **MPreis Supermarket** (⏲ 6am-9pm) in the main train station and a large indoor food market by the river in **Markthalle** (Herzog Siegmund Ufer; ⏲ 8am-4pm Mon-Fri, Sat morning).

Drinking

Elferhaus (☎ 582 875; Herzog-Friedrich Strasse 11) Tunnelling into a slab of rock, this cool *Bierhaus* (beerhouse) has a vibe that gets lively late when the mostly college crowd shows up.

Jimmy's (☎ 570 473; Wilhelm Greil Strasse 17) Very cool, very industrial looking, the hub of Innsbruck's hip nightlife is here. It features lots of metal and exposed stone, and a Buddha on the wall that oversees the proceedings.

Krah Vogel (☎ 5801 4971; Anichstrasse 12) Red-walled, festive, Krah Vogel is a favourite student haunt. Stop in for a beer after 10pm when it gets busy.

360 Bar (☎ 566 550; 7th fl, Maria Theresien Strasse 18; ⏲ Mon-Sat) Like the name says, it's all about the views. This hip wine bar across from Lichtblick has perhaps the best views of the city. Relax in the plush surroundings and lounge in style swathed in ultramodern comfort with excellent service.

Entertainment

The tourist office sells tickets for 'Tirolean evenings' (€32 for alpine music, folk dancing, yodelling and one drink), classical concerts and performances in the **Landestheater** (Rennweg 2). For more entertainment options, pick up a copy of *Innsider*, found in cafés across town.

Bacchus (☎ 940 210; Salurnerstrasse 14) A mixed/gay club that attracts what German speakers succinctly call *ein gemischtes Publikum* (all ages, all tastes and all looks).

Cinematograph (☎ 578 500; Museumstrasse 31) Screens independent films in their original language.

Couch Club (Anichstrasse 7; Thu-Sat) Come to the hip Couch Club for clubbing.

Treibhaus (☎ 586 874; Angerzellgasse 8) The arty, community-minded Treibhaus hosts live music ranging from urban groove to ska, short-film festivals and the like. On Sunday there's a 'jazz breakfast' from 10.30am and 'five o'clock tea'.

Getting There & Away

Austrian Airlines has three flights a week from London Gatwick to **Innsbruck airport** (INN; ☎ 22 525). Tyrolean Airways flies daily to Amsterdam, Frankfurt, Paris, Vienna and Zürich.

The A12 and the parallel Hwy 171 are the main roads to the east and west respectively. Hwy 177 heads north to Germany and Munich. The A13 motorway is a toll road (€8) southwards through the Brenner Pass to Italy; it includes the impressive Europabrücke (Europe Bridge), several kilometres south of the city. Toll-free Hwy 182 follows the same route, passing under the bridge.

Fast trains depart seven times daily for Bregenz (€25.10, 2¾ hours) and every two hours to Salzburg (€29.50, two hours). Connections are hourly to Kitzbühel (€12.20, 1¼ hours). On many trains to Lienz, people travelling on Austrian rail passes must pay a surcharge for travelling through Italy. Ask before boarding or call ☎ 05-17 17, available 24 hours.

Getting Around

The airport is 4km west of the city centre. To get there, take bus F, which departs from opposite the main train station half-hourly (hourly on Saturday afternoon and Sunday) and passes through Maria Theresien Strasse. A taxi from the main train station to the airport costs around €10.

Single bus tickets, including to the airport, cost €1.80. A 24-hour pass is €3.50.

Street parking is very limited in the city centre. Parking garages (eg under the Old Town) cost €10 and upwards per day.

MAYRHOFEN

☎ 05285 / pop 4000

Run barefoot in meadows and inhale the purified, brisk mountain air surrounded by the beautiful Zillertal (Ziller) Valley, where unspoilt landscapes and the power of the piste dominate your periphery. Old farmhouses alongside elegant hotels make for a quaint contrast in this mountain chalet village. Have a glass of schnapps when you arrive – it has been a symbol of hospitality welcoming visitors to the Ziller for centuries. There's also a little test in this: how you drink it may foretell your experience in Mayrhofen. Gulp it and your holiday may be action packed and exhilarating, or sip it and enjoy a more relaxed and serene alpine paradise.

The **Europa House tourist office** (☎ 67 60; www.mayrhofen.at; Europahaus; 8am-6pm Mon-Fri, 9am-noon & 2-6pm Sat, 10am-noon Sun) has loads of comprehensive information, basically from A-Z for both summer and winter. It's free and written in English. There are good **walks** originating from the village; ask at the tourist office for maps or about guided trips. Mayrhofen is home to the steepest piste in Austria, known as the HariKari. There is year-round **skiing** on the Hintertux Glacier. A pass costs €33/29 per day in winter/summer; inquire at the tourist office.

To work your taste buds instead of your legs, visit **Erlebnis Sennerei** (☎ 62 713; www.cennerei-zillertal.at; Hollenzen 116; adult/child €11/free; 10am-3pm), a grass-roots dairy. See how local cheeses are made on the production facility tour and then enjoy the chance to taste them.

For sleeping, try the **Hotel Neue Post** (☎ 62 131; www.neue-poast.at; Hauptstrasse 400; s/d from €51/86; P). It's a lavish affair that's surprisingly well priced – although rates vary with the season and are higher in winter. It has a fabulous indoor swimming pool, and a great spa, sauna and solarium.

Our favourite local eating and drinking spot is **Mo's** (☎ 63 435; Hauptstrasse 417; mains €6-20), on the town's main street. The food is quite good, although the mix of cuisines is a bit strange – it encompasses the Mediterranean, Caribbean and American South. It also showcases live music.

To reach Mayrhofen catch a train to Jenbach from Innsbruck (€10, 1½ hours, hourly). From Jenbach (€5, 45 minutes) there are multiple trains daily to Mayrhofen, which is the last stop on the rail line.

AUSTRIA

AUSTRIA

KITZBÜHEL

☎ 05356 / pop 8600

Kitzbühel began life in the 16th century as a silver and copper mining town and today continues to preserve a charming medieval centre despite its other persona – as a fashionable and prosperous winter resort. It's renowned for the white-knuckled Hahnenkamm downhill ski race in January and the excellence of its slopes.

Orientation & Information

From the main train station to the town centre is 1km. You emerge from the train station onto Bahnhofstrasse and walk straight ahead and then turn left into Josef Pirchl Strasse; take the right fork (no entry for cars), which is still Josef Pirchl Strasse, and continue past the post office. Following this road will eventually take you to the **tourist office** (☎ 62 155-0; www.kitzbuehel.com; Hinterstadt 18; 🕑 8.30am-6pm Mon-Fri, 9am-6pm Sat).

Activities

SKIING

In winter there is good intermediate skiing on Kitzbüheler Horn to the north and Hahnenkamm to the south of town. A one-day ski pass costs around €35, though some *pensions*/hotels offer 'Ski Hit' reductions before mid-December or after mid-March.

HIKING

Dozens of summer hiking trails surround the town; the tourist office gives free maps and free guided hikes. Get a head start to the heights with a one- or three-day cable-car pass for €15/35.

There is an alpine flower garden (free) on the slopes of the Kitzbüheler Horn (a toll road for drivers). The scenic Schwarzsee is a fine location for summer swimming.

Sleeping

Prices quoted for *pensions* and hotels are for the winter high season.

Pension Hörl (☎/fax 63 144; Josef Pirchl Strasse 60; s/d €20/40, with shared bathroom €18/36) Conveniently close to the train station, this *pension* is cheap, friendly and more comfortable than the jumble-sale décor first suggests.

Pension Schmidinger (☎ 63 134; Ehrenbachgasse 3; s/d from €35/70) The spotless rooms here are decorated in a pleasant country style and have new bathrooms.

Pension Mühlbergerhof (☎ 62 835; fax 64 488; Schwarzseestrasse 6; s/d from €35/70) The colour scheme in the public areas of this *pension* is somewhat darker than Schmidinger, but the rooms are light and airy. The owners serve breakfast featuring fresh produce from their farm.

Eating

Asia Markt (Josef Pirchl Strasse 16; meals €4.50-6.50; 🕑 Mon-Sat) This grocery store serves light weekday lunches and early evening meals.

La Fonda (☎ 73 673; Hinterstadt 13; mains €5-12; 🕑 dinner) The kitschy Tex-Mex décor makes this place a popular choice, plus the kitchen is open until midnight for those wanting to dine late.

Huberbräu Stüberl (☎ 65 677; Vorderstadt 18; mains €6.50-12.50) This is a Kitzbühel 'must', although so many diners come for the Austrian food and beer that the service is sometimes rather off-hand.

Zinnkrug (☎ 62 613; Bichlstrasse 9; mains €6-17.50) A typically Austrian inn, Zinnkrug is known for its pork spare ribs and fondue (€15.60).

For self-caterers, there's a **Spar supermarket** (🕑 Mon-Sat) on Bichlstrasse (corner of Ehrenbachgasse).

Getting There & Away

Direct trains to Innsbruck (€12.20, one to two hours, depending on the service) only leave Kitzbühel every two hours or so, but there are hourly services to Wörgl, where you can change for Innsbruck. Trains to Salzburg (€20.80, two hours) leave roughly hourly. Slower trains stop at Kitzbühel-Hahnenkamm, which is closer to the town centre than the main Kitzbühel stop.

Getting to Lienz by public transport is awkward. The train is slow and the bus is infrequent (€12.50, two hours). There are four bus departures Monday to Friday and two each on Saturday and Sunday.

Heading south to Lienz, you pass through some marvellous scenery. Hwy 108 (the Felber Tauern Tunnel) and Hwy 107 (the Grossglockner mountain road; closed in winter) both have toll sections.

LIENZ

☎ 04852 / pop 13,000

The piste-filled outline of the Dolomite mountain range engulfing the southern skyline beckons visitors to the capital of East

Tirol. Lienz serves mostly as a stopover for skiers and hikers passing through or on the way to the Hohe Tauern National Park, which is Europe's largest national park.

Orientation & Information

The town centre is within the junction of the Isel and Drau Rivers. To reach Hauptplatz from the train station cross the road (or take the 'Zur Stadt' exit) and follow the street past the post office. The **tourist office** (☎ 65 265; www.lienz-tourismus.at; Europaplatz 1; 🕒 8am-6pm Mon-Fri, 9am-noon Sat, 9am-noon Sun summer & winter high season) will find rooms free of charge, or you can use the hotel board (free telephone) outside.

Sights & Activities

There is downhill skiing on the nearby **Zettersfeld** and **Hochstein** peaks. A one-day ski pass covering both is €30. However, the area around Lienz is more renowned for its cross-country skiing; the town fills up for the annual **Dolomitenlauf** cross-country skiing race in mid-January.

In summer there's good hiking in the mountains. The cable cars are closed during the low season (April, May, October and November).

Sleeping & Eating

There are ADEG supermarkets on Hauptplatz and Tiroler Platz.

Comfort-Camping Falken (☎ 64 022; Eichholz 7; camp site without/with electricity €8/10.50, adult €6; 🕒 mid-Dec–Oct) Just south of town, this camping ground has good washing facilities, a restaurant and mountain views.

Altstadthotel Eck (☎ 64 785; altstadthotel.eck@utanet.at; Hauptplatz 20; s/d from €55/110) Atmospheric and spacious, it provides all the comfort you'd expect from one of the town's leading hotels.

Pick Nick Ossi (☎ 71 091; Europaplatz 2; snacks €3-7) Salads, pizza and other fast food are on offer here.

Adlerstüberl (☎ 62 550; Andrä Kranz Gasse 5; mains from €8) Daily specials are featured at this eatery, which does the usual assortment of Austrian dishes with varying results.

Getting There & Away

Except for the 'corridor' route through Italy to Innsbruck, trains to the rest of Austria connect via Spittal Millstättersee to the east. Trains to Salzburg (€26.90) take at least three hours. Villach, between Spittal and Klagenfurt, is a main junction for rail routes to the south. To head south by car, you must first divert west or east along Hwy 100.

HOHE TAUERN NATIONAL PARK

You wouldn't guess from its small stature, but little Austria actually contains the largest national park in the Alps. Straddling Tirol, Salzburg and Carinthia, the Hohe Tauern National Park stretches over 1786 sq km. At the heart of this protected oasis of flora and fauna (including marmots and some rare ibexes) lies the **Grossglockner** (3797m), Austria's highest mountain. The Grossglockner towers over the 10km-long Pasterze Glacier, which is best seen from the outlook at **Franz Josef's Höhe**.

Although camping is not allowed in the park, there are mountain huts and hiking trails. Ask the tourist office in Lienz (left) for details. If you're on foot, the most direct public transport into the park from Lienz is by bus to Franz Josef's Höhe. This goes via Heiligenblut, where you'll find the **Hotel Senger** (☎ 22 15; www.romantic.at; Hof 23; s/d from €40/80; P ⊠ 💻). Located in a charming old farmhouse, it lends a real feel for being up in the mountains (think stone floors, open fireplaces, and plenty of nooks and crannies in which to relax). The whole place has the friendly, sociable atmosphere of a ski chalet.

Buses run from mid-June to late September, but infrequently and on a very complicated and confusing schedule, so ask the Lienz tourist office *and* your bus driver before boarding in front of the train station. The return fare from Lienz is €10.20, plus a park toll of €2.70.

The portion of the **Grossglockner Hochalpenstrasse** (Hwy 107; www.grossglockner.at, in German) running through the park is considered one of the most scenic in the world. It winds upwards 2000m past waterfalls, glaciers and Alpine meadows. The highway runs between Lienz and Zell am See, and if you catch a bus from Lienz to Franz Josef's Höhe, you'll be traversing the southern part of this route. If you want to travel further north, ask your driver, or the **Kärtnen tourist office** (☎ 04824-200 121) just up the road from the bus stop in Heiligenblut about current bus schedules.

If you have your own vehicle, you'll have more flexibility. However, beware that the road is open only between May and mid-

September, and you must pay tolls (at least €26/17 for a car/motorcycle, but more if you take a circular route).

At the northern end of the park, turn west along Hwy 168 (which becomes Hwy 165) to reach the spectacular, triple-level **Krimml Falls**.

VORARLBERG

Vorarlberg is Austria's 'wild west', occupying the country's furthest western reaches and separated from it by the Arlberg massif. Over the centuries its isolation has helped cultivate an individual identity (right down to the language) and it still often associates itself more with neighbouring Switzerland than Vienna.

Alluringly beautiful, this region is an aesthetic mix of mountains, hills and valleys. Trickling down from the Alps to the shores of Lake Constance (Bodensee), Vorarlberg is a destination in its own right, attracting everyone from classical-music buffs to skiers. It's also a gateway, by rail or water, to Germany, Liechtenstein or Switzerland.

BREGENZ

☎ 05574 / pop 27,500

Ritzy Bregenz sits pretty on the shores of Lake Constance and emits a decidedly posh vibe – go window shopping for Dior and Louis Vuitton at one of the designer shops gracing its quaint Old Town streets. Visit in summer, during the annual Bregenzer Festspiele (Bregenz Festival), to catch this provincial capital at its most boisterous.

Orientation

Bregenz is on Lake Constance's eastern shore. Turn left at the main train station exit and take Bahnhofstrasse to the city centre (five minutes). Buses for the city leave from outside the train station.

Information

Cockpit Café (Seegalerie, Bahnhofstrasse 10; per 15 min €1.20; 🕑 5pm-midnight) Offers Internet access.

Post Office (Seestrasse 5; 🕑 7am-7pm Mon-Fri, 8am-noon Sat)

Tourist Office (☎ 49 59-0; www.bregenz.at, in German; Bahnhofstrasse 14; 🕑 9am-noon & 1-5pm Mon-Fri, to noon only Sat, to 7pm Mon-Sat during the Bregenz Festival) Also offers free Internet access.

Sights & Activities

Most tourists who arrive in Bregenz are drawn almost instinctively to the **Bodensee**, a major summer holiday destination for Austrians, Swiss and Germans, all of whom take advantage of the many water sports and attractions lining its banks.

Other highlights around the Bodensee include the **Zeppelin Museum** (Friedrichshafen), Meersburg's picturesque half-timbered houses built in classical German style and its two castles, the **Cathedral of St Nicholas** (Überlinge), the **flower island** of Mainau and the Gothic cathedral of Konstanz.

Bregenz offers spectacular views from its **Pfänder** mountain; a **cable car** (☎ 421 600; www.pfaenderbahn.at, in German; admission €10; 🕑 9am-7pm, closed 2 weeks in Nov) carries you up and back. There are hiking trails at the top.

Bregenz is also of interest to architecture fans. The most notable modern building is the shimmering art-gallery block, the **Kunsthaus**, by award-winning Swiss architect Peter Zumthor.

Festivals & Events

A feature that makes the **Bregenzer Festspiele** (Bregenz Festival) in July and August so remarkable is its setting. During the four-week programme, operas and classical works are performed from a floating stage on the lake's edge. For tickets, contact the **Kartenbüro** (☎ 407-6; www.bregenzerfestspiele.com; Postfach 311, A-6901) about nine months beforehand, or ask about cancellations on the day.

Sleeping & Eating

The tourist office has a list of private homes that let rooms for €20 to €30 per person if none of the following options sound appealing. Expect prices during the festival to be higher than those quoted here.

Jugendgästehaus Bregenz (☎ 42867; www.jgh.at/bregenz; Mehrerauerstrasse 5; dm from €20; Ⓟ 💻) In a former needle factory, this HI hostel is a lively place, with larger than average dorms boasting only six beds plus en suite. There's also a decent restaurant on the premises. The hostel is near the skateboard park; take the 'Zum See' exit from the train station and pass the casino.

Pension Sonne (☎ 42 572; Kaiserstrasse 8; s/d from €35/66) This family-run *pension* is rather basic (the wooden floors can feel a little cold), but it is the most central accommodation option around. Ask to see a few rooms; some have nicer décor than others. The cheapest rooms share bathrooms.

Gästehaus am Tannenbauch (☎ 44 174; Im Gehren 1; s/d €40/80; ⏰ May-Oct; Ⓟ) Travellers with a taste for something different might prefer this quirky guesthouse. From the outside it looks like a normal house; inside it explodes into an ornate display of baroque kitsch. The highlight is the regal breakfast room.

Deuring-Schlössle (☎ 47 800; www.deuring-schloessle.com; Ehregutaplatz 4; s/d €135/210; Ⓟ) Bregenz's best rooms are found in this fabulously renovated old castle. Each one is decorated differently, but all have loads of medieval charm and grace. Its restaurant (mains from €20) is also the best in Bregenz, with a sophisticated look and a gourmet menu.

Gösserbräu (☎ 42 467; Anton Schneider Strasse 1; mains €8-12; ⏰ 9am-1pm Tue-Sun) Solid Austrian fare, simple and hearty, but not too stodgy, is served in a number of uniquely decorated dining rooms. The vegetarian mushroom goulash with dumplings is divine.

Getting There & Away

Trains to Munich (€36, 2½ hours) go via Lindau. There are also regular departures to St Gallen and Zürich. Trains to Innsbruck (€27, 2¾ hours) depart every two hours.

Boat services operate from late May to late October, with a reduced schedule from early March. For information, call ☎ 42 868. Bregenz to Lake Constance by boat via Friedrichshafen takes about 3½ hours and there are about seven departures daily. Special boat passes offer discounts.

ARLBERG REGION

The Arlberg region, shared by Vorarlberg and neighbouring Tirol, has some of the best skiing in Austria. Summer is less busy and many bars are closed.

St Anton am Arlberg is the largest resort, where you're as likely to hear a cheery antipodean 'G'day' or Scandinavian *God dag*, as you are to hear an Austrian *Grüss' Di*. There are good intermediate to advanced runs here, as well as nursery slopes on Gampen and Kapall. The **tourist office** (☎ 05446-22 690; www.stantonamarlberg.com; ⏰ 9am-5pm Mon-Fri), on the main street, has details. Head diagonally left from the train station to find it.

A ski pass valid for 83 ski lifts in St Anton and neighbouring St Christoph Lech, Zürs and Stuben costs €45 for one day and €180 for six days (reductions for children and seniors).

There are nearly 600 accommodation options in and around St Anton, 80% of which are open during summer. Even with all this choice, it can be hard to find somewhere to stay over winter without booking ahead (note that short stays of a couple of days will usually incur a surcharge).

Haus Wannali (☎ 05446-23 50; Arlberg Strasse 509; s/d €40/80) is a central spot, with a friendly atmosphere and entertaining regulars. Some of the best views in town are enjoyed from the relatively spick-and-span **Pension Strolz Christian** (☎ 05446-30 119; Ing Gomperz Strasse 606; s/d €40/80).

When hunger hits, there is a Spar supermarket on the main road, and decent pizza and pasta dishes at **Pomodoro** (☎ 33 33; Fussgängerzone 70; mains from €8; ⏰ dinner Dec-Apr). The food isn't great but the atmosphere is lively.

Loud, bawdy and very English, **Piccadilly** (☎ 221 32 76; Fussgängerzone 55) often has live music. For an après-ski cocktail or two head to **Krazy Kanguruh** (☎ 26 33), a longtime favourite bar on the lower slopes.

Getting There & Away

St Anton is on the main railway route between Bregenz (€14.50) and Innsbruck (€13.60), less than 1½ hours from both cities. St Anton is close to the eastern entrance of the Arlberg Tunnel, the toll road connecting Vorarlberg and Tirol. The tunnel toll is €9.45/7.25 for cars/motorcycles. You can avoid the toll by taking the B197, but no vehicles with trailers are allowed on this winding road.

AUSTRIA DIRECTORY

ACCOMMODATION

Reservations are recommended at Christmas, Easter and during summer. They are binding on both parties, so if you don't take a reserved room, the price could still be deducted from your credit card. Hostels tend to be more flexible; however, small groups booking into hostels might find their reservation for a four-bed room translated into four separate beds on arrival.

Tourist offices can supply lists of all types of accommodation and will generally make reservations – sometimes for a small fee.

Many resort towns hand out a *Gästekarte* (guest card) to people staying overnight. This card is funded by a resort tax of around €1 to €2 per night, added to the accommodation tariff, and it offers useful discounts on transport, sporting facilities and museums. Check with the tourist office if you're not offered one at your resort accommodation. In smaller towns, the first night's accommodation can cost slightly more than subsequent nights.

There are more than 500 camping grounds in Austria, but most close in winter. If you pitch a tent outside an established camping ground you need the property owner's approval; on public land it's illegal. Outside Vienna, Tirol and protected areas, free camping is allowed in a campervan, but only if you don't set up equipment outside the van. The **Austrian Camping Club** (Österreichischer Camping Club; Map p64; ☎ 01-71 199-1272; Schubertring 1-3, A-1010 Vienna) has information.

In the mountains, hikers can take a break from camping by spending the night in an alpine hut. See below for further details.

Two HI-affiliated hostelling associations operating within the country are **Österreichischer Jugendherbergsverband** (Map p64; ☎ 01-533 53 53; www.oejhv.or.at; 01, Schottenring 28, A-1010 Vienna) and **Junge Hostels Austria** (Map p64; ☎ 01-533 18 33; www.jungehotels.at; 01, Helferstorferstrasse 4, Vienna). Prices are generally €13 to €20 per night.

It's quite common for house owners to rent out rooms in their home (€15 to €30 per person, per night). Look out for the ubiquitous *Zimmer frei* (room vacant) signs.

The cheapest budget hotels start at around €25/40 for singles/doubles with a shared bathroom, and €35/60 for those with private facilities. Most midrange hotels start at around €50/80 for rooms with private facilities.

For this chapter we've defined places costing less than €40 as budget, while midrange options cost €40 to €80 and top-end hotels start at €80 per person.

Accommodation prices quoted in this chapter are for the high summer season (or winter in ski resorts) and include all taxes. Unless otherwise stated, all rooms have private facilities and breakfast is included.

ACTIVITIES

Hiking & Mountaineering

Walking and climbing are popular with visitors and Austrians alike, and most tourist offices sell maps of hiking routes. Mountain paths have direction indicators and often markers indicating their level of difficulty. Those with a red-white-red marker mean you need sturdy hiking boots and a pole; a blue-white-blue marker indicates the need for mountaineering equipment. There are 10 long-distance national hiking routes, while three European routes pass through Austria. Options include the northern Alpine route from Lake Constance to Vienna, via Dachstein, or the central route from Feldkirch to Hainburger Pforte, via Hohe Tauern National Park.

Don't try mountaineering without the proper equipment or experience. The **Österreichischer Alpenverein** (ÖAV; Austrian Alpine Club; Map p95; ☎ 0512-587 828; office@alpenverein-ibk.at; Wilhelm Greil Strasse 15, A-6010 Innsbruck) has touring programmes and also maintains a list of alpine huts in hill-walking regions. These provide inexpensive accommodation and often have meals or cooking facilities. Members of the club take priority but anyone can stay. It's a good idea to book huts. Listing your next intended destination in the hut book on departure provides you with an extra measure of safety, as search-and-rescue teams will be alerted should a problem arise.

Skiing & Snowboarding

Austria has some of the world's best skiing and snowboarding. The most popular regions are Vorarlberg and Tirol, but Salzburg province and Carinthia offer cheaper possibilities. Unusually, skiing is possible year-round at the famous Stubai Glacier near Innsbruck.

The skiing season starts in December and lasts well into April at higher-altitude resorts. Count on spending €20 to €38 for a daily ski pass (to ride the ski lifts). Rental generally starts at €16 for downhill equipment or €14 for cross-country skis; rates drop for multiple days.

Spa Resorts

There are spa resorts throughout the country, identifiable by the prefix *Bad* (bath), eg Bad Ischl. While perfect for the self-indulgent pampering that stressed-out city-dwellers today so often crave, they also promise more traditional healing cures for respiratory, circulatory and other ailments. The **Austrian National Tourist Office** (www.austria-tourism.at) can provide details, as can the **Österreichischer**

Heilbäder & Kurortverband (Austrian Thermal Baths & Spa Association; ☎ 01-512 19 04; oehkv@newsclub.at).

BOOKS

Lonely Planet has guides to both *Austria* and *Vienna*, as well as the *German Phrasebook*.

Graham Greene's evocative spy story *The Third Man* is set in Vienna, as is John Irving's *Setting Free the Bears*. Numerous travel writers, from the masterful Patrick Leigh Fermor *(A Time of Gifts)* to the amusing Bill Bryson *(Neither Here Nor There)*, have passed through the city.

BUSINESS HOURS

Shops usually open 9am to 6pm Monday to Friday, and 9am to 1pm or 5pm on Saturday. However, grocery stores might open as early as 6am, and other shops don't close their doors until 7.30pm. In smaller cities, there's sometimes a two-hour closure over lunch.

Banks keep short hours, usually 9am to 12.30pm and 1.30pm to 3pm Monday to Friday, with 'late' (5.30pm) closing on Thursday. Information offices are generally open from 9am to 5pm Monday to Saturday. Restaurants generally open around 11am and stop serving food around 10pm. Most bars open sometime around noon, while clubs don't start rocking until after 10pm.

EMBASSIES & CONSULATES

Austrian Embassies & Consulates

Following is a list of Austrian diplomatic missions abroad.

Australia (☎ 02-6295 1533; www.austriaemb.org.au; 12 Talbot St, Forrest, Canberra, ACT 2603)
Canada (☎ 613-789 1444; www.austro.org; 445 Wilbrod St, Ottawa, ON K1N 6M7)
France Embassy (☎ 01 40 63 30 63; www.aussenministerium.at/paris; 6, rue Fabert, 75007 Paris); Consulate (☎ 01 40 63 30 90; 17, ave de Villars, 75007 Paris) Visas only at the consulate.
Germany (☎ 30-202 87-0; www.oesterreichische-botschaft.de; Stauffenbergstrasse 1, D-10785 Berlin)
Ireland (☎ 01-269 4577; dublin-ob@bmaa.gv.at; 93 Ailesbury Rd, Dublin 4)
Netherlands (☎ 070-324 54 70; den-haag-ob@bmaa.gv.at; van Alkemadelaan 342, 2597 AS Den Haag)
New Zealand (☎ 04-499 6393; diessl@ihug.co.nz, Level 2, Willbank House, 587 Willis St, Wellington)
UK (☎ 020-7235 3731; www.austria.org.uk; 18 Belgrave Mews West, London SW1X 8HU)
USA (☎ 202-895 6700; www.austria.org; 3524 International Court NW, Washington, DC 20008)

Embassies & Consulates in Austria

Only *Botschaften* (embassies) and *Konsulate* (consulates) in Vienna issue visas. In case of an emergency, you might be redirected to a limited-hours consulate in a nearer city. The following diplomatic missions are located in Vienna unless otherwise stated:

Australia (Map p64; ☎ 01-50 674-0; www.australian-embassy.at; 04, Mattiellistrasse 2-4)
Canada (Map p64; ☎ 01-53 138-3000; www.kanada.at; 01, Laurenzerberg 2)
Croatia (☎ 01-484 87 83-0; 17, Heubergg 10)
Czech Republic (Map p60; ☎ 01-894 37 41; 14, Penzingerstrasse 11-13)
France (Map p64; ☎ 01-50 275-0; www.ambafrance-at.org; 04, Technikerstrasse 2)
Germany (Map p60; ☎ 01-71 154-0; 03, Metternichgasse 3)
Hungary (Map p64; ☎ 01-53 780-300; 01, Bankgasse 4-6)
Ireland (Map p64; ☎ 01-715 42 46-0; 01, Rotenturmstrasse16-18)
Italy (Map p60; ☎ 01-712 51 21-0; 03, Rennweg 27)
Netherlands (Map p64; ☎ 01-58 939; 01, Opernring 5)
New Zealand (☎ 01-318 85 05; Salesianergasse 15/3)
Slovakia (☎ 01-318 90 55-200; 19, Armbrustergasse 24)
Slovenia (Map p64; ☎ 01-586 13 09; 01, Niebelungengasse 13)
Switzerland (Map p60; ☎ 01-79 505-0; 03, Prinz Eugen Strasse 7)
UK (Map p60; ☎ 01-71 613-0; www.britishembassy.at; 03, Jaurèsgasse 12)
USA Embassy (Map p60; ☎ 01-31 339-0; www.usembassy.at; 09, Boltzmanngasse 16); Consulate (Map p64; ☎ 512 58 35; 01, Gartenbaupromenade 2) Visas at the consulate only.

FESTIVALS & EVENTS

The Austrian National Tourist Office Vienna (ANTO; www.austria-tourism.at) has a list of annual and one-off events on its website; just click on 'Events'. Following is a list of major festivals.

February

Fasching This Shrovetide carnival before Lent involves parties, waltzes and a parade; celebrated countrywide.

May/June

Festwochen (Vienna) The Vienna Festival focuses on classical music, theatre and other performing arts.
Lifeball (Vienna; www.lifeball.org) One of the final balls of the season, this is a huge gay/straight AIDS fundraising gala attracting celebrity guests.

July

Bregenzer Festspiele (Bregenz) Opera with a difference – performed on a floating stage on Lake Constance.
Salzburger Festspiele (Salzburg) Austria's leading classical music festival attracts major stars, like Simon Rattle and Placido Domingo.
Love Parade (Vienna) Austria hosts its own version of the popular techno street parade.

September

Ars Electronica Festival (Linz) This is a celebration of weird and wonderful technological art and computer music.
Bruckner Fest (Linz) This highbrow classical music festival pays homage to native Linz son Bruckner.

November

Christmas Markets (particularly Vienna and Salzburg) Quaint stalls selling traditional decorations, foodstuffs, mulled wine and all manner of presents heralding the arrival of the festive season.

December

Krampus (Innsbruck and elsewhere) St Nicholas, his friend Krampus (Black Peter) and an array of masked creatures cause merriment and mischief in a parade that harks back to pagan celebrations.
Kaiserball (Vienna) The Imperial Ball kicks off Vienna's three-month season of balls, combining glamour and high society with camp decadence.

GAY & LESBIAN TRAVELLERS

Public attitudes to homosexuality are less tolerant than in most other Western European countries, except perhaps in Vienna. A good information centre/meeting point in Vienna is **Rosa Lila Villa** (Map p60; ☎ 01-586 81 50; 06, Linke Wienzeile 102). The age of consent for gay men is 18; for everyone else it's 14. Vienna has a Pride march, the Rainbow Parade, on the last Saturday in June.

HOLIDAYS

New Year's Day 1 January
Epiphany 6 January
Easter Monday March/April
May Day 1 May
Ascension Five and a half weeks after Easter
Whit Monday Seven weeks after Easter
Corpus Christi 10 days after Whit Monday
Assumption of the Virgin Mary 15 August
National Day 26 October
All Saints' Day 1 November
Immaculate Conception 8 December
Christmas Day 25 December
Boxing Day 26 December

INTERNET RESOURCES

The **Austrian National Tourist Office** (ANTO; www.austria-tourism.at) is a comprehensive starting point, with general information and details on different attractions and types of holidays.

Train times and fares are available from **Österreiche Bundesbahnen** (ÖBB; Austrian Railways; www.oebb.at).

Herold (www.herold.at) maintains an online telephone book. Budget travellers might also find quite useful the *Mensa* (university canteen; www.mensen.at, in German) listing.

LANGUAGE

Although Austrians understand Hochdeutsch ('high' or received German), they use different words and some even speak a dialect. Apart from using the expressions *Grüss Gott* (hello), *Servus!* (hello and goodbye) and *Ba Ba* (bye bye), they join their Bavarian cousins in forming the diminutive with 'erl' instead of the northern German 'chen'. Therefore when Austrians say *ein Bisserl,* they mean *ein Bisschen* (a little), and they use the word *Mäderl* (girl) instead of *Mädchen.*

Some expressions of time are also unique. *Heuer* means 'this year' and Austrians talk not of the German *Januar* but of *Jänner* (January).

MONEY

The currency is the euro, although you will still hear some references to its Austrian predecessor, the Schilling. Straight conversion of prices from Schilling to euro is the reason for occasionally strange prices – eg €3.63 for a phone card or €2.91 for a cup of coffee.

Major train stations have currency offices, and there are plenty of banks, *bureaux de change* and *Bankomats* (ATMs) across the country.

Costs

Expenses in Austria are average for Western Europe, with prices highest in big cities and ski resorts. Budget travellers can possibly scrape by on €40 a day, after rail-card costs; double this amount if you intend to avoid self-catering or staying in hostels. The minimum you can expect to pay per person is €13/25 for a hostel/hotel and €5/10 for a lunch/dinner.

Taxes & Refunds

Value-added tax (*Mehrwertsteuer* or MwSt) is charged at either 10% (eg travel, food and museum entry) or 20% (drinks and luxury goods). Prices always include taxes. For purchases over €75, non-EU residents can reclaim the MwSt either upon leaving the EU or afterwards. (Note that one-third of your refund will be absorbed in charges.) Ensure the shop has the forms to be filled out at the time of purchase, and present the documentation to customs on departure for checking and stamping.

The airports at Vienna, Salzburg, Innsbruck, Linz and Graz have counters for instant refunds, as do some land crossings. You can also reclaim by post.

Tipping & Bargaining

Austrian waiters aren't renowned for friendly or speedy service, but it's still rude not to round off the bill so that it includes a 10% tip. Pay it directly to the server; don't leave it on the table. Taxi drivers will also expect tips of 10%. Bargaining is unheard of.

POST

Post office hours vary: typical hours in smaller towns are 8am to noon and 2pm to 6pm Monday to Friday (money exchange to 5pm), and 8am to 11am Saturday, but a few main post offices in big cities are open daily until late, or even 24 hours. Stamps are also available in *Tabak* (tobacco) shops. Postcards and standard letters (up to 20g) cost €0.55 both within Austria and to Europe.

TELEPHONE

Don't worry if a telephone number you are given has only four digits, as many as nine digits, or some odd number in between. The Austrian system often adds direct-dial (DW) extensions to the main number after a hyphen. Thus, say ☎ 12 345 is a main number, ☎ 12 345-67 will be an extension, which could be a phone or fax. Generally, a -0 will give you the switchboard operator.

From a public phone, it costs €0.12 per minute to call anywhere in Austria, be it next door or across the country.

Mobile Phones

Mobile phones in Austria operate on GSM 900/1800, which is compatible with other European countries and Australia, but not with the North American GSM 1900 system or the system used in Japan.

If you're staying for a while, it's possible to get a prepaid phone in Austria, or strike a deal where you pay for calls and line rental but get your handset free. Try **Max.Mobil** (Map p60; ☎ 0676-20 00; 03, Kelsenstrasse 5-7) or **Mobilkom** (☎ 0800-664 300).

Phonecards

The minimum tariff in phone boxes is €0.20. Some boxes will only accept phonecards (Telefon-Wertkarte), which can be bought from post offices in two denominations – €3.60 and €6.90.

TIME

Austria operates on Central European Time (GMT/UTC plus one hour). Clocks go forward one hour on the last Saturday night in March and back again on the last Saturday night in October.

TOURIST INFORMATION

Tourist offices (usually called *Kurverein*, *Verkehrsamt* or *Tourismusverband*) tend to adjust their hours from one year to the next, so the hours listed in this chapter are a guide only and may have changed slightly by the time you arrive.

The **Austrian National Tourist Office** (ANTO; www.austria-tourism.at) has a number of overseas offices, including those in the following list. Some of these offices are not open to personal callers, so phone first. There is a comprehensive listing on the ANTO website.

Australia (☎ 02-9299 3621; info@antosyd.org.au; 1st fl, 36 Carrington St, Sydney, NSW 2000)
UK (☎ 020-7629 0461; info@anto.co.uk; 14 Cork St, London W1S 3NS)
USA (☎ 212-944 6880; info@oewnyc.com; PO Box 1142, New York, NY 10108-1142)

VISAS

Visas are not required for EU, US, Canadian, Australian or New Zealand citizens. Visitors may stay a maximum of three months (six months for Japanese citizens). There are no time limits for European Union and Swiss nationals, but they should register with the police before taking up residency. Most African and Arab nationals require a visa.

TRANSPORT IN AUSTRIA

GETTING THERE & AWAY

Air

The national carrier, Austrian Airlines, has an excellent safety record and specialises in linking numerous Eastern European cities to the West via Vienna.

Low-cost airlines also serve Austria. Ryanair flies from London to Graz, Klagenfurt, Linz and Salzburg; Air Berlin flies to Vienna from Germany; and German Wings has limited services from Düsseldorf and Stuttgart. Central European low-cost carrier Sky Europe flies to many destinations, including Croatia, France, Hungary, Italy and Poland. Be warned, however, that its 'Vienna' airport is far from the city – in Slovakia, actually.

Following are the key international airports in Austria:

Graz (GRZ; ☎ 0316-29 02-0; www.flughafen-graz.at, in German)
Innsbruck (INN; ☎ 0512-22 525-0; www.innsbruck-airport.com, in German)
Klagenfurt (KLU; ☎ 0463-41 500; www.klagenfurt-airport.com)
Linz (LNZ; ☎ 07221-600-0; www.flughafen-linz.at)
Salzburg (SZG; ☎ 0662-85 80-100; www.salzburg-airport.com, in German)
Vienna (VIE; ☎ 01-7007 22333; www.viennaairport.com)

Major international airlines, reputable regional carriers and low-cost airlines flying to and from Austria include:

Air Berlin (code AB; ☎ 0820-400 011; www.airberlin.com)
Air France (code AF; ☎ 01-50 222-2400; www.airfrance.com)
Alitalia (code AZ; ☎ 01-505 17 07; www.alitalia.com)
Austrian Airways (code OS; ☎ 05-17 66; www.aua.com)
British Airways (code BA; ☎ 01-79 567-567; www.ba.com)
Croatia Airlines (code OU; ☎ 01-70 07-36163; www.croatiaairlines.com)
CSA (code OK; ☎ 01-512 38 05-0; www.czechairlines.com)
German Wings (code 4U; ☎ 01-50 291-0070; www.germanwings.com)
Iberia (code IB; ☎ 01-795 67 61-2; www.iberia.com)
KLM (code KL; ☎ 0900-359 556; www.klm.com)
LOT Polish Airlines (code LO; ☎ 01-961 08 85; www.lot.com)
Lufthansa (code LH; ☎ 0810-1025 8080; www.lufthansa.com)
Ryanair (code FR; ☎ 0900-210 240; www.ryanair.com)
SAS Scandinavian Airlines (code SK; ☎ 01-68 055-4466; www.scandinavian.net)
SkyEurope Airlines (code NE; ☎ 01-9985 5555; www.skyeurope.com)
Swiss International Air Lines (code LX; ☎ 0810-810 840; www.swiss.com)

Land

BORDER CROSSINGS

There are many entry points from the Czech Republic, Hungary, Slovakia, Slovenia and Switzerland; main border crossings are open 24 hours. There are usually no border controls to/from Germany and Italy.

BUS

Buses leave Austria for as far afield as England, the Baltic countries, the Netherlands, Germany and Switzerland. But most significantly, they provide access to Eastern European cities small and large – from the likes of Belgrade, Sofia and Warsaw, to Banja Luka, Mostar and Sarajevo.

Services operated by **Eurolines** (www.eurolines.at) leave from Vienna (see p73) and from several regional cities.

CAR & MOTORCYCLE

Austria levies fees for its entire motorway network. Therefore tourists need to choose between a 10-day pass (motorcycle/car €4.30/7.60), a two-month pass (€10.90/21.80) or a yearly pass (€29/72.60) and then clearly display the chosen toll label *(Vignette)* on their vehicle. Passes are available at borders, on freeways or from service stations. Without one, you will face an on-the-spot fine of up to €220 or, if you don't pay up immediately, a €2180 fine. See **Asfinag** (www.oesag.at, in German) for details .

TRAIN

The main rail services in and out of the country include the route from Vienna's Westbahnhof to Munich, via Salzburg and Bregenz. Trains to the Czech Republic leave from Südbahnhof in Vienna. Express services to Italy go via Innsbruck or Villach; trains to Slovenia are routed through Graz.

For Austrian rail passes that extend into other countries, see p1121.

River & Lake

Hydrofoils run to Bratislava and Budapest from Vienna (see p73). Germany and Switzerland can be reached from Bregenz (see p101).

GETTING AROUND

Air

Austrian Airlines and its subsidiary, Tyrolean Airlines, operate regular internal flights, but train, bus and car travel usually suffices in such a small country.

Bicycle

Private operators and hostels hire bikes; expect to pay anything from €7 to €10 per day. Vienna has cut-price city bikes (p74).

You can pay separately to take your bike on slow trains (€2.90/7.50/22.50 for a daily/weekly/monthly ticket); on fast trains it costs €6.80 per day, if space allows. Booking is advisable, because if there's no space in the passenger carriages, you will have to send your bike as registered luggage (€21.40). If a group of you are travelling with bikes, ask about the '1-Plus Freizeitticket' (passenger plus bike).

Boat

Services along the Danube are mainly scenic pleasure cruises, but provide a leisurely way of getting from A to B. For more information on boat services along the river, see p73.

Bus

Both *Postbuses* and *Bahnbuses* are now operated by the railways, ÖBB. Bus services are generally limited to less-accessible regions, such as the Salzkammergut or Hohe Tauern National Park. Between major cities in environmentally friendly Austria, only train services exist.

Buses are single class, clean, efficient and run on time. Generally you can only buy tickets from the drivers. Call ☎ 01-71 101 for inquiries.

Car & Motorcycle

AUTOMOBILE ASSOCIATIONS

The **Austrian Automobile Club** (Map p64; Österreichischer Automobil, Motorrad und Touring Club; ÖAMTC; ☎ 01-71 199-0; Schubertring 1-3, A-1010 Vienna) provides emergency breakdown assistance via its **24-hour phone line** (☎ 120). It charges non-members an initial call-out fee of €95/135 per day/night, on top of other service charges.

EMERGENCY NUMBERS

- Alpine Rescue ☎ 140
- Ambulance ☎ 144
- Fire ☎ 122
- Police ☎ 133

BRING YOUR OWN VEHICLE

Cars can be transported on trains; Vienna is linked by a daily motorail service to Innsbruck, Salzburg and Villach.

DRIVING LICENCE

Visitors from the EU and the USA can drive using their home driving licence; those from elsewhere require an International Driving Permit.

FUEL & SPARE PARTS

Motorway service stations are found at regular intervals. Basic spare parts are widely available. Ordering more specialised parts, especially for non-European models, takes time and can be costly.

HIRE

Multinational car-hire firms **Avis** (www.avis.at), **Budget** (www.budget.at), **Europcar** (www.europcar.co.at) and **Hertz** (www.hertz.at) all have offices in major cities; ask at tourist offices for details. The minimum age for hiring small cars is 19 years, or 25 years for larger, 'prestige' cars. Customers must have held a driving licence for at least a year. Many contracts forbid customers to take cars outside Austria, particularly into Eastern Europe.

ROAD CONDITIONS

Roads are generally good, but care is needed on difficult mountain routes. Snow chains are highly recommended in winter. There are tolls (usually €2.50 to €10) for some mountain tunnels.

ROAD RULES

Vehicles drive on the right-hand side, and you must give way to traffic on the right. On mountain roads, buses always have priority; otherwise, priority lies with uphill traffic. The usual speed limits are 50km/h in towns, 130km/h on motorways and 100km/h on other roads. There's a steep on-the-spot fine for drink-driving (over 0.05% blood-alcohol content) and your driving licence may be confiscated. If you plan to drive on motorways, you must pay a tax and affix a *Vignette* to your windscreen (see p106).

Many city streets have restricted parking (called 'blue zones') during shopping hours. Parking is unrestricted on unmarked streets.

Motorcyclists must have their headlights on during the day, and crash helmets are compulsory for riders and passengers.

Hitching

It's illegal to hitchhike on Austrian motorways (and for minors under 16 years of age to hitch anywhere in Burgenland, Upper Austria, Styria and Vorarlberg).

Train

The efficient state network, ÖBB, is supplemented by a few private lines. Eurail and Inter-Rail passes (see p1121) are always valid on the state network, but only valid sometimes on private lines. There is no supplement on Eurail and Inter-Rail passes for national travel on faster EC (Eurocity) and IC (Intercity) trains. Tickets purchased on the train cost about €3 extra. Fares quoted in this chapter are for 2nd-class tickets.

Before arriving in Austria, EU residents can buy a Eurodomino Pass (see p1122) for Austria for €104 for three days and €10 for each extra day for up to eight days in total.

Available to non-EU residents are the Austrian rail pass (US$119 for three days; US$18 for each extra day up to eight days in total) and the European Eastpass (US$158 for five days; US$23 for each extra day up to 10 days in total) for travel within Austria, the Czech Republic, Hungary, Poland and Slovakia. Both are valid for a month. The Austria & Switzerland Pass (US$270/228 over/under 26 years for four days, and $32/27 for each extra day up to 10 days in total) is valid for two months.

Within Austria, anyone can buy a Vorteils-card (adult/under 26 years/senior €99.90/19.90/26.90), which reduces fares by 45% and is valid for a year.

Nationwide train information can be obtained by dialling ☎ 05-17 17 (local rate) or by going online at **ÖBB** (www.oebb.at).

Belgium

Now really! How did Belgium ever get labelled 'boring'? In a country where fine food is mandatory, beer and chocolates unbeatable and café culture common, how could anyone find it dull? And that's without even mentioning Belgium's history, arts, fashion or clubbing.

België to Flemish speakers and La Belgique to the nation's French speakers is an eccentric little country that takes time to know. Don't make the mistake of judging it on day one or, worse still, in the first hour. Granted, you won't be texting about the landscape or all of those little red-brick houses. But hang around awhile (it usually takes only two days) and you'll soon reschedule your travel plans.

FAST FACTS

- **Area** 30,000 sq km
- **Capital** Brussels
- **Currency** euro (€); A$1 = €0.60; ¥100 = €0.67; NZ$1 = €0.50; UK£1 = €1.48; US$1 = €0.78
- **Famous for** chocolate, beer, WWI battlefields, tennis greats, *Tintin*
- **Official Languages** Flemish, French, German
- **Population** 10.4 million
- **Phrases** *goeiendag/bonjour* (hello; Flemish/French); *tot ziens/au revoir* (goodbye; Flemish/French); *bedankt/merci* (thanks; Flemish/French)
- **Telephone Codes** country code ☎ 32; international access code ☎ 00; reverse-charge code ☎ 1224

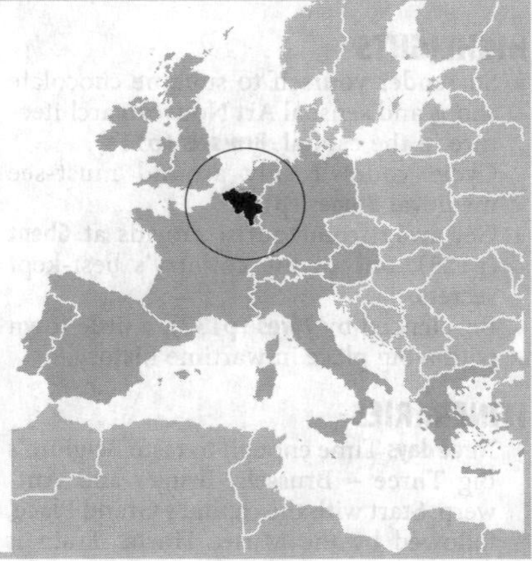

HIGHLIGHTS

- Surrender yourself to sublime chocolate shops and sensual Art Nouveau architecture in the capital, **Brussels** (p114).
- Cycle yourself silly around must-see medieval **Bruges** (p129).
- Get away from tourist crowds at **Ghent** (p125), one of the country's best-kept secrets.
- Be silenced by **Ypres** (p132), a little town with a big place in wartime history.

ITINERARIES

- **Three days** Time enough to taste Belgium's Big Three – Brussels, Bruges and Antwerp. Start with the capital's Grand Place, followed by the Musée Horta. Train it to Bruges and within an hour you'll be wandering along canals. Follow Flanders' flat landscape to Antwerp – you'll see the spire of the fabulous Onze Lieve Vrouwkathedraal well before arrival.
- **One week** Use the three-day itinerary, but add an extra night in both Brussels and Bruges. A day trip to Ypres is also a must. Put your French to practice in the Ardennes towns of Rochefort or La Roche-en-Ardennes – both good chill-out zones.

CLIMATE & WHEN TO GO

Belgium's weather is fickle. To avoid major dampness, visit between May and September. 'Wretched' best describes the winter months from November to March – the days are grey and wet with occasional light snow.

In need of a splurge at discount rates? Brussels is the place to do it – on weekends. Many top-end hotels in the capital cut prices on Friday and Saturday nights to make up for the absence of Eurocrats. We've noted weekend rates in the relevant reviews.

HISTORY

Bruges, Ghent and Ypres were Belgium's first major cities, booming in the 13th and 14th centuries due to the cloth trade. Their craftspeople established powerful guilds (organisations to stringently control arts and crafts), whose elaborate guildhalls you'll see in many cities – the most famous are those on Brussels' Grand Place (p115).

When Protestantism swept Europe in the 16th century, the Low Countries (present-day Belgium, the Netherlands and Luxembourg, often referred to as the Benelux) embraced it, much to the chagrin of their ruler, the fanatically Catholic Philip II of Spain. He ordered the Inquisition to enforce Catholicism, a move that led to the Iconoclastic Fury, in which Protestants ran riot ransacking churches, including Antwerp's Onze Lieve Vrouwkathedraal (p121), Belgium's finest Gothic cathedral. Inevitably, in 1568, war broke out. It lasted 80 years and, in the end, roughly laid the region's present-day borders. Holland and its allied provinces victoriously expelled the Spaniards, while Belgium and Luxembourg stayed under their rule.

For the next 200 years Belgium remained a battlefield for successive foreign powers. After the Spaniards came the Austrians, and, in turn, the French. Napoleon was trounced in 1815 at Waterloo (p120), near Brussels. In 1830 the Catholic Belgians won independence from Holland and finally formed their own kingdom.

The ensuing years saw the start of Flemish nationalism, with tension growing between Flemish (Dutch) and French speakers that has continued to this day.

Then, from 1885 came Belgium's most shadowy period – King Léopold II's rule of the Congo (see p121).

Despite Belgium's neutrality, the Germans invaded in 1914 and the town of Ypres was destroyed. Tours of the Ypres Salient (p133) offer poignant WWI reminders.

HOW MUCH?

- **Midrange hotel double** €80-150
- **Restaurant meal** €15-35
- **Baguette sandwich** €3.20
- **Cinema ticket** €6
- **1 kg of pralines** €30-58

LONELY PLANET INDEX

- **1L petrol** €1.40
- **1L bottled water** €0.80
- **Bottle of Trappist beer** €3.30
- **Souvenir T-shirt** €14
- **Frites (fries)** €1.80

During WWII the country was taken over within three weeks of a surprise German attack in May 1940. Controversy over the questionable early capitulation by King Léopold III led to his abdication in 1950 in favour of his son, King Baudouin, whose popular reign ended with his death in 1993. Childless, Baudouin was succeeded by his brother, the present King Albert II.

Although the headquarters of the EU and the North Atlantic Treaty Organization (NATO), Belgium kept a low profile on the international arena until the end of the 20th century, when it became best known for poisoned chickens and paedophiles. Sick of mismanagement and neglect, the nation turned to radical political reform and, in 1999, booted out the Christian Democrat party after 40 years in power.

In came Liberal prime minister Guy Verhofstadt, who sought to raise public morale by reinventing Belgium with robust foreign policies and new moral freedoms. Belgium is the second country (following the Netherlands) to legalise gay marriage and euthanasia. In 2003 the country sided with France and Germany against the US-led war in Iraq. During the same year a failed attempt was made to prosecute former US president George Bush in the Belgian courts for war crimes.

In the last year or two things have quietened on the home front. Belgians, it seems, have gone back to sipping a beer while watching their girls slam the greats in world tennis (see p113).

PEOPLE

Belgium's population is basically split in two: the Flemish and the Walloons. Language is the dividing factor, made official in 1962 when a linguistic divide was drawn across the country, cutting it almost equally in half. To the north of the divide lies Flanders (Vlaanderen), whose Flemish speakers make up 60% of Belgium's 10.2 million population. South of the divide is Wallonia (La Wallonie), where French-speaking Walloons make up most of the remaining population. A tiny percentage of Belgians speak German and live in an enclave in the far east, an area known as the Eastern Cantons.

RELIGION

Christianity was established early and today Catholicism reigns supreme – roughly 75% of the population is Roman Catholic. While church attendance has dropped dramatically in recent decades, religious traditions remain strong and influence many aspects of daily life including politics and education. Belgium also has sizeable Protestant, Jewish and Muslim communities.

ARTS

Literature

Inspector Maigret fans would know Belgium's the birthplace of Liège novelist Georges Simenon.

Comic strips are a Belgian forte. *Tintin* by Georges Remi, aka Hergé, is unquestionably the best-known internationally, but all comic art is high profile here (see p115).

Hugo Claus' *The Sorrow of Belgium* weaves a story based on Nazi collaboration during WWII.

Music

Jazz is right at home in Belgium. Adolphe Sax invented the saxophone and octogenarian Toots Thielemans still enthrals audiences with his legendary harmonica playing. For information on the Brussels Jazz Marathon, see Festivals & Events (p140).

In the 1950s Jacques Brel took the French-speaking world by storm and is still much loved in his homeland. Also from this era is French rock idol Johnny Hallyday, who maintains ties with his father's home country.

Arno Hintjens is the godfather of Belgian rock. Love or loathe him, Helmut Lotti is also Belgian (not German), and pumps out crooners.

K's Choice, dEUS, Axelle Red and Hooverphonic are among contemporary names to look out for.

For details about the Concours Musical International Reine Élisabeth de Belgique (Queen Elisabeth International Musical Competition), see Festivals & Events (p139). The best place to catch opera or classical music is La Monnaie/De Munt (p119).

Architecture

Many of Belgium's earliest buildings are on Unesco's World Heritage list. These include mighty belfries such as those in Bruges (p129) and Tournai (p135), many Flemish *begijnhoven* (see Bruges' Begijnhof, p129) and, of course, Brussels' famous Grand Place (p115).

On the flip side, there's little in the way of exciting modern architecture. Swathes of Brussels have gone under the demolition ball to make way for the EU quarter's boring glass buildings. But in other old art cities, designers have realised that modern structures can sit harmoniously alongside ancient, as seen in Bruges' new Concertgebouw (p132) and bOb Van Reeth's Zuiderterras café (p124) in Antwerp.

Not to be missed is Belgium's Art Nouveau architecture, best seen at Brussels' Musée Horta (p115) and the Old England building (p115). Art Nouveau swept across Europe at the end of the 19th century and blended architecture with daily aspects of life. Check out guided tours by the Atelier de Recherche et d'Action Urbaine (p115).

Visual Arts

Belgium's rich art heritage began in Bruges in the late Middle Ages with painters known as the Flemish Primitives. Their works greatly influenced the course of European art and, centuries later, still astonish viewers. Key players included Jan Van Eyck and Hans Memling; their paintings are best viewed at Bruges' Groeningemuseum (p129) and Hospitaalmuseum St Janshospitaal (p129), and also at Ghent's St Baafskathedraal (p125).

The greatest 16th-century Flemish painter was Pieter Breugel the Elder, who lived and worked in Brussels. The capital's Musées Royaux des Beaux-Arts (p115) holds an excellent range of his works.

BELGIUM

Antwerp held the cultural high ground during the 17th century, mainly thanks to Flemish baroque painter Pieter Paul Rubens. Some of his famous altarpieces adorn the city's Onze Lieve Vrouwkathedraal (p121).

The 19th-century's James Ensor was a pioneer of expressionism. See his work at Antwerp's Koninklijk Museum voor Schone Kunsten (p122).

Surrealism, a movement that developed in Paris in the 1920s, found fertile ground here. Works by René Magritte and Paul Delvaux are displayed at Brussels' Musées Royaux des Beaux-Arts (p115).

Belgium's best-known contemporary artist is the avant-garde Panamarenko. His bizarre sculptures can be seen at Ghent's Stedelijk Museum voor Actuele Kunst (p125).

Theatre & Dance

Belgium's dynamic contemporary dance scene centres on two companies – **Rosas** (www.rosas.be) in Brussels and **Charleroi Danses/Plan K** (www.charleroi-danses.be), based in Charleroi. To see Belgium's only classical-dance company, the Royal Flanders Ballet, visit the Koninklijk Ballet van Vlaanderen (p125). For information on Brussels' KunstenFestivaldesArts, combining theatre and dance, see p139.

SPORT

If it weren't for Kim Clijsters and Justine Henin-Hardenne, there would be almost nothing to say here. But in 2003 Belgium's tennis aces became the world's top two female tennis players – a feat that no other country, except the USA, has managed. Since then the pair has continued to play lead roles in top international tournaments.

ENVIRONMENT

Belgium's environmental picture is ugly and the scene is not getting rosier – the country's two green political parties were catapulted out of government in the last general election (2003). The only nationally protected reserves are the Hautes Fagnes Nature Reserve (p135) and the Hoge Kempen in Limburg. Water and noise pollution, urbanisation and waste management are the most pressing environmental issues.

FOOD & DRINK

Belgians love food. They are reputed to dine out, on average, more than any other people in the world. Expect to pay €14 or less for a main course in eateries listed as budget in this chapter; midrange restaurants charge between €15 and €30; anything over €30 is top end.

Staples & Specialities

Meat and seafood are abundantly consumed and, although there are traditional regional dishes such as Ghent's *waterzooi* (a cream-based chicken stew), the most popular dishes have crossed local boundaries. Brussels' dining scene is eminently international, reflecting its status as the EU capital, but around the countryside things are less diverse.

Belgium's national dish is *mosselen/moules* (mussels cooked in white wine) served in steaming cauldrons with a mountain of chips. Offal is big on menus, and you'll also come across *paardenfilet/steack de cheval* (horse steak) and *filet américain.* Don't be deceived, the latter is not a succulent American steak but a blob of minced beef served raw.

Belgians swear they invented *frieten/frites* (chips or fries) and, judging by the availability, it's a claim few would contest. Every village has at least one *frituur/friture* where *frites* are served smothered until unrecognisable with thick mayonnaise.

A *belegd broodje/sandwich garni* (half a baguette with a prepared filling) is an immensely popular snack food.

And then there's chocolate. The Belgians have been quietly making some of the world's finest chocolate for well over a century. Filled chocolates, or pralines (*prah*-leens), are the nation's forte.

On the drinking scene, beer rules. No country in the world boasts a brewing tradition as rich and diverse as Belgium. And nowhere else will you find the quantity of quality beers offered by this little nation. Somewhere between 400 and 800 beers exist. Try a dark Trappist beer made by monks, potent golden nectars such as Duvel (named after the devil himself) or the acquired taste of tangy, fruity *lambics* (champagne-style beers brewed in and around Brussels). For the latter, don't miss Brussels' Musée Bruxellois de la Gueuze (p115).

Where to Eat & Drink

Any place, any time, you'll find honest food being served at much-loved eateries.

At lunchtime many restaurants offer a *dagschotel/plat du jour* (dish of the day), which often represents excellent value. Also watch for a *dagmenu/menu du jour* (menu of the day). These menus comprise three courses and work out cheaper than selecting individual courses à la carte.

Those here to drink will be spoiled for choice. All cafés serve alcohol and many stay open until the last person leaves. True beer lovers should head to specialist cafés – see right for some highlights in Beer Top Five.

Vegetarians & Vegans

Fear not! Belgium may be carnivore kingdom but vegetarians are catered for, albeit reluctantly at times. Vegans, on the other hand, will go hungry almost everywhere except at Antwerp's zany Lombardia (p124).

> **BEER TOP FIVE**
>
> **Bierhuis Kulminator** (p124) Over 700 brews in this specialist pub.
>
> **De Biertempel** (p119) Shop 'til you drop among hundreds of beers.
>
> **Musée Bruxellois de la Gueuze** (opposite) Unlike any brewery you've ever smelt.
>
> **'t Brugse Beertje** (p132) Beer pub known far beyond Belgium's borders.
>
> **Westmalle Triple** Arguably the nation's best beer. Brewed by Trappist monks at their abbey near Antwerp (not open to visitors) and packs a 9% punch.

BRUSSELS

pop 1,000,000

Defining Brussels (Brussel in Flemish, Bruxelles in French) is no easy task. Walk the streets here, the best way to get around, and you'll soon understand why. Quirky, secretive, surreal – Brussels, like the country it represents, pulls multiple identities into one enigmatic core. Home to superb Art Nouveau architecture, the EU headquarters, shabby suburbs and more restaurants, pubs and chocolate shops than you could possibly visit, Brussels subtly slides under your skin.

ORIENTATION

The Grand Place, Brussels' imposing 15th-century market square, is the city's chief landmark. It sits dead centre in the Petit Ring, a pentagon of boulevards enclosing central Brussels. The city centre is divided into the Lower Town (comprising the medieval core and atmospheric quarters such as Ste Catherine, St Géry and the Marolles) and the Upper Town, home to major museums and chic shopping precincts based around the Sablon and Ave Louise.

East of the Petit Ring is the real-life Gotham City of the EU.

Gare Centrale, Brussels' most central train station, is about five-minutes' walk from the Grand Place; Gare du Midi, where international trains arrive, is 2.5km from the famous square.

Unlike anywhere else in Belgium, Brussels is officially bilingual. Everything – from the names of streets to train stations – is written in both Flemish and French. We have used the French versions.

INFORMATION

Money-changing facilities can be found on and around the Grand Place, at Gare du Midi and Brussels National Airport.

Belgian Tourist Information Centre (☎ 02 504 03 90; www.visitflanders.com, www.belgique-tourisme.net; Rue du Marché aux Herbes 63; 🕑 9am-6pm Mon-Fri, 9am-1pm & 2-6pm Sat & Sun, 9am-1pm Sun Jan-Feb; 🚊 Bourse/ Ⓜ Gare Centrale) Supplies national tourist information.

Brussels International (☎ 02 513 89 40; www.brusselsinternational.be; Grand Place; 🕑 9am-6pm Easter-Oct, 9am-6pm Mon-Sat, 10am-2pm Sun Nov-Dec, 9am-6pm Mon-Sat Jan-Easter; 🚊 Bourse/ Ⓜ Gare Centrale) The City of Brussels' tiny tourist office is located inside the town hall and is usually crammed.

Brussels International – Tourism (Gare du Midi; 🕑 8am-8pm Sat-Thu, 8am-9pm Fri May-Sep, 8am-5pm Mon-Thu, 8am-8pm Fri, 9am-6pm Sat, 9am-2pm Sun Oct-Apr; Ⓜ Gare du Midi) For visitors arriving by Eurostar or Thalys.

BXL (☎ 02 502 99 80; Pl de la Vieille Halle aux Blés 46; per 15 min/1 hr €1/2; 🕑 noon-midnight; Ⓜ Gare Centrale) Groovy café/bar with Internet access.

Helpline (☎ 02 648 40 14; 🕑 24hr) Assistance line run by Community Help Service.

Hôpital St Pierre (☎ 02 535 31 11, emergency 02 535 40 51; cnr Rue Haute & Rue de l'Abricotier; 🕑 24hr; Ⓜ Hôtel des Monnaies) Central hospital offering emergency assistance.

Main post office (☎ 02 226 97 00; Blvd Anspach; 🕑 8am-6pm Mon-Fri, 10.30am-4.30pm Sat; Ⓜ De Brouckère)

SIGHTS

Brussels' magnificent central square, **Grand Place**, tops every newcomer's itinerary. Here you'll find the splendid Gothic-style **Hôtel de Ville**, the only building to escape bombardment by the French in 1695 – ironic considering that it was the target. The square's splendour is due largely to its antique frame of **guildhalls**, erected by merchant guilds and adorned with gilded statues and symbols.

Galeries St Hubert, one block northeast of Grand Place, is a European first and a must-visit. Opened in 1847, this *grande dame* of Brussels' shopping arcades contains an eclectic mix of shops, as well as a cinema, restaurant and cafés. Off one of the galleries is **Rue des Bouchers** (see p118).

The **Musées Royaux des Beaux-Arts** (☎ 02 508 32 11; www.fine-arts-museum.be; Rue de la Régence 3; adult/concession €5/3.50; 🕑 10am-5pm Tue-Sun; Ⓜ Parc) houses Belgium's premier collections of ancient and modern art, and is well endowed with works by Pieter Breugel the Elder, Rubens and the Belgian surrealists. To get here, walk up from the Lower Town, or use the metro or tram 92, 93 or 94.

A superb introduction to the Art Nouveau movement is the **Musée Horta** (☎ 02 543 04 90; www.hortamuseum.be; Rue Américaine 25; adult/concession/child €5/3.50/2.50; 🕑 2-5.30pm Tue-Sun; Ⓜ Horta). It occupies two adjoining houses in St Gilles that Horta designed in 1898. To get here, take tram 91 or 92 from Pl Louise.

The **Musée des Instruments de Musique** (☎ 02 545 01 30; www.mim.fgov.be; Rue Montagne de la Cour 2; adult/concession/child €5/3.50/free; 🕑 9.30am-5pm Tue-Fri, 10am-5pm Sat & Sun; Ⓜ Gare Centrale) boasts one of the world's biggest collections of instruments. It's located in the **Old England building**, a former department store and Art Nouveau showpiece built in 1899 by Paul Saintenoy.

Anyone with even a vague interest in Belgian beers must not miss the excellent **Musée Bruxellois de la Gueuze** (☎ 02 521 49 28; www.cantillon.be; Rue Gheude 56; adult/concession €4/3; 🕑 9am-5pm Mon-Fri, 10am-5pm Sat; Ⓜ Gare du Midi). It's about 800m from Gare du Midi – head to Pl Bara, take Rue Limnander and then cross into Rue Gheude.

An absolutely anonymous, suburban yellow-brick house – that's the façade of the **Musée Magritte** (☎ 02 428 26 26; www.magrittemuseum.be; Rue Esseghem 135; adult/concession €7/6; 🕑 10am-6pm Wed-Sun), where Belgium's most famous surrealist artist lived from 1930 to 1954. To get there, take the metro to Simonis and then tram 19.

The **Centre Belge de la Bande Dessinée** (☎ 02 219 19 80; www.cbbd.be, in Flemish & French; Rue des Sables 20; adult/concession/child €7/6/3; 🕑 10am-6pm Tue-Sun; Ⓜ Botanique) is a tour through the country's vibrant comic-strip culture. It's housed in a Horta-designed Art Nouveau building, and is a 10-minute walk from Grand Place.

Despite being a national symbol the **Manneken Pis** fountain – a little boy cheerfully taking a leak into a pool – never fails to disappoint visitors because of its diminutive size. It's three blocks from the Grand Place, on the corner of Rue de l'Étuve and Rue du Chêne.

The newly renovated **Atomium** (☎ 02 475 47 77; www.atomium.be; Sq Atomium; adult/concession/child €9/6/free; 🕑 10am-5.30pm; Ⓜ Heyzel) is a space-age leftover from the 1958 World Fair – a model of an iron molecule enlarged 165 billion times. Take the metro or, more scenically, tram 81.

BRUSSELS IN TWO DAYS

On day one, the **Grand Place** (left) is not to be missed. Neither is **Galeries St Hubert** (left). Head next to the Upper Town for the **Musées Royaux des Beaux-Arts** (left), then stock up on pralines at **Pierre Marcolini** (p119) before tramming it to **Musée Horta** (left). By night trawl **Rue des Bouchers** (p118) and then hit the **pubs/cafés** (p118).

On day two, visit the **Koninklijk Museum voor Midden-Afrika** (see Léopold II & the Congo, p121). In the afternoon, wind down with a stroll along Rue Antoine Dansaert, home to fashion shops like **Stijl** (p119), then devote time to Brussels' unique *lambic* beer at cosy **À La Bécasse** (p119).

TOURS

Atelier de Recherche et d'Action Urbaine (ARAU; ☎ 02 219 33 45; www.arau.org; Blvd Adolphe Max 55; Ⓜ De Brouckère), a heritage conservation group, runs tours offering entry into some of Brussels' private Art Nouveau showpieces.

SLEEPING

Budget

Beersel Camping (☎ 02 331 05 61; campingbeersel@pandora.be; Steenweg op Ukkel 75; adult/tent/car €3/2/1.50; 🕑 year-round) Small ground in Beersel, south of Brussels. Tram 55 (direction Uccle) stops

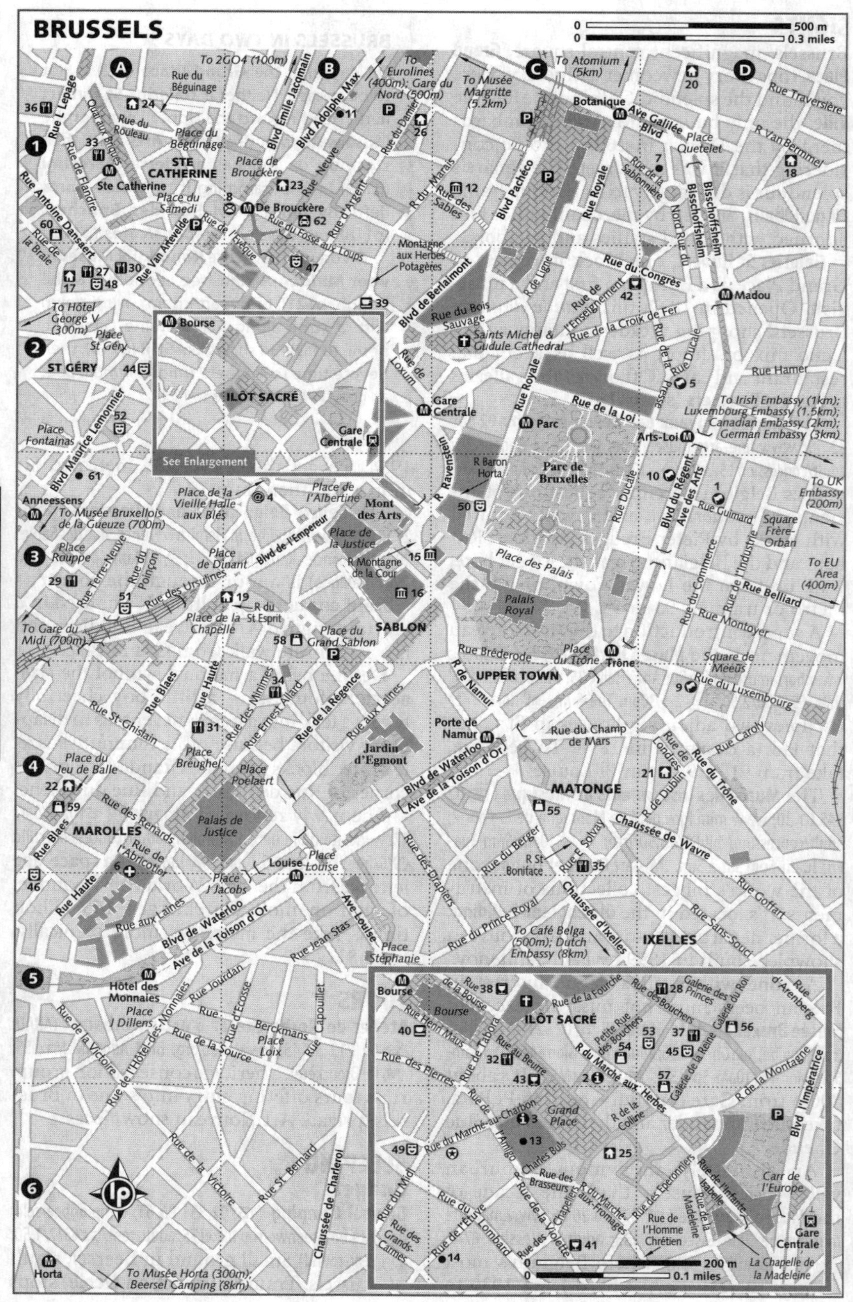
BRUSSELS
STE CATHERINE
ST GÉRY
ILÔT SACRÉ
See Enlargement
SABLON
UPPER TOWN
MAROLLES
MATONGE
IXELLES
Parc de Bruxelles
Palais Royal
Palais de Justice
Jardin d'Egmont
Mont des Arts
Grand Place
Saints Michel & Gudule Cathedral
Gare Centrale
To Atomium (5km)
To Musée Margritte (5.2km)
To Eurolines (400m); Gare du Nord (500m)
To 2GO4 (100m)
To Hôtel George V (300m)
To Musée Bruxellois de la Gueuze (700m)
To Gare du Midi (700m)
To Irish Embassy (1km); Luxembourg Embassy (1.5km); Canadian Embassy (2km); German Embassy (3km)
To UK Embassy (200m)
To EU Area (400m)
To Café Belga (500m); Dutch Embassy (8km)
To Musée Horta (300m); Beersel Camping (8km)
BELGIUM

INFORMATION
Australian Embassy....................1 D3
Belgian Tourist Information Centre....................2 C5
Brussels International....................3 C6
BXL....................4 B3
French Embassy....................5 D2
Hôpital St Pierre....................6 A4
Les Auberges de Jeunesse....................7 D1
Main Post Office....................8 B1
New Zealand Embassy....................9 D4
US Embassy....................10 D3

SIGHTS & ACTIVITIES
Atelier de Recherche et d'Action Urbaine (ARAU)....................11 B1
Centre Belge de la Bande Dessinée....................12 C1
Galeries St Hubert....................(see 56)
Hôtel de Ville....................13 C6
Manneken Pis....................14 C6
Musée des Instruments de Musique....................15 B3
Musées Royaux des Beaux-Arts..16 B3
Old England Building....................(see 15)

SLEEPING
Atlas....................17 A2
B&B Phileas Fogg....................18 D1
Bruegel....................19 B3
Centre Vincent Van Gogh....................20 D1
Chambres en Ville....................21 D4
Hôtel Galia....................22 A4
Hôtel Métropole....................23 B1
Hôtel Noga....................24 A1
Hôtel Saint Michel....................25 C6
Sleep Well....................26 B1

EATING
Bonsoir Clara....................27 A2
Chez Léon....................28 D5
Comme Chez Soi....................29 A3
Comocomo....................30 A2
Easy Tempo....................31 A4
GB Express....................32 C5
Jacques....................33 A1
Le Perroquet....................34 B4
L'Ultime Atome....................35 C4
Picnik....................36 A1
Taverne du Passage....................37 D5

DRINKING
À la Bécasse....................38 C5
À la Mort Subite....................39 B2
Falstaff....................40 B5
Goupil le Fol....................41 C6
Le Bier Circus....................42 C2
Le Roy d'Espagne....................43 C5

ENTERTAINMENT
AB....................44 A2
Arenberg Galeries....................45 D5
Fuse....................46 A5
La Monnaie/De Munt....................47 B2
L'Archiduc....................48 A2
Le Belgica....................49 B6
Musée du Cinéma....................50 C3
Recyclart....................51 A3
Tels Quels....................52 A2
Théâtre Royal de Toone....................53 D5

SHOPPING
De Biertempel....................54 C5
Galerie d'Ixelles....................55 C4
Galeries St Hubert....................56 D5
Manufacture Belge de Dentelles....................57 D5
Pierre Marcolini....................58 B3
Place du Jeu-de-Balle Fleamarket....................59 A4
Stijl....................60 A1

TRANSPORT
Hertz....................61 A3
Taxi Stop....................62 B1

3km away, from where you take bus UB (direction Halle).

Sleep Well (☎ 02 218 50 50; www.sleepwell.be; Rue du Damier 23; dm/s/d/tr with shared bathroom €17/28/50/67; ⊠ 🖳; Ⓜ Rogier) Bright, modern hostel-cum-hotel close to brash Rue Neuve, Brussels' main shopping thoroughfare. Handy central location and inside it's all very polished.

Hôtel Galia (☎ 02 502 42 43; www.hotelgalia.com; Pl du Jeu-de-Balle 15; s/d/tr €60/65/70; ⊠; Ⓜ Porte de Hal/ 🚊 Lemonnier) The only frills in this well-maintained little place are the comic-strip embellishments. Overlooking Brussels' well-known flea-market square, it has good-sized clean rooms (tiny bathrooms) and is handy to nightlife.

Also recommended:

Centre Vincent Van Gogh (☎ 02 217 01 58; www.chab.be; Rue Traversière 8; dm/s/d/q €13.50/28/42/66, bed sheets €4; ⊠ 🖳; Ⓜ Botanique) Brussels' cheapest dorms are offered in this clean, well-run and laid-back hostel. Bar, terrace and kitchen facilities are available.

Bruegel (☎ 02 511 04 36; www.jeugdherbergen.be; Rue du St Esprit 2; dm/s/d €19/33/62; ⊠ 🖳; Ⓜ Gare Centrale) Most central of Brussels' three HI hostels.

2GO4 (☎ 02 219 30 19; www.2GO4.be; Blvd Émile Jacqmain 99; dm/s/d/q €21/43/59/99; ⊠ 🖳; Ⓜ Rogier) The city's newest hostel offers a central location, contemporary décor and a free morning coffee. Breakfast is not included.

Midrange & Top End

Most of Brussels' B&B accommodation is organised by **Bed & Brussels** (☎ 02 646 07 37; www.bnb-brussels.be).

Chambres en Ville (☎ 02 512 92 90; www.chez.com/chambreenville, in French; Rue de Londres 19; s/d €60/80, one-night supplement per room €15; Ⓜ Trône) Revolting façade on a poky backstreet just metres away from the EU's gleaming quarter – arrive at this B&B and you'll wonder what you're in for. Once inside, it's obvious. In a word: lovely.

Hôtel Saint Michel (☎ 02 513 64 79; www.hotelsaintmichel.be; Grand Place 11; s/d/tr €65/100/125, with view €113/133/156; Ⓜ Gare Centrale) Now this is choice real estate – the *only* hotel smack bang on Brussels' famous square. The royal entrance downgrades to ordinary rooms that are comparatively overpriced but, hey, outside your window is the Grand Place! Weekend discounts often available.

B&B Phileas Fogg (☎ 02 217 83 38; www.phileasfogg.be; Rue Van Bemmel 6, St Josse; s/d/tr/f €75/85/100/120; ⊠; Ⓜ Madou) Exotic B&B run by an exuberant young mother and avid traveller. All the rooms have private bathrooms, though two share a toilet. The Blue Room is a favourite.

Hôtel Noga (☎ 02 218 67 63; www.nogahotel.com; Rue du Béguinage 38; s/d/tr €85/105/130; Ⓟ 🖳; Ⓜ Ste Catherine) Sixty years old and still going strong, this little gem in Ste Catherine mixes modern and old in a self-assured feast for the eyes. It's child and baby friendly, and parking costs €10.

Hôtel Métropole (☎ 02 217 23 00, reservations 02 214 24 24; www.metropolehotel.com; Pl de Brouckère 31; s/d/ste from €330/360/500, weekend r from €120; P ⊠ ; M De Brouckère) The *grande dame* of Brussels' hotel scene and perfect for a weekend splurge that won't cost an arm or leg. The lavish French Renaissance–style foyer contrasts with the soberly furnished rooms. A regal buffet breakfast is included.

Also recommended:

Hôtel George V (☎ 02 513 50 93; www.george5.com; Rue 't Kint 23; s/d/tr/q €64/75/86/97; Bourse) This family-run hotel on the edge of St Géry has prices that are a snip for this funky part of town.

Atlas (☎ 02 502 60 06; www.atlas.be; Rue du Vieux Marché aux Grains 30; s/d/tr/duplex €110/125/155/175; P ; Bourse/ M Ste Catherine) Central hotel with kitchen-equipped, split-level duplex apartments; good for families.

EATING

Restaurants of all persuasions abound in Brussels and if they don't make the grade, they don't last. The exception to this rule are those on Rue des Bouchers, a must-see street lined with barking hawkers and tacky tourist restaurants – great for a wander, but eat elsewhere. Rue Antoine Dansaert offers ample choice.

GB Express (Rue au Beurre 25; 8am-10pm, 8am-9pm Sun; Bourse) For self caterers, essentials are sold at this little supermarket near the Grand Place.

Easy Tempo (☎ 02 513 54 40; Rue Haute 146; pizza €7-11; lunch Tue-Sun, dinner Tue-Sat; M Porte de Namur) Marolles pizza joint with an ultra-friendly crew and a protected wall. The closest metro is Porte de Namur, but it's just as easy to walk the 1km from the Grand Place.

Picnik (☎ 02 217 34 84; Rue de Flandre 109; soup €2-3, dagschotel €8; 11.30am-4pm Mon-Fri; M Ste Catherine) This tiny organic lunch bar is in Ste Catherine.

Le Perroquet (☎ 02 512 99 22; Rue Watteeu 31; light meals €8-10; noon-1am; M Porte de Namur) Art Nouveau café in the affluent Sablon. Salads and stuffed pitas, including vegetarian options, are the mainstay.

Comocomo (☎ 02 503 03 30; Rue Antoine Dansaert 19; 3/6/9 tapas €8.50/14/19; lunch & dinner; Bourse) Relative newcomer Comocomo is an ultra-trendy, modern-day tapas eatery.

Chez Léon (☎ 02 513 04 26; www.chezleon.be; Rue des Bouchers 18; mains €13-20; noon-11pm; ⊠; M Gare Centrale) Great for families with free Belgian-style meals for under 12s (provided there are two paying adults).

L'Ultime Atome (☎ 02 513 13 67; Rue St Boniface 14; mains €11-20; 11am-midnight; M Porte de Namur) Just one of many great eateries in this Ixelles backstreet. An eclectic crowd keeps this brasserie buzzing day and night, and there's a wide range on offer, including vegetarian fare.

Taverne du Passage (☎ 02 512 37 31; www.tavernedupassage.com; Galerie de la Reine 30; mains €15-20; noon-midnight daily Aug-May, Fri-Tue Jun & Jul; M Gare Centrale) Consistently keen service, faithful Belgian meals and a fabulous location inside Galeries St Hubert are the pivotal points of this Brussels institution. Kids are genuinely welcomed.

Bonsoir Clara (☎ 02 502 09 90; Rue Antoine Dansaert 18; mains €17-25; lunch Mon-Fri, dinner daily; Bourse) This restaurant is one of the capital's enduring success stories.

Jacques (☎ 02 513 27 62; Quai aux Briques 44; mussels €22, mains €15-25; lunch & dinner Mon-Sat; M Ste Catherine) A down-to-earth seafood restaurant that has been around for over 60 years. Locals love it.

Comme Chez Soi (☎ 02 512 29 21; Pl Rouppe 23; mains €40-60, 4-course menu from €67; lunch & dinner Tue-Sat; ⊠ ; Anneessens) Chef Pierre Wynants' innovative cuisine will bite a good chunk out of your holiday budget, but it'll be worth every cent. Reservations essential.

DRINKING

Café culture is ingrained in Brussels. Hardly a street in the city centre doesn't have at least one pub, café or bar.

Le Roy d'Espagne (☎ 02 513 08 07; Grand Place 1; M Gare Centrale) Sit and sip (pricey beers) the splendour of the Grand Place in this former guildhall. And, yes, those are inflated dried pigs' bladders above your head.

À la Mort Subite (☎ 02 513 13 18; Montagne aux Herbes Potagères 7; ⊠; M Gare Centrale) Long café with wood panelling, mirrored walls and brusque service. One of the country's many brews is named after it (the name means 'instant death' but the beer itself is not that strong) and it ranks as one of the city's institutions. A must.

Falstaff (☎ 02 511 87 89; Rue Henri Maus 17; 10am-2am; Bourse) Art Nouveau *grand* *café* designed by Horta disciple Houbion. Exotic world of mirrors, glass and fluidity.

Goupil le Fol (☎ 02 511 13 96; Rue de la Violette 22; ⌚ 8pm-5am; Ⓜ Gare Centrale) Bastion of French chanteuse…you'll only hear the likes of Édith Piaf and Brussels' own Jacques Brel in this kooky café.

Also recommended:

Le Bier Circus (☎ 02 218 00 34; Rue de l'Enseignement 89; ⌚ noon-2.30pm Mon-Fri, 6pm-midnight daily; Ⓜ Madou) For serious beer buffs.

À La Bécasse (☎ 02 511 00 06; Rue de Tabora 11; ⌚ 10am-1am; Ⓣ Bourse) Come for a jug of draught *lambic*.

ENTERTAINMENT

Get past the cafés and Brussels offers everything from unique folkloric pageants to stunning contemporary dance. The English-language magazine *Bulletin* has a 'What's On' guide with excellent entertainment coverage. Also check *Le Soir* on Wednesday.

Cinemas

Arenberg Galeries (☎ 02 512 80 63; www.arenberg.be; Galerie de la Reine 26; ⌚ from 2pm; Ⓜ Gare Centrale) Remodelled Art Deco cinema located inside Galeries St Hubert. Foreign and art-house films are the staples.

Musée du Cinéma (☎ 02 507 83 70; Rue Baron Horta 9; admission €2.50; ⌚ from 5pm; Ⓜ Gare Centrale) One to make cinema buffs swoon. Two auditoriums: silent movies with live piano accompaniment are screened in one every night of the year; the other is devoted to classic talkies. It's expected to reopen after renovations soon after this book's publication.

Gay & Lesbian Venues

Tels Quels (☎ 02 512 32 34; www.telsquels.be, in French; Rue du Marché-au-Charbon 81; ⌚ 5pm-late Sun-Tue, Thu & Fri, 2pm-late Wed & Sat; Ⓣ Anneessens) The group's headquarters is home to a café-cum-information centre, the only meeting place in town aimed at both lesbians and gay men.

Le Belgica (www.lebelgica.be; Rue du Marché-au-Charbon 32; ⌚ 10pm-3am Thu-Sat, 7pm-3am Sun; Ⓣ Bourse) Despite the unassuming façade, this is one of the city's oldest and best gay pubs.

Live Music, Dance & Theatre

L'Archiduc (☎ 02 512 06 52; Rue Antoine Dansaert 6; ⌚ 4pm-late; Ⓣ Bourse) Exclusive Art-Deco bar built in the 1930s and located on one of the city's hippest streets. It has jazz concerts every weekend.

AB (☎ 02 548 24 00; www.abconcerts.be; Blvd Anspach 110; Ⓣ Bourse) Great venue smack in the heart of the city. AB, or Ancienne Belgique, has two auditoriums accommodating international and home-grown bands.

La Monnaie/De Munt (☎ 07 023 39 39; www.demunt.be; Pl de la Monnaie; Ⓜ De Brouckère) Brussels' premier venue for opera and theatre is also the place to catch contemporary dance by Anne Teresa De Keersmaeker's innovative company, Rosas. Check their website, www.rosas.be/rosas, for performance details.

Théâtre Royal de Toone (☎ 02 511 71 37; www.toone.be; Petite Rue des Bouchers 21; admission €10; ⌚ 8.30pm Thu-Sat; Ⓜ Gare Centrale) Famous marionette theatre.

Nightclubs

Fuse (☎ 02 511 97 89; www.fuse.be; Rue Blaes 208; depending on DJs admission €3-12; ⌚ 11pm-7am Sat; Ⓜ Porte de Hal) The Marolles house club that put Brussels on the international circuit. Now more than a decade old, its two floors attract some 2000 dancers, all going strong.

Recyclart (☎ 02 502 57 34; www.recyclart.be; Gare de la Chapelle, Rue des Ursulines 25; Ⓣ Anneessens) An occasional club for those in the know located in a disused train station in the Marolles. Dance nights are listed online.

SHOPPING

Chocolate, beer, fashion, lace and bric-a-brac…Brussels has these and many other lines covered.

De Biertempel (☎ 02 502 19 06; Rue du Marché aux Herbes 56; Ⓣ Bourse) Stocks 550 Belgian brews plus matching glasses.

Gare du Midi market (⌚ 6am-1pm Sun; Ⓜ Gare du Midi) Brussels' biggest general market sprawls next to the train lines and has a distinctly Mediterranean feel.

Pierre Marcolini (☎ 02 514 12 06; Pl du Grand Sablon 39; Ⓜ Porte de Namur) For Belgium's most expensive pralines (€58 per kg).

Stijl (☎ 02 512 03 13; Rue Antoine Dansaert 74; Ⓜ Ste Catherine) The shop that changed this part of the city. Home to top fashion designers, including members of the Antwerp Six (p126).

Place du Jeu-de-Balle fleamarket (Pl du Jeu-de-Balle; ⌚ 7am-2pm; Ⓜ Porte de Hal) The Marolles' famous *brocante* (second-hand) market.

Manufacture Belge de Dentelles (☎ 02 511 44 77; Galerie de la Reine 6-8; Ⓜ Gare Centrale) Lace specialist shop inside Galeries St Hubert.

Browse a stately *galerie,* such as **Galeries St Hubert** (Ⓜ Gare Centrale), or pick up some dried grasshoppers at **Galerie d'Ixelles** (Chaussée d'Ixelles; Ⓜ Porte de Namur), the pulse of Brussels' African community, located just off Chaussée de Wavre.

GETTING THERE & AWAY

Air

For details on air services to and from Brussels, see p140.

Bus

The **Eurolines** (☎ 02 274 13 50; www.eurolines.be; Rue du Progrès 80) office is located at Gare du Nord, from where its buses arrive and depart. For information on services, see p141.

Car & Motorcycle

See p142 for information on various car-hire companies.

Train

Brussels three main train stations are Gare du Midi (South Station), Gare Centrale (Central Station) and Gare du Nord (North Station).

Gare du Midi (☎ 02 528 28 28) is the main station for international connections: the Eurostar and Thalys fast trains stop here only. Call the train station for any international and national enquiries.

For more on international train services, including Eurostar and Thalys trains, see p141. For information on getting to other destinations in Belgium, see the Getting There & Away sections throughout the chapter.

GETTING AROUND

To/From the Airport

The Airport City Express train runs between the airport and the city's three main train stations – Gare du Nord, Gare Centrale and Gare du Midi (one way €2.80). The service runs every 15 minutes from 5.30am to 11.30pm and the trip takes 15 to 25 minutes (depending on the station's location).

A taxi between the airport and central Brussels costs €29.

For details on shuttle buses between Brussels and Charleroi airport, see p135.

Public Transport

Brussels' efficient public-transport system is operated by **Société des Transports Intercommunaux Bruxellois** (☎ 02 515 20 00; www.stib.irisnet.be, French only), and comprises buses, trams, metro and *prémetro* (trams that travel underground). Single tickets cost €1.50, a book of 10 tickets is €10.50 and a one-day card costs €4. Services run from 6am until midnight.

Taxi

Call **Taxis Bleus** (☎ 02 268 00 00) or **Taxis Verts** (☎ 02 349 49 49). Taxes are officially included in the meter price, so ignore requests for extra service charges.

AROUND BRUSSELS

Leuven

pop 89,700

If you've ever downed a Stella Artois, this is the place from where it came. Leuven (Louvain in French) is Flanders' premier university town, as well as home to the beer that discerning Belgians balk at. The town is within easy striking distance of Brussels by train (€4.30, 35 minutes, five hourly) and its main attractions – a flamboyant 15th-century **Stadhuis** (town hall; ☎ 01 621 15 40; Grote Markt; admission €2) and the **Groot Begijnhof** (Great Beguinage; admission free) – are well worth a day trip.

Leuven is also famed for **Rock Werchter** (www.rockwerchter.be), held for three days over the first weekend of July. Together with Glastonbury (England), this is one of Europe's biggest 'field' rock festivals.

Waterloo

pop 29,000

Waterloo, the battleground where Napoleon was defeated in 1815 and European history changed its course, is 18km south of Brussels. Unless you are a war or history buff, it is fairly staid. What's more, the most important sites are spread out over several kilometres, making it quite tedious to get around using public transport. You'll need to catch TEC bus W from Ave Fosny at Brussels' Gare du Midi train station; ask the driver for a day card (€6).

On arrival, the best place to start is at Waterloo's **Office du Tourisme** (☎ 02 352 09 10; www.waterloo-tourisme.be; Chaussée de Bruxelles 218; ⏲ 9.30am-6.30pm Apr-Sep, 10.30am-5pm Oct-Mar). Bus W stops here and tourist staff will assist with timetables for getting around the area.

FLANDERS

The only thing flat about Flanders is typography. Belgium's Flemish-speaking northern region is the country's powerhouse, home to vibrant cities, historic gems and contemporary culture.

ANTWERP

pop 446,500

Cosmopolitan, confident and full of contrasts, Antwerp (Antwerpen in Flemish, Anvers in French) is an essential stop. Appreciated by art and architecture lovers, mode moguls, club queens and diamond dealers, Belgium's second-biggest city once again revels in fame and fortune.

Orientation

Antwerp's historic centre, based around the Grote Markt, is 1km from the impressive Centraal Station. The two are linked by the pedestrianised Meir (pronounced 'mare'), a bustling shopping thoroughfare. The city basically ends at the Scheldt River, Antwerp's economic lifeline.

Information

2Zones (☎ 03 232 24 00; Wolstraat 15; per hr €4.50; 🕑 11am-midnight) Cool Internet bar.
Main post office (Groenplaats 43)
Main tourist office (☎ 03 232 01 03; www.visitantwerpen.be; Grote Markt 13; 🕑 9am-6pm Mon-Sat, 9am-5pm Sun)
St Elisabethgasthuis (☎ 03 234 41 11, emergency 03 234 40 50; Leopoldstraat 26; 🕑 24hr) Central hospital.
Tourist office (Centraal Station; 🕑 9am-6pm Mon-Sat, 9am-5pm Sun)

Sights

Antwerp's epicentre is the **Grote Markt**, a pedestrianised market square presided over by the Renaissance-style **Stadhuis** and lined by Renaissance-style **guildhalls**, most of which were reconstructed in the 19th century. Rising from a rough pile of rocks at its centre is the voluptuous, baroque **Brabo Fountain**.

Just a steeple's fall away is Belgium's largest Gothic cathedral, **Onze Lieve Vrouwkathedraal** (☎ 03 213 99 51; Handschoenmarkt; adult/concession €2/1.50; 🕑 10am-5pm Mon-Fri, 10am-3pm Sat, 10am-4pm Sun). Built between 1352 and 1521, it houses four early canvases by Rubens including the *Descent from the Cross* (1612).

LÉOPOLD II & THE CONGO

In 1885 Belgium's King Léopold II personally acquired the Congo in Africa, an area almost 100 times the size of his homeland. Between then and 1908, when the Belgian state stripped the king of his possession, it is estimated up to 10 million Africans died because of starvation, overwork or murder carried out in Léopold's quest for rubber, ivory and other commodities.

A BBC TV documentary, aired in Belgium in 2004, shone this period of history squarely into Belgian faces – and some didn't like what they saw. Outspoken foreign minister Louis Michel retaliated, saying it was biased and didn't take into account the social context of that time.

It is impossible to know for sure the number of people who died. On Léopold's orders, the Congo archives were destroyed. According to Adam Hochschild in his book *King Léopold's Ghost*, the furnaces in the Congo offices in Brussels burnt for over a week. But what is sure is that the booty from this barbarity was enormous. Brussels' landmarks – such as the Arcade du Cinquantenaire – were built on these proceeds. So, too, was the **Koninklijk Museum voor Midden-Afrika** (Royal Museum for Central Africa; ☎ 02 769 52 30; www.africamuseum.be; Leuvensesteenweg 13, Tervuren; adult/concession €4/1.50; 🕑 10am-5pm Tue-Fri, 10am-6pm Sat & Sun). This monumental museum makes for an easy half-day excursion that won't be readily forgotten.

Located at Tervuren, a Flemish-speaking town 14km east of Brussels, the museum houses the world's most impressive array of African artefacts. But up until recently, the permanent exhibition was one big imperialistic showpiece, mirroring views from the 1960s when it was established, but way off centre with current thinking. Since 2001 museum director Guido Gryseels has been overhauling the entire museum, a process due to be completed for centennial celebrations in 2010. In the meantime temporary exhibitions aim to inform visitors that there was more than just one story in the Congo during Léopold's reign.

To get to the museum, take the metro to Montgomery then tram 44 (20 minutes); the fare is covered by a one-day card (€4).

The prestigious **Rubenshuis** (☎ 03 201 15 55; Wapper 9-11; adult/concession €5/2.50; 10am-5pm Tue-Sun) was the home and studio of Pieter Paul Rubens, northern Europe's greatest baroque artist. Little more than a ruin when acquired by the city in 1937, it has been superbly restored along original lines. Unfortunately, only a handful of Rubens' lesser works are displayed.

To immerse yourself in Rubens, head to the **Koninklijk Museum voor Schone Kunsten** (☎ 03 238 78 09; www.antwerpen.be/cultuur/kmska; Leopold De Waelplaats, 't Zuid; adult/concession/child €6/4/free, last Wed of the month free; 10am-5pm Tue-Sat, 10am-6pm Sun). This fine arts museum houses an impressive permanent collection, from Flemish Primitives to contemporary styles. The best sections are the 17th-century Flemish baroque masters and the section on Ensor. To get here, take tram 8 from Groenplaats or bus 1 or 23 (direction Zuid) from Centraal Station.

Fashion followers must start with Antwerp's mode museum, **MoMu** (☎ 03 470 27 70; www.momu.be; Nationalestraat 28; adult/concession €7/5; 10am-6pm Tue-Sun). It's located in the much-celebrated **Modenatie** (www.modenatie.com) complex, home also to the Flanders Fashion Institute.

Down on the Scheldt is **Zuiderterras**, a raised promenade built decades ago alongside the city's main dock. It offers a steepled skyline plus an essential pit stop (see p124).

Wander the length of Zuiderterras to arrive at **St Jansvliet**, a small tree-lined square and entry to **St Annatunnel**. This 570m-long pedestrian tunnel, dug under the Scheldt in the 1930s, links the city centre with the **Linkeroever**, or Left Bank, from where there's a fab city panorama.

Zurenborg, about 2km southeast of Centraal Station, is famed for the eclectic architecture found in a handful of streets. The showcase is **Cogels-Osylei**, where affluent citizens went wild a century ago. Tram 11 (direction Eksterlaar) runs along Cogels-Osylei.

Sleeping

To explore the city's burgeoning B&B scene, check out **The Association of Antwerp Guestrooms** (www.bedandbreakfast-antwerp.com).

BUDGET

Camping De Molen (☎ 03 219 81 79; Thonetlaan; adult/car/tent €1.80/1/2.50; Apr-Sep) The pick of Antwerp's two camping grounds, located on the Linkeroever; take bus 81 or 82 (direction Linkeroever).

Hostel Op Sinjoorke (☎ 03 238 02 73; www.jeugdhergergen.be; Eric Sasselaan 2; dm/s/d €14.50/29/42; Jan-Nov; P ⊠) This run-of-the-mill HI-affiliated hostel is nearly 3km south of the city centre. To get there, take tram 2 (direction Hoboken).

Den Heksenketel (☎ 03 226 71 64; www.heksenketel.org; Pelgrimstraat 22; dm €19) The only cheap accommodation in the heart of the city and located on a street with an unbeatable cathedral view. Three simple but fresh dorms are situated above a small folk-music club (concerts Monday, jam sessions Thursday). Take *premetro* tram 2 or 15 to Groenplaats.

MIDRANGE & TOP END

Hotel Scheldezicht (☎ 03 231 66 02; www.hotelscheldezicht.be; St Jansvliet 2; s/d/tr from €45/65/85; 💻) Quaint old-style hotel, well situated on a tree-lined square in the historic centre. The spacious modern rooms have private shower cubicles, but the toilets are shared. Take *premetro* tram 2 or 15 to Groenplaats.

Bed, Bad & Brood (☎ 03 248 15 39; www.bbantwerp.com; Justitiestraat 43; 2 night-minimum s/d/f €50/60/85) Wooden floors and old-fashioned furniture are the salient features of this spacious and charming B&B. It's 1.5km from the Grote Markt, or take tram 12 or 24 from Franklin Rooseveltplaats (direction Zuid) and get off at the Gerechtshof stop.

Aan de Leien B&B (☎ 03 288 66 95; www.europeholidayhomes.info; Britselei 49 bte 6; s/d €55/62, penthouse €100; ⊠) Quality B&B on the top floor of a modern apartment block. With extra euros to spend, go for the penthouse – it's sublime. From Centraal Station take bus 23 to Nationale Bank stop.

Floatel Diamond Princess (☎ 03 227 08 15; www.diamondprincess.be; Bonapartedok; s/d/ste €57/77/139; P ❄) Former 1952 Norwegian passenger ship turned hotel. Though hard to believe, there are 52 cabins on board: all pretty small but pleasantly decorated. It's about 1km north of the Grote Markt – take bus 1 or 13 from the corner of De Keyserlei and Frankrijklei.

Keizerstraat, a quite backstreet half-way between Centraal Station and the Grote Markt, has several options including **Hotel Prinse** (☎ 03 226 40 50; www.hotelprinse.be; Keizerstraat 63; s/d/tr €104/122/140 Sun-Thu, €95/116/140

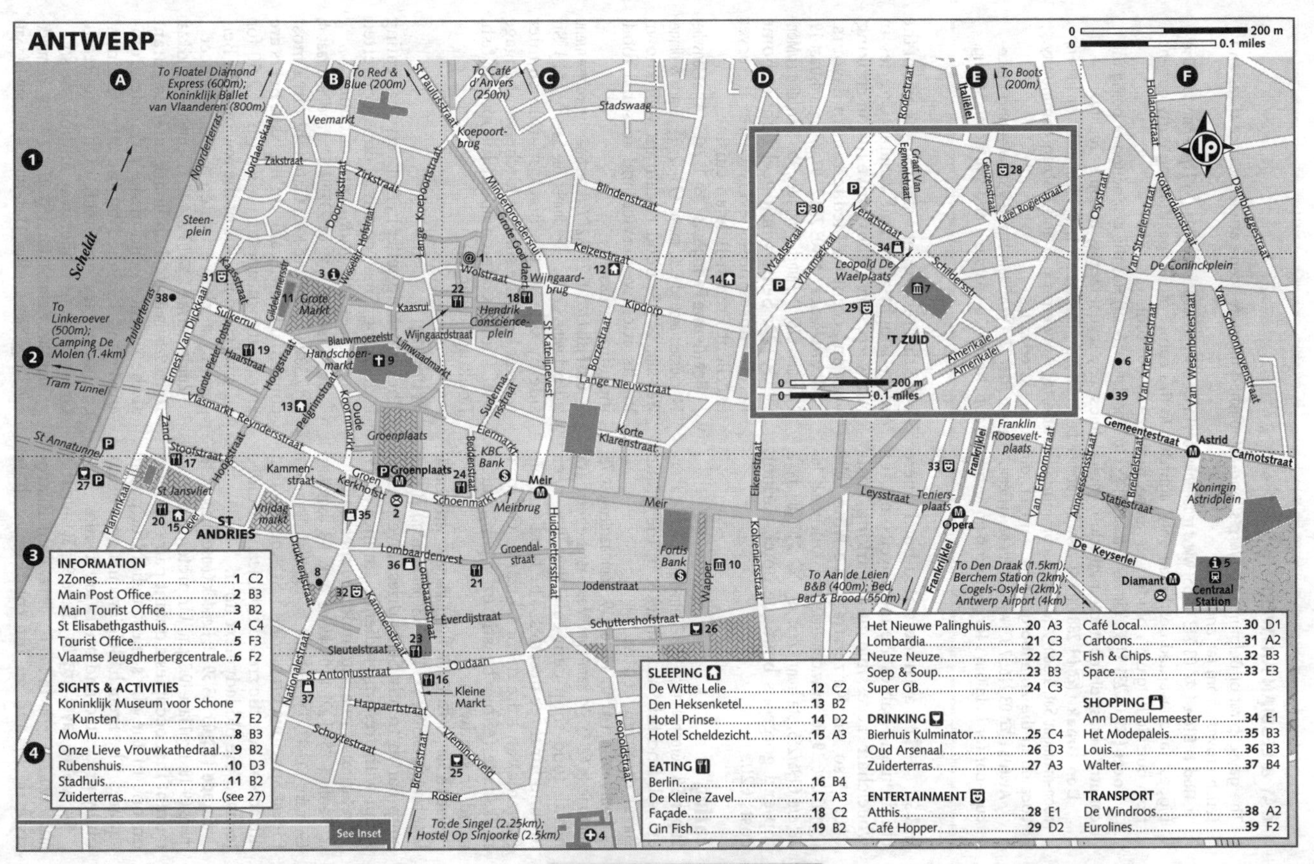
ANTWERP
0 200 m
0 0.1 miles
INFORMATION
2Zones....1 C2
Main Post Office....2 B3
Main Tourist Office....3 B2
St Elisabethgasthuis....4 C4
Tourist Office....5 F3
Vlaamse Jeugdherbergcentrale..6 F2
SIGHTS & ACTIVITIES
Koninklijk Museum voor Schone Kunsten....7 E2
MoMu....8 B3
Onze Lieve Vrouwkathedraal....9 B2
Rubenshuis....10 D3
Stadhuis....11 B2
Zuiderterras....(see 27)
SLEEPING
De Witte Lelie....12 C2
Den Heksenketel....13 B2
Hotel Prinse....14 D2
Hotel Scheldezicht....15 A3
EATING
Berlin....16 B4
De Kleine Zavel....17 A3
Façade....18 C2
Gin Fish....19 B2
Het Nieuwe Palinghuis....20 A3
Lombardia....21 C3
Neuze Neuze....22 C2
Soep & Soup....23 B3
Super GB....24 C3
DRINKING
Bierhuis Kulminator....25 C4
Oud Arsenaal....26 D3
Zuiderterras....27 A3
ENTERTAINMENT
Atthis....28 E1
Café Hopper....29 D2
Café Local....30 D1
Cartoons....31 A2
Fish & Chips....32 B3
Space....33 E3
SHOPPING
Ann Demeulemeester....34 E1
Het Modepaleis....35 B3
Louis....36 B3
Walter....37 B4
TRANSPORT
De Windroos....38 A2
Eurolines....39 F2
See Inset

BELGIUM

GAY & LESBIAN ANTWERP

The gay capital of Belgium, Antwerp's long-established nightlife scene attracts dance divas and fetish crowds from far and wide.

Red & Blue (☎ 03 213 05 55; www.redandblue.be; Lange Schipperskapelstraat 11; 11pm-7am Sat) The biggest (and awarded best) men-only nightclub in this corner of Europe, drawing party queens from outside Belgium's borders to house, techno, rap and soul.

Boots (☎ 03 231 34 83; Van Aerdtstraat 22; 10.30pm-late Fri & Sat) Has the distinction of being the country's most disreputable nightclub, where almost any sexual fantasy becomes reality.

Den Draak (☎ 03 288 00 84; www.hetrozehuis.be, in Flemish; Draakplaats 1; 3pm-midnight Tue-Fri, noon-midnight Sat & Sun) Café and community centre for Antwerp's gay and lesbian community. Located in the Zurenborg – take tram 11 (direction Eksterlaar).

Atthis (☎ 03 216 37 37; www.atthis.be, in Flemish; Geuzenstraat 27; 8.30pm-late Fri & Sat) Meeting-place-cum-bar for Belgium's longest-running lesbian group. Nearly 30 years old and still going strong.

Fri & Sat; P), an understated hotel where children and babies are most welcome. It's wheelchair accessible and parking costs €10. Also on Keizerstraat, **De Witte Lelie** (☎ 03 226 19 66; www.dewittelelie.be; Keizerstraat 16-18; s/d €195/265, ste from €275; P) is a top-end gorgeous boutique hotel. Parking costs €20.

BELGIUM

Eating

Super GB (Groenplaats; 8.30am-8pm) Self caterers will find this supermarket in the Grand Bazar shopping centre.

Lombardia (☎ 03 233 68 19; Lombaardenvest 78; light meals €4-8; 8am-6pm Mon-Sat) Legendary health-food-shop-cum-café that has been around for three decades. The food's all *bio* (organic) and the décor's bizarre. Go for a milkshake (either beastie or vegan), juice, salad or sandwich.

Soep & Soup (☎ 03 707 28 05; Kammenstraat 89; small/large bowl €4.25/5.50; 11am-6.30pm Mon-Sat) Buzzy soup bar in trendy St Andries. Five pots of soup, with fresh ingredients, simmer away. Vegetarians can ask to hold the meatballs.

Berlin (☎ 03 227 11 01; Kleine Markt 1-3; dagschotel €9, mains €12-17; 7.30am-1am Mon-Wed, 10am-3am Fri-Sun) Spacious brasserie in St Andries that attracts an eclectic crowd from jeans-minded teens to the old lady next door.

Façade (☎ 03 233 59 31; Hendrik Conscienceplein 18; mains €9-18; 11am-10.30pm) Unpretentious restaurant that occupies a quaint pair of houses on one of the city's most delightful public squares. The French/Belgian cuisine is beautifully presented and prices are a snip.

De Kleine Zavel (☎ 03 231 96 91; Stoofstraat 2; mains €20-27; lunch Sun-Fri, dinner daily) Bistro-style décor and an informal atmosphere belie this restaurant's standing as one of the most sought-after and reliable eateries in Antwerp, serving inventive fusion cooking, with an accent on Mediterranean flavours.

Neuze Neuze (☎ 03 232 27 97; Wijngaardstraat 19-21; mains €25; lunch Mon, Tues, Thu & Fri, dinner Mon-Sat) Dr Seuss would feel right at home here – noses noses everywhere. It serves excellent French-Belgian cuisine.

Het Nieuwe Palinghuis (☎ 03 231 74 45; St Jansvliet 14; mussels around €20, mains €25-32; lunch & dinner Wed-Sun) Seafood restaurant well known for its attentive service and seasonal food, including mussels.

Gin Fish (☎ 03 231 32 07; Haarstraat 9; 4-course menu incl/excl wine €75/60; dinner Tue-Sat) Sit side-by-side at the black marble counter overlooking the sunken kitchen and engage chef Didier Garnich about his love of fish. Bookings essential.

Drinking

The only thing better in Antwerp than eating is drinking. Small convivial pubs, converted warehouses and *grand cafés* abound.

Oud Arsenaal (☎ 03 232 97 54; Pijpelincxstraat 4; 7.30am-7.30pm Wed-Mon) Catch the city's most congenial brown café while it lasts. Beers are among the cheapest in town (just €2.50 for a Duvel) and it's one of the few pubs in Belgium to stock Westvleteren Trappist beer.

Zuiderterras (☎ 03 234 12 75; Ernest van Dijckkaai 37; 9am-midnight) Landmark café/restaurant at the southern end of the riverside promenade and designed by the city's eminent contemporary architect, bOb Van Reeth. Great place to while away an hour or so.

Bierhuis Kulminator (☎ 03 232 45 38; Vleminckveld 32; 8pm-late Mon, 11am-late Tue-Fri, 5pm-late Sat)

Boasts more than 700 types of beer – just open the menu and point.

Entertainment

Café Hopper (☎ 03 248 49 33; Leopold De Waelstraat 2) Cosy café in 't Zuid that doubles as the city's best jazz venue; performances are on Sunday, Monday and Wednesday.

Cartoons (☎ 03 232 96 32; Kaasstraat 4-6) Art-house movies and quality foreign films are screened in three auditoriums.

deSingel (☎ 03 248 28 28; www.desingel.be; Desguinlei 25) Antwerp's chief venue for classical music, international theatre and modern dance.

Koninklijk Ballet van Vlaanderen (☎ 03 234 34 38; www.kbvv.be; Westkaai 16, 't Eilandje) The Royal Flanders Ballet is the nation's only classical-dance company.

Getting There & Away

BUS

Buses arrive and depart from the **Eurolines** (☎ 03 233 86 62; Van Straelenstraat 8) office near Franklin Rooseveltplaats. For information on services, see p141.

TRAIN

Antwerp's beautiful **Centraal Station** (☎ 02 528 28 28) is about 1.5km from the historic centre. The station has undergone a massive upgrade in recent years to accommodate Thalys high-speed trains linking Belgium and the Netherlands. Work on the new underground lines is due to finish at the end of 2007. From then on, the journey time between Antwerp and Amsterdam will be about 2½ hours. National connections include IC trains every half-hour to Brussels (€6, 35 minutes) and Ghent (€7.80, 45 minutes), and hourly trains to Bruges (€12.40, 70 minutes).

Getting Around

A good network of buses, trams and a *premetro* is run by **De Lijn Antwerpen** (☎ 07 022 02 00; www.delijn.be). The main bus hubs are Franklin Rooseveltplaats and Koningin Astridplein.

In summer bikes can be hired from **De Windroos** (☎ 03 480 93 88; Steenplein 1a) for €2.50/12.50 per one hour/day.

GHENT

pop 229,000

Ghent (known as Gent in Flemish and Gand in French) is Flanders' unsung city. Sandwiched between Brussels, Bruges and Antwerp, this crisp stylish and well-organised city has long been overlooked by visitors on the traditional art-town hop between Belgium's big three. If you're into exploring Flanders without the tourist hordes, Ghent's the go.

Orientation

The city's medieval core contains not one but three central squares. The westernmost square, the Korenmarkt, is the main hub – it's 2km north of the main train station, St Pietersstation.

Information

Coffeelounge (☎ 09 329 39 11; Botermarkt 6; per hr €2; 10am-7pm Wed-Mon) Offers Internet access.

Main post office (Lange Kruisstraat 55)

Tourist office (☎ 09 266 52 32; www.visitgent.be; Botermarkt 17; 9.30am-6.30pm Apr-Oct, 9.30am-4.30pm Nov-Mar)

Sights

Though **St Baafskathedraal** (☎ 09 269 20 45; St Baafsplein; 8.30am-6pm Apr-Oct, 8.30am-5pm Nov-Mar) is unimpressive from the outside, formidable queues form to see the **Adoration of the Mystic Lamb** (adult/child €3/1.50; 9.30am-4.30pm Mon-Sat, 1-4.30pm Sun Apr-Oct, 10.30am-3.30pm Mon-Sat, 1-3.30pm Sun Nov-Mar). This lavish representation of medieval religious thinking is one of the earliest-known oil paintings, executed in 1432 by Flemish Primitive artist Jan Van Eyck. It's not to be missed. It's wheelchair accessible.

The 14th-century **Belfort** (☎ 09 233 39 54; Botermarkt; adult/child €3/free; 10am-12.30pm & 2-5.30pm Easter–mid-Nov) affords spectacular views of the city and can be climbed either by a lift or, if you're so inclined, stairs.

The **Gravensteen** (☎ 09 225 93 06; St Veerleplein; adult/concession/child €6/2.50/1.50; 9am-6pm Apr-Sep, 9am-5pm Oct-Mar), located smack in the heart of the city, belonged to the 12th-century counts of Flanders and is the quintessential castle.

Ghent's highly regarded **SMAK** (Stedelijk Museum voor Actuele Kunst; ☎ 09 221 17 03; www.smak.be; Citadelpark; adult/concession/child €5/3.80/free, 10am-1pm Sun free; 10am-6pm Tue-Sun) contains works by Karel Appel, Pierre Alechinsky and Panamarenko – three of Belgium's best-known contemporary artists – as well as works by international celebrities.

The **Museum voor Vormgeving** (Design Museum; ☎ 09 267 99 99; www.designmuseum.gent.be;

Jan Breydelstraat 5; adult/concession/child €2.50/1.20/free, 10am-1pm Sun free; 10am-6pm Tue-Sun) is one of Ghent's little-known gems, with a mix of furnishings from the Renaissance through to contemporary styles.

Formerly a Middle Ages meat market, the **Groot Vleeshuis** (☎ 09 267 86 07; Groentenmarkt 7; 10am-6pm Tue-Sun) is now a tasting hall for local products.

Ghent's **Museum voor Schone Kunsten** (☎ 09 240 07 00; www.mskgent.be; Citadelpark) was being renovated at the time of research. In the meantime some of its collection is exhibited in St Baafskathedraal and at SMAK.

Festivals & Events

Time a visit with **De Gentse Feesten** (www.gentsefeesten.be), an annual 10-day festival held in mid-July that transforms the city into a party of music and theatre. The festival includes **10 Days Off** (www.10daysoff.be), one of Europe's biggest techno parties.

Sleeping

Complete B&B listings and a booking service are organised by **Bed & Breakfast Ghent** (www.bedandbreakfast-gent.be).

Camping Blaarmeersen (☎ 09 266 81 60; camping.blaarmeersen@gent.be; Zuiderlaan 12; adult/tent/car €4.50/4.50/2.50) The only camping ground in the vicinity of the city, this spot is a long way west of the centre. Take bus 9 (direction Mariakerke) from St Pietersstation to the Europabrug stop, then bus 38 or 39, which stops out the front.

De Draecke (☎ 09 233 70 50; www.vjh.be; St Widostraat 11; dm/tw €16.60/42; ☒) This is one of Belgium's best HI-affiliated hostels, occupying

SHOPPERS & CLUBBERS UNITE!

Shop until you drop, dine into dark, then club the night away…that's Antwerp. As an avant-garde fashion capital snapping at the heels of Milan and New York, and the top spot on the clubbing circuit between Amsterdam and Paris, this city's a magnet for shoppers and clubbers alike.

The best known of the city's fashion designers are the 'Antwerp Six' – Ann Demeulemeester, Dries Van Noten, Walter Van Beirendonck, Dirk Van Saene, Dirk Bikkembergs and Marina Yee. For designer fashions wander Schuttershofstraat and Huidevettersstraat; retro and streetwear groove on in Kammenstraat. Oh, and don't miss **MoMu** (☎ 03 470 27 70; www.momu.be; Nationalestraat 28; adult/concession €7/5; 10am-6pm Tue-Sun); for details, see p122.

Some recommended fashion shops:

Ann Demeulemeester (☎ 03 216 01 33; Verlatstraat 38) Stocks her complete line of men's and women's clothing.

Het Modepaleis (☎ 03 470 25 10; Nationalestraat 16) Headquarters and shop of Dries Van Noten.

Louis (☎ 03 232 98 72; Lombaardstraat 4) Great introduction to various Belgian players, including newer designers such as Véronique Branquinho and Olivier Theyskens.

Walter (☎ 03 213 26 44; St Antoniusstraat 12) Van Beirendonck's outlet looks more like an ultramodern art gallery than somewhere to buy clothes.

On the clubbing circuit, Antwerp's scene melds permanent with one-off in a mix that holds both mainstream and alternative. Trance and experimental electronica are big – check out **Noctis.com** (www.noctis.com) to track down clubs, one-off parties or festivals. Alternatively, pick up fliers at **Fish & Chips** (☎ 03 227 08 24; 36-38 Kammenstraat).

A good place to start is **Café d'Anvers** (☎ 03 226 38 70; www.café-d-anvers.com; Verversrui 15; 11pm-7.30am Fri & Sat). This legendary club does funk and house, disco and soul in a refurbished church in the city's red-light district. Many of Belgium's top DJs started here.

Red & Blue (☎ 03 213 05 55; www.redandblue.be; Lange Schipperskapelstraat 11; 11pm-7am Sat) is men only on Saturday nights but goes mixed on Friday. **Space** (Frankrijklei 53; admission €8; 6am-2pm Sat, Mon & Tue, 8am-6am Sun) is the after-club club. Dancing starts when the streetlights go out. **Café Local** (www.cafélocal.be; Waalsekaai 25; 10pm-late Thu-Sat) is another long-time favourite, previously known for its techno parties but these days preferring salsa and global grooves.

Well-established events to watch out for include **Antwerp is Burning** (www.antwerpisburning.be), a one-night, once-a-year affair combining seven clubs, and **Clubland**, an extravaganza that takes over open fields on the Linkeroever (Left Bank) for a night in summer.

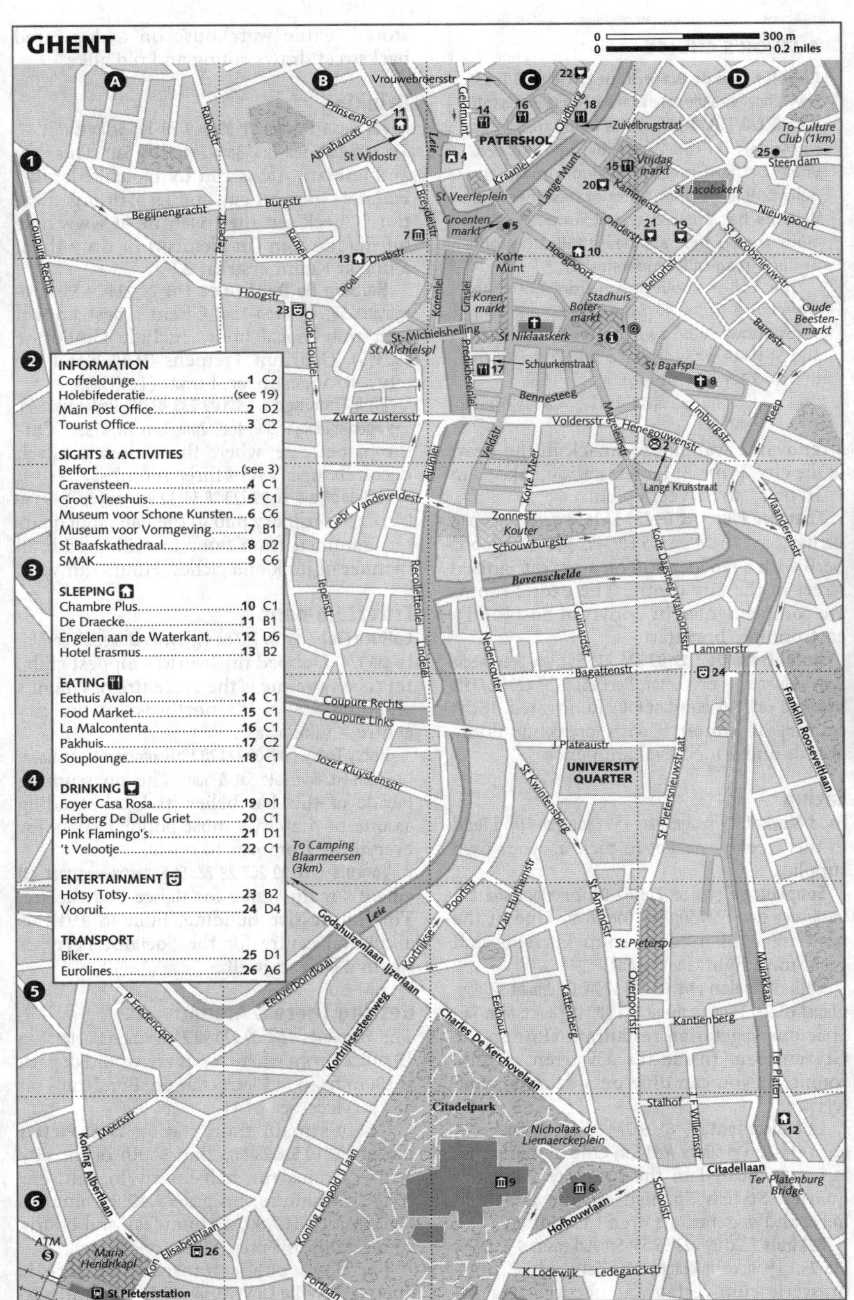
GHENT
0 300 m
0 0.2 miles
INFORMATION
Coffeelounge....1 C2
Holebifederatie....(see 19)
Main Post Office....2 D2
Tourist Office....3 C2
SIGHTS & ACTIVITIES
Belfort....(see 3)
Gravensteen....4 C1
Groot Vleeshuis....5 C1
Museum voor Schone Kunsten....6 C6
Museum voor Vormgeving....7 B1
St Baafskathedraal....8 D2
SMAK....9 C6
SLEEPING
Chambre Plus....10 C1
De Draecke....11 B1
Engelen aan de Waterkant....12 D6
Hotel Erasmus....13 B2
EATING
Eethuis Avalon....14 C1
Food Market....15 C1
La Malcontenta....16 C1
Pakhuis....17 C2
Souplounge....18 C1
DRINKING
Foyer Casa Rosa....19 D1
Herberg De Dulle Griet....20 C1
Pink Flamingo's....21 D1
't Velootje....22 C1
ENTERTAINMENT
Hotsy Totsy....23 B2
Vooruit....24 D4
TRANSPORT
Biker....25 D1
Eurolines....26 A6
PATERSHOL
UNIVERSITY QUARTER
To Culture Club (1km)
To Camping Blaarmeersen (3km)
Citadelpark
St Pietersstation
ATM
Vrouwebroersstr
Prinsenhof
Abrahamstr
St Widostr
Geldmunt
Leie
Oudburg
Zuivelbrugstraat
Kraanlei
Lange Munt
Vrijdag markt
Kammerstr
Steendam
St Jacobskerk
Nieuwpoort
Onderstr
St Jacobsnieuwstr
St Veerleplein
Groenten markt
Korte Munt
Hoogpoort
Belfortstr
Begijnengracht
Burgstr
Rabotstr
Peperstr
Ramen
Drabstr
Poel
Hoogstr
Coupure Rechts
Oude Houtlei
J Breydelstr
Korenlei
Graslei
Koren-markt
Stadhuis
Boter-markt
St-Michielshelling
St Michielspl
St Niklaaskerk
Predikherenlei
Schuurkenstraat
St Baafspl
Oude Beesten-markt
Barrestr
Reep
Limburgstr
Bennesteeg
Zwarte Zustersstr
Voldersstr
Magaleinstr
Henegouwenstr
Lange Kruisstraat
Veldstr
Korte Meer
Ajuinlei
Gebr Vandeveldestr
Zonnestr
Kouter
Schouwburgstr
Vlaanderenstr
Korte Dagsteeg
Walpoortsstr
Bovenschelde
Iepenstr
Recollettenlei
Lindelei
Nederkouter
Guinardstr
Lammerstr
Bagattenstr
Franklin Rooseveltlaan
Coupure Rechts
Coupure Links
J Plateaustr
Jozef Kluyskensstr
St Kwintensberg
St Pietersnieuwstraat
Van Hulthemstr
Poortstr
St Amandstr
St Pieterspl
Godshuizenlaan
Ijzerlaan
Kortrijkse
Edverbondkaai
Eekhout
Kattenberg
Overpoortstr
Muinkkaai
Kantienberg
P Fredericqstr
Kortrijksesteenweg
Charles De Kerchovelaan
Ter Platen
Stalhof
J F Willemsstr
Meersstr
Koning Albertlaan
Koning Leopold II laan
Nicholaas de Liemaerckeplein
Citadellaan
Ter Platenburg Bridge
Hofbouwlaan
Schoolstr
Maria Hendrikapl
Kon Elisabethlaan
K Lodewijk
Ledeganckstr
Fortlaan
BELGIUM

AUTHOR'S CHOICE

Engelen aan de Waterkant (☎ 09 223 08 83; www.engelenaandewaterkant.be; Ter Platen 30; s/d/tr €110/120/150; ⊠ 💻) The name translates to 'Angels on the Waterside' and, indeed, you'd be hard pressed to find a more angelic B&B in Belgium. Interior designer Ann Willems has created two luxuriously spacious rooms that are beautifully thought out and magically understated.

The B&B is about 1.5km from both the city centre (tram 40 from the Korenmarkt stops about 500m away at Ter Platenbrug) and St Pietersstation (take bus 70 to 79 to the stop Ter Platenbrug).

a renovated warehouse smack in the heart of the city. From St Pietersstation, take tram 1, 10 or 11 to St Veerleplein.

Chambre Plus (☎ 09 225 37 75; www.chambreplus.be; Hoogpoort 31; s/d/ste €65/80/140; ⊠) Gorgeous B&B with a fab location on a pedestrianised street in the city centre. The exotic rooms are complemented by convivial hosts and a gastronomic breakfast.

Hotel Erasmus (☎ 09 224 21 95; www.proximedia.com/web/hotel-erasmus.html; Poel 25; s/d/f €75/95/150, luxury s/d €85/110, breakfast €10) Renovated 16th-century townhouse with creaking floorboards and a medieval ambience.

Eating

Food Market (Vrijdagmarkt; 🕒 8am-2pm Fri) Head to this weekly market to pick up your own supplies.

Souplounge (☎ 09 223 62 03; Zuivelbrugstraat 6; small/large soup €3/4.50; 🕒 10am-7pm) One of the new breed of modern soup kitchens and great for a light, fast meal.

Eethuis Avalon (☎ 09 224 37 24; Geldmunt 32; dagschotel €8.50, 3-course menu €11.50; 🕒 lunch Mon-Sat) Spacious vegetarian restaurant close to the Gravensteen. Inside it's a warren of little rooms, or you can dine outside on a small terrace.

La Malcontenta (☎ 09 224 18 01; Haringsteeg 7; mains €14-20; 🕒 dinner Wed-Sat) One of many restaurants located in the intimate Patershol quarter. Stylish Spanish cuisine is served here, and vegetarians aren't forgotten.

Pakhuis (☎ 09 223 55 55; Schuurkenstraat 4; mains €15-25; 🕒 noon-midnight Mon-Sat) This huge brasserie-cum-restaurant occupying a restored textile warehouse on a dog-eared backstreet draws young and old alike.

Drinking

Foyer Casa Rosa (☎ 09 269 28 12; Belfortstraat 39; 🕒 3pm-1am Sun-Thu, 3pm-2am Fri & Sat) This gay and lesbian café is run by Holebifederatie, Flanders' biggest gay and lesbian organisation. Check out their website at www.holebifederatie.com (in Flemish) or drop them a line at Kammerstraat 22.

Herberg De Dulle Griet (☎ 09 224 24 55; Vrijdagmarkt 50; 🕒 noon-1am) Ghent's best-known beer pub. Local brews include Guillotine (9.3%), Delirium Tremens (9.5%) and the city's strongest beer, Piraat (10.5%).

Pink Flamingo's (☎ 09 233 47 18; Onderstraat 55; 🕒 noon-midnight Sun-Thu, 2pm-3am Fri & Sat) Off-the-planet café, where the authentic kitsch décor changes every three months.

't Velootje (☎ 09 223 28 34; Kalversteeg 2; 🕒 9pm-late) Extraordinary pub in the Patershol quarter crammed from floor to ceiling with all manner of junk and riches. Hours can vary.

Entertainment

Culture Club (☎ 09 267 64 41; www.cultureclub.be; Afrikalaan 174) Dubbed the 'world's hippest club', this classy venue is the epicentre of Ghent's clubbing scene. It's northeast of the city centre – take a taxi.

Hotsy Totsy (☎ 09 224 20 12; Hoogstraat 1; 🕒 noon-late Mon-Fri, 8pm-late Sat & Sun) The unassuming façade of this bar belies its local standing as one of the city's most popular spots for everything from jazz to poets.

Vooruit (☎ 09 267 28 28; St Pietersnieuwstraat 23) Ghent's main venue for dance and theatre. This impressive building, built in 1912 as a cultural centre for the Socialist Party, is worth a look in itself.

Getting There & Around

The **Eurolines** (☎ 09 220 90 24; Koningin Elisabethlaan 73) office, from where buses arrive and depart, is 100m from St Pietersstation. For details on bus services, see p141.

Ghent's main train station is **St Pieters station** (☎ 02 528 28 28), 2km south of the city centre. Trains run half-hourly to Antwerp (€7.80, 45 minutes), Bruges (€5.40, 20 minutes) and Brussels (€7.80, 45 minutes), and hourly connections to Ypres (€9.50, one hour).

The city's public transport network is operated by **De Lijn** (☎ 09 210 93 11). Trams to

BELGIUM

the city centre (1, 10, 11, 12 and 13) depart from the tram station in the tunnel to the right as you exit the train station.

Bikes can be hired from the **train station** (☎ 02 528 28 28) for €9.50 per day (plus €12.50 deposit), or from **Biker** (☎ 09 224 29 03; Steendam 16; per half-/full-day €6.50/9; 9am-12.30pm & 1.30-6pm Tue-Fri, until 5pm Sat).

BRUGES

pop 117,000

Touristy, overcrowded and a tad fake. Describe any other city in these terms and it would be left for dead. But not Bruges (Brugge in Flemish, Bruges in French). This Flemish city is Belgium's most popular destination and, despite the crowds, it's not to be missed.

Suspended in time centuries ago because of misfortune that drove the townsfolk away, Bruges is one of Western Europe's most-visited medieval cities and dreamily evokes a world long since gone. But its reputation as one of the most perfectly preserved cities is in part fabrication. While what you see reflects that of centuries ago, much of the architecture dates only to the 19th and 20th centuries.

Orientation

Central Bruges is neatly encased in an egg-shaped series of canals, at the heart of which is the picturesque Markt, the city's central square. The train station is 1.5km south of the Markt.

Information

Coffee Link (☎ 05 034 99 73; www.thecoffeelink.com; Mariastraat 38; 11am-6pm Thu-Tue) Atmospheric Internet café inside the precincts of the former St Janshospitaal.

In & Uit Brugge (☎ 05 044 46 46; www.brugge.be; 't Zand; 10am-6pm Fri-Wed, 10am-8pm Thu) Tourist office located inside the Concertgebouw.

Main post office (☎ 05 033 14 11; Markt 5)

Train station tourist office (9.30am-12.30pm & 1-5pm Tue-Sat)

Sights

Bruges' nerve centre is the historic **Markt**, a large square from which rises Belgium's most famous **Belfort** (Belfry; Markt; adult/concession €5/3; 9.30am-5pm Tue-Sun, last tickets sold 4.15pm). The 366 steps to the top are worth the squeeze.

Smaller but arguably more impressive than the Markt is the adjoining **Burg.** This square is home to the **Heilig-Bloedbasiliek** (Basilica of the Holy Blood; 9.30-11.50am & 2-5.50pm Apr-Sep, 10-11.50am & 2-3.50pm Oct-Mar), where a few coagulated drops of Christ's blood are kept and cherished. This phial is paraded annually in the elaborate Heilig-Bloedprocessie (Holy Blood Procession) on Ascension Day (17 May in 2007 and 1 May in 2008).

Belgium's oldest and arguably most beautiful **Stadhuis** (Town Hall; admission €2.50; 9.30am-5pm Tue-Sun) also rises from the Burg. Tours take in the Gotishe Zaal (Gothic Hall), with its polychromatic ceiling.

Bruges' prized collection of art dating from the 14th to 20th centuries is housed in the small **Groeningemuseum** (Dijver 12; adult/concession €8/5; 9.30am-5pm Tue-Sun). A controversial make-over of the museum a few years ago means you now need to start in Room 2 – which presents the Flemish Primitives – then backtrack to Room 1 to view things chronologically.

The **Hospitaalmuseum St Janshospitaal** (Mariastraat 38; adult/concession €8/5; 9.30am-5pm Tue-Sun) is home to a handful of masterpieces by Hans Memling, plus many works by lesser-known painters of his time. Don't miss Memling's reliquary of St Ursula – the attention to detail is stunning.

The **Onze Lieve Vrouwekerk** (Church of Our Lady; Mariastraat; adult/concession €2.50/1.50; 9.30am-5pm Tue-Sat, 1.30-5pm Sun) has one remarkable art treasure – Michelangelo's *Madonna and Child* (1504). This small marble statue was the only work of art by Michelangelo to leave Italy during his lifetime. Although pinched several times by occupying forces, it has always been returned.

The **Begijnhof** (admission free; 9am-6.30pm) was home to a 13th-century religious community of unmarried or widowed women, known as *Begijnen* (Beguines). One of Bruges' quaintest spots, it's a 10-minute walk south of the Markt.

Choco-Story (☎ 05 061 22 37; www.choco-story.be; Wijnzakstraat 2; adult/child €6/4; 10am-5pm) is devoted to telling the story of chocolate, and is Bruges' newest attraction. It's well done.

De Halve Maan/Straffe Hendrik (☎ 05 033 26 97; www.halvemaan.be; Walplein 26; admission €4.50; 11am-4pm Apr-Sep, 11am-3pm Oct-Mar) is a family brewery offering crowded guided tours (45 minutes) that finish with a beer.

BELGIUM

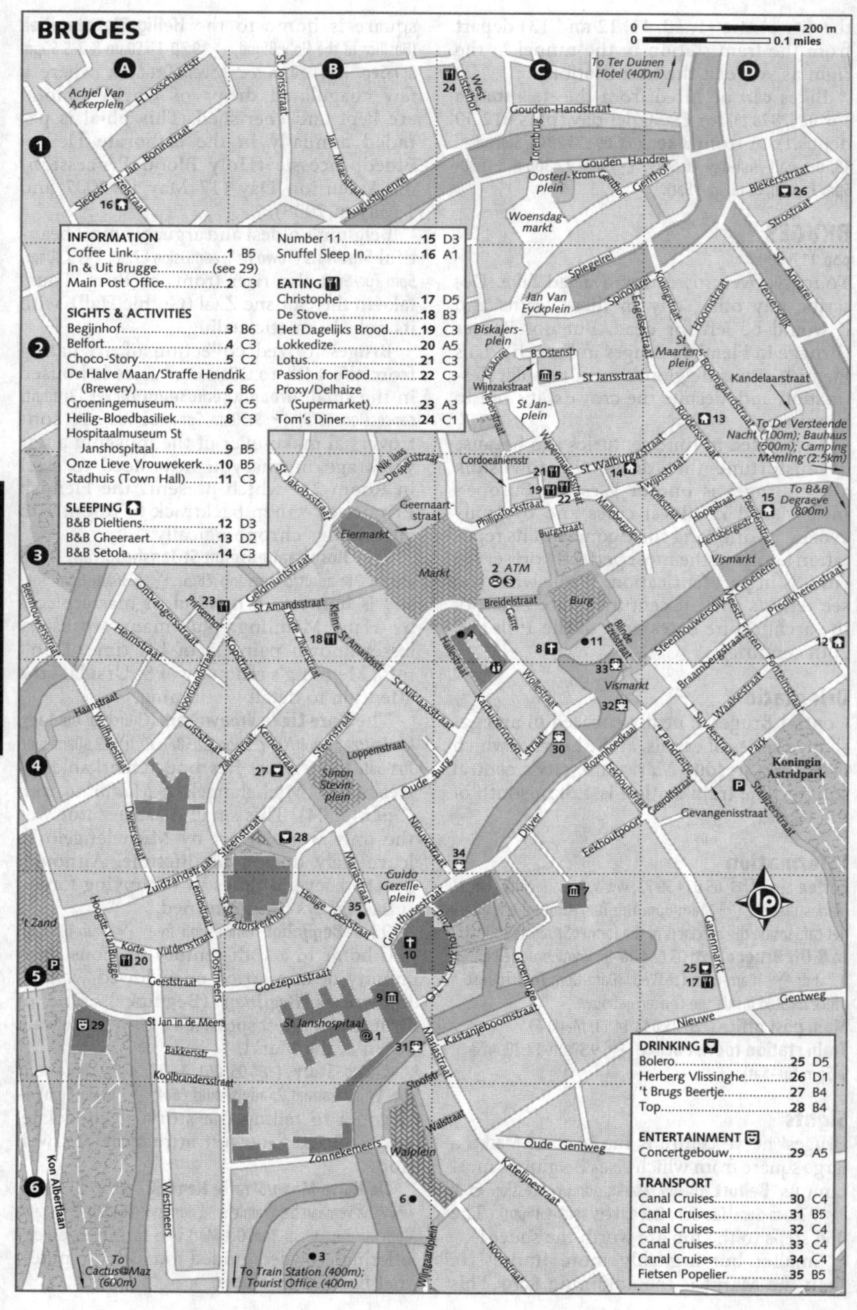
BRUGES
0 200 m
0 0.1 miles
A
B
C
D
1
2
3
4
5
6
INFORMATION
Coffee Link....................1 B5
In & Uit Brugge...............(see 29)
Main Post Office..............2 C3
SIGHTS & ACTIVITIES
Begijnhof.......................3 B6
Belfort...........................4 C3
Choco-Story....................5 C2
De Halve Maan/Straffe Hendrik (Brewery)........6 B6
Groeningemuseum............7 C5
Heilig-Bloedbasiliek...........8 C3
Hospitaalmuseum St Janshospitaal..................9 B5
Onze Lieve Vrouwekerk.....10 B5
Stadhuis (Town Hall).........11 C3
SLEEPING
B&B Dieltiens.................12 D3
B&B Gheeraert.................13 D2
B&B Setola......................14 C3
Number 11.......................15 D3
Snuffel Sleep In................16 A1
EATING
Christophe.......................17 D5
De Stove..........................18 B3
Het Dagelijks Brood...........19 C3
Lokkedize.........................20 A5
Lotus...............................21 C3
Passion for Food...............22 C3
Proxy/Delhaize (Supermarket)..............23 A3
Tom's Diner.......................24 C1
DRINKING
Bolero.................................25 D5
Herberg Vlissinghe...............26 D1
't Brugs Beertje....................27 B4
Top......................................28 B4
ENTERTAINMENT
Concertgebouw.....................29 A5
TRANSPORT
Canal Cruises........................30 C4
Canal Cruises........................31 B5
Canal Cruises........................32 C4
Canal Cruises........................33 C4
Canal Cruises........................34 C4
Fietsen Popelier......................35 B5
To Ter Duinen Hotel (400m)
To De Versteende Nacht (100m); Bauhaus (500m); Camping Memling (2.5km)
To B&B Degraeve (800m)
To Cactus@Maz (600m)
To Train Station (400m); Tourist Office (400m)
Achjel Van Ackerplein
H Losschaertstr
Jan Boninstraat
Sledestr
Ezelstraat
St Jorisstraat
Jan Miraelstraat
Augustijnenrei
West Gistelhof
Gouden-Handstraat
Torenbrug
Gouden Handrei
Oosterlingenplein
Krom Genthof
Genthof
Woensdagmarkt
Blekersstraat
Strostraat
Spiegelrei
St Annarei
Verversdijk
Jan Van Eyckplein
Spinolarei
Koningstraat
Engelsestraat
Hoornstraat
Biskajersplein
St Maartensplein
Boomgaardstraat
Kandelaarstraat
B Ostenstr
Kraanrei
Wijnzakstraat
St Jansstraat
Ieperstraat
St Janplein
Riddersstraat
Cordoeaniersstr
Wapenmakersstraat
St Walburgastraat
Twijnstraat
Nik laas Despasstraat
St Jakobsstraat
Geernaartstraat
Philipstockstraat
Mallebergplein
Kelkstraat
Hoogstraat
Peerdenstraat
Eiermarkt
Burgstraat
Hertsbergestr
Markt
ATM
Vismarkt
Geldmuntstraat
Breidelstraat
Burg
Groenerei
Predikherenstraat
Beenhouwersstraat
Ontvangersstraat
Prinsenhof
St Amandsstraat
Kleine St Amandsstr
Korte Zilverstraat
Garre
Blinde Ezelstraat
Steenhouwersdijk
Meestraat
Helmstraat
Kopstraat
Hallestraat
Noordzandstraat
St Niklaasstraat
Wollestraat
Braambergstraat
Fonteinstraat
Haanstraat
Wulfhagestraat
Gistsstraat
Zilverstraat
Kemelstraat
Steenstraat
Kartuizerinnenstraat
J Suveestraat
Waalsestraat
Loppemstraat
Rozenhoedkaai
't Pandreitje
Park
Koningin Astridpark
Simon Stevinplein
Oude Burg
Eekhoutstraat
Gevangenisstraat
Stalijzerstraat
Dweersstraat
Nieuwstraat
Dijver
Eekhoutpoort
Gerolfstraat
Zuidzandstraat
Steenstraat
Lendestraat
St Salvatorskerkhof
Mariastraat
Guido Gezelleplein
Heilige Geeststraat
Gruuthusestraat
Pl. Z. O.L.V. Kerkhof Z.
Groeninge
Garenmarkt
't Zand
Hoogste Van Brugge
Korte Vuldersstraat
Geeststraat
Goezeputstraat
Oostmeers
Gentweg
Nieuwe
St Jan in de Meers
St Janshospitaal
Kastanjeboomstraat
Bakkersstr
Koolbrandersstraat
Stoofstr
Walstraat
Oude Gentweg
Zonnekemeers
Walplein
Katelijnestraat
Kon Albertlaan
Westmeers
Wijngaardplein
Noordstraat
BELGIUM

Tours

Quasimundo (☎ 05 033 07 75; www.quasimundo.com; adult/under 26/under 8 €18/16/free, with your own bike €12; ⏲ mid-Mar–mid-Oct) offers excellent half-day bike tours of Bruges and/or the surrounding countryside. Bookings are necessary.

Canal tours (adult/child €5.70/2.80; ⏲ 10am-6pm Mar–mid-Nov) are touristy, but what isn't here? Viewing Bruges from the water gives it a totally different feel than by foot. Boats depart every 20 minutes from jetties south of the Burg, including Rozenhoedkaai and Dijver, and tours last 30 minutes.

The clip-clop of hooves hitting cobblestones resounds constantly in the streets of Bruges. **Horse-drawn carriages** (5 passengers €30) leave from the Markt, and their well-trodden route takes 35 minutes.

Quasimodo (☎ 05 037 04 70; www.quasimodo.be; incl lunch adults/under 26 yr €50/40) offers two excellent bus day trips – a 'Triple Treat' tour of Bruges or a tour of the Ypres Salient's famous WWI battlefields (see p132).

Sleeping

Despite an abundance of offerings, Bruges' accommodation scene gets booked way in advance. Reserve early if you want the pick of the crop.

BUDGET

Camping Memling (☎ 05 035 72 50; www.camping-memling.be; Veltemweg 109, St Kruis; tent/car €12/5; ⏲ year-round) The quietest local campground is located 2.5km east of the city centre. Take bus 11 from the train station to the Vossensteert stop and walk 400m back in the direction of Bruges.

Snuffel Sleep In (☎ 05 033 31 33; www.snuffel.be; Ezelstraat 47-49; dm/d €15/36; ⊠) Funky place that's been around for years. It has basic but original rooms, friendly staff, a kitchen and a bar. From the train station take bus 3 or 13.

Bauhaus (☎ 05 034 10 93; www.bauhaus.be; Langestraat 135; hostel section dm/d/tr per person €15/18/17, hotel section s/d/tr €26/40/57) Big and bustling hostel with separate budget hotel section next door. A popular hangout for young travellers, though the blue rooms hardly fuel the imagination. The bar's lively and the adjoining café has cheap meals. Take bus 6 or 16 from the train station.

B&B Degraeve (☎ 05 034 57 11; www.stardekk.com/bedbreakfast; Kazernevest 32; s/d/tr €33/45/58) Located in a quiet, untouristed part of the city and run by a zany woman who has filled the two spacious rooms with bizarre décor.

AUTHOR'S CHOICE

B&B Dieltiens (☎ 05 033 42 94; www.users.skynet.be/dieltiens; Waalsestraat 40; s/d/tr €50/60/90; ⊠) This classical mansion was featured on the first map of Bruges published in the 16th century. Lovingly restored by Koen and Annemie Dieltiens, this B&B has three gorgeous guestrooms with polished wooden floors and subtle warm tones. Inquire also about their studio apartment in a 17th-century house.

MIDRANGE & TOP END

B&B Gheeraert (☎ 05 033 56 27; www.users.skynet.be/brugge-gheeraert; Riddersstraat 9; s/d/tr €50/60/80, 1-night stay extra €10; ⊠ 💻) Curl around the steep spiral staircase and arrive at the three lofty rooms in this delightful B&B. The two nicest, at the rear, look out over a garden. All have white décor, polished timber floors and a large en suite bathroom. Children and babies (cot and highchair available) are welcome.

B&B Setola (☎ 05 033 49 77; www.bedandbreakfast-bruges.com; St Walburgastraat 12; s/d/tr/f €50/60/80/100, 1-night stay extra €10; ⊠) Get away from old world and *brocante* in this mansion dating from 1740. The three 2nd-floor guestrooms have cool, clean vibes, and the woman who runs this place is a charm. Can't get a better location, and the buffet breakfast is fab.

Ter Duinen Hotel (☎ 05 033 04 37; www.terduinenhotel.be; Langerei 52; s/d from €98/105; Ⓟ ❄) Beautifully executed hotel facing a canal about 1km north of the Markt. The neat rooms have a refined, romantic air and the staff are efficient and friendly.

Number 11 (☎ 05 033 06 75; www.number11.be; Peerdenstraat 11; d €115-140, ste €215; ⊠ 💻) There's no mincing words: this B&B is a stunner. The three rooms – 'Vanilla', 'Grey' and 'Chocolate' – harmoniously blend modern and medieval styles. Ask about the kookiest chandelier you'll ever see.

Eating

From cosy *estaminets* (taverns) to 1st-class restaurants, Bruges has all bases covered.

Passion for Food (☎ 047 740 17 14; Philipstockstraat 39; soup €4-6, salad €6-13; ⏲ lunch & dinner Wed-Mon)

BELGIUM

Great Mediterranean flavours at this laid-back eatery. Sip a fresh juice on the terrace.

Het Dagelijks Brood (☎ 05 033 60 50; Philipstockstraat 21; snacks €5-11; 🕑 7am-6pm Wed-Mon; ☒) Smoke-free tearoom offering pies and *boterhammen* (sandwiches), plus the essential big table. This Belgian success story now has branches worldwide.

Lokkedize (☎ 05 033 44 50; Korte Vuldersstraat 33; dishes €8-10; 🕑 7pm-late Wed & Thu, 6pm-late Fri-Sun) One of the city's most convivial *eetcafés* (eating cafés) and a great spot for a late-night bite (kitchen open till midnight).

Tom's Diner (☎ 05 033 33 82; West Gistelhof 23; mains €10-15; 🕑 6.30pm-1am Wed-Mon) To the north of the city, a little way out of the tourist centre and all the better for it. Stylish food at very affordable prices. Locals love it.

De Stove (☎ 05 033 78 35; Kleine St Amandsstraat 4; mains €18-28; 🕑 lunch Sat-Tue, dinner Fri-Tue) Charming restaurant tucked away on a pedestrian lane. The eight tables are arranged around an old stove, the service is intimate and the food – fish specialities – is excellent.

Also recommended:

Lotus (☎ 05 033 10 78; Wapenmakerstraat 5; meals €10; 🕑 11.45am-2pm Mon-Sat) Excellent lunchtime vegetarian restaurant.

Christophe (☎ 05 034 48 92; Garenmarkt 34; mains €14-23; 🕑 7pm-1am Thu-Mon) Cool late-night bistro.

Proxy/Delhaize (Geldmuntstraat) Supermarket for self-caterers.

BELGIUM

Drinking

Herberg Vlissinghe (☎ 05 034 37 37; Blekersstraat 2; 🕑 11am-late Wed-Sun) Someone has been pouring beer at Bruges' oldest café since 1515 – mind-blowing really.

't Brugs Beertje (☎ 05 033 96 16; Kemelstraat 5; 🕑 4pm-1am Thu-Tue) Belgium's most famous beer pub is a tiny place situated on a poky backstreet. About 250 national brews are on offer, listed by brewery.

Top (St Salvatorskerkhof 5; 🕑 9pm-late Tue-Sat, 10pm-late Sun) Cool bar, and one of the few places in Bruges that does dance music after midnight. Opens late and moves until morning.

Bolero (☎ 05 033 81 11; Garenmarkt 32; 🕑 10pm-4am Thu-Mon) The only gay and lesbian bar in town.

Entertainment

Concertgebouw (☎ 05 047 69 99; www.concertgebouw.be; 't Zand 34) Contemporary comes to Bruges in the form of this concert hall, the newest building on the city's skyline. Opened in 2002 to celebrate Bruges' stint as the European City of Culture, its minimal design incorporates the city's three famous towers.

Cactus@MaZ (☎ 05 071 68 40; www.cactusmusic.be; Magdalenastraat 27) The city's premier venue for contemporary and world music – either live or DJ.

Getting There & Away

Bruges' **train station** (☎ 02 528 28 28) is about 1.5km south of the Markt. Trains run every half-hour to Brussels (€11.80, one hour) and Ghent (€5.40, 20 minutes), and hourly trains to Antwerp (€12.40, one hour 10 minutes). For Ypres (Ieper in Flemish; €10.10, two hours) take the train to Kortrijk, from where there are hourly connections.

Getting Around

A small network of buses operated by **De Lijn** (☎ 05 956 53 53) covers destinations in and around Bruges. To get from the train station to the Markt, take any bus marked 'Centrum'.

Bruges is great for cyclists. Hire a bike from **Fietsen Popelier** (☎ 05 034 32 62; Mariastraat 26; 🕑 10am-8pm Jul & Aug, 10am-6pm Sep-Jun) for €3.50/7/10 per hour/half-day/full day or a tandem for €8/15/22.

YPRES

pop 35,200

Only the hardest are not moved by Ypres (Ieper in Flemish). Ypres and its surrounding area were the last bastion of Belgian territory unoccupied by the Germans in WWI. As such, the region was a barrier to a German advance towards the French coastal ports around Calais. More than 300,000 Allied soldiers were killed here during four years of fighting that left the medieval town flattened. Convincingly rebuilt, the town and its surrounds, known as the Ypres Salient, are dotted with cemeteries and memorials. Unless you've got a car, the best way to visit is by guided tour (opposite).

Information

Post office (Diksmuidsestraat 33)

Ypres Visitors Centre (☎ 05 723 92 20; www.ieper.be; Grote Markt 34; 🕑 9am-6pm Mon-Fri, 10am-6pm Sat & Sun Apr-Sep, 10am-5pm Oct-Mar)

Sights

Ypres' hub, the **Grote Markt**, is dominated by the enormous **Lakenhalle** (Cloth Hall) with its 70m-high belfry. This hall testifies to Ypres importance, alongside Bruges and Ghent, as a medieval cloth town. Attached to the eastern end of the Lakenhalle is the Renaissance-style **Stadhuis**, noted for its lovely arcade gallery.

On the 1st floor of the Lakenhalle is **In Flanders Fields Museum** (☎ 05 723 92 20; www.inflandersfields.be; Grote Markt 34; admission €7.50; 🕑 10am-6pm Apr-Sep, 10am-5pm Tue-Sun Oct-Mar) which honours ordinary people experiencing wartime horrors.

The **Menin Gate** (Meensestraat) is one of the saddest reminders of the town's past. The huge white gate is inscribed with the names of 54,896 British and Commonwealth troops who were lost in the quagmire of the trenches and who have no graves. Every evening at 8pm traffic is halted while buglers sound the Last Post.

Tyne Cot Cemetery, on a plateau about 8km northeast of Ypres, is the largest British Commonwealth war cemetery in the world. Its name comes from the Northumberland infantrymen who tried to take this ridge – they fancied the German bunkers positioned on the hillside looked like Tyneside cottages. In all, 11,956 soldiers are buried here. The cemetery is best visited by guided tour (below).

Tours

Visit on a cold grey day when the lifeless fields are no more than muddy bogs and fog drapes the graves of the dead, and you'll have little difficulty conjuring up the scene of almost a century ago. Two companies offer good bus tours of the Ypres Salient. Book at least a day or two in advance.

Quasimodo (☎ 05 033 07 75; www.quasimundo.com; adult/under 26/under 8 €18/16/free, with your own bike €12; 🕑 mid-Mar–mid-Oct) Located in Bruges (see p131).

Salient Tours (☎ 05 721 46 57; www.salienttours.com; 2½/4hr tour €20/25; 🕑 Thu-Tue Mar-Nov) Run by an Englishman based in Ypres.

Sleeping & Eating

Jeugdstadion (☎ 05 721 72 82; info@jeugdstadion.be; Bolwerkstraat 1; adult/car €4.50/4.50; 🕑 mid-Mar–Oct) Basic campground attached to a youth centre, 900m southeast of Grote Markt.

B&B Hortensia (☎ 05 721 24 06; info@guesthouse-ieper.be; Rijselsestraat 196; s/d €51/61) In the heart of town with modern, sober rooms. No fuss or bother.

Hotel Regina (☎ 05 721 88 88; www.hotelregina.be; Grote Markt 45; s/d €75/100) Smack on the Markt and overlooking the Lakenhalle, this is Ypres' most atmospheric hotel. The cheaper rooms are old and ordinary; the most expensive ones are large and rustic.

In het Klein Stadhuis (☎ 05 721 55 42; Grote Markt 32; mains €10-15; 🕑 daily Jun-Sep, Mon-Sat Oct-May) Smooth, split-level café tucked away in a quaint guildhall next to the Stadhuis. Offers good-value meals day and night.

De Stoove (☎ 047 922 92 33; Surmont de Volsbergstraat 12; mains under €20; 🕑 lunch Thu-Tue, dinner Thu-Mon) Just a few streets away from the Lakenhalle, this fish restaurant has a relaxed ambience.

Getting There & Around

From Ypres **train station** (☎ 02 528 28 28) there are hourly trains direct to Kortrijk (€4.30, 30 minutes) and Ghent (€9.50, one hour). For Brussels (€14.60, 1½ hours), Bruges (€10.10, 1¼ hours) and Antwerp (€16.30, two hours), change at Kortrijk.

Regional buses leave from the bus station to the left outside the train station.

Hire bikes from **Jeugdstadion** (☎ 05 721 72 82; info@jeugdstadion.be; Bolwerkstraat 1; 🕑 mid-Mar–Oct) for €5 per day.

WALLONIA

Brush up on your French – you'll need it in Wallonia. Stepping across the linguistic divide into Belgium's French-speaking southern half is akin to entering a different country. Gone are the flat fields and affluent art cities of the north, replaced instead by a rolling forested landscape hiding intimate villages, mighty citadels, patriotic cities and industrial decay. Burrow down in Wallonia's southeastern corner, an area known as the Ardennes, and you'll find ancient castles nestled in river valleys below forested plateaus – all very beguiling.

LIÈGE

pop 185,500

Love or loathe it, Liège (Luik in Flemish) always makes an impression. Sprawled along the Meuse River, about 90km east of Brussels, Liège is the Ardennes' largest city – a gritty place that takes time to know. For

Simenon fans, this is George's birthplace and his primary place of homage (though there's little to see).

The main tourist office is **Maison du Tourisme** (☎ 04 237 92 92; www.liege.be; Pl St Lambert 35; 9am-6pm Jun-Sep, 9.30am-5.30pm Oct-May).

Sights

For a city panorama, start with **Montagne de Bueren** (Hors Château), a flight of 373 stairs leading up to a former citadel.

The excellent **Musée d'Art Réligieux et d'Art Mosan** (Museum of Religious Art & Art from the Meuse Valley; ☎ 04 221 42 25; Rue Mêre Dieu; adult/child €3.80/2; 11am-6pm Tue-Sat, 11am-4pm Sun) is chock-full of well-preserved regional religious relics.

Life as it was for some during the 18th century is depicted in the beautiful **Musée d'Ansembourg** (☎ 04 221 94 02; Féronstrée 114; adult/child €3.80/2; 1-6pm Tue-Sun). If you've just come from the previous museum, you'll find this rich, Regency-styled mansion wonderfully uncluttered.

The **Musée de l'Art Wallon** (☎ 04 221 92 31; Féronstrée 86; adult/child €3.80/2; 1-6pm Tue-Sat, 11am-4.30pm Sun) accommodates art by French-speaking Belgians including surrealists René Magritte and Paul Delvaux.

Sleeping & Eating

Auberge de Jeunesse (☎ 04 344 56 89; www.laj.be; Rue Georges Simenon 2; dm/s/d €16.60/29/42;) To get to this modern HI-affiliated hostel on Outremeuse take bus 4 from Gare Guillemins to Pl St Lambert and change to bus 18.

Hôtel Les Acteurs (☎ 04 223 00 80; www.lesacteurs.be, in French; Rue des Urbanistes 10; s/d €50/65, breakfast €6; P) Comfy modern hotel that tries hard to be artistic. It's well located, and buses 1 and 4 stop about 200m away.

As Ouhès (☎ 04 223 32 25; Pl du Marché 21; mains €12-20, menu €25) Liège institution that specialises in rich Walloon cuisine. Note the apt logo – a gluttonous man sitting on a mound of hams, sausages and waffles.

Getting There & Away

Buses operated by **Eurolines** (☎ 04 222 36 18; Rue des Guillemins 94) leave 100m from the main train station. See p141 for details on services.

The principal train station is **Gare Guillemins** (☎ 02 528 28 28), 2km south of Pl St Lambert, the city's heart. Train connections include to Brussels (€12.40, one hour, half-hourly), Namur (€7.40, 50 minutes, half-hourly), Spa (€4.30, 50 minutes, hourly), Tongeren (€3.80, 30 minutes, hourly) and Luxembourg City (€32.20, 2½ hours, every two hours).

AROUND LIÈGE

Tongeren

pop 29,500

Tongeren, 20km north of Liège in Flanders, is Belgium's oldest city. The original locals put up considerable resistance under the leadership of Ambiorix when the area was besieged by Roman troops in 15 BC. The **Gallo-Roman Museum** (☎ 01 267 03 30; www.galloromeinsmuseum.be, in French & Flemish; Kielenstraat 15) has many findings from these times, however, it's closed until spring 2008.

Tongeren is also well known for its Sunday **Antique Market** (Veemarkt) and the elegant **Onze Lieve Vrouwbasiliek** (Basilica of Our Lady; Grote Markt; adult €2.50; 10am-noon & 1.30-5pm Apr-Sep), which is undergoing archaeological excavation but is still worth a visit.

For more information, head to the **tourist office** (☎ 01 239 02 55; www.tongeren.be, in Flemish; Stadhuisplein 9; 8.30am-5pm Jul-Aug, 8.30am-noon & 1-5pm Mon-Fri, 10am-4pm Sat & Sun Sep-Easter, 8.30am-noon & 1-5pm Mon-Fri, 9.30am-5pm Sat & Sun Easter-Sep).

WORTH A TRIP

There's no bursting its bubble. For centuries Spa, Europe's oldest health resort, has embraced royalty and the wealthy who came to drink, bathe and cure themselves in the mineral-rich waters that bubble forth here. These days a new generation interested in wellbeing is taking to the town's palatial hill-top complex, the **Thermes de Spa** (☎ 08 777 25 60; www.thermesdespa.com; 10am-9pm). Spend a couple of hours in one of the hydrotherapy pools (€17), or submerse yourself for days.

Spa is 40km southeast of Liège and connected by regular trains (€4.30, 50 minutes). The **Office du Tourisme** (☎ 08 779 53 53; www.spa-info.be, in French & Flemish; Pl Royale 41; 9am-6pm Mon-Fri, 10am-6pm Sat & Sun) can help with inquiries.

BELGIUM

Hautes Fagnes Nature Reserve

The Hautes Fagnes, or High Fens, is a plateau of swampy heath, woods and windswept moors that sweeps over to Germany's Eifel hills. The area is popular with walkers and cyclists.

Start a visit at the **Botrange Nature Centre** (☎ 08 044 03 00; www.centrenaturebotrange.be, in French & Flemish; Route de Botrange 131; ⏲ 10am-6pm), located 2.5km from the sturdy stone **Signal de Botrange** that marks Belgium's highest point (694m).

It takes at least 1¼ hours to arrive here on public transport from Liège: take the train to Verviers (€3.40, 20 minutes, hourly) and then bus 390 (€3.60, 30 minutes, five daily) to Rocherath.

CHARLEROI

pop 200,600

A city on the edge – Charleroi, born of coal, iron and glass, flanks the formerly coal-rich Sambre Valley and was the powerhouse of the steel industry up until the 1970s. These days it's surrounded by a blackened industrial landscape with belching chimneys and old slag heaps – hardly fuel for tourists.

The city's **airport** (CRL; www.charleroi-airport.com), sometimes called Brussels–Charleroi or Brussels' South, is 6km north of the city and is serviced by Ryanair flights from Ireland, Britain and several European destinations. Frequent shuttle buses connect the airport with Brussels' main train station, Gare du Midi (€10.50 one way, one hour). Buses arrive and depart from the corner of Rue de France and Rue de l'Instruction near the Thalys exit at Gare du Midi.

Should you want to explore Charleroi, bus A and 68 run from the airport to Charleroi train station.

TOURNAI

pop 67,400

As provincial towns in Wallonia go, Tournai (Doornik in Flemish) is decidedly pleasant. Situated on the Scheldt River (L'Escaut in French), just 10km from the French border and 80km from Brussels, it offers a World Heritage–listed belfry and cathedral, plus a cache of enjoyable museums.

Follow your nose to the belfry to find the **Office du Tourisme** (☎ 06 922 20 45; www.tournai.be; Vieux Marché aux Poteries 14; ⏲ 8.30am-6pm Mon-Fri, 9.30am-noon & 2-5pm Sat, 10am-noon & 2.30-6pm Sun).

Sights

The five towers of the striking but sober **Cathédrale Notre Dame** (Grand Place; admission free; ⏲ 9.30am-noon & 2-5.30pm) have long been the trademark of Tournai's skyline. Pummelled by a freak tornado in 1999, major works to realign the towers mean some parts of the cathedral are still off limits to tourists.

Tournai's 72m-high **belfry** (☎ 06 922 20 45; Grand Place; adult/child €2/1; ⏲ 10am-1pm & 2-6.30pm Tue-Sun Mar-Oct, 10am-noon & 2-5pm Tue-Sat, 2-5pm Sun Nov-Feb) is Belgium's oldest, dating from 1188. Climb the 256 steps.

The **Musée des Beaux-Arts** (☎ 06 922 20 43; Enclos St Martin; adult/child €3/2; ⏲ 9.30am-12.30pm & 2-5.30pm Wed-Mon Apr-Oct, 10am-12 noon & 2-5pm Wed-Mon Nov-Feb) is the city's little gem. Housed in a building designed by Victor Horta, it contains paintings and sculptures by local, national and international artists.

Tapestry lovers should not miss the **Musée de la Tapisserie** (☎ 06 984 20 73; Pl Reine Astrid; admission €2.50; ⏲ 9.30am-12.30pm & 2-5.30pm Wed-Mon).

Sleeping & Eating

Auberge de Jeunesse (☎ 06 921 61 36; www.laj.be; Rue St Martin 64; dm/s/d €16.60/29/42) A pleasant, modern hostel around the corner from the Musée des Beaux-Arts. It's a 20-minute walk from the train station: take bus 4 (direction Baisieux).

Hôtel d'Alcantara (☎ 06 921 26 48; hotelalcantara@hotmail.com; Rue des Bouchers St Jacques 2; s/d from €75/85; Ⓟ) Not the most expensive hotel in town but certainly the most charming. Attentive service and 15 well-priced, modern rooms are set behind a discreet courtyard. Parking costs €7.50.

Le Giverny (☎ 06 922 44 64; Quai du Marché au Poisson 6; mains €13-20, menus €40-56; ⏲ lunch Tue-Fri & Sun, dinner Tue-Sat) Occupies an old bakery and is a lovely eating space with great French food.

Getting There & Away

Tournai's **train station** (☎ 02 528 28 28) is about 900m from the heart of town, the Grand Place. There are regular trains to Brussels (€10.70, one hour) and Ypres (€7.80, one hour).

NAMUR

pop 106,200

The capital of Wallonia, Namur (Namen in Flemish) is an excellent jumping-off point for exploring the forested Ardennes. Some 60km southeast of Brussels, it's a picturesque town, built at the confluence of the Meuse and Sambre rivers and presided over by a citadel that, in times gone by, ranked as one of Europe's mightiest.

The **Office du Tourisme** (☎ 08 124 64 49; www.pays-de-namur.be; Sq Léopold; 9.30am-6pm) is near the train station.

Sights

What remains of Namur's once-mighty **citadel** (Route Merveilleuse) is slung high above the town on a rocky outcrop. It covers a huge area, though only towers, tunnels and much of the outer walls still exist. Take the **tourist train** (☎ 08 124 64 49; €1; 10am-5pm hourly Jun–mid-Sep, Sat & Sun Apr, May & mid-Sep–Oct), which departs hourly from the tourist office, for easy access or, alternatively, walk up.

Don't miss the **Trésor du Prieuré d'Oignies** (☎ 08 125 43 00; Rue Julie Billiart 17; adult/child €2/1; 10am-noon & 2-5pm Tue-Sat, 2-5pm Sun & Mon), a one-room hoard of Gothic treasures housed in a modern convent. Ring the bell and a nun will guide you.

The **Musée Félicien Rops** (☎ 08 122 01 10; www.ciger.be/rops; Rue Fumal 12; admission €3; 10am-6pm daily Jul & Aug, 10am-6pm Tue-Sun Sep-Jun) is devoted to works by the 19th-century, Namur-born artist Félicien Rops (1833–98), who fondly illustrated erotic lifestyles and macabre scenes.

Sleeping & Eating

Camping Les 4 Fils Aymon (☎ 08 158 02 94; Chaussée de Liège; tent, car & 2 people €6.20; Apr-Sep) Pleasant camping ground located about 8km east of Namur; bus 12 leaves hourly from the bus station.

Auberge de Jeunesse (☎ 08 122 36 88; www.laj.be; Ave F Rops 8; dm/s/d €16.60/29/42; P ⊠ 💻) Attractive riverfront hostel about 3km southwest of the train station. Buses 3 and 4, which both depart hourly from Pl de la Station, stop nearby.

Hôtel Les Tanneurs (☎ 08 124 00 24; www.tanneurs.com; Rue des Tanneries 13; s €45-200, d €60-215, breakfast €10; P ✣ 💻) Unique hotel situated on a shabby street in the heart of town. Unites modern comfort with 17th-century charm. Book well ahead.

Le Pain Quotidien (☎ 08 122 16 66; Rue du Collège 5; light meals €5-11; 7.30am-5.30pm; ⊠) Atmospheric option for a light bite at any time of the day.

Brasserie Henry (☎ 08 122 02 04; Pl St Aubain 3; mains €10-27; noon-midnight Mon-Thu, noon-1am Fri & Sat) Sociable brasserie and an institution among Namur's late-night diners.

La Bonne Fourchette (☎ 08 123 15 36; Rue Notre Dame 112; mains €15-18, menu du chef €25; dinner daily, lunch Sat & Sun) Intimate Belgian/French restaurant, located near the casino, with plum décor and hovering angels.

Getting There & Away

BUS

Local and regional buses are operated by **TEC** (☎ 08 125 35 55; Pl de la Station; 7am-7pm). Regional buses leave from either the bus station near the C&A department store or from Pl de la Station. Details of bus services to regional destinations are given in the Getting There & Away section in each of the following towns.

TRAIN

Namur is a major rail hub in this part of Belgium and boasts a gleaming **train station** (☎ 02 528 28 28). Regional connections include Brussels (€7.40, one hour), Dinant (€3.90, 30 minutes), Jemelle (€7.40, 40 minutes), Liége (€7.40, one hour) and Marloie (€6.70, 35 minutes).

DINANT

pop 12,700

Pressed between rock and river, Dinant is one of the Ardennes' tourist hot spots. About 28km south of Namur, its bulbous cathedral, **Église Notre Dame** (Pl Reine Astrid; admission free), competes for attention with the cliff-front **citadel** (☎ 08 222 36 70; www.citadellededinant.be; Le Prieuré 25; adult/child €6.50/4; 10am-6pm Apr-Oct, 10am-4pm Sat-Thu Nov-Mar) and in summer the town almost chokes with tourists and traffic. Good for a pit stop but there are better places deeper in the Ardennes to kick back.

The **tourist office** (☎ 08 222 28 70; www.dinant-tourisme.be; Ave Cadoux 8; 8.30am-7pm Mon-Fri, 9.30am-7pm Sat, 10am-6pm Sun) is on the opposite side of the river from the cathedral.

ROCHEFORT & HAN-SUR-LESSE

pop 15,600

As a base in this part of the Ardennes, Rochefort's hard to beat. Together with its neighbour Han-sur-Lesse, Rochefort is famed for the millennia-old underground limestone grottoes that attract families from all over

Belgium. The caves at Han are the more spectacular of the two, but Han itself is a tourist trap; stay in Rochefort and commute between the towns.

Rochefort is also well known for the Trappist beer of the same name that's brewed by local monks. There's no shortage of watering holes for sampling.

The Rochefort **tourist office** (☎ 08 434 51 72; www.valdelesse.be; Rue de Behogne 5; 8am-6pm Mon-Fri, 9.30am-5pm Sat & Sun Jul & Aug, 8am-5pm Mon-Fri, 10am-5pm Sat & Sun Sep-Jun) is in the centre of town.

Sights & Activities

The impressive **Grottes de Han** (☎ 08 437 72 13; www.grotte-de-han.be; Rue Lamotte 2; adult/child €12/7; 10am-noon & 1.30-5.30pm Apr-Oct, 11.30am-4pm Nov, Dec & Mar) is a series of caves dripping with stalactites and stalagmites a little way out of Han. Excursions here start with a toy-train ride, followed by a long walk through cold tunnels and finally a boat trip on an underground lake. Rochefort's cave, **Grotte de Lorette** (☎ 08 421 20 80; Drève de Lorette; adult/child €7.25/4.70; 10.30am-4.30pm Mar-Oct), is smaller but also worth seeing.

The area is a great base for **walking** and **cycling**. One trail for cyclists is **RAVeL**, an 18km stretch of disused train line linking Rochefort and the village of Houyet. Buy a map of the local trails from the tourist office and hire a bike from **Cycle Sport** (☎ 08 421 32 55; Rue de Behogne 59; 9.30am-noon & 1.30-6.30pm Tue-Sat, 9.30am-noon Sun) for €10/15/20 per morning/afternoon/full day.

Sleeping & Eating

The following options are all in Rochefort.

Camping Communal (☎ 08 421 19 00; Rue du Hableau; adult €2, car & tent €3; Easter-Oct) Next to the Lomme River, immediately below the main part of town, the facilities here are very basic, but it's well located and there's a large playground and pool nearby.

Le Vieux Moulin (☎ 08 421 46 04; www.giterochefort.be; Rue du Hableau 25; demi pension 25 yr & under/26 yr & over €18.50/21.25; year-round) Pleasant *gîte d'étape* (basic hostel-style accommodation) in the heart of town. The overnight price includes breakfast and one meal.

Hôtel La Malle Poste (☎ 08 421 09 86; www.malleposte.be; Rue de Behogne 46; s/d Maison du Cocher €60/85, Les Thermes from €75/100) The best address in town. Two beautifully restored buildings offer a variety of accommodation – opt for a night in the quaint old stagecoach quarter, Maison du Cocher, or choose a more stylish room (complete with jacuzzi) in the new Les Thermes section.

La Bella Italia (☎ 08 422 15 20; Rue de Behogne 50; pizza €7.50-12) Enjoy excellent pizza at this busy Italian restaurant in the heart of town.

La Gourmandise (☎ 08 421 09 86; Rue de Behogne 24; mains €9-21) Stop in for a Rochefort beer or stay for dinner – excellent local cuisine, such as chicken in Trappist sauce, is served.

Getting There & Away

Rochefort is linked by bus to Han-sur-Lesse and the train stations of Jemelle and Houyet. To get here from Namur, take the train to Jemelle (€7.40, 40 minutes, hourly) and from there bus 29 to Rochefort (€1.20, seven minutes, hourly), which continues on to Han (€1.20, seven minutes).

LA ROCHE-EN-ARDENNE

pop 4250

La Roche is a vibrant little town hidden in a deep valley, crowned by a ruined castle and surrounded by verdant hills. One of the Ardennes' most popular summer resorts, it hums with Belgian holidaymakers buying up big on smoked hams and getting into outdoor pursuits. All in all, a great family destination.

The **tourist office** (☎ 08 436 77 36; www.la-roche-tourisme.com; Pl du Marché 15; 9am-5pm) is on the main street.

Sights & Activities

La Roche's picture-postcard medieval **castle** (adult/child €4/2; 10am-7pm Jul & Aug, 10am-noon & 2-5pm Apr-Oct, 1.30-4.30pm Mon-Fri, 10am-noon & 1.30-4.30pm Sat & Sun Nov-Mar), perched on a crag above town, is accessed from steps leading up from the main street.

Kayaking is big business here. The most popular excursion, a 25km paddle along the Ourthe River (€20, six hours), is organised by **Ardenne-Aventures** (☎ 08 441 19 00; www.ardenne-aventure.be; Rue du Hadja 1), next to the bridge at the northern end of town. It also hires out mountain bikes (half-/full day €17/22) for exploring the many marked hiking/biking trails that crisscross the surrounding hills.

Sleeping & Eating

Camping Le Vieux Moulin (☎ 08 441 13 80; www.strument.com; Petite Strument 62; adult/child/campsite

€2.50/2.50/8; Easter-Oct) Draped for what seems an eternity along a stream next to the Hôtel Moulin de la Strument. Great site.

Domaine des Olivettes (☎ 08 441 16 52; www.lesolivettes.be; Chemin des Soeret 12; dm €12, s/d from €35/55) Hotel-cum-hostel-cum-equestrian centre, perched on a hill above town. The hotel rooms are pleasant, alternatively there's a separate *auberge* (hostel) with dormitory-style accommodation.

Hôtel Moulin de la Strument (☎ 08 441 15 07; www.strument.com; Petite Strument 62; s/d €65/75; Feb-Dec; P) La Roche's most agreeable hotel is part of an old mill and is nestled in a secluded wooded valley next to a babbling stream. There's a good restaurant on site.

Maison Bouillon & Fils (☎ 08 441 18 80; Pl du Marché 6; snacks €5-10) Where but the Belgian Ardennes would a butcher's shop boast its own café? Dine in with an *assiette ardennaise* (plate of mixed local charcuterie, €10) or takeaway from this must-see boucherie.

Le Clos René (☎ 08 441 26 17; Rue Châmont 30; snacks €6-10; 11am-11pm daily Jul & Aug, Fri-Wed Sep-Jun) Escape sausages and smoked hams in this tasteful crêperie. Kids welcome.

BELGIUM

Getting There & Away

Buses are the only form of public transport to La Roche. If you're coming from either Namur or Luxembourg, the nearest rail junction is Marloie, from where bus 15 goes to La Roche (€3.50, 35 minutes, six per day). From Liège, take the Liège–Jemelle train to Melreux and then bus 13 to La Roche (€3.50, 30 minutes, seven a day).

BASTOGNE

pop 14,000

It was in Bastogne, close to the Luxembourg border, that thousands of soldiers and civilians died during WWII's Battle of the Bulge. Today this little town is full of wartime reminders.

The main square – a parking lot adorned with a tank – has been renamed Pl McAuliffe after the famous American general whose reply to the German call to surrender was 'Nuts!'. Here, too, you'll find the **Maison du Tourisme** (☎ 06 121 27 11; www.paysdebastogne.be; Pl McAuliffe; 9am-6pm mid-Jun–mid-Sep, 9.30am-12.30pm & 1-5.30pm mid-Sep–mid-Jun).

Most visitors head straight to the star-shaped **American Memorial** that stands on a hill just outside town. Next to the memorial is the **Bastogne Historical Centre** (☎ 06 121 14 13; Colline du Mardasson; adult/child €8.50/6; 9.30am-6pm Jul-Aug, 9.30am-5pm May-Jun & Sep, 10am-4.30pm Mar-Apr & Oct-Dec), where war footage recounts the battle.

For overnighters, **Hôtel Caprice** (☎ 06 121 81 40; www.horest.be; Pl McAuliffe 25; s/d/tr €55/70/95; P) has saccharine-sweet pink rooms and **Restaurant Léo** (☎ 06 121 14 41; Rue du Vivier 4; mains €12-20; 11.30am-9.30pm Tue-Sun) does an excellent *assiette ardennaise* (11 types of charcuterie).

To get to Bastogne, the closest rail junction is Libramont, from where bus 163b (€3.50, 45 minutes) departs every two hours.

BELGIUM DIRECTORY

ACCOMMODATION

Prices listed in reviews are for rooms with attached bathroom unless otherwise specified.

Camping and caravanning facilities are plentiful and at their best in the Ardennes. Rates vary widely – expect to pay €10 to €20 for two adults, a tent and vehicle.

Belgium has many youth hostels (*jeugdherbergen* in Flemish, *auberges de jeunesse* in French) affiliated with Hostelling International (HI), as well as a small number of private hostels offering slightly cheaper accommodation. HI hostels charge €14.50 to €17.60 per night in a dorm, including breakfast and sheets, or €29/42 in a single/double room. Contact **Vlaamse Jeugdherbergcentrale** (☎ 03 232 72 18; www.jeugdherbergen.be; Van Stralenstraat 40, B-2060 Antwerp) for hostels in Flanders and **Les Auberges de Jeunesse** (☎ 02 219 56 76; www.laj.be; Rue de la Sablonnière 28, B-1000 Brussels) for Wallonia.

In Wallonia's rural areas you'll occasionally come across *gîtes d'étapes,* basic hostel-style places mostly set up for large groups, though individual travellers are welcome.

B&Bs *(gastenkamers/chambres d'hôtes)* usually represent excellent value. Spacious rooms, private bathrooms, breakfast feasts and vibrant hosts are the salient features. Prices start at €35/45 per single/double, rising to around €50/65 for midrange options and levelling out at €100 to €160 at the top end.

The cheapest hotels charge €35 to €45 for a single room and €50 to €60 for doubles. Expect shared bathroom facilities. Midrange hotel prices average €70 to €100 for singles and €80 to €150 for doubles. Top-end establishments start at €150. Many hotels in Brussels offer weekend discounts – see p110 for details.

ACTIVITIES

Canoeing & Kayaking

The Ardennes is the place to ride rivers. Kayaks and canoes can be hired at La Roche-en-Ardenne (p137), but don't expect rapids of any magnitude.

Cycling

Belgians are passionate about cycling. There are two genres: in flat Flanders, bikes are a popular means of everyday travel and many roads have dedicated cycle lanes; in Wallonia, the hilly terrain is favoured by mountain-bike (VTT, or *vèlo tout-terrain* in French) enthusiasts.

Bikes are not allowed on motorways but can be taken on trains (one way/return €5/8). Hire them from private operators or from most train stations for around €6.50/9.50 per half-/full day or €55 per week. You may be required to pay a deposit (€20) and/or show your passport or credit card. For more on cycling, see p142.

Walking

Walkers are spoilt for choice, with easy, flat terrain in Flanders or the more inspiring hills of the Ardennes in Wallonia. Local tourist offices have copious information about paths and they sell regional hiking maps.

BUSINESS HOURS

Banks open from 9am to 3.30pm or as late as 5pm Monday to Friday. Tourist office hours vary – see the individual city and town sections throughout this chapter for more details.

Restaurants generally open from 11.30am until 2pm or 3pm and from 6.30pm to 11pm. Brasseries are open from 11am to 1am.

Pubs and cafés open from 10am or 11am to 1am or 2am (some stay open until dawn). Clubs open from 11pm to 6am Friday to Sunday.

Shops open from 9am to 6pm Monday to Saturday; supermarkets stay open until 9pm. Shops in major cities also open from 10am to 4pm on Sunday. Shops in smaller towns close for lunch (noon to 2pm).

EMBASSIES & CONSULATES

Belgian Embassies & Consulates

Australia (☎ 02-6273 2501; fax 6273 3392; 19 Arkana St, Yarralumla, ACT 2600)
Canada (☎ 613-236 7267; fax 236 7882; Constitution Sq, Ste 820, 360 Albert St, Ottawa ON K1R 7X7)
France (☎ 01 44 09 39 39; fax 47 54 07 64; rue de Tilsitt 9, Paris F-75840 Cedex 17)
Germany (☎ 49-3020 6420; fax 3020 642 200; Jägerstrasse 52-53, Berlin D-10117)
Ireland (☎ 01-205 7100; fax 283 9403; 2 Shrewsbury Rd, Ballsbridge, Dublin 4)
Luxembourg (☎ 25 43 251; fax 45 42 82; rue des Girondins 4, Luxembourg City L-1626)
Netherlands (☎ 070-312 34 56; fax 364 55 79; Alexanderveld 97, Den Haag NL-2585 DB)
New Zealand (☎ 09-575 6202; ismackenzie@xtra.co.nz; 15A Rarangi Rd, St Heliers, Auckland)
UK (☎ 020-7470 3700; fax 7470 3795; 103-105 Eaton Sq, SW1W 9AB)
USA (☎ 202-333 6900; fax 333 5457; 3330 Garfield St, NW, Washington, DC, 20008)

Embassies & Consulates in Belgium

The following diplomatic missions are all embassies and all are located in or around Brussels:

Australia (☎ 02 286 05 00; fax 02 230 68 02; Rue Guimard 6, B-1040)
Canada (☎ 02 741 06 11; fax 02 741 06 43; Ave de Tervuren 2, B-1040)
France (☎ 02 548 87 11; fax 02 513 68 71; Rue Ducale 65, B-1000)
Germany (☎ 02 787 18 00; fax 02 787 28 00; Rue Jacques de Lalaing 8-14, B-1040)
Ireland (☎ 02 235 66 76; fax 02 235 66 71; Rue Wiertz 50, B-1050)
Luxembourg (☎ 02 735 57 00; fax 02 737 57 10; Ave de Cortenbergh 75, B-1000)
Netherlands (☎ 02 679 17 11; fax 02 679 17 75; Ave Herrmann-Debroux 48, B-1160)
New Zealand (☎ 02 512 10 40; fax 02 513 48 56; 7th fl, Sq de Meeus 1, B-1100)
UK (☎ 02 287 62 11; fax 02 287 63 55; Rue d'Arlon 85, B-1040)
USA (☎ 02 508 21 11; fax 02 511 27 25; Blvd du Régent 27, B-1000)

FESTIVALS & EVENTS

Belgium buzzes with music, pageantry and parades.

Concours Musical International Reine Élisabeth de Belgique (Queen Elisabeth International Musical Competition; www.concours-reine-elisabeth.be) Held in May, this is Belgium's most prestigious classical-music event.

KunstenFESTIVALdesArts (www.kunstenfestivaldesarts.be) Held in Brussels over three weeks in May, big names in the worlds of music, dance, theatre and opera combine for an international festival to rival all others.
Brussels Jazz Marathon (www.brusselsjazzmarathon.be) The second-last weekend in May brings nonstop jazz to Brussels.
Rock Werchter (www.rockwerchter.be) Held in Leuven, near Brussels, for three days over the first weekend of July. Together with Glastonbury (England), this is one of Europe's biggest 'field' rock festivals.
De Gentse Feesten (www.gentsefeesten.be) An annual 10-day festival in mid-July that transforms the city into a party of music and theatre (see p126).
Pageant of the Golden Tree (www.comitevoorinitiatief.be) Famous Bruges procession that retells the history of Flanders. Held every five years – check the website for dates.

HOLIDAYS

Following is a list of the public holidays observed in Belgium:
New Year's Day 1 January
Easter Monday March/April
Labour Day 1 May
Ascension Day Fortieth day after Easter
Whit Monday Seventh Monday after Easter
Festival of the Flemish Community 11 July (Flanders only)
National Day 21 July
Assumption 15 August
Walloon Community 27 September (Wallonia only)
All Saints' Day 1 November
Armistice Day 11 November
Christmas Day 25 December

MONEY

Banks are the best place to exchange money. Outside banking hours, exchange bureaux (*wisselkantoren* in Flemish, *bureaux d'échange* in French) operate at Brussels National Airport and at main train stations. ATMs are widespread.

Tipping is optional, as service and VAT is included in hotel and restaurant prices.

POST

Mail can be sent either *prior* (priority) or *nonprior* (nonpriority) but, given the delays experienced with priority mail, don't even consider sending things nonpriority. Letters under 50g to European countries cost €0.60 and to non-European countries €0.65.

Poste restante attracts a €0.40 fee and you may need to show your passport. Following are some useful addresses:
Poste Restante Hoofdpostkantoor, Groenplaats, B-2000 Antwerp
Poste Restante Hoofdpostkantoor, Markt 5, B-8000 Bruges
Poste Restante Bureau de Poste Central, Blvd Anspach 1, B-1000 Brussels

TELEPHONE

Belgium's international access code is ☎ 00. The country code is ☎ 32. Call ☎ 1234 for an international operator.

Local phone calls are metered and cost a minimum of €0.25. Telephone numbers prefixed with 0900 or 070 are pay-per-minute numbers (€0.17 to €0.45 per minute). Numbers prefixed with 0800 are toll-free calls. Those prefixed with 0472 to 0479, 0482 to 0489 and 0492 to 0499 are mobile numbers. Note also that a call to directory assistance (☎ 1405) costs €3.

TIME

Belgium runs on Central European Time (GMT/UTC plus one hour). During daylight-savings time Central European Time is GMT/UTC plus two hours.

VISAS

There are no entry requirements or restrictions on EU nationals visiting Belgium. Citizens of Australia, Canada, Israel, Japan, New Zealand and the USA don't need visas to visit as tourists for up to three months. Except for people from a few other European countries (such as Switzerland), everyone else must have a visa issued by a Belgian embassy or consulate.

For up-to-date visa information, check **Federal Public Service Foreign Affairs Belgium** (www.diplomatie.be).

TRANSPORT IN BELGIUM

GETTING THERE & AWAY

Air

SN Brussels Airlines has flights from Brussels National Airport to European and African destinations. VLM Airlines flies from Brussels National and Antwerp airport to London.

Belgium's main international airports:
Antwerp (ANR; ☎ 03 285 65 00; www.antwerpairport.be)
Brussels National Airport (BRU; ☎ 09 007 00 00; www.brusselsairport.be)
Charleroi (CRL; www.charleroi-airport.com)
Liège (LGG; ☎ 04 234 84 11; www.liegeairport.com)

BELGIUM

Airlines flying to and from Belgium:

Aer Lingus (code EI; ☎ 02 548 98 48; www.airlingus.com)
Air France (code AF; ☎ 02 526 12 70; www.airfrance.com)
British Airways (code BA; ☎ 02 717 32 17; www.british airways.com)
KLM (code KL; ☎ 07 022 27 47; www.klm.be)
Lufthansa (code LH; ☎ 07 035 30 30; www.lufthansa.be)
Ryanair (code FR; ☎ 09 028 80 07; www.ryanair.com)
SN Brussels Airlines (code SN; ☎ 07 035 11 11; www.flysn.com)
Virgin Express (code TV; ☎ 07 035 36 37; www.virgin-express.com)
VLM Airlines (code VG; ☎ 03 287 80 80; www.flyvlm.com)

Check the following for cheap airlines flying into Belgium: **Wizz Air** (www.wizzair.com), **Welcome Air** (www.welcomeair.com), **Sky Europe** (www.skyeurope.com), **Condor – Born to Fly** (www.condor.com) and **Aer Arann** (www.aerarann.com).

Land

BUS

Eurolines (☎ 02 274 13 50; www.eurolines.be) operates international bus services to and from Belgium.

Depending on the destination and the time of year, Eurolines buses stop in Brussels, Antwerp, Ghent, Leuven and Liège. Tickets can be bought from its offices in these cities or from travel agencies – for details see the relevant city's Getting There & Away section.

Services from Brussels include Amsterdam (€18, 3¾ hours, six daily), Frankfurt (€34, 5¼ hours, one daily), London (€38, 8½ hours, six daily), Luxembourg City (€15, 3¼ hours, one or two daily) and Paris (€25, 3¾ hours, nine daily).

One Busabout service also passes through Belgium, stopping in Bruges as part of its Northern Loop. For details, see p1117.

CAR & MOTORCYCLE

The main motorways into Belgium are the E19 from the Netherlands, the E40 from Germany, E411 from Luxembourg, and the E17 and E19 from France. There are no controls at border crossings. From Luxembourg, fill up before you leave as petrol is more expensive in Belgium. For road rules, see p142.

TaxiStop (☎ 07 022 22 92; www.taxistop.be; Rue du Fossé aux Loups 28, Brussels) is a travel agency that matches long-distance travellers and drivers headed for the same destination for a reasonable fee.

EMERGENCY NUMBERS

- Ambulance ☎ 100
- Fire ☎ 100
- Police ☎ 101
- EU-wide emergency hotline ☎ 112
- Touring Secours breakdown service ☎ 07 034 47 77 (24-hour assistance)

TRAIN

Trains operated by **Eurostar** (☎ 02 528 28 28; www.eurostar.com) travel between Brussels' Gare du Midi station and London's Waterloo station (two hours 20 minutes, 10 trains Monday to Friday, seven Saturday and Sunday) through the Eurotunnel. Standard semi-flexible, 2nd-class fares start from €200 return, though cheaper fares are available (21-day advance fare €40). Fares include travel to any train station in Belgium (eg continue from Brussels' Gare du Midi to Bruges at no extra cost).

For details on **Eurotunnel** (☎ 07 022 32 10; www.eurotunnel.com) services between the UK and France, see p278 and p415.

Thalys (☎ 07 066 77 88; www.thalys.com) fast trains link various cities in Belgium with destinations in France, the Netherlands and Germany. In Brussels, Thalys trains depart from Gare du Midi. Flexible one-way fares, known as Librys tickets, include Brussels to Paris (€74.50, 1½ hours, hourly), Cologne (€40, 2¼ hours, six daily) and Amsterdam (€44, 2¾ hours, five daily). Cheaper non-flexible return fares (eg Paris/Cologne/Amsterdam €49/29/32), known as Smilys, are also available. Discounted adult fares are also offered on weekends and for trips booked well in advance. Travellers aged 12 to 26 get a 50% discount and seniors a 30% reduction.

Sea

Two overnight car-ferry services exist:

P&O (☎ Belgium 02 710 64 44, UK 0870-520 2020; www.poferries.com) Sails overnight from Zeebrugge in Belgium to Hull in the UK (14 hours) and charges from €162/245 one way/return for two passengers, a car and cabin.

Superfast Ferries (☎ Belgium 05 025 22 52, UK 0870-234 0870; www.superfast.com) Ultramodern ferry sails three times per week between Zeebrugge in Belgium and Rosyth in Scotland (18 hours). Fares start at €92/165 one way/return for a car. Adult passengers pay from €60 one way.

BELGIUM

GETTING AROUND

Bicycle

Cycling is a great way to get around in Flanders. The countryside is riddled with cycling routes and if you hire a bike (or buy a second-hander), it's easy to cycle from destination to destination, or go from city to city by train, using the bike to explore once you're there.

Those serious about a cycling holiday should get the multilingual *Topogids Vlaanderen Fietsroute*. This book details the 800km Flanders Cycle Route, plus shorter circuits. It's available from the **Belgian Tourist Information Centre** (☎ 02 504 03 90; www.visitflanders.com, www.belgique-tourisme.net; Rue du Marché aux Herbes 63; 9am-6pm Mon-Fri, 9am-1pm & 2-6pm Sat & Sun, 9am-1pm Sun Jan-Feb; Ⓜ Gare Centrale).

For more on cycling, see p139.

Bus

Buses are a secondary means of getting around as the rail network is so widespread. The exception is the Ardennes region in Wallonia. Here train lines run to bigger settlements, but many smaller places are connected only by bus. Without a car, you'll find relatively short distances can involve long waits as bus routes are often sparsely serviced.

Following are the major bus companies:

De Lijn (☎ 01 631 37 11; www.delijn.be, in Flemish) Buses in Flanders.

Société des Transports Intercommunaux de Bruxelles (☎ 02 515 20 00; www.stib.irisnet.be, in French & Flemish) Buses in Brussels.

Transport en Commun (☎ 01 023 53 53; www.infotec.be, in French) Buses in Wallonia.

Car & Motorcycle

Foreign drivers don't need an international driving licence in Belgium; your driving licence from home will suffice. Road rules are easy to understand, although the peculiar give-way-to-the-right law takes getting used to. Standard international signs are used and motorways are toll-free. The speed limit is 50km/h in towns, 90km/h outside towns and 120km/h on motorways. The blood alcohol limit is 0.05%. Fuel prices per litre are around €1.40 for unleaded and €1.10 for diesel.

Major car-hire companies have offices in central Brussels, as well as offices at Brussels National Airport and Gare du Midi, the city's main train station. Hire cars from either the airport or Gare du Midi cost considerably more because of additional taxes.

Following are some recommended car-hire companies:

Avis (☎ 02 537 12 80; www.avis.be; Rue Américaine 145, Brussels)

Budget (☎ 02 646 51 30; www.budget.com; Ave Louise 327b, Brussels)

Hertz (☎ 02 513 28 86; www.hertz.be; Blvd Maurice Lemonnier 8, Brussels)

Hitching

It's illegal to hitch on Belgian motorways.

Train

Taking the train is the best way to get around. Belgium built Continental Europe's first train line (between Brussels and Mechelen) in the 1830s and has since developed an extremely dense network. Trains are run by the **Belgische Spoorwegen/Société National des Chemins de Fer Belges** (Belgian Railways; ☎ 02 528 28 28; www.b-rail.be). Major train stations have information offices, open until about 7pm (later in large cities).

There are four levels of service: InterCity (IC) trains (the fastest), InterRegional (IR), local (L) and peak-hour (P) commuter trains. Depending on the line, there will be an IC and IR train every half-hour or hour.

Trains have 1st- and 2nd-class compartments; both are completely nonsmoking.

COSTS

Second-class tickets are 50% cheaper than 1st-class tickets. On weekends return tickets to anywhere within Belgium are 50% cheaper than on weekdays. Children under 12 travel for free when accompanied by an adult, provided the journey starts after 9am. Seniors over 65 (including visitors) pay only €4 for a return 2nd-class trip anywhere in Belgium (not on weekends from mid-May to mid-September).

If you intend on doing day excursions, investigate discounted packages known as B-Excursions. They're always good value.

TRAIN PASSES

Benelux Tourrail Allows five days' travel in one month in Belgium, Luxembourg and the Netherlands, and costs €160/120 in 1st/2nd class (under 26 years €90, 2nd class only). It can be purchased in Belgium or Luxembourg but not in the Netherlands (though it's valid for use there).

Go Pass Provides 10 one-way trips anywhere in Belgium for people under 26 (€45, 2nd class only).

Rail Pass Gives 10 one-way trips anywhere in Belgium. Valid for one year and costs €104/68 in 1st/2nd class.

BELGIUM

Britain

Neophyte visitors to Western Europe's third-most populous nation often arrive expecting warm beer, teetering double-decker buses and red telephone boxes on every street corner. Instead they discover a country that has dramatically moved on from its clichéd stereotypes and is riding a wave of latter-day economic and cultural confidence.

But just because the double-deckers are disappearing and the telephone boxes have taken on a steely grey hue (room-temperature beer can still be found if you head to the right pub), doesn't mean that Britain has abandoned the qualities that still make it great for travellers.

Cosmopolitan London remains one of the most exciting cities in the world, with rising post-industrial challengers like Manchester, Bristol and Glasgow jostling for the mantle of Britain's second-most vibrant metropolis. For nature-huggers, there are plenty of remote areas of jaw-dropping beauty, including the desolate Devon moors, the craggy Scottish Highlands and the pretty, sheep-strewn Cotswolds. And for those who like their history served on a platter with its heart still beating, almost every town in the country has an ancient market square and a clutch of centuries-old pubs and churches that are still in use to this day.

Whether it's history, nature or contemporary culture that attracts you to Britain's shores, it's clear that leaving your preconceptions at the border is a good idea. This diverse yet easily travelled land is ideal for wandering off the beaten path. And if you happen to find a double-decker bus along the way, don't forget to take a photo.

FAST FACTS

- **Area** 240,000 sq km (149,000 sq miles)
- **Capital** London
- **Currency** pound sterling (£); A$1 = £0.40; ¥100 = £0.47; NZ$1 = £0.33; US$1 = £0.52; €1 = £0.68
- **Famous for** historic sites, rolling countryside, haggis, tea, football, Shakespeare, royal family
- **Official Languages** English, Gaelic, Welsh
- **Phrases** where's the toilet?; can I have the bill please?; one overseas postcard stamp please
- **Population** 60 million
- **Telephone Codes** country code ☎ 44; international operator for overseas reverse-charges calls ☎ 155; international access code ☎ 00

HIGHLIGHTS

- Take in some of London's bustling **markets** (p176), saving room for a strolling smorgasbord of great food.
- Stroke your chin with artistic understanding at contemporary galleries, like Newcastle's **Baltic** (p228), Bristol's **Arnolfini** (p204) and London's **Tate Modern** (p163).
- Tramp through the mist and aim for the desolate summit of **Snowdon** (p271), the highest peak in Wales.
- Laugh yourself silly with a gaggle of comedy shows at the gargantuan **Edinburgh Fringe Festival** (p247).
- Duck down the historic back alley 'shuts' of **Shrewsbury** (p213), Britain's greatest Tudor town.

ITINERARIES

Depending on the duration of your stay, consider the following itineraries:

- **One week** Travel west from London to Winchester, England's ancient capital, then continue to Salisbury for a saunter around Stonehenge. Head northwest to Bath, a World Heritage city, then drop into Bristol for its contemporary vibe. End your stay in Glastonbury, overlooking the countryside from the hilltop Tor.
- **Two weeks** Drive north from London to the dreamy spires of Cambridge, then continue to York, the ancient Viking capital. Next stop is Durham, with its stunning cathedral, followed by miles of gorgeous Northumbrian countryside. Head across the border into Scotland and make for Edinburgh before continuing via the Grampians to Inverness, the gateway to the Highlands.

CLIMATE & WHEN TO GO

Although Britain's climate is generally mild and its annual rainfall unspectacular, grey, overcast skies can make for depressing days any time of year. Average July temperatures in London are 22°C (71°F) and the average January temperature is 4°C (39°F). Further north it's cooler. For more information, see Climate Charts (p1100).

July and August are the busiest months for tourism, often leading to headache-inducing crowds at major attractions. Flights and accommodation can be prohibitively expensive during this period. You are just as likely to enjoy fine weather in late spring and early autumn, so May to June and September to mid-October are recommended as alternative times to visit.

HOW MUCH?

- **Hostel bed** £16
- **Restaurant main** £8
- **Loaf of bread** £0.65
- **Local phone call** £0.20
- **Cappuccino** £2

LONELY PLANET INDEX

- **1L petrol** £0.90
- **1L bottled water** £0.50
- **Pint of beer** £2.25
- **Souvenir T-shirt** £10
- **Takeaway fish and chips** £4

HISTORY

See individual England (p148), Scotland (p240) and Wales (p266) history sections in this chapter for in-depth information on Britain's colourful past.

PEOPLE

With a population of 60 million, Britain is one of the world's most densely populated nations. Despite this, there are a myriad of distinct regional identities: it's common to travel less than 50 miles and find a completely different accent with its own special vocabulary. Southerners will tell you they don't understand a word uttered by the Geordies, while northerners will happily tease the Welsh over the way they speak. For the most part, this regional rivalry is fairly friendly – although it's wise to avoid calling someone 'English' if they come from Scotland or Wales. Indeed, the independent-minded Scots and Welsh often view themselves as separate races from the English.

RELIGION

In the nation's most recent census, 72% of Brits identified themselves as Christians, with Muslims being the second-biggest group at 3%. The remaining largest faiths were Hindus, Sikhs, Jews and Buddhists. Around 16% said they had no religion – a

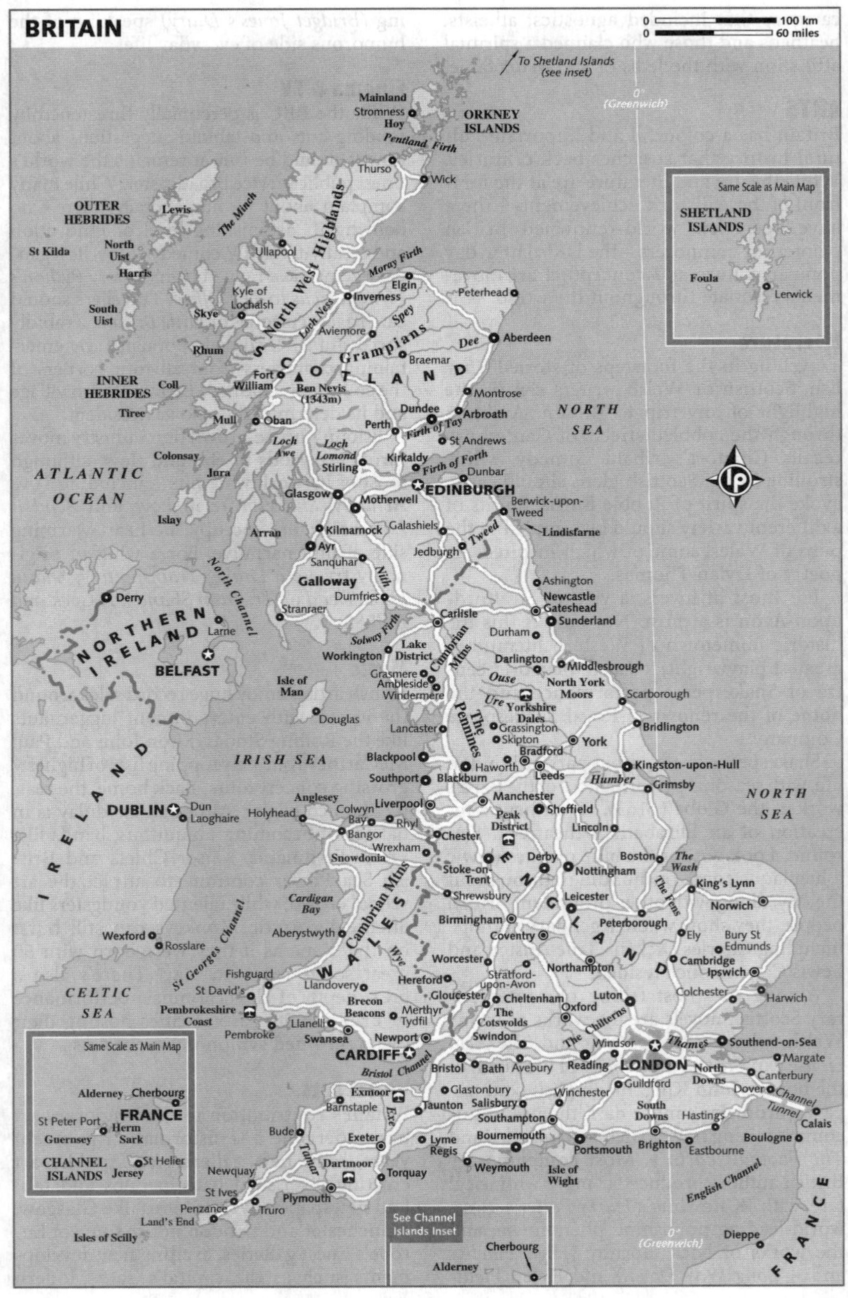
BRITAIN
0 100 km
0 60 miles
To Shetland Islands (see inset)
0° (Greenwich)
Same Scale as Main Map
SHETLAND ISLANDS
Foula
Lerwick
Mainland
Stromness
Hoy
ORKNEY ISLANDS
Pentland Firth
Thurso
Wick
OUTER HEBRIDES
Lewis
The Minch
St Kilda
North Uist
Harris
South Uist
Ullapool
North West Highlands
Moray Firth
Elgin
Peterhead
Inverness
Kyle of Lochalsh
Skye
Loch Ness
Spey
Aviemore
Grampians
Dee
Aberdeen
Rhum
Braemar
SCOTLAND
Fort William
Ben Nevis (1343m)
INNER HEBRIDES
Coll
Tiree
Montrose
NORTH SEA
Dundee
Arbroath
Mull
Oban
Perth
Firth of Tay
St Andrews
Loch Awe
Loch Lomond
Colonsay
Kirkaldy
Stirling
Firth of Forth
Dunbar
ATLANTIC OCEAN
Jura
Glasgow
EDINBURGH
Motherwell
Berwick-upon-Tweed
Islay
Arran
Kilmarnock
Galashiels
Lindisfarne
Tweed
Ayr
Jedburgh
Sanquhar
North Channel
Nith
Galloway
Ashington
Dumfries
Newcastle
Gateshead
Derry
Stranraer
Carlisle
Sunderland
NORTHERN IRELAND
Larne
Solway Firth
BELFAST
Durham
Lake District
Workington
Cumbrian Mtns
Darlington
Middlesbrough
Isle of Man
Grasmere
Ambleside
Windermere
Ouse
North York Moors
Scarborough
Ure
Yorkshire Dales
Douglas
The Pennines
Grassington
Lancaster
Bridlington
Skipton
York
IRISH SEA
Bradford
Blackpool
Haworth
Leeds
Kingston-upon-Hull
Southport
Blackburn
Humber
Grimsby
NORTH SEA
Anglesey
Manchester
IRELAND
DUBLIN
Dun Laoghaire
Holyhead
Colwyn Bay
Liverpool
Sheffield
Rhyl
Peak District
Lincoln
Bangor
Chester
Wrexham
Snowdonia
Boston
The Wash
Derby
Stoke-on-Trent
Nottingham
ENGLAND
The Fens
King's Lynn
Shrewsbury
Cardigan Bay
Leicester
Norwich
Cambrian Mtns
WALES
Birmingham
Peterborough
Wexford
Rosslare
Aberystwyth
Coventry
Ely
Bury St Edmunds
St Georges Channel
Wye
Worcester
Cambridge
Northampton
Fishguard
Stratford-upon-Avon
Ipswich
Llandovery
Hereford
CELTIC SEA
St David's
Gloucester
Cheltenham
Luton
Colchester
Harwich
Pembrokeshire Coast
Brecon Beacons
Merthyr Tydfil
The Cotswolds
Oxford
The Chilterns
Llanelli
Pembroke
Swansea
Newport
Swindon
Windsor
Thames
Southend-on-Sea
CARDIFF
LONDON
Margate
Bristol Channel
Bristol
Bath
Avebury
Reading
North Downs
Canterbury
Same Scale as Main Map
Alderney
Cherbourg
FRANCE
Exmoor
Glastonbury
Winchester
Guildford
Dover
Channel Tunnel
Barnstaple
Taunton
Salisbury
Exe
South Downs
St Peter Port
Herm
Southampton
Hastings
Calais
Guernsey
Sark
Bude
Exeter
Lyme Regis
Bournemouth
Brighton
Boulogne
CHANNEL ISLANDS
St Helier
Jersey
Tamar
Portsmouth
Eastbourne
Dartmoor
Weymouth
Isle of Wight
Newquay
Torquay
English Channel
St Ives
Plymouth
Penzance
Truro
See Channel Islands Inset
Land's End
Isles of Scilly
0° (Greenwich)
Dieppe
FRANCE
Cherbourg
Alderney

category that included agnostics, atheists, heathens and those who claimed a spiritual affiliation with the Jedis of *Star Wars* fame.

ARTS

Britain has a colourful and important cultural history that stretches back centuries. While theatre and literature are at the forefront of these historic achievements – there have been few world-renowned British painters or composers – the UK's latter-day popular culture and conceptual art movements resonate throughout the world.

Literature

Travelling in the footsteps of storied English, Scottish or Welsh writers can be the highlight of any trip to Britain. Ambling through the cobbled streets of Canterbury recalls Chaucer's ribald comedy, while strolling in the Scottish glens should easily evoke the spirit of Robbie Burns. Spirits of a different variety should be sampled in the pubs of Wales, some of which inspired the poetry of Dylan Thomas.

For most lit lovers, a visit to Stratford-upon-Avon is a must. Not only is this the historic hometown of Western literature's greatest playwright, it's also the world centre of Shakespeare performance and the home of the renowned Royal Shakespeare Company.

Shakespeare is also a big part of London life, with seasonal performances of the Bard's work at the Globe (p163), an authentic recreation of an Elizabethan theatre-in-the-round. Look out for the blue plaques (www.blueplaque.com) on buildings throughout the city; along with other prominent British people, they show where legendary authors, including Charles Dickens, Jane Austen and Lewis Carroll, once resided.

Among the most telling of contemporary Scottish novels are the works of Irvine Welsh, whose *Trainspotting* and *The Acid House* explore the underbelly of life north of the border. John King, his English counterpart, chronicles similar dark themes in uncompromising novels such as *Skinheads* and *The Football Factory*. Most contemporary British authors produce far more whimsical fare, with JK Rowling's *Harry Potter* series a world-leading publishing phenomena, and the works of Nick Hornby (*High Fidelity* and *A Long Way Down*) and Helen Fielding (*Bridget Jones's Diary*) speaking of the humorous side of everyday life.

Cinema & TV

While the BBC is perennially threatened by funding cuts and tabloid suggestions about how it should be run, it remains the world's finest public service broadcaster. While many complain about its bureaucracy, there's no denying its astonishing level of innovation and creativity. In TV comedy alone, its legendary gems have ranged from *Monty Python's Flying Circus* to *The Office*. Travellers should catch a few episodes of *Little Britain*, a rabidly successful BBC comedy populated by entertaining characters from all four corners of the country, including a certain Welsh village and its determinedly solo gay resident.

Britain's home-grown film industry moves through periods of ebb and flow, although most of its worldwide hits – including *Love Actually, Shakespeare in Love* and *Bend it Like Beckham* – occupy the heart-warming side of film narrative. For a whiff of originality try *Vera Drake, Trainspotting, Shaun of the Dead* or *Tristram Shandy: A Cock and Bull Story*.

Music

British artists enjoy huge record sales around the world, with entertainment juggernauts like the Rolling Stones, Elton John and Paul McCartney routinely topping lists of highest-grossing concert tours. Back home, the reality is much edgier. Although Coldplay is in danger of becoming ubiquitous, bands like Franz Ferdinand, Kaiser Chiefs and British Sea Power continue to attract the art school crowd, while talented youngsters like Sheffield's Arctic Monkeys can still burst on the scene as if they were born with 50 great songs ready to play. There's also a great depth of classical music performance in Britain, with several cities hosting their own renowned symphony orchestras.

Visual Arts

Britain's contribution to contemporary art has undergone a transformation in recent years, with new galleries and public art creating feverish debate in pubs and tabloid newspapers. While cities like Glasgow, Manchester and London house some of Europe's finest galleries, exciting new developments such as the capital's Tate Modern

LIGHTS, CAMERA, ACTION...

With Hollywood relying on clever set construction to make its movies, filmmakers in Britain can simply step outside. From untouched rolling vistas and dark London streets to castles, cathedrals and villages that have remained unchanged for centuries, the country is a giant outdoor movie set waiting to happen. For visitors, this means the fun of identifying familiar or not-so-familiar backdrops from favourite movies.

Among recent epics, the latest version of *Pride and Prejudice* brought Keira Knightley to the windswept vistas and handsome country houses of Lincolnshire (p220), Derbyshire and the Peak District (p215), while the 2006 movie version of *The Da Vinci Code* scoured the country for historic sites. Among its real-life sets – some of them standing in for other locations named in the book – were Winchester Cathedral (p188), the National Gallery (p159) and the story's climatic Rosslyn Chapel in Edinburgh.

The *Harry Potter* movie series is the most prominent user of British locations. From train stations to suburban streets and even London Zoo, these films stretch across England, with the magical Hogwarts School of Witchcraft and Wizardry being comprised from interiors and exteriors at Gloucester Cathedral, Wiltshire's Lacock Abbey, Northumberland's Alnwick Castle and Oxford's Christ Church College (p206). The most popular site for visitors, though, is Hogsmead Station. Played in the movie by the charming Goathland Station (p225) on the North York Moors, it has barely changed since opening in 1865.

Not surprisingly, London remains England's movie location capital with hundreds of films shot in and around the city since directors first began yelling 'action' more than a century ago. Celebrated movies shot here include *Elizabeth* (Tower of London), *Notting Hill* (have a guess), *Lock Stock and Two Smoking Barrels* (Staples Market and Borough Market), *The Madness of King George* (St Paul's Cathedral and Royal Naval College, Greenwich) and *Shakespeare in Love* (Marble Hill House and the Thames River near Barnes). Also check out *28 Days Later:* it includes some incredibly eerie scenes of empty London streets.

(p163) and Newcastle's Baltic (p228) have become dramatic and incredibly popular showcases for the most recent artistic movements.

Public art has also taken on a new role, with the *Angel of the North* – a giant metal sculpture known locally as the Gateshead Flasher – becoming a symbol of northern pride, while arguments over what should occupy an empty Trafalgar Square plinth show that artistic debate remains surprisingly strong. Britain's contemporary artists can always make the front pages of the tabloids, with guerrilla artist Banksy regularly stoking the fires of controversy by smuggling his works onto the walls of august galleries or depositing his installations in prominent public places.

ENVIRONMENT

The Land

At less than 600 miles from north to south and under 300 miles at its widest point, Britain is roughly the same size as New Zealand or half the size of France. There's a huge array of landscapes, including the craggy Snowdonia mountains in northwest Wales (p271), the rolling Yorkshire Dales in England (p224) and the barren, windswept islands off western Scotland (p264).

Wildlife

Mostly famous for being run over on roads, hedgehogs are commonly found throughout Britain, including in urban settings where they scavenge for food at night. Another night-time scavenger, although a far rarer sight, is the red fox. While deer occupy large estates, particularly in the north, you are much more likely to see a grey squirrel. This ubiquitous tree-hopper may look cute but it was originally an interloper from North America and has pushed the smaller, indigenous red squirrel closer to extinction.

While it might seem that pigeons dominate the skies, Britain's colourful and varied birdlife includes river-dwelling herons, coastal guillemots and the ever-popular red-breasted robin. In the wilds of Scotland, you may spot a golden eagle, Britain's largest bird of prey.

Environmental Issues

Farming methods adopted after WWII saw the swift demolition of much of Britain's archetypal patchwork landscape, replacing stone walls, ancient wetlands and centuries-old hedgerows with vast, open fields. These hedgerows – knotty shrubs and bushes that sheltered some of Britain's most vulnerable flowers, insects and small mammals – have almost disappeared in some regions, taking their rare flora and fauna with them.

While experiments with alternative energy have seen wind and solar farms emerging across the UK, there remains a not-in-my-backyard rejection from many communities to these developments, leading the government to seriously suggest a new generation of nuclear power plants to meet the nation's future energy requirements.

FOOD & DRINK

The words 'British' and 'cuisine' never used to be uttered in the same sentence without a nervous laugh or gagging reflex. Those days are long gone and there's now a rich variety of well-prepared regional dishes alongside an impressive array of cosmopolitan options, reflecting the nation's burgeoning ethnic diversity.

Staples & Specialities

While the rib-sticking breakfast fry-up has changed little over the years, Britain's other traditional dishes have been reinvented for foodies at some of the nation's finest restaurants. These newly revered dishes – still available in less gourmet fashion at pubs across the land – include fish and chips, bangers and mash, steak and kidney pie, Sunday roast and ploughman's lunch: a salad heavily reliant on pickles, cheese and cold pies rather than fresh vegetables.

Most Brits have also embraced a huge variety of ethnic cuisines, with Chinese and Indian restaurants now more common than traditional English chippies. Indeed, curry from the Indian subcontinent is the most popular food in Britain, with cities like Glasgow, Birmingham and Manchester vying to be the nation's curry capital.

Where to Eat & Drink

There's a good variety of eateries in most towns, with vegetarians catered for on many menus. Cities often have vegan and vegetarian-only restaurants if you prefer not to sit with the meat-eating crowd. While not every pub serves food, most provide inexpensive, filling meals. It's also the perfect opportunity to try some regional beers. If you've been raised on lager, a traditional bitter or ale is a bit of a shock – not as cold or as effervescent. Keep in mind that Scotland has introduced a nonsmoking ban in pubs and restaurants, with England and Wales set to introduce similar bans in 2007.

ENGLAND

When the government's Department for Culture launched a campaign to discover England's enduring icons in 2006, they kicked-off with a top 12 of well-worn classics. Spitfire war planes, the FA Cup and *Alice in Wonderland* made the cut, while chestnuts like Stonehenge and cups of tea rounded out the numbers.

But when organisers opened the list to public nomination, they were overwhelmed with suggestions for icons they hadn't even thought of, creating a collage of self-reflection from the population about what being English really means. Eschewing the obvious, suggestions included gin, Penguin books, the *Teletubbies,* regional accents, John Cleese's silly walk and closed-circuit TV cameras in public places.

With Scotland and Wales gaining more power to run their own affairs in recent years, the 'idea' of England – as opposed to Britain – is clearly back on the agenda. For visitors, the debate indicates the surprising level of diversity they can expect to experience here. Rolling hills, thatch-roofed cottages and olde-world pubs are a given, but latter-day England is also stuffed with exciting cities like Bristol, Manchester and Newcastle; dripping with excellent beaches from Whitby to Newquay; and coloured by accessible outdoor adventure in regions like Exmoor, the Peak District and the North York Moors.

HISTORY

Celts & Romans

Populated by bands of hunter-gatherers for centuries, England was shaken from its stupor around 4000 BC when modern Europeans, wielding new-fangled stone tools,

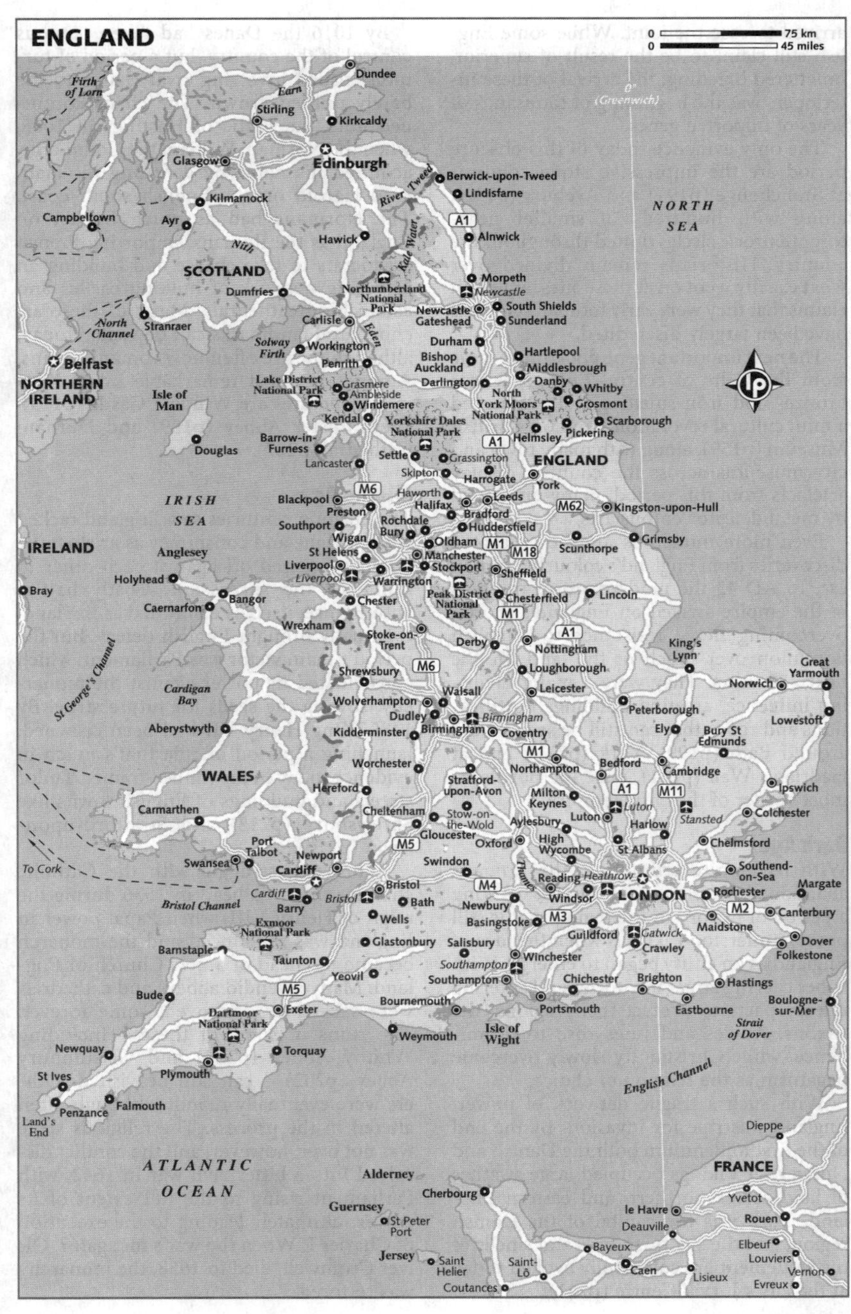
ENGLAND
0 75 km
0 45 miles
0° (Greenwich)
NORTH SEA
IRISH SEA
ATLANTIC OCEAN
English Channel
Strait of Dover
Bristol Channel
Cardigan Bay
St George's Channel
Solway Firth
Firth of Lorn
North Channel
To Cork
SCOTLAND
ENGLAND
WALES
NORTHERN IRELAND
IRELAND
FRANCE
Dundee
Earn
Stirling
Kirkcaldy
Edinburgh
Glasgow
Berwick-upon-Tweed
River Tweed
Lindisfarne
Kilmarnock
Campbeltown
Ayr
A1
Alnwick
Hawick
Nith
Kale Water
Morpeth
Northumberland National Park
Newcastle
Dumfries
Newcastle
Gateshead
South Shields
Sunderland
Stranraer
Carlisle
Eden
Belfast
Workington
Durham
Hartlepool
Penrith
Bishop Auckland
Middlesbrough
Isle of Man
Lake District National Park
Grasmere
Ambleside
Windermere
Darlington
Danby
Whitby
North York Moors National Park
Grosmont
Kendal
Yorkshire Dales National Park
Scarborough
Douglas
Barrow-in-Furness
Helmsley
Pickering
Lancaster
Settle
Grassington
Skipton
Harrogate
York
M6
Blackpool
Haworth
Leeds
Preston
Halifax
Bradford
M62
Kingston-upon-Hull
Rochdale
Southport
Bury
Huddersfield
Grimsby
Wigan
Oldham
M1
M18
Scunthorpe
Anglesey
St Helens
Manchester
Liverpool
Stockport
Liverpool
Warrington
Sheffield
Holyhead
Bray
Bangor
Chester
Peak District National Park
Chesterfield
Lincoln
Caernarfon
Wrexham
Stoke-on-Trent
Derby
Nottingham
King's Lynn
Loughborough
Shrewsbury
Great Yarmouth
Norwich
Walsall
Leicester
Wolverhampton
Peterborough
Lowestoft
Dudley
Birmingham
Aberystwyth
Kidderminster
Birmingham
Coventry
Ely
Bury St Edmunds
Northampton
Bedford
Worchester
Cambridge
Stratford-upon-Avon
Hereford
Milton Keynes
Ipswich
M11
Carmarthen
Luton
Cheltenham
Stow-on-the-Wold
Aylesbury
Luton
Stansted
Colchester
Harlow
Gloucester
High Wycombe
Port Talbot
Oxford
Chelmsford
M5
St Albans
Newport
Swansea
Cardiff
Swindon
Southend-on-Sea
Reading
Heathrow
Bristol
M4
Thames
Margate
Cardiff
Barry
Bristol
Bath
Newbury
Windsor
LONDON
Rochester
M2
Canterbury
Wells
Basingstoke
M3
Maidstone
Exmoor National Park
Guildford
Gatwick
Dover
Glastonbury
Salisbury
Crawley
Folkestone
Barnstaple
Winchester
Taunton
Southampton
Yeovil
Southampton
Chichester
Brighton
Hastings
Bude
Bournemouth
Portsmouth
Eastbourne
Boulogne-sur-Mer
Exeter
Dartmoor National Park
Weymouth
Isle of Wight
Newquay
Torquay
Plymouth
St Ives
Penzance
Falmouth
Land's End
Dieppe
Alderney
Cherbourg
Yvetot
Guernsey
le Havre
St Peter Port
Deauville
Rouen
Elbeuf
Bayeux
Jersey
Saint Helier
Saint-Lô
Louviers
Caen
Lisieux
Vernon
Coutances
Evreux

BRITAIN

arrived to case the joint. While some English still claim to be the result of superior, unfettered breeding, the arrival of these interlopers was the beginning of thousands of years of imported genes.

The only evidence today of this obscure period are the impressive stone columns at Stonehenge (p191) and Avebury (p192), along with hundreds of smaller near-forgottenrock circles dotted throughout the country. Historians remain divided over what exactly went on at these sites, although claims that they were early football stadiums have been largely discredited.

The next important gene pool influx came from the Celts of central Europe, whose bronze- and iron-smelting skills launched a mini cultural revolution. London's British Museum (p159), along with many town and city museums across the country, display artefacts from this period, many unearthed by metal detector enthusiasts.

Even more numerous are the excavated discoveries from England's colourful Roman era. In AD 43 the modern storm troopers of the empire arrived on England's shores, overcoming fierce resistance to establish dominion over much of the land for the next 350 years. They were a major civilising influence, creating buildings, fortifications and roads that can still be seen in and around Bath (p199), York (p221), and at Hadrian's Wall (p231), once the northernmost border of the entire empire.

Dark Ages

With its empire crumbling, the Romans abandoned the island around 410, sparking a period of history in the region that is still poorly understood. This is when the idea of England as an entity began to emerge. With tribes carving larger territories and entering uneasy pacts to protect their regions, the Saxons, Angles and Jutes rose to prominence, while Christianity slowly overcame paganism as the religion of choice.

With such a fragile network of power, England was ripe for invasion. By the end of the first millennium both the Danish and Norwegian Vikings occupied large swathes of land across northern and eastern England. York was the capital of the Danish region, and the sights, sounds and smells of the settlement are colourfully evoked today at the city's Jorvik Centre (p221).

By 1016 the Danes had taken tenuous control of the country, but a period of turmoil ensued involving rival claims to the barely unified crown. The chaos continued until the Battle of Hastings in 1066, when the Norman, William the Conqueror, acquired his name by defeating his main rival Harold on the English south coast. The Normans had as much impact on England as the Romans, importing French aristocrats to take charge and building an imposing network of hulking castles and astonishing cathedrals. Many of these architectural landmarks can be visited today, although they're often now romantic ruins. Among the most remarkable intact Norman structures are Windsor Castle (p179), Westminster Abbey (p159) and Durham Cathedral (p227).

Middle Ages

The ensuing centuries saw England racked with intrigue and conspiracy as aristocratic families squared off against each other to influence the succession. Costly battles with France, itself as disunified as England, eventually brought English defeat. But the period's main victor was Parliament, which consolidated its power against the monarchy, sowing the seeds for future strife. By 1485, King Henry VII had been crowned, launching a period of rule that's much in evidence today in the timber-framed Tudor streets and buildings of English towns like Shrewsbury (p213) and Stratford-upon-Avon (p210).

A brewing struggle with the Catholic church came to a head in 1536 during the reign of Henry VIII, when Papal power in England was renounced and the monarch became the head of a new Church of England. Many splendid abbeys and cathedrals were sacked or destroyed, some forever. The ruins of some of these – including Whitby Abbey (p226) and Glastonbury Abbey (p202) – can still be visited. Others were eventually rebuilt, although often altered in the process. The religious strife was not over, however, and the conflict dissolved into a bitter civil war in 1642, with Parliament rising to the full extent of its power, ultimately leading to the execution of Charles I. When the war's instigator, Oliver Cromwell, died in 1658, the monarchy was restored.

Victorian Age

The monarchy and Parliament were never the same again. By the 18th century the new position of prime minister began to assume greater power while the monarchy, soon represented by Queen Victoria, sank into a largely ceremonial role.

By the 19th century England had built a formidable global empire and was using its territories to fuel immense commercial expansion. The country was perfectly positioned to launch the Industrial Revolution, which tied machine innovation to the population explosion. The lasting cultural impact of the Victorian era is still evident throughout the country in the enormous 19th-century, glass-roofed train stations and magnificent public buildings that can be found in cities such as London, Newcastle and Manchester.

New Labour, New Millennium

England's 20th century was a period of war and end-of-empire followed by cultural and economic resurgence. Two world wars brought the nation almost to its knees, although many still recall the 1940 Battle of Britain, when the English resisted a three-month air attack from Germany, as its finest hour. Many former colonies were restored to independence after WWII and the nation's manufacturing industries entered a period of slow, painful decline.

By the 1990s, though, England had bounced back and entered the new millennium with one of the world's strongest economies. Its role on the world stage was exemplified by its relationship with the USA and participation in military campaigns in Afghanistan and Iraq. Echoing a history of protest, millions took to the streets of London and other major English cities to protest the nation's involvement. In 2005, terrorist bombs killed dozens on public transit in the capital, a direct reaction to Britain's support for the War on Terror.

With the country's Labour Prime Minister Tony Blair coming towards the end of his final term in office, Britain's political future is entering a period of uncertainty. Dour Gordon Brown is preparing to take over and square-off against a slowly regrouping Conservative Party that is itching to repeat the hold on power it enjoyed under Margaret Thatcher.

PEOPLE

With 49.5 million residents, England dominates the numbers when it comes to Britain's population. But there is great cultural diversity throughout the country's many regions, with most areas retaining a distinct identity, complete with specific accents and vocabulary. Many English towns and cities – particularly London, Birmingham and Manchester – have large and vibrant Asian communities. For an insight into the English psyche, flick through Kate Fox's entertaining *Watching the English: The Hidden Rules of English Social Behaviour*.

LONDON

☎ 020 / pop 7.4 million

Like a mid-sized country on its own, London has enough history, vitality and cultural drive to keep most visitors occupied for weeks. But while first-timers come thinking they'll spend their time snapping photos of red double-decker buses and Trafalgar Square pigeons, they discover the city that accounts for almost a sixth of England's total population has moved on from its clichéd persona.

In recent years this most cosmopolitan of world capitals has led international trends in music, fashion and the arts, riding a wave of 21st-century British confidence that has washed into areas of the city that were formerly dark and depressing. Adding to established tourist-haven neighbourhoods like Westminster, Knightsbridge and the City, reinvented areas of London like Clerkenwell and the South Bank have become visitor-friendly. It's a process that, with the Olympic Games rolling into town in 2012, will continue to alter London's tourist landscape. The downside of this gentrification, of course, is increasing cost: London is now Europe's most expensive city for visitors.

But while popular attractions like the London Eye (p163) and the Tower of London (p162) remain expensive, there are dozens of excellent free or nearly free sights that can help keep travel budgets down. These include the Tate Modern (p163), the National Gallery (p159) and the Victoria & Albert Museum (p161). And just wandering the streets of London (stopping only for a cheap lunch-time sandwich to scoff in a nearby

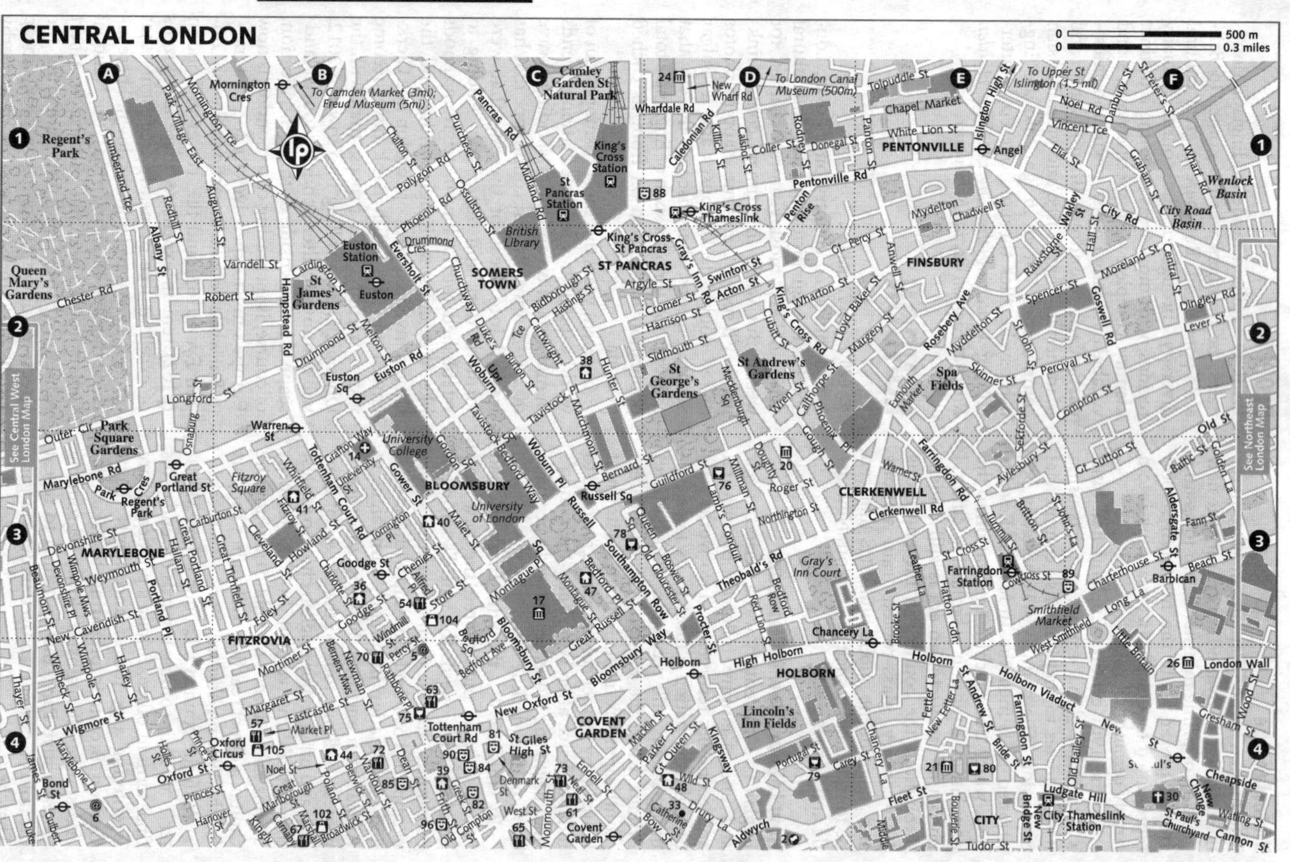
CENTRAL LONDON
0 500 m
0 0.3 miles
See Central West London Map
See Northeast London Map
To Camden Market (3mi); Freud Museum (5mi)
To London Canal Museum (500m)
To Upper St Islington (1.5 mi)
Regent's Park
Queen Mary's Gardens
Park Square Gardens
Camley Garden St Natural Park
King's Cross Station
St Pancras Station
King's Cross Thameslink
King's Cross-St Pancras
Euston Station
Euston
Euston Sq
Warren St
Great Portland St
Regent's Park
British Library
St James' Gardens
St George's Gardens
St Andrew's Gardens
Spa Fields
University College
University of London
Fitzroy Square
Gray's Inn Court
Lincoln's Inn Fields
Smithfield Market
Farringdon Station
Barbican
City Thameslink Station
Wenlock Basin
City Road Basin
PENTONVILLE
FINSBURY
ST PANCRAS
SOMERS TOWN
BLOOMSBURY
CLERKENWELL
MARYLEBONE
FITZROVIA
HOLBORN
COVENT GARDEN
CITY
Angel
Russell Sq
Goodge St
Tottenham Court Rd
Oxford Circus
Bond St
Holborn
Chancery La
Covent Garden
St Paul's
Pentonville Rd
Euston Rd
Hampstead Rd
Tottenham Court Rd
Gower St
Gray's Inn Rd
King's Cross Rd
Farringdon Rd
Clerkenwell Rd
Goswell Rd
City Rd
Rosebery Ave
Theobald's Rd
High Holborn
Holborn Viaduct
New Oxford St
Oxford St
Kingsway
Southampton Row
Aldersgate St
Fleet St
Ludgate Hill
Cheapside
London Wall
Aldwych

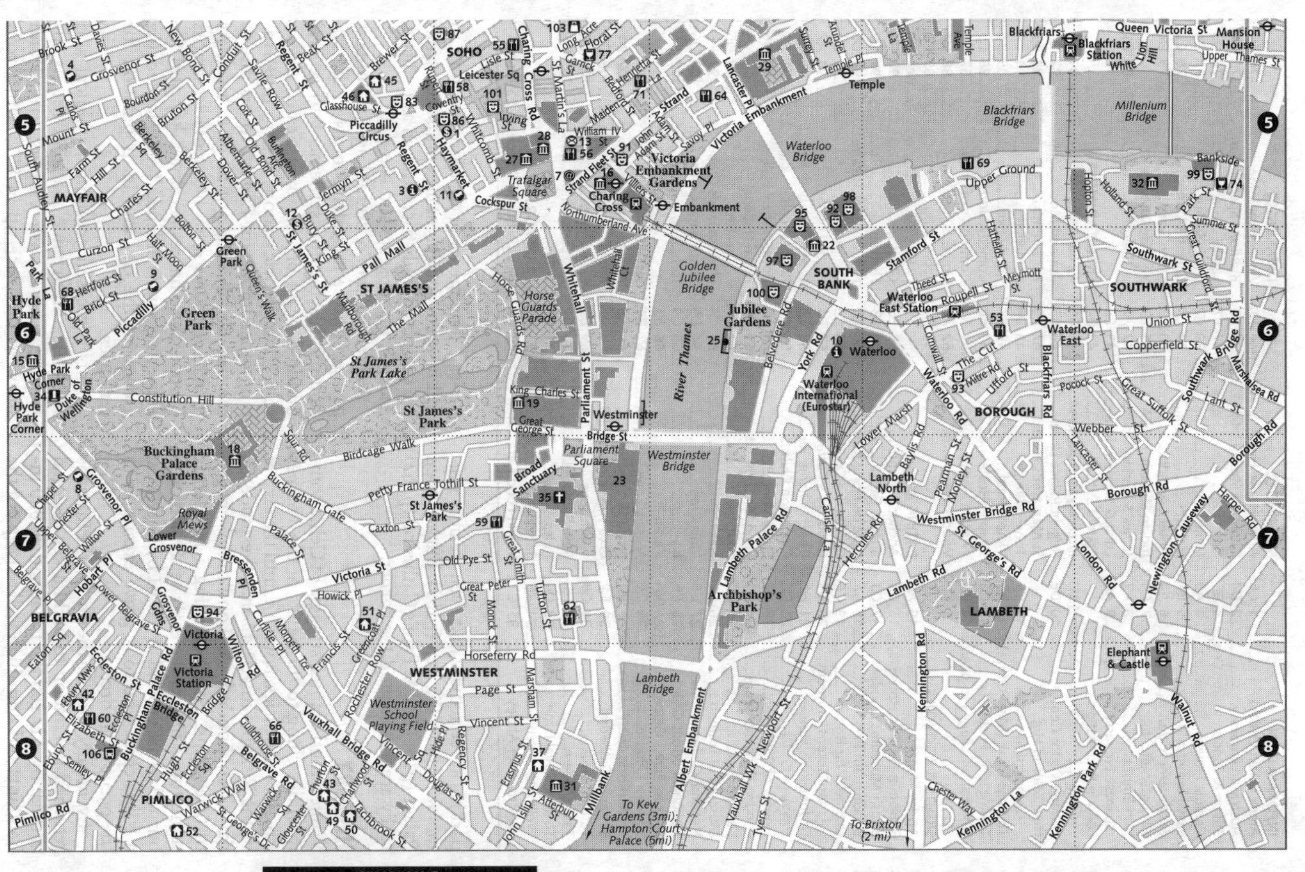
SOHO
MAYFAIR
ST JAMES'S
SOUTHWARK
SOUTH BANK
BOROUGH
LAMBETH
WESTMINSTER
BELGRAVIA
PIMLICO
River Thames
Millenium Bridge
Blackfriars Bridge
Waterloo Bridge
Golden Jubilee Bridge
Westminster Bridge
Lambeth Bridge
Green Park
St James's Park
St James's Park Lake
Buckingham Palace Gardens
Royal Mews
Jubilee Gardens
Victoria Embankment Gardens
Archbishop's Park
Westminster School Playing Field
Horse Guards Parade
Trafalgar Square
Parliament Square
Piccadilly Circus
Leicester Sq
Charing Cross
Embankment
Temple
Blackfriars
Blackfriars Station
Mansion House
Waterloo
Waterloo East
Waterloo East Station
Waterloo International (Eurostar)
Lambeth North
Elephant & Castle
Westminster
Hyde Park Corner
Victoria
Victoria Station
Piccadilly
Pall Mall
The Mall
Whitehall
Parliament St
Strand
Haymarket
Regent St
Charing Cross Rd
Victoria Embankment
Albert Embankment
Millbank
Waterloo Rd
Blackfriars Rd
Westminster Bridge Rd
Kennington Rd
Lambeth Rd
Lambeth Palace Rd
Borough Rd
London Rd
Newington Causeway
Southwark Bridge Rd
Southwark St
Victoria St
Vauxhall Bridge Rd
Buckingham Palace Rd
Constitution Hill
Birdcage Walk
Horse Guards Rd
Kennington Park Rd
Kennington La
To Kew Gardens (3mi); Hampton Court Palace (5mi)
To Brixton (2 mi)
BRITAIN

INFORMATION
- Amex (Main Office) 1 C5
- Australian Embassy 2 D4
- Britain & London Visitor Centre 3 B5
- Canada House 4 A5
- easyInternetcafe 5 B4
- easyInternetcafe 6 A4
- easyInternetcafe 7 C5
- Irish Embassy 8 A7
- Japanese Embassy 9 A6
- London Information Centre (see 101)
- London Visitor Centre 10 D6
- New Zealand High Commission 11 C5
- Thomas Cook (Main Office) 12 B5
- Trafalgar Sq Post Office 13 C5
- University College Hospital 14 B3

SIGHTS & ACTIVITIES
- Apsley House 15 A6
- Benjamin Franklin House 16 C5
- British Museum 17 C3
- Buckingham Palace 18 B7
- Cabinet War Rooms 19 C6
- Charles Dickens Museum 20 D3
- Dr Johnson's House 21 E4
- Hayward Gallery 22 D6
- Houses of Parliament 23 C7
- London Canal Museum 24 D1
- London Eye 25 D6
- Museum of London 26 F4
- National Gallery 27 C5
- National Portrait Gallery 28 C5
- Shakespeare's Globe (see 99)
- Somerset House 29 D5
- St Martin-in-the-Fields (see 56)
- St Paul's Cathedral 30 F4
- Tate Britain 31 C8
- Tate Modern 32 F5
- Theatre Royal Drury Lane 33 D4
- Wellington Arch 34 A6
- Westminister Abbey 35 C7

SLEEPING
- Arran House Hotel (see 40)
- Charlotte Street Hotel 36 B3
- City Inn 37 C8
- Generator 38 C2
- Hazlitt's 39 C4
- Hotel Cavendish 40 C3
- Indian Student YMCA 41 B3
- James & Cartref Houses 42 A8
- Luna & Simone Hotel 43 B8
- Oxford St YHA 44 B4
- Piccadilly Backpackers 45 B5
- Regent Palace Hotel 46 B5
- St Margaret's Hotel 47 C3
- Travelodge 48 D4
- Victor Hotel 49 B8
- Victoria Hostel 50 B8
- Wigram House 51 B7
- Windermere Hotel 52 A8

EATING
- Anchor & Hope 53 E6
- Busaba Eathai 54 B3
- Café de Hong Kong 55 C5
- Café in the Crypt 56 C5
- Carluccio's Caffe 57 B4
- Chuen Cheng Ku 58 C5
- Cinnamon Club 59 C7
- Ebury Wine Bar 60 A8
- Food for Thought 61 C4
- Footstool 62 C7
- Hakkasan 63 C4
- India Club 64 D5
- Ivy 65 C4
- Kazan 66 B8
- Masala Zone 67 B4
- Nobu 68 A6
- Oxo Tower Restaurant & Brasserie 69 E5
- Rasa Sumudra 70 B4
- Rules 71 C5
- Satsuma 72 B4
- World Food Café 73 C4

DRINKING
- Anchor Bankside 74 F5
- Bradley's Spanish Bar 75 B4
- Lamb 76 D3
- Lamb & Flag 77 C5
- Queen's Larder 78 C3
- Seven Stars 79 D4
- Ye Olde Cheshire Cheese 80 E4

ENTERTAINMENT
- 12 Bar Club 81 C4
- Amused Moose Soho 82 C4
- Bar Rhumba 83 B5
- Borderline 84 C4
- Candy Bar 85 B4
- Comedy Store 86 C5
- Compton's of Soho 87 C5
- Cross 88 D1
- Fabric 89 F3
- Fiction (see 88)
- Ghetto 90 C4
- Heaven 91 C5
- National Film Theatre 92 D5
- Old Vic 93 E6
- Pacha London 94 A7
- Queen Elizabeth Hall 95 D5
- Ronnie Scott's 96 C4
- Royal Festival Hall 97 D6
- Royal National Theatre 98 D5
- Shakespeare's Globe 99 F5
- South Bank Centre 100 D6
- tkts 101 C5

SHOPPING
- Agent Provocateur 102 B4
- Muji 103 C5
- Paperchase 104 C3
- Top Shop 105 B4

TRANSPORT
- Victoria Coach Station 106 A8

park) is a free activity that even wealthy visitors will enjoy: Big Ben (p159), Buckingham Palace (p161) and St Paul's Cathedral (p162) really are just around the corner.

HISTORY

While a mud-stained straggle of Celtic communities clung to the banks of the Thames River for centuries, it wasn't until the arrival of the Romans in AD 43 that the modern-day idea of London – or 'Londinium' – began to take shape. Foreshadowing a frequently tumultuous future, the early settlement was burned to the ground in AD 61 by Boudicca, a tribal chief who took grave exception to the occupying forces.

Eventually quelling the unrest, the Romans returned to London to build a key regional capital. By AD 200 the town had 30,000 inhabitants and a 6m-high wall to keep out the riff-raff. Fragments of this fortification can still be seen, and the names of its four gates are preserved in districts known as Ludgate, Aldgate, Bishopsgate and Newgate.

With their empire crumbling, the Romans gave up on the ungrateful locals in the 5th century, leaving the settlement to several hundred years of less-sophisticated Saxon rule. 'Lundenwic' soon began outstripping other important English towns due to the trading advantage of its giant river. As merchant routes grew like tentacles across Europe, the Thames became a key port for delivering goods inland. Trade fuelled the growth of the city and its population for centuries.

This increased economic, political and symbolic importance made invasions inevitable. The Danish Vikings arrived and smashed the place up in 851, with Saxon

King Alfred taking 25 years to retake and rebuild the city. A period of short-lived Saxon prosperity ensued, but the persistent Vikings finally appointed a Danish king in 1016, naming London their capital. In 1042 the Viking-friendly Saxon, Edward the Confessor, took the throne. He built Westminster Abbey – where British monarchs are still crowned – but died a few years before a turning point in English history.

The power vacuum created by Edward's death led to an international struggle for control over the country. Following a series of skirmishes, the 1066 Battle of Hastings enabled the Norman King William the Conqueror to march into London, build his citadel at the Tower of London (p162) and underline the city's pre-eminent role as capital.

With this foundation, London grew prosperous and increased in global importance throughout the medieval period, surviving devastating challenges like the 1665 Plague and 1666 Great Fire that would have gutted other cities. Instead, London simply shrugged and reinvented itself – many of the city's landmarks were built at this time by visionary architect Christopher Wren. By 1720 London had 750,000 inhabitants and was the centre of a growing world empire. Fuelled by mercantile wealth, the Victorian era was the city's golden age.

In contrast, WWII was London's darkest hour, with the city on the edge of destruction after relentless bombing. Several museums recall this period, still fresh in the memory of many locals. The ugly postwar rebuilding phase of the 1950s gave way to the cultural renaissance of the 1960s when London was the planet's undisputed swinging capital.

A couple of decades in the doldrums ensued, but today's London is both economically and culturally pre-eminent, as hip as it was in the '60s, and almost as rich as it was in the Victorian era, creating a self-confidence that fuelled its selection as 2012 Olympic Games host. But for every period of success, tragedy has never been far away. The day after winning its Olympic bid, four terrorist bombs killed dozens of people on buses and underground trains around the city. While deep anxiety initially gripped many Londoners, most soon returned to their daily routines – a response mirrored throughout the capital's turbulent history.

ORIENTATION

The Thames River, London's main geographic feature, divides the city roughly into north and south. Many of London's must-see attractions – including Buckingham Palace (p161), Big Ben (p161) and the Houses of Parliament (p161) – are located surprisingly close to each other, to north of the river in the highly walkable Westminster area.

The easy-to-use London Underground system ('the tube') is the essential method for finding your way to everything else – pick up a colour-coded underground map to navigate your way around the extensive network. Don't worry if you take a wrong turn or head in the wrong direction: getting a little bit lost on the tube is a rite of passage and it is easy to retrace your steps and find your way back to your point of origin. Many of the city's main attractions lie within the loop of the Circle Line (colour-coded yellow).

Among London's other popular districts for visitors, the West End includes major theatres, a small Chinatown, and Covent Garden's markets and buskers. The chichi Kensington and Knightsbridge areas feature pricey boutiques, major national museums and the verdant Hyde Park. The area known as the City is home to St Paul's Cathedral (p162) and a plethora of fantastic old pubs. It is also a short hop from the Tower of London (p162). The South Bank includes gentrified riverside back alleys, in addition to the Globe theatre (p163), London Eye (p163) and the Tate Modern (p163). The East End houses up-and-coming, formerly grungy areas packed with street markets and great ethnic restaurants. Heading east along the river, you will witness the dramatic revival of the Docklands and experience the colourful history of Greenwich. Turning west upriver you'll stumble upon the green havens of Richmond Park, Kew Gardens (p164) and imposing Hampton Court Palace (p165).

Major main-line train stations are dotted throughout the capital at Victoria, Waterloo, Euston, King's Cross, Paddington and Marylebone. The main bus and coach hub is Victoria Station, due south of Buckingham Palace. Pick up a *London A-Z* map book: it's the definitive street guide and comes in a handy pocket-sized version.

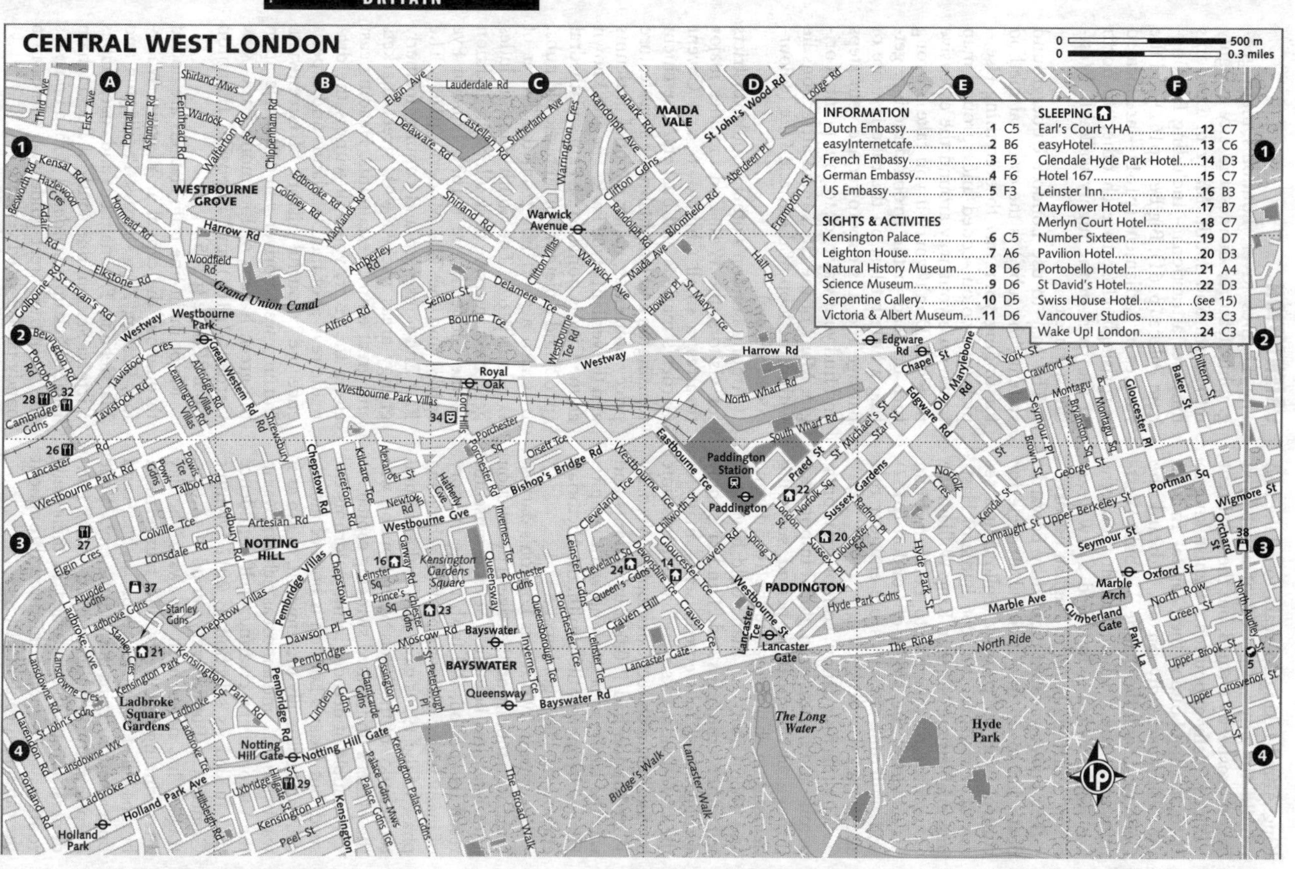
CENTRAL WEST LONDON
0 500 m
0 0.3 miles
INFORMATION
Dutch Embassy 1 C5
easyInternetcafe 2 B6
French Embassy 3 F5
German Embassy 4 F6
US Embassy 5 F3
SIGHTS & ACTIVITIES
Kensington Palace 6 C5
Leighton House 7 A6
Natural History Museum 8 D6
Science Museum 9 D6
Serpentine Gallery 10 D5
Victoria & Albert Museum 11 D6
SLEEPING
Earl's Court YHA 12 C7
easyHotel 13 C6
Glendale Hyde Park Hotel 14 D3
Hotel 167 15 C7
Leinster Inn 16 B3
Mayflower Hotel 17 B7
Merlyn Court Hotel 18 C7
Number Sixteen 19 D7
Pavilion Hotel 20 D3
Portobello Hotel 21 A4
St David's Hotel 22 D3
Swiss House Hotel (see 15)
Vancouver Studios 23 C3
Wake Up! London 24 C3
MAIDA VALE
WESTBOURNE GROVE
PADDINGTON
BAYSWATER
NOTTING HILL
Hyde Park
The Long Water
Grand Union Canal
Paddington Station
Ladbroke Square Gardens
Kensington Gardens Square

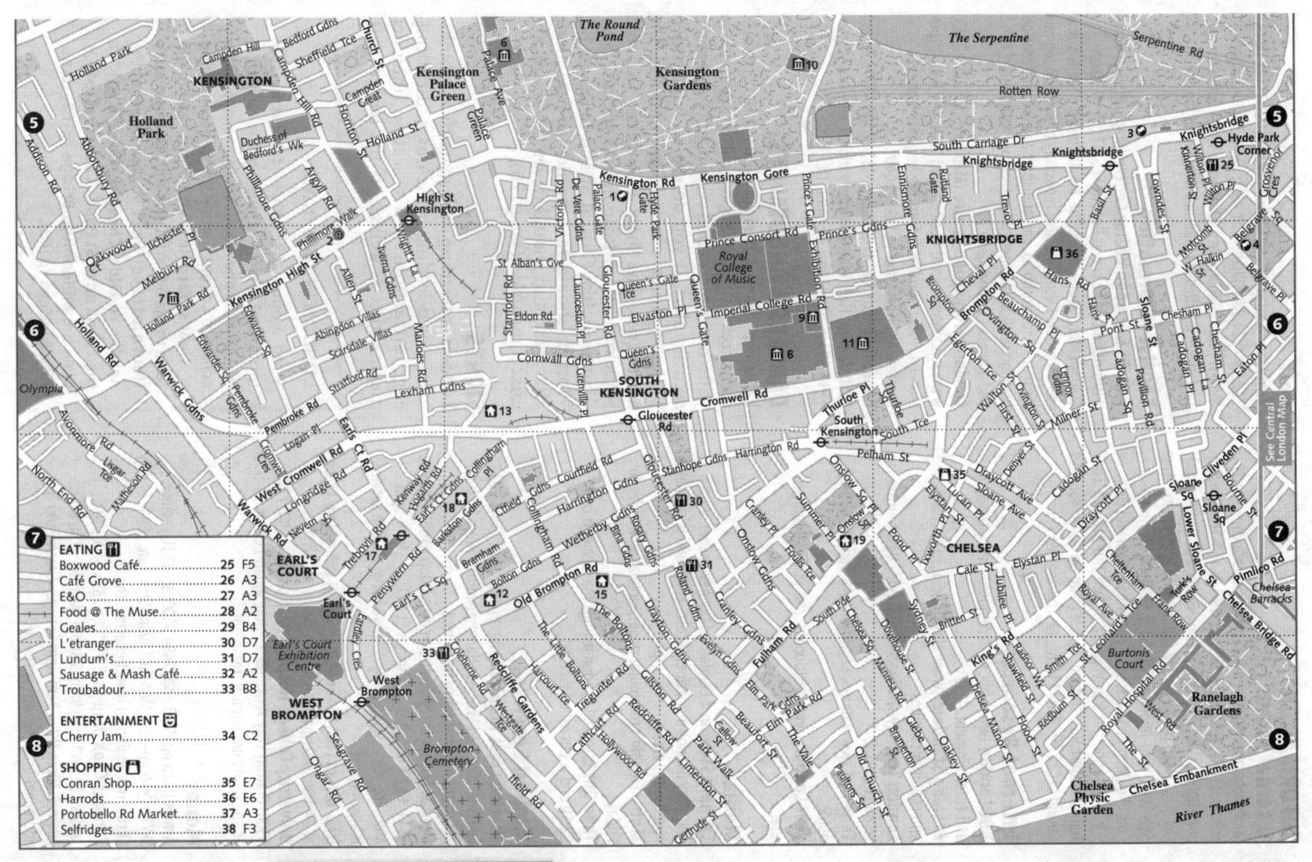

See Central London Map
EATING
Boxwood Café 25 F5
Café Grove 26 A3
E&O 27 A3
Food @ The Muse 28 A2
Geales 29 B4
L'etranger 30 D7
Lundum's 31 D7
Sausage & Mash Café 32 A2
Troubadour 33 B8
ENTERTAINMENT
Cherry Jam 34 C2
SHOPPING
Conran Shop 35 E7
Harrods 36 E6
Portobello Rd Market 37 A3
Selfridges 38 F3
KENSINGTON
KNIGHTSBRIDGE
SOUTH KENSINGTON
CHELSEA
EARL'S COURT
WEST BROMPTON
Kensington Gardens
The Serpentine
The Round Pond
Holland Park
Kensington Palace Green
Royal College of Music
Ranelagh Gardens
Chelsea Physic Garden
Burtons Court
Brompton Cemetery
Earl's Court Exhibition Centre
Olympia
River Thames
Chelsea Embankment
Hyde Park Corner
Knightsbridge
Sloane Sq
South Kensington
Gloucester Rd
High St Kensington
Earl's Court
West Brompton
Cromwell Rd
Brompton Rd
Kensington Rd
Kensington Gore
Old Brompton Rd
Fulham Rd
King's Rd
Kensington High St
Warwick Rd
Holland Rd

INFORMATION

Internet Access

easyInternetcafé (www.easyInternetcafé.com; per 20 min from £1); Kensington (Map pp156-7; 160-166 Kensington High St W8; 7am-11pm; High St Kensington); Oxford St (Map pp152-3; 358 Oxford St W1; 8am-11pm Sun-Wed, 8am-midnight Thu-Sat; Bond St); Tottenham Court Rd (Map pp152-3; 9-16 Tottenham Court Rd W1; 8am-midnight Sun-Wed, 8am-2am Thu-Sat; Tottenham Court Rd); Trafalgar Square (Map pp152-3; 456-459 Strand WC2; 8am-11pm; Charing Cross).

Internet Resources

BBC London (www.bbc.co.uk/london) News, transport and entertainment.
Evening Standard (www.thisislondon.co.uk) News and entertainment listings.
London Town (www.londontown.com) Vast tourism resource portal.
Time Out (www.timeout.com/london) Superior listings guide.
Visit London (www.visitlondon.com) Official tourism site.

Media

Evening Standard London's daily newspaper, with Thursday listings magazine. It costs £0.45 and is circulated Monday to Friday.
Metro Free slim commuter paper, circulated Monday to Friday.
Time Out Essential London listings magazine. It costs £2.50 and is published weekly.

Medical Services

Charing Cross Hospital (Map pp152-3; ☎ 8846 1234; Fulham Palace Rd W6; Hammersmith) Offers 24-hour accident and emergency treatment.
Dental Emergency Care Service (Map p160; ☎ 7188 0511; Guy's Hospital, St Thomas St SE1; 9am-5pm Mon-Fri; London Bridge) Arrive early: walk-in service is always busy.
NHS Direct (☎ 0845 4647; 24hr) Call for latest roster of 24-hour pharmacies.
University College Hospital (Map pp152-3; ☎ 7387 9300; Grafton Way WC1; Euston Square) Offers 24-hour accident and emergency treatment.

Money

Amex (Map pp152-3; ☎ 7484 9600; 30-31 Haymarket SW1; 9am-6pm Mon-Sat, 10am-5pm Sun; Piccadilly Circus) Has additional branches across the city.
Thomas Cook (Map pp152-3; ☎ 7853 6400; 30 St James's St SW1; 9am-5.30pm Mon, Tue, Thu & Fri, 10am-5.30pm Wed, 9am-4pm Sat; Green Park) Has additional branches across the city.

Post

Trafalgar Square Post Office (Map pp152-3; ☎ 0845 722 3344; 24-28 William IV St WC2; 8.30am-6.30pm Mon-Fri, 9am-5.30pm Sat; Charing Cross) Busy central post office; hundreds of branches throughout the city.

Tourist Information

Britain & London Visitor Centre (Map pp152-3; www.visitbritain.com; 1 Lower Regent St SW1; 9.30am-6.30pm Mon, 9am-6.30pm Tue-Fri, 10am-4pm Sat & Sun; Piccadilly Circus) Massive repository of free London and UK maps and brochures, plus transport and accommodation booking service, Internet computers (per 15 minute £1) and a bureau de change.
London Information Centre (Map pp152-3; 7292 2333; www.londontown.com; 1 Leicester Sq WC2; 8am-11pm Mon-Fri, 10am-6pm Sat & Sun; Leicester Square) Located in the Leicester Sq ticket booth.
London Visitor Centre (Map pp152-3; ☎ 7620 1550; Arrivals Hall, Waterloo International Terminal SE1; 8.30am-10pm) Late-opening TIC.

DANGERS & ANNOYANCES

London has considerable antiterrorist measures in place. As a visitor *never* leave your bag unattended – you may trigger a security alert. If you do see an unattended package, don't touch it and inform the authorities. The main annoyance to avoid is pickpockets, whose haunts include bustling areas like Oxford St and Leicester Sq. Women should take particular care alone after dark and should never take minicabs unaccompanied (see p178).

SIGHTS

London is teeming with magnificent buildings, world-leading museums and cutting-edge attractions. This section includes major sights as well as off-the-beaten-path

LONDON IN TWO DAYS

Stroll around the sights of **Westminster** (opposite) before enjoying the artworks of the **National Gallery** (opposite). Walk across to Covent Garden for some shopping in **Neal's Yard** (p175), before taking the tube to Blackfriars. Duck into **Dr Johnson's House** (p162) off Fleet St, grab a beer at the nearby **Ye Olde Cheshire Cheese** (p172), then stroll up to **St Paul's Cathedral** (p162). Walk the **Millennium Bridge** (p163) to the **Tate Modern** (p163).

BRITAIN

attractions that are well worth a visit. The listings are grouped by district.

The West End

NATIONAL GALLERY

Occupying a handsome promontory overlooking Trafalgar Square, the **National Gallery** (Map pp152-3; ☎ 7747 2885; www.nationalgallery.org.uk; Trafalgar Square WC2; admission free; 🕑 10am-6pm Mon-Tue & Thu-Sun, 10am-9pm Wed; ⊖ Charing Cross) is Britain's leading public art space. Seminal paintings from every epoch in art history are here, including works by Giotto, Leonardo da Vinci, Michelangelo and Van Gogh. Arrive early and take your time or target your visit to a particular period.

CHARLES DICKENS MUSEUM

London's most celebrated novelist is fondly remembered at the **Charles Dickens Museum** (Map pp152-3; ☎ 7405 2127; www.dickensmuseum.com; 48 Doughty St WC1; adult/child £5/3; 🕑 10am-5pm Mon-Sat, 11am-5pm Sun; ⊖ Russell Square), which occupyies the modest town house residence where he worked on *Pickwick Papers, Oliver Twist* and *Nicholas Nickleby.* The museum's Aladdin's cave of glass-encased Dickensia includes writing quills and the tiny wooden desk where he penned many of his great works.

NATIONAL PORTRAIT GALLERY

The excellent **National Portrait Gallery** (Map pp152-3; ☎ 7306 0055; www.npg.org.uk; 2 St Martin's Pl WC2; admission free; 🕑 10am-6pm Mon-Wed, Sat & Sun, 10am-9pm Thu & Fri; ⊖ Charing Cross) is the place to put faces to the famous and infamous names of Britain's past and present. The ground floor is the most fun, focusing on contemporary figures from popular culture, including Harry Potter actor Daniel Radcliffe – the gallery's youngest non-Royal portrait.

BENJAMIN FRANKLIN HOUSE

The recently opened **Benjamin Franklin House** (Map pp152-3; ☎ 7930 6602; www.benjaminfranklinhouse.org; 36 Craven St WC2; adult/child £8/5; 🕑 hourly tours 10am-5pm Wed-Sun; ⊖ Charing Cross) is tucked in the backstreets of Charing Cross. The Founding Father's only remaining residence in the world, entry into this steep-staired town house is by costumed tour only. You'll learn about Franklin's colourful life in London, including his predilection for standing naked at his window to 'take the air'.

ST MARTIN-IN-THE-FIELDS

There was a church on this site long before Trafalgar Square arrived out the front. Today's incarnation of **St Martin-in-the-Fields** (Map pp152-3; ☎ 7766 1100; www.stmartin-in-the-fields.org; Trafalgar Square WC2; admission free; 🕑 8am-6.30pm; ⊖ Charing Cross) was completed in 1726 and is renowned for its neoclassical and baroque flourishes. It's a busy parish church with plenty to attract visitors, including classical music concerts (tickets from £5), brass rubbing (£3 to £15) and an atmospheric crypt café.

SOMERSET HOUSE

The magnificent Georgian courtyard of **Somerset House** (Map pp152-3; ☎ 7845 4600; www.somerset-house.org.uk; Strand WC2; admission free; ⊖ Temple/Covent Garden) is a lively ice rink in winter and a concert venue in summer. Its visitor-friendly cultural collections include the **Courtauld Gallery** (☎ 7848 2526; adult/child £5/free, free 10am-2pm Mon; 🕑 10am-6pm), famous for its impressionist paintings; the **Gilbert Collection** (☎ 7420 9410; adult/child £5/free; 🕑 10am-6pm), with its decorative arts exhibitions; and the **Hermitage Rooms** (☎ 7845 4630; adult/child £5/free; 🕑 10am-6pm), with its treasures from St Petersburg's State Hermitage Museum. Combined entry tickets are available (two collections/three collections £12/8).

BRITISH MUSEUM

Founded in 1753, the **British Museum** (Map pp152-3; ☎ 7323 8299; www.thebritishmuseum.ac.uk; Great Russell St WC1; admission free; 🕑 10am-5.30pm Sat-Wed, 10am-8.30pm Thu & Fri; ⊖ Russell Square/Tottenham Court Rd) houses one of the world's oldest and finest cultural collections. With some seven million items – the result of judicious acquisition and the controversial plundering of the empire – its highlights include rooms stuffed with Egyptian, Mesopotamian, Greek and Roman antiquities. A latter-day wonder, the museum's spectacular **Great Court** is the largest covered public square in Europe.

Westminster, St James's & Pimlico

WESTMINSTER ABBEY

London's leading religious attraction, **Westminster Abbey** (Map pp152-3; ☎ 7222 5152; www.westminster-abbey.org; 20 Dean's Yard SW1; adult/child £10/6; 🕑 9.30am-4.45pm Mon-Tue & Thu-Fri, 9.30am-8pm Wed, 9.30am-2.45pm Sat, worship only Sun; ⊖ Westminster) is where most British monarchs have been crowned since Christmas Day 1066. Once

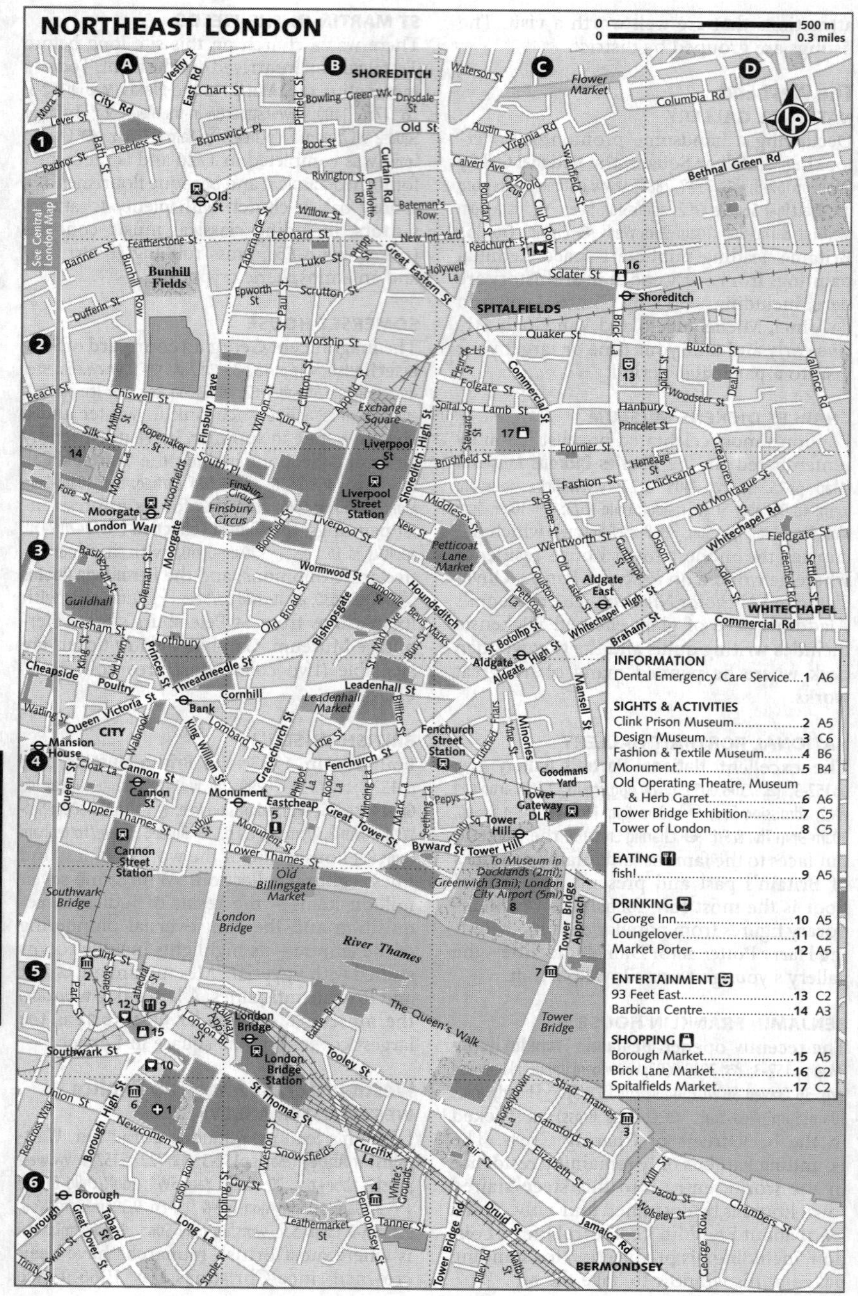
NORTHEAST LONDON
0 500 m
0 0.3 miles
A
B
C
D
1
2
3
4
5
6
SHOREDITCH
SPITALFIELDS
WHITECHAPEL
CITY
BERMONDSEY
See Central London Map
City Rd
Old St
Bethnal Green Rd
Great Eastern St
Commercial St
Shoreditch High St
Bishopsgate
Houndsditch
Whitechapel Rd
Whitechapel High St
Commercial Rd
London Wall
Moorgate
Finsbury Pave
Liverpool St
Wormwood St
Old Broad St
Threadneedle St
Cornhill
Leadenhall St
Fenchurch St
Queen Victoria St
Cannon St
Cheapside
Poultry
Lombard St
King William St
Gracechurch St
Eastcheap
Great Tower St
Byward St
Tower Hill
Upper Thames St
Lower Thames St
Minories
Mansell St
Aldgate High St
Brick La
Hanbury St
Fashion St
Wentworth St
Middlesex St
Brushfield St
Folgate St
Worship St
Chiswell St
Featherstone St
Leonard St
Luke St
Scrutton St
Redchurch St
Sclater St
Quaker St
Buxton St
Columbia Rd
Tooley St
St Thomas St
Borough High St
Southwark St
Union St
Long La
Newcomen St
Snowsfields
Druid St
Jamaica Rd
Tower Bridge Rd
Bermondsey St
Crucifix La
Shad Thames
Gainsford St
Tower Bridge Approach
River Thames
The Queen's Walk
London Bridge
Southwark Bridge
Tower Bridge
Bunhill Fields
Finsbury Circus
Exchange Square
Guildhall
Petticoat Lane Market
Leadenhall Market
Old Billingsgate Market
Flower Market
Goodmans Yard
Liverpool Street Station
Fenchurch Street Station
Cannon Street Station
London Bridge Station
Moorgate
Bank
Monument
Mansion House
Aldgate
Aldgate East
Tower Hill
Tower Gateway DLR
Shoreditch
Borough
To Museum in Docklands (2mi); Greenwich (3mi); London City Airport (5mi)
INFORMATION
Dental Emergency Care Service....1 A6
SIGHTS & ACTIVITIES
Clink Prison Museum....2 A5
Design Museum....3 C6
Fashion & Textile Museum....4 B6
Monument....5 B4
Old Operating Theatre, Museum & Herb Garret....6 A6
Tower Bridge Exhibition....7 C5
Tower of London....8 C5
EATING
fish!....9 A5
DRINKING
George Inn....10 A5
Loungelover....11 C2
Market Porter....12 A5
ENTERTAINMENT
93 Feet East....13 C2
Barbican Centre....14 A3
SHOPPING
Borough Market....15 A5
Brick Lane Market....16 C2
Spitalfields Market....17 C2
BRITAIN

a monastery, its highlights include cloistered courtyards, the fan-vaulted Henry VII chapel, and a gaggle of monuments to famous statesmen, scientists and poets.

CABINET WAR ROOMS

The evocative **Cabinet War Rooms** (Map pp152-3; ☎ 7930 6961; http://cwr.iwm.org.uk; Clive Steps, King Charles St SW1; adult/child £11/free; 9.30am-6pm; ⊖ Westminster) are the mothballed underground bunkers where Winston Churchill and his advisors ran Britain's war effort. Check out the tiny bed from where he held morning meetings and the Transatlantic Telephone Room where he called President Roosevelt. The new **Churchill Museum** adjunct delves even deeper into the war leader's life and times.

TATE BRITAIN

Ever in the shadow of its rambunctious sibling, **Tate Britain** (Map pp152-3; ☎ 7887 8000; www.tate.org; Millbank SW1; admission free; 10am-5.50pm; ⊖ Pimlico) features a world-leading collection of British art from the 16th century to the late 20th century. Keep an eye out for works by Blake, Constable, Hockney, Bacon and Moore. The Turner collection is also particularly comprehensive. There is a **boat service** (p178) to the Tate Modern from here.

APSLEY HOUSE

An 18th-century masterpiece with a multicolumned exterior and gilded, highly ornate interiors, **Apsley House** (Map pp152-3; ☎ 7499 5676; 149 Piccadilly W1; adult/child £5.10/2.60; 10am-5pm Tue-Sun Apr-Oct, 10am-4pm Tue-Sun Nov-Mar; ⊖ Hyde Park Corner) is the historic home of the Duke of Wellington – his descendants still live here. Check out the giant dinner services on the ground floor: they show that money was no substitute for taste. An excellent audioguide handset is included.

> **TOP FIVE LONDON HOUSE MUSEUMS**
>
> - Freud Museum (p164)
> - Dr Johnson's House (p162)
> - Charles Dickens Museum (p159)
> - Benjamin Franklin House (p159)
> - Leighton House (right)

BUCKINGHAM PALACE

Built for the Duke of Buckingham in 1703, **Buckingham Palace** (Map pp152-3; ☎ 7766 7300; Buckingham Palace Rd SW1; state rooms adult/child £14/8; 9.45am-6pm Aug & Sep, changing of the guard 11.30am daily May-Jul, alternate days Aug-Apr; ⊖ Green Park) has been the monarch's main London pad since 1837. The gaudily furnished **State Rooms** are open in summer for the hordes of Royal-loving tourists, but it's more fun watching the **changing of the guard** outside.

OTHER SIGHTS

The neatest and most royal of London's royal parks, **St James's Park** (Map pp152-3; The Mall SW1; 5am-dusk; ⊖ St James's Park) is also one of the city's most tranquil picnic spots.

Visit **Wellington Arch** (Map pp152-3; ☎ 7230 2726; Hyde Park Corner W1; 10am-6pm Wed-Sun Apr-Sep, 10am-5pm Wed-Sun Oct, 10am-4pm Wed-Sun Nov-Mar; ⊖ Hyde Park Corner), a restored 19th-century archway with an historic exhibition.

More impressive from the outside (especially the soaring, crenulated tower known as Big Ben), tours of the **Houses of Parliament** (Map pp152-3; ☎ 7219 3000; www.parliament.uk; Parliament Sq SW1; tour adult/child £7/5; Jul & Aug; ⊖ Westminster) are also available during MPs' summer hols.

Kensington & Knightsbridge

VICTORIA & ALBERT MUSEUM

The **Victoria & Albert Museum** (Map pp156-7; ☎ 7942 2000; www.vam.ac.uk; Cromwell Rd SW7; admission free; 10am-5.45pm Mon-Tue & Thu-Sun, 10am-10pm Wed; ⊖ South Kensington) is the world's greatest repository of decorative arts. Spread over nearly 150 galleries, it's bursting with everything from furniture to fashion and ceramics to sculpture. Regular temporary exhibitions – including recent Art Deco shows – are often must-see blockbusters.

LEIGHTON HOUSE

The home of leading Victorian artist Lord Fredric Leighton, the highlight of **Leighton House** (Map pp156-7; ☎ 7602 3316; 12 Holland Park Rd W1; adult/child £3/1; 10am-5.45pm Mon-Tue & Thu-Sun, 10am-10pm Wed; ⊖ High St Kensington) is the astonishing ground-floor Arab Hall. An homage to both ancient Islamic motifs and 19th-century English aesthetics, it's covered with swirling marble and peacock blue tiles, while its elaborate domed ceiling is awash with gold leaf. Many of Leighton's canvases line the sunlit studio upstairs.

NATURAL HISTORY MUSEUM

Fascinating interactive exhibits ensure the **Natural History Museum** (Map pp156-7; ☎ 7942 5000; www.nhm.ac.uk; Cromwell Rd SW7; admission free; 🕑 10am-5.50pm Mon-Sat, 11am-5.50pm Sun; ⊖ South Kensington) is a favourite for both kids and adults. Highlights include the Darwin Centre, with 22 million plant and animal specimens, and the Kobe earthquake simulator. Miss the towering dinosaur skeletons and the ginormous blue whale at your peril.

SCIENCE MUSEUM

The **Science Museum** (Map pp156-7; ☎ 0870 870 4868; www.sciencemuseum.org.uk; Exhibition Rd SW7; admission free; 🕑 10am-6pm; ⊖ South Kensington) does a terrific job of bringing to lustrous life a subject that can be impenetrable. Curiously, although it's stuffed with hi-tech simulators and a five-storey IMAX cinema, kids crowd in awe around the low-tech steam engines and Industrial Revolution machinery. Escape the crowds at the museum's lounge-style **Dana Centre**, an adults-only bar and café.

OTHER SIGHTS

Charming **Kensington Palace** (Map pp156-7; ☎ 0870 751 5170; www.hrp.org.uk; Kensington Gardens W8; adult/child £10.80/7.20; 🕑 10am-5pm Mar-Oct, 10am-4pm Nov-Feb; ⊖ High St Kensington/Notting Hill Gate) is the smaller royal palace that was Princess Diana's last home.

At 145 hectares **Hyde Park** (Map pp156-7; ☎ 7298 2000; 🕑 5am-dusk; ⊖ Hyde Park Corner) is a sprawling green space, with its own gallery, lake and Speakers Corner of nut-bar orators.

The City

MUSEUM OF LONDON

The underrated **Museum of London** (Map pp152-3; ☎ 0870 444 2852; www.museumoflondon.org.uk; 150 London Wall EC2; admission free; 🕑 10am-5.50pm Mon-Sat, noon-5.50pm Sun; ⊖ Barbican/St Paul's) is a recommended introduction to the city's rich history, starting with a set of 300,000-year-old flint tools found in Piccadilly. The rest is a fascinating smorgasbord of Romans, royals and rooms re-creating London's historic epochs. Don't miss the dramatic Fire of London simulation and check the museum's lively roster of temporary exhibitions.

DR JOHNSON'S HOUSE

The 18th-century residence of this most famous of Londoners, **Dr Johnson's House** (Map pp152-3; ☎ 7353 3745; www.drjh.dircon.co.uk; 17 Gough Sq EC4; adult/child £4.50/1.50; 🕑 11am-5.30pm Mon-Sat May-Sep, 11am-5pm Mon-Sat Oct-Apr; ⊖ Blackfriars) is hidden along an alleyway off Fleet St. The handsome, creaky-floored property contains the rotund raconteur's drinking chair, where he entertained pals like actor David Garrick and philosopher Edmund Burke, and the top-floor garret is where he researched his monumental *Dictionary of the English Language.*

TOWER OF LONDON

Despite the coach parties and surrounding tower blocks, it is still possible to back into a corner at the **Tower of London** (Map p160; ☎ 0870 756 6060; www.hrp.org.uk; Tower Hill EC3; adult/child £15/9.50; 🕑 9am-6pm Tue-Sat, 10am-6pm Sun-Mon Mar-Oct, 9am-5pm Tue-Sat, 10am-5pm Sun-Mon Nov-Feb; ⊖ Tower Hill) and find uninterrupted views of the crenulated medieval buildings. After the obligatory **Crown Jewels** visit, take some time to explore the walls, dungeons and museum rooms. Reserve ahead well ahead of time (see www.hrp.org.uk) for the 9.30pm **Ceremony of the Keys**, the tower's 700-year-old lock-up routine.

ST PAUL'S CATHEDRAL

Christopher Wren's grand masterpiece, the recently renovated **St Paul's Cathedral** (Map pp152-3; ☎ 7246 8350; www.stpauls.co.uk; Ludgate Hill EC4; adult/child £9/3.50; 🕑 8.30am-4pm Mon-Sat, services only Sun; ⊖ St Paul's) is the proud bearer of the capital's largest church dome. Attractions include the golden ceiling mosaics and the **Whispering Gallery** – if you talk close to the wall it carries your words around to the opposite side. VIPs remembered by their tombs and monuments here include Nelson, Joshua Reynolds and Christopher Wren himself.

OTHER SIGHTS

Iconic London landmark **Tower Bridge** (Map p160; ☎ 7403 3761; www.towerbridge.org.uk; Tower Bridge SE1; adult/child £5.50/3; 🕑 10am-6.30pm Apr-Sep, 9.30am-6pm Oct-Mar; ⊖ Tower Hill) houses a small exhibition.

The **Monument** (Map p160; ☎ 7626 2717; Monument St EC3; adult/child £2/1; 🕑 9.30am-5.30pm; ⊖ Monument) is a 65m (202ft) Doric column designed by Wren to commemorate the Great Fire of 1666. Climb the spiral staircase for some good views.

Along the South Bank

TATE MODERN

The hugely popular **Tate Modern** (Map pp152-3; ☎ 7887 8008; www.tate.org.uk; Bankside SE1; admission free; 10am-6pm Sun-Thu, 10am-11pm Fri & Sat; ⊖ Blackfriars) exhibits 20th-century art in an evocative former power station shed. The permanent collection, ranging from Rothko to Lichtenstein, is impressive, while temporary installations in the Turbine Hall and regular special exhibitions draw locals back for more. The **café** on level seven has great views over the Thames, and there's a boat to Tate Britain (p178).

OLD OPERATING THEATRE

Near St Thomas's Hospital, the excellent **Old Operating Theatre, Museum and Herb Garret** (Map p160; ☎ 7188 2679; www.thegarret.org.uk; 9a St Thomas's St SE1; adult/child £4.75/3.75; 10.30am-5pm; ⊖ London Bridge) contains a herbal workshop where an 18th-century apothecary compounded natural remedies, some of which may even have worked. The main attraction is a later surgical theatre where gruesome procedures were performed – check out the large 'decapitating hook' on display.

SHAKESPEARE'S GLOBE

An authentic 1997 rebuild of the original London theatre where many Shakespeare plays were performed, the **Globe** (Map pp152-3; ☎ 7902 1500; www.shakespeares-globe.org; 21 New Globe Walk SE1; adult/child £8.50/7; 10am-5.45pm; ⊖ Mansion House/Southwark/London Bridge) has become a pilgrimage destination for fans of the Bard. Within its circular wood-framed walls, outdoor plays are performed 'in the round' from early May to early October (p173). The rest of the year, there are a colourful exhibition and popular theatre tours.

> **ROUTEMASTERS RULE**
>
> Decommissioned after more than 50 years of public service, London's charming red double-decker Routemaster buses have begun a new lease of life travelling on two heritage routes. Bus 9 trundles from the Royal Albert Hall to Aldwych via Piccadilly Circus, while bus 15 runs from Trafalgar Square to Tower Hill via Fleet St. Standard fares apply (see p178) and they run every 15 minutes from 9.30am to 6pm.

CLINK PRISON MUSEUM

The darkened Bankside alleyways are the perfect location for the gruesome **Clink Prison Museum** (Map p160; ☎ 7403 0900; www.clink.co.uk; 1 Clink St SE1; adult/child £5/3.50; 10am-6pm Mon-Fri, 10am-9pm Sat & Sun; ⊖ London Bridge), which illuminates the gory history of a hellish dungeon that occupied this area from the 12th century. With its shadowy, sawdust-floored rooms populated by mannequins sporting the latest line in face sores, torture features heavily, with terrifying 'iron boots' and 'scold's bridles' on prominent display.

DESIGN MUSEUM

The **Design Museum** (Map p160; ☎ 0870 833 9955; www.designmuseum.org; 28 Shad Thames SE1; adult/child £7/free; 10am-5.45pm; ⊖ London Bridge/Tower Hill) celebrates the look of leading contemporary products from shoes to motorway signage to furniture. Not surprisingly, it has an excellent shop of irresistible trinkets, and its chichi restaurant overlooking the Thames is popular with chin-stroking aesthetes and those pretending to be architects.

LONDON EYE

On a clear day, from the **London Eye** (Map pp152-3; ☎ 0870 500 0600; www.londoneye.com; Jubilee Gardens SE1; adult/child £13/6.50; 10am-9pm Jun-Sep, 10am-8pm Oct-May; ⊖ Westminster/Waterloo) you can see for 25 miles in every direction. The 32 glass-enclosed gondolas of the world's largest Ferris wheel take 30 minutes to completely rotate, so passengers (up to 25 in each capsule) really get time to take in the experience. Consider a night 'flight' for more sparkly views. It's a good idea to book tickets in advance via the website – especially in summer, when everyone wants a ride.

OTHER SIGHTS

Walk across the **Millennium Bridge** (Map pp152-3; ⊖ St Paul's/Blackfriars), the 'Blade of light' footbridge over the Thames linking the Tate Modern and St Paul's Cathedral.

On the **Golden Jubilee Bridge** (Map pp152-3; ⊖ Embankment/Waterloo), two hi-tech, pedestrian walkways straddle the Thames between Embankment tube station and the South Bank.

Kooky British designer Zandra Rhodes' **Fashion & Textile Museum** (Map p160; ☎ 7407 8664; 83 Bermondsey St SE1; adult/child £5/free; 10am-4.15pm Tue-Sat, noon-4.15pm Sun; ⊖ London Bridge) showcases fashion from 1950 to the present day.

The justly revered contemporary art space, **Hayward Gallery** (Map pp152-3; ☎ 7960 4242; www.hayward.org.uk; Belvedere Rd, South Bank SE1; adult/child £8/free; 10am-6pm Mon & Thu-Sun, 10am-8pm Tue-Wed; Waterloo/Embankment), has been revamped with a swish new foyer and glass pavilion. The main attraction, though, is the wealth of temporary exhibitions that pass through, illuminating blockbuster as well as little-known artists and movements.

North London

FREUD MUSEUM

Celebrating the life and work of the father of psychoanalysis, the **Freud Museum** (☎ 7435 2002; www.freud.org.uk; 20 Marsefield Gardens NW3; adult/child £5/free; noon-5pm Wed-Sun; Finchley Rd) occupies the home where Sigmund Freud lived his final years. Combining glimpses into his everyday life with fascinating insights into his theories, the highlight is the ground-floor study – complete with cushion-covered analyst couch – where it's easy to imagine Freud gently questioning his patients. A series of remarkable home movies runs in an upstairs TV room.

LONDON CANAL MUSEUM

The capital's near-forgotten network of waterways is brought to life at the tranquil **London Canal Museum** (Map pp152-3; ☎ 7713 0836; www.canalmuseum.org.uk; 12-13 New Wharf Rd N1; adult/child £3/1.50; 10am-4.30pm Tue-Sun; King's Cross), situated alongside a Regent's Canal section jostling with brightly painted narrow boats. Along with the treasure trove of boat ephemera, scale models and a walk-in re-creation of an old barge, there's an exhibition on the 19th-century ice trade, when huge blocks were imported from Norway and transported via canal to London's iceboxes.

South London

GREENWICH

Worthy of its own maritime-themed day trip, Greenwich's highlights start with the **Cutty Sark** (☎ 8858 2698; www.cuttysark.org.uk; King William Walk SE10; adult/child £5/3.70; 10am-5pm; DLR Cutty Sark), a lovely old tea-and-wool clipper ship. It's a short walk to the complex of handsome Greenwich palaces that includes the **National Maritime Museum** (☎ 8312 6565; www.nmm.ac.uk; Park Row SE10; admission free; 10am-6pm Jul-Aug, 10am-5pm Sep-Jun) and the baroque **Old Royal Naval College** (☎ 8269 4747; www.oldroyalnavalcollege.org; King William Walk SE10; admission free; 10am-5pm). Climb the nearby hill to the **Royal Observatory** (☎ 8312 6565; www.rog.nmm.ac.uk; Greenwich Park SE10; admission free; 10am-6pm Jul-Aug, 10am-5pm Sep-Jun). A brass strip in the courtyard here marks the Prime Meridian, dividing the world into eastern and western hemispheres.

ELTHAM PALACE

London's most beautiful Art Deco home, **Eltham Palace** (☎ 8294 2548; www.elthampalace.org.uk; Court Yard SE9; adult/child £7.30/3.70; 10am-5pm Sun-Wed Apr-Oct, 10am-4pm Sun-Wed Nov-Mar), off Court Rd, is worth an afternoon of anyone's time. In the grounds of a 12th-century royal estate – the ruin-strewn gardens remain from centuries past – a large new house was built in the 1930s, reflecting the best of cutting-edge design. Concealed lighting and under-floor heating were the hot mod cons but the curved wooden walls, marble-lined dining room and glass-domed roof remain breathtaking to this day.

MUSEUM IN DOCKLANDS

Housed in a 200-year-old brick warehouse once used to store rum and sugar, the **Museum in Docklands** (☎ 0870 444 3857; www.museumindocklands.org.uk; West India Quay, Hertsmere Rd E14; adult/child £5/free; 10am-6pm; Canary Wharf) illuminates the intriguing ebb and flow of two millennia of Thames River history. Displays include Roman figurines, along with a striking scale model of the medieval London Bridge. Save time for a scurvy stroll around Sailortown, an evocative walk-through re-creation of the area's 18th-century streets, complete with recorded sounds of drunken sailors and cackling hags.

West of London

KEW GARDENS

The verdant Royal Botanic **Kew Gardens** (☎ 8332 5655; www.rbgkew.org.uk; Richmond TW9; adult/child £10/free; 9.30am-6pm Mon-Fri, 9.30am-7pm Sat & Sun Apr-Aug, 9.30am-5.30pm Sep & Oct, 9.30am-3.45pm Nov-Jan, 9.30am-5pm Feb & Mar; Kew Gardens) covers 120 hectares and grows more species than any other in the world. A haven of tranquillity, the stunning variety of flora and the magnificent conservatories are a respite from the city streets. Following an extensive

10-year renovation, the handsome **Kew Palace** (☎ 0870 751 5179; www.hrp.org.uk; adult/child £5/3.50; 🕑 10am-5.45pm Tue-Sun), which has been home to generations of royals since 1728, reopened in 2006.

HAMPTON COURT PALACE

Britain's grandest Tudor pile, **Hampton Court Palace** (☎ 0870 752 7777; www.hrp.org.uk; East Molesey, Surrey; adult/child £3.50/2.50; 🕑 10.15am-5.15pm Mon, 9.30am-5.15pm Tue-Sun Apr-Oct, 9.30am-3.45pm Nov-Mar) fuses Henry VIII's splendid Great Hall, Christopher Wren's later King's Apartments and the entertaining Tudor Kitchens, complete with animal carcasses and giant fireplaces. Costumed interpreters roam the grounds on most days, offering colourful insights into everyday life at the palace. Save time to stroll the immaculate gardens, which include the wizened Great Vine – the oldest vine in the world – and the Privy Garden, recently restored to its early-18th-century glory. Twice-hourly trains arrive at Hampton Court station (change at Surbiton) from London Waterloo (£4.80, 30 minutes), and a boat travels here (p178).

TOURS

London is crisscrossed with great walking tours that scratch below the surface of the city's rich history.

Back Passages of Spitalfields (☎ 7729 4816; www.backpassageswalks.co.uk; adult/child £6/5; 🕑 6.30pm first 2 Sun of every month Apr-Oct) For a less-conventional approach, the tour combines comic street theatre and eye-opening stories on this infamous East End enclave.

London Walks (☎ 7624 3978; www.walks.com; adult/child £6/free) History-huggers will enjoy these strolls, which expertly cover a huge array of subjects, including Haunted London, Hidden Pubs and the Da Vinci Code.

Theatre Royal Drury Lane (Map pp152-3; ☎ 7850 8791; Catherine St; adult/child £10.50/8.50; 🕑 2.15pm & 4.45pm Mon, Tue, Thu & Fri, 10.15am Sat; ⊖ Covent Garden) Theatre lovers can peek behind the curtain on a colourful backstage tour, which brings to life notable characters from London theatrical lore.

FESTIVALS & EVENTS

University Boat Race (www.theboatrace.org) Traditional Oxford versus Cambridge row-off in March from Putney to Mortlake along the Thames River.

London Marathon (www.london-marathon.co.uk) Held in April, this is the capital's giant annual jog-a-thon from Greenwich Park to The Mall.

Trooping the Colour (www.royal.gov.uk) The Queen's 'other birthday', celebrated with pomp, pageantry and parades at Horse Guards Pde in mid-June.

Lawn Tennis Championships (www.wimbledon.org) World's leading tennis event, held at Wimbledon from late June.

Pride Parade (www.pridelondon.org) From Oxford St, gays and lesbians paint the town pink in July.

Notting Hill Carnival (www.lnhc.org.uk) Enormous multicultural party and street parade in mid-August.

London Film Festival (www.lff.org.uk; National Film Theatre, South Bank) Showing the best of British and international arthouse films in October.

Lord Mayor's Show (www.lordmayorsshow.org; City of London) Held in November, this is a giant colourful street procession in the City.

New Year's Eve Celebration From 31 December to 1 January, countdown to midnight in Trafalgar Square.

SLEEPING

Staying in London is an expensive business, but there are ways to cut your costs without sleeping on the streets. Hostels increasingly offer private rooms and colleges offer good-value summer accommodation – contact **Venuemasters** (☎ 0114 249 3090; www.venuemasters.com), which represents many of London's universities. It's also worth trying a B&B homestay: check your options with the **London Bed & Breakfast Agency** (☎ 7586 2768; www.londonbb.com).

In the midrange market, chain hotels like Premier Travel Inn and Holiday Inn Express offer some of London's most reliable and best-value accommodation. Contact London's official **hotel bookings service** (☎ 0845 644 3010; www.visitlondonoffers.com) for up-to-date sleepover bargains throughout the city.

West End

The centre of the action charges a premium for convenience, but it can also be a noisy place to spend the night.

BUDGET

Piccadilly Backpackers (Map pp152-3; ☎ 7434 9009; www.piccadillybackpackers.com; 12 Sherwood St W1; dm/s/tw £12/36/52; 💻; ⊖ Piccadilly Circus) This giant, cheap and cheerful spot is as bright as a kindergarten art class. Along with pod-style dorm beds, high-speed Internet (per hour £1) and a travel shop for local and onward vacation planning, there's a rowdy on-site bar. This is a party hostel, so don't expect to get far with your copy of *War and Peace*.

Oxford St YHA (Map pp152-3; ☎ 0870 770 5894; oxfordst@yha.org.uk; 14 Noel St W1; dm £23.50; ⊠ 🖳; ⊖ Oxford Circus) The most central of London's YHA hostels is basic, clean, welcoming and loud. All the dorms are small – there's a maximum of four beds per room – and there's a TV lounge and large kitchen. It's a great location for nearby pubs, clubs and theatres.

MIDRANGE

Travelodge (Map pp152-3; ☎ 0870 850 950; www.travelodge.co.uk; 10 Drury Lane WC2; r from £49; ⊖ Covent Garden/Holborn) On the northern fringes of Covent Garden, price is the main selling point at this functional chain hotel. The rooms are clean but institutional – perfect if you're planning to be out all day and just need a well-located place to crash.

Regent Palace Hotel (Map pp152-3; ☎ 0870 400 8703; www.regentpalacehotel.co.uk; Glasshouse St W1; s/d/tr from £64/89/99; ⊠ 🖳; ⊖ Piccadilly Circus) Particularly convenient for shops, pubs and restaurants, this central hotel has 888 rooms. Less than half are en suite – the shower complexes on each floor are reminiscent of a hostel – and most have standard facilities and humdrum furnishings. The proximity to major sights is hard to beat, though.

TOP END

Hazlitt's (Map pp152-3; ☎ 7434 1771; www.hazlittshotel.com; 6 Frith St W1; s/d/ste from £175/255/300; ❄; ⊖ Tottenham Court Rd) Named after essayist William Hazlitt, there is a strong tradition of famous writers staying at this wonky-walled rustic charmer. Filled with antique furniture, it has all the modern flourishes of a chic boutique property – including triple-glazed windows to keep out the sounds of the passing Soho rabble.

Bloomsbury & Fitzrovia

A quieter, more residential area than the rabble-rousing West End, prices are usually more reasonable here.

BUDGET

Generator (Map pp152-3; ☎ 7388 7666; www.generatorhostels.com; Compton Pl WC1; dm/s/tw from £12.50/35/46; ⊠ 🖳; ⊖ Russell Square) Don't be fooled by the industrial, factory-floor interiors here: this hostel, off 37 Tavistock Pl, is not about work but about serious hedonism. There are nearly 900 beds, an on-site travel agency and an Internet suite, but it's the late-opening bar that sees the most action. There's no kitchen, so you'll have to have beer for breakfast.

Indian Student YMCA (Map pp152-3; ☎ 7387 0411; www.indianymca.org; 41 Fitzroy Sq W1; dm/s/d £22/35/50; ⊠ 🖳; ⊖ Warren St) For all nationalities and not just students, this good-value YMCA has clean, good-sized rooms, laundry facilities and an excellent gym. Prices include breakfast and a tasty curry dinner, and there are attractive discounts for longer stays.

MIDRANGE

St Margaret's Hotel (Map pp152-3; ☎ 7636 4277; www.stmargaretshotel.co.uk; 26 Bedford Pl WC1; s/d from £55/82; ⊠; ⊖ Russell Square/Holborn) This smashing family-run town house hotel is among the most homey sleepovers in central London. The rooms are simply furnished but comfortable, and the bathrooms – mostly shared – are spotless. Ask for a back room if you're craving tranquillity and you'll be overlooking a small garden.

Arran House Hotel (Map pp152-3; ☎ 7636 2186; www.arranhotel-london.com; 77-79 Gower St WC1; dm/s/d from £18.50/55/72; 🖳; ⊖ Goodge St) This good-value, hotel has dorm and private accommodation, and is a short walk from the British Museum. The cosy double rooms have Art Deco fireplaces and the rose garden is a pleasant summer bonus. Free wi-fi.

Also recommended:

Hotel Cavendish (Map pp152-3; ☎ 7636 9079; www.hotelcavendish.com; 75 Gower St WC1; s/d/tr £75/90/130; ⊠; ⊖ Goodge St) Simple B&B hotel with some heritage flourishes.

TOP END

Charlotte St Hotel (Map pp152-3; ☎ 7806 2000; www.firmdale.com; 15-17 Charlotte St W1; s/d/ste from £195/230/340; Ⓟ ⊠ ❄ 🖳; ⊖ Goodge St) This superior property combines traditional furnishings with contemporary art flourishes but doesn't sacrifice service for looks. Popular with visiting media types, its sumptuous rooms and suites include granite and oak bathrooms with TVs. The chichi bar has a colourful Alexander Hollweg wall mural.

Westminster, Pimlico & Victoria

Not the most attractive part of London, Victoria's budget hotels are better value than those in Earl's Court. Pimlico is more residential but convenient for the Tate Britain area.

BUDGET

Victoria Hostel (Map pp152-3; ☎ 7834 3077; www.astorhostels.com; 71 Belgrave Rd SW1; dm £15-18, d & tw £50; 💻; ⊖ Pimlico) This warm and welcoming backpacker joint has 200 beds in mostly mid-sized dorms. Facilities include two kitchens and a TV lounge with DVDs. Thursday nights are reserved for group dinners, and rates include continental breakfast. Beware the hostel guitar and take down anyone who looks ready to play it.

Wigram House (Map pp152-3; ☎ 7834 1169; www.wmin.ac.uk/comserv; 84-99 Ashley Gardens SW1; s/tw £35/56; ⊖ Victoria) One of seven University of Westminster student residences available from June to September, this six-storey Victorian mansion has basic study rooms (all with sinks), shared bathrooms, large kitchens and laundry facilities. Located in a quiet residential area near St James's Park.

MIDRANGE

Luna & Simone Hotel (Map pp152-3; ☎ 7834 5897; www.lunasimonehotel.com; 47-49 Belgrave Rd SW1; s/d/tr from £35/65/90; ⊠ 💻; ⊖ Victoria) In a street crowded with B&Bs of widely varying quality, this is a shining example of a basic good-value option. The bright, spotless rooms have satellite TV and most are en suite (love those power showers). Wi-fi is available on the ground and 1st floors.

James House & Cartref House (Map pp152-3; ☎ 7730 7338/7730 6176; www.jamesandcartref.co.uk; 108 & 129 Ebury St SW1; s/d/tr from £52/70/95; ⊠ 💻; ⊖ Victoria) The best in the area for the budget, these two handsome town house B&Bs face each other across the street. Run by a friendly couple with a good knowledge of the area, the rooms (some with shared bathrooms) are clean and bright, and the cooked breakfast is hearty enough to keep you going until the afternoon.

Also recommended:

Victor Hotel (Map pp152-3; ☎ 7592 9853; www.victorhotel.co.uk; 51 Belgrave Rd SW1; s/d £50/60; ⊖ Victoria) Standard town house B&B (continental breakfast only), with easy access to major attractions.

Windermere Hotel (Map pp152-3; ☎ 7834 5163; www.windermere-hotel.co.uk; 142-144 Warwick Way SW1; s/d from £89/114; ⊠ 💻; ⊖ Victoria) Elegant 22-room character B&B with free high-speed Internet.

TOP END

City Inn (Map pp152-3; ☎ 7630 1000; www.cityinn.com/london; 30 John Islip St SW1; r from £264; 🅿; ⊖ Pimlico) One of the largest hotels built in London for decades when it opened in 2003, the clean, contemporary lines of this top-end sleepover mirror London's recent style renaissance. Flat-screen TVs, DVD players and minimalist furnishings fill the rooms – some of which have floor-to-ceiling windows – and the on-site Millbank Lounge is *the* place to watch the local pseuds unwind.

Kensington & Earl's Court

Close to Hyde Park, major museums and a busy shop-lined High St, Kensington is a good base with a wide range of accommodation options. Adjacent Earl's Court mines the budget end of the spectrum, but the quality here can vary enormously.

BUDGET

Earl's Court YHA (Map pp156-7; ☎ 0870 770 5804; earlscourt@yha.org.uk; 38 Bolton Gardens SW5; dm £19.50; ⊠ 💻; ⊖ Earl's Court) Situated in a large, recently refurbished Victorian town house, this immaculate and spacious hostel has mainly four-bed dorms and very helpful staff. There is a well-equipped self-catering kitchen and a large lounge with satellite TV. Bike hire is available (per day £9.50).

easyHotel (Map pp156-7; ☎ 7216 1717; www.easyhotel.com; 14 Lexham Gardens W8; r from $30; ⊠; ⊖ Earl's Court/Gloucester Rd) The first of a planned chain of orange-hued no-frills properties, the rooms here are 'small', 'very small' or 'tiny' and most are windowless. Each has a double bed, aeroplane-style cubicle bathroom and wall-mounted TV (£5 extra). On the plus side, it's clean, well located and, if you book far enough ahead, an exceptional deal.

MIDRANGE

Swiss House Hotel (Map pp156-7; ☎ 7373 2769; www.swiss-hh.demon.co.uk; 171 Old Brompton Rd SW5; B&B s/d/tw/tr from £58/95/95/135; ⊖ Gloucester Rd) Graceful, relaxed and uncluttered, this family-friendly guesthouse is a breath of fresh air on a street of otherwise dull options. Its large, light-filled rooms have laminated floors and a simple, contemporary décor, and the hosts are happy to point you in the direction of the attractions you want to visit.

Mayflower Hotel (Map pp156-7; ☎ 7370 0991; mayflowerhotel.co.uk; 26-28 Trebovir Rd SW5; s/d/tr from £65/85/105; 💻; ⊖ Earl's Court) Yet another white-stucco, former town house hotel, the Mayflower distinguishes itself by offering rooms with a refreshing Indonesian theme, including lovely teak furnishings and colourful fabric flourishes. The bathrooms, with floor-to-ceiling tiles, are equally impressive. There's a juice bar in the lobby, and the continental breakfast includes cheese, waffles and fresh fruit.

Also recommended:

Merlyn Court Hotel (Map pp156-7; ☎ 7370 1640; www.merlyncourthotel.com; 2 Barkston Gardens SW5; B&B s/d/tr/q from £38/55/65/70, with shared bathroom from £30/45/60/65; ⊠; ⊖ Earl's Court) Lovely family-run B&B with rooms for up to four people.

Hotel 167 (Map pp156-7; ☎ 7373 3221; www.hotel167.com; 167 Old Brompton Rd SW5; s/d from £79/99; ⊖ Gloucester Rd/South Kensington) Colourful B&B with plenty of quirky character.

TOP END

Number Sixteen (Map pp156-7; ☎ 7589 5232; www.numbersixteenhotel.co.uk; 16 Sumner Pl SW7; s/d from £95/170; ⊠ ❄; ⊖ South Kensington) This luxury boutique hotel, with tranquil interiors and choice art throughout, is a tasteful respite from the bustling city streets. Each high-ceilinged room has a calming, individually designed colour scheme and some overlook the private gardens at the back. The idyllic conservatory and sumptuous drawing room compete for attention.

Bayswater, Paddington & Notting Hill

This area has a good selection of inexpensive accommodation, with some funky options at the higher price range around Notting Hill.

BUDGET

Wake Up! London (Map pp156-7; ☎ 7262 4471; www.wakeuplondon.co.uk; 1 Queen's Gardens W2; dm/s/d/tw from £11/18/30/35; ⊠ 💻; ⊖ Paddington) The spartan mid-sized dorms at this colourful Australian-owned hostel are complemented by a plethora of facilities that include laundry facilities, Internet access, a well-stocked kitchen and an on-site travel agency. The subterranean bar specialises in getting you as drunk as possible for the least amount of money.

Leinster Inn (Map pp156-7; ☎ 7229 9641; www.astorhostels.com; 7-12 Leinster Sq W2; dm/s/d from £14/26.50/41; ⊠ 💻; ⊖ Bayswater) In a large, old house northwest of Bayswater tube station and close to Portobello Rd Market, this friendly, well-established hostel has an Internet café, late-opening bar and regular themed party nights. Prices include continental breakfast.

MIDRANGE

St David's Hotel (Map pp156-7; ☎ 7723 3856; www.stdavidshotels.com; 16-20 Norfolk Sq W2; s/d/tr from £35/59/80; ⊖ Paddington) A warm welcome makes this 19th-century hotel property one of the best on the block. Rooms have satellite TV and are clean and comfortable, with calming creamy colours and dark wood furniture.

Vancouver Studios (Map pp156-7; ☎ 7243 1270; www.vancouverstudios.co.uk; 30 Prince's Sq W2; s/d/tw £75/99/110; ⊠; ⊖ Paddington) Don't be fooled by its typical Victorian exterior: Vancouver Studios is a cut above everything else on the street. All rooms have kitchenettes (so you can save a bundle on eating) and the house cat (ambitiously named Panther) will likely follow you to the ivy-covered garden for a chat. Rooms are a kaleidoscope of different styles but all are beautifully maintained and feature large shower rooms.

Also recommended:

Glendale Hyde Park Hotel (Map pp156-7; ☎ 7706 4441; www.ghphotel.com; 8 Devonshire Tce W2; s/d/tw/tr from £45/55/55/60; ⊠ 💻; ⊖ Paddington) Comfortable, pastel-coloured guesthouse B&B.

Pavilion Hotel (Map pp156-7; ☎ 7262 0905; www.pavilionhoteluk.com; 34-36 Sussex Gardens W2; s £60-85, d/tr £100/120; ⊖ Paddington) Funky, trinket-packed art hotel with theme rooms ranging from 'Casablanca Nights' to 'Honky Tonk Afro'.

TOP END

Portobello Hotel (Map pp156-7; ☎ 7727 2777; www.portobello-hotel.co.uk; 22 Stanley Gardens W11; s/d/tw from £135/180/200; ⊠ ❄ 💻; ⊖ Notting Hill Gate) From the Sex Pistols to Kate Moss, this exclusive Notting Hill sleepover has been a firm favourite of discerning stars for years. Its public spaces are bright and theatrical but the rooms are tastefully decorated with high ceilings, colourful fabrics and unforgettable beds, some of them four-poster. There's a 24-hour bar and restaurant and free Internet access – but if you can afford to stay here, that's probably not an issue.

EATING

It's hard *not* to find somewhere to eat in London. All-you-can-eat pizza bars abound, pubs serve heaping grub by the tonne and street markets dish up home-cooked nosh for the price of a Starbucks latte. But quality varies enormously and it's easy to drop £20 on a meal and walk away feeling dissatisfied. Pick up *Time Out* or visit the restaurant

BRITAIN

review website of the **Evening Standard** (www.esrestaurants.co.uk) for news on the latest foodie hotspots. The following reviews are grouped by district and price category.

West End

Soho is one of London's gastronomic centres, with plenty of worthy choices along Old Compton and Dean Sts. Chinatown offers plenty of set-menu bargains here, while a 10-minute stroll to Covent Garden delivers options for trendy vegetarian scoffers.

BUDGET

Café de Hong Kong (Map pp152-3; ☎ 7534 9898; 47-49 Charing Cross Rd WC2; lunch combo £5.80; lunch & dinner; ⊖ Leicester Square) This clamorous Chinese cafeteria is full every lunch time with noisy Asian students comparing mobile-phone images and sipping bubble tea. The fast-food approach delivers great value, though, with dozens of rice or noodle combos for under £6.

Food for Thought (Map pp152-3; ☎ 7836 9072; 31 Neal St WC2; mains £4-8; 9.30am-8.30pm Mon-Sat, noon-5pm Sun; ⊠; ⊖ Covent Garden) Crammed among Neal St's trendy boutiques, this tiny vegetarian nook is good value. Its ever-changing menu of hearty dishes includes excellent stir-fries and substantial salads plus the kind of cakes your granny would make, if she was into GM-free cooking.

Also recommended:

Café in the Crypt (Map pp152-3; ☎ 7839 4342; St Martin-in-the-Fields, Duncannon St WC2; mains £4-9; 8am-8pm Mon-Wed, 8am-10.30pm Thu-Sat, noon-8pm Sun; ⊖ Charing Cross) Under the shadowy church arches, this is a great spot for coffee and a cake.

Chuen Cheng Ku (Map pp152-3; ☎ 7437 1398; 17 Wardour St W1; combo lunch £8.80; lunch & dinner; ⊖ Leicester Square) Arrive early at this giant Cantonese restaurant: it's hugely popular.

MIDRANGE

Masala Zone (Map pp152-3; ☎ 7287 9966; 9 Marshall St W1; mains £6-12; lunch & dinner Mon-Sat, dinner Sun; ⊠; ⊖ Oxford Circus) The industrial, canteen-like design, juxtaposed against terracotta walls and Indian artworks, fits perfectly with the modern approach to Indian cuisine here. Dishes range from street hawker snacks to noodle bowls and curries, but there are some good-value combos that allow you to flex your taste buds without exhausting your cash.

World Food Café (Map pp152-3; ☎ 7379 0298; 1st fl, 14 Neal's Yard WC2; mains £6-12; 11.30am-4.30pm Mon-Fri, 11am-5pm Sat; ⊠; ⊖ Covent Garden) Accompanied by world music and colourful artwork, this friendly vegetarian eatery overlooking funky Neal's Yard offers wholesome, generously portioned dishes from several regions. There are excellent Mexican and West African meals, along with Thai curries and Turkish meze.

Satsuma (Map pp152-3; ☎ 7437 8338; 56 Wardour St W1; mains £6-12; lunch & dinner; ⊖ Piccadilly Circus) Don't be put off by the modern Japanese chain restaurant look of this place; the food includes excellent handmade sushi and more good-value combo options than you can shake a stick at. The fresh tempura plates are recommended, as well as the takeout bento boxes – a perfect picnic lunch.

Also recommended:

India Club (Map pp152-3; ☎ 7836 0650; 2nd fl, Strand Continental Hotel, 143 Strand WC2; set meal £12; lunch & dinner Mon-Sat; ⊖ Temple) The food comes first at this shabby upstairs canteen, specialising in home-style Indian dishes.

Rules (Map pp152-3; ☎ 7836 5314; 35 Maiden Lane WC2; mains £18-26; lunch & dinner; ⊠; ⊖ Covent Garden) One of London's oldest restaurants, specialising in gamey British cuisine.

TOP END

Ivy (Map pp152-3; ☎ 7836 4751; 1 West St WC2; mains £12-25; lunch & dinner; ⊖ Leicester Square) Sitting in the heart of London's theatre district, the ritzy Ivy remains a top draw for visiting glitterati, who come to relive their humble backgrounds by scoffing delightfully gourmet versions of traditional British dishes, like kedgeree and shepherd's pie. You'll have to book far in advance here, preferably before your birth.

Bloomsbury & Fitzrovia

Prices are generally lower in this area, but there are some expensive chichi pockets lurking around many corners.

BUDGET

Carluccio's Caffe (Map pp152-3; ☎ 7636 2228; 8 Market Pl W1; mains £6-12; lunch & dinner; ⊖ Oxford Circus) Among the family-owned Italian restaurants in the backstreets behind Oxford St, this lunch-time shopping pit stop serves satisfying pasta and risotto dishes. The good-value menu includes daily-changing specials and the hearty desserts are prepared with care. Sit outside in summer to watch the locals rush by.

MIDRANGE

Busaba Eathai (Map pp152-3; ☎ 7299 7900; 22 Store St W1; mains £5-11; lunch & dinner; ; Goodge St) A happening Thai eatery with the communal bench seating arrangements favoured by many of London's new wave Asian restaurants. But the aesthetics are only part of the equation here. Generous, innovative dishes, like butternut pumpkin curry and prawns pomelo on betel leaves, bring the office workers back for more.

Rasa Samudra (Map pp152-3; ☎ 7637 0222; 5 Charlotte St W1; mains £6-12; lunch & dinner Mon-Sat, dinner Sun; Goodge St) Ignore the neon-pink exterior of this lip-smacking South Indian restaurant and head straight for the Keralan fish and shellfish menu. There are plenty of well-priced mains, but if you can stretch to £30, indulge in the Seafood Feast, a banquet of entrées, curries and desserts that covers the kitchen's main highlights, including the excellent crab curry. A Vegetarian Feast is also available.

TOP END

Hakkasan (Map pp152-3; ☎ 7907 1888; 8 Hanway Pl W1; mains £6-35; lunch & dinner; Tottenham Court Rd) You don't have to spend much to eat here but it helps. The first Chinese restaurant in London to receive a Michelin star, this sleek, sophisticated haunt serves exquisite reinventions of traditional dishes in its haughty dining room. If you would rather soak up the atmosphere without making your credit card sweat, drop by for lunch or just linger at the cocktail bar.

Westminster, Pimlico & Victoria

Not exactly a smorgasbord of great dine-out options – the pubs are a popular alternative here – there are a few midrange restaurants worth pulling up a chair at in this area.

Footstool (Map pp152-3; ☎ 7222 2779; St John's, Smith Sq SW1; mains £8-18; lunch Mon-Fri; Westminster) Set in an atmospheric brick-vaulted church crypt, the buffet lunch is deservedly popular and focuses on traditional British and Mediterranean fare. Check out the shady character in the corner – he's probably an MP from the nearby House of Commons. Dinner is also served when there are concerts in the upstairs church, usually several times per week; call for evening opening hours.

Cinnamon Club (Map pp152-3; ☎ 7222 2555; 30 Great Smith St SW1; mains £11-29; breakfast & lunch Mon-Fri, dinner Mon-Sat; St James's Park) Britain's love affair with Indian cuisine is nowhere more apparent than at this sumptuous restaurant, housed in a restored Victorian library. Classic regional dishes receive a pioneering contemporary twist, while a new Indian breakfast menu attracts the adventurous.

Also recommended:

Kazan (Map pp152-3; ☎ 7233 7100; 93 Wilton Rd SW1; mains £8-14; lunch & dinner; Victoria) Minimalist Turkish restaurant with authentic cuisine.

Ebury Wine Bar (Map pp152-3; ☎ 7730 5447; 139 Ebury St SW1; mains £10-20; lunch & dinner; ; Victoria) Unpretentious spot serving traditional Brit nosh–like beef and ale sausages.

Kensington, Knightsbridge & Earl's Court

From finger-licking cheap eats to credit card–busting Michelin stars, this area caters well to most budgets.

BUDGET

Troubadour (Map pp156-7; ☎ 7341 6333; 265 Old Brompton Rd SW5; mains £6-13; breakfast, lunch & dinner; West Brompton/Earl's Court) This wood-floored bohemian hang-out is exactly what a great café should be: tons of trinkety character, servers who encourage you to linger and a menu focused on comfort food. A great place for breakfast – it serves boiled eggs with soldiers – the menu classics include Cajun chicken and bangers and mash, with an emphasis on organic ingredients.

MIDRANGE

Lundum's (Map pp156-7; ☎ 7373 7774; 117 Old Brompton Rd SW7; mains £4.50-14; lunch & dinner Mon-Sat, lunch Sun; Gloucester Rd/South Kensington) Set in a beautiful Edwardian building with bright and airy interiors, this Danish eatery serves authentic Scandinavian dishes like hearty pork meatballs and succulent grilled salmon. The lunch special – two courses for £13.50 – is a good deal, allowing you to dip into marinated herrings without gagging at the price.

Nobu (Map pp152-3; ☎ 7447 4747; Metropolitan Hotel, 19 Old Park Lane W1; mains £6-28; lunch & dinner Mon-Sat, dinner Sun; Hyde Park Corner) Overlooking Hyde Park, this strong contender for London's best Japanese restaurant has a comfortably minimalist décor, anonymously efficient service, and is out of this world when it comes to exquisitely prepared and presented sushi and sashimi. The bento boxes include a chocolate version.

L'etranger (Map pp156-7; ☎ 7584 1118; 36 Gloucester Rd SW7; mains £15-26; ⏲ lunch & dinner; ⊖ Gloucester Rd) This elegant contemporary restaurant focuses on French cuisine with an Indochinese twist. The service can be a bit snooty but the food is usually worth the hassle: the caramelised black cod is excellent and the wine list has some great tipples from around the world – there's a wine shop next door if you fancy a takeout.

TOP END

Boxwood Café (Map pp156-7; ☎ 7235 1010; Wilton Pl SW1; mains £10-26; ⏲ lunch & dinner; ⊠; ⊖ Hyde Park Corner) The stylish interiors of this Gordon Ramsay restaurant belie a surprisingly comfortable eatery with an excellent menu of contemporary British dishes. The seasonal offerings focus on simple preparations that reveal naturally complex flavours, hence dishes like steamed wild sea bass and fried oysters with fennel and lemon. A nonsnooty way to enjoy a top-class meal in haughty Knightsbridge.

Notting Hill

Increasingly a London food-lovers paradise, Notting Hill combines cheap ethnic takeaways, quirky cafés and some seriously trendy restaurants.

BUDGET

Sausage & Mash Café (Map pp156-7; ☎ 8968 8898; 268 Portobello Rd W10; mains £6-8; ⏲ 9am-11pm Mon-Thu, 9am-11.30pm Fri & Sat, 9am-10pm Sun; ⊖ Ladbroke Grove) Wittily known as the S&M café, this place does an upmarket version of the rib-sticking English favourite. There are 20 sausage varieties to choose from (including vegetarian options), with wild boar and mushroom and tarragon recommended. The excellent puddings include treacle tart and sherry trifle.

Café Grove (Map pp156-7; ☎ 7243 1094; 253a Portobello Rd W11; mains £5-9.50; ⏲ 10am-5pm Sun-Fri, 10am-6pm Sun; ⊖ Ladbroke Grove) This no-frills neighbourhood eatery has been attracting the locals for decades. They come for all-day breakfasts (the eggs Benedict are worth dropping in for), as well as heaping pasta dishes, large salads and jaw-stretching sandwiches. There's a large terrace overlooking the nearby market.

MIDRANGE

Geales (Map pp156-7; ☎ 7727 7528; 2 Farmer St W8; mains £10; ⏲ lunch & dinner Mon-Sat, dinner Sun; ⊖ Notting Hill Gate) Decked out in maritime blue and white, Geales is as close to the seaside as many Notting Hill locals ever get. A cut above the area's greasy chip shops, its chefs know exactly how to prepare the best seasonal catches. If you must try fish and chips in London, this is *the* place to do it. Grab one of the tables outside in summer for a bonus tan at no extra cost.

Food @ The Muse (Map pp156-7; ☎ 7792 1111; 269 Portobello Rd W11; mains £8-14; ⏲ lunch & dinner Tue-Sat, dinner Sun & Mon; ⊖ Notting Hill Gate) Part of the Muse Gallery, this sleek, modern restaurant focuses on contemporary European cuisine. Its dishes are eclectic and adventurous, with the hot and sour green mango salad with roast peanuts particularly recommended. Although its stark white interiors make it look a little cold, there's a comfortable, laidback vibe.

E&O (Map pp156-7; ☎ 7229 5454; 14 Blenheim Cres W11; mains £6-22; ⏲ lunch & dinner; ⊖ Notting Hill Gate/Ladbroke Grove) Its long name is 'Eastern & Oriental' but the trendy E&O has moved way beyond most fusion restaurants with dishes that defy categorisation. Come for a culinary adventure and you'll find yourself mixing Japanese, Chinese and West Coast–influenced courses. Book ahead: it's always popular.

South Bank & Bankside

Reflecting this area's growing gentrification, there are some good midrange 'gastropubs' and a few swanky new restaurants.

Anchor & Hope (Map pp152-3; ☎ 7928 9898; 36 The Cut SE1; mains £11-16; ⏲ lunch Tue-Sat, dinner Mon-Sat; ⊖ Southwark/Waterloo) One of London's most-celebrated gastropubs, the mainly British fare includes delicacies like pigeon and pig's heart. It's not all offal, though, with Lancashire hot pot and steak and ale pie catering to more conventional tastes. It also roasts a vegetarian every Sunday – just kidding.

fish! (Map p160; ☎ 7407 3803; Cathedral St SE1; mains £11-17; ⏲ lunch & dinner; ⊖ London Bridge) Situated in an incongruous glass pavilion overlooking Borough Market, this contemporary brasserie specialises in fresh, sustainably sourced fish dishes. Among the exquisitely prepared, seasonal offerings, the seared scallops with roast tomatoes is recommended, while a side order of Thai crab cakes is a good idea.

Oxo Tower Restaurant & Brasserie (Map pp152-3; ☎ 7803 3888; 8th fl, Barge House St SE1; mains £11-26; 🕐 lunch & dinner Mon-Sat; ⊖ Blackfriars/Waterloo) For a splurge with a view, it's hard to beat these twin Thameside restaurants located in one of London's leading Art Deco landmarks. The restaurant is on the pricey side, so head to the brasserie: the views are the same and the menu features plenty of tempting French-themed treats.

DRINKING

Booze has flown through London like a second Thames River since the wine-quaffing Romans set up shop here almost 2000 years ago. But while the capital has more old-school pubs than you can shake a yard of ale at, a new breed of lounge-style bars has also slid onto the scene in recent years. The following are some of our favourite London drinking holes.

Ye Olde Cheshire Cheese (Map pp152-3; ☎ 7353 6170; 145 Fleet St EC4; ⊖ Blackfriars) One of the granddaddies of London pubs, this 17th-century multiroomed maze is stacked over several levels. Head downstairs to find a brick-lined vault fringed with stone arches and dimly lit corners – it's the kind of place villains from Dickens might have come to plan their nefarious shenanigans. There's also a great selection of Samuel Smith ales.

Market Porter (Map p160; ☎ 7407 2495; 9 Stoney St SE1; ⊖ London Bridge) Nestled in the backstreets near Borough Market, the exterior of this real-ale pioneer is decked with flowers in spring and summer. A little less fragrant inside, its hardwood floors and upturned barrel tables are the perfect setting for a pint of Otter Bitter or the splendidly named Slater's Top Totty.

Bradley's Spanish Bar (Map pp152-3; ☎ 7636 0359; 44 Hanway St W1; ⊖ Tottenham Court Rd) Shabby, small and charming, this roguish bohemian haunt can still pack in the alternative types on most nights. Head downstairs for dimly lit alcoves, red velvet seats and a diverse selection of draught European beers or just plug some money into the jukebox. It's stocked with classics by Nirvana, Pearl Jam *et al.*

Queen's Larder (Map pp152-3; ☎ 7837 5627; 1 Queen Sq WC1; ⊖ Russell Square) Used by Queen Charlotte to store delicacies for George III, this old pub has been whitewashed of much of its colourful history. It's still a tranquil retreat from the London hubbub, though – especially in summer, when you can sit outside in the lovely square.

Lamb & Flag (Map pp152-3; ☎ 7497 9504; 33 Rose St WC2; ⊖ Covent Garden) Tucked in the narrow backstreets of Covent Carden, this old charmer has hardly changed in decades. The wood floors are still painted black, the tables are chipped and wobbly, and the shadowy backroom still contains an open fireplace. For those who like to eat with their beer, it also offers a celebrated gourmet cheese selection.

Anchor Bankside (Map pp152-3; ☎ 7407 1577; 34 Park St SE1; ⊖ London Bridge) With a large patio on the edge of the Thames, this is the perfect spot to watch the pleasure boats slide by. On rainy days the main pub building – a handsome brick and timber construction, garnished with red window frames and bright blue shutters – is a cosy gem, with an array of Shakespearean ephemera indicating the area's link to the Bard.

Loungelover (Map p160; ☎ 7012 1234; 1 Whitby St E1; ⊖ Shoreditch) With its menagerie of interior quirks – think stuffed hippo's heads and Victorian chandeliers – this eccentric drinking hole has been popular with hipsters since it opened. Despite the determinedly wacky aesthetics, it's still cosy and has a kick-ass selection of cocktails. There's also live music on Friday nights.

Seven Stars (Map pp152-3; ☎ 7242 8521; 53-54 Carey St W12; ⊖ Holborn) There's not much elbow room at this eccentric sliver of a pub that combines the history of several centuries with movie-buff wall displays and some serious gastropub dining. Built in the early 1600s, it has a continental ambience, a surprisingly good wine list and a roster of sturdy high-end scotches.

George Inn (Map p160; ☎ 7407 2056; Talbot Yard, 77 Borough High St SE1; ⊖ London Bridge) Dating from 1676, London's last surviving galleried coaching inn, with its low ceilings and dark-panelled rooms, is mentioned in Dickens' *Little Dorrit*. Now owned by the National Trust, it has become something of a history theme pub – which explains the coach parties that roll up in summer.

AUTHOR'S CHOICE

Lamb (Map pp152-3; ☎ 7405 0713; 94 Lamb's Conduit St WC1; ⊖ Russell Square) Residing on the strangely named Lambs Conduit St, this classic old-school boozer is like walking into a Victorian pub museum. A heritage award winner, the Lamb celebrates several bar-room features that were once standard across the land. High-backed banquettes are finished in green leather, small tables are topped with brass rails to keep pints from toppling and the polished, U-shaped counter is topped with dozens of etched glass 'snob screens' located at eye level. These small revolving panels were designed to close so that drinkers could conceal their identity while drinking at the bar. While the screens are rarely used today, the Lamb is a warm and welcoming spot and a good bar to sample distinctive tipples, including the honey-sweet Waggle Dance, the fruity St George's Ale and the surprisingly light Triple A – a good beer for first-time bitter drinkers.

ENTERTAINMENT

By day and night London hosts a lively, vibrant mix of welcome distractions. It's a world leader in live theatre, a catalyst for new music and a hub of great clubs. Following are some of the city's recommended entertainment highlights.

Theatre

While juggernaut musicals that never seem to end and vanity projects starring Hollywood glitterati like Nicole Kidman draw the headlines, London's theatreland is far more diverse than it's often given credit for. A glimpse at the depth of what's on offer in the West End and beyond is available at the **Official London Theatre website** (www.officiallondontheatre.co.uk), which provides comprehensive listings and regular discounts.

There are many hole-in-the-wall businesses advertising cheap tickets but Leicester Sq's **tkts** (Map pp152-3; www.tkts.co.uk; 🕓 10am-7pm Mon-Sat, noon-3pm Sun; ⊖ Leicester Square) is the only one that's consistently reputable. Arrive in the morning to see what's on offer for the day (booking fee £2.50). If you're in town during the low season – mid-January to mid-March – dozens of theatres take part in **Get Into London Theatre** (☎ 0870 040 0039; www.getintolondontheatre.com), a discount promotion with tickets for top shows running from £15 to £30.

Royal National Theatre (Map pp152-3; ☎ 7452 3000; www.nt-online.org; South Bank SE1; tickets £7-35; ⊖ Waterloo) Running its own discount promotion in summer, with tickets selling for £10 during the annual Travelex promotion, the National is Britain's flagship repertory. Located on the South Bank, this three-stage theatre combines innovative new plays and sparkling revivals of important dramas.

Shakespeare's Globe (Map pp152-3; ☎ 7401 9919; www.shakespeares-globe.org; 21 New Globe Walk SE1; 🕓 May-Oct; ⊖ Mansion House/Southwark/London Bridge) Fans of the bearded Bard will love taking in a performance at the Globe, a near-perfect replica of the building where his plays were staged from 1598 to 1611. This is alfresco theatre-in-the-round, so make sure you bring something warm to wear on cooler evenings. Tours and exhibitions are also offered (p163).

Old Vic (Map pp152-3; ☎ 0870 060 6628; www.oldvictheatre.com; Waterloo Rd SE1; ⊖ Waterloo) London theatre buffs are enjoying watching the controversial 10-year tenure of Hollywood hot shot Kevin Spacey at this venerable playhouse, which was on its last legs until the late 1990s. Its famous white knight has not been given an easy ride, though: several shows have been panned and its future is far from assured.

Live Music

London's live rock, pop, indie and classical music scenes hit the stage at dozens of venues around the city. Pick up a copy of *Time Out*, which lists hundreds of gigs every week. The following are among the notable venues:

Brixton Academy (☎ 7771 3000; www.brixton-academy.co.uk; 211 Stockwell Rd SW9; ⊖ Brixton) Top venue for hot bands.

Shepherd's Bush Empire (☎ 8534 3300; www.shepherds-bush-empire.co.uk; Shepherds Bush Green W12; ⊖ Shepherd's Bush) Leading larger rock and pop venue.

12 Bar Club (Map pp152-3; ☎ 7916 6989; www.12barclub.com; Denmark St WC2; ⊖ Tottenham Court Rd) Intimate, with an emphasis on singer-songwriters.

Borderline (Map pp152-3; ☎ 7734 5547; www.meanfiddler.com; Orange Yard, Manette St WC2; ⊖ Tottenham Court Rd) Subterranean space with rock edge.

Garage (☎ 8963 0940; www.meanfiddler.com; 20-22 Highbury Corner N5; ⊖ Highbury & Islington) Focused on indie acts.

Ronnie Scott's (Map pp152-3; ☎ 7439 0747; www.ronniescotts.co.uk; 47 Frith St W1; ⊖ Leicester Square) Old-school jazz favourite.

Barbican Centre (Map p160; ☎ 7638 8891; www.barbican.org.uk; Silk St EC2; ⊖ Moorgate/Barbican) Home of the London Symphony Orchestra.

South Bank Centre (Map pp152-3; ☎ 0870 380 0400; www.rfh.org.uk; Belvedere Rd SE1; ⊖ Waterloo) Classical venue with Royal Festival Hall, Queen Elizabeth Hall and Purcell Room stages.

Nightclubs

Not surprisingly, London hosts an astonishing array of clubs, from noisy warehouse-sized dance stadiums to intimate house and hip-hop fests where fans immerse themselves in the latest groove. While 'superclubs' can charge anywhere up to £20 for entry on Friday and Saturday nights, admission on a wet Monday in January at one of the smaller joints can be free. The following is a tasting menu of what's on offer.

93 Feet East (Map p160; ☎ 7247 3293; 150 Brick Lane E1; admission free-£10; 🕑 5-11pm Mon-Thu, 5pm-1am Fri, noon-1am Sat, noon-10.30pm Sun; ⊖ Liverpool St) Hosting Hoxton's finest, this excellent club has three rooms, a swish downstairs bar and an appealing outdoor courtyard for cooling off. Hip-hop, soul and house are the mainstays, but there's an eclectic mix of additional happenings to keep the smart crowd interested.

Bar Rhumba (Map pp152-3; ☎ 7287 2715; 26 Shaftesbury Ave W1; admission free-£12; 🕑 10.30pm-3am Mon & Wed, 8.30pm-3am Tue, Thu & Fri, 9pm-5am Sat, 8pm-1.30am Sun; ⊖ Piccadilly Circus) This intimate subterranean club in the heart of Soho has been packing them in for more than 10 years. The crowds come for theme nights like Barrio Latino, focusing on salsa and urban Latin beats, and Sportswear Jam, where Adidas-clad funksters party to house music.

Fabric (Map pp152-3; ☎ 7336 8898; 77a Charterhouse St EC1; admission £12-15; 🕑 9.30pm-5am Fri, 10pm-7am Sat; ⊖ Farringdon) This former meat-cellar venue attracts an international crowd to its three packed dance floors, including the kidney-shaking 'Bodysonic' floor. Focuses include electro and house, but Friday night's Fabriclive event is a heart-racing mix of everything from hip-hop to drum'n'bass.

Pacha London (Map pp152-3; ☎ 7834 4440; admission £15-20; Terminus Pl SW1; 🕑 10pm-4am Fri, 10pm-6am Sat; ⊖ Victoria) Large, loud and mainstream, this ever-popular London nightspot combines wood panelling, upholstered booths and an amazing stained-glass ceiling. The music is pop, soul and house, and there are regular monthly theme nights.

Also recommended:

Cross (Map pp152-3; ☎ 7837 0828; 27-31 King's Cross Goods Yard; admission £12-15; 🕑 10.30pm-5am Fri & Sat, 10.30pm-4am Sun; ⊖ King's Cross) House with an Ibizan flavour; located off York Way N1.

Cherry Jam (Map pp156-7; ☎ 7727 9950; 58 Porchester Rd W2; admission £5-8; 🕑 7pm-1.30am Thu-Sat; ⊖ Royal Oak) Latin to deep-house, plus live bands and readings.

Gay & Lesbian Venues

Soho is the heart of gay London – head for the main strip of Old Compton St where there are plenty of bars and cafés, and pick up free listings like *Boyz* and *QX*. More serious papers and magazines include *Diva* and *Gay Times*. The annual Pride Parade is in July (p165). Recommended popular pubs, bars and clubs:

Candy Bar (Map pp152-3; ☎ 7494 4041; 4 Carlisle St W1; 🕑 5-11.30pm Mon-Thu, 5pm-2am Fri & Sat, 5-11.30pm Sun; ⊖ Tottenham Court Rd) London's best lesbian bar.

Compton's of Soho (Map pp152-3; ☎ 7479 7961; 51-53 Old Compton St W1; ⊖ Leicester Square) Popular cruising bar for the boys.

Fiction (Map pp152-3; ☎ 7749 1199; 27-31 King's Cross Goods Yard; admission £9-15; 🕑 11pm-5am Fri; ⊖ King's Cross) Weekly gay night at the Cross nightclub, off York Way N1.

Ghetto (Map pp152-3; ☎ 7287 3726; 5-6 Falconberg Ct W1; admission £2-7; 🕑 10.30pm-3am Mon-Thu, 10.30pm-4am Fri, 10.30pm-5am Sat, 10pm-3am Sun; ⊖ Tottenham Court Rd) Club for fashionable glitterati.

Heaven (Map pp152-3; ☎ 7930 2020; The Arches, Villiers St WC2; admission £1-12; 🕑 10.30pm-3am Mon & Wed, 10.30am-6pm Fri, 10pm-5am Sat; ⊖ Charing Cross) Legendary London gay club.

Sport

Football is at the heart of English culture and London has 11 professional teams – more than any other city in the world. While Premiership high-flyers like **Chelsea** (☎ 7915 2951; www.chelseafc.com; Stamford Bridge Stadium, Fulham Rd SW6; admission £38-48; ⊖ Fulham Broadway) and **Arsenal** (☎ 7704 4040; www.arsenal.com; Avenell Rd N5; admission £28-50; ⊖ Arsenal) attract the lion's share of the crowds, it's easy (and cheaper) to catch a game at one of the smaller London clubs, like **Queen's Park Rangers**

A SPOT OF TEE-HEE

Bored with sleepy old pubs and nightclubs that won't play that obscure Kraftwerk single for you? London's booming comedy-club scene offers an alternative night out where you can rub shoulders with the locals and practise your understanding of the eclectic British sense of humour.

Some shows are staged in purpose-built clubs, while many more take place in spare pub rooms. There's always plenty of beer flowing to keep the audience well lubricated, and there are usually at least three stand-up comics ready to take the stage and launch their candid observations on an unsuspecting world – don't sit too close to the front or you'll be one of the main observations. If you think you're funnier, some venues have open-mic nights where you can tell all your best jokes in a drunken stupor.

Among the best clubs, the **Comedy Store** (Map pp152-3; ☎ 0870 060 2340; www.thecomedystore.co.uk; 1a Oxendon St SW1; admission £13-15; ⊖ Leicester Square/Piccadilly Circus) is the most established, while **Downstairs at the King's Head** (☎ 8340 1028; www.downstairsatthekingshead; 2 Crouch End Hill N8; admission £4-8; ⊖ Finsbury Park), **Amused Moose Soho** (Map pp152-3; ☎ 8341 1341; www.amusedmoose.co.uk; 17 Greek St W1; admission £5-12; ⊖ Leicester Square) and **Headliners** (☎ 8566 4067; www.headlinerscomedy.biz; The George IV, 185 Chiswick High Rd W4; admission £10; ⊖ Turnham Green) are always good for a few guffaws. For information on upcoming shows, check *Time Out* or visit **Chortle** (www.chortle.co.uk).

(☎ 0870 112 1967; www.qpr.co.uk; Loftus Rd Stadium W12; admission £22-28; ⊖ Shepherd's Bush).

Wembley Stadium (☎ 8795 9000; www.wembleystadium.com; Empire Way, Wembley; ⊖ Wembley Stadium) This new 80,000-seat, state-of-the-art stadium in northwest London was not finished at the time of research, but will be the country's premier venue for football matches and the host stadium for the 2012 Olympic Games.

Twickenham (☎ 8892 2000; www.rfu.com; Rugby Rd, Twickenham; ⊖ Hounslow East then bus 281, or rail Twickenham) The shrine of English rugby union.

Lord's (☎ 7432 1000; www.lords.org; St John's Wood Rd NW8; admission £5-50; ⊖ St John's Wood) One of the city's two major cricket venues.

Brit Oval (☎ 7582 7764; www.surreycricket.com; Kennington Oval SE11; admission £5-50; ⊖ Oval) The city's other venerable cricket ground.

All England Lawn Tennis Club (☎ 8944 1066; www.wimbledon.org; Church Rd SW19; admission £15-60; ⊖ Southfields) Watch tennis and eat strawberries and cream at Wimbledon's tennis club (see p165).

Walthamstow Stadium (☎ 8531 4255; www.wsgreyhound.co.uk; Chingford Rd E4; admission £1-6; ⊖ Walthamstow Central, then bus 97 or 215) You can rub shoulders with the working classes on a cheap and cheerful greyhound racing night out here.

SHOPPING

Manically crowded Oxford St is lined with generic high street chains, but it's far more fun to duck down London's backstreets for some less mainstream shopping. Among the more enjoyable shopping areas are Covent Garden's Neal's Yard for youthful shoe shops and clothing boutiques; the Charing Cross Rd area between Tottenham Court Rd and Leicester Sq for general and specialist bookshops; King's Rd for designer knick-knacks and home accessories; and Knightsbridge for credit card–breaking top-end designers. While simply wandering around these areas until you find something you like is highly recommended, the following London shops are on the top of our list.

Agent Provocateur (Map pp152-3; ☎ 7439 0229; 6 Broadwick St W1; ⊖ Oxford Circus) This playful designer lingerie shop manages to produce an air of tasteful eroticism without the sleaze factor of less classy outfits. Founded by designer Vivienne Westwood's son, it has become a major success with matching outfits across the capital.

Conran Shop (Map pp156-7; ☎ 7589 7401; 81 Fulham Rd N1; ⊖ Angel) Before IKEA, there was Brit-design guru Terence Conran. This eminently browsable store – one of a small chain across the capital – has lots of large furnishings that are unlikely to fit in your suitcase, but there are legions of small, must-have vases, clocks and picture frames that are hard to resist.

Harrods (Map pp156-7; ☎ 7730 1234; 87-135 Brompton Rd SW1; ⊖ Oxford Circus) London's temple to indulgent shopping, this legendary megalithic department store has acres of designer goods that are outside the budgets of most London visitors. The colourful ground-floor

HOT MARKETS

Brick Lane is still the best place for a morning fried-egg sandwich, sold from a rusting roadside van held together with layers of old cooking fat. But there's much more to London's eclectic street markets than a heart attack waiting to happen. The following are five great market recommendations.

Borough Market (Map p160; 8 Southwark St SE1; noon-6pm Fri, 9am-4pm Sat; London Bridge) 'London's Larder', this original 13th-century farmers market is a smorgasbord of quality fresh food and produce. Come here hungry: you'll want to snack on treats like rustic pork pies and succulent chorizo sandwiches. If you get thirsty, grab a beer in the nearby Market Porter pub (p172).

Brick Lane Market (Map p160; Brick Lane E2; 8am-2pm Sun; Aldgate East) This sprawling East End pearl is a real hotchpotch of fake designer T-shirts, cheap razor blades and socks that are as thin as paper. But it's just as much fun to watch as it is to buy: there are still a few old-school market hawkers here and their lively banter is always entertaining. Arrive early to avoid the bottleneck crowds.

Camden Market (Camden High St NW1; 10am-6pm; Camden Town) A cosmopolitan grab bag of several markets lining the High St, this colourful area is great for local arts, trendy crafts and cheap souvenirs. There are some excellent outdoor food stands serving heaping ethnic dishes for just a few quid along with fun vintage clothes stalls under the railway arches.

Portobello Rd Market (Map pp156-7; Portobello Rd W10; 8am-6pm Mon-Wed, Fri & Sat, 8am-1pm Thu; Notting Hill Gate/Ladbroke Grove) Like a giant open-air bric-a-brac museum, this clutch of markets specialises in browsable used goods, including vintage clothes and funky costume jewellery. Since this is chichi Notting Hill, there are also plenty of tasty takeout treats that are a cut above the burger stands of other markets.

Spitalfields Market (Map p160; Commercial St, E1; 10am-5pm Mon-Fri & Sun; Liverpool St) A favourite among Londoners, there's a youthful, intelligent vibe to this lovely covered Victorian market between Brushfield and Lamb Sts. You'll find cool stuff like funky new fashions and retro furniture alongside jewellery and handmade soaps. The twice-weekly food market (Wednesday and Sunday) is a delightful feast of organic beer, piquant cheeses and chocolate croissants.

food court is worth a stroll – it has lots of cheap Harrods-label teas and biscuits you can buy as souvenirs for your poor friends back home.

Muji (Map pp152-3; ☎ 7379 0820; 135 Long Acre WC2; Covent Garden) Homesick language students and budget-conscious young locals flock to this Japanese general store whenever they have a few pennies to spare. Despite the generally low prices, everything – from basic sweatshirts to stainless-steel business-card holders – has a minimalist flair. There are outlets throughout the city.

Paperchase (Map pp152-3; ☎ 7467 6200; 213-215 Tottenham Court Rd W1; Goodge St) Those who drool over stationery won't want to miss this three-storey flagship store. It's bristling with clever notepads, quirky journals, slick pens and designer desk storage units.

Selfridges (☎ 7636 7700; 36-38 Great Castle St W1; Bond St/Marble Arch) Trendier than its Harrods department-store rival, Selfridges' expansive clothing floors cover a kaleidoscope of designers from Paul Smith to Karen Millen. The annual January sale is an orgy of cut-price designer wear.

Topshop (Map pp152-3; ☎ 7636 7700; 36-38 Great Castle St W1; Oxford Circus) This giant flagship store is a bit of a revelation to those who think they know this chain from its high street locations across Britain. Funky designer copies, hipster disposable fashions and low, low prices are the reasons it's always crowded.

GETTING THERE & AWAY

As the country's major transport gateway, much of the information about arriving in London is covered in this chapter's Transport in Britain section (p277).

Air

Along with the region's much larger Heathrow, Gatwick, Stansted and Luton airports, **London City Airport** (LCY; ☎ 7646 0088; www.londoncityairport.com) services an expanding roster of UK, European and international destinations. Mainly used by business travellers, it's in Docklands, 6 miles east of central London. Its domestic routes include regular Flybe flights from Edinburgh (from £50, 1¼ hours).

Bus

Most long-distance bus services terminate at **Victoria Coach Station** (Map pp152-3; ☎ 7730 3466; 184 Buckingham Palace Rd SW1; ⊖ Victoria).

The array of National Express buses arriving here includes daily direct services from Oxford (£12, 1¾ hours), Cambridge (£10, two hours), Birmingham (from £1, three hours), Manchester (from £1, four to five hours), Cardiff (from £3, three to four hours) and Glasgow (from £5, eight to nine hours).

Megabus runs direct services to Victoria from Birmingham (from £1, three hours), Cardiff (from £1, three hours), Edinburgh (from £3, eight to nine hours), Liverpool (£3.50, five hours) and Plymouth (from £1, three hours).

Train

High-speed **Eurostar** (☎ 0870 518 6186; www.eurostar.com) trains arrive in London from Paris (from £59, three hours) and Brussels (from £59, 2½ hours) via the Channel Tunnel. There are regular direct services from Lille, Avignon and Disneyland Paris, with additional connections from across Europe. Eurostar services currently arrive at London Waterloo, but will begin arriving at a swanky new St Pancras terminal, due to open in 2007, once a high-speed rail link has been completed across the city. The new line will shave 30 minutes from travel times.

Frequent daily train routes into the city include Oxford to London Paddington (£16.50, one hour), Manchester to London Euston (from £12.50, 2½ hours), Edinburgh to London King's Cross (from £12.50, 4½ to 5½ hours), Newcastle to London King's Cross (from £10, three hours) and Cardiff to London Paddington (from £24, two hours). Megatrain discount services into the city include Salisbury to London Waterloo (from £1, 1½ hours), Portsmouth to London Waterloo (from £1, 1½ hours) and Bath to London Waterloo (from £1, 2½ hours).

GETTING AROUND

To/From the Airports

HEATHROW

Fifteen miles west of central London, Heathrow is accessible by main-line train, tube and bus. Arriving every 15 minutes between 5.25am and 11.55pm at London Paddington, the **Heathrow Express** (☎ 0845 600 1515; www.heathrowexpress.co.uk) is the fastest transit option (£14.50, 20 minutes). The Piccadilly Line underground train service also picks up at Heathrow and stops at several central London stations, including Knightsbridge, Hyde Park Corner, Piccadilly Circus and Leicester Square (£6.20, one hour). The service runs every few minutes from 5.30am to 11.45pm. Frequent National Express buses from Heathrow arrive at London Victoria through the day (£10, one hour).

GATWICK

Some 30 miles south of London, Gatwick airport is accessible by main-line train and bus services. Arriving at London Victoria every 15 or 30 minutes between 5.50am and 2.10am, the **Gatwick Express** (☎ 0845 850 1530; www.gatwickexpress.co.uk) is the most efficient option (£14, 30 minutes). Frequent National Express buses from Gatwick arrive at Victoria during the day (£6.60, one to two hours).

STANSTED

About 35 miles northeast of central London, Stansted is London's third-busiest international gateway. It's accessible by main-line train and bus. Arriving at London Liverpool St every 15 to 45 minutes between 6.15am and 1.15am, the **Stansted Express** (☎ 0845 748 4950; www.standstedexpress.com) is the fastest route into London (£15, 45 minutes). Frequent direct National Express buses from Stansted arrive at London Victoria throughout the day (£10, 1½ hours).

LONDON CITY

Six miles east of central London, London City Airport is in Docklands. With the demise of its shuttle bus service, the best way to get to central London is via the Docklands Light Railway (DLR). The station is 50m from the airport terminal and services run regularly to Bank (£3, 22 minutes), Canning Town (£3, eight minutes) and Canary Wharf (£3, 14 minutes). You can link with the underground system at any of these stations.

LUTON

About 35 miles north of London, Luton is a growing London airline link for domestic and international routes. It's accessible by main-line train and bus. Regular direct train services arrive from Luton at London King's Cross throughout the day (£11.20, one hour). Frequent National Express buses from Luton arrive at London Victoria throughout the day (£8, one to 1½ hours). **easyBus** (www.easybus.co.uk) runs a frequent daily minibus service from the airport to London's Regent's Park area (from £2, one to two hours).

Boat

New boat services are popping up all the time around London. If you have a Travelcard (see Bus & Tube, right), you'll get one-third off all fares listed here. The following options are the most useful for visitors.

Tate-to-Tate (☎ 7887 8888; www.tate.org.uk/tatetotate; 🕒 10am-5pm) ferries operate between Bankside pier at Tate Modern and the new Milbank pier at sister museum Tate Britain, stopping en route at the London Eye (one-way/day ticket £4.30/7.30).

City Cruises (☎ 7740 0400; www.citycruises.com) links Greenwich and Westminster (one-way/return £7/9), as well as Tower Pier and the London Eye (one-way/return £6/7). A popular all-day Red Rover pass is available (£9.50), and the company also offers lunch and dinner cruises.

Westminster Passenger Service Association (☎ 7930 2062; www.wpsa.co.uk; 🕒 Apr-Oct) operates a regular up-river service from Westminster to Kew Gardens (one-way/return £10.50/16.50, 1½ hours) and Hampton Court (one-way/return £13.50/19.50, two hours).

Car & Motorcycle

We do not advise driving in London: traffic jams are common, parking space is at a premium and there are annoyingly dutiful traffic wardens. If you bring your car into central London from 7am to 6.30pm on a weekday, you'll need to pay a £5 per day **congestion charge** (☎ 0845 900 1234; www.cclondon.com). You know you are entering the chargeable zone when you see a large letter 'C' painted on the road.

Public Transport

For information on London's bus, underground (tube), DLR and main-line train services, contact **Transport for London** (☎ 7222 1234; www.tfl.gov.uk). Its website has a useful journey planner engine.

For the lowest fares on public transport, buy an Oyster prepaid fare card. Purchased at tube stations (£3 returnable deposit), you charge the card with cash, swipe it on buses or at tube/train station barriers and the fare is deducted from your balance. Oyster fares are lower than the regular fares charged to passengers buying single tickets.

BUS & TUBE

London's extensive bus and tube systems generally run from early morning (typically 7am for buses and 5.30am for the tube) until around midnight. The single adult fare on buses is £1.50 (£0.80 to £1 with Oyster). Depending on the length of your trip, single adult fares on the tube cost £3 to £6.20 (£1 to £5.50 with Oyster).

Travelcards allow all-day, unlimited access to bus, tube, DLR and many main-line London train services. The adult one-day Travelcard costs £4.30 to £6.20, depending on the areas you will be travelling in and the time of day you will be travelling. If you use an Oyster card for all-day travel, the card is capped so that you will never pay more than the price of a Travelcard no matter how many trips you take.

When the regular bus and tube services stop for the night, a system of night buses (prefixed with the letter 'N') rolls into action. Trafalgar Square, Tottenham Court Rd and Oxford Circus are its main terminals. They stop by request only, so make sure you have your arm outstretched when the bus turns up. These services run every 10 to 20 minutes and they accept your previous day's Travelcard up until 4.30am.

DLR & TRAIN

The monorail-like, driverless Docklands Light Railway (DLR) runs from Bank and Tower Hill underground stations to Canary Wharf, Stratford, Beckton, Greenwich and Lewisham. Fares operate the same way as on the tube and your Travelcard is valid on the DLR network. Main-line trains are the primary means of transport to much of London's suburbia. Main-line stations interchange with the tube and you can use your Travelcard for any parts of the journey within London.

Taxi

The city's famous black cabs now come in a variety of colours and can be hailed when their 'for hire' sign is lit. They're not the cheapest way to travel and there are extra charges for more than five passengers. You can tip taxi drivers up to 10% but most people round up to the nearest pound. To book a taxi in advance, call **Dial-a-Cab** (☎ 7253 5000). It runs a 24-hour service.

Minicabs can carry up to four people and tend to be cheaper than black cabs. Be aware that there is a problem with unlicensed minicabs in London. Do not get into a minicab if you are unsure whether it is legitimate. Transport for London estimates that unlicensed minicab drivers commit 10 sexual assaults in the capital every month. Visit its website at www.tfl.gov.uk for a search engine of accredited operators. These operators include **Lady Cabs** (☎ 7272 3300), which employs women drivers and is recommended for women travelling alone, and **Green Tomato Cars** (☎ 8748 8881), which uses energy-efficient vehicles.

AROUND LONDON

When you're tired of London, you're tired of life, opined arch 18th-century Londoner Samuel Johnson. But he wasn't living in an age when a day out on the airless tube system can leave you exhausted and grouchy. Luckily, the capital is surprisingly close to some excellent day-out escapes. Excluding well-known day-trip haunts like Brighton, Oxford and Stonehenge, here are some historic gems closer to home.

Windsor & Eton

☎ 01753 / pop 31,000

One of Britain's largest and most imposing medieval palaces, **Windsor Castle** (☎ 020-7766 7304; adult/child £13.50/7.50; ⏰ 9.45am-5.15pm Mar-Oct, 9.45am-4.15pm Nov-Feb) is still in use by the Queen. But that doesn't mean visitors have to content themselves with peering through the gates outside. Instead, you can enter large sections of the complex, now fully restored after the devastating 1992 fire. Highlights include Queen Mary's giant dolls' house, designed by Sir Edward Lutyens, and St George's Chapel, containing the tombs of several monarchs, including Henry VIII (interred with third wife, Jane Seymour). The surrounding Victorian town is also worth checking out, particularly for its traditional tea rooms. Make sure you put the milk in the cup before the tea or they'll know you're a tourist.

A short walk along Thames St and across the river brings you to **Eton College** (☎ 671177; www.etoncollege.com; adult/child £4/3.20; ⏰ 10.30am-4.30pm mid-Mar–mid-Apr, 2-4.30pm mid-April–Jun, 10.30am-4.30pm Jul-Aug, 2-4.30pm Sep), that famous public school that has educated 18 prime ministers and any number of royals. Several buildings date from when Henry VI founded the school in the mid-15th century. Entry includes a free tour and admission to the **Museum of Eton Life**, which focuses on the world of the public schoolboy past and present.

Direct trains from London Waterloo arrive at Windsor and Eaton Riverside twice hourly (£7, one hour).

Hatfield House

Home to the 7th Marquess of Salisbury, **Hatfield House** (☎ 01707-287010; www.hatfield-house.co.uk; adult/child £8.50/4; ⏰ noon-5pm Wed-Sun Apr-Sep) is England's most celebrated Jacobean edifice – a graceful stone and red-brick mansion teeming with period tapestries, paintings and furniture. The largest private estate in Hertfordshire, it's surrounded by 800 hectares of tranquil woodland. Its attractions include a national collection of **model soldiers** and dozens of rural trails, and it's a great place to bring a picnic and spend the day.

The entrance to the grounds is just across the street from Hatfield train station. Direct trains arrive from London King's Cross every 15 minutes (£6.80, 20 minutes).

SOUTHEAST ENGLAND

Traditionally a day-trip playground for Londoners looking to escape the capital's overcrowded streets, the southeast offers fascinating historic towns, sweeping green-belt vistas and some of the country's most vibrant seaside resorts – most less than a 60-minute train ride from the city.

With a disproportionately large swathe of the UK population living in one of the five 'Home Counties' here – these are the miserable commuters you'll see silently clutching their daily newspapers on the train ride into London – even the southeast's small towns can feel busy.

This is especially true on summer weekends, when street markets burst into life and high street shopping becomes a clamorous contact sport. Luckily, respite is never more than a few miles away in the sleepy pub-strewn villages, handsome castle complexes and patchwork rolling hills that colour the region. For visitor information, contact **Tourism South East** (☎ 023-8062 5400; www.visitsoutheastengland.com).

CANTERBURY

☎ 01227 / pop 43,552

With its jaw-dropping, multispired cathedral surrounded by cobbled medieval streets, this Unesco World Heritage city has been a popular pilgrimage site for Christians and tourists for centuries. Latter-day visitors – they just about overwhelm the area during summer – come to immerse themselves in religious and secular history, including Thomas Becket's murder and the bawdy works of Geoffrey Chaucer. But this is no mothballed outdoor museum: Canterbury is a surprisingly vibrant centre, and a good base for exploring the region's quaint villages, gentle valleys and colourful coastline.

Orientation & Information

Almost enclosed by a medieval wall and fully surrounded by a modern ring road, the historic centre of Canterbury is compact enough to explore on foot, which is just as well since many of its ancient streets are closed to cars. The bus station is within the old city walls on St George's Lane, but the two train stations – Canterbury East and Canterbury West – are a few minutes' walk from the ancient perimeter.

The **TIC** (☎ 378100; www.canterbury.co.uk; 12-13 Sun St; 9.30am-5pm Mon-Sat Easter-Oct, 10am-4pm Mon-Sat Nov-Easter, 10am-4pm Sun Easter-Dec) is opposite the cathedral. Free Internet access is available at the **library** (☎ 463608; High St; 9.30am-6pm Mon, Wed & Thu, 9.30am-7pm Tue, 8.30am-7pm Fri, 9am-5pm Sat).

Sights & Activities

Barely surviving major fires in 1067 and 1174, **Canterbury Cathedral** (☎ 762862; www.canterbury-cathedral.org; adult/child £6/4.50; 9am-6.30pm Mon-Sat, 9am-2.30pm & 4.30-5.30pm Sun Apr-Oct, 9am-5pm Mon-Sat, 10am-2pm & 4.30-5.30pm Sun Nov-Mar) embodies Britain's tumultuous and frequently bloody religious history. Following the 1170 martyrdom of Thomas Becket in the northwest transept, the site became Europe's top spot for pilgrims and remains the spiritual centre of today's Church of England. It's easy to spend a couple of hours marvelling at the Early English architecture here, but it's worth taking a one-hour tour (adult/child £4/2) to hear the stories behind the stonework.

Illuminating the city's earlier history, Canterbury's **Roman Museum** (☎ 785575; Butchery Lane; adult/child £2.90/1.80; 10am-5pm Mon-Sat year-round, 1.30-5pm Sun Jun-Oct) is located underground at the level of the original settlement. A fascinating mix of excavated artefacts and clever reconstructions – check out the mosaic remains and the smells in the Roman kitchen – visitors are encouraged to handle some of the displays and use their deductive skills as archaeologists.

The gloriously cheesy **Canterbury Tales** (☎ 479227; www.canterburytales.org.uk; St Margaret's St; adult/child £7.25/5.25; 10am-5pm Mar-Jun & Sep-Oct, 9.30am-5pm Jul & Aug, 10am-4.30pm Nov-Feb) is a kid-friendly 3-D evocation of scenes from Geoffrey Chaucer's ribald 17,000-line prose and verse epic. The *Knight's Tale, Miller's Tale* and *Wife of Bath's Tale* are among those given the moving puppet treatment, while the final display is a reconstruction of St Thomas Becket's shrine.

Those craving a tranquillity break from the hordes should consider a chauffeured **punt** (☎ 07816-760869; adult/child £7/4; 10am-dusk Easter-Oct) along the Stour River. Pick up a boat near West Gate Tower and sit back and watch the ancient city slip by. The sleepy trawl lasts around 40 minutes, and highlights include miles of tree-lined river bank and acres of grassy meadows.

Sleeping

Summer is uber-crowded in Canterbury, so booking ahead is essential.

BUDGET

YHA Hostel (☎ 462911; www.yha.org.uk; 54 New Dover Rd; dm £17.50; P ⊠ 🖳) A splendid Victorian Gothic pile that looks as though it should be haunted, this 69-bed YHA is now open year-round. Located less than a mile from Canterbury East train station, the ambience is at this hostel is typically institutional and the facilities – including a TV lounge, games room, shop and cycle storage – are a couple of notches above basic. The leafy garden is a nice bonus and is used for barbecues in summer.

Kipps Independent Hostel (☎ 786121; www.kipps-hostel.com; 40 Nunnery Fields; dm/s/d £14/19/33; P ⊠ 💻) A good-value backpacker joint located a few minutes' walk from the city centre, Kipps combines the warmth of a family-run property with facilities that create a comfortable home-from-home. Internet access (per 30 minutes £1), a games room and a tuck shop are available, and there's a wide array of rooms types – dorms have a maximum of eight beds and camping spots are offered (£6.50 per person).

MIDRANGE

Cathedral Gate Hotel (☎ 464381; www.cathgate.co.uk; 36 Burgate; s £26-60, d £50-90; ⊠) An amazing location, just a hop, skip and jump from the cathedral to this labyrinthine 15th-century property. The rooms offer a grab bag of historic quirks – giant interior beams and wonky floors are common – but all have fairly modern, if slightly worn furnishings. The basic budget rooms on the 3rd floor have shared facilities but are a bargain.

White House (☎ 761836; www.canterburybreaks.co.uk; 6 St Peter's Lane; s/d £50/70; ⊠) Reputedly the retirement home of Queen Victoria's coachman, this lovely Regency-era town house is a five-minute walk from the cathedral. All rooms have mostly modern furnishings surrounded by pastel and flower-patterned décor – not everyone's cup of tea but certainly comfortable. A family-run property, the hosts are warm and welcoming, and they serve a hearty breakfast.

Greyfriars House (☎ 456255; www.greyfriars-house.co.uk; 6 Stour St; s £35-55, d £55-70; P) Once the gatehouse to a Franciscan monastery, this centrally located 12th-century guesthouse backs onto the river, enabling guests to enjoy a tranquil waterfront garden. Rooms are furnished in a modern, floral-patterned style. There's a vegetarian breakfast for noncarnivorous travellers.

Also recommended:

Tudor House (☎ 765650; 6 Best Lane; s £25-35, d £48-55; ⊠)

Acacia Lodge & Tanglewood Cottage (☎ 769955; www.acacialodge.com; 39 London Rd; s £32-48, d £48-60; P ⊠)

TOP END

Abode Canterbury (☎ 766266; www.abodehotels.co.uk; High St; s & d from £99; P) The former County Hotel, this handsome timber-framed property in the heart of the city was undergoing renovations when we visited and was due to relaunch as a chichi boutique property by the time you read this. If all goes to plan, it will be the city's most sought-after sleepover.

Eating & Drinking

The streets of Canterbury are full of coffee and sandwich shops offering cheap eats, but there's also an array of quality dining options for those with the time and money for something a little fancier. With history on its side, the number of olde-world pubs is satisfyingly large.

Café St Pierre (☎ 456791; 41 St Peter's St; baguettes £3.50; 🕑 8am-6pm Mon-Sat, 9am-5.30pm Sun) This welcoming French eatery – with popular people-watching seating out the back – has fresh-baked pastries, baguettes and quiches. It's perfect for a mid-morning snack or lunch to go as you meander towards the cathedral.

Thomas Becket (☎ 464384; 21 Best Lane; mains £5-9) Probably Canterbury's best traditional bar, this textbook English pub comes complete with a roaring fireplace and a coterie of copper pots. A good spot to hunker in a corner and work your way through the local ales.

Café des Amis du Mexique (☎ 464390; 93-95 St Dunstan's St; mains £7-14; 🕑 lunch & dinner) A popular and laid-back Mexican restaurant, this spot serves superior burritos and enchiladas, along with a side dish of tequilas and Latin music. Despite the Southwestern US artwork and blue and white tiles adorning the walls, the menu also includes mashed potatoes.

Goods Shed (☎ 459153; Station Rd; mains £8.50-22; 🕑 market 10am-7pm Mon-Sat, restaurant noon-2.30pm & 6-9pm Tue-Sun; ⊠) Adjacent to Canterbury West train station, this converted Victorian warehouse is a must-visit for those craving great food. Sourcing fine seasonal ingredients from its on-site daily farmers market, the restaurant's ever-changing menu has a rustic brasserie approach.

Getting There & Away

Regular direct National Express buses arrive throughout the day from London Victoria (£11.40, two hours) and Dover (£4.30, 40 minutes). The **Stagecoach East Kent** (☎ 0870 243 3711) bus 115 service also arrives hourly (less frequently on Sunday) from Dover (£2.90, 35 minutes). Train services from London Victoria (£18.30, 90 minutes) arrive at either

BRITAIN

Canterbury West or Canterbury East stations, while services from London Charing Cross and London Waterloo (£18.30, 90 minutes) arrive only at Canterbury West. Trains from Dover Priory (£5.20, 15 to 30 minutes) arrive at Canterbury East twice an hour.

DOVER

☎ 01305 / pop 34,087

The definition of a 'gateway town', the brightest thing about Dover is its signature white cliffs. The rest – aside from a visit-worthy medieval castle – is a grey, uninspiring, run-down melange of access routes to the ferry port.

Orientation & Information

Ferry departures are from the Eastern Docks, while Dover Priory train station is a short walk west of the city centre, just off Folkestone Rd. The bus station is more central, on Pencester Rd. The city centre **TIC** (☎ 205108; www.whitecliffscountry.org.uk; Old Town Gaol, Biggin St; 9am-5.30pm Mon-Fri, 10am-4pm Sat & Sun) provides accommodation, and ferry and bus booking services.

Sights & Activities

One of England's mightiest medieval fortresses, **Dover Castle** (☎ 211067; adult/child £9.50/4.80; 10am-6pm Apr-Jul & Sep, 9.30am-6.30pm Aug, 10am-5pm Oct, 10am-4pm Mon-Fri Nov-Jan, 10am-4pm Feb & Mar) occupies a spectacular hilltop promontory dripping with history. There are Roman, Saxon and Norman remains here, but it's the site's more recent past that attracts many visitors. Expanded during WWII, the castle's labyrinth of secret Napoleonic tunnels was used as an Allied command post during the evacuation of Dunkirk. Entry includes a colourful 50-minute underground tour of this fascinating complex.

Make some time to visit the **White Cliffs of Dover** (☎ 202756; Langdon Cliffs, Upper Rd; admission free; 10am-5pm Mar-Oct, 11am-4pm Nov-Feb) and take a windy stroll along its protected 5-mile stretch of marked coastal trail. The visitor centre introduces some of the flora and fauna to look out for while you're on this gentle hike. The cliff top is a fantastic spot to run towards your partner at full speed, but make sure you don't fall over the edge.

BRITAIN

Sleeping

Castle St and Maison Dieu Rd are B&B hotspots but there are plenty of other options throughout the town.

Dover YHA (☎ 0870 770 5798; dover@yha.org.uk; 306 London Rd; dm £17.50;) This slightly run-down Georgian town house is a 15-minute walk from the bus and train stations. Home to a wide configuration of room sizes, the most popular are its three two-bed dorms. There are no laundry facilities, but cycle storage, a games room and a café serving evening meals are useful extras. Rates include breakfast.

East Lee Guest House (☎ 210176; www.eastlee.co.uk; 108 Maison Dieu Rd; s/d from £35/52;) This lovely, flower-fronted Victorian heritage house – home of local 19th-century artist William Henry East – offers a warm welcome and a selection of chintz-themed rooms. Vegetarians can enjoy a cooked breakfast but the continental – featuring fresh fruit and cheese – is also recommended (the hosts will pack it up for you if you have to leave in a rush).

Churchill Hotel (☎ 203633; www.bw-churchillhotel.co.uk; Waterfront; s/d £68/90; P) Set in an attractive curve of Regency town houses, some of the Churchill's rooms have great sea views. All rooms are decorated in a comfortable, if uninspired business hotel manner. There's a useful on-site gym for those who want to work up a sweat before their cross-channel ferry trip, and a buffet breakfast is available (£9) in the brasserie.

Eating & Drinking

Dover has never been a culinary hotspot but there are a couple of foodie haunts almost worth missing your ferry for.

Coastguard Pub & Restaurant (☎ 853176; The Bay, St Margaret's Bay; mains £6-18; lunch & dinner) The closet pub to France in Britain, the Coastguard is a perfect summer spot to quaff a few beers while overlooking the gleaming white cliffs. Among the traditional brews, Dogbolter and Seasider are recommended. The rustic restaurant is also worth a splurge, and is renowned for its hearty seafood dishes and 30-variety cheese menu: good fuel for the 5-mile trek back to the city centre.

Cullin's Yard (☎ 211666; 11 Cambridge Rd; mains £6-20; lunch & dinner) Popular with the locals, this waterfront bistro specialises in regional seafood but also serves traditional British dishes, like beef and ale casserole, with a dash of gourmet flair. A lively, friendly place on most days, there's the added bonus of live music on most weekends.

Getting There & Away

For details of ferry services from mainland Europe, see p279.

National Express buses arrive twice hourly from London Victoria (£11.50, three hours) and also several times a day from Canterbury (£4.30, 40 minutes). Regular Stagecoach East Kent buses arrive from Brighton (£5.50, three hours) throughout the day.

Train services arrive several times an hour at Dover Priory station from London Victoria (£22, two hours) and hourly from London Charing Cross (£22, two hours).

HEVER CASTLE

Anne Boleyn's childhood home, the grounds of **Hever Castle** (☎ 01732-865224; www.hever-castle.co.uk; adult/child £9.80/5.30; ⏲ noon-5pm Mar-Oct, noon-3.30pm Nov), near Edenbridge, Kent, have a moat, a 13th-century castle and a 15th-century Tudor manor house. Despite their royal provenance, the castle fell into disrepair during the 18th century only to be rescued by an extensive renovation in the early 1900s, which included 'new' Edwardian interiors. The stunning Italian Garden, complete with sculptures, secret grottoes and a forest of flowers, is at least as attractive as the buildings, while the yew and water mazes ensure families are kept well occupied. There's also a meticulous display of model houses depicting homes from 1086 to 1901.

Hourly trains arrive from London Victoria (£7.70, 50 minutes, change at East Croydon) at Hever station, a 1-mile walk from the castle.

LEEDS CASTLE

One of Britain's most-visited historic attractions, **Leeds Castle** (☎ 01622-765400; www.leeds-castle.com; adult/child £13/9; ⏲ 10am-5pm Apr-Oct, 10am-3.30pm Nov-Mar) does not disappoint. A magnificent and romantically alluring site near Maidstone, Kent situated on two islands surrounded by formidable woodlands, the castle began life as a Norman stronghold before housing six of England's medieval queens. In private ownership until the 1970s, the castle is stuffed with medieval furnishings, has an aviary of endangered birds and even displays an odd collection of antique dog collars. Save time for the elaborate maze – if you solve it, you're rewarded with panoramic views of the surrounding park.

National Express runs a daily direct bus to the castle from London Victoria (£18 return, 90 minutes). The coach leaves London at 9am and departs from the castle at 3.05pm. The price includes admission.

BRIGHTON & HOVE

☎ 01273 / pop 247,820

While many of England's crumbling seaside resorts are paint-peeled reminders of an era when all Brits used to vacation at local beaches, Brighton – which merged with nearby Hove in 2000 – has successfully moved on from its past of deck chairs and donkey rides. Now one of the country's hippest cities, it has a vibrant cultural scene and a youthful bohemian edge that make up for a seven-mile stretch of beach completely covered with stones. The beach has never been the main attraction, though, and today's visitors are happiest hitting the city's eccentric tangle of quirky backstreets or indulging in the biggest annual arts festival south of Hadrian's Wall.

Orientation & Information

The seafront is a 10-minute downhill stroll from the train station along Queen's Rd and West St. When you arrive at the beach, the near-derelict West Pier is to your right while the bustling Brighton Pier is to your left. Between the piers, a few streets back from the front, you'll find the Lanes and North Laine shopping areas. Hove is west of the city centre.

The **TIC** (☎ 292590; www.visitbrighton.com; Bartholomew Sq; ⏲ 9am-5pm Mon-Fri, 10am-5pm Sat, 10am-4pm Sun) has maps, listings magazines and an accommodation booking service. Between Hove and Brighton, **Internet Junction** (109 Western Rd; per hr £2.50; ⏲ 10am-9pm Mon-Fri, 10am-8pm Sat, 11am-6pm Sun) offers Internet access with 20 computers on two floors.

Sights

Built between 1815 and 1822 for the playboy Prince Regent, the onion-domed **Royal Pavilion** (☎ 290900; www.royalpavilion.org.uk; adult/child £6.10/3.60, guided tours £1.25; ⏲ 9.30am-5.45pm

Apr-Sep, 10am-5.15pm Oct-Mar, tours 11.30am & 2.30pm) is a jaw-dropping fusion of faux Asian interiors and over-the-top period furnishings. Among the gold-slathered surfaces, multichandeliered ceilings and near-obscene displays of languid decadence, there's a comparatively discreet tearoom and a new permanent exhibition on the palace's turbulent conservation history.

Brighton's original fishing-village heart is now known as **The Lanes**, a narrow, cobblestone web of 17th-century cottages housing a cornucopia of independent shops, restaurants and pubs. Renowned for its one-of-a-kind eateries, it is more gentrified than the adjacent **North Laine** area, which has a funkier, alternative vibe. Along streets of multicoloured shops, this avant-garde area offers used record stores, vegetarian cafés and retro skater fashions to local hipster types.

Formerly named Palace Pier, the landmark **Brighton Pier** (☎ 609361; www.brightonpier.co.uk; admission free; 🕑 10am-10pm Mon-Thu, 10am-11pm Fri-Sun) is a suitably brash reminder of England's simple, seaside-loving past. Its white-painted exterior houses noisy arcades, greasy takeout food stands, and – like a fairground on a stick – a clutch of thrill rides and traditional attractions, including a stripy helter-skelter and a cheesy ghost train. The skeletal remains of the nearby **West Pier** shimmer in the haze, but are now just a giant perching post for flocks of visiting starlings.

Festivals

For the final three weeks of every May, **Brighton Festival** (☎ 709709; www.brightonfestival.org) takes over the city with a bewildering cavalcade of more than 700 dance, music, theatre and book events. Highlights of England's largest arts festival include free performances on almost every street corner, and a weird and wacky fringe festival that mirrors the city's colourful eccentricity.

Sleeping

Traditional B&Bs line the streets radiating from Brighton Pier, but there are also some new boutique properties and a good selection of backpacker joints. Book ahead during summer and Brighton Festival season, and be aware that some local hotels have a minimum two-night stay on weekends.

BUDGET

St Christopher's Inn (☎ 020-7407 1856; www.st-christophers.co.uk; 10-12 Grand Junction Rd; dm £10-27; ⊠ 💻) A great waterfront location near Brighton Pier for this bustling, party-lovers hostel. Along its brightly painted corridors, the dorms have up to 10 beds and all have en suite facilities. There's no kitchen – free continental breakfast is included – but there are good food and drinks specials at the hopping downstairs bar. Guests with extra money can upgrade to a hotel room on the property's upper floors (singles/doubles from £25).

Baggies Backpackers (☎ 733740; 33 Oriental Pl; dm/d £12/30; ⊠) A popular, laid-back budget option with a good vibe, Baggies has a communal feel and is close to the seafront. Attracting long-termers as well as short-stop visitors, most areas are a little worn but everything is clean and functional. Dorms are mostly small but shower rooms are shared, which may be an issue for shy travellers.

MIDRANGE

Paskins Town House (☎ 601203; www.paskins.co.uk; 18-19 Charlotte St; s & d per person from £27.50; ⊠) This excellent 19-room boutique B&B occupies two Victorian town houses and has a commendable eco-friendly stance that includes properly feeding vegetarian guests; the organic traditional or veggie breakfasts (including homemade sausages) are almost worth the price of staying. Its eminently comfortable rooms are designed in Regency, pop culture or Art Deco styles, and some have four-poster beds.

Genevieve Hotel (☎ 681653; www.genevievehotel.co.uk; 18 Madeira Pl; s/d from £40/70; ⊠ 💻) This clean, well-maintained heritage establishment with a friendly proprietor has a central location near Brighton Pier. The 13 rooms are fairly sparse – two have four-poster beds – but all include free wi-fi.

George IV Hotel (☎ 321196; www.georgeivhotel.co.uk; 34 Regency Sq; s £40-50, d £60-120; ⊠) This recently refurbished gem combines high ceilings, elegant furnishings and a juke box in reception. The warm welcome includes a slew of borrowable DVDs and board games, and the accommodation highlight is a balcony room with a commanding view of the ghostly West Pier. There's no dining room, but basket breakfasts can be ordered for morning delivery.

BRITAIN

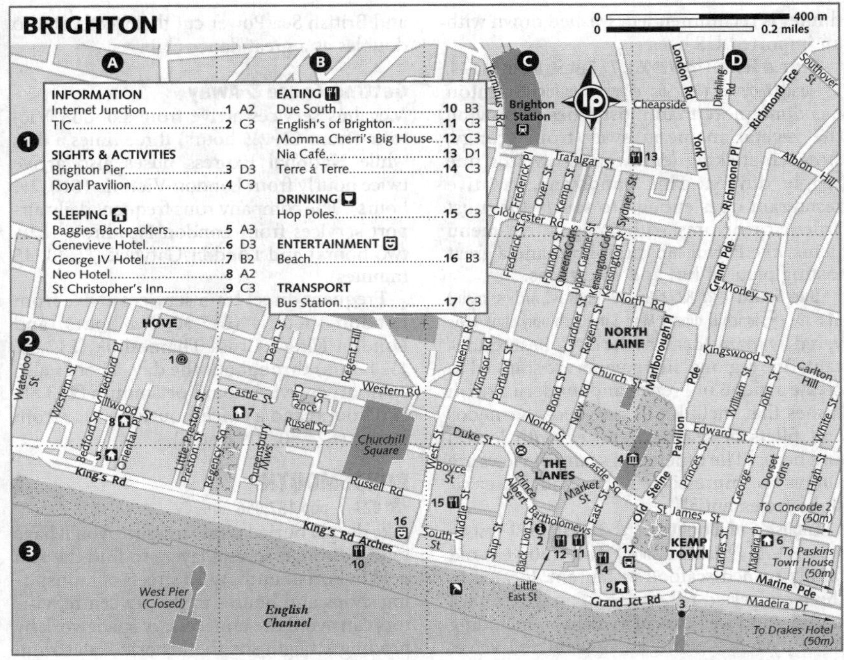

Neo Hotel (☎ 711104; www.neohotel.com; 19 Oriental Pl; s/d from £45/85; ⊠ 🖳) At the forefront of Brighton's new wave of boutique properties, this artsy, sophisticated spot near the West Pier combines modern Asian design flourishes with cosy home comforts. The mostly en suite bathrooms feature chrome and matte black finishes, and the breakfasts here – check out the pancakes – are clearly made with love. Neo Hotel may well represent the future of the venerable British B&B.

TOP END

Drakes Hotel (☎ 696934; www.drakesofbrighton.com; 44 Marine Pde; s/d from £95/125; Ⓟ ⊠ ✣) Sumptuous and ultra-fashionable, the 20-room Drakes has justifiably been hailed as one of Britain's top boutique hotels. While the immaculate design aesthetic is easy to achieve with enough money, it's the service element that puts this sleepover in the big league: unlike many snooty UK hotels, it manages to be both top-end and laid-back. The rooms are effortlessly swanky and most have great views over the seafront.

Eating

Unlike most British seaside resorts, Brighton has more to offer than limp fish and chips. The Lanes is a good area for adventurous foodie exploring but there are eye-opening culinary surprises in many other parts of the city, too.

Nia Café (☎ 6711371; 87 Trafalgar St; mains £6-14; ⏲ 9am-11pm Mon-Sat, 9am-6pm Sun) A smashing lunch spot for those craving more than a vacuum-packed sandwich – sesame chicken fillet is recommended – this funky spot attracts chin-stroking trendies to its school-desk interiors and popular outdoor seating area. It also makes for a good afternoon cappuccino spot but beware of the tempting cake selection.

Momma Cherri's Big House (☎ 325305; 2-3 Little East St; mains £8-11; ⏲ lunch & dinner) Recently moved to its second location after a TV-show makeover, Momma's is a riot of colourful interiors and exuberant dishes guaranteed to spice up the coldest seaside day. The Southern-style jerk chicken and jambalaya are great, but for those who haven't eaten in a month, the two-course 'Soul in a Bowl' dinner is recommended, washed down with an imported US beer.

Terre a Terre (☎ 729051; 71 East St; mains £12-14; lunch & dinner Wed-Sun, dinner only Tue) Brighton has done more than most cities in moving the vegetarian menu away from grungy, stomach-sticking lentil roasts towards fine veggie dining. This handsome, creative restaurant does enough to satisfy the most ardent carnivores with imaginative menu items, like Parmesan dumplings and a great tasting plate of hot and cold tapas.

Due South (☎ 821218; 139 Kings Rd Arches; mains £11-19; lunch & dinner Mon-Sat, lunch only Sun) Revered by many locals as the city's best restaurant, fine regional ingredients are sourced to create a menu of French and modern British dishes that includes Sussex beef tournedos and fillets of sea bass stuffed with lemon and herbs. The unfettered seafront views are almost as impressive as the food. Reservations are essential.

English's of Brighton (☎ 327980; 29-31 East St; mains £11-25; lunch & dinner) This 150-year-old family-owned seafood restaurant, located in three converted fisherman's cottages, serves unfussy and well-executed dishes – including great oysters – amid an opulent red velvet décor. It's the best place in the Lanes to sample local fish without a coating of deep-fried batter.

Drinking & Entertainment

It would be criminal to come to Brighton and not sample the ever-happening nightlife, which ranges from some of the region's best pubs to a wide array of live music and clubbing options. Pick up the Friday *Argus* newspaper for its listings guide.

Hop Poles (☎ 710444; 13 Middle St) Among the pubs, this place has an artsy, laid-back vibe and attracts the city's chattering smarty-pants crowd. Its gastropub menu is a plus but there's also a selection of candy behind the bar for those who like to nibble chocolate with their cask ale.

Beach (☎ 722272; 171-181 Kings Rd Arches; admission £3-10) For clubbers, this is welcoming, mainstream – think '70s and house nights – and massively popular: arrive early on weekends because the queues can be enormous.

Concorde 2 (☎ 673311; www.concorde2.co.uk; Maderia Shelter Hall, Maderia Dr; admission £4-14) Live music aficionados should appreciate this club, where Brighton luminaries like Fat Boy Slim and British Sea Power cut their teeth. It also doubles as a great dance club.

Getting There & Away

Megabus services arrive from London Victoria (from £1, 2½ hours) three times a day, while National Express buses also arrive twice hourly from London Victoria (£10, 2½ hours). The company runs frequent daily airport services from London Heathrow (£20, two hours) and London Gatwick (£6.40, 45 minutes).

Frequent direct train services arrive from London Victoria (£17.30, 1½ hours) and London King's Cross Thameslink (£13.50, 1½ hours) throughout the day. There's also an hourly service from Portsmouth (£13.80, two hours) and a twice-hourly service from Dover (£24.50, 2½ hours).

PORTSMOUTH

☎ 023 / pop 187,056

Like deeply buried pirate treasure, you'll have to dig through several layers to find the real gold in Portsmouth. With streets of uninspiring shops and houses in its city centre, visitors can avoid the unnecessary spadework by heading straight for the historic waterfront. The spiritual home of Britain's Royal Navy, much of the ancient docks here have been polished to a gentrified hue in recent years, but their salty, richly storied past is still much in evidence.

Orientation & Information

Portsmouth's southern Southsea district houses many of the city's best restaurants, pubs and accommodations, but the harbourfront area on the west side – site of the bus station and the end of the train line from London – is its historic heart. Known as The Hard, this cobblestoned patch is the site of Portsmouth's major maritime attractions and its main **TIC** (☎ 9282 6722; www.visitportsmouth.co.uk; The Hard; 9.30am-5.45pm Apr-Sep, 9.30am-5.15pm Oct-Mar), which has an accommodation booking service (£2). The **Central Library** (☎ 9281 9311; Guildhall Sq; 9am-7pm Mon-Fri, 9am-5pm Sat, 12.30-4pm Sun) offers free Internet access.

Sights & Activities

Dripping with seafaring heritage, Portsmouth's **Historic Dockyard** (☎ 9286 1512; www.flagship.org.uk; all-inclusive ticket adult/child £15.50/12.50;

BRITAIN

(🕑 10am-5.30pm Apr-Oct, 10am-5pm Nov-Mar) is the final resting place for a gaggle of prized vessels. The remains of the **Mary Rose** (adult/child £9.70/8), Henry VIII's favourite warship, provide an object lesson in shipwreck preservation. In contrast, the handsome, fully intact decks of **HMS Victory** (adult/child £9.70/8), Lord Nelson's Battle of Trafalgar flagship, memorialises Britain's greatest naval hero and his famous win against the French. Lacking the historic provenance of the other two vessels, **HMS Warrior** (adult/child £9.70/8), the world's first all-iron battleship, colourfully evokes life on board in the Victorian era.

Taking to the water without getting your feet wet is recommended on a 45-minute **Harbour Tour** (☎ 9283 9766; adult/child £3.50/2) around Portsmouth's leading maritime sights. Aside from the aforementioned old warships, you'll likely glimpse the Royal Navy's latter-day hardware – this is home to Britain's three aircraft carriers and a coterie of steely grey frigates and destroyers. They're enough to shiver anyone's timbers.

Literary history is also part of the picture in Portsmouth, where the off-the-beaten-path **Charles Dickens' Birthplace Museum** (☎ 9282 7261; www.charlesdickensbirthplace.co.uk; 393 Old Commercial Rd; admission £2.50; ☎ 10am-5pm Apr-Oct) celebrates the surprising fact that Britain's leading 19th-century novelist was born here in 1812. Rooms are decorated with Regency-era furnishings, and displays evoke Dickens' later life with a smattering of his inkwells and snuff boxes. Ghoulish visitors will enjoy seeing the couch where he died in 1870.

Sleeping

Southsea's crumbling Victorian town houses are a hotbed of B&B action, but there are also a couple of good options on the Point (also known as Spice Island) in Old Portsmouth.

Southsea Backpackers Lodge (☎ 9283 2495; www.portsmouthbackpackers.co.uk; 4 Florence Rd, Southsea; dm £13, d £30-34; ⊠ 💻) A quiet, cosy atmosphere permeates this large, labyrinthine Victorian house in a residential side street near the seafront. The wooden-bedded dorms are mostly small, and there's coin-operated Internet access (per 30 minutes £1) in the satellite TV–equipped lounge. The garden area is a popular summer barbecue spot.

Sailmaker's Loft (☎ 9282 3045; 5 Bath Sq; s/d £25/55; ⊠ 💻) This small, recently renovated B&B is run by a retired merchant seaman with plenty of salty stories about old Portsmouth. Located on a cobblestone seafront promontory of character taverns and ancient houses, you'll likely awake to the sound of seagulls hovering overhead. Mostly en suite, some of the rooms have great views across the harbour.

Queen's Hotel (☎ 9282 2466; www.bw-queenshotel.co.uk; Clarence Pde, Southsea; s/d from £45/90; P ⊠ 💻) If Dickens' Miss Haversham was a hotel, this is what she'd look like: a faded former aristocrat that still has more character than anything around her. Behind the Victorian wedding cake architecture, the rooms are comfortable but a bit worn; some face the windswept waterfront. Wi-fi is available.

Eating & Drinking

Sallyport Tea Rooms (☎ 9281 6265; 35 Broad St; mains £2.50-5.50; 🕑 10am-5pm; ⊠) This charmingly old-fashioned tea nook is an ideal respite from the rain and wind. Tuck into a large pot of Earl Grey and a tea bun while some gentle jazz tunes drone in the background. It's also a good spot for lunch – the fresh-made sandwiches are a treat – but it can get crowded so consider eating early or late.

Spice Island Inn (☎ 9282 4293; 65 Broad St; mains £6-14; ⊠) Occupying a handsome corner plot on this historic waterfront elbow, this large gentrified pub has the best outdoor seating of any in the area. Order some fish and chips and a couple of pints and head to a table overlooking the water. Watch the boats slip by as you fend off the seagulls.

Bistro Montparnasse (☎ 9281 6754; 103 Palmerston Rd, Southsea; 2-/3-course lunch £14.50/17.50, 2-/3-course dinner £22.50/27.50; 🕑 lunch & dinner Tue-Sat; ⊠) Along a street of generic Indian and Chinese restaurants, this oasis of Mediterranean comfort food is worth a splurge, especially with lovingly created desserts like banana and butterscotch pancakes. The hardwood floors and Tuscan-orange walls are a perfect, chilled-out accompaniment.

Getting There & Away

BOAT

Portsmouth services a wide array of passenger routes to and from France, Spain and the Channel Islands. These include an Isle of Wight car ferry provided by **Wightlink** (☎ 0870 582 7744; www.wightlink.co.uk) throughout the day (£15.20 day return, 15 minutes); a service from Bilbao on **P&O Ferries** (☎ 08705

980 333; www.poferries.com) two to three times per week (from £152); and a daily **Brittany Ferries** (☎ 08703 665 333; www.brittany-ferries.co.uk) route from Cherbourg (from £52, three to five hours).

BUS & TRAIN

National Express buses arrive throughout the day from London Victoria (£14, two to three hours) and Heathrow Airport (£14, two to four hours). There are also regular services from Brighton (£3.20, 3½ hours) and Southampton (£3, 50 minutes). Megabus services arrive from London Victoria (from £1, 2½ hours); the discount operator also offers cheap Portsmouth train services under its Megatrain banner from London Waterloo (from £1, 2½ hours). There are regular-priced train services every 10 minutes or so from London Victoria and London Waterloo (from £23, 1½ to 2½ hours). Additional trains also arrive hourly from Brighton (£13.80, 1½ hours).

WINCHESTER

☎ 01962 / pop 107,213

Dripping with ancient attractions, the capital of Saxon England is a history-lovers dream. With a grand cathedral, frisson of Arthurian legend and dozens of centuries-old buildings lining its streets, it's like stepping into a time capsule. Far from being a sleepy museum piece, though, Winchester has a busy city centre, plenty of bustling shops and some smashing old pubs.

Orientation & Information

Winchester's compact centre is easy to explore on foot, but make sure you duck down the backstreets behind the chain stores to find the historic gems. The train station is a 10-minute walk west of the city centre, and the bus station is on Broadway, opposite the **TIC** (☎ 840500; www.visitwinchester.co.uk; Guildhall, Broadway; 9.30am-5.30pm Mon-Sat, 11am-4pm Sun May-Sep, 10am-5pm Mon-Sat Oct-Apr), which provides regular guided tours (adult/child £3/free) of the city. **Jamie's Internet Cafe** (☎ 870880; 10 Parchment St; per hr £3; 10am-5pm Mon-Sat) offers Internet access.

Sights

Glorious **Winchester Cathedral** (☎ 857200; www.winchester-cathedral.org.uk; 1 The Close; suggested donation £4, tours free; 8.30am-6pm Mon-Sat, 8.30am-5.30pm Sun, tours 10am-3pm Mon-Sat) features a magnificent, multicolumned melange of architectural styles and is the final resting place of Jane Austen, whose discreet gravestone resides on the north side of the nave. Duck down to the chilly crypt for the modern Anthony Gormley figure. It stands spookily reflected in several inches of water during the basement's regular floods.

Nearby flint-walled **Great Hall** (☎ 846476; www.hants.gov.uk/discover/places/great-hall.html; Castle Ave; admission free; 10am-5pm Mar-Oct, 10am-4pm Nov-Feb) is all that remains of a gargantuan 11th-century castle destroyed by Oliver Cromwell in 1651. It now houses the giant, multicoloured **King Arthur's Round Table**, a medieval commemorative artefact created to celebrate the legendary monarch long after his reputed reign.

Step into the past over at the **Hospital of St Cross** (☎ 851375; www.stcrosshospital.co.uk; St Cross Rd; adult/child £2.50/0.50; 9.30am-5pm Mon-Sat, 1-5pm Sun Apr-Oct, 10.30am-3.30pm Mon-Sat Nov-Mar), Britain's oldest charitable institution. This still-working almshouse is home to 25 elderly gents who reside in a row of picturesque stone cottages. Visitors receive the Wayfarer's Dole – some bread and sherry – and can check out a magnificent Norman church whose walls are more than 1m thick.

Festivals & Events

The outlandish **Winchester Hat Fair** (☎ 849841; www.hatfair.co.uk), held from late June to early July, bills itself as Britain's longest-running festival of street theatre. Combining clowns, comedy, live music and buskers (hence the hat reference in the title), it's the town's annual excuse for putting a smile on its face.

Sleeping

With the recent closure of Winchester's YHA hostel, budget accommodation is hard to come by here. Ask at the TIC for recommendations.

Mrs Blockley's (☎ 852073; roseyblockley@uwclub.net; 54 St Cross Rd; s £30, d £52-60; P ⊠) A 10-minute walk from the city centre, this homy but good-quality B&B is a great deal for budget travellers. Its three cosy rooms share a large bathroom, and wi-fi is available. The emphasis is on quiet, since the friendly hosts live on-site.

Bethany House (☎ 862188; www.bethanyhousebandb.co.uk; 114 Christchurch Rd; s/d £45/65; P ⊠)

It's well worth the 15-minute walk from the city centre to this large former convent that's been expertly renovated with a rustic chic ambience. The three themed bedrooms – ask for the White Room if you want a tranquillity fix – have modernist en suites and there's ample off-road parking.

Wessex Hotel (☎ 861611; www.wessex-hotel.co.uk; Paternoster Row; s/d from £65/120; P ⊠) A bland 1960s exterior contrasts sharply with handsome rooms that look like they've been imported from a country manor. Ask for a cathedral view – the hotel backs onto the ancient site – and you can lay in bed and count the windows when you wake up. It has an unbeatable central location.

Hotel du Vin (☎ 841414; www.hotelduvin.com; Southgate St; d/ste from £125/185) Set in a thoroughly updated 18th-century Georgian town house, Winchester's smartest boutique property has 23 stylish rooms with luxe touches, like monsoon showers and Egyptian linen. There's a lovely walled garden, and a popular on-site bistro serving French and British specialities.

Eating & Drinking

Forte Tea Rooms (☎ 856840; 78 Parchment St; mains £3-7; 9am-5.30pm Mon-Sat) This chatter-filled upstairs nook offers well-priced home-style dishes, a warming atmosphere and a small shelf of well-thumbed travel books. There's a large finger-licking sandwich selection but it's the cakes that draw most visitors – hot fruit scones and a pot of tea never tasted better.

Black Boy (☎ 861754; 1 Wharf Hill; mains from £5; lunch & dinner) A wood-fired hearth scents the air while a wide selection of regional beers takes care of the palate at this unabashedly traditional hilltop pub. It's hard to beat a pint of Cheriton sipped slowly over a giant weekend newspaper here, but the food – due to a newly installed gourmet chef – is also a big draw.

Wykeham Arms (☎ 853834; 75 Kingsgate St; mains £5-13; lunch & dinner) Winchester's favourite pub is a charming combination of olde-world atmosphere, fine regional ales, well-stocked wine and a diverse, locally sourced menu that's far above the usual pub fare. Check out the beef and bitter sausages. Arrive early if you want an evening table.

Cafe De Paris (☎ 860006; 5 Jewry St; mains £4-21; 10-11.30am, noon-2pm & 7-11pm Mon-Sat) An authentic Parisian ambience permeates this spick and span French brasserie, where the impressive menu of meticulously prepared dishes runs from light baguette lunch sandwiches to serious dinner cuisine, including swordfish, steak and oysters.

Getting There & Away

National Express buses arrive in the city centre several times a day from London Victoria (£12.60, two hours), while Megabus services run from London Victoria to St Catherine's Park & Ride (from £1, 1½ hours) four times daily. The park and ride is a 10-minute local bus ride from the city centre. **Stagecoach Hampshire** (☎ 0845 121 0180) provides additional local bus links from Salisbury, Southampton and Portsmouth. Trains arrive several times daily from London Waterloo (£22, one hour), Southampton (£4.30, 20 minutes) and Portsmouth (£7.90, one hour).

CHANNEL ISLANDS

Closer to the French coast, the Channel Islands – Jersey, Guernsey, Herm, Sark and Alderney – are a strangely exotic hybrid of English and French culture. Though a bit sleepy for visitors under 50, they are characterised by their rugged coastlines, sandy bays and multiflowered vistas: a direct result of the balmier climate enjoyed by the islanders. With their own stamps and currency (which has the same value as sterling but can't be used on the mainland), taxes are low and there's no value-added tax (VAT).

Jersey, the biggest and busiest of the islands, is the best one to visit. Its main attraction is **Jersey Zoo** (☎ 01534-860000; Les Augres Manor, Trinity; adult/child £11.50/7.40; 9.30am-5pm), which was founded by Gerald Durrell and focuses on rare animal conservation. The **Jersey War Tunnels** (☎ 01534-860808; adult/child £9/5; 10am-6pm) are also worth a visit. Housed in a German underground hospital, the site colourfully explores the island's past as an occupied region during WWII.

For more information on visiting Jersey, contact **Jersey Tourism** (☎ 01534-500700; www.jersey.com; Liberation Sq, St Helier; 8.30am-6pm, reduced hr in winter). For information on visiting any of the other islands, contact **Guernsey Tourism** (☎ 01481-723552; www.visitguernsey.com; North Plantation, St Peter Port; 9am-5pm Mon-Fri, 9am-4pm Sat, 9.30am-12.30pm Sun).

Getting There & Away

There are daily flights to the Channel Islands from several mainland UK airports, including London Gatwick, London Stansted, Birmingham and Manchester. Fares vary considerably but range from £49 to £200, so it pays to shop around. Airlines serving the islands include **British Airways** (☎ 0870 850 9850; www.ba.com), **Flybe** (☎ 0870 567 6676; www.flybe.com) and **Aurigny Air Services** (☎ 01481-822886; www.aurigny.com).

Regular high-speed boat services operated by **Condor Ferries** (☎ 0870 243 5140; www.condorferries.co.uk) arrive in Jersey from Poole (£53, 4½ hours) and Weymouth (£47, 3½ hours), with similar rates for routes to Guernsey.

SOUTHWEST ENGLAND

With two of England's best moorland national parks – South Devon's Dartmoor and North Devon's Exmoor – as well as some superbly craggy Cornish coastal walks dripping with sandy bays and the occasional palm tree, the balmy southwest is one of England's most naturally attractive regions. But it's not all about the outdoors here. History fans will find it hard to leave Salisbury, where the past resides on every street corner, and nearby Stonehenge and Avebury recall the mysteries of past civilisations. It's even more difficult to tear yourself away from Bath, England's most handsome Georgian city. But the region's other main towns – Bristol and Exeter – also have their charms and are enlivened by their more youthful, student-driven populations. For information on visiting the region, contact **South West Tourism** (☎ 0870 442 0880; www.visitsouthwest.co.uk).

SALISBURY

☎ **01722 / pop 43,355**

While you can't throw a brick in Salisbury without hitting a preserved antique pile, this charming city is far from being a mothballed historic theme park. Amid its winding thoroughfares and implausibly leaning pubs, the streets are constantly buzzing with rushing locals studiously ignoring their pretty surroundings. Along with its stirring cathedral – its soaring architecture is enough to convert hardened atheists – two of Britain's leading prehistoric sites lie on the city's doorstep.

Orientation & Information

A 10-minute walk from the train station along Fisherton St, Salisbury city centre is easily negotiated on foot and radiates from its busy Market Sq focal point. Behind the square's hulking Guildhall, you'll find a welcoming **TIC** (☎ 334956; www.visitsalisbury.com; Fish Row; 🕒 9am-5pm Mon-Sat year-round, 10.30am-4.30pm Sun May-Sep), with a free accommodation booking service. Walk to the square's opposite corner – a circuitous route during the Tuesday and Saturday markets – for free Internet access at the **library** (☎ 324145; Market Pl; 🕒 10am-7pm Mon, 9am-7pm Tue, Wed & Fri, 9am-5pm Thu & Sat).

Sights & Activities

Beneath its soaring wedding-cake spire, **Salisbury Cathedral** (☎ 555120; www.salisburycathedral.org.uk; suggested donation adult/child £4/2; 🕒 7.15am-6.15pm) is one of Britain's finest 13th-century Gothic churches. Free tours run throughout the day and illuminate the intricate stonework interior of flying buttresses and arching vaulted ceilings. Restore the crick in your neck in the octagonal chapter house, where one of only four original Magna Carta documents is displayed, before heading out into Cathedral Close, an impressive medieval perimeter of small museums and restored period houses.

Find out what happened to the region's first cathedral with a 10-minute bus ride (bus 3, 5, 6, 8 or 9) to **Old Sarum Castle** (☎ 335398; adult/child £2.90/1.50; 🕒 10am-4pm Mar & Oct, 10am-5pm Apr-Jun & Sep, 9am-6pm Jul-Aug, 11am-3pm Nov-Feb), an Iron Age settlement abandoned due to overcrowding in 1217. Bricks from the church that once stood here were used to build Salisbury's 'new' cathedral, and the area is now a tranquil grassy knoll that's perfect for soft hiking and summer picnicking.

Sleeping

Not short of heritage-hugging B&Bs and character hotels, Salisbury's accommodation options can quickly diminish in summer when the Stonehenge-bound coach parties roll into town. Use the TIC's free booking service for assistance.

Salisbury YHA Hostel (☎ 327572; salisbury@yha.org.uk; Milford Hill; dm £17.50-20.50, s/d with shared bathroom £20.50/40.50; P ⊠ 💻) A leafy, winding driveway opens out onto this surprisingly large country house, offering solid institutional YHA facilities and a bonus cooked breakfast. Most dorms are mercifully small and private rooms with shared facilities are also available. It's a five-minute downhill walk into the city centre.

Spire House (☎ 339213; lois.faulkner@talk21.com; 84 Exeter St; d/tw/f £60/80/100; P ⊠) Ask for a front room at this well-restored period B&B and you'll be treated to a view of the cathedral, looking like a pale ghost behind its night-time floodlights. The surfeit of home comforts here includes brass, mostly four-poster beds, sparkling-clean bathrooms and heaping breakfasts, with several vegetarian options available.

Red Lion Hotel (☎ 323334; www.the-redlion.co.uk; Milford St; s/d £97/126; P) Opened in 1220, and reputedly England's oldest purpose-built hotel, the Red Lion is a heritage-lovers dream. Antiques colour the public areas, while discreet mod cons, including newly added en suites, ensure guests don't have to live in the past. If you fancy a pint, look no further than the timber-beamed downstairs bar.

Eating & Drinking

There are plenty of cafés and sandwich bars in central Salisbury. Head along Fisherton St for a wide selection of dinner options.

Suzette's Pancake Café (☎ 326966; 4 Fish Row; mains £3-4; 🕑 9am-6pm Mon-Sat, 10am-5.30pm Sun) An ideal cheap-eat spot with a bonus outdoor seating area, the crepe-wrapped light meals have sweet and savoury ingredients, like brie, bacon and bananas – although not necessarily together. The Fair Trade coffee is a nice touch.

Anokaa (☎ 414142; 60 Fisherton St; mains £7-15; 🕑 lunch & dinner) The Anokaa's popular lunch buffet (£7.25) is great value, while its stylish, loungy décor is enough to make you forget all about the flock wallpaper and sitar music ambience of most British Indian eateries. Drop by for dinner and choose from dishes with a contemporary twist, like sea bass and lamb rack.

Haunch of Venison (☎ 411313; 1 Minster St; mains £6-16; 🕑 lunch & dinner) Combines perhaps the city's best olde-worlde bar – check out the warming hearth, wonky walls and low-ceilinged nooks – with a great upstairs restaurant serving finger-licking gastropub versions of Brit faves. The venison sausages with mash and red onion marmalade is recommended.

TOP FIVE SOUTHERN ENGLAND CHURCHES

- **Winchester Cathedral** (p188)
- **Salisbury Cathedral** (opposite)
- **Bath Abbey** (p199)
- **Exeter Cathedral** (p192)
- **Wells Cathedral** (p202)

Getting There & Away

Three direct National Express buses arrive daily from London Victoria (£14, three to 3½ hours) via Heathrow (£14, two to 2½ hours). One daily service also arrives from Bath (£8.30, 1½ hours) and another from Bristol (£8.30, two hours).

Salisbury train services arrive every 30 minutes from London Waterloo (£24.20, 1½ hours). There's also an hourly service from Portsmouth (£12.50, 1½ hours, hourly) and frequent services throughout the day from Bath (£11.20, one hour) and Exeter (£22.70, two hours).

Getting Around

Local bus services run by **Wilts and Dorset Bus Company** (☎ 336855; www.wdbus.co.uk) are reasonably well organised and link Salisbury with Stonehenge and Avebury. Bikes can be hired from **Hayball Cyclesport** (☎ 411378; 26-30 Winchester St; 🕑 9am-5.30pm Mon-Sat) for £10 per day.

STONEHENGE

Looking like a ring of giant stone dominoes and cursed by poor site management, **Stonehenge** (☎ 0870 333 1181; www.english-heritage.org.uk/stonehenge; adult/child £5.90/3; 🕑 9.30am-6pm mid-March–May, 9am-7pm Jun-Aug, 9.30am-6pm Sep–mid-Oct, 9.30am-4pm mid-Oct–mid-Mar) can be a distinctly underwhelming experience. Most visitors come hoping to feel the site's spooky mysticism or marvel at the unfathomable prehistoric engineering project that brought these huge rocks from a Welsh quarry up to 5000 years ago. The reality is a stubbly field next to a noisy main road housing a roped-off area where the ring – which may be an ancient calendar or place of pagan worship – sits sullen and unloved. Plans to reroute the road and transform the experience for the coachloads of perplexed tourists arriving daily collapse every few years. The best time

BRITAIN

to arrive is early morning when the crowds are at their smallest: watching the sun filter between the upright stones can still create a flicker of eeriness, especially if you pan around and count the number of ancient burial mounds dotting the landscape on the otherwise pancake-flat Salisbury Plain.

Wilts and Dorset public buses from Salisbury bus and train stations arrive at Stonehenge every 15 minutes in summer (bus 3, £6.50 return). The company also runs seasonal double-decker guided tours to the site (adult/child £15/8). But the best deal is the one-day Explorer bus pass (£6.50), enabling you to take in the superior Avebury after your Stonehenge disappointment.

AVEBURY

Older and more eerily tranquil than its over-touristed neighbour, Avebury's **stone circle** (☎ 01672-539250; admission free) is one of the largest megalithic monuments in Britain, completely encircling the pretty village of the same name that has resided here for centuries. The 100 stones are smaller than Stonehenge's, but the site is far bigger and visitors can move around it without restriction. The northwest corner has the most complete cluster of standing rocks, including the massive Swindon Stone, one of the few never to have been toppled by Christians during the medieval era. For some useful context, check out the fascinating **Alexander Keiller Museum** (☎ 01672-539250; adult/child £4.20/2.10; 🕑 10am-6pm Apr-Oct, 10am-4pm Nov-Mar), which carefully explains the history of the stones and the region's mysterious spiritual past. This includes the ancient, pyramid-shaped **Silbury Hill** nearby. The height of Nelson's Column, it's Europe's largest human-made prehistoric construction.

Wilts and Dorset public buses from Salisbury arrive every hour in Avebury (buses 5 and 6, £6.50 return).

EXETER

☎ 01392 / pop 111,078

A half-destroyed red stone church on Catherine St recalls what Exeter looked like before WWII bombing raids decimated much of the historic city centre. A bland postwar rebuilding programme created a grey, New Town look and latter-day visitors have to search a little to uncover the area's charms. A large student population, reinvented Quay and attractive Cathedral Green are the heart of the city today.

Orientation & Information

St David's train station is a 15-minute walk northwest of the city centre. While Exeter Central station is much closer, most intercity trains don't stop there. The large Paris St bus and coach station is near the eastern end of the High St, just a few minutes' walk from Cathedral Green, Exeter's historic centre. Follow the signs south of the cathedral for the downhill stroll to the Quay on the River Exe.

The **TIC** (☎ 265700; www.exeter.gov.uk/tourism; Civic Centre, Dix's Field; 🕑 9am-5pm Mon-Sat year-round, 10am-4pm Sun Apr-Oct), near the bus and coach station, is the staging point for a wide array of free **walking tours** (☎ 265203), including one covering Exeter's little-known underground catacombs. The **Central Library** (☎ 384201; Castle St; 🕑 9.30am-7pm Mon, Tue, Thu & Fri, 10am-5pm Wed, 9.30am-4pm Sat, 11am-2.30pm Sun) offers free 30-minute Internet sessions for nonmembers.

Sights & Activities

Nestled on a close of historic houses, **Exeter Cathedral** (☎ 255573; www.exeter-cathedral.org.uk; The Close; suggested donation £3.50; 🕑 7.30am-6.30pm Mon-Sat, 7.30am-5pm Sun) has a grand, statue-covered entrance that historians believe was once painted in vibrant colours. Grab the mobile wheelie-mirror inside and check out the gold bosses that stud the vaulted ceilings, before comparing the tiny chapels that punctuate the interior. Like many English cathedrals, there's plenty of evidence of Victorian renovation but some of the best ancient quirks remain, including carvings of a man standing on his head and an angel playing bagpipes.

The **Quay** area is a highlight of any visit to Exeter. Situated on a curving elbow of the Exe River, this cobbled, quaintly gentrified former port area is crowded with lazy, leisure-minded locals in summer. Its refurbished brick warehouses are home to galleries, cafés and pubs, and on sunny days, everyone can find an outdoor seating spot here.

Those who prefer to be more active should pack a picnic and rent a bike or canoe from the area's **Saddles & Paddles** (☎ 424241; www.sadpad.com; 4 King's Wharf; bikes/canoes per day £13/15; 🕑 9.30am-5.30pm) before heading downriver to spot herons and kingfishers.

Sleeping

There is a clutch of mid-priced B&Bs on St David's Hill between the train station and city centre. There are several more clustered around the Clock Tower near Exeter Central station.

Exeter YHA Hostel (☎ 0870 770 5826; exeter@yha.org.uk; 47 Countess Wear Rd; dm £15.50; P ⊠ 💻) This large 17th-century house overlooking the Exe River is 3 miles southeast of the city centre and offers dorm rooms with up to eight beds (most have four), as well as a café, games room and bike-hire service. There's a large lounge-worthy garden. Take bus K or T from the High St or bus 57 or 85 from the bus station, alight at School Lane and follow the signs.

Raffles Hotel (☎ 270200; www.raffles-exeter.co.uk; 11 Blackall Rd; s/d from £38/60; P) A superior town house B&B with a good location near the city centre, the Raffles is all about its antiques. Each high-ceilinged room is stuffed with period features, adding a quiet understated elegance that keeps some guests coming back for more. The owners are also committed to serving their guests organic produce and offer a good breakfast option for starving vegetarian travellers.

Clock Tower Hotel (☎ 424545; www.clocktowerhotel.co.uk; 16 New North Rd; s £42, d £58-68; P) Among a row of adjoining B&Bs on New North Rd, this clean and comfortable Georgian town house has some titchy single rooms and can be a little noisy when full. But all rooms are newly furnished, and it's just a few minutes' walk from Exeter Central station and the city's main action. In summer guests can sit on the landscaped patio and watch the world go by.

Eating

Exeter has a good selection of cafés to feed its cosmopolitan student population and a couple of worthy top-end establishments for those who want to splurge. The Quay is the hotspot for alfresco summer dining.

Mango's Café Bar (☎ 438538; Cellar 3, King's Wharf, The Quay; mains £4-6; 🕑 10am-6pm, 10am-10pm in summer) A funky yellow cave interior, friendly staff and quality fresh-made dishes make this low-cost eatery feel like an expensive treat. In fact, it couldn't be much cheaper, with hearty wraps and panini sandwiches around the £5 mark. The soups – try the carrot and coriander – will have you licking the plate for more and there are plenty of options for vegetarians.

Milkmaid Restaurant (☎ 277438; 15 Catherine St; mains £5-8; 🕑 breakfast & lunch) An Exeter legend that has reinvented itself several times over the years, the well-located Milkmaid has fancied up its menu with yuppie ingredients like feta and ricotta. But it's the fish and chips and farmhouse grills that its mainly elderly defenders keep coming back for – some of these old women would come here to order their daily Welsh Rarebit even if the place closed down.

Red Square (☎ 411292; Rougemount House, Castle St; mains £9-16; 🕑 lunch Mon-Sat, dinner Tue-Sat) Causing a bit of a revolution in Exeter's conservative dining scene, this excellent Russian restaurant is well worth a night out. Rather than covering its walls with Soviet kitsch, the staid dining room focuses on delivering ethnic fusion dishes, like stroganoff-style calamari and aubergine caviar.

Getting There & Away

Nine direct National Express buses arrive at Paris St station from London Victoria daily (£21.50, four to five hours). There are five daily direct arrivals from Plymouth (£8.90, one to two hours), four from Bristol (£11.60, two hours) and two from Penzance (£22, 4½ hours). Megabus runs one daily bus from London Victoria (from £1, four hours). Train services from Paddington arrive at St David's station hourly (£26.50, 2½ hours). Services also arrive from Bristol (£17.60, 1½ hours), Salisbury (£22.70, two hours) and Penzance (£21.50, three hours).

PLYMOUTH

☎ 01752 / pop 243,795

Bypassing its ugly post-WWII city centre and heading for the salty, olde-worlde charms of the Hoe and Barbican areas is the best way to experience Plymouth. With a rich maritime history that includes the Pilgrim Fathers and Francis Drake, visitors can spend a couple of days here communing with the spirits of sea dogs past.

Orientation & Information

Plymouth's grey, shop-heavy city centre is south of the train station. Continue south (and uphill) to the headland Hoe for commanding views of Plymouth Sound and most of the city's best accommodation options. Downhill and to the east of here is the cobbled Barbican area, stuffed with restaurants, attractions and the city's **TIC** (☎ 304849; www.visitplymouth.co.uk; 3-5 The Barbican; 🕑 9am-5pm Mon-Fri, 9am-4pm Sat). Back in the city centre, **Plymouth Internet Café** (☎ 221777; 32 Frankfort Gate; per hr £4; 🕑 9am-5pm Mon-Sat, 10am-4pm Sun) offers adequate but expensive Internet access.

Sights & Activities

The utterly charming tangle of Elizabethan streets that makes up the **Barbican** has undergone a recent renaissance that's added seafront cafés and galleries to Plymouth's top pubs and restaurants. It's also home to the city's best and newest attractions, including **Plymouth Mayflower** (☎ 306330; 3-5 The Barbican; adult/child £4/2; 🕑 10am-6pm Apr-Oct, 10am-5pm Nov-Mar), an entertaining hi-tech exploration of the Pilgrim Fathers' departure for America; the **National Marine Aquarium** (☎ 600301; www.national-aquarium.co.uk; Rope Walk, Cox Side; adult/child £9.50/5.75; 🕑 10am-6pm Apr-Oct, 10am-5pm Nov-Mar), an excellent interpretive centre dripping with live exhibits; and the **Plymouth Dry Gin Distillery** (☎ 665292; 60 Southside St; tour £5; 🕑 tours 10.30am-4.30pm in summer, call head at other times), a tipple-happy historic production facility where the tours include some warming samples.

Sleeping & Eating

Head to the Hoe – especially Citadel Rd – for a plethora of good-value B&Bs, but make sure you shop around: while rates may be similar, there are wide disparities between the facilities on offer. For dining to suit all budgets, stroll down to the Barbican.

Globe Backpackers Plymouth (☎ 225158; www.backpackers.co.uk/plymouth; 172 Citadel Rd; dm/d £12/30) Grubby and a bit chaotic, Plymouth's only backpacker option could use some competition to keep it on its toes. Located in a crumbling pink-painted town house on the Hoe, facilities include a large lounge and small dorms, as well as a few private double rooms. The staff mean well and the property is close to all the historic action.

Jewell's Hotel (☎ 254760; 220 Citadel Rd; s £25, d £45-60; Ⓟ) Among the dozens of good-value, traditional B&Bs around the Hoe's labyrinthine northern tip, this superb property stands out. Elegant but comfortable rooms include welcoming extras like hairdryers and hot-water bottles and the hosts' pudgy lapdog offers a friendly personal greeting to anyone arriving at the door.

Platters (☎ 227262; 12 The Barbican; mains £4-15; 🕑 lunch & dinner) Carved fish leap from the timber beams in this character-packed Barbican favourite. The locally sourced, freshly cooked fish and chips are second-to-none, while more adventurous diners can feast on turbot, red mullet and the small but well-chosen wine list. Watch out for the tempting dessert menu, a largely health-free zone.

Himalayan Spice (☎ 252211; 31 New St; mains £7-11; 🕑 lunch daily, dinner Mon-Sat) Incongruously located in a 16th-century stone cottage in a Barbican back alley, this excellent Indian and Nepalese restaurant is a local favourite, with plenty of vegetarian options. Try the flour-rolled, deep-fried Himalayan Chicken followed by a jog up the hill to the Hoe to work it off.

Getting There & Away

Seven direct National Express buses arrive from London Victoria daily (£27.50, five to seven hours), while four buses arrive from Bristol (£24.50, three to four hours) and five from Exeter (£8.90, one to two hours). Megabus runs a daily service from London Victoria (from £1, 5½ hours). Hourly train services arrive in the city from London Paddington (3½ hours), while frequent services arrive from Penzance (£11.40, two hours), Exeter (£4.90, one hour) and Bristol (£42.50, 2½ hours).

DARTMOOR NATIONAL PARK

If existentialism was a landscape, this is what it would look like: bleak, wasted, wild vistas are the norm here, and it's one of the few places in England where you can feel utterly alone, despite wandering pockets of sheep and semiwild Dartmoor ponies. This menacing emptiness was the main reason why Arthur Conan-Doyle set *The Hound of the Baskervilles* here. But there's an undeniably haunting beauty to this south Devon moor that encourages trek-loving visitors to quietly commune with the barren tableland, jutting tors and scrubby gorse as if they're meeting Mother Nature face-to-face.

Orientation

This 368-sq-mile park is a hiker's paradise, but with changeable weather and visibility-crushing fog it's not a place to stroll unprepared. Thankfully, there are some excellent resources for those planning a visit.

Information

Princetown, the moor's largest village, houses the region's main **High Moorland Visitor Centre** (☎ 01822-890414; Tavistock Rd; 10am-5pm, 10am-4pm in winter), which can assist with maps, accommodation and activities, like cycling and horse riding.

There are additional, smaller information centres at **Haytor** (☎ 01364-665120; 10am-5pm Easter-Oct, 10am-4pm Sat & Sun only in winter), **Postbridge** (☎ 01822-880272; 10am-5pm Easter-Oct, 10am-4pm Sat & Sun only in winter) and **Newbridge** (☎ 01364-631303; 10am-5pm Easter-Oct, 10am-4pm Sat & Sun only in winter), the last of which is also the arrival point for many summer coach parties. The majority of visitors stick to the eastern side of the park where the main settlements are, while serious hikers prefer to get away from it all on the western edge.

Keep in mind that the **Ministry of Defence** (☎ 0800 458 4858; www.dartmoor-ranges.co.uk) has three well-marked live firing ranges in the park's north section: phone ahead for an update on firing schedules. For further visitor information, contact the **Dartmoor Tourist Association** (☎ 01822-890567; www.discoverdartmoor.com) or **Dartmoor National Park Authority** (☎ 01626-832093; www.dartmoor-npa.gov.uk).

Sleeping

B&Bs are plentiful in the larger settlements on the edge of the park (like Buckfastleigh, Okehampton and Tavistock), but Dartmoor is also well served with hostelling and camping options. Most of the area is privately owned, but it's generally acceptable to camp so long as you stick to the area's Backpacking Code: don't camp on moorland enclosed by walls, within sight of roads or houses, or near heavily trafficked areas.

Plume of Feathers (☎ 01822-890240; www.plumeoffeathers-dartmoor.co.uk; Princetown; camp sites from £5, bunkhouse from £6, d from £55; P) One of Princetown's best-value accommodation options, this large, friendly stone pub offers 75 camp sites with a shower and toilet block, basic but cheap dorm bunkhouses and comfortable but not luxurious private B&B rooms. It's busy in summer, so call ahead.

Bellever YHA Hostel (☎ 0870 770 5692; bellever@yha.org.uk; Bellever; dm £13.95; P ⊠) This imposing stone farmhouse hostel in the heart of the park offers basic but tranquil accommodation in its mostly small dorms. It's an outdoor-lovers favourite, with hiking trails, Dartmoor ponies and open moorland just outside the windows. There's a £1 discount for those arriving on foot and by bike or bus – bus 82 from Plymouth to Exeter stops in nearby Postbridge.

Okehampton YHA Hostel (☎ 0870 770 5978; okehampton@yha.org.uk; Klondyke Rd, Okehampton; dm £15.50; P ⊠) On the northern edge of the park, this charming Victorian railway goods shed is an activity-centre hostel combining standard but well-maintained facilities, with programs in archery, pony trekking and gorge scrambling. It's also a good base for hitting the park's many hiking trails.

Lydgate House (☎ 01822-880209; www.lydgatehouse.com; Postbridge; s per person £55, d per person £60-70; Apr-Oct; P ⊠) This lovely country house overlooking a river valley in the centre of Dartmoor is highly recommended. Relaxed and adult-oriented, its seven rooms are eminently comfortable and tastefully decorated, while the peaceful terrace is a good spot to view herons and house martins.

Getting There & Around

Transmoor Link bus 82 (three daily Monday to Saturday, five Sunday, weekends only in winter) runs across Dartmoor between Plymouth and Exeter via Postbridge, Princetown and Yelverton. Pick up a copy of the *Discovery Guide to Dartmoor by Bus and Train* from local information centres or contact **Devon Bus** (☎ 01392-382800; www.devon.gov.uk/buses) for information. An alternative to the buses is to hire a bike from Tavistock's **Dartmoor Cycle Hire Centre** (☎ 01822-618178; West Devon Business Park) for £6/12 per half-/full day.

EXMOOR NATIONAL PARK

North Devon's Exmoor is smaller than Dartmoor, its national park cousin to the south, but it makes up for its lack of size with some uniquely breathtaking scenery. Within its 265 sq miles, it offers lovely beaches, dramatic sea cliffs, tree-lined copses, verdant hidden valleys, and romantically expansive moorland crisscrossed by tumbling streams, horned sheep and England's last herd of wild red deer.

There are a number of particularly attractive villages in the region: Lynton and

Lynmouth are joined by a water-operated railway; pretty Porlock, at the edge of the moor in a beautiful valley, is studded with thatch-roofed cottages; Dunster, dominated by its handsome Victorian-restored castle, is a picturesque survivor from the 13th century; and Selworthy, a National Trust village that's so stuffed with rustic charm that it's often used as an olde-worlde movie set.

Orientation

Well-marked walking paths crisscross Exmoor. One of the best and easiest sections of the region's Southwest Coast Path runs through the park between Minehead and Padstow. This is also excellent horse-riding country – ask at visitor centres for local stables.

Information

The five visitor information centres include the main facility in **Dulverton** (☎ 01398-323841; Fore St; ⌚ year-round), as well as outposts in **Combe Martin** (☎ 01271-883319; 13 Cross St; ⌚ Apr-Oct), **County Gate** (☎ 01598-741321; A39 Countisbury; ⌚ Apr-Oct), near Lynton, **Dunster** (☎ 01643-821835; Dunster Steep; ⌚ Apr-Oct) and **Lynmouth** (☎ 01598-752509; The Esplanade; ⌚ Apr-Oct). For visitor information, contact **Greater Exmoor Tourism** (www.visit-exmoor.info) or the **Exmoor National Park Authority** (☎ 01398-323665; www.exmoor-nationalpark.gov.uk).

Sleeping

Greater Exmoor Tourism's online accommodation site **Exmoor Coast & Country** (www.exmoorholidayguide.co.uk) is a good place to start your research. For those on a tight budget, there are comfortable but basic YHA hostels in **Lynton** (☎ 0870 770 5942; lynton@yha.org.uk; dm £11.95; ⌚ Apr-Oct; P ⊠), **Exford** (☎ 0870 770 5828; exford@yha.org.uk; Exe Mead; dm £12.95; P ⊠) and **Minehead** (☎ 0870 770 5968; minehead@yha.org.uk; Alcombe Combe; dm £11.95; P ⊠).

Quaint B&Bs and guesthouses are scattered throughout Exmoor. Recommendations include Lynton's charming **Sinai House** (☎ 01598-753227; www.sinaihouse.co.uk; Lynway; s & d per person £27-36; P ⊠), Porlock's delightfully thatch-roofed **Myrtle Cottage** (☎ 01643-862978; bob.steer@virgin.net; High St; s/d per person £20/30; P ⊠) and Dunster's classically medieval **Luttrell Arms** (☎ 01643-821555; www.bhere.co.uk; High St; s/d from £65/95; ⊠).

Getting There & Around

Planning transport to Exmoor requires a little creativity. Three direct National Express buses arrive daily from London Victoria (£27.50, 5½ hours) in Barnstaple, outside the park's western edge. From here you can take local bus 307 (1¼ hours) to Dulverton, or bus 309 or 310 to Lynton (one hour). Frequent trains arrive in Exeter from London Paddington (from £26.50, two to three hours). From here you can pick up the pretty Tarka Line train service to Barnstaple (£10.80, one hour, 12 daily Monday to Saturday, six daily Sunday). Active travellers can rent mountain bikes at several spots around the park, including Minehead's **Pompy's Cycles** (☎ 01643-704077; www.pompyscycles.co.uk; Mart Rd) for £12.50 per day.

CORNWALL

Penzance

☎ 01736 / pop 20,260

Lacking the idyllic quaintness of nearby St Ives, Penzance – the end of the train line from London – is larger and a bit scruffier than its Cornish neighbours. But beyond the derelict reminders of the town's bustling port days, there are several latter-day reasons to drop by, including some smashing old pubs, a sea-bound historic castle and a dramatic coastal cliff hike. The **TIC** (☎ 362207; www.visit-westcornwall.com; Station Approach; ⌚ 9am-5.30pm Mon-Fri, 9am-5pm Sat, 10am-1pm Sun May-Aug, 9am-5pm Mon-Sat, 10am-1pm Sun Sep, 9am-5pm Mon-Fri, 10am-1pm Sat Oct-Apr) is opposite the train station.

St Michael's Mount (☎ 710507; www.stmichaelsmount.co.uk; Marazion; adult/child £6/3; ⌚ 10.30am-5.30pm Sun-Fri Mar-Oct), a dramatic 12th-century castle complex on a lush tree-covered island just off the coast, is well worth a visit. Echoing the palatial Mont St-Michel off Normandy, the Cornish version houses beautiful baronial rooms, a lovely priory church and some verdant subtropical hanging gardens. You can walk across at low tide and there are ferries at high tide in summer.

Walkers should also check out the 17-mile stretch of the **South West Coast National Trail** (☎ 01752-896237; www.southwestcoastpath.com) between Penzance and Land's End. Head west along the windswept cliffs towards the tip of England's crenulated boot for some achingly beautiful bays, a symphony of crashing waves and an accompanying chorus of cawing seabirds. Before you hit the Land's

End crowds, you'll spot the seafront Minnick Theatre, Bishop's Rock lighthouse and the shimmering Isles of Scilly.

Penzance's accommodation includes characterful B&Bs and rooms above old-school pubs. A popular spot is **Penzance YHA Hostel** (☎ 0870 770 5992; penzance@yha.org.uk; Castle Horneck, Alverton; dm £15.50; ⊠ 💻), 1.5 miles from the train station on the edge of town. This solid Georgian mansion has great views of the coastline. The facilities are predictably institutional, but include a TV lounge, bike storage and a small library. There's also a wooded garden and some spots for camping.

For those with a little more to spend, **Chy-an-Mor Hotel** (☎ 363411; www.chyanmoor.co.uk; Regent Tce; s £36-43, d £60-93; P ⊠) is a charming listed town house B&B with 10 elegantly decorated guest rooms, including some with four-poster beds. Most rooms enjoy views across Mount's Bay, while the rear-facing accommodation looks over the peaceful, palm-fringed vista of St Mary's Church. It's a 10-minute walk to the town centre.

Aside from the ubiquitous Cornish pasty shops – don't knock 'em until you've tried 'em – Penzance town centre has some good eating alternatives. Among these, **Yam Parlour** (☎ 366740; 36 Causewayhead; mains £5-8.50; 🕒 lunch & dinner, also breakfast Sat) is a vegetarian café where nonveggies are happy to eat. This highly convivial wood-floored nook has a laid-back vibe and a serious commitment to hearty, locally sourced ingredients. The changing menu can range from mushroom ravioli to squash and coconut curry, and there's a money-saving dinnertime bring-your-own-beer option.

A 10-minute walk away, the **Union Hotel** (☎ 362319; www.unionhotel.co.uk; Chapel St; mains £8-16; 🕒 lunch & dinner), opposite the architecturally splendid Egyptian House, houses the snug Nelson Bar, which serves some distinctive local brews in an atmospheric sea-dog setting. Great food is also part of the attraction at the hotel's wood-lined Hamilton Restaurant, where locally caught fish is a particular menu highlight. There are also 28 guest rooms (singles/doubles £35/58) here – a fact that Charles Dickens made use of during a brief visit.

Five direct National Express buses arrive in Penzance daily from London Victoria (£35.50, nine hours), while two direct services also arrive from Exeter (£22, 4½ hours), two from Newquay (£5, 1½ hours) and two from Bristol (£37, 6½ hours). Hourly direct train services arrive from London Paddington (£67, 5½ hours) throughout the day, while there are also frequent direct services from Exeter (£28.40, three hours) and Plymouth (£11.40, two hours).

Land's End

☎ 01736

The jagged sea-battered cliffs that surround it would warn off most visitors but many still manage to get through and dive into **Legendary Land's End** (☎ 0870 458 0099; www.landsend-landmark.co.uk; admission £10; 🕒 10am-3pm, later in summer), a slick, seaside-style complex of campy attractions, pricey fast-food joints and 'Last in Britain' gift shops. Fans of the tacky will enjoy the 'multi-sensory' Last Labyrinth, a 'spooky' light-show menagerie of witches, pirates and monsters. Consider avoiding it entirely and pick your way across the rocks to check out the end of Britain as it crumbles into the sea. On a clear day, you can spot the Isles of Scilly in the distance.

If you're feeling adventurous, continue along the coastal path for about 3 miles to Porthcurno's **Minack Theatre** (☎ 810181; www.minack.com; adult/child £2.50/1; 🕒 9.30am-5.30pm Apr-Oct, 10am-4pm Nov-Mar). Dramatically carved into a cliff overlooking the bay, this outdoor amphitheatre is open year-round for curious visitors, and stages a varied roster of musicals, Shakespearean classics and popular dramas from May to September (tickets £6 to £7.50). Bus 1 to Penzance stops at Porthcurno and provides a late-night escape after the shows in summer.

Accommodation in the area includes hostels and family-run B&Bs. Among the highlights are **Land's End YHA Hostel** (☎ 0870 770 5906; Letcha Vean, St Just-in-Penwith; dm £14; 🕒 Apr-Oct, by appointment Nov-Mar), a remote property with small dorms and commanding sea views but no laundry facilities, and **Whitesand's Lodge** (☎ 871776; www.whitesandslodge.co.uk; Sennen; tent sites £6.50, dm £12.50, s/d £22/44; P 💻), an uber-relaxing, recently refurbished holiday spot offering tent pitches, dorm accommodation and B&B private rooms. There's a hearty menu in its vegetarian-friendly restaurant, and an array of guest activities are available, including surfing, yoga and horse riding.

St Ives

☎ 01736 / pop 9870

The train from St Erth to St Ives delivers curving sandy bays and paradise-blue waters before drawing towards a higgle-piggle of stone cottages rising invitingly from the sea. Combining steep, rock-hewn streets with a friendly, artist-dominated cultural scene and a surprisingly sophisticated array of restaurants, this may be Cornwall's prettiest village. Ask at the **TIC** (☎ 796297; www.visit-westcornwall.com; Guildhall, Street-an-Pol; 🕑 9am-5.30pm Mon-Fri, 9am-5pm Sat, 10am-4pm Sun Jun-Sep, 9am-5pm Mon-Fri, 10am-1pm Sat May-Oct) for gallery and dining guides.

Like a tasty, overstuffed Cornish pasty, the streets of St Ives are full of tiny artist-run galleries, but it's the **Tate St Ives** (☎ 796226; www.tate.org.uk; Porthmeor Beach; adult/child £5.50/free; 🕑 10am-5.30pm Mar-Oct, 10am-4.30pm Nov-Feb) that is the focal point. From its striking beachfront setting, the southwest satellite of the popular London gallery showcases the works of local legends like Barbara Hepworth and John Wells. There's a panoramic top-floor café, and an array of free talks and tours that keep the place livelier than a seagull with a live catch.

For those who'd like to try surfing, consider taking lessons from **Shore Surf** (☎ 755556; www.shoresurf.com; lessons half-/full day £20/35) in nearby Hayle – it operates a free minibus to get you around the area. Popular surfing beaches include **Porthminster** and **Porthmeor**.

Among the area's sleepover options, **St Ives International Backpackers** (☎ 799444; www.backpackers.co.uk/st-ives; The Stennack; dm £11-17; 💻) is a large, 70-bed hostel occupying a former Wesleyan chapel opposite the town cinema. There's nothing holy about its grungy interior, funky coloured walls and basic rooms. A surf-loving party joint in summer, board fans are always welcome – board and wetsuit storage is available.

In contrast, the **Anchorage** (☎ 797135; www.theanchoragebandb.co.uk; 5 Bunkers Hill; per person £30-38; ⊠), among the dozens of tiny, period B&Bs tucked in the backstreets behind Wharf Rd, is a real charmer. Its friendly, dedicated owners are continually improving a cosy property that already features dark timber ceilings and sparkling bathrooms. Breakfast includes several vegetarian options.

Not surprisingly, fish is a local dine-out speciality, and a highlight is the **Seafood Café** (☎ 794004; 45 Fore St; mains £5-15; 🕑 lunch & dinner), a modern, good-value bistro lunch spot near the harbourfront. One of the best places in town to sample locally caught seafood, it becomes a gourmet dinner spot every evening but never loses its low-key, informal approach. Try the sea bream and herb-roasted new potatoes for a taste of local marine life.

If you've had your fill of fish, try **St Andrews Street Bistro** (☎ 797074; 16 St Andrews St; mains £4-14; 🕑 lunch & dinner), a chilled-out, rather eclectic restaurant lined with works by local artists. The artistry carries over to the menu, which brings piquant Moroccan influences to the preparation of locally sourced ingredients. There are always good vegetarian options, too.

Newquay

☎ 01637 / pop 19,570

The UK's surfing capital, noisy Newquay seems like a giant, open-air nightclub in summer when party-loving drinkers throng the streets. If you're just here for the waves, you'll meet plenty of like-minded souls on the 11 sandy stretches around town, especially the ever-popular **Fistral Beach** to the west and the learner-friendly **Watergate Bay** to the east.

The **TIC** (☎ 854020; www.newquay.co.uk; Marcus Hill; 🕑 9.30am-5.30pm Mon-Sat, 9.30am-1pm Sun, reduced hr in winter) is near the bus station and there are surf shops dotted around the town, including the recommended **Offshore Extreme** (☎ 877083; www.offshore-extreme.co.uk; 6 Pentire Ave; per day equipment rental from £6, lessons & equipment rental from £12).

Newquay has many competing surf-happy independent hostels, including the bright and modern town centre **Reef Surf Lodge** (☎ 879058; www.reefsurflodge.info; 10-12 Berry Rd; per person £15-30; 🅿 💻). Most of its dorms, each with CD players and TVs, are tiny but the facilities are superior to other local hostels, with a bar, licensed restaurant and regular live music shows. Twin and en suite rooms are available for those who want to upgrade, but watch out for the somewhat annoying muzak playing almost permanently through the corridors.

Other budget recommendations:

Original Backpackers (☎ 874668; www.originalbackpackers.co.uk; 16 Beachfield Ave; dm £8-17) This comfortable 25-year-old backpacker joint, complete with cosy 1970s interiors, overlooks Towan Beach.

BRITAIN

Boarding House (☎ 873258; www.theboardinghouse.co.uk; 32 Headland Rd; dm £18-25) Close to Fistral Beach, this superior hostel has a great sundeck and an on-site surfing school.

BATH

☎ **01225 / pop 90,144**

Getting lost is the first thing any visitor to Bath, the UK's most handsome city, should do. Its lovely, honey-coloured stone streets and higgle-piggle of teeming back alleys are a stroller's delight and encourage unplanned exploration. But while it's tempting to just keep walking, there are some sights in England's only Unesco World Heritage city that are well worth stopping for.

History

Bath's enduring popularity for visitors is based on a stroke of geological luck. It's the site of the only hot springs in the country, which is why tribal Brits established a settlement here almost 3000 years ago. The restorative waters are also the main reason the Romans arrived in AD 44. Creating the town of Aquae Sulis, an enormous complex of baths and temples dedicated to Sulis-Minerva, they laid the foundations for the modern city. But instead of lounging around in hot baths after the departure of the Romans, the later medieval era was one of monastic devotion with the town becoming a religious centre and the site of an important abbey. The hot springs were rediscovered in the early 18th century when, fed by wool trade wealth, Bath began expanding and attracting the fashionable glitterati for restorative sojourns. The present-day city owes much of its appearance to this golden age.

Orientation & Information

Bath's bus and train stations face each other on the southern edge of town in a bend of the Avon River. The main historic attractions occupy a fan-shaped area north of this point, with the landmark Abbey just five minutes' walk away.

The **TIC** (☎ 0906 711 2000; www.visitbath.co.uk; Abbey Chambers, Abbey Churchyard; per min £0.50; 9.30am-5pm Mon-Sat, 10am-4pm Sun Oct-May, 9.30am-6pm Mon-Sat, 10am-4pm Sun Jun-Sep) is on the southern side of the Abbey. Internet access is available at **Click** (☎ 481008; 13a Manvers St; per 20 min £1; 10am-10pm) across from the train station.

Sights & Activities

ROMAN BATHS

The unmissable heart of any visit here, the **Roman Baths** (☎ 477785; www.romanbaths.co.uk; Abbey Churchyard; adult £10-11, child £6; 9.30am-5pm Jan & Feb, 9am-5pm Mar-Jun, 9am-9pm Jul & Aug, 9am-5pm Sep & Oct, 9.30am-4.30pm Nov & Dec) are a tangible link with the UK's ancient past. While you won't want to dive into the steaming, sickly green pools, check out the largely intact Roman engineering on display and you'll get a glimpse of what it was like to be a Roman in Britain. Note the number of coins thrown into some of the pools – it should be enough to make this attraction free. It's always crawling with tourists in summer, so arrive late or early to beat the crowds.

JANE AUSTEN CENTRE

Celebrating the life and times of Bath's most famous resident – she only lived here for five years but keep that to yourself – the bright, **Jane Austen Centre** (☎ 443000; www.janeausten.co.uk; 40 Gay St; adult/child £5.95/2.95; 10am-5.30pm Mon-Sat, 10.30am-5.30pm Sun) is a must for lit lovers. Visits start with a 15-minute introductory talk, before you're let loose in rooms of artefacts and educational displays. Visit the top-floor teahouse where you can sink your teeth into Mr Darcy (the cake), and enquire about the centre's popular 90-minute walking tours (adult/child £4.50/3.50) at 11am on Saturday and Sunday.

BATH ABBEY

Off Cheap St, do not miss **Bath Abbey's** (☎ 422462; suggested donation £3; 9am-6pm Mon-Sat, 1-2.30pm & 4.30-5.30pm Sun Apr-Oct, 9am-5.30pm Mon-Sat, 1-2.30pm Sun Nov-Mar) extraordinary exterior of angels ascending and descending heavenly ladders before you duck inside this lovely medieval edifice. Compact compared to many of England's cathedrals, highlights of the well-scrubbed interior include a spider web–style vaulted ceiling and some impressively intricate stained-glass windows. Head to the onsite **Heritage Vaults** (adult/child £2.50/free; 9am-4pm Mon-Sat) for an exhibition of the Abbey's centuries-old stone carvings.

OTHER ATTRACTIONS

Other recommended attractions and activities:

Bizarre Bath Comedy Walk (☎ 335124; www.bizarrebath.co.uk; adult/child £7/5; 8pm Apr-Sep) Like a

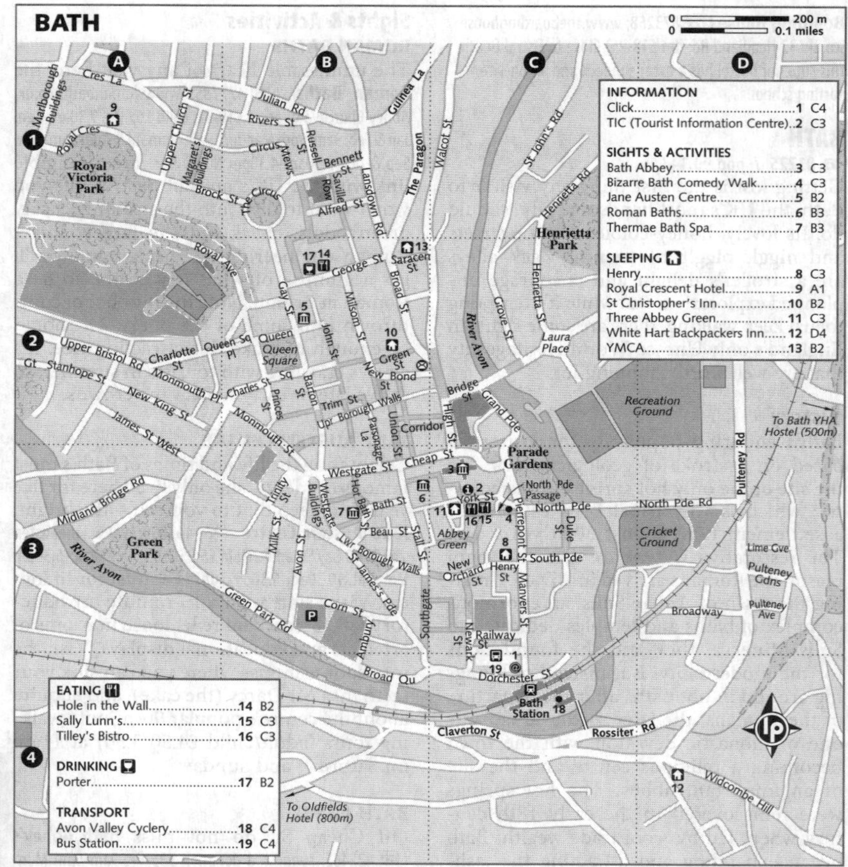

fringe-festival show on legs, this irreverent and highly entertaining 90-minute trawl around the city is great fun. It departs from Huntsman Inn, North Parade Passage.

Thermae Bath Spa (☎ 335678; www.thermaebathspa.com; Hetling Pump Room, Hot Bath St; spa sessions 2hr/4hr/full day £19/29/45) Limping towards completion at the time of research, this giant modern-day reinvention of the Bath bath experience promises a smorgasbord of spa treatments.

Sleeping

Sleepover bargains are hard to find in summertime Bath when the tourists arrive en masse. Book ahead or suffer the consequences.

BUDGET

YMCA (☎ 325900; www.bathymca.co.uk; International House, Broad St Pl; dm £13-15, s £24-28, tw £36-44; P ⊠ 💻) Bath's largest hostel is bright, cheerful and right in the city centre. The dorms are somewhat institutional, but the compact private rooms are great value. Facilities include laundry facilities and an on-site gym and continental breakfast is thrown in (not literally).

White Hart Backpackers Inn (☎ 313985; www.whitehartbath.co.uk; Widcombe Hill; dm £14, s £25, d £40-60; ⊠) Modern furnishings in a recently renovated pub heritage building five minutes' south of the train station, this cosy property combines good-value private rooms with a corridor of mid-sized dorms. Most rooms share bathrooms, and guests can have their free continental breakfast in the pretty pub garden. The downstairs pub has a great atmosphere and some super Mediterranean-influenced dishes (mains £9 to £12).

Other recommended budget options:

Bath YHA Hostel (☎ 0870 770 5688; bath@yha.org.uk; Bathwick Hill; dm £12.50; ⊠ 💻) A 25-minute uphill climb from the city centre brings you to this typical YHA hostel in a rambling Italianate mansion.

St Christopher's Inn (☎ 481444; www.st-christophers.co.uk; 9 Green St; dm £16; 💻) Party-lovers hostel in the heart of the city.

MIDRANGE

Henry (☎ 424052; www.thehenry.com; 6 Henry St; s £35, d £60-65; ⊠) Smashing guesthouse with a strong claim to being Bath's best sleep-over deal. The warren of recently renovated rooms – with shared bathrooms – successfully combine period features with IKEA-esque furnishings. Wi-fi is available, and extra beds can be added to some rooms.

Oldfields Hotel (☎ 317984; www.oldfields.co.uk; 102 Wells Rd; s £45-69, d £65-115; P ⊠) This elegant hilltop property overlooking Bath's Georgian splendour is surprisingly affordable. The service is excellent, and the rooms combine reproduction antiques and Jacuzzi-style baths. The cooked vegetarian breakfast is a nice touch. It's a 10-minute downhill stroll to the city centre – a bit of a hike on your way back.

Three Abbey Green (☎ 428558; www.threeabbeygreen.com; 3 Abbey Green; d/tw/tr £95/95/125; ⊠ 💻) A 17th-century town house in a quiet square near the Abbey, this immaculate period property has been recently renovated to a high standard. The wide configuration of rooms tastefully combine new and antique furnishings. There are original hearths in some rooms but also a bright, modern subterranean breakfast room. There's a computer for free Internet access.

TOP END

Royal Crescent Hotel (☎ 823333; www.royalcrescent.co.uk; 16 Royal Cres; d £290-390; P ⊠) Bath's signature hotel, the gloriously refined Royal Crescent combines beautiful, antique-lined rooms with an air of nonpompous pampering. The hedonistic on-site spa is popular with chichi guests, while the tranquil gardens are perfect for a spot of afternoon tea.

Eating & Drinking

There are plenty of eating options lining the main streets of Bath, but it's worth exploring the back alleys for something unexpected. The TIC has a couple of good dine-out guides.

Sally Lunn's (☎ 461634; 4 North Parade Passage; mains £5-10; 🕑 brunch, lunch & dinner) This chatty 17th-century tearoom is a local favourite. Sample the Georgian-era Sally Lunn Bun, a triumph of historic marketing that's actually a giant bread roll with sweet or savoury toppings (the real reason for its popularity). Try not to bang your head as you manoeuvre down the wonky stairs to the little on-site museum of excavated artefacts.

Porter (☎ 424104; 15 George St; mains £3-6; 🕑 lunch & dinner) An old-school pub with an unusual twist, Porter's good-value menu is entirely vegetarian, with hearty burgers, crepes and large salads well represented. Students make up much of the clientele, which is attracted by a nightly roster of eclectic live music (cover £3 to £5). Sunday is comedy night, and there are regular beer and wine specials.

Tilley's Bistro (☎ 484200; 3 North Parade Passage; mains £6-17; 🕑 lunch & dinner Mon-Sat; ⊠) This centrally located, French-influenced characterful restaurant is a cosy lunch spot and a romantic dinner destination. There's a large selection of small dishes that diners can mix and match, including recommended garlic escargots and Cornish white crab salad. Vegetarians are also well served with a good range of options, including finger-licking wild mushroom pancakes.

Hole in the Wall (☎ 425242; 16 George St; mains £10-18; 🕑 lunch & dinner Mon-Sat, dinner Sun; ⊠) There's a gastropub feel to this lovely British bistro where seasonal, locally sourced ingredients are de rigueur. Ask for one of the discreet alcove tables and have a couple of tipples from the impressively large wine list before tucking into the recommended pan-fried Gloucester beef.

Getting There & Around

Bath is eminently walkable, but bike rentals are also available from **Avon Valley Cyclery** (☎ 442442; Bath train station; 🕑 9am-5.30pm Mon-Sat) for £10/15 per half-/full day.

Ten direct National Express buses arrive daily from London Victoria (£16.50, 3½ hours), while one arrives direct from Salisbury (£8.30, 1½ hours) and two from Bristol (£3.50, 50 minutes). There's also a frequent nondirect service from Glastonbury (£6.50, three hours). Direct train services from

London Paddington (from £19, 1½ hours) arrive twice hourly, while hourly direct services arrive from Cardiff (£12.90, one hour). There's also a four-times-an-hour service from Bristol (£5.20, 15 minutes).

WELLS

☎ 01749 / pop 10,406

This Somerset gem is one of England's smallest cities, but it has more medieval charm than settlements many times its size. Named after the springs rising around several of its ancient buildings, its marvellous cathedral alone draws visitors from far and wide. With some great pubs, a bustling street market (on Wednesday and Saturday) and its proximity to popular Glastonbury, it's an ideal base for exploring the region – unless you're travelling by train: Wells has no train station. The **TIC** (☎ 672552; www.wells.gov.uk; Town Hall, Market Pl; 9.30am-5.30pm Apr-Oct, 10am-4pm Nov-Mar) offers historic walking tours in summer.

Sights

The jaw-dropping west front of **Wells Cathedral** (☎ 674483; www.wellscathedral.org.uk; suggested donation adult/child £5/2; 7am-7pm Apr-Sep, 7am-6pm Oct-Mar) would satisfy most visitors, with its vast menagerie of 300 medieval sculptures representing bishops, angels and biblical scenes. But the structure's impressive interior should not be missed. Its highlights include the **scissor arches**, a clever medieval solution to subsidence, a 14th-century **mechanical clock** with jousting knights and an octagonal **chapter house** that's dripping with ecclesiastical atmosphere. Save some time to wander the nearby **Vicar's Close**, a clutch of pretty houses completed in 1363 for the men of the choir. It's reportedly one of the oldest continuously inhabited streets in Europe.

Beyond the cathedral is the **Bishop's Palace** (☎ 678691; adult/child £5/1; 10.30am-6pm Mon-Fri, noon-6pm Sun Apr-Oct), surrounded by a moat where boiling oil might once have flowed. Highlights include Jacobean staircases, Gothic staterooms and a ruined, but imposing, Great Hall. It's worth strolling through the beautiful gardens – avoid the swans that regard it as their territory.

Sleeping & Eating

Bay Tree House (☎ 677933; www.baytree-house.co.uk; 85 Portway; s/d £28/42; P ⊠) With no dedicated budget accommodation, one of the city's best sleepover deals is Bay Tree House, a few minutes' walk from the city centre. The rooms are simply decorated with modern pine furnishings, there's a pretty garden at the back and vegetarian breakfasts are available.

Canon Grange B&B (☎ 671800; www.canongrange.co.uk; Cathedral Green; s & d from £52; ⊠) Set in a near-perfect location, this 15th-century, antique-strewn B&B has impeccable views of the cathedral's west front. The best room is the Walnut Suite, with its lavish interior, high ceilings and exposed beams.

Good Earth (☎ 678600; 4 Priory Rd; mains £4-7; 9am-5pm Mon-Sat) Near the bus station, this eatery serves hearty home-made soups, chunky pizza and healthy salads.

Fountain Inn & Boxers Restaurant (☎ 672317; 1 St Thomas St; mains £8-14; lunch & dinner) A gastropub delight, combining a cosy old-school bar with a restaurant featuring clever reinventions of traditional game and fish ingredients. Curd fans are well looked after, with plates of regional cheese prominent on the menu.

Getting There & Away

Without a train service to call its own, a once-daily direct National Express bus arrives from London Victoria (£18, 3½ hours) at the Princess Rd bus park. You can also use local transport to connect from the far busier National Express stops in Bristol and Bath. From Bristol, take the frequent bus 376 or 377 (one hour), and from Bath take bus 173 or 403 (1¼ hours). There's also the hourly bus 163 service from Glastonbury (15 minutes).

GLASTONBURY

☎ 01458 / pop 8429

Druidic mysticism and straggle-haired young hippies converge like ley lines on this pretty Somerset town that has reinvented itself as a New Age capital. The **TIC** (☎ 832954; www.glastonburytic.co.uk; 9 High St; 10am-5pm Sun-Thu, 10am-5.30pm Fri & Sat Apr-Sep, 10am-4pm Sun-Thu, 10am-4.30pm Fri & Sat Oct-Mar) is used to fielding rapid-fire questions about recommended veggie restaurants as well as the supposed remains of King Arthur.

There is only one daily direct National Express bus from London Victoria (£18, four hours), so it's best to hook up with the numerous services running to Bristol. Buses

376 and 377 connect Glastonbury with Bristol (hourly, 1½ hours) throughout the day. There is no Glastonbury train station.

Sights & Activities

While the town is reputed (on tenuous evidence) to be the birthplace of English Christianity, its main attraction is the romantically ruined **Glastonbury Abbey** (☎ 832267; www.glastonburyabbey.com; adult/child £4.50/3; ⌚ 9.30am-6pm Apr-Sep, 9.30am-5pm Oct, 9.30am-4.30pm Nov-Jan, 10am-5pm Feb & Mar), where intricately carved arch and pillar remnants indicate a once-stunning structure. Most visitors spend a couple of minutes reflecting in front of an area fancifully marked in the grass as King Arthur's grave. As with many of Glastonbury's attractions, faith is the key. But even if you don't believe that Glastonbury Tor, a derelict hilltop church tower on the edge of town, is a gateway to the underworld, it's a lovely spot to bring a picnic and spend a few hours enjoying the inquisitive sheep and panoramic views.

Festivals & Events

The town's youthful summer vibe is exemplified by **Glastonbury Festival** (☎ tickets 0870 120 0332; www.glastonburyfestivals.co.uk), a long weekend of music, theatre and New Age shenanigans that's one of England's favourite outdoor events. More than 100,000 turn up to writhe around in the fields at Pilton, 8 miles east of Glastonbury. Three-day admission is by advance ticket (£125) and the late-June extravaganza takes place annually – except in 2006, when it took a long-overdue year off.

Sleeping & Eating

Glastonbury Backpackers (☎ 833353; www.glastonburybackpacker.com; 4 Market Pl; dm/d £12/30; 🖳) This bright and lively backpackers is perfectly central and has a popular bar with regular live music. Try to snag one of the good-value private rooms or you'll be stuck in a cramped dorm. Book ahead: it's very busy in summer.

AppleTree House (☎ 830803; www.appletreehouse.org.uk; 27 Bere Lane; s/d £30/60; ⊠) Experience B&B perfection at AppleTree House, where you can borrow movies for your VCR, relax in the poppy-covered garden or hang out in your calming, pastel-coloured room while contemplating the mysteries of the cosmos.

Café Galatea (☎ 834284; 5a High St; mains £8-10; ⌚ lunch Mon, lunch & dinner Wed-Sun; 🖳) Recommended for an array of carnivore-pleasing vegetarian meals, along with a menu of Spanish and Italian favourites, this café has an Internet café and a boutique where you can pick up those essential crystals.

BRISTOL

☎ 0117 / pop 420,556

The most exciting city in the southwest, this once-decrepit port town is characterised by a hip cultural scene, trend-setting populace and a wealth of historic and modern attractions. This new Bristol is exemplified by the city's Harbourside: a cool Euro-plaza of street cafés and waterfront restaurants, complete with hi-tech museums and funky galleries. With public artworks, cobbled squares and cleaned-up urban waterways, this regenerated area – reminiscent of central Amsterdam – is contemporary Bristol's latter-day heart.

Orientation & Information

The Harbourside is a 15-minute walk west of Temple Meads train station, in an elbow of the Floating Harbour, a system of locks and docks that snakes through the city and looks like a river. The hilly city centre is a few minutes' north of this area, while further north on Marlborough St is the busy bus and coach station.

Ask at the **TIC** (☎ 0906 711 2191; www.visitbristol.co.uk; Wildscreen Walk, Harbourside; per min £0.50; ⌚ 10am-6pm Mar-Oct, 10am-5pm Nov-Feb) for maps, walking trails and an excellent free vegan guide. **Internet Exchange** (☎ 945 9926; 27-29 Baldwin St; per hr £4; ⌚ 10am-8pm Mon-Fri, 11am-7pm Sat, 1-5pm Sun) provides convenient Internet access near the Harbourside.

Sights

@Bristol (☎ 0845 345 1235; www.at-bristol.org.uk; Harbourside; combined admission Explore & Wildwalk adult/child £15/11, Explore & IMAX adult/child £14/10.50, Wildwalk & IMAX adult/child £13/10; ⌚ 10am-5pm Mon-Fri, 10am-6pm Sun) is a triumvirate of popular hi-tech attractions that includes **Explore** (adult/child £9/6.50), a kids-of-all-ages hands-on science centre; **IMAX** (adult/child £7/5.50), mostly showing eye-popping documentary flicks, and **Wildwalk** (adult/child £8/6), a fun-but-educational trawl through the natural world, which includes some mesmerising leafcutter ants.

 Book accommodation online at www.lonelyplanet.com

For those with more intellectual pursuits in mind, the **Arnolfini** (☎ 917 2300; www.arnolfini.org.uk; 16 Narrow Quay; admission free; ⏲ 10am-8pm Fri-Wed, 10am-6pm Thu), Bristol's version of London's Tate Modern, is a funky, recently reopened arts centre in an atmospheric dockyard venue. Alongside revolving exhibitions of contemporary art in its high-ceilinged gallery rooms, there's an arthouse cinema and a roster of cutting-edge dance performances. Head to the cool ground-floor café-bar to hang out with Bristol's young creative types. It's open until 2am on Friday.

Restored to its former glory for the recent bicentenary of its local designer, Isembard Kingdom Brunel's **SS Great Britain** (☎ 929 1843; www.ssbritain.org; Great Western Dockyard; adult/child £8.95/4.95; ⏲ 10am-5.30pm Apr-Oct, 10am-4.30pm Nov-Mar) is a must-see feat of Industrial Revolution engineering. Mounted on a shimmering glass 'sea', visitors can clamber up the gangway to compare the luxury of 1st class with the cramped steerage accommodation.

Check out the **British Empire & Commonwealth Museum** (☎ 925 4980; www.empiremuseum.co.uk; Clock Tower Yard, Temple Meads Station; adult/child £6.95/3.95; ⏲ 10am-5pm) for its fascinating evocation of British colonialism around the globe.

Brunel's other great local landmark is the **Clifton Suspension Bridge** (☎ 974 4664; Clifton).

Sleeping

Bristol is characterised by conservative, old-fashioned B&Bs and business hotels, but there are a few good sleepover options around the city. Check out the St Paul's Rd area for its plethora of guesthouses.

Bristol Backpackers (☎ 925 7900; www.bristolbackpackers.co.uk; 17 St Stephen's St; dm/tw/tr £14/36/45; 💻) A character-stuffed joint with its own dungeon-style bar, the predominantly mid-sized dorms are cramped but comfortable. There's free wi-fi – plus a few on-site computers for those travelling sans laptop – and the central location is highly desirable.

Bristol YHA Hostel (☎ 0870 770 5726; bristol@yha.org.uk; 14 Narrow Quay; dm/tw £19.95/44; ⊠ 💻) An excellent warehouse renovation in the heart of the Harbourside, the rooms here – mostly four-bed, en suite dorms – have been refurbished with new carpets and furnishings. A free cooked breakfast is now included and there's an on-site cosy café that also serves beer.

Arches Hotel (☎ 924 7398; www.arches-hotel.co.uk; 132 Cotham Brow; s/d £35/58; Ⓟ ⊠) Go green at this friendly, nine-room guesthouse committed to recycling, low-energy lighting and no genetically modified foods. There are several vegan and vegetarian-only breakfast options available: the continental is free, the cooked costs £3 extra.

Washington Hotel (☎ 973 3980; www.cliftonhotels.com; St Paul's Rd; s £30-64, d £50-80; Ⓟ) Among the dozen or so B&Bs occupying faded Georgian town houses on this pretty curve of St Paul's Rd, the Washington is perhaps the best value. Spread over three knocked-together houses, there's a variety of room configurations (the cheapest singles don't have en suites) but all have high ceilings, standard furnishings and welcome packs of fresh fruit.

Also recommended:

Toad Lodge (☎ 924 7080; www.toadlodge.com; 12 Cotham Park; s/d £25/35) It's a 20-minute walk from the city centre to this great-value B&B.

Brigstow Hotel (☎ 929 1030; www.brigstowhotel.com; Welsh Back; r £149-250; Ⓟ ⊠ 💻) Cool waterside location for this stylish designer sleepover.

Eating

There are good cafés and restaurants lining the Harbourside – the alfresco dining areas here are especially popular in summer – but it's also worth strolling uphill via Park Row to Whiteladies St, where you'll find a full menu of worthy alternatives.

St Nicholas Market (922 4017; entrances High St, Corn St & St Nicholas St; ⏲ 9.30am-5.30pm Mon-Sat) A smashing undercover Victorian market full of gourmet, deli-style takeouts. Make a circuit to check out home-made options, like olive bread, Stilton pasties and Caribbean delicacies, before deciding what you're in the mood for. Then top it off with some vintage clothes shopping.

Mud Dock Café (☎ 934 9734; 40 The Grove; mains £7-18; ⏲ breakfast, lunch & dinner) Occupying an industrial-chic renovation of an old red-brick harbour building, Mud Dock offers modern Brit cuisine (check out the lamb cutlet topped with chicken and blue-cheese mousse) and a lively, laid-back ambience. The top-floor patio enjoys fab summertime views of the busy waterfront.

Hullaballoos (☎ 923 9212; 46 Whiteladies Rd; 2-course lunch £9.75, dinner mains £12-18; ⏲ lunch daily, dinner Mon-Sat) This chilled-out British brasserie offers excellent service and the kind of perfectly prepared food with gourmet flourishes usually found on more expensive menus.

The lunch soups are superb, while mains like grilled salmon or pork and leek sausages are deservedly popular. Bringing your own beer is encouraged, but there's also a good wine menu.

Also recommended:

Clifton Sausage (☎ 973 1192; 1 Chandos Rd; mains £8.50-14; lunch & dinner) Eight types of banger are the cornerstone of this gourmet comfort-food classic.

Red Snapper (☎ 973 7999; 7-9 Portland St; mains £11-19.50; lunch daily, dinner Mon-Sat) Fish-lovers paradise with a veritable smorgasbord of options – anyone for gurnard?

Entertainment

As one of Britain's leading contemporary music incubators, Bristol has some great live venues. Pick up a copy of *Venue* (£1.30), the region's glossy weekly listings magazine, to find out what's on.

Fleece (☎ 945 0996; wwww.fleecegigs.co.uk; 12 St Thomas St; admission from £4) Features local indie faves and quality cover bands that move expertly from Manic Street Preachers to Massive Attack.

Croft (☎ 987 4144; www.the-croft.com; 117-119 Stokes Croft; admission from £3) If you're interested in seeing the next big thing before it hits MTV, head to this venue in the city's funky Stokes Croft area.

Getting There & Away

AIR

Bristol International Airport (BRS; ☎ 0870 121 2747; www.bristolairport.co.uk) is 7 miles southwest of the city. It services an expanding roster of routes from Europe, including Prague, Berlin, Dublin and Amsterdam. Domestic routes include regular easyJet flights from Edinburgh (from £15, 1¼ hours), Glasgow (from £15, 1¼ hours) and Newcastle (from £12, one hour). Regular Air Southwest services arrive from Leeds Bradford (from £19, one hour), Manchester (from £19, one hour) and Norwich (from £19, one hour).

BUS

Eighteen daily direct National Express buses arrive in Bristol from London Victoria (from £7, 1½ hours), as well as three direct services from Cardiff (£6.50, one hour), four from Exeter (£11.60, two hours) and two from Penzance (£37, seven hours). Megabus runs five daily services from London Victoria (from £1, three hours).

TRAIN

Half-hourly trains arrive from London Paddington (from £20, 1½ hours) daily, with frequent services arriving from Bath (£5.20, 15 minutes), Cardiff (£7.80, 45 minutes) and Exeter (from £8, 1½ hours).

Getting Around

The Bristol International Flyer bus is the most cost-effective way to travel from the airport to the city (adult/child £5/4, 30 minutes, half-hourly 5am to 11pm). Visit the excellent **Travel Bristol Info Centre** (www.travelbristol.org; 11 Colston Ave; 8.30am-5.30pm Mon-Fri, 8.30am-1pm Sat) for further information on regional buses, ferries, trains and bike routes.

CENTRAL ENGLAND

The geographic heartland of England is a grab bag of wildly differing scenes that represent Britain in miniature. There are flower-decked villages studded with ancient cottages in the Cotswolds, windswept rocky vistas in the hiking-friendly Peak District, history around every corner in fascinating towns like Stratford-upon-Avon, Oxford and Shrewsbury, and rejuvenated former industrial cities like Birmingham that are as vital as almost any in the country. For information on visiting the region, contact **Heart of England Tourism** (☎ 01905-761100; www.visitheartofengland.com).

OXFORD

☎ 01865 / pop 143,016

A crowded tourist hotspot in summer, Oxford lives up to its advance billing as a colourful, history-flavoured sleepover – especially if you bypass the jostling tour groups and turn up early or late in the season. The celebrated university's ancient buildings dominate the city centre, but it's not quite as pretty as Cambridge, its comparatively quaint rival to the northeast. However, it more than makes up for this by being a far more vibrant, cosmopolitan spot, with a wider array of attractions and activities.

History

Oxford University is the oldest university in Britain, with the first of its 39 colleges built for the country's chin-stroking intellectuals in the early 13th century. Its colourful history includes a 14th-century riot over the quality of a local innkeeper's wine, which suggests that students have changed little over the centuries, and its plethora of notable graduates includes William Morris, Oscar Wilde, Lewis Carroll and, allegedly, Sherlock Holmes. Women were not admitted to Oxford's closeted halls until 1878 and were not allowed to receive degrees until the 1920s. All colleges are now coeducational, except St Hilda's, which accepts only women.

Orientation & Information

Surrounded by rivers on its eastern, southern and western edges, pedestrian-friendly Oxford is best explored on foot or by bike – keep an eye out for zooming cyclists when crossing the streets. The train station is just an easy 10-minute stroll west of the city centre along George St and Hythe Bridge St – you will pass by the bus station on Gloucester Green (there's no green) along the way.

Ever-busy **TIC** (☎ 726871; 15-16 Broad St; www.visitoxford.org; 9.30am-5pm Mon-Sat, 10am-4pm Sun Apr-Oct) is packed with maps and brochures on the region, which is just as well since the harried staff will probably be too busy to talk to you. Pick up an Oxford Visitor Card (£2.50) while you're there for attraction and eat-out discounts across the city. Web access is available at **Mic@s Internet** (☎ 726364; 118 High St; per 30 min £1; 9am-11pm Mon-Sat, 10am-11pm Sun).

Sights & Activities

OXFORD UNIVERSITY

It is impossible to miss Oxford's crenulated college buildings, some of which are surrounded by fortress-like walls presumably intended to keep out intellectual inferiors. Fool the dons by assuming a foppish haircut, wearing a stripy shirt, and clutching some weighty tomes under your arm as you stroll purposely around the town. The following are some of the university's must-see college highlights. Keep in mind that colleges can be closed to visitors on any given day, so call ahead.

The most spectacular of Oxford's colleges, the main entrance to **Christ Church** (☎ 286573; www.visitchristchurch.net; Broadwalk; adult/child £4.50/3.50; 9am-5.30pm Mon-Sat, 1-5.30pm Sun) is **Tom Tower**, with its postcard-perfect Christopher Wren–designed dome. Save time for a look at the **Great Hall**, which was copied for the *Harry Potter* movie series, and check out **Christ Church Cathedral**, the smallest in Britain. It has some lovely stained-glass windows.

Arguably Oxford's prettiest college, **Magdalen** (☎ 276000; www.magd.ox.ac.uk; High St; adult/child £3/2; noon-6pm Jul-Sep, 1-6pm Oct-Jun) combines a collection of stately buildings with a verdant tapestry of landscaped grounds. The architectural highlight is the **cloister**. Surrounding a lovely quadrangle, it features fantastical carvings of hippos, jesters and dancers that are said to have inspired CS Lewis during his time here.

One of Oxford's oldest colleges, the main highlight of **Merton** (☎ 276310; www.merton.ox.ac.uk; Merton St; admission free; 2-4pm Mon-Fri, 10am-4pm Sat & Sun) is the 14th-century **Old Library**, the oldest continuously operating college library in the world. Summer tours (£2) of the building are offered from July to September for curious bookworms.

The following Oxford attractions are also well worth a visit: **Bodleian Library** (☎ 277224; www.bodley.ox.ac.uk; tour £5; 9am-4.45pm Mon-Fri, 9am-12.30pm Sat), one of the world's oldest public libraries (enter on Broad or Catte Sts); **Radcliffe Camera** (Radcliffe Sq), a circular architectural gem and Oxford landmark (no public access inside); and **Sheldonian Theatre** (☎ 277299; www.sheldon.ox.ac.uk; 10am-12.30pm & 2-4.30pm Mon-Sat), a magnificent Christopher Wren–designed edifice with a joyously colourful interior (enter on Broad or Catte Sts).

MUSEUMS

Founded in 1683, Britain's oldest museum is also one of its best. The highlights of the vast **Ashmolean** (☎ 278000; www.ashmol.ox.ac.uk; Beaumont St; admission free; 10am-5pm Tue-Sat, noon-5pm Sun) collection include a wealth of Chinese, Egyptian and European artworks and antiquities. There's also a collection of modern British paintings in the Sands Gallery and an ever-changing roster of fascinating temporary exhibitions (also free).

In its magnificent Victorian Gothic home, the **University Museum of Natural History** (☎ 272950; www.oum.ox.ac.uk; Parks Rd; admission free; noon-5pm) deftly illuminates the natural sciences, with wide-eyed visitors inexorably drawn to the hulking dinosaur skeletons. The adjacent **Pitt Rivers Museum** (☎ 270927; www.prm.ox.ac.uk; admission free; noon-4.30pm Mon-Sun) is a bewildering menagerie of collected artefacts

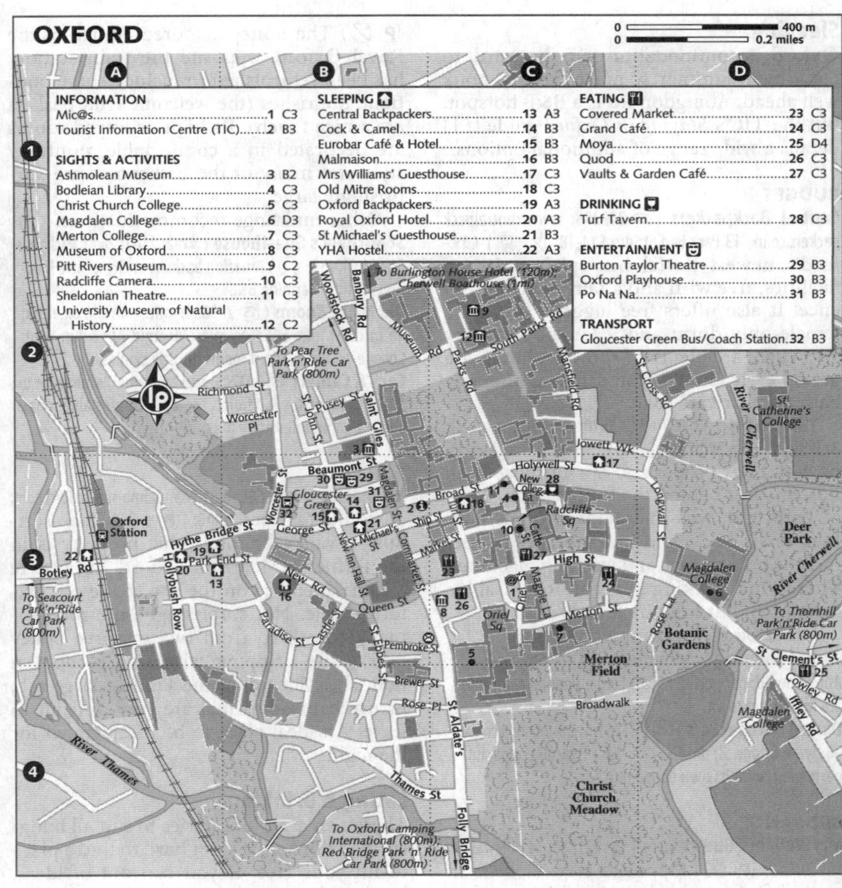

ranging from shrunken heads to stuffed animals. It's like a vast fairground sideshow of the wild and wacky. For an introduction to the city's history, the **Museum of Oxford** (☎ 252761; St Aldgate's; adult/child £2/0.50; 🕑 10am-4.30pm Tue-Fri, 10am-5pm Sat, noon-4pm Sun) is well worth a visit. Its evocation of the university's early days – including re-created rooms and college treasures – is illuminating.

PUNTING

Consider hiring a punt at **Cherwell Boathouse** (☎ 515978; Bardwell Rd; per hr £10-12). You can spend a leisurely couple of hours winding along the river honing your pole-wielding skills while drinking in the pretty college buildings. Remember that punting is not as easy as it looks – make sure you bring a picnic for relief if the going gets too tough.

Tours

The TIC offers an array of good walking tours, including a **City and College Tour** (adult/child £6.50/3), an **Inspector Morse Tour** (adult/child £7/3) and a **Ghost Tour** (adult/child £5/3). A popular night-time option is the **Pub Tour** (£6.50), which winds its merry way, with plenty of quaffing time, through several atmospheric local hostelries. Times and frequency for these tours vary through the year, so call ahead. Downloadable MP3 tours from **Tourist Tracks** (www.tourist-tracks.com; £5) are also available for those loners who prefer to amble at their own pace.

Sleeping

Oxford accommodation can be hard to come by in summer, so make sure you book well ahead. Abingdon Rd is a B&B hotspot, but the TIC's *Staying in Oxford* guide (£1) details a wide range of additional options.

BUDGET

Central Backpackers (☎ 242288; www.centralbackpackers.co.uk; 13 Park End St; dm £14-18; ☒ ☐) Oxford's newest hostel has spick-and-span facilities, free wi-fi and a fairly quiet ambience. It also offers free luggage storage, a female-only dorm and a lounge with Sky TV. There are plenty of showers, but if you get up early enough you can snag the only bath for a private soak.

YHA Hostel (☎ 0870 770 5970; oxford@yha.org.uk; 2a Botley Rd; dm £20.95; ☒ ☐) One of England's newest YHA properties, this purpose-built hostel is just behind the train station. Most of its bright, well-maintained rooms have four to six beds, and its range of facilities include bike storage and washing machines. There's no parking (except for disabled travellers), but rates include breakfast.

Other budget recommendations:

Oxford Camping International (☎ 246551; 426 Abingdon Rd; per person £9.25) Large, popular camp site 1.5 miles from town.

Oxford Backpackers (☎ 721761; www.hostels.co.uk; 9a Hythe Bridge St; dm £14-16; ☐) Typically colourful party joint, with its own happening bar.

MIDRANGE

Mrs Williams' Guesthouse (☎ 721880; 14 Holywell St; s/d £35/50; P ☒) Opposite New College in central Oxford, this homy and immaculate property has a panelled dining room and a romantic fireplace to add to its tranquil feel. Book far in advance, as there are only four rooms. The hearty breakfast is excellent.

Eurobar Café & Hotel (☎ 725087; www.eurhotels.co.uk; 48 George St; s/d £35/50; P ☒) Well located with plenty of nearby pubs and restaurants, the comfortable Eurobar Café & Hotel has the look of a continental pub with the rooms of a standard British B&B: most of them are slightly chintzy and not all come with en suites. The bar itself is worth a visit even if you are not staying here: the food is cheap and cheerful, and they have a good selection of real ales.

Royal Oxford Hotel (☎ 248432; www.royaloxfordhotel.co.uk; Park End St; s/d/tr/tw from £75/80/80/90; P ☒) The honey-coloured edifice of the Royal Oxford, opposite the train station, has been refurbished to include some boutique flourishes (the welcome fruit baskets are a nice touch). Its high-ceilinged rooms are decorated in a comfortable, nonfussy style and many of the bathrooms are surprisingly large.

Other midrange recommendations:

St Michael's Guesthouse (☎ 242101; 26 St Michael's St; s/d £40/55; ☒) Amazing backstreet city-centre location for this charming B&B.

Old Mitre Rooms (☎ 279821; mitre@lincoln.ox.ac.uk; 4b Turl St; r from £45; ⌚ mid-Mar–mid-Apr & Jun-Sep) College-owned student rooms, mostly singles.

Cock & Camel (☎ 203705; cockandcamel@youngs.co.uk; 24-26 George St; s & d from £75; ☒) Comfortable rooms above a sometimes noisy pub.

TOP END

Malmaison (☎ 268400; www.malmaison-oxford.com; 3 Oxford Castle; r from £110; P ☒) This seriously swanky boutique-chic property is in the former HM Prison Oxford, an austere Victorian edifice on the site of the old Oxford Castle. Not surprisingly, the rooms – many converted from two or three pokey cells – are dripping with stylish modern flourishes, including the kind of large-tub, luxury bathrooms that are very difficult to leave. An ideal place to be incarcerated for the night.

Eating & Drinking

There's an array of eateries to suit all budgets in Oxford, so it's not hard to find a place to fill your face. If you run out of ideas, head to the nearest bar for traditional pub grub and a pint of regional ale.

Covered Market (Market St; snacks from £1.50; ⌚ 8am-5.30pm Mon-Sat) Not everything is for eating in this large, airy market hall, but it's hard to shake the idea that you're wondering around a gourmet smorgasbord. From samosas to sausages and olives to sticky buns, the quality is a cut above standard market fare. A good spot to bring a newspaper and grab a strong morning coffee.

Turf Tavern (☎ 243235; 4 Bath Pl; mains £4-8; ⌚ lunch & dinner) There's excellent pub grub at this recommended 16th-century watering hole that's hidden along a back alley between Holywell St and New College Lane. Welcoming a mix of students, locals and tourists under its low-beamed ceilings, drinkers spill out into the adjoining courtyards in summer. Allegedly the spot where Bill Clinton 'didn't inhale' cannabis in his student days.

Vaults & Garden Café (☎ 279112; St Mary's Church, Radcliffe Sq; mains £5-8; 🕑 10am-5pm) The handsome city-centre church of St Mary's is home to this chatty, wholesome spot, which specialises in organic and vegetarian dishes – the tasty pancakes and large salads are recommended. In summer pick up a cold organic beer and sit outside in the shadow of Radcliffe Camera.

Moya (☎ 200111; 97 St Clement's St; mains £5-11; 🕑 lunch & dinner) This sleek, contemporary Slovak restaurant serves an array of well-priced, carnivore-friendly dishes, including richly sauced venison medallions and an excellent goulash. There's plenty of menu space for vegetarians, too: check out the goats cheese devil's toast.

Grand Café (☎ 204463; 84 High St; mains £6-14; 🕑 9am-7pm) The grande dame of Oxford coffeehouses, this elegant, multicolumned 1920s room is a little past its prime, but it recalls an age of elegance now almost forgotten. Potted palms abound and the gilded arms protruding from the walls are a little alarming, but the menu of tasty sandwiches, dainty salads and decadent desserts is popular with locals and visitors.

Quod (☎ 202505; 92-94 High St; mains £8-17; 🕑 lunch & dinner) This modern European brasserie includes specials like duck confit with celeriac, bacon and prunes and succulent slow-roasted lamb shank. The room, with its exposed brick walls, high ceilings and large windows, is bright and welcoming, and the curved bar is a good spot for an end-of-day cocktail. Large paintings by young British artists line the walls.

Entertainment

Leaflets and posters paper the streets of Oxford announcing all sorts of events at the colleges and around town – you don't have to be a student to partake.

Po Na Na (☎ 249171; 13 Magdalen St) A hip, late-opening bar-cum-nightclub.

Oxford Playhouse (☎ 305305; www.oxfordplayhouse.com; 11-12 Beaumont St) The city's leading theatre, music and dance stage.

Burton Taylor Theatre (☎ 305305; www.burtontaylor.co.uk; Gloucester St) The Playhouse's studio hotspot for offbeat productions.

Getting There & Away

BUS

Oxford is an easy bus hop from London, and there are several companies servicing this route. Direct National Express buses arrive every 20 minutes from London Victoria (£12, 1½ hours), with five additional direct services from Birmingham (£10.20, one to two hours) and one from Bristol (£13, three hours). Megabus services arrive from London Victoria (from £1, 1½ hours) every 15 minutes. **Oxford Tube** (☎ 772250; www.oxfordtube.com) bus services arrive throughout the day from London Victoria (£11, 1½ hours), offering a 24-hour service and discounts for students and young people. **Oxford Express** (☎ 785400; www.oxfordbus.co.uk) operates a similar service with competing times and prices. **Stagecoach Express** (☎ 01234-212852) runs an hourly X5 service from Cambridge (£7, 3½ hours).

TRAIN

Direct trains arrive from London Paddington (from £9.50, 55 minutes) every 30 minutes. Direct trains also arrive twice hourly from Birmingham (from £8, one hour). Nondirect trains arrive regularly from Bath (£10.40, 1½ hours) and Bristol (£13.40, 1¼ hours); both trains change at Didcot Parkway.

Getting Around

Oxford is best explored on foot – almost everything is within easy reach if you hoof it. But this is also a highly bike-friendly town, so consider renting from **Cycloanalysts** (☎ 424444; www.cycloanalysts.com; 150 Cowley Rd; 🕑 9am-6pm Mon-Sat, 10am-4pm Sun) from £10 per day and pick up a map of bike routes from the TIC.

BLENHEIM PALACE

Britain's largest stately pile, still lived in by the latest Duke of Marlborough, **Blenheim Palace** (☎ 0870 060 2080; Woodstock; adult/child £14/8.50; 🕑 10.30am-5.30pm mid-Feb–Oct, 10.30am-5.30pm Wed-Sun Nov–mid-Dec) is arguably the nation's finest baroque masterpiece. Built from the proceeds of a large reward paid to John Churchill by Queen Anne for his role in defeating Louis XIV, the extravagant 18th-century home was the historic birthplace of Winston Churchill in 1874. The detailed **Churchill Exhibition** explores the life of this decorated and still-revered wartime leader. Additional highlights include the aptly named

BRITAIN

Long Library, the painted ceilings of the **Great Hall** and the **private apartments** of the sitting duke, accessible via a special 30-minute tour. Save plenty of time for the beautifully landscaped **gardens**. Partly designed by 'Capability' Brown, they include a maze, greenhouse and a picturesque human-made lake. Time your visit correctly and you'll hit the colourful annual **Jousting Tournament** in late April. Bus 20 (£4.20 return, 30 minutes, twice hourly) from Oxford train and bus stations stops in Woodstock village, in the shadow of the palace.

STRATFORD-UPON-AVON

☎ 01789 / pop 111,474

Stratford teeters on the edge of theme-park madness in summer, when coachloads of tourists descend on the town to pay camera-wielding, gift shop–hogging homage to England's leading dead playwright. But if you can circumvent the crowds by arriving early or late in the season, it's still possible to celebrate Shakespeare's life and works without jostling for space on every street corner. Whatever you do, remember that the play's the thing and make sure you catch a performance by the resident Royal Shakespeare Company. It will remind you what all the fuss is about, 450 years after the Bard shuffled off this mortal coil.

Orientation & Information

Stratford's compact old centre is easily explored on foot. The train station is a 15-minute walk (or £5 taxi ride) west and the Avon River abuts the town centre's eastern edge. Head south along the river bank to find the main theatres and Holy Trinity Church, Shakespeare's final resting place.

You can book accommodation, buy theatre tickets and exchange currency at the **TIC** (☎ 293127; www.shakespeare-country.co.uk; Bridgefoot; 🕑 9am-5pm Mon-Sat, 10am-3pm Sun Oct-Mar, 9am-5.30pm Mon-Sat, 10am-4pm Apr-Sep). For Internet access, head to **Cyber Junction** (☎ 263400; 28 Greenhill St; per 30 min £3; 🕑 10am-5.30pm Mon-Sat).

Sights & Activities

Much like mothballed artefacts in glass cases, there's an unreal quality to the five timber-framed Shakespeare-related houses on Stratford's mostly modern streets. The most worthy of a visit is **Shakespeare's Birthplace** (Henly St; adult/child £7/2.75), a scrubbed-clean Tudor building where chatty interpreters explain the history of the house. Reputed to be the spot where the Bard entered the world mewling and puking, the upstairs bedroom has been a pilgrimage site for Shakespeare fans – including Dickens and Thomas Hardy – for centuries. Located a mile from the town centre, **Anne Hathaway's Cottage** (adult/child £5.50/2) is an idyllic thatch-roofed farmhouse where Shakespeare's wife was raised. It's often crowded in summer so take a breather in the cottage garden, which includes sculptures of Shakespearian characters and a Yew maze. All five houses are administered by the **Shakespeare Birthplace Trust** (☎ 204016; www.shakespeare.org.uk), which sells two good-value combined-entry ticket options (three houses adult/child £11/5.50, five houses £14/6.50).

You can see where the Bard is now at the immaculate **Holy Trinity Church** (☎ 266316; www.stratford-upon-avon.org; Old Town; suggested donation £1.50; 🕑 8.30am-6pm Mon-Sat, 12.30-5pm Sun Apr-Oct, 9am-4pm Mon-Sat, 12.30-5pm Sun Nov-May), accessed via a handsome tree-lined avenue and a tiny doorway through which almost everyone has to stoop. The high altar and stained-glass windows are highlights, but most people come for the grave in the chancel, a discreet stone slab in the floor marked with a blue chord.

The man himself is brought back to life at Stratford's newest attraction. **Shakespearience** (☎ 290111; www.shakespearience.co.uk; Waterside; adult/child £7.25/6.25; 🕑 10.30am-5pm Apr-Sep, 11am-5pm Oct-Mar) is a surprisingly entertaining hi-tech extravaganza that uses holograms to stage highlights from nine plays inside a re-creation of a traditional Elizabethan theatre. 'Shakespeare' even makes a messianic appearance himself to explain his philosophies on life.

Check out some real theatre performed by the world-leading **Royal Shakespeare Company** (☎ 0870 609 1110; www.rsc.org.uk; tickets £5-55; 🕑 box office 9.30am-8pm Mon-Sat) where tickets for plays are often available on performance day. The company's Royal Shakespeare Theatre (RST) is closed for redevelopment until 2010. Its plays will be temporarily transferred to the new Courtyard Theatre. The company's other theatre, the Swan, will be closed for refurbishment in 2008 and 2009. It will not produce any plays during this period.

BRITAIN

Sleeping

Grove Rd and Evesham Pl, between the train station and town centre, is B&B central. Be aware that many places charge per person rather than per room.

YHA Hostel (☎ 0870 770 6052; stratford@yha.org.uk; Hemmingford House, Alveston; dm £19.95; P 💻) Nearly 2 miles from the town centre, this splendid white stucco Georgian mansion contains mostly small dorms and good facilities. The cycle storage and games room are a nice touch, but it's the 1.2 hectares of verdant grounds that stand out. Take bus X18 or 77 to Alveston from Stratford's Bridge St.

Hamlet House (☎ 204386; www.hamlethouse.com; 52 Grove Rd; s/d from £22.50/45; P ⊠ 💻) All rooms at this exceptionally comfortable B&B are scrupulously clean and some include video libraries alongside their TVs. Breakfast options include a gourmet omelette choice and cooked vegetarian alternative. Broadband access is free – you can borrow the house computer if you don't have a laptop – and guests can freely loan a couple of mountain bikes.

White Swan (☎ 297022; www.thewhiteswanstratford.co.uk; Rother St; s £60-70, d £80-100; P ⊠) A characterful pub near the centre of the action, the accommodation combines modern and olde-worlde flourishes, with all rooms en suite. Ask for a heritage room and you'll have wonky ceiling beams, creaky floors and a four-poster bed (some rooms only). The downstairs bar contains a good menu of traditional pub food.

Falcon Hotel (☎ 0870 832 9905; www.legacy-hotels.co.uk; Chapel St; s £54-105, d £80-145; P) Like two hotels in one, there are beautifully maintained, wood-beamed rooms with leaded windows here but also some modern chichi suites for those who prefer 21st-century living. Either way, the Falcon is a well-located, larger property sitting atop a warren of atmospheric bars and restaurants.

Also recommended:

Quilts & Croissants (☎ 267629; www.quiltcroissants.co.uk; 33 Evesham Pl; s £18-40, d £36-52; P ⊠) Charming, family-run B&B a short walk from the town centre.

Moonraker House (☎ 268774; www.moonrakerhouse.com; 40 Alcester Rd; s £40, d £68-75; P) Lovely, indulgently comfortable B&B with friendly owners.

Eating & Drinking

Sheep St is Stratford's restaurant row, but aside from the pie and cake shops there's a paucity of cheap eats in town.

Baguette Barge (☎ 0796 395 6720; Barncroft Gardens, Waterside; sandwiches £2-3; 🕑 lunch & dinner) This charming barge moored on the Avon River serves superior good-value takeout sarnies and baguettes. Expect to wait up to 10 minutes for a burger – they're actually cooked from scratch.

Garrick Inn (☎ 292186; 25 High St; mains £4-9; 🕑 lunch & dinner) A smashing Tudor pub, complete with low ceilings and leaded windows, the Garrick also has a large and varied menu of hearty pub food, with more than the usual share of vegetarian options. Baked potatoes – with more toppings than you can shake a stick at – are the best deal and will likely fill you up for the day.

Dirty Duck (☎ 297312; Southern Lane; mains £6-14; 🕑 lunch & dinner) This great Flowers brewery pub on the banks of the Avon River has an excellent menu of gastropub delights, including slow-cooked Welsh lamb, prime beef and ale pie, and Duchy of Cornwall pork and herb sausages. If you're not hungry, decamp to the patio with a beer and watch the world float by.

Lambs (☎ 292554; 12 Sheep St; mains £11-19; 🕑 lunch & dinner) Combining a smart and sassy menu fusing traditional ingredients with new influences with a charming exposed beam interior, Lambs offers mouthwatering reinterpretations of steak, lamb and pasta classics. It is worth dining here for the ambience alone: this 16th-century building is one of Stratford-Uopn-Avon's oldest structures.

Also recommended:

Thespians (☎ 267187; 27 Sheep St; mains £6-12; 🕑 lunch & dinner) Good-value South Indian restaurant with plenty of vegetarian options.

Malbec (☎ 296106; 6 Union St; 2-course lunch £10, 3-course dinner £26; 🕑 lunch & dinner Tue-Sat) Low-key modern British brasserie with gourmet flourishes.

Getting There & Away

Four direct National Express buses arrive daily from London Victoria (£15, 2½ to 3½ hours), while two direct buses arrive from Birmingham (£6.50, one hour) and two from Oxford (£8.30, one hour). Every two hours a direct train arrives in Stratford from London Marylebone (from £10.50, 2¼ hours). In addition, the Shakespeare Line is a direct hourly train service from Birmingham Snow Hill to Stratford (£5.40, 50 minutes).

THE COTSWOLDS

A delightful higgle-piggle of implausibly pretty villages – think charming stone churches, thatch-roofed homes and hearth-lit pubs – set in a postcard-perfect sea of rolling hills studded with dozy sheep, the Cotswolds is classic English countryside. Built on the medieval wool trade, the region is popular with hikers and bikers but also attracts convoys of tour buses in summer.

Orientation & Information

Running north from Bath for around 100 miles, the Cotswolds is easily divided into southern and northern areas, with the northern half attracting most visitors. With its own train station, Moreton-in-Marsh is a good northern access point for visiting the more attractive nearby villages of Chipping Campden and Stow-on-the-Wold. In the south, Cheltenham is a handsome spa town with excellent train and bus access. For more information on planning a visit, contact the **Cotswold Tourist Board** (☎ 01452-426280; www.cotswolds.com, www.the-cotsworlds.org).

Getting There & Around

Five nondirect (change at Cirencester) National Express buses arrive daily from London Victoria at Moreton-in-Marsh (£18.60, three to four hours) and Stow-on-the-Wold (£18.60, 3½ to 4½ hours). Eleven direct daily London Victoria bus services also arrive in Cheltenham (from £4, three hours). Direct daily train services arrive every two hours from London Paddington at Moreton-in-Marsh (£23.30, 1½ hours). Regular direct and nondirect trains also arrive at Cheltenham from London Paddington throughout the day (from £19, two to 2½ hours).

Getting around the Cotswolds by public transport isn't easy. If you're trying anything ambitious, contact Traveline. Bike fans can also rent in Chipping Campden from **Cotswold Country Cycles** (☎ 01386-438706; www.cotswoldcountrycycles.com; Longlands Farm Cottage; per day £12). It also offers some popular bike tours of the region (from £195) that include accommodation.

Chipping Campden

☎ 01386 / pop 1943

The breathtaking, historically intact **High St** here is worth a visit alone, with its combination of handsome wool-trade public buildings and nearby fringe of beautiful thatch-roofed cottages, many with immaculate gardens. Among the highlights are the 17th-century **Market Hall** and the lovely Perpendicular Gothic **St James Church**, possibly the finest church in the Cotswolds. For a town map (£0.20) and more recommendations, visit the **TIC** (☎ 841206; www.visitchippingcampden.com; Old Police Station, High St; 10am-5.30pm Apr-Oct, 10am-5pm Nov-Mar).

There are no hostels here, but the **Eight Bells** (☎ 840371; www.eightbellsinn.co.uk; Church St; s/d from £50/85; ☒) is among the best sleepovers with its modern-decorated pub rooms. The **Kings Arms** (☎ 840256; www.thekingsarmshotel.com; The Square; s/d from £75/85; ☒) is a slightly pricier alternative, with more traditional interiors. Both have good restaurants that are a cut above the usual pub offerings (mains from £8), and they serve great beers like Hook Norton and Tangle Foot.

Stow-on-the-Wold

☎ 01451 / pop 2074

Known colloquially as Stow, this elegant town is dripping with twee teashops and pricey boutique galleries serving the strolling tourists that descend here en masse in summer. The lovely Georgian-era **Square** is worth a visit, complete with its historic **Market Cross**. The nearby 15th-century **St Edward's Church** is notable for the tombstones of wool-trade bigwigs that line its floor. The **TIC** (☎ 831082; www.stowonthewold.net; Hollis House, The Square; 9.30am-5.30pm Mon-Sat Mar-Oct, 9.30am-4.30pm Mon-Sat Nov-Feb) can assist with further recommendations.

The central **YHA Hostel** (☎ 0870 770 6050; stow@yha.org.uk; The Square; dm £15; P ☒ 🖳) is popular with families and has top-notch facilities. For those with greater budgets, there's the historic **Stow Lodge Hotel** (☎ 830485; www.stowlodgehotel.co.uk; The Square; s/d from £75/95; P ☒), which has large rooms and its own gardens. Its popular on-site restaurant serves traditional British dishes with a gourmet flourish (three-course dinner £22).

Cheltenham

☎ 01242 / pop 98,875

This large and elegant spa town is the biggest settlement in the southern Cotswolds. It's worth visiting for its central **Promenade**, the only place to be seen in summer, its **Art Gallery & Museum** (popular with Arts and Crafts fans) and its handsome Regency-era

Pittville Pump Room, the heart of the town's spa claim to fame. Horse-racing fans make a beeline here every March, when the **Cheltenham Festival** – England's top steeplechase event – hits town. Contact the **TIC** (☎ 522878; www.visitcheltenham.info; 77 Promenade; 9.30am-5.15pm Mon-Sat) for its free accommodation booking service.

For budget travellers, it will likely recommend the **YMCA** (☎ 524024; www.cheltenhamymca.org; 6 Vittoria Walk; dm/s £16.50/25), with small dorms and single rooms; breakfast is included in the rates. For those with more money, the **Hotel Kandinsky** (☎ 527788; www.aliashotels.com; Bayshill Rd; s/d £75/105) is the coolest sleepover in town, with its eclectic antique and arty interiors.

BIRMINGHAM

☎ 0121 / pop 970,892

Britain's second-largest city, Birmingham has lagged behind post-industrial rivals like Glasgow and Manchester and their successful rebranding as hip urban centres. But while 'Brum' appears on the surface to be just a vast, open-air shopping centre, its increasing cultural vibrancy, space-age new architecture and undoubted cosmopolitan charms make it a city on the rise.

For maps, brochures and a free accommodation booking service, contact the **TIC** (☎ 0870 428 1859; www.beinbirmingham.co.uk; The Rotunda, 150 New St; 9.30am-5.30pm Mon-Sat). There are free computers with Internet access on every floor of the grubby **Central Library** (☎ 303 4511; Chamberlain Sq; 9am-8pm Mon-Fri, 9am-5pm Sat).

Sights

For a fascinating glimpse into Birmingham's tenement-housing past, check out the **Back to Backs** (☎ 666 7671; 50-54 Inge St; adult/child £4.50/2.20; 10am-5pm Tue-Sun), a preserved courtyard of 19th-century working-class homes illustrating what life was like here from the 1840s to the 1970s.

Take a crash course in the cool new Birmingham, over at **IKON Gallery** (☎ 248 0708; www.ikon-gallery.co.uk; 1 Oozells Sq, Brindleyplace; admission free; 11am-6pm Tue-Sun), a nest of rooms with an ever-changing roster of contemporary artworks.

Along with its comprehensive selection of chain stores, Birmingham is a market-lovers mecca, with several overlapping indoor and outdoor **markets** centred around the Bull Ring area near the cathedral. Visiting magpies will also want to check out the charming **Jewellery Quarter**, with its walkable streets of 100 shiny gem shops.

Sleeping & Eating

Billy's International Backpackers (☎ 07951-745102; 58 Coventry St, Digbeth; dm from £17) Opened in early 2006, this is one of the city's first hostel-style sleepover spots. Located above a pub in the city centre, it has 30 beds and each room has an en suite shower (toilets are shared). Breakfast and a free luggage room are included, and some twin rooms are available.

The midrange chains offer some of the best prices and locations in central Birmingham. They include **Ibis** (☎ 622 6010; www.ibishotel.com; Ladywell Walk; r £49-85; P) and **Holiday Inn Express** (☎ 0870 400 9670; www.hiexpress.co.uk; 65 Lionel St; r £49-75; P).

Birmingham's eating-out options have vastly improved in recent years with some good restaurants slowly emerging on the local scene. Reflecting its large Asian population, the city's Balti Triangle area is a must-do pilgrimage for curry connoisseurs. Excellent baltis (Pakistani curries made and served in a flat-bottomed pan) are proffered at the laid-back **Royal Al Faisel** (☎ 449 5695; 136 Stoney Lane; buffet £6; lunch & dinner), the ornate **Punjab Paradise** (☎ 449 4110; 377 Ladypool Rd; mains from £7; dinner) and the ever-popular **Al Frash** (☎ 753 3120; 186 Ladypool Rd; mains from £7; dinner).

Getting There & Away

Direct National Express buses arrive twice hourly from London Victoria (from £2, 2¾ hours). Five direct services arrive daily from Oxford (from £1, two hours) and eight from Bristol (from £1, two hours). Nine daily direct Megabus services arrive from London Victoria (from £1, three hours). Twice-hourly direct train services arrive at Birmingham New Street from London Euston (from £10, 1½ hours) and Birmingham Snow Hill from London Marylebone (from £10, 2½ hours).

SHREWSBURY & AROUND

☎ 01743 / pop 67,150

With justifiable claim to being England's finest Tudor town (there are more than 50 handsome medieval black-and-white buildings around this curve of the Severn River) Shrewsbury is a history-lovers dream. But the secret to really enjoying the town is to duck along the ancient passageways (known locally as 'shuts') behind the preserved mansions. Shrewsbury is also a great base for exploring the breathtaking Shropshire countryside. For information on visiting the wider region, contact **Shropshire Tourism** (☎ 462462; www.shropshiretourism.info).

Orientation & Information

Eminently explorable on foot, Shrewsbury's olde-worlde town centre is a five-minute uphill walk from the bus and train stations. The **TIC** (☎ 281200; www.visitshrewsbury.com; The Square; 9.30am-5.30pm Mon-Sat, 10am-4pm Sun Apr-Sep, 10am-5pm Mon-Sat, 10am-4pm Sun Oct-Mar) is in the Music Hall on the ancient market square. It's the starting point for a roster of entertaining historic walks. Free Internet access is available at the **Reference Library** (☎ 255380; 1a Castle St; 9.30am-5pm Mon-Sat, 1-4pm Sun).

Sights & Activities

Wandering Shrewsbury's winding medieval streets is the best way to spend an afternoon here. But while marvelling at teetering 15th-century masterpieces like **Ireland's Mansion** and **Abbot's House**, there are some hidden gems that do warrant further exploration. Head down **Grope Lane** – a narrow alleyway that was once sex-trade central – and you will find dozens of markings scored into the wood by craftsmen from centuries past. Drop into the **King's Head** pub to take a look at a recently uncovered medieval wall painting. And stroll around the back of the **Nag's Head** to see the shell of a near-derelict Tudor building.

WORTH A TRIP

A 30-minute bus 96 ride from Shrewsbury brings you to **Ironbridge** (☎ 01952-884391; www.ironbridge.org.uk; single-attraction ticket adult £1.50-9, child £1-6, combined-attraction ticket adult/child £14/9.50; 10am-5pm), a World Heritage–designated cluster of 10 Industrial Revolution themed museums. Head first to the **TIC** (☎ 01952-884391; www.visitironbridge.co.uk; Tollhouse; 9am-5pm Mon-Fri, 10am-5pm Sat & Sun) to plan your visit. It's tricky to make the best of Ironbridge without transport, so arrive on the weekend when a shuttle bus operates between the museums (£0.50 per trip).

Originally founded after the Battle of Hastings and 'modernised' in the 13th and 19th centuries, **Shrewsbury Abbey** (☎ 232723; www.shrewsburyabbey.com; Abbey Foregate; admission free; 10am-4.45pm Apr-Oct, 10.30am-3pm Nov-Mar) is a magnificent sandstone edifice. Once the centrepiece of a complex of monastic buildings, it survived the Dissolution by becoming a parish church. It houses Norman-era arches and a technicolour Victorian altar.

Located in one of the town's finest Tudor structures, **Shrewsbury Museum & Art Gallery** (☎ 361196; Barker St; admission free; 10am-4pm Tue-Sat) exhibits fascinating artefacts from the nearby Roman settlement of Viroconium. Look for temporary exhibitions on Charles Darwin leading up to 2009, when the city celebrates the birth of its famous son.

Sleeping & Eating

Shrewsbury's youth hostel has closed, but there are several pubs offering cheap B&B rates for visitors.

Lion & Pheasant Hotel (☎ 236288; lionandpheasant@aol.com; 49-50 Wyle Cop; s £25-45, d £50-55; P) This clean, comfortable and well-maintained 17th-century guesthouse is a warren of 27 mostly en suite rooms in a wide array of sizes. Most are fairly modern but some have character features, like old fireplaces and exposed beams. There's an excellent Sunday roast in the downstairs pub restaurant (£8.50).

Tudor House (☎ 351735; www.tudorhouseshrewsbury.com; 2 Fish St; from s/d £69/79; ☒) A superior 15th-century pub classic with immaculate accommodation, on a quiet cobbled backstreet in the town centre. The rooms have been tastefully modernised with sinks and LCD TVs but have lost none of their Tudor charm. This family-run sleepover spot also cooks up organic cooked breakfasts.

Prince Rupert Hotel (☎ 499955; www.prince-rupert-hotel.co.uk; Butcher Row; s/d £85/105; ☒) Ask for a room in the historic 12th-century Mansion House wing and you can live out all your medieval role-playing fantasies. Many of the hotel's other rooms are markedly more modern, but there's a cosy, maiden aunt feel throughout. With three on-site restaurants – the Royalist is the best – there's no excuse for going hungry. It has a great location right in the heart of town.

Good Life Wholefood Restaurant (☎ 350455; Barracks Passage; mains £2-5; 9.30am-4.30pm Mon-Fri, 9.30am-4.30pm Sat) Tucked along a quiet 'shut' off Wyle Cop, this great-value vegetarian and vegan eatery is well worth a visit. Every meal has a home-cooked feel and there's an ever-changing roster of daily specials. Regulars include hearty quiches – the broccoli and Stilton is recommended – along with curries and large salads.

Three Fishes (☎ 344793; 4 Fish St; mains £5-9; ⏲ lunch & dinner Mon-Sat) This affable, multi-beamed Tudor tavern serves quite decent pub grub, but most visitors are here for the ale. Start slowly, and make sure you try the Adnams, White Monk and award-winning Timothy Taylor's Landlord.

Owens Brasserie (☎ 363633; 18 Butcher Row; mains £7-14; ⏲ lunch & dinner) This contemporary bistro with a Mediterranean-influenced, locally sourced menu has a good outside seating area. The goat's cheese with walnut crumb, served with piquant cranberries, is a recommended lunch, while finger-licking larger mains include pan-fried Barbary duck. There's an impressive wine selection and regular live music.

Getting There & Away

Two direct National Express buses arrive from London Victoria (£16.50, 4½ hours) daily, while one arrives from Wrexham (£4.50, 1½ hours) and two from Birmingham (£5, 1½ hours). Frequent nondirect train services (change at Crew or Birmingham New Street) arrive from London Euston (from £10, two to three hours) throughout the day. Hourly direct services also arrive from Wrexham (£5, 40 minutes), Swansea (£27.80, three hours) and Cardiff (£27, two hours).

PEAK DISTRICT NATIONAL PARK

Squeezed between the industrial Midlands to the south, Manchester to the west and Sheffield to the east, the 555-sq-mile Peak District is one of England's wildest and windiest outdoor spots. That's not to say it's inhospitable. In fact, the 'peaks' here are often fairly gentle hills, and there are plenty of soft hiking and biking routes for those who prefer not to break a sweat when heading out for the day.

Orientation

The region is divided into the wilder and more dramatic scenery of the Dark Peak area in the north and the gentler, low-lying meadows and dales of the White Peak area in the south. Buxton to the west or Matlock to the east are good bases for exploring the park, or you can stay right in the centre at Bakewell or Castleton. There are also prehistoric sites, limestone caves and the fine stately homes of Chatsworth and Haddon Hall to keep you occupied. From Edale, the Pennine Way starts its 250-mile meander northwards.

Information

There are 10 well-resourced visitor information centres in and around the park, including those at **Bakewell** (☎ 01629-813227; Old Market Hall, Bridge St), **Buxton** (☎ 01298-25106; The Crescent), **Edale** (☎ 01433-670207; Main St) and **Castleton** (☎ 01433-620679; Buxton Rd). For further information, check out the region's official visitor website **Peak District** (www.visitpeakdistrict.com). It has search engines for accommodation and activities.

Sleeping

For those on a tight budget, there are popular YHA hostels in **Castleton** (☎ 0870 770 5758; castleton@yha.org.uk; dm £14; ⊠) and **Bakewell** (☎ 0870 770 5682; bakewell@yha.org.uk; Fly Hill; dm £14; ⊠), and a recommended but often very busy YHA Activity Centre hostel in **Edale** (☎ 0870 770 5808; edale@yha.org.uk; Rowland Cote, Nether Booth; dm £12.50; Ⓟ ⊠), where you can try your hand at caving, kayaking, climbing and abseiling.

B&Bs and pub sleepovers are scattered throughout the Peak District. Recommendations include Edale's charming **Stonecroft Guest House** (☎ 01433-670262; www.stonecroftguesthouse.co.uk; Stonecroft, Grindsbrook; r £64-74; Ⓟ ⊠), Buxton's ancient **Old Hall Hotel** (☎ 01298-22841; www.oldhallhotelbuxton.co.uk; The Square; s/d £70/105) and Bakewell's handsome **Rutland Arms Hotel** (☎ 01629-812812; www.bakewell.demon.co.uk; The Square; s/d £65/120; Ⓟ) is reputedly the historic home of the venerable Bakewell pudding (or tart as everyone else calls it).

Getting There & Around

One direct National Express bus arrives in Buxton from London Victoria (£21, five hours) and another from Manchester (£6.20, one hour) daily. One daily direct service also arrives in Bakewell from Derby (£6.50, 50 minutes) and another from Manchester (£7.30, 1¼ hours). Hourly nondirect (change at Stockport) train services arrive in Buxton from London Euston (from £13.50, three hours). A direct service also arrives every two hours from Sheffield in Edale (£4.25, 33 minutes) and another arrives hourly from Manchester in Buxton (£6.35, one hour).

The local and regional bus system serves the park surprisingly well. Many visitors use the hourly Trent Barton Transpeak service that cuts across the Peak District from Nottingham and Derby to Manchester via Matlock, Bakewell and Buxton. Additional well-used routes include the First South Yorkshire bus 272 Sheffield to Castleton, Bowers bus 58 Macclesfield to Bakewell and Trent Barton bus 199 Manchester Airport to Buxton. Visit the useful online route planner at **Derbyshire County Council** (www.derbyshire.gov.uk/buses) for more information.

EAST ENGLAND

Despite the bustling tourist magnet of Cambridge, few visitors to the UK ever make it to the wilds of Norfolk and Lincolnshire, a clutch of picturesque counties that remain a mystery even to the majority of Brits. This absence of tourists belies a region that is well worth exploring. East England is where you'll find pretty market towns, gently undulating farm-strewn landscapes, swathes of beautifully desolate coastline and gallons of colourful history.

A founding economic powerhouse of the industrial revolution – wool and weaving made Norwich one of England's most prominent cities, and King's Lynn a major port in centuries past – the region's restaurants and accommodation scenes have undergone a quiet revolution in recent years, surprising those who come here to salve their curiosity. For information on visiting the area, including a great selection of cycling route maps, contact the **East of England Tourist Board** (☎ 0870 225 4800; www.visiteastofengland.com).

CAMBRIDGE

☎ 01223 / pop 117,717

Hallowed home of one of the world's most prestigious centres of learning, pretty Cambridge is steeped in crenulated history and scholarly ambience. The 31-college university, which dominates the city centre, was founded by a 13th-century splinter group that broke off from Oxford – still known locally as the 'other place' – to set up their own competing academic bastion. The rivalry has been barely concealed ever since. Yet Cambridge does not rest only on its swotty laurels. It is also a lively city with enough designer boutiques and trendy cafés to keep its compact centre teeming with locals and visitors.

Orientation & Information

Pedestrian-friendly Cambridge is easily explored on foot by even the laziest of walkers. Like Oxford, it's also a great city for cyclists. The main university buildings occupy the city centre in a wide bend of the Cam River. The bus station is also in the city centre on Drummer St, but the train station is a 20-minute walk or £5 taxi ride to the southeast. The most revered colleges and the Backs – a popular stretch of the river and grasslands at the 'back' of these colleges – are west of Sidney St.

Crowded in summer, the **TIC** (☎ 0871 226 8006; www.visitcambridge.org; The Old Library, Wheeler St; 🕑 10am-5.30pm Mon-Fri, 10am-5pm Sat Oct-Mar, 10am-5.30pm Mon-Fri, 10am-5pm Sat, 11am-4pm Sun Apr-Oct) sells a £2.50 Official Visitor Card that provides small discounts at sights, activities and restaurants. Between the train station and the city centre, **Budget Internet Café** (☎ 464625; 30 Hills Rd; per hr from £0.90; 🕑 9am-11pm) offers the cheapest Internet access in Cambridge.

Sights & Activities

CAMBRIDGE UNIVERSITY

There's an uneasy relationship between some of the colleges and the tourists that overrun the city in summer. Visitors are not simply allowed to run free in the halls of academe, and each of the five main colleges – King's, Queen's, Clare, Trinity and St John's – charges entry fees of up to £5. Colleges frequently close to visitors at short notice, so call ahead if you want to follow in the footsteps of VIP alums like Tennyson, Isaac Newton and Prince Charles.

Among the university's unmissable highlights is **King's College Chapel** (☎ 331212; www.kings.cam.ac.uk/chapel; King's Pde; adult/child £4.50/3; 🕑 9.30am-3.30pm Mon-Fri, 9.30am-3.15pm Sat, 1.15-2.15pm Sun term-time, 9.30am-4.30pm Mon-Sat, 10am-5pm Sun outside term-time), a dazzling Tudor testament to Christian devotion that has the power to make the most ardent atheist think twice. If you can un-crick your neck after

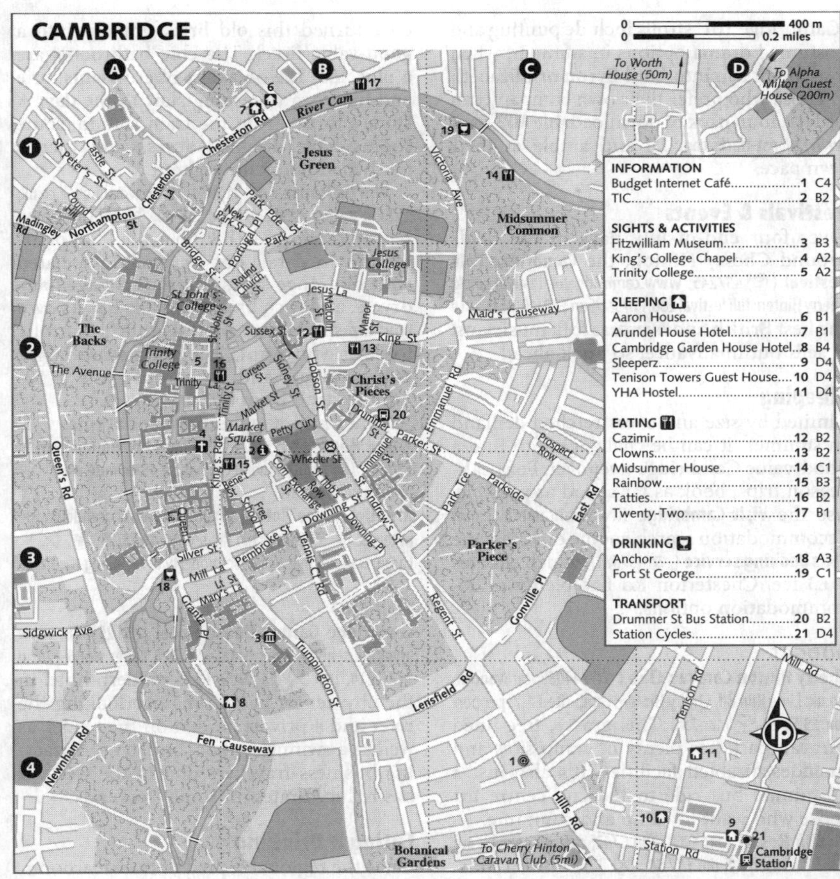

staring at the astonishing **fan-vaulted ceiling**, check out the intricately carved **wooden screen** contributed by Henry VIII.

Nearby **Trinity College** (☎ 338400; adult/child £2.20/1.30; ⏲ 10am-5pm) is one of the university's grandest and most attractive academic piles. Founded in 1546, it includes the **Great Court**, with acres of manicured lawns, broad pathways and palatial historic buildings. Don't miss the **Wren Library** (☎ 338488; admission free; ⏲ noon-2pm Mon-Fri year-round, 10.30am-12.30pm Sat term-time). Its collection includes AA Milne's original *Winnie the Pooh*.

Echoing its history as a centre of discovery, many Cambridge colleges have their own museums covering themes such as archaeology, anthropology and polar research. But the university's leading cultural light is the **Fitzwilliam Museum** (☎ 332900; www.fitzmuseum.cam.ac.uk; Trumpington St; admission free; ⏲ 10am-5pm Tue-Sat, noon-5pm Sun), one of Britain's most important collections of art and antiquities. Founded in 1816, highlights include Egyptian, Greek and Roman artefacts, a kaleidoscope of artworks from Titian, Rembrandt and Monet, and a treasure trove of ceramics, glass and silver ware. Don't miss the breathtaking William Morris edition of *The Works of Geoffrey Chaucer*.

Tours

Time-challenged visitors should consider a TIC-arranged **walking tour** (☎ 457574; adult £7-9, child £4.50; ⏲ 10.30am Mon-Sat Jul & Aug, 11.30am Mon-Sat Apr-Sep, 1.30pm daily year-round). These

'Cambridge 101' strolls include punting and costumed drama options in summer, when you might run into Lord Byron or Elizabeth I. Those who prefer their own company can order a four-pack of downloadable **MP3 tours** (www.tourist-tracks.com; £5) and amble at their own pace.

Festivals & Events

Over four end-of-July days in the fields around Cherry Hinton, the **Cambridge Folk Festival** (☎ 457245; www.cambridgefolkfestival.co.uk; Cherry Hinton; full festival £86, Fri/Sat/Sun £29/40/4) hosts the best British and overseas folk musicians. It sells out in advance, so book ahead.

Sleeping

Limited by size and overstretched demand in summer, it can be challenging to find a good-value Cambridge sleepover. For peak-season trips, book as far ahead as possible, use the **Visit Cambridge** (www.visitcambridge.org) accommodation search engine or access the **TIC's booking service** (☎ 457581), which charges a £3 fee. Chesterton Rd has plenty of accommodation options.

BUDGET

Cherry Hinton Caravan Club (☎ 244088; caravanclub.co.uk; Lime Kiln Rd, Cherry Hinton; camp site £4-7, per person £3.50-5; Mar-Jan) This grassy, tree-lined caravan park has plenty of camp sites and includes disabled facilities. It's also just a 10-minute bus ride to the city centre for those who want to camp and commute.

YHA Hostel (☎ 0870 770 5742; cambridge@yha.org.uk; 97 Tenison Rd; dm £17.50;) Fifteen minutes from both the city centre and the train station, this red-brick Victorian town house is a typically institutional YHA effort, with plenty of solid 1970s furniture. Happily, most dorms are small (including 10 two-bed rooms) and bike storage is available.

Other budget recommendations:

Alpha Milton Guest House (☎ 311625; www.alphamiltonguesthouse.co.uk; 61-63 Milton Rd; s/d from £20/40; P) Comfortable, family-run B&B with some en suite rooms.

Tenison Towers Guest House (☎ 363924; www.cambridgecitytenisontowers.com; 148 Tenison Rd; s/d £30/55) Clean, great-value B&B five minutes from the train station.

MIDRANGE

Sleeperz (☎ 304050; www.sleeperz.com; Station Rd; s/tw/d £39/49/59; P) A minimalist makeover turned this old brick granary into a good-value hotel. The chic bathrooms are a plus, and the breakfast of croissants, brie and ham is a refreshing start to the day. A stone's throw from the train station, some rooms have disabled access and there's hardwood floors throughout.

Worth House (☎ 316074; www.worthhouse.co.uk; 152 Chesterton Rd; s £35-45, d £55-60;) This cosy, recently renovated B&B has the kind of attention to detail not normally associated with midrange spots. All rooms have hairdryers, and each breakfast table has its own toaster so you can scoff as much Marmite toast as you want. The rooms are larger than average, and the property is a 10-minute stroll from the city centre.

Other midrange recommendations:

Aaron House (☎ 314723; 71 Chesterton Rd; s/d from £30/48; P) Traditional B&B that's a 15-minute walk from the city centre.

Arundel House Hotel (☎ 367701; www.arundelhousehotels.co.uk; 53 Chesterton Rd; s/d from £75/95; P) Large, tranquil manor-house property overlooking the Cam.

TOP END

Cambridge Garden House Hotel (☎ 259988; www.moathousehotels.com; Granta Pl, Mill Lane; s £86-179, d £172-214; P) This modern hotel in the city centre has rooms overlooking the river and a private garden on the banks, as well as a swimming pool and gym. Attracting business travellers during the week, it has reduced rates on some weekends.

Eating & Drinking

Once the regional capital of twee tearooms, Cambridge now has a cosmopolitan selection of cafés, bars and restaurants to suit most tastes and budgets.

Clowns (☎ 355711; 54 King St; mains £3-6.50; 8am-midnight Mon-Sat, 8am-11pm Sun) If the creepy Clown-themed décor doesn't scare you off, this cosy café is well worth a look. It can be crowded with students at peak times, but its toasted sandwiches, hearty pasta dishes and hot chocolate make it a comfortable spot to peruse the local papers.

Cazimir (☎ 355156; 13 King St; mains £4-8; 8.30am-5.30pm Mon-Fri, 8.30am-7pm Sat, noon-5pm Sun) The antithesis of the Starbucks chain that permeates many streets here, Cazimir is lined with works by local artists and serves a darn good sandwich. The daily soup specials are hearty enough for most travellers.

BRITAIN

Rainbow (☎ 321551; 9a Kings Pde; mains £7-9; ⏲ 10am-10pm Tue-Sat; ⊠) Near the gates of King's College, this inviting subterranean vegetarian bistro fuses influences from around the world to keep its menu enticing, even for those not traditionally interested in a meat-free diet. There are also plenty of vegan options and the service is excellent.

Fort St George (☎ 354327; Midsummer Common; mains £6-12; ⏲ lunch & dinner) The city's best pub, this lovely 16th-century spot is ideal for sitting outside in summer watching the world float by. There's a hearty selection of real ales and the menu combines well-prepared pub standards with some veggie-friendly options. If you don't drink too much, you can rent a punt outside.

Twenty-Two (☎ 351880; 22 Chesterton Rd; set menu dinners £25-30; ⏲ dinner Tue-Sat) In a quiet neighbourhood near Jesus Green, this tiny town house restaurant is one of the city's best. The seasonal menu of English and French modern classics, often incorporating Asian influences, changes monthly but frequently includes sumptuously prepared partridge, sea bass or spring lamb.

Also recommended:

Tatties (☎ 323399; 11 Sussex St; mains £1-4; ⏲ 8.30am-6pm Mon-Fri, 10am-5pm Sun) Local budget legend specialising in baked potatoes and baguettes.

Anchor (☎ 353554; Silver St; mains £5-9 ⏲ lunch & dinner) This traditional pub has lovely views over the Cam's willow trees and bobbing punts.

Midsummer House (☎ 369299; Midsummer Common; set menu lunch £30, set menu dinner £50; ⏲ lunch Fri & Sat, dinner Tue-Sat) A sophisticated two Michelin–starred dining room serving exquisite French/Mediterranean meals.

Getting There & Away

Fourteen daily direct National Express buses arrive from London Victoria (£10, two hours), while one daily direct service arrives from King's Lynn (£7, two hours). There are two late-night direct services from Norwich (£13.40, two hours) and several nondirect services from the city throughout the day. National Express Airport runs 20 daily services from Stansted Airport (£9.70, 50 minutes) and 29 daily services from Heathrow Airport (£25, two to three hours). **Stagecoach Express** (☎ 01234-212852) runs an hourly X5 service from Oxford (£7, 3½ hours).

Direct trains arrive every 30 minutes from London King's Cross (£17.50, 50 minutes) and London Liverpool St (£17.50, one hour). There are also regular direct services from Norwich (£13.30, one hour), Ely (£4.10, 15 minutes) and King's Lynn (£9.30, 50 minutes).

Getting Around

Cambridge has a good local bus network, with **Stagecoach in Cambridge** (☎ 423578; www.stagecoachbus.com/cambridge) dominating the services. It offers a £2.50 unlimited Dayrider pass on all of its routes. If you're wanting to zip around the city centre or plan to check out the surrounding countryside, hire a bicylce from **Station Cycles** (☎ 307125; www.stationcycles.co.uk; Station Rd; ⏲ 8.30am-6pm Mon-Fri, 9am-5pm Sat, 10am-4pm Sun Mar-Oct) for £8/16 per day/week.

ELY

☎ 01353 / pop 13,954

Pronounced 'eelee', this pretty Cambridgeshire town was once an inland island surrounded by eel-infested waters. Ely remains at the centre of the Fens (a flat, marshy area that is both desolate and hauntingly attractive) and is notable for its lovely Georgian houses and history-lined winding streets. For information on the town, visit the **TIC** (☎ 662062; www.tourism.eastcambs.gov.uk; 29 St Mary's St; ⏲ 10am-5.30pm Apr-Oct, 10am-5pm Sat, 11am-4pm Sun Nov-Mar). Visit the website for comprehensive local accommodation listings.

The town's chief attraction is the imposing **Ely Cathedral** (☎ 667735; www.ely.org.uk/cath.htm; adult/concession £5.20/4.50; ⏲ 7am-7pm May-Sep, 7.30am-6pm Mon-Sat, 7.30am-5pm Sun Oct-Mar), a wondeful example of Norman Romanesque architecture built between 1081 and 1189. Known as the 'Ship of the Fens', its highlights include the lovely **Octagon Tower** and the palatial **Lady Chapel**, which attracts choirs from around the world. Free general tours are offered daily, with additional paid tours of the Octagon and West towers available from March to November (£5 or £3.20 with cathedral admission).

Buses X11 and X12 run half-hourly from Cambridge (£2.50, one hour). There are also regular direct train services from London King's Cross (£20.50, one hour), and frequent direct train services from Cambridge (£4.10, 15 minutes), Norwich (£12.20, 50 minutes) and King's Lynn (£5.60, 30 minutes).

LINCOLNSHIRE

Lincoln

☎ 01522 / pop 85,963

Since it's not on the main tourist drag, many visitors bypass this historic city, missing the hilltop 900-year-old **Lincoln Cathedral** (☎ 544544; www.lincolncathedral.com; adult/child £4/1; 7.15am-8pm Mon-Fri, 7.15am-6pm Sat & Sun Jun-Aug, 7.15am-6pm Mon-Sat, 7.15am-5pm Sun Sep-May) in the process. Its magnificent triptych of towers – including the 81m central tower – dominate the landscape and invite visitors to check out the rewarding building and its surrounding tangle of medieval streets. Nearby **Lincoln Castle** (☎ 511068; adult/child £3.50/2; 9.30am-5.30pm Mon-Sat, 11am-5pm Sun, 4pm closing in winter) is a history-lovers dream where you can learn about the old Roman town, the public executions once staged here and the Magna Carta, a copy of which is on display.

For further local information and accommodation options, visit the **TIC** (☎ 873213; www.visitlincolnshire.com; 9 Castle Hill; 9.30am-6pm Mon-Sat, 10.30am-4.30pm Sun Jul-Sep, 9.30am-5.30pm Mon-Thu, 9.30am-5pm Fri, 10am-5pm Sat & Sun Oct-Jun).

National Express runs one daily direct service from London Victoria (£19.60, 4½ hours) and one daily direct service from Birmingham (£13, three hours). Train travellers have to change at Newark North Gate for the hourly rail service from London King's Cross (from £17, two hours).

NORFOLK

Norwich

☎ 01603 / pop 174,047

East England's largest city (it was even bigger than London in the Middle Ages), Norwich has undergone a quiet renaissance in recent years, transforming it from a forgotten backwater into a surprisingly vibrant centre that's well worth a visit. Part of its attraction is its young university population, but it also has a Championship soccer team, an international airport and a foundation of attractive historic buildings. For information and accommodation tips, contact the **TIC** (☎ 727927; www.visitnorwich.co.uk; The Forum, Millennium Plain; 10am-6pm Mon-Sat, 10.30am-4pm Sun Apr-Oct, 10am-5.30pm Mon-Sat Nov-Mar).

Opened in 2001, the horseshoe-shaped **Forum** (☎ 727950; www.theforumnorwich.co.uk; admission free; 7am-midnight) is a swanky, lottery-funded edifice housing public services as well as **Origins** (☎ 727922; adult/child £5.95/3.95; 10am-5.15pm Mon-Sat, 11am-4.45pm Sun), a multimedia, hands-on introduction to the region that makes the formation of Norfolk seem like an experiment hatched by hi-tech whiz-kids. It's also worth dropping by the University of East Anglia's newly renovated **Sainsbury Centre for Visual Arts** (☎ 593199; www.scva.org.uk; 11am-5pm Tue-Sun), which displays an excellent collection of contemporary works by the likes of Francis Bacon and Henry Moore.

Norwich International Airport (NWI; ☎ 411923; www.norwichinternational.com) is just a 15-minute drive from the city centre. Flights arrive from Dublin (1½ hours), Manchester (55 minutes), Cardiff (one hour) and Edinburgh (1½ hours). National Express runs five daily direct buses from London Victoria (£14, three hours) and one daily direct service from King's Lynn (£6.80, 1½ hours). There are twice-hourly trains from London Liverpool Street (from £19.50, two hours) and Ely (£12.20, one hour).

King's Lynn

☎ 01553 / pop 40,921

A once-vital English port, King's Lynn is a sleepy Norfolk town clinging to the banks of the Great Ouse River. Still busy on market days (Tuesday, Friday and Saturday), it's worth an afternoon of wandering for those looking for a quiet break. For information and accommodation recommendations, contact the **TIC** (☎ 0870 770 5902; www.west-norfolk.gov.uk; Custom House, Purfleet Quay; 10am-5pm Mon-Sat, noon-5pm Sun Apr-Sep, 10.30am-4pm Mon-Sat, noon-4pm Sun Oct-Mar). There's a small, well-located **YHA Hostel** (☎ 772461; kingslynn@yha.org.uk; College Lane; dm £11.95; Apr-Oct) with basic facilities. Hourly direct trains arrive from London King's Cross (£25.50, 1½ hours) and Cambridge (£9.30, 45 minutes).

NORTHEAST ENGLAND

By turns wild, pretty, historic and urban, this corner of England offers excellent walking and hiking country, great expanses of empty beach, two of England's most vibrant cities – historic York and resurgent post-industrial Newcastle – plus a hoard of world-class relics and ruins dating back two turbulent millennia. Highlights include the magnificent York Cathedral, Newcastle's buzzing arts, entertainment and party scenes, Roman emperor Hadrian's vast wall straddling England's narrow neck, the haunting monastery island of Lindisfarne and countless hiking and cycling options around the area's many national parks, such as the Yorkshire Dales and along the ever-popular, 268-mile Pennine Way. For general information on visiting the region, check **North East England** (www.visitnorthumbria.com) and **Yorkshire Tourist Board's** (www.yorkshirevisitor.com) official website. For art, theatre and heritage information visit www.culturalyorkshire.com.

YORK

☎ 01904 / pop 180,000

A well-preserved time capsule, York has been a settlement of military, political, religious and commercial eminence dating as far back as Roman times right up to the Industrial Revolution. Visitors from York's medieval past would recognise, even today, much of its wonderfully preserved heritage, such as the spectacular Minster and the stout medieval wall girdling the city's ancient alleyways, although they might be surprised at the modern profusion of gift shops and tea rooms, not to mention the sheer mass of sightseeing visitors. Despite this press of people, York wears its popularity well and retains an undiluted appeal. This bustling, tourist-friendly city, easily explored on foot, is one of England's finest urban attractions.

Orientation

Although the city is relatively small, York's streets are a confusing medieval tangle, further confused by the fact that 'gate' means street, and 'bar' means gate. There are five major landmarks: the walkable 2.5 miles of city wall; the Minster at the northern corner; Clifford's Tower, a 13th-century fortification and mound at the southern end; the Ouse River that cuts the city centre in two; and the train station just outside the western corner.

Information

City Screen (☎ 541155; 13-17 Coney St; per 30 min £2; 🕑 10am-5pm)

Post Office (Lendal; 🕑 8.30am-5.30pm Mon-Fri, 8.30am-6pm Sat)

TIC (☎ 621756; www.thisisyork.co.uk/www.visityork.org; De Grey Rooms, Exhibition Sq; 🕑 9am-5pm Mon-Sat, 10am-4pm Sun Nov-Mar, 9am-6pm Mon-Sat, 10am-5pm Sun Apr-Oct) The website is useful for accommodation listings and special offers. There's also a small tourist information office at the train station.

What's on York (www.whatsonyork.com) Up-to-date events listings.

Sights

YORK MINSTER

Northern Europe's largest Gothic cathedral, **York Minster** (☎ 557216; Minster Yard; adult/concession £5/4; 🕑 9am-5pm Mon-Sat, noon-6.30pm Sun) is the city's highlight and a 1000-year-old treasure house of architecture and richly coloured stained glass, especially the giant **Great Eastern Window**, whose 117 detailed panels cost just £58 to create in 1408. Take an audio tour of the **Undercroft** (adult/concession £3/2, combined ticket £7/5) for subterranean Roman, Norman and Viking remains and treasure, and the atmospheric crypt. The view past gargoyles and over the city atop the Minster's 275-step **tower** is spectacular.

JORVIK CENTRE

Offering a time-machine ride through Viking streets, the **Jorvik Centre** (☎ 543402; Coppergate; adult/concession/child £7.20/6.10/5.10; 🕑 10am-5pm Apr-Oct, 10am-4pm Nov-Mar), York's most popular visitor attraction, is entertainingly cheesy. The animatronic dioramas conjuring the sights, sounds and unfortunate smells of the era are a tad tired by now, although a planned revamp with talking Viking ghosts, a new gallery and a new display of artefacts from the era should have pepped things up by the time you read this.

NATIONAL RAILWAY MUSEUM

In a big train shed near the train station, the **National Railway Museum** (☎ 621261; Leeman Rd; admission free; 🕑 10am-6pm) is one giant train set offering you the chance to get up close to dozens of steam-age leviathans, including the legendary *Mallard* and *Flying Scotsman*, the liveried splendour of various royal trains and a Japanese bullet train. There are good interactive displays and a fully working locomotive turntable. Even for nontrainspotters it's surprising fun.

YORK CASTLE MUSEUM

The **York Castle Museum** (☎ 687687; Castle Area, Eye of York; adult/child £6.50/4; 🕑 9.30am-5pm Apr-Oct, 9.30am-4.30pm Nov-Mar) contains a labyrinth of rooms exploring 600 years of British life from medieval prisons to Victorian parlours. There's a less-than-homely prison cell where you can try the bed of York's most famous prisoner, the notorious highwayman Dick Turpin.

Tours

The **Association of Voluntary Guides** (10.15am & 2.15pm Apr-Oct, 6.45pm Jun-Aug) offers free two-hour walking tours, departing across the street from the TIC. There's fierce competition among the city's cut-throat ghost-tour operators, which befits a city reputed to be Europe's most haunted. Among the best is the **Ghost Hunt of York** (608700; The Shambles; adult/child £4/2.50; 8pm), a 75-minute tour led by a top-hatted guide offering an entertaining mix of horror and hilarity.

Sleeping

York is always crowded in summer and finding a bed can be trying. Use the TIC's accommodation booking service (£3).

BUDGET

Marmadukes Hostel (0870 066 0156; www.marmadukeshostels.com; St Peter's Grove; dm £10-18, d from £18;) Easily the best hostel in town, newcomer Marmadukes offers modern surroundings, small dorms (the largest holds 10 beds) and plush doubles with wood floors. There's also a summer garden and a cosy little bar-café in this solid old house, a five-minute walk from the city walls.

York Youth Hotel (625904; www.yorkyouthhotel.com; 11-13 Bishophill Senior; dm £12-18) Located in a smart Georgian town house, this popular, if basic, hostel offers decent four-, six- and eight-bed dorms, and a comfortable bar serving hearty pub grub.

York International Youth Hostel (0870 770 6102; york@yha.org.uk; 42 Water End, Clifton; dm £13.50-18.50;) Large and busy, this hostel is reached via a riverside footpath from the city centre. Most rooms have four beds, and there's a good café-bar and private garden. Book in advance to avoid the summer crush.

York Backpackers (627720; www.yorkbackpackers.co.uk; 88-90 Micklegate; dm £13-14, d £35;) This group-oriented place offers spartan dorm accommodation beneath elaborately corniced ceilings in a splendid 18th-century historic house. The wooden bunks are rickety and there's one huge, sleep-defying 36-bed dorm. On the plus side, it's one of the city's most sociable hostels thanks to its lively bar and cheap beer.

MIDRANGE & TOP END

A gaggle of B&Bs cluster along Bootham and Grosvenor Tces, parallel to the train line and a quick walk from the city centre.

Marmadukes (0870 066 0156; www.marmadukesworld.com; St Peter's Grove; d £25-50;) Next door to Marmadukes Hostel and run by the same enthusiastic owners, this new guesthouse offers cut-price boutique chic, with serene, minimalist décor and good-quality fittings. It's terrific value.

Bar Convent (464902; www.bar-convent.org.uk; 17 Blossom St; s/d with shared bathroom £30/55, d & tw £66;) Inside this 17th-century convent you'll find a serene, welcoming atmosphere and appropriately monastic (but comfortable) accommodation.

Jorvik Hotel (653511; Marygate; s/d/ste £40/65/70) The central, charmingly old-fashioned Jorvik, a short amble from the city walls, might not win any prizes for its perfectly adequate, if somewhat dated, furnishings but it just might win hearts with its excellent cooked breakfast.

Four High Petergate (658516; www.fourhighpetergate.co.uk; 4 High Petergate; s/d/tw from £65/90/100) Just inside the city walls, this elegant town house is wonderfully equipped to pamper with solid teak furniture, soft, silky bed linen, goose-down pillows, posh bathrooms and flat-screen TVs, although the standard rooms are on the small side. There's a great bistro downstairs (see opposite).

Also recommended:

23 St Mary's (622738; www.23stmarys.co.uk; 23 St Mary's, Bootham; s/d £34/60) Award-winning hospitality, good-sized rooms, lots of character and ever-helpful owners.

Arnot House (641966; www.arnothouseyork.co.uk; 17 Grosvenor Tce; r £65-70;) A cosy, quirky B&B with Victorian-era furnishings, five minutes from the city walls.

Eating

Food lovers will be spoilt for choice; York is awash with individual and inexpensive little tearooms serving light lunches and snacks. There's a vast array of restaurants, too.

Betty's (659142; St Helen's Sq; lunch mains £6-8, cream tea £7; 9am-9pm) A high-class treat complete with a pianist tickling the ivories, this refined tearoom serves excellent lunches and breakfasts, along with dainty pastries and great cream teas.

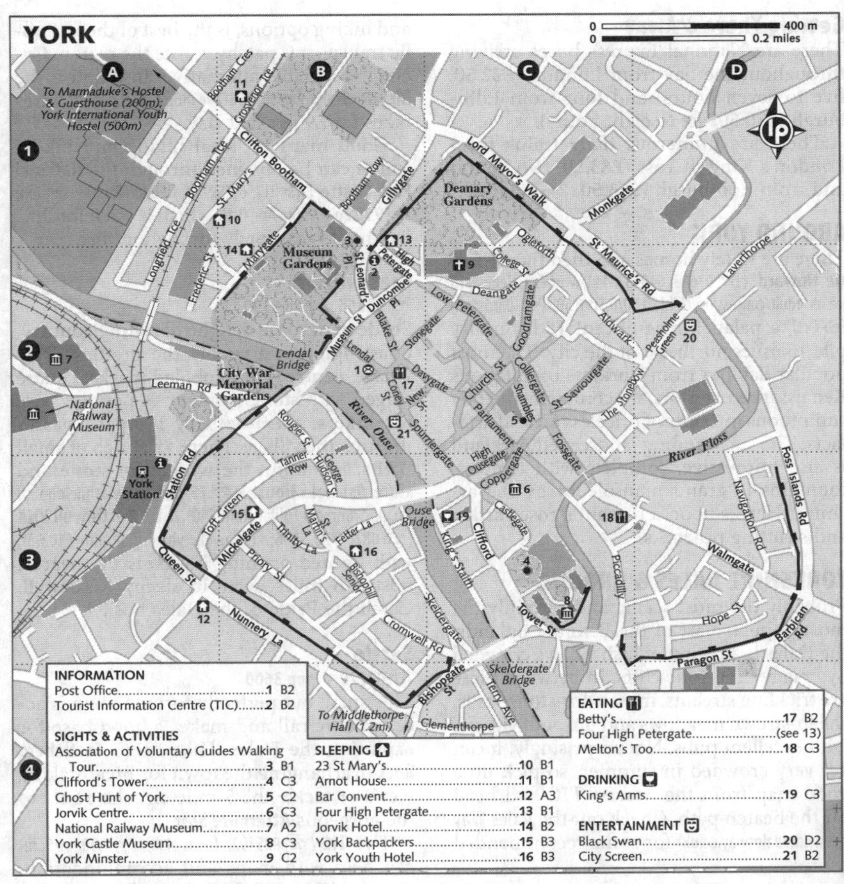

Melton's Too (☎ 629222; 25 Walmgate; tapas £3-5, mains £7.50-12; ⏰ 10.30am-10pm) Sister restaurant to the foodies' favourite Meltons, this is a slightly more casual, keenly priced place specialising in unpretentiously prepared and presented (and often locally sourced) British fare, such as Yorkshire steak and kidney and Whitby smoked haddock croquettes. Good tapas, too.

Four High Petergate (☎ 658516; www.fourhighpetergate.co.uk; 4 High Petergate; mains £12-15; ⏰ lunch & dinner) Let's let the dishes speak for themselves: how about caramelised fennel and tomato tart or crisp ham hock and baby pear salad, or maybe scrumpy marinated loin of wild boar with warm aduki bean salad, chorizo and cherry apples?

Drinking & Entertainment

Forget the clubbing scene, York is hardly party central, but the profusion of atmospheric city-centre pubs more than compensates.

Black Swan (☎ 686911; Peasholme Green) A rambling, higgledy-piggledy Tudor boozer that serves great cask ales, and hosts live blues and jazz on Sunday.

King's Arms (☎ 659435; King's Staith) The enduringly popular riverside King's Arms really does come into its own over the summer months.

City Screen (☎ 541144; 13-17 Coney St; admission from £4) A great little independent arthouse cinema that also hosts regular live music and comedy gigs.

Getting There & Away

There are National Express buses arriving throughout the day from London (£22.50, five to seven hours) and four from Edinburgh (£30.50, six to eight hours).

There are numerous daily trains from London's King's Cross (£83.50, two hours) and from Edinburgh (£63.50, 2½ hours).

AROUND YORK

There are stately homes and then there's **Castle Howard** (☎ 01653-648333/444; www.castlehoward.co.uk; adult/concession/child £9.50/8.50/6.50; ⏰ 10am-4pm Feb-Oct), a palatial, magnificent 18th-century pile 15 miles northeast of the city. The most popular day out from York, its ostentatious Renaissance exteriors are complemented by sumptuous interiors of priceless art and artefacts. The surrounding landscaped parkland is also impressive, complete with temples, fountains, a grand mausoleum by the architect Hawksmoor, a romantic rose garden and strutting peacocks.

YORKSHIRE DALES & AROUND

Probably the most scenic and certainly the most popular part of the Pennine uplands, the Dales is a region of lush valleys crowned by craggy limestone cliffs. In between there are trickling streams, mossy dry-stone walls, sheep-strewn meadows and unspoilt villages with excellent pubs. Not surprisingly, it can get very crowded in summer, so pick up a good map from the nearest TIC and head off the beaten path. Check out the **Dales Way** (www.thedalesway.co.uk) for some recommended routes.

Orientation & Information

The 700-sq-mile Yorkshire Dales National Park is best explored from Grassington, home of the region's main TIC. For orientation, the Dales can be broken into northern and southern halves. In the north, the main dales run parallel and east to west, and include Wensleydale, Teesdale and Swaledale. In the southern half, the north to south Ribblesdale with its famous viaduct is the route of the Leeds–Settle–Carlisle (LSC) railway. Pretty Wharfedale is parallel to the east.

Getting Around

Unless you're driving, the LSC is the best way to get to those places along its route. Settle, which offers good accommodation and hiking options, is the best of these. Public transport is patchy across the region. Cycling is a viable alternative. In Skipton, the **Bicycle Shop** (☎ 01756-794386; 3-5 Water St) hires bikes for £9 per half-day.

Good maps on local hiking and biking routes can be obtained through the **National Park Centre** (☎ 01756-752774; Hebdon Rd, Grassington; ⏰ 9.30am-5.15pm Apr-Oct), which is open for limited hours seasonally throughout the year.

Grassington

☎ 01756 / pop 1100

Set deep in some delightful rolling country, Grassington is arguably the prettiest Dale village, centred on a cobbled market square ringed with stone cottages. A popular base for hikers, the **Dales Way** footpath passes through the village. There's a clutch of small B&Bs, including the wonderful stone and slate **Ashfield House** (☎ 752584; www.ashfieldhouse.co.uk; Summers Fold; r from £40), but **Kettlewell YHA** (☎ 0870 770 5896; kettlewell@yha.org.uk; dm £10.60), with limited opening hours, is the nearest hostel, 6 miles away in sleepy Kettlewell. Catch the Pride of the Dales bus 74.

Settle

☎ 01729 / pop 3600

This small but perfectly formed town is accessible by rail and makes a good base for exploring the Dales. Hike up to **Castleberg Rock** overhanging the town for breathtaking views or tackle the 5-mile circular route to the gorgeous **Attermire Scar.**

The **TIC** (☎ 825192; Town Hall; ⏰ 9.30am-5pm) can help with maps and accommodation. Try the YHA **Stainforth Youth Hostel** (☎ 0870 770 6046; stainforth@yha.org.uk; dm £13.95), a Georgian house near rivers and wooded glades (opening times are limited so call ahead), or the **Golden Lion Hotel** (☎ 01524-251240; bookings@goldenlionyorks.net; Duke St; s/d £40/72, with shared bathroom £33/60), with chintzy but comfy rooms and a cosy pub restaurant downstairs.

Skipton

☎ 01756 / 14,300

Skipton is worth a visit for its excellent **castle** (☎ 792442; adult/concession/child £5.40/4.80/2.90; ⏰ 10am-6pm Mon-Sat, noon-6pm Sun), which is one of Britain's best-preserved medieval fortresses. The giant complex was besieged for three years and finally captured during the Civil War. On market days (Monday,

Wednesday, Friday and Saturday) the town comes alive with stalls and shoppers. The **TIC** (☎ 792809; 35 Coach St; 10am-5pm Mon-Sat, 11.30am-3.30pm Sun) has comprehensive information on the town and surrounding area. There are B&Bs aplenty on Keighley Rd, and the town is served by frequent trains from Leeds.

Haworth

☎ 01535 / pop 6078

Even without its literary heritage the captivatingly pretty cobbled streets and hillside vistas in Haworth make it well worth a visit. Being the home of the legendary Bronte sisters, it's also a hugely popular literary shrine to Emily, Anne and Charlotte. A summer tourist magnet, the **Bronte Parsonage Museum** (☎ 642323; Church St; adult/concession/child £4.90/3.60/1.60; 10am-5.30pm Apr-Sep, 11am-5pm Oct-Mar) offers a fascinating trip back in time for literature buffs. The **TIC** (☎ 642329; www.haworth-village.org.uk; Main St; 9am-5pm) can help with accommodation, but good bets include the former Victorian stately home **Haworth Youth Hostel** (☎ 0870 770 5858; Haworth@yha.org.uk; Longlands Dr, Lees Lane; dm £13.95; Feb-Oct), which should be your first option. There are frequent buses from Keighley, which has train connections with Leeds.

NORTH YORK MOORS NATIONAL PARK

Wilder and more dramatic than the Dales but no less beautiful, the brooding North York Moors cover 550 sq miles of wild and wonderful terrain coloured by purple heather (between July and September) dotted with old stone farmhouses and romantic ruins; the perfect setting in which to imagine star-crossed Bronte heroes and heroines in a clinch.

Orientation & Information

The moors run east to west, from the craggy coastline that includes Whitby and Scarborough to the gentle rolling hills and steep cliffs of Hambleton and Cleveland Hills. There are several TICs in the area, but the **Moors Centre** (☎ 01439-772737; Lodge Lane, Danby; 10am-5pm Apr-Oct, 11am-4pm Nov-Dec & Mar, 11am-4pm Sat & Sun only Jan-Feb) is the best of them. The official park website, **North York Moors National Park** (www.moors.uk.net), is an excellent resource for planning your exploration of the area.

Activities

A network of trails snakes through the park, making walking the best way to experience the area. The 110-mile **Cleveland Way** from Helmsley to Filey will take you via as many of its hills and coastal vistas as you can handle. The steam trains of the **North Yorkshire Moors Railway** (NYMR; ☎ 01751-473799; 1-day pass adult/concession/child £14/12/7; Apr-Oct, limited winter services) offer a more sedate way to traverse the region, running the picturesque 18 miles between Pickering and Grosmont – look out for **Goathland Station**, transformed into Hogsmead Station for the *Harry Potter* movies.

Getting Around

The **Moorbus** (☎ 01845-597426; www.moors.uk.net; Moorslink) services a network of stops (daily June to September, Sunday April to October) throughout the region.

Helmsley & Around

☎ 01439 / pop 1500

Starting point for the **Cleveland Way**, Helmsley's 13th-century ruined **castle** (☎ 770442; adult/concession/child £4/3/2; 10am-6pm Apr-Sep, to 4pm Oct-Mar) is the town's top visitor attraction. The locals focus more on the **market place**, where stallholders set up shop every Friday. The nearby town hall houses the **TIC** (☎ 770173; 9.30am-5.30pm Mar-Oct, 10am-4pm Fri-Sun Nov-Feb).

Among Britain's most impressive monastic ruins is the 13th-century **Rievaulx Abbey** (☎ 798228; adult/concession/child £4.20/3.20/2.10; 10am-6pm Apr-Sep, 10am-4pm Oct-Mar), about 3 miles west of Helmsley. The abbey's soaring arches and intricate decorative flourishes are a testament to the wealth and power of the monks who once lived here. The fanciful fake 18th-century temples at nearby **Rievaulx Terrace & Temples** (☎ 01969-640382; admission £4; variable Mar-Nov) offer glorious views overlooking the abbey (although it's a steep, mile-long slog uphill from the abbey).

Helmsley has several atmospheric B&Bs and coaching inns, including historic coaching inn **Feathers** (☎ 770275; feathershotel@aol.com; s/d from £40/70). **Helmsley Youth Hostel** (☎ 0870 770 5860; helmsley@yha.org.uk; Carlton Lane; dm £13.95) is a friendly backpacker option, with varying opening hours.

Scarborough & District buses (☎ 01723-507300) runs an hourly service from Scarborough via Pickering (£3.55, 90 minutes) on bus 128.

Pickering

☎ 01751 / pop 6600

An excellent gateway to the moors, this bustling little market town's atmospheric train station, restored to its 1930s glory, is a suitably charming terminus for the steam locomotives of the North Yorkshire Moors Railway, the best way to explore the area without a car. The well-preserved ruins of Pickering's Norman **castle** (☎ 474989; adult/concession £3/2.30; 10am-6pm Apr-Sep, 10am-4pm Oct) are also well worth a visit, as are the 15th-century frescoes in the nearby **Church of St Peter and St Paul**. Pickering's helpful **TIC** (☎ 473791; The Ropery; 9.30am-6pm Mon-Sat, 9.30am-5pm Sun Mar-Oct, 10am-4.30pm Mon-Sat Nov-Feb) can assist with accommodation bookings.

You'll find several B&Bs on Eastgate (the road to Scarborough), including **Eden House** (☎ 472289; www.edenhousebandb.co.uk; s/d £30/56), a pretty little flower-bedecked stone cottage.

Whitby

☎ 01947 / pop 14,100

We challenge you not to fall in love with Whitby, Yorkshire's most rewarding coastal town, the moment you set eyes on it. Dominated by a forbidding cliff-top abbey ruin, threaded with steep, narrow streets winding down to pretty harbour quays stacked high with lobster pots and lined with pubs and excellent seafood restaurants, it's well worth putting on your itinerary.

Whitby has a compelling history, too; the young Captain James Cook was apprenticed to a Whitby shipowner and HMS *Endeavour* was built here, but much of the town's renown is based on the fictional character of Dracula: for Whitby is where Bram Stoker's creation makes landfall (follow in his great undead footsteps with the TIC's *Dracula Trail* leaflet; £0.60).

The **TIC** (☎ 602674; 9am-6pm May-Sep, 10am-4.30pm Oct-Apr) is across from the train station.

SIGHTS

Burial place of Anglo Saxon saints and kings, venerable **Whitby Abbey** (☎ 603568; adult/concession/child £4/3/2; 10am-6pm Apr-Sep, 10am-5pm Oct, 10am-4pm Nov-Mar), accessible via 199 stone steps and through the graveyard of the church next door, is an evocative wind-whipped spot with a history dating back to AD 657, engagingly explained at the **visitor centre**. Hold onto your hat for a wind-blasted 5.5-mile cliff-top walk south to beautiful **Robin Hood's Bay**.

SLEEPING

The helpful staff at the TIC will book accommodation for free.

Whitby Backpackers (☎ 601794; www.thewhitbybackpackers.co.uk; 28 Hudson St; dm £10-15; Mar-Nov) Centrally located in a Victorian house, this is the town's best hostel, combining a friendly atmosphere with good-sized rooms and superior facilities.

Harbour Grange Backpackers Whitby (☎ 600817; backpackers@harbourgrange.co.uk; Spital Bridge; dm from £12; ⊠) Roll out of your bunk and you're

TOP FIVE YORKSHIRE WALKS

The best way to explore this lovely part of the country is to get its measure with your own feet. Most of the following walks can be split into day-long sections. Be sure to take the right gear and sensible precautions, as the weather can close in suddenly. For detailed information on these paths, consult **Outdooryorkshire.com** (www.outdooryorkshire.com) or Lonely Planet's *Walking in Britain*.

- **The Cleveland Way** Along 109 miles of rugged coast and high moorland through the North York Moors National Park (see p225).
- **The Dales Way** Heading into the Lake District from Ilkely to Windermere over some wonderfully remote hills.
- **The Herroit Way** A 52-mile track over the northern Dales of Wensleydale and Swaledale.
- **The Kirklees Way** Easily split into manageable day-trip chunks, this 72-mile path takes in some varied Pennine terrain.
- **The Pennine Way** The 268-mile daddy of them all, creeping up the backbone of England from Derbyshire, through three national parks and into the Scottish Borders.

almost in the harbour at this small, basic backpackers. The only small downside is the 11.30pm curfew.

White Horse & Griffin (☎ 604857; www.whitehorseandgriffin.co.uk; 87 Church St; s/d from £35/60) A fantastic mix of olde-worlde charm and modern creature comforts with an excellent and popular restaurant attached. It's the pick of Whitby's accommodation.

Also recommended:

Riviera Hotel (☎ 602533; www.rivierawhitby.com; 4 Crescent Tce; B&B s/d £31/52) Pay a little extra for a grand four-poster or a mesmerising view across the bay.

Langley Hotel (☎ 604250; www.langleyhotel.com; 16 Royal Cres; s/d £35/66) Some chintz horrors, but it's comfortable and offers good value, with panoramic sea views.

EATING

Grapevine Bistro (☎ 820275; 2 Grape Lane; tapas £4-6, mains £7-11; ⏲ lunch & dinner) Creditable tapas by day, with slightly more substantial Mediterranean flavours by night, including a couple of good veggie options.

Magpie Café (☎ 602058; 14 Pier Rd; mains £7-14; ⏲ 11.30am-9pm) Join the line snaking outside this crowded Whitby institution for what may be Yorkshire's best seafood. The fish and chips live up to their reputation, but the long selection of finer fare is worth considering. There's a window for takeaway fish and chips if you can't be bothered waiting.

GETTING THERE & AWAY

Trains arrive via Middlesbrough, so you have to change if you're coming from York or Durham. It's a long journey, but worth it for the hypnotic panorama of the Dales scrolling past along the way. Regular buses arrive from York and Scarborough.

DURHAM

☎ 0191 / pop 100,000

Worth a day trip at the least, Durham is a magnificent natural hill fortress defended on three sides by a loop of the Wear River. Crowned by a magnificent castle and Britain's finest Norman cathedral, it's an atmospheric towndown to the cobbles of its medieval streets. It's also a lively place packed with busy pubs and bars.

Orientation & Information

The compact town centre is best explored on foot and it's hard to get lost with the cathedral looming above. The train station is above and northwest of the cathedral, while the bus station is on the western side.

The **TIC** (☎ 384 3720; www.durhamtourism.co.uk; Millennium Pl; ⏲ 9.30am-5.30pm Mon-Sat, 10am-4pm Sun) books accommodation for free. Internet access is available at no cost at **Clayport Library** (☎ 386 4003; Millennium Pl; ⏲ 9.30am-7pm Mon-Fri, 9am-5pm Sat), but photo ID is required and there is a 30-minute limit at peak times.

Sights

If you need one good reason to visit the city, that reason is the part church, part fortress of **Durham Cathedral** (☎ 386 4266; Palace Green; admission free; ⏲ 9.30am-6pm Mon-Sat, 12.30-5pm Sun, 9.30am-8pm mid-Jun–Sep). A magnificent Unesco-listed landmark, its ornate, rib-vaulted architecture was an engineering breakthrough for its time and the soaring structure remains an architectural marvel today. Climb the 66m **tower** (adult/child £3/1.50) for spectacular city views or take an illuminating tour (adult/child £3.50/free); call ahead for times.

The stout **Durham Castle** (☎ 334 3800; Palace Green; adult/child £5/2.50; ⏲ 10am-12.30pm & 2-4.30pm Jul-Sep) nearby, also a World Heritage Site, was completed in 1072 and was the university's first home 800 years later. Don't miss the beautifully preserved Norman chapel.

Sleeping

Accommodation options abound online at www.visitbritain.com, although vacancies are virtually nonexistent during university graduation in late June. During holidays 11 **colleges** (☎ 334 5878; www.dur.ac.uk/conference_tourism; r per person from £20) – including the castle's medieval University College – offer a variety of rooms outside term-time.

There's no youth hostel, so the best budget bet is to stay with the friendly **Mrs Metcalfe** (☎ 384 1020; 12 The Ave; s £22). There are only two cosy rooms, so book ahead.

Court Inn (☎ 384 7350; Court Lane; s/d £50/70) The three spacious rooms above this cosy, central little pub have lots of character and are more like mini-apartments. Well worth considering.

Farnley Tower (☎ 375 0011; www.farnley-tower.co.uk; The Ave; s/d £65/75, s with shared bathroom £55; 💻) A five-minute walk from town, this former country house (with castle and cathedral views from many rooms) is our pick for atmosphere, pleasant grounds and a great breakfast.

Eating & Drinking

Almshouse (☎ 386 1054; Palace Green; dishes £3-7; 9am-5pm) Right on Palace Green you'll find good-value, hearty, made-on-the-premises soups, light lunch and café fare here.

Brown Sugar Bistro (☎ 386 5050; 81-83 New Elvet; dishes £4-7; 7am-11pm) This great little bar, café and bistro is great for filling breakfasts and good *ciabatta* sandwiches.

It may be a student town, but don't expect wild nightlife from Durham. There are plenty of good clubs and bars, though, including the low-key **Shakespeare** (63 Saddler St) and **Varsity** (46 Saddler St), a bright, backpacker-friendly three-level pub offering a good beer selection, cheap bar food and a covered garden.

Getting There & Around

Six National Express buses run from London daily (£27.50, six to eight hours) and three arrive from Edinburgh (£21.50, four to five hours). The Arriva X1 service runs throughout the day to Newcastle, excluding Sunday. On the main London–Edinburgh line, trains arrive from London (£90.40, three hours) and Edinburgh (£44, two hours) throughout the day. Trains also arrive every few minutes from York (£18.90, 45 minutes).

For local bus information, call ☎ 0870 608 2608.

NEWCASTLE-UPON-TYNE

☎ 0191 / pop 470,000

Once synonymous with post-industrial decline and decay, these days Newcastle is brimming with confidence and a hedonistic yen to have fun. All of a sudden, it seems, this unfailingly friendly city, with its distinctive Geordie accent thicker than molasses, has kick-started a vibrant arts and entertainment scene (although its riotous nightlife is a bit more of an established tradition). Then there's the city's captivating riverside vista, a press of solid 19th-century and futuristic 21st-century architecture, with a mini Sydney Harbour Bridge stuck in the middle of it, all lit at night like a classic 1940s movie.

Orientation & Information

Newcastle's compact city centre is easy to navigate on foot and it has an excellent public transport system, including a metro system circling the centre and connecting the suburbs. The Central train and bus station is just south of the city centre. Packed with chain stores, indoor markets and giant £1 shops, it's partly pedestrianised around Grainger St. A surprising number of buildings here are formidable 19th-century classical structures, with almost half-heritage listed. Tourist information is available at the **TIC** (☎ 277 8000; www.visitnewcastlegateshead.com; Market St; 9.30am-5.30pm Mon-Sat).

Sights

Make sure you take a stroll down by the riverside where many of Newcastle's great buildings and structures will jostle for your attention – although those on the south bank technically fall within neighbouring Gateshead).

BALTIC

A contemporary art centre housed in a vast former flourmill, **Baltic** (☎ 478 1810; Gateshead Quay; admission free; 10am-7pm Mon-Sat, 10am-5pm Sun; M Gateshead) is the North's answer to London's Tate Modern. It's reached from the Newcastle side of the river via the Gateshead Millennium Bridge, a bowed pedestrian walkway that opens like an eye for passing ships.

SAGE MUSIC CENTRE

To call the **Sage Music Centre** (☎ 443 4666; www.thesagegateshead.org; Gateshead Quays; 10am-11.30pm; M Gateshead) a live music venue hardly does justice to this terrific building, designed by celebrated architect Sir Norman Foster, although the splendid concert halls are acoustically excellent. Even if you're not attending a gig or a concert (every genre is represented), it's well worth wandering the vast lobby just for a peep at the building, lingering for a coffee or snack at the excellent café, and listening to the jazz and classical music listening posts.

LIFE SCIENCE CENTRE

It's dedicated to explaining genetics, but if this sounds dull, think again, because **Life** (☎ 243 8210; Times Sq; adult/concession £6.95/5.50; 10am-6pm Mon-Sat, 11am-6pm Sun; M Central Station) is a brilliantly realised audiovisual treat with great simulated rides that take you on hair-raising taxi rides through Newcastle and bungee jumping off its bridge (although what that has to do with genetics isn't immediately clear).

ANGEL OF THE NORTH

A short drive from the city south along the A1 (you can't miss it), the most potent symbol of restored Northeast pride is the towering, rusting, forbidding, welcoming, redemptive, apocalyptic **Angel of the North** (☎ 478 4222; A1, Gateshead; admission free) sculpture, with a 54m wingspan and built from 200 tonnes of steel by artist Antony Gormley.

Sleeping

There has long been a dearth of good accommodation, although things are slowly improving.

Newcastle YHA (☎ 0870 770 5972; www.yha.org.uk; 107 Jesmond Rd; dm £12; Ⓜ Jesmond) A basic but clean YHA property in quiet Jesmond. It fills up quickly, so book ahead.

Albatross Backpackers (☎ 233 1330; www.albatrossnewscastle.com; 51 Grainger St; dm £16.50-19.50, s/d £45/47; 💻; Ⓜ Central Station) Finally the city centre has some good budget accommodation in this smart new backpackers, with no curfew and 24-hour reception. Light sleepers beware, the chances of sharing with groups of drunken snorers are high.

Premier Lodge (☎ 0870 990 6530; www.premierlodge.com; Quayside; r from £45; Ⓜ Central Station) This McHotel chain is your best (almost only) midrange bet in the city centre. The rooms are uniformly bland, the clientele are business folk in the week and stag and hen party animals on weekends, but on the plus side, it's smack dab in the middle of the quayside action.

Adelphi Hotel (☎ 281 3109; theadelphihotelnewcastle.co.uk; 63 Fern Ave, Jesmond; s/d £40/60; Ⓜ Jesmond) This is a cosy B&B, in a leafy Newcastle suburb a short metro ride from the city centre and away from the hubbub.

Eating

New restaurants have sprouted like mushrooms around the city centre in recent years. Grey St and the general Quayside area are good places to follow your nose. Many Newcastle restaurants have early-bird dinner specials.

Blake's Coffee House (☎ 261 5463; 53 Grey St; breakfast £2-4; 🕑 9am-6pm; Ⓜ Monument) This central, popular, high-ceilinged café is the perfect spot to while away a morning over the papers and gently recover from the night before.

El Torero (☎ 233 1122; The Side, Quayside; mains £4-6; 🕑 noon-11pm Mon-Sat; Ⓜ Central Station) Decent tapas served right in the city centre, perfect for a light lunch or a later beer ballast pit stop.

Paradiso Caffe Bar (☎ 221 1240; 1 Market Lane; mains £5-17; 🕑 11am-10.30pm Mon-Fri, 12.30-3.30pm Sun; Ⓜ Monument) An atmospheric location in an old print-works factory and a decent bistro menu make the Paradiso an enduring hit with locals. There's also a great balcony for relaxing alfresco dining.

Drinking & Entertainment

Newcastle may be trying to shed its image as a late-night, open-air vomitorium but, well, it still is if you wander round at throwing out (and up) time. If you like the idea, as so many locals do, of staggering from one packed drinking shed to another to chase the seemingly eternal happy hour, simply head to the Bigg Market and Quayside areas. More discerning revellers will have to look a little harder, but there are some excellent little bars, clubs and pubs if you know where to go. The local listings magazine *The Crack* has the latest clubbing intelligence.

Sage Music Centre (☎ 443 4666; www.thesagegateshead.org; Gateshead Quays; 🕑 10am-11.30pm; Ⓜ Gateshead) For live music and concerts, do not forget to consult the programme at this excellent centre.

Trent House Soul Bar (☎ 261 2154; 1-2 Leazes Lane; Ⓜ Haymarket) Easy-going and run by the World Headquarters folk (which explains the fantastic jukebox), this is a great place to kick off the night.

Crown Posada (31 The Side; Ⓜ Central Station) In the midst of the Quayside throngs, this low-key pub offers relative repose and some decent real ale.

World Headquarters (☎ 261 7007; Curtis Mayfield House, Carliol Sq; Ⓜ Monument) Fantastic sounds ranging from funk, soul and old-school R&B to rare groove, northern soul and a smattering of house are the auditory treats on offer at Newcastle's coolest nightclub.

Baja Beach Club (☎ 477 6205; Hillgate Quay; Ⓜ Gateshead) The pumping pop, bikini-clad barmaids, tropical theming and roaring drunken crowd take this place so far over the top (and that's saying something for this town) it's compelling (in a multicar pile-up kind of way).

Getting There & Away

AIR

Located 20 minutes from the city centre, daily flights to **Newcastle International Airport** (NCL; www.newcastleairport.com) arrive from London's Heathrow and Gatwick airports, as well as Amsterdam and Paris, with other cities served on a less regular basis. Low-cost favourites **Ryanair** (☎ 0870 156 9569; www.ryanair.com) and **easyJet** (☎ 0870 600 0000; www.easyjet.com) ply their trade here, so check their websites for the latest deals.

BOAT

Regular ferries arrive at Royal Quays from Norway, Sweden and the Netherlands. For more information, see p279.

BUS

National Express coaches arrive from many major UK cities, including London (£25.50, 6½ hours) and Edinburgh (£11, 2½ hours). The excellent-value Explorer Northeast ticket (£6) is valid on most local regional services. Bus 505 arrives from Berwick-upon-Tweed, and bus 685 comes from Hexham and Haltwhistle for Hadrian's Wall.

TRAIN

There are frequent trains from Edinburgh (£39, 1¾ hours), York (£19.50, one hour) and London (£90.40, three hours). Berwick-upon-Tweed and Alnmouth (for Alnwick) are also served.

Getting Around

The city centre is surprisingly easy to navigate on foot, and the excellent metro is quicker and more efficient than many local buses. Unlimited travel for one day costs £3.20.

NORTHUMBERLAND

Relatively unknown to international visitors and for that matter a good number of Brits, Northumberland offers wild, empty spaces, a rugged coastline, acres of empty beaches and some magical little islands. Inland you'll find vast expanses of forested land, much of it a dedicated national park, its horizons dotted with the jagged remains of immense fortifications that speak of centuries of bloody conflict, mostly with the Scots.

The most significant of these ruins is Hadrian's Wall. Brainchild of Roman Emperor Hadrian in AD 122, it stretches from Newcastle to Bowness-on-Solway near Carlisle and was the northern frontier of the empire for almost 300 years. It was superseded in Norman times by dozens of castles and fortified houses, some of which remain largely intact. You'll stumble upon some of these by hiking in the wild and empty **Cheviot Hills** in **Northumberland National Park**, but take good care, these are wild regions and the weather can turn nasty. Check **Visit Northumberland** (www.visitnorthumberland.com) for further regional information.

Berwick-Upon-Tweed & Around

☎ 01289 / pop 26,000

A good stopover before heading up to Scotland, Berwick-upon-Tweed sits on the northern tip of England. The historic site of Scottish–English strife for centuries, it's now a peaceful market town set amid some beautiful countryside. Tourist information is available from the **TIC** (☎ 330733; www.berwickonline.org.uk; 106 Marygate; ⏲ 10am-5pm Mon-Sat, 11am-4pm Sun), which has a free town guide with accommodation listings.

SIGHTS & ACTIVITIES

While the town is pretty and its intact Elizabethan **wall** offers a scenic walk, the best attractions lie outside.

Dominating the coastal skyline, the stunning **Bamburgh Castle** (☎ 01668-214515; adult/concession/child £6/5/2.50; ⏲ 11am-5pm Mar-Oct) was the seat of Northumbria's Angle kings and remains one of the most impressive castles in the British isles. The present 11th-century structure (restored in the 19th century) was a Norman stronghold that survived many sieges, and holds an interesting collection of art and weaponry.

SLEEPING & EATING

Berwick is the main accommodation hub in the area.

Berwick Backpackers (☎ 331481; www.berwickbackpackers.co.uk; 56 Bridge St; dm/d £15/20) Occupying a top location only five minutes from the bus and train stations and close to several good restaurants and pubs, this recently refurbished place is a great budget option.

Old Vicarage Guest House (☎ 306909; www.oldvicarageberwick.co.uk; Church Rd, Tweedmouth; B&B s/d £30/50) Just south of the river, this friendly place offers cosy, if slightly old-fashioned, rooms.

BRITAIN

Amaryllis (☎ 331711; 5-7 West St; lunch mains £4-7, dinner mains £10-16) A cosy café and a creditable restaurant offering fresh home-made fare, including some decent veggie options such as wild mushroom risotto.

GETTING THERE & AWAY

Berwick is on the main London to Edinburgh train line and several trains arrive daily from each city (from London £109, 3½ hours; from Edinburgh £16, 45 minutes). The main local bus for travellers is bus 501, which runs to/from Alnwick via Bamburgh; call ☎ 0870 608 2608 for information.

Alnwick

☎ 01665 / pop 7700

A good alternative Northumberland base to Berwick is the pretty market town of Alnwick with an endearing, cobbled town centre, a **TIC** (☎ 510665; 2 The Shambles) that's open year-round and a huge medieval **castle** (☎ 510777; adult/child £7.50/free; ⏲ 11am-5pm Apr-Oct), which contains a sumptuous interior and a surprisingly good collection of Italian art including Titians and Canalettos. The TIC can help with accommodation in the area and there are several B&Bs along Bondgate without.

Hadrian's Wall

Rome's most ambitious engineering project, the surviving sections of this 73-mile wall, built to repel marauding tribes from Scotland, are mightily impressive to this day. The most spectacular section of this World Heritage Site is between Hexham and Brampton. You can now walk and cycle its length along Hadrian's Wall Path. Local TICs sell guides with full details and maps of the path.

Chesters Roman Fort (☎ 01434-681379; adult/concession £3.80/2.90; ⏲ 9.30am-6pm Apr-Sep, 10am-4pm Oct-Mar), near Chollerford, is a well-preserved fortification that includes an impressive bathhouse. Its museum displays a fascinating array of Roman sculptures and drawings found in the area.

Housesteads Roman Fort (☎ 01434-344363; adult/concession £3.80/2.90; ⏲ 10am-6pm Apr-Sep, 10am-4pm Oct-Mar), northeast of Bardon Mill, is the area's most dramatic and popular ruin. The carefully preserved foundations include a famous latrine, which offered ancient users some great views over the Northumbrian countryside.

Roman Army Museum (☎ 01697-747485; adult/concession £3.90/3.50; ⏲ from 10am, seasonal closing times Feb-Nov) offers a graphic reconstruction of military life, including a cool virtual reality flight over a reconstructed Hadrian's Wall.

SLEEPING

Corbridge, Hexham, Brampton and Haltwhistle make ideal bases for exploring the wall, and are stuffed with B&Bs and a number of cheap, convenient YHA hostels. The following selection starts in the east.

Greenhead Youth Hostel (☎ 016977-47401; greenhead@yha.org.uk; Greenhead, Brampton; dm £11.95; ⏲ Apr-Oct) A charming chapel-conversion beside a babbling brook, with better facilities than most. It's 3 miles west of Haltwhistle station, and is also served by the trusty bus 685 and the White Star bus 185 from Carlisle. Opening hours vary, so call ahead.

Once Brewed Youth Hostel (☎ 0870 770 5980; oncebrewed@yha.org.uk; Military Rd, Bardon Mill; dm £13.95; ⏲ daily Feb-Nov, Mon-Sat Feb & Oct, Mon Mar & Nov)

WORTH A DETOUR

While you're near the coast make time for two of Northumberland's islands if you can. The star attraction is the holy island of **Lindisfarne**, a serene, enchanting place with some important religious and historical heritage, including a castle and an ancient **Benedictine Priory** (☎ 01289-389200; adult/concession £3.60/2.70; ⏲ 10am-6pm Apr-Sep, 10am-4pm Oct-Jan, 10am-4pm Sat & Sun only Feb-Mar).

An early site of Christian worship in the British Isles, it was also one of the early victims (AD 793) of the Viking raids. The island is reached by a causeway at low tide (see www.lindisfarne.org.uk for tide times). Although often overrun with tourists in summer, this seat of Anglo-Saxon Christianity rediscovers its tranquillity at most other times.

Also worth a trip are the **Farne Islands**, a seabird sanctuary teeming with puffins, guillemots, razorbills, terns, shags, cormorants and eider ducks, oh, and a large colony of grey seals. For information on a range of excellent tours contact **Billy Shiel's Boat Trips** (☎ 01665-720308).

Modern, equipped, next to a TIC and 3 miles from Housesteads Roman Fort. Northumbria bus 685 (from Hexham or Haltwhistle stations) drops you at Henshaw.

Holmhead Guest House (☎ 016977-47402; www.bandbhadrianswall.com; Castle Farm, Hadrian's Wall; s/d £43/66) A picturesque old farmhouse built from stones pillaged from the wall. The rooms are on the small side, but the hosts are experts on local Roman life and can help you plan trips around the area.

GETTING THERE & AWAY

The Newcastle to Carlisle train line has stations at Hexham, Haydon Bridge, Bardon Mill, Haltwhistle and Brampton, but not all trains stop at all stations. There are hourly buses from Carlisle and Newcastle on bus 685. From June to September the hail-and-ride Hadrian's Wall Bus links Hexham, Haltwhistle and Carlisle with the main sites. Call Hexham **TIC** (☎ 01434-652220).

NORTHWEST ENGLAND

Popular culture, the arts, music and big nights out on the town are the major attractions in the southern part of this decidedly urban corner of England, a sprawl of conurbations that sprang from the Industrial Revolution running from Merseyside (Liverpool) to the Humber River. The area was, and in many ways still is, the working-class heartland of England. It's a decidedly urban landscape dominated by the bright lights of Liverpool and Manchester, although there are some important exceptions, including historic walled Chester, which makes a good starting point for North Wales and the Lake District, the latter a complete contrast and the most beautiful corner of England.

MANCHESTER

☎ **0161 / pop 390,000**

Two historical double acts neatly encapsulate Manchester's modern history, for this is where Mr Rolls met Mr Royce and where Mr Marx worked with Mr Engels on the *Communist Manifesto*. The former duo epitomises Manchester's key role as a centre of innovation and engineering excellence since the early days of the Industrial Revolution, while the latter highlights the labour often harshly exploited to realise its achievements. Manchester's era as the crucible of industrialisation and political ferment is long behind it, however, and what remains is a lively, modern city with ample public space and art, strikingly juxtaposed modern and Victorian architecture, and a buzzing nightlife, including a vibrant gay scene. Visitors will find plenty to do and see, and can get around easily by foot or public transport.

Orientation & Information

The University of Manchester lies to the south of the city centre (on Oxford St/Rd). To the west of the university is Moss Side, a ghetto still dogged with high unemployment and a thriving drug trade – avoid. Victoria train station caps the city in the north.

The **TIC** (☎ 0871 222 8223; www.visitmanchester.com; Town Hall Extension, Lloyd St, St Peter Sq; 🕑 10am-5.30pm Mon-Sat, 10.30am-4.30pm Sun & bank holidays) also has branches in Terminals 1 and 2 at the airport. Internet access is available at **easyEverything** (☎ 832 9200; St Anne's Sq).

Sights & Activities

Explore the city centre on foot and you'll find some grand Victorian architecture, most notably in Albert Sq, home of the enormous Victorian Gothic Town Hall, designed by Albert Waterhouse (of London's Natural History Museum fame) in 1876.

Further south, the Castlefield district offers a pleasing mosaic of solid old civic structures, warehouses, Roman ruins, serene canalside paths and pubs next to soaring modern skyscrapers, such as the new Hilton tower.

The area also contains the excellent **Museum of Science & Industry** (☎ 832 2244; Liverpool Rd, Castlefield; admission free, exhibitions adult/child £5/3; 🕑 10am-5pm), offering vivid, interactive displays on the city's once proud textile and engineering industries, and featuring some excellent live demonstrations of industrial weaving and working steam engines. If you only visit one museum in Manchester, make it this one.

The **Manchester Art Gallery** (☎ 234 1456; cnr Nicholas & Mosley Sts; admission free; 🕑 10am-5pm Tue-Sun) houses an impressive collection covering everything from early Italian, Dutch and Flemish painters to Gainsborough, Blake, Constable and the Pre-Raphaelites.

Out in Manchester's rapidly regenerating **Quays** area (take the Metrolink to either

Broadway or Harbour City), the excellent and free **Imperial War Museum** (☎ 836 4000; Trafford Wharf Rd, Trafford Park; 10am-6pm; Harbour City Metrolink) is a cut above the usual armoury for war anoraks, projecting 20ft-high short films on the walls that explore the impact of war on the lives of everyday people.

Also in the Quays is the architecturally bold **Lowry Complex**, with two theatres and a number of free galleries (one devoted to the complex's namesake LS Lowry, visual chronicler of urban working-class landscapes and their 'matchstick' denizens).

You may begin to understand why fans of the city's most famous football club treat its home as hallowed ground if you head to the **Manchester United Football Museum** (☎ 0870 442 1994; www.manutd.com; Old Trafford stadium; museum only adult/child £5.50/3.75, with tour £7.50/5). The entertaining hour-long tours of changing rooms and sacred turf run every 10 minutes. Call or email ahead, as tour times depend on match days and times. Your only chance of getting a ticket to an actual game is to go to the box office early on match day and wait with thousands for the handful of cancelled tickets to be released.

Sleeping

The TIC can arrange accommodation for a £2.50 booking fee, plus a 10% deposit.

YHA Manchester (☎ 839 9960; manchester@yha.org.uk; dm adult/under 18yr £20.95/15.95) Across the road from the Museum of Science & Industry in the Castlefield area (well signposted), this hostel has over 140 beds and full facilities.

Hatters (☎ 236 9500; www.hattersgroup.com; 50 Newton St; dm £15-17, s/d £30/45;) The best low-priced option is equidistantly located between the train and coach stations in the city centre, and offers 200 beds, cheap high-speed Internet access, no lockout, plus a full restaurant and laundry facilities.

Ox (☎ 839 7740; www.theox.co.uk; 71 Liverpool Rd; d from £45) Next to the Museum of Science & Industry you'll find reasonably priced rooms upstairs from this pub/restaurant. The rooms nearest the bar can be noisy.

Mitre Hotel (☎ 834 4128; www.mitrehotel.com; Cathedral Gates; s/d/f £52/65/85) The location (beside Manchester Cathedral and Arndale) and the charm (sloping 200-year-old floors and simple, plain but welcoming rooms) make this family-owned place your best midrange bet in town.

Eating

The most distinctive restaurant zones are Chinatown in the city centre and Rusholme in the south, called the Curry Mile for its plethora of Indian restaurants, but cafés and restaurants cover the city centre, as well.

Chinatown is bounded by Charlotte, Portland, Oxford and Mosley Sts, and it has a number of restaurants, mostly, but not exclusively, Chinese.

Basement (☎ 237 1832; 24 Lever St; mains £2-3; noon-6pm Wed-Sat, noon-3pm Sun) Ludicrously cheap organic and vegan fare, including tasty jacket potatoes and fresh juices, are the reason to come to this excellent community-run, not-for-profit café. That and the free Internet access. Don't forget to tip your volunteer staff.

Café And (☎ 834 1136; 74-76 High St; sandwiches £3) A café, record store and quirky interiors shop in the up-and-coming Northern Quarter, Café And serves fresh, inexpensive wraps and warming soups.

Tampopo (☎ 819 1966; 16 Albert Sq; mains £6.50-9) Near the Town Hall in smart, contemporary surroundings you'll find this excellent Pan-Asian canteen serving affordable noodle, dumpling, yakitori and satay dishes.

Le Mont (☎ 605 8282; Levels 5 & 6, Urbis, City Gardens; 2-course lunch £15, mains £21-26; lunch & dinner Mon-Fri, lunch Sat) For dinner with a view and few compromises on ingredients, quality (or price). Dishes might include butter-fried skate wings with Morecombe Bay shrimps, or saffron risotto with lobster pieces in a cognac cream sauce.

Drinking

There are several places to drink close to the canal in Castlefield. We recommend:

Dukes 92 (☎ 839 8646; 2 Castle St) High ceilings and outdoor seating for sunny days.

Britons Protection (☎ 236 5895; 50 Great Bridgewater St) A convivial little pub serving a selection of real ales and an extensive range of single malt whisky.

Bar Centro (☎ 835 2863; 72 Tib St) In the ever-cool Northern Quarter, this bar has an alternative vibe and makes a great place to kick off a big night out.

Entertainment

The glory days of acid house, ecstasy-fuelled house and the loose-limbed, guitar-backed Madchester sound may have faded, but Manchester still parties hard and offers a huge choice to clubbers.

Following are two abiding Manchester stalwarts (by the ephemeral standards of clubland).

Music Box (☎ 236 9971; 65 Oxford St; admission £5-12; 🕑 Wed-Sat) An intimate club, leaning towards jagged, hard-edged house.

Sankey's Soap (☎ 661 9085; Jersey St, Ancoats; admission free-£11; 🕑 Fri & Sat) Much larger and slightly more mainstream, Sankey's hosts the biggest names from the international clubbing firmament.

Getting There & Away

Manchester International Airport (MAN; 489 3000; www.manchesterairport.co.uk) is 10 miles south of the city centre and has flights to more than 100 destinations, including Amsterdam, Berlin, Dublin, Nice, Paris and Prague. Domestic services with **BMI** (www.bmi.co.uk) include London Heathrow (from £28, 50 minutes), Aberdeen (from £48, one hour) and Inverness (from £60, one hour).

There are many coach links with the rest of the country. National Express operates out of Chorlton St train station in the city centre to almost anywhere you'll want to go, including London's Victoria Station (£21 return, 4½ hours, seven to nine daily) and Edinburgh (£24.50, 6½ hours, about five daily).

Piccadilly is the main station for trains to and from the rest of the country, although Victoria serves Halifax and Bradford. Both train stations are linked by **Metrolink** (☎ 0845 748 4950). There are frequent services to London (£92, 2¾ hours, hourly) and Liverpool (£8.30, 45 minutes to one hour, three hourly).

Getting Around

The free buses 1 and 2 make travelling anywhere in the city centre a breeze. Routes and schedules are available from the TIC. For general inquiries about local transport, including night buses, phone ☎ 228 7811 from 8am to 8pm. A Day Saver ticket (£3) covers travel throughout the Great Manchester area on bus, train and Metrolink. Manchester's Metrolink light-railway (tram) makes frequent connections between Victoria and Piccadilly train stations and G-Mex (for Castlefield). Buy tickets from machines on the platforms.

CHESTER

☎ 01244 / pop 80,000

One of the oldest cities in England, Chester oozes historical appeal and is well worth a day trip. Ringed by the most complete city walls in Britain (much of its 2 miles is the original Roman construction), its streets are lined with ancient timber-framed houses. Make time to stroll the walls and to nose around the unusual two-level shopping streets (known as the Rows, and thought to date back as far as the post-Roman period). Unsurprisingly, Chester attracts hordes of summer visitors, but it's big and bustling enough in its own right to avoid being hollowed out entirely by tourism.

Orientation & Information

Built in a bow formed by the Dee River, the walled city centre is now surrounded by suburbs. The train station is a 15-minute walk from the city centre; go up City Rd, then turn right onto Foregate at the large roundabout.

The **TIC** (☎ 402111; www.chestercc.gov.uk; Town Hall) is just opposite the cathedral, while the **Chester Visitor Centre** (☎ 351609; tis@chestercc.gov.uk; Vicar's Lane) can book your accommodation, and then keep you busy for days with guided walks, brass rubbing, ghost hunting and even a wall patrol with fully clad Roman legionaries.

Sights & Activities

The present **Chester Cathedral** (☎ 324756; admission £2) was originally a Saxon minster, and with its cloisters, showcases the most complete monastic complex in Britain.

The **Dewa Roman Experience** (☎ 343407; Pierpoint Lane; adult/concession/child £3.95/3.50/2.25; 🕑 9am-5pm) is an interactive museum. Its simulated archaeological dig and reconstruction of typical Roman street life is especially great for kids, but, honestly, who doesn't want to try on a set of Roman armour?

Sleeping & Eating

Sleeping options inside the city walls are rare, although numerous good-value B&Bs line Hoole Rd, the road into the city from the M53/M56.

Chester Backpackers (☎ 400185; www.chesterbackpackers.co.uk; 67 Boughton St; dm/s/d £14/20/38; 💻) The only real budget choice in Chester, five minutes from both the train station and the city centre, is small, friendly but rather

BRITAIN

cramped (the tiny 18-bed dorm in particular). The en suite singles and doubles are basic but good value.

Recorder House Hotel (☎ 326580; www.recorderhotel.co.uk; 19 City Walls; s/d/tr from £45/70/85) Top spot in town, right on the city walls, this delightful Georgian inn overlooks the Dee River. Some of the homy rooms feature four-poster bedsteads.

Katie's Tea Room (☎ 400322; 38 Watergate St; tea & scones £3, lunches £4-6; 9am-5pm Tue-Sat) A cosy, stone-walled, wood-beamed little nook ideal for a light refreshment break.

Francs (☎ 317952; 14 Cuppin St; dinner mains £8-10, 3-course lunch £11; lunch & dinner) Rib of sirloin, mustard roasted and served with a red wine gravy or rustic, hearty 'rillettes de porc' with onion chutney are typical of the honest, flavoursome fare served in this avowedly Francophone little 'coin de France'.

Getting There & Around

Chester has excellent transport connections, especially to and from North Wales.

National Express has numerous connections with Chester, including Birmingham (£10.20, 2½ hours, four daily), and on to London (£21, 5½ hours), Manchester (£6.20, 1¼ hours, three daily), Liverpool (£6.10, one hour, four daily) and Llandudno (£9, 1½ hours, departs once daily at 4.55pm). For many destinations in the south or east, it's necessary to change at Birmingham; for the north, change at Manchester.

For information on local bus services ring **Chester City Transport** (☎ 602666). Local buses leave from Market Sq behind the Town Hall.

Any bus from the train station goes into the city centre. There are numerous trains to Manchester (£10.30, one hour, hourly); Liverpool (£4.30, 40 minutes, half-hourly); Holyhead (£16.40, two hours, approximately hourly), via the North Wales coast, for ferries to Ireland; Shrewsbury (£7.10, one hour, hourly in the morning); and London's Euston station (£56.20, 2½ to three hours, almost hourly, last one at 7.30pm). Phone ☎ 0845 748 4950 for details.

LIVERPOOL

☎ 0151 / pop 510,000

Visually more striking than Manchester, with some fantastic architecture, a grand waterfront facing the broad Mersey estuary, towering cathedrals and a busy nightlife, infectiously friendly Liverpool is on the up. Formerly a down-at-heel city trying to evolve from economic depression following its industrial and maritime decline, Europe's City of Culture for 2008 is busily polishing and patching itself for the occasion. Of all northern England's cities, Liverpool has perhaps the strongest sense of its own identity, one closely tied with the sporting totems of Liverpool and Everton football teams, and, of course, with its most famous sons, the Beatles.

Orientation & Information

Lime St, the main train station, is just to the east of the city centre. The National Express coach station is on the corner of Norton and Islington Sts, slightly northeast of the train station. The bus station is in the city centre on Paradise St. The city is fairly compact, but a steepish hill lies between the Albert Dock and the eastern part of the city centre.

Occupying the same building as the information centre in charge of the 2008 Year of Culture celebrations, the **TIC** (☎ 233 2008; www.visitliverpool.com; The 08 Place Whitechapel; 9am-5.30pm Mon-Sat, 10.30am-4.30pm Sun) also has a branch inside the Maritime Museum (both book accommodation). You can log on at **CafféLatte.net** (☎ 709 9683; 4 South Hunter St; per 30 min £1; 9am-6pm).

Sights & Activities

A £100 million renovation helped make **Albert Dock** (☎ 708 8854; all museums admission free; from 10am), deservedly, Liverpool's number one tourist attraction, housing several outstanding museums.

The **Merseyside Maritime Museum** (☎ 4784499; 10am-5pm) is Liverpool's best museum, with several absorbing exhibition spaces on the city's maritime heritage. Don't miss the ones covering the slave trade and the Atlantic War against the Nazis.

Tate Gallery Liverpool (☎ 702 7400; 10am-6pm Tue-Sun & bank holiday Mon) won't thrill if you've already visited its London counterpart, but it's well represented by a roll call of 20th-century artistic talent all the same.

For many, a visit to Liverpool wouldn't be complete without a Beatles pilgrimage. A sanitised version of the rise of Liverpool's most famous sons it may be, but the **Beatles Story** (☎ 709 1963; Britannia Vaults, Albert Dock; adult/

child £7.95/5.45; 10am-5.50pm) still pulls in the punters and includes a re-creation of the famous Cavern Club, which also hosts live music. It's also the departure tour for the rather more worthwhile **Magical Mystery Tour** (709 3285; www.caverncitytours.com; tickets £11.95; tours from the main TIC/Beatles Story 2.10pm/2.30pm, also 11.40am/noon during summer, weekends & holidays), which takes passengers by a psychedelic bus to the actual Penny Lane and Strawberry Fields (you know, where the banker never wore a mac in the pouring rain).

Liverpool's two cathedrals, looming either side of Hope St, are both well worth visiting. The modern concrete lantern, brightly lit at night, of the **Metropolitan Cathedral of Christ the King** (709 9222; Mount Pleasant; 8am-6pm Mon-Sat, 8am-5pm Sun) contains a wonderfully serene and uplifting space for worship, washed with a celestial blue when the sun lights the stained glass. The massive neo-Gothic **Liverpool Cathedral** (709 6271; Hope St; 8am-6pm) is the largest church in England, and offers unrivalled views across the city and estuary from its 100m-high **tower** (adult/child £4.25/2.50; 11am-5pm Mon-Sat).

Sleeping

Swanky new boutique independents and international chains just keep coming but, alas, the choices are still pretty limited at the mid and budget ranges. For help with accommodation, ring 0845 601 1125.

Embassie Hostel (707 1089; www.embassie.com; 1 Falkner Sq; dm 1st night £13.50, subsequent nights £12.50) Named for its former life as the Venezuelan consulate, this comfortable hostel is a labour of love for its owners, a former backpacker and his father, who provide a comfortable environment, summer barbecues on the patio, and free coffee, tea and toast.

YHA Liverpool International (0870 770 5924; liverpool@yha.org.uk; 25 Tabley St, Wapping; dm adult/under 18yr £20.95/15.95; P) Large, smart, modern and boasting a full complement of facilities including 24-hour Internet access, games room and laundry, this hostel also occupies a handy location right near all the sights, bars and museums in and around Albert Dock.

International Inn (709 8135; www.internationalinn.co.uk; 4 S Hunter St; dm/tw £15/36; P) Close to the city centre, off Hardman St, the International is well equipped with a café, kitchen and games room.

Aachen Hotel (709 3477; www.aachenhotel.co.uk; 89 Mount Pleasant; s/d £42/50, s with shared bathroom £32) The decidedly old-fashioned rooms (and often rather tacky fittings) are more than compensated for by the friendly service and the generous breakfasts. Reasonable value overall.

Feathers Hotel (709 9655; feathershotel@feathers.co.uk; 117 Mount Pleasant; s/d £47/75) Part of a chain but managing to avoid feeling too much like one, Feathers offers spacious, burgundy-carpeted, beechwood-panelled rooms and a good buffet breakfast.

Eating

Good new places, from inexpensive cafés to fine dining restaurants, are springing up all the time and dining out in Liverpool has never been better. The area around Hope St is really buzzing, as is the up-and-coming Ropewalks/Chinatown district.

Flannagan's Apple (231 1957; 18 Mathew St; pub meals £5) In the city centre, the famed Flannagan's Apple won't win culinary prizes, but it's cheap and fun.

Everyman Bistro (708 9545; 5-9 Hope St; mains £6-8; noon-midnight Mon-Sat) With freshly made food, this eatery offers great value with soups and salads starting at £2, a reasonable list of beers and wines and some good veggie options.

Tea Factory (708 7008; Fleet St; snacks £2.50-4.50, mains £6-11; 11am-midnight Mon-Sat) Iron girders, brick walls and a long, long bar lend this bar-cum-bistro in a former tea factory an air of cool. The international menu is wide and eclectic, including bangers and mash, steak and chips, lamb tagine, pizza and chilli con carne.

Alma De Cuba (709 7097; St Peter's Church; tapas £2.50-5, mains £11-21; lunch & dinner Mon-Sat) A wonderfully atmospheric space in a stylishly converted church with a very cool bar and Latin American flavours, such as jalapeno rib-eye steak or calamari with saffron rice and grilled prawns.

60 Hope St (707 6060; 60 Hope St; 2-course set lunch £14, mains £15-24; lunch Mon-Fri, dinner Mon-Sat) Featuring modern European food, such as confit duck leg with garlic mash, or foie gras ballotine with apple jelly and toasted brioche, 60 Hope St is one of Liverpool's premier restaurants. It offers a fine dining menu as well as good-value bistro lunch deals.

PARTY TIME IN LIVERPOOL

The city has spent the last few years limbering up for two years of cultural events, carnivals, races, celebrations and some good, hard partying. It all starts in 2007, when it will celebrate its 800th birthday (based on exactly what event isn't clear). This is just the preamble, however, to 2008 when Liverpool celebrates its status as European City of Culture, a partly EU-funded year extravaganza of art, dance, performance, music and theatre events, led by former–artistic director Robyn Archer. In 2008 world-renowned conductor Sir Simon Rattle will return to the Royal Liverpool Philharmonic Orchestra. The start of the 2008 Tall Ships Race will also begin here in 2008. For more details of the events in store and the artistic programme, visit **08 Liverpool** (www.liverpool08.com).

Drinking & Entertainment

The old Beatles stamping ground of Mathew St is still a good place to go for a night out. Slightly southwest of Bold, Seel and Slater Sts you'll stumble on an amazing array of clubs and pubs catering to most punters.

Philharmonic Dining Room (☎ 709 1163; cnr 36 Hope & Hardman Sts) Built in 1900 by the shipwrights who fitted out the ocean-going liner *Lusitania,* the Philharmonic is one of Britain's most extraordinary pubs. The interior is resplendent with etched glass, stained glass, wrought iron, mosaics and ceramic tiling, and wingback armchairs. Even the men's loo is a heritage-listed marble marvel.

Baby Cream (☎ 702 5823; Atlantic Pavillion) Down at Albert Dock the cool-and-it-knows-it Baby Cream is a great style bar despite its rather sniffy airs and graces. You can select your own compilation CD from a menu of tracks to take home.

Heebie Jeebies (☎ 708 7001; 80-82 Seel St; admission £4-7; Mon-Sat) Depending on the night, you'll find house, techno, '50s rock and roll and funk. Admission is free on Thursday, when you get a bit of everything.

Everyman Theatre (☎ 709 4776; Hope St) One of the best repertory theatres in England, with a proud roll call of past and present talent.

Getting There & Away

Liverpool John Lennon International Airport (LPL; 0870 129 8484; www.liverpooljohnlennonairport.com) is 7 miles southeast of the city centre and operates services to more than 50 destinations. European destinations include Amsterdam, Barcelona, Dublin, Madrid, Nice, Paris and Rome, while domestic routes include Aberdeen and Inverness with Ryanair (both from £12, one hour), Southampton (from £22, 1¼ hours) with Flybe and Belfast with easyJet (from £15, 35 minutes).

There are National Express coach services linking Liverpool to most major towns, including London's Euston station (£22, 5¼ hours, four daily), Manchester (£5.80, 1½ hours, hourly) and Chester (£4.70, 45 minutes, half-hourly).

Direct trains head to London's Euston station (£94.50, three hours, hourly) and Chester (£4.30, 45 minutes, half-hourly).

Getting Around

The 500 bus service runs at least twice an hour (£2.80 one-way) between Liverpool's Lime St station and the airport. After midnight the N86 service links the airport with the main bus station at Queen Sq.

Public transport in the region is coordinated by **Merseytravel** (☎ 236 7676). For day visitors, a Saveaway ticket costs £3.70; it offers all-day off-peak travel on buses, trains and ferries throughout the region.

Liverpool has no less than 18 bus companies operating, and these change every few months. Most services are quite frequent. Check the Queen St Travel Centre in the main TIC for up-to-date information.

The ferry across the Mersey, started 800 years ago by Benedictine monks but made famous by Gerry & the Pacemakers, still offers one of the best views of Liverpool. Boats depart from Pier Head ferry terminal, just north of Albert Dock. Special 50-minute commentary cruises (adult/concession/child £4.95/3.60/2.75) run year-round, departing hourly from 10am to 3pm Monday to Friday and until 6pm Saturday and Sunday. Phone **Mersey Ferries** (☎ 330 1444) for more information.

LAKE DISTRICT

A dramatic landscape of dizzying ridges and huge lakes gouged out by the slow march of Ice Age glaciers, the Lake District is the most beautiful corner of England. It may not be the wildest place on earth but for bucolic England it's as extreme as it gets. The Lake District is home to both the highest peak (Scaffell; 978m) and the wettest inhabited place (Seathwaite; over 3m of rain a year), so take the changeable weather conditions seriously if you venture into the hills.

Even in summer, hikes on the mountains – with their swiftly changing microclimates – have proved fatal to experienced hikers. Before heading out, prepare thoroughly and check the **Weatherline** (☎ 0870 055 0575).

The lakes are easily England's most popular wilderness, attracting 14 million-plus visitors yearly who come for some serious hiking or to potter gently around the tea shops, stone cottages and souvenir shops of the countless pretty Lakeland villages.

The awe-inspiring geography of the place shaped Wordsworth's real and literary persona, and resonates powerfully in his poetry. His houses, Dove Cottage at Grasmere and Rydal Mount, between Ambleside and Grasmere, are literary shrines.

Orientation & Information

The two principal bases for the Lake District are Keswick in the north (particularly for walkers) and Windermere/Bowness in the south. Kendal, Coniston, Ambleside, Grasmere and Cockermouth are less-hectic alternatives. All these towns have hostels, numerous B&Bs and places to eat.

Ullswater, Grasmere, Windermere, Coniston Water and Derwent Water are usually considered the most beautiful lakes, but they also teem with boats. Wastwater, Crummock Water and Buttermere are equally spectacular and less crowded.

The shelves of the local TICs groan with guidebooks and brochures, and both Windermere and Keswick have decent information centres with free accommodation booking services. If you're staying for a few days, buy any one of the dozens of books featuring information on walking, bicycling, travelling with children or driving. Those interested in Wordsworth's life might enjoy reading his sister Dorothy's *Grasmere Journals*.

The numerous walking/climbing shops in the region, particularly in Ambleside and Keswick, are good sources of local information. **George Fisher** (☎ 01768-772178; 2 Borrowdale Rd, Keswick) is an excellent shop for stocking up on equipment.

There are over 25 YHA hostels in the region, many of which can be linked by foot. The YHA also runs a shuttle-bus between eight of the Lake District hostels during summer. Call ☎ 0870 770 5672 for more information.

Getting There & Away

National Express buses have direct connections from Windermere to Preston (£9.90, two hours, two daily) and Keswick to Birmingham (£31, 3½ hours, two daily).

For all public transport inquiries, contact Traveline. There are several important bus services in the Lake District, including bus 555, which runs about once an hour year-round and links Lancaster with Carlisle, via Kendal, Windermere, Ambleside, Grasmere and Keswick. Bus 599 is an open-top bus that runs during the summer between Windermere and Ambleside, via Grasmere. Bus 505 runs from Ambleside to Coniston via Hawkshead. Ask about Day Ranger (£7.50) and Explorer tickets (four/seven days £17/25), which can offer better value than single tickets.

Windermere is at the end of a spur off the main train line between London's Euston station and Glasgow. Trains arriving include from London (£109, four hours, at least six daily) and Manchester (£13.30, two hours, 15 daily).

Getting Around

Walking or cycling are the best ways to get around, but bear in mind that conditions can be treacherous and the going can be very, very steep. **Country Lanes** (☎ 01539-444544; www.countrylanes.co.uk; train station, Windermere) rents many bike sizes from £15 per day.

Windermere, Bowness & Around

☎ 015394 / pop 8500

Thanks to the railway, the Windermere/Bowness conglomerate is the largest tourist town in the Lake District. The two towns are quite strung out, with lakeside Bowness a 30-minute downhill walk from Windermere. The excellent **TIC** (☎ 46499; Victoria St, Windermere) is conveniently located near the train station at the northern end of town, and also offers Internet access for £3 per 30 minutes.

Offering beds in small rooms and plenty of camaraderie, **Lake District Backpackers Lodge**

(☎ 46374, 44725; High St; dm £12.50) is 200m from the train station. Call ahead for reservations. Popular with families, **Windermere YHA** (☎ 0870 770 6094; High Cross, Bridge Lane, Troutbeck; dm adult/under 18yr £13.95/9.95) commands a scenic spot on Lake Windermere in the Troutbeck Valley. Two miles from the train station, numerous buses run past Troutbeck Bridge, and in summer the hostel sends a minibus to meet trains.

Windermere is dry stone wall-to-wall with B&Bs, which the TIC can book for you. The great-value **Bendan Chase** (☎ 45638; www.placetostaywindemere.co.uk; 1 College Rd; s/d from £25/40; P) is close to the train station and offers an excellent cooked breakfast. Almost opposite, **Applegarth Hotel** (☎ 43206; www.lakesapplegarth.co.uk; College Rd; s/d from £40/80) offers Victorian wood-panelled splendour and comfort. Guests have free use of a nearby country club pool, gym, sauna and gym.

There are plenty of decent cafés and tearooms in town, but the steady flow of visitors means the restaurants in both townships don't have to try very hard to win custom, so they don't. The **Bowness Kitchen** (☎ 45529; 4 Grosvenor Tce, Bowness) serves tasty toasted sandwiches for £3, while **Old England** (☎ 42444; Church St; afternoon tea £11) offers a refined riverside spot for afternoon tea. If you have wheels, your best bet for a square meal is to head up into pretty Troutbeck, about 5 miles north of Windermere for excellent food, roaring fires and lip-smackingly good cask ale at the **Queen's Head** (☎ 31274; www.queensheadhotel.com; mains £6-10, 3-course set menu £11).

Grasmere

☎ 015394 / pop 2700

Occupying a graceful spot amid meadows, woods and water, Grasmere is a delight. Unsurprisingly, in summer it's completely overrun. Information can be found at the **TIC** (☎ 35245; Red Bank Rd; ⌚ 9.30am-5.30pm).

The homes of poet William Wordsworth are the major attractions here. **Dove Cottage & Museum** (☎ 35544; adult/concession/child £6.20/5/3.90; ⌚ 9.30am-5.30pm) is where Wordsworth wrote much of his most important work, including *The Prelude*, his powerful, exultant paean to an awakening mind nurtured by and mirrored in the natural drama of the area. The admission price includes a worthwhile guided tour. Just south of Grasmere, it's accessible by bus 555 or 599 (in summer).

Grasmere Butharlyp How YHA (☎ 0870 770 5836; grasmere@yha.org.uk; Easedale Rd; dm adult/under 18yr £15.50/10.95) is just north of the village. The lovely **How Foot Lodge** (☎ 35366; www.howfoot.co.uk; d from £64) is right next to Dove Cottage, which is on the main A591 Kendal–Keswick Rd, just south of Grasmere village.

Keswick

☎ 017687 / pop 5000

Keswick is an important walking centre, and although the town centre lacks the green charm of Windermere, the lake is beautiful. The **TIC** (☎ 72645), in the middle of the pedestrianised town centre, books accommodation and runs guided tours of the area.

The **Youth Hostel** (☎ 0870 770 5894; keswick@yha.org.uk; dm adult/under 18yr £17.50/13.95), a short walk down Station Rd from the TIC, is open most of the year. Station Rd has a number of B&Bs, most charging around £26 per person.

Kendal

☎ 01539 / pop 27,100

On the eastern outskirts of the Lake District National Park, Kendal is a lively town and makes for a good base from which to explore the region. The **TIC** (☎ 725758; Highgate) is in the Town Hall.

Kendal Youth Hostel (☎ 0870 770 5892; kendal@yha.org.uk; 118 Highgate; dm adult/under 18yr £17.50/13.95; ⌚ daily mid-Apr–Aug, Tue-Sat Sep-early Apr) is right next door to the Brewery, a wonderful arts complex with a theatre, cinema and bar/bistro.

Kendal is on the branch train line from Windermere to Oxenholme, with connections north to Manchester and south to Lancaster and Barrow-in-Furness.

Ambleside

☎ 015394 / 2600

Towards the northern end of Windermere, Ambleside is a good base for both hikers and village amblers.

Rydal Mount (☎ 33002; adult/student/child £4.50/3.50/1.50; ⌚ 9.30am-5pm Mar-Oct, 10am-4pm Nov-Feb), where Wordsworth lived for 37 years, still contains many effects from the poet's life.

Right beside the water, the vast **Ambleside YHA** (☎ 32304; www.yha.org.uk; Waterhead; dm/d £20/38) is an excellent flagship hostel, with a few (very popular) doubles, some family rooms and a full range of facilities, including a shuttle bus service to carry you or your rucksack around the area.

At the tip of Windermere, the **Wateredge Inn** (☎ 32332; www.wateredgeinn.co.uk; s/d from £50/70) offers some great accommodation housed in two converted 17th-century fishermen's cottages.

CARLISLE

☎ **01228 / pop 73,000**

Most visitors pass quickly through unremarkable Carlisle, a transport hub for five scenic railway journeys (see the boxed text, below) to Northumberland, Dumfries & Galloway, the Borders (the beautiful Scottish border counties) and the Lake District.

The well-stocked **TIC** (☎ 625600; Old Town Hall; 9.30am-5.30pm Mon-Sat, 10am-4pm Sun May-Aug & Easter, shorter hr Mon-Sat & closed Sun rest of year) has information for visiting Hadrian's Wall. A general information office at the train station is open until 7.30pm.

National Express coaches have services to London (£30.50, 6½ hours, two daily), Edinburgh (£15.60, 3¾ hours, three daily), Glasgow (£15.40, two hours, 10 daily) and Manchester (£21.50, three hours, three daily). A Rail Link coach service runs to Galashiels in the Scottish Borders.

You can get almost anywhere easily by rail from Carlisle, most notably London's Euston station (£99, four hours, 15/10 daily in summer/winter).

SCOTLAND

Don't make the mistake of thinking Scotland is just a continuation of England. It's a dramatically different, proudly independent country that's worth making as much time as you possibly can for in your itinerary. Its vast wilderness areas of wild coast, remote islands, high moorland, vast lochs, stone-hewn villages and snow-capped mountains are an obvious draw outshining and outsizing anything in England or Wales. The array of terrain makes it an outward-bound and adventure-sport enthusiast's playground, and one that's easily accessible from its cities. The principal cities, Edinburgh and Glasgow, are important and thriving centres rich with historical, cultural and social interest.

HISTORY

Scotland's early history is evoked by the ancient standing stones on Lewis (p264), but almost nothing is known about those who lived here around 3000 BC. Roman chroniclers were the first to record the presence of fierce and dogged tribes here who repelled their advance from England after their arrival in 55 BC. After decades of clashes, Emperor Hadrian built his eponymous fortified wall to contain these restive clans.

THE NORTHWEST'S SCENIC RAILWAYS

Carlisle is the terminus for six famous scenic railways that are well worth riding on just for the sheer pleasure of watching such great scenery roll past. Part of the main rail network, they also connect with some important destinations. Most of the following have Day Ranger tickets that allow unlimited travel. Phone ☎ 08457-484950 for timetable details and information on Day Ranger passes.

- **Cumbrian Coast Line** Hugs the coast in a great arc around to Lancaster, with views over the Irish Sea and back to the Lake District.
- **Glasgow–Carlisle Line** The main route north to Glasgow goes through Lockerbie and takes in some grand scenery.
- **Lake District Line** You think the landscape on the north–south main line is the most beautiful yet and then the line branches west just outside Kendal, taking you towards Windermere (your destination) and things get even better.
- **Leeds–Settle–Carlisle Line** (LSC) One of the great engineering achievements of the Victorian railway age, this famous line cuts southeast across the Yorkshire Dales through beautiful countryside. Several stations make good starting points for walks in the Yorkshire Dales National Park.
- **Tyne Valley Line** This scenic line follows Hadrian's Wall to and from Newcastle.

SCOTLAND: EUROPE'S ADVENTURE SPORT CAPITAL?

Scotland is trying to play down its dowdy tartan-and-shortbread image and recast itself as Europe's thrusting young adrenaline sport destination, a kind of New Zealand of the northern hemisphere. While there may be some stiff competition elsewhere, Scotland offers more than enough outdoor thrills to stake a serious claim to the title.

Bored with merely hiking in all that spectacular scenery? Want to gorge jump, surf, snow hole, mountain bike, sea kayak, dive with basking sharks, ice climb, dog sled, kite surf or white-water raft? It's all on offer somewhere in Scotland. Two important centres for such horseplay and rough housing are Aviemore and Fort William.

At the foot of the Cairngorms, about 25 miles southeast of Inverness, **Aviemore** offers great trekking, biking, white-water rafting and, yes, dog sledding. The adventure centre at **Glenmore Lodge** (☎ 01479-861256; www.glenmorelodge.org.uk) is a good place to start.

Fort William is fast becoming an important centre. It has hosted the Mountain Bike World Cup, the Wilderness Arc adventure race and the annual run, yes run, up Ben Nevis. Nearby Kinlocheven boasts an excellent climbing centre, the **Ice Factor** (☎ 01855-831100; www.icefactor.co.uk), complete with climbing walls and a massive indoor freezer containing 9m of ice wall to get your crampons into. For these and other activities in the area, see **Outdoor Capital of the UK** (www.outdoorcapital.co.uk).

The west coast is another good area for adventure sports, including **Oban**, offering some excellent wreck diving and sea kayaking. Contact the local TIC for further details (see p260). A good general resource may be found at **Adventure in Scotland** (www.visitscotland.com/adventure).

Scandinavian tribes, who dominated northern Europe for much of the first millennium, were the next big threat, causing the Celts from Ireland to arrive and form an alliance with the local Picts. The alliance began a unifying process that evolved into the concept of nationhood. Scone became the first capital, and the Stone of Destiny, now at Edinburgh Castle (p246), was launched into legend as a symbol of Scottish nationhood.

By the start of the next millennium the Normans had conquered England, but all they could do in Scotland was influence affairs. The outlying regions remained a law unto themselves, culminating in the first full-scale invasion from England in 1296. The resulting 1328 Treaty of Northampton recognised Robert the Bruce as king of an independent country.

By the 16th century Scotland was a strongly nationalistic society with its own close links to Europe and a visceral hatred of the English. It boasted universities at St Andrews, Glasgow, Edinburgh and Aberdeen (there were only two in England at the time), reflecting a rigorous and pioneering intellectual climate. The period's distinctive and imposing architecture can be seen today at palaces at Holyrood (p246) and Stirling (p256).

When the childless Queen Elizabeth I died in 1603, Mary Stuart's son united the crowns of Scotland and England, becoming James I of England and James VI of Scotland. In 1707, after complex bargaining and a modicum of double-dealing, England's government persuaded the Scottish Parliament to agree to the formal union of the two countries under a single parliament. But after a rebellion was suppressed at the Battle of Culloden (1746), the English set out to destroy the clans, prohibiting Highland dress, weapons and military service. They also cleared entire villages from the land to make way for sheep grazing, forcing thousands of families to abandon their traditional homes – the remains of destroyed houses from this time can still be seen throughout the Highland region.

While its political power had been forcibly removed, Scotland's cultural and intellectual life flourished throughout the 18th century, and Edinburgh in particular became an important centre of Enlightenment thinking. Philosophers Adam Smith and David Hume along with seminal Scottish poet Robert Burns influenced generations of thinkers, and the city became one of Europe's most beautiful examples of the new rational approach to architecture. Much of this heritage is still intact, making modern-day Edinburgh one of the world's most picturesque cities.

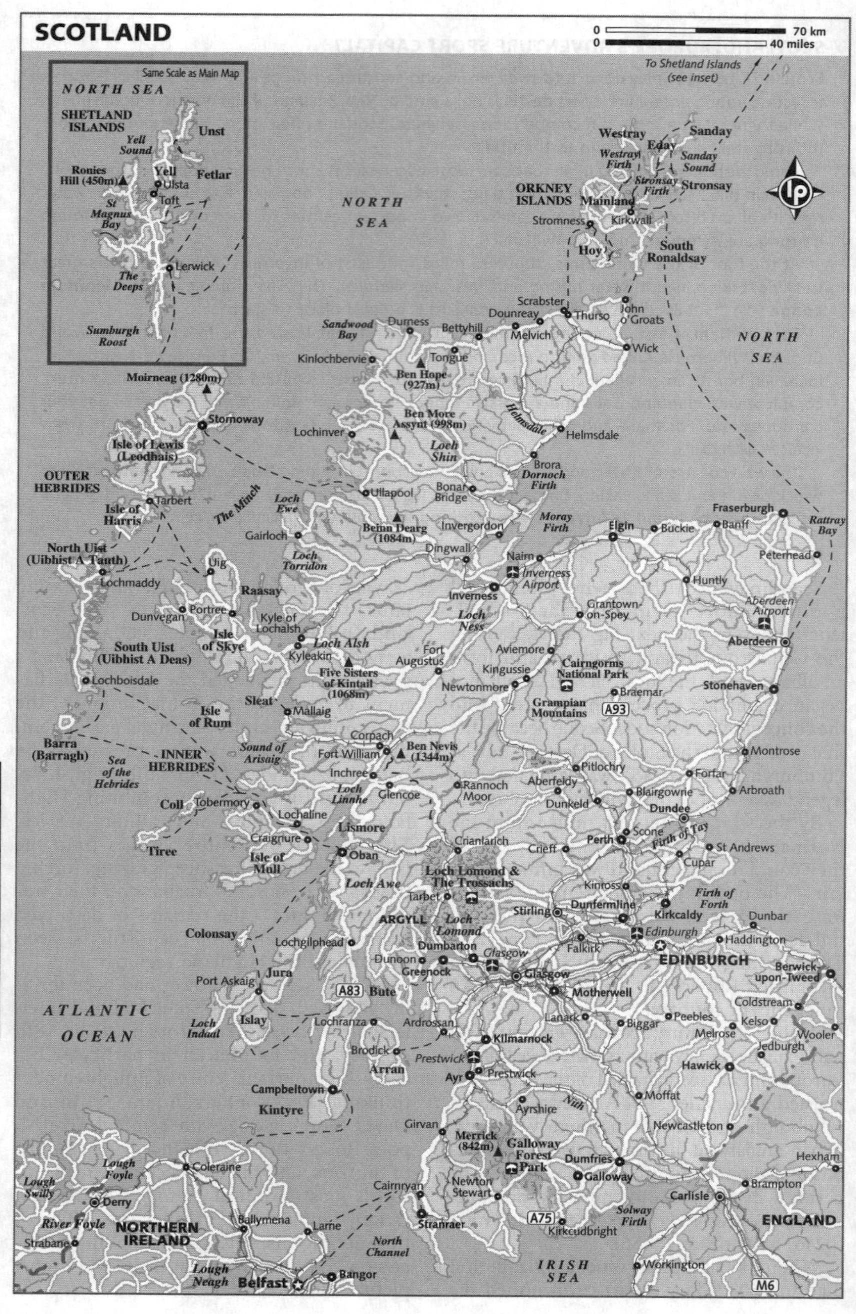
SCOTLAND
0 70 km
0 40 miles
Same Scale as Main Map
NORTH SEA
SHETLAND ISLANDS
Unst
Yell Sound
Ronies Hill (450m)
Yell
Fetlar
Ulsta
Toft
St Magnus Bay
Lerwick
The Deeps
Sumburgh Roost
To Shetland Islands (see inset)
Westray
Eday
Sanday
Westray Firth
Sanday Sound
Stronsay Firth
Stronsay
ORKNEY ISLANDS
Mainland
Kirkwall
Stromness
Hoy
South Ronaldsay
NORTH SEA
Scrabster
Thurso
Dounreay
John o'Groats
Durness
Bettyhill
Melvich
Wick
Sandwood Bay
Kinlochbervie
Tongue
Ben Hope (927m)
Moirneag (1280m)
Stornoway
Ben More Assynt (998m)
Lochinver
Loch Shin
Helmsdale
Isle of Lewis (Leodhais)
Brora
Dornoch Firth
OUTER HEBRIDES
Ullapool
Bonar Bridge
Tarbert
Isle of Harris
The Minch
Loch Ewe
Beinn Dearg (1084m)
Invergordon
Moray Firth
Elgin
Buckie
Banff
Fraserburgh
Rattray Bay
Gairloch
Dingwall
Nairn
Peterhead
North Uist (Uibhist A Tauth)
Uig
Loch Torridon
Inverness Airport
Huntly
Lochmaddy
Raasay
Inverness
Grantown-on-Spey
Aberdeen Airport
Dunvegan
Portree
Kyle of Lochalsh
Loch Ness
Isle of Skye
Aberdeen
South Uist (Uibhist A Deas)
Loch Alsh
Fort Augustus
Aviemore
Cairngorms National Park
Kyleakin
Kingussie
Lochboisdale
Five Sisters of Kintail (1068m)
Newtonmore
Braemar
Stonehaven
Sleat
Grampian Mountains
A93
Isle of Rum
Mallaig
Barra (Barragh)
INNER HEBRIDES
Sound of Arisaig
Corpach
Fort William
Ben Nevis (1344m)
Montrose
Sea of the Hebrides
Pitlochry
Inchree
Aberfeldy
Forfar
Loch Linnhe
Glencoe
Rannoch Moor
Blairgowrie
Arbroath
Coll
Tobermory
Dunkeld
Dundee
Lochaline
Lismore
Scone
Tiree
Craignure
Crianlarich
Crieff
Perth
Firth of Tay
St Andrews
Isle of Mull
Oban
Cupar
Loch Awe
Loch Lomond & The Trossachs
Kinross
Tarbet
Firth of Forth
ARGYLL
Loch Lomond
Stirling
Dunfermline
Kirkcaldy
Dunbar
Colonsay
Edinburgh
Lochgilphead
Dumbarton
Falkirk
Haddington
Glasgow
EDINBURGH
Dunoon
Greenock
Berwick-upon-Tweed
Port Askaig
Jura
Glasgow
A83
Bute
Motherwell
ATLANTIC OCEAN
Coldstream
Loch Indaal
Islay
Lochranza
Lanark
Peebles
Biggar
Kelso
Ardrossan
Melrose
Wooler
Kilmarnock
Jedburgh
Brodick
Arran
Prestwick
Hawick
Ayr
Prestwick
Campbeltown
Nith
Moffat
Kintyre
Ayrshire
Girvan
Newcastleton
Merrick (842m)
Galloway Forest Park
Lough Foyle
Coleraine
Dumfries
Hexham
Lough Swilly
Galloway
Cairnryan
Newton Stewart
Brampton
Derry
Carlisle
River Foyle
NORTHERN IRELAND
Ballymena
Larne
Stranraer
A75
Solway Firth
ENGLAND
Strabane
Kirkcudbright
North Channel
Lough Neagh
IRISH SEA
Workington
Belfast
Bangor
M6

The 19th century saw Scotland take a leading role in the Industrial Revolution, with Glasgow becoming an international powerhouse of commerce and the 'second city' in the British Empire after London. While generations of Scots now turned to heavy industry for their employment, Scottish industrialists moved around the world, leaving a lasting legacy as far afield as Canada and Australia.

Scotland escaped much of the devastation that saw English cities reduced to rubble in WWII. A gradual industrial decline followed the war, along with a growing feeling that England was increasingly treating its brother nation as a second-class citizen.

Nationalistic fervour grew in the 1970s, with the Scottish Nationalist Party (SNP) using its newly won seats in the British Parliament as a soapbox to call for devolution. Separatist demands became louder throughout the 1980s following economic recession and cuts to government services. Following through on its election promise, Britain's new Labour government of 1997 announced a referendum on devolution among the Scots. The result was overwhelmingly in favour.

Representatives to the new Scottish Parliament – which has limited but increasing law-making powers – were elected in 1999. Plans for a new parliament building (p246) were quickly announced. Massively over budget, woefully late and dogged by serious subsequent teething troubles – Scotland's electorate must be praying the story of its parliament building isn't a sign of things to come in the brave new world of devolved government.

ENVIRONMENT

The Land

The Scottish landscape is divided into the Southern Uplands, Central Lowlands and the Highlands. The first is characterised by low, heather-covered hills; the second by the coal and oil deposits that fuelled the country's economic growth; and the third by sword-shaped lochs, broad valleys and dramatic mountain peaks. Loch Awe is the longest loch (24 miles), Ben Nevis is the highest peak (1343m) and there are 790 islands around the coast. While Scotland covers only half as much landmass as England (about 491,000 sq miles), almost 80% of Britain's coastline lies north of the English border.

Wildlife

Scotland is blessed with some amazing wildlife, from red deer, the endangered red squirrel, otters and an array of rare bird life, including ospreys, golden eagles, kites and puffins. There are even reindeer (introduced into the Cairngorms) and the odd fierce (but small and reclusive) wildcat. Not so wild, but hugely endearing, are Scotland's Highland Cattle (imagine a normal cow, but dressed up in a thick rug of ginger shag pile and sporting giant comedy Viking horns).

National Parks & Conservation Areas

Huge areas of Scotland are naturally beautiful and 12.8% of the country is designated as areas of Specific Scientific Interest (SSI). This includes several categories of protected land, including 73 National Nature Reserves, 40 National Scenic Areas and 51 Wetlands Areas of International Importance. There are also two national parks, Cairngorms National Park (p258) and Loch Lomond & the Trossachs National Park. In addition, Scotland houses several Unesco-designated World Heritage Sites, including Edinburgh, New Lanark and Orkney.

Environmental Issues

Despite its outstanding natural beauty, Scotland has historically suffered serious challenges to its natural environment. Native forests and traditional farms were cleared by the English to make way for sheep grazing in the 18th century, and the 1980s witnessed the introduction of giant non-native conifer plantations that destroyed huge areas of delicate ecosystems.

While the long-term effects of these are difficult to calculate, global warming is already taking its toll: Scotland's tentative skiing industry is further under threat due to decreasing snowfalls; the Cairngorm Railway (p258), built to service the slopes despite a huge environmentalist outcry, may become a white elephant if snowfall levels continue to decrease.

Blessed with endless opportunities to generate power through tidal, hydro and wind power, Scotland offers huge potential to generate renewable energy. While hydroelectric power generation has been well established here, harnessing tidal power is at the early experimental stages and the increased use of wind power is being held back by controversy over planning, in addition to objections from those who see the wind turbines as an intrusion on the landscape.

PEOPLE

The Scottish regard themselves as a separate race occupying the same island as the English and Welsh. While the English proudly label themselves British, the Scots rarely do and mistakenly calling them English won't make you any friends.

Scotland's strong sense of nationalistic pride is partly based on the many influential and conspicuous achievers in its past, including poet Robert Burns, novelist Sir Walter Scott, and an incredible roster of inventors and innovators.

Scotland's population is five million (25 million around the world claim Scottish lineage), with more than 80% living in towns and cities in the Central Lowlands. Only 9% of Britain's population lives in Scotland.

LANGUAGE

Gaelic is spoken here by 80,000 people, mainly in the Highlands and Islands, while Lallans, or Lowland Scots, is spoken (theoretically at least) in the south. It's not unusual to see bilingual road signs, Gaelic shows on TV and Gaelic words used in English conversation. For example, ceilidh (pronounced kay-lay), which translates as 'visit' but now means an evening of dance and live music, is in wide usage. There's an online Scots dictionary at www.scots-online.org.

EDINBURGH

☎ 0131 / pop 440,000

Scotland's proud and historic capital city is a visual delight. Built on a grand scale around two hills, one topped by its impressive castle, the other, called Arthur's Seat, a big chunk of undeveloped mountain seemingly helicoptered in for effect. Among the large, well-proportioned Georgian buildings and the tangle of arches and walkways you'll find a rich haul of excellent museums, galleries, pubs, and entertainment options to suit every taste and budget. History jumps out at you from every turn and every building seems to have its own ghost story. And with the UK's most popular and comprehensive summer festival scene, visitors who plan a brief stopover often end up staying longer.

Orientation

Edinburgh's two most distinctive landmarks are Arthur's Seat, the 251m-high rocky peak southeast of the city centre, and the castle, which dominates Princes St Gardens. The Old and New Towns are separated by Princes St Gardens and Waverley train station. Buildings are restricted to the northern side of Princes St, lined with high-street chains. At the eastern end, Calton Hill is crowned by several monuments, including an incomplete war memorial modelled on the Parthenon, and a tower honouring Nelson. The Royal Mile (Lawnmarket, High St and Canongate) is Princes St's parallel equivalent in the Old Town. The bus station is in the New Town, off the northeastern corner of St Andrew Sq, north of Princes St.

Information

EMERGENCY

Edinburgh Rape Crisis Centre (☎ 556 9437)

INTERNET ACCESS

connect@edinburgh (☎ 473 3800; 3 Princes St; per 15 min £0.50; 🕒 9am-8pm Jul & Aug, 9am-5pm Sep-Jun) Inside the TIC near Waverley train station.

e-Corner (☎ 558 7858; 54 Blackfriars St; per 30 min £1; 🕒 10am-9pm Mon-Sat, 11am-9pm Sun) Fast Internet access.

INTERNET RESOURCES

Eventful Ed (www.eventful-edinburgh.com) Guide to city festivals.

The List (www.list.co.uk) Local listings magazine's events site.

MEDICAL SERVICES

Chemists and pharmacies operate standard shop hours, with 24-hour opening arranged on a rotating basis. Check information in chemist shop windows when closed.

Minor Injuries Unit (☎ 537 1330; Western General Hospital, Crew Rd South; 🕒 9am-9pm) Walk-in clinic for the slightly afflicted.

Royal Infirmary (☎ 536 1000; 51 Little France Cres, Old Dalkeith Rd; 🕒 24hr) For accident and emergency treatment.

MONEY

Amex (☎ 718 2501; 69 George St; 🕒 9am-5pm Mon, Tue & Thu-Sat, 9.30am-5pm Wed)

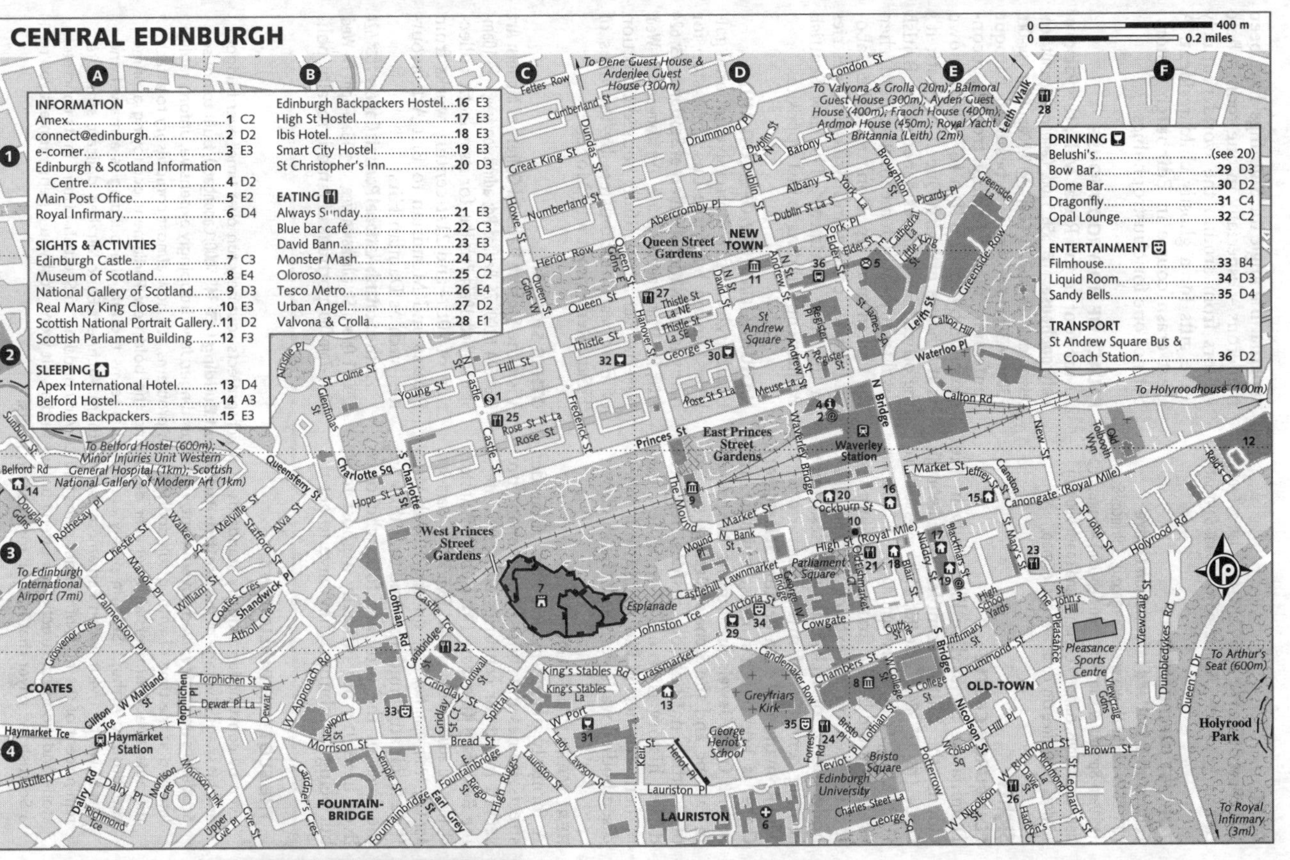
CENTRAL EDINBURGH
0 400 m
0 0.2 miles
INFORMATION
Amex....1 C2
connect@edinburgh....2 D2
e-corner....3 E3
Edinburgh & Scotland Information Centre....4 D2
Main Post Office....5 E2
Royal Infirmary....6 D4
SIGHTS & ACTIVITIES
Edinburgh Castle....7 C3
Museum of Scotland....8 E4
National Gallery of Scotland....9 D3
Real Mary King Close....10 E3
Scottish National Portrait Gallery..11 D2
Scottish Parliament Building....12 F3
SLEEPING
Apex International Hotel....13 D4
Belford Hostel....14 A3
Brodies Backpackers....15 E3
Edinburgh Backpackers Hostel....16 E3
High St Hostel....17 E3
Ibis Hotel....18 E3
Smart City Hostel....19 E3
St Christopher's Inn....20 D3
EATING
Always Sunday....21 E3
Blue bar café....22 C3
David Bann....23 E3
Monster Mash....24 D4
Oloroso....25 C2
Tesco Metro....26 E4
Urban Angel....27 D2
Valvona & Crolla....28 E1
DRINKING
Belushi's....(see 20)
Bow Bar....29 D3
Dome Bar....30 D2
Dragonfly....31 C4
Opal Lounge....32 C2
ENTERTAINMENT
Filmhouse....33 B4
Liquid Room....34 D3
Sandy Bells....35 D4
TRANSPORT
St Andrew Square Bus & Coach Station....36 D2
To Dene Guest House & Ardenlee Guest House (300m)
To Valvona & Crolla (20m); Balmoral Guest House (300m); Ayden Guest House (400m); Fraoch House (400m); Ardmor House (450m); Royal Yacht Britannia (Leith) (2mi)
To Holyroodhouse (100m)
To Belford Hostel (600m); Minor Injuries Unit Western General Hospital (1km); Scottish National Gallery of Modern Art (1km)
To Edinburgh International Airport (7mi)
To Arthur's Seat (600m)
To Royal Infirmary (3mi)
NEW TOWN
OLD-TOWN
COATES
FOUNTAIN-BRIDGE
LAURISTON
Queen Street Gardens
East Princes Street Gardens
West Princes Street Gardens
St Andrew Square
Waverley Station
Haymarket Station
Holyrood Park
Pleasance Sports Centre
Greyfriars Kirk
George Heriot's School
Edinburgh University
Bristo Square
Parliament Square
Esplanade
Princes St
George St
Queen St
Rose St
Thistle St
Leith Walk
Leith St
N Bridge
S Bridge
Waterloo Pl
Calton Rd
Canongate (Royal Mile)
High St (Royal Mile)
Holyrood Rd
Cowgate
Grassmarket
Lothian Rd
Queensferry St
Nicolson St
Lauriston Pl
Candlemaker Row
Johnston Tce
The Mound
Waverley Bridge
Dalry Rd
Haymarket Tce
Morrison St
Shandwick Pl
Palmerston Pl
Heriot Row
Dundas St
Great King St
Cumberland St
Fettes Row
Drummond Pl
London St
Broughton St
Albany St
Abercromby Pl
York Pl
Greenside Row
The Pleasance
St Leonard's St
Dumbiedykes Rd
Queen's Dr
Viewcraig St
Potterrow
Chambers St
Earl Grey St
Fountainbridge
W Approach Rd
Charlotte Sq

POST

Main Post Office (☎ 0845 722 3344; St James Centre, Leith St; 8.30am-5.30pm Mon-Fri, 8.30am-6pm Sat)

TOURIST INFORMATION

Edinburgh & Scotland Information Centre (☎ 0845 225 5121; www.edinburgh.org; 3 Princes St; 9am-8pm Jul & Aug, 9am-5pm Sep-Jun) Accommodation reservations, currency exchange and coach booking services. Offers free city guide and pocket map.

Sights

EDINBURGH CASTLE

Dominating the skyline like a city in the clouds, the hilltop complex of **Edinburgh Castle** (☎ 225 9846; Castle Hill; adult/concession/child £10.30/8.50/4.50; 9.30am-6pm Apr-Oct, 9.30am-5pm Nov-Mar) should be the first stop for any visitor. Perched on an extinct volcano, it's a hodge-podge of architectural styles, representing centuries of myriad historic uses. The Romanesque 11th-century **St Margaret's Chapel** is Edinburgh's oldest building, the **Scottish Crown Jewels** are among the oldest in Europe and the **Stone of Destiny**, symbol of Scottish nationhood, resides here. It's darker history is recorded in a new permanent **Prisoners of War** exhibition, where disembodied wails permeate the shadows.

REAL MARY KING CLOSE

A formerly plague-ridden nest of hidden streets, homes and shops built over and preserved intact for centuries comes to life at the **Real Mary King Close** (☎ 430160; 2 Warriston's Cl, High St; adult/concession/child £8/6/5; 10am-9pm Apr-Oct, 10am-4pm Nov-Mar) on the Royal Mile. It's a fascinating underground tour through the lives of the ordinary folk who once lived here. It's not officially a ghost tour, but being Edinburgh, they have to get the supernatural angle in. 'Sightings' have been numerous – especially in one room where visitors from around the world routinely leave gifts for a ghostly child resident. A great crash course in Edinburgh history, but not one for claustrophobics.

PALACE OF HOLYROODHOUSE

At the foot of the Royal Mile, the **Palace of Holyroodhouse** (☎ 556 5100; Canongate; adult/concession/child £8.80/7.70/4.80; 9.30am-6pm Apr-Oct, 9.30am-4.30pm Nov-Mar) is a beautiful baroque confection mostly dating from a reconstruction by Charles II in 1671. Best known as the home of Mary Queen of Scots, it's the official Scottish residence of the British royal family – which means it's closed when the Queen turns up. Don't miss the elaborate plaster ceiling and Brussels tapestries in the **State Apartments**. The new Scottish Parliament Building is just opposite.

NATIONAL GALLERY OF SCOTLAND

Edinburgh has five impressive national galleries, linked by a free bus. First stop for many is the **National Gallery of Scotland** (☎ 624 6200; The Mound; admission free; 10am-5pm Fri-Wed, 10am-7pm Thu), a beautifully housed collection of European blockbusters by the likes of Titian, Rembrandt and Monet.

OTHER SIGHTS

Visit the **Scottish National Gallery of Modern Art** (☎ 624 6200; 75 Belford Rd; admission free; 10am-5pm Fri-Wed, 10am-7pm Thu) for its eclectic collection of 20th- and 21st-century works from Picasso and Mondrian to Brit Art favourites, such as Damian Hirst.

At the **Scottish National Portrait Gallery** (☎ 624 6200; 1 Queen St; admission free; 10am-5pm Fri-Wed, 10am-7pm Thu) portraits of famous royalty, poli-

THE SCOTTISH PARLIAMENT

Even by construction industry standards in which projects routinely run over time, over budget and hit snags, the saga of the **Scottish Parliament Building** (☎ 348 5000; Canongate), built to house Scotland's newly devolved government, was a humdinger. Jaw-droppingly expensive, unforgivably late and at the time of writing still dogged with problems, it's now almost compulsory to attach the adjective 'controversial' whenever describing the bold new Parliament occupying a prime site close to Arthur's Seat. In purely architectural terms though, the building is a marvel and is well worth a visit (when Parliament is not sitting). Architect Enric Miralles' delicate structure, reminiscent of the hulls of slender ships and cleverly nodding to Scottish history in its concrete, stone and wood construction, is utterly unique and a visit won't cost you a penny (unless you're a Scottish tax payer that is). Call for opening hours.

ticians and celebrities from Mary Queen of Scots to Sean Connery are exhibited.

The **Museum of Scotland** (☎ 247 4422; Chambers St; admission free; ⏲ 10am-5pm Mon-Sat, noon-5pm Sun) offers a thorough telling of Scotland's story from its days as volcanic magma to devolution.

Far from being the gin palace you might expect, the Royal Family's now retired luxury boat, the **Royal Yacht Britannia** (☎ 555 5566; Ocean Terminal, Leith; adult/child £9/5; ⏲ 9.30am-4.30pm Apr-Sep, 10am-3.30pm Oct-Mar), offers some surprisingly clean, elegant Art Deco lines and some insights into Royal life.

Festivals & Events

Unrivalled anywhere else in the UK, the **Edinburgh International Festival** (☎ 473 2000; www.eif.co.uk) takes over the city in August with three weeks of world-class music, dance, drama and opera.

Sitting alongside the official Edinburgh International Festival is the **Edinburgh Festival Fringe** (☎ 226 0000; www.edfringe.com), a semi-alternative arts festival focusing on theatre, comedy and music.

Just to make sure every bed within a 40-mile radius is taken for the whole of August, there's also the **Edinburgh Film Festival** (☎ 228 4051; edfilmfest.org.uk) and a book festival, plus the magnificent **Edinburgh Military Tattoo** (☎ 0870 555 1188; www.edinburgh-tattoo.co.uk), a stirring celebration of pipe bands and pageantry (no really, it's excellent).

While booking ahead is advised for the International Festival and Military Tattoo, tickets for many Fringe shows can often be purchased on the day.

Sleeping

It's essential to book for festival, New Year and peak summer periods, and it's never too early to do so. The TIC can help with reservations (£3); it also has a good free listings brochure, and plenty of options online at **Edinburgh – Inspiring Capital** (www.edinburgh.org/accommodation). Almost all the hostels have better locations than the B&Bs and guesthouses, which are mostly outside the city centre.

BUDGET

St Christopher's Inn (☎ 226 1446; www.st-christophers.co.uk; 9-13 Market St; dm £13-19; 💻) With two bars and proximity to city-centre nightlife, St Christopher's Inn is the party hostel. There is swipe-card entry providing additional security, all dorms have en suite bathrooms and a continental breakfast is included. In addition to all of this, there is a good-value restaurant attached. Book online to receive a discount.

Smart City Hostel (☎ 0870 892 3000; www.smartcityhostels.com; 50 Blackfriars St; dm/tw from £16.50/28.50) This huge new hostel was still a building site when we visited but should be worth checking out by the time you read this. The owners promise a high-end, 620-bed hostel. Should be good, they're spending £10m on it. Facilities include women-only dorms, laundry and café. Linen is included in the price.

Brodies Backpackers (☎ 556 6770; www.brodieshostels.co.uk; 12 & 93 High St, Royal Mile; dm £10-19.50, s/d £35/40; 💻) Brodies occupies two sites (go for the slightly smarter one at number 93, which also has the private rooms). Otherwise the dorms are fine, with superior mattresses and themed rooms that range from *Trainspotting* to traditional tartan, although new carpets in the older block wouldn't hurt.

Edinburgh Backpackers Hostel (☎ 220 1717; www.hoppo.com; 65 Cockburn St; dm £14-20, d/tr/q from £50/64/78) Bright and friendly, close to pubs and nightlife, this hostel is a good bet, with a large TV and pool room, and a few quiet doubles over the road. The shower/bed ratio could be higher.

Also recommended:

High St Hostel (☎ 557 3984; www.scotlands-top-hostels.com; 8 Blackfriars St; dm £11-12.50) With luck a major renovation programme will see the old carpets chucked out and the lingering aroma of stale socks banished forever.

Belford Hostel (☎ 225 6209; www.hoppo.com; 6/8 Douglas Gardens; dm incl breakfast £15-17, d/tr/q from £40/58/79; 💻) A church conversion with an excellent bar lounge. Close to two major galleries and a 10-minute walk from the city centre.

MIDRANGE & TOP END

Dene Guest House (☎ 556 2700; deneguesthouse@yahoo.com; 7 Eyre Pl; s £30-45, d £50-80) Very quiet and rather grand, this guesthouse is located in a high-ceilinged Georgian town house in New Town, about a mile's walk from the city centre.

Ardenlee Guest House (☎ 556 2838; info@ardenlee.co.uk; 9 Eyre Pl; s £30-59, d £50-90) Ardenlee is a short walk from the city centre in a listed Victorian town house. Family-run and informal, breakfast includes vegetarian options.

Ibis Hotel (☎ 240 7000; www.ibishotel.com; 6 Hunter Sq; r £55-77; ❄) Great value for its location, rooms are clean and well equipped (satellite TV, wi-fi), if a little impersonal. It's always popular, so book well ahead at peak times.

Apex International Hotel (☎ 0845 365 0000; reservations@apexhotels.com; 31-35 Grassmarket; r £120-145; P ❄) A cannonball's shot from the castle and close to the lively pubs and restaurants of Grassmarket, the Apex offers plush, modern rooms, with muted décor, wood floors, large beds, and splashes of colour from the throws and cushions. There's also a smart spa, gym and 15m pool.

Lined with solid Georgian town houses, Pilrig St, a 10-minute walk from the city centre, offers about a dozen B&Bs. We recommend:

Balmoral Guest House (☎ 554 1857; www.balmoralguesthouse.co.uk; 32 Pilrig St; s/d from £30/45) Our favourite. Quiet, friendly and homy, with comfortable beds and attractive period décor.

Ayden Guesthouse (☎ 554 2187; www.ayden-edinburgh.com; 70 Pilrig St; s/d from £45/60) Contemporary chic in chocolate and cream tones, with a gourmet breakfast.

Ardmor House (☎ 554 4944; www.ardmorhouse.com; 74 Pilrig St; s/d £45/65) A lovely interior design job, with charming hosts.

Fraoch House (☎ 554 1353; www.fraochhouse.com; 66 Pilrig St; r from £60;) Appealing, with free Internet and wi-fi access and DVD players.

Eating

Offering by far the best selection of dining options in Scotland, Edinburgh has food to satisfy most tastes, although finding real bargain budget food in the city centre isn't easy. The dining scene is quite diffuse and far flung, so there's no one defined foodie area in which to stroll and browse. Many of the city's 700 bars also offer good budget to mid-price meals.

RESTAURANTS

David Bann (☎ 556 5888; 56-58 St Mary's St; mains £8-12; 11am-midnight Tue-Sun) A mastery of flavour and texture, with Asian, Indian and Middle Eastern influences, together with great service in smart, softly lit surroundings make this vegetarian place one of the best restaurants, meat or no meat, in Edinburgh. Vegan options, too.

Urban Angel (☎ 225 6215; www.urban-angel.co.uk; 121 Hanover St; mains £7-13; 8am-midnight Mon-Sat) Fresh bistro and café food, often locally sourced, including pastries, light lunches, brunches and more substantial and polished dishes, such as pheasant with Puy lentils, Savoy cabbage and beetroot salsa. Good veggie options, too.

Blue bar café (☎ 221 1222; 10 Cambridge St; mains £11-16; noon-3pm & 6-10.30pm Mon-Sat) Continental influences with British favourites, creating a menu that mixes Toulouse cassoulet with sticky toffee pudding, although not on the same plate. It's popular with visitors from the Traverse Theatre downstairs.

Oloroso (☎ 226 7614; 33 Castle St; mains £14-24; noon-2.30pm & 6-10.30pm) Accessed via a lift in an anonymous street-level foyer, Oloroso is an Edinburgh foodie favourite, with a smart bar and the best views in town – especially from the terrace. The ever-changing menu features delicately prepared versions of Scottish fare, salmon and game.

CAFÉS

Always Sunday (☎ 622 0667; 170 High St, Royal Mile; mains £4-6; 8am-6pm Mon-Fri, 9am-6pm Sun) This elegant, modern café is the best on offer along the Royal Mile, serving Fair Trade coffee, wheat-free dishes, good light lunches and plenty of vegetarian options.

Monster Mash (☎ 225 7069; 4 Forrest Rd; mains £5-9; 8am-10pm) The greasy spoon café reinvented, Monster Mash serves generous portions of Brit comfort food – fried breakfasts, sausage and mash, shepherd's pie, steak pie – fast and without fuss.

SELF-CATERING

Valvona & Crolla (☎ 556 6066; 19 Elm Row, Leith Walk; 8am-6pm Mon-Sat, 11am-4.30pm Sun) The makings of a luxury picnic, including a great array of cheeses, bread and deli goodies, such as Spanish ham and Scottish smoked salmon, await at this atmospheric old providore.

Self-caterers have easy access to a couple of small urban supermarkets, including **Tesco Metro** (94 Nicolson St; 7am-midnight).

Drinking

The array of pubs and bars is vast, as you might expect from a capital city, tourist hotspot and student town. If you just want to wander, the area around Grassmarket has a few good places in close proximity.

Dragonfly (☎ 228 4543; West Port) A quirky, glam little cocktail bar just far enough off the beaten path to make you feel like you've stumbled on a hidden gem. The bar staff know their cocktails, and the crowd is smart, youngish and friendly.

Dome Bar (☎ 624 8624; 14 George St) Occupying a palatial former bank, the Dome is by far the most magnificent eating and drinking space in town. The food is forgettable, but it's a great place for a drink. The quieter, Art Deco cocktail bar linked to the main bar is great, too. If only the cocktail list were better.

Belushi's (☎ 226 1446; 9-13 Market St; 🕑 noon-1am) Attached to St Christopher's Inn, this place has a ready client base of young party-goers, but the late licence, live music and pumping DJ sets make it worth considering even if you're not sleeping upstairs.

Bow Bar (☎ 226 7667; 80 The West Bow, Victoria St) Small and popular, with a slightly older crowd than other nearby places, you'll find a good real ale and single malt whisky selection at the bar.

Opal Lounge (☎ 226 2275; 51a George St; 🕑 noon-3am) A subterranean-style bar with house beats on the sound system. It's been around a while, but remains as cool as ever, with good wine and cocktail lists. Dress up.

Entertainment

Edinburgh has a frenetic arts and entertainment scene that stretches well beyond the traditional festival period. Pick up fortnightly local magazine the *List* (£2.20) for the latest information on Edinburgh and Glasgow happenings. It usually includes a few coupons with two-for-one offers.

Sandy Bells (☎ 225 2751; 25 Forrest Rd; 🕑 11.30am-1am Mon-Sat, 12.30-11.30pm Sun) This tiny pub is the best spot in the city to experience traditional Scottish music. It has free performances almost nightly and on Sunday afternoons. It fills up quickly on weekends.

Liquid Room (☎ 225 2564; 9c Victoria St; admission £4-8; 🕑 10.30pm-3am Mon-Sat, 11pm-3am Sun) Popular mid-sized club, the subterranean Liquid Room has the best indie night in town on Friday. It's also a good live venue attracting some big rock acts.

Filmhouse (☎ 228 2688; www.filmhousecinema.com; 88 Lothian Rd; admission £5.50) A great independent cinema, Filmhouse's eclectic programme runs the gamut of the classic to the down-right weird. It's also home to the August Edinburgh International Film Festival.

Getting There & Away

AIR

More than 50 airlines, including BA, KLM, Ryanair, easyJet, Flybe and BMI Baby, operate out of **Edinburgh International Airport** (EDI; ☎ 333 1000; www.edinburghairport.com). The number of connections between Edinburgh and other European cities is increasing all the time, including to Amsterdam, Paris and Madrid, while US flights also arrive from New York. There are many arrivals from the rest of the UK – via such hubs as London, Bristol, Birmingham, Cardiff, Luton and Manchester – and from other Scottish cities, including Aberdeen and Inverness.

BUS

National Express and Scottish Citylink services arrive from a multitude of locations throughout the UK at **St Andrew Square Bus & Coach station** (St Andrew Sq), north of Princes St. Citylink arrives from Aberdeen (£17.20, 3¼ hours, hourly), Glasgow (£4.20, 1¼ hours, every 20 minutes) and Inverness (£16.70, four hours, hourly) among others, while National Express services arrive from destinations, such as London (£31, nine to 12 hours, seven daily), Newcastle (£15.20, three hours, three daily) and York (£30.50, 5½ to nine hours, four daily).

New kid on the block, **Megabus** (☎ 01738-639095; www.megabus.com) runs frequent refurbished double-decker bus services to Edinburgh from three Scottish cities (Glasgow, 1½ hours; Dundee, two hours; Perth, 1½ hours). Fares are as low as £1 (plus £0.50 booking fee).

TRAIN

Up to 20 trains run daily from London's King's Cross station (4½ to 5½ hours) and fares vary considerably (for details, see p281). **ScotRail** (☎ 0845 748 4950; www.firstgroup.com/scotrail) runs two northern lines to Edinburgh from Inverness (£34.90, 3½ hours) and Aberdeen (£34.90, 2½ hours), with trains throughout the day. There are trains every 15 minutes from Glasgow (£9.90, 45 minutes).

Getting Around

An Airlink service operated by **Lothian Buses** (www.lothianbuses.co.uk) shuttles between the airport and the city centre (£3, 30 minutes, every 15 minutes). Local buses for travel around the city are operated by Lothian Buses and **First Edinburgh** (www.firstedinburgh.co.uk). Adult fares start at £1; exact change is required. For full information – including details on the night bus system – pick up a free *Edinburgh Travelmap* from the TIC or call Traveline. For a taxi call **Central Taxis** (☎ 229 2468).

GLASGOW

☎ **0141 / pop 630,000**

Not as picturesque as its richer neighbour Edinburgh, the former industrial powerhouse of Glasgow is grittier, edgier and arguably more fun for it. Overflowing with fine museums and galleries, the best nightlife in Scotland and a lively arts scene (kept vibrant and cutting edge by the presence of a good art school), Glasgow also makes a good jumping-off point for the Highlands.

Orientation

The two train stations (Central and Queen St), Buchanan St bus station and the TIC are all within a couple of blocks of George Sq, the city's main public space. Running along a ridge in the northern part of the city, Sauchiehall (*sokky*-hall) St is a busy pedestrian mall, with high street shops at its eastern end and pubs and restaurants to the west. In front of the Royal Concert Hall, it connects with Buchanan St, a second major pedestrian thoroughfare where shops, restaurants and coffee bars collide. The nearby Merchant City area contains street cafés, swanky restaurants and popular bars.

Information

Amex (☎ 222 1401; 115 Hope St; 🕑 8.30am-5.30pm Mon-Fri, 9am-noon Sat)
Central Post Office (47 St Vincent St; 🕑 8.30am-5.45pm Mon-Fri, 9am-5.30pm Sat) Also has currency exchange.
easyInternet (☎ 222 2364; 57 St Vincent St; per hr £1.40; 🕑 24hr)
Glasgow Museums (www.glasgowmuseums.com) A great guide to city museums.
Glasgow Royal Infirmary (☎ 211 4000; 84-86 Castle St; 🕑 24hr) For accident and emergency treatment.
Glasgow TIC (☎ 204 4400; www.seeglasgow.com; 11 George Sq; 🕑 9am-6pm Mon-Sat Oct-Apr, 9am-7pm Mon-Sat, 10am-6pm Sun May, Jun & Sep, 9am-8pm Mon-Sat, 10am-6pm Sun Jul & Aug) Also has currency exchange.
Munro (☎ 339 0012; 693 Great Western Rd; 🕑 9am-9pm) Late-opening chemist.

Sights

KELVINGROVE ART GALLERY & MUSEUM

Closed for what feels like forever, **Kelvingrove Art Gallery & Museum** (☎ 287 2699; Argyle St; admission free; 🕑 10am-5pm Mon-Thu & Sat, 11am-5pm Fri & Sun) reopened in 2006. Contained in this Victorian fairy-tale of a stately home is a magpies' nest of oddities – suits of armour, a giraffe, a Spitfire fighter plane hanging from the ceiling. There's also a lot of serious art – Renaissance art from the likes of Botticelli, plenty of impressionists, including Van Gogh, Whistler and Monet, works from local boy Charles Rennie Mackintosh and, in pride of place, Salvador Dali's *Christ of St John of the Cross*. If you only visit one museum in Glasgow, make it this one.

GALLERY OF MODERN ART

Glasgow's **Gallery of Modern Art** (☎ 229 1996; Queen St; admission free; 🕑 10am-5pm Mon-Thu & Sat, 11am-5pm Fri & Sun) is a most accessible and very popular collection of works housed in a beautiful neoclassical building in the city centre. It's a good introduction to some of Scotland's finest contemporary artists and has some quirky, humorous installations. There is art here for both aesthetes and people who wouldn't normally set foot in a gallery.

ST MUNGO'S MUSEUM OF RELIGIOUS LIFE & ART

At **St Mungo's** (☎ 553 2557; 2 Castle St; admission free; 🕑 10am-5pm Mon-Thu & Sat, 11am-5pm Fri & Sun) you'll find a fascinating exploration of major world religions, including medieval and modern stained-glass windows and a magnificent bronze sculpture of Shiva. The **Gallery of Religious Life** illuminates disparate beliefs relating to birth, marriage, death and the afterlife.

GLASGOW NECROPOLIS

Looming on a hill above the nearby cathedral, Glasgow's 'City of the Dead' **Necropolis** (☎ 287 3961; Wishart St; admission free; 🕑 dawn-dusk) is like no other cemetery in Scotland. Undulating turf and minor headstones on its lower reaches give way to giant Victorian temples built to house some of the city's great and good in the afterlife. A fascinating glimpse into the vanity and wealth of a bygone age, there are also some of the best views of the city from between the crooked tombs at the top.

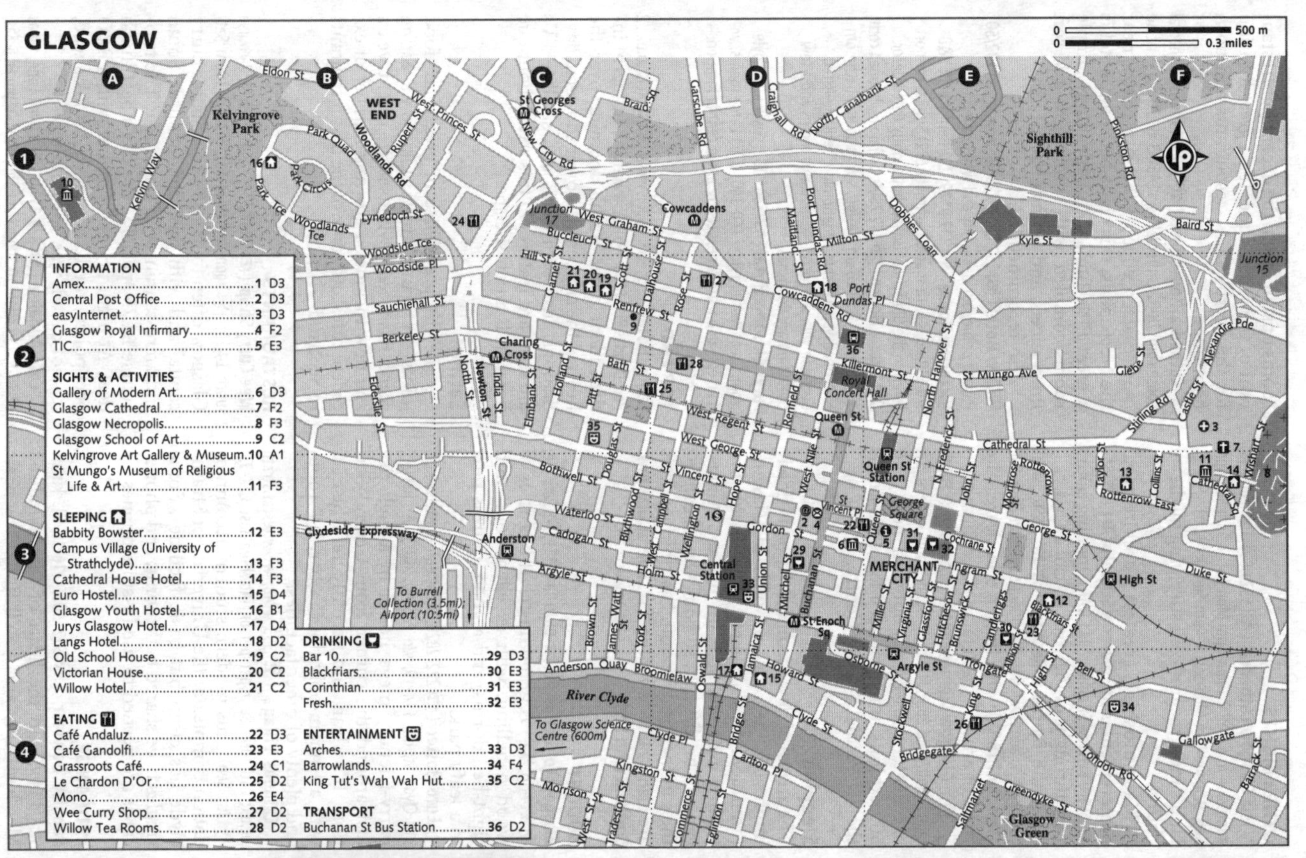
GLASGOW
0 500 m
0 0.3 miles
INFORMATION
Amex....1 D3
Central Post Office....2 D3
easyInternet....3 D3
Glasgow Royal Infirmary....4 F2
TIC....5 E3
SIGHTS & ACTIVITIES
Gallery of Modern Art....6 D3
Glasgow Cathedral....7 F2
Glasgow Necropolis....8 F3
Glasgow School of Art....9 C2
Kelvingrove Art Gallery & Museum....10 A1
St Mungo's Museum of Religious Life & Art....11 F3
SLEEPING
Babbity Bowster....12 E3
Campus Village (University of Strathclyde)....13 F3
Cathedral House Hotel....14 F3
Euro Hostel....15 D4
Glasgow Youth Hostel....16 B1
Jurys Glasgow Hotel....17 D4
Langs Hotel....18 D2
Old School House....19 C2
Victorian House....20 C2
Willow Hotel....21 C2
EATING
Café Andaluz....22 D3
Café Gandolfi....23 E3
Grassroots Café....24 C1
Le Chardon D'Or....25 D2
Mono....26 E4
Wee Curry Shop....27 D2
Willow Tea Rooms....28 D2
DRINKING
Bar 10....29 D3
Blackfriars....30 E3
Corinthian....31 E3
Fresh....32 E3
ENTERTAINMENT
Arches....33 D3
Barrowlands....34 F4
King Tut's Wah Wah Hut....35 C2
TRANSPORT
Buchanan St Bus Station....36 D2
To Burrell Collection (3.5mi); Airport (10.5mi)
To Glasgow Science Centre (600m)
River Clyde
Kelvingrove Park
Sighthill Park
Glasgow Green
WEST END
MERCHANT CITY

BRITAIN

OTHER SIGHTS

Visit **Glasgow Cathedral** (☎ 552 6891; Cathedral Sq; admission free; 9.30am-6pm Mon-Sat, 1-5pm Sun Apr-Sep, 9.30am-4pm Mon-Sat, 1-4pm Sun Oct-Mar), Scotland's most magnificent surviving medieval church.

Mackintosh's greatest architectural achievement is the **Glasgow School of Art** (☎ 353 4526; 167 Renfrew St; adult/child £5/4). Opening hours vary throughout the year, so call ahead.

At the **Burrell Collection** (☎ 287 2550; Pollok Country Park; admission free; 10am-5pm Mon-Thu & Sat, 11am-5pm Fri & Sat) you'll find an eclectic treasure trove of artworks, artefacts and ephemera.

The **Glasgow Science Centre** (☎ 420 5000; Pacific Quay; adult/child £6.95/4.95; 10am-6pm) offers an excellent, hands-on day out with more than 500 exhibits in its Science Mall. Don't miss the 3D Virtual Science Centre.

Sleeping

The arrival of new accommodation is slowly improving the range on offer in Glasgow (admittedly from a pretty low base), but finding a decent B&B in July and August can still be difficult, so book well ahead for the summer peak season. Last-minute deals are also available via the TIC site at **Glasgow: Scotland with Style** (www.seeglasgow.com).

BUDGET

Glasgow Youth Hostel (☎ 0870 004 1119; 7-8 Park Tce; dm £14-16;) A grand hostel. It has acres of wood panelling, with excellent four- and eight-bed dorms, and a good address next to a leafy park.

Euro Hostel (☎ 222 2828; www.euro-hostels.co.uk; 318 Clyde St; dm £14-19, s/d £35/40;) A large, party-friendly mega hostel in a high-rise just around the corner from Central Station. It's clean and recently refurbished, with a women-only floor, a bar, TV room and plenty of other facilities.

Campus Village (☎ 553 4148; www.rescat.strath.ac.uk; Cathedral St; r per person incl breakfast £27-33; Jun-Sep) This modern student accommodation complex at the University of Strathclyde has clean but basic facilities. Some singles have shared bathrooms, and phonecards are needed to use in-suite phones.

MIDRANGE

Babbity Bowster (☎ 552 5055; 16-18 Blackfriars St; s/d £40/55) In the heart of the revitalised Merchant City area you'll find a few basic rooms upstairs from the decent pub/restaurant of the same name. It's a great location for the nearby cafés, restaurants and posh boutiques.

Cathedral House Hotel (☎ 552 3519; www.cathedralhouse.com; 28-32 Cathedral Sq; s £45-53, d £70-85) At the quiet eastern edge of the city centre near the Necropolis, this eight-bedroom hotel is a great little find, with appealingly simple rooms complete with comfy beds and soft linen sheets, and a plush bar.

Also recommended:

Willow Hotel (☎ 332 2323; 228 Renfrew St; s/d £32/50) Past its prime, but clean, tidy and well located.

Victorian House (☎ 332 0129; 212 Renfrew St; B&B s/d £39/60, s with shared bathroom £32) Similar comfort levels to the Old School House, but slightly dated décor.

Old School House (☎ 332 7600; oschoolh@hotmail.com; 194 Renfrew St; B&B s/d £40/60, s with shared bathroom £32) Good-value accommodation in a heritage-listed Georgian villa with quiet, comfortable rooms and a few contemporary flourishes.

Jurys Glasgow Hotel (☎ 334 8161; www.jurysdoyle.com; Great Western Rd; r £60-140;) Large rooms, wi-fi access, an on-site fitness centre and a central location.

TOP END

Langs Hotel (☎ 333 1500; www.langshotels.co.uk; 2 Port Dundas Pl; r £100-195) A swanky, modern, independent hotel brashly looming over the heart of the city centre. Power showers, PlayStations, lush bathrooms and satellite TVs are standard features in this stylish boutique hotel, as is an on-site spa.

Eating

Despite the prevalence of greasy fast-food joints on many streets, Glasgow's eating scene has been revitalised in recent years and now includes a growing number of excellent cafés and some of the best restaurants in Scotland.

RESTAURANTS

Wee Curry Shop (☎ 353 0777; 7 Buccleuch St; 2-course lunch £4.75; noon-2pm Mon-Sat, 5.30-10.30pm Sat) Glasgow often touts itself as Britain's curry capital and with this fabulous little South Indian restaurant who can argue? The two-course £4.75 special is the city's best lunch deal. At night prices jump, but with a BYO beer policy, you'll save anyway. Book ahead, it's not called 'wee' for nothing.

Café Andaluz (☎ 339 1111; 2 Cresswell Lane; tapas £2.75-5; noon-10.30pm Mon-Thu, noon-11pm Fri & Sat,

6-10.30pm Sun) Once you've fashioned some earplugs from the Manchego cheese to keep out the interminable muzak, you'll be ready to enjoy the hot and cold tapas among ersatz (but impressive all the same) Moorish surroundings.

Mono (☎ 552 9458; 12 King's Ct; mains £2.50-6; ⌚) The sign on the beer tap reading 'Fosters is not vegan, sorry' says it all at this endearing, scruffy and inexpensive veggie café, bar, health-food shop and left-field record store. Tofu jerk with basmati rice, hummus, falafel and veggie burgers are some of the options. Skip the Fosters for the excellent Fraoch Heather Ale. Mono is off King's St.

Café Gandolfi (☎ 552 6813; 64 Albion St; mains £6-14; 9am-11pm Mon-Sat, 11am-11pm Sun) A Glasgow institution serving fine European brasserie food (made with Scottish produce), good breakfasts, coffee and pastries, and now with a new bar upstairs. Mains might include smoked venison with daupinoise potatoes, or pancakes with Stornoway black pudding and mushrooms. It's popular, so book ahead for dinner.

Le Chardon D'Or (☎ 248 3801; 176 West Regent St; 2-/3-course lunch £15.50/18.50, dinner mains £12-18; ⌚ lunch Mon-Fri, dinner Mon-Sat) The flavoursome old-school French cuisine, such as fried scallops with pancetta lardons or confit of lamb with linguine and thyme jus, make sense when you know that chef Brian Maule (who's name you'll see emblazoned everywhere among the towering lilies, dark brown leather banquettes and crisp white linen) is the former head chef at London's estimable Le Gavroche.

CAFÉS

Willow Tea Rooms (☎ 332 0521; 217 Sauchiehall St; lunches £3-7; ⌚ 9am-5pm Mon-Sat, 11am-4.30pm Sun) Designed by Charles Rennie Mackintosh, this must-see Art Nouveau café is often packed at peak times, so plan to eat early or late to avoid the crowds. The afternoon tea is a local legend. The deluxe room is the place to sit, with its high-backed Mackintosh chairs.

Grassroots Café (☎ 333 0534; 93-97 St Georges Rd; mains £5-12; ⌚ 10am-10pm) A laid-back restaurant using mainly organic ingredients on its eclectic vegetarian menu. Homy comfort dishes like veggie bangers and mash are popular, with the daily soup special often worth checking out. Organic beers – including the delicious Lomond Gold – or filling fruit smoothies are the perfect accompaniments.

Drinking

Glasgow has plenty of street cafés – the piazza around the Gallery of Modern Art is a great spot for sitting outside and watching the world go by – and it's full of great pubs, too. There are dozens of interesting spots just waiting to be discovered.

Fresh (☎ 552 5532; 51-53 Cochrane St; juices & smoothies £2.50; ⌚ 8am-7pm Mon-Fri, 9am-6pm Sat, 11am-6pm Sun) The city centre's only fresh juice bar has the décor of a day spa to complement its wide range of fruity pick-me-ups.

Blackfriars (☎ 552 5924; 36 Bell St; ⌚ noon-midnight Mon-Sat, 12.30pm-midnight Sun) Glasgow's best traditional pub couldn't be more laid-back, attracting a healthy mix of locals, students and visitors.

Corinthian (☎ 552 1101; 191 Ingram St; ⌚ 11am-3am) Even if you don't want a drink, pop in for the amazing, lofty, elaborate Victorian interior of this former bank. It's an incredible statement of the wealth and status Glasgow enjoyed in its heyday as second world city of the British Empire. These days three stylish bars and a nightclub occupy this incredible space.

Bar 10 (☎ 572 1448; 10 Mitchell Lane; ⌚ 10am-midnight Mon-Sat, noon-midnight Sun) The brainchild of Ben Kelly, creator of Manchester's legendary Hacienda Club, this older venue still beats most of Glasgow's would-be trendy drinking holes. Capturing the essence of a busy, metropolitan Euro-bar, there are drinks specials and DJs on most nights.

Entertainment

Glasgow is Scotland's entertainment and nightlife capital, and you can plug in to what's on by picking up the *List* (£2.20) or scanning local newspapers (especially the *Herald* and the *Evening Times*) throughout the week. The monthly *Gig Guide*, available free in many pubs, lists upcoming music concerts. Tickets can be booked via **Ticket Scotland** (☎ 204 5151; www.ticketsscotland.com).

LIVE MUSIC & NIGHTCLUBS

King Tut's Wah Wah Hut (☎ 221 5279; 272a St Vincent St; ⌚ noon-midnight Mon-Sat, 6pm-midnight Sun) A legendary live music spot where the early indie versions of Oasis and Radiohead started out. There's live music nightly.

Barrowlands (☎ 552 4601; www.glasgow-barrowland.com; 244 Gallowgate) Legendary old dance-hall venue where some of the larger visiting bands crack open their guitar cases. Check online and book ahead.

Arches (☎ 565 1000; 253 Argyle St; admission £5-12; 11pm-3am Wed-Sat) A fantastic, modular club space that can turn from intimate little multivenue to pumping mega club depending on the night and bill. Carl Cox and Laurent Garnier are some of the recent DJs to drop in. There's also live music and an excellent bar and café (11am until late Monday to Saturday) under one of the high brick arches.

Getting There & Away

AIR

Ten miles west of the city, **Glasgow International Airport** (GLA; ☎ 887 1111; www.glasgowairport.com) receives flights from the UK and the rest of the world. Several no-frills airlines, including easyJet, bmiBaby and Ryanair, provide domestic services from London and other cities. For more details, see p277. Don't confuse GIA with Glasgow Prestwick, a much smaller airport, much, much further out.

BUS

All long-distance buses arrive and depart from **Buchanan St bus station** (☎ 333 3708; Killermont St), and there are a number of competing services that keep prices down.

Silver Choice (☎ 01355-230403; www.silverchoicetravel.co.uk) offers the best deal from London (£25, 8½ hours). There are daily departures at 10pm from London Victoria, but book well in advance because it's a popular service.

Seven National Express services arrive daily from London (single £31, 8½ to 10 hours). National Express also runs regular coaches from Birmingham (£42.50, seven to nine hours), Carlisle (£15.60, two hours) and York (£30.50, seven to 10 hours), among others.

Coaches run by **Scottish Citylink** (☎ 0870 550 5050; www.citylink.co.uk) arrive in Glasgow from most of Scotland's towns and cities. Services include the popular route from Edinburgh that runs every 20 minutes (£4.20, 1¼ hours). There are also daily arrivals from Aberdeen (£17.20, four hours), Fort William (£14, three hours), Inverness (£16.70, four hours), Oban (£13.10, three hours), Skye (£24.80, 6¼ hours) and Stirling (£4.20, 45 minutes).

Daily refurbished double-decker buses owned by **Megabus** (☎ 01738-639095; www.megabus.com) run to Glasgow from three Scottish cities: Dundee (two to three hours), Edinburgh (1½ hours) and Perth (two hours). Fares are as low as £1 (plus £0.50 booking fee) if you order far enough in advance.

TRAIN

As a general rule, Glasgow's Central train station serves southern Scotland, England and Wales, while Queen St train station serves the north and east. Trains arrive throughout the day from London Euston and London King's Cross stations. A much more comfortable ride than a long-haul bus trek, prices can vary considerably (from £25) for the five-hour direct trip.

The West Highland train line north to Oban and Fort William is run by **ScotRail** (☎ 0845 748 4950; www.firstgroup.com/scotrail), with direct links from Dundee (£23.10, 1½ hours), Aberdeen (£34.90, 3¼ to four hours) and Inverness (£34.90, 3½ hours). There are numerous trains from Edinburgh (from £9.90, 50 minutes) to Glasgow.

Getting Around

TO/FROM THE AIRPORT

The bus 905 shuttle service travels between Glasgow International Airport and Buchanan St bus station (£3.30) from 6am Monday (from 7am Sunday) to midnight Saturday. It runs every 10 to 15 minutes during the week and every 30 minutes on weekends. A taxi on the same route costs £12 to £17.

BUS

The city is covered by a good bus system, but passengers often need exact change when purchasing tickets. The main operator is **First Glasgow** (☎ 423 6600; www.firstglasgow.com), whose city-centre fares average £0.90. For multiple trips, the company's FirstDay ticket, purchased from the driver, allows unlimited all-day travel after 9.30am for £2.45. There are also several night bus routes, mostly alighting in George Sq.

TRAIN

There's an extensive suburban train network in Glasgow, which connects to the highly efficient **SPT subway** (☎ 0870 608 2608; www.spt.co.uk) loop at Buchanan St bus station. Serving 15 stations in the city centre, west and south of the city, single SPT tickets cost £1. For travel after 9.30am, there's an unlimited-trip Discovery Ticket for £1.90. Alternatively, the Roundabout Glasgow ticket (£4.50) covers travel on all train and subway routes in the city for one day.

SOUTHWEST SCOTLAND

Southwest Scotland offers some fine Scottish scenery – bare hills, moors, woods and a craggy coastline – without the attendant tour buses and crowds you might find in the Highlands. Warmed by Gulf Stream currents, it also enjoys the region's mildest climate (we're speaking relatively here). This was also the home of Robbie Burns, Scotland's national poet.

Ayrshire is immediately southwest of Glasgow, while Dumfries & Galloway covers the southern half of this western elbow. There are many notable historic and prehistoric attractions linked by the Solway Coast Heritage Trail. The Southern Upland Way links the region coast-to-coast. This is also great cycling country. Visit a local TIC for extensive information on these routes.

Isle of Arran

☎ 01770 / pop 4800

The region's best walking country, Arran is often described as 'Scotland in miniature' because of its compact reflection of a variety of scenery. This includes sheep-strewn farmland, rock-sheltered beaches, looming peaks, such as **Goat Fell**, and a coastal road that's perfect for cycling.

The main **TIC** (☎ 303774; www.ayrshire-arran.com; The Pier, Brodick; ⌚ 9am-5pm Mon-Thu & Sat, 9am-7.30pm Fri, 10am-5pm Sun May-Sep, 9am-5pm Mon-Sat Oct-Apr) is helpfully stocked with information on how to experience the region, which includes the highly recommended **Brodick Castle** (☎ 302202; adult/child £10/7; ⌚ 11am-4.30pm Apr-Sep, 11am-3.30pm Oct), 2.5 miles north. It's a magnificent 13th-century sandstone pile full of silver, porcelain and hunting trophies of the stuffed-head variety. The landscaped gardens, featuring many exotic plants, are excellent.

Call the TIC for accommodation assistance or head for the **Belvedere Guest House** (☎ 302397; stb@vision-unlimited.co.uk; Alma Rd; s/d £20/40). The nearest **SYHA hostel** (☎ 0870 004 1140; dm £12-14; ⌚ Mar-Oct) is 14 miles north in Lochranza.

GETTING THERE & AROUND

Conveniently accessible from Glasgow, Brodick is only an hour's ferry ride by **CalMac** (☎ 302166; www.calmac.co.uk) from Ardrossan (passenger/car £5/36.50, four to six daily). Six buses run daily from Brodick to Lochranza (£2, 45 minutes, Monday to Saturday) and there are complete services around the island. Ask for additional transport information at the TIC, or consider renting a bike for your visit from **Mini Golf Cycle Hire** (☎ 07968-024040; Shore Rd).

Stranraer & Cairnryan

☎ 01776 / pop 11,500

These port towns a few miles apart are transport hubs rather than destinations in themselves. The bus and train stations, as well as the TIC and some accommodation options, are huddled around the sea terminals. At less than 2½ hours away, Stranraer offers the shortest link to Northern Ireland.

The **TIC** (☎ 702595; 28 Harbour St) specialises in booking Citylink/National Express journeys, as well as day trips across the Irish Sea. Frequent **Stena Line** (☎ 0870 570 7070; www.stenaline.co.uk) services arrive from Belfast.

For an economical bed for the night, try **Ivy House** (☎ 704176; www.ivyplace.worldonline.co.uk; 3 Ivy Pl; r per person £22).

National Express coach services arrive from London, while **Stagecoach Western** (☎ 704484) runs services from Glasgow (£8.35, three hours, six daily). ScotRail trains arrive from Glasgow throughout the day (£15, 2½ hours).

SOUTHEAST SCOTLAND

The ancient abbeys, lush glens and proud forests of the Scottish Borders have a unique beauty and romance that's often missed by travellers rushing through on their way to Edinburgh. Those who do stop discover the lovely valley of the Tweed River and a host of dramatic ruins, charming stone towns and villages. This is a great region to explore on foot or by bike: check local TICs for maps and options, or head straight for the signposted **Tweed Cycleway** between Biggar and Berwick-upon-Tweed.

Located between England's Cheviot Hills and Scotland's Pentland, Moorfoot and Lammermuir Hills, the Scottish Borders has a good network of local buses. **First** (☎ 01896-752237) runs numerous services from

Galashiels, Melrose and Edinburgh, and it offers a Rover ticket for unlimited travel in the region (£6.45).

Jedburgh & Around

☎ 01835 / pop 4000

The best base for exploring the Scottish Borders, Jedburgh is a bustling wee town that's well worth checking out on foot. Its **TIC** (☎ 863170; Murray's Green; 9am-7pm Mon-Sat, 10am-6pm Jul & Aug, variable hr rest of year) has plenty of maps and transport information for exploring the region but your first stop should be **Jedburgh Abbey** (☎ 863925; adult/concession/child £4.50/3.50/2; 9.30am-6.30pm Apr-Sep, 9.30am-4.30pm Mon-Sun Oct-Mar). The most complete of the ruined Border abbeys, this 12th-century red sandstone masterpiece was founded by David I as an Augustinian priory.

Local bus services arrive from Melrose (£3, 30 minutes, five daily Monday to Saturday). Munro bus services from Edinburgh arrive throughout the day (£5.90, two hours, eight daily Monday to Saturday, five on Sunday).

Melrose & Around

☎ 01896 / pop 1650

Another popular base for exploring the Borders, Melrose is a pretty little village clustered around a perfectly formed market square, with a good selection of cafés and restaurants. Check in with the **TIC** (☎ 0870 608 0404; Abbey St; 10am-5pm year-round, 10am-2pm Sun Apr-Oct) for local B&B options, or head to the **Melrose Youth Hostel** (☎ 0870 004 1141; Priorwood; dm from £13;), a quiet, well-maintained place in a rather grand Georgian mansion overlooking the abbey.

The main attraction here is **Melrose Abbey** (☎ 822562; adult/concession/child £3.50/2.50/1.20; 9.30am-6.30pm Apr-Sep, 9.30am-4.30pm Mon-Sat, 2-4.30pm Sun Oct-Mar). Repeatedly attacked by the English in the 14th century, the abbey's highly decorative red sandstone shell is a potent symbol for many Scots. Rebuilt by Robert the Bruce – whose heart is reputedly buried here – this Gothic gem has great views from the top of the tower. Next to the Abbey, **Marmion's** (☎ 822245; Buccleuch St; snacks £3-5, mains £7-13; lunch & dinner Mon-Sat) is a good bet, serving coffee, pastries, light lunches and decent restaurant food in the evening. The owners of Marmion's also run the nearby **Fauhope Country House** (☎ 823184; fauhope@bordernet.co.uk; d £70), a fabulous country home in a great spot near the Tweed River.

Buses arrive in Melrose throughout the day from Jedburgh (£3, 30 minutes, 11 daily Monday to Saturday, five on Sunday) and Edinburgh (£5.20, 2¼ hours, eight daily Monday to Saturday).

CENTRAL SCOTLAND

North of the big cities, but before the Highlands start their climb north, this area of gently rolling hills is home to some of Scotland's most important secondary towns, including striking and historic Stirling. On the coast near Dundee, the ancient university town of St Andrews, spiritual home of the game of golf, is well worth the detour.

Stirling

☎ 01786 / pop 45,000

Commanding spectacular views over the surrounding plains and across to snow-capped mountains, Stirling Castle must be one of the two most spectacular Scottish fortifications and it's the main reason for a visit to this lively little university town. The castle has played a huge role in the town's blood-drenched history – key victories over the English at the Battle of Stirling Bridge (1297) and the Battle of Bannockburn (1314) both happened in this area.

Head up the steep streets from the train station and you'll find some fascinating old stone buildings, the SYHA hostel and the windswept castle itself. Take a slight detour to the **TIC** (☎ 08707-200620; 41 Dumbarton Rd; 9am-7.30pm Mon-Sat, 9.30am-6.30pm Sun Jul & Aug, variable hr rest of year) for local information.

The thick, grey walls of **Stirling Castle** (☎ 450000; adult/concession/child £8/6/2; 9.30am-6pm Apr-Oct, 9.30am-5pm Nov-Mar), perched dramatically on an extinct volcano, contain some excellent sights and experiences, including an absorbing guided tour and a top-rate military museum. The current complex was conceived as a fortress in the 14th century when a succession of Stuart monarchs began their residency.

One of Scotland's best SYHA properties, **Stirling Youth Hostel** (☎ 0870 004 1149; St John St; dm £14-15, tw £35;) occupies a large old church building near the castle. Rooms are small and each has en suite facilities. The huge dining room/lounge area is a great hang-out.

BRITAIN

Munro Guesthouse (☎ 472695; www.munroguesthouse.com; 14 Princes St; s/d £35/48) is a homy little B&B right in the heart of town. If you're after refreshment, **Peckham's** (☎ 447047; 52 Port St; mains £7-9; 🕑 10am-10pm) is a great delicatessen with an inexpensive bistro and café attached serving good-value wines. You're likely to run into a castle employee who'll regale you with some great insider stories.

Scottish Citylink buses arrive throughout the day from Aberdeen (£14.50, 3½ hours, four daily), Edinburgh (£6.20, one hour, three daily), Glasgow (£4.20, 45 minutes, hourly) and other towns and cities. ScotRail services arrive from Dundee (£13.70, 50 minutes), Edinburgh (£5.90, 50 minutes, twice hourly), Glasgow (£6.10, 40 minutes, every two hours) and other cities throughout the day.

St Andrews

☎ 01334 / pop 14,200

Another university town, St Andrews is better known for its affiliations with the game of golf and is something of a pilgrimage for golfers. Its fascinating history casts a long shadow over its cobbled streets and ancient terrace cottages. Scotland's former ecclesiastical capital, the ruins of a cavernous cathedral and moody, seafront castle lurk on its outskirts. The university, founded in 1410, is the country's oldest. While 6000 students fill St Andrews during term, golfers annually flock here in even bigger numbers for the area's nine courses – especially the legendary Old Course, the sport's spiritual home.

The **TIC** (☎ 472021; www.visit-standrews.co.uk; 70 Market St; 🕑 9.30am-5pm Mon-Sat Oct-Mar, 9.30am-5pm daily Apr-Sep) has a free town guide with a street map.

The turmoil of the Reformation reduced Scotland's largest-ever church, **St Andrews Cathedral** (☎ 472563; The Pends; adult/child incl castle £6/2.70; 🕑 9.30am-6.30pm Apr-Sep, 9.30am-4.30pm Oct-Mar), to rubble in 1559. Half-eaten walls detail its past splendour, while a visitor centre explains its turbulent history. The 12th-century tower offers spectacular views – watch out for seals bobbing offshore. A short, windswept walk away is the ruined **St Andrews Castle** (☎ 477196; The Scores; adult/child incl cathedral £4/1.25; 🕑 9.30am-6.30pm Apr-Sep, 9.30am-4.30pm Oct-Mar). Perched on coastal rocks, this is a great spot for storm-watching. In contrast, the **British Golf Museum** (☎ 460046; Bruce Embankment; adult/child £5/2.75; 🕑 9.30am-5.30pm Easter–mid-Oct, 11am-3pm mid-Oct–Easter) offers a lively, light-hearted account of the evolution and history of the game. Those who don't know their mashie niblick from their brassie spoon, however, won't miss much if they skip it.

Golf fans take over the town's accommodation during major tournaments and throughout summer, so make peak bookings well in advance. Five minutes' from the bus station, the only hostel in town, **St Andrews Tourist Hostel** (☎ 479911; www.standrewshostel.com; St Mary's Pl; dm £12-16; 🕑 7am-11pm), is clean, basic and friendly, with only a few bunks per room. Guesthouses are numerous, with **Brownlees Guest House** (☎ 473868; www.brownlees.co.uk; 7 Murray Pl; r per person £25-32) being a good budget option that serves a rib-sticking breakfast.

There are some good eating options, including the **Eating Place** (☎ 475671; 177-179 South St; mains £4-7; 🕑 9.30am-5pm Mon-Sat, 11am-5pm Sun), which serves sweet and savoury Scottish pancakes and tapas upstairs. The **Vine Leaf Restaurant** (☎ 477497; 131 South St; 2-course dinner £19.95; 🕑 from 7pm Tue-Sat) serves inventive seafood and meat options, such as oh-so-tender eight-hour lamb.

The **Central Bar** (☎ 478296; Market St) is the town's top pub for real ale and quiet chats, while **Ma Bells** (☎ 472611; 40 The Scores) is where students and backpackers spend most of their drinking time.

Leuchars, the nearest train station, is a £10 taxi or £2.10 bus (96 or 99) ride away, with direct links to/from Aberdeen, Dundee, Edinburgh and Inverness. **Stagecoach Fife** (☎ 01334-474238) runs buses from Edinburgh (£7, two hours, hourly) and Dundee (£3.10, 30 minutes, half-hourly).

EASTERN HIGHLANDS

Like a craggy nose jutting defiantly into the North Sea, the land between Perth and the Firth of Tay in the south and Inverness and Moray Firth in the north offers great expanses of empty beach, craggy cliffs teeming with seabirds, tiny stone fishing villages and the bare shoulders of the Cairngorm Mountains – oh, and two of Scotland's biggest cities, Aberdeen and Dundee.

Orientation & Information

The Grampian Mountains march from Oban in a great arc northeastwards, becoming the

Cairngorm Mountains in the eastern region. The Cairngorms are as dramatic and demanding as any of the Scottish ranges, and the coastline, especially from Stonehaven to Buckie, is exceptional. Aberdeen is the region's biggest city, providing the main ferry port for Shetland. Reflecting the division between the Eastern and Western Highlands, there are few links between Perth and Inverness, the capital of the Highlands.

There are information centres in towns and cities throughout the region and a useful website from the **Highlands of Scotland Tourism Board** (www.visithighlands.com).

Perthshire & Cairngorms

One of the region's most important towns (it's on the main train line from Edinburgh and Inverness), Perth became Scotland's capital in the 12th century. It's now a bustling settlement that celebrates its heritage without resting idly on it.

With its excellent visitor amenities, Aviemore makes a good base for exploring the region and is regarded as the gateway to the Cairngorms. This is where hikers, bikers and climbers congregate to take on the Scottish outdoors and in winter it's the centre of the country's skiing and snowboarding action. While the season traditionally runs from December until April, recent light snowfalls have seen closures as early as February. Check **Ski Scotland** (ski.visitscotland.com) for the latest conditions.

The **Cairngorms National Park** (www.cairngorms.co.uk), Britain's newest, is a wildly beautiful place combining wild mountain tundras, secluded old pinewoods, ancient castles, unique wildlife and lush colours year-round. There are plenty of attractions and activities here, with the **Cairngorm Mountain Railway** (☎ 01479-861261; Cairngorm Ski Area; adult/concession £8.75/7.50; ⏲ 10am-4.30pm), the UK's highest and longest funicular, a popular, though pricey, trip.

The modern **Aviemore Youth Hostel** (☎ 0870 004 1104; 25 Grampian Rd; dm £12-14; 💻) is well equipped with small dorms, and is close to both the local TIC and village centre.

Aberdeen

☎ 01224 / pop 205,000

Founded in part on the demand for oil – whale oil that is – today granite-hewn Aberdeen is again booming from oil, this time black gold from deep under the North Sea. This busy working town and harbour lacks the historical charms of other Scottish towns of its size, and is really only worth visiting if you're heading on to another part of the nearby coast or some of the remote northern isles. That said, there are a couple of good museums, and a fairly lively nightlife and cultural scene supported by Aberdeen's large university population.

ORIENTATION & INFORMATION

The city is built on a ridge that runs east–west to the north of the Dee River. Union St, the main shopping street, runs along the crest of this ridge. The train and bus stations are next to each other off Guild St, and the **TIC** (☎ 288828; www.aberdeen-grampian.com; 23 Union St; ⏲ 9am-6.30pm Mon-Sat, 10am-4pm Sun Jul & Aug, variable hr rest of year) is on the corner of Union St and Shiprow. The Old Town, with its cobbled streets, old university and ecclesiastical buildings, is a mile north of the city centre.

SIGHTS

There's a fascinating modern exploration of the region's long association with the sea at **Aberdeen Maritime Museum** (☎ 337700; Shiprow; admission free; ⏲ 10am-5pm Mon-Sat, noon-3pm Sun). There's plenty of hi-tech, touch-screen action, the chance to pilot a mini-sub, a three-storey replica of a North Sea oilrig, and plenty of well-presented information about ships and drilling for oil. Also worth a look is **Aberdeen Art Gallery** (☎ 523700; Schoolhill; admission free; ⏲ 10am-5pm Mon-Sat, 2-5pm Sun), the city's third-oldest surviving home, with a surprisingly good collection of 19th-, 20th- and 21st-century art, including work from bad boy double act Gilbert & George.

SLEEPING

The booming oil economy means beds fill up in the week when oilfield workers monopolise much of the city's accommodation. Their presence keeps many hotel prices artificially high, although weekend deals are available almost everywhere. Clusters of B&Bs line Bon Accord St and Springbank Tce (both close to the city centre).

SYHA Aberdeen Youth Hostel (☎ 0870 004 1100; 8 Queen's Rd; dm £13-15; 💻) An imposing granite house a mile west of the train station. It's clean and welcoming but a bit too clinical to be truly cosy.

Dunrovin Guest House (☎ 586081; 186 Bon Accord St; s/d £30/50, with shared bathroom £27/40) This place gets our vote for its hearty Scottish breakfast (with fresh fruit and vegetarian options), for the enthusiastic hosts and for their tongue-in-cheek brochure likening the place to Edgar Allen Poe's *Haunted Palace* ('Everything about it was evil…it reeked of human depravity – but what of its occupants, what of them?'). Book ahead.

Highland Hotel (☎ 583685; www.highlandhotel.net; 91-5 Crown St; r from £70, guesthouse s/d Mon-Thu from £45/58, Fri-Sun £37.50/50) A comfortable hotel with cheerful, if rather neutral, rooms and some cheaper guesthouse accommodation nearby.

EATING & DRINKING

Close to the TIC and just off Union St, the refurbished Belmont St houses some of Aberdeen's best cafés, bars and restaurants.

Prince of Wales (☎ 640597; 7 St Nicholas Lane; mains £5) The best pub for a cheap and cheerful lunch. This institution offers some great Scottish ales to help the chips slip down.

Ashvale Fish Restaurant (☎ 596581; 42-48 Great Western Rd; takeaway £3, mains £6-9; 11.45am-11pm) Outside the city centre, you'll find this quality, award-winning fish-and-chip joint.

Foyer Restaurant (☎ 582277; 82a Crown St; light dishes £5.50-7, mains £10.50-16; 10am-11pm Tue-Sat) A glass and beechwood interior with natural light and an inventive, hearty dishes, like mushroom and onion suet pudding or grilled sea bass with fennel sauerkraut, make this the fine-dining pick. It's a laudable not-for-profit community venture, too.

GETTING THERE & AWAY

Air

Six miles northeast of the city centre, **Aberdeen Airport** (ABZ; ☎ 0870 040 0006; www.aberdeenairport.com) receives flights from 34 destinations in 21 countries. Ryanair and easyJet offer competitive and highly variable fares from London and other UK cities. There are also regular but expensive **Loganair** (☎ 0870 850 9850; www.loganair.co.uk) flights from Orkney and Shetland.

Boat

The passenger ferry terminal is a short walk east of the train and bus stations. **NorthLink Ferries** (☎ 0845 600 0449; www.northlinkferries.co.uk) runs services to Orkney (passenger only one way from £15.60, car from £61.50, six hours, daily) and Shetland (passenger only one way from £20.40, car from £82.80, 12½ hours, three weekly).

Bus

There are National Express buses from London (£40, two hours, five daily) in addition to which Scottish Citylink runs frequent services from Edinburgh (£17.20, three hours), Glasgow (£17.20, four hours) and other Scottish cities.

Train

Services from London King's Cross (£122.50, 7½ hours) and Scottish destinations, including Dundee (£20.70, one hour) and Inverness (£21.50, 2¼ hours), arrive throughout the day.

GETTING AROUND

From the airport, **First Aberdeen's** (☎ 650065) bus 27 (£1.30, 35 minutes) arrives frequently on Union St. The company runs an extensive service throughout the city and offers an unlimited one-day adult pass for £2.50.

WESTERN HIGHLANDS

If you were to explore just one part of Scotland's vast wilderness, make it this one. Stretching from Rannoch Moor past Fort William on the west coast, this is a majestically wild region of mist-covered glens, ice-cold lochs and towering snow-covered mountains, including Ben Nevis, Britain's highest peak. To the south lies Loch Lomond, the largest lake in Scotland, to the west the rugged Isle of Mull. The 95-mile **West Highland Way** between Fort William and Glasgow is one of Britain's best hiking trails (for moderately accomplished ramblers).

Orientation & Information

Fort William, at the southern end of the Great Glen, is the region's main base for visitors. Oban, on the west coast, is the key ferry port for the Inner Hebrides (Mull, Coll, Tiree, Colonsay, Jura and Islay), and the Outer Hebridean islands of South Uist and Barra.

There's a reasonable scattering of SYHA accommodation and some independent hostels in some locations, including Glencoe, Oban, Tobermory, Crianlarich, Inchree and Corpach. Call in at the Fort William TIC for details.

Fort William

☎ 01397 / pop 9500

Situated on the banks of Loch Linnhe and at the bottom of the great Caledonian Canal, Fort William is no great shakes as a destination itself but is a useful base for exploring the local mountains. There's at least one of everything here that a visitor might need – including hiking shops, cafés, pubs and accommodation. For local information, visit the **TIC** (☎ 703781; Cameron Sq; 9am-8pm Mon-Sat, 10am-6pm Sun) or check **Discover Fort William** (www.discover-fortwilliam.com).

The lively, convivial **Fort William Backpackers** (☎ 700711; www.scotlands-top-hostels.com; Alma Rd; dm £12;) is a short walk from the bus and train stations, and has impressive hillside views. **Bank St Lodge** (☎ 700070; www.accommodation-fortwilliam.com; dm/d/tr/q £13/45/55/65) is a tad sterile but very central.

Scottish Citylink buses travel from Glasgow (£14, three hours, four daily) and Edinburgh (£19.90, 3¼ hours, two daily), both via Glencoe. The spectacular West Highland train line runs three daily trains from Glasgow (£20.30, 3¾ hours).

Some local buses are run by **Rapsons/Highland Country** (☎ 702373; www.rapsons.co.uk), but call ahead for timetables since services are seasonal. **Off-Beat Bikes** (☎ 704008; 117 High St; 9am-5.30pm) rents bikes from £10 per half-day.

Oban

☎ 01631 / pop 8500

A hub for holiday-makers every summer, Oban is a traditional resort town combining pretty bay-front vistas with a raft of visitor amenities. The bus and train station and ferry terminal are together beside the harbour, and the **TIC** (☎ 563122; Argyll Sq; Mon-Sat May-Sep) is in a former church nearby.

Oban Backpackers Lodge (☎ 562107; www.scotlands-top-hostels.com; Breadalbane St; dm £12-13;) is less than a mile from the train station and has a welcoming ambience, including a friendly lounge area. The SYHA **Oban Youth Hostel** (☎ 0870 004 1144; Corran Esplanade; dm £13-15, s/d £17.50/35;) is a little more institutional, but has great views across the bay and a smart new block of private rooms. There are several B&Bs along Corran Esplanade, but these can fill up quickly in summer. The best spot for food is **Ee-Usk** (☎ 565666; North Pier; mains £10-20; lunch & dinner), serving excellent seafood, including delicious smoked haddock chowder (£3.95) and yummy desserts.

There are Scottish Citylink buses from Glasgow (£13.10, three hours, four daily), Fort William (£8.20, 1½ hours, four daily) and other Scottish destinations. There are also three daily trains from Glasgow (£16.80, three hours). **CalMac** (☎ 566688; www.calmac.co.uk) ferries link Oban with the Inner and Outer Hebrides.

Isle of Mull

Scotland's third-largest island abounds with great mountain views and pretty seascapes, drawing thousands of visitors to its charming shores every summer, offering a field day to the especially bloodthirsty strain of Mull midge (thankfully only a pest in summer). While most visitors arrive at the Craignure ferry terminal, many quickly head north to Tobermory, a picture-perfect fishing port that's also the capital, with its quaysides lined with houses in cheerful primary colours and cosy pubs.

There are TICs in both towns, but only **Craignure's** (☎ 01680-812377; 8.30am-7pm Mon-Thu, 8.30am-5.15pm Fri, 9am-5pm Sat, 10am-5pm Sun) is open year-round. Call ahead for accommodation options.

Don't expect to turn up and easily find a bed in summer, when accommodation is often booked out. Call in advance for the tiny SYHA **Tobermory Youth Hostel** (☎ 0870 004 1151; Main St; dm £12.50), which fills up quickly, or **Highland Cottage** (☎ 01688-302030; Breadalbane St), quite simply a cute little cottage B&B in the centre of town.

For a filling pub lunch or weekend evening of live music, **MacGochan's** (☎ 01688-302350; Ledaig, Tobermory; mains £3.50-6) is popular with locals and visitors.

NORTHERN HIGHLANDS & ISLANDS

One of Europe's last great wildernesses, this breathtakingly beautiful swathe of endless moors, glassy lochs and buffeted coastal cliffs is as close to nature as anyone could wish to be. It's also the ancient homeland of Gaelic culture.

It's easy to underestimate the size of the region, so give yourself extra time to explore via air, bus, train or ferry. Public transport outside the main centres can be as rare as a wild haggis sighting and some services are severely curtailed out of season. Contact the **Highlands of Scotland Tourist Board** (☎ 0845 225 5121; www.visithighlands.com) for transport and accommodation advice throughout the region, or drop by one of the local TICs that dot the area.

Inverness

☎ 01463 / pop 61,000

The capital of the Highlands, rapidly expanding Inverness is the perfect base for plotting a trip through the region. It's an attractive town straddling the Ness River, although it has few attractions of its own (even the red, baronial-style castle is closed to visitors), but it's just 6 miles from Loch Ness and few visit here without making an excursion to this vast, deep body of water reputed to be the home of the famous monster, Nessie.

ORIENTATION & INFORMATION

The town centre resides on the river's eastern bank, along with the bus and train stations, new Eastgate shopping centre and several hostels.

The **TIC** (☎ 234353; Castle Wynd; 9am-6pm Mon-Sat, 10am-5pm Sun) is near the castle and has probably the friendliest tourism bureau staff in Scotland. It can help with information on the entire Highlands region, and offers currency exchange and an Internet access terminal (per 20 minutes £1).

SIGHTS

No visit to Inverness is complete without a trek to **Loch Ness**. While tourists by the coach load roll up here every few minutes in summer, there's no doubt that a half-day excursion is worth the Citylink bus fare (adult £7.30 return). The romantic ruin of **Urqhuart Castle** (☎ 01456-450551; adult/concession/child £6/4.50/1.20; 9.30am-6.30pm Apr-Sep, 9.30am-4.30pm Mon-Sat, 2-4.30pm Sun Oct-Mar) commands a great spot over the loch. Entry includes a movie presentation on the castle history.

Nearby Drumnadrochit earns an often tacky living from the cult of the monster. **Loch Ness 2000** (☎ 01456-450573; adult/concession/child £5.95/4.50/3.50; 9am-8pm Jul & Aug, 9am-6pm Jun & Sep, 9am-5.30pm Oct, 9.30am-5pm Easter-May, 10am-3.30pm Nov-Easter) traces the historic hunts for Nessie. A good way to see a bit more of the Loch and surrounding area is aboard the *Loch Ness Express* (see p262).

SLEEPING

Inverness has plenty of budget options and a good range of B&Bs and guesthouses, but the town fills quickly in summer, so book ahead. If you're thinking about staying longer, **Wilderness Cottages** (☎ 01456-486358; www.wildernesscottages.co.uk) is a good website for booking longer stays in some great locations around the Highlands. There are also several midrange and top-end options along the banks of Loch Ness and on Old Edinburgh Rd.

Bazpackers Backpackers Hostel (☎ 717663; 4 Culduthel Rd; dm £10-15; 💻) Clean and compact, with great views across the river. The homy feel is enhanced by a wood-burning stove.

Inverness Millburn Youth Hostel (☎ 0970 004 2227; Victoria Dr; dm £11.50-13.50; ⊠) A large, modern property that's one of the SYHA's best, although the location set far back from the river on the other side of the town centre is not ideal.

Inverness Tourist Hostel (☎ 241962; 24 Rose St; dm £13-14; 💻) Located right at the bus station, the town's newest backpacker option has a swanky fitted kitchen and black leather couches, and a helpful band of staff.

Eastgate Backpackers Hostel (☎ 718756; www.eastgatehostel.com; 38 Eastgate; dm £10-16) This well-situated, lively hostel offers power showers, metal bunks, and mixed and single-sex dorms.

Bluebell House (☎ 238201; www.bluebell-house.co.uk; 31 Kenneth St; s/d from £30/54) This delightful place, set just back from the northern side of the Ness, has three good-value rooms decorated with care by the charming landlady, who has an eye for interiors and antiques.

King's Highway (☎ 251800; invernesslodge@jdwetherspoon.co.uk; 72-74 Church St; r £44) Modern, uniform and located above the town's Wetherspoon chain pub. At this flat rate year-round, it's very good value, especially the family rooms.

Ivybank Guest House (☎ 232796; ivybank@talk21.com; 28 Old Edinburgh Rd; s £25-60, d £50-65) A neatly kept stone lodge with a pleasant garden on a quiet road.

Rocpool Reserve (☎ 240089; www.rocpool.com; Culduthel Rd; s/d from £95/130) The finest address in Inverness, this slinky little style hotel aims to pamper and please, with terrific contemporary furnishings, broadband access, plasma TVs, spa-like bathrooms and fluffy gowns. There's a good bar and restaurant (p262).

BRITAIN

EATING & DRINKING

Castle Restaurant (☎ 230925; 41-43 Castle St; mains £4-7; ⌚ 8am-8.30pm Mon-Sat) A backpacker favourite, this cheap and cheery café serves heaping plates of simple comfort food that provide enough fuel for a giant hike around the region. Mountains of chips come accompanied with fried fish or crusty meat pies.

Mustard Seed (☎ 220220; 16 Fraser St, mains £8-15; ⌚ noon-3pm & 6-10pm) The queen of Inverness restaurants until Rocpool came along, but still holding its own by focusing on traditional French and Scottish produce prepared with a modern flare, such as seared wild halibut in lobster oil.

Rocpool Reserve (☎ 240089; www.rocpool.com; Culduthel Rd; mains £10-19) Beneath bold swathes of contemporary art, you'll find modern European food (chargrilled lamb with polenta and sea bass ravioli with a seafood carpaccio) and surprisingly reasonable lunch deals. For summer browsing, there's a delightful terrace overlooking the river.

Hootannay Cèilidh CaféBar (☎ 233651; 67 Church St; ⌚ noon-midnight) This excellent, sociable and folk music–friendly pub easily wins the prize for best boozer in town. A host of Scottish beer specials are on offer, with the rust-coloured Red Kite from Black Isle Brewery particularly recommended. There's rip-roaring traditional music on the ground floor nightly and a host of rock and comedy events upstairs almost as regularly. Shows are free throughout the week; there's a £2 charge, covering both floors, on Friday and Saturday.

GETTING THERE & AROUND

Ten miles east of town, **Inverness Airport** (INV; ☎ 01667-464000) receives flights from Edinburgh, Glasgow, London, Orkney and Shetland, among other destinations.

National Express coach services arrive from London (£40, 13 hours, four daily), while Citylink buses travel from Edinburgh (£16.70, four hours, hourly), Fort William (£8.80, two hours, six daily), Glasgow (£15.50, four hours, hourly) and other Scottish destinations.

There are several daily train services from London (£122, eight to 10 hours), including the overnight *Caledonian Sleeper*, along with services from Glasgow (£34.90, 3½ hours) and Edinburgh (£34.90, 3¼ hours). The highly picturesque Kyle of Lochalsh (£15.90, 2½ hours, two to four daily) line delivers passengers from the bridge across to the Isle of Skye, while the line from Thurso (£14, 3½ hours, two to three daily) connects with the ferry from Orkney.

Highland Country (☎ 710555; www.rapsons.com) operates local buses, with information and advice available at the TIC. A Rover ticket costs £6 for unlimited one-day travel.

Fort Augustus

☎ 01320 / pop 1500

At the far southern end of Loch Ness, halfway between Inverness and Fort William, the pretty village of Fort Augustus is a good place to stop and take it easy. The village marks an important staging post of the Caledonian Canal, an engineering triumph that carves its way through the Highlands from the North Sea to the Atlantic. At Fort Augustus a series of locks raises boats up to the level of the next loch. Potter about, relax and watch the goings on around the lock gates. Its 'high street' is the quayside, and it's lined with good pubs and cafés.

The **TIC** (☎ 366367) can help with finding and booking B&B accommodation in the village, or there's **Stravaigers Lodge** (☎ 366257; Glendoe Rd; dm from £15, tw £30), a new backpackers just near the old Abbey (closed to visitors). Your best bet for food and drink is the **Bothy** (☎ 366736; mains £6-12; ⌚ lunch & dinner), serving reasonable pub grub right by the swing bridge over the canal.

GETTING THERE & AWAY

Citylink buses connect Fort Augustus with Inverness (£8, 45 minutes, six daily) and Fort William (£8.20, one hour, six daily). Much more fun, but far less frequent, the **Loch Ness Express** (☎ 0800 328 6426; www.lochnessexpress.com) steams the length of Loch Ness to Fort Augustus (£13, two hours, twice daily May to October, once daily November and December) from Dochgarroch (with a bus transfer into and out of the centre of Inverness), stopping at Urqhuart Castle and Foyers along the way.

Orkney Islands

☎ 01856 / pop 19,250

Just 6 miles off the northern coast of Scotland, this magical group of islands is reknowned for its dramatic coastal scenery (which ranges from soaring cliffs to white, sandy beaches), abundant marine bird life and a plethora of mysterious prehistoric finds. If you find yourself in the area around mid-June, do not miss the **St Magnus Arts Festival** (www.stmagnusfestival.com), which is a lively celebration of arts, performance and music.

Sixteen of the 70 Orkney Islands are inhabited, but Kirkwall is the main town and Stromness is the major port. They're both on Mainland, the largest island. Contact Kirkwall's **TIC** (☎ 872856; 6 Broad St; Mon-Sat Oct-Apr, daily May-Sep) for more information, or check **Visit Orkney** (www.visitorkney.com) for some pretrip resources.

Stenness, a small village that is a short bus ride from Kirkwall or Stromness, is the most accessible spot for exploring prehistoric Orkney. The **Standing Stones of Stenness**, **Barnhouse Neolithic Village** and **Skara Brae**, a 5000-year-old village uncovered 150 years ago, are all quite close by. Particularly recommended, though, is **Maes Howe** (☎ 761606; adult/child £3/1; 9.30am-6.30pm Apr-Sep, 9.30am-4.30pm Mon-Sat, 2-4.30pm Sun Oct-Mar), a 5000-year-old earth-mound tomb, which is an impressive engineering feat by any standards and a wonderfully atmospheric place.

There's a good selection of low-priced B&Bs in the area – especially on Mainland – and numerous hostels dot the region. In Stromness, **Brown's Hostel** (☎ 850661; 45 Victoria St; dm £11) is popular and close to the ferry, while **Rickla** (☎ 761575; www.rickla.co.uk; Harray; d from £70) offers sumptuous B&B accommodation, with well-equipped rooms overlooking the hills of Hoy and near all the prehistoric monuments.

GETTING THERE & AWAY

Flights run by **Loganair** (☎ 0845 773 3377) arrive daily in Kirkwall from Aberdeen (from £147, one hour), Glasgow (from £184, 1¾ hours) and a number of other Scottish cities. Meanwhile British Airways provides affiliated connections to London, Manchester and throughout the rest of the United Kingdom.

Services operated by **NorthLink Ferries** (☎ 0845 600 0449; www.northlinkferries.co.uk) run from Aberdeen, Scrabster and the Shetlands, while **John o'Groats Ferries** (☎ 01955-611353; www.jogferry.co.uk) also operates a passenger-only run from the mainland.

Shetland Islands

☎ 01595 / pop 23,000

Sixty miles north of Orkney, the Shetland Islands remained under Norse rule until 1469, when they were given to Scotland as part of a Danish princess's dowry. Even today these remote, windswept, treeless islands are almost as much a part of Scandinavia as Britain. Lerwick, the capital, is less than 230 miles from Bergen in Norway. For some pretrip information, check **Visit Shetland** (www.shetland-tourism.co.uk).

Much bleaker than Orkney, Shetland is famous for its varied bird life, its rugged coastline and 4000-year-old archaeological heritage. It's worth taking a **boat** (☎ 01950-431367) to the astounding and mysterious prehistoric engineering marvel of **Mousa Broch**, an amazingly preserved lookout tower on a tiny island south of Lerwick.

Small ferries connect a handful of the smaller islands. Contact the **TIC** (☎ 693434; 8am-6pm Mon-Fri, 8am-4pm Sat, 10am-1pm Sun Apr-Sep, 9am-5pm Mon-Fri Oct) for information on B&Bs and camping barns, or you can stay at **Lerwick Youth Hostel** (☎ 692114; King Harald St; dm £11; mid-Apr–Sep), which has a good café attached.

NorthLink Ferries (☎ 01856-851144; www.northlinkferries.co.uk) runs services from Aberdeen to Lerwick and Kirkwall to Lerwick.

North Coast

The coast from Dounreay to Ullapool is spectacular. Everything you see is on a massive scale: vast emptiness, enormous lochs and snow-capped mountains. Unreliable weather and the limited public transport system are the only drawbacks.

From the tiny town of **Durness**, you can make forays out to the savagely beautiful **Cape Wrath**, play extreme golf (at the most northerly course in mainland Britain) or explore mile after mile of empty beach. The Durness **TIC** (☎ 01971-511259) can help with accommodation and sightseeing.

Getting to Thurso by bus or train is no problem, but from there your troubles start. From June to September **Rapsons/Highland Country Buses** (☎ 01847-893123; www.rapsons.co.uk) runs its Northern Explorer service once daily (except Sunday) from Thurso to Durness (£7.75, 2½ hours). The rest of the year, there are Monday to Saturday services from Thurso to Bettyhill.

West Coast

Ullapool is the jumping-off point for the Isle of Lewis; contact its **TIC** (☎ 01854-612135; 6 Argyle St; ⏲ daily Apr-Sep, Mon-Sat Oct, Mon-Fri Nov-Mar) for information. The coastline keeps getting better round to Gairloch, along Loch Maree, and down to the Kyle of Lochalsh and Skye. From there you're back in the land of the tour bus; civilisation (and main roads) can be a shock after all the empty space.

Kyle of Lochalsh ('Kyle') is a small village that overlooks the lovely island of Skye across narrow Loch Alsh. There's a **TIC** (☎ 01599-534276; ⏲ 9am-5.30pm Mon-Sat Easter-Oct) beside the seafront car park, but the nearest hostels are on Skye. Kyle can be reached by bus and train from Inverness, and also by direct Citylink buses from Glasgow (£22.40, 5½ hours).

Isle of Skye

pop 8850

Skye is a large, rugged island, 50 miles north to south and 25 miles east to west. It's ringed by stunning coastline and dominated by the magnificent Cuillin Hills. The remote west coast is especially beautiful and is teeming with wildlife; seals and otters are frequently sighted. You can contact the **Portree TIC** (☎ 01478-612137; Bayfield Rd) for more information.

SLEEPING & EATING

There are more than a dozen SYHA and independent hostels on the island and numerous B&Bs. The SYHA hostels most relevant to ferry users are at **Uig** (☎ 0870 004 1155; dm £12; ⏲ Apr-Sep) for the north and the Outer Hebrides (Western Isles), and **Armadale** (☎ 0870 004 1103; dm £12; ⏲ Apr-Sep) for Mallaig.

Skye Backpackers (☎ 01599-534510; www.scotlands-top-hostels.com; Kyleakin; dm £12-13) The best independent hostel is this welcoming backpackers, a short walk from the Skye Bridge.

Portree House Hotel (☎ 01478-613713; Home Farm Rd; s £24-28, d £50-70) In Portree, this hotel offers a homy kind of comfort.

Bosville Hotel (☎ 01478-612846; www.macleodhotels.co.uk/bosville; 9-11 Bosville Tce; s/d from £75/90) Also in Portree, the Bosville Hotel offers the plushest lodgings, and a good restaurant and bistro.

Kinloch Lodge (☎ 01471-833214; www.kinloch-lodge.co.uk; mains £6.50-13.50; ⏲ lunch) Run by acclaimed food writer Claire Macdonald, this is the undisputed gourmet destination on the island.

GETTING THERE & AWAY

A road bridge connects Skye to the mainland. **CalMac** (☎ 08705-650000; www.calmac.co.uk) operates a ferry service from the mainland between Mallaig and Armadale (passengers/cars £2.60/15.05, 30 minutes, four daily). It's wise to book, especially during the summer.

Outer Hebrides (Western Isles)

The Outer Hebrides are bleak, remote and treeless. The climate is fierce – the islands are completely exposed to the gales sweeping in from the Atlantic, and it rains more than 250 days of the year. Some people find the landscape mournful, but others are captivated by the stark beauty and isolated world of the crofters. Check **Visit Hebrides** (www.witb.co.uk) for resources. Home to Harris Tweed, the windiest place in Britain, and prehistoric standing stones and brochs, there's more to these islands than you might think.

Lewis is reached by ferry from Ullapool, and its largest town, Stornoway, has a **TIC** (☎ 01851-703088; 26 Cromwell St) as well as several banks. On Harris (which can be reached from Uig on Skye), the **TIC** (☎ 01859-502011; Pier Rd) is in Tarbert. North Uist sports a **TIC** (☎ 01876-500321) in Lochmaddy, while South Uist has a **TIC** (☎ 01878-700286) in Barra.

WALES (CYMRU)

You don't have to go far from the urban southeastern corner of Wales to hit its vast rolling hills and mountains and its sparsely populated coastline. For all the charm of its capital city, Cardiff, you'll get the most from a visit by heading into Wales' great outdoors, tramping some of its glorious national-park wildernesses, and exploring remote inland and coastal towns and villages.

It's in these remote spots you'll get a feel for the distinctive Welsh culture and history, as well as its language, one of the oldest in Europe, and one that's tentatively regaining in popularity. Millennia-long literary and musical traditions live on in some villages and towns, many of them represented at the annual Eisteddfod (see p272).

Despite a tumultuous history as the whipping boy of European invaders and English

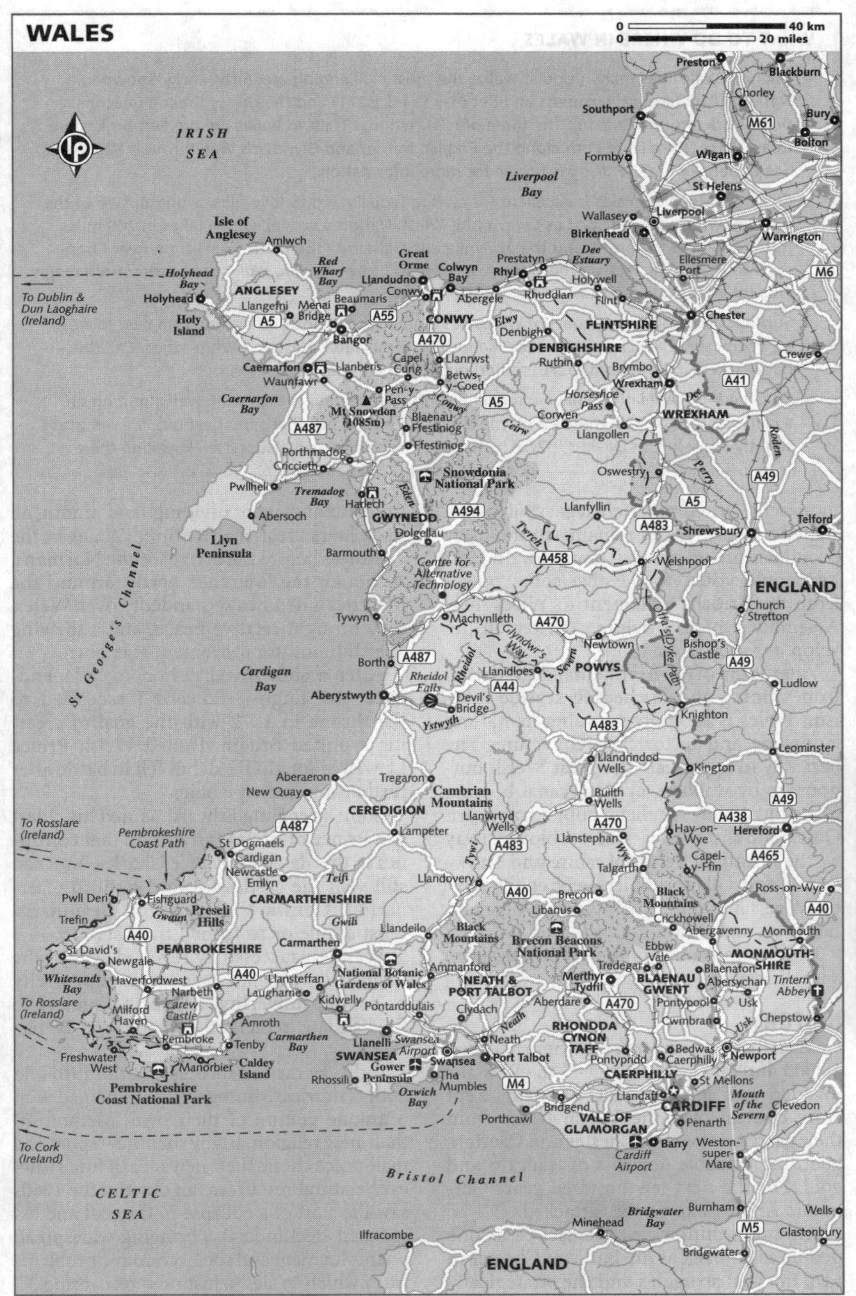
WALES
0 40 km
0 20 miles
IRISH SEA
Liverpool Bay
Isle of Anglesey
Amlwch
Red Wharf Bay
Holyhead Bay
ANGLESEY
To Dublin & Dun Laoghaire (Ireland)
Holyhead
Holy Island
Llangefni
Menai Bridge
Beaumaris
Bangor
A5
A55
Great Orme
Llandudno
Conwy
Colwyn Bay
Abergele
Prestatyn
Rhyl
Rhuddlan
Dee Estuary
Holywell
Flint
CONWY
Elwy
Denbigh
FLINTSHIRE
DENBIGHSHIRE
A470
Caernarfon
Llanberis
Capel Curig
Llanrwst
Betws-y-Coed
Waunfawr
Pen-y-Pass
Conwy
Caernarfon Bay
Mt Snowdon (1085m)
A5
Blaenau Ffestiniog
Ffestiniog
A487
Porthmadog
Criccieth
Pwllheli
Tremadog Bay
Harlech
Abersoch
Llyn Peninsula
Snowdonia National Park
Eden
GWYNEDD
A494
Dolgellau
Barmouth
Centre for Alternative Technology
Tywyn
Machynlleth
Borth
A487
Cardigan Bay
Rheidol Falls
Rheidol
Aberystwyth
Devil's Bridge
Ystwyth
A44
St George's Channel
Ruthin
Corwen
Ceirw
Llangollen
Horseshoe Pass
Brymbo
Wrexham
WREXHAM
Dee
Oswestry
Llanfyllin
Twrch
A458
Welshpool
A470
Glyndwr's Way
Newtown
Severn
Llanidloes
POWYS
A483
Offa's Dyke Path
Knighton
Llandrindod Wells
Builth Wells
Kington
Aberaeron
New Quay
Tregaron
Cambrian Mountains
CEREDIGION
Llanwrtyd Wells
A470
A487
Lampeter
A483
Llanstephan
Wye
Tywi
To Rosslare (Ireland)
Pembrokeshire Coast Path
St Dogmaels
Cardigan
Newcastle Emlyn
Teifi
CARMARTHENSHIRE
Llandovery
A40
Brecon
Talgarth
Libanus
Pwll Deri
Fishguard
Gwaun
Preseli Hills
Trefin
A40
PEMBROKESHIRE
Gwili
Llandeilo
Black Mountains
Brecon Beacons National Park
St David's
Newgale
Carmarthen
Whitesands Bay
Haverfordwest
A40
Llansteffan
National Botanic Gardens of Wales
Ammanford
NEATH & PORT TALBOT
Narbeth
Laugharne
Kidwelly
Pontarddulais
Clydach
To Rosslare (Ireland)
Milford Haven
Carew Castle
Amroth
Carmarthen Bay
Llanelli
Swansea Airport
Neath
Pembroke
Tenby
SWANSEA
Swansea
Port Talbot
Freshwater West
Manorbier
Caldey Island
Gower Peninsula
Rhossili
The Mumbles
Oxwich Bay
Pembrokeshire Coast National Park
M4
Porthcawl
Bridgend
To Cork (Ireland)
CELTIC SEA
Bristol Channel
Ilfracombe
ENGLAND
Minehead
Bridgwater Bay
Preston
Blackburn
Chorley
Southport
M61
Bury
Bolton
Formby
Wigan
St Helens
Wallasey
Liverpool
Birkenhead
Warrington
Ellesmere Port
M6
Chester
Crewe
A41
Roden
Perry
A49
A5
A483
Shrewsbury
Telford
ENGLAND
Church Stretton
Bishop's Castle
A49
Ludlow
Leominster
A49
A438
Hay-on-Wye
Hereford
A465
Capel-y-Ffin
Black Mountains
Ross-on-Wye
A40
Crickhowell
Abergavenny
Monmouth
MONMOUTH-SHIRE
Ebbw Vale
Tredegar
Blaenafon
Merthyr Tydfil
BLAENAU GWENT
Abersychan
Tintern Abbey
Aberdare
A470
Pontypool
Usk
RHONDDA CYNON TAFF
Cwmbran
Chepstow
Usk
Bedwas
Newport
Pontypridd
Caerphilly
CAERPHILLY
St Mellons
Llandaff
CARDIFF
Mouth of the Severn
Clevedon
Penarth
VALE OF GLAMORGAN
Barry
Cardiff Airport
Weston-super-Mare
Burnham
Wells
M5
Glastonbury
Bridgwater

BRITAIN

WHAT TO DO WHERE IN WALES

- Hiking – Wales has many popular walks; the most challenging are in the rocky Snowdonia National Park (around Llanberis and Betws-y-Coed, p271) and the grassy Brecon Beacons National Park (around Brecon). The three official National Trails in Wales are the Pembrokeshire Coast Path, Offa's Dyke Path along the English border and Glyndwr's Way through Mid Wales. See Lonely Planet's *Walking in Britain* for more information.
- Cycling – Much of Wales is excellent for cycling (you'll need to love hills, though). Two of the best-known routes are Lon Las Cymru (the Welsh National Route), which takes in 260 miles from Holyhead to Cardiff, and the 227-mile Lon Geltaidd ('the Celtic Trail') from near Chepstow to Fishguard. Pick up the Wales Tourist Board's free *Cycling Wales* publication from major TICs for an introduction to these and other routes.
- Surfing – The southwest coast of Wales has a number of good surf spots. From east to west, try Porthcawl, Oxwich Bay, Rhossili, Manorbier, Freshwater West and Whitesands. Call the backpackers in Fishguard (p270) to find out which are the best breaks.
- Coasteering – A relatively new adrenaline sport, coasteering is the art of, well, jumping off a cliff into the sea (OK, there's a bit more to it than that, but that's the best bit). It's wet and slightly scary fun. St David's (p270) is the place to go. You can also try sea kayaking there.

monarchs (leaving a rich legacy of stout-walled castles), Wales remains an intensely proud nation, no more so than now. In 1997 its people voted to devolve some power from the British Parliament to Wales' new Assembly, which is helping the region develop its voice as a nation.

After years of environmental degradation from mining and unchecked seaside tourism, Wales is carefully guarding its natural landscape and historical architecture. The best way to appreciate the great Welsh outdoors is by walking, cycling, canal-boating or using Wales' excellent public transport. Outdoors enthusiasts will be blown away by the beauty of Pembrokeshire and Snowdonia, and village amblers will enjoy Hay-on-Wye, Brecon, St David's, Dolgellau, Llanberis and Betws-y-Coed.

Check information online at **VisitWales** (www.visitwales.com).

HISTORY

Celtic tribes settled here some time between 10,000 and 5000 BC. In AD 43 the Romans invaded and for the next 400 years kept close control over the Welsh tribes from their garrison towns at Chester and Caerlon, guarding valuable deposits of lead, tin and gold. For the next few hundred years Germanic Anglo-Saxon tribes attacked.

Although thinking of themselves as one people as far back as the Battle of Chester in 616, internal struggles and the strategically unfortunate law of dividing land among all male heirs created a fractured Wales in the centuries before the arrival of the Normans. Although the 'Marcher Lords' around the Marches ruled heavy-handedly over Wales, they brought relative peace, and a thriving Welsh literature movement was born.

After a short-lived period of independence, the English Edward I ascended to the throne in 1272 with the goal of creating a united Britain. Famed Welsh Prince Llewellyn fought hard, but fell in battle after further internal squabbles.

Soon after King Edward named his eldest son Prince of Wales, a tradition that continues to this day with Prince Charles. You can still visit the castles Edward built in Caernarfon, Conway, Harlech and Beaumaris, most a mile or so from a train station.

Wales unsuccessfully revolted against the English crown, but having no capital city or central university, and being subject to English law, reluctantly accepted its British status.

Industry thrived throughout the 19th and 20th centuries. Mining villages emerged with a unique culture of their own, Methodism their new religion, rugby their new sport and male voice choirs their new idea of fun. However, natural resources ran out and the 1960s saw the start of a collapse in the coal and associated steel industry, bringing widespread unemployment and socioeconomic problems from which Wales is just now recovering.

In 1997 the people of Wales voted to be governed by a Welsh Assembly rather than from the House of Commons in London. In a self-confident step towards greater political autonomy, the first Assembly was put in place in May 1999, and it now meets in a fantastic new Assembly building at Cardiff Bay (p268).

ENVIRONMENT

The Land

Wales has two major mountain systems: the Black Mountains and Brecon Beacons in the south, and the more dramatic mountains of Snowdonia in the northwest. The population is concentrated in the southeast along the coast between Cardiff (the capital) and Swansea and the old mining valleys that run north into the Brecon Beacons. Wales is approximately 170 miles long and 60 miles wide. About 20% of the country is designated as three national parks: Snowdonia, Pembrokeshire and Brecon Beacons.

Wildlife

Keep an eye open for peregrine falcons around Brecon Beacons, and dolphins and seals off the coast of Pembrokeshire.

Environmental Issues

Wales is committed to preserving its natural heritage. The national parks use a 'park and ride' system where drivers can hop on and hop off buses after leaving their cars in car parks. In Snowdonia try the Snowdon Sherpa (p271), or the Puffin Shuttle in Pembrokeshire along the coast path.

PEOPLE

Wales has a population of 2.9 million people, around 5% of the total population of Britain.

LANGUAGE

Welsh is spoken by over 20% of the population, mainly in the north. Recent efforts have been made to reverse its decline. Every Welsh person speaks English, but there's been a national push for Welsh TV and radio programmes and a more aggressive education policy, and most signs are now bilingual.

At first sight, Welsh looks impossibly difficult to get your tongue around. Once you know that 'dd' is pronounced 'th', 'w' can also be a vowel pronounced 'oo', 'f' is 'v' and 'ff' is 'f', and you have had a native speaker teach you how to pronounce 'll' (roughly 'cl'), you will be able to ask the way to Llanfairpwllgwyngyllgogerychwyrndrobwllllantysiliogogogoch (a village in Anglesey reputed to have Britain's longest place name – no joke) and be understood. Try out the following (pronunciation in brackets) for practice:

- *Bore da* (bora-da) good morning
- *Peint o gwrw* (paint-o-guru) pint of beer
- *Diolch* (diolkh) thank you

GETTING THERE & AWAY

Wales is pretty easily accessible from Chester, Liverpool and Shrewsbury in the north, and from Bristol in the south. Regular ferries depart from Swansea, Fishguard and Holyhead for Cork, Rosslare and Dublin in Ireland.

GETTING AROUND

Wales is committed to creating better public transport, but in the meantime you might have difficulty getting around, especially in the more rural areas. Call the eternally helpful **Traveline** (☎ 0870 608 2608; www.traveline.org.uk), which will give you everything you need to know about buses and trains (except prices).

Travel Passes

Four excellent passes allow free travel in designated regions of Wales and immediately adjacent areas of England, and on all rail routes and nearly all intercity bus routes. Following are the passes, with high-/low-season prices (high season is late May to September and Christmas):

4 in 8 Flexi-pass Eight days' bus travel plus any four days' train travel throughout Wales (£55/45).

8 in 15 Flexi-pass Fifteen days' bus travel plus any eight days' train travel throughout Wales (£92/75).

Freedom of North and Mid Wales 7-day Flexi Rover Any three days out of seven of bus and train travel in north and Mid Wales (£35/30).

Freedom of South Wales 7-day Flexi-Rover Seven days' bus travel plus any three days' train travel in south Wales (£35/30).

These passes are sold online at **Freedom of Wales Flexipass** (www.walesflexipass.co.uk), over the counter at most train stations and at many TICs.

Bus

Some 70 private bus companies operate in Wales. The biggest intercity operators are Arriva Cymru, First Cymru and Stagecoach. For all public transport information call the UK-wide Traveline.

Train

Wales has some fantastic train lines, both main-line services (☎ 0845 748 4950) and narrow-gauge and steam-train survivors. See the **Great Little Trains of Wales** (www.greatlittletrainsofwales.co.uk) for more information on nine narrow-gauge railways.

Tours

Several backpacker bus companies run three- to seven-day trips throughout Wales:

Bus Wales (☎ 0800 328 0284; www.buswalestours.com) Leaves from Cardiff, Bath and Bristol, and offers three-day All Wales Tours (£75).

Dragon Tours (☎ 01874-658124; www.dragonbackpackertours.co.uk) Picks up at Cardiff (including hostels and train and bus stations). Trips usually leave Monday and include the six-day All-Wales Circuit (£175), four-day Welsh Highlights (£125) and three-day Weekend Mountain Breaks (£110).

Shaggy Sheep (☎ 07919-244549; www.shaggysheep.com) Leaves from London and offers three-day Merlin Backpacker weekends (£69, plus £39 kitty) and a four-day Dragon All-Wales Tour (£79, plus £59 kitty).

SOUTH WALES

The villages that form a continuous chain along the valleys have their own stark beauty. The traditional market town of **Abergavenny** is worth a stop.

Nestled in a beautiful valley is the breathtaking **Tintern Abbey** (☎ 051-562650; adult/concession £2.50/2; ⏲ 9.30am-6pm, shorter hr in winter), Cistercian ruins on a grand scale, and immortalised in poetry by Wordsworth.

The **Big Pit** (☎ 01495-790311; admission free), near Blaenafon, closed as a coal mine in 1980. These days it gives you a chance to experience life underground, and the guided tours conducted by former miners are highly recommended.

CARDIFF (CAERDYDD)

☎ 029 / pop 285,000

Poor Cardiff. There's absolutely nothing wrong with it. It's a handsome town, with a castle, a large park, pleasant riverside walks, a few good museums and galleries, some interesting civic architecture and a reasonably lively cultural scene (helped by the presence of a university). The trouble is that these parts add up to a less than compelling whole and there's little to keep you here for long. Do make time to explore the new Cardiff Bay area if you're in town, though.

Stock up on maps and information at the **TIC** (☎ 2022 7281; www.visitcardiff.info; The Hayes) for all of Wales. Free Internet access is available at **Cardiff Central Library** (☎ 2038 2116; Frederick St).

Sights

The gargoyle-like animals guarding the outer walls give some clue to the lavish Victorian interior at **Cardiff Castle** (☎ 2087 8100; Castle St); it's more Hollywood than medieval. Nearby, the **National Museum & Gallery of Wales** (☎ 2039 7951; Cathays Park; admission free; ⏲ 10am-5pm Tue-Sun & bank holidays) offers a good crash course in Welsh culture and one of the finest collections of impressionist art in Britain.

The port area at **Cardiff Bay**, about 2 miles from the city centre, is well worth making an afternoon for and is also a good place to stop for lunch. Here you'll find the imposing, modern, slate-sided performance and arts space of the **Wales Millennium Centre**, and the glass and wood marvel, with a roof

WORTH A TRIP

In the early 1970s a group of folk interested in an alternative and above all sustainable way of living set up home in a Welsh quarry. What looked like an eccentric experiment by a bunch of hippies and dreamers then looks like a prescient move today, as oil prices soar and climate change accelerates alarmingly. Still an endearingly idealistic bunch but communicating a serious and practical message, their **Centre for Alternative Technology** (☎ 01654-702400; www.cat.org.uk; adult/concession & child summer £8/4, winter £6/4; ⏲ 10am-5.30pm, 10am-4pm in winter) is home to three interactive hectares of experimentation and information about renewable energy and sustainable living. It's an inspiring place and full of ideas that you can apply in your own life. Courses and residential visits are available, as well as countless special events. Great for kids.

like an upturned boat, that is the new **Welsh Assembly Building**. You can find out about it at the **Pierhead** (☎ 2089 8477; admission free; 9.30am-4.30pm Mon-Fri, 10.30am-4.30pm Sat & Sun).

Sleeping

The city's beds can fill up when there's a big rugby match in town.

YHA Cardiff (☎ 0870 770 5750; cardiff@yha.org.uk; 2 Wedal Rd; dm £14.90; bus 28 or 29) Located in a hip student area.

Cardiff Backpacker (☎ 2034 5577; www.cardiffbackpacker.com; 98 Neville St, Riverside; dm from £17.70; P) A lively backpackers, a five- to 10-minute walk from most sights in the city centre.

Riverbank (☎ 2037 8866; www.sleepcheap.co.uk; 53-59 Despenser St, Riverside; s/d £40/50;) This good, central newcomer is an excellent, central budget guesthouse and close to the Millennium Centre.

Big Sleep Hotel (☎ 2063 6363; www.thebigsleephotel.com; Bute Tce; r from £45; P) Top spot in town for value and interior cool, the high-rise big sleep is really great value given the amazingly stylish rooms occupying a former office block.

Cathedral Rd, which runs alongside the Taff River, is lined with B&Bs occupying large, solid houses. The following are recommended:

Church Hotel (☎ 340881; 126 Cathedral Rd; s/d/f from £30/50/60) A homy place run, apparently, by famed Welsh singer Charlotte Church's mum.

Town House (☎ 2023 9399; www.thetownhousecardiff.co.uk; 70 Cathedral Rd; s/d £45/62; P) A solid old Victorian house, comfortable and quiet.

Eating

Finding good, fresh food that's not out of a fryer or from familiar chain outlets is surprisingly hard in the city centre. Your best bet is to head to Cardiff Bay, which offers lots of options.

Norwegian Church (☎ 2045 4899; mains £3-5; 10am-6pm) A scenic spot for a snack overlooking the water is at this cosy café inside the pretty, white-weatherboard church close to the Assembly Building.

Bayside Brasserie (☎ 2035 8440; mains £5-11; lunch & dinner) For a full-blown meal, this brasserie serves good, reasonably priced modern European dishes. The fish, which you select before it's cooked, is particularly tasty.

Getting There & Away

National Express buses travel to/from London (£19, 3¼ hours, seven daily) and Bristol (£6.50, 50 minutes, every half-hour). Trains come from all over the southeast and head west to Swansea and as far as Haverfordwest.

Brecon Beacons National Park

The Brecon Beacons National Park covers 519 sq miles of high bare hills, surrounded on the northern flanks by a number of attractive market towns; Llandovery, Brecon, Crickhowell, Talgarth and Hay-on-Wye make good bases. The railhead is at Abergavenny (with a Norman castle). A 55-mile cycleway/footpath, the Taff Trail, connects Cardiff with Brecon.

The **National Park Visitor Centre** (☎ 01874-623366; www.visitbreconbeacons.com), near Libanus, is close to many walking trails. Other information offices are in **Brecon** (☎ 01874-622485) and **Llandovery** (☎ 01550-720693; Kings Rd). All make B&B bookings.

Brecon (Aberhonddu)

☎ 01874 / pop 7800

Brecon is an attractive, historic market town that provides an excellent base for walking in the magnificent surrounding countryside. There's also a **cathedral** dating from the 13th century, a market held on Tuesday and Friday, and a highly acclaimed jazz festival in August.

The **TIC** (☎ 622485; brectic@powys.gov.uk) can help with further information and offers a useful mini-guide to the national park. The **YHA Brecon** (☎ 0870 770 5718; brecon@yha.org.uk; Groesffordd) is popular with trekkers and cyclists. The walker-friendly **Bridge Café** (☎ 622024; www.bridgecafé.co.uk; 7 Bridge St; mains £4-8; r £40-50; café 11am-6pm Wed-Sat) offers delicious, fresh, creative home-made food and a couple of appealing, comfortable rooms. A shade upmarket is the enchanting and central **B&B Cantre Selyf** (☎ 622904; www.cantreselyf.co.uk; Lion St; s £48, d £60-72;), which occupies a spacious Georgian town house, with décor that harks back to the 17th century, scrubbed floors and a lovely garden.

Brecon has no train station, but there are regular bus links. **Stagecoach Red & White** (☎ 01685-385539) has regular buses to Swansea and Abergavenny, and to Hereford via Hay-on-Wye.

Hay-on-Wye

☎ 01497 / pop 1600

At the northeastern tip of the Black Mountains is Hay-on-Wye, an eccentric market village that is now known as the world centre for **second-hand books** – there are over 35 shops and more than one million books, everything from first editions costing £1000 to books by the yard (literally).

Contact the **TIC** (☎ 820144; www.haye-on-wye.co.uk; Craft Centre, Oxford Rd; 11am-1pm & 2-4pm) for information on the excellent restaurants and B&Bs in the area. **Capel-y-Ffin Youth Hostel** (☎ 0870 770 5748) is 8 miles south of Hay on the road to Abergavenny. The walk here from Hay follows part of Offa's Dyke and is highly recommended. Get away from it all at the **Barn** (☎ 01873-890477; www.thebarn-wales.co.uk; Pen-y-Maes; s/d £25/50, with shared bathroom £40/45) in a peaceful remote valley 8 miles from Hay.

SOUTHWEST WALES

The coastline northeast of St David's to Cardigan is particularly beautiful and, as it is protected by Pembrokeshire National Park, it remains delightfully unspoilt. The Pembrokeshire Coast Path begins at Amroth, north of Tenby, on the western side of Carmarthen Bay, and continues to St Dogmaels to the west of Cardigan. Tenby is an attractive holiday destination, a little overrun at times.

Carmarthen Bay is more often referred to as Dylan Thomas Country; **Dylan's boathouse** (☎ 01994-427420; adult/concession £3/2; 10am-5.30pm May-Oct, 10.30am-3.30pm Nov-Apr) at Laugharne, where he wrote *Under Milk Wood,* is a moving memorial preserved exactly as he left it. Llanstephan has a beautiful Norman castle above sandy beaches. On west-facing beaches, there's good surf.

From Pembroke Dock **Irish Ferries** (☎ 08705-171717) leaves for Rosslare in Ireland; ferries connect with buses from Cardiff and destinations east. **Stena Line** (☎ 08705-707070) has ferries from Fishguard to Rosslare, from where buses and trains connect.

BRITAIN

Pembrokeshire Coast National Park

The national park protects a narrow band of magnificent coastline, broken only by the more dense development around Pembroke and Milford Haven. The only significant inland portion is the mystical Preseli Hills to the southeast of Fishguard. There are National Park Information Centres and TICs at **Tenby** (☎ 01834-842402), **St David's** (☎ 01437-720392) and **Fishguard** (☎ 01348-873484). The free *Coast to Coast* has detailed local information or check out the Pembrokeshire Coast National Park Authority's website at www.pcnpa.org.uk. Apart from hostels, there are loads of B&Bs from around £20. Contact Traveline for bus information.

St David's (Tyddewi)

☎ 01437 / pop 1450

The linchpin for the southwest is beautiful St David's, one of Europe's smallest 'cities', referred to as such because of its cathedral. There's a web of interesting streets and, concealed in the Vale of Roses, beautiful **St David's Cathedral** (☎ 720517; 8am-6pm Mon-Sat, shorter hr in winter) is spectacularly well preserved. Contact the **TIC** (☎ 720392; www.stdavids.co.uk; High St) for more information. **TYF Adventure** (☎ 721611; 1 High St) offers a range of outdoor adrenaline fun including coasteering, sea kayaking, surfing and rock climbing.

There are several handy youth hostels: near **St David's** (☎ 0870 770 6042); at **Trefin** (☎ 0870 770 6074), 11 miles from St David's; and the superb little **Pwll Deri** (☎ 0870 770 6004), on the cliffs 8 miles from Trefin and just over 4.5 miles from Fishguard.

There are regular **Richards Bros** (☎ 01239-613756) buses to/from Fishguard (45 minutes, every two hours Monday to Saturday). The closest train station is Haverfordwest, from where bus 411 runs hourly into St David's.

Fishguard (Abergwaun)

☎ 01348 / pop 3200

Fishguard is on a beautiful bay, and the old part of town, Lower Fishguard, was the location for the 1971 film version of *Under Milk Wood,* starring Richard Burton and Elizabeth Taylor. The train station and harbour (for ferries to Rosslare) are at Goodwick, a 20-minute walk from the town proper.

There's a **TIC** (☎ 873484; www.fishguardonline.com; daily summer), but the **Hamilton Guest House & Backpackers Lodge** (☎ 874797; www.fishguard-backpackers.com; 21 Hamilton St; dm/d £12/30) is even more helpful, and has a sauna.

MID WALES

Most visitors to Wales head either for the easily accessible south or the scenically more dramatic north, leaving the quiet valleys of Mid Wales to the Welsh.

The 120-mile **Glyndwr's Way** national trail visits sites associated with the Welsh hero between Knighton (on Offa's Dyke Path) and Welshpool via picturesque villages, such as Machynlleth, and stunning natural scenery. Leaflets are available from TICs in the area and are invaluable, as route-finding is difficult in places.

Machynlleth is an attractive market town and a good base for exploring Mid Wales. Check with the **TIC** (☎ 01654-702401; mactic@mail.powys.gov.uk) for local information.

A remarkably pleasant coastal university town, **Aberystwyth** has good transport connections. Contact the **TIC** (☎ 0197-612125; www.aberystwyth-online.co.uk) for B&Bs. **Borth Youth Hostel** (☎ 0870 770 5708; yha.org.uk; dm adult/child £11.95/9.95) is 8 miles north of Aberystwyth, near a wide sandy beach.

Running through the Vale of Rheidol to Devil's Bridge are **steam trains**, offering spectacular views of the waterfall.

NORTH WALES

North Wales is dominated by the Snowdonia Mountains, which loom over the beautiful coastline. The Red Rover day ticket (£16.90) covers most of the region. For information call Traveline.

Holyhead (Caergybi)

☎ 01407 / pop 12,500

Holyhead is a grey and daunting ferry port. Both **Irish Ferries** (☎ 08705-171717) and **Stena Line** (☎ 08705-707070) run ferries to Dublin. Stena Line also sails to Dun Laoghaire, just outside Dublin.

The **TIC** (☎ 762622; holyhead@nwtic.com) is in ferry terminal 1. In the nearby township there's a batch of B&Bs that are used to dealing with late ferry arrivals (check ahead with the TIC). Trains come from all over Britain, including London, Chester, Birmingham and Llandudno.

Llandudno

☎ 01492 / pop 22,000

Developed as a Victorian holiday town, Llandudno has retained much of its 19th-century architecture and antiquated atmosphere, and seethes with visitors in summer. There's a wonderful **pier & promenade** and donkeys on the beach.

Llandudno is situated on its very own peninsula nestled between two sweeping beaches, and dominated by the spectacular limestone headland, the **Great Orme**, with the mountains of Snowdonia providing the backdrop. The Great Orme, with its **tramway** (adult/child £3.95/2.80), superb views and Bronze Age mine, is fascinating.

There are hundreds of guesthouses, but it can be difficult to find somewhere to stay in the peak July/August season. Contact the **TIC** (☎ 876413; www.llandudno-tourism.co.uk; 1/2 Chapel St) for more information.

Conwy

☎ 01492 / pop 3900

Conwy has been revitalised since the through traffic on the busy A55 was consigned to a tunnel, which burrows under the estuary of the Conwy River. It's a picturesque and interesting little town, dominated by superb **Conwy Castle** (☎ 592358; adult/concession £4.50/4; 🕑 9.30am-6pm Jun-Sep, 9.30am-4pm Oct-May), one of the grandest of Edward I's castles and a medieval masterpiece.

The **TIC** (☎ 592248; conwy.tic@virgin.net; Conwy Castle Visitor Centre) is located in the castle. About 3 miles south of Llandudno, Conwy is linked to Llandudno by several buses hourly and a few trains. There are, however, numerous trains from Llandudno to Llandudno Junction, a 15-minute walk from Conwy.

Snowdonia National Park

Although the Snowdonia Mountains are fairly compact, they loom over the coast and offer easily the most spectacular scenery in Wales. The most popular region is in the north around Mt Snowdon, at 1085m the highest peak in Britain south of the Scottish Highlands. Hikers must be prepared to deal with hostile conditions at any time of the year. Check **Mount Snowdon** (www.visitsnowdonia.info) or **Snowdonia National Park** (www.snowdonia-npa.gov.uk) for more information.

There are several National Park Information Centres, including **Betws-y-Coed** (☎ 01690-710426; ticbetws@hotmail.com), **Blaenau Ffestiniog** (☎ 01766-830360) and **Harlech** (☎ 01766-780658). They all have a wealth of information, and all make B&B bookings.

The beautiful, if crowded, hamlet of **Betws-y-Coed** is a lovely base from which to explore Snowdonia. The nearest hostel is **Capel Curig** (☎ 0870 770 5746; capelcurig@yha.org.uk; dm adult/child £16/12.50), 5 miles west.

Bed and breakfasts, and hotels, are plentiful. The intimate **Henllys Guest House** (☎ 01690-710534; www.jhaddy.freeserve.co.uk; Old Church Rd; per person from £15) is housed in a converted Victorian magistrate's court set next to the Conwy River. Another historic building is the homey, welcoming **Royal Oak Hotel** (☎ 01690-710219; www.royaloakhotel.net; r per person £40-60; P), a former coaching inn located right in the heart of the village.

Snowdon Sherpa buses run along the major mountain routes within the national park, and have connections to Llandudno from Betws-y-Coed, to Caernarfon from Waunfawr and to Caernarfon/Bangor from Llanberis.

In Llanberis, you can take the **Snowdon Mountain Railway** (☎ 0870 458 0033; www.snowdonrailway.co.uk) for the ride to the top and back (adult/child £21/14). The **TIC** (☎ 01286-870765; www.llanberis.org; 41a High St) is helpful.

The best hostel in the area is the **Pen-y-Pass Youth Hostel** (☎ 0870 770 5990; penypass@yha.org.uk; Nantgwynant, Caernarfon; dm adult/child £13.95/9.95), 6 miles up the valley situated in a spectacular site at the start of one of the paths up Snowdon. **Pete's Eats** (☎ 01286-870358; mains £2-5) is a warm café opposite the TIC where hikers swap information over large portions of hearty food, like chip butties, and big mugs of tea. In the evening, climbers hang out in the **Heights** (☎ 01286-871179; www.heightshotel.co.uk; 74 High St; dm/d £14/50, f £60-100; P), a hotel/hostel that has a pub and restaurant that will arrange outdoor adventures for guests.

Llangollen

☎ 01978 / pop 2600

Famous for its **International Musical Eisteddfod** (☎ 862001; www.international-eisteddfod.co.uk), Llangollen is just 8 miles from the English border. This six-day music, song and dance festival, held in July, attracts folk groups from around the world.

The town makes an excellent base for outdoor activities, such as walks to ruined **Valle Crucis Abbey** and the Horseshoe Pass, horse-drawn canal-boat trips and canoeing on the Dee River.

The **Llangollen Youth Hostel & Activity Centre** (☎ 0870 770 5932; llangollen@yha.org.uk; Tyndwr Rd; adult/under 18yr £11.95/8.95) is 1.5 miles from the town centre. Contact the **TIC** (☎ 860828) for B&Bs.

BRITAIN DIRECTORY

ACCOMMODATION

Reflecting the wide array of sleepover options available in Britain, accommodation in this chapter has been listed in budget order, with the lowest-priced first. Budget listings are usually hostels or backpacker joints, midrange options are often B&Bs or small guesthouses and top-end spots are typically swish hotels. Remember that local TICs will find and book accommodation for you ahead of your arrival if you tell them your budget and what you're looking for. This service is sometimes free but usually costs around £3.

Most budget listings in this chapter are under £30 per person, while midrange options are generally under £60. Top-end accommodation ranges upwards of £60. London prices are often higher in these categories. Typically, breakfast is included in midrange and top-end options and may also be included in budget accommodation.

Free camping is rarely possible in Britain, except in remote areas, but there's a surfeit of pay-per-pitch sites across the country. Rates can range from £2 to £15 per night, depending on location and season, and facilities can run from shared cold-water taps to hot showers and laundry facilities. The best-selling and comprehensive *AA Caravan and Camping Britain & Ireland* (£9.99) guide is widely available. Also visit **UK Campsite** (www.ukcampsite.co.uk) for thousands of listings and user-reviews.

The separate Youth Hostel Associations (YHA) for **England & Wales** (☎ 0870 770 8868; www.yha.org.uk) and **Scotland** (☎ 0870 155 3255; www.syha.org.uk) offer dorm bed rates from £9 to £20 per night. Their facilities vary from institutionalised basic to IKEA-chic modern, with some larger hostels now offering private rooms and free breakfasts to compete with independent operators. Prices in this chapter are for adults, but per-night discounts are available to all under 18s (usually about 25%) and Hostelling International (HI) members (usually £1 to £2). Not all hostels are open year-round, so book or call ahead before you arrive.

There's a growing array of independent hostels and backpackers across Britain, varying widely in quality, facilities and price (typically from £10 to £25). Some are quiet and cosy, while others are for serious party travellers. The online **Independent Hostel Guide** (www.independenthostelguide.co.uk) is a listing resource for tracking down some of these hostels. For Scotland only, check **Scottish Independent Hostels** (www.hostel-scotland.co.uk) for online listings.

Many universities offer student accommodation to visitors during Christmas, Easter and summer holidays. Usually in basic single study rooms, rates typically range from £15 to £35 per person. For information, contact **Venuemasters** (☎ 0114 249 3090; www.venuemasters.com), which represents 100 British universities and offers online bookings.

A British institution and often the best-value accommodation in town, B&Bs and guesthouses can range from £15 per person for a bedroom in a family home to more than £50 for a warm and fuzzy stay in a characterful heritage house. The common link is the heaping cooked breakfast intended to keep you fuelled well into the afternoon. For comprehensive listings, pick up the *AA Bed & Breakfast Guide* (£12.99).

Hotels can run from poky pub rooms (£20 to £50) to a night of luxury in a sleek boutique property (upwards of £75). In between is a growing roster of competitive mid-range chains, including **Ibis** (www.ibishotel.com) and **Premier Travel Inn** (www.premiertravelinn.com). Often in convenient city-centre locations, they provide modern, good-value rooms for flat rates (from £40). Note that most B&Bs, guesthouses and hotels charge per room but some charge per person – make sure you know what you're paying before you unpack your bag.

ACTIVITIES

Britain is a great destination for outdoor enthusiasts, from daredevil rock climbers to beach-bum surfer dudes and leisurely day hikers. There are clubs and associations across the land, and useful brochures and maps available from **Visit Britain** (www.visitbritain.com). Its website has some good recommendations and links under its Get Active section.

Cycling

Compact Britain is an excellent destination to explore by bike. Not all cities are cycle-friendly (Oxford, Bristol and Bath are among the best) but there are plenty of designated routes through some of the nation's best countryside. Popular routes and regions include the Yorkshire Dales Cycleway, Derbyshire's Peak District and the Scottish Borders. The 10,000-mile **National Cycle Network** (☎ 0845 113 0065; www.nationalcyclenetwork.org.uk) crisscrosses Britain with one-day and multi-day rides, and is actively expanding. Contact the network for excellent maps and other cycling resources. The **Cyclists' Touring Club** (☎ 0870 873 0060; www.ctc.org.uk) is the leading national organisation for biking enthusiasts, and they can help out with route information and general inquiries about cycling throughout Britain. Hiring bicycles is easy in the UK, with prices typically ranging from £6 for a half-day to £60 for a week – book ahead for summer rentals.

Hiking

Britain's cornucopia of picturesque terrains makes for great hiking country. Day hikes are a popular and accessible way to escape from the crowded cities, and there are hundreds of longer routes waiting for more adventurous travellers. Popular hiking trails include the 191-mile **Coast to Coast Walk** (www.coast2coast.co.uk) across three northern England national parks, the 100-mile **Cotswold Way** (www.cotswold-way.co.uk) between Bath and Chipping Campden, and the 84-mile **Dales Way** (www.thedalesway.co.uk) through Yorkshire's charming countryside. Other routes crisscross Exmoor and Dartmoor National Parks, Pembrokeshire National Park in Wales, and the highlands and islands of Scotland. Many of these are mentioned throughout this chapter.

Ramblers Association (☎ 020-7339 8500; www.ramblers.org.uk) is a voluntary organisation with a wealth of experience on hiking and walking across Britain. It produces dozens of maps, guides and accommodation listings for local and visiting hoofers. For additional information and resources (some for free download), check out **National Trails** (www.nationaltrails.co.uk).

Water Sports

Surrounded by water and dripping with lakes, lochs and canals, Britain offers a brimming bucket full of coastal and inland water-based activities.

The Devon and Cornwall region is England's surfing mecca, with rideable swells at ore than 100 closely linked beaches, including Newquay's ever-popular Fistral Beach. Scotland is opening up to its surfing potential, with the north coast proving popular among adventurous board fans. Southwest Wales also has some great waves around Newgale and Whitesands. Equipment hire centres are widespread. The **British Surfing Association** (☎ 0870 011 4240; www.britsurf.org) should be your first stop for information and resources. Windsurfers can also check out Brit-based options via the **Royal Yachting Association** (☎ 0845 345 0400; www.rya.org.uk).

With hundreds of shipwrecks strewn around its coast, diving is also popular. Some of the best wetsuit haunts are along the English south coast, where hapless medieval and WWII vessels jostle for space. The **British Sub-Aqua Club** (☎ 0151 350 6200; www.bsac.com) offers courses and information for dive fans.

BOOKS

For detailed country guides pick up the latest Lonely Planet editions of *Great Britain, England, Scotland* and *Wales*. Among the legions of travel literature on the British Isles, Bill Bryson's *Notes from a Small Island* is hugely entertaining, while AA Gill's acidic *The Angry Island* is great fun. For an alternative take on the country's kitschest attractions, read *Bollocks to Alton Towers*, a celebration of day trips out to off-beat attractions such as the Cumberland Pencil Museum.

BUSINESS HOURS

Standard office hours are from 9am to 5pm Monday to Friday. Most banks are open 9.30am to 5pm during the week, with larger branches also opening on Saturday morning. Shops open from at least 9am to 5pm Monday to Saturday, while opening from 10am to 4pm on Sunday is also increasingly common at larger shops. Many will also stay open late one night per week, usually Thursday or Friday. Some city-centre supermarkets are open 24 hours. Restaurants often open daily for lunch from 11am to 3pm, then reopen for dinner from 6pm to 10pm, but specific hours can vary widely. Traditional pub opening hours are from 11am to 11pm Monday to Saturday and from noon to 10.30pm Sunday, however, a recent relaxing of the licensing laws means that many – particularly those ones in the cities – will stay open later, especially on weekends.

EMBASSIES & CONSULATES

British Embassies & Consulates Abroad

For more British embassies, visit the website of the **Foreign & Commonwealth Office** (www.fco.gov.uk).

Australia (☎ 02-6270 6666; www.britaus.net; Commonwealth Ave, Yarralumla, Canberra, ACT 2600)
Canada (☎ 613-237 1530; www.britainincanada.org; 80 Elgin St, Ottawa, ON K1P 5K7)
France (☎ 01 44 51 31 00; www.amb-grandebretagne.fr; 35 rue du Faubourg St Honoré, 75383 Paris Cedex 08)
Germany (☎ 030-204 570; www.britischebotschaft.de; Wilhelmstrasse 70, 10117 Berlin)
Ireland (☎ 01-205 3700; www.britishembassy.ie; 29 Merrion Rd, Ballsbridge, Dublin 4)
Japan (☎ 03-5211 1100; www.uknow.or.jp; 1 Ichiban-cho, Chiyoda-ku, Tokyo 102-8381)
Netherlands (☎ 070 427 04 27; www.britain.nl; Lange Voorhout 10, 2514 ED, The Hague)
New Zealand (☎ 04-924 2888; www.britain.org.nz; 44 Hill St, Wellington 1)
USA (☎ 202-588 6500; www.britainusa.com; 3100 Massachusetts Ave NW, Washington, DC 20008)

Embassies & Consulates in Britain

For more embassies, visit the website of the **Foreign & Commonwealth Office** (www.fco.gov.uk).

Australia (Map pp152-3; ☎ 020-7379 4334; www.australia.org.uk; Australia House, Strand, London, WC2B 4LA)
Canada (Map pp152-3; ☎ 020-7258 6600; Macdonald House, 1 Grosvenor Sq, London, W1K 4AB)
France (Map pp156-7; ☎ 020-7073 1200; www.ambafrance-uk.org; 58 Knightsbridge, London, SW1X 7JT)
Germany (Map pp152-3; ☎ 020-7824 1300; www.german-embassy.org.uk; 23 Belgrave Sq, London, SW1 8PZ)
Ireland (Map pp152-3; ☎ 020-7235 2171; 17 Grosvenor Pl, London, SW1X 7HR)
Japan (Map pp152-3; ☎ 020-7465 6500; www.uk.emb-japan.go.jp; 101-104 Piccadilly, London, W1J 7JT)
Netherlands (Map pp156-7; ☎ 020-7590 3200; www.netherlands-embassy.org.uk; 38 Hyde Park Gate, London, SW7 5DP)
New Zealand (Map pp152-3; ☎ 020-7930 8422; www.nzembassy.com; 80 Haymarket, London, SW1Y 4TQ)
USA (Map pp152-3; ☎ 020-7499 9000; www.usembassy.org.uk; 24 Grosvenor Sq, London, W1A 1AE)

FESTIVALS & EVENTS

There are countless diverse special events held around Britain throughout the year,. Many of them are based on traditional customs initiated centuries ago. Some of the more prominent festivals and events include:

January

Hogmanay/New Year (www.edinburghshogmanay.org; Princess St, Edinburgh) Huge, raucous party from 31 December to 1 January echoed by smaller versions throughout the UK.

April

Grand National (www.aintree.co.uk) Britain's top annual horse race. Held in Aintree, Liverpool, in early April.

May

FA Cup Final (www.thefa.com) Nail-biting conclusion to England's annual knock-out football club competition at Wembley Stadium in London. Held in mid-May.

June

Glastonbury Festival (www.glastonburyfestivals.co.uk) Giant open-air music extravaganza at Somerset in late June.

July

Llangollen International Musical Eisteddfod (www.international-eisteddfod.co.uk) In Llangollen, Wales, a 60-year-old celebration of international folk music and dance. Held in early July.
T in the Park (www.tinthepark.com) Scotland's leading open-air music festival, held in Glasgow in mid-July.
Farnborough International Air Show (www.farnborough.com) In Farnborough, Surrey, the world's largest aeroplane display. Held in mid-July.

August

Edinburgh Fringe Festival (www.edfringe.com) Sprawling, three-week comedy and avant-garde performance fest in Edinburgh from early August.
Brecon Jazz Festival (www.breconjazz.co.uk) In mid-August, indoor and outdoor jazz concerts in the Welsh countryside.
Reading Festival (www.readingfestival.com) Popular annual live music (and camping) fest in Reading, Berkshire. Held in late August.

September

Braemar Gathering (www.braemargathering.org) Held in early September, haggis scoffing and caber tossing in the Scottish Highlands of Braemar, Deeside, attended by a kilted Royal Family.

November

Guy Fawkes Night Bonfires and fireworks recalling failed antigovernment plot from the 1600s. Held nationwide on 5 November.

GAY & LESBIAN TRAVELLERS

Most major cities have 'out' gay and lesbian scenes – especially London, Brighton, Manchester and Glasgow – but there can still be some mindless intolerance in smaller towns and tabloid newspapers. **Visit Britain** (www.visitbritain.com) has introductory information and an e-newsletter for gay travellers on its website, while the website of the **Gay Britain Network** (www.gaybritain.co.uk) provides links to searchable databases and offers gay-friendly travel information. **Gay Times** (www.gaytimes.co.uk) and **Diva** (www.divamag.co.uk) provide resources and information in their print and online versions, while the **National Gay & Lesbian Switchboard** (☎ 020-7837 7324; www.llgs.org.uk) offers a 24-hour support service for residents and visitors throughout Britain.

HOLIDAYS

Public Holidays

Called bank holidays in Britain, these affect most businesses, although larger shops increasingly remain open. The following is a list of the main public holidays:

New Year's Day 1 January
New Year's Holiday 2 January (Scotland only)
Good Friday March/April, Friday before Easter
Easter Monday March/April (except Scotland)
May Day First Monday in May
Spring Bank Holiday Last Monday in May
Summer Bank Holiday First Monday in August (Scotland only)
Summer Bank Holiday Last Monday in August (England and Wales only)
Christmas Day 25 December
Boxing Day 26 December

MEDIA

Britain has some of the world's best and worst newspapers. At the top end, it's hard to beat the *Guardian, Telegraph, Times* and *Independent*, most of which now come in handy tabloid sizes. At the bottom of the barrel, the *Sun, Star* and *Mirror* continue to mine their puerile fascination with sex and celebrities – a recipe that has made the *Sun* Britain's most widely read newspaper. The magazine sector is equally diverse, with classy *GQ* and *Vogue* only dreaming they could reach the massive circulation of *Viz*, Britain's adults-only comic strip.

On TV and radio, the public service British Broadcasting Corporation (BBC) continues to provide high-quality news, entertainment and sports services. Along with the BBC's two free-to-air TV channels, there are three additional free channels available on regular TV sets. A massive expansion in cable and satellite services has also delivered dozens of new channels to viewers who pay for decoders and/or packages.

MONEY

Still refusing to adopt the euro (€) – it's accepted at some major tourist attractions, larger hotels and at increasing numbers of businesses in London and the southeast – Britain's currency remains the pound sterling (£), split among a variety of coins and banknotes each bearing the Queen's image. Scotland and Northern Ireland also issue banknotes, which are legal tender across the UK: if you have trouble using them in England, exchange them at any bank for free.

ATMs

It's not hard to find an ATM – usually called 'cashpoints' – in Britain, where they're often located outside banks, building societies and large supermarkets. They accept a wide variety of cards, including Visa, MasterCard and American Express (Amex). Some cashpoints, particularly those in unusual locations like pubs, charge extra fees for withdrawals.

Credit Cards & Debit Cards

MasterCard and Visa are the most acceptable cards in Britain, with Amex not far behind. Britain recently launched 'Chip & Pin', a debit and credit card payment system that requires a security number to be entered. This system does not apply to traditional cards issued overseas: you will be able to use your card in the usual manner.

Moneychangers

Be careful with bureaux de change: they may advertise good exchange rates but sometimes levy outrageous fees and commissions. Always ask what the 'extras' are before making a transaction. Banks are a safe money-changing option and some larger post offices will also exchange your foreign dosh.

Travellers Cheques

An inconvenient method of payment in Britain – they are rarely accepted at businesses and have to be exchanged for cash at banks or exchanges – travellers cheques have been largely superseded by credit and debit cards.

POST

Most post offices are open from 9am to 5pm Monday to Friday and until noon on Saturday. Within the UK, 1st-class mail is quicker and more expensive (£0.32 per letter) than 2nd-class mail (£0.23). Postcards sent overseas cost £0.44 (Europe) and £0.50 (outside Europe). Stamp-vending machines are located outside some post offices, and larger newsagents and supermarkets sell them in books of four or 10. Single stamps are often available at larger attractions and some TICs.

STUDYING

There are thousands of language schools throughout Britain, not just the ones advertised on the postcards handed out along Oxford St in London. Unfortunately, some of the outfits are scams preying on the impressionable. The **British Council** (www.britishcouncil.org) administers an accreditation scheme for schools and its website provides a good introduction to studying in Britain. **English UK** (www.englishuk.com) offers an even more specific service, and is a one-stop shop for information on classes, visas and regions for study.

TELEPHONE

Call boxes, mostly operated by British Telecom (BT), are a common enough sight on UK streets. Most take coins, credit cards, phonecards or a combination of all three. Coin phones do not give change and they charge a minimum of £0.20. Local calls are charged by time, while national calls are by time and distance: it's cheaper to call before 8am or after 6pm Monday to Friday or any time on weekends. Many hotels charge high fees for in-room phone usage – you may need to sell your body if you want to make an international call.

EMERGENCY NUMBERS

For almost any type of emergency, dial ☎ 999. You will be connected to the nearest coastguard, fire service, mountain rescue, ambulance or police via this number.

BRITAIN

Mobile Phones

Mobile phones are ubiquitous in Britain, with text messaging a national pastime. Britain uses the GSM 900/1800 network, covering Europe, Australia and New Zealand. It's not generally compatible with North America. Ask your service provider if you can use your phone in Britain. If mobile access is important to you, consider buying a pay-as-you-go phone here for as little as £50. It has its own number and you buy top-up cards to stay in credit. Mobile phone numbers usually begin with ☎ 07.

Phone Codes

For international direct calls, dial ☎ 00 followed by the country code, area code (drop the first zero if there is one) and local number. Dial ☎ 155 for the international operator. For calls within Britain, dial ☎ 100 for operator assistance and ☎ 118118 for directory enquiries. Useful codes to know include:

☎ 0800 – free call
☎ 0845 – local rate call
☎ 0870 – national rate call
☎ 0871 – local rate call
☎ 0891 – premium rate call
☎ 0906 – premium rate call

TOURIST INFORMATION

The website of **Visit Britain** (www.visitbritain.com) is stuffed with resources and staff are ever-eager to send brochures and information on request. **England** (www.enjoyengland.com), **Scotland** (www.visitscotland.com) and **Wales** (www.visitwales.com) also have dedicated tourism agencies. Most regions and many towns and cities have their own visitor websites – they are listed throughout this chapter. Britain also has a good network o. local TICs.

TRAVELLING WITH DISABILITIES

While newer businesses and attractions are user-friendly for disabled people, there are many old buildings in Britain that are not. Wheelchair travellers, in particular, are not well served by traditional pubs and B&Bs. Ibis and Premier Travel Inn hotels provide well-designed disabled rooms, while many banks and ticket offices are fitted with hearing loops. Newer buses have ramps for wheelchair access – one of the reasons for the demise of London's old Routemasters – and train networks usually provide personal ramps and attendants if you call ahead. Contact **National Rail Enquiries** (☎ 08457-484950; www.nationalrail.co.uk) for further details. **RADAR** (☎ 020-7250 3222; www.radar.org.uk) publishes an invaluable guide on disabilities holidays in Britain, while **Holiday Care** (☎ 0845 124 9971; www.holidaycare.org.uk) provides lists of accessible accommodation.

VISAS

You don't need a visitor visa if you are a citizen of Australia, Canada, New Zealand, South Africa or the USA. Tourists are generally permitted to stay for up to six months, but are prohibited from working. All other nationalities should apply for a visitor visa through their nearest British diplomatic mission. These currently cost around £50. For more information, visit **UK Visas** (www.ukvisas.gov.uk).

Current worldwide security issues mean that immigration officials at all ports of entry are stricter now than ever before. Be prepared to answer questions about your reasons for entering Britain and the date you expect to leave – show your outbound travel ticket if necessary.

WORK

The Working Holidaymaker scheme allows Commonwealth citizens aged 17 to 27 years to live and work here for up to two years, but arrangements must be made in advance via a British embassy overseas. Visiting full-time students from the USA are eligible to apply to work in Britain for up to six months. Contact the **British North America Universities Club** (☎ 020-7251 3472; www.bunac.org.uk) for details. Nationals from most EU countries can live and work freely in Britain, but there may be restrictions on citizens from newer member nations. For more information, visit **Working in the UK** (www.workingintheuk.gov.uk).

TRANSPORT IN BRITAIN

GETTING THERE & AWAY

Air

Britain is a hectic airline hub, with London, Manchester and Glasgow in particular receiving frequent flights from around the world. A plethora of regional airports has also sprung up in recent years, servicing busy routes from Europe and beyond.

Consider some of these as alternatives to the main airports; they may be cheaper and more convenient, depending on where you plan to stay in Britain. The following are among the key international airports:

Birmingham (BHM; ☎ 0870 733 5511; www.bhx.co.uk)
Bristol (BRS; ☎ 0870 121 2747; www.bristolairport.co.uk)
Cardiff (CWL; ☎ 01446-711111; www.cwlfly.com)
Edinburgh (EDI; ☎ 0870 040 0007; www.edinburghairport.com)
Glasgow (GGW; ☎ 0870 040 0008; www.glasgowairport.com)
Liverpool John Lennon (LPL; ☎ 0870 129 8484; www.liverpooljohnlennonairport.com)
London Gatwick (LGW; ☎ 0870 000 2468; www.gatwickairport.com)
London Heathrow (LHR; ☎ 0870 000 0123; www.heathrowairport.com)
London Luton (LTN; ☎ 01582-405100; www.london-luton.co.uk)
London Stansted (STN; ☎ 0870 000 0303 www.stanstedairport.com)
Newcastle (NCL; ☎ 0870 122 1488; www.newcastleairport.com)
Manchester (MAN; ☎ 0161 489 3000; www.manchesterairport.co.uk)
Southampton (SOU; ☎ 08700 4020 0009; www.southamptonairport.com)

Following are some of the busiest airlines flying to/from Britain, including their UK contact details:

Aer Lingus (code EI; ☎ 0845 876 5000; www.flyaerlingus.com)
Air Canada (code AC; ☎ 0871 220 1111; www.aircanada.com)
Air France (code AF; ☎ 0870 142 4343; www.airfrance.com)
American Airlines (code AA; ☎ 0845 778 9789; www.aa.com)
British Airways (code BA; ☎ 0870 850 9850; www.ba.com)
British Midland/BMI (code BD; ☎ 0870 6070 555; www.flybmi.com)
Cathay Pacific (code CX; ☎ 020-8834 8888; www.cathaypacific.com)
easyJet (code EZY; ☎ 0870 600 0000; www.easyjet.com)
KLM (code KLM; ☎ 0870 507 4074; www.klm.com)
Lufthansa (code LH; ☎ 0870 833 7747; www.lufthansa.com)
Qantas (code QF; ☎ 0845 774 7767; www.qantas.com/au)
Ryanair (code FR; ☎ 0871 246 0000; www.ryanair.com)
United (code UA; ☎ 0845 844 4777; www.united.com)
Virgin Atlantic (code VS; ☎ 0870 574 7747; www.virgin-atlantic.com)

Land

BUS

Servicing a vast network of long-distance routes, **Eurolines** (☎ 0870 514 3219; www.eurolines.com; 52 Grosvenor Gardens, Victoria, London) is an umbrella company linking 32 regional bus/coach operators. Popular direct daily services to London Victoria arrive from Amsterdam (from £10, two hours, three daily), Paris (from £15, nine hours, four daily) and Dublin (from £24, 12 hours, two daily), among many others. There are also Eurolines services to cities outside London. You can book tickets online, through any UK National Express office or at many larger travel agencies.

CAR & MOTORCYCLE

Visitors can bring cars or motorbikes to Britain from Europe via ferry services or the Channel Tunnel. For specific information on these routes, refer to Sea (opposite) and for tips on driving in Britain, see p280. If hiring, check with the company regarding insurance requirements and drop-off charges for travelling from mainland Europe to Britain.

TRAIN

Regular **Eurostar** (☎ 0870 518 6186; www.eurostar.com) high-speed services arrive from France (£59, three hours) and Belgium (£59, 2½ hours) throughout the day. Currently, these terminate at London Waterloo but this will switch to London St Pancras when a new terminal is opened in 2007. Youth discounts are available to travellers under 26 years.

An alternative to Eurostar is the vehicle train service operated by **Eurotunnel** (☎ 0870 535 3535; www.eurotunnel.com). These carry cars and their passengers through the Channel Tunnel between Folkestone in the UK and Calais in France. Trains depart up to four times an hour in each direction between 6am and 10pm, and hourly from 10pm to 6am. A car plus passengers can cost up to £220 but advertised promotions can bring this down to £39. The journey takes 35 minutes.

Rail/ferry links involve trains at either end and a ferry or high-speed catamaran across the Channel. It's usually cheaper but much slower than travelling by Eurostar. Contact **Rail Europe** (www.raileurope.com) for routes, information and prices. Eurail passes are not valid for travel to or around Britain, but Eurostar discounts are offered to Eurail pass holders.

Sea

With a bewildering array of marine services linking Britain and Europe, prices can change rapidly to reflect the intense competition. Shop around for bargains via operators' websites and keep an eye on national newspapers for summer promotions. The shortest crossing from mainland Europe is Calais to Dover on the English south coast. Some key routes and operators are listed following. Contact operators for additional routes and information.

Brittany Ferries (☎ 0870 366 5333; www.brittanyferries.co.uk) From France, operates between Cherbourg and Portsmouth (£29, six to nine hours, daily); from Spain, operates between Santander and Plymouth (from £48, 24 hours, twice weekly).

DFDS Seaways (☎ 0870 252 0524; www.dfds.co.uk) From the Netherlands, operates between Amsterdam and Newcastle (from £110, 15 hours, daily); from Sweden, operates between Gothenburg and Newcastle (from £105, 17 hours, twice weekly).

P & O (☎ 0870 242 4999; www.poferries.com, www.poirishsea.com) From France, operates between Calais and Dover (from £18, 75 minutes, every 45 minutes); from Ireland, operates between Dublin and Liverpool (£99, seven hours, twice daily); from Spain, operates between Bilbao and Portsmouth (from £150, 31 hours, two to three times weekly).

Stena Line (☎ 0870 570 7070; www.stenaline.com) From Ireland, operates between Rosslare and Fishguard, south Wales (from £65, 1½ to three hours, twice daily); from the Netherlands, operates between the Hook of Holland and Harwich (from £59, 3½ hours, three daily).

Superfast Ferries (☎ 0870 234 0870; www.superfast.com) From Belgium, operates between Zeebrugge and Rosyth near Edinburgh (from £99, 17½ hours, daily).

GETTING AROUND

Buses, trains and cheap airlines form a dense transport network across much of Britain, but these services dwindle to almost nothing in remote areas where populations are low. With some creative thinking, visitors can get almost anywhere – especially if they deploy a bike or the odd hiking trail. Hire cars are also an option, but they are rarely cost-effective unless travelling in a group or to areas not well served by other transport methods.

Contact **Traveline** (☎ 0870 608 2608; www.traveline.org.uk, www.travelinescotland.com; 🕑 8am-8pm) for information on local and regional bus and train options, or visit the website of **Transport Direct** (www.transportdirect.info) for longer journeys – the website has car route maps, and a useful tool for comparing flight, bus and train options between cities.

Air

No-frills airlines offer some of the best potential bargains for travelling around Britain – especially between London and Scotland – but you'll have to be flexible to get the best deals (flights from £1, excluding taxes and fees) and factor in the cost of travelling to and from airports. There are sometimes extortionate penalties for ticket changes and some airlines now charge for hold luggage.

AIRLINES IN BRITAIN

The following airlines operate domestic flights:

Air Scotland (code GRE; ☎ 0141 222 2363; www.air-scotland.com) Serving Birmingham, Edinburgh, Glasgow, Manchester and Newcastle.

Air Southwest (code WOW; ☎ 0870 241 8202; www.airsouthwest.com) Serving Bristol, Cardiff, Jersey, Leeds Bradford, London Gatwick, Manchester, Newquay, Norwich and Plymouth.

BA Connect (code TH; ☎ 0870 850 9850; www.ba.com/baconnect) Serving Birmingham, Bristol, Edinburgh, Glasgow, Inverness, London Gatwick, London Luton, London City, Manchester and Southampton.

BmiBaby (code WW; ☎ 0870 224 0224; www.bmibaby.com) Serving Birmingham, Cardiff, Edinburgh, Glasgow, London Gatwick, Manchester and Newquay.

easyJet (code EZY; ☎ 0870 600 0000; www.easyjet.com) Serving Aberdeen, Bristol, Edinburgh, Glasgow, Inverness, Liverpool, London Gatwick, London Luton, London Stansted and Newcastle.

Flybe (code BE; ☎ 0871 700 0535; www.flybe.com) Serving Aberdeen, Birmingham, Bristol, Edinburgh, Exeter, Glasgow, Jersey, Leeds Bradford, Liverpool John Lennon, London City, London Gatwick, London Luton, Manchester, Newcastle, Newquay, Norwich and Southampton.

Ryanair (code FR; ☎ 0871 246 0000; www.ryanair.com) Serving Aberdeen, Birmingham, Blackpool, Bristol, Cardiff, Edinburgh, Glasgow, Inverness, Leeds Bradford, Liverpool John Lennon, London Gatwick, London Luton, London Stansted, Manchester, Newcastle and Newquay.

Scot Airways (code CB; ☎ 0870 606 0707; www.scotairways.com) Serving Dundee, Edinburgh, London City and Southampton.

Bicycle

Compact Britain is a bike-friendly destination, with urban and countryside routes attracting plenty of pedal pushers. Helmets are not compulsory here but they are advisable since some routes – particularly in cities – can be overly crowded. While the best roads for cycling are country lanes, many urban centres have designated bike paths. Cost-effective bike rentals (from £6 per half-day) are available in larger towns. See Cycling (p273) for further information.

Bus

Buses are the cheapest way to get around in Britain but they can be slow, with some services dawdling interminably before reaching their destination. While local services operate in each region, there's also a network of intercity buses (usually referred to as coaches) covering longer distances. It's advisable to make coach reservations in advance during July and August, either online, by phone or at larger bus stations.

Britain's dominant coach operator is **National Express** (☎ 0870 580 8080; www.nationalexpress.com), along with its north-of-the-border subsidiary **Scottish Citylink** (☎ 0870 550 5050; www.citylink.co.uk). **Megabus** (☎ 0900 160 0900; www.megabus.com) is its no-frills rival, with a growing roster of services between major cities. It's worth checking out for a bargain (book early for fares from £1) but keep in mind that National Express frequently offers low 'funfares' to compete on Megabus routes.

Traveline (☎ 0870 608 2608; www.traveline.org.uk, www.travelinescotland.com; 8am-8pm) has a comprehensive online search engine covering bus and coach options throughout Britain.

BUS PASSES

The National Express Brit Xplorer pass comes in Hobo (seven-day), Footloose (14-day) and Rolling Stone (28-day) versions, allowing for unlimited travel across more than 1000 destinations. It is only available to non-Brits but can be purchased in the UK. It also offers an annual NX2 discount card for all under 26s (£10, ID required, 30% discount on regular fares). They have a similar card for over 50s. Scottish Citylink offers three-day, five-day and eight-day passes (£35/59/79) for both locals and visitors.

Car & Motorcycle

Often the quickest, most convenient way to travel around Britain is by motorbike or car – particularly in remote areas and for groups of two or more. Cars are often inconvenient in city centres where parking can be troublesome and expensive. Petrol is also pricey in Britain, especially compared with North America.

DRIVING LICENCE

Your overseas driving licence is valid in Britain for up to 12 months from your date of entry.

HIRE

Vehicle hire is expensive within Britain and it is often better to make arrangements in your home country for a fly/drive deal. Larger operators charge up to £275 per week for a tiny car but rates will vary considerably based on a number of factors, including the pick-up and drop-off locations, whether or not you are picking up on the weekend and how long you are renting the vehicle for. Ask for any special offers and mention that you are shopping around for the best rate. It is also worth considering smaller independent operators in larger cities, as they're usually more open to negotiation.

Following are the major hire companies:

Avis (☎ 0870 010 0287; www.avis.co.uk)
Budget (☎ 0870 153 9170; www.budget.co.uk)
EasyCar (☎ 0906 333 3333; www.easycar.com)
Europcar (☎ 0845 758 5375; www.europecar.co.uk)
Hertz (☎ 0870 844 8844; www.hertz.co.uk)
Thrifty (☎ 01494-751600; www.thrifty.co.uk)

PURCHASE

For longer treks, it may be more cost-effective to buy an older car or a camper van, especially if you split the cost with fellow travellers. Roadworthy near-wrecks cost anywhere from £500 but for something with seats you should budget for around £1000. Make sure the vehicle comes with a logbook and has passed its Ministry of Transport (MOT) test before you hand over any money. Additional costs before you set out on your road trip will include road tax (up to £105 for six months) and third party insurance (often around £400). Check out what's available in the used market via **Autotrader** (www.autotrader.co.uk) and **Exchange and Mart** (www.exchangeandmart.co.uk) magazines.

ROAD RULES

The *Highway Code*, available in most bookshops, contains everything you need to know about Britain's road rules. Vehicles drive on the left-hand side; seat belts are compulsory in the front seats (also in the back, where they are fitted); and the speed limit is 30mph around built-up areas, 60mph on single carriageways and 70mph on dual carriageways. Remember to give way to your right at roundabouts. The maximum blood-alcohol level for driving is 35mg (100mL). A yellow line along the edge of the road indicates parking restrictions – look for a sign nearby stating exact limits. Motorcyclists must wear helmets. In England and Wales, brown road signs guide you to attractions and places of interest, while blue signs do the same thing in Scotland.

Train

Travelling by train in Britain is far better than flying if you actually want to see the country you are visiting. Train travel also has the added convenience of dropping you right into the centre of town, rather than making you struggle in from an airport out in the middle of nowhere. But with new trains and faster rail services in recent years (redressing decades of underinvestment) fares can be expensive. There are two ways to circumvent this expense: book your tickets early and be flexible on dates you wish to travel so that you can shop around for the best deal, or consider buying either a discount or unlimited-travel train pass. While the network is extensive, covering all cities and most towns, it can be somewhat difficult to use the train to reach remote areas. For comprehensive fare, route and timetable information, contact the **National Rail Enquiry** (☎ 0845 748 4950; www.nationalrail.co.uk).

Consider adding almost unlimited one-day regional bus travel at both ends of your train trip by booking a combined bus and train **Plusbus** (www.plusbus.org.uk) ticket. This can be useful for outbound and onward travel to your accommodation.

CLASSES & COSTS

Many but not all trains have two classes: 1st-class tickets are up to 50% more expensive than standard-class tickets and have separate carriages on the trains. There are myriad ticketing options within standard class and the system is needlessly complex on some routes. Following are some of the options available:

Apex The cheapest option for long-distance outward and return journeys on different days. Must be booked at least 48 hours in advance; availability is limited.

Cheap Day Return For outward and return journeys on the same day (usually limited to travel after 9.30am); often costs little more than a one-way fare and is a great deal for day-trippers.

SuperSaver Return ticket, but with weekday peak time travel, Friday travel and holiday travel not allowed.

Keep in mind that there are dozens of train operators in Britain, many servicing the same routes. Frequent promotions are advertised, especially during low or shoulder seasons, and these can dramatically reduce fares. While the no-frills, low-cost approach has not yet deeply infiltrated the train market, Megabus subsidiary **Megatrain** (☎ 0900 120 0300; www.megatrain.com) recently launched routes between London, Bath, Exeter, Portsmouth and Salisbury. If you book these tickets far enough in advance, fares can be as low as £1.

RESERVATIONS

Reserving you tickets is recommended for travel during summer, in peak times and on popular routes. Advance tickets can be purchased at any train station, or online via **QJump** (www.qjump.co.uk) or **Trainline** (www.thetrainline.com).

TRAIN PASSES

The Young Persons Railcard (£20), Senior Railcard (£20) and Disabled Persons Railcard (£14) are each valid for up to 12 months and provide a one-third discount on most trips within Britain. Check out the various options at the **Railcard website** (www.railcard.co.uk). Applications can be processed over the counter at the larger stations: you will need to show proof of age or student enrolment to get the Young Persons or Senior Railcards, and proof of entitlement for the Disabled Persons Railcard. Some regions will also offer their own discount train passes, with the southeast's Network Card (£20) being a particularly popular choice.

The most convenient, cost-effective option for extensive train travel is the **BritRail** (www.britrail.com) pass. You must buy them in your home country via the BritRail or **Rail Europe** (www.raileurope.com) websites or from larger travel agents. With a validated pass, you do not need to pick up tickets: just step on the train and show your pass to the attendant. You might consider paying that little bit extra for a 1st-class pass, especially if you plan on travelling during the crowded summer season. Winter discounts are offered on some BritRail passes.

Pass options include the popular BritRail Consecutive Pass (unlimited four- to 31-day travel for US$218 to US$702) and the BritRail Flexipass (four-, eight- or 15-day travel over a two-month period for US$275 to US$604). England-only and Scotland-only versions of these passes are cheaper. There are also popular nonconsecutive London passes (US$70 to US$176). Remember that Eurail passes are not valid in Britain.

France

She might be a grand old dame in many ways, but *douce France* (sweet France) is still one of the belles of the European ball. Even if you've never set foot on French soil, it's a place that already seems familiar – every time you've gazed at an impressionist painting, watched a New Wave film or sipped sparkling champagne, you've been letting a little bit of Gallic flair seep into your soul.

It's certainly a place where you can enjoy the finer things in life, whether that means wandering around one of France's world-class museums or sitting down to indulge in some of the fabulous cuisine for which the country is justly famous. But modern-day France is a real melting pot, shot through with streaks of Celtic, Basque and North African culture, as well as a reputation for artistic invention and a fondness for the architectural avant-garde. At times, it can make for a volatile mix – something that was clearly demonstrated during the innercity riots and student demonstrations that swept the country in 2005 and 2006.

But with so much history, culture and *joie de vivre* behind her, France always finds her feet again before too long. From the broad boulevards of Paris to the grand chateaux of the Loire Valley, this is the country for which the word 'chic' was invented – seductive and aloof, old-fashioned and forward-looking, enthralling and exasperating in equal measures, but always characterised by a certain *je ne sais quoi*.

FAST FACTS

- **Area** 551,000 sq km
- **Capital** Paris
- **Currency** euro (€); A$1 = €0.60; ¥100 = €0.67; NZ$1 = €0.50; UK£1 = €1.48; US$1 = €0.78
- **Famous for** croissants, cheese, the Eiffel Tower, strikes, terrible driving
- **Official Language** French
- **Phrases** *merci* (thank you); *parlez-vous Anglais?* (do you speak English?); *excusez-moi* (excuse me); *s'il vous plaît* (please)
- **Population** 60.2 million
- **Telephone Codes** country code ☎ 33; international access code ☎ 00

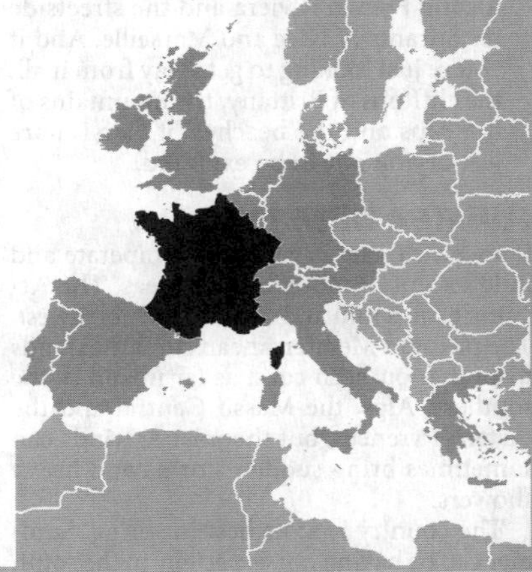

HIGHLIGHTS

- Delve into the delights of France's unforgettable capital, **Paris** (p291).
- Catch some surf along the coast around **Biarritz** (p355).
- Hit the wine trail in **Burgundy** (p360) or **Bordeaux** (p350).
- Indulge your senses (and your stomach) on the **Côte d'Azur** (p388).
- Escape the crowds in the spectacular surrounds of the **Jura** (p378).

ITINERARIES

- **One week** First stop has to be Paris, the unique and utterly unmissable City of Lights, with its grand streets, chichi boutiques and cultural sights. You'll only have time to scratch the surface in a week, but whatever you do make sure you've ticked off Notre Dame, the Louvre, the Musée d'Orsay, Montmartre and of course the Eiffel Tower before you leave. Then for the rest of the week you'll have time for day trips to Versailles, Chartres and possibly Rouen.
- **Two weeks** After Paris, the rest of France is your oyster – so hop on a TGV (*trains à grande vitesse;* high-speed train) and head for whichever region most takes your fancy. The Loire Valley is crammed with some of the country's finest chateaux, while the Dordogne is littered with fabulous prehistoric cave art. If it's Gallic gastronomy you're after, then make a beeline for the vineyards of Burgundy and the Côte d'Or before swinging south for the French Riviera and the streetside restaurants of Nice and Marseille. And if you're just looking to get away from it all, the clifftops of Brittany, the mountains of the Alps and the beaches of Corsica are just crying out to be explored.

CLIMATE & WHEN TO GO

France's climate is generally temperate and mild except in mountainous areas. The Atlantic brings rain and wind to the northwest. The pleasant Mediterranean climate extends from the southern coast as far inland as the southern Alps, the Massif Central and the eastern Pyrenees, but the mistral winds can sometimes bring sudden storms and heavy showers.

The country is at its best in spring. Summer can be baking hot, especially in the south away from the coast. Even Paris can swelter in July and August. It can also be a crowded, traffic-choked and expensive time to travel, especially around the Mediterranean. Autumn by contrast is mellow and pleasant everywhere, and swimming and sunbathing are often viable until October. Winter provides excellent winter sport opportunities in the mountains.

HOW MUCH?

- **Bottle of table wine** €4
- **Half-/full-day bicycle hire** €10/15
- **Restaurant meal** €20-30
- **Espresso** €0.90
- **Public transport ticket** €1.40

LONELY PLANET INDEX

- **1L petrol** €1.30
- **1L bottled water** €0.80
- **25cL beer – at a bar** €3.50
- **Souvenir T-shirt** €10
- **Crepe** €2

HISTORY

Prehistory

Neanderthals were the first to live in France (about 90,000 to 40,000 BC). Cro-Magnons followed 35,000 years ago and left behind cave paintings and engravings, especially around the Vézère Valley (p359). Neolithic people (about 7500 to 4000 years ago) created France's incredible *menhirs* (standing stones) and *dolmens* (monolithic tombs), best seen around Carnac in Brittany (p334).

The Celtic Gauls arrived between 1500 and 500 BC. They were superseded by the Romans for around five centuries after Julius Caesar took control around 52 BC, until the Franks (thus the name 'France') and the Alemanii overran the country from the east.

The Frankish Merovingian and Carolingian dynasties ruled from the 5th to the 10th century AD. In 732 Charles Martel defeated the Moors, preventing France from falling under Muslim rule. Martel's grandson, Charlemagne (742–814), extended the power and boundaries of the kingdom and was crowned Holy Roman Emperor in 800.

The Early French Kings

The tale of how William the Conqueror and his Norman forces occupied England in 1066 (making Normandy and, later, England, a formidable rival of France) is told in the Bayeux Tapestry (p329). The rivalry between France and England lasted three centuries, reaching its height during the Hundred Years' War (1337–1453).

Following the occupation of Paris by the English allied dukes of Burgundy, John Plantagenet was made regent of France on behalf of England's King Henry VI in 1422. Less than a decade later he was crowned king at Paris' Notre Dame (p298).

Luckily for the French, a 17-year-old warrior called Jeanne d'Arc (Joan of Arc) came along in 1429. She persuaded Charles VII that she had a divine mission from God to expel the English from France and bring about Charles' coronation in Reims. Following her capture by the Burgundians and subsequent sale to the English in 1430, Joan was convicted of witchcraft and heresy and burned at the stake in Rouen, on the site now marked by the city's cathedral (p327).

The arrival of Italian Renaissance culture during the reign of François I (r 1515–47) saw the construction of some of France's finest chateaux, especially in the Loire Valley (p338).

The 30-year period from 1562 to 1598 was one of the bloodiest periods in French history. Ideological disagreement between

FRANCE

the Huguenots (French Protestants) and the Catholic monarchy escalated into full-scale war – a conflict known as the Wars of Religion.

The Sun King

Louis XIV, Le Roi Soleil (Sun King) ascended the throne in 1643, and spent the next sixty years in a series of wars that gained territory, terrified neighbours and nearly bankrupted the treasury. He also constructed the fabulous palace at Versailles (p312).

Louis XV ascended to the throne in 1715 and shifted the royal court back to Paris. As the 18th century progressed, the *ancien régime* (old order) became increasingly out of step with the needs of the country. Antiestablishment and anticlerical ideas expressed by Voltaire, Rousseau and Montesquieu further threatened the royal regime.

Revolution to Republic

Social and economic crisis marked the 18th century. The general mood of discontent among the French populace, and Louis' refusal to address their concerns, flared into violence when a Parisian mob stormed the prison at Bastille (now a busy roundabout; p300). France was declared a constitutional monarchy but before long, the moderate republican Girondins lost power to the radical Jacobins. Louis XVI was publicly guillotined in January 1793 on Paris' place de la Concorde (p300).

The Reign of Terror between September 1793 and July 1794 saw religious freedoms revoked, churches closed, cathedrals turned into 'Temples of Reason' and thousands beheaded. In the chaos a dashing young Corsican general named Napoleon Bonaparte (1769–1821) stepped from the shadows.

Napoleon Bonaparte

In 1799 Napoleon assumed power and in 1804 Pope Pius VII crowned him emperor of France at Notre Dame. Napoleon waged several wars in which France gained control over most of Europe. Two years later, Allied armies entered Paris, exiled Napoleon to Elba and restored the House of Bourbon to the French throne at the Congress of Vienna (1814–15).

In 1815 Napoleon escaped, entering Paris on 20 May. His glorious 'Hundred Days' back in power ended with the Battle of Waterloo and his exile to the island of St-Helena, where he died in 1821.

Second Republic to Second Empire

The subsequent years were marked by civil strife and political unrest, with monarchists and revolutionaries vying for power. Louis-Philippe (r 1830–48), a constitutional monarch, was subsequently chosen by parliament, only to be ousted by the 1848 Revolution. The Second Republic was established and Napoleon's nephew, Louis Napoleon Bonaparte, was elected president. But in 1851 Louis Napoleon led a coup d'état and proclaimed himself Emperor Napoleon III of the Second Empire (1852–70).

France enjoyed significant economic growth at this time. Paris was transformed under urban planner Baron Haussmann (1809–91) who, among other things, created the 12 huge boulevards radiating from the Arc de Triomphe (p300). But Napoleon III embroiled France in various catastrophic conflicts, including the Crimean War (1853–56) and the Franco-Prussian War (1870–71), which ended with Prussia taking the emperor prisoner. Upon hearing the news, defiant Parisian masses took to the streets demanding a republic be declared – the Third Republic.

The Great War

A trip to the Somme (p327) battlefields goes some way to revealing the unimaginable human cost of WWI. Of the eight million French men called to arms, 1.3 million were killed and almost one million crippled. Much of the war took place in northeastern France – trench warfare using thousands of soldiers as cannon fodder to gain a few metres of territory.

WWII

In 1939, following the invasion of Poland, France joined Britain in declaring war on Germany. Despite constructing a lavish series of defences along its German border (the so-called Maginot Line), by June 1940 France had been overrun and surrendered. Germany divided France into an Occupied Zone (in the north and west) and a puppet state in the south, centred on the spa town of Vichy.

The British Army were driven from France during the Battle of Dunkirk (p326) in 1940. Four years later, on 6 June 1944, Allied forces stormed the coastline of Normandy (p331) in the largest invasion ever mounted, now known as D-Day. The bloody Battle of Normandy followed and Paris was finally liberated on 25 August.

The Fourth Republic

In the first postwar election in 1945, the wartime leader of the Free French, Général Charles de Gaulle, was appointed head of the government, but quickly sensed that the tide was turning against him and in 1946 he resigned.

Progress rebuilding France's shattered economy and infrastructure was slow. By 1947 France was forced to turn to the USA for loans as part of the Marshall Plan to rebuild Europe. The economy gathered steam in the 1950s but the decade marked the end of French colonialism in Vietnam and in Algeria. The Algerian War (1954–62) was particularly brutal, characterised by torture and massacre meted out to nationalist Algerians.

The Fifth Republic

De Gaulle assumed the presidency again in 1958 and drafted a new constitution – the Fifth Republic – which gave considerable powers to the president at the expense of the National Assembly.

Georges Pompidou (1911–74), prime minister under de Gaulle, stepped onto the podium as president and was followed by Valéry Giscard d'Estaing (b 1926). In 1981 he was ousted by long-time head of the Parti Socialiste (Socialist Party), François Mitterrand (1916–96).

By 1986 the economy was weakening and in parliamentary elections that year the right-wing opposition led by Jacques Chirac (Paris mayor since 1977) won a majority in the National Assembly.

Presidential elections in 1995 ushered in Jacques Chirac, who was re-elected with an overwhelming majority in 2002 (hardly surprising considering his opponent was the National Front leader Jean-Marie Le Pen).

In May 2005, a national referendum on the European Constitution was rejected by French voters, causing huge embarrassment to the government, and placing a considerable question mark over the country's pro-European future.

In October and November 2005, the country was rocked by several weeks of running battles between police and gangs of young people across France. The riots were sparked by the deaths of two teenagers of North African descent who were electrocuted while attempting to hide from the police, and began in the poor, ethnically diverse *banlieue* (suburbs) of Paris, but quickly spread to several of the country's major cities.

More recently, in early 2006, huge student demonstrations hit the streets in protest against a law designed to shake up France's rigidly protected labour market. After several weeks of unrest, the government was forced into an embarrassing U-turn, and the proposed legislation was shelved, leaving the continuing question of France's high unemployment rate (at the time of writing one of the worst in Europe) unanswered.

PEOPLE

France is relatively sparsely populated – 107 people inhabit every square kilometre – although 20% of the national population is packed into the Paris area.

The last 10 years have seen rural and suburban areas steadily gaining population; and Paris and the northeast (except Alsace) losing inhabitants to southern France, where populations are predicted to rise by 30% over the next 30 years.

For much of the last two centuries, the birth-rate in France has been steadily falling, but that trend now seems to have reversed. By 2050 the population of mainland France is expected to reach 64 million – five million more than in 2000.

Multicultural France has always drawn immigrants from the rest of Europe and its former colonies, especially those in North Africa. Immigrants today form 7.4% (4.3 million) of the population yet only 36% have French citizenship, which is not conferred automatically at birth. Racial tensions – so clearly on display during the 2005 riots – are fuelled by the extreme-right Front National (National Front), headed by the politician Jean-Marie Le Pen.

RELIGION

Since the Revolution, secular France has maintained a rigid distinction between church and state. Some 55% of French identify themselves as Catholic, but no more than 10% attend church regularly. Another one million are Protestant, while France's Muslim community is around 5 million. Over half of France's 600,000-strong Jewish population (Europe's largest) lives in and around Paris.

ARTS

Literature

France has made huge contributions to European literature. The philosophical work of Voltaire (1694–1778), and Jean-Jacques Rousseau, dominated the 18th century. A century later the poems and novels of Victor Hugo – *Les Misérables* and *Notre Dame de Paris* (The Hunchback of Notre Dame) among them – became landmarks of French Romanticism.

In 1857 two literary landmarks were published: *Madame Bovary* by Gustave Flaubert (1821–80) and Charles Baudelaire's collection of poems, *Les Fleurs du Mal* (The Flowers of Evil). Émile Zola (1840–1902) meanwhile strove to convert novel-writing from an art to a science in his series, *Les Rougon-Macquart*.

Symbolists Paul Verlaine (1844–96) and Stéphane Mallarmé (1842-98) aimed to express mental states through their poetry. Verlaine's poems, with those of Arthur Rimbaud (1854–91) are seen as French literature's first modern poems.

After WWII, the existentialist movement developed around the lively debates of Jean-Paul Sartre (1905–80), Simone de Beauvoir (1908–86) and Albert Camus (1913–60) over coffee and cigarettes in Paris' Left Bank cafés.

Contemporary authors include Françoise Sagan, Pascal Quignard, Jean Auel, Emmanuel Carrère and Stéphane Bourguignon. Also popular are Frédéric Dard (alias San Antonio), Léo Malet and Daniel Pennac.

Cinema

Cinematographic pioneers, the Lumière brothers, shot the world's first-ever motion picture in March 1895 and French film flourished in the following decades. The post-WWII *nouvelle vague* (New Wave) filmmakers, such as Claude Chabrol, Jean-Luc Godard and François Truffaut, pioneered the advent of modern cinema, using fractured narratives, documentary camerawork and highly personal subjects.

Big-name stars, slick production values and nostalgia were the dominant motifs in the 1980s, as filmmakers switched to costume dramas, comedies and 'heritage movies'. Claude Berri's depiction of prewar Provence in *Jean de Florette* (1986), Jean-Paul Rappeneau's *Cyrano de Bergerac* (1990) and *Bon Voyage* (2003), set in 1940s Paris – all starring France's best-known (and biggest-nosed) actor Gérard Depardieu – found huge audiences in France and abroad.

Two of France's most recent cinematic successes couldn't be more different. *La Haine* (1995) directed by Mathieu Kassovitz, documented the bleak reality of life in the Parisian suburbs, and looks even more relevant in the wake of the recent ethnic riots. At the other end of the spectrum, *Le Fabuleux Destin de Amélie Poulain* (*Amélie;* 2001) is a feel-good story about a Parisian do-gooder, directed by Jean-Pierre Jeunet, and was a massive international hit.

Music

There's more to French music than accordions and Édith Piaf.

French musical luminaries – Charles Gounod (1818–93), César Franck (1822–90) and *Carmen*-creator Georges Bizet (1838–75) among them – were a dime a dozen in the 19th century. Claude Debussy (1862–1918) revolutionised classical music with *Prélude à l'Après-Midi d'un Faune* (Prelude to the Afternoon of a Faun); while Maurice Ravel (1875–1937) peppered his work, including *Boléro,* with sensuousness and tonal colour.

Jazz hit 1920s Paris, which post-WWI hoisted the likes of Sidney Bechet, Kenny Clarke, Bud Powell and Dexter Gordon.

The *chanson française* (a tradition dating from the troubadours of the Middle Ages) was revived in the 1930s by Piaf and Charles Trenet. In the 1950s the Left Bank cabarets nurtured *chansonniers* (cabaret singers) such as Léo Ferré, Georges Brassens, Claude Nougaro, Jacques Brel and Serge Gainsbourg.

French pop music has evolved massively since the 1960s *yéyé* (imitative rock) days of Johnny Hallyday. Particularly strong is world music, from Algerian *rai* and other North African music (artists include Natacha Atlas) to Senegalese *mbalax* (Youssou N'Dour) and West Indian *zouk* (Kassav, Zouk Machine). One musician who combines many of these elements is Paris-born Manu Chao.

Another hot musical export is Parisian electronic music from bands such as Daft

Punk and Air. French rap was spearheaded in the 1990s by Senegal-born Paris-reared rapper MC Solaar, and today is a popular genre in its own right; hard-core rappers include Parisian heavyweights Booba of Senegalese origin and Rohff (whose fourth album, *Au delà de mes Limites*, released in 2005, sold 30,000 copies in the first week).

And for some inexplicable reason, the French still absolutely *love* Johnny Hallyday. Go figure.

Architecture

Southern France is the place to find France's Gallo-Roman legacy, especially at the Pont du Gard (p403), and the amphitheatres in Nîmes (p402) and Arles (p388).

Several centuries later, architects adopted Gallo-Roman motifs in *roman* (Romanesque) masterpieces such as Poitier's Église Notre Dame la Grande (p347).

Impressive 12th-century Gothic structures include Avignon's massive pontifical palace (p387), the seminal cathedral at Chartres (p313), and of course, Notre Dame Cathedral in Paris (p298).

Under Napoleon, many of Paris' best-known sights – the Arc de Triomphe, the Arc du Carrousel at the Louvre and the Assemblée Nationale building – were designed.

Art Nouveau (1850–1910) combined iron, brick, glass and ceramics in new ways. See it for yourself at Paris' metro entrances and in the Musée d'Orsay (p294).

French political leaders have long sought to immortalise themselves by building public edifices. Georges Pompidou commissioned the once-reviled – now much-revered – Centre Beaubourg (p299) in Paris while François Mitterrand commissioned several contemporary architectural landmarks, including IM Pei's glass pyramid (p299) at the Louvre.

Painting

An extraordinary flowering of artistic talent occurred in 19th- and 20th-century France. The impressionists, who endeavoured to capture the ever-changing aspects of reflected light, included Edouard Manet, Claude Monet, Edgar Degas, Camille Pisarro, and Pierre-Auguste Renoir.

They were followed by the likes of Paul Cézanne, Paul Gauguin and Georges Seurat. A little later the Fauves, the most famous of whom was Henri Matisse, became known for their radical use of vibrant colour. France was also where cubism was pioneered, principally by Pablo Picasso and Georges Braque.

ENVIRONMENT

The Land

France, Western Europe's largest country, is hugged by water or mountains along each side except its northeastern boundary, a relatively flat frontier abutting Germany, Luxembourg and Belgium. Inland, five major river systems cross the country.

Europe's highest peak, Mt Blanc (4807m), spectacularly tops the French Alps which stagger along France's eastern border from Lake Geneva to the Côte d'Azur. North of Lake Geneva the gentle Jura Range runs along the Swiss frontier, while the rugged Pyrenees lace France's 450km-long border with Spain.

The ancient Massif Central covers one-sixth (91,000 sq km) of the country and is renowned for its chain of extinct volcanoes.

Wildlife

France is blessed with a rich variety of flora and fauna, with more mammals (around 110) than any other country in Europe. Couple this with its 363 bird species, 30 amphibian types, 36 varieties of reptiles and 72 kinds of fish, and wildlife watchers are in paradise.

The Alps and Pyrenees shelter the marmot, the nimble chamois (mountain antelope) and the *bouquetin* (Alpine ibex). Red and roe deer and wild boar are common in lower-altitude forested areas.

The wolf, which disappeared from France in the 1930s, was seen in the Parc National du Mercantour in 1992. The brown bear disappeared from the Alps in the mid-1930s. The 300-odd bears living in the Pyrenees at that time have dwindled to one orphaned cub following the controversial shooting of its mother – the last female bear of Pyrenean stock – by a hunter in 2004. However another 12 to 18 bears of Slovenian origin also call the Pyrenees home.

National Parks

The proportion of land protected in France is low relative to the country's size: six small *parcs nationaux* (national parks) fully protect just 0.8% of the country. Another 7%

is protected by 42 *parcs naturals régionaux* (regional parks) and a further 0.4% by 136 smaller *réserves naturelles* (nature reserves).

Environmental Issues

Summer forest fires are an annual hazard. Wetlands, essential for the survival of a great number of species, are shrinking. More than two million hectares – 3% of French territory – are considered important wetlands, but only 4% of this land is protected.

France generates around 80% of its electricity from nuclear power stations – the highest ratio in the world – with the rest coming from carbon-fuelled power stations and renewable resources (mainly wind farms and hydro-electric dams).

FOOD & DRINK

Staples & Specialities

France is rightly renowned across the world for its cuisine. There's an enormous range of cuisine that can be broadly classed as 'French', from the rich, classic dishes of Burgundy, Périgord, Lyon and Normandy to the Mediterranean flavours of Provence, Languedoc and Corsica. Broadly speaking, the hot south tends to favour olive oil, garlic and tomatoes, while the cooler north favours cream and butter. Coastal areas specialise in mussels, oysters and saltwater fish. Wherever you choose to eat, one thing's for sure – you certainly won't go hungry.

Nothing is more French than *pain* (bread). More than 80% of all French people eat it at every meal. The classic French bread is the long, thin baguette (and the similar but fatter *flûtes*), but there are countless other varieties.

France has nearly 500 varieties of *fromage* (cheese). The choice on offer at a *fromagerie* (cheese shop) can be overwhelming, but *fromagers* (cheese merchants) always allow you to sample and are usually happy to advise.

Traditionally charcuterie is made only from pork, though a number of other meats – from beef and veal to chicken and goose – are used in making sausages, blood puddings, hams and other cured and salted meats. Pâtés, terrines and *rillettes* (potted meats) are essentially charcuterie and are prepared in many different ways.

The traditional French breakfast is usually coffee, French bread and jam, occasionally accompanied by a croissant or a *pain au chocolat* (chocolate croissant). Meats, yogurts, cereals and fresh fruit are also sometimes eaten at breakfast.

Drinks

There are dozens of wine-producing regions throughout France, but the principal regions are Alsace, Bordeaux, Burgundy, Champagne, Languedoc-Roussillon, the Loire region and the Rhône. Areas such as Burgundy comprise many well-known districts, including Chablis, Beaujolais and Mâcon, while Bordeaux encompasses Médoc, St-Émilion and Sauternes among many others.

The *bière à la pression* (draft beer) is served by the *demi* (about 33cL). Northern France and Alsace produce some excellent local beers.

The most popular nonalcoholic beverages consumed in France are coffee and mineral water. If you prefer tap water rather than bottled water, ask for *une carafe d'eau* (a jug of water).

The most common coffee is espresso. A small espresso, served without milk, is called *un café noir, un express* or simply *un café*. *Café crème* is espresso with steamed milk or cream.

Where to Eat & Drink

BISTROS & BRASSERIES

A bistro (often spelled *bistrot*) can be simply a pub or bar with snacks and light meals, or a fully fledged restaurant. Brasseries – which can look very much like cafés – serve full meals, drinks and coffee from morning till late at night.

RESTAURANTS

The restaurant comes in many guises. Generally they specialise in a particular variety of food (eg regional, traditional, Vietnamese). You can generally get an excellent French meal for under €30.

Restaurants almost always have a *carte* (menu) posted outside. Most offer at least one fixed-price, multicourse meal, known as a *menu* or *menu du jour* (daily *menu*). This usually offers an entrée, such as salad, pâté or soup; a main dish, including the *plat du jour* (daily special); and a final course (cheese or dessert).

Boissons (drinks) cost extra unless the *menu* says *boisson comprise* (drink included), in which case you may get a beer or a glass of mineral water. If the *menu* has *vin compris* (wine included), you'll probably be served a 25cL *pichet* (jug) of house wine.

Vegetarians & Vegans

Vegetarians and vegans will have a tough time in many parts of France. Specialist vegetarian restaurants are few and far between, and most menus are still very meat-heavy, although vegetarian choices and *produits biologiques* (organic products) are becoming more and more common.

PARIS

pop 2.15 million

What can be said about the sexy, sophisticated City of Lights that hasn't already been said a thousand times before? Quite simply, this is one of the world's great metropolises, a trend-setter, market-leader and cultural capital for over a thousand years and still going strong. This is the place that gave the world the cancan and the cinematograph, a city that reinvented itself during the Renaissance, bopped to the beat of the Jazz Age and positively glittered during the *belle époque* (beautiful era). As you might expect, Paris is strewn with historic architecture, glorious galleries and cultural treasures galore, but the modern-day city is much more than just a museum piece. It's a heady hotchpotch of cultures and ideas – a place to stroll the boulevards, shop till you drop or just do as the Parisians do and watch the world buzz by from a streetside café. Savour every moment.

HISTORY

The Parisii, a tribe of Celtic Gauls, settled the Île de la Cité in the 3rd century BC. In 508 AD, Clovis I made Paris his seat in the newly united Gaul. Paris prospered during the Middle Ages and flourished during the Renaissance when many of city's most famous buildings were erected.

The excesses of Louis XVI and his queen, Marie-Antoinette, led to an uprising of Parisians on 14 July 1789 and the storming of the Bastille prison – kick-starting the French Revolution.

In 1851 Emperor Napoleon III oversaw the building of a more modern Paris, with wide boulevards, sculptured parks and a sewer system. Following the disastrous Franco-Prussian War and the establishment of the Third Republic, Paris entered perhaps its most resplendent period, the *belle époque*, famed for its Art Nouveau architecture and artistic and scientific advances. By the 1930s, Paris had become a centre for the artistic avant-garde, an era cut short by the Nazi occupation of 1940–44.

The compact city centre is surrounded by the *banlieue*, a network of sprawling suburbs mostly occupied by Paris' ethnic communities. In late 2005, the city was rocked by violent clashes between police and angry youths from the *banlieue*; the violence spread to many other French cities and took several weeks to bring under control.

ORIENTATION

Central Paris is quite small: around 9.5km (north to south) by 11km (east to west). Excluding the Bois de Boulogne and the Bois de Vincennes, its total area is 105 sq km. The Seine River flows east–west through the city; the Rive Droite (Right Bank) is north of the river, while the Rive Gauche (Left Bank) is to the south.

Paris is divided into 20 arrondissements (districts), which spiral clockwise from the centre. City addresses always include the number of the arrondissement.

The city has 372 metro stations and there is almost always one within 500m of where you need to go.

INFORMATION

Discount Cards

Carte Musées-Monuments (Museums-Monuments Card; ☎ 01 44 61 96 60; 1/3/5 days €18/36/54) Includes entry to some three dozen sights in Paris – including the Louvre, the Centre Pompidou and the Musée d'Orsay – and another 22 in the Île de France, including parts of the chateaux at Versailles. It's available from tourist offices, Fnac outlets, RATP information desks and major metro stations.

Internet Access

Phonecard-operated Internet terminals are dotted all over Paris. A 120-unit *télécarte* buys two hours' connection while a 50-unit one is worth about 50 minutes.

Internet cafés are also liberally scattered around the city:

Cyber Cube (Map pp292-3; ☎ 01 56 80 08 08; www.cybercube.fr; 9 rue d'Odessa, 14e; per min €0.15, per 5/10hr €30/40; 🕑 10am-10pm; Ⓜ Montparnasse Bienvenüe)

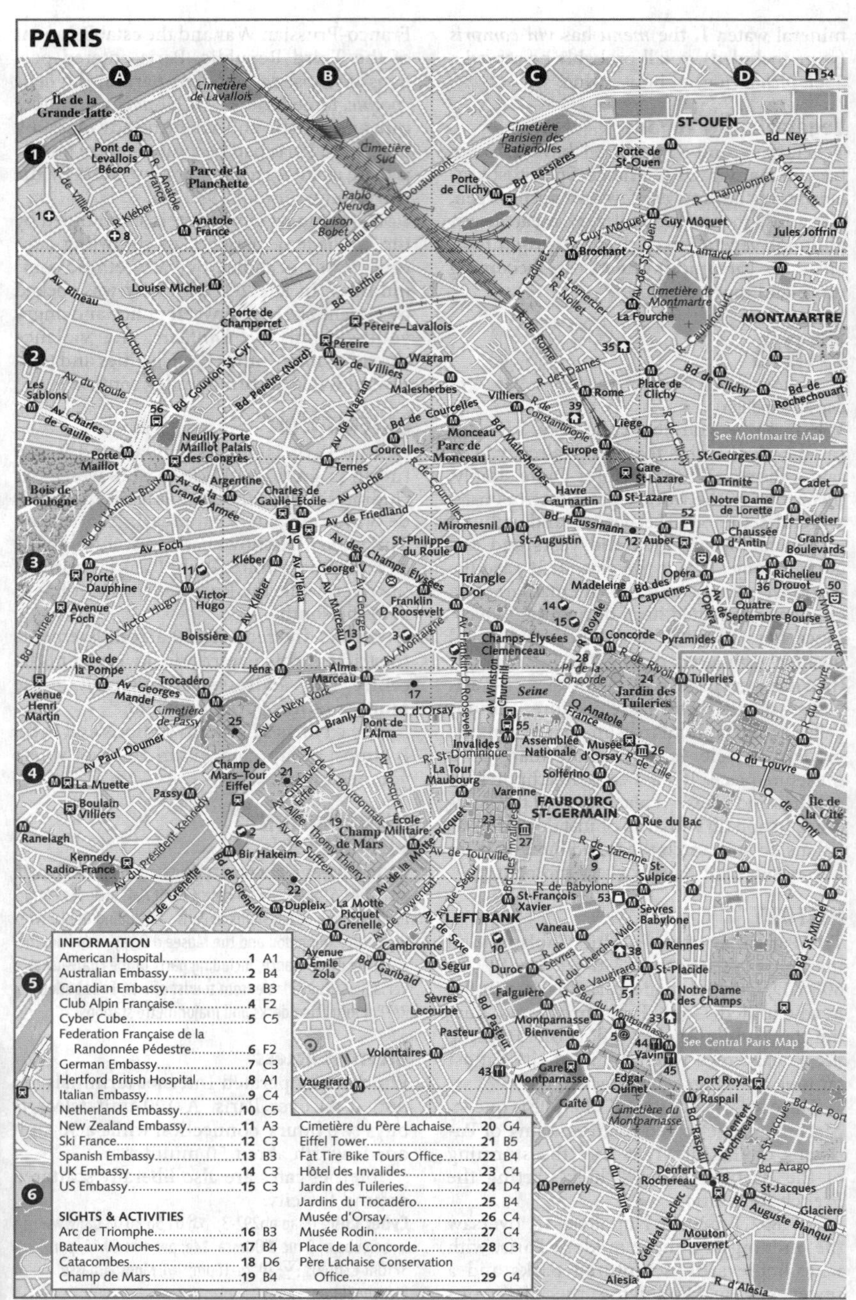
PARIS
INFORMATION
American Hospital 1 A1
Australian Embassy 2 B4
Canadian Embassy 3 B3
Club Alpin Française 4 F2
Cyber Cube 5 C5
Federation Française de la Randonnée Pédestre 6 F2
German Embassy 7 C3
Hertford British Hospital 8 A1
Italian Embassy 9 C4
Netherlands Embassy 10 C5
New Zealand Embassy 11 A3
Ski France 12 C3
Spanish Embassy 13 B3
UK Embassy 14 C3
US Embassy 15 C3
SIGHTS & ACTIVITIES
Arc de Triomphe 16 B3
Bateaux Mouches 17 B4
Catacombes 18 D6
Champ de Mars 19 B4
Cimetière du Père Lachaise 20 G4
Eiffel Tower 21 B5
Fat Tire Bike Tours Office 22 B4
Hôtel des Invalides 23 C4
Jardin des Tuileries 24 D4
Jardins du Trocadéro 25 B4
Musée d'Orsay 26 C4
Musée Rodin 27 C4
Place de la Concorde 28 C3
Père Lachaise Conservation Office 29 G4
Île de la Grande Jatte
Parc de la Planchette
Bois de Boulogne
ST-OUEN
MONTMARTRE
See Montmartre Map
Cimetière de Montmartre
Parc de Monceau
Triangle D'or
Seine
Jardin des Tuileries
FAUBOURG ST-GERMAIN
LEFT BANK
Champ de Mars
See Central Paris Map
Cimetière du Montparnasse
Île de la Cité

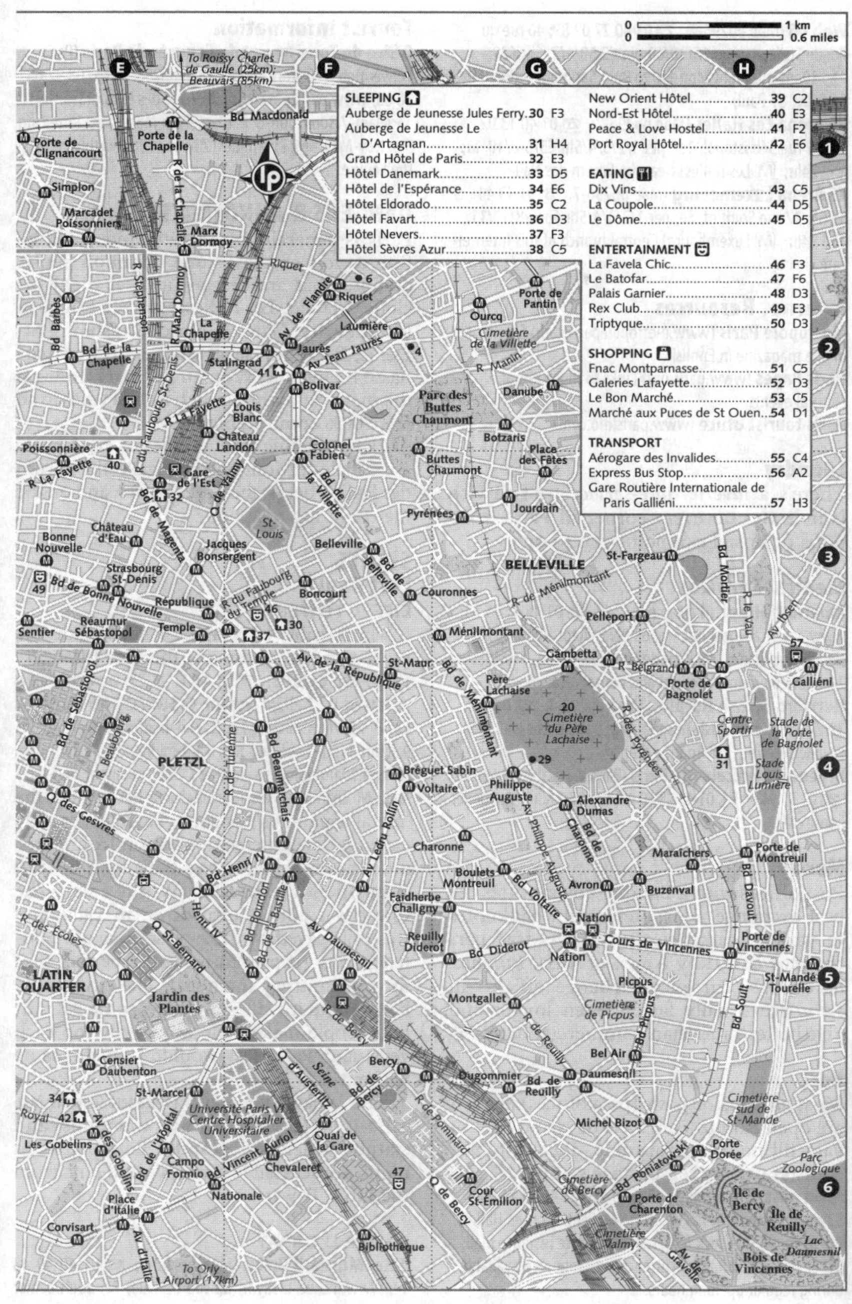
0 1 km
0 0.6 miles
E
F
G
H
1
2
3
4
5
6
To Roissy Charles de Gaulle (25km); Beauvais (85km)
SLEEPING
Auberge de Jeunesse Jules Ferry.....30 F3
Auberge de Jeunesse Le D'Artagnan.....31 H4
Grand Hôtel de Paris.....32 E3
Hôtel Danemark.....33 D5
Hôtel de l'Espérance.....34 E6
Hôtel Eldorado.....35 C2
Hôtel Favart.....36 D3
Hôtel Nevers.....37 F3
Hôtel Sèvres Azur.....38 C5
New Orient Hôtel.....39 C2
Nord-Est Hôtel.....40 E3
Peace & Love Hostel.....41 F2
Port Royal Hôtel.....42 E6
EATING
Dix Vins.....43 C5
La Coupole.....44 D5
Le Dôme.....45 D5
ENTERTAINMENT
La Favela Chic.....46 F3
Le Batofar.....47 F6
Palais Garnier.....48 D3
Rex Club.....49 E3
Triptyque.....50 D3
SHOPPING
Fnac Montparnasse.....51 C5
Galeries Lafayette.....52 D3
Le Bon Marché.....53 C5
Marché aux Puces de St Ouen.....54 D1
TRANSPORT
Aérogare des Invalides.....55 C4
Express Bus Stop.....56 A2
Gare Routière Internationale de Paris Galliéni.....57 H3
Bd Macdonald
Porte de Clignancourt
Porte de la Chapelle
Simplon
Marcadet Poissonniers
R de la Chapelle
Marx Dormoy
R Riquet
R Stephenson
Bd Barbès
R Marx Dormoy
La Chapelle
Bd de la Chapelle
Av de Flandre
Riquet
Laumière
Jaurès
Stalingrad
Av Jean Jaurès
Bolivar
Porte de Pantin
Ourcq
Cimetière de la Villette
R Manin
Parc des Buttes Chaumont
Danube
Botzaris
Buttes Chaumont
Place des Fêtes
Jourdain
Pyrénées
Louis Blanc
R La Fayette
Château Landon
R du Faubourg St-Denis
Colonel Fabien
Bd de la Villette
Poissonnière
Gare de l'Est
Q de Valmy
Bd de Magenta
St-Louis
Château d'Eau
Bonne Nouvelle
Jacques Bonsergent
Belleville
Bd de Belleville
BELLEVILLE
St-Fargeau
Bd Mortier
R le Vau
Av Ibsen
Strasbourg St-Denis
Bd de Bonne Nouvelle
République
R du Faubourg du Temple
Goncourt
Couronnes
R de Ménilmontant
Pelleport
Réaumur Sébastopol
Sentier
Temple
Ménilmontant
Gambetta
R Belgrand
Porte de Bagnolet
Gallièni
Av de la République
St-Maur
Bd de Ménilmontant
Père Lachaise
Cimetière du Père Lachaise
R des Pyrénées
Centre Sportif
Stade de la Porte de Bagnolet
Stade Louis Lumière
Bd de Sébastopol
R Beaubourg
PLETZL
R de Turenne
Bd Beaumarchais
Bréguet Sabin
Voltaire
Philippe Auguste
Alexandre Dumas
Bd de Charonne
R Philippe Auguste
Av Ledru Rollin
Q des Gesvres
Charonne
Maraîchers
Porte de Montreuil
Bd Henri IV
Boulets Montreuil
Bd Voltaire
Avron
Buzenval
Bd Davout
Q Henri IV
Bd Bourdon
Bd de la Bastille
Faidherbe Chaligny
Nation
R des Écoles
Q St-Bernard
Av Daumesnil
Reuilly Diderot
Bd Diderot
Cours de Vincennes
Porte de Vincennes
LATIN QUARTER
Jardin des Plantes
St-Mandé Tourelle
Picpus
Montgallet
Cimetière de Picpus
R de Bercy
R de Reuilly
Bd Picpus
Bd Soult
Censier Daubenton
Bercy
Q d'Austerlitz
Seine
Bel Air
Dugommier
Bd de Reuilly
Daumesnil
St-Marcel
Bd de Bercy
R de Pommard
Cimetière sud de St-Mandé
Royal
Université Paris VI Centre Hospitalier Universitaire
Michel Bizot
Les Gobelins
Av des Gobelins
Bd de l'Hôpital
Quai de la Gare
Porte Dorée
Parc Zoologique
Campo Formio
Bd Vincent Auriol
Chevaleret
Bd Poniatowski
Nationale
Q de Bercy
Cour St-Émilion
Cimetière de Bercy
Porte de Charenton
Île de Bercy
Île de Reuilly
Place d'Italie
Corvisart
Bibliothèque
Cimetière Valmy
Av de Gravelle
Lac Daumesnil
Bois de Vincennes
Av d'Italie
To Orly Airport (17km)
FRANCE

Web 46 (Map pp296-7; ☎ 01 40 27 02 89; 46 rue du Roi de Sicile, 4e; per 15/30/60min €2.50/4/7, 5hr €29; 10am-midnight Mon-Fri, to 9pm Sat, noon-midnight Sun; M St-Paul)
XS Arena Les Halles (Map pp296-7; ☎ 01 40 13 02 60; 31 rue Sébastopol, 1er; per 1/2/3/4/5hr €3/6/8/10/11; 24hr; M Les Halles) Near the Forum des Halles.
XS Arena Luxembourg (Map pp296-7; ☎ 01 43 44 55 55; 17 rue Soufflot, 5e; per 1/2/3/4/5hr €3/6/8/10/11; 24hr; M Luxembourg) Central branch of this Internet-café chain.

Internet Resources
Metropole Paris (www.metropoleparis.com) Excellent online magazine in English.
Paris Pages (www.paris.org) Links to museums and cultural events.
Paris tourist office (www.parisinfo.com)

Laundry
There's a *laverie libre-service* (self-service laundrette) on every corner in Paris; your hotel or hostel can point you to one.

Medical Services
American Hospital (Map pp292-3; ☎ 01 46 41 25 25; www.american-hospital.org; 63 blvd Victor Hugo, 92200 Neuilly-sur-Seine; M Pont de Levallois Bécon) Provides 24-hour emergency medical and dental care.
Hertford British Hospital (Map pp292-3; ☎ 01 46 39 22 22; www.british-hospital.org; 3 rue Barbès, 92300 Levallois-Perret; M Anatole France)
Urgences Médicales de Paris (Paris Medical Emergencies; ☎ 01 53 94 94 94, 01 48 28 40 40) Runs 24-hour emergency house calls.

Money
Post offices with a Banque Postale offer the best exchange rates, and accept banknotes in various currencies as well as travellers cheques issued by Amex or Visa. *Bureaux de change* (currency-exchange offices) in Paris are usually faster, open longer and give better rates than commercial banks.

Post
Most *bureaux de poste* (post offices) in Paris are open 8am to 7pm weekdays and 8am or 9am till noon on Saturday. *Tabacs* (tobacconists) usually sell postage stamps.
Main post office (Map pp296-7; ☎ 01 40 28 76 00; 52 rue du Louvre, 1er; 24hr; M Sentier or Les Halles) Opens round the clock for letters and poste restante mail. Other services, including currency exchange, are available during regular opening hours.

Tourist Information
Office de Tourisme et de Congrès de Paris (Paris Convention & Visitors Bureau; Map pp296-7; ☎ 08 92 68 30 00; www.parisinfo.com; 25-27 rue des Pyramides, 1er; 9am-7.30pm Jun-Oct, 10am-7pm Mon-Sat, 11am-7pm Sun Nov-May; M Pyramides) About 500m northwest of the Louvre.

DANGERS & ANNOYANCES
Paris is generally a safe city, and you'll be fine if you employ some common sense. Stations that are best avoided at night include Châtelet-Les Halles; Château Rouge in Montmartre; Gare du Nord; Strasbourg St-Denis; Réaumur Sébastopol; and Montparnasse Bienvenüe. Women *do* travel alone on the metro at night, though not all who do so feel 100% comfortable.

Pickpocketing is a problem – notorious areas include Montmartre, Pigalle, the Forum des Halles, below the Eiffel Tower, and on the metro during rush hour.

SIGHTS
Left Bank
EIFFEL TOWER
It's impossible to imagine Paris without its most famous landmark, the **Tour Eiffel** (Eiffel Tower; Map pp292-3; ☎ 01 44 11 23 23; www.tour-eiffel.fr; lifts to 1st/2nd/3rd platform €4.50/8/11, children 3-11yr €2.50/4.50/6, stairs to 1st & 2nd platforms €4; lifts 9.30am-11pm Sep–mid-Jun, 9am-midnight mid-Jun–Aug, stairs 9.30am-6pm Sep–mid-Jun, 9am-midnight mid-Jun–Aug; M Champ de Mars-Tour Eiffel or Bir Hakeim), but the 'metal asparagus', as some Parisians snidely called it, faced fierce opposition from Paris' artistic elite when it was built for the 1889 Exposition Universelle (World Fair). The tower was almost torn down in 1909, and was only saved by the new science of radiotelegraphy (it proved to be the perfect spot for transmitting antennas). The city should be thankful it's still standing – some 5.8 million people make their way to the top each year, and Paris just wouldn't be the same without it.

The **Jardins du Trocadéro** (Trocadero Gardens; Map pp292-3; M Trocadéro), whose fountains and statue garden are grandly illuminated at night, are accessible across Pont d'Iéna from the Eiffel Tower.

MUSÉE D'ORSAY
The **Musée d'Orsay** (Map pp292-3; ☎ 01 40 49 48 14; www.musee-orsay.fr; 62 rue de Lille, 7e; adult/senior

& 18-25yr €7.50/5.50, under 18yr & 1st Sun of month free; 9.30am-6pm Tue, Wed, Fri-Sun, to 9.45pm Thu; M Musée d'Orsay or Solférino), housed in a turn-of-the-century train station facing the Seine, displays France's national collection of paintings, sculptures and objets d'art produced between the 1840s and 1914. Many visitors head straight to the upper level to see the impressionist paintings by Monet, Pissarro, Renoir, Sisley, Degas and Manet and the postimpressionist works by Cézanne, Van Gogh, Seurat and Matisse, but there's also lots to see on the ground floor, including some early works by Manet, Monet, Renoir and Pissarro. The middle level has some superb Art Nouveau rooms.

Tickets remain valid all day, so you can come and go as you please. The reduced entrance fee of €5.50 applies to everyone after 4.15pm (8pm on Thursday) and all day Sunday.

PANTHÉON

The domed landmark now known as the **Panthéon** (Map pp296-7; ☎ 01 44 32 18 00; www.monum.fr; place du Panthéon, 5e; adult/18-25yr €7.50/5, under 18yr & 1st Sun Oct-Mar free; 10am-6.30pm Apr-Sep, to 6.15pm Oct-Mar; M Luxembourg) was commissioned as an abbey church in 1750, and was completed in 1789. The crypt houses the tombs of Voltaire, Jean-Jacques Rousseau, Victor Hugo, Émile Zola, Jean Moulin and Nobel Prize–winner Marie Curie, among many others. Inside the Panthéon you'll find a working model of Foucault's Pendulum, which demonstrates the rotation of the earth; it wowed the scientific establishment when it was presented here in 1851.

CATACOMBES

The problems posed by Paris' overflowing cemeteries were solved in 1785 by exhuming the bones and storing them in the tunnels of three disused quarries. One, created in 1810, is now known as the **Catacombes** (Map pp292-3; ☎ 01 43 22 47 63; www.catacombes.paris.fr, in French; 1 av Colonel Henri Roi-Tanguy, 14e; adult/senior & student/14-25yr €5/3.50/2.50, under 14 free; 10am-5pm Tue-Sun; M Denfert Rochereau). After descending 20m (130 steps) below street level, visitors will follow 1.6km of underground corridors stacked with the bones and skulls of millions of Parisians. Spooky, but super.

MUSÉE RODIN

The **Musée Rodin** (Map pp292-3; ☎ 01 44 18 61 10; www.musee-rodin.fr; 77 rue de Varenne, 7e; adult/senior & 18-25yr €7/5, under 18 & 1st Sun free, garden only €1; 9.30am-5.45pm Tue-Sun Apr-Sep, to 4.45pm Tue-Sun Oct-Mar; M Varenne), is both a sublime museum and one of the most relaxing spots in the city, with a lovely garden full of sculptures and shade trees. The museum houses casts of some of Rodin's most celebrated works, including *The Thinker* and *The Kiss*.

MUSÉE NATIONAL DU MOYEN ÂGE

The **Musée National du Moyen Âge** (National Museum of the Middle Ages; Map pp296-7; ☎ 01 53 73 78 16, 01 53 73 78 00; www.musee-moyenage.fr; Thermes & Hôtel de Cluny, 6 place Paul Painlevé, 5e; adult/senior, student & 18-25yr €6.50/4.50, under 18yr & 1st Sun of month free; 9.15am-5.45pm Wed-Mon; M Cluny-La Sorbonne or St-Michel) is housed in two structures: the frigidarium (cooling room) and Gallo-Roman baths dating from around AD 200, and the late-15th-century Hôtel de Cluny, considered the finest example of medieval civil architecture in Paris. The spectacular displays at the museum include statuary, illuminated manuscripts, armaments, furnishings and objects made of gold, ivory and enamel.

JARDIN DU LUXEMBOURG

When the weather is fine Parisians flock to the terraces and chestnut groves of the 23-hectare **Jardin du Luxembourg** (Luxembourg Garden; Map pp296-7; 7am-9.30pm Apr-Oct, 8am-sunset Nov-Mar; M Luxembourg) to relax and sunbathe.

HÔTEL DES INVALIDES

The **Hôtel des Invalides** (Map pp292-3; M Varenne or La Tour Maubourg) was built in the 1670s by Louis XIV as housing for 4000 *invalides* (disabled war veterans). On 14 July 1789, a mob forced its way into the building and seized 28,000 rifles before heading to the prison at Bastille, starting the revolution.

CHAMP DE MARS

Running southeast from the Eiffel Tower, the grassy **Champ de Mars** (Field of Mars; Map pp292-3; M Champ de Mars-Tour Eiffel or École Militaire), named after the Roman god of war, was originally a parade ground for the nearby 18th-century École Militaire (Military Academy). This vast, French-classical building (1772) counted Napoleon among its graduates.

CENTRAL PARIS

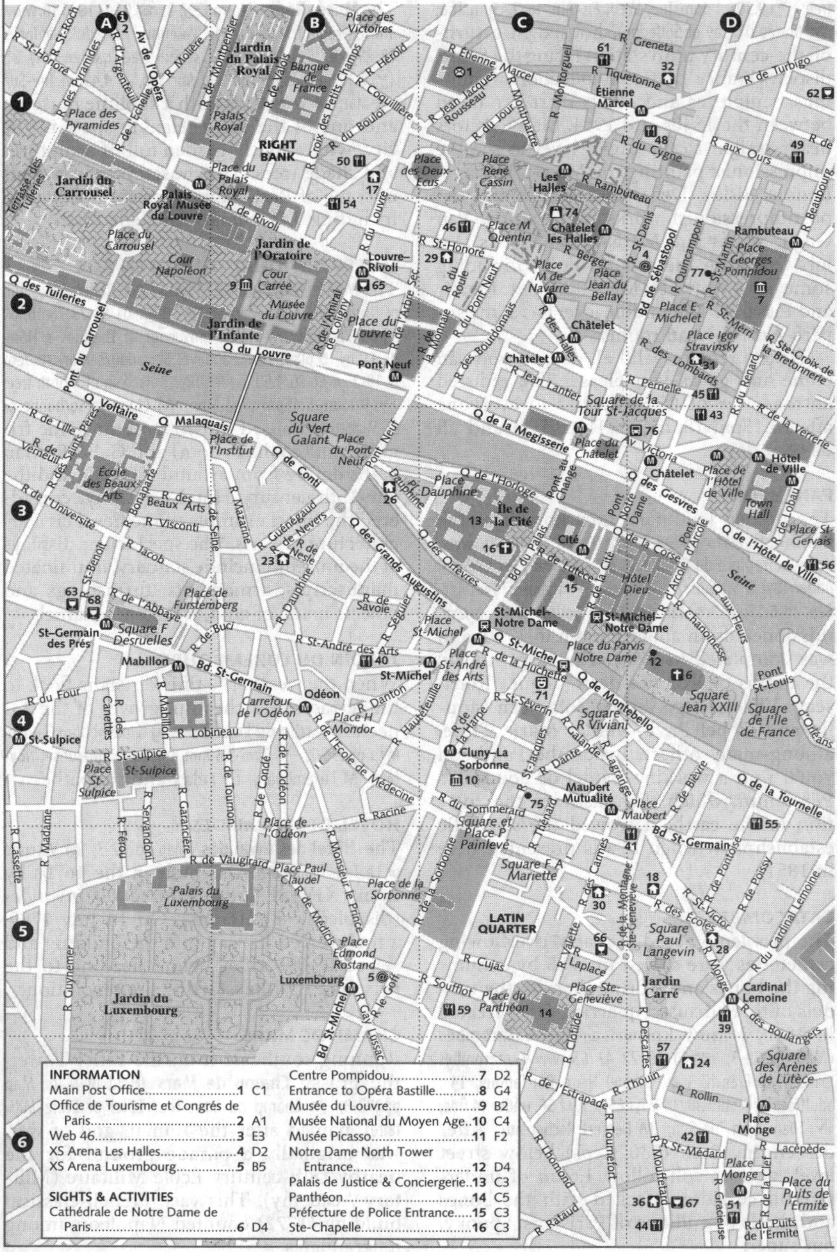

INFORMATION

- Main Post Office....1 C1
- Office de Tourisme et Congrés de Paris....2 A1
- Web 46....3 E3
- XS Arena Les Halles....4 D2
- XS Arena Luxembourg....5 B5

SIGHTS & ACTIVITIES

- Cathédrale de Notre Dame de Paris....6 D4
- Centre Pompidou....7 D2
- Entrance to Opéra Bastille....8 G4
- Musée du Louvre....9 B2
- Musée National du Moyen Age....10 C4
- Musée Picasso....11 F2
- Notre Dame North Tower Entrance....12 D4
- Palais de Justice & Conciergerie....13 C3
- Panthéon....14 C5
- Préfecture de Police Entrance....15 C3
- Ste-Chapelle....16 C3

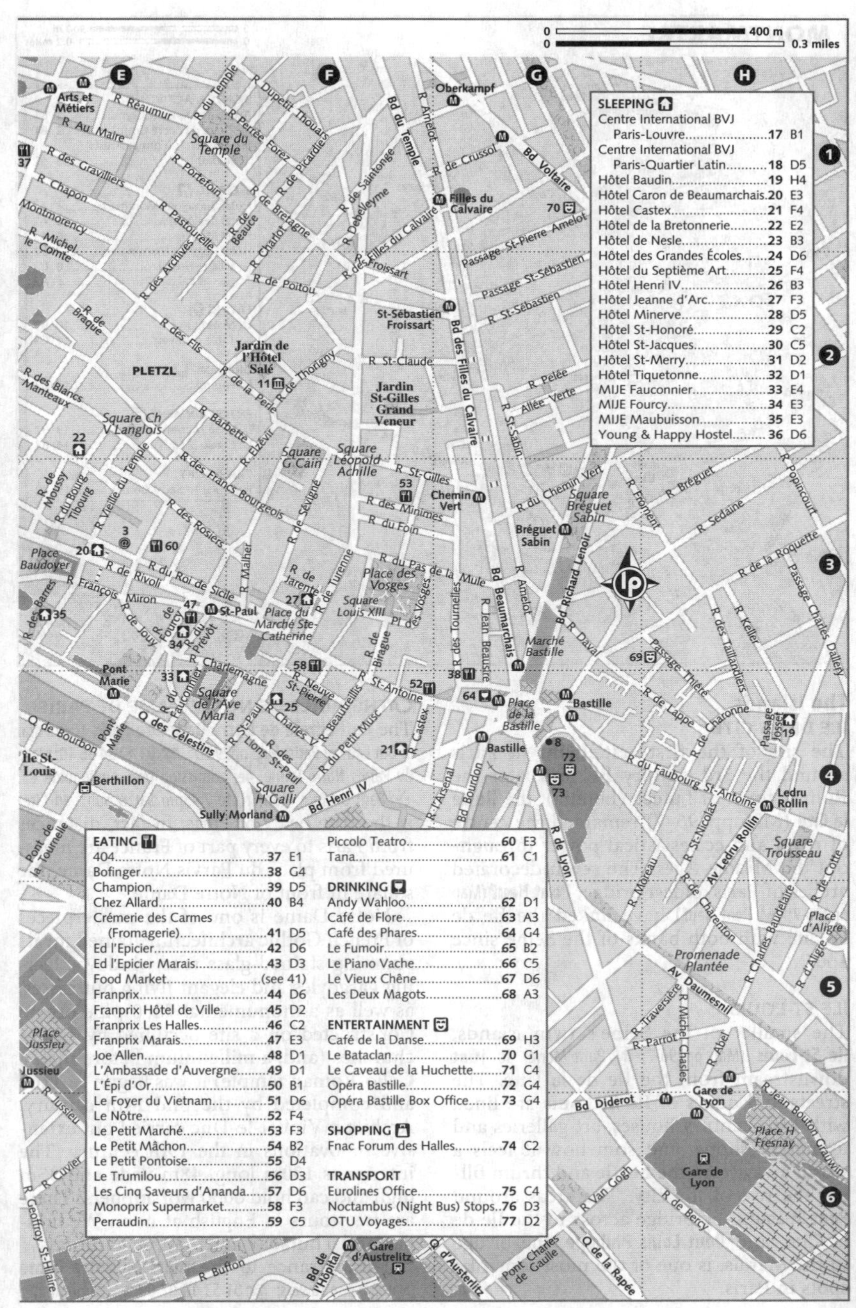
0 400 m
0 0.3 miles
SLEEPING
Centre International BVJ Paris-Louvre 17 B1
Centre International BVJ Paris-Quartier Latin 18 D5
Hôtel Baudin 19 H4
Hôtel Caron de Beaumarchais 20 E3
Hôtel Castex 21 F4
Hôtel de la Bretonnerie 22 E2
Hôtel de Nesle 23 B3
Hôtel des Grandes Écoles 24 D6
Hôtel du Septième Art 25 F4
Hôtel Henri IV 26 B3
Hôtel Jeanne d'Arc 27 F3
Hôtel Minerve 28 D5
Hôtel St-Honoré 29 C2
Hôtel St-Jacques 30 C5
Hôtel St-Merry 31 D2
Hôtel Tiquetonne 32 D1
MIJE Fauconnier 33 E4
MIJE Fourcy 34 E3
MIJE Maubuisson 35 E3
Young & Happy Hostel 36 D6
EATING
404 37 E1
Bofinger 38 G4
Champion 39 D5
Chez Allard 40 B4
Crémerie des Carmes (Fromagerie) 41 D5
Ed l'Epicier 42 D6
Ed l'Epicier Marais 43 D3
Food Market (see 41)
Franprix 44 D6
Franprix Hôtel de Ville 45 D2
Franprix Les Halles 46 C2
Franprix Marais 47 E3
Joe Allen 48 D1
L'Ambassade d'Auvergne 49 D1
L'Épi d'Or 50 B1
Le Foyer du Vietnam 51 D6
Le Nôtre 52 F4
Le Petit Marché 53 F3
Le Petit Mâchon 54 B2
Le Petit Pontoise 55 D4
Le Trumilou 56 D3
Les Cinq Saveurs d'Ananda 57 D6
Monoprix Supermarket 58 F3
Perraudin 59 C5
Piccolo Teatro 60 E3
Tana 61 C1
DRINKING
Andy Wahloo 62 D1
Café de Flore 63 A3
Café des Phares 64 G4
Le Fumoir 65 B2
Le Piano Vache 66 C5
Le Vieux Chêne 67 D6
Les Deux Magots 68 A3
ENTERTAINMENT
Café de la Danse 69 H3
Le Bataclan 70 G1
Le Caveau de la Huchette 71 C4
Opéra Bastille 72 G4
Opéra Bastille Box Office 73 G4
SHOPPING
Fnac Forum des Halles 74 C2
TRANSPORT
Eurolines Office 75 C4
Noctambus (Night Bus) Stops 76 D3
OTU Voyages 77 D2
Arts et Métiers
Oberkampf
Filles du Calvaire
St-Sébastien Froissart
Chemin Vert
Bréguet Sabin
St-Paul
Pont Marie
Sully Morland
Bastille
Ledru Rollin
Gare de Lyon
Gare d'Austerlitz
Jussieu
PLETZL
Jardin de l'Hôtel Salé
Jardin St-Gilles Grand Veneur
Place des Vosges
Place de la Bastille
Square du Temple
Île St-Louis
Berthillon
Promenade Plantée
Bd Henri IV
Bd Beaumarchais
Bd des Filles du Calvaire
Bd du Temple
Bd Voltaire
Bd Diderot
Av Daumesnil
Av Ledru Rollin
R du Faubourg St-Antoine
R St-Antoine
R de Rivoli
Q des Célestins
Q de la Rapée
FRANCE

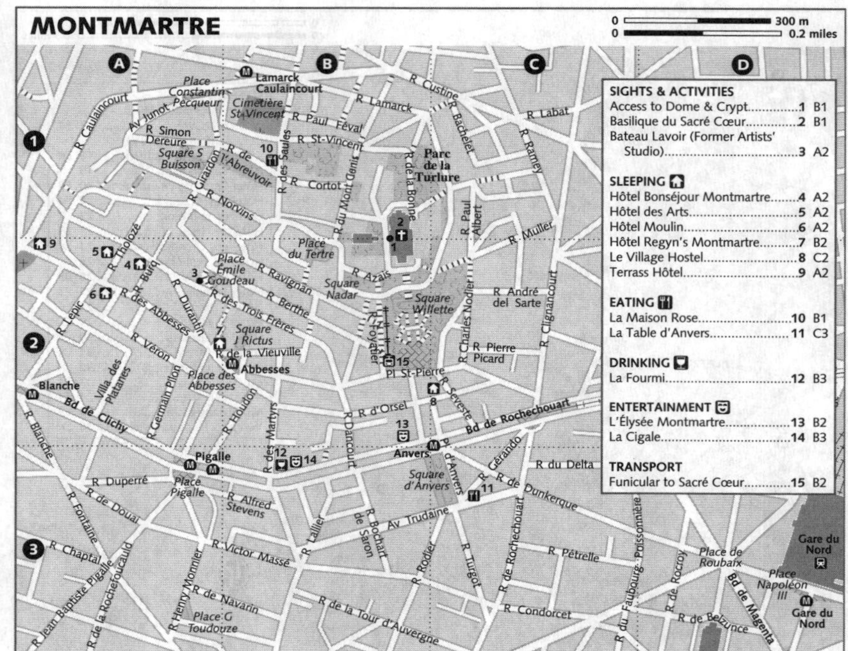

The Islands

ÎLE DE LA CITÉ

The site of the first settlement in Paris around the 3rd century BC and later the Roman town of Lutèce (Lutetia), the **Île de la Cité** (Map pp296–7) remained the centre of royal and ecclesiastical power throughout the Middle Ages. The seven decorated arches of Paris' oldest bridge, **Pont Neuf** (Map pp296-7; Ⓜ Pont Neuf) have linked the Île de la Cité with both banks of the Seine since 1607.

ÎLE ST-LOUIS

The smaller of the Seine's twin islands, **Île St-Louis** (Map pp296-7; Ⓜ Pont Marie) is just downstream from the Île de la Cité. The streets and quays of Île St-Louis are lined with 17th-century houses, art galleries and upmarket shops, and somehow it feels a world away from the hustle and thrum filling the rest of the city. The areas around **Pont St-Louis**, the bridge across to the Île de la Cité, and **Pont Louis Philippe**, the bridge to the Marais, is one of the most romantic spots in Paris.

CATHÉDRALE DE NOTRE DAME DE PARIS

The **Cathédrale de Notre Dame de Paris** (Cathedral of Our Lady of Paris; Map pp296-7; ☎ 01 42 34 56 10; place du Parvis Notre Dame, 4e; admission free, audioguide €5; 🕒 8am-6.45pm Mon-Fri, to 7.45pm Sat & Sun; Ⓜ Cité) is the true heart of Paris; in fact, distances from Paris to every part of France are measured from place du Parvis Notre Dame, the square in front of Notre Dame.

Notre Dame is one of the masterpieces of French Gothic architecture, famed for its stunning stained-glass rose windows, leering gargoyles and elegant flying buttresses, as well as a monumental 7800-pipe organ. Constructed on a site occupied by earlier churches (and, a millennium before that, a Gallo-Roman temple) it was begun in 1163 and completed by the mid-14th century. Architect Viollet-le-Duc carried out extensive renovations in the 19th century. The interior is 130m long, 48m wide and 35m high and can hold 6000 worshippers. There are free tours in English at noon Wednesday and Thursday and 2.30pm Saturday.

The entrance to the **tours de Notre Dame** (Notre Dame towers; ☎ 01 53 10 07 00; www.monum.fr;

rue du Cloître Notre Dame; adult/student & 18-25yr €7.50/5, under 18yr & 1st Sun Oct-Mar free; 9.30am-7.30pm Apr-Jun & Sep, 9am-7.30pm Mon-Fri, 9am-11pm Sat & Sun Jul & Aug, 10am-5.30pm Oct-Mar), is from the North Tower. The 387 spiralling steps bring you to the top of the west façade, where you'll come face-to-face with the 13-tonne bell Emmanuel in the South Tower and will have a spectacular view of Paris. No hunchbacks, though, despite what you may have heard from Victor Hugo.

STE-CHAPELLE

The most exquisite of Paris' Gothic monuments, **Ste-Chapelle** (Map pp296-7; 01 53 40 60 97; www.monum.fr; 4 blvd du Palais, 1er; adult/18-25yr €6.50/4.50, under 18yr & 1st Sun Oct-Mar free; 9.30am-6pm Mar-Oct, 9am-5pm Nov-Feb; Cité), is tucked within the walls of the Palais de Justice (Law Courts). Built in just under three years, Ste-Chapelle was consecrated in 1248. The chapel was conceived by Louis IX to house his collection of sacred relics, now kept in the treasury of Notre Dame.

Right Bank

MUSÉE DU LOUVRE

The vast Palais du Louvre was constructed as a fortress by Philippe-Auguste in the early 13th century and rebuilt in the mid-16th century. In 1793, the Convention turned it into the **Musée du Louvre** (Louvre Museum; Map pp296-7; 01 40 20 53 17; www.louvre.fr; permanent collections/permanent collections & temporary exhibits €8.50/13, after 6pm Wed & Fri €6/11, under 18yr & from 6pm Fri under 26yr permanent collections free, 1st Sun of month free; 9am-6pm Mon, Thu, Sat & Sun, to 9.45pm Wed & Fri; Palais Royal-Musée du Louvre), one of France's (if not the world's) finest museums.

When the museum opened in the late 18th century it contained some 2500 paintings, sculptures and objets d'art; today a staggering 35,000 exhibits are on display. The collection is mind-bogglingly diverse, ranging from Islamic artworks and Egyptian artefacts through to one of the world's greatest collections of Greek and Roman antiquities (including the *Venus de Milo* and the *Winged Victory of Samothrace*). But it's the Louvre's astonishingly rich collection of paintings that draws most visitors; highlights include signature works by Raphael, Botticelli, Delacroix and Titian, Géricault's *The Raft of the Medusa* and of course Leonardo da Vinci's mischievous *La Joconde*, better known as the *Mona Lisa*. If you have time, don't miss the section devoted to objets d'art, which houses a series of fabulously extravagant salons and rooms, including the lavish apartments of Napoleon III's Minister of State.

The museum is divided into four sections: the Sully, Denon and Richelieu Wings and the Hall Napoleon. You'll only scratch the surface in a single day's visit, and museum fatigue can be a real problem at the Louvre – you'll enjoy it much more if you don't try and pack too much into one day.

The main entrance and ticket windows in the Cour Napoleon are covered by the 21m-high glass **Grande Pyramide**. The queues are always heavy at the main entrance; the smaller entrances at the Carrousel du Louvre, 99 rue de Rivoli, or from the Palais Royal-Musée du Louvre metro station are usually quieter. You can avoid the queues completely by buying tickets in advance from the ticket machines in the Carrousel du Louvre, by ringing 08 92 68 36 22 or 08 25 34 63 46, or by booking online at www.louvre.fr. Tickets are also available at Fnac (p307) for an extra €1.50. Tickets remain valid for the whole day.

JARDIN DES TUILERIES

The formal, 28-hectare **Jardin des Tuileries** (Tuileries Garden; Map pp292-3; 01 40 20 90 43; 7am-9pm late Mar-late Sep, to 7.30pm late Sep-late Mar; Tuileries or Concorde) was laid out in its present form – more or less – in the mid-17th century by André Le Nôtre, who also created the gardens at Versailles (p312). The Tuileries soon became the most fashionable spot in Paris for parading about in one's finery; today it is a favourite of joggers. It forms part of the Banks of the Seine World Heritage site as listed by Unesco in 1991.

CENTRE POMPIDOU

The **Centre National d'Art et de Culture Georges Pompidou** (Georges Pompidou National Centre of Art & Culture; Map pp296-7; 01 44 78 12 33; www.centrepompidou.fr; place Georges Pompidou, 4e; Rambuteau) is the most successful art and cultural centre in the world.

The Centre Pompidou, also known as the Centre Beaubourg, has amazed visitors since it was inaugurated in 1977, not only for its outstanding collection of modern art, but also for its radical architectural statement; it was among the first buildings to have its 'insides' turned outside. But it all began to look somewhat *démodé* by the late 1990s, hence the recent €85-million renovation, complete with theatre, cinema and dance spaces and a super-stylish restaurant.

The 4th and 5th floors are occupied by the **Musée National d'Art Moderne** (MNAM, National Museum of Modern Art; adult/senior & 18-25yr €10/8, under 18 & 1st Sun of month free; 11am-9pm Wed-Mon), France's national collection of art dating from 1905 onwards. If you're into surrealism, cubism or contemporary art, this is the place to head for.

HÔTEL DE VILLE

Gutted during the Paris Commune of 1871, Paris' **Hôtel de Ville** (City Hall; Map pp296-7; ☎ 08 20 00 75 75, 01 42 76 50 49; www.paris.fr; place de l'Hôtel de Ville, 4e; Ⓜ Hôtel de Ville) was rebuilt in the neo-Renaissance style (1874–82). There's a **Salon d'Accueil** (Reception Hall; 29 rue de Rivoli, 4e; 10am-7pm Mon-Sat), which dispenses copious amounts of information and brochures and is used for temporary exhibitions, usually with a Paris theme. The Hôtel de Ville faces the majestic place de l'Hôtel de Ville, used from the Middle Ages to the 19th century to stage many of Paris' celebrations, rebellions, book burnings and public executions.

MUSÉE PICASSO

The **Musée Picasso** (Map pp296-7; ☎ 01 42 71 25 21; www.musee-picasso.fr; 5 rue de Thorigny, 3e; adult/18-25yr €7/5.50 Wed-Sat & Mon, admission for all Sun €5.50, under 18 & 1st Sun of month free; 9.30am-6pm Wed-Mon Apr-Sep, to 5.30pm Wed-Mon Oct-Mar; Ⓜ St-Paul or Chemin Vert), housed in the mid-17th-century Hôtel Salé, is one of Paris' best-loved art museums and includes more than 3500 of the master's works. You can also view paintings from his collection, including work by Cézanne, Matisse, Modigliani and Degas.

PLACE DE LA BASTILLE

The Bastille, built during the 14th century as a fortified royal residence, is the most famous monument in Paris that no longer exists; the notorious prison was demolished by a revolutionary mob on 14 July 1789. The **place de la Bastille** (Map pp296-7; Ⓜ Bastille) in the 12e, where the prison once stood, is now a busy traffic roundabout.

ÉTOILE & CHAMPS-ÉLYSÉES

A dozen avenues radiate from the world's largest traffic roundabout, **place de l'Étoile** (Map pp292-3; Ⓜ Charles de Gaulle Étoile) – officially called place Charles de Gaulle; first among these is the av des Champs-Elysées. This broad boulevard, whose name refers to the 'Elysian Fields' of Greek mythology, links place de la Concorde with the Arc de Triomphe. Symbolising the style and *joie de vivre* of Paris since the mid-19th century, the avenue remains one of the city's swankiest shopping districts.

ARC DE TRIOMPHE

The **Arc de Triomphe** (Triumphal Arch; Map pp292-3; ☎ 01 55 37 73 77; www.monum.fr; viewing platform adult/18-25yr €8/6, under 18yr & 1st Sun of month Oct-Mar free; 10am-11pm Apr-Sep, to 10.30pm Oct-Mar; Ⓜ Charles de Gaulle-Étoile) is 2.2km northwest of place de la Concorde. Commissioned in 1806 by Napoleon to commemorate his victories, it remained unfinished when he started losing battles and then entire wars, and wasn't completed until 1836. Since 1920, the body of an **unknown soldier** from WWI has lain beneath the arch; his fate and that of countless others is commemorated by a memorial flame rekindled each evening around 6.30pm.

The **viewing platform** (up 284 steps) affords fine views of the dozen surrounding avenues, many named after Napoleonic generals (including ultra-exclusive av Foch, Paris' widest boulevard).

PLACE DE LA CONCORDE

Place de la Concorde (Map pp292-3; Ⓜ Concorde) was laid out between 1755 and 1775. The 3300-year-old pink granite obelisk in the middle of the square once stood in the Temple of Ramses at Thebes (today's Luxor); Muhammad Ali, viceroy and pasha of Egypt, gave it to France in 1831.

MONTMARTRE & PIGALLE

During the late 19th and early 20th centuries bohemian **Montmartre** (Map p298; Ⓜ Anvers or Abbesses) attracted numerous writers and artists, including Picasso, who lived at the studio called **Bateau Lavoir** (Map p298; 11bis Émile Goudeau; Ⓜ Abbesses) from 1908 to 1912. Montmartre retains an upbeat ambience that all the tourists in the world couldn't spoil.

A few blocks southwest of Montmartre is neon-drenched **Pigalle** (Map p298; Ⓜ Pigalle), 9e and 18e, a red-light district that also boasts plenty of trendy nightspots, clubs and cabarets (including the original Moulin Rouge).

BASILIQUE DU SACRÉ CŒUR

The **Basilique du Sacré Cœur** (Basilica of the Sacred Heart; Map p298; ☎ 01 53 41 89 00; www.sacre-coeur-montmartre.com; place du Parvis du Sacré Cœur, 18e; 6am-11pm; M Anvers), perched at the top of the Butte de Montmartre (Montmartre Hill), was built from contributions pledged by Parisian Catholics after the humiliating Franco-Prussian War of 1870–71. Some 234 spiralling steps lead to the spectacular panorama from the basilica's **dome** (admission €5; 9am-7pm Apr-Sep, to 6pm Oct-Mar).

CIMETIÈRE DU PÈRE LACHAISE

The world's most-visited graveyard, **Cimetière du Père Lachaise** (Père Lachaise Cemetery; Map pp292-3; ☎ 01 55 25 82 10; admission free; 8am-6pm Mon-Fri, 8.30am-6pm Sat, 9am-6pm Sun mid-Mar–early Nov; 8am-5.30pm Mon-Fri, 8.30am-5.30pm Sat, 9am-5.30pm Sun early Nov–mid-Mar; M Philippe Auguste, Gambetta or Père Lachaise) opened its one-way doors in 1804. Among the 800,000 people buried here are Chopin, Molière, Balzac, Proust, Gertrude Stein, Colette, Pissarro, Seurat, Modigliani, Sarah Bernhardt, Yves Montand, Delacroix, Édith Piaf and even the 12th-century lovers, Abélard and Héloïse. The graves of **Oscar Wilde** (Division 89) and **Jim Morrison** (Division 6) are perennially popular. Free maps are available from the **conservation office** (Map pp292-3; 16 rue du Repos, 20e).

TOURS

Fat Tire Bike Tours (Map pp292-3; ☎ 01 56 58 10 54; www.fattirebiketoursparis.com; 24 rue Edgar Faure, 15e; tours adult/student €24/22; office 9am-7pm; M Dupleix) Offers four-hour English-language tours of the city at 11am March to November, with additional tours mid-May to July. Night tours are also available; check the website.

Bateaux Mouches (Map pp292-3; ☎ 01 42 25 96 10; www.bateauxmouches.com, in French; Port de la Conférence, 8e; adult/concession €8/4, under 4 free; every 15-30min mid-Mar–mid-Nov; M Alma Marceau) Based on the Right Bank near the Pont de l'Alma, this is the most famous riverboat company in Paris. Cruises on 1000-seat boats run at 11am, 2.30pm, 4pm, 6pm and 9pm from mid-November to mid-March, with additional winter cruises depending on demand.

SLEEPING

The student travel agency **OTU Voyages** (Map pp296-7; ☎ 01 40 29 12 22; www.otu.fr, in French; 119 rue St-Martin, 4e; 9.30am-6.30pm Mon-Fri, 10am-6pm Sat; M Rambuteau), opposite Centre Pompidou, can *always* find you accommodation, even in summer. The finder's fee is €15.

Alcôve & Agapes (☎ 01 44 85 06 05; www.bed-&-breakfast-in-paris.com) arranges B&B accommodation in Paris for between €60 and €195 for a double.

Louvre & Les Halles

BUDGET

Centre International BVJ Paris-Louvre (Map pp296-7; ☎ 01 53 00 90 90; www.bvjhotel.com; 20 rue Jean-Jacques Rousseau, 1er; dm €25, d per person €28; M Louvre-Rivoli) This modern hostel run by the Bureau des Voyages de la Jeunesse has single-sex rooms for two to eight people. There's usually space (even in summer) if you stop by early, but you must be under 35 and there are no kitchen facilities.

Hôtel Tiquetonne (Map pp296-7; ☎ 01 42 36 94 58; fax 01 42 36 02 94; 6 rue Tiquetonne, 2e; s €30-40, d €50; M Étienne Marcel) If you're looking for good-value digs smack in the middle of party town, this vintage 47-room cheapie is clean and comfortable and some rooms are quite large.

MIDRANGE

Hôtel St-Honoré (Map pp296-7; ☎ 01 42 36 20 38; paris@hotelsthonore.com; 85 rue St-Honoré, 1er; s/d/tw/q €59/74/83/92; M Châtelet) Between the Palais Royal and the Seine and at the eastern end of a very upmarket shopping street, this offers some fairly cramped rooms and a few more spacious ones for three and four people.

Marais & Bastille

BUDGET

Hôtel Baudin (Map pp296-7; ☎ 01 47 00 18 91; hotelbaudin@wanadoo.fr; 113 av Ledru Rollin, 11e; s €29-52, d €35-62, tr €40-76; M Ledru Rollin) This old-fashioned hostelry has 17 brightly coloured rooms, ranging from ultra cheap (with hand basins and hall showers) to slightly more expensive (with private shower or bath and toilet). Reception is on the 1st floor.

Maison Internationale de la Jeunesse et des Étudiants (MIJE; ☎ 01 42 74 23 45; www.mije.com; dm €27, s/tw/tr per person €42/32/28;) runs three hostels in renovated *hôtels particuliers* (private mansions) in the heart of the Marais, and you won't find a better budget deal in Paris. Costs are the same for all three; reservations at any of the MIJE hostels can be made via the central switchboard or emailing; they'll hold you a bed till noon. The annual membership fee costs €2.50.

MIJE Fourcy (Map pp296-7; 6 rue de Fourcy, 4e; M St-Paul) The largest MIJE hostel with 185 beds. A three-course *menu* at the in-house restaurant costs €10.50; two-courses cost €8.50. Both *menus* include a drink.

MIJE Fauconnier (Map pp296-7; 11 rue du Fauconnier, 4e; Ⓜ St-Paul or Pont Marie) A 122-bed hostel two blocks south of MIJE Le Fourcy.

MIJE Maubuisson (Map pp296-7; 12 rue des Barres, 4e; Ⓜ Hôtel de Ville or Pont Marie) The pick of the three hostels, half a block south of the *mairie* (town hall) of the 4e.

MIDRANGE

Hôtel Jeanne d'Arc (Map pp296-7; ☎ 01 48 87 62 11; www.hoteljeannedarc.com; 3 rue de Jarente, 4e; s €58-96, d €82-96, tr €115, q €145; Ⓜ St-Paul) This cosy, 36-room hotel near place du Marché Ste-Catherineis ideally located for the museums, bars and restaurants of the Marais and has a country-tinged atmosphere – but everyone knows about it, so book early.

Hôtel Castex (Map pp296-7; ☎ 01 42 72 31 52; www.castexhotel.com; 5 rue Castex, 4e; s €85-115, d & tw €95-140, ste €160-220; ; Ⓜ Bastille) Equidistant from Bastille and the Marais, the 30-room Castex retains some of its 17th-century elements, including a vaulted stone cellar-cum–breakfast room and Toile de Jouy wallpaper. Try to get one of the independent rooms (1 and 2) off the patio.

Hôtel du Septième Art (Map pp296-7; ☎ 01 44 54 85 00; hotel7art@wanadoo.fr; 20 rue St-Paul, 4e; s & d €85-135, tw €90-135; ; Ⓜ St-Paul) This film-themed hotel has a black-and-white movie motif running throughout, right down to the tiled floors and bathrooms. The 23 guest rooms spread over five levels (no lift) are sizeable and imaginatively decorated.

Hôtel de la Bretonnerie (Map pp296-7; ☎ 01 48 87 77 63; www.bretonnerie.com; 22 rue St-Croix de la Bretonnerie, 4e; s & d €116-149, tr & q €174, ste €180-205; ; Ⓜ Hôtel de Ville) This charming hotel in the heart of the Marais has a touch of old-world class – each of the 22 guestrooms and seven suites is richly decorated in its own individual style; some have four-poster and canopy beds.

Hôtel Caron de Beaumarchais (Map pp296-7; ☎ 01 42 72 34 12; www.carondebeaumarchais.com; 12 rue Vieille du Temple, 4e; s & d €125-162; ; Ⓜ St-Paul) This 18th-century–style hotel has to be seen to be believed. The lavish lobby, with its pianoforte, gilded mirrors and candelabra, sets the tone – the idea is to recreate the atmosphere of an upmarket 18th-century townhouse, and although some of the rooms are a bit small, you'll feel every inch the aristocrat.

TOP END

Hôtel St-Merry (Map pp296-7; ☎ 01 42 78 14 15; www.hotelmarais.com; 78 rue de la Verrerie, 4e; d & tw €160-230, tr €205-275, ste €335-407; Ⓜ Châtelet) This medieval number in the Marais is housed in the former presbytery of the Église St-Merry, complete with beamed ceilings, church pews and wrought-iron candelabra. The rich Gothic atmosphere is fantastic – but on the downside, there's no lift, no air-con and no TVs.

The Islands

BUDGET*

Hôtel Henri IV (Map pp296-7; ☎ 01 43 54 44 53; 25 place Dauphine, 1er; s €27-34, d €35-72, tr €47; Ⓜ Pont Neuf or Cité) Perched on the tip of the Île de la Cité, this rickety old hotel has 20 tattered and worn rooms, but you won't often find something this romantic at such a knockdown price in Paris. Hall showers cost €2.50 and breakfast is included.

Latin Quarter & Jardin des Plantes

The Latin Quarter offers the best value on the Left Bank, especially compared with the sky-high prices of the hotels in the neighbouring 6e.

BUDGET

Young & Happy Hostel (Map pp296-7; ☎ 01 47 07 47 07; www.youngandhappy.fr; 80 rue Mouffetard, 5e; dm €21-23, d per person €24-26; ; Ⓜ Place Monge) It's a little rough around the edges, but this friendly hostel in the Latin Quarter remains popular with an old-school backpacking crowd. Dorms are small and sleep two to eight people; arrive before 8am if you want a bed in summer. The 2am curfew is strictly enforced.

Centre International de Séjour BVJ Paris-Quartier Latin (Map pp296-7; ☎ 01 43 29 34 80; www.bvjhotel.com; 44 rue des Bernardins, 5e; dm €26, s/d per person €35/28; ; Ⓜ Maubert Mutualité) This 100-bed hostel on the Left Bank is a branch of the Centre International BVJ Paris-Louvre and has the same rules. All rooms have showers and telephones.

MIDRANGE

Port Royal Hôtel (Map pp292-3; ☎ 01 43 31 70 06; www.portroyal.fr; 8 blvd de Port Royal, 5e; s €41-89, d €52.50-89; Ⓜ Les Gobelins) It's hard to imagine that this 46-room hotel, managed by the same family for three generations, still only bears one star. The spotless, quiet rooms overlook either the street or a small glassed-in courtyard.

Hôtel St-Jacques (Map pp296-7; ☎ 01 44 07 45 45; www.hotel-saintjacques.com; 35 rue des Écoles, 5e; s €52-80, d €90-118, tr €145; ⊠ 💻; Ⓜ Maubert Mutualité) This stylish 38-room hotel has balconies overlooking the Panthéon. The décor has been thoroughly updated since *Charade* was filmed here in the 1960s, but a few 19th-century features (trompe l'œil ceilings, iron staircase) still remain.

Hôtel de l'Espérance (Map pp292-3; ☎ 01 47 07 10 99; www.hoteldelesperance.fr; 15 rue Pascal, 5e; s €71-79, d €79-87, tw €87, tr €102; 💻; Ⓜ Censier Daubenton) The 'Hotel of Hope', just south of lively rue Mouffetard, is a quiet, immaculately kept 38-room place with faux antique furnishings.

Hôtel Minerve (Map pp296-7; ☎ 01 43 26 26 04; www.hotel-paris-minerve.com; 13 rue des Écoles, 5e; s €84-132, d €98-132, tr €150-152; ❄ 💻; Ⓜ Cardinal Lemoine) This 54-room hotel is owned by the same family who runs the Familia Hôtel. The reception is kitted out with Oriental carpets and antique books, and some rooms have French frescoes and reproduction 18th-century wallpaper. Eight rooms have views of Notre Dame, and a couple have their own tiny courtyards.

Hôtel des Grandes Écoles (Map pp296-7; ☎ 01 43 26 79 23; www.hotel-grandes-ecoles.com; 75 rue du Cardinal Lemoine, 5e; s & d €105-130, tr €125-150; Ⓟ ⊠; Ⓜ Cardinal Lemoine or Place Monge) This wonderful, welcoming hotel has one of the loveliest situations in the Latin Quarter, tucked away in a courtyard off a medieval street with its own garden. Rooms 29 to 33 have direct access to the garden.

St-Germain, Odéon & Luxembourg

The well-heeled St-Germain des Prés is the quintessential place to stay in central Paris, but you'll need to bring your spare change – budget places just don't exist in this part of town.

> **AUTHOR'S CHOICE**
>
> **Hôtel Danemark** (Map pp292-3; ☎ 01 43 26 93 78; www.hoteldanemark.com; 21 rue Vavin, 6e; s €115-132, d €132-152; ⊠ ❄ 💻; Ⓜ Vavin) The eclectic rooms at this chic boutique hotel southwest of the Jardin de Luxembourg are an imaginative mix of contemporary décor and period character – think slinky lighting, modern art and hip bathrooms, offset by the occasional spot of exposed stonework.

MIDRANGE

Hôtel de Nesle (Map pp296-7; ☎ 01 43 54 62 41; www.hoteldenesleparis.com; 7 rue de Nesle, 6e; s €55-75, d €75-100; Ⓜ Odéon or Mabillon) A relaxed, colourfully decorated hotel with 20 rooms, half of which are painted with murals taken from (mostly French) literature. Even better is the huge back garden complete with pathways, trellis and a small pond.

Hôtel Sèvres Azur (Map pp292-3; ☎ 01 45 48 84 07; www.hotelsevresazur.com; 22 rue de l'Abbé Grégoire, 6e; s €85-95, d €90-115, tr €135; 💻; Ⓜ St-Placide) On a quiet street between Montparnasse and St-Germain, this 31-room hotel offers great value. The modern, bedrooms are bold and brightly shaded – choose from street or courtyard views.

Clichy & Gare St-Lazare

BUDGET

Hôtel Eldorado (Map pp292-3; ☎ 01 45 22 35 21; www.eldoradohotel.fr; 18 rue des Dames, 17e; s €25-50, d & tw €45-70, tr €50-80; Ⓜ Place de Clichy) This bohemian place is one of Paris' grooviest finds, with 40 colourfully decorated rooms in the main building and a pleasant garden annexe.

MIDRANGE

New Orient Hôtel (Map pp292-3; ☎ 01 45 22 21 64; www.hotel-paris-orient.com; 16 rue de Constantinople, 8e; s €82-105, d €99-105, tw €105-130, tr & q €140; ⊠ ❄ 💻; Ⓜ Europe) A personality-packed hotel with 30 cosy, ever-so-slightly twee rooms, some of which have small balconies.

Hôtel Favart (Map pp292-3; ☎ 01 42 97 59 83; www.hotel-paris-favart.com; 5 rue Marivaux, 2e; s €89-110, d €110-135, tr €130-160, q €155-176; ⊠ ❄; Ⓜ Richelieu Drouot) With 37 rooms facing the Opéra Comique, the Favart is a stylish Art Nouveau hotel that feels like it never let go of the *belle époque*. It's especially handy for the department stores on blvd Haussmann.

Gare du Nord, Gare de l'Est & République

The areas around the Gare du Nord and Gare de l'Est are far from the prettiest parts of Paris, but you will find plenty of decent-value hotels. Place de la République is convenient for the nightlife areas of Ménilmontant.

BUDGET

Peace & Love Hostel (Map pp292-3; ☎ 01 46 07 65 11; www.paris-hostels.com; 245 rue La Fayette, 10e; dm €17-21, d per person €21-26; 💻; Ⓜ Jaurès or Louis Blanc) This modern-day hippy hang-out is a groovy (if overcrowded) hostel with beds in 20 smallish, shower-equipped rooms for two to four people. There's a great kitchen and eating area, but most of the action revolves around the ground floor bar (open till 2am).

Auberge de Jeunesse Jules Ferry (Map pp292-3; ☎ 01 43 57 55 60; www.fuaj.fr; 8 blvd Jules Ferry, 11e; dm €20, d per person €20; ⊠ ❄ 💻; Ⓜ République or Goncourt) This official hostel, three blocks east of place de la République, is decidedly institutional and the two- to six-person rooms could use a refit but, on the upside, there's no curfew. You'll pay an extra €2.90 per night without an HI card.

Auberge de Jeunesse Le D'Artagnan (Map pp292-3; ☎ 01 40 32 34 57; www.fuaj.fr; 80 rue Vitruve, 20e; dm €21.50; Ⓜ Porte de Bagnolet) With 435 beds on seven levels, this is the largest hostel in France. Dorms have two to eight beds, and there's a bar, cinema and laundry facilities.

Hôtel Nevers (Map pp292-3; ☎ 01 47 00 56 18; www.hoteldenevers.com; 53 rue de Malte, 11e; s & d €35-53, tr €66-78; 💻; Ⓜ Oberkampf) This family-run budget hotel is around the corner from place de la République. The 32 guestrooms are sparsely furnished, but cat-lovers will appreciate the friendly feline welcome.

MIDRANGE

Nord-Est Hôtel (Map pp292-3; ☎ 01 47 70 07 18; hotel.nord.est@wanadoo.fr; 12 rue des Petits Hôtels, 10e; s/d/tr/q €63/73/97/123; 💻; Ⓜ Poissonnière) This unusual 30-room hotel, charmingly located on the 'Street of Little Hotels', is set back from the street and fronted by a small terrace.

Grand Hôtel de Paris (Map pp292-3; ☎ 01 46 07 40 56; grand.hotel.de.paris@gofornet.com; 72 blvd de Strasbourg, 10e; s/d/tr/q €77/83/102/119; Ⓜ Gare de l'Est) The Grand Hôtel de Paris is just south of the Gare de l'Est on blvd de Strasbourg. It has 49 soundproofed rooms and makes a pleasant bolthole if you're in the area.

Montmartre & Pigalle

Montmartre is one of the most charming neighbourhoods in Paris, with a clutch of midrange and top-end hotels. The area east of Sacré Cœur can be rough; it might be prudent to avoid Château Rouge metro station at night.

BUDGET

Le Village Hostel (Map p298; ☎ 01 42 64 22 02; www.villagehostel.fr; 20 rue d'Orsel, 18e; dm €20-23, d per person €23-27, tr per person €21.50-25; ⊠ 💻; Ⓜ Anvers) 'The Village' is a fine 25-room hostel with beamed ceilings and views of Sacré Cœur. Beds are in rooms for four to six people, all with showers and toilets. Kitchen facilities are available, and there's a popular bar too. Curfew is 2am.

Hôtel Bonséjour Montmartre (Map p298; ☎ 01 42 54 22 53; www.hotel-bonsejour-montmartre.fr; 11 rue Burq, 18e; s €25, d €32-48, tr €59; Ⓜ Abbesses) The 'Good Stay' at the top of a quiet street is a perennial budget favourite. It's a simple place – no lift, linoleum or parquet floors – but it's welcoming and at the time of research was receiving a much needed face-lift. Some rooms have little balconies and at least one room offers a fleeting glimpse of Sacré Cœur. Hall showers cost €2.

MIDRANGE

Hôtel Moulin (Map p298; ☎ 01 42 64 33 33; www.hotelmoulin.com; 3 rue Aristide Bruant, 18e; s €55-63, d €59-67, tw €67-70; 💻; Ⓜ Abbesses or Blanche) There are 27 good-sized, well-equipped rooms in a main building and a garden annexe at this quiet little hotel, owned by a welcoming Korean family.

Hôtel des Arts (Map p298; ☎ 01 46 06 30 52; www.arts-hotel-paris.com; 5 rue Tholozé, 18e; s €68, d & tw €82, tr €97; 💻; Ⓜ Abbesses or Blanche) The 'Arts Hotel' is a friendly and attractive 50-room place convenient to both place Pigalle and Montmartre, nestled near the Moulin de la Galette, one of Montmartre's old-style windmills.

Hôtel Regyn's Montmartre (Map p298; ☎ 01 42 54 45 21; www.paris-hotels-montmartre.com/hotel_regyns; 18 place des Abbesses, 18e; s €72-92, d & tw €84-104, tr €104-124; ⊠ 💻; Ⓜ Abbesses) This 22-room hotel should be one of your first choices if you want to stay in old Montmartre and not break the bank. It's just opposite the metro station, and some of the dinky rooms have views over Paris.

TOP END

Terrass Hotel (Map p298; ☎ 01 46 06 72 85; www.terrass-hotel.com; 12 rue Joseph de Maistre, 18e; s €208-280, d 248-320, ste €360; ⊠ ❄ 💻; Ⓜ Blanche) This sedate and stylish hotel at the southwestern corner of Montparnasse Cemetery has 100 spacious, impeccably designed rooms and suites. For the ultimate Parisian experience, junior suite 703 has stunning views of the Eiffel Tower from the Jacuzzi and 802 boasts its own private terrace.

EATING

Paris likes to think of itself as the culinary capital of France, and the city has a plethora of classically French cafés, bistros and brasseries. But modern-day Paris is a gastronomic melting-pot, and you'll find some of the city's best food at tiny restaurants serving traditional Vietnamese, Caribbean and North African cuisine.

Louvre & Les Halles

Tana (Map pp296-7; ☎ 01 42 33 53 64; 36 rue Tiquetonne, 2e; mains €9-20; ⏲ dinner; Ⓜ Étienne Marcel) In a street where each restaurant is more original than the next, Tana takes the tart. The mixed hors d'oeuvre for two and the *homok pla* (fish steamed in banana leaf, €10) are both excellent.

Joe Allen (Map pp296-7; ☎ 01 42 36 70 13; 30 rue Pierre Lescot, 1er; mains €13-16.50, lunch menu €13; ⏲ noon-1am; Ⓜ Étienne Marcel) An American-style favourite in Paris for some 35 years, Joe Allen is little bit of New York in Paris. Ribs (€16.50) are a speciality.

Le Petit Mâchon (Map pp296-7; ☎ 01 42 60 08 06; 158 rue St-Honoré, 1er; mains €14-22, lunch menu €16.50; ⏲ lunch & dinner Tue-Sun; Ⓜ Palais Royal-Musée du Louvre) An upbeat bistro with Lyon-inspired specialities. Try the *saucisson de Lyon* (Lyon sausage) studded with pistachios.

L'Épi d'Or (Map pp296-7; ☎ 01 42 36 38 12; 25 rue Jean-Jacques Rousseau, 1er; mains €16-22, 2-/3-course menu €18/22; ⏲ lunch & dinner Mon-Fri, dinner Sat; Ⓜ Louvre-Rivoli) This oh-so-Parisian bistro serves classic dishes such as *gigot d'agneau* (leg of lamb), lovingly cooked for seven hours.

Self-catering options include **Franprix Les Halles** (Map pp296-7; 35 rue Berger, 1er; ⏲ 8.30am-7.50pm Mon-Sat; Ⓜ Châtelet) and **Ed l'Épicier Marais** (Map pp296-7; 80 rue de Rivoli, 4e; Ⓜ Hôtel de Ville).

Marais & Bastille

The Marais is one of Paris' premier neighbourhoods for eating out. If you're looking for quick eats, check out the small noodle shops along rue Au Maire, 3e (Map pp296–7, Ⓜ Arts et Métiers) or the falafel and shwarma (kebabs) restaurants along rue des Rosiers, 4e (Map pp296–7; Ⓜ St-Paul).

Piccolo Teatro (Map pp296-7; ☎ 01 42 72 17 79; 6 rue des Écouffes, 4e; mains €9-12, lunch menu €9-15; ⏲ lunch & dinner; Ⓜ St-Paul) This intimate restaurant serves excellent vegetarian food in a stone-walled dining room packed with cosy little tables.

Le Trumilou (Map pp296-7; ☎ 01 42 77 63 98; 84 quai de l'Hôtel de Ville, 4e; mains €13-21, menus €17.50 & €19; Ⓜ Hôtel de Ville) This no-frills bistro is a Parisian institution; if you're looking for an authentic French menu at reasonable prices, you won't do better. The *confit de canard* (duck preserve) is excellent.

L'Ambassade d'Auvergne (Map pp296-7; ☎ 01 42 72 31 22; 22 rue du Grenier St-Lazare, 3e; mains €14-21, menu €27; ⏲ lunch & dinner; Ⓜ Rambuteau) The 100-year-old 'Auvergne Embassy', is the place to head to if you are really hungry. The sausages and hams of the Auvergne are famous throughout France, as are the lentils from Puy.

Le Petit Marché (Map pp296-7; ☎ 01 42 72 06 67; 9 rue Béarn, 3e; mains €14-19, lunch menu €14; ⏲ lunch & dinner; Ⓜ Chemin Vert) This great little bistro just up from the place des Vosges attracts a mixed crowd with its hearty cooking and friendly service.

404 (Map pp296-7; ☎ 01 42 74 57 81; 69 rue des Gravilliers, 3e; couscous & tajines €14-24, lunch menu €17; ⏲ lunch Mon-Fri, dinner daily, brunch to 4pm Sat & Sun; Ⓜ Arts et Métiers) As comfortable a Maghreb (North African) caravanserai as you'll find in Paris, the 404 has excellent couscous and *tajines* (Moroccan casseroles) and superb grills (€12 to €22).

Bofinger (Map pp296-7; ☎ 01 42 72 87 82; 5-7 rue de la Bastille, 4e; mains €16.50-37.50, 2-/3-course menu €23/30; ⏲ lunch & dinner Mon-Fri, dinner Sat & Sun; Ⓜ Bastille) Founded back in 1864, this place is reputedly the oldest brasserie in Paris. Bofinger specialises in Alsatian-inspired *choucroute* (sauerkraut with assorted meats; €17.50 to €19).

There are food shops, convenience stores and delicatessens along rue St-Antoine. There's also a branch of the famous delicatessen **Le Nôtre** (Map pp296-7; ☎ 01 53 01 91 91; 10 rue St-Antoine, 4e; ⏲ 9.30am-10pm Mon-Fri, 9am-10pm Sat & Sun; Ⓜ Bastille).

There are a few supermarkets in the area:

Franprix Hôtel de Ville (Map pp296-7; 87 rue de la Verrerie, 4e; ⏲ 9am-9pm Mon-Sat; Ⓜ Hôtel de Ville)
Franprix Marais (Map pp296-7; 135 rue St-Antoine, 4e; ⏲ 9am-8.30pm Mon-Sat; Ⓜ St-Paul)
Monoprix (Map pp296-7; 71 rue St-Antoine, 4e; ⏲ 9am-9pm Mon-Sat; Ⓜ St-Paul)

Latin Quarter & Jardin Des Plantes

Rue Mouffetard, 5e (Map pp296–7; Ⓜ Place Monge or Censier Daubenton), and the surrounding streets are filled with cheap restaurants, sandwich shops and crepe stalls, but whatever you do, avoid the area around rue de la Huchette (locally known as 'Bacteria Alley').

Le Foyer du Vietnam (Map pp296-7; ☎ 01 45 35 32 54; 80 rue Monge, 5e; mains €6-8.50, menu €8.50 & €12.50; lunch & dinner Mon-Sat; Ⓜ Place Monge) A favourite meeting spot for the capital's Vietnamese community, serving simple meals such as 'Saigon' or 'Hanoi' soup (noodles, soya beans and pork flavoured with lemon grass, coriander and chives).

Les Cinq Saveurs d'Ananda (Map pp296-7; ☎ 01 43 29 58 54; 72 rue du Cardinal Lemoine, 5e; mains €9.50-15; lunch & dinner Tue-Sun; Ⓜ Cardinal Lemoine) Set back from the place de la Contrescarpe, this semivegetarian restaurant is extremely popular with health-food lovers. All ingredients are farm-fresh and 100% organic.

Le Petit Pontoise (Map pp296-7; ☎ 01 43 29 25 20; 9 rue de Pontoise, 5e; mains €15-25; lunch & dinner; Ⓜ Maubert Mutualité) This busy brasserie features a blackboard menu full of seasonal delights, ranging from foie gras with figs (€12) to *poulet fermier avec pommes purée* (roasted farm chicken served with mashed potato; €13).

Perraudin (Map pp296-7; ☎ 01 46 33 15 75; 157 rue St-Jacques, 5e; mains €15-29, lunch menu €18; lunch & dinner Mon-Fri; Ⓜ Luxembourg) Perraudin has hardly changed since it first opened its doors in 1910, and makes the perfect place to try classics such as *bœuf bourguignon* (beef marinated and cooked in red wine with mushrooms, bacon, onions and carrots; €15), *gigot d'agneau* (€16) or *confit de canard* (€16).

Chez Allard (Map pp296-7; ☎ 01 43 26 48 23; 41 rue St-André des Arts, 5e; mains €19-35, 2-/3-course menu €24/32; lunch & dinner Mon-Sat; Ⓜ St-Michel) A charming bistro where the staff couldn't be kinder (a welcome surprise in Paris) and the food is superb. Try the *canard aux olives vertes* (duck with green olives).

Place Maubert, 5e, becomes a lively food market on Tuesday, Thursday and Saturday mornings. There are provisions shops nearby, including a great cheese shop called **Crémerie des Carmes** (Map pp296-7; ☎ 01 43 54 50 93; 47ter blvd St-Germain, 5e; 7.30am-1pm & 3.30-8pm Mon-Fri, to 1pm Sat; Ⓜ Maubert Mutualité).

Supermarkets include the following:

Champion (Map pp296-7; 34 rue Monge, 5e; 8.30am-9pm Mon-Sat; Ⓜ Cardinal Lemoine)

Ed l'Épicier (Map pp296-7; 37 rue Lacépède, 5e; 9am-1pm & 3-7.30pm Mon-Fri, 9am-7.30pm Sat; Ⓜ Place Monge)

Franprix (Map pp296-7; 82 rue Mouffetard, 5e; 8.30am-8.50pm Mon-Sat; Ⓜ Censier Daubenton or Place Monge)

Montparnasse

Since the 1920s the area around blvd du Montparnasse has been one of the city's premier avenues for enjoying that most Parisian of pastimes: sitting in a café and checking out the scenery on two legs.

La Coupole (Map pp292-3; ☎ 01 43 20 14 20; 102 blvd du Montparnasse, 14e; mains €12.50-32, lunch menu €15; 8am-1am Sun-Thu, to 1.30am Fri & Sat; Ⓜ Vavin) This 450-seat brasserie (est 1927) has hardly changed since the days of Sartre, Soutine, Man Ray and Josephine Baker. Book for lunch, but you'll have to queue for dinner.

Dix Vins (Map pp292-3; ☎ 01 43 20 91 77; 57 rue Falguière, 15e; lunch menu €20; lunch & dinner Mon-Fri; Ⓜ Pasteur) This tiny little restaurant is so popular you will probably have to wait at the bar even if you've booked. Excellent value, good service and stylish décor.

Montmartre & Pigalle

Montmartre's restaurants vary widely in quality, especially during the busy summer season, so choose carefully.

La Maison Rose (Map p298; ☎ 01 42 57 66 75; 2 rue de l'Abreuvoir, 18e; mains €14.50-16.50, menu €16.50; lunch & dinner to 11pm Mar-Oct, lunch Thu-Mon, dinner to 9pm Mon, Thu-Sat Nov-Feb; Ⓜ Lamarck Caulaincourt) The tiny 'Pink House', just north of place du Tertre, is the quintessential intimate Montmartre bistro.

AUTHOR'S CHOICE

Le Dôme (Map pp292-3; ☎ 01 43 35 25 81; 108 blvd du Montparnasse, 14e; mains €29-56; lunch & dinner; Ⓜ Vavin) An Art Deco extravaganza dating from the 1930s, and still a quintessential Parisian dining experience, Le Dôme is a monumental place for a meal, with the emphasis on the freshest seafood such as *huitres* (oysters) and *sole meunière* (sole sautéed in butter and garnished with lemon and parsley).

La Table d'Anvers (Map p298; ☎ 01 48 78 35 21; 2 place d'Anvers, 9e; mains €18, 2-/3-course lunch menu €15/23; lunch Tue-Fri, dinner Mon-Sat; M Anvers) This local favourite serves up great Mediterranean/Provençal dishes in addition to boasting some very decent fixed-price *menus*.

DRINKING

Paris is justly famous for its café culture, but these days there's a huge range of drinking establishments, especially in the Marais and along the Grands Boulevards. Happy hour sometimes lasts till around 9pm, but remember you'll always pay more in the central arrondissements than in the outskirts.

Louvre & Les Halles

Le Fumoir (Map pp296-7; ☎ 01 42 92 00 24; 6 rue de l'Amiral Coligny, 1er; 11am-2am; M Louvre-Rivoli) 'The Smoking Room' is a huge colonial-style bar-café just opposite the Louvre. It's a fine place to sip top-notch gin from quality glassware while nibbling on olives; during happy hour (6pm to 8pm) cocktails are all around half-price at €6.

Marais & Bastille

Andy Wahloo (Map pp296-7; ☎ 01 42 71 20 38; 69 rue des Gravilliers, 3e; noon-2am; M Arts et Métiers) Casablanca meets candy store in this trendy, multicoloured cocktail lounge. During happy hour (5pm to 8pm) a cocktail/beer is €5/3 – after that it doubles.

Café des Phares (Map pp296-7; ☎ 01 42 72 04 70; 7 place Bastille, 4e; 7am-3am Sun-Thu, to 4am Fri & Sat; M Bastille) If you like Camus with your coffee, head for the city's original philocafé. Debates take place at 11am Sundays.

Latin Quarter & Jardin des Plantes

Le Piano Vache (Map pp296-7; ☎ 01 46 33 75 03; 8 rue Laplace, 5e; noon-2am Mon-Fri, 9pm-2am Sat & Sun; M Maubert Mutualité) Just down the hill from the Panthéon, 'The Mean Piano' is a grungy underground venue with regular bands and DJs playing mainly rock, reggae and pop.

Le Vieux Chêne (Map pp296-7; ☎ 01 43 37 71 51; 69 rue Mouffetard, 5e; 4pm-2am Sun-Thu, to 5am Fri & Sat; M Place Monge) 'The Old Oak' is supposedly the oldest bar in Paris, and it's still popular with students and jazz fans. Happy hour lasts till 9pm, with half-pints for €2.50 (usually €3.50).

St-Germain, Odéon & Luxembourg

Café de Flore (Map pp296-7; ☎ 01 45 48 55 26; 172 blvd St-Germain, 6e; 7.30-1.30am; M St-Germain des Prés) The Flore is an Art Deco café where the red upholstered benches, mirrors and marble walls haven't changed since the days when Sartre, de Beauvoir, Camus and Picasso bent their elbows here.

Les Deux Magots (Map pp296-7; ☎ 01 45 48 55 25; 170 blvd St-Germain, 6e; 7-1am; M St-Germain des Prés) This erstwhile literary haunt is best known as the favoured hangout of Sartre, Hemingway, Picasso and André Breton. Everyone has to sit on the terrace at least once for a coffee (€4), beer (€5.50) or the famous hot chocolate served in porcelain jugs (€6).

Montmartre & Pigalle

La Fourmi (Map p298; ☎ 01 42 64 70 35; 74 rue des Martyr, 18e; 8am-2am Mon-Thu, 10am-4am Fri-Sun; M Pigalle) A perennial Pigalle favourite, the 'Ant' buzzes all day and night; it's hip without being overly pretentious.

ENTERTAINMENT

For the low-down on Paris after dark, pick up *Pariscope* (€0.40) or *Officiel des Spectacles* (€0.35), both published on Wednesday. **Zurban** (www.zurban.com, in French; €1), also published on Wednesday, offers a fresher look at entertainment in the capital.

For up-to-date listings on clubs and venues, pick up a copy of *LYLO* (*Les Yeux, Les Oreilles,* literally 'Eyes and Ears'), available at cafés, bars and clubs across town.

Radio FG (www.radiofg.com, in French; 98.2MHz FM) and **Radio Nova** (www.novaplanet.com, in French; 101.5MHz FM) are also good sources of information, or for club listings check out www.france-techno.fr (in French) or www.parissi.com (in French).

You can buy tickets for cultural events at many ticket outlets, including **Fnac** (☎ 08 92 68 36 22; www.fnac.com) and at most **Virgin Megastore branches** (www.virginmega.fr), for a small commission.

Cinemas

Expect to pay up to €9 for a first-run film. Students, and those under 18 and over 60 will usually receive discounts of about 25% except on Friday nights and weekends. On Wednesday (and sometimes Monday) cinemas give discounts of 20% to 30% to everyone.

Live Music

OPERA & CLASSICAL

Opéra National de Paris (ONP; ☎ 08 92 89 90 90; www.opera-de-paris.fr, in French) This opera splits its season between the Palais Garnier, its original home built in 1875, and the Opéra Bastille, which opened in 1989. Both opera houses also stage ballets and classical music concerts. The season runs from September to July.

Opéra Bastille (Map pp296-7; 2-6 place de la Bastille, 12e; Ⓜ Bastille) Tickets are available from the **box office** (Map pp296-7; 130 rue de Lyon, 12e; 10.30am-6.30pm Mon-Fri; Ⓜ Bastille) two weeks before the date of the performance, but are often sold out well in advance. Operas and ballets cost anywhere between €6 and €114; seats with limited visibility are often available from the box office for €6 to €9. Students, and people under 26 and over 65 can purchase any unsold tickets for just €20 15 minutes before curtains-up.

Palais Garnier (Map pp292-3; place de l'Opéra, 9e; box office 11am-6.30pm Mon-Sat; Ⓜ Opéra) Tickets and prices at the box office of the city's original opera house are similar to those at the Opéra Bastille.

ROCK, POP & INDIE

Le Bataclan (☎ 01 43 14 00 30; 50 blvd Voltaire, 11e; admission €15-50; box office 3-7pm Mon-Sat; Ⓜ Oberkampf or St-Ambroise) Built in 1864, this small concert hall is one of Paris' most eclectic venues, hosting rock, dance, comedy and techno acts from France and further afield.

La Cigale (Map p298; ☎ 01 49 25 89 99; 120 blvd de Rochechouart, 18e; admission €22-45; box office noon-7pm Mon-Fri; Ⓜ Anvers or Pigalle) An enormous old music hall seating up to 2000 people, with a regular programme of live gigs and international artists.

L'Élysée Montmartre (Map p298; ☎ 01 55 07 16 00; www.elyseemontmartre.com; 72 blvd de Rochechouart, 18e; admission €10-35; Ⓜ Anvers) This huge old music hall has an impressive domed roof and is one of the better venues to go to in Paris for one-off rock and indie concerts. There are club nights and big-name DJs at the weekend.

Café de la Danse (Map pp296-7; ☎ 01 47 00 57 59; www.cafédeladanse.com, in French; 5 Passage Louis-Philippe, 11e; admission €8-30; box office noon-6pm Mon-Fri; Ⓜ Bastille) Reliable venue for modern dance and rock, world-music and folk gigs.

JAZZ & BLUES

After WWII, Paris was Europe's most important jazz centre and it is again very much à la mode; the city's better clubs attract top international stars.

Le Caveau de la Huchette (Map pp296-7; ☎ 01 43 26 65 05; 5 rue de la Huchette, 5e; adult Sun-Thu €11, Fri & Sat €13, student €10; 9pm-2.30am Sun-Thu, to 4am Fri & Sat; Ⓜ St-Michel) Housed in a medieval *caveau* (cellar), this club is where virtually all the jazz greats have played since the end of WWII.

Nightclubs

Paris has a thriving club scene, and there are some mighty fine DJs based here, but the scene moves fast, so check local listings for the latest tips.

Le Batofar (Map pp292-3; ☎ 01 56 29 10 33; www.batofar.net, in French; admission free-€15; 9pm-midnight Mon & Tue, 9pm or 10pm-4am to 6am Wed-Sun; Ⓜ Quai de la Gare or Bibliothèque) A long-standing club housed inside an old tugboat opposite 11 quai François Mauriac, 13e. Expect electronica and techno for the most part, as well as some big-name DJs.

Triptyque (Map pp292-3; ☎ 01 40 28 05 55; www.letryptique.com; 142 rue Montmartre, 2e; admission €3-10; 9pm-2am Sun-Wed, to 5am Thu-Sat; Ⓜ Grand Boulevards) A vast club split over three underground rooms, with a play list spanning electro, hip-hop and funk, as well as jazz and live acts.

Rex Club (Map pp292-3; ☎ 01 42 36 10 96; 5 blvd Poissonnière, 2e; admission €8-13; 11.30pm-6am Wed-Sat; Ⓜ Bonne Nouvelle) The Rex reigns supreme in the house and techno scene and regularly hosts local and international DJs.

La Favela Chic (Map pp292-3; ☎ 01 40 21 38 14; www.favelachic.com, in French; 18 rue du Faubourg du Temple, 10e; admission €10; 7.30pm-2am Tue-Fri, 9.30pm-4am Sat; Ⓜ République) The ambience is more shantytown than chic in this restobar-cum-dancehall, which shimmies to the sound of samba and classic Brazilian pop.

SHOPPING

Le Bon Marché (Map pp292-3; ☎ 01 44 39 80 00; www.bonmarche.fr; 24 rue de Sèvres, 7e; 9.30am-7pm Mon-Wed & Fri, 10am-9pm Thu, 9.30am-8pm Sat; Ⓜ Sèvres Babylone) Opened by Gustave Eiffel as Paris' first department store in 1852.

Galeries Lafayette (Map pp292-3; ☎ 01 42 82 34 56; www.galerieslafayette.com; 40 blvd Haussmann, 9e; 9.30am-7.30pm Mon-Wed, Fri & Sat; to 9pm Thu;

(M) Auber or Chaussée d'Antin) Paris' premier department store features a wide selection of fashion and accessories.

Marché aux Puces de St-Ouen (Map pp292-3; www.les-puces.com; rue des Rosiers, av Michelet, rue Voltaire, rue Paul Bert & rue Jean-Henri Fabre, 18e; 9am or 10am-7pm Sat-Mon; (M) Porte de Clignancourt) Paris' *marchés aux puces* (flea markets) are an essential shopping stop – you might even find a few gems among all the tat and bric-a-brac. This is one of the largest, grouped into 10 separate areas (eg Marché Serpette and Marché Biron for antiques, Marché Malik for second-hand clothing).

GETTING THERE & AWAY

Air

AÉROPORT D'ORLY

The small **Orly airport** (ORY; ☎ 01 49 75 15 15, flight info 08 92 68 15 15; www.adp.fr) is about 18km south of the city.

AÉROPORT PARIS-BEAUVAIS

The international airport at **Beauvais** (BVA; ☎ 03 44 11 46 86; www.aeroportbeauvais.com), 80km north of Paris, is used by Ryanair for its European flights, including those between Paris and Dublin, Shannon and Glasgow.

AÉROPORT ROISSY CHARLES DE GAULLE

Roissy Charles de Gaulle (CDG; ☎ 01 48 62 22 80, 08 92 68 15 15; www.adp.fr) is Paris' main international airport, 30km northeast of Paris. Terminals (Aérogares) 1 and 25 are used by international and domestic carriers.

Bus

Eurolines links Paris with destinations in Western and central Europe, Scandinavia and Morocco. The main **Eurolines office** (Map pp296-7; ☎ 01 43 54 11 99; www.eurolines.fr; 55 rue St-Jacques, 5e; 9.30am-6.30pm Mon-Fri, 10am-1pm & 2-6pm Sat; (M) Cluny-La Sorbonne) is in the city centre.

Gare Routière Internationale de Paris-Galliéni (Map pp292-3; ☎ 08 92 89 90 91; 28 av du Général de Gaulle, 93541 Bagnolet; 8am-10pm; (M) Gallieni), the city's international bus terminal, is in the suburb of Bagnolet.

Train

Paris has six major train stations, each handling traffic to different parts of France and Europe.

Gare d'Austerlitz (Map pp292-3; blvd de l'Hôpital, 13e; (M) Gare d'Austerlitz) Spain and Portugal; Loire Valley and non-TGV trains to southwestern France (eg Bordeaux and Basque Country).

Gare de l'Est (Map pp292-3; blvd de Strasbourg, 10e; (M) Gare de l'Est) Luxembourg, Switzerland (Basel, Lucerne, Zurich), southern Germany (Frankfurt, Munich) and points further east; areas east of Paris (Champagne, Alsace and Lorraine).

Gare de Lyon (Map pp296-7; blvd Diderot, 12e; (M) Gare de Lyon) Parts of Switzerland (eg Bern, Geneva, Lausanne), Italy and points beyond; TGV Sud-Est trains to areas southeast of Paris, including Dijon, Lyon, Provence, the Côte d'Azur and the Alps.

Gare du Nord (Map p298; rue de Dunkerque, 10e; (M) Gare du Nord) The UK, Belgium, northern Germany, Scandinavia, Moscow; terminus of the high-speed Thalys trains to/from Amsterdam, Brussels, Cologne and Geneva and Eurostar to London; trains to northern France, including TGVs to Lille and Calais.

Gare Montparnasse (Map pp292-3; cnr av du Maine & blvd de Vaugirard, 15e; (M) Montparnasse Bienvenüe) Brittany and places en route from Paris (eg Chartres, Angers, Nantes); TGVs to Tours, Nantes, Bordeaux and southwestern France.

Gare St-Lazare (Map pp292-3; cnr rue St-Lazare & rue d'Amsterdam, 8e; (M) St-Lazare) Normandy (eg Dieppe, Le Havre, Cherbourg).

GETTING AROUND

To/from the Airports

AÉROPORT D'ORLY

Getting to and from Orly airport is easy; there are lots of buses shuttling between the airport and the city. Apart from RATP bus 183, all services call at both terminals. Tickets are sold on board. Children under 11 usually pay half-price.

Air France Bus 1 (☎ 08 92 35 08 20; www.cars-airfrance.com, in French) This *navette* (shuttle bus; single/return €8/12, 30 to 45 minutes, every 15 minutes from 6am to 11pm) runs to/from Gare Montparnasse (Map pp292–3) and Aérogare des Invalides (Map pp292–3) in the 7e. The bus also stops at Porte d'Orléans or Duroc metro stations on request.

Noctilien Bus 31 (☎ 08 92 68 77 14, 08 92 68 41 14 in English) Part of the RATP night service, Noctilien bus No 31 links Gare de Lyon, Place d'Italie and Gare d'Austerlitz in Paris with Orly-Sud (€5.60, one hour, every hour from 12.30am to 5.30pm).

Orlybus (☎ 08 92 68 77 14) This RATP bus (€5.80, 30 minutes, every 15 to 20 minutes from 6am to 11.30pm from Orly, 5.35am to 11pm to Orly) runs to/from Denfert Rochereau metro stations (Map pp292–3) in the 14e and makes several stops in the eastern 14e.

Orlyval (☎ 08 92 68 77 14) This RATP service links Orly with the city centre via a shuttle train and the RER (€9.05,

35 to 40 minutes, every four to 12 minutes from 6am to 11pm). A shuttle train runs between the airport and Antony RER station (eight minutes) on RER line B; to get to Antony from the city (26 minutes), take line B4 towards St-Rémy-lès-Chevreuse. Orlyval tickets are valid on the RER and for metro travel within the city.

RATP Bus 183 (☎ 08 92 68 77 14) This is a slow public bus that links Orly-Sud (only) with Porte de Choisy metro station (€1.40 or one metro/bus ticket, one hour, every 35 minutes from 5.35am to 8.35pm).

RER C (☎ 08 90 36 10 10) An Aéroports de Paris (ADP) shuttle bus links the airport with RER line C at Pont de Rungis-Aéroport d'Orly RER station (€5.65, 50 minutes every 15 to 30 minutes from 5.35am to 11.30pm from Orly, 5.06am to 12am to Orly). From the city, take a C2 train towards Pont de Rungis or Massy-Palaiseau. Tickets are valid for onward travel on the metro.

Private shuttle buses provide door-to-door service for about €26 for a single person (from €17 per person for two or more). Book in advance and allow for numerous pick-ups and drop-offs.

Allô Shuttle (☎ 01 34 29 00 80; www.alloshuttle.com)
Paris Airports Service (☎ 01 46 80 14 67; www.parisairportservice.com)
Shuttle Van PariShuttle (☎ 08 00 69 96 99; www.parishuttle.com)
World Shuttle (☎ 01 46 80 14 67; www.world-shuttles.com)

A taxi between central Paris and Orly will cost €40 to €45 and take 30 minutes.

AÉROPORT PARIS-BEAUVAIS

Express Bus (☎ 08 92 68 20 64) leaves Parking Pershing (Map pp292–3; Ⓜ Porte Maillot) at 1 blvd Pershing in the 17e, just west of Palais des Congrès de Paris, three hours before Ryanair departures and leaves the airport 20 to 30 minutes after each arrival, dropping off just south of Palais des Congrès on place de la Porte Maillot (€16.90, one to 1¼ hours, 8.05am to 10.40pm from Beauvais, 5.45am to 8.05pm to Beauvais). Tickets can be bought from the **Ryanair** (☎ 03 44 11 41 41) counter at the airport or from a kiosk in the car park.

A taxi between central Paris and Beauvais will cost €110 during the day and €150 at night and on Sundays.

AÉROPORT ROISSY CHARLES DE GAULLE

Roissy Charles de Gaulle has two train stations, CDG1 and CDG2. Both stations are served by RER line B3. A free shuttle bus links each of the terminals with the train stations.

There are a number of public-transport options running between Aéroport Roissy Charles de Gaulle and central Paris. Tickets for public buses can be purchased on board.

Air France bus 2 (☎ 08 92 35 08 20; www.cars-airfrance.com, in French) This service (single/return €12/18, 35 to 50 minutes, every 15 minutes from 5.45am to 11pm) links the airport with the Arc de Triomphe just outside 2 av Carnot in the 17e (Map pp292–3; Ⓜ Charles de Gaulle-Étoile) and the Palais des Congrès de Paris (Map pp292-3; Ⓜ Porte Maillot) at blvd Gouvion St-Cyr in the 17e.

Air France bus 4 (☎ 08 92 35 08 20; www.cars-airfrance.com, in French) This service (single/return €12/18, 45 to 55 minutes, every 30 minutes 7am to 9pm) links the airport with Gare de Lyon (Map pp296–7) and Gare Montparnasse (Map pp292–3).

Noctilien Bus 121 & 140 (☎ 08 92 68 77 14, 08 92 68 41 14, in English) Part of RATP's night service. Links Montparnasse, Châtelet and Gare du Nord with Roissy Charles de Gaulle (€7, every hour from 12.30am to 5.30pm) and bus No 140 links Gare du Nord and Gare de l'Est with the airport.

RATP Bus 350 (☎ 08 92 68 77 14) This bus (€4.20 or three metro/bus tickets, 1¼ hours, every 30 minutes from 5.45am to 7pm) links Aérogares 1 and 2 with Gare de l'Est (Map pp292–3) and Gare du Nord (Map p298).

RATP Bus 351 (☎ 08 92 68 77 14) Links place de la Nation (Map pp292–3; Ⓜ Nation) at av du Trône in the 11e, with Roissy Charles de Gaulle (€4.20 or three metro/bus tickets, 55 minutes, every 30 minutes from 7am to 9.30pm from Roissy Charles de Gaulle, 8.30am to 8.20pm to Roissy Charles de Gaulle).

RER B (☎ 08 90 36 10 10) RER line B3 links CDG1 and CDG2 with the city (€8, 30 minutes, every four to 15 minutes from 4.56am to 12.15am from Roissy Charles de Gaulle, 4.56am to 11.56pm to Roissy Charles de Gaulle). Take any RER line B train whose four-letter destination code begins with E (eg EIRE); a shuttle bus (every five to eight minutes) will ferry you to the appropriate terminal.

Roissybus (☎ 08 92 68 77 14) This direct bus links both terminals with rue Scribe (Ⓜ Opéra) in the 9e (€8.40, one hour, every 15 to 20 minutes from 5.45am to 11pm).

The four shuttle-van companies listed in the Orly section (p309) will take you from Roissy Charles de Gaulle to your hotel for €25 for one person or €17 per person for two or more people. Book these shuttles in advance.

Taxis to/from the city centre cost from €40 to €55, depending on the traffic and time of day.

Car & Motorcycle

You'll need nerves of steel to drive in Paris, but it can be done. The fastest way across the city by car is usually via the *boulevard périphérique*, the ring road that encircles the city.

In many parts of Paris you pay €1.50 to €2 an hour for street parking. Municipal parking garages usually charge €4 per hour and about €25 for 24 hours. Beware of Paris' notoriously ticket-happy traffic wardens.

Car rental companies:

Avis (☎ 08 02 05 05 05; www.avis.fr)
Budget (☎ 08 25 00 35 64; www.budget.fr, in French)
Europcar (☎ 08 25 35 83 58; www.europcar.fr, in French)
Hertz (☎ 08 25 86 18 61; www.hertz.fr)

Smaller agencies can offer much more attractive deals. Check the *Yellow Pages* under 'Location d'Automobiles: Tourisme et Utilitaires'.

Public Transport

Paris' public transit system is mostly operated by the **RATP** (Régie Autonome des Transports Parisians; ☎ 08 92 68 77 14; www.ratp.fr).

The same RATP tickets are valid on the metro, the RER, buses, the Montmartre funicular and Paris' three tram lines. They cost €1.40 per ticket or €10.70 (€5.35 for children aged four to 11) for a *carnet* (book of tickets) of 10. Tickets and transport maps are available at all metro stations.

BUS

Paris' bus system runs between 5.45am and 12.30am Monday to Saturday. Services are reduced on Sunday and public holidays (when buses run from 7am to 8.30pm) and from 8.30pm to 12.30am daily when a *service en soirée* (evening service) of 20 buses operates.

After the metro lines have closed, 35 Noctilien (www.noctilien.fr) night buses kick in, departing every hour from 12.30am to 5.30am. The buses serve the main train stations and cross the major arteries of the city. Many routes pass through place du Châtelet (1er) west of the Hôtel de Ville. Look for blue 'N' or 'Noctilien' signs at bus stops.

Short bus rides (ie rides in one or two bus zones) cost one metro/bus ticket (€1.40); longer rides require two tickets. Remember to cancel *(oblitérer)* it in the *composteur* next to the driver. A single ride on a Noctilien bus costs €2.80.

METRO & RER NETWORK

Paris' underground network consists of two interlinked systems: the **Métropolitain** (metro) with 14 lines and 372 stations; and the **RER** (Réseau Express Régional), a network of suburban train lines.

Each metro train is known by the name of its terminus. On lines that split into several branches (such as line 3, 7 and 13), the terminus is indicated on the cars with back-lit panels, and often on electronic signs on the station platforms. The last train on each line begins its run between 12.35am and 1.04am. The metro starts up again around 5.30am.

The RER is faster than the metro, but the stops are further apart. Some of Paris' attractions, particularly those on the Left Bank, can be reached more easily by the RER than by metro.

RER lines are known by an alphanumeric combination – the letter (A to E) refers to the line, the number to the spur it will follow to the suburbs.

Always keep your ticket until you exit from your station; you may be stopped by a *contrôleur* (ticket inspector) and fined (€25 to €45).

TOURIST PASSES

The Mobilis card and its coupon allows unlimited travel for one day in two to eight zones (€5.40 to €18.40), but you'd need to make at least six metro trips in a day (based on the *carnet* price) to break even on this pass.

Paris Visite passes offer discounted entry to certain museums and activities and discounts on transport fares. The version covering one to three zones costs €8.35/13.70/18.25/26.65 for one/two/three/five days.

TRAVEL PASSES

The cheapest way to use public transport in Paris is to get a Carte Orange, a combined metro, RER and bus pass. A weekly Carte Orange *(coupon hebdomadaire)* costs €15.70 for zones 1 and 2 and is valid from Monday to Sunday. To buy your first Carte Orange, take a passport-size photograph to any metro or RER ticket window.

Taxi

The *prise en charge* (flag-fall) in a Parisian taxi is €2. Within the city limits, it costs

€0.77 per kilometre for travel between 7am and 7pm Monday to Saturday, and €1.09 per kilometre from 7pm to 7am at night, all day Sunday and on public holidays. Each piece of baggage over 5kg costs €1 extra, as do pick-ups from stations.

Twenty-four-hour taxi companies include the following:

Abeille Radio Taxi (☎ 01 42 70 00 42)
Alpha Taxis (☎ 01 45 85 85 85)
ASTC (☎ 01 42 88 02 02)
Taxis Bleus (☎ 01 49 36 10 10)
Taxis-Radio Étoile (☎ 01 42 70 41 41)

AROUND PARIS

Bordered by five rivers – the Epte, Aisne, Eure, Yonne and Marne – the area around Paris is rather like a giant island, which explains why it's often referred to as the Île de France. In past centuries, this was where you'd find the country retreats of the French kings – most notably at the extravagant chateaux of Versailles and Fontainebleu. These days the royal castles have been joined by a kingdom of a rather more magic kind.

DISNEYLAND PARIS

In 1992, Mickey Mouse, Snow White and friends set up shop on reclaimed sugar-beet fields 32km east of Paris, at a cost of €4.6 billion. Though not quite as over-the-top as its American cousins, **Disneyland Paris** (☎ 08 25 30 60 30, UK 0 870 503 0305, USA 407-WDISNEY, 407-934 7639; www.disneylandparis.com; adult/child €42/34, Passe-Partout ticket adult/child €51/43, under 3 free) is still capable of packing in the crowds – some 12 million visitors strolled through its gates last year.

One-day admission fees to either the main Disneyland theme park or Walt Disney Studios Park include unlimited access to rides and activities. A Passe-Partout ticket allows entry to both parks for one day.

VERSAILLES

pop 85,300

The prosperous, leafy and ever-so bourgeois suburb of Versailles, 21km southwest of Paris, is the site of the grandest and most famous chateau in France. It served as the kingdom's political capital and royal court for more than a century, from 1682 to 1789 – the year revolutionary mobs massacred the palace guard and dragged Louis XVI and Marie-Antoinette back to Paris where they eventually had their heads lopped off.

Sights

The **Château de Versailles** (Versailles Palace; ☎ 01 30 83 77 88; www.chateauversailles.fr; admission to the palace adult/under 18yr €8/free, admission to Grand & Petit Trianon €5/free, joint ticket incl guided tour high/low season €20/15.50; 🕑 9am-6.30pm Tue-Sun Apr-Oct, to 5.30pm Tue-Sun Nov-Mar) was built in the mid-17th century during the reign of Louis XIV – the Roi Soleil (Sun King) – to project the absolute power of the French monarchy. Jointly designed by the architect Louis Le Vau (later replaced by Jules Hardouin-Mansart), the painter and interior designer Charles Le Brun, and the landscape artist André Le Nôtre, it's a fabulous monument to the wealth and ambition of the French aristocracy.

The 580m-long palace itself is split into several wings, each with its own astonishing array of grand halls, wood-panelled corridors and sumptuous bedchambers, including the **Grand Appartement du Roi** (King's Suite) and the **Galerie des Glaces** (Hall of Mirrors), a 75m-long ballroom with 17 huge mirrors on one side. Outside the main palace are the vast **landscaped gardens**, filled with canals, pools and neatly trimmed box hedges, and two outbuildings, the **Grand Trianon** and the **Petit Trianon**.

There are **guided tours** (1/1½/2hr adult €5/7/8, 10-17yr €4/5.50/7; 🕑 9am-4pm Tue-Sun Apr-Oct, to 3.45pm Tue-Sun Nov-Mar) around parts of the chateau not otherwise open to the public, although you'll need to book ahead in the high season.

Alternatively, the **Office de Tourisme de Versailles** (☎ 01 39 24 88 88; www.versailles-tourisme.com; 2bis av de Paris; 🕑 10am-6pm Mon, 9am-7pm Tue-Sun Apr-Sep, 9am-7pm Tue-Sat, to 6pm Sun Oct-Mar) offers tours (€8) of the chateau year-round.

Sleeping

Royal Hôtel (☎ 01 39 50 67 31; www.royalhotelversailles.com; 23 rue Royale; d €58-67, tr €85) In the delightful St-Louis neighbourhood, this hotel displays some character and a deep fondness for patterned wallpaper. The smallish rooms are on the verge of being pretty, with an odd mix of bulk furnishings and old-fashioned touches.

Hôtel d'Angleterre (☎ 01 39 51 43 50; www.hotel-angleterre-versailles.com; 2bis rue de Fontenay; s €55-66, d & tw €72-87) Less than 300m from the chateau entrance, and around the corner from the

Jeu de Paume, is this charming 18-room hotel. The clean, attractive rooms are very modern – aside from the red velvet curtains and squishy mattresses. Some rooms are considerably smaller and pokier than others.

À la Ferme (☎ 01 39 53 10 81; 3 rue du Maréchal Joffre; starters €6-10, mains €10.50-15, lunch/dinner menu €14.50/21.80; ⏰ lunch & dinner Wed-Sun) 'At the Farm' specialises in grilled meats and the cuisine of southwestern France. It's cheaper and more relaxed than a lot of restaurants in the area.

Crêperie St-Louis (☎ 01 39 53 40 12; 33 rue du Vieux Versailles; menus €10-15; ⏰ lunch & dinner) A warm little Breton place that's very popular at lunch, with sweet and savoury crepes (€3 to €8.50).

If you're entering outdoor **Marché Notre Dame** (place du Marché Notre Dame; ⏰ 7.30am-1.30pm Tue, Fri & Sun) from the tourist office, enter via passage Saladin (33 av de St-Cloud). There are also **food halls** (⏰ 7am-1pm & 3.30-7.30pm Tue-Sat, 7am-2pm Sun) surrounding the marketplace.

Getting There & Away

RER line C5 (€2.55) takes you from Paris' Left Bank RER stations to Versailles–Rive Gauche station, which is only 700m southeast of the chateau. The last train to Paris leaves shortly before midnight.

SNCF operates up to 70 trains a day from Paris' Gare St-Lazare (€3.40) to Versailles–Rive Droite, which is 1.2km from the chateau. The last train to Paris leaves just after midnight.

CHARTRES

pop 40,250

The magnificent 13th-century cathedral of Chartres, crowned by twin spires – one Gothic, the other Romanesque – is arguably the most famous and most beautiful in France, rivalled only by Notre Dame and Rouen in terms of scale and spectacle. Surrounded by farmland 88km southwest of Paris, the cathedral completely dominates the medieval town and the surrounding countryside, and makes a great day trip from Paris.

The **Office de Tourisme de Chartres** (☎ 02 37 18 26 26; www.chartres-tourisme.com; place de la Cathédrale; ⏰ 9am-7pm Mon-Sat, 9.30am-5.30pm Sun Apr-Sep, 10am-6pm Mon-Sat, to 1pm & 2.30-4.30pm Sun Oct-Mar) rents **audioguide tours** (per 1/2 people €5.50/8.50) of the medieval city (1½ hours).

Sights

The 130m-long cathedral **Cathédrale Notre Dame de Chartres** (Cathedral of Our Lady of Chartres; ☎ 02 37 21 22 07; www.cathedrale-chartres.com, in French; place de la Cathédrale; ⏰ 8.30am-6.45pm), is one of the crowning architectural achievements of Western civilisation. The original Romanesque cathedral was devastated in a fire in 1194, but remnants of it remain in the **Portail Royal** (Royal Portal) and the 103m-high **Clocher Vieux** (Old Bell Tower, also known as the South Tower). The rest of the cathedral predominantly dates from the 13th century, including many of the 172 glorious **stained-glass windows**, which are renowned for the depth and intensity of their blue tones.

A platform emerges some 70m up the 112m-high **Clocher Neuf** (New Bell Tower or North Tower; adult/concession €6.50/4.50, under 18 & 1st Sun of certain months free; ⏰ 9.30am-noon & 2-5.30pm Mon-Sat, 2pm-5.30pm Sun May-Aug, 9.30am-noon & 2-4.30pm Mon-Sat, 2-4.30pm Sun Sep-Apr), with superb views of the cathedral's three-tiered flying buttresses and 19th-century copper roof.

Eating

Le Grill Pélagie (☎ 02 37 36 07 49; 1 av Jehan de Beauce; mains €10-15, menu €11.50-18.50; ⏰ lunch & dinner Mon-Fri, dinner Sat) This is a popular place specialising in grills and Tex-Mex dishes such as quesadillas (€6.50) and fajitas (€14 to €16).

Café Serpente (☎ 02 37 21 68 81; 2 Cloître Notre Dame; dishes €13.50-15; ⏰ 10am-11pm) This atmospheric brasserie and *salon de thé* (tearoom) is conveniently located opposite the cathedral.

Le Tripot (☎ 02 37 36 60 11; 11 place Jean Moulin; mains €13.50-24, lunch menu €15; ⏰ lunch Tue-Sun, dinner Mon-Sat) This wonderful little place just down from the cathedral is one of the best bistros in Chartres.

There's a **covered market** (place Billard; ⏰ 7am-1pm Sat), just off rue des Changes south of the cathedral. It dates from the early 20th century; there are many food shops surrounding it.

Getting There & Away

Some 30 SNCF trains a day (20 on Sunday) link Paris' Gare Montparnasse (€12.40, 55 to 70 minutes) with Chartres, all of which pass through Versailles-Chantiers (€10.10, 45 to 60 minutes).

CHAMPAGNE

The rural countryside of Champagne is, of course, best-known for producing the world's bubbly supply. Although there are many pretenders to the crown, only wine produced in designated local areas (known as *appellations*), then aged, bottled and labelled according to strict regulations, can be labelled as true champagne. The town of Épernay, south of Reims, is home to many of the region's most famous vintages, and the top place for a spot of *dégustation* (tasting).

REIMS

pop 206,000

Along with Épernay, the neat, orderly town of Reims (pronounced something like 'rance') is one of the most important centres of champagne production. From 816 until 1825, French monarchs began their reigns with a coronation ceremony in Reims' famed cathedral, which remains the city's most impressive landmark. Like much of the rest of the city, the cathedral has been heavily restored since the devastating bombardments that laid waste to Reims during WW1.

Orientation & Information

The train station is about 1km northwest of the cathedral, across square Colbert from place Drouet d'Erlon, the city's major nightlife centre. Virtually every street in the city centre is one-way.

There's Internet access in the courtyard of a shopping arcade at **Clique et Croque Cybercafé** (27 rue de Vesle; per min €0.07; 🕑 10am-12.30am Mon-Sat, 2-9pm Sun). The **tourist office** (☎ 03 26 77 45 00; www.reims-tourisme.com; 2 rue Guillaume de Machault; 🕑 9am-7pm Mon-Sat, 10am-6pm Sun & holidays mid-Apr–mid-Oct, 9am-6pm Mon-Sat, 11am-4pm Sun & holidays mid-Oct–mid-Apr) sells Le Pass Citadine (€12), which includes a champagne house tour, an all-day bus ticket, entry to all four municipal museums and a box of *biscuits roses* (pink biscuits), traditionally nibbled with champagne. There's also a **branch post office** (2 rue Cérès).

Sights & Activities

The **Cathédrale Notre Dame** (🕑 approx 7.30am-7.30pm, closed Sun morning Mass), a Gothic edifice begun in 1211 and completed around a century later, was for centuries the venue for all French royal coronations – including that of Charles VII, who was crowned here on 17 July 1429, with Joan of Arc at his side.

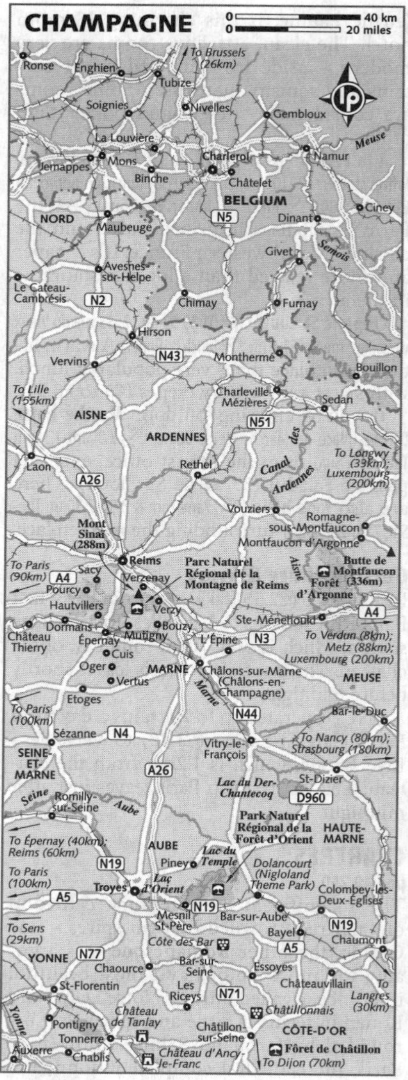

Following the extensive damage caused during WW1, the cathedral was restored with funds donated largely by John D Rockefeller; reconsecration took place in 1938, just in time for the next war. Today, the 138m-long cathedral is more interesting for its dramatic history than for its heavily restored architectural features. Notable sights include the western façade's 12-petalled **great rose window**, a 15th-century **astronomical clock**, and decorative windows designed by painter Marc Chagall.

CHAMPAGNE CELLARS

Some of the most celebrated names in Champagne production have their base in Reims, complete with *caves* (cellars) and tasting tours.

Taittinger (☎ 03 26 85 84 33; www.taittinger.com; 9 place St-Niçaise; tours adult/under 12yr €7/free) An excellent place to come for a clear, straightforward presentation on how champagne is actually made – no clap-trap about 'the champagne mystique' here!

Mumm (pronounced moom; ☎ 03 26 49 59 70; www.mumm.com; 34 rue du Champ de Mars; tours adult/under 16yr €7.50/free) Founded in 1827 and now the world's third-largest producer (eight million bottles a year).

Pommery (☎ 03 26 61 62 55; www.pommery.com; 5 place du Général Gouraud; tours adult/student & 12-17yr/under 12yr €8/6/free) Cellar tours take you 30m underground to Gallo-Roman quarries and 25 million bottles of bubbly.

Sleeping

Centre International de Séjour (CIS; ☎ 03 26 40 52 60; www.cis-reims.com; chaussée Bocquaine; 1-/2-/3-bed dm €20/13.50/12, with shower & toilet €32/18/14.50; 24hr;) The 85 brightly painted rooms are institutional and pretty drab, but this friendly hostel makes a decent budget base. To get there take bus B, K, M or N to the Comédie stop or bus H to the Pont de Gaulle stop.

Hôtel de la Cathédrale (☎ 03 26 47 28 46; hoteldelacathedrale@wanadoo.fr; 20 rue Libergier; d/q from €60/80) Charm, graciousness and some very shiny brass greet guests at this family-run two-star place, whose 17 tasteful rooms are smallish but pleasingly chintzy.

Grand Hôtel de l'Univers (☎ 03 26 88 68 08; www.hotel-univers-reims.com, in French; 41 blvd Foch; d from €78) This venerable three-star place has 42 large rooms, tastefully appointed, with high ceilings and bathrooms big enough to do jumping jacks in.

Eating & Drinking

Place Drouet d'Erlon, the focal point of Reims' nightlife, is lined with pizzerias, brasseries and sandwich places.

L'Apostrophe (☎ 03 26 79 19 89; 59 place Drouet d'Erlon; 2-course weekday menu €14, mains €13-21.50) This stylish café/brasserie specialises in highbrow chatter and mean *piscines* (enormous multiperson cocktails), along with excellent French and international cuisine.

Brasserie Le Boulingrin (☎ 03 26 40 96 22; 48 rue de Mars; menu €17.50-24; Mon-Sat) Offers a mini-trip back in time with original 1920s décor, including an old-time zinc bar. The culinary focus is on meat and fish.

Le Continental (☎ 03 26 47 01 47; 95 place Drouet d'Erlon; menu €22-55; meals noon-2.30pm & 7-11.30pm) Built in the early 20th century, this classy, marble-floored place serves up panoramic views and classic French dishes such as *magret de canard* (duck breast fillet). It opens all afternoon for drinks.

Self-caterers should try the **food market** (place du Boulingrin; to 1.30pm Wed) or **Monoprix supermarket** (21 rue de Chativesle; 9am-8pm Mon-Sat).

Getting There & Away

Direct services link Reims with Épernay (€5.50, 24 to 46 minutes, 23 daily weekdays, 14 daily weekends) and Paris' Gare de l'Est (€21.60, 1¾ hours, 10 to 15 daily). In town, tickets and information are available at the **Boutique SNCF** (9.30am-7pm Mon-Fri, to 6pm Sat) inside the Centre Bourse shopping centre. Journeys to Paris will take just 45 minutes once the long-awaited TGV Est Européen line starts running in June 2007.

ÉPERNAY

pop 26,000

Home to a number of the world's most famous champagne houses, well-to-do Épernay, 25km south of Reims, is the best place in Champagne for sampling a bit of the bubbly. Beneath the streets of the town, some 200 million of bottles of champagne are slowly being aged, just waiting around to be popped open for some fizz-fuelled celebration.

Orientation

Mansion-lined av de Champagne, where many of Épernay's champagne houses are based, stretches eastwards from the town's commercial heart around place des Arcades, rue Général Leclerc and rue St-Thibault.

Information

Cyberm@nia (11 place des Arcades; per hr €3; 11am-midnight Mon-Sat, 2-8pm Sun) Internet access.

Main post office (place Hugues Plomb)

Tourist office (☎ 03 26 53 33 00; www.ot-epernay.fr, in French; 7 av de Champagne; 🕑 9.30am-12.30pm & 1.30-7pm Mon-Sat, 11am-4pm Sun & holidays mid-Apr–mid-Oct, 9.30am-12.30pm & 1.30-5.30pm Mon-Sat mid-Oct–mid-Apr) Has details on cellar visits and walking routes in the area.

Champagne Houses

Dignified razzle-dazzle is the name of the game at Épernay's many champagne houses. Several *maisons* (houses) offer informative tours, followed by tasting and a visit to the factory-outlet champagne shop.

Moët & Chandon (☎ 03 26 51 20 20; www.moet.com; adult/12-17yr €8/4.70; 18 av de Champagne; 🕑 tours 9.30-11.15am & 2-4.15pm, closed Sat & Sun mid-Nov–Mar) Arguably the number-one name in the world of champagne production. A Methusalem of vintage 1995 Dom Perignon is a snip at €6000.

De Castellane (☎ 03 26 51 19 11; www.castellane.com, in French; 64 av de Champagne; adult/10-17yr €7/5; 🕑 tours 10.30-11.15am & 2.30-5.15pm mid-Mar–Dec, Sat & Sun Jan–mid-Mar, closed 3 weeks Jan) Tours take in the *maison*'s bubbly museum, dedicated to the *méthode champenoise*.

Mercier (☎ 03 26 51 22 22; www.champagnemercier.com; 68-70 av de Champagne; adult/12-17yr €6.50/3; 🕑 tours 9.30-11.30am & 2-4.30pm mid-Feb–mid-Dec, closed Tue & Wed mid-Feb–early-Mar & mid-Nov–mid-Dec) The most popular marque in France has the flashiest tour – highlights include a 160,000L champagne barrel and a lift that plummets 30m underground into the musty champagne cellars.

Sleeping

Hôtel St-Pierre (☎ 03 26 54 40 80; hotel.saintpierre@wanadoo.fr; 1 rue Jeanne d'Arc; d €36, with hand basin €24) In an early 20th-century mansion that has hardly changed in half a century, this one-star place has 15 simple rooms that retain the charm and atmosphere of yesteryear.

Hôtel Les Berceaux (☎ 03 26 55 28 84; www.lesberceaux.com; 13 rue des Berceaux; d €77-86) This three-star institution, founded in 1889, has 27 comfortable rooms, each different and all with a modern Champenoise ambience.

Le Clos Raymi (☎ 03 26 51 00 58; www.closraymi-hotel.com; 3 rue Joseph de Venoge; d from €130) Staying at this delightful three-star place is like being a personal guest of Monsieur Chandon of champagne fame, whose luxurious home this was over a century ago. The seven romantic rooms have giant beds, 3.7m-high ceilings, ornate mouldings and parquet floors.

Eating

La Cave à Champagne (☎ 03 26 55 50 70; 16 rue Gambetta; menu €15-36; 🕑 Thu-Tue) Well-regarded by locals for its Champenoise cuisine, including *potée à la Champenoise* (poultry and pork oven-baked with cabbage).

Places to pick up picnic supplies include the **covered market** (Halle St-Thibault; rue Gallice; 🕑 8am-noon Wed & Sat), and **Traiteur** (9 place Hugues Plomb; 🕑 8am-12.45pm & 3-7.30pm, closed Sun & Wed).

The Hôtel Les Berceaux has two in-house eateries: **Restaurant Patrick Michelon** (menu €30-64; 🕑 Wed-Sun), a gastronomic restaurant whose specialities include truffles (in season) and blackcurrant sorbet; and **Le Sept** (menu €16-22), a more popularly priced bistro with traditional French fare.

Getting There & Around

The **train station** (place Mendès-France) has direct services to Nancy (€25.10, two hours, five or six daily), Reims (€5.50, 24 to 46 minutes, 23 daily weekdays, 14 daily weekends) and Paris' Gare de l'Est (€18.60, 1¼ hours, eight to 13 daily).

TROYES

pop 123,000

Troyes has an old city graced with some of the finest Renaissance and medieval architecture in France. The streets are lined with half-timbered houses and gabled buildings, though few would be familiar to Chrétien de Troyes, who penned courtly romances here in the 12th century – the city was almost totally rebuilt after a 1524 fire.

Orientation & Information

The main commercial street is rue Émile Zola. Most of the city's sights and activities are in the Old City, centred on the 17th-century town hall and Église St-Jean.

The main **tourist office** (☎ 03 25 73 36 88; rue Mignard; 🕑 10am-7pm Jul–mid-Sep, 9am-12.30pm & 2-6.30pm Mon-Sat, 10am-noon & 2-5pm Sun & holidays Apr-Jun & mid-Sep–Oct) is in the city centre, and there's a second **annexe** (☎ 03 25 82 62 70; 16 blvd Carnot; 🕑 9am-12.30pm & 2-6.30pm Mon-Sat except holidays year-round, 10am-1pm Sun & holidays Nov-Mar) at the train station.

Sights

The best way to explore Troyes' old town is on foot. You'll find some of the oldest buildings along **rue Paillot de Montabert**, **rue**

Champeaux and **rue de Vauluisant**. Just off rue Champeaux (between No 30 and 32) is the narrow **ruelle des Chats** (Alley of the Cats), which feels like a time hole into the 16th century.

The **Cathédrale St-Pierre et St-Paul** (10am-7pm Jul & Aug, 10am-1pm & 2-6pm Mon-Sat, to 5pm Sun & holidays Sep-Jun, closed Mon Nov-Mar) is something of an architectural mishmash, incorporating elements from every period of Champenoise architecture. In 1429, Joan of Arc and Charles VII stopped here on their way to his coronation in Reims.

The **Musée d'Art Moderne** (03 25 76 26 80; place St-Pierre; adult/student under 25yr €5/free; 11am-6pm, closed Mon & hols) features works by Derain, Dufy, Matisse, Modigliani, Picasso, Soutine and local favourite Maurice Marinot, amassed by local entrepreneurs Pierre and Denise Lévy, who founded the Lacoste chain.

The **Musée St-Loup** (03 25 76 21 68; 1 rue Chrestien de Troyes; adult/student under 25yr €4/free; 10am-noon or 1pm & 2-6pm, closed Tue & holidays), has a varied collection of medieval sculpture, archaeology and natural history.

Also worth a look is the **Apothicairerie de l'Hôtel-Dieu-le-Comte** (03 25 80 98 97; quai des Comtes de Champagne), a wood-panelled pharmacy from the early 1700s.

Sleeping

Hôtel Le Trianon (03 25 73 18 52; 2 rue Pithou; d with hand basin/shower €25/34; reception 11am-8pm Mon, 6.30am-8pm Tue-Sat, 9am-1pm Sun) At this gay-friendly place the rainbow flag flies proudly from the balcony. The eight rooms, above a jaunty yellow bar, are spacious, if a little ordinary.

Hôtel Les Comtes de Champagne (03 25 73 11 70; www.comtesdechampagne.com; 56 rue de la Monnaie; d/q from €47/63, s/d with hand basin from €30/35, s with shower from €41) For centuries, the same massive wooden ceiling beams have kept this super-welcoming place from collapsing into a pile of toothpicks. A huge and very romantic double goes for €69.

Hôtel Arlequin (03 25 83 12 70; www.hotelarlequin.com; 50 rue de Turenne; d from €53.50, with shower €39.50; reception 8am-12.30pm & 2-10pm Mon-Sat, 8am-12.30pm & 6.30-10pm Sun & holidays) The 22 cheerful rooms at this charming, custard-yellow hostelry come with antique furnishings, high ceilings and commedia dell'arte playfulness.

Eating

Pizzeria Giuseppino (03 25 73 92 44; 26 rue Paillot de Montabert; pasta & pizzas €7-9.50; Tue-Sat) Serves crispy, ultra-thin pizza widely considered to be Troyes' best.

Le Jardin Gourmand (03 25 73 36 13; 31 rue Paillot de Montabert; menu €16.50; closed Mon lunch & Sun) Elegant without being overly formal this places boasts a decent wine list including 25 vintages available by the glass; there is a terrace in summer.

La Mignardise (03 25 73 15 30; 1 ruelle des Chats; menu €19-45; closed dinner Sun & Mon) An elegant restaurant whose traditional French cuisine is served under ancient wood beams, 19th-century mouldings and ultra-modern halogen lamps.

Valentino (03 25 73 14 14; 35 rue Paillot de Montabert; menu €22-46; noon-1.30pm & 7.30-9.30pm, closed lunch Sat, dinner Sun & Mon) A modern fusion restaurant, combining classic French ingredients and savoir-faire with East Asian flavours.

For self-catering try the **covered market** (8am-12.45pm & 3.30-7pm Mon-Thu, 7am-7pm Fri & Sat, 9am-12.30pm Sun) or the **Monoprix supermarket** (71 rue Émile Zola; 8.30am-8pm Mon-Sat).

Getting There & Away

The **bus station office** (03 25 71 28 42; 8.30am-12.30pm & 2-6.30pm Mon-Fri), run by Courriers de l'Aube, is in a corner of the train station building. Troyes is on the rather isolated line linking Basel (Bâle; Switzerland) and Mulhouse (Alsace) with Paris' Gare de l'Est (€21.10, 1½ hours, 12 to 14 daily).

ALSACE & LORRAINE

Perched on the border between France and Germany, the neighbouring regions of Alsace and Lorraine are where the worlds of Gallic and Germanic culture meet head-on, but despite its Teutonic overtones, this is still very much part of France.

STRASBOURG

pop 427,000

To most people, Strasbourg is best known as one of Europe's main seats of power. The European parliament, the Council of Europe and the European Court of Human Rights are all based here (when they're not busy in Brussels), and despite its rather bureaucratic image, you'll find Strasbourg a

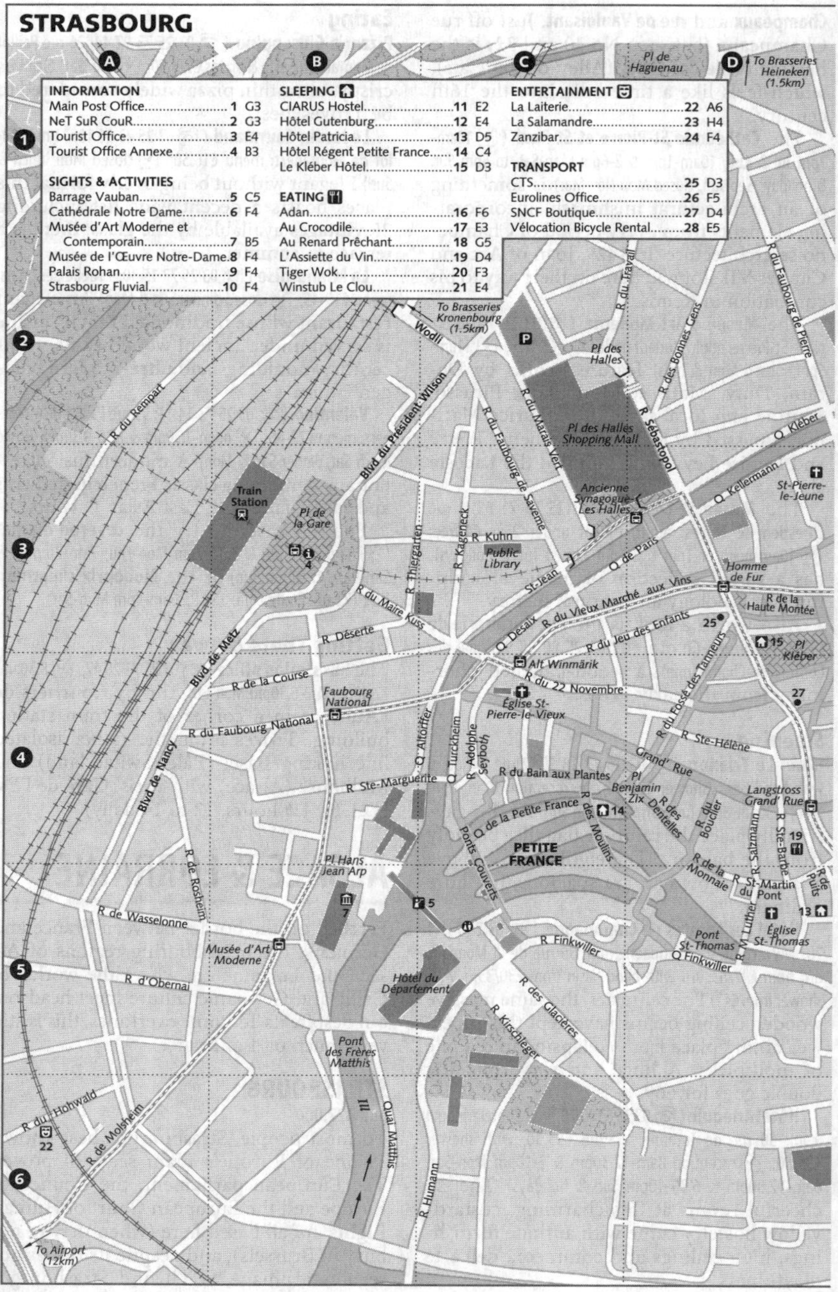
STRASBOURG
A
B
C
D
1
2
3
4
5
6
INFORMATION
Main Post Office........1 G3
NeT SuR CouR........2 G3
Tourist Office........3 E4
Tourist Office Annexe........4 B3
SIGHTS & ACTIVITIES
Barrage Vauban........5 C5
Cathédrale Notre Dame........6 F4
Musée d'Art Moderne et Contemporain........7 B5
Musée de l'Œuvre Notre-Dame........8 F4
Palais Rohan........9 F4
Strasbourg Fluvial........10 F4
SLEEPING
CIARUS Hostel........11 E2
Hôtel Gutenburg........12 E4
Hôtel Patricia........13 D5
Hôtel Régent Petite France........14 C4
Le Kléber Hôtel........15 D3
EATING
Adan........16 F6
Au Crocodile........17 E3
Au Renard Prêchant........18 G5
L'Assiette du Vin........19 D4
Tiger Wok........20 F3
Winstub Le Clou........21 E4
ENTERTAINMENT
La Laiterie........22 A6
La Salamandre........23 H4
Zanzibar........24 F4
TRANSPORT
CTS........25 D3
Eurolines Office........26 F5
SNCF Boutique........27 D4
Vélocation Bicycle Rental........28 E5
Pl de Haguenau
To Brasseries Heineken (1.5km)
To Brasseries Kronenbourg (1.5km)
Wodli
R du Travail
R des Bonnes Gens
R du Faubourg de Pierre
Pl des Halles
R du Marais Vert
R Sébastopol
Pl des Halles Shopping Mall
R du Faubourg de Saverne
Blvd du Président Wilson
R du Rempart
Q Kléber
Q Kellermann
St-Pierre-le-Jeune
Ancienne Synagogue-Les Halles
Train Station
Pl de la Gare
R Kuhn
R Kageneck
R Thiergarten
Public Library
Q de Paris
St-Jean
Homme de Fur
R de la Haute Montée
R du Maire Kuss
Q Desaix
R du Vieux Marché aux Vins
R du Jeu des Enfants
Pl Kléber
R Déserte
Alt Winmärik
R du 22 Novembre
Blvd de Metz
R de la Course
Faubourg National
Église St-Pierre-le-Vieux
R du Fossé des Tanneurs
R du Faubourg National
Q Altorffer
Q Turckheim
R Adolphe Seyboth
R Ste-Hélène
Grand' Rue
Blvd de Nancy
R Ste-Marguerite
R du Bain aux Plantes
Pl Benjamin Zix
R des Dentelles
R du Bouclier
Langstross Grand' Rue
Q de la Petite France
R des Moulins
R Salzmann
R Ste-Barbe
PETITE FRANCE
R de la Monnaie
R St-Martin
du Pont
R du Puits
Pl Hans Jean Arp
R de Rosheim
Ponts Couverts
Église St-Thomas
R de Wasselonne
Musée d'Art Moderne
R Finkwiller
Pont St-Thomas
Q Finkwiller
R M Luther
R d'Obernai
Hôtel du Département
R des Glacières
R Kirschleger
Pont des Frères Matthis
Ill
Quai Matthis
R du Hohwald
R de Molsheim
R Humann
To Airport (12km)

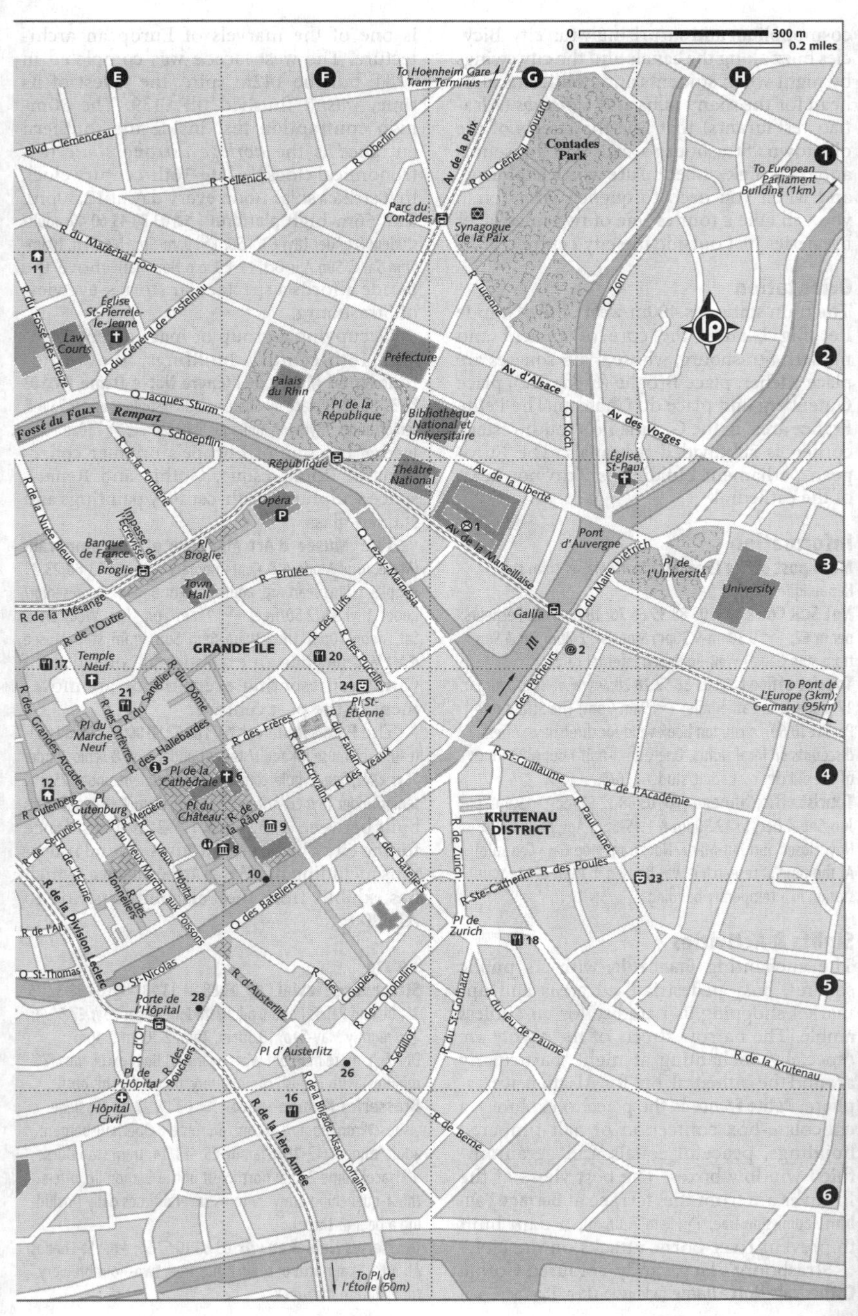
0 300 m
0 0.2 miles
E
F
G
H
1
2
3
4
5
6
To Hoenheim Gare Tram Terminus
To European Parliament Building (1km)
To Pont de l'Europe (3km); Germany (95km)
To Pl de l'Étoile (50m)
Blvd Clemenceau
R Sellénick
R Oberlin
Av de la Paix
R du Général Gourard
Contades Park
Parc du Contades
Synagogue de la Paix
R du Maréchal Foch
R Turenne
Q Zorn
Église St-Pierre-le-Jeune
Law Courts
R du Fossé des Treize
R du Général de Castelnau
Préfecture
Av d'Alsace
Av des Vosges
Palais du Rhin
Pl de la République
Q Jacques Sturm
Fossé du Faux Rempart
Q Schoepflin
Bibliothèque National et Universitaire
Q Koch
République
Théâtre National
Av de la Liberté
Église St-Paul
R de la Fonderie
R de la Nuée Bleue
Opéra
Impasse de l'Écrevisse
Banque de France
Broglie
Pl Broglie
Q Lezay-Marnésia
Av de la Marseillaise
Pont d'Auvergne
Q du Maire Dietrich
Pl de l'Université
University
Town Hall
R Brulée
R de la Mésange
R de l'Outre
Gallia
Ill
Temple Neuf
GRANDE ÎLE
R des Juifs
R des Pucelles
R du Dôme
R du Sanglier
Q des Pêcheurs
Pl St-Étienne
R des Grandes Arcades
Pl du Marché Neuf
R des Orfèvres
R des Hallebardes
R des Frères
R du Faisan
R des Écrivains
R des Veaux
R St-Guillaume
R de l'Académie
Pl de la Cathédrale
Pl Gutenberg
R Gutenberg
R Mercière
Pl du Château
R de la Râpe
R Paul Janet
KRUTENAU DISTRICT
R de Serruriers
R de l'Écurie
R du Vieux Marché aux Poissons
R du Vieux Hôpital
R des Tonneliers
R des Bateliers
R de Zurich
R Ste-Catherine
R des Poules
R de la Division Leclerc
Q des Bateliers
R de l'Ail
Pl de Zurich
Q St-Thomas
Q St-Nicolas
R des Couples
R des Orphelins
R du St-Gothard
R du Jeu de Paume
R d'Austerlitz
Porte de l'Hôpital
R d'Or
R des Bouchers
Pl d'Austerlitz
R Sédillot
R de la Krutenau
Pl de l'Hôpital
Hôpital Civil
R de la Brigade Alsace Lorraine
R de la 1ère Armée
R de Berne
1
2
3
6
8
9
10
11
12
16
17
18
20
21
23
24
26
28

FRANCE

cosmopolitan and surprisingly fun city. Bicycles buzz along the canals and the city swings by night when students and politicians alike head for the many pubs and *winstubs* (Alsatian restaurants) that line the streets of the old town. Strasbourg's excellent museums and rosy-pink cathedral are worth exploring, and when you need to quench your thirst, you can take a tour of one of two huge lager breweries just outside the city centre.

Orientation

The train station is 400m west of the Grande Île (Big Island), the core of ancient and modern Strasbourg, whose main squares are place Kléber, place Broglie (*broag*-lee), place Gutenberg and place du Château. The Petite France area, in the Grande Île's southwestern corner, is subdivided by canals. The European parliament building is 2km northeast of the cathedral.

Information

Main post office (5 av de la Marseillaise; tram stop République)

NeT SuR CouR (☎ 03 88 35 66 76; 18 quai des Pêcheurs; per hr €2; ⌚ 9.30am-9.30pm Mon-Fri, 2-8pm Sat & Sun; tram stop Gallia) Well-equipped Internet café.

Tourist office (☎ 03 88 52 28 28; www.ot-strasbourg.fr; 17 place de la Cathédrale; ⌚ 9am-7pm) The Strasbourg Pass (€10.60), a coupon book valid for three days, offers discounts on local sights. One-and-a-half-hour MP3 tours of the old city cost adult/student €6/3.

Tourist office annexe (☎ 03 88 32 51 49; ⌚ 9am-7pm Jun-Sep & Dec, to 12.30pm & 1.45-6pm Apr, May, Oct & Nov, closed Sun Jan-Mar & Nov; tram stop Gare Centrale) At the time of research it was housed in front of the train station in a temporary building.

Sights & Activities

The enchanting **Grande Île,** with its public squares, busy pedestrianised areas and upmarket shopping, is paradise for an aimless amble. The narrow streets of the **old city** are especially enchanting at night, particularly around the cathedral, but for Alsatian atmosphere, **Petite France** is the place to explore – a chocolate-box confection of half-timbered buildings, peaceful canals and geranium-filled window boxes. The best views of the Ill River are from the terrace at **Barrage Vauban** (admission free; ⌚ 9am-7.30pm), a dam built to prevent river-borne attacks on the city.

Strasbourg's lacy, candy-coloured Gothic **Cathédrale Notre Dame** (admission free; ⌚ 7am-7pm) is one of the marvels of European architecture. The west façade was completed in 1284, but the 142m spire, the tallest of its time, wasn't finished till 1439. The 30m-high contraption just inside the southern entrance is the *horloge astronomique* (astronomical clock), a late-16th-century clock that strikes solar noon every day at 12.30pm. The 66m-high **platform** (☎ 03 88 43 60 40; adult/student & under 18yr €3/1.50; ⌚ 9am-5pm Mon-Fri, 10am-5pm Sat & Sun Apr-Oct, to 4.30pm Nov-Mar) above the façade affords a spectacular stork's-eye view of Strasbourg.

Occupying a group of magnificent 14th- and 16th-century buildings, the world-renowned **Musée de l'Œuvre Notre-Dame** (☎ 03 88 32 88 17; 3 place du Château; adult/student under 25yr & senior/under 18yr with audioguide €4/2/free; ⌚ 10am-6pm Tue-Sun) has one of Europe's premier collections of Romanesque, Gothic and Renaissance sculptures, 15th-century paintings and stained glass.

The **Musée d'Art Moderne et Contemporain** (Museum of Modern & Contemporary Art; ☎ 03 88 23 31 31; place Hans Jean Arp; adult/student under 25yr & senior/under 18yr €5/2.50/free; ⌚ 11am-7pm Tue, Wed, Fri & Sat, noon-10pm Thu, 10am-6pm Sun; tram stop Musée d'Art Moderne) has an exceptional collection of works representing every major art movement of the past century.

The **Palais Rohan** (☎ 03 88 52 50 00; 2 place du Château; each museum adult/student under 25yr & senior/under 18yr €4/2/free, whole complex adult/student under 25yr & senior/under 18yr €6/3/free; ⌚ 10am-6pm Wed-Mon) was built between 1732 and 1742 as a residence for the city's bishops. It houses several museums including the **Musée Archéologique**, which has exhibits from the Palaeolithic period to AD 800.

Tours

Strasbourg Fluvial (☎ 03 88 84 13 13, ☎ 03 88 32 75 25; behind Palais Rohan; adult/student under 25yr €7.50/4; ⌚ nightly May-Sep, 10.30am, 1pm, 2.30pm & 4pm Dec-Feb, more frequent when warmer) Boat excursions (70 minutes) with English commentary are run by this outfit.

Brasseries Kronenbourg (☎ 03 88 27 41 59; siege.visites@kronenbourg-fr.com; 68 route d'Oberhausbergen; adult/student/12-18yr/family €5/4/3/14; tram stop Ducs d'Alsace) Some 2.5km northwest of the Grande Île, offers thirst-quenching brewery tours several times daily (including a beer or three).

Brasseries Heineken (☎ 03 88 19 57 55; 4 rue St-Charles) About 1.5km north of town it has free, two-hour brewery tours during the week.

Call or email either of the breweries to make a reservation, and remember to ask when tours are conducted in English.

Sleeping

It is *extremely* difficult to find last-minute accommodation from Monday to Thursday when the European parliament is in session (generally for one week each month) – contact the tourist office for dates. Many hotels apply high-season rates during European parliament sessions and in May, June, September, October and December.

CIARUS Hostel (☎ 03 88 15 27 88; www.ciarus.com; 7 rue Finkmatt; 8-/4-/2-bed dm incl breakfast €20/24/26.50; 💻) This welcoming, 101-room hostel is so stylish it even counts a number of European parliament members among its regular clients. By bus, take No 2, 4 or 10 to the Place de Pierre stop.

Hôtel Patricia (☎ 03 88 32 14 60; www.hotelpatricia.fr; 1a rue du Puits; d from €43, with hand basin €32, hall shower €2; 🕑 reception 8am-8pm Mon-Sat, 8am-2pm Sun; ⊠) The dark, rustic interior, simple furnishings and Vosges sandstone floors of this former convent make for an atmospheric night's sleep.

Le Kléber Hôtel (☎ 03 88 32 09 53; www.hotel-kleber.com; 29 place Kléber; d €52-75; ⊠) The 30 rooms are named after fruits, spices, pastries and other high-calorie treats and are decorated accordinglyMeringue is all white, of course, while Noisette is light brown and makes you feel like you're inside a giant hazelnut. Dieters might want to avoid Pavlova or Kougelopf.

Hôtel Gutenberg (☎ 03 88 32 17 15; www.hotel-gutenberg.com; 31 rue des Serruriers; d €65-98; ⊠ ❄) One of the city's best-value two-star hotels, just two blocks from the cathedral. The 42 tasteful rooms have antique touches and sparkling, all-tile bathrooms.

Hôtel Régent Petite France (☎ 03 88 76 43 43; www.regent-hotels.com; 5 rue des Moulins; d from €255, ste €350-465; ⊠ ❄) Guests of this luxurious four-star hotel enjoy romantic watery views, a sauna, and marble bathrooms worthy of a Roman emperor.

Eating & Drinking

Strasbourg is a gastronomer's dream. Just south of place Gutenberg, rue des Tonneliers and nearby streets are lined with midrange restaurants of all sorts. Inexpensive eateries can be found along rue des Frères, especially towards place St-Étienne.

Au Renard Prêchant (☎ 03 88 35 62 87; 33 place de Zurich; mains €9.50-16.50; 🕑 closed Sun & lunch Sat) A stuffed, bespectacled *renard* (fox) presides over this warm, woody and very Alsatian restaurant, housed in a 16th-century chapel. *Gibier* (game) bagged by Molsheim-area hunters is a winter speciality.

Adan (☎ 03 88 35 70 84; www.adan.fr, in French; 6 rue Sédillot; menu €12.50; 🕑 lunch Mon-Sat) An informal vegetarian-organic restaurant with tasty soups, salads and quiches.

Tiger Wok (☎ 03 88 36 44 87; 8 rue du Faisan; dinner €14, all-you-can-eat €23; 🕑 lunch & dinner) Locals tired of pigs' knuckles and fois gras flock to this wokkery, where you choose your ingredients (veggies, fish, meat) and then watch them being stir-fried by your own personal *wokeur*.

Winstub Le Clou (☎ 03 88 32 11 67; 3 rue du Chaudron; mains from €20; 🕑 closed Sun, holidays & lunch Wed) A typical *winstub* (literally 'wine room'), where diners sit together at long tables with paisley tablecloths. Specialities include *baeckeoffe* (meat stew) and *wädele braisé au pinot noir* (ham knuckles in wine).

L'Assiette du Vin (☎ 03 88 32 00 92; 5 rue de la Chaîne; lunch menu with wine €23; 🕑 dinner daily, lunch Tue-Fri) The décor changes with the seasons as does the French cuisine, inspired by what's available fresh in the marketplace. The award-winning wine list encompasses 250 vintages.

Au Crocodile (☎ 03 88 32 13 02; www.au-crocodile.com; 10 rue de l'Outre; 2-/3-course lunch menu €56/78, with wine €83/110; 🕑 Tue-Sat) This superb restaurant has the hushed solemnity of a true temple of French gastronomy. Specialities include *foie de canard cuit en croûte de sel* (duck liver cooked in a crust of salt; €55). Reservations are a good idea, especially on Friday and Saturday. Look out for the eponymous stuffed croc suspended above the foyer.

Entertainment

Strasbourg's nightlife is both busy and buzzy. Details on cultural events appear in the free monthly *Spectacles* (www.spectacles-publications.com, in French), available at the tourist office.

Zanzibar (☎ 03 88 36 66 18; 1 place St-Étienne; concerts usually €4-6; 🕑 4pm-4am, may be closed Aug) A laid-back bar in the heart of the Grande Île's student quarter, with regular gigs held in the Dantesque cellar.

La Laiterie (☎ 03 88 23 72 37; www.artefact.org, in French; 11-13 rue du Hohwald; 🕑 closed Jul, Aug &

Christmas-early Jan; tram stop Laiterie) One kilometre southwest of the station, this is Strasbourg's most vibrant venue for live music.

La Salamandre (☎ 03 88 25 79 42; www.lasalamandre-strasbourg.fr, in French; 3 rue Paul Janet; admission Fri & Sat €5, other nights €3-4; ⏰ 9pm-4am Wed-Sun Oct-Apr, 10pm-4am Wed-Sat May-Sep) Billed as a *bar-club-spectacles*, this disco has theme nights each Friday (salsa, 1980s etc).

Getting There & Away

Strasbourg's **airport** (SXB; ☎ 03 88 64 67 67; www.strasbourg.aeroport.fr) is 12km southwest of the city centre (towards Molsheim) near the village of Entzheim. The **Navette Aéroport**, run by CTS, links the Baggersee tram stop with the airport (€5 incl tram, 15 minutes, thrice hourly until at least 10.30pm).

Eurolines buses stop 2.5km south of the **Eurolines office** (☎ 03 90 22 14 60; 6D place d'Austerlitz; ⏰ 10am-12.30pm & 2-6.30pm Mon-Fri, 10am-12.30pm Sat; tram stop Lycée Couffignal) near Stade de la Meinau (the city's main football stadium), on rue du Maréchal Lefèbvre.

Train tickets are available at the **SNCF Boutique** (5 rue des France-Bourgeois; ⏰ 10am-7pm Mon-Fri, to 5pm Sat). The train station (at the time of research undergoing a major refit) is linked to Metz (€20.40, 1¼ to 1¾ hours, four to eight daily), Nancy (€19.70, 1¼ hours, 10 to 17 daily) and Paris' Gare de l'Est (€50.30, four to 4¾ hours, nine to 13 daily), as well as various local destinations.

Getting Around

Four tram lines form the centrepiece of Strasbourg's public transport network, run by **CTS** (☎ 03 88 77 70 70; 56 rue du Jeu des Enfants). The main hub is at place de l'Homme de Fer. Single bus/tram tickets, sold by bus drivers and the ticket machines, cost €1.20. The Tourpass (€3.20), valid for 24 hours, is sold at tourist offices and tram stops.

Strasbourg is one of Europe's most bike-friendly cities. The city's **Vélocation system** supplies bikes (per half-/whole day €4/7, Monday-to-Friday €10, plus €100 deposit) from various outlets:

City centre (☎ 03 88 24 05 61; 10 rue des Bouchers; ⏰ 9.30am-noon & 2-6.30pm or 7pm May-Sep, 10am-5pm Mon-Fri Oct-Apr; tram stop Porte de l'Hôpital)

Train station (☎ 03 88 23 56 75; 4 rue du Maire Kuss; ⏰ 9.30am-7pm Mon-Fri, 9.30am-noon & 2-7pm Sat, also open 9.30am-noon & 2-7pm Sun & holidays Jun-Aug; tram stop Alt Winmärik)

MASSIF DES VOSGES

The **Parc Naturel Régional des Ballons des Vosges** covers about 3000 sq km in the south of the Vosges range. In the warm months, the gentle, rounded mountains, deep forests, glacial lakes and rolling pastureland are a paradise for cyclists, with an astounding 10,000km of marked trails.

For information contact the **Maison du Parc** (☎ 03 89 77 90 34; www.parc-ballons-vosges.fr, in French; 1 cour de l'Abbaye; ⏰ 10am-noon & 2-6pm Tue-Sun Jun–mid-Sep, 2-6pm Mon-Fri mid-Sep–May, also open 10am-noon Mon-Fri during school holidays) in Munster.

NANCY

pop 331,000

Delightful Nancy has an air of refinement found nowhere else in Lorraine. With a magnificent central square, several fine museums and sparkling shop windows, the former capital of the dukes of Lorraine seems as opulent today as it did in the 16th to 18th centuries, when much of the city centre was built.

Orientation & Information

Pedestrians-only place Stanislas connects the medieval Vieille Ville (Old Town), centred on the Grande Rue, with the 16th-century Ville Neuve (New Town) to the south. The train station is 800m southwest of place Stanislas.

The **tourist office** (☎ 03 83 35 22 41; www.ot-nancy.fr; place Stanislas; ⏰ 9am-7pm Mon-Sat, 10am-5pm Sun & holidays Apr-Oct, 9am-6pm Mon-Sat, 10am-1pm Sun & holidays Nov-Mar) is inside the Hôtel de Ville.

Sights

Neoclassical **place Stanislas**, whose 250th anniversary was celebrated with great fanfare in 2005, is one of the most beautiful public spaces in Europe. The rococo fountains, gilded gateways and opulent buildings that surround the square form one of the finest ensembles of 18th-century architecture anywhere in France.

The highlight of a visit to Nancy is the brilliant **Musée de l'École de Nancy** (School of Nancy Museum; ☎ 03 83 40 14 86; 36-38 rue du Sergent Blandan; adult/student & senior €6/4; ⏰ 10.30am-6pm Wed-Sun), which brings together a heady collection of furnished rooms and curvaceous glass produced by the Art Nouveau (Jugendstil) movement.

The **Musée des Beaux-Arts** (Fine Arts Museum; ☎ 03 83 85 30 72; 3 place Stanislas; adult/student & senior

€6/4; ⌚ 10am-6pm Wed-Mon) includes a superb collection of Daum-made Art Nouveau glass and a rich selection of 14th- to 18th-century paintings.

The 16th-century Palais Ducal, former residence of the dukes of Lorraine, now houses the **Musée Historique Lorrain** (Lorraine Historical Museum; ☎ 03 83 32 18 74; 64 & 66 Grande Rue; adult/student €5/3.50, Wed students free; ⌚ 10am-12.30pm & 2-6pm Wed-Mon), dedicated to fine arts and to regional art and folklore.

Sleeping

Hôtel des Portes d'Or (☎ 03 83 35 42 34; www.hotel-lesportesdor.com; 21 rue Stanislas; d €50-60) This cosy two-star hostelry, superbly situated near place Stanislas, has 20 charming rooms with upholstered doors. It's often full so call ahead.

Hôtel de Guise (☎ 03 83 32 24 68; www.hoteldeguise.com; 18 rue de Guise; d €59-95; ⊠) A grand stone staircase leads to extra-wide hallways and 48 bright, spacious rooms at this old hotel, partly dating from the 17th century. The bathrooms are as modern as the 18th-century hardwood floors are charmingly creaky.

Hôtel des Prélats (☎ 03 83 30 20 20; www.hoteldesprelats.com; 56 place Monseigneur Ruch; d €92; ⊠ ❄; tram stop Cathédrale) In a grand building that's been a hotel since 1906, this two-star hotel, completely renovated in 2005, has 41 rooms with parquet floors, huge beds and antique furnishings.

Eating & Drinking

Rue des Maréchaux is lined with reasonably priced eateries. There are lots of cheapies around the covered market along rue St-Dizier and rue des Quarte Égises.

NANCY FANCIES

Bergamotes de Nancy are hard candies made with bergamot, a citrus fruit – used to flavour Earl Grey tea – that grows on the slopes of Mt Etna (Sicily). The only confectioner allowed to sell *bergamottes* (with two Ts) is **Lefèvre-Lemoine** (Au Duché de Lorraine; 47 rue Henri Poincaré; ⌚ 9.30am-7pm Mon-Sat, to 12.30pm Sun; tram stop Nancy Gare), founded in 1840. One of its old-fashioned sweets tins made a cameo appearance in the film *Amélie*.

Aux Délices du Palais (☎ 03 83 30 44 19; 69 Grande Rue; 1st course or dessert €4, mains €8; ⌚ Mon-Fri) Billing itself as *bistronomique*, this informal place serves everything from chicken *tajine* to beef fajitas to endive tartes.

Brasserie Excelsior (☎ 03 83 35 24 57; 50 rue Henri Poincaré; after-10pm menu €19/29; ⌚ 8am-12.30am Mon-Sat, 8am-11pm Sun, lunch noon-3pm & dinner 7pm-closing time; tram stop Nancy Gare) Built in 1910, this sparkling brasserie's Art Nouveau décor is unforgettable, and the food's pretty good, too.

Le Ch'timi (*shtee*-mee; ☎ 03 83 32 82 76; 17 place St-Epvre; ⌚ 9am-2am Mon-Sat, 9am-8pm Sun) *The* place to go for beer, with 150 brews, including 16 on tap.

There's a **covered market** (place Henri Mangin; ⌚ 7am-6pm Tue-Thu, to 6.30pm Fri & Sat; tram stop Point Central) and a **Monoprix supermarket** (⌚ 8.30am-8.30pm Mon-Sat).

Getting There & Away

The **train station** (place Thiers; tram stop Nancy Gare) is on the line from Paris' Gare de l'Est (€37.80, 2¾ to 3¼ hours, 13 to 17 daily) to Strasbourg (€19.70, 1¼ hours, 10 to 17 daily). Tickets can be purchased at the **SNCF office** (18 place St-Epvre; ⌚ 12.30-6pm Mon, 9.30am-1pm & 2-6pm Tue-Fri).

NORTHERN FRANCE

Tucked into the northeast corner of France, this is one of the most densely populated and industrial areas in the country and the site of many of the most notorious battlefields of WWI. The region is made up of three separate areas – Flanders (Flandre or Flandres), Artois and Picardy (Picardie).

LILLE

pop one million

In recent decades the once-grimy industrial city of Lille has transformed itself – with generous government help – into a glittering and self-confident cultural and commercial hub. Highlights for the visitor include an attractive old town with a strong Flemish accent, three renowned art museums, stylish shopping, some fine dining and a cutting-edge nightlife scene.

Orientation

Place du Général de Gaulle separates Lille's main shopping precinct (around pedestrianised rue Neuve) from the narrow streets of Vieux Lille (Old Lille) to the north. Lille's two train stations, old-fashioned Gare Lille-Flandres and ultramodern Gare Lille-Europe, are 400m apart on the eastern edge of the city centre.

Information

4 Players (9 rue Maertens; per 10min/1hr prepaid €0.50/3; 11am-10.30pm Mon-Fri, 10am-11.30pm Sat, 2-10pm Sun) Internet café.

Post office (8 place de la République) Changes money and has a Cyberposte.

Tourist office (☎ 08 91 56 20 04; www.lilletourism.com; place Rihour; 9.30am-6.30pm Mon-Sat, 10am-noon & 2-5pm Sun & holidays) A brochure (€2) outlines four walking tours. City maps cost €0.30.

Sights

Vieux Lille, which begins north of place du Général de Gaulle, is justly proud of its restored 17th- and 18th-century houses. The old brick residences along **rue de la Monnaie** now house chic shops and boutiques. Other intriguing buildings include the ornate 17th-century **Vieille Bourse** (Old Stock Exchange; place du Général de Gaulle) and the Art Deco home of *La Voix du Nord* (1932), the leading regional daily newspaper.

Lille's world-renowned **Palais des Beaux-Arts** (☎ 03 20 06 78 00; place de la République; adult/12-25yr/under 12yr €4.60/3/free; 2-6pm Mon, 10am-6pm Wed-Sun; Ⓜ République Beaux Arts) possesses a first-rate collection of 15th- to 20th-century paintings, including works by Rubens, Van Dyck and Manet.

If Paris can turn a disused train station into a world-class museum, why not take an Art Deco municipal swimming pool (built 1927–32) and transform it into a temple of the arts? **La Piscine Musée d'Art et d'Industrie** (☎ 03 20 69 23 60; 23 rue de l'Espérance, Roubaix; adult €3; 11am-6pm Tue-Thu, 11am-8pm Fri, 1-6pm Sat & Sun; Ⓜ Gare Jean Lebas), 11km northeast of central Lille, showcases fine arts and sculpture in a delightfully watery environment.

Sleeping

Auberge de Jeunesse (☎ 03 20 57 08 94; lille@fuaj.org; 12 rue Malpart; dm with breakfast €16; closed 24 Dec-late Jan; Ⓜ Mairie de Lille) This spartan former maternity hospital now houses 165 beds in three- to seven-bed dorms. Toilets and showers are down the hall.

Hôtel Le Globe (☎ 03 20 57 29 58; 1 blvd Vauban; d €38, with shower €34) The large rooms have French windows that look out on the Citadelle and (in most cases) chimneys that add a dollop of old-fashioned charm – just try and ignore the lumpy pillows.

Hôtel de France (☎ 03 20 57 14 78; hotel.de.france .lille@wanadoo.fr; 10 rue de Béthune; s/d from €45/50) You can't get much more central than this two-star place, whose 33 rooms are awkwardly laid out but functional. Some of the top-floor rooms have great views but there's no lift.

Hôtel Brueghel (☎ 03 20 06 06 69; www.hotel -brueghel.com; 5 parvis St-Maurice; s/d €74/80) The two-star rooms are a mix of modern and antique, though they don't have as much Flemish charm as the lobby. The wood-and-wrought-iron lift dates from the 1920s.

Grand Hôtel Bellevue (☎ 03 20 57 45 64; www .grandhotelbellevue.com; 5 rue Jean Roisin; d from €125) This three-star Best Western was grandly built at the turn of the century. A creaky *belle époque* lift trundles guests to the 60 spacious rooms, which have high ceilings and antique-style French furnishings.

Eating

Vieux Lille has a varied selection of restaurants, many of them serving Flemish specialities such as *carbonnade* (braised beef stewed with beer and brown sugar).

La Source (☎ 03 20 57 53 07; 13 rue du Plat; 2-course menu €8-13; lunch Mon-Sat, dinner Fri) An organic food shop founded way back in 1979 and now a Lille institution, great for vegetarian, fowl and fish *plats du jour*.

La Voûte (☎ 03 20 42 12 16; 4 rue des Débris St-Étienne; menu €10.50-18.50; closed Sun & Mon) Regional dishes such as *carbonnade* (€13) and *lapin à la flamande* (rabbit in a white-wine and prune sauce, €13), are served in this bistro-cum-*estaminet* (tavern).

Le Palais (☎ 03 20 74 53 47; 4 rue du Palais de Justice; mains €11-15; closed Sun & dinner Mon) Serves solid French-Flemish cuisine at fair prices, including *potjevlesch* (a gelled pâté made with pork, rabbit, fowl and veal).

À l'Huîtrière (☎ 03 20 55 43 41; www.huitriere.fr; 3 rue des Chats Bossus; lunch menu €44, menu dégustation €110; noon-2pm & 7-9.30pm, closed dinner Sun & about 21 Jul-22 Aug) On the 'Street of the Hunchback Cats', this venerable seafood restaurant is packed with Art Deco atmosphere, and has held a Michelin star since 1930. Book ahead on Friday, Saturday and holidays.

Lille's **covered food market** (place Nouvelle Aventure; 8am-2pm Tue-Thu, to 8pm Fri & Sat, to 3pm Sun

& holidays; Ⓜ Gambetta) is about 1.2km southwest of the centre in the Wazemmes district. Right outside, the city's largest **outdoor market** (⏰ 7am-1.30pm or 2pm Tue, Thu & Sun) is at its liveliest on Sunday. The largest supermarket is **Carrefour** (Euralille shopping centre; ⏰ 9am-10pm Mon-Sat).

Drinking

Chocolaterie Vandyck (☎ 03 28 82 07 72; 4 rue des Bouchers; ⏰ 2-7pm Tue & Wed, 10am-7pm Thu-Sat, 3-7.30pm Sun) Hot chocolate (€4.50 to €7.50) and chocolate pralines are the highlights at this delightful *salon de chocolat* (chocolate room).

Café Citoyen (Citizen Café; ☎ 03 20 13 15 73; http://cafecitoyen.org, in French; 7 place du Vieux Marché aux Chevaux; plat du jour €8.30; ⏰ noon-midnight Mon-Fri, 2-7pm Sat) This volunteer-run ethical café is relaxed and very friendly – Internet access is free if you order an organic beer or a cup of fair-trade coffee.

L'Illustration Café (☎ 03 20 12 00 90; 18 rue Royale; ⏰ 2pm-2am Sun-Thu, to 3am Fri & Sat) This mellow, smoky bar attracts artists and intellectuals in the mood to exchange weighty ideas or just shoot the breeze.

Café Le Relax (☎ 03 20 54 67 34; 48 place de la Nouvelle Aventure; ⏰ 10.30am-at least midnight Tue-Sun; Ⓜ Gambetta) A genuine, unadulterated *café de quartier* (neighbourhood café) where locals pop by for a cup of espresso or a cold Pelforth blonde, and to run into friends, especially after exploring nearby Wazemmes market.

Getting There & Away

Eurolines (☎ 03 20 78 18 88; 23 parvis St-Maurice; ⏰ 9.30am-6pm Mon-Fri, 1-6pm Sat, longer hr Jul-Aug) serves Brussels (€14, 1½ to two hours), Amsterdam (€41, six hours) and London (€34, six hours). Buses depart from blvd de Leeds, to the left as you arrive at Gare Lille-Europe from av Le Corbusier.

Lille's two train stations are one stop apart on metro line 2. Gare Lille-Flandres is used by regional services and TGVs to Paris' Gare du Nord (€35.40, at peak hours €48.40, 64 minutes, 23 daily Monday to Friday, 15 daily Saturday and Sunday). Gare Lille-Europe handles everything else, including Eurostars to London (1¾ hours), TGVs/Eurostars to Brussels (weekday/weekend €24/15.50, 40 minutes, 11 to 13 daily) and TGVs to Nice (€110.30 or €130.40, 7¼ hours, two direct daily).

Getting Around

Lille's two speedy metro lines, two tramways and bus lines – several of which cross into Belgium – are run by **Transpole** (☎ 08 20 42 40 40), which has an **information window** (⏰ closed Sunday) in the Gare Lille-Flandres metro station.

CALAIS

pop 75,000

You have to feel sorry for poor old Calais – it's one of the most visited towns in France, thanks to the daily mass of cross-Channel ferry traffic, but almost no-one stops for longer than it takes to exit the ferry terminal and hightail it out of town. You can't really blame them – apart from some pleasant restaurants and Rodin's *The Burghers of Calais*, there's not much to keep even the most enthusiastic visitor entertained for more than a few hours.

Orientation & Information

The train station is located 650m south of the main square, place d'Armes, and 700m north of Calais' commercial district, which is centred around blvd Léon Gambetta and place du Théâtre. On foot, the car ferry terminal is 1.5km northeast of place d'Armes. The Channel Tunnel's vehicle loading area is approximately 6km southwest of the town centre.

The **tourist office** (☎ 03 21 96 62 40; www.calais-cotedopale.com; 12 blvd Georges Clemenceau; ⏰ 10am-1pm & 2-6.30pm Mon-Sat, also open 10am-1pm Sun Jul & Aug) provides all the usual information.

Sights

Calais' Flemish Renaissance-style **town hall** (1911–25) houses the town's main sight – Rodin's famous sculpture *Les Bourgeois de Calais* (1895), honouring six local citizens who, in 1347, held off the besieging English forces for more than eight months. When he eventually conquered the city, Edward III was so impressed by their efforts (and the entreaties of his consort Philippa) he spared both the Calaisiens and their six leaders.

Original WWII artefacts fill the **Musée de la Guerre** (☎ 03 21 34 21 57; adult/student/family of 5 incl audioguide €6/5/14; ⏰ 10am-6pm May-Sep, 11am-5pm Wed-Mon Feb-Apr, noon-5pm Wed-Mon Oct & Nov), housed in a concrete bunker that used to be German naval headquarters.

Sleeping

Auberge de Jeunesse (☎ 03 21 34 70 20; www.auberge-jeunesse-calais.com; av Maréchal de Lattre de Tassigny; dm €16.50, s €21; 🕑 24hr) Modern, well equipped and just 200m from the beach, this 87-bed hostel is served by bus 3 or 9.

Hôtel La Sole Meunière (☎ 03 21 96 86 66; 53 rue de la Mer; s/d/q €47/54/80) A family-run two-star place named after the ground-floor restaurant, which – you guessed it – specialises in butter-sautéed sole. The best rooms have views of the port.

Hôtel Richelieu (☎ 03 21 34 61 60; www.hotelrichelieu-calais.com, in French; 17 rue Richelieu; d/q €55/110) Fifteen cheery rooms, each one outfitted with antique furniture redeemed by the owner from local markets.

Eating

Rue Royal and place d'Armes are lined with touristy restaurants.

Au Cadre Vert (☎ 03 21 34 69 44; 3 rue André Gerschell; mains €8-12; 🕑 closed Sun, lunch Sat & lunch Wed) A family-run French restaurant known for its generous portions and reasonable prices. Specialities include *magret de canard* in raspberry sauce and *côte de bœuf sauce peurotte* (beef ribs in mushroom sauce).

Aux Mouettes (☎ 03 21 34 67 59; 10 rue Jean Pierre Avron; menu €16-32; 🕑 closed Mon & dinner Sun) Fisherfolk sell their daily catch across the street at the quay, so this restaurant unsurprisingly specialises in the very freshest seafood.

For self-catering there is a **food market** (place d'Armes; 🕑 Wed & Sat morning) and a **Match supermarket** (place d'Armes; 🕑 9am-7.30pm Mon-Sat year-round, to noon Sun Jun-Aug). Outside the city centre are several monumental *hypermarchés* (large supermarkets) catering for cross-Channel shoppers, including **Cité Europe** (☎ 03 21 46 47 48; www.cite-europe.com; boulevard du Kent; 🕑 10am-8pm Mon-Thu, to 9pm Fri, 9am-8pm Sat).

Getting There & Around

BOAT

Every day, 32 to 40 car ferries from Dover dock at Calais' busy car ferry terminal, about 1.5km northeast of place d'Armes.

P&O Ferries Car ferry terminal (☎ 03 21 46 10 10; 🕑 6am-10pm); Calais town centre (41 place d'Armes)
SeaFrance Car ferry terminal (☎ 03 21 46 80 05; 🕑 5.45am-10.45pm); Calais town centre (☎ 03 21 19 42 42; 2 place d'Armes)

Buses (€1.50 or £1, hourly from about 10am to 7pm or 7.30pm) link both Gare Calais-Ville and place d'Armes with the car ferry terminal.

Hoverspeed, the company that pioneered the use of cross-Channel hovercraft, ceased operations in late 2005.

BUS

Cariane Littoral (☎ 03 21 34 74 40; 10 rue d'Amsterdam) operates express BCD services from Calais to Boulogne (€6.90, 40 minutes, four daily Monday to Friday, twice Saturday) and Dunkirk (€7.40, 45 minutes, 12 daily Monday to Friday, thrice Saturday).

CAR & MOTORCYCLE

To reach the Channel Tunnel's vehicle loading area at Coquelles, follow the road signs on the A16 to the Tunnel Sous La Manche (Tunnel under the Channel) at exit 13.

TRAIN

Calais has two train stations: Gare Calais-Ville in the city centre; and Gare Calais-Fréthun, a TGV station 10km southwest of town near the Channel Tunnel entrance. They are linked by the free Navette TER, a bus service operated by Cariane Littoral.

Gare Calais-Ville is linked to Boulogne (€6.90, 28 to 48 minutes, 17 daily Monday to Saturday, nine on Sunday), Dunkirk (€7.40, 50 minutes, six daily on weekdays, three or four daily on weekends) and Lille-Flandres (€14.70, 1¼ hours, 19 daily on weekdays, 10 daily on weekends).

Calais-Fréthun is served by TGVs to Paris' Gare du Nord (€37.20 or €50.60, 1½ hours, six daily Monday to Saturday, thrice Sunday) as well as the Eurostar to London.

DUNKIRK

pop 209,000

Dunkirk (Dunkerque), made famous and flattened almost simultaneously during the Allied evacuation of 1940, was rebuilt in a utilitarian and pretty uninspiring fashion after the war. Charming it may not be, but the port has an interesting maritime museum and a pleasant beach resort, perfect for a leisurely stroll on a summer's day.

Orientation & Information

The train station is 600m southwest of Dunkirk's main square, place Jean Bart. The beach and esplanade are 2km northeast of the centre in Malo-les-Bains.

Dunkirk's **tourist office** (☎ 03 28 66 79 21; www.lesdunesdeflandre.fr; rue de l'Amiral Ronarc'h; 🕑 9am-12.30pm & 1.30-6.30pm Mon-Sat, 10am-noon & 2-4pm Sun & holidays, no midday closure Jul & Aug) is inside a 58m-high **belfry** (adult €3).

Sights

The **Musée Portuaire** (Harbour Museum; ☎ 03 28 63 33 39; www.museeportuaire.com; 9 quai de la Citadelle; adult/student €4/3; 🕑 10am-12.45pm & 1.30-6pm Wed-Mon, no midday closure Jul & Aug) will delight ship-model lovers of all ages. Forty-five-minute **guided tours** (€6/5, incl museum €8/6.50) take visitors aboard several historic water-craft, including the *Duchesse Anne*, built for the German merchant marine in 1901.

The faded seaside resort of **Malo-les-Bains** is 2km northeast of Dunkirk's city centre. Its promenade-lined beach, **Plage des Alliés**, is named in honour of the Allied troops evacuated from here in 1940. The **British Memorial** (route de Furnes), honouring more than 4500 British and Commonwealth soldiers missing in action from 1940, is 1.5km southeast of the tourist office.

Getting There & Away

For links to Calais, see opposite. Most trains to Lille stop at Lille-Flandres (€12.20, 35 to 70 minutes, 15 to 30 daily).

Ferries run by **Norfolk Line** (☎ in the UK 0870-870 1020, in France 03 28 28 95 50; www.norfolkline.com) link the car ferry port, 20km west of the town centre, with Dover.

BATTLE OF THE SOMME MEMORIALS

The Battle of the Somme, a WWI Allied offensive waged northeast of Amiens, was designed to relieve pressure on the beleaguered French troops at Verdun. On 1 July 1916, British, Commonwealth and French troops went 'over the top' in a massive assault along a 34km front. But German positions proved virtually unbreachable, and on the first day alone, 21,392 Allied troops were killed and another 35,492 were wounded.

By the time the offensive was called off in mid-November, some 1.2 million lives had been lost on both sides. The British had advanced 12km, the French 8km. The Battle of the Somme has become a metaphor for the meaningless slaughter of war and its killing fields have become a site of pilgrimage.

NORMANDY

The land of Camembert and Calvados (an apple-flavoured apéritif), Normandy is a largely rural region where cows far outnumber their two-legged neighbours. Dotted with lush fields and winding hedgerows, Normandy is where you'll find the historic beaches of D-Day, the soaring spires of the Mont St-Michel and the stunning Bayeux Tapestry – the world's largest comic strip.

ROUEN

pop 108,750

With its elegant spires and soaring Gothic cathedral – one of the most stunning in northern France – the ancient city of Rouen is one of Normandy's highlights. Badly damaged during WWII, the city has since been lavishly restored, and the medieval quarter is filled with half-timbered houses and punch-drunk, polished-up buildings. The young French heroine Joan of Arc (Jeanne d'Arc) was tried for heresy and burned at the stake in the central square in 1431. Rouen makes an ideal base for exploring northern Normandy and Monet's home in Giverny.

Orientation

The main train station (Gare Rouen-Rive Droite) is at the northern end of rue Jeanne d'Arc, the main thoroughfare running south to the Seine. The old city is centred around rue du Gros Horloge between the place du Vieux Marché and the cathedral.

Information

Cybernet (☎ 02 35 07 73 02; 47 place du Vieux-Marché; per hr €4; 🕑 10am-10pm) Internet café.

Main post office (45 rue Jeanne d'Arc) Has a Cyberposte terminal.

Tourist office (☎ 02 32 08 32 40; www.mairie-rouen.fr; 25 place de la Cathédrale; 🕑 9am-7pm Mon-Sat, 9.30am-12.30pm & 2-6pm Sun May-Sep, 9am-6pm Mon-Sat, 10am-1pm Sun Oct-Apr) Opposite the west façade of the cathedral.

Sights

The main street of the old city, rue du Gros Horloge, runs from the cathedral to **place du Vieux Marché**, where 19-year-old Joan of Arc was executed in 1431. An iron cross outside the futuristic **Église Jeanne d'Arc** (🕑 10am-12.15pm & 2-6pm, closed Fri & Sun morning) marks the site.

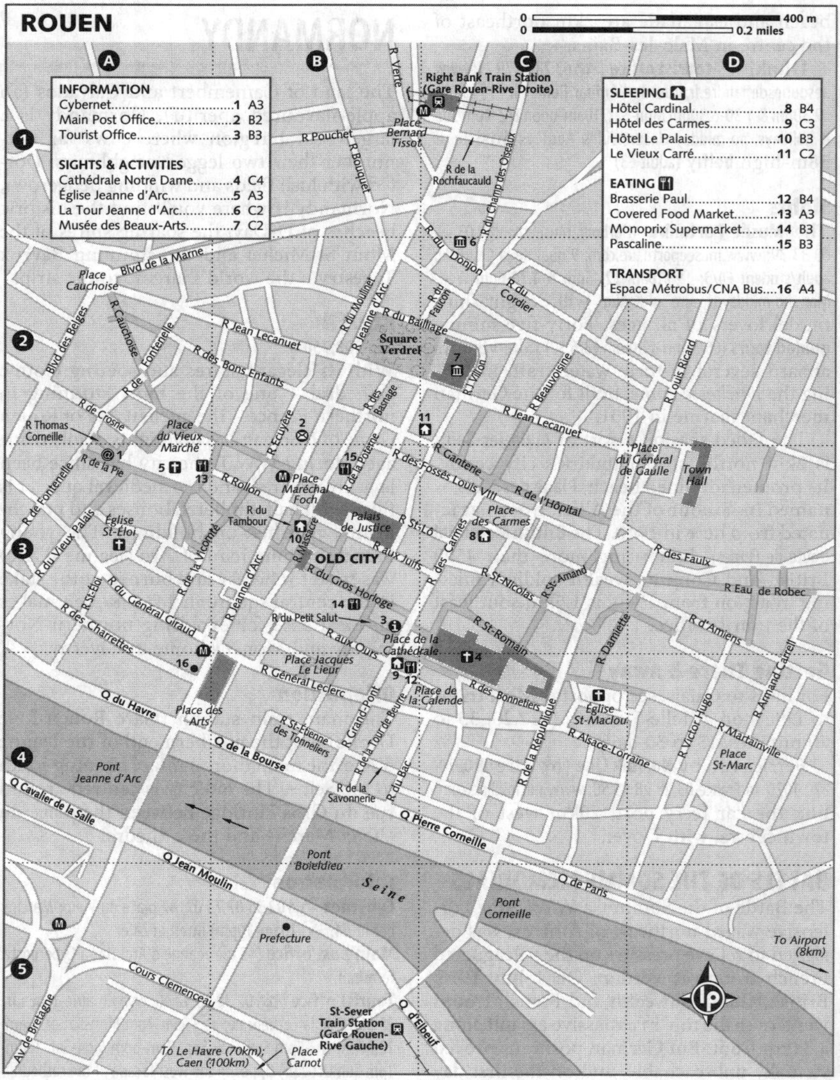

ROUEN

INFORMATION

- Cybernet ... 1 A3
- Main Post Office ... 2 B2
- Tourist Office ... 3 B3

SIGHTS & ACTIVITIES

- Cathédrale Notre Dame ... 4 C4
- Église Jeanne d'Arc ... 5 A3
- La Tour Jeanne d'Arc ... 6 C2
- Musée des Beaux-Arts ... 7 C2

SLEEPING

- Hôtel Cardinal ... 8 B4
- Hôtel des Carmes ... 9 C3
- Hôtel Le Palais ... 10 B3
- Le Vieux Carré ... 11 C2

EATING

- Brasserie Paul ... 12 B4
- Covered Food Market ... 13 A3
- Monoprix Supermarket ... 14 B3
- Pascaline ... 15 B3

TRANSPORT

- Espace Métrobus/CNA Bus ... 16 A4

Rouen's **Cathédrale Notre Dame** (8am-6pm Tue-Sun, 2-6pm Mon) is a masterpiece of French Gothic architecture, and is the famous subject of a series of paintings by Monet. From June to mid-September, as dusk falls over the square, Monet's canvases are projected onto the front of the cathedral as part of a dazzling light show. Best of all, it's free.

The **Musée des Beaux-Arts** (02 35 71 28 40; 26bis rue Jean Lecanuet; adult/student €3/2; 10am-6pm Wed-Mon) features paintings from the 15th to the 20th centuries, including work by Caravaggio, Rubens, Modigliani and (of course) a painting of Rouen Cathedral by Monet.

La Tour Jeanne d'Arc (02 35 98 16 21; rue du Donjon; adult €1.50; 10am-12.30pm & 2-6pm Wed-Sat &

Mon, 2-6.30pm Sun Apr-Sep, 10am-12.30pm & 2-5pm Wed-Sat & Mon, 2-5.30pm Sun Oct-Mar) is where Joan of Arc was imprisoned before her execution.

Sleeping

The 'Bon Weekend' scheme offers two weekend nights for the price of one in some hotels, but you must book eight days ahead.

Hôtel Le Palais (☎ 02 35 71 41 40; 12 rue du Tambour; r from €30) Top hotel for value in town, bang in the middle of things near the Palais de Justice and the Gros Horloge. Don't expect too many spoils – the rooms are basic and not all have bathrooms, but Rouen is on your doorstep.

Hôtel des Carmes (☎ 02 35 71 92 31; www.hoteldescarmes.fr.st, in French; 33 place des Carmes; r €45-61; P) This sweet little streetside hotel offers imaginative rooms, decked out with patchwork quilts and vibrant colours.

Le Vieux Carré (☎ 02 35 71 67 70; www.vieux-carre.fr; 34 rue Ganterie; d €55-57) This half-timbered hotel is a fantastic find. Downstairs there's an old-fashioned *salon de thé*, crammed with faded photos and overloaded bookshelves, and upstairs you'll find smartly styled rooms with garden or courtyard views.

Hôtel Cardinal (☎ 02 35 70 24 42; www.cardinal-hotel.fr; 1 place de la Cathédrale; s €47-59, d €58-72) What this modern hotel lacks in character, it more than makes up for in location – the Cardinal sits in a fantastic spot right opposite the cathedral, and the top-floor rooms have balconies overlooking the square.

Eating

Au Temps des Cerises (☎ 02 35 89 98 00; 4-6 rue des Basnage; lunch menu €10.50, dinner menu from €15; closed Sun, Mon & lunch Sat) There's no better place to check out Normandy's famous cheeses than this ever-popular restaurant. Choose your cheesy poison – the menu is packed with *tartiflette* (potato tart), fondue and endless varieties of *croûtes* (pies) – and tuck in.

Pascaline (☎ 02 35 89 67 44; 5 rue de la Poterne; menus €13-16) This bustling bistro serves up traditional cuisine in typically French surroundings – net curtains, wooden tables and chuffing coffee machines abound.

Brasserie Paul (☎ 02 35 71 86 07; 1 place de la Cathédrale; mains €10-25) The classic Rouennaise brasserie – think starchy service, plush red seats and overhead fans (there's even a self-playing pianola). The menu is crammed with regional dishes, including Simone de Beauvoir's favourite smoked duck salad.

Dairy products, fish and fresh produce are on sale at the **covered food market** (place du Vieux Marché; 6am-1.30pm Tue-Sun), and there's a **Monoprix supermarket** (65 rue du Gros Horloge).

Getting There & Away

Regional bus information is dispensed by **Espace Métrobus** (☎ 02 35 52 92 00; 9 rue Jeanne d'Arc). Buses leave from quai du Havre and quai de la Bourse.

Trains to Paris' Gare St-Lazare (€18.50, 70 minutes, six to eight daily), Caen (€20.70, two hours, 12 daily) and Dieppe (€9, 45 minutes, 12 to 15 daily) depart from Gare Rouen-Rive Droite. The Gare Rouen-Rive Gauche south of the river handles regional services.

BAYEUX

pop 15,000

There's one reason why several million visitors descend on Bayeux every year – a 70m-long piece of embroidered cloth known to the French as *La Tapisserie de la Reine Mathilde*, and to the rest of the world as the Bayeux Tapestry. Bayeux' winding streets are crammed with higgledy-piggledy period buildings, including a fine Gothic cathedral and lots of wooden-framed Norman houses, and the city makes a perfect launching pad for exploring the invasion beaches just to the north.

Orientation & Information

The Cathédrale Notre Dame, the major landmark in the centre of Bayeux and visible throughout the town, is 1km northwest of the train station.

Just off the northern end of rue Larcher is the **tourist office** (☎ 02 31 51 28 28; www.bayeux-tourism.com; pont St-Jean; 9am-7pm Mon-Sat, 9-1pm & 2-6pm Sun Jun-Aug, 9.30-12.30pm & 2-6pm daily Apr-May & Sep-Oct, 9.30am-12.30pm & 2-5.30pm Mon-Sat Nov-Mar).

Sights

The **Bayeux Tapestry** was commissioned by Bishop Odo of Bayeux, William the Conqueror's half-brother, to commemorate the opening of Bayeux' cathedral in 1077. The 70m-long tapestry recounts the story of the Norman conquest of England in 1066 across 58 remarkable scenes – look out for Halley's comet and the graphic scenes of the battle itself, complete with severed limbs and lopped-off heads.

The tapestry is housed in the **Musée de la Tapisserie de Bayeux** (☎ 02 31 51 25 50; rue de

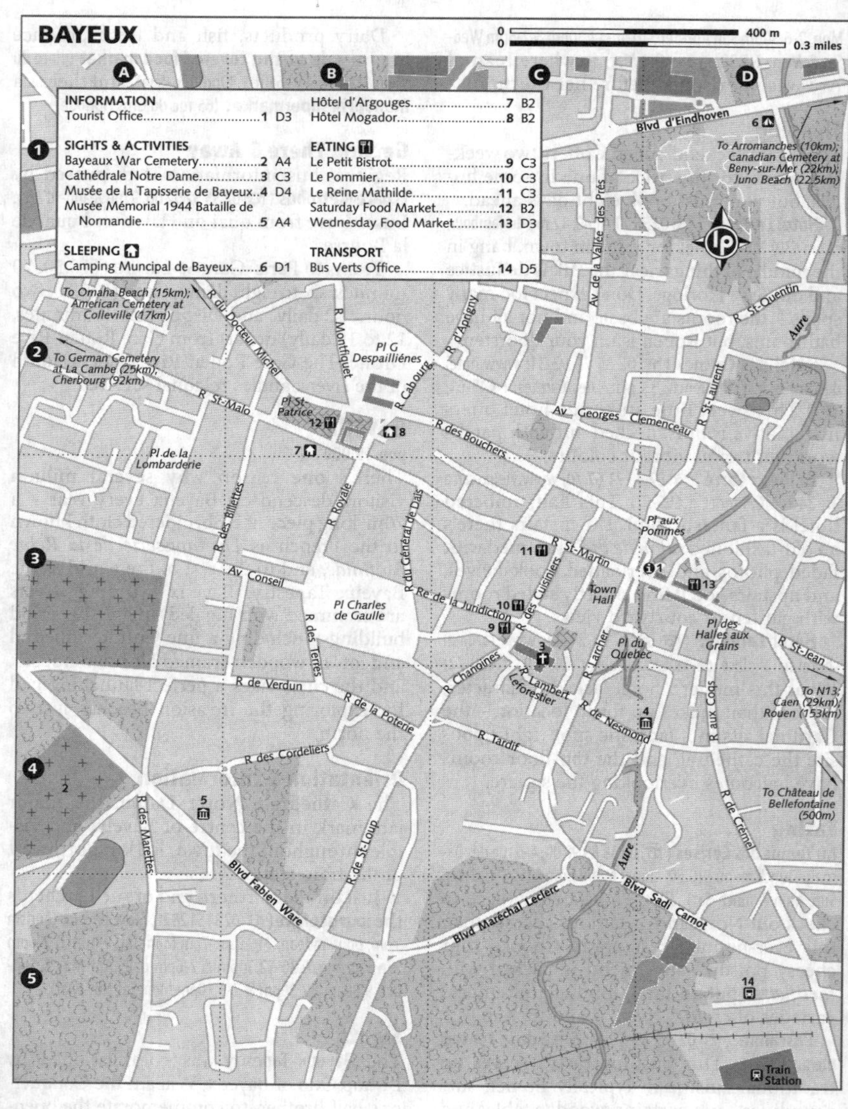

Nesmond; adult/student incl admission to Musée Baron Gérard €8/3; 9am-6.30pm mid-Mar–Apr & Sep-Nov, 9.30am-12.30pm & 2-6pm Dec–mid-Mar, 9am-7pm May-Aug). An audioguide is included.

The spectacular **Cathédrale Notre Dame** (place de la Liberté; 8.30am-6pm Oct-Jun, to 7pm Jul-Sep) is a fine example of Norman Gothic architecture, dating from the 13th century.

The recently refurbished **Musée Mémorial 1944 Bataille de Normandie** (02 31 92 93 41; blvd Fabien Ware; adult/student €6/3; 9.30am-6.30pm May–mid-Sep, 10am-12.30pm & 2-6pm mid-Sep–Apr), houses one of Normandy's main collections of D-Day memorabilia, including tanks, vintage weapons, documents, photos and lots of military hardware.

The **Bayeaux war cemetery** (☎ 02 21 21 77 00; blvd Fabien Ware), west of the war museum, is the largest of the Commonwealth military cemeteries in Normandy. It contains 4868 graves of soldiers from the UK and 10 other countries (including Germany). 1807 other Commonweath soldiers whose bodies were never found are commemorated on the memorial across the road.

Sleeping

Camping Municipal de Bayeux (☎ 02 31 92 08 43; blvd d'Eindhoven; camp sites per adult/site €3.50/4; 🕑 mid-Mar–mid-Nov) This camping ground is about 2km north of the town centre. Bus 3 stops three times daily at nearby Les Cerisiers.

Hôtel Mogador (☎ 02 31 92 24 58; hotel.mogador@wanadoo.fr; 20 rue Alain Chartier; d €46-51; Ⓟ) A reliable if slightly run-down hotel on the main market square. Floral curtains and the odd exposed beam conjure up some character, and there's a small garden courtyard that makes a lovely spot for morning croissant.

Hôtel d'Argouges (☎ 02 31 92 88 86; dargouges@aol.com; 21 rue St-Patrice; d €80-100; Ⓟ) This stately 18th-century mansion is now a graceful hotel, centred around an enclosed carriage-yard. The more expensive rooms are packed with old furniture and period features.

Château de Bellefontaine (☎ 02 31 22 00 10; www.hotel-bellefontaine.com; 49 rue de Bellefontaine; s €60-90, d €90-135, ste €120-180; Ⓟ ☒) Surrounded by 2 hectares of groomed parkland just outside Bayeux, this majestic 18th-century castle is top of the heap in terms of luxury. If you can afford them, the beautifully appointed park-view suites are the rooms to choose.

Eating

Open-air food markets are held on rue St-Jean on Wednesday mornings, and on place St-Patrice on Saturday mornings.

La Reine Mathilde (☎ 02 31 92 00 59; 47 rue Saint-Martin; cakes €3-6) This sumptuous *patissier* and *salon de thé* serves the kind of wickedly indulgent cakes that would send Marie-Antoinette into overdrive.

Le Petit Bistrot (☎ 02 31 51 85 40; 2 rue du Bienvenu; mains €14-22; 🕑 closed Sun & Mon Sep-Jun) An excellent spot for down-to-earth regional cooking, served in a tiny dining room decked out with sunny colours, plain wooden tables and terracotta floor tiles.

Le Pommier (☎ 02 31 21 52 10; 40 rue des Cuisiniers; menus €21.50-28.50; 🕑 closed Tue & Wed low season) For something more upmarket, this smart restaurant dishes up Norman specialities such as roast duck in apple sauce and steamed rabbit, as well as a selection of classic French dishes.

Getting There & Away

Bus Verts (☎ 08 10 21 42 14), opposite the train station, runs daily buses to Caen, leaving from the train station and place St-Patrice. Bus Verts also runs regular buses to the D-Day beaches (see below).

There are regular trains to Caen (€5.30, 20 minutes) and Cherbourg (€14, one hour), as well as direct services to Paris' Gare St-Lazare (€30.40, five daily).

D-DAY BEACHES

The D-Day landings, code-named 'Operation Overlord', were the largest military operation in history. Early on 6 June 1944, Allied troops stormed ashore along 80km of beaches north of Bayeux, code-named (from west to east) Utah, Omaha, Gold, Juno and Sword. The landings on D-Day – called Jour J in French – were followed by the Battle of Normandy, which ultimately lead to the liberation of Europe from Nazi occupation. Caen's **Mémorial museum** (below) provides the best overview of the Battle of Normandy, and there are many small D-Day museums dotted around the area. Once on the coast, several well-signposted routes link the main battle sites.

The most brutal fighting on D-Day took place 15km northwest of Bayeux along the stretch of coastline now known as **Omaha Beach**. Dune-lined **Juno Beach**, 12km east of

CAEN MÉMORIAL

Caen's hi-tech museum, **Mémorial – Un Musée pour la Paix** (Memorial – A Museum for Peace; ☎ 02 31 06 06 44; www.memorial-caen.fr, in French; adult/student & 10-18yr €17.50/16, WWII veterans free; 🕑 9am-7pm Feb-Sep, to 6pm Oct-Dec, closed Jan) uses sound, lighting, film, animation and lots of fantastic exhibits to vividly explore the events of WWII, the D-Day landings and the ensuing Cold War. Tickets remain valid for 24 hours, so you can split your visit over two days. The museum also runs tours (p332) of the D-Day beaches.

Arromanches, was stormed by Canadian troops on D-Day. Little remnants of the fighting remains on the beaches apart from the occasional concrete bunker – these days they're as popular with summer holiday-makers as history buffs.

To make it possible to unload cargo without having to capture one of the heavily defended Channel ports, the Allies established two prefabricated breakwaters code-named Mulberry Harbours. One of them, Port Winston, can still be viewed at low tide at **Arromanches**, a seaside town 10km northeast of Bayeux.

Perched above Omaha Beach, the **American Military Cemetery** (☎ 02 31 51 62 00; 🕒 9am-6pm mid-Apr–Sep, 9am-5pm Oct–mid-Apr) at Colleville-sur-Mer, 17km northwest of Bayeux, is the largest American cemetery in Europe, containing the graves of 9387American soldiers and a memorial to 1557 others whose remains were never found.

Tours

Caen Mémorial (☎ 02 31 06 06 45; www.memorial-caen.fr; afternoon tour adult/under 18yr & veteran €67.50/54, morning tour per person €54; 🕒 tours 9am & 1pm Apr-Sep, 1pm Oct-Mar) The museum conducts minibus tours around the landing beaches. The price includes entry to the museum.

D-Day Tours (☎ 02 31 51 70 52; www.d-daybeaches.com; BP 48525, 14400 Bayeux; adult/student/under 10yr €75/65/40) Offers day tours of the main D-Day sites.

Getting There & Away

From Bayeux, bus No 70, run by **Bus Verts** (☎ 08 10 21 42 14), goes west to Colleville-sur-Mer, Omaha Beach, Pointe du Hoc and Grandcamp-Maisy. Bus 74 (75 during summer) serves Arromanches, Gold and Juno Beaches, and Courseulles. The company runs several extra routes around the D-Day beaches during the summer months.

MONT ST-MICHEL

pop 42

The slender towers and sky-scraping turrets of the abbey of Mont St-Michel are one of the classic postcard images of Northern France. Rising from flat white sands, the abbey sits atop a small island encircled by stout ramparts and battlements, connected to the mainland by an old causeway. Legend has it that the abbey was founded in the 8th century, when Aubert, the bishop of Avranches, was visited by the archangel Michael in a dream.

There are a few expensive hotels on the Mont itself, but most people choose to stay at Beauvoir, opposite the Mont, or Pontorson, about 9km inland from the bay.

Information

Mont St-Michel tourist office (☎ 02 33 60 14 30; www.ot-montsaintmichel.com; 🕒 9am-7pm Jul & Aug, to noon & 2-5.30pm Sep-Jun) Up the stairs to the left inside Porte de l'Avancée. A detailed map of the Mont is available for €3.50.

Pontorson tourist office (☎ 02 33 60 20 65; mont.st.michel.pontorson@wanadoo.fr; place de l'Église; 🕒 9am-noon & 2-7pm Mon-Fri, 10am-noon & 3-6pm Sat, 10am-noon Sun Apr-Sep, 9am-noon & 2-6pm Mon-Fri, 10am-noon & 3-6pm Sat Oct-Mar) Has information about walking tours and local events.

Sleeping & Eating

Camping Haliotis (☎ 02 33 68 11 59; www.camping-haliotis-mont-saint-michel.com; Pontorson; camp sites per adult/site €4.50/4; 🕒 Apr-Nov; 🏊) Just off blvd Général Patton, this complex has a heated pool, bike hire, tennis courts and an on-site bar.

Centre Duguesclin (☎/fax 02 33 60 18 65; aj@ville-pontorson.fr; blvd du Général Patton, Pontorson; dm €11-14; 🕒 year-round) One kilometre west of the train station, this modern, renovated hostel offers four- to six-bed rooms and kitchen facilities. The hostel closes from 10am to 6pm, but there's no curfew.

Hôtel de Bretagne (☎ 02 33 60 10 55; www.lebretagnepontorson.com; 59 rue du Couësnon, Pontorson; s €35-48, d €39-64) This timber-fronted hotel looks shabby from the outside, but the flowery bedspreads and frilly curtains add a touch of brightness to the bedrooms themselves. The downstairs restaurant offers local specialities such as oysters with Camembert and scallops cooked in cider (lunch *menu* €11, dinner *menu* €15 to €38).

Hôtel Montgomery (☎ 02 33 60 00 09; www.hotel-montgomery.com; 13 rue du Couësnon, Pontorson; s €47-55, d €57-160, ste €115-250; P) This 16th-century mansion boasts a vine-covered Renaissance façade and a selection of quirky rooms along its creaky wood-panelled corridors. The most expensive have huge four-poster beds and hefty Renaissance furniture. The downstairs restaurant is the best in Pontorson for French cuisine (dinner *menu* €16 to €25).

La Mère Poulard (☎ 02 33 89 68 68; Grande Rue; lunch menu €29-39, dinner menu €45-65; 🕒 11am-10pm) At the base of the Mont, this tourist institution churns out its famous *omelettes à la Mère Poulard* (soufflé omelettes) at astronomical prices. Autographed photos of visiting film stars and politicians adorn the walls.

Getting There & Away

Courriers Bretons (☎ 02 33 60 11 43) runs between Pontorson and Mont St-Michel (€1.80, 15 minutes, seven to 10 daily) and also to/from St-Malo (€8, one hour).

Local trains from Pontorson include Caen (€21.70, 2¼ hours, two daily) and Cherbourg (via Lison, €23.30, 2½ to three hours, two daily).

BRITTANY

Flung out on the far west of France, Brittany is in many ways a nation apart, thanks to its status as the last outpost of traditional Celtic culture in the country. With its own unique language – closely related to other Celtic languages such as Cornish and Welsh – and a calendar packed with colourful festivals and events, Brittany is one of France's most fascinating regions – it's also blessed with lots of beautiful beaches and the oldest standing stones this side of Stonehenge.

QUIMPER

pop 59,400

Small enough to feel like a village with its timbered houses and cobblestone streets, and large enough to serve as a centre for Breton culture and arts, Quimper (*kam*-pair) is Finistère's thriving capital. Derived from the Breton word *kemper*, meaning 'confluence', Quimper sits at the juncture of the small Odet and Steïr Rivers.

The **tourist office** (☎ 02 98 53 04 05; www.quimper-tourisme.com, in French; place de la Résistance; 🕒 9am-7pm Mon-Sat, 10am-12.45pm & 3-5.45pm Sun Jul & Aug, 9.30am-12.30pm & 1.30-6pm or 6.30pm Mon-Sat Sep-Jun, 10am-12.45pm Sun Jun & 1-15 Sep) arranges weekly guided tours in July and August.

Sights

Quimper's **Cathédrale St-Corentin** (🕒 9.30-noon & 1.30-6.30pm Mon-Sat May-Oct, 9am-noon & 1.30-6.30pm Mon-Sat Nov-Apr, 1.30-6.30pm Sun year-round) was begun in 1239 but only completed in the 1850s, with the addition of its dramatic twin spires.

The **Musée Départemental Breton** (☎ 02 98 95 21 60; 1 rue du Roi Gradlon; adult/child €4/2.50; 🕒 9am-6pm Jun-Sep, 9am-noon & 2-5pm Tue-Sat & 2-5pm Sun Oct-May) is housed in the former bishop's palace. Superb exhibits showcase the area's history, furniture, costumes, crafts and archaeology. Adjoining the museum is the **Jardin de l'Evêché** (Bishop's Palace Garden; admission free; 🕒 9am-5pm or 6pm).

Quimper's local crafts include exquisite faïence pottery, best seen at the **Musée de la Faïence** (☎ 02 98 90 12 72; 14 rue Jean-Baptiste Bousquet; adult/child €4/2.50; 🕒 10am-6pm Mon-Sat mid-Apr–mid-Oct).

The **Musée des Beaux-Arts** (☎ 02 98 95 45 20; 40 place St-Corentin; adult/child €4/2.50; 🕒 10am-7pm Jul & Aug, 10am-noon & 2-6pm Wed-Mon Apr-Jun & Sep-Oct, 10am-noon & 2-6pm Wed-Sat & Mon, 2-6pm Sun Nov-Mar), in the town hall, displays European paintings from the 16th to early 20th centuries.

Sleeping

Camping Municipal (☎/fax 02 98 55 61 09; av des Oiseaux; camp sites from €8.50; 🕒 Apr-Sep) An attractive wooded camping ground 1km west of the old city. Take bus 1 from the train station to the Chaptal stop.

Auberge de Jeunesse (☎ 02 98 64 97 97; quimper@fuaj.org; 6 av des Oiseaux; dm incl breakfast €14.50, bedding €3; 🕒 Apr-Sep) Beside Camping Municipal, Quimper's seasonal youth hostel has self-catering facilities.

Hôtel TGV (☎ 02 98 90 54 00; www.hoteltgv.com; 4 rue de Concarneau; d €36-46) The best bet of several hotels around the train station, the TGV has 22 small but bright rooms. Light sleepers beware: the adjacent bar can be noisy at night.

Hôtel Gradlon (☎ 02 98 95 04 39; www.hotel-gradlon.com; 30 rue de Brest; d €69-155; 🕒 closed 20 Dec-20 Jan) Quimper's most charming hotel is this former 19th-century coach house, recently renovated and set around a rose garden.

Eating

Crepes are king in Quimper, but fine-diners won't be disappointed either.

Crêperie du Sallé (☎ 02 98 95 95 80; 6 rue du Sallé; galettes €3-9; 🕒 lunch & dinner Tue-Sat) Locals crowd into this traditional restaurant for Breton crepes including *saucisse fumée* (smoked sausage) and *Forestiére* (made with mushrooms, fatty bacon and cheese).

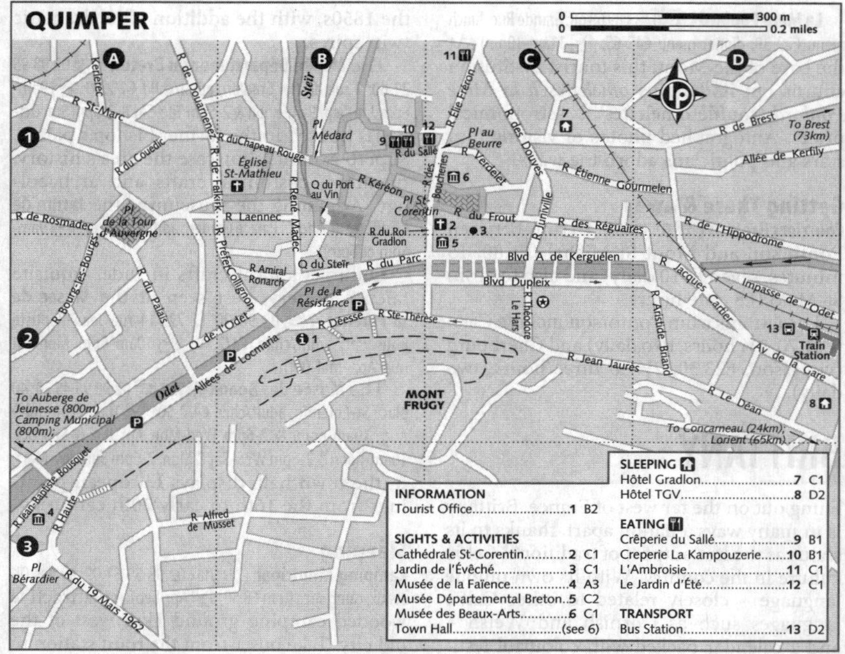

Crêperie La Krampouzerie (☎ 02 98 95 13 08; 9 rue du Sallé; mains from €7; ⏰ closed Sun & Mon) This rustic restaurant creates crepes and *galettes* puff-pastry cakes) using local ingredients such as *algues d'Ouessant* (seaweed from the Île de Ouessant) and homemade ginger caramel.

Le Jardin d'Eté (☎ 02 98 95 33 00; 15 rue du Sallé; lunch menu €14, dinner menu €23-27.50; ⏰ lunch & dinner Tue-Sat) Occupying a glassed-in terrace strung with lanterns, 'the summer garden' is strictly for gourmands, with specialities including duck mousse and coquilles St-Jacques (scallops).

L'Ambroisie (☎ 02 98 95 00 02; www.ambroisie-quimper.com; 49 rue Elie Fréron; menu €22-60; ⏰ lunch & dinner Tue-Fri, lunch Sat, closed mid-Jun–mid-Jul) Quimper's most celebrated gastronomic restaurant makes the most of regional produce in dishes such as quail in cider sauce and almond cake with strawberries.

Getting There & Away

CAT/Connex Tourisme (☎ 02 98 90 68 40) bus destinations include Brest (€6, 1¼ hours) and Douarnenez (€2, 35 minutes, six to 10 daily).

Caoudal (☎ 02 98 56 96 72) runs buses to Concarneau (€2, 45 minutes, seven to 10 daily).

There are frequent trains to Brest (€14, 1¼ hours, up to 10 daily), Rennes (€30.10, 2½ hours, five daily) and Paris (Gare Montparnasse; €68.20, 4¾ hours, eight daily).

CARNAC

pop 4600

Stand aside, Stonehenge – Carnac (Garnag in Breton) has the world's greatest concentration of megalithic sites. Predating Stonehenge by around 100 years, there are more than 3000 of these upright stones, most around thigh-high, erected between 5000 and 3500 BC.

Situated about 32km west of Vannes, Carnac has two parts: the old stone village, Carnac-Ville, and, 1.5km south, the seaside resort of Carnac-Plage.

Information

Tourist office (☎ 02 97 52 13 52; www.ot-carnac.fr; 74 av des Druides, Carnac-Plage; ⏰ 9am-7pm Mon-Sat, 3-7pm Sun Jul & Aug, 9am-noon or 12.30pm & 2-6pm Mon-Sat Sep-Jun)

Tourist office annexe (☎ 02 97 52 13 52; place de l'Église, Carnac-Ville; 9.30am-12.30pm & 2-6pm Apr-Sep & school holidays)

Sights

Carnac's mighty **megaliths** stretch some 13km north from Carnac-Ville to the village of Locmariaquer. No-one's quite sure what purpose these cromlech cairns served, although theories abound – depending on which book you read, the Carnac stones signify just about everything from sun worship to a phallic fertility cult. Even more mysterious is the thorny question of their construction – just *how did* the builders hew and haul these vast granite blocks several millennia before the wheel arrived in Brittany, let alone the JCB.

With no less than 1099 stones, the **Alignements du Ménec**, 1km north of Carnac-Ville, is the largest menhir field. Some 1.5km northeast are the **Alignements de Kermario**, and 500m further on the **Alignements de Kerlescan**. Between June and September, seven buses a day run between the two sites and both Carnac-Ville and Carnac-Plage.

Between 10am and 5pm from October to May, you can wander freely through many sites, but during the rest of the year, you can only visit on a 1½-hour **guided tour** (€4), organised by the **Maison des Mégalithes** (☎ 02 97 52 89 99; route des Alignements; admission free; 9am-8pm Jul & Aug, to 5.15pm Sep-Apr, to 7pm May-Jun).

Sleeping & Eating

Camping des Menhirs (☎ 02 97 52 94 67; www.lesmenhirs.com; 7 allée St-Michel, Carnac-Plage; camp sites €29; May-late Sep) There are more than 15 camping grounds in and around Carnac, including this luxury complex 300m north of the beach, complete with sauna (€4), and cocktail bar.

Auberge Le Ratelier (☎ 02 97 52 05 04; www.le-ratelier.com; 4 Chemin du Douet, Carnac-Ville; d €43-55; Feb-Dec) This rustic eight-room hotel – a former farmhouse with low ceilings with traditional timber furnishings – is in a quiet street southwest of place de l'Église. Feast on gourmet seafood at its wood-beamed restaurant (*menu* €17 to €40; open lunch and dinner May to September, closed Wednesday October to December and February to April).

Hôtel Le Bateau Ivre (☎ 02 97 52 19 55; fax 02 97 52 84 94; 71 blvd de la Plage, Carnac-Plage; s €64-114, d €83-160; P) The Bateau Ivre is one of Carnac's more upmarket hotels. All rooms have a balcony and overlook the beach, which is lined with jaunty yellow-and-white bathing tents in summer.

Crêperie au Pressoir (☎ 02 97 52 01 86; village du Ménec; galettes €3-7.50; lunch & dinner Easter-Aug) This artisan creperie is in a traditional long Breton house, right in the middle of a 70-strong *chromlec'h* (circle of menhirs).

Getting There & Away

The main bus stops are in Carnac-Ville outside the police station on rue St-Cornély and in Carnac-Plage beside the tourist office. **Cariane Atlantique** (☎ 02 97 47 29 64) buses go to Auray (€3.80), Vannes (€6.30) and Quiberon (€3.80).

The nearest year-round train station is in Auray, 12km to the northeast. SNCF has an office in the Carnac-Plage tourist office.

Getting Around

Hire bikes for around €9/17 per half-/full day from **Lorcy** (☎ 02 97 52 09 73; 6 rue de Courdiec, Carnac-Ville) and **Le Randonneur** (☎ 02 97 52 02 55; 20 av des Druides, Carnac-Plage).

ST-MALO

pop 52,700

The port of St-Malo, battered by swelling seas and encircled by sturdy ramparts, became a key port during the 17th and 18th centuries, and an important base for merchant ships and government-sanctioned privateers (otherwise known as pirates). These days St-Malo is a summertime haven, especially for British tourists, for whom the city is just a short cross-Channel ferry-hop away.

Orientation

St-Malo consists of the harbour towns of St-Malo and St-Servan plus the suburbs of Paramé and Rothéneuf to the east. The old walled city of St-Malo is known as Intra-Muros (within the walls) or Ville Close. From the train station, it's a 15-minute walk westwards along av Louis Martin.

Information

Cyberm@lo (☎ 02 99 56 07 78; 68 chaussée de Sillon; per 15min/1hr €1.50/4; 10am-1am Mon-Sat, 11am-11pm Sun mid-Jun–mid-Sep, 11am-9pm Tue-Thu, to 11pm Fri & Sat, 3-8pm Sun mid-Sep–mid-Jun) Internet access along the seafront.

Main post office (1 blvd de la République)
Tourist office (☎ 08 25 13 52 00, 02 99 56 64 43; www.saint-malo-tourisme.com; esplanade St-Vincent; 9am-7.30pm Mon-Sat, 10am-6pm Sun Jul & Aug, 9am-12.30pm & 1.30-6pm or 6.30pm Mon-Sat Sep-Jun, 10am-12.30pm & 2.30-6pm Sun Easter-Jun & Sep)

Sights

For the best views of the walled city, stroll along the **ramparts**, constructed at the end of the 17th century under military architect Vauban. You can make a complete circuit (around 2km), and there's access at several places, including all the city gates. From their northern stretch, look across to the remains of **Fort National** (admission free; Jun-Sep). You can also walk to the rocky islet of Île du Grand Bé, where 18th-century writer Chateaubriand is buried. Check tide times with the tourist office, as the island is accessible for around six hours around high tide.

The battle to drive German forces out of St-Malo destroyed around 80% of the old city during August 1944; damage to the **Cathédrale St-Vincent** (place Jean de Châtillon; 9.30am-6pm except during Mass), was particularly severe.

Other attractions in St-Malo include the **Musée International du Long Cours Cap-Hornier** (Museum of the Cape Horn Route; ☎ 02 99 40 71 58; adult/child €5/2.50; 10am-noon & 2-6pm Apr-Sep, Tue-Sun Oct-Mar), which explores of the lives of the leather-skinned sailors who plied the Cape Horn route, and the excellent **Grand Aquarium** (☎ 02 99 21 19 00; av Général Patton; adult/child €14/10; at least 10am-6pm Feb-Dec, to 8pm Jul & Aug), 4km south of the city. If you're hardy enough to brave the Atlantic swells, there are also several pleasant **beaches** around St-Malo.

Sleeping

Camping Aleth (☎ 02 99 81 60 91; camping@ville-saint-malo.fr; allée Gaston Buy, St-Servan; camp sites €11.50; May-Sep) Next to Fort de la Cité, Camping Aleth has panoramic 360-degree views and is close to the beaches. Take bus 1 in July and August or No 3 year-round.

Auberge de Jeunesse Ethic Etapes (☎ 02 99 40 29 80; www.centrevarangot.com; 37 av du Père Umbricht; dm incl breakfast €12.50-16.50;) This efficient place has a self-catering kitchen and sports facilities. Take bus No 5 from the train station or 1 (July and August only) from the bus station.

Hôtel les Chiens du Guet (☎ 02 99 40 87 29; www.leschiensduguet.com, in French; 4 place du Guet; d €37-48, tr €47-53) This welcoming no-star place is near Porte St-Pierre, which opens directly onto the beach. The 12 simple, sunlit rooms are homy if somewhat snug.

Hôtel France et Chateaubriand (☎ 02 99 56 66 52; www.hotel-fr-chateaubriand.com; place Chateaubriand; s €41-79, d €48-95) Opposite the chateau entrance, this grand place houses 80 rooms that combine a rarefied traditional French atmosphere with a relaxed seaside ambience.

Hôtel San Pedro (☎ 02 99 40 88 57; www.sanpedro-hotel.com; 1 rue Ste-Anne; s €43-49, d €53-65; Feb-Nov;) Tucked away in the old city, the San Pedro has cool, crisp neutral-toned décor with subtle splashes of colour, friendly service, and superb sea views.

Eating

Pain de Campagne (☎ 02 99 20 11 26, 7 rue Ste-Barbe; meals €5-9; lunch Thu-Tue, dinner Thu-Sat, Mon & Tue Sep-Jun, noon-2am daily Jul & Aug) The locals' choice for sandwiches and light lunches.

Crêperie Margaux (☎ 02 99 20 26 02; 3 place du Marché aux Légumes; menu €12; closed Tue & Wed) You can watch the owner of this wonderful little creperie hand-making traditional crepes.

Côté Jardin (☎ 02 99 81 63 11, 36 rue Dauphine, St-Servan; menu €18-24; lunch Tue-Sun, dinner Tue & Thu-Sun) This charming restaurant presents regional and traditional cuisine, and boasts a terrace overlooking the marina and city.

Marché Plus (cnr rue St-Vincent & rue St-Barbe; 7am-9pm Mon-Sat, 7am-noon Sun), in the old city, is good for picnic supplies, while **Bordier** (9 rue de l'Orme; Tue-Sat) is the best cheese and dairy shop in town. Just down the street is the covered market, **Halle au Blé** (8am-noon Tue & Fri).

Getting There & Away

Brittany Ferries (☎ in France 08 25 82 88 28, in the UK 0870 556 1600; www.brittany-ferries.com) sail between St-Malo and Portsmouth and **Condor Ferries** (☎ in France 08 25 13 51 35, in the UK 0870 243 5140; www.condorferries.co.uk) run to both Poole and Weymouth via Jersey or Guernsey. Ferries leave from the Gare Maritime du Naye.

From April to September, **Compagnie Corsaire** (☎ 08 25 13 80 35) and **Etoile Marine Excursions** (☎ 02 23 18 02 04, www.etoile-marine-excursions.com) run a Bus de Mer (Sea Bus; adult/child return €6/4, 10 minutes, hourly) shuttle service between St-Malo and Dinard.

Courriers Bretons (☎ 02 99 19 70 80) serves Pontorson (€2.50, one hour) and Mont St-Michel (€4.30, 1½ hours, three to four daily).

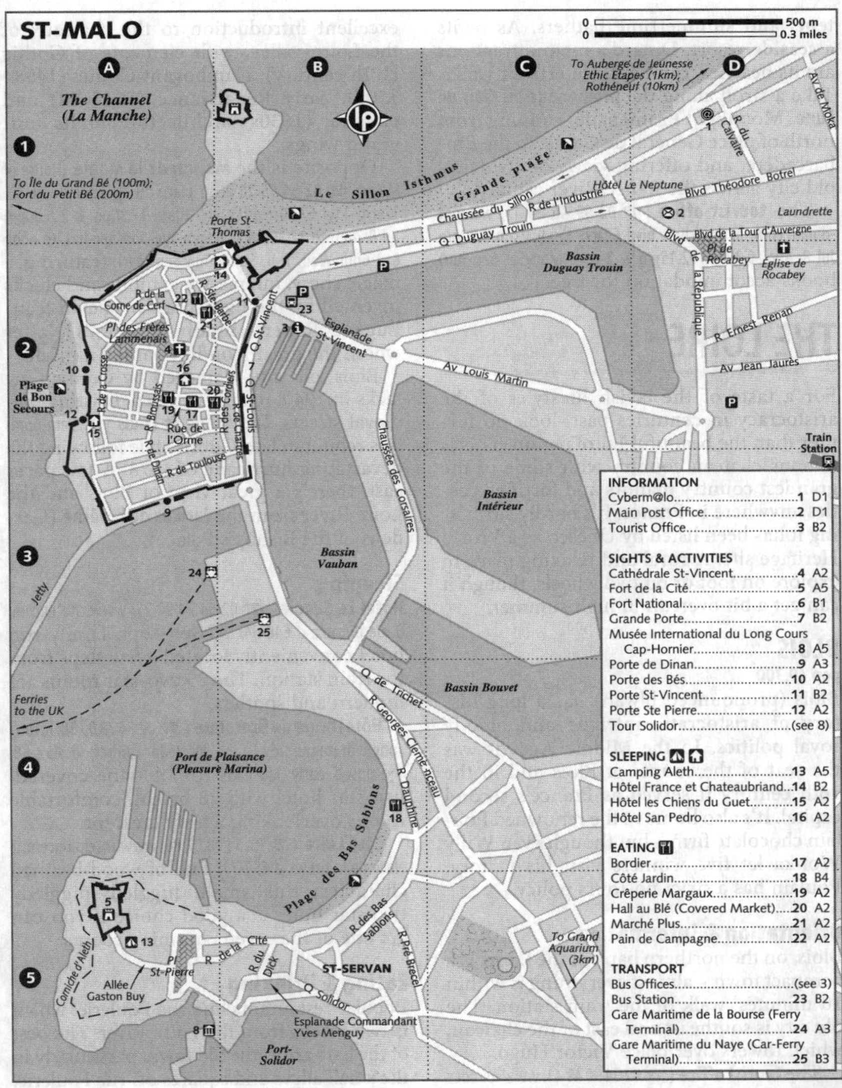

TIV (☎ 02 99 82 26 26) has buses to Dinard (€1.50, 30 minutes, hourly) and Rennes (€3, one to 1½ hours, three to six daily).

TGV trains services run frequently between St-Malo and Rennes (€11.60, one hour), and there is also a direct service to Paris' Gare Montparnasse (€58, three hours).

AROUND ST-MALO

Dinard

pop 10,100

Visiting Dinard 'in season' is like stepping into one of the canvases Picasso painted here in the 1920s. *Belle époque* mansions built into the cliffs preside over the beach, dotted with blue-and-white-striped bathing tents and summertime bathers. As befits a seaside resort, Dinard's main attractions are its beaches, cafés and waterfront walks. Take a stroll along the **promenade du Clair de Lune** (Moonlight Promenade) running from north of place Général de Gaulle to the Embarcadère, and offering views of St-Malo's old city across the Rance River estuary.

The **tourist office** (☎ 02 99 46 94 12; www.ot-dinard.com, in French; 2 blvd Féart; 9.30am-7.30pm Jul & Aug, 9.30am-12.15pm & 2-6pm Mon-Sat Sep-Jun) books accommodation for free.

THE LOIRE

For a taste of the lavish lifestyles of the aristocracy in centuries past, look no further than the beautiful Loire region. This is famous chateau country with some of the grandest country manors and fortified castles anywhere in France. It's hardly surprising it has been listed by Unesco as a World Heritage site. A rural and relaxing place to explore on foot or on two wheels, though it can get a bit overrun in high summer.

BLOIS

pop 49,300

Blois (pronounced blwah) has a long history of aristocratic intrigue and bloody royal politics. In the Middle Ages it was the seat of the counts of Blois and in the 16th century it served as France's second capital. It's also home to the renowned Poulain chocolate firm – but though even Willy Wonka let five winners visit his factory, Poulain has a strict no-tours policy.

Orientation & Information

Blois, on the northern bank of the Loire, is a compact town – almost everything is within 10 minutes' walk of the train station. The old city is southeast and east of the chateau, which towers over place Victor Hugo.

The **tourist office** (☎ 02 54 90 41 41; www.loiredeschateaux.com; 23 place du Château; 9am-7pm Mon-Sat, 10am-7pm Sun Apr-Sep, 9am-12.30pm & 2-6pm Mon-Sat, 9.30am-12.30pm Sun Oct-Mar) supplies free walking brochures.

Sights

The **Château de Blois** (☎ 02 54 90 33 32; adult/student/6-17yr €6.50/5/3; 9am-7pm Jul & Aug, to 6pm Apr-Jun, Sep & Oct, to 12.30pm & 2-5.30pm Nov-Mar) makes an excellent introduction to the chateaux of the Loire valley, with elements of Gothic (13th century); Flamboyant Gothic (1498–1503), early Renaissance (1515–24) and classical (1630s) architecture in its four grand wings.

Opposite is the **Maison de la Magie** (House of Magic; ☎ 02 54 55 26 26; 1 place du Château; adult/12-17yr/6-11yr €7.50/6.50/5; 10am-12.30pm & 2-6.30pm Jul & Aug, to 12.30pm & 2-6pm Tue-Sun Apr-Jun, to noon & 2-6pm Wed, Thu, Sat & Sun Sep-Mar) featuring a magic show, interactive exhibits and clocks invented by the Blois-born magician Jean-Eugène Robert-Houdin (1805–71), after whom the great Houdini named himself.

Blois' old city, damaged by German attacks in 1940, retains its steep, twisting medieval streets. **Cathédrale St-Louis** (9am-6pm) was rebuilt in late-Gothic style following the devastating hurricane of 1678. A few paces east, there's a great view of Blois and the Loire River from the **Jardins de l'Évêché** (Gardens of the Bishop's Palace).

Sleeping

Hôtel Le Savoie (☎ 02 54 74 32 21; www.citotel.com; 6 rue Ducoux; d €48-54) A well-kept, family-run hotel conveniently located a few steps from the train station. The 25 two-star rooms are modern and spotless.

Hôtel Anne de Bretagne (☎ 02 54 78 05 38; http://annedebretagne.free.fr; 31 av Jean Laigret; d €52-58; closed early Jan-early Feb) A vine-covered, two-star hotel with 28 bright, comfortable rooms overlooking a leafy crescent.

Côté Loire (☎ 02 54 78 07 86; www.coteloire.com; 2 place de la Grève; d €53-72) Full of wood-beamed character, this small, higgledy-piggledy two-star hotel is a good choice if you can get one of the seven charming rooms.

Eating & Drinking

Popular restaurants line rue Foulerie, which is two blocks from the Loire River. The best of the bars are in the old town, particularly in the small alleys and squares off rue Foulerie.

Le Bistrot (☎ 02 54 78 47 74; 12 rue Henry Drussy; 8am-midnight Mon-Thu, to 2am Fri & Sat, also Sun approx Apr-Sep, to 2am daily May-Aug) An informal bar-brasserie–wine bar serving steaks (€11.50 to €13.50), salads (€8.50) and hot open sandwiches (€8.50).

Les Banquettes Rouges (☎ 02 54 78 74 92; 16 rue des Trois Marchands; menu €13.50-37.50; noon-1.45pm & 7-9.45pm Tue-Sat) Hearty French favourites,

FRANCE

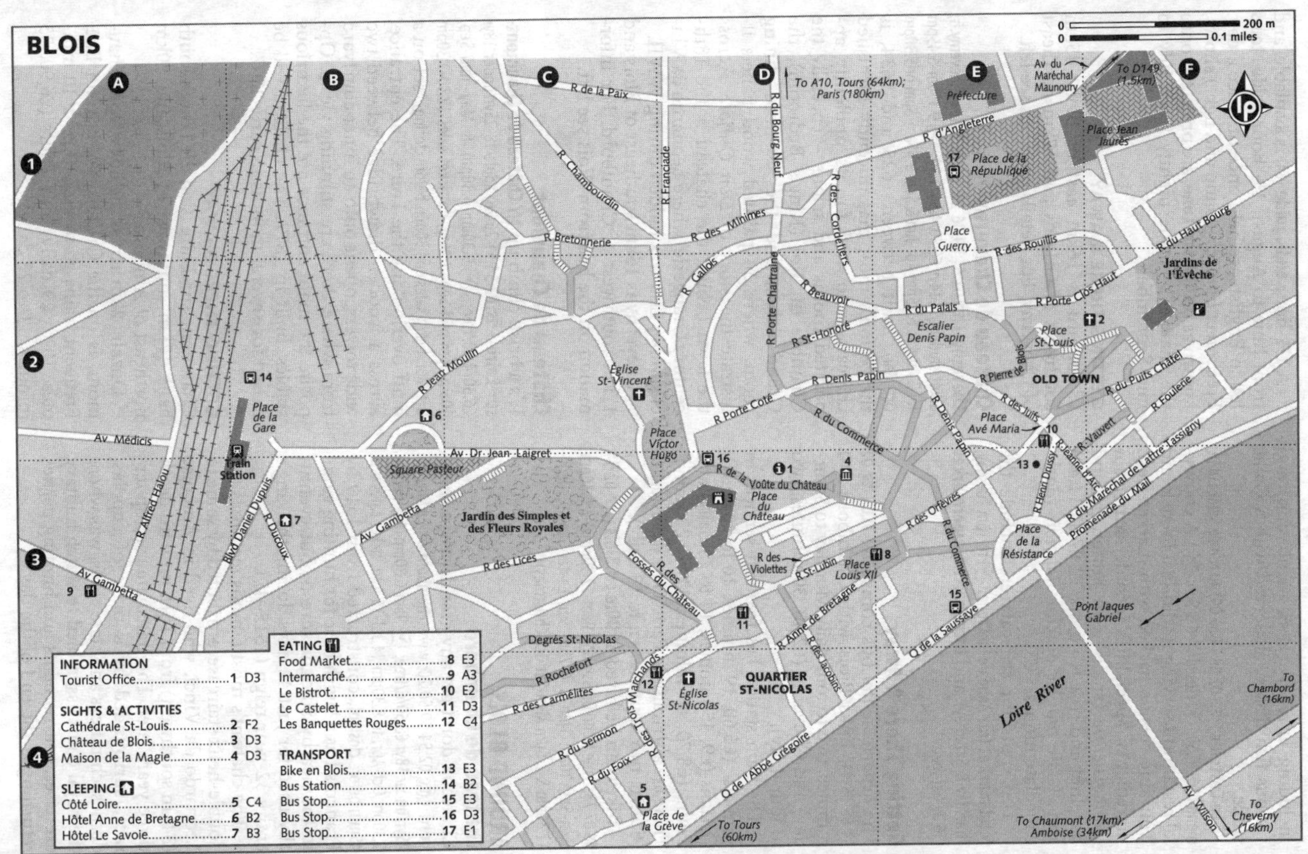
BLOIS
0 200 m
0 0.1 miles
INFORMATION
Tourist Office 1 D3
SIGHTS & ACTIVITIES
Cathédrale St-Louis 2 F2
Château de Blois 3 D3
Maison de la Magie 4 D3
SLEEPING
Côté Loire 5 C4
Hôtel Anne de Bretagne 6 B2
Hôtel Le Savoie 7 B3
EATING
Food Market 8 E3
Intermarché 9 A3
Le Bistrot 10 E2
Le Castelet 11 D3
Les Banquettes Rouges 12 C4
TRANSPORT
Bike en Blois 13 E3
Bus Station 14 B2
Bus Stop 15 E3
Bus Stop 16 D3
Bus Stop 17 E1
OLD TOWN
QUARTIER ST-NICOLAS
Loire River
Jardins de l'Évêche
Jardin des Simples et des Fleurs Royales
Square Pasteur
Place de la République
Place Jean Jaurès
Préfecture
Place Louis XII
Place du Château
Place Victor Hugo
Place de la Gare
Train Station
Place de la Résistance
Place St-Louis
Place Avé Maria
Place Guerry
Place de la Grève
Escalier Denis Papin
Église St-Vincent
Église St-Nicolas
Pont Jaques Gabriel
Promenade du Mail
Degrés St-Nicolas
To A10, Tours (64km); Paris (180km)
To D149 (1.5km)
Av du Maréchal Maunoury
To Chambord (16km)
To Cheverny (16km)
To Chaumont (17km); Amboise (34km)
To Tours (60km)
Av Wilson
Av Gambetta
Av Médicis
Av Dr Jean Laigret
R Alfred Halou
Blvd Daniel Dupuis
R Ducoux
R Jean Moulin
R Bretonnerie
R Chambourdin
R de la Paix
R Franciade
R des Minimes
R Gallois
R du Bourg Neuf
R Porte Chartraine
R des Cordeliers
R Beauvoir
R St-Honoré
R Denis Papin
R du Commerce
R Porte Côté
R de la Voûte du Château
R du Palais
R d'Angleterre
R des Rouillis
R Porte Clos Haut
R du Haut Bourg
R du Puits Châtel
R Fouierie
R Vauvert
R Pierre de Blois
R des Juifs
R Henri Drussy
R Jeanne d'Arc
R du Maréchal de Lattre de Tassigny
R des Orfèvres
R St-Lubin
R Anne de Bretagne
R des Jacobins
R des Violettes
R des Fossés du Château
R des Trois Marchands
R des Lices
R Rochefort
R des Carmélites
R du Sermon
R du Foix
Q de la Saussaye
Q de l'Abbé Grégoire

including *jarret d'agneau* (lamb shin) and various fish dishes, all served with a Gallic smile.

Le Castelet (☎ 02 54 74 66 09; 40 rue de Saint Lubin; menu €16-26.50; closed Wed & Sun;) A convivial restaurant serving traditional French and Touraine cuisine packed with market-fresh ingredients. Specialities include *escargots à l'amboisienne* (snails with butter, ground hazelnut and rosé wine; six/12 €7.80/11.40) and classic *mousse au chocolat noir* (dark-chocolate mousse; €5).

Top spots for self-caterers include the **food market** (rue Anne de Bretagne; to 1pm Tuesday, Thursday & Saturday) and **Intermarché supermarket** (16 av Gambetta).

Getting There & Away

The *départemental* bus company, **TLC** (☎ 02 54 58 55 44) links Blois with Chambord (40 minutes, two to four daily Monday to Saturday) and Cheverny (€2.40, 30 minutes, two to four daily).

The train station has frequent services to Amboise (€5.60, 19 minutes, 10 to 20 daily), Orléans (€9, 45 minutes, 14 to 28 daily) and Tours (€8.70, 40 minutes, 11 to 22 daily). There are also trains to Paris' Gare d'Austerlitz (€22.10, two hours, seven to 13 daily).

Bikes can be hired at **Bike en Blois** (☎ 02 54 56 07 73; 8 rue Henri Drussy; 9am-12.30pm & 2-6.30pm Mon-Sat, 10am-1pm & 6-7pm Sun Easter-Sep, 9.30am-12.30pm & 2-6pm Mon-Sat Oct-Christmas).

AROUND BLOIS

Château de Chambord

Chateaux don't get any grander than **Chambord** (☎ 02 54 50 50 20; www.chambord.org; adult/18-25yr/under 18yr €8.50/6/free; 9am-6.30pm May-Sep, to 5.30pm Oct-Apr, to 8.30pm 14 Jul-15 Aug, ticket sales end 45min before closing), constructed from 1519 by François I as a lavish base for hunting game in the nearby Sologne forests, but eventually used for just 42 days during the king's entire 32-year reign (1515–47).

The chateau's most famous feature is the double-helix staircase, attributed by some to Leonardo da Vinci, who lived in Amboise (34km southwest) from 1516 until his death three years later. The Italianate rooftop terrace, surrounded by a maze of cupolas, domes, chimneys and slate roofs, was where the royal court assembled to watch military exercises, tournaments and hunting parties returning at the end of the day.

A 1½-hour **audioguide** (€4) is available, and from June to August, 1½-hour **guided tours** (€4) in English are held once or twice a day. Free *son et lumière* (sound and light) shows, known as **Les Clairs de Lune**, are projected onto the chateau's façade nightly from July to mid-September.

GETTING THERE & AWAY

Chambord is 16km east of Blois, 45km southwest of Orléans and 17km northeast of Cheverny. For details on buses see left.

Château de Cheverny

Cheverny (☎ 02 54 79 96 29; www.chateau-cheverny.fr; adult/student/7-14yr €6.50/4.50/3.50; 9.15am-6.45pm Jul & Aug, to 6.15pm Apr-Jun & Sep, 9.45am-5pm or 5.30pm Oct-Mar), built between 1625 and 1634, is the region's most magnificently furnished chateau, renowned for its opulently appointed rooms and salons – epecially the Chambre du Roi (King's Bedroom), the Grand Salon, and the 1st-floor dining room, where 34 painted wood panels illustrate the story of *Don Quijote*. Across the lawn behind the chateau is the 18th-century Orangerie, where Leonardo da Vinci's *Mona Lisa* was hidden during WWII.

Cheverny is 16km southeast of Blois and 17km southwest of Chambord. For information on the bus from Blois see left.

Château de Chaumont

It's a brisk climb up to **Château de Chaumont-sur-Loire** (☎ 02 54 51 26 26; adult/18-25yr/under 18yr €6.50/4.50/free; 9.30am-6.30pm 8 May–mid-Sep, 10am-5pm mid-Sep–7 May, no ticket sales 12.30-1.30pm Oct-Mar, ticket sales end 30min before closing), set on a bluff overlooking the Loire. The entrance, across a wooden drawbridge between two wide towers, opens onto an inner courtyard from where there are stunning views. Opposite the main entrance are the luxurious stables, built in 1877. The chateau will be closed for several months in early 2007.

GETTING THERE & AWAY

Chaumont-sur-Loire is on the Loire's south bank 17km southwest of Blois and 20km northeast of Amboise.

Onzain, 2km across the Loire from Chaumont, is on the Orléans–Tours train line. Frequent trains go to Blois (€2.90, 10 minutes, 10 to 20 daily) and Tours (€6.90, 35 minutes, 11 to 22 daily).

The Chaumont-sur-Loire **tourist office** (☎ 02 54 20 91 73; 24 rue du Maréchal Leclerc; 🕒 9.30am-12.30pm & 2-7pm Mon-Sat May-Sep, plus Sun & holidays Jun-Aug, to 12.30pm & 1.30-5pm or 5.30pm, closed Sun & holidays Feb-Apr & Oct-late Dec) rents bikes for €5/10 per half-/full day.

TOURS

pop 270,000

Lively Tours has the cosmopolitan, bourgeois air of a miniature Paris, with wide 18th-century avenues, formal public gardens, café-lined boulevards and a thriving university with 25,000 students. The French spoken in Tours is said to be the purest in France.

Orientation & Information

The focal point is place Jean Jaurès, where the city's major thoroughfares – rue Nationale, blvd Heurteloup, av de Grammont and blvd Béranger – meet. The train station is 300m east of place Jean Jaurès. The old city is centred on place Plumereau, 400m west of rue Nationale.

For the local low-down head for the **tourist office** (☎ 02 47 70 37 37; www.ligeris.com; 78-82 rue Bernard Palissy; 🕒 8.30am-7pm Mon-Sat, 10am-12.30pm & 2.30-5pm Sun & holidays mid-Apr–mid-Oct, 9am-12.30pm & 1.30-6pm Mon-Sat, 10am-1pm Sun & holidays mid-Oct–mid-Apr).

Sights

In an impressive 17th- to 18th-century archbishop's palace, the **Musée des Beaux-Arts** (☎ 02 47 05 68 73; 18 place François Sicard; adult/student/under 13yr €4/2/free; 🕒 9am-12.45pm & 2-6pm Wed-Mon) has an excellent collection of paintings, furniture and objets d'art from the 14th to 20th centuries.

Tours' Gothic-style **Cathédrale St-Gatien** (🕒 9am-7pm) dates from the 13th to 16th centuries, although the domed tops of the two 70m-high towers are from the Renaissance. The cathedral's interior is renowned for its 13th- to 15th-century stained-glass windows.

The city's archaeological museum, **Musée de l'Hôtel Goüin** (☎ 02 47 66 22 32; 25 rue du Commerce; adult/child €3.50/3; 🕒 9.30am-12.30pm & 1.15-6.30pm Apr-Sep, to 12.30pm & 2-5.30pm Oct-Mar), is housed in an impressive Renaissance residence built for a wealthy merchant around 1510.

About 1.6km west of place Jean Jaurès, the **Jardin Botanique** (blvd Tonnelle; admission free; 🕒 7.45am-sunset) has a tropical greenhouse, medicinal herb garden and petting zoo. There are also emus and kangaroos bouncing around. To get there, it's a short walk or take Bus 4 along blvd Béranger.

Sleeping

Auberge de Jeunesse du Vieux Tours (☎ 02 47 37 81 58; www.ajtours.org, in French; 5 rue Bretonneau; s, d or tr per person incl breakfast €17; 🕒 reception 8am-noon & 5-10pm Oct-Mar, 8am-noon & 6-11pm Apr-Sep; 💻) A well-equipped, 146-room hostel near the old town. There are eight kitchens for cooking and three lounges for hanging out – you can also rent bikes (€10 per day) or for that extra touch of luxury, your very own minifridge (€0.50 a day).

Hôtel Val de Loire (☎ 02 47 05 37 86; hotel.val.de.loire@club-Internet.fr; 33 blvd Heurteloup; s/d €33/42,with hand basin €22/31) This two-star hotel, in a bourgeois home built in 1870, has heaps of charm. The ceilings get lower the higher up you go but all the rooms boast real parquet floors and antique furniture.

Hôtel du Cygne (☎ 02 47 66 66 41; http://perso.wanadoo.fr/hotelcygne.tours; 6 rue du Cygne; d €44-74; P) A pretty 18-room hotel on a quiet side street, with wooden-shuttered windows, blooming flowerboxes, high ceilings and the odd chandelier.

Hôtel Mondial (☎ 02 47 05 62 68; www.hotelmondialtours.com; 3 place de la Résistance; s/d from €46/50) A postwar two-star option with 19 immaculate, carpeted rooms overlooking a public square. There's a sunny room on the 2nd floor to enjoy the buffet breakfast.

Eating

In the old city, place Plumereau, rue du Grand Marché and rue de la Rôtisserie are loaded with restaurants and cafés. Further east, cheap eats are available along rue Colbert.

Comme Autre Fouée (☎ 02 47 05 94 78; 11 rue de la Monnaie; lunch menu €10, other menu from €16-19.50; 🕒 lunch Fri & Sat, dinner Tue-Sat, lunch Tue-Thu mid-May–mid-Sep) Comme Autre Fouée specialises in *fouée* (or *fouaces*), an age-old regional speciality that is created by baking a small, flat disc of dough in a wood-fired oven. Served piping hot, these minipitta breads are then filled with pork *rillettes*, *haricots blancs* (butterbeans) or fresh goat's cheese. When in doubt, *fouée* make a hearty, all-you-can-eat meal.

Le Bœuf' Salad (☎ 02 47 66 70 58; 19 rue du Grand Marché; menu €14-22; 🕒 sometimes closed Tue & Wed)

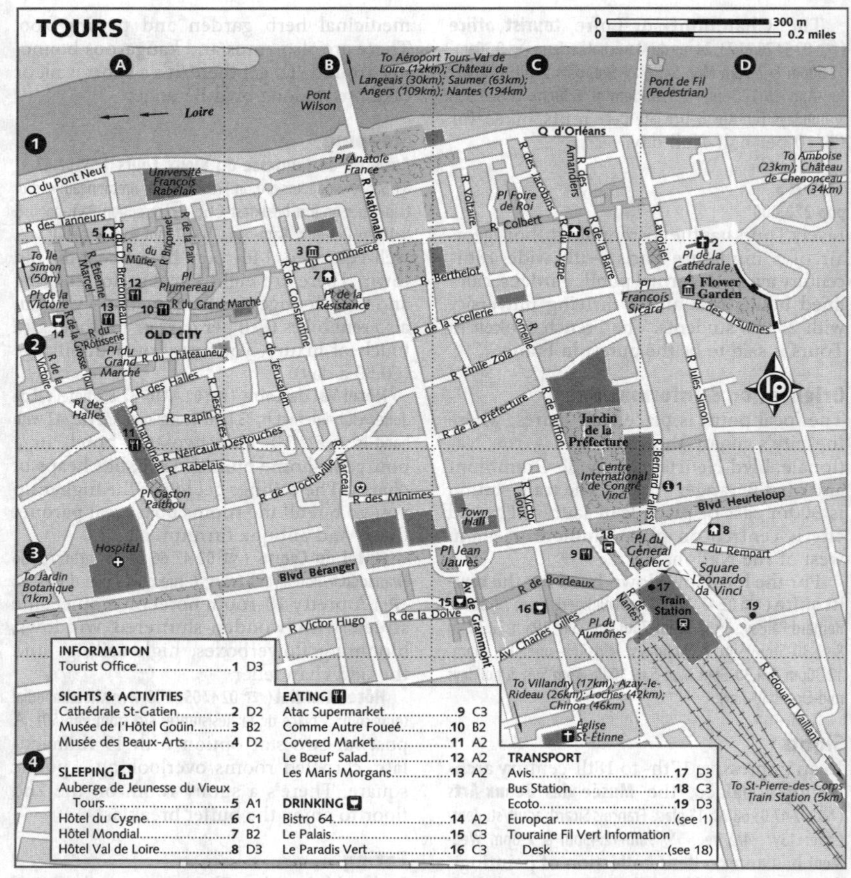

An informal French eatery, decked out in white and blue, serving Tours' cheapest steak-and-fries platter (€7, available October to May).

Les Maris Morgans (☎ 02 47 64 95 34; 6 rue de la Rôtisserie; menu €16-29; ⏰ dinner Thu-Tue) This innovative eatery specialises in meat and fish dishes that you cook yourself on a *pierre chaude* (hot rock); and *bisquines*, a creamy seafood smorgasbord served on a cork platter.

The best place for fresh produce is **Les Halles** (covered market; place Gaston Pailhou; ⏰ 7am-7pm). General supplies are sold at two **Atac supermarkets** (place du Général Leclerc ⏰ 7.30am-8pm Mon-Sat; place Jean Jaurès **shopping arcade**; ⏰ 9am-7.30pm Mon-Sat).

Drinking & Entertainment

The old town is full of bars – a good starting point is place Plumereau, which fills to bursting in the summer, and nearby rue du Grand Marché.

Le Palais (☎ 02 47 61 48 54; 15 place Jean Jaurès; ⏰ 7am-2am, closed Sun Nov-Mar) Every Monday night, this trendy bar-brasserie hosts a *café des langues,* where you can chat to linguistically motivated locals in English (and lots of other languages).

Bistro 64 (64 rue du Grand Marché; ⏰ 11am-2am Mon-Sat) An intimate bar choked with smoke from cigarettes and the candles on the tiny tables. Jazz usually provides the background score, although there's live music on Thursday nights.

Le Paradis Vert (☎ 02 47 66 00 94; 9 rue Michelet; adult/student billiard table per hr €10/8; 🕑 10am-2am) France's largest pool hall with 36 tables. The Monday night tournament (7.30pm to 1am) is open to all comers.

Getting There & Away

Aéroport Tours-Val de Loire (TUF; ☎ 02 47 49 37 00; www.tours-aeroport.com) is linked to London Stansted by Ryanair. A **shuttle bus** (€5) links Tours' bus station with all Ryanair flights.

Buses operated by **Touraine Fil Vert** (☎ 02 47 47 17 18; www.touraine-filvert.com, in French) serve destinations including Amboise (€2.10, 45 minutes, seven daily Monday to Saturday). There's an **information desk** (☎ 02 47 05 30 49; 🕑 7am-7pm Mon-Sat) at the bus station on place du Général Leclerc.

The regional train station is linked to St-Pierre-des-Corps, Tours' TGV train station, by frequent shuttle trains. Trains run 13 to 20 times a day between Tours and Orléans (€15.90, one to 1½ hours), stopping en route at Blois (€8.70, 35 minutes). SNCF lines go to Angers (€14.70, one hour, eight to 14 daily) and Chenonceau (€5.50, 30 minutes, four to six daily) as well as various other local destinations.

TGVs travel to Paris' Gare Montparnasse (€37.60 or €50.30, 1¼ hours, 13 to 15 daily), Bordeaux (€40.40, 2½ hours) and La Rochelle (€31.30, two to three hours). Slower corail services travel to Gare d'Austerlitz (€28.50, two to 2¾ hours, nine to 14 daily), Poitiers (€16.70 or €13.80, 40 to 60 minutes) and Nantes (€26.70 or €23.80, about two hours).

Car-rental companies include **Avis** (☎ 02 47 20 53 27), inside the train station; **Europcar** (☎ 02 47 64 47 76; 76 blvd Bernard Palissy); and **Ecoto** (☎ 02 47 66 75 00; www.ecoto.fr; 8 rue Marcel Tribut).

AROUND TOURS

Some of the Loire's finest **chateaux** can be visited on a day trip from Tours. The tourist office in Tours has details of *son et lumières* and other spectacles performed at the chateaux during summer.

With its moat, drawbridge, towers and turrets, the 16th-century **Château de Chenonceau** (☎ 08 20 20 90 90; www.chenonceau.com; adult/student & child €8/6.50; 🕑 9am-7pm mid-Mar–mid-Sep, to 4.30pm rest of year) is everything a fairy-tale castle should be, although the chateau's antique-stuffed interior is overshadowed by the glorious landscaped gardens that surround the castle. There's even a fabulous yew tree *labyrinthe* (maze) in which to get thoroughly lost.

The grand fortifications and turrets of the **Château Azay-le-Rideau** (☎ 02 47 45 42 04; adult/18-25yr/under 18yr €7.50/5/free; 🕑 9.30am-7pm Jul & Aug, to 6pm Apr-Jun & Sep, 10am-12.15pm & 2-5.15pm Oct-Mar) were designed to indicate the rank and prestige of the castle's owners. The chateau's most impressive feature is an extraordinary staircase with ornamented loggias on each floor.

The crenellated **Chateau de Langeais** (☎ 02 47 96 72 60; adult/10-17yr/under 10yr €7.50/4/free; 🕑 9.30am-7pm Jul & Aug, to 6.30pm Feb-Jun & Sep–mid-Nov, 10am-5pm mid-Nov–Jan) is the most authentic of the valley's chateaux, with an atmospheric interior packed with period furnishings, tapestries and original 15th-century floor tiles. There's even a working drawbridge and a ruined 10th-century donjon (keep), thought to be the oldest in France.

Perched above the Vienne River, the mostly ruined medieval **Château de Chinon** (☎ 02 47 93 13 45; adult/student €6/4.50; 🕑 9am-7pm Apr-Sep, 9.30am-5pm Oct-Mar), consists of three sections separated by waterless moats: the 12th-century Fort St-Georges, the Château du Milieu (the Middle Castle), and, at the western tip, the 13th-century Fort du Coudray. Superb views are on offer from the 14th-century clock tower, and four of the castle's rooms are dedicated to Joan of Arc, who in 1429 picked out Charles VII from among a crowd of courtiers in the *Salle du Trône* (Throne Room).

Getting There & Away

Many chateaux are accessible by train or SNCF bus from Tours, including Chenonceau, Villandry, Azay-le-Rideau, Langeais, Amboise, Chaumont, Chinon and Saumur, but touring the chateaux by public transport can be slow and expensive.

An organised bus tour is a better option. There are several operators offering English-language tours of the main chateaux; typical prices are €18 to €31 for a half-day trip in a minibus for up to eight people. Stops at each chateau last between 45 minutes and one hour, and you'll usually be entitled to discounted entry fees if you're part of an organised group. Reservations can be made at the Tours tourist office.

Acco-Dispo (☎ 06 82 00 64 51; www.accodispo-tours.com)
Quart de Tours (☎ 06 85 72 16 22; www.quartdetours.com)
Services Touristiques de Touraine (STT; ☎ 02 47 05 46 09; www.stt-millet.fr) Runs full-sized coaches for individuals rather than groups from April to mid-October.
St-Eloi Excursions (☎ 02 47 37 08 04; www.saint-eloi.com)

AMBOISE

pop 11,000

The picturesque town of Amboise, nestling under its fortified chateau on the southern bank of the Loire River, reached its peak during the decades around 1500, when luxury-loving Charles VIII enlarged the chateau and François I held raucous parties there. These days the town makes the most of its association with Leonardo da Vinci, who lived out his last years here under the patronage of François I.

Amboise makes a convenient base for visiting the chateaux between Tours and Blois.

The **tourist office** (☎ 02 47 57 09 28; www.amboise-valdeloire.com; 🕒 9.30am-1pm & 2-6pm Mon-Sat, 10am-1pm & 2-6pm Sun Apr-Jun & Sep, 9am-8pm Mon-Sat & 10am-6pm Sun Jul & Aug, 10am-1pm & 2-6pm Mon-Sat & 10am-1pm sometimes Sun Oct-Mar) stocks maps for walking (*Balades Royales,* €4) and cycling (*5 Circuits Vélos,* €2) and supplies a free English-language brochure for a walking tour of Amboise.

Amboise's **royal chateau** (☎ 02 47 57 00 98; place Michel Debré; adult/15-25yr/7-14yr €8/7/5; 🕒 9am-7pm Jul & Aug, 9am-6pm or 6.30pm mid-Mar–Jun, Sep & Oct, 9am-noon & 2-4.45pm Nov–mid-Mar) sits high above town on a rocky outcrop, affording panoramic views of the town and the Loire.

Charles VIII (r 1483–98), who was born and brought up here, enlarged the chateau in 1492 after a visit to Italy that left him deeply impressed by that country's artistic creativity and luxurious lifestyle. Today, just a few of the chateau's 15th- and 16th-century structures survive, including the Flamboyant Gothic Chapelle St-Hubert, said to be the final resting place of Leonardo da Vinci; and the Salle des États (Estates Hall), where a group of Protestant conspirators were tried before being hanged from the balcony in 1560.

Leonardo da Vinci came to Amboise in 1516 at the invitation of François I. Until his death three years later at the age of 67, he lived and worked at **Le Clos Lucé** (☎ 02 47 57 00 73; www.vinci-closluce.com; 2 rue du Clos Lucé; adult/student/6-15yr Apr–mid-Nov €12/9.50/7, mid-Nov–Mar €9/7/6; 🕒 9am-8pm Jul & Aug, 9am-7pm Apr, Jun, Sep & Oct, 9am-6pm Nov, Dec, Feb & Mar, 9am-5pm Jan, ticket sales end 1hr before closing), a brick manor house that now houses scale models of his inventions, including a proto-automobile, armoured tank, parachute and hydraulic turbine.

Sleeping

Camping Municipal de l'Île d'Or (☎ 02 47 57 23 37; Île d'Or; camp sites per adult/site €2.50/3.50; 🕒 Apr-early Oct) Has trans-river views of the chateau; the municipal swimming pool is next door.

Centre Charles Péguy-Auberge de Jeunesse (☎ 02 47 30 60 90; www.mjcamboise.fr, in French; dm €11, bedding €4; 🕒 reception 2-8pm Mon-Fri, usually 5.30-7.30pm Sat & Sun) A smart, efficient 72-bed youth hostel on the Île d'Or, with rooms for one to six people.

Hôtel La Brèche (☎ 02 47 57 00 79; www.labreche-amboise.com; 26 rue Jules Ferry; d with breakfast €66; 🕒 Mar-Oct) Near the train station, this 14-room place is comfortable and full of charm. The owner is full of local knowledge.

Le Clos d'Amboise (☎ 02 47 30 10 20; www.leclosamboise.com; 27 rue Rabelais; r €79-170; 🕒 closed late Nov–mid-Feb; 🅿) This grand 17th-century ecclesiastical residence boasts a tranquil walled garden and a fantastic selection of lavishly appointed rooms.

Château de Pintray (☎ 02 47 23 22 84; www.chateau-de-pintray.com; d with breakfast €96) Six kilometres west of Amboise in Lussault-sur-Loire, this small 16th-century chateau has five traditionally furnished rooms and a delightful garden. You can taste and buy wines produced on the estate.

Eating

The southern side of place Michel Debré is lined with eateries; more restaurants and food shops line rue Nationale.

L'Épicerie (☎ 02 47 57 08 94; 46 place Michel Debré; lunch menu €11, dinner menu €19.50-37.50; 🕒 Wed-Sun, also open Mon & Tue Jul-Sep, closed late Oct–mid-Dec) A quaint little restaurant with traditional French dishes, including *tournedos de canard aux baies poivrées* (duck breast in a sauce of pink peppercorns and red Chinon wine, €16.50).

Le Pavillon des Lys (☎ 02 47 30 01 01; 9 rue d'Orange; menu €22-33; 🕒 closed Tue Dec-Feb; ⊠) An elegant French restaurant which makes the perfect end to a hard day of chateau sightseeing.

Self-caterers can head for the **Marché Plus supermarket** (5 quai du Général de Gaulle; 7am-9pm Mon-Sat, 10am-2pm Sun) or the **open-air food market** (8am-1pm Fri & Sun).

Getting There & Away

Touraine Fil Vert's line C1 links Amboise's post office with Tours' bus terminal (€2.10, 45 minutes, seven daily Monday to Saturday).

The **train station** (blvd Gambetta), across the river from the town centre, is served by trains from Paris' Gare d'Austerlitz (€24.20, 2¼ to three hours, 11 daily), Blois (€5.60, 20 minutes, 10 to 20 daily) and Tours (€4.50, 15 minutes, 10 to 20 daily).

Hire mountain bikes at **Cycles Richard** (02 47 57 01 79; 2 rue de Nazelles; per day €15; 9am-noon & 2.30-7pm Tue-Sat).

SOUTHWESTERN FRANCE

Though the Côte d'Azur is the most popular beach spot in France, the many seaside resorts along the Atlantic Coast are fast catching up. If you're a surf-nut or a beach bum, then the sandy bays around Biarritz and Bayonne will be right up your alley, while oenophiles can sample the fruits of the vine in the high temple of French wine-making, Bordeaux. Towards the Pyrenees you'll find the Basque Country, which in many ways is closer to the culture of northern Spain than to the rest of France.

NANTES

pop 550,000

Spirited and innovative, the university city of Nantes is France's sixth-largest metropolis. In the 18th century Nantes was France's foremost port, and in the 19th – following the abolition of slavery – it was a cutting-edge industrial centre. The shipyards have been relocated to St-Nazaire, but Nantes is enjoying a renaissance as a cultural hub, with plenty of museums, a lively biscuit factory–turned–cultural centre, and a museum in the city's magnificent medieval castle.

Orientation

On the Loire's northern bank, central Nantes' two main arteries, both served by tram lines, are the partly pedestrianised cours des 50 Otages and a broad east–west boulevard that connects the train station with quai de la Fosse. They intersect near the Gare Centrale bus/tram hub. The old city is to the east, between cours des 50 Otages and the Château des Ducs de Bretagne.

Information

Cyber City (02 40 89 57 92; 14 rue de Strasbourg; per hr €3; 10am-1am Mon-Sat, 11am-midnight Sun) Internet access.
Main post office (place de Bretagne)
Main tourist office (02 72 64 04 79; www.nantes-tourisme.com; cours Olivier de Clisson; 10am-6pm Mon-Wed, Fri & Sat, 10.30am-6pm Thu, closed Sun)
Tourist office annexe (2 place St-Pierre; 10am-1pm & 2-6pm Tue, Wed & Fri-Sun, 10.30am-1pm & 2-6pm Thu, closed Mon)

Sights

The **Château des Ducs de Bretagne** (Castle of the Dukes of Brittany; 02 51 17 49 00; adult/child each for museum/exhibitions €5/3 or for both €8/5, admission to grounds free; 9am-7pm mid-May–mid-Sep, 10am-6pm Wed-Mon mid-Sep–mid-May) has reopened after renovation, and houses a multimedia-rich museum covering the city's history.

Showcasing one of the finest collections of French paintings outside Paris, Nantes' **Musée des Beaux-Arts** (Fine Arts Museum; 02 51 17 45 00; 10 rue Georges Clemenceau; adult/child €3.50/2; 10am-6pm Wed-Mon, to 8pm Thu) displays works by Chagall, Monet, Picasso and Kandinsky.

Overlooking the river, the **Musée Jules Verne** (02 40 69 72 52; www.julesverne.nantes.fr, in French; 3 rue de l'Hermitage; adult/student & child €3/1.50; 10am-noon & 2-6pm Mon & Wed-Sat, 2-6pm Sun) is a magical place dedicated to the works of the great author, who was born in Nantes in 1828. Exhibits include first-edition books, manuscripts, and interactive displays.

Inside the Flamboyant Gothic **Cathédrale St-Pierre et St-Paul** (place St-Pierre), the tomb of François II (r 1458–88), duke of Brittany, and his second wife, Marguerite de Foix, is a masterpiece of Renaissance art.

The 19th-century **Jardin des Plantes** is one of the most exquisite botanical gardens in France and makes a beautiful spot for a stroll or an afternoon picnic.

Sleeping

Auberge de Jeunesse La Manu (02 40 29 29 20; nanteslamanu@fuaj.org; 2 place de la Manu; dm incl breakfast €15; early Jan-late Dec;) About 600m east of the train station's northern entrance in a converted factory, this well-equipped hostel is a 15-minute walk from the centre. Take tram 1 to the Manufacture stop.

Hôtel St-Daniel (☎ 02 40 47 41 25; www.hotel-saintdaniel.com; 4 rue du Bouffay; s €32-40, d €45, tr & q €50; ⊠) Peacefully situated overlooking the St-Croix church courtyard in the heart of the old town, this clean, cheery place has a variety of well-priced rooms.

Hôtel Renova (☎ 02 40 47 57 03; 11 rue Beauregard; www.hotel-renova.com; s €34-43, d €38-48, tr & q €55; ⊠) There are six steep mosaic-tiled flights of stairs at this narrow hotel of 24 rooms which has an absolutely superstar location in a pedestrianised street in the old city.

Hôtel Pommeraye (☎ 02 40 48 78 79; www.hotel-pommeraye.com; 2 rue Boileau; s €45-64, d €53-84; 💻) Sleek and chic, the colourful rooms at this boutique place on the corner of Nantes' smartest shopping street are sized like clothes (M, L, XL, XXL), with prices to match.

Hôtel des Colonies (☎ 02 40 48 79 76; www.hotel descolonies.fr; 5 rue du Chapeau Rouge; s €56-64, d €63-71; ⊠ 💻) Local art exhibitions are displayed in the lobby of this cherry-red place, and upstairs you'll find snazzy rooms decked out with boldly coloured walls and boxy resin light fittings.

Hôtel La Pérouse (☎ 02 40 89 75 00; www.hotel-la perouse.fr; 3 allée Duquesne; s €81-95, d €91-133; ⊠ ❄ 💻) Styled to reflect the city's shipbuilding traditions, this stunning pad is Nantes' hottest choice for design-conscious travellers, with 46 rooms kitted out with zigzag chairs, canvas curtains, and glass sinks.

Eating

Nantes' most cosmopolitan dining is in the medieval Bouffay quarter. Breton creperies are plentiful throughout town. West of cours des 50 Otages, rue Jean-Jacques Rousseau and rue Santeuil are lined with eateries.

Ma Saison Préfeŕe (☎ 02 40 47 13 12; 10 rue de Chateaux; dishes €6-7; 🕑 10am-8pm Mon-Sat) Though not exclusively vegetarian, this little lemon-and-lime-coloured hole in the wall is a great place for homemade vegetable tarts and lasagnes.

Rêve Marins (☎ 02 40 47 00 96; 2 rue du Roi Albert; mains €7.50-12; 🕑 lunch & dinner Tue-Sat) This much-lauded place combines classic crepes and buckwheat *galettes* with very un-classic fillings like chicken curry, or kangaroo and Muscadet grapes.

Brasserie La Cigale (☎ 02 51 84 94 94; 4 place Graslin; mains €7.50-14, brunch €20; 🕑 7.30am-12.30am) No visit to Nantes is complete without a coffee, cake or all-out feast at this Art Nouveau showpiece, with several salons decorated by 1890s gilded tile work and frescoed ceilings.

Le Bistrot de l'Écrivain (☎ 02 51 84 15 15; 15 rue Jean Jacques Rousseau; menu €17; 🕑 lunch & dinner Mon-Sat) With checked-clothed tables and wine bottles lining the walls, Le Bistrot de l'Écrivain serves authentic Nantaise cuisine like *sandre au beurre blanc* (pike in white sauce).

Sardines are sold at street stalls throughout town between March and November.

Stock up on supplies at the huge marketplace, **Marché de Talensac** (rue Talensac; 🕑 7.30am-1pm Tue-Sun), **Monoprix supermarket** (2 rue du Calvaire; 🕑 9am-9pm Mon-Sat), or the basement at **Galeries Lafayette** (rue de la Marne; 🕑 9am-7.30pm Mon-Sat).

Drinking

La Maison (☎ 02 40 37 04 12; 4 rue Lebrun; 🕑 3pm-2am) You have to see to believe this trip of a place, decorated room by room like a home furnished in *bad* 1970s taste.

Café Cult (☎ 02 40 47 18 49; www.lecult.com; place du Change; 🕑 2pm-2am Mon & Sat, noon-2am Tue-Fri) Squeezed in a smoky half-timbered house bohemian Café Cult draws students.

Le Bar du Coin (☎ 02 40 47 55 05; 21 rue de la Juiverie; 🕑 11am-2am Apr-Oct, closed Sun Nov-Mar) This neighbourhood bar in the heart of the medieval Bouffay quarter is where most Nantais nights out get started.

Entertainment

Listings of cultural events appear in *Nantes Poche* and *Pil'* (both €0.50). *Le Mois Nantais*, available at the tourist office and *tabacs*, has day-by-day details of cultural events. Good what's-on websites include www.leboost.com, in French. The six-screen **Cinéma Katorza** (☎ 02 51 84 90 60; 3 rue Corneille) screens *v.o.* (*version originale;* foreign movies subtitled in French) films.

Getting There & Away

AIR

Aéroport Nantes-Atlantique International (NTE; ☎ 02 40 84 80 00; www.nantes.aeroport.fr) is 12km southeast of town. The public bus TAN-Air links the airport with the Gare Centrale bus/tram hub and the train station's southern entrance (€6, 20 minutes) from about 5.30am until 9pm.

BUS

The southbound **bus station** (☎ 08 25 08 71 56) is used by CTA buses serving areas of the Loire-Atlantique *département* south of the Loire River. The northbound **bus office** (☎ 08 25 08 71 56; 1 allée Duquesne, on cours des 50 Otages), run by Cariane Atlantique, handles buses to destinations north of the Loire.

Eurolines (☎ 02 51 72 02 03; allée de la Maison Rouge; 9.30am-12.30pm & 1.30-6pm Mon-Sat) has an office in town.

CAR

Budget, Europcar and Hertz are located outside the train station's southern entrance.

TRAIN

The **train station** (☎ 36 35; 27 blvd de Stalingrad) is well connected. Destinations include Paris' Gare Montparnasse (€49.10 to €61.40, 2¼ hours, 15 to 20 daily), Bordeaux (€37, four hours, three or four daily) and La Rochelle (€21, 1¾ hours, three or four daily).

Tickets and information are also available at the **SNCF ticket office** (La Bourse, 12 place de la Bourse; 10am-7pm Mon, 9am-7pm Tue-Sat).

Getting Around

The **TAN network** (☎ 08 01 44 44 44; www.tan.fr, in French) includes three modern tram lines that intersect at the Gare Centrale (Commerce), the main bus/tram transfer point. Buses run from 7.15am to 9pm. Night services continue until 12.30am.

Bus/tram tickets (€1.20) can be purchased from bus (but not tram) drivers and at tram-stop ticket machines. They're valid for one hour after being time-stamped. A 24-hour Ticket Journalier costs €3.30.

POITIERS

pop 120,000

The cobblestoned city of Poitiers is packed with history. Founded by the Pictones, a Gaulish tribe, and lexpanded by the Romans, Poitiers was the capital of Poitou, governed by the Counts of Poitiers in the Middle Ages. Poitiers has one of the oldest universities in France, first established in 1432 and a lynchpin of this city today.

Orientation & Information

The train station is 600m downhill (west) from the old city, which begins just north of Poitiers' main square, place du Maréchal Leclerc, and stretches northeast to Église Notre Dame la Grande. Rue Carnot heads south from place du Maréchal Leclerc.

The **tourist office** (☎ 05 49 41 21 24; www.ot-poitiers.fr; 45 place Charles de Gaulle; 10am-11pm Mon-Sat, to 6pm & 7-11pm Sun 21 Jun-Aug, to 10pm Mon-Sat, to 6pm & 7-10pm Sun 1-17 Sep, to 6pm Mon-Sat 18 Sep-20 Jun) is near Église Notre Dame. Check your email at **Virtual 86** (☎ 05 49 53 63 42; 13 rue Magenta; per 15min/1hr €0.50/2; 10am-2am daily).

Sights

Strolling Poitiers' streets is the best way to get a feel for the city's past. Along the footpaths, red, yellow, and blue lines correspond with three **self-guided walking tours** detailed on a free map handed out by the tourist office.

The earliest parts of the **Église Notre Dame la Grande** (place Charles de Gaulle; 8.30am-7pm Mon-Sat, 2-7pm Sun) date from the 11th century, while the chapels were added in the 15th and 16th centuries. A few 12th- or 13th-century frescoes can be seen on the U-shaped dome above the choir.

The 13th century stained-glass window of the Crucifixion at the **Cathédrale St-Pierre** (rue de la Cathédrale; 8am-6pm) is among the oldest in France.

The **Musée Ste-Croix** (☎ 05 49 41 07 53; www.musees-poitiers.org; 3 rue Jean Jaurès; adult/child €3.50/free; 1.15-6pm Mon, 10am-noon & 1.15-6pm Tue-Fri, to noon & 2-6pm Sat & Sun Jun-Sep, 2-5pm Mon-Sun Oct-May) has exhibits on the history of Poitou from prehistoric times to the 19th century.

Sleeping & Eating

Hôtel Central (☎ 05 49 01 79 79; www.centralhotel86.com; 35 place du Maréchal Leclerc; d €34-51) Facing directly onto place du Maréchal, this two-star place is a terrific bargain, with snug, sunlit rooms and a handy lift.

Hôtel de l'Europe (☎ 05 49 88 12 00; www.hotel-europe-poitiers.com; 39 rue Carnot; d €49.50-79; P) This elegant hotel, with its sweeping staircase, oversized rooms and refined furnishings, dates from 1710. The annexe has modern rooms for the same price.

Le Grand Hôtel (☎ 05 49 60 90 60; www.grandhotelpoitiers.fr; 28 rue Carnot; s €65.50-68, d €80.50-83; P) Poitiers' premier hotel certainly lives up to its name. Faux Art Deco furnishings and fittings fill the public areas with character, and rooms are spacious and well-equipped.

Aux 40 Gourmands (☎ 05 49 37 01 37; 40 rue Carnot; mains €10.50-12.50; lunch & dinner Tue-Sat)

FRANCE

This relaxed place serves sumptuous *moules et frites* (mussels and fries); try them with crème fraîche and Pineau des Charentes, a sweet white wine with a Cognac base.

La Serrurerie (☎ 05 49 41 05 14; 28 rue des Grandes Écoles; mains €11-16, weekend brunch €14.50; ⌚ 8am-2am) Decked out with mosaics, steel balustrades and retro toys, this vibrant bistro-bar is Poitier's communal lounge/dining room. Specialities include pastas and a *crème brûlée* you'll be dreaming about for days.

The covered **Marché Notre Dame** (⌚ 7am-1pm Tue-Sat) is next to Église Notre Dame la Grande; an open-air market is held outside from 7am to 1pm on Saturdays. The **Monoprix supermarket** (⌚ 9am-7.30pm Mon-Sat) is across from 29 rue du Marché Notre Dame (behind the Palais de Justice).

Getting There & Away

The **train station** (☎ 08 36 35 35 35; blvd du Grand Cerf) has links to Bordeaux (€30.30, 1¾ hours), La Rochelle (€19.30, 80 minutes), Nantes (€24.40, 3¼ hours) and other cities. TGV tickets from Paris' Gare Montparnasse (1½ hours, 12 daily) cost from €46.40.

AROUND POITIERS

Piercing the countryside with gleaming domes, pods and towers, **Futuroscope** (☎ 05 49 49 30 80; www.futuroscope.com; Jaunay-Clan; adult 1 day/2 days €31/59, under 16 €24/44; ⌚ 10am-approx 10pm, closed Jan-early Feb) is a futuristic theme park with 22 whizz-bang attractions. Schedules change annually, as do many of the attractions – present highlights include **Digitalworld**, an action-packed 3D trip; **Zoo Safari**, starring a giant robotic giraffe; and **Cosmos**, a trip through the solar system and beyond. Allow at least five hours to see the major attractions.

Futuroscope is 10km north of Poitiers in Jaunay-Clan. TGV trains link the park's TGV station with Paris (from €46.40, 1½ hours) and Bordeaux (€31.20, 1¾ hours).

Local **STP buses** (☎ 05 49 44 66 88) Nos 9, 16 and 17 (€1.20, 30 minutes) link Futuroscope (Parc de Loisirs stop) with Poitiers' train station; there are hourly buses from 6.15am until 7.30pm or 9pm.

LA ROCHELLE

pop 120,000

Known as *La Ville Blanche* (White City), La Rochelle's luminous limestone façades are topped by 14th- and 15th-century towers glowing white in the bright coastal sunlight.

One of France's foremost seaports from the 14th to 17th centuries, La Rochelle is now a pleasure port and sailing centre, and boasts one of the largest marinas in the country. The city's arcaded walkways, half-timbered houses and ghoulish gargoyles are reminders of La Rochelle's seafaring past.

Orientation & Information

La Rochelle is centred on the Vieux Port (Old Port). The old city unfolds to its north. To the southeast, the train station is linked to the Vieux Port by the av du Général de Gaulle, with the tourist office tucked in the Le Gabut quarter halfway between.

The **post office** (6 rue de l'Hôtel de Ville) has exchange services and a Cyberposte. The **tourist office** (☎ 05 46 41 14 68; larochelle-tourisme.com; Le Gabut; ⌚ 9am-8pm Mon-Sat, 11am-5.30pm Sun Jul & Aug; 9am-7pm Mon-Sat, 11am-5pm Sun Jun & Sep; 10am-12.30pm & 1.30-6pm Mon-Sat, 10am-1pm Sun Oct-May) sells the *Pass Rochelais*, offering discounts on public transport, sights and activities. The Internet café, **Akromicro** (☎ 05 46 34 07 94; rue de l'Aimable Nanette; per hr €2; ⌚ 10am-midnight), is behind the tourist office.

Sights & Activities

An enormous defensive chain used to be stretched between the two 14th-century stone towers at the harbour entrance. **Tour de la Chaîne** and **Tour St-Nicolas** both have fine views across the harbour.

West of Tour de la Chaîne, the medieval wall leads to the steeple-topped, 15th-century **Tour de la Lanterne** – look closely and you might spot some graffiti carved by English privateers held here during the 18th century.

The three **towers** (☎ 05 46 34 11 81; admission per tower adult/18-25yr/child €5/3.50/free; ⌚ 10am-7pm Jul & Aug, to 12.30pm & 2-6.30pm 15 May-Jun & 1-15 Sep, to 12.30pm & 2-5.30pm Tue-Sun Oct-May) can be visited individually or on a combined ticket (€10/6.50).

La Rochelle's state-of-the-art **Aquarium** (☎ 05 46 34 00 00; adult/student & child €12.50/10, with audioguide €16/13; ⌚ 9am-11pm Jul & Aug, to 8pm Apr-Jun & Sep, 10am-8pm Oct-Mar) is home to fish, sea flora and some mean-looking bull sharks.

The flat **Île de Ré**, 9km west of La Rochelle, boasts 70km of coastline, including lots of fine-sand beaches (one or two of which are favourite spots for local naturists). Its western half curves around the Fier d'Ars, a bay lined with *marais salants* (salt evaporation pools), saltwater marshes and a bird reserve, **Lilleau des Niges**. Year-round, **Rébus** (☎ 05 46 09 20 15) runs buses from La Rochelle (the train station car park, Tour de la Grosse Horloge and place de Verdun) to all the major towns on the island.

Sleeping

Camping du Soleil (☎ 05 46 44 42 53; av Marillac; camp sites per adult/tent €8.50/8.50; ⌚ late Jun-late Sep) This is the closest camping ground to the city. Take bus 10 to get there.

Centre International de Séjour-Auberge de Jeunesse (☎ 05 46 44 43 11; www.fuaj-aj-larochelle.fr.st; av des Minimes; dm incl breakfast €14-16, tw incl breakfast €34; ⌚ closed Christmas period) This popular hostel is 2km southwest of the train station in Les Minimes.

Hôtel Terminus Vieux Port (☎ 05 46 50 69 69; www.tourisme-francais.com/hotel/terminus; 7 rue de la Fabrique; d €46-68; Ⓟ) Bedecked with navy-blue awnings, this welcoming hotel has 32 freshly renovated rooms, each named after one of the islands offshore from La Rochelle.

Hôtel La Marine (☎ 05 46 50 51 63; www.hotel-marine.com, in French; 30 quai Duperré; d €55-95; ⊠) For captivating views of La Rochelle's iconic towers, try for rooms 1, 6, 9 or 13 of this exquisite boutique hotel in the northwest corner of the Vieux Port. Each of the 13 rooms is individually fitted out with cool décor and smart designer furniture.

Hôtel François 1er (☎ 05 46 41 28 46; www.hotelfrancois1er.fr; 15 rue Bazoges; d €60-106; Ⓟ) A number of 15th and 16th century French kings stayed in this building set back behind a cobbled courtyard. The 40 rooms are atmospheric if a bit heavy handed with the heritage décor. King-size rooms cost proportionately more.

Eating

Teatro Bettini (☎ 05 46 41 07 03; 3 rue Thiers; mains from €9.50; ⌚ lunch & dinner Tue-Sat) Part Italian diner, part Rochelais restaurant, this decades-old eatery is an old favourite for hearty lasagne and seafood.

Café de la Paix (☎ 05 46 41 39 79; 54 rue Chaudrier; mains €11-20; ⌚ 7am-10pm Mon-Sat) A *belle époque* brasserie-bar serving traditional cuisine including beef, fish and foie gras, as well as bountiful breakfasts and afternoon teas.

André (☎ 05 46 41 28 24; www.bar-andre.com; 8 place de la Chaîne; mains €15-30; ⌚ noon-4pm & 7pm-midnight) This renowned seafood place first opened in the 1950s as a small seafood café, and has now grown into a maze of interconnecting dining rooms, each with its own individual maritime ambience.

Le Comptoir des Voyages (☎ 05 46 50 62 60; www.coutanceau.com; 22 rue St-Jean du Perot; menu €26) This chic restaurant done out with rattan chairs, palms and red walls takes you on a stylish world tour of international flavours using the best regional produce.

The lively, 19th-century **covered market** (place du Marché; ⌚ 7am-1pm) seethes with stalls selling fresh fish, meat, fruit and vegetables.

In the old city there's a **Monoprix supermarket** (30-36 rue du Palais; ⌚ 8.30am-8pm Mon-Sat), and freshly-baked breads and pastries are available at **Boulangerie Fillon** (18 quai Louis Durand; ⌚ 6am-9pm Mon & Thu-Sat, 6am-8pm Tue, 6am-1pm Sun).

Getting There & Away

La Rochelle airport (LRH; ☎ 05 46 42 30 26; www.larochelle.aeroport.fr, in French), north of city centre off the N237, has flights to destinations throughout France as well as London Stansted (with Ryanair) and Southampton and Birmingham (with Flybe). Bus 7 runs from the airport to the town centre (€1.20).

From the bus station at place de Verdun, **Océcars** (☎ 05 46 00 95 15) runs services to regional destinations, including the Île de Ré.

Eurolines ticketing is handled by **Citram Littoral** (☎ 05 46 50 53 57; 30 cours des Dames; ⌚ closed Mon morning, Sat afternoon & Sun).

The **train station** (☎ 08 36 35 35 35) is linked by TGV to Paris' Gare Montparnasse (€57.60, three hours, five or six direct daily). Other destinations served by regular trains include Nantes (€22.30, two hours), Poitiers (€19.30, 1½ hours), and Bordeaux (€23.80, two hours).

Getting Around

The innovative public transport system, **RTCR** (☎ 05 46 34 02 22), has a main bus hub and **information office** (place de Verdun; ⌚ 7.30am-6.30pm Mon-Fri, 8am-6.30pm Sat). Most lines run until sometime between 7.15pm and 8pm. Tickets cost €1.20.

The city's distinctive yellow bikes can be rented at **Les Vélos Autoplus** (☎ 05 46 34 02 22; ⌚ 9am-7pm Jul & Aug, 9am-12.30pm & 1.30-7pm May, Jun & Sep, 9.15am-12.15pm & 1.50-6pm Mon-Sat Oct-Apr). The first two hours are free; after that bikes cost €1 per hour.

BORDEAUX

pop 735,000

The city long known as *La Belle Au Bois Dormant* (Sleeping Beauty) is well and truly awake after years of slumber. The millennium was a major turning point for Bordeaux, when former mayor, controversial ex–Prime Minister Alain Juppé roused this graceful city, pedestrianising its boulevards, restoring its neoclassical architecture, and implementing a hi-tech public transport system. These days, bolstered by its high-spirited student population, *La Belle* Bordeaux never seems to sleep at all.

Orientation

The city centre lies between the flower-filled place Gambetta and the Garonne River. From place Gambetta, place de Tourny is 500m northeast, from where the tourist office is 400m to the east. Bordeaux' train station, Gare St-Jean, is about 3km southeast of the city centre.

Information

Bordeaux Monumental (☎ 05 56 48 04 24; 28 rue des Argentiers; ⏲ 10am-1pm & 2-6pm Mon-Sat, 2-6pm Sun) Specialist tourist office dedicated to the city's history.

Cyberstation (☎ 05 56 01 15 15; 23 cours Pasteur; per hr €3; ⏲ 9.30am-2am Mon-Sat, 2pm-2am Sun) Internet café.

Main post office (37 rue du Château d'Eau) Currency exchange and Cyberposte.

Tourist office (☎ 05 56 00 66 00; www.bordeaux-tourisme.com; 12 cours du 30 Juillet; ⏲ 9am-7.30pm Mon-Sat, to 6.30pm Sun Jul & Aug, 9am-7pm Mon-Sat, 9.30am-6.30pm Sun May, Jun, Sep & Oct, 9am-6.30pm Mon-Sat, 9.45am-4.30pm Sun Nov-Apr) Runs city and regional tours, and sells the *Plan Guide du Patrimoine* (€1) with four walking itineraries around the city.

Train station tourist office (⏲ 9am-noon & 1-6pm Mon-Sat, 10am-noon & 1-3pm Sun May-Oct, 9.30am-12.30pm & 2-6pm Mon-Fri Nov-Apr).

Sights

Looming above the city is **Cathédrale St-André** (☎ 05 56 81 26 25; admission free; ⏲ 7.30am-6pm Tue-Fri, 9am-7pm Sat, 9am-6pm Sun, 2-6pm Mon). A Unesco World Heritage Site, the cathedral's oldest section dates from 1096, but it mostly dates from the 13th and 14th centuries. It's particularly renowned for its elaborate masonry carvings, best seen in the north portal. Behind the choir, the 50m-high belfry, 15th-century **Tour Pey-Berland**, has a panoramic view at the top of 232 narrow steps.

Bordeaux' museums have free entry for permanent collections; temporary exhibits cost €5 for adults and €2.50 for children.

Occidental art buffs can trace its evolution from the Renaissance to the mid-20th century at Bordeaux' exceptional **Musée des Beaux-Arts** (Museum of Fine Arts; ☎ 05 56 10 20 56; 20 cours d'Albret; ⏲ 11am-6pm Wed-Mon). More recent works are on display at the **Musée d'Art Contemporain** (Museum of Contemporary Art; ☎ 05 56 00 81 50; Entrepôt 7, rue Ferrére; ⏲ 11am-6pm Tue, Thu-Sun, to 8pm Wed), in a former colonial warehouse.

Gallo-Roman statues and prehistoric relics dating back 25,000 years are highlights of the impressive **Musée d'Aquitaine** (☎ 05 56 01 51 00; 20 cours Pasteur; ⏲ 11am-6pm Tue-Sun).

Exquisite faïence pottery, porcelain, gold, iron, glasswork and furniture are displayed at the **Musée des Arts Décoratifs** (Museum of Decorative Arts; ☎ 05 56 00 72 50; 39 rue Bouffard; ⏲ museum 2-6pm Wed-Mon, temporary exhibits from 11am Mon-Fri).

The landscaped **Jardin Public** (cours de Verdun), established in 1755 and laid out in the English style a century later, includes the meticulously catalogued **Jardin Botanique** (☎ 05 56 52 18 77; admission free; ⏲ 8.30am-6pm), founded in 1629 and at its present site since 1855; and the nearby **Musée d'Histoire Naturelle** (Natural History Museum; ☎ 05 56 48 29 86; ⏲ 11am-6pm Mon & Wed-Fri, 2-6pm Sat & Sun).

Pretty **place Gambetta**, a central open area ringed by shady benches, wasn't always so peaceful – during the Reign of Terror that followed the Revolution, a guillotine placed here severed the heads of 300 alleged counter-revolutionaries.

Sleeping

Auberge de Jeunesse (☎ 05 56 33 00 70; www.centres-animation.asso.fr; 22 cours Barbey; dm incl bedding & breakfast €20; ⊠ 💻) Bordeaux' only hostel is housed in a lino-and-glass building with a self-catering kitchen and four-bed dorms, each with their own bathroom.

Hôtel Boulan (☎ 05 56 52 23 62; fax 05 56 44 91 65; 28 rue Boulan; s €20-28, d €25-32) Situated on a secluded little side street, but still handy for a slew of Bordeaux' sights.

Hôtel Touring (☎ 05 56 81 56 73; le-touring@wanadoo.fr; 16 rue Huguerie; s €25-42, d €30-50, tr €57) This budget hotel run by a friendly family has impeccable rooms furnished with 1940s and '50s furniture including school-style desks and club chairs. The cheapest rooms have showers but share toilet facilities.

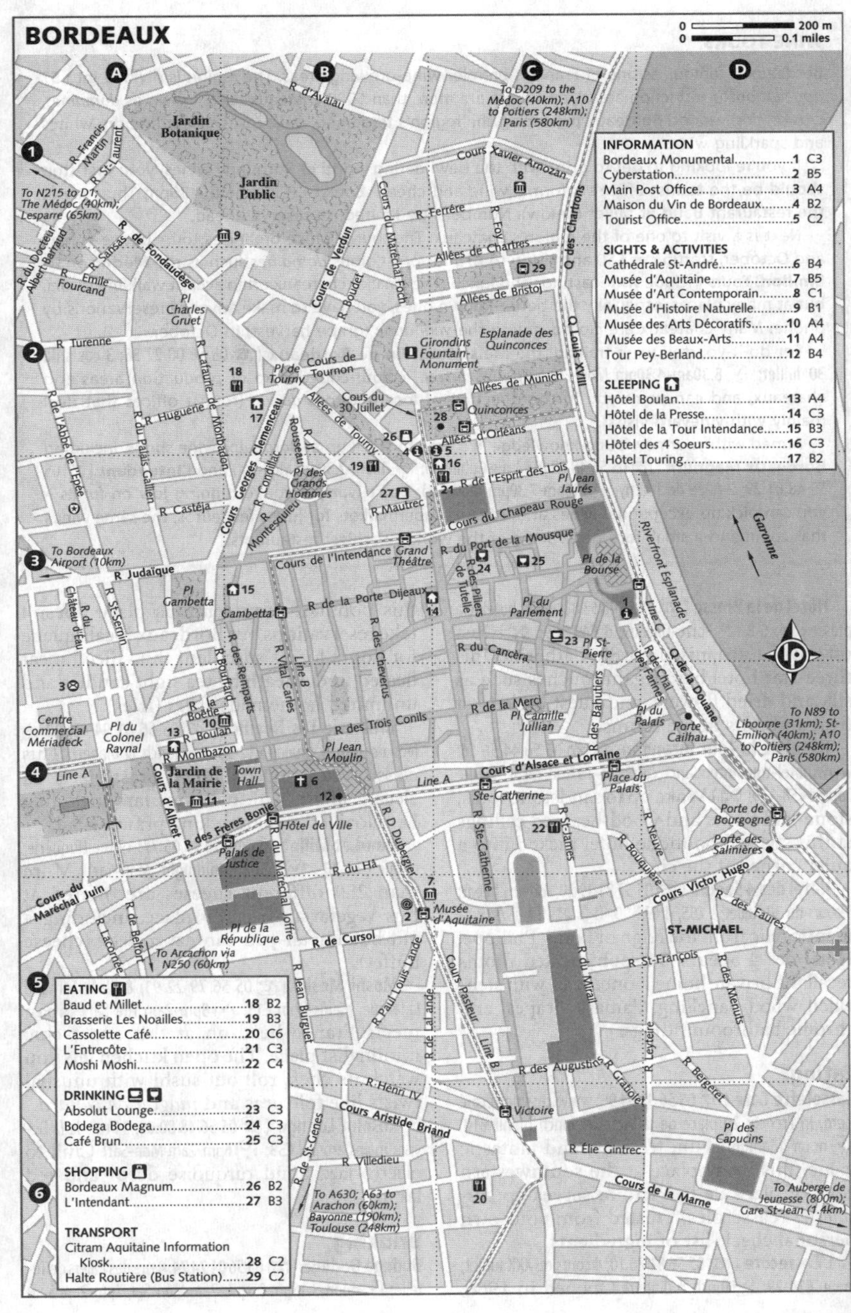
BORDEAUX
0 200 m
0 0.1 miles
A
B
C
D
1
2
3
4
5
6
INFORMATION
Bordeaux Monumental......1 C3
Cyberstation......2 B5
Main Post Office......3 A4
Maison du Vin de Bordeaux......4 B2
Tourist Office......5 C2
SIGHTS & ACTIVITIES
Cathédrale St-André......6 B4
Musée d'Aquitaine......7 B5
Musée d'Art Contemporain......8 C1
Musée d'Histoire Naturelle......9 B1
Musée des Arts Décoratifs......10 A4
Musée des Beaux-Arts......11 A4
Tour Pey-Berland......12 B4
SLEEPING
Hôtel Boulan......13 A4
Hôtel de la Presse......14 C3
Hôtel de la Tour Intendance......15 B3
Hôtel des 4 Soeurs......16 C3
Hôtel Touring......17 B2
EATING
Baud et Millet......18 B2
Brasserie Les Noailles......19 B3
Cassolette Café......20 C6
L'Entrecôte......21 C3
Moshi Moshi......22 C4
DRINKING
Absolut Lounge......23 C3
Bodega Bodega......24 C3
Café Brun......25 C3
SHOPPING
Bordeaux Magnum......26 B2
L'Intendant......27 B3
TRANSPORT
Citram Aquitaine Information Kiosk......28 C2
Halte Routière (Bus Station)......29 C2
Jardin Botanique
Jardin Public
To D209 to the Médoc (40km); A10 to Poitiers (248km); Paris (580km)
To N215 to D1; The Médoc (40km); Lesparre (65km)
To Bordeaux Airport (10km)
To N89 to Libourne (31km); St-Emilion (40km); A10 to Poitiers (248km); Paris (580km)
To Arcachon via N250 (60km)
To A630; A63 to Arachon (60km); Bayonne (190km); Toulouse (248km)
To Auberge de Jeunesse (800m); Gare St-Jean (1.4km)
Garonne
Riverfront Esplanade
Esplanade des Quinconces
Girondins Fountain-Monument
Quinconces
Grand Théâtre
Gambetta
Pl Gambetta
Pl de Tourny
Pl Charles Gruet
Pl des Grands Hommes
Pl Jean Jaurès
Pl de la Bourse
Pl du Parlement
Pl St-Pierre
Pl du Palais
Porte Cailhau
Pl Camille Jullian
Pl Jean Moulin
Pl du Colonel Raynal
Centre Commercial Mériadeck
Jardin de la Mairie
Town Hall
Hôtel de Ville
Palais de Justice
Pl de la République
Ste-Catherine
Place du Palais
Porte de Bourgogne
Porte des Salinières
ST-MICHAEL
Pl des Capucins
Victoire
Musée d'Aquitaine
Line A
Line B
Line C
Cours Xavier Arnozan
Cours de Verdun
Cours du Maréchal Foch
Q des Chartrons
Q Louis XVIII
Q de la Douane
Allées de Chartres
Allées de Bristol
Allées de Munich
Allées d'Orléans
Allées de Tourny
Cours de Tournon
Cours du 30 Juillet
Cours Georges Clemenceau
Cours de l'Intendance
Cours du Chapeau Rouge
Cours d'Alsace et Lorraine
Cours d'Albret
Cours du Maréchal Juin
Cours Victor Hugo
Cours Pasteur
Cours Aristide Briand
Cours de la Marne
R d'Avalau
R Francis Martin
R St-Laurent
R de Fondaudège
R du Docteur Albert Barraud
R Sansas
R Emile Fourcand
R Turenne
R Lafaurie de Monbadon
R Huguerie
R du Palais Gallien
R de l'Abbé de l'Epée
R Castéja
R Condillac
R Montesquieu
R JJ Rousseau
R Mautrec
R de l'Esprit des Lois
R du Port de la Mousque
R des Piliers de Tutelle
R Judaïque
R du Château d'Eau
R St-Sernin
R de la Porte Dijeaux
R des Remparts
R Bouffard
R Vital Carles
R des Cheverus
R du Cancéra
R de Chai des Farines
R des Bahutiers
R de la Merci
R des Trois Conils
R la Boëtie
R Boulan
R Montbazon
R des Frères Bonie
R du Maréchal Joffre
R D Dubergier
R Ste-Catherine
R St-James
R Neuve
R Bouquière
R des Faures
R du Hâ
R de Cursol
R de Belfort
R Lacornée
R Jean Burguet
R Paul Louis Lande
R de Lalande
R du Mirail
R St-François
R des Menuts
R Leyteire
R Bergeret
R des Augustins
R Gratiolet
R Henri IV
R Elie Gintrec
R Villedieu
R de St-Genès
R Ferrère
R Foy
R Boudet

FRANCE

WINE TOURS

Bordeaux is famous as one of France's premier wine-growing areas. The region is divided into 57 *appellations* (production areas), and there are more than 5000 chateaux (also known as *domaines*, *crus* or *clos*) around Bordeaux producing the region's trademark reds, rosés, sweet and dry whites and sparkling wines.

If you're looking to get to grips with the bewildering world of Burgundy wines, your first stop should be the tourist office's informal wine and cheese courses (€22), held 4.30pm Thursday at the restaurant Baud et Millet (below). Numbers are limited, so reserve ahead.

Next is a visit to one of the region's chateaux. The tourist office organises tours between May and October, starting at €50 and rising to €75 for prestigious *domaines* such as the **Médoc** or **St-Emilion**. Tours include wine tastings and lunch. The smaller chateaux often accept walk-in visitors, but at many places, especially the better-known ones, you have to make advance reservations by phone. Many chateaux are closed during the *vendange* (grape harvest) in October.

For do-it-yourself wine trailing, the **Maison du Vin de Bordeaux** (☎ 05 56 00 22 88; 3 cours du 30 Juillet; ⏲ 8.30am-4.30pm Mon-Fri) supplies a free, colour-coded map of production areas and chateaux, and can point you in the direction of local *maisons du vin* (tourist offices that deal mainly with vineyard visits).

Armed with your newfound knowledge, it's time to stock up at Bordeaux' wine shops, including **Bordeaux Magnum** (☎ 05 56 48 00 06; 3 rue Gobineau; ⏲ 10am-7.30pm Mon-Sat) and **l'Intendant** (☎ 05 56 48 01 29; 2 Allée de Tourny; ⏲ 10am-7.30pm Mon-Sat). Don't worry if you're running low on funds – you can pick up exceptional wines at Bordeaux' supermarkets for just a few euros, the same wines that command a small fortune at some of the world's flashiest restaurants.

Hôtel de la Presse (☎ 05 56 48 53 88; www.hoteldelapresse.com; 6-8 rue Porte-Dijeaux; d €49-109; ❄) Just off the pedestrianised rue Ste Catherine, this three-star hotel has elegant touches such as silk and dried flowers, and guest baskets of fruit and nuts in the rooms.

Hôtel de la Tour Intendance (☎ 05 56 44 56 56; www.hotel-tour-intendance.com; 14-16 rue de la Vieille Tour; d €58-129; ❄) Wake up to sandstone walls, stone-laid floors and wood-beamed ceilings at this stylised boutique hotel tucked into a quiet corner of the city.

Hôtel des 4 Soeurs (☎ 05 57 81 19 20; 4soeurs.free.fr; 6 cours du 30 Juillet; s €65, d €75-90; ⊠ ❄ 💻) A romantic relic from the reign of Louis-Philippe, Hôtel des 4 Soeurs' 34 sophisticated rooms recall the private home it once was, with stencilled wood-panelling, damask drapes, and chrome bathroom fittings.

Eating

Cassolette Café (☎ 05 56 92 94 96; www.cassolettecafé.com, in French; 20 place de la Victoire; lunch menu €10; ⏲ noon-midnight) Fun, friendly, and fantastic value, this lively place at the southwestern edge of place de la Victoire serves up *cassolettes* (casseroles) created from your own personal check-list of ingredients.

L'Entrecôte (☎ 05 56 81 76 10; 4 cours du XXX Juillet; menu €14-29; ⏲ lunch & dinner) Opened in 1966, this popular, unpretentious place doesn't take reservations but Bordeaux locals queue for hours for its succulent thin-sliced meat heated underneath by tea-light candles and unlimited homemade *frites* (fries).

Brasserie Les Noailles (☎ 05 56 81 94 45; 12 allèes de Tourny, mains €12-30; ⏲ lunch & dinner) This classic velour-filled French brasserie is an elegant affair, with delicious fare including Les Noailles' signature king prawn salad.

Baud et Millet (☎ 05 56 79 05 77; 19 rue Huguerie; menu €15-30; ⏲ 9.30am-midnight Mon-Sat) More than 250 different cheeses are offered at this vegetarian-friendly place, including a gut-busting all-you-can-eat *raclette* (cheese buffet).

Moshi Moshi (☎ 05 56 79 22 91; 8 place Fernand Lafargue; mains from €15; ⏲ 8pm-2am Tue-Sat) Japan meets France head-on at this super-chic minimalist place. The open kitchen lets you watch its chefs roll out sushi with unusual twists like foie gras and *magret de canard*.

Absolut Lounge (☎ 05 56 48 80 00; 14 rue de la Devise; mains around €33; ⏲ 6pm-2am Mon-Sat) Chill to electro-jazz amid turquoise décor and red lamps.

Drinking

Bodega Bodega (☎ 05 56 01 24 24; 4 rue des Piliers de Tutelle; ⏲ noon-3.15pm & 7pm-2am Mon-Sat, 7pm-2am Sun)

The biggest and best Spanish bar in town has two levels of tapas, tunes and trendy types.

Café Brun (☎ 05 56 52 20 49; 45 rue St-Rémi; ⌚ 10am-2am) This bar-bistro with a warm atmosphere and cool jazz is great for an evening apéritif.

Entertainment

Bordeaux buzzes by night. Details of events appear in the free publications *Bordeaux Plus* and *Clubs & Concerts* (www.clubsetconcerts.com, in French), available at the tourist office.

Getting There & Away

Bordeaux airport (BOR; ☎ 05 56 34 50 50; www.bordeaux.aeroport.fr) is in Mérignac, 10km west of the city centre, with domestic and international services. The train station and place Gambetta are connected to the airport by **Jet'Bus** (☎ 05 56 34 50 50; single/return €6.50/11), which runs till around 9.30pm. A taxi from the airport costs about €20.

Citram Aquitaine runs most buses to destinations in the Gironde and has an **information kiosk** (☎ 05 56 43 68 43; ⌚ 1-8pm Mon-Fri, 9am-1.30pm & 5-8pm Sat) at esplanade des Quinconces.

Eurolines (☎ 05 56 92 50 42; 32 rue Charles Domercq; ⌚ 7am-7.30pm Mon-Fri, 9am-7pm Sat) faces the train station.

Bordeaux is one of France's major rail hubs. The station, **Gare St-Jean**, is 3km from the city centre. Destinations include Paris' Gare Montparnasse (€63.70, three hours, at least 16 daily), Bayonne (€25.70, 1¾ hours), Nantes (€39.60, four hours), Poitiers (€30.30, 1¾ hours), La Rochelle (€23.80, two hours) and Toulouse (€31.60, 2¼ hours).

ARCACHON

pop 11,800

A long-time oyster harvesting area on the tranquil, triangular Bassin d'Arcachon (Arcachon Bay), this seaside town lured bourgeois Bordelaise at the end of the 19th century. Its four little quarters are romantically named for each of the seasons, and are filled with grand villas evoking the town's golden past. Arcachon seethes with sunseekers in summer, but you'll find practically deserted beaches a short bike ride away.

The **tourist office** (☎ 05 57 52 97 97; www.arcachon.com; place Président Roosevelt; ⌚ 9am-7pm Jul & Aug, to 6.30pm Mon-Fri, to 5pm Sat, 10am-noon & 1-5pm Sun Apr-Jun & Sep, 9am-6pm Mon-Fri, to 5pm Sat Oct-Mar) is a few hundred metres from the train station.

In the **Ville d'Été** (Summer Quarter), Arcachon's sandy beach, **Plage d'Arcachon**, is flanked by two piers. Lively **Jetée Thiers** is at the western end. A **pedestrian promenade** runs from the Plage d'Arcachon to **Plage Péreire**, **Plage des Abatilles** and the **Dune du Pilat**.

Cycle paths link Arcachon with the Dune du Pilat and Biscarosse, and around the Bassin d'Arcachon to Cap Ferret.

Sleeping & Eating

La Forêt (☎ 05 56 22 73 28; www.campinglaforet.fr; route de Biscarosse; camp sites €12.50-26.50; ⌚ Apr–mid-Oct; 🏊) A well-run, three-star camping ground, 'the forest' has shady pine trees and spotless amenities.

Hôtel La Paix (☎ 05 56 83 05 65; fax 05 56 83 05 65; 8 av de Lamartine; s/d €33.50/36.50, with shared bathroom €26/29, half-board d €54-62; ⌚ May-Sep) Many of the simple rooms at this hotel, 200m from the beach, have scrubbed timber floors and open onto a sunny courtyard. Upstairs are three self-contained apartments (€152.50 to €487) available from Easter to November.

Hôtel le Dauphin (☎ 05 56 83 02 89; www.dauphin-arcachon.com; 7 av Gounod; tw €52-79, d €57-88, tr €64-95, q €71-107; P ✖ 🏊) You can't miss this late-19th-century gingerbread place thanks to its patterned red-and-cream brickwork and twin semicircular staircases. Several eras have left their legacy, with a '50s marble foyer, '70s glass- and cork-panelled walls, plus '80s pine furniture.

St-Christaud (☎ 05 56 83 38 53; 8 allée de la Chapelle; menu from €12.50; ⌚ lunch & dinner Jun-Aug, by reservation Sep-May; ⊠) Opening on a sun-baked courtyard overlooking the beachfront, this authentic family-run place serves just one hearty *plat* a day, but it's always top-notch.

La Calypso (☎ 05 56 83 65 08; 84 blvd de la Plage; menu €20; ⌚ closed Wed & Thu Sep-Jun) With beamed ceilings, red tablecloths and a cosy open fire in the chillier months, this is the best place to try delicious bouillabaisse Arcachonnaise.

Getting There & Around

Frequent trains between Bordeaux and Arcachon (€9, 50 minutes) coordinate with TGVs from Paris' Gare Montparnasse.

Bikes can be hired at **Locabeach** (☎ 05 56 83 39 64; www.locabeach.com; 326 blvd de la Plage; ⌚ 9am-12.30pm & 2.30-7pm) and **Dingo Vélos** (☎ 05 56 83 44 09; www.dingovelos.com; rue Grenier; ⌚ 9.30am-6.30pm Apr-Sep, to midnight Jul & Aug).

BAYONNE

pop 42,000

Bayonne (Baiona' in Basque) is bordered by its twin rivers, the Adour and the Nive, which provide a picturesque backdrop for the town's narrow streets, shuttered buildings and waterside restaurants. The cultural and economic capital of the French Basque country, Bayonne is famous for its marzipan and prime smoked ham; it's also rumoured to be the place where the *baïonnette* (bayonet) was developed in the early 17th century.

Orientation

The Adour and Nive Rivers split Bayonne into three: St-Esprit, the area north of the Adour; Grand Bayonne, the oldest part of the city, on the western bank of the Nive; and the very Basque Petit Bayonne quarter to its east.

Information

Post office (21 blvd Alsace-Lorraine)

Taxiphone (1 place Ste-Ursule; per hr €2; ⌚ 11am-10pm) Internet café that also does cheap international phone calls.

Tourist office (☎ 05 59 46 01 46; www.bayonne-tourisme.com; place des Basques; ⌚ 9am-7pm Mon-Sat, 10am-1pm Sun Jul & Aug, 9am-6.30pm Mon-Fri, 10am-6pm Sat Sep-Jun) Supplies the useful listings brochure *Fêtes* and lots of brochures on local activities.

Sights

The twin towers of Bayonne's Gothic **cathedral** (⌚ 8am-noon & 3-7pm Mon-Sat) soar above the city. Construction began in the 13th century, when Bayonne was ruled by the Anglo-Normans, and was completed after France assumed control in 1451. It has three Renaissance-era stained-glass windows.

The **Musée Basque et de l'Histoire de Bayonne** (☎ 05 59 46 61 90; 37 quai des Corsaires; www.musee-basque.com, in French; adult/student/under 18yr €5.50/3/free; ⌚ 10am-6.30pm Tue-Sun May-Oct, 10am-12.30pm & 2-6pm Tue-Sun Nov-Apr) is an excellent introduction to the Basque people and their culture.

Musée Bonnat (☎ 05 59 59 08 52; 5 rue Jacques Lafitte; adult/student/child €5.50/3/free; ⌚ 10am-6.30pm Wed-Mon May-Oct, 10am-12.30pm & 2-6pm Wed-Mon Nov-Apr) contains canvases by El Greco, Goya, Ingres and Degas, and a roomful of works by Rubens. A **combined ticket** (adult/student €9/4.50) admits you to both museums.

The town's premier fiesta is the five-day **Fêtes de Bayonne** in early August – like Pamplona's 'running with the bulls', only with cows. There's also a **chocolate festival** in May.

Sleeping

Auberge de Jeunesse (☎ 05 59 58 70 00; www.hibiarritz.org; 19 route des Vignes, Anglet; B&B €16.50; ⌚ Apr-Oct) In the town of Anglet, complete with a Scottish pub, this hostel is lively and popular. Reservations are essential in summer. The hostel also has a small camping area (per person with breakfast €10.50).

Hôtel Paris-Madrid (☎ 05 59 55 13 98; sorbois@wanadoo.fr; place de la Gare; d/tr €32/47, r with shower €27, s/d with shared bathroom €18/24; P) You can tumble off the train straight into this highly recommended hotel, where the owners speak English and the rooms surround a peaceful patio.

Adour Hôtel (☎ 05 59 55 11 31; www.adourhotel.net; 13 place Ste-Ursule; d/tr from €55/70) Near the station, this friendly family establishment has bright, airy rooms, comprehensively renovated in 2005. Each one is decorated with a Basque theme – bullfighting, rugby, chocolate, cuisine and more.

Hôtel Loustau (☎ 05 59 55 08 08; www.hotel-loustau.com; 1 place de la République; s/d/tr/q from €77/84/89/94; ⊠ ❄) This tall, attractive 18th-century building on the St-Esprit side of the town has comfortable rooms. On the southern side of the building, the full-length windows open out onto views of the Adour River.

Eating & Drinking

Numerous reasonably priced restaurants surround the covered market and quai Amiral Jauréguiberry.

Bistrot Ste-Cluque (☎ 05 59 55 82 43; 9 rue Hugues; mains €9.50-15) There's only one *menu* here – a large blackboard that's propped up before you. Noisy, smoky and bustling with busy waiters, it makes a wonderful and unpretentious spot for a meal.

Le Chistera (☎ 05 59 59 25 93; 42 rue Port Neuf; mains €10-14, menu €15; ⌚ Thu-Sun, lunch Tue & lunch Wed) This authentically Basque restaurant features in many a French gastronomic guide. The *chistera* is the basket that pelota players strap to their wrists, and the restaurant is decorated with motifs from the sport.

Bar-Restaurant du Marché (☎ 05 59 59 22 66; 39 rue des Basques; ⌚ lunch Mon-Sat) You can fill yourself to bursting point with homely Basque cooking at this unpretentious place, and all for under €15.

La Grange (☎ 05 59 46 17 84; 26 quai Galuperie; mains €14-22; ⌚ Mon-Sat) With a shady outside terrace, this popular place overlooks the Nive River. Basque music plays sotto voce in the cosy interior, hung with hanks of dried peppers and garlic. Traditional flavours and seafood are the order of the day.

The **covered market** (quai Commandant Roquebert) occupies an imposing riverside building. There are a number of tempting food shops and delicatessens along rue Port Neuf and rue d'Espagne.

Most pubs and bars are in the Petit Bayonne area, especially along rue Pannecau, rue des Cordeliers and quai Galuperie. Two lively night-time spots are **Café-Bar Le Patio** (38 rue Pannecau) and **Massaï Café** (14 rue des Cordeliers).

Getting There & Away

The **Biarritz-Anglet-Bayonne airport** (BIQ; ☎ 05 59 43 83 83; www.biarritz.aeroport.fr) is 5km southwest of Bayonne and 3km southeast of Biarritz. Ryanair flies daily to London Stansted and three times weekly to Dublin. Air France has daily flights to Paris (Orly and Roissy Charles de Gaulle) and Lyon.

The hourly bus 6 links Bayonne and Biarritz with the airport. A taxi from the town centre costs around €15.

From place des Basques, **ATCRB buses** (☎ 05 59 26 06 99) runs nine services daily to St-Jean de Luz (€3, 40 minutes) with connections for Hendaye (€3, one hour). Transportes Pesa buses leave twice a day for Bilbao in Spain, calling by Irún and San Sebastián.

Eurolines is represented by **Voyages Domejean** (☎ 05 59 59 19 33; 3 place Charles de Gaulle). Buses stop in the square, opposite the office.

TGVs run between Bayonne and Paris' Gare Montparnasse (€75.60, five hours, eight daily). There are frequent services to Biarritz (€2.20, 10 minutes) and the French–Spanish border towns of Hendaye (€6.20, 40 minutes) and Irún (€6.50, 45 minutes).

There are also trains to Bordeaux (€24.90, 2¼ hours, at least 10 daily) and Toulouse (€35.50, 3¾ hours, five daily).

BIARRITZ

pop 30,000

The stylish coastal town of Biarritz, 8km west of Bayonne, took off as a popular seaside resort in the mid-19th century when Napoleon III and his Spanish-born wife, Eugénie, visited regularly. Nowadays, everyone from Parisian weekenders to beach bums in camper vans flock to this lovely seaside town, renowned for its beaches and some of Europe's best surfing.

Orientation

Place Clemenceau, the heart of town, is south of the main beach (Grande Plage). Pointe St-Martin, topped with a lighthouse, rounds off Plage Miramar, the northern continuation of the Grande Plage. The train station and airport are about 3km southeast of the centre.

Information

Form@tic (☎ 05 59 22 12 79; 15 av de la Marne; per hr €4; ⌚ 10am-8pm Jul-Sep, 10am-7pm Mon-Sat Oct-Jun, closed Sat afternoon Nov-May) Internet access.

Main post office (rue de la Poste)

Tourist office (☎ 05 59 22 37 00; www.biarritz.fr; square d'Ixelles; ⌚ 8am-8pm Jul & Aug, 9am-6pm Mon-Sat, 10am-5pm Sun Sep-Jun) Publishes a free monthly what's-on guide.

Tourist office annexe At the train station; open July and August.

Sights & Activities

Biarritz' **Musée de la Mer** (Sea Museum; ☎ 05 59 22 33 34; www.museedelamer.com; Esplanade du Rocher de la Vierge; adult/child €7.50/5; ⌚ 9.30am-12.30pm & 2-6pm daily Apr-Oct, closed Mon Nov-Mar) has 24 tanks seething with underwater life from the Bay of Biscay (Golfe de Gascogne). Tickets are €1 cheaper at the tourist office.

Biarritz' fashionable beaches are end-to-end bodies on hot summer days. In the high season, the **Grande Plage** and also **Plage Miramar** to its north are lined with striped bathing tents. North of Pointe St-Martin, the superb surfing beaches of **Anglet** stretch northwards for more than 4km. Take eastbound bus 9 from place Clemenceau.

If you fancy hitting the surf, boards and lessons are available at the Auberges de Jeunesse in Biarritz and Anglet, the **Rip Curl Surf Shop** (☎ 05 59 24 38 40; 2 av de la Reine Victoria) or the **Quiksilver Surf School** (☎ 05 59 22 03 12; www.biarritz-boardriders.com, in French).

Sleeping

Biarritz Camping (☎ 05 59 23 00 12; www.biarritz-camping.fr; 28 rue d'Harcet; camp sites €15-21.50; ⌚ mid-May–mid-Oct; 🅿) This camping ground, 2km southwest of the centre, has spacious, shady pitches. Take westbound bus 9 to the Biarritz Camping stop.

FRANCE

Auberge de Jeunesse (☎ 05 59 41 76 00; www.hibiarritz.org; 8 rue Chiquito de Cambo; B&B €17.50; ⌚ year-round) This popular hostel, with rooms for two to four, offers outdoor activities such as surfing, sailing and guided walks. From the train station, follow the railway westwards for 800m.

Hôtel Palym (☎ 05 59 24 16 56; www.le-palmarium.com; 7 rue du Port Vieux; d €50-55, d/tr with shared bathroom €42/52; ⌚ mid-Jan–mid-Nov) This welcoming 20-room family-run place occupies a brightly painted town house on a street packed with hotels. Bedrooms are colourful though the bathrooms are a squeeze.

Hôtel St-Julien (☎ 05 59 24 20 39; www.saint-julien-biarritz.com, in French; 20 av Carnot; s €60-80, d €66-99; Ⓟ) The new owners have renovated this late-19th-century villa, with its attractive shuttered façade and original parquet flooring. The 3rd-floor rooms have views of both mountain and sea.

Maison Garnier (☎ 05 59 01 60 70; www.hotel-biarritz.com, in French; 29 rue Gambetta; r €95-130) The seven rooms of this elegant mansion are delightfully decorated and furnished. The attic rooms (especially No 5) have a special charm.

Hôtel Plaza (☎ 05 59 24 74 00; www.groupe-segeric.com; 20 av Édouard VII; s/d from €105/125; Ⓟ ⊠ ⊠) The Plaza is an Art Deco delight overlooking Grande Plage. Refurbished to great effect, the original 1930s glass-fronted lift and plenty of decorative detail throughout give the feel of a glamorous hotel in its heyday.

Eating

Le Corsaire (☎ 05 59 24 63 72; Port des Pêcheurs; mains €11-15; ⌚ lunch & dinner Tue-Sat) It's all about seafood here at the water's edge, with dishes including *dorade à l'espagnole* (Spanish sea bream) and grilled cod with chorizo.

Tikia (☎ 05 59 24 46 09; 1 place Ste Eugénie; menu €13-20; ⌚ lunch & dinner) 'Tikia' is the Basque word for small. The restaurant's indeed modestly sized, though the same can't be said of the *brochettes* – giant skewers of duck, steak or seafood.

Le Clos Basque (☎ 05 59 24 24 96; 12 rue Louis-Barthou; menu €24, mains €12; ⌚ Tue-Sat) With its tiles and exposed stonework this tiny place could have strayed in from Spain. The cuisine, however, is emphatically Basque, traditional with a contemporary twist or two.

Le Vivier des Halles (☎ 05 59 24 58 57; 8 rue du Centre; menu €25; ⌚ daily Jul-Sep, Tue-Sun Oct-Jun) The fish could almost flap their way up the road from the nearby covered market to this place, where the seafood is reasonably priced and the fish soup a special delight.

Downhill from Biarritz' covered market, **La Table de Don Quichotte** (12 av Victor Hugo) sells Spanish hams, sausages, pickles and wines. The **Épicerie Fine du Port Vieux** (41bis rue Mazagran) is another excellent delicatessen.

Drinking & Entertainment

There are several good bars along rue du Port Vieux and the streets radiating from it.

Le Surfing (☎ 05 59 24 78 72; 9 blvd Prince des Galles) Surf-themed bar which makes the perfect place to discuss waves and wipe-outs.

Ventilo Caffe (rue du Port Vieux; ⌚ Wed-Sun Sep-May, daily Jun-Aug) This café attracts a young crowd and gets packed to the gills on summer nights.

Two discos near the town centre are **Le Caveau** (☎ 05 59 24 16 17; 4 rue Gambetta; ⌚ 11pm-5am) and **Biarritz Latino** (☎ 05 59 22 77 59; ⌚ 11pm-5am Tue-Sat).

Getting There & Away

Stopping on av Jean Petit, nine daily **ATCRB buses** (☎ 05 59 26 06 99) follow the coast southwestwards to St-Jean de Luz (€3, 30 minutes) and Hendaye (€3, one hour). For other destinations, it's better to go from Bayonne.

Biarritz-La Négresse train station is 3km from the town centre. Destinations and fares are similar to Bayonne (see p355). Bus 2 and 9 connect the two stations. **SNCF** (13 av du Maréchal Foch; ⌚ Mon-Fri) has a town-centre office.

For flights to **Biarritz-Anglet-Bayonne airport**, see p355. To get to the airport from Biarritz, take STAB bus 6 or, on Sunday, line C to/from Biarritz' Hôtel de Ville.

LOURDES

pop 15,000 / elevation 400m

Lourdes was a sleepy market town until 1858, when Bernadette Soubirous, a 14-year-old peasant girl, saw the Virgin Mary in a series of 18 visions that came to her in a grotto. Nowadays Lourdes is one of the world's most important Catholic pilgrimage sites, descended upon annually by some five million visitors – and although the town has more than its fair share of tacky souvenirs, it's still an intriguing place to visit.

Orientation

Lourdes' two main streets are rue de la Grotte and blvd de la Grotte, both leading to the Sanctuaires Notre Dame de Lourdes. The principal north–south thoroughfare, av Général Baron Maransin, connects the train station with place Peyramale.

Information

Micro Point Com (8 place du Champ Commun; per hr €4; 2-7pm Mon, 9.30am-noon & 2-7pm Tue-Sat) Internet access.

Post office (1 rue de Langelle)

Tourist office (05 62 42 77 40; www.lourdes-infotourisme.com; place Peyramale; 9am-7pm Mon-Sat, 10am-6pm Sun Jul & Aug, 9am-6.30pm Mon-Sat, 10am-12.30pm Sun Apr-Jun & Sep, 9am-noon & 2-6pm Mon-Sat Oct-Mar)

Sights

The development of the **Sanctuaries of Our Lady of Lourdes** began within a decade of the miraculous events of 1858. The most revered site is the **Grotte de Massabielle** (Massabielle Cave), lit by flickering candles left by the thousands of pilgrims who visit the cave every year. The 19 holy baths are said to cure all kinds of diseases and ailments – the most recent confirmed case was that of an Italian, Anna Santaniello, who was apparently cured of chronic rheumatism in 2005.

The main 19th-century section of the sanctuaries includes the neo-Byzantine **Basilique du Rosaire** (Basilica of the Rosary), the **crypt** and above it the spire-topped, neo-Gothic **Basilique Supérieure** (Upper Basilica).

From Palm Sunday to mid-October, there are **torchlight processions** nightly at 9pm from the Massabielle Grotto, while at 5pm there's the **Procession Eucharistique**, where pilgrims bearing banners process along the Esplanade des Processions.

All four places of worship open from 6am to 10pm in summer and 7am to 7pm in winter.

Sleeping & Eating

Camping de la Poste (05 62 94 40 35; 26 rue de Langelle; camp sites per person/pitch €2.80/4; Easter–mid-Oct) Right in the heart of town, it's tiny, friendly – and often full. It also rents eight excellent-value rooms with bathroom (d/tr/q €26/35/44).

Hôtel Cazaux (05 62 94 22 65; hotelcazaux@yahoo.fr; 2 chemin des Rochers; s/d €30/35; Easter–mid-Oct) This small 20-room hotel is a converted private house. It's friendly, a true bargain and really cosy.

Grand Hôtel de la Grotte (05 62 94 58 87; www.hotel-grotte.com; 66 rue de la Grotte; s/d/tr from €64/72/88 Apr-Oct; P) This charming *fin de siècle* place has a gorgeous garden, bar and a couple of prestige restaurants, and makes an excellent choice for those who like comfort and old-world courtesy.

Hôtel Gallia et Londres (05 62 94 35 44; www.hotelgallialondres.com; 26 av Bernadette Soubirous; s €73-78, d €86-96; Apr-Oct; P) The spacious bedrooms are each individually and attractively decorated à la Louis XVI – get ready to gasp at the chandeliers and wooden panelling of the dining room.

Lourdes' covered market occupies most of place du Champ Commun.

Le Cardinal (05 62 42 05 87; 11 place Peyramale; salads €5-5.50; Mon-Sat) Le Cardinal is an unpretentious bar-brasserie where you can tuck into steak, pork or chicken, garnished with chips and salad for only €6.

L'Ardiden (05 62 94 30 55; 48 av Peyramale; lunch menu €11, dinner menu €12.50-16, mains €8-14; Wed-Sun) A pleasantly sited neighbourhood restaurant, especially strong on pizza and pasta.

Restaurant le Magret (05 62 94 20 55; 10 rue des Quatre Frères Soulas; menus €26 & €33, mains €17-23; Tue-Sun Feb-Dec) This rustic restaurant offers an innovative menu with a pronounced regional flavour.

Getting There & Away

The **bus station** (place Capdevieille) has services northwards to Pau (€7.40, 1¼ hours, four to six daily).

Lourdes is well connected by train to cities all over France, including Bayonne (€18.90, 1¾ hours, up to four daily) and Toulouse (€22.20, 1¾ hours, six daily). There are four daily TGVs to Paris' Gare Montparnasse (€91.80, six hours).

THE DORDOGNE

The Dordogne – better known to the French as Périgord – is one of the most popular areas of France, and it's easy to see what attracts visitors here in their thousands every year. Littered with ancient chateaux, sparkling rivers and quintessentially French countryside villages, the Dordogne region is for many people the picture of rural France. It's also renowned as one of the world's most important prehistoric sites – the Vézère Valley is littered with some of the most spectacular cave art ever found.

SARLAT-LA-CANÉDA

pop 10,000

Nestled at the bottom of a sheltered valley, Sarlat-la-Canéda is one of the most attractive medieval towns in France. It's certainly one of the best-restored – a maze of cobbled alleyways, unexpected cul-de-sacs and snaking lanes, hemmed in by the town's distinctive honey-bricked buildings and elegant mansions. Unsurprisingly, it's also hugely popular, and the summer crowds can take the shine off things. Sarlat makes an excellent base for exploring the prehistoric sites of the Vézère Valley.

Orientation & Information

The heart-shaped Cité Médiévale (Medieval Town) is bisected by the rue de la République (La Traverse), which joins up with the main roads north and south from town. The train station is 2km from the Cité Médiévale, which is centred around place de la Liberté, rue de la Liberté and place du Peyrou.

Sarlat's **tourist office** (☎ 05 53 31 45 45; www.ot-sarlat-perigord.fr; rue Tourny; ⌚ 9am-7pm Mon-Sat, 10am-noon Sun Apr-Oct, 9am-noon & 2-7pm Mon-Sat Nov-Mar) is in a building attached to the cathedral and books accommodation for a small fee.

Sleeping & Eating

Hôtel Les Récollets (☎ 05 53 31 36 00; www.hotel-recollets-sarlat.com; 4 rue Jean-Jacques Rousseau; d €43-63) Lost in the narrow alleys of the Medieval Town, this great-value hotel has bags of period appeal (think quirky layouts and exposed brickwork) and colourful bedrooms.

Hôtel St-Albert (☎ 05 53 31 55 55; www.sarlathotel.com; place Pasteur; r €45-58; Ⓟ) This cosy little hotel lies slightly outside the busy streets of the old town, and offers 25 snug rooms decked out in sunny tones and a calm, convivial atmosphere.

La Maison des Peyrat (☎ 05 53 59 00 32; www.maisondespeyrat.com; Le Lac de la Plane; r €47-95) This beautifully renovated 17th-century house, formerly a nuns' hospital and aristocratic hunting lodge, is set on a hill 1.5km from the town centre. The 11 rooms have lots of country-tinged charisma; the best have views over the gardens and the countryside beyond.

Getting There & Away

Bus services from Sarlat are practically nonexistent – about the only destination is Périgueux (€7.10, 1½ hours) via Montignac. There's no bus station – departures are from the train station, place Pasteur or place de la Petite Rigaudie.

The **train station** (☎ 05 53 59 00 21) is 1.3km south of the old city on av de la Gare. Destinations include Périgueux (via Le Buisson; €12.60, 1¾ hours, two daily), Les Eyzies (change at Le Buisson; €7.90, 50 minutes to 2½ hours, two daily) and Bordeaux (€21.20, 2½ hours, five to seven direct daily).

LES EYZIES DE TAYAC

pop 850

Two museums in the one-street touristy village of Les Eyzies de Tayac provide an excellent introduction to the valley's prehistoric legacy. The excellent **Musée National de Préhistoire** (National Museum of Prehistory; ☎ 05 53 06 45 45; adult/18-25yr/under 18yr €5/3.50/free, adult Sun €3; ⌚ 9.30am-6.30pm Jul & Aug, to 6pm Wed-Mon Jun & Sep, to noon & 2-5.30pm Wed-Mon Oct-May) contains the most comprehensive collection of prehistoric finds in France, including stone-age tools and a famous bas-relief carving of a bison licking its flank.

About 250m north of Musée National de Préhistoire along the cliff face is the **Abri Pataud** (☎ 05 53 06 92 46; www.semitour.com; adult/6-12yr €5.50/3.50; ⌚ 10am-7pm Jul-Sep, to 12.30pm & 2-6pm Mon-Sat Sep-Jun) a Cro-Magnon *abri* (shelter) inhabited over a period of 15,000 years starting some 37,000 years ago.

MONTIGNAC

pop 3101

The previously peaceful town of Montignac, 25km northeast of Les Eyzies, achieved sudden fame after the discovery of the nearby Grotte de Lascaux (Lascaux Caves; see opposite).

The **tourist office** (☎ 05 53 51 82 60; www.bienvenue-montignac.com, in French; place Bertrand de Born; ⌚ 9am-7pm Jul-Sep, 9am-noon & 2-6pm Mon-Sat Apr-Jun & Sep-Oct; 10am-noon & 2-5pm Mon-Sat Nov-Mar) is next to the 14th-century Église St-Georges le Prieuré.

You won't find better value in Montignac than sweet little **Hôtel de la Grotte** (☎ 05 53 51

ANCIENT HISTORY

The Vézère Valley is renowned for its fantastic prehistoric **caves**, many of which contain the finest examples of cave art ever found.

Of the Vézère Valley's 175 known sites, the most famous ones include the **Grotte de Font de Gaume** (☎ 05 53 06 86 00; www.leseyzies.com/grottes-ornees; adult/18-25yr/under 18yr €6.50/4.50/free; 9.30am-5.30pm May-Sep, 9.30am-12.30pm & 2-5.30pm Sep-May, closed Sat), 1km northeast of Les Eyzies, where you can see around two-dozen prehistoric paintings of mammoths, bison, horses, fish, reindeer and bears, created some 14,000 years ago.

Eight kilometres east of Les Eyzies is the **Abri du Cap Blanc** (☎ 05 53 59 21 74; adult/7-15yr €6/3.50; 9.30am-7pm Jul & Aug, 10am-noon & 2-6pm Apr-Jun & Sep-Nov), which is unusual in that it only contains carved sculptures, rather than the combinations of engravings and cave paintings you'll see elsewhere.

The spectacular, 1200m-long **Grotte de Pech Merle** (☎ 05 65 31 27 05; www.pechmerle.com; adult/5-18yr mid-Jun–mid-Sep €7.50/4.50, mid-Sep–mid-Jun €6/4; 9.30-noon & 1.30-5pm Apr-Nov), 30km northeast of Cahors, has dozens of stunning cave paintings created some 16,000 to 20,000 years ago, as well as the haunting sight of a human footprint, clearly imprinted into the muddy clay floor.

Most famous of all are the **Lascaux Caves** (☎ 05 53 51 95 03; www.semitour.com; adult/6-12yr €8/5, joint ticket with Le Thot adult/child €10/7; 9am-8pm Jul & Aug, 10am-noon & 2-5.30pm Apr-Jun & Sep-Oct, 10am-12.30pm & 2-5.30pm Tue-Sat Feb-Mar & Nov-Dec, closed Jan), 2km southeast of Montignac. The cave's walls are covered with an astonishing menagerie of animals and figures, including oxen, deer, horses, reindeer and mammoth, as well as an amazing 5.5m bull, the largest cave drawing ever found. The original cave was closed to the public in 1963 to prevent damage to the paintings, but the most famous sections have been meticulously re-created in a second cave nearby – a massive undertaking that required some 20 artists and took 11 years.

Most of the caves are closed in winter, and get very busy in summer. Visitor numbers are also strictly limited, so you'll need to reserve well ahead during busy periods.

80 48; hoteldelagrotte@wanadoo.fr; place Tourny; d €49-57), which, with its red-and-white striped awnings and chichi furnishings, seems to have dropped out of a time hole to the 1930s.

Splendid **La Roseraie** (☎ 05 53 50 53 92; www.laroseraie-hotel.com; 11 place des Armes; s €81-96, d €92-152, s with half-board €105-130, d with half-board €150-194; P), housed in one of the town's grandest mansions overlooking place des Armes, is the top choice in town, with plenty of plumped-up cushions, floral wallpaper and polished furniture. Half-board is compulsory on weekends, and in July and August.

QUERCY

Southeast of the Dordogne *département* lies the warm, unmistakably southern region of Quercy, many of whose residents still speak Occitan (Provençal). The dry limestone plateau in the northeast is covered with oak trees and riddled with canyons carved by the serpentine Lot River. The main city of Cahors is surrounded by some of the region's finest vineyards.

CAHORS

pop 21,432

There's something unmistakeably Mediterranean about the laid-back town of Cahors, former capital of the Quercy region – a reminder that the sunbaked regions of Toulouse and Languedoc lie just to the south.

The main commercial thoroughfare is the north–south blvd Léon Gambetta. It divides Vieux Cahors (Old Cahors) to the east, from the new quarters to the west. Place François Mitterrand is home to the **tourist office** (☎ 05 65 53 20 65; cahors@wanadoo.fr; place François Mitterrand; 9am-6.30pm Mon-Sat, 10am-1pm Sun Jul & Aug, 9am-12.30pm & 1.30-6pm Sep-Jun).

Sights

Encircled by a hairpin loop in the Lot River and ringed by hills, the city has been inhabited since Roman times, but its most celebrated landmark is the three-towered medieval **Pont du Valentré**, which spans the river on the west side of the city.

The old **medieval quarter** is east of blvd Léon Gambetta, which cuts through the centre of the modern city. In the Middle Ages Cahors was a prosperous commercial and financial centre, and reminders of the city's wealth are clearly visible along the narrow streets and alleyways of the old city, densely packed with elegant houses and merchant's mansions.

Sleeping & Eating

Auberge de Jeunesse (☎ 05 65 35 64 71; fjt46@wanadoo.fr; 20 rue Frédéric Suisse; dm €9.50; 24hr;) The town's 40-bed youth hostel. The hostel's staff is helpful and efficient and there's a cheap canteen. There are a few private rooms and four- to 10-bed rooms; reservations are advisable.

Hôtel de la Paix (☎ 05 65 35 03 40; www.hoteldelapaix-cahors.com; 30 place St-Maurice; s €48, d €54-70, ste €75) Inside a tall, pale-pink building on place St-Maurice, the rooms at this small hotel are a little hit-and-miss, but most are roomy and freshly decorated.

Marché Couvert (place des Halles; 7.30am-12.30pm & 3-7pm Tue-Sat, 9am-noon Sun & most holidays) A covered market also known as Les Halles.

Le Lamparo (☎ 05 65 35 25 93; 76, rue Georges Clémenceau; menu €11.50-26) This popular bistro caters for all moods, from pizza, pasta and gourmet salads through to regional fish and meat dishes.

Getting There & Away

Cahors' **train station** (place Jouinot Gambetta, aka place de la Gare) is on the main SNCF line linking Paris' Gare d'Austerlitz (€60.90, five hours, four to eight daily). To get to Sarlat-la-Canéda, take a train to Souillac and an SNCF bus from there (€13, three hours, twice daily).

BURGUNDY & THE RHÔNE

Burgundy is the spiritual heartland of two of France's *raisons d'être* – food and wine. The vineyards along the Côte d'Or and the Côte des Nuits are littered with some of the most prestigious names in French wine-making. It's also renowned for rich, meaty cooking – this is the place to try quintessentially Burgundian dishes such as *bœuf bourguignon* and *escargots* (snails). But it's not just a place to fill your stomach – the historic city of Dijon is famous for its glorious Renaissance architecture and excellent museums, and the city of Beaune is home to the country's finest medieval hospital.

DIJON

pop 230,000

Dijon, mustard capital of the universe, is one of France's most appealing provincial cities. Filled with some of France's most elegant medieval and Renaissance buildings, the lively centre is wonderful for strolling, especially if you like to leaven your cultural enrichment with good food and shopping, and the city's 25,000 students help keep the nightlife scene snappy.

Orientation

Dijon's main thoroughfare, known for much of its length as rue de la Liberté, stretches from the train station eastwards past the tourist office and the Palais des Ducs to Église St-Michel. The main shopping precinct is around rue de la Liberté and perpendicular rue du Bourg. The focal point of the old town is place François Rude.

Information

Laundrettes 41 rue Auguste Comte (6am-9pm); 28 rue Berbisey (6am-8.30pm); 8 place de la Banque (7am-8.30pm)

Main post office (place Grangier) Cyberposte and currency exchange.

Netwave (10 rue de la Liberté; per hr €4; 10am-9pm Mon-Sat, to 10pm Jun-Aug) Internet access.

Tourist office (☎ 08 92 70 05 58; www.dijon-tourism.com; place Darcy; 9am-7pm May–mid-Oct, 10am-6pm mid-Oct–Apr) The *Owl's Trail* (€2) details a walking tour whose route is marked on the footpath with bronze triangles.

Sights & Activities

MEDIEVAL & RENAISSANCE ARCHITECTURE

Once home to the region's rulers, the elaborate **Palais des Ducs et des États de Bourgogne** complex lies at the heart of old Dijon. The eastern wing houses the Musée des Beaux-Arts. The 15th-century **Tour Philippe le Bon** (Tower of Philip the Good; ☎ 03 80 74 52 71; adult/student/under 12yr €2.50/1.50/free; guided visits every 45-60min 9am-noon & 1.45-5.30pm Easter-late Nov, 9am-11am & 1.30-3.30pm Wed, Sat & Sun late Nov-Easter) affords fantastic views over the city.

Many of Dijon's finest **hôtels particuliers** are north of the Palais des Ducs on and around rues Verrerie, Vannerie and des Forges. The 17th-century **Maison des Cariatides** (28 rue Chaudronnerie), is particularly impressive.

FRANCE

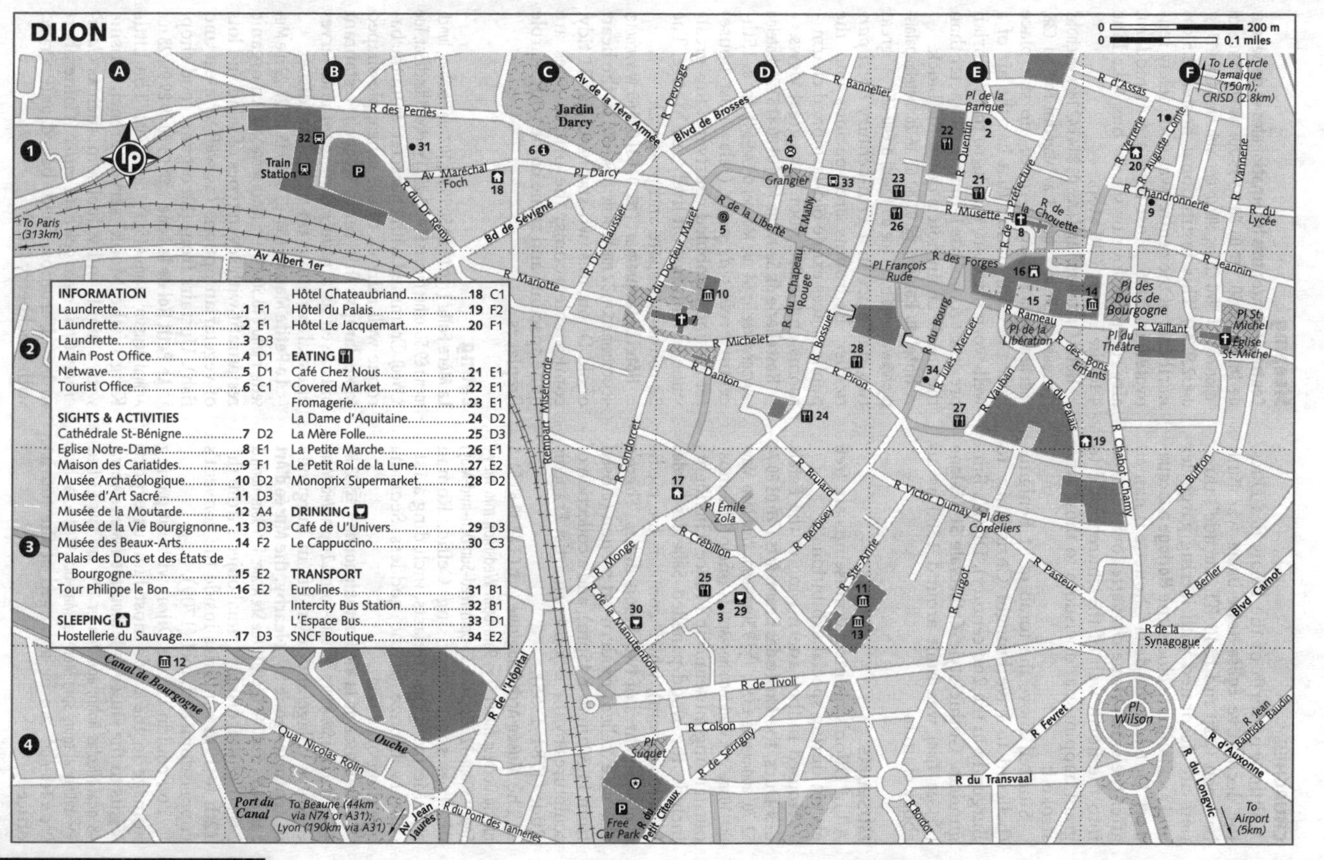
DIJON
0 200 m
0 0.1 miles
INFORMATION
Laundrette 1 F1
Laundrette 2 E1
Laundrette 3 D3
Main Post Office 4 D1
Netwave 5 D1
Tourist Office 6 C1
SIGHTS & ACTIVITIES
Cathédrale St-Bénigne 7 D2
Eglise Notre-Dame 8 E1
Maison des Cariatides 9 F1
Musée Archaéologique 10 D2
Musée d'Art Sacré 11 D3
Musée de la Moutarde 12 A4
Musée de la Vie Bourgignonne 13 D3
Musée des Beaux-Arts 14 F2
Palais des Ducs et des États de Bourgogne 15 E2
Tour Philippe le Bon 16 E2
SLEEPING
Hostellerie du Sauvage 17 D3
Hôtel Chateaubriand 18 C1
Hôtel du Palais 19 F2
Hôtel Le Jacquemart 20 F1
EATING
Café Chez Nous 21 E1
Covered Market 22 E1
Fromagerie 23 E1
La Dame d'Aquitaine 24 D2
La Mère Folle 25 D3
La Petite Marche 26 E1
Le Petit Roi de la Lune 27 E2
Monoprix Supermarket 28 D2
DRINKING
Café de U'Univers 29 D3
Le Cappuccino 30 C3
TRANSPORT
Eurolines 31 B1
Intercity Bus Station 32 B1
L'Espace Bus 33 D1
SNCF Boutique 34 E2
To Paris (313km)
Train Station
R des Perrières
Av Maréchal Foch
R du Dr Rémy
Bd de Sévigné
Av Albert 1er
Jardin Darcy
Av de la 1ère Armée
R Devosge
Blvd de Brosses
Pl Darcy
R Dr Chaussier
R du Docteur Maret
R de la Liberté
R Mariotte
R Bannelier
Pl Grangier
R Mably
R du Chapeau Rouge
R Michelet
R Danton
R Bossuet
R Piron
Pl François Rude
R des Forges
R du Bourg
R Jules Mercier
Pl de la Banque
R Quentin
R Musette
R de la Préfecture
R de la Chouette
R Rameau
Pl de la Libération
R des Bons Enfants
R Vauban
R du Palais
Pl des Ducs de Bourgogne
Pl du Théâtre
R Vaillant
Pl St-Michel
Église St-Michel
R d'Assas
R Verrerie
R Auguste Comte
R Chandronnerie
R Vannerie
R du Lycée
R Jeannin
To Le Cercle Jamaïque (150m); CRISD (2.8km)
Rempart Miséricorde
R Condorcet
R Brulard
Pl Émile Zola
R Crébillon
R Berbisey
R Monge
R de la Manutention
R Ste-Anne
R Victor Dumay
Pl des Cordeliers
R Chabot Chamy
R Buffon
R Pasteur
R Turgot
R Berlier
Blvd Carnot
R de la Synagogue
R de Tivoli
R Colson
Pl Suquet
R de Serrigny
R du Transvaal
R Fevret
Pl Wilson
R Jean Baptiste Baudin
R d'Auxonne
R du Longvic
To Airport (5km)
R Bordot
R de l'Hôpital
Canal de Bourgogne
Quai Nicolas Rolin
Ouche
Port du Canal
To Beaune (44km via N74 or A31); Lyon (190km via A31)
Av Jean Jaurès
R du Pont des Tanneries
R du Petit Cîteaux
Free Car Park

CHURCHES

A little way north of the Palais des Ducs, the decorative **Église Notre-Dame** was built between 1220 and 1240. The façade's three tiers are decorated with leering gargoyles and an elaborate clock, the **Horloge à Jacquemart**. Outside, rue de la Chouette is named after the small stone *chouette* (owl) carved into the north wall of the church, said to grant happiness and wisdom to those who stroke it.

Situated above the tomb of St Benignus (believed to have brought Christianity to Burgundy in the 2nd century), Dijon's Burgundian Gothic-style **Cathédrale St-Bénigne** (9am-7pm) was built around 1300 as an abbey church.

MUSEUMS

All of Dijon's municipal museums are free except during special exhibitions.

Housed in the eastern wing of the Palais des Ducs, the **Musée des Beaux-Arts** (☎ 03 80 74 52 70; audioguide €3.90; 9.30am-6pm Wed-Mon May-Oct, 10am-5pm Wed-Mon Nov-Apr) is one of the most outstanding museums in France. Highlights include the wood-panelled **Salle des Gardes** (Guards' Room), which contains the medieval sepulchres of two Valois dukes. There's also an excellent modern-art section (closed from 11.30am to 1.45pm), and a collection of sculptures by the Dijon-born artist François Rude (1784–1855).

The **Musée Archéologique** (☎ 03 80 30 88 54; 5 rue du Docteur Maret; 9am-6pm Wed-Mon mid-May–Sep, 9.30am-12.30pm & 1.35-6pm Wed-Sun Oct–mid-May) displays some surprising Celtic, Roman and Merovingian artefacts, including a 1st-century bronze of the goddess Sequana standing on a boat.

The **Musée de la Vie Bourguignonne** (☎ 03 80 44 12 69; 17 rue Ste Anne; 9am-noon & 2-6pm Wed-Mon) explores village and town life in Burgundy in centuries gone by. Nearby, the **Musée d'Art Sacré** (☎ 03 80 44 12 69; 15 rue Ste Anne; 9am-noon & 2-6pm Wed-Mon) displays ritual objects from the 12th to 19th centuries inside the convent's copper-domed chapel (1709).

You couldn't leave Dijon without paying homage to the city's most famous export. Visits to the **Musée de la Moutarde** (Musée Amora; 48 quai Nicolas Rolin; adult/under 12yr incl tour €3/free; bilingual tours 3pm Mon-Sat May-Oct, Wed & Sat Nov, Dec & Feb-Apr) can be arranged at the tourist office.

Sleeping

Centre de Rencontres Internationales et de Séjour de Dijon (CRISD; ☎ 03 80 72 95 20; www.auberge-cri-dijon.com; 1 blvd Champollion; dm with breakfast €17, s/d €32.50/43) This institutional hostel, 2.5km northeast of the centre, was completely renovated in 2006. Most beds are in modern, airy rooms of four or six. By bus, take Line 4 to the Epirey CRI stop.

Hôtel Chateaubriand (☎ 03 80 41 42 18; www.hotelchateaubriand.fr, in French; 3 av Maréchal Foch; d €38, with hand basin €34) A 23-room, no-star place near the train station that has the air of a well-worn dive but, thanks to the Victorian breakfast room, has far more character than the sterile chain hotels down the block.

Hôtel du Palais (☎ 03 80 67 16 26; hoteldupalais-dijon@wanadoo.fr; 23 rue du Palais; d €40-68) A great two-star place in a 17th-century *hôtel particulier*. Bedrooms are spacious and the public spaces exude old-fashioned charm – rooms on the 3rd floor have great views.

Hostellerie du Sauvage (☎ 03 80 41 31 21; hoteldusauvage@free.fr; 64 rue Monge; d €44-54) In a 15th-century *relais de poste* (relay post house) set around a cobbled courtyard, this great-value hotel is just off lively rue Monge. The 22 rooms are spare and practical.

Hôtel Le Jacquemart (☎ 03 80 60 09 60; www.hotel-lejacquemart.fr; 32 rue Verrerie; d €47-60) In the heart of old Dijon, this two-star hotel has 31 tidy, comfortable rooms; the pricier ones are quite spacious and some come with marble fireplaces.

Eating

La Mère Folle (☎ 03 80 50 19 76; 102 rue Berbisey; lunch menu €9.50, other menus €14.50-23; closed lunch Sat, Tue & Wed) Crammed with character, from the baroque wall mirrors to the pineapple-shaped table lamps, this camp French restaurant bills itself as a *resto extravagant* and serves unusual variations on traditional dishes.

La Petite Marche (☎ 03 80 30 15 10; 27-29 rue Musette; menu €10.50-14; lunch Mon-Sat) An organic restaurant with seven types of salad and lots of vegetarian options (as well as meat and fish). Upstairs from the organic food shop.

Le Petit Roi de la Lune (☎ 03 80 49 89 93; 28 rue Amiral Roussin; mains €15; closed Sun) 'The Little King of the Moon' serves French cuisine with a highly individual spin, such as *Camembert frit avec gelée de mûre* (Camembert in bread crumbs, fried, baked and served with blackberry jelly).

La Dame d'Aquitaine (☎ 03 80 30 45 65; 23 place Bossuet; lunch menu €15-21.50, dinner menu €32.50-39; closed Sun & lunch Mon) Excellent Burgundian and southwestern French cuisine served under the vaulted bays of a 13th-century cellar.

Self-caterers should check out the **covered market** (Halles du Marché; rue Quentin; 6am-1pm Tue-Sat), the **Monoprix supermarket** (11-13 rue Piron; 9am-8.45pm Mon-Sat) and the excellent **fromagerie** (28 rue Musette; closed Mon morning & Sun).

Drinking & Entertainment

For the latest on Dijon's cultural scene, pick up *Spectacles*, available free from the tourist office. Dijon's club scene is centred on place de la République, and there are lots of bars along rue Berbisey.

Café Chez Nous (☎ 03 80 50 12 98; impasse Quentin; 10am-2am, closed Mon morning & Sun) A quintessentially French *bar du coin* (neighbourhood bar), down a tiny alleyway from the covered market. The *plat du jour* chalked up daily on the blackboard costs €6.50 to €9.

Le Cercle Jamaïque (☎ 03 80 73 52 19; 14 place de la République; admission free; 2pm-5am Tue-Sat) Decked out in lovably tacky baroque decor, this nightclub has live music (Cuban, flamenco, jazz, rock and roll) nightly from 11pm to 3.30am. Rum-based cocktails are the speciality. The downstairs disco (open 11pm to 5am Thursday to Saturday) plays everything but techno.

Le Cappuccino (☎ 03 80 41 06 35; 132 rue Berbisey; 5pm-2am Mon-Sat) Despite the name, beer rather than coffee is the mainstay at this popular bar – there are more than 100 brews to choose from, including Mandubienne, the only beer brewed in Dijon.

Café de l'Univers (☎ 03 80 30 98 29; 47 rue Berbisey; 5pm-2am) One of many convivial café-bars along rue Berbisey, with live music at weekends and a small downstairs dance floor (open roughly 8pm to 2am Thursday to Sunday).

Getting There & Away

Five kilometres southeast of the city centre, **Dijon-Bourgogne airport** (DIJ; ☎ 03 80 67 67 67) has regular flights to many French cities, as well as to Amsterdam.

The bus station is in the train station complex, where there's a **Transco information counter** (☎ 03 80 42 11 00; 6am-8pm Mon-Fri, 7am-2pm & 3-6pm Sat, 10am-1pm & 4-8pm Sun).

Transco bus 60 (12 to 17 daily Monday to Saturday, two Sunday) links Dijon with the northern Côte de Nuits wine villages (30 minutes). Other Transco buses travel to various destinations around Burgundy.

International bus travel is handled by **Eurolines** (☎ 03 80 68 20 44; 53 rue Guillaume Tell; Mon-Fri & Sat morning).

Train services include Lyon (€23.80, two hours, 14 to 17 daily), Nice (€72.40, six hours, two daily), Paris' Gare de Lyon (€49 by TGV; 1¾ hours, 15 daily weekdays, eight to 10 weekends) and Strasbourg (€40, four hours, three or four nondirect daily). In the city centre tickets can be purchased at the **SNCF boutique** (55 rue du Bourg; 12.30-7pm Mon, 10am-7pm Tue-Sat).

Getting Around

Details on Dijon's bus network, operated by Divia, are available from **L'Espace Bus** (☎ 08 00 10 20 04; www.divia.fr, in French; place Grangier; 7.30am-6.45pm Mon-Fri, 8.30am-6.30pm Sat). Single tickets, sold by drivers, cost €0.90 and are valid for an hour; a Forfait Journée ticket costs €3 (available from the tourist office or L'Espace Bus).

The tourist office rents bikes year-round for €12/17 per half-/full day, €50 for three days. Helmets are free.

CÔTE D'OR VINEYARDS

Burgundy's most renowned vintages come from the vine-covered Côte d'Or (Golden Hillside), a range of hills made of limestone, flint and clay that runs south from Dijon for about 60km. The northern section, the **Côte de Nuits**, stretches from Marsannay-la-Côte south to Corgoloin and produces reds known for their robust, full-bodied character. The southern section, the **Côte de Beaune**, lies between Ladoix-Serrigny and Santenay and produces great reds and great whites.

Tours

Bourgogne Randonnées (☎ 03 80 22 06 03; www.bike-in-france.com; 7 av du 8 Septembre, Beanue; day tour incl lunch & tastings €65; 9am-noon & 1.30-7pm Mon-Sat, 10am-noon & 2-7pm Sun Apr-Oct) Arranges tailor-made bike tours around the Côte d'Or. Bikes can be rented for €15/69/170 per day/week/month.

Wine & Voyages (☎ 03 80 61 15 15; www.wineandvoyages.com; 2/3hr tours €50/60; Mar–mid-Dec) Runs minibus tour of the Côte de Nuits vineyards. Reservations can be made by phone or Internet, or last-minute at the Dijon tourist office.

BEAUNE

pop 22,000

Beaune (pronounced similarly to bone), 44km south of Dijon, is the unofficial capital of the Côte d'Or. This thriving town's *raison d'être* is wine – making it, tasting it, selling it, but, most of all, drinking it. Consequently Beaune is one of the best places in France for wine-tasting. The jewel of Beaune's old city is the magnificent Hôtel-Dieu, France's most splendid medieval charity hospital.

Orientation

The old city, enclosed by ramparts and a stream, is encircled by a one-way boulevard with seven names. The tourist office and the commercial centre are about 1km west of the train station.

Information

Laundrette (19 rue du Faubourg St-Jean; ⌚ 6am-9pm)
Post office (7 blvd St Jacques)
Tourist office (☎ 03 80 26 21 30; www.beaune-burgundy.com) 1 rue de l'Hôtel-Dieu (⌚ 9am or 10am-1pm & 2-7pm Jun-3rd weekend Nov, to 6pm late Mar-May, to 5pm 4th week in Nov-late Mar); 6 blvd Perpreuil (⌚ same hr but midday closure is noon-1pm)

Sights & Activities

Founded in 1443 and used as a hospital until 1971, the celebrated Gothic **Hôtel-Dieu des Hospices de Beaune** (☎ 03 80 24 45 00; rue de l'Hôtel-Dieu; adult/student/under 18yr €6/5/3; ⌚ ticket counter 9am-6.30pm Easter–mid-Nov, to 11.30am & 2pm-5.30pm mid-Nov–Easter, interior closed 1hr later) is topped by ornate turrets and pitched rooftops covered in multicoloured tiles. Highlights include the barrel-vaulted **Grande Salle**, an 18th-century **pharmacy**, the huge **kitchens**, and the disturbing **Polyptych of the Last Judgement**, an apocalyptic altar-piece by the Flemish painter Roger van der Weyden.

Underneath Beaune's streets and buildings, millions of dusty bottles of wine are being aged to perfection in cool, dark, cobweb-lined cellars. You can sample and compare fine Burgundy wines at several places around town.

Using a *tastevin* (a flat silvery cup) you can sample a whopping 16 wines at **Marché aux Vins** (☎ 03 80 25 08 20; www.marcheauxvins.com, in French; 2 rue Nicolas Rolin; admission €10; ⌚ visits begin 9.30-11.30am & 2-5.30pm, no midday closure mid-Jun–Aug), the former Église des Cordeliers.

During the 45-minute tour of the cobweb-covered cellar at **Reine Pédauque** (☎ 03 80 22 23 11; www.reine-pedauque.com, in French; rue de Lorraine; admission €7.50; ⌚ tours 10.30am, 11.30am, 2.30pm, 3.30pm & 4.30pm, also at 5.30pm Mar-Nov, closed Mon Dec-Feb), visitors sample at least one white, two reds and Belen, an apéritif.

Patriarche Père et Fils (☎ 03 80 24 53 78; www.patriarche.com; 5 rue du Collège; audioguide tour €10; ⌚ 9.30-11.30am & 2-5.30pm) are the largest cellars in Beaune, and are like Paris' Catacombs, except that the corridors are lined with dusty wine bottles instead of human bones. You get to sample and compare 13 of them.

Sleeping

Camping ground (☎ 03 80 22 03 91; 10 rue Auguste Dubois; camp sites per adult/tent €3.50/4.50; ⌚ mid-Mar–Oct) A four-star camping ground 700m north of the centre.

Hôtel Rousseau (☎ 03 80 22 13 59; 11 place Madeleine; d €52, s/d/tr/q with hand basin from €25/32/48/56, hall shower €3) An endearingly shabby, 12-room hotel run since 1959 by a woman *d'un certain âge*. Some of the old-fashioned rooms have showers or toilets. The best budget bet.

Hôtel de la Cloche (☎ 03 80 24 66 33; www.hotel-cloche-beaune.com, in French; 40-42 place Madeleine; d €55-70) The 32 rooms at this veteran three-star establishment mix old-fashioned character with contemporary comfort.

Abbaye de Maizières (☎ 03 80 24 74 64; www.abbayedemaizieres.com, in French; 19 rue Maizières; d €77-107) A quirky three-star hotel inside a 12th-century chapel with 13 rooms that make use of the old brickwork and wooden beams.

Hôtel des Remparts (☎ 03 80 24 94 94; www.hotel-remparts-beaune.com; 48 rue Thiers; d €91-105; ⊠ ⊡) Set around two delightful courtyards, this 17th-century townhouse has 22 rooms with red tile floors, antique furniture and luxurious bathrooms.

Eating

Most cafés and restaurants are around place Carnot, place Félix Ziem and place Madeleine.

Caves Madeleine (☎ 03 80 22 93 30; 8 rue du Faubourg Madeleine; menu €12-22; ⌚ closed Thu, Sun & lunch Fri) A convivial Burgundian restaurant with long wooden tables and regional classics such as *bœuf bourguignon*, *cassolette d'escargots* and *jambon persillé* (jellied moulded ham).

Le Bistrot Bourguignon (☎ 03 80 22 23 24; 8 rue Monge; menu €13-27; ⌚ closed Sun & Mon) A bistro-style restaurant and wine bar that serves good-value cuisine billed as *régionale et originale* and 15 Burgundian wines by the glass (€3 to €8).

Ma Cuisine (☎ 03 80 22 30 22; passage Ste Hélène; menu €19; 12.15-1.30pm & 7.30-9pm Mon, Tue, Thu & Fri) An intimate place whose traditional French and Burgundian dishes include *pigeon de Bresse entier rôti au jus* (whole Bresse pigeon roasted in its juices, €25).

The covered market at place de la Halle hosts a **food market** (to 12.30pm Sat) and a smaller **marché gourmand** (gourmet market; Wed morning). The nearest *fromagerie* is **Alain Hess Fromager** (7 place Carnot; Tue-Sat). **Casino supermarket** (28 rue du Faubourg Madeleine; 8.30am-7.30pm Mon-Sat) is through an archway on rue Faubourg Madeleine.

Getting There & Away

Bus 44, run by **Transco** (☎ 03 80 42 11 00), links Beaune with Dijon (€5.95, one hour, seven weekdays, four Saturday, two Sunday and holidays), stopping at Côte d'Or wine villages such as Vougeot, Nuits-St-Georges and Aloxe-Corton. Buses serve villages south of Beaune, including Pommard, Volnay, Meursault and La Rochepot (three daily weekdays, one or two daily weekends).

Beaune has frequent trains to Dijon (€6.20, 20 minutes, 16 to 22 daily) via the Côte d'Or village of Nuits-St-Georges (€2.90, 10 minutes). Other destinations include Paris' Gare de Lyon (€42.70, two TGVs daily), and Lyon (€20.50, two hours, 11 to 17 daily).

LYON

pop 415,000

Commercial, industrial and banking powerhouse for the past 500 years, grand old Lyon (Lyons in English) is the focal point of a prosperous urban area of almost two million people, France's second-largest conurbation. Outstanding art museums, a dynamic cultural life, a busy clubbing and drinking scene, not to mention a thriving university and fantastic shopping, lend the city a distinctly sophisticated air.

Information

Commercial banks are a dime a dozen on rue Victor Hugo (2e), rue du Bât d'Argent (1er) and rue de la République (1er).

AOC Exchange (20 rue Gasparin, 2e; 9.30am-6.30pm Mon-Sat; Ⓜ Bellecour) Currency exchange off place Bellcour.

Espace Internet (☎ 04 78 39 72 41; cnr rue Romarin & rue Terraille, 1er; per hr €2; 10am-8.30pm Mon-Sat; Ⓜ Hôtel de Ville) Internet access.

Lav'+ (rue Terme, 1er; 6am-9pm; Ⓜ Hôtel de Ville) Laundrette.

Laverie de la Fresque (1 rue de la Martinière, 1er; 6am-10pm; Ⓜ Hôtel de Ville) Laundrette.

Main post office (10 place Antonin Poncet, 2e; Ⓜ Bellecour)

Raconte-Moi La Terre (☎ 04 78 92 60 22; www.raconte-moi.com; 38 rue Thomassin, 2e; per hr €4; 10am-7.30pm Mon-Sat; Ⓜ Cordeliers) Internet access.

Tourist office (☎ 04 72 77 69 69; www.lyon-france.com; place Bellecour, 2e; 10am-5.30pm Mon-Sat; Ⓜ Bellecour) The Lyon City Card (one/two/three days per adult €18/28/38, per four- to 18-year-old €9/14/19) covers admission to every museum in Lyon, a guided tour, a river excursion (between April and October) and unlimited travel on public transport.

Sights

VIEUX LYON

Old Lyon, with its cobblestone streets and **medieval and Renaissance houses** below Fourvière hill, is divided into three quarters: St-Paul at the northern end, St-Jean in the middle and St-Georges in the south.

Lovely old buildings languish on **rue du Bœuf**, **rue St-Jean** and **rue des Trois Maries**. The partly Romanesque **Cathédrale St-Jean** (place St-Jean, 5e; Ⓜ Vieux Lyon), seat of Lyon's 133rd bishop, was built from the late 11th to the early 16th centuries. The **astronomical clock** in the north transept arm chimes at noon, 2pm, 3pm and 4pm.

FOURVIÈRE

More than two millennia ago, the Romans built the city of Lugdunum on the slopes of Fourvière. Today, Lyon's 'hill of prayer' – topped by a basilica and the **Tour Métallique** – affords spectacular views of the city and its two rivers. Footpaths wind uphill but the funicular departing from place Édouard Commette is the least taxing way up; use a metro ticket or buy a return ticket (€2.20).

Crowning the hill is the **Basilique Notre Dame de Fourvière** (www.lyon-fourviere.com, in French), a typically over-the-top example of 19th-century ecclesiastical architecture. You can climb to the top on your own, or there are **guided tours** (☎ 04 78 25 86 19; adult/under 16yr €5/3; 2.30pm & 4pm Mon-Sun Jun-Sep, 2.30pm & 4pm Wed & Sun Oct, Apr & May, 2.30pm & 3.30pm Wed & Sun Nov) which end up at the **Tour de l'Observatoire**

(Observatory Tower; adult/under 16yr €2/1; 10.30am-noon & 2-6.30pm Wed-Sun Mar-Sep).

Roman artefacts and several sumptuous mosaics are displayed in the **Musée de la Civilisation Gallo-Romaine** (Museum of Gallo-Roman Civilisation; 04 72 38 81 90; www.musees-gallo-romains.com, in French; 17 rue Cléberg, 5e; adult/18-25yr/under 18yr €4/2.50/free, Thu free; 10am-6pm Tue-Sun; Fourvière funicular station). Next door, the **Théâtre Romain**, built around 15 BC and enlarged in AD 120, once seated an audience of 10,000.

PRESQU'ÎLE

The centrepiece of beautiful **place des Terreaux** (M Hôtel de Ville) is the 19th-century fountain sculpted by Frédéric-Auguste Bartholdi, creator of New York's Statue of Liberty.

Next door, the **Musée des Beaux-Arts** (04 72 10 17 40; 20 place des Terreaux, 1er; adult/under 18yr €6/free; 10am-6pm Wed-Thu & Sat-Mon, 10.30am-6pm Fri; M Hôtel de Ville) showcases one of France's finest collection of sculpture and painting outside Paris.

Lyonnais silks, French and Asian textiles, and carpets are showcased at the **Musée des Tissus** (Textile Museum; 04 78 38 42 00; www.musee-des-tissus.com, in French; 34 rue de la Charité, 2e; adult/under 18yr €5/free; 10am-5.30pm Tue-Sun; M Ampère). Next door, the **Musée des Arts Décoratifs** (Decorative Arts Museum; free with Textile Museum ticket; 10am-5.30pm Tue-Sun) displays 18th-century furniture, tapestries, ceramics and silver.

OTHER ATTRACTIONS

Lyon's graceful 117-hectare **Parc de la Tête d'Or** (04 72 69 47 60; blvd des Belges, 6e; 6am-11pm mid-Apr–mid-Oct, to 9pm mid-Oct–mid-Apr; M Masséna), landscaped in the 1860s, is graced by a lake, botanic garden with greenhouses, an alpine garden, rose garden and zoo.

At the northern edge of the park is the brick-and-glass **Cité Internationale**, which houses the **Musée d'Art Contemporain** (04 72 69 17 17; www.moca-lyon.org; 81 quai Charles de Gaulle, 6e; adult/under 18yr variable depending on exhibition/free; noon-7pm Wed-Sun).

The WWII headquarters of Gestapo commander Klaus Barbie house the evocative **Centre d'Histoire de la Résistance et de la Déportation** (CHRD; 04 78 72 23 11; 14 av Berthelot, 7e; adult/under 18yr €4/free; 9am-5.30pm Wed-Sun; M Perrache or Jean Macé), which explores the exploits of the French resistance during WWII.

Film buffs should head for the **Musée Lumière** (04 78 78 18 95; www.institut-lumiere.org; 25 rue du Premier Film, 8e; adult/under 18yr €6/5; 11am-6.30pm Tue-Sun; M Monplaisir-Lumière), housed inside the Art Nouveau home (1899–1902) of Antoine Lumière who, with his sons Auguste and Louis, shot the world's first motion picture, *La Sortie des Usines Lumières* (Exit of the Lumières Factories) in 1895.

Today classic films are screened in the **Hangar du Premier Film** – the film set for *La Sortie des Usines Lumières* – that somehow escaped demolition when the rest of the Lumière factories were bulldozed in the 1970s.

Festivals & Events

Les Nuits de Fourvière (www.nuitsdefourviere.fr, in French) brings a multitude of fabulous open-air concerts to Fourvière's Théâtre Romain mid-June to early August.

For several days around 8 December, Lyon is lit up by the **Fête des Lumières** (Festival of Lights), marking the Feast of the Immaculate Conception.

Sleeping

Auberge de Jeunesse du Vieux Lyon (04 78 15 05 50; lyon@fuaj.org; 41-45 montée du Chemin Neuf, 5e; dm €13; reception 7am-1pm & 9pm or 10pm-1am; M Vieux Lyon) Rates include breakfast at this superbly located hostel above Vieux Lyon. Its 180 beds are split between rooms for two to seven people.

Hôtel de la Poste (04 78 28 62 67; 1 rue Victor Fort, 4e; s/d/tr/q €39/44/58/70, with shared bathroom €37/35/45/66; reception 7am-9pm Mon-Fri, 8am-9pm Sat & Sun; M Croix Rousse) Price – not prettiness – pulls in the punters at this bright but basic hotel overlooking the lovely central square in Croix Rousse.

Hôtel Iris (04 78 39 93 80; hoteliris@freesurf.fr; 36 rue de l'Arbre Sec, 1er; s/d €45/47, with shared bathroom €37/39; M Hôtel de Ville) The location of this two-star number inside a four-centuries-old convent couldn't be better, so get in quick to snag one of its simple courtyard rooms.

Hôtel St-Vincent (04 78 37 75 79; www.hotel-saintvincent.com, in French; 9 rue Pareille, 1er; s/d/tr €45/55/65; M Hôtel de Ville) High beamed ceilings, giant windows, old stone walls and original wooden floors make this three-level, 32-room hotel a fine place for lapping up authentic Lyonnais atmosphere.

Hôtel St-Antoine (04 78 92 91 91; www.hotel-saintantoine.fr; 1 rue du Port du Temple, 2e; s/d €63/69; ; M Cordeliers) A stylish mix of old and new greets guests at this thoroughly modern

LYON
0 400 m
0 0.2 miles
To modernartcafé (800m)
Jardin des Plantes
To Hôtel de la Poste (600m); Croix Rousse Markets (750m)
To N83; N84; La Dombes (25km); Pérouges (27km)
To L'Ouest (3km); Colonges-au-Mont-D'Or (10km)
To Cité Internationale & Musée d'Art Contemporain (2km)
To Les Halles de Lyon (1km)
To St-Just Funicular Station
To Musée Lumière (2.5km); Hangar du Premier Film (3km)
To Beaujolais (40km); A6 to Paris (460km)
To Marseille (315km via A7)
To A43 to Lyon St-Exupéry Airport (25km); Grenoble (110km)
Saône
Rhône
FOURVIÈRE HILL
ST-PAUL
VIEUX LYON
ST-JEAN
ST-GEORGES
MERCIDRE-ST-ANTOINE
PRESQU'ÎLE
QUARTIER AUGUSTE COMTE
Town Hall
Pl des Terreaux
Pl Louis Pradel
Pl de la Bourse
Pl Francisque Regaud
Cordeliers
Pl de la République
Pl des Jacobins
Pl des Célestins
Pl Bellecour
Bellecour
Pl Antonin Poncet
Pl Ampère
Ampère
Pl Carnot
Perrache
Gare de Perrache
Gare St-Paul
Pl St-Paul
Palais de Justice
Pl St-Jean
Pl Édouard Commette
Fourvière
Vieux Lyon
Minimes
Théâtre Romain
Pont Morand
Pont Lafayette
Pont Wilson
Pont Alphonse Juin
Pont Bonaparte
Pont de Gallieni
Cours Gambetta
Av Berthelot
Cours de Verdun

INFORMATION
AOC Exchange 1 C4
Espace Internet 2 C1
Lav' + 3 C1
Laverie de la Fresque 4 B1
Main Post Office 5 C4
Raconte-Moi La Terre 6 D3
Tourist Office 7 C4

SIGHTS & ACTIVITIES
Basilique Notre Dame de Fourviére 8 A3
Cathédrale St-Jean 9 B3
Centre d'Histoire de la Résistance et de la Déport 10 C6
Musée de la Civillisation Gallo-Romaine 11 A3
Musée des Arts Décoratifs (see 13)
Musée des Beaux-Arts 12 C2
Musée des Tissus 13 C5
Tour Métallique 14 A2

SLEEPING
Auberge de Jeunesse du Vieux Lyon 15 A4
Collége Hôtel 16 B2
Hôtel Iris 17 D2
Hôtel St-Antoine 18 C3
Hôtel St-Vincent 19 B1
Sofitel Royal Lyon 20 C6

EATING
Brasserie Georges 21 B6
Café des Fédérations 22 C2
Commanderie des Antonins 23 C3
Food Market 24 C3
Gaston Restaurant Agricole 25 C3
Jim-Deli 26 C3
La Halle de la Martiniére 27 B1
Le Pain Quotidien 28 C3
Le Petit Léon 29 C2
Oxalis 30 D1

DRINKING
Bauhaus Bar 31 B1
Ké Pêcherie 32 C2
Le Bar 33 D2

TRANSPORT
Bus Station 34 B6
Centre d'Échange (see 34)
Eurolines (see 34)
Intercars (see 34)
Linebus (see 34)
SNCF Boutique 35 C4

FRANCE

hotel, inside an 18th-century townhouse a pebble's throw from the Saône.

Collège Hotel (☎ 04 72 10 05 05; www.college-hotel.com; 5 place St-Paul, 5e; undergraduate/graduate/postgraduate d €105/125/140; ; M Vieux Lyon) The stark minimalism of this cutting-edge hotel comes as something of a shock, but most have flat-screen TVs and private balconies. Breakfast is served in the *salle de classe petit dejeuner* (breakfast classroom), bedecked like a classroom of yesteryear.

Eating

RESTAURANTS

Gaston Restaurant Agricole (☎ 04 72 41 87 86; 41 rue Mercière, 2e; 2-/3-course menu €11.50/14.50; lunch & dinner Mon-Sat; M Cordeliers) Pack a giant-sized appetite before venturing into this feisty agricultural restaurant, complete with rusty old tractor, farm tools and veggie-filled wheelbarrows.

Commanderie des Antonins (☎ 04 78 37 19 21; www.commanderie-antonins.fr; 30 quai St-Antoine, 2e; mains €7-13.50, menu €20; lunch & dinner; M Bellecour) This meat-lover's paradise cooks meat the old-fashioned way – slowly over a low heat in a wood-burning oven – and serves it with a flourish in a medieval banquet hall.

Le Petit Léon (☎ 04 72 10 11 11; www.leondelyon.com; 3 rue Pléney, 1er; plat du jour €11.50, menu €18.50; lunch Tue-Sat; M Hôtel de Ville) Tables are highly sought after at this soulful old-world bistro, the affordable arm of Michelin-starred big brother Léon de Lyon around the corner.

Oxalis (☎ 04 72 07 95 94; www.lessardinesfilantes.fr, in French; 23 rue de l'Arbre Sec, 1er; lunch menu €15, dinner menus €28-35; lunch & dinner Mon-Fri; M Hôtel de Ville) Lyon-born chef Sonia Ezgulian fuses Mediterranean with Asian and African at her truly globe-spanning restaurant – she also runs cooking courses.

Brasserie Georges (☎ 04 72 56 54 54; www.brasseriegeorges.com; 30 cours de Verdun, 2e; mains €15-20, menus €21.50 & €24.50; 8am-11.15pm Sun-Thu, 8am-12.15am Fri & Sat; M Perrache) In fashion since 1836, the original Art Deco interior is breathtaking – as is the sheer size of the place. Food is a mix of onion soup, mussels, sauerkraut, seafood platters and Lyon specialities.

Café des Fédérations (☎ 04 78 28 26 00; www.lesfedeslyon.com, in French; 8 rue Major Martin, 1er; lunch/dinner menu €19.50/23; lunch & dinner Mon-Fri; M Hôtel de Ville) In Lyon a *bouchon* is a small, local bistro that cooks up traditional city cuisine, and this is one of the city's old favourites, especially for its *caviar de la Croix Rousse* (lentils in a creamy sauce).

For quick eats at lunch time, try the following:

Le Pain Quotidien (☎ 04 78 38 29 84; 13-15 rue des Quatre Chapeaux, 2e; tartines €6-8, salads €12; 7am-10.30pm Mon-Sat, 7am-7pm Sun; M Hôtel de Ville) Great for *tartines* (thick toast with topping) and rustic lunches.

Jim-Deli (☎ 04 78 38 31 67; 14 rue des Quatre Chapeaux, 2e; pasta €7-13; M Hôtel de Ville) Authentic Italian *panini* (bread rolls), *carpaccio* (raw beef with olive oil, lemon juice and spices), pasta and salads.

SELF-CATERING

Central Lyon has two **outdoor food markets** (Tue-Sun morning; Presqu'île quai St-Antoine, 2e; M Bellecour or Cordeliers; Croix Rousse blvd de la Croix Rousse, 4e; M Croix Rousse).

Les Halles de Lyon (102 cours Lafayette, 3e; 7am-noon & 3-7pm Tue-Sat, to noon Sun; M Part-Dieu) and **La Halle de la Martinière** (24 rue de la Martinière, 1er; 8am-7.30pm Tue-Sun; M Hôtel de Ville) are the main indoor food markets.

Drinking

The bounty of café-terraces on place des Terreaux (1er, metro station Hôtel de Ville) buzz with drinkers day and night.

Ké Pêcherie (☎ 04 78 28 26 25; quai de la Pêcherie, 1er; 7am-1.30am; M Hôtel de Ville) Seemingly open all hours, this ever-changing bar spans the drinking spectrum: daytime café drifts into lounge bar come late afternoon, followed by heaving venue after dark.

Le Bar (☎ 04 78 31 51 08; 10bis rue de la Bourse, 1er; 11am-3am; M Hôtel de Ville) A striking minimalist interior and imaginative cocktails are on offer at this cocktail bar, one of Lyon's most chic.

modernartcafé (☎ 04 72 87 06 82; www.modernartcafé.net; 65 blvd de la Croix Rousse, 4e; 11.30am-2am Mon-Fri, 3.30pm-2am Sat, 11am-2am Sun, shorter hr winter & rain; M Croix Rousse) Retro furnishings, contemporary art, and multimedia events make this art bar one cool place to lounge. There's even a pocket-sized beach.

Bauhaus Bar (☎ 04 72 00 87 22; 17 rue Sergent Blandant, 1er; M Hôtel de la Ville) Tiny and trendy, this chic bar attracts a cool crowd with its authentic Bauhaus furnishings.

Entertainment

The tourist office knows most about Lyon's dynamic entertainment scene. Local listings guides include weekly *Lyon Poche* (www.lyonpoche.com, in French; €1 at newsagents) and the free weekly *Le Petit Bulletin* (www.petit-bulletin.fr, in French) available on street corners and at the tourist office.

Getting There & Away

Flights to/from dozens of European cities land at **Aéroport Lyon-St-Exupéry** (LYS; ☎ 08 26 80 08 26; www.lyon.aeroport.fr), 25km east of the city. **Satobus** (☎ 04 72 68 72 17; www.satobus.com) links the airport with the city centre (single/return €8.40/14.90, every 20 minutes from 5am to midnight).

In the Perrache complex, **Eurolines** (☎ 04 72 56 95 30), **Intercars** (☎ 04 78 37 20 80) and **Linebus** (☎ 04 72 41 72 27) have offices on the bus-station level of the Centre d'Échange (follow the 'Lignes Internationales' signs).

Lyon has two main-line train stations: **Gare de la Part-Dieu** (Ⓜ Part-Dieu), which handles long-haul trains; and **Gare de Perrache** (Ⓜ Perrache), a stop for both long-distance and regional trains. Tickets are sold in town at the **SNCF Boutique** (2 place Bellecour, 2e; ⌚ 9am-6.45pm Mon-Fri, 10am-6.30pm Sat; Ⓜ Bellecour).

Destinations by TGV include Paris' Gare de Lyon (€58.70 to €76.30, two hours, every 30 to 60 minutes), Lille-Europe (€77.20, 3¼ hours, nine daily), Nantes (€72.20, 4½ hours, five daily), Beaune (€20.50, 2¼ hours, up to nine daily), Dijon (€23.40, 2¾ hours, at least 12 daily) and Strasbourg (€45.60, 5¼ hours, five daily).

Getting Around

Lyon's buses, trams, metro and funiculars are run by **TCL** (☎ 08 20 42 70 00; www.tcl.fr, in French; Vieux Lyon place Commette, 5e; ⌚ 10am-12.30pm & 2-5pm Mon-Fri, 10am-12.30pm & 1.30-5pm Sat; Ⓜ Vieux Lyon; Presqu'île 5 rue de la République, 1er; ⌚ 7.30am-6.30pm Mon-Fri, 9am-noon & 1.30-5pm Sat; Ⓜ Bellecour). Tickets cost €1.50/12.20 for one/10 and are available from bus and tram drivers and from machines at metro entrances. Two-hour/day tickets cost €2.10/4.30. Public transport runs from around 5am to midnight.

THE FRENCH ALPS

The spiritual home of winter sports, the French Alps form one of the most stunning mountain ranges in Europe. The snowy peaks and ice-capped spires of this region are famous for their downhill thrills and fresh powder, but there are also some fascinating towns to explore, including Annecy, which sits in a spectacular spot surrounded by sawtooth mountains and a sparkling lake, and elegant Grenoble, the undisputed capital of the Alps.

CHAMONIX

pop 10,000 / elevation 1037m

Grungy and gritty, Chamonix is where the serious Alpine action kicks in. This is France's legendary mountaineering centre, where world-class skiers, boarders and climbers push themselves to extremes on Europe's most challenging pistes and rock faces. It's also renowned for its lively après-ski scene, and for having the world's highest (and most terrifying) cable car.

Information

There are several seasonal currency-exchange places between the tourist and post offices.

Banque de Savoie (☎ 04 50 53 30 25; 1 place Balmat; ⌚ 9am-1pm & 3-7pm May, Jun & early Sep-Nov, 8am-8pm Jul-early Sep & Dec-Apr) Exchange bureau with competitive rates.

Laverie Automatique (174 av de l'Aiguille du Midi; 7/16kg wash €5.50/10; ⌚ 9am-8pm) Laundrette.

Le Bureau (☎ 04 50 90 68 37; 7/13 quai du Vieux Moulins; per 10min/1hr €1/4.50; ⌚ 10am-10pm Mon-Fri, noon-9pm Sat & Sun) Internet access.

Maison de la Montagne (190 place de l'Église) Your first port of call for finding out everything about the Mont Blanc area.

Office de Haute Montagne (OHM; ☎ 04 50 53 22 08; www.ohm-chamonix.com) Information on trails, hiking conditions and *refuges* (mountain huts).

Post office (89 place Balmat)

Tourist office (☎ 04 50 53 00 24; www.chamonix.com; 85 place du Triangle de l'Amitié; ⌚ 8.30am-12.30pm & 2-7pm mid-Dec–Mar & mid-Jun & Sep, 9am-12.30pm & 2-6.30pm Mon-Sat Apr–mid-Jun, 8.30am-12.30pm & 1.30-7pm early Jul, 8.30am-7.30pm mid-Jul–mid-Aug, 8.30am-7pm mid-end Aug) Accommodation and activity information; also sells ski passes.

Sights

AIGUILLE DU MIDI

A jagged pinnacle of rock rising above glaciers, snowfields and rocky crags, 8km from the domed summit of Mont Blanc, the **Aiguille du Midi** (3777m) is one of Chamonix' most famous landmarks. If you can handle the height, the panoramic views from the summit are unforgettable.

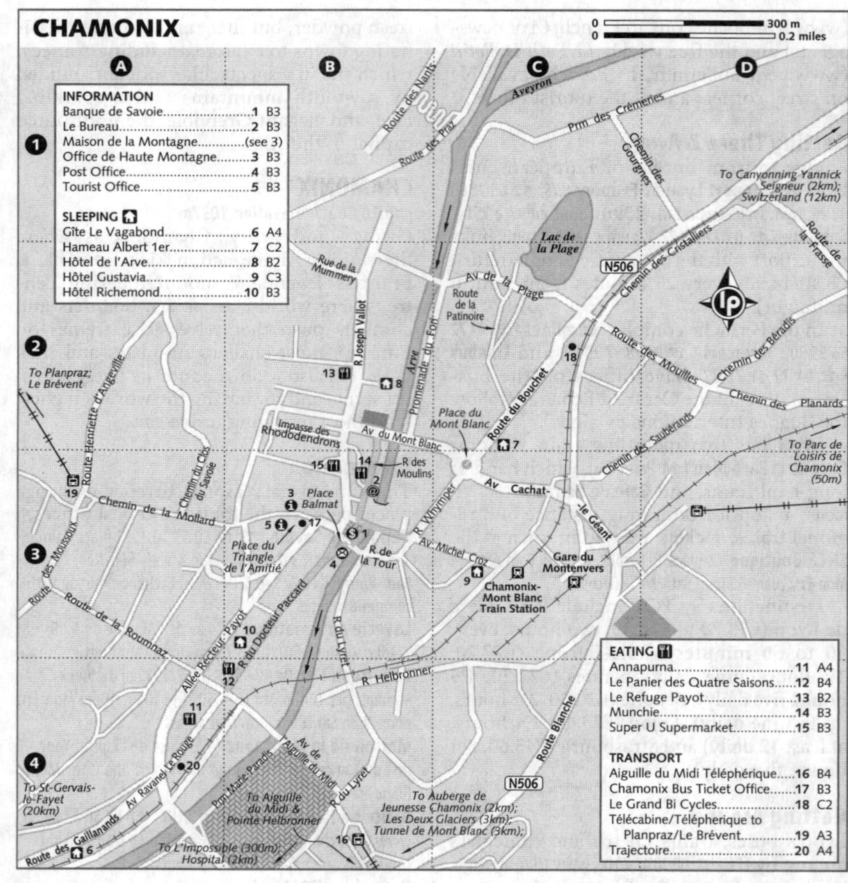

The **Téléphérique du l'Aiguille du Midi** (Aiguille du Midi cable car; ☎ 04 50 53 30 80, advance reservations 24hr ☎ 08 92 68 00 67; 100 place de l'Aiguille du Midi; adult/12-15yr/4-11yr return €36/31/25.50, adult/12-15yr/4-11yr return to midstation Plan de l'Aiguille €16/14/11.50; 7am-5.40pm Jun-Nov, 8.30am-4pm mid-Dec–Jan, 8.10am-4pm Feb & Mar, 8.10am-4.30pm Apr, 8.30am-5pm May) links Chamonix with the Aiguille du Midi. Be prepared for long queues.

From the Aiguille du Midi, a second cable car, the **Télécabine Panoramic Mont Blanc**, travels to Pointe Helbronner (3466m) on the French–Italian border.

LE BRÉVENT

The highest peak on the western side of the valley, **Le Brévent** (2525m) has fabulous views of the Mont Blanc massif and a fabulous summit restaurant.

Reach it via the **Télécabine du Brévent** (☎ 04 50 53 13 18; 29 rte Henriette d'Angeville; Chamonix-Brévent adult/12-15yr/4-11yr return €17/15/14, Chamonix-Planpraz adult/12-15yr/4-11yr return €12/10.50/8.50; 8am-5.45pm Jun-Sep, 8.45am-4.45pm mid-Dec–Apr), from the end of rue de la Mollard to midstation **Planpraz** (2000m), from where another cable car travels to the top.

MER DE GLACE

The **Mer de Glace** (Sea of Ice), the second-largest glacier in the Alps, is 14km long, 1800m wide and up to 400m deep. The glacier moves 45m a year at the edges, and up to 90m a year in the centre, and has become

FRANCE

a popular tourist attraction thanks to the rack-and-pinion railway line built between 1897 and 1908.

Since 1946, the **Grotte de la Mer de Glace** (late May-late Sep) – an ice cave – has been carved every spring. Work commences in February and takes up to three months. The interior temperature is between -2°C and -5°C. Take a look down the slope for last year's cave to see how far the glacier has moved.

A mountain train links **Gare du Montenvers** (04 50 53 12 54; 35 place de la Mer de Glace; adult/12-15yr/4-11yr return €16/14/11.50; 10am-4.30pm mid-Dec–Apr, 8.30am-5.30pm May-Jun & Sep, 8am-6.30pm Jul & Aug) in Chamonix with Montenvers (1913m), from where a cable car transports tourists in summer down to the glacier and cave. A combined ticket for the train, cable car and cave costs €22.50/19.50/16 per adult/12- to 15-year-old/four- to 11-year-old.

Sleeping

BUDGET

Les Deux Glaciers (04 50 53 15 84; glaciers@clubInternet.fr; 80 rte des Tissières; camp sites per 2 adults, tent & car €13; mid-Dec–mid-Nov) Chamonix has some 13 camping grounds in summer, but this is the only one which opens year-round. Ride the train to Les Bossons or the Chamonix bus to the Tremplin-le-Mont stop.

Auberge de Jeunesse Chamonix (04 50 53 14 52; chamonix@fuaj.org; 127 montée Jacques Balmat; dm mid-Apr–Oct/Dec–mid-Apr €17/22; reception 8am-noon, 5-7.30pm & 8.30-10pm; Dec-Oct) This hostel is 2km south of Chamonix in Les Pélerins. There's no kitchen but there's a decent snack bar. Package stays are available in summer and winter. Take the Chamonix-Les Houches bus line and get off in Les Pélerins d'en Haut.

Gîte Le Vagabond (04 50 53 15 43; www.gitevagabond.com; 365 av Ravanel-le-Rouge; dm €14.50, with breakfast €19.50, with half-board €31.50, d with breakfast €62; reception 8-10am & 4.30-10pm;) This legendary hangout is where cool dudes free-ride by day and eat, drink and party by night. Beds are in four- or six-person dorms, and doubles have their own bathroom.

MIDRANGE

During July, August and the ski season, most hotels are heavily booked, so reserve ahead.

Hôtel Gustavia (04 50 53 00 31; www.hotel-gustavia.com; 272 av Michel Croz; s/d/tr/q from €46/74/102/180) *'Une belle addresse'* since 1890, this charming manor-house hotel with bottle-green wooden shutters and wrought-iron balconies oozes soul, and has a great après-ski bar.

Hôtel Richemond (04 50 53 08 85; www.richemond.fr; 228 rue du Docteur Paccard; s €56-64, d €87-102, tr €108-130, q €123-145) The same family has run this ginger-shuttered hotel with wrought-iron balconies facing Mont Blanc since 1914. Most of the two-star rooms tout flower-power wallpaper, lurid carpets and other kitsch 1960s furnishings which just about qualify for a 'retro' tag.

Hôtel de l'Arve (04 50 53 02 31; www.hotelarve-chamonix.com; 60 impasse des Anémones; d €58-83;

ALPINE ADVENTURES

Chamonix is obviously known for its fantastic skiing and snowboarding, but there's much more to this part of the Alps than simply hurtling downhill strapped to a couple of matchsticks.

From late spring until October, 310km of **walking trails** open up in the mountains around Chamonix. For walking information, contact **Chamonix Guide** (04 50 55 66 47, 06 03 60 21 03; www.chamonixguide.com; 840 rte des Chavants) or the **Compagnie des Guides** (04 50 53 00 88; www.chamonix-guides.com; 190 place de l'Église), who also run **rock-climbing** and **cycling** expeditions.

Canyoning and **white-water rafting** trips are organised by **Cham' Aventure** (04 50 53 55 70; www.cham-aventures.com; 190 place de l'Église) and **Canyonning Yannick Seigneur** (06 77 88 24 50; www.canyoning-chamonix.com; 44 chemin de l'Ordon).

Paragliding above the valley is popular; starter flights from Planpraz cost €90, or €220 from the Aiguille du Midi. Paragliding schools include **Summits** (04 50 53 50 14, 06 84 01 26 00; www.summits.fr; 27 allée du Savoy) and **Les Ailes du Mont Blanc** (04 50 53 92 76, 06 20 46 55 57; www.lesailesdumontblanc.com; 24 av de la Plage).

Down in the valley, there's a **summer luge track** at the **Parc de Loisirs de Chamonix** (04 50 53 08 97; www.planards.com; 1/6 descents €5/25; 1.30-6pm Sat & Sun May & Oct, 1.30-6pm Jun & Sep, 10am-7.30pm Jul & Aug).

mid-Dec–mid-Oct) The Arve is one of the last great family-run hotels left in Chamonix, handed down through four generations since 1890. The best rooms look down the valley to Mont Blanc.

Hameau Albert 1er (04 50 53 05 64; www.hameaualbert.fr; 38 rte du Bouchet; d €115-150;) This exquisite hotel is a hamlet of traditional Savoyard farms and wooden chalets bizarrely placed in the centre of town. Interiors are rustic and the futuristic swimming pool is a dream.

Eating

A food market fills place du Mont-Blanc on Saturday morning.

Le Panier des Quatre Saisons (04 50 53 98 77; 24 Galerie Blanc Neige; mains €15; dinner Thu, lunch & dinner Fri-Tue Dec-May & mid-Jun–Oct) A firm favourite, the Basket of Four Seasons cooks up a veritable feast of season-driven, quintessentially French dishes.

Annapurna (04 50 55 81 39; planetguddoy@aol.com; 62 av Ravanel-Le Rouge; mains €15) Authentic Indian dishes – biryani, tandoori etc – as well as more unusual dishes like curried lobster tail (€38).

Munchie (04 50 53 45 41; 87 rue des Moulins; mains €17-25; dinner Mon-Sun) Think fusion at this trendy hang-out with great pan-Asian food. Mains include blackened salmon *sashimi* (slices of raw fish), sushi, and a couple of imaginative vegetarian dishes.

L'Impossible (04 50 53 20 36; 9 chemin du Cry; lunch/dinner menus €20/24.50 & €29.50) An 18th-century barn, located near the Aiguille du Midi cable car, has been transformed into this rustic eatery with wood, wicker and warm lighting, and a deliciously upmarket French *menu*.

Self-caterers can choose from **Le Refuge Payot** (04 50 53 18 71; www.refugepayot.com; 166 rue Joseph Vallot) for deli supplies and the **Super U** (117 rue Joseph Vallot) supermarket for everything else.

Getting There & Away

From **Chamonix bus station** (04 50 53 07 02; www.altibus.com; 6.45am-10.30am & 1.25-4.45pm Mon-Fri, 6.45am-11am Sat & Sun), at the train station, there are buses to Geneva airport and bus station (www.sat-montblanc.com; single/return €34/55, 1½ to 2¼ hours, three daily) and Courmayeur (single/return €10/18, three daily).

Chamonix-Mont Blanc **train station** (04 50 53 12 98; place de la Gare) is on the line between St-Gervais-le-Fayet, 23km west of Chamonix, and Martigny, 42km north of Chamonix in Switzerland. There are nine to 12 daily trains and a return Chamonix-St-Gervais fare is €9 (40 minutes).

From St-Gervais-le-Fayet, there are trains to most major French cities.

Getting Around

Local buses are run by **Chamonix Bus** (04 50 53 05 55; chamonixbus@transdev.fr; 591 promenade Marie-Paradis; 7am-7pm Sep-Apr, 8am-noon & 2-7pm Jun-Aug).

Le Grand Bi Cycles (04 50 53 14 16; 240 av du Bouchet; 9am-7pm Jul & Aug, 9am-7pm Tue-Sat Jun) and **Trajectoire** (04 50 53 18 95; 91 av Ravanel le Rouge) rent bikes for €10 to €15 a day.

ANNECY

pop 50,000 / elevation 448m

Chic Annecy, capital of the Haute-Savoie, is perfect for a good old mosey. Nestled around the northwestern end of Lake Annecy against a pretty backdrop of Alpine peaks, the town is crisscrossed with ancient canals, geranium-covered bridges, medieval houses and arched alleyways perfect for meandering. This is *the* hot spot to kick back and relax after the high-altitude and attitude-fuelled Alpine resorts – except in summer when bumper-to-bumper traffic makes it a tad taxing.

Orientation

The train and bus stations are 500m northwest of Vieil Annecy, also called the Vieille Ville (Old Town), which is huddled around the Thiou River (split into Canal du Thiou to the south and Canal du Vassé to the north). The town centre is between the post office and the purpose-built Centre Bonlieu, near the shores of Lac d'Annecy.

Information

Internet – Red Sector Café (04 50 45 39 75; 3bis av de Chevêne; per 15min/1hr €1/4; 10am-7pm Fri-Wed)
Lav'Confort Express (6 rue de la Gare; 7am-9pm) Laundrette.
Post office (4bis rue des Glières) Has a Cyberposte.
Tourist office (04 50 45 00 33; www.lac-annecy.com; 1 rue Jean Jaurès, Centre Bonlieu; 9am-12.30pm & 1.45-6pm Mon-Sat mid-Sep–mid-May, 9am-6.30pm Mon-Sat mid-May–mid-Sep, Sun Mar-Oct)

FRANCE

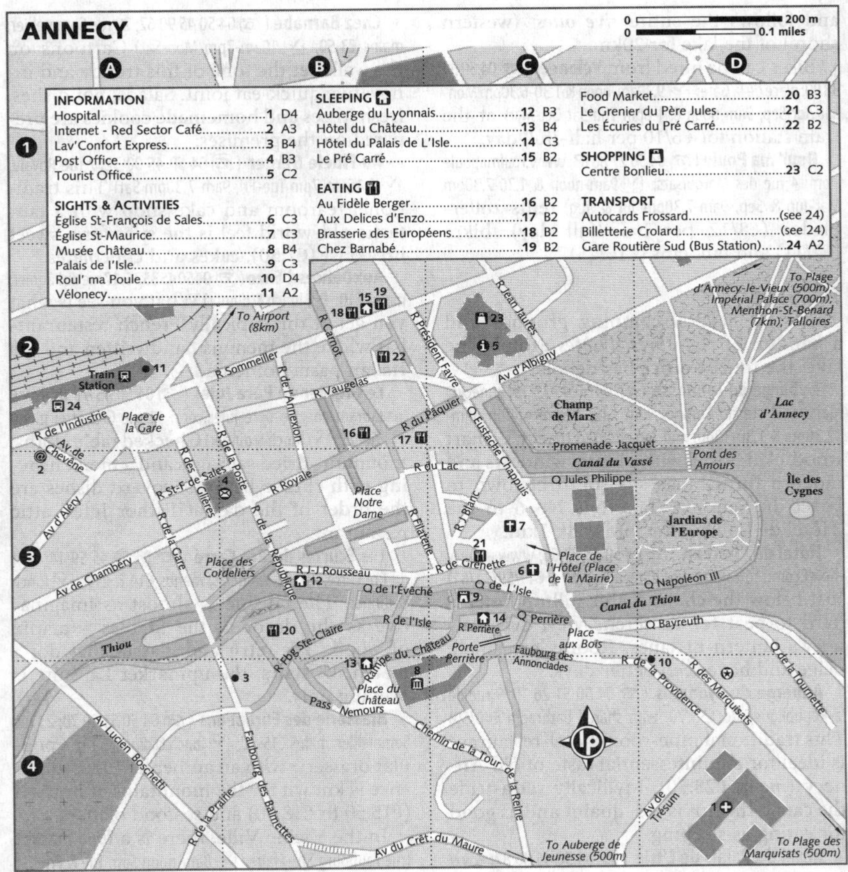

Sights & Activities

Wandering around the Vieille Ville and lakefront are the essence of Annecy. Just east, behind the town hall, are the **Jardins de l'Europe**, linked to the park of **Champ de Mars** by the poetic arch of **Pont des Amours** (Lovers' Bridge).

The old town retains much of its 17th-century appearance, with a warren of narrow streets, canals and colonnaded passageways. On the central island, the **Palais de l'Isle** (☎ 04 50 33 87 31; 3 passagede l'Île; adult/student/under 12yr €3.50/1.50/free, free 1st Sun of month Oct-May; ⏲ 10.30am-6pm Jun-Sep, 10am-noon & 2-5pm Wed-Mon Oct-May) was a prison, but now hosts local-history displays.

In the 13th- to 16th-century castle above town, the **Musée Château** (☎ 04 50 33 87 30; adult/student/under 12yr €5/2/free; ⏲ 10.30am-6pm Jun-Sep, 10am-noon & 2-5pm Wed-Mon Oct-May) explores traditional Savoyard art and Alpine natural history. A combined ticket covering palace and castle costs €6.

Parks and grassy areas line the lakefront. **Plage d'Annecy-le-Vieux** (admission free; ⏲ Jul & Aug) is 1km east of Champ de Mars. Somewhat closer to town, the privately run **Plage Impérial** (admission €3; ⏲ Jul & Aug) slumbers in the shade of the elegant pre-WWI **Impérial Palace**. You'll find **Plage des Marquisats** (admission free; ⏲ Jul & Aug) 1km south along rue des Marquisats.

Biking and blading are big in Annecy. A two-way cycling track – equally popular with roller-bladers – starts in Annecy-le-Vieux and follows the entire *rive ouest* (western shore) of the lake for 20km.

Bikes can be hired from **Vélonecy** (☎ 04 50 51 38 90; place de la Gare; ⌚ 9.30am-noon & 1.30-6.30pm Mon-Sat Apr-Sep, 9am-noon & 1-6pm Thu-Sat Oct-Mar) at the train station for €6/10 per half-/full day.

Roul' ma Poule (☎ 04 50 27 86 83; www.roulmapoule.com; 4 rue des Marquisats; ⌚ 9am-noon & 1.30-7.30pm Mar-Jun & Sep, 9am-7.30pm Jul & Aug) rents rollerblades (€8/12 per half-/full day), bikes (€7/11) and tandems (€16/25).

Sleeping

There are several camping grounds and a handful of *chambres d'hôtes* around the lake; the tourist office has details.

Auberge de Jeunesse (☎ 04 50 45 33 19; annecy@fuaj.org; 4 rte du Semnoz; dm €12; ⌚ reception 8am-12.30pm & 1.30-10pm mid-Jan–Nov) Annecy's smart wood-clad hostel with picture windows and modern furnishings sits south of town in Forêt du Semnoz. Take bus No 6 to the 'Hôtel de Police' stop and walk 1km.

Hôtel du Château (☎ 04 50 45 27 66; www.annecy-hotel.com; 16 rampe du Château; s/d/tr/q €49/59/71/81) Just below the chateau, this hilltop hotel is hard to beat for its serene view over Annecy's lantern-lit lanes. Rooms are small, beige and have seen better days.

Auberge du Lyonnais (☎ 04 50 51 26 10; 9 rue de la République; s/d €55/70, with shared bathroom €40/50) This traditional nine-room hotel-restaurant is ideal for a quintessential taste of old Annecy (*menu* €28.50). Idyllically set astride the canal, the inn is old, quaint and as good for eating as sleeping.

Hôtel du Palais de L'Isle (☎ 04 50 45 86 87; www.hoteldupalaisdelisle.com; 13 rue Perrière; s/d from €62/76; 💻) Guests slumber in the heart of Vieille Ville action at this old 18th-century house where the crisp contemporary décor is an oasis of peace after the tourist mayhem outside.

Le Pré Carré (☎ 04 50 52 14 14; www.hotel-annecy.net; 27 rue Sommellier; s/d €125/135; 💻) The contemporary interior of this modern four-star hotel makes a refreshing change from the older norm. Service is impeccable and the sauna is a dream.

Eating

In the Vieille Ville, the quays along both sides of Canal du Thiou are lined with cafés and restaurants. There are lots of cheap places along rue du Pâquier.

Chez Barnabé (☎ 04 50 45 90 62; 29 rue Sommellier; mains €3.50; ⌚ 10am-7pm Mon-Sat) Cartoons on the walls set the tone of this trendy and innovative quick-eat joint. Salads, hot dishes, fresh juices and homemade cookies are prepared on the premises.

Au Fidèle Berger (☎ 04 50 45 00 32; 2 rue Royale; ⌚ 9.15am-7pm Tue-Fri, 9am-7.30pm Sat) This traditional tearoom and cake shop with a fantastic old-world feel is the spot for a sweet breakfast (€7.50), cakes and chocolates.

Aux Delices d'Enzo (☎ 04 50 45 35 36; 17 rue du Pâquier; mains €10; ⌚ lunch & dinner) What you see is what you get at this typically French restaurant-bar where the menu is handwritten and the Italian pasta homemade.

Le Grenier du Père Jules (☎ 04 50 45 41 18; www.restaurant-chez-le-pere-jules.com; 11 rue Grenette; menu €11.50-21; ⌚ lunch & dinner) Checked table cloths, mountain-dried sausages and a menu heaving with cheese-heavy Savoyard dishes are the order of the day at Father Jules' attic restaurant.

Les Écuries du Pré Carré (☎ 04 50 45 59 14; cour du Pré Carré, 10 rue Vaugelas; menus €14 & €19; ⌚ lunch & dinner) The cuisine is almost as imaginative as the décor at the Stables – a mix of wood, '70s retro and glasses that don't match. Upstairs, the upmarket La Suite is evening only.

Brasserie des Européens (☎ 04 50 51 30 70; 23 rue Sommeiller; mains €15-20; ⌚ lunch & dinner) This popular brasserie with an authentic 1920s ambience is known for the mountains of mussels (€15.50 to €18.50) and seafood platters.

In the Vieille Ville, there is a **food market** (rue Faubourg Ste-Claire; ⌚ 8am-noon Sun, Tue & Fri).

Getting There & Away

From Annecy's small **airport** (NCY; ☎ 04 50 27 30 06; 8 route Côte Merle) north of the city in Meythet, Air France operates daily flights to/from Paris' Orly Ouest (€220, 1¼ hours).

From the **bus station** (Gare Routière Sud; rue de l'Industrie), adjoining the train station, the **Billetterie Crolard** (☎ 04 50 45 08 12; www.voyages-crolard.com; ⌚ 7.15am-12.30pm & 1.45-7.30pm Mon-Sat, Sun in peak seasons) sells bus tickets to lakeside destinations including Menthon (€2.10, 20 minutes) and Talloires (€2.90, 30 minutes). It also runs up to five daily buses to/from Lyon-St-Exupéry airport (single/return €30/45).

Next door, **Autocars Frossard** (☎ 04 50 45 73 90; ⌚ 7.45-11am & 2-7.15pm Mon-Fri, 7.45am-1pm Sat) sells tickets for Geneva (€10.30, 1¾ hours, up to 12 daily) and a bus four times weekly to/from Nice (€66.50, 9¼ hours) via Grenoble (€16.60, two hours).

From the **train station** (place de la Gare), there are frequent trains to Chambéry (€8.20, 50 minutes), Lyon (€20.50, 2¼ hours) and Paris' Gare de Lyon (€109, 3¾ hours).

GRENOBLE

pop 156,000

Elegant Grenoble is the Alps' economic soul. Spectacularly sited in a broad valley surrounded by snow-capped mountains, it sits in the centre of the Dauphiné region. Shops thrive, boulevards are broad and architecturally fine, and a gregarious student population adds a big-city buzz to the air.

Orientation

The old city is centred around place Grenette and place Notre Dame, both 1km east of the train and bus stations. The main university campus is a couple of kilometres east of the old centre on the southern side of the Isère River.

Information

Arobase (☎ 04 76 19 08 49; 22 rue de la Poste; per 15/30/60min €1/1.50/2.50; 🕑 10am-11pm Mon-Sat, 1-9pm Sun) Internet access.

Au 43 Viallet (43 rue Viallet; 🕑 7am-8pm) Laundrette.

Laverie Berriat (88 cours Berriat; 🕑 7am-8pm) Laundrette.

Neptune Internet (☎ 04 76 63 94 18; 2 rue de la Paix; per hr €2.50; 🕑 9am-9pm Mon-Fri, 10am-8pm Sat, 1-8pm Sun) Internet access.

Post office (rue de la République) Next to the tourist office.

Tourist office (☎ 04 76 42 41 41; www.grenoble-isere.info; 14 rue de la République; 🕑 9am-6.30pm Mon-Sat, 10am-1pm Sun, longer hr Jun-Aug) Inside the Maison du Tourisme. Sells maps and guides, arranges city tours.

Sights

Looming above the old city on the northern side of the Isère River, the grand 16th-century **Fort de la Bastille** is Grenoble's best known landmark. The views are spectacular, with vast mountains on every side and the grey waters of the Isère River below.

To get to the fort, hop into one of the pods of the **Téléphérique Grenoble Bastille** (☎ 04 76 44 33 65; quai Stéphane Jay; adult/student/under 5yr €4/3.50/free, adult/student return €6/5). Unsurprisingly, it gets crowded in summer – leave early to avoid the worst queues.

The sleek glass-and-steel exterior of Grenoble's boldest museum stands at the southern end of place Notre Dame. Also called Musée des Beaux-Arts, **Musée de Grenoble** (☎ 04 76 63 44 44; www.museedegrenoble.fr; 5 place de Lavalette; adult/student €5/2, free 1st Sun of month; 🕑 10am-6.30pm Wed-Mon) is renowned for its modern collection, including works by Chagall, Matisse, Modigliani, Monet, Picasso, Pissaro, Gauguin among others.

The **Musée Dauphinois** (☎ 04 76 85 19 01; www.musee-dauphinois.fr, in French; 30 rue Maurice Gignoux; admission free; 🕑 10am-7pm Wed-Mon Jun-Sep, to 6pm Oct-May) documents the cultures, crafts and traditions of Alpine life, including a fantastic exhibition devoted to the region's skiing history.

This moving **Musée de la Résistance et de la Déportation de l'Isère** (Resistance & Deportation Museum; ☎ 04 76 42 38 53; www.resistance-en-isere.com, in French; 14 rue Hébert; admission free; 🕑 9am-6pm Mon & Wed-Fri, 1.30-6pm Tue, 10am-6pm Sat & Sun Sep-Jun, 10am-7pm Mon & Wed-Sun, 1.30-7pm Tue Jul & Aug) examines the deportation of Jews and other 'undesirables' from Grenoble to Nazi camps during WWII, and explores the role of the Vercors region in the French Resistance.

Considered one of Europe's leading centres of contemporary art, **Le Magasin** (☎ 04 76 21 95 84; www.magasin-cnac.org; 155 cours Berriat; adult/student/under 10yr €3.50/2/free; 🕑 2-7pm Tue-Sun) is housed in a vast warehouse built by employees of Gustave Eiffel. There are two exhibition areas – a permanent 1000-sq-metre space with a huge glass roof called 'The Rue' and a flexible space of about 900 sq metres known as 'The Galleries'. Charles Saatchi would be green with envy.

On place Notre-Dame the imposing **Cathédrale Notre Dame** and adjoining 14th-century Bishops' Palace – home to Grenoble's bishops until 1908 – form the **Musée de l'Ancien Évêché** (☎ 04 76 03 15 25; www.ancien-eveche-isere.com, in French; 2 rue Très Cloîtres; admission free; 🕑 9am-6pm Wed-Sat & Mon, 10am-7pm Sun).

Activities

For information on activities, the main outdoor organisations are in the **Maison de la Montagne** (☎ 08 25 82 55 88; 3 rue Raoul Blanchard; 🕑 9am-6pm Mon-Fri, 10am-1pm & 2-5pm Sat), including the **Bureau Info-Montagne** (☎ 04 76 42 45 90; www.grande-traversee-alpes.com, in French) which has information on hiking routes, *gîtes* (country accommodations) and *refuges*.

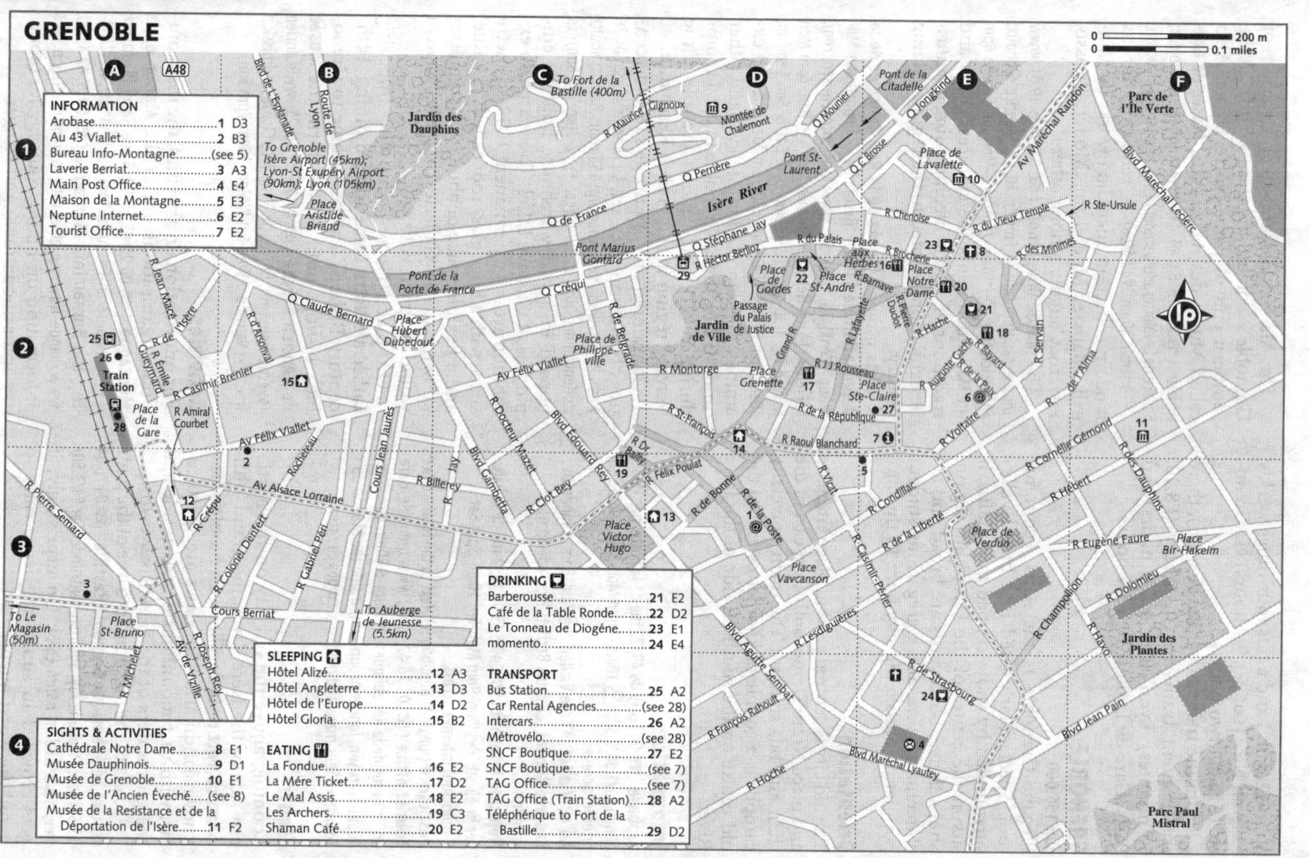
GRENOBLE
INFORMATION
Arobase....1 D3
Au 43 Viallet....2 B3
Bureau Info-Montagne....(see 5)
Laverie Berriat....3 A3
Main Post Office....4 E4
Maison de la Montagne....5 E3
Neptune Internet....6 E2
Tourist Office....7 E2
SIGHTS & ACTIVITIES
Cathédrale Notre Dame....8 E1
Musée Dauphinois....9 D1
Musée de Grenoble....10 E1
Musée de l'Ancien Évêché....(see 8)
Musée de la Resistance et de la Déportation de l'Isère....11 F2
SLEEPING
Hôtel Alizé....12 A3
Hôtel Angleterre....13 D3
Hôtel de l'Europe....14 D2
Hôtel Gloria....15 B2
EATING
La Fondue....16 E2
La Mére Ticket....17 D2
Le Mal Assis....18 E2
Les Archers....19 C3
Shaman Café....20 E2
DRINKING
Barberousse....21 E2
Café de la Table Ronde....22 D2
Le Tonneau de Diogéne....23 E1
momento....24 E4
TRANSPORT
Bus Station....25 A2
Car Rental Agencies....(see 28)
Intercars....26 A2
Métrovélo....(see 28)
SNCF Boutique....27 E2
SNCF Boutique....(see 7)
TAG Office....(see 7)
TAG Office (Train Station)....28 A2
Téléphérique to Fort de la Bastille....29 D2

Sleeping

Auberge de Jeunesse (☎ 04 76 09 33 52; grenoble@fuaj.org; 10 av du Grésivaudan; B&B €12; reception 7.30am-11pm) Five kilometres south of the train station in the Echirolles district. From Cours Jean Jaurès, take bus 1 to the Quinzaine stop (look for the Casino supermarket).

Hôtel Alizé (☎ 04 76 43 12 91; www.hotelalize.com; 1 rue Amiral Courbet; s with hand basin €28, d with hand basin/shower/shower & toliet €30/35/39, tr €47) The major drawcard of this simple one-star pad opposite the train station is its cheapness; book in advance to snag one of its 35 rooms.

Hôtel Gloria (☎ 04 76 46 12 93; hotelgloria@wanadoo.fr; 12 rue Aristide Berges; s/d €46/50) Gloria is a simple number, tucked down an appealing side street in the train station area. The hotel's heyday is long-gone, but it's still an atmospherically old-fashioned place to stay.

Hôtel de l'Europe (☎ 04 76 46 16 94; www.hoteleurope.fr; 22 place Grenette; s/d from €52/56, s with hand basin/shower €29/39) This late-17th-century Grenoblois building on place Grenette is among the city's oldest hotels. The 45 comfortable rooms are fantastic value – the front ones have balconies with mountain views.

Hôtel Angleterre (☎ 04 76 87 37 21; www.hotel-angleterre-grenoble.com; 5 place Victor Hugo; d €98-170;) Hotel England – the pick of several three-star hotels in the area – has a lovely outlook over tree-shaded place Victor Hugo. Rooms are luxurious, if a little small.

Eating

Les Archers (☎ 04 76 46 27 76; 2 rue Docteur Bailly; mains €10-15; 11am-2am Tue-Sat, to 1am Sun & Mon) This busy brasserie has a great outside terrace, cosy red leather banquette seating inside and a shellfish repertoire that's hard to beat.

Shaman Café (☎ 04 38 37 23 56; 1 place Notre Dame; menu from €11; 8am-midnight) Submerge yourself in oriental opulence at this cavernous restaurant-cum-bar with low lighting and a cuisine that flits between India, Japan, Morocco and Italy.

La Fondue (☎ 04 76 15 20 72; 5 rue Brocherie; fondue per person €12.50-22.50; dinner Mon, lunch & dinner Tue-Sat) Leave your waistline worries at the door at Grenoble's fondue hot spot, which offers more than 15 flavours of fondue as well as traditional *tartiflette* and *raclette*.

Le Mal Assis (☎ 04 76 54 75 93; 9 rue Bayard; mains €15; dinner Tue-Sat) 'The Badly Seated' is a cosy upmarket restaurant favoured by a cultured crowd. Cuisine is very much old-school bourgeois; think traditional mains and *gratin dauphinois* (potatoes in nutmeg-spiced cream).

La Mère Ticket (☎ 04 76 44 45 40; 13 rue Jean-Jacques Rousseau; menus €18.50 & €24; lunch & dinner Mon-Sat) Traditional cooking is on offer at this endearingly old-fashioned French restaurant, with its checked table cloths, lace curtains and handwritten menu.

Drinking

Le Tonneau de Diogène (☎ 04 76 42 38 40; 6 place Notre Dame; menu from €8; 11.30am-midnight) Grenoble's best known philo-café is a cramped atmospheric place, decked out with polished wood, leather booths, tightly packed tables and an academic crowd.

Café de la Table Ronde (☎ 04 76 44 51 41; www.cafétableronde.com, in French; 7 place St-André; lunch/dinner menu €10/22; 7am-midnight Mon-Sat) This historic café from 1739 was a favoured haunt of Stendhal and Rousseau, and its old-world atmosphere has hardly changed since the 19th century. In summer its tables and chairs spill onto place St-André, the city's liveliest drinking square.

momento (☎ 04 76 26 21 59; 2 rue Beccaria; to 1am Sun-Wed, to 2am Thu-Sat) Steel and neon mingle with a well-dressed set at this lounge bar, where tapas whets appetites and DJs spin vinyl from 10.30pm.

Barberousse (☎ 04 76 57 14 53; www.barberousse.com, in French; 8 rue Hache; 6pm-2am Tue-Sat) There are 70-odd types of aromatic rum (cherry, apple and papaya etc) at this superbly hip shooter bar hidden down an alley.

Getting There & Away

AIR

A clutch of budget airlines, including Ryanair and easyJet, flies to/from **Grenoble-Isère airport** (GNR; ☎ 04 76 65 48 48; www.grenoble-airport.com), 45km northwest of Grenoble, from London, Bristol, Stockholm, Warsaw and Rome.

BUS

The **bus station** (☎ 04 76 87 90 31; rue Émile Gueymard) is next to the train station. Bus companies including **VFD** (☎ 08 20 83 38 33; www.vfd.fr, in French) and **Transisère** (☎ 04 76 87 90 31; www.transisere.fr, in French) serve many Alpine destinations, including the Vercors ski stations.

Intercars (☎ 04 76 46 19 77; www.intercars.fr, in French; 9am-noon & 2-6pm Mon-Fri, 9am-noon & 2-5pm Sat) handles international destinations.

TRAIN

From the **train station** (rue Émile Gueymard), next to the Gare Europole tram stop, trains run to/from Paris' Gare de Lyon (from €86, three hours), Chambéry (€9.50, one hour, 10 to 13 daily) and Lyon (€17.30, 1¾ hours, five daily). Train tickets are sold at the station and in town at the **SNCF boutique** (15 rue de la République; 9am-6.30pm Mon-Fri, 10am-6pm Sat).

Getting Around

TO/FROM THE AIRPORT

Shuttle buses run by **Trans-Isère** (04 76 87 90 31) to/from Grenoble-Isère airport use the bus station (single/return €4/8, 45 minutes, four to eight daily).

BICYCLE

Métrovélo (08 20 22 38 38; 7am-8pm Mon-Fri, 9am-noon & 2-7pm Sat & Sun), underneath the train station, rents out bikes for €1.20/3/5 per hour/half-day/full day.

BUS & TRAM

Grenoble's three pollution-free tram lines – called A, B and C – run through the heart of town. A bus and tram ticket costs €1.30 from drivers or the ticket machines at tram/bus stops. Time-stamp tickets in the blue machines at stops before boarding. *Carnets* of 10/20 tickets (€10.50/19.50) can be bought at the **TAG office** (04 76 20 66 66; 8.30am-6.30pm Mon-Fri, 9am-6pm Sat) inside the tourist office or next to the train station. Trams run from 5am to midnight; buses stop between 6pm and 9pm.

CAR

All the major car-rental agencies are in the Europole complex underneath the train station.

THE JURA

The dark wooded hills and granite plateaus of the Jura Mountains stretch for 360km along the French–Swiss border from the Rhine to the Rhône. Part of the historic Franche-Comté region, the Jura is one of the least explored regions in France, which makes it a fine place to escape the Alpine crowds. If you're looking for a taste of traditional mountain life, the Jura makes a far better destination than the ruthlessly modernised and tourist-orientated resorts elsewhere in the Alps.

The Jura – from a Gaulish word meaning 'forest' – is an important agricultural area, best known for its unique wines and cheeses. It is also France's premier cross-country skiing area and popular for its superb hiking and nature trails.

BESANÇON

pop 125,000

Old town, young heart: that's Besançon, capital of the Franche-Comté region. One of France's most liveable cities, Besançon boasts one of the country's largest foreign student populations and an innovative spirit that finds full expression in an old town humming with hip bars and bistros. Since the 18th century, Besançon has been a noted clock-making centre, and Victor Hugo and the film-pioneering Lumière brothers were all born on place Victor Hugo in the old town.

Orientation

The old city is enclosed by the curve of the Doubs River (Boucle du Doubs). The tourist office and train station sit just outside this loop. The Battant quarter straddles the northwest bank of the river around rue Battant. Grande Rue, the pedestrianised main street, slices through the old city from the river to the gates of the citadel.

Information

Blanc-Matic (14 rue de la Madeleine; 7am-8pm) Laundrette.

ID PC (28 rue de la République; per hr €3; 9.30am-noon & 2-7pm Tue-Sat) Computer shop with Internet terminal.

Post office (23 rue Proudhon; 8am-7pm Mon-Fri, 8am-noon Sat)

Tourist office (03 81 80 92 55; www.besancon-tourisme.com; 2 place de la 1ère Armée Française; 9.30am-7pm Mon-Sat, 10am-5pm Sun Jun-Sep, 9.30am-6pm Mon-Sat, 10.30am-12.30pm Sun Apr, May & Oct, 9.30am-12.30pm & 1.30-5.30pm Mon-Sat, 10.30am-12.30pm Sun Nov-Mar) Sells city maps and guides.

Sights

Built by Vauban for Louis XIV between 1688 and 1711, Besançon's **citadel** (03 81 87 83 33; www.citadelle.com; rue des Fusillés de la Résistance; adult/4-14yr €8/4.50; 9am-7pm Jul & Aug, 9am-6pm Apr-Jun, Sep & Oct, 10am-5pm Nov-Mar) is a steep 15-minute walk from **Porte Noire** (Black Gate; rue de la Convention), a triumphal arch left over from the city's Roman days. Inside the citadel are three museums: the **Musée Comtois** zooms in on local traditions, the **Musée d'Histoire Naturelle** covers natural history, and the **Musée de la Résistance et de la Déportation** examines the rise of Nazism and the French Resistance movement. There's also an animal park with an insect house, aquarium and small zoo.

Thought to be France's oldest museum, the **Musée des Beaux-Arts** (☎ 03 81 87 80 49; 1 place de la Révolution; adult/student €3/free; ⏰ 9.30am-noon & 2-6pm Wed-Mon) has an impressive art collection and displays on Franche-Comté's long history of clock-making.

Housed in the 18th-century **Cathédrale St-Jean** (rue de la Convention; adult/under 18yr €2.50/free; ⏰ 7 guided tours daily Wed-Mon Apr-Sep, Thu-Mon Oct-Mar), the city's incredible *Horloge Astronomique* (astronomical clock) has 30,000 moving parts and tells the time in 16 places, the tides in eight different ports, and the time of sunrise and sunset. It really has to be seen to be believed.

Sleeping

Auberge de Jeunesse Les Oiseaux (☎ 03 81 40 32 00; 48 rue des Cras; dm incl breakfast €20) The city's hostel is two kilometres east of the train station. Rates include breakfast and bedding; subsequent nights cost €2 less. Take bus 7 from the tourist office in the direction of Orchamps and get off at Les Oiseaux.

Hôtel du Nord (☎ 03 81 81 34 56; www.hotel-du-nord-besancon.com; 8 rue Moncey; s/d/tr from €35/38/48) This excellent-value hotel, strung with wrought-iron balconies and flower boxes, sits on a smart street in the old quarter. The pricier rooms have huge bathrooms.

Hôtel de Paris (☎ 03 81 81 36 56; www.hotel-deparis.com; 33 rue des Granges; d €50-64; 💻) The Paris prides itself on being the city's oldest hotel where a clutch of celebrities stayed, including Colette and George Sand in 1932. Skip breakfast in the hotel and head for the grand Brasserie du Commerce next door instead.

Hôtel Castan (☎ 03 81 65 02 00; www.hotelcastan.fr; 6 square Archéologique Castan; d €110-170; 💻) Monumental fireplaces, canopy beds, stags' heads and ornate grandfather clocks add a touch of period authenticity to Besançon's loveliest boutique hotel.

Eating

Au Gourmand (☎ 03 81 81 40 56; 5 rue Mégevand; menu from €9; ⏰ lunch & dinner Tue-Fri, lunch Sat) Going strong for 22 years, this legendary bistro is loved by everyone – students, couples and old ladies alike. The house speciality is *les parmentières* (mashed potato bespeckled with various fillings).

Au Petit Polonais (☎ 03 81 81 23 67; 81 rue Granges; menu €11-14.50; ⏰ lunch & dinner Mon-Fri, lunch Sat) One of Besançon's oldest restaurants, founded in 1870 by Polish émigrés, this place still pulls in the punters with its delicious cooked meats, fondues and sausages.

Apéro et dînatoire – apéritif and a light casual dinner – is what trendy **MI:AM** (☎ 03 81 82 09 56; 8 rue Morand; mains €15; ⏰ 11.30am-midnight Tue-San) is best at. Snag a seat on the busy buzzing street terrace if you can. The same set run **La Femme du Boulanger** (☎ 03 81 82 86 93; 6 rue Morand; salads €10; ⏰ 8am-7pm Mon-Sat), a paradise for cake and tart lovers, next door.

Self-caterers can food shop at the **indoor market** (cnr rue Paris & rue Claude Goudimel) or **outdoor market** (place de la Révolution).

Drinking

Nightlife is concentrated in the old Battant quarter and around the river; Besançon's most happening street is rue Claude Pouillet (along with parallel quai Vauban).

La Crémerie (☎ 03 81 83 55 00; 9 rue Claude Pouillet; ⏰ 5pm-1am Tue-Thu, to 2am Fri & Sat) Hotshot venue on the city's buzziest street. Bars are constantly coming and going along this ramshackle strip, but the Dairy has long been strong.

Carpé Diem (☎ 03 81 83 11 18; 2 place Jean Gigoux) Drink, smoke and hang out with a student set at this small, rough-and-ready café-bar through which a decidedly bohemian air blows.

Les Passagers du Zinc (☎ 03 81 81 54 70; 5 rue de Vignier; ⏰ 5pm-1am Tue-Fri, 5pm-2am Sat & Sun) A grungy bar and club that hosts tapas nights and live bands. Step through the bonnet of an old Citröen DS to reach the cellar.

Getting There & Away

From the **bus station** (9 rue Proudhon), there are daily services to Ornans and Pontarlier.

From **Besançon Gare Viotte**, 800m uphill from the city centre, there are trains to/from Paris' Gare de Lyon (€86, 2¾ hours, three daily), Dijon (€14.40, 50 minutes, 20 daily), Lyon (€24.10, 2¾ hours, seven daily) and local destinations. Buy tickets at the train station or from the **Boutique SNCF** (44 Grand Rue; ⏰ 9am-7pm Mon-Fri, 9am-6pm Sat) in town.

Getting Around

Borrow a bicycle to cruise around town – free with a valid bus ticket – from local bus company office, **Boutique Ginko** (☎ 08 25 00 22 44; www.ginkobus.com; 4 place du Huit Septembre; 🕑 10am-7pm Mon-Sat). Bus tickets cost €1.05/3.20/8.90 for a single ticket/day ticket/*carnet* of 10.

AROUND BESANÇON

Saline Royal

Envisaged by its designer, Claude-Nicolas Ledoux, as the 'ideal city', the 18th-century **Saline Royale** (Royal Salt Works; ☎ 03 81 54 45 45; www.salineroyale.com; adult/16-25yr/6-15yr €7/4.50/3; 🕑 9am-7pm Jul-Aug, 9am-noon & 2-6pm Apr-Jun, Sep & Oct, 10am-noon & 2-5pm Nov-Mar) in **Arc-et-Senans** (pop 1400), 30km southwest of Besançon, is a showpiece of early Industrial Age town planning. Although his urban dream was never realised, Ledoux' semicircular saltworks is now listed as a Unesco World Heritage Site.

Regular trains link Besançon (€5.60, 35 minutes, up to 10 daily) and Arc-et-Senans.

Route Pasteur & Route du Vin

Nearly every town in the Jura seems has a street, square or garden (sometimes all three) named after Louis Pasteur, the great 19th-century chemist, born and raised in the Jura, who invented pasteurisation and developed the first rabies vaccine.

Pasteur grew up in **Arbois**, a rural community 35km east of Dole. His laboratory and workshops in Arbois are on display at **La Maison de Louis Pasteur** (☎ 03 84 66 11 72; 83 rue de Courcelles; adult/7-15yr €5.50/3; guided tours 🕑 9.45am, 10.45am, 11.45am & hourly 2-6pm Jun-Sep, hourly 2.15-5.15pm Apr, May & 1-15 Oct). The house is still decorated with its original 19th-century fixtures and fittings.

No visit to Arbois, Jura's wine capital, would be complete without a glass of *vin jaune*. The history of this nutty 'yellow wine', matured for six years in oak casks, is told in the **Musée de la Vigne et du Vin** (☎ 03 84 66 26 14; museevignevin@wanadoo.fr; adult/child €3.50/2.50; 🕑 10am-noon & 2-6pm Wed-Mon Mar-Jun, Sep & Oct, 10am-12.30pm & 2-6pm Jul & Aug, 2-6pm Wed-Mon Nov-Feb).

The Arbois **tourist office** (☎ 03 84 66 55 50; www.arbois.com; rue de l'Hôtel de Ville; 🕑 9.30am-noon & 2-6pm Sep-Apr, 9am-12.30pm & 2-6.30pm May-Sep) has cycling information and a list of *caves* where you can try the local vintage.

Trains link Arbois and Besançon (€7.70, 45 minutes, eight to 10 daily).

PARC NATUREL RÉGIONAL DU HAUT-JURA

Experience the Jura at its rawest in the Parc Naturel Régional du Haut-Jura, an area of 757 sq km filled with glacial lakes, mountains and low-lying valleys.

Highlights include **Les Rousses** (pop 2850, elevation 1100m) the park's main sports hub, both in winter (for skiing) and summer (for walking and mountain biking) and the incredible views from the **Telesiège Val Mijoux** (chairlift; return €6; 🕑 9.30am-12.30pm & 2-6pm Jul & Aug), which travels from the ski resort of Mijoux all the way to Mont Rond (elevation 1533m). Even more stunning is the view from the **Col de la Faucille**, 20km south of Les Rousses.

The **Château de Voltaire** (☎ 04 50 40 53 21; allée du Château; 🕑 Tue-Sat mid-May–mid-Sep) where the great writer lived from 1759 until his return to Paris and death in 1778, is also worth visiting. Guided tours take in the chateau, chapel and surrounding 7-hectare park.

Public transport in the park is almost non-existent, so you'll need your own wheels.

PROVENCE

It's impossible not to be swept up by the sights – and smells – of picture-perfect Provence. Whether wandering through the region's lavender-filled fields or drinking in the spicy aromas of Marseille's markets, you'll discover Provence is an assault on the senses. With tiny hamlets, hilltop villages and brightly coloured fields, it made the ideal canvas for artists such as Cézanne and van Gogh, who both lived and worked here and made Provence the subject of some of their most famous paintings.

MARSEILLE

pop 807,071

The gritty, grimy and gloriously real city of Marseille is France's oldest and largest after Paris. It's far less genteel than its Provençal counterparts, but its rough-and-tumble edginess and litter-swirled streets have an irresistible pull. Pulsing to a sultry Mediterranean tempo, Marseille also beats to the drum of neighbouring northern Africa. Its fusion of cultures is best experienced at its thronging street markets, where spice stands and Moroccan craft-shops sit side by side with stalls selling fish straight off the boats.

Orientation

The city's main thoroughfare, blvd La Canebière, stretches eastwards from the Vieux Port (Old Port). The train station is north of La Canebière at the northern end of blvd d'Athènes. A few blocks south of La Canebière is the cours Julien, a large pedestrianised square. The ferry terminal is west of place de la Joliette, a few minutes' walk north of the Nouvelle Cathédrale. Addresses below include arrondissements (1er being the most central).

Information

There are banks and exchange bureaus on La Canebière near the Vieux Port.

Canebière Change (39 La Canebière, 1er) Currency-exchange service.

Info Cafe (☎ 04 91 33 74 98; 1 quai du Rive Neuve, 1er; per 30min/1hr €2/3.50; 9am-10pm Mon-Sat, 2.30-7.30pm Sun) Internet access.

Laverie des Allées (15 allées Léon Gambetta, 1er; 8am-8pm) Laundrette.

Laverie Self-Service (5 rue Justice Breteuil, 1er) Laundrette.

Main post office (1 place de l'Hôtel des Postes, 1er) Offers currency exchange.

Tourist office (☎ 04 91 13 89 00; www.marseille-tourisme.com; 4 La Canebière, 1er; 9am-7pm Mon-Sat, 10am-5pm Sun, mid-Jun–mid-Sep) Sells the Marseille City Pass (for one/two days €18/25), which includes access to the city's museums, unlimited travel on public transport, a guided city tour and a boat trip to either Île d'If or Îles due Frioul.

Tourist office annexe (☎ 04 91 50 59 18; Gare St-Charles train station; 10am-1pm & 2-6pm Mon-Sat)

Dangers & Annoyances

Forget everything you may have heard about Marseille – it's no more dangerous than many other French cities. In fact, its ingrained integration of cultures meant Marseille got off lightly during the riots that swept the country in 2005. But as with any big city, keep your wits about you, and don't leave anything of value in a parked car, even in the boot. At night, take extra care in the Belsunce area, southwest of the train station.

Sights

MUSEUMS

The courtyard of the **Centre de la Vieille Charité** (Old Charity Cultural Centre; ☎ 04 91 14 58 80; 2 rue de la Charité, 2e; admission €3; 10am-5pm Tue-Sun Oct-May, 11am-6pm May-Sep) incorporates the **Musée d'Archéologie** (☎ 04 91 14 58 80; admission €2) and **Musée des Arts Africains, Océaniens & Amérindiens** (Museum of African, Oceanic & American Indian Art; ☎ 04 91 14 58 38; admission €2), which has a diverse collection of primitive art, including masks from the Americas, Africa and the Pacific. A combined ticket to all the museums costs €4.

The **Musée d'Histoire de Marseille** (☎ 04 91 90 42 22; ground fl, Centre Bourse shopping centre, 1er; adult/child/under 12yr €2/1/free; noon-7pm Mon-Sat) offers an overview of the city's history, including the remains of a 3rd-century vessel discovered in the Vieux Port in 1974.

BASILIQUE NOTRE DAME DE LA GARDE

Be blown away by the celestial views and knock-out 19th-century architecture at the hilltop **Basilique Notre Dame de la Garde** (☎ 04 91 13 40 80; admission free; basilica & crypt 7am-8pm May-Sep, 7am-10pm mid-Jun–mid-Aug, 7am-7pm Oct-Apr), the resplendent Romano-Byzantine basilica 1km south of the Vieux Port that dominates Marseille's skyline. The domed basilica was built between 1853 and 1864 and is ornamented with coloured marble, murals and mosaics restored in 2006.

CHÂTEAU D'IF

Immortalised in Alexandre Dumas' 1840s novel *Le Comte de Monte Cristo* (The Count of Monte Cristo), the 16th-century fortress-turned-prison **Château d'If** (☎ 04 91 59 02 30; adult/student €5/3.50; 9.30am-6pm Mon-Sat Sep-Mar, 9.30am-6.30pm Jun-Aug) sits on a 30-sq-km island 3.5km west of the Vieux Port. Political prisoners of all persuasions were incarcerated here, including the revolutionary hero Mirabeau, and the Communards of 1871.

GACM (☎ 04 91 55 50 09, www.answeb.net/gacm; 1 quai des Belges, 1er) runs boats to the Château d'If at 9am, 10.30am, noon, 2pm, and 3.30pm (€9 return, 20 minutes).

Sleeping

Generally, the better hotels cluster around the old port (where budget options are pretty much nonexistent) and as you head east out of the centre along the corniche.

Auberge de Jeunesse de Bonneveine (☎ 04 91 17 63 30; fax 04 91 73 97 23; impasse du Docteur Bonfils, 8e; dm €15-16, d €34-36, both incl bedding & breakfast; Feb-Dec;) A fair hike from the centre, this HI makes up for it with its proximity to the beach, and outdoor terrace and bar. Take bus 44 from the Rond Point du Prado metro stop and get off at the place Bonnefons stop.

Le Richelieu (☎ 04 91 31 01 92; www.lerichelieu-marseille.com; 52 corniche Président John F Kennedy, 7e; d €34-53) With a breezy, beach-house vibe and marine-themed rooms, this artists' haven is built onto the rocks next to the plage des Catalans.

Hôtel St-Louis (☎ 04 91 54 02 74; www.hotel-st-louis.com; 2 rue des Récollettes, 1er; d €45-47, tw €52, tr €63) This charmingly simple pied-à-terre is in the heart of Marseille's chic shopping district. Most rooms have towering ceilings, terracotta-tiled floors and charming balconies even Juliet would admire.

Hôtel Lutetia (☎ 04 91 50 81 78; www.hotelmarseille.com; 38 allées Léon Gambetta, 1er; s/d/tr from €55/60/69) Awaken to the cacophony of church bells ringing on Sunday mornings from Les Rèformès, the distinctive twin-steepled church just up the street from the sweet, petite Hôtel Lutetia.

Hôtel Péron (☎ 04 91 31 01 41; www.hotel-peron.com; 119 corniche John F Kennedy, 7e; d €69.50-72.50, tw €78-97; 💻) The faded exterior of this authentic 1920s period piece conceals bedrooms with original Art Deco bathrooms and parquet floors. Many rooms are angled to accentuate the sea views, and all have balconies.

Hôtel du Palais (04 91 37 78 86; www.hotelmarseille.com; 26 rue Breteuil, 6e; d €80-100; ⊠ ❄ 💻) For a stylish sleep, head south from the Vieux Port to this chic little place of 22 intimate rooms done out in designer shades, with chrome minibars, free wi-fi, a sleek red lobby, and cachet to spare.

Eating

African, Middle Eastern and Mediterranean cuisines, along with Provençal specialities, are the mainstays of Marseille's restaurants. Marseille is also the place to try authentic bouillabaisse (fish stew) – check out the restaurants around the old port.

Chez Madie Les Galinettes (☎ 04 91 90 40 87; 138 quai du Port, 2e; mains €10-28; 🕓 lunch & dinner Mon-Sat, closed Sat lunch Jun-Aug) Decked out with pop art and mural panels, this portside place is top for bouillabaisse (€35). Order a day ahead if you're stopping by for lunch.

Le Souk (☎ 04 91 91 29 29; 98 quai du Port, 2e; menu €20-30; 🕓 lunch Tue-Sun, dinner Tue-Sat Sep-Jun, lunch Sat & Sun, dinner Sun Jul & Aug) Try the authentic *tajine* amid Moroccan mosaic walls, iron furniture, and tiny candles.

Au Bord de l'Eau (☎ 04 91 72 68 04; 15 rue des Arapèdes, port de la Madrague Montredon, 8e; menu €25-30; 🕓 daily Jul-Aug) This little harbourside restaurant is literally 'at the water's edge' of the Calanques, but the fantastic seafood is worth the trip. Catch bus No 83, then bus 19.

Lemongrass (☎ 04 91 33 97 65; 8 rue Fort-Notre-Dame, 1e; menu €30; 🕓 closed Sun) Spice up your day (or night) at this refreshing fusion place. Lemongrass serves lush *menus* of Asian/French fare such as curried lobster and coconut rice pudding.

Chez Fonfon (☎ 04 91 52 14 38; 140 rue du Vallon des Auffes, 7e; mains around €40; 🕓 closed Mon lunch & Sun) Another place famed for its bouillabaisse, with a lush list of local rosés and crisp Cassis white wines.

Stock up at **Marché des Capucins** (place des Capucins, 1er; 🕓 Mon-Sat), one block north of La Canebière, or the **fruit and vegetable market** (cours Pierre Puget, 6e; 🕓 Mon-Sat). The **fish market** (quai des Belges; 🕓 8am-1pm) is a daily fixture at the Vieux Port docks.

Drinking & Entertainment

Cultural events are covered in Wednesday's *L'Hebdo* (in French; €1) available around town. The website www.marseillebynight.com, in French, also has listings.

Options for a coffee or something stronger abound on and around the Vieux Port. Students and artists congregate at the alternative cafés and bars of cours Julien and its surrounding streets.

Le Bar de la Marine (☎ 04 91 54 95 42; 15 quai de Rive Neuve, 1er; 🕓 7am-1am) This Marseille institution draws drinkers from every walk of life.

Au Petit Nice (☎ 04 91 48 43 04; 28 place Jean Jaurès; 🕓 6am-2am) This cosy Brit boozer-type place is a local favourite.

Pelle Mêle (☎ 04 91 54 85 26; 8 place aux Huiles, 1er; 🕓 7pm-1am Mon-Sat) Jive to jazz at this lively bistro near the port. Bands start from 10pm.

L'Intermediaire (☎ 04 91 47 01 25; 39 cours Julien; 🕓 7pm-2am Mon-Sat) Groovers gather at this artsy place for new bands (from 10.30pm most nights).

Getting There & Away

AIR

The **Marseille-Provence airport** (MRS; ☎ 04 42 14 14 14), also known as the Marseille-Marignane airport, is 28km northwest of the city in Marignane. It's a Ryanair minihub and has flights across Europe.

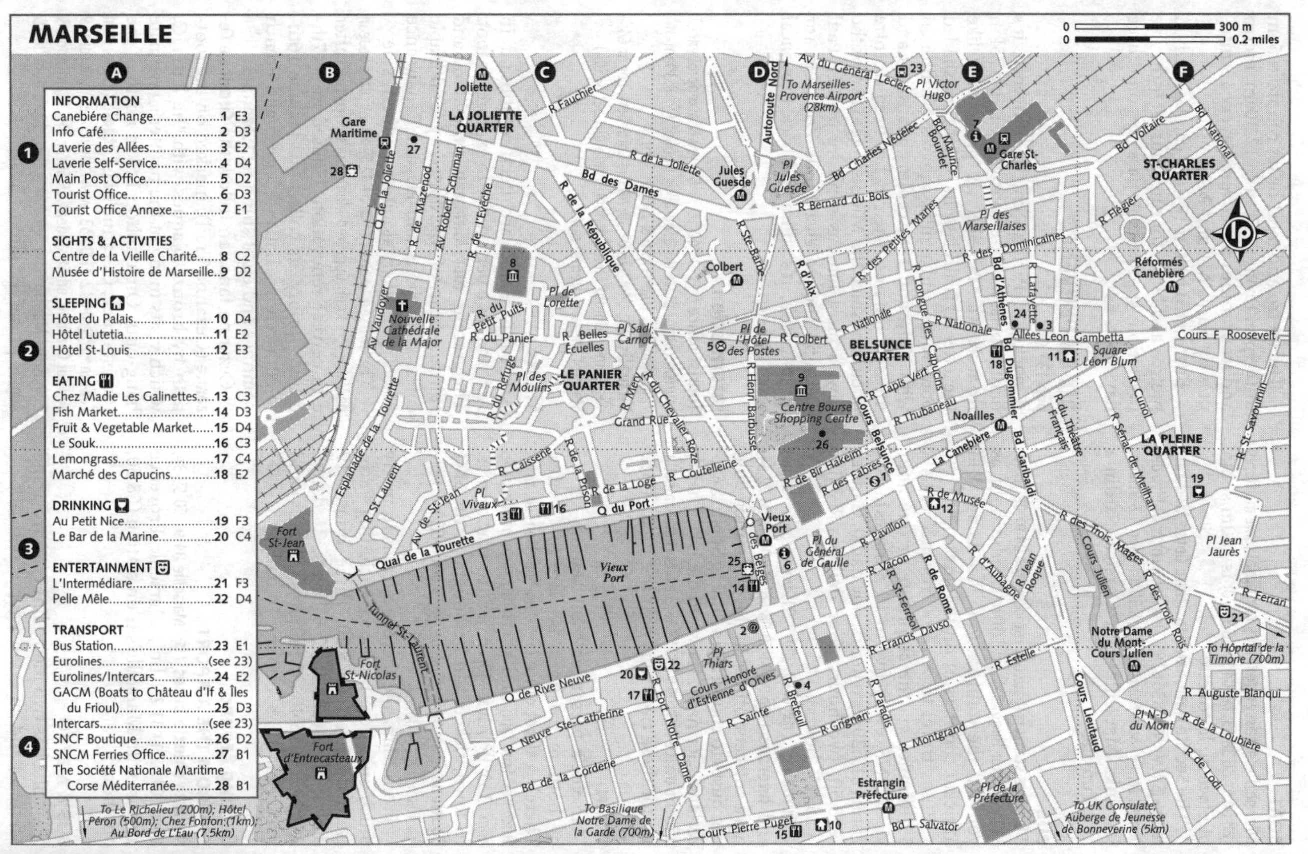
MARSEILLE
0 300 m
0 0.2 miles
INFORMATION
Canebiére Change 1 E3
Info Café 2 D3
Laverie des Allées 3 E2
Laverie Self-Service 4 D4
Main Post Office 5 D2
Tourist Office 6 D3
Tourist Office Annexe 7 E1
SIGHTS & ACTIVITIES
Centre de la Vieille Charité 8 C2
Musée d'Histoire de Marseille 9 D2
SLEEPING
Hôtel du Palais 10 D4
Hôtel Lutetia 11 E2
Hôtel St-Louis 12 E3
EATING
Chez Madie Les Galinettes 13 C3
Fish Market 14 D3
Fruit & Vegetable Market 15 D4
Le Souk 16 C3
Lemongrass 17 C4
Marché des Capucins 18 E2
DRINKING
Au Petit Nice 19 F3
Le Bar de la Marine 20 C4
ENTERTAINMENT
L'Intermédiare 21 F3
Pelle Mêle 22 D4
TRANSPORT
Bus Station 23 E1
Eurolines (see 23)
Eurolines/Intercars 24 E2
GACM (Boats to Château d'If & Îles du Frioul) 25 D3
Intercars (see 23)
SNCF Boutique 26 D2
SNCM Ferries Office 27 B1
The Société Nationale Maritime Corse Méditerranée 28 B1
To Le Richelieu (200m); Hôtel Péron (500m); Chez Fonfon (1km); Au Bord de L'Eau (7.5km)
To Basilique Notre Dame de la Garde (700m)
To UK Consulate; Auberge de Jeunesse de Bonneverine (5km)
To Marseilles-Provence Airport (28km)
To Hôpital de la Timone (700m)

FRANCE

BOAT

Marseille's **passenger ferry terminal** (gare maritime; ☎ 04 91 56 38 63; fax 04 91 56 38 70) is 250m south of place de la Joliette (2e).

The **Société Nationale Maritime Corse Méditerranée** (SNCM; ☎ 08 36 67 95 00; www.sncm.fr; 61 blvd des Dames, 2e; 8am-6pm Mon-Fri, 8.30am-noon & 2-5.30pm Sat) links Marseille with Corsica, Sardinia and Tunisia.

BUS

The **bus station** (gare des autocars; ☎ 04 91 08 16 40; 3 place Victor Hugo, 3e) is 150m to the right as you exit the train station. Tickets are sold at ticket counters or on the bus.

Buses travel to Aix-en-Provence (€4.40, 35 minutes via the autoroute or one hour via the N8, every five to 10 minutes), Avignon (€17.20, two hours, one daily), Cannes (€23.50, two hours, four daily) and Nice (€25, 2¾ hours).

Eurolines (☎ 0892 289 9091, www.eurolines.com) and **Intercars** (☎ 04 91 50 08 66; fax 04 91 08 72 34) have adjacent offices in the bus station, and run buses to countries including Spain, Switzerland, Germany, Italy and the UK. There's a joint **office** (☎ 04 91 50 57 55; 3 allées Léon Gambetta, 1er) for these two firms near the Vieux Port.

TRAIN

Marseille's passenger train station, served by both metro lines, is Gare St-Charles. There's a **ticket office** (9am-8pm Mon-Sat; ticket purchases 4am-1am) and a **left-luggage office** (rates from €3.50; 7.30am-10pm) next to platform A. In town, tickets can be bought at the **SNCF Boutique** (9 rue Montgrand, 6e; 9.30am-6.30pm Mon-Fri, 10am-6pm Sat).

From Marseille there are trains to pretty much anywhere in France including Paris' Gare de Lyon (€75.20, three hours, 17 daily), Nice (€26.40, 2½ hours, 21 daily), Avignon (€16.40, 30 minutes, 27 daily) and Lyon (€43.10, 3¼ hours, 16 daily).

Getting Around

TO/FROM THE AIRPORT

Navette shuttle buses (☎ Marseille 04 91 50 59 34, airport 04 42 14 31 27) link Marseille-Provence airport with Marseille's train station (€8.50, one hour).

BUS & METRO

Marseille has two metro lines (Métro 1 and Métro 2) and an extensive bus network.

The metro and most buses run from 5am until 9pm. From 9.25pm to 12.30am, metro and tram routes are covered every 15 minutes by buses M1 and M2.

Bus/metro tickets (€1.60) can be used on metros and buses for one hour after they've been time-stamped. A pass for one/three days costs €4/9.50.

AIX-EN-PROVENCE

pop 137,067

A pocket of Parisian chic in Provence, it's hard to believe Aix-en-Provence is just 25km from chaotic Marseille. Aix (pronounced like the letter X) is all class: its plane-tree–shaded boulevards and public squares are littered with 17th- and 18th-century mansions and mossy fountains. The city has been a centre of culture since the Middle Ages (two of the town's most famous sons are painter Paul Cézanne and novelist Emile Zola) but for all its polish, it's still a laid-back Provençal town at heart.

Information

Tourist office (☎ 04 42 16 11 61; www.aixenprovencetourism.com; 2 place du Général de Gaulle; 8.30am-7pm Mon-Sat, 10am-1pm & 2-6pm Sun)

Virtualis (☎ 04 42 26 02 30; 40 rue Cordeliers; per hr €4; 9am-midnight Mon-Fri, noon-midnight Sat & Sun) State-of-the-art Internet café.

Sights

Art, culture, and architecture abound in Aix, and it's a perfect city to explore on foot. The graceful **cours Mirabeau** is the literal and spiritual heart of Aix, dotted by fashionable cafés, stone lions and elegant Renaissance *hôtels particuliers* along its southern side.

The **Musée Granet** (☎ 04 42 52 88 32; place St-Jean de Malte; 11am-6pm Wed-Mon) has reopened after a three-year renovation. Housed in a 17th-century priory, its collections include 16th- to 20th-century Italian, Flemish and French paintings and eight stunning Cézannes.

Cézanne fans can follow the **Circuit de Cézanne** (Cézanne Trail), marked on the footpath by bronze plaques with the letter C, which visits many of the painter's favourite hang-outs. On a hilltop 1.5km north of the tourist office, Cézanne's last **studio** (Atelier Paul Cézanne; ☎ 04 42 21 06 53; www.atelier-cezanne.com; 9 av Paul Cézanne; adult/student €5.50/2; 10am-noon & 2-5pm Oct-Mar, to 6pm Apr-Jun & Sep, 10am-6pm Jul & Aug) is preserved almost as he left it.

Sleeping

Camping Arc-en-Ciel (☎ 04 42 26 14 28; route de Nice; camp sites €17.50; Apr-Sep) This four-star campground is bordered by wooded hills and a busy motorway. Take bus 3 to Les Trois Sautets – it's 2km southeast of town.

Auberge de Jeunesse du Jas de Bouffan (☎ 04 42 20 15 99; fax 04 42 59 36 12; 3 av Marcel Pagnol; dm incl breakfast & sheets €16; 7am-1pm & 5pm-midnight, closed 20 Dec-9 Feb) Flash and cyclist-friendly, with a bar and tennis courts, this HI hostel is 2km west of the centre. Take bus 4 from La Rotonde to the Vasarely stop.

Hôtel Le Manoir (☎ 04 42 26 27 20; www.hotelmanoir.com; 8 rue d'Entrecasteux; d €57-85, tr €78-85; closed Jan; P) In a 14th-century cloister with its own leafy garden, Le Manoir has 40 antique-furnished rooms in a secluded but super-central wedge of the old town.

Hôtel Cardinal (☎ 04 42 38 32 30; fax 04 42 26 39 05; 24 rue Cardinale; s/d €58/68, self-catering ste €80) Beneath stratospheric ceilings, the romantic rooms are beautifully furnished with antiques, tasselled curtains and bathrooms.

Eating & Drinking

Aix excels for Provençal cuisine, and is also renowned for its colourful markets.

Charlotte (☎ 04 42 26 77 56; 32 rue des Bernardines; 2-/3-course menu €13/16; lunch & dinner Tue-Sat) Townspeople congregate like a big extended family at this bustling place, turning out delicious, simple home cooking from the open kitchen.

Le Zinc d'Hugo (☎ 04 42 27 69 69; 22 rue Lieutaud; mains €14-18; lunch & dinner Tue-Sat) This rustic French bistro boasts stone walls, wooden tables and a daily changing blackboard *menu*.

Les Deux Garçons (☎ 04 42 26 00 51; 53 cours Mirabeau) Aix' best café has been in business since 1792 and is still resplendent. Cèzanne and Zola used to hang out here. Take a seat in its gilded salon or outdoor terrace and wait for your white-aproned waiter to arrive.

Trestle tables set up each morning for the produce market on place Richelme, displaying olives, goat's cheese, honey and lots of other Provençal products. Another **food market** (place des Prêcheurs) takes place on Tuesday, Thursday and Saturday morning.

Aix' sweetest treat is calisson, a small, diamond-shaped delicacy made with ground almonds and fruit syrup. Traditional *calissonniers* include **Roy René** (☎ 04 42 26 67 86; www.calisson.com; 10 rue Clémenceau).

Getting There & Away

Aix' **bus station** (☎ information office 08 91 02 40 25; av de l'Europe) is a 10-minute walk southwest from La Rotonde. Buses run to Marseille (€4.40, 35 minutes, every 10 minutes Monday to Saturday, every 20 minutes on Sunday), Arles (€10, 1¾ hours, five daily), and Avignon (€13.90, one hour, six daily).

The tiny **train station** (5am-9.15pm Mon-Fri, 6am-9.15pm Sat & Sun, information office 9am-7pm) is at the southern end of av Victor Hugo. There are frequent services to Marseille (€6.20, 35 minutes, at least 18 daily), from where there are connections to just about everywhere.

Aix' bus station is linked to the TGV station (€3.90) and Aéroport Marseille-Provence (€7.90) by the half-hourly **Navette** (☎ 04 42 93 59 13).

AVIGNON

pop 88,312

Looped by 4.3km of stone ramparts, this graceful city is the belle of Provence's ball. Its turn as the papal seat of power has bestowed Avignon with a treasury of magnificent art and architecture, none grander than the massive Palais des Papes. Famous for its annual performing arts festival, Avignon is also renowned for its fabled bridge, the Pont St-Bénézet, aka the Pont d'Avignon.

Orientation

The café-clad central square place de l'Horloge is 300m south of place du Palais, which abuts the Palais des Papes. The city gate nearest the train station is Porte de la République, while the city gate next to Pont Édouard Daladier, which leads to Villeneuve-lès-Avignon, is Porte de l'Oulle.

Information

Lavmatic (27 rue du Portail Magnanen; 7am-7.30pm) Laundrette.

Post office (cours Président Kennedy) Currency exchange and Cyberposte.

Tourist office (☎ 04 32 74 32 74; www.avignon-tourisme.com; 41 cours Jean Jaurès; 9am-6pm Mon-Sat, 10am-5pm Sun Apr-Jun & Aug-Oct, 9am-6pm Mon-Fri, 9am-5pm Sat, 10am-noon Sun Nov-Mar, 9am-7pm Mon-Sat, 10am-5pm Sun Jul) Ask about the Avignon Passion museum pass, which entitles you to special discounts.

Webzone (☎ 04 32 76 29 47; 3 rue St Jean le Vieux; per 30/60min €2/3.50; 10am-10pm)

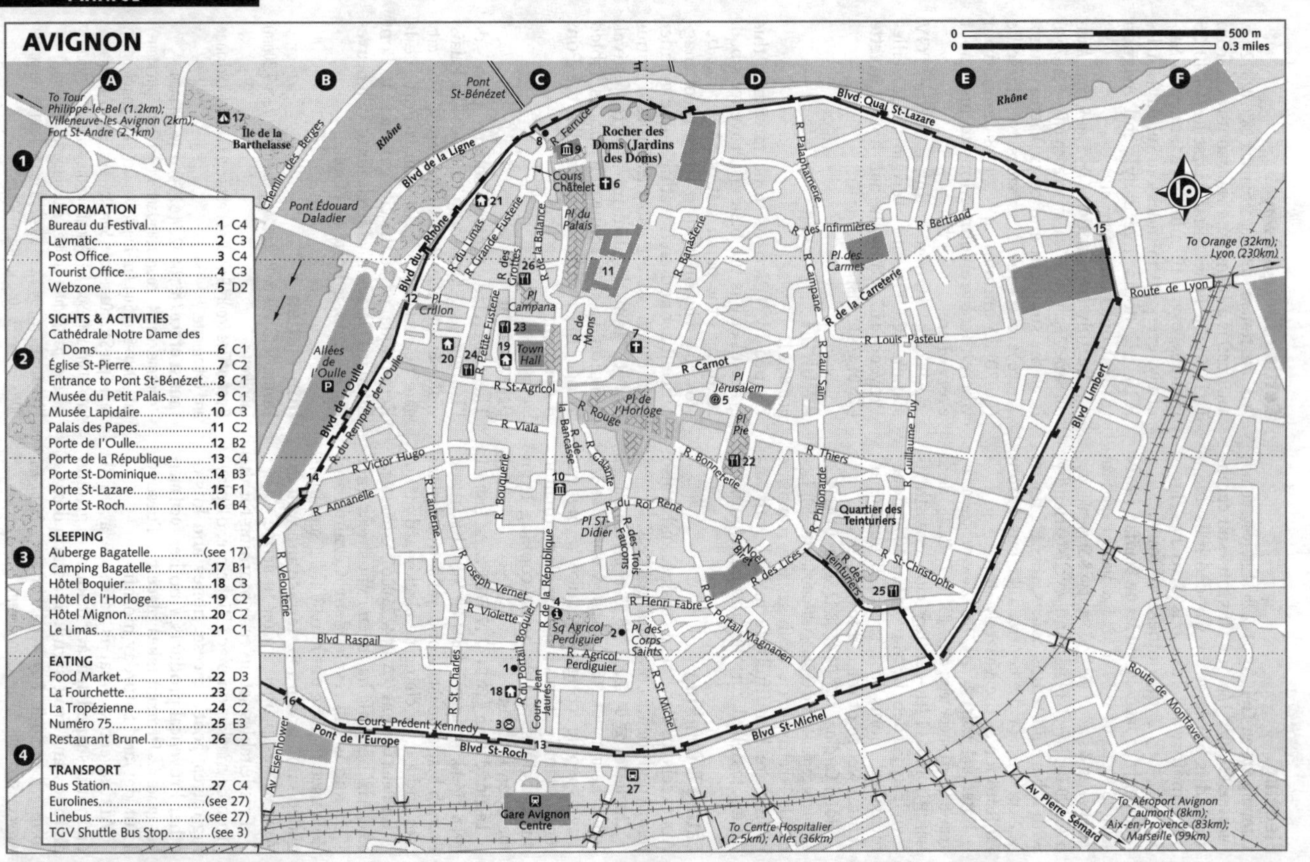
AVIGNON
INFORMATION
Bureau du Festival 1 C4
Lavmatic 2 C3
Post Office 3 C4
Tourist Office 4 C3
Webzone 5 D2
SIGHTS & ACTIVITIES
Cathédrale Notre Dame des Doms 6 C1
Église St-Pierre 7 C2
Entrance to Pont St-Bénézet 8 C1
Musée du Petit Palais 9 C1
Musée Lapidaire 10 C3
Palais des Papes 11 C2
Porte de l'Oulle 12 B2
Porte de la République 13 C4
Porte St-Dominique 14 B3
Porte St-Lazare 15 F1
Porte St-Roch 16 B4
SLEEPING
Auberge Bagatelle (see 17)
Camping Bagatelle 17 B1
Hôtel Boquier 18 C3
Hôtel de l'Horloge 19 C2
Hôtel Mignon 20 C2
Le Limas 21 C1
EATING
Food Market 22 D3
La Fourchette 23 C2
La Tropézienne 24 C2
Numéro 75 25 E3
Restaurant Brunel 26 C2
TRANSPORT
Bus Station 27 C4
Eurolines (see 27)
Linebus (see 27)
TGV Shuttle Bus Stop (see 3)
To Tour Philippe-le-Bel (1.2km); Villeneuve-les Avignon (2km); Fort St-Andre (2.1km)
To Orange (32km); Lyon (230km)
To Aéroport Avignon Caumont (8km); Aix-en-Provence (83km); Marseille (99km)
To Centre Hospitalier (2.5km); Arles (36km)
Rocher des Doms (Jardins des Doms)
Quartier des Teinturiers
Gare Avignon Centre
Île de la Barthelasse
Pont St-Bénézet
Pont Édouard Daladier

Sights

The **Pont St-Bénézet** (St Bénézet's Bridge; ☎ 04 90 27 51 16; full price/pass €4/3.30; 9am-7pm Apr-Jun, Oct & Nov, 9am-8pm Jul-Sep, 9.30am-5.45pm Nov-Mar, to 9pm theatre festival Jul) is a fabled 900m wooden bridge – the subject of a famous French nursery rhyme – and was completed in 1185, and repaired several times before all but four of its 22 spans were washed away in the mid-1600s. The best views of the bridge are from the Rocher des Doms or Pont Édouard Daladier, or across the river on the Île de la Barthelasse's promenade des Berges.

The **Palais des Papes** (Palace of the Popes; ☎ 04 90 27 50 00; place du Palais; full price/pass €9.50/7.50; 9am or 9.30am-6.30pm or 7pm Oct-Jun, 9am-8pm Jul-Sep, to 9pm theatre festival Jul) was built during the 14th century as a fortified palace for the papal court. It's the largest Gothic palace in the world, but its undecorated rooms are all but empty, except during occasional art exhibitions.

The **Musée du Petit Palais** (☎ 04 90 86 44 58; place du Palais; full price/pass €6/3; 10am-1pm & 2-6pm Wed-Mon Jun-Sep, 9.30am-1pm & 2-5.30pm Wed-Mon Oct-May) houses an outstanding collection of Italian religious paintings including works by Botticelli, Carpaccio and Giovanni di Paolo.

Museum buffs on a budget will appreciate the **Musée Lapidaire** (☎ 04 90 86 33 84; 27 rue de la République; full price/pass €2/1; 10am-1pm & 2-6pm Wed-Mon), with a random but interesting collection of Egyptian, Roman, Etruscan and Early Christian pieces.

Avignon's encircling ramparts were built between 1359 and 1370, and restored during the 19th century, minus their original moats. The best views of the walled city are from the **Tour Philippe-le-Bel** (☎ 04 32 70 08 57; full price/pass €2/1; 10am-12.30pm & 2-6.30pm, closed Mon mid-Sep–mid-Jun), across the Rhône in the 13th-century town of Villeneuve-lès-Avignon.

Festivals & Events

More than 600 *spectacles* (performances) take to the stage and streets during the **Festival d'Avignon** (Bureau du Festival; ☎ 04 90 27 66 50; www.festival-avignon.com; Espace St-Louis, 20 rue du Portail Boquier), founded in 1946 and held annually from early July to early August. The fringe event, **Festival Off** (Avignon Public Off; ☎ 01 48 05 01 19; www.avignon-off.org), has an eclectic – and cheaper – programme of experimental performances.

Sleeping

You'll need to book months ahead for a room during the festival. Many places close for a few weeks midwinter.

Camping Bagatelle (☎ 04 90 86 30 39; camping.bagatelle@wanadoo.fr; Île de la Barthelasse; camp sites €9-15.50; reception 8am-9pm) A shady camping ground just north of Pont Édouard Daladier, 850m from the walled city.

Auberge Bagatelle (☎ 04 90 85 78 45; auberge.bagatelle@wanadoo.fr; Île de la Barthelasse; dm €15, s €29-33, d €35-37) Adjoining the camping ground, this hostel has 180 beds in a mix of two- to eight-bed rooms, plus snazzier private digs in its adjoining hotel.

Hôtel Mignon (☎ 04 90 82 17 30; www.hotel-mignon.com; 12 rue Joseph Vernet; s €36, d €40-55;) Cute and comfy, this 16-room place within the walled city is a favourite for its pastel rooms, helpful staff, and a decent breakfast of croissants and rolls (€5).

Hôtel Boquier (☎ 04 90 82 34 43; www.hotel-boquier.com; 6 rue du Portail Boquier; d €45-62) Handy for the train and bus stations, this 18th-century manor has rooms inspired by distant destinations such as southern Africa and India. A little wrought-iron gate opens to the wood-beamed café (for guests only; €7).

Hôtel de l'Horloge (☎ 04 90 16 42 00; www.hotels-ochre-azur.com; place de l'Horloge; s €72-122, d €82-132;) On Avignon's main square, refined rooms are tastefully decorated in natural fabrics and fibres, with muslin curtains overlaid by stone-coloured checked linen drapes and lustrous chocolate-brown carpet.

Le Limas (☎ 04 90 14 67 19; www.le-limas-avignon.com; 51 rue du Limas; d €86-135, tr €139-165, all incl breakfast;) Behind its discreet entrance 50m from the papal palace, this chic B&B in an 18th-century mansion is like something out of *Vogue Living*, with four white-on-white rooms with hardwood floors.

Eating

Place de l'Horloge is a riot of restaurants and cafés from Easter until mid-November.

Numéro 75 (☎ 04 90 27 16 00; 75 rue Guillaume Puy; mains from €10; lunch & dinner Mon-Sat, daily during the festival) This place in a lovely old house (where Pernod was first concocted in 1870) is now one of Avignon's 'in' spots for Mediterranean cuisine, best savoured on the €15 'chef's suggestion' *menu*.

Restaurant Brunel (☎ 04 90 27 16 00; 46 rue de la Balance; mains €10-18; lunch & dinner Tue-Sat)

A local favourite for authentic Provençal food, especially at lunch, when the outside terrace is always packed.

La Fourchette (☎ 04 90 85 20 93; 17 rue Racine; menu from €28; ⏲ Mon-Fri) An enduring classical French restaurant west of place de l'Horloge, La Fourchette has a fixed-price *menu* dotted with house specialities such as sardines and a sinful ice-cream meringue with praline.

More than 40 outlets fill Les Halles' **food market** (place Pie; ⏲ 7am-1pm Tue-Sun). St-Tropez' famous cream-and-cake concoction, *tarte Tropézienne,* is best tasted at **La Tropézienne** (☎ 04 90 86 24 72; 22 rue St-Agricol; ⏲ 8.30am-7.30pm Mon-Sat).

Getting There & Away

BUS

The **bus station** (halte routière; ☎ 04 90 82 07 35; blvd St-Roch; ⏲ information window 10.15am-1pm & 2-6pm Mon-Fri) is in the basement of the building down the ramp to the right as you exit the train station.

Local services include Aix-en-Provence (€13.90, one hour), Arles (€7.10, 1½ hours), Marseille (€20, 35 minutes), Nice (€37) and Nîmes (€7.60, 1¼ hours). Most lines operate on Sunday at reduced frequency.

Long-haul bus companies **Linebus** (☎ 04 90 85 30 48) and **Eurolines** (☎ 04 90 85 27 60; www.eurolines.fr) have offices at the far end of the bus platforms.

TRAIN

The **main train station** (⏲ information counters 9am-6.15pm Mon-Sat) is located across blvd St-Roch from Porte de la République. The TGV station is a few kilometres from town. A shuttle bus (€2, half-hourly from 5.30am to 10.50pm) links the TGV station to the bus stop outside the main post office.

There are trains to Arles (€5.70, 20 minutes, 14 to 18 daily); Marseille (€15.50, 40 minutes); Nice (€38.80, three hours); Nîmes (€7.40, 30 minutes, 15 daily); and, by TGV, Paris' Gare de Lyon (€67, 2½ hours) and Lyon (€29.60, one hour).

AROUND AVIGNON

Arles

pop 51,614

If the winding streets, stone squares, and colourful houses of Arles seem familiar, it's hardly surprising – the town featured in some of the most celebrated canvases by Vincent van Gogh, who lived and worked here for much of his life in a yellow house on place Lamartine. Unfortunately the yellow house was destroyed during WWII, but you can still follow in Vincent's footsteps on the **Van Gogh Trail**, marked out by footpath plaques and an accompanying brochure handed out by the **tourist office** (☎ 04 90 18 41 20; www.tourisme.ville-arles.fr; esplanade Charles de Gaulle; ⏲ 9am-6.45pm Apr-Sep, to 4.45pm Mon-Sat, 10am-1pm Sun Oct-Mar).

Contemporary artists, including the likes of David Hockney, Francis Bacon and Fernando Botero pay homage to van Gogh's distinctive painting style at the appropriately named **Fondation Vincent van Gogh** (☎ 04 90 49 94 04; 24bis Rond Point des Arènes; adult/student €7/5; ⏲ 10am-7pm Jul-Sep, 10am-6pm Apr-Jun, 11am-5pm Tue-Sun Oct-Mar).

Two millennia ago, Arles was the region's major port and a major Roman settlement. The town's 12,000-seat theatre and a 20,000-seat amphitheatre, known as the **Arénes** and the **Théâtre Antique**, are still standing – today they are still used for cultural events and bullfights.

The **bus station** (☎ information office 08 10 00 08 16; 24 blvd Georges Clemenceau; ⏲ 7.30am-4pm Mon-Sat) is served by companies including **Telleschi** (☎ 04 42 28 40 22), which runs services to Aix-en-Provence (€9.80, 1¾ hours).

Arles' **train station** (⏲ information office 9am-12.30pm & 2-6.30pm Mon-Sat) is just across from the bus station. Major rail destinations include Nîmes (€6.90, 30 minutes), Marseille (€12.20, 45 minutes) and Avignon (€6, 20 minutes).

CÔTE D'AZUR

The Côte d'Azur, otherwise known as the French Riviera, has been synonymous with chic elegance and lofty living for well over a century, however, its heyday was during the 1950s and '60s, when practically everyone who was anyone seemed to have upped sticks and bought a duplex apartment along its pebble-strewn shores. It's still a playground for the rich and beautiful, especially at stylish resorts such as Nice, Cannes, St-Tropez, and of course the epitome of extravagance, Monte Carlo – but less well-heeled visitors will find plenty to entertain them too.

NICE

pop 345,892

Naughty Nice is certainly one of the highlights of the French Riviera. Sun-seekers sip cocktails while reclining on the parasoled lounges lining its pebbled shores, children splash in azure seas and roller-bladers cruise the promenade des Anglais – but Nice is more than just a beacon for fun in the sun. You'll find some major art museums, the reamins of a ruined Roman city and a glorious old town to discover, as well as some of the best restaurants, bars and markets on the Mediterranean. The city is a great base from which to explore the rest of the Côte d'Azur, with some great-value hotels and handy travel links to the rest of the Riviera.

Orientation

Avenue Jean Médecin runs south from near the Gare Nice Ville (the main train station) to place Masséna. You will find the modern city centre north and west of place Masséna. The bus station is located three blocks east. The promenade des Anglais follows the gently arced beachfront right from the city centre to the airport, which is 6km west. Vieux Nice (Old Nice) is delineated by blvd Jean Jaurès, quai des États-Unis and, towards the east, the hill known as Le Château.

Information

Barclays Bank (2 rue Alphonse Karr) There's a change counter here.

Cyberpoint (☎ 04 93 92 70 63; 10 av Félix Faure; per hr €4; 🕑 10am-10pm Mon-Sat, 3-9pm Sun) Organised internet cafe with English keyboards.

Le Change (☎ 04 93 88 56 80; 17 av Thiers; 🕑 7.30am-8pm) Currency exchange; opposite the Gare Nice Ville.

Main post office (23 av Thiers)

Main tourist office (☎ 0892 70 74 07; 5 promenade des Anglais; 🕑 8am-8pm Mon-Sat, 9am-7pm Sun Jun-Sep, 9am-6pm Mon-Sat Oct-May) Right by the beach.

Nice Ferber tourist office annexe (☎ 04 93 83 32 64; promenade des Anglais; 🕑 8am-8pm Mon-Sat, 9am-7pm Sun Jun-Sep, 9am-6pm Mon-Sat Oct-May) Towards town from the airport.

Post office (2 rue Louis Gassin) In Vieux Nice.

Taxi Lav rue Pertinax (22 rue Pertinax; 🕑 7am-9pm) Vieux Nice (13 rue du Pont Vieux; 🕑 7am-9pm) Laundrette.

Train station tourist office (☎ 08 92 35 35 35; av Thiers; 🕑 8am-8pm Mon-Sat, 9am-7pm Sun Jun-Sep, 8am-7pm Mon-Sat, 9am-6pm Sun Oct-May)

Sights

VIEUX NICE

Go off-map in the old town's tangle of tiny 18th-century pedestrian passages and alleyways, where you'll find several historic churches including the baroque **Cathédrale Ste-Réparate** (place Rossetti) and the mid-18th-century **Chapelle de la Miséricorde**, next to place Pierre Gautier.

At the eastern end of quai des États-Unis, steep steps and a **cliffside lift** (€0.70; 🕑 10am-5.30pm Oct-Mar, 9am-7pm Apr, May & Sep, 9am-8pm Jun-Aug) climb to the **Parc du Château**, a beautiful hilltop park with great views over the old city and the beachfront. The chateau itself was razed by Louis XIV in 1706 and never rebuilt.

MUSEUMS

The excellent **Musée d'Art Moderne et d'Art Contemporain** (Marmac; ☎ 04 93 62 61 62; www.mamac-nice.org; av St-Jean Baptiste; adult/student €4/2.50; 🕑 10am-6pm) is worth a visit for its stunning architecture alone, but it also houses some fantastic avant-garde art from the 1960s to the present, including iconic pop art from Roy Lichtenstein, and Andy Warhol's 1965 *Campbell's Soup Can*.

The largest public collection of works by the Russian-born artist Marc Chagall is housed at the **Musée National Message Biblique Marc Chagall** (Marc Chagall Biblical Message Museum; ☎ 04 93 53 87 20; permanent collection adult/student €5.50/4, temporary exhibitions additional €1.50; 🕑 10am-6pm Wed-Mon Jul-Sep, to 5pm Oct-Jun), freshly renovated in 2006.

Heading northeast from the Chagall museum (about 2.5km from the city centre) brings you to the **Musée Matisse** (☎ 04 93 81 08 08; www.musee-matisse-nice.org; 164 av des Arènes de Cimiez; adult/student €4/2.50; 🕑 10am-6pm Wed-Mon), which contains a fantastic collection of exhibits and paintings spanning Matisse's entire career, including his famous paper cut-outs *Blue Nude IV* and mixed-media *Woman with Amphora*.

RUSSIAN ORTHODOX CATHEDRAL OF ST-NICOLAS

Crowned by six onion domes, the multi-coloured **Cathédrale Orthodoxe Russe St-Nicolas** (Russian Orthodox Cathedral of St-Nicolas; ☎ 04 93 96 88 02; av Nicolas II; 🕑 9am-noon & 2.30-6pm, closed Sun morning), was built between 1902 and 1912 in early-17th-century style, and is the largest outside Russia. It's an easy 15-minute walk from Gare Nice Ville; shorts, miniskirts and sleeveless shirts are forbidden.

BEACHES

Free sections of beach alternate with 15 sun-lounge–lined **plages concédées** (private beaches; ⏰ late Apr/early May-15 Sep), for which you have to pay by renting a chair (around €11 a day) or mattress (around €9).

On the beach, operators hire catamarans, paddleboats, sailboards and jet skis; you can also parascend, water-ski, or paraglide. There are outdoor showers on every beach, and indoor showers and toilets opposite 50 promenade des Anglais.

Tours

Trans Côte d'Azur (☎ 04 92 00 42 30; www.trans-cote-azur.com; quai Lunel) runs cruises in summer to the Îles de Lérins (adult/child €25/17), St-Tropez (adult/child €45/27) and Monaco (adult/child €20/15).

Festivals & Events

Flower-covered floats and impressive fireworks light up the city during the **Carnaval de Nice** (Nice Carnival; www.nicecarnaval.com) in mid-February. In mid-July, Nice swings to the week-long **Nice Jazz Festival** (www.nicejazzfest.com).

Sleeping

Nice has lots and lots of hotels, ranging from bargain-bucket to superchic. Sea-views and a beachfront location obviously come at a considerable surcharge – you'll find better value in the city centre, around the main train station, and along rue d'Angleterre, rue d'Alsace-Lorraine and av Durante.

BUDGET

Villa Saint-Exupéry (☎ 04 93 84 42 83; www.vsaint.com; 22 av Gravier; dm €18-22, s €30, d €52 incl breakfast; 🅿 ⊠ 💻) In a lovely former monastery, this palatial independent hostel is fit for St-Exupéry's little prince, and worth the 3km trip from the city centre. Treats include a slate-and-steel kitchen, a barbecue terrace, a 24-hour common room/bar, and terrazzo-tiled, mostly en-suite dorms and rooms, some with magical views across Nice to the Mediterranean. Take bus 1, direction Saint Sylvestre, along av Jean Médecin to the Gravier stop and follow the steps up to the hostel.

Auberge de Jeunesse – Les Camèllias (☎ 04 93 62 15 54; www.fuaj.org; 3 rue Spitalieri; dm incl breakfast €20, bedding €3; ⊠ 💻) Flash backpacking. The four- to eight-bed dorms (136 beds all-up) have space-age metallic bunks and in-room showers, and there's a self-catering kitchen. A funky citrus-coloured bar stays open to 11pm, and there's no curfew.

MIDRANGE & TOP END

Hôtel Wilson (☎ 04 93 85 47 79; www.hotel-wilson-nice.com; 39 rue de l'Hôtel des Postes; s/d/tr €45/50/60.50, with shared bathroom €27/33.50/43.50) Owner and multilingual *bon vivant* Jean-Marie Martinez lives in this rambling old apartment building and shares his dining table, books and classical music with his guests. Some rooms have small balconies.

Villa la Tour (☎ 04 93 80 08 15; www.villa-la-tour.com; 4 rue de la Tour; s €45-127, d €48-135, ❄) This intimate *chambre d'hôte*–style hotel in Nice's old town has organza curtains framing rustic rooms with fragrant Fragonard Perfumery soaps and quirky details such as bedside lamps designed like chic little paper shopping bags. There's also a petite rooftop patio.

Hôtel de la Buffa (☎ 04 93 88 77 35; www.hotel-buffa.com; 56 rue de la Buffa; d €48-73; ❄ 💻) Up a spiral staircase in a character-filled building, old-fashioned corridors with ornate cornices and baskets of dried and silk flowers open to 13 bright, airy, sun-washed rooms with lofty ceilings and angular bathrooms.

Hôtel Acanthe (☎ 04 93 62 22 44; www.hotel-acanthe-nice.cote.azur.fr; 2 rue Chauvain; d €57-61) Facing the fountained Albert I gardens, this place is perfectly positioned for the beach and old town. Behind its peach-coloured curved façade, the pick are the four 'round' rooms, which have semicircular balconies.

Hôtel Lépante (☎ 04 93 62 20 55; www.hotellepante.com; 6 rue de Lépante; s €59-99, d €59-109; ❄) Renovated in a palette of Mediterranean colours, this homy, unpretentious hotel is housed in a landmark 1915 *belle époque* building. Two rooms have balconies just big enough for a tiny tables and chairs.

Hôtel Armenonville (☎ 04 93 96 86 00; www.hotel-armenonville.com; 20 av des Fleurs; d €74-96, with shower or bath only €49-61; 💻) Graced by grand Grecian-style columns, this dove-white 1905 pavilion is secluded in gardens filled with citrus trees. A marble staircase leads to rooms in romantic hues such as rose and olive.

FRANCE

Villa Victoria (☎ 04 93 88 39 60; www.villa-victoria.com; 33 blvd Victor Hugo; s €75-155, d €90-170;) How many inner-city hotels can boast their own botanic garden (complete with a fairy-lit gazebo overlooked by a marble breakfast room flanked by five sets of French doors)? This is one of the few.

Hôtel Hi (☎ 04 97 07 26 26; www.hi-hotel.net; s from €165, d €185-395;) Imagine you're invited to stay with ultra-connected, urbanite friends in their techno-funky, futuristic pad designed in part by Philippe Starck; with a panoramic rooftop splash pool, and in-room surround-sound stereos programmed by DJ Laurent Garnier. The party vibe here means (for a price!), you are.

Eating

Niçoise nibbles include *socca* (a thin layer of chickpea flour and olive oil batter fried on a large griddle, served with pepper), niçoise salad, ratatouille and *farcis* (stuffed vegetables). Generally, you'll find the most authentic restaurants in the back streets of Vieux Nice.

Chez René Socca (☎ 04 93 92 05 73; 2 rue Miralhéti; dishes from €2; 9am-9pm, to 10.30pm Jul & Aug, closed Mon & Nov) The cheapest fare in town and it's good. Split into two sides (order food on one and drinks on the other), this is a great, casual place for tapas-style bites such as spiced fish cakes, washed down with local wine.

Fenocchio (☎ 04 93 80 72 52; 2 place Rossetti; ice creams from around €2.50; 9am-midnight Feb-Oct) The best ice cream in Nice, made on the premises in scores of unique flavours such as lavender and thyme.

Lou Pilha Leva (place Centrale; dishes from €3; 11am-10pm) Seated at wooden tables under an awning, this down-to-earth place is great for vegetarians, especially for *soupe au pistou* (soup of vegetables, noodles, beans, basil and garlic).

Nissa Socca (☎ 04 93 80 18 35; 5 rue Ste-Réparate; dishes from €6, menu €13; closed Sun & lunch Mon) Locals love this inexpensive *socca* joint in Nice's ambient old town, and it's a prime location for taste-testing authentic Niçoise cuisine.

La Table Alziari (☎ 04 93 80 34 03, 4 rue François Zanin, mains €8-14; noon-2pm & 7.30-10pm Tue-Sat) In the heart of old Nice, this tiny, traditional Provençal place has no *carte*, just a blackboard with a daily selection of seasonal dishes.

Zucca Magica (☎ 04 93 56 25 27; 4bis quai Papacino; lunch/dinner menu €18/22; lunch & dinner Tue-Sat) The Italian-vegetarian 'magic pumpkin' is always packed full of regulars. Book ahead, and bring your appetite: lunch comprises four set dishes plus dessert (five for dinner), and depends on what turns up at the daily market.

Chantecler (☎ 04 93 16 64 00; 37 promenade des Anglais; most mains €30-70; closed Mon, Tue & Jan) Up there in the fame stakes, along with the historic hotel in which it's housed, is the Negresco's crimson-coloured, Michelin-starred restaurant.

Pack the ultimate picnic hamper from cours Saleya's fruit and vegetable market, and pick up fresh-caught fish from the **fish market** (place St-François; 6am-1pm Tue-Sun).

Drinking & Entertainment

Vieux Nice's little streets are jammed with bars and cafés in which to sip a perfect *pastis* (a 90-proof anise-flavoured alcoholic drink).

Cave de la Tour (☎ 04 93 80 03 31; 3 rue de la Tour; 7am-7pm Tue-Sat, 7am-noon Sun) An utterly untouristy old-town treasure that combines a wonderful wine shop and a café-bar. It also serves food for around €7.50 for a main meal.

La Banane (☎ 06 03 18 61 40; 6 rue de la Poissonnerie; dishes €3.50-9; 9am-9pm Mon, Wed & Thu, 9am-midnight Fri-Sun) This hidden little bolt-hole is a chic spot to grab a drink or a *croque banane*.

Le Bar des Oiseaux (☎ 04 93 80 27 33; 5 rue St-Vincent; noon-midnight Tue-Sat Jun-Aug, 6pm-12.30am Tue-Sat Sep-May) Artistic types flock to this bohemian bar (and adjoining theatre) for live jazz, blues and cabaret. There's a cover charge of about €5 when entertainment's on the bill.

Chez Wayne's (☎ 04 93 13 46 99; 15 rue de la Préfecture) A magnet for carousing locals and visitors alike, this raucous watering hole has live bands every night.

Les Trois Diables (☎ 04 93 92 93 37; 2 cours Saleya; 5pm-3.15am) The 'three devils' tempts a mainly local crowd with trip-hop, house and electro.

L'Ôdace (☎ 04 93 82 37 66; 29 rue Alphonse Karr; until late Thu-Sat Jul & Aug, Fri & Sat Sep-Jun) The vast industrial-style party temple formerly known as Le Grand Escurial is now even hipper after its relaunch.

NICE
A
B
C
D
1
2
3
4
5
6
INFORMATION
Barclays Bank....1 D4
Cyberpoint....2 E4
Le Change....3 C3
Main Post Office....4 C3
Main Tourist Office....5 D5
Post Office....6 E5
Taxi Lav....7 D2
Taxi Lav....8 G2
Train Station Tourist Office....9 D3
SIGHTS & ACTIVITIES
Cathédrale Ste-Réprate....10 G2
Chapelle de la Miséricorde....11 G2
Cliffside Lift....12 F5
Flower Market....13 E5
Musée d'Art Moderne et d'Art Contemporain....14 F4
Musée National Message Biblique Marc Chagall....15 E2
Russian Orthodox Cathedral of St-Nicolas....16 B3
Trans Côte d'Azur....17 G5
WWI Memorial....18 G6
SLEEPING
Auberge de Jeunesse - Les Camèllias..19 E3
Hôtel Acanthe....20 E4
Hôtel Armenonville....21 B4
Hôtel de la Buffa....22 B5
Hôtel Hi....23 B4
Hôtel Lépante....24 E3
Hôtel Négresco....25 B5
Hôtel Wilson....26 E4
Villa la Tour....27 H1
Villa Victoria....28 C4
EATING
Chantecler....(see 25)
Chez René Socca....29 H1
Fenocchio....30 G2
Fish Market....31 H1
Fruit & Vegetable Market....32 D2
La Table Alziari....33 H1
Lou Pilha Leva....34 G2
Nissa Socca....35 G2
Zucca Magica....36 G4
DRINKING
Cave de la Tour....37 H1
Chez Wayne's....38 F5
La Banane....39 G3
ENTERTAINMENT
L'Ôdace....40 D4
Le Bar des Oiseaux....41 G2
Les Trois Diables....42 G3
TRANSPORT
Budget....43 C3
Corsica Ferries Terminal....44 H5
Corsica Ferries Terminal....45 G5
Corsica Ferries Ticket Office....46 G5
Eurolines....(see 49)
Ferry Terminal....47 H6
Holiday Bikes....48 C3
Intercars....(see 49)
Intercity Bus Station....49 G1
JML....(see 43)
Ligne d'Azur Information Office....50 E4
SNCM Office....(see 47)
To Blvd Auguste Reynaud; Autoroute A8
To Villa Saint-Exupery (3km)
Blvd Auguste Raynaud
Av Borrigilione
R Fl Raiberti
Pl Général de gaulie
Blvd Joseph Garnier
R A Binet
Gare du Sud
Av Villermont
Av Malaaussena
Av Raymond Comboul
Av George V
R Clément Roassal
Av Mirabeau
R Marceau
Blvd Gambetta
R Vernier
R Trachel
Blvd Raimbaldi
R Assalit
Gare Nice Ville
R Pertinax
R Lamartine
R Miron
R de Paris
R de Belgique
R d'Alsace-Lorraine
Av Notre Dame
Blvd du Parc Impérial
Av Nicolas II
Blvd du Tzaréwich
Av Primerose
R Cuvier
Av Thiers
R Gounod
Av Auber
R Paganini
R d'Angleterre
R d'Italie
R E Tiranty
Av Maréchal
Av Georges Clemenceau
R Berlioz
R de Châteauneuf
R de Russie
R Paul Déroulède
R Rossini
R Guiglia
Av Jean Médecin
Av Robert Schuman
R F Passy
R Verdi
Av Durante
R Alphonse Karr
R Caffarelli
R Maccarani
Blvd Victor Hugo
R de la Liberté
Pa Emile Négrin
To Cannes (34km)
Av des Fleurs
R du Maréchal Joffre
Pl Magenta
Blvd François Grosso
Av des Orangers
Pl Grimaldi
R Massena
R Bottero
R Cronstadt
R de la Buffa
R Dalpozzo
R du Congrès
R Halévy
R Paradis
Av de Suède
To Nice Ferber Office (5km); Airport (5.5km)
R Meyerbeer
R de France
R Massenet
Av de Verdun
Jardin Albert Ier
R de Rivoli
Promenade des Anglais

FRANCE

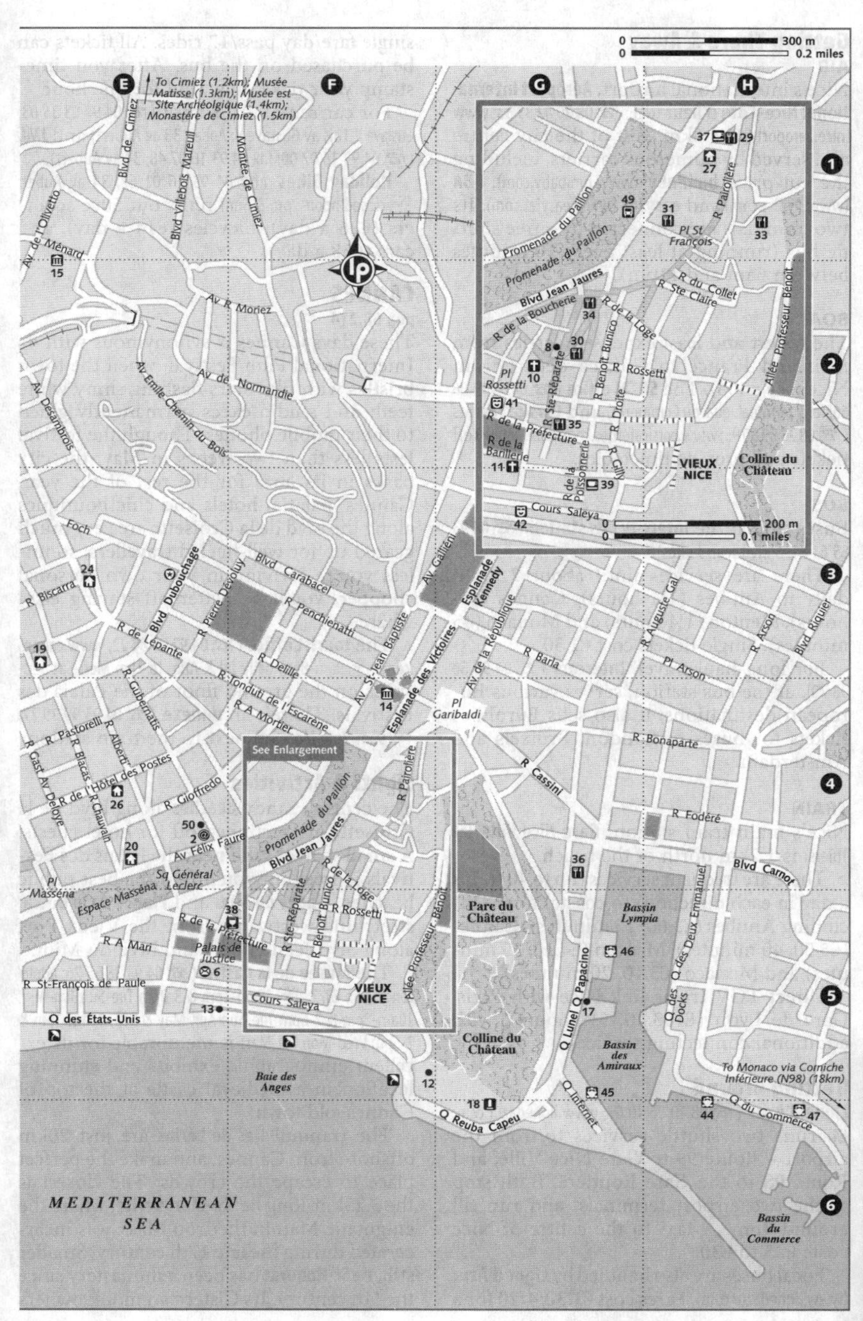
To Cimiez (1.2km); Musée Matisse (1.3km); Musée est Site Archéolgique (1.4km); Monastère de Cimiez (1.5km)
See Enlargement
VIEUX NICE
Colline du Château
Parc du Château
Pl Garibaldi
Pl Masséna
Bassin Lympia
Bassin des Amiraux
Bassin du Commerce
Baie des Anges
MEDITERRANEAN SEA
To Monaco via Corniche Inférieure (N98) (18km)
Promenade du Paillon
Blvd Jean Jaures
Esplanade des Victoires
Esplanade Kennedy
Cours Saleya
Q des États-Unis
Q Reuba Capeu
Q Lunel
Q Papacino
Q Infernet
Q du Commerce
Blvd Carnot
Blvd Dubouchage
Blvd Carabacel
Av Jean Médecin
Av de la République
Av Félix Faure
Palais de Justice
Sq Général Leclerc
Espace Masséna
300 m
0.2 miles
200 m
0.1 miles

Getting There & Away

AIR

Nice's international airport, **Aéroport International Nice-Côte d'Azur** (NCE; ☎ 08 20 42 33 33; www.nice.aeroport.fr), is 6km west of the city centre and served by numerous carriers, including the cut-price **bmiBaby** (www.bmibaby.com), **DBA** (www.flydba.com) and **easyJet** (www.easyjet.com). Its two terminals are connected by a free shuttle bus (running at least every 10 minutes between 6am and 11pm).

BOAT

The fastest and least expensive ferries from mainland France to Corsica depart from Nice (see p406). The **SNCM office** (☎ 04 93 13 66 66; ferry terminal, quai du Commerce) and **Corsica Ferries** (☎ 08 25 09 50 95; www.corsicaférries.com; quai Lunel) sell tickets and provide timetables.

BUS

Buses stop at the **intercity bus station** (☎ 04 93 85 61 81; 5 blvd Jean Jaurès).

There are services until about 7.30pm daily to Antibes (1¼ hours), Cannes (1½ hours), Menton (1¼ hours) and Monaco (45 minutes). Single tickets cost €1.30.

For long-haul travel, **Intercars** (☎ 04 93 80 08 70), at the bus station, serves various European destinations; it also sells Eurolines tickets for buses to London, Brussels and Amsterdam.

TRAIN

Nice's main train station, **Gare Nice Ville** (av Thiers) is 1.2km north of the beach.

There are frequent services (up to 40 trains a day in each direction) to coastal towns including Antibes (€3.60, 25 minutes), Cannes (€5.50, 40 minutes), Menton (€4.10, 35 minutes) and Monaco (€3.10, 20 minutes).

Direct TGV trains link Nice with Paris' Gare de Lyon (€103.20, 5½ hours), with additional connecting services.

Getting Around

Ligne d'Azur (☎ 08 10 06 10 07; www.lignedazur.com; €4) runs two shuttle services to/from the airport – Route 99 to Gare Nice Ville, and Route 98 to the Gare Routière. Both stop at the two airport terminals, and run till around 9pm. A taxi to the centre of Nice costs €25 to €30.

Local buses are also handled by **Ligne d'Azur** (www.lignedazur.com). Fares cost €1.30/4/20 for a single fare/day pass/17 rides. All tickets can be purchased on the bus. After you time-stamp your ticket, it's valid for one hour.

For car rental, try **Budget** (☎ 04 97 03 35 03; Gustave V 1bis av Gustave V; Aubert 38 av Aubert) and **JML** (☎ 04 93 16 07 00; fax 04 93 16 07 48; 34 av Aubert).

Holiday Bikes (☎ 04 93 16 01 62; 34 av Auber; 🕑 closed noon-2pm & Sun) rents out 50cc scooters (€26 a day), bicycles (€14 a day), and cars (€58 a day).

CANNES

pop 68,214

These days Cannes is synonymous with its International Film Festival, when the town bristles with film stars flashing shiny white teeth and studio execs permanently glued to their mobile phones. Though the festival lasts less than two weeks in May, the city basks in its aura for the rest of the year. Cannes' palatial hotels and chic boutiques along the blvd de la Croisette are very much geared up for well-heeled travellers, so unless you're arriving in your own personal chopper, you'll be better off staying elsewhere.

The **tourist office** (☎ 04 92 99 84 22; www.cannes.com; 🕑 9am-8pm daily Jul & Aug, to 7pm Mon-Sat Sep-Jun) is on the ground floor of the Palais des Festivals. There's an **annexe** (☎ 04 93 99 19 77; 🕑 9am-7pm Mon-Sat) next to the train station.

Sights & Activities

The central, sandy **beaches** along blvd de la Croisette are sectioned off for hotel guests. A small strip of sand near the Palais des Festivals is free, but you'll find the best public beaches, **Plages du Midi** and **Plages de la Bocca**, stretching westwards from the Vieux Port along blvd Jean Hibert and blvd du Midi.

The **Musée de la Castre** (☎ 04 93 38 55 26; adult/concession €3/2; 🕑 10am-1pm & 3-7pm Tue-Sun Jun-Aug, 10am-1pm & 2-6pm Tue-Sun Apr, May & Sep, 10am-1pm & 2-5pm Wed-Mon Oct-Mar) is memorable for its excellent ethnographic exhibits and stunning location in a medieval castle at the top of Cannes' old town.

The tranquil **Îles de Lérins** are just 20km offshore from Cannes, and make the perfect place to escape the crowds. The closest is the 3.25km-long **Île Ste-Marguerite**, where the enigmatic Man in the Iron Mask was incarcerated during the late 17th century. Smaller still, **Île St-Honorat** has been a monastery since the 5th century. Its Cistercian monk owners welcome visitors to their community and seven small chapels.

Boats, operated by several companies, leave from quai des Îles on the western side of the harbour. **Compagnie Maritime Cannoise** (CMC; ☎ 04 93 38 66 33) runs ferries to Île Ste-Marguerite (€11 return), while **Compagnie Estérel Chanteclair** (☎ 04 93 39 11 82) operates boats to Île St-Honorat (€12 return), with skeleton schedules in winter. **Trans Côte d'Azur** (☎ 04 92 98 71 30; www.trans-cote-azur.com; quai St-Pierre) charges €10 for trips to/from Ste-Marguerite.

Sleeping

Hotel prices in Cannes fluctuate wildly according to the season, and soar during the film festival, when you'll need to book months in advance.

Parc Bellevue (☎ 04 93 47 28 97; www.parcbellevue.com; 67 av Maurice Chevalier, Cannes-La Bocca; camp sites per 2 adults, tent & car €24; Apr-Sep) Five-and-a-half kilometres west of the city, this is the closest camping ground to Cannes. The No 9 bus from the bus station on place Bernard Cornut Gentille stops 400m away.

Le Chalit (☎ 04 93 99 22 11; www.le-chalit.com; 27 av du Maréchal Galliéni; dm from €20, bedding €3) Just 300m northwest of the station, this independent hostel has a self-catering kitchen, wi-fi, and no curfew.

Le Chanteclair (☎/fax 04 93 39 68 88; 12 rue Forville; d from €50, with shower from €37; closed mid-Oct–early Jan) Right in the heart of the Le Suquet old town and just moments from the Forville Provençal market, this sweet, simple 15-room place has an enchanting courtyard garden, and is handy for the harbourside restaurants.

Hôtel Molière (☎ 04 93 38 16 16; www.hotel-moliere.com; 5 rue Molière; d from €80) This elaborately colonnaded pretty-in-pink period piece has restrained, subtle rooms. Most have balconies looking over the manicured gardens lined with conifers. Rates include a classic continental breakfast.

Hôtel Atlantis (☎ 04 93 39 18 72; www.cannes-hotel-atlantis.com; 4 rue de 24 Août; d from €80; P) This cheerful place offers outstanding bang for your buck. Top-notch amenities include a lift, guest spa and sauna, plus cheaper use of two different private beaches (€9).

Hôtel 3.14 (☎ 04 92 99 72 00; www.3-14hotel.com; 5 rue François Einesy; d from €120) Otherwise known as *trois-quatorze* (three-fourteen) or more often, Pi, this is the hottest design choice in Cannes. Each individually perfumed floor is themed after an aspect of a continent such as North America's '70s psychedelia. Lounge around on the private beach or by the rooftop swimming pool.

Eating

La Tarterie (☎ 04 93 39 67 43; 33 rue Bivouac Napoléon; most dishes €3-9; 8.30am-4.30pm) Fashionistas and backpackers jostle for stellar salads and specialities such as *clafoutis* – a fruit tart baked in sweet batter.

Mantel (☎ 04 93 39 13 10; 22 rue St-Antoine; lunch menu €23, dinner menu €32-70; closed lunch & dinner Wed & Thu lunch) With a charming owner who may well also be your waiter, this cosy little gem of a restaurant dishes up gastronomic bliss. Don't miss Mantel's signature crepe suzette for dessert.

Barbarella (☎ 04 92 99 17 33; 16 rue St-Dizier; mains €23-38; 7-11.30pm Tue-Sun) At the top of the old town in a trompe l'œil–painted building with groovy, upbeat interiors, this camp place (named after the sci-fi '60s flick) does fusion food such as roasted duck fillet glazed in coffee sauce.

Auberge Provençale (☎ 04 92 99 27 17; 10 rue St-Antoine; mains €24-38; lunch & dinner) Established in 1860, Cannes' oldest restaurant is a time-honoured tradition for classic Provençal lunches accompanied by very fine bottles of wine.

Astoux & Brun (☎ 04 93 39 21 87; 21 rue Félix Faure; menu from €28; 10am-1am) If you're a seafood connoisseur, this world-renowned place needs no introduction. Oysters, scallops and mussels just don't come any fresher.

AUTHOR'S CHOICE

Hôtel Negresco (☎ 04 93 16 64 00; www.hotel-negresco-nice.com; 37 promenade des Anglais; r €250-525) Built in 1912 and now a protected historical site, the pink-domed Negresco houses priceless art and architecture (including one of only three Hyacinthe Rigaud Louis XIV portraits – the others are in the Louvre and Versailles; and the Gustave Eiffel–designed stained-glass Salon Royale, bears a 1-tonne Baccarat crystal chandelier). Two hundred and fifty staff are on hand-and-foot to attend to your every whim, and there's even a private beach. High living.

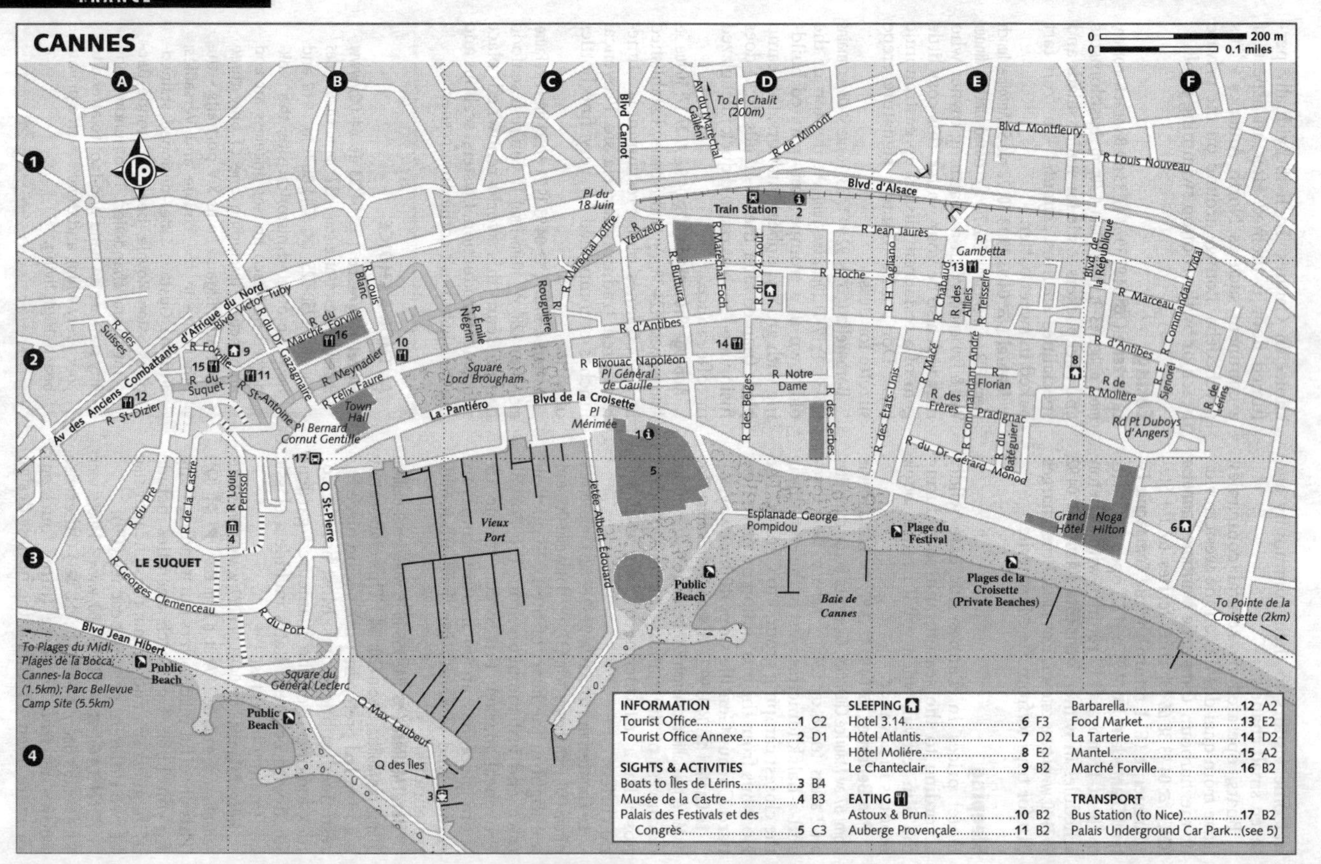
CANNES
0 200 m
0 0.1 miles
Train Station
Blvd d'Alsace
Blvd Carnot
Blvd Montfleury
R Louis Nouveau
R Jean Jaurès
R Hoche
R d'Antibes
Blvd de la Croisette
La Pantiéro
Pl Gambetta
Square Lord Brougham
Town Hall
Vieux Port
Jetée Albert Édouard
Esplanade George Pompidou
Plage du Festival
Public Beach
Baie de Cannes
Plages de la Croisette (Private Beaches)
Grand Hôtel
Noga Hilton
LE SUQUET
Q St-Pierre
Q Max Laubeuf
Q des Îles
Blvd Jean Hibert
Av des Anciens Combattants d'Afrique du Nord
R Georges Clemenceau
To Le Chalit (200m)
To Pointe de la Croisette (2km)
To Plages du Midi; Plages de la Bocca; Cannes-la Bocca (1.5km); Parc Bellevue Camp Site (5.5km)
INFORMATION
Tourist Office 1 C2
Tourist Office Annexe 2 D1
SIGHTS & ACTIVITIES
Boats to Îles de Lérins 3 B4
Musée de la Castre 4 B3
Palais des Festivals et des Congrès 5 C3
SLEEPING
Hotel 3.14 6 F3
Hôtel Atlantis 7 D2
Hôtel Molière 8 E2
Le Chanteclair 9 B2
EATING
Astoux & Brun 10 B2
Auberge Provençale 11 B2
Barbarella 12 A2
Food Market 13 E2
La Tarterie 14 D2
Mantel 15 A2
Marché Forville 16 B2
TRANSPORT
Bus Station (to Nice) 17 B2
Palais Underground Car Park (see 5)

The daily **food market** (place Gambetta; closed Mon Dec-Feb) is one of Cannes' main markets. **Marché Forville** (rue du Marché Forville) comes to life every morning except Monday (when a flea market takes its place).

Getting There & Away

Regular buses service Nice (€1.30, 1½ hours), Nice airport (€12.90, 40 minutes, hourly from 8am to 7pm) and other local destinations.

Trains run to Nice (€5.50, 30 minutes) and Marseille (€23.60, two hours), as well as St-Raphaël (€5.70, 30 minutes), from where you can get buses to St-Tropez and Toulon.

ST-TROPEZ

pop 5542

At the turn of the century St-Tropez was still a quaint fishing port favoured by a few artists, intellectuals and writers. But since the 1950s, when Brigitte Bardot shimmied along its streets in *Et Dieu Créa la Femme (And God Created Woman)*, St-Tropez has been transformed into the high temple of Riviera chic, crammed with the kind of upmarket boutiques and designer restaurants that would put most Parisian boulevards to shame. St-Tropez is at its worst in high summer, when the streets are jammed with nose-to-trail traffic and red-faced sightseers, but visit off-season and you'll be able to glimpse a much quieter, prettier side to sexy St-Tropez.

Orientation

The beaches where A-listers lounge start about 4km southeast of the town. The village itself is at the tip of a petite peninsula on the southern side of the Bay of St-Tropez, across from the Massif des Maures. The old town sits snugly between quai Jean Jaurès (the main quay of the luxury yacht-packed Vieux Port), place des Lices (an elongated square a few blocks back from the port) and a lofty 16th-century citadel overlooking the town from the northeast edge.

Information

Kreatik Café (☎ 04 94 97 40 61; 19 av Gal Lerclerc; 10am-9pm, closed Mon Dec-Feb) State-of-the-art Internet access.
Laverie du Port (quai de l'Épi; 7am-10pm) Close to the car park near the port.
Post office (place Celli) One block from the port.
Tourist office (☎ 04 94 97 45 21; www.ot-saint-tropez com; quai Jean Jaurès; 9.30am-8.30pm Jul & Aug, 9.30am-12.30pm & 2-7pm Apr-Jun, Sep & Oct, 9.30am-12.30pm & 2-6pm Nov-Mar)

Sights & Activities

The **Musée de l'Annonciade** (☎ 04 94 97 04 01; place Grammont, Vieux Port; adult/student €4.50/2.50; 10am-noon & 3-7pm Wed-Mon Jun-Sep, 10am-noon & 2-6pm Wed-Mon Oct-May, closed Nov) houses an impressive collection of works by Matisse, Bonnard, Dufy and especially Signac, who lived and worked in St-Tropez.

The best views of St-Tropez' bay are from the 17th-century **Citadelle de St-Tropez** (☎ 04 94 97 59 43; adult/concession €4/2.50; 10am-12.30pm & 1.30-6.30pm Apr-Sep, to 5.30pm Oct-Mar) above the town.

The town's best beach is **Plage de Tahiti**, which morphs into the 5km-long **Plage de Pampelonne**. For a spot of full-body sunbathing, there are lots of *naturiste* (nudist) beaches around St-Tropez, including **La Moutte**, 4.5km east of town, and **Plage de l'Escalet** on the southern side of Cap Camarat. There's a bus to nearby Ramatuelle from St-Tropez, but you'll have to walk the 4km southeast to the beach.

Sleeping & Eating

Hôtel La Méditerranée (☎ 04 94 97 00 44; www.hotelmediterranee.org; 21 blvd Louis Blanc; d €90-170;) The kind of unpretentious, old-fashioned place you hoped still existed in St-Trop. The Méditerranée has 16 charming rooms and a courtyard restaurant beneath the trees (mains €16 to €20).

Hôtel Sube (☎ 04 94 97 30 04; www.hotel-sube.com; 15 quai Suffren; d €90-250; closed early Jan-early Feb;) This nautically styled hotel is perched above the old port. Portside rooms cost more, but they are worth it for the view of the fabulous floating palaces pulled up out the front.

La Maison Blanche (☎ 04 94 97 52 66; www.hotellamaisonblanche.com; place des Lices; d €221-374; closed Feb;) Behind a hedged courtyard, the nine white-on-white rooms are a statement in chic minimalism. There's an outdoor champagne bar in summer; breakfast is served in a marquee.

Sénéquier (☎ 04 94 97 00 90; cnr quai Jean Jaurès & place aux Herbes; dishes €5-12.50; 8am-2am Apr-Oct, to 6pm Nov-Mar) This quintessential St-Trop quaiside café is the place to splurge on stellar coffee, elaborate ice creams, and homemade nougat (€8 for 200gm).

Le Petit Charron (☎ 04 94 97 73 78; 5 rue Charrons; mains €18-22; ⌚ dinner Tue-Sat) Off place des Lices in a charming little lane, this traditional restaurant is certainly small, with a tiny dining room and itty-bitty terrace, but it's worth trying to sample its classical Provençal *menus*.

The place des Lices market is held on Tuesday and Saturday mornings. There's also a centuries-old **fish market** (⌚ to noon Tue-Sat) on place aux Herbes. There are four supermarkets in the village including **Prisunic** (9 av du Général Leclerc; ⌚ 8am-8pm Mon-Sat).

Getting There & Away

St-Tropez **bus station** (av Général de Gaulle) is on the southwestern edge of town on the main road. There's an **information office** (☎ 04 94 54 62 36; ⌚ 8am-noon & 2-6pm Mon-Fri, to noon Sat) at the station. **Sodetrav** (☎ in Hyères 04 94 12 55 12) has eight buses daily from St-Raphaël-Valescure train station to St-Tropez bus station.

Trans Côte d'Azur (p390 and p394) runs boat trips from Nice and Cannes between Easter and September.

MENTON

pop 29,266

East of Monaco, the pastel-shaded, seaside town of Menton is within walking distance of the Italian border. Bordered by gardens and lemon groves it has a pretty beach and charming old town, and attracts fewer tourists than the rest of the Côte d'Azur. Menton's has the highest temperatures on the coast – it's not unusual for it to be snowing in Ventimiglia when the sun's shining here.

The **tourist office** (☎ 04 92 41 76 76; www.menton.fr; 8 av Boyer; ⌚ 9am-7pm Jun-Aug, 8.30am-12.30pm & 1.30-6pm Mon-Fri, 9am-noon & 2-6pm Sat Sep-May) is inside the Palais de l'Europe.

The early-17th-century **Église St-Michel** (Church of St Michael; ⌚ 10am-noon & 3-5.15pm, closed Sat morning), the grandest and possibly prettiest baroque church in this part of France, is perched in the centre of the Vieille Ville.

Since the 1930s, local citrus growers have congregated in Menton for the annual **Fête des Citrons** (Lemon Festival), which zings into action in February.

Sleeping

Camping Saint Michel (☎ 04 93 35 81 23; route des Ciappes de Castellar; camp sites per 2 adults, tent & car around €15; ⌚ 1 Apr-15 Oct) Five hundred metres from the hostel.

Auberge de Jeunesse (☎ 04 93 35 93 14; www.fuaj.org; Plateau St-Michel; dm €16, bedding €3; ⌚ reception 7am-10am & 5-10pm, closed Nov-Jan; P) Menton's HI hostel is a 1.5km hike uphill from the train station; or take the (infrequent) bus 6 to the stop at Camping Saint Michel.

Hôtel Richelieu (☎ 04 93 35 74 71; www.hotelrichelieumenton.com; 26 rue Partouneaux; s €39-48, d €49-89) Some of lofty-ceilinged rooms here have air-conditioning, and all have modernised bathrooms and floating floors. There's nearby public parking.

Hôtel des Arcades (☎ 04 93 35 70 62; fax 04 93 35 35 97; 41 av Félix Faure; s €40-61, d with hand basin €51-74) Fifty metres from the sea, this colonnaded ochre hotel with pale-blue shutters has basic but character-filled rooms with TVs and phones.

Getting There & Away

The **bus station** (☎ 04 93 28 43 27, information office 04 93 35 93 60) has links to Monaco (€2.20 return, 30 minutes) and Nice (€5.20 return, 1¼ hours). There are also buses to the Nice-Côte d'Azur airport (€16.40, 1½ hours) run by **Bus RCA** (☎ 04 93 85 64 44).

There are frequent trains to Monaco (€1.70, 10 minutes) and Nice (€5, 45 minutes).

MONACO

pop 30,000

Squeezed into 1.95 sq km, making it the world's second-smallest country after the Vatican, this pint-sized principality is a sovereign state, with its own red-and-white flag, national holiday (19 November) and Monégasque dialect. Ruled by the Grimaldi family since 1297, Monaco's manicured streets are presided over by palaces, fountained parks and one of the world's highest concentrations of plain-clothes policemen and CCTV cameras.

Monaco is best-known for its casino, Formula 1 Grand Prix and high-rolling lifestyle. It's also notorious as a tax-free haven. Many of Europe's richest businessmen, celebrities and sportsmen have a part-time home here in order to dodge paying their dues to the taxman.

Recently Monaco mourned the loss of its beloved monarch, Prince Rainier (1923–2005), who was married to the Hollywood actress Grace Kelly (1929–82) in 1956, and ruled from 1949 until his death on 6 April

2005. Their son, Albert (b 1958) was enthroned on 19 November 2005.

ORIENTATION

Monaco is made up of six areas: Monaco Ville, with its narrow, fairy-tale streets leading to the Palais du Prince (Prince's Palace) on the southern side of the port; the capital, Monte Carlo, north of the port; La Condamine, the flat area southwest of the port; Fontvieille, the industrial area southwest of Monaco Ville; Moneghetti, the hillside suburb west of La Condamine; and Larvotto, the beach area north of Monte Carlo, from where the French town of Beausoleil is just three streets uphill.

INFORMATION

Calls between Monaco and France are international calls. To call Monaco from France or elsewhere, dial ☎ 00 377; to phone France from Monaco, dial ☎ 00 33.

Monaco-imprinted euro coins are rarely spotted in circulation, and are quickly pocketed by collectors. There are (of course!) numerous banks near the casino.

Change Bureau (Jardins du Casino; 9am-7.30pm)

Direction du Tourisme et des Congrès de la Principauté de Monaco (☎ 92 16 61 16; www.monaco-tourisme.com; 2a blvd des Moulins; 9am-7pm Mon-Sat, 10am-noon Sun) From mid-June to late-September tourist information kiosks open around the harbour and the train station.

Laverie Laundrette (1 Escalier de la Riviera, Beausoleil; 7am-7pm) Near the border of Monaco and France.

Main post office (1 av Henri Dunant) In Monte Carlo, inside the Palais de la Scala. Monégasque stamps must be used to post mail in Monaco; rates are the same as France.

Stars 'n' Bars (☎ 93 50 95 95; www.starsnbars.com; 6 quai Antoine, 1er; per 15min €2; 11am-midnight) There's an Internet corner and wi-fi inside this rockin' restaurant-bar.

SIGHTS & ACTIVITIES

The changing of the guard, enacted with comical solemnity every day at 11.55am sharp, takes place outside the **Palais du Prince** (☎ 93 25 18 31), at the southern end of rue des Remparts in Monaco Ville. You can also visit the **state apartments** (adult/child €4/2; 9.30am-6.30pm Jun-Sep, 10am-5pm Oct, closed Nov-May) with a 10-language audioguide.

The 1910-built **Musée Océanographique de Monaco** (☎ 93 15 36 00; av St-Martin, Monaco Ville; adult/student €11/6; 9.30am-7pm Jul & Aug, to 6.30pm Apr-Jun & Sep) houses one of the world's best aquariums, with coral, sharks and plenty of tropical fish. It's a hilly walk along the cliff from Monte Carlo; alternatively take bus 1 or 2.

Prince Rainier and Princess Grace are buried inside the 1875 Romanesque-Byzantine **Cathédrale de Monaco** (4 rue Colonel). Monaco's boys' choir, Les Petits Chanteurs de Monaco, sings Sunday Mass at 10am between September and June.

Flowering year-round, more than a thousand species of cacti and exotic plants tumble down the slopes of the **Jardin Exotique** (☎ 93 15 29 80; 62 blvd du Jardin Exotique; adult/student €7/3.50; 9am-7pm mid-May–mid-Sep, to 6pm mid-Sep–mid-May).

FESTIVALS & EVENTS

As well as the much-hyped **Formula 1 Grand Prix**, which hits Monaco's streets in late May, there's also the **International Circus Festival of Monaco** (www.montecarlofestivals.com) held late January.

SLEEPING

Relais Internationale de la Jeunesse Thalassa (☎ 04 93 78 18 58; blvd de la Mer; dm €14; closed Nov-Mar) This is the closest hostel to Monaco, in a beautiful spot right by the sea on Cap d'Ail.

Hôtel de France (☎ 93 30 24 64; fax 92 16 13 34; 6 rue de la Turbie; s/d/tr €70/80/93) Your best bet for bargain accommodation in Monaco is this well-located place near the old city and the casino. Appealing rooms have cable TV, telephones and hairdryers.

Hôtel Helvetia (☎ 93 30 21 71; www.monte-carlo.mc/helvetia; 1bis rue Grimaldi; s €73-83, with shared bathroom €56-70, d €78-91, with shared bathroom €68-78) Overlooking the alfresco cafés of rue Princesse Caroline, the Helvetia's simple rooms have an old-fashioned charm.

Hôtel Alexandra (☎ 93 50 63 13; fax 92 16 06 48; 35 blvd Princesse Charlotte; s €95-115, d €120-150, tr €160-180;) This turn-of-the-century hotel is the closest thing to a midrange place in Monaco. It's in a great Monte Carlo location near the train station, and its 56 rooms are spacious, comfy and modern.

EATING

Decent-priced restaurants congregate in La Condamine along place d'Armes and rue Caroline; you'll find sandwich bars along quai Albert, 1er.

Bilig (☎ 97 98 20 45; 11bis rue Princesse Caroline; mains €5-10.50; to 6pm Oct-Apr, to 10pm May-Sep, closed Sun) This small creperie has a cute wooden outdoor deck and cosy interior and serves superior savoury and sweet crepes.

La Cigale di Mare (☎ 97 77 14 64; 4 rue Baron de Ste-Suzanne; mains €9-20; noon-3pm & 7.30-11pm Mon-Fri) As unpretentious as it gets, this pink-tableclothed, family-run place specialises in scrumptious seafood/pasta combinations such as fusili with baby octopus, or gnocchi with red mullet.

Huit & Demi (☎ 93 50 97 02; cnr rue Langlé & rue Princesse Caroline; mains €12-27; noon-3pm & 7-11pm, closed Sat lunch & Sun) Dine on tasty Italian dishes surrounded by crimson curtains and black-and-white posters of movie stars. The pavement terrace is prime when the weather's warm.

Café de Paris (☎ 92 16 20 20; place du Casino; mains €17-53; 7am-2am) Adjacent to the opulent Monte Carlo Casino, this is a fabulous spot for classy French fare, and for limo-spotting from the sprawling 300-seat terrace.

GETTING THERE & AWAY

Buses to France leave from various stops around the city; the tourist office has schedules and maps.

A train trip along the coast offers mesmerising views of the Med. There are frequent trains to Nice (€3.10, 25 minutes) and Menton (€1.70, 10 minutes).

LANGUEDOC-ROUSSILLON

Languedoc-Roussillon is really three separate regions rolled into one. Bas Languedoc (Lower Languedoc) is known for bullfighting, rugby and robust red wines and is home to all the major sights, including the Roman amphitheatre at Nîmes and the turret-topped town of Carcassonne. Inland is the mountainous region of Haut Languedoc (Upper Languedoc), while Roussillon sits beside the rugged Pyrenees and shares more than just a border with nearby Catalonia.

CARCASSONNE

pop 46,250

From afar, Carcassonne looks like some fairy-tale medieval city. Bathed in late-afternoon sunshine and highlighted by dark clouds, the old walled city (La Cité) is truly breathtaking. But with an estimated 3.5-million annual visitors, it can be a tourist hell in high summer – but even then you'll have to be fairly stone-hearted not to be moved.

Information

Main tourist office (☎ 04 68 10 24 30; www.carcassonne-tourisme.com; 28 rue de Verdun; 9am-7pm Jul & Aug, 9am-6pm Mon-Sat, 9am-noon Sun Sep-Jun)

Tourist office annexe (Porte Narbonnaise; year-round) In La Cité.

Sights

La Cité, enclosed by two rampart walls dotted with 52 stone towers, is one of Europe's largest city fortifications. But only the lower sections of the walls are original; the rest, including the anachronistic witches'-hat roofs, were stuck on by Viollet-le-Duc in the 19th century. It's lit up in spectacular fashion after dark.

Entry to the 12th-century **Château Comtal** (adult/student/under 18 €6.50/4.50/free; 9.30am-6.30pm Apr-Sep, 9.30am-5pm Oct-Mar) includes a 30-minute guided tour of both castle and ramparts.

Sleeping

Camping de la Cité (☎ 04 68 25 11 77; www.campeole.fr; camp sites €16-21.50, for walkers €9-11; mid-Mar–mid-Oct) A walking and cycling trail leads from the site to both La Cité and the Ville Basse. From mid-June to mid-September, bus 8 connects the camping ground with La Cité and the train station.

Auberge de Jeunesse (☎ 04 68 25 23 16; carcassonne@fuaj.org; rue Vicomte Trencavel; B&B €16; Feb–mid-Dec) Carcassonne's cheery HI-affiliated hostel, in the heart of La Cité, has rooms sleeping four to six. It has a kitchen, snack bar, great outside terrace and an Internet station, and rents bikes (per day €8).

Hôtel Astoria (☎ 04 68 25 31 38; www.astoriacarcassonne.com, in French; 18 rue Tourtel; d/tr/q €45/52/66; Mar-Jan; P) Rooms are fresh and pleasant, each with tiles or parquet, both at this midrange hotel and its agreeable annexe. Bathrooms are a bit pokey but it's very good value.

Hôtel du Pont Vieux (☎ 04 68 25 24 99; www.hoteldupontvieux.com, in French; 32 rue Trivalle; d €77-82; P) Bedrooms, most with a bathtub, have attractively rough-hewn walls. On the 3rd floor, rooms 18 and 19 have unsurpassed views of La Cité and there's a small terrace, accessible to all guests.

Eating

Restaurant des Musées (☎ 06 17 05 24 90; 17 rue du Grand Puits; menu €8.50-18) This simple, unpretentious place has three rear terraces with views of the ramparts. It bakes its own organic bread and offers excellent-value meals, including a couple of vegetarian *menus* (€9.50). No booze, but you can bring your own wine.

Au Bon Pasteur (☎ 04 68 25 49 63; 29 rue Armagnac; menu €15-28; closed Sun & Mon Jul & Aug, Sun & Wed Sep-Jun) At this intimate family restaurant, the simple wooden tables and chairs belie the sophistication of the cooking. Year-round, its *menu classique* (€15) and *formules de midi* (lunch specials; €10 to €11.50) both represent excellent value.

Restaurant Gil (☎ 04 68 47 85 23; 32 route Minervoise; menu €18-28, mains €9-18; ⏲ Tue-Sat) Head downstairs, below street level, for quality, Catalan-influenced cuisine. A particular strength is its fresh seafood and grilled fish (€10 to €15).

There's a **covered market** (rue du Verdun; ⏲ Mon-Sat) and an **open-air market** (place Carnot; ⏲ Tue, Thu & Sat). **L'Art Gourmand** (13 rue St-Louis) sells scrummy chocolate and 33 types of ice cream.

Getting There & Away

Ryanair flies daily from London Stansted and Brussels Charleroi to Carcassonne's **airport** (CCF; ☎ 04 68 71 96 46), 5km from town. There are also flights to Dublin, Liverpool and UK East Midlands at least three times weekly.

Carcassonne is on the main train line to Toulouse (€12.70, 50 minutes, frequent).

NÎMES

pop 134,000

Plough your way through the traffic-clogged outskirts of Nîmes to reach its true heart, still beating where the Romans established their town over two millennia ago. Here, you will find some of France's best-preserved classical buildings, together with some stunning modern constructions. The city also boasts one of France's best-preserved Roman amphitheatres, but is perhaps most well-known for its contribution to world fashion – this is the original home of *serge de Nîmes,* nowadays more often called denim.

For information, drop in to the **tourist office** (☎ 04 66 58 38 00; www.ot-nimes.fr; 6 rue Auguste; ⏲ 8am-8pm Mon-Sat, 10am-6pm Sun Jul & Aug; 8.30am-7pm Mon-Sat, 10am-5pm or 6pm Sun Sep-Jun).

Sights

A **combination ticket** (adult/child €9/7) admits you to Les Arènes, La Maison Carrée and Tour Magne.

LES ARÈNES

This superb Roman **amphitheatre** (adult/under 16yr/under 11yr €8/6/free with audioguide; ⏲ 9am-7pm Jun-Aug, to 5.30pm Mar-May, Oct & Sep, 9.30am-4.30pm Nov-Feb), built around AD 100 to seat 24,000 spectators, is wonderfully preserved, even retaining its upper storey, unlike its counterpart in Arles.

MAISON CARRÉE

This well-preserved rectangular Roman temple, today called the **Maison Carrée** (Square House; adult/11-16yr/under 11yr €4.50/3.50/free; ⏲ 9am-7pm Jun-Aug, to 5.30pm Mar-May, Oct & Sep, 9.30am-4.30pm Nov-Feb) was built around AD 5 to honour Emperor Augustus' two adopted sons. It has survived the centuries as a medieval meeting hall, private residence, stable, church and, after the Revolution, archive.

The striking glass and steel building across the square, designed by the British architect Sir Norman Foster, is the **Carré d'Art** (Square of Art), housing the municipal library and **Musée d'Art Contemporain** (Contemporary Art Museum; place de la Maison Carrée; adult/11-16yr/under 11yr €5/3.50/free).

TOUR MAGNE

Nîmes' other Roman monuments enrich the elegant Jardins de la Fontaine (Fountain Gardens). A 15-minute uphill walk brings you to the crumbling 30m-high **Tour Magne** (adult/11-16yr/under 11yr €3/2.50/free; ⏲ 9am-7pm Jun-Aug, to 5.30pm Mar-May, Oct & Sep, 9.30am-4.30pm Nov-Feb), the largest of a chain of towers that once punctuated the city's Roman ramparts. From here, there's a magnificent view of Nîmes and the surrounding countryside.

Festivals & Events

Nîmes becomes more Spanish than French during its *férias* (festivals). The five-day **Féria de Pentecôte** (Whitsuntide Festival) in June, and the three-day **Féria des Vendanges**, are both marked by daily *corridas* (bullfights). The **Bureau de Locations des Arènes** (☎ 04 66 02 80 90; 2 rue de la Violette) sells tickets.

Sleeping

Camping Domaine de la Bastide (☎ 04 66 62 05 82; www.camping-nimes.com; camp sites €13; ⏲ year-round) is 4km south of town on the D13. Take bus D and get off at La Bastide, the terminus.

Auberge de Jeunesse (☎ 04 66 68 03 20; www.hinimes.com; 257 chemin de l'Auberge de Jeunesse, la Cigale; dm €12, d/q €27.50/47) This hostel has everything from dorms to cute houses for two to six in its extensive grounds, 3.5km northwest of the train station. There's also bike hire (per day €14) and camping (per person €6). Take bus I, and get off at the Stade stop.

Hôtel Amphithéâtre (☎ 04 66 67 28 51; hotel-amphitheatre@wanadoo.fr; 4 rue des Arènes; s €34-39, d €44-61; ⏲ Feb-Dec; ⊠ ⊡) The Amphithéâtre, once a pair of 18th-century mansions, has 15 rooms decorated in warm, woody colours. Each is named after a writer or painter – the nicest are Montesquieu or Arrabal (€61), both large and with a balcony overlooking pedestrian place du Marché.

Hôtel Central (☎ 04 66 67 27 75; www.hotel-central.org; 2 place du Château; d/tr/q €45/55/65, r with shared bathroom €35; P) With its creaky floorboards and bunches of wild flowers painted on each bedroom door, this friendly hotel is full of character. Room 20, up on the top (5th) floor, has great rooftop views.

Royal Hôtel (☎ 04 66 58 28 27; rhotel@wanadoo.fr; 3 blvd Alphonse Daudet; s €45-65, d €60-85) New owners have preserved the raffishly bohemian atmosphere of this hotel, popular with visiting artistes. Some of the imaginatively furnished rooms overlook pedestrian place d'Assas, which can be noisy on summer nights.

Eating

Nîmes' gastronomy owes as much to Provence as it does to Languedoc. Spicy southern delights, such as aïoli and *rouille* (a spicy mayonnaise of olive oil, garlic and chilli peppers), are as abundant as cassoulet.

There are colourful Thursday markets in the old city in July and August. The covered food market is in rue Général Perrier.

La Truye qui Filhe (☎ 04 66 21 76 33; 9 rue Fresque; menu €9.50; noon-2pm Mon-Sat, closed Aug) Within the vaults of a restored 14th-century inn is the best bargain in Nîmes, blending a self-service format with a regional *menu*.

Côte Bleue (☎ 04 66 67 36 12; rue du Grand Couvent; menu €17, mains €9-13; Mon-Sat Jun-Sep, lunch Mon-Sat, dinner Fri & Sat Oct-May) Decked out in blues and yellows, the Blue Coast is as attractive inside as out, and serves excellent, generous portions of Provençal cooking.

Getting There & Away

Nîmes' **airport** (FNI; ☎ 04 66 70 49 49), 10km southeast of the city, is served by Ryanair, which flies to/from London (Stansted and Luton), Liverpool and Nottingham East Midlands.

The **bus station** (☎ 04 66 29 52 00; rue Ste-Félicité) connects with the train station. Regional destinations include Pont du Gard (€6.20, 30 minutes, up to six daily).

There's an **SNCF sales office** (11 rue de l'Aspic). At least eight TGVs daily run to/from Paris' Gare de Lyon (€72.70 to €88.80, three hours). There are frequent services to Arles (€6.90, 30 minutes), Avignon (€7.70, 30 minutes) and Marseille (€17.20, 1¼ hours).

AROUND NÎMES

Pont du Gard

The Pont du Gard, a Unesco World Heritage Site, is an exceptionally well-preserved, three-tiered Roman aqueduct that was once part of a 50km-long system of canals built about 19 BC by the Romans to bring water from near Uzès to Nîmes. The scale is huge: the 35 arches of the 275m-long upper tier, running 50m above the Gard River, contain a watercourse designed to carry 20,000 cubic metres of water per day and the largest construction blocks weigh over five tonnes.

From car parks (€5) either side of the Gard River, you can walk along the road bridge, built in 1743 and running parallel to the aqueduct's lower tier. The best view of the Pont du Gard is from upstream, beside the river, where you can swim on hot days.

CORSICA

Corsica is separated from the rest of France by more than just the blue waters of the Mediterranean. This wild, proud and defiantly individual island has only been French for under 250 years, and would have remained an independent nation if the revolutionary Pascale Paoli had had his way. As it was, Corsica became part of France in 1769, but retains much of its island identity, with a distinctive language, culture and way of life. It's dotted with beautiful beaches, quaint fishing ports and mountain villages, as well as one of the country's most challenging walking routes (including the leg-shredding GR20) so it's packed to bursting in high summer.

Dangers & Annoyances

When Corsica makes headlines, it's often because nationalist militants have turned nasty (previous acts include bombings, bank robberies and the murder of the prefect). The violence isn't targeted at visitors and they need not worry about their safety.

BASTIA

pop 37,800

With its colourful jumble of tenement buildings and atmospheric old port, Bastia is like a miniature version of mainland Marseille: a thriving, lively city that's not overprettified for tourists. Basking beneath the Mediterranean sun, the city's narrow streets are crowned by a crumbling 15th-century citadel.

Information

Cyber Space (☎ 04 95 30 70 83; 3 blvd Paoli; per 15min/1hr €1/3.80; 9am-midnight Mon-Sat, 4pm-midnight Sun)
Post office (av Maréchal Sébastiani; 8am-7pm Mon-Fri, to noon Sat)
Tourist office (☎ 04 95 54 20 40; www.bastia-tourisme.com; place St-Nicolas; 8.30am-noon & 2-6pm Mon-Sat)

Sights & Activities

Bastia can be covered in a half-day stroll starting with **place St-Nicolas**, a vast seafront esplanade laid out in the 19th century. The square is lined with trees and cafés, and at the southern end, a bizarre statue of **Napoleon Bonaparte** depicted as a muscle-bound Roman emperor stands guard.

Between place St-Nicolas and the old port lies **Terra Vecchia**, a historic neighbourhood of old houses and tumbledown tenement blocks.

The **old port** is an atmospheric jumble of boats, restaurants and crumbling buildings, dominated by the twin towers of the **Église St-Jean-Baptiste**, which loom over the north side of the harbour.

Bastia's most historic quarter juts out above the old port. The **citadel** (Terra Nova), built by the Genoese between the 15th and 17th centuries to protect Bastia's harbour, can be reached by climbing the stairs through **Jardin Romieu**, the hillside park on the southern side of the harbour.

Sleeping

Camping San Damiano (☎ 04 95 33 68 02; www.campingsandamiano.com; camp sites per tent & vehicle €5-7, per person €5-7; Apr-Oct) Served by the airport bus, this is a pine-forested camping ground 5km south of Bastia; furnished bungalows are available.

Hôtel Posta Vecchia (☎ 04 95 32 32 38; www.hotel-postavecchia.com; quai des Martyrs de la Libération; d €40-47, tr €70-95, q €80-105;) The best option within walking distance of the old port, with bright décor and floating timber floors. An extra €10 buys sea views.

Hôtel Central (☎ 04 95 31 71 12; www.centralhotel.fr; 3 rue Miot; s €55-60, d €65-90, apt €85-105;) Charming (and central), the terracotta-tiled corridors of this old hotel lead to airy rooms with timber floors, checked curtains and pretty prints of sailing boats. The pick of the rooms have balconies overlooking a courtyard garden.

Hôtel Les Voyageurs (☎ 04 95 34 90 80; www.hotel-lesvoyageurs.com; 9 av Maréchal Sébastiani; s €63, d €73-83, tr €83-93; P) Bastia's best hotel, chicly decorated with Matisse prints, lemon walls, wrought-iron furniture and all-white bathrooms.

Eating

Cafés and restaurants line place St-Nicolas, the old port, quai des Martyrs and place de l'Hôtel de Ville.

A Casarella (☎ 04 95 32 02 32; rue du Dragon; mains €9-28; lunch Mon-Fri, dinner Mon-Sat) Artistically decorated with contemporary paintings and navy tablecloths, this restaurant combines classical Corsican produce with imaginative cuisine.

Petite Marie (☎ 04 95 32 47 83; 2 rue des Zéphyrs; mains €13-20; lunch Tue-Fri, dinner Mon-Sat) Squeezed into a cross-vaulted room just back from the port, this little restaurant serves *plats du jour* of the freshest seafood imaginable, as well as exceptional paella.

Osteria U Tianu (☎ 04 95 31 36 67; 4 rue Rigo; menu €19; 7pm-2am Mon-Sat, closed Aug) For a memorable taste of Corsica – culturally as well as culinary – climb the narrow wooden stairs to this quarter-of-a-decade-old restaurant, lined with posters of Che Guevara, old banknotes and hunting rifles.

Pick up fresh supplies at the lively morning **food market** (place de l'Hôtel de Ville; Tue-Sun). The large **Spar supermarket** (rue César Campinchi) is the most convenient place for staples.

Getting There & Away

AIR

Aéroport Bastia-Poretta (BIA; ☎ 04 95 54 54 54; www.bastia.aeroport.fr) is 24km south of the city. Buses (€8, seven to nine daily, fewer on Sunday) depart from outside the Préfecture building. The tourist office has schedules, and timetables are posted at the bus stop. A taxi to the airport costs around €30.

BOAT

The southern ferry terminal is at the eastern end of av François Pietri. The vehicle entrance is 600m north.

FRANCE

There's an **SNCM office** (☎ 04 95 54 66 81; www.sncm.com; 🕑 8-11.45am & 2-5.45pm Mon-Fri, 8am-noon Sat) in the southern terminal. Tickets are sold two hours before departure in the Corsica Marittima section of the terminal building.

Moby Lines (☎ 04 95 34 84 94; www.mobylines.it; 4 rue du Commandant Luce de Casabianca) has a bureau in the ferry terminal, open two hours before each sailing.

The **Corsica Ferries office** (☎ 04 95 32 95 95; www.corsicaferries.com; 15bis rue Chanoine Leschi; 🕑 8.30am-noon & 2-6pm Mon-Fri, 9am-noon Sat) is across the road from the ferry terminal.

BUS

Bastia's buses leave from several locations around town. The tourist office can provide timetables and show you where to catch your bus.

Eurocorse (☎ 04 95 31 73 76) travels to Ajaccio (€20, three hours) via Corte (€11, two hours) twice daily except on Sundays.

Les Beaux Voyages (☎ 04 95 65 11 35) travels to Île Rousse and Calvi (€15, two hours) daily except Sunday. Buses leave from outside the train station.

Les Rapides Bleus (☎ 04 95 31 03 79; 1 av Maréchal Sébastiani) runs buses to Porto Vecchio (€20 plus €1 per item of baggage), with connections to Bonifacio and Sartène.

TRAIN

The **train station** (☎ 04 95 32 80 61; av Maréchal Sébastiani; 🕑 6am-8.30pm Mon-Sat, 8.30am-8.30pm Sun) is beside the large roundabout on Square Mal Leclerc. Main destinations include Ajaccio (€20.70, four hours, four daily) via Corte, and Calvi (€15.70, three hours, three or four daily) via Île Rousse.

CALVI

pop 4800

There's a sliver of Mediterranean chic at Calvi, curving around a crescent-shaped bay, beneath the snowy peaks of Monte Cinto (2706m). Watching over the town, the citadel remains as a relic of the town's past as a strategic military outpost, with a huddle of 13th-century hilltop houses cosseted by 15th-century bastions.

In 1794, a British expeditionary fleet assisting Pasquale Paoli's Corsican nationalist forces besieged and bombarded the Genoese stronghold. In the course of the battle, Captain Horatio Nelson was wounded by rock splinters and lost the use of his right eye.

Orientation & Information

The citadel – also known as the Haute Ville (Upper City) – sits on a rocky promontory northeast of the Basse Ville (Lower City). Boulevard Wilson, the major thoroughfare through town, is uphill from the marina.

The **main tourist office** (☎ 04 95 65 16 67; www.balagne-corsica.com; 🕑 9am-noon & 3-7pm Mon-Fri, 9am-12.30 & 2.30-6.30 Sat & Sun Jul & Aug, 9am-noon & 2-6pm Mon-Sat Apr, May & Sep, 9am-noon & 2-6pm Mon-Fri Oct-Mar) is opposite the marina.

Sights & Activities

Calvi's 15th-century **citadel** dominates the harbour skyline. The **Palais des Gouverneurs** (Governors' Palace; place d'Armes), once the seat of power for the Genoese administration, now serves as a base for the French Foreign Legion.

Uphill from Caserne Sampiero is the 13th-century **Église St-Jean Baptiste**, rebuilt in 1570.

Calvi's 4km of beach begins at the marina and stretches east around the Golfe de Calvi. Other good beaches are west of town, including **Algajola**.

Sleeping

Most of Calvi's hotels are closed in winter.

Camping Les Castors (☎ 04 95 65 13 30; www.castors.fr; route de Pietra Maggiore; camp sites per adult €8-9.50, tent €3-4, car €2.50-3.50; 🕑 May-Sep;) An 800m stroll southeast of town, this three-star camping ground rents studios and mobile homes from €290 per week.

Hôtel Le Belvedere (☎ 04 95 65 01 25; www.resa-hotels-calvi.com; place Christophe Colomb; d €45-115, tr €70-130;) Both the standard and deluxe rooms at this pleasant two-star place have views over the sparkling blue Golfe de Calvi.

Hôtel Le Rocher (☎ 04 95 65 20 04; www.hotel-le-rocher.com, in French; blvd Wilson; d €70-170, mezzanine r €105-200; 🕑 Apr-Sep;) Elegant and well-equipped, this three-star hotel also has mezzanine family rooms sleeping up to four people, where crimson fabrics contrast with soothing neutral furnishings.

Eating

A Cantina (☎ 06 25 78 10 42; quai Landry; tapas dishes €3-7, plates €10; 🕑 7pm-2am Apr-Nov, plus lunch May-Sep) On a portside terrace this cantina serves 'Corsican tapas' and more than 150 Corsican wines.

U Minellu (☎ 04 95 65 05 52; Traverse à l'Église; menu from €14; ⏰ daily Mar-Nov, Mon-Sat Dec-Feb) This is a delightful family restaurant that serves up Corsican dishes such as *brocciu* (cheese made from goat's or sheep's milk) cannelloni, Corsican pork, and chestnut and apple cake.

Île de Beauté (☎ 04 95 65 00 46; quai Landry; menu €20-50, mains €12-35; ⏰ mid-Mar–Dec) Straight out of St-Tropez, with bright red chairs covering its waterfront terrace, this eminently stylish café specialises in fish and Corsican cuisine.

The **marché couvert** (covered market; ⏰ 8am-noon Mon-Sat) is near Église Ste-Marie Majeure. **Annie Traiteur** (rue Clemenceau; ⏰ Apr-Oct) sells Corsican products, or for general supplies there's the **Casino Supermarket** (av Christophe Colomb), and, next door, a **Super-U supermarket** (av Christophe Colomb).

Getting There & Away

AIR

Southeast of town (7km) is **Aéroport Calvi-Ste-Catherine** (CLY; ☎ 04 95 65 88 88; www.calvi.aeroport.fr), with flights to Nice, Marseille, Lyon and other French cities. **Taxis** (☎ 04 95 65 03 10) from the airport cost around €20.

BOAT

From Calvi there are express **NGV ferries** to Nice (2½ hours, five per week). SNCM tickets are handled by **Tramar** (☎ 04 95 65 01 38; quai Landry; ⏰ 9am-noon & 2-5pm Mon-Fri, 9am-noon Sat). Tickets for Corsica Ferries are handled by **Les Beaux Voyages** (☎ 04 95 65 15 02; place de la Porteuse d'Eau).

BUSES

Buses to Bastia (€15, 2¼ hours) are run by **Les Beaux Voyages** (☎ 04 95 65 15 02; place de la Porteuse d'Eau).

TRAIN

Calvi's **train station** (☎ 04 95 65 00 61; ⏰ until 7.30pm) is off av de la République. There are two departures daily to Ajaccio (€24.10), Bastia (€15.70) and the stations between.

From April to October, the single-car trains of CFC's **Tramway de la Balagne** make 19 stops along the coast between Calvi and Île Rousse (45 minutes). The line is divided into three sectors – you need one ticket for each sector. *Carnets* of six tickets (€8) are sold at stations.

LES CALANQUES

One of Corsica's most stunning natural sights is about 85km south of Calvi: Les Calanques de Piana (E Calanche in Corsican), a spectacular landscape of red granite cliffs and spiky outcrops, carved into bizarre shapes by the forces of wind, water and weather. Less rocky areas support pine and chestnut forests, whose green foliage contrasts dramatically with the technicoloured granite.

AJACCIO

pop 60,000

If you didn't already know that Napoleon Bonaparte was born in Ajaccio (pronounced Ajaxio) you will within a few minutes' of arriving here. With a glittering harbourfront, designer boutiques and fashionable restaurants, Corsica's cosmopolitan capital honours its famous son with street names, statues, and several stellar museums.

Orientation

Ajaccio's main street is cours Napoléon, stretching from place de Gaulle north to the train station and beyond. The old city is south of place Foch. The port is on the east side of town, from where a tree-lined promenade leads west along plage St-Francois.

Information

Absolut Game (☎ 04 95 21 56 60; av de Paris; per hr €3; ⏰ 9am-2am) Internet café.
Lavomatique (rue Maréchal Ornano; ⏰ 8am-10pm) Laundrette.
Main post office (13 cours Napoléon)
Tourist office (☎ 04 95 51 53 03; www.ajaccio-tourisme.com; 3 blvd du Roi Jérôme; ⏰ 8am-7pm Mon-Sat, 9am-1pm Sun) Free Internet.

Sights

You can't walk far in Ajaccio without stumbling across the Ajaccio-born boy who became Emperor of France. In fact, Napoleon spent little of his adult life in Corsica. After crowning himself Emperor of France in 1804, he never returned.

The saga begins at the **Musée National de la Maison Bonaparte** (☎ 04 95 21 43 89; rue St-Charles; adult/concession €5/3.50; ⏰ 9am-11.30am & 2-5.30pm Tue-Sun, 2-5.50pm Mon Apr-Sep, 10-11.30am & 2-4.15pm Tue-Sun, 2-4.15pm Mon Oct-Mar), the grand building in the old city where Napoleon was born and spent the first nine years of his childhood.

Established by Napoleon's uncle, the exceptional **Musée Fesch** (☎ 04 95 21 48 17; 50-52 rue du Cardinal Fesch; adult/student €5.50/4; 2-6pm Mon, 9.30am-6pm Tue-Thu, 2-2.30pm Fri, 10.30am-6pm Sat & Sun Jul & Aug, 9.30am-noon & 2-6pm Tue-Sun Apr-Jun & Sep, 9.30am-noon & 2-6pm Tue-Fri & Sun Oct-Mar) has the finest collection of 14th-to-19th-century Italian art outside the Louvre (mostly looted during Napoleon's foreign campaigns), including works by Titian, Botticelli, Raphael, Poussin and Bellini.

Sleeping

Hôtel Kallisté (☎ 04 95 51 34 45; www.hotel-kalliste-ajaccio.com, in French; 51 cours Napoléon; s €45-56, d €52-69, tw €58-76, tr €69-89) With clean lines and 50 contemporary rooms, this stylish city hotel – complete with a glass lift, terracotta-tiled floors and exposed brickwork – is a fantastic deal.

Hôtel Fesch (☎ 04 95 51 62 62; www.hotel-fesch.com; 7 rue du Cardinal Fesch; s €56-79, d €61-89; closed mid-Dec–mid-Jan) Presiding over one of Ajaccio's oldest pedestrianised streets, numerous shops and restaurants are at your doorstep at this grand, old-fashioned 77-room hotel.

Hôtel Napoléon (☎ 04 95 51 54 00; www.hotel-napoleon-ajaccio.com; 4 rue Lorenzo Vero; s €65-89, d €75-105) Just off cours Napoléon, rooms at this smart hotel aren't large, but they're tastefully decorated in cool neutral tones, and come with crisp white-tiled bathrooms and free wi-fi.

Eating

Le Papacionu (☎ 04 95 21 27 86; 16 rue St-Charles; mains €7.50-18, pizza €9-12; ⌚ dinner Mon-Sat, closed Nov-Feb) Ajaccio's best pizza is served on bright pink, purple and cobalt-blue plates at this fabulous, funky little hole in the wall eatery.

Le 20123 (☎ 04 95 21 50 05; 2 rue du Roi de Rome; menu €26; ⌚ dinner Tue-Sun) This Corsican bistro started life in the village of Pila Canale (postcode 20123). When the owner upped sticks, he decided to re-create his old restaurant – village square, water-pump, washing lines and all.

Le Grand Café Napoléon (☎ 04 95 21 42 54; 10 cours Napoléon; menu €28-45, mains €23-30; ⌚ Mon-Sat) This place is home to Ajaccio's grandest dining room, replete with soaring cream arches, black-and-white terrazzo floors and red tablecloths, and a much-loved streetside café.

Ajaccio's **open-air food market** (square Campinchi; ⌚ to noon, closed Mon) fills the area with Corsican atmosphere every morning. The daily fish market is in the building behind the food market.

Getting There & Away

AIR

Aéroport d'Ajaccio-Campo dell'Oro (AJA; ☎ 04 95 23 56 56) is 8km east of the city centre. Transports Corse d'Ajaccio (TCA) bus 8 links the airport with Ajaccio's train and bus stations (€4.50).

BOAT

Boats depart from the combined bus and ferry **Terminal Maritime et Routier** (quai l'Herminier). The **SNCM ticket office** (☎ 04 95 29 66 99; 3 quai l'Herminier; ⌚ 8am-8pm Tue-Fri, to 6pm Mon, to 1pm Sat) is across the street. Inside the terminal, the SNCM bureau sells tickets a few hours before departure for evening ferries.

BUS

Bus companies operate from Terminal Maritime et Routier on quai l'Herminier. Most have ticket kiosks on the right as you enter the station.

Eurocorse (☎ 04 95 21 06 30) travels to Bastia (€18, three hours, two daily), Bonifacio (€19.50, four hours, two or three daily) and Calvi (€19.85, change at Ponte Leccia). Services run daily except Sundays.

CAR

The main car-rental companies also have airport bureaus.

Budget (☎ 04 95 21 17 18; 1 blvd Lantivy)
Europcar (☎ 04 95 21 05 49; 16 cours Grandval)
Hertz (☎ 04 95 21 70 94; 8 cours Grandval)

TRAIN

The **train station** (☎ 04 95 23 11 03; place de la Gare) operates services to Bastia (€20.70, four hours, three to four daily), Corte (€11, two hours, three to four daily) and Calvi (€24.10, five hours, two daily; change at Ponte Leccia).

BONIFACIO

pop 2700

The most vivid view of Bonifacio is from aboard a boat in the sapphire-blue Bouches de Bonifacio (Strait of Bonifacio). This stunning 12km strait channels between Corsica's southernmost tip and the Italian island of Sardinia. From the water, the tall, sun-bleached buildings of Bonifacio's citadel appear to morph seamlessly into the serrated white limestone cliffs rising up from the sea. Within the clifftop citadel is a charming maze of alleyways with a distinct medieval feel.

The **tourist office** (☎ 04 95 73 11 88; www.bonifacio.fr; 2 rue Fred Scamaroni; ⌚ 9am-8pm Jul & Aug, to 7pm May, Jun & Sep, to noon & 2-6pm Mon-Fri Oct-Apr) is in the Haute Ville.

Sights

The steps linking rue St-Érasme with Porte de Gênes are known as Montée Rastello then become Montée St-Roch further up. At the top of Montée St-Roch you will find the **Porte de Gênes**. Just inside the gateway, you can stroll through the **Bastion Memorial** (admission €2.50; ⌚ 9am-7pm mid-Apr–Sep), which features permanent exhibits on Bonifacio's history.

Along the ramparts, fabulous panoramic views unfold from **place du Marché** and **place Manichella**.

Crisscrossed by meandering alleyways lined with tall stone houses, the old city has a distinctly medieval feel. **Rue des Deux Empereurs** is so named because Charles V and Napoleon once slept in the houses at Nos 4 and 7. **Église Ste-Marie Majeure**, a 14th-century Romanesque church, is known for its loggia (roofed porch).

From the citadel, the **Escalier du Roi d'Aragon** (Staircase of the King of Aragon; admission €2; 9am-6pm Mon-Sat Apr-May & Sep-Oct, daily Jul & Aug) leads down the cliff.

Sleeping

Camping L'Araguina (04 95 73 02 96; av Sylvère Bohn; camp sites from €13.50; Mar-Oct) Near the Hôtel des Étrangers, shaded by olive trees and only a short walk into town.

Hôtel des Étrangers (04 95 73 01 09; hoteldes etrangers.ifrance.com; av Sylvère Bohn; d €37-74; Apr-Oct; P) Bonifacio's best deal is just 300m outside town, a rambling hotel with 30 light, airy, old-fashioned soundproofed rooms with cable TVs.

Hotel du Roy d'Aragon (04 95 73 03 99; www.royaragon.com; 13 quai Jérôme Comparetti; d €49-145, ste €127-197;) The pick of places to stay on the crowded quay. This sophisticated three-star place has minimalist rooms furnished in blond wood; higher-priced rooms come with port views and balconies.

Eating

L'Archivolto (04 95 73 17 58; rue de l'Archivolto; plats du jour €7-14; dinner Mon-Sat mid-Mar–Oct) Specialities such as chicken in Pietra beer and a fresh herb tart with *brocciu* are long-standing favourites at this wonderfully quirky restaurant-cum–antique shop in the citadel.

Cantina Doria (04 95 73 50 49; 27 rue Doria; menu €12-15; Apr-Oct) Sit with locals on wooden benches, surrounded by copper pots, photos and rusty signs, for classic *soupe Corse* and *gateau à la châtaigne* (chestnut cake).

U Castille (04 95 73 04 99; rue Simon Varsi; mains €13-23, pizzas €7.50-11.50; lunch & dinner Tue-Sat Nov-Feb, daily Mar-Oct) Four separate dining premises run by the same family, but the Corsican menu, wood-fired pizzas and excellent wine list is interchangeable among all.

Getting There & Away

AIR

Bonifacio's airport, **Aéroport de Figari** (FSC; 04 95 71 10 10), is 21km north of town. An airport bus runs from the town centre in July and August (€7 to €8).

BOAT

In summer, ferries to Santa Teresa in Sardinia are operated by **Saremar** (04 95 73 00 96; www.saremar.it, in Italian) and **Moby Lines** (04 95 73 00 29; www.mobylines.it) from Bonifacio's ferry port (50 minutes, two to seven daily). Fares start from €8 one-way, plus taxes (around €6.20 one-way).

BUS

Eurocorse (Porto Vecchio 04 95 70 13 83) runs two buses to Ajaccio (€19.50, four hours) via Sartène from Monday to Saturday. For Bastia, change at Porto Vecchio (€6.50, 45 minutes, two to four buses daily).

FRANCE DIRECTORY

ACCOMMODATION

Accommodation is listed in this chapter in order of price. Generally you'll be able to find a budget room for under €40 (€50 in Paris). Most are equipped with a hand basin but have communal baths and showers.

Hotels listed under 'midrange' are usually €40 to €100 for a double (up to €150 in Paris) and have en-suite bathroom facilities. Top-end accommodation will cost more than €100 (€150 in the capital). Prices for midrange and top-end accommodation include private bathroom unless stated. Prices given are for the high season.

During periods of heavy domestic or foreign tourism, popular destinations are packed out – particularly in July and August, when the French tend to take their summer holidays. Tourist offices will often reserve rooms (generally for a fee).

Camping & Caravan Parks

Camping is immensely popular in France, and many of the thousands of camping grounds are near rivers, lakes or oceans. Most close from October or November to March or April. Hostels sometimes let travellers pitch tents in their grounds. Gîtes de France coordinates farm camping and publishes an annual guide *Camping à la Ferme*.

Camping in nondesignated spots, or *camping sauvage*, is usually illegal.

Gîtes Ruraux & B&Bs

A *gîte rural* is a self-contained holiday cottage (or part of a house) in a village or on a farm. A *chambre d'hôte*, basically a B&B (bed and breakfast), is a room in a private house, rented by the night. The website www.bbfrance.com is useful for B&Bs and vacation rentals.

Ask about Gîtes de France brochures and guides at local tourist offices, or contact the **Fédération Nationale des Gîtes de France** (☎ 01 49 70 75 75; www.gites-de-france.fr).

Hostels & Foyers

A dormitory bed in an *auberge de jeunesse* (hostel) costs €25 in Paris, and anything from €10 to €35 in the provinces. Breakfast/dinner is often available for €3/10; bedding (ie, sheets) costs extra.

Guests need to purchase an annual Hostelling International card (€10.70/15.25 for people under/over 26) or a nightly Welcome Stamp (€1.50) to stay at hostels run by French hostelling associations **Ligue Française pour les Auberges de la Jeunesse** (LFAJ; ☎ 01 44 16 78 78; www.auberges-de-jeunesse.com; 7 rue Vergniaud, 13e, Paris; Ⓜ Glacière) and **Fédération Unie des Auberges de Jeunesse** (FUAJ; ☎ 01 48 04 70 30; www.fuaj.org; 9 rue de Brantome, 3e, Paris; Ⓜ Rambuteau).

Hotels

French hotels vary greatly in quality. In practically every major city you'll be able to find everything from low-budget no-starrers to full-blown pleasure palaces catering to your every whim, but what you get for your money can be quite variable.

In general there are a few rules shared by most hotels. A double room has one double bed – if you prefer twin beds you'll need to ask for *deux lits séparés*. Remember that French hotels almost never include breakfast in their advertised nightly rates; you can cut costs by steering clear of the hotel breakfast and picking up some croissants from a local *boulangerie* (bakery) instead. Hotels usually ask for a credit card number to confirm a reservation. Look out for great weekend deals to 33 cities and towns at www.bon-week-end-envilles.com.

ACTIVITIES

From the peaks, rivers and canyons of the Alps to the mountains and volcanic peaks of the Massif Central – not to mention 3000km of coastline stretching from the Med to the Dover Straits – France lends itself to exhilarating outdoor adventures by the mountain load.

Adventure Sports

France is a top spot for adventurous activities. In big cities and picturesque places, especially the Côte d'Azur and the Alps, local companies offer high adrenaline pursuits such as canyoning, paragliding, white-water rafting and bungy jumping.

Cycling

The French take cycling very seriously – the country practically grinds to a halt during the annual Tour de France. Mountain bikes are called *vélo tout-terrain* (VTT) in France. A *piste cyclable* is a cycling path.

Top cycling spots include Annecy in the Alps, the Dordogne and the Loire Valley.

Hiking

The countryside is crisscrossed by a staggering 120,000km of *sentiers balisés* (marked walking paths), which pass through every imaginable terrain in every region of the country. No permit is needed to hike.

The *sentiers de grande randonnée* (GRs) are long-distance footpaths that cover huge areas of France – some are several hundred kilometres long.

The **Fédération Française de la Randonnée Pédestre** (FFRP; French Ramblers' Association) has an **information centre** (Map pp292-3; ☎ 01 44 89 93 93; www.ffrp.asso.fr, in French; 14 rue Riquet 19e, Paris; Ⓜ Pernety) in Paris, as does the **Club Alpin Français** (CAF; Map pp292-3; ☎ 01 53 72 87 00; www.ffcam.fr, in French; 24 av de Laumière, 19e, Paris; Ⓜ Laumière).

Lonely Planet's *Walking in France* is packed with essential practical information.

Skiing

France has more than 400 resorts in the Alps, the Jura, the Pyrenees, the Vosges, the Massif Central and the mountains of Corsica. The season lasts from mid-December to late March or April. January and February tend to have the best conditions, but the slopes get very crowded during the February-March school holidays.

The Alps have some of Europe's finest ski facilities. Much cheaper and less glitzy, smaller low-altitude stations are in the Pyrenees and the Massif Central.

Ski de fond (cross-country skiing) is possible at high-altitude resorts but is usually much better in the valleys. Undoubtedly some of the best trails are in the Jura range.

Prearranged package deals are by far the cheapest way to ski. Paris-based **Ski France** (☎ 01 47 42 23 32; www.skifrance.fr; 61 blvd Haussmann 8e, Paris; Ⓜ Opéra) has information and an annual brochure covering more than 50 ski resorts.

Water Sports

France has fine beaches along all its three coasts. The sandy beaches stretching along the Atlantic Coast (eg near La Rochelle) are less crowded than their pebbly counterparts on the Côte d'Azur. Corsica has some magnificent spots. Brittany and the north coast are also popular, albeit cooler, beach destinations.

The best surfing in France is on the Atlantic coast around Biarritz (p355) where waves reach heights of 4m. White-water rafting, canoeing and kayaking are practised on many French rivers, especially in the Dordogne and the Alps. Contact the **Fédération Française de Canoë-Kayak** (FFCK; ☎ 01 45 11 08 50; www.ffck.org, in French).

BUSINESS HOURS

French business hours are usually 9am or 9.30am to 7pm or 8pm, often with a midday break from noon or 1pm to 2pm or 3pm (except in Paris). Most businesses close on Sunday; exceptions include grocery stores, *boulangeries*, cake shops and florists.

Restaurant hours vary, but they are generally open for lunch between noon and 2pm and for dinner from 7.30pm. Cafés open from early morning until around midnight. Bars usually open early evening and close at 1am or 2am.

Banks usually open from 8am or 9am to 11.30am or 1pm and then 1.30pm or 2pm to 4.30pm or 5pm, Monday to Friday or Tuesday to Saturday. Post offices generally open from 8.30am or 9am to 5pm or 6pm on weekdays (often with a midday break) and on Saturday mornings from 8am to noon.

Supermarkets open Monday to Saturday from about 9am or 9.30am to 7pm or 8pm; some open on Sunday morning.

TOP TIP

In France, computer keyboards are laid out differently, which can make typing quite difficult. To change the keyboard language, hold down Alt and the Maj (majiscule) button – and hey presto, you can type away to your heart's content.

EMBASSIES & CONSULATES

French Embassies & Consulates

France's diplomatic and consular representatives abroad are listed on the website www.france.diplomatie.fr.

Australia Canberra (☎ 02-6216 0100; www.ambafrance-au.org; 6 Perth Ave, Yarralumla, ACT 2600); Sydney Consulate (☎ 02-9261 5779; www.consulfrance-sydney.org; Level 26, St Martin's Tower, 31 Market St, Sydney, NSW 2000)

Canada Ottowa (☎ 613-789 1795; www.ambafrance-ca.org; 42 Sussex Drive, Ottawa, Ont K1M 2C9); Toronto Consulate (☎ 416-925 8041; www.consulfrance-toronto.org; 2 Bloor Est, Suite 2200, Toronto M4W 1A8)

Germany Berlin (☎ 030-590 039 000; www.botschaft-frankreich.de; Pariser Platz 5, Berlin 10117); Munich Consulate (☎ 089-419 4110; www.consulfrance-munich.de; Heimeranstrasse 31, Level 3, Munich 80339)

Italy (☎ 06-686 011; www.ambafrance-it.org; Piazza Farnese 67, 00186 Rome)

Netherlands Amsterdam Consulate (☎ 020-530 6969; www.consulfrance-amsterdam.org; Vijzelgracht 2, 1017 HR Amsterdam); The Hague (☎ 070-312 5800; www.ambafrance-nl.org; Smidsplein 1, 2514 BT Den Haag)

New Zealand (☎ 04-384 2555; www.ambafrance-nz.org; Level 13, Rural Bank Bldg, 34-42 Manners St, PO Box 11-343, Wellington)

Spain Barcelona Consulate (☎ 93-270 3000; www.consulfrance-barcelone.org; Ronda Universitat 22, 08007 Barcelona); Madrid (☎ 91-423 8900; www.ambafrance-es.org; Calle de Salustiano Olozaga 9, 28001 Madrid)

UK London Consulate (☎ 020-7073 1200; www.consulfrance-londres.org; 21 Cromwell Rd, London SW7 2EN); London Embassy (☎ 020-7073 1000; www.ambafrance-uk.org; 58 Knightsbridge, London SW1X 7JT); London Visa Section (☎ 020-7073 1250; 6A Cromwell Place, London SW7 2EW)

USA New York Consulate (☎ 212-606 3600; www.consulfrance-newyork.org; 934 Fifth Ave, New York, NY 10021); Washington (☎ 202-944 6000; www.ambafrance-us.org; 4101 Reservoir Rd NW, Washington, DC 20007)

Embassies & Consulates in France

All foreign embassies can be found in Paris. Many countries – including the United States, Canada and a number of European countries – will also have consulates in other major cities.

Australia (Map pp292-3; ☎ 01 40 59 33 00; www.austgov.fr; 4 rue Jean Rey, 15e; Ⓜ Bir Hakeim)

Canada (Map pp292-3; ☎ 01 44 43 29 00; www.amb-canada.fr; 35 av Montaigne, 8e; Ⓜ Franklin D Roosevelt)

Germany (Map pp292-3; ☎ 01 53 83 45 00; www.amb-allemagne.fr; 13-15 av Franklin D Roosevelt, 8e; Ⓜ Franklin D Roosevelt)

Italy (Map pp292-3; ☎ 01 49 54 03 00; www.amb-italie.fr; 51 rue de Varenne, 7e; Ⓜ Rue du Bac)
Netherlands (Map pp292-3; ☎ 01 40 62 33 00; www.amb-pays-bas.fr; 7 rue Eblé, 7e; Ⓜ St-François Xavier)
New Zealand (Map pp292-3; ☎ 01 45 01 43 43; www.nzembassy.com; 7ter rue Léonard de Vinci, 16e; Ⓜ Victor Hugo)
Spain (Map pp292-3; ☎ 01 44 43 18 00; www.amb-espagne.fr; 22 av Marceau, 8e; Ⓜ Alma Marceau)
UK (Map pp292-3; ☎ 01 44 51 31 00; www.amb-grandebretagne.fr; 35 rue du Faubourg St-Honoré, 8e; Ⓜ Concorde)
USA (Map pp292-3; ☎ 01 43 12 22 22; www.amb-usa.fr; 2 av Gabriel, 8e; Ⓜ Concorde)

FESTIVALS & EVENTS

Most French cities, towns and villages have at least one major arts festival each year.

May/June

May Day Workers' day is celebrated countrywide on 1 May with trade union parades, and diverse protests. People give each other *muguet* (lilies of the valley) for good luck. No-one works (except waiters and muguet sellers).
Cannes Film Festival (www.festival-cannes.com) The stars walk the red carpet at Cannes in mid-May, the epitome of see-and-be-seen cinema events in Europe.
Fête de la Musique (www.fetedela musique.culture.fr) Bands, orchestras, crooners, buskers and spectators take to the streets for this national celebration of music on 21 June.

July

National Day On 14 July fireworks, parades and all-round hoo-ha to commemorate the storming of the Bastille in 1789, symbol of the French Revolution.
Gay Pride (www.gaypride.fr) Effervescent street parades, performances and parties through Paris and other major cities.

August/September

Festival Interceltique de Lorient (www.festival-interceltique.com, in French) Huge Celtic festival attracting people from all over Brittany and the UK.

December

Christmas Markets Alsace is the place to be for a traditional-style festive season, with world-famous Christmas markets, decorations and celebrations.

GAY & LESBIAN TRAVELLERS

France is one of Europe's most liberal countries when it comes to homosexuality, in part because of a long tradition of public tolerance towards people who choose not to live by conventional social codes. Paris has been a thriving gay and lesbian centre since the late 1970s. Montpellier, Lyon, Toulouse, Bordeaux and many other towns also have significant active communities. Attitudes tend to become more conservative in the countryside and villages.

Online, www.gayscape.com has hundreds of links, while www.france.qrd.org is a 'queer resources directory' for gay and lesbian travellers.

HOLIDAYS

The following *jours fériés* (public holidays) are observed in France.

New Year's Day (Jour de l'An) 1 January – parties in larger cities; fireworks are subdued by international standards.
Easter Sunday & Monday (Pâques & lundi de Pâques) Late March/April.
May Day (Fête du Travail) 1 May – traditional parades.
Victoire 1945 8 May – the Allied victory in Europe that ended WWII.
Ascension Thursday (Ascension) May – celebrated on the 40th day after Easter.
Pentecost/Whit Sunday & Whit Monday (Pentecôte & lundi de Pentecôte) May/June – celebrated on the seventh Sunday after Easter.
Bastille Day/National Day (Fête Nationale) 14 July – *the* national holiday.
Assumption Day (Assomption) 15 August.
All Saints' Day (Toussaint) 1 November.
Remembrance Day (L'onze Novembre) 11 November – celebrates the WWI armistice.
Christmas (Noël) 25 December.

LEGAL MATTERS

French police have wide powers of stop-and-search and can demand proof of identity at any time. Foreigners must be able to prove their legal status in France (eg passport, visa, residency permit). If the police stop you, be polite, remain calm and don't argue. Don't leave baggage unattended at airports or train stations: suspicious objects will be summarily blown up.

MONEY

The official currency of France is the euro.

Bureaux de change are available in most major cities, and most large post offices offer currency exchange and cash travellers cheques. Commercial banks charge a stiff fee for changing money – generally it's cheaper to use the *distributeurs automatiques de billets* (DAB, otherwise known as ATMs). Most ATMs are linked to the Cirrus, Plus and Maestro networks – check with your bank back home for overseas fees.

Visa and MasterCard (Access or Eurocard) are widely accepted at most shops, restaurants and hotels, although you'll need to know your *code* (PIN number).

For lost cards, call:

Amex (☎ 01 47 77 72 00)
Diners Club (☎ 08 10 31 41 59)
MasterCard, Eurocard & Access (Eurocard France; ☎ 08 00 90 13 87, 01 45 67 84 84)
Visa (Carte Bleue; ☎ 08 00 90 20 33)

POST

France's 17,000 post offices are marked with a yellow or brown sign reading 'La Poste'. Since La Poste also has banking, finance and bill-paying functions, queues can be very long, but there are automatic machines for postage.

Postal Rates

Domestic letters of up to 20g cost €0.53. For international post, there are three different zones: a letter/package under 20g/2kg costs €0.55/12.50 to Zone A (EU, Switzerland, Iceland, Norway); €0.75/14 to Zone B (the rest of Europe and Africa); and €0.90/20.50 to Zone C (North and South America, Asia and the Middle East, Australasia).

Receiving Mail

Picking up poste-restante mail costs €0.50; you must show your passport or national ID card. Mail will be kept 15 days. Poste-restante mail not addressed to a particular branch goes to the city's main post office.

TELEPHONE

International Dialling

To call someone outside France, dial the international access code (☎ 00), the country code, the area code (without the initial zero if there is one) and the local number.

EMERGENCY NUMBERS

- Ambulance (SAMU) ☎ 15
- EU-wide emergency hotline ☎ 112
- Fire ☎ 18
- Police ☎ 17
- Rape crisis hotline ☎ 08 00 05 95 95

To make a reverse-charges (collect) call *(en PCV)* or a person-to-person call *(avec préavis)*, dial ☎ 3123 or ☎ 08 00 99 00 11 (for the USA and Canada) and ☎ 08 00 99 00 61 for Australia.

Phonecards offer much better international rates than Country Direct services (which allow you to be billed by the long-distance carrier you use at home).

Mobile Phones

France uses GSM 900/1800, compatible with the rest of Europe and Australia but not with the North American or Japanese systems. The three major networks are **SFR** (☎ 08 00 10 60 00; www.sfr.com), **Bouygues** (☎ 08 10 63 01 00; www.bouygtel.com) and **Orange** (☎ 08 00 83 08 00; www.orange.fr). If you have a compatible phone, you can buy a 'prepaid' kit that includes a SIM-card and a set number of calls. When these run out you purchase a recharge card at most *tabacs*.

Mobile phone numbers in France always begin 06.

National Dialling Areas

France has five telephone dialling areas; the full 10-digit number is used no matter where you are. There are five regional area codes.

☎ 01 Paris region
☎ 02 the northwest
☎ 03 the northeast
☎ 04 the southeast (including Corsica)
☎ 05 the southwest

For international directory inquiries, dial ☎ 3212. The cost is about €2.50. Emergency numbers and 08 00 numbers are free.

Public Phones & Telephone Cards

Public phones in France are card-operated. *Télécartes* (phonecards) cost €8 or €15 at post offices, *tabacs* and anywhere you see a sticker saying *'télécarte en vente ici'*.

Cartes à code (with a free access number and a scratch-off code) offer better rates than *cartes à puce* (cards with a magnetic chip). They can be used from private as well as public phones, and often have good international rates.

VISAS

EU nationals and citizens of Switzerland, Iceland and Norway need a passport or national identity card to enter France. Citizens of Australia, the USA, Canada, New Zealand, Japan and Israel don't need visas for stays up to three months; nor do citizens of EU candidate countries (except Turkey).

TRANSPORT IN FRANCE

GETTING THERE & AWAY

Air

AIRLINES

Most of the world's major carriers fly to Paris and other French cities.

Air Canada (code AC; ☎ 08 25 88 08 81; www.aircanada.ca; hub Toronto)
Air France (code AF; ☎ 08 20 82 08 20; www.airfrance.com; hub Paris)
Alitalia (code AZ; ☎ 08 20 31 53 15; www.alitalia.com; hub Rome)
American Airlines (code AA; ☎ 08 10 87 28 72; www.americanairlines.com; hub Dallas)
BMI BritishMidland (code BD; ☎ short haul 0870 6070 555, long haul 0870 6070 555; www.flybmi.com; hub London)
British Airways (code BA; ☎ 08 25 82 54 00; www.britishairways.com; hub London)
KLM (code KL; ☎ 08 90 71 07 10; www.klm.com; hub Amsterdam)
Lufthansa (code LH; ☎ 08 20 02 00 30; www.lufthansa.com; hub Frankfurt)
Qantas (code QF; ☎ 08 20 82 05 00; www.qantas.com; hub Sydney)

There are numerous budget airline serving France.

bmiBaby (www.bmibaby.com) Budget subsidiary of BMI.
easyJet (www.easyjet.com) Main UK budget carrier.
Flybe (www.flybe.com) Regional UK budget carrier.
Ryanair (www.ryanair.com) Mainly UK destinations.
Transavia (www.transavia.com) Budget subsidiary of KLM.

AIRPORTS

France's main international airports are **Roissy Charles de Gaulle** (CDG; ☎ 01 48 62 12 12) and **Orly** (ORY; ☎ 01 49 75 15 15); see p309. France's other main airports include the following:

Bordeaux (BOD; ☎ 05 56 34 50 50; www.bordeaux.aeroport.fr)
Lille (LIL; ☎ 03 20 49 68 68; www.lille.aeroport.fr, in French)
Lyon (LYS; ☎ 08 26 80 08 26; www.lyon.aeroport.fr)
Marseille (MRS; ☎ 04 42 14 14 14; www.mrsairport.com)
Nantes (NTE; ☎ 02 40 84 80 00; www.nantes.aeroport.fr)
Nice (NCE; ☎ 08 20 42 33 33; www.nice.aeroport.fr)
Strasbourg (SXB; ☎ 03 88 64 67 67; www.strasbourg.aeroport.fr)
Toulouse (TLS; ☎ 08 25 38 00 00; www.toulouse.aeroport.fr)

Land

If you're travelling around Europe, look for discount bus and train passes, which can be combined with discount air fares.

BUS

Buses are slower and less comfortable than trains, but are cheaper, especially if you qualify for discount rates (people under 26, over 60, teachers and students).

Eurolines (☎ 08 92 69 52 52, 01 43 54 11 99; www.eurolines.com) groups together 32 European coach operators and links points across Europe, Morocco and Russia. Eurolines' website has information on fares, routes and bookings. Return tickets cost about 20% less than two singles.

French coach company **Intercars** (☎ 08 92 89 80 80; www.intercars.fr, in French) links France with other European cities, notably Eastern Europe and Russia. The office in **Paris** (☎ 01 49 03 40 63; 139bis rue de Vaugirard, 15e; Ⓜ Falguière) links with European destinations such as Prague (€56, 16 hours) and Warsaw (€90, 28 hours). From **Lyon** (☎ 04 78 37 20 80; Perrache bus station) you can reach Naples, Porto, Minsk or Zagreb. From **Nice** (☎ 04 93 80 08 70; Nice bus station) you can reach San Sebastian, Casablanca and Venice.

CAR & MOTORCYCLE

At some border points you may be asked for passport or identity card (your driving licence will not be sufficient). Police searches are not uncommon for vehicles entering France, particularly from Spain and Belgium. See p416 for details about driving in France.

Channel Tunnel

The Channel Tunnel, inaugurated in 1994, is the first dry-land link between England and France since the Ice Age.

High-speed **Eurotunnel trains** (☎ in the UK 0870 535 3535, in France 03 21 00 61 00; www.eurotunnel.com) whisk cars, motorcycles and coaches from Folkestone through the Channel Tunnel to Coquelles, 5km southwest of Calais. Shuttles run 24 hours a day, with up to five an hour during peak periods.

Prices start from UK£49 one-way for a car including all passengers, unlimited luggage and taxes; discounts for advance bookings are often available on the website.

TRAIN

Rail services link France with every country in Europe. You can book tickets and get information from **Rail Europe** (www.raileurope.com) up to two months ahead. In France, ticketing is handled by the **SNCF** (☎ 08 92 35 35 35; www.sncf.com).

Eurostar

The **Eurostar** (☎ in France 08 92 35 35 39, in the UK 08705 186 186; in France www.voyages-sncf.com, in the UK www.eurostar.com) travels between London and Paris in just 2½ hours. There are direct daily services between London and Ashford (Kent) and Paris, Brussels, Lille, Disneyland Paris and Calais-Fréthun. Extra seasonal routes operate during ski season.

A standard 2nd-class one-way ticket from London to Paris costs UK£149, or €223.50 in the opposite direction. Discounts are available if you book 14 or seven days ahead, and if you're under 25 or a student.

Sea

Regular ferries travel to France from Italy, the UK, Channel Islands and Ireland.

FROM IRELAND

Eurail pass holders pay 50% of the adult pedestrian fare for crossings between Ireland and France on Irish Ferries (make sure you book ahead).

Irish Ferries (☎ in Republic of Ireland 0818 300 400, in Northern Ireland 0035 381 830 0400, in France 01 44 88 54 504; www.irishferries.ie) has overnight services from Rosslare to Cherbourg (18½ hours) or Roscoff (16 hours) every other day (three weekly from mid-September to October). A foot passenger/car and driver costs from €56/99. There's no fee if you book online.

Brittany Ferries (☎ in the UK 0870 366 5333, in France 08 25 82 88 28; www.brittany-ferries.com) operates car ferries on Saturdays (April to October) from Cork to Roscoff (13 hours) and on Friday in the other direction.

FROM ITALY

From April to mid-October, the **Société Nationale Maritime Corse Méditerranée** (SNCM; ☎ in France 08 25 88 80 88; www.sncm.fr) has five or six car ferries per week from Marseille or Toulon to Porto Torres on Sardinia. The crossing takes about 11 hours; one-way fares are around €118 without a cabin.

Several ferry companies ply the waters between Corsica and Italy.

FROM UK

Fares vary hugely according to the season and day of travel – a Friday night ferry can cost much more than a Sunday morning one, and July and August are always more expensive. Special return fares, often requiring advance booking, are sometimes cheaper than a standard one-way fare. Check out **Ferry Savers** (☎ 0870 990 8492; www.ferrysavers.com), which guarantees the lowest prices on Channel crossings.

Brittany

From mid-March to mid-November, **Brittany Ferries** (☎ in the UK 0870 366 5333, in France 08 25 82 88 28; www.brittany-ferries.com) links Plymouth to Roscoff (six hours, one to three daily). The one-way fare for foot passengers ranges from UK£23 to UK£73. There's also a daily crossing to St-Malo (8¾ hours); pedestrians pay from UK£48 one-way.

From April to September, **Condor Ferries** (☎ in the UK 0845 345 2000, in France 02 99 20 03 00; www.condorferries.com) has at least one daily ferry linking Weymouth with St-Malo (UK£41, seven to 10 hours).

Normandy

Transmanche Ferries (☎ 0800 917 1201; www.transmancheferries.com) operate the Newhaven–Dieppe route. The crossing (up to three daily) takes four hours. A one-way foot-passenger fare starts at UK£12; the one-way fare for a car and two adults starts from UK£33.

There's a 4¼-hour crossing (two or three per day) from Poole to Cherbourg with **Brittany Ferries** (☎ in the UK 0870 366 5333, in France 08 25 82 88 28; www.brittany-ferries.com). Foot passengers pay from UK£48 one-way.

Brittany Ferries and Condor Ferries also operate two or three car ferries a day (five hours by day, eight hours overnight) between Portsmouth and Cherbourg, and two faster catamarans a day from April to September. Foot passengers pay from UK£38 one-way.

Brittany Ferries also has car-ferry services from Portsmouth to Caen (Ouistreham, six hours, three per day). Tickets cost the same as for Poole–Cherbourg.

Northern France

The Dover–Calais crossing (70 minutes to 1½ hours, 15 daily) is handled by **SeaFrance** (☎ in the UK 0870 571 1711, in France 08 04 04 40 45; www.seafrance.com). Foot passenger fares start at UK£6 to UK£12 return. Fares for a car and up to nine passengers cost from UK£24 to UK£45 one-way. **P&O Ferries** (☎ in the UK 0870 598 0555, in France 08 25 01 30 13; www.poferries.com) also operates a Dover–Calais service (one to 1½ hours, 29 daily) from UK£18 one-way for foot passengers and €55 one-way including a small car.

Ferries run by **Norfolk Line** (☎ 03 28 59 01 01; www.norfolkline.com) link Loon Plage, about 25km west of Dunkirk (Dunkerque), with Dover from UK£19 one-way for a vehicle and up to nine passengers, while **Speed Ferries** (☎ in the UK 0130 420 3000, in France 03 21 10 50 00; www.speedferries.com) offers an ultrafast catamaran service between Boulogne and Dover from UK£19 one-way for a vehicle and up to five passengers (50 minutes, five daily).

GETTING AROUND

Air

Air France (☎ 08 20 82 08 20; www.airfrance.com) controls the lion's share of France's long-protected domestic airline industry, although the British budget carrier easyJet has flights linking Paris with Marseille, Nice and Toulouse.

Cheaper deals are available on weekdays and for bookings made at least three weeks in advance. Significant discounts are available to children, young people, families and seniors. Last-minute offers are posted on the Air France website every Wednesday.

Bus

For travel between regions, a train is your best bet since inter-regional bus services are limited. Buses are used quite extensively for short-distance travel within *départements*, especially in rural areas with relatively few train lines (eg Brittany and Normandy) – but services are often slow and few and far between.

Car & Motorcycle

Having your own wheels gives you exceptional freedom and allows you to visit more remote parts of France. Unfortunately it can be expensive and, in cities, parking and traffic are frequently a major headache. Motorcyclists will find France great for touring, with winding roads of good quality and lots of stunning scenery. Just make sure your wet-weather gear is in good nick.

DRIVING LICENCE & DOCUMENTS

All drivers must carry a national ID card or passport; a valid driving licence (*permis de conduire;* most foreign licences can be used in France for up to a year); car-ownership papers, known as a *carte grise* (grey card); and proof of third party (liability) insurance.

FUEL & TOLLS

Essence (petrol or gasoline), also known as *carburant* (fuel) costs from around €1.30 per litre for 95 unleaded. Petrol stations on the autoroutes are often more expensive than those in towns. You'll have to factor in the cost of tolls on many of France's autoroutes, based on the distance travelled.

HIRE

To hire a car you'll usually need to be over 21 and in possession of a valid driving licence and a credit card. Major rental companies include the following:

ADA (☎ 08 25 16 91 69; www.ada.fr, in French)
Avis (☎ 08 20 05 05 05; www.avis.com)
Budget (☎ 08 25 00 35 64; www.budget.com)
Easycar (☎ 090 63 33 33 33; www.easycar.com)
Europcar (☎ 08 25 35 83 58; www.europcar.com)
Hertz (☎ 08 25 34 23 43; www.hertz.com)
OTU Voyages (☎ 01 40 29 12 12; www.otu.fr, in French) For students.

Cheap deals can be found online, or through **Auto Europe** (☎ 1-888 223 5555; www.autoeurope.com) in the US, or **Holiday Autos** (☎ 0870 530 0400; www.holidayautos.co.uk) in the UK.

Automatic transmissions are *very* rare in France – you'll need to order one well in advance.

INSURANCE

Unlimited third party liability insurance is mandatory in France. Third party liability insurance is provided by car-rental companies, but collision-damage waivers (CDW) vary between companies. When comparing rates check the *franchise* (excess), which is usually €350 for a small car. Your credit card may cover CDW if you use it to pay for the car rental.

ROAD RULES

Cars drive on the right in France. All passengers must wear seat belts, and children who weigh less than 18kg must travel in backward-facing child seats. The speed limits on French roads are as follows:

- 50km/h in built-up areas
- 90km/h (80km/h if it's raining) on N and D highways
- 110km/h (100km/h if it's raining) on dual carriageways
- 130km/h (110km/h if it's raining) on autoroutes

Under the *priorité à droite* (priority to the right) rule, any car entering an intersection (including a T-junction) from a road on your right has the right-of-way, unless the intersection is marked *'vous n'avez pas la priorité'* (you do not have right of way) or *'cédez le passage'* (give way).

It is illegal to drive with a blood-alcohol concentration over 0.05% – the equivalent of two glasses of wine for a 75kg adult. Mobile phones may only be used when accompanied by a hands-free kit or speakerphone.

Riders of any type of two-wheeled vehicle with a motor (except motor-assisted bicycles) must wear a helmet.

Train

France's superb rail network is operated by the state-owned SNCF (www.sncf.com). Many towns and villages not on the SNCF train network are served by supplementary buses.

The flagship trains on French railways are the superfast TGVs, which operate on the following routes:

TGV Atlantique Sud-Ouest & TGV Atlantique Ouest These link Paris' Gare Montparnasse with western and southwestern France, including Brittany (Rennes, Quimper, Brest), Nantes, Tours, Poitiers, La Rochelle, Bordeaux, Biarritz and Toulouse.

TGV Est Under construction. This line will connect Paris with Strasbourg and Germany. The first sections are due to open in mid-2007.

TGV Nord, Thalys & Eurostar These link Paris' Gare du Nord with Arras, Lille, Calais, Brussels, Amsterdam, Cologne and, via the Channel Tunnel, Ashford and London Waterloo.

TGV Sud-Est & TGV Midi-Méditerranée These link Paris' Gare de Lyon with the southeast, including Dijon, Lyon, Geneva, the Alps, Avignon, Marseille, Nice and Montpellier.

A non-TGV train is referred to as a *corail* or TER *(train express régional)*.

Special deals are available at www.sncf.com. Last-minute deals are published online every Tuesday. Reduced fares are available with the **Carte 12-25** (€49) for travellers aged 12 to 25; the **Carte Enfant Plus** (€65) for one to four adults travelling with a child aged four to 11; and a **Carte Sénior** (€50) for those over 60. A **Carte Escapades** (€99) for 26- to 59-year-olds guarantees savings of 25% on a return journey of at least 200km including a Saturday night away.

The France Railpass allows unlimited travel on SNCF trains for four days over a one-month period. In 2nd class it costs US$229; each additional day costs US$30. The France Youthpass allows four days of travel in a month. In 2nd class it costs US$169, plus US$23 for each extra day. These passes can be purchased from travel agents or travel websites such as www.raileurope.com.

Before boarding the train you must time-stamp your ticket in a *composteur*, one of those orange posts at the start of the platform. If you forget, find a conductor so they can punch it for you to avoid being fined.

ROAD RULES

Cars drive on the right in France. All passengers must wear seat belts, and children who weigh less than 18kg must travel in backward-facing child seats. The speed limits on French roads are as follows:

- 50km/h in built-up areas
- 90km/h (80km/h if it's raining) on N and D highways
- 110km/h (100km/h if it's raining) on dual carriageways
- 130km/h (110km/h if it's raining) on autoroutes

Under the *priorité à droite* (priority to the right) rule, any car entering an intersection (including a T-junction) from a road on your right has right of way, unless the intersection is marked *vous n'avez pas la priorité* (you do not have right of way) or *cédez le passage* (give way).

It's illegal to drive with a blood-alcohol concentration over 0.05% – the equivalent of two glasses of wine for a 75kg adult. Mobile phones may only be used when accompanied by a hands-free kit or speakerphone.

Riders of any type of two-wheeled vehicle with a motor (except motor-assisted bicycles) must wear a helmet.

Train

France's superb rail network is operated by the state-owned SNCF (www.sncf.com). Many rural towns and villages not on the SNCF train network are served by SNCF buses.

The flagship trains on the rail system are the super-fast TGVs, which operate on the following routes:

TGV Atlantique Sud-Ouest & TGV Atlantique Ouest These link Paris' Gare Montparnasse with western and southwestern France, including Brittany, Rennes, Quimper, Brest, Nantes, Tours, Poitiers, La Rochelle, Bordeaux, Biarritz and Toulouse.

TGV Est Under construction, this line will connect Paris with Strasbourg and Germany; the first section are due to open in 2007.

TGV Nord, Thalys & Eurostar These link Paris' Gare du Nord with Arras, Lille, Calais, Brussels, Amsterdam, Cologne and, via the Channel Tunnel, Ashford and London Waterloo.

TGV Sud-Est & TGV Midi-Méditerranée These link Paris' Gare de Lyon with the southeast, including Dijon, Lyon, Geneva, the Alps, Avignon, Marseille, Nice and Montpellier.

A non-TGV train is referred to as a *corail* or TER (*train express régional*).

Special deals are available at www.sncf.com; last-minute deals are published online every Tuesday. Reduced fares are available with the **Carte 12-25** (€49) for travellers aged 12 to 25, the **Carte Enfant Plus** (€65) for one to four adults travelling with a child aged four to 11, and a **Carte Senior** (€50) for those over 60. A **Carte Escapades** (€85) for 26- to 59-year-olds guarantees savings of 25% on a return journey of at least 200km including a Saturday night away.

The France Railpass allows unlimited travel on SNCF trains for four days over a one-month period. In 2nd class it costs US$220; each additional day costs US$30. The France Youthpass allows four days of travel over a one-month period in 2nd class; it costs US$169, plus US$23 for each extra day. These passes can be purchased from travel agents or travel websites such as www.raileurope.com.

Before boarding the train you must time-stamp your ticket in a *composteur*, one of those orange posts at the start of the platform. If you forget, find a conductor so they can punch it for you to avoid being fined.

Germany

The more you know about Germany the less you understand it. Think Germans only drink beer? Wait until you spend a week drinking nothing but excellent white wines in cute little wine bars. Think the food is all about sausage? Wait until you find your meal choices span the globe with nary a wurst in sight. Think Germans are closed minded and cold? Wait until one chats you up and you experience their good-natured humility and progressive world view.

What Churchill called Russia, 'a riddle wrapped in a mystery inside an enigma' could just have easily applied to Germany. Dismiss everything you think you know about it and start from scratch. As you travel Germany's regions you'll find that given all their differences they might as well be separate countries. And that's the real fun of visiting Germany – first having your stereotypes blown away and then trying to make sense of what you've found.

From the ongoing reinvention of Berlin to the celebration of tradition in Munich you will find contradictions everywhere. Your best course of action is to savour the richly financed museums and culture, revel in the nation's soul (the land) and join in the serious pursuit of consumption – be it beer, wine and yes, sausage, or something exotic. Through experience you'll relish one of Europe's richest cultures.

FAST FACTS

- **Area** 356,866 sq km (138 Luxembourgs, two-thirds of France)
- **Capital** Berlin
- **Currency** euro (€); A$1 = €0.60; ¥100 = €0.67; NZ$1 = €0.50; UK£1 = €1.48; US$1 = €0.78
- **Famous for** sausages, beer, culture, cars, history
- **Official Language** German
- **Phrases** *Guten Tag* (good day); *Auf Wiedersehen* (goodbye); *Ja/Nein* (yes/no); *Danke* (thank you); *Sprechen Sie Englisch?* (Do you speak English?)
- **Population** 83 million
- **Telephone Codes** country code ☎ 49; international access code ☎ 00

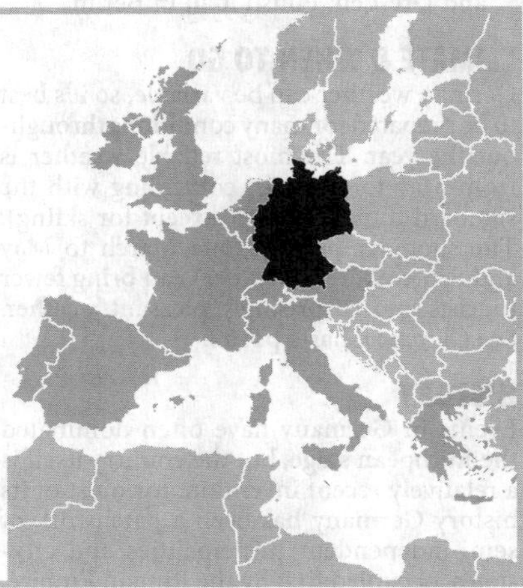

HIGHLIGHTS

- Party day and night in **Berlin** (p428); save sleep for somewhere else as there's no time what with the clubs, museums, bars and mind-blowing culture.
- Time your journey for **Oktoberfest** (p477), Munich's big booze up, or just hang out in a beer garden.
- Seek out the villages less visited in the **Moselle Valley** (p507) home to the crisp white wine of the same name.
- Go cuckoo in the **Black Forest** (p499), discovering its chilly crags, misty peaks and endless trails.
- Get into the vibe of **Leipzig** (p453), the surprisingly vibrant star of the east.

ITINERARIES

- **One week** Starting in Berlin spend three days in and around the city, then head south through the wonderful little Bavarian town of Bamberg before ending up in Munich.
- **One month** Start in Munich for some Bavarian joy, then head up to the goofy castles in Füssen. Take in some of the Bavarian Alps and Lake Constance before the fun of Freiburg. Explore the Black Forest, soak up Baden-Baden and settle in for a boat voyage down the Rhine in Mainz. Detour up the Moselle to Trier and then hit Cologne. Pop up to Hamburg and Lübeck before heading back to Bavaria and Bamberg. Head north into the old East and Weimar and then enjoy Leipzig and Dresden. Finish it all in Berlin.

CLIMATE & WHEN TO GO

German weather can be variable, so it's best to be prepared for many conditions throughout the year. The most reliable weather is from May to October, coinciding with the standard tourist season (except for skiing). The shoulder periods (late March to May and September to October) can bring fewer tourists and surprisingly pleasant weather. See Climate Charts p1100.

HOW MUCH?

- **Budget hotel room** €50
- **Tasty sausage meal** €6
- **Baden-Baden spa** €21
- **Bottle of Rhine wine** €6
- **U-Bahn ticket** €1.80

LONELY PLANET INDEX

- **1L petrol** €1.35
- **1L bottled water** €1
- **Beer (0.3L local Pils)** €2
- **Souvenir T-shirt** €15
- **Döner kebab** €2

HISTORY

Events in Germany have often dominated the European stage, but the country itself is a relatively recent invention: for most of its history Germany has been a patchwork of semi-independent principalities and city-states, occupied first by the Roman Empire, then the Holy Roman Empire and finally the Austrian Habsburgs. Perhaps because of this, many Germans retain a strong regional identity, despite the momentous events that have occurred since.

The most significant medieval events in Germany were pan-European in nature – Martin Luther brought on the Protestant Reformation with his criticism of the Catholic Church in Wittenberg in 1517, a movement that sparked the Thirty Years' War. Germany became the battlefield of Europe,only regaining stability after the Napoleonic Wars with increasing industrialisation and the rise of the Kingdom of Prussia. In 1866 legendary Prussian 'Iron Chancellor' Otto von Bismarck brought the German states together, largely by force, and a united Germany emerged for the first time in 1871, under Kaiser Wilhelm I.

WWI & the Rise of Hitler

With the advent of the 20th century, Germany's rapid growth soon overtaxed the political talents of Kaiser Wilhelm II and led to mounting tensions with England, Russia and France. When war broke out in 1914, Germany's only ally was a weakened Austria-Hungary. Gruelling trench warfare on two fronts sapped the nation's resources, and by late 1918 Germany sued for peace. The kaiser abdicated and escaped to the Netherlands. Amid widespread public anger and unrest a new republic, which became known as the Weimar Republic, was proclaimed.

GERMANY
0 100 km
0 60 miles
DENMARK
SWEDEN
COPENHAGEN
Bornholm
NORTH SEA
BALTIC SEA
Sylt Island
Amrum Island
North Frisian Islands
Schleswig
Rügen Island
Sassnitz
Binz
Heide
Kiel
Stralsund
Warnemünde
Rostock
SCHLESWIG-HOLSTEIN
East Frisian Islands
Cuxhaven
Lübeck
Wismar
MECKLENBURG-WESTERN POMERANIA
Wilhelmshaven
Hamburg
Schwerin
HAMBURG
A24
A241
A19
A1
Bremen
BREMEN
A7
Elbe River
A11
NETHERLANDS
POLAND
BRANDENBURG
Oder
A31
LOWER SAXONY
SAXONY-ANHALT
A1
A19
BERLIN
Potsdam
Frankfurt/Oder
Hanover
A2
A12
A30
A2
Hameln
Magdeburg
River
A13
Badenwerder
Goslar
Wernigerode
Lutherstadt Wittenberg
NORTH RHINE-WESTPHALIA
Rhine
Clausthal-Zellerfeld
Quedlinburg
Dessau
A15
A9
A44
Dortmund
Göttingen
A13
A7
Nordhausen
Halle
Leipzig
Meissen
Görlitz
Kassel
A4
Düsseldorf
THURINGIA
Naumburg
Dresden
Cologne
Eisenach
Erfurt
Weimar
A4
A4
Aachen
A45
Marburg
SAXONY
Bonn
A5
61
HESSE
A9
A72
BELGIUM
River
Cochem
Koblenz
Frankfurt-am-Main
A3
A7
A48
PRAGUE
RHINELAND-PALATINATE
River
Wiesbaden
Hanau
Rüdesheim
Mainz
Marktredwitz
LUXEMBOURG
Trier
Würzburg
Bamberg
A3
CZECH REPUBLIC
SAARLAND
Mannheim
Heidelberg
Nuremberg
Moselle
Saarbrücken
Rothenburg/Tauber
A6
BAVARIA
Dinkelsbühl
A19
Karlsruhe
Regensburg
Danube
A3
River
Baden-Baden
Stuttgart
Nördlingen
Passau
River
A8
A92
A5
BADEN-WÜRTTEMBERG
Ulm
Augsburg
Rhine
A81
FRANCE
Freiburg
A7
Munich
Donaueschingen
AUSTRIA
A95
A8
Constance
Berchtesgaden
Lake Constance
Lindau
Füssen
Garmisch-Partenkirchen
Oberstdorf
LIECHTENSTEIN
SWITZERLAND

The Treaty of Versailles in 1919 chopped huge areas off Germany and imposed heavy reparation payments. These were impossible to meet, and when France and Belgium occupied the Rhineland to ensure continued payments, the subsequent hyperinflation and miserable economic conditions provided fertile ground for political extremists. One of these was Adolf Hitler, an Austrian drifter, would-be artist and German army veteran.

Led by Hitler, the National Socialist German Workers' Party (or Nazi Party) staged an abortive coup in Munich in 1923. This landed Hitler in prison for nine months, during which time he wrote *Mein Kampf*.

From 1929 the worldwide economic Depression hit Germany hard, leading to unemployment, strikes and demonstrations. The Communist Party under Ernst Thälmann gained strength, but wealthy industrialists began to support the Nazis and police turned a blind eye to Nazi street thugs.

The Nazis increased their strength in general elections and in 1933 replaced the Social Democrats as the largest party in the Reichstag (parliament), with about one-third of the seats. Hitler was appointed chancellor and one year later assumed absolute control as *Führer* (leader).

WWII & the Division of Germany

From 1935 Germany began to re-arm and build its way out of depression with strategic public works such as the autobahns. Hitler reoccupied the Rhineland in 1936, and in 1938 annexed Austria and, following a compromise agreement with Britain and France, parts of Czechoslovakia.

All of this took place against a backdrop of growing racism at home. The Nuremberg Laws of 1935 deprived non-Aryans – mostly Jews and Roma (sometimes called Gypsies) – of their German citizenship and many other rights. On 9 November 1938, the horror escalated into *Kristallnacht* ('night of broken glass'), in which synagogues and Jewish cemeteries, property and businesses across Germany were desecrated, burnt or demolished.

In September 1939, after signing a pact that allowed both Stalin and himself a free hand in the east of Europe, Hitler attacked Poland, which led to war with Britain and France. Germany quickly occupied large parts of Europe, but after 1942 began to suffer increasingly heavy losses. Massive bombing reduced Germany's cities to rubble, and the country lost 10% of its population. Germany accepted unconditional surrender in May 1945, soon after Hitler's suicide.

At the end of the war, the full scale of Nazi racism was exposed. 'Concentration camps', intended to rid Europe of people considered undesirable according to Nazi doctrine, had exterminated some six million Jews and one million more Roma, communists, homosexuals and others in what has come to be known as the Holocaust, history's first 'assembly line' genocide.

At conferences in Yalta and Potsdam, the Allies (the Soviet Union, the USA, the UK and France) redrew the borders of Germany, making it around 25% smaller than it had become after the Treaty of Versailles 26 years earlier. Germany was divided into four occupation zones.

In the Soviet zone of the country, the communist Socialist Unity Party (SED) won the 1946 elections and began a rapid nationalisation of industry. In September 1949 the Federal Republic of Germany (FRG) was created out of the three western zones; in response the German Democratic Republic (GDR) was founded in the Soviet zone the following month, with (East) Berlin as its capital.

From Division to Unity

As the West's bulwark against communism, the FRG received massive injections of US capital, and experienced rapid economic development (the *Wirschaftswunder* or 'economic miracle') under the leadership of Konrad Adenauer. The GDR, on the other hand, had to pay US$10 billion in war reparations to the Soviet Union and rebuild itself from scratch.

A better life in the west increasingly attracted skilled workers away from the miserable economic conditions in the east. As these were people the GDR could ill afford to lose, it built a wall around West Berlin in 1961 and sealed its border with the FRG.

In 1971 a change to the more flexible leadership of Erich Honecker in the east, combined with the *Ostpolitik* (East Politics) of FRG chancellor Willy Brandt, allowed an easier political relationship between the two Germanys. In the same year the four occupying powers formally accepted the division of Berlin.

Honecker's policies produced higher living standards in the GDR, yet East Germany barely managed to achieve a level of prosperity half that of the FRG. After Mikhail Gorbachev came to power in the Soviet Union in March 1985, the East German communists gradually lost Soviet backing.

Events in 1989 rapidly overtook the GDR government, which resisted pressure to introduce reforms. When Hungary relaxed its border controls in May 1989, East Germans began crossing to the west. Tighter travel controls resulted in would-be defectors taking refuge in the FRG's embassy in Prague. Meanwhile, mass demonstrations in Leipzig spread to other cities and Honecker was replaced by his security chief, Egon Krenz, who introduced cosmetic reforms. Then suddenly on 9 November 1989, a decision to allow direct travel to the west was mistakenly interpreted as the immediate opening of all GDR borders with West Germany. That same night thousands of people streamed into the west past stunned border guards. Millions more followed in the next few days, and the dismantling of the Berlin Wall began soon thereafter.

The trend at first was to reform the GDR but, in East German elections held in early 1990, citizens voted clearly in favour of the proreunification Christian Democratic Union (CDU). A Unification Treaty was drawn up to integrate East Germany into the Federal Republic of Germany, enacted on 3 October 1990. All-German elections were held on 2 December that year and, in the midst of national euphoria, the CDU-led coalition, which strongly favoured reunification, soundly defeated the Social Democrat opposition. CDU leader Helmut Kohl earned the enviable position of 'unification chancellor'.

Into the Millennium

In 1998 a coalition of Social Democrats, led by Gerhard Schröder, and Bündnis 90/die Grünen (the Greens party) took political office from Kohl and the CDU amid allegations of widespread financial corruption in the unification-era government.

Schröder and the SDP-Greens only narrowly managed to retain office in the 2002 general election. In 2004 things looked even worse. The slashing of university funding brought students out in protest for several weeks, and a botched reform of the public health insurance system was one of the most unpopular pieces of legislation ever, resulting in massive gains for the supposedly discredited CDU at subsequent local elections.

These advances paid off in September 2005 as a fumbling Schröder went down in national elections, although just barely. The winner by a very narrow margin was Angela Merkel and the CDU. Not only is Merkel the first woman chancellor in German history but she is also the first one who grew up in the old GDR.

A trained physicist who studied quantum chemistry, Merkel may find a use for her old training in her government. Because of the CDU's narrow victory it was forced into a 'grand coalition' with the SDP in which the latter gets half of the cabinet seats. Truly it's a situation where unexpected and unwanted reactions could be the norm.

Surprisingly, however, despite her tiny margin of victory, Merkel's popularity soared in the months after she took power. Perhaps it was her unusual background or her straight-talking style that had Germans of all stripes intrigued by what they saw. But with unemployment hitting 12% in 2006, Merkel and her unlikely coalition have their work cut out for them.

PEOPLE

Germany has a population of around 83 million, making it the most populous in Europe after Russia. Germany's main native minority is the tiny group of Slavonic Sorbs in the eastern states of Saxony and Brandenburg, who maintain their own folk traditions. In political and economic terms, Germany is Europe's most decentralised nation, but considerable variation in population density exists. The Ruhr district in the northern Rhineland has Germany's densest concentration of people and industry, while Mecklenburg-Western Pomerania in the northeastern corner is relatively sparsely settled. About one-third of the population lives in 84 cities, each with more than 100,000 people.

Immigration compensates for the extremely low birth rate among the established German population, and more than seven million foreigners now live in Germany. Most hail from Turkey, Italy, Greece and the former Yugoslavia, and have arrived as 'guest workers' in the FRG since the early 1960s to work in lower-paid jobs. In 1999 archaic immigration laws dating back to 1913 were changed to make it easier for residents without German ancestry to gain citizenship. Integration is generally fairly successful, although larger immigrant communities tend to stick together.

RELIGION

The majority religions in Germany are Protestantism and Catholicism, which claim roughly equal numbers of followers. Some regions have higher concentrations of one branch – Bavaria is staunchly Catholic, for example.

The most significant minority religion is Islam, with about 1.8 million adherents, many of them immigrants. Around 60,000 Jews also live in Germany, little more than a tenth of pre-WWII numbers. Many are actually from the former Soviet Union, attracted by the relaxed immigration and citizenship deals offered around the time of reunification.

Germans who belong to a registered denomination have to pay a church tax on top of their income tax, usually around 10% of their salary. Unsurprisingly, fewer and fewer people are choosing to declare their religious affiliation!

ARTS

Germany's meticulously creative population has made major contributions to international culture, particularly during the 18th century when the Saxon courts at Weimar and Dresden attracted some of the greatest minds of Europe. With such rich traditions to fall back on, inspiration has seldom been in short supply for the new generations of German artists, despite the upheavals of the country's recent history.

Literature

The undisputed colossus of the German arts was Johann Wolfgang von Goethe: poet, dramatist, painter, politician, scientist, philosopher, landscape gardener and perhaps the last European to achieve the Renaissance ideal of excellence in many fields. His greatest work, the drama *Faust,* is the definitive version of the legend, showing the archetypal human search for meaning and knowledge.

Goethe's close friend Friedrich Schiller was a poet, dramatist and novelist. His most famous work is the dramatic cycle *Wallenstein,* based on the life of a treacherous general of the Thirty Years' War who plotted to make himself arbiter of the empire. Schiller's other great play, *William Tell,* dealt with the right of the oppressed to rise against tyranny.

On the scientific side, Alexander von Humboldt contributed much to environmentalism through his studies of the relationship of plants and animals to their physical surroundings. His contemporary, the philosopher Georg Wilhelm Friedrich Hegel, created an all-embracing classical philosophy that is still influential today.

Postwar literature in both Germanys was influenced by the politically focused Gruppe 47. It included writers such as Günter Grass, winner of the 1999 Nobel Prize for Literature, whose modern classic, *Die Blechtrommel* (The Tin Drum), humorously follows German history through the eyes of a young boy who refuses to grow up. Christa Wolf, an East German novelist and Gruppe 47 writer, won high esteem in both Germanys. Her 1963 story *Der geteilte Himmel* (Divided Heaven) tells of a young woman whose fiancé abandons her for life in the West.

A wave of recent novelists has addressed modern history in a lighter fashion. *Helden wie wir* (Heroes Like Us) by Thomas Brussig, an eastern German, tells the story of a man whose penis brings about the collapse of the Berlin Wall, while the GDR's demise is almost incidental to the eponymous barfly in Sven Regener's *Herr Lehmann* (Mr Lehmann). Also from Berlin is Russian-born Wladimir Kaminer, whose books document the stranger-than-fiction lives of his many friends and acquaintances in the capital. He's currently *the* hot author and *Russian Disco* has been translated into English. There's also acclaim for Robert Löhr's *Der Schachautomat* (The Chess Automat), a novel about a 19th-century puppet that plays chess.

Cinema & TV

Since the foundation of the UFA studios in Potsdam in 1917, Germany has had an active and successful film industry. Marlene Dietrich (1901–92) became the country's first international superstar and sex symbol, starting out in silent films and later moving to Hollywood. Director Fritz Lang also made a name for himself, with complex films like *Metropolis* (1926) and *M* (1931).

During the Third Reich, the arts were devoted mainly to propaganda, with grandiose projects and realist art extolling the virtues of German nationhood. The best-known Nazi-era director was Leni Riefenstahl (1902–2003) whose *Triumph of the Will* (1934), depicting the Nuremberg rallies, won great acclaim but later rendered her unemployable. The controversy surrounding her personal politics dogged her for much of her life.

The 1960s and 1970s saw a great revival of German cinema, spearheaded by energetic, politically aware young directors such as Rainer Werner Fassbinder, Wim Wenders, Volker Schlöndorff and Margarethe von Trotta.

Most recently, Wolfgang Becker's GDR comedy *Good Bye Lenin!* (2003) was a surprise smash hit worldwide. One of the most powerful recent movies has been Marc Rothemund's *Sophie Scholl: The Final Days* (2006). It's a harrowing true story about a woman who protested against the Nazis in Munich and paid the ultimate price.

Meanwhile, German TV still shows a real predilection for showing musical variety shows long on hokum and schmaltz. After a few beers they're a hoot.

Music

Forget brass bands and oompah music – few countries can claim the impressive musical heritage of Germany. Even a partial list of household names would have to include Johann Sebastian Bach, Georg Friedrich Händel, Ludwig van Beethoven, Richard Strauss, Robert Schumann, Johannes Brahms, Felix Mendelssohn-Bartholdy, Richard Wagner and Gustav Mahler, all of whom are celebrated in museums, exhibitions and festivals around the country.

These musical traditions continue to thrive: the Berlin Philharmonic, Dresden Opera and Leipzig Orchestra are known around the world, and musical performances are hosted almost daily in every major theatre in the country.

Germany has also made significant contributions to the contemporary music scene. Internationally renowned artists include punk icon Nina Hagen, '80s balloon girl Nena, and rock bands from the Scorpions to Die Toten Hosen and current darlings Wir sind Helden. Gothic and hard rock are disproportionately well-followed in Germany, largely thanks to the success of death-obsessed growlers Rammstein.

For real innovation, though, the German dance music scene is second to none, particularly in Frankfurt-am-Main and Berlin. Kraftwerk pioneered the original electronic sounds, which were then popularised in raves and clubs such as Berlin's Tresor in the early '90s. Paul van Dyk was among the first proponents of euphoric trance, which pushed club music firmly into the commercial mainstream; DJs such as Ian Pooley, Westbam and Ellen Allien now play all over the world. Producers and remixers Jazzanova also have a great worldwide reputation on the more jazzy, down tempo side of things.

Meanwhile what's old is new. Max Raabe and his Palast Orchester have been touring the country to sold out performances of the classic Berlin cabaret-style music of the 1920s and 1930s. Less old but still new, many local groups such as Wir sind Helden, Silbermond, Tomte and Kettcar have attracted a loyal following by playing the festival circuit with German-language rock.

Architecture

The scope of German architecture is such that it could easily be the focus of an entire visit. The first great wave of buildings came with the Romanesque period (800–1200), examples of which can be found at Trier Cathedral, the churches of Cologne and the chapel of Charlemagne's palace in Aachen.

The Gothic style (1200–1500) is best viewed at Freiburg's Münster cathedral, Cologne's Dom (cathedral) and the Marienkirche in Lübeck. Red-brick Gothic structures are common in the north of Germany, with buildings such as Schwerin's Dom and Stralsund's Nikoliakirche.

For classic baroque, Balthasar Neumann's superb Residenz in Würzburg, the magnificent cathedral in Passau and the many classics of Dresden's old centre are must-sees. The neoclassical period of the 19th century was led by Karl Friedrich Schinkel, whose name crops up all over Germany.

In 1919 Walter Gropius founded the Bauhaus movement in an attempt to meld theoretical concerns of architecture with the practical problems faced by artists and craftspeople. The Bauhaus flourished in Dessau, but with the arrival of the Nazis, Gropius left for Harvard University.

Albert Speer was Hitler's favourite architect, known for his pompous neoclassical buildings and grand plans to change the face of Berlin. Most of his epic works ended up unbuilt or flattened by WWII.

Frankfurt shows Germany's take on the modern highrise. For a glimpse of the future of German architecture, head to Potsdamer Platz, Leipziger Platz and the new government area north of the Reichstag in Berlin, which are becoming glitzy swathes of glass, concrete and chrome.

Visual Arts

The Renaissance came late to Germany but flourished once it took hold, replacing the predominant Gothic style. The draughtsman Albrecht Dürer of Nuremberg was one of the world's finest portraitists, as was the prolific Lucas Cranach the Elder, who worked in Wittenberg for more than 45 years. The baroque period brought great sculpture, including works by Andreas Schlüter in Berlin, while romanticism produced some of Germany's most famous paintings, best exemplified by Caspar David Friedrich and Otto Runge.

At the turn of the 20th century, expressionism established itself with great names like Swiss-born Paul Klee and the Russian-born painter Wassily Kandinsky, who were also associated with the Bauhaus design school. By the 1920s, art had become more radical and political, with artists like George Grosz, Otto Dix and Max Ernst exploring the new concepts of Dada and surrealism. Käthe Kollwitz is one of the era's few major female artists, known for her social realist drawings.

The only works encouraged by the Nazis were of the epic style of propaganda artists like Mjölnir; nonconforming artists such as sculptor Ernst Barlach and painter Emil Nolde were declared 'degenerate' and their pieces destroyed or appropriated for secret private collections.

Since 1945 abstract art has been a mainstay of the German scene, with key figures like Joseph Beuys, Monica Bonviciniand and Anselm Kiefer achieving worldwide reputations. Leipzig has recently emerged as a hotspot for art. Figurative painters like Neo Rauch are generating much acclaim.

Theatre & Dance

In the 1920s Berlin was the theatrical capital of Germany; its most famous practitioner was the poet and playwright Bertolt Brecht (1898–1956). Brecht introduced Marxist concepts into his plays, aiming to encourage moral debate by detaching the audience from what was happening on stage.

Today Berlin once again has the most dynamic theatre scene in the country, as Volksbühne director Frank Castorf vies with Schaubühne head Thomas Ostermeier to capture the attention of young audiences neglected by the major stages, choosing mainly modern, provocative works. Dance, too, is undergoing a renaissance – although it is in Frankfurt. American William Forsythe has put together what is possibly the world's most innovative dance troupe, the Forsythe Company, which tours almost constantly.

SPORT

Football (soccer) is the number one spectator sport in Germany, as in most other European countries. Germany hosted the cup in 2006 in new or rebuilt stadiums all over the country. Although Germany finished third (Italy beat France in the final in Berlin), it was widely praised for hosting a fantastic series of matches and many Germans took great pride in their time on the world stage.

The German national team actually did better than many expected, even if it couldn't add another World Cup victory to its previous two. The Bundesliga is the top national league, with seasons running from September to June; notable top-flight teams include Bayern München, Borussia Dortmund and Hertha BSC (Berlin's major team). The DFB (www.dfb.de) is the national body responsible for all levels of the game.

International sports are also very well-attended, especially when the relevant national teams are in form; major tennis, athletics, Grand Prix, swimming, cycling and water polo events are all features of the German sporting calendar.

ENVIRONMENT

The Land

Germany covers 356,866 sq km and can be divided from north to south into several geographical regions.

The Northern Lowlands are a broad expanse of flat, low-lying land that sweeps across the northern third of the country from the Netherlands into Poland. The landscape is characterised by moist heaths interspersed with pastures and farmland.

The complex Central Uplands region divides northern Germany from the south. Extending from the deep schisms of the Rhineland massifs to the Black Forest, the Bavarian Forest, the Ore Mountains and the Harz Mountains, these low mountain ranges are Germany's heartland. The Rhine and Main Rivers, important waterways for inland shipping, cut through the southwest of this region. With large deposits of coal as well as favourable transport conditions, this was one of the first regions in Germany to undergo industrialisation.

The Alpine Foothills, wedged between the Danube and the Alps, are typified by subalpine plateaus and rolling hills, and moors in eastern regions around the Danube.

Germany's Alps lie entirely within Bavaria and stretch from the large, glacially formed Lake Constance in the west to Berchtesgaden in Germany's southeastern corner. Though lower than the mountains to their south, many summits are well above 2000m, rising dramatically from the Alpine Foothills to the 2962m Zugspitze, Germany's highest mountain.

Wildlife

Few species of flora and fauna are unique to Germany. Unique, however, is the importance Germans place on their forests, the prettiest of which are mixed-species deciduous forests planted with beech, oak, maple and birch. You'll find that many cities even have their own *Stadtwald* (city forest). Alpine regions bloom in spring with orchids, cyclamen, gentians, edelweiss and more; and the heather blossom on the Lüneburg Heath, north of Hanover, is stunning in August.

Apart from human beings, common mammals include deer, wild pigs, rabbits, foxes and hares. The chances of seeing these in summer are fairly good, especially in eastern Germany. On the coasts you will find seals and, throughout Germany, falcons, hawks, storks and migratory geese are a common sight.

National Parks

Berchtesgaden (in the Bavarian Alps), the Wattenmeer parks in Schleswig-Holstein, Lower Saxony and Hamburg, and the Unteres Odertal, a joint German-Polish endeavour, are highlights among Germany's 13 national parks. There are also a number of Unesco-listed sites in Germany, including the Wartburg castle in Eisenach.

Environmental Issues

Germans are fiercely protective of their natural surroundings. Households and businesses participate enthusiastically in waste-recycling programmes. A refund system applies to a wide range of glass bottles and jars, while containers for waste paper and glass can be found in each neighbourhood. The government is a signatory of the major international treaties on climate change and runs its own campaigns to save energy and reduce CO2 emissions domestically; a controversial 'eco-tax' was recently added to the price of petrol.

FOOD & DRINK

Staples & Specialities

Wurst (sausage), in its hundreds of forms, is by far the most universal main dish. Regional favourites include bratwurst (spiced sausage), *Weisswurst* (veal sausage) and *Blutwurst* (blood sausage). Other popular main dishes include *Rippenspeer* (spare ribs), *Rotwurst* (black pudding), *Rostbrätl* (grilled meat), *Putenbrust* (turkey breast) and many forms of schnitzel (breaded pork or veal cutlet).

Potatoes feature prominently in German meals, as *Bratkartoffeln* (fried), *Kartoffelpüree* (mashed), Swiss-style *Rösti* (grated then fried) or *Pommes Frites* (french fries); a Thuringian speciality is *Klösse*, a ball of mashed and raw potato that is then cooked into a dumpling. A similar Bavarian version is the *Knödel*. *Spätzle*, a noodle variety from Baden-Württemberg, is a common alternative.

Germans are keen on rich desserts. Popular choices are the *Schwarzwälder Kirschtorte* (Black Forest cherry cake) – one worthwhile tourist trap – as well as endless varieties of

Apfeltasche (apple pastry). In the north you're likely to find berry *mus*, a sort of compote. Desserts and pastries are also often enjoyed during another German tradition, the 4pm coffee break.

DRINKS

Beer is the national beverage and it's one cultural phenomenon that must be adequately explored. The beer is excellent and relatively cheap. Each region and brewery has its own distinctive taste and body.

Vollbier is 4% alcohol by volume, *Export* is 5% and *Bockbier* is 6%. *Helles Bier* is light, while *dunkles Bier* is dark. *Export* is similar to, but much better than, typical international brews, while the *Pils* is more bitter. *Alt* is darker and more full-bodied. A speciality is *Weizenbier*, which is made with wheat instead of barley malt and served in a tall, 500mL glass. Nonalcoholic beers such as *Clausthaler* are also popular.

Eastern Germany's best beers hail from Saxony, especially Radeberger from near Dresden and Wernesgrüner from the Erzgebirge on the Czech border. *Berliner Weisse* is a low-alcohol wheat beer mixed with woodruff or raspberry syrup, seen as a bit of a tourist drink by locals. The breweries of Cologne produce *Kölsch*, always served in 200mL glasses to keep it fresh; in Bamberg *Schlenkerla Rauchbier* is smoked to a dark-red colour.

German wines are exported around the world, and for good reason. They are inexpensive and typically white, light and intensely fruity. A *Weinschorle* or *Spritzer* is white wine mixed with mineral water. The Rhine and Moselle Valleys are the classic wine-growing regions.

The most popular nonalcoholic choices are mineral water and soft drinks, coffee and fruit or black tea. Bottled water almost always comes bubbly *(mit Kohlensäure)* – order *ohne Kohlensäure* if you're bothered by bubbles.

Where to Eat & Drink

Increasingly, German towns of any size have bright and modern bistro-type restaurants serving a wide range of fresh and creative food. In addition you'll find no shortage of ethnic foods; Italian, Turkish, Greek and Chinese are all popular. Most pubs serve basic German food. If you're on a low budget, you can get a feed at stand-up food stalls *(Schnellimbiss* or *Imbiss)*. The food is usually reasonable and filling, ranging from döner kebabs to traditional German sausages with beer.

Much of the German daily and social life revolves around daytime cafés, which often serve meals and alcohol as well as coffee. The late-opening variety are great places to meet people.

For self-caterers, supermarkets are inexpensive and have a decent range. Make a point of buying your drinks in supermarkets if your budget is tight.

Students can eat cheaply (though not always well) at university *Mensa* (caféterias). ID is not always checked.

Vegetarians & Vegans

Most German restaurants will have at least a couple of vegetarian dishes on the menu, although it is advisable to check anything that doesn't specifically say it's meat-free, as bacon and chicken stock both seem to be common undeclared ingredients in German cuisine. Asian and Indian restaurants will generally be quite happy to make vegetarian dishes on demand. Vegans may find themselves having to explain exactly what they do and don't eat to get something suitable.

Habits & Customs

Restaurants always display their menus outside with prices, but watch for daily or lunch specials chalked onto blackboards. Lunch is the main meal of the day; getting a main meal in the evening is never a problem, but you may find that the dish or menu of the day only applies to lunch.

Rather than leaving money on the table, tip when you pay by stating a rounded-up figure or saying *'es stimmt so'* (that's the right amount). A tip of 10% is generally more than sufficient.

BERLIN

☎ 030 / pop 3.45 million

Apologies to Samuel Johnson, who coined the compliment to London, but in the 21st century it's he, or she, who is tired of *Berlin* who is tired of life. Even the English capital can't currently compete with the pace of change in its reborn German counterpart.

Just two decades ago this was still a divided city, split between the rival Cold War blocs of communist east and capitalist west. Today it's the European Shanghai, where building cranes watch over the skyline, and world-beating architectural icons – Norman Foster's Reichstag dome, Daniel Libeskind's Jewish Museum and Peter Eisenman's Holocaust Memorial – pop up every few years.

Renowned for its diversity and tolerance, its alternative culture, its night-owl stamina and its affordability it might be. But the best thing about the German capital is the way it reinvents itself and isn't shackled by its powerful – and still palpable – history.

Tills ring in the halls of the gleaming Potsdamer Platz complex just down the road from Hitler's bunker, university stallholders sell novels opposite the site of a major book-burning and bits of the 'Berlin Wall' (they're not) are hawked everywhere alongside döner kebabs and Wurst.

Students rub shoulders with Russian émigrés, fashion boutiques inhabit monumental GDR buildings, and the nightlife has long left the American sector, as clubbers watch the sun rise in the city's east.

In short, all human life is here, and don't expect to get much sleep.

HISTORY

United, divided, united again, Berlin has a rollercoaster past. The merger of two medieval trading posts, it enjoyed its first stint as a capital when in 1701 it became the leading city of the state of Brandenburg-Prussia. Under Prussian King Friedrich I and his son, Friedrich II, it flourished culturally and politically.

The Industrial Revolution, when commercial giants like Siemens emerged, also boosted the city. As workers flooded to Berlin's factories, its population doubled between 1850 and 1870. 'Deutschland' was a latecomer to the table of nationhood, but in 1871 Berlin was again proclaimed a capital, this time of the newly unified Germany.

By 1900 the city was home to almost two million people, but it fell into decline after WWI. Defeated and left to pay heavy war reparations, Germany suffered economic crisis and hyperinflation. There was a brief, early communist uprising in the capital, led by Karl Liebknecht and Rosa Luxemburg (whose names now adorn East Berlin streets). However, that was quickly quashed and during the following Weimar Republic (1919–1933) Berlin gained a reputation for decadence. Cabaret, the savage political theatre of Bertolt Brecht (see p443), expressionist art and jazz all flourished as Berliners partied to forget their troubles.

Worse horrors arose with Hitler and the Third Reich. Berlin became a showground for Nazi power from the mid-1930s – including during the 1936 Olympics – and so suffered heavily during WWII. During the 'Battle of Berlin' from August 1943 to March 1944, British bombers hammered the city nightly. The Soviets also shelled Berlin and invaded from the east.

In August 1945 the Potsdam Conference (see Schloss Cecilienhof, p446) split the capital into zones occupied by the four victorious powers – the USA, Britain, France and the Soviet Union. In June 1948 the three Western Allies introduced a separate currency and administration in their sectors. In response, the Soviets blockaded West Berlin. Only a huge airlift by the Allies managed to keep the city stocked with food and supplies. In October 1949 East Berlin became the capital of the GDR.

The Berlin Wall, built in August 1961, was originally intended to prevent the drain of skilled labour from the East, but soon became a Cold War symbol. For decades, East Berlin and West Berlin developed separately, until Hungarians breached the Iron Curtain in May 1989 and the Berlin Wall followed on 9 November. By 1 July 1990, when the western Deutschmark was adopted in the GDR, the Wall was being hacked to pieces. The Unification Treaty signed on 3 October that year designated Berlin the official capital of Germany, and in June 1991 the parliament voted to move the seat of government from Bonn back to Berlin. In 1999, that was finally achieved.

Not everything has been plain sailing since. Without the huge national subsidies provided during the decades of division, the newly unified Berlin has struggled economically. In 2001 the centre-right mayor resigned amid corruption allegations, leaving the city effectively bankrupt. Current centre-left mayor Klaus Wowereit is popular but has made few inroads into the crisis, and the city's public debts now exceed €58 billion. Wowereit tries to look on the bright

BERLIN IN TWO DAYS

Investigate the **Brandenburg Gate** (opposite) area, including the **Reichstag** (p434) and the **Holocaust Memorial** (p434). Walk east along Unter den Linden, stopping at the **Bebelplatz book-burning memorial** (p435). Veer through the **Museumsinsel** (p435) for window-shopping and café-hopping through **Hackescher Markt** (p435). In the evening, explore the bars of Prenzlauer Berg, along Kastanieanallee, Pappelallee and the 'LSD' triangle between Lette-, Stargarder- and Dunckerstrasse. Stop in **Wohnzimmer** (p444).

Start the next day at the **East Side Gallery** (p437) remnant of the Berlin Wall, before heading for **Checkpoint Charlie** (p437) and the nearby **Jewish Museum** (p437). Take the U-Bahn to **Kurfürstendamm** (p437) and catch a scenic bus 100 back to the **Fernsehturm** (p436). Later, explore Friedrichshain nightlife around Simon-Dach-Strasse and Boxhagener Platz and perhaps go clubbing – **Watergate** (p443) is good. Alternatively head for the **Philharmonie** (p443) or the **Berliner Ensemble** (p443).

side, once famously declaring, 'Berlin is poor, but sexy'. He got that right, at least.

ORIENTATION

Standing at Berlin's Brandenburg Gate, on the former east–west divide, you can see many major sights. Looking east, your eye follows the road Unter den Linden, past the Museumsinsel (Museum Island) in the Spree River, to the needle-shaped Fernseh turm (TV tower) at Alexanderplatz.

If you turn west, you face the golden Siegessäule (Victory Column) along the equally huge thoroughfare of Strasse des 17 Juni, which cuts through the middle of Berlin's central park, the Tiergarten. To your right, just near the Brandenburg Gate, is the glass-domed Reichstag (Parliament) and beyond that the new government district and even newer Hauptbahnhof (main train station). The cluster of skyscrapers diagonally off to the left, with the unusual, circus-tent roof, is Potsdamer Platz.

On the other, far west side of the Tiergarten, out of sight near Zoo station, lies the one-time centre of West Berlin, including the shopping street of the Kurfürstendamm (or 'Ku'damm').

Although wealthier, more mature Berliners still happily frequent the west, the eastern districts are the most vibrant. Even 'Mitte', or the centre, now lies east of the former Wall. As Mitte heads northeast, it merges into the trendy district of Prenzlauer Berg. Friedrichshain, another nightlife hotspot, is found several kilometres east of the centre, around Ostbahnhof.

Kreuzberg, south of Mitte, was the alternative hub of West Berlin and is still hanging in there, with some interesting restaurants and bars. So, too, are the better-heeled southwestern districts of Charlottenburg, Schöneberg and Wilmersdorf.

Maps

Excellent free maps of the centre are available from tourist offices and many hotels. If you're heading to the suburbs, newsagents and bookshops sell full-size maps from publishers Falk, Michelin and ADAC.

INFORMATION

Bookshops

Dussman (Map pp432-3; ☎ 205 1111; Friedrichstrasse 90; 🕑 10am-10pm Mon-Sat; Ⓜ S-Bahn Friedrichstrasse) Books (including in English), CDs and DVDs over five huge floors.

Discount Card

Berlin-Potsdam Welcome Card (48/72hr card €16/22) Free public transport, plus museum and entertainment discounts.

Internet Access

@ Internet (Map p438; ☎ 2977 6270; 1st fl, main hall, Ostbahnhof; per 15 min €1; 🕑 10am-10pm)

Al Hamra (Map pp432-3; ☎ 4285 0095; Raumerstrasse 16; per 15 min €1; 🕑 from 10am; Ⓜ Eberswalder Strasse)

easyInternetcafé (Map p439; ☎ 7870 6446; www.easyInternetcafe.com; Kurfürstendamm 224; 🕑 6.30am-2am; Ⓜ Kurfürstendamm/Zoologischer Garten) One of several throughout the city.

Surf & Sushi (Map pp432-3; ☎ 2838 4898; Oranienburger Strasse 17; per 30 min €2.50; 🕑 from noon Mon-Sat, from 1pm Sun; Ⓜ Oranienburger Strasse/Hackescher Markt)

Laundry

Schnell und Sauber (€5; 6am-11pm) Charlottenburg (Map p439; Uhlandstrasse 53); Mitte (Map pp432-3; Torstrasse 115)

Medical Services

Kassenärztliche Bereitschaftsdienst (Public Physicians' Emergency Service; ☎ 310 031) Phone referral service.

Post

Post office (Map pp432-3; Georgenstrasse 12; 8am-10pm) Inside Friedrichstrasse station.

Tourist Information

Berlin Tourismus Marketing (☎ 250 025; www.berlin-tourist-information.de) Europa-Center (Map p439; Budapester Strasse 45; 10am-7pm Mon-Sat, 10am-6pm Sun); Brandenburger Tor (Map pp432-3; 10am-6pm); Fernsehturm (Map pp432-3; 10am-6pm)

EurAide (Map p439; www.euraide.de; Zoo Station; 8.30am-noon Mon-Sat Jun-Oct, 1-4.45pm Mon-Fri Nov-May) English-language service.

DANGERS & ANNOYANCES

Berlin is generally safe and tolerant. Walking alone at night on city streets isn't risky. Begging on the street and in the U-Bahn is increasing, but aggressive demands are rare. Take the usual precautions against theft in major stations.

SIGHTS

Unless otherwise indicated, where sights are grouped together they are all accessed by the same station listed at the beginning of the section.

Brandenburg Gate

Finished in 1791 as one of 18 city gates, the neoclassical **Brandenburger Tor** (Map pp432-3; Pariser Platz; Ⓜ S-Bahn Unter den Linden) became an east–west crossing point after the Wall was built in 1961. A symbol of Berlin's division, it was a place US presidents loved to grandstand. John F Kennedy passed by in 1963. Ronald Reagan appeared in 1987 to appeal to the Russian leader, 'Mr Gorbachev, tear down this wall!'. In 1989, more than 100,000 Germans poured through it, as the Wall fell. Five years later, Bill Clinton somewhat belatedly noted: 'Berlin is free'. The crowning Quadriga statue, a winged

MITTE & PRENZLAUER BERG

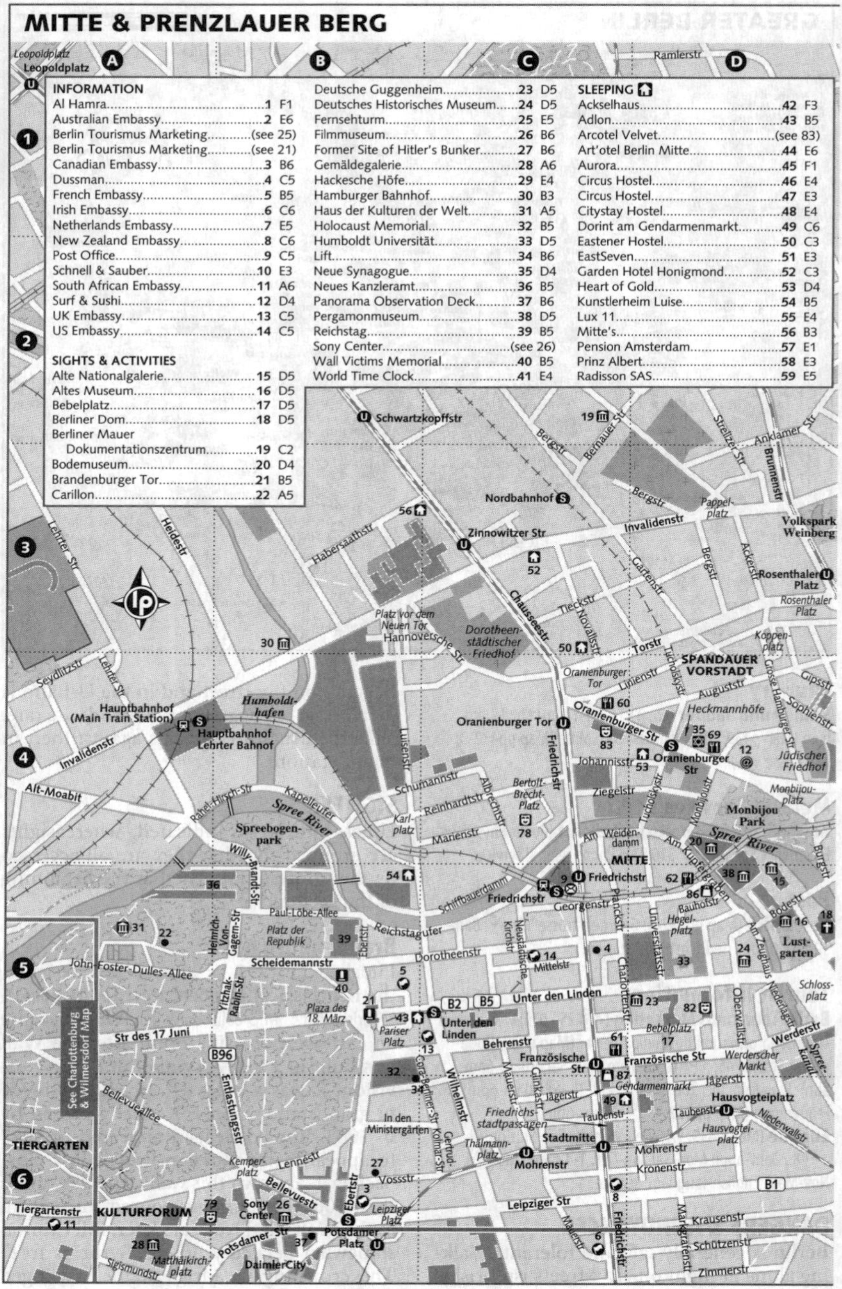

INFORMATION

Al Hamra	1	F1
Australian Embassy	2	E6
Berlin Tourismus Marketing	(see 25)	
Berlin Tourismus Marketing	(see 21)	
Canadian Embassy	3	B6
Dussman	4	C5
French Embassy	5	B5
Irish Embassy	6	C6
Netherlands Embassy	7	E5
New Zealand Embassy	8	C6
Post Office	9	C5
Schnell & Sauber	10	E3
South African Embassy	11	A6
Surf & Sushi	12	D4
UK Embassy	13	C5
US Embassy	14	C5

SIGHTS & ACTIVITIES

Alte Nationalgalerie	15	D5
Altes Museum	16	D5
Bebelplatz	17	D5
Berliner Dom	18	D5
Berliner Mauer Dokumentationszentrum	19	C2
Bodemuseum	20	D4
Brandenburger Tor	21	B5
Carillon	22	A5
Deutsche Guggenheim	23	D5
Deutsches Historisches Museum	24	D5
Fernsehturm	25	E5
Filmmuseum	26	B6
Former Site of Hitler's Bunker	27	B6
Gemäldegalerie	28	A6
Hackesche Höfe	29	E4
Hamburger Bahnhof	30	B3
Haus der Kulturen der Welt	31	A5
Holocaust Memorial	32	B5
Humboldt Universität	33	D5
Lift	34	B6
Neue Synagogue	35	D4
Neues Kanzleramt	36	B5
Panorama Observation Deck	37	B6
Pergamonmuseum	38	D5
Reichstag	39	B5
Sony Center	(see 26)	
Wall Victims Memorial	40	B5
World Time Clock	41	E4

SLEEPING

Ackselhaus	42	F3
Adlon	43	B5
Arcotel Velvet	(see 83)	
Art'otel Berlin Mitte	44	E6
Aurora	45	F1
Circus Hostel	46	E4
Circus Hostel	47	E3
Citystay Hostel	48	E4
Dorint am Gendarmenmarkt	49	C6
Eastener Hostel	50	C3
EastSeven	51	E3
Garden Hotel Honigmond	52	C3
Heart of Gold	53	D4
Kunstlerheim Luise	54	B5
Lux 11	55	E4
Mitte's	56	B3
Pension Amsterdam	57	E1
Prinz Albert	58	E3
Radisson SAS	59	E5

See Charlottenburg & Wilmersdorf Map

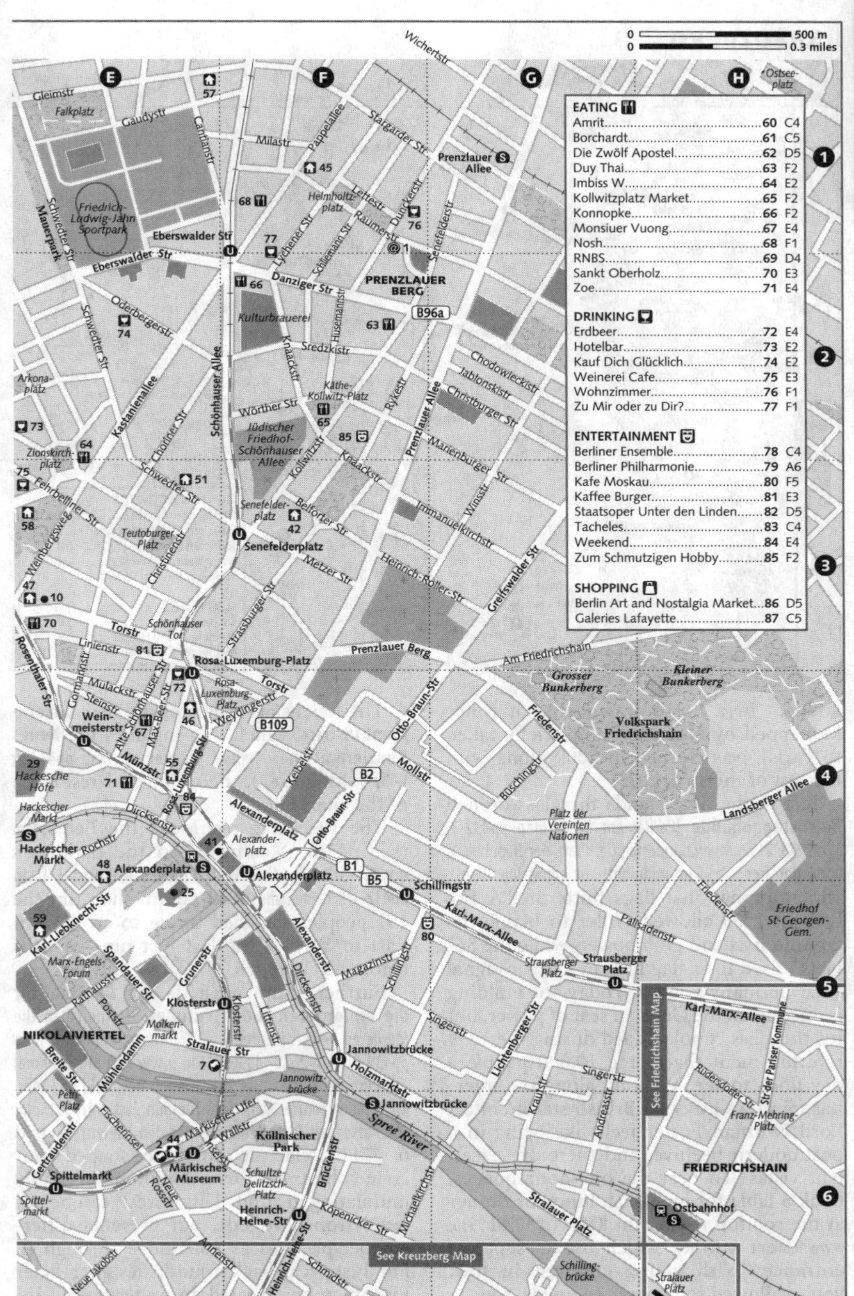
0 500 m
0 0.3 miles
E
F
G
H
1
2
3
4
5
6
EATING
Amrit....60 C4
Borchardt....61 C5
Die Zwölf Apostel....62 D5
Duy Thai....63 F2
Imbiss W....64 E2
Kollwitzplatz Market....65 F2
Konnopke....66 F2
Monsiuer Vuong....67 E4
Nosh....68 F1
RNBS....69 D4
Sankt Oberholz....70 E3
Zoe....71 E4
DRINKING
Erdbeer....72 E4
Hotelbar....73 E2
Kauf Dich Glücklich....74 E2
Weinerei Cafe....75 E3
Wohnzimmer....76 F1
Zu Mir oder zu Dir?....77 F1
ENTERTAINMENT
Berliner Ensemble....78 C4
Berliner Philharmonie....79 A6
Kafe Moskau....80 F5
Kaffee Burger....81 E3
Staatsoper Unter den Linden....82 D5
Tacheles....83 C4
Weekend....84 E4
Zum Schmutzigen Hobby....85 F2
SHOPPING
Berlin Art and Nostalgia Market....86 D5
Galeries Lafayette....87 C5
Wichertstr
Ostseeplatz
Gleimstr
Falkplatz
Gaudystr
Cantianstr
Milastr
Pappelallee
Stargarder Str
Prenzlauer Allee
Friedrich-Ludwig-Jahn Sportpark
Mauerpark
Schwedter Str
Eberswalder Str
Helmholtzplatz
Lettestr
Raumerstr
Dunckerstr
Lychener Str
Schliemann Str
Senefelderstr
PRENZLAUER BERG
Danziger Str
B96a
Oderbergerstr
Kulturbrauerei
Husemannstr
Sredzkistr
Knaackstr
Schönhauser Allee
Kastanienallee
Arkonaplatz
Chodowieckistr
Jablonskistr
Christburger Str
Rykestr
Käthe-Kollwitz-Platz
Wörther Str
Jüdischer Friedhof-Schönhauser Allee
Kollwitzstr
Choriner Str
Zionskirchplatz
Fehrbelliner Str
Marienburger Str
Immanuelkirchstr
Winsstr
Senefelderplatz
Belforter Str
Teutoburger Platz
Christinenstr
Weinbergsweg
Metzer Str
Heinrich-Roller-Str
Greifswalder Str
Strassburger Str
Torstr
Schönhauser Tor
Linienstr
Rosenthaler Str
Prenzlauer Berg
Am Friedrichshain
Rosa-Luxemburg-Platz
Gormannstr
Mulackstr
Steinstr
Alte Schönhauser Str
Max-Beer-Str
Weydingerstr
Weinmeisterstr
B109
Otto-Braun-Str
Grosser Bunkerberg
Kleiner Bunkerberg
Volkspark Friedrichshain
Friedenstr
Hackesche Höfe
Münzstr
Rosa-Luxemburg-Str
Keibelstr
B2
Mollstr
Büschingstr
Landsberger Allee
Hackescher Markt
Dircksenstr
Alexanderplatz
Platz der Vereinten Nationen
Rochstr
B1
B5
Schillingstr
Karl-Liebknecht-Str
Karl-Marx-Allee
Friedhof St-Georgen-Gem.
Palisadenstr
Marx-Engels-Forum
Spandauer Str
Grunerstr
Alexanderstr
Magazinstr
Strausberger Platz
Rathausstr
Poststr
Klosterstr
Littenstr
Molkenmarkt
NIKOLAIVIERTEL
Stralauer Str
Singerstr
Lichtenberger Str
Jannowitzbrücke
Holzmarktstr
Breite Str
Mühlendamm
Petriplatz
Fischerinsel
Märkisches Ufer
Spree River
Wallstr
Köllnischer Park
Krautstr
Andreasstr
Rüdersdorfer Str
Str der Pariser Kommune
Franz-Mehring-Platz
See Friedrichshain Map
FRIEDRICHSHAIN
Gertraudenstr
Spittelmarkt
Märkisches Museum
Neue Rossstr
Schultze-Delitzsch-Platz
Brückenstr
Heinrich-Heine-Str
Köpenicker Str
Michaelkirchstr
Stralauer Platz
Ostbahnhof
Annenstr
See Kreuzberg Map
Neue Jakobstr
Schmidstr
Schillingbrücke

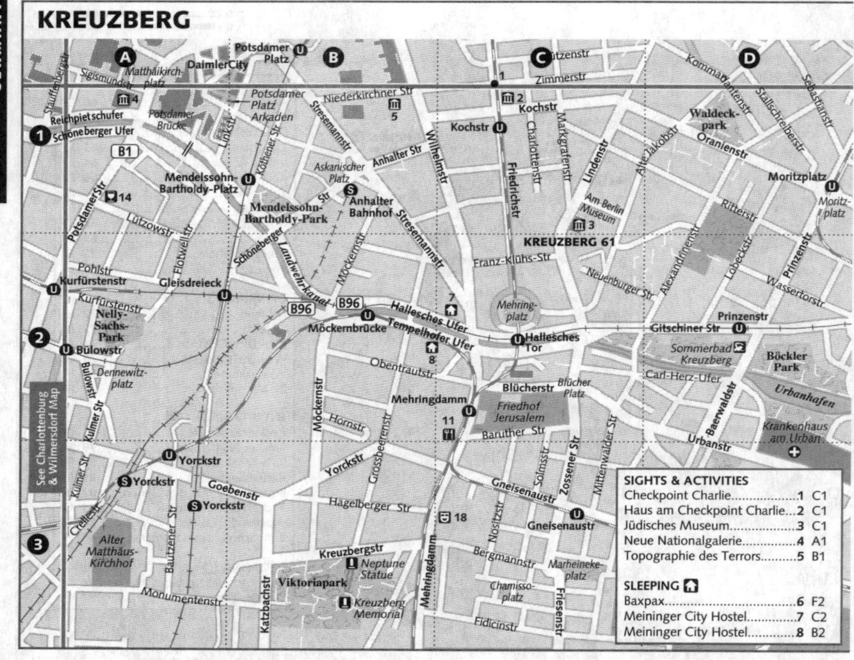

goddess in a horse-drawn chariot (once kidnapped by Napoleon and briefly taken to Paris), was cleaned in 2000 along with the rest of the structure.

Just to the west stands the glass-domed **Reichstaggebäude** (Parliament Bldg; Map pp432-3; ☎ 2273 2152; www.bundestag.de; Platz der Republik 1; admission free; 🕑 8am-midnight, last admission 10pm), with four national flags fluttering. A fire here in 1933 allowed Hitler to blame the communists and grab power, while the Soviets raised their flag here in 1945 to signal Nazi Germany's defeat. Today, the building is once again the German seat of power, but it's the glass cupola added during the 1999 refurbishment that some 10,000 people a day flock to see. Walking along the internal spiral walkway by British star architect Lord Norman Foster feels like being in a postmodern beehive, and there are excellent vistas. To beat the one-hour queues, book a table for breakfast, lunch or dinner at the rooftop restaurant **Käfer** (☎ 2262 9935; www.feinkost-kaefer.de), which uses a separate entrance. With young children in tow, you're allowed to bypass the queue, too.

The Reichstag is part of the new **Government District**, which also includes the **Neues Kanzleramt** (New Federal Chancellery; Map pp432-3; Willy-Brandt-Strasse 1), the office and residence of the chancellor.

The Reichstag overlooks the **Tiergarten** (see p436). Meanwhile to the building's south stands the **Wall Victims Memorial** (Map pp432-3; Scheidemannstrasse), commemorating the 191 people who died trying to cross from East to West – the last just nine months before the Wall fell.

Further south again is the **Denkmal für die ermordeten Juden Europas** (Memorial to the Murdered Jews of Europe or Holocaust Memorial; Map pp432-3; ☎ 2639 4336/4311; www.stiftung-denkmal.de; Cora-Berliner-Strasse 1; admission free; field 🕑 24hr, information centre 10am-8pm Tue-Sun, last entry 7.15pm; Ⓜ Potsdamer Platz/S-Bahn Unter den Linden) a grid of 2711 'stelae' or differently shaped concrete columns set over 19,000m2 of gently undulating ground. This 'forest' can be entered from any side, but presents different perspectives as you move through it. For historical background, designer Peter Eisenman has created an underground in-

formation centre in the southeast corner of the site. Weekly **English tours** (€3; 4pm Sun) meet near the **lift** (Map pp432-3) here.

Unter den Linden

Celebrated in literature and lined with lime (or linden) trees, the street **Unter den Linden** (M S-Bahn Unter den Linden) was the fashionable avenue of old Berlin. Today, after decades of communist neglect, it's been rebuilt and regained that status. The thoroughfare stretches east from the Brandenburger Tor to the Museumsinsel, passing shops, embassies, operas, the **Deutsche Guggenheim** (Map pp432-3; ☎ 202 0930; www.deutsche-guggenheim.de; Unter den Linden 13-15; adult/concession €4/3, free Mon; 11am-8pm, to 10pm Thu; M Französische Strasse) and the **Humboldt Universität** (Map pp432-3; M S-Bahn Friedrichstrasse).

Stop by **Bebelplatz** (Map pp432-3; M Französische Strasse), opposite the university, where there's a **book-burning memorial** – a reminder of the first major Nazi book-burning, which occurred in May 1933. A transparent window tile in the stone pavement reveals empty bookshelves below.

SAVE ON MUSEUMS ENTRY

With some leading Berlin museums costing €8 each, don't ignore the **SchauLust Museen Berlin Pass** (☎ 250 025). Available from tourist offices for €12, it allows you free admission to more than 70 museums (not including Checkpoint Charlie or the Jewish Museum) over three days. Without any pass, all museums listed on www.smb.museum are free on Thursday for four hours before closing time.

Museumsinsel

The so-called **Museums Island** (Map pp432-3; ☎ all museums 2090 5577; www.smb.museum; adult/concession €8/4 each, or €12/6 all; 10am-6pm Tue-Sun, to 10pm Thu; M S-Bahn Hackescher Markt) lies in the Spree River. On it stands the **Pergamonmuseum** (Map pp432-3; Am Kupfergraben; M S-Bahn Hackescher Markt), which is to Berlin what the British Museum is to London: a feast of Mesopotamian, Greek and Roman antiquities looted by archaeologists. The museum takes its name from the Pergamon Altar inside, but the real highlight of the collection is the Ishtar Gate from Babylon.

Meanwhile, the **Alte Nationalgalerie** (Old National Gallery; Map pp432-3; Bodestrasse 1-3; M S-Bahn Hackescher Markt) houses 19th-century European sculpture and painting; the **Altes Museum** (Map pp432-3; Am Lustgarten; M S-Bahn Hackescher Markt) has art from ancient Rome and Greece; and the reopened **Bodemuseum** (Map pp432-3; Monbijoubrücke; M S-Bahn Hackescher Markt) houses sculpture, Byzantine art and painting from the Middle Ages to the 19th century. Watch for special exhibitions at each.

Overlooking the 'island' is the **Berliner Dom** (Berlin Cathedral; Map pp432-3; adult/concession/under 14 €5/3/free). The nearby **Deutsches Historisches Museum** (German History Museum; Map pp432-3; ☎ 203 040; www.dhm.de; Unter den Linden 2; admission €4, free Mon; 10am-6pm) has a new permanent exhibition on national history, but is still arguably most notable for the glass-walled spiral staircase by modernist architect IM Pei (creator of the Louvre's glass pyramid).

Hackescher Markt

A complex of shops and apartments around eight courtyards, the **Hackesche Höfe** (Map pp432-3; M S-Bahn Hackescher Markt) is Germany's largest live/work space and a major attraction of 21st-century Berlin. Despite increasing commercialisation – Adidas, Puma and, gulp, Hugo Boss recently opened stores – the neighbourhood retains sufficient cutting-edge streetwear boutiques to woo savvy young consumers.

Shops, cafés and restaurants are the main draw here, but you'll also find the **Neue Synagogue** (Map pp432-3; ☎ 8802 8451; www.cjudaicum.de; Oranienburger Strasse 28-30; adult/concession €3/2; 🕒 10am-8pm Sun & Mon, to 6pm Tue-Thu, to 5pm Fri, reduced hr Nov-Apr), with its history of local Jewish life. Plus, there's the counter-cultural cum shopping centre of **Tacheles** (Map pp432-3; ☎ 282 6185; Oranienburger Strasse 54-56) in a bombed-out department store.

Further north, the spectacular gallery of the **Hamburger Bahnhof** (Map pp432-3; ☎ 3978 3439; www.smb.museum; Invalidenstrasse 50, Mitte; adult/concession €6/3; 🕒 10am-6pm Tue-Fri, 11am-6pm Sat & Sun; Ⓜ Hauptbahnhof/Lehrter Stadtbahnhof) showcases works by Warhol, Lichtenstein, Rauschenberg and Joseph Beuys.

TV Tower

Call it Freudian or call it *Ostalgie* (nostalgia for the communist East or *Ost*), but Berlin's once-mocked socialist **Fernsehturm** (Map pp432-3; ☎ 242 3333; www.berlinerfernsehturm.de; adult/concession €7.50/3.50; 🕒 10-1am; Ⓜ Alexanderplatz) is fast becoming its most-loved symbol. Originally erected in 1969 and the city's tallest structure, its central bauble was decorated as a giant football for the 2006 Fifa World Cup™, while its 368m outline still pops up in numerous souvenirs. That said, ascending 207m to the revolving (but musty) Telecafé is a less singular experience than visiting the Reichstag dome.

The Turm dominates **Alexanderplatz**, a former livestock and wool market that became the lowlife district chronicled by Alfred Döblin's 1929 novel *Berlin Alexanderplatz* and then developed as a 1960s communist showpiece.

Even in a city so often described as one big building site, today's Alexanderplatz is an unusual hive of construction activity as it is transformed into the next Potsdamer Platz-style development. However, its communist past still echoes through the retro **World Time Clock** (Map pp432-3) and along the portentous **Karl-Marx-Allee**, which leads several kilometres east from the square to Friedrichshain.

Tiergarten

From the Reichstag (see p434), the Tiergarten park's **carillon** (Map pp432-3; John-Foster-Dulles-Allee; bus 100 or 200) and the **Haus der Kulturen der Welt** (House of World Cultures; Map pp432-3; John-Foster-Dulles-Allee) are clearly visible. The latter was the US contribution to the 1957 International Building Exposition and it's easy to see why locals call it the 'pregnant oyster'.

Further west, the wings of the **Siegessäule** (Victory Column; Map p439; bus 100 or 200) were the *Wings of Desire* in that famous Wim Wenders film. This golden angel was built to commemorate Prussian military victories in the 19th century. Today, as the end point of the annual Christopher Street Parade, she's also a gay icon. However, there are better views than those at the column's peak.

A short walk south from here is a cluster of interesting embassy buildings and museums, including the **Bauhaus Archiv** (off Map pp434-5; ☎ 254 0020; www.bauhaus.de; Klingelhöferstrasse 14; adult/concession €6/3; 🕒 10am-5pm Wed-Mon; Ⓜ Nollendorfplatz), with drawings, chairs and other Modernist objects from the famous Bauhaus school of design – as well as a very tempting shop. The school itself survives in Dessau (see p464).

The **Berliner Philharmonie**, founded in 1961, (see p443) and yet more museums are found a little east in the **Kulturforum** (Map pp432-3; Ⓜ S-Bahn Potsdamer Platz). These include the spectacular **Gemäldegalerie** (Picture Gallery; Map pp432-3; ☎ 266 2951; www.smb.museum; Matthäiskirchplatz 4-6; adult/concession €6/3; 🕒 10am-6pm Tue-Sun, to 10pm Thu) showing European painting from the 13th to the 18th centuries. Nearby is the **Neue Nationalgalerie** (Map pp434-5; ☎ 266 2951; www.smb.museum; Potsdamer Strasse 50; adult/concession €6/3; 🕒 10am-6pm Tue-Fri, to 10pm Thu, 11am-6pm Sat & Sun). Housing 19th- and 20th-century works by Picasso, Klee, Miró and many German expressionists, it was built by Bauhaus director Ludwig Mies van der Rohe.

Potsdamer Platz

The lid was symbolically sealed on capitalism's victory over socialism in Berlin when this postmodern temple to mammon was erected in 2000 over the former death strip. Under the big-top, glass-tent roof of the **Sony Center** (Map pp432-3; Ⓜ or S-Bahn Potsdamer Platz) and along the malls of the Lego-like **DaimlerCity** (Map pp432-3; Ⓜ or S-Bahn Potsdamer Platz), people swarm in and around shops, restaurants, offices, loft apartments, clubs, a cinema, a luxury hotel and a casino – all revitalising what was the busiest square in prewar Europe.

During the Berlin Film Festival (see p438), Potsdamer Platz welcomes Hollywood A-listers. In between, you can rub shoulders with German cinematic heroes – particularly Marlene Dietrich – at the **Filmmuseum** (Map pp432-3; ☎ 300 9030; www.filmmuseum-berlin.de; Potsdamer Strasse 2, Tiergarten; adult/concession €6/4; 🕑 10am-6pm Tue-Sun, to 8pm Thu). There's also 'Europe's fastest' lift to the **Panorama Observation Deck** (Map pp432-3; www.panoramapunkt.de; adult/concession €3.50/2.50; 🕑 11am-8pm).

But, as ever in Berlin, the past refuses to go quietly. Just north of Potsdamer Platz lies the former site of **Hitler's Bunker** (Map pp432-3). A little southeast lies the **Topographie des Terrors** (Map pp434-5; ☎ 2548 6703; www.topographie.de; Niederkirchner Strasse; admission free; 🕑 10am-8pm May-Sep, to dusk Oct-Apr), a sometimes shockingly graphic record of the Gestapo and SS headquarters that once stood here.

Jewish Museum

The Daniel Libeskind building that's the **Jüdisches Museum** (Map pp434-5; ☎ 2599 3300; www.juedisches-museum-berlin.de; Lindenstrasse 9-14; adult/concession €5/2.50; 🕑 10am-10pm Mon, to 8pm Tue-Sun, last entry 1hr before closing; Ⓜ Hallesches Tor) is as much the attraction as the Jewish-German history collection within. Designed to disorientate and unbalance with its 'voids', cul-de-sacs, barbed metal fittings, slit windows and uneven floors, this still-somehow-beautiful structure swiftly conveys the uncertainty and sometime terror of past Jewish life in Germany. It's a visceral experience, after which the huge collection itself demands your concentration. A highlight is the Garden of Exile, with tall concrete columns like trees and an uneven floor. The building's footprint is a ripped-apart Star of David.

Kurfürstendamm

West Berlin's legendary shopping thoroughfare, the Ku'damm has lost some of its cachet since the Wall fell, but is worth visiting. You will find the **Kaiser-Wilhelm-Gedächtniskirche** (Map p439; ☎ 218 5023; Breitscheidplatz; Memorial Hall 🕑 10am-4pm Mon-Sat, Hall of Worship 🕑 9am-7.30pm) here, which remains in ruins – just as British bombers left it on 22 November 1943 – as an antiwar memorial. Only the broken west tower still stands.

Stasi Museum

The one-time secret police headquarters now houses the **Stasi Museum** (Map p431; ☎ 553 6854; House 1, Ruschestrasse 103; adult/concession €3/2; 11am-6pm Tue-Fri, 2-6pm Sat & Sun; Ⓜ Magdalenenstrasse). It's largely in German, but worth it to see the cunning surveillance devices and communist paraphernalia.

Tours

Guided tours are phenomenally popular; you can choose Third Reich, Wall, bunker, communist, boat or bicycle tours, as well as guided pub-crawls. Most cost €10 to €12 each.

TRACING THE BERLIN WALL

Just as the infamous Wall snaked across Berlin, so today's remnants are scattered across the city. The longest surviving stretch is the so-called **East Side Gallery** (Map p438; www.eastsidegallery.com; Mühlenstrasse; Ⓜ S-Bahn Warschauer Strasse) in Friedrichshain. Panels along this 1.3km of graffiti and art include the famous portrait of Soviet leader Brezhnev kissing GDR leader Erich Hönecker and a Trabant car seemingly bursting through the (now crumbling) concrete.

Climbing the tower at the **Berliner Mauer Dokumentationszentrum** (Berlin Wall Documentation Centre; Map pp432-3; ☎ 464 1030; Bernauer Strasse 111; admission free; 🕑 10am-5pm; Ⓜ S-Bahn Nordbahnhof) you overlook a memorial across the street – an artist's impression of the death strip behind an original stretch of wall. Photos and eyewitness testimonies are also on show.

In Kreuzberg, the famous sign at **Checkpoint Charlie** (Map pp434-5) still boasts 'You are now leaving the American sector'. But it and the reconstructed US guardhouse are just a bit of fun now. To learn about the seriously tragic past, visit **Haus am Checkpoint Charlie** (Map pp434-5; ☎ 253 7250; www.mauer-museum.com; Friedrichstrasse 43-45; adult/concession €9.50/5.50; 🕑 9am-10pm; Ⓜ Kochstrasse/Stadtmitte). Tales of spectacular escape attempts include through tunnels, in hot-air balloons and even using a one-man submarine.

New Berlin (☎ 017-9973 0397; www.newberlintours.com) even offers free (yup, free) 3½-hour introductory tours. These leave at 11am and 1pm outside the Starbucks that's rather controversially located in Pariser Platz near the Brandenburg Gate. Guides are enthusiastic, knowledgeable… and accept tips.

Alternatively, you can beetle around Berlin in a Trabant car. **Trabi Safari** (☎ 275 2273; www.trabi-safari.de; €25-35) operates from Gendarmenmarkt.

Other operators include:

Brewer's Berlin Tours (☎ 017-7388 1537; www.brewersberlintours.com).

Insider Tours (☎ 692 3149; www.insidertour.com)

Original Berlin Walks (☎ 301 9194; www.berlinwalks.com)

FESTIVALS & EVENTS

International Film Festival Berlin (☎ 259 200; www.berlinale.de) The Berlinale, held in February, is Germany's answer to the Cannes and Venice film festivals.

Christopher Street Day (☎ 017-7277 3176; www.csd-berlin.de) On the last weekend in June, this is Germany's largest gay event.

Love Parade (☎ 308 8120; www.loveparade.net) At the time of research, Berlin's huge techno street parade was making a comeback, hopefully sustainable.

SLEEPING

Mitte & Prenzlauer Berg

BUDGET

Berlin's independent hostels far outdo the DJH (www.jugendherberge.de) offerings in the city.

Circus Hostels (Map pp432-3; ☎ 2839 1433; www.circus-hostel.de; Rosa-Luxemburg-Strasse 39 & Weinbergsweg 1a; dm €15-20, s/d €32/48, 2/4-person apt €75/130; 💻; Ⓜ U-Bahn Rosenthaler Platz) These two are widely regarded as the best hostels in town, with great central locations, efficient staff, good bars and upbeat, tastefully decorated rooms in cheerful colours.

Citystay Hostel (Map pp432-3; ☎ 2362 4031; www.citystay.de; Rosenstrasse 16; dm €15-20, s/d €34/48; 💻; Ⓜ S-Bahn Alexanderplatz/Hackescher Markt) Tucked away on a quiet street between the Fernsehturm and Hackescher Markt, this loft-style establishment uses expensive finishes and bright colours to create an upbeat atmosphere. Showers (none ensuite) are clean, but the sparse rooms lack cupboards.

Heart of Gold (Map pp432-3; ☎ 2900 3300; www.heartofgold-hostel.de; Johannisstrasse 11; dm €14-19, s/d €40/60, apt €120-160, d without bathroom €48; 💻; Ⓜ Oranienburger Tor) Even if you're not into the subtle *Hitchhiker's Guide to the Galaxy* theming, this new building in Mitte still offers comfortable accommodation and a convenient location. A nice touch is the stylish tiled niches with stainless-steel sinks.

EastSeven (Map pp432-3; ☎ 9362 2240; www.eastseven.de; Schwedter Strasse 7; dm €17-23, s/d €35/55, bedding €3; 💻; Ⓜ Senefelder Platz) It sounds like a boy band and this wonderful, cosy place *is* squeaky clean. Even the retro '70s look that emulates many nearby Prenzelberg bars has been achieved with the help of IKEA(!). The kitchen adjoins a lovely garden perfect for summer barbecues.

Aurora (Map pp432-3; ☎ 4699 5524; www.aurora-hostel.com; Pappelallee 21; s/d with bathroom €42/66, s/d/tr €26/48/64; 💻; Ⓜ Eberswalder Strasse) The way of the future, this sleek streamlined pad straddles the gulf between budget and boutique hotel. Decorated in neutral tones, it even has customisable coloured lighting, as in some famous Phillipe Starck abodes.

Pension Amsterdam (Map pp432-3; ☎ 448 0792; www.pension-amsterdam.de; Gleimstrasse 24; s €36.50, d €70-90, tr €75-120; 💻; Ⓜ Schönhauser Allee) There's plenty to like about this contemporary *pension*: big apartments, full kitchens, rooms with four-poster beds and a buzzy downstairs café popular with a mixed gay crowd.

Other recommendations:

Eastener Hostel (Map pp432-3; ☎ 017-5112 3515; www.eastener-hostel.de; Novalisstrasse 15; dm €15-20, s/d €30/44; ☒) Small quiet, unassuming-looking hostel, where guests rave about the personal touch.

Mitte's (Map pp432-3; ☎ 2839 0965; www.backpacker.de; Chausseestrasse 102; dm €15-19, d €44-66; 💻; Ⓜ Zinnowitzer Strasse) and **Baxpax** (Map pp434-5; ☎ 6951 8322; www.baxpax.de; Skalitzer Strasse 104; Ⓜ Görlitzer Bahnhof) These sister establishments are a bit ramshackle, especially Mitte's, but fun and funky, with rooms themed by nationality in Baxpax.

MIDRANGE

Arcotel Velvet (Map pp432-3; ☎ 278 7530; www.arcotel.at; Oranienburger Strasse 52; s €60-100, d €70-110; Ⓟ ☒; Ⓜ Oranienburger Tor) Floor-to-ceiling windows give front rooms a bird's-eye view of the bustling street and, combined with bathrooms separated only by gauze curtains, create a feeling of loft living. Back rooms are more traditional.

Prinz Albert (Map pp432-3; ☎ 293 833; www.prinzalbert-berlin.de; Veteranenstrasse 10; s €65-85, d €90-110; ⊠; M Rosenthaler Platz) Although minutes from hipster-central Kastanienallee, this sweet, gay-friendly hotel has a neighbourhood feel. Six of the seven generously sized, neutrally decorated rooms overlook the pleasant Weinbergspark, and there's a restaurant downstairs.

Kunstlerheim Luise (Map pp432-3; ☎ 284 480; www.kuenstlerheim-luise.de; Luisenstrasse 19; s/d from €85/120, s/d without bathroom €50/80; P ⊠; M Friedrichstrasse) A room with Andy Warhol-style bananas and golden crowns, another with a giant bed and yet another with Edward Hopper-style murals – every room in the wonderful Kunstlerheim Luise is a work of art, and those on the top floors (no lift) are quite affordable too.

Ackselhaus (Map pp432-3; ☎ 4433 7633; www.ackselhaus.de; Belforter Strasse 21; s €85-120, d €95-160; M Senefelder Platz) A Mediterranean oasis in Prenzlauer Berg, this relaxing and elegant terrace comes with a garden and Italian or African apartments (with kitchens). Its sister three doors down boasts various 'blue' themes, plus all-day restaurant Club del Mar.

Garden Hotel Honigmond (Map pp432-3; ☎ 2844 5577; www.honigmond-berlin.de; Invalidenstrasse 122; s €90-110, d €115-160; P ⊠; M Zinnowitzer Strasse/S-Bahn Nordbahnhof) This classic, romantic hotel is kitted out with such flair that even urban hipsters will be enchanted. Creaky wooden floors, some four-poster beds and the lush garden make it feel worlds away from the busy street.

Lux 11 (Map pp432-3; ☎ 936 2800; www.lux-eleven.com; Rosa-Luxemburg-Strasse 9-13; r from €115, ste from €135; ⊠; M Weinmeisterstrasse/Alexanderplatz) A liberal use of white – off-white, cream, beige and light grey –make this slick, streamlined hotel a haven of calm in Mitte. Its restaurant, Shiro I Shiro, is also winning plaudits for its innovative cuisine and striking white-and-blue interior.

TOP END

Art'otel Berlin Mitte (Map pp432-3; ☎ 240 620; www.arthotel.de; Wallstrasse 70-73; s/d from €130/260; P ⊠ ✣ 💻; M Märkisches Museum) This Georg Baselitz-inspired Art'otel was the first of Berlin's new-generation hotels, and its highlight remains the breakfast/dining room. Here, new building meets old in an inner courtyard, and you realise what a broad, but still cool, mix of people you're staying with.

Dorint am Gendarmenmarkt (Map pp432-3; ☎ 203 570; www.dorint.de; Charlottenstrasse 50-52; s/d from €160/190, breakfast €25; ⊠; M Französische Strasse) The Adlon notwithstanding, this is some people's Berlin favourite. Frosted glass, chocolate brown tones and a wonderful enclosed terrace in the top-floor spa area show real style. However, it's the sly hint of fun – the old gym rings, for example – that's always won us over.

Both the prestigious **Hotel Adlon** (Map pp432-3; ☎ 226 10; www.hotel-adlon.de, www.kempinski.com; Am Pariser Platz, Unter den Linden 77; s/d from €280/325; P ⊠ ✣ 🏊) and the new **Radisson SAS** (Map pp432-3; ☎ 238 280; www.radissonsas.com; Karl-Liebnecht-Strasse 1-3; r €130-350; P ⊠ 🏊), with its giant aquarium lobby, are themselves sightseeing attractions. Breakfast is not included at the Radisson.

Friedrichshain & Kreuzberg

Eastern Comfort Hostelboot (Map p438; ☎ 6676 3806; www.eastern-comfort.com; Mühlenstrasse 73-77; dm €14-18, s/d from €42/46, bedding €5; 💻; M S-Bahn Warschauer Strasse) This floating hostel near the last standing bit of Wall is refreshingly unusual. Upper cabins enjoy river views here and there's a nicely designed bar at the back, where Captain Edgar and crew organise regular events and gigs. Campers can pitch a tent on the deck for €10 a night.

Other recommendations:

Odyssee Globetrotter Hostel (Map p438; ☎ 2900 0081; www.globetrotterhostel.de; Grünberger Strasse 23; dm €10-16, s/d from €29/39; 💻; M S-Bahn Warschauer Strasse) Popular party hostel in bohemian Friedrichshain.

Meininger City Hostel (Map pp434-5; ☎ 6663 6100; www.meininger-hostels.de; Hallesches Ufer 30; dm €13.50-25, s/d €49/66; P ⊠ 💻) Dorms are clean but spartan, while cheerfully furnished doubles and singles stand out. Branches at Tempelhofer Ufer 10 (Map pp434-5) and Meininger Strasse 10 (Map p439).

Charlottenburg & Schöneberg

Pension Kettler (Map p439; ☎ 883 4949; Bleibtreustrasse 19; s €50-75, d €60-90; M Uhlandstrasse) If you want quirk and true Berlin character, you'll find heaps of it at this nostalgic retreat, strewn with objects best described as 'esoterica'. The place's most eccentric and memorable feature, though, is its owner!

Propellor Island City Lodge (off Map p439; ☎ 891 9016; www.propeller-island.de; Albrecht-Achilles-Strasse

58; s €65-125, d €90-195; ⊠; Ⓜ Adenauer Platz) Berlin's most eccentric hotel is the brainchild of artist/musician Lars Stroschen, who crafted these 30 unique environments. Here walls slant, beds seemingly hang above the floor, wardrobes hide showers, and there are other surreal features.

Hotel-Pension Art Nouveau (Map p439; ☎ 327 7440; www.hotelartnouveau.de; Leibnizstrasse 59; s €95-140, d €110-165; ⊠; Ⓜ Adenauer Platz/S-Bahn Savignyplatz) A rickety bird-cage lift drops you off on the 4th floor in one Berlin's best *pensions*, with handpicked antiques and creative use of colour. The owners are its greatest asset, though, treating guests like family friends.

Askanischer Hof (Map p439; ☎ 881 8033; www.askanischer-hof.de; Kurfürstendamm 53; s €100-110, d €125-145; ⊠; Ⓜ Adenauer Platz/S-Bahn Savignyplatz) Decorated in decadent 1920s style (with a few other eras thrown in), it's little surprise this became David Bowie's favourite hotel in the creative cradle of 1970s West Berlin. It's still an artistic meeting spot.

EATING

Berliners love eating out and you needn't walk far for a feed. Restaurants usually open from 11am to midnight, with varying *Ruhetage* or rest days; many close during the day from 3pm to 6pm. Cafés often close around 8pm, though equal numbers stay open until 2am or later.

Berlin is a snacker's paradise, with Turkish (your best bet), Wurst (sausage), Greek, Italian, Chinese, even Sudanese *Imbiss* stalls throughout the city.

Self-caterers will find Aldi, Lidl, Plus and Penny Markt discount supermarkets throughout Berlin. There's the excellent organic **Kollwitzplatz market** (Map pp432-3; 🕑 9am-4pm Sat & Sun) and the **Winterfeldtplatz farmer's market** (Map p439; 🕑 Wed & Sat).

Mitte & Prenzlauer Berg

Konnopke (Map pp432-3; Schönhauser Allee 44a; 🕑 5.30am-8pm Mon-Fri; Ⓜ Eberswalder Strasse) Even former chancellor Gerhard Schröder has eaten Wurst here under the S-Bahn tracks in Prenzelberg.

RNBS (Map pp432-3; ☎ 540 2505; Oranienburger Strasse 50; mains €2-4; Ⓜ Oranienburger Strasse/Hackescher Markt) We can't vouch for the 'beauty tea' (sadly didn't work for us), but the Asian soups and noodle dishes served up by this tiny orange-and-white outlet are as delicious as they are healthy: no preservatives, no MSG, no artificial flavourings.

Sankt Oberholz (Map pp432-3; ☎ 2408 5586; Rosenthaler Strasse 72a; dishes €3.50-5; Ⓜ Rosenthaler Platz) Not so much a café as a hilarious social experiment, where Berlin's '*Urbanen Pennern*' (office-less, self-employed creatives) flock with their laptops for the free wi-fi access. The deli fare of soups, lasagne and savoury polenta cake is pretty good too.

Monsieur Vuong (Map pp432-3; ☎ 3087 2643; Alte Schönhauser Strasse 46; mains €6.50; Ⓜ Weinmeisterstrasse/Rosa-Luxemburg-Platz/Alexanderplatz) Because this Vietnamese is where everyone says you should eat, this is where everyone is. Arrive early to avoid queuing. Mr Vuong himself shakes regulars' hands in the red-lacquer room, and the soups are toothsome.

Nosh (Map pp432-3; ☎ 4404 0397; Pappelallee 77; mains €6-13, 🕑 dinner only in winter; Ⓜ Eberswalder Strasse) Relaxed diner style eatery, with a daily changing blackboard menu and staples of spring rolls, Asian and European dishes. Sunday brunch is a great time to come.

Zoe (Map pp432-3; ☎ 2404 5635; Rochstrasse 1; mains €8-18, 2-course lunch menus €6-7; Ⓜ Weinmeisterstrasse/Alexanderplatz) The all-white fittings and trendy customers fortunately don't denote a case of style over substance here. Mediterranean and Asian flavours are skilfully mixed to create a piquant tang. Excellent lunch deals.

Borchardt (Map pp432-3; ☎ 8188 6250; Französische Strasse 47; mains €13-20; Ⓜ Französische Strasse) On every Berlin *promi*'s (celeb's) speed-dial list, this refined French-German bistro also tolerates ordinary civilians.

Other recommendations:

Imbiss W (Map pp432-3; ☎ 4849 2657; Kastanienallee 49; mains €3-6; Ⓜ Rosenthaler Platz) Canadian-run joint offering Southeast Asian food and naan pizzas.

Duy Thai (Map pp432-3; ☎ 4431 7116; Kollwitzstrasse 89; mains €5-14; Ⓜ Eberswalder Strasse) Dishes are made to order in this relaxed canteen.

Die Zwölf Apostel (The 12 Apostles; Map pp432-3; ☎ 201 0222; Georgenstrasse; mains €9-16; Ⓜ Friedrichstrasse) Ecclesiastical décor and huge pizzas, including a 'Judas'. Good weekday lunch deals.

Friedrichshain & Kreuzberg

Curry 36 (Map pp434-5; ☎ 881 4710; Mehringdamm 36; 🕑 9am-5pm; Ⓜ Mehringdamm) This is Kreuzberg's – some believe Berlin's – best sausage stand.

Frittiersalon (Map p438; Boxhagener Strasse 104; Ⓜ Frankfurter Tor) The enormous choice here includes Wurst, organic fries, tofu and even a Camembert burger.

Hasir (Map pp434-5; Adalbertstrasse 10; 24hr; Kottbusser Tor) The birthplace (yes, really) of the döner kebab is a sit-down restaurant, too.

Café V (Map pp434-5; 612 4505; Lausitzer Platz 12; dishes €5.50-9.50; Görlitzer Bahnhof) Yellow, red and gilt trimmings greet you as you enter this old-school veggie/vegan café. Everything comes with a soya/caffeine-free/tofu alternative, although you can also choose straight-up dishes like pizza or Thai fish curry.

Schneeweiss (Map p438; 2904 9704; Simplonstrasse 16; day menu €5.50-11, dinner mains €13-20; dinner only Mon-Fri, all day Sat & Sun; S-Bahn Warschauer Strasse) Subtly embossed vanilla wallpaper, rectangular glass lights along the long, central table and parquet flooring keep neutral 'Snow White' feeling more après-ski than icy. The vaguely Swiss/Austrian 'Alpine' food is a '70s throwback, but still enjoyable. Evenings here are megafashionable, so book.

Amrit Kreuzberg (Map pp434-5; 612 5550; Oranienstrasse 202; dishes €7-14.50; Görlitzer Bahnhof); Mitte (Map pp432-3; 2888 4840; Oranienburger Strasse 45; Oranienburger Tor); Schöneberg (Map p439; 2101 4640; Winterfeldstrasse 40; Nollendorfplatz) One of three busy Amrits around town, that serve the same tasty pan-Indian cuisine.

Pi-Bar (Map p438; 2936 7581; Gabriel-Max-Strasse 17; mains €7-17; S-Bahn Warschauer Strasse) A salubrious Friedrichshain stalwart that has seen off countless pretenders, Pi continues to serve a tasty combination of vegetarian and fish-based cuisine, plus great breakfasts. The comfy sofas remain, but the walls have a new lick of red/tangerine paint.

Weltrestaurant Markthalle (Map pp434-5; 617 5502; Pücklerstrasse 34; mains €8-15; Görlitzer Bahnhof) This wood-lined, century-old pub draws a mixed clientele of ageing hipsters and neighbourhood folk with its relaxed vibe and simple no-nonsense food.

Charlottenburg & Schöneberg

Raststätte Gnadebrot (Map p439; 2196 1786; Marin-Luther-Strasse 202; mains €3.50-6; Victoria-Luise-Platz/Nollendorfplatz) An ironic, retro '70s take on a motorway roadhouse, this wins loyal fans for its friendly atmosphere (you share bench seats) and good, cheap food and drinks.

Schwarzes Café (Map p439; 313 8038; Kantstrasse 148; dishes €4.50-9; S-Bahn Zoo/Savignyplatz) Founded in 1978, this 24-hour food'n'booze institution must have seen half of Berlin pass through it (or out in it) at some point. Interesting toilets, too.

Mutter (Map p439; 216 4990; Hohenstaufenstrasse 4; mains €4-14; Nollendorfplatz) Sushi, Thai soups and often wonderfully presented Asian dishes are complemented by a list of cocktails that includes coconut-flavoured *Muttermilch* (mother's milk) in this opulent, gold-bedecked café.

Engelbecken (off Map p439; 615 2810; Witzlebenstrasse 31; mains €8-16; dinner only Mon-Sat, lunch & dinner Sun; Sophie Charlotte Platz) Come here for what many rate as Berlin's best Bavarian food, with Schweinsbraten, schnitzels, dumplings and sauerkraut. All meats are organic.

DRINKING

After dark, each Berlin district offers something different, but for the past decade, the hottest action has lain east. Prenzlauer Berg was the first GDR sector to develop a happening nightlife and still attracts student, creative and gay customers. Later, more clubs and bars sprang up in Mitte around Hackescher Markt, catering to a cool, slightly older and wealthier crowd. The area around Simon-Dach-Strasse and Boxhagener Platz in Friedrichshain is the latest to have emerged.

In the west, Kreuzberg remains alternative, becoming grungier as you move east. Charlottenburg and Winterfeldtplatz are fairly upmarket and mature, but liberal.

Bars without food open between 5pm and 8pm and may close as late as 5am (if at all).

Astrobar (Map p438; 2966 1615; Simon-Dach-Strasse 40; S-Bahn Warschauer Strasse) One of the first on the Friedrichshain scene and still going strong, the Astro offers the future as it looked in the 1960s, with spaceships, robots and classic computer games in the back room.

Erdbeer (Map pp432-3; Max-Beer-Strasse 56; Rosa-Luxemburg-Platz) A warren of interconnected rooms, this rambling cocktail bar derives its name not only from its red colour scheme, but also its customers' favourite brand of daiquiri (*Erdbeer*, or strawberry).

Kumpelnest 3000 (Map pp434-5; 8891 7960; Lützowstrasse 23; Kurfürstenstrasse) Once a brothel, always an experience – the Kumpelnest has been famed since the '80s for its wild, inhibition-free nights. Much of the original whorehouse décor remains intact. According to some locals, your bag may not (remain intact, that is) unless you keep a beady eye on it.

Hotelbar (Map pp432-3; ☎ 4432 8577; Zionkirchstrasse 5; Ⓜ Rosenthaler Platz) This cosy subterranean bar has a broad music policy, with jazz, latin beats and electropop to things like 'balkandub', 'Hammondorgel' and even spoken word.

Green Door (Map p439; ☎ 215 2515; Winterfeldtstrasse 50; Ⓜ Nollendorfplatz) Ring the doorbell to get them to open the namesake green door and let you into this tiny neighbourhood bar. Cocktails are on offer.

Other recommendations:

Möbel Olfe (Map pp434-5; ☎ 6165 9612; Reichenberger Strasse 177; closed Mon; Ⓜ Kottbusser Tor) Sparsely furnished beer hall good for Polish beer and table football.

Tabou Tiki Room (Map pp434-5; Maybuchufer 39; closed Mon; Ⓜ Schönleinstrasse) A slice of kitschy '60s Hawaii in Berlin. Exotic cocktails.

ENTERTAINMENT

Berlin's legendary nightlife needs little introduction. Whether alternative, underground, cutting-edge, saucy, flamboyant or even highbrow, it all crops up here.

Nightclubs

Clubs rarely open before 11pm (though earlier 'after-work' clubs and Sunday sessions are also popular) and stay open well into the early hours – usually sunrise at least. As the scene changes so rapidly, it's always wise to double-check listings magazines or ask locals. Admission charges, when they apply, range from €5 to €15.

Berghain/Panorama Bar (Map p438; www.berghain.de; Wrienzer Bahnhof; from midnight Thu-Sat; Ⓜ Ostbahnhof) Techno fans from across the world pump it up in a huge cathedral-like former railway workshop, or chill out in the quieter Panorama Bar upstairs. Cutting-edge sounds in industrial surrounds.

Café Moskau (off Map pp432-3; ☎ 2463 1626; www.das-moskau.com; Karl-Marx-Allee 34; Ⓜ Schillingstrasse) It doesn't really matter what's on, this onetime GDR restaurant is the epitome of retro Soviet kitsch and has to be seen. At the time of research, intermittent funk/reggae events were the order of the day, although the WMF techno/house evenings might return.

Kaffee Burger (Map pp432-3; ☎ 2804 6495; www.kaffeeburger.de; Torstrasse 60; Ⓜ Rosa-Luxemburg-Platz) A cornerstone of Berlin's so-bad-it's-good alternative scene, decked out in original GDR '60s wallpaper. Come here for indie, rock, punk and cult author Wladimir Kaminer's fortnightly *Russendisko* (Russian disco; www.russendisko.de).

Kosmos (Map p438; ☎ 4004 8130; www.kosmos-berlin.de; Karl-Marx-Allee 131a; from 10am; Ⓜ Frankfurter Tor) This monolithic GDR cinema has been reborn as one of Berlin's newest club/bar/bistros, with a huge main floor.

Spindler & Klatt (Map p438; ☎ 609 3702; www.spindlerklatt.com; Köpenicker Strasse 16-17; from 8pm Wed-Sun; Ⓜ Ostbahnhof/Schlesisches Tor) Unusually upmarket for Berlin, this club's combination of horizontal loungers and food service (hiccup!) has garnered plenty of headlines. In summer, there's a nice terrace.

Watergate (Map p438; ☎ 6128 0394; www.water-gate.de; Falckensteinstrasse 49a; from 11pm Fri & Sat; Ⓜ Schlesisches Tor) Watch the sun rise over the Spree River through the floor-to-ceiling windows of this fantastic lounge. The music is mainly electro, drum'n'bass and hip-hop.

Weekend (Map pp432-3; www.week-end-berlin.de; Am Alexanderplatz 5; from 11pm Thu-Sat; Ⓜ Alexanderplatz) Tear your eyes from the beautiful people and gaze through the 12th-floor windows, across the *Blade-Runner* landscape of dug-up Alexanderplatz and over Berlin. (Alexanderplatz 5 is the one with the Sanyo logo.)

Berlin also has a thriving scene of no-holds-barred sex clubs. The notorious **KitKat Club** (off Map p439: ☎ 7889 9704; Bessemerstrasse 14; Ⓜ Alt-Tempelhof) is the original and best.

Music & Theatre

Berliner Philharmonie (Map pp432-3; ☎ information 254 880, tickets 2548 8999; www.berliner-philharmoniker.de; Herbert-von-Karajan Strasse 1; Ⓜ Potsdamer Platz) Director Sir Simon Rattle has consolidated the orchestra's supreme musical reputation and the hall is praised for its acoustics, too.

Staatsoper Unter den Linden (Map pp432-3; ☎ information 203 540, tickets 2035 4555; www.staatsoper-berlin.de; Unter den Linden 5-7; Ⓜ S-Bahn Unter den Linden) This is the handiest and most prestigious of Berlin's three opera houses, where unsold seats go on sale cheap an hour before curtains-up.

Berliner Ensemble (Map pp432-3; ☎ information 284 080, tickets 2840 8155; www.berliner-ensemble.de; Bertolt-Brecht-Platz 1; Ⓜ Friedrichstrasse) *Mack the Knife* had its first public airing here, during the *Threepenny Opera's* premiere in 1928. Bertolt Brecht's former theatrical home continues to present his plays.

IN BERLIN'S LIVING ROOM

Berlin was once famous for its ramshackle squat bars. And while many snow-white nightlife venues are going upmarket, others have been trying to reclaim that anarchic legacy. A spate of new bars exists decorated like 1950s, 1960s or 1970s domestic living rooms. They feature flock wallpaper, bead curtains and mismatched, sometimes threadbare, sofas seemingly rescued from the rubbish tip.

The most famous exponent of this 'second-hand design' is the dimly lit pub/café called **Wohnzimmer** (Living Room; Map pp432-3; ☎ 445 5458; Lettestrasse 6; 🕑 10am-4am; Ⓜ Eberswalder Strasse). In hip Prenzlauer Berg, it combines styles from Louis XVI to, primarily, GDR c 1950.

Weinerei Cafe (Map pp432-3; ☎ 440 6983; cnr Veteranenstrasse & Fehrbellinerstrasse; 🕑 10am-midnight; Ⓜ Eberswalder Strasse) feels even more ad hoc, like stepping into someone's house. On Friday and Saturday nights, you simply rent a wine glass for €1, enjoy as many refills as you want and pay what you think is appropriate at the evening's end. (Be fair, otherwise they'll go broke!)

Zu Mir oder zu Dir? (Your place or mine?; Map pp432-3; Lychener Strasse 15; 🕑 from 8pm; Ⓜ Eberswalder Strasse) is a slightly more plush and trendy bar, with a double bed and some eye-catching pop-art features.

In two venues, **Kaufbar** (Buy-Bar or Purchasable; Map p438; ☎ 464 1030; Gärtnerstrasse 4; 🕑 11am-1am; Ⓜ S-Bahn Warschauer Strasse) and the sunny ice-cream café **Kauf Dich Glücklich** (Shop Yourself Happy; Map pp432-3; ☎ 4435 2182; Oderberger Strasse 44; 🕑 noon-midnight; Ⓜ Eberswalder Strasse), even the furniture is on sale. As you enjoy one of the latter's famous waffles, just pray someone doesn't come in and snap up the chair or table you're using.

SHOPPING

Department store **KaDeWe** (Map p439; Tauentzienstrasse 21; Ⓜ U-Bahn Wittenbergplatz) is Germany's most renowned retail emporium, equivalent to Harrods. The 6th-floor gourmet food halls are extraordinary, and the store is near the principal western shopping thoroughfare of Kurfürstendamm. Famous Parisian store **Galeries Lafayette** (Map pp432-3; ☎ 209 480; Friedrichstrasse 76-78; 🕑 10am-8pm Mon-Sat; Ⓜ S-Bahn Friedrichstrasse) also has a ritzy branch in Mitte.

While **Hackescher Markt** (p435) is increasingly commercial, plenty of cutting-edge boutiques are found in Prenzlauer Berg, especially along Kastanienallee (nicknamed 'casting alley' for its beautiful people) and Stargarder Strasse.

With flea markets across town, the **Berlin Art & Nostalgia Market** (Map pp432-3; Georgenstrasse, Mitte; 🕑 8am-5pm Sat & Sun; Ⓜ S-Bahn Friedrichstrasse) is heavy on collectibles, books, ethnic crafts and GDR memorabilia.

GETTING THERE & AWAY

Air

The plan is to turn Schönefeld into the city's main hub, Berlin-Brandenburg-International (BBI). That won't be for several years, however, and presently **three airports** (www.berlin-airport.de) operate.

Schönefeld (SXF) is the furthest from the centre but increasingly the busiest, with flights to/from Europe, Israel and North Africa, including easyJet (www.easyjet.com) services to the UK and Netherlands.

Tegel (TXL) has a similarly European focus and is the Air Berlin (www.airberlin.com) hub. Direct Delta Airlines (www.delta.com) services to/from New York also rotate out of here.

The landing hub for Allied airlifts during the Berlin blockade of 1948–49, **Tempelhof** (THF) today serves domestic and Danish destinations only.

Bus

Berlin is well connected to the rest of Europe by a network of long-distance buses. Most buses arrive at and depart from the **Zentraler Omnibusbahnhof** (ZOB; off Map p439; ☎ 302 5361; Masurenallee 4-6; Ⓜ Kaiserdamm/Witzleben), opposite the Funkturm radio tower. Tickets are available from travel agencies or at the bus station.

Car

Lifts can be organised by **ADM Mitfahrzentrale** (ride-share agencies; ☎ 194 40); Zoo station (Map p439; 🕑 9am-8pm Mon-Fri, 10am-6pm Sat & Sun); Alexanderplatz U-Bahn (Map pp432-3; 🕑 10am-6pm Mon-Fri, 11am-4pm Sat & Sun).

Train

Regular long-distance services arrive at the new Hauptbahnhof (also called Lehrter Bahnhof), with many continuing east to Ostbahnhof and Lichtenberg. You'll probably need to switch to local services to get to the former major terminus of Berlin Zoo (although local petitioning *might* change this). ICE and IC trains leave hourly to every major city in Germany and there are connections to central Europe. Sample fares include to Leipzig (€36, 1¼ hours), Hamburg (€48 to €58, 1½ to two hours), Stralsund (€32.30, three hours) and Prague (€53.80, five hours).

GETTING AROUND

Berlin's public transport system is excellent and much better than driving around the city. The comprehensive network of U-Bahn and S-Bahn trains, buses, trams and ferries covers most corners.

To/From the Airport

There are two principal ways of reaching Schönefeld. The half-hourly S9 travels through all the major downtown stations, taking 45 minutes from Friedrichstrasse. Faster 'Airport Express' trains (mainly RE4, RE5) travel the same route, also half-hourly, taking 31 minutes from the Hauptbahnhof, 21 minutes from Alexanderplatz and 15 minutes from Ostbahnhof. A taxi costs up to €35. The airport station is 400m from the terminal, linked by covered walkway.

Tegel airport is connected by bus 109 to Zoo station, via Kurfürstendamm and Luisenplatz. JetExpress Bus TXL (€4.10) goes via Unter den Linden, Potsdamer Platz and the Reichstag. A taxi between Tegel airport and Zoo station will cost around €20.

Tempelhof airport is reached by the U6 (Platz der Luftbrücke) and by bus 119 from Kurfürstendamm via Kreuzberg. A taxi costs around €15.

Car & Motorcycle

Although garage parking is expensive (about €1.50 per hour), it makes sense to ditch your wheels as soon as possible in Berlin. Few hotels have their own garages.

Public Transport

One type of ticket is valid on all transport – including the U-Bahn, buses, trams and ferries run by **Berliner Verkehrsbetriebe** (☎ 194 49; www.bvg.de) as well as the S-Bahn and regional RE, SE and RB trains operated by **Deutsche Bahn** (www.bahn.de).

Three tariff zones exist – A, B and C. Unless venturing to Potsdam or the outer suburbs, you'll only need an AB ticket. The following are available:

Ticket type	AB	BC	ABC
Single	€2.10	€2.30	€2.60
Day Pass	€5.80	€5.70	€6
Group Day Pass (up to 5 people)	€14.80	€14.30	€15
7-Day Pass	€25.40	€26.20	€31.30

Most tickets are available from vending machines located in the stations, but must be validated before use. If you're caught without a validated ticket, there's a €50 on-the-spot fine.

GAY & LESBIAN BERLIN

Up there with Amsterdam as one of the gayest cities in Europe, Berlin boasts a wild scene reminiscent of the anything-goes 1920s. Venues are concentrated around Nollendorfplatz in Schöneberg and Schönhauser Allee station in northern Prenzlauer Berg. Consult gay and lesbian freebie *Siegessäule* to bone up (oo-er) on the scene.

Dance club SchwuZ (Map pp434-5; ☎ 693 7025; www.schwuz.de; Mehringdamm 61; 🕑 from 11pm Fri & Sat; Ⓜ Mehringdamm) is one of the longest-running mixed institutions; there's a café here all week too.

SO36 (Map pp434-5; ☎ 6140 1307; Oranienstrasse 190; Ⓜ Kottbusser Tor) is a thrashy punk venue also popular with gays and lesbians.

Men cruise at **Grosse Freiheit** (Map p438; Boxhagener Strasse 114; 🕑 from 10pm; Ⓜ Frankfurter Tor) and lesbians hang out at **Schokofabrik** (Map pp434-5; ☎ 615 1561; Mariannenstrasse 6; Ⓜ Kottbusser Tor).

A popular new bar, attracting a mixed crowd is **Zum Schmutzigen Hobby** (Map pp432-3; Rykestrasse 45; 🕑 from 5pm; Ⓜ Eberswalder Strasse) run by well-known drag queen Nina Queer.

U-Bahn and S-Bahn services operate from 4am until just after midnight on weekdays, with many *Nachtbus* (night bus) services in between. At weekends, major U-Bahn lines run every 15 minutes all night, while most S-Bahns operate hourly.

Taxi

Taxi stands are located at all main train stations and throughout the city. Ring **TAXIfon** (☎ 0800-8001 1554) or **Funk Taxi** (☎ 0800-026 1026).

BRANDENBURG

Despite its proximity to Berlin, Brandenburg has suffered from a poor reputation since reunification. Many western Germans still think of Brandenburgers as archetypal Ossis, ambivalent about the demise of the GDR and perhaps even a touch xenophobic. However, even the most sneering Wessi will happily go to Potsdam on a day trip.

POTSDAM

☎ 0331 / pop 131,000

With ornate palaces and manicured gardens dotted around a huge riverside park, the Prussian royal seat of Potsdam is the most popular day trip from Berlin. Elector Friedrich Wilhelm of Brandenburg laid the ground for the town's success when he made it his second residence in the 17th century. But Friedrich II (Frederick the Great) commissioned most of the palaces in the mid-18th century.

In August 1945, the victorious WWII Allies chose nearby Schloss Cecilienhof for the Potsdam Conference, which set the stage for the division of Berlin and Germany into occupation zones.

In the suburb of Babelsberg is the site of a historic – and now once again functioning – film studio (with less historic theme park).

Orientation

Potsdam Hauptbahnhof is just southeast of the city centre, across the Havel River. As this is still quite a way – 2km – from Sansoucci Park, you might like to change here for a train going one or two stops to Charlottenhof (for Schloss Sanssouci) or Sanssouci (for Neues Palais). Some RB trains from Berlin stop at all three stations.

Information

Potsdam Information (☎ 275 580; www.potsdamtourismus.de; Brandenburger Strasse 3; 🕑 9.30am-6pm Mon-Fri, 9.30am-4pm Sat & Sun Apr-Oct, 10am-6pm Mon-Fri, 9.30am-4pm Sat & Sun Nov-Mar) Near the Hauptbahnhof.

Sanssouci Besucherzentrum (☎ 969 4202; www.spsg.de; An der Orangerie 1; 🕑 8.30am-5pm Mar-Oct, 9am-4pm Nov-Feb) Near the windmill and Schloss Sanssouci.

Sights

SANSSOUCI PARK

At the heart of **Sanssouci Park** (adult two-day pass incl all interiors €15; 🕑 dawn-dusk) lies a celebrated rococo palace, **Schloss Sanssouci** (☎ 969 4190; mandatory tour adult/concession €8/5; 🕑 9am-5pm Tue-Sun Apr-Oct, to 4pm Nov-Mar). Built in 1747, it has some glorious interiors. Only 2000 visitors are allowed entry each day (a Unesco rule), so tickets are usually sold by 2.30pm, even in quiet seasons. Tours run by the tourist office guarantee entry.

The late-baroque **Neues Palais** (New Palace; ☎ 969 4255; adult/concession €5/4; 🕑 10am-5pm Sat-Thu) was built in 1769 as the royal family's summer residence. It's one of the most imposing buildings in the park and the one to see if your time is limited. The tour takes in about a dozen of its 200 rooms.

The **Bildergalerie** (Picture Gallery; ☎ 969 4181; adult/concession €2.50/1.50; 🕑 10am-5pm Tue-Sun 15 May-15 Oct) contains a rich collection of 17th-century paintings by Rubens, Caravaggio and other big names.

Many consider the **Chinesisches Haus** (Chinese Teahouse; ☎ 969 4222; admission €1; 🕑 10am-5pm Tue-Sun 15 May-15 Oct) to be the pearl of the park. It's a circular pavilion of gilded columns, palm trees and figures of Chinese musicians and animals, built in 1757. Look out for a monkey with Voltaire's face!

NEUER GARTEN

When outgoing British PM Winston Churchill and his accompanying successor Clement Attlee arrived at **Schloss Cecilienhof** (☎ 969 4244; tours adult/concession €4/3; 🕑 9am-5pm Tue-Sun) in 1945 they must have immediately felt at home. Located in the separate New Garden, northeast of the centre on the bank of the Heiliger See, this is an incongruously English-style country manor in rococo-heavy Potsdam.

Churchill and Attlee, along with US President Truman and Soviet leader Stalin, were

here for the Potsdam Conference on administering postwar Germany. Large photos of the participants are displayed inside.

FILMPARK BABELSBERG

Germany's small retort to Hollywood, the **UFA Film Studios** (☎ 721 2755; www.filmpark.de; Grossbeerenstrasse; adult/concession/child €17/15.50/12.50; ⏲ 10am-6pm 15 Mar-2 Nov) was where Fritz Lang's *Metropolis* was shot, FW Murnau filmed the first Dracula movie, *Nosferatu*, and Marlene Dietrich starred in *The Blue Angel*. Since a relaunch in 1999, it's helped Berlin regain its film-making crown, with Jean-Jacques Annaud's *Enemy at the Gates* and Roman Polanski's *The Pianist* also made here. However, the visitor experience is not that thrilling – just par-for-the-course theme-park rides and a studio tour. The studios are east of the city centre.

ALTSTADT

In April 1945, Royal Air Force bombers devastated the historic centre of Potsdam, including the City Palace on Alter Markt. Fortunately some features – and the palaces of Sanssouci Park – survived undamaged.

The **Brandenburger Tor** (Brandenburg Gate) at the western end of the old town on Luisenplatz isn't a patch on that in Berlin but it is older, dating from 1770. From here, pedestrian Brandenburger Strasse runs due east, providing the town's main eating strip.

Standing out from its surrounds is the pretty **Holländisches Viertel** (Dutch Quarter). Towards the northern end of Friedrich-Ebert-Strasse, it has 134 gabled red-brick houses, built for Dutch workers who came to Potsdam in the 1730s at the invitation of Friedrich Wilhelm I. The homes have been well restored and now house all kinds of interesting galleries, cafés and restaurants.

Tours

Boats belonging to **Weisse Flotte** (☎ 275 9210; www.schiffahrt-in-potsdam.de; Lange Brücke 6; 🕒 8.45am-4.15pm Apr-Oct) cruise the Havel and the lakes around Potsdam, departing regularly from the dock near Lange Brücke, with frequent trips to Wannsee (€8/10 one way/return) and around the castles (€9). Sister company **Haveldampfschiffahrt** (☎ 275 9233; www.schiffahrt-in-potsdam.de; Lange Brücke 6; tours from €9.50) has equivalent steamboat tours.

Getting There & Away

S-Bahn line S7 links central Berlin with Potsdam Hauptbahnhof about every 10 minutes. Some regional (RB/RE) trains from Berlin stop at all three stations in Potsdam. Your ticket must cover Berlin Zones A, B and C (€2.60) to come here.

Getting Around

Potsdam is part of Berlin's S-Bahn network but has its own trams and buses; these converge on Lange Brücke near the Hauptbahnhof. A two-zone ticket costs €1.60 and a day pass €3.70.

SACHSENHAUSEN CONCENTRATION CAMP

In 1936 the Nazis opened a 'model' *Konzentrationslager* (concentration camp) for men in a disused brewery in Sachsenhausen, some 35km north of Berlin. By 1945 about 220,000 prisoners had passed through the gates – labelled, as at Auschwitz in Poland, *Arbeit Macht Frei* (Work Sets You Free). About 100,000 were murdered here.

After the war, the Soviets and the communist leaders of the new GDR set up Speziallager No 7 (Special Camp No 7) for political prisoners, ex-Nazis, monarchists and other 'misfits', jailing 60,000 and killing up to 12,000.

The **Sachsenhausen Memorial and Museum** (☎ 03301-200 200; 🕒 8.30am-6pm Tue-Sun Apr-Sep, 8.30am-4.30pm Oct-Mar) consists of several parts. The **Neues Museum** (New Museum) includes a history of anti-Semitism and audiovisual material. East of it are **Barracks 38 & 39**, reconstructions of two typical huts housing most of the 6000 Jewish prisoners brought to Sachsenhausen after Kristallnacht (9–10 November 1938). Number 38 was rebuilt after being torched by neo-Nazis in September 1992.

The easiest way to get to Sachsenhausen from Berlin is to take the frequent S1 to Oranienburg (€2.60, 50 minutes). The walled camp is a signposted 20-minute walk from Oranienburg station.

SAXONY

Saxony is in many ways the most successful of the old East German states. Leipzig is a growing city with a dynamic centre. Dresden is a major tourist draw and is nearing the culmination of decades of rebuilding. Linked to the latter by the fabled Elbe River, Meissen is a gem of a medieval town with a palace and cathedral high on a hill.

With a long history dating back to the Germanic tribes of over 1000 years ago, Saxony embodies many of the classic qualities associated with Germany. Its two main cities have a long tradition in the arts and are today centres of culture. And even though the local dialect can be impenetrable to those with mere schoolbook German, that same classic German traces its roots right back here.

The state is fairly compact and highspeed rail links make the region easily accessible from all corners of Germany.

DRESDEN

☎ 0351 / pop 483,000

In death, Dresden became even more famous than in life. In life, she was famous throughout Europe as 'Florence on the Elbe', owing to the efforts of Italian artists, musicians, actors and master craftsmen who flocked to the court of Augustus the Strong, bestowing countless masterpieces upon the city. Shortly before the end of WWII, Allied bombers blasted and incinerated much of the historic centre, a beautiful jewel-like area dating from the 18th century. More than 35,000 died and in bookstores throughout town you can you can see books showing the destruction (or read about it in Kurt Vonnegut's classic *Slaughterhouse Five*).

Rebuilding began under the communist regime in the 1950s and accelerated greatly after reunification. The city celebrated its 800th anniversary in 2006 and the event was capped by opening Frauenkirche, an icon that had been a pile of rubble for the previous five decades. With a beautiful baroque centre and vibrant nightlife, Dresden is a major tourist attraction that's best enjoyed outside of the peak summer season.

Orientation

The Elbe River splits the town in a rough V-shape, with the Neustadt to the north and the Altstadt to the south.

Dresden has two main train stations: the Hauptbahnhof on the southern side of town, and the contemporary Dresden-Neustadt north of the river. Most trains stop at both. Dresden-Mitte is little more than a forlorn platform between the two.

From the Hauptbahnhof, pedestrian-only Prager Strasse leads north into the Altstadt. Here there's a mix of communist-era triumphalism and modern-day commercialism. The lovely Brühlsche Terrasse runs along the Elbe between the Albertinum and the Zwinger, with boat docks below.

In the Neustadt, home to much of the city's nightlife, the main attractions for visitors are the Albertplatz and Antonstadt quarters. In and around Louisenstrasse you'll find all manner of shops, galleries, funky boutiques and dozens of cafés, bars and clubs. Hauptstrasse is pedestrianised and connects Albert platz with the Augustusbrücke.

Information

Dresden Information Prager Strasse 21 (☎ 4919 2100; www.dresden.de); Theaterplatz 2 (🕑 10am-6pm Mon-Fri, 10am-4pm Sat & Sun) Discount cards from €19.

E@sy Internet (☎ 017-2579 5652; Pfarrgasse 1; per hr €4; 🕑 9am-midnight) Note that wi-fi access and Internet terminals are common in Dresden's cafés.

Haus Des Buches (☎ 497 369; Dr-Külz-Ring 12) Bookshop with huge selection on local history and culture.

Sights

MONUMENTS & LANDMARKS

One of Dresden's most beloved icons, the **Frauenkirche** (Church of Our Lady; ☎ 439 3934; www.frauenkirche-dresden.org; Neumarkt; 🕑 10am-6pm) was rebuilt in time for city's 800th anniversary celebrations. Built between 1726 and 1743 under the direction of baroque architect George Bähr, it was Germany's greatest Protestant church until February 1945, when bombing raids flattened it. The communists decided to leave the rubble as a war memorial; after reunification, calls for reconstruction prevailed and the huge project began in 1992.

Look for the very few blackened stones on the exterior, these were salvaged from the rubble of the original. Otherwise – not surprisingly – the church feels brand new, especially inside. Most moving is the melted cross from the original. You can also climb to the top for good views. The surrounding Neumarkt is part of a massive redevelopment designed to evoke prewar Dresden.

The neo-Renaissance opera house, **Semperoper** (☎ 491 1496; www.semperoper.de; Theaterplatz; tour adult/child €6/3; 🕑 varies), designed by Gustav Semper, *is* Dresden. The original building opened in 1841 but burned down less than three decades later. Rebuilt in 1878, it was pummelled in WWII and reopened in 1985 after the communists invested millions restoring it. The best way to appreciate it is through one of the many performances.

The **Schloss** (☎ 491 4619; Schlossplatz), a massive neo-Renaissance palace, has ongoing restoration projects. Its many features include the **Hausmannsturm** (Servants' Tower; adult/child €2.50/1.50; 🕑 10am-6pm Wed-Mon) and the baroque Catholic **Hofkirche** (🕑 9am-5pm Mon-Thu, 1-5pm Fri, 10am-5pm Sat, noon-4pm Sun), which contains the heart of Augustus the Strong. Outside, you'd need a really wide-angle lens to get a shot of Wulhelm Walther's amazing 102m-long tiled mural, the **Fürstenzug** (Procession of Princes; Augustusstrasse), on the wall of the former Stendehaus (Royal Stables). The scene, a long row of royalty on horses, was painted in 1876 and then transferred to some 24,000 Meissen porcelain tiles in 1906. The Schloss also houses museums, see below.

MUSEUMS

For information on most of Dresden's museums, see the website www.skd-dresden.de. Allow at least two full days for a sampling of what's on offer.

The imposing block, **Albertinum** (☎ 491 4619; Brühlsche Terrasse; adult/child €5/2.50; 🕑 10am-6pm Wed-Mon), houses many of Dresden's art treasures, including the **Münzkabinett** collection of antique coins and medals, and the **Skulpturensammlung**, which includes classical and Egyptian works. The **Galerie Neue Meister**, with renowned 19th- and 20th-century paintings from leading French and German impressionists, was closed during 2006 for expansion and renovation.

Dresden's elaborate 1728 fortress **Zwinger** (☎ 491 4622; Theaterplatz 1; 🕒 10am-6pm Tue-Sun) is an attraction in its own right, with a popular ornamental courtyard, and also houses six major museums. The most important are the **Rüstkammer** (armoury; adult/child €3/2), with its superb collection of ceremonial weapons, and the **Galerie Alte Meister** (adult/child €6/3.50,

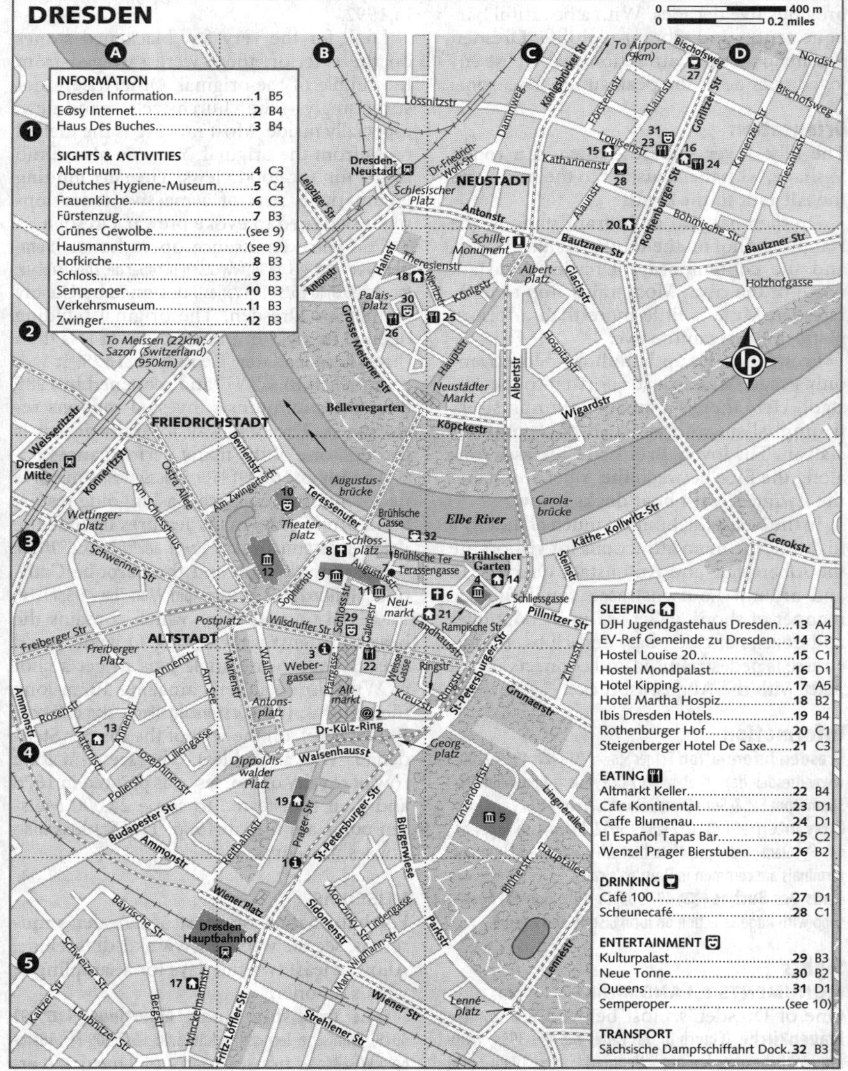

incl entry to Rüstkammer), which features masterpieces including Raphael's *Sistine Madonna*. The dazzling **Porzelansammlung** (Porcelain Collection; adult/child €5/3) is another highlight.

Located in the Schloss, the **Grünes Gewölbe** (Green Vault; adult/child €6/3.50; 10am-6pm Wed-Mon) is one of the world's finest collections of jewel-encrusted precious objects. Treasures include the world's biggest green diamond, tiny pearl sculptures and a stunning group of 137 gem-studded figures by Johann Melchior Dinglinger, court jeweller of Augustus the Strong.

Also in the Schloss, the **Verkehrsmuseum** (Transport Museum; ☎ 864 40; Augustusstrasse 1; adult/child €3/1.50; 10am-5pm Tue-Sun) is fittingly located in the Johanneum, the old stables. Motoring back towards the 20th century, this is a fascinating collection including penny-farthings, trams, dirigibles and carriages. Included in the admission is a great 40-minute film with original black-and-white footage of 1930s Dresden.

One of the oddest museums is the product of a mouthwash baron. The **Deutsches Hygiene-Museum** (☎ 484 6670; Lingnerplatz 1; adult/child €6/3; 10am-6pm Tue-Sun) is awash in displays relating to the ravages of venereal disease, the theory of eugenics and reasons to bathe.

Tours

Cruise the Elbe on the world's oldest fleet of paddle-wheel steamers with **Sächsische Dampfschiffahrt** (☎ 866 090; www.saechsische-dampfschiffahrt.de; adult/child €11/5.50). Ninety-minute tours leave from the Terrassenufer dock at 11am, 1pm, 3pm and 5pm daily. There's also service to villages along the river.

Sleeping

Accommodation in Dresden can be very expensive in the high season. Luckily, several good-value budget places can be found in the lively Neustadt. New luxury hotels are opening as the Altstadt is renovated.

BUDGET

DJH Jugendgästehaus Dresden (☎ 492 620; jghdresden@djh-sachsen.de; Maternistrasse 22; dm €17;) This tower block was once a Communist Party training centre; now it's a great hostel, with 480 beds in small dorms and a bistro (breakfast included). Take tram 7 or 10 to the corner of Ammonstrasse and Freiberger Strasse.

Hostel Louise 20 (☎ 889 4894; www.louise20.de; Louisenstrasse 20; dm/s/d €15/30/40;) Rooms are divided between two buildings here. Basic ones are off a courtyard at the back while more expensive – and stylish – units are up front. Families can rent entire suites of rooms. There are kitchen facilities; most rooms share baths.

Hostel Mondpalast (☎ 804 6061; www.mondpalast.de; Louisenstrasse 77; dm/s/d €15/39/50;) The Moon Palace has rooms decorated by theme (Australia, Greece, space travel – see the website) and a great bar/café. It's one of many good value places in this fun-filled neighbourhood.

EV-Ref Gemeinde zu Dresden (☎ 438 230; www.ev-ref-gem-dresden.de; Brühlscher Garten 4; s/d €45/70) Amazing value in a great location – right across from the Albertinum and on the river. This historic retirement home makes rooms available for travellers whenever a resident has permanently 'checked out'. Rooms have baths and TV and often great views, although obviously they'd prefer you keep quiet.

MIDRANGE

Hotel Kipping (☎ 478 500; www.hotel-kipping.de; Winckelmannstrasse 6; s/d from €75/90;) Just south of the Hauptbahnhof, this is a family-run, family-friendly hotel that comes with 20 comfortable rooms in a house right out of the *Addams Family*. The bar and café are especially appealing and there's wi-fi.

Ibis Dresden Lilienstein (☎ 4856 6663; www.ibishotel.com; Prager Strasse 13; r €50-120;) Together with the adjoining Ibis Dresden Bastei and the Ibis Dresden Königstein, this huge communist-era complex has over 900 rooms. The décor has been redone in 'cheap and cheerful' and pluses include wi-fi and a good chance at a vacancy in summer. The breakfast buffet is vast.

Hotel Martha Hospiz (☎ 817 60; www.vch.de; Nieritzstrasse 11; r €54-120;) Quiet reigns in this 50-room inn with country furnishings, built over 100 years ago by a church. The location is central and it has many amenities, including wi-fi.

Rothenburger Hof (☎ 812 60; www.rothenburger-hof.de; Rothenburger Strasse 15-17; r €75-140;) In the middle of Neustadt you'll find this well-appointed 26-room place in a renovated 1865 mansion. It offers many health treatments in its spa and sauna.

TOP END

Steigenberger Hotel De Saxe (☎ 438 60; www.desaxe-dresden.steigenberger.com; Neumarkt 9; r from €200; ☒ ☒ ☐) This 178-room grand hotel opened in 2006 on the site of a historic hotel of the same name. It's part of the scheme to recreate the prewar Neumarkt around the Frauenkirche. The hotel offers a spa, sauna, wi-fi and many more luxuries.

Eating

It's no problem finding somewhere to eat in the Neustadt, with oodles of cafés and restaurants found along Königstrasse and the streets north of Albertplatz. This is definitely the most interesting part of town at night. South of the river, look near the Altmarkt, and Münzgasse/Terrassengasse, between Brühlsche Terrasse and the Frauenkirche, for restaurants representing all kinds of local and international cuisine.

Cafe Kontinental (☎ 801 3531; Görlitzer Strasse 1; mains €5-15; 24hr; ☐) A bustling place open around the clock, this trendy café caters to a broad swath of Neustadt characters.

Caffe Blumenau (☎ 802 6502; Louisenstrasse 67; mains €5-15; 8am-2am; ☐) Flowers abound in this beautiful café and bar, which also has a sunny back patio. A long breakfast menu is served through the day as well as sandwiches, salads, pasta and cakes.

Wenzel Prager Bierstuben (☎ 804 2010; Königstrasse 1; mains €7-20; 11am-midnight) This busy beer hall serves up oceans of Czech lager under arched brick ceilings. Always crowded, the menu leans towards traditional meaty mains. The garlic soup is sublime, the cured pork with horseradish a delight.

El Español Tapas Bar (☎ 804 8670; An der Dreikönigskirche 7; meals €7-20; 11am-1am) On a leafy square overlooking the newly restored Three Kings Church, this tapas place glows with good seasoning and good cheer. When it's warm dine on the square, when it's cold settle into the woodsy interior. The tapas menu is long and varied.

Altmarkt Keller (☎ 481 8130; Altmarkt 4; mains €8-25; 11am-midnight) The foods of Saxony and neighbouring Bohemia (in the Czech Republic) are featured in this underground restaurant. Look for lots of hearty pork and beef dishes and as well as all manner of dumplings. On many nights there's live music that gets the tourist toes a-tapping.

Drinking & Entertainment

As elsewhere, many of the places listed under Eating above are also good just for a drink.

Dresden is synonymous with opera, and performances at the spectacular **Semperoper** (☎ 491 1496; www.semperoper.de; Theaterplatz) are brilliant. Tickets cost from €10, but they're usually booked out well in advance. Some performances by the renowned philharmonic are also held there, but most are in the communist-era **Kulturpalast** (☎ 486 60; www.kulturpalast-dresden.de; Schlossstrasse 2), which hosts a wide range of concerts and events.

Neue Tonne (☎ 802 6017; www.jazzclubtonne.de; Königstrasse 15; entry free-€15) This well-known place has live music almost nightly.

Scheunecafé (☎ 802 6619; Alaunstrasse 36-40; mains €7-12) Set back from the street, Indian food, a vast beer garden, live music and deejays all combine here for a fun and funky stew.

Café 100 (☎ 801 7729; Alaunstrasse 100) Off a courtyard, you'll pass hundreds of empty bottles on the way in, a foreshadowing of the lengthy wine list and delights that follow. Candles give the underground space a romantic yet edgy glow.

Queens (☎ 810 8108; Görlitzerstrasse 3) This hopping gay bar/lounge/disco is a good first stop to find out what's happening locally.

Getting There & Around

Dresden's **airport** (DRS; www.dresden-airport.de), served by Lufthansa, DBA, Air Berlin among others, is 9km north of the city centre, on S-Bahn line 2 (€1.70, 30 minutes). The Airport City Liner bus serves Dresden-Neustadt (€3) and the Hauptbahnhof (€4), with stops at key points in town. A taxi to the Hauptbahnhof is about €15.

Dresden is well linked to the regular service through the day to Leipzig (€26, 70 minutes), Berlin-Hauptbahnhof by IC/EC train (€30.20, 2¼ hours) and Frankfurt-am-Main (€76, 4½ hours).

Dresden's **public transport network** (www.dvbag.de) charges €1.70 for a single ticket; day tickets cost €4.50. Tram 3, 6, 7 and 8 provide good links between the Hauptbahnhof and Neustadt.

AROUND DRESDEN

Meissen

☎ 03521 / pop 29,000

Some 27km northwest of Dresden, Meissen is a compact, perfectly preserved old town and the centre of a rich wine-growing region. It makes for a good day trip out of Dresden by train or boat and beguiles with its red-tiled roofs and historic charm.

Meissen's medieval fortress, the Albrechtsburg, crowns a ridge high above the Elbe River and contains the former ducal palace and Meissen Cathedral, a magnificent Gothic structure. Augustus the Strong of Saxony created Europe's first porcelain factory here in 1710. The town celebrated its 1075th anniversary in 2004.

Like Dresden, Meissen straddles the Elbe River, with the old town on the western bank and the train station on the eastern. Both sides were struck by record flood levels in 2002, with water pushing quite a distance into the Altstadt; look out for plaques marking the highest points. Cafés line the streets and are popular on warm days.

The tourist office is at **Meissen-Information** (☎ 419 40; www.touristinfo-meissen.de; Markt 3; ⌚ 10am-6pm Mon-Fri, to 4pm Sat & Sun, to 4pm Mon-Fri, to 3pm Sat Nov-Mar). Staff can help find accommodation.

Steep stepped lanes lead up to Meissen's towering 13th-century **Albrechtsburg Cathedral** (☎ 452 490; Domplatz 7; adult/child €3.50/2; ⌚ 10am-6pm Mar-Oct, 10am-4pm Nov-Feb), which contains an altarpiece by Lucas Cranach the Elder.

Beside the cathedral is the remarkable 15th-century **palace** (☎ 470 70; Domplatz 1; adult/child €3.50/2.50; ⌚ 10am-6pm Mar-Oct, to 5pm Nov-Feb), widely seen as the birthplace of Schloss architecture, with its ingenious system of internal arches. A combined ticket for both buildings costs adult/child €5/2.50.

Meissen has long been renowned for its chinaware, with its trademark insignia of blue crossed swords. The Albrechtsburg palace was originally the manufacturing site, but the factory is now 1km southwest of the Altstadt in an appropriately beautiful building, the **Porzellan Manufaktur** (Porcelain Factory; ☎ 468 700; Talstrasse 9; adult/child €8/4; ⌚ 9am-6pm May-Oct, 9am-5pm Nov-Apr), which dates to 1916. There are often long queues for the workshop demonstrations, but you can view the porcelain collection upstairs at your leisure.

GETTING THERE & AWAY

Half-hourly S-Bahn trains run from Dresden's Hauptbahnhof and Neustadt train stations (€5.10, 45 minutes). To visit the porcelain factory, get off at Meissen-Triebischtal (one stop after Meissen).

A more interesting way to get here is by steamer (between May and September). Boats leave from the Sächsische Dampfschiffahrt (see p451) dock in Dresden at 9.45am and head back at 2.45pm (€16.10 return, two hours).

Saxon Switzerland

Sächsische Schweiz (Saxon Switzerland) is a 275 sq km national park 50km south of Dresden, near the Czech border. Its wonderfully wild, craggy country is dotted with castles and tiny towns along the mighty Elbe. The landscape varies unexpectedly and radically: its forests can look deceptively tropical, while the worn cliffs and plateaus recall the parched expanses of New Mexico or central Spain (generally without the searing heat).

The highlight of the park is the **Bastei** lookout, on the Elbe some 28km southeast of Dresden. One of the most breathtaking spots in the whole of Germany, it features towering outcrops 305m high and unparalleled views of the surrounding forests, cliffs and mountains, not to mention a magnificent sightline right along the river itself.

LEIPZIG

☎ 0341 / pop 498,000

Leipzig is the busiest city in Saxony, a livelier alternative to Dresden. Although it lacks the capital's bus-load of museums, Leipzig in many ways feels more vibrant in an everyday sense. It's not weighed down by the past and like its shopping passages, invites exploration.

Leipzig also has some of the finest classical music and opera in the country, and its art and literary scenes are flourishing. Once home to Bach, Wagner and Mendelssohn, and to Goethe (who set a key scene of *Faust* in the cellar of his favourite watering hole), it more recently earned the sobriquet *Stadt der Helden* (City of Heroes) for its leading role in the 1989 democratic revolution.

The city has a compact centre worth wandering and a growing arts scene. It's definitely worth a day or two of your travels.

Orientation

Leipzig's centre lies within a ring road that outlines the town's medieval fortifications. To reach the city centre from the Hauptbahnhof, cross Willy-Brandt-Platz and continue south along Nikolaistrasse for five minutes.

The central Markt (square), which was being redeveloped for a new station at the time of research, is a couple of blocks southwest, and east down Grimmiasche Strasse is the massive Augustusplatz, home to some of the city's most important (if not prettiest) GDR-era buildings and also the modern MDR Tower.

The Hauptbahnhof contains a modern mall with over 140 shops and (radically for Germany) it is open from 6am to 10pm daily. You'll find good bookshops, a post office, banks and much more. There's wi-fi in the DB Lounge.

Information

Internetcafé (☎ 993 9530; Reichsstrasse 18; per 15 min €1; 🕑 10am-10pm) A full service shop for CD burning and Internet.

Leipzig Tourist Service (☎ 710 4260; www.leipzig.de; Richard-Wagner-Strasse 1; 🕑 9am-7pm Mon-Fri, 9am-4pm Sat, 9am-2pm Sun) One of the most helpful in Germany, with discount cards from €7.40.

Sights

Don't rush from sight to sight – wandering around Leipzig is a pleasure in itself, with many of the blocks around the central Markt crisscrossed by old internal shopping passages. Four good ones: **Steibs Hof** (100-year-old blue tiles and classic cafés), **Specs Hof** (soaring atrium, bookshops, cafés), **Jägerhofpassage** (galleries, theatre, antiques) and the classic **Mädlerpassage** (grand design, the famous Auerbachs Keller, see p456).

MONUMENTS & LANDMARKS

Off the southern ring road is the 108m-high tower of the baroque **Neues Rathaus** (new town hall; ☎ 1230; Martin-Luther-Ring; 🕑 7am-4.30pm Mon-Fri). Though the origins date to the 16th century, its current manifestation was completed in 1905. The interior makes it one of the finest municipal buildings in Germany; the lobby houses rotating art exhibitions, mostly on historical themes.

Located 4km southeast of the centre, the **Völkerschlachtdenkmal** (Battle of Nations Monument; Strasse des 18 Oktober; adult/child €3/1.50; 🕑 10am-6pm Apr-Oct, to 4pm Nov-Mar) is a massive 91m-high monument commemorating the decisive victory here by the combined Prussian, Austrian and Russian forces over Napoleon's army in 1813. Climb the 500 steps for a view of the region. Take tram 15 from the station (direction Meusdorf).

MUSEUMS

Leipzig's finest museum, the **Museum der Bildenden Künste** (Museum of Fine Arts; ☎ 216 990; Grimmaische Strasse 1-7; adult/child €5/3.50; 🕑 10am-6pm Tue & Thu-Sun, 10am-8pm Wed), is housed in a stunning new building that provides both a dramatic – and echoey – backdrop to its collection, which spans old masters and the latest efforts of local artists.

Haunting and uplifting by turns, the **Zeitgeschichtliches Forum** (Forum of Contemporary History; ☎ 222 20; Grimmaische Strasse 6; admission free; 🕑 9am-6pm Tue-Fri, 10am-6pm Sat & Sun) tells the story of the GDR from division and dictatorship to resistance and reform. It does a good job of chronicling the 1989 revolution, which started here and it captures the tragic drama of the original Iron Curtain division.

Former headquarters of the East German secret police, the **Stasi Museum** (☎ 961 2443; Dittrichring 24; admission free; 🕑 10am-6pm) has exhibits on propaganda, amazingly hokey disguises, surveillance photos and other forms of 'intelligence'. There are also mounds of papier-mâché that were created when officers shredded and soaked secret documents before the fall of the GDR.

Opposite the Thomaskirche, is the **Bach Museum** (☎ 964 110; Thomaskirchhof 16; adult/child €3/2; 🕑 10am-5pm), where JS Bach worked from 1723 until his death in 1750. This collection focuses on the composer's busy life in Leipzig. There are portraits, manuscripts and other Bach memorabilia.

ART

Leipzig has a thriving art scene thanks to the Art Academy of Leipzig, a famous old school where figurative painting never went out of style. Now the efforts of its many local grads such as Neo Rauch, Tim Eitel and Tilo Baumgärtel are all the rage. You can see some of the best works at the Museum der Bildenden Künste (see above) or you can go out to the many **galleries** found along Spinnereisstrasse, 2km west of the centre (take tram 14 to stop S-Bf. Miltitzer Allee). The tourist office has useful gallery information.

Sleeping

Leipzig Tourist Service (see left) offers free booking in private homes near the centre. Average cost is €30 to €45.

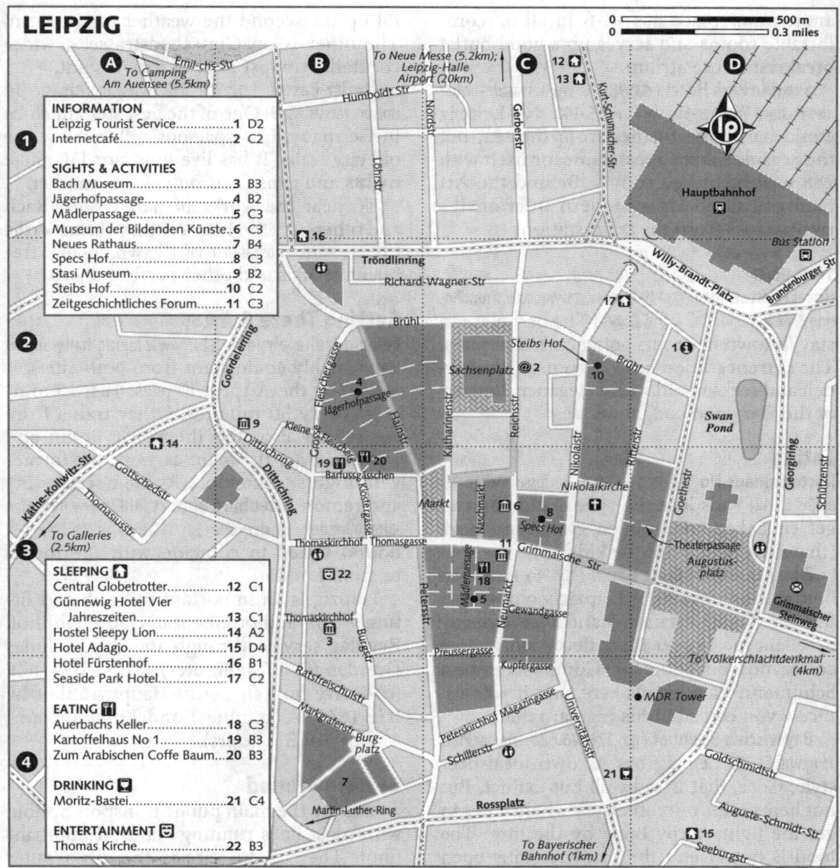

BUDGET

Camping Am Auensee (☎ 465 1600; www.motel-auensee.de; Gustav-Esche-Strasse 5; camp sites per person from €3, cabins €28-35) This camping ground is in a pleasant wooded spot on the city's northwestern outskirts (take tram 10 or 28 to Wahren). The cabins are A-frame bungalows.

Central Globetrotter (☎ 149 8960; www.globetrotter-leipzig.de; Kurt-Schumacher-Strasse 41; dm €14, s/d €24/36; 💻) In a busy location just north of the train station, this 80-room hostel offers bare-bones accommodation, although some rooms boast murals, albeit ones that won't win any scholarships to the Art Academy of Leipzig.

Hostel Sleepy Lion (☎ 993 9480; www.hostel-leipzig.de; Käthe-Kollwitz-Strasse 3; dm €15, s/d €28/40; ⊠ 💻) All rooms have their own baths at this 59-room facility in a renovated building. Some come with fake trees as well.

MIDRANGE

Midrange accommodation in the centre is fairly unexciting and usually the preserve of the big chains (particularly the many Accor brands).

Hotel Adagio (☎ 216 699; www.hotel-adagio.de; Seeburgstrasse 96; r €72-95; ⊠) The 32 rooms here are smartly decked out with a black-and-white theme. You can take breakfast in the garden and there's a certain intimate charm.

Günnewig Hotel Vier Jahreszeiten (☎ 985 10; www.gunnewig.de; Kurt-Schumacher-Strasse 23; r €60-130; ⊠ 💻) Close to the train station, this anonymous place has wi-fi in all 67 comfortable rooms and serves up a good buffet breakfast in the atrium.

Seaside Park Hotel (☎ 985 20; www.seaside-hotels.de; Richard-Wagner-Strasse 7; r €95-140;) Leipzig could hardly be further from the sea, but the Seaside makes a real name for itself with 288 well-furnished rooms. Behind the Art Nouveau façade is a modern interior. It's right across from the train station.

TOP END

Hotel Fürstenhof (☎ 1400; www.starwood.de; Tröndlinring 8; r €135-350;) The best place to stay in town has roots going back 200 years. The current edition has 92 rooms, a fine garden and reeks of old world elegance. It's part of the Starwood conglomerate.

Eating

Kartoffelhaus No 1 (☎ 960 4603; Barfussgässchen 12; mains €6-12) Kids love the spuds, and you can get 'em baked, fried, boiled, grilled and more (that's the tubers not the kids).

Zum Arabischen Coffe Baum (☎ 965 1321; Kleine Fleischergasse 4; mains €6-15) Leipzig's oldest coffee bar has a restaurant and café offering excellent meals over three floors, plus a free coffee museum at the top. Composer Robert Schumann met friends here, and if you ask nicely you can sit at his regular table.

Bayerischer Bahnhof (☎ 124 5760; Bayerischer Platz 1; mains €7-20) Leipzig has its own local beer style, Gose, that is sadly all but extinct. But not here at this microbrewery where you can get the light, herby brew by the litre. The food is hearty and the place remains open while the real train station is rebuilt next door. Take tram 9, 10 or 16.

Auerbachs Keller (☎ 216 100; www.auerbachs-keller-leipzig.de; Mädlerpassage; mains €14-22) Founded in 1525, Auerbachs Keller is one of Germany's classic restaurants, serving typically hearty fare. Goethe's *Faust – Part I* includes a scene here, in which Mephistopheles and Faust carouse with some students before they ride off on a barrel. The historic section of the restaurant includes the Goethe room and the Fasskeller; note the carved tree-trunk in the latter, depicting the whole barrel-riding adventure.

Drinking & Entertainment

Barfussgässchen and Kleine Flieschergasse, west of the Markt, form one of Leipzig's two 'pub miles', packed with outdoor tables that fill up the second the weather turns warm. The other is on Gottschedstrasse, a wider cocktail strip just west of the Altstadt.

Moritz-Bastei (☎ 702 590; www.moritzbastei.de; Universitätsstrasse 9) One of the best student clubs in Germany, in a spacious cellar below the old city walls. It has live music or DJs most nights and runs films outside in summer.

To hear the works of native-born Bach and others, try the 18th-century **Thomaskirche** (☎ 212 4676; Thomaskirchhof 18), which has frequent recitals and other performances.

Getting There & Away

Leipzig-Halle airport (LEJ; www.leipzig-halle-airport.de), roughly equidistant from both cities, is served by the Airport Express (€4, 15 minutes) every 30 minutes. Other trains from the region also stop there. Air Berlin and Lufthansa are the main carriers, the former with flights to London. Ryanair serves tiny and remote **Altenburg airport** (ADC; www.flughafen-altenburg.de). There's a shuttle bus (€14, 1¾ hours) timed to coincide with the flights to/from London.

Leipzig is an important rail hub and fittingly has a monumental Hauptbahnhof. Regular service through the day includes Dresden (€26, 70 minutes), Munich by ICE (€74, five hours), Berlin-Hauptbahnhof by ICE (€36, 70 minutes) and Frankfurt-am-Main (€61, 3½ hours).

Getting Around

Trams are the main public transport option, with most lines running via the Hauptbahnhof. The S-Bahn circles the city's outer suburbs. A single ticket costs €1.70 and a day card €4.90. A vast project of building an S-Bahn line under the city centre is due for completion in 2009.

THURINGIA

Thuringa likes to trade on its reputation as the 'Green Heart' of Germany, an honour helped by the former GDR's dodgy economy, which limited development. These days its main towns of Erfurt, Weimar and Eisenach are popular for their historic centres and deserve visits, even if it's just a break in a train journey.

While the communist era may have been relatively benign, the previous decades were not. The Nazis had numerous concentration camps here including the notorious Buchenwald and the nightmare of Mittelbau Dora. But yet again, in contrast, Weimar was the place where Germany tried a liberal democracy in the 1920s and in previous centuries it was home to notables such as Bach, Schiller, Goethe, Thomas Mann and many more.

ERFURT

☎ 0361 / pop 202,000

Thuringia's capital was founded by St Boniface as a bishopric in 742. In the Middle Ages the city shot to prominence and prosperity as an important trading post. The Altstadt's many well-preserved 16th-century and later buildings attest to its wealth.

During WWII, damage was extensive, and the GDR regime did little to restore the city's former glories. Over the past decade, however, Erfurt has spiffed up what it has and a stroll through the old streets and across the rivers is a delight.

Orientation

Most of the car traffic is routed around the Altstadt via two ring roads, making it a pleasure to walk between the main sights. The train and bus stations are just beyond the southeastern edge of the town centre, and were undergoing a massive reconstruction at the time of research. It's a five-minute walk north along Bahnhofstrasse to Anger, the main shopping and business artery. The little Gera River bisects the Altstadt, spilling off into numerous creeks.

Information

Erfurt Tourismus (☎ 664 00; www.erfurt-tourist-info.de; Benediktsplatz 1; ⌚ 10am-7pm Mon-Fri, to 4pm Sat & Sun) Has a discount card from €9.90.

Internettreff (☎ 262 3834; Ratskellerpassage, Fischmarkt 5; per hr €1.50; ⌚ 1-8pm Mon-Sat) Has Internet access.

Sights

It's hard to miss Erfurt's cathedral, **Dom St Marien** (☎ 646 1265; Domplatz; tours adult/child €2.50/1.50; ⌚ 9am-5pm Mon-Fri, to 4pm Sat, 1-5pm Sun, less in winter), which casts its massive shadow over Domplatz from an artificial hill built specially to hold it. Ironically, it was originally only planned as a simple chapel in 752; by the time it was completed it was the rather strange, huge amalgam you see today (if only a divine hand could reach down and rearrange things a bit…). In July the stone steps leading up to the cathedral are the site of the **Domstufenfestspiele**, where operas are performed against the dramatic background.

Next to the cathedral, the 1280 **Severikirche** (☎ 576 960; ⌚ 9am-12.30pm & 1.30-5pm Mon-Fri, less in winter) is an impressive five-aisled church hall boasting a stone Madonna (1345) and a 15m-high baptismal font (1467), as well as the sarcophagus of St Severus, whose remains were brought to Erfurt in 836.

The **Augustinerkloster** (☎ 576 600; Augustinerstrasse; adult/child €6/5; ⌚ tours 10am-noon & 2-5pm Tue-Sat, 11am-2pm Sun), now a nunnery, has a strong pedigree: Martin Luther was a monk here from 1505 to 1511 and, after being ordained beneath the chapel's stained-glass windows, read his first mass. You can view Luther's cell and an exhibit on the Reformation. The grounds and church are free.

North of the Dom complex and west of Andreasstrasse, many of the city's lesser churches were demolished to erect the impressively tough-looking **Citadelle Petersberg** (Petersberg fortress; ☎ 211 5270) – hence the reason why Erfurt has so many steeples without churches attached. There is a fascinating series of subterranean tunnels within the thick walls, which can only be seen on a guided tour from the tourist office.

Unique in this part of Europe, the medieval **Krämerbrücke** (Merchants' Bridge) is an 18m-wide, 120m-long curiosity spanning the Gera River. Quaint houses and shops line both sides of the narrow road.

Sleeping

Jugendherberge Hochheimerstrasse (☎ 6013 2600; www.djh.de; Hochheimer Strasse 12; dm from €17; ⊠ 💻) This modern 200-bed hostel is 2km south of the city (take tram 5 to Steigerstrasse).

Pension am Dom (☎ 55048660; www.pension-am-dom-erfurt.de; Lange Brücke 57; r €29-69; ⊠) True to its name, this friendly little central *pension* has superb views of the cathedral from the breakfast room and terrace. Rooms are light and airy with natural wood floors. It's located over some trendy stores.

InterCity Hotel (☎ 560 00; www.intercityhotel.com; Willy-Brandt-Platz 11; r €60-120; ⊠ ❄ 💻) Part of the new train station complex, this modern and comfortable abode has good views of the choo-choos and is convenient for the centre. It has wi-fi.

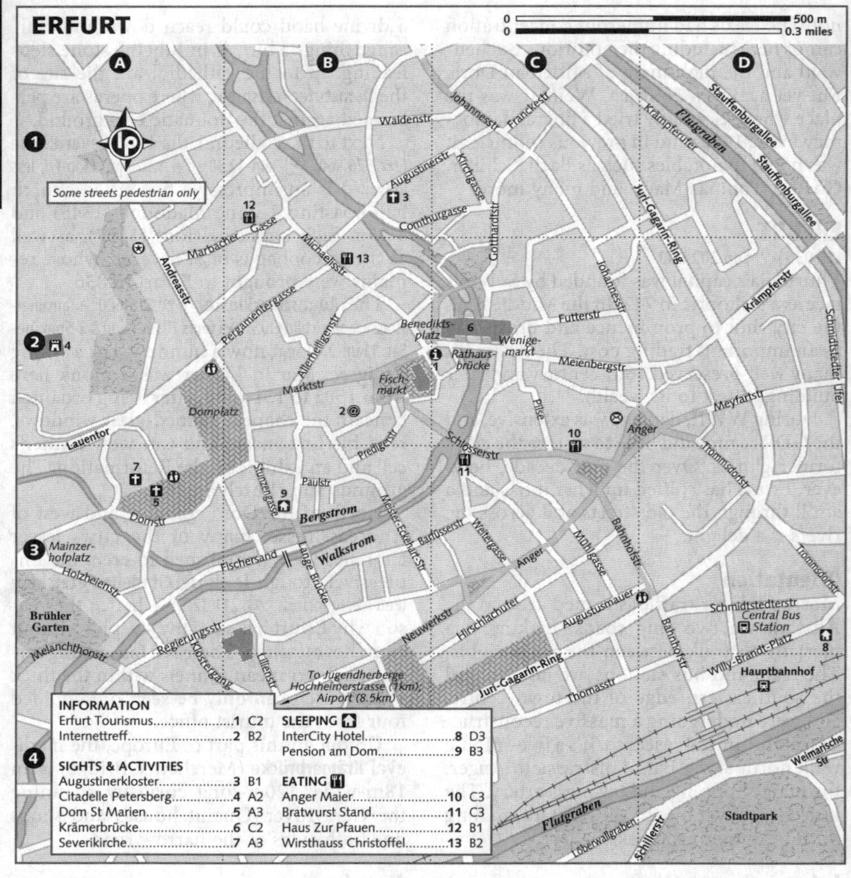

Eating

Look for interesting and trendy restaurants and cafés along Michaelisstrasse and Marbacher Gasse. For a quick treat, have a *Thuringer Bratwurst* hot off the grill from a **stand** (☎ 793 5250; Schlösserstrasse; meal €1.50) near a small waterfall.

Wirsthauss Christoffel (☎ 262 6943; Michaelisstrasse 41; mains €6-11) History oozes out of the wooden walls at this quaint little café. As the name implies, local sausage is a house specialty. On some nights films are shown in the basement.

Anger Maier (☎ 566 1058; Schlösserstrasse 8; mains €6-12) This tunnel-like restaurant is an Erfurt institution, with cheap, quality eats in a busy, smoky old warren.

Haus Zur Pfauen (☎ 211 5209; Marbacher Gasse 12; mains €7-10) An atmospheric microbrewery with a large beer garden and tasty brews. If you're reduced to crawling, you might just head upstairs to the simple rooms (accommodation from €45).

Getting There & Around

Erfurt's Hauptbahnhof is on a line with frequent service linking Leipzig (€25, one hour), Weimar (€7, 15 minutes) and Eisenach (€9 to €17, 30 to 50 minutes). Hourly ICE/IC service goes to Frankfurt (€46, 2½ hours) and Berlin-Hauptbahnhof (€47, 2¾ hours).

Public transport in the city centre costs €1.50 but you're likely to just walk.

AROUND ERFURT

Eisenach is home to the Wartburg, the only German castle to be named a Unesco World Heritage Site. Composer Johann Sebastian Bach was born here but he plays second fiddle to the amazing edifice in stone and half-timber high on the hill.

The small town has a good **tourist office** (☎ 792 30; www.eisenach.de; Markt 9; ⏰ 10am-6pm Mon, 9am-6pm Tue-Fri, 10am-2pm Sat & Sun), which can help you find accommodation if your day trip gets extended.

The **Wartburg** (☎ 2500; www.wartburg-eisenach.de; tour adult/child €6/3; ⏰ tours 8.30am-5pm), parts of which date to the 11th century, is perched high above the town on a wooded hill, is said to go back to Count Ludwig der Springer (the Jumper); you'll hear the story of how the castle got its name many times, but listen out for how Ludwig got his peculiar moniker as well.

The castle owes its huge popularity to Martin Luther, who went into hiding here from 1521 to 1522 after being excommunicated; during this time he translated the entire New Testament from Greek into German, contributing enormously to the development of the written German language. His modest, wood-panelled **study** is part of the guided tour (available in English), which is the only way to view the interior. The **museum** houses the famous Cranach paintings of Luther and important Christian artefacts from all over Germany. Most of the rooms you'll see here are extravagant 19th-century impressions of medieval life rather than original fittings; the re-imagined Great Hall inspired Richard Wagner's opera *Tannhäuser*. Between Easter and October, crowds can be horrendous; arrive before 11am.

Frequent direct trains run to Erfurt (€9 to €17, 30 to 50 minutes) and most continue on the short distance to Weimar.

WEIMAR

☎ **03643** / **pop 64,000**

The city of Goethe is not impressive on first glance. There are no vast cathedrals or palaces, nor are there any world-renowned museums. But spend a little time wandering its very attractive old streets and visiting its fascinating little museums and historic houses and soon you will understand the allure. You'll feel the presence of notables like Luther, Schiller and Liszt and you'll begin to understand the remarkable cultural accomplishments achieved in Weimar over the centuries.

Because of its historical significance, Weimar has received particularly large handouts for the restoration of its many fine buildings, and in 1999 it was the European Capital of Culture. While the city can sometimes feel like a giant museum teeming with tourists, it is one of Germany's most fascinating places and should not be missed.

Orientation

Weimar's compact and walkable centre is a 20-minute jaunt downhill from the station.

Information

There are scores of little book and music shops in town.

Tourist Information (☎ 240 00; www.weimar.de; Markt 10; ⏰ 9.30am-6pm Mon-Fri, 9.30am-4pm Sat & Sun) Discount cards good for most admissions from €13.

Vobis (☎ 902 925; Schwanseestrasse; per hr €2; ⏰ 10am-8pm) Internet access.

Sights

A good place to begin a tour is in front of the neo-Gothic 1841 **Rathaus** on the Markt. For in-depth museum information and high-end souvenirs try the **Stiftung Weimarer Klassik** (Weimar Classics Foundation; ☎ 545 401; www.swkk.de; Frauentorstrasse 4; ⏰ 10am-6pm).

Those who visit the **Goethe Nationalmuseum** (☎ 545 347; Frauenplan 1; adult/child €6.50/5; ⏰ 9am-6pm Tue-Sun) expecting to learn all about the great man of letters will probably be disappointed. Rather than focusing on Goethe himself, the museum offers a broad overview of German classicism, from its proponents to its patrons.

The adjoining **Goethe Haus**, where such works as *Faust* were written, focuses much more on the man himself. He lived here from 1775 until his death in 1832. Goethe's original 1st-floor living quarters are reached via an expansive Italian Renaissance staircase decorated with sculpture and paintings brought back from his travels to Italy. You'll see his dining room, study and the bedroom with his deathbed. Because demand often exceeds capacity, you'll be given a time slot to enter. Once inside, you can stay as long as you want. The **Faustina café** has a controversial Christoph Hodgson mural depicting Weimar's famous and infamous.

The Bauhaus school and movement were founded in Weimar in 1919 by Walter Gropius, who managed to draw top artists including Kandinsky, Klee, Feininger and Schlemmer as teachers. The exhibition at the **Bauhaus Museum** (☎ 545 961; Theaterplatz; adult/child €4.50/3.50; ⏰ 10am-6pm) chronicles the evolution of the group, explains its innovations and spotlights the main players. In 1925 the Bauhaus moved to Dessau and in 1932 to Berlin, where it was dissolved by the Nazis the following year.

Housed in the **Stadtschloss**, the former residence of the ducal family of Saxe-Weimar, the **Schlossmuseum** (☎ 545 960; Burgplatz 4; adult/child €5/4; ⏰ 10am-6pm Tue-Sun Apr-Oct, 10am-4pm Nov-Mar) displays encompass sculpture, paintings and arts-and-craft objects. Highlights include the Cranach Gallery, several portraits by Albrecht Dürer and collections of Dutch masters and German romanticists. Several restored residence rooms can also be seen.

Goethe's fellow dramatist Friedrich von Schiller lived in Weimar from 1799 until his early death in 1805; unlike his mentor, he had to buy his own house, now known as **Schiller Museum** (☎ 545 350; Schillerstrasse 12; adult/child €6.50/5; ⏰ 9am-6pm Wed-Mon). The study at the end of the 2nd floor contains the desk where he penned *Wilhelm Tell* and other works, and also holds his deathbed.

Liszt Haus (☎ 545 388; Marienstrasse 17; adult/child €2.50/2; ⏰ 10am-6pm Tue-Sun Apr-Oct) is on the western edge of **Ilm Park**. Composer and pianist Franz Liszt lived here in 1848 and again from 1869 to 1886, when he wrote *Hungarian Rhapsody* and *Faust Symphony*.

Sleeping

The tourist office can help find accommodation, especially at busy times. There are many *pensions* scattered about the centre, which is where you should try to stay.

Hababusch (☎ 850 737; www.hababusch.de; Geleitstrasse 4; dm €10, s/d €15/24) Get in touch with the town's past at this unrestored 19th-century house. Conditions are, well, historic, but if you're looking for atmosphere this is it. The charming fountain out front is dedicated to the city.

Jugendherberge Germania (☎ 850 490; www.djh.de; Carl-August-Allee 13; dm from €17; ⊠ 💻) The 121-bed Germania, south of the station, is convenient for a quick getaway but a little far from the centre.

Hotel Fürstenhof (☎ 833 231; www.fuerstenhof-weimar.de; Rudolf-Breitscheid-Strasse 2; r €46-100; 💻) A nice modern alternative to the ubiquitous 'period' décor elsewhere, the 17 rooms boast abstract prints. There's a vivid yellow breakfast room.

Ringhotel Kaiserin Augusta (☎ 2340; www.hotel-kaiserin-augusta.de; Carl-August-Allee 17; r €66-140; ⊠ 💻) Directly across from the train station, this 242-bed business hotel offers many services and well-equipped rooms with wi-fi. It has a good terrace and breakfast buffet.

Hotel Elephant (☎ 8020; www.starwood.com; Markt 19; r €100-250; ⊠ 💻) A true classic, the marble Bauhaus-Deco splendour of the 99-room Elephant has seen most of Weimar's great and good come and go; just to make the point, a golden Thomas Mann looks out over the Markt from a balcony in front. Its **Elephantenkeller** restaurant is also a local institution. Was that Goethe you just saw stroll past? The terrace is a delight.

Eating

Residenz-Café (☎ 594 08; Grüner Markt 4; mains €5-15) Known as the 'Resi' by regulars, this is one of Weimar's most popular haunts and has been for more than 160 years. The food is hearty and local, look for filling, starchy treats. The Sunday brunch draws hordes.

Johanns Hof (☎ 493 617; Scherfgasse 1; mains €6-14) Large windows punctuate the maroon walls in this historic and stylish café. The long wine list specialises in German white wines. Creative dishes include a fine garlic soup.

Zum Zwiebel (☎ 502 375; Teichgasse 6; mains €7-13; ⏰ dinner) Look for the cute statue and logo at this unassuming place with exposed brick walls. The menu combines potatoes, sausage and, of course, onions. Yum.

Köstritzer Schwarzbierhaus (☎ 779 337; Scherfgasse 4; mains €7-18) Fans of dark beer and substantial traditional Thuringian cooking are in exactly the right place here – the listed half-timbered house has been converted into a restaurant and *pension* (double €80).

Entertainment

Deutsches Nationaltheater (German National Theatre; ☎ 755 334; www.nationaltheater-weimar.de; Theaterplatz; ⏰ closed Jul-Aug) This historic venue was used to draft the constitution of the ill-fated Weimar Republic in 1919. Expect a mix of classic and contemporary plays, plus ballet, opera and classical concerts.

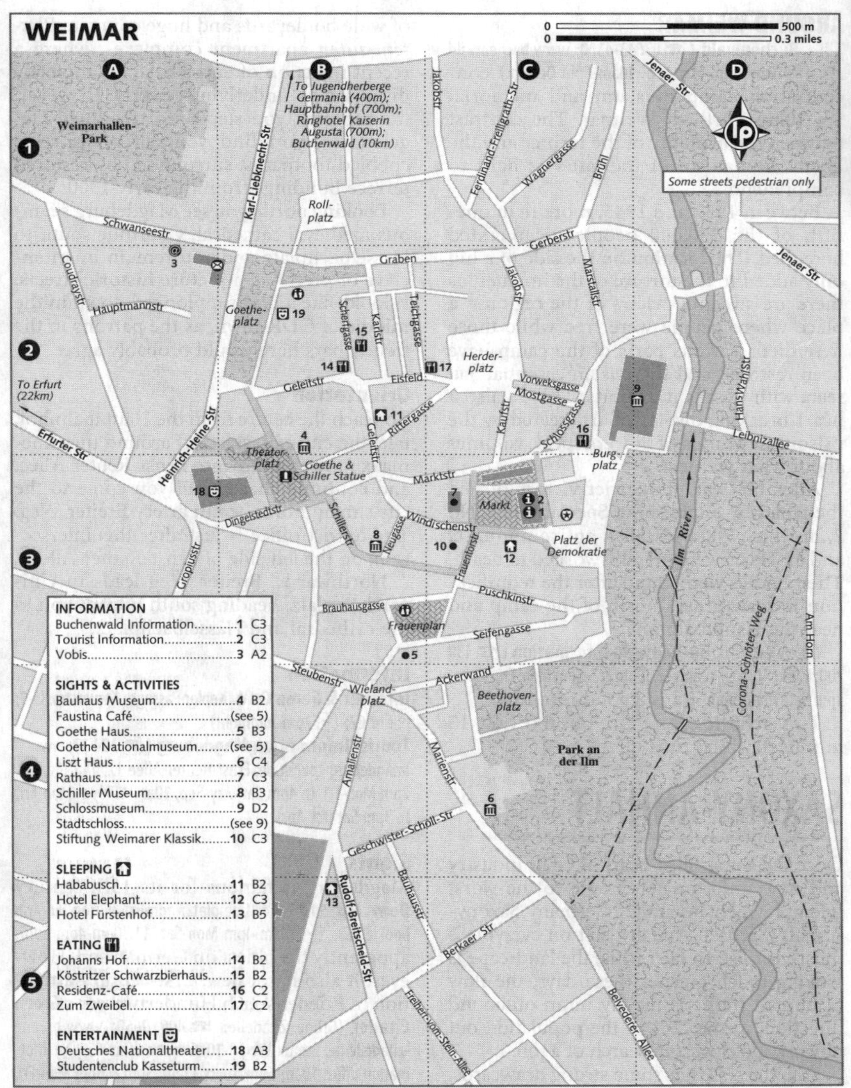

Studentenclub Kasseturm (☎ 851670; www.kasseturm.de; Goetheplatz 10; 6pm-late) A classic, the Kasseturm is a historic round tower with three floors of live music, DJs and cabaret.

Getting There & Away

Weimar's Hauptbahnhof is on a line with frequent service linking Leipzig (€22, one hour) and Erfurt (€7, 15 minutes). Hourly ICE/IC services go to both Frankfurt (€49, 2½ hours) and Berlin-Hauptbahnhof (€44, 2½ hours).

The town centre is a 20-minute walk south of the Hauptbahnhof. Most buses serve Goetheplatz, on the northwestern edge of the Altstadt.

AROUND WEIMAR

The **Buchenwald** (☎ 03643-4300; www.buchenwald.de; ⌚ 10am-6pm May-Sep, 10am-5pm Oct-Apr) concentration camp museum and memorial are 10km north of Weimar. The contrast between the brutality of the former and the liberal humanism of the latter is hard to comprehend.

Between 1937 and 1945, more than one-fifth of the 250,000 people incarcerated here died. The location on the side of a hill only added to the torture of the inmates, as there are sweeping views of the region – a place where people were free while those here died. Various parts of the camp have been restored and there is an essential **museum** with excellent exhibits. There's also a heart-breaking display of art created by the prisoners. Murals of flowers speak volumes about what was lost.

After the war, the Soviet victors turned the tables by establishing Special Camp No 2, in which 7000 so-called anticommunists and ex-Nazis were literally worked to death. Their bodies were found after the reunification in mass graves north of the camp and near the Hauptbahnhof.

In Weimar, **Buchenwald Information** (☎ 430 200; Markt 10; ⌚ 10am-12.30pm & 1-5pm Mon-Fri, 10am-3pm Sat, 10am-2pm Sun) is a good resource.

To reach the camp, take bus 6 (€1.60, 15 minutes), which runs often.

SAXONY-ANHALT

Once the smog-filled heart of GDR industry and now unfortunately home to the worst unemployment in a united Germany, Saxony-Anhalt (Sachsen-Anhalt) isn't on everyone's must-visit list. In fact, while the landscape is looking much greener these days, the flow of human traffic is mainly in an outbound direction, as the 25% of the population out of work looks west in search of a job.

Still, the state has some strong drawcards, making it worthwhile venturing in, especially Dessau's Bauhaus legacy and the wonderful bordering landscape of the Harz region.

MAGDEBURG

☎ 0391 / pop 228,000

Sometimes, just turning the corner in Magdeburg can take you back 100 years. Generally, Saxony-Anhalt's capital is a city of wide boulevards and huge concrete *Plattenbauten* apartment complexes, where a recent injection of euros hasn't completely disguised an underlying poverty. However, the moment you step onto tree-lined Hegelstrasse, you find yourself on pristine cobbled footpaths, surrounded by restored terrace buildings from the early 1900s.

Looking north, you see Magdeburg's famous medieval cathedral. Continue south to Hasselbachplatz and you remain in an enclave of pretty-as-a-picture historic streets. It looks like a film set plonked down in the middle of GDR-town, as the patrons in the trendy bars here would probably agree.

Orientation

To reach the centre from the Hauptbahnhof, take the city exit, skirt left around the Cinemaxx movie theatre into Ernst-Reuter-Allee, and continue ahead until you come to the city's main north–south artery Breiter Weg. The tourist office is just after this intersection, on the left side of Ernst-Reuter-Allee.

Northwards, Breiter Weg leads to Universitätsplatz; heading south it takes you to the cathedral and Hasselbachplatz.

Information

Internet & Game Café (Kepler Passage, Keplerstrasse 9; per hr €2; ⌚ 2pm-midnight)

Tourist Information Magdeburg (☎ 194 33; www.magdeburg-tourist.de; Ernst-Reuter-Allee 12; ⌚ 10am-7pm Mon-Fri, to 4pm Sat May-Sep, 10am-6.30pm Mon-Fri, to 3pm Sat Oct-Apr)

Sights

Magdeburg is famous for its 13th-century **Dom** (☎ 543 2414; Domplatz; admission free, English booklet €3; ⌚ 10am-4pm Mon-Sat, 11.30am-4pm Sun), apparently the oldest on German soil. However, it also has a new, 21st-century attraction in Friedensreich Hundertwasser's **Green Citadel** (Grüne Zitadelle; ☎ 400 9650; www.gruene-zitadelle.de; Breiter Weg 8-10; German tours €5; ⌚ information office 10am-6pm, tours 11am, 3pm & 5pm Mon-Fri, hourly 10am-5pm Sat & Sun). The last design by the famous Austrian architect, this apartment and shopping complex was completed in 2005, five years after his death. It evinces all his signature features – irregular windows, free-form walls and golden domes. The building's pink, but derives its name from its natural architecture and grass-covered roof.

WORTH A TRIP: MITTELBAU DORA

From late 1943, thousands of slave labourers – mostly Russian, French and Polish prisoners of war toiled under horrific conditions to dig enormous tunnels in the chalk hills north of Nordhausen. From a 20km labyrinth of immense proportions, they produced the V1 and V2 rockets that rained destruction on London, Antwerp and other cities late in the war.

The camp, **Mittelbau Dora** (☎ 03631-495 820; www.buchenwald.de; 🕓 10am-6pm Tue-Sun May-Sep, 10am-4pm Oct-Apr), was created as a satellite of the Buchenwald concentration camp after British bombers destroyed the missile plants in far northeastern Germany. During the last two years of WWII, at least 20,000 prisoners died at Dora.

A museum with permanent exhibits of this horror opened in 2006. The grounds are open during daylight hours but to see the tunnels – many still filled with partially assembled rockets, you need to take a **tour** (🕓 11am & 2pm Tue-Fri, 11am, 1pm & 3pm Sat & Sun).

During the GDR era Dora mouldered away, with but a couple of small memorials to mark the site. Since reunification, recognition of what happened at Dora has been slowly growing, with visitors only allowed into the tunnels since 1995. The horrible truth of the place belies any need for extensive facilities and a visit to the camp may be among the most unforgettable experiences you have in Germany.

Getting There & Away

Mittelbau Dora is 5km north of Nordhausen, an unfortunate town you'll want to visit only to change trains. The Harzquerbahn (www.hsb-wr.de) train line links Nordhausen to Wernigerode (see 'Bewitching Harz' p464). The stop closest to Mittelbau Dora is Nordhausen-Krimderode, 11 minutes by almost hourly trains (€4) from tracks adjacent to the DB station. From the stop it is a 20-minute walk to the memorial.

Nordhausen is linked to Halle and Göttingen (both €15, 1½ hours) by frequent trains.

The historic area surrounding **Hasselbachplatz** is an attraction in its own right and full of bars, clubs and restaurants. Just wander or check listing magazine *Dates* for tips.

Sleeping & Eating

DJH Jugendherberge Magdeburg (☎ 532 101; www.jugendherberge.de; Leiterstrasse 10; dm junior/senior €18/21; P ⊠ 🖳) The smart, modern premises, generous space, good facilities and quiet but central location make this a winner. The staff are friendly and there's a late curfew.

Green Citadel (☎ 620 780; www.hotel-zitadelle.de; Breiter Weg 9; r from €105; P ⊠) One of only two Hundertwasser hotels in the world and certainly the cheaper, this allows you to savour up-close the architect's penchant for uneven, organic forms. The attached café (dishes €3.50 to €4.50, 🕓 7am to 7pm) is open to the public, serving breakfast and light meals.

Bingöl 2 (☎ 744 8640; Breiter Weg 226; mains €2-8.50; 🕓 10am-midnight, to 6am Fri & Sat) This superior döner kebab shop has a large sit-down section and a menu that includes falafel, Turkish pizza, börek and dishes from the grill.

Liebig (☎ 555 6754; Liebigstrasse 1-3; snacks €3-9, meals €5-16; 🕓 10am-1am) Private alcoves and pleated curtains lining the walls create a feeling of warmth and privacy amid this trendy bar/café/restaurant. Mediterranean fare, curries and steaks are all served.

Getting There & Away

There are trains to/from Berlin (€22, one hour and 40 minutes, hourly), while regular IC and RE trains run to Leipzig (€19 to €23, 1¼ to two hours, twice hourly).

DESSAU

☎ **0340 / pop 79,500**

'Less is more' and 'form follows function' – both these dictums were taught in Dessau, home of the influential Bauhaus school. Between 1925 and 1932, some of the century's greatest artists and architects breathed life into the ground-breaking principles of modernism here, among them Walter Gropius, Paul Klee, Wassily Kandinsky and Ludwig Mies Van der Rohe. Their legacy still stands proud, in the immaculate Bauhaus school building, the lecturers' purpose-built homes and other pioneering constructions.

BEWITCHING HARZ

The **Harz Mountains** constitute a mini-Alpine region straddling Saxony-Anhalt and Lower Saxony. Here, medieval castles overlook fairy-tale historic towns, while there are caves, mines and numerous hiking trails to explore.

The region's highest – and most famous – mountain is the Brocken, where one-time visitor Johann Wolfgang von Goethe set the 'Walpurgisnacht' chapter of his play *Faust*. His inspiration in turn came from folk tales depicting Walpurgisnacht as an annual witches' coven. Every 30 April to 1 May it's celebrated enthusiastically across the Harz region, particularly in Thale.

Goslar

Goslar is a truly stunning 1000-year-old city with beautifully preserved half-timbered buildings and an impressive **Markt.** The town's **Kaiserpfalz** is a reconstructed Romanesque 11th-century palace. Just below there's the restored **Domvorhalle**, which displays the 11th-century 'Kaiserstuhl' throne, used by German emperors.

One way to reach the **Brocken's summit** is to take a bus (810) or train (faster) from Goslar to Bad Harzburg and then a bus (820) to Torfhaus, where the 8km Goetheweg trail begins.

The **tourist office** (☎ 05321-780 60; www.goslar.de, in German; Markt 7; ⏰ 9.15am-6pm Mon-Fri, 9.30am-4pm Sat, to 2pm Sun May-Oct; 9.15am-5pm Mon-Fri, 9.30am-2pm Sat Nov-Apr) can help with accommodation, which includes a **DJH Hostel** (☎ 05321-222 40; www.jugendherberge.de; Rammelsbergerstrasse 25; dm junior/senior €16.50/19.50; P) and hotels **Die Tanne** (☎ 05321-343 90; www.die-tanne.de; Bäringerstrasse 10; s €40-65, d €65-100) and **Kaiserworth** (☎ 05321-7090; www.kaiserworth.de; Markt 3; s €70-100, d €120-180) .

As well as being serviced by buses (www.rbb-bus.de), Goslar is connected by train to Hanover (€13.40, one hour and 10 minutes) and Wernigerode (€7.60, 50 minutes).

Wernigerode

Flanked by the foothills of the Harz Mountains, Wernigerode boasts colourful half-timbered houses, many with uniquely distinctive features. A fairy-tale ducal castle – one of the most-visited in Germany – watches above. The town is the northern terminus of the steam-powered **Harzquerbahn railway** (☎ 03943-5580; www.hsb-wr.de), which chugs to the summit of the Brocken from here.

Wernigerode Tourismus (☎ 03943-633 035; www.wernigerode-tourismus.de; Nicolaiplatz 1; ⏰ 9am-7pm Mon-Fri, 10am-4pm Sat, 10am-3pm Sun May-Oct, slightly reduced hr winter) can provide more details.

The Bauhaus was born in Weimar in 1919, and it sought brief respite in Berlin (see p436) before being disbanded by the Nazis in 1933. But as the site of the movement's heyday and the 'built manifesto of Bauhaus ideas', Dessau is the true keeper of the flame.

Orientation

The leading Bauhaus sights are west of the Hauptbahnhof, clearly signposted and within easy walking distance. The town centre lies east, also reachable on foot.

Information

Bauhaus Foundation (☎ 650 8251; www.bauhaus-dessau.de; Gropiusallee 38; ⏰ 10am-6pm Mon-Fri) Has info on, and tours of, Bauhaus buildings, including in English.

Tourist office (☎ 204 1442, accommodation reservations 220 3003; www.dessau-tourismus.de; Zerbster Strasse 2c; ⏰ 9am-6pm Mon-Fri, 9am-1pm Sat Apr-Oct, 9am-5pm Mon-Fri, 10am-1pm Sat Nov-Mar) Offers city tours and sells a three-day discount card.

Sights

Bauhaus founder Walter Gropius considered architecture the ultimate creative expression. So his first realised project, the **Bauhaus Building** (Bauhaus Gebäude; ☎ 650 8251; www.bauhaus-dessau.de; Gropiusallee 38; exhibition hall adult/concession €4/3, with Meisterhäuser €8/5, tours €4/3; ⏰ 10am-6pm, German tours 11am & 2pm, extra tours Sat & Sun), is extremely significant. Once home to the Institute for Design (Hochschule für Gestaltung) where the architect and colleagues taught, the recently renovated building today houses a postgraduate college but remains open to the public. You can visit the changing exhibitions and wander through a small section. However,

Accommodation options include a private **Jugendgästehaus** (☎ 03943-632 061; Friedrichstrasse 53; dm junior/senior €16.50/20; P) and **Altwernigeroder Aparthotel** (☎ 03943-949 260; www.appart-hotel.de, in German; Marktstrasse 14; s/d €45/75, apt from €85; P ⊠)

Direct buses run to most major towns in the region. For trains to Quedlinburg (€7.60, 50 minutes) and Thale (€9.10, one hour and 10 minutes), change at Halberstadt.

Quedlinburg

Quedlinburg's spectacular castle district, perched on a 25m-high plateau above its historic half-timbered buildings, was established during the reign of Heinrich I, from 919 to 936. The present-day Renaissance **Schloss** dates from the 16th century. Its centrepiece is the restored baroque **Blauer Saal** (Blue Hall).

Contact **Quedlinburg-Tourismus** (☎ 03946-905625; www.quedlinburg.de; Markt 2; ⏲ 9am-7pm Mon-Fri, 10am-4pm Sat & Sun Apr-Oct; 9.30am-5.30pm Mon-Fri, to 2pm Sat Nov-Mar) for more information. Lodgings include a **DJH hostel** (☎ 03946-811 703; www.jugendherberge.de; Neuendorf 28; dm junior/senior €14/18, bedding €3; P) and the hotels **Zum Alten Fritz** (☎ 03946-704 880; Pölkenstrasse 18; s/d €45/65; P) and **Romantik Hotel Theophano** (☎ 03946-963 00; www.hoteltheophano.de; Markt 13-14; s/d from €70/100).

There are frequent trains to Thale (€1.80, 11 minutes) and Magdeburg (€11.70, one hour, hourly).

Thale

Two rugged outcrops, the **Hexentanzplatz** and **Rosstrappe**, flank the sensational **Bode Valley**, which is a hikers' favourite. There's a cable car to the rather overdeveloped Hexentanzplatz. Meanwhile, the Rosstrappe, reached by chairlift, bears a strange hoof imprint, supposedly left when the mythological Brunhilde jumped the gorge on horseback to escape her unloved husband Bode. (He fell to his death.) Both outcrops become bacchanalian party sites on Walpurgisnacht.

Thale Tourismus (☎ 03947-2597; www.thale.de; Rathausstrasse 1; ⏲ 9am-5pm Mon-Fri, 10am-3pm Sat & Sun) can help with accommodation, which includes a **DJH Hostel** (☎ 03947-2881; www.jugendherberge.de; Bodetal-Waldkater; dm junior/senior €14.50/17.50, s/d from €19.50/24.50; P) and **Hoffmanns Gästehaus** (☎ 03947-2881; www.hoffmanns-gaestehaus.de; s €50-65, d €65-75, f €75-105).

There are trains and buses to Wernigerode and Quedlinburg, as well as trains from Magdeburg (€13.40, 1½ hours).

taking a tour is best; it gets you into otherwise closed rooms, even if you don't understand German.

Since a key Bauhaus aim was to 'design for living', the three white, concrete **Master Craftsmen's Houses** (Meisterhäuser; www.meisterhaeuser.de; Ebertallee 63-71; admission to all three adult/concession €5/3; ⏲ 10am-6pm Tue-Sun summer, to 5pm winter), are a fascinating isnsight into the style. These villas were built by Gropius for senior institute staff, including himself, Klee, Kandinsky, Laszlo Moholy-Nagy and Lyonel Feininger. In addition to this, Marcel Breuer – creator of the iconic steel frame chair – ocassionally meddled in the homes' interior design.

The many other Bauhaus buildings include the world's first housing estate **Törten**. Take tram 1 to Dessau Süd, alighting at Damashckestrasse.

Sleeping & Eating

In Dessau, you really can eat, drink and sleep Bauhaus. For a different diet, investigate the main thoroughfare of Zerbster Strasse.

Bauhaus dorms (☎ 650 8318; oede@bauhaus-dessau.de; Gropiusallee 38; r per person from €28; P ⊠) Since the Bauhaus school was renovated in 2006, you can really live the modernist dream, by hiring the former students' dorms inside. If the main building's booked out, opt for a taste of the GDR instead, by reserving a cheaper bed (€15) in a 1970s *Plattenbau* apartment complex at Heidestrasse 33.

An den 7 Säulen (☎ 619 620; www.pension7saeulen.de, in German; Ebertallee 66; s €47-52, d €65-72; P ⊠) This relaxed *pension* has a spa and a glass-fronted breakfast room overlooking the Master Craftsmen's Houses across the leafy street.

Bauhaus Klub (☎ 650 8444; Gropiusallee 38; dishes €3-7) Starting to see a pattern here? The occasional cool dude in black polo-neck jumper and horn-rimmed glasses can be seen among the broad mix of people in this basement bar of the Bauhaus school.

Kornhaus (☎ 640 4141; Kornhausstrasse 146; mains €7-13) Treat yourself to traditional local specialities and a refined evening in the curved Bauhaus dining room, with its striking 1930s carpet. Or, enjoy a light meal on the balcony overlooking the Elbe River.

Getting There & Away

IC and RE trains run to Berlin every two hours (€22, 1½ hours). Dessau is equidistant from Leipzig and Magdeburg (both €9.10, one hour), with frequent services to each.

MECKLENBURG-WESTERN POMERANIA

Mecklenburg-Vorpommern combines historic Hanseatic-era towns like Schwerin, Wismar and Stralsund with holiday areas such as Warnemünde and Rügen Island. It is off the path for many travellers but in summer it seems like half the country is here in some state of undress lolling on the sands. Outside of these somewhat mild times (this is a region where the beaches are dotted with large wicker beach baskets to provide shelter) the intrepid visitor is rewarded with journeys far from the maddening crowds.

SCHWERIN

☎ 0385 / pop 97,000

State capital Schwerin has a modest dignity befitting its status. The oldest city in Mecklenburg-Western Pomerania, it has numerous lakes, including one that is the town's centrepiece. Buildings are an interesting mix of 16th- to 19th-century architecture. It's small enough to explore on foot and if you're on the move, you can see it as part of a half-day break on a train journey. But Schwerin's beauty and charm are invariably infectious, and few people regret spending extra time here.

Orientation

The Altstadt is a 10-minute walk south from the Hauptbahnhof along Wismarsche Strasse. A couple of blocks east of the Hauptbahnhof is the rectangular Pfaffenteich, a pretty artificial pond with the garish apricot-coloured 1840 Arsenal (now government offices) at its southwest corner. Heading east from here will take you to the central Markt.

Information

In-Ca Internet (☎ 500 7883; Wismarsche Strasse 123; per hr €3; 10am-midnight)

Schwerin-Information (☎ 592 5212; www.schwerin.de; Markt 14; 9am-7pm Mon-Fri, 10am-6pm Sat & Sun, reduced hr winter)

Sights

Southeast of the Alter Garten, over the causeway on the Burginsel (Burg Island), Schwerin's superb neo-Gothic palace, the **Schloss Schwerin** (☎ 525 2920; www.schloss-schwerin.de; adult/child €4/2.50; 10am-6pm 15 Apr-14 Oct, 10am-5pm Tue-Sun 15 Oct-15 Apr), was built in the mid-1800s around the chapel of a 16th-century ducal castle and is quite rightly the first attraction visitors head to upon arrival. The causeway is overlooked by a statue of **Niklot**, an early Slavic prince, who was defeated by Heinrich der Löwe in 1160. The huge, graphic picture of his death is a highlight of the castle's interior.

You don't get better examples of north German red-brick architecture than this 14th-century Gothic **Dom** (☎ 565 014; Am Dom 4; tower €1; 10am-5pm Mon-Fri, noon-5pm Sun), towering above the Markt. You can climb up to the platform in the 19th- century tower.

The enormous neoclassical building in the Alter Garten, the **Staatliches Museum** (☎ 595 80; Alter Garten 3; adult/child €6/4; 10am-8pm Tue, 10am-6pm Wed-Sun), couldn't really be anything other than a museum, and the contents fit the imposing exterior well: the permanent displays showcase old Dutch masters including Rembrandt, Rubens and Brueghel, as well as oils by Lucas Cranach the Elder and collections of more modern works by Marcel Duchamp and Ernst Barlach.

Sleeping & Eating

There are numerous cafés in the pedestrianised centre.

DJH Jugendherberge (☎ 326 0006; www.djh.de; Waldschulweg 3; dm from €17) This hostel is about 4km south of the city centre, just opposite the zoo. Take bus 14, which has stops at the Hauptbahnhof and Marienplatz.

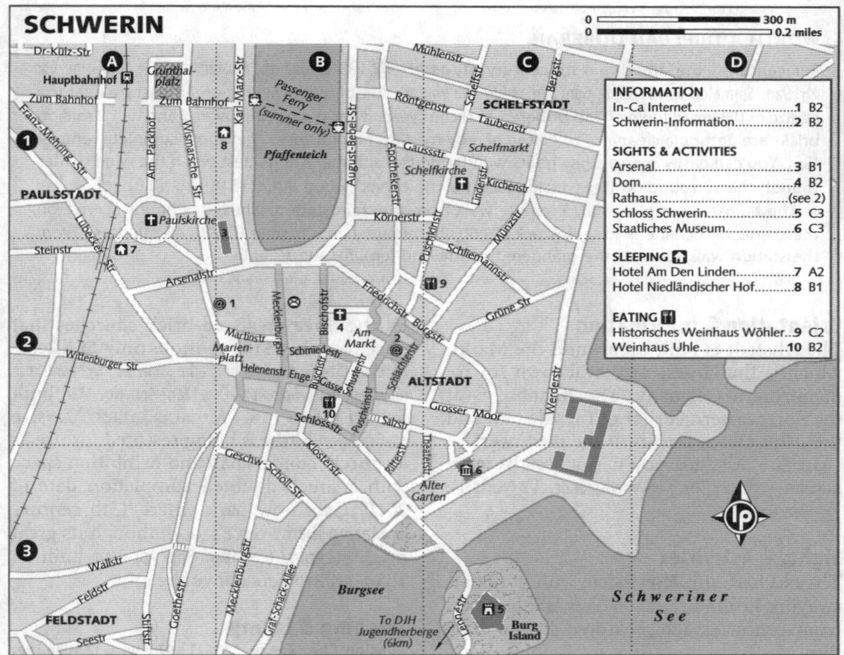

Hotel Am Den Linden (☎ 512 084; Franz-Mehring-Strasse 26; s/d €64/77) Close to the train station and the centre, this dignified 25-room hotel looks onto the impressive Paulskirche. Rooms are comfortable and there is a good breakfast.

Hotel Niederländischer Hof (☎ 591 100; www.niederlaendischer-hof.de; Karl-Marx-Strasse 12-13; s/d from €90/118; P) You can't beat the Pfaffenteich location or the swank rooms and marble bathrooms at this exceedingly classy hotel. There's even a library with an open fire for those contemplative German winters.

Historisches Weinhaus Wöhler (☎ 555 830; Puschkinstrasse 26; mains €8-16) The stained-glass windows framed in lead tell you that this place is indeed historic. Opened in 1895, the building dates to the 18th century. The food is classic German and on weekends you can enjoy live music. The beer garden is alluring and you can sleep it off in the comfortable rooms (€80 to €130) upstairs.

Weinhaus Uhle (☎ 562 956; Schusterstrasse 13-15; mains €9-24) This long-standing traditional family wine merchant (the building is from the 18th century) has vaulted ceilings in the downstairs restaurant and a lovely *weinstube* upstairs. As you'd guess, the wine list is long.

Getting There & Away

Schwerin is on the line linking Hamburg (€23, one hour) with Stralsund (€28, two hours). Service to Rostock (€13.40 to €17, one hour) is frequent, as is that to Wismar (€6.20, 30 minutes). There are RE trains to Berlin-Hauptbahnhof (€29, 2½ hours).

WISMAR

☎ **03841 / pop 46,000**

Wismar, a Hanseatic gem that's fast being discovered, is about halfway between Rostock and Lübeck. It joined the powerful trading league in the 13th century – the first town east of Lübeck to do so. For centuries it was in and out of Swedish control, and traces of that rule can still be seen, particularly in the 'Swedish heads' all over town. Quieter than Rostock or Stralsund, Wismar can fill up with visitors quickly in high season; it's definitely worth an overnight stay, and is also the gateway to **Poel Island**, a lovely little piece of green to the north.

WORTH A TRIP: BAD DOBERAN

For centuries the amazing 13th-century **Munster** (☎ 038203-627 16; Klosterstrasse 2; admission €3; ⌚ 9am-6pm Mon-Sat, 11.30am-6pm Sun, reduced hr winter) slumbered away in a green pasture near the centre of the small town of Bad Doberan. In recent years it has been rediscovered and its 1.2 million bricks are getting a cleaning, while the nearby medieval monastery is getting a complete renovation. You can easily spend a few hours wandering this site that's at its best when the wind rustles though the surrounding trees. Inside look for the carved wood alter (1310) from Lübeck.

The Munster complex is a 15-minute walk from the train station, which has hourly service on the scenic branchline linking Rostock (€2.60, 20 minutes) and Wismar (€6.20, 45 minutes). From the station walk towards the mannered centre and look for the steeple.

Orientation & Information

The Altstadt is built up around the Markt, which is the largest medieval town square in northern Germany. The Bahnhof is at the northeastern corner of the Altstadt and the Alter Hafen port is in the northwest.

In the Altstadt you'll find **tourist information** (☎ 251 3025; www.wismar.de; Am Markt 11; ⌚ 9am-6pm).

Sights & Activities

The old harbour, **Alter Hafen**, with old boats swaying in the breeze, evokes trading days from centuries ago. Featured in the 1922 film *Nosferatu* it is still a focal point of activity in Wismar. **Clermont Reederei** (☎ 224 646; www.reederei-clermont.de; adult/child €7/6) operates hour-long harbour cruises five times daily from April to October, leaving from Alter Hafen. Daily boats also go to Poel Island (€14/7 return). Various other companies run tours on historic ships during summer; contact the harbour for details.

Running through town, the **Grube** (channel) is the last artificial medieval waterway in the north and should be a part of any stroll through the historic quarter. The **Wasserkunst** is a 12-sided well from 1602 that anchors a corner of the attractive **Markt**.

The town's historical museum **Schabbellhaus** (☎ 282 350; www.schabbellhaus.de; Schweinsbrücke 8; adult/child €2/1, free Fri; ⌚ 10am-8pm Tue-Sun May-Oct, to 5pm Nov-Apr) has taken over a former Renaissance brewery (1571), just south of the Nikolaikirche across the canal. The museum's pride and joy is the large tapestry *Die Königin von Saba vor König Salomon* ('The Queen of Sheba before King Solomon'; 1560–75).

CHURCHES

Wismar was a target for Anglo-American bombers just weeks before the end of WWII. Of the three great red-brick churches that once rose above the rooftops only **St-Nikolai-Kirche** (St-Nikolai-Kirchhof; admission €1; ⌚ 8am-8pm May-Sep, 10am-6pm Apr & Oct, 11am-4pm Nov-Mar), built from 1381 to 1487, remains intact. Massive **St-Georgen-Kirche** is being restored for use as a church, concert hall and exhibition space with a much-doubted completion date of 2010. Cars now park where 13th-century **St-Marien-Kirche** once stood, though its great brick **steeple**, (⌚ 10am-8pm Apr-Oct), built in 1339, still towers above the city.

Sleeping & Eating

Pension Chez Fasan (☎ 213 425; www.pension-chez-fasan.de; Bademutterstrasse 20a; r €21-50) The best budget deal in town. Rooms in the three-building complex come with baths, satellite TV and a great central location.

Hotel Reuterhaus (☎ 222 30; www.hotel-reuterhaus.de; Am Markt 19; r €60-90) With views over the Wasserkunst from many of the 10 rooms, this family-run hotel makes for an atmospheric stay. The restaurant here is good and there are tables on the Markt when the sun shines.

Fischerklause (☎ 252 850; Fischerreihe 4; mains €7-13; ⌚ lunch & dinner Tue-Sat) A small place popular with locals that serves up the catch brought into the nearby Alter Hafen. The place swims with character.

Brauhaus am Lohberg (☎ 250 238; Kleine Hohe Strasse 15; mains €7-13) Spread over a series of warehouses dating back to the 16th century, this popular spot is honouring Wismar's long tradition of brewing by once again making its own beer. There's a good seafood menu.

Getting There & Away

Trains travel the coastal branchlines to Rostock (€9.10, 65 minutes, hourly) and Schwerin (€6.20, 30 minutes, hourly).

ROSTOCK & WARNEMÜNDE

☎ 0381 / pop 198,000

Rostock, the largest city in sparsely populated northeastern Germany, is a major Baltic port and shipbuilding centre. Its chief suburb – and chief attraction – is Warnemünde, 12km north of the centre. Counted among eastern Germany's most popular beach resorts, it's hard to see it as a small fishing village these days, but the boats still bring in their catches, and some charming streets and buildings persist amid the tourist clutter.

First mentioned in 1161 as a Danish settlement, Rostock began taking shape as a German fishing village around 1200. In the 14th and 15th centuries, it was an important Hanseatic trading city; parts of the city centre, especially along Kröpeliner Strasse, retain the flavour of this period.

Orientation & Information

The city begins at the Südstadt (Southern City), south of the Hauptbahnhof, and extends north to Warnemünde on the Baltic Sea. Much of the city is on the western side of the Warnow River, which creates a long shipping channel due north to the sea.

The Altstadt is an oval area approximately 1.5km north of the Hauptbahnhof. Rosa-Luxemburg-Strasse runs north from the station to Steintor, which unofficially marks the southern boundary of the old town.

Tourist Information (☎ 381 2222; www.rostock.de; Neuer Markt 3; ⏰ 10am-7pm Mon-Fri, 10am-4pm Sat & Sun May-Sep, closed Sun Oct-Apr)

Warnemünde-Information (☎ 548 000; www.warnemuende.de; Am Strom 59; ⏰ 10am-6pm Mon-Fri, 10am-3pm Sat & Sun)

Sights

Lined with 15th- and 16th-century burghers' houses, Kröpeliner Strasse is a lively, cobbled pedestrian street that runs west from Neuer Markt to the **Kröpeliner Tor**, a 55m-high tower, which contains the **Regional History Museum** (☎ 454 177; adult/child €3/1.50; ⏰ 10am-6pm Wed-Sun).

The mostly intact **Kloster Zum Heiligen Kreuz** (Holy Cross convent; ☎ 203 590; Klosterhof 18), was established in 1270 by Queen Margrethe I of Denmark; today it houses the **Cultural History Museum** (adult/child €3/1.50; ⏰ 9am-6pm Tue-Sun), with an excellent and varied collection including sculptures by Ernst Barlach and large numbers of everyday items used by locals over the centuries.

Rostock's pride and joy, the **Marienkirche** (☎ 453 325; Am Ziegenmarkt; admission €2; ⏰ 10am-4pm Mon-Sat, 11.15am-noon Sun), built in 1290, was the only one of Rostock's four main churches to survive WWII unscathed. The long north-south transept was added after the ceiling collapsed in 1398. Notable features include the 12m-high astrological clock (1470–72), the Gothic bronze baptismal font (1290), the baroque organ (1770) and some fascinating tombstones in the floor.

The crowded seafront promenade to the north at **Warnemünde**, lined with hotels and restaurants, is where the tourists congregate. Its broad, sandy beach stretches west from the **lighthouse** (1898) and the **Teepott** exhibition centre, and is chock-a-block on hot summer days with bathers.

Sleeping

Accommodation in Warnemünde can be like gold dust in summer. For private rooms, contact the tourist office. At other times – especially in the spring and fall – it is a lovely alternative to Rostock.

Baltic-Freizeit Camping und Ferienpark (☎ 04544-800 30; www.baltic-freizeit.de; Dünenweg 27, Markgrafenheide; camp sites per person €9-17) On the east side of Warnow River, this enormous city-run affair has 1200 sites. Take tram 4 to Dierkower Kreuz, then bus 18 (45 minutes).

City-Pension (☎ 252 260; www.city-pension-rostock.de; Krönkenhagen 3; r €40-90) A small family *pension* occupying a lovely quiet street near the harbour, in the heart of the old-fashioned northern Altstadt. Rooms are simple but comfortable.

Hotel Kleine Sonne (☎ 497 3153; www.die-kleine-sonne.de; Steinstrasse 7; r €60-100; ⊠ 💻) The bargain offshoot of the swanky Hotel Sonne across the street, this is actually a fine place in its own right, with a very modern style and art by landscape painter Nils Ausländer.

InterCity Hotel (☎ 495 00; www.intercityhotel.de; Herweghstrasse 51; r €85-120; ⊠ 💻) Right by the train station, the InterCity has wi-fi and 174 comfortable modern rooms. Ask for one with a view other than the lightwell however.

Eating

On many mornings fish-smokers set up shop on the Neuer Markt, as well as Warnemünde's harbour. Kröpliner Strasse in Rostock is a good place to find cafés. Warnemünde abounds in stands selling fish and chips, ice cream and other gut-popping fare.

Krahnstöver Likörfabrik (☎ 252 3551; Grosse Wasserstrasse 30/Grubenstrasse 1; mains €5-12) This late-15th-century old liquor factory is an excellent example of late Gothic architecture. The wine bar has an inventive menu; around the corner, the Kneipe seems as old as the building and dishes up hearty fare.

Zum Alten Fritz (☎ 208 780; Warnowufer 65; mains €7-18) This locally popular pub/restaurant honours two Rostock traditions at its harbourside location: seafaring and brewing. Lucky sailor! The creative menu feature organic ingredients.

Seekist zur Krim (☎ 521 14; Am Strom 47, Warnemünde; mains €9-20) On a tree-shaded and quiet stretch of Am Strom, this restaurant serves steaks, schnitzel and seafood. Try a platter of the latter for €15. There's a nice patio.

Getting There & Around

Rostock is on the busy line linking Hamburg (€28 to €35, two hours) to Stralsund (€12, one hour). Services to Schwerin (€13.40 to €17, one hour) are frequent as is the branch line to Wismar (€9.10, 70 minutes, hourly). There are RE trains to Berlin Hauptbahnhof (€32, three hours, every two hours).

Various ferry companies operate from Rostock seaport. **Scandlines** (☎ 673 1217; www.scandlines.de) has daily services to Trelleborg in Sweden (€20, 5¾ hours) and Gedser in Denmark (€5 to €10, two hours). **TT-Line** (☎ 670 790; www.ttline.de) departs for Trelleborg several times daily (€20 to €30, three to six hours).

There's frequent S-Bahn service linking Rostock to Warnemünde (€1.40, 20 minutes). In Rostock tram lines 5 and 6 link the train station with the centre. The entire area lends itself to bike touring. **Radstation** (☎ 252 3990; Hauptbahnhof; per day from €15; ⏰ 10am-6pm Mon-Fri, to 1pm Sat) is very convenient for rentals.

STRALSUND

☎ 03831 / pop 59,000

Possessing an unmistakable medieval profile, Stralsund was the second-most powerful member of the medieval Hanseatic League, after Lübeck. In 1648 Stralsund, Rügen and Pomerania came under the control of Sweden, which had helped in their defence. The city remained Swedish until it was incorporated into Prussia in 1815.

An attractive town of imposing churches and elegant townhouses, Stralsund boasts more examples of classic red-brick Gothic gabled architecture than almost anywhere else in northern Germany. It has some good, growing museums and is great place if you want to feel the culture of the Baltic.

Orientation

The Altstadt is effectively on its own island, surrounded by lakes and the sea. Its main hubs are Alter Markt in the north and Neuer Markt in the south. The Hauptbahnhof is across the Tribseer Damm causeway, west of the Neuer Markt. The harbour is on the Altstadt's eastern side.

Information

Toffi's Web Cafe (☎ 309 385; Lobshagen 8a; per min €0.05; ⏰ noon-10pm) This groovy place has a long list of coffees, tea and beers to help lubricate your surfing.

Tourismuszentrale (☎ 246 90; www.stralsundtourismus.de; Alter Markt 9; ⏰ 9am-7pm Mon-Fri, to 2pm Sat, 10am-2pm Sun May-Sep, 9am-5pm Mon-Fri, 10am-2pm Sat Oct-Apr)

Sights

One of the two structures dominating the Alter Markt is the gorgeous 14th-century **Rathaus**, with its late-Gothic decorative façade. The upper portion has slender copper turrets and gables that have openings to prevent strong winds from knocking over the façade; this ornate design was Stralsund's answer to its rival city, Lübeck, which has a similar town hall. The sky-lit gallery overhanging the vaulted walkway is held aloft by shiny black pillars on carved and painted bases.

Exit through the eastern walkway to the main portal of the other dominant presence in the Alter Markt, the 1270 **Nikolaikirche** (☎ 299 799; Alter Markt; ⏰ 10am-noon & 2-4pm). Modelled after the Marienkirche in Lübeck (p541) and bearing a fleeting resemblance to Notre Dame, it's filled with art treasures. Also worth a closer look are the **high altar** (1470), 6.7m wide and 4.2m tall, showing Jesus' entire life, and the mostly inaccurate **astronomical clock** (1394), allegedly the oldest in the world.

The Neuer Markt is dominated by the massive 14th-century **Marienkirche** (☎ 298 965; Neuer Markt; ⏰ 10am-7pm May-Oct, 10am-noon, 2-4pm

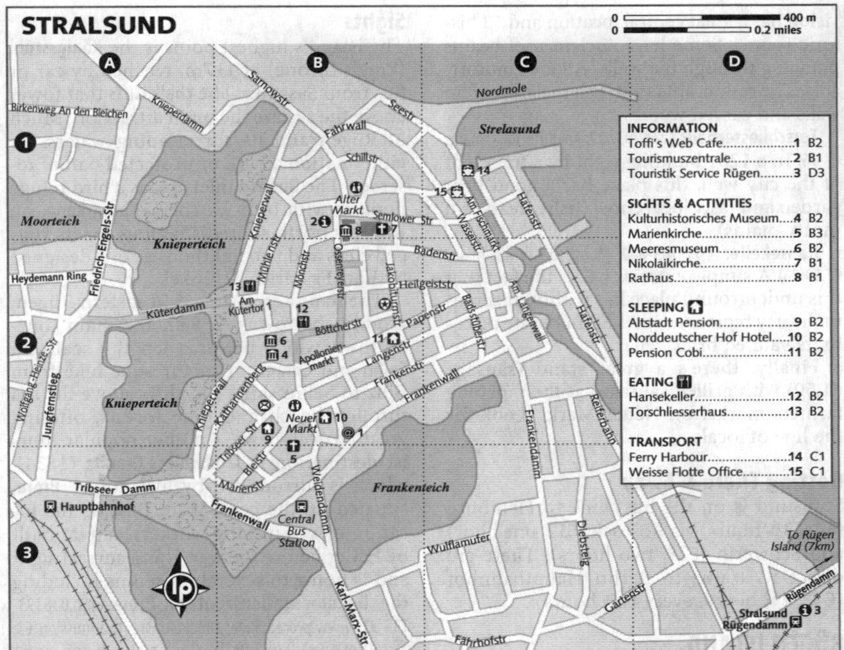

Nov-Apr), another superb example of north German red-brick construction. Check out the huge **F Stellwagen organ** (1659), festooned with music-making cherubs. You can climb the steep wooden steps up the **tower** (admission €1) for a sweeping view of the town and Rügen Island. Ongoing renovations through to 2010 are intended to restore the church to its original look.

MUSEUMS

North of Neuer Markt, a 13th-century convent church is now the **Meeresmuseum** (Oceanographic Museum; ☎ 265 010; www.meeresmuseum.de; Katharinenberg 14-20; adult/child €6.50/4.50; ⏲ 10am-6pm Jun-Sep, 10am-5pm Oct-May). It has extensive displays on local sealife and the people who catch it. A major new addition opening in 2008 will focus on the Baltic and have several huge tanks of live fish.

Stralsund's cultural history museum, **Kulturhistorisches Museum** (☎ 287 90; Mönchstrasse 25-27; adult/child €3/1.50; ⏲ 10am-5pm Tue-Sun), has a large historical collection, paintings by Caspar David Friedrich and Philipp Otto Runge, *faïence* (tin-glazed earthenware), playing cards and Gothic altars, as well as various outlying exhibitions in restored houses.

Tours

Ferries operate seven times daily by **Weisse Flotte** (☎ 0180-321 2120; www.weisse-flotte.com; Fährstrasse 16; one way €2.30; ⏲ May-Oct) to the scenic fishing village of Altefähr on Rügen. One-hour **harbour cruises** depart four times daily (€6) in summer.

Sleeping & Eating

Pension Cobi (☎ 278 288; www.pension-cobi.de; Jakobiturmstrasse 15; s/d €32/46) In the shadow of the Jakobikirche, this is a great location for exploring the Altstadt, and also offers bike hire to get a bit further afield. The 14 rooms are smart, clean and some have balconies.

Altstadt Pension (☎ 303 580; Tribseer Strasse 15; s/d €45/65; ⊠) This 12-room inn is on the main drag into town and is popular with touring cyclists. The modern rooms contrast with the vintage building and precinct. There's a sunny terrace for breakfast or a drink.

Norddeutscher Hof Hotel (☎ 293 161; www.nd-hof.de; Neuer Markt 22; r €40-90) This maroon vision has a great central location and 13 historic rooms. Some have ancient roof beams plunging through the walls. All are comfortable. The restaurant is a stylish melange of tin walls and carved wood.

Torschliesserhaus (☎ 293 032; Am Kütertor 1; mains €7-16) In a 1281 building right by a fragment of the city wall, this place has a good beer garden and tasty local chow (fishy treats and meaty mains).

Hansekeller (☎ 703 840; Mönchstrasse 48; mains €7.50-13) A simple exterior belies the fact that this underground place lies within. It serves up hearty regional dishes at moderate prices in its vaulted brick cellar.

Finally, there's a great stand (sausage €1.50) with grilled sausages at the morning farmers market on Neuer Markt. Look for the line of locals.

Getting There & Away

Stralsund is on the busy line to Hamburg (€44, 3¼ hours) via Rostock (€12, one hour) and Schwerin (€28, two hours). There are direct IC trains to Berlin Hauptbahnhof (€42, 2¾ hours, every two hours).

RÜGEN ISLAND

Germany's largest island, Rügen has 574km of coast. It is at times hectic, relaxed, barren, windblown and naked. If you don't mind losing a little epidermis to the scouring sands, you can have a very German beach holiday here. Otherwise, it makes a good day trip out of Stralsund, especially if you have your own car.

The resort tradition here reflects all aspects of Germany's recent past. In the 19th century, luminaries such as Einstein, Bismarck and Thomas Mann came to unwind in the fashionable coastal resorts. Later, both Nazi and GDR regimes made Rügen the holiday choice for dedicated comrades.

From the bridge near Stralsund that links the mainland and Rügen, the island is easily traversed by numerous well-marked roads.

Information

Tourismus Rügen (☎ 03838-807 70; www.ruegen.de; Am Markt 4, Bergen) Has extensive accommodation listings.

Touristik Service Rügen (☎ 03831-285 70; www.insel-ruegen.com; Bahnhof Rügendamm, Werftstrasse 2; 🕒 8am-9pm Mon-Fri, 9am-8pm Sat, 10am-7pm Sun) The place for information in Stralsund.

Sights

The island's highest point is the **Königsstuhl** (king's throne) at 117m, reached by car or bus from Sassnitz. The **chalk cliffs** that tower above the sea are the main attraction. Much of Rügen and its surrounding waters are either national park or protected nature reserves. The **Bodden** inlet area is a bird refuge popular with bird-watchers. **Kap Arkona**, on Rügen's north shore, is famous for its rugged cliffs and two lighthouses, one designed by Karl Friedrich Schinkel.

The main resort area is in eastern Rügen, around the towns of **Binz**, the main tourist town which boasts a lengthy seafront, **Sellin** and **Göhren**. A picturesque hike from Binz to Sellin skirts the cliffs above the sea through beech and pine forests, offering great coastal views. Another popular tourist destination is **Jagdschloss Granitz** (1834), which is surrounded by lush forest. **Prora**, situated up the coast from Binz, is the location of a 2km-long workers' retreat built by Hitler before the war. It is a surreal sight and is home to several museums including the **Dokumentationszentrum Prora** (☎ 038393-139 91; www.proradok.de; Objektstrasse 1; admission €3; 🕒 10am-6pm), which looks at the huge construction's history.

Getting There & Around

Trains from Stralsund reach Sassnitz (€9.10, 50 minutes, hourly) and Binz (€12, 45 minutes, every two hours). Trains from the latter also serve Hamburg (€51, four hours).

To get around the island however and really appreciate it, you'll need a car.

Scandlines (☎ 0381 543 50; www.scandlines.de) car ferries run from Sassnitz Mukran, several kilometres south of Sassnitz, to Trelleborg in Sweden (one way €12 to €15, 3¾ hours, five daily). The port is linked to the train station by bus.

BAVARIA

For many, Bavaria (Bayern) is every German stereotype rolled into one. Lederhosen, beer halls, oompah bands and romantic castles are just some Bavarian clichés associated with Germany as a whole. But as any Bavarian will tell you, the state thinks of itself as Bavarian first and German second. And as any German outside of Bavaria will tell you, the *Bavarian* stereotypes aren't representative of the rest of Germany. It's a mostly Catholic place and the politics are often conservative (almost 90 years ago this was the land of beer hall putsches), even if people drink serious quantities of beer.

Bavaria was ruled for centuries as a duchy under the line founded by Otto I of Wittelsbach, and eventually graduated to the status of kingdom in 1806. The region suffered amid numerous power struggles between Prussia and Austria and was finally brought into the German empire in 1871 by Bismarck. The last king of Bavaria was Ludwig II (1845–86), who earned the epithet 'the mad king' due to his obsession with building fantastic fairy-tale castles at enormous expense. He was found drowned in Starnberger See in suspicious circumstances and left no heirs.

Bavaria draws visitors year-round. If you only have time for one part of Germany after Berlin, this is it. Munich, the capital, is the heart and soul. The Bavarian Alps, Nuremberg and the medieval towns on the Romantic Road are other important attractions.

MUNICH

☎ 089 / pop 1.25 million

Munich (München) is truly the capital of all things Bavarian. It's a heady mix of world-class museums, historic sites, cosmopolitan shopping, exhausting nightlife, trendy restaurants, roaring beer halls, vast parks and, of course, Oktoberfest.

It can easily occupy several days of your time and it will indeed be time well spent. The efficient public transport system can whisk you around town – although if you stay above ground you might be surprised at how compact the centre really is. Against all this urban life is the backdrop of the Alps, peaks that exude an allure that many locals – and visitors – find inescapable.

It is hard to imagine any visit to Germany feeling complete without at least some time spent in this vibrant city.

History

Originally settled by monks from the Benedictine monastery at Tegernsee in the 7th and 8th century, the city itself wasn't founded until 1158 by Henry the Lion. In 1255 Munich became the home for the Wittelsbach dukes, princes and kings who ruled for the next 700 years. The city suffered through the Black Plague first in 1348 and again in 1623, when two-thirds of the population died.

Munich has been the capital of Bavaria since 1503, but didn't really achieve prominence until the 19th century under the guiding hand of Ludwig I. Ludwig became more conservative and repressive, and carried on an affair with the actress and dancer Lola Montez. He was forced to abdicate in favour of his son, Maxmilian II, who started a building renaissance, promoting science, industry and education.

At the turn of the last century there were half a million residents, but in the aftermath of WWI Munich became a hotbed of right-wing political ferment. Hitler staged a failed coup attempt in Munich in 1923 but the National Socialists seized power only a decade later. WWII brought bombing and more than 6000 civilian deaths until American forces entered the city in 1945. Then, in 1972, the Munich Olympics turned disastrous when 11 Israeli athletes were murdered.

Today it is the centre of Germany's hitech industries, besides being the home of Siemens and BMW.

Orientation

The main train station is just west of the city centre. From the station, head east along Bayerstrasse, through Karlsplatz, and then along Neuhauser Strasse and Kaufingerstrasse to Marienplatz, the hub of Munich.

North of Marienplatz are the Residenz (the former royal palace), Schwabing (the famous student section) and the parklands of the Englischer Garten through which the Isar River runs. East of Marienplatz is the Platzl quarter for beer houses and restaurants, as well as Maximilianstrasse, a fashionable street that is ideal for simply strolling and window-shopping.

Information

For late-night shopping and services such as pharmacies and currency exchange, the Hauptbahnhof's multilevel shopping arcades cannot be beat.

BOOKSHOPS

Hugendubel Marienplatz (☎ 484 484; Marienplatz 22); Salvatorplatz (☎ 484 484; Salvatorplatz 2) Has a good selection of guides and maps and the Salvatorplatz outlet has all English titles.

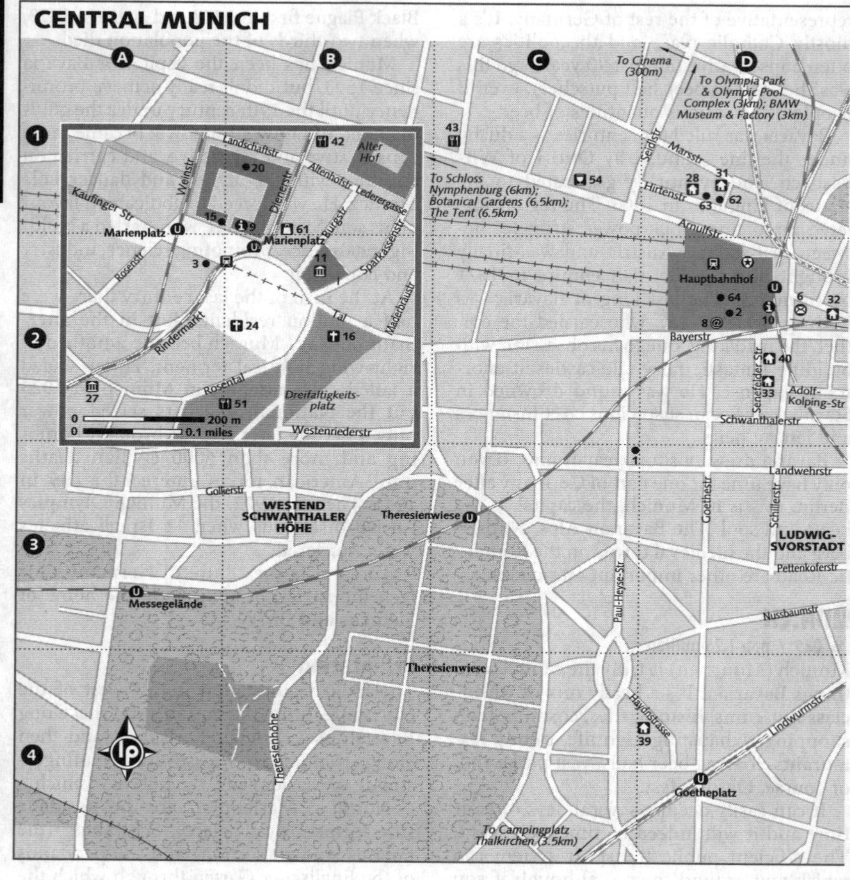

Max&Milian (☎ 260 3320; Ickstattstrasse 2) Gay bookshop and unofficial community centre.

INTERNET ACCESS

easyInternetcafé (☎ 5599 9696; Bahnhofplatz 1; per 80 min €2; 🕑 24hr) In the post office building, part of a chain of Internet cafés. Has hundreds of terminals and is normally packed with cyber surfers.

Internet Café (☎ 2070 2737; Tal 31; per 30 min €1; 🕑 24hr) Full service shop.

Times Square Internet Cafe (☎ 5126 2600; Hauptbahnhof; per 5 min €0.50; 🕑 7.30am-1am) Large bar and restaurant across from track 11.

LAUNDRY

City SB-Waschcenter (Paul-Heysestrasse 21; 🕑 7am-11pm; €4) Close to the Hauptbahnhof.

MEDIA

Expats in Bavaria (www.expats-in-bavaria.com) Quirky, colourful and useful site for all manner of local info.

Munich Found (www.munichfound.de; €3) Long-running English language local magazine with a good website. Good entertainment coverage.

Munich Transport (www.mvv-muenchen.de/en) Everything you need to know about Munich's transport system.

Municipal Website (www.muenchen.de) The city government's site is stuffed with useful info and links.

Toytown Munich (www.toytowngermany.com) Irreverent English-language recommendations from locals and expats. Good bar and club reviews.

POST

Main post office (Bahnhofplatz 1; 🕑 7.30am-8pm Mon-Fri, 9am-4pm Sat) The poste restante address is:

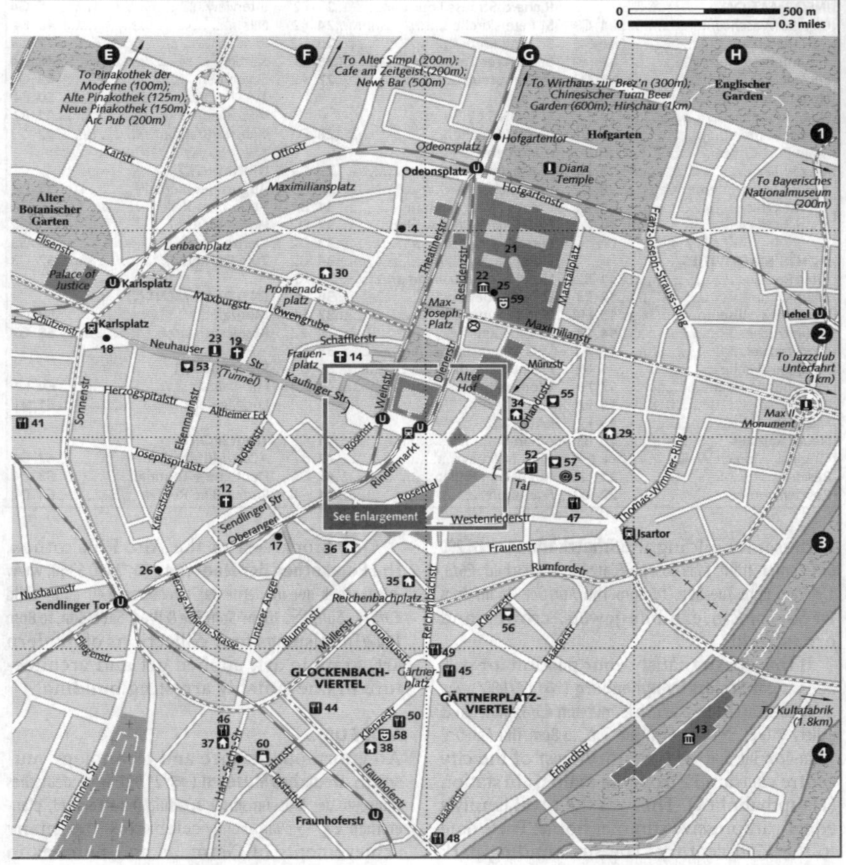

Hauptpostlagernd (Poste Restante), Bahnhofplatz 1, 80074 München.

TOURIST INFORMATION

EurAide (☎ 593 889; www.euraide.com; Hauptbahnhof; 🕑 8am-noon & 1-4pm Jun) Next to platform 11 at the main train station, EurAide validates rail passes, sells train tickets and tours and dispenses savvy advice in English.

Tourist office (☎ 2333 6500; www.muenchen-tourist.de) Main tourist office (Hauptbahnhof; 🕑 9am-8pm Mon-Sat, 10am-6pm Sun); branch office (Marienplatz; 🕑 10am-8pm Mon-Fri, 10am-4pm Sat) Both offices sell the Munich Welcome Card (from €7.50), which allows one to three days unlimited travel on public transport, plus discounts for many museums, galleries and other attractions. The main tourist office is to the right as you exit the Hauptbahnhof via the eastern entrance; its room-finding service is free. The branch office is beneath the Neues Rathaus. Be sure to ask for the excellent and free guide *Young and About in Munich*.

TRAVEL AGENCIES

DER Reisebüro (☎ 120 40; Hauptbahnhof)

Sights

PALACES

The huge **Residenz** (Max-Joseph-Platz 3) housed Bavarian rulers from 1385 to 1918 and features more than 500 years of architectural history. Apart from the palace itself, the **Residenzmuseum** (☎ 290 671; www.schloesser.bayern.de; Residenzstrasse 1; adult/child €6/5; 🕑 9am-6pm Tue-Sun, to 8pm Thu Apr-Oct, 10am-4pm Tue-Sun Nov-Mar) has an extraordinary array of 100 rooms containing no end of treasures and artworks.

INFORMATION
City-SB Waschcenter....1 C3
DER Reisebüro....(see 64)
easyInternetcafe....(see 6)
EurAide....2 D2
Hugendubel....3 A2
Hugendubel....4 F1
Internet Cafe....5 G3
Main Post Office....6 D2
Max&Milian....7 F4
Times Square Internet Cafe....8 D2
Tourist Office....9 B1
Tourist Office....10 D2

SIGHTS & ACTIVITIES
Altes Rathaus....11 B2
Asamkirche....12 F3
Deutsches Museum....13 H4
Frauenkirche....14 F2
Glockenspiel....15 A1
Heiliggeistkirche....16 B2
Jüdisches Museum....17 F3
Karlstor....18 E2
Michaelskirche....19 F2
Neues Rathaus....20 B1
Original Munich Walks....(see 64)
Residenz....21 G2
Residenzmuseum....22 G2
Richard Strauss Fountain....23 E2
St Peterskirche....24 B2
Schatzkammer....25 G2
Sendlinger Tor....26 E3
Stadtmuseum....27 A2

SLEEPING
4 you München....28 D1
Apartments & Hotel Maximilian....29 G2
Bayerischer Hof....30 F2
Creatif Hotel Elephant....31 D1
Easy Palace Station Hotel....32 D2
Euro Youth Hotel....33 D2
Hotel Alcron Garni....34 G2
Hotel am Viktualienmarkt....35 F3
Hotel Blauer Bock....36 F3
Hotel Olympic....37 F4
Pension am Gärtnerplatztheater....38 F4
Pension Haydn....39 D4
Wombat's....40 D2

EATING
Alhambra....41 E2
Alois Dallmayr....42 B1
Augustiner Keller....43 C1
Fraunhofer....44 F4
Interview....45 G4
Nil....46 F4
Riva....47 G3
Santini....48 G4
Seven Fish....49 G4
Two In One....50 F4
Viktualienmarkt....51 B2
Weisses Brauhaus....52 G3

DRINKING
Augustiner Bierhalle....53 E2
Augustiner Keller....54 C1
Hofbräuhaus....55 G2
Klenze 17....56 G3
Zum Dürnbrau....57 G3

ENTERTAINMENT
Morizz....58 F4
Residenztheater....59 G2

SHOPPING
Fuckuall....60 F4
Ludwig Beck....61 B1

TRANSPORT
ADM-Mitfahrzentrale....62 D1
Deutsche – Touring....63 D1
Radius Bike Rentals....64 D2

In the same building, the **Schatzkammer** (☎ 290 671; enter from Max-Joseph-Platz 3; adult/child €6/3; 9am-6pm Tue-Sun, to 8pm Thu Apr-Oct, 10am-4pm Tue-Sun Nov-Mar) exhibits jewels, crowns and ornate gold.

If this doesn't satisfy your passion for palaces, visit **Schloss Nymphenburg** (☎ 179 080; www.schloesser.bayern.de; adult/child museum €5/4, museum & gallery €10/8; 9am-6pm Tue-Sun, to 8pm Thu Apr-Oct, 10am-4pm Tue-Sun Nov-Mar), northwest of the city centre via tram 17 from the main train station (Hauptbahnhof). This was the royal family's equally impressive summer home. Parts date to the 17th century. The surrounding park deserves a long, regal stroll.

ART GALLERIES

A treasure-house of European masters from the 14th to 18th centuries, recently renovated **Alte Pinakothek** (☎ 238 052 16; www.alte-pinakothek.de; Barer Strasse 27; adult/child €5.50/4, €1 Sun; 10am-8pm Tue, 10am-5pm Wed-Sun), a stroll northeast of the city, includes highlights such as Dürer's Christ-like *Self Portrait* and his *Four Apostles*, Rogier van der Weyden's *Adoration of the Magi* and Botticelli's *Pietà*.

Immediately north of the Alte Pinakothek, the **Neue Pinakothek** (☎ 238 051 95; www.neue-pinakothek.de; Barer Strasse 29; adult/child €5.50/4, €1 Sun; 10am-8pm Wed, to 5pm Thu-Mon) contains mainly 19th-century works, including Van Gogh's *Sunflowers*, and sculpture.

One block east of the Alte Pinakothek, the **Pinakothek der Moderne** (☎ 2380 5360; www.pinakothek-der-moderne.de; Barer Strasse 40; adult/child €9/5, €1 Sun; 10am-5pm Tue & Wed, Sat & Sun, to 8pm Thu & Fri) displays four collections of modern art, graphic art, applied art and architecture in one suitably arresting building.

MUSEUMS

An enormous science and technology museum, **Deutches Museum** (☎ 217 91; www.deutsches-museum.de; Museumsinsel 1; adult/child €8.50/3, planetarium €2; 9am-5pm) celebrates the many achievements of Germans and humans in general. Kids become gleeful kids as they interact with the exhibits. So do adults. Many get a charge out of the shocking electrical displays. Take the S-Bahn to Isartor.

The **Bayerisches Nationalmuseum** (☎ 211 2401; www.bayerisches-nationalmuseum.de; Prinzregentenstrasse 3; adult/child €5/4; 10am-5pm Tue-Sun, to 8pm Thu), east of the Hofgarten, houses an impressive collection of Bavarian and southern German artefacts.

Tracing the lives of local Jews before, during and after the Holocaust, the **Jüdisches Museum** (☎ 2332 8189; www.juedisches-museum.muenchen.de; St Jakobsplatz 16) is moving to an impressive new space in March 2007. It promises to document a culture once important to Munich that was almost wiped out by the Nazis.

North of the city, auto-fetishists can thrill to the **BMW Museum** (☎ 3822 3307; www.bmwmobiletradition.de), adjacent to the BMW headquarters. As part of the recent corporate image arms race among German car-makers (see p492), BMW is opening a vast new celebration of its brand in mid-2007. Take the U3 to Olympiazentrum.

PARKS & GARDENS

One of the largest city parks in Europe, the **Englischer Garten**, west of the city centre, is a great place for strolling, especially along the Schwabinger Bach. In summer, nude sunbathing is the rule rather than the exception. It's not unusual for hundreds of naked people to be in the park during a normal business day, with their clothing stacked primly on the grass. If they're not doing this, they're probably drinking merrily at one of the park's three **beer gardens** (p482).

Munich's beautiful **Botanical Gardens** (☎ 1786 1350; adult/child €3/2; ⏰ varies with season, generally 9am-6pm) are two stops past Schloss Nymphenburg on tram 17.

OLYMPIA PARK COMPLEX

If you like heights, then take a ride up the lift of the 290m **Olympiaturm** (tower) situated in the **Olympia Park complex** (☎ 672 750; www.olympiapark-muenchen.de; adult/child €4/3.50; ⏰ tower 9am-midnight). And if you fancy a swim, then the **Olympic Pool Complex** (☎ 3067 2290; Olympic Park; admission €3.50; ⏰ 7am-11.15pm) will have you feeling like Mark Spitz while you imagine seven gold medals around your neck – or just work on your breast stroke. Take the U3 to Olympia zentrum.

Tours

The hordes of visitors and plethora of sights mean there's lots of people willing to show you around – an excellent way to gain background and context on what you see.

Mike's Bike Tours (☎ 2554 3987; www.mikesbiketours.com; tours from €24) Enjoyable (and leisurely) city cycling tours in English. Tours depart from the archway at the Altes Rathaus on Marienplatz.

Munich Walk Tours (☎ 2070 2736; www.munichwalktours; Tal 31; tours from €10) Walking tours of the city and a tour focused on 'beer, brewing and boozing'.

Original Munich Walks (☎ 5502 9374; www.radiusmunich.com; Hauptbahnhof near track 32; tours from €10) Runs English-language tours: a two-hour walk of the city heart and an excellent tour of Third Reich sites.

Festivals & Events

Hordes come to Munich for **Oktoberfest** (www.oktoberfest.de) running the 15 days before the first Sunday in October. Reserve accommodation well ahead and go early in the day so you can grab a seat in one of the hangar-sized beer 'tents'. The action takes place at the Theresienwiese grounds, about a 10-minute walk southwest of the Hauptbahnhof. While there is no entrance fee, those €7 1L steins of beer add up fast. Although its origins are in the marriage celebrations of Crown Prince Ludwig in 1810, there's nothing regal about this beery bacchanalia now; expect mobs, expect to meet new and drunken friends, expect decorum to vanish as night sets in and you'll have a blast.

Sleeping

Munich has no shortage of places to stay – except at Oktoberfest or during some busy summer periods, when the wise (meaning those with a room) will have booked. Many of the budget and midrange places can be found in the anonymous streets around the train station. There's no good reason to stay here if you can avoid it as you'll find more charm and genuine fun elsewhere.

BUDGET

Munich's youth hostels that are DJH and HI affiliated do not accept guests over age 26, except group leaders or parents accompanying a child.

Campingplatz Thalkirchen (☎ 7243 0808; www.camping-muenchen.de; Zentralländstrasse 49; camp sites per person/tent €4.50/4, heated cabin per person €11; ⏰ mid-Mar–end Oct) To get to this camping ground, southwest of the city centre, take the U3 to Thalkirchen and then catch bus 57 (about 20 minutes).

The Tent (☎ 141 4300; www.the-tent.com; In den Kirschen 30; bed in main tent €9, camp sites per tent/person €5.50/5.50; ⏰ Jun-Sep) Pads and blankets provided for the bagless, bring your own lock for the lockers. Take tram 17 to the Botanic Gardens then follow the signs to a legendary international party.

Euro Youth Hotel (☎ 5990 8811; www.euro-youth-hotel.de; Senefelderstrasse 5; dm €15-18, r €39-60; 💻) The party never stops at the friendly Euro Youth Hotel, where happy noncampers work on international relationships in the bar and lounge. Rooms and facilities in this classic old building are well maintained.

4 you München (☎ 552 1660; www.the4you.de; Hirtenstrasse 18; dm €17-25, r €34-54; 💻) The 4 you is proud of its ecofriendly practices (check out the virgin wool blankets). Dorms have four to 12 beds while the private rooms have their own baths.

Wombat's (☎ 599 8918; www.wombats-hostels.com; Senefelderstrasse 1; dm €19, d €62; 💻) Despite the name this 300-bed hostel is refreshingly free of Aussie shtick. Dorms have six to eight beds. There's a fun and relaxed vibe at this well-run place.

Easy Palace Station Hotel (☎ 558 7970; www.easypalace.com; Schützenstrasse 7; dm €20, r €29-69; 💻) This once-sedate midrange hotel has been converted into a budget haven (you can still see traces of its past stodgy life). Dorm rooms have four to six beds. Singles and doubles have both shared and private baths.

MIDRANGE

Pension Haydn (☎ 5440 4703; www.pension-haydn.de; Haydnstrasse 9; r €38-95) Not far from Goetheplatz U-Bahn station on a quiet residential street, the Haydn's rooms are tended with care. More money buys private bathrooms.

Hotel am Viktualienmarkt (☎ 225 014; www.hotel-am-viktualienmarkt.de; Utzschneiderstrasse 14; r €40-150; 💻) Near the Viktualienmarkt (duh!), the 27 renovated rooms have a nice, light feel. It's good value in a great location.

Creatif Hotel Elephant (☎ 555 785; www.munich-hotel.net; Lämmerstrasse 6; r €50-150; ⊠ 💻) The Creatif is a delightful and friendly place bursting with flowers. Its 44 rooms are stylish and comfortable, in an Ikea sort of way and there's free wi-fi.

Hotel Alcron Garni (☎ 228 3511; www.hotel-alcron.de; Ledererstrasse 13; r €60-100; ⊠ 💻) Nicely located near the Marienplatz, the 14 rooms here are furnished with vintage furniture. It's a good place to crash in the very middle of town.

Hotel Blauer Bock (☎ 231 780; www.hotelblauerbock.de; Sebastiansplatz 9; r €60-102, with shared bathroom €41-79; ⊠) This hotel traces its hostelry roots back more than a century. The 75 rooms now are modern and comfortable and the location on a quieter side street is excellent.

Pension am Gärtnerplatztheater (☎ 202 5170; www.pension-gaertnerplatztheater.de; Klenzestrasse 45; r €65-180; 💻) An antique-filled classic just down the street from hip and happening Gärtnerplatz. The 10 rooms have a timeless air, although that scent is wood polish.

TOP END

Hotel Olympic (☎ 231 890; www.hotel-olympic.de; Hans-Sachs-Strasse 4; r €90-180; 💻) This hotel has classy yet with unfussy decor that highlights the many fine antiques and artworks. There are 38 very nice, spacious rooms and they have wi-fi. You can't beat the relatively quiet location.

Apartments & Hotel Maximilian (☎ 242 580; www.maximilian-munich.com; Hochbrückenstrasse 18; r €130-300; ⊠ ❄ 💻) This new and stylish place has 54 studios and apartments in a great location. All units come with kitchen facilities and wi-fi. There's a garden out back and the staff are truly lovely. This is a great place for longer stays or for those sick of hotel rooms. Look for deals.

Bayerischer Hof (☎ 212 00; www.bayerischerhof.de; Promenadeplatz 2-6; r from €210; ⊠ ❄ 💻 🏊) Opened in 1841, generations of world leaders have made the Bayerischer Hof their home in Munich. The beautiful glass domed atrium, marble and gold leaf details and bustling efficiency are just some of the exquisite details. Breakfast on the top-floor terrace is a sublime treat.

Eating

Clusters of restaurants can be found anywhere there's pedestrian life. The streets in and around Gärtnerplatz and Glockenback-Viertel are the flavour-of-the-moment. You can always do well in and around Marienplatz and the wonderful Viktualienmarkt, while Schwabing is always full of eating delights.

RESTAURANTS

Riva Bar Pizzeria (☎ 220 240; Tal 44; mains €7-12) Straight from fashionable Milan, this authentic pizza place packs 'em in for wood-fired treats. Wait for a table inside or out at the long bar up front, toss a *ciao* or two to the cheery chefs.

Fraunhofer (☎ 266 460; Fraunhoferstrasse 9; mains €7-14; 💻) The always-crowded Fraunhofer serves up good Bavarian cuisine from a changing menu. The setting is old and the patrons young at this hip place.

Wirthaus zur Brez'n (☎ 390 092; Leopoldstrasse 72; mains €7-15) Tradition abounds at this Bavarian beer hall and restaurant. Of the many levels, go for the *keller* (basement) for real authenticity. There's season brews on tap and choice menu items like duck. Look for the bad jokes on the walls.

MUNICH WALKING TOUR

The pivotal **Marienplatz** is a good starting point for a walking tour of Munich. Dominating the square is the towering neo-Gothic **Neues Rathaus** (new town hall; Marienplatz), with its ever-dancing **Glockenspiel** (carillon), which performs at 11am and noon (also at 5pm from March to October), bringing the square to an expectant standstill (note the fate of the Austrian knight…). Two important churches are on this square: the baroque star **St Peterskirche** (Rindermarket 1; tower €1.50; 9am-7pm Apr-Oct, to 6pm Nov-Mar) and, behind the **Altes Rathaus**, the often forgotten **Heiliggeistkirche** (Tal 77; 7am-6pm). Head west along shopping street Kaufingerstrasse to the landmark of Munich, the late-Gothic **Frauenkirche** (Church of Our Lady; 423 457; Frauenplatz; tower adult/child €3/1.50; tower 10am-5pm Mar-Oct) with its then-trendy 16th-century twin onion domes. Go inside and join the hordes gazing at the grandeur of the place, or climb the tower for majestic views of Munich. Continue west to the large grey 16th-century **Michaelskirche** (609 0224; Neuhauserstrasse 52; 8am-7pm), Germany's earliest and grandest Renaissance church.

Further west is the **Richard Strauss Fountain** and the medieval **Karlstor**, an old city gate. Double back towards Marienplatz and turn right onto Eisenmannstrasse, which becomes Kreuzstrasse and converges with Herzog-Wilhelm-Strasse at the medieval gate of **Sendlinger Tor**. Go down the shopping street Sendlinger Strasse to the **Asamkirche** (Sendlinger Strasse 34), a flamboyant 17th-century church designed by brothers Cosmas Damian and Egid Quirin Asam. The ornate marble façade won't prepare you for the opulence inside, where scarcely an inch is left unembellished.

Continue along Sendlinger Strasse and turn right on Hermann-Sack-Strasse to reach the **Stadtmuseum** (233; St-Jakobs-Platz 1; adult/child €4/2; 10am-6pm Tue-Sun), where a mixed but good bag of exhibits cover beer brewing, fashion, musical instruments, photography and puppets (who *don't* get top billing).

Santini (202 2658; Fraunhoferstrasse 43; mains €8-15) Jaunty red-and-white checked tablecloths set the mood at this cheery pizzeria and pasta place. There are tables outside and candles providing a romantic glow inside.

Seven Fish (2300 0219; Gärtnerplatz 6; mains €8-20) Outside there's a stylish café, inside it's a higher-end stylish restaurant with blue accents on exposed brick walls. As the name implies, fish is the specialty here and the line-up depends on what's fresh.

Alhambra (5488 1741; Schwanthaler Strasse 13; meals €9-18) A great place near the Hauptbahnhof, this stylish tapas place serves up Mediterranean and Spanish treats that range from hummus to tortillas. There's a great long bar.

Weisses Brauhaus (290 1380; Tal 7; mains €9-20) The place for classic Bavarian fare in an ancient beer-hall setting. Everything from *weissewurst* (beloved local white sausage) to hearty traditional fare such as boiled ox cheeks is on offer.

CAFÉS

Two in One (2024 4595; Klenzestrasse 39; snacks €3-6; 10am-7.30pm Tue-Sat) That amazing smell may be the fresh cut flowers or the fine tea. It's hard to tell at this florist-cum-tea shop near Gärtnerplatz. Have a cake at one of the tiny tables and try to decide.

News Bar (281 787; Amalienstrasse 55; sandwiches €5;) Besides food and drinks, newspapers and magazines are available at this popular Schwabing hang-out. Enjoy the *Herald-Tribune* with a latte.

Café am Zeitgeist (2865 6873; Türkenstrasse 74; meals €6-12) This casual place stretches back off the street so you can enjoy an outside table without exhaust. There are toys for the kids and treats like *flammenkuchen* for one and all.

Nil (265 545; Hans-Sachs-Strasse 2; meals €7-12; 8am-4am) Right in trendy Glockenback-Viertel, this hip place draws a straight and gay crowd in the know. Tables outside are packed when the sun shines, inside it's packed all night long.

Interview (202 1646; Gärtnerplatz 1; mains €7-15) Patrons at this thriving and trendy café are more interested in eyeing each other than their food. Too bad, as the breakfasts served to 5pm (as well as the pastas, salads and more) are worth more than a glance.

SELF-CATERING

Viktualienmarkt, just south of Marienplatz, is a large open-air market open daily except

Saturday afternoon and Sunday, where you can put together a picnic feast to take to the Englischer Garten. The fresh produce, cheese and baked goods are hard to resist. Or relax here under the trees, at tables provided by one of the many beer and sausage vendors.

Alois Dallmayr (☎ 213 50; Dienerstrasse 14) One of the world's great delicatessens, behind the mustard-yellow awnings you'll find sparkling cases filled with fine foods. This is the place to come if you want a pet crayfish (see their fountain home).

Drinking

Apart from the beer halls and gardens, Munich has no shortage of lively pubs. Schwabing and Glockenback-Viertel are good places to follow your ears. Many serve food.

Alter Simpl (☎ 272 3083; Türkenstrasse 57) On a quieter Schwabing street than most, this historic pub exudes atmosphere. Thomas Mann hung out here 100 years ago and probably still would today.

Arc Pub (☎ 0178-3256423; Schraudolphstrasse 24) A popular sports bar with expats and travellers who want to catch live broadcasts of the action from home – wherever that may be. Popular and lively.

Klenze 17 (☎ 228 5795; Klenzestrasse 17) The extensive whisky selection is almost as large as Klenze 17's two small rooms, usually populated with young folks, many scarfing down nachos at midnight.

Entertainment

CINEMAS & THEATRE

Munich is one of the cultural capitals of Germany; the publications and websites listed on p474 can guide you to the best events. For tickets, try **Munchën Ticket** (☎ 5481 8154; www.muenchenticket.de).

Residenztheater (☎ 2185 1920; Max-Joseph-Platz 2) Home of the Bavarian State Opera (www.staatsoper.de) and the site of many cultural events (particularly during the opera festival in July).

Cinema (☎ 555 255; www.cinema-muenchen.com; Nymphenburger Strasse 31) Current films in English are screened here. Take the U1 to Stiglmaier Platz, exit at Nymphenburgerstrasse.

NIGHTCLUBS

Jazzclub Unterfahrt (☎ 448 2794; Einsteinstrasse 42-44) Near the Max-Weber-Platz U-Bahn station. It has live music from 7.30pm nightly, and open jam sessions on Sunday night. Things often go until 3am.

Kultafabrik (www.kultafabrik.de; Grafingerstrasse 6; 🕑 8pm-6am or later) From potatoes to clubbing. This former spud factory has been reborn as a vast playground of clubs. There's over 25 that you can sample before you end up mashed or fried. The themes range from live rock to techno (of course) to post-Soviet squalor. It's close to the Ostbahnhof station.

GAY & LESBIAN VENUES

Much of Munich's gay and lesbian nightlife is around Gärtnerplatz and the Glockenback-Viertel. Any of the places in this area listed above (such as Nil) will have a mixed crowd. *Our Munich* and *Sergej* are monthly guides easily found in this neighbourhood. Another good resource is Max&Milian (p473).

Morizz (☎ 201 6776; Klenzestrasse 43) is a popular haunt for gay men that takes it cue from a classic Paris nightspot. It has a long wine and cocktail list and goes until dawn.

Shopping

All shoppers converge on the Marienplatz to buy designer shoes or kitschy souvenirs. The stylish department store **Ludwig Beck** (☎ 236 910; Marienplatz 11) has something for everyone. Bypass Calvin et al for more unusual European choices.

For the well-heeled, check out the *haute couture* shops on Maxmilianstrasse. Meanwhile Schwabing boasts its fair share of quirky, artistic boutiques, especially along Hohenzollernstrasse.

The edgy, trendy culture of Glockenback-Viertel is exemplified by **Fuckuall** (☎ 2323 1816; Jahnstrasse 6), a purveyor of German gangsta clothing and whose distinctive and declarative logo is pasted up all over town.

Christkindlmarkt (Marienplatz) in December is large and well stocked but often expensive, so buy a warm drink and just wander around. A huge flea market, the **Auer Dult** (Mariahilfplatz), has great buys and takes place during the last weeks of April, July and October.

Getting There & Away

AIR

Munich's sparkling white **airport** (MUC; www.munich-airport.de) is second in importance only to Frankfurt-am-Main for international and national connections. Flights will take you to all major destinations worldwide. Main German cities are serviced by at least half a dozen flights daily. easyJet and DBA are major budget carriers here.

BUS

Munich is linked to the Romantic Road by the popular **Deutsche-Touring** (☎ 889 895 13; www.deutsche-touring.com; Hirtenstrasse 14) Munich-Frankfurt service (see p482). Buses stop along the northern side of the train station on Arnulfstrasse.

CAR & MOTORCYCLE

Munich has autobahns radiating out on all sides. Take the A9 to Nuremberg, the A92 to Passau, the A8 east to Salzburg, the A95 to Garmisch-Partenkirchen and the A8 to Ulm or Stuttgart. The main rental companies have counters together on the second level of the Hauptbahnhof. For arranged rides, the **ADM-Mitfahrzentrale** (☎ 194 40; www.mitfahrz.org; Lämmerstrasse 6; 8am-8pm) is near the Hauptbahnhof. The cost is split with the driver and you can reach most parts of Germany for well under €40.

TRAIN

Train services to/from Munich are excellent. There are rapid connections at least every two hours to all major cities in Germany, as well as daily EC trains to other European cities such as Paris (€105, nine hours), Vienna (€68, four hours) and Zurich (€59, 4½ hours).

High-speed ICE services from Munich include Frankfurt (€75, 3¾ hours, hourly), Hamburg (€115, six hours, hourly) and Berlin (€96, six hours, every two hours).

Getting Around

TO/FROM THE AIRPORT

Munich's international airport is connected by the S8 and the S1 to Marienplatz and the Hauptbahnhof (€8.80). The service takes about 40 minutes and there is a train every 10 minutes from 4am until around 12.30am. The S8 route is slightly faster.

Taxis make the long haul for at least €60.

BICYCLE

Pedal power is popular in relatively flat Munich. **Radius Bike Rental** (☎ 596 113; www.radiusmunich.com; Hauptbahnhof near track 32; 10am-6pm May-Sep) rents out two-wheelers from €17 per day.

CAR & MOTORCYCLE

It's not worth driving in the city centre – many streets are pedestrian only. The tourist office has a map that shows city parking places (€2 or more per hour).

PUBLIC TRANSPORT

Munich's excellent public transport network (MVV; www.mvv-muenchen.de) is zone-based, and most places of interest to tourists (except Dachau and the airport) are within the 'blue' inner zone (Innenraum; €2.20). MVV tickets are valid for the S-Bahn, U-Bahn, trams and buses, but they must be validated before use. The U-Bahn stops operating around 12.30am Monday to Friday and 1.30am on Saturday and Sunday, but there are some later buses and S-Bahns. Rail passes are valid exclusively on the S-Bahn.

Kurzstrecke (short rides) cost €1.10 and are good for no more than four stops on buses and trams, and two stops on the U- and S-Bahns. *Tageskarte* (day passes) for the inner zone cost €4.80, while three-day tickets cost €11.80, or €20 for two adults travelling together (partner ticket).

TAXI

Taxis are expensive (€2.80 flag fall, plus €1.50 per kilometre) and not much more convenient than public transport. For a radio-dispatched taxi dial ☎ 216 10.

DACHAU

The first Nazi concentration camp was **Dachau** (☎ 08131-669 970; www.kz-gedenkstaette-dachau.de; Alte-Roemerstrasse 75; admission free; 9am-5pm Tue-Sun), built in March 1933. Jews, political prisoners, homosexuals and others deemed 'undesirable' by the Third Reich were imprisoned in the camp. More than 200,000 people were sent here; more than 30,000 died at Dachau and countless others died after being transferred to other death camps. An English-language documentary is shown at 11.30am and 3.30pm. A visit includes camp relics, memorials and a very sobering museum. Take the S2 (direction Petershausen) to Dachau and then bus 726 or 724 to the camp. A Munich XXL day ticket (€6.50) will cover the trip.

ROMANTIC ROAD

The popular and schmaltzily named Romantic Road (Romantische Strasse) links a series of picturesque Bavarian towns and cities. It's not actually one road per se but rather a 353km route chosen to highlight as many quaint towns and cities as possible in western Bavaria.

From north to south it includes the following major stops:

- Würzburg – Starting point and featuring 18th-century artistic splendour among the vineyards.
- Rothenburg ob der Tauber – The medieval walled hub of cutesy picturesque Bavarian touring.
- Dinkelsbühl – Another medieval walled town replete with moat and watchtowers, a smaller Rothenberg. The town is best reached by the Romantic Road by bus or car.
- Augsburg – A medieval and Renaissance city with many good places for a beer.
- Wieskirche – This Unesco World Heritage **church** (☎ 08862 932 930; www.wieskirche.de; ⏰ 8am-5pm) is a truly amazing work of 18th-century rococo excess. It towers over a tiny village 25km northeast of Füssen. The church is best reached by the Romantic Road bus or car.
- Füssen – The southern end of the route and the cute and over-run home of mad King Ludwig's castles.

In addition to these principal stops, more than a dozen more little towns clamour for attention – and your money.

Getting There & Around

The principal cities and towns listed above are all easily reached by train – see the individual listings for details. But to really explore the route, you are best off with your own transportation. The entire length is copiously marked with brown signs in German, English and Japanese. With a car, you can blow through places of little interest and linger at those that attract.

A popular way to tour the Romantic Road is the **Deutsche-Touring Romantic Road bus** (www.deutsche-touring.com). Starting in Frankfurt in the north and Munich in the south, a bus runs in each direction each day covering the entire route between Würzburg and Füs-

BEER HALLS & BEER GARDENS

Beer-drinking is not just an integral part of Munich's entertainment scene, it's a reason to visit. Germans drink an average of 130L of the amber liquid each per year, while Munich residents manage to drink much more. Locals will be happy to help ensure that you don't bring down the average.

Beer halls can be vast boozy affairs seating thousands or much more modest neighbourhood hang-outs. The same goes for beer gardens. Both come in all shapes and sizes. What's common is a certain camaraderie among strangers, huge litre glasses of beer (try putting one of those in your carry on) and lots of cheap food – the saltier the better. Note that in beer gardens tradition allows you to bring your own food, a boon if you want an alternative to pretzels, sausages and the huge white radishes served with, you guessed it, salt.

On a warm day there's nothing better than sitting and sipping among the greenery at one of the Englischer Garten's classic beer gardens. **Chinesischer Turm** (☎ 383 8730) is justifiably popular while the nearby **Hirschau** (☎ 369 942) on the banks of Kleinhesseloher See is less crowded.

Augustiner Keller (☎ 594 393; Arnulfstrasse 52) Only five minutes from the Hauptbahnhof, the Keller has a large and leafy beer garden and a fine cavernous hall when the weather keeps you indoors.

Augustiner Bierhalle (☎ 5519 9257; Neuhauser Strasse 27) What you probably imagine an old-style Munich beer hall looks like, filled with laughter, smoke and clinking glasses.

Zum Dürnbrau (☎ 222 195; Tal 21) Tucked into a corner off Tal, this is a great and authentic little alternative to the Hofbräuhaus. There's a small beer garden and drinkers of dark drafts enjoy pewter-topped mugs.

Hofbräuhaus (☎ 2901 3610; Am Platzl 9) The ultimate cliché of Munich beer halls. Tourists arrive by the busload but no-one seems to mind that this could be Disneyland (although the theme park wasn't once home to Hitler's early speeches, like this place was).

sen. However, seeing the entire route in one day is only for those with a love of buses and unusual fortitude. Stops are brief (15 minutes for Wieskirche, *Schnell!* 30 minutes for Rothenburg, *Schnell!* etc) so you'll want to choose places where you can break the trip for a day (stopovers are allowed). But of course this leads you to decide between a 30-minute visit and a 24-hour one.

The buses depart April to October from Frankfurt Hauptbahnhof at 8am and from Munich Hauptbahnhof at 8.15am and take about 13 hours. The total fare (tickets are bought on board) is a pricey €139. Railpass holders get a 60% discount and flexipass holders do not need to use a travel day for the discount. You can also just ride for individual segments (eg Rothenberg to Augsburg costs €27).

WÜRZBURG

☎ 0931 / pop 133,000

Nestled among river valleys lined with vineyards, Würzburg beguiles even before you reach the city centre. Three of the four largest wine growing estates in all of Germany are here and most of the delicate whites produced locally never leave the region – the locals will always reach for a wine glass first. Over 1300 years old, Würzburg was rebuilt after bombings late in the war (it took only 17 minutes to almost completely destroy the city). Today it's a centre of art, beautiful architecture and delicate wines.

The **tourist office** (☎ 372 335; www.wuerzburg.de; Oberer Markt; 10am-6pm Mon-Fri, 10am-2pm Sat & Sun May-Oct, reduced hr & closed Sun other times), in the rococo masterpiece Haus zum Falken.

Sights

The magnificent, sprawling **Residenz** (☎ 355 170; www.schloesser.bayern.de; Residenzplatz 2; adult/child €5/4; 9am-6pm Apr-Oct, 10am-4pm Nov-Mar), a baroque masterpiece by Neumann, took a generation to build and boasts the world's largest ceiling fresco (graphic artists take note: he didn't need no stinking Photoshop); the **Hofgarten** at the back is a beautiful spot. The interior of the **Dom St Kilian** (☎ 386 261; Kiliansplatz; admission €5; 10am-7pm Tue-Sun Apr-Oct, to 5pm Tue-Sun Nov-Mar) and the adjacent **Neumünster**, an 11th-century church in the old town housing the bones of St Kilian – the patron Saint of Würzburg – continue the baroque themes of the Residenz.

Neumann's fortified **Alter Kranen** (old crane), which serviced a dock on the riverbank south of Friedensbrücke, is now the **Haus des Frankenweins** (☎ 390 1111; Kranenkai 1), where you can taste Franconian wines (for around €3 per glass).

The medieval fortress **Marienberg**, across the river on the hill, is reached by crossing the 15th-century stone **Alte Mainbrücke** (bridge) from the city and walking up Tellstiege, a small alley. It encloses the **Fürstenbau Museum** (☎ 438 38; admission €4; 9am-6pm Tue-Sun Apr-Oct, 10am-4pm Tue-Sun Nov-Mar) featuring the Episcopal apartments, and the regional **Mainfränkisches Museum** (☎ 430 16; adult/child €3/1.50; 10am-5pm Tue-Sun Apr-Oct, to 4pm Nov-Mar). See both on a combined card (€5). For a simple thrill, wander the walls enjoying the panoramic views.

Sleeping & Eating

Würzburg's many *Weinstuben* are excellent places to sample the local vintages. Look for crests of gilded grapes over entrances. Sanderstrasse has a good strip of lively bars.

Kanu-Club (☎ 725 36; Mergentheimer Strasse 13b; camp sites per person/tent €5/5; Apr-Sep) A camping ground on the west bank of the Main; take tram 3 or 5 to Jugendbühlweg.

Hostel Babelfish (☎ 3040430; www.babelfish-hostel.de; Prymstrasse 3; dm/d from €16/45;) Close to the centre, this new hostel is ultra-clean and well run. Dorms have four to 10 beds each. From the train station walk east 200m.

Pension Spehnkuch (☎ 547 52; www.pension-spehnkuch.de; Röntgenring 7; s/d from €29/60) Located by the train station, the seven simple rooms are kept spotless by the charming family.

Hotel Till Eulenspiegel (☎ 355 840; www.hotel-till-eulenspiegel.de; Sanderstrasse 1a; s/d from €63/85;) Oxygen-lovers celebrate: this is a non-smoking hotel. Run by the gregarious Johannes, the 18 rooms are comfortable and some have sunny balconies. There's also a small but good *weinstube* and a pub serving unusual Bavarian microbrews.

Karma X (☎ 329 4149; Kardinal-Fraulhaber-Platz 4; meals €4-8; 7am-7.30pm Mon-Sat;) A kind of Danish modern café done up in creams and orange – sort of like fresh-squeezed orange juice (which you can order). This upscale deli offers breakfasts, soups, salads, sandwiches, desserts and picnics to go.

Weinstuben Juliusspital (☎ 540 80; Juliuspromenade 19; meals €8-20) This rambling place serves from a long list of wines. You can have a meal or just a drink at one of the many old wooden tables.

Zum Stachel (☎ 527 70; Gressengasse 1; mains €12-25) This cosy *weinstube* traces its roots back to the 15th century. The ambitious menu has numerous local specialities including excellent beef and seafood dishes. There's a garden seating area and the ceiling inside is decorated with murals showing a *stachel* (mace) in action. Book ahead.

Getting There & Away

Würzburg is served by frequent trains from Frankfurt (€21 to €28, one to two hours) and one hour from Nuremberg (€14 to €19, 40 minutes to one hour). It's a major stop for the ICE trains on the Hamburg–Munich line. It is also on the Deutsche-Touring Romantic Road bus route (€14, 2¼ hours to/from Rothenburg). The stop is in front of the train station.

BAMBERG

☎ 0951 / pop 70,000

Off the major tourist routes, Bamberg is celebrated by those in the know. It boasts an amazing and preserved collection of 17th- and 18th-century buildings, palaces and churches. It is bisected by a large canal and a fast-flowing river that are spanned by cute little bridges and it even has its own local style of beer. No wonder it has been recognised by Unesco as a World Heritage Site. Could it be the best town in Germany?

The **tourist office** (☎ 871 161; www.bamberg.info; Geyerswörthstrasse 3; 🕑 9.30am-6pm Mon-Fri, to 2.30pm Sat year-round & Sun May-Oct) is on an island in the Regnitz River.

Sights

Bamberg's main appeal is its fine buildings – their sheer number, their jumble of styles and the ambience this creates. Most attractions are spread either side of the Regnitz River, but the colourful **Altes Rathaus** (Obere Brücke; 🕑 9.30am-4.30pm Tue-Sun Apr-Sep, 10am-4pm Tue-Sun Oct-Mar) is actually precariously perched on its own islet.

The princely and ecclesiastical district is centred on Domplatz, where the Romanesque and Gothic **cathedral** (Domplatz; 🕑 8am-6pm Apr-Sep, 8am-5pm Oct-Mar), housing the statue of the chivalric king-knight, the *Bamberger Reiter*, is the biggest attraction. Across the square, the imposing 17th-century **Neue Residenz** (☎ 519 390; Domplatz 8; adult/child €3/2; 🕑 9am-6pm Apr-Sep, 10am-4pm Oct-Mar) is filled with treasures and opulent décor.

Above Domplatz is the former Benedictine monastery of St Michael, at the top of Michaelsberg. The **Kirche St Michael** (Franziskanergasse 2; 🕑 9am-6pm) is a must-see for its baroque art and the herbal compendium painted on its ceiling. The garden terraces afford another marvellous overview of the city's splendour.

Sleeping & Eating

Bamberg's unique style of beer is called *Rauchbier*, which literally means smoked beer. With a bacon flavour at first, it is a smooth brew that goes down easy. Happily, many of the local breweries also rent rooms.

Campingplatz Insel (☎ 563 20; www.campinginsel.de; Am Campingplatz 1; camp sites per person/tent €3.50/6) A well-equipped place in a tranquil spot right on the river. Take bus 18 to Campingplatz.

Jugendherberge Wolfsschlucht (☎ 560 02; www.djh.de; Oberer Leinritt 70; dm €15; 🕑 closed mid-Dec–mid-Jan) On the river's west bank, take bus 18 to Rodelbahn, walk northeast to the riverbank, then turn left to this cute 92-bed hostel.

Brauerei Spezial (☎ 243 04; www.brauerei-spezial.de; Obere Königstrasse 10; r €20-55, meals €8-15) Across from Fässla, this half-timbered brewery has cosy drinking and dining areas featuring old tile stoves. The seven rooms are quite simple but comfortable.

Petrolthof Fässla (☎ 265 16; www.faessla.de; Obere Königstrasse 19-21; s/d €37/55) It's a dream come true – a bed in a brewery. The 21 rooms are large, clean and comfy. Look for the keg over the door.

Hotel Alte Post (☎ 980 260; Heiliggrabstrasse 1; r €38-100; 💻) A five-minute walk from the train station, this 40-room place has simple rooms that come with wi-fi.

Teegiesserei (☎ 297 2595; Pfahlplätzchen 2; meals €6-10; 🕑 11am-7.30pm Tue-Sun) Like an upscale home featured in a Sunday supplement, this stylish café at first seems all style over substance. But sample the many cakes and teas and you'll see the depths of its goodness.

Schlenkerla (☎ 560 60; Dominikanerstrasse 6; meals €7-15) This ancient half-timbered building is *the* place to sample Rauchbier. The traditional menu boasts many a porky platter and there's always seasonal specials.

Getting There & Away

There are hourly trains to/from both Würzburg (€15.50, one hour) and Nuremberg (€10, one hour). Bamberg is also served by ICE trains running between Munich (€48, 2½ hours) and Berlin (€69, four hours) every two hours.

ROTHENBURG OB DER TAUBER

☎ 09861 / pop 12,000

In the Middle Ages, Rothenburg's town fathers built strong walls to protect the town from siege; today they are the reason the town is under siege from tourists. The most stereotypical of all German walled towns, Rothenburg can't help being so cute.

Granted 'free imperial city' status in 1274, it's a confection of twisting cobbled lanes and pretty architecture enclosed by towered stone walls. The **tourist office** (☎ 404 92; www.rothenburg.de; Marktplatz 2; 9am-noon, 1-5pm Mon-Fri, 10am-2pm Sat) can help you find a room, which might be a good idea because after dark the streets are quiet and the underlying charm comes out.

Note that the gaggle of Christmas shops and 'museums' are quite wiley – once in you have to walk the entire labyrinth in order to escape.

Sights

The **Rathaus on Markt** was commenced in Gothic style in the 14th century but completed in Renaissance style. The **tower** (admission €1) gives a majestic view over the town and the Tauber Valley. According to legend, the town was saved during the Thirty Years' War when the mayor won a challenge by the Imperial general Tilly and downed more than 3L of wine at a gulp. The **Meistertrunk** scene is re-enacted by the clock figures on the tourist office building (eight times daily in summer). Actors re-enact other famous scenes from the past (but not the mythical assault on the tour bus by fudge vendors) at 6.30pm Friday, May to September.

Totally uncommercial, **Jakobskirche** (☎ 700 60; Klingengasse 1; adult/child €2/1; 9am-4pm) is sober and Gothic. Marvel at the carved *Heilige Blut Altar* (Holy Blood Altar).

The **Reichsstadt Museum** (☎ 939 043; Klosterhof 5; adult/child €3/1.50; 9.30am-5.30pm Apr-Oct, 1-4pm Nov-Mar), in the former convent, features the superb *Rothenburger Passion* in 12 panels and the Judaica room, with a collection of gravestones with Hebrew inscriptions.

Sleeping & Eating

Resist the temptation to try a *Schneeball*, a crumbly ball of bland dough with the taste and consistency of chalk – surely one of Europe's worst 'local specialities'.

Das Lädle (☎ 6130; www.das-laedle.de; Spitalgasse 18; r €22-48) A good budget option, with light, modern rooms in a central location.

Hotel & Cafe Uhl (☎ 4895; www.hotel-uhl.de; Plölein 8; r €35-70, meals €6-10; ☒) Downstairs there's a nice bakery and café with views, upstairs the 12 rooms are bright and modern.

Altfrankische Weinstube (☎ 6404; Klosterhof 7; r €48-70; mains €7-15) Vine covered and cosy, the Altfrankische Weinstube is justifiably popular, with a varied and well-priced menu, and a fantastic atmosphere set by the wine barrels out front. The rooms are simple and comfortable.

Getting There & Away

There are hourly trains to/from Steinach, a transfer point for service to Würzburg (total journey €10, 70 minutes). Rothenburg is a cross-road for tourist buses. The Deutsche-Touring Romantic Road bus pauses here for 30 minutes. A companion bus serving the Castle Road route provides daily links May to September to Heidelberg (€46, three hours) and Nürnberg (€14, two hours).

NUREMBERG

☎ 0911 / pop 494,000

Levelled during the war, Nuremberg has spent the last few decades rebuilding itself. It's hard to sense that the town was once a half-timbered medieval wonder but that's OK, as the current version has charms of its own. The narrow backstreets reward wanderers, who can take sustenance at places grilling up the town's seductive namesake sausage. Germanisches Nationalmuseum is a reason to not just get off the train but to make the journey. In winter the famous Christmas market draws hordes.

Nuremberg played a major role during the Nazi years, as documented in Leni Riefenstahl's film *Triumph of Will* and during the war crimes trials afterwards. It has done an admirable job of confronting this ugly past with museums and exhibits.

Orientation

The main train station is just outside the city walls of the old town. The main artery, the mostly pedestrian Königstrasse, takes you through the old town and its major squares. Breite Gasse, Königsstrasse and Karolinenstrasse are the main shopping streets.

Information

Both tourist offices sell the two-day Nürnberg Card (€18), which provides free public transport and entry to all museums and attractions, including those in nearby Fürth.

Netzkultur (☎ 211 0782; 3rd fl, Maximum Bldg, Färberstrasse 11; per hr €3.50; 🕑 9-1am) Burn CDs, surf the Internet.

Post office (Bahnhofplatz 1)

Schnell und Sauber Laundry (☎ 180 9400; Sulzbacher Strasse 86; per load €4; 🕑 6am-midnight) Tram 8 to Deichslerstrasse.

Tourist offices (www.tourismus.nuernberg.de) Main office (☎ 233 6132; Königstrasse 93; 🕑 9am-7pm Mon-Sat); branch office (☎ 233 6135; Hauptmarkt 18; 🕑 9am-6pm Mon-Sat, 10am-4pm Sun May-Sep)

Sights

The stunning **Germanisches Nationalmuseum** (☎ 133 10; www.gnm.de; Kartäusergasse 1; adult/child €5/4; 🕑 10am-6pm Tue-Sun, 10am-9pm Wed) is the most important general museum of German culture. It displays works by German painters and sculptors, an archaeological collection, arms and armour, musical and scientific instruments and toys. Look for the globe dating from 1492.

Close by, the sleek and harmonious **Neues Museum** (☎ 240 200; Luitpoldstrasse 5; adult/child €4/3; 🕑 10am-8pm Tue-Fri, to 6pm Sat & Sun) contains a superb collection of contemporary art and design.

The scenic **Altstadt** is easily covered on foot. On Lorenzer Platz there's the **St Lorenzkirche**, noted for the 15th-century tabernacle that climbs like a vine up a pillar to the vaulted ceiling.

To the north is the bustling **Hauptmarkt**, where the most famous Christkindlesmarkt in Germany is held from the Friday before Advent to Christmas Eve. The church here is the ornate **Pfarrkirche Unsere Liebe Frau**; the clock's figures go strolling at noon. Near the Rathaus is **St Sebalduskirche**, Nuremberg's oldest church (dating from the 13th century), with the shrine of St Sebaldus.

Climb up Burgstrasse to the enormous 15th-century **Kaiserburg complex** (☎ 225 726; Burg 13; adult/child €5/4; 🕑 9am-6pm Apr-Sep, 10am-4pm Oct-Mar) for good views of the city. The walls spread west to the tunnel-gate of **Tiergärtnertor**, where you can stroll behind the castle to the gardens. Nearby is the renovated **Albrecht-Dürer-Haus** (☎ 231 2568; Albrecht-Dürer-Strasse 39; adult/child €5/2.50; 🕑 10am-5pm Tue-Sun, to 8pm Thu), where Dürer, Germany's renowned Renaissance draughtsman, lived from 1509 to 1528.

Nuremberg's role during the Third Reich is well known. The Nazis chose this city as their propaganda centre and for mass rallies, which were held at **Luitpoldhain**, a (never completed) sports complex of megalomaniac proportions. After the war, the Allies deliberately chose Nuremberg as the site for the trials of Nazi war criminals. Not to be missed is the **Dokumentationzentrum** (☎ 231 5666; www.museen.nuernberg.de; Bayernstrasse 110; adult/child €5/2.50; 🕑 9am-6pm Mon-Fri, 10am-6pm Sat & Sun) in the north wing of the massive unfinished Congress Hall, which would have held 50,000 people for Hitler's spectacles. The museum's absorbing exhibits trace the rise of Hitler and the Nazis and the important role Nuremberg played in the mythology. Take tram 9 or 6 to Doku-Zentrum.

Sleeping

Lette'm Sleep (☎ 992 8128; www.backpackers.de; Frauentormauer 42; dm €16-20, r with shared bathroom €44-52; 💻) Dorms are available, as well as quirky private rooms designed with colour and flair not often seen in hostels.

Pension Sonne (☎ 227 166; Königstrasse 45; s/d with shared bathroom €30/60) It's a steep climb up three flights of stairs to the cosy and bright rooms with high ceilings.

Hotel Lucas (☎ 227 845; www.hotel-lucas.de; Kaiserstrasse 22; r €50-90; ⊠ 💻) Some of the 11 tidy rooms here have balconies, others have small adjoining rooms for doing work – which for you might mean scrutinising a guidebook. The location is very central.

Merian-Hotel (☎ 214 6 90; www.merian-hotel.de; Unschlittplatz 7; r €85-130) The 21 rooms here are simply decorated but that means there's no competition for your attention, which should be focused on the nearby fast-flowing Pegnitz River. The hotel has a good outdoor café in this attractive and quiet part of the old town.

Hotel Agneshof (☎ 214440; www.agneshof-nuernberg.de; Agnesgasse 10; r €100-250; ⊠ 💻) In the middle of Nuremberg's well-preserved historic centre, the Agneshof has 74 bright and well-appointed rooms with wi-fi. The small sauna is a plus.

Eating

Don't leave Nuremberg without trying its famous finger-sized grilled sausages. Order 'em by the dozen with *Meerrettich* (horseradish) on the side.

Bratwursthäusle (☎ 227 695; Rathausplatz 2; meals €6-10) Here the local sausages are flame-grilled and scrumptious. Get them with *Kartoffelsalat* (potato salad). There are also nice tree-shaded tables outside.

Zwinger (☎ 220 48; Lorenzer Strasse 33; mains €6-12) Up front you can have a meal of local favourites at this popular meeting place. In back there's live music or DJs until late.

Kettensteg (☎ 221 081; Maxplatz 35; mains €7-15) Right by the river and with its own suspension bridge to the other side, this beer garden and restaurant is fine on a summer day and cosy in winter. The basic fare is tasty and absorbs lots of beer.

Lindbergh (☎ 214 25 95; Burgstrasse 1; mains €8-15) This contemporary café and bar has huge windows overlooking the St Sebalduskirche. There's a good wine list and smattering of creative continental hits on the varied menu.

Getting There & Around

Nuremberg's **airport** (NUE; www.airport-nuernberg.de) is a hub for budget carrier Air Berlin, which has service throughout Germany, as well as flights to European capitals including London, Paris and Rome. There's frequent service to the airport on the S-2 line (€1.80, 20 minutes).

The city is also a hub for train service. ICE trains run to/from Berlin-Hauptbahnhbf (€77, 4½ hours, every two hours), Frankfurt-am-Main (€39, two hours, hourly) and on the new fast line to Munich (€41, 79 minutes, hourly). Trains run hourly to Stuttgart (€28, 2¼ hours).

Tickets on the bus, tram and U-Bahn system cost €1.80 each. Day passes are €3.60.

REGENSBURG

☎ 0941 / pop 129,000

On the wide Danube River, Regensburg has relics of all periods as far back as the Romans, yet doesn't have the tourist mobs you'll find in other equally attractive German cities. Oh well, their loss. The centre escaped the war's carpet bombing and Renaissance towers that could be in Florence mix with half-timbered charm. Throngs of students keep things from getting too mouldy.

Orientation & Information

From the main train station, you walk up Maximillianstrasse for 10 minutes to reach the centre. There's Internet access at coin-operated terminals (per 15 minutes €1) on the top level of the train station.

Tourist office (☎ 507 4410; www.regensburg.de; Altes Rathaus; 9am-6pm Mon-Fri, to 4pm Sat & Sun)

Sights

Dominating the skyline are the twin spires of the Gothic **Dom St Peter** (☎ 597 1002; Domplatz; admission free; tours in German adult/child €2.50/1.50; tours 10am, 11am, 2pm Mon-Sat, 1 & 2pm Sun May-Oct; 11am Mon-Fri & 1pm Sun Dec-Apr) built during the 14th and 15th centuries from unusual green limestone.

The **Altes Rathaus** (Rathausplatz 1; guided tours €6; tours in German through the day, tours in English 3.30pm Mon-Sat May-Sep) was progressively extended from medieval to baroque times and remained the seat of the Reichstag for almost 150 years.

The **Roman wall**, with its **Porta Praetoria** arch, follows Unter den Schwibbögen onto Dr-Martin-Luther-Strasse.

Lavish **Schloss Thurn und Taxis** (☎ 504 8133; Emmeramsplatz 6; adult/child €11.50/9; 11am-5pm Mon-Fri, 10am-5pm Sat & Sun) is near the train station and includes the castle proper (Schloss) and the royal stables (Marstall). The adjoining **Basilika St Emmeram** (☎ 510 30; Emmeramsplatz; 9am-5pm) is a riot of rococo and has a perfect cloister.

Sleeping & Eating

Azur-Camping (☎ 270 025; fax 299 432; Weinweg 40; camp sites per person/site €5/6) Bus 6 from the train station goes to the entrance.

DJH Hostel (☎ 574 02; www.djh.de; Wöhrdstrasse 60; dm €17;) Regensburg's modernised hostel is in a beautiful old building on Unterer Wöhrd island about a 10-minute walk north of the Altstadt. Take bus 3 from Albertstrasse to Eisstadion.

Spitalgarten Hotel (☎ 847 74; www.spitalgarten.de; St Katharinenplatz 1; s/d €23/46) Across the river is the Spitalgarten, with basic rooms in a large imposing building. A beer garden is attached.

Hotel Am Peterstor (☎ 545 45; www.hotel-am-peterstor.de; Fröliche-Türkenstrasse 12; s/d €40/55)

The 36 clean, basic rooms are simply decorated in an attractive and unfussy way.

Hotel Kaiserhof (☎ 585 350; www.kaiserhof-am-dom.de; Kramgasse 10-12; r €60-125; 💻) The best rooms at this 30-room inn face the Dom. The décor is understated, which adds to the feeling of spaciousness. Ask for a room with a new bathroom.

Roter Hahn (595 090; www.roter-hahn.com; Rote-Hahnen-Gasse 10; s/d from €80/90; ⊠ 💻) Look for the namesake red cock as you penetrate the narrow cobblestone streets in the heart of the old town. The 30 rooms have an edgy contemporary feel and wi-fi. The café (mains €7 to €15) has a creative modern fusion menu.

Historische Wurstküche (☎ 466 210; Thundorferstrasse 3; meals €6) The Danube rushes past this little house that's been cooking up the addictive local version of Nuremberg sausages (slightly spicier) for centuries.

Bodega (☎ 584 0486; Vor der Grieb 1a; meals €8-16) Hidden in a little alley, this contemporary tapas bar has an array of tempting dishes on display in glass cases. Sample the long wine list while hanging out outside or settle in inside for a trip to Spain.

Getting There & Away

Regensburg is on the train line between Nuremberg (€16 to €21, one hour, hourly) and Austria. There are hourly trains to Munich (€21, 1½ hours).

AUGSBURG

☎ 0821 / pop 259,000

Originally established by the Romans, Augsburg later became a centre of Luther's Reformation. Today it's a lively provincial city, criss-crossed by little streams, that has an appealing ambience and vitality. It makes a good day trip from Munich.

The **tourist office** (☎ 502 0724; www.augsburg-tourismus.de; Maximilian Strasse 57; 🕒 9am-5pm Mon-Fri, 10am-2pm Sat) can help with accommodation.

Sights

Look for the very impressive onion-shaped towers on the **Rathaus** (☎ 3240; Rathausplatz; 🕒 10am-6pm) and the adjacent **Perlachturm**. North of here is the 11th-century **Dom Maria Heimsuchung** (Hoher Weg; 🕒 10am-6pm Mon-Sat), which has more 'modern' additions, such as the 14th-century doors showing scenes from the Old Testament.

The Fuggers – a 16th-century banking family – left their mark everywhere. They have lavish tombs inside **St Anna Kirche** (Annastrasse; 🕒 10am-12.30pm & 3-6pm Tue-Sat, noon-6pm Sun), a place also known for being a Martin Luther bolthole. The 16th-century **Fuggerei** (no laughing!) was built with banking riches to house the poor. The excellent **museum** (☎ 319 881; Mittlere Gasse 13; adult/child €2/1; 🕒 10am-6pm) shows how they lived.

Sleeping & Eating

Jakoberhof (☎ 510 030; www.jakoberhof.de; Jakoberhofstrasse 41; s/d €49/64, with shared bathroom €26/39) Rooms at this dignified inn are sparsely decorated, which makes it easier not to lose something. Look for this temple of good value under its own onion dome.

Dom Hotel (☎ 343 930; www.domhotel-augsburg.de; Frauentorstrasse 8; s/d from €67/76; ⊠ 💻) The 52 comfortable rooms here are modern and have wi-fi. Some have their own solariums, while some attic rooms have open beams and great views.

König von Flandern (☎ 158 050; Karolinenstrasse 12; meals €6-10) This underground brewery is always packed. The food is tasty and goes well with the many house beers on tap. Try the piquant Alligator döppelbock.

Getting There & Away

Trains between Munich and Augsburg are frequent (€10 to €18, 40 minutes). The Deutsche-Touring Romantic Road bus stops at the train station and the Rathaus.

FÜSSEN

☎ 08362 / pop 14,000

Close to the Austrian border and the foothills of the Alps, Füssen has some splendid baroque architecture, but it is primarily visited for the two castles in nearby Schwangau associated with King Ludwig II. The **tourist office** (☎ 938 50; www.fuessen.de; Kaiser-Maximillian-Platz 1; 🕒 9am-5pm Mon-Fri, 10am-2pm Sat) is often overrun.

Sights

Neuschwanstein and **Hohenschwangau castles** provide a fascinating glimpse into the romantic king's state of mind (or lack thereof) and well-developed ego. Hohenschwangau is where Ludwig lived as a child, but more interesting is the adjacent Neuschwanstein, his own creation (albeit with the help of a theatrical designer). Although it was unfinished when he died in 1886, there is plenty of evidence of Ludwig's twin obsessions: swans and Wagnerian operas. The sugary pastiche of architectural styles, alternatively overwhelmingly beautiful and just a little-too-much, reputedly inspired Disney's Fantasyland castle.

Tickets may only be bought from the **ticket centre** (☎ 930 830; www.ticket-center-hohenschwangau.de; Alpseestrasse 12; each castle adult/child €9/free, both €17/free; 🕑 9am-6pm mid-Apr–mid-Oct, 10am-4pm mid-Oct–mid-Apr). In summer it's worth the €1.60 surcharge to reserve ahead. To walk to Hohenschwangau takes 10 minutes while Neuschwanstein is a 30-minute steep hike. Horse-drawn carriages (€5) and shuttle buses (€2) shorten but don't eliminate the hike.

Take the bus from Füssen train station (€1.55, eight minutes, hourly) or share a taxi (☎ 7700; €8.50 for up to four people). Go early to avoid the worst of the rush.

Sleeping & Eating

A pavilion near the tourist office has a computerised list of vacant rooms in town; most of the cheapest rooms, at around €15 per person, are in private homes just a few minutes from the Altstadt. Füssen is a pretty quiet place after dark and most people will stay only long enough to see the castles. There are a couple of cafés in the centre to grab lunch at.

DJH Hostel (☎ 7754; www.djh.de; Mariahilferstrasse 5; dm €16; 💻) It gets a bit loud when the 134 beds are full, but otherwise it's quiet and only a signposted 10-minute walk from the train station.

Hotel Sonne (☎ 9080; www.hotel-sonne.de; Reichenstrasse 37; r from €80; ⊠) Just across from the tourist office, the pastel-coloured Sonne is hard to miss. The 32 rooms are comfortable, if not exactly as bright as the name.

Getting There & Away

Trains to Munich (€20, two hours) run every two hours. Füssen is the start of the Romantic Rd. Deutsche-Touring buses start in Munich and are the best way to reach Wieskirche (€6, 50 minutes) if you don't have a car.

RVO bus 9606 (www.rvo-bus.de) connects Füssen, via Oberammergau, with Garmisch-Partenkirchen (€8, two hours, five to six daily).

BAVARIAN ALPS

While not quite as high as their sister summits further south in Austria and Switzerland, the Bavarian Alps (Bayerische Alpen) are really a bunch of drama queens, owing to their abrupt rise from the rolling Bavarian foothills. Stretching westward from Germany's southeastern corner to the Allgäu region near Lake Constance, the Alps take in most of the mountainous country fringing the southern border with Austria.

Getting There & Around

While the public transport network is good, the mountain geography means there are few direct routes between main centres; sometimes a short cut via Austria is quicker (such as between Füssen and Garmisch). Road rather than rail routes are often more practical. For those driving, the German Alpine Rd (Deutsche Alpenstrasse) is a scenic way to go.

BERCHTESGADEN

☎ 08652 / pop 8300

Berchtesgaden is easily the most dramatically scenic corner of the Bavarian Alps, which hang down into Austria like an appendix here. The views over the steep valleys and craggy peaks go on forever. To reach the centre from the train station, cross the footbridge and walk up Bahnhofstrasse. The helpful **tourist office** (☎ 9670; www.berchtesgaden.de; Königsseer Strasse 2; 🕑 8am-6pm Mon-Fri, to 5pm Sat, 9am-3pm Sun mid-Jun–Sep) is just across the river from the train station.

Sights & Activities

A tour of the **Salzbergwerk** (☎ 600 220; Bergwerkstrasse 83; adult/child €13/8; 🕑 9am-5pm May–mid-Oct, 12.30-3.30pm mid-Oct–Apr) combines history with a carnival. Visitors descend into the salt mine for a 1½-hour tour.

Nearby **Obersalzberg** is an innocent-looking place with an ugly legacy as the second seat of government for the Third Reich. Hitler, Himmler, Goebbels and the rest of the Nazi bigwigs all maintained homes here. The **Dokumentation Obersalzberg Museum** (☎ 947 960; www.obersalzberg.de; Salzbergstrasse 41; adult/child €2.50/free; 🕑 9am-5pm April-Oct, 10am-3pm Tue-Sun Nov-Mar) documents their time in the area, as well as the horrors their policies produced, through photos, audio and film. The admission fee also gets you into the creepy **Hitler's bunker**. Catch bus 9538 (€5 return, nine minutes, hourly) from the Nazi-constructed Berchtesgaden train station to 'Dokumentation'.

Kehlstein (☎ 2969; admission €13.50; ⌚ May-Oct) is a spectacular meeting house built for, but seldom used by, Hitler. Despite its reputation as the **'Eagle's Nest'**, it's a popular destination because of stunning views. Entry includes transport on special buses, which link the summit with Obersalzberg-Hintereck between 8.55am to 4.50pm, as well as the 120m lift through solid rock to the peak. Or you can make the steep ascent or descent on foot in two to three hours.

The best way to see Obersalzberg and Kehlstein is with **Eagle's Nest Tours** (☎ 649 71; www.eagles-nest-tours.com; €40), which has tours in English lasting four hours and covering the entire history of the area during WWII.

You can forget the horrors of war at the **Königssee**, a beautiful alpine lake situated 5km south of Berchtesgaden (and linked by hourly buses in summer). There are frequent boat tours across the lake to the picture-perfect chapel at St Bartholomä (€12), or all the way to Obersee (€16).

The wilds of Berchtesgaden National Park offer some of the best **hiking** in Germany. A good introduction to the area is a 2km path up from St Bartholomä beside the Königssee to the Watzmann-Ostwand, a massive 2000m-high rock face where scores of overly ambitious mountaineers have died.

Sleeping & Eating

Of the five camping grounds around Berchtesgaden, the nicest are at Königssee.

Grafenlehen (☎ 4140; www.camping-grafenlehen.de; camp sites per person/site €5.50/6) This place has a playground and mountain views.

DJH Hostel (☎ 943 70; www.djh.de; Gebirgsjägerstrasse 52; dm €14; ⌚ closed Nov & Dec) Take bus 9539 to Jugendherberge and this swarming 307-bed hostel.

Hotel Floriani (☎ 660 11; www.hotel-floriani.de; Königsseer Strasse 37; s/d from €35/58) The cheerful, homey rooms all have spectacular vistas plus cable TV and access to the kitchen.

InterContinental Resort Berchtesgaden (☎ 975 50; www.ichotelsgroup.com; Hintereck 1; r from €160; ⊠ ✲ 💻 🏊) You might say this beautiful new 138-room resort is a silk purse made from a sow's ear. It's built right in Obersalzberg next to the Dokumentation Museum and is an ambitious attempt to reclaim the area's stunning beauty from the stain of the Nazis.

Getting There & Away

There is hourly service to Berchtesgaden from Munich (€30, 2¾ hours), which usually requires a change in Frilassing. There's direct service to nearby Salzburg in Austria (€7.60, one hour, hourly).

GARMISCH-PARTENKIRCHEN

☎ 08821 / pop 27,000

The towns of Garmisch and Partenkirchen were merged by Hitler for the 1936 Winter Olympics. Munich residents' favourite getaway spot, this often-snooty, year-round resort is also a big draw for skiers, snowboarders, hikers and mountaineers.

The **tourist office** (☎ 180 700; www.garmisch-partenkirchen.de; Richard Strauss Platz 2; ⌚ 8am-6pm Mon-Sat, 10am-noon Sun) is in the centre of town. Check the Internet at **Play Maxx** (☎ 943 4086; Hindenburgstrasse 30; per 30 min €2; ⌚ 10am-1am).

Sights & Activities

The huge **ski stadium** outside town hosted the Olympics. From the pedestrian Am Kurpark, walk up Klammstrasse, cross the tracks and veer left on the first path to reach the stadium and enjoy the spectacular views.

An excellent short hike from Garmisch is to the **Partnachklamm gorge**, via a winding path above a stream and underneath the waterfalls. You take the Graseck cable car and follow the signs.

An excursion to the **Zugspitze** summit, Germany's highest peak (2962m), is a popular outing from Garmisch. There are various ways up, including a return trip by the **Bayerische Zugspitzbahn rack-railway** (www.zugspitz.de; day pass from €36), just west of the main train station, summit cable car or Eibsee cable car, or you can scale it in two days. For detailed information concerning guided hiking or mountaineering courses, check with **Bergsteigerschule Zugspitze** (☎ 589 99; www.bergsteigerschule-zugspitze.de; Dreitorspitzstrasse 13, Garmisch).

Garmisch is bounded by three separate ski areas – **Zugspitze plateau** (the highest), **Alpspitze/Hausberg** (the largest) and **Eckbauer** (the cheapest). Day ski passes range from €18 for

Eckbauer to €36 for Zugspitze. The hopefully named Happy Ski Card is a pass for the entire region (from €86 for three days). A web of cross-country ski trails runs along the main valleys.

Flori Wörndle (☎ 583 00; www.skischule-woerndle.de) has ski-hire outlets at the Alpspitze and Hausbergbahn lifts. The tourist office has detailed information on the many local ski schools.

Sleeping & Eating

DJH Hostel (☎ 2980; www.djh.de; Jochstrasse 10; dm €20; closed mid-Nov–Dec) Situated in the suburb of Burgrain, this hostel has 200 beds. From the train station take bus 3 or 4 to the Burgrain stop.

Hotel Schell (☎ 957 50; www.hotel-schell.de; Partnachauenstrasse 3; s/d from €30/50;) In a quaint and fairly modest house a short walk from the train station, the Schell has 25 compact well-maintained rooms.

Hotel Zugspitze (☎ 9010; www.hotel-zugspitze.de; Klammstrasse 19; r €76-105;) The 48 cosy timber-lined rooms and an elegant indoor pool make you feel at home – a very nice home.

Bistro Mukkefuck (☎ 734 40; Zugspitzstrasse 3; meals €6-12) If you can get past the curious name, an outdoor beer garden and a tasty menu of salads, sandwiches and pastas awaits.

Getting There & Away

From Garmish there is train service to Munich (€16, 80 minutes, hourly) and to Innsbruck via Mittenwald (€13, 80 minutes, every two hours). RVO bus 9606, from in front of the train station, links Garmisch with Füssen (€8, two hours, five to six daily) via Oberammergau.

HOT & COLD FUN IN THE ALPS

The Bavarian Alps are extraordinarily well organised for outdoor pursuits, with skiing, snowboarding and hiking being the most popular. The ski season usually runs from mid-December to April. Ski gear is available for hire in all the resorts, with the lowest daily/weekly rates including skis, boots and stocks at around €15/50. Five-day skiing courses start from €100.

During the warmer months, the activities include hiking, canoeing, rafting, biking and paragliding.

OBERSTDORF

☎ 08322 / pop 10,400

Over in the western Bavarian Alps, Oberstdorf sits in a pretty flat meadow below the peaks. Besides skiing, it offers superb hiking. At busy times, car use in the centre is restricted – a good thing.

The main **tourist office** (☎ 7000; www.oberstdorf.de; Bahnhofplatz 3; 8.30am-6pm Mon-Fri, 9.30am-noon Sat) is near the train station.

Savvy skiers value Oberstdorf for its friendliness, its reasonable prices and the generally uncrowded slopes. The village is surrounded by several ski areas: the **Nebelhorn** (www.dashoechste.de), **Fellhorn/Kanzelwand** (www.dashoechste.de) and **Söllereck** (www.soellereckbahn.de). Combined daily/weekly ski passes that include all three areas (plus the adjoining Kleinwalsertal lifts on the Austrian side) cost €34/174. Check with the tourist office for information on schools and equipment rental.

For an exhilarating day **hike**, ride the Nebelhorn cable car to the upper station then walk down via the Gaisalpseen, two lovely alpine lakes.

There's a **camping ground** (☎ 6525; www.camping-oberstdorf.de; Rubingerstrasse 16; camp sites per tent €3-5, per person €5-5.50) 2km north of the station beside the train line.

The **DJH Hostel** (☎ 2225; www.djh.de; Kornau 8; dm €15) is on the outskirts of town near the Söllereck chairlift – take the Kleinwalsertal bus to the Reute stop.

Hotel Kappeler Haus (☎ 96860; www.kappeler-haus.de; Am Seeler 2; s/d from €38/74) has 47 spacious rooms with nice views right near the centre. There's on-site parking and many of the rooms have wrap-around balconies. The breakfast is tops.

Südtiroler Sonnenkeller (☎ 3140; Weststrasse 5; meals €6-12) is a great basement restaurant with a large number of beers on tap and well-prepared regional foods. Try the Südtiroler Schlutzkrapfen for an amazing local take on ravioli.

There are hourly RB trains to/from Immenstadt where you connect to Lindau (€15, 1¾ hours). Munich has direct trains (€25, 2½ hours, hourly). On weekdays, bus connections to Füssen go via Pfronten (€9.30, 2½ hours, two daily).

BADEN-WÜRTTEMBERG

With the exception of cuckoo clocks in the Black Forest, Baden-Württemberg runs distant second in the cliché race to Bavaria. But that's really all the better, as it is a rich and varied place with just about everything that might inspire a visit to Germany – plus a few surprises.

OK, so on the top of the hour the Black Forest goes, well, cuckoo. But it is also a pretty land of hills, trees and cute villages that rewards exploration. If you want a big and quaint German village with lots of history, then there's Heidelberg. Baden-Baden is the sybaritic playground for spa-goers and Freiburg has youthful vibrance in an intriguing package. Finally, Lake Constance is a misty redoubt bordering Switzerland that has all the pleasures a large body of water can offer.

The prosperous modern state of Baden-Württemberg was created in 1951 out of three smaller regions: Baden, Württemberg and Hohenzollern (thank goodness the names stopped at two).

STUTTGART

☎0711 / pop 590,000

Hemmed in by grape-covered hills, residents of prosperous Stuttgart enjoy a high quality of life. Just watch them zip about in their Mercedes. Nevertheless it is Baden-Württemberg's state capital and the hub of its industries. At the forefront of Germany's economic recovery from the ravages of WWII, Stuttgart started life less auspiciously in 950 as a horse stud farm. About 80% of the city centre was destroyed in the war, but there are a few historical buildings left and – no surprise – car museums. Mostly however, it is a good hub for exploring other parts of the state.

Information

Call & Internet C@fé (☎ 259 9103; Esslingerstrasse; per hr €2; 🕑 9.30am-11pm)

Post office (Bolzstrasse 3)

Tourist office (☎ 222 80; www.stuttgart-tourist.de; Königstrasse 1a; 🕑 9am-8pm Mon-Fri, to 6pm Sat, 11am-6pm Sun) Opposite the main train station on the main pedestrian strip, the office sells the three-day StuttCard (€17.50), which allows free public transport and free entry to some museums.

Waschsalon (☎ 241 275; Hohenheimer Strasse 33; per load €7.50; 🕑 8am-6.30pm Mon-Fri, to 1pm Sat) Self-serve and drop-off.

Sights

The tower at the grotty main train station sports the three-pointed star of the Mercedes-Benz. It's also an excellent vantage point for the sprawling city and surrounding hills, and is reached via a **lift** (admission free; 🕑 10am-10pm Tue-Sun).

Stretching southwest from the Neckar River to the city centre is the **Schlossgarten**, an extensive strip of parkland divided into three sections (Unterer, Mittlerer and Oberer), complete with ponds, swans, street entertainers and modern sculptures. At their northern edge the gardens take in the **Wilhelma Zoo & Botanical Gardens** (☎ 540 20; Neckarstrasse; adult/child €11/5.50; 🕑 8.15am-6pm May-Aug, reduced hr winter). At the gardens' southern end they encompass the sprawling baroque **Neues Schloss** (Schlossplatz) and the Renaissance **Altes Schloss**, which houses a **regional museum** (☎ 279 3400; Schillerplatz 6; adult/child €3/free; 🕑 10am-5pm Tue-Sun) where exhibits include Roman-era discoveries.

Next to the Altes Schloss is the city's oldest square, Schillerplatz, with its monument to the poet **Schiller**, and the 12th-century **Stiftskirche** (Stiftstrasse 12; 🕑 9am-5.30pm Mon-Wed, Fri & Sun, noon-5.30pm Thu). Adjoining the park you'll find the **Staatsgalerie** (☎ 212 4050; Konrad-Adenauer-Strasse 30; adult/child €4.50/2.50; 🕑 10am-6pm Tue-Sun, to 9pm Thu), which houses an excellent collection from the Middle Ages to the present. It's especially rich in old German masters from the surrounding Swabia region.

Next door there's the **Haus der Geschichte** (House of History; ☎ 212 3950; Urbansplatz 2; admission €3). This is an eye-catching postmodern museum that covers the past 200 years of the Baden-Württemburg area in film, photography, documents and multimedia.

MOTOR MUSEUMS

An arms race has broken out among the local auto companies, with both building new and costly monuments to themselves.

The motor car was first developed by Gottlieb Daimler and Carl Benz at the end of the 19th century. The impressive new-for-2006 **Mercedes-Benz Museum** (☎ 172 2578; Mercedesstrasse 137; admission €8; 🕑 9am-5pm Tue-Sun)

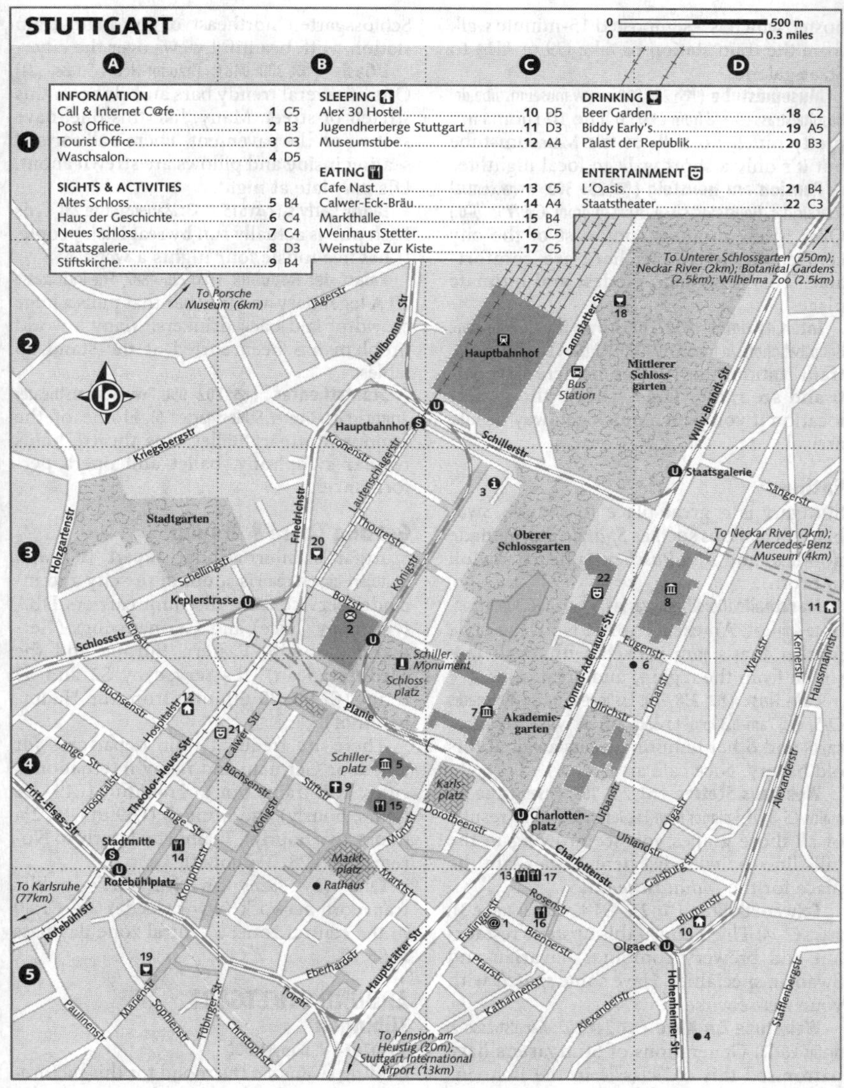

is in the suburb of Bad-Cannstatt; take S-Bahn 1 to Neckarstadion. For even faster cars, cruise over to the striking new-for-2007 **Porsche Museum** (☎ 911 5685; Porscheplatz 1; 🕑 9am-4pm Mon-Fri, to 5pm Sat & Sun); take S-Bahn 6 to Neuwirtshaus, north of the city. Admission prices for the new place were not set but expect them to rival Mercedes.

Sleeping

Alex 30 Hostel (☎ 838 8950; www.alex30-hostel.de; Alexanderstrasse 30; dm/s/d from €19/20/25; 💻) Tidy and orderly in an interesting neighbourhood. Take U-Bahn lines 5, 6 or 7 to Olgaeck.

Jugendherberge Stuttgart (☎ 241 583; www.jugendherberge-stuttgart.de; Haussmannstrasse 27; dm €17-23) It's a steep climb to this modern hostel, which is a signposted 15-minute walk from the train station or take U9 or U14 to Staatsgalerie.

Museumstube (☎ 296 810; www.museumstube.de; Hospitalstrasse 9; s/d from €35/55) The 10 rooms are pretty much no-frills at the Museumstube but it's only a short walk to local nightlife.

Pension am Heusteig (☎ 239 300; www.central-classic.de; Heusteigstrasse 30; s/d from €59/75; 💻) Only a few minutes southeast of the city centre, the 14 rooms here are comfortable. This is a small, modest and intimate place.

InterCity Hotel (☎ 222 8233; www.intercityhotel.com; Hauptbahnhof; s/d from €70/100; ⊠ 💻) Right in the train station, the 101 rooms here have wi-fi and are rather large. This is the perfect location if you plan a quick getaway or late arrival.

Eating

Stuttgart is a great place to sample Swabian specialities such as *Spätzle* (homemade noodles) and *Maultaschen* (a hearty ravioli in broth).

Markthalle (Dorotheenstrasse 4; 🕑 7am-6.30pm Mon-Fri, to 4pm Sat) An excellent Art Nouveau-style market that's jam-packed with fresh fare (often from the region) and great cafés.

Cafe Nast (☎ 238 970; Esslinger Strasse 40; snacks €2-5; 🕑 7am-6.30pm, to 3pm Sat) A vast array of tarts and other tempting treats await at this old bakery. Nice café area.

Weinhaus Stetter (☎ 240 163; Rosenstrasse 32; mains €5-8; 🕑 dinner Mon-Fri, lunch Sat) The results of all those grapes you see growing in the hills line the wine list here. Locals jam the place for the *Maultaschen*.

Calwer-Eck-Bräu (☎ 222 494 40; Calwerstrasse 31; mains €7-14) The menu at this upstairs restaurant and brewery combines Bavarian and Swabian specialties. Have some *spätzle* with your *weissewurst*.

Weinstube Zur Kiste (☎ 244 002; Kanalstrasse 2; mains €8-17) Generations of Stuttgarters have patronised this old classic in the Bohnenviertel (Bean Quarter). Enjoy local chow and wines in the creaky old building or at tables outside.

Drinking & Entertainment

Though in German, *Lift Stuttgart* (€1), a comprehensive guide to local entertainment and events is useful. There's a **beer garden** (☎ 226 1274; Canstatterstr 18) in the Mittlerer Schlossgarten northeast of the main train station, with beautiful views over the city.

L'Oasis (☎ 300 0481; Theodor-Heuss-Strasse 21) One of several trendy bars and clubs on this stretch of street. Many, like this one, have seating on the pavement. There's all sorts of seating inside and pillows are strewn about. DJs play late at night.

Biddy Early's (☎ 615 9853; Marienstrasse 28) This Irish pub is actually run by real Irish people. It has live music four nights a week.

Palast der Republik (☎ 226 4887; Friedrichstrasse 27) A legendary and tiny bar that pulls a huge crowd of laid-back drinkers. Many a world problem has been sorted at the stand-up tables.

Staatstheater (☎ 202 090; www.staatstheater.stuttgart.de; Oberer Schlossgarten 6) Home of the famous Stuttgart Ballet, this theatre holds regular symphony, ballet and opera performances.

Getting There & Around

Stuttgart's international **airport** (SGT; www.stuttgart-airport.com) is south of the city and includes service from discount carriers DBA (Germany, Nice) and Germanwings (Germany, London, Eastern Europe and the Mediterranean). It's served by S2 and S3 trains (€2.90, 30 minutes from the Hauptbahnhof).

There are frequent train departures for all major German, and many international, cities. ICE trains run to Frankfurt (€49, 1½ hours, hourly) and Munich (€39 to €46, 2¼ hours, two hourly). Trains run hourly to Nuremberg (€28, 2¼ hours).

One-way fares on Stuttgart's public transport network (www.vvs.de) are €1.80 in the central zone; a central zone day pass is €5.10.

AROUND STUTTGART

Tübingen

☎ 07071 / pop 83,000

Gliding swans set the mood for this picturesque town. It's a perfect place to spend a day wandering along winding alleys of half-timbered houses and old stone walls, and taking a boat ride down the Neckar River. Given that the local university has 22,000 students, there's an appealing edge to it all.

The **tourist office** (☎ 913 60; www.tuebingen-info.de; An der Neckarbrücke; 🕑 9am-7pm Mon-Fri, to 5pm Sat) is beside the bridge.

On **Marktplatz**, the centre of town, is the 1435 **Rathaus** with its baroque façade and astronomical clock. The nearby late-Gothic **Stiftkirche** (Am Holz-markt; 9am-5pm Feb-Oct, to 4pm Nov-Jan) houses the tombs of the Württemberg dukes and has excellent medieval stained-glass windows. From the heights of the Renaissance **Schloss Hohentübingen** (Burgsteig 11), now part of the university, there are fine views over the steep, red-tiled rooftops of the old town. Inside, the **museum** (297 7384; 10am-5pm Wed-Sun) covers local history.

The **Jugendherberge Tübingen** (230 02; www.djh.de; Gartenstrasse 22/2; dm €20-24;) has a delightful location by the river.

Hotel Am Schloss (929 40; www.hotelamschloss.de; Burgsteige 18; s/d from €51/86) is an attractive hotel with 37 simple and pleasant rooms. Its restaurant serves over two dozen varieties of *Maultaschen*, the local stuffed pasta (€6 to €10).

Boulanger (233 45; Collegiumsgasse 2; meals €6-10) is a classic old student bar and café. There are several more of this type nearby on Kornhausstrasse.

Neckarmuller (278 48; Gartenstrasse 4) is a brewery with a terrace on the river. It has good weisse beer.

There are hourly RE trains between Tübingen and Stuttgart (€10, one hour).

HEIDELBERG

06221 / pop 143,000

The French destroyed Heidelberg in 1693; they may have been the last visitors to dislike this charming town on the Neckar River. Its castle ruins and medieval town are irresistible drawcards for most travellers in Germany. Mark Twain recounted his succinct observations in *A Tramp Abroad*. Britain's JMW Turner loved the place and it inspired him to produce some of his finest landscape paintings. Throw in nice weather and lively pubs, and you understand why many of Heidelberg's students (attending the oldest university in the country) rarely graduate on time. But be warned: this place seethes with tourists during July and August.

Orientation

Heidelberg's captivating old town starts to reveal itself after a 15-minute walk that will interest few west of the main train station, along the Kurfürsten-Anlage. Hauptstrasse is the pedestrian way leading eastwards through the heart of the Altstadt from Bismarckplatz via Marktplatz to Karlstor.

Information

Buchhandlung Schmitt & Hahn (845 196; Hauptstrasse 8) Classy bookshop with lots of English titles.
Post office (Sophienstrasse 8-10) Near the Altstadt.
Tourist office (194 33; www.cvb-heidelberg.de; Willy-Brandt-Platz 1; 9am-7pm Mon-Sat year-round, 10am-6pm Sun Apr-Nov) Outside the train station. The €14 Heidelberg Card offers free public transport and free admission to many sights.
Waschtrommel (485 775; Rohrbacher Strasse 10; 8.30am-9.30pm Mon-Fri, to 8.30pm Sat) A self-service laundry (per load €4) *and* an Internet café (per 30 min €1).

Sights

Heidelberg's imposing **Schloss** (538 421; adult/child €3/1.50, tours €4; 10am-5.30pm) is one of Germany's finest examples of grand Gothic-Renaissance architecture. The building's half-ruined state actually adds to its romantic appeal (Twain called it 'the Lear of inanimate nature'). Seen from anywhere in the Altstadt, this striking red-sandstone castle dominates the hillside. The entry fee covers the castle, the **Grosses Fass** (Great Vat), an enormous 18th-century keg capable of holding 221,726L, and the **Deutsches Apothekenmuseum** (German Pharmaceutical Museum; 258 80; Schlosshof 1; adult/child €3/1.50; 10am-5.30pm).

You can take the **funicular railway** (adult/child return €5/4; 9am-5pm) to the castle from lower Kornmarkt station, or enjoy an invigorating 10-minute walk up steep, stone-laid lanes. The funicular continues up to the **Königstuhl,** where there are good views.

Dominating Universitätsplatz are the 18th-century **Alte Universität** and the **Neue Universität**. Nearby there's the **Studentenkarzer** (student jail; 543 554; Augustinergasse 2; adult/child €2.50/2; 10am-noon & 2-5pm Tue-Sat Apr-Oct, 10am-2pm Tue-Fri Nov-Mar). From 1778 to 1914 this jail was used for misbehaved students. Sentences (usually two to 10 days) were earned for 'heinous' crimes such as drinking, singing and womanising. The **Marstall** is the former arsenal, now a student *mensa*.

The **Kurpfälzisches Museum** (Palatinate Museum; 583 402; Hauptstrasse 97; adult/child €3/2; 10am-5pm Tue-Sun, to 9pm Wed) contains paintings, sculptures and the jawbone of the 600,000-year-old Heidelberg Man.

The Heidelberg region has been a major global supplier of printing equipment, much

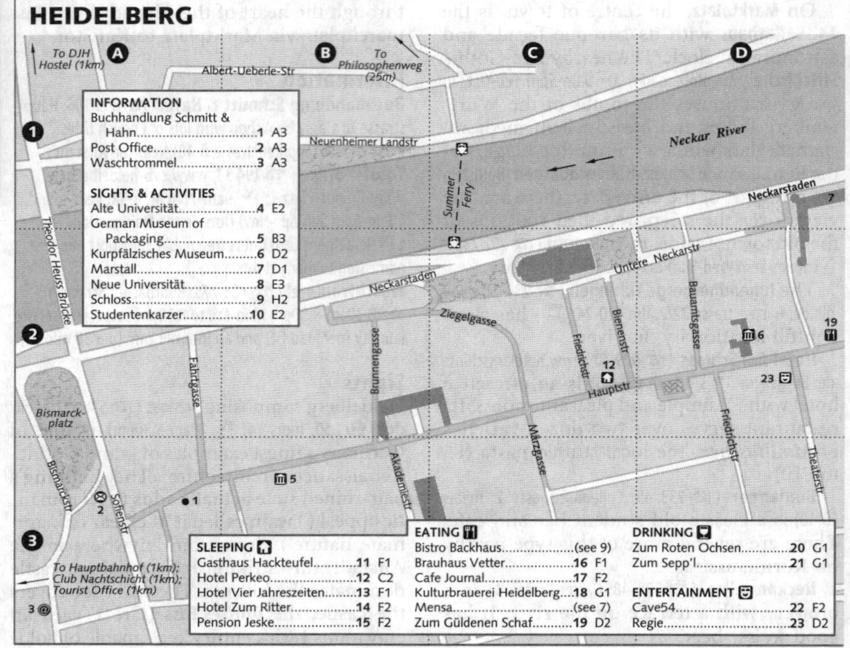

of it used to create packaging for products. The **German Museum of Packaging** (Deutsches Verpackungs-Museum; ☎ 213 61; Hauptstrasse 22; adult/child €4/2; ⏲ 1-6pm Wed-Fri, 11am-6pm Sat & Sun) celebrates classic packages such as the Nivea jar and the Coke bottle, all from an era when a package was *not* a plastic clamshell requiring access via chain saw.

A stroll along the **Philosophenweg**, north of the Neckar River, gives a welcome respite from Heidelberg's tourist hordes.

Sleeping

Finding any accommodation during Heidelberg's high season can be difficult. Arrive early in the day or book ahead.

Camping Haide (☎ 802 506; www.camping-heidelberg.de; Schlierbacher Landstrasse 151; camp sites per person €5.50, tent €2.50-6) These grounds are in a pretty spot on the river. Take bus 35 to Orthopädische Klinik.

DJH Hostel (☎ 651 190; www.djh.de; Tiergartenstrasse 5; dm €15-20; 💻) This hostel is across the river from the train station, and has 487 beds. From the station or Bismarckplatz, take bus 33 towards Ziegelhausen.

Pension Jeske (☎ 237 33; www.pension-jeske-heidelberg.de; Mittelbadgasse 2; r per person from €25) The four rooms at this backpacker favourite are squirreled away in a 250-year-old house. The Altstadt's pleasures are just outside.

Hotel Vier Jahreszeiten (☎ 241 64; www.4-jahreszeiten.de; Haspelgasse 2; s/d from €60/100) Goethe himself reputedly once slumbered here, so you know it's old. Things have been spiffed up since, although the palette tends towards beige in the 22 rooms.

Gasthaus Hackteufel (☎ 905 380; www.hackteufel.de; Steingasse 7; s/d from €80/120; 💻) Each of the 12 rooms is distinctive and full of character at the Hackteufel, in the middle of the romantic old town.

Hotel Perkeo (☎ 141 30; Hauptstrasse 75; s/d from €90/120; ⊠ 💻) The 24 rooms here are bright and have wi-fi. Many have views of the surrounding hills. Look for the little statue of a thirsty gatekeeper on the façade. The café is a good place to take in some of the street action.

Hotel Zum Ritter (☎ 1350; www.ritter-heidelberg.de; Hauptstrasse 178; s/d from €90/150; 💻) Ornate Hotel Zum Ritter is close to the cathedral

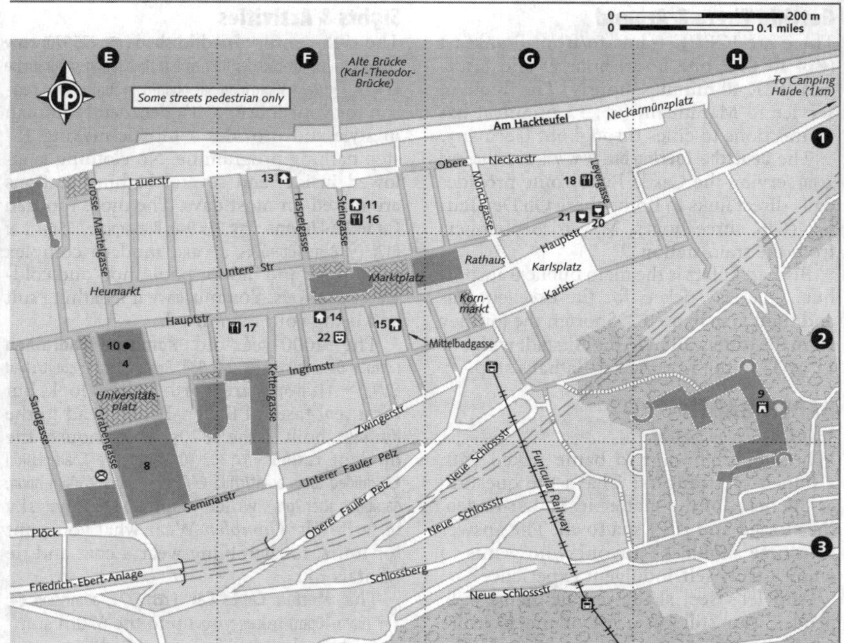

and provides grand accommodation in 39 ornate rooms. It survived the French destruction of 1693.

Eating

The Zum Güldenen Schaf is one of many Altstadt restaurants that cater exclusively to tourists. The only locals are washing dishes.

Cafe Journal (☎ 161 712; Hauptstrasse 162; meals €4-8) A classic café with a good view of the passing mobs. It's a place to linger over your own journal while enjoying coffee and a meal.

Bistro Backhaus (☎ 979 70; Im Schlosshof; meals €5-9) Worth the jaunt to the Schloss, this surprisingly hype-free place has good local favourites and at reasonable prices. There are several grilled sausages, yum.

Brauhaus Vetter (☎ 165 850; Steingasse 9; mains €5-12) A popular brewery that serves up lots of hearty fare to absorb the suds. The copper kettles gleam. Groups of six or more can order the Brewer's feast, a sausage, pretzels, radishes, meat and cheese smorgasbord.

Kulturbrauerei Heidelberg (☎ 502 980; Leyergasse 6; mains €8-15) The classic-looking Kulturbrauerei has an excellent beer garden. It's a big, bright and airy place and is always busy.

Also useful is the **Mensa** (Universitätsplatz; meals €3), which caters to students.

Drinking & Entertainment

This being a uni town, you won't have to go far to find a happening backstreet bar. Lots of the action centres on Unterestrasse. Two ancient pubs, **Zum Roten Oschen** (☎ 209 77; Hauptstrasse 213) and **Zum Sepp'l** (☎ 230 85; Hauptstrasse 217), are now filled with tourists reliving the uni days they never had.

Regie (☎ 652 226; Theaterstrasse 2; meals €6-10) What better way to deal with the tourist invasion than with a takeaway cocktail from this stylish and large café. There are tables outside and a good menu.

Club Nachtschicht (☎ 438 550; Bergheimer Strasse 147) A classic club near the train station. There's a mix of DJs, house, pop, soul and more. Big with locals.

Cave54 (☎ 278 40; www.cave54.de; Krämerpetrolse 2; Thu-Sun) For live jazz and blues, head to this stone cellar that oozes character. There are regular jam sessions.

Getting There & Around

There are ICE/IC trains to/from Frankfurt (€14 to €17, one hour, hourly) and Stuttgart (€21, 40 minutes, hourly) The frequent service to Mannheim (€5, 15 minutes) has connections to cities throughout Germany.

The **Deutsche-Touring bus** (www.deutsche-touring.com) serving the Castle Road route provides daily direct links to Rothenberg Ob Der Tauber (€46, three hours, May to September) from the train station.

Bismarckplatz is the main public transport hub. One-way tickets for the excellent bus and tram system are €2. Shorten the journey from the train station to the Altstadt with bus 11 or 33 to the Kornmarkt/Rathaus stop.

BADEN-BADEN

☎ 07221 / pop 54,000

Who wouldn't want to bathe naked with a bunch of strangers? That's the question at the heart of the matter in Baden-Baden, the storied and ritzy spa town. The answer of course should be anyone who wants to enjoy a truly self-indulgent experience.

And let's see, shall we call them, well, prudes, can still get a bit of the pleasure while staying suited and segregated. The natural hot springs have attracted visitors since Roman times, but this small city only really became fashionable in the 19th century. It is a stately, closely cropped and salubrious place. As noted sybarite Bill Clinton said: 'Baden-Baden is so nice you had to name it twice'.

Orientation & Information

The train station is 7km northwest of town. Leopoldplatz and Sophienstrasse are the hubs. North of here are the baths, the Stiftskirche and the Neues Schloss. Across the little river to the west you will find the Trinkhalle (pump room) and the tourist office, and past Goetheplatz both the Kurhaus and Spielhalle (casino). Unless noted, everything listed below is within the centre.

The **tourist office** (☎ 275 200; www.baden-baden.com; Kaiserallee 3; ⌚ 10am-5pm Mon-Sat, 2-5pm Sun) is in the Trinkhalle. There is a spa *Kurtaxe* (visitors' tax) of €3.10, entitling you to a *Kurkarte* from your hotel that brings various discounts. Drink from the source of it all here for €0.20 (it's warm and salty).

Surf the Web at **Internet & C@llshop** (☎ 398 400; Lange Strasse 54; per hr €2; ⌚ 10am-10pm).

Sights & Activities

The 19th-century **Friedrichsbad** (☎ 275 920; www.roemisch-irisches-bad.de; Römerplatz 1; bathing programme €21-29; ⌚ 9am-10pm Mon-Sat, noon-8pm Sun) is the reason for your journey. It's decadently Roman in style and provides a muscle-melting 16-step bathing programme. No clothing is allowed inside, and several bathing sections are mixed on most days. The more modern **Caracalla-Therme** (☎ 275 940; Römerplatz 11; per 2 hr €12; ⌚ 8am-10pm) is a vast, modern complex of outdoor and indoor pools, hot- and cold-water grottoes. You must wear a bathing suit and bring your own towel.

The 2000-year-old **Römische Badruinen** (Roman Bath Ruins; ☎ 275 934; Römerplatz 1; adult/child €2/1; ⌚ 11am-5pm) are worth a quick look, but for a real taste of Baden-Baden head to the **Kurhaus**, built in the 1820s, which houses the opulent **casino** (☎ 302 40; Kaiserallee 1; admission €3, guided tours adult/child €4/2; ⌚ tours 9.30am-noon; gambling after 2pm), which inspired Dostoyevsky to write *The Gambler*. Wear what you want for tours, for gambling wear a coat and tie (rentals €11).

The **Merkur Cable Car** (☎ 2771; admission €4; ⌚ 10am-10pm) takes you up to the 670m summit, where there are fine views and numerous walking trails (bus 204 or 205 from Leopoldplatz takes you to the cable-car station).

Sleeping & Eating

DJH Hostel (☎ 522 23; www.djh.de; Hardbergstrasse 34; dm €18-22) This modern three-storey hostel is on a hillside 3km northwest of the centre – it's a steep hike up a long flight of stairs to the entrance. Take bus 201 to Grosse Dollenstrasse then walk for 10 minutes.

Hotel Bischoff (☎ 223 78, www.hotelsbaden-baden.de; Römerplatz 2; s/d €50/70; 💻) Centrally located close to the spas, the Bischoff has 50 comfortable rooms spread over four floors, some with balconies.

Steigenberger Europäischer Hof (☎ 9330; www.steigenberger.de; Kaiserallee 2; s/d from €120/180; ⊠ ❄ 💻) A true grand hotel, this regal beauty has its own little park across from the Kurhaus. Luxuries abound and the breakfast is worth an hour or two. Look for excellent off-season specials.

Hirsch's (☎ 281 110; Kaiserallee 4; mains €7-12) This candle-lit corner specialises in great Swabian dishes. It's a low-key bargain by local standards and there's a good range of beers on tap (you'll sweat them out tomorrow).

Leo's (☎ 380 81; Luisenstrasse 8; lunch special €9) A great spot for a leisurely meal. It's justifiably popular, has a varied menu and a large terrace.

Garibaldi (☎ 302 840; Luisenstrasse 4; mains €12-20) A stylish Italian bistro with pavement tables. A good wine list, pasta and fresh seafood are the features.

Getting There & Around

Baden Airpark (FKB; www.badenairpark.de) is the local airport. It has daily Ryanair service (Barcelona, Dublin, London and Rome) but like many tiny airports served by the budget carrier, getting to/from the airport can be a challenge. Consult the airport website for details on the sketchy service.

Baden-Baden is on the busy Mannheim-Basel train line. Local trains serve Karlsruhe (€7, 15 minutes) frequently and Offenburg (€8, 30 minutes, hourly), from where you can make connections to much of Germany.

Bus 201, 205 and 216 run frequently to/from Leopoldsplatz (€2).

BLACK FOREST

The Black Forest (Schwarzwald) gets its name from the dark canopy of evergreens, though it's also dotted with open slopes and farmland. Although some parts heave with visitors, a 20-minute walk from even the most crowded spots will put you in quiet countryside interspersed with enormous traditional farmhouses and patrolled by amiable dairy cows. It's not nature wild and remote, but bucolic and picturesque.

The Black Forest is east of the Rhine between Karlsruhe and Basel. It's shaped like a bean, about 160km long and 50km wide. From north to south there are four good bases for your visit: Freudenstadt, Schiltach, Triberg and Titisee. Each has good train links.

Those with a car will find their visit especially rewarding, as you can wander the rolling hills and deep valleys at will. One of the main tourist roads is the Schwarzwald-Hochstrasse (B500), which runs from Baden-Baden to Freudenstadt and from Triberg to Waldshut. Other thematic roads with maps provided by tourist offices include Schwarzwald-Bäderstrasse (spa town route), Schwarzwald-Panoramastrasse (panoramic view route) and Badische Weinstrasse (wine route). Whatever you do, make certain you have an excellent commercial regional road map with you.

And, yes, there are many, many places to buy cuckoo clocks (you pay at least €150 for a good one).

Regional specialities include *Schwarzwälderschinken* (ham), which is smoked and served in a variety of ways. Rivalling those ubiquitous clocks in fame (but not price), *Schwarzwälderkirschtorte* (Black Forest cake) is a chocolate and cherry concoction. Most hotels and guesthouses have restaurants serving traditional hearty (but expensive) German fare.

FREUDENSTADT

Freudenstadt is a good base for exploring the northern Black Forest and hikes into the surrounding countryside. It's most notable feature is a vast **marketplace** that is the largest in the country. The **tourist office** (☎ 07441-8640; www.freudenstadt.de; Am Markt-platz; 🕑 10am-6pm Mon-Fri, to 2pm Sat & Sun Mar-Nov, 10am-5pm Mon-Fri, to 1pm Sat & Sun Dec-Feb) has Internet access and is especially helpful with ideas for local walks.

The **DJH Hostel** (☎ 07441-7720; www.djh.de; Eugen-Nägele-Strasse 69; dm from €18) has 138 beds in a central and classic 1960s building. **Pension Traube** (☎ 07441-917 450; fax 853 28; Markt 41; s/d €35/70) has 26 rooms right in the midst of everything. The Markt has many excellent cafés, some with wi-fi.

From Freudenstadt, train lines run south to Schiltach (€5, 30 minutes) and north to the important transfer point of Karlsruhe (€14, two hours).

SCHILTACH

The prettiest town in the Black Forest is easily Schiltach, where there is the always underlying roar of the Kinzig and Schiltach Rivers, which meet here. Half-timbered buildings lean at varying angles along the crisscrossing hillside lanes.

The **tourist office** (☎ 07836-5850; www.schiltach.de; Hauptstrasse 5; 🕑 10am-5pm Mon-Fri, to 2pm Sat) can help with accommodation and has a lot of English-language information. Be sure not to miss the **Schüttesäge-museum** (Hauptstrasse 1; 🕑 11am-5pm Tue-Sun Apr-Oct), which is part of an old mill built on the river. It shows what water power could do. The **Markt** (square) has several tiny museums that cover local

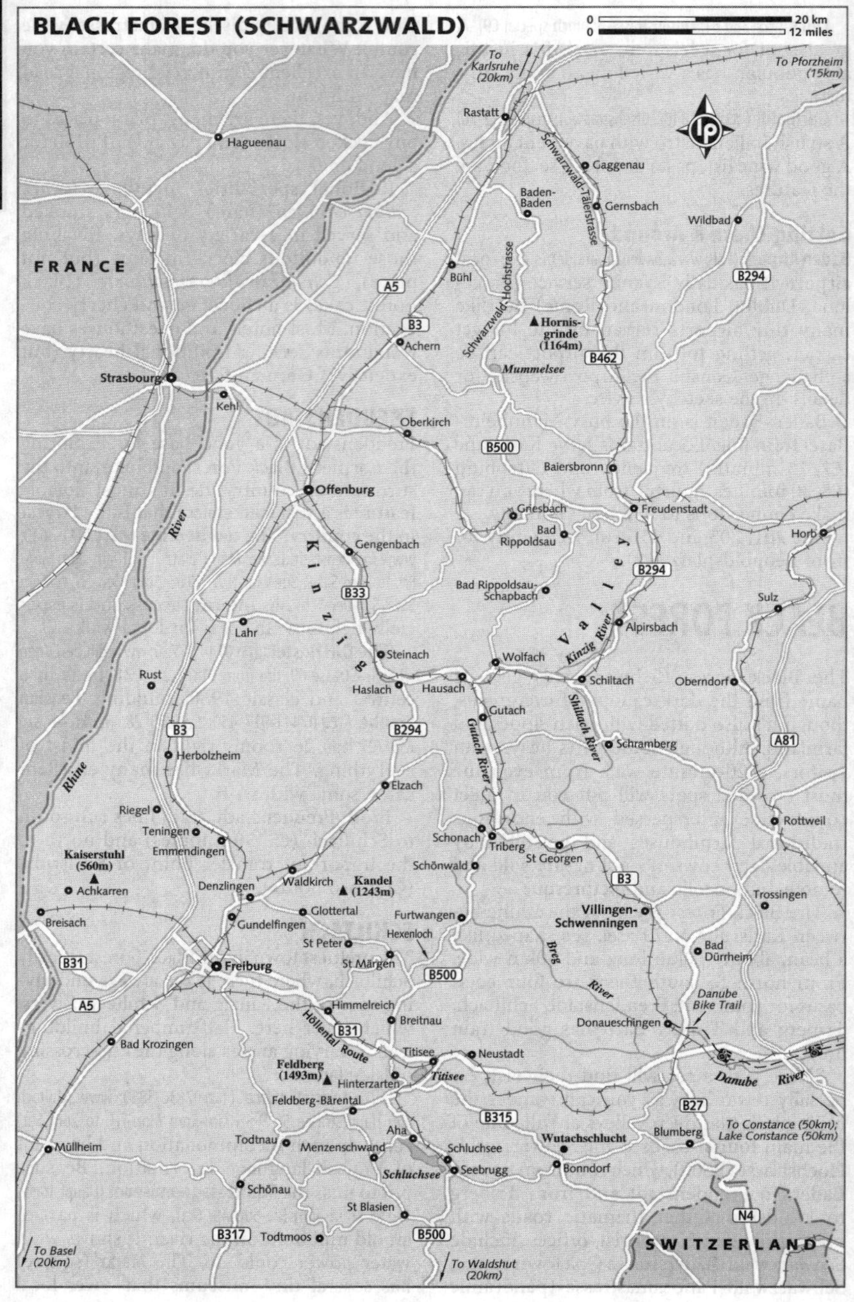
BLACK FOREST (SCHWARZWALD)
0 20 km
0 12 miles
To Karlsruhe (20km)
To Pforzheim (15km)
Rastatt
Hagueenau
Schwarzwald-Tälerstrasse
Gaggenau
Baden-Baden
Gernsbach
Wildbad
FRANCE
Bühl
A5
B294
Schwarzwald-Hochstrasse
B3
Hornisgrinde (1164m)
Achern
B462
Mummelsee
Strasbourg
Kehl
Oberkirch
B500
Baiersbronn
Offenburg
Griesbach
Freudenstadt
River
Bad Rippoldsau
Horb
Kinzig Valley
Gengenbach
B294
Bad Rippoldsau-Schapbach
B33
Sulz
Kinzig River
Alpirsbach
Lahr
Steinach
Wolfach
Rust
Schiltach
Oberndorf
Haslach
Hausach
Gutach
Shiltach River
B3
B294
Schramberg
A81
Herbolzheim
Gutach River
Rhine
Elzach
Riegel
Rottweil
Teningen
Schonach
Triberg
Emmendingen
St Georgen
Kaiserstuhl (560m)
Schönwald
Waldkirch
Kandel (1243m)
B3
Achkarren
Denzlingen
Trossingen
Villingen-Schwenningen
Breisach
Glottertal
Furtwangen
Gundelfingen
Hexenloch
St Peter
Bad Dürrheim
B31
Freiburg
St Märgen
Breg River
B500
A5
Danube Bike Trail
Himmelreich
Breitnau
Donaueschingen
Höllental Route
B31
Bad Krozingen
Titisee
Neustadt
Feldberg (1493m)
Hinterzarten
Titisee
Danube River
Feldberg-Bärental
B27
B315
To Constance (50km); Lake Constance (50km)
Aha
Wutachschlucht
Blumberg
Todtnau
Müllheim
Menzenschwand
Schluchsee
Seebrugg
Bonndorf
Schluchsee
Schönau
St Blasien
N4
B317
Todtmoos
B500
SWITZERLAND
To Basel (20km)
To Waldshut (20km)

history and culture. Most are open in the afternoons during the tourist season.

There are numerous hotels and restaurants in the compact centre. **Zum Weyssen Rössle** (☎ 07836-387; www.weysses-roessle.de; Schenkenzeller Strasse 42; s/d from €47/69; 💻) dates from 1590 and has nine lovely rooms with four-poster beds and wi-fi. The excellent restaurant serves creative versions of local fare. **Zur alten Brücke** (☎ 07836-20 36; www.altebruecke.de; Schramberger Strasse 13; s/d from €35/62) is another cosy choice and has a restaurant serving various maultaschen.

Schiltach is on a small train line linking Offenburg (€8, 45 minutes) via Hausach to Freudenstadt (€5, 30 minutes) with hourly service.

Around Schiltach

Alpirsbach, 10km north of Schiltach, is a small town that is worth a trip for its 12th-century **Benedictine abbey** (adult/child €3/1.50; 🕑 10am-4.30pm Mon-Sat, 11am-4.30pm Sun). It's often uncrowded and if you find yourself alone in the large Romanesque complex it can be quite eerie. The cloisters are impressive, as is the small museum that documents the lives of those who lived here.

Alpirsbach is a stop for the hourly trains linking Schiltach and Freudenstadt.

TRIBERG

Framed by three mountains – hence the name – Triberg has two duelling cuckoo clocks that claim to be the world's largest – it's a close call on these house-sized oddities.

It has an appealing old centre and plenty of chances to go for a stroll. There's a one-hour walk to a roaring **waterfall** that starts near the **tourist office** (☎ 07722-866490; www.triberg.de; Wallfahrtstrasse 4; 🕑 10am-5pm). In the same building is the **Schwarzwaldmuseum** (☎ 07722-4434; adult/child €4/3; 🕑 10am-5pm, Sat & Sun only Nov-Apr) with displays of local crafts.

The **DJH Hostel** (☎ 07722-4110; www.djh.de; Rohrbacher Strasse 35; dm from €18) has 128 beds and spectacular views from its peak location. Take any bus from the train station to Markt and then walk 1.2km uphill.

Hotel Pfaff (☎ 07722-44 79; www.hotel-pfaff.com; Hauptstrasse 85; s/d €38/72) offers comfortable lodgings near the waterfall; some rooms have balconies with views. There is also a fine restaurant.

Triberg is midway on the Karlsruhe (€20, 1½ hours) to Konstanz (€20, 1½ hours) train line. There's hourly service and good connections. Change at Hausach for Schiltach and Freudenstadt. The station is 1.7km from the centre, take any bus to Markt.

STRETCHING YOUR LEGS IN THE BLACK FOREST

With more than 7000km of marked trails, hiking possibilities during summer are, almost literally, endless. Three classic long-distance **hiking trails** run south from the northern Black Forest city of Pforzheim as far as the Swiss Rhine: the 280km Westweg to Basel; the 230km Mittelweg to Waldhut-Tiengen; and the 240km Ostweg to Schaffhausen.

The southern Black Forest, especially the area around the 1493m Feldberg summit, offers some of the best hiking; small towns such as Todtmoos or Bonndorf serve as useful bases for those wanting to get off the more heavily trodden trails. The 10km Wutachschlucht (Wutach Gorge) outside Bonndorf is justifiably famous.

Around Triberg

In Furtwangen, 17km south of Triberg, visit the **Deutsches Uhrenmuseum** (German Clock Museum; ☎ 07723-920 117; Gerwigstrasse 11; adult/child €4/2.50; 🕑 9am-6pm Apr-Oct, 10am-5pm Nov-Mar) for a look at the traditional Black Forest skill of clock-making. A fun demo shows what puts the 'cuc' and the 'koo' in the namesake clock.

TITISEE

The iconic glacial **lake** here draws no shortage of visitors to the busy village of Titisee. Walking around Titisee or paddle-boating across it are major activities. But if you can drive into the surrounding rolling meadows to see some of the truly enormous traditional house-barn combos.

The **tourist office** (☎ 07651-980 40; www.titisee.de; Strandbadstrasse 4, Kurhaus; 🕑 8am-noon & 1.30-5.30pm Mon-Fri year-round, 10am-noon Sat & Sun May-Oct) can help you arrange a farm stay.

Terrassencamping Sandbank (☎ 07651-8243; fax 8286; Seerundweg; camp sites per person €5-6, site €5.50-8; 🕑 Apr-Oct) is one of four camping grounds on the Titisee.

The **DJH Hostel** (☎ 07652-238; www.djh.de; Bruderhalde 27; dm from €18) is in a huge farmhouse and is reached by bus 7300 from Titisee.

WORTH A TRIP: HEAVEN & HOLE

Just south of Furtwangen, look for a tiny road off to the west evocatively called the **Hexenloch** (Witch's Hole). This narrow road penetrates deep into a narrow valley of rushing white water and tall trees. It alone is worth the cost of a car rental – which is the only way to enjoy the hole. Even on warm days it's cold as a witch's… you know what, down here. The road follows the bends in the river and you'll see shaded banks of snow months after it has melted elsewhere. Look for small roadhouses with little spinning water wheels.

West of the south end of the Hexenloch road, **St Peter** is a tiny town that offers redemption with a big church. Two onion-domed towers mark the town's namesake old abbey. It's an 18th-century vision in gold, glitter and gilt that would do any Las Vegas designer proud. You can ponder your own place in heaven at the cute little cafés out front.

Hotel Sonneneck (☎ 07651-8246; fax 881 74; Parkstrasse 2; s/d €39/72) provides spacious comfort near the lake and boasts an excellent restaurant downstairs.

Titisee is linked to Freiburg by frequent train service (€9, 40 minutes). To reach Triberg to the north, there are very scenic hourly connections via Neustadt and Donaueschigen (€14, two hours).

Around Titisee

The Black Forest **ski season** runs from late December to March. While there is good downhill skiing, the area is more suited to cross-country skiing. The centre for winter sports is around Titisee, with uncrowded downhill ski runs at **Feldberg** (www.liftverbund-feldberg.de; day passes €23; rental equipment available) and numerous graded cross-country trails.

In summer you can use the lifts to reach the summit of Feldberg (1493m) for a wondrous panorama that stretches to the Alps.

Feldberg is 15km south of Titisee. It can be reached by bus 7300 from Titisee (€4, 12 minutes, hourly).

FREIBURG

☎ 0761 / pop 213,000

Nestled between hills and vineyards, Freiburg im Breisgau is a delightful place, thanks to the city's large and thriving university community. There's a sense of fun here best exemplified by the tiny medieval canals *(bächle)* running right down the middle of streets.

Founded in 1120 and ruled for centuries by the Austrian Habsburgs, Freiburg has retained many traditional features, although major reconstruction was necessary following WWII. The monumental 13th-century cathedral is the city's key landmark but the real attractions are the vibrant cafés, bars and street-life, plus the local wines. The best times for tasting are July for the four days of *Weinfest* (Wine Festival), or August for the nine days of *Weinkost* (wine tasting).

Orientation

The city centre is a convenient 10-minute walk from the train station. Walk east along Eisenbahnstrasse to the tourist office, then continue through the bustling pedestrian zone to Münsterplatz, dominated by the red-stone cathedral.

Information

Main post office (Eisenbahnstrasse 58-62)

Tourist office (☎ 388 1880; www.freiburg.de; Rotteckring 14; 9.30am-8pm Mon-Fri, to 5pm Sat, 10am-noon Sun Jun-Sep, 9.30am-6pm Mon-Fri, to 2.30pm Sat, 10am-noon Sun Nov-Apr) Amazingly helpful and loads of information on the Black Forest.

Wash & Tours (☎ 288 866; Salzstrasse 22; wash €4, Internet per 30 min €2; 9am-7pm Mon-Fri, to 6pm Sat, Sun closed) There's a drop-off laundry downstairs and an Internet café upstairs. How's that spin your web?

Sights

The major sight in Freiburg is the 700-year-old **Münster** (Cathedral; Münsterplatz; steeple adult/child €1.50/1.00; 9.30am-5pm Mon-Sat, 1-5pm Sun year-round), a classic example of both high and late-Gothic architecture that looms over Münsterplatz, Freiburg's market square. Ascend the west tower to the stunning pierced spire for great views of Freiburg and, on a clear day, the Kaiserstuhl wine region and the Vosages Mountains to the west. South of the Münster stands the picturesque **Kaufhaus**, the 16th-century merchants' hall.

The bustling **university quarter** is northwest of the **Martinstor** (one of the old city gates).

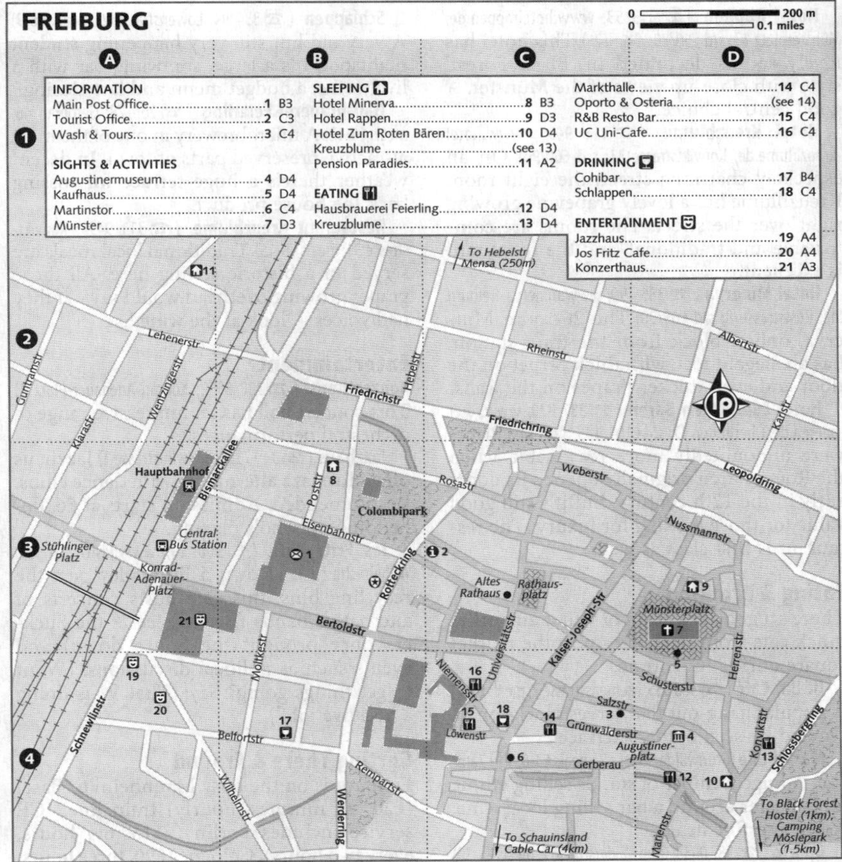

Freiburg's main museum, the **Augustinermuseum** (☎ 201 2531; Salzstrasse 32; 🕑 10am-5pm Tue-Sun) has a fine collection of medieval art. Through 2007 the main building is being restored and much of the collection is in storage. Until completion only a few notable pieces are on exhibit and admission is free.

The popular trip by **cable car** (one way/return €7.50/10.70, concession €4.50/6.50; 🕑 9am-5pm Jan-Jun, to 6pm Jul-Sep, 9.30am-5pm Oct-Dec) to the **Schauinsland peak** (1284m) is a quick way to reach the Black Forest highlands. Numerous easy and well-marked trails make the Schauinsland area ideal for day walks. From Freiburg take tram 4 south to Günterstal and then bus 21 to Talstation.

Sleeping

Camping Möslepark (☎ 767 9333; www.camping-freiburg.com; Waldseestrasse 77; camp sites per person/tent €6/3) To reach this camping ground take tram 1 to Stadthalle (direction: Littenweiler), turn right under the road, go over the train tracks and follow the bike path.

Black Forest Hostel (☎ 881 7870; www.blackforest-hostel.de; Kartäuserstrasse 33; dm/s/d €13/23/28) Take tram 1 to Oberlinden (direction: Littenweiler) for this hostel.

Pension Paradies (☎ 273700; www.paradies-freiburg.de; Friedrich-Ebert-Platz; r €35-80; 💻) This is a real find over the train tracks (take tram 4). The rooms are simple but stylish. There is a vast café with vegetarian specials and a large terrace.

Hotel Rappen (☎ 313 53; www.hotelrappen.de; Münsterplatz 13; s/d €60/80; ⊠ 💻) This hotel has lovely rooms decorated in 'Black Forest' style with close-up views of the Münster. A good central choice.

Hotel Kreuzblume (☎ 311 9495; www.hotel-kreuzblume.de; Konviktstrasse 31; s/d €60/90) On an especially charming street, the eight-room Kreuzblume has a lovely grapevine growing right over the street. The rooms are comfortable and traditional, and the restaurant is excellent.

Hotel Minerva (☎ 386 490; www.minerva-freiburg.de; Poststrasse 8; s/d €69/90) The 26-room Minerva, only a block from the train station, has an elegant feel, with thick carpet on the floor and even thicker drapes on the walls.

Hotel Zum Roten Bären (☎ 387 870; www.roter-baeren.de; Oberlinden 12; s/d €105/145; ⊠ 💻) Prices were undoubtedly more reasonable when the Roten Bären originally opened its doors early in the 12th century, but it's still good value for those looking for luxury. The restaurant is first class as well.

Eating & Drinking

There's a good selection of wurst and other quick eats from stalls set up in the market square during lunchtime.

UC Uni-Café (☎ 383 355; Niemensstrasse 7; meals €3-7) A popular hang-out that serves snacks on its see-and-be-seen outdoor terrace.

Markthalle (Grünwälderstrasse 2; meals €3-8; 🕑 7am-7pm) A huge number of stands selling ethnic food cluster around a bar selling local wine. A fun and fine deal.

Oporto (☎ 387 0038; Grünwälderstrasse 2; meals €5-10) This gorgeous wine bar and café looks like a classic from the 19th century. The bar and dining area are richly detailed. In the rear, the adjoining Osteria is all exposed brick and mimes an Italian wine cellar.

Cohibar (☎ 767 8550; Milchstrasse 9; snacks €3-5) Mellow and candlelit, this café doesn't close till 3am at weekends. At any time it's the kind of place where you may be inspired to work on your novel. Besides booze it has good coffees.

R & B Resto Bar (☎ 217 2204; Universitätstrasse; meals €6-10) In the heart of the university café district, this chic place serves fresh and creative soups, salads and sandwiches as well as pasta. In the back there's a funky bar with jazzy music. Grab a table outside and order breakfast any time.

Schlappen (☎ 334 94; Lowenstrasse 2; meals €6-9) A very old but still very happening student nightspot. It's a large, sprawling bar with a lively vibe, a budget menu and late closing.

Hausbrauerei Feierling (☎ 266 78; Gerberau 46; meals €6-12) A microbrewery in one of the most attractive preserved parts of town. In decent weather there's a huge terrace for tossing back the house product.

Restaurant Kreuzblume (☎ 311 9495; Konviktstrasse 31; meals €8-15) Traditional local meals are served in a historic setting here. All those grapes growing overhead would say – if they had voices – 'look at the wine list'.

Entertainment

Konzerthaus (☎ 388 8552; Konrad-Adenauer-Platz 1) This concert hall has an impressive range of orchestral performances.

Jazzhaus (☎ 349 73; Schnewlinstrasse 1) Jazzhaus offers live jazz alternating with dance clubs. Recommended. Admission starts at €6, depending on who's playing.

Jos Fritz Cafe (☎ 300 19; www.josfritzcafé.de; Wilhelmstrasse 15) Down a little alley past the recycling bins, this café hosts concerts of alternative bands (Bernadetee & the Suckers once brought the house down) and events such as political discussions. (Want to get things going? Say: 'That W is doing a heckuva job!')

Getting There & Around

Freiburg is on the busy Mannheim to Basel (€20, 45 minutes, hourly) train line. ICE service includes Berlin (€115, 6½ hours, every two hours), Cologne (€90, three hours, every two hours) and Frankfurt (€54, two hours, hourly). Freiburg is linked to Titisee by frequent trains (€9, 40 minutes).

Single rides on the efficient local bus and tram system cost €2. A 24-hour pass costs €4.80. Trams depart from the bridge over the train tracks.

LAKE CONSTANCE

Lake Constance (Bodensee) is an oasis in landlocked southern Germany. Even if you never make contact with the water, this giant bulge in the sinewy course of the Rhine can offer a splash of refreshment. There are many historic towns around its periphery, which can be explored by boat or bicycle and on foot. While sun is nice, the lake is best on one of the many misty days when it is shrouded in mystery.

Constance's southern side belongs to Switzerland and Austria, where the snow-capped Alps provide a perfect backdrop when viewed from the northern shore. The German side of Lake Constance features three often-crowded tourist centres in Constance, Meersburg and the island of Lindau. It's essentially a summer area, when it abounds with aquatic joy.

Getting There & Around

Trains link Lindau and Constance, and buses fill in the gaps to places like Meersburg. By car, the B31 hugs the northern shore of Lake Constance, but it can get rather busy. The Constance-Meersburg car ferry (p506) provides a vital link for those who don't want to circumnavigate the entire lake.

The most enjoyable, albeit slowest, way to get around is on the **Bodensee-Schiffsbetriebe boats** (BSB; www.bsb-online.com) which, from Easter to late October, call several times a day at the larger towns along the lake; there are discounts for rail pass-holders.

The **Erlebniskarte** (3 days/1 week €69/89) is a handy pass that allows free boat travel and free access to a host of activities around the lake. Numerous other discount cards are available. Ask at tourist information offices.

CONSTANCE

☎ 07531 / pop 81,000

Constance (Konstanz) sits right on the Swiss border. It's a tidy lake town and is a good place for gazing across the waters. Its main attraction is fittingly named Mainau Island.

It achieved historical significance in 1414, when the Council of Constance convened to try to heal huge rifts in the Catholic Church. The consequent burning at the stake of the religious reformer Jan Hus as a heretic, and the scattering of his ashes over the lake, did nothing to block the Reformation.

The **tourist office** (☎ 133 030; www.konstanz.de/tourismus; Bahnhofplatz 13; 9am-6.30pm Mon-Fri, to 4pm Sat, 10am-1pm Sun Apr-Oct; 9.30am-12.30pm, 2-6pm Mon-Fri Nov-Mar) is 150m to the right from the train station exit. **Clixworkx.net** (☎ 991 211; Bodanstrasse 21; per 15 min €1; 10am-7pm Mon-Sat) has Internet access.

WHEELING AROUND LAKE CONSTANCE

A 270km international bike track circumnavigates Lake Constance through Germany, Austria and Switzerland, tracing the often-steep shoreline beside vineyards and pebble beaches. The route is well signposted, but you may want one of the many widely sold cycling maps. The tourist booklet *Rad Urlaub am Bodensee* lists routes, rental places and a wealth of other information about the region.

In Constance, **Kultur-Rädle** (☎ 07531-273 10; Bahnhofplatz 29; bike rental per day from €10; 9am-12.30pm & 2.30-6pm Mon-Fri, 10am-4pm Sat year-round, 10am-12.30pm Sun Apr-Oct) rents out bikes and organises cycling tours.

Sights & Activities

The city's most visible feature is the Gothic spire of the cathedral, added in 1856 to a church that was started in 1052, which has excellent views over the old town. Visit the **Niederburg** quarter or relax in the parklands of the **Stadtgarten**. Head across to **Mainau Island** (☎ 3030; www.mainau.de; adult/child €12; 7am-8pm mid-Mar–Nov, 9am-6pm Nov–mid-Mar), with its baroque castle set in vast and gorgeous gardens that include a butterfly house. Take bus 4 (€2, 25 minutes) or a BSB ferry from the harbour behind the station. Five **beaches** are open from May to September, including the Strandbad Horn, with bush-enclosed nude bathing. Take bus 5 or walk for 20 minutes around the shore.

Sleeping & Eating

Campingplatz Bodensee (☎ 330 57; www.dkv-camping.de; Fohrenbühlweg 45; camp sites per person/tent €4/5) This is a lovely spot to camp. Take bus 1 to the car-ferry terminal, then walk south along the shore for 10 minutes.

Jugendherberge Konstanz (☎ 322 60; www.jugendherberge-konstanz.de; Zur Allmannshöhe 16; dm €21-24) To reach Jugendherberge Konstanz take bus 1 or 4 from the station to the Jugendherberge stop and stay in this converted water tower.

Hotel Goldener Sternen (☎ 252 28; www.hotel-goldener-sternen.de; Bodanplatz 1; s/d from €50/80) The 20 rooms are basic but comfortable at this modest place right near the train station.

Hotel Barbarossa (☎ 128 990; www.barbarossa-hotel.com; Obermarkt 8-12; s/d from €48/88; ☒ 💻) Charming old place has been carefully restored (although the floors still creak). White walls set off beautiful wooden antiques. There's a good restaurant (mains €8 to €20) downstairs with local specialities.

Hafenalle Biergarten (☎ 211 26; Hafenstrasse 10) A perfect spot for a beer garden, Hafenalle catches the breeze off the lake. There's the usual array of pretzels and sausages.

Aran (☎ 365 2556; Marktstätte 6; meals €4-7; 🕑 7am-5pm) The current star of Constance cafés, Aran has a stylish interior where you can buy garden plants, cute décor items and excellent soups, salads and sandwiches. The bread is from its bakery.

Getting There & Away

Constance has trains to Offenburg via Triberg in the Black Forest (€26, 2¼ hours, hourly) and connections via Singen to Stuttgart (€35, 2¼ hours, hourly). There are good connections into Switzerland including Zurich (€16, one hour, hourly).

BSB Ferries on various schedules serve numerous destinations including Meersburg (€4.20, 30 minutes) and Lindau (€11.20, three to four hours).

MEERSBURG

☎ 07532 / pop 5300

Constance is the big city compared to Meersburg across the lake. The winding cobblestone streets, vine-patterned hills and a sunny lakeside promenade make it a good stop if travelling by ferry or car.

The helpful **tourist office** (☎ 440 400; www.meersburg.de; Kirchstrasse 4; 🕑 9am-noon & 2-6pm Mon-Fri, 10am-2pm Sat) is in the Altstadt and can help find accommodation if you decide to stay.

Steigstrasse is lined with delightful half-timbered houses, each boasting a gift shop. The 11th-century **Altes Schloss** (☎ 800 00; adult/child €6/4; 🕑 9am-6.30pm) is the oldest structurally intact castle in Germany.

The useful Constance to Meersburg **car ferry** (☎ 07531-803 666; person/car €2/7.20, 30 min) runs every 15 minutes year-round from the northeastern Constance suburb of Staad. BSB ferries stop on their shore-hugging voyages between Constance (€4.20, 30 minutes) and Lindau (€10.50, 2½ to three hours).

LINDAU

☎ 08382 / pop 26,500

A forgotten corner of Bavaria, most people assume the lovely little island-city is part of Baden-Württemberg but it's not. Here you'll see the blue and white Bavarian state colours and maybe it's just us, but there's a renewed emphasis on beer compared to the wine-drinkers elsewhere on the lake.

The **tourist office** (☎ 260 030; www.lindau-tourismus.de; Ludwigstrasse 68; 🕑 9am-6pm Mon-Fri, 10am-2pm Sat & Sun Jun-Sep, reduced hr winter) is directly opposite the train station. **Internet Cafe Salem** (☎ 943 1297, Bahnhofplatz 08, per 15 min €1; 🕑 10am-7pm Mon-Fri, 11am-5pm Sat & Sun) is close to the station.

Connected to the nearby lakeshore by bridges, key sights of this oh-so-charming island town have murals: **Altes Rathaus** (Reichsplatz), the **city theatre** (Barfüsser-platz) and the harbour's **Seepromenade**, with its Bavarian Lion monument and lighthouse. When the haze clears, the Alps provide a stunning backdrop for photos.

Park Camping Lindau am See (☎ 722 36; www.park-camping.de; Fraunhoferstrasse 20; camp sites per person/tent €6/2.50) is on the foreshore 3km southeast of Lindau. Take bus 1 or 2 to the bus station, then bus 3.

The attractive-looking façade of **Hotel Gasthof Goldenes Lamm** (☎ 5732; www.goldenes-lamm-lindau.de; Schafgasse 3; s/d from €47/84) is mirrored by the 21 comfortable rooms inside. The restaurant is good and has many fish dishes.

The maroon **Alte Post** (☎ 934 60; www.alte-post-lindau.de; Fischergasse 3; s/d €44/80) has 19 beautifully maintained rooms. The restaurant (mains €7 to €18) serves Bavarian/Austrian fare and has a large terrace. Guests can use bikes for free.

The personality begins over the door at **Zurtischerin Galerie und Weinstube** (☎ 5428; Ludwigstrasse 50; snacks under €4; 🕑 5pm-2am); look for the big fish. Inside there's local art on the walls and some of the characters who painted it might just let you buy them a drink. Regional wines are featured.

Lindau has trains to/from Ulm on the Munich–Stuttgart line (€20, 1¾ hours, hourly), Munich (€33, 2¼ hours, four times daily). There are hourly RB trains to/from Immenstadt where you connect to Oberstdorf (€15, 1¾ hours). Trains to nearby Bregenz (€3.20, nine minutes, hourly) let you connect to the rest of Austria.

BSB Ferries on various schedules serve destinations including Meersburg (€10.50, 2½ to three hours) and Constance (€11.20, three to four hours).

RHINELAND-PALATINATE

Rhineland-Palatinate (Rheinland-Pfalz) has an unsettled topography characterised by thinly populated mountain ranges and forests cut by deep river valleys. Created after WWII from parts of the former Rhineland and Rhenish Palatinate regions, its turbulent history goes all the way back to the Romans, as seen in Trier (p508). In recent centuries it was hotly contested by the French and a variety of German states.

This land of wine and great natural beauty reaches its apex in the verdant Moselle Valley towns such as Cochem, and along the heavily touristed Rhine, where rich hillside vineyards provide a backdrop for noble castles and looming medieval fortresses. For this part of Germany, focus your attention on the water and the land it courses through.

MOSELLE VALLEY

Exploring the vineyards and wineries of the Moselle (Mosel) Valley is an ideal way to get a taste of German culture and people – and, of course, the wonderful wines. Take the time to slow down and savour a glass or two.

The Moselle is bursting at the seams with historical sites and picturesque towns built along the river below steep rocky cliffs planted with vineyards (they say locals are born with one leg shorter than the other so that they can easily work the vines). It's one of the country's most romantically scenic regions, with stunning views rewarding the intrepid hikers who brave the hilly trails.

Many wine-makers have their own small *pensions* but accommodation is hard to find in May, on summer weekends or during the local wine harvest (mid-September to mid-October). Note also that much of the region – like the vines themselves – goes into a deep slumber from November to March.

Getting There & Around

The most scenic part of the Moselle Valley runs 195km northeast from Trier to Koblenz; it's most practical to begin your Moselle Valley trip from either of these two.

It is not possible to travel the banks of the Moselle River via rail. Local and fast trains run every hour between Trier and Koblenz, but the only riverside stretch of this line is between Cochem and Koblenz (however it's a scenic dandy). Apart from this run – and the scenic Moselweinbahn line taking tourists between Bullay and Traben-Trarbach – travellers must use buses, ferries, bicycles or cars to travel between most of the upper Moselle towns.

Moselbahn (☎ 0651-147 750; www.moselbahn.de) runs eight buses on weekdays (fewer at weekends) between Trier and Bullay (three hours each way), a very scenic route following the river's winding course and passing through numerous quaint villages. Buses leave from outside the train stations in Trier and Bullay.

A great way to explore the Moselle in the high season is by boat. Between May and early October, **Köln-Düsseldorfer (KD) Line** (☎ 0221-208 8318; www.k-d.com) ferries sail daily between Koblenz and Cochem (€22.40 one way, 4¾ hours). Various smaller ferry companies also operate on the Moselle from some of the towns. Eurail and German Rail passes are valid for all normal KD Line services, and travel on your birthday is free.

The Moselle is a popular area among cyclists, and for much of the river's course there's a separate 'Moselroute' bike track. Most towns have a rental shop or two, ask at the tourist offices. Many of the Moselbahn buses also carry bikes.

Koblenz

☎ 0261 / pop 109,000

Koblenz is an important ferry and train junction at the confluence of the Rhine and Moselle Rivers. The **tourist office** (☎ 303 880; www.koblenz.de; Bahnhofsplatz 7; 9am-6pm Mon-Sat year-round, 10am-6pm Sun Apr-Oct) is in a very modern building in front of the Hauptbahnhof.

The **Deutsches Eck** is a park at the dramatic meeting point of the rivers. It's dedicated to German unity and is a good reason for a riverside stroll.

South of Koblenz, at the head of the beautiful Eltz Valley, **Burg Eltz** (☎ 02672-950 500; adult/child €6/4.50; 9.30am-5.30pm Apr-Nov) is not to be missed. Towering over the surrounding hills, this superb medieval castle has frescoes, paintings, furniture and ornately decorated rooms. Burg Eltz is best reached by train to Moselkern, from where it's a 50-minute walk up through the forest. Alternatively, you can drive via Münster-Maifeld to the nearby car park.

In town, Altenhof and the area around Münzplatz in the Altstadt offer a variety of good eating options. The small towns in either river valley offer more salubrious accommodation than that locally.

The busy KD line ferry dock is a 10-minute walk from the train station. Trains fan out in all directions. Up the Moselle to Trier (€17, 1½ hours, hourly) via Cochem and Bullay, north along the Rhine to Cologne (€18, one hour, two hourly) and south on the Rhine to Mainz (€18, one hour, two hourly).

Cochem

☎ 02671 / pop 5400

This pretty German town has narrow alleyways and one of the most beautiful castles in the region. It's also a good base for hikes into the hills. The staff are very helpful in Cochem's **tourist office** (☎ 600 40; www.cochem.de; Endertplatz), next to the Moselbrücke bridge.

For a great view, head up to the **Pinnerkreuz** with the chairlift on Endertstrasse (€5). The stunning **Reichsburg Castle** (☎ 255; 9am-5pm mid-Mar–mid-Nov) is just a 15-minute walk up the hill from town. There are regular daily tours (adult/child €3.50/2) and English translation sheets are available.

Cochem's **HH Hieronimi** (☎ 221; Stadionstrasse 1-3), just across the river is one of many friendly, family-run vineyards that offers tours.

Campingplatz Am Freizeitszentrum (☎ 4409; Stadionstrasse; camp sites per person/tent/car €5/4/6) is downstream from the northern bridge, alongside the river.

Moseltal-Jugendherberge (☎ 8633; www.djh.de; Klottener Strasse 9; dm €17-24) is beautifully situated on the banks of the river, the 148 beds are in spotless four-bed rooms.

Hotel-Pension Garni Villa Tummelchen (☎ 910 520; www.villa-tummelchen.com; Schlossstrasse 22; s/d from €47/80) is a bit up the hill from town and thus has sweeping Moselle views. It's worth an extra couple of euros to get a room with a balcony and a view.

This is the terminus for KD Line boats from Koblenz. Trains run twice hourly to Bullay (€4, 10 minutes), where you can pick up the Moselbahn bus.

Cochem to Trier

Take the train – or a boat – from Cochem to Bullay where you can catch the Moselbahn bus for the little river towns the rest of the way to Trier.

Full of fanciful Art Nouveau villas, the double town of **Traben-Trarbach** is a welcome relief from the 'romantic-half-timbered-town' circuit. Pick up a map of the town at the **tourist office** (☎ 839 80; www.traben-trarbach.de; Bahnstrasse 22).

The twin town of **Bernkastel-Kues** is at the heart of the middle Moselle region. On the right bank, Bernkastel has a charming **Markt**, a romantic ensemble of half-timbered houses with beautifully decorated gables. For a primer on the local vino – one of many, try Bernkastel's **Weingut Dr Willkomm** (☎ 8054; Gestade 1). Located in a lovely old arched cellar, the vineyard also distils its own brandy. The **tourist office** (☎ 4023; www.bernkastel-kues.de; Am Gestade 6) is on the Bernkastel side.

TRIER

☎ 0651 / pop 100,000

Trier is touted as Germany's oldest town and you'll find more Roman ruins here than anywhere else north of the Alps. Although settlement of the site dates back to 400 BC, Trier itself was founded in 15 BC as Augusta Treverorum, the capital of Gaul, and was second in importance only to Rome in the Western Roman Empire. Its proximity to France can be tasted in its cuisine, while its large student population injects life among the ruins.

Orientation & Information

From the main train station head west along Bahnhofstrasse and Theodor-Heuss-Allee to the Porta Nigra, where you'll find Trier's nearby **tourist office** (☎ 978 080; www.trier.de; 9am-6pm Mon-Sat, 10am-3pm Sun May-Oct; reduced hr winter). There are good two-hour guided **city walking tours** (adult/child €6/3; 1.30pm Sat May-Oct) in English. The Trier-Card (€12) is a combined ticket for the city's main attractions and public transport. From Porta Nigra, walk along Simeonstrasse's pedestrian zone to Hauptmarkt, the heart of the old city. Most of the sights are within this area of roughly 1 sq km. Several places around the station offer Internet access.

Sights

The town's chief landmark is the **Porta Nigra** (adult/child €2.10/1; 9am-6pm Apr-Sep, to 5pm Mar & Oct, to 4pm Nov-Feb), the imposing city gate on

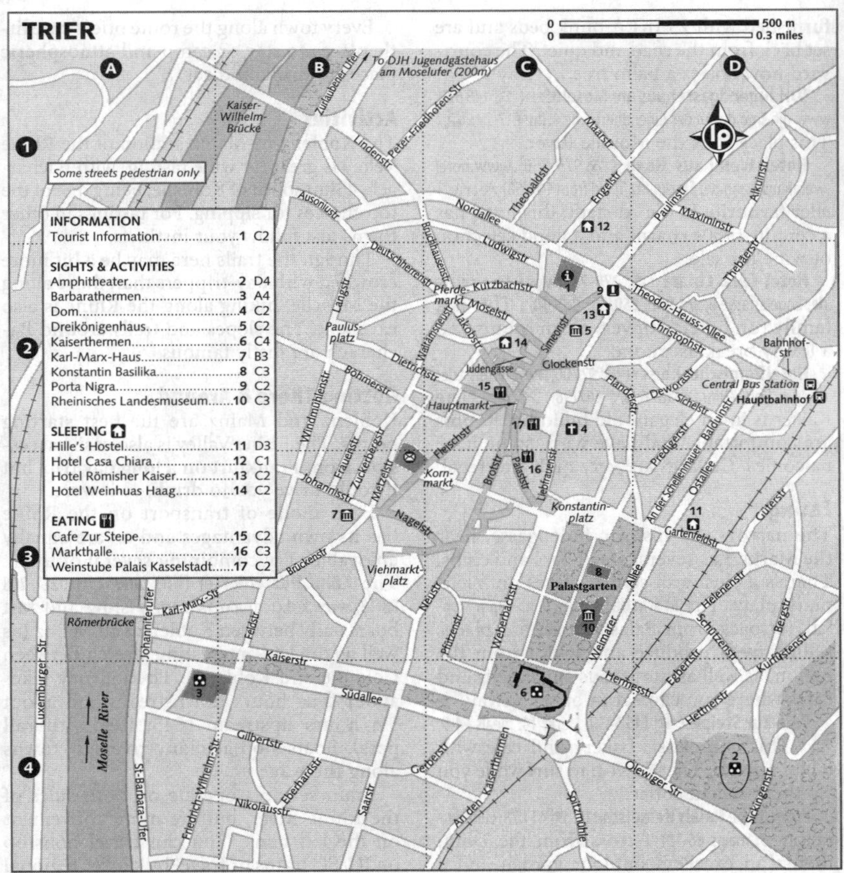

the northern edge of the town centre, which dates back to the 2nd century AD. The interesting **Rheinisches Landesmuseum** (Weimarer Allee 1; adult/child €2.50/0.50; 9.30am-5pm Tue-Fri, 10.30am-5pm Sat & Sun, 9.30am-5pm Mon May-Oct) puts the Roman era into context.

Trier's massive (and massively restored) Romanesque **Dom** (www.dominformation.de; Liebfraustrasse 12; 6.30am-6pm Apr-Oct, to 5.30pm Nov-Mar) shares a 1600-year history with the nearby and equally impressive **Konstantin Basilika** (☎ 724 68; Konstantinplatz; tours by appt €25; 10am-6pm Mon-Fri, noon-6pm Sun Apr-Oct). Also worth visiting are the Roman **Amphitheater** (Olewigerstrasse), the **Kaiserthermen** (Im Palastgarten) and **Barbarathermen** (Roman baths; Südallee). The early-Gothic **Dreikönigenhaus** (Simeonstrasse 19) was built around 1230 as a protective tower; the original entrance was on the second level, accessible only by way of a retractable rope ladder.

The **Karl Marx Haus Museum** (☎ 970 680; Brückenstrasse 10; adult/child €3/1.50; 10am-6pm Apr-Oct, to 5pm & closed Mon Nov-Mar) is the suitably modest birthplace of the man. It is a major pilgrimage stop for the growing numbers of mainland Chinese tourists to Europe.

Sleeping

Camping Treviris (☎ 869 21; Luxemburger Strasse 81; camp sites per person/tent/car €6/4/4; Apr-Oct) This camping ground is central and beside the Moselle River.

Hille's Hostel (☎ 710 2785; www.hilles-hostel-trier.de; Gartenfeldstrasse 7; dm €15) The rooms here are furnished with 25 IKEA bunk beds and are set back from the road and quiet. The courtyard now boasts a palm tree.

DJH Jugendgästehaus am Moselufer (☎ 146 620; www.djh-info.de; An der Jugendherberge 4; dm €17-24; 💻) This place is by the Moselle River.

Hotel Weinhaus Haag (☎ 975 750; www.hotel-weinhaus-haag.de; Stockplatz 1; s/d from €47/50) A traveller favourite in the Altstadt, this hotel has a certain 1950s charm and a good selection of wine for sale.

Hotel Casa Chiara (☎ 270 730; www.casa-chiara.de; Engelstrasse 8; s/d from €50/80; ⊠ 💻) This is a family run hotel with very clean rooms and a lovely breakfast room.

Hotel Römischer Kaiser (☎ 97700; www.hotels-trier.de; Am Porta-Nigra-Platz 6; s/d €67/98; ⊠ 💻) The Kaiser is in an elegant old building. Rooms are comfortable and have wi-fi; some have balconies. Ceilings are very high and regal.

Eating

The narrow and historic Judengasse, near the Markt, has several small bars and clubs. There's a cluster of stylish places on Viehmarktplatz. The **Markthalle** (🕐 9am-10pm Mon-Sat), set back from Palaststrasse, has places selling fresh produce and wines from the region, as well as numerous small delis and cafés where you can eat in or take away.

Cafe Zur Steipe (☎ 145 5456; Markt 14; meals €4-9; 💻) This is a classic bakery and café with tables outside. There's wi-fi to surf while you sip the excellent coffee.

Weinstube Palais Kesselstadt (☎ 411 78; Liebfrauenstrasse 9; mains €6-10) Across from the Dom, there's an excellent outdoor garden and a long list of local wines on offer here. The food is creative.

Getting There & Away

Trier has a train service to Koblenz (€17, 1½ hours, hourly) via Bullay and Cochem, as well as to Luxembourg (€13, 45 minutes, hourly).

RHINE VALLEY – KOBLENZ TO MAINZ

A trip along the Rhine is on the itinerary of most travellers, as it should be. The section between Koblenz and Mainz offers vistas of steep vineyard-covered mountains punctuated by scores of castles. It's really rather magical. Spring and autumn are the best times to visit; in summer it's overrun and in winter most towns go into hibernation. For information on Koblenz, see p507.

Every town along the route offers cute little places to stay or camp and atmospheric places to drink and eat.

Activities

The Koblenz-to-Mainz section of the Rhine Valley is great for wine tasting, with Bacharach, 45km south of Koblenz, being one of the top choices for sipping. For tastings in other towns just follow your instincts.

Though the trails here may be a bit more crowded with day-trippers than those along the Moselle, hiking along the Rhine is also excellent. The slopes and trails around Bacharach are justly famous.

Getting There & Around

Koblenz and Mainz are the best starting points. The Rhine Valley is also easily accessible from Frankfurt on a long day trip, but it could drive you to drink, as it were.

Each mode of transport on the Rhine has its own advantages and all are equally enjoyable. Try combining several of them. The **Köln- Düsseldorfer (KD) Line** (☎ 0221-208 83 18; www.k-d.com) runs many slow and fast boats daily between Koblenz and Mainz (as well as the less-interesting stretch between Cologne and Koblenz). The journey takes about four hours downstream and about 5½ hours upstream (€45, free with rail pass). Boats stop at many riverside towns along the way.

Train services operate on both sides of the Rhine River, but are more convenient on the left bank. You can travel nonstop on IC/EC trains or travel by slower regional RB or RE services. The ride is amazing, sit on the right heading north and on the left heading south.

Touring the Rhine Valley by car is also ideal. The route between Koblenz and Mainz is short enough for a car to be rented and returned to either city. There are no bridge crossings between Koblenz and Rüdesheim, but there are several ferry crossings.

St Goar/St Goarshausen

☎ 06741

These two towns are on opposite sides of the Rhine, St Goar is on the left bank. One of the most impressive castles on the river is **Burg Rheinfels** (☎ 383; adult/child €4/2; 🕐 9am-6pm Apr-Oct, 11am-5pm Sat & Sun in good weather Nov-Mar) in St Goar. An absolute must-see, the labyrinthine ruins reflect the greed and ambition of Count Dieter V of Katzenelnbogen, who built the castle in 1245 to help levy tolls on passing ships ('African or European?'). Across the river, just south of St Goarshausen, is the Rhine's most famous sight, the **Loreley Cliff**. Legend has it that a maiden sang sailors to their deaths against its base. It's worth the trek to the top of the Loreley for the view.

For camping **Campingplatz Loreleyblick** (☎ 2066; camp sites per person/site €3/2.50; Mar-Oct) is on the banks of the Rhine, opposite the legendary rock.

St Goar's **Jugendherberge** (☎ 388; www.djh.de; Bismarckweg 17; dm €13) is right below the castle. You can sip the house wine here in a rural atmosphere. The **Schlosshotel Rheinfels** (☎ 8020; www.schlosshotel-rheinfels.de; s/d from €95/145;) in the castle is the top address in town. Rooms are posh and the views sublime.

Bacharach

☎ 06743 / pop 2400

Walk beneath one of its thick-arched gateways in Bacharach's medieval walls and you'll find yourself in a beautifully preserved medieval village. Drop by the **tourist office** (☎ 919 303; www.bacharach.de; Oberstrasse 45; 9am-5pm Mon-Fri, 10am-4pm Sat Apr-Oct) for information on Bacharach's sights and lodging.

Bacharach's **Jugendherberge** (☎ 1266; www.djh.de; dm €17) is a legendary facility housed in the Burg Stahleck castle. In town, **Hotel Kranenturm** (☎ 1308; www.kranenturm.com; Langstrasse 30; s/d from €40/55) is charming and offers an array of neat rooms, some with river views.

Zum Grünen Baum (☎ 1208; Oberstrasse 63; mains €6-10) is a wonderful place to sample Rhine wines.

Mainz

☎ 06131 / pop 183,000

A short train ride from Frankfurt, Mainz has an attractive old town that makes for a good day trip. Though it can't compare to the compact beauty of the nearby towns along the Rhine, Mainz impresses with its massive **Dom** (cathedral; ☎ 253 412; Domstrasse 3; 9am-6.30pm Mon-Fri, 10am-4pm Sat, 12.45-3pm Sun), which has a smorgasbord of architecture: Romanesque, Gothic and baroque. **St Stephanskirche** (Weisspetrolse 12; 10am-noon, 2-5pm) has stained-glass windows by Marc Chagall. Mainz's museums include the

> **RHINE TOWNS**
>
> Besides those listed in this section, here's the low-down on some other towns along the route. All have train and boat service.
>
> **Boppard** Roman walls and ruins (left bank).
>
> **Oberwesel** Numerous towers and walkable walls of a ruined castle (left bank).
>
> **Assmannshausen** Small relatively untouristed village with nice hotels and sweeping views; good hikes (right bank).
>
> **Rüdesheim** Overrated and over-visited town of trinkets and hype.

Gutenberg Museum (☎ 122 640; Liebfrauenplatz 5; adult/child €3.50/1.50; 9am-5pm Tue-Sat, 11am-3pm Sun), which contains two namesake copies of the first printed Bible. For more information on attractions in Mainz, visit the **tourist office** (☎ 286 210; www.mainz.de; Brückenturm am Rathaus; 9am-6pm Mon-Fri, 10.30am-2.30pm Sat).

Trains along the Rhine to Koblenz (€18, one hour) run twice hourly. Heidelberg (€18, one hour, hourly) is an easy trip as is Frankfurt via the Frankfurt airport (€9, 35 minutes, several per hour).

HESSE

The Hessians, a Frankish tribe, were among the first to convert to Lutheranism in the early 16th century. Apart from a brief period of unity in that same century under Philip the Magnanimous, Hesse (Hessen) remained a motley collection of principalities and, later, of Prussian administrative districts until proclaimed a state in 1945. Its main cities are Frankfurt-am-Main, Kassel and the capital, Wiesbaden.

As well as being a transport hub, Frankfurt-am-Main offers its own diversions, although you'll most likely soon leave the state entirely.

FRANKFURT-AM-MAIN

☎ 069 / pop 643,000

Called 'Mainhattan' and 'Bankfurt', and much more, Frankfurt is on the Main (pronounced 'mine') River, and, after London, it is Europe's centre of finance. Both sobriquets also refer to the city's soaring skyline of skyscrapers, a profile found nowhere else on the continent.

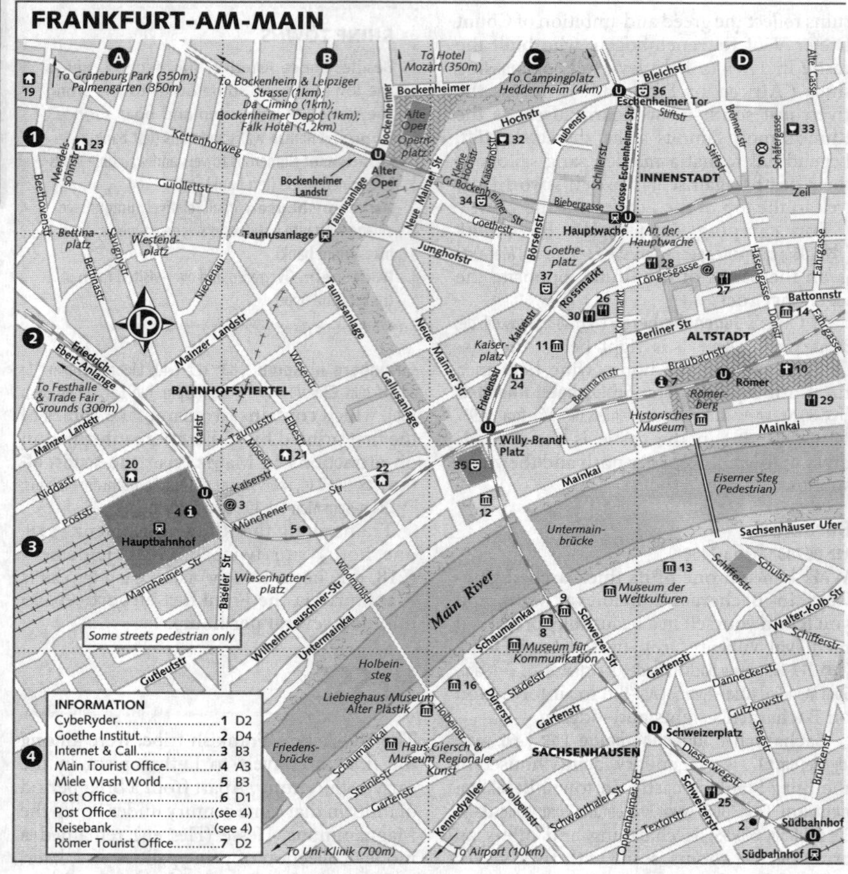

But while all seems cosmopolitan, it is often just a small town at heart. Things tend to get quiet in the evenings and the long list of museums is devoid of any really outstanding stars. Then again, is has cute old pubs you would only ever find in a small town. Mind you, when a major trade fair is in town, it feels as bustling as any metropolis.

Frankfurt-am-Main is Germany's most important transport hub for air, train and road connections, so you will probably end up here at some point. Note that it is generally referred to as Frankfurt-am-Main, or Frankfurt/Main, since there is another Frankfurt (Frankfurt-an-der-Oder) located near the Polish border.

Orientation

The airport is 11 minutes by train southwest of the city centre. The Hauptbahnhof is on the western side of the city, but it's still within walking distance of the city centre.

The best route to the city centre through the sleazy train station area is along Kaiserstrasse. This leads to Kaiserplatz and on to a large square called An der Hauptwache. The area between the former prison/police station (Hauptwache), and the Römerberg, in the tiny vestige of Frankfurt's original old city, is the centre of Frankfurt. The Main River flows just south of the Altstadt, with several bridges leading to one of the city's livelier areas, Sachsenhausen. Its

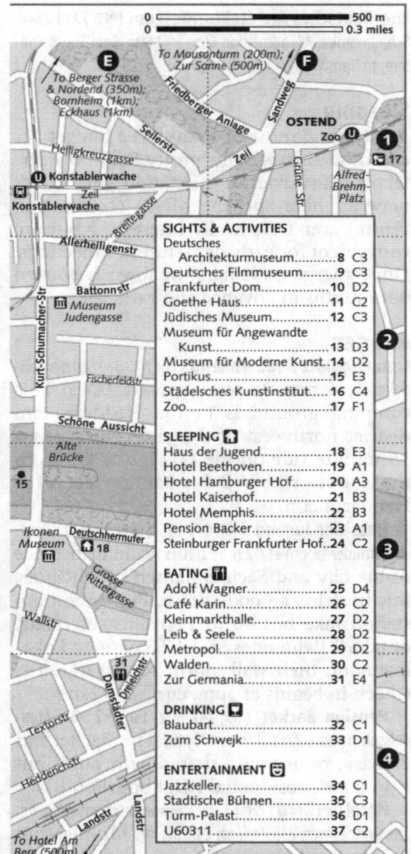

northeastern corner, known as Alt-Sachsenhausen, is full of quaint old houses and narrow alleyways.

Information

BOOKSHOPS

The Hauptbahnhof is an excellent place to go book shopping. Stores near tracks 9 and 17 have scores of English language books and periodicals, as well as guidebooks and maps.

INTERNET ACCESS

CybeRyder (☎ 396 754; Töngesgasse 31; per 30 min €2; ⏲ 9am-8pm Mon-Sat) Full service shop.
Internet & Call (☎ 2424 7939; Kaiserstrasse 81; per hr €2; ⏲ 9am-11pm)

LAUNDRY

Miele Wash World (Moselstrasse 17; wash/dry €4/1; ⏲ 6am-11pm) Near the train station.

MEDICAL SERVICES

Doctor Referral Service (☎ 192 92; ⏲ 24hr)
Uni-Klinik (☎ 630 10; Theodor Stern Kai, Sachsenhausen; ⏲ 24hr)

MONEY

Reisebank Train station (⏲ 6.30am-10pm); airport (Terminal 1, arrival hall B; ⏲ 6am-11pm) The train station branch is near the southern exit at the head of platform 1.

POST

Post office (Zeil 90; ground fl, Karstadt department store; ⏲ 9.30am-8pm) Hauptbahnhof (⏲ 7am-7.30pm Mon-Fri, 8am-4pm Sat); airport (departure lounge B; ⏲ 7am-9pm)

TOURIST INFORMATION

Main tourist office (☎ 212 388 00; www.frankfurt-tourismus.de; ⏲ 8am-9pm Mon-Fri, 9am-6pm Sat, Sun) In the main hall of the train station. For its efficient room-finding service the charge is €3. Römer branch (Römerberg 27; ⏲ 9.30am-5.30pm Mon-Fri, 10am-4pm Sat & Sun) Northwest corner of the Römerberg square. The Frankfurt-am-Main Card (one day/two days €8/12) gives 50% off admission to important attractions and unlimited travel on public transport.

Sights

About 80% of the old city was wiped off the map by two Allied bombing raids in March 1944, and postwar reconstruction was subject to the hurried demands of the new age. Rebuilding efforts were more thoughtful in the **Römerberg**, the old central area of Frankfurt west of the cathedral, where restored 14th- and 15th-century buildings provide a glimpse of the beautiful city this once was. The old town hall, or **Römer**, is in the northwestern corner of Römerberg and consists of three 15th-century houses topped with Frankfurt's trademark stepped gables.

East of Römerberg, behind the Historischer Garten (which has the remains of Roman and Carolingian foundations), is the **Frankfurter Dom** (Domplatz 14; tour adult/child €2/1; ⏲ 9am-noon Mon-Thu, Sat & Sun, 2.30-6pm daily), the coronation site of Holy Roman emperors from 1562 to 1792. It's dominated by the elegant 15th-century Gothic **tower** – one of the few structures left standing after the 1944 raids.

Anyone with an interest in German literature should visit **Goethe Haus** (☎ 138 800; Grosser Hirschgraben 23-25; adult/child €5/3; 9am-6pm Mon-Fri Apr-Sep, to 4pm Mon-Fri Oct-Mar, 10am-4pm Sat & Sun year-round). Johann Wolfgang von Goethe was born in this house in 1749.

A little further afield, there's the botanical **Palmengarten** (☎ 2123 6689; Siesmayerstrasse 63; adult/child €5/2; 9am-6pm), next door to **Grüneburg Park**. The **Frankfurt Zoo** (☎ 212 337 35; Alfred-Brehm-Platz 16; adult/child €8/4; 9am-7pm, to 5pm Oct-Apr) is also a good place to unwind. It is also a nice 40-minute walk from the zoo east along the south bank of the Main River to the **lock** in Offenbach – just before it there's a good beer garden.

There's a great **flea market** (8am-2pm Sat) along Museumsufer.

MUSEUMS

Frankfurt's museum list is long but a mixed bag. To sample them all, buy a 48-hour Museumsufer ticket (€12). North of the cathedral, the excellent **Museum für Moderne Kunst** (☎ 2123 0447; Domstrasse 10; adult/child €6/3; 10am-5pm Tue & Thu-Sun, to 8pm Wed) features works of modern art by Joseph Beuys, Claes Oldenburg and many others.

For more modern art, check out the new **Portikus** (☎ 9624 4540; www.portikus.de; Alte Brücke 2 Maininsel; admission free; 11am-6pm Tue & Thu-Sun, to 8pm Wed) in a dramatic building on an island in the river.

Also on the north bank there's the **Jüdisches Museum** (Jewish Museum; ☎ 2123 5000; Untermainkai 14-15; adult/child €4/2; 10am-5pm Tue & Thu-Sun, to 8pm Wed), a huge place with exhibits on the city's rich Jewish life before WWII.

Numerous museums line the south bank of the Main River along the so-called *Museumsufer* (Museum Embankment). Pick of the crop is the **Städelsches Kunstinstitut** (☎ 605 0980; Schaumainkai 63; adult/child €8/6; 10am-5pm Tue, Fri-Sun, to 9pm Wed & Thu), with a world-class collection of paintings by artists from the Renaissance to the 20th century, including Botticelli, Dürer, Van Eyck, Rubens, Rembrandt, Vermeer, Cézanne and Renoir.

Other highlights include the **Deutsches Filmmuseum** (☎ 2123 8830; Schaumainkai 41; adult/child €2.50/1.30; 10am-5pm Tue, Thu & Fri, to 7pm Wed & Sun, 2-7pm Sat); the fascinating, design-oriented **Museum für Angewandte Kunst** (Museum of Applied Arts; ☎ 2123 4037; Schaumainkai 17; admission €5; 10am-5pm Tue & Thu-Sun, to 9pm Wed); and the **Deutsches Architekturmuseum** (☎ 2123 8844; Schaumainkai 43; admission €6; 11am-6pm Tue & Thu-Sun, to 8pm Wed).

Sleeping

Predictably, most of Frankfurt's budget accommodation is in the grotty Bahnhofsviertel, which surrounds the station. The streets between here and the Messe (convention centre) aren't especially interesting but are convenient for early departures or meetings. During large trade fairs the town is booked out months in advance and rates soar.

BUDGET

Campingplatz Heddernheim (☎ 570 332; An der Sandelmühle 35; camp sites per site/person/car €4/6/5) This camping ground is in the Heddernheim district northwest of the city centre. It's a 15-minute ride on the U1, U2 or U3 from the Hauptwache U-Bahn station – get off at Heddernheim.

Haus der Jugend (☎ 610 0150; www.djh.de; Deutschherrnufer 12; dm €17-22) Within walking distance of the city and Sachsenhausen's nightspots, this hostel is a good choice. From the train station take bus 46 to Frankensteinerplatz, or take S-Bahn lines S3, S4, S5 or S6 to Lokalbahnhof, then walk north for 10 minutes. Check-in begins at 1pm, curfew is 2am.

Pension Backer (☎ 747 992; fax 747 900; Mendelssohnstrasse 92; s/d from €25/40) The Backer has 25 basic rooms with shared bathrooms but is in a nice residential neighbourhood.

Hotel Am Berg (☎ 612 021; www.hotel-am-berg-ffm.de; Grethenweg 23; s/d from €40/50; ⊠) In pleasant Sachsenhausen, this 21-room hotel is in a pretty old sandstone building. Rooms come in all shapes and sizes.

MIDRANGE

Hotel Memphis (☎ 242 6090; www.memphis-hotel.de; Münchenerstrasse 15; s/d from €60/80; ⊠ 💻) The stylish modern rooms here are fully equipped and the front desk staff are trained to assist with all your needs, business or otherwise.

Hotel Kaiserhof (☎ 256 1790; www.kaiserhof-frankfurt.de; Kaiserstrasse 62; s/d from €65/80; ⊠ 💻) This remodelled hotel three minutes from the Hauptbahnhof has 42 rooms that are easy on the eyes and have wi-fi. Those on the top floor have a small terrace.

Hotel Hamburger Hof (☎ 2713 9690; www.hamburgerhof.com; Poststrasse 10-12; s/d €69/79) An excellent choice, the Hamburger Hof's 60 rooms are done up in stark, contrasting colours. There's wi-fi in all and a good level of service from the staff.

Hotel Beethoven (☎ 746 091; www.hotelbeethoven.de; Beethovenstrasse 44; s/d €80/120; ⊠ 🖳) The elegant Beethoven is in a quiet neighbourhood north of the train station. The 31 rooms are a bit regal.

Falk Hotel (☎ 719 188 70; www.hotel-falk.de; Falkstrasse 38; r €80-180; ⊠) In the fun neighbourhood of Bockenheim, this pleasant hotel has 29 rooms decorated in comfortable yet minimalist style.

TOP END

Hotel Mozart (☎ 156 8060; www.hotelmozart.de; Parkstrasse 17; s/d from €95/150; ⊠ 🖳) A 10-minute walk north from the Alter Opera (opera house), the Mozart is nicely furnished, has excellent breakfasts and is directly across the street from peaceful Grüneburg Park. The 35 rooms are spacious and have wi-fi.

Steigenberger Frankfurter Hof (☎ 215 02; www.steigenberger.de; Am Kaiserplatz; s/d from €150/200; ⊠ ⁘ 🖳) Schopenhauer used to lunch here but his pessimism is unlikely to dampen your enthusiasm for this cosmopolitan and elegant 19th-century neo-Renaissance institution. The 131 rooms are traditionally luxurious.

Eating

Known to the locals as Fressgasse (Munch-Alley), the Kalbächer Petrolse and Grosse Bockenheimer Strasse area, between Opernplatz and Börsenstrasse, has some medium-priced restaurants and fast-food places with outdoor tables in summer.

The area around the main train station has lots of ethnic eating options. Baseler Strasse in particular has a Middle Eastern tone. Wallstrasse and the surrounding streets in Alt-Sachsenhausen also have lots of ethnic mid-priced restaurants.

Another good place for ravenous hunters and gatherers is the cosmopolitan Berger Strasse and Nordend areas north of the Zeil.

RESTAURANTS

Da Cimino (☎ 771 142; Abdelstrasse 28; pizza €5-9) Customers flock here for the tasty pizza, possibly the best in town.

Leib & Seele (☎ 281 529; Kornmarkt 11; mains €6-12) Modern yet old-fashioned at the same time, Leib & Seele has large windows, a terrace and tables lit with candles. The menu extends beyond Germany and features many seasonal specials.

Eckhaus (☎ 491 197; Bornheimer Landstrasse 45; meals from €7) This is a relaxed restaurant and bar that serves well-priced salads and main dishes well into the evening. Nice outside area. Take the U-4 to Merianplatz.

CAFÉS

Walden (☎ 9288 2700; Kleiner Hirschgraben 7; meals €6-12) An über-trendy café near the centre. Breakfast is served until 5pm and you can go right from eggs to the lengthy cocktail list. At night there are DJs, soul and jazz.

Metropol (☎ 288 287; Weckmarkt 13-15; mains €7) Near the Dom, this popular place serves up café fare until late. Savour a coffee for hours with a book.

Café Karin (☎ 295 217; Grosser Hirschgraben 28; mains €9-15) Breakfast and whole-grain baked goods are the specialities at this understated place near the Zeil. The coffee is a treat as well.

APPLE-WINE TAVERNS

Apple-wine taverns are a Frankfurt's great local tradition. They serve *Ebbelwoi* (Frankfurt dialect for *Apfelwein*), an alcoholic apple cider, along with local specialities like *Handkäse mit Musik* (literally, 'hand-cheese with music'). This is a round cheese soaked in oil and vinegar and topped with onions; your bowel supplies the music. Some good *Ebbelwoi* are situated in Alt-Sachsenhausen.

Zur Germania (☎ 613 336; Textorstrasse 16; meals €7-15) This Sachsenhausen apple-wine tavern has a good outdoor area and is well-known for its huge pork roasts.

Zur Sonne (☎ 459 396; Berger Strasse 312; mains €7-16) This place has a fine yard for fair-weather imbibing in Bornheim. The schnitzels are excellent. Take the U4 to Bornheim-Mitte to get there

Adolf Wagner (☎ 612 565; Schweizer Strasse 71; meals €8-15; 🕑) This old place has one of the most atmospheric interiors in Sachsenhausen. The garden is appealing as well.

SELF-CATERING

Off Hasenpetrolse, **Kleinmarkthalle** (Hasengasse 5-7; 🕑 7.30am-6pm Mon-Fri, to 3pm Sat) is a great produce market with loads of fruit, vegetables, meats and hot food.

Drinking

Many of the places listed under Eating are good for a drink, especially the apple wine joints.

Blaubart (☎ 282 229; Kaiserhofstrasse 18-20) In a large basement, the ceiling here is arched bricks. The long tables are lined with jolly beer-drinkers.

Zum Schwejk (☎ 293 166; Schäfferpetrolse 20) This is a popular gay bar. It is one of several on this street. Look for the blue mannequins out front.

Entertainment

Ballet, opera and theatre are strong features of Frankfurt's entertainment scene. Free *Frizz* has good listings (in German) of what's on in town. For information and bookings, go to **Städtische Bühnen** (☎ 134 0400; Willy-Brandt-Platz).

Forsythe Company (☎ 2123 7586; www.theforsythecompany.de; Bockenheimer Depot; Carlo-Schmid-Platz 1) Easily the world's most talked-about dance company right now; the work of William Forsythe is often on tour.

Turm-Palast (☎ 281 787; Am Eschenheimer Turm) This is a multiscreen cinema with films in English.

Jazzkeller (☎ 288 537; Kleine Bockenheimer Strasse 18a) This club attracts top acts.

Mousonturm (☎ 4058 9520; Waldschmidtstrasse 4) Arty rock, dance performances and politically oriented cabaret are on tap at this converted soap factory in Bornheim.

U60311 (☎ 297 060 311; Rossmarkt 6) A top local club for techno, U60311 draws the best talent from around Europe. It's underground, literally.

Getting There & Away

AIR

Germany's largest airport is **Frankfurt airport** (FRA; ☎ 6901; www.airportcity-frankfurt.com), a vast labyrinth with connections throughout the world. It's served by most major airlines, although not many budget ones.

Only cynics like Ryanair would say that Frankfurt has another airport. **Frankfurt-Hahn airport** (HHN; www.hahn-airport.de) is 70km west of Frankfurt. Buses from Frankfurt's Hauptbahnhof take about two hours – longer than the flight from London. Given the journey time it's fitting the bus company is called **Bohr** (☎ 06543-501 90; www.bohr-omnibusse.de; adult/child €12/6; ⏲ hourly).

BUS

The Deutsche-Touring Romantic Road bus (see p482) leaves from the south side of the Hauptbahnhof.

CAR

Frankfurt-am-Main features the famed Frankfurter Kreuz, the biggest autobahn intersection in the country. All the main car rental companies have offices in the main hall of the train station and at the airport.

TRAIN

The Hauptbahnhof handles more departures and arrivals than any station in Germany. Among the myriad of services: Berlin (€98, four hours, hourly), Hamburg (€93, 3½ hours, hourly) and Munich (€75, 3¾ hours). For Cologne take the fast (75 minutes) ICE line or the slower and more scenic line along the Rhine (€40, 2½ hours, hourly).

Many long-distance trains also stop at the airport. This station is beyond the S-Bahn station under Terminal 1.

Getting Around

TO/FROM THE AIRPORT

S-Bahn lines S8 and S9 run every 15 minutes between the airport and Frankfurt Hauptbahnhof (€3.35, 4.15am to 1am, 11 minutes), usually continuing via Hauptwache and Konstablerwache. Taxis (about €30) take 30 minutes without traffic jams.

The airport train station has two sections: platforms 1 to 3 (below Terminal 1, hall B) handle S-Bahn connections, while IC and ICE connections are in the long-distance train station 300m distant.

AUTHOR'S CHOICE

Why not enjoy Frankfurt's iconic apple wine while seeing the city? The **Ebbelwei-Express** (€5, apple wine extra; ⏲ 1.30-5.30pm Sat & Sun) is a special tram that makes a circuit of all the city's principal sights every weekend year-round. The trams are decades old but the wood seats are the perfect venue for quaffing, munching a fresh pretzel and enjoying the sites. There's a reason every time you see one of these go by everyone on board has a huge grin. The trams stop all over town; get a schedule from the tourist offices.

PUBLIC TRANSPORT

Both single or day tickets for Frankfurt's excellent transport network (RMV; www.traffiQ.de) can be purchased from automatic machines at almost any train station or stop. The peak period short-trip tickets *(Kurzstrecken)* cost €1.35, single tickets cost €1.90 and a *Tageskarte* (24-hour ticket) costs €4.90 (€7.40 with the airport).

TAXI

Taxis are slow compared to public transport and expensive at €2.50 flag-fall plus a minimum of €1.60 per kilometre. There are numerous taxi ranks throughout the city, or you can book a cab (☎ 230 001, 25 00 01, 54 50 11).

NORTH RHINE-WESTPHALIA

One quarter of Germany's population, and an even larger chunk of its heavy industry, is crammed into the Rhine-Ruhr region. This is not only Germany's economic powerhouse, but also one of the most densely populated conurbations in the world. Though the area has some bleak industrial centres, Cologne and some other cities are steeped in history.

COLOGNE

☎ 0221 / pop 1 million

Cologne (Köln) seems almost ridiculously proud to be home to Germany's largest cathedral; the twin-tower shape of its weather-beaten Gothic hulk adorns the strangest souvenirs – from egg cosies and slippers to glassware and expensive jewellery. However, this bustling Rhine-side metropolis has much more to offer than its most recognisable and ubiquitous symbol. As early as the first century AD, Colonia Agrippinensis was an important Roman trading settlement. Today it's one of Germany's most multicultural spots, with a vibrant nightlife only partly fuelled by the local *Kölsch* beer.

Almost completely destroyed in WWII – except a fortuitously unscathed cathedral – Cologne has been rebuilt and meticulously restored since. *Et es, wie et es* (it is how it is) runs a familiar motto in the city dialect. Well, how is it exactly? *Joot* (good)!

Orientation

It's hard to miss the cathedral (Dom) on the doorstep of the main train station. From this, the centre of the tourist action, the pedestrianised and hideously congested Hohe Strasse runs south through the old town. Alternatively, there's a pleasant riverfront stroll 500m to the east.

The nightlife hubs of the Belgisches Viertel (tram 3, 4 or 5 to Friesenplatz) and the Zülpicher Viertel (trams 8 or 9 to Zülpicher Viertel/Bahnhof Süd) are several kilometres southwest.

Information

Future-Point (☎ 206 7251; Richmodstrasse 13; per 10 min €1; 🕒 10.30am-9pm Mon-Fri, 11.30am-8pm Sat & Sun) Internet access inside the trendy Café Lichtenberg.

Internet Café Colony (☎ 272 0630; per 10 min €0.40; Zülpicher Strasse 38-40; 🕒 10am-2am Mon-Sat, 11am-2am Sun) Wide range of services, including online laptop connection.

Köln Welcome Card (€9/14/19 for 24/48/72hr) Free public transport and discounted museum admission.

Main post office (☎ 01802-3333; WDR Centre, Breite Strasse 6-26; 🕒 9am-7pm Mon-Fri, 9am-2pm Sat)

Tourist office (☎ 2213 0400; www.koelntourismus.de; Unter Fettenhennen 19; 🕒 9am-9pm Mon-Sat, 10am-6pm Sun & hols Oct-Jun; 9am-10pm Mon-Sat, 10am-6pm Sun & hols Jul-Sep)

Sights & Activities

DOM

As easy as it is to get church-fatigue in Germany, the huge **Kölner Dom** (www.koelner-dom.de; admission free; 🕒 6am-7.30pm, no visitors during services) is one you shouldn't miss. Blackened with age, this gargoyle-festooned Gothic cathedral has a footprint of 12,470 sq metres, with twin spires soaring to 157m. Although its ground stone was laid in 1248, stop-start construction meant it wasn't finished until 1880, as a symbol of Prussia's drive for unification. Just over 60 years later it escaped WWII's heavy night-bombing largely intact. (No miracle, by the way. Allied pilots used it to navigate in an era before reliable radar.)

Sunshine filtering softly through stained-glass windows and the weak glow of candles are the only illumination in the moody, high-ceilinged interior.

Behind the altar lies the cathedral's most precious reliquary, the **Shrine of the Three Magi** (c 1150–1210), which reputedly contains the bones of the Three Wise Men.

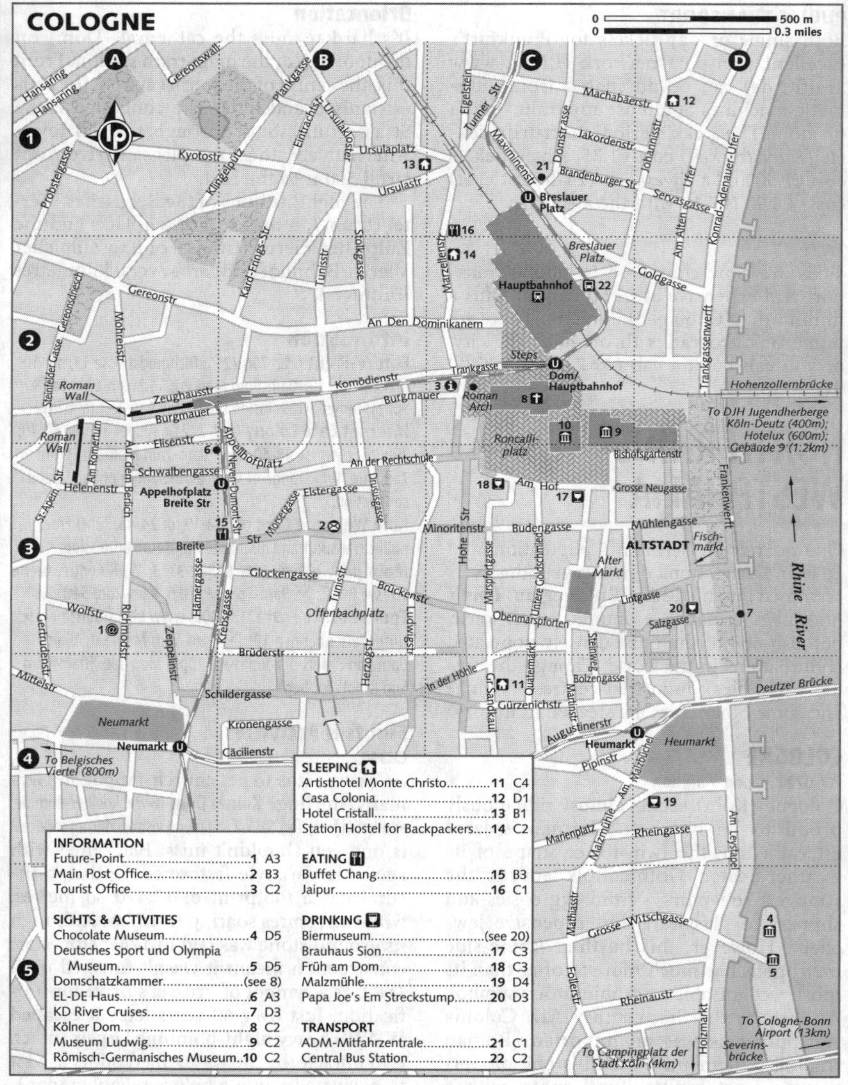

Brought to Cologne from Milan in the 12th century, it can just be glimpsed through the gates to the inner choir – although even this is impossible during Confession, when the entire choir is shut.

To see the shrine properly, you need to take a **guided tour** (adult/concession €4/2; 🕑 10.30am & 2.30pm Mon-Sat, 2.30pm Sun in English). Groups meet inside the main portal and tours in German (same price) are more frequent.

Alternatively, you can embark on the seriously strenuous endeavour of climbing the 509 steps of the Dom's **south tower** (adult/concession €2/1; 🕑 9am-5pm Mar-Sep, to 4pm Oct-Feb). You pass the 24-tonne **Peter Bell**, the world's largest working clanger, before emerging at 98.25m to magnificent views.

The renovated cathedral **treasury** (☎ 1794 0300; www.domschatzkammer-koeln.de; adult/concession €4/2; 10am-6pm) has a glittering collection of crowns and reliquaries.

MUSEUMS

South along the riverbank is the glass-walled **Chocolate Museum** (☎ 931 8880; www.schokoladenmuseum.de; Rheinauhafen; adult/concession €6/3.50; 10am-6pm Tue-Fri, 11am-7pm Sat & Sun, last entry 1hr before closing), famous for its fountain of liquid chocolate, whose aroma permeates the entire exhibition.

The neighbouring **Deutsches Sport und Olympia Museum** (☎ 336 090; www.sportmuseum-koeln.de, in German; Rheinauhafen 1; adult/concession €5/2.50; 10am-6pm Tue-Fri, 11am-7pm Sat & Sun) engagingly tells the history of the games with original souvenirs and multimedia displays.

Two prominent museums next to the cathedral might also take your fancy. The **Römisch-Germanisches Museum** (Roman Germanic Museum; ☎ 2212 2304; www.museenkoeln.de; Roncalliplatz 4; adult/concession €4/2; 10am-5pm Tue-Sun) displays artefacts from the Roman settlement in the Rhine Valley. The **Museum Ludwig** (☎ 2212 6165; www.museenkoeln.de; Bischofsgartenstrasse 1; adult/concession €7.50/5.50; 10am-6pm Tue-Sun, closed during Carnival) has an astoundingly good collection of 1960s Pop Art, German expressionism and Russian avant-garde painting, as well as photography.

The sombre **EL-DE Haus** (☎ 2212 6331; Appellhofplatz 23-25; adult/concession €2.50/1; 10am-4pm Tue-Fri, 11am-4pm Sat & Sun) documents Cologne's Nazi era.

Tours

Day cruises and Rhine journeys can be organised through **KD River Cruises** (☎ 208 8318; www.k-d.com; Frankenwerft 35). Day trips (10am, noon, 2pm and 6pm) cost €6.80. Sample one-way fares are €11.40 to Bonn and €35.60 to Koblenz.

Festivals & Events

Held just before Lent in late February or early March, Cologne's **Carnival** (Karneval) rivals Munich's Oktoberfest for exuberance, as people dress in creative costumes and party in the streets. Things kick off the Thursday before the seventh Sunday before Easter and last until Monday *(Rosenmontag)*, when there are formal and informal parades.

Sleeping

Accommodation prices in Cologne increase by at least 20% when fairs are on. For more options, the tourist office offers a room-finding service (€3).

BUDGET

Campingplatz der Stadt Köln (☎ 831 966; camp sites per person/site €4/4; Easter–mid-Oct) This place is on the riverbank on Weidenweg in Poll, 5km southeast of the city centre. There are excellent kitchen facilities and a small shop. Take the U16 to Marienburg and cross the Rodenkirchener bridge.

Jugendherberge Köln-Deutz (☎ 814 711; www.jugendherberge.de; Siegesstrasse 5a; dm €20) This is a behemoth of a hostel and while there's not much character in its green-grey rooms, those on the top floors have great views. Plus, everything feels clean and spanking new. It's a relatively easy 15-minute walk east from the main train station over the Hohenzollernbrücke.

Station Hostel for Backpackers (☎ 912 5301; www.hostel-cologne.de; Marzellenstrasse 44-56; dm €17-22, s €28-35, d €42-50, breakfast €3;) Brightly patterned curtains can't quite disguise the basic quality of the dorms here. However, the place is convenient and the staff friendly and knowledgeable. It's a great spot to meet people.

Pension Jansen (☎ 251 85; www.pensionjansen.de; 2nd fl, Richard Wagner Strasse 18; s/d with shared bathroom from €40/65) This cute, well-cared-for *pension* has six individually decorated rooms with cheerful colours and motifs. Details like handmade wreaths hanging on aqua walls – or a big red rose screen-printed on the bed linen – convey a homey atmosphere. Book early.

MIDRANGE

Casa Colonia (☎ 160 6010; www.casa-colonia.de; Machabäerstrasse 63; s/d from €50/70) The young new owners plan to have this cosy Mediterranean charmer transformed into a cheap(ish) design hotel from early 2007, with sleek, minimalist rooms at affordable prices. Check the website for the latest details.

Artisthotel Monte Christo (☎ 277 4883; www.artisthotel-monte-christo.com; Grosse Sandkaul 24-26; s/d

€50/70) Above a club (ear-plugs provided) and with 5pm check-out, this louche hotel attracts dedicated bohemians, from Russian architecture professors to struggling DJs. The décor is camp and kitsch, with bright walls, plastic flowers, glitter-sprayed animal trophies and religious icons arranged in ways the Vatican probably wouldn't approve.

Hotel Chelsea (☎ 207 150; www.hotel-chelsea.de; Jülicher Strasse 1; s €70-160, d €80-175, ste €170-230; P 💻) Another long-standing 'art' hotel, the Chelsea has an eye-catching roof extension. Its interior detailing is a little ordinary and nonsmokers might wish its rooms were aired more, but the overall vibe is good.

Hotel Cristall (☎ 163 00; www.hotelcristall.de; Ursulaplatz 9-11; s/d €70/90; P 💻) The design here is a sort of womb-like, modern baroque, with low lighting and a gilt-framed romantic portrait of a woman in every room, but it also has black-and-white bathrooms and wooden floors (or black-and-white carpet tiles). Angular red, orange and purple sofas also greet you in the lobby.

Hotel Hopper et cetera (☎ 924 400; www.hopper.de; Brüsseler Strasse 26; s/d from €90/120; P ⊠ 💻) Parquet flooring, white linen and red chairs lend an elegant simplicity to this former monastery's rooms. The package is rounded off with a bar and sauna in separate parts of the vaulted cellar.

Eating

Cologne's beer halls serve meals but the city overflows with restaurants, especially around the Belgisches and Zülpicher Viertels.

Habibi (☎ 271 7141; Zülpicher Strasse 28; dishes €3-8; 🕑 11am-1am, to 3am Fri & Sat) A takeaway/restaurant with sturdy wooden tables and a smattering of decorated tiles, 'Beloved' it truly is among its young customers. Falafel joins kebabs, schawarma, halloumi cheese, hubbi (mince and almonds), mint tea on the house, and sweets.

Feynsinn (☎ 240 9210; Rathenauplatz 7; mains €5-10) The glint of artfully arranged glasses behind the mirrored bar will catch your eye from the street, as will the broken-glass chandeliers. Inside under murals, students, creative types and tourists tuck into curries, stews and other fare.

Alcazar (☎ 515 733; Bismarckstrasse 39; snacks €4-9, mains €9-15) The food and atmosphere are both hearty and warming at this old-school, slightly hippie pub. The changing menu always has one veggie option.

Hotelux (☎ 241 136; Von-Sandt Platz 10; €9-17; 🕑 dinner only) Soviet leader Lenin and sailors from the Battleship Potemkin overlook the proceedings in this fun, red-lined restaurant. There's a 'metro' underground train compartment while the food runs the gamut from Russian and Georgian to Ukrainian and Armenian.

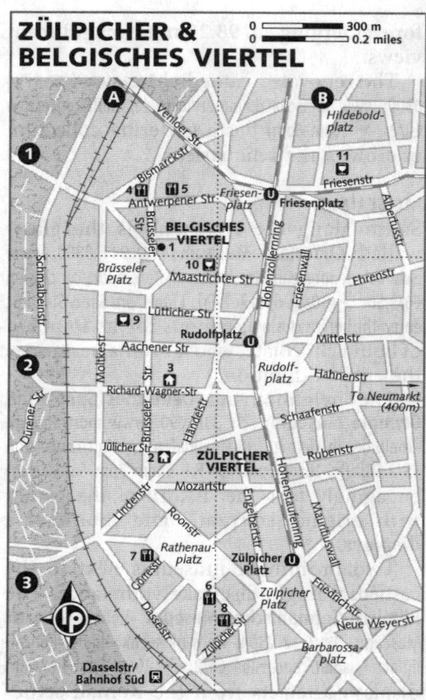

INFORMATION
Cleanicum....1 A1

SLEEPING
Hotel Chelsea....2 A2
Pension Jansen....3 A2

EATING
Alcazar....4 A1
CurryCologne....5 A1
Feynsinn....6 A3
Fischermann's....7 A3
Habibi....8 B3

DRINKING
Hallmackenreuther....9 A2
M20....10 A2
Päffgen....11 B1

Jaipur (☎ 137 322; Marzellenstrasse 50-56; mains €9-18) The food is as authentic as the décor is excessive in Cologne's best Indian restaurant.

Fischermanns' (☎ 283 6285; Rathenauplatz 21; mains €10-17, 3-course set menu €26; 🕑 dinner only) Elegant, with well-executed Eurasian cuisine, Fischermanns' is a favourite with locals celebrating a twenty- or thirty-something birthday or trying to impress a first-time date. But who needs an excuse to indulge?

Other recommendations:

CurryCologne (☎ 589 4556; Antwerperstrasse 5; dishes €2.50-6; 🕑 11am-11pm Mon-Thu, 11.30am-midnight Fri & Sat, 1-11pm Sun) A Wurst outlet goes designer and trendy.

Buffet Chang (☎ 250 9909; top fl, DuMont Carré Centre, Breite Strasse 80-90; all-you-can-eat buffet €6; 🕑 11am-9pm Mon-Sat, noon-7pm Sun) Plastic-and-formica Chinese canteen offering great value.

Drinking

As in Munich, beer in Cologne reigns supreme. More than 20 local breweries turn out a variety called *Kölsch,* which is relatively light and slightly bitter. The breweries run their own beer halls and serve their wares in skinny 200ml glasses.

BEER HALLS

Früh am Dom (☎ 258 0394; Am Hof 12-14) This three-storey beer hall and restaurant (including cellar bar) is the most central, with black-and-white flooring, copper pans and tiled ovens keeping it real, despite the souvenir shop. It's open for breakfast.

Päffgen (☎ 135 461; Friesenstrasse 64-66) Another favourite, this thrumming wood-lined room has its own beer garden. It's not far from the bars of the Belgisches Viertel.

Malzmühle (☎ 210 117; Heumarkt 6) Attracting more locals than most, possibly because of the 10L 'Pittermännchen' kegs that customers can roll home.

Brauhaus Sion (☎ 257 8540; Unter Taschenmacher 9) A traditional-looking, low-lit option, with Wurst sold by the metre.

BARS

For more options, take a tram to Zülpicher Platz and explore.

Biermuseum (☎ 257 7802; Buttermarkt 39) This is a good-time place with 18 varieties of the amber liquid on tap but not one iota of class.

Papa Joe's Em Streckstrump (☎ 257 7931; Buttermarkt 37) Live New Orleans jazz provides the soundtrack in this intimate pub, serving beer in larger than normal glasses for Cologne.

Hallmachenreuther (☎ 517 970; Brüsseler Platz 9) Oatmeal, white and lilacs are used in this popular café bar's retro interior. Good for a late breakfast or a late drink.

Hotelux (☎ 350 0870; Rathenauplatz 22) The little sister of the Hotelux restaurant (see Eating) serves cocktails and 'Soviet water' (ie vodka) in a similarly themed environment.

> **MY BEAUTIFUL LAUNDRETTE**
>
> No, even we can't quite believe we're enthusing about a self-service laundrette here. However, there can't be many better places to air your dirty laundry than Cologne's **Cleanicum** (www.cleanicum.de; Brusseler Strasse 74-76; loads from €3; 🕑 10am-1am Mon-Fri, 9am-1am Sat, 11am-10pm Sun). Its washing machines and dryers sit in the middle of a 'lounge' establishment that also includes sofas, magazines, a TV area, Internet terminals, a retro 1970s cocktail bar and a vibrating massage chair (€1 for 15 minutes). There's even a double bed should doing the housework make you particularly tired or frisky.
>
> A similar, albeit less central, operation exists in Hamburg, too (p536).

Entertainment

Gebäude 9 (☎ 814 637; Deutz-Mülheimer Strasse 127-129) Once a factory, this is now a Cologne nightlife stalwart, with clubbing, concerts, a cinema and theatre. Expect anything from drum'n'bass, indie pop, gypsy music and '60s trash to film noir and puppets.

M20 (☎ 519 666; Maastricher Strasse 20) This popular retro cocktail bar sports cube-shaped lights and brown leather sofas. Regular DJ evenings favour indie guitar rock, but some live acts play more laid-back Latin music.

Getting There & Away

AIR

Cologne-Bonn airport (CGN; www.airport-cgn.de) is growing in importance. There are now direct flights to New York, while budget airline German Wings (www.germanwings.com) uses this as its hub, notably offering cheap flights to Moscow and St Petersburg, among others.

CAR

The city is on a main north–south autobahn route and is easily accessible for drivers and hitchhikers. The **ADM-Mitfahrzentrale** (☎ 194 40; www.citynetz-mitfahrzentrale.de; Maximinen Strasse 2) is near the train station.

TRAIN

There are frequent RE services operating to both nearby Bonn (€6, 18 minutes) and Düsseldorf (€10 to €16, 25 to 30 minutes) as well as to Aachen (€12.50, 45 to 50 minutes). Frequent EC, IC, or ICE trains go to Hanover (€56, three hours), Frankfurt-am-Main (€55, 1¼ hours, three hourly) and Berlin (€93, 4¼ hours, hourly). Frequent Thalys high-speed services connect Cologne to Paris (€85.50, four hours) via Aachen and Brussels; rail pass-holders get only a small discount on this.

Getting Around

S-Bahn 13 runs between Cologne/Bonn airport and the main train station every 15 minutes from 5.30am to 11.20pm daily (€2.20, 20 minutes). Key in code 2000 for Köln Hauptbahnhof. Bus 670 goes to Bonn every half-hour.

Buses and trams serve the inner city, with local trains handling trips up to 50km away, including Bonn. A one-day pass costs €6 if you're staying near the city (one or two zones), €9 for most of the Cologne area (four zones); and €13.30 including Bonn (seven zones). Single city trips cost €1.20, while 1½-hour two-zone tickets are €2.20.

AROUND COLOGNE

Bonn

☎ 0228 / pop 293,000

South of Cologne on the Rhine's banks, Bonn became West Germany's temporary capital in 1949. But exactly 50 years later it was demoted when most (but not quite all) government departments returned to Berlin.

The city's brief tenure as capital, however, has left it with an excellent collection of museums. These, plus its status as Beethoven's birthplace and some 18th-century baroque architecture, make it worth a day trip.

The **tourist office** (☎ 775 000; www.bonn-regio.de; Windeckstrasse 1; ⏰ 9am-6.30pm Mon-Fri, to 4pm Sat, 10am-2pm Sun) is a three-minute walk along Poststrasse from the Hauptbahnhof, and can fill you in with any extra details.

Ludwig van Beethoven fans will head straight to the **Beethoven-Haus** (☎ 981 7525; www.beethoven-haus-bonn.de; Bonngasse 24-26; adult/concession €4/3; ⏰ 10am-6pm Mon-Sat, 11am-5pm Sun Apr-Oct, closing at 5pm Nov-Mar), where the composer was born in 1770. The house contains memorabilia concerning his life and music, including his last piano, with an amplified sounding board to accommodate his deafness. There's a new multimedia section and a shop selling kitschy souvenirs tinnily chiming the Ninth Symphony. The annual Beethoven Festival takes place September to October.

The **Haus der Geschichte der Bundesrepublik Deutschland** (FRG History Museum; ☎ 916 50; www.hdg.de; Willy-Brandt-Allee 14; admission free; ⏰ 9am-7pm Tue-Sun) presents Germany's postwar history. It is part of the **Museumsmeile**, four museums that also includes the **Kunstmuseum** (☎ 776 260; Friedrich-Ebert-Allee 2; adult/concession €5/2.50; ⏰ 10am-6pm Tue-Sun, to 9pm Wed); and the **Kunst-und Ausstellungshalle der Bundesrepublik Deutschland** (☎ 917 1200; Friedrich-Ebert-Allee 2; adult/concession €7/3.50; ⏰ 10am-9pm Tue & Wed, 10am-7pm Thu-Sun).

Those wanting to go a bit further might consider combining their trip to Bonn with a visit to the spa town of Bad Godesberg.

From Cologne, it's quicker to take an RE train to Bonn (€6, 18 minutes) than a tram (€13.30 day pass, 55 minutes each way). For river trips, see p519.

DÜSSELDORF

☎ 0211 / pop 571,000

'D-Town' or 'The City D', as local magazine editors like to call Düsseldorf, is Germany's fashion capital. But that means Jil Sander and Wolfgang Joop rather than cutting-edge streetwear, as you'll soon discover observing fur-clad *Mesdames* with tiny dogs along the ritzy shopping boulevard of the Königsallee.

Indeed, this elegant and wealthy town could feel stiflingly bourgeois if it weren't for its lively old-town pubs, its position on the Rhine, its excellent art galleries and the postmodern architecture of its Mediahafen. Fortunately, those are more than enough to make up for its pretensions.

Orientation

The train station lies at the southeastern edge of the old town, about 1km west of the Rhine River. The Mediahafen and Rheinturm are much further south, on the riverbank.

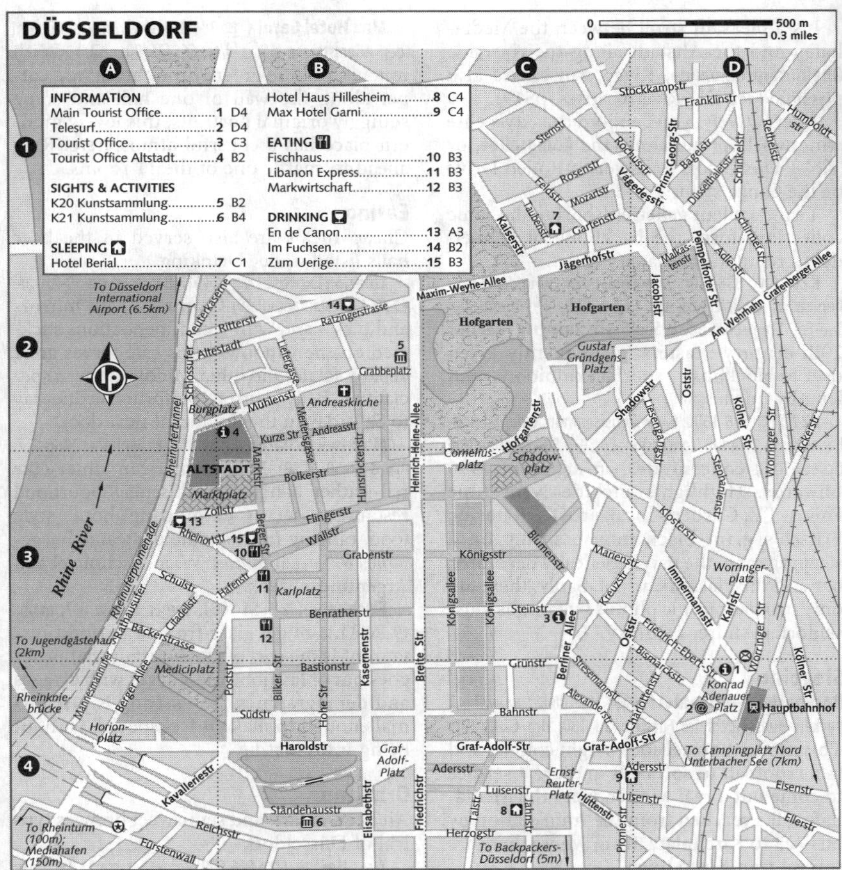

Information

Telesurf (Graf-Adolf-Strasse 102; per 15 min €0.50; 🕒 10am-4am Mon-Sat, 10am-midnight Sun) Minutes left of the train station.

Tourist office (www.duesseldorf-tourismus.de) Main office (☎ 172 0222; Immermannstrasse 65B; 🕒 10am-6pm Mon-Sat); branch office (☎ 602 5753; Burg Platz; 🕒 noon-6pm) branch office (☎ 300 4897; Sparkasse bldg, Berliner Allee 33; 🕒 10am-6pm Mon-Sat)

Sights & Activities

Düsseldorf has a lively **Altstadt** (old town), filled with enough restaurants, beer halls and pubs to have earned it the slightly exaggerated title of the 'longest bar in the world'. In the central **Marktplatz** you'll find a statue of the former ruler, or elector, Jan Wellem.

What really sets the city apart, however, is the contemporary architecture of its **Mediahafen**. Here, in the city's south, docks have been transformed into an interesting commercial park, most notably including the **Neuer Zollhof**, three typically curved and twisting buildings by Bilbão Guggenheim architect Frank Gehry. You'll find a map of the park on a billboard behind (ie on the street side of) the red-brick Gehry building.

For a bird's-eye view of the Mediahafen, and indeed all of Düsseldorf, catch the express elevator to the 168m viewing platform of the neighbouring **Rheinturm** (adult/child €3.50/1.50; 🕒 10am-11.30pm). There's also a revolving restaurant and cocktail bar a level above, at 172.5m.

It's a pleasant stroll between the Mediahafen and the Altstadt along the riverside **Rheinuferpromenade**. River cruises are also possible (see KD River Cruises, p519).

Alternatively, you can join the city's elite window-shopping along the **Königsallee**, or 'Kö' – Düsseldorf's answer to Rodeo Drive or the Ginza strip.

Two excellent galleries, sharing the same collection, form the backbone of Düsseldorf's reputation as a city of art.

K20 (☎ 838 10; www.kunstsammlung.de; Grabbeplatz 5; adult/concession €6.50/4.50; 10am-6pm Tue-Fri, 11am-6pm Sat & Sun), containing earlier 20th-century masters, is frequently given over to blockbuster special exhibitions with lengthy queues.

K21 (☎ 838 1600; www.kunstsammlung.de; Ständehausstrasse 1; adult/concession €6.50/4.50, combination ticket €10/8) concentrates on art from 1990 onwards. Highlights include Nam June Paik's TV Garden, local artist's Katarina Fritsch's giant black mouse sitting on a sleeping man, the psychedelically decorated bar and the glassed-in roof. Sadly, there are only two panoramic photos by famous Düsseldorfer Andreas Gursky.

Sleeping

Backpackers-Düsseldorf (☎ 302 0848; www.backpackers-duesseldorf.de; Fürstenwall 180; dm €20;) This modern hostel adds bright colours and table football to soft beds and great service to come out a real winner. Near the Mediahafen, it's reached from the train station by bus 725 to Kirchplatz, from where there are several trams into town.

Jugendgästehaus (☎ 557310; www.jugendherberge.de; Düsseldorfer Strasse 1; dm €22, s/d from €26/48) On the other bank of the Rhine in posh Oberkassel, this will remain open while undergoing renovation until 2008.

Hotel Haus Hillesheim (☎ 386 860; www.hotel-hillesheim.de; Jahnstrasse 19; s/d €60/70, with shared bathroom €40/55; P) Crammed with animal trophies, plants and all manner of bric-a-brac, this dimly lit pub has homey rooms both above it and quieter ones in the garden behind.

Hotel Berial (☎ 490 0490; Gartenstrasse 30; www.hotelberial.de; s/d €60/80;) A youthful ambience reigns here, thanks to the staff and the contemporary furnishings. Décor features lots of blue, blond wood, glass bathroom doors and some bright prints.

Max Hotel Garni (☎ 386 800; www.max-hotelgarni.de; Adersstrasse 65; s/d/tr €65/75/90;) With touches of lime green, up-lighting, red carpet along the wall of one hall and some squiggly original portraits, this lovely modern place has a cheerful atmosphere. Ring ahead to snaffle one of the 11 rooms.

Eating

Cheap meals are also served in the beer halls listed under Drinking.

Libanon Express (☎ 134 917; Berger Strasse 19-21; café €2.50-13, restaurant €8-19) Crammed with mirrors and tiles – and with recommendations stickered on the window – this café serves great kebabs, falafel and other Middle-Eastern specialities. Belly dancers perform Wednesday to Saturday in the restaurant next door.

Marktwirtschaft (☎ 860 6848; Benrather Strasse 7; mains €6.50-14.50) With American diner–like red-leather banquettes, this neighbourhood restaurant serves comforting home-style food, ranging from a plate of steamed vegetables to Dutch *matjes*, Wiener schnitzel and Argentinean steak.

Fischhaus (☎ 854 9864; Berger Strasse 3-7; mains €9-26) This huge, glass-fronted seafood restaurant is the sort of classic affair that never goes out of fashion, and buzzes with all ages and demographics. The setting is just formal enough to make it feel special, without being intimidating.

Drinking

Alt beer, a dark and semisweet brew, is typical of Düsseldorf.

Zum Uerige (☎ 866 990; Berger Strasse 1) In this noisy, cavernous place, the trademark Uerige Alt beer flows so quickly that the waiters just carry around trays and give you a glass whenever they spy one empty.

Im Fuchsen (☎ 828 955; Ratzingerstrasse 28) The 'Little Fox' is a typically rumbustious Rheinish beer hall, with *Schweinhaxe* (knuckle of pork) and other local fare.

En de Canon (☎ 329 798; Zollstrasse 7) This centuries-old tavern is popular in summer for its beer garden.

Getting There & Away

From **Düsseldorf International** (DUS: www.duesseldorf-international.de), trains go directly to other German cities, while frequent S-Bahn services (1 and 7) head to Düsseldorf train station.

Low-cost carrier Ryanair uses **Niederrhein (Weeze) airport** (NRN; www.flughafen-niederrhein.de) and it is the usual wheeze. The **shuttle bus** (☎ 06543-501 90; www.bohr-omnibusse.de) to Düsseldorf (€11; 1¼ hours) leaves soon after the plane's scheduled arrival.

The many train services from Düsseldorf include to Cologne (€10 to €16, 25 to 30 minutes), Frankfurt-am-Main (€65, two hours), Hanover (€46 to €49, 2¾ hours) and Hamburg (€63 to €73, 3½ to four hours).

Getting Around

The metro, trams and buses are useful to cover Düsseldorf's distances. Up to three stops *(Kurzstrecke)* costs €1.10, a ticket for the centre €2 and for the greater city €3.80. Day-passes start at €4.70

AACHEN

☎ 0241 / pop 244,000

If you fancy an indulgent mini-break, Aachen has the perfect recipe. Before reaching its relaxing thermal baths, you'll find yourself wandering narrow cobbled streets past quirky fountains, shops full of gingerbread, one of Germany's most famous cafés, and a small but perfectly formed cathedral.

The town's curative thermal springs were the reason the great Frankish conqueror Charlemagne (Karl der Grosse) made this his capital in 794, and the cathedral he built consolidated its fame. Its proximity to the Netherlands and Belgium gives Aachen – Aken or Aix La Chappelle in Dutch or French – a dynamic international personality, while its large student population saves it from being too touristy and twee.

Orientation

Aachen's compact centre is contained within two ring roads roughly tracing the old city walls. The inner ring road, or Grabenring, changes names – most ending in 'graben' – and encloses the old city proper. To get to the tourist office from the Hauptbahnhof, cross Römerstrasse, follow Bahnhofstrasse north and then go left along Theaterstrasse to Kapuzinergraben.

Information

The Web (☎ 997 9210; Kleinmarschierstrasse 74-76; per 10 min €0.50; 🕑 10am-11pm Mon-Thu, to 3am Fri & Sat, 11am-10pm Sun)

Tourist office (☎ 180 2960/1; www.aachen.de; Atrium Elisenbrunnen, Kapuzinergraben; 🕑 9am-6pm Mon-Fri, to 2pm Sat year-round, plus 10am-2pm Sun Apr-Dec)

Sights

OLD TOWN & FOUNTAINS

Next to the tourist office is the **Elisenbrunnen**, the only town fountain with drinkable water; despite its sulphuric 'rotten eggs' smell, it's supposedly good for the digestion.

In the far left-hand corner of the park behind the Elisenbrunnen, you'll find the **Geldbrunnen**, which represents the circulation of money. The comical figures around the pool clutch their coins or purses while the water is sucked down the central plughole (jokingly known as 'the taxman').

Head east along the top of the park here, towards Forum M, and turn left into Buchkremerstrasse. Soon you'll reach a fountain with a scary-looking creature. This is the mythological **Bahkauv**, which was rumoured to jump on the backs of those returning late

THE DEVIL'S IN THE DETAIL

If the devil has all the best music, he also has the funniest myths. Aachen lore, for example, has it that you haven't really visited the town unless you've touched the thumb of hell's black prince.

The legend goes that a mysterious benefactor appeared when the town needed more money to finish its cathedral. Locals recognised him as Lucifer by his cloven hoofs, but being *lues* (cunning and crafty, in the local dialect) hatched a plan to deal with him. They agreed when he asked to be paid with the soul of the first being to enter the cathedral, and when the time came released a wolf into the building. Satan pounced on the creature, but flew into a rage on realising he'd been cheated. Storming out of the cathedral, he slammed the door so hard he trapped his thumb.

Today, a statue of the wolf (or Roman bear) stands in the cathedral's antechamber, with a hole in its chest from where its soul was ripped. Meanwhile, 'the devil's thumb' remains stuck in the main cathedral doors – between the side doors currently used. Inside the lion's head on the right-hand door, you can feel, well, a digit-shaped something.

from the pub and demand a lift all the way home.

Buchkremerstrasse becomes Buchel. Turn left just past **Leo van den Daele** (see right), then right again, you'll come to Hühnermarkt, with its **Hühnerdiebbrunnen** (Chicken thief fountain). The hasty thief hasn't noticed one of his stolen chickens is a rooster and is about to unmask him by crowing.

From here, Aachen's main **Markt** is visible just to the northeast. The 14th-century **Rathaus** (adult/concession €2/1; 10am-5pm Mon-Fri, to 1pm & 2-5pm Sat & Sun) overlooks the Markt, while a fountain statue of **Charlemagne** is in the middle.

Head back down the hill along Krämerstrasse until you come to the **Puppenbrunnen** (Puppet fountain), where you're allowed to play with the movable bronze figures.

Continuing in the same direction for 50m, you'll arrive at Aachen's famous Dom.

DOM

While Cologne's cathedral wows you with its size and atmosphere, Aachen's similarly Unesco-listed **Dom** (Kaiserdom or Münster; www.aachendom.de; 7am-7pm) impresses with its shiny neatness. The small, Byzantine-inspired **octagon** at the building's heart dates from 805 but was refurbished in 2003, so its ceiling mosaics glitter and its marble columns gleam.

The building's historical significance stems not just from Charlemagne's having ordered it built, but that 30 Holy Roman emperors were crowned here from 936 to 1531.

The brass **chandelier** hanging in the centre was donated by Emperor Friedrich Barbarossa in 1165. Meanwhile, standing at the main altar and looking back towards the door, it's just possible to glimpse Charlemagne's simple marble throne. The man himself lies in the golden **shrine** behind the altar. The cathedral became a site of pilgrimage after his death; there's a major pilgrimage at the start of June 2007.

Multilingual leaflets in the antechamber provide a concise cathedral guide.

THERMAL BATHS

The 8th-century Franks were first lured to 'Ahha' (water) for its thermal springs. And just over 1200 years later, the state-of-the-art **Carolus Thermen** (Carolus Thermal Baths; ☎ 182 740; www.carolus-thermen.de; Stadtgarten/Passstrasse 79; without/with sauna from €9.50/19) are still reeling them in.

That's hardly surprising, for the complex is part therapeutic spa – good for rheumatism etc – and part swimming centre. Quirky currents whiz you around one pool, water jets bubble up in another and taps pour out cold water in yet another (under which single travellers might wish to shove the many canoodling couples…). Only diehard fans should pay for the sauna, as there's – bizarrely – a steam room accessible to all.

The baths are in the city garden, northeast of the centre.

Sleeping

Jugendgästehaus (☎ 711 010; www.jugendherberge.de; Maria-Theresia-Allee 260; dm €22, s/d €36.50/54; P) This modern DJH outpost sits on a hill overlooking the city, and gets lots of school groups. Take bus 2 to Ronheide.

Hotel Marx (☎ 375 41; www.hotel-marx.de; Hubertusstrasse 33-35; s/d €50/75, with shared bathroom from €35/60) There's a garden with pond out of the back of this traditional family-run place. Inside the rooms are decent, even if the bathrooms are a little cramped.

Hotel Domicil (☎ 705 1200; www.domicilaachen.de; Lütticher Strasse 27; s €75-85, d €100-110; P) This elegant, neutrally decorated hotel feels like an apartment complex. It's set across two 19th-century terrace houses with its own garden in a quiet district, yet just 10 minutes on foot from the centre.

Hotel Drei Könige (☎ 483 93; www.h3k-aachen.de; Büchel 5; s €80-90, d €110-120, ste from €120;) The renovated Drei Könige has classy rooms with iron-frame beds (some four-poster) and different Mediterranean colour schemes in each, from cool pale green to sienna red.

Eating & Drinking

Aachen's students have their own 'Latin Quarter' along **Pontstrasse**, with dozens of bars and cheap eats. The street heads northeast off the Markt and runs for nearly a kilometre.

Vitaminbar (☎ 409 3912; Alexaniergraben 13-15; dishes €2.50-6.50) Exotic options like Iranian and Russian are among this café's dozens of tasty sandwich fillings. The salads are just as diverse.

Leo van den Daele (☎ 357 24; Büchel 18; dishes €4.50-8.50) A warren of 17th-century rooms linked by crooked stairs across four merchants' homes, this nationally renowned café specialises in gingerbread, or Printen. Yet you can also enjoy light meals – soups, sandwiches, quiches and *pastetchen* (vol au vents) – among its tiled stoves and antique knick-knacks.

Rose am Dom (☎ 287 82; Fischmarkt 1; mains €8-16) Being stationed in the cathedral's former kitchen gives this place a medieval atmosphere, although its partly seasonal menu is more modern and international. When mussels are on, it's hard to believe you're not in Belgium.

Getting There & Away

There are twice-hourly trains to Cologne (€12.50, 45 to 50 minutes) and Liège (€9.90, 40 minutes), as well as transfers from Düsseldorf and Köln-Bonn airports. The high-speed Thalys train passes through regularly on its way to Brussels and Paris (€80.50, 3½ hours). There's also a frequent bus to Maastricht. The bus station is at the north-eastern edge of Grabenring on the corner of Kurhausstrasse and Peterstrasse.

Getting Around

Most points of interest are easily reached on foot, although the baths are a bit of a hike. Buses cost €1.45 (trip of a few stops), €2 (regular single) or €5 (day pass).

LOWER SAXONY

Lower Saxony (Niedersachsen) likes to make much of its half-timbered towns. Hamelin is certainly a true fairy-tale beauty, and leaning Lüneberg is quite unlike any other you'll see. However, the state is also home to the famous Volkswagen car company, while even the business-minded capital, Hanover, has its diversions. See also 'Bewitching Harz', p464.

HANOVER

☎ 0511 / pop 523,000

German comedians – yes, they do exist – like to dismiss Hanover as 'the autobahn exit between Göttingen and Walsrode'. However, the capital of Lower Saxony is nowhere near that grim. While it's famous for hosting trade fairs, particularly the huge CEBIT computer show in March, it also boasts acres of greenery in the Versailles-like Herrenhäuser Gärten (gardens).

Parts of the central Altstadt (old town) look medieval, but few of them are. They're mostly clever fakes built after intense WWII bombing.

Information

Hannover Tourismus (☎ information 1234 5111, ☎ room reservations 1234 555; www.hannover.de; Ernst-August-Platz 8; ⏲ 9am-6pm Mon-Fri, 9am-2pm Sat)

Teleklick Hannover (Schillerstrasse 23; ⏲ 10am-11pm Mon-Sat, noon-10pm Sun) Internet access.

Sights & Activities

The enormous **Grosser Garten** (Large Garden; admission €3, free in winter) is the highlight of the **Herrenhäuser Gärten** (☎ 1684 7576; www.hannover.de/herrenhausen/start.htm; ⏲ 9am-sunset). It has a small maze and Europe's tallest fountain. Check the website in summer for Wasserspiele, when all fountains are synchronised, and the night-time **Illuminations**. The **Niki de Saint Phalle Grotto** is a magical showcase of the artist's work. She was French – her colourful figures adorn the famous Stravinsky fountain outside the Centre Pompidou in Paris – but developed a special relationship with Hanover. There's a popular beer garden in the Grosser Garten. Alternatively, the flora of the **Berggarten** (Mountain Garden; €2, combined entry with Grosser Garten €4) is interesting.

The **Neues Rathaus** (new town hall) was built between 1901 and 1913. Town models in the foyer reveal the extent of WWII devastation. There's a pleasant lakeside café and, if you don't mind queuing, a **curved lift** (adult/child €2/1.50; ⏲ 10am-6pm Apr-Nov) to a 98m viewing platform.

Beside the Leine River since 1974, are **Die Nanas**, three fluorescent-coloured, earth-mama sculptures by de Saint Phalle. Although major Hanover landmarks, they're best seen on Saturday, when there's a flea market at their feet.

In summer, the **Machsee** (lake) has **ferries** (crossing €3, tour €6) and numerous boats for hire. There's a free public **swimming beach** on the southeast shore.

Sleeping

The tourist office only finds private rooms during trade fairs but can arrange hotel bookings year-round for a fee.

Jugendherberge (☎ 131 7674; www.jugendherberge.de; Ferdinand-Wilhelm-Fricke-Weg 1; dm junior/senior from €18/21; (P) (💻)) This large space-lab

MORE FAIRY-TALE TOWNS

Kids in particular will love Hamelin, just one of 60 towns situated on Germany's so-called **Märchenstrasse** (Fairytale Road; ☎ 0561-707 707; www.deutsche-maerchenstrasse.de; Obere Königsstrasse 15, Kassel). Many Grimms' fairy tales originated along this meandering route, which stretches 600km north from Hanau to Bremen. Polle boasts 'Cinderella's castle' for example, the Rapunzel tale hails from a tower in Trendelburg, and Puss in Boots first stepped out in Oedelsheim. For more details, visit the comprehensive multilingual website.

looking structure houses a modern hostel with breakfast room and terrace bar overlooking the river. Take U3 or U7 to Fischerhof, cross the Lodemannbrücke bridge and turn right.

GästeResidenz PelikanViertel (☎ 399 90; www.gaesteresidenz-pelikanviertel.de; Pelikanstrasse 11; s €40-230, d €60-260, tr €80-280; Ⓟ) Upmarket student residence meets budget hotel, this huge complex has a wide range of plain but very pleasant rooms, all with kitchenettes. Prices fluctuate wildly, so try to avoid trade fair periods. Take U9 to Pelikanstrasse.

City Hotel Flamme (☎ 388 8004; www.cityhotelflamme.de; Lammstrasse 3; s €50-65, d €75-90; Ⓟ) Rooms are arranged around a light-filled courtyard with a glass curtain-wall frontage, and the owners will pick you up from the nearby train station.

Lühmanns Hotel am Rathaus (☎ 326 268; www.hotelamrathaus.de; Friedrichswall 21; s €60-85, d €75-90, f €120-140; ⊠ 💻) Arty posters and even the odd original work of art fill this comfy, tasteful choice. Although it is located on a busy street, double glazing keeps the noise at bay.

Other recommendations:

City Hotel am Thielenplatz (☎ 327 691; www.smartcityhotel.de; Thielenplatz 2; s €40-50, d €50-60; Ⓟ ⊠ 💻) Could be fabulous when a retro 1950s conversion is finished.

Etap Hotel (☎ 235 5570; www.etaphotel.com; Runde Strasse 7; s/d €40/50; 💻) Garish but comfortable chain hotel, right near the train station.

Eating & Drinking

Markthalle (Karmarschstrasse 49; dishes €3.50-8) This huge covered market of food stalls and gourmet delicatessens is a no-nonsense place for a quick bite – both carnivorous and vegetarian.

Maestro (☎ 300 8575; Sophienstrasse 2; mains €4.50-8) This atmospheric subterranean restaurant offers an all-you-can-eat vegetarian buffet (€7) at lunch daily. Its tucked-away courtyard beer garden (shh!) is perfect in summer.

Mr Phung Kabuki (☎ 215 7609; Friedrichswall 10; sushi €2-6, most mains €7-14) Boats bob by on the water-based sushi chain, but you can order all manner of pan-Asian and wok dishes in this airy, trendy restaurant with an enormous range of spirits.

Pier 51 (☎ 807 1800; Rudolf von Bennigsen Ufer 51; mains €6-18) This atmospheric glass-walled cube juts out into the Maschsee, and has an outside 'Piergarten' with old-fashioned covered straw seats. Cuisine is modern and international.

Brauhaus Ernst August (☎ 365 950; Schmiedestrasse 13a) A local institution, the Brauhaus Ernst August brews its own Hannöversch beer.

Getting There & Around

Hanover's **airport** (HAJ; www.hannover-airport.de) has many connections, including on low-cost carrier Air Berlin (www.airberlin.com).

There are frequent train services to Hamburg (€36, 1¼ hours), Berlin (€53, 1½ hours), Cologne (€56, three hours) and Munich (€101, five hours), among others.

U-Bahn lines from the Hauptbahnhof are boarded in the station's north (follow the signs towards Raschplatz), except the U10 and U17, which are overground trams leaving near the tourist office.

Most visitors only travel in the central 'Hannover' zone. Single tickets are €1.90 and day passes €3.60.

The S-Bahn (S5) takes 16 minutes to the airport (€3.20).

AROUND HANOVER

Hamelin

☎ 05151 / pop 59,000

Some German towns just look like they came straight from a fairy story. Thanks to the Brothers Grimm, others are even more inextricably linked. In the 19th century, the two brothers documented national folklore, and their subsequent collection of tales means the name Hamelin (Hameln in German) will be forever associated with 'the Pied Piper of'.

Of course, according to the story, this quaint, ornate town got rid of all its rats when the piper *(Der Rattenfänger)* lured them into the Weser River in the 13th century – and then lost all its children when it refused to pay him. However, you wouldn't really know it. Today, rat-shaped bread, marzipan-filled *Rattenfängertorte* (Pied Piper cake) and fluffy rat toys fill the shops, while 'the Pied Piper' himself can be seen in various tourist guide guises, mesmerising onlooking children with haunting tunes.

The train station is about 800m east of the centre. To get to **Hameln Tourist Information** (☎ 957 823; www.hameln.de/touristinfo; Diesterallee 1; 9am-6pm Mon-Fri year-round; 9.30am-4pm Sat, 9.30am-1pm Sun May-Sep, 9.30am-1pm Sat Oct-Apr) take bus 2, 3, 4, 12, 21, 33 or 34.

The best way to explore is to follow the **Pied Piper trail** – the line of white rats drawn on the pavements. There are information posts at various points. They're in German, but at least you know when to stop to admire the various restored 16th- to 18th-century half-timbered houses.

The **Rattenfängerhaus** (Rat Catcher's House; Osterstrasse 28), from 1602, is perhaps the finest example, with its steep and richly decorated gable. Also not to be missed is the **Hochzeitshaus** (1610–17) at the Markt (square) end of Osterstrasse. The **Rattenfänger Glockenspiel** at the far end chimes daily at 9.35am and 11.35am, while a **carousel of Pied Piper figures** twirls at 1.05pm, 3.35pm and 5.35pm.

Frequent S-Bahn trains (S5) head from Hanover to Hamelin (€9.10, 50 minutes). By car, take the B217 to/from Hanover.

WOLFSBURG

☎ 05361 / pop 124,000

There's no doubt in Wolfsburg that Volkswagen is king – from the huge VW emblem adorning the company's global headquarters (and a factory the size of a small country) to the insignia on almost every vehicle. 'Golfsburg', as it's nicknamed after one of it's most successful models, does a nice sideline in modern architecture. But here in 'the capital of Volkswagen', a brave-new-world theme park called Autostadt is top of the bill.

LÜNEBURG: THE WOBBLY TOWN

With an off-kilter church steeple, buildings leaning on each other and houses with swollen 'beer-belly' façades, it's as if charming Lüneburg has drunk too much of the Pilsener lager it used to brew.

Of course, the city's wobbly angles and uneven pavements have a more prosaic cause. For centuries until 1980, Lüneburg was a salt-mining town, and as this 'white gold' was extracted from the earth, ground shifts and subsidence knocked many buildings sideways. Inadequate drying of the plaster in the now-swollen façades merely added to this asymmetry.

But knowing the scientific explanation never detracts from the pleasure of being on Lüneburg's comic-book crooked streets.

Between Hanover (€23, one hour; or €17 return Niedersachsen Ticket for 1¾-hour ME services) and Hamburg (€11, 30 minutes), the city's an undemanding day trip from either. From the train station, head west into town towards the highly visible, 14th-century **St Johanniskirche**, whose 106m-high spire leans 2.2m off true. Local legend has it that the architect tried to kill himself by jumping off it. (He fell into a hay cart and was saved, but celebrating his escape later in the pub drank himself into a stupor, fell over, hit his head and died after all.)

The church stands at the eastern end of the city's oldest square, **Am Sande**, full of typically Hanseatic stepped gables. At the western end stands the beautiful black-and-white **Industrie und Handelskammer** (Trade and Industry Chamber).

Continue one block past the Handelskammer and turn right into restaurant-lined Schröderstrasse, which leads to the **Markt**, where the **ornate Rathaus** contains the **tourist office** (☎ 207 6620; www.lueneburg.de; 9am-5pm Mon-Fri, to 4pm Sat & Sun May-Sep, 9am-5pm Mon-Fri, to 2pm Sat Oct-Apr).

Admire the square, before continuing west along Waagestrasse and down our favourite Lüneburg street, **Auf dem Meere**, en route to the **St Michaeliskirche**. Here the wonky façades and wavy pavements are like something from the 1919 German expressionist movie *The Cabinet of Dr Caligari,* or out of a Tim Burton film. Just look at the steps leading to the church!

It's too late now to regain your equilibrium, so head for the pubs along **Am Stintmarkt** on the bank of the Ilmenau River.

Orientation & Information

Wolfsburg's centre lies just southeast of the Hauptbahnhof. Autostadt is north across the train tracks. Head through the 'tunnel' under the Phaeno science centre, and you'll see the footbridge.

Wolfsburg tourist office (☎ 899 930; www.tourismus-wolfsburg.de, for English www.wolfsburg.de; Willy Brandt-Platz 3; 🕑 9am-7pm) In the train station.

Sights & Activities

AUTOSTADT

Spread across 25 hectares, **Autostadt** (Car City; ☎ 0800-2886 782 38; www.autostadt.de; Stadtbrücke; adult/concession/child/family €14/11/6/38; 🕑 9am-8pm Apr-Oct, 9am-6pm Nov-Mar) is a celebration of all things VW – so no muttering about the company's recent boardroom scandals up the back there, please! Exhibitions run the gamut of automotive design and engineering, the history of the Beetle and the marketing of individual marques, including VW itself, Audi, Bentley, Lamborghini, Seat and Skoda.

Included in the admission price are 45-minute shuttle **tours** (🕑 9am-6pm Mon-Fri, every 15 min, in English 1.30pm daily) of the enormous Volkswagen factory. The place is larger than Monaco, so you only get to see a snippet on the tour.

Most excitingly, there are **obstacle courses** and **safety training** (€25 each) if you have a valid licence and are comfortable with a left-hand drive car. Ring ahead to organise an English-speaking instructor.

Two hours before closing time, there's a discounted *Abendticket* (€6).

AUTOMUSEUM

For diehard fans not sated by Autostadt, the **AutoMuseum** (☎ 520 71; Dieselstrasse 35; adult/concession/family €6/3/15; 🕑 10am-5pm) has a collection of classic VW models. The collection includes *Herbie, the Love Bug,* a beetle made of wood, one of lace iron and the original 1938 Cabriolet presented to Adolf Hitler on his 50th birthday. Take bus 208 from the main bus station to AutoMuseum.

PHAENO

The space-age building beside the train station is **Phaeno** (☎ 0180-106 0600; www.phaeno.de; Willy Brandt-Platz 1; adult/concession/family €11/7/25; 🕑 10am-6pm Tue-Sun), an expensive new science centre designed by British-based Iraqi architect Zaha Hadid and frequently populated by hundreds of teenage school children on physics outings. Some 250 hands-on exhibits and experiments – wind up your own rocket, watch thermal images of your body – provide hours of fun. It's very physical, but also requires concentration. Instructions and explanations come in German and English.

Sleeping & Eating

DJH hostel (☎ 133 37; Lessingstrasse 60; dm junior/senior €16.50/19.50; Ⓟ 💻) Slightly cramped and fairly old, with pine furniture and checked linen, this hostel is nevertheless friendly and extremely central.

Hotel Wolf (☎ 865 60; www.alterwolf.de; Schlossstrasse 21; s/d from €35/50, f €75-85; Ⓟ) While the rooms inside this attractive, black-and-white half-timbered house aren't particularly fashionable, some are huge. Handy for families, but not for the city's nightlife, it's in a quiet, leafy part of town just behind Autostadt and the city castle.

Cityhotel Journal (☎ 292662; www.cityhotel-journal.de; Kaufhofpassage 2; s/d from €40/70) Above a pub on the city's main drinking strip, this must get pretty noisy in summer. However, if you're not planning on an early night, it's friendly, homey and convenient.

Global Inn (☎ 2700; www.globalinn.de; Kleistrasse 46; s €45-65, d €90; Ⓟ ⊠) Some cheaper single rooms are small in this central hotel, but all are of a comfortable corporate standard. There's a very popular Italian restaurant on site, too.

Other recommendations are the **Penthouse Hotel** (☎ 2710; www.penthouse-hotel.de; Schachtweg 22; s apt €45, d apt €55-65; f apt €75), where apartments all have kitchenettes, or the five-star **Ritz Carlton** (☎ 607 000; www.ritzcarlton.com; Autostadt; r from €200; Ⓟ ⊠ ⛝).

There are eight **Autostadt restaurants** within the park, ranging from a cheap American diner (Cylinder) to an upmarket Mediterranean (Chardonnay).

Kebab shops are dotted all along Porschestrasse and there are wall-to-wall bar/cafés along the Kaufhofpassage. Other convenient options include the Italian and pizzeria **Aalto Bistro** (☎ 891 689; Porschestrasse 1; mains €10-15; 🕑 dinner Mon-Sat) and the more upmarket **Walino** (☎ 255 99; Kunstmuseum, Porschestrasse 53; mains €16-17.50 or per person 3-courses for 2 €18.50; 🕑 closed Mon) located high up in the Kunstmuseum.

Getting There & Around

Frequent ICE train services go to Hanover (€19, 30 minutes) and Berlin (€39, one hour). If you use RE services from Hanover (one hour), a Niedersaschsen ticket will get you to Wolfsburg and back in a day for €17.

Most major sights are easily reached on foot, although a free shuttle bus also runs from the train station down Porschestrasse to the town centre.

For longer journeys, single bus tickets cost €1.70. A day pass costs €4. The major bus transfer point (ZOB) is at the northern end of Porschestrasse.

BREMEN

☎ 0421 / pop 550,000

Bremen is what Germans call *schön klein,* the equivalent of good things coming in small packages. You can easily travel on foot between the main attractions of its red-brick market place, Art-Deco Böttcherstrasse and the dollhouse-sized Schnoor district.

Best known from the fairy tale of the *Town Musicians of Bremen* – four animals who ran away from their owners to find fame here – Bremen is predictably cute and pretty. But the waterfront promenade along the Weser River is a wonderful place to enjoy a drink and the student district along Ostertorsteinweg is just downright alternative.

ORIENTATION

Head south (straight ahead) from the train station to reach the centre, on banks of the Weser River. The Schlachte waterfront promenade is west of the centre; the Schnoor district lies just east. The student and nightlife district is further east still, along Ostertorsteinweg.

INFORMATION

ErlebnisCARD (adult & 2 children 1/2 days €6.50/8.50) Free public transport and discounts on sights.

Internet.Center Bremen (☎ 277 6600; Bahnhofsplatz 22-28; per hr €5; ⏲ 10am-10pm Mon-Sat, noon-8pm Sun)

Tourist office (☎ 01805-101030; www.bremen-tourism.de; Hauptbahnhof; ⏲ 9am-7pm Mon-Fri, to 6pm Sat & Sun) Organises daily city tours; branch office (Obernstrasse/Liebfrauenkirchhof; ⏲ 10am-6.30pm Mon-Fri, to 4pm Sat & Sun)

SIGHTS & ACTIVITIES

Bremen's **Markt** is striking, particularly its ornate, gabled **Rathaus** (town hall). In front stands a 13m-tall medieval statue of the knight **Roland**, Bremen's protector. On the building's western side, you'll find a sculpture of the **Town Musicians of Bremen** (1951). Local artist Gerhard Marcks has cast them in their most famous pose, scaring the robbers who invaded their house, with the rooster atop the cat, perched on the dog, on the shoulders of the donkey.

Also on the Markt is the twin-towered **Dom St Petri** (cathedral), whose most interesting – and slightly macabre – feature is its **Bleikeller** (Lead Cellar; ☎ 365 0441; adult/concession €1.50/1; ⏲ 10am-5pm Mon-Fri, 10am-2pm Sat, noon-5pm Sun Apr-Oct) Here, open coffins reveal eight corpses that have mummified in the dry underground air. The Bleikeller has its own entrance, south of the main cathedral door.

If the Markt is memorable, then nearby **Böttcherstrasse** is unique. It's an opulent Art-Deco alley commissioned by Ludwig Roselius, the inventor of decaffeinated coffee and founder of the company Hag. He later managed to save it from the Nazis, who thought it 'degenerate'. Under the golden relief you enter a world of tall brick houses, shops, galleries, restaurants, a **Glockenspiel** and several museums (which can easily be skipped). If you can, peek in the back door of 'Haus Atlantis' (aka the Hilton hotel), for its phantasmagorical, multicoloured, glass-walled **spiral staircase**.

The maze of narrow winding alleys known as the **Schnoorviertel** was once the fishermen's quarter and then the red-light district. Now its dollhouse-sized cottages are souvenir shops and restaurants. The cute **Schnoor Teestübchen** (Teashop; Wüste Stätte 1) serves Frisian tea and cakes.

With more time, make a visit to the oyster-shaped **Universum Science Center** (☎ 334 60; www.usc-bremen.de; Wiener Strasse 2; adult/concession & child €11/7; ⏲ 9am-6pm Mon-Fri, 10am-7pm Sat & Sun, last entry 90 min before closing), or the **Beck's Brewery** (☎ 5094 5555; Am Deich 18-19; tours in German & English €7.50; ⏲ 10am-5pm Tue-Sat, to 3pm Sun, in English 2pm Tue-Sun).

SLEEPING

Camping Stadtwaldsee (☎ 841 0748; www.camping-stadtwaldsee.de; Hochschulring 1; camp sites per adult/tent/car €7/4/1.50) Totally rebuilt in late 2005, this

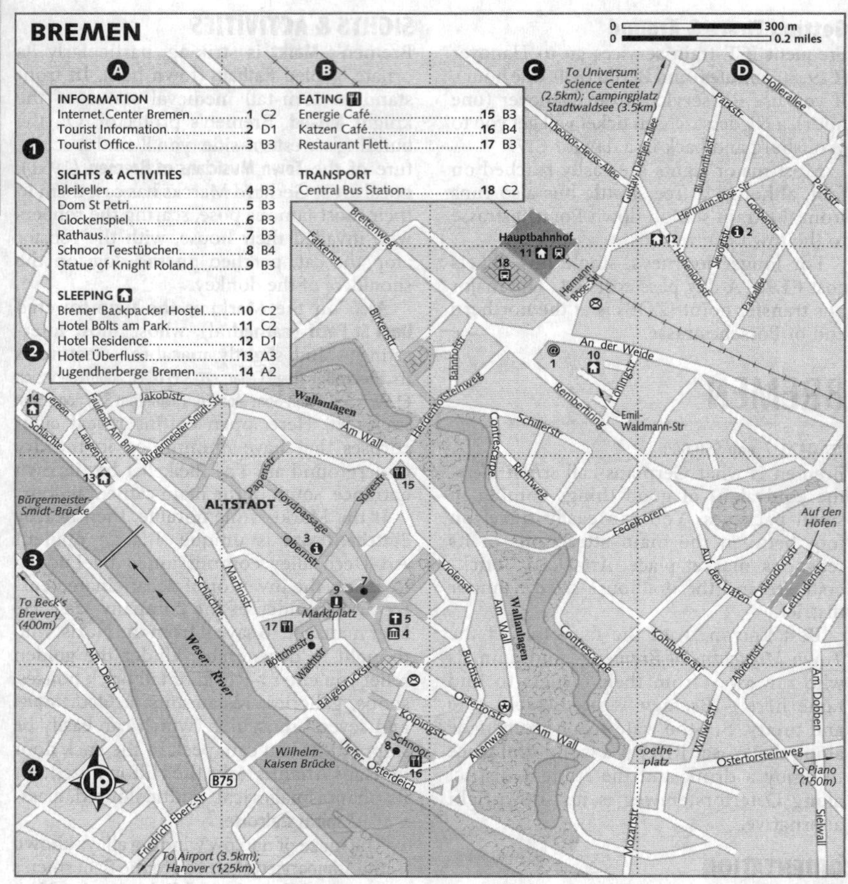

camping ground features modern amenities, a supermarket and café with a lakeside terrace. By car, take the A27 to the university exit in Bremen Nord. Tram 6 will get you close and bus 28 is on the doorstep.

Jugendherberge Bremen (☎ 163 820; www.jugendherberge.de; Kalkstrasse 6; dm junior/senior €21/24, s/d €32/56; ⊠ 💻) Like a work of art from the exterior, with a yellow and orange Plexiglas façade and slit rectangular windows, this refurbished building is even better inside. Comfortable dorms are all ensuite, there's a bar/breakfast room with huge glass windows overlooking the Weser River, and a rooftop terrace. Take tram 3 or 5 to Am Brill.

Bremer Backpacker Hostel (☎ 223 8057; www.bremer-backpacker-hostel.de; Emil-Waldmannstrasse 5-6; dm €16, s/d €27/44, bedding €3; Ⓟ 💻) Five minutes from the train station, tucked away on a quiet street, you'll find simply furnished but spotless rooms, a kitchen and living room. The communal showers are all on the ground floor – thanks to low water pressure, we presume from the taps on the first floor.

Hotel Bölts am Park (☎ 346 110; www.hotel-boelts.de; Slevogtstrasse 23; s/d €50/80; Ⓟ) This family-run hotel in a leafy neighbourhood has real character, from the old-fashioned breakfast hall to its well-proportioned rooms. A few singles with hall showers and toilets cost €40.

Hotel Residence (☎ 348 710; www.hotelresidence.de; Hohlenstrasse 42; s €65-100, d €80-140; Ⓟ ⊠)

Some rooms in this century-old terrace are a bit snug, but all are modern, comfortable and clean, while the best doubles – rooms 12 and 22 – have balconies overlooking a quiet street. A sauna, solarium and bar complete the package.

Hotel Überfluss (☎ 322 860; www.hotel-ueberfluss.com; Langenstrasse 72/Schlachte; s/d €135/180; ⊠ ✿ ▣) Dragging quaint Bremen into the 21st century is this jaw-dropping design hotel. It's all green-tinted windows overlooking the Weser River, black bathrooms and glowing fibre-optic curtains imported from Las Vegas. However, the friendly staff prevent it from ever becoming intimidating.

EATING

The student quarter in and around Ostertorsteinweg, **Das Viertel**, is full of restaurants and cafés. The waterfront promenade, **Schlachte**, is more expensive and mainstream, but pleasant nonetheless.

Piano (☎ 785 46; Fehrfeld 64; mains €5.50-9.50) One of the most enduringly popular cafés in the student quarter, Piano serves pizza, pasta, steaks and veggie casseroles. Breakfast can also be enjoyed until 4pm.

Energie Café (☎ 277 2510; cnr Sögestrasse & Am Wall; mains €3.50-12.50; ⏲ closed Sun) A delightfully upbeat café run by a local power company, this one serves delicious cut-price lunches and solid evening meals. Amuse yourself while waiting between by watching the model surfer on the wave-motion display.

Restaurant Flett (☎ 320 995; Böttcherstrasse 3-5; mains €7-15) Come here for local specialities like *Labskaus* (a hash of beef or pork with potatoes, onion and herring) or *Knipp* (fried hash and oats). Slightly touristy it might be, but it's hard to take against the photo-bedecked room, featuring first-hand snaps of celebs from Elvis to Clinton to Gerhard Schröder.

Katzen Café (☎ 326 621; Schnoor 38; mains €8.50-16.50, 3-course menu €19.50) This Moulin Rouge-style restaurant opens out into a rear sunken terrace bedecked with flowers. The menu runs the gamut from Alsatian to Norwegian, with seafood a strong theme.

GETTING THERE & AWAY

Flights from **Bremen airport** (BRE: www.airport-bremen.de) include easyJet (www.easyjet.com) flights to London-Luton.

Frequent trains go to Hamburg (€18.30 to €22, one hour), Hanover (€18.70 to €27, one hour to one hour and 20 minutes) and Cologne (€52, three hours). Some IC trains run direct to Frankfurt-am-Main (€76, 3¾ hours) and Munich (€100, six hours) daily.

GETTING AROUND

Tram 6 leaves the airport frequently, heading to the centre (€2.05, 15 minutes). Other trams cover most of the city. With single bus/tram tickets costing €2.05, a day pass (€5 for one adult and two children) is excellent value.

HAMBURG

☎ 040 / pop 1.7 million

Water, water everywhere – Germany's leading port city has always been outward-looking. Its dynamism, multiculturalism and hedonistic red-light district, the Reeperbahn, all arise from its maritime history.

Joining the Hanseatic League trading bloc in the Middle Ages, Hamburg has been enthusiastically doing business with the rest of the world ever since. In the 1960s, it nurtured the musical talent of the Beatles. Nowadays, it's also a media capital and the wealthiest city in Germany.

The Alster Lakes, the Elbe River and the canals between the Speicherstadt warehouses are all perfect for leisure cruises. Haggling at the rowdy fish market early on a Sunday is also an unrivalled experience.

ORIENTATION

The Hauptbahnhof is quite central, near the Binnenalster and Aussenalster (Inner and Outer Alster Lakes); the Speicherstadt and port lie south/southwest of these, on the Elbe River. The nightlife districts of St Pauli (containing the Reeperbahn) and the Schanzenviertel are further west. The city's sprawl means using public transport is necessary.

INFORMATION

EMERGENCY

Police Hauptbahnhof (Kirchenallee exit); St Pauli (Davidwache, Spielbudenplatz 31; Ⓜ Reeperbahn)

INTERNET ACCESS

Internet Café (☎ 2800 3898; Adenauerallee 10; per hr €2; ⏲ 10am-midnight Mon-Sat, to 1pm Sun; Ⓜ Hauptbahnhof)

Tele-Time (☎ 4131 4730; Schulterblatt 39; per hr €3; ⏲ 10am-midnight; Ⓜ Feldstrasse/Sternschanze)

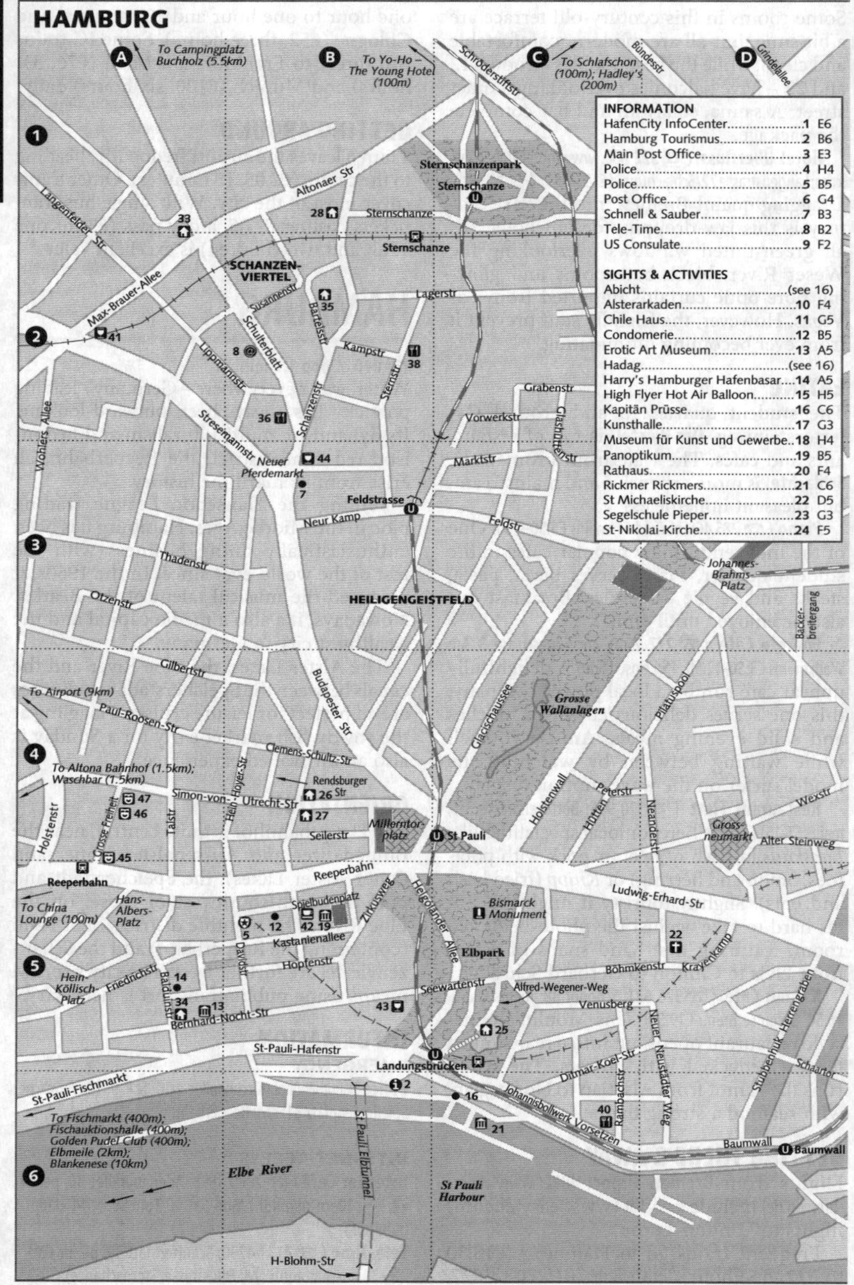
HAMBURG
To Campingplatz Buchholz (5.5km)
To Yo-Ho – The Young Hotel (100m)
To Schlafschon (100m); Hadley's (200m)
INFORMATION
HafenCity InfoCenter....................1 E6
Hamburg Tourismus....................2 B6
Main Post Office....................3 E3
Police....................4 H4
Police....................5 B5
Post Office....................6 G4
Schnell & Sauber....................7 B3
Tele-Time....................8 B2
US Consulate....................9 F2
SIGHTS & ACTIVITIES
Abicht....................(see 16)
Alsterarkaden....................10 F4
Chile Haus....................11 G5
Condomerie....................12 B5
Erotic Art Museum....................13 A5
Hadag....................(see 16)
Harry's Hamburger Hafenbasar....................14 A5
High Flyer Hot Air Balloon....................15 H5
Kapitän Prüsse....................16 C6
Kunsthalle....................17 G3
Museum für Kunst und Gewerbe....................18 H4
Panoptikum....................19 B5
Rathaus....................20 F4
Rickmer Rickmers....................21 C6
St Michaeliskirche....................22 D5
Segelschule Pieper....................23 G3
St-Nikolai-Kirche....................24 F5
Schröderstiftstr
Bundesstr
Grindelallee
Sternschanzenpark
Sternschanze
Altonaer Str
Langenfelder Str
Max-Brauer-Allee
SCHANZEN-VIERTEL
Susannenstr
Bartelsstr
Schulterblatt
Lagerstr
Kampstr
Sternstr
Lippmannstr
Schanzenstr
Stresemannstr
Wohlers Allee
Neuer Pferdemarkt
Grabenstr
Vorwerkstr
Glashüttenstr
Marktstr
Feldstrasse
Neur Kamp
Feldstr
Johannes-Brahms-Platz
Thadenstr
Otzenstr
HEILIGENGEISTFELD
Backerbreitergang
Gilbertstr
Budapester Str
Glacischaussee
Grosse Wallanlagen
Pilatuspool
To Airport (9km)
Paul-Roosen-Str
Clemens-Schultz-Str
To Altona Bahnhof (1.5km); Waschbar (1.5km)
Rendsburger Str
Simon-von-Utrecht-Str
Holstenstr
Grosse Freiheit
Talstr
Hein-Hoyer-Str
Millerntorplatz
Seilerstr
St Pauli
Holstenwall
Peterstr
Hütten
Neanderstr
Wexstr
Grossneumarkt
Alter Steinweg
Reeperbahn
To China Lounge (100m)
Hans-Albers-Platz
Spielbudenplatz
Zirkusweg
Helgoländer Allee
Bismarck Monument
Ludwig-Erhard-Str
Davidstr
Kastanienallee
Hopfenstr
Elbpark
Krayenkamp
Hein-Köllisch-Platz
Friedrichstr
Balduinstr
Bernhard-Nocht-Str
Seewartenstr
Alfred-Wegener-Weg
Böhmkenstr
Venusberg
St-Pauli-Hafenstr
Landungsbrücken
Ditmar-Koel-Str
Neuer Neustädter Weg
Stubbenhuk
Herrengraben
Schaartor
St-Pauli-Fischmarkt
Johannisbollwerk
Vorsetzen
Rambachstr
Baumwall
To Fischmarkt (400m); Fischauktionshalle (400m); Golden Pudel Club (400m); Elbmeile (2km); Blankenese (10km)
Elbe River
St Pauli Elbtunnel
St Pauli Harbour
H-Blohm-Str

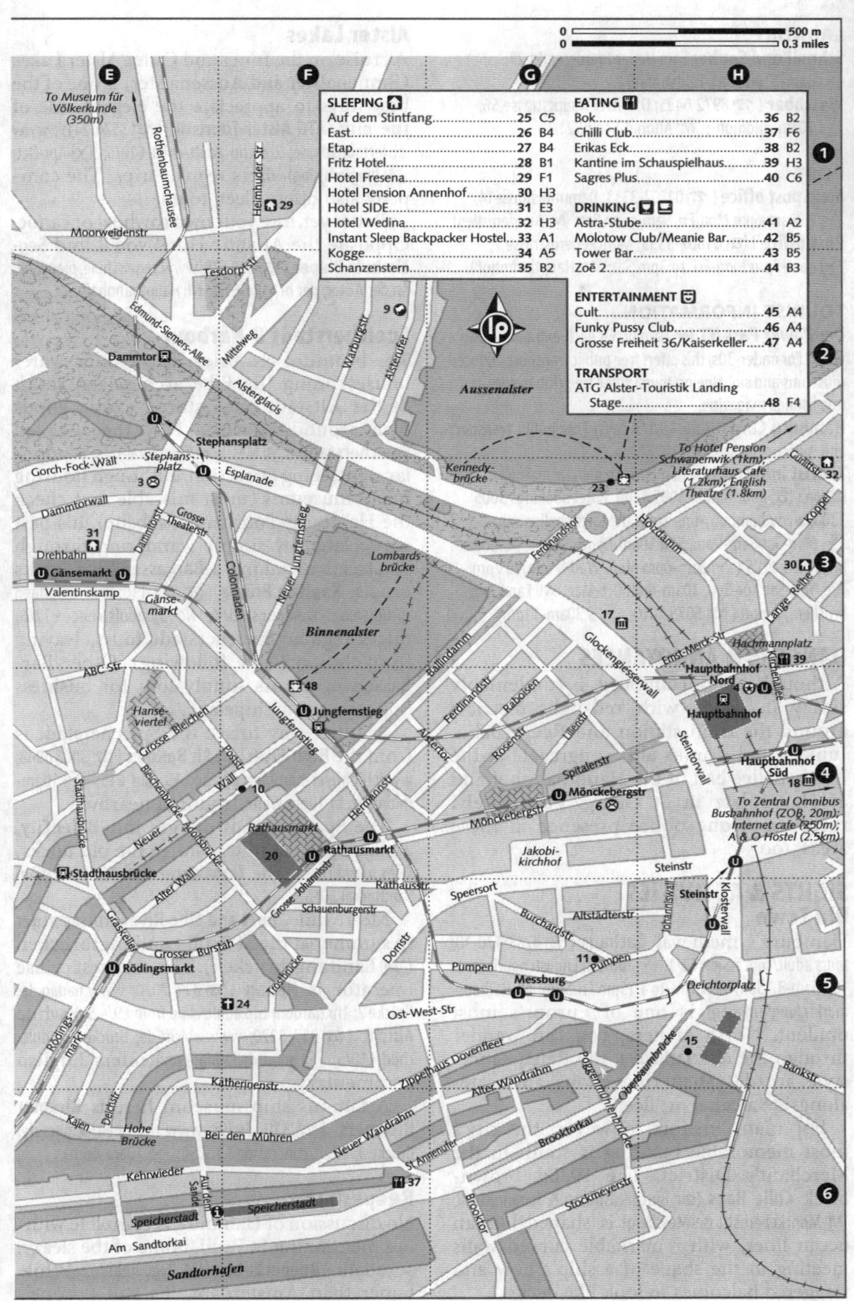
0 500 m
0 0.3 miles
SLEEPING
Auf dem Stintfang....25 C5
East....26 B4
Etap....27 B4
Fritz Hotel....28 B1
Hotel Fresena....29 F1
Hotel Pension Annenhof....30 H3
Hotel SIDE....31 E3
Hotel Wedina....32 H3
Instant Sleep Backpacker Hostel....33 A1
Kogge....34 A5
Schanzenstern....35 B2
EATING
Bok....36 B2
Chilli Club....37 F6
Erikas Eck....38 B2
Kantine im Schauspielhaus....39 H3
Sagres Plus....40 C6
DRINKING
Astra-Stube....41 A2
Molotow Club/Meanie Bar....42 B5
Tower Bar....43 B5
Zoë 2....44 B3
ENTERTAINMENT
Cult....45 A4
Funky Pussy Club....46 A4
Grosse Freiheit 36/Kaiserkeller....47 A4
TRANSPORT
ATG Alster-Touristik Landing Stage....48 F4
To Museum für Völkerkunde (350m)
Rothenbaumchausee
Heimhuder Str
Moorweidenstr
Tesdorpfstr
Edmund-Siemers-Allee
Mittelweg
Warburgstr
Alsterufer
Dammtor
Alsterglacis
Aussenalster
Stephansplatz
Gorch-Fock-Wall
Esplanade
Dammtorwall
Dammtorstr
Grosse Theaterstr
Kennedybrücke
To Hotel Pension Schwanenwik (1km); Literaturhaus Cafe (1.2km); English Theatre (1.8km)
Curtiusstr
Koppel
Holzdamm
Ferdinandstor
Drehbahn
Gänsemarkt
Valentinskamp
Colonnaden
Neuer Jungfernstieg
Lombardsbrücke
Lange Reihe
Binnenalster
Ballindamm
Glockengiesserwall
Ernst-Merck-Str
Hachmannplatz
Kirchenallee
ABC Str
Hauptbahnhof Nord
Hauptbahnhof
Jungfernstieg
Ferdinandstr
Raboisen
Hanseviertel
Grosse Bleichen
Poststr
Alstertor
Rosenstr
Lilienstr
Steintorwall
Hauptbahnhof Süd
Stadthausbrücke
Bleichenbrücke
Adolfsbrücke
Neuer Wall
Hermannstr
Spitalerstr
Mönckebergstr
To Zentral Omnibus Busbahnhof (ZOB, 20m); Internet cafe (250m); A & O Hostel (2.5km)
Rathausmarkt
Jakobikirchhof
Alter Wall
Grosse Johannisstr
Rathausstr
Steinstr
Schauenburgerstr
Speersort
Burchardstr
Altstädterstr
Johanniswall
Klosterwall
Graskeller
Grosser Burstah
Rödingsmarkt
Trostbrücke
Domstr
Pumpen
Messburg
Deichtorplatz
Ost-West-Str
Rödingsmarkt
Zippelhaus Dovenfleet
Alter Wandrahm
Poggenmühlenbrücke
Oberbaumbrücke
Bankstr
Katharinenstr
Deichstr
Kajen
Hohe Brücke
Bei den Mühren
Neuer Wandrahm
St Annenufer
Brooktorkai
Kehrwieder
Auf dem Sande
Speicherstadt
Brooktor
Stockmeyerstr
Am Sandtorkai
Sandtorhafen

LAUNDRY

Schnell und Sauber (Am Neuer Pferdemarkt 27; 6am-11pm; Feldstrasse)

Waschbar (8972 6425; Ottenser Hauptstrasse 56; 10am-midnight; Altona) See p521.

POST

Main post office (01802-3333; Dammtorstrasse14; 8.30am-6pm Mon-Fri, 9am-noon Sat; Jungfernstieg)

Post office (01802-3333; Mönckebergstrasse 7; 9am-7pm Mon-Fri, to 3pm Sat; Hauptbahnhof)

TOURIST INFORMATION

Der Power Pass (€7 for 1st day, €3 each extra day up to a week) For under-30s, this offers free public transport, reduced museums and sightseeing tours, some free club entries and a free listings magazine.

Hamburg Card (€7.50/15 1/3 days) Free public transport and museums discounts.

Tourist information Hamburg Tourismus main train station (information 3005 1200, hotel bookings 3005 1300; www.hamburg-tourismus.de; Kirchenallee exit; Mon-Sat 8am-9pm, Sun 10am-6pm); Landungsbrücken, btwn piers 4 & 5 (8am-6pm Mon, Wed & Sun, to 7pm Tue, Thu-Sat Apr-Sep, 10am-6pm Oct-Mar; Landungsbrücken); airport (5075 1010; 5.30am-11pm)

DANGERS & ANNOYANCES

Although safe, Hamburg is undeniably sleazy in parts, with red-light districts around the train station and Reeperbahn. Junkies and drunks also congregate at the Kirchenallee exit of the Hauptbahnhof and at Hansaplatz in St Georg. Fortunately, there's a strong police presence in these areas, too.

SIGHTS & ACTIVITIES

Old Town

Hamburg's medieval **Rathaus** (4283 120 10; tours adult/concession €2/1, tours in English hourly from 10.15am-3.15pm Mon-Thu, to 1.15pm Fri-Sun; Rathausmarkt/Jungfernstieg) is one of Europe's most opulent. North of here, you can wander through the **Alsterarkaden**, the Renaissance-style arcades sheltering shops and cafés alongside a canal or 'fleet'.

For many visitors, however, the city's most memorable building is south in the Merchant's District. The 1920s, brown-brick **Chile Haus** (cnr Burchardstrasse & Johanniswall; Mönckebergstrasse/Messberg) is shaped like an ocean liner, with remarkable curved walls meeting in the shape of a ship's bow and staggered balconies to look like decks.

Alster Lakes

A cruise on the Inner and Outer Alster Lakes (Binnenalster and Aussenalster) is one of the best ways to appreciate the elegant side of the city. **ATG Alster-Touristik** (3574 2419; www.alstertouristik.de; 2hr trip adult/child €10/5; Apr-Oct; Jungfernstieg) offers regular trips. The company also offers 'fleet' tours.

Better yet, hire your own rowboat or canoe. Opposite the Atlantic Hotel you'll find **Segelschule Pieper** (247 578; www.segelschule-pieper.de; An der Alster; per hr from €12; Hauptbahnhof).

Speicherstadt & Harbour

The beautiful red-brick, neo-Gothic warehouses lining the Elbe archipelago south of the Altstadt once stored exotic goods from around the world. Now the so-called **Speicherstadt** (Messberg/Baumwall) is a popular sightseeing attraction. Although housing many museums (most missable, but check the Hamburg Tourismus website), it's best appreciated by simply wandering through its streets or taking a **Barkassen** boat up its canals. **Kapitän Prüsse** (313 130; www.kapitaen-pruesse.de; Landungsbrücke No 3; adult/child €12/6) offers regular Speicherstadt tours, leaving from the port (see following). Other Barkassen operators simply tout for business opposite the archipelago.

Another way to see the Speicherstadt is from the **High-Flyer Hot Air Balloon** (3008 6968; www.highflyer-hamburg.de; per 15 min €15; 10am-midnight, to 10pm winter) moored nearby.

The Speicherstadt merges into **HafenCity**, a major project to transform the old docks. Get details at the **InfoCenter** (3690 1799; Am Sandtorkai 30).

Meanwhile, **port and Elbe River cruises** start in summer at the St Pauli Landungsbrücken (Landungsbrücken). The cheapest cruise operator is **Hadag** (311 7070; www.hadag.de; Brücke 2; 1hr harbour trip adult/child from €9/4.50), while **Abicht** (317 8220; www.abicht.de; Brücke 1; adult/child €10/5; noon daily Mar-Nov) offers English commentary.

A famous ship museum here is **Rickmer Rickmers** (319 5959; www.rickmer-rickmers.de; Brücke 1; adult/concession €3/2.50; 10am-6pm).

Reeperbahn

No discussion of Hamburg is complete without mentioning St Pauli, home of the sleazy, sexadelic **Reeperbahn** (Reeperbahn). While tamer than Amsterdam, it's still Europe's biggest red-light district – a kind of Champs Elyseés of sex shops, peep shows, dim bars and raucous clubs.

Among the 'sights' are the men-only **Herbertstrasse**, the **Erotic Art Museum** (☎ 317 4757; www.eroticartmuseum.de; Bernhard-Nocht-Strasse 69; adult/concession €8/5; ⏰ noon-10pm, to midnight Fri & Sat), and the **Condomerie** (Spielbudenplatz 18), with its extensive collection of prophylactics and sex toys.

Harry's Hamburger Hafenbasar (☎ 312 482; www.hafenbasar.de; cnr Balduinstrasse & Erichstrasse; adult/child €2.50/1.50, redeemable against any purchase; ⏰ noon-6pm Tue-Sun) is bursting with African statues, Asian masks and other ephemera shipped back from abroad.

Fischmarkt

Here's the perfect excuse to stay up all Saturday night. Every Sunday between 5am and 10am, curious tourists join locals of every age and walk of life at the famous Fischmarkt in St Pauli. The market has been running since 1703, and its undisputed stars are the boisterous *Marktschreier* (market criers) who hawk their wares at full volume. Live bands also entertainingly crank out cover versions of ancient German pop songs in the adjoining *Fischauktionshalle* (Fish Auction Hall). Take bus 112 to Hafentreppe.

Blankenese

The upmarket western district of **Blankenese** (Ⓜ Blankenese, then bus 48 to Krögers Treppe or Weseberg), a former fishing village, is wonderful to explore, as are its fine houses also set on a hillside labyrinth of narrow, cobbled streets. There's a network of **58 stairways** (4864 steps total!). The best views of the broad Elbe River and the container ships putting out to sea are enjoyed from the 75m-high **Süllberg** hill.

Museums

Three of Hamburg's dozens of museums stand out. The Hamburger **Kunsthalle** (☎ 428 131 200; www.hamburger-kunsthalle.de; Glockengiesserwall; adult/concession €8.50/5; ⏰ 10am-6pm Tue-Sun, to 9pm Thu; Ⓜ Hauptbahnhof) consists of two buildings – and old one housing 20th-century art, and a new white concrete cube of contemporary works – linked by a memorable underground passage.

The **Museum für Kunst und Gewerbe** (Museum of Arts & Crafts; ☎ 428 542 732; www.mkg-hamburg.de; Steintorplatz 1; adult/concession €8/5, both from 4pm Tue & 5pm Thu €5; ⏰ 10am-6pm Tue-Sun, to 9pm Thu; Ⓜ Hauptbahnhof) isn't quite so exalted, but its posters, ornaments and temporary exhibitions are always lots of fun.

The **Museum für Völkerkunde** (Museum of Ethnology; ☎ 01805-308 888; www.voelkerkundemuseum.com; Rothenbaumchaussee 64; adult/concession €6/3, Fri all €3; ⏰ 10am-6pm Tue-Sun, to 9pm Thu; Ⓜ Hallerstrasse) demonstrates sea-going Hamburg's acute awareness of the outside world. The giant statues from Papua New Guinea at the top of the stairs are unforgettable.

Churches

From the tower of the **St Michaeliskirche** (tower adult/concession €3/1.50; ⏰ 10am-6pm Apr-Oct, to 5pm Nov-Mar; Ⓜ Stadthausbrücke) you have panoramic views.

The WWII-damaged **St-Nikolai-Kirche** (Ost-West-Strasse; adult/child €2/1; ⏰ 11am-5pm; Ⓜ Rödingsmarkt) is now an antiwar memorial, with some chilling photos of the then-bombed-out city.

SLEEPING

Budget

For private rooms, contact **Bed & Breakfast** (☎ 491 5666; www.bed-&-breakfast.de), which has singles from €27 to €45 and doubles from €40 to €70.

Campingplatz Buchholz (☎ 540 4532; www.camping-buchholz.de; Kieler Strasse 274; camp sites per person/car €5/5, tent €8-11; Ⓜ Hamburg-Stellingen/Hagenbecks Tierpark) This small, family-run site has decent washing facilities, lots of shade and now some private hotel rooms. It's well connected to the city. When driving, take the A7/E45 and take exit 26 to Hamburg-Stellingen.

A & O Hostel (☎ 2104 0294; www.aohostel.com; Hammer Landstrasse 170; dm €12, s/d €29/32, breakfast €5, bedding €3; Ⓟ ⊠ 💻; Ⓜ Hammer Kirche) Typical of the A & O chain – new and clean, but a trifle bland – the Hamburg branch has a slightly out-of-the-way location.

Instant Sleep Backpacker Hostel (☎ 4318 2310; www.instantsleep.de; Max-Brauer-Allee 277; dm €15-20, s/d €28/44; 💻; Ⓜ Sternschanze) Brightly painted murals distract you from this place's relatively spartan surrounds. It's friendly, though, and in the happening Schanzenviertel.

Auf dem Stintfang (☎ 313 488; www.jugendherberge.de; Alfred-Wegener-Weg 5; dm €19-22, d €47; Ⓟ ⊠ 💻; Ⓜ Landungsbrücken) Modern, clean and convenient (head out of the U-Bahn station, up some steps and you're at the front door), this DJH hostel overlooks the Elbe and the harbour. With lots of large, noisy school groups, however, it's very keen on rules, and you're locked out part of the day.

Hotel Pension Annenhof (☎ 243 426; www.hotelannenhof.de; Lange Reihe 23; s/d €40/70; Ⓜ Hauptbahnhof) Behind the grubby façade, Annenhof's surprisingly attractive rooms have polished wooden floorboards and bright colour schemes, but no breakfast.

Other recommendations:

Schanzenstern (☎ 439 8441; www.schanzenstern.de; Bartelsstrasse 12; dm €18, s/d/tr €36/52/62; ⊠ 💻; Ⓜ Sternschanze) Backpackers' hostel with older rooms and healthy café.

Kogge (☎ 312 872; www.kogge-hamburg.de; Bernhard-Nocht-Strasse 59; s/d €29.50/48.50; Ⓜ Reeperbahn) Quirkily themed rock and roll pub with 5pm check-out.

Etap (☎ 306 220; www.etaphotel.com; Simon-von-Utrecht Strasse 64; s/d €44/52; 💻; Ⓜ St Pauli) Unusually central location for this budget chain.

Midrange

Schlafschön (☎ 4135 4949; www.schlafschoen.de; Monetastrasse 4; s with shared bathroom €55-75, d with shared bathroom €85; Ⓟ; Ⓜ Schlump). In the same former hospital as Hadley's, you'll find this separate B&B, where sunny beach-house colours are complemented by Turkish throws and Moroccan tiles. The centrepiece is a huge breakfast room, with a courtyard balcony. Look for the door saying 'Schwesterhaus' on the left side of the street near Beim Schlump.

Hotel Fresena (☎ 410 4892; www.hotelfresena.de; Moorweidenstrasse 34; s €56-70, d €84; Ⓟ ⊠; Ⓜ Dammtor) Bright walls, 1970s graphic-design posters, and vaguely Oriental touches and a largely nonsmoking policy make this an excellent choice in the five-floor, five-*pension* Dammtorpalais. Breakfast is extra.

Hadley's (☎ 417 871; www.bed-&-breakfast-hamburg.de; Beim Schlump 85; s/d from €60/70; Ⓟ; Ⓜ Schlump) This B&B's beds are set on a mezzanine platform (reached by ladder) above living areas mostly decorated in grey-blue tones. Most rooms have shared bathrooms. The place is set in a former hospital and while you can order breakfast in your room (€5 extra), we recommend heading to Hadley's warmly decorated café, just around the corner in the totally transformed ER.

Yo-Ho – The Young Hotel (☎ 284 1910; www.yoho-hamburg.de; Moorkamp 5; s/d €70/90; Ⓟ; Ⓜ Schlump/Christuskirche) Fashionable without being pretentious, the Yo-Ho is an exotic mix of ascetic, vaguely Japanese rooms, a magnificent 1001-nights breakfast room and a great Syrian restaurant. Under-26s get €20 off room rates.

Hotel Wedina (☎ 280 8900; www.wedina.de; Gurlittstrasse 23; s €75-145, d €110-165; Ⓟ; Ⓜ Hauptbahnhof) JK Rowling and Michel Houellebecq (now, that would be an interesting conversation) are just two authors who've been billeted in this arty relaxed hotel when doing public readings in the nearby Literaturhaus. There's 'urban living' in the green, blue and yellow-schemed houses. The group- and family-friendly red house also takes longer bookings.

Other recommendations:

Fritz Hotel (☎ 822 2283 0; www.fritzhotel.com; Schanzenstrasse 101-103; s/d €60/90; Ⓜ Sternschanze) This stylish townhouse hotel, decorated in white and grey with touches of red, is convenient but a tad noisy at the front.

Hotel-Pension Schwanenwik (☎ 220 0918; www.hotel-schwanenwik.de; Schwanenwik 29; s/d €70/90; Ⓟ; Ⓜ Hauptbahnhof, then bus 6 to Mundsburger Brücke) Well-run place overlooking the Aussenalster. Also has some rooms with shared facilities (s/d €45/65).

Top End

Hamburg has many ritzy hotels, both designer and traditional, but you could do worse than starting with these.

East (☎ 309 933; Simon-von-Utrecht-Strasse 31; r €150-375; Ⓟ ⊠; Ⓜ St Pauli) Pillars, walls and lamps emulate organic forms in the public areas of this warm, richly decorated design hotel. Floors are themed by plants and spices.

SIDE (☎ 309 990; www.side-hamburg.de; Drehbahn 49; r €190-230; Ⓟ ❄; Ⓜ Stephansplatz/Gänsemarkt) Italian designer Matteo Thun has created a space-age millionaire's bachelor pad here.

EATING

The **Schanzenviertel** (Ⓜ Feldstrasse/Schanzenstern) swarms with cheap eateries; try **Schulterblatt** for Portuguese outlets or **Susanenstrasse** for Asian and Turkish. Conversely, be aware that many fish restaurants around the Landungsbrücken are rather over-rated and quite touristy.

Erikas Eck (☎ 433 545; Sternstrasse 98; dishes €4.50-7.50; 🕑 7-2pm; Ⓜ Feldstrasse/Sternschanze) Hamburg's night-owls flock to this red-eye specialist, which starts serving breakfast at 1am.

Kantine im Schauspielhaus (☎ 2487 1239; Kirchenallee 39; lunches €4.50-7.50; 🕑 noon-3pm Mon-Fri;

THE ELBMEILE

Hamburg's western riverfront from Altona to Övelgönne – the Elbmeile or Elbe Mile – is Germany's hottest dining scene. Best known is **Das Weisse Haus** (☎ 390 9016; Neumühlen 50; menus €28 & €36), owned by TV chef Tim Mälzer, a sort of local Jamie Oliver. However, serious restaurant critics tip **Le Canard** (☎ 8812 9531; www.lecanard-hamburg.de; Elbchaussee 139; mains €16-28) for an out-of-this-world experience. Both restaurants serve modern international cuisine.

More relaxed is **Lust auf Italien** (☎ 382 811; Grosse Elbstrasse 133; mains €7-17), with its communal wooden benches. The completely informal venues are the summertime 'beach' clubs. There's one along Grosse Elbstrasse not far from Lust auf Italien, or try the kiosk **Strandperle** (Schulberg 2), further west from Das Weisse Haus.

Ⓜ Hauptbahnhof) There's as much theatre in this bustling basement restaurant as there is on the stage above, as waiters patrol between the tables calling out ready orders of pasta, salad or meat, and thespians gossip between rehearsals over the almost obligatory glass of house red.

Literaturhaus Café (☎ 220 1300; Schwanenwik 38; dishes €5-15; Ⓜ Hauptbahnhof) With golden walls and heavy chandeliers, this stunningly baroque café positively glows, as you will too after partaking of its Mediterranean bistro fare.

Chilli Club (☎ 3570 3580; Am Sandtorkai 54; dishes €4-20; Ⓜ Baumwall) This trendy noodle bar is tucked away in the industrial-looking Hafen City. Asian tapas, dim sum and sushi are also served within the restaurant's red-and-black interior.

Bok (☎ 4318 3597; Schulterblattt 3; mains €9-15; Ⓜ Feldstrasse/Sternschanze) Thai, Korean and Japanese food is on the menu at this cool but casual pan-Asian restaurant in the Schanzenviertel. It's large, and if fully booked has at least three sister outlets nearby to direct you to.

DRINKING & ENTERTAINMENT

Zoë 2 (Neuer Pferdemarkt 17; 🕑 from noon; Ⓜ Feldstrasse) The battered sofas, rough-hewn walls and old lampshades here prove that the ad-hoc, second-hand look so popular in Berlin is a Hamburg hit, too. Bottled beers and cocktails provide all the sophistication needed.

Astra-Stube (☎ 4325 0626; www.astra-stube.de; Max-Brauer-Allee 200; 🕑 from 9.30pm; Ⓜ Reeperbahn) This is a lo-fi DJ bar with some live bands that pulls in curious tourists and all types and ages from the St Pauli neighbourhood or 'Kiez'.

Tower Bar (☎ 311 137 0450; Seewartenstrasse 9; 🕑 from 6pm; Ⓜ Landungsbrücken) For a more elegant, mature evening, repair to this 14th-floor eerie of the Hotel Hafen for unbeatable harbour views.

Meanie Bar/Molotow Club (☎ 310 845; www.molotowclub.com; Spielbudenplatz 5; 🕑 from 6pm; Ⓜ Reeperbahn) One of the few venues along the Reeperbahn with real local cred, the retro Meanie Bar sits above the Molotow Club, where an alternative, independent music scene thrives by hosting the likes of the White Stripes, the Hives, the Kills and the Bravery.

Cult (☎ 2982 2180; Grosse Freiheit 2; 🕑 from 11pm Thu-Sat; Ⓜ Reeperbahn) Claiming to be Hamburg's most beautiful club, Cult serves up an unintimidating, good-time mix of '70s and '80s music in its shiny, cathedral-like main room.

Grosse Freiheit 36/Kaiserkeller (☎ 3177 7811; Grosse Freiheit 36; 🕑 from 10pm Tue-Sat; Ⓜ Reeperbahn) Wedged between live sex theatres and peep shows, this is popular for live rock and pop, particularly as the Beatles played in the basement Kaiserkeller.

Funky Pussy Club (☎ 314 236; Grosse Freiheit 34; 🕑 from 11pm Thu-Sat; Ⓜ Reeperbahn) Despite the dreadful name, this artistically decorated place is a hit for its mainstream chart-toppers and hip-hop, dance and house. Most drinks are €1 on a Thursday.

China Lounge (☎ 3197 6622; Nobistor 14; 🕑 from 11pm Thu-Sat; Ⓜ Reeperbahn) This leading club has four areas playing electro, house, hip-hop and R&B – the main floor is under a huge laughing Buddha. Thursday is students' evening.

Golden Pudel Club (☎ 3197 9930; Fischmarkt 27; 🕑 from 10pm; bus 112 to Hafentreppe) In a ramshackle fisherman's hut near the waterfront, this underground bar/club plays an eclectic mix of, electronica, hip-hop, R'n'B and reggae to a mixed crowd.

GETTING THERE & AWAY

Air

Hamburg's **airport** (HAM: www.flughafen-hamburg.de) has frequent flights to domestic and European cities, including on low-cost carrier Air Berlin (www.airberlin.com).

For flights to/from Ryanair's so-called 'Hamburg-Lübeck' see p542.

Bus

The **Zentral Omnibus Busbahnhof** (ZOB, central bus station; ☎ 247 5765; Adenauer Allee 78; 🕑 6.30am-9pm) is southeast of the Hauptbahnhof and most popular for services to central and eastern Europe. **Eurolines** (☎ 4024 7106; www.eurolines.com) has buses to Prague (one way/return €55/98) and Warsaw (one way/return €55/86), for example. However, if you call or visit, you'll find several specialist operators.

Autokraft (☎ 208 8660) travels to Berlin frequently for €24/39 one way/return. Elsewhere, **Berlin Linienbus** (☎ 030-861 9331; www.berlinlinienbus.de) and **Rainbow Tours** (☎ 3209 3309; www.rainbowtours.de, in German) are both very good options for travelling to Berlin or London, respectively.

Car & Motorcycle

The A1 (Bremen–Lübeck) and A7 (Hanover–Kiel) cross south of the Elbe River.

Train

When reading train timetables, remember that there are two main train stations: Hamburg Hauptbahnhof and Hamburg-Altona. There are frequent RE/RB trains to Lübeck (€10, 45 minutes), as well as various services to Hanover (€36, 1¼ hours) and Bremen (€18.30 to €22, one hour). In addition there are EC trains to Berlin (€48 to €58, 1½ to two hours), Cologne (€68 to €78, four hours) and Munich (€111, six to nine hours). Overnight train services also travel to international destinations such as Copenhagen and Paris.

GETTING AROUND

To/From the Airport

The **Airport Express** (☎ 227 1060; www.jasper-hamburg.de) runs between the Hauptbahnhof and airport (€5; 25 minutes, every 15 to 20 minutes, 🕑 6am-11pm). You can also take the U1 or S1 to Ohlsdorf, then change to bus 110.

Public Transport

There is an integrated system of buses, U-Bahn and S-Bahn trains. Day tickets, brought from machines before boarding, cost €5.80, or €4.90 after 9am. From midnight to dawn the night-bus network takes over from the trains, converging on the main metropolitan bus station at Rathausmarkt.

SCHLESWIG-HOLSTEIN

Sandwiched between the North and Baltic seas, Schleswig-Holstein is Germany's answer to the Côte d'Azur. Of course, the northern European weather here on the Danish border often makes it a pretty funny sort of answer, as dark clouds and strong winds whip in across this flat peninsula. Still, people flock to the beaches on the coasts and the countryside in between has a stark beauty.

LÜBECK

☎ 0451 / pop 215,000

Oh, how the mighty have fallen! But Lübeck doesn't look like she cares. Once the 'queen' of the Hanseatic League – a powerful medieval trading bloc – she's now just a provincial town, yet she still boasts an extraordinary appearance.

The two pointed cylindrical towers of Lübeck's Holstentor (gate) lean towards each other across the stepped gable that joins them, behind which the streets are lined with medieval merchants' homes and spired churches forming the city's so-called 'crown'. It's hardly surprising that this 12th-century gem is on Unesco's World Heritage List. The place looks so good you could eat it – especially the colourful displays of its famous marzipan, which you actually can.

Orientation & Information

Lübeck's old town is set on an island ringed by the canalised Trave River, a 10-minute walk east of the main train station. Leaving the station, head through the bus station and veer left along Hansestrasse. The tourist office is just across the Puppenbrücke (Doll Bridge), near the Holstentor. There are billboard maps all over town and signs in English.

Lübeck Travemünde Tourismus (☎ 01805 882 233; www.lubeck-tourism.de; Holstentorplatz 1; 🕑 9.30am-7pm Mon-Fri, 10am-3pm Sat, 10am-2pm Sun Jun-Sep,

9.30am-6pm Mon-Fri, 10am-3pm Sat Oct-May) With café and Internet terminals, staff can organise city tours and sell discount cards.

Sights

The impossibly cute city gate or **Holstentor** (☎ 122 4129; adult/concession €5/3; 🕑 10am-5pm Tue-Sun Apr-Sep, 10am-4pm Tue-Sun Oct-Mar) serves as Lübeck's museum as well as its symbol. It's been under renovation, but should be out of its clever *trompe l'oeil* wraps by now. The six gabled brick buildings east of the Holstentor are the **Salzspeicher**, once used to store the salt (from Lüneburg, p529) that was pivotal to Lübeck's Hanseatic trade.

Behind these warehouses, the Trave River forms a moat around the old town, and if you do one thing in Lübeck in summer, it should be a **boat tour**. From April to September, **Maak-Linie** (☎ 706 3859; www.maak-linie.de) and **Quandt-Linie** (☎ 777 99; www.quandt-linie.de) depart regularly from either side of the Holstentorbrücke. Prices are adult/student/child €7/5.50/3.50.

Each of Lübeck's seven churches offer something different. The shattered bells of the **Marienkirche** (Schüsselbuden 13; 🕑 10am-6pm Apr-Sep, to 5pm Oct, to 4pm Tue-Sun Nov-Mar) still lie on the floor where they fell after a bombing raid. There's also a little devil sculpture outside, with an amusing fairy tale (in English). The tower lift in the **Petrikirche** (Schmiedstrasse; adult/concession €2.50/1.50; 🕑 11am-4pm Tue-Sun, to 6pm mid-Nov–mid-Dec, closed Feb) affords superb views.

The **Rathaus** (town hall; ☎ 122 1005; Breite Strasse 64; adult/concession €3/1.50; tours 🕑 11am, noon & 3pm Mon-Fri) is ornate, but the tours are in German and, frankly, most visitors will prefer a visit to **JG Niederegger** (Breite Strasse 89) opposite. This is Lübeck's mecca of chocolate-coated **marzipan**, with lots of sweet gifts and an adjoining café.

Lübeck has some 90 lovely *Gänge* (walkways) and *Höfe* (courtyards) tucked away behind its main streets, the most famous being the **Füchtingshof** (Glockengiesserstrasse 25; 🕑 9am-noon & 3-6pm) and the **Glandorps Gang** (Glockengiesserstrasse 41-51).

Both of these are near the **Günter Grass-Haus** (☎ 122 4192; www.guenter-grass-haus.de; Glockengiesserstrasse 21; adult/concession €4/2.50, 'Kombi' card with Buddenbrookhaus €7/4; 🕑 10am-6pm Apr-Dec, 11am-5pm Nov-Mar). The author of *The Tin Drum* (*Die Blechtrommel*) has lived in town for years. Fellow Nobel Prize-winning author Thomas *(Death in Venice)* Mann was born in Lübeck and he's commemorated in the award-winning **Buddenbrookhaus** (☎ 122 4190; www.buddenbrookhaus.de; Mengstrasse 4; adult/concession €5/3; 'Kombi' card with Buddenbrookhaus €7/4; 🕑 10am-6pm Apr-Dec, 11am-5pm Nov-Mar).

For children, there's a fantastic **Marionettentheater** (Puppet Theatre; ☎ 700 60; cnr Am Kolk & Kleine Petersgrube; 🕑 Tue-Sun). Alternatively, ask the tourist office about the nearby seaside resort of **Travemünde**.

Sleeping

BUDGET

Campingplatz Schönböcken (☎ 893 090; fax 892 287; Steinrader Damm 12; camp sites per person/tent/car €4.50/3.50/1; 🕑 Apr-Oct) This modern camping ground has a kiosk, entertainment room and children's playground, although two readers have complained about the lack of shade in summer. It's 15 minutes by bus west of the city centre (take bus 7).

Jugendgästehaus Altstadt (☎ 702 0399; www.jugendherberge.de; Mengstrasse 33; dm junior/senior €18/21) If you prefer convenience, opt for this central DJH hostel. It isn't particularly new, but it's cosy and comfortable enough.

Vor dem Burgtor (☎ 334 33; www.jugendherberge.de; Am Gertrudenkirchhof 4; dm junior/senior €17/20; P 💻) Those fussier about their furnishings might prefer the huge, modern Vor dem Burgtor, however, it's popular with school groups, and outside the old town – just.

Hotel zur Alten Stadtmauer (☎ 737 02; www.hotelstadtmauer.de; An der Mauer 57; s/d €45/75, with shared bathroom from €38/65; P) With pine furniture and splashes of red or yellow, this simple 25-room hotel is bright and cheerful. The wooden flooring means sound carries, but customers tend not to be the partying type. Back rooms overlook the river.

Two very cheap and basic places are **Sleep-Inn** (☎ 719 20; www.cvjm-luebeck.de/cvjm; Grosse Petersgrube 11; dm €12.50; 🕑 mid-Jan–mid-Dec) and the **Rucksackhotel** (☎ 706 892; www.rucksackhotel-luebeck.de; Kanalstrasse 70; dm €13-15, d €34-40, bedding €3; 💻). The latter has a vegetarian café open to the public.

MIDRANGE & TOP END

Hotel Lindenhof (☎ 872 100; www.lindenhof-luebeck.de; Lindenstrasse 1a; s €65-80, d €85-110, f €100-135; P ☒) Its rooms are business-like and small, but a healthy breakfast buffet, friendly service and little extras, (free biscuits, newspapers, and a 6am to midnight snack service) propel the Lindenhof into a superior league.

Hotel Jensen (☎ 702 490; www.hotel-jensen.de; An der Obertrave 4-5; s €65-85, d €85-110) Classic and romantic, this old Patrizierhaus (mansion house) is conveniently located facing the Salzspeicher across the Trave River. Its seafood restaurant, Yachtzimmer, is also excellent.

Klassik Altstadt Hotel (☎ 702 980; www-klassik-altstadt-hotel.de; Fischergrube 52; s/d €75/130, ste from €135; P ⊠) Each room here is dedicated to a different, mostly German, writer or artist (somehow Russia's Nikolai Gogol creeps in). It's a token gesture, though, and the overwhelming impression is of a decent, traditionally furnished hotel.

Radisson SAS Senator Hotel (☎ 1420; www.senatorhotel.de, Willy-Brandt-Allee 6; s/d €135/160; P ⊠ ✣ 💻 🏊) The Senator's three rectangular brick wings are spectacularly cantilevered out into the Trave River, like something from *War of the Worlds*. Rooms are newly refurbished in opulent Southeast Asian colonial style, and there are wonderful restaurant views.

Eating

Suppentopf (☎ 400 8136; Fleischerstrasse 36; soups €3.50; ⏲ 11am-4pm Mon-Fri, closed Jul & Aug) Join Lübeck's office workers for a stand-up lunch of delicious, often spicy soup, in this progressive modern kitchen.

Tipasa (☎ 706 0451; Schlumacherstrasse 12-14; mains €4-16) Pizzas, curries and other budget meals are served below the faux caveman frescos of animals and Australian Aboriginal dot paintings.

Nui (☎ 203 7333; Beckergrube 72; sushi €2-16, mains €9-17; ⏲ dinner only Sat, closed Sun) Tempting smells waft from the artfully organised designer plates in this trendy but relaxed Thai-cum-Japanese restaurant.

Schiffergesellschaft (☎ 767 76; Breite Strasse 2; mains €10-23) The fact it's a tourist magnet can't detract from this 500-year-old guildhall's thrilling atmosphere. Ships' lanterns, a gilded chandelier and orange Chinese-style lamps with revolving maritime silhouettes all join 17th-century ship models in hanging from the painted, wooden-beamed ceiling. Staff in long white aprons serve fishy Frisian specialities and local beer.

Getting There & Away

Lübeck's **airport** (LBC; www.flughafen-luebeck.de) is linked to London by budget carrier Ryanair (www.ryanair.com) and to Gdansk in Poland by Hungarian low-cost carrier Wizz-Air (www.wizzair.com).

To head into town, catch scheduled bus 6 to the Hauptbahnhof and the neighbouring central bus station. If you're flying on Ryanair to 'Hamburg-Lübeck' there are synchronised shuttle buses direct to Hamburg (one way €8, 1¼ hours).

Otherwise, trains head to Hamburg at least once an hour (€10, 45 minutes) and there are frequent services to Schwerin (€11.70, 1¼ hours). Trains to/from Copenhagen also stop here.

Getting Around

Frequent double-decker buses run to Travemünde (€3.50, 45 minutes) from the central bus station. City buses also leave from here; a short journey of a few stops costs €1.40, a normal single costs €1.90 and a trip from the airport is €2.15.

NORTH FRISIAN ISLANDS

Germany's North Frisian Islands are a strange proposition. Hearing of their long grass-covered dunes, shifting sands, bird colonies and rugged cliffs, you'd imagine them as the domain of hardy nature-lovers. Instead, they're a favourite of the German jetset and actually feel more like Martha's Vineyard. Traditional reed-thatched cottages now house luxury goods stores, such as Cartier and Louis Vuitton, while car parks on Sylt are frequently crammed with Mercedes and Porsches.

Still, bicycle-riding nobodies can still be seen taking in the pure sea air in the remoter corners of glamorous Sylt. Amrum and Föhr are more peaceful still.

SYLT

☎ 04651 / pop 21,600

Even on Sylt, the most accessible and hence busiest island, it's possible to get back to nature. Admittedly not in Westerland, which is the largest town and Sylt's Miami Beach. Here high-rises obscure views of the beach, although some of the **world's best windsurfing** is off this shore.

However, even by the time you reach Kampen things are changing. Kampen might resemble St Tropez, with ritzy restaurants and celebrity guests. But it's also home to the 52.5m-tall **Uwe Dune**. Climb the wooden steps to the top for a 360-degree view.

Towards List, on the island's northern tip, is the popular **Wanderdünengebiet**, where people hike between grass-covered dunes. Or try List's **beach-side sauna**.

Inside the Westerland train station, there's an **information pavilion** (☎ 846 1029; ⏰ 9am-4pm in summer, reduced hr winter) or try **Westerland Tourism** (☎ 9980 or 0180 550 9980; www.westerland.de; ⏰ 9am-5pm Mon-Thu, to 2pm Fri).

Accommodation is at a premium in summer, but ask the tourist office about cheaper private rooms. Beware that credit cards are not always accepted – even in some mid-range hotels. A small *Kurtaxe,* or resort tax, will be added to your bill.

Campingplatz Kampen (☎ 420 86; Möwenweg 4; camp sites per person/tent/car €3.50/4.50/1.50; ⏰ Easter-Oct) Admittedly with more caravans than tents, this is still beautifully set amid dunes near Kampen, 500m from the beach.

Hostels include the Hörnum **Jugendherberge** (☎ 880 294; www.jugendherberge.de; Friesenplatz 2; dm €15.50), in the south of the island, and List's **Jugendherberge** (☎ 870 397; www.jugendherberge.de; List; dm €19). Neither is very central, but bus services bring you close.

Hotel Gutenberg (☎ 988 80; www.hotel-gutenberg.de; Friedrichstrasse 22, Westerland; s €65-75, d €115-135; ⊠) Sea-green stained wood sets the tone for this clean, friendly and light-filled place. The hotel takes credit cards. The Cheaper doubles (€100) share spotless facilities.

Hotel Wünschmann (☎ 5025; www.hotelwunschmann.de; Andreas-Dirks-Strasse, Westerland; s €80-140, d €120-250; Ⓟ) The foyer has a modern designer ambience and more traditionally decorated rooms, some with seaside balconies.

Gosch (fish sandwiches €2-3.50, meals €6-10) The Gosch fast-fish chain has colonised mainland Germany, but it originated in Sylt and remains here in force.

Kupferkanne (☎ 410 10; Stapelhooger Wai, Kampen; meals €5.50-9) Giant mugs of coffee and huge slices of cake are served outdoors at this *Alice in Wonderland*-style café, where wooden tables surrounded by a maze of low bramble hedges overlook the Wadden Sea. Meals are served in the attached Frisian house.

Sansibar (☎ 964 646; Hörnumer Strasse 80; Rantum; mains €6-32) This large grass-roof pavilion on the beach north of Hörnum is ideal for a drink or dinner at sunset.

Getting There & Around

Sylt is connected to the mainland by a narrow causeway exclusively for trains. Regular services travel from Hamburg (Altona and Hauptbahnhof) to Westerland (€39, three hours).

If driving, you must load your vehicle onto a **car train** (☎ 995 0565; www.syltshuttle.de; one way €43) in Niebüll near the Danish border. There are constant crossings (usually at least once an hour) in both directions, and no reservations can be made.

There's also a **car ferry** (☎ 0180-310-3030; www.sylt-faehre.de; one way per person/car €6/38.50) from Rømøin Denmark to List in the north.

Air Berlin (www.airberlin.com) has several services a week from Berlin and Düsseldorf to **Sylt/Westerland airport** (GWT; www.flughafen-sylt.de), Hapag-Lloyd Express (www.hlx.com) flies from Hannover, Köln-Bonn and Stuttgart, and Lufthansa (www.lufthansa.com) arrives from Frankfurt, Hamburg and Munich, among others.

Sylt's two north–south bus lines run every 20 to 30 minutes, and three other frequent lines cover the rest of the island.

AMRUM & FÖHR

Tiny Amrum is renowned for its fine white *Kniepsand*. There's a 10km stroll from the tall **lighthouse** at Wittdün to the village of Norddorf, and an 8km return hike along the beach. The **tourist office** (☎ 04682-194 33; fax 04682-940 394; ferry landing, Wittdün) can provide accommodation information.

The 'green isle' of Föhr is interesting for its Frisian culture. Its main village, Wyk,

WALK ON WATER

Okay, that's an exaggeration. You can't quite play Jesus in the North Frisian Islands, but you can walk between the islands at low tide. The best *Wattwandern,* as this activity is called (the same as Dutch *Wadlopen*), is between the islands of Amrum and Föhr, a full-day excursion (€25.50) also involving boat and bus trips. Contact **Adler-Schiffe** (☎ 04651-987 00; www.adler-schiffe.de).

boasts plenty of windmills, there are 16 northern hamlets tucked behind dikes up to 7m tall, and there's the large 12th-century church of **St Johannis** in Nieblum. The **Föhr information service** (☎ 04681-3040; fax 04681-3068; Wyk harbour) can help with more details. There is no camping here.

Getting There & Around

WDR (☎ 800; www.wdr-wyk.de) has ferries to Föhr (€5.50, 45 minutes) and Amrum (€7.80, 1½ hours) from Dagebüll Hafen (change in Niebüll).

Adler-Schiffe (☎ 04651-987 00; www.adler-schiffe.de; Boysenstrasse 13, Westerland; return adult/child €22/12) offers day cruises from Hörnum harbour in Sylt, and has quicker journeys on its *Adler Express* ship.

On Amrum, there are buses between the ferry terminal in Wittdün and Norddorf.

GERMANY DIRECTORY

ACCOMMODATION

Local tourist offices are great resources for accommodation in Germany – almost all offer a *Gastgeberverzeichnis* (accommodation list) and a *Zimmervermittlung* (room-finding service), and staff will usually go out of their way to find something in your price range.

In this book, options are listed by price, with the cheapest first. Accommodation usually includes breakfast, except in camping grounds and holiday apartments. Prices include private bathrooms unless otherwise specified.

Germany has more than 2000 organised camping grounds, several hundred of which stay open throughout the year. Prices are around €3 to €5 for an adult, plus €3 to €7 for a car and/or tent. Look out for ecologically responsible camping grounds sporting the Green Leaf award from the ADAC motoring association.

Deutsches Jugendherbergswerk (DJH; www.djh.de) coordinates the official Hostelling International (HI) hostels in Germany. Guests must be members of an HI-affiliated organisation, or join the DJH when checking in. The annual fee is €12/20 for junior/senior, which refers to visitors below/above 26 years old. Bavaria is the only state that enforces a strict maximum age of 26 for visitors. A dorm bed ranges from around €15 to €20 for juniors and €16 to €25 for seniors. Camping at a hostel (where permitted) is generally half-price. Sheet hire costs from €2.50 to €4.

Private rooms and guesthouses can be excellent value, especially for lone travellers, with prices starting as low as €25. Budget hotels and *pensions* typically charge under €70 for a double room (under €50 with shared bathroom), while good-value midrange options come in around €70 to €140. Anything over €140 can generally be considered top end, and should offer enough amenities to justify the price – spa facilities are a common extra.

Renting an apartment for a week or more is a popular option, particularly for small groups. Again, tourist offices are generally the best source of information, or have a look in newspaper classifieds under *Ferienwohnungen (FeWo)* or *Ferien-Apartments.* Rates vary widely but decrease dramatically with the length of stay. Local *Mitwohnzentralen* (accommodation-finding services) can help in finding shared houses and longer-stay rentals.

ACTIVITIES

Germany, with its rugged Alps, picturesque uplands and fairy-tale forests, is ideal for hiking and mountaineering. There are well-marked trails crisscrossing the countryside, especially in popular areas such as the Black Forest (see p499), the Harz Mountains (p464), the Saxon Switzerland area (p453) and the Thuringian Forest. The Bavarian Alps (p489) offer the most dramatic and inspiring scenery, however, and are the centre of mountaineering in Germany. Good sources of information on hiking and mountaineering are: **Verband Deutscher Gebirgs-und Wandervereine** (Federation of German Hiking Clubs; ☎ 0561-938 730; www.wanderverband.de); and **Deutscher Alpenverein** (German Alpine Club; ☎ 089-140 030; www.alpenverein.de).

The Bavarian Alps are the most extensive area for winter sports. Cross-country skiing is also good in the Black Forest and Harz Mountains. Ski equipment starts at around €15 per day, and daily ski-lift passes start at around €15. Local tourist offices are the best sources of information.

Cyclists will often find marked cycling routes, and eastern Germany has much to offer in the way of lightly travelled back roads. There's an extensive cycling trail along the Elbe River, and islands like Rügen Island (p472) are also good for cycling. For more details and tips, see Getting Around on (p549).

BOOKS

For a more detailed guide to the country, pick up a copy of Lonely Planet's *Germany*. Lonely Planet also publishes *Bavaria*, and *Berlin* and *Munich* city guides.

The German literary tradition is strong and there are many works that provide excellent background to the German experience. Mark Twain's *A Tramp Abroad* is recommended for his comical observations on German life.

For a more modern analysis of the German character and the issues that are facing Germany, dip into *Germany and the Germans* by John Ardagh.

BUSINESS HOURS

By law, shops in Germany may open from 6am to 8pm on weekdays and until 4pm on Saturday. In practice, however, only department stores and some supermarkets and fashion shops stay open until 8pm. But this is changing and in large cities more places are finding ways to stay open later and even on Sunday.

Banking hours are generally 8.30am to 1pm and 2.30pm to 4pm weekdays, but many banks remain open all day, and until 5.30pm on Thursday. government offices close for the weekend at 1pm or 3pm on Friday. Museums are often closed on Monday; opening hours vary greatly, although many are open later one evening per week.

Restaurants are usually open from 11am to midnight, with varying *Ruhetage* or closing days; many close for lunch during the day from 3pm to 6pm. Cafés often close around 8pm, though equal numbers stay open until 2am or later. Bars that don't serve food open between 5pm and 8pm and may close as late as 5am (if at all) in the larger cities.

DANGERS & ANNOYANCES

Although the usual cautions should be taken, theft and other crimes against travellers are relatively rare in Germany. Africans, Asians and southern Europeans may encounter racial prejudice, especially in eastern Germany, where they can be singled out as convenient scapegoats for economic hardship. However, the animosity is usually directed against immigrants, not tourists.

DISCOUNT CARDS

Many cities offer discount cards. These cards will usually combine up to three days' free use of public transport with free or reduced admission to major local museums and attractions. They're generally a good deal if you want to fit a lot in; see the Information section under the relevant destination and ask at tourist offices for full details.

EMBASSIES & CONSULATES

German Embassies & Consulates

Australia (☎ 02-6270 1911; 119 Empire Circuit, Yarralumla, ACT 2600)

Canada (☎ 613-232 1101; 1 Waverley St, Ottawa, Ont K2P 0T8)

France (☎ 01-53 83 45 00; 13-15 Ave Franklin Roosevelt, 75008 Paris)

Ireland (☎ 01-269 3011; 31 Trimleston Ave, Booterstown, Dublin)

New Zealand (☎ 04-473 6063; 90-92 Hobson St, Wellington)

The Netherlands (☎ 070-342 0600; Groot Hertoginnelaan 18-20, 2517 EG The Hague)

UK (☎ 020-7824 1300; 23 Belgrave Square, London SW1X 8PZ)

USA (☎ 202-298 4000; 4645 Reservoir Rd, NW Washington, DC 20007-1998)

Embassies & Consulates in Germany

The following embassies are all in Berlin. Many countries also have consulates in cities such as Frankfurt-am-Main and Munich.

Australia (Map pp432-3; ☎ 880 0800; Wallstrasse 76-78)

Canada (Map pp432-3; ☎ 203 120; Leipziger Platz 17, Tiergarten)

France (Map pp432-3; ☎ 590 039 000; Pariser Platz 5)

Ireland (Map pp432-3; ☎ 220 720; Friedrichstrasse 200)

New Zealand (Map pp432-3; ☎ 209 560; Friedrichstrasse 60)

South Africa Map pp432-3; ☎ 220 730; Tiergartenstrasse 18)

The Netherlands (Map pp432-3; ☎ 209 560; Klosterstrasse 50)

UK (Map pp432-3; ☎ 204 570; Wilhelmstrasse 70-71)

USA (Map pp432-3; ☎ 238 5174; Neustädtische Kirchstrasse 4-5)

FESTIVALS & EVENTS

January-February

Carnival season Shrovetide – also known as '*Fasching*' or '*Karneval*' – sees many Carnival events begin in large cities, most notably Cologne, Munich, Düsseldorf and Mainz. The partying hits a peak just before Ash Wednesday.
International Film Festival Held in Berlin (see p438).

March

Frankfurt Music Fair
Frankfurt Jazz Fair
Spring Fairs Held throughout Germany.
Bach Festival

April

Munich Ballet Days
Mannheim May Fair
Stuttgart Jazz Festival
Walpurgisnacht Festivals Held the night of 30 April/1 May in the Harz Mountains.

May

Dresden International Dixieland Jazz Festival
Dresden Music Festival Held in last week of May into first week of June.
Red Wine Festival Held in Rüdesheim.

June

Händel Festival Held in Halle.
International Theatre Festival Held in Freiburg.
Moselle Wine Week Held in Cochem.
Munich Film Festival
Sailing regatta Held in Kiel.

July

Berlin Love Parade See p438.
Folk festivals Held throughout Germany.
International Music Seminar Held in Weimar.
Kulmbach Beer Festival
Munich Opera Festival
Richard Wagner Festival Held in Bayreuth.

August

Heidelberg Castle Festival
Wine festivals Held throughout the Rhineland area.

September

Berlin Festival of Music & Drama
Oktoberfest Held in Munich (see p477).

October

Bremen Freimarkt
Berlin Jazzfest
Frankfurt Book Fair

November-December

Christmas fairs Held throughout Germany, most famously in Munich, Nuremberg, Berlin, Essen and Heidelberg.
St Martin's Festival Held throughout Rhineland and Bavaria.
Silvester New Year's Eve, celebrated everywhere.

GAY & LESBIAN TRAVELLERS

German people are generally fairly tolerant of homosexuality, but gays (*Schwule*) and lesbians (*Lesben*) still don't enjoy the same social acceptance in Germany as in some other northern European countries. Most progressive are the larger cities, particularly Berlin, Frankfurt-am-Main and Munich, which have dozens of gay and lesbian bars and meeting places. The age of consent is 18 years. Christopher Street Day, in June, is the biggest Pride festival in Germany, with events held in Berlin and many other major towns.

HOLIDAYS

Germany has many public holidays, some of which vary from state to state. Holidays include:
New Year's Day 1 January
Easter March/April
Labour Day 1 May
Ascension Day 40 days after Easter
Whitsun/Pentecost May/June
Day of German Unity 3 October
All Saints' Day 1 November
Day of Prayer & Repentance 18 November
Christmas 24–26 December

MEDIA

Magazines

Germany's most popular magazines are *Der Spiegel, Focus* and *Stern*. *Die Zeit* is a weekly publication about culture and the arts.

Newspapers

The most widely read newspapers in Germany are *Die Welt, Frankfurter Allgemeine,* Munich's *Süddeutsche Zeitung* and the left-leaning *Die Tageszeitung (Taz)*. *Bild* is Germany's favourite sensationalist tabloid, part of the Axel Springer publishing empire.

Radio

German radio sticks to a fairly standard diet of news and discussion or Europop, inane chatter and adverts, though most regions and cities have their own stations so quality can vary. The BBC World Service (on varying AM wavelengths) broadcasts in English.

TV

Germany's two national TV channels are the government-funded ARD and ZDF. They are augmented by a plethora of regional broadcasters, plus private cable channels such as Pro7, SAT1 and RTL, which show a lot of dubbed US series and films with long ad breaks. You can catch English-language news and sports programmes on cable or satellite TV in most hotels and *pensions*.

MONEY

The easiest places to change cash in Germany are the banks or foreign exchange counters at airports and train stations, particularly those of the Reisebank. The main banks in larger cities generally have money-changing machines for after-hours use, although they don't often offer reasonable rates. Some local Sparkasse banks have good rates and low charges.

There are international ATMs virtually everywhere in Germany. Typically, withdrawals over the counter against cards at major banks cost a flat €5 per transaction. Check other fees and the availability of services with your bank before you leave home.

Travellers cheques can be cashed at any bank and the most widely accepted are Amex, Thomas Cook and Barclays. A percentage commission (usually a minimum of €5) is charged by most banks on any travellers cheque, even those issued in euros.

POST

Standard post office hours are 8am to 6pm weekdays and to noon on Saturday. Many train station post offices stay open later or offer limited services outside these hours.

Within Germany and the EU, standard-sized postcards cost €0.45 and a 20g letter is €0.55. Postcards to North America and Australasia cost €1, a 20g airmail letter is €1.55. Surface-mail parcels up to 2kg within Europe are €8.20, €12.30 to destinations elsewhere. Airmail parcels up to 1kg are €10.30/21 within Europe/elsewhere.

TELEPHONE

Calling from a private phone is most expensive between 9am and 6pm. From telephone boxes, city calls cost €0.10 per minute, calls to anywhere else in Germany €0.20 per minute.

EMERGENCY NUMBERS

- Ambulance ☎ 112
- Fire ☎ 112
- Police ☎ 110
- ADAC breakdown service ☎ 0180-222 2222

Expensive reverse-charge (collect) calls can be made to some countries through home-direct services. Check with your long-distance carrier or phone company before you leave home. The best bet is to have somebody at home use their cheap rates to call you.

For directory assistance within Germany call ☎ 118 33 (☎ 118 37 in English); both cost €0.25 plus €0.99 per minute. International information is ☎ 118 34 (€0.55 per 20 seconds).

Mobile Phones

Mobile phones ('handies') are ubiquitous in Germany; the main operators are T-Mobile, Vodafone, O2 and E-Plus. You can pick up a pre-pay SIM card for around €30; top-up cards are available from kiosks, various shops and vending machines. Mobile numbers generally begin with a ☎ 016 or ☎ 017 prefix. Calling from a landline costs up to €0.54 per minute.

Phone Codes

The country code for Germany is ☎ 49. To ring abroad from Germany, dial ☎ 00 followed by the country code, area code and number.

An operator can be reached on ☎ 0180-200 1033.

Phonecards

Most pay phones in Germany accept only phonecards, available for €5, €10 and €20 at post offices, news kiosks, tourist offices and banks. One call unit costs a little more than €0.06 from a private telephone and €0.10 from a public phone.

TIME

Germany runs on Western European time, one hour ahead of GMT.

TRAVELLERS WITH DISABILITIES

Germany is fair at best (but better than much of Europe) for the needs of physically disabled travellers, with access ramps for wheelchairs and/or lifts in some public buildings.

Deutsche Bahn operates a **Mobility Service Centre** (☎ 01805-512 512; 8am-8pm Mon-Fri, 8am-2pm Sat) whose operators can answer questions about station and train access. With one day's notice, they can also arrange for someone to meet you at your destination.

VISAS

Citizens of the European Union and some other Western European countries can enter Germany on an official identity card. Americans, Australians, Canadians, Israelis, Japanese, New Zealanders and Singaporeans require only a valid passport (no visa). Germany is also part of the Schengen visa scheme (see p1109). Three months is the usual limit of stay, less for citizens of some developing countries.

WORK

With unemployment always high, Germany offers limited prospects for employment unless you have high-level specialist skills such as IT expertise. EU citizens can work in Germany with an *Aufenthaltserlaubnis* (residency permit); non-EU citizens require a work permit as well.

TRANSPORT IN GERMANY

GETTING THERE & AWAY

Air

The main arrival and departure points in Germany used to be Frankfurt-am-Main, and Munich. But with the explosion of budget carriers, almost any town with a tarmac seems to be getting a few flights. Places such as Düsseldorf, Berlin, Nuremberg and even Baden-Baden have cheap flights to parts of Europe. See p1112 for details on how you can find cheap flights within Europe.

Ryanair, easyJet, Air Berlin, DBA and Germanwings are among the foremost cheap options in Germany, but don't count Lufthansa out: it has been aggressively competing on price as well.

The following airlines all fly to/from Germany:

Air Berlin (code AB; ☎ 01805-737 800; www.airberlin.de)
Alitalia (code AZ; ☎ 01805-074 747; www.alitalia.it)
British Airways (code BA; ☎ 01805-266 522; www.britishairways.com)
Czech Airlines (code OK; ☎ 01805-006 737; www.csa.cz)
DBA (code DI; ☎ 0900 1100322; www.flydba.com)
easyJet (code BH; ☎ 01803-654 321; www.easyjet.com)
Germania Express (code ST; ☎ 01805-737 100; www.gexx.de)
Germanwings (code 4U; ☎ 01805-955 855; www.germanwings.com)
Iberia (code IB; ☎ 01803-000 613; www.iberia.es)
LOT (code LO; ☎ 01803-000 336; www.lot.com)
Lufthansa (code LH; ☎ 01803-803 803; www.lufthansa.com)
Ryanair (code FR; ☎ 0190-170 100; www.ryanair.com)
SAS (code SK; ☎ 01803-234 023; www.scandinavian.net)
Wizzair (code W6; www.wizzair.com)

Land

BUS

Travelling by bus between Germany and the rest of Europe is cheaper than by train or plane, but journeys will take a lot longer.

Eurolines is a consortium of national bus companies operating routes throughout the continent. Sample one-way fares and travel times include: London–Frankfurt (€80, 16 hours); Amsterdam–Frankfurt (€39, eight hours); Paris–Hamburg (€69, 11½ hours); Paris–Cologne (€39, 6½ hours); Prague–Berlin (€29, seven hours) and Barcelona–Frankfurt (€89, 20 hours). Eurolines has a discounted youth fare for those under-26 that saves you around 10%. Tickets can be purchased throughout Germany at most train stations. Eurolines' German arm is **Deutsche-Touring** (☎ 069-790 350; www.deutsche-touring.com).

CAR & MOTORCYCLE

Germany is served by an excellent highway system. If you're coming from the UK, the quickest option is the Channel Tunnel. Ferries take longer but are cheaper. You can be in Germany three hours after the ferry docks.

Within Europe, autobahns and highways become jammed on weekends in summer and before and after holidays. This is especially true where border checks are still carried out, such as going to/from the Czech

Republic and Poland. For details on road rules when driving in Germany, see p550.

TRAIN

A favourite way to get to Germany from elsewhere in Europe is by train.

Long-distance trains between major German cities and other countries are called EuroCity (EC) trains. The main German hubs with the best connections for major European cities are Hamburg (Scandinavia); Cologne (Thalsys trains to France, Belgium and the Netherlands, with Eurostar connections from Brussels going on to London); Munich (southern and southeastern Europe) and Berlin (Eastern Europe).

Often longer international routes are served by at least one day train and often a night train as well.

Sea

If you're heading to/from the UK or Scandinavia, port options include Hamburg, Lübeck, Rostock, Sassnitz and Kiel. The Puttgarden–Rodbyhavn ferry to Copenhagen is popular. In eastern Germany, ferries run daily between Trelleborg (Sweden) and Sassnitz, on Rügen Island (p472).

There are daily services between Kiel and Gothenburg (Sweden) and Oslo (Norway). The Kiel–Gothenburg trip takes 13½ hours and costs from €37 to €85. A ferry between Travemünde (near Lübeck) and Trelleborg (Sweden) runs one to four times daily. The journey takes seven hours and costs from €20 to €40. Car-ferry service is good from Gedser (Denmark) to Rostock.

GETTING AROUND

Air

There are lots of flights within the country, many by budget carriers such as Air Berlin, DBA and Germanwings. See opposite for additional details. Note that with check-in times and the like, flying is often not as efficient as a fast train.

Bicycle

Radwandern (bicycle touring) is very popular in Germany. Pavements are often divided into separate sections for pedestrians and cyclists – be warned that these divisions are taken very seriously. Favoured routes include the Rhine, Moselle, Elbe and Danube Rivers and the Lake Constance area. Of course, cycling is strictly *verboten* (forbidden) on the autobahns. Hostel-to-hostel biking is an easy way to go, and route guides are often sold at DJH hostels. There are well-equipped cycling shops in almost every town, and a fairly active market for used touring bikes.

Simple three-gear bicycles can be hired from around €10/35 per day/week, and more robust mountain bikes from €15/50. DB publishes *Bahn&Bike*, an excellent annual handbook (in German) covering bike rental and repair shops, routes, maps and other resources. **DB** (☎ 0180-515 14 14; www.bahn.de/bahnundbike) also has extensive live information on bike rentals and carriage.

A separate ticket must be purchased whenever you carry your bike on trains (generally €3 to €6). Many trains (excluding ICEs) have at least one 2nd-class carriage with a bicycle compartment.

Germany's main cycling organisation is the **Allgemeiner Deutscher Fahrrad Club** (ADFC; ☎ 0421-346 290; www.adfc.de).

Boat

Boats are most likely to be used for basic transport when travelling to or between the Frisian Islands, though tours along the Rhine, Elbe and Moselle Rivers are also popular. During summer there are frequent services on Lake Constance but, with the exception of the Constance–Meersburg and the Friedrichshafen–Romanshorn car ferries, these boats are really more tourist crafts than a transport option. From April to October, excursion boats ply lakes and rivers in Germany and can be a lovely way to see the country.

Bus

The bus network in Germany functions primarily in support of the train network. That is, they go to destinations that are not serviced by trains. Bus stations or stops are usually located near the train station in any town. Consider using buses when you want to cut across two train lines and avoid long train rides to and from a transfer point. A good example of where to do this is in the Alps, where the best way to follow the peaks is by bus.

Within Germany **Eurolines** (☎ 069-790 350) operates as Deutsche-Touring GmbH; services include the Romantic and Castle Roads buses in southern Germany, as well as organised bus tours of Germany lasting a week or more.

Car & Motorcycle

AUTOMOBILE ASSOCIATIONS

Germany's main motoring organisation is the Munich-based **Allgemeiner Deutscher Auto mobil Club** (ADAC; ☎ 089-767 60; www.adac.de), which has offices in all major cities.

DRIVING LICENCE

Visitors do not need an international driving licence to drive in Germany; technically you should carry an official translation of your licence with you, but in practice this is rarely necessary.

FUEL & SPARE PARTS

Prices for fuel vary from €1.30 to €1.35 per litre for unleaded regular. Avoid buying fuel at the more expensive autobahn filling stations. Petrol stations are generally easy to find, although they can be scarce in the centres of many towns.

HIRE

You usually must be at least 21 years of age to hire a car in Germany. You'll need to show your licence and passport, and make sure you keep the insurance certificate for the vehicle with you at all times.

Germany's four main rental companies are **Avis** (☎ 0180-555 77; www.avis.de), **Europcar** (☎ 0180-580 00; www.europcar.de), **Hertz** (☎ 0180-533 3535; www.hertz.de) and **Sixt** (☎ 0180-526 0250; www.sixt.de).

INSURANCE

You must have third-party insurance to enter Germany with a vehicle.

ROAD CONDITIONS

The autobahn system of motorways runs throughout Germany. Road signs (and most motoring maps) indicate national autobahn routes in blue with an 'A' number, while international routes have green signs with an 'E'. Though efficient, the autobahns are often busy, and visitors frequently have trouble coping with the high speeds. Secondary roads (usually designated with a 'B' number) are easier on the nerves and much more scenic, but can be slow going.

Cars are impractical in urban areas. Vending machines on many streets sell parking vouchers which must be displayed clearly behind the windscreen. Leaving your car in a central *Parkhaus* (car park) costs roughly €10 per day or €1.25 per hour.

ROAD RULES

Road rules are easy to understand and standard international signs are in use. You drive on the right, and most cars are right-hand drive. Right of way is usually signed, with major roads given priority, but on unmarked intersections traffic coming from the right always has right of way.

The usual speed limits are 50km/h in built-up areas and 100km/h on the open road. The speed on autobahns is unlimited, though there's an advisory speed of 130km/h; exceptions are clearly signposted.

The blood-alcohol limit for drivers is 0.05%. Obey the road rules carefully: the German police are very efficient and issue heavy on-the-spot fines. Germany also has one of the highest concentrations of speed cameras in Europe.

Local Transport

Public transport is excellent within big cities and small towns, and is generally based on buses, *Strassenbahn* (trams), S-Bahn and/or U-Bahn (underground trains). Tickets cover all forms of transit; fares are determined by zones or time travelled, sometimes both. Multiticket strips and day passes are generally available offering better value than single-ride tickets.

Make certain that you have a ticket when boarding – only buses and some trams let you buy tickets from the driver. In some cases you will have to validate it on the platform or once aboard. Ticket inspections are frequent (especially at night and on holidays) and the fine is a non-negotiable €30 or more.

Train

Operated almost entirely by Deutsche Bahn (DB; www.bahn.de), the German train system is the finest in Europe, and is generally the best way to get around the country.

Trains run on an interval system, so wherever you're heading, you can count on a service at least every two hours. Schedules are integrated throughout the country so that connections between trains are time-saving and tight, often only five minutes. Of course this means that when a train is late, connections are missed and you can find yourself stuck waiting for the next train.

CLASSES

It's rarely worth buying a 1st-class ticket on German trains; 2nd class is usually quite comfortable. There's more difference between the train classifications – basically the faster a train travels, the plusher (and more expensive) it is.

Train types include:

ICE InterCityExpress services run at speeds up to 300km/h. The trains are very comfortable and feature restaurant cars.
IC/EC Called InterCity or EuroCity, these are the premier conventional trains of DB. When trains are crowded, the open-seating coaches are much more comfortable than the older carriages with compartments.
RE RegionalExpress trains are local trains that make limited stops. They are fairly fast and run at one- or two-hourly intervals.
RB RegionalBahn are the slowest DB trains, not missing a single cow town.
S-Bahn These DB-operated trains run frequent services in larger urban areas. Not to be confused with U-Bahns, which are run by local authorities who don't honour rail passes.
EN, ICN, D These are night trains, although an occasional D may be an extra daytime train.

COSTS

Standard DB ticket prices are distance-based. You will usually be sold a ticket for the shortest distance to your destination.

Sample fares for one-way, 2nd-class ICE travel include Hamburg–Munich €115, Frankfurt-am-Main–Berlin €98 and Frankfurt-am-Main–Munich €75. Tickets are good for four days from the day you tell the agent your journey will begin, and you can make unlimited stopovers along your route during that time. In this chapter train fares given between towns are all undiscounted second class.

There are hosts of special fares that allow you to beat the high cost of regular tickets. DB is now selling tickets like airlines (ie trains with light loads may have tickets available at a discount). The key is to ask at the ticket counters. Most DB personnel are happy to help you sort through the thicket of ticket prices.

The following are among the most popular train fares offered by DB (2nd class):

BahnCard 25/50/100 Only worthwhile for extended visits to Germany, these discount cards entitle holders to 25/50/100% off regular fares and cost €50/200/3000.
Schönes Wochenende 'Good Weekend' tickets allow unlimited use of RE, RB and S-Bahn trains on a Saturday or Sunday between midnight and 3am the next day, for up to five people travelling together, or one or both parents and all their children/grandchildren for €28. They are best suited to weekend day trips from urban areas.
Sparpreis Round-trip tickets offered at major discounts.
Surf&Rail As the name implies these are bargains found online. Think €59 round-trip Munich-Berlin.

RESERVATIONS

Nearly all DB stations offer the option of buying tickets with credit cards at machines for long-haul trips; these usually have English-language options, but if in doubt consult the ticket window. Buying a ticket or supplement *(Zuschlag)* from a conductor carries a penalty (€1.50 to €4.50). If you're stuck you can *technically* use a credit card on the train, but in practice it may not be possible.

On some trains there are no conductors at all, and roving inspectors enforce compliance. If you are caught travelling without a valid ticket the fine is €30, no excuses.

During peak periods, a seat reservation (€3) on a long-distance train can mean the difference between squatting near the toilet or relaxing in your own seat. Express reservations can be made at the last minute.

SCHEDULE INFORMATION

The DB website (www.bahn.de) is excellent. There is extensive info in English and you can use it to sort out all the discount offers and schemes. In addition it has an excellent schedule feature that works not just for Germany but the rest of Europe.

For a phone schedule and fare information (available in English), call ☎ 01805-996 633 (€0.13 per minute).

TRAIN PASSES

Agencies outside Germany sell German Rail passes for unlimited travel on all DB trains for a number of days in a 30-day period. Sample 2nd-class prices for adults/under 26 are €160/130 for four days. Most Eurail and Inter-Rail passes are valid in Germany.

Greece

There *is* something magical about Greece. It's the alluring combination of the magnificent archaeological sites that vividly recall Greece's rich past and the magnetism of more than 1400 islands harbouring breathtaking beaches that guarantee you a deep tan while soaking up a chilled-out vibe. It's a combination that makes for guilt-free travel – a slice of history served alongside a healthy slice of hedonism – and that makes Greece one of the most popular destinations on the planet.

While this is the Greece for most tourists, there's plenty to occupy travellers with more adrenalin-focussed activities in mind. Intrepid visitors can mountain climb, hike, windsurf and even hit the ski slopes. No matter what your aspirations, you cannot wander far without stumbling across a broken column, a crumbling bastion or a tiny Byzantine church, each neglected and forgotten but retaining an aura of their former glory.

Perhaps, though, the true allure of Greece is due to less tangible attributes – the dazzling clarity of the light, the floral aromas that permeate the air, the spirit of the place – for there is hardly a grove, mountain or stream that is not sacred to a deity, and the ghosts of the past still linger everywhere.

Among the myriad attractions, travellers to Greece inevitably end up with a favourite site they long to return to – get out there and find yours.

FAST FACTS

- **Area** 131,944 sq km
- **Capital** Athens
- **Currency** euro (€); A$1 = €0.60; ¥100 = €0.67; NZ$1 = €0.50; UK£1 = €1.48; US$1 = €0.78
- **Famous for** ancient ruins, beautiful beaches
- **Official Language** Greek
- **Phrases** *yasas* (hello); *andio* (goodbye); *parakalo* (please); *efharisto* (thank you); *ne* (yes); *ohi* (no)
- **Population** 11 million
- **Telephone Codes** country code ☎ 30; international access code ☎ 00; reverse-charge code ☎ 161

HIGHLIGHTS

- In Athens, savour your first glimpse of the **Acropolis** (p564), the most important monument of the ancient world.
- Meander through the atmospheric streets of the largest inhabited medieval town in Europe, **Rhodes** (p615).
- Dash off a quick 100m at ancient **Olympia** (p580), the evocative birthplace of the games.
- Experience the dramatic **volcanic caldera** (p604) of incomparable Santorini, arguably the most spectacular Greek dot on the map.
- Sip sunset drinks on the seafront in the beautiful Venetian town of **Nafplio** (p576), one of Greece's most romantic destinations.

ITINERARIES

- **One week** Explore Athens' museums and ancient sites on day one before spending a couple of days in the Peloponnese visiting Nafplio, Mycenae and Olympia, followed by four days in the Cyclades.
- **One month** Give yourself some more time in Athens and the Peloponnese, then island-hop through the Ionians for a few days. Explore the Zagoria villages before travelling back to Athens via Meteora and Delphi. Take a ferry from Piraeus to Chios, then island-hop through the northeastern Aegean Islands, the Dodecanese and the Cyclades over a couple of weeks.

HOW MUCH?

- **Local telephone call** €0.25 per min
- **Minimum taxi fare** €3
- **International Herald Tribune newspaper** €2
- **Coffee** €2.50-3.50
- **Can of soft drink** €1

LONELY PLANET INDEX

- **1L petrol** €1-1.20
- **1L bottled water** €1.30
- **Bottle of beer** €2.50
- **Souvenir T-shirt** €13
- **Gyros** €2

CLIMATE & WHEN TO GO

Greece's climate is typically Mediterranean with mild, wet winters followed by very hot, dry summers. Spring and autumn are the best times to visit – the weather is fine and the beaches uncrowded. Winter is quiet; the islands are in hibernation between late November and early April. Easter is when Greece starts repainting and rolling up the shutters, and from late June until mid-September it's sheer summer madness – while party people will enjoy this, vacant rooms and stretches of sand are rare.

HISTORY

With its strategic position at the crossroads of Europe and Asia, Greece has endured a long and turbulent history. During the Bronze Age (3000–1200 BC in Greece), the advanced Cycladic, Minoan and Mycenaean civilisations flourished. The Mycenaeans were swept aside in the 12th century BC by the warrior-like Dorians, who introduced Greece to the Iron Age. The next 400 years are often referred to as the dark ages, a period about which little is known.

By 800 BC, when Homer's *Odyssey* and *Iliad* were first written down, Greece was undergoing a cultural and military revival with the evolution of the city-states, the most powerful of which were Athens and Sparta. Greater Greece, Magna Graecia, was created, with southern Italy as an important component. The unified Greeks repelled the Persians twice, at Marathon (490 BC) and Salamis (480 BC). Victory over Persia was followed by unparalleled growth and prosperity known as the classical (or Golden) age.

The Golden Age

During this period, Pericles commissioned the Parthenon, Sophocles wrote *Oedipus the King* and Socrates taught young Athenians to think. The Golden Age ended with the Peloponnesian War (431–404 BC), when the militaristic Spartans defeated the Athenians. They failed to notice the expansion of Macedonia under King Philip II, who easily conquered the war-weary city-states.

Philip's ambitions were surpassed by those of his son, Alexander the Great, who marched triumphantly into Asia Minor, Egypt, Persia and what are now parts of Afghanistan and India. In 323 BC he met an untimely death at the age of 33, and his generals divided his empire between themselves.

Roman Rule & the Byzantine Empire

Roman incursions into Greece began in 205 BC. By 146 BC, Greece and Macedonia had become Roman provinces. After the subdivision of the Roman Empire into eastern and western empires in AD 395, Greece became part of the eastern (Byzantine) Empire, based at Constantinople.

In the centuries that followed, Venetians, Franks, Normans, Slavs, Persians, Arabs and, finally, Turks took turns chipping away at the Byzantine Empire.

The Ottoman Empire & Independence

After the end of the Byzantine Empire in 1453, when Constantinople fell to the Turks, most of Greece became part of the Ottoman Empire. Crete was not captured until 1670, leaving Corfu as the only island not occupied by the Turks. By the 19th century the Ottoman Empire was in decline. The Greeks, seeing nationalism sweep through Europe, fought the War of Independence (1821–32). The great powers – Britain, France and Russia – intervened in 1827, and Ioannis Kapodistrias was elected the first Greek president.

Kapodistrias was assassinated in 1831 and the European powers stepped in once again, declaring that Greece should become a monarchy. In January 1833, Otho of Bavaria was installed as king. His ambition, called the Great Idea, was to unite all the lands of the Greek people to the Greek motherland. In 1862 he was peacefully ousted and the Greeks chose George I, a Danish prince, as king.

During WWI, Prime Minister Venizelos allied Greece with France and Britain. King Constantine (George's son), who was married to the Kaiser's sister Sophia, disputed this and left the country.

Smyrna & WWII

After the war, Venizelos resurrected the Great Idea. Underestimating the newfound power of Turkey under the leadership of Atatürk, he sent forces to occupy Smyrna (the present-day Turkish port of İzmir), with its large Greek population. The army was heavily defeated and this led to a brutal population exchange between the two countries in 1923.

In 1930 George II, Constantine's son, was reinstated as king and appointed the dictator General Metaxas as prime minister. Metaxas' grandiose ambition was to combine aspects of Greece's ancient and Byzantine past to create a Third Greek Civilisation. However, his chief claim to fame is his celebrated *ohi* (no) to Mussolini's request to allow Italian troops into Greece in 1940.

Greece fell to Germany in 1941 and resistance movements, polarised into royalist and communist factions, staged a bloody civil war lasting until 1949. The civil war was the trigger for a mass exodus that saw almost one million Greeks head off to places such as Australia, Canada and the USA. Entire villages were abandoned as people gambled on a new start in cities such as Melbourne, Toronto, Chicago and New York.

The Colonels' Coup

Continuing political instability led to the colonels' coup d'etat in 1967. King Constantine (son of King Paul, who succeeded George II) staged an unsuccessful countercoup and fled the country. The colonels' junta distinguished itself with its appalling brutality, repression and political incompetence. In 1974 they attempted to assassinate Cyprus' leader, Archbishop Makarios, and when he escaped the junta replaced him with the extremist Nikos Samson, prompting Turkey to occupy North Cyprus. The continued Turkish occupation of Cyprus remains one of the most contentious issues in Greek politics. The junta had little choice but to hand back power to the people. In November 1974 a plebiscite voted against restoration of the monarchy. Greece became a republic with the right-wing New Democracy (ND) party taking power.

The Socialist 1980s

In 1981 Greece entered the European Community (now the EU). Andreas Papandreou's Panhellenic Socialist Movement (Pasok) won the next election, giving Greece its first socialist government. Pasok promised the removal of US air bases and withdrawal from NATO, but delivered only rising unemployment and spiralling debt.

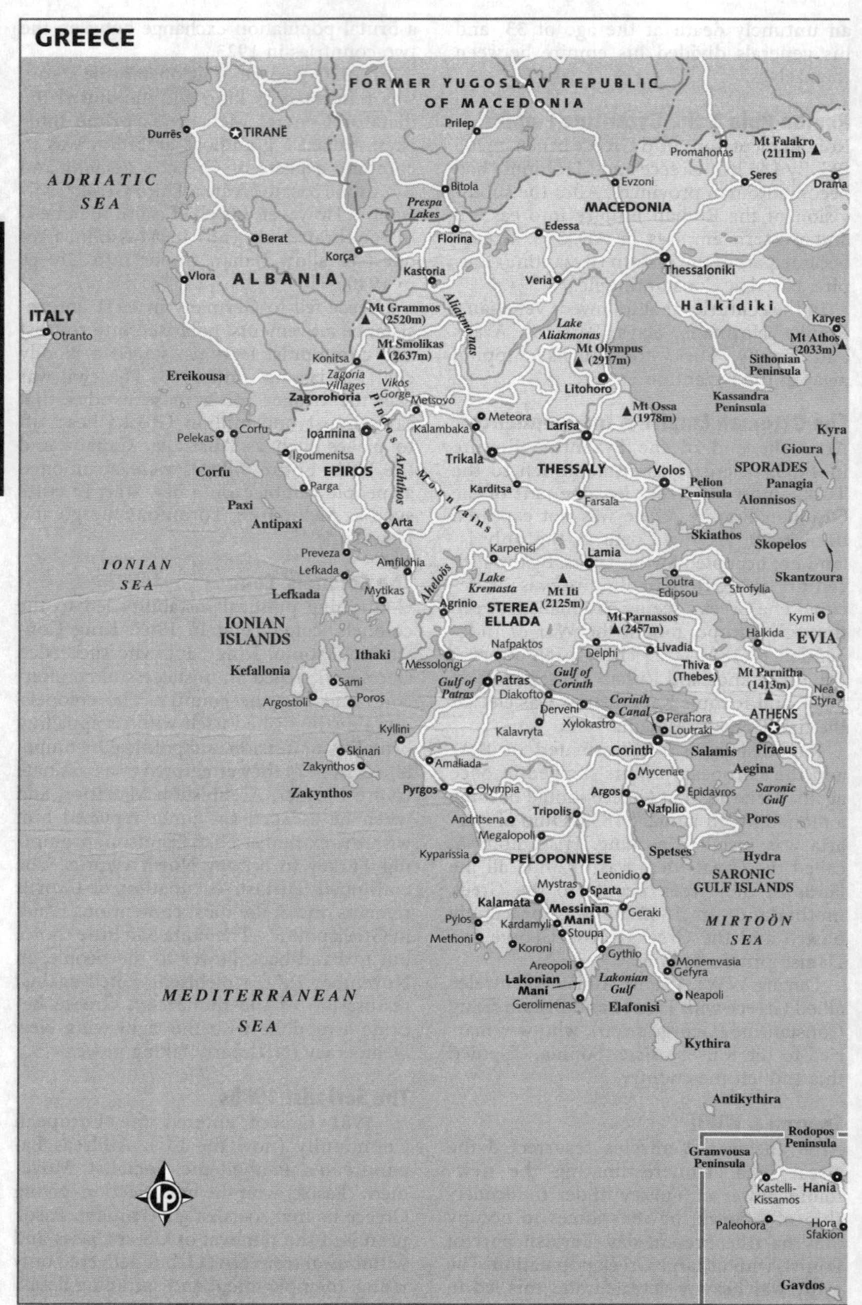
GREECE
FORMER YUGOSLAV REPUBLIC OF MACEDONIA
Durrës
TIRANË
Prilep
Mt Falakro (2111m)
Promahonas
ADRIATIC SEA
Bitola
Evzoni
Seres
Drama
Prespa Lakes
MACEDONIA
Berat
Edessa
Florina
Korça
Thessaloniki
Kastoria
Vlora
ALBANIA
Veria
ITALY
Otranto
Mt Grammos (2520m)
Aliakmonas
Halkidiki
Lake Aliakmonas
Karyes
Mt Smolikas (2637m)
Mt Olympus (2917m)
Mt Athos (2033m)
Konitsa
Sithonian Peninsula
Ereikousa
Zagoria Villages
Vikos Gorge
Litohoro
Zagorohoria
Metsovo
Kassandra Peninsula
Mt Ossa (1978m)
Pindos
Meteora
Pelekas
Corfu
Ioannina
Kalambaka
Larisa
Kyra
Gioura
Igoumenitsa
Trikala
SPORADES
Corfu
EPIROS
THESSALY
Volos
Arahthos
Mountains
Panagia
Parga
Karditsa
Pelion Peninsula
Alonnisos
Paxi
Farsala
Antipaxi
Arta
Skiathos
Skopelos
Preveza
Karpenisi
Lamia
IONIAN SEA
Lefkada
Amfilohia
Skantzoura
Lake Kremasta
Mt Iti (2125m)
Loutra Edipsou
Strofylia
Lefkada
Mytikas
Aheloös
Agrinio
STEREA ELLADA
Kymi
IONIAN ISLANDS
Mt Parnassos (2457m)
Halkida
EVIA
Nafpaktos
Ithaki
Livadia
Messolongi
Delphi
Thiva (Thebes)
Kefallonia
Mt Parnitha (1413m)
Gulf of Patras
Patras
Gulf of Corinth
Sami
Nea Styra
Diakofto
Argostoli
Poros
Corinth Canal
Derveni
ATHENS
Perahora
Xylokastro
Kalavryta
Loutraki
Kyllini
Corinth
Salamis
Piraeus
Skinari
Amaliada
Aegina
Zakynthos
Mycenae
Pyrgos
Olympia
Argos
Epidavros
Saronic Gulf
Zakynthos
Nafplio
Tripolis
Poros
Andritsena
Megalopoli
Spetses
Kyparissia
PELOPONNESE
Hydra
Leonidio
SARONIC GULF ISLANDS
Mystras
Sparta
Kalamata
Messinian Mani
Geraki
MIRTOÖN SEA
Pylos
Kardamyli
Stoupa
Methoni
Koroni
Gythio
Monemvasia
Areopoli
Gefyra
Lakonian Mani
Lakonian Gulf
MEDITERRANEAN SEA
Gerolimenas
Neapoli
Elafonisi
Kythira
Antikythira
Rodopos Peninsula
Gramvousa Peninsula
Kastelli-Kissamos
Hania
Paleohora
Hora Sfakion
Gavdos

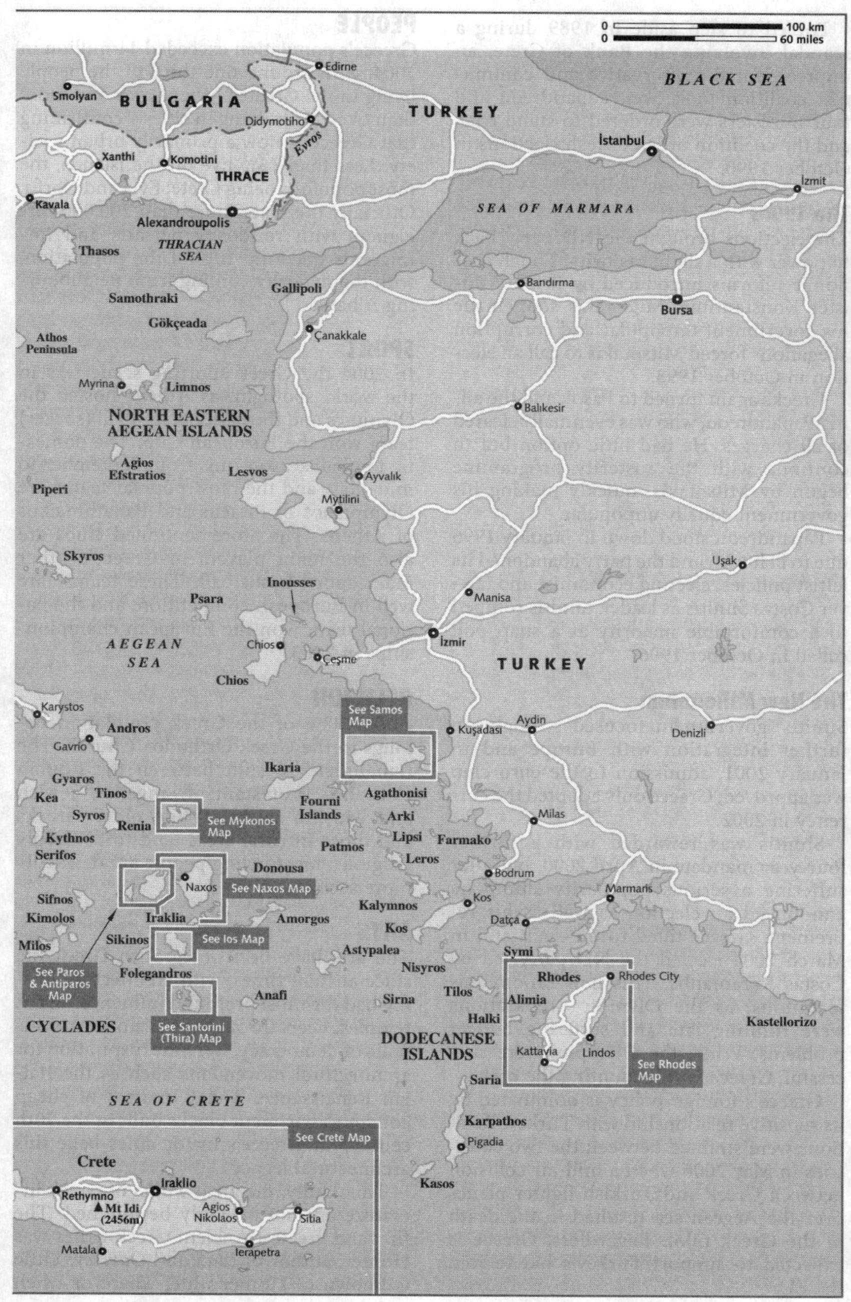
0 100 km
0 60 miles
BLACK SEA
Edirne
Smolyan
BULGARIA
TURKEY
Didymotiho
Evros
İstanbul
Xanthi
Komotini
THRACE
İzmit
Kavala
Alexandroupolis
SEA OF MARMARA
THRACIAN SEA
Thasos
Samothraki
Gallipoli
Bandırma
Bursa
Gökçeada
Athos Peninsula
Çanakkale
Myrina
Limnos
NORTH EASTERN AEGEAN ISLANDS
Balıkesir
Agios Efstratios
Lesvos
Ayvalık
Piperi
Mytilini
Skyros
Uşak
Inousses
Psara
Manisa
AEGEAN SEA
Chios
İzmir
Çeşme
TURKEY
Chios
Karystos
See Samos Map
Andros
Kuşadası
Aydin
Denizli
Gavrio
Ikaria
Gyaros
Agathonisi
Kea
Tinos
Fourni Islands
Arki
Syros
Renia
See Mykonos Map
Milas
Kythnos
Lipsi
Farmako
Serifos
Patmos
Leros
Donousa
Bodrum
Naxos
See Naxos Map
Sifnos
Marmaris
Kos
Kimolos
Iraklia
Amorgos
Kalymnos
Datça
Kos
Milos
Sikinos
See Ios Map
Astypalea
Symi
See Paros & Antiparos Map
Folegandros
Nisyros
Rhodes
Rhodes City
Anafi
Tilos
Alimia
Sirna
Halki
Kastellorizo
CYCLADES
See Santorini (Thira) Map
DODECANESE ISLANDS
Kattavia
Lindos
See Rhodes Map
Saria
SEA OF CRETE
Karpathos
See Crete Map
Pigadia
Crete
Kasos
Iraklio
Rethymno
Mt Idi (2456m)
Agios Nikolaos
Sitia
Matala
Ierapetra

GREECE

Forced to step aside in 1989 during a scandal involving the Bank of Crete, an unprecedented conservative and communist coalition took over. Papandreou and four ministers were ordered to stand trial, and the coalition ordered fresh elections in October 1990.

The 1990s

The elections brought the ND party back to power with a slight majority. Tough economic reforms introduced by Prime Minister Konstantinos Mitsotakis soon made his government unpopular and corruption allegations forced Mitsotakis to call an election in October 1993.

Greeks again turned to Pasok and the ailing Papandreou, who was eventually cleared of all charges. He had little option but to continue with the austerity programme begun by Mitsotakis, quickly making his government equally unpopular.

Papandreou stood down in January 1996 due to ill health and the party abandoned its leftist policies, electing economist and lawyer Costas Simitis as leader. Simitis romped to a comfortable majority at a snap poll called in October 1996.

The New Millennium

Simitis' government focused strongly on further integration with Europe and in January 2001, admission to the euro club was approved; Greece duly adopted the currency in 2002.

Simitis was rewarded with a further four-year mandate in April 2000, but after suffering a serious popularity slump he announced an election as well as his retirement. Greece tilted to the right and in March 2004 elected the ND party led by Costas Karamanlis. This new broom was fortuitous, as the Olympic preparations were running late and suffering budget problems. While the Olympics were successful, Greece is still counting the cost.

Greece's foreign policy is dominated by its sensitive relationship with Turkey. Relations were strained between the two countries in May 2006 when a mid-air collision between Greek and Turkish fighter planes over the Aegean sea resulted in the death of the Greek pilot. Regardless, Greece is expected to support Turkey's bid to join the EU.

PEOPLE

Greece's population exceeded 11 million in 2004, with around one-third of the people living in the Greater Athens area and more than two-thirds living in cities – confirming that Greece is now a primarily urban society. Less than 15% live on the islands, the most populous being Crete, Evia and Corfu. Officially there are more than 200,000 foreigners with residency permits and immigrants make up 10% of the population, with the majority coming from neighbouring Albania.

SPORT

In 2004 the Greek sporting scene was in the world spotlight, as Athens hosted the Olympics and the national football (soccer) team won the European Cup. The domestic football season runs from September to mid-May, and the most popular teams are Olympiakos of Piraeus and Panathinaikos of Athens. The aforementioned clubs are also the main players in Greece's other main sport, basketball. These teams fare well in European competition, and the national team won the European championships in 2005.

RELIGION

About 98% of the Greek population belongs to the Greek Orthodox Church. The remainder are split between the Roman Catholic, Protestant, Evangelist, Jewish and Muslim faiths. While older Greeks and those in rural areas tend to be deeply religious, most young people are decidedly more secular.

ARTS

The arts have been integral to Greek life since ancient times, with architecture having had the most profound influence. Greek temples, seen throughout history as symbolic of democracy, were the inspiration for architectural movements such as the Italian Renaissance. Today, masses of cheap concrete apartment blocks built in the 20th century in Greece's major cities belie this architectural legacy.

Thankfully, the great works of Greek literature are not as easily besmirched. The first and greatest Ancient Greek writer was Homer, author of *Iliad* and *Odyssey*. Little is known of Homer's life; where or when he lived, or whether, as it is alleged, he was blind.

Pindar (c 518–438 BC) is regarded as the pre-eminent lyric poet of ancient Greece and was commissioned to recite his odes at the Olympic Games. The great writers of love poetry were Sappho (6th century BC) and Alcaeus (5th century BC), both of whom lived on Lesvos. Sappho's poetic descriptions of her affections for women gave rise to the term 'lesbian'.

The Alexandrian, Constantine Cavafy (1863–1933), revolutionised Greek poetry by introducing a personal, conversational style. Later, poet George Seferis (1900–71) won the Nobel Prize for literature in 1963, as did Odysseus Elytis (1911–96) in 1979. Nikos Kazantzakis, author of *Zorba the Greek* and numerous novels, plays and poems, is the most famous of 20th-century Greek novelists. Contemporary novelists' works are rarely translated into English.

Greece's most famous painter was a young Cretan called Domenikos Theotokopoulos, who moved to Spain in 1577 and became known as the great El Greco. Famous painters of the 20th century include Konstantinos, Partenis and later, George Bouzianis, whose work can be viewed at the National Art Gallery in Athens.

Music has been a facet of Greek life since ancient times. When visiting Greece today, your trip will inevitably be accompanied by the plucked-string sound of the ubiquitous bouzouki. The bouzouki is one of the main instruments of *rembetika* music – which is in many ways the Greek equivalent of the American blues and has its roots in the sufferings of the refugees from Asia Minor in the 1920s. Alongside the bouzouki, *rembetika* music is accompanied by guitar, violin and accordion.

Dance is also an integral part of Greek life. Whether at a wedding, nightclub or village celebration, traditional dance is widely practised. If you don't see any on your travels, try to catch the Dora Stratou Dance Company (p569) in Athens.

Drama continues to feature in domestic arts, particularly in Athens and Thessaloniki. In summer, Greek dramas are staged in the ancient theatres where they were originally performed.

Greek film has for many years been associated with the work of filmmaker Theo Angelopoulos, who won Cannes' Palme d'Or in 1998 with *An Eternity and One Day*. Since the late '90s, Greek cinema has witnessed a minor renaissance, with films such as *Safe Sex* (2000) luring Greek movie-goers back to the cinema.

Greek TV is dominated by chat shows, sport and foreign movies, only to be interrupted by localised versions of the latest American 'reality TV' hit.

ENVIRONMENT

The Land

Greece sits at the southern tip of the Balkan Peninsula. Of its 1400 islands only 169 are inhabited. The land mass is 131,944 sq km and Greek territorial waters cover a further 400,000 sq km.

Around 80% of Greece is mountainous. The Pindos Mountains in Epiros are the southern extension of the Dinaric Alps, which run the length of former Yugoslavia. The range continues through central Greece and the Peloponnese, and re-emerges in Crete. Less than a quarter of the country is suitable for agriculture.

Greece lies in one of the most seismically active regions in the world; it recorded more than 20,000 earthquakes in the last 40 years – most of them very minor. The activity occurs because the eastern Mediterranean lies at the meeting point of three continental plates: the Eurasian, African and Arabian.

Wildlife

The variety of flora in Greece is unrivalled in Europe, with a dazzling array of spectacular wild flowers best seen in the mountains of Crete and the southern Peloponnese.

You won't encounter many animals in the wild, mainly due to hunting. Wild boar, still found in the north, is a favourite target. Squirrels, rabbits, hares, foxes and weasels are all fairly common on the mainland. Reptiles are well represented by snakes, including several poisonous viper species.

Lake Mikri Prespa in Macedonia has the richest colony of fish-eating birds in Europe, while the Dadia Forest Reserve in Thrace counts such majestic birds as the golden eagle and the giant black vulture among its residents.

The brown bear, Europe's largest land mammal, still survives in very small numbers in the mountains of northern Greece, as does the grey wolf.

Europe's rarest mammal, the monk seal, once very common in the Mediterranean Sea, is now on the brink of extinction in Europe. There are about 400 left in Europe, half of which live in Greece. About 40 frequent the Ionian Sea and the rest are found in the Aegean.

The waters around Zakynthos are home to Europe's last large sea turtle colony, that of the loggerhead turtle *(Careta careta)*. The **Sea Turtle Protection Society of Greece** (☎/fax 21052 31342; www.archelon.gr) runs monitoring programmes and is always on the look-out for volunteers.

National Parks

While facilities in Greek national parks aren't on par with many other countries, all have refuges and some have marked hiking trails. The most visited parks are Mt Parnitha, north of Athens, and the Samaria Gorge on Crete. The others are Vikos-Aoös and Prespa national parks in Epiros; Mt Olympus on the border of Thessaly and Macedonia; and Parnassos and Iti national parks in central Greece. There is also a national marine park off the coast of Alonnisos, and another around the Bay of Laganas area off Zakynthos.

Environmental Issues

Greece is belatedly becoming environmentally conscious but, regrettably, it's too late for some regions. Deforestation and soil erosion are problems that go back thousands of years, with olive cultivation and goats being the main culprits. Forest fires are also a major problem, with an estimated 25,000 hectares destroyed every year. Epiros and Macedonia in northern Greece are the only places where extensive forests remain.

General environmental awareness remains at a depressingly low level, especially where litter is concerned. The problem is particularly bad in rural areas, where roadsides are strewn with aluminium cans and plastic packaging hurled from passing cars.

FOOD & DRINK

Staples & Specialities

SNACKS

Greece has a great range of fast-food options. Foremost among them are the gyros and the souvlaki. The gyros is a giant skewer laden with seasoned meat that grills slowly as it rotates, the meat being steadily trimmed from the outside. Souvlaki are small cubes of meat cooked on a skewer. Both are served wrapped in pitta bread with salad and lashings of tzatziki (a yogurt, cucumber and garlic dip). Other snacks are pretzel rings, spanakopitta (spinach and cheese pie) and *tyropitta* (cheese pie).

STARTERS

Greece is famous for its appetisers, known as *mezedes* (literally, 'tastes'; meze for short). Standards include tzatziki, *melitzanosalata* (aubergine dip), taramasalata (fish-roe dip), *dolmades* (stuffed vine leaves), *fasolia* (beans) and *oktapodi* (octopus). A selection of three or four starters represents a good meal and makes an excellent vegetarian option.

MAIN DISHES

You'll find moussaka (layers of aubergine and mince, topped with béchamel sauce and baked) on every menu, alongside a number of other taverna staples. They include *moschari* (oven-baked veal and potatoes), *keftedes* (meatballs), *stifado* (meat stew), *pastitsio* (baked dish of macaroni with minced meat and béchamel sauce) and *yemista* (either tomatoes or green peppers stuffed with minced meat and rice).

Kalamaria (fried squid) is the most popular (and cheapest) seafood, while *barbouni* (red mullet) and *sifias* (swordfish), sold by the kilogram, tend to be more expensive than meat dishes.

Fortunately for vegetarians, salad is a mainstay of the Greek diet. The most popular is *horiatiki salata,* normally listed on English-language menus as Greek salad. It's a delicious mixed salad comprising cucumbers, peppers, onions, olives, tomatoes and feta cheese and is perfect on a hot day.

DESSERTS

Most Greek desserts are Turkish in origin and are variations on pastry soaked in honey, such as baklava (thin layers of pastry filled with honey and nuts). Delicious Greek yogurt also makes a great dessert, especially with Greek honey – easily the best in the world.

DRINKS

Bottled mineral water is cheap and available everywhere, as are soft drinks and packaged juices. Greece is traditionally a wine-drinking society. Retsina, wine flavoured with pine tree resin, is somewhat of an acquired taste. Fortunately, Greece also produces an increasingly good range of wines from traditional grape varieties.

Mythos, in its distinctive green bottle, is the most common Greek beer, but in many places the choice is either Amstel or Heineken. You can expect to pay about €1 for a can in a supermarket or kiosk, €2 in a restaurant and from €5 for a glass in a club. The most popular aperitif is the aniseed-flavoured ouzo, which is mixed with water to taste.

Where to Eat & Drink

The most common variety of restaurant in Greece is the taverna, traditionally an extension of the Greek home table. *Estiatorio* is Greek for restaurant and often has the same dishes as a taverna but with higher prices. A *psistaria* specialises in charcoal-grilled dishes while a *psarotaverna* specialises in fish. *Ouzeria* (ouzo bars) often have such a range of *mezedes* that they can be regarded as eateries.

Kafeneia are the smoke-filled cafés where men gather to drink 'Greek' coffee, play backgammon and cards, and engage in heated political discussion. Every Greek town you'll visit now has at least one café-bar where Greece's youth while away hours over a Nescafé Frappé.

Buying and preparing your own food is easy in Greece – every town of consequence has a supermarket, as well as fruit-and-vegetable shops.

ATHENS ΑΘΗΝΑ

pop 3.7 million

Ancient Athens, named after the goddess of wisdom, Athena, is up there with Rome for its archaeological treasures, classical mythology, sense of history and grandeur, and its lasting influence on Western civilisation. It's just as well it wasn't named after the god of love, Eros, as, until its 2004 Olympics facelift, it was a city few fell for.

The Olympics, while putting a huge dent in the city's bank balance, showed the world that Athens was a city of style and culture, and worthy of more attention than most gave it. Although much of Athens was given a makeover, she's still no beauty, and increasingly suffers from traffic congestion, pollution and urban sprawl.

Take the time to look beneath her skin and you will discover a complex city full of contradictions as only a place with such a long history as hers can be. Funky new cafés sit beside atmospheric neighbourhood *ouzeria,* stylish Michelin-star restaurants sit next door to traditional family tavernas, and *rembetika* is performed at one bar while at a club across the street a DJ spins trance.

Athens is worth visiting just as much for its ancient wonders and splendid artefacts as it is for its contemporary style and buzzy social life.

ORIENTATION

Athens is a sprawling city but most sights are within a manageable distance. Syntagmatos Sq, or Syntagma (*syn*-tag-ma), is the city's heart. Surrounded by luxury hotels, banks, and airline and travel offices, it's dominated by the Greek parliament building. Omonia Sq (Plateia Omonias) is to the north of Syntagma; Gazi, Psyrri and Monastiraki Sq (Plateia Monastirakiou) are to its west; the Plaka district borders it to the south; and Kolonaki is at its east.

ATHENS IN TWO DAYS

Head to the **Acropolis** (p564) early to beat the crowds before exploring the atmospheric Plaka district. Have lunch at **Byzantino** (p568) on the leafy square, before spending the heat of the afternoon at the **National Archaeological Museum** (p565). Enjoy Parthenon views over dinner at **Pil Poul** (p568) or have gyros at **Viasos** (p567).

On the second day, visit the wonderful **Benaki Museum** (p566) or **Museum of Cycladic Art** (p566). Lunch at **Eat** (p568) before shopping Plaka, then rest up for a night out drinking (try **Brettos**, p569), eating (**Taverna tou Psara, p568**) and dancing (hit **Lava Bore**, p569).

GREECE

CENTRAL ATHENS

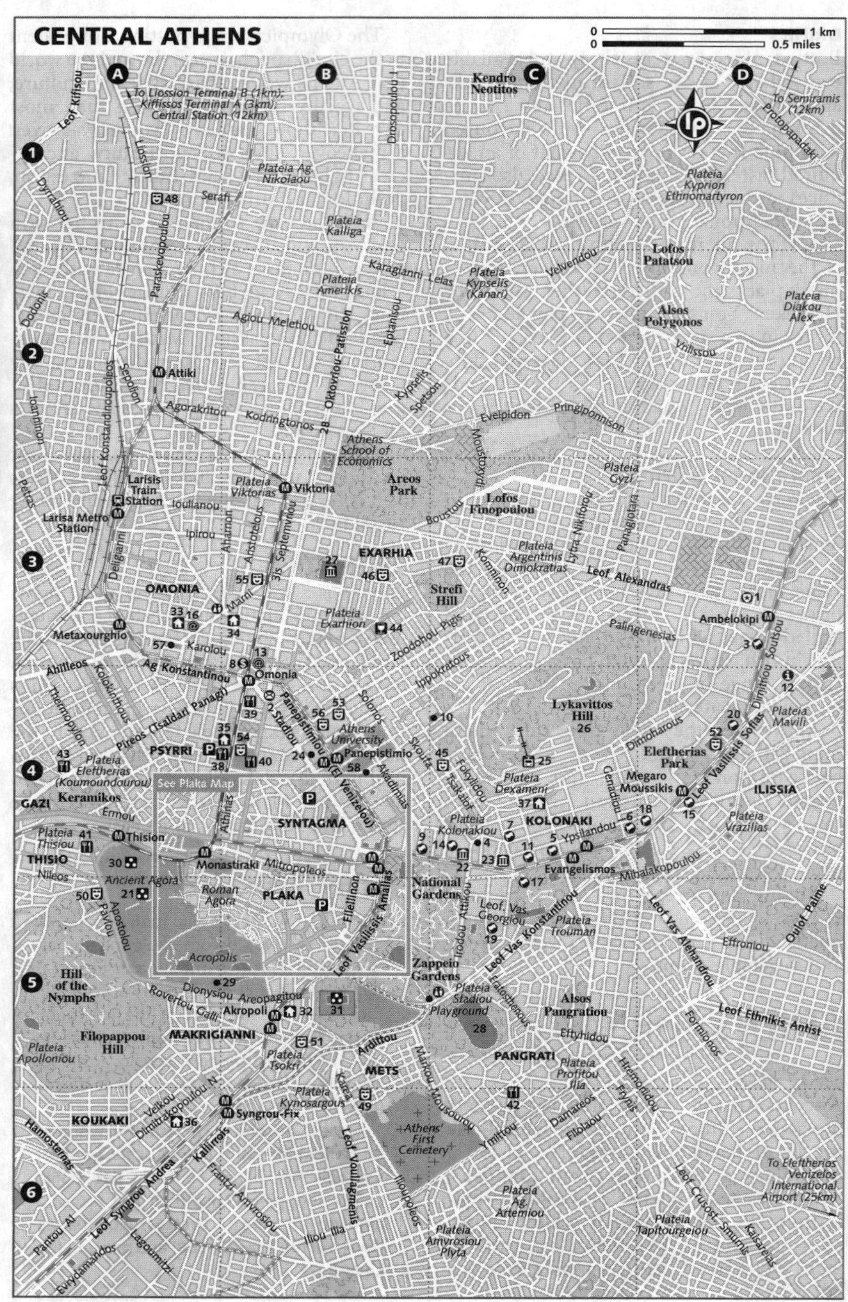

INFORMATION		SIGHTS & ACTIVITIES			
Aliens Bureau	(see 1)	Ancient Agora	21 A5	Marinopoulos Supermarket	39 B4
Athens Police Station	1 D3	Benaki Museum	22 C4	Meat Market	40 B4
Athens' Central Post Office	2 B4	Goulandris Museum of Cycladic & Ancient Greek Art	23 C4	Pil Poul	41 A4
Australian Embassy	3 D3	Hellenic Festival Box Office	24 B4	Spondi	42 C6
British Council	4 C4	Lykavittos Funicular Railway	25 C4	Varoulko	43 A4
British Embassy	5 C4	Lykavittos Hill	26 C4	**DRINKING**	
Canadian Embassy	6 C4	National Archaeological Museum	27 B3	Wonderbar	44 B3
Cypriot Embassy	7 C4	Panathenaic Stadium	28 C5	**ENTERTAINMENT**	
Eurochange	8 B3	Stoa of Eumenes	29 A5	Alekos' Island	45 C4
French Embassy	9 B4	Temple of Hephaestus	30 A4	Aroma	46 B3
French Institute of Athens	10 C4	Temple of Olympian Zeus	31 B5	Decadence	47 C3
German Embassy	11 C4	**SLEEPING**		Gagarin 205 Club	48 A1
Greek National Tourist Organisation/EOT Head Office	12 D4	Athens Backpackers	32 B5	Half Note Jazz Club	49 B6
Internet Cyberzone	13 B3	Athens International Youth Hostel Victor Hugo	33 A3	Kirkis	50 A5
Italian Embassy	14 C4	Elysium Design Hotel	34 B3	Lamda Club	51 B5
Japanese Embassy	15 D4	Fresh	35 B4	Megaron Mousikis	52 D4
Mocafé	16 A3	Marble House Pension	36 A6	Olympia Theatre	53 B4
New Zealand Embassy	17 C4	Periscope	37 C4	Rembetika Stoa Athanaton	54 B4
South African Embassy	18 D4	**EATING**		Rodon Club	55 B3
Tourist Police	(see 12)	Fruit & Vegetable Market	38 B4	Ticket House	56 B4
Turkish Embassy	19 C5			**TRANSPORT**	
US Embassy	20 D4			OSE Office	57 A3
				OSE Office	58 B4

The city's major landmarks, the Acropolis and Lykavittos Hill, serve as good reference points as they're visible from most places.

Omonia is home to pickpockets, prostitutes and drug dealers. Spruced up for the Olympics, its central square is surrounded by commercial franchises and fast-food joints. All of Athens' major central streets meet here. Panepistimiou (El Venizelou) and Stadiou run parallel southeast to Syntagma, while Athinas heads south to the market district of Monastiraki and the nightlife area of Psyrri.

Monastiraki is linked to Syntagma by the pedestrianised shopping street Ermou and Mitropoleos, which skirts the northern edge of Plaka. Plaka, a charming old neighbourhood of labyrinthine streets (now dominated by souvenir shops and tavernas) is nestled on the northeastern slope of the Acropolis with most ancient sites nearby.

INFORMATION

Bookshops

The bigger *periptera* (kiosks) stock a good range of English-language magazines and international newspapers.

Compendium Books (Map p570; ☎ 210 322 1248; Nikis 28, Plaka) Specialises in English-language books and offers an excellent selection of Greek history and literature.

Eleftheroudakis Books Plaka (Map p570; ☎ 210 322 9388; Nikis 20); Syntagma (Map p570; ☎ 210 325 8440; Panepistimiou 17) English-language books. At the Plaka branch, travel guides (including Lonely Planet) are downstairs.

Cultural Centres

These centres hold arts and cultural events, run language courses and screen films. Check the *Kathimerini* supplement in the *International Herald Tribune* for detailed listings.

British Council (Map p562; ☎ 210 369 2333; www.britishcouncil.gr; Plateia Kolonaki 17, Kolonaki)

French Institute of Athens (Map p562; ☎ 210 362 4301; www.ifa.gr; Sina 31, Kolonaki)

Goethe Institut (Map p570; ☎ 210 366 1008; www.goethe.de/athen; Omirou 14-16, Kolonaki)

Emergency

Athens police station (Map p562; ☎ 210 725 7000; Syntagma Sq, Syntagma)

Fire brigade (☎ 199)

First-aid service (☎ 166)

Police emergency (☎ 100)

Tourist police (☎ 171; 24hr) General tourist info and emergency help.

Internet Access

Internet cafés in Athens charge anything from €1.50 to €4 per hour.

Arcade Internet Café (Map p570; ☎ 210 321 0701; Stadiou 5, Syntagma; per hr €3; 9am-10pm Mon-Fri, 10am-10pm Sat) Wide range of services and dedicated ADSL laptop connections.

Internet Cyberzone (Map p562; ☎ 210 520 3939; Satovriandou 7, Omonia; per hr €2.50; 24hr) Prices drop after midnight.

Mocafé (Map p562; ☎ 210 522 7717; cnr Marni & Veranzerou 49, Omonia; per hr €3, laptop per hr €2; 8am-1am) Handily placed near the Youth Hostel Victor Hugo (p566), with wireless.

Laundry

Plaka Laundrette (Map p570; ☎ 210 321 3102; Angelou Geronta 10, Plaka; 5kg wash & dry €9; 8am-7pm Mon-Sat, to 1pm Sun)

Left Luggage

Most hotels store luggage free for guests but this may mean leaving your bags unsecured in a hallway, so check ahead if you need to leave luggage long-term. Facilities are available at the airport and train station.

Medical Services

The *Kathimerini* supplement in the *International Herald Tribune* gives details for hospitals and pharmacies.

Ambulance (☎ 166)

Duty doctor (☎ 105; 2pm-7am)

Duty hospitals (☎ 1434)

Duty pharmacy (☎ 107)

SOS Doctors (☎ 1016; 24hr) Call-out service with multilingual doctors.

Money

Most banks have branches around Plateia Syntagmatos. Both banks and currency exchanges change travellers cheques.

Acropole Foreign Exchange (Map p570; ☎ 210 331 2765; Kydathineon 23, Plaka; 11.30am-6.30pm Mon-Sat) Also offers Western Union services and has an ATM.

Post

Athens' Central Post Office (Map p562; Eolou 100, Omonia; 7.30am-8pm Mon-Fri, to 2pm Sat) All poste restante is sent here unless specified otherwise.

Parcel post office (Map p570; Stadiou 4, Syntagma; 7.30am-2pm Mon-Fri) Parcels over 2kg going abroad must be taken here, unwrapped for inspection.

Syntagma post office (Map p570; ☎ 210 331 9500; cnr Mitropoleos & Plateia Syntagmatos, Syntagma; 7.30am-8pm Mon-Fri, to 2pm Sat, 9am-1.30pm Sun) If staying in Plaka, get poste restante sent here.

Telephone

Public phones are everywhere and take phonecards, readily available from kiosks. See p638 for card denominations.

Toilets

Public toilets are thin on the ground, but fast-food outlets have toilets and you can test the hospitality of tourist-tired Athenians by trying bars or cafés.

Tourist Information

City of Athens Info Line (☎ 195) Info booths are set up in Syntagma Sq during summer.

Greek National Tourist Organisation/EOT Head office (Map p562; ☎ 210 870 7000; www.gnto.gr; Tsoha 7; 9am-2pm Mon-Fri); EOT info desk (☎ 210 353 0445; Arrivals Hall, Eleftherios Venizelos International airport; 9am-8pm Mon-Fri, 10am-7pm Sat & Sun); EOT tourist office (Map p570; ☎ 210 331 0392; Amalias 26; 9am-8pm Mon-Fri, 10am-7pm Sat & Sun)

DANGERS & ANNOYANCES

Like any big city, Athens has its irritations. Many footpaths are marble, which get slippery when wet – ridged rubber soles work best.

Pickpockets are a problem. Be on your guard on the metro, around Omonia, and at the Sunday market. Don't keep valuables in the outer pocket of your day-pack. Better still, don't use a day-pack: they scream 'tourist'!

When taking taxis, establish whether the driver's going to use the meter or negotiate a fair price before you get in. Always ignore drivers' stories that the hotel you've directed them to is closed or full – they're angling for a commission from another hotel that you'll end up paying for. Insist on going where you want.

Bar scams are commonplace, particularly in Plaka and Syntagma. They go something like this: friendly Greek approaches solo male traveller, discovers traveller is new to Athens, and reveals that he, too, is from out of town. However, friendly Greek knows a great bar where they order drinks and equally friendly owner offers another drink. Women appear, more drinks are served and the crunch comes at the end of the night when traveller is hit with an exorbitant bill.

SIGHTS

Acropolis

Athens' most iconic symbol, the **Acropolis** (Map p570; ☎ 210 321 0291; sites & museum adult/concession €12/6, free Sun; 8am-7.30pm Apr-Oct, 8.30am-3pm Nov-Mar) is arguably the most important

CHEAPER BY THE HALF-DOZEN

The €12 admission charge at the Acropolis includes entry to the other significant ancient sites: Ancient Agora, Roman Agora, Keramikos, Temple of Olympian Zeus and the Theatre of Dionysos. The ticket is valid for four days.

ancient monument in the Western world – something not lost on the multitudes of tourists who converge on it every day, so visit early morning or late afternoon.

Pericles commissioned most of its buildings in the 5th century BC, Athens' Golden Age. The entrance is through the **Beule Gate**, a Roman arch added in the 3rd century AD. Beyond this is the **propylaea**, the monumental gate that was the city's entrance in ancient times. Damaged in the 17th century when lightning set off a Turkish gunpowder store, it's since been restored. South of the propylaea is the small, graceful **Temple of Athena Nike** (not accessible).

It's the **Parthenon**, however, that epitomises the glory of ancient Greece. Completed in 438 BC, it's unsurpassed in grace and harmony. To achieve perfect form, its lines were ingeniously curved to counteract optical illusions. The base curves upward slightly towards the ends, and the columns become slightly narrower towards the top – effects that make them look straight. Above the columns are the remains of a Doric frieze, partly destroyed by Venetian shelling in 1687. The best surviving pieces are the controversial Elgin Marbles, carted off to Britain by Lord Elgin in 1801.

To the north is the **Erechtheion** and its much-photographed Caryatids, the six maidens who support its southern portico. These are plaster casts – the originals (except for the one taken by Lord Elgin) are in the **Acropolis Museum** (Map p570; 11am-4.30pm Mon, 8am-4.30pm Tue-Sun Apr-Oct, 11am-2.30pm Mon, 8.30am-3.30pm Tue-Sun Nov-Mar).

South of the Acropolis

The importance of theatre in the everyday lives of Athenians is evident from the dimensions of the enormous **Theatre of Dionysos** (Map p570; ☎ 210 322 4625; adult/concession €2/1; 8am-7pm Apr-Oct, to 3pm Nov-Mar); enter via Dionysiou Areopagitou and Thrasillou Sts. Built between 340 BC and 330 BC on the site of an earlier theatre (dating to the 6th century BC), it held 17,000 people. The **Stoa of Eumenes**, built as a shelter and promenade for theatre audiences, runs west to the **Theatre of Herodes Atticus**, built in Roman times. It's used for performances, but is closed at other times.

Ancient Agora

The **Ancient Agora** (Map p562; ☎ 210 321 0185; Adrianou 24; adult/concession €4/2; 8am-7pm Apr-Oct, to 5pm Nov-Mar) was the marketplace of ancient Athens and the focal point of civic and social life. Socrates spent time here expounding his philosophy. The main monuments are the well-preserved **Temple of Hephaestus** (Map p562), the 11th-century **Church of the Holy Apostles** (Map p570) and the reconstructed **Stoa of Attalos** (Map p570), which houses the site's museum.

Roman Agora

The Romans built their **agora** (Map p570; ☎ 210 324 5220; cnr Pelopida Eolou & Markou Aureliou; adult/concession €2/1; 8am-7pm Apr-Oct, to 5pm Nov-Mar) just east of the ancient Athenian Agora. The wonderful **Tower of the Winds** was built in the 1st century BC by a Syrian astronomer, Andronicus. Each side represents a point of the compass and has a relief carving depicting the associated wind.

Temple of Olympian Zeus

Begun in the 6th century BC, Greece's largest **temple** (Map p562; ☎ 210 922 6330; adult/concession €2/1; 8am-7pm Apr-Oct, to 5pm Nov-Mar), behind Hadrian's Arch, took more than 700 years to build, with Emperor Hadrian overseeing its completion in AD 131. It's impressive for the sheer size of its 104 Corinthian columns – 17m high with a base diameter of 1.7m. East of the temple, the **stadium**, built in the 4th century BC as a venue for the Panathenaic athletic contests, hosted the first modern Olympic Games in 1896.

National Archaeological Museum

One of the world's great museums, the **National Archaeological Museum** (Map p562; ☎ 210 821 7717; www.culture.gr; 28 Patission 44; adult/concession €6/3; 12.30-7pm Mon, 8am-7pm Tue-Fri, 8.30am-3pm Sat & Sun Apr-Oct, 11am-5pm Mon, 8am-5pm Tue-Fri, 8am-3pm Sat & Sun Nov-Mar) contains important finds

GREECE

from major archaeological sites around the country. The crowd-pullers are the exquisite gold artefacts from Mycenae and spectacular Minoan frescoes from Santorini. There are also wonderful collections of sculpture and intricate Cycladic figurines.

Benaki Museum

This superb **museum** (Map p562; ☎ 210 367 1000; www.benaki.gr; cnr Leof Vasilissis Sofias & Koumbari 1, Kolonaki; adult/concession €6/3; 🕑 9am-5pm Mon, Wed, Fri & Sat, to midnight Thu, to 3pm Sun) houses the sumptuous collection of Antoine Benaki, the son of an Alexandrian cotton magnate. The splendid collection includes ancient sculpture, Persian, Byzantine and Coptic objects, Chinese ceramics, icons, El Greco paintings and a fabulous collection of traditional costumes.

Goulandris Museum of Cycladic & Ancient Greek Art

This wonderful private **museum** (Map p562; ☎ 210 722 8321; www.cycladic-m.gr; Neofytou Douka 4; adult/concession €5/2.50; 🕑 10am-4pm Mon & Wed-Fri, to 3pm Sat) was custom-built to display its extraordinary collection of Cycladic art, with an emphasis on the early Bronze Age. It's easy to see how the graceful marble statues influenced the art of Modigliani and Picasso.

Lykavittos Hill

Pine-covered **Lykavittos** (Hill of Wolves; Map p562) is the highest of the eight hills dotted around Athens. From the summit, there are stunning views of the city, the Attic basin and the islands of Salamis and Aegina (pollution permitting of course) that are enchanting at sunset. The open-air Lykavittos Theatre is used for concerts in summer.

The main path to the summit starts at the top of Loukianou, or you can take the **funicular railway** (Map p562; one way/return €2/4; 🕑 9.15am-11.45pm) from the top of Ploutarhou.

Changing of the Guard

The traditionally costumed *evzones* (guards) guarding the **Tomb of the Unknown Soldier** (Map p570), in front of the parliament building on Syntagma, change every hour on the hour. On Sundays at 10.45am, a whole platoon marches down Vasilissis Sofias to the Tomb, accompanied by a band.

FESTIVALS & EVENTS

The annual **Hellenic Festival** (www.greekfestival.gr) is the city's most important cultural event, running from mid-June to August. It features a line-up of international music, dance and theatre at venues across the city. The programme is available online and tickets can be booked at the **festival box office** (Map p562; ☎ bookings 210 327 2000, information 210 928 2900; info@greekfestival.gr).

SLEEPING

Athenians go out late and like to party, so most of these sleeping options are close to the action but quiet. Plaka is popular due to its proximity to the sights, but Omonia's cheap sleeps are still close enough to keep budget travellers happy. Book well ahead for July and August. Most hotels give good discounts in the off season and for longer stays.

Budget

Athens International Youth Hostel Victor Hugo (Map p562; ☎ 210 523 2049; fax 210 523 2540; Victor Hugo 16; large dm/q €8/15) While it's no longer a member of HI (Hostelling International), this hostel (undergoing renovations) is still popular. The dodgy location is a drawback – women shouldn't walk alone here at night.

Student & Travellers' Inn (Map p570; ☎ 210 324 4808; www.studenttravellersinn.com; Kydathineon 16, Plaka; dm €15, 4-person dm/d €28/70, 4-person dm/d with shared bathroom €24/65; ❄ 💻) Travellers like to chill in the courtyard of this well situated hostel. Rooms may be spartan, but extras (breakfast/snacks, laundry, left luggage, travel service and tours) make up for this.

Athens Backpackers (Map p562; ☎ 210 922 4044; www.backpackers.gr; Makri 12, Makrigianni; dm €18-25, 2-/4-person studio with kitchen €100/120; ❄ 💻) Athens' most popular hostel has a rooftop party bar with Acropolis views, a sports bar, a café, a kitchen, daily movies, and its Aussie management hosts (free!) barbecues. Breakfast and nonalcoholic drinks are included, and long-term storage, airport pick-up and tours are also available.

Marble House Pension (Map p562; ☎ 210 922 8294; www.marblehouse.gr; Zini 35, Koukaki; s/d/tr €42/48/55, d/tr with shared bathroom €42/49; ❄) This is a long-standing Athens favourite, located on a quiet cul-de-sac just 10 minutes' walk from Plaka. All rooms have fridges, ceiling fans and safety boxes. Breakfast costs €5.

Tempi Hotel (Map p570; ☎ 210 321 3175; www.travelling.gr/tempihotel; Eolou 29, Monastiraki; d/tr €60/75, s/d with shared bathroom €40/54) This quiet, friendly, family-run hotel, on the pedestrian part of Eolou, overlooks Plateia Agia Irini. A communal kitchen and nearby markets make it ideal for self-caterers.

Midrange

Hotel Adonis (Map p570; ☎ 210 324 9737; www.hotel-adonis.gr; Kodrou 3, Plaka; s/d from €59/86;) This spotlessly clean hotel is one of the best deals around. Guests return for the friendly welcome, great location and super Acropolis views from the rooftop breakfast room-cum-bar. Rooms have satellite TV and include breakfast.

Hotel Cecil (Map p570; ☎ 210 321 7079; www.cecil.gr; Athinas 39, Monastiraki; s/d €63/89;) Looking rather worn around the edges these days, this hotel, in a fine old classical building with high ceilings and wooden floors, is close to the Psyrri nightlife and sights. Rooms come with TV and breakfast.

Elysium Design Hotel (Map p562; ☎ 210 523 4601; info@elysium-hotels.com; Aristotelous 3, Omonia; s/d €68/73;) This 'cheap and chic' boutique hotel may be Best Western–branded, but it has style – including Philippe Starck Kartell chairs and other funky features. Rooms are tiny, but come with free wi-fi and ADSL, coffee makers, TV and fridge.

Hotel Acropolis House (Map p570; ☎ 210 322 2344; hotel@acropolishouse.gr; Kodrou 6-8, Plaka; s/d/tr from €78/83/107, d with shared bathroom €72;) This well-situated hotel in a 19th-century house feels more *pension* (guesthouse) than hotel, with communal areas and hospitable management. Rooms are clean and come with TV.

Central Athens Hotel (Map p570; ☎ 210 323 4357; www.centralhotel.gr; Apollonos 21, Plaka; s/d €99/121;) This is one of the best midrange deals around: spacious stylish rooms have satellite TV, fridge, breakfast included, balconies (many with Acropolis views) and Internet access. There are wonderful vistas from the rooftop where you can sunbake and relax in the Jacuzzi.

Hotel Hermes (Map p570; ☎ 210 323 5514; www.hermeshotel.gr; Apollonos 19, Plaka; s/d €120/145;) Next to the Central, this hotel has a similar level of style and services (breakfast included, minifridge, satellite TV etc).

Top End

Periscope (Map p562; ☎ 210 729 7200; www.periscope.gr; Haritos 22, Kolonaki; r from €150;) A hip hotel with a cool edgy look (and Mini Cooper seats for chairs in the ground floor café-bar), this place has comfortable minimalist rooms with all the mod cons and a quiet location in chic Kolonaki.

Fresh (Map p562; ☎ 210 524 8511; www.freshhotel.gr; Sophocleous 26; d incl breakfast from €158;) The rooftop lounge-bar and lap pool with Acropolis views are the highlight at this funky hotel, with white light-filled interiors, lots of dark wood, and orange and fuchsia features. The minimalist rooms are small but comfortable and the buffet breakfast expansive.

Semiramis (☎ 210 628 4400; www.semiramisathens.com; Char Trikoupi 48, Kifissia-Kefalari; d from €200;) While the upmarket Kifissia location, overlooking leafy Kefalari park, might not suit first-time visitors to Athens, design hotel fans will love this contemporary hotel by designer Karim Rashid. The retro, hi-tech, candy-coloured rooms with DVD library and wi-fi; the curvaceous swimming pool with sundeck; and the cosmopolitan restaurant are hard to leave.

EATING

For travellers, eating in Athens has been traditionally associated with a taverna meal in Plaka, yet the city's eating scene is now more diversified and sophisticated. While every visitor should experience the traditional taverna or *ouzeria* meal, there's also some wonderful fine dining and Asian food on offer. Athens also has plenty of places where you can eat and run. Locals in a hurry tend to grab a gyros or a coffee and snack from the ubiquitous Flocafé. Note that some restaurants don't accept credit cards.

Monastiraki & Thysio

Savas (Map p570; ☎ 210 324 5048; Mitropoleos 86-88, Monastiraki; gyros €2) Without a doubt, this place serves the tastiest gyros (pork, beef or chicken) in Athens. You can take away or sit down in what becomes one of the city's busiest eat streets late at night. The souvlaki, kebabs and grilled-meat plates are enormous.

Viasos (Map p570; ☎ 210 321 2256; Adrianou 19, Monastiraki; gyros €2) Popular with a young local

AUTHOR'S CHOICE

Spondi (Map p562; ☎ 210 752 0658; www.spondi.gr; Pyrronos 5, Pangrati; mains €20-35; ⏰ 8pm-midnight) While there are now other highly fancied fine-dining restaurants in Athens, Spondi is the only Athenian restaurant that could offer a money-back guarantee. Dining in its vaulted cellar or in its courtyard in summer is quite a relaxed affair, however the staff is clearly working hard to give you an experience worthy of its Michelin star. The chef uses local Greek ingredients and imported produce to create a cuisine that stays true to French technique but embodies Greek flavours. And for those who still sneer at Greek wines, the wine list is a revelation – as are the sublime desserts.

Greek crowd that comes here to socialise over juicy gyros and generous serves of *mezedes*, salads, mixed grills and ouzo, this place is on what has become one of Athens' most atmospheric pedestrian areas, particularly late at night with the glorious ruins glowing near you.

Pil Poul (Map p562; ☎ 210 3423 665; Apostolou Pavlou 51, Thisio; mains €30; ⏰ closed Sun) While the Franco-Mediterranean menu and service here sometimes fail to match the sublime Acropolis views, this is still arguably the most romantic dinner spot in Athens.

Psyrri & Gazi

Pica Pica: Tapas Stories (Map p570; ☎ 210 325 1663; Ag Anargyron, Psyrri; mains €2.50-20) If you're tired of Greek food, head here for tasty authentic Spanish tapas, including tortilla, *patatas bravas* (spicy potatoes), *gambas* (prawns), *pulpo* (octopus) and the like. While you can wash it down with sangría, we suggest a delicious Peloponnese chardonnay instead.

Taverna tou Psiri (Map p570; ☎ 210 321 4923; Eshylou 12, Psyrri; mains €5-12) This atmospheric taverna is popular with locals who come for the daily specials menu. It's tucked away off Plateia Iroon; look for the apt mural of a drunk leaning against a lamppost.

Varoulko (Map p562; ☎ 210 522 8400; Pireos 80, Gazi; mains €22-30; ⏰ closed Sun) This Michelin-starred seafood restaurant has remained popular with Athenian celebrities and food tourists since moving from Piraeus. While dishes such as the squid-ink soup and smoked swordfish are sublime, it gave us the distinct impression of a restaurant simply going through the motions.

Plaka

Byzantino (Map p570; ☎ 210 322 7368; Kydathineon 18, Plaka; mains €3-16) If you must eat in the heart of Plaka (everyone wants to do it once), this is one of the better choices for hearty traditional cuisine and a good range of daily specials. It's also in a pleasant shady spot that's great for people-watching.

Eden Vegetarian Restaurant (Map p570; ☎ 210 324 8858; Lyssiou 12, Plaka; mains €4-10) This long-standing favourite serves up vegetarian versions of Greek classics and organic wine and beer.

Taverna tou Psarra (Map p570; ☎ 210 321 8734; Eretheos 16, Plaka; mains €5-18) On a path leading up towards the Acropolis, this gem of a taverna is one of Plaka's best, serving scrumptious *mezedes* and excellent fish and meat classics on a terrace under the plane trees.

O Platanos (Map p570; ☎ 210 322 0666; Diogenous 4, Plaka; mains €7; ⏰ noon-4.30pm & 7.30pm-midnight Mon-Sat, noon-4.30pm Sun) Laid-back O Platanos (Plane Tree) serves tasty, home cooked-style Greek cuisine. The lamb dishes are delicious and we love the leafy courtyard.

Noodle Bar (Map p570; ☎ 210 331 8585; Apollonos 11, Plaka; mains €8) The pick of several Asian restaurants around Plaka, Noodle Bar serves up tasty noodles and soups (we love the laksa) at honest prices.

Eat (Map p570; ☎ 210 324 9129; Adrianou 91, Plaka; mains €8-17) A sleek alternative to the endless traditional tavernas, Eat serves interesting salads and pastas and modern interpretations of Greek classics.

Self-Catering

You'll find the best selection of fresh produce at the **fruit and vegetable market** (Map p562) on Athinas, opposite the **meat market** (Map p562), where some wonderful stores sell delicious olives in barrels. In the surrounding streets, pastry shops sell delicious *pitas* (pies). Decent supermarkets in central Athens include **Marinopoulos** (Map p562; Athinas 60, Omonia) and **Vasilopoulou** (Map p570; Stadiou 19, Syntagma).

DRINKING

Athens has more than its fair share of drinking establishments, from casual, grungy student hang-outs to Irish pubs for expats. Outside summer, the bars of Psyrri are the most popular, although during summer most of the action heads to the islands. Some bars open from morning until late, while others (noted below) don't open until late.

Bars & Pubs

Brettos (Map p570; ☎ 210 323 2110; Kydathineon 41, Plaka) This distillery, bottle shop and bar is dark and dingy, but once the sun goes down, its eye-catching, back-lit collection of coloured bottles gives the place a certain magic. Watch those shots of Brettos-brand spirits – they're lethal.

Mooi (Map p570; ☎ 210 321 2624; cnr Miaouli & Themidos, Psyrri; closed Mon) Formerly known as Bee, cool Mooi is mellow by day but late at night attracts a party crowd that spills out onto the street.

Sobar (Map p570; ☎ 210 322 2205; Navarhou Apostoli 5, Psyrri; 10pm-3.30am Sun-Thu, to 6am Fri & Sat) This funky bar is low-key until around 1am when it goes off, while weekends frequently see some dancing on the bar.

Wonderbar (Map p562; ☎ 210 381 8577; Themistokleous 80, Exarhia) Relaxed by day, packed by night, this lounge bar attracts hip young Athenians who come for some of Athens' best DJs.

Cafés

Athens' cafés have some of the highest prices for coffee in Europe, yet if you do what the locals do and sit on a frappé (frothy ice coffee) all day, you can do the café scene relatively cheaply. Kolonaki has a mind-boggling array of cafés off Plateia Kolonakiou, on Skoufa and Tsakalof Streets.

ENTERTAINMENT

The *Kathimerini* supplement inside the *International Herald Tribune* has daily event listings and a cinema guide.

Nightclubs

Athenians don't head to clubs until after midnight. Cover charges apply late and when there's a guest DJ, and drinks are more expensive than at bars.

Decadence (Map p562; ☎ 210 882 3544; cnr Pouliherias & Voulgaroktonou 69, Lofos Strefi; admission €6-8) For indie and alternative music lovers, Decadence has two levels, with a quieter bar scene on the lower floor and a club located upstairs.

Lava Bore (Map p570; ☎ 210 324 5335; Filellinon 25, Plaka; cover varies) This fun dance club is popular with a young international globetrotting crowd.

Live Music

POP, ROCK & JAZZ

Get tickets for concerts at **Ticket House** (Map p562; ☎ 210 360 8366; Panepistimiou 42). Popular venues:

Rodon Club (Map p562; ☎ 210 524 7427; Marni 24, Omonia; from 10pm) You'll either love or hate this grungy club – the city's main venue for rock and metal – but die-hard fans and visiting rock musos swear by it.

Gagarin 205 Club (Map p562; ☎ 210 854 7601; Liossion 205; from 9.30pm) The city's coolest space attracts the most interesting international and local acts, along with Athens' most interesting people.

Half Note Jazz Club (Map p562; ☎ 210 921 3310; Trivonianou 17, Mets; from 10.30pm) Jazz buffs won't be disappointed – this dark, smoky club is the main venue for serious jazz.

REMBETIKA

Traditional *rembetika* is hard to catch during the summer months when most of the authentic venues close, but you can see a popularised version at some tavernas in Psyrri.

Rembetika Stoa Athanaton (Map p562; ☎ 210 321 4362; Sofokleous 19; 3.30-7pm & 11pm-late Mon-Sat Oct-May) Located in the meat market, this is still *the* place to listen to *rembetika*.

Classical Music, Opera & Dance

Dora Stratou Dance Company (Map p570; ☎ 210 921 6650; www.grdance.org; Filopappos Hill; tickets €15; from 9.30pm Tue-Sat & 8.15pm Sun May-Sep) This traditional folk-dancing show features more than 75 musicians and dancers.

Megaron Mousikis (Athens Concert Hall; Map p562; ☎ 210 728 2333; www.megaron.gr; Leof Vasilissis Sofias; tickets €10-60) Tickets can be purchased online for performances by local and international artists at this superb concert venue.

Olympia Theatre (Map p562; ☎ 210 361 2461; www.nationalopera.gr; Akadimias 59, Exarhia; tickets from box office €20-52; 9am-9pm) The Greek National Opera season of classical opera, ballet and orchestral concerts runs from November to June.

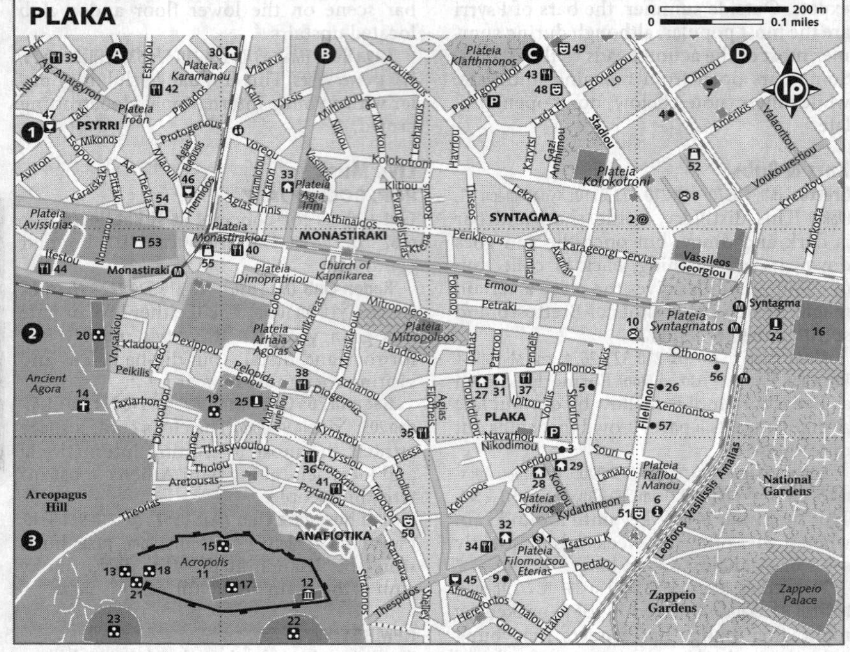

Cinemas

Most cinemas show recent releases in English and admission prices are around €8. Two of the major cinemas in central Athens are **Apollon** (Map p570; ☎ 210 323 6811; Stadiou 19) and the **Astor** (Map p570; ☎ 210 323 1297; Stadiou 28).

Gay & Lesbian Venues

You'll find the greatest number of gay bars in Makrigianni, south of the Temple of Olympian Zeus, and Exarhia. Most don't get moving until midnight. Check out www.gay.gr.

Alekos' Island (Map p562; Sarri 41, Psyrri) This long-standing gay bar attracts a more mellow older crowd.

Aroma (Map p562; ☎ 210 381 9615; Tsamadou 15, Exarhia) Athens' most popular lesbian dance club plays both mainstream and Greek music.

Kirkis (Map p562; ☎ 210 346 6960; Apostolou Pavlou 31, Thisio) Head to this hip gay and lesbian hang-out to find out what's hot in Athens when you're visiting.

Lamda Club (Map p562; ☎ 210 942 4202; Lembesi 15, Makrigianni) Athens' best gay dance club gets crowded late.

SHOPPING

Athens is the place to shop for cool jewellery, hippy-chic clothes and leather shoes, as well as some great souvenirs, such as backgammon sets, hand-woven textiles, traditional cross-stitched blouses, olive soap and olive oil skin products, worry beads and colourful ceramics. You'll find boutiques on Ermou; designer brands in Kolonaki; and souvenirs, folk art and leather in Plaka and Monastiraki.

Attica department store (Map p570; ☎ 211 180 2600; Panepistimiou 9) This store has several floors of funky fashion from around the globe, including Greek designers, along with accessories, cosmetics and travel goods.

Stavros Melissinos' Store (Map p570; ☎ 210 321 9247; Aghias Theklas 2, Monastiraki) Sandal wearers should head here for some custom-made sandals and poetry from the poet sandal maker.

If you are in Athens on a weekend, it is obligatory to visit the **Sunday market** (Map p570; ⏲ 7am-2pm) near the **Monastiraki flea market** (Map p570), which starts at Plateia Monastirakiou.

INFORMATION		
Acropole Foreign Exchange	1	C3
Arcade Internet Café	2	D1
Compendium Books	3	C2
Eleftheroudakis Books	4	D1
Eleftheroudakis Books	5	C2
EOT Tourist Office	6	D3
Goethe Institut	7	D1
Parcel Post Office	8	D1
Plaka Laundrette	9	C3
Syntagma Post Office	10	D2
SIGHTS & ACTIVITIES		
Acropolis	11	A3
Acropolis Museum	12	B3
Beule Gate	13	A3
Church of the Holy Apostles	14	A2
Erechtheion	15	B3
Parliament Building	16	D2
Parthenon	17	B3
Propylaia	18	A3
Roman Agora	19	A2
Stoa of Attalos	20	A2
Temple of Athena Nike	21	A3
Theatre of Dionysos	22	B3
Theatre of Herodes Atticus	23	A3
Tomb of the Unknown Soldier (Changing of the Guard)	24	D2
Tower of the Winds	25	B2
Trekking Hellas	26	D2
SLEEPING		
Central Athens Hotel	27	C2
Hotel Acropolis House	28	C3
Hotel Adonis	29	C3
Hotel Cecil	30	B1
Hotel Hermes	31	C2
Student & Travellers' Inn	32	C3
Tempi Hotel	33	B1
EATING		
Byzantino	34	C3
Eat	35	B3
Eden Vegetarian Restaurant	36	B3
Noodle Bar	37	C2
O Platanos	38	B2
Pica Pica: Tapas Stories	39	A1
Savas	40	B2
Taverna tou Psarra	41	B3
Taverna tou Psiri	42	A1
Vasilopoulou	43	C1
Viasos	44	A2
DRINKING		
Brettos	45	C3
Mooi	46	A1
Sobar	47	A1
ENTERTAINMENT		
Apollon	48	C1
Astor	49	C1
Dora Stratou Dance Company	50	B3
Lava Bore	51	C3
SHOPPING		
Attica Department Store	52	D1
Monastiraki Flea Market	53	A2
Stavros Melissinos' Store	54	A1
Sunday Market	55	A2
TRANSPORT		
Aegean Airlines	56	D2
Olympic Airlines	57	D2

GETTING THERE & AWAY

Air

Athens is serviced by **Eleftherios Venizelos International Airport** (ATH; ☎ 210 353 0000; www.aia.gr) at Spata, 27km east of Athens. Facilities are excellent, with a good selection of reasonably priced cafés and decent duty-free shopping, including local products. For phone numbers for international airlines in Athens, see p639.

The majority of domestic flights are handled by Greece's much maligned national carrier, **Olympic Airlines** (code OA; Map p570; ☎ 210 926 4444; www.olympicairlines.com; Filellinon 15, Syntagma).

Crete-based **Aegean Airlines** (code A3; Map p570; ☎ 210 331 5502; www.aegeanair.com; Othonos 10, Syntagma) offers flights to many of the same destinations as Olympic.

Bus

Athens has two main intercity **KTEL** (www.ktel.org) bus stations, about 5km to 7km north of Omonia. KTEL timetables are online. **EOT** (www.gnto.gr) also has online schedules for both stations.

Kifissos Terminal A (☎ 210 512 4910; Kifissou 100) has buses running to the Peloponnese, Igoumenitsa, Ionian Islands, Haldiki, Florina, Ioannina, Kastoria, Edessa and Thessaloniki, among other destinations. Get here on bus 015 from the junction of Zinonos and Menandrou, near Plateia Omonia.

Liossion Terminal B (☎ 210 831 7153; Liossion 260) has departures to Trikala (for Meteora), Delphi, Larissa, Thiva, Volos and other destinations. To get here take bus 024 from outside the main gate of the National Gardens on Amalias. Get off the bus at Liossion 260, turn right onto Gousiou and you'll see the terminal.

Car & Motorcycle

Syngrou Rd, south of the Temple of Olympian Zeus, is packed solid with car-rental firms. National Rd 1 is the main route north from Athens, starting at Nea Kifissia: take Vasilissis Sofias from Syntagma and follow the signs. National Rd 8, which begins beyond Dafni, is the road to the Peloponnese: take Agiou Konstantinou from Omonia.

Ferry

See p641 for information on ferries travelling to and from the islands.

Train

Larissa Station is Athens' main train station. Suburban and intercity train services pass through here. Timetables are available from www.isap.gr.

More information on services is available from **OSE offices** (Omonia Map p562; ☎ 210 524 0647; Karolou 1; 8am-6pm Mon-Fri, to 3pm Sat; Syntagma Map p562; ☎ 210 362 4402; Sina 6; 8am-3.30pm Mon-Fri, to 3pm Sat). Both offices handle advance bookings.

GREECE

GETTING AROUND

The metro system makes getting around central Athens and to Piraeus easy, but Athens' road traffic is still horrendous. A 24-hour travel pass (€2.90) is valid for all forms of public transport.

To/From the Airport

BUS

Bus X94 (25 minutes, every 10 minutes 7.30am to 11.30pm) operates daily between the airport and metro Line 3 at Ethniki Amyna.

Bus X95 (60 to 90 minutes, every 30 minutes over 24 hours) operates between the airport and Plateia Syntagma. The Syntagma stop is on Othonos St.

Bus X96 (60 to 90 minutes, every 20 minutes over 24 hours) operates between the airport and Plateia Karaiskaki in Piraeus.

Tickets for all these services cost €2.90.

METRO

Line 3 of the metro links the airport to the city centre in around 30 minutes; it operates from Monastiraki from 5.50am to 10.50pm, and from the airport from 6.30am to 11.30pm. Tickets cost €6.

TAXI

Taxi fares vary according to the time of day and level of traffic, but you should expect to pay from €20 to €30 from the airport to the city centre, and from €20 to €25 from the airport to Piraeus, depending on traffic conditions. Both trips can take up to an hour.

Bus & Trolleybus

Blue-and-white suburban buses operate every 15 minutes from 5am to midnight. Route numbers and destinations are listed on the free EOT map. Timetables can be obtained from the **GNTO** (www.gnto.gr), at EOT tourist offices, or at the **Athens Urban Transport Organisation** (OASA; ☎ 210 883 6076; www.oasa.gr). The EOT map identifies the routes of the yellow trolleybuses too, which also run from 5am to midnight.

Special buses to Piraeus operate 24 hours, running every 20 minutes, from 6am to midnight, and then hourly until 6am. Bus 040 leaves from the corner of Syntagma and Filellinon, and bus 049 leaves from the Omonia end of Athinas.

Tickets for all services cost €0.45 and must be purchased before boarding from a ticket booth or a *periptero*. The same tickets can be used on either buses or trolleybuses and must be validated as you board.

Metro

The metro operates from 5am to midnight. Trains run every three minutes during peak periods and every 10 minutes at other times. For metro timetables visit www.ametro.gr. Travel within one section costs €0.60 and a journey covering two or more sections costs €0.75. Tickets must be validated before travelling.

Taxi

Athenian taxis are yellow. The flag fall is €0.75 and there's an additional surcharge of €0.80 from ports and train and bus stations, as well as a €3 surcharge from the airport. After that, the day rate (tariff 1 on the meter) is €0.28 per kilometre. The rate doubles between midnight and 5am (tariff 2 on the meter). Baggage is charged at the rate of €0.30 per item over 10kg. The minimum fare is €3.

AROUND ATHENS

Piraeus Πειραιάς

pop 175,697

Greece's main port, Piraeus, is the hub of the Aegean ferry network. It takes around 25 minutes to get here from the centre of Athens by metro (avoid taking a bus or taxi – the streets are even more clogged than they are in Athens), so there's no reason to stay in shabby Piraeus. However, a trip to tranquil Mikrolimano (Small Harbour), with its cafés and fish restaurants, reveals another side to Piraeus.

ORIENTATION & INFORMATION

Piraeus consists of a peninsula surrounded by harbours. The largest of its three harbours is the Megas Limin (Great Harbour) on the western side, where all the ferries leave from, along with hydrofoil and catamaran services to Aegina and the Cyclades. Zea Marina (Limin Zeas) and Mikrolimano, on the eastern side of the peninsula, are for private yachts. **Internet Center** (☎ 210 411 1261; Akti Poseidonos 24; per hr €2.50; 🕑 10am-11pm) is an Internet café on the main road, across from the main harbour.

EATING

If you're in Athens for more than a few days, a seafood meal on the harbour at Mikrolimano is a must.

Jimmy & the Fish (☎ 210 412 4417; Koumoundourou 46; mains €16; ⏰ 1pm-1am) This is the most reliable of the harbour-front restaurants, serving up excellent seafood in stylish surrounds. There is also a couple of good cafés along this strip. Trolleybus 20 runs past the harbour.

GETTING THERE & AWAY

Bus

Two 24-hour bus services operate between central Athens and Piraeus. Bus 049 runs from Omonia to the bus station at the Great Harbour, and bus 040 runs from Syntagma to the tip of the Piraeus peninsula. Bus 040 is the service to catch from Athens for Zea Marina (get off at the Hotel Savoy), though the trip can take well over an hour in bad traffic. The fare is €0.45 for each service.

Ferry

The following information is a guide to ferry departures between June and mid-September. There are fewer ferries running in April, May and October, and they are radically reduced in winter – especially to smaller islands. The main branch of EOT in Athens (p564) has a reliable schedule, updated weekly. All ferry companies make

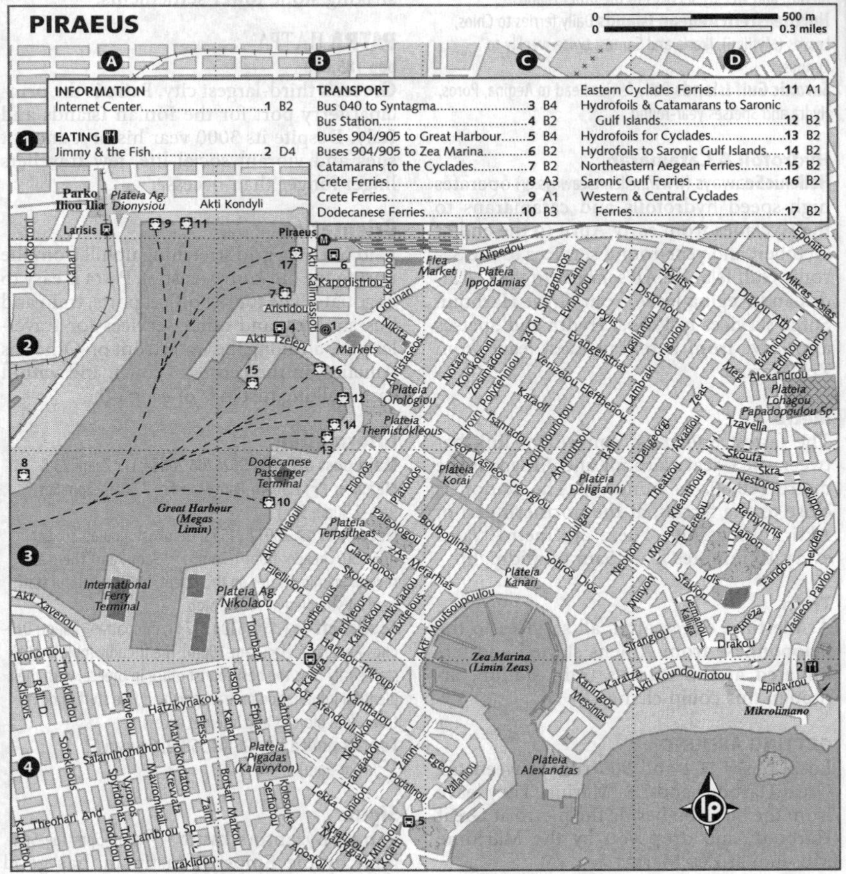

timetables available online (see p641). The departure points for ferry destinations are shown on the Piraeus map (see p573). When buying your ticket, confirm the departure point. See the Getting There & Away sections for each island for more details.

Crete There are two boats a day to Hania and Iraklio, a daily service to Rethymno, and three a week to Agios Nikolaos and Sitia.

Cyclades There are daily ferries to Amorgos, Folegandros, Ios, Kimolos, Kythnos, Milos, Mykonos, Naxos, Paros, Santorini, Serifos, Sifnos, Sikinos, Syros and Tinos; two or three ferries a week to Iraklia, Shinoussa, Koufonisi, Donoussa and Anafi; and none to Andros or Kea.

Dodecanese There are daily ferries to Kalymnos, Kos, Leros, Patmos and Rhodes; three a week to Karpathos and Kassos; and weekly services to the other islands.

Northeastern Aegean Islands Daily ferries to Chios, Lesvos (Mytilini), Ikaria and Samos; twice weekly to Limnos.

Saronic Gulf Islands Daily ferries head to Aegina, Poros, Hydra and Spetses year-round.

Hydrofoil & Catamaran

Hellenic Seaways (www.hellenicseaways.gr) operates high-speed hydrofoils and catamarans to the Cyclades from early April to the end of October, and year-round services to the Saronic Gulf Islands. All services to the Cyclades and Aegina leave from Great Harbour. Some services to Poros, Hydra and Spetses also leave from here, but most leave from Zea Marina.

Metro

The fastest and most convenient link between the Great Harbour and Athens is the metro (€0.60, 24 minutes). The station is close to the ferries, at the northern end of Akti Kalimassioti. There are metro trains every 10 minutes from 5am to midnight.

Train

At the time of research, all services to the Peloponnese from Athens started and terminated at the Piraeus train station, although this could change.

GETTING AROUND

Local buses 904 and 905 run between the Great Harbour and Zea Marina. They leave from the bus stop beside the metro at Great Harbour, and drop you by the Maritime Museum at Zea Marina.

THE PELOPONNESE ΠΕΛΟΠΟΝΝΗΣΟΣ

The Peloponnese is ruggedly beautiful, breathtaking at its best. Home to Olympia, birthplace of the Olympic Games; the ancient archaeological sites of Mycenae, Epidavros and Corinth; the ruined Byzantine city of Mystras; and ancient Sparta; it has played a significant role in Greek history.

Two of Greece's most gorgeous towns grace its shores – Venetian-style Nafplio and romantic Monemvasia. The isolated Mani Peninsula is blanketed with spectacular wildflowers in spring and dotted with striking stone tower settlements.

PATRA ΠΑΤΡΑ

pop 185,670

Greece's third-largest city, Patra is the principal ferry port for the Ionian Islands and Italy. Despite its 3000 year history, ancient sites and vibrant social life, few travellers linger longer than necessary.

Orientation

Laid out on a grid stretching uphill from the port to the old *kastro* (castle), Patra is easy to negotiate. The tourist office, ports, train and bus stations, and other services for travellers, are all along the waterfront on Othonos Amalias, in the centre of town, and within easy walking distance of each other.

Information

Main post office (☎ 26106 20644; cnr Zaimi 23 & Mezonos; 🕑 7.30am-8pm Mon-Fri, 7.30am-2pm Sat, 9am-1.30pm Sun)

Netp@rk (☎ 26012 21553; Gerokostopoulou 36; per hr €1.50, cheaper from 1-7am; 🕑 9am-7am) There are several 'gaming' cafés on this street, but the helpful staff here let you plug in your laptop.

Tourist office (☎ 26104 61741; infopatras@hol.gr; Othonos Amalias 6; 🕑 8am-10pm) The friendly multilingual staff easily runs the best tourist office in Greece, with their plentiful information on transport and free stuff to do in town, free bicycles and Internet access.

Tourist police (☎ 26104 55833; Gounari 52; 🕑 7am-9pm)

Sights

Patra's Byzantine **kastro** (🕑 8am-5pm Tue-Sun), built by the Emperor Justinian, has good

GREECE

views to the Ionion Islands. Patra's **museum** (☎ 26102 75070; Mezonos 42; 8.30am-3pm Tue-Sun) has a small archaeological collection from the Mycenaean, Hellenic and Roman eras. The impressive **Roman Odeon** (cnr Germanou & Sotiriadou; 8am-3pm Tue-Sun) is a magical spot to see a performance.

Sleeping

Pension Nicos (☎ 26106 23757; cnr Patreos & Agiou Andreou 121; s/d/tr €20/35/45, d/tr with shared bathroom €30/40) This place is spotlessly clean and the best budget choice.

Hotel Saint George (☎ 26102 25092; Agiou Andreou 73; s/d €50/75) With a central location, you'll find clean rooms here, some with port views.

Eating & Drinking

Scores of stylish cafés and fast-food eateries lie between Kolokotroni and Ermou, while Aghios Nikolaos and Radinou (off Riga Fereou) are the places for drinking. Pedestrianised Trion Navarhon is lined with tavernas.

Europa Centre (☎ 26104 37006; Othonos Amalias 10; mains €4-8; 7am-midnight) Convenient to all transport, this place serves Greek standards and also has a left-luggage service.

Mythos (☎ 26103 29984; cnr Trion Navarhon 181 & Riga; mains €5-12; 7pm-late) Settle into this atmospheric taverna for a range of good home-cooked Greek classics.

Dia Discount Supermarket (Agiou Andreou 29) This supermarket is ideally located for travellers wanting to purchase provisions for their journey.

Getting There & Away

From **Patras train station** (☎ 26106 39108; Othonos Amalias 27) there are seven trains a day to Athens via Corinth, terminating at Piraeus or the airport. Four are InterCity express trains (€12, 3½ hours), while three are slow trains (€6, four to seven hours). Between four and eight trains run south daily to Pyrgos (for Olympia, €6, two hours) and Kalamata (€8, five hours).

The **KTEL Achaia bus station** (☎ 26106 23886; cnr Zaimi 2 & Othonos Amalias) has regular services to Athens (€13, three hours, half-hourly) via Corinth, with less frequent services to Ioannina (€18, 4½ hours, two daily), Thessaloniki (€33, 10 hours, four daily), Pyrgos (€8, two hours, nine to 10 daily), Tripoli (€12, 3½ hours, two daily) and Kalamata (€17, four hours, two daily). There are 10 buses daily to Pyrgos (for Olympia). Buses to the Ionian islands, via the port of Kyllini, leave from the **KTEL Zakynthos bus station** (☎ 26102 20993/22224; Othonos Amalias 47) or nearby **KTEL Keffalonia bus station** (☎ 26102 74938; Othonos Amalias 58).

Ionion Ferries depart for Zakynthos (€6, 1½ hours, four to five daily). Strintzis and Ionian Ferries head to Kefallonia (€7 to €12, 1½ to 2½ hours, nine daily). Strintzis also goes to Ithaki (€12, 3½ hours, two daily), and Minoan Lines and ANEK Lines sail to Corfu (€26 to €30, seven hours, two daily). For services to Italy see p640. The tourist office (opposite) can provide you with timetables. Numerous ticket agencies line the waterfront.

DIAKOFTO–KALAVRYTA RAILWAY ΔΙΑΚΟΦΤΟ–ΚΑΛΑΒΡΥΤΑ

This spectacular rack-and-pinion line crawls up the deep gorge of the Vouraikos River from the small coastal town of Diakofto to the mountain resort of Kalavryta, 22km away. It's a thrilling one-hour journey, with dramatic scenery best viewed from 1st class (€5) rather than 2nd (€4). There are five trains a day in each direction. Diakofto is one hour east of Patra on the main train line to Athens. It can be tough to get a ticket, so buy in advance from any train station in Greece.

CORINTH ΚΟΡΙΝΘΟΣ

pop 29,787

Modern Corinth (*ko*-rin-thoss), 6km west of the Corinth Canal, is an uninspiring town, largely due to devastating earthquakes, but it makes a convenient base for visiting ancient Corinth.

At Lecheon, about 4km west of Corinth, **Blue Dolphin Camping** (☎ 27410 25766; www.camping-blue-dolphin.gr; per adult/tent €6/6;) is close to the ancient Corinth turn-off. It has a beach and decent facilities and it offers tours. Buses from Corinth to Lecheon stop here.

Hotel Apollon (☎ 27410 22587; www.hotelapollongr.com; Damaskinou 2; s/d €50/60;) is handily situated near the bus and train stations and offers good discounts; it is the best accommodation option in town. Well-equipped rooms come with minibar and TV (some also have DVD players).

GREECE

Buses to Athens (€6, 1½ hours, half-hourly) and Lecheon and ancient Corinth (€0.90, 20 minutes, hourly) leave from the **KTEL Korinthos bus station** (☎ 27410 75425; Dimocratias 4) opposite the train station, while buses to Nafplio leave from **Argolis bus station** (cnr Ethnikis Antistaseos & Aratou).

It's more convenient to take the train to Patra and Athens. There are 14 daily, four of which are InterCity services. Trains also head to Kalamata (€6, 4½ hours, three daily) via Argos (for Nafplio, €2, one hour, five daily) and Tripoli (€3, 2½ hours, three daily).

ANCIENT CORINTH & ACROCORINTH ΑΡΧΑΙΑ ΚΟΡΙΝΘΟΣ & ΑΚΡΟΚΟΡΙΝΘΟΣ

The ruins of **ancient Corinth** (☎ 27410 31207; site & museum €6; 8am-7.30pm Apr-Oct, to 5pm Nov-Mar) lie at the edge of the village of ancient Corinth, and 7km southwest of Corinth's modern town. It was one of ancient Greece's wealthiest cities, but earthquakes and invasions have left little standing. The only ancient Greek monument remaining is the imposing **Temple of Apollo**; the others are Roman. Towering over the site is **Acrocorinth**, the ruins of an ancient citadel built on a massive outcrop of limestone.

The great-value digs at **Tasos Taverna & Rooms** (☎ 27410 31225; fax 27410 31183; centre of town, 200m from museum; s/d/q €25/35/50;) consist of spotlessly clean rooms above an excellent taverna serving home-style Greek classics. Rooms have TV and most have a fridge, balcony and views. Breakfast is available for €6. There are discounts during the low season.

NAFPLIO ΝΑΥΠΛΙΟ

pop 14,500

With majestic Palamidi Fortress presiding over it, and breezy lanes lined with elegant Venetian houses and neoclassical mansions dripping with crimson bougainvillea, atmospheric Nafplio is one of Greece's prettiest towns. Add to that one of the liveliest waterfront café scenes – sublime for sunset watching – along with a vibrant nightlife and you've got a great place to spend a few days.

Information

Kasteli Travel & Tourist Agency (☎ 27520 29395; 38 Vass Konstantinou; 9am-2pm year-round & 6-8pm summer) The friendly English-speaking staff here books rooms, rents cars and sells air and ferry tickets.

Municipal tourist office (☎ 27520 24444; 25 Martiou; 9am-1.30pm & 4-8pm) Unhelpful, providing more information about other Greek destinations rather than Nafplio.

Odyssey Bookshop (☎ 27520 23430; Plateia Syntagmatos) Excellent range of international papers, magazines and novels.

Posto Café (☎ 27520 21508; Sidiras Merarhias; per hr €3; 10am-late) Has an upstairs Internet café with fast connections. Plug in your laptop for an extra €0.50.

Tourist police (☎ 27520 28131; Kountouridou 16)

Sights

There are spectacular views of the town and surrounding coast from the magnificent hilltop **Palamidi Fortress** (☎ 27520 28036; admission €4; 8am-6.45pm summer, to 5pm at other times), built by the Venetians between 1711 and 1714. The **Vasilios Papantoniou Museum** (☎ 27520 28379; 1 Vas Alexandrou St; adult/concession €4/2; 9am-2.30pm year-round & 6-9pm summer) is one of Greece's best small museums, with its displays of vibrant regional costumes. The museum shop is worth a peek for its quality souvenirs.

Sleeping

The old town is *the* place to stay, with plenty of *pensions*, but limited budget options. Midweek prices are significantly lower than weekend rates (Friday to Sunday). In the high season it's necessary to book ahead. While cheaper rooms can be found on the road to Argos and Tolo, you'll have transport costs into town.

Hotel Economou (☎ 27520 27721; Argonafton 22; dm/d/tr €10/30/35) Nafplio's only budget hotel may be quite a walk from the old town, but backpackers appreciate its clean rooms and accommodating management.

Kapodistrias (☎ 27520 29366; www.hotelkapodistrias.gr; Kokinou 20; s/d €50/75, breakfast €5;) These beautiful rooms, many with elegant canopy beds, come with sea or old-town views.

Hotel Victoria (☎ 27520 27420; fax 27520 27517; Spiliadou 3; s/d €65/80;) This characterless but clean hotel in an excellent location offers good discounts when it's quiet. Some rooms have citadel views.

Andromeda (☎ 27520 96480; www.andromeda-pension.com; Ipsilantou 13; s/d incl breakfast €80/100;) This stylish family-owned *pension* has spacious rooms equipped with ADSL, flat-screen TV, minibar, fresh flowers, polished floorboards and Korres products. It offers discounts of up to 30% midweek and in the off season.

Hotel Grande Bretagne (☎ 27520 96200; www.grandebretagne.com.gr; Filellinon Sq; s/d incl breakfast €160/220) In the heart of Nafplio's café action and overlooking the sea, this splendidly restored hotel, built in 1878, is Nafplio's most luxurious, with high ceilings, antiques and chandeliers.

Eating

Nafplio's old-town streets are full of restaurants; the tavernas on Staïkopoulou and those overlooking the port on Bouboulinas get jam-packed on weekends.

To Kenitrikon (☎ 27520 29933; Plateia Syntagmatos; mains €3-10) This is *the* place to head for breakfast. Relax under the shady trees on this pretty square and enjoy the expansive 'Kenitrikon breakfast'.

Taverna O Vassilis (☎ 27520 25334; Staïkopoulou 20-24; mains €4-8.50) The busiest taverna on this atmospheric eating strip is equally as popular with locals as it is with tourists, who all come for the delicious home-style classics.

Taverna Aeolos (☎ 27520 26828; V Olgas 30; mains €4-11) This busy taverna with outdoor seating is always packed with locals who share the generous mixed-grill plates for €8.50. It has great live music during summer.

Shopping

Nafplio shopping is a delight, with jewellery workshops, boutiques and wonderful regional products, such as honey, wine and handicrafts.

Metallagh (☎ 27520 21267; Sofrani 3; 🕒 10am-3pm & 6-10pm summer, 8am-5pm autumn-spring) Here, young jeweller Maria Koitsoidaki handcrafts her wonderful organic jewellery from silver and fine metals, gems and stones.

Komboloi Museum (☎ 27520 21618; Staikopolou 25; 🕒 10am-8pm) This is actually a shop specialising in beautiful worry beads, including the owner's antique worry bead collection.

Getting There & Away

The **KTEL Argolis bus station** (☎ 27520 27323; Syngrou 8) has hourly buses to Athens (€10, 2½ hours) via Corinth. It also has services to Argos (for Peloponnese connections) and Mycenae and Epidavros; these all cost from €1 to €2 and take around 30 to 45 minutes.

EPIDAVROS ΕΠΙΔΑΥΡΟΣ

World Heritage–listed **Epidavros** (☎ 27530 22006; admission €6; 🕒 8am-7pm Apr-Oct, to 5pm Nov-Mar) was the sanctuary of Asclepius, god of medicine. The **theatre** is spectacular, but don't miss the peaceful **Sanctuary of Asclepius**, once a flourishing spa and healing centre. Epidavros is best visited by bus as a day trip from Nafplio (€2, 40 minutes, four daily).

MYCENAE ΜΥΚΗΝΕΣ

Although settled as early as the 6th millennium BC, **Ancient Mycenae** (☎ 27510 76585; admission €8; 🕒 8am-7pm Apr-Oct, to 5pm Nov-Mar) was at its most powerful from 1600 to 1200 BC. Mycenae's entrance, the **Lion Gate**, is Europe's oldest monumental sculpture. Described by Homer as being 'rich in gold', excavations of **Grave Circle A** by Heinrich Schliemann in the 1870s uncovered magnificent gold treasures, such as the Mask of Agamemnon, now on display at the National Archaeological Museum (p565).

Most people visit on day trips from Nafplio, but the historic **Belle Helene Hotel** (☎ 27510 76225; fax 27510 76179; Christou Tsounta; s/d €35/50) on the main street, is where Schliemann stayed during the excavations.

There are three buses daily to Mycenae from Argos (€1.50, 30 minutes) and Nafplio (€2, 45 minutes).

SPARTA ΣΠΑΡΤΗ

pop 19,550

Modern, laid-back Sparta (*spar*-tee) is at odds with its ancient Spartan image of discipline and deprivation. Although there's little to see, the town makes a convenient base from which to visit Mystras.

Sparta's street grid system sees Palaeologou running north–south through the town, and Lykourgou running east–west.

Hellas Net (☎ 27310 21500; Palaeologou 34; 🕒 8.30am-11pm) is located above a DVD/games store on Palaeologou. The **tourist police** (☎ 27310 20492; Theodoritou 20) can provide information. The **post office** (Archidamou 10; 🕒 7.30am-2pm Mon-Fri) is at Archidamou.

Camping Paleologou Mystras (☎ 27310 22724; fax 27310 25256; per adult/tent €4/3.50; 🕒 year-round; 🏊), 2km west of Sparta on the road to

Mystras, has good facilities, and buses travelling to Mystras will drop you there.

Hotel Cecil (☎ 27310 24980; fax 27310 81318; Palaeologou 125; s/d €35/45; ❄) has long been popular with travellers who come for its clean rooms with balcony and TV, decent breakfasts, and parking.

Refurbished **Menelaion Hotel** (☎ 27310 22161/5; www.menelaion.com; Palaeologou 91; s/d/tr €79/106/135; ❄ 🏊) is in an elegant neoclassical building and has a welcome courtyard swimming pool. The rooms, while comfortable, are characterless. Ask for discounts in the low season.

Restaurant Elysse (☎ 27310 29896; Palaeologou 113; mains €4.50-10), run by a friendly Greek-Canadian family, serves up good Greek standards and a few Lakonian specialities, although next-door's **Café Ouzeri** (☎ 27310 081565; mains €2.50-10) has more character.

Sparta's **KTEL Lakonias bus station** (☎ 27310 26441; cnr Lykourgou & Thivronos) services Athens via Corinth (€14, 3½ hours, 10 daily), Gythio (€4, one hour, five daily), Monemvasia (€7, two hours, three daily) and other destinations. Frequent buses to Mystras take 30 minutes (€0.90).

MYSTRAS ΜΥΣΤΡΑΣ

Magical **Mystras** (☎ 27310 83377; adult/concession €6/3; 🕒 8am-7.30pm Apr-Oct, to 3.30pm Nov-Mar) was once the effective capital of the Byzantine Empire. Today its streets are lined with ruins of palaces, monasteries and churches, most of them dating from between 1271 and 1460.

Allow half a day to explore the site. While only 7km from Sparta, staying in the village nearby allows you to get to the site early before it heats up. **Hotel Byzantion** (☎ 27310 83309; byzanhtl@otenet.gr; s/d €40/60; ❄ 🏊), near the main square, has rooms with views, satellite TV and a swimming pool.

GEFYRA & MONEMVASIA ΓΕΦΥΡΑ & ΜΟΝΕΜΒΑΣΙΑ

pop 1,320

The atmospheric Byzantine walled village of Monemvasia occupies one side of a great rock, dramatically rising from the sea, which was separated from mainland Gefyra by an earthquake in AD 375.

While mass tourism blights the town during the day, it hasn't lessened the thrill of arriving – you enter a narrow tunnel on foot, from where you emerge in the magical town of cobblestone streets and stone houses. Signposted steps lead up to the ruins of a **fortress** built by the Venetians in the 16th century, and the Byzantine **Church of Agia Sophia**, perched precariously on the edge of the cliff. The views are spectacular.

Sleeping & Eating

To truly appreciate Monemvasia, stay overnight and explore after the day-trippers leave or before they arrive. If you're on a tight budget it's best to stay in Gefyra.

Hotel Aktaion (☎ 27320 61234; fax 27320 63026; s/d €30/40) This modern hotel, on the Gefyra end of the causeway, is popular with budget travellers for its clean rooms with balconies and views of the sea and 'the rock'.

Hotel Malvasia (☎ 27320 61113/61160; fax 27320 61722; d from €80, apt €160; ❄) The best 'hotel' in Monemvasia, this place has a variety of atmospheric, traditionally decorated rooms and apartments (most with sea views) scattered in stone buildings around the old town.

To Kanoni (☎ 27320 61387; Monemvasia; mains €6-12) While the interior here is charmingly decorated, on a balmy night the small terrace is the spot to eat excellent seafood and Greek classic meals.

Taverna O Botsalo (☎ 27320 61491; Gefyra; mains €6-23.50) O Botsalo serves up tasty meals overlooking the port in Gefyra.

Getting There & Away

Buses stop at the friendly **Malvasia Travel** (☎ 27320 61752) where you can buy tickets for buses and ferries. Four daily buses travel to Athens (€23, 5½ hours) via Corinth and Sparta (€8).

GYTHIO ΓΥΘΕΙΟ

pop 4489

Gythio (*yee*-thih-o) was once the port of ancient Sparta. Now it's a picturesque fishing town on the Lakonian Gulf and is the gateway to the rugged Mani Peninsula.

Pretty **Marathonisi islet**, linked to the mainland by a causeway, is said to be ancient Cranae, where Paris (prince of Troy) and Helen (the wife of Menelaus of Sparta) consummated the love affair that sparked the Trojan War. You'll find the **Museum of Mani History** (☎ 27330 24484; admission €1.50; 🕒 9am-7pm) here in an 18th-century tower.

Sleeping & Eating

Camping Meltemi (☎ 27330 22833; www.campingmeltemi.gr; per adult/tent €5/4.50; year-round;) This camping ground is situated behind silver olive groves on the beach 3km south of Gythio, and has a big swimming pool, bungalows and summer beauty contests! The Areopoli bus stops here.

Xenia Karlaftis Rooms to Rent (☎ 27330 22719; s/d/tr €25/35/40) Clean rooms and kitchen access make this a good budget option opposite Marathonisi, but there are a dozen places nearby of similar quality if you can't get in here.

Hotel Aktaion (☎ 27330 23500/1; fax 27330 22294; Vassilis Pavlou 39; s/d €40/60;) While the interior of this elegant neoclassical building had a charmless renovation in 1995, the clean rooms have TV and phone, but better yet, balconies with sea views.

The waterfront areas on the harbour and port are lined with fish tavernas and cafés.

I Gonia (☎ 27330 24024; Vassilis Pavlou; mains €3-7; 10am-late) This is a cheap option for tasty taverna standards and tables on the sea. It's on the corner, opposite the port.

Isalos (☎ 27330 24024; Vassilis Pavlou; mains €4.50-22; 11am-late) This place, close to Hotel Aktaion, has won awards for its quality seafood and pasta, and creative flair.

Getting There & Away

The **KTEL Lakonias bus station** (☎ 27330 22228; cnr Vasileos Georgios & Evrikleos) has buses to Athens (€18, 4½ hours, five daily), Sparta (€4, one hour, four daily), Areopoli (€2, 30 minutes, four daily) and the Diros Caves (€3, one hour, one daily). **ANEN Lines** (www.anen.gr) runs five ferries weekly to Kissamos, Crete (€21, seven hours), via Kythira (€10, 2½ hours) in summer. The schedule changes so check first with **Rozakis Travel** (☎ 27330 22207) on the waterfront.

THE MANI H MANH

The beautiful Mani occupies the central peninsula of the southern Peloponnese and is divided into two regions: the Lakonian (inner) Mani in the south and Messinian (outer) Mani in the northwest near Kalamata. The area is best explored by car.

Lakonian Mani

The wild and remote Lakonian Mani is dotted with striking stone-tower houses, and is loveliest in spring when the barren countryside bursts into life with a spectacular display of wildflowers.

Areopoli, some 30km southwest of Gythio, has a number of lovely towers on the narrow, cobbled streets of its old town. Nearby are the stunning **Diros Caves** (☎ 27330 52222; adult/concession €12/6; 8am-5.30pm Jun-Sep, to 3pm Oct-May), where a subterranean river flows. **Gerolimenas**, 20km further south, is a tranquil fishing village on a sheltered bay.

Tsimova Rooms (☎ 27330 51301; Kapetan Matepan, Areopoli; s/d €35/50, apt €65) has cosy rooms in a renovated tower tucked behind the Church of Taxiarhes, while **Pyrgos Kapetanakas** (☎ 27330 51233; fax 27330 51401; access off Kapetan Matepan, Areopoli; s/d/tr €50/70/90;) is another comfortable option in a splendid tower house, built by the powerful Kapetanakas family at the end of the 18th century.

Nicola's Corner Taverna (☎ 27330 51366; Plateia Athanaton, Areopoli; mains €4-9), on the central square, is a longstanding favourite for its delicious Greek classics.

The **bus station** (☎ 27330 51229; Plateia Athanaton) services Gythio (€2, 30 minutes, four daily), Itilo (for the Messinian Mani, €1, 20 minutes, three daily) and the Diros Caves (€1, 15 minutes, one daily).

Messinian Mani

The Messinian Mani runs along the coast from Kalamata to Itilo and has some of Greece's most dramatic countryside: beautiful aquamarine swimming coves surrounded by silver olive groves and set against the Taygetos Mountains.

The enchanting seaside village of **Kardamyli**, 37km south of Kalamata, was made famous by travel writer Sir Patrick Leigh Fermor, who wrote about his rambles in *Mani: Travels in the Southern Peloponnese*. Trekkers come for the magnificent **Vyros Gorge**. Walks are well organised and colour-coded.

Kardamyli has a good choice of small hotels and *domatia* (rooms usually in private homes) to suit all budgets: all are well signposted and easy to find, but book ahead for summer.

Olympia Koumounakou Rooms (☎ 27210 73623; s/d €25/30) is basic but clean and popular with backpackers who like the communal kitchen.

Notos Hotel (☎ 27210 73730; www.notoshotel.gr; studio €100, apt €125-150;) is really a boutique hamlet of individual stone houses, furnished in a contemporary rustic style, with fireplaces, fully equipped kitchens, and verandas and balconies with fab sea views.

Lela's Rooms (☎ 27210 73541/73730; fax 27210 64130; s/d/f €50/60/70;), run by Lela, former housekeeper to Patrick Leigh Fermor, who lived in Kardamyli for many years, has basic charming rooms, while **Lela's Taverna** (☎ 27210 73541) serves up tasty home-style Greek cuisine with sublime sea views.

Kardamyli is on the main bus route from Itilo to Kalamata and two to three buses stop daily at the central square. The hotels above will help with tickets and flagging the busses down.

OLYMPIA ΟΛΥΜΠΙΑ

pop 1475

In ancient times, Olympia was a sacred place of temples, priests' dwellings and public buildings, as well as being the venue for the quadrennial Olympic Games. The first Olympics were staged in 776 BC, reaching the peak of their prestige in the 6th century BC. The city-states were bound by a sacred truce to stop fighting for three months and compete. The site of ancient Olympia lies 500m beyond the modern town of the same name.

You can check email at the excellent wireless **Ep@thlon C@fé** (☎ 26240 23894; Stefanopoulou; per 30min €2; 10am-late); use its laptops or take your own.

Ancient Olympia (☎ 26240 22517; adult/concession €6/3, site & museum €9/5; 8am-7.30pm May-Oct, to 3pm Nov-Apr) is dominated by the immense ruined **Temple of Zeus**, to whom the games were dedicated. Don't miss the statue of **Hermes of Praxiteles**, a classical sculpture masterpiece, at the **museum** (adult/concession €6/3; 12.30-7.30pm Mon, 8am-7.30pm Tue-Sun).

Camping Diana (☎ 26240 22314; fax 26240 22425; per adult/tent €6/4; year-round;) is the best situated of Olympia's camping grounds (250m west of town); it has lovely leafy grounds with good facilities.

Pension Achilleys (☎ 26240 22562; Stefanopoulou 4; s/d/tr €25/35/40) is rather worn around the edges but **Pension Posidon** (☎ 26240 22567; Stefanopoulou 9; s/d/tr €30/40/50) is a sparkling clean, family-run place.

Best Western Europa (☎ 26240 22650/23850; www.hoteleuropa.gr; Drouva 1; s/d €85/125;) is an excellent family-ran hotel on a hill overlooking town with a wonderful large swimming pool – perfect after a tiring Olympics. Ask for one of their fab split-level rooms, but all come with satellite TV, minibar and buffet breakfast.

Taverna Gefsis Melathron (☎ 26240 22916; ant.xri@yahoo.gr; George Douma 3; mains €3-7) is by far the best place to eat in town. This friendly family-run taverna (mum is chef, daughter handles the floor and dad provides the organic wines) serves delicious traditional cuisine, including scrumptious vegetarian options, such as fried baby zucchini balls.

There are four buses a day to Athens (€23, 5½ hours) and regular buses to Pyrgos (€1.60, 30 minutes) and Tripoli (€10, 2½ hours) that leave from the centre of town. Two InterCity trains run daily to Corinth (€12, two hours) via Pyrgos (€3, 30 minutes) and Patra (€12, 45 minutes).

CENTRAL GREECE ΚΕΝΤΡΙΚΗ ΕΛΛΑΔΑ

This dramatic landscape of deep gorges, rugged mountains and fertile valleys is home to the magical mountaintop monasteries of Meteora and the ruins of ancient Delphi, where Alexander the Great sought advice from the Delphic Oracle.

DELPHI ΔΕΛΦΟΙ

pop 1500

The setting of Delphi, overlooking the Gulf of Corinth from the slopes of Mt Parnassos, is stunning, making ancient Delphi a very special place to visit.

The bus station, post office, OTE, banks and **EOT** (☎ 22650 82900; Vasileon Pavlou 44; 7.30am-2.30pm Mon-Fri) are all on modern Delphi's main street, Vasileon Pavlou.

By the 6th century BC, **ancient Delphi** (☎ 22650 82312; site or museum €6 year-round, combined adult/concession €9/5 year-round, free Sun Nov-Mar; 7.30am-7.30pm Apr-Oct, 8.30am-7pm Tue-Fri, 8.30am-2.45pm Sat, Sun & holidays Nov-Mar) had become the Sanctuary of Apollo. Thousands of pilgrims flocked there to consult the (middle-aged female) oracle, who sat at the mouth of a fume-emitting chasm. After sacrificing a sheep or goat, pilgrims would ask a question, and a priest would translate the oracle's response made incoherent by her writhing and shuddering. Wars, voyages and business transactions were undertaken on the strength of these prophecies. From the entrance, take the **Sacred Way** up to the **Temple of Apollo**, where the oracle supposedly sat. From here the path continues to the **theatre** and **stadium**.

Opposite the main site and down the hill some 100m is the **Sanctuary of Athena** and the much-photographed **Tholos** – a 4th-century-BC columned rotunda of Pentelic marble.

Apollon Camping (☎ 22650 82762; apollon4@otenet.gr; per adult/tent €5/3.50;) is 1.5km west of town; it has good facilities, including a restaurant, minimarket and barbecue.

The welcoming **Hotel Hermes** (☎ 22650 82318; www.delphihotels.gr; Vasileon Pavlou-Friderikis 27; s/d €55/70;) in the town centre has spacious rooms with balcony, stunning valley views and breakfast included.

Taverna Epikouros (☎ 22650 83250; Vasileon Pavlou-Friderikis 33; mains €4-12) has wonderful valley views, unobtrusive service and serves up scrumptious *mezedes*, such as cheese croquettes, imaginative salads and generous portions of tasty regional dishes (try the lamb with eggplant purée).

From the **bus stop** (☎ 22660 82317) on the main road there are six buses a day to Athens (€12, three hours).

METEORA ΜΕΤΕΩΡΑ

Magical Meteora (meh-*teh*-o-rah), with its magnificent late-14th-century monasteries perched atop enormous rocky pinnacles, is one of Greece's most extraordinary sights.

While there were once monasteries on all 24 pinnacles, only six are still occupied: **Megalou Meteorou** (Grand Meteoron; 9am-5pm Wed-Mon), **Varlaam** (9am-2pm & 3.20-5pm Fri-Wed), **Agiou Stefanou** (9am-2pm & 3.30-6pm Tue-Sun), **Agias Triados** (Holy Trinity; 9am-12.30pm & 3-5pm Fri-Wed), **Agiou Nikolaou Anapafsa** (9am-3.30pm Sat-Thu) and **Agias Varvaras Rousanou** (9am-6pm). Admission is €2 for each monastery and strict dress codes apply (women must wear skirts below their knees, and men long trousers and sleeves).

The tranquil village of **Kastraki**, 2km from Kalambaka, is the best base for visiting Meteora.

Vrachos Camping (☎ 24320 22293; camping-kastraki@kmp.forthnet.gr; per adult/tent €5/5;) has great views, a good taverna, a barbecue and a pool, and is a short stroll from Kastraki.

While the rooms at gregarious hosts Thanassis and Toula Nakis' **Dupiani House** (☎ 24320 75326; doupiani-house@kmp.forthnet.gr; s/d/tr €30/45/55), 500m from town, are simple, travellers book well ahead for the panoramic views (ask for a room with a balcony, and reconfirm your booking). Skip the underwhelming €5 breakfast.

Taverna Gardenia (☎ 24320 22504; Kastrakiou St; mains €3-8) serves up the freshest Greek food, along with excellent service; the splendid views of Meteora and fragrant scent of gardenias here are a bonus. The owners also have good-value and spacious rooms

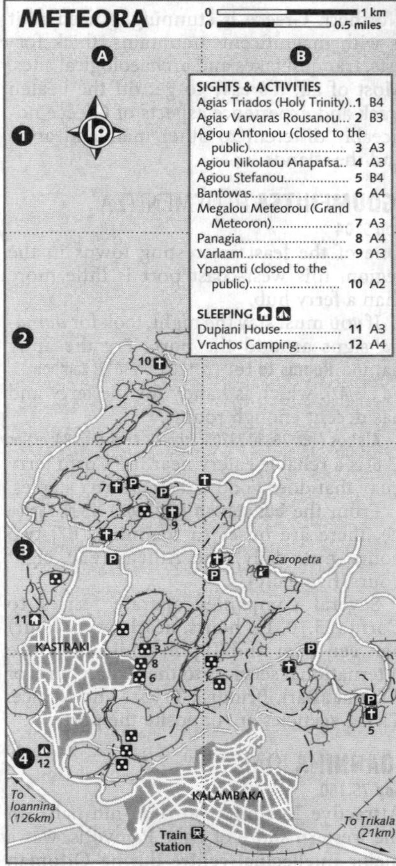

(some with views) at **Plakjas** (☎ 24320 22504; s/d/tr €30/45/55), behind the restaurant.

Local buses shuttle between Kalambaka and Kastraki. Hourly buses from Kalambaka go to the transport hub of Trikala (€1.50, 30 minutes), from where there are buses to Ioannina (€9, three hours, two daily) and Athens (€21, 5½ hours, eight daily). From Kalambaka, there are also express trains to Athens (€20, five hours, two daily), and Thessaloniki (€11, four hours, two daily) via Paliofarsalos.

NORTHERN GREECE ΒΟΡΕΙΑ ΕΛΛΑΔΑ

Northern Greece is stunning, graced as it is with magnificent mountains, thick forests, tranquil lakes and archaeological sites. Most of all, it's easy to get off the beaten track and experience aspects of Greece noticeably different to other mainland areas and the islands.

IGOUMENITSA ΗΓΟΥΜΕΝΙΤΣΑ

pop 9104

One of the least interesting towns in the region, this west-coast port is little more than a ferry hub.

If you must stay the night, look for *domatia* signs around the port. Try the aptly named **Rooms to Let** (☎ 26650 23612; Xanthou 12; s/d €35/42), which is handy for the ferry and has decent enough rooms.

Alekos (☎ 26650 23708; Ethnikis Andistasis 84; mains €3-6) is a reliable eatery near the Corfu ferry quay that does good Greek taverna staples.

From the **bus station** (☎ 26650 22309; Kyprou 29), there are buses to Ioannina (€7, two hours, nine daily) and Athens (€30, eight hours, five daily).

Several companies operate ferries to Corfu (€5.10, 1½ hours, nearly every hour) between 5am and 10pm, while there are international services to the Italian ports of Ancona, Bari, Brindisi, Trieste and Venice. Ticket agencies are opposite the port.

IOANNINA ΙΩΑΝΝΙΝΑ

pop 75,180

Attractive Ioannina (ih-o-*ah*-nih-nah) on the western shore of Lake Pamvotis, was a major intellectual centre during Ottoman rule. Today it's a thriving university town with a lively waterfront café scene.

The main streets meet in the town centre, around Plateia Dimokratias. There's Internet access at the **Web** (☎ 26510 26813; Pyrsinella 21; per hr €2.50; 24hr) and regional tourist information at **EOT** (☎ 26510 41142; Dodonis 39; 7.30am-2.30pm).

Sights

The pleasant **old town** sits on a small peninsula jutting into the lake. Within its impressive fortifications is the **kale**, an inner citadel with lovely grounds and lake views, and home to the **tomb of Ali Pasha** and splendid **Fetiye Cami** (Victory Mosque), built in 1611. The **nisi** (island) sits serenely in the middle of the lake, with four monasteries set among the trees. Ferries (€1, half-hourly summer, hourly winter) to the island leave from near the waterfront cafés.

Sleeping & Eating

Limnopoula Camping (☎ 26510 20541; fax 26510 38060; Kanari 10; per adult/tent €5/3; Apr-Oct) This shady camping ground must have one of the nicest spots of any in Greece; it's right on the edge of the lake 2km northwest of town.

Hotel Kastro (☎ 26510 22866; www.epirus.com/hotel-kastro; Andronikou Paleologou 57; s/d incl breakfast €65/75;) This charming restored hotel is in a traditional building across from the Kale.

Kale (☎ 26510 64206; Kastro; mains €3-7) While scores of cafés line the waterfront, there are few lovelier places to sit with a cold beer on a sunny day than at atmospheric Kale, in an old stone building in the kale. It serves up good sandwiches, salads and pastas.

Taberna To Manteio (☎ 26510 25452; Plataia Georgiou 15; mains €3-9) The deliciously simple, fresh Greek *mezedes,* salads and grills ensure this place is always packed with locals, particularly on weekends when families come to linger over lunch.

Getting There & Away

Aegean Airlines (code A3; ☎ 26510 64444) and **Olympic Airlines** (code OA; ☎ 26510 26518) fly twice a day to Athens, and Olympic has a daily flight to Thessaloniki.

The **main bus station** (☎ 26510 26404; Zossimadon), 300m north of Plateia Dimokratias, services Athens (€27, 7½ hours, 10 daily), Igoumenitsa (€7, 2½ hours, nine daily),

Thessaloniki (€22, seven hours, five daily) and Trikala (€10, 3½ hours, two daily).

ZAGORIA VILLAGES & VIKOS GORGE ΤΑ ΖΑΓΟΡΟΧΩΡΙΑ & ΧΑΡΑΔΡΑ ΤΟΥ ΒΙΚΟΥ

The spectacular Zagoria region, with its deep gorges, raging rivers, dense forests and snow-capped mountains, covers a large expanse of the Pindos Mountains north of Ioannina. Some 46 charming villages, famous for their grey-slate architecture, and known collectively as the Zagorohoria, are sprinkled across the mountains.

Delightful **Monodendri** is a popular departure point for treks through dramatic **Vikos Gorge**, with its sheer limestone walls. It's a strenuous 7½-hour walk along well-marked paths from here to the atmospheric twin villages of **Megalo Papingo** and **Mikro Papingo**. Get information on the walks from Ioannina's EOT office (opposite).

In Monodendri, the atmospheric **Archontiko Zarkada** (☎ 26530 71305; www.monodendri.com; s/d incl breakfast €35/45) is one of Greece's best (and best-value) small hotels, with friendly service and spacious, comfortable rooms including TV, DVD/CD player, minibar, spa-showers and valley views. Its taverna serves delicious regional specialities.

In Megalo Papingo, **Lakis** (☎ 26530 41087; fax 26530 41120; d €50) is a *domatia,* taverna and store all in one, while Mikro Papingo's rustic **Xenonas Dias** (☎ 26530 41257; s/d €50/65) also has a restaurant that serves tasty meals.

There are buses from Ioannina to Megalo and Mikro Papingo (€5, two hours, three weekly) and to Monodendri (€3, one hour, twice daily).

THESSALONIKI ΘΕΣΣΑΛΟΝΙΚΗ

pop 800,764

Thessaloniki (thess-ah-lo-*nee*-kih), also known as Salonica (Saloniki), was the second city of Byzantium and is the second city of modern Greece with countless Byzantine churches, a smattering of Roman ruins, engaging museums, shopping to rival Athens, fine restaurants, a lively café scene and a vibrant nightlife.

Orientation

Laid out on a grid system, the main thoroughfares of Tsimiski, Egnatia and Agiou Dimitriou run parallel to Leof Nikis, on the waterfront. Plateias Eleftherias and Aristotelous, both off Leof Nikis, are the main squares.

Information

Bianca Laundrette (Panagias Dexias 3; per 6kg load €6; 8am-8.30pm Tue, Thu & Fri, 8.30am-3pm Mon, Wed & Sat)
First-aid centre (☎ 23105 30530; Navarhou Koundourioti 10) Near the port.
In Spot: the Internet Place (☎ 23109 68173; Patriarchou Ioakim 28; per hr €2.50, unlimited hr midnight-noon €6; 24hr)
Main post office (Aristotelous 26; 7.30am-8pm Mon-Fri, 7.30am-2.15pm Sat, 9am-1.30pm Sun)
Tourist information office (☎ 23102 21100; the-info_office@gnto.gr; Tsimiski 136; 8am-2.45pm Mon-Fri, to 2pm Sat)
Tourist police (☎ 23105 54871; 5th fl, Dodekanisou 4; 7.30am-11pm)

Sights

The award-winning **Museum of Byzantine Culture** (☎ 23108 68570; Leoforos Stratou 2; admission €4; 10.30am-5pm Mon, 8.30am-3pm Tue-Fri) is one of Greece's best, with splendid sculptures, mosaics, ceramics, jewellery, icons and other intriguing artefacts beautifully displayed. The **Archaeological Museum** (☎ 23108 30538; Manoli Andronikou 6; admission €4; 10.30am-5pm Mon, 8.30am-3pm Tue-Sun) houses some finds from Northern Greece, including splendid Macedonian gold from Alexander the Great's time. The compelling **Thessaloniki Centre of Contemporary Art** (☎ 23105 46683; admission free; 11am-7pm) and small **Museum of Photography** (☎ 23105 66716; admission free; 11am-7pm Mon-Fri, to 9pm Sat & Sun) beside the port, are worth an hour of your time.

Sleeping

Acropol Hotel (☎ 23105 36170; fax 23105 28492; Tandalidou 4; s/d with shared bathroom €18/26) The best budget option in town has spartan but clean rooms.

Hotel Pella (☎ 23105 24221; pellahot@otenet.gr; Ionos Dragoumi 63; s/d with shared bathroom €35/50) This family-run hotel has spotless rooms with TVs, and breakfast is included.

Hotel Tourist (☎ 23102 70501; fax 23102 26865; Mitropoleos 21; s/d incl breakfast €55/70;) In an old neoclassical hotel, Hotel Tourist has comfortable rooms with TV and air-con.

City Hotel (☎ 23102 69421; ww.cityhotel.gr; Komninon 11; s/d €85/105;) This contemporary,

GREECE

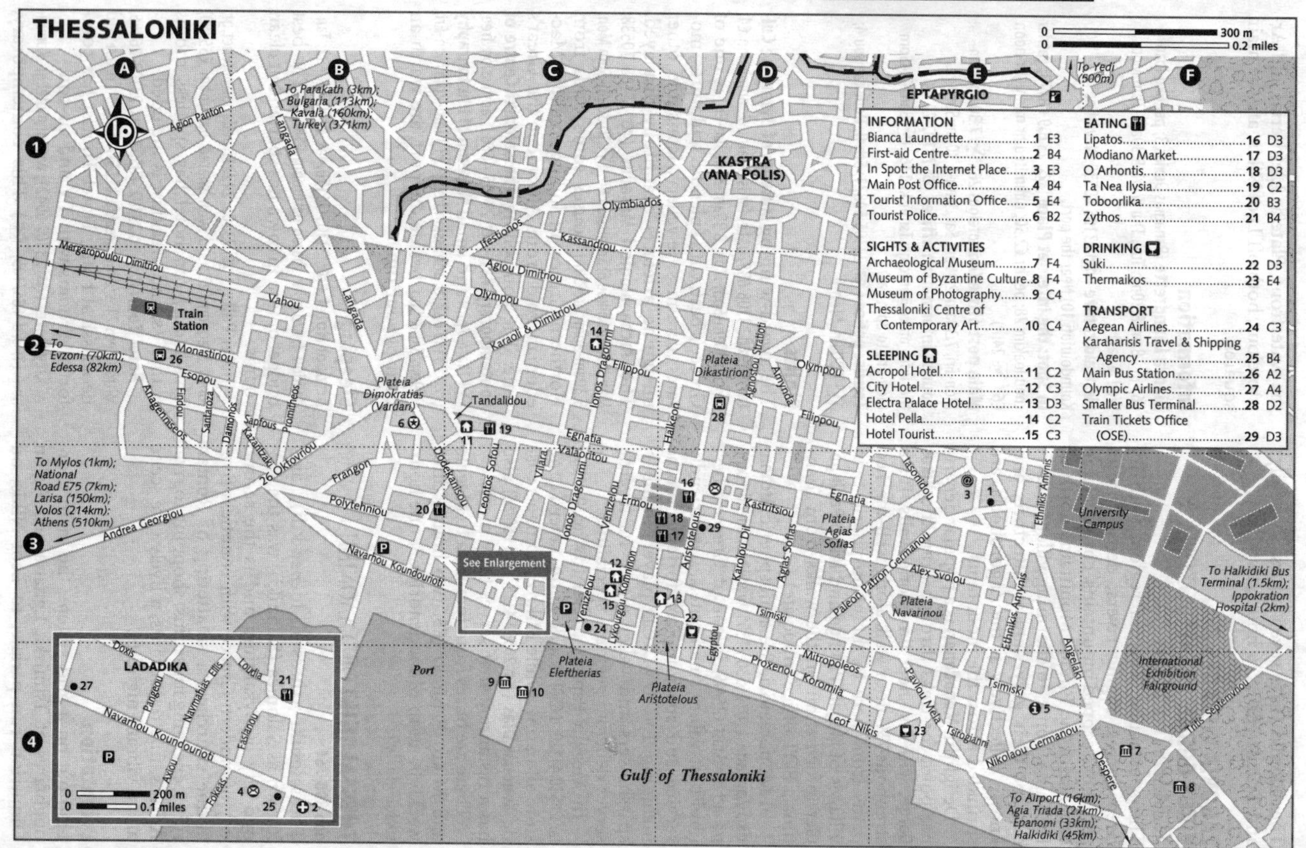
THESSALONIKI
0 300 m
0 0.2 miles
INFORMATION
Bianca Laundrette 1 E3
First-aid Centre 2 B4
In Spot: the Internet Place 3 E3
Main Post Office 4 B4
Tourist Information Office 5 E4
Tourist Police 6 B2
SIGHTS & ACTIVITIES
Archaeological Museum 7 F4
Museum of Byzantine Culture 8 F4
Museum of Photography 9 C4
Thessaloniki Centre of Contemporary Art 10 C4
SLEEPING
Acropol Hotel 11 C2
City Hotel 12 C3
Electra Palace Hotel 13 D3
Hotel Pella 14 C2
Hotel Tourist 15 C3
EATING
Lipatos 16 D3
Modiano Market 17 D3
O Arhontis 18 D3
Ta Nea Ilysia 19 C2
Toboorlika 20 B3
Zythos 21 B4
DRINKING
Suki 22 D3
Thermaikos 23 E4
TRANSPORT
Aegean Airlines 24 C3
Karaharisis Travel & Shipping Agency 25 B4
Main Bus Station 26 A2
Olympic Airlines 27 A4
Smaller Bus Terminal 28 D2
Train Tickets Office (OSE) 29 D3
To Parakath (3km); Bulgaria (113km); Kavala (160km); Turkey (371km)
To Yedi (500m)
EPTAPYRGIO
KASTRA (ANA POLIS)
Train Station
To Evzoni (70km); Edessa (82km)
To Mylos (1km); National Road E75 (7km); Larisa (150km); Volos (214km); Athens (510km)
To Halkidiki Bus Terminal (1.5km); Ippokration Hospital (2km)
To Airport (16km); Agia Triada (27km); Epanomi (33km); Halkidiki (45km)
University Campus
International Exhibition Fairground
Plateia Dimokratias (Vardari)
Plateia Dikastirion
Plateia Agias Sofias
Plateia Navarinou
Plateia Eleftherias
Plateia Aristotelous
Port
Gulf of Thessaloniki
See Enlargement
LADADIKA
0 200 m
0 0.1 miles

stylish hotel, in an excellent central location, has comfortable rooms with wireless Internet and a buffet breakfast.

Electra Palace Hotel (☎ 23102 32221; www.electrahotels.gr; Plateia Aristotelous 9; s/d from €120/150;) This luxurious five-star hotel is Saloniki's finest, with impeccable service, plush rooms, a rooftop bar, indoor and outdoor swimming pools, and a *hammam* (Turkish bath).

Eating & Drinking

O Arhontis (☎ 23102 80202; Ermou 26; mains €4; 10am-8pm) Eat delicious grilled sausages, potatoes and salads off butcher's paper at this popular working-class eatery at Modiano market.

Ta Nea Ilysia (☎ 23105 36996; Leontos Sofou 17; mains €6) This no-nonsense taverna serves enormous portions of traditional dishes to a local clientele.

Toboorlika (☎ 23105 48193; Naomahia Limbou 14; mains €6) This authentic *ouzeri*, decorated with musical instruments, gets packed with locals who come for the fresh seafood and to watch the two owners (cousins) perform *rembetika*.

Zythos (☎ 23105 40284; www.zythos.gr; Katouni 5; mains €8) Popular with locals, the friendly staff at this excellent taverna serves up delicious traditional Greek food, interesting regional specialities, good wines by the glass and beers on tap.

Suki (☎ 23102 34027; Plateia Aristotelous 4; noon-3am) Of all the funky bars on Plateia Aristotelous this is the most interesting, with its friendly androgynous staff, whimsically decorated interior (think pink chandeliers and lace brolly lamps), and dance music.

Thermaikos (☎ 23102 39842; Leof Nikis 21; noon-late) This retro-cool bar is the most bohemian of the many Leof Nikis bars, playing funk, jazz and alternative music, and attracting a young arty crowd.

Head to Modiano market for fresh fruit and vegetables, olives and bread; **Lipatos** (☎ 23108 55866; Plateia Aristotelous 23) has the best selection of pitta bread, breads and biscuits hot out of the oven.

Getting There & Away

The train station is on Monastiriou, the westerly continuation of Egnatia beyond Plateia Dimokratias. Thessaloniki's **Makedonia airport** (SKG; ☎ 23104 73700) is 16km southeast of the centre. **Olympic Airlines** (code OA; ☎ 23103 68666; Koundourioti 3) and **Aegean Airlines** (code A3; ☎ 23102 80050; Venizelou 2) have several flights a day to Athens. Between them they fly to Ioannina, Lesvos, Limnos, Corfu, Iraklio, Mykonos, Chios, Hania, Samos, Crete, Rhodes and Santorini.

The **main bus station** (☎ 23105 95408; Monastiriou 319) services Athens (€32, seven hours, 12 daily) and Ioannina (€23, six hours, five daily) among other destinations. Buses to the Halkidiki Peninsula leave from the smaller **bus terminal** (☎ 23109 24445; Karakasi 68).

Weekly ferries go to Limnos (€21, eight hours), Lesvos (€32, 13 hours) and Chios (€32, 18 hours) throughout the year. **Karaharisis Travel & Shipping Agency** (☎ 23105 24544; fax 23105 32289; Navarhou Koundourioti 8) handles tickets for all ferries and hydrofoils.

From the **train station** (☎ 23105 17517; Monastiriou) there are seven daily express services to Athens (€28, six hours) and two fast trains to Alexandroupolis (€17, 5½ hours). All international trains from Athens (to Belgrade, Sofia, Istanbul etc) stop at Thessaloniki. Get schedules from the **train tickets office** (OSE; ☎ 23105 98120; Aristotelous 18) or the train station.

Bus 78 plies the airport bus route (slowly), while a taxi to/from the airport costs around €15 and takes about 20 minutes.

MT OLYMPUS ΟΛΥΜΠΟΣ ΟΡΟΣ

Greece's highest mountain, Mt Olympus, was the ancient home of the gods. The highest of its eight peaks is Mytikas (2918m), popular with trekkers, who use Litohoro (5km inland from the Athens–Thessaloniki highway) as their base. The **EOS office** (☎ 23520 84544; Plateia Kentriki; 9.30am-12.30pm & 6-8pm Mon-Sat, Jun-Sep) has information on various treks. The main route to the top takes two days, with a stay overnight at one of the refuges (open May to October). Good protective clothing is essential, even in summer. If you trek outside the official season, you do so at your own risk.

Olympos Beach Camping (☎ 23520 22111/2; www.olympos-beach.gr; Plaka Litohoro; per adult/tent €6/7; Apr-Oct) is an excellent camping ground, with decent bungalows, a good taverna, a funky waterfront lounge bar and disco, and a pleasant beach.

An atmospheric old hotel, **Hotel Aphroditi** (☎ 23520 81415; fax 23520 83646; Plateia Kentriki; d/tr

GREECE

incl breakfast €30/40) has four-poster beds, balconies with views of Olympus, and a cosy bar with a fireplace.

Gastrodromio El Olympio (☎ 23520 21300; www.gastrodromio.gr; Plateia Kentriki; mains €4-11) One of Greece's best country restaurants, with specialities such as *soutzoukakia* (minced meat with cumin and mint), and delicious wild mushrooms, an impressive list of regional wines, and lovely views of Olympus.

From the **bus stop** (☎ 23520 81271) there are 18 buses daily to Thessaloniki (€7, 1½ hours) via Katerini, and three to Athens (€25, 5½ hours).

GREECE

HALKIDIKI ΧΑΛΚΙΔΙΚΗ

Beautiful pine-covered Halkidiki is a three-pronged peninsula that extends into the Aegean Sea, southeast of Thessaloniki. It has splendid sandy beaches around its 500km of coastline. The middle **Sithonia Peninsula** is the most spectacular, with pine forests and pretty beaches (and rooms to rent everywhere) and is more suited to independent travellers than the overdeveloped **Kassandra Peninsula**. You'll need your own wheels to explore the Halkidiki properly.

Mt Athos Αγιος Ορος

Halkidiki's third prong is occupied by the all-male Monastic Republic of Mt Athos (known in Greek as the Holy Mountain), where monasteries full of priceless treasures stand amid an impressive landscape of gorges, wooded mountains and precipitous rocks. While the process for obtaining a four-day visitor permit is becoming easier, only 10 foreign adult males may enter Mt Athos per day, so the summer waiting list is long. Start by contacting the **Mt Athos Pilgrims' Office** (☎ 23102 52578; fax 23108 22424; gikastheo@yahoo.gr; Egnatia 109, Thessaloniki; 🕑 8.30am-1.30pm & 6-8pm Mon, Tue, Thu & Fri) to make a booking. Fax your passport copy and, if you are Orthodox, certified evidence of your religion. Once the reservation is confirmed, visit the office to collect your visa (adult/student €35/25). If it's confirmed two weeks in advance, you can proceed straight to the port of Ouranoupolis (the departure point for boats to Mt Athos) and collect the permit there. You can visit 20 monasteries on foot, but you can only stay one night at each of the monasteries you've booked.

ALEXANDROUPOLIS ΑΛΕΞΑΝΔΡΟΥΠΟΛΗ

pop 49,176

Alexandroupolis has very few sights, but its lively student atmosphere makes for a pleasant stopover on the way to Turkey or Samothraki.

Hotel Mitropolis (☎ 25510 26443; fax 25510 89608; Atanasiou Diakou 11; s/d €35/40) is the best budget option, with spotlessly cleans rooms that have a TV and fridge. The 4th-floor rooms have enormous terraces. Discounts are offered out of season.

To Nisiotiko (☎ 25510 20990; G Zarifi 1; mains €3-12) is an atmospheric taverna/*ouzeri* with traditional blue-and-white décor and fresh flowers. Specialising in seafood, it serves up some of the tastiest food in Greece – try some flaming feta (€3), a plate of grilled octopus (€6) and a bottle of chardonnay from Drama and you'll be in heaven.

Locals seem to do more drinking than eating. A young crowd frequents the scores of café-bars on Leof Dimokratias between Ionos Dragoumi and Mitropolitou Kaviri, the university students hang out at the bars on Nikiforou Foka, while the older folk like the waterfront places.

Head to **Vatitsis Shipping Agency** (☎ 25510 26721; a_vati@otenet.gr; Kyprou 5) for local ferries and tickets to Samothraki and Limnos. **Sever Travel** (☎ 25510 22555; sever1@otenet.gr; Megalou Alexandrou 24) handles long-distance and international ferries, along with airlines. There are a few flights a day to Athens. To Thessaloniki, there are trains (€10, seven hours, six daily) and buses (€20, six hours, six daily). To Istanbul (Turkey) there's a daily train (€22, 10 hours) and a daily OSE bus (€16, five to seven hours), while to Svilengrad (Bulgaria) there's a daily train (€5, four to six hours).

SARONIC GULF ISLANDS ΝΗΣΙΑ ΤΟΥ ΣΑΡΩΝΙΚΟΥ

These islands are scattered about the Saronic Gulf, named after the mythical King Saron of Argos, a keen hunter who drowned while chasing a deer that had swum into the gulf to escape. They are the closest island group to Athens and their proximity to the congested capital makes them a popular escape. Accommodation is scarce between mid-June and September, and at weekends year-round.

AEGINA ΑΙΓΙΝΑ

pop 13,500

Once a major player in the Hellenic world, thanks to its strategic position at the mouth of the gulf, Aegina (*eh*-yee-nah) is close enough to Athens for workers to commute. A popular destination for day trips, the island also enjoys its position as Greece's premier producer of pistachios.

Bustling **Aegina Town**, on the west coast, is the island's capital and main port. There is no official tourist office, but there are plenty of booking agencies along the waterfront that will be keen to help you out. Further information can be gleaned at www.aeginagreece.com. **Nesant Internet Café** (☎ 22970 24053; Afeas 13; per 10min €1; 10am-2am) provides Internet access.

Lovely **Temple of Aphaia** (☎ 22970 32398; adult/concession €4/2; 8am-6:30pm), a well-preserved Doric temple 12km east of Aegina Town, served as a model for the construction of the Parthenon. Standing on a pine-clad hill with imposing views out over the gulf, it is well worth a visit. Buses from Aegina Town to the small resort of Agia Marina can drop you at the site.

In Aegina Town, **Hotel Plaza** (☎ 22970 25600; s/d €30/40) is a popular budget choice. More up-market is **Aeginitiko Archontiko** (☎ 22970 24968; www.aeginitikoarchontiko.gr; s/d €60/70;) in a 19th-century sandstone building. Book ahead, especially at weekends.

A flotilla of ferries (€5.90, 70 minutes) and hydrofoils (€10, 35 minutes) plies the waters between Aegina and Piraeus with great regularity. There is a good public bus service on the island.

HYDRA ΥΔΡΑ

pop 2700

Considered the most stylish destination of the group, Hydra (*ee*-drah) has a fine natural horseshoe-shaped harbour with gracious white and pastel stone mansions stacked up the rocky hillsides that surround it. Since the 1950s the island has been a haven for artists, celebrities and writers.

Hydra's main attraction is its tranquillity. There are no motorised vehicles – apart from sanitation and construction vehicles – and the main forms of transport are by foot and donkey.

Hydra Town is on the island's north coast. There is no tourist office, but check out www.greeka.com/saronic/hydra for more detailed information. **Satis Tours** (☎ 22980 52184) on the waterfront has a helpful free guide called *Holidays in Hydra*, while just around the corner on Tombazi, **Flamingo Internet Café** (☎ 22980 53485; per 15min €3; 11am-midnight) has Internet access.

Pension Erofili (☎ 22980 54049; www.pensionerofili.gr; Tombazi; s/d/tr €40/50/60;) is a popular place to stay, with clean, comfortable rooms, including TV and fridge, and a sizeable inner courtyard. It's about 300m from the harbour. **Hotel Miranda** (☎ 22980 52230; www.mirandahotel.gr; Miaouli; s/d/tr incl breakfast €80/110/165;) is worth a splurge. Originally built in 1810 as the mansion of a wealthy Hydriot sea captain, this stylish place retains much of its historical character.

There are two ferry (€9.80, 3½ hours) and six hydrofoil (€18.10, 1½ hours) services daily between Hydra and Piraeus. The ferries go via Aegina (€6.50, two hours), while the hydrofoils mostly go via Poros (€7.90, 30 minutes).

SPETSES ΣΠΕΤΣΕΣ

pop 4000

Spetses is an attractive island that is packed with visitors in summer. Known in antiquity as Pityoussa (meaning 'pine-covered'), the original pine forests disappeared long ago. The island's present attractiveness is largely thanks to Spetses-born philanthropist Sotirios Anargyrios, who made a fortune in the US after emigrating in 1848. Anargyrios returned in 1914, bought two-thirds of the then-barren island, planted Aleppo pines, financed the island's road system, and commissioned many of the town's grandest buildings.

Spetses Town, the main port, sprawls along half the northeast coast of the island. The **old harbour**, ringed by old Venetian buildings and filled with colourful boats of every shape and size, is a delightful place to explore. The island's coastline is speckled with coves and small, perfect pine-shaded beaches.

GREECE

There is no tourist office, but **Mimoza Travel** (☎ 22980 75170) on the waterfront in Spetses Town can help with accommodation and other services. Take a look at www.spetsesdirect.com for more information. **1800 Net Café** (☎ 22980 29498; per hr €3; ⌚ 9am-midnight) provides Internet access.

Villa Marina (☎ 22980 72646; s/d €40/56; ❄), located just off Plateia Agios Mamas, beyond the row of restaurants, is a small place with tidy rooms containing a fridge, and there's also a well-equipped communal kitchen.

A daily ferry connects Spetses to Piraeus (€13.50, four hours) via Hydra (€4.90, one hour) and Aegina (€10.10, three hours). There are at least six hydrofoils daily to Piraeus (€23.90, 2½ hours). There are also boats to Kosta, Ermioni and Porto Heli on the Peloponnese mainland.

CYCLADES ΚΥΚΛΑΔΕΣ

The Cyclades (kih-*klah*-dez) are the islands you picture in your mind's eye when you think of the Greek Islands. Named after the rough *kyklos* (circle) they form around the island of Delos, they are rugged outcrops of rock in the azure Aegean, speckled with white cubist buildings and blue-domed Byzantine churches. Throw in sun-blasted golden beaches and a fascinating culture and it's easy to see why many find the Cyclades irresistible.

Some of the islands, such as Mykonos, Ios and Santorini, have seized tourism with great enthusiasm, so you should prepare to battle the crowds if you turn up at the height of summer. Others are little more than clumps of rock, each with a village, secluded coves and a few curious tourists. Ferry services rarely run in winter, while from July to September the Cyclades are vulnerable to the *meltemi*, a fierce northeasterly wind that can cull ferry schedules.

History

The Cyclades enjoyed a flourishing Bronze Age civilisation (3000–1100 BC), more or less concurrent with the Minoan civilisation. Between the 4th and 7th centuries AD, the islands, like the rest of Greece, suffered a series of invasions and occupations. During the Middle Ages they were raided by pirates – hence the labyrinthine character of their towns, which was meant to confuse attackers. On some islands the whole population moved into the mountainous interior to escape the pirates, while on others they braved it out on the coast. Consequently, the *hora* (main town) is on the coast on some islands, while on others it is inland.

The Cyclades became part of independent Greece in 1827. During WWII they were occupied by the Italians. Before the revival of the islands' fortunes by the tourist boom that began in the 1970s, many islanders lived in poverty and many more headed for the mainland or emigrated to America and Australia in search of work.

MYKONOS ΜΥΚΟΝΟΣ

pop 9300

Sophisticated Mykonos shamelessly survives on tourism, but does it well. The island has something for everyone with marvellous beaches, romantic sunsets, chic boutiques, excellent restaurants and bars, and its long-held reputation as a mecca for gay travellers. The maze of white-walled streets in Mykonos Town was designed to confuse pirates, and it certainly manages to captivate and confuse the crowds that consume the island's capital in summer.

Orientation & Information

Mykonos Town has two ferry quays. The old quay, where most of the conventional ferries and some fast ferries dock, is 400m north of the town waterfront. The new quay is 2.5km north of town, where buses meet arriving ferries.

There is no tourist office, but at the old port, the same building houses the **Hoteliers Association of Mykonos** (☎ 22890 24540; www.mykonosgreece.com; ⌚ 8am-midnight) and the **Association of Rooms, Studios & Apartments** (☎ 22890 26860; ⌚ 9am-10pm). Both can book accommodation. **Island Mykonos Travel** (☎ 22890 22232; www.discovergreece.org), on Taxi Sq, where the port road meets the town, is helpful for travel information.

Angelo's Internet Café (☎ 22890 24106; Xenias; per hr €3.50) is on the road between the southern bus station and the windmills.

(Continued on page 597)

GRANT DIXON

Hiker surveying the Highlands (p259), Scotland

Musicians in Dublin bar (p660), Ireland

DOUG MCKINLAY

Low energy house at the Centre for Alternative Technology (p268), Wales

PATRICK HORTON

Chatsworth House (p215), England

GLENN BEANLAND

JEAN-BERNARD CARI

Basilique du Sacré Cœur (p301), Paris

Mont St-Michel (p332), France

MARK DAFFEY

Fresh produce from the Loire Valley (p338), France

GREG E

JOHN ELK III

Cycling through the Netherlands (p843)

PASCALE BEROUJON

Vieux Port (p381), Marseille, France

NEIL SETCHFIELD

Bruges (p129), Belgium

Luxembourg City (p832), Luxembourg

GLENN VAN DER KNIJFF

WAYNE WALTON

Santiago de Compostela (p990), Spain

Street scene in Coimbra (p911), Portugal

ANDERS BLOMQVIST

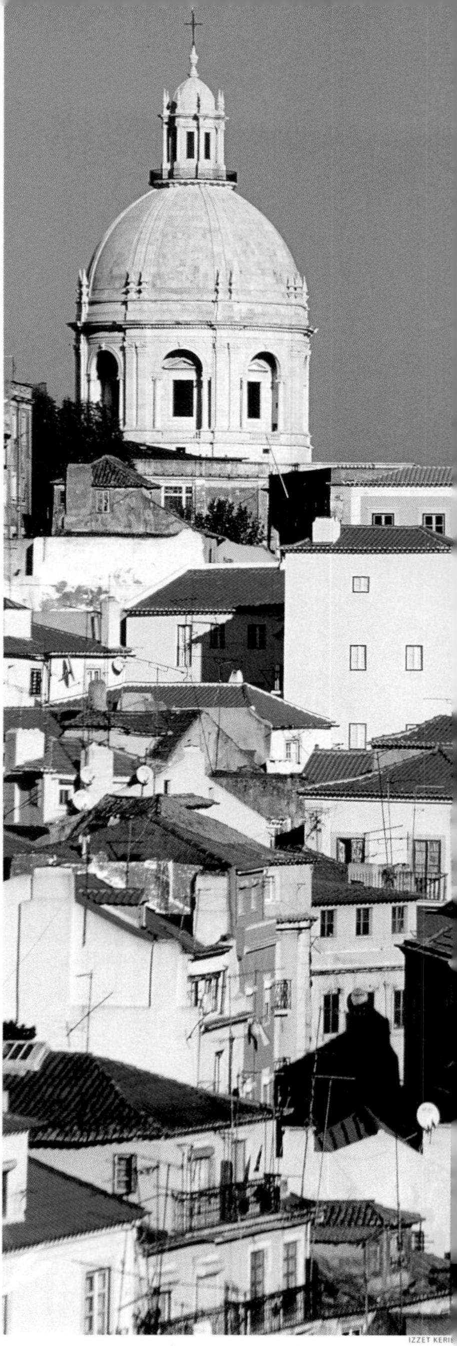

IZZET KERI

Alfama (p893), Lisbon, Portugal

DALLAS STRIBLEY

Local favourites in San Sebastián (p982), Spain

Tranquil courtyard in Seville (p1008), Spain

OLIVER STREWE

Alcázar and cathedral (p954), Segovia, Spain

DAVID TOMLINSON

CHRIS MELLOR

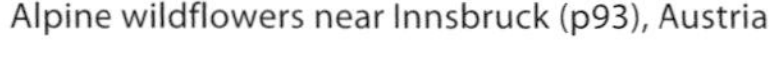

Alpine wildflowers near Innsbruck (p93), Austria

DENNIS JOHNS

Waterfall in Black Forest (p499), Germany

Grossglockner peak, Hohe Tauern National Park (p99), Austria

MARK HON

GLENN VAN DER KNIJFF

Zermatt (p1062), Switzerland

Harvesting grapes in the Moselle Valley (p507), Germany

JONAS KALTENBACH

Dining in Bern (p1045), Switzerland

GLENN BEANLAND

BETHUNE CARMICHAEL

Ancient Greek ruins in Sicily (p800), Italy

WAYNE WALT

Boat moored before Mykonos Town (p588), Greece

DAMIEN SIMO

Festa del Redentore (p755), Italy

Santorini (p604), Greece

DIANA MAYFI

(Continued from page 588)

Sights & Activities

A stroll around Mykonos Town, shuffling through snaking streets with blinding white walls and balconies of flowers is a must for any visitor. **Little Venice**, where the sea laps up to the edge of the restaurants and bars, and Mykonos' famous hilltop row of **windmills** should be included in the spots-to-see list.

The island's most popular beaches are on the southern coast. **Platys Gialos** has wall-to-wall sun lounges, while nudity is not uncommon at **Paradise Beach**, **Super Paradise**, **Agrari** and gay-friendly **Elia**. The less-squashy beaches, further from town, are **Kalo Livadi** and **Kalafatis** in the southeast, and **Panormos** on the northern coast. All can be accessed by bus or *caiques* (small fishing boats).

Sleeping

Rooms in town fill up quickly in the high season. Outside July and August though, they are as cheap as chips.

Mykonos has two camping areas, both on the south coast. Minibuses from both meet the ferries and buses go regularly into town.

Paradise Beach Camping (☎ 22890 22852; www.paradisemykonos.com; per person/tent €8/4;) There are lots of options here, including beach cabins and apartments, as well as bars, a swimming pool, games etc. It is skin-to-skin mayhem in summer with a real party atmosphere.

Mykonos Camping (☎ 22890 24578; www.mycamp.gr; per person/tent €8/4) This place, right on Paraga Beach, also has plenty of options, ranging from tents to dorm rooms to apartments. There's a minimarket, self-service restaurant and bar.

Hotel Apollon (☎ 22890 22223; fax 22890 24237; Paralia, Mykonos Town; s/d with shared bathroom €50/65) Prepare for some old-world Mykonian charm in the middle of the main waterfront. Rooms are traditional and well-kept, and the owner is friendly.

Hotel Philippi (☎ 22890 22294; chriko@otenet.gr; 25 Kalogera, Mykonos Town; s/d €60/75) In the heart of the *hora*, Philippi has spacious, bright, clean rooms that open onto a railed veranda overlooking a lush garden. An extremely pleasant place to stay.

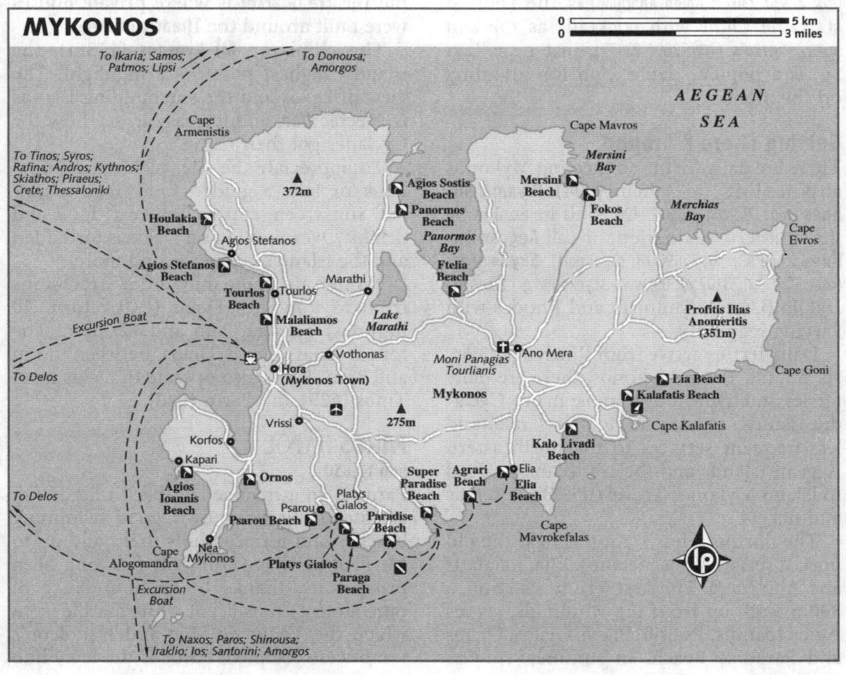

Eating & Drinking

There is no shortage of places to eat and drink in Mykonos Town.

Antonini's (☎ 22890 22319; Taxi Sq; dishes €3.50-12.50) A local hang-out with standard, but reliable Greek food, Antonini's offers a different view from its terrace overlooking Taxi Sq.

Madupas (☎ 22890 22224; Paralia; dishes €5-12) On the waterfront, Madupas serves a mean Mykonian sausage and is a great spot to chill out with a Mythos and watch the parade of passers-by.

Katerina's Bar (☎ 22890 23084; Agion Anargion) In Little Venice, this place has superb views from its balcony and water lapping below your feet.

Cavo Paradiso (☎ 22890 27205; www.cavoparadiso.gr; admission from €20) For those who want to go the whole hog, this club 300m above Paradise Beach picks up around 2am and boasts a pool the shape of Mykonos. A bus transports clubbers from town in summer.

Long feted as a gay travel destination, Mykonos has plenty of gay-centric clubs and hang-outs. In Little Venice, **Kastro** (☎ 22890 23072; Agion Anargion) is the spot to start the night with cocktails as the sun sets. **Pierro's** (☎ 22890 22177), just near Taxi Sq, is a popular dance club for rounding off the night.

Getting There & Around

There are daily flights connecting Mykonos airport (JMK) to Athens (€94). **Olympic Airlines** (code OA; ☎ 22890 22490; Plateia Remezzo) is by the southern bus station, or call **Aegean Airlines** (code A3; ☎ 22890 28720; airport). **Sky Express** (code SEH; ☎ 28102 23500; www.skyexpress.gr) flies to Iraklio (Crete), Santorini and Rhodes with varying regularity.

Daily ferries arrive from Piraeus (€23.60, six hours). From Mykonos, there are daily ferries and hydrofoils to most major Cycladic islands, regular services to Crete, and less-frequent services to the northeastern Aegean Islands and the Dodecanese. Head to Island Mykonos Travel (p588) for details and tickets.

The northern bus station is near the old port. It serves Agios Stefanos, Elia, Kalafatis and Ano Mera. The southern bus station, a 300m walk up from the windmills, serves Agios Ioannis, Psarou, Platys Gialos, Ornos and Paradise Beach. In summer, *caiques* from Mykonos Town and Platys Gialos putter to Paradise, Super Paradise, Agrari and Elia beaches.

DELOS ΔΗΛΟΣ

Southwest of Mykonos, the island of **Delos** (☎ 22890 22259; sites & museum €5; 🕘 9am-3pm Tue-Sun) is the Cyclades' archaeological jewel, and the opportunity to clamber among the ruins shouldn't be missed.

According to mythology, Delos was the birthplace of Apollo – the god of light, poetry, music, healing and prophecy. The island flourished as an important religious and commercial centre from the 3rd millennium BC, reaching its apex of power in the 5th century BC.

Ruins include the **Sanctuary of Apollo**, containing temples dedicated to him, and the **Terrace of the Lions**. These proud beasts were carved in the early 6th century BC using marble from Naxos to guard the sacred area. The original lions are in the island's museum, with replicas on the original site. The **Sacred Lake** (dry since 1926) is where Leto supposedly gave birth to Apollo, while the **Theatre Quarter** is where private houses were built around the **Theatre of Delos**.

The climb up **Mt Kynthos** (113m), the island's highest point, is a highlight. The view of Delos and the surrounding islands is spectacular, and it's easy to see how the Cyclades got their name.

To appreciate the site, pick up a guidebook or take a guided tour. Take a sunhat, sunscreen, sturdy footwear, food and drinks. Overnighting on Delos is forbidden and the island's cafeteria is no more.

Numerous companies offer excursions from Mykonos to Delos (€10 return, 30 minutes) between 9am and 12.50pm. The return boats leave Delos between noon and 3pm. Boats also operate to Delos from Tinos (€25) and Paros (€40).

PAROS ΠΑΡΟΣ

pop 12,850

Paros is an attractive laid-back island with an interesting main town, good swimming beaches and terraced hills that build up to Mt Profitis Ilias (770m). It has long been prosperous, thanks to an abundance of pure almost-translucent white marble from which the *Venus de Milo* and Napoleon's tomb were sculpted. Paros is the ferry hub for the Cyclades, so you may pass through, even if you're not intending to stay.

Orientation & Information

Paros' main town and port is Parikia, on the west coast. Opposite the ferry terminal, on the far side of Windmill roundabout, is Plateia Mavrogenous, the main square. Agora, also known as Market St, the main commercial thoroughfare, runs southwest from the far end of the square.

There is no tourist office, but travel agencies such as **Santorineos Travel** (☎ 22840 24245; bookings@santorineos-travel.gr), on the waterfront near Windmill roundabout, oblige with information. Check also www.parosweb.com. Opposite the ferry quay, to the left, is **Memphis.net** (☎ 22840 23768; per 15min €1; 9am-midnight), which provides Internet access.

Sights & Activities

Panagia Ekatontapyliani (Our Lady of the Hundred Gates; ☎ 22840 21243; 7.30am-9.30pm), known for its beautiful ornate interior, is one of the most impressive churches in the Cyclades, dating from AD 326. Within the church compound, the **Byzantine Museum** (Parikia; admission €1.50; 9:30am-2pm & 6-9pm) has an interesting collection of icons and other artefacts.

A great option on Paros is to rent a scooter at one of the many outlets in Parikia and ride around the island. There are sealed roads the whole way around, and the opportunity to explore villages such as **Naoussa**, **Marpissa** and **Aliki**, and swim at beaches such as **Logaras**, **Punda** and **Golden Beach**. Naoussa is a cute little fishing village on the northeastern coast that is all geared up to welcome tourists.

Less than 2km from Paros, the small island of **Antiparos** has fantastic beaches, which have made it wildly popular. The chief attraction is its **cave** (admission €3.50; 10.15am-3pm Jun-Sep), considered to be one of Europe's best.

Sleeping

The **Rooms Association** (☎ 22840 22722; 9am-1am) has a helpful kiosk on the quay. There's loads of camping around Paros, with charges of around €6 per person and €4 per tent.

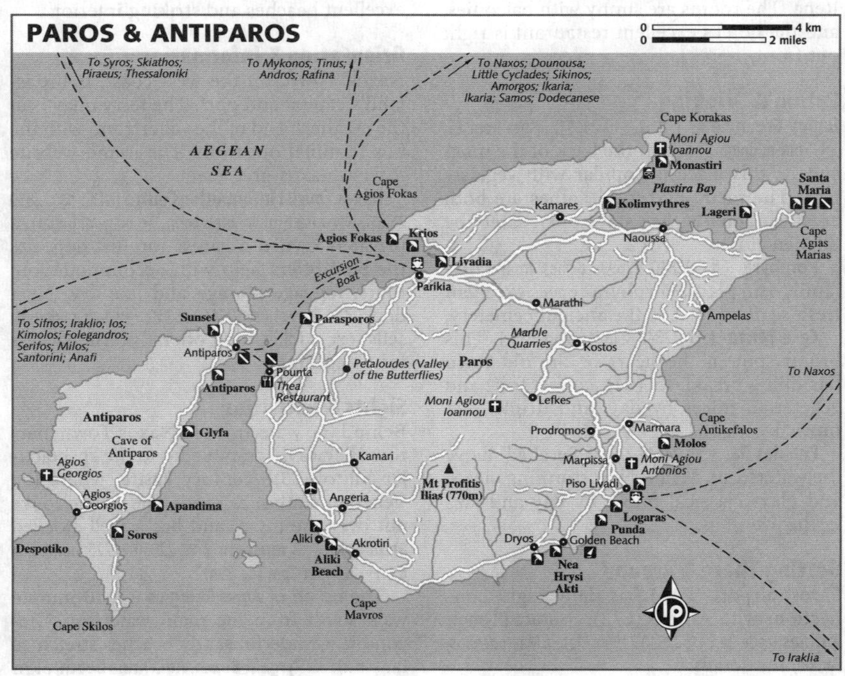

Koula Camping (☎ 22840 22081; www.campingkoula.gr) At Livadia beach, this campground is about 500m north of Parikia's waterfront. There is a restaurant and a minimarket here.

Naoussa Camping (☎ 22840 51595; http://campingnaoussa.parosweb.com) On the north coast at Kolimvythres Beach near Naoussa, this place provides free transport from the port or airport.

Rooms Mike (☎ 22840 22856; roommike@otenet.gr; s/d/tr €25/35/45) A popular place with backpackers, Mike's offers good value, a shared kitchen, a roof terrace and friendly local advice. Walk 100m east from the port and it's next to Memphis.net.

Rooms Rena (☎ 22840 22220; www.cycladesnet.gr/rena; Epitropakis; s/d/tr €25/40/50; ❄) One of the top choices in town, the quiet and well-kept rooms here are excellent value. To get here, turn left from the pier then right at the ancient cemetery.

Hotel Argonauta (☎ 22840 21440; www.argonauta.gr; s/d/tr €57/68/81; ❄) On the main square of the old town, the recently renovated Argonauta has a more traditional feel then Rena. The rooms are sunny with balconies, and the hotel's excellent restaurant is right out front.

Eating & Drinking

Happy Green Cows (☎ 22840 24691; dishes from €5; 🕑 7pm-midnight) Just off the back of the main square, this place is popular with vegetarians. The menu and meal names are both creative, and the bar stays open after the kitchen closes.

Porphyra (☎ 22840 22693; dishes from €5) A family-run place, Porphyra serves excellent fresh seafood next to the ancient cemetery.

Café Micro (☎ 22840 24674; Market St) This bright spot in the heart of the old town has filling breakfasts (€4), coffee, fruit and vegetarian juices by day, and drinks and music by night.

Pebbles Bar (☎ 22840 22283) Perched above the waterfront, Pebbles has stunning views, and plays classical music by day and jazz in the evenings.

Getting There & Around

Paros' airport (PAS) has daily flight connections with Athens (€72); contact **Olympic Airlines** (code OA; ☎ 22840 21900; Plateia Mavrogenous, Parikia) for details.

Parikia is a major ferry hub with daily connections to Piraeus (€23.40, five hours) and frequent ferries and catamarans to Naxos, Ios, Santorini, Mykonos and Crete. The fast boats generally take half the time but are more expensive, eg a fast boat to Piraeus costs €39.10. The Dodecanese and the northeastern Aegean Islands are also well serviced from here. Head to Santorineos Travel (p599) for tickets.

From Parikia there are frequent bus services to the entire island. In summer there are hourly excursion boats to Antiparos from Parikia port, or you can catch a bus to Pounta and ferry it across.

NAXOS ΝΑΞΟΣ

pop 18,200

Naxos, the biggest and greenest of the Cyclades, enjoys its reputation as a family destination. Deeply fertile, Naxos produces olives, figs, citrus, corn and potatoes, and, unlike many of its neighbouring islands, could probably survive without tourism. The island is well worth taking the time to explore with its fascinating main town, excellent beaches and striking interior.

Orientation & Information

Naxos Town, on the west coast, is the island's capital and port. The ferry quay is at the northern end of the waterfront, with the bus terminal out front. The island website is www.naxos-greece.net.

Naxos Tourist Information Centre (NTIC; ☎ 22850 25201; www.naxostownhotels.com; 🕑 8am-midnight), a privately owned organisation just opposite the port offers help with accommodation, tours, luggage storage and laundry. Next door, **Zas Travel** (☎ 22850 23330; 🕑 8am-midnight) sells ferry tickets and offers Internet access for €4 an hour.

Sights & Activities

Behind the waterfront in Naxos Town, narrow alleyways scramble up to the spectacular hilltop 13th-century **kastro**, where the Venetian Catholics lived. The *kastro* looks out over the town, and has a well-stocked **archaeological museum** (☎ 22850 22725; admission €3; 🕑 8.30am-3pm Tue-Sun).

The beach of **Agios Georgios** is a 10-minute walk south from the main waterfront. Beyond it, wonderful sandy beaches stretch as far south as **Pyrgaki Beach**. **Agia Anna Beach**, 6km from town, and **Plaka Beach** are lined with accommodation and packed in summer.

A rental car or scooter will help reveal Naxos' dramatic landscape. The **Tragaea region** has tranquil villages, churches atop rocky crags and huge olive groves. **Filoti**, the largest inland settlement, perches on the slopes of **Mt Zeus** (1004m), the highest peak in the Cyclades.

In **Apollonas** there's the mysterious 10.5m **kouros** (naked male statue), constructed c 7th century, lying abandoned and unfinished in an ancient marble quarry.

Sleeping

Owners of *domatia* and camping grounds meet ferries, picking up those with a booking and competing for those without. There are good beachside camping grounds south of town, charging around €5 per person.

Camping Maragas (☎ 22850 42552; www.maragascamping.gr/naxos-camping.htm) On Agia Anna Beach, this place has all sorts of options, including camping, rooms and studios, and there is a restaurant and minimarket on site.

Plaka Camping (☎ 22850 42700; www.plakacamping.gr) At Plaka Beach (8km from town), this camping ground is on a long beautiful sandy white beach and offers a restaurant, Internet access and a minimarket.

Hotel Grotta (☎ 22850 22215; www.hotelgrotta.gr; s/d incl breakfast €50/70; P) Overlooking

GREECE

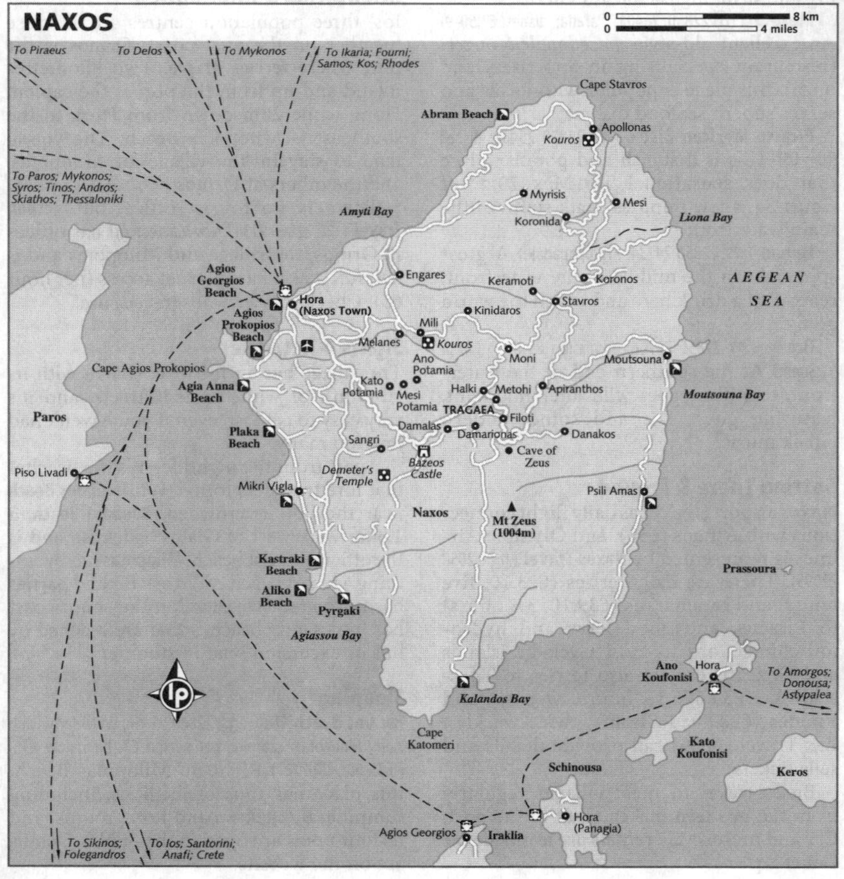

Grotta Beach at the northern end of town, this modern hotel has comfortable and immaculate rooms, and offers great sea views.

Pension Sofi (☎ 22850 23077; www.pensionsofi.gr; d & tr €30-60) and **Studios Panos** (☎ 22850 26078; www.studiospanos.com; Agios Georgios Beach; d & tr €30-60;) are both in town and run by members of the friendly Koufopoulos family. All guests are met with a glass of family-made wine or ouzo, and rooms are immaculate and have bathroom and kitchen. Highly recommended; rates at both places halve out of the high season.

Eating & Drinking

Naxos Town's waterfront is lined with eating and drinking establishments.

Meze 2 (☎ 22850 26401; Paralia; dishes €2.50-9) An excellent old-style *mezedopoleio-ouzeri* (restaurant specialising in appetisers and ouzo), this place is popular with locals and serves superb seafood dishes.

Picasso Mexican Bistro (☎ 22850 25408; dishes from €5) This is a stylish and popular place that does sensational Tex-Mex 20m off Court Sq, a few minutes' walk south of the main waterfront.

Lemon (☎ 22850 24734; Protopapadaki) A great spot right in the middle of the waterfront, relax with a drink here and watch the world go by.

Ocean (☎ 22850 26766; admission €5-8; from 11:30pm) At the southern end of the waterfront, this place goes wild after midnight, featuring guest DJs and some modern Greek music.

Getting There & Around

Naxos airport (JNX) has daily flight connections with Athens (€56), and Olympic Airlines is represented by **Naxos Travel** (☎ 22850 22095). There are daily ferries (€23.10, five hours) and catamarans (€39.10, 3¾ hours) to Piraeus, and good ferry and hydrofoil connections to most Cycladic islands and Crete. There are also ferries to Thessaloniki (€34.50, 15 hours, weekly) and Rhodes (€22.80, 14 hours, twice weekly). Zas Travel (p600) can provide details and sells tickets.

Buses travel to most villages regularly from the bus terminal in front of the port. Car and motorcycle rentals are available off Court Sq.

IOS ΙΟΣ

pop 1850

While some would like to see Ios shake off its tag of 'Party Island', for others partying is the prime reason for going there. There are wall-to-wall bars and nightclubs in 'the village' (Hora) that thump all night, and fantastic fun facilities at Milopotas Beach that entertain all day.

But there's more to Ios than just hedonistic activities. British poet and novelist Lawrence Durrell thought highly of Ios as a place of poetry and beauty, and there is an enduring claim that Homer was buried on Ios, with his alleged tomb in the north of the island.

Orientation & Information

Ios' three population centres are all close together on the west coast. Ormos is the port where ferries arrive. Two kilometres inland and up from the port is the capital, Hora, while 2km down from Hora to the southeast is Milopotas Beach. The young tend to stay in 'the village' or Milopotas, and the others at Ormos.

There is no tourist office, but **Acteon Travel** (☎ 22860 91343; www.acteon.gr) has offices in Ormos, the village and Milopotas and is helpful. It also has Internet access (per hour €5). Check out www.iosgreece.com.

Sights & Activities

The village has an intrinsic charm with its labyrinth of white-walled streets, and it's very easy to get lost, even if you haven't had one too many.

Apart from the nightlife, it 's the beaches that lure travellers to Ios. While **Gialos Beach** near the port is crowded, **Koubara Beach**, a 1.3km walk west of Gialos, is less so and is the official nudist beach. **Milopotas** has everything a resort beach could ask for and parties hard. Isolated **Manganari** on the south coast has four sandy beaches that are reached by bus or excursion boat in summer.

Sleeping

Far Out Beach Club (☎ 22860 91468; www.faroutclub.com; Milopotas; camping per person €7, bungalow €15, r €25-60;) Right on Milopotas Beach, this place has tons of facilities, including camping, bungalows and hotel rooms, and its four pools are open to the public. Details are on the website.

Francesco's (☎ 22860 91223; www.francescos.net; Hora; dm/s/d €11/30/40;) A lively meeting place in the village with superlative views from its terrace bar, Francesco's is convenient for party-going and rates halve out of the high season. The party spirit rules here.

Hotel Nissos Ios (☎ 22860 91610; www.nissosioshotel.gr; Milopotas; dm/s/d €25/45/65;) This bright, cheerful place is on Milopotas Beach. Rooms feature massive colourful wall murals, and there is a good restaurant on site.

Hotel Poseidon (☎ 22860 91091; www.poseidonhotelios.gr; Ormos; s/d/tr €65/75/95;) Near the ferry quay in Ormos, the Poseidon offers superb views, spacious rooms and a refreshing pool for a quieter stay on Ios.

Eating & Drinking

There are numerous places to get cheap eats such as gyros in the village.

Porky's (☎ 22860 91143; Hora) Just off the main square, this place is legendary for its good-value tasty toasties and hamburgers.

Susana (☎ 22860 51108; Ormos; dishes from €2.50) Down at the port, Susana is regularly full of locals. Its pastas and pizzas are particularly popular.

Ali Baba's (☎ 22860 91558; Hora; dishes €6-10) Long an Ios favourite, Ali Baba's parties until late. Upbeat service complements the funky ambience. The meals are of humungous proportions, especially the Dinosaur Ribs.

At night, the compact little village erupts with bars. Its tiny central square gets so packed that by midnight you won't be able to fall over even if you want to. Perennial favourites include **Red Bull** (☎ 22860 91019), **Slammers** (☎ 22860 92119) and **Blue Note** (☎ 22860 92271).

Getting There & Around

Ios has daily ferry connections with Piraeus (€21, seven hours) and there are frequent hydrofoils and ferries to the major Cycladic islands and Crete. There are buses every 15 minutes between the port, the village and Milopotas Beach until early morning, and two to three a day to Manganari Beach (€6, 45 minutes). Head to Acteon Travel (opposite) for details and tickets.

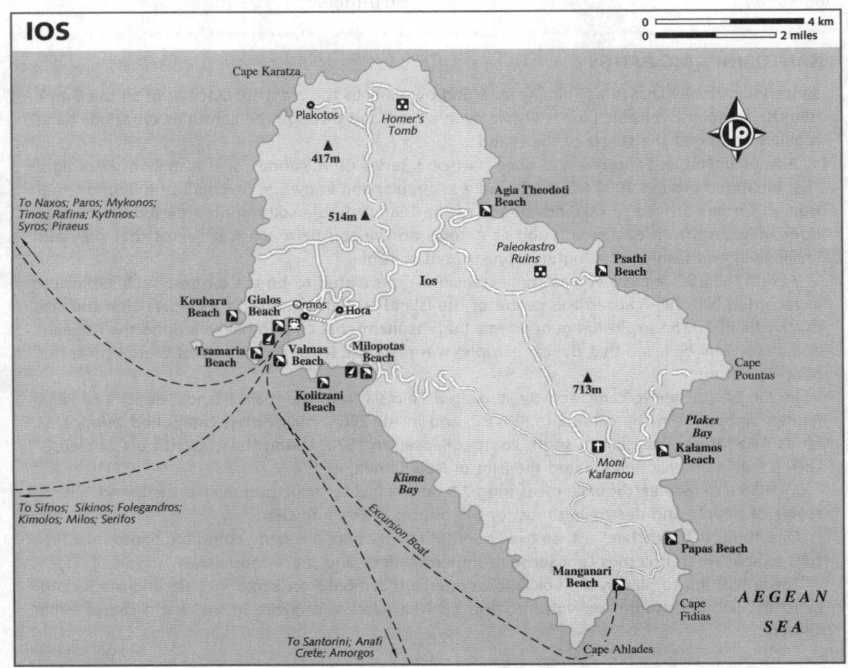

GREECE

SANTORINI (THIRA)
ΣΑΝΤΟΡΙΝΗ (ΘΗΡΑ)

pop 13,400

Stunning Santorini, shaped like a doughnut with a bite taken out of its southwestern side, is unique and should not be missed. Viewed from a boat in the doughnut's hole, the startling sight of the submerged caldera almost encircled by sheer lava-layered cliffs – topped off by clifftop towns that look like a dusting of icing sugar – will grab your attention and not let it go. If you turn up in the high season though, be prepared for relentless crowds and commercialism because Santorini survives on tourism.

Orientation & Information

Santorini's capital, Fira, perches on top of the caldera on the west coast, with the new port of Athinios, where most ferries dock, 10km south by road. The old port of Fira Skala, used by cruise ships and excursion boats, is directly below Fira and accessed by cable-car (adult/child €3/1.50 one way), donkey (€3; up only) or by foot (588 steps).

The bus station and taxi station are located just south of Fira's main square, Plateia Theotokopoulou.

Dakoutros Travel (☎ 22860 22958; www.dakoutrostravel.gr; ⏰ 8.30am-10pm), opposite the taxi station, is extremely helpful, and there is a batch of other agencies around the square. Internet access is available at **PC World** (☎ 22860 25551; Central Sq; per 30min €2.10). The post office is one block south of the taxi station.

Sights & Activities

FIRA

The stunning caldera views from Fira are unparalleled.

The exceptional **Museum of Prehistoric Thira** (☎ 22860 23217; admission €3; ⏰ 8.30am-3pm Tue-Sun), which has wonderful displays of artefacts predominantly from ancient Akrotiri, is two blocks south of the main square. **Megaron Gyzi Museum** (☎ 22860 22244; admission €3; ⏰ 10.30am-1.30pm & 5-8pm Mon-Sat, 10.30am-4.30pm Sun), behind the Catholic cathedral, houses local memorabilia, including photographs of Fira before and after the 1956 earthquake.

SANTORINI'S BIG BANGS

Santorini, officially known as Thira, is regarded by many as the most spectacular of all the Greek islands. Its violent volcanic past is visible everywhere, and through the centuries eruptions have regularly changed the shape of the island.

Always unstable, Santorini was once part of a series of volcanoes over a million years ago. First inhabited around 3000 BC, the island was circular and known as Strongili (the Round One). Human settlers arrived to take advantage of the island's fertile soil during a period of volcanic dormancy, and from evidence found at Akrotiri on the southern coast, it seems that they led idyllic lives and fashioned a highly sophisticated culture.

About 1650 BC, a massive volcanic explosion – speculated to be the biggest such explosion in recorded history – caused the centre of the island to sink, producing a caldera that the sea quickly filled in. The explosion generated a huge tsunami that caused havoc around the Aegean, and it is widely believed that the catastrophe was responsible for the demise of Crete's powerful Minoan culture.

In 236 BC further volcanic activity separated Thirasia from the main island. The islet of Palia Kameni appeared in the caldera in 197 BC, and in AD 726 a major blast catapulted pumice as far as Asia Minor. The island's south coast collapsed in 1570, taking the ancient port of Eleusis with it, while an eruption created the islet of Nea Kameni in 1707.

In 1956 a savage earthquake measuring 7.8 on the Richter scale pummelled the island, killing scores of people and destroying most of the houses in Fira and Oia.

One thing is for certain – it isn't over yet. Minor tremors are fairly common. Santorini is incomparable when it comes to a sense of impermanence and precariousness.

Those wishing to play in the volcanic wonderland can bake on Santorini's sizzling black-sand beaches, clamber around on volcanic lava on Nea Kameni or swim in the warm sea at Palia Kameni.

AROUND THE ISLAND

Santorini's black-sand **beaches** of **Perissa** and **Kamari** sizzle – beach mats are essential. It's a strange feeling to walk over black sand then out onto smooth lava when going for a dip.

Excavations in 1967 uncovered the remarkably well-preserved Minoan settlement of **Akrotiri** at the south of the island with its remains of two- and three-storey buildings. A section of the roof collapsed in 2005 killing one visitor, and at the time of research, the site's future as a visitor attraction was up in the air.

On the north of the island, the flawless village of **Oia** (ee-ah), famed for its postcard sunsets, is less hectic than Fira and a must-visit. Its caldera-facing tavernas are superb spots for brunch. There's a path from Fira to Oia along the top of the caldera that takes about three hours to walk.

Of the surrounding islets, only **Thirasia** is inhabited. Visitors can clamber around on volcanic lava on **Nea Kameni** then swim into warm springs in the sea at **Palia Kameni**; there are various excursions available to get you there.

Sleeping

Decide where you want to stay before the aggressive accommodation owners who meet the boats try to decide things for you. Fira has spectacular views, but is miles from the beaches. Perissa has a great beach but is on the southeast coast, away from the caldera views.

Santorini Camping (☎ 22860 22944; www.santorinicamping.gr; Fira; per person €8; P) This place, 500m east of Fira's main square, is the cheapest option. There is a restaurant, bar, minimarket and swimming pool, but no caldera views.

Maria's Rooms (☎ 22860 25143; Agiou Mina, Fira; d €60;) On the southern edge of town, Maria's has small but immaculate rooms, and stunning caldera views from its terrace.

Stelio's Place (☎ 22860 81860; www.steliosplace.com; Perissa; d/tr/q €60/75/100; P) Stelio's is an excellent option just back from Perissa's black-sand beach on the southeast coast. There's a refreshing pool, very friendly service, and free port and airport transfers. Rates more than halve out of the high season.

Hotel Keti (☎ 22860 22324; www.hotelketi.gr; Agiou Mina, Fira; d/tr €75/97.50; ❄) Just to the north of Maria's Rooms, with caldera views to die for, Hotel Keti has satellite TV and refrigerators in each of its immaculate rooms.

Eating & Drinking

Cheap eateries are in abundance around the square in Fira.

Taverna Lava (☎ 22860 81776; Perissa; dishes €3-8) On Perissa's waterfront, this island-wide favourite has a mouth-watering menu. You can visit the kitchen and pick what looks good.

Naoussa (☎ 22860 24869; Erythrou Stavrou, Fira; dishes €3-20) This restaurant serves excellent-value Greek classics.

Nikolas (☎ 22860 24550; Erythrou Stavrou, Fira; dishes €5-10) This long-established traditional place serving Greek cuisine in the heart of Fira receives rave reviews from diners. From the main square, head straight up the pedestrian mall (Danezi) and take the first right.

Most of the more popular bars and clubs in Fira are clustered along Erythrou Stavrou.

Kira Thira (☎ 22860 22770) Opposite Nikolas restaurant, Kira Thira is Fira's oldest bar and plays smooth jazz, ethnic sounds and occasional live music.

Full Moon Bar (☎ 22860 81177; ⏲ 9pm-late) On the main street in Perissa, this lively nightspot goes off until the wee hours.

Getting There & Around

Santorini airport (JTR) has daily flight connections with Athens (€94). Call **Olympic Airlines** (code OA; ☎ 22860 22493) or **Aegean Airlines** (code A3; ☎ 22860 28500) for details. **Sky Express** (code SEH; ☎ 28102 23500; www.skyexpress.gr) has connections with Crete, Mykonos and Rhodes with varying regularity.

There are daily ferries (€27.80, nine hours) and fast boats (€45, 5¼ hours) to Piraeus; daily connections in summer to Mykonos, Ios, Naxos, Paros and Iraklio; and ferries to the smaller islands in the Cyclades. Large ferries use Athinios port, where they are met by buses (€1.20) and taxis. Get your tickets from Dakoutros Travel (p604).

Buses go frequently to Oia, Kamari, Perissa and Akrotiri from Fira. Port buses usually leave Fira, Kamari and Perissa one to 1½ hours before ferry departures. A rental car or scooter is a great option on Santorini.

CRETE ΚΡΗΤΗ

pop 540,000

Greece's largest and most southerly island, Crete, with its dramatic landscape and unique cultural identity, is a delight to explore. Its size and distance from the rest of Greece gives Crete the feel of a different country.

The island is split by a spectacular chain of mountains running east to west. Major

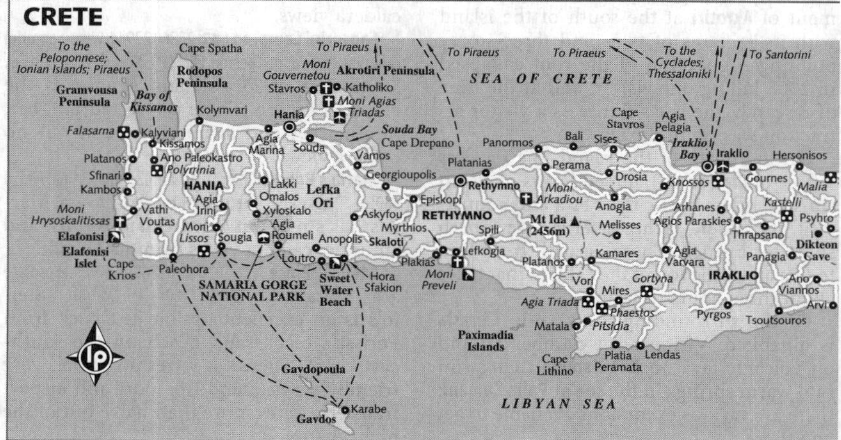

towns are on the more hospitable northern coast, while most of the southern coast is too precipitous to support large settlements. The rugged mountainous interior, dotted with caves and sliced by dramatic gorges, offers rigorous trekking and climbing.

While Crete's proud, friendly and hospitable people have enthusiastically embraced mass tourism, they continue to fiercely protect their traditions and culture – and it is the people that remain a major part of the island's appeal.

For more detailed information, snap up a copy of Lonely Planet's *Crete*. Good websites on Crete include www.interkriti.org, www.infocrete.com and www.explorecrete.com.

History

Crete was the birthplace of Minoan culture, Europe's first advanced civilisation, which flourished between 2800 and 1450 BC. Very little is known of Minoan civilisation, which came to an abrupt end, possibly destroyed by Santorini's volcanic eruption in around 1650 BC. Later, Crete passed from the warlike Dorians to the Romans, and then to the Genoese, who in turn sold it to the Venetians. Under the Venetians, Crete became a refuge for artists, writers and philosophers who fled Constantinople after it fell to the Turks. Their influence inspired the young Cretan painter Domenikos Theotokopoulos, who moved to Spain and there won immortality as the great El Greco.

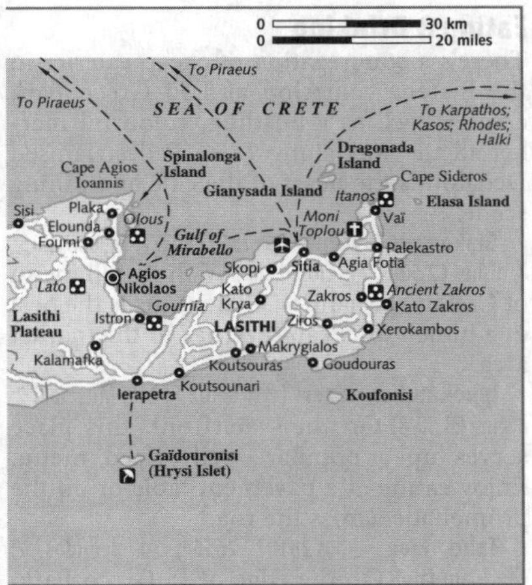

The Turks conquered Crete in 1670. In 1898 it became a British protectorate after a series of insurrections and was united with independent Greece in 1913. There was fierce fighting during WWII when a German airborne invasion defeated Allied forces in the 10-day Battle of Crete. A fierce resistance movement drew heavy German reprisals, including the slaughter of whole villages.

IRAKLIO ΗΡΑΚΛΕΙΟ

pop 131,000

Iraklio (ee-*rah*-klee-oh; often spelt Heraklion), Crete's capital, is a bustling modern city and the fifth-largest in Greece. It has a lively city centre, an excellent archaeological museum and is close to Knossos, Crete's major visitor attraction. The city has undergone a significant makeover in recent years, partly due to being chosen as an Olympic city, but mostly because of increasing prosperity.

Orientation & Information

Iraklio's harbours face north into the Sea of Crete. The old harbour is instantly recognisable as it is protected by the old Venetian fortress. The new harbour is 400m east. Plateia Venizelou, the main square, is the heart of the city, 400m south of the old harbour, up a main drag called 25 Avgoustou.

There is no official tourist office, but there is good information at www.heraklion-city.gr. **KTEL** (www.ktel.org), which runs the buses on Crete, has useful tourist information inside Bus Station A.

Skoutelis Travel (☎ 28102 80808; www.skoutelis.gr; 25 Avgoustou 20), between Plateia Venizelou and the old harbour, handles airline and ferry bookings, and rents cars. **Gallery Games** (☎ 28102 82804; www.gallerygames.net; Korai 14; per hr €1.50; 🕑 24hr) has high-speed Internet access.

Sights

Iraklio's **archaeological museum** (☎ 28102 26092; Xanthoudidou 2; adult/student €6/3; 🕑 12.30-7pm Mon, 8am-7pm Tue-Sun) has an outstanding Minoan collection, second only to the national museum in Athens.

Protecting the old harbour is the impressive fortress **Rocca al Mare** (☎ 28102 46211; adult/student €2/1; 🕑 8.30am-3pm Tue-Sun), which, like

GREECE

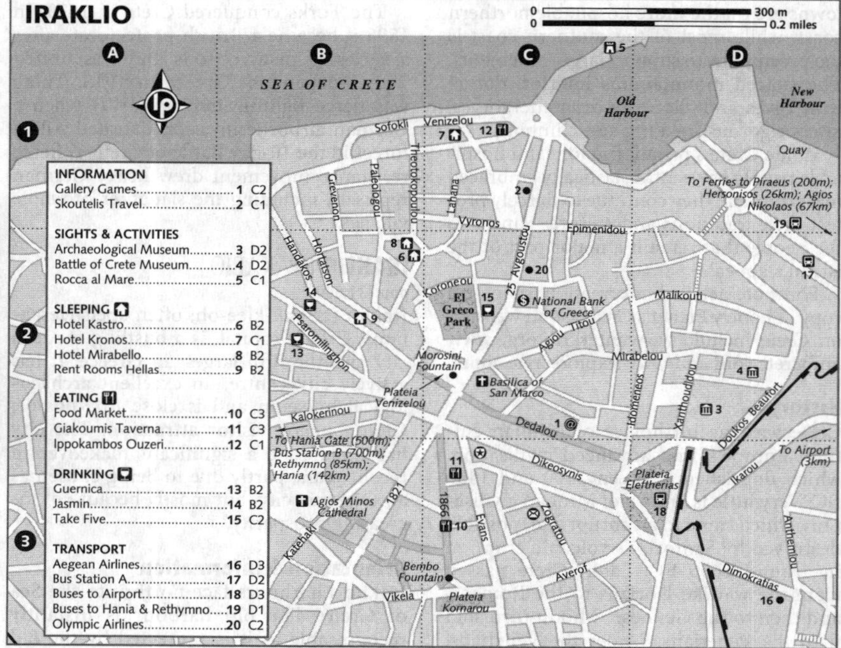

the city walls, was built by the Venetians in the 16th century.

The **Battle of Crete Museum** (☎ 28103 46554; cnr Doukos Beaufort & Hatzidaki; admission free; ⏲ 8am-3pm) chronicles the historic WWII battle with photographs, letters, uniforms and weapons.

Sleeping

Rent Rooms Hellas (☎ 28102 88851; Handakos 24; dm/d/tr with shared bathroom €10/30/40) A popular budget choice, this place has a lively atmosphere, packed dorms, a rooftop bar and a bargain breakfast (€2.50).

Hotel Mirabello (☎ 28102 85052; www.mirabello-hotel.gr; Theotokopoulou 20; s/d €37/40; ❄) A pleasant, relaxed budget hotel on a quiet street in the centre of town, this place is run by an ex–sea captain who has travelled the world. Check out the excellent website.

Hotel Kronos (☎ 28102 82240; www.kronoshotel.gr; Sofokli Venizelou 2; s/d €49/65; ❄ 💻) Down by the old harbour, this well-maintained older hotel has large, airy rooms that come with phone and TV. Ask for a room with a sea view.

Hotel Kastro (☎ 28102 84185; www.kastro-hotel.gr; Theotokopoulou 22; s/d €110/135; ❄ 💻) Next to Hotel Mirabello, this upmarket place has large rooms with fridges and satellite TV. A 35% discount is offered for Internet reservations.

Eating & Drinking

There's a congregation of cheap eateries in the Plateia Venizelou and El Greco Park area, as well as a bustling, colourful market all the way along 1866. Pedestrianised Dedalou is the heart of the café and dining scene.

Giakoumis Taverna (☎ 28102 80277; Theodosaki 5-8; dishes €2.50-8; ⏲ closed Sun) With its full menu of Cretan specialities, Giakoumis is the best of a bunch of cheap tavernas in the market area.

Ippokambos Ouzeri (☎ 28102 80240; Mitsotaki 2; dishes €3.50-8) On the waterfront, this place serves up a popular, well-priced menu. Enjoy eating at a pavement table or on the promenade across the road.

Take Five (☎ 28102 26564; Akroleondos 7; ⏲ 10am-late) On the edge of El Greco Park, this gay-friendly place has low-key music and ambience. The outside tables fill up after sundown.

Jasmin (☎ 28102 88880; Handakos 45; ⏰ noon-late) A soothing spot for herbal teas and hot chocolate by day, and alcohol and world music by night, Jasmin has a pleasant back terrace.

Guernica (☎ 28102 82988; Apokoronou Kritis 2; ⏰ 10am-late) In a rambling old building with a delightful terrace garden, Guernica combines traditional décor and contemporary music exquisitely.

Getting There & Around

There are many flights daily from Iraklio's Nikos Kazantzakis airport (HER) to Athens (€83) and, in summer, regular flights to Thessaloniki and Rhodes. Get your tickets from **Olympic Airlines** (code OA; ☎ 28102 44824; 25 Avgoustou 27) or **Aegean Airlines** (code A3; ☎ 28103 44324; Leof Dimokratias 11). **Sky Express** (code SEH; ☎ 28102 23500; www.skyexpress.gr) has connections with Santorini, Mykonos and Rhodes with varying regularity.

Daily ferries service Piraeus (€29.50, seven hours), and most days boats go to Santorini and continue on to other Cycladic islands. Head to Skoutelis Travel (p607) for schedules and tickets.

Iraklio has two bus stations. Bus Station A is just inland from the new harbour and serves eastern Crete (Agios Nikolaos, Ierapetra, Sitia, Malia and the Lasithi Plateau). The Hania and Rethymno terminal is opposite Bus Station A.

Bus Station B, 50m beyond the Hania Gate, serves the southern route (Phaestos, Matala and Anogia). Check out www.ktel.org for long-distance bus information.

Bus 1 travels between the airport and city centre (€0.70) every 15 minutes from 6am to 1am. It stops at Plateia Eleftherias, across the road from the archaeological museum.

KNOSSOS ΚΝΩΣΣΟΣ

Five kilometres south of Iraklio, **Knossos** (☎ 28102 31940; admission €6; ⏰ 8am-7pm Apr-Oct, to 5pm Nov-Mar) was the capital of Minoan Crete, and is now the island's major tourist attraction.

Knossos (k-nos-*os*) is the most famous of Crete's Minoan sites and is the inspiration for the myth of the Minotaur. According to legend, King Minos of Knossos was given a magnificent white bull to sacrifice to the god Poseidon, but decided to keep it. This enraged Poseidon, who punished the king by causing his wife Pasiphae to fall in love with the animal. The result of this odd union was the Minotaur – half-man and half-bull – who lived in a labyrinth beneath the king's palace, munching on youths and maidens.

In 1900 Arthur Evans uncovered the ruins of Knossos. Although archaeologists tend to disparage Evans' reconstruction, the buildings – incorporating an immense palace, courtyards, private apartments, baths, lively frescoes and more – give a fine idea of what a Minoan palace might have looked like.

A whole day is needed to see the site and a guidebook is essential. Arrive early to avoid the jam. From Iraklio, local bus 2 goes to Knossos (€0.95) every 10 minutes from Bus Station A.

GREECE

PHAESTOS & OTHER MINOAN SITES ΦΑΙΣΤΟΣ

Phaestos (☎ 29820 42315; admission €4; ⏰ 8am-7pm May-Oct, to 5pm Nov-Apr), 63km southwest of Iraklio, is Crete's second-most important Minoan site. While not as impressive as Knossos, Phaestos (fes-*tos*) is still worth a visit for its stunning views of the surrounding Mesara plain and Mt Psiloritis. The layout is similar to Knossos, with rooms arranged around a central courtyard. Eight buses a day head to Phaestos from Iraklio's Bus Station B (€4.50, 1½ hours).

Other important Minoan sites can be found at **Malia**, 34km east of Iraklio, where there's a palace complex and adjoining town, and **Zakros**, 40km southeast of Sitia, the last Minoan palace to have been discovered in 1962.

RETHYMNO ΡΕΘΥΜΝΟ

pop 29,000

Rethymno (*reth*-im-no), Crete's third-largest town, is one of the island's architectural treasures, due to its stunning fortress and mix of Venetian and Turkish houses in the old quarter. A compact town, most spots of interest are within a small area around the old Venetian harbour.

The old quarter is on a peninsula that juts out into the Sea of Crete; the fortress sits at the head of the peninsula, while the

Venetian harbour, ferry quay and beach are on its eastern side. El Venizelou is the main strip along the waterfront and beach. Running parallel behind it is Arkadiou, the main commercial street.

The **municipal tourist office** (☎ 28310 29148; Eleftheriou Venizelou; ⌚ 9am-2pm Mon-Fri), on the beach side of El Venizelou, is convenient and helpful. **Ellotia Tours** (☎ 28310 24533; elotia@ret.forthnet.gr; Arkadiou 161) will answer all transport, accommodation and tour inquiries. **Galero Café** (☎ 28310 54345; per hr €3), beside the Rimondi fountain with its spouting lion heads, has Internet access.

Rethymno's 16th-century **Venetian fortress** (fortezza; ☎ 28310 28101; Paleokastro Hill; admission €3; ⌚ 8am-8pm) is the site of the city's ancient acropolis and affords great views across the town and mountains. The main gate is on the eastern side of the fortress, opposite the interesting **archaeological museum** (☎ 28310 54668; admission €1.50; ⌚ 8.30am-3pm Tue-Sun), which was once a prison.

Happy Walker (☎ 28310 52920; www.happy-walker.com; Tombazi 56) runs an excellent programme of daily walks in the countryside (€25 per person), and also longer walking tours.

Elizabeth Camping (☎ 28310 28694; www.camping-elizabeth.com; per person/tent €6.50/4.50) is situated on Mysiria Beach, 4km east of town, and is accessible by the bus that goes to and from Iraklio. It has a taverna, snack bar and minimarket. **Rethymno Youth Hostel** (☎ 28310 22848; www.yhrethymno.com; Tombazi 41; dm €8) is a well-run place with crowded dorms, free hot showers and no curfew. **Sea Front** (☎ 28310 51981; www.rethymnoatcrete.com; Arkadiou 159; s/d €30/35; ❄) has all sorts of options and is ideally positioned with beach views and spacious rooms. **Hotel Fortezza** (☎ 28310 55551; www.fortezza.gr; Melissinou 16; s/d incl breakfast €57/69; P ❄ 🏊) is more upmarket; with a refreshing pool, it's in a refurbished old building in the heart of the old town.

There are plenty of eating options, but **Samaria** (☎ 28310 24681; El Venizelou 39; mains €3.50-8) is one of the few waterfront tavernas where you'll see local families eating. The soups and grills are excellent. **Restaurant Symposium** (☎ 28310 50538; www.symposium-kriti.gr; dishes from €3.50), near the Rimondi fountain, takes its food seriously (check out the website) but has good prices. Near the same fountain, **Mona Liza** (☎ 28310 23082; Paleologou 36) is legendary for its '*crema*' ice cream made from sheep's milk.

There are daily ferries between Piraeus and Rethymno (€24, nine hours). Buses depart regularly to Iraklio (€5.90, 1½ hours), Hania (€5.55, one hour) and Agia Galini.

HANIA XANIA

pop 53,500

Hania (hahn-*yah;* often spelt Chania) is the former capital of Crete and the island's second-largest city. It is also Crete's most romantic and alluring town, with a rich mosaic of Venetian and Ottoman architecture, particularly in the area of the old harbour which lures tourists in droves. Modern Hania retains the exoticism of a city caught between East and West. Hania is an excellent base for exploring nearby idyllic beaches and a spectacular mountainous interior.

Orientation & Information

Hania's bus station is on Kydonias, two blocks southwest of Plateia 1866, one of the city's main squares. From Plateia 1866, the old harbour is a short walk up Halidon.

The **tourist information office** (EOT; ☎ 28210 36155; Plateia 1866 16-18; ⌚ 8am-2.30pm) is helpful and provides practical information and maps. The city's website at www.chania.gr is worth a look for more information and upcoming events. **Tellus Travel** (☎ 28210 91500; Halidon 108; ⌚ 8am-11pm) can help with schedules and ticketing, and also rents out cars. **Manos Internet Cafe** (☎ 28210 94156; Zambeliou 24; per hr €4), at Hotel Manos, provides Internet access.

Sights & Activities

A stroll around the **old harbour** is a must for any visitor to Hania. It is worth the 1.5km walk around the sea wall to get to the Venetian **lighthouse** at the entrance to the harbour.

The **archaeological museum** (☎ 28210 90334; Halidon 30; admission €2; ⌚ 8.30am-3pm Tue-Sun) is in a 16th-century Venetian Church that the Turks made into a mosque. The building became a movie theatre in 1913, then was a munitions depot for the Germans during WWII.

Hania's covered **food market**, in a massive cross-shaped building, is definitely worth a wander.

If you're interested in activities such as trekking or mountain biking in Crete's rugged Lefka Ori (White Mountains) south of Hania, contact **Trekking Plan** (☎ 28210 60861; www.cycling.gr), located 8km west of Hania in Agia Marina, or **Alpine Travel** (☎ 28210 50939; www.alpine.gr; Boniali 11-19; 9am-2pm Mon-Fri).

Sleeping

There is a swath of sleeping options around the old harbour, many in restored Venetian buildings.

Camping Hania (☎ 28210 31138; per person/tent €5/3.50) Take the Kalamaki Beach bus from the east corner of Plateia 1866 (every 15 minutes) to get to this camping ground, which is located 3km west of town on the beach. There is a restaurant, bar and mini-market.

Pension Lena (☎ 28210 86860; www.travelling-crete.com/lena; Ritsou 5; s/d €32/50;) A friendly *pension* in an old Turkish building near the mouth of the old harbour, Lena's has an old-world feel and a cosy atmosphere. Help yourself to a room if Lena isn't there.

Hotel Manos (☎ 28210 94156; www.manoshotel.gr; Zambeliou 24; s/d €45/55;) One of the oldest small waterfront hotels, Manos has great views from its harbour-facing rooms. The rooms are clean and spacious, and there is an Internet café.

Amphora Hotel (☎ 28210 93224; www.amphora.gr; Parodos Theotokopoulou 20; s/d €75/90;) Hania's most historically evocative hotel, Amphora

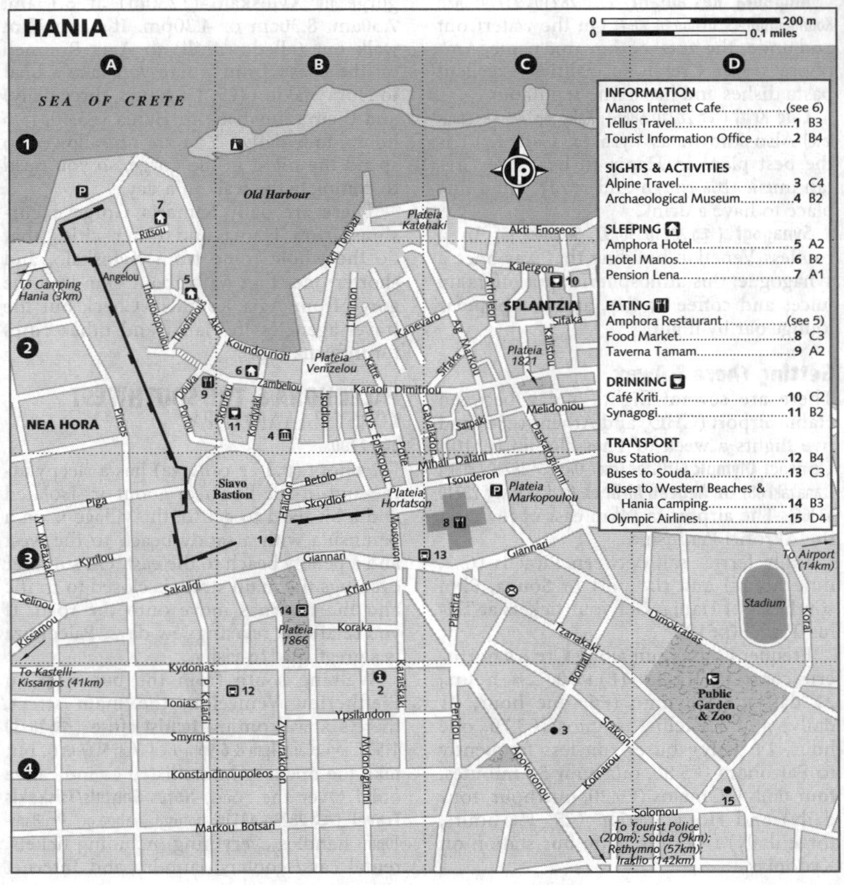

is in an immaculately restored Venetian mansion with elegantly decorated rooms around a courtyard.

Eating & Drinking

The entire waterfront of the old harbour is lined with restaurants and tavernas, many of which qualify as tourist traps. Watch out for touts trying to reel you in.

For cheap traditional cuisine, the tavernas in the food market offer excellent quality and prices.

Taverna Tamam (☎ 28210 58639; Zambeliou 49; mains €4-6.50; 🕑 1pm-12.30am) A taverna in an old converted Turkish bathhouse, this place has tasty soups and a superb selection of vegetarian specialities.

Amphora Restaurant (☎ 28210 93224; Akti Koundourioti 49; mains €4.50-7) On the waterfront and under the hotel of the same name, Amphora serves Cretan specialities, excellent pasta dishes and has a fine reputation.

Café Kriti (☎ 28210 58661; Kalergon 22; 🕑 8pm-late) Also known as Lyrakia, Café Kriti is the best place in Hania to hear live Cretan music. It's rough-and-ready, but a fine place to have a drink.

Synagogi (☎ 28210 96797; Skoufou 15) In a roofless Venetian building that was once a synagogue, this atmospheric spot offers up juices and coffee by day, and is a popular lounge bar by night.

Getting There & Away

There are several flights a day between Hania airport (CHQ) and Athens (€86) and five flights a week to Thessaloniki (€110). Contact **Olympic Airlines** (code OA; ☎ 28210 58005; Tzanakaki 88) or **Aegean Airlines** (code A3; ☎ 28210 63366). The airport is 14km east of town on the Akrotiri Peninsula.

Daily ferries sail between Piraeus (€22, nine hours) and the port of Souda, 9km southeast of Hania. Get your tickets at Tellus Travel (p610).

Frequent buses run along Crete's northern coast to Iraklio (€11.50, 2¾ hours, 21 daily), Rethymno (€6, one hour, 21 daily) and Kastelli-Kissamos (€3.70, one hour, 14 daily); buses run less frequently to Paleohora (€5.80, our hour 50 minutes, four daily), Omalos (€5.20, one hour, four daily) and Hora Sfakion (€5, 1¼ hours, three daily) from the main bus station on Kydonias.

Buses for Souda's port (€0.90) leave daily from outside the food market. Buses for the beaches west of Hania leave from the eastern side of Plateia 1866.

SAMARIA GORGE
ΦΑΡΑΓΓΙ ΤΗΣ ΣΑΜΑΡΙΑΣ

The **Samaria Gorge** (☎ 28250 67179; admission €5; 🕑 6am-3pm May–mid-Oct) is one of Europe's most spectacular gorges and a 'must-do'. Walkers should take rugged footwear, food, drinks and sun protection for this strenuous five- to six-hour trek.

You can do the walk as part of an excursion tour, or do it independently by taking the Omalos bus from the main bus station in Hania (€5, one hour) to the head of the gorge at Xyloskalo (1230m) at 6.15am, 7.30am, 8.30am or 4.30pm. It's a 16.7km walk out (all downhill) to Agia Roumeli on the coast, from where you take a boat to Hora Sfakion (€5, 1¼ hours, three daily) and then a bus back to Hania (€5.40, two hours, four daily). You are not allowed to spend the night in the gorge, so you need to complete the walk in a day.

There are daily Samaria Gorge excursions from Hania and other cities that do the whole route from Xyloskalo, and shorter ones that walk about 4km into the gorge from Agia Roumeli. Check out the travel agencies in Hania and other cities for information.

PALEOHORA & THE SOUTHWEST COAST ΠΑΛΑΙΟΧΩΡΑ

pop 2200

Paleohora (pal-ee-o-*hor*-a) has a sleepy at-the-end-of-the-line feel about it. Isolated and a bit hard to get to, the village is on a peninsula with a sandy beach to the west and a pebbly beach to the east. On summer evenings the main street is closed to traffic and the tavernas move onto the road. If you're after a relaxing few days, Paleohora is a great spot to visit.

Walking south from the bus stop on Eleftheriou Venizelou, the main street, there's a welcoming **tourist office** (☎ 28230 41507; 🕑 10am-1pm & 6-9pm Wed-Mon May-Oct), but take the opening hours listed as indicative only! Over the road, **Notos Rentals/Tsiskakis Travel** (☎ 28230 42110; notosgr@yahoo.gr; 🕑 8am-10pm) handles everything including tickets, rental cars/scooters, laundry and Internet

BEAT THE CROWDS

The Samaria Gorge walk is extremely popular and can get quite crowded, especially in summer. Most walkers are on a day trip from Hania and other northern-coast cities, and are heading back there that day.

If you've got a bit of time on your hands, an excellent option is to let the sprinters go and to take your time trekking through this stupendous gorge. When you hit the coast at Agia Roumeli, down a cool beer, take a dip in the refreshing Libyan Sea, savour the tasty Cretan specials at **Farangi Restaurant & Rooms** (☎ 28250 91225; s/d/tr €18/30/35;) and stay the night in the tidy rooms above the restaurant. There are plenty of other eating and sleeping options in this seaside village should Farangi be full. The next day you can take a ferry either west to Sougia or Paleohora, or east to Loutro or Hora Sfakion.

access (€4.40 per hour). The **ferry quay** is a tad further south, two blocks left, at the end of the pebbly beach.

The ruins of the 13th-century **Venetian castle** are worth clambering over, although there's not much left after the fortress was destroyed by the Turks, the pirate Barbarossa in the 16th-century and then the Germans during WWII.

Camping Paleohora (☎ 28230 41120; per person/tent €4/2.50) is 1.5km northeast of town, near the pebble beach. There's a taverna and nightclub here. **Homestay Anonymous** (☎ 28230 41509; www.anonymoushomestay.com; s/d/tr with shared bathroom €22/25/28) is a great option with its warm service and communal kitchen. Manolis, the owner, is an excellent source of local information. Across the road from the sandy beach, **Poseidon Hotel** (☎ 28230 41374; www.interkriti.net/hotel/paleohora/poseidon; s/d/apt €30/35/40;) has a mix of tidy double rooms, studios and apartments. There is also a good café on site.

There are plenty of eating options on the main street. Vegetarians rave about **Third Eye** (☎ 28230 41234; mains €4-6), just inland from the sandy beach. Specialities include a tempting range of Greek-Asian fusion dishes. On the pebble beachside, **Calypso** (☎ 28230 83019; dishes €5-8;) has tasty daily specials, and runs alternative-cuisine theme nights, with everything from Indian to Mexican.

Further east along Crete's southwest coast are **Sougia**, **Agia Roumeli** (at the mouth of the Samaria Gorge; see the boxed text, above), **Loutro** and **Hora Sfakion**. No road links the coastal resorts, but a daily boat from Paleohora to Sougia (€4.30, one hour), Agia Roumeli (€6.80, two hours), Loutro (€7.50, 2½ hours) and Hora Sfakion (€8.50, three hours) connects the villages in summer. The ferry leaves Paleohora at 9.45am and returns from Hora Sfakion at 1pm.

There are at least five buses daily between Hania and Paleohora (€5.40, two hours). A bus for Samaria Gorge hikers (see opposite) leaves for Omalos (€8.10, 1½ hours) each morning at 6am.

LASITHI PLATEAU
ΟΡΟΠΕΔΙΟ ΛΑΣΙΘΙΟΥ

The impressive mountain-fringed Lasithi Plateau in eastern Crete is laid out like an immense patchwork quilt. At 900m above sea level, it is a vast flat expanse of orchards and fields, which was once dotted with thousands of stone windmills with white canvas sails. There are still plenty of windmills, but most are now of the metal variety.

There are 20 villages around the periphery of the plain, the largest being Tzermiado (population 750), Agios Georgios (population 550) and Psyhro (population 210). The perimeter of the plateau is a popular bike route, though cycling up to the plateau is not an easy matter.

The **Dikteon Cave** (☎ 28440 31316; admission €4; 8am-6.30pm) is where, according to mythology, Rhea hid the newborn Zeus from Cronos, his offspring-gobbling father. The cave is 1km from the village of Psyhro, which is the most convenient place to stay. **Zeus Hotel** (☎ 28440 31284; s/d €25/30) is near the start of the Dikteon Cave road. On the main street, **Stavros** (☎ 28440 31453; dishes €5-8) serves tasty home-style Cretan dishes with produce mostly from the family farm.

There are daily buses to the area from Iraklio (€5, two hours) and Agios Nikolaos (€6.30, 2½ hours), though having your own wheels would make life a lot easier.

AGIOS NIKOLAOS
ΑΓΙΟΣ ΝΙΚΟΛΑΟΣ

pop 11,000

Agios Nikolaos (*ah*-yee-os nih-*ko*-laos) is a cute former fishing village on Crete's northeast coast. Most of the action is around the picturesque **Voulismeni Lake**, about 200m north from the main square Plateia Venizelou. The lake is ringed with cafés and tavernas, and is linked to the sea by a short canal. The ferry port is 150m past the canal.

The very helpful **municipal tourist office** (☎ 28410 22357; www.agiosnikolaos.gr; 8am-9.30pm Apr–mid-Nov) is on the north side of the bridge over the canal and does a good job of finding sleeping options. **Polyhoros Internet Café** (☎ 28410 24876; 28 Oktovriou 13; per hr €4; 9am-2am) has Internet access just up from the canal.

The two nice little beaches in town, **Kytroplatia Beach** and **Ammos Beach**, get a bit crowded in summer. **Almyros Beach**, about 1km south, gets less so. Agios Nikolaos acts as a base for excursion tours to **Spinalonga Island**. The island's massive fortress was built by the Venetians in 1579, but taken by the Turks in 1715. It later became a leper colony, but nowadays is a fascinating place to explore. Tours run for around €20.

Afrodite Rooms (☎ 28410 28058; Korytsas 27; s/d with shared bathroom €18/25) is a convenient comfortable budget option. There's a tiny communal kitchen. **Pergola Hotel** (☎ 28410 28152; Sarolidi 20; s/d €25/35;) is a friendly family-run place out near the ferry port, with clean rooms, balconies and sea views.

Finding a place to eat will not be a problem. **Itanos** (☎ 28410 25340; Kyprou 1; mains €3-10), tucked away on a back street off the main square, is superb and has reasonable prices. **Migomis** (☎ 28410 24353; N Plastira 20; mains €8-15) overlooks the lake from high on the south side, providing superb ambience and views.

Ferries depart for Rhodes (€25.80, 11 hours) via Sitia, Kasos, Karpathos and Halki three times a week. There are also three weekly ferries to Piraeus (€27, 12 hours). Buses to Iraklio run every 30 minutes (€5, 1½ hours) and to Sitia (€5.50, 1½ hours, six times daily). Catch them from the bus station at the southern end of Sofias Venizelou.

SITIA ΣΗΤΕΙΑ

pop 8500

Sitia (si-*tee*-a) is a lovely little town in the northeastern corner of Crete that has escaped much of the tourism frenzy along the north coast. It is on an attractive bay flanked by mountains, and is an easy place to unwind.

The helpful **tourist office** (☎ 28430 28300; Karamanli; 9.30am-2.30pm), on the waterfront, has town maps. The main square, Plateia Iroon Plytehniou, is in the corner of the bay, recognisable by its palm trees and statue of a dying soldier. The ferry port is about 500m to the northeast. Internet access is available at Itanos Hotel (below).

Porto Belis Travel (☎ 28430 22370; www.portobelis-crete.gr; Karamanli Aven 34; 9am-8.30pm), on the waterfront just before the start of the town beach, is a one-stop shop, handling ticketing, rental cars and scooters, and accommodation bookings in town. It also runs **Porto Belis House** (☎ 28430 22370; d/q €34/57;) above the travel agency. These rooms are immaculate, have kitchens and look straight out onto the beach. Check out the website.

Hotel Arhontiko (☎ 28430 28172; Kondylaki 16; s/d with shared bathroom €28/32), two blocks uphill from the port, has spotless rooms in a beautifully maintained neoclassical building. **Itanos Hotel** (☎ 28430 22900; www.itanoshotel.com; Karamanli 4; s/d incl breakfast €35/60;) is an upmarket establishment next to the square. There's a 10% discount if you book on the Internet and, if you're staying in the hotel, it includes a drink with dinner if you eat at its excellent **Itanos Taverna** (dishes €3-12), on the waterfront outside the front door.

The waterfront is lined with tavernas. Popular with locals is **Gato Negro** (☎ 28430 25873; dishes €6-12), serving Cretan specialities using produce from the owner's farm. It's the closest taverna to the ferry quay. **Kali Kardia** (☎ 28430 22249; Foundalidou 22; mains €4-6), a couple of streets back from the waterfront, is also excellent.

Sitia airport (JSH) has four flights a week to Athens (€66) with **Olympic Airlines** (code OA; ☎ 28430 22270; 4 Septemvriou 3). There are regular ferries from Piraeus to Sitia (€27.50, 14 hours), and three ferries per week via Kasos, Karpathos and Halki to Rhodes (€23, 10 hours). Porto Belis Travel (above) has details and sells tickets. There are five buses daily to Iraklio (€10, 3½ hours) via Agios Nikolaos (€5.50, 1½ hours).

DODECANESE ΔΩΔΕΚΑΝΗΣΑ

Due to their geographic proximity to the coast of western Turkey, the 18 islands of the Dodecanese have suffered a turbulent past of invasions and occupations that has endowed them with a fascinating diversity.

In 1291, the Knights of St John, having fled Jerusalem, came to Rhodes and established themselves as masters of the Dodecanese. In 1522, Süleyman I staged a massive attack and took Rhodes Town, claiming the Dodecanese for the Ottoman Empire. In 1912 it was the Italians who ousted the Turks, and in 1944 the Germans took over. The following year Rhodes was liberated by British and Greek commandos. In 1947 the Dodecanese became part of Greece. These days, tourists rule.

The islands themselves range from the verdant and mountainous to the rocky and dry. While Rhodes and Kos host highly developed tourism, the more remote islands await those in search of traditional island life.

RHODES ΡΟΔΟΣ

pop 98,000

Rhodes (Rodos in Greek) is the largest island in the Dodecanese. According to mythology, the sun god Helios chose Rhodes as his bride and bestowed light, warmth and vegetation upon her. The blessing seems to have paid off, for Rhodes produces more flowers and sunny days than most Greek islands. Throw in an east coast of virtually uninterrupted sandy beaches and it's easy to understand why sun-starved northern Europeans flock here.

Rhodes Town

pop 56,000

Rhodes' capital is Rhodes Town, on the northern tip of the island. Almost everything of interest lies in its World Heritage–listed Old Town, the largest inhabited medieval town in Europe, enclosed within massive walls. The New Town to the north is a monument to package tourism.

The main port, Commercial Harbour, is east of the Old Town, and north of here is Mandraki Harbour, the supposed site of the Colossus of Rhodes, a 32m-high bronze statue of Apollo built over 12 years (294–282 BC). The statue stood for a mere 65 years before being toppled by an earthquake. There are no remains and no tangible evidence that it actually existed, but these days you will see it on a lot of souvenir T-shirts.

INFORMATION

For information about the island, visit www.rodosisland.gr.

Mango Café Bar (☎ 22410 24877; www.mango.gr; Plateia Dorieos 3, Old Town; per hr €5; ⌚ 9.30am-midnight) Has Internet access.

Tourist information office (EOT; ☎ 22410 35226; cnr Makariou & Papagou; ⌚ 7.30am-3pm Mon-Fri) Has brochures, maps and *Rodos News,* a free English-language newspaper.

Triton Holidays (☎ 22410 21690; www.tritondmc.gr; 1st fl, Plastira 9, Mandraki) In the New Town, this place is extremely helpful, handling accommodation bookings, ticketing and rental cars.

SIGHTS & ACTIVITIES

The Old Town is reputedly the world's finest surviving example of medieval fortification, with 12m-thick walls. The Knights of St John lived in the Knights' Quarter in the northern end of the Old Town.

The cobbled **Odos Ippoton** (Avenue of the Knights) is lined with magnificent medieval buildings, the most imposing of which is the **Palace of the Grand Masters** (☎ 22410 23359; admission €6; ⌚ 8.30am-7.30pm Tue-Sun), which was restored, but never used, as a holiday home for Mussolini.

The 15th-century Knight's Hospital now houses the **archaeological museum** (☎ 22410 27657; Plateia Mousiou; admission €3; ⌚ 8am-4pm Tue-Sun). The splendid building was restored by the Italians and has an impressive collection that includes the ethereal marble statue *Aphrodite of Rhodes*.

The pink-domed **Mosque of Süleyman,** at the top of Sokratous, was built in 1522 to commemorate the Ottoman victory against the knights, then rebuilt in 1808.

SLEEPING

Mango Rooms (☎ 22410 24877; www.mango.gr; Plateia Dorieos 3, Old Town; s/d €30/45; ❄ 💻) Mango has a restaurant, bar and Internet café down

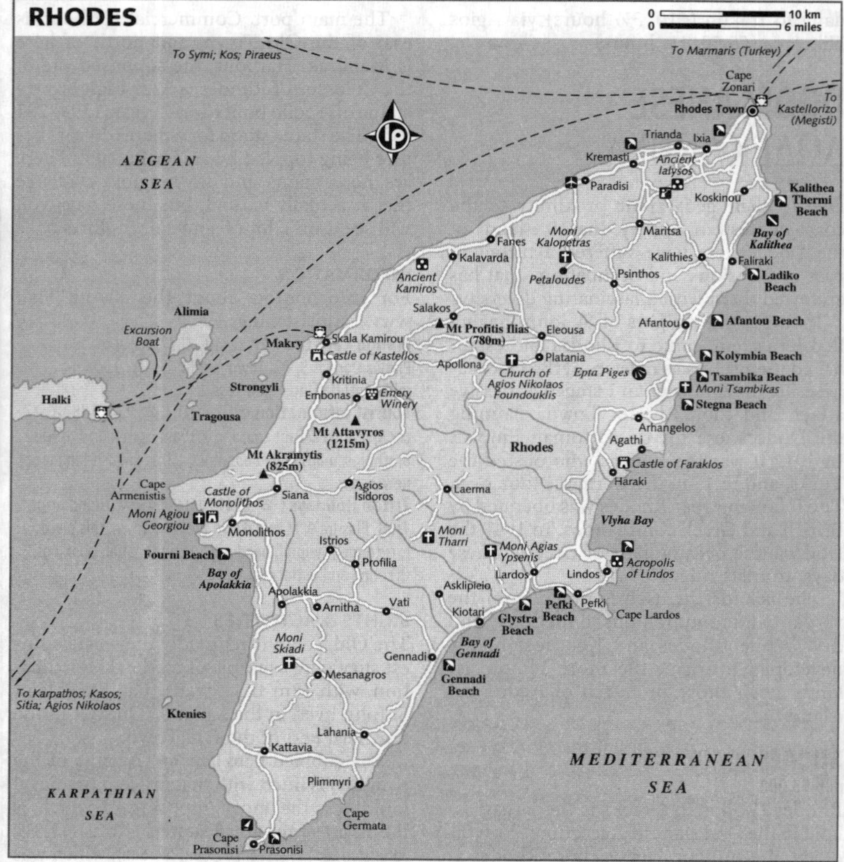

below, six well-kept rooms above, and a superb sun terrace on top. This is a good-value one-stop-shop near the back of the Old Town.

Pink Elephant Pension (☎ 22410 22469; www.pinkelephantpension.com; Timakida 9, Old Town; d €30-50) Down a side street at the back of the Old Town, this *pension* has cosy, compact and clean rooms around a communal courtyard.

Hotel Spot (☎ 22410 34737; www.spothotelrhodes.com; Perikleous 21, Old Town; s/d/tr incl breakfast €35/60/80; ❄) Convenient and exceptionally clean, the Spot offers a small book exchange, left-luggage facilities and tastefully decorated rooms.

Hotel Andreas (☎ 22410 34156; www.hotelandreas.com; Omirou 28d, Old Town; s/d €50/60; ❄) This place has individually decorated rooms and terrific views from its roof-terrace. The price changes by the room, all of which can be checked out online. Choose your room before you go.

EATING & DRINKING

There is food and drink every way you look in Rhodes. Outside the city walls, there are a lot of cheap places in the New Market, at the southern end of Mandraki Harbour.

Taverna Kostas (☎ 22410 26217; Pythagora 62, Old Town; mains €5-10) This good-value spot has stood the test of time and can't be beaten for its quality grills and fish dishes.

Kasbah (☎ 22410 78633; Platonos 4-8; mains from €11; 🕑 dinner) If you want a break from Greek

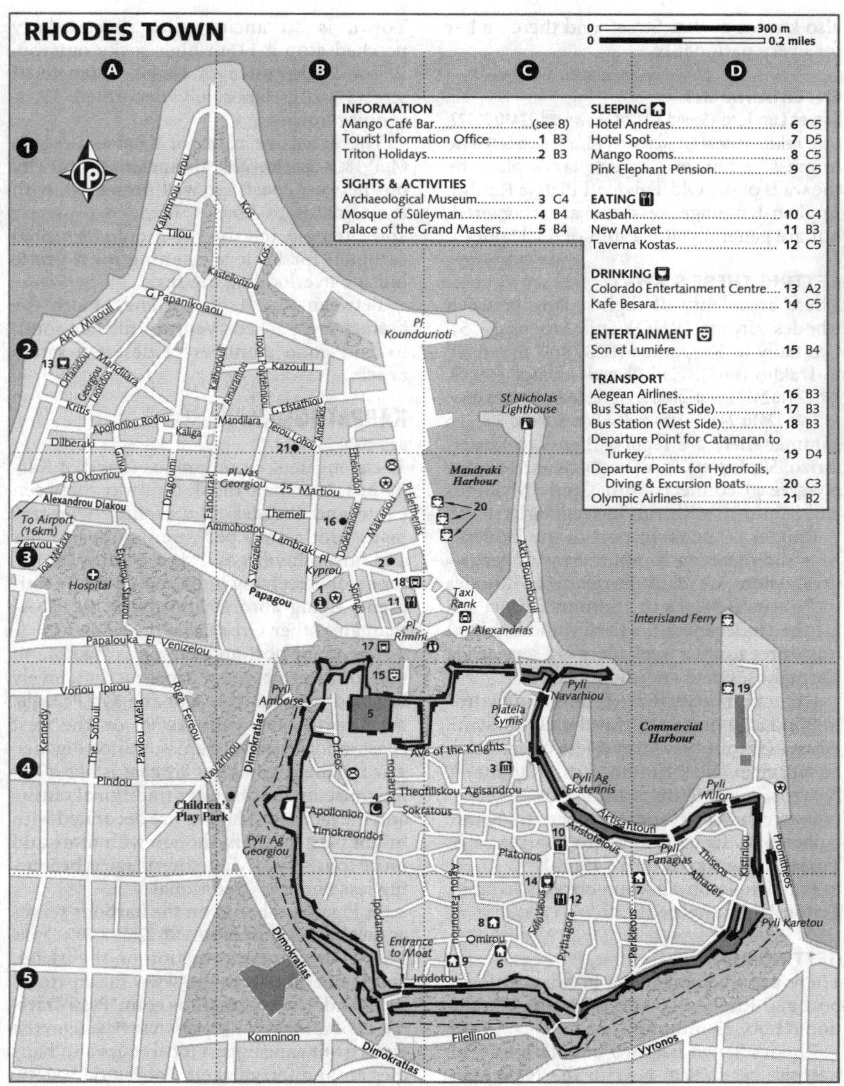

food, try Kasbah, which serves Moroccan-influenced meals in a refined atmosphere.

Kafe Besara (☎ 22410 30363; Sofokleous 11, Old Town) This Aussie-owned establishment is one of the Old Town's liveliest bars and a great spot to hang out.

Mango Café Bar (☎ 22410 24877; Plateia Dorieos 3, Old Town) If you're staying at Mango Rooms, you've only got to climb the stairs to get home. Mango claims to have the cheapest drinks in town and is the preferred haunt of local expats and die-hard travellers.

Colorado Entertainment Centre (☎ 22410 75120; www.coloradoclub.gr; Orfanidou 57) This enormous palace of hype has six venues in one in the northwest of the New Town. Orfanidou is also known as 'Bar Street' and there's a bar for every nationality.

ENTERTAINMENT

Son et Lumiére (Sound & Light Show; ☎ 22410 21922; www.hellenicfestival.gr; admission €6; Mon-Sat) The impressive Son et Lumière takes place by the walls of the Old Town off Plateia Rimini. English-language sessions are staggered, but are generally at 9.15pm or 11.15pm.

GETTING THERE & AWAY

There are plenty of flights daily between Rhodes airport (RHO) and Athens (€75), two daily to Karpathos (€28) and one daily to Iraklio (€65). Call **Olympic Airlines** (code OA; ☎ 22410 24571; Ieru Lohou 9) or **Aegean Airlines** (code A3; ☎ 22410 24400; Ethelondon Dodekanision 20). In summer there are regular flights to Kastellorizo. **Sky Express** (code SEH; ☎ 28102 23500; www.skyexpress.gr) connects with Crete, Mykonos and Santorini with varying regularity.

Rhodes is the main port of the Dodecanese and there is a complex array of departures. There are daily ferries from Rhodes to Piraeus (€38, 15 to 18 hours). Most sail via the Dodecanese north of Rhodes, but at least three times a week there is a service via Karpathos, Crete and the Cyclades.

Excursion boats (€22 return) and hydrofoils (€12.50 one way) travel daily to Symi. Ferries (€8 one way) travel less often. Similar services also run to Kos, Kalymnos, Nisyros, Tilos, Patmos and Leros.

Between April and October, there are daily boats from Rhodes to Marmaris in Turkey (one way/return €45/60).

For details on all your options, contact Triton Holidays (p615).

GETTING AROUND

There are frequent buses between the airport and Rhodes Town's west-side bus station (€1.50, 25 minutes).

Rhodes Town has two bus stations. The **west-side bus station**, next to the New Market, serves the airport, Kamiros (€4.10, 55 minutes) and the west coast. The **east-side bus station** (Plateia Rimini) serves the east coast, Lindos (€4.60, 1½ hours) and the inland southern villages.

Around the Island

The **Acropolis of Lindos** (☎ 22440 31258; admission €6; 8.30am-6pm Tue-Sun), 47km from Rhodes Town, is an ancient city spectacularly perched atop a 116m-high rocky outcrop. Below is the town of **Lindos**, a tangle of streets with elaborately decorated 17th-century houses.

The extensive ruins of **Kamiros** (admission €4; 8am-5pm Tue-Sun), an ancient Doric city on the west coast, are well preserved, with the remains of houses, baths, a cemetery and a temple, but the site should be visited as much for its lovely setting on a gentle hillside overlooking the sea.

Between Rhodes Town and Lindos the **beaches** are packed. Venture further south to find good stretches of deserted sandy beach.

KARPATHOS ΚΑΡΠΑΘΟΣ

pop 6000

The elongated, mountainous island of Karpathos (*kar*-pah-thos), midway between Crete and Rhodes, is a scenic, hype-free place with a cosy port, numerous beaches and unspoilt villages. It is a wealthy island, reputedly receiving more money from emigrants living abroad (mostly in the USA) than any other Greek island.

The main port and capital is **Pigadia**, on the southeast coast. Karpathos has lovely beaches, particularly **Apella** and **Kyra Panagia**, both north of Pigadia, **Lefkos** on the west coast, and **Ammoöpi**, 8km south of Pigadia. The northern village of **Olymbos** is like a living museum. Locals wear traditional outfits and the façades of houses are decorated with bright plaster reliefs, though with more and more tourists arriving, the village is becoming less and less 'traditional'.

In Pigadia, a booth on the harbour serves as **municipal tourist office** (☎ 22450 23835; Jul & Aug). For more information on the island, check out the websites www.inkarpathos.com and www.karpathos.com. **Possi Travel** (☎ 22450 22148; possitvl@hotmail.com; Pigadia) on the waterfront can suggest local tours and handles air and ferry tickets. **Pot Pourri** (☎ 22450 29073; Apodimon Karpathion, Pigadia; per hr €3; 7am-1am & 6pm-1am), on the western side of the harbour, offers Internet access.

Elias Rooms (☎ 22450 22446; www.eliasrooms.com; Dimokratias Pigadia; s/d €20/25) is an excellent accommodation option. Owner Elias is a mine of information and his rooms have great views while being in a quiet part of town. **Hotel Titania** (☎ 22450 22144; www.titania

karpathos.gr; Dimokratias, Pigadia; s/d €38/48;) is in the centre of Pigadia and has spacious rooms with fridge, phone and TV.

Try the Karpathian goat *stifado* at **To Helliniko** (22450 23932; Pigadia; dishes €3-8) on the waterfront. Head for **Taverna I Orea Karpathos** (22450 22501; Pigadia; mains €4-6) near the quay for traditional Karpathian dishes.

In summer, Karpathos airport (AOK), 13km southwest of town, has daily flights to Rhodes (€28) and Athens (€79). The **Olympic Airlines** (code OA; 22450 22150) office is on the central square in Pigadia. There are three ferries a week to Rhodes (€18.50, four hours) and four to Piraeus (€33, 19 hours) via Crete and the Cyclades. The ferries between Rhodes and Crete stop at Pigadia and the small northern port of Diafani on Karpathos. In summer there are daily excursion boats from Pigadia to Apella and Kyra Panagia beaches.

There are also excursions from Pigadia to Diafani that include a bus trip to Olymbos. Local buses drop you at Lefkos and Ammoöpi beaches.

SYMI ΣΥΜΗ

pop 2600

Symi is an inviting, rocky, dry island 24km north of Rhodes. The port town of Gialos is a Greek treasure, with pastel-coloured mansions heaped up the hills surrounding the protective little harbour. Symi is swamped by day-trippers from Rhodes, and it's worth staying over to enjoy the island in cruise control. The town is divided into Gialos, the port, and the tranquil *horio* (village) above it, accessible by taxi, bus or 360 steps from the harbour.

There is no tourist office. The best source of information is the free, widely available monthly English-language *Symi Visitor* (www.symivisitor.com), which includes maps of the town. **Kalodoukas Holidays** (22460 71077; www.symi-greece.com) handles accommodation bookings, ticketing and has a book of walking trails on the island. For Internet access head to **Roloï Bar** (22460 71595; per hr €4; 9am-3am), a block back from the waterfront.

Budget accommodation is scarce. **Rooms Katerina** (22460 71813, 69451 30112; d €25-30) is excellent, but get in quick as there are only three rooms. There is a communal kitchen with breathtaking views down over the port. **Pension Catherinettes** (22460 72698; marina-epe@rho.forthnet.gr; d €32-50) has airy rooms on the north side of the harbour. It's where the treaty surrendering the Dodecanese to the Allies was signed in 1945. Located back from the excursion boats is **Hotel Albatros** (22460 71707; www.albatrosymi.gr; d incl breakfast €50), a small family-run place where breakfast is served in the friendly lounge.

Taverna Neraida (22460 71841; mains from €5), back from the waterfront by the square, serves solid Greek dishes and features intriguing old photos of Symi on its walls. **Vapori Bar** (22460 72082) is open all day. Drop by to use the Internet (per hour €4) or read the free newspapers by day, or for drinks and cruising at night.

There are frequent ferries and hydrofoils between Rhodes and Kos that stop at Symi, as well as daily excursion boats from Rhodes. Small taxi boats visit inaccessible east-coast beaches daily in summer, including spectacular **Agios Georgious**, backed by a 150m sheer cliff.

KOS ΚΩΣ

pop 17,900

A long, fertile island with a mountainous spine, Kos is only 5km from the Turkish peninsula of Bodrum. Hippocrates, the father of medicine, was born on Kos, but that's as Greek as this place gets. Package tourists turn up in droves, and with its palm-lined streets, neon cafés, pulsing clubs and tourist trains, Kos Town, the main town and port, exudes a mini–Las Vegas aura.

Orientation & Information

Kos Town is based around a circular harbour protected by the imposing Castle of the Knights on its southeastern side. The ferry quay is north of the castle. Akti Koundourioti is the main drag around the harbour.

The **municipal tourist office** (22420 24460; www.kosinfo.gr; Vasileos Georgiou 1; 8am-2.30pm & 3-10pm Mon-Fri, 9am-2pm Sat) is on the waterfront directly south of the port and provides maps and accommodation information. **Exas Travel** (22420 28545), near the archaeological museum in the heart of town to the southwest of the harbour, handles schedules, ticketing and excursions.

Café Del Mare (22420 24244; www.cybercafe.gr; Megalou Alexandrou 4; per half-hr €3; 9am-1am) is a well-equipped Internet café near the harbour.

Sights & Activities

The focus of the **archaeological museum** (☎ 22420 28326; Plateia Eleftherias; adult/student €3/2; 🕑 8am-2.30pm Tue-Sun) is sculpture from excavations around the island.

The **ancient agora**, with the ruins of the **Shrine of Aphrodite** and **Temple of Hercules**, is just off Plateia Eleftherias. North of the agora is the **Hippocrates Plane Tree**, under which the man himself is said to have taught his pupils.

The **Castle of the Knights** (☎ 22420 27927; admission €4; 🕑 8am-2.30pm Tue-Sun), built in the 14th century, protected the knights from the encroaching Ottomans, and was originally separated from town by a moat. That moat is now Finikon, a major street.

On a pine-clad hill, 4km southwest of Kos Town, stand the extensive ruins of the renowned healing centre of **Asklipieion** (☎ 22420 28763; adult/student €4/3; 🕑 8.30am-6pm Tue-Sun), where Hippocrates practised medicine.

Sleeping

Kos Camping (☎ 22420 23275; per adult/tent €4.50/2.50) This camping ground, 3km along the eastern waterfront, has good shade and a minimarket. Hop on any bus to Agios Fokas from the harbour Kleopatras 2.

Pension Alexis (☎ 22420 28798; fax 22420 25797; Irodotou 9; s/d €25/30; ❄) This highly recommended place has long been a budget favourite with travellers. It has large rooms and shared facilities. Try the legendary feta omelette for breakfast. It's back behind Dolphin Sq.

Hotel Afendoulis (☎ 22420 25321; afendoulishotel@kos.forthnet.gr; Evripilou 1; s/d €35/50; ❄ 💻) In a pleasant, quiet area about 500m south of the ferry quay, this well-kept hotel won't disappoint. Run by the charismatic English-speaking Alexis, this is a great place to relax and enjoy Kos.

Eating & Drinking

Restaurants line the central waterfront, but you might want to hit the backstreets for value. There are a dozen discos and clubs around the streets of Diakon and Nafklirou, just north of the agora.

Barbas (☎ 22400 27856; Evripilou 6; mains €3-5) Opposite Hotel Afendoulis, Barbas specialises in grills and has a mouth-watering chicken souvlaki. Sit at the streetside tables and watch the locals pass by.

Olympiada (☎ 22420 23031; Kleopatras 2; mains €3.50-4) Back in the ruins area, behind the Olympic Airlines office, Olympiada serves up reliable unpretentious Greek dishes.

Fashion Club (☎ 22420 22592; Kanari 2) Off Dolphin Sq, this monster establishment has three bars and is a long-time favourite.

Kalua (☎ 22420 24938; Akti Zouroudi 3) Head around to the beach to the north of the harbour where there is no shortage of bars. An outdoor venue with a swimming pool, Kalua is popular.

Getting There & Around

There are daily flights to Athens (€93) from Kos' **Ippokratis airport** (KGS) with **Olympic Airlines** (code OA; ☎ 22420 28330). The airline runs buses (€3) to the airport, which is 28km southwest of Kos Town.

There are frequent ferries from Rhodes to Kos that continue on to Piraeus (€38, 12 to 15 hours) via Kalymnos, Leros and Patmos. Less-frequent ferries head to Nisyros, Tilos, Symi and Samos. In summer, ferries depart daily for Bodrum in Turkey (€34 return, one hour). Get details and tickets at Exas Travel, near the archaeological museum (p619).

Buses for Agios Fokas leave from opposite the town hall on the harbour; all other buses leave from the bus station on Kleopatras, near the ruins at the back of town.

Next to the tourist office is a blue minitrain for Asklipion (€3 return, hourly) and a green minitrain that does city tours (€3, 20 minutes).

PATMOS ΠΑΤΜΟΣ

pop 3050

Patmos is a great place to unwind, and for the religiously motivated it is a place not to be missed. Orthodox and Western Christians have long made pilgrimages to Patmos, for it was here that St John wrote his revelations.

Orientation & Information

The main town and port of Skala is about halfway down the east coast of Patmos, with a protected harbour. Towering above Skala to the south is the *hora,* crowned by the immense Monastery of St John the Theologian.

The **tourist office** (☎ 22470 31666; ⌚ 8am-6pm Mon-Fri Jun-Sep), post office and police station are in the white building at the port in Skala. For further information on the island, visit www.patmosweb.gr or www.patmos-island.com. **Apollon Travel** (☎ 22470 31324; apollontravel@stratas.gr), on the waterfront, handles schedules and ticketing. **Blue Bay Internet Café** (☎ 22470 31165; per hr €5; ⌚ 9am-2pm & 4-8pm) is 200m south from the port in the Blue Bay Hotel.

Sights & Activities

The **Cave of the Apocalypse** (☎ 22470 31234; admission free, treasury €3; ⌚ 8am-1.30pm daily & 4-6pm Tue, Thu & Sun), where St John wrote his divinely inspired *Book of Revelations*, is halfway between the port and *hora*. Take a bus from the port or hike up the **Byzantine path**, which starts from a signposted spot on the Skala–*hora* road.

The **Monastery of St John the Theologian** (☎ 22470 31398; admission free; ⌚ 8am-1.30pm daily & 4-6pm Tue, Thu & Sun) looks more like a castle than a monastery and tops Patmos like a crown. It exhibits all kinds of monastic treasures.

Patmos' coastline provides secluded coves, mostly with pebble beaches. The best is **Psili Ammos**, in the south, reached by excursion boat from Skala port. **Lambi Beach**, on the north coast, is a pebble-beach–lover's dream come true.

Sleeping & Eating

Stefanos Camping (☎ 22470 31821; per person/tent €6/3) On the pleasant tree-shaded Meloi Beach, 2km northeast of Skala, this spot has a minimarket and café-bar.

Hotel Australis (☎ 22470 31576; www.patmosweb.gr/australishotel; d incl breakfast €40-60) This place, at the northern end of Skala, has private facilities, a family church on site and an oasis-like garden that has featured in *Garden Design* magazine. Australis also has apartments in town.

Blue Bay Hotel (☎ 22470 31165; www.bluebay.50g.com; s/d/tr €72/109/135; ❄ 💻) At the quieter southern end of Skala, this waterfront hotel has superb rooms, Internet access, and breakfast included in its rates (which tumble out of the high season).

Grigoris Taverna (☎ 22470 31515; mains €3-5) Opposite the port gate, this is a popular spot with tasty *mayirefta* (precooked, oven-baked dishes) and grills.

Kipos Garden Restaurant (☎ 22470 31884; dishes €3-8) Head into the heart of Skala for home-grown vegetable dishes such as fried aubergines.

Getting There & Away

Patmos is well connected, with ferries to Piraeus (€30.50, eight hours, two weekly) and south to Rhodes (€27, 7½ hours, two weekly). In summer, daily Flying Dolphin hydrofoils head south to Kos and Rhodes, and north to Samos. Apollon Travel (left) has details and tickets.

GREECE

NORTHEASTERN AEGEAN ISLANDS ΤΑ ΝΗΣΙΑ ΤΟΥ ΒΟΡΕΙΟ ΑΝΑΤΟΛΙΚΟ ΑΙΓΑΙΟΥ

One of Greece's best-kept secrets, these far-flung islands are strewn across the northeastern corner of the Aegean, closer to Turkey than mainland Greece. They harbour unspoilt scenery, welcoming locals, fascinating independent cultures, and remain relatively calm even when other Greek islands are sagging with tourists at the height of summer. Turkish influence is barely visible, despite the islands being part of the Ottoman Empire until 1912. Island-hopping isn't as easy as in other islands groups due to distances and a relative scarcity of ferries.

SAMOS ΣΑΜΟΣ

pop 32,800

A lush mountainous island only 3km from Turkey, Samos has a glorious history as the legendary birthplace of Hera, wife and sister of god-of-all-gods, Zeus. Samos was an important centre of Hellenic culture, and the mathematician Pythagoras and storyteller Aesopus are among its sons. The island has beaches that bake in summer, and a hinterland that is superb for hiking. Spring brings with it pink flamingos, wildflowers, and orchids that the island grows for export, while summer brings throngs of package tourists.

Samos has two main ports: Vathy (Samos Town) in the northeast and Pythagorio on the southeast coast. Those coming from the south generally arrive in Pythagorio. Big ferries use Vathy. Once you're on Samos and have onward tickets, double-check where your boat is leaving from. Buses between the two take 25 minutes. **By Ship Travel** (☎ 22730 25065; www.byshiptravel.gr) has offices at both ports that handle schedules and ticketing.

Pythagorio Πυθαγόρειο

pop 1300

Pretty Pythagorio, where you'll disembark if you've come from Patmos, is small and enticing. The town stands on the site of the World Heritage–listed ancient city of Samos. Although the settlement dates from the Neolithic era, most of the remains are from Polycrates time (around 550 BC).

The cordial **municipal tourist office** (☎ 22730 61389; deap5@otenet.gr; 8am-9.30pm) is two blocks from the waterfront on the main street, Lykourgou Logotheti. By Ship Travel is next door. Across the street, **Digital World** (☎ 22730 62722; per hr €4; 11am-10:30pm) provides Internet access. The bus stop is two blocks further inland on the same street, next to the post office.

The 1034m-long **Evpalinos Tunnel** (☎ 22730 61400; adult/student €4/2; 8.45am-2.45pm Tue-Sun), built in the 6th century BC, was dug by political prisoners and used as an aqueduct to bring water from the springs of Mt Ampelos (1140m). In the Middle Ages, locals used the tunnel as a hideout during pirate raids. Part of it can still be explored. It's a 20-minute walk north of town. If you feel like reminiscing about maths study, there's an excellent **statue of Pythagoras** and his triangle on the waterfront opposite the ferry quay.

Hotel Evripili (☎ 22730 61096; Konstantinou Kanari; s/d €45/60), just back from the waterfront, is a friendly hotel in a stone building with cosy rooms, some with balcony. On the waterfront, **Polixeni Hotel** (☎ 22730 61590; d €65;) is a homely place with nicely furnished, clean and comfortable rooms; it's a good option.

At **Espirides Garden-Tavern** (☎ 22730 61767; Pythagora; mains from €5) 'Mama's Plate of the Day' is the stuff legends are made of, while the food at **Poseidonas Neptune Taverna** (☎ 22730 62530; mains from €5), on the small town beach, past the jetty with the Pythagoras statue on it, is superb.

Vathy (Samos) Βαθύ Σάμος

pop 2025

Busy Vathy, 25 minutes north of Pythagorio by bus, is an attractive working port town. Most of the action is along Themistokleous Sofouli, the main street that runs along the waterfront. The main square, Plateia Pythagorou, in the middle of the waterfront, is recognisable by its four palm trees and statue of a lion.

The rarely open and hard-to-find **tourist office** (☎ 22730 28530; Jun-Sep) is in a side street one block north of the main square. **ITSA Travel** (☎ 22730 23605; www.itsatravel.com), opposite the quay, is helpful with travel inquiries, excursions, accommodation and luggage storage. To get to Vathy's bus station, follow the waterfront south and turn left onto Lekati, 250m south of Plateia Pythagorou (just before the police station). **Diavlos NetCafé** (☎ 22730 22469; per hr €4; 8.30am-11.30pm), near the bus station, offers Internet access.

The **archaeological museum** (☎ 22730 27469; adult/student €3/2; 8.30am-3pm Tue-Sun), by the municipal gardens, is first rate. The highlight is a 5.5m *kouros* statue.

Pythagoras Hotel (☎ 22730 28601; www.pythagorashotel.com; Kallistratou 12; dm/s/d €15/20/35;) is a friendly, great-value place with a convivial atmosphere run by English-speaking Stelio. There is a restaurant, bar, satellite TV and Internet access on site. Facing inland, the hotel is 400m to the left of the quay. Call ahead for free pick up on arrival. **Pension Dreams** (☎ 22730 24350; Areos 9; d €30), back up to the left behind the main square and overlooking the harbour, is another good option.

Garden Taverna (☎ 22730 24033; Manolis Kalomiris; mains €4-9) serves good Greek food in a lovely garden setting; it's also up to the left behind the main square. **Ovaga** (☎ 22730 25476; Kefalopoulou 13) is an excellent waterfront bar with outstanding views; it's to the north of the port on the way to Pythagoras Hotel.

Around Samos

Ireon (☎ 22730 95277; adult/student €3/2; 8.30am-3pm Tue-Sun), the legendary birthplace of the goddess Hera, is 8km west of Pythagorio. The temple at this World Heritage site was enormous – four times the Parthenon – though only one column remains.

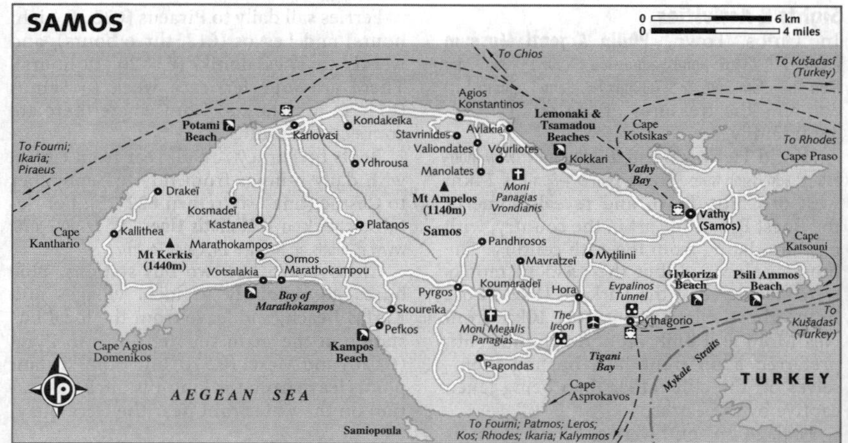

The captivating villages of **Vourliotes** and **Manolates**, on the slopes of imposing Mt Ampelos, northwest of Vathy, are excellent walking territory and have many marked pathways.

Choice beaches include **Tsamadou** on the north coast, **Votsalakia** in the southwest and **Psili Amos** to the east of Pythagorio.

Getting There & Around

There are daily flights to Athens (€73) from **Samos airport** (SMI), 4km west of Pythagorio, and five weekly to Thessaloniki (€149) with **Olympic Airlines** (code OA; ☎ 22730 27237; cnr Kanari & Smyrnis, Vathy).

There are daily ferries for Piraeus (€26, 13 hours), but only four a week head north to Chios (€11.70, four hours). Others head west to the Cyclades. Daily hydrofoils ski south to Patmos (€13.50, 1¼ hours), carrying on to Leros, Kalymnos and Kos (€23, 3½ hours). There are daily ferries to Kuşadası (for Ephesus) in Turkey (€47 return plus €10 port taxes). Day excursions are also available from April to October.

You can get to most of the island's villages and beaches by bus. Rental cars and scooters are readily available around the island.

CHIOS ΧΙΟΣ

pop 54,500

Due to its thriving shipping and mastic industries (mastic produces the resin used in chewing gum), Chios (*hee*-os) has never really bothered much with tourism. If you are an off-the-beaten-track type of Greek Island traveller, you'll find Chios all the more appealing.

One great attraction lies in exploring the island's inland villages, including some 20 *mastihohoria* (mastic villages) that were spared during an 1822 Turkish massacre because of the sultan's fondness for chewing gum.

Orientation & Information

Chios Town, on the island's eastern coast, is a working port and home to half the island's inhabitants. A main street runs in a semicircle around the port, with most ferries docking at its northern end. The *kastro* (old Turkish quarter) is to the north of the ferry quay, and Plateia Vounakiou, the main square, is just south and inland from the quay.

The **municipal tourist office** (☎ 22710 44389; infochio@otenet.gr; Kanari 18; 🕒 7am-10pm Apr-Oct, to 4pm Nov-Mar) is on the street that runs inland to the main square. It is extremely helpful and provides information on accommodation, schedules and rentals. The publication *Hiking Routes on Chios* is available there.

Agean Travel (☎ 22710 41277; aegeantr@otenet.gr; Leof Aigaiou 14) on the waterfront handles ticketing, while **Enter Internet Café** (☎ 22710 41058; Leof Aigaiou 48; per hr €3.50), in an impressive upstairs place on the southern waterfront, has internet access.

Sights & Activities

In Chios Town, **Philip Argenti Museum** (☎ 22710 23463; Korais; admission €1.50; 🕑 8am-2pm Mon-Thu, 8am-2pm & 5-7.30pm Fri, 8am-12.30pm Sat) contains the treasures of the wealthy Argenti family.

World Heritage–listed **Nea Moni** (New Monastery; admission free; 🕑 8am-1pm & 4-8pm) is 14km west of Chios Town and reveals some of the finest Byzantine art in the country, with mosaics dating from the 11th century. The mosaics survived, but the resident monks were massacred by the Turks in 1822. Those in the ghost village of **Anavatos**, 10km from Nea Moni and built on a precipitous cliff, preferred a different fate, hurling themselves off the cliff rather than being taken captive by the Turks.

Pyrgi, 24km southwest of Chios Town, is one of Greece's most unusual villages. The façades of the town's dwellings are decorated with intricate grey-and-white geometric patterns and motifs. The tiny medieval town of **Mesta**, 10km from Pyrgi and nestled within fortified walls, has four entry gates, two ornate churches and cobbled streets connected by overhead arches.

Sleeping & Eating

Chios Rooms (☎ 22710 20198; www.chiosrooms.gr; Leoforos Aigaiou 110, Chios Town; s/d/tr with shared bathroom €25/35/45) A top location to stay, this place is upstairs in a restored neoclassical house on the waterfront at the southern end of the harbour. It has bright, airy rooms and is lovingly being restored by its Kiwi owner Don.

Hotel Kyma (☎ 22710 44500; kyma@chi.forthnet.gr; Evgenias Chandris 1, Chios Town; s/d/tr incl breakfast €61/78/97; ❄) Around the corner from Chios Rooms, this place occupies a charismatic century-old mansion and has helpful owners. Ask for a room overlooking the sea.

To Meliotiko Ouzeri (☎ 22710 40407; Chios Town; dishes from €4) On the waterfront to the right of the ferry quay, this is a place to bring a healthy appetite as the servings of Greek classics are massive.

Getting There & Around

There are daily flights from Chios airport (JKH) to Athens (€69) and five per week to Thessaloniki (€110) with **Olympic Airlines** (code OA; ☎ 22710 20359). The airport is 4km south of Chios Town.

Ferries sail daily to Piraeus (€22.50, eight hours) and Lesvos (€12, three hours), and weekly to Thessaloniki (€34.20, 18 hours). There are four ferries a week to Samos (€11.70, four hours) from where there are connections south.

Boats to Turkey run all year from Chios, with daily sailings from July to September to Çeşme (one way/return €22/25). For details, check out **Miniotis Lines** (☎ 22710 24670; www.miniotis.gr; Neorion 24, Chios Town).

Chios Town has two bus stations. Blue buses go regularly to local villages and Karfas Beach, and leave from the local bus station at the main square. Buses to Pyrgi (€2.20) and Mesta (€2.70) and other distant points leave from the long-distance bus station on the waterfront near the ferry quay.

LESVOS (MYTILINI) ΛΕΣΒΟΣ (ΜΥΤΙΛΗΝΗ)

pop 93,500

The third-largest of the Greek islands after Crete and Evia, fertile Lesvos is mountainous and presents excellent hiking and birdwatching opportunities. Lesvos has always been a centre of philosophy and artistic achievement and to this day is a spawning ground for innovative ideas in the arts and politics. Spoil yourself with a taste of the island's prized olive oil, ouzo and sardines, or relax in its therapeutic hot springs. An excellent source of information on the island is www.greeknet.com.

The two main towns on the island are the capital of Mytilini on the southeast coast, and attractive Mithymna on the north coast.

Mytilini Μυτιλήνη

pop 27,250

The capital and main port, Mytilini, is built between two harbours (north and south) with an imposing fortress and forest of pines on the promontory to the east. All ferries dock at the southern harbour, and most of the town's action is around this waterfront. With a large university campus, Mytilini is a lively place, even out of season.

The **tourist office** (☎ 22510 42511; 6 Aristarhou; 🕑 9am-1pm Mon-Fri), 50m up Aristarhou inland from the quay, offers brochures and maps, but its opening hours are limited. The **tourist police** (☎ 22510 22776) are at the en-

SAPPHO, LESBIANS & LESVOS

One of Greece's great ancient poets, Sappho, was born on the island of Lesvos during the 7th century BC, in the town of Eresos. Her poetry became famous for its lyrically evocative style and richly sumptuous imagery. Most of Sappho's work was devoted to love and desire, and the objects of her affection were often female. Owing to this last fact, her name and birthplace have come to be associated with female homosexuality.

These days, Lesvos is visited by many lesbians paying homage to Sappho. The whole island is very gay friendly, in particular the southwestern beach resort of Skala Eresou, which is built over ancient Eresos. The village is well set up to cater to lesbian needs and has a 'Women Together' festival held annually in September. Check out www.sapphotravel.com for details.

There is an excellent statue of Sappho taking pride of place in the main square on the waterfront in Mytilini.

trance to the quay and are helpful if you're outside tourist-office hours. **Samiotis Tours** (☎ 22510 42574; samiotistours@hotmail.com; Kountourioti 43) on the waterfront, handles flights, boat schedules, ticketing and excursions to Turkey.

Sponda (☎ 22510 41007; Komninaki; per hr €3) has impressive Internet access a block back from the waterfront in a pool bar.

SIGHTS & ACTIVITIES

Mytilini's excellent neoclassical **archaeological museum** (☎ 22510 22087; 8 Noemvriou; adult/child €3/2; 8am-7.30pm) has a fascinating collection from Neolithic to Roman times. Follow the signposts from the ferry.

A superb place for a stroll or a picnic is the pine forest surrounding Mytilini's impressive **fortress** (adult/student €2/1; 8am-2.30pm Tue-Sun), which was built in early Byzantine times and enlarged by the Turks.

Theophilos Museum (☎ 22510 41644; admission €2; 9am-2.30pm & 6-8pm Tue-Sun), 4km south of Mytilini in Varia village, is a shrine to the prolific folk painter Theophilos.

Five kilometres from Mytilini, on the Gulf of Yera, are the **Therma Yera hot springs** (☎ 22510 24575; admission €2.50; 8am-6pm), where you can bathe in a steamy white room overlooking the water and mountains. The experience is highly recommended.

SLEEPING

Pension Thalia (☎ 22510 24640; Kinikiou 1; s/d €25/30) This *pension* has clean, bright rooms in a large house. It is about a five-minute walk north of the main square, up Ermou, the road that links the south and north harbours. Follow the signs from the corner of Ermou and Adramytiou.

Pension Iren (☎ 22510 22787; Komninaki 41; d/tr incl breakfast €30/35) One block back from the waterfront, rooms here are simple but clean. It's easy to find and not far from the ferry quay should you be arriving late at night.

Porto Lesvos Hotel (☎ 22510 41771; www.portolesvos.gr; Komninaki 21; s/d €60/90) This is a stylish hotel with superb rooms and service – right down to robes and slippers – in a restored building one block further north from Pension Iren.

EATING & DRINKING

Restaurant Averof (☎ 22510 22180; Ermou 52; mains from €4) Greek staples such as *patsas* (tripe soup) are dished up at this no-nonsense traditional place just back from the main square.

Kalderimi (☎ 22510 46577; Thasou 3; mains from €6) Popular with locals, Kalderimi has an excellent ambience with tables in a vine-covered pedestrian street just back from the Sappho statue on the main harbour.

Ocean Eleven Bar (Kountourioti 17) In the corner on the waterfront, this is a superb spot to relax with a drink and partake in some Mytilini people-watching.

GETTING THERE & AROUND

Written up on flight schedules as Mytilene, Lesvos' Odysseas airport (MJT) has daily connections with Athens (€78) and Thessaloniki (€88), and two a week to Chios (€28) with **Olympic Airlines** (code OA; ☎ 22510 28659) and **Aegean Airlines** (code A3; ☎ 22510 61120).

In summer, there are daily boats to Piraeus (€27.90, 12 hours), some via Chios and Mykonos, and one boat a week to Thessaloniki (€30.20, 13 hours). There are four ferries a week to Ayvalik in Turkey (one way/return €30/45). Stop by Samiotis Tours (p625) for ticketing and schedules.

Mytilini has two bus stations. For local buses, head along the waterfront to the main square, where buses leave regularly for Therma Yera. For long-distance buses, walk 600m from the ferry along the waterfront to El Venizelou and turn right until you reach Agia Irinis park, which is next to the station. There are regular services in summer to Mithymna, Petra, Agiasos, Skala Eresou, Mantamados and Agia Paraskevi.

Mithymna Μήθυμνα

pop 1500

The gracious, preserved town of Mithymna (known by locals as Molyvos) is 62km north of Mytilini. Cobbled streets canopied by flowering vines wind up the hill below the impressive castle. The town is full of cosy tavernas and genteel stone cottages.

ORIENTATION & INFORMATION

From the bus stop, walk straight ahead towards the town for 100m to the helpful **municipal tourist office** (☎ 22530 71347; www.mithymna.gr; 8am-9pm Mon-Fri, 9am-7pm Sat & Sun), which has good maps. Some 50m further on, the cobbled main thoroughfare of 17 Noemvriou heads up to the right. Going straight at this point will take you to the colourful fishing port. There are three Internet cafés along the port road. **Panatella Holidays** (☎ 22530 71520; www.panatella-holidays.com) handles bookings and local trips.

SIGHTS & ACTIVITIES

The noble **Genoese castle** (☎ 22530 71803; admission €2; 8am-7pm Tue-Sun) sits above the town like a crown and affords tremendous views out to Turkey.

Pebbly **Mithymna Beach** sits below the town and is good for swimming. Don't forget to stroll down to the harbour.

Eftalou hot springs (☎ 22530 71245; public/private bath per person €3.50/5; public bath 10am-2pm & 4-8pm, private bath 9am-6pm), 4km from town on the beach, is a superb bathhouse complex with a whitewashed dome and steaming, pebbled pool. There are also private baths where you don't need a bathing suit.

SLEEPING & EATING

Nassos Guest House (☎ 22530 71432; www.nassosguesthouse.com; Arionis; d & tr €20-35) An airy, friendly place with shared facilities and a communal kitchen, this guesthouse is in an old Turkish house oozing with character. With rapturous views, it's highly recommended. To get there, head up 17 Noemvriou and take the second right (a sharp switchback).

Hotel Sea Horse (☎ 22530 71630; www.seahorse-hotel.com; d incl breakfast €75;) Down at the old harbour, this hotel in a renovated old stone building is right on the water. The rooms are clean and comfortable, and the Sea Horse Café is open daily from 8am until late.

Betty's Restaurant (☎ 22530 71421; Agora; mains from €5) Betty's has superb home-style Greek food, views and atmosphere in a building that was once a notorious bordello. Ask Betty about the old photos on the wall. Take the downhill fork after passing through the uphill tunnel on 17 Noemvriou.

GETTING AROUND

In summer, buses go regularly to Petra Beach and Eftalou. Buses to Mytilini (€5) take 1¾ hours. Car- and scooter-hire outlets line the port road.

Around the Island

East of Mithymna, the traditional picturesque villages surrounding Mt Lepetymnos (**Sykaminia**, **Mantamados** and **Agia Paraskevi**) are worth a visit if you have time.

Southern Lesvos is dominated by **Mount Olympus** (968m) and the very pretty day-trip destination of **Agiasos**, which has good artisan workshops making everything from handcrafted furniture to pottery.

Western Lesvos is known for its petrified forest, with petrified wood at least 500,000 years old, and for the gay-friendly town of Skala Eresou, the birthplace of Sappho (see p625).

SPORADES ΣΠΟΡΑΔΕΣ

Scattered to the southeast of the Pelion Peninsula, to which they were joined in prehistoric times, the 11 islands that make up the Sporades group have mountainous terrain and dense vegetation. Skiathos has the best beaches and a throbbing tourist scene, while Skopelos is more relaxed, with a postcard waterfront, sandy bays and lush forest trails. Alonnisos is far less visited and retains more local character. The National Marine Park of Alonnisos, encompassing seven islands, is aimed at protecting the Mediterranean monk seal, and many island residents are dedicated to preserving the region's delicate ecology.

The main ports for the Sporades are Volos and Agios Konstantinos on the mainland.

SKIATHOS ΣΚΙΑΘΟΣ

pop 6150

Lush and green, Skiathos has a beach-resort feel about it. An international airport has brought loads of package tourists, but the island still oozes enjoyment. Skiathos Town and some excellent beaches are on the hospitable south coast, while the north coast is precipitous and less accessible.

Orientation & Information

Skiathos Town's main thoroughfare is Papadiamanti, running inland opposite the quay. There's a **tourist information booth** (☎ 24270 23172) to the left as you leave the port, but it opens irregularly. The helpful **tourist police** (☎ 24270 23172; ⌚ 8am-9pm), about halfway along Papadiamanti next to the high school, can provide information and maps.

Heliotropio Travel (☎ 24270 22430; helio@skiathos.gr), opposite the ferry quay, handles ticketing. It also has rental cars, and runs excellent excursions, including full-/half-day trips around the island (€17/12), and a day trip that takes in Skopelos and Alonnisos (€20). **Internet Zone Café** (☎ 24270 22767; Evangelistrias 28; per hr €4.40; ⌚ 9am-1am) is 30m from the post office.

Sights

Skiathos has superb beaches, particularly on the south coast. **Koukounaries** is popular with families. A stroll over the headland, **Big Banana Beach** is stunning, but if you want an all-over tan, head a tad further to **Little Banana Beach**, where bathing suits are a rarity.

Sleeping

The **Rooms to Let** (☎ 24270 22990) bookings kiosk on the waterfront opens when ferries and hydrofoils arrive. *Domatia* owners also meet incoming ferries. Accommodation is scarce in July and August, but prices can as much as halve out of the high season.

Camping Koukounaries (☎ 24270 49250; per person/tent €7/3) This place, 30 minutes away from town by bus at Koukounaries Beach, has good facilities, a minimarket and a taverna.

Pension Pandora (☎ 24270 24357, 69791 56019; Paleokastro; s/d/q €30/45/60; P ❄) Run by the effervescent Georgina, this family-run place is 10 minutes' walk north of the quay. The spotless rooms have TV, kitchens and balconies. Georgina also has two exceptional apartments just off Papadiamanti.

Villa Orsa (☎ 24270 22430; s/d incl breakfast €70/80; ❄) Perched above the old harbour, this mansion features traditionally styled rooms and a courtyard terrace overlooking the sea.

Eating & Drinking

Skiathos Town is brimming with eateries. Nightlife sprawls along Polytehniou; to find it, turn left off Papadiamanti at Evangelistrias and walk 100m.

Psaradika Ouzeri (☎ 24270 23412; Paralia; mains €3.50-10) By the fish market at the far end of the old port, Psaradika is the seafood winner, specialising in fresh fish at decent prices.

Taverna Dionysos (☎ 24270 22675; Panora; menus from €7) Heading up Papadiamanti, turn right opposite the National Bank to find this place, which has tasty three-course menus. Taverna Dionysos presents you with an ouzo before dinner, and a *metaxa* (Greek brandy) with coffee to finish. Bring your appetite.

Maria's Pizza (☎ 24270 22292; Syngrou 6; mains €8-12) Above the old port, this popular hole-in-the-wall place offers tasty handmade pizzas, pastas and salads.

Kahlua Bar (☎ 24270 23205; Polytehniou) On the club strip at the eastern waterfront end of town, Kahlua is popular and pulses with mainstream DJ sets and dancing drinkers.

Entertainment

Cinema Attikon (☎ 24270 22352; admission €7) On Papadiamanti, this excellent open-air cinema features recent English-language movies that you can watch while sipping a beer.

Getting There & Around

In summer, there is a daily flight from Athens to Skiathos (€53). There is an **Olympic**

Airlines office (code OA; ☎ 24270 22200) at Skiathos airport (JSI).

There are frequent daily hydrofoils to/from the mainland ports of Volos (€21.10, 1¼ hours) and Agios Konstantinos (€23.20, 1½ hours), as well as cheaper ferries. The hydrofoils head to and from Skopelos (€10, 35 minutes) and Alonnisos (€14.20, one hour). In summer, there is a daily hydrofoil to Thessaloniki (€35.30, 3½ hours).

Crowded buses ply the south-coast road between Skiathos Town and Koukounaries every 30 minutes between 7.30am and 11pm year-round, stopping at all the beaches along the way. The bus stop is at the eastern end of the harbour.

SKOPELOS ΣΚΟΠΕΛΟΣ

pop 4700

A mountainous island, Skopelos is covered in pine forests, vineyards, olive groves and fruit orchards. While the northwest coast is exposed with high cliffs, the southeast is sheltered and harbours pleasant pebbled beaches. The island's main port and capital of Skopelos Town, on the east coast, skirts a semicircular bay and clambers in tiers up a hillside, culminating in a ruined fortress.

Velanio Beach on the south coast is the island's nudie spot. On the west coast, pebbled **Panormos Beach**, with its sheltered emerald bay surrounded by pine forest, is superb. The 2km stretch of **Milia Beach**, a few kilometres further on, is considered the island's best for swimming.

In Skopelos Town, there is no tourist office, but **Thalpos Leisure & Services** (☎ 24240 22947; www.holidayislands.com), on the waterfront between the ferry quay and the excursion-boat quay, is handy for accommodation and tours. Head 50m up the road opposite the port entrance to find Platanos Sq. Along Doulidi, the street to the left after Gyros.gr, is the **Skopelos Internet Café** (☎ 24240 23093; per hr €3.50), post office and a stack of popular nightspots. The bus station is next to the port.

Pension Sotos (☎ 24240 22549; www.skopelos.net/sotos; s/d €25/50; ❄), in the middle of the waterfront, has big rooms in an enchanting old Skopelete building. There's also a communal kitchen, terrace and courtyard. Check out individual rooms and their different prices online before you go. **Perivoli Studios** (☎ 24240 58022; www.skopelos.net/perivoli; d/tr €60/70; P ❄) are studio-apartments in what used to be a traditional stone building used for roasting plums. About 100m from the new quay, each studio has a well-equipped kitchen and terrace.

Head to Souvlaki Sq, 100m up from the dock, for cheap eats such as gyros and souvlaki. The top spot in town to chill out is under the huge plane tree at **Platanos Jazz Bar** (☎ 24240 23661), opposite the excursion-boat quay. It's open all day, serves a mean omelette (€3) for breakfast, and plays wicked jazz and blues until the late hours. It's the ideal place to recover from, or prepare for, a hangover. Next door is **Taverna Ta Kimata O Angelos** (☎ 24240 22381; mains from €4), a traditional taverna that is the oldest one on the island.

On Doulidi, there is a clutch of popular bars, including **Panselinos** (☎ 24240 24488; 🕑 10pm-3am), which mixes Greek pop sounds with live performances.

In summer, there are daily ferries to Volos (€16.90, 3½ hours) and Agios Konstantinos (€31.60, 3½ hours) that also call at Skiathos. Flying Dolphin hydrofoils dash several times a day to Skiathos (€10.30, 45 minutes), Alonnisos (€7.70, 20 minutes), Volos (€26.30, 2¼ hours) and Agios Konstantinos (€27.40, 2½ hours). Most hydrofoils also call in at Loutraki, the port below Glossa on the northwest coast of the island. For schedules and tickets, visit **Skopelos Ferry Office** (☎ 24240 22767), opposite the port. There are frequent buses from Skopelos Town to Glossa (€3.20, one hour) stopping at all beaches along the way.

ALONNISOS ΑΛΟΝΝΗΣΟΣ

pop 2700

Green, serene, attractive Alonnisos is at the end of the line and is thereby the least visited of the Sporades' main islands. The west coast is mostly precipitous cliffs, but the east coast is speckled with pebble-and-sand beaches. The seas surrounding the island have been declared a marine park and reputedly have the cleanest waters in the Aegean.

The port village of Patitiri isn't particularly attractive. Its concrete buildings were slapped together in 1965 after an earthquake destroyed the hilltop capital of Alonnisos Town. There are two main thoroughfares; facing inland from the ferry quay, Pelasgon is to the left and Ikion Dolopon is to the far right.

There is no tourist office or tourist police, but the post office, police and Internet access at **Techno Plus** (☎ 24240 29100; per hr €3; 9am-2pm & 5-9pm) are on Ikion Dolopon. On the waterfront itself, **Alonnisos Travel** (☎ 24240 65188; www.alonnisostravel.gr) handles boat scheduling and ticketing. **Ikos Travel** (☎ 24240 65320; www.ikostravel.com) runs a popular round-the-island excursion. The bus stop is on the corner of Ikion Dolopon and the waterfront.

The tiny *hora*, **Old Alonnisos**, is a few kilometres inland. Its streets sprout a profusion of plant life, alluring villas of eclectic design and dramatic vistas.

Alonnisos is ideal for walking. Waterfront travel agencies offer guided tours or there's an excellent trail guide called *Alonnisos on Foot: A Walking & Swimming Guide* by Bente Keller & Elias Tsoukanas, which is available at newsstands for €9.

The **Rooms to Let service** (☎ 24240 66188; fax 24240 65577; 9.30am-2pm & 6.30-10.30pm), opposite the quay, books accommodation all over the island. **Camping Rocks** (☎ 24240 65410; per person €5) is a shady, basic camping ground. It is a steep hike about 1.5km from the port; go up Pelasgon and take the first road on your left. **Pension Pleiades** (☎ 24240 65235; pleiades@Internet.gr; s/d €35/50;) looks out over the harbour and is visible from the quay. The rooms are immaculate, balconied, bright and cheerful. **Paradise Hotel** (☎ 24240 65213; www.paradise-hotel.gr; s/d/tr €63/80/99; P) is an excellent-value place featuring a swimming pool and including a buffet breakfast in its prices. Follow the stairway opposite the National Bank.

To Kamaki Ouzeri (☎ 24240 65245; Ikion Dolopon; mains €4-10) is a traditional island eatery. Check the ready-to-eat dishes out in the kitchen. **Café Flisvos** (☎ 24240 65307; mains from €5) is the pick of the waterfront restaurants, under the canopy opposite the dock.

There are ferries with varying regularity connecting Alonnisos to Volos (€14.80, 4½ hours) and Agios Konstantinos (€31.30, four hours) via Skopelos and Skiathos. Flying Dolphin hydrofoils provide the most regular schedules between the islands. They travel several times a day to Skopelos Town (€7.70, 20 minutes), Skiathos (€14.70, 1½ hours), Volos (€27.80, 2½ hours) and Agios Konstantinos (€31.30, 2¾ hours).

The local bus (€1) runs to the *hora* every hour. Car- and scooter-hire outlets are on Pelasgon and Ikion Dolopon, but only one main road spans the island!

IONIAN ISLANDS ΤΑ ΕΠΤΑΝΗΣΑ

The idyllic cypress- and fir-covered Ionian islands stretch down the western coast of Greece from Corfu in the north to Kythira, off the southern tip of the Peloponnese. Mountainous, with dramatic cliff-backed beaches, soft light, and turquoise-coloured water, they're more Italian in feel, offering a contrasting experience to other Greek islands.

CORFU ΚΕΡΚΥΡΑ

pop 109,540

Corfu is the second-largest and most important island in the group and many consider it to be Greece's most beautiful island.

Corfu Town

pop 39,048

Built on a promontory and wedged between two fortresses, Corfu's old town is a tangle of narrow alleyways of shuttered Venetian buildings. The elegant Liston, in the centre of town, is a row of arcaded buildings inspired by the Rue de Rivoli in Paris.

The town's Palaio Frourio (Old Fortress) stands on an eastern promontory, separated from the town by parks and gardens known as the Spianada. The Neo Frourio (New Fortress) lies to the northwest. Ferries dock at the new port, just west of the Neo Frourio. The **long-distance bus station** (Avrami) is inland from the port. The **tourist police** (☎ 26610 30265; 3rd fl, Samartzi 4) provide helpful info. Check email at **On Line Internet Café** (Kapodistria 28; per hr €4).

SIGHTS

The **archaeological museum** (☎ 26610 30680; P Vraila 5; admission €3; 8.30am-3pm Tue-Sun) houses a collection of finds from Mycenaean to classical times. The **Church of Agios Spiridon** (Agios Spiridonos) has a richly decorated interior and displays the remains of St Spiridon, paraded through town four times a year.

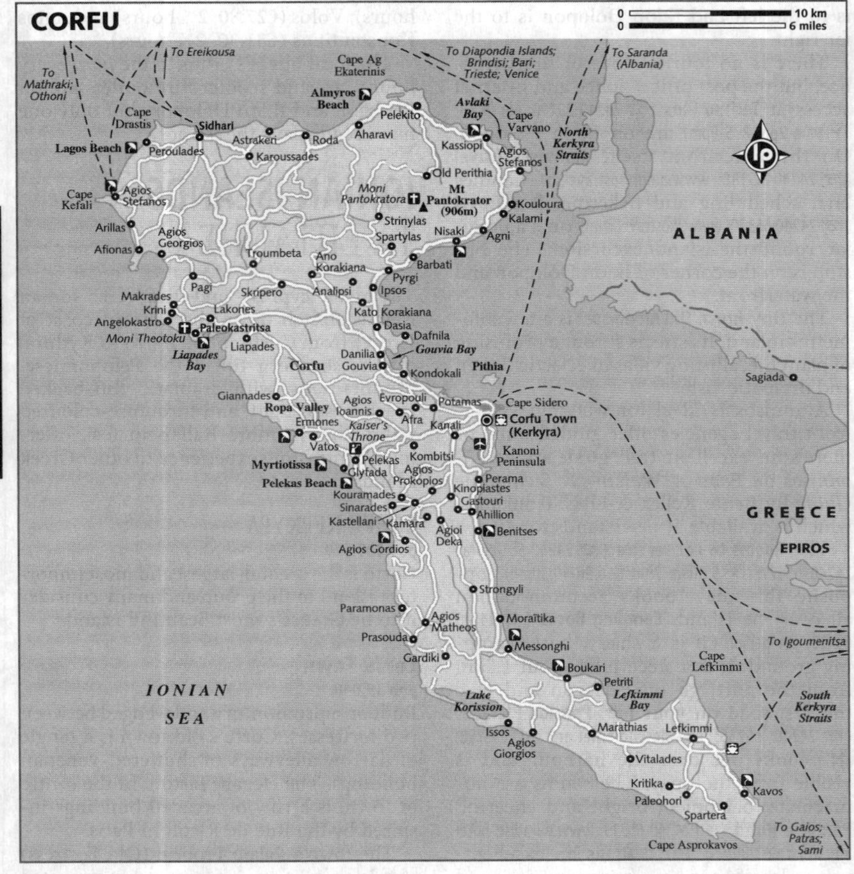

SLEEPING & EATING

Hotel Hermes (☎ 26610 39268/39321; fax 26610 31747; G Markora 14; s/d €30/40, with shared bathroom €20/30) While this hotel has seen better days, it's one of the best deals in town and is popular with backpackers who hang out in the cool lobby to escape the summer heat.

Hotel Konstantinoupolis (☎ 26610 48716; www.konstantinoupolis.com.gr; K Zavitsianou 1, Old Port; s/d/tr €70/98/116;) The breezy rooms at this well-maintained old hotel are clean and come with TV, minibar and wi-fi. Book a front room overlooking the lovely harbour. Prices drop by €20 out of the high season.

To Tsipouzadiko (☎ 26610 82240; mains €3-8; dinner) This big atmospheric place, with old 45 *rembetika* records on its walls, serves up generous portions of fresh (cheap) Greek food. Its lovely garden terrace hums till late with the chatter of locals. It's on the lane behind courthouse and Hotel Konstantinoupolis in Old Port.

La Famiglia (☎ 26610 30270; Maniarisi Arlioti 16; mains €6-14; 8pm-late) Unusual for Greece, as it's equally popular with tourists (who eat around 8pm) and locals (who pack the place late). This Italian eatery has authentic pastas, buzzy atmosphere and great music.

To Dimarchio (☎ 26610 39031; Plateia Dimarchio; mains €7-20) One of the city's best restaurants on an attractive square, this place serves high quality (and occasionally inventive) Italian and Greek dishes, prepared with the freshest ingredients.

Café Liston (☎ 26610 45514; Eleftherias 10) There's nothing like starting the day with an espresso under the arcades of the Liston. This is our pick for quality and people-watching, although local frappé-drinking teens prefer roadside **Libro d'Oro** (The Liston).

Around the Island

The main resort on the west coast is **Paleokastritsa**, set around a series of gorgeous cypress-backed bays. Further south, there are good beaches around the small village of **Agios Gordios**. Between Paleokastritsa and Agios Gordios is the hilltop village of **Pelekas**, a good place to watch the sunset.

Sunrock (☎ 26610 94637; www.geocities.com/sunrock_corfu; Pelekas Beach; per person with shared bathroom/full board €18/24;) is a resort popular with backpackers because of its great facil ities, activities and pick-up service.

Getting There & Away

Corfu's **Ioannis Kapodistrias airport** (CFU; ☎ 26610 30180) is 3km from Corfu Town. **Olympic Airlines** (code OA; ☎ 26610 38694; Polila 11, Corfu Town) and **Aegean Airlines** (code A3; ☎ 26610 27100) offer several flights daily to Athens, while Olympic also flies to Thessaloniki a few times a week. There are hourly ferries to Igoumenitsa (€6, 1½ hours), a daily ferry to Paxi, and in summer there are daily services to Patra (€21 to €25, six hours) on the international ferries (see p640 for more details). Daily buses to Athens (€30, 8½ hours) and Thessaloniki (€29, eight hours) leave from the Avrami terminal.

Getting Around

Buses for villages close to Corfu Town leave from Plateia San Rocco. Services to other destinations leave from Avrami terminal. A taxi from the airport to the old town costs around €10.

LEFKADA ΛΕΥΚΑΔΑ

pop 22,500

Joined to the mainland by a narrow isthmus, fertile Lefkada with its pine forests and olive groves, also boasts many pretty bays, splendid beaches, and one of the hottest windsurfing spots in Europe.

Lefkada Town

Most travellers' first port of call, laid-back Lefkada Town is popular with yachties and windsurfers heading south. The town has an earthquake-resistant corrugated-iron style of architecture that's quite unique, an attractive marina, pleasant waterfront areas and a vibrant pedestrian thoroughfare with some very funky jewellery and fashion boutiques.

SLEEPING & EATING

Pension Pirofani (☎ 26450 25844; Marina Dorpfeld; d/tr €70/85) This great-value *pension* with balconied clean rooms is in prime people-watching territory.

Hotel Ianos (☎ 26450 22217; Marina Lefkada; www.ianoshotel.gr; s/d/tr €100/130/150;) While the décor of this hotel was dated before it opened, rooms have minibars and TV, there's a the swimming pool, and the marina location is unbeatable. Prices drop considerably outside of the high season.

Gustoso (☎ 26450 24603; Agelou Sikelianou, western seafront; mains €6-20) This attractive Italian pizzeria is the pick of a dozen eateries and cafés lining the waterfront for its delicious salads and best wood-fired-oven pizzas outside of Napoli.

Around the Island

With its lovely bay and pleasant waterfront, **Nydri** is somewhat blighted by tacky souvenir shops and touristy tavernas. Tiny **Agios Nikitas** is a typically atmospheric Greek town with a laid-back ambience, but gets very crowded in summer.

Eucalyptus-scented **Vasiliki**, with its pretty village, relaxed style, seaside eateries and long beach, is just the place to spend a few days. Popular with windsurfers, it's possible to organise windsurfing lessons (and book hotels) through **Club Vass** (☎ UK 01920 484121; www.clubvass.com) or guided treks, sea kayaking and other outdoor activities through **Trekking Hellas** (☎ 26450 31130; www.trekking.gr). Overlooking the bay, **Pension Holidays** (☎ 26450 31426; d €55;) has great-value rooms near the village centre.

Getting There & Around

Four Island Ferries operates daily ferries between Nydri, Frikes (Ithaki), Fiskardo (Kefalonia) and Vasiliki. Most trips take about 90 minutes and tickets cost €5 per person and €27 per car. Get times and tickets from **Borsalino Travel** (☎ 26450 92528; Nydri) or **Samba Tours** (☎ 26450 31520; Vasiliki).

ITHAKI ΙΘΑΚΗ

pop 3052

Odysseus' long lost home in Homer's *Odyssey*, Ithaki, or ancient Ithaca, is a verdant island blessed with cypress-covered hills and beautiful turquoise coves for swimming.

Kioni

The tiny village of Kioni has a laid-back vibe, a magical waterfront location and is a wonderful place to chill for a few days. It's possible to walk to nearby coves to swim, but it's best to explore the island with your own wheels.

SLEEPING & EATING

Hamilton House (☎ 26740 31654; marina waterfront; r €40) Although it has a shabby charm, the cluttered interior of this traditional stone house, right on the village waterfront, won't be to everyone's taste. For the price, the location and sea views are unbeatable.

Captain's Apartments (☎ 26740 31481; www.captains-apartments.gr; studio/apt €45/65;) Owned by an affable former merchant navy captain, these clean, spacious apartments are well-equipped for self-catering, and have satellite TV and balconies overlooking the valley and village. Well-signposted, it's easy to find.

Kalipso (☎ 26740 31066; mains €5-35) If the yachts are anchored at the marina, head here early for a waterfront table and hearty traditional Greek dishes, as it's liable to run out of food – although the well-meaning staff might make it up to you with a nightcap on the house!

Around the Island

The tiny relaxed port of **Frikes**, where the ferries dock, is a cheaper alternative to Kioni and there are rooms to rent – ask at the waterfront tavernas and shops. While the capital **Vathy** is attractive with elegant mansions rising from around its bay, it has a big-town feel after Kioni.

Getting There & Around

Four Island Ferries operates daily ferries between Frikes, Fiskardo (Keffalonia), and Nydri and Vasiliki (Lefkada). Tickets can be purchased at the Frikes dock just before departure. Most trips take an average of 90 minutes and tickets cost €5 per person and €27 per car. Call **Delas Tours** (☎ 26740 32104; www.ithaca.com.gr; Vathy) for times. You really need a car to explore the island.

KEFALLONIA ΚΕΦΑΛΛΟΝΙΑ

pop 45,000

Tranquil cypress- and fir-covered Kefallonia has fortunately not succumbed to package tourism to the extent the other Ionian islands have, despite being thrust under the spotlight following its starring role in *Captain Corelli's Mandolin*. The largest Ionian island is breathtakingly beautiful in parts and remains low-key outside the resort areas.

Fiskardo

Pretty Fiskardo, with its pastel-coloured Venetian buildings set around a picturesque bay, was the only Kefallonian village not to be destroyed by the 1953 earthquake. Despite its popularity with European yachties and upmarket package tourists, it's still laid-back enough to appeal to independent travellers, and is a sublime spot to chill for a few days. There are lovely walks and sheltered coves for swimming.

SLEEPING & EATING

Regina's Rooms (☎ 26740 41355; www.myrtoscorp.com; d €50-60) On the car park, this is a budget bargain and ideal for self-caterers. All of its colourful breezy rooms have TV, fridge and balconies, some with gorgeous bay views, and some with kitchenettes or access to a communal kitchen. Friendly Regina gives good discounts for long stays and when it's quiet.

Faros Suites (☎ 26740 41355; d from €120;) A super-comfortable family-owned boutique hotel successfully fusing Greek and African style, the hospitable South African–Greek owners here make you feel at home. The spacious suites are more like apartments with fully equipped kitchens and balconies with sea views.

Café Tselenti (☎ 26740 41344; mains €5-20) This is the most elegant dining option in town, and while the focus is Italian, it also serves some superb Greek classics.

Vasso's (☎ 26740 41276; mains €6-25) Vasso's waterside location, with sailing boats bobbing up and down beside your table, is romantic. It's the place to head for exceptional seafood, whether it's fresh grilled fish or pasta with crayfish.

Around the Island

Straddling a slender isthmus on the north west coast, the petite pastel-coloured village of **Assos** watches over the ruins of a Venetian fortress perched upon a pine-covered peninsula. Popular with upmarket package tourists, there are several tavernas on the waterfront, but little else to interest independent travellers. Splendid **Myrtos Beach**, 13km south of Assos, is spellbinding from both above, where the postcard views are breathtaking, and below, where you'll think you've discovered the perfect beach – until you try to clamber across the painful pebbles that is!

A car is best for exploring Kefallonia. **Pama Travel** (☎ 26740 41033; www.pamatravel.com; waterfront, Fiskardo) rents cars and boats, books accommodation, sells tickets and has Internet access. Across the bay, **Nautilus Travel** (☎ 26740 41440; fax 26740 41470) sells tickets for ferries.

Getting There & Around

There are daily flights to Athens (€65) from **Keffalonia airport** (EFL; ☎ 26710 41511), 9km south of Argostoli. Four Island Ferries operates daily ferries between Fiskardo, Frikes (Ithaki), and Nydri and Vasiliki (Lefkada). Get tickets from Nautilus Travel or the dock before departure. Most trips average 90 minutes and cost €5 per person and €27 per car. In the high season, there are ferries from Pesada to Agios Nikolaos (Zakynthos). Daily ferries operate from Sami to Patra (€11.50, 2½ hours), and from Argostoli and Poros to Kyllini (the Peloponnese).

ZAKYNTHOS ΖΑΚΥΝΘΟΣ

pop 39,000

The beautiful island of Zakynthos, or Zante, has stunning coves, dramatic cliffs and laid-back beaches, but unfortunately is over-run by package tourist groups, so only a few special spots warrant your time.

Zakynthos Town

The island's capital and port is an attractive Venetian town that was painstakingly reconstructed after the 1953 earthquake. Its elegant arcades and lively café scene make it the best base from which to explore the island.

Along the waterfront, Lombardou and its surrounding streets are home to touristy tavernas, travel agencies and car-rental agencies. Plateia Agiou Markou is the buzzy main square, off which runs Alexandrou Roma, the main pedestrian shopping street, with everything from fashion boutiques to souvenir shops (with a mind-boggling array of loggerhead turtle souvenirs). Look out for the traditional sweet stores on and around Eleftheriou Venizelou selling *mandolato,* the local soft nougat.

SLEEPING & EATING

Hotel Strada Marina (☎ 26950 42761; www.stradamarina.gr; Lombardou 14; s/d €75/120; ❄ 🅿) The rooms may be uninspiring and the rooftop swimming pool filled only in summer, but this hotel is well situated, and portside rooms have balconies with sea views. Rates can drop by half when it's quiet.

Avoid eating on the touristy Plateia Agiou Markou and do what the locals do – hit Alexandrou Roma for cheap eats.

2D (☎ 26950 27008; Alexandrou Roma 32; gyros from €2.50) Owned by two guys called Dionysus, 2D does the most delicious gyros and juicy roast chickens in town, and they even home deliver!

Arekia (☎ 26950 26346; Krioneriou 92; mains €3-10) Take a short stroll north of the centre along the waterfront for a memorable night out at this atmospheric taverna. The exuberant musical entertainment, delicious Greek food, and warm friendly service make for one of the most memorable experiences you'll have in Greece.

Around the Island

Most people head to Zakynthos for the famous **Shipwreck Beach** in the northwest. While Zakynthos is best explored by car, for a sea-level look take a boat from Cape Skinari near Agios Nikolaos, Porto Vromi or Alykes.

Continue south to gorgeous **Limnionas** where you can swim in crystal-clear turquoise coves. Arrive early as there's barely enough space for a few people to sunbathe on the rocks. The only eatery at the cove, **Taverna Porto Limnionas** (☎ 26950 48650; mains €3-12) serves up delicious Greek classics (try the excellent *mezedes* plate) in a sublime setting overlooking the sea.

Cape Keri near the island's southernmost point has spectacular views of sheer cliffs and splendid beaches. It's possible to swim at pleasant **Keri Beach** nearby, but it's nothing to write home about. The **Bay of Laganas** has been declared a national marine park by the Greek government in order to protect the endangered loggerhead turtles that come ashore to lay their eggs in August – the peak of the tourist invasion. While the pleasant beaches are worth a look, it's best not to risk one more beach umbrella piercing an unborn baby turtle's shell, and soak up some sun elsewhere.

Zakynthos' **airport** (ZTH; ☎ 26950 28322) is 6km from Zakynthos Town. **Olympic Airlines** (code OA; ☎ 26950 28322; airport) has daily flights to Athens and other Ionion Islands. There are hourly ferries to Igoumenitsa (€6, 1½ hours), including car ferries (€27 per car), and several daily bus-ferry services to Patra (€5, 3½ hours). As bus services are poor, to explore the island it's best to hire a car. Try **Europcar** (☎ 26950 41541; Plateia Agiou Louka, Zakynthos Town).

GREECE

GREECE DIRECTORY

ACCOMMODATION

Greece has a wide range of accommodation options from excellent camping grounds to flashy designer hotels and everything in-between. However, if you're travelling extensively you'll find that in some towns you might have to move up or down a category for a night or two. Prices quoted in this book are for the high season (many destinations from June to September, but always July to August) and include an attached bathroom, unless otherwise stated. Budget rooms cost up to €60, midrange from €60 to €150, while top-end rooms start at €150. Prices are about 40% cheaper between October and May, but note that some towns virtually board up during winter. Greek accommodation is subject to strict price controls, and by law a notice must be displayed in every room stating the category of the room and the seasonal price. If you think there's something amiss, contact the tourist police.

Greece has around 340 camping grounds, many of them in wonderfully scenic locations. They're generally open from April to October. The **Panhellenic Camping Association** (www.panhellenic-camping-union.gr) has detailed information on camping grounds around Greece. Standard facilities include hot showers, kitchens, restaurants and minimarkets – and often a swimming pool. Prices vary according to facilities, but reckon on €5 to €7 per adult, €3 to €4 for children aged four to 12, €4 for a small tent, €5 for a large one and €6 upwards for a caravan.

Greece has more than 50 mountain refuges, which are listed in the booklet *Greece Mountain Refuges & Ski Centres*, available free of charge at EOT and EOS (Ellinikos Orivatikos Syndesmos, the Greek Alpine Club) offices.

You'll find youth hostels in most major towns and on some islands. Most hostels throughout Greece are affiliated with the **Greek Youth Hostel Organisation** (☎ 21075 19530; y-hostels@otenet.gr), including hostels in Athens, Olympia, Patra, Thessaloniki, and on the islands of Crete and Santorini. Most charge €8 to €11 for a dorm bed, and you don't have to be a member to stay.

Domatia are the Greek equivalent of a bed and breakfast – minus the breakfast. Initially consisting of little more than spare rooms rented out in summer, *domatia* nowadays are often purpose-built additions to the family house, but can still represent good value. Expect to pay about €25 to €35 for a single and €40 to €50 for a double. Don't worry about finding them – owners will find you as they greet ferries and buses shouting 'room!'.

Hotels in Greece are classified as deluxe, or A, B, C, D or E class. The ratings seldom seem to have much bearing on the price, but expect to pay about €18/25 for singles/doubles in D and E class, and anything from €35/45 to €60/80 for singles/doubles with a private bathroom in a decent C-class place. Some places are classified as *pensions* and are rated differently. Both hotels and *pensions* are allowed to levy a 10% surcharge for stays of less than three nights, but they seldom do.

ACTIVITIES

Diving & Snorkelling

Snorkelling can be enjoyed just about anywhere along Greece's magnificent coastlines. Corfu, Mykonos and Santorini are just some of the good areas to snorkel. Diving, however, must take place under the supervision of a diving school to protect the antiquities still in the deep.

Skiing
Greece offers inexpensive European skiing with more than a dozen resorts dotted around the mainland, mainly in the north. It's no Switzerland, however, and the resorts are basic, catering mainly to Greek skiers. The main areas are Mt Parnassos (195km northwest of Athens) and Mt Vermio (110km west of Thessaloniki). A good season starts in early January and goes through to April. Take a look at www.snowreport.gr for snow reports and web cams.

Trekking
Greece could be a trekkers' paradise if trekking organisations received better funding. Outside the main popular routes, the trails are generally overgrown and poorly marked. Several companies run organised treks; the biggest is **Trekking Hellas** (Map p570; ☎ 210 331 0323; www.outdoorsgreece.com; Filellinon 7, Athens).

Windsurfing
Greece is a fantastic windsurfing destination and sailboards are widely available for hire, priced at €12 to €15 per hour. The top spots for windsurfing are Hrysi Akti on Paros, and Vasiliki on Lefkada, which is a popular place to learn.

Yachting
Set aside your prejudices about deck shoes and cardigans knotted around necks: yachting is a brilliant way to see the Greek Islands. All you need is a couple of certified sailors in your group and you can hire a 28ft bare boat (no crew) that sleeps six for around €1000 per week, although hiring a skipper will nearly double that price.

BUSINESS HOURS
Banks are open from 8am to 2pm Monday to Thursday, and to 1.30pm Friday. Some banks in the larger cities and towns are also open from 3.30pm to 6.30pm and on Saturday (8am to 1.30pm). Post offices are open from 7.30am to 2pm Monday to Friday; in major cities they're open until 8pm and also open from 7.30am to 2pm on Saturday.

In summer, shops are generally open from 8am to 1.30pm and 5.30pm to 8.30pm on Tuesday, Thursday and Friday, and 8am to 2.30pm on Monday, Wednesday and Saturday. Shops generally open 30 minutes later during winter. *Periptera* will often be your saviour: open from early morning to late at night, they sell everything from beer to bus tickets.

Restaurants in tourist areas generally open at 11am and stay open through to midnight; normal restaurant hours are 11am to 2pm and from 7pm to midnight or 1am. Cafés tend to open between 9am and 10am and stay open until midnight. Bars open around 8pm and close late, and while discos might open at 10pm, you'll drink alone until midnight. Nightclubs generally close around 4am, but many go through to dawn during summer.

CHILDREN
Greece is an easy destination to travel through with children. Hotels and restaurants (plenty of kids' menus) are used to having children around and the Greeks, being so family-oriented, are very welcoming. However, the summer heat can be challenging, and running around poorly maintained tourist sites (such as ruins), requires a watchful eye – as does crossing any road in Greece!

CUSTOMS
You may bring the following into Greece duty-free: 200 cigarettes or 50 cigars; 1L of spirits or 2L of wine; 50g of perfume; and 250mL of eau de Cologne.

DANGERS & ANNOYANCES
Greece has the lowest crime rate in Europe, however, you might doubt that statistic if you head down the wrong street in Omonia, Athens. See the Athens section (p564) for more information on this as well as a common con that travellers fall for.

EMBASSIES & CONSULATES
Greek Embassies & Consulates
Greek diplomatic missions abroad include the following:

Australia (☎ 02-6273 3011; 9 Turrana St, Yarralumla, ACT 2600)

Canada (☎ 613-238 6271; 76-80 Maclaren St, Ottawa, Ontario K2P 0K6)

Cyprus (☎ 02-680 670/1; Byron Bvld 8-10, Nicosia)

France (☎ 01-47 23 72 28; www.amb-grece.fr/presse; 17 Rue Auguste Vaquerie, 75116 Paris)

Germany (☎ 30-20 62 60; www.griechische-botschaft.de; Jaegerstrasse 54-55, 10117 Berlin-Mitte)

GREECE

Italy (☎ 06-853 7551; www.greekembassy.it; Viale G Rossini 4, Rome 00198)
Japan (☎ 03-3403 0871/2; www.greekemb.jp; 3-16-30 Nishi Azabu, Minato-ku, Tokyo 106-0031)
New Zealand (☎ 04-473 7775; 5-7 Willeston St, Wellington)
South Africa (☎ 12-430 7351; 1003 Church St, Arcadia, Pretoria 0083)
Spain (☎ 01-564 4653; Av Doctor Arce 24, Madrid 28002)
Turkey (☎ 312 448-0647; Ziya-ul-Rahman Caddesi 9-11, Gaziosmanpasa 06700, Ankara)
UK (☎ 020-7229 3850; www.greekembassy.org.uk; 1a Holland Park, London W11 3TP)
USA (☎ 202-939 1300; www.greekembassy.org; 2221 Massachusetts Ave NW, Washington, DC 20008)

Embassies & Consulates in Greece

All foreign embassies in Greece are in Athens and its suburbs.

Australia (Map p562; ☎ 210 645 0404; Dimitriou Soutsou 37, GR-115 21)
Canada (Map p562; ☎ 210 727 3400; Genadiou 4, GR-115 21)
Cyprus (Map p562; ☎ 210 723 7883; Irodotou 16, GR-106 75)
France (Map p562; ☎ 210 361 1663; Leof Vasilissis Sofias 7, GR-106 71)
Germany (Map p562; ☎ 210 728 5111; cnr Dimitriou 3 & Karaoli, Kolonaki GR-106 75)
Italy (Map p562; ☎ 210 361 7260; Sekeri 2, GR-106 74)
Japan (Map p562; ☎ 210 775 8101; Athens Tower, Leoforos Messogion 2-4, GR-115 27)
New Zealand (Map p562; ☎ 210 687 4701; Kifissias 268, Halandri)
South Africa (Map p562; ☎ 210 680 6645; Kifissias 60, Maroussi, GR-151 25)
Turkey (Map p562; ☎ 210 724 5915; Vasilissis Georgiou 8, GR-106 74)
UK (Map p562; ☎ 210 723 6211; Ploutarhou 1, GR-106 75)
USA (Map p562; ☎ 210 721 2951; Leoforos Vasilissis Sofias 91, GR-115 21)

FESTIVALS & EVENTS

In Greece, it is probably easier to list the dates when festivals and events are *not* on! Some festivals are religious, some cultural and others seemingly just an excuse to party. It is worth timing at least part of your trip to coincide with one fesitval or event, as you will be warmly invited to join in the revelry. The following list is by no means exhaustive and more details can be found at www.cultureguide.gr.

January

Epiphany (Blessing of the Waters) Christ's baptism is celebrated on the 6th when seas, lakes and rivers are blessed. The largest ceremony occurs at Piraeus.

February

Carnival Season The three-week period before the beginning of Lent is celebrated all over Greece with fancy dress, feasting and traditional dance.

March

Independence Day On 25 March, parades and dancing mark the anniversary of the hoisting of the Greek flag that started the War of Independence.

April

Easter The most important festival of the Greek Orthodox religion. The emphasis is on the Resurrection rather than the Crucifixion so it's a celebratory event. The most significant part of the event is midnight on Easter Saturday when candles are lit (symbolising the Resurrection) and a fireworks and candle-lit procession hits the streets.

May

May Day The celebrations on 1 May see a mass exodus from towns to the countryside to picnic and gather wildflowers, with which to make wreaths for adorning homes.

June

Hellenic Festival The most important of summer festivals, events are staged throughout Greece; however, the Theatre of Herodes Atticus in Athens and the Theatre of Epidavros, near Nafplio, are venues for traditional events.

July

Feast of Agia Marina (St Marina) This feast day is celebrated on 17 July in many parts of Greece, and is a particularly important event on the Dodecanese island of Kasos.

August

Feast of the Assumption Greeks celebrate this day (15 August) with family reunions and many expats head back to their home town for the festivities.
Samothraki World Music Festival The northeastern Aegean island of Samothraki plays host to Greece's biggest rave party for a week starting at the end of August.

September

Genesis tis Panagias The birthday of the Virgin Mary is celebrated on 8 September with religious services and feasting.

October

Feast of Agios Dimitrios This feast day, on 26 October, is celebrated in Thessaloniki with much revelry.

Ohi (No) Day Metaxas' refusal to allow Mussolini's troops free passage through Greece in WWII is commemorated on 28 October with parades, folk dancing and feasting.

GAY & LESBIAN TRAVELLERS

In a country where the church plays a significant role in shaping society's views on issues such as sexuality, it's not surprising that homosexuality is generally frowned upon. While there is no legislation against homosexual activity, it is wise to be discreet and to avoid open displays of togetherness. Greece is a popular destination for gay travellers. Athens has a busy gay scene that packs up and heads to the islands for summer. Mykonos has long been famous for its bars, beaches and hedonism and a visit to Eresos on Lesvos has become something of a pilgrimage for lesbians.

HOLIDAYS

New Year's Day 1 January.
Epiphany 6 January.
First Sunday in Lent February.
Greek Independence Day 25 March.
Good Friday/Easter Sunday March/April.
Spring Festival/Labour Day 1 May.
Feast of the Assumption 15 August.
Ohi Day 28 October.
Christmas Day 25 December.
St Stephen's Day 26 December.

INTERNET ACCESS

Greece still lags behind the rest of Europe for travellers looking for Internet access, however, we've listed cafés under the Information heading for cities and islands where available. Charges differ wildly (as does the speed of access) – from €1.50 per hour in big cities to up to €10 per hour on some of the islands. Some midrange and most top-end hotels offer some form of Internet connection (occasionally wi-fi), but laptop-wielding visitors will often find this a frustrating and expensive business.

INTERNET RESOURCES

Culture Guide (www.cultureguide.gr) Plenty of information about contemporary culture and the arts.

Greek Ferries (www.greekferries.org) Get all your ferry information from the source. Covers international and domestic ferries.

Greek National Tourist Organisation (www.gnto.gr) Concise tourist information.

LonelyPlanet.com (www.lonelyplanet.com) Has postcards from other travellers and the Thorn Tree bulletin board, where you can pose those tricky questions or help answer other travellers' questions on your return.

Ministry of Culture (www.culture.gr) Information on ancient sites, art galleries and museums.

LANGUAGE

Greeks are naturally delighted if you can speak a little of their language, but you don't need Greek to get around the major tourism sites. Many Greeks have lived abroad, usually in Australia or the USA, and English is widely spoken, but venturing to remote villages can prove more of a challenge.

MONEY

Banks will exchange all major currencies, in either cash or travellers cheques and also Eurocheques. Post offices charge less commission than banks, but won't cash travellers cheques. For a country with so many tourists, credit cards are not as widely accepted as you'd expect in Greece. Always check that an establishment accepts cards and always have cash handy. ATMs are located everywhere except the smallest villages.

Greece is still a cheap destination by northern European standards, but it's no longer dirt-cheap. A daily budget of €40 would entail staying in youth hostels or camping, staying away from bars, and only occasionally eating in restaurants or taking ferries. Allow at least €80 per day if you want your own room and plan to eat out regularly and see the sights. If you really want a holiday (comfortable rooms and restaurants all the way) you'll need closer to €120 per day.

Your money will go a lot further if you travel in the quieter months, as accommodation is generally much cheaper outside the high season when there are more opportunities to negotiate better deals.

Greece adopted the euro in 2002, and the Greek drachma disappeared after a two-month period of dual circulation. Value-added tax (VAT) varies from 15% to 18%. A tax-rebate scheme applies at a restricted number of shops and stores; look for a Tax Free sign. You must fill in a form at the shop and then present it with the receipt at the airport on departure. A cheque will (hopefully) be sent to your home address.

In restaurants the service charge is included on the bill, but it is the custom to leave a small tip – just round up the bill. Accommodation is nearly always negotiable outside peak season, especially for longer stays. While souvenir shops will generally bargain, prices in other shops are normally clearly marked and non-negotiable.

POST

Tahydromia (post offices) are easily identified by the yellow sign outside. Regular post boxes are yellow; red post boxes are for express mail. The postal rate for postcards and airmail letters within the EU is €0.60, to other destinations it's €0.65. Post within Europe takes five to eight days and to the USA, Australia and New Zealand, nine to 11 days. Some tourist shops also sell stamps, but with a 10% surcharge.

Mail can be sent poste restante to any main post office and is held for up to one month. Your surname should be underlined and you will need to show your passport when you collect your mail. Parcels are not delivered in Greece – they must be collected from a post office.

SOLO TRAVELLERS

Greece is a great destination for solo travellers, particularly during summer when the islands are full of travellers meeting and making friends. Hostels, as well as other backpacker-friendly accommodation, are excellent places to meet other travellers. Solo women are quite safe – which is not to say that problems don't occur, but violent offences are rare.

TELEPHONE

The Greek telephone service is maintained by Organismos Tilepikoinonion Ellados, a public corporation always referred to by its acronym OTE (o-*teh*). Public phones are easy to use and pressing the 'i' button brings up the operating instructions in English. Public phones are everywhere and all use phonecards.

For directory inquiries within Greece, call ☎ 131 or ☎ 132; for international directory inquiries, it's ☎ 161 or ☎ 162.

Mobile Phones

Mobile phones have become the must-have accessory in Greece. If you have a compatible GSM phone from a country with a global roaming agreement with Greece, you will be able to use your phone there. Make sure you have global roaming activated before you leave your country of residence. There are several mobile service providers in Greece; **Cosmote** (www.cosmote.gr/) has the best coverage. You can purchase a Greek SIM card for around €20 and cards are available everywhere to recharge the SIM card.

EMERGENCY NUMBERS

- Ambulance ☎ 166
- Fire ☎ 199
- Police ☎ 100
- Roadside Assistance (ELPA) ☎ 104
- Tourist Police ☎ 171

Phone Codes

Telephone codes are part of the 10-digit number within Greece. The landline prefix is 2 and for mobiles it's 6.

Phonecards

All public phones use OTE phonecards, sold at OTE offices and *periptera*. These cards are sold in €3, €5 and €9 versions, and a local call costs €0.30 for three minutes. There are also excellent discount-card schemes available that offer much better value for money.

TOURIST INFORMATION

Tourist information is handled by the Greek National Tourist Organisation (GNTO), known as EOT in Greece. There is either an EOT office or a local tourist office in almost every town of consequence and on many of the islands. Popular destinations have tourist police who can also provide information.

Tourist Offices Abroad

Australia (☎ 02-9241 1663-5; hto@tgp.com.au; 37-49 Pitt St, Sydney, NSW 2000)
Canada (☎ 416-968 2220; grnto.tor@on.aibn.com; Suite 102, 1500 Don Mills Rd, Toronto, Ontario M3B 3K4)
France (☎ 1-42 60 65 75; eot@club-Internet.fr; 3 Ave de l'Opéra, Paris 75001)
Germany Berlin (☎ 30-217 6262; Wittenbergplatz 3a,

10789 Berlin 30); Frankfurt (☎ 69-236 561; info@gzf-eot.de; Neue Mainzerstrasse 22, 60311 Frankfurt); Hamburg (☎ 40-454 498; info-hamburg@gzf-eot.de; Neurer Wall 18, 20254 Hamburg); Munich (☎ 89-222 035/6; Pacellistrasse 5, 2W 80333 Munich)
Italy Milan (☎ 02-860 470; Piazza Diaz 1, 20123 Milan); Rome (☎ 06-474 4249; Via L Bissolati 78-80, Rome 00187)
Japan (☎ 03-350 55 917; gnto-jpn@t3.rim.or.jp; Fukuda Bldg West, 5th fl 2-11-3 Akasaka, Minato-ku, Tokyo 107)
UK (☎ 020-7495 9300; www.gnto.co.uk; 4 Conduit St, London W1R ODJ)
USA Chicago (☎ 312-782 1084; www.greektourism.com; Suite 600, 168 North Michigan Ave, Chicago, IL 60601); Los Angeles (☎ 213-626 6696; Suite 2198, 611 West 6th St, Los Angeles, CA 92668); New York (☎ 212-421 5777; Olympic Tower, 645 5th Ave, New York, NY 10022)

TRAVELLERS WITH DISABILITIES

If mobility is a problem, the hard fact is that most hotels, museums and ancient sites are not wheelchair accessible. While facilities in Athens are steadily improving – such as at the Acropolis (p564), which now has a wheelchair lift – elsewhere the uneven terrain is an issue even for able-bodied people.

Useful information on travelling with disabilities is available on the Internet at www.sath.org and www.access-able.com.

VISAS

Visitors from most countries don't need a visa for Greece. The list of countries whose nationals can stay in Greece for up to three months include Australia, Canada, all EU countries, Iceland, Israel, Japan, New Zealand and the USA. For longer stays, apply at a consulate abroad or at least 20 days in advance to the **Aliens Bureau** (Map p562; ☎ 210 770 5711; Leoforos Alexandras 173, Athens; 8am-1pm Mon-Fri) at the Athens Central Police Station. Elsewhere in Greece, apply to the local authority.

TRANSPORT IN GREECE

GETTING THERE & AWAY

Air

There are more than a dozen international airports in Greece, but most of them handle only summer charter flights to the islands. **Eleftherios Venizelos airport** (ATH; ☎ 210 353 0000; www.aia.gr), near Athens, handles the vast majority of international flights, including all intercontinental ones, and has regular scheduled flights to all the European capitals.

Thessaloniki is also well served by **Macedonia airport** (SKG; ☎ 23104 73700), and there are scheduled flights to/from Iraklio (Crete) from **Nikos Kazantzakis airport** (HER; ☎ 28102 28401).

Airlines that fly to and from Greece include the following:
Air France (code AF; ☎ 2109 601 100; www.airfrance.com)
British Airways (code BA; ☎ 8011 156 000; www.britishairways.com)
Delta Airlines (code DL; ☎ 00 800 4412 9506; www.delta.com)
easyJet (code EZY; ☎ 2103 530 300; www.easyjet.com)
Emirates (code EK; ☎ 2019 333 400; www.emirates.com)
Japan Airlines (code JL; ☎ 2103 248 211; www.jal.com)
KLM (code WA; ☎ 2109 110 000; www.klm.com)
Lufthansa (code IH; ☎ 2106 175 200; www.lufthansa.com)
Olympic Airlines (code OA; ☎ 8011 144 444; www.olympic-airways.gr)
Virgin Express (code TV; ☎ 2109 490 777; www.virgin-express.com)

Land

BORDER CROSSINGS

From Albania

There are four crossing points between Greece and Albania. Kakavia, 60km northwest of Ioannina, is the main one. Others are Sagiada (near Igoumenitsa), Mertziani (near Konitsa) and Krystallopigi (near Kotas).

From Bulgaria

There are two Bulgarian border crossings: one at Promahonas (109km northeast of Thessaloniki) and the other at Ormenio (in northeastern Thrace).

From Former Yugoslav Republic of Macedonia (FYROM)

There are three border crossings here: Evzoni (68km north of Thessaloniki); Niki; and Doïrani.

From Turkey

The crossing points for Turkey are at Kipi, 43km east of Alexandroupolis, and, less conveniently, at Kastanies, 139km northeast of Alexandroupolis.

BUS

The Hellenic Railways Organisation (OSE) operates an overnight bus between Athens (500m west of the Larisis train station) and Tirana, Albania (€35.20, 16 hours, daily) via Ioannina and Gjirokastra. To Bulgaria, the OSE operates an Athens–Sofia bus (€45.50, 15 hours, daily except Monday), as well as a Thessaloniki–Sofia service (€19, 7½ hours, four daily). To Turkey, the OSE operates from Athens to Istanbul (€67.50, 22 hours, daily except Wednesday). This stops at Thessaloniki (€44) and Alexandroupolis (€15).

CAR & MOTORCYCLE

You can drive or ride through the border crossings listed (p639) with your own transport, but if you are in a hire car, make sure that your insurance can cover this, and find out whether the car-hire company has roadside assistance coverage in these countries.

TRAIN

There are three daily trains from Sofia to Athens (€30.65, 18 hours) via Thessaloniki (€17.90, six to seven hours), where you need to change trains. There are daily trains between Istanbul and Thessaloniki (€42.50, around 14 hours). To the FYROM, there are two trains daily from Thessaloniki to Skopje (€14.50, three hours).

Sea

You'll find all the latest information about ferry routes, schedules and services online. For an overview try www.greekferries.gr. Most of the ferry companies have their own websites, including the following:

Agoudimos Lines (www.agoudimos-lines.com)
ANEK Lines (www.anek.gr)
Blue Star Ferries (www.bluestarferries.com)
Fragline (www.fragline.gr)
Hellenic Mediterranean Lines (www.hml.gr)
Minoan Lines (www.minoan.gr)
Superfast (www.superfast.com)
Ventouris Ferries (www.ventouris.gr)

The following ferry services are for the high season (July and August), and prices are for one-way deck class. Prices are about 30% less in the low season.

ALBANIA

Corfu-based Petrakis Lines has daily ferries to the Albanian port of Saranda (€15, 25 minutes), plus a weekly service to Himara (€25, 1¼ hours).

CYPRUS & ISRAEL

Passenger services from Greece to Cyprus and Israel have been suspended indefinitely.

ITALY

There are ferries to the Italian ports of Ancona, Bari, Brindisi, Trieste and Venice from Patra, Igoumenitsa, Corfu and Kefallonia. If you want to take a vehicle across, it's a good idea to make a reservation beforehand.

Ancona

Blue Star Ferries and Superfast Ferries run two boats daily to Patra (€60 to €70, 19 hours or 21 hours via Igoumenitsa). Tickets are available through **Morandi & Co** (☎ 071-20 20 33; Via XXIX Settembre 2/0). Superfast accepts Eurail passes. **ANEK Lines** (☎ 071-207 23 46; Via XXIX Settembre 2/0) does the trip daily (€70) in 19½ hours via Igoumenitsa.

Bari

Minoan Lines (☎ 080 52 10 266; Via Latilla 14) and **Superfast Ferries** (☎ 080 52 11 416; Corso de Tullio 6) have daily sailings to Patra via Igoumenitsa. **Ventouris Ferries** (☎ 080 521 7609) has daily boats to Corfu (10 hours) and Igoumenitsa (11½ hours) for €45.

Brindisi

The trip from Brindisi operates only between April and early October. **Hellenic Mediterranean Lines** (☎ 0831-548001; Costa Morena) offers services to Patra (€50), calling at Igoumenitsa, Corfu, Kefallonia, Paxi and Zakynthos on the way. **Agoudimos Lines** (☎ 0831-550180; Via Provinciale per Lecce 29) and **Fragline** (☎ 0831-54 85 40; Via Spalato 31) sail only to Igoumenitsa.

Trieste

ANEK Lines (☎ 040-32 20 561; Via Rossini 2) has boats to Patra (€68, 32 hours) every day except Thursday, calling at Corfu and Igoumenitsa.

Venice

Minoan Lines (☎ 041-24 07 177; Stazione Marittima 123) has boats to Patra (€75, 29 hours) every day except Wednesday, calling at Corfu and Igoumenitsa. **Blue Star Ferries** (☎ 041-277 0559; Stazione Marittima 123) sails the route four times weekly for €64.

TURKEY

Five regular ferry services operate between Turkey's Aegean coast and the Greek Islands. Tickets for all ferries to Turkey must be bought a day in advance. For more information about these services, see Rhodes (p618), Chios (p624), Kos (p620), Lesvos (p625) and Samos (p623).

GETTING AROUND

Greece is a relatively straightforward destination to travel around thanks to its comprehensive transport system. On the mainland, buses travel to just about every town on the map and trains offer a good alternative where available. Island-hopping is what most people think of when travelling within Greece and there are myriad ferries that crisscross the Adriatic and Aegean Seas. If you are in a hurry, there is also an extensive and well-priced domestic air network. Note that timetables are seasonal and change in at least some way every year.

Air

The vast majority of domestic flights are handled by Greece's much-maligned national carrier, **Olympic Airlines** (code OA; ☎ 801 114 4444; www.olympicairlines.com).

Crete-based competitor **Aegean Airlines** (code A3; ☎ 80111 20000; www.aegeanair.com) is the sole survivor of the deregulation of domestic air travel. It offers flights to many of the same destinations as Olympic, and has the same fares, but Aegean often has great discount fares as well as youth and senior discounts.

Bicycle

Given Greece's hilly terrain, stifling summer heat and rather wayward four-wheeled friends, cycling is not that popular a form of transport. You can hire bicycles at most tourist centres, but these are generally for pedalling around town rather than for serious riding. Prices generally range from €5 to €12 per day. If you wish to do a cycling tour of Greece, bicycles are carried for free on ferries.

Boat

CATAMARAN

High-speed catamarans have become an important part of the island travel scene. They are just as fast as hydrofoils, if not faster, and are much more comfortable. They are also much less prone to cancellation in rough weather and the fares are generally the same as hydrofoils. The main players are Hellas Flying Dolphins and Blue Star Ferries.

FERRY

Every island has a ferry service of some sort, although in winter these are pared back. Services pick up from April, and during July and August Greece's seas are a mass of wake and wash. The ferries come in all shapes and sizes, from the state-of-the-art 'superferries' that run on the major routes to the ageing open ferries that operate local services to outlying islands.

The main ferry companies operating in Greece include:

ANEK (☎ 21041 97420; www.anekgr)
Blue Star Ferries (☎ 21089 19800; www.bluestarferries.com)
GA Ferries (☎ 21041 99100; www.gaferries.com)
Hellenic Seaways (☎ 21041 99000; www.hellenicseaways.gr)
LANE Lines (☎ 21042 74011; www.lane.gr)
Minoan Lines (☎ 21041 45700; minoan.gr)
NEL Lines (☎ 22510 26299; www.nel.gr)

Classes

Large ferries usually have four classes: 1st class has air-con cabins and a decent lounge and restaurant; 2nd class has smaller cabins and sometimes a separate lounge; tourist class gives you a berth in a shared four-berth cabin; and the last class, 3rd, is 'deck', which gets you a seat, restaurant, lounge/bar and (drum roll) the deck.

Deck class is an economical way to travel and is the class that most travellers use; 1st class is almost the same price as the equivalent air fare on some routes. Children under four travel free, those between four and 10 years pay half-fare. Children over 10 pay full fare. When buying tickets you will automatically be given deck class.

Costs

Fares are fixed by the government. The small differences in price you may find

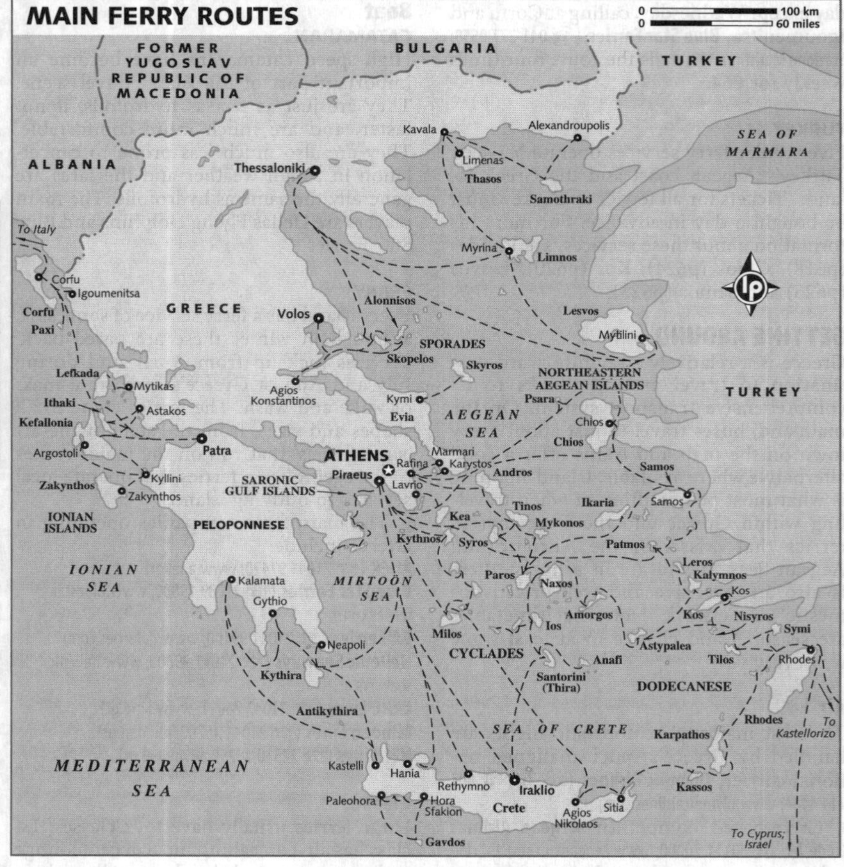

between ticket agencies are the result of some agencies sacrificing part of their designated commission to qualify as a discount service. The discount offered seldom amounts to much. Tickets can be bought at the last minute from quayside tables set up next to the boats.

Routes

The hub of the vast ferry network is Piraeus, the main port of Athens. It has ferries to the Cyclades, Crete, the Dodecanese, the Saronic Gulf Islands and the northeastern Aegean Islands. Patra is the main port for ferries to the Ionian Islands, while Volos and Agios Konstantinos are the ports for the group of islands called Sporades.

HIGH-SPEED FERRY

High-speed ferries are slashing travel times on some of the longer routes. **NEL Lines** (☎ 22510 26299; www.nel.gr), for example, does Piraeus to Chios in 4½ hours – nearly half the time of a normal ferry (and twice the price).

HYDROFOIL

Hydrofoils offer a faster sea-based alternative to ferries on some routes, in particular on those running to/from the islands closest to the mainland. They take half the time, but cost twice as much. Most routes will operate only during the high season. **Hellenic Seaways** (☎ 21041 99000; www.hellenicseaways.gr) travels from Piraeus to the Saronic Gulf Islands and the ports of the eastern Peloponnese, as well as to the Sporades from Agios Konstantinos and Volos. **Aegean Hydrofoils** (☎ 22410 24000), based in Rhodes, serves the Dodecanese and provides connections to the northeastern Aegean Islands of Ikaria and Samos as well as other routes.

Tickets for hydrofoils must be bought in advance and there is often seat allocation.

Bus

All long-distance buses on the mainland and the islands are operated by regional collectives known as **KTEL** (Koino Tamio Eispraxeon Leoforion; www.ktel.org). Fares are fixed by the government and service routes can be found on the company's website. (We've rounded fares up to the nearest euro.)

Greece's buses are comfortable, they run on time and there are frequent services on all the major routes. The buses are reasonably priced, with journeys costing about €4 per 100km. Fares and journey times on a couple of the major routes are Athens–Thessaloniki (€31, 7½ hours) and Athens–Patra (€14, three hours). Tickets should be bought at least an hour in advance to ensure a seat. Buses don't have toilets and refreshments, but stop around every three hours for those needs.

Car & Motorcycle

A great way to explore areas in Greece that are off the beaten track is by car. However, it's worth bearing in mind that Greece has the highest road-fatality rate in Europe. The road network has improved dramatically in recent years and places that were little more than a one-lane dirt track masquerading as a road have now been widened and asphalted. Driving from Athens to Thessaloniki, you'll rack up about €24 in freeway tolls.

Almost all islands are served by car ferries, but they are expensive. For example, the cost for a vehicle from Igoumenitsa to Corfu is €27, while from Piraeus to Mykonos it's €76. Petrol in Greece is expensive at around €1 per litre in the big cities, but you'll pay up to €0.20 more in remote areas.

The Greek automobile club, **ELPA** (www.elpa.gr), offers reciprocal services to members of other national motoring associations. If your vehicle breaks down, dial ☎ 104.

You can bring a vehicle into Greece for four months without a Carnet – provided you have a Green Card (international third party insurance).

HIRE

Rentals cars are available just about anywhere in Greece. The major multinational companies are represented in Athens and in most major tourist destinations. You can generally get a much better rate with local companies. Their advertised rates are about 25% lower and they're often willing to bargain. Make sure to check the insurance waivers on these companies closely and check how they can assist in case of a breakdown.

High-season weekly rates with unlimited kilometres start at about €280 for the smallest models, dropping to €200 in winter – and that's without tax and extras. Major companies will request a credit-card deposit. The minimum driving age in Greece is 18, but most car-hire firms require a driver of 21 or over.

Mopeds and motorcycles are available for hire everywhere, however, regulations stipulate that you need a valid motorcycle licence stating proficiency for the size of motorcycle you wish to rent – from 50cc upwards.

Motorcycles are a cheap way to travel around Greece. Mopeds and 50cc motorcycles range from €10 to €15 per day or from €25 per day for a 250cc motorcycle. Outside the high season, rates drop considerably. Ensure the bike is in good working order and the brakes work well.

If you plan to hire a motorcycle or moped, check that your travel insurance covers you for injury resulting from motorcycle accidents.

ROAD RULES

While it sometimes appears that there aren't any road rules in Greece, you are apparently supposed to drive on the right and overtake on the left. No casual observer would ever guess that it is compulsory to wear seat belts in the front seats of vehicles, and in the back if they are fitted.

The speed limit for cars is 120km/h on toll roads, 90km/h outside built-up areas and 50km/h in built-up areas. For motorcycles up to 100cc, the speed limit outside built-up areas is 70km/h and for larger motorbikes, 90km/h. Drivers exceeding the speed limit by 20/40% receive a fine of €60/160, however, most tourists escape with a warning.

Drink-driving laws are strict; a blood alcohol content of 0.05% incurs a fine of around €150 and over 0.08% is a criminal offence.

Public Transport

BUS

Most Greek towns are small enough to get around on foot. All major towns have local bus systems, but the only places that you're likely to need them are Athens, Kalamata and Thessaloniki.

METRO

Athens is the only city large enough to warrant a metro system – and it finally has one. See p572 for details.

TAXI

Taxis are widely available in Greece and they are reasonably priced. Yellow city cabs are metered. Flag fall is €0.75, followed by €0.28 per kilometre in towns and €0.53 per kilometre outside towns. The rate doubles from midnight to 5am. Additional charges are €3 from airports; €0.80 from ports, bus stations and train stations; and €0.30 per luggage item over 10kg.

Taxi drivers in Athens are gifted in their ability to make a little extra with every fare. If you have a complaint, note the cab number and contact the tourist police. In rural areas taxis don't have meters, so make sure you agree on a price before you get in – drivers are generally honest, friendly and helpful.

Train

The main problem with train travel in Greece is that there are only two main lines: north to Thessaloniki and Alexandroupolis, and to the Peloponnese. In addition there are a number of branch lines, such as the Pyrgos–Olympia line and the spectacular Diakofto–Kalavryta mountain railway. There are two distinct levels of service: the painfully slow, dilapidated trains that stop at all stations, and the faster, modern intercity trains.

Inter-Rail and Eurail passes are valid in Greece, but you still need to make a reservation. In summer, make reservations at least two days in advance.

Ireland

It's about time…' reads a recent Dublin Tourism tagline, and nothing could be truer. Sure, at face value it's just another tourism bureau slogan, but looking deeper you realise that these three words illuminate much of what it means to be Ireland at the beginning of the 21st century. Thanks to a sky-rocketing economy, the Celtic Tiger has burst from the fog and rain of its battered history to become one of Europe's most prosperous countries. The land of Stone Age tombs, rolling green hills, medieval castles and towering cliffs that the word 'Ireland' conjures, still exists, but today it shares space with things of this century, like beachfront holiday homes and the M1 motorway.

The slogan is also indicative of who the Irish are as a people. Centuries of conquest, famine and emigration have left them surprisingly friendly yet expectedly cynical, a combination that makes for a wickedly dark sense of humour. If you ask the fellow sitting next to you at the pub what he thinks of the Celtic Tiger, or the staggering rate of new immigrants or the declining power of the Catholic Church in Ireland, he might just say, 'It's about feckin time!'

This sentiment rings just as true for Northern Ireland, which remains part of the UK. If you ask a person up North what she thinks about the new climate of peace, chances are she'll tell you…well, you know what she'll say.

FAST FACTS

- **Area** 84,421 sq km
- **Capitals** Dublin, Belfast (Northern Ireland)
- **Currency** euro (€), Republic/pound sterling (£) NI; €1 = £0.69; £1 = €1.44; A$1 = €0.58/£0.40; ¥100 = €0.68/£0.47; NZ$1 = €0.47/£0.33; US$1 = €0.83/£0.54
- **Famous for** U2, St Patrick, Guinness, green hills
- **Official Languages** English, Irish Gaelic
- **Population** 3.9 million
- **Phrases** *craic* (good time); bleedin' (bloody); *sláinte* (cheers); shorts (shots); deadly (brilliant)
- **Telephone Codes** country code ☎ 353; Northern Ireland ☎ 44 28; international access code ☎ 00

HIGHLIGHTS

- Gallivant through the many museums, pubs and literary haunts of frenetic **Dublin** (p652), and ask a local, 'Where's the *craic*?'
- Enjoy bohemian **Galway** (p683), with its hip cafés and live music venues.
- Walk along the walls of **Derry** (p698) and learn about the volatile history of Northern Ireland.
- Drive, cycle or hitch to haunting **Kells Priory** (p668) and hang out among the ruins and the sheep.

ITINERARIES

- **One week** Spend a couple days in Dublin ambling through the excellent national museums, and gorging yourself on Guinness and other tourists in Temple Bar. Get medieval in Kilkenny before heading on to Cork and discovering why they call it 'The Real Capital'. Meander through lush, idyllic West Cork and take in the friendly spirit and melodious accents of its denizens.
- **Two weeks** Follow the one-week itinerary, then make your way from West Cork up to touristy Killarney and the Ring of Kerry on your way to bohemian Galway. Using Galway as your base, go and explore the alluring Aran Islands and the awesome Cliffs of Moher. Finally, allow yourself to be seduced by the mirror-like lakes, pale mountains and lonely valleys of the Connemara.

HOW MUCH?

- **Cup of coffee** €2.50
- **Irish Times (newspaper)** €1.50
- **Umbrella** €10
- **Cinema ticket** €9
- **Aran sweater** €50+

LONELY PLANET INDEX

- **1L petrol** €1.10
- **1L bottled water** €1.50
- **Pint of Guinness** €4
- **Souvenir T-shirt** €15
- **Pub sandwich** €4

CLIMATE & WHEN TO GO

Ireland has a relatively mild climate. Average temperatures range from 4°C to 7°C in January and February, and from 14°C to 16°C in July and August. Snow is scarce, but rain is plentiful – about 1000mm annually.

The tourist season begins the weekend before St Patrick's Day (17 March) and is in full swing from Easter onwards. Crowds are at their biggest – and prices at their highest – in July and August.

HISTORY

Very Early Irish, Celts & Vikings

Our tale begins around 10,000 years ago, as the last ice caps melted and the rising sea level cut Ireland off from Britain. Hunter-gatherers may first have traversed the narrowing land bridge, but many more crossed the Irish Sea in small boats. Farming did not reach Ireland until around 4000 BC.

The Celtic warrior tribes who influenced Irish culture came from central Europe. They had conquered large sections of southern Europe and plundered Rome in the 4th century AD. Known as 'Galli' (Gauls) by the Romans and 'Keltoi' by the Greeks, they were feared by both.

The Celts probably reached Ireland from mainland Europe around 300 BC and were well ensconced by 100 BC. Christian monks, including St Patrick, arrived in Ireland around the 5th century AD and, as the Dark Ages enveloped Europe, Ireland became an outpost of European civilisation. A land of saints, scholars and missionaries, its thriving monasteries produced beautiful illuminated manuscripts, some of which survive to this day.

From the end of the 8th century the rich monasteries were targets of raids by Vikings. At the height of their power the Vikings ruled Dublin, Waterford and Limerick, but were eventually defeated by legendary Celtic hero Brian Ború, the king of Munster, at the Battle of Clontarf in 1014.

The British Arrive

In 1169 the Norman conquest of England spread to Ireland when Henry II, fearful of the Irish kingdoms' power, dispatched forces to the island.

Oppression of the Catholic Irish got seriously under way in the 1500s when Elizabeth I gave loads of Irish land to Protestant

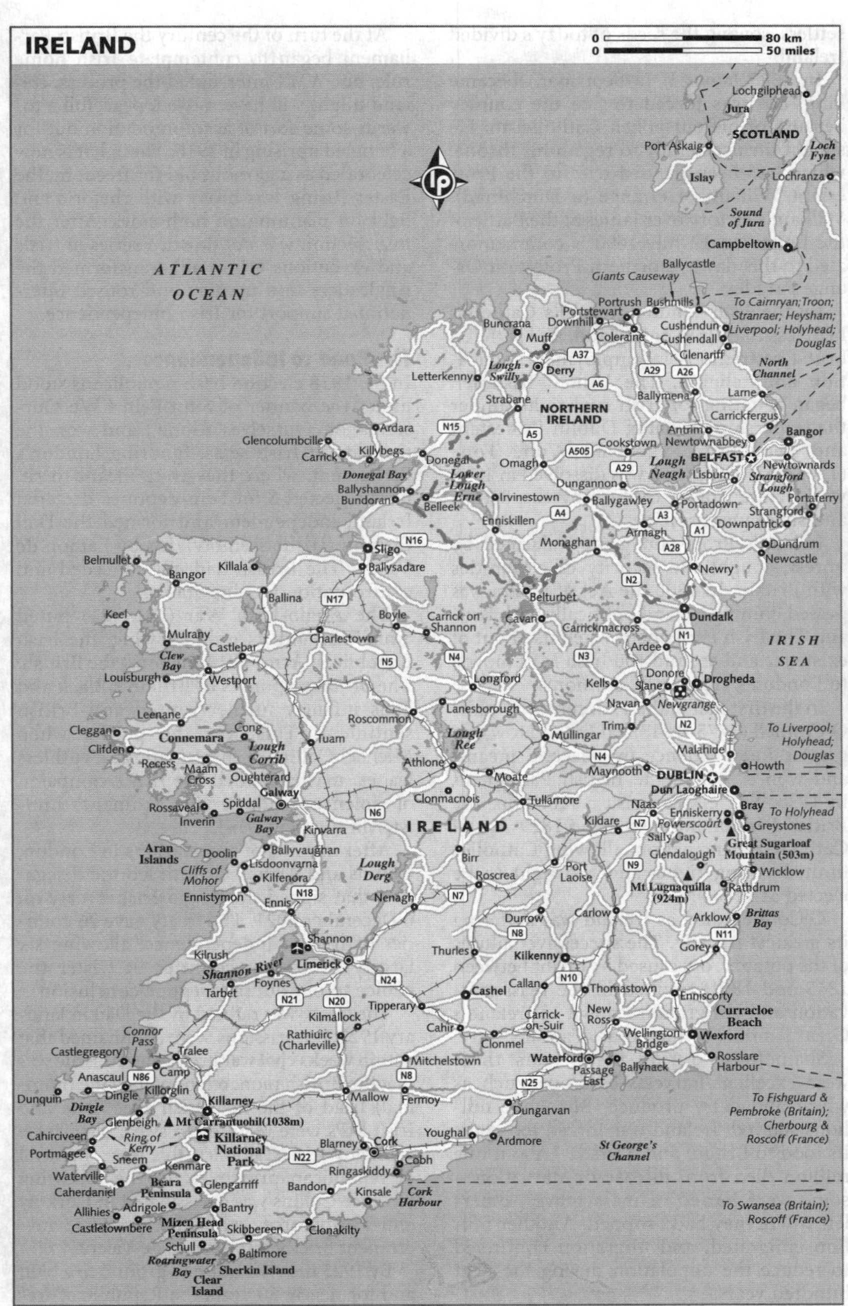
IRELAND
0 80 km
0 50 miles
ATLANTIC OCEAN
IRISH SEA
NORTHERN IRELAND
IRELAND
SCOTLAND
Jura
Islay
Lochgilphead
Port Askaig
Loch Fyne
Lochranza
Sound of Jura
Campbeltown
Ballycastle
Giants Causeway
Portrush
Bushmills
Portstewart
Downhill
Coleraine
Buncrana
Muff
Cushendun
Cushendall
Glenariff
To Cairnryan; Troon; Stranraer; Heysham; Liverpool; Holyhead; Douglas
North Channel
Lough Swilly
Derry
Letterkenny
Strabane
Ballymena
Larne
Carrickfergus
Antrim
Newtownabbey
Bangor
BELFAST
Newtownards
Lisburn
Strangford Lough
Portaferry
Strangford
Downpatrick
Dundrum
Newcastle
Newry
Portadown
Armagh
Lough Neagh
Cookstown
Omagh
Dungannon
Ballygawley
Monaghan
Enniskillen
Irvinestown
Lower Lough Erne
Belleek
Ballyshannon
Bundoran
Donegal
Donegal Bay
Killybegs
Carrick
Glencolumbcille
Ardara
Sligo
Ballysadare
Belmullet
Bangor
Killala
Ballina
Keel
Mulranny
Clew Bay
Castlebar
Westport
Louisburgh
Charlestown
Boyle
Carrick on Shannon
Belturbet
Cavan
Carrickmacross
Dundalk
Ardee
Donore
Slane
Drogheda
Newgrange
Kells
Navan
Trim
Longford
Lanesborough
Roscommon
Lough Ree
Mullingar
Athlone
Moate
Maynooth
Malahide
Howth
DUBLIN
Dun Laoghaire
To Liverpool; Holyhead; Douglas
Leenane
Cleggan
Clifden
Connemara
Cong
Lough Corrib
Recess
Maam Cross
Oughterard
Galway
Tuam
Rossaveal
Inverin
Spiddal
Galway Bay
Clonmacnois
Tullamore
Naas
Kildare
Enniskerry
Powerscourt
Bray
To Holyhead
Greystones
Great Sugarloaf Mountain (503m)
Sally Gap
Glendalough
Wicklow
Rathdrum
Mt Lugnaquilla (924m)
Arklow
Brittas Bay
Gorey
Aran Islands
Doolin
Cliffs of Mohor
Lisdoonvarna
Kilfenora
Ballyvaughan
Kinvarra
Lough Derg
Birr
Roscrea
Port Laoise
Ennistymon
Ennis
Nenagh
Durrow
Carlow
Shannon
Kilrush
Shannon River
Limerick
Foynes
Tarbet
Thurles
Kilkenny
Callan
Thomastown
Enniscorty
Cashel
Tipperary
Kilmallock
Rathluirc (Charleville)
Cahir
Clonmel
Carrick-on-Suir
New Ross
Curracloe Beach
Wellington Bridge
Wexford
Rosslare Harbour
Waterford
Passage East
Ballyhack
Connor Pass
Castlegregory
Tralee
Camp
Anascaul
Dingle
Dunquin
Killorglin
Dingle Bay
Killarney
Glenbeigh
Mt Carrantuohil (1038m)
Cahirciveen
Ring of Kerry
Killarney National Park
Portmagee
Sneem
Kenmare
Waterville
Caherdaniel
Beara Peninsula
Glengarriff
Allihies
Adrigole
Bantry
Castletownbere
Mizen Head Peninsula
Skibbereen
Schull
Baltimore
Roaringwater Bay
Sherkin Island
Clear Island
Mitchelstown
Mallow
Fermoy
Blarney
Cork
Cobh
Ringaskiddy
Bandon
Kinsale
Cork Harbour
Clonakilty
Youghal
Ardmore
Dungarvan
St George's Channel
To Fishguard & Pembroke (Britain); Cherbourg & Roscoff (France)
To Swansea (Britain); Roscoff (France)
A37
A29
A26
A6
A5
A505
A29
A4
A3
A1
A28
N15
N16
N17
N2
N1
N3
N4
N5
N2
N4
N6
N7
N9
N18
N7
N8
N11
N10
N24
N21
N20
N8
N25
N86
N22

settlers, sowing the seeds of today's divided Ireland.

In 1685 James II (a Scotsman) became king, but was forced to flee the country because of his outspoken Catholicism. He sought unsuccessfully to regain his throne, which had been handed over to the Protestant William of Orange (a Dutchman). William's victory over James at the Battle of the Boyne on 12 July 1690 is commemorated to this day by northern Protestant Orange Parades.

By the 18th century Ireland's Catholics held less than 15% of the land, and suffered brutal restrictions in employment, education and religion. The United Irishmen began agitating for Irish civil rights under the leadership of young Dublin Protestant and Republican, Theobald Wolfe Tone (1763–98). The group was dissolved in 1798 with Wolfe Tone's capture by the British and subsequent suicide.

Ireland's Protestant gentry, alarmed by unrest, sought the security of closer ties with Britain. In 1800 the Act of Union was passed, joining Ireland politically with Britain. The Irish Parliament voted itself out of existence and around 100 Irish MPs moved to London's House of Commons.

In the first half of the 19th century Daniel O'Connell (1775–1847) led Ireland towards greater independence by peaceful means, and won a seat in the British Parliament in 1828. Rather than risk a rebellion, the British Parliament passed the 1829 Act of Catholic Emancipation, allowing Catholics limited voting rights and the right to be elected as MPs.

O'Connell died as Ireland was suffering its greatest tragedy. The successive failures of the potato crop, caused by blight between 1845 and 1851, resulted in the mass starvation and emigration known as Ireland's Great Famine, or the Potato Famine.

Shamefully, during these years there were excellent harvests of crops, such as wheat and dairy produce. But while millions starved, Ireland was forced to export its food to Britain and overseas. About one million died from disease or starvation – some were buried in mass graves, others left where they had dropped. Another million emigrated, and migration continued to reduce the population during the next hundred years.

At the turn of the century the British Parliament began to contemplate Irish home rule, but WWI interrupted the process. Ireland might still have moved, peacefully, towards some sort of accommodation but for a bungled uprising in 1916. Though it is now celebrated as a glorious bid for freedom, the Easter Rising was heavy with rhetoric and light on planning on both sides. After the insurrection was put down, a series of trials and executions (15 in all) transformed the ringleaders into martyrs and roused international support for Irish independence.

The Road to Independence

In the 1918 election Irish republicans stood under the banner of Sinn Féin ('We Ourselves' or 'Ourselves Alone') and won the majority of Irish seats. Ignoring London's Parliament, where they were meant to sit, newly elected Sinn Féin deputies declared Ireland independent and formed the Dáil Éireann (Irish assembly), led by Eamon de Valera. The British had not conceded and confrontation was inevitable.

The Anglo-Irish War (1919–21) pitted Sinn Féin and its military wing, the Irish Republican Army (IRA), against the British. The brutal responses of Britain's Black and Tans infantry further roused anti-British sentiment. This was the period when Michael Collins, a charismatic and ruthless leader, masterminded the IRA's campaign of violence (while serving as finance minister in the new Dáil).

After months of negotiations in London, Collins and Arthur Griffith led the delegation that signed the Anglo-Irish Treaty on 6 December 1921. The treaty gave 26 counties of Ireland independence, allowing six largely Protestant counties in Ulster the choice to opt out (a foregone conclusion).

The treaty was ratified by the Dáil in January 1922, but passions were so inflamed that within weeks civil war broke out. At issue was that the British monarch remained the (nominal) head of the new Irish Free State and Irish MPs were required to swear allegiance. To many Irish Catholics, this was a betrayal of republican principles. In the following violence Collins was assassinated in Cork by anti-Treaty forces, while the Free State government briefly imprisoned de Valera.

By 1923 the civil war had ground to a halt, and for nearly 50 years the Republic of Ireland was relatively peaceful. After boycotting the Dáil for a number of years, de Valera founded Fianna Fáil (Warriors of Ireland), which won a majority in the 1932 election. De Valera introduced a new constitution in 1937 that abolished the oath of British allegiance and claimed sovereignty over the six counties of Ulster. In 1948 the Irish government declared the country a republic and, in 1949, left the British Commonwealth.

The Troubles

According to the Anglo-Irish Treaty, six counties in the North were to be governed by a Northern Irish Parliament sitting at Stormont, near Belfast, from 1920 until 1972.

The Protestant majority made its rule absolute by systematically excluding Catholics from power. This led to the formation of a nonsectarian civil rights movement in 1967 to campaign for fairer representation for Northern Irish Catholics. In January 1969 civil rights marchers walked from Belfast to Derry to demand a fairer division of jobs and housing. Just outside Derry, a Protestant mob attacked the mostly Catholic marchers. Further marches, protests and violence followed. Far from keeping the two sides apart, Northern Ireland's mainly Protestant police force, the Royal Ulster Constabulary (RUC), became part of the problem.

Finally, in August 1969 British troops were sent into Derry and (two days later) Belfast to maintain law and order. Though Catholics initially welcomed the army, it was soon seen as a tool of the Protestant majority. The peaceful civil rights movement lost ground and the IRA, which had been hibernating, found new, willing recruits for an armed independence struggle.

Thus the so-called Troubles rolled back and forth throughout the 1970s and into the 1980s. Passions reached fever pitch in 1972 when 13 unarmed Catholics were shot dead by British troops in Derry on 'Bloody Sunday' (30 January). Then in 1981 IRA prisoners in Northern Ireland went on a hunger strike to demand the right to be recognised as political prisoners (rather than as terrorists). Ten of them fasted to death, the best known being an elected MP, Bobby Sands.

The waters were further muddied by the IRA splitting into 'official' and 'provisional' wings, from which sprang even more violent republican organisations. Protestant paramilitary organisations, such as the Ulster Volunteer Force (UVF), sprang up in opposition to the IRA and its splinter groups, and violence was met with violence.

Giving Peace a Chance

The 1985 Anglo-Irish Agreement gave the Dublin government an official consultative role in Northern Irish affairs for the first time. The Downing St Declaration of December 1993, signed by Britain and the Republic, moved matters forward, with Britain declaring it had no 'selfish, economic or military interest' in preserving the division of Ireland.

In August 1994 a 'permanent cessation of violence' by the IRA, announced by Sinn Féin's leader Gerry Adams, offered the prospect of peace in Ulster. When Protestant paramilitary forces responded with their own cease-fire in October 1994, most British troops were withdrawn to barracks and roadblocks were removed.

In 1995 the British and Irish governments published two 'framework documents' to lay the groundwork for all-party peace talks. The subsequent negotiations stalled when Britain's Conservative prime minister John Major refused to allow all-party talks to start until the IRA decommissioned its weapons. An IRA bomb in the Docklands area of London shattered the negotiations in February 1996. In June, with the IRA's refusal to restore its cease-fire, 'all-party' talks on Ulster's future convened without Sinn Féin.

The peace process regained momentum with the landslide victory in May 1997 of Tony Blair's Labour Party, its massive majority enabling it to act with a freer hand than the previous Conservative government. In June 1997 Britain's new Northern Ireland secretary, Dr Mo Mowlam, promised to admit Sinn Féin to all-party talks following any new cease-fire, which the IRA declared on 20 July 1997.

These talks produced the Good Friday Agreement on 10 April 1998. This agreement allows the people of Northern Ireland to decide their political future by majority vote and commits its signatories to 'democratic and peaceful means of resolving differences on political issues'. It established a new Northern Irish Parliament and high-level political links between the Republic and Northern Ireland. In simultaneous referendums in May 1998 the agreement was approved by 71% of voters in the North and 94% in the South. However, despite these moves towards peace, later that year a bomb planted by the 'Real IRA' killed 28 people in Omagh.

The IRA then volunteered to 'decommission' some of its weapons stockpiles, but devolution was again suspended in October 2002 following allegations of spying by the IRA. November 2003 elections did not bode well for further negotiations, despite the IRA making peaceful steps by destroying even more weapons.

Then in 2004 a permanent peace agreement was just hours away when the negotiations fell apart due to lack of trust. Many people began to question the IRA's devotion to peace when they were fingered for both a £26.5 million bank robbery in December 2004 and a January 2005 killing.

Suddenly on 28 July 2005 the IRA had big news; they announced the official end to the armed campaign. Two months later the independent arms decommissioning body verified that the IRA had in fact destroyed all its weapons.

Today a cautious optimism prevails and, despite lingering animosity and occasional flare-ups, most agree that the 'war' is finally over.

PEOPLE

Ireland's total population is around 5.6 million people: 3.9 million in the Republic and 1.7 million in Northern Ireland. Prior to the 1845–51 Great Famine, the population was around eight million; death and emigration reduced it to around six million, and emigration continued at high levels for the next hundred years. It wasn't until the 1960s that the population began to recover.

Thanks to the EU, Ireland has seen a modest influx of immigrants, mostly from Eastern Europe, within the past five years.

RELIGION

Religion has played a pivotal role in Irish history. About 90% of residents in the Republic are Roman Catholic, followed by 3% Protestant, 0.1% Jewish and the rest with no professed religious belief. In the North 53% are Protestant and 44% Catholic.

The Catholic Church has traditionally opposed attempts to liberalise laws governing contraception, divorce and abortion. Today condom machines can be found all over Ireland and divorce is legal, but abortion remains illegal in the Republic. Though still wielding considerable influence in the South, the Church has been weakened recently by drastically declining attendance at church services, falling numbers of people entering religious life and by paedophile sex scandals. It's now treated with a curious mixture of respect and derision by various sections of the community.

ARTS

Literature

The Irish have made an enormous impact on world literature. Important writers include Jonathan Swift, Oscar Wilde, WB Yeats, George Bernard Shaw, James Joyce, Sean O'Casey, Samuel Beckett and Roddy Doyle, whose *Paddy Clarke Ha Ha Ha* won the Booker Prize in 1993. The Ulster-born poet Seamus Heaney was awarded the Nobel Prize for Literature in 1995. Earlier Irish Nobel laureates include Shaw (1925), Yeats (1938) and Beckett (1969). Frank McCourt became a world favourite with his autobiographical *Angela's Ashes,* which won the Pulitzer Prize, and *'Tis.*

Music

Traditional Irish music – played on instruments such as the *bodhrán* (a flat, goatskin drum), *uilleann* (or 'elbow') pipes, flute and fiddle – is an aspect of Irish culture impossible to miss. Of Irish groups, perhaps the best known are the Chieftains, the Dubliners and the Pogues. Popular Irish singers/musicians who have made it on the international stage include Van Morrison, Enya, Sinéad O'Connor, Bob Geldof, U2, the Cranberries, The Corrs and Westlife.

Architecture

Ireland is packed with archaeological sites that are reminders of its long and dramatic history. You may encounter the following terms:

Cashel A stone *ring fort* or *rath.*

Dolmen A portal tomb or Stone Age grave consisting of stone 'pillars' supporting a stone roof or capstone.

Passage tomb A megalithic mound-tomb with a narrow stone passage that leads to a burial chamber.

Ring fort or **rath** A circular fort, originally constructed of earth and timber, but later made of stone.

THE GAELTACHT

Killarney was lovely, but it's time to move on, so you pack up the car and head out for Dingle, a town you've heard only great things about. As you drive along, you're thinking about how *Lonely Planet* said that in Dingle you can swim with a dolphin and about how cool that would be, when you look up to check the road sign and wonder, 'What the f*ck does that say?'

Well my friend that sign says that you've officially entered the Gaeltacht, one of the Irish (or Gaelic as it is sometimes called) speaking regions in Ireland. But since the sign telling you this is in Irish, it could really say 'Swimming with dolphins prohibited', and you wouldn't know the difference.

Other than the Dingle Peninsula, the Aran Islands, the Connemara and Donegal are other areas where you may find the domination of the language in street signs less than romantic. A Celtic language closely related to Scottish Gaelic (and less so to Welsh), Irish is an attractive but difficult tongue with a unique orthographic system. For example, 'mh' is pronounced like 'v', 'bhf' is a 'w' and 'dh' is like 'g'. In pockets of the Republic it remains, at least in theory, the first language of communication and commerce among the majority of the population.

Technically English and Gaelic are both the official languages of the Republic (even though Mandarin Chinese is actually the second most-spoken language), so children are required to study Gaelic for up to 12 years in school. Truthfully, though, most Irish citizens who don't live in the Gaeltacht can only speak it on a remedial level, and of the 90,000 people who do live there, only 55.6% of adults speak Irish on a daily basis.

So if you've got your heart set on swimming with Fungie the dolphin, just stop and ask for directions.

Round tower A tall tower or belfry built as a lookout and place of refuge from the Vikings.

Theatre

Ireland has a rich theatrical history. Dublin's first theatre was founded in Werburgh St in 1637. The literary revival of the late 19th century resulted in the establishment of Dublin's Abbey Theatre, now Ireland's national theatre, which presents works by former greats – WB Yeats, George Bernard Shaw and Sean O'Casey – and promotes modern Irish dramatists. One of the most outstanding playwrights of the last two decades is Frank McGuinness (born 1956), whose plays explore the consequences of 1972's Bloody Sunday on the people of Derry. Other playwrights to watch out for are Martin McDonagh, Brian Friel (of *Dancing at Lughnasa* fame), Conor McPherson, Donal O'Kelly and Enda Walsh.

ENVIRONMENT

Ireland is divided into 32 counties: 26 in the Republic and six in Northern Ireland. The island measures 84,421 sq km (about 83% is the Republic) and stretches 486km north to south and 275km east to west. The jagged coastline extends for 5631km. The midlands of Ireland are flat, rich farmland with huge swathes of peat (which is rapidly being depleted for fuel).

Carrantuohill (1038m) on the Iveragh Peninsula, County Kerry, is the highest mountain on the island. The Shannon River, the longest in Ireland, flows for 259km before emptying into the Atlantic west of Limerick.

Ireland's rivers and lakes are well stocked with fish, and the island is home to some three-dozen mammal species. The Office of Public Works (OPW) maintains five national parks and 76 nature reserves in the Republic; the Department of the Environment owns or leases more than 40 nature reserves in Northern Ireland.

FOOD & DRINK

In Irish B&B accommodation, breakfasts almost inevitably include 'a fry', a plate consisting of fried eggs, bacon, sausages, black pudding (a blood sausage) and tomatoes. Traditional meals (like Irish stew, often found in pubs) can be cheap and hearty. Potatoes are everywhere, colcannon and champ being two of the tastiest mashes. Seafood is often excellent, especially in the west, and there are some good vegetarian restaurants in cities and larger towns. The *panini,* an Italian type of sandwich, is so popular here you would think it was a traditional dish.

In Ireland a drink means a beer, either lager or stout. Stout is usually Guinness, although in Cork it can mean a Murphy's or a Beamish. If you haven't developed a taste for stout, a wide variety of lagers are available, including Harp and Smithwicks (don't pronounce the 'w'!). Asking for a Guinness will get you a pint (570mL); if you want a half-pint, ask for a 'glass' or a 'half'.

If someone suggests visiting a pub for its good *craic,* it means a good time with convivial company. In the Republic, cigarettes are not part of the mix: smoking in all public places was banned in March 2004. The same ban will go into effect in the North soon after this book's publication.

DUBLIN

☎ 01 / pop 1.1 million

Sitting in a tapas restaurant on Great Georges St, nursing a Guinness or a hangover (or both), you think about what your favourite experience has been in Dublin so far. Was it drinking in Temple Bar with people from dozens of other countries or was it buying fresh veggies at the Asian food market? Was it admiring the Georgian houses along St Stephen's Green or was it wandering the grounds of Trinity College? You never come to an answer, but you do realise that, just as the waters on the banks of the Liffey River seem to rise every day, so does your affection for this city.

The roar of prosperity and the advent of the EU have made it so that all roads lead to Dublin. Visitors swarm in droves like moths to a light bulb – for the historic museums, top-class attractions and Georgian architecture, while immigrants from Eastern Europe, Asia and Africa set up new lives for their families, thus adding even more depth and complexity to an already rich cultural tapestry. Add a hard partying nightlife to this mixture and what you get is a city that's constantly changing, and having a splendid time doing it.

ORIENTATION

Dublin is neatly divided by the Liffey River into the more affluent 'south side' and the less prosperous 'north side'.

North of the river important landmarks are O'Connell St, the shopping thoroughfare, and Gardiner St, with its B&Bs and guesthouses. Henry St, the main shopping precinct, , runs west off O'Connell. Busáras, the main bus station, and Connolly station, one of the main train stations, are near the southern end of Gardiner.

Immediately south of the river is the bustling, raucous, Temple Bar district, Dame St, Trinity College and, just below it, the lovely St Stephen's Green. Pedestrianised Grafton St and its surrounding streets and lanes are crammed with shops and are always busy. About 2km west is Heuston station, the city's other main train station.

INFORMATION

Bookshops

Easons (Map p657; ☎ 873 3811; 40 O'Connell St) One of the biggest magazine stockists in Ireland.

Hodges Figgis (Map p657; ☎ 677 4754; 56-58 Dawson St) Offers a large selection of books on things Irish.

Sinn Féin Bookshop (Map pp654-5; ☎ 872 7096; 44 West Parnell Sq) The place to get items Sinn Fein–related.

Internet Access

Dublin has more Internet cafés than you can shake a stick at; Talbot St and Crampton Quay are lined with them. These are some of the better ones.

Cyborg (Map pp654-5; ☎ 855 3163; 44 Talbot St; per hr €1; 🕑 9am-11pm)

Surf Centre One (Map pp654-5; ☎ 855 2560; 43 Lower Gardiner St; per hr €1.50)

Medical Services

Eastern Regional Health Authority (Map pp654-5; ☎ 679 0700; www.erha.ie; Dr Steevens' Hospital, 138 Thomas St) Opposite Heuston train station; can advise you on a suitable doctor from 9am to 5pm Monday to Friday.

Doctors on Call (☎ 453 9333; 🕑 24hr) Request a doctor to come to your accommodation (€60 to €75).

O'Connell's Pharmacy (Map p657; ☎ 873 0427; 55-56 O'Connell St; 🕑 7.30am-10pm Mon-Fri, 8am-10pm Sat, 10am-10pm Sun)

Well Woman Clinic (Map p657; ☎ 872 8051, 688 3714; www.wellwomancentre.ie; 35 Lower Liffey St; 🕑 Mon, Thu & Fri 9.30am-7.30pm, Tue & Wed 8am-7.30pm, Sat 10am-4pm, Sun 1-4pm) Handles women's health issues and can supply contraception.

Money

The Dublin airport and Dublin Tourism Centre have currency-exchange counters, and numerous banks around the city centre have exchange facilities. The central bank offers the best exchange rates, while the airport and ferry terminal bureaus offer the worst. ATMs are everywhere.

Post

Dublin's famous **General Post Office** (GPO; Map p657; ☎ 705 7000; O'Connell St; 🕑 8am-8pm Mon-Sat) is north of the river. South of the river are post offices on Anne St South (Map pp654–5) and St Andrew's St (Map p657).

Tourist Information

All Dublin tourist offices provide walk-in services only.

Dublin Tourism City Centre (Map pp654-5; 14 O'Connell St; 🕑 9am-5pm Mon-Sat); Dun Laoghaire (Dun Laoghaire ferryport; 🕑 10am-1pm & 2-6pm)

Dublin Tourism Centre (Map p657; ☎ 605 7700; www.visitdublin.com; St Andrew's Church, 2 Suffolk St; 🕑 9am-7pm Mon-Sat, 10.30am-3pm Sun Jul & Aug, 9am-5.30pm Mon-Sat, 10.30am-3pm Sun Sep-Jun) A sort of tourist information complex. Services include accommodation bookings, car hire, maps, and tickets for tours, concerts and more. Ask about the Dublin Pass (www.dublinpass.ie), which allows entrance into over 30 of Dublin's attractions, as well as tours and special offers.

Fáilte Ireland (☎ 1850 230 330; www.ireland.ie; Baggot St; 🕑 9am-5pm Mon-Fri) Less conveniently situated about 500m southeast of the city centre, but much less crowded than the other centres.

Northern Ireland Tourist Board (NITB; Map p657; ☎ 679 1977; www.discovernorthernireland.com; 16 Nassau St; 🕑 9.15am-5.30pm Mon-Fri, 10am-5pm Sat) Offers information and free booking services.

Temple Bar Information Centre (Map p657; ☎ 677 2255; www.templebar.ie; 12 East Essex St; 🕑 9am-7pm Mon-Fri, 10am-6pm Sat, noon-6pm Sun Jun-Sep, 9am-5.30pm Mon-Fri, 10am-6pm Sat, noon-4pm Sun Oct-May) Provides free maps, guides and information on sights within the Temple Bar district.

SIGHTS

Trinity College & Book of Kells

Ireland's premier university was founded by Elizabeth I in 1592. Its full name is the University of Dublin, but **Trinity College** (Map p657; College Green) is the institution's sole college. Until 1793 the students were all Protestants, but today most of them are Catholic. Women were admitted in 1903.

Walking tours (per person €9) take place every 40 minutes from 10.45am to 3.40pm Monday to Saturday and 10.15am to 3pm Sunday from mid-May to September. Departures are from College St, inside the main gate on College Green. The tour is a good deal since it includes the fee to see the *Book of Kells*, an elaborately illuminated manuscript dating from around AD 800, and one of Dublin's prime attractions. It's displayed in the East Pavilion of the **Colonnades** (Map p657; adult/concession €8/7; 🕑 9.30am-5pm Mon-Sat year-round, 9.30am-4.30pm Sun Jun-Sep, noon-4.30pm Sun Oct-May), together with the 9th-century *Book of Armagh*, the even older *Book of Durrow* (AD 675) and the harp of Brian Ború, who led the Irish against the Vikings in the Battle of Clontarf.

Trinity's other big attraction is the **Dublin Experience** (Map p657; ☎ 608 1688; admission €5, adult/concession incl Book of Kells €11/8.50; 🕑 10am-5pm mid-May–Sep), a 45-minute audiovisual introduction to the city.

Museums

Among the highlights of the impressive **National Museum** (Map pp654-5; ☎ 667 7444; www.museum.ie; Kildare St; admission by donation; 🕑 10am-5pm Tue-Sat, 2-5pm Sun) are the superb Bronze Age, Iron Age and medieval gold objects in the treasury, the skeleton of a once-tall, mighty Viking and the incredibly well-preserved 'Bog Body'. Other exhibits focus on the Viking period, the 1916 Easter Rising and the struggle for Irish independence. The nearby **Natural History Museum** (Map pp654-5; ☎ 677 7444; www.museum.ie; Merrion St; admission free; 🕑 10am-5pm Tue-Sat, 2-5pm Sun), aka the 'dead

DUBLIN IN...

Two Days

Start by heading to **Trinity College** (left) where the tour allows you entrance to the Book of Kells. Afterwards window shop your way down Grafton St while en route to **Havana** (p660) for lunch. Walk off those tapas while marvelling at the Georgian architecture surrounding **St Stephen's Green** (p658) before you party your arse off in **Temple Bar** (p660). Then go sleep it off at the gorgeous **Grafton Guesthouse** (p659). Begin your next day with a hearty Irish breakfast before venturing off to view the fine art at the **National Gallery** (p656). Top off your visit by having the best beer of your life at the **Guinness Brewery** (p658).

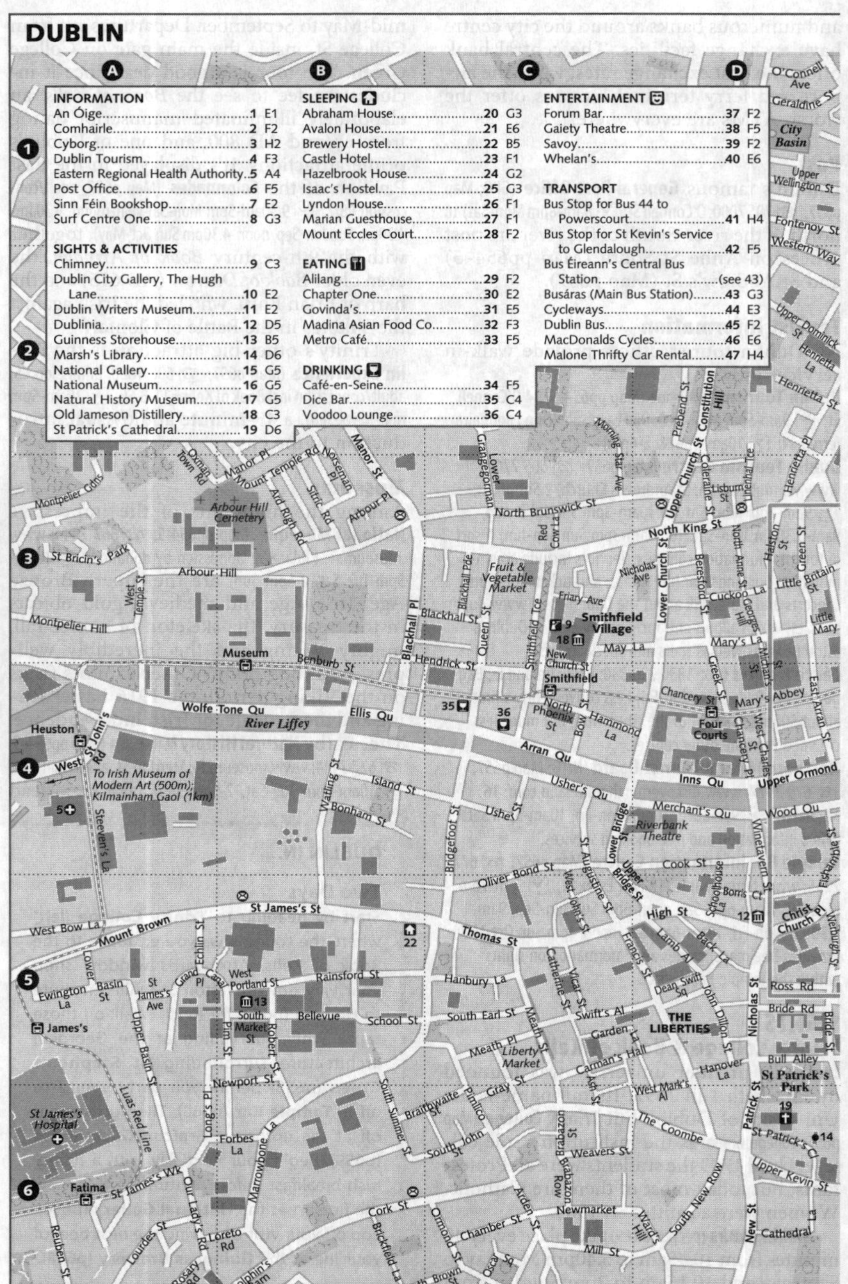

DUBLIN
A
B
C
D
1
2
3
4
5
6
INFORMATION
An Óige....1 E1
Comhairle....2 F2
Cyborg....3 H2
Dublin Tourism....4 F3
Eastern Regional Health Authority..5 A4
Post Office....6 F5
Sinn Féin Bookshop....7 E2
Surf Centre One....8 G3
SIGHTS & ACTIVITIES
Chimney....9 C3
Dublin City Gallery, The Hugh Lane....10 E2
Dublin Writers Museum....11 E2
Dublinia....12 D5
Guinness Storehouse....13 B5
Marsh's Library....14 D6
National Gallery....15 G5
National Museum....16 G5
Natural History Museum....17 G5
Old Jameson Distillery....18 C3
St Patrick's Cathedral....19 D6
SLEEPING
Abraham House....20 G3
Avalon House....21 E6
Brewery Hostel....22 B5
Castle Hotel....23 F1
Hazelbrook House....24 G2
Isaac's Hostel....25 G3
Lyndon House....26 F1
Marian Guesthouse....27 F1
Mount Eccles Court....28 F2
EATING
Alilang....29 F2
Chapter One....30 E2
Govinda's....31 E5
Madina Asian Food Co....32 F3
Metro Café....33 F5
DRINKING
Café-en-Seine....34 F5
Dice Bar....35 C4
Voodoo Lounge....36 C4
ENTERTAINMENT
Forum Bar....37 F2
Gaiety Theatre....38 F5
Savoy....39 F2
Whelan's....40 E6
TRANSPORT
Bus Stop for Bus 44 to Powerscourt....41 H4
Bus Stop for St Kevin's Service to Glendalough....42 F5
Bus Éireann's Central Bus Station....(see 43)
Busáras (Main Bus Station)....43 G3
Cycleways....44 E3
Dublin Bus....45 F2
MacDonalds Cycles....46 E6
Malone Thrifty Car Rental....47 H4
O'Connell Ave
Geraldine St
City Basin
Upper Wellington St
Fontenoy St
Western Way
Upper Dominick St
Henrietta La
Henrietta St
Henrietta Pl
Arbour Hill Cemetery
Arbour Hill
Montpelier Gdns
St Bricin's Park
Montpelier Hill
Manor St
North Brunswick St
North King St
Upper Church St
Constitution Hill
Fruit & Vegetable Market
Smithfield Village
Smithfield
Museum
Benburb St
Wolfe Tone Qu
River Liffey
Ellis Qu
Arran Qu
Inns Qu
Upper Ormond
Four Courts
Heuston
To Irish Museum of Modern Art (500m); Kilmainham Gaol (1km)
Usher's Qu
Merchant's Qu
Wood Qu
Riverbank Theatre
Oliver Bond St
St James's St
Thomas St
High St
Mount Brown
Rainsford St
Bellevue
School St
THE LIBERTIES
Liberty Market
St Patrick's Park
James's
St James's Hospital
Luas Red Line
Fatima
The Coombe
Newmarket
Cork St
Upper Kevin St
Cathedral La
Bride Rd
Bull Alley
Christ Church Pl

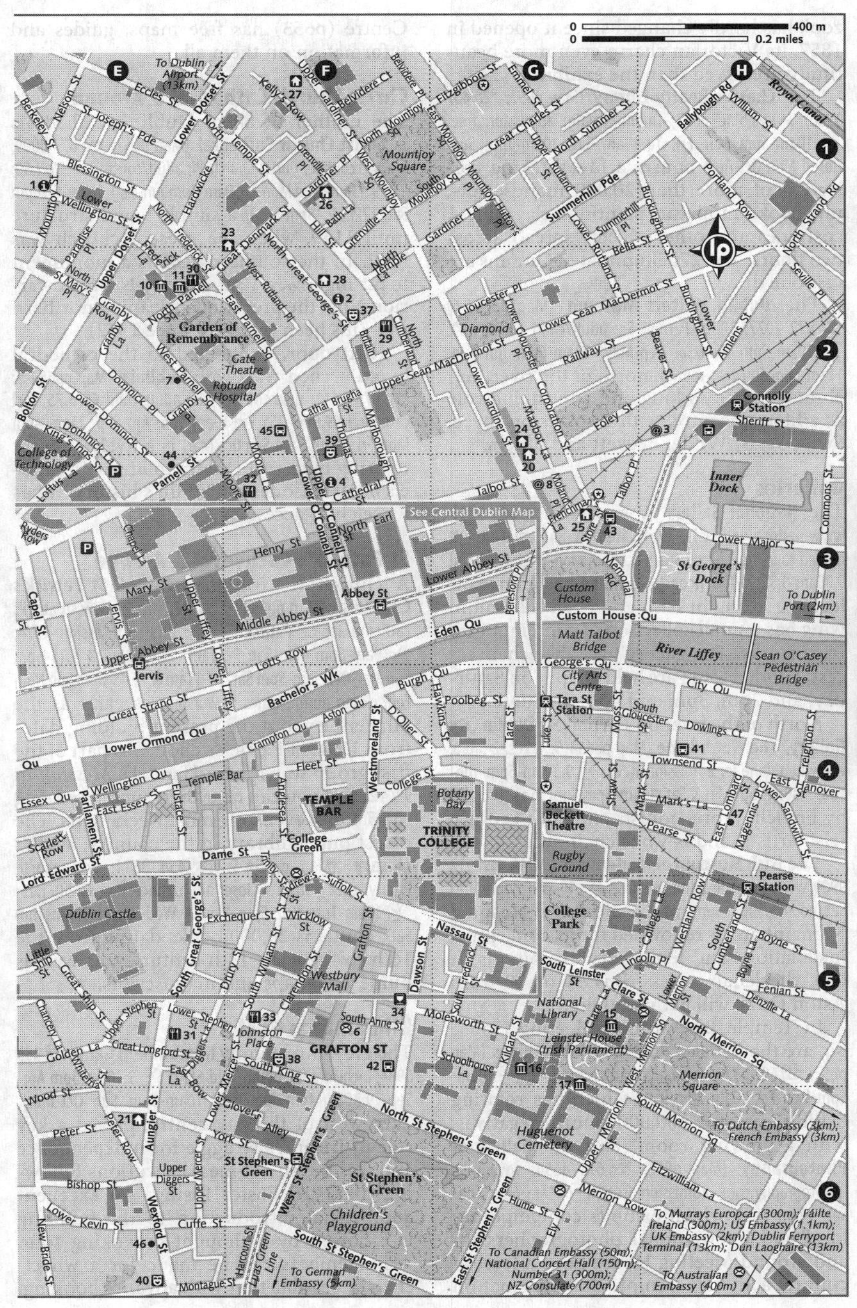
0 400 m
0 0.2 miles
To Dublin Airport (13km)
Mountjoy Square
Garden of Remembrance
Gate Theatre
Rotunda Hospital
College of Technology
Diamond
Connolly Station
Inner Dock
St George's Dock
Custom House
To Dublin Port (2km)
Matt Talbot Bridge
River Liffey
Sean O'Casey Pedestrian Bridge
City Arts Centre
Tara St Station
See Central Dublin Map
Abbey St
Jervis
TEMPLE BAR
TRINITY COLLEGE
Botany Bay
College Green
Samuel Beckett Theatre
Rugby Ground
College Park
Pearse Station
Dublin Castle
Westbury Mall
National Library
Leinster House (Irish Parliament)
Merrion Square
Johnston Place
GRAFTON ST
Huguenot Cemetery
St Stephen's Green
Children's Playground
Upper Diggers St
To Dutch Embassy (3km); French Embassy (3km)
To Murrays Europcar (300m); Fáilte Ireland (300m); US Embassy (1.1km); UK Embassy (2km); Dublin Ferryport Terminal (13km); Dun Laoghaire (13km)
To Canadian Embassy (50m); National Concert Hall (150m); Number 31 (300m); NZ Consulate (700m)
To Australian Embassy (400m)
To German Embassy (5km)
Luas Green Line
Royal Canal
IRELAND

zoo', has hardly changed since it opened in 1857, its Victorian charm even more beautifully preserved than the exhibits.

The **Chester Beatty Library** (Map p657; ☎ 407 0750; www.cbl.ie p657; Dublin Castle; admission free; 🕑 10am-5pm Mon-Fri, 10-11am Sat, 10am-1pm Sun, closed Mon Oct-Apr) houses a breathtaking collection of more than 20,000 manuscripts, rare books, miniature paintings, clay tablets, costumes and other objects spread across two floors. The 270 illuminated Qur'ans are just one draw.

The **Dublin Writers Museum** (Map pp654-5; ☎ 872 2077; 18-19 Parnell Sq; adult/child €6.70/4.20; 🕑 10am-5pm Mon-Sat Sep-May, 10am-6pm Jun-Aug, 11am-5pm Sun year-round), north of the river, celebrates the city's long and continuing role as a literary centre, with displays on Joyce, Swift, Yeats, Wilde, Beckett and others.

Galleries

The **National Gallery** (Map pp654-5; ☎ 661 5133; www.nationalgallery.ie; West Merrion Sq; admission & guided tours free; 🕑 9.30am-5.30pm Mon-Wed, Fri & Sat, 9.30am-8.30pm Thu, noon-5.30pm Sun) has a fine collection, strong in Irish art. The Millennium wing has a small collection of contemporary Irish works. The gallery has wheelchair access. Guided tours are held at 2pm on Saturday, and 2pm, 3pm and 4pm on Sunday.

North of the river on Parnell Sq **Dublin City Gallery, The Hugh Lane** (Map pp654-5; ☎ 222 5550; www.hughlane.ie; admission free; 🕑 9.30am-6pm Tue-Thu, 9.30am-5pm Fri & Sat, 11am-5pm Sun) has works by French impressionists and 20th-century Irish artists, and is wheelchair accessible.

The **Irish Museum of Modern Art** (IMMA; ☎ 612 9900; www.imma.ie; admission free; 🕑 10am-5.30pm Tue-Sat, noon-5.30pm Sun), at the old Royal Hospital Kilmainham, is renowned for its conceptual installations and temporary exhibitions. It has wheelchair access. Bus 51 or 79 from Aston Quay will get you there.

In Temple Bar, around Meeting House Sq, are the **National Photographic Archives** (Map p657; ☎ 603 0374; www.nli.ie; admission free; 🕑 10am-5pm Mon-Fri, 10am-2pm Sat), which has rotating exhibitions and 300,000 photo negatives, with a viewing room, and the **Gallery of Photography** (Map p657; ☎ 671 4654; www.irish-photography.com; admission free; 🕑 11am-6pm Tue-Sat, 1-6pm Sun), which exhibits contemporary local and international photographers. In and around Meeting House Sq is a feast of cultural activities. Temple Bar Information Centre (p653) has free maps, guides and information on them all.

Christ Church Cathedral & Around

The mother of all of Dublin's cathedrals is **Christ Church Cathedral** (Map p657; ☎ 677 8099; www.cccdub.ie; Christ Church Pl; adult/concession €5/2.50; 🕑 9.45am-5pm Mon-Fri, 9am-5pm Jun-Aug, 10am-6.30pm Sat, 12.45-2.45pm Sun), a simple wood structure until 1169, when the present church was built. In the southern aisle is a monument to Strongbow, a 12th-century Norman warrior. Note the precariously leaning northern wall (it's been that way since 1562).

Next door, connected to the cathedral by an arched walkway, **Dublinia** (Map pp654-5; ☎ 679 4611; www.dublinia.ie; adult/child €6/3.75, incl cathedral €9.95/5.75; 🕑 10am-5pm Apr-Sep, 11am-4pm Mon-Fri, 10am-4pm Sun Oct-Mar) is a lively attempt to bring medieval Dublin to life, with models of 10 episodes in Dublin's history. It has wheelchair access.

St Patrick's Cathedral & Around

A church was on the site of **St Patrick's Cathedral** (Map pp654-5; ☎ 475 4817; www.stpatrickscathedral.ie; St Patrick's Close; adult/concession €5/4; 🕑 9am-6pm Mon-Sat, 9-11am, 12.45-3pm & 4.15-6pm Sun Mar-Oct, 9am-5pm Sat, 10-11am & 12.45-3pm Sun Nov-Feb, closed during times of worship) as early as the 5th century, but the present building dates from 1191. St Patrick's choir was part of the first group to perform Handel's *Messiah* in 1742, and you can hear their successors sing the 5.45pm evensong most weeknights. The oldest public library in the country, **Marsh's Library** (Map pp654-5; ☎ 454 3511; www.marshlibrary.ie; St Patrick's Close; adult/concession €2.50/1.25; 🕑 10am-1pm & 2-5pm Mon & Wed-Fri, 10.30am-1pm Sat), contains 25,000 books dating from the 16th to the early 18th centuries, as well as numerous maps and manuscripts.

Kilmainham Gaol

The grey, threatening **Kilmainham Gaol** (☎ 453 5984; Inchicore Rd; adult/child €5/2; 🕑 9.30am-5pm Apr-Sep, 9.30am-4pm Mon-Sat, 10am-5pm Sun Oct-Mar), 2km west of the city centre, played a key role in Ireland's struggle for independence and was the site of mass executions following the 1916 Easter Rising. An excellent audiovisual introduction to the building is followed by a thought-provoking tour. Arrangements can be made for a wheelchair-accessible tour with advance booking.

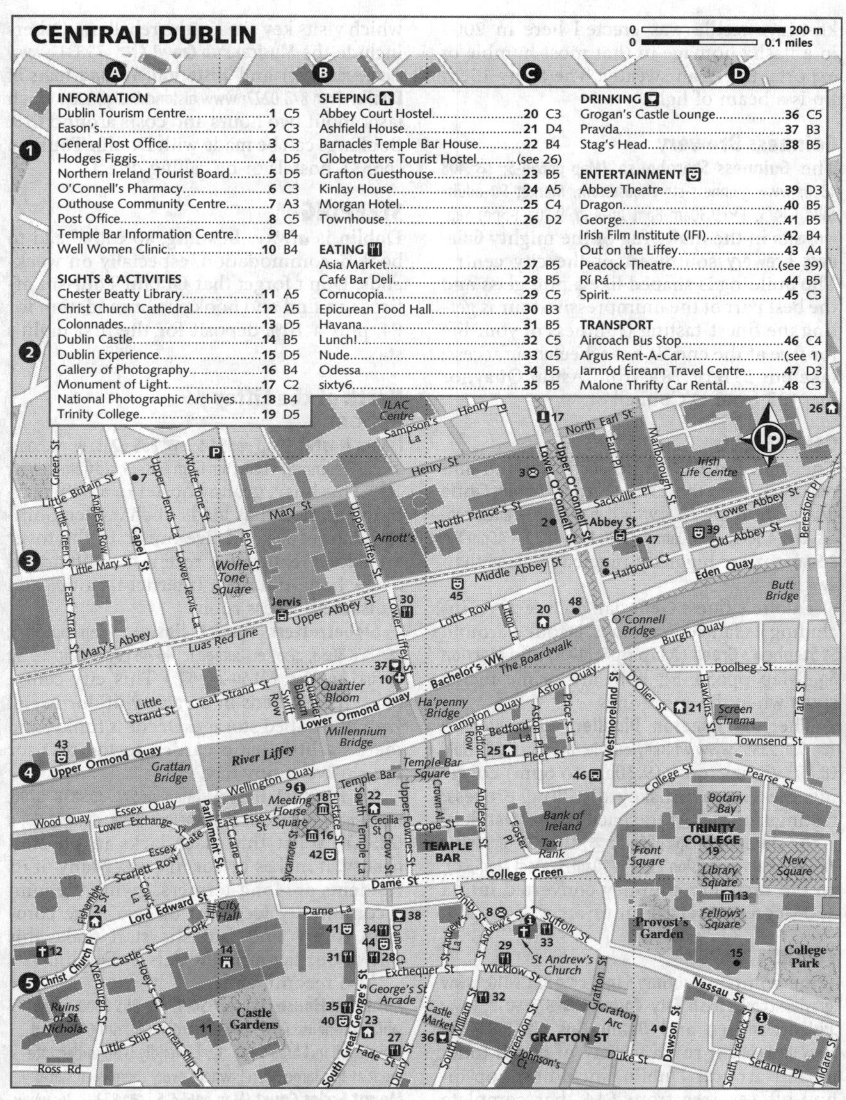

Buses 79, 78A, 51B and 51C from Aston Quay all pass by here.

O'Connell St

The 1815 **General Post Office** (GPO; Map p657; ☎ 705 7000; O'Connell St; 🕒 8am-8pm Mon-Sat) is an important landmark because, during the 1916 Easter Rising, the Irish Volunteers used it as a base for attacks against the British army. After a fierce battle the GPO was almost totally destroyed. Upon surrendering, the leaders of the Irish rebellion and 13 others were taken to Kilmainham Gaol and executed.

The nearby **Monument of Light** (Map p657; O'Connell St), better known as 'The Spire', soars 120m over O'Connell St. The gigantic knitting needle was erected here in 2003 in a flashy homage to that most humble of exports, the Aran sweater. The teeny 15cm tip is a beam of light.

Guinness Brewery

The **Guinness Storehouse** (Map pp654-5; ☎ 408 4800; www.guinness-storehouse.com; Market St; adult/child €14/5; ⏲ 9.30am-8pm Jul-Aug, 9.30am-5pm Sep-Jun) sits in the malty fug of the mighty **Guinness brewery** southwest of the city centre. The building is shaped like a pint glass and the best part of the unimpressive tour is getting the finest-tasting Guinness of your life for free at the end. It has wheelchair access; take bus 51B or 78A from Aston Quay, or bus 123 from O'Connell St.

Other Sights

The centre of British power in Ireland and dating back to the 13th century, **Dublin Castle** (Map p657; ☎ 677 7129; www.dublincastle.ie; adult/concession €4.50/2; ⏲ 10am-4.45pm Mon-Fri, 2-4.45pm Sat & Sun) is more higgledy-piggledy palace than castle.

Dublin's finest Georgian architecture, including its famed doorways, is found around **St Stephen's Green** (Map pp654–5) and **Merrion Sq** (Map pp654–5); both are prime picnic spots when the sun shines.

The **Old Jameson Distillery** (Map pp654-5; ☎ 807 2355; www.whiskeytours.ie; Bow St; adult/child €8.75/3.95) has tours (9.30am to 6pm) covering the entire whiskey-distilling process; tastings follow. At the back of the distillery is the **Chimney** (Map pp654-5; ☎ 817 3838; Smithfield Village; adult/concession €5; ⏲ 10am-5.30pm Mon-Sat), an old distillery chimney converted into a 360-degree observation tower.

TOURS

Tour companies **Gray Line** (☎ 872 9010; www.grayline.com), **Irish City Tours** (☎ 872 9010; www.irishcitytours.com) and **Dublin Bus** (☎ 873 4222; www.dublinbus.ie) run a variety of coach tours in and around Dublin, including hop-on hop-off services from €14 that complete 1½-hour city circuits with commentary.

It's worth considering one of the many walking tours and pub crawls of the city. Two of the best are the **Dublin Literary Pub Crawl** (☎ 670 5602; www.dublinpubcrawl.com), led by actors performing pieces from Irish literature, and the well-reviewed **1916 Rebellion Walking Tour** (☎ 086-858 3847; www.1916rising.com), which visits key sites in the rebellion. Others include the **Musical Pub Crawl** (☎ 475 3313; www.discoverdublin.ie) and **Historical Walking Tours of Dublin** (☎ 878 0227; www.historicalinsights.ie). Each lasts about two hours and costs around €10. Bookings can be made with Dublin Tourism (p653), hostels or by calling direct.

SLEEPING

Dublin is *always* bustling, so call ahead to book accommodation, especially on weekends. Don't forget that Dublin Tourism offices can find and book accommodation for €4, plus a 10% deposit for the first night's stay.

North of the Liffey

BUDGET

Isaacs Hostel (Map pp654-5; ☎ 855 6215; www.isaacs.ie; 2-5 Frenchman's Lane; dm from €18-25, s/d from €39/36; 💻) This busy, grungy hostel in a 200-year-old wine vault has loads of character. Summer barbecues and live music in the foyer are added features. A recent face-lift added a new hang-out area, Internet facilities and a disabled-access room.

Globetrotters Tourist Hostel (Map pp654-5; ☎ 878 8088; gtrotter@indigo.ie; 46-48 Lower Gardiner St; dm incl breakfast €21.50-24; 💻) This city-centre place has 94 beds in a variety of dorms, all with under-bed storage. Décor is funky, and there's a little patio garden to the rear for the elusive sunny day.

Abbey Court Hostel (Map p657; ☎ 878 0700; www.abbey-court.com; 29 Bachelor's Walk; dm €21-29, d €88; 💻) What this place lacks in physical beauty, it makes up for in *craic*. Many of its residents are long-termers, giving the joint a community feel, and its two large common rooms and fantastic staff make this one of our favourite hostels in Dublin.

Also recommended:

Abraham House (Map pp654-5; ☎ 855 0600; www.abraham-house.ie; 83 Lower Gardiner St; dm €13-34, d €38-46, all incl breakfast; 💻) Friendly is an understatement at this large hostel, where every room is en suite.

Mount Eccles Court (Map pp654-5; ☎ 873 0826; www.eccleshostel.com; 42 Nth Great George's St; dm €13.50-26, d €33.50-35.50; 💻) The snack machines are almost as big as the TV room at this pristine place on a beautiful street.

MIDRANGE & TOP END

Hazelbrook House (Map pp654-5; ☎ 836 5003; www.hazelbrookhouse.ie; 85-86 Lower Gardiner St; s/d/tr €55/90/135; 🅿) Situated in a fine grey Georgian house, the basic but comfortable Hazelbrook serves a complete Irish breakfast that could keep a person full until dinner.

Townhouse (Map pp654-5; ☎ 878 8808; www.townhouseofdublin.com; 47-48 Lower Gardiner St; s/d from €67/110) Elegant without pretension, the Townhouse has all the hallmarks of a great guesthouse. With monikers like 'The Gambler's Secret', each of the individually designed rooms is named after plays by the famous playwrights who once occupied the houses, Dion Boucicault (1829–90) and Lafcadio Hearn (1850–1904).

Castle Hotel (Map pp654-5; ☎ 874 6949; www.castle-hotel.ie; Great Denmark St; s/d €80/135; P) Established in 1809, this hotel claims to be Dublin's oldest. Many rooms are decent-sized, and retain their Georgian cornicing and proportions. The house, though rough around the edges, still feels like a 19th-century home.

Modest options in the Upper Gardiner St area (north of the city centre) include:

Marian Guesthouse (Map pp654-5; ☎ 874 4129; www.marianguesthouse.ie; 21 Upper Gardiner St; s/d from €35/60; P)

Lyndon House (Map pp654-5; ☎ 878 6950; www.lyndonhouse.net; 26 Gardiner Pl; s/d €50/100; P)

South of the Liffey

BUDGET

Avalon House (Map pp654-5; ☎ 475 0001; www.avalon-house.ie; 55 Aungier St; dm/s/d from €17/37/70; 💻) A megahostel near St Stephen's Green, with four-, 12- and 20-bed mixed dorms on two levels, offering some privacy. There's a large kitchen, several lounges and a pool room.

Barnacles Temple Bar House (Map p657; ☎ 671 6277; www.barnacles.ie; 19 Temple Lane; dm/d from €17.50/78; 💻) Plenty bright and immaculately clean, Barnacles' location in the heart of Temple Bar makes it a great place to stay if you don't mind the sound of drunken revellers vomiting outside your window.

Ashfield House (Map p657; ☎ 679 7734; www.ashfieldhouse.ie; 19-20 D'Olier St; dm/d/q from €15/80/140; 💻) A stone's throw from Temple Bar and O'Connell Bridge, this modern hostel has one 14-bed dorm; its 25 other rooms include four-bed rooms and doubles. It feels more like a small hotel than a hostel.

Also recommended:

Kinlay House (Map p657; ☎ 679 6644; www.kinlayhouse.ie; 2-12 Lord Edward St; dm/d from €20/70; 💻) Huge, mixed 24-bed dorms and smaller rooms. Not for the faint-hearted.

Brewery Hostel (Map pp654-5; ☎ 453 8600; www.irish-hostel.com; 22-23 Thomas St; dm/d from €20/78; P 💻) Small and family run, with a patio out the back.

MIDRANGE & TOP END

Grafton Guesthouse (Map p657; ☎ 679 2041; www.graftonguesthouse.com; 26-27 Sth Great George's St; s/d €75/120) An absolute find, this gorgeous guesthouse has 16 individually decorated rooms, and is perfect for a couple of nights with that special someone…wink, wink.

Number 31 (☎ 676 5011; www.number31.ie; 31 Leeson Close; s/d/tr from €80/120/220; P) The coach house and former dwelling of architect Sam Stephenson (of Central Bank fame) still feels like a 1960s home, with sunken sitting room, leather sofas, mirrored bar and floor-to-ceiling windows. A hidden oasis of calm, five-minutes' walk from St Stephen's Green. Children under 10 are not permitted.

Morgan Hotel (Map p657; ☎ 643 7000; www.themorgan.com; 10 Fleet St; s/d from €140/295; 💻) Falling somewhere between *Alice in Wonderland* and a cocaine and hooker fuelled rock and roll fantasy, the Morgan is absolutely uber-cool. The sexy colour scheme of white floors and walls with dark blue and pink lighting extends into the bar, the rooms and even the cigar patio.

EATING

Dubliners' recent increased spending power has encouraged many excellent new restaurants to take root, while the city's influx of immigrants has created a market for ethnically diverse eateries. The number of good restaurants and cafés north of the Liffey is growing. Many midrange options are concentrated around the southern side of the city centre, and Temple Bar is awash with eateries of mixed quality.

North of the Liffey

Madina Asian Food Co (Map pp654-5; ☎ 087-925 2485; 20-21 Moore St; 🕑 9.30am-8pm Mon-Sat, 11.30am-7pm Sun) Located on diverse Moore St, this great little market is perfect if you're in the mood to cook food from India, Turkey, the Philippines or beyond. It even has a *halal* butcher.

Epicurean Food Hall (Map p657; Lower Liffey St; mains €4-15; 🕑 9.30am-5.30pm Mon-Sat) You'll be spoilt for choice in this refurbished arcade that has almost every imaginable type of food stall. The quality varies, but good choices include Itsabagel, Kaffe Moka and Istanbul House.

Alilang (Map pp654-5; ☎ 874 6766; 102 Parnell St; mains €6-15; ⌚ noon-2.30pm Mon-Fri, 5.30-11.30pm Mon-Thu, 5.30pm-midnight Sat & Sun) With Parnell St quickly becoming a Chinatown of sorts, Alilang's delicious mix of Chinese, Japanese and Korean cuisine gives it a leg up on the competition. Tasty dishes, like *padun* (seafood pancake), cod and tofu hotpot, or barbecued meats brought to your table with gas burner, skillet and spicy marinade, make the food a talking piece.

Chapter One (Map pp654-5; ☎ 873 2266; 18-19 Nth Parnell Sq; mains €30-34; ⌚ 12.30-2.30pm Tue-Fri, 6-11pm Tue-Sat) Savour classic French cuisine, like foie gras, duck confit or rabbit cassoulet, to the tinkle of the grand piano in the vaulted basement of the Dublin Writers Museum. This is one of the city's top 10 restaurants. Get there before 7pm for the three-course Pre-Theatre Special (€32.50).

South of the Liffey

BUDGET

Asia Market (Map p657; ☎ 677 9764; 18 Drury St; ⌚ 10am-7pm) Self-caterers should wander the aisles here and try to figure out what all the products are. You'll find heaps of fresh produce and stir-fry sauces, in addition to the usual Asian grocery stand-bys.

Metro Café (Map pp654-5; ☎ 679 4515; 43 Sth William St; mains €4-8; ⌚ 8am-8pm Mon, Tue, Fri & Sat, 8am-9pm Wed, 8am-10pm Thu, 10.15am-7pm Sun) Funky music and cartoonish art make this bright café seem like it snuck out of Paris. The fresh food and daily quote board are enough to warrant regular visits, as is the friendly staff.

Lunch! (Map p657; ☎ 677 1546; 63 Sth William St; mains €5.80-6.15; ⌚ 8am-7pm Mon-Wed, 8am-9pm Thu-Sat, 9am-9pm Sun) If you can handle the sea-green colour scheme, this 'calzone café' has a tasty menu, including a create-your-own sandwich option. Note the neat little fish tank above the door.

Nude (Map p657; ☎ 677 4804; 21 Suffolk St; snacks €5-8; ⌚ 7.30am-9pm Mon-Wed & Fri, 7.30am-10pm Thu, 8am-9pm Sat, 10am-8pm Sun) This ultracool place (owned by Bono's brother) just off Grafton St is very popular, serving tasty wraps with all kinds of Asian fillings. You can eat in or take away, but be sure to try one of the freshly squeezed fruit juices.

Govinda's (Map pp654-5; ☎ 475 0309; 4 Aungier St; mains €5-9; ⌚ noon-9pm Mon-Sat) The soup at this branch of the Hare Krishna chain is so subtle and flavourful you'll think Krishna cooked it himself. The place is totally vegetarian, with a wholesome mix of salads and Indian-influenced hot daily specials.

Cornucopia (Map p657; ☎ 677 7583; 19 Wicklow St; mains €9.50-11; ⌚ 8.30am-8pm Mon-Wed, Fri & Sat, 8.30am-9pm Thu) For those escaping the Irish cholesterol habit, Cornucopia is a popular, mostly vegan café turning out scrumptious healthy goodies. There's even a hot vegetarian breakfast as an alternative to muesli.

MIDRANGE & TOP END

Havana (Map p657; ☎ 400 5990; Sth Great George's St; tapas €6.50-12.50; ⌚ 11.30am-10.30pm Mon-Wed, 11.30am-11.30pm Thu & Fri, 1-11.30pm Sat, 3-10.30pm Sun) It always feels like a party in this lively tapas place across from Café Bar Deli. Stop in Monday, Tuesday or Wednesday when any two tapas cost just €12.

Café Bar Deli (Map p657; ☎ 677 1646; 12-13 Sth Great George's St; mains €9-13; ⌚ 12.30-11pm Mon-Sat, 2-10pm Sun) Having to choose between fresh salads, giant bowls of pasta or pizza with imaginative toppings, like crab and buttered leek, is the only bad part of eating at Café Bar Deli. The rest of the experience is just divine.

sixty6 (Map p657; ☎ 400 5878; 66-67 Sth Great George's St; lunch €10-15.50, dinner €11.50-20; ⌚ 8am-10.30pm Mon-Wed, 8am-11pm Thu-Sat, 11am-10.30pm Sun) This excellent new kid on the block came on the scene packing a mighty punch. With a full veggie menu, extensive wine list and attached grocer, sixty6 is definitely one of the most comprehensive and tasty eateries in all of Ireland.

Odessa (Map p657; ☎ 670 7634; 13 Dame Ct; mains €15-25; ⌚ dinner 6pm-late daily, brunch 11.30am-4.30pm Sat & Sun) Just off Exchequer St, Odessa's loungy atmosphere with comfy sofas and retro standard lamps attracts Dublin's hipsters, who flock in for its brunch (€8 to €15), home-made burgers, steaks or daily fish specials. You might not escape the sofa after a few of Odessa's renowned cocktails, quaffed over a game of backgammon.

DRINKING

Temple Bar, Dublin's 'party district', is almost always packed with obnoxious stag/hen parties, girls in very little clothing, and loud guys from Ohio wearing Guinness T-shirts. If you're just looking to get smashed and snog with someone from another country, there is no better place in Ireland. If that's not your style, there's plenty to do beyond

Temple Bar. In fact, most of the best old-fashioned pubs are outside the district.

Grogan's Castle Lounge (Map p657; ☎ 677 9320; 15 Sth William St) Grogan's has long been a favourite haunt of Dublin's writers and painters, as well as others from the bohemian, alternative set.

Café en-Seine (Map pp654-5; ☎ 677 4567; 40 Dawson St) The best way to describe Café en-Seine is faux-Parisian Left Bank Victorian decadence…seriously. The only thing missing is absinthe. Rumour has it that this posh, four-level nightspot cost around €17 million to renovate; it looks it, too.

Stag's Head (Map p657; ☎ 679 3701; 1 Dame Ct) Built in 1770, and remodelled in 1895, the Stag's Head is possibly the best traditional pub in Dublin (and therefore the world). You may find yourself philosophising in the ecclesiastical atmosphere, as James Joyce did. Some of the fitters that worked on this pub probably also worked on churches in the area, so the stained-wood-and-polished-brass similarities are no accident.

Hipster spots include **Dice Bar** (Map pp654-5; ☎ 674 6710; 79 Queen St), the decadent **Voodoo Lounge** (Map pp654-5; ☎ 873 6013; 37 Arran Quay), the hip-hop **Forum Bar** (Map pp654-5; ☎ 878 7084; 144 Parnell St) and the north side's USSR-style **Pravda** (Map p657; ☎ 874 0076; 35 Lower Liffey St).

ENTERTAINMENT

For events, reviews and club listings, pick up a copy of the bimonthly freebie **Event Guide** (www.eventguide.ie) or the weekly *In Dublin,* available at cafés and hostels. Thursday's *Irish Times* has a pull-out section called 'The Ticket' that has reviews and listings of all things arty.

Cinemas

Irish Film Institute (IFI; Map p657; ☎ 679 5744; www.irishfilm.ie; 6 Eustace St) The fantastic IFI has two screens showing classic and arthouse films. Wheelchair access is available.

Savoy (Map pp654-5; ☎ 874 6000; Upper O'Connell St) The Savoy, a traditional four-screen first-run cinema, has late-night shows on weekends.

Gay & Lesbian Venues

Central Dublin has the feeling of a city just coming out of the closet – people are ready to party and they don't care who knows.

George (Map p657; ☎ 478 2983; 89 Sth Great George's St) An excellent cruising spot and the patriarch of Dublin's gay and lesbian clubs, the venerable George has different themes, including bingo and karaoke, most nights of the week.

Dragon (Map p657; ☎ 478 1590; 64-65 Sth Great George's St) Dublin's hottest queer nightspot is upscale and loungy, with giant booths, crazy lighting and a bouncing dance floor.

Out on the Liffey (Map p657; ☎ 872 2480; 27 Upper Ormond Quay) A 'harder' rough and ready pub, popular with the biker or butch set of both sexes.

Many other nightspots have weekly gay and lesbian nights.

Rí Rá (Map p657; ☎ 671 1220; www.rira.ie; Dame Ct; ⌚ Mon-Sat)

Spirit (Map p657; ☎ 877 9999; www.spiritdublin.com; 57 Middle Abbey St)

Nightclubs

Whelan's (☎ 478 0766; www.whelanslive.com; 25 Wexford St) A Dublin institution; there is almost no better place to see live music, especially singer/songwriters.

Spirit (Map p657; ☎ 877 9999; www.spiritdublin.com; 57 Middle Abbey St) Spanning three floors, this club-kid fantasy covers all the bases. One floor pounds out house music, while another bumps funky soul, and yet another acts as a chill-out room with a classical cellist and massage therapists.

Rí Rá (Map p657; ☎ 671 1220; www.rira.ie; Dame Ct; ⌚ Mon-Sat) One of the friendlier clubs in the city centre, Rí Rá is full nearly every night with a diverse crowd who come for the mostly funk music downstairs, or more laid-back lounge tunes and movies upstairs.

Theatre & Classical Music

Abbey Theatre (Map p657; ☎ 878 7222; www.abbeytheatre.ie; Lower Abbey St) The famous Abbey Theatre is Ireland's national theatre, putting on new Irish works as well as revivals of Irish classics.

Peacock Theatre (Map p657; ☎ 878 7222; www.abbeytheatre.ie; Lower Abbey St) Part of the same complex as the Abbey Theatre, Peacock Theatre is committed to new plays and contemporary dramas.

Gaiety Theatre (Map pp654-5; ☎ 677 1717; www.gaietytheatre.com; Sth King St) This popular theatre hosts, among other things, a programme of classical concerts, opera and musicals.

National Concert Hall (☎ 417 0000; www.nch.ie; Earlsfort Tce) Just south of the city centre, Ireland's premier orchestral hall hosts a variety of concerts year-round, including a series of lunch-time concerts from 1.05pm to 2pm on Tuesday from June to August.

GETTING THERE & AWAY

Air

About 13km north of the city centre, **Dublin airport** (DUB; ☎ 814 1111; www.dublinairport.com) is Ireland's major international gateway airport, with direct flights from Europe, North America and Asia. Budget airlines, like Ryanair and Flybe, land here. See p705 for more details.

Boat

There are two direct services from Holyhead on the northwestern tip of Wales – one to Dublin Port and the other to Dun Laoghaire at the southern end of Dublin Bay. Boats also sail direct to Dublin Port from Liverpool and from Douglas, on the Isle of Man. See p706 for more details.

Bus

Busáras (Map pp654-5; ☎ 836 6111; www.buseireann.ie; Store St), Dublin's main bus station, is just north of the Liffey. Standard one-way fares from Dublin include Belfast (€12, three hours, 16 daily), Cork (€10, 3½ hours, six daily), Galway (€14, 3¾ hours, 16 daily) and Rosslare Harbour (€15.50, three hours, 13 daily).

The private company **Citylink** (☎ 626 6888; www.citylink.ie) has daily services to Galway for €14.

Aircoach (Map p657; ☎ 844 7118) offers a service that can be caught at the airport and will take you to Belfast for €7 to €12, depending on the day. It can also be caught from in front of Boyle Sports on Westmoreland St and will take you to Cork for the same price.

Train

North of the Liffey is **Connolly station** (Map pp654-5; ☎ 703 2358), the station for Belfast, Derry, Sligo, other points north and Wexford. **Heuston station** (Map pp654-5; ☎ 703 3299), south of the Liffey and west of the city centre, is the station for Cork, Galway, Killarney, Limerick, Waterford, and most other points to the south and west. For travel information and tickets, contact the **Iarnród Éireann Travel Centre** (Map p657; ☎ 836 6222, bookings 703 4070; www.irishrail.ie; 35 Lower Abbey St). Regular one-way fares from Dublin include Belfast (€34.50, two hours, up to eight daily), Cork (€54.50, three hours, up to nine daily) and Galway (€29, three hours, five daily).

GETTING AROUND

To/From the Airport

A frequent Airlink Express service is available with **Dublin Bus** (Bus Átha Cliath; Map pp654-5; ☎ 873 4222; www.dublinbus.ie; 59 O'Connell St) to/from Busáras, Heuston train station and various points around the city (€5, 30 to 40 minutes from the stations). Alternatively, take the slower bus 41, 41B, 16 or 746 (€1.80, one hour). A taxi to the city centre should cost around €22. Some Dublin airport taxi drivers can be unscrupulous, so make sure the meter is on and mention up front that you'll need a meter receipt.

To/From the Ferry Terminals

Buses 53 and 53A go to Busáras from the **Dublin Ferryport terminal** (☎ 855 2222; Alexandra Rd) after all ferry arrivals (€2.50). Buses also run from Busáras to meet Irish Ferries departures. To travel between Dun Laoghaire's ferry terminal and Dublin, take bus 46A to Fleet St in Temple Bar, bus 7 to Eden Quay, or the Dublin Area Rapid Transport (DART) train service to Pearse station (for south Dublin) or Connolly station (for north Dublin).

Bicycle

Most bike-hire outlets open during the high season only, and daily hire costs can reach €25 per day. Try **MacDonalds Cycles** (☎ 475 2586; 38 Wexford St), south of the city centre, or **Cycleways** (Map pp654-5; ☎ 873 4748; 185-186 Parnell St).

Car

All the major car-hire companies have offices at Dublin airport and in the city centre. See p707 for details.

Public Transport

Dublin Bus local buses cost €0.95 for one to three stages, up to a maximum of €1.90 (23 or more stages). You must tender exact change when boarding; drivers can't give change.

One-day passes cost €5 for bus services (including Airlink), or €8.50 for travel on both bus and DART. Late-night Nitelink buses (€4) operate from the College St/ Westmoreland St/D'Olier St triangle, south of the Liffey, until 4.30am on Thursday, Friday and Saturday nights.

DART (www.dart.ie) provides quick rail access as far north as Howth (€1.95) and south to Bray (€2.30). Pearse station is handy for central Dublin. Bicycles cannot be taken on DART, but may travel on suburban trains.

LUAS (www.luas.ie), from the Irish word for 'light', is a light rail system that is currently running on two (unconnected) lines; the green line runs from the eastern side of St Stephen's Green southeast to Sandyford, and the red line runs from Tallaght to Connolly station, with stops at Heuston station, the National Museum and Busáras. Single fares range from €1.25 to €1.90 depending on how many zones you travel through.

Taxis in Dublin are expensive, and flag fall costs €2.75. For taxi service, call **National Radio Cabs** (☎ 677 2222).

AROUND DUBLIN

Dun Laoghaire

☎ 01

Dun Laoghaire (pronounced dun-leary), only 13km south of central Dublin, is a popular resort and busy harbour with ferry connections to Britain. The B&Bs are slightly cheaper than in central Dublin, and the fast and frequent train connections make it a convenient stay.

On the southern side of the harbour is the **Martello Tower**, where James Joyce's epic novel *Ulysses* opens. It now houses the **James Joyce Museum** (☎ 280 9265; adult/child €6.50/4; 🕑 10am-1pm & 2-5pm Mon-Sat, 2-6pm Sun Mar-Oct, by arrangement only Nov-Feb). If you fancy a cold salt-water dip, Dun Laoghaire's **Forty Foot Pool** is the place.

The Rosmeen Gardens area south of the ferry pier is packed with B&Bs. To get there, walk south along George's St, the main shopping strip; Rosmeen Gardens is the first street after Glenageary Rd Lower.

Bus 7, 7A or 46A or the DART rail service (€3.50 return, 20 minutes) will take you from Dublin to Dun Laoghaire. For information on Dun Laoghaire ferries, see p706.

Malahide Castle

☎ 01

Despite the vicissitudes of Irish history, the Talbot family managed to keep **Malahide Castle** (☎ 846 2184; adult/child €6.50/4; 🕑 10am-5pm Mon-Sat, 11am-6pm Sun Apr-Sep, 11am-5pm Sun Nov-Mar) from 1185 through to 1973. The castle is packed with furniture and paintings, and Puck, the family ghost, is still in residence. The extensive **Fry Model Railway** (☎ 846 2184; adult/child €6.70/4.20; 🕑 10am-1pm & 2-5pm Mon-Thu & Sat, 2-6pm Sun Apr-Sep, closed Oct-Mar) in the castle grounds covers 240 sq metres and re-creates Ireland's rail and public transport system (it's actually better than it sounds). Combined admission tickets and wheelchair access are available.

To reach Malahide from Dublin, take bus 42 from beside Busáras, or a Drogheda-bound suburban train or DART from Connolly station. Malahide is 13km northeast of Dublin.

Brú na Bóinne

☎ 041

A thousand years older than Stonehenge, the extensive Neolithic necropolis known as Brú na Bóinne (Boyne Palace) is one of the most extraordinary sites in Europe. Its tombs date from about 3200 BC, predating the great pyramids of Egypt by some six centuries. The complex, including the Newgrange and Knowth passage tombs, can only be visited on a tour run by the **Brú na Bóinne visitor centre** (☎ 988 0300; Donore; adult/student visitor centre only €2.75/1.50, visitor centre & Newgrange €5.50/2.75, visitor centre & Knowth €4.25/1.50; 🕑 9.30am-7pm May-Sep, 9.30am-5.30pm Oct & Mar-Apr, 9.30am-5pm Nov-Feb). At 8.20am during the winter solstice the rising sun's rays shine directly down Newgrange's long passage and illuminate the chamber for a magical 17 minutes. Arrive early in the summer months as tours tend to fill up.

Day tours run by **Mary Gibbons** (☎ 01-283 9973; www.newgrangetours.com; tour & admission fees €35; 🕑 Mon-Fri) are stellar.

Bus Éireann's service to Donore (via Drogheda; €16 return, 1½ hours, five daily) stops at the gates of the visitor centre.

THE SOUTHEAST

Simply put, the southeast is a hell of a lot sunnier and dryer than the rest of Ireland. It's probably why the Vikings settled here, and certainly a reason why people love to visit. But the weather isn't the only reason people come in droves to the southeast – the area is littered with early-Christian ruins like Glendalough and impressive castles like Powerscourt. There's also the Wicklow Way, one of many rugged hiking trails which allow you to explore the region's plentiful waterfalls, beaches and mountains. Combine this with artsy towns like medieval Kilkenny and seaside Wexford, and you have a region not only diverse, but also bathed in sunlight and warmth, by Irish standards at least.

COUNTY WICKLOW

County Wicklow, less than 20km south of Dublin, has three contenders for the 'best in Ireland': best garden (at Powerscourt), best monastic site (at Glendalough) and best walk (the Wicklow Way). Pleasant seaside resorts and beaches sit between Bray and Arklow, especially at Brittas Bay. West towards Sally Gap and due south from here is a sparsely populated mountainous wasteland, which includes the black waters of Lough Tay.

Powerscourt

☎ 01

In 1974, after major renovations, the 18th-century mansion at **Powerscourt Estate** (☎ 204 6000; www.powerscourt.ie; house & gardens adult/child €9/5; 9.30am-5.30pm Mar-Oct, 9.30am-dusk Nov-Feb) burned to the ground when a bird's nest in a chimney caught fire. One wing of the building remains, now revamped with an exhibition room, café and shop, but people come for the 19th-century, 20-hectare formal gardens with views east to the Great Sugar Loaf Mountain (575m).

The estate is 500m south of Enniskerry's main square and about 22km south of Dublin, and is wheelchair accessible. Dublin Bus 44 runs regularly from Townsend St in Dublin to Enniskerry (€2, one hour, every 20 minutes).

From the estate, a scenic 6km trail leads to **Powerscourt Waterfall** (☎ 204 6000; adult/child €4.50/4; 9.30am-7pm Mar-Oct, 10.30am-dusk Nov-Feb), at 121m the highest in Ireland. You can reach the waterfall by road (5km), following signs from the estate entrance.

Glendalough

☎ 0404 / pop 280

Nestled between two lakes, haunting Glendalough (Gleann dá Loch, pronounced glen-da-lock) is one of the most historically significant monastic sites in Ireland and one of the loveliest spots in the country.

It was founded in the late 6th century by St Kevin, a bishop who established a monastery on the Upper Lake's southern shore and about whom there is much folklore.

During the Middle Ages, when Ireland was known as 'the island of saints and scholars', Glendalough became a monastic city catering to thousands of students and teachers. The site is entered through the only surviving monastic gateway in Ireland.

The **Glendalough Visitor Centre** (☎ 45325; adult/child €2.90/1.30; 9.30am-5.15pm mid-Mar–mid-Oct, 9.30am-4.15pm mid-Oct–mid-Mar), opposite the Lower Lake car park, overlooks a round tower, a ruined cathedral and the tiny Church of St Kevin. It has historical displays and a good 20-minute audiovisual, and staff can help plan half-hour to half-day hikes. From the visitor centre a trail leads 1.5km west to the panoramic Upper Lake, with a car park and more ruins nearby.

Visitors swarm to Glendalough in summer, so it's best to arrive early and/or stay late, preferably on a weekday, as the site is free and open 24 hours. The lower car park gates are locked when the visitor centre closes.

SLEEPING

Glendalough Hostel (☎ 45342; glendaloughyh@ireland.com; dm/d €22.50/50; P) Lying just 600m west of the visitor centre this modern and pristine hostel can sleep up to 118 people. Because of its location, it attracts interesting outdoorsy types from all over the world, especially during summer. It has great wheelchair accessibility.

Glendalough Hermitage (☎ 45777; www.hermitage.dublindiocese.ie; St Kevin's Parish Church; s/tw bungalows €45/65, minimum 2 nights; P) Designed for contemplation, these modest, self-catering dwellings are open to people of all faiths.

The Glendalough area also has plenty of moderately priced B&Bs.

GETTING THERE & AWAY

Daily services are available with **St Kevin's Bus Service** (☎ 01-281 8119) to Glendalough (one-way/return €11/18, 1½ hours) from outside the Mansion House on Dawson St in Dublin. Buses leave Monday to Saturday at 11.30am and 6pm (11.30am and 7pm on Sunday), returning to Dublin at 7.15am and 4.30pm Monday to Friday (9.45am and 4.30pm on Saturday and 9.45am and 5.30pm on Sunday).

The Wicklow Way

Running for 132km from Marlay Park, Rathfarnham, in southern County Dublin through to County Carlow, the Wicklow Way is the oldest and most popular of Ireland's long-distance walks. The route is clearly signposted and is documented in leaflets and guidebooks; one of the better ones is *The Complete Wicklow Way* by JB Malone. Much of the trail traverses countryside above 500m, so pack boots with grip, a walking stick and clothing for Ireland's fickle weather.

The most attractive section of the walk is from Enniskerry to Glendalough (three days). Camping is possible along the route, but you'll need to ask permission from local farmers. An Óige's **Knockree Hostel** (☎ 01-276 7892; dm €15; ⌚ closed 10am-5pm; P) is a tranquil farmhouse with lovely views, 7km west of Enniskerry. The village of Roundwood, a good stopover, has a camp site and some B&Bs.

WEXFORD

☎ 053 / pop 9443

A fine example of Ireland's new prosperity, Wexford's tiny streets sit lined with a mixture of old-time pubs, modern boutiques and an ever-increasing number of upscale restaurants. The town's rich and bloody history includes being founded by the Vikings, and being nearly obliterated by Oliver Cromwell.

Wexford is a convenient stopover for those travelling to France or Wales via the Rosslare Harbour ferry port, 21km south-east of town. Wexford's more colourful draw, though, is its world-famous opera festival, held every October (see right).

Orientation & Information

The train and bus stations are at the northern end of town, on Redmond Pl. Follow the Slaney River 700m south along the waterfront quays to reach the **tourist office** (☎ 23111; www.southeastireland.com; The Crescent; ⌚ 9am-6pm Mon-Sat May-Sep, 9am-5pm Oct-Apr). The curiously tight North Main and South Main Sts are a block inland and parallel to the quays.

The main post office is northwest of the tourist office on Anne St. Internet access is available in the youth centre at the **Megabytes** (☎ 23262; Francis St; per hr €3; ⌚ 9am-9.30pm Mon-Thu, 9am-5pm Fri, noon-4pm Sat).

Sights

Of the six original town gates, only the 14th-century **West Gate** (Slaney St) survives. Nearby is **Selskar Abbey**, founded by Alexander de la Roche in 1190 after a crusade to the Holy Land. Its present ruinous state is a result of Cromwell's 1649 visit. The **Bullring**, on the corner of Cornmarket and Nth Main St, was the site of one of Cromwell's massacres, but it gets its name from the now-defunct sport of bull-baiting. Today a **market** is held here on Friday and Saturday mornings.

About 4km northwest of Wexford, on the Dublin–Rosslare (N11) road at Ferrycarrig, the **Irish National Heritage Park** (☎ 20733; www.inhp.com; adult/concession €7.50/6; ⌚ 9.30am-6.30pm) is a theme park that re-creates dwellings and life from the Stone Age to the early Norman period. Last admission is 1½ hours before closing. Taxis from town cost about €6.

Festivals & Events

Wexford hosts the **Wexford Festival Opera** (☎ 22400; www.wexfordopera.com; Theatre Royal, 27 High St) in late October. The 18-day extravaganza presents rarely performed operas and shows to packed audiences.

Sleeping & Eating

Ferrybank Camping & Caravan Park (☎ 42611; info@wexfordcorp.ie; camp site €12; ⌚ May-Oct; ♿) Location and luxury, this campground is right across the river from the town centre.

Westgate House (☎ 22167; www.wexford-online.com/westgate; s/d €45/75; P) With Selskar Abbey and West Gate right across the road you won't lack for a good view from this refurbished family guesthouse.

Cappuccino's (☎ 23669; 25 North Main St; mains €5-12; ⌚ 8am-6pm Mon-Fri, 8am-6.30pm Sat, 10am-6.30pm Sun) The hot food in this three-level eatery, with exposed bricks, is mouth-watering.

South 51 (☎ 74559; 52 South Main St; mains €10-19; ⌚ 10.30am-9pm Mon-Fri, 10.30am-7pm Sat, 12.30-6pm Sun) A California-style bistro, South 51 has enough different menus to please anyone with an appetite.

Drinking

Sky & the Ground (☎ 21273; 112-113 South Main St) A popular place to eat and drink, this family establishment has traditional music nightly.

Thomas Moore Tavern (☎ 24348; Cornmarket) Locals call this an 'old man's pub', meaning it's good for a quiet drink and a chat.

Entertainment

Wexford Arts Centre (☎ 23764; www.wexfordartscentre.ie; Cornmarket) Theatre and dance productions are put on here year-round.

Getting There & Away

On the Dublin–Rosslare line is Wexford's **O'Hanrahan train station** (☎ 22522), which is served by three trains daily in each direction. The three-hour trip to Dublin costs €21 (more on weekends); to Rosslare Harbour (30 minutes) it's €5.50. **Bus Éireann** (☎ 23939, 051-879 000) runs from the train station to Rosslare Harbour (€4.30, 30 minutes, approximately hourly Monday to Saturday, 10 on Sunday), Dublin (€12, 2¼ hours, 13 Monday to Saturday, 10 on Sunday) and beyond.

WATERFORD

☎ 051 / pop 44,504

Waterford (Port Láirge) is a busy port and commercial centre, retaining vestiges of its Viking and Norman past in its narrow streets and town walls. Today Waterford is famed for its crystal but little else, apart from a few lively pubs. Despite a recent face-lift, it's an unlovely town with little to offer beyond a couple of mildly interesting heritage sites. Budget travellers, beware: Waterford has no hostels.

Orientation & Information

The main shopping street runs directly back from the Suir River, beginning as Barronstrand St and changing names as it runs south to intersect with Parnell St, which runs northeast back up to the river and becoming The Mall on the way.

The very helpful **tourist office** (☎ 870 800; www.southeastireland.com; The Granary, 41 Merchant's Quay; 🕓 9am-6pm Mon-Fri, 10am-6pm Sat May-Sep, 11am-5pm Sun Jul & Aug, 9.15am-5pm Mon-Sat Oct-Apr) is near the river.

Sights & Activities

Waterford Crystal Factory Visitor Centre (☎ 373 311; www.waterfordvisitorcentre.com; 🕓 8.30am-4.15pm Mar-Oct, 9am-3.15pm Nov-Feb) is 2km out along the road to Cork (N25). A tour (adult/student €9/6.50) will take you through the factory to see glass blowers and fragile exhibits. Bus 3 runs from the Clocktower to the Waterford Crystal Factory every 15 minutes (€2.50 return).

Sleeping & Eating

Mayor's Walk House (☎ 855 427; mayorswalkbandb@eircom.net; 12 Mayor's Walk; s/d €27/48) This quiet B&B serves up big welcomes and bigger breakfasts. It's near the police station, about a 10-minute walk out of town.

Rice Guesthouse (☎ 371 606; www.riceguesthouse.com; 35-36 Barrack St; s/d/tr €55/100/120) Located just minutes from the town centre, this guesthouse has remarkably comfortable beds, especially if you've been on the road for a while.

Haricot's Wholefood (☎ 841 299; 11 O'Connell St; mains €8-10; 🕓 9am-8pm) Haricot's serves generous portions of vegetarian and meat dishes. The chocolate cake is a gooey delight.

47 The Bistro (☎ 844 774; 47 Patrick St; mains €7-13; 🕓 11.30am-9.30pm Mon-Sat, noon-9pm Sun) With delightful food and a sharp interior, this place could easily be passed off as a Manhattan bistro. Its homemade desserts are superb.

Getting There & Around

Seven kilometres south of the city at Killowen, **Waterford airport** (☎ 875 589) has daily flights with Aer Arann to Luton airport, outside London, Manchester and Lorient in France. See p705 for contact details.

The **train station** (☎ 873 401) is across the river from the town centre. Trains run regularly to Dublin (€23, three hours, five daily), Rosslare Harbour (€14.50, 1½ hours, two daily), Kilkenny (€9.50, 45 minutes, five daily) and Cork (€28.50, three to five hours, four daily), via Limerick Junction.

From the **Bus Éireann** (☎ 879 000) depot, opposite the tourist office, plenty of buses run daily to Dublin (€11, three hours), Wexford (€12, 1½ hours), Rosslare Harbour (€14, 1½ hours), Kilkenny (€19, one hour) and Cork (€14, 2¼ hours). **Rapid Express Coaches** (☎ 872 149; Parnell St) runs several services daily to Dublin (€11) and Dublin airport (€15).

BnB Cycles (☎ 870 356; 22 Ballybricken), up Patrick St and past the police station, rents bikes for €15 per day.

KILKENNY

☎ 056 / pop 18,696

Beautiful Kilkenny (Cill Chainnigh) is impossible to forget once you've seen its medieval streets. Nestled in lush grounds overlooking the river, Kilkenny Castle will imprint itself upon your mind, while the town's excellent selection of pubs and eateries will make you wish your taste buds had a memory as well. Kilkenny is also renowned for its devotion to the arts, and hosts several world-class festivals throughout the year.

Orientation & Information

Most places of interest can be found on or close to Parliament St and its continuation (High St), which runs parallel to the Nore River, and along Rose Inn St, which becomes John St, as it leads away from the river to the northeast. The **tourist office** (☎ 775 1500; www.southeastireland.com; Rose Inn St; 9am-6pm Mon-Fri, 10am-6pm Sat May-Sep, 11am-5pm Sun Jul & Aug, 9.15am-5pm Mon-Sat Oct-Apr) is a short walk from the castle. Internet access is plentiful; the **Kilkenny e.centre** (☎ 776 0093; 26 Rose St; per hr €5; 10am-8pm Mon-Sat, 11am-7pm Sun) is comfy and central.

Sights & Activities

KILKENNY CASTLE

Stronghold of the powerful Butler family, **Kilkenny Castle** (☎ 772 1450; adult/child incl tour €5/2; 9.30am-7pm Jun-Aug, 10am-6.30pm Sep, 10.30am-5pm Apr-May, 10.30am-12.45pm Oct-Mar) has a history dating back to 1172, when the legendary Anglo-Norman Strongbow erected a wooden tower on the site.

The **Long Gallery**, with its vividly painted ceiling and extensive portrait collection of Butler family members, is quite remarkable.

The castle hosts contemporary art exhibitions in the **Butler Gallery** (☎ 776 1106; www.butlergallery.com; admission free).

ST CANICE'S CATHEDRAL

The approach on foot from Parliament St leads over Irishtown Bridge and up **St Canice's Steps**, which date from 1614. Around the **cathedral** (☎ 776 4971; www.cashel.anglican.org; adult/concession €3/2; 9am-6pm Mon-Sat, 2-6pm Sun Jun-Aug, 10am-1pm & 2-5pm Mon-Sat, 2-6pm Sun Apr-May & Sep, 10am-1pm & 2-4pm Mon-Sat, 2-4pm Sun Oct-Mar) is a wheelchair-accessible **round tower** (which you can climb – if you're over 12 – for €2). Although the present cathedral dates from 1251, it has a much lengthier history.

OTHER ATTRACTIONS

Rothe House (☎ 772 2893; Parliament St; adult/child €5/3; 10.30am-5pm Mon-Sat, 3-5pm Sun Apr-Oct, 11am-4pm Mon-Sat Nov-Mar) is a restored 1594 Tudor house. Original owner, wealthy John Rothe, lived here with his wife and 12 children.

Tynan walking tours (☎ 087-265 1745; www.tynantours.com; adult/student €6/5) conducts hour-long tours of Kilkenny, departing from the tourist office several times a day (weekends only November to March).

Sleeping

Tree Grove Caravan & Camping Park (☎ 777 0302; www.camping-ireland.ie; camp site €15; Mar–mid-Nov) You can walk into town along the river from this full-facilities park. By car, it's 1.5km south of Kilkenny on the New Ross (R700) road.

Kilkenny Tourist Hostel (☎ 776 3541; kilkennyhostel@eircom.net; 35 Parliament St; dm/tw €16/40) This central, creaky hostel has loads of character and a turf fire. Check the information board for happenings.

Bregagh Guesthouse (☎ 772 2315; www.bregaghhouse.com; Dean St; s/d €45/90) Funky bedspreads and a hearty breakfast are two of the many enjoyable things about this centrally located spot.

Lacken House (☎ 776 1085; www.lackenhouse.ie; Dublin Rd; s/d €140/250; P) Just out of town, this beautiful 1847 Victorian guesthouse is absolutely luxurious, and the breakfast is superb. Make sure to try its stellar restaurant as well (p668).

Eating

Halal Center (☎ 778 6389; 6 Irishtown; mains €5.50-12; 10am-11pm Sun-Wed, 10am-midnight Thu-Sat) Boasting a menu of over 100 items, including veggie options, this tandoori takeaway/delivery joint is one of the best and most slept-upon places in town. It also doubles as a newsagent/corner store.

Marble City Bar (☎ 776 1143; 66 High St; lunch €6.50-9.50, dinner €10.50-14.50; 10am-9pm) The food is impeccably presented in this slick Gotham-esque bar that looks more expensive than it is.

Lacken House (☎ 776 1085; Dublin Rd; mains €25-30, 5-course menu €50; 🕑 6.30-10pm) The celebrated Lacken House dishes out such appetising original creations as pork with cider potato, and ostrich fillet with caviar.

Gourmet Store (☎ 777 1727; 56 High St; 🕑 9am-6pm Mon-Sat) A good option for classy picnickers and hostellers.

Drinking & Entertainment

John Cleere's (☎ 776 2573; 22 Parliament St) Cleere's often has good alternative bands – and the occasional poetry reading – in its theatre out the back.

Kyteler's Inn (☎ 772 1064; 27 St Kieran's St) The old house of Dame Kyteler (aka the Witch of Kilkenny) is a tourist magnet, but atmospheric all the same.

Watergate Theatre (☎ 776 1674; www.watergatekilkenny.com; Parliament St) The Watergate hosts musical and theatrical productions throughout the year.

Getting There & Away

The **McDonagh train station** (☎ 772 2024; Dublin Rd) is east of the town centre via John St. At least four trains daily travel from Dublin's Heuston station to Kilkenny (€21.50) and then on to Waterford (€9). Fares are higher on Friday and Saturday.

Bus Éireann (☎ 776 4933, 051-879 000) operates from the train station. There are six buses a day to Dublin (€10.50, 2¼ hours), three to Cork (€16, two on Sunday), and a couple to Wexford, Waterford and Rosslare Harbour.

AROUND KILKENNY

Kells Priory

Kells Priory might be one of the neatest off-the-beaten-path attractions in Ireland. Only 13km south of Kilkenny, this awe-inspiring monastic site sits among rolling fields and beside a babbling brook. Since these 12th- and 15th-century ruins have no admission fee and there are no set opening hours, you may find yourself completely alone here (except for the sheep), making it a fine place for howling at the moon. The site is difficult to get to, so unless you have a car, you'll have to take a taxi (about €20 from Kilkenny) or thumb it.

THE SOUTHWEST

The southwest is the part of Ireland people fantasise about. Strewn with remnants of Ireland's many different pasts, its verdant hills and fields stretch out towards the ocean, where small towns dot the seaside like the jewels of a crown. Alternatively, Cork city buzzes and whirs with the kind of energy and cultural cool that's just shy of being considered a renaissance. From Kinsale's culinary zeal to the Ring of Kerry's beauty to Glengarriff's rustic appeal, the southwest encapsulates all the lustre that draws people to Ireland.

CORK

☎ 021 / pop 123,062

There's a reason the locals call Cork (Corcaigh) 'The Real Capital' or 'The People's Republic of Cork'; something special is going on here. The Irish Republic's second-biggest city has transformed itself into a place humming with the type of cultural currency found only in cities with art and music scenes as vibrant as this one. While Dublin may still be the actual capital of the Republic, at least Cork spent all of 2005 as Europe's Capital of Culture.

Cork has long been a significant city in Ireland, not least during the Anglo-Irish War. The Black and Tans were at their most brutal in Cork. The city was also a centre for the civil war that followed independence (Irish leader Michael Collins was ambushed and killed nearby). Today Cork is noted for its sports teams and, of course, its rivalry with Dublin.

Orientation & Information

The city centre is an island between two channels of the Lee River. Oliver Plunkett St and the curve of St Patrick's St are the main shopping/eating/drinking areas. The train station and several hostels are north of the river; MacCurtain St and Glanmire Rd Lower are the main thoroughfares there.

Send emails at the **Webworkhouse.com** (☎ 427 3090; www.webworkhouse.com; 8a Winthrop St; per hr €1.50-5; 🕑 24hr) or snail mail at the **main post office** (Oliver Plunkett St; 🕑 9am-5.30pm). There are also plenty of other Internet cafés all over Cork.

The **tourist office** (☎ 425 5100; www.corkkerry.ie; Grand Pde; 🕒 9.15am-5pm Sep-May, 9am-6pm Mon-Sat Jun, 9am-7pm Mon-Sat, 10am-3.40pm Sun Jul-Aug), awash in souvenirs, has plenty of brochures, books and maps about the city and county.

Sights

Housed in a building combining the 18th-century Cork Customs House with 21st-century Dutch design, the **Crawford Municipal Art Gallery** (☎ 490 7855; www.crawfordartgallery.com; Emmet Pl; admission free; 🕒 10am-5pm Mon-Sat) is a must see for anyone who enjoys art, architecture or both. Pieces by Irish artists like Jack Yeats and Cork's James Barry sit among a fine permanent collection that includes artists from Continental Europe as well. The museum has wheelchair access.

Just south of the city centre sits the Protestant **St Fin Barre's Cathedral** (☎ 496 3387; www.cathedral.cork.anglican.org; Bishop St; adult/child €3/1.50; 🕒 9.30am-5.30pm Mon-Fri Apr-Sep, 10am-12.45pm & 2-5pm Mon-Fri Oct-Mar). Built in 1879, this beautiful Gothic Revival structure has a multitude of notable features, including a Golden Angel who sits on the eastern side of the cathedral, and whose job it is to blow her horn at the onset of the Apocalypse.

Structurally less impressive but with a fantastic moniker, 'The Four Faced Liar' or **St Anne's Church** (☎ 450 5906; www.shandonbells.org; John Redmond St; adult/student €6/5; 🕒 9.30am-4.30pm Mon-Sat) sits perched upon a hill a little north of the river. Admission lets you climb the tower, ring the Shandon Bells (which aren't always in tune) and watch an audiovisual presentation about the Shandon area.

The **Cork Public Museum** (☎ 427 0679; museum@corkcity.ie; Fitzgerald Park; admission free; 🕒 11am-1pm & 2.15-5pm Mon-Fri, 3-5pm Sun Sep-May, 3-6pm Sun-Fri Jun-Aug) has a fine collection of artefacts that trace Cork's history from prehistory to the present, including the city's role in the fight for independence. Bus 8 goes to the University College Cork (UCC) main gates nearby.

Originally serving as a jail from the years 1824–1923, the **Cork City Gaol** (☎ 430 5022; www.corkcitygaol.com; adult/child €6/3.50; 🕒 9.30am-6pm Mar-Oct, 10am-5pm Nov-Feb) is now a terrific museum about a terrifying subject. Restored cells, mannequins representing both prisoners and guards, and an impressive 35-minute taped tour make this attraction intriguing. Also housed in the same location is the **National Radio Museum** (adult/child €6/3.50), which details the history of broadcast radio in Cork. The jail is off Sunday's Well Rd.

Festivals & Events

The **Cork International Jazz Festival** (www.corkjazzfestival.com) and the **International Film Festival** (www.corkfilmfest.org) both take place in October.

Sleeping

BUDGET

Kinlay House Shandon (☎ 450 8966; www.kinlayhouse.ie; Bob & Joan's Walk; dm €13-17, s/d with shared bathroom incl breakfast €38/48, d €52; 💻) This hostel has loads of personality. The kitchen and dining room are both big, and if you're around on a sunny day, it has great barbecues.

Cork International Hostel (☎ 454 3289; corkyh@gofree.indigo.ie; 1-2 Redclyffe, Western Rd; dm €15-19, tw €42; 💻) The cheerful staff at this bright and busy An Óige hostel do a great job coping with the flow of young travellers and lively groups. Bus 8 stops outside.

Brú Bar & Hostel (☎ 455 9667; www.bruhostel.com; 57 MacCurtain St; 6-/4-bed dm €16.50/21, d €50; P 💻) Cork's newest and funkiest hostel also has a bar and an Internet café on the premises. This clean and friendly triple treat can be a rocking good time, especially on the weekends, so be sure to make reservations as the place gets packed. It's wheelchair accessible.

Sheila's Hostel (☎ 450 5562; www.sheilashostel.ie; 4 Belgrave Pl; dm €15-17, s €30-32, d €46-52; 💻) Sheila's sauna, cinema room and super-friendly staff make up for its occasional dinginess. It's also a great place to meet travellers from all over the world.

AUTHOR'S CHOICE

Garnish House (☎ 427 5111; www.garnish.ie; Western Rd; s €60-80, d €90-140; P) With charming rooms (think flowers and fresh fruit), gourmet breakfasts and hosts who are eager to please, Garnish House is possibly the perfect B&B. From the moment you arrive and are greeted with tea and goodies, until the moment you leave, you will experience nothing short of absolute attentiveness. There is no mistaking that the secret ingredient here is love.

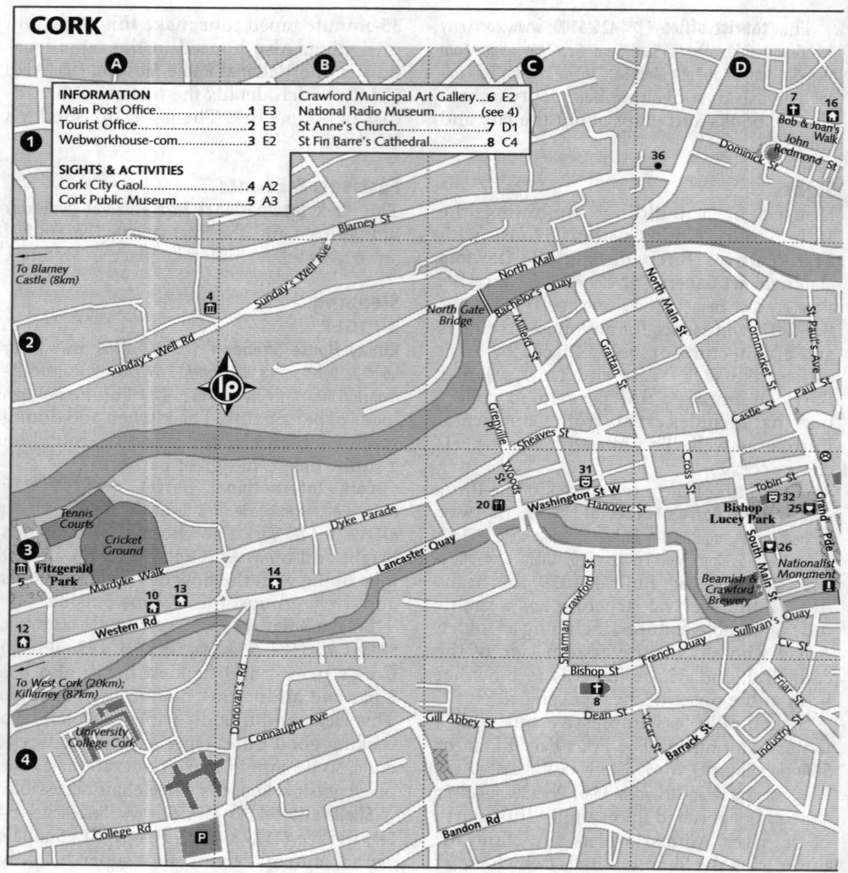

MIDRANGE & TOP END

Victoria Hotel (☎ 427 8788; www.thevictoriahotel.com; St Patrick's St; r per person €38-75) Boasting such esteemed former guests as Charles Stuart Parnell and James Joyce, the independently owned Victoria is one of Cork's oldest hotels, as well as one of its most centrally located. Its modest rooms are comfortable, and some of them sleep a family of up to six.

Gresham Metropole (☎ 450 8122; www.gresham-hotels.com; MacCurtain St; s/d €110/140; P) Following a total refurbishment, the Metropole allows you to pad around on lush carpets and feel comfortably corporate in the lavish rooms, swimming pool, health club, and elegant bars and restaurant. One room is wheelchair accessible.

Close to the train station at the north-eastern end of town there is a handful of quite basic but perfectly fine B&Bs, including:

Oaklands (☎ 450 0578; oaklandsbandb@o2.ie; Glanmire Rd Lower; s/d €40/64)

Auburn House (☎ 450 8555; auburnhouse@eircom.net; Wellington Rd; s/d €50/74, with shared bathroom €40/66; P).

Over at the other end of town is a string of high-quality B&Bs along Western Rd, leading towards the university. Some of the better ones are **Crawford House** (☎ 427 9000; crawford@indigo.ie; Western Rd; s/d €65/90), which has great Jacuzzis, and the very crisp and clean **Blue Dolphin** (☎ 427 4908; www.bluedolphin.ie; 3 College View, Western Rd; s/d €50/70).

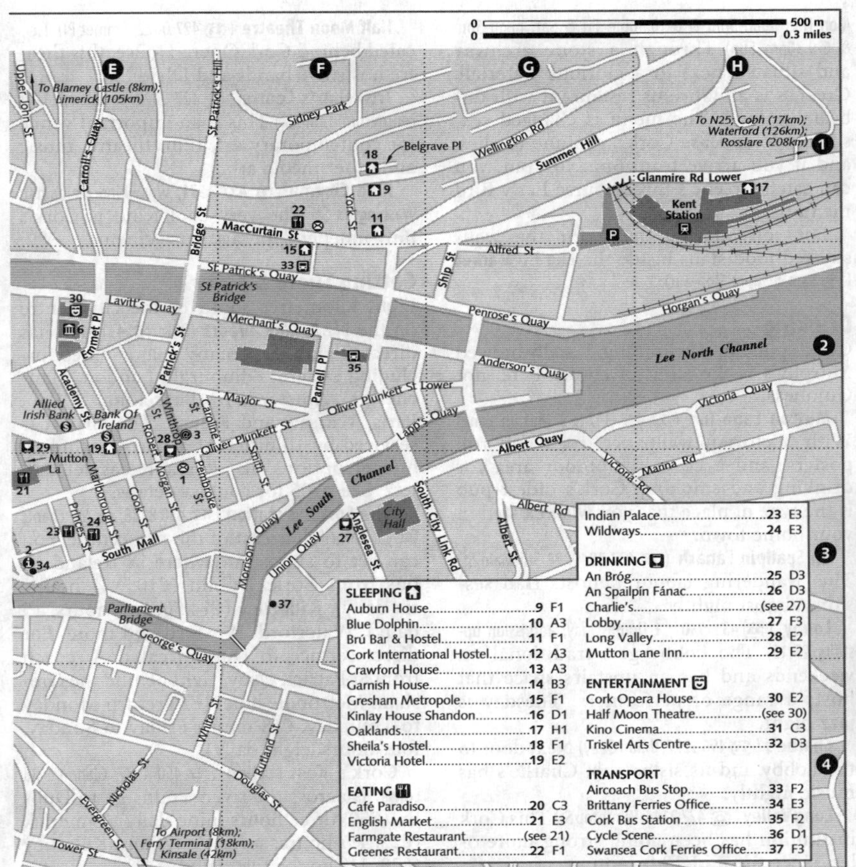

Eating

Wildways (☎ 427 2199; 21 Princes St; snacks €3-7.50; 🕒 8am-5pm Mon-Fri, 9am-4.30pm Sat & Sun) Cork's first organic soup and sandwich bar serves such a variety of delicious and healthy food that even the pickiest of eaters can find something scrumptious. If you're around for breakfast, make sure to try the excellent chocolate-chip pancakes.

Farmgate Restaurant (☎ 427 8134; English Market; mains €8.50-12; 🕒 8.30am-5pm Mon-Sat) An unmissable Cork experience at the heart of the English Market. Filling breakfasts, coffee and lunches draw a regular Cork clientele to the Farmgate's balcony, which overlooks the market below, source of the food on your plate.

Indian Palace (☎ 427 3690; 31 Princes St; mains €8.50-18.50; 🕒 12.30-2.30pm & 5pm-midnight Mon-Sat, 4pm-midnight Sun) If you like incredible Indian food, superb service and an interesting ambience, Indian Palace isn't for you…just kidding! This place is excellent, especially if you want a romantic candlelit dinner.

Café Paradiso (☎ 427 7939; 16 Lancaster Quay; mains €16-22; 🕒 12.30-3pm & 6.30-10.30pm Tue-Sat) Top-class vegetarian dishes that will seduce the most committed carnivore make this cheerful restaurant a busy place. Creativity maintains the standard of dishes, and the wine list is terrific.

Greenes Restaurant (☎ 455 2279; 48 MacCurtain St; lunch €10-13, dinner €18-33; 🕒 noon-5pm & 6-10pm

Mon-Thu, noon-5pm & 6-10.30pm Fri & Sat, noon-5pm & 6-9.30pm Sun) Through a stone archway and situated next to a glorious waterfall, Greenes is a luxurious restaurant with unbeatable food. The menu is changed seasonally to appease Cork's geniune foodies, and if you arrive from 6pm to 7pm, you can catch Greene's three-course Early Bird menu (€25).

For self-catering, head for the well-stocked food stalls inside the **English Market** (🕓 9am-5.30pm Mon-Sat).

Drinking

Cork's pub life is brimming. Locally brewed Murphy's is the stout of choice here, not Guinness.

Mutton Lane Inn (☎ 427 3471; 3 Mutton Lane) With Victorian wallpaper, rock and roll posters, and a covered outdoor area for drinking and smoking, Cork's oldest pub is the type of place that you wish existed in your home town.

An Spailpín Fánach (☎ 427 7949; 28 Sth Main St) The 'wandering labourer' hosts trad sessions almost nightly.

Lobby (☎ 431 9307; 1 Union Quay; admission upstairs €5-15) The Lobby gets traditional on weekends and has an upstairs space that hosts a range of performers. Tuesday is jazz night.

Charlie's (☎ 496 5272; Union Quay) Next door to the Lobby and its sister pub, Charlie's has music nightly.

Long Valley (☎ 427 2144; Winthrop St) This Cork institution has been going strong more or less since the mid-19th century.

An Bróg (☎ 427 0074; 72 Oliver Plunkett St) This is *the* spot for Cork's 20-something crowd, with excellent live indie music and/or DJs nightly.

Entertainment

Cork's cultural life is generally of a high calibre. To see what's happening grab *WhazOn?* or *Totally Cork,* which are free monthly publications available from the tourist office, newsagencies, shops, hostels and B&Bs.

Cork Opera House (☎ 427 0022; www.corkoperahouse.ie; Emmet Pl) Staging everything from opera to stand-up, the Opera House productions vary from the vibrant African singer Oumou Sangaré to *Carmen* and the *Vagina Monologues.* It has wheelchair access.

Half Moon Theatre (☎ 427 0022; Emmet Pl) Located behind Cork Opera House, this theatre hosts live bands and DJs.

Triskel Arts Centre (☎ 427 2022; www.triskelartscentre.com; Tobin St) This is an important venue for contemporary art, film, theatre, music and other media arts.

Kino Cinema (☎ 427 1571; www.kinocinema.net; Washington St) The very cool Kino is Cork's only independent arthouse cinema.

Getting There & Away

Eight kilometres south of the city centre on the N27, **Cork airport** (ORK; ☎ 431 3131) has direct flights into many major cities, including Dublin, Edinburgh, London, Manchester, Amsterdam, Barcelona, Milan, Paris, Warsaw and Prague. The airport is serviced by 10 different airlines, including budget options like Ryanair, easyJet and Jet2. See p705 for contact details.

The **Cork bus station** (☎ 450 8188; cnr Merchants Quay & Parnell Pl) is east of the city centre. You can get to almost anywhere in Ireland by bus from Cork: Dublin (€10, 4¼ hours, six daily), Killarney (€14.50, two hours, 15 daily), Waterford, Wexford and more. For direct service to Dublin, catch Aircoach from St Patrick Quay, right behind the Gresham Metropole hotel (€15 return Monday to Thursday, €18 return Friday to Sunday, four hours, eight daily).

Cork's **Kent station** (☎ 450 4777; Glanmire Rd Lower) is across the river. Trains go to Dublin (€50, three hours, nine daily), Limerick (€22, 1½ hours, seven daily) and Killarney (€20, 1½ hours, five daily).

Cork's ferry terminal, with regular boats to Swansea and Roscoff (France), is at Ringaskiddy, about 15 minutes by car southeast of the city centre along the N28. **Swansea Cork Ferries** (☎ 483 6000; 14 Union Quay) and **Brittany Ferries** (☎ 427 7801; 42 Grand Pde) both have city-centre offices. See p706 for more details.

Getting Around

Frequent buses head from the bus station to the airport (€3.70, 25 minutes) from April to September (fewer in the low season). Otherwise, a taxi costs around €15. Buses also run fairly often to the ferry terminal (€5.50, 40 minutes).

Parking discs are sold at newsagencies for €1.80 per hour.

Cycle Scene (☎ 430 1183; 396 Blarney St) has bikes for hire from €16/80 per day/week. Return them almost anywhere in the country for another €25.

AROUND CORK

Blarney

☎ 021 / pop 2146

Lying just northwest of Cork, the village of Blarney (An Bhlarna) receives a *bazillion* visitors a year, for one sole reason, **Blarney Castle** (☎ 438 5252; www.blarneycastle.ie; adult/child €8/2.50; 9am-7pm Mon-Sat, 9.30am-5.30pm Sun Jun-Aug, 9am-6.30pm Mon-Sat May & Sep, 9am-6pm or to sunset Mon-Sun Oct-Apr). If you're not germaphobic and don't mind putting your lips where millions of others have (and where locals are rumoured to urinate), you can kiss the castle's legendary **Blarney Stone** on the battlements and get the 'gift of the gab'. Queen Elizabeth I, exasperated with Lord Blarney's ability to talk endlessly without actually agreeing to her demands, invented the term. Bending over backwards to kiss the rock requires a head for heights, although there's someone there to hold you in position. Getting there at opening time is one way to beat crowds.

B&Bs surround the castle, including the **White House** (☎ 438 5338; www.thewhitehouseblarney.com; s/d €50/70; P), which tends to fill up quickly. The upscale **Blarney Woollen Mills Hotel** (☎ 438 5011; www.blarneywoollenmillshotel.com; s/d €70/140; P), almost directly in the centre of town, has a pub, restaurant, workout room and multiple shops, all on the premises.

Buses run regularly from the Cork bus station (€4.90 return, 30 minutes).

Cobh

☎ 021 / pop 6767

The pretty town of Cobh (pronounced cove) is a day trip with your sweetie type of place, where you can go for a walk, snog a little and take photos for your holiday snaps. Its picture-perfect looks and rich maritime history make it enjoyable for the rest of us, too. Be sure to visit the excellent **Cobh, The Queenstown Story** (☎ 481 3591; www.cobhheritage.com; adult/child €6/3; 9.30am-6pm May-Oct, 9.30am-5pm Nov-Apr) heritage centre in the town's old train station. It tells the story of the migrants who sailed from here, and of the town's links with the *Titanic* and the *Lusitania*. Last admission is one hour before closing, and the centre has wheelchair access.

Cobh is 24km southeast of Cork via the N25. Hourly trains (€5.10 return, 30 minutes) also connect with Cork.

Kinsale

☎ 021 / pop 2257

Beautiful and scenic, Kinsale (Cionn tSáile) is one of the many gems that dot the coastline of County Cork. Its reputation as a gourmet paradise is deserved, but a word to the wise: watch where you walk, the locals are far from diligent with regards to cleaning up after their dogs.

The **tourist office** (☎ 477 2234; www.corkkerry.ie; 1 Pier Rd; 9.15am-7pm Mon-Sat, 10.15am-5pm Sun Jul-Aug, 9.15am-6pm Mon-Sat Jun & Sep-Oct, 9.15am-5pm Mon-Sat Apr-May, 9.15am-5pm Tue-Sat Jan-Mar & Nov-Dec) is in the centre of town.

Southeast of Kinsale, a scenic 2.5km walk from the town centre, stand the stout ruins of **Charles Fort** (☎ 477 2263; www.heritageireland.ie; adult/student €3.70/1.30; 10am-6pm mid-Mar–Oct, 10am-5pm Nov–mid-Mar). Built in the 1670s, and with lovely views, This is one of the best-preserved star forts in Europe.

SLEEPING

Guardwell Lodge (☎ 477 4686; www.guardwelllodge.com; Guardwell; dm €17-19, s/d €29/55;) Guardwell Lodge is a great place to stay, with hardwood floors, a comfy lounge and a clean kitchen. It's the only budget option around the town centre.

White House (☎ 477 2125; www.whitehouse-kinsale.ie; Pearse St; s/d €65/130, breakfast per person extra €10) A solid guesthouse in the town centre, the White House has spacious rooms and lovely giant beds. The attached restaurant is also quite delectable and not to be missed.

Pier House (☎ 477 4475; www.pierhousekinsale.com; Pier Rd; s/d €100/150) This immaculate B&B sits among a well-manicured garden, and has big rooms, luxurious bathrooms, a sauna and a hot tub. It also serves as gallery space for a few local artists. Combine all that with friendly hosts, and you have yourself a fantastic place to stay.

EATING

Patsy's Corner (☎ 086-865 8143; Market Sq; snacks €3-7; 9am-5.30pm Mon-Sat) Serving home made soups and pastries alongside fresh sandwiches and salads, Patsy's holds its own as a great corner café in a town full of gourmet restaurants.

Man Friday (☎ 477 2260; www.man-friday.net; cnr River & High Rds, Scilly; mains €19.50-28.50; 🕑 6.30-10.15pm Mon-Sat) A five-minute walk east of the town centre brings you to this well-respected, tropically themed restaurant with a view. Bring a big appetite because the portions are heaping and the food is excellent.

Vintage Restaurant (☎ 477 2502; www.vintagerestaurant.ie; 50 Main St; mains €30-40; 🕑 6.30-9.30pm Tue-Sat) One cannot talk about Kinsale's gourmet food scene without discussing the Vintage Restaurant. Easily one of the town's best and most creative places, it specialises in seafood dishes so good that you won't regret forking over a fistful of euros.

GETTING THERE & AWAY

Buses connect Kinsale with Cork (€6.90 return, 45 minutes, 10 daily Monday to Saturday, five on Sunday) and stop near the tourist office. To head west by bus you'll have to go back to Cork, from where there are plenty of connections (see p672).

WEST CORK

Travelling west by public transport from Cork can be tough. There are at least two daily bus services in summer connecting towns, but some routes are not serviced at all during the rest of the year. The trick is to plan ahead at Cork, have the timetables committed to memory, and be prepared to change buses and backtrack. Make friends with **Bus Éireann** (☎ in Cork 021-450 8188; www.buseireann.ie). If you're so inclined, hitchhiking is another lovely way to get around West Cork.

Baltimore

☎ 028 / pop 383

Just 13km down the Ilen River from Skibbereen, sleepy Baltimore has a population of around 380 that swells enormously during summer. Its main attraction is its proximity to Sherkin and Clear Islands. The **tourist office** (☎ 21766; skibbereen@skibbereen.corkkerrytourism.ie; 🕑 9.15am-5.15pm Mon-Fri Oct-May, 9am-6pm Mon-Sat Jun & Sep, 9am-7pm Jul & Aug) in Skibbereen can handle questions about the area. The **Baltimore Diving Centre** (☎ 20300; www.baltimorediving.com; Harbour Dr) arranges diving expeditions (€90 for two dives, including gear).

Baltimore has plenty of B&Bs, plus the excellent and gay-friendly IHH **Rolf's Hostel** (☎ 20289; www.rolfsholidays.com; dm €13-15, d €40-60; Ⓟ); follow the signs up a hill about 1km east of town. Whether or not you're staying, Rolf's café/restaurant/wine bar/art gallery (mains €8.50 to €21, open 8.30am to 9.30pm, closed Monday and Tuesday in winter) is a terrific place to grab a bite.

Clear & Sherkin Islands

☎ 028

Clear Island, or Cape Clear as the locals call it, is the most southerly point of Ireland (apart from Fastnet Rock, 6km to the southwest). Clear Island is a Gaeltacht area, with about 120 Irish-speaking inhabitants, one shop, three pubs and its own website, **Oileán Chléire** (Cape Clear Island; www.oilean-chleire.ie). There's also a wonderful **storytelling festival** each year in early September.

The **camping ground** (☎ 39119; per person €7; 🕑 Jun-Sep) is signposted from the shop. An Óige's basic **Cape Clear Island Hostel** (☎ 41968; anoige@fenlon.net; dm €17; 💻) is a short walk from the pier. **Cluain Mara** (☎ 39153; www.capeclearisland.com; Nth Harbour; s/d €30/60; Ⓟ) and **Ard Na Goithe** (☎ 39160; The Glen; s/d €30/60; Ⓟ) are both amazingly friendly places in typical island houses. They can be reached by taking the 'bus', a silver minivan, from the pier for €2.

The ferry **Naomh Ciarán II** (☎ 39159; www.capeclearferry.info) sails between Baltimore and Cape Clear (weather permitting) three to four times daily in summer and less frequently in the low season. The trip takes 45 minutes and costs €12 return (bikes go free). In summer boats to Clear Island also leave from Schull (opposite).

If Cape Clear seems a long ride, consider heading to tiny Sherkin Island, its friendly neighbour, with a couple of convivial pub/restaurants, several decent B&Bs and a few good beaches. Sherkin is known for its delicious oysters.

The homy **Horseshoe Cottage B&B** (☎ 20598; chris@sherkintefl.com; s/d €35/70) has bay views and one wheelchair-accessible room, and does summer boat trips on a 45ft schooner. Try the **Jolly Roger Tavern** (☎ 20379) for fresh mussels and a great atmosphere.

Ferries (☎ 20218) sail from Baltimore nine times daily in summer and reasonably frequently in winter (€7 return, 10 minutes).

Mizen Head Peninsula

☎ 028

Mizen Head is an alternative to the better known and more touristy Ring of Kerry and Dingle Peninsula to the north.

At least two buses a day leave Cork (via Skibbereen) for the small village of **Schull** at the foot of Mt Gabriel (407m). In summer Schull's pubs and restaurants are packed with tourists, but the rest of the year it's blissfully quiet.

Schull Backpackers' Lodge (☎ 28681; www.schullbackpackers.com; Colla Rd; camp site per person €10, d €48, dm/s/d with shared bathroom €15/20/44; 💻) is excellent and has wheelchair access. It rents bikes (€11), and organises diving, kayaking and horse-riding trips. **Glencairn** (☎ 28007; susanglencairn@yahoo.ie; Ardmanagh Dr; s/d €40/70), on a cul-de-sac just 100m off Main St, serves up a mighty Irish breakfast.

During July and August **boats** (☎ 28138) leave from Schull's pier for Clear Island at 10am, 2.30pm and 4.30pm, returning at 11am, 3.30pm and 5.30pm. In June and September one boat leaves at 2.30pm and returns at 5.30pm. The one-way/return fare is €8/13.

The road south from Schull leads to **Mizen Head** and its 1910 **signal station**, now a **visitors centre** (☎ 35115; www.mizenhead.net; adult/child €6/4.50; 🕒 10am-6pm Jun-Sep, 10.30am-5pm mid-Mar–May & Oct, 11am-4pm Sat & Sun Nov–mid-Mar), which is on a small island connected to the mainland by a 45m-high suspension bridge. From here you can look down on pounding sea, striking rock formations and maybe the odd seal.

Beara Peninsula

☎ 027

Via Bantry, the N71 follows the coast northwest to Glengarriff, from where the R572 runs southwest to the Beara Peninsula, a wild, handsome, rocky landscape that's ideal for exploring by foot or bike. It's possible to drive the 137km 'Ring of Beara' in one day, although that would be missing the point. It's also possible to thumb-it around the Ring, which will definitely take more than a day. If you're driving or cycling (leg power permitting), don't miss the beautiful Healy Pass.

Walkers might like to tackle the ruggedly beautiful Hungry Hill, made famous by Daphne Du Maurier's book of the same name, just outside the pleasant fishing town of Castletownbere, itself a good place to stop for a bite or a pint.

Murphy's Village Hostel (☎ 63555; murphyshostel@eircom.net; Main St; dm/d €17/40; Ⓟ) in the heart of Glengarriff is cheerful, bright and wheelchair accessible. The **Cottage Bar & Restaurant** (☎ 63226; www.cottagebar.com; Main St; s/d €50/90) is a quiet and comfortable place which includes breakfast, dinner and a glass of wine in its rates.

Garranes Hostel (☎ 73147; dm/s €14/19) between Castletownbere and Allihies has a breathtaking location high above Bantry Bay. The atmosphere is quiet and meditative here, appropriately so as it's run by the **Dzogchen Buddhist Retreat Centre** (☎ 73032; www.dzogchenbeara.ie) next door. Guests can join daily meditation sessions. Given the atmosphere, this isn't a place to party. Inquire first by phone.

Among the copper mines surrounding the village of **Allihies** is the newly remodelled **Village Allihies Hostel** (☎ 71307; allihieshostel@eircom.net; dm/s/d €18/25/45; Ⓟ 💻). Also in Allihies is the welcoming **Sea View Guesthouse** (☎ 73004; www.seaviewallihies.com; s/d €35/70; Ⓟ).

Bus Éireann's bus 46 runs from Cork to Castletownbere, via Bantry, Glengarriff and Adrigole, once or twice a day. Bus 282 serves Castletownbere and Kenmare with a stop at Lauragh twice a day, Monday to Saturday, from mid-June to August only. Though most people walk or hitch to Allihies, it's served by the privately run **O'Donoghue bus company** (☎ 70007).

KILLARNEY

☎ 064 / pop 12,087

Though its tourist trade is healthy all year, Killarney becomes a strange orgy of hypertourism and over-the-top 'Irishness' during summer. Unlike most tourist traps, however, Killarney's popularity is justly deserved. Not only is it a lovely town, but it also has a national park and three lakes at its doorstep, providing endless escapes for walkers and cyclists. It's a convenient base for touring the Ring of Kerry (p678) and also a transport hub for the area.

Information

Guide Killarney (€5) is a good monthly 'what's on' guide, available at B&Bs, hostels and the tourist office.

IRELAND

Killarney Library (☎ 32655; Rock Rd; 10am-5pm Mon, Wed, Fri & Sat, 10am-8pm Tue & Thu) Internet access is free, but you should book ahead.

Main Post Office (☎ 31461; New St)

Rí Rá (☎ 38729; 3 Plunkett St; per hr €2.95; 10am-10pm Mon-Sat Mar-Oct, 9am-9pm Mon-Sat Nov-Feb, noon-9pm Sun year-round) Offers the cheapest Internet access.

Tourist Office (☎ 31633; www.corkkerry.ie; Beech Rd; 9am-8pm Mon-Sat, 10am-6pm Sun Jul-Aug, 9am-6pm Mon-Sat, 10am-6pm Sun Sep & Jun, 9.15am-5pm Mon-Sat Oct-May) Killarney's tourist office is busy.

Sights

WITHIN KILLARNEY

Most of Killarney's attractions are just outside the town, not actually in it. The 1855 **St Mary's Cathedral** (☎ 31014; Port Rd) is worth a look, as is the **Museum of Irish Transport** (☎ 34677; Scott's Gardens, East Ave Rd; adult/child €5/2; 10am-6pm Mar-Oct, 11am-4pm Sep-Oct), which has an interesting assortment of old cars and bikes, and is wheelchair accessible.

KILLARNEY NATIONAL PARK

The backdrop of mountains (well, big hills) beyond town are part of Killarney's huge 10,236-hectare national park. Within the park are beautiful Lough Leane, Muckross Lake and Upper Lake. There's a pedestrian entrance opposite St Mary's Cathedral, and a drivers' entrance off the N71.

Besides ruins and ex-gentry housing, the park also has much to explore by foot, bike or boat – plenty of options to last a day or longer. The *Killarney Area Guide* (€1.90 at the tourist office) has some ideas.

The restored 14th-century **Ross Castle** (☎ 35851; www.heritageireland.ie; adult/concession €5/2; 9am-6.30pm Jun-Aug, 10am-6pm Sep & May, 10am-5pm Tue-Sun Oct, 10am-5pm Apr) is a 2.5km walk from St Mary's Cathedral. Hour-long **cruises on Lough Leane** (adult/child €8/5) leave the castle daily in summer; make bookings at the tourist office. From late September to May boats depart only on demand.

Inisfallen Island, Lough Leane's largest, is where the 13th-century *Annals of Inisfallen* were written. The annals, now in the Bodleian Library at Oxford, remain a vital source of information about early Irish history. From Ross Castle you can hire a boat and row to the island to inspect the ruins of a 12th-century **oratory**. Alternatively, boatmen charge around €8 per person for the trip.

The core of Killarney National Park is **Muckross Estate** (☎ 31440; www.muckross-house.ie; adult/child €5.75/2.35; 9am-6pm), donated to the government in 1932. You can walk around the estate's rooms and view the 19th-century fittings free of guided tours. The estate is 5km from central Killarney, set in beautiful gardens; in summer a tourist bus (€8) leaves for the house at 1.45pm from O'Connor's pub (High St), returning at 5.15pm.

GAP OF DUNLOE

In summer the Gap, a heather-clad valley at the foot of Purple Mountain (832m), is Killarney tourism at its ugliest. Rather than following the hordes on one-hour horse-and-trap rides through the Gap (about €50), consider hiring a bike and cycling to Ross Castle. From there take a boat across to Lord Brandon's Cottage and cycle through the Gap and back into town via the N72. This should cost about €25, including bike hire.

Sleeping

Wherever you stay, book ahead from June to August. Hostels often hire bikes and offer discounted tours.

BUDGET

Fleming's White Bridge Caravan & Camping Park (☎ 31590; www.killarneycamping.com; White Bridge, Ballycasheen Rd; camp site €19; Apr-Oct) This camping ground is about 2.5km from town on the banks of the Flesk River. To get here, head south out of Killarney along Muckross Rd and turn left at Woodlawn.

Flesk Muckross Caravan & Camping Park (☎ 31704; www.campingkillarney.com; Muckross Rd; camp site €19; mid-Apr–Sep) About 1.5km from the town centre on Kenmare road (N71), this campground has great views of the mountains and an on-site supermarket.

Súgán Hostel (☎ 33104; www.killarneysuganhostel.com; Lewis Rd; dm/d €16/35) Resembling a hobbit hole, this homy hostel has warm hosts and an equally warm fire. The atmosphere is nothing short of familial, which makes leaving a hard task. Bicycle hire is €12 a day.

Killarney Railway Hostel (☎ 35299; railwayhostel@eircom.net; Fair Hill; dm/s/d €16/30/38; P) This bright, clean hostel is conveniently located near the train and bus stations, and the town centre. It has a good kitchen and a lounge full of leather chair comfy-ness, and has wheelchair access.

IRELAND

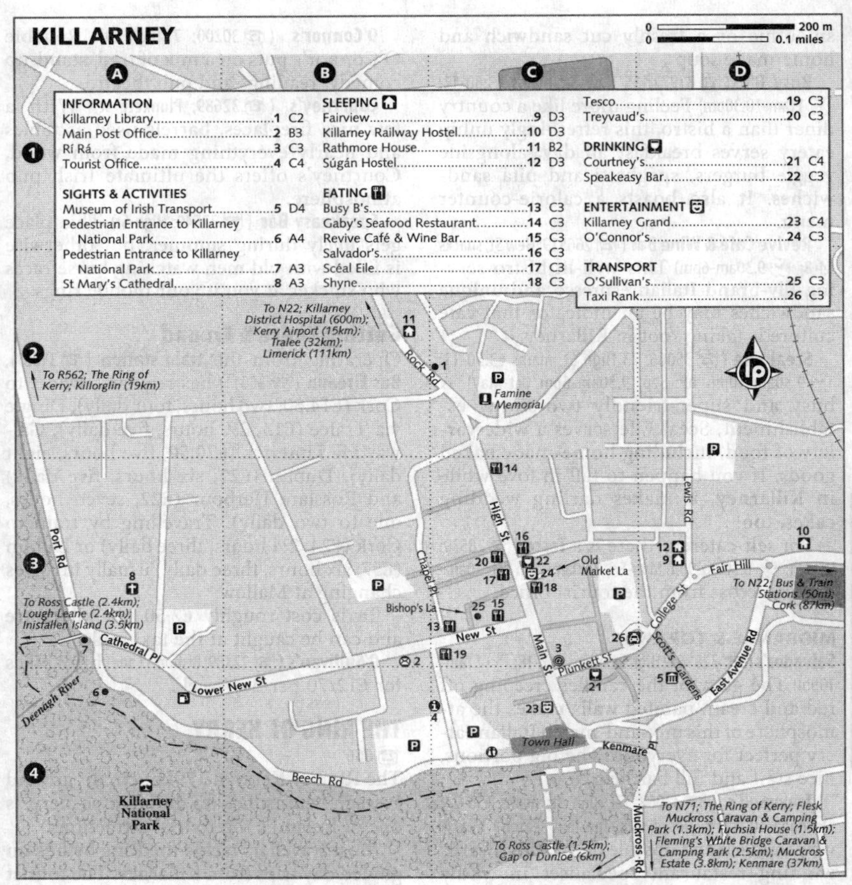

MIDRANGE & TOP END

Finding a room can be tricky during the high season, so it may be worth the €4 fee to have the tourist office do the hunting.

Rathmore House (☎ 32829; rathmorehousekly@iol.ie; Rock Rd; s/d €42/70; P) There's a real Irish welcome at this long-established, family-run B&B at the entrance to town.

Fuchsia House (☎ 33743; www.fuchsiaguesthouse.com; Muckross Rd; s/d €65/110; P) Rooms are huge, with plush carpets, sparkling bathrooms (with towel warmers), antique furniture and elegant, original décor. Some look out over the back yard, a lush garden in rich greens and pinks.

Fairview (☎ 34164; www.fairviewkillarney.com; Lewis Rd; s/d €130/180; P) Having received more awards than humanly imaginable, the incredible Fairview has been wooing visitors for the past 25 years. The lavish interior is enhanced by luxurious little touches, like plasma TVs and Jacuzzis in most of the rooms. The host, James, is possibly the most attentive in Killarney. Rates are substantially discounted in the low season, and wheelchair access is available.

Eating

BUDGET

Shyne (☎ 32686; 1 Old Market Rd; smoothies €3.60-5, snacks €3-8; 9.30am-10pm Jun-Sep, 9.30am-6pm Oct-May) Feel like a healthier alternative to all the crap food and booze you've been consuming? Drop by Shyne and get a delicious smoothie or a freshly cut sandwich and home-made soup.

Busy B's (☎ 31972; 15 New St; mains €3.50-11; 🕑 11am-10.30pm) Feeling more like a country diner than a bistro, this refreshingly unhip eatery serves breakfast all day, alongside veggie burgers, spaghetti and pita sandwiches. It also boasts a calorie-counter menu.

Revive Café & Wine Bar (☎ 266519; New St; snacks €4-8; 🕑 9.30am-6pm) This well-lit bistro serving Illy-brand Italian espresso and unique sandwiches may be an indicator that café culture is taking root in Killarney.

Scéal Eile (☎ 35066; 73 High St; mains €3.50-11; 🕑 9.30am-10pm Jun-Sep, 9.30am-6pm Oct-May) A busy and super-friendly two-storey establishment, Scéal Eile serves a wide variety of food, including home-made baked goods. If you happen to fall in love while in Killarney, it makes darling wedding cakes, too!

For self-caterers, there is a **Tesco** (☎ 28530; New St; 🕑 8.30am-9pm Mon-Fri, 8.30am-7pm Sat, 10am-6pm Sun) across from the tourist office.

IRELAND

MIDRANGE & TOP END

Salvador's (☎ 32816; 9 High St; mains €12-18; 🕑 11am-10pm) The glow of the candles creeping off red and cream painted walls makes the atmosphere of this mix-and-match Italian eatery perfect for everyone. The big portions, nice staff and full bar help, too.

Treyvaud's (☎ 33062; 62 High St; mains €15-24; 🕑 noon-10.30pm, closed Mon-Tue low season) With very modern and upscale décor, this award-winning restaurant specialises in wildly exotic meats such as kangaroo, alligator and ostrich.

Gaby's Seafood Restaurant (☎ 32519; High St; mains €24.50-48; 🕑 6-10pm Mon-Sat) Gaby's is the place to go if someone else is footing the bill. Its sophisticated yet unpretentious nautical theme fits perfectly, allowing you to sit back, relax and enjoy the delicious lobster or steak that (hopefully) someone else is paying for.

Drinking & Entertainment

Killarney Grand (☎ 31159; Main St) A great place for authentic music, if you can hear it over the boisterous crowd, the Grand has interesting takes on the traditional thing from 9pm. At 11pm modern bands take over (€6 cover).

O'Connor's (☎ 30200; 7 High St) Reliable O'Connor's puts on a mix of trad, stand-up comedy, readings and pub theatre.

Courtney's (☎ 32689; Plunkett St) With a few nice fireplaces, barrels used as tables and nearly everything made from wood, Courtney's offers the ultimate Irish pub atmosphere.

Speakeasy Bar (☎ 32540; High St) This place gets lively during summer, but otherwise is filled with old men watching horse races who snicker at you if your mobile rings.

Getting There & Around

Operating from the **train station** (☎ 31067), **Bus Éireann** (☎ 30011) has regular services to Cork (€14.50, two hours, four daily), Dingle via Tralee (€13, 2½ hours, five daily), Galway via Limerick (€20.50, five hours, eight daily), Dublin (€22, six hours, five daily) and Rosslare Harbour (€22, seven hours, one to two daily). Travelling by train to Cork (€24, 2¼ hours, three daily) or Dublin (€57, six hours, three daily) usually involves changing at Mallow.

Taxis cost roughly €2.50 per kilometre and can be caught at the taxi rank.

O'Sullivan's (☎ 22389; Bishop's Lane) hires bikes for €12/70 per day/week.

THE RING OF KERRY

☎ 066

The Ring of Kerry, a 179km circuit around Iveragh Peninsula with dramatic scenery, is one of Ireland's top tourist attractions.

Most travellers tackle the Ring by bus on guided day trips from Killarney. The tourist buses approach the Ring in an anticlockwise direction, and in summer it's hard to know which is more unpleasant – driving or cycling behind the buses or travelling in the opposite direction and meeting them on blind corners.

Eliminate some of these frustrations by leaving the main highway. The **Ballaghbeama Pass** cuts across the peninsula's central highlands, and has spectacular views and little traffic.

The shorter **Ring of Skellig**, at the end of the peninsula, has fine views of the Skellig Rocks and is less touristy. You can forgo roads completely by walking the **Kerry Way**, which winds through the Macgillycuddy's Reeks mountains past Carrantuohill (1038m), Ireland's highest mountain.

Sights

Daniel O'Connell (see p646) was born near **Cahirciveen**, one of the Ring's larger towns. The excellent, wheelchair-accessible **Barracks Heritage Centre** (☎ 947 2777; adult/student €4/3; 10am-5pm Mon-Sat, 1-5pm Sun May-Sep) off Bridge St occupies what was once an intimidating Royal Irish Constabulary (RIC) barracks. Exhibits focus on O'Connell and moving material on the famine's local impact. From here you can follow signs to see a couple of impressive **ring forts** and the dilapidated **Ballycarbery Castle**. All three are on private land, but there are many gaps in the fences.

South of Cahirciveen the R565 branches west to the 11km-long **Valentia Island**, a jumping-off point for an unforgettable experience: the **Skellig Rocks**, two tiny islands 12km off the coast. The vertiginous climb up uninhabited Skellig Michael inspires an awe that monks could have clung to life in the meagre beehive-shaped stone huts that stand on the only flat strip of land on top.

Calm seas permitting, boats run from spring to late summer from Portmagee, just before the bridge to Valentia, to Skellig Michael. The standard fare is around €35 return. Advance booking is essential; contact **Joe Roddy & Sons** (☎ 947 4268; www.skelligtrips.com) or **Des Lavelle** (☎ 947 6124; lavelles@indigo.ie).

The **Skellig Experience** (☎ 947 6306; www.skelligexperience.com; adult/child €4.40/2.20; 10am-6pm Apr-May & Sep-Nov, 10am-7pm Jun-Aug), on Valentia Island across from Portmagee, has exhibits on the life and times of the monks who lived on Skellig Michael from the 7th to the 12th centuries. It is wheelchair accessible.

Sleeping

There are scores of hostels and great B&Bs along the Ring. It's wise to book your next night as you make your way around, as some places are closed out of season and others fill up quickly.

Cáitín Hostel (☎ 947 7614; Kells; dm €13) A no-frills hostel in the middle of nowhere.

Royal Pier (☎ 947 6144; dm €18-25, d €45-50) This large Victorian hotel/hostel in Knightstown, on Valentia Island, once actually hosted Queen Victoria. It was in the process of changing hands and being renovated at the time of research.

Riverside House (☎ 976 1184; www.riversidehousebnb.com; Killorglin; s/d €43.50/65; Mar-Nov; P) This gorgeous B&B has panoramic gardens, a patio balcony, and a dining room that overlooks the river.

O'Shea's B&B (☎ 947 2402; osheasbnb@eircom.net; Church St; s/d €35/70; P) Directly in the centre of Cahirciveen, across from the bus stop, O'Shea's is a friendly B&B, with a nice view from the back of the house.

Ballinskelligs Inn (☎ 947 9106; www.ballinskelligsinn.com; Ballinskelligs; s/d €35/70; P) Hosting people for over 100 years, this seaside inn is a comfortable place to spend the night after a long day of cycling, hiking or driving. The attached pub/restaurant is rip-roaring fun during summer.

Getting There & Around

If you're not really up to cycling, **Bus Éireann** (☎ 064-30011) has a Ring of Kerry bus service daily from late May to mid-September. In June buses leave Killarney at 8.30am and 1.45pm, and stop at Killorglin, Glenbeigh, Kells, Cahirciveen, Waterville, Caherdaniel and Sneem, before returning to Killarney (the 3.45pm service terminates at Waterville).

Travel agencies in Killarney, including **Destination Killarney Tours** (☎ 064-32638; Scott's Gardens) and **O'Connor's Tours** (☎ 32456; 7 High St), offer daily tours of the Ring for about €20. Hostels in Killarney arrange tours for around €18.

THE DINGLE PENINSULA

☎ 066

The Dingle Peninsula is far less crowded and just as beautiful as the Ring of Kerry, with narrow roads that discourage heavy bus traffic.

The region's main hub, Dingle Town (An Daingean), is a workaday fishing village with some of Ireland's most interesting pubs. The western tip of the peninsula, noted for its extraordinary number of ring forts and high crosses, is predominantly Irish-speaking.

The **tourist office** (☎ 915 1188; www.corkkerry.ie; 9am-7pm Mon-Sat, 10am-5pm Sun Jun-Aug, 9.15am-1pm & 2-5.15pm Tue & Thu-Sat Sep-May) is at the Dingle Town pier. **Dingle Internet Café** (☎ 915 2478; Lower Main St; per hr €5; 10am-8pm Mon-Sat, 1-6pm Sun, closed Sun Nov-Feb, 10am-10pm Mar-Oct) also offers cheap international calling.

Dingle Town

pop 1647

In the winter of 1984 fisherfolk noticed a bottlenose dolphin that followed their vessels and sometimes leapt over their boats. **Dingle Boatmen's Association** (☎ 915 2626) leaves Dingle's pier for one-hour trips to find Fungie the dolphin. The cost is €12 (or free if Fungie doesn't show, but he usually does). You can swim with him for €25; wetsuit hire is extra. The **Peig Sayers** (☎ 915 1344; www.greatblasketisland.com) also leaves from the harbour for the Blasket Islands (€30 return).

Dingle Oceanworld (☎ 915 2111; www.dingle-oceanworld.ie; adult/child €10.50/6.25; 10am-6pm, 10am-8.30pm in summer), opposite the harbour, has a walk-through tunnel and touch pool, and it's wheelchair accessible. It was renovated in 2005 and is now a top-notch experience.

Ride a horse through the peninsula for €20 per hour with **Dingle Horse Riding** (☎ 915 2199; www.dinglehorseriding.com), or learn to surf by contacting Jamie at **Westcoast Surf School** (☎ 086-306 7053) for €30/25 per adult/child, including equipment.

East of Dingle

From Tralee the N86 heads west along the coast. The 'quick' route to Dingle Town is southwest from Camp via Anascaul and the N86. The scenic route follows the R560 northwest crossing the wildly scenic **Connor Pass** (456m).

West of Dingle

From Dingle follow signs for the 'Slea Head Drive', a scenic coastal stretch of the R559. To the southwest, **Slea Head** offers some of the peninsula's best views.

Ferries (☎ 915 6422, 915 4864) run from Dunquin to the bleak, uninhabited (since 1953) **Blasket Islands** (€20 return, 20 minutes), off the tip of the peninsula. Subtly powerful exhibits at Dunquin's excellent, wheelchair-accessible **Blasket Centre** (☎ 915 6444; adult/child €3.50/1.25; 10am-7pm Jul-Aug, 10am-6pm Apr-Jun & Sep) feature the lives of the islanders, many of them celebrated musicians, storytellers and writers.

Sleeping

Grapevine Hostel (☎ 915 1434; Dykegate St, Dingle Town; dm €15-17, d €40-45) On a small street in the centre of town, the Grapevine is a well-run hostel, whose lack of TV encourages guitar singalongs around the fireplace.

An Capall Dubh (☎ 915 1105; Green St, Dingle Town; s/d €70/90; P) Sitting on a cobbled courtyard and accessed through a 19th-century stone-built coach entrance, this delightful B&B is a great place to relax after a long day in the outdoors, or a long night at the pubs.

Dingle Bay Hotel (☎ 915 1231; www.dinglebayhotel.com; Strand St, Dingle Town; s/d €90/180; P) An upscale, modern place on the water, the Dingle Bay has all the amenities a hotel of this calibre should have, including Internet access for your laptop. It's also wheelchair accessible.

Hostels east of Dingle include the IHH **Dingle Gate Hostel** (☎ 915 7150; fuchsia@eircom.net; camp site per person €5, dm/s/d €12/17/34), in Anascaul, and the IHH **Connor Pass Hostel** (☎ 713 9179; dm €14; Apr-Oct) in Stradbally.

West of Dingle, in Dunquin, look for the following recommended options:

Black Cat Hostel (☎ 915 6286; dm/d €12/24) An IHO hostel in Ballyferriter.

Ballybeag Hostel (☎ 915 9876; dm/d €15/30;) In Ventry, this fantastic hostel offers bike hire, cheap laundry facilities, wheelchair access and a swing in the garden.

Dun Chaion Hostel (☎ 915 6121; dm €13-16, d €34; closed 10am-5pm; P) An Óige's hostel, across from the Blasket Centre.

Eating

An Café Liteártha (☎ 915 2204; Dykegate Lane, Dingle Town; snacks €3-7; 9am-6pm) Allow the spirit of literary Dingle to engulf you as you eat your soup in this café, nestled at the back of an excellent bookshop that specialises in local history and Irish-language books.

Homely House (☎ 915 2431; Dick Mack's Yard, Green St, Dingle Town; snacks €4-9.50; noon-5pm Mon-Sat) Owned by an expat from Los Angeles, this tiny restaurant is probably the closet thing you'll get to authentic Mexican food in all of Ireland. Also note that the back of the menu is laugh-out-loud funny.

Blue Zone (☎ 915 0303; Green St, Dingle Town; mains €6-16; 6pm-1am Tue-Sat) Chill out to some Miles Davis and enjoy a Thai-gingered chicken and lime pizza with a glass of California Pinot Noir in Dingle's only 'Jazz, Pizza & Wine Bar'.

Drinking

An Droichead Beag (☎ 915 1723; www.thesmallbridge.com; Main St, Dingle Town; 10am-11.30pm Mon-Thu, 10am-12.30am Fri & Sat, noon-11pm Sun) Now this is a pub! Filled with snugs, odd woodwork and a couple of bars, this great cavernous place has 'mighty' trad sessions nightly.

Foxy John's (☎ 915 1316; Main St) Half hardware store, half old-school pub, stop into Foxy John's for a pint, some nails and some good *craic*. You can also hire a bike here for €10 a day.

Dick Mack's (☎ 915 1960; Green St) Vestiges of its previous incarnation as a pub and cobbler line the walls, while drunken revellers sing songs and pat each other's backs. Although shoes are no longer repaired here, rumour has it that belts still are.

Getting There & Around

Buses stop outside the car park at the back of the Super Valu store in Dingle Town. Killarney–Tralee–Dingle buses run four times daily Monday to Saturday (€13, 2½ hours). Dingle has several bike-hire places. **Paddy Walsh** (☎ 915 2311; Dykegate St), near the Grapevine Hostel, has bikes for €12/70 per day/week.

LIMERICK

☎ 061 / pop 54,023

Trying to shake off both the dubious nickname 'Stab-City' and the backlash from the squalor depicted in Frank McCourt's *Angela's Ashes*, Limerick (Luimneach) finally seems to be getting its act together. With a growing number of good restaurants and a lively music scene, Limerick might be as cool as Cork or Galway if you give it a few years.

Orientation & Information

The main street through town changes name from Rutland St to Patrick St, then O'Connell St, The Crescent and Quinlan St as it runs south. The train and bus station are to the southeast, off Parnell St. The **tourist office** (☎ 317522; www.shannonregiontourism.ie; Arthur's Quay; ⏰ 9am-6pm Mon-Fri, 9.30am-5.30pm Sat & Sun Jul-Aug, 9.30am-5.30pm Mon-Fri, 9.30am-1pm Sat Nov-Apr, 9.30am-5.30pm Mon-Sat May-Jun & Sep-Oct) is near the Shannon River.

Sights

The fascinating **Hunt Museum** (☎ 312833; www.huntmuseum.com; Rutland St; adult/child €7.20/3.50; ⏰ 10am-5pm Mon-Sat, 2-5pm Sun) has contemporary art shows, and a superb collection of Bronze Age, Celtic and medieval artefacts. Half the fun of this museum is opening the drawers, where much of the collection is kept, to discover random treasures within. It's also wheelchair accessible.

The lofty, echoing rooms of the restored **Georgian House** (☎ 314130; 2 Perry Sq; adult/child €6/3; ⏰ 10.30am-4.30pm) are charmingly eerie. The back garden leads to a coach house that contains a photographic memoir of Limerick and a small but evocative **Ashes Exhibition**, including a reconstruction of Frank McCourt's childhood home.

Across the Shannon is the sturdy but underwhelming **King John's Castle** (☎ 360788; Nicholas St; adult/child €7.95/4.75; ⏰ 10.30am-4.30pm Nov-Mar, 10am-5.30pm Apr-Oct). Limerick's oldest building, **St Mary's Cathedral** (☎ 310293; admission €2; ⏰ 9am-4pm Mon-Fri, 9am-1pm Sat, 9am-4pm Sat Jun-Sep), was founded in 1168; parts of the original survive.

Sleeping & Eating

Cherry Blossom (☎ 469449; www.cherryblossomlimerick.com; 3 Alexandra Tce, O'Connell Ave; dm/s/d/q €20/30/50/72) Your best budget option in town is small and friendly, and has only one dorm room, a single-sex six-bedder.

Railway Hotel (☎ 413653; www.railwayhotel.ie; Parnell St; s/d €45/90) There is something classic and lean about this hotel, like you could imagine a horror film taking place here, in a good way (if that makes any sense). The Irish breakfast is great after a long night on the town, and the attached bar is a nice place to meet other travellers. It's opposite the bus and train station.

Java's Café & Wine Bar (☎ 418077; 5 Catherine St; mains €6-8; ⏰ 9am-10pm Mon-Sat, 10.30am-8pm Sun) Stylish Java's has loads of teas and coffees and fresh wraps and salads at good prices. The walls are red, and it's all very hip and busy.

Aubars (☎ 317799; 49-50 Thomas St; mains €8.50-24; ⏰ 8pm-midnight Sun-Thu, 8pm-2am Fri & Sat) The coloured lighting, mirrored walls and Continental Europe and bistro fare of this bar/restaurant are definite signs that Limerick is pulling itself out of its mired past.

Getting There & Around

Twenty-four kilometres from Limerick, **Shannon airport** (SNN; ☎ 712000) handles domestic and international flights. Some budget airlines that land here are Ryanair and easyJet. See p705 for contact details.

Bus Éireann (☎ 313333) services operate from Colbert train station, with hourly connections to Dublin (€12, 1¼ hours), Cork (€14.60, two hours) and Galway (€14.60, 2½ hours). Direct buses also run from the airport to Dublin, Cork and Killarney. By **train** (☎ 315555) it costs €41.50 to Dublin (10 daily) and €22 to Cork (seven daily). Hourly buses connect Shannon with the bus and train station (€5.70).

Emerald Alpine Cycles (☎ 416983; 1 Patrick St) hires bikes for €20/80 per day/week. For an extra €25, return or pick up the bike in any other town nationwide.

THE WEST COAST

There's an ineffable, almost magic quality that draws us to Ireland's west coast. It could be the way that Galway so unexpectedly sweeps us off our feet, or the way that the Burren looks like a large lunar landscape littered with flowers. Some might say that it's the solemn Aran Islands that pull us in, or those ancient fortresses that call out to us. Regardless of its source, there's no denying that something is there, and it keeps pulling millions of us to it year after year.

IRELAND

THE BURREN

The harsh and haunting Burren stretches across west County Clare like a time capsule melted into magma. *Boireann* is Irish for 'Rocky Country', and the name is no exaggeration. Unwelcoming from the surface, the Burren transforms upon entering into a complex landscape littered with ancient dolmens, ring forts, round towers, high crosses and a surprisingly diverse range of flora, while rocky foreshores and splendid cliffs line its coast.

Tim Robinson's excellent *Burren Map & Guide* is available at bookshops or tourist offices. If you're stuck for transport, a number of bus tours leave the Galway tourist office every morning for the Burren and Cliffs of Moher, including **O'Neachtain Tours** (☎ 091-553188; www.oneachtaintours.com). They all cost around €25. A much better way to explore the Burren, however, is on foot: **Burren Hill Walks** (☎ 065-707 7168) based in Ballyvaughan and **Burren Wild** (☎ 087-877 9565; www.burrenwalks.com) near Kinvara both offer half-day guided walks for €20 per person.

Doolin

☎ 065 / pop 200

Tiny Doolin, famed for its music pubs, is a convenient base for exploring the Burren and the awesome Cliffs of Moher. It's also a gateway for boats to Inisheer, the easternmost and smallest of the Aran Islands. In summer it can be difficult to get a bed in Doolin, so book ahead. Some of the hostels hire bikes for around €10 a day, plus deposit.

Doolin's reputation for topnotch traditional Irish music has spread like wildfire; summer nights find the three pubs packed with an appreciative cosmopolitan crowd.

SLEEPING & EATING

Aille River Hostel (☎ 707 4260; www.esatclear.ie/~ailleriver; dm/d/tr €14/33/52.50; closed Jan; P) In a picturesque spot by the river in the upper village this converted 17th-century farmhouse is the best budget choice. It has turf fires, hot showers, free laundry facilities and good company.

Daly's House (☎ 707 4242; www.dalys-doolin.com; s/d €30/60; P) What makes B&Bs special is that someone is bringing you into their home, and here Susan Daly makes you feel truly welcome. Situated 100m off Fisher St, Daly's House has panoramic views of the Cliffs of Moher, a comfy lounge area and even babysitting options.

Doolin Cafe (☎ 707 4795; Roadford; lunch €3.50-9.50, dinner €17-22.50; noon-3pm & 6-10pm) There's great atmosphere – homy but elegant – at this friendly café. With the fantastic food, from steaks to veggie options, it could be pretentious, but chooses not to be.

Lazy Lobster (☎ 707 4390; Roadford; mains €15.50-25; 5-10pm Thu-Sat, noon-3pm & 5-9pm Sun) Considering Doolin's proximity to the sea, this award-winning restaurant is hard to resist. Ummm…fresh lobster!

GETTING THERE & AWAY

There are direct buses to Doolin from Limerick, Ennis, Galway and even Dublin; the main Bus Éireann stop is across from Paddy Moloney's Doolin Hostel. For information on ferries to and from the islands, see p686.

Cliffs of Moher

About 8km south of Doolin are the towering 203m Cliffs of Moher, one of Ireland's most famous natural features. In summer the cliffs are overrun by day-trippers, so consider staying in Doolin and hiking or biking along the Burren's quiet country lanes, where the views are superb and crowds are never a problem. Either way, be careful along these sheer cliffs, especially in wet or windy weather.

Near the **Cliffs of Moher tourist centre** (☎ 065-708 1171; 9.30am-5.30pm May-Sep) is **O'Brien's Tower**, which you can climb for €1. Apparently, local landlord Cornelius O'Brien (1801–57) raised it to impress 'lady visitors'. From the tower walk south or north and the crowds soon disappear. You can also avoid the crowds – and the €5 charge for the car park – by visiting after the tourist centre closes.

GALWAY

☎ 091 / pop 65,832

Galway glows. Hip, happening, there's something going on here; you don't walk down Shop St, you glide. There's an energy here that you can feel and you just know there is no place like it in the rest of Ireland. As you creep through medieval streets, bouncing between pubs, restaurants and shops, the city seems to whisper, 'Whatever it is that you want, we've got it baby'. Galway also acts as a gateway for the Aran Islands.

Orientation & Information

Galway's tightly packed city centre is spread evenly on both sides of the Corrib River. The bus and train stations are within a stone's throw of Eyre Sq.

The **tourist office** (☎ 537700; www.irelandwest.ie; Forster St; 9am-5.45pm Jun-Oct, 9am-5.45pm Mon-Sat, 9am-12.45pm Sun Jan-May & Nov-Dec) is a short way off Eyre Sq. In summer there can be a long wait to make accommodation bookings.

Send mail at the **main post office** (Eglington St) and email at **net@ccess** (☎ 569 772; Old Malt Shopping Arcade, High St; per hr €2.50; 9am-11pm).

Sights

Set to be finished with restoration by the time you read this, **Eyre Sq**, the city centre's eastern focal point, will be a fine place for people-watching. In the centre of the square is **Kennedy Park**, honouring a visit by John F Kennedy in 1963. Southwest of the square, the **Collegiate Church of St Nicholas of Myra** (Shop St) dates from 1320 and has several tombs.

Also on Shop St, parts of **Lynch Castle**, now a bank, date back to the 14th century. Lynch, so the story goes, was a mayor of Galway in the 15th century who, when his son was condemned for murder, personally acted as hangman. The stone façade that is the **Lynch Memorial Window** (Market St) marks the spot of the deed.

Across the road, in the Bowling Green area, is the **Nora Barnacle House Museum** (☎ 564743; www.norabarnacle.com; 8 Bowling Green; admission €2.50; 10am-5pm mid-May–mid-Sep or by appointment), the former home of the wife and lifelong muse of James Joyce. The small museum is dedicated to the couple.

Little remains of Galway's old city walls apart from the **Spanish Arch**, right beside the river mouth. The **Spanish Arch Museum** (Spanish Pde) is set to open by this book's publication and will house, among other things, the controversial statue of Galway-born writer and hell-raiser Pádraic O'Conaire (1883–1928), which was previously in Eyre Sq.

Feel like petting slimy sea creatures? Stop by the **Atlantaquaria** (☎ 585100; www.nationalaquarium.ie; Salthill Promenade; adult/child €8/5; 10am-5pm Wed-Sun Oct-Mar, 9am-6pm Apr-Sep) and see the hands-on exhibit at Ireland's National Aquarium. It's roughly 2km from the city centre.

Festivals & Events

In July the **Galway Arts Festival** (www.galwayartsfestival.com) is a big event. The **Galway Oyster Festival** (www.galwayoysterfest.com), going strong for 50 years, draws thousands each autumn.

Sleeping

BUDGET

Salthill Caravan Park (☎ 523972; www.salthillcaravanpark.com; camp site per person €8; Apr-Sep; P) Just west of Salthill, off Salthill Rd, is this scenic spot right on the water. A bus runs the 4km into the city centre every half-hour.

Barnacle's Quay Street House (☎ 568644; www.barnacles.ie; 10 Quay St; dm €16.50-23, d €56;) In a repurposed 16th-century townhouse, Barnacle's is at the heart of the action, surrounded by all the pubs, cafés and restaurants you came to Galway for. Unfortunately, this also makes it very loud, especially when the 7am street sweeper cleans up the previous night's *craic*.

Kinlay House (☎ 565244; www.kinlayhouse.ie; Merchant's Rd; dm €17.50-26, d €52-57;) The modern,

IRELAND

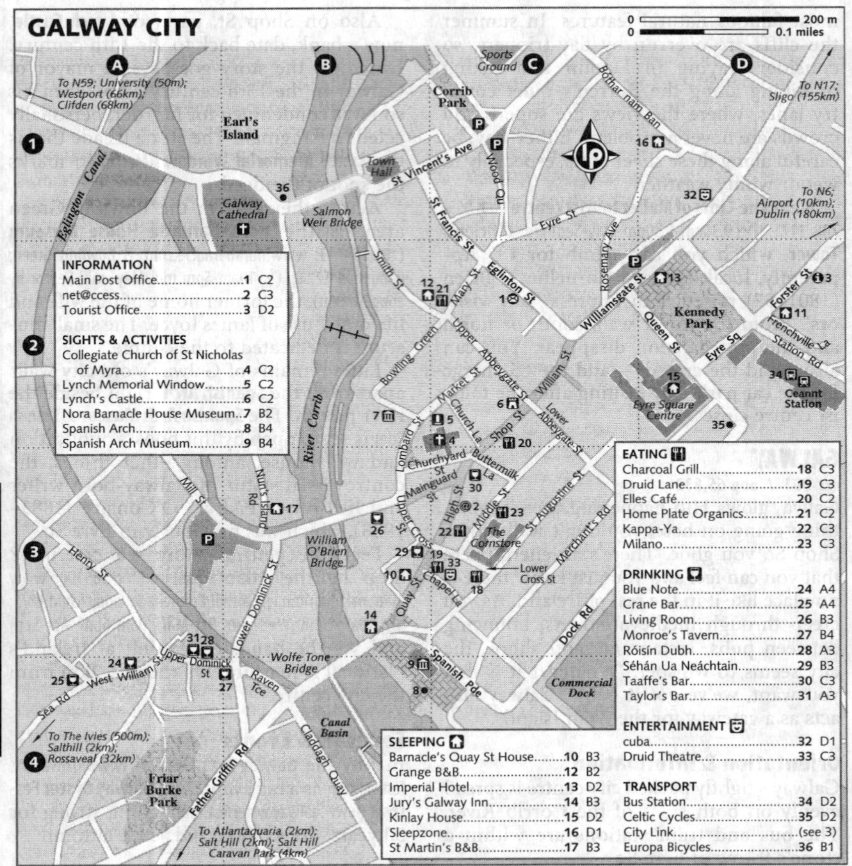

large, wheelchair-accessible Kinlay House is a convenient base half a block off Eyre Sq. It has clean, spacious rooms and a huge eating/lounge area, which can see all-night revelry. You can book discounted bus tours and Aran Islands ferries at reception.

Also recommended:

Galway Hostel (☎ 566959; www.galwaycityhostel.com; Frenchville Lane; dm €18-23, s/d €60/62; 💻) Newly refurnished, the Galway Hostel is a no-frills, but friendly, place to stay, right across from the bus station.

Sleepzone (☎ 566999; www.sleepzone.ie; Bóthar nam Ban, Wood Quay; dm €19.50-25, s/d €50/64; P 💻) This very large, clean hostel is painted in bright pastels and has large kitchen and dining areas, where all the action happens. Make sure to look at the whiteboard to see what's going on in Galway when you visit.

MIDRANGE & TOP END

St Martin's B&B (☎ 568286; 2 Nun's Island Rd; s/d €37.50/75) St Martin's is in an ideal spot, with back-window views overlooking the William O'Brien Bridge and a simple garden on the banks of the Corrib. It's in a well-kept, older townhouse, and the home cooking, comfortable rooms, friendliness and central location put it above everything else.

Grange B&B (☎ 530160; Smith St; s/d €43/65) Nestled nicely above a Mexican food joint and just two minutes' walk from both Shop St and Eyre Sq, Grange's prime location is perfect for anyone who plans on cavorting around Galway.

Jury's Galway Inn (☎ 566444; www.bookajurysinn.com; Quay St; r €112; P) Overlooking the Corrib and Wolfe Tone Bridge, this is a completely modern, full-service hotel. Rooms can accommodate three adults or a family of four at no additional charge. It's also wheelchair accessible.

Imperial Hotel (☎ 563033; www.imperialhotelgalway.ie; Eyre Sq; s/d €90/150; 💻) Sitting right on Eyre Sq, this delightful three-star hotel has everything you might need during your stay, including a bar/restaurant on the premises. It also has incredibly comfortable beds.

Eating

Home Plate Organics (☎ 561475; 13 Mary St; mains €5-10; 🕑 noon-8pm) Home Plate is smart and homy, and serves high-quality meals in heaping quantities. It's the best deal in town, whether you crave roasted meat, a *ciabatta* sandwich or a veggie omelette.

Kappa-Ya (☎ 086-354 3616; 4 Middle St; mains €5-15; 🕑 11am-5pm) A welcome addition to an already fine culinary scene, Kappa-Ya is Galway's first sushi restaurant. The service is as friendly as the food is good.

Milano (☎ 568488; Middle St; mains €8-13; 🕑 noon-10.30pm) This classy place offers a good variety of dishes, including exquisite salads, gourmet pizza and plenty of veggie options.

Druid Lane (☎ 563015; 9 Quay St; mains €14.95-24; 🕑 5-10.30pm, lunch 12.30-3pm Jun-Aug) Druid Lane's unique menu, coupled with its extensive wine list, make chef/owner Camilla Cutler seem like a culinary genius. The tasteful decorations and loquacious staff only add to the enjoyment of the meal.

Also recommended:

Elles Café (☎ 569585; 12 Shop St; snacks €3.50-8; 🕑 8am-6pm) Smart café selling tasty smoothies, sandwiches and fair-trade coffee.

Charcoal Grill (☎ 087-683 8367; Lower Cross St; snacks €1.70-10; 🕑 noon-3am Sun-Thu, noon-4am Fri-Sat) A fantastic late-night Turkish chipper whose creamy garlic sauce you'll taste halfway through the next day.

Drinking & Entertainment

The free *Galway Advertiser* includes listings of what's on in the city. It's available on Thursday at the tourist office and newsstands around town.

LIVE MUSIC

Blue Note (☎ 589116; 3 West William St) Do you like soul music? How about funk or Afrobeat? Rather, do you like music so good, you can't help but move? We thought so. The Blue Note has different DJs playing excellent music nightly. If that weren't enough, it also has an outside heated smoking area, and serves free hot dogs on Tuesday, Wednesday and Sunday.

Róisín Dubh (☎ 586540; www.roisindubh.net; Upper Dominick St) Appearing like a reliable local boozer, Róisín Dubh is better known as *the* place to see new rock and roll talents before they get too big.

Séhán Ua Neáchtain (☎ 568820; 17 Upper Cross St) Known simply as Neáchtains, this dusty old pub has a truly fabulous atmosphere and attracts an eccentric, mixed crowd.

Good spots to hear trad sessions include **Monroe's Tavern** (☎ 583397; Upper Dominick St), which has set dancing on Tuesday, **Taaffe's Bar** (☎ 564066; 19 Shop St), **Taylor's Bar** (☎ 587239; Upper Dominick St) and the **Crane Bar** (☎ 587419; 2 Sea Rd).

NIGHTCLUBS

Living Room (☎ 563804; www.thelivingroom.ie; Bridge St) Hip, cool and funky, if this place could walk, it would swagger. Its 1970s-style wallpaper, couches and low, coloured lighting make it virtually irresistible.

cuba (☎ 565991; www.cuba.ie; Eyre Sq) Exuding Latin swank and attracting exuberant crowds, cuba has three cavernous floors with soulful DJs and live bands, often going simultaneously.

THEATRE

Druid Theatre (☎ 568660; Chapel Lane) The long-established Druid is famed for its experimental works by young Irish playwrights.

Getting There & Around

The **bus station** (☎ 562000) is just behind the Great Southern Hotel, off Eyre Sq, and next to the **Ceannt train station** (☎ 561444). Bus Éireann operates services to Doolin (€13, 1½ hours, seven daily Monday to Saturday in summer, twice on Sunday), Dublin (€14, 3¾ hours, 15 daily), Killarney (€20.50, 4¾ hours, three daily), Limerick, Sligo and beyond.

Private bus companies, generally a bit cheaper than Bus Éireann, also operate from Galway. **Citylink** (☎ 564163; www.citylink.ie) runs 17 buses daily to Dublin airport (€19) via the city centre (€14).

Four or more trains run to and from Dublin (€29, €40.50 on Friday and Sunday,

2¾ hours, six daily). You can connect with other trains at Athlone.

Celtic Cycles (☎ 566606; Queen St), a Raleigh rent-a-bike outlet, hires bikes for €20/80 per day/week. **Europa Bicycles** (☎ 563355), on Earl's Island opposite Galway Cathedral, charges €10/50 per day/week.

ARAN ISLANDS

☎ 099

In recent years the windswept Aran Islands have become one of western Ireland's major attractions. Apart from natural beauty, the Irish-speaking islands have some of the country's oldest Christian and pre-Christian ruins.

On tiny **Inisheer**, the abundance of stone walls is almost absurd, with countless kilometres of them separating every patch of rocky land. Though seemingly inhospitable, the islands were actually settled much earlier than the mainland, since agriculture was easier to pursue here than in the densely forested Ireland of the pre-Christian era.

There are three main islands in the group, all inhabited year-round. Most visitors head for long and narrow (14.5km by a maximum 4km) **Inishmór** (or Inishmore). The land slopes up from the relatively sheltered northern shores of the island and plummets on the southern side into the raging Atlantic. **Inishmaan** and **Inisheer** are much smaller and receive far fewer visitors.

The islands can get crowded at holiday times (St Patrick's Day, Easter) and in July and August, when accommodation is at a premium and advance reservations are advised.

Orientation & Information

The **tourist office** (☎ 61263; ⌚ 10am-5pm Easter-1 Jun & Oct, 10am-6pm Jun & Sep, 10am-7pm Jul & Aug, 11am-5pm Mon-Thu, 10am-5pm Fri-Sun Nov-Easter) operates year-round on the waterfront at Kilronan, the arrival point and major village of Inishmór. You can leave your luggage and change money here. Around the corner is Spar Supermarket, which has an ATM, and about 150m to the north is a small post office. The Ionad Árann heritage centre has Internet access.

JM Synge's *The Aran Islands* is the classic account of life on the islands and is readily available in paperback. A much less accessible (but more recent) tribute to the islands is map-maker Tim Robinson's *Stones of Aran*. For detailed exploration, pick up a copy of his *The Aran Islands: A Map and Guide*.

Getting There & Away

AIR

If time is important or if seasickness is a concern, you could fly to the islands and back with **Aer Arann** (☎ 091-593034; www.aerarannislands.ie) for €45. Flights operate to all three islands at least seven times daily (less in the low season) and take less than 10 minutes. The mainland departure point is Connemara regional airport at Minna, near Inverin, 38km west of Galway. A connecting bus from outside the Galway tourist office costs €3 one-way.

BOAT

All three islands are served year-round by **Island Ferries** (☎ 091-568903; www.aranislandferries.com); the trip takes around 40 minutes (adult/child €25/13 return). Unfortunately the boat leaves from Rossaveal, 37km west of Galway. It's an extra €6 to catch an Island Ferries bus from outside the tourist office in Galway. Buses leave 1½ hours before ferry departure times and are scheduled to meet arriving ferries. If you have a car, you can go straight to Rossaveal and leave it in the car park there for free.

InisMór Ferries (☎ 091-566535; www.queenofaran2.com), billed as the islanders' ferry company, runs a nearly identical operation.

Another option is to leave from Doolin in County Clare. **Doolin Ferries** (☎ 065-707 4455, 091-567676; www.doolinferries.com) runs to Inishmór (55 minutes) and Inisheer (40 minutes) for €35 from Doolin.

Inter-island services are very limited in winter.

Getting Around

Inisheer and Inishmaan are small enough to explore on foot, but on larger Inishmór bikes are definitely the way to go. **Aran Cycle Hire** (☎ 61132), just up from Kilronan's pier, is one of many bike shops that hire bikes for €10 per day. The islands are tough on bikes, so check your cruiser carefully before hiring.

Plenty of small operators offer island bus tours for around €10.

IRELAND

Inishmór

The 'Big Island' has four impressive stone forts thought to be 2000 years old. Halfway down the island and about 8km west of Kilronan, semicircular **Dún Aengus** (☎ 61008; adult/child €2.10/1.10; ⌚ 10am-6pm Mar-Oct, 10am-4pm Nov-Feb), perched on the edge of the sheer cliffs, is the best known of the four. It's an amazing place, but take great care near the cliff edge as there are no guard rails.

About 1.5km north is **Dún Eoghanachta**, while halfway back to Kilronan is **Dún Eochla**; both are smaller, perfectly circular ring forts. Directly south of Kilronan and dramatically perched on a promontory is **Dún Dúchathair**, surrounded on three sides by cliffs.

Ionad Árann (☎ 61355; www.visitaranislands.com; adult/child €3.50/2, incl film €5.50/4; ⌚ 10am-7pm Jun-Aug, 10am-5pm Apr-May & Sep-Oct), just off the main road leading out of Kilronan, introduces the geology, wildlife, history and culture of the islands. Robert Flaherty's 1934 film *The Man of Aran* is shown five times daily.

SLEEPING & EATING

An Aharla (☎ 61305; dm/d €12/34) In a laid-back former farmhouse, positioned in a grove of trees (a rarity on these islands), An Aharla has three four-bed dorms and lots of good vibes.

Mainistir House (☎ 61169; www.mainistirhousearan.com; dm/s/d €15/20/35; 💻) This colourful 60-bed hostel is in a scenic spot on the main road north of Kilronan. The shuttle from the pier costs €2.50. Book ahead for the great-value organic, largely vegetarian buffet dinners (€15; served 8pm to closing in summer, from 7pm in winter).

Lios Aengus (☎ 61030; snacks €5-8; ⌚ 9.30am-5pm) A simple coffee shop with OK soups and sandwiches.

Man of Aran Cottage (☎ 61301; lunch from €6, set dinner €35; ⌚ 11.30am-7.30pm Mar-Oct) Serves fresh fish and organic veggies and herbs from the owners' garden. Bookings are essential.

Inishmaan

The least visited of the three islands is Inishmaan (Inis Meáin, or 'Middle Island'). High stone walls border its fields, and it's a delight to wander the lanes, taking in some of the tranquillity. The main archaeological site is **Dún Chonchúir**, a massive oval-shaped stone fort built on a high point and offering views of the island.

There are no hostels on Inishmaan, but B&Bs are relatively cheap, at about €35 per person.

Inisheer

The smallest island, only 8km off the coast from Doolin, is Inisheer (Inis Oírr, or 'Eastern Island'). The 15th-century **O'Brien Castle** (Caislea'n Uí Bhriain) overlooks the beach and harbour.

Brú Radharc Na Mara (☎ 75024; maire.serraigh@oceanfree.net; dm/d €15/40; ⌚ Mar-Oct) is an IHH hostel near the pier with ocean views. Also near the pier, **Ard Mhuire B&B** (☎ 75005; s/d €30/60) has home-baked goods, a lovely garden and a comfy sitting room.

CONNEMARA

☎ 095

Between placid, mirror-like lakes, pale mountains, lonely valleys and more than occasional rainbows, the northwestern corner of Galway, called the Connemara, is so gorgeous that it hurts your brain. Connemara's isolation has allowed Irish to thrive and the language is widely spoken here; the lack of English signposting can be confusing at times.

The most scenic routes through Connemara are Oughterard–Recess (via the N59), Recess–Kylemore Abbey (via the R344) and the Leenane–Louisburgh route (via the R335). From Galway, **Lally Tours** (☎ 091-562905; www.lallytours.com) and **O'Neachtain Tours** (☎ 091-553188; www.oneachtaintours.com) run daylong bus trips through Connemara for roughly €25.

Sights & Activities

Aughnanure Castle (☎ 091-552214; adult/child €2.75/1.25; ⌚ 9.30am-6pm 31 Mar-30 Sep), 3km east of Oughterard, is a 16th-century tower house overlooking Lough Corrib.

Just west of **Recess** (Straith Salach) on the N59, the turn north at the R334 takes you through the stunning Lough Inagh Valley. At the end of the R334 is the equally scenic **Kylemore Abbey** (☎ 41146; www.kylemoreabbey.com; adult/child €11/free; ⌚ 9.30am-5.30pm mid-Mar–Nov, 10.30am-4.30pm Nov–mid-Mar) and its adjacent lake. The neo-Gothic abbey is run by nuns.

From Kylemore, take the N59 east to Leenane (An Líonán), then detour north on the R335 to Louisburgh and onwards to Westport (below); or travel 17km southwest along the N59 to **Clifden** (An Clochán), Connemara's largest town. Like many small west Irish towns, Clifden has recently seen amazing growth, and now has loads of art galleries among its pubs and restaurants. The **Connemara Walking Centre** (☎ 1850 266 636; www.walkingireland.com; Island House, Market St) runs guided walking trips from €20.

Sleeping

Ben Lettery Hostel (☎ 51136; www.anoige.ie; Ballinafad; dm €12-15.50; Mar-Nov; P) Sitting in the heart of Connemara's wilderness, this excellent and super-friendly An Óige hostel is on the N59 halfway between Recess and Clifden.

Clifden Town Hostel (☎ 21076; Market St, Clifden; dm/d €16/36; P) The friendly Clifden Town Hostel has a lovely view of the river, two clean kitchens and is in the centre of town.

Canrawer House Hostel (☎ 091-552 388; www.oughterardhostel.com; Oughterard; dm/d €17/38; Feb-Oct; P) This attractive place at the Clifden end of town is just over 1km down a signposted turning. It offers fishing trips for those who stay.

Central Hotel (☎ 21430; centralhotelclifden@hotmail.com; Main St, Clifden; s/d €30/60) This homy hotel/B&B is obviously loved and well taken care of, since each room is individually decorated. The pub downstairs has music nightly.

Getting There & Away

Galway–Westport buses stop in Clifden, as well as Oughterard, Maam Cross and Recess; a few lines also stop in Cong and Leenane. There are four express buses daily between Clifden and Galway (two on Sunday).

WESTPORT

☎ 098 / pop 5314

The beautiful town of Westport (Cathair na Mairt) is a popular stop on the way to/from Sligo or Donegal. It has a tree-lined mall running along the Carrowbeg River, handsome Georgian buildings and a few good pubs.

North over the Carrowbeg is a small **tourist office** (☎ 25711; www.irelandwest.ie; James St; 9am-6pm Jul-Aug, 9am-5.45pm Mon-Sat May-Jun & Sep, 9am-5.45pm Mon-Fri, 10am-1pm Sat Oct-Apr).

Sights

Westport's major attraction, **Croagh Patrick**, 7km west of the town, is the hill from which St Patrick performed his snake expulsion (Ireland has been serpent-free ever since). Climbing the 765m peak is a ritual for thousands of pilgrims on the last Sunday of July.

Sleeping

Old Mill Hostel (☎ 27045; www.oldmillhostel.com; dm €16.50-17.50, d €22.50) In a courtyard off James St sits the 18th-century former brewery that now houses the Old Mill Hostel. The friendly staff, relaxed atmosphere and comfortable beds make it a lovely stay.

St Anthony's (☎ 28887; www.st-anthonys.com; Distillery Rd; s €50, d €75-80; P) Simplicity is the theme at this cosy B&B, where breakfast is delicious and the hosts are gracious. All six rooms have a classic feel, but only two have Jacuzzis.

Olde Railway Hotel (☎ 25166; www.anu.ie/railwayhotel; The Mall; s/d from €100/180; P) Chock-full of various antiques and bric-a-brac, the Olde Railway doesn't seem much changed since English novelist William Thackeray stayed here in 1834.

Getting There & Away

Buses depart from Mill St for just about everywhere, including Cork (€24, six hours, two daily), Dublin (€17, four hours, six daily), Galway (€14.50, two hours, six daily) and Sligo (€15.50, two hours, two daily), where there are connections to Belfast (€27.50). Bus Éireann has a counter at the tourist office. The **train station** (☎ 25253; Altamount St) is southeast of the town centre. Rail connections to Dublin (€28, €44 on Friday and Sunday, 3½ hours) go via Athlone.

THE NORTHWEST

Way under the tourism radar, Ireland's northwest is a veritable paradise for anyone seeking to get off the beaten path. WB Yeats' poetry still echoes through the sleepy towns and prehistoric sites of rustic County Sligo, while the wild and remote beaches of County Donegal reign as some of the best surf spots in Europe. It's only a matter of time before the crowds descend on the northwest, but for now, it's our little secret.

SLIGO

☎ 071 / pop 18,473

William Butler Yeats (1865–1939) was born in Dublin and educated in London, but his poetry is infused with the landscapes, history and folklore of his mother's native Sligo (Sligeach). He returned many times, and reminders of his presence in this sweet, sleepy town are plentiful.

The **North West Regional Tourism office** (☎ 916 1201; www.irelandnorthwest.ie; Temple St; 9am-5pm Mon-Sat Jun-Aug, 9am-5pm Mon-Fri Sep-May) is just south of the town centre. The **main post office** (Wine St) is east of the train and bus station. **Café Online** (☎ 914 4892; Stephen St; per hr €3; 10am-11pm Mon-Sat, noon-1pm Sun), across from the library, has Internet access.

Sligo's two major attractions are outside town. **Carrowmore**, 5km to the southwest, is the site of a **megalithic cemetery** (☎ 916 1534; carrowmoretomb@duchas.ie; adult/child €2/1; 10am-6pm Easter-Oct), with more than 60 stone rings, passage tombs and other Stone Age remains. It's one of the largest Stone Age necropolises in Europe.

Don't miss the hilltop cairn-grave **Knocknarea**, a few kilometres northwest of Carrowmore. About 1000 years younger than Carrowmore, it's said to be the grave of the legendary Maeve, 1st century AD Queen of Connaught. Several trails lead to the 328m summit, which commands unrivalled views over the surrounding country and shore.

The shabby but convenient IHH **White House Hostel** (☎ 914 5160; Markievicz Rd; dm €14; P) is just north of the town centre. The excellent **Eden Hill Holiday Hostel** (☎ 914 3204; http://homepage.eircom.net/~edenhill; Perse Rd; dm €13-15, d €36-40; P) is about 1.5km from the train station and is the best hostel in Sligo. Pick-up can be arranged. **Clarence Hotel** (☎ 914 2211; fax 914 5823; Wine St; s/d €65/115; P) is one of Sligo's best, even though the rooms are decorated in standard business-hotel style.

Café Bar Deli (☎ 914 0100; 15-16 Rear Stephen St; mains €6.50-15; 6-10pm Wed-Sun), a popular pasta-and-pizza place, is upstairs from the equally popular music venue **Left Bank** (www.leftbank.ie; mains €4-10; food served noon-5pm), which serves food from upstairs or outside on the river if the weather agrees. **Bistro Bianconi** (☎ 914 1744; 44 O'Connell St; mains €9-30; noon-2.30pm & 5.30-11.30pm Mon-Sat) serves pizza from its wood-fired oven, as well as fresh pasta and steak dishes.

Getting There & Around

Flights to Dublin run from **Sligo airport** (☎ 916 8280). **Bus Éireann** (☎ 916 0066) has six services daily to/from Dublin (€17, four hours). The Galway–Sligo–Donegal–Derry service runs five times daily; it's €14 and 2½ hours to Galway, and €16.50 and 2½ hours to Derry. Buses operate from below the **train station** (☎ 916 9888), which is just west of the town centre along Lord Edward St. Trains to Dublin (€25, three hours, three daily) pass by Boyle, Carrick-on-Shannon and Mullingar.

DONEGAL

Bundoran

☎ 071 / pop 1678

Heeding the siren's call of some of Europe's most perfect waves, surfers from all over the world have made Bundoran (Bun Dobhráin) a bona fide beach town. If you don't plan on surfing though, bring a pocket full of change because Bundoran's streets are lined with kitschy casinos, tacky rides and enough crappy arcades to make Coney Island blush.

The seasonal **tourist office** (☎ 984 1350; bundoran@irelandnorthwest.ie; Main St; 10am-5pm Mon-Sat Jun-Aug, 11am-3pm Sat & Sun Sep-May) is opposite the Holyrood Hotel. The post office is a further 120m south.

If outdoor activity is what you crave, the **Donegal Adventure Centre** (☎ 984 2418; www.donegal-holidays.com; Bay View Ave) can sort you out with kayaking, ropes courses and surf lessons. Surf lessons cost €35/25 for an adult/child, while kayak lessons cost €40. Those interested in riding pretty ponies should contact **Donegal Equestrian Holidays** (☎ 984 1288; www.donegalequestrianholidays.com; Bayview Ave); you can trot along trails by day, and stay at either its hostel or four-star accommodation by night.

Once the holiday home of Viscount Enniskillen, the nearly 300-year-old building housing the **Homefield Hostel** (☎ 984 1288; homefieldhouse@eircom.net; Bayview Ave; dm/d €20/40; P) now hosts world travellers year-round. A lovely B&B option is the **Setanta House** (☎ 984 1599; www.setantahouse.com; Drumacrin Rd; s/d €37/60; P), whose location 450m from the main street makes it an easy amble after a day of surfing or gambling.

Main St has no shortage of greasy diners and pubs, but for a better bite, venture into **La Sabbia Restaurant** (☎ 984 2253; Homefield Hostel,

Bayview Ave; mains €10-20) for impeccable Italian food, or the **Central Bar** (☎ 984 2722; Grand Central Hotel, Main St; mains €7-14) for sensational pub grub.

Bus Éireann (☎ 074-912 1309) buses stop on Main St. There are direct daily services to Sligo (€8.20, 45 minutes), Galway (€18, 2¼ hours), Donegal (€6.80, 40 minutes) and more. **Ulsterbus/Translink** (☎ 028-9066 6630; www.ulsterbus.co.uk) has one daily service Monday to Friday to Belfast via Enniskillen. **Feda O'Donnell** (☎ 074-954 8114) buses stop two to three times daily, en route to Galway, at the Holyrood Hotel.

Donegal Town

☎ 074 / pop 2453

Donegal Town (Dún na nGall) is not the major centre in County Donegal, but it's pleasant and well worth a visit.

The triangular Diamond is the centre of Donegal; a few steps south along the Eske River is the **tourist office** (☎ 972 1148; www.irelandnorthwest.ie; Quay St; 🕒 9am-5pm Mon-Sat Jun-Aug, 9am-5pm Mon-Fri Sep-May).

Donegal Castle (☎ 972 2405; donegalcastle@duchas.ie; adult/child €3.50/1.25; 🕒 10am-6pm mid-Mar–Oct, 9.30am-4.30pm Fri-Sun Nov-Dec), on a rocky outcrop over the Eske River, stands in ruins but is impressive all the same. About 2.4km out of town is the unique **Donegal Craft Village** (☎ 972 2225; donegalcraftvillage@eircom.net; Ballyshannon Rd; 🕒 9am-6pm Mon-Sat, 11am-6pm Sun), where you can purchase everything from metalwork to hand-blown glass, all made on the premises.

The comfortable IHH/IHO **Donegal Town Independent Hostel** (☎ 972 2805; www.donegalhostel.com; dm/d €13/31; Ⓟ) is 1km northwest of town on the Killybegs road (N56). The three-star **Abbey Hotel** (☎ 972 1014; www.whites-hotelsireland.com; the Diamond; s/d €90/150) doesn't have a whole lot of personality, but does sit right in the centre of town.

Busy **Blueberry Tearoom** (☎ 972 2933; the Diamond; mains €6.50-9; 🕒 9am-7pm) has substantial sandwiches, excellent baked goods, and home-made jams and marmalades. The **Famous Donegal Chipper** (☎ 972 1428; Upper Main St; fish & chips from €7; 🕒 12.30-11pm Mon-Tue, 12.30-11.30pm Thu-Sun) isn't kidding: it's well known throughout the area for its fabulous fish and chips.

Bus Éireann (☎ 972 1101) goes to Derry (€12.50, 1½ hours, seven daily), Enniskillen (€9.70, 1¼ hours, six daily), Sligo (€12, one hour, five daily), Galway (€18, four hours, five daily) and Dublin (€17.50, 4¼ hours, five daily). The bus stop is on the Diamond, outside the Abbey Hotel.

Around County Donegal

The awe-inspiring cliffs at **Slieve League**, dropping 300m straight into the Atlantic Ocean, are absolutely recommended. To drive to the cliff edge, take the Killybegs–Glencolumbcille road (R263) and, at Carrick, take the turn-off signposted 'Bunglas'. Continue beyond the narrow track signposted for Slieve League (this trail is good for hikers) to the one signposted for Bunglas. Starting from Teelin, experienced walkers can spend a day walking via Bunglas and the somewhat terrifying One Man's Path to Malinbeg, near Glencolumbcille.

IHH's **Derrylahan Hostel** (☎ 973 8079; derrylahan@eircom.net; camp site per person €6, dm/s/d €12/16/36; Ⓟ), on a working farm 2km southeast of Carrick and 3km northwest of Kilcar, is a convenient base for walkers. Call for free pick-up from Kilcar or Carrick.

Daily Bus Éireann coaches (three daily in summer) stop in Kilcar and Carrick on the Donegal–Glencolumbcille route.

NORTHERN IRELAND

☎ 028 / pop 1.7 million

When you cross from the Republic into Northern Ireland you immediately notice two big differences; the street signs are in miles and the roads are well maintained. Soon enough though, you find that these aren't the only differences; the accent here is distinctly different, the currency is pounds sterling (making everything more expensive) and you remark once more about how nicely maintained the roads are. Yes, you are now in the UK.

From the looming city walls of Derry to the breathtaking scenery along the Causeway Coast to the architecture in Queen Victoria's pet city of Belfast, Northern Ireland has always had a bevy of things to attract visitors. Unfortunately, decades of guerrilla warfare deterred most tourists and it wasn't until within the past five or 10 years that they finally started to return.

Today Northern Ireland seems rejuvenated. Belfast is a happening place with a stellar nightlife and an excellent culinary scene, while Derry appears to be coming into its own as a cool, artistic city. The stunning Causeway Coast and its namesake, the geologically anomalistic Giant's Causeway, get more and more visitors each year, while lesser-known towns like Enniskillen are suddenly finding that they have a decent tourist trade, too.

That's not to say that the scars of the Troubles have healed, but at least people are getting along, which at this point in time is all that anyone can ask for.

BELFAST

pop 277,390

It's a new era in Belfast. Optimism floats through this marvellous Victorian city like a virus you can't help but catch; the peace process has finally bore its fruit and the war is officially over.

Each time you go out to the university pubs on Botanic Ave, the posh shops along Donegall Sq or the fine restaurants on Great Victoria St, you can feel the exuberance of a city on the rise, literally. Just look east towards the river and you can see all the new structures, built or being built, that suggest a cultural reawakening of a city long in slumber.

That being said, Belfast's harsh past isn't one that can ever be forgotten; reminders like the 'Peace Wall' that divides the city are everywhere. But maybe it's these reminders of the past that will keep the people of the present pushing towards a very bright future.

Orientation

The city centre is compact, with the imposing City Hall in Donegall Sq as the central landmark. Belfast's principal shopping district is north of the square. North of that, around Donegall St and St Anne's Cathedral, is the bohemian Cathedral Quarter.

South of the square lies the Golden Mile, a restaurant- and pub-filled stretch of Dublin Rd, Shaftesbury Sq, Bradbury Pl and Botanic Ave. To the east, most of Belfast's smart new hotel, leisure and arts developments line the banks of the Lagan. East of the river rise the huge yellow cranes of the Harland & Wolff shipyards.

Information

Belfast Welcome Centre (☎ 9023 9026; www.gotobelfast.com; 47 Donegall Pl; 🕑 9am-7pm Mon-Sat, 11am-4pm Sun Jun-Sep, 9am-5pm Mon-Sat, 11am-4pm Sun Oct-May) Efficient and extremely helpful.

Fáilte Ireland (☎ 9026 5500; www.ireland.ie; 53 Castle St; 🕑 9am-5pm Mon-Fri year-round, 9am-12.30pm Sat Jun-Aug) Has information on the Irish Republic.

Hostelling International Northern Ireland (HINI; ☎ 9032 4733; www.hini.org.uk; 22-32 Donegall Rd) At the Belfast International Youth Hostel.

Internet Café (☎ 9043 4058; per hr £3; 🕑 9am-7pm Mon-Sat, 11am-4pm Sun Jun-Sep, 9am-5pm Mon-Sat, 11am-4pm Sun Oct-May) Send email and have a coffee; next to the Belfast Welcome Centre.

Main Post Office (Castle Pl) There is also a smaller branch at the top end of Botanic Ave by Shaftesbury Sq, and a branch on University Rd.

Sights

CITY CENTRE

The wheelchair-accessible Renaissance-style **City Hall** (☎ 9027 0456; Donegall Sq; admission free; 🕑 guided tours 11am, 2pm & 3pm Mon-Fri & 2.30pm Sat Jun-Sep, 11am & 2.30pm Mon-Fri & 2.30pm Sat Oct-May), completed in 1906, is a testament to the city's Industrial Revolution success. At the northeastern corner is a statue of Sir Edward Harland – the Yorkshire-born engineer who founded Belfast's Harland & Wolff shipyards – whose famous yellow twin cranes **Samson and Goliath** tower above the city. The yards' most famous construction was the *Titanic*, the 'unsinkable' ship that sank in 1912. A memorial to the disaster stands on the eastern side of City Hall.

City Hall is fronted by an especially dour statue of Queen Victoria. To the northeast – between High St and Queen's Sq – the queen's consort, Prince Albert, also makes his Belfast appearance at the slightly leaning **Albert Memorial Clocktower** (1867).

Across from the Europa Hotel, the famed **Crown Liquor Saloon** (☎ 9027 9901; 46 Great Victoria St; 🕑 11.30am-11pm Mon-Sat, 12.30-10pm Sun) was built by Patrick Flanagan in 1885 and displays Victorian architecture at its most extravagant. The snugs are equipped with bells that once connected to a board behind the bar, enabling customers to order drinks without leaving their seats. The Crown was lucky to survive a 1993 bomb that devastated the (now fully restored) **Grand Opera House** (☎ 9024 1919; www.goh.co.uk; Great Victoria St) across the road.

MUSEUMS & GARDENS

Belfast's biggest tourist attraction, the **Ulster Folk & Transport Museums** (☎ 9042 8428; www.magni.org.uk; adult/child 1 museum £5/3, both museums £6.50/3.50; 10am-5pm Mon-Fri, 10am-6pm Sat, 11am-6pm Sun Mar-Jun, 10am-6pm Mon-Sat, 11am-6pm Sun Jul-Sep, 10am-4pm Mon-Fri, 10am-5pm Sat, 11am-5pm Sun Oct-Feb), one of Northern Ireland's finest museums, is 11km northeast of the city centre beside the Bangor road (A2) near Holywood. The 30 buildings on the 60-hectare site range from urban terrace homes to thatched-roof farm cottages. A bridge crosses the A2 to the Transport Museum, a sort of automotive zoo, which contains various Ulster-related vehicles, including a prototype of the vertical take-off and landing (VTOL) aircraft. From Belfast take Ulsterbus 1 or any Bangor-bound train that stops at Cultra station.

The excellent **Ulster Museum** (☎ 9038 3000; www.magni.org.uk), in the **Botanic Gardens** (☎ 9032 4902; admission free; 8am-sunset) near the university, is being renovated and will reopen in 2008. The gardens themselves are well worth a wander, though.

W5 (☎ 9046 7700; www.w5online.co.uk; 2 Queen's Quay; adult/child/concession £6/4/4.50; 10am-5pm Mon-Thu, 10am-6pm Fri & Sat, noon-6pm Sun Sep-Jun, 10am-6pm Mon-Sat, noon-6pm Sun Jul-Aug), aka the whowhatwherewhenwhy, is an interactive science centre with fun exhibits, such as a laser harp, a lie detector and a wind tunnel. The centre is wheelchair accessible.

FALLS & SHANKILL RDS

The Catholic Falls Rd and the Protestant Shankill Rd have been battlefronts since the 1970s. Even so, these areas are quite safe and worth venturing into, if only to see the large **murals** expressing local political and religious passions. King Billy riding to victory in 1690 on his white steed and hooded IRA gunmen are two of the more memorable images.

If you don't fancy an organised tour (see right), the best way to visit the sectarian zones of Falls and Shankill Rds is by what is known locally as the 'people's taxi'. These black former London cabs run a buslike service up and down their respective roads from terminuses in the city. Shankill Rd taxis go from North St, and Falls Rd taxis from Castle St. The Falls Rd taxis occupy the first line at the Castle St taxi park, with signs in Gaelic. Taxis depart when full, dropping off and picking up passengers as they go; fares on both services cost £1 per person.

Tours

Both **Black Taxi Tours** (☎ 9064 2264; www.belfasttours.com) and **Original Belfast Black Taxi Tours** (☎ 0800-032 2003) offer organised 'people taxi' tours. An even-sided account of the Troubles is given in a refreshingly down-to-earth way. Running daily, prices are £8 per person based on a group of four sharing, and pick-up can be arranged.

Mini Coach (☎ 9031 5333; www.minicoachni.co.uk; 22 Donegall Rd) conducts two-hour city tours (£8 per person) that include Falls and Shankill Rds, St Anne's Cathedral and Harland & Wolff shipyards. Tours leave at 10.30am daily and 12.30pm Monday to Friday from the Belfast International Youth Hostel (p694).

There are a number of walking tours available, including the two-hour **Bailey's Historical Pub Tour** (☎ 9268 3665). It costs £6, and begins at Flanagan's (above the Crown Liquor Saloon on Great Victoria St) on Thursday at 7pm and Saturday at 4pm.

The Belfast Welcome Centre also hands out maps for the **Titanic Trail** and **In the Footsteps of C.S. Lewis**, both of which are self-guided walking tours. The doomed ship *Titanic* and famed author CS Lewis are both products of Belfast.

Festivals & Events

Belfast Film Festival (☎ 9032 5913; www.belfastfilmfestival.org) This festival shows a wonderful variety of independent and classic films at the end of March each year.

Between the Lines (www.crescentarts.org) This literary festival takes place each March at the Crescent Arts Centre.

Cathedral Quarter Arts Festival (☎ 9023 2403; www.cqaf.com) This fantastic festival, in early May, attracts pioneering writers, comedians, musicians and artists, and theatre productions.

City Dance (www.crecentarts.org) This dance festival occurs each June at the Crescent Arts Centre.

Festival at Queen's (☎ 9066 7687; www.belfastfestival.com) For three weeks in late October and early November, Belfast hosts this arts festival, the second largest in the UK, in and around Queen's University.

Sleeping

BUDGET

Linen House (Paddy's Backpackers; ☎ 9058 6400; www.belfasthostel.com; 18-20 Kent St; dm £6.50-10, tw £24; P ⊠ 💻) In a former linen factory in the

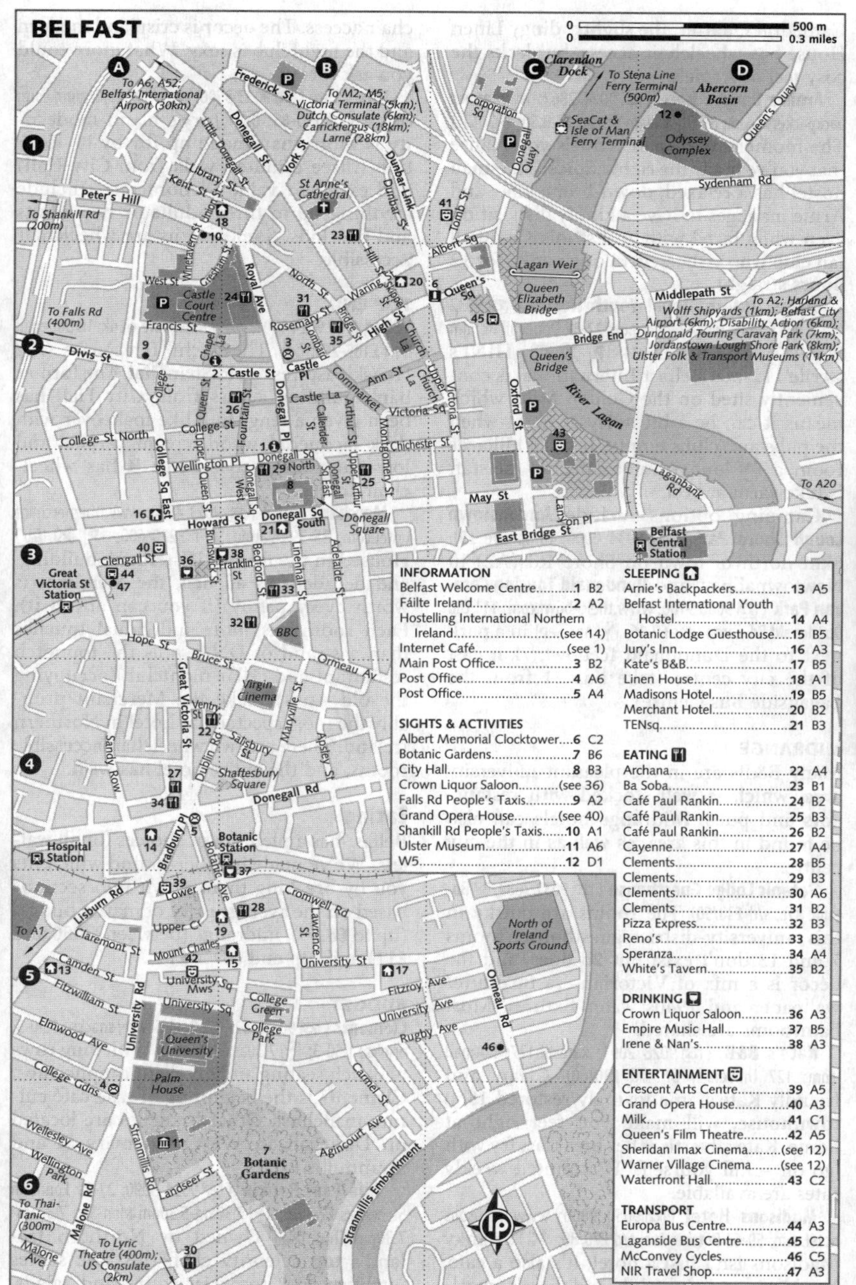
BELFAST
0 500 m
0 0.3 miles
A
B
C
D
1
2
3
4
5
6
To A6; A52; Belfast International Airport (30km)
To M2; M5; Victoria Terminal (5km); Dutch Consulate (6km); Carrickfergus (18km); Larne (28km)
To Stena Line Ferry Terminal (500m)
Clarendon Dock
Abercorn Basin
Corporation Sq
SeaCat & Isle of Man Ferry Terminal
Odyssey Complex
Queen's Quay
Donegall Quay
Sydenham Rd
Frederick St
Donegall St
Little Donegall St
York St
Dunbar Link
Dunbar St
Tomb St
Library St
Kent St
Peter's Hill
To Shankill Rd (200m)
Union St
St Anne's Cathedral
Albert Sq
Lagan Weir
Queen Elizabeth Bridge
Middlepath St
To A2; Harland & Wolff Shipyards (1km); Belfast City Airport (6km); Disability Action (6km); Dundonald Touring Caravan Park (7km); Jordanstown Lough Shore Park (8km); Ulster Folk & Transport Museums (11km)
Bridge End
Queen's Bridge
River Lagan
Winetavern St
Gresham St
West St
Castle Court Centre
Royal Ave
North St
Hill St
Waring St
Skipper St
Queen's Sq
To Falls Rd (400m)
Francis St
Rosemary St
Lombard St
Bridge St
High St
Church La
Divis St
Chapel La
Castle St
Castle Pl
Ann St
Upper Church La
Victoria St
Oxford St
College Ct
Queen St
Fountain St
Donegall Pl
Castle La
Callender St
Arthur St
Cornmarket
Victoria Sq
Montgomery St
Chichester St
College St
College St North
Upper Queen St
Wellington Pl
Donegall Sq North
Donegall Sq West
Donegall Sq East
Upper Arthur St
College Sq East
Howard St
Donegall Sq South
Donegall Square
May St
Lanyon Pl
East Bridge St
Laganbank Rd
To A20
Belfast Central Station
Glengall St
Great Victoria St Station
Brunswick St
Franklin St
Bedford St
Linenhall St
Adelaide St
BBC
Hope St
Bruce St
Ormeau Av
Virgin Cinema
Great Victoria St
Ventry St
Maryville St
Salisbury St
Apsley St
Sandy Row
Dublin Rd
Shaftesbury Square
Donegall Rd
Bradbury Pl
Botanic Station
Hospital Station
Lower Cr
Botanic Ave
Cromwell Rd
Lisburn Rd
Upper Cr
Lawrence St
North of Ireland Sports Ground
To A1
Claremont St
Mount Charles
Camden St
University Sq Mws
University St
Fitzroy Ave
Ormeau Rd
Fitzwilliam St
University Rd
University Sq
College Green
University Ave
Elmwood Ave
Queen's University
College Park
Rugby Ave
College Gdns
Palm House
Carmel St
Wellesley Ave
Stranmillis Rd
Agincourt Ave
Wellington Park
Botanic Gardens
Landseer St
Stranmillis Embankment
To Thai-Tanic (300m)
Malone Rd
To Lyric Theatre (400m); US Consulate (2km)
Malone Ave
INFORMATION
Belfast Welcome Centre....1 B2
Fáilte Ireland....2 A2
Hostelling International Northern Ireland....(see 14)
Internet Café....(see 1)
Main Post Office....3 B2
Post Office....4 A6
Post Office....5 A4
SIGHTS & ACTIVITIES
Albert Memorial Clocktower....6 C2
Botanic Gardens....7 B6
City Hall....8 B3
Crown Liquor Saloon....(see 36)
Falls Rd People's Taxis....9 A2
Grand Opera House....(see 40)
Shankill Rd People's Taxis....10 A1
Ulster Museum....11 A6
W5....12 D1
SLEEPING
Arnie's Backpackers....13 A5
Belfast International Youth Hostel....14 A4
Botanic Lodge Guesthouse....15 B5
Jury's Inn....16 A3
Kate's B&B....17 B5
Linen House....18 A1
Madisons Hotel....19 B5
Merchant Hotel....20 B2
TENsq....21 B3
EATING
Archana....22 A4
Ba Soba....23 B1
Café Paul Rankin....24 B2
Café Paul Rankin....25 B3
Café Paul Rankin....26 B2
Cayenne....27 A4
Clements....28 B5
Clements....29 B3
Clements....30 A6
Clements....31 B2
Pizza Express....32 B3
Reno's....33 B3
Speranza....34 A4
White's Tavern....35 B2
DRINKING
Crown Liquor Saloon....36 A3
Empire Music Hall....37 B5
Irene & Nan's....38 A3
ENTERTAINMENT
Crescent Arts Centre....39 A5
Grand Opera House....40 A3
Milk....41 C1
Queen's Film Theatre....42 A5
Sheridan Imax Cinema....(see 12)
Warner Village Cinema....(see 12)
Waterfront Hall....43 C2
TRANSPORT
Europa Bus Centre....44 A3
Laganside Bus Centre....45 C2
McConvey Cycles....46 C5
NIR Travel Shop....47 A3

Cathedral Quarter, the slightly dingy Linen House has wheelchair access, but lacks the cosy feel of Arnie's.

Arnie's Backpackers (☎ 9024 2867; www.arniesbackpackers.co.uk; 63 Fitzwilliam St; dm £7-9.50; ⊠ 💻) The moment you enter Arnie's you realise that you've made the right choice. The small hostel has a relaxed, down-home vibe, and Arnie manages to have a kindly disposition even when faced with an Estonian football fan club who've been drinking vodka for 12 hours straight.

Belfast International Youth Hostel (☎ 9032 4733, 9031 5435; www.hini.org.uk; 22-32 Donegall Rd; dm £9.50-12.75, s £18-24, d £26-34; Ⓟ ⊠ 💻) HINI's sterile 112-bed Belfast International is conveniently sited on the Golden Mile, which means it can be a bit noisy at night when the pubs and clubs empty. It has a billiards room, a TV lounge and a café, but the staff is lukewarm at best.

Camping options include **Jordanstown Lough Shore Park** (☎ 9034 0000; camp site £9), 8km north of town on Shore Rd (A2) in Newtownabbey, and **Dundonald Touring Caravan Park** (☎ 9080 9100; www.theicebowl.com; 111 Old Dundonald Rd; camp sites £9-16; 🕑 Apr-Sep) in a park next to the Dundonald Icebowl, 7km east of the city centre (take bus 21 from the Laganside Bus Centre).

MIDRANGE

Many B&Bs are in the pleasant university area, which is well stocked with restaurants and pubs. Midrange hotels can also be found in this area, as well as in the city centre.

Botanic Lodge Guesthouse (☎ 9032 7682; 87 Botanic Ave; s/d £30/50) The rooms are quirky in this university-district guesthouse; rooms 7 and 13 don't exist but 2b does, and the décor is a mix of Victorian-era furniture/wallpaper and 1940s water fixtures. Most bathrooms are shared.

Kate's B&B (☎ 9028 2091; katesbb127@hotmail.com; 127 University St; s/d £30/60) Clean and friendly Kate's, in a lovingly restored 1860 townhouse, will make you feel right at home. Kate advertises her breakfast fry with 'go on – kill yourself!' Discounted weekly rates are available.

Madisons Hotel (☎ 9050 9800; www.madisonshotel.com; 59-63 Botanic Ave; s/d £70/80; ⊠) Swanky Madisons isn't just a hotel, it's also a café, bar, bistro and nightclub, and there's wheelchair access. The décor is crisp and modern and the nightclub is sexy. What more could you ask for?

Jury's Inn (☎ 9053 3500; www.bookajurysinn.com; College Sq; r £75-85; ⊠) Jury's bland modernity is more than made up for by its location (three minutes' walk from City Hall) and excellent value – room rates include anything up to three adults or two adults and two kids. Some rooms are wheelchair accessible.

TOP END

TENsq (☎ 9024 1001; www.tensquare.co.uk; 10 Donegall Sq; r £165-250; ⊠) The chichi 'Ten square' (*not* 'Tensk') aspires to old Shanghai. The former bank building across from City Hall has been given a feng shui–like makeover with dark lacquered wood, cream carpets and low-slung futon-style beds. It has wheelchair access.

Merchant Hotel (☎ 9023 4888; www.themerchanthotel.com; 35-39 Waring St; r £220-600; Ⓟ ⊠ 💻) Housed in the former Ulsterbank building, and decadent as all hell, the Merchant is worth every penny (if you can afford it). Each room has more individual touches than a strand of DNA, plus the topnotch restaurant and cellar nightclub (occupying the old vault) make the Merchant probably the most spectacular hotel in Northern Ireland. There are two wheelchair accessible rooms, and the entire hotel has wi-fi.

Eating

Belfast has a plethora of choices for all wallets. We've made it easier to find which fits you by breaking them down into sections based on the average price of mains: budget (up to £8.50), midrange (between £8.50 and £11) and top end (over £11).

BUDGET

Clements (☎ 9033 1827; 62 Botanic Ave; snacks £1.50-5, drinks £1.50-3; 🕑 7.30am-10.30pm) With long rows of couch seating and excellent cappuccinos, Clements is the beginning of true café culture in Belfast. Other branches are located on Donegall Sq West, Rosemary St and Stranmillis Rd.

Café Paul Rankin (☎ 9031 5090; 27-29 Fountain St; snacks £2.30-6; 🕑 7.30am-5.30pm Mon-Sat, 7.30am-7.30pm Thu; ⊠) Owned by Northern Ireland's top celebrity chef, this café serves quality cakes, focaccia, soups and salads, with comfy benches and sofas for lounging on. Other branches are at 12 Upper Arthur St (☎ 9031 0108) and the Castle Court Centre.

Pizza Express (☎ 9032 9050; 25-27 Bedford St; mains £5.15-8; noon-11pm Mon-Wed, noon-11.30pm Thu-Sat, noon-10.30pm Sun) With flowers on all the tables and a wide open kitchen, Pizza Express looks a lot more expensive than it actually is. The food is very good and the staff is exceptionally accommodating.

White's Tavern (☎ 9024 3080; 1-4 Wine Cellar Entry; mains £6-7; food served noon-6pm Mon-Sat) Historic White's, on a cobbled alley off High St, is a popular lunch-time meeting spot, serving down-to-earth pub food, such as baked potatoes, fish dishes, Irish stew, and sausage and champ.

Thai-Tanic (☎ 9066 8811; 2 Eglantine Ave; mains £6.50-8.50; 5-11pm Tue-Sun) Despite the cheesy name, tiny Thai-Tanic serves killer food and does deliveries within a 5km radius.

MIDRANGE

Ba Soba (☎ 9058 6868; 38 Hill St; mains £6-10; noon-3pm Tue-Fri, 5.30-10pm Mon-Thu, 5.30-11pm Fri & Sat) This bright and breezy Asian noodle bar dishes up fragrant bowls of Japanese *ramen* (noodle broth), prawn tempura, Thai warm salad and a host of other Asian dishes.

Archana (☎ 9032 3713; 53 Dublin Rd; mains £6-11; noon-2pm & 5.30-11pm Mon-Fri, 5-11pm Sat & Sun) It's actually disturbing how good Archana is. There is plenty to choose from, whether you eat meat or not, and the lunch specials are unbeatable at only £5 to £7.50. Seriously, do yourself a favour and eat here.

TOP END

Speranza (☎ 9023 0213; 16-19 Shaftesbury Sq; mains £9-13; 5-11.30pm Mon-Sat, 5-11pm Fri & Sat, 3-10pm Sun; ☒) A local institution – it's been around for more than 20 years – Speranza is a buzzing Italian restaurant that complements traditional pastas with more sophisticated dishes.

Reno's (☎ 9031 1026; 34-36 Bedford St; lunch £5-10, dinner £9-15; 8am-9.45pm Mon-Fri, 11am-9.45pm Sat, noon-6pm Sun, bar until 1am Mon-Sat) Billing itself as a 'food & entertainment emporium', Reno's serves fine food all day long. Stop in on weekend nights for live music, or drop by earlier for its pre-theatre menu.

Cayenne (☎ 9033 1532; 7 Ascot House, Shaftesbury Sq; mains £13-19; noon-2.30pm Mon-Fri, 6-10.15pm Mon-Thu, 6-11.15pm Fri & Sat) Behind an anonymous frosted-glass façade lurks this award-winning restaurant serving quality Irish produce prepared with an Asian or Mediterranean twist. Cayenne is owned by TV celebrity chef Paul Rankin. Reservations recommended.

Drinking

Pubs are generally open until 11pm Monday to Saturday, though pubs with an entertainment licence stay open to 1am or 1.30am and until 11pm Sunday.

Crown Liquor Saloon (☎ 9024 9476; 46 Great Victoria St) Beautiful enough to bring a drunk from any era to tears, Belfast's most famous bar has a wonderfully ornate Victorian interior with discreet panelled snugs.

Irene & Nan's (☎ 9023 9123; 12 Brunswick St) Although no one is quite sure where the name came from, there's no mistake that Irene & Nan's 1950s retro theme is dripping with designer chic. It's a laid-back place though, and its in-bar bistro will tempt your taste buds.

Empire Music Hall (☎ 9024 9276; 42 Botanic Ave) Residing in a converted Victorian church, the epic Empire has three floors of entertainment, including a basement jazz club, and has a weekly stand-up comedy night.

Entertainment

The Belfast Welcome Centre issues *Whatabout?*, a free monthly guide to Belfast events. Another useful guide is **wheretotonight.com** (www.wheretotonight.com).

CINEMAS

Queen's Film Theatre (QFT; ☎ 9097 1097; www.queensfilmtheatre.com; 20 University Sq) The QFT is a two-screen arthouse cinema, close to the university, and a major venue for the Belfast Film Festival in March.

The Odyssey Complex has two monster cinemas:

Sheridan Imax Cinema (☎ 9046 7000; www.belfastimax.com) This is Ireland's only 3D and 2D large-format cinema.

Warner Village Cinemas (☎ 0871-224 0240; www.theodyssey.co.uk) Belfast's biggest multiplex, with 12 screens and stadium seats throughout.

LIVE MUSIC & NIGHTCLUBS

Crescent Arts Centre (☎ 9024 2338; www.crescentarts.org; 2 University Rd) The Crescent puts on fine concerts, from New York jazz to top-rate

Irish music. It also stages a literary festival called Between the Lines each March, and the City Dance festival in June.

Waterfront Hall (☎ 9033 4455; www.waterfront.co.uk; Lanyon Pl) The impressive 2235-seat Waterfront is Belfast's flagship concert venue, hosting local, national and international performers from pop stars to symphony orchestras.

Milk (☎ 9027 8876; www.clubmilk.com; 10-14 Tomb St; admission £2-10) Milk is one of Belfast's hottest and most sophisticated clubs. Monday is gay night, with cabaret acts hosted by Baroness Titty Von Tramp.

THEATRE

Grand Opera House (☎ 9024 1919; www.goh.co.uk; 2-4 Great Victoria St) This grand old venue plays host to a mixture of opera, popular musicals and comedy shows.

Lyric Theatre (☎ 9038 1081; www.lyrictheatre.co.uk; 55 Ridgeway St) The Lyric, south of the city, stages serious drama; Hollywood star Liam Neeson first trod the boards here.

Getting There & Away

For all Ulsterbus, Northern Ireland Railways (NIR) and local bus information call **Translink** (☎ 9066 6630; www.translink.co.uk). The **NIR Travel Shop** (☎ 9024 2420; Great Victoria St station; 9am-5pm Mon-Fri, 9am-12.30pm Sat) can book and provide information on trains, buses and ferries.

AIR

There are flights from some regional airports in Britain to the convenient **Belfast City Airport** (BHD; ☎ 9093 9093; www.belfastcityairport.com; Airport Rd), 6km northeast of the city centre, but everything else, including flights from the Republic, Britain, Amsterdam, Brussels and New York, goes to **Belfast International Airport** (BFS; ☎ 9448 4848; www.belfastairport.com), 30km north of the city in Aldergrove by the M2. Some of the budget airlines that land at these airports are Ryanair and Flybe. For more information, see p705.

BOAT

For details on ferries to/from Northern Ireland, see p706. Four main ferry routes connect Belfast to Stranraer, Liverpool and the Isle of Man.

Steam Packet/SeaCat (☎ 0870 552 3523; www.steam-packet.com) catamaran car ferries dock at Donegall Quay, a short walk north of the city centre. **P&O European** (☎ 0870 242 4777; www.poirishsea.com) ferries travelling to and from Scotland dock at Larne, 30km north of Belfast.

Norfolkline Irish Sea Ferries (☎ 0870 600 4321) to Liverpool leave from Victoria terminal, 5km north of central Belfast; take a bus from Europa Bus Centre or catch a taxi (£5). **Stena Line** (☎ 0870 570 7070; www.stenaline.co.uk) services to Stranraer leave from Corry Rd, near the city centre.

BUS

Belfast has two separate bus stations. The smaller of the two is the **Laganside Bus Centre** (Oxford St), near the river, with bus connections to Counties Antrim, Down and Derry. Buses to everywhere else in Northern Ireland, the Republic, Belfast International Airport and the Larne ferries leave from the bigger **Europa Bus Centre** (Glengall St). Regional bus timetables are free at the bus stations.

Ulsterbus has hourly Belfast–Dublin buses that take about three hours and start at £8.30 one-way. The service to Derry (£9.40, 1¾ hours) is even more frequent.

Depending on the day, **Aircoach** (☎ 0870 225 7555; www.aircoach.ie) leaves Jury's Hotel hourly for Dublin airport (£7 to £12, 2½ hours). At the airport you can catch a local bus into town.

TRAIN

Belfast has two main train stations: Great Victoria St, next to the Europa Bus Centre, and the **Belfast Central** (East Bridge St), east of the city centre.

Destinations served from Belfast Central include Derry and Dublin. Belfast–Dublin trains (£24/35 one-way/return, two hours) run up to eight times daily (five on Sunday). From Belfast Central, a free (with your bus or train ticket) Centrelink bus to Donegall Sq in the city centre leaves every 10 minutes. A local train also connects with Great Victoria St.

Great Victoria St station has services to Derry (£9.80, 2¼ hours, about every two hours) and Larne Harbour (£4.70, one hour, hourly).

Getting Around

Airbus buses link Belfast International Airport with the Europa Bus Centre every half-hour (£6, 30 minutes). Alternatively, a taxi costs about £25.

The Belfast City Airport is only 6km northeast of the city centre. Take a shuttle bus from the terminal to the Sydenham Halt station, from where trains (£1.30, every half-hour) run to Belfast Central station, Botanic station or Great Victoria St station. The taxi fare is about £8.

A short trip on a bus costs £1 to £1.60. Most local bus services depart from Donegall Sq, near the City Hall, where there's a ticket kiosk.

If you're driving, be fastidious about where you park; car theft is a serious problem here. The tourist office has a free leaflet showing all the multistorey car parks.

McConvey Cycles (☎ 9033 0322; www.mcconveycycles.com; 182 Ormeau Rd) hires bikes for £15/60 per day/week. A deposit is required.

THE BELFAST–DERRY COASTAL ROAD

Ireland isn't short of fine stretches of coast, but the Causeway Coast stretching from Portstewart in County Derry to Ballycastle in County Antrim, and the Antrim Coast stretching from Ballycastle to Belfast, taking in the striking rock formations of the Giant's Causeway, are as magnificent as they come.

From late May to late September Ulsterbus' Antrim Coaster bus 252 operates twice daily (except Sunday) between Belfast and Coleraine (four hours), stopping at all the main tourist sights. An open-topped Bushmills Bus (bus 177) runs from the Giant's Causeway to Coleraine seven times daily in July and August. The trip takes just over an hour. Bus 172 runs year-round along the coast between Ballycastle and Portrush. **Translink** (☎ 9066 6630; www.translink.co.uk) handles all bookings and inquiries.

Carrickfergus

pop 28,000

Only 13km northeast of Belfast is Carrickfergus and its impressive Norman **castle** (☎ 9335 1273; adult/child £3/1.50; 🕑 10am-6pm Mon-Sat, 2-6pm Sun Jun-Aug, 10am-6pm Mon-Sat, 2-6pm Sun Apr-May & Sep, 10am-4pm Mon-Fri, 2-4pm Sun Oct-Mar), which was built in 1180 by John de Courcy and overlooks the harbour where William III landed in 1690. A small museum documents the castle's long history (it was occupied until 1928).

There are no hostels in Carrickfergus; a fine B&B is **Langsgarden** (☎ 9336 6369; 72 Scotch Quarter; s/d £23/48; P ⊠).

Glens of Antrim

Between Larne and Ballycastle, the nine Glens of Antrim are extremely picturesque stretches of woodland and downland where streams cascade into the sea. The port of **Cushendall** has been dubbed the 'Capital of the Glens', while **Glenariff**, a few kilometres to the south, is 'Queen of the Glens'. Between Cushendun and Ballycastle, eschew the main A2 road for the narrower and more picturesque B92, and take the turn-off down to sweeping Murlough Bay.

A good bet for a budget bed, and possibly a bedtime story, is at the modern **Ballyeamon Camping Barn** (☎ 2175 8699; www.taleteam.demon.co.uk; dm £8; P ⊠ 💻) near Cushendall on the B14. The proprietor is a professional storyteller.

Ballycastle

pop 4000

Ballycastle, where the Atlantic Ocean meets the Irish Sea, is a quiet harbour town and a natural base for exploring the coasts to the west or south.

The IHH/IHO **Castle Hostel** (☎ 2076 2337; www.castlehostel.com; 62 Quay Rd; dm/d £9/24; P ⊠) is just past the Marine Hotel. It's clean, welcoming and spacious, with wheelchair access. The IHO **Ballycastle Backpackers** (☎ 2076 3612; www.bcbackpackers.com; 4 North St; dm £8, d £20-30; P ⊠) is near the waterfront and the main bus stop.

Carrick-a-Rede Island

The 20m - **rope bridge** (☎ 2076 9839; adult/child £2/1; 🕑 10am-6pm Mar-Sep), connecting Carrick-a-Rede Island to the mainland and swaying some 25m above pounding waves, is fun to stagger across. The island is the site of a salmon fishery and a nesting ground for gulls and fulmars. It's a scenic 1.25km walk from the car park to the bridge. Note that the bridge is closed in high winds.

Giant's Causeway

Chances are you have seen pictures of the Giant's Causeway (Clochán an Aifir), Northern Ireland's main tourist attraction. The hexagonal basalt columns, all 38,000 of them (counting the ones underwater), are amazingly uniform. Legend has it that the giant in question, Finn McCool, built the Causeway to get to Scottish rival giant Benandonner on the Scottish island of Staffa (which has similar rock formations).

The more prosaic explanation is that lava erupted from an underground fissure and crystallised some 60 million years ago. The phenomenon is explained in an audiovisual (£1) at the **Causeway Visitors Centre** (☎ 2073 1855; www.giantscausewaycentre.com; ⌚ 10am-5pm Mar-Jun & Sep-Oct, 10am-6pm Jul-Aug, 10am-4.30pm Nov-Feb).

It costs nothing to visit the site, but car parking is an exorbitant £5. It's an easy 10- to 15-minute walk downhill to the Causeway itself. A better approach, though, is to follow the cliff-top path northeast for 2km to the Chimney Tops headland, which has excellent views of the Causeway and the coastline. For the less mobile or the downright lazy, a minibus shuttles from the visitors centre to the Causeway for £1.60 return.

Bus 172 runs about four times daily (more often in summer and fewer on Sunday) between Portrush and Ballycastle, passing by the Giant's Causeway. If you can, try to visit the Causeway midweek or out of season to avoid the crowds and experience it at its most evocative.

IRELAND

Bushmills

Bushmills, 4km southwest of the Giant's Causeway, is a small town off the A2 between Portrush and Ballycastle. The town makes a good base for visits to the Causeway Coast, but its real attraction is the **Old Bushmills Distillery** (☎ 2073 3218; www.bushmills.com; adult/child £5/2.50; ⌚ 9.30am-5.30pm Mon-Sat, noon-5.30pm Sun), 500m south of the main square. After a noisy tour of the industrial process (it's quieter on weekends, when production is halted), there's a whiskey-tasting session. Tours are held at 10.30am, 11.30am, 1.30pm, 2.30pm and 3.30pm Monday to Friday, and 1.30pm, 2.30pm and 3.30pm Saturday and Sunday from November to March; the last tour is at 4pm from April to October.

The excellent HINI **Mill Rest Hostel** (☎ 2073 1222; 49 Main St; dm/s/tw £13/18.50/33; ⌚ closed 10am-5pm Sep-Jun; ⊠ 💻) has small dorms and one wheelchair-friendly twin room (reserve in advance).

Dunluce Castle

Abandoned in 1641, the ruins of 14th-century **Dunluce Castle** (☎ 2073 1938; adult/child £2/1; ⌚ 10am-5.30pm Apr-Sep, 10am-4.30pm Oct-Mar), between Bushmills and Portrush, are dramatically sited right on the cliff edge – so close, in fact, that the castle's kitchen once collapsed into the sea. Perched 30m above the sea, the castle was of obvious military value, and the extensive remains inside the walls give a good idea of what life was like here.

Portstewart & Downhill

These seaside resorts are only a few kilometres apart. Pleasant Portstewart has a slightly decayed, early-20th-century feel to it, while Downhill has a lovely long stretch of beach.

Portstewart's friendly **Causeway Coast Hostel** (☎ 7083 3789; 4 Victoria Tce; dm/d £9/28; ⊠ 💻) is at the eastern end of town, and is wheelchair accessible. The Belfast–Portrush bus 218 stops about 100m away.

Harder to get to, but well worth the effort, is the **Downhill Hostel** (☎ 7084 9077; www.downhillhostel.com; 12 Mussenden Rd; dm/d £9/30; P ⊠), a lovely converted period house on the beach, with open fires and a good library of books and vinyl. Pick-up can be arranged from Castlerock train station. The Coleraine–Limavady bus 134 also passes nearby.

DERRY

pop 107,000

Derry. Londonderry. The name you use for Northern Ireland's second-largest city can be a political statement, but today most people just call it Derry, whatever their politics. The 'London' prefix was added after settlers from London Guilds built the city walls and were granted much of the land in the area by James I.

In the '60s resentment at the long-running Protestant domination of the city council boiled over in the (Catholic-dominated) civil rights marches of 1968. In August 1969 fighting between police and local youths in the poor Catholic Bogside district prompted the UK government to send British troops into Derry. In January 1972 'Bloody Sunday' resulted in the deaths of 13 unarmed Catholic civil rights marchers in Derry at the hands of the British army, an event that marked the beginning of the Troubles in earnest. Inquiry into the events of Bloody Sunday is still continuing in Derry's Guildhall.

Today Derry is as safe to visit as anywhere else in Northern Ireland, while the Bogside and the inner city have been redeveloped. The city's long, dramatic history is still palpable – in the 17th-century city walls, in the captivating Bogside murals – but it's also a laid-back place with a well-founded reputation for musical excellence, from traditional to cutting-edge contemporary, and a lively arts scene that thrives in the city's many innovative venues.

Orientation

The old centre of Derry is the small, walled city on the western bank of the Foyle River. The heart of the walled city is The Diamond, intersected by four main roads: Shipquay St, Ferryquay St, Bishop St Within and Butcher St. The Catholic Bogside area is below the walls to the northwest. To the south is a Protestant estate known as the Fountain. The Waterside district across the river is mostly Protestant.

Information

Central Library (☎ 7127 2310; 35 Foyle St; per hr £3; 🕒 9.15am-5.30pm Tue, Wed & Fri, 9.15am-8pm Mon & Thu, 9.15am-5pm Sat) Internet access is available.

Claude's Café (☎ 7127 9379; 4 Shipquay St; per hr £5; 🕒 9am-5.30pm) Offers Internet access.

Derry Visitor & Convention Bureau (☎ 7126 7284; www.derryvisitor.com; 🕒 9am-5pm Mon-Fri, 10am-5pm Sat mid-Mar–Jun & Oct, 9am-7pm Mon-Fri, 10am-6pm Sat, 10am-5pm Sun Jul-Sep, 9am-5pm Nov–mid-Mar) Handles all of Northern Ireland and the Republic, as well as Derry. The office may be relocated in the next couple of years.

Main Post Office (Custom House St) Just north of the Tower Museum.

Sights

Derry's magnificent **city walls**, built between 1613 and 1618, were the last to be constructed in Europe, and are Ireland's only city walls to survive almost intact. They're about 8m high, 9m thick and encircle the old city for 1.5km. The walls make for a fantastic walk, and the gates give an excellent overview of Bogside (itself worth a closer look on foot) and its defiant **murals**, one notably proclaiming 'You Are Now Entering Free Derry'. From the city walls between Butcher's Gate and the army barracks you are able to see many of the darkly beautiful building-side murals.

Just inside Coward's Bastion to the north, O'Doherty's Tower is home to the excellent **Tower Museum** (☎ 7137 2411; tower.museum@derrycity.gov.uk; admission £3; 🕒 10am-4.30pm Mon-Sat), which traces the story of Derry from the days of St Columbcille to the present. The newly renovated museum was expanded to include an interactive Spanish Armada exhibition. The **Harbour Museum** (☎ 7137 7331; Harbour Sq; admission free; 🕒 10am-1pm & 2-4.30pm Mon-Fri) has interesting displays on Derry's maritime tradition and Victorian past. The deeply moving **Museum of Free Derry** (☎ 7136 0880; www.museumoffreederry.org; 55-61 Glenfada Park; 🕒 9.30am-4pm Mon-Thu, 9.30am-3pm Fri, 1-4pm Sat) exhibits all things related to The Troubles, Civil Rights, Bloody Sunday and everything in between. It screens an excellent 45-minute film about Bloody Sunday. At the time of research no fees had been set.

The fine red-brick **Guildhall** (☎ 7137 7335; admission free; 🕒 9am-5pm Mon-Fri), just outside the city walls, was originally built in 1890 and is noted for its stained-glass windows. Guided tours are available in July and August.

Austere **St Columb's Cathedral** (☎ 7126 7313; requested donation £1; 🕒 9am-5pm Mon-Sat Apr-Oct, 9am-4pm Nov-Mar) dates from 1628 and stands at the southern end of the walled city, off Bishop St Within.

Tours

Both **Derry Visitor & Convention Bureau** (☎ 7126 7284; www.derryvisitor.com; 44 Foyle St; 🕒 9am-5pm Mon-Fri, 10am-5pm Sat mid-Mar–Jun & Oct, 9am-7pm Mon-Fri, 10am-6pm Sat, 10am-5pm Sun Jul-Sep, 9am-5pm Nov–mid-Mar) and **City Tours** (☎ 7127 1996; www.irishtourguides.com; 11 Carlisle Rd) offer walking tours of the city walls for around £4. **Free Derry Tours** (☎ 0779 328 5972; www.freederry.net) also does a fantastically informative tour and its founder, Ruairi O'Heara, might very well be Derry's most fascinating tour guide.

Sleeping

Derry City Independent Hostel (☎ 7128 0542; www.derryhostel.com; 44 Great James St; dm/d incl breakfast £11/32; ⊠ 💻) Every hostel should strive to engender the warm atmosphere that Steve and Kylie have created at Derry City Independent. It is a little cramped but it's funky and fun, with an eating nook covered in Indian paintings and pillows. There's free Internet access, no checkout time and the fifth night is free.

Saddler's House (☎ 7126 9691; www.thesaddlershouse.com; 36 Great James St; s/d £30/45; P ⊠) Everything in this centrally located Victorian townhouse, from the sharp-witted hosts to their bulldog Bertie, is absolutely lovable. It's almost worth visiting Derry just to stay here or at its sister B&B, Merchant's House.

Merchant's House (☎ 7126 9691; 16 Queen St; s £20-30, d £45-50) A Georgian-style townhouse around the corner from Saddler's House. The marble fireplace, antique furniture and home-made marmalade are just a few of the little touches that make a stay here utterly enjoyable.

Tower Hotel (☎ 7137 1000; www.towerhotelderry.com; Butcher St; s/d £89/125; P ⊠) The Tower is the only hotel within the city walls, with plush wheelchair-accessible rooms, a fitness centre and a good restaurant.

Eating

An Bácús (☎ 7126 4678; 37 Great James St; snacks £2-4; 🕑 7.30am-5pm Mon-Fri, 9am-5pm Sat) The bilingual menu at this Irish-language café is a little confusing to read, but you will learn the Irish words for egg *(ubh)* and Coke (Cóca). It's a cute place for a coffee and a pastry or sandwich.

Flaming Jacks (☎ 7126 6400; 29-35 Strand Rd; lunch £5-6, dinner £7-14; 🕑 noon-2.30pm & 5-10.30pm Mon-Thu, noon-4.30pm Fri & Sat, noon-4pm Sun) It could be the sultry modern interior or the extensive wine list that brings droves of people to Flaming Jacks, or it could be the fact that it's probably the only place in Ireland that gives free soft drink refills. You be the judge.

Mange 2 (☎ 7136 1222; 2 Clarendon St; lunch £7, dinner £10-16; 🕑 noon-2.45pm & 5.30pm-late daily, breakfast from 10.30am Sat & Sun) The fine food and service in this candlelit, Georgian-style dining room make it a nice place to drop a few pounds, sterling that is. The interesting fusion menu includes a handful of good veggie options.

For self-caterers, **Tesco** (Strand Rd) has a large supermarket in the Quayside Shopping Centre.

Drinking

Peadar O'Donnell's (☎ 7126 2318; 63 Waterloo St) Peadar's goes for traditional music sessions nightly from around 11pm.

Sandino's (☎ 7130 9297; 1 Water St) This alternative Latin American–themed venue (named after Nicaraguan guerrilla leader Augusto Sandino) is popular with up-and-coming bands and visiting musicians. It hosts regular theme nights, and various fund-raising and political events.

Entertainment

Millennium Forum (☎ 7126 4455; www.millenniumforum.co.uk; New Market St) Ireland's biggest theatre auditorium has wheelchair-accessible spaces for dance, drama, concerts, opera and musicals.

Nerve Centre (☎ 7126 0562; www.nerve-centre.org.uk; 7-8 Magazine St) The ever-expanding Nerve Centre is a multimedia venue for music, and has an arthouse cinema, café and bar. It also has workshops and studios for animation, film and music.

Getting There & Away

About 13km east of Derry along the A2, the **City of Derry airport** (LDY; ☎ 7181 0784; www.cityofderryairport.com) has direct flights daily to London Stansted, Dublin, Glasgow, Manchester and Birmingham. Some of the budget airlines that land here are Ryanair and Aer Arann. See p705 for contact details.

The **bus station** (☎ 7126 2261) is just outside the city walls, on Foyle St near the Guildhall. Ulsterbus' bus 212, the *Maiden City Flyer*, is the fastest service between Belfast and Derry (£9.40, 1¾ hours, every half-hour, less on Sunday). Bus 234 runs to Portrush and Portstewart in July and August (£6.50, 1½ hours, four daily). Five buses daily (four on Sunday) go to Dublin (£12.80, 4¼ hours).

Lough Swilly Bus Service (☎ 7126 2017), with an office upstairs at the Ulsterbus station, serves County Donegal across the border.

Air Porter Buses (☎ 7126 9996; www.airporter.co.uk) runs 13 daily services (six on weekends) between Belfast International Airport, Belfast City Airport and Derry's Quayside Shopping Centre for £15.

Derry's **Waterside train station** (☎ 7134 2228) lies across the Foyle River from the city centre, but is connected to it by a free

Linkline bus that leaves the bus station 15 minutes before each train departure. Nine trains run daily (four on Sunday) to Belfast (£9.40, three hours) via Portrush.

ENNISKILLEN & LOUGH ERNE

Enniskillen, the main town of County Fermanagh, is handy for activities on Upper and Lower Lough Erne. Enniskillen itself has only one notable sight, **Enniskillen Castle** (☎ 6632 5000; www.enniskillencastle.co.uk; adult/child £2.50/1.50; ⏰ 10am-5pm Tue-Fri, 2-5pm Sat-Mon, closed Sun Sep-May, closed Sat Oct-Apr), home to the Fermanagh County Museum, with displays on the county's history and landscape, and the Museum of the Royal Inniskilling Fusiliers.

The town centre is on an island in the Erne River, which connects the upper and lower lakes. The very helpful **tourist office** (☎ 6632 3110; Wellington Rd; ⏰ 9am-7pm Mon-Fri Jul-Aug, 9am-5.30pm Sep-Jun, 10am-6pm Sat & 11am-5pm Sun Easter-Sep) is about 100m from the town centre.

Between May and September – from the Round 'O' Jetty at Brook Park – the **MV Kestrel waterbus** (☎ 6632 2882) operates 1½-hour tours (£8) of the lower lough, which include a visit to **Devenish Island**, with its 9th-century church and one of the best round-towers in Ireland.

White Island, close to the eastern shore of the lough, has a line of six mysterious statues, dating from around the 6th century. On weekends from April to September, and daily in July and August, a ferry runs across to White Island from the Castle Archdale marina, 20km north of Enniskillen on the Kesh road. The return fare is £4. Contact the tourist office for bookings.

The modern and spotless **Bridges Hostel** (☎ 6634 2806; Belmore St; dm/tw £13/26; ⊠ 💻) is part of the Bill Clinton Peace Centre in central Enniskillen. Two twin rooms are wheelchair accessible. Roughly 3km down the A4 sits the lovely **Dromard House B&B** (☎ 6638 7250; www.dromardhouse.com; Tamalght; s/d £25/50), a traditional Ulster farmhouse on a working farm.

Getting There & Around

Enniskillen's **Ulsterbus station** (☎ 6632 2633; Shore Rd) is across from the tourist office. There are up to 10 services daily (fewer on weekends) to Belfast via Dungannon (£9.40, 2½ hours). Buses also run to Derry (£13, 2½ hours, once daily Monday to Friday) via Omagh. Bus Éireann has services to Dublin via Ballygawley (£17.60, three hours, three daily, fewer on weekends).

IRELAND DIRECTORY

ACCOMMODATION

Sleeping listings in this chapter include the high-season price. Low-season rates are 15% to 25% less. Most budget listings in this chapter are under €30 per person, while midrange options are generally under €65. Top-end places range upwards of €65.

Booking ahead is essential in peak season. Fáilte Ireland (Irish Tourist Board) will book accommodation for a 10% room deposit and a fee of €4. The **Northern Ireland Tourist Board** (NITB; www.discovernorthernireland.com) books accommodation at no cost with a 10% room deposit. This is handy when it may take numerous calls to find a room. Accommodation for the Republic and the North may also be booked online, via the **Gulliver booking service** (www.gulliver.ie). A deposit of 10% and a €4 fee is payable.

B&Bs

Bed and breakfasts are as Irish as it gets. It sometimes seems that every other house is a B&B, and you'll find them in the strangest locations. Typical costs are around €35 per person a night, though more-luxurious B&Bs can cost upwards of €55 per person. Most B&Bs are small, so in summer they quickly fill up.

Camping & Hostels

Commercial camping grounds typically charge €12 to €18 for a tent and two people, and some hostels have space for tents. Unless otherwise indicated, prices given in this chapter for 'camp site' are for a tent plus two people.

Hostels in Ireland can be booked heavily in summer. An Óige (meaning 'youth') and Hostelling International Northern Ireland (HINI) are branches of Hostelling International (HI); An Óige has 33 hostels in the Republic, while HINI has seven in the North. Other hostel associations include Independent Holiday Hostels (IHH), a cooperative group with about

120 hostels throughout the island, and the Independent Hostels Owners (IHO) association, which has over 100 members around Ireland.

From June to September nightly costs at most hostels are €15 to €20, except for the more expensive hostels in Dublin, Belfast and a few other places.

An Óige (Map pp654-5; ☎ 01-830 4555; www.anoige.ie; 61 Mountjoy St, Dublin 7)

Hostelling International Northern Ireland (HINI; ☎ 028-9032 4733; www.hini.org.uk; Belfast International Youth Hostel, 22-32 Donegall Rd, Belfast BT12 5JN)

Independent Holiday Hostels (IHH; ☎ 01-836 4700; www.hostels-ireland.com)

Independent Hostel Owners in Ireland (IHO; ☎ 074-973 0130; www.holidayhound.com/ihi; Dooey Hostel, Glencolumbcille, County Donegal)

ACTIVITIES

Ireland is great for outdoor activities, and tourist boards put out a wide selection of information sheets covering bird-watching (County Donegal and County Wexford), surfing (great along the west coast), scuba diving (West Cork), rock climbing, fishing, horse riding, sailing, canoeing and many other activities.

Walking is particularly popular, although you must come prepared for wet weather. There are now well over 20 way-marked trails throughout Ireland, one of the most popular being the 132km Wicklow Way.

BOOKS

Lonely Planet's *Ireland, Dublin, Cycling Ireland, Walking in Ireland* and *World Food Ireland* guides offer comprehensive coverage of the island and its most-visited city.

McCarthy's Bar by Pete McCarthy is laugh-out-loud funny and a must-read for anyone travelling in Ireland.

BUSINESS HOURS

Offices are open 9am to 5pm Monday to Friday, shops a little later. On Thursday and/or Friday shops stay open later; although the closing time varies from shop to shop, they would be unlikely to be open after 9pm. Many shops also open on Saturday. In winter tourist attractions are often open shorter hours, fewer days per week or may be shut completely. In Northern Ireland some tourist attractions are closed on Sunday morning.

Restaurants north and south tend to close around 9pm or 10pm. In the Republic pubs close at 11.30pm Monday to Thursday, 12.30am Friday and Saturday, and at 11pm on Sunday; some pubs have licences allowing them to stay open until 2.30am Thursday to Saturday. In Northern Ireland pubs close at 11pm Monday to Saturday and 10pm on Sunday; those holding late licences generally stay open until 1am Monday to Friday and until midnight on Sunday.

EMBASSIES & CONSULATES

Irish Embassies & Consulates

Irish diplomatic missions overseas include the following:

Australia (☎ 02-6273 3022; irishemb@cyberone.com.au; 20 Arkana St, Yarralumla, ACT 2600) There is also a consulate in Sydney.

Canada (☎ 613-233 6281; embassyofireland@rogers.com; Suite 1105, 130 Albert St, Ottawa, Ontario K1P 5G4)

France (☎ 01 44 17 67 00; paris@iveagh.irlgov.ie; 4 rue de Paris, 75116 Paris)

Germany (☎ 030-220 720; Friedrichstrasse 200, D-10117 Berlin)

Netherlands (☎ 070-363 09 93; www.irish embassy.nl; Dr Kuyperstraat 9, 2514 BA The Hague)

New Zealand (☎ 09-977 2252; consul@ireland.co.nz; 6th fl, 18 Shortland St, 1001 Auckland)

UK (☎ 020-7235 2171; 17 Grosvenor Pl, London SW1X 7HR) There are consulates in Edinburgh and Cardiff.

USA (☎ 202-462 3939; 2234 Massachusetts Ave NW, Washington, DC 20008-2849) Boston, Chicago, New York and San Francisco have consulates.

Embassies & Consulates in Ireland

The following countries have diplomatic offices in Dublin:

Australia (☎ 01-676 1517; www.australianembassy.ie; 2nd fl, Fitzwilton House, Wilton Tce, Dublin 2)

Canada (☎ 01-478 1988; www.canada.ie; 4th fl, 65-68 St Stephen's Green, Dublin 2)

France (☎ 01-277 5000; www.ambafrance.ie; 36 Ailesbury Rd, Dublin 4)

Germany (☎ 01-269 3011; www.germanembassy.ie; 31 Trimleston Ave, Booterstown, Co Dublin)

Netherlands (☎ 01-269 3444; www.netherlands embassy.ie; 160 Merrion Rd, Dublin 4)

New Zealand (☎ 01-660 4233; 37 Leeson Park, Dublin 6)

UK (☎ 01-205 3700; www.britishembassy.ie; 29 Merrion Rd, Ballsbridge, Dublin 4)

USA (☎ 01-668 7122; www.dublin.usembassy.gov; 42 Elgin Rd, Ballsbridge, Dublin 4)

In Northern Ireland, nationals of most countries should contact their embassy in London. Consulates in the North include:

Germany (☎ 028-7034 0403; Hillman's Way, Ballycastle Rd, Coleraine)
Netherlands (☎ 028-9037 0223; fax 9037 1104; 14-16 West Bank Rd, Belfast BT3 9JL)
New Zealand (☎ 028-9264 8098; The Ballance House, 118A Lisburn Rd, Glenavy BT29 4NY)
USA (☎ 028-9038 6100; www.americanembassy.org.uk; Danesfort House, 223 Stranmillis Rd, Belfast BT9 5GR)

FESTIVALS & EVENTS

St Patrick's Day is a cacophony of parades, fireworks and light shows for three days around 17 March in Dublin; Cork, Armagh and Belfast also have parades. The All-Ireland hurling and football finals both take place in Dublin in September. There are great regional cultural events around the island, like the Galway Arts Festival (p683) in late July and the Kilkenny Arts Festival in late August. In Dublin, Leopold Bloom's Joycean journey around the city is marked by various events on Bloomsday (16 June). The Dublin International Film Festival in April is also a highlight. In Northern Ireland July is marching month and every Orangeman in the country hits the streets on the 'glorious 12th'. Other events include the Galway Oyster Festival in September and the Belfast Festival at Queen's in November.

GAY & LESBIAN TRAVELLERS

Despite the decriminalisation of homosexuality for people over 17 years of age (Northern Ireland in 1982 and the Republic in 1993), gay life is generally neither acknowledged nor understood. Only Dublin and, to a lesser extent, Belfast, Cork, Galway, Waterford and Limerick have open gay and lesbian communities. The monthly **Gay Community News** (www.gcn.ie), available at bars and cafés, is a free publication of the **National Lesbian & Gay Federation** (☎ 01-671 9076; Unit 2, Scarlet Row, West Essex St, Dublin 8). Information is also available from **Outhouse Community Centre** (Map p657; ☎ 01-873 4932; www.outhouse.ie; 105 Capel St, Dublin 1), a gay, lesbian and transgender community centre.

HOLIDAYS

Following is a list of the main public holidays in the Republic, Northern Ireland or both:

New Year's Day 1 January
St Patrick's Day 17 March
Easter (Good Friday to Easter Monday inclusive) March/April
May Holiday 1 May
Christmas Day 25 December
St Stephen's Day (Boxing Day) 26 December

NORTHERN IRELAND

Spring Bank Holiday Last Monday in May
Orangemen's Day 12 July
August Bank Holiday First Monday in August

REPUBLIC

June Holiday First Monday in June
August Holiday First Monday in August
October Holiday Last Monday in October

INTERNET RESOURCES

Ireland is well wired, so there's a lot of useful information available online. **CIE Group** (www.cie.ie) and **Translink** (www.translink.co.uk) are handy for planning transport in the South and North, respectively.

Entertainment Ireland (www.entertainmentireland.ie) Countrywide listings for clubs, theatres, festivals, cinemas, museums and much more.
Irish Times (www.ireland.com) Get up to speed on the latest news before you leave home with Ireland's largest daily newspaper.
Irish Tourist Board (www.ireland.ie) The Republic's tourist information site has heaps of practical information. It features a huge accommodation database with photos.
Lonely Planet (www.lonelyplanet.com) Comprehensive travel information and advice.
Northern Ireland Tourism (www.discovernorthernireland.com) Northern Ireland's official tourism information site is particularly strong on activities and accommodation.
Office of Public Works (www.heritageireland.ie) The Republic's heritage sites – castles, churches and abbeys, parks, cemeteries and the like.

MAPS

Good-quality maps of Ireland include Lonely Planet's *Dublin City Map*, Michelin *Ireland Motoring Map* No 923 (1:400,000) and Ordnance Survey's (OS) four Ireland *Holiday Maps* (1:250,000). The more-detailed OS *Discovery* series (1:50,000) covers the entire country with 89 maps.

MONEY

The Irish Republic uses the euro, while Northern Ireland uses the British pound sterling (£). Banks offer the best exchange rates; exchange bureaus, open longer, have worse rates and higher commissions. Post offices generally have exchange facilities and are open on Saturday morning.

In Northern Ireland several banks issue their own Northern Irish pound notes, which are equivalent to sterling but not readily accepted in Britain. At the time of research ATMs in Northern Ireland were not accepting certain debit/credit cards from the USA.

Ireland is expensive, marginally more than Britain, but prices vary around the island. Prices for sites and museums are usually 20% to 50% lower for children, students and senior citizens (OAPs).

For budget travellers, €65 per day should cover hostel accommodation, getting around, a restaurant meal and just enough for a pint.

Fancy hotels and restaurants usually add a 10% or 15% service charge onto bills. Simpler places usually don't add service; if you decide to tip, just round up the bill (or add 10% at most). Taxi drivers do not have to be tipped, but if you do, 10% is more than generous.

POST

The post offices (An Post) throughout the Republic are generally open 9am to 5.30pm Monday to Friday, and 9am to 1pm Saturday; smaller offices close for lunch.

Letters weighing less than 50g cost €0.60 to Britain and €0.65 to Continental Europe and the rest of the world.

Post-office hours and postal rates in Northern Ireland are the same as Britain. Mail can be addressed to poste restante at post offices, but is officially held for only two weeks. Writing 'hold for collection' on the envelope may help.

TELEPHONE

Local telephone calls from a public phone in the Republic cost €0.50 for three minutes (around €0.60 to a mobile). In Northern Ireland a local call costs a minimum of £0.30. Some payphones in the North take euros. Prepaid phonecards by Eircom or private operators, available in newsagencies and post offices, work from all payphones and dispense with the need for coins.

To call Northern Ireland from the Republic, you do not use ☎ 0044 as for the rest of the UK. Instead, dial ☎ 048 and then the local number.

You can dial direct to your home-country operator and then reverse charges (collect) or charge the call to a local phone-credit card. From the Republic dial the following codes, then the area code and the number you want. Your home-country operator will come on the line before the call goes through.

Australia ☎ 1800 550061
France ☎ 1800 551033
New Zealand ☎ 1800 550064
UK (BT) ☎ 1800 550044
USA (AT&T) ☎ 1800 550000
USA (MCI) ☎ 1800 551001
USA (Sprint) ☎ 1800 552001

Reverse-charge calls can also be made from the North using the same numbers as from the UK.

Mobile Phones

The mobile (cell) phone network in Ireland runs on the GSM 900/1800 system compatible with the rest of Europe and Australia, but not the USA. Ireland's three service providers are Vodafone (087), O2 (086) and Meteor (085). A new SIM for your mobile will cost from around €10, but may be free after the standard phone-credit refund. Pay-as-you-go phones cost from €100.

TOURIST INFORMATION

The Irish tourist board, **Fáilte Ireland** (www.failteireland.ie), and the **Northern Ireland Tourist Board** (NITB; www.discovernorthernireland.com) operate separate offices. Both are well organised and helpful, though Fáilte Ireland will not provide any information on places (such as B&Bs and camping grounds) that it has not approved. Every town big enough to have half-a-dozen pubs will have a tourist office, although smaller ones may close in winter. Most will find you a place to stay for a fee of €2 to €4.

Tourism Ireland (www.tourismireland.com) handles tourist information for both tourist boards overseas.

Tourist Offices Abroad

Following are overseas offices of Tourism Ireland:

Australia (☎ 02-9299 6177; 5th fl, 36 Carrington St, Sydney, NSW 2000)

Canada (☎ 1 800 223 6470; Ste 3403, 2 Bloor St W, Toronto M4W 3E2)
New Zealand (☎ 09-977 2255; Level 6, 18 Shortland St, Private Bag, 92136 Auckland)
UK (☎ 0800 039 7000; Nations House, 103 Wigmore St, London W1U 1QS)
USA (☎ 1 800 223 6470; 345 Park Ave, New York, NY 10154)

TRAVELLERS WITH DISABILITIES

Guesthouses, hotels and sights throughout Ireland are increasingly being adapted for people with disabilities. In Northern Ireland this became compulsory under the Disability Discrimination Act of 1995, and service providers across the North worked to make the necessary adjustments by the 2004 deadline. Fáilte Ireland's various accommodation guides indicate which places are wheelchair accessible, and the NITB publishes *Accessible Accommodation in Northern Ireland*. Comhairle publishes detailed accessibility information in the Republic and the North. Travellers to Northern Ireland should also check out **All Go Here** (www.everybody.co.uk).

Comhairle (Map pp654-5; ☎ 01-605 90 00; www.comhairle.ie; 7th fl, Hume House, Ballsbridge, Dublin 4)
Disability Action (☎ 028-9029 7880; www.disabilityaction.org; Portside Business Park, 189 Airport Rd West, Belfast BT3 9ED)

VISAS

Citizens of the EU, Australia, Canada, New Zealand and the US don't need a visa to visit either the Republic or Northern Ireland. EU nationals are allowed to stay indefinitely, while other visitors can usually remain for three to six months. UK nationals born in Britain or Northern Ireland don't need a passport, but should carry some identification.

TRANSPORT IN IRELAND

GETTING THERE & AWAY

Air

The Fáilte Ireland **online tourist office** (www.ireland.ie) has information on getting to Ireland from a number of countries. International departure tax is normally included in the price of your ticket.

There are nonstop flights from Britain, Continental Europe and North America to Dublin and Shannon, and nonstop connections from Britain and Europe to Cork.

International airports in the Republic include the following:

Cork (ORK; ☎ 021-431 3131; www.corkairport.com)
Dublin (DUB; ☎ 01-814 1111; www.dublinairport.com)
Kerry (KIR; ☎ 066-976 4644; www.kerryairport.ie; Farranfore)
Knock (NOC; ☎ 094-67222; www.knockairport.com)
Shannon (SNN; ☎ 061-712000; www.shannonairport.com)
Waterford (WAT; ☎ 051-875589; www.flywaterford.com)

International airports in Northern Ireland include the following:

Belfast City (BHD; ☎ 028-9093 9093; www.belfastcityairport.com) Serves Britain.
Belfast International (BFS; ☎ 028-9448 4848; www.belfastairport.com) Serves Britain, Europe and the USA.
Derry (LDY; ☎ 028-7181 0784; www.cityofderryairport.com) Serves Britain.

For a comprehensive list of airlines serving Ireland from outside Western Europe, see p1112. Airlines flying to and from Ireland include the following:

Aer Arann (code RE; ☎ 01-814 5240; www.aerarann.ie) A small carrier that operates flights within Ireland and also to Britain.
Aer Lingus (code EI; ☎ 01-886 8844; www.aerlingus.com) The Irish national airline, with direct flights to Britain, Continental Europe and the USA.
Air France (code AF; ☎ 01-605 0383; www.airfrance.com)
Alitalia (code AZ; ☎ 01-844 6035; www.alitalia.com)
American Airlines (code AA; ☎ 01-602 0550; www.aa.com)
BMI British Midland (code BD; ☎ in the UK 01332-854 854; www.flybmi.com)
British Airways (code BA; ☎ in the UK 0845 773 3377; www.ba.com)
Continental Airlines (code CO; ☎ 1890 925 252; www.continental.com)
Delta Airlines (code DL; ☎ 1800 768 080; www.delta.com)
easyJet (code EZY; ☎ 048-9448 4929; www.easyjet.com)
Finnair (code AY; ☎ 01-844 6565; www.finnair.com)
Flybe (code BEE; ☎ in the UK 0870-567 6676; www.flybe.com)
Iberia (code IB; ☎ 01-407 3017; www.iberia.com, in Spanish)

EMERGENCY NUMBERS

These numbers apply in both the Republic and Northern Ireland:

- Ambulance ☎ 999
- Fire ☎ 999
- Police ☎ 999

Jet2 (code LS; ☎ 0818-200 017; www.jet2.com)
KLM (code KLM; ☎ 01-663 6900; www.klm.nl)
Lufthansa (code LH; ☎ 01-844 5544; www.lufthansa.com)
Ryanair (code FR; ☎ 01-609 7800; www.ryanair.com) Ireland's budget carrier, flying to Britain and Continental Europe.
Scandinavian Airlines (code SK; ☎ 01-844 5888; www.scandinavian.net)
US Airways (code US; ☎ 1890 925 065; www.usairways.com)

Land

Because of cheap flights, getting to Ireland by land is not very popular. National Express and Bus Éireann's Eurolines operate services direct from London and other UK centres to Dublin, Belfast and other cities. For details in London, contact **National Express** (☎ 0870-514 3219; www.nationalexpress.com); in Dublin contact **Bus Éireann** (☎ 01-836 6111; www.buseireann.ie). London to Dublin by bus takes about 12 hours and costs £28/41 one-way/return (more for the evening bus). To Belfast it takes 13 hours and costs £29/42.

Sea

There's a variety of ferry services from Britain and France to Ireland. Prices vary depending on season, time of day, day of the week and length of stay. One-way fares for an adult foot passenger can be as little as £20, but can exceed £60 in summer. For a car plus driver and up to four adult passengers, prices can cost £130 to £250.

Keep an eye out for special deals, discounted return fares and other money savers. And plan ahead – some services are booked up months in advance.

BRITAIN

Regular ferry services run to ports in the Republic and Northern Ireland from Scotland (Cairnryan–Larne, Stranraer–Belfast, Troon–Belfast and Troon–Larne), England (Heysham–Belfast, Liverpool–Belfast and Liverpool–Dublin), Wales (Fishguard–Rosslare Harbour, Holyhead–Dublin, Holyhead–Dun Laoghaire, Pembroke–Rosslare Harbour and Swansea–Cork) and from the Isle of Man (Douglas–Dublin and Douglas–Belfast).

Irish Ferries (☎ 0818-300 400, 01-638 3333, in the UK 0870 517 1717; www.irishferries.com) For ferry and fast-boat services from Holyhead to Dublin (two or 3¼ hours), and ferry services from Pembroke to Rosslare Harbour (3¾ hours).
Isle of Man Steam Packet Company/Sea Cat (☎ 1800-805 055, in the UK 0870 552 3523; www.steam-packet.com) Ferry and fast-boat services from Douglas (Isle of Man) to Belfast (2¾ hours, Easter to September) and Dublin (2¾ hours, Easter to September); Liverpool to Dublin (3¾ hours, February to October); and Troon to Belfast (2½ hours).
Norfolkline Irish Sea Ferries (☎ 01-819 2999, in the UK 0870 600 4321; www.norfolkline-ferries.co.uk/en/is-passenger/) Ferries from Liverpool to Belfast (eight hours), and from Dublin to Liverpool (seven hours).
P&O European Ferries (☎ 01-407 3434, in the UK 0870 242 4777; www.poirishsea.com) Ferry and fast-boat services from Cairnryan to Larne (one or 1¾ hours), Troon to Larne (1¾ hours, March to October) and Liverpool to Dublin (eight hours).
Stena Line (☎ 01-204 7777, in the UK 0870 570 7070; www.stenaline.co.uk) Ferry and fast-boat services from Holyhead to Dublin (three hours) and Holyhead to Dun Laoghaire (1¾ hours); Fishguard to Rosslare Harbour (1¾ or 3½ hours); and Stranraer to Belfast (1¾ or 3¼ hours).
Swansea Cork Ferries (☎ 021-427 6000, in the UK 01792-456116; www.swanseacorkferries.com) Ferry services from Swansea to Cork (10 hours).

FRANCE

Ferries run between Roscoff and Cherbourg to Rosslare Harbour and Cork.

Brittany Ferries (☎ in Ireland 021-427 7801, in France 02 98 29 28 00; www.brittanyferries.com) Services from Roscoff to Cork once weekly (13 hours, April to September).
Irish Ferries (☎ in France 01 43 94 46 94) Ferries from Roscoff/Cherbourg to Rosslare Harbour (17½ or 20½ hours, April to December).
P&O European Ferries Services from Cherbourg to Rosslare Harbour (19 hours).

GETTING AROUND

Travelling around Ireland looks simple, as the distances are short and there's a dense network of roads and railways. But in Ireland, from A to B is seldom a straight line, and public transport can be expensive (particularly trains), infrequent or both. For these reasons having your own transport – either car or bicycle – can be a major advantage.

Air

There are flights within Ireland between Dublin and Belfast, Cork, Derry, Donegal, Galway, Kerry, Shannon and Sligo, as well as a Belfast–Cork service. Most domestic flights take 30 to 50 minutes. For the list of airlines, see p705.

Bicycle

Ireland is a great place for cycling, despite inconsistent roads and inclement weather. You can either bring your bike with you on the ferry or plane, or hire one in Ireland. Typical hire costs are €10 to €20 per day or around €50 to €100 a week. Bags and other equipment can also be hired. Raleigh Rent-a-Bike agencies are all over Ireland. Contact them at **Eurotrek** (☎ 01-465 9659; www.eurotrekraleighgroup.com). Like many local bike shops, they offer one-way hire for an extra charge.

Bicycles can be transported by bus if there is enough room onboard; it usually costs €10 per trip. On trains, costs start at €2.50 for a one-way journey, but bikes are not allowed onboard on certain routes, including the Dublin Area Rapid Transit (DART).

Bus

The Republic of Ireland's national bus line, **Bus Éireann** (☎ 01-836 6111; www.buseireann.ie), operates services all over the Republic and into Northern Ireland. Fares are much cheaper than train fares. Return trips are usually only slightly more expensive than one-way fares, and special deals (eg same-day returns) are often available. Most intercity buses in Northern Ireland are operated by **Ulsterbus** (☎ 028-9066 6630; www.translink.co.uk).

Car & Motorcycle

AUTOMOBILE ASSOCIATIONS

Automobile association members should ask for a Card of Introduction entitling you to services offered by sister organisations, usually free of charge.

Automobile Association (AA; www.aaireland.ie) Northern Ireland (☎ 0870-950 0600, breakdowns 0800-667 788); The Republic (☎ 01-677 9481, breakdowns 1800-667788)

Royal Automobile Club (RAC; www.rac.ie) Northern Ireland (☎ 0800-029 029); The Republic (☎ 1800-483 483)

HIRE

Car hire in Ireland is expensive, so you're better off booking a package deal from home. In the high season it's wise to book ahead. Extra fees may apply if you cross the North–South border. Automatic cars are more expensive.

PASSES & DISCOUNT

Eurail passes are valid for train travel in the Republic of Ireland but not in Northern Ireland, and will get you a 50% discount on Irish Ferries crossings to France. InterRail passes give you a 50% reduction on train travel within Ireland and on Irish Ferries and Stena Line services. Both Bus Éireann and Iarnród Éireann offer discounts to ISIC holders.

Britrail has an option to add on Ireland for an extra fee. The pass also covers ferry transit.

Irish Rambler tickets are available from Bus Éireann for bus-only travel in the Republic. They cost €53 (for travel on three out of eight consecutive days), €116 (eight out of 15 days) or €168 (15 out of 30 days). The similar Open Road pass costs €45 for travel on three out of six consecutive days and is extendable.

Irish Rover tickets combine services on Bus Éireann and Ulsterbus. They cost €70 (for three days' travel out of eight consecutive days), €158 (eight out of 15 days) and €235 (15 out of 30 days).

For train-only travel within the Republic, Iarnród Éireann Explorer tickets cost €127 (five days' travel out of 15). It costs €157 (five days' travel out of 15) to include Northern Ireland.

Irish Explorer Rail and Bus tickets (€194) allow you eight days' travel out of 15 consecutive days on trains and buses in the Republic.

In Northern Ireland the Freedom of Northern Ireland ticket is good for unlimited travel on Ulsterbus and Northern Ireland Railways for one day (£14), three days' travel out of eight (£34) or seven consecutive days (£50).

People under 21 cannot hire a car; for most hire companies you must be at least 23 and have had a valid driving licence for one year. Some companies will not hire to those aged over 70 or 75. Your own local licence is usually sufficient to hire a car for up to three months.

In the Republic typical weekly high-season hire rates – with insurance, VAT, unlimited distance and collision-damage waiver – cost €300 for a small car to €450 for a larger one. **Nova Car Hire** (www.rentacar-ireland.com) acts as an agent for Alamo, Budget, European and National, and offers greatly discounted rates.

The international hire companies and the major local operators have offices all over Ireland. Recommended Dublin-based operators:

Argus Rent-A-Car (Map p657; ☎ 01-490 4444, 862 3811; www.argusrentals.com; Dublin Tourism Centre, Suffolk St)

Malone Thrifty Car Rental (☎ 01-874 5844; www.thrifty.ie) Dublin (Map pp654-5; 26 East Lombard St); Central Dublin (Map p657; 33 Bachelors Walk)

Murrays Europcar (☎ 01-614 2800, 812 0410; www.europcar.com; Baggot St Bridge) Just southeast of the city.

ROAD RULES

Driving is on the left-hand side and you should only overtake (pass) to the right of the vehicle ahead of you. The driver and passengers must wear safety belts, and children under 12 cannot sit in the front. Motorcyclists and passengers must wear helmets; headlights should be dipped.

Minor roads can be potholed and narrow, but the traffic is rarely heavy, except through tourist or commercial towns. Speed limits in both Northern Ireland and the Republic appear in kilometres, miles or both: 112km/h (70mph) on the motorways, 96km/h (60mph) on other roads and 48km/h (30mph) or as signposted in towns. On quiet, narrow, winding rural roads it's foolish to speed. Ireland's blood-alcohol limit is 0.08% and strictly enforced.

Car parks and other specified areas in Ireland are regulated by 'pay and display' tickets or disc parking. Available from most newsagencies, discs are good for one hour and cost around €1.50 each. In Northern Ireland beware of Control Zones in town centres where, for security reasons, cars must not be left unattended. Double yellow lines by the roadside mean no parking at any time, while single yellow lines indicate restrictions (which will be signposted).

Train

The Republic of Ireland's railway system, **Iarnród Éireann** (☎ 1850-360 222, 01-836 6222; www.irishrail.ie), has routes fanning out from Dublin. Tickets can be twice as expensive as the bus, but travel times may be dramatically reduced. Special fares are often available, and a midweek return ticket sometimes costs just a bit more than the single fare; the flip side is that fares may be significantly higher on Friday or Sunday. A 1st-class ticket costs an extra €10. **Northern Ireland Railways** (☎ in Dublin 028-9066 6630, 01-679 1977; www.translink.co.uk) has four routes from Belfast, one of which links up with the Republic's rail system.

IRELAND

Italy

Known to Italians as *il Bel Paese* (the Beautiful Country), Italy hits the senses hard. It's impossibly beautiful one minute, comically chaotic the next; it's colourful, noisy and highly theatrical. The food is superb and its passion utterly disarming.

It's also a nation with a lot to live up to. Many of its sights seem so familiar that the risk of disappointed expectations is a real one. Fortunately, though, no photo can portray the thrill of exploring the Colosseum in Rome or seeing Michelangelo's *David* in Florence. The unique atmosphere of Venice's haunting canals or Verona's romantic lanes can never be felt on film.

Away from the cities, Italy's ancient landscape provides a wealth of outdoor opportunities. You can walk the Amalfi Coast, ski in the Dolomites or simply soak up the sun on Sicily and Sardinia's golden beaches.

Of course, there's more to Italy than the obvious. To list every beautiful hill town in Umbria, or to review every great trattoria in Puglia or Tuscan vineyard would require a tome heavier than an airline luggage allowance. The art to visiting Italy is to get out there and discover it for yourself – sooner or later you'll find a corner you can call your own.

ITALY

FAST FACTS

- **Area** 301, 230 sq km
- **Capital** Rome
- **Currency** euro (€); A$1 = €0.60; ¥100 = €0.67; NZ$1 = €0.50; UK£1 = €1.48; US$1 = €0.78
- **Famous for** food and wine, Roman ruins, Renaissance art, Tuscany
- **Official Language** Italian
- **Phrases** *buon giorno* (hello); *grazie* (thanks); *mi scusi* (excuse me); *quanto costa?* (how much is it?)
- **Population** 57.8 million
- **Telephone Codes** country code ☎ 39; international access code ☎ 00; reverse-charge code ☎ 170

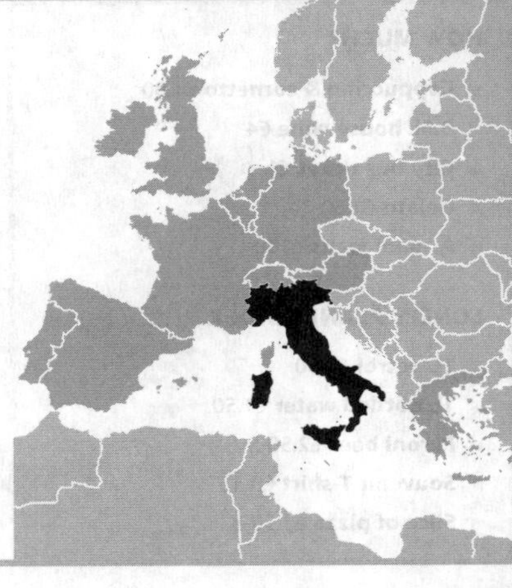

HIGHLIGHTS

- Throw yourself into the boiling chaos of **Rome** (p716), Italy's most compelling city.
- Savour the spectacular scenery along the **Cinque Terre** (p742) and **Amalfi Coast** (p795).
- Give your imagination a workout in the ancient Greek amphitheatre of **Syracuse** (p807).
- Lap up the romance in **Verona** (p750), Romeo and Juliet's hometown.
- Scramble among **Matera's sassi** (p797), a stark reminder of Italy's lost peasant culture.

ITINERARIES

- **One week** After climbing Pisa's Leaning Tower immerse yourself in Florence for a couple of days. Sated on the Renaissance, stop off at Siena en route to three days in Rome, time enough for its greatest hits.
- **Two weeks** After two days in Venice and a day in Verona start heading south. Gorge yourself on food in Bologna and art in Pisa, Florence and Siena as you make for Rome. Spend two days in the capital and then move on to Naples and the Amalfi Coast. Spend your final two days in the sun on Sicily, in Palermo and Taormina.

CLIMATE & WHEN TO GO

Italian summers are long, hot and often uncomfortably humid. Winters can be surprisingly severe, even in the south where snow in the mountainous hinterland is an annual fixture. November is Italy's wettest month.

The best times to visit are from April to June or in early autumn (September and October) – at these times the weather's sunny without being scorching and the crowds are bearable. Avoid beaches in August as prices skyrocket and much of the coastline is infested with sun-beds, booked and paid for months in advance. Winter is a peaceful and cost-effective time to visit the cities.

See p1100 for climate charts.

HOW MUCH?

- **Cappuccino & cornetto** €1.80
- **0.5L house wine** €4
- **City bus ticket** €1
- **Gelato** €1.50-3
- **Armani jeans** €180

LONELY PLANET INDEX

- **1L petrol** €1.30
- **1L bottled water** €1.50
- **Peroni beer** €2.50-5
- **Souvenir T-shirt** €8-15
- **Slice of pizza** €1.50-3

HISTORY

Little is known about the origins of the Etruscans but by the 7th century BC they had grown into the dominant force in central Italy, rivalled only by the Greeks on the south coast. Since the 8th century BC Greek traders had been settling in Italy founding a number of independent city-states, collectively known as Magna Graecia. Both groups thrived until the 3rd century BC when Rome's rampaging legionnaires crashed in.

Rise & Fall of the Romans

Whether or not you believe that Romulus founded Rome in 753 BC, Remus' twin brother is generally acknowledged as the first of Rome's seven kings. The last, the Etruscan Tarquinius, was ousted in 509 BC and replaced by the Roman Republic.

The fledgling republic got off to a shaky start but once it had survived a Gallic invasion in 390 BC, it began to spread its wings. It colonised much of the Mediterranean and, under Julius Caesar, Gaul. Caesar, the last of the republic's consuls, was assassinated in 44 BC, sparking a power struggle between his great-nephew Octavian and Mark Antony (Cleopatra's lover). Octavian prevailed and in 27 BC was hailed as Augustus Caesar, Rome's first emperor.

Rome's golden age came in the 2nd century AD, but by the 3rd century economic decline and the spread of Christianity was fuelling discontent. Diocletian tried to stop the rot by splitting the empire into eastern and western halves, but when his successor, Constantine (the first Christian emperor), moved his court to Constantinople, Rome's days were numbered. Sacked by the Goths in 410 and plundered by the Vandals in 455, the Western Empire finally fell in 476.

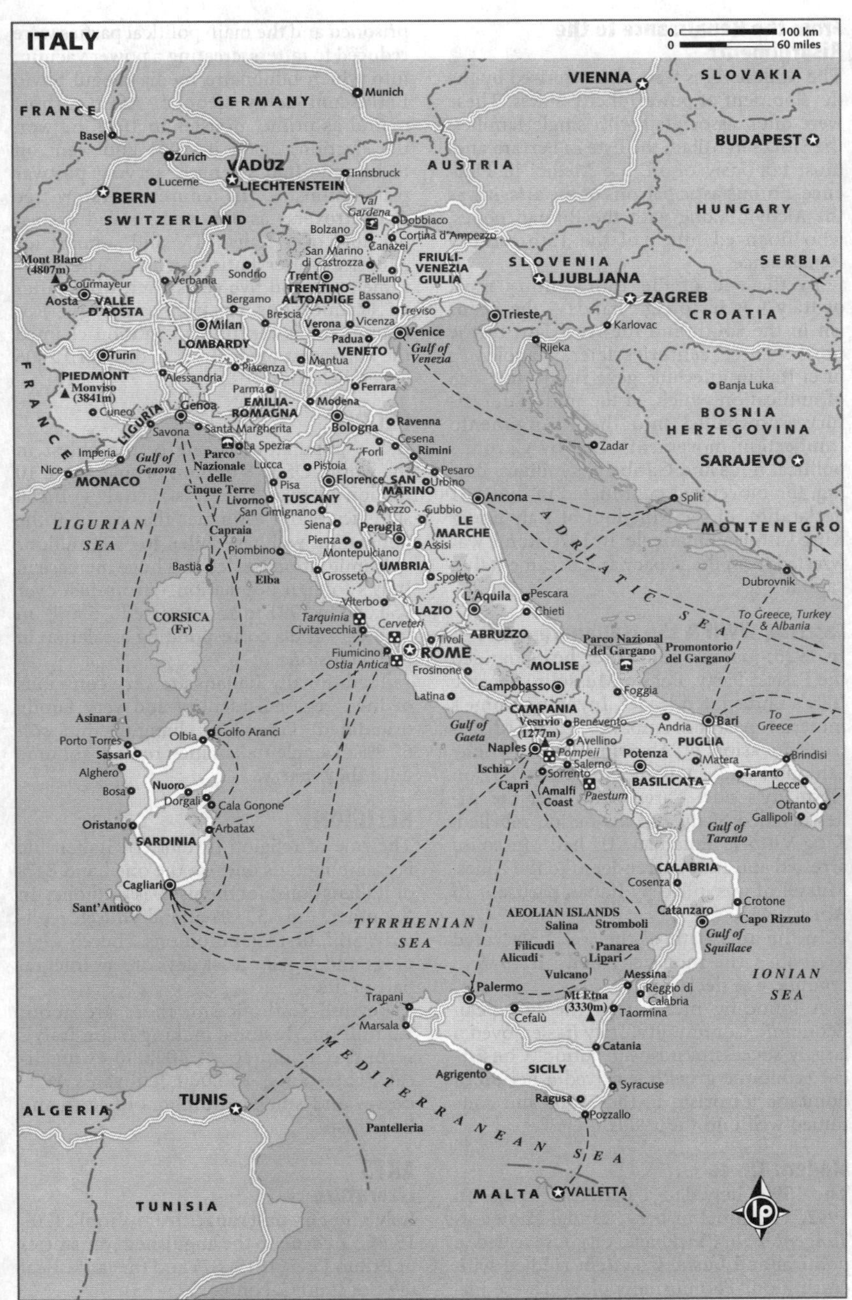
ITALY
0 100 km
0 60 miles
FRANCE
GERMANY
Munich
VIENNA
SLOVAKIA
BUDAPEST
Basel
Zurich
VADUZ
LIECHTENSTEIN
Innsbruck
AUSTRIA
Lucerne
BERN
SWITZERLAND
HUNGARY
Val Gardena
Dobbiaco
Bolzano
Cortina d'Ampezzo
Canazei
San Marino di Castrozza
FRIULI-VENEZIA GIULIA
SLOVENIA
SERBIA
Mont Blanc (4807m)
Courmayeur
Aosta
VALLE D'AOSTA
Sondrio
Verbania
Trent
TRENTINO-ALTOADIGE
Belluno
Bassano
LJUBLJANA
ZAGREB
CROATIA
Bergamo
Brescia
Treviso
Trieste
Karlovac
Milan
Verona
Vicenza
Venice
LOMBARDY
Padua
VENETO
Gulf of Venezia
Rijeka
Turin
Mantua
Piacenza
Alessandria
PIEDMONT
Monviso (3841m)
Parma
Ferrara
Banja Luka
EMILIA-ROMAGNA
Modena
Cuneo
Genoa
LIGURIA
Bologna
Ravenna
BOSNIA HERZEGOVINA
Savona
Santa Margherita
Cesena
Imperia
La Spezia
Forlì
Rimini
Zadar
Nice
MONACO
Gulf of Genova
Parco Nazionale delle Cinque Terre
Lucca
Pistoia
Pesaro
Urbino
SARAJEVO
Pisa
Florence
SAN MARINO
Livorno
TUSCANY
Ancona
Split
San Gimignano
Arezzo
Gubbio
LIGURIAN SEA
Capraia
Siena
Perugia
LE MARCHE
MONTENEGRO
Pienza
Assisi
Piombino
Montepulciano
Bastia
UMBRIA
Elba
Grosseto
Spoleto
ADRIATIC SEA
Dubrovnik
L'Aquila
Pescara
Viterbo
CORSICA (Fr)
LAZIO
Chieti
Tarquinia
Civitavecchia
Cerveteri
Tivoli
ABRUZZO
To Greece, Turkey & Albania
Parco Nazional del Gargano
Promontorio del Gargano
Fiumicino
ROME
Ostia Antica
Frosinone
MOLISE
Campobasso
Foggia
Latina
Asinara
CAMPANIA
Vesuvio (1277m)
Benevento
Gulf of Gaeta
Andria
Bari
To Greece
Porto Torres
Olbia
Golfo Aranci
Sassari
Avellino
Naples
Pompeii
PUGLIA
Alghero
Ischia
Salerno
Potenza
Matera
Brindisi
Nuoro
Sorrento
Taranto
Bosa
Capri
BASILICATA
Lecce
Dorgali
Amalfi Coast
Paestum
Cala Gonone
Oristano
Otranto
Gallipoli
Arbatax
SARDINIA
Gulf of Taranto
CALABRIA
Cagliari
Cosenza
Crotone
Sant'Antioco
AEOLIAN ISLANDS
Salina
Stromboli
Catanzaro
Capo Rizzuto
TYRRHENIAN SEA
Filicudi
Alicudi
Panarea
Lipari
Gulf of Squillace
Vulcano
Messina
IONIAN SEA
Palermo
Trapani
Reggio di Calabria
Mt Etna (3330m)
Cefalù
Taormina
Marsala
Catania
SICILY
Agrigento
Syracuse
MEDITERRANEAN SEA
ALGERIA
TUNIS
Ragusa
Pozzallo
Pantelleria
MALTA
VALLETTA
TUNISIA

ITALY

From the Renaissance to the Risorgimento

The Middle Ages were characterised by the development of powerful city-states. These were often associated with single families: the Sforza in Milan, the Este in Ferrara and, most famously of all, the Medici in Florence. Enthusiastic patrons of the arts, it was the Medici, along with the Roman popes, who financed much of the 15th-century Renaissance.

By the end of the 16th century most of Italy was in foreign hands – the Spanish in the south and the Austrians in the north. Three centuries later, Napoleon's brief Italian interlude gave rise to the idea of unification which, in the mid-19th century, snowballed into the Risorgimento (unification movement). Led by Cavour's political nous and Garibaldi's military daring, the movement culminated in the 1861 declaration of the Kingdom of Italy under King Vittorio Emanuele. In 1870 Rome was wrested from the papacy and became Italy's capital.

Fascism, WWII & the Italian Republic

In 1925, just six years after he'd founded the Fascist Party, Benito Mussolini became Italy's undisputed leader. Invoking Rome's imperial past he embarked on a disastrous invasion of Abyssinia (modern-day Ethiopia) and, in 1940, entered WWII on Germany's side. Three years later the Allies invaded Sicily and his nation rebelled: King Vittorio Emanuele III had Mussolini arrested and Italy surrendered to the Allies. Mussolini was killed by Italian partisans in April 1945.

In the aftermath of the war Italy voted to abolish the monarchy and, in 1946, a republic was declared.

A founding member of the European Economic Community, Italy has enjoyed a largely successful postwar period. Consistent economic growth survived a period of domestic terrorism in the 1970s and continued well into the 1980s.

Modern Times

The 1990s heralded a period of crisis. In 1992, a national bribery scandal known as *Tangentopoli* ('kickback city') revealed a political and business system riddled with corruption. Top business players were imprisoned and the main political parties were reduced to tatters, creating a power vacuum into which billionaire media-mogul Silvio Berlusconi deftly stepped. After a short period as prime minister in 1994, he won the elections again in 2001 and went on to become Italy's longest serving postwar prime minister. His tenure was rarely free of controversy as opponents railed against his hold over Italian TV and support for American intervention in Iraq. The party came to an end five years later, when, after an acrimonious election campaign, Romano Prodi's centre-left coalition claimed the narrowest of victories in the April 2006 general election.

PEOPLE

Italy's population is one of the oldest in the world. Of 57.8 million people, some 10 million are over 65, and Istat (Italy's official statistics body) estimates that by 2050 the population will have fallen to 55.8 million.

Immigration has led to a huge increase in Italy's foreign population – from just over 350,000 in 1991 to an estimated 2.6 million in 2004 – and a corresponding escalation in racial tensions.

Traditionally Italians are very conscious of their regional identity and very family orientated. Times are changing, but still 67.9% of single Italian men remain at home until they marry.

RELIGION

The role of religion in modern Italian life is an ambiguous one: on the one hand 84% of Italians consider themselves Catholic; on the other, only 33.9% attend church regularly. Still, first Communions, church weddings and regular feast days are an integral part of life.

Beyond Catholicism, there are about 1.3 million Muslims, making Islam Italy's second religion, about 400,000 evangelical Protestants, 350,000 Jehovah's Witnesses and smaller numbers of Jews and Buddhists.

ARTS

Literature

Italy's literary past ranges from Virgil's (70–19 BC) *Aeneid*, to the anguished war stories of Primo Levi (1919–87) and the fantastical tales of Italo Calvino (1923–85).

THE MAFIA

It takes a pretty big story to knock a general election off the headlines before a winner's even been declared. But that's exactly what happened on 11 April 2006 when it was announced that after 43 years on the run, the Sicilian mafia boss, Bernardo Provenzano, had been arrested. A huge PR victory for the Italian police, the arrest was an important breakthrough in the fight against organised crime; just how important remains to be seen.

Italy's mafia comprises five distinct groups: the original Cosa Nostra in Sicily; the Neapolitan Camorra; the 'Ndrangheta in Calabria, and the two Puglian groups, the Sacra Corona Unita and La Rosa. Together they have an annual turnover estimated at €100 billion or 10% of Italy's GDP.

Of the five it's the Calabrian 'Ndrangheta that's been attracting the most attention in recent months. Said to control distribution of Colombian cocaine in Europe, it sent shivers through Calabria's political hierarchy when, in October 2005, it gunned down the region's vice president. The murder, before witnesses and in broad daylight, was widely interpreted as a declaration of inviolability. That the killers were subsequently caught did little to dent the pervading sense of pessimism.

The mafia groups are deeply entrenched in their territories and with the power to impose silence through fear, they are as healthy now as they've ever been, their profits never healthier. To their traditional activities of trafficking (cigarettes, drugs, arms, bootleg CDs), racketeering and profiteering on public works contracts, they've added the hugely lucrative business of illegal waste disposal. The Italian environmental organisation Legambiente estimates that the ecomafia has made up to €132 billion in the last 10 years, burying or burning everything from asbestos to toxic liquid.

Dante (1265–1321), whose *Divina Commedia* (Divine Comedy) dates to the early 1300s, was one of three 14th-century greats, the others being Petrarch (1304–74) and Giovanni Boccaccio (1313–75), considered the first Italian novelist.

Just over a century later Machiavelli (1469–1527) established his name with his political classic, *The Prince*.

In more recent times Sicily has proved a fertile literary soil. Giuseppe Tomasi di Lampedusa (1896–1957) depicts the island's wary mentality in *Il Gattopardo* (The Leopard), a theme that Leonardo Sciascia (1921–89) later returned to. Andrea Camilleri's (1925–) whodunits starring maverick detective Montalbano are hugely popular.

Cinema

For a moment in the early 2000s, it looked like Italian cinema was about to enjoy a Renaissance. Roberto Benigni (1952–) had recently won an Oscar for *La Vita è Bella* (Life is Beautiful; 1997) and Gabriele Muccino (1967–) was winning rave reviews for his smash hit *L'Ultimo Bacio* (The Last Kiss; 2001). Unfortunately, the moment passed and little came of the hope.

The heyday of Italian cinema was the post-WWII period, when the neorealists Roberto Rossellini (1906–77), Vittorio de Sica (1901–74) and Luchino Visconti (1907–76) turned their cameras onto the war-weary Italians. Classics of the genre include *Ladri di Biciclette* (Bicycle Thieves; 1948) and *Roma Città Aperta* (Rome Open City; 1945).

Federico Fellini (1920–94) created his own highly visual style and won an international audience with films such as *La Dolce Vita* (The Sweet Life; 1959).

Of Italy's contemporary directors, Nanni Moretti (1953–) can usually be relied on for an idiosyncratic take on Italian life. His thinly disguised attack on Berlusconi, *Il Caimano* (The Cayman; 2006), caused controversy when it was released in the middle of the 2006 election campaign.

Music

Emotional and highly theatrical, opera has always appealed to the Italians. Verdi (1813–1901) might be the most famous of Italian composers, but Puccini (1858–1924), Bellini (1801–35), Donizetti (1797–1848) and Rossini (1792–1868) are hardly unknowns. Tenor Luciano Pavarotti (1935–) enjoyed critical acclaim and popular support during his singing career, while Andrea Bocelli (1958–) continues to sell CDs by the box load.

TOP TEN ITALY

- Top Museums – Museo e Galleria Borghese, Rome (p723); Museo Archeologico Nazionale, Naples (p787)
- Top Medieval Centre – Urbino (p785)
- Top Architecture – Baroque Lecce (p799); Florence's Duomo (p772)
- Top Ruins – Pompeii (p792); Agrigento, Sicily (p808)
- Top Festivals – Il Palio, Siena (p780); Carnevale, Venice (p755)
- Top Walks – Dolomites (p767); Cinque Terre (p742)
- Top Coastline – Amalfi Coast (p795)
- Top Pizza – Da Michele, Naples (p790)
- Top Coffee – San Tommaso 10, Turin (p745)
- Top Drinking Piazzas – Campo de'Fiori, Rome (p734); Campo Santa Margherita, Venice

But it's not all opera. Antonio Vivaldi (1675–1741) created the concerto in its present form and wrote one of classical music's greatest hits *Le Quattro Stagione* (The Four Seasons). Whether the hits of Eros Ramazzotti (1963–) will be played in 300 years' time is a matter of debate.

Architecture & Visual Arts

Everywhere you go in Italy you're faced with reminders of the country's convoluted past. In the south, where the Greeks left an indelible mark, there are well-preserved temples in the Valley of the Temples in Agrigento (p808), Sicily. Pompeii (p792) offers insights into the day-to-day lives of Romans, while the Byzantine mosaics of Ravenna (p766), Venice (p752) and Palermo (p801) reflect eastern influences.

During the 15th century, artists and architects flourished, particularly in Florence and Rome. Filippo Brunelleschi (1377–1446) defied the architectural laws of the day in creating what was considered the greatest artistic feat of the day – the dome on Florence's Duomo (p772). His achievement was later overshadowed by the works of Michelangelo Buonarrotti (1475–1564), the greatest of the High Renaissance (1490–1520) artists. Contemporaries Leonardo da Vinci (1452–1519) and Raphael (1483–1520) further brightened the scene.

Controversial and highly influential, Michelangelo Merisi da Caravaggio (1573–1610) dominated the late 16th century. More than one of his paintings was rejected by religious patrons on the grounds that it was blasphemous. There were few such problems in the ensuing baroque era when art was put at the service of the church. The result was highly decorative – witness the Roman works of rivals Gianlorenzo Bernini (1598–1680) and Francesco Borromini (1599–1667) or, further south, the excesses of Lecce's *centro storico* (historic centre; p799).

Signalling a return to the sober lines of classical art, neoclassicism was the predominant movement of the late 18th and early 19th centuries. Its most famous Italian exponent was Canova (1757–1822), who carved a name for himself with his smooth sensual style. Rome's Spanish Steps (p725) and Trevi Fountain (p725) both date to this period.

But if neoclassicism owed everything to the past, Italian futurism provided a rallying cry for modernism. Inspired by Umberto Boccioni (1882–1916), painters like Giacomo Balla (1871–1958) were hugely influential. Caught up in the modernist spirit, the 1920s *razionalisti* (rationalists) provided the architectural vision behind the EUR district in Rome. Built for the Esposizione Universale di Roma in 1942, from which it takes its name, EUR is a suburb in the south of Rome, an area of wide boulevards and huge linear buildings – unlike anywhere else in the ancient city.

ENVIRONMENT

Bound on three sides by four seas (the Adriatic, Ligurian, Tyrrhenian and Ionian), Italy has more than 8000km of coastline. Inland, about 75% of the peninsula is mountainous – the Alps curve 966km around the country's northern border while the Apennines extend 1350km from north to south.

Italy and its surrounding seas harbour a rich fauna. You're unlikely to meet them, but 80 Marsican brown bears roam free in the Parco Nazionale d'Abruzzo, Lazio e Molise. To the north, the Parco Nazionale dei Monti Sibillini is home to more than 50 species of mammal, including the wolf and wildcat, and over 150 types of bird. Swordfish, tuna and dolphins are common along the coastline and although white sharks are known to exist, attacks are rare.

Italy has 21 national parks, covering about 5% of the country, and over 400 nature reserves, natural parks and wetlands. Major parks include the Parco Nazionale del Gran Paradiso (Piedmont/Valle d'Aosta), Parco Nazionale d'Abruzzo, Lazio e Molise, Parco Nazionale del Pollino (Basilicata/Calabria) and Parco Nazionale dei Monti Sibillini (Umbria/Le Marche).

Italy also has 40 World Heritage sites, more than any other country. These range from the historic centres of Siena, Naples, Pienza and Florence, to sites of natural beauty such as the Amalfi Coast, Cinque Terre and Aeolian Islands.

Of Italy's environmental challenges, air pollution is the most obvious. A feature of many city centres, it's largely caused by car emissions. Traffic restrictions are helping but still a lot needs to be done.

In the countryside, tree clearing and illegal building have led the Worldwide Fund for Nature (WWF) to claim that a third of Italy's coastline is threatened by erosion. There are also natural hazards: landslides, floods, earthquakes and volcanic eruptions.

FOOD & DRINK

Italians are serious, knowledgeable and highly opinionated about food. However, *la cucina italiana* is something that only foreigners talk about. Italians discuss Tuscan cuisine or Neapolitan pizzas, Piedmontese wine or Puglian pasta. In short, Italian cooking is regional. Local specialities abound – pesto in Liguria, pizza in Naples, *ragù* (bolognese sauce) in Bologna. It's the same with wine – Piedmont produces Italy's great reds, Barolo, Barbaresco and Dolcetto, while Tuscany's famous for its Chianti, Brunello and white Vernaccia. Peroni is the national beer; for a draft, order it *alla spina*.

As a rule it always pays to eat local food prepared with seasonal produce. Vegetarians will find delicious fruit and veg in the hundreds of daily markets. Few restaurants cater specifically to vegetarians but most serve vegetable-based antipasti (starters), pastas, contorni (side dishes) and salads. Popular antipasti include fried vegetables and vegetables marinated in olive oil. Pasta is often served with mushrooms, courgettes or eggplant.

Where to Eat & Drink

Dining options are divided into several categories. At the most basic level a *tavola calda* (literally 'hot table') offers canteen-style food. Pizzerias, the best of which have a *forno a legna* (wood-fired oven), serve the obvious but often a full menu as well. For takeaway, a *rosticceria* sells cooked meats and a *pizza al taglio*, pizza by the slice.

To sample wine make for an *enoteca*, a wine bar that will often serve light snacks (cheeses and cold meats) and a couple of hot dishes. Alternatively, most bars/cafés serve *tramezzini* (sandwiches) and *panini* (bread rolls). Another option is to go to one of the many *alimentari* (delicatessens) and ask them to make a panino with the filling of your choice. At a *pasticceria* you can buy pastries, cakes and biscuits. *Forni* (bakeries) are another good choice for a cheap snack.

For a full meal you'll want a trattoria, an *osteria* or a *ristorante*. Traditionally, *trattorie* were family-run places that served a basic menu of local dishes at affordable prices. Thankfully, a few still do. *Ristoranti* offer more choice and smarter service. An *osteria* is usually a small trattoria or wine bar serving a limited food menu.

Restaurants, all of which are nonsmoking, usually open for lunch from noon to 3pm and for dinner from 7.30pm, earlier in tourist areas. For more on opening times see the Italy Directory, p816.

Most eateries charge a *pane e coperto* (cover charge), ranging from €1 to €4, and a *servizio* (service charge) of 10% to 15%. If a service charge isn't included, tourists are expected to round up the bill or leave 10%.

Habits & Customs

A full Italian meal consists of an antipasto, a *primo piatto* (first course), a *secondo piatto* (second course) with an *insalata* (salad) or *contorno* (vegetable side dish), and *dolci* (dessert). When eating out it's perfectly acceptable to order, say, a *primo* followed by an *insalata* or *contorno*.

Italians don't tend to eat a sit-down *colazione* (breakfast), preferring instead a cappuccino and *cornetto* (croissant) at a bar. *Pranzo* (lunch) is traditionally the main meal of the day, although this is changing as office hours reduce many people to a light lunch and large *cena* (evening meal). Italians are late diners, often not eating until after 9pm.

ROME

pop 2.6 million

Rome. Just the name conjures up 2700 years of Western civilisation. After three millennia of exerting influence over the world's politics, religion, architecture, transportation and social morays, Rome might now be filled with more foreigners carrying maps of Rome than actual Roman citizens. However, its storied past and legendary buildings overpower and captivate even the most jaded visitors. From the iconic Colosseum to the medieval winding streets of Trastevere, practically every centimetre of Rome is saturated in history or artistically inspired, or both. Even the air feels just a tiny bit more significant here.

Modern Rome stands up to its past. It is at once traditional and avant-garde, chaotic and fashionable. It is a thriving metropolis, the seat of many an international organisation, but with nary a skyscraper in sight. Its moniker, the *Città Eterna* (Eternal City), speaks as much to its future as its past.

HISTORY

Rome's earliest origins displayed nothing of the greatness it would later attain. It started out as a settlement of Etruscan, Latin and Sabine tribes, but the legendary founding dates to 21 April 753 BC. The noble twins Romulus and Remus had been sent down the Tiber River as babies by their rival great uncle Amulius. Nursed by a she-wolf and raised by shepherds, the strong and brave twins eventually learned of their noble birth and returned to the village, where they deposed Amulius, taking back control of the village. Soon after establishing the future empire on Palatine Hill, Romulus killed Remus in a quarrel and named the burgeoning settlement after himself.

In just a few hundred years, the village grew into an almost omnipotent superpower and, at one point, controlled most of the Mediterranean and European world, from Britain to Egypt. Up until the decline and eventual fall of the Roman Empire in AD 476, the city was the grandest the Western world would ever know.

In the fourth century, a new force spread. The apostles Peter and Paul had been slowly gaining Christian converts since their visits in the 1st century AD, but it was Emperor Constantine who helped inextricably link Rome and Christianity by making it the official religion. In AD 312, Constantine reportedly had a vision of the cross before winning a battle. Impressed with the power of this Christian God (and, perhaps even more impressed with the power of institutionalising a state religion of his own choosing), Constantine became the religion's most ardent patron. He stopped crucifixions (in favour of hanging), got rid of pagan sacrifices and temples, Christianised the Eastern city of Byzantium (which became Constantinople and is now modern-day Istanbul), and initiated the Council of Nicaea, which voted to confirm the divinity of Jesus.

ORIENTATION

Rome is surprisingly small. Most sights are between the Roma Termini train station and the Vatican on the other side of the Tevere (Tiber) River, just three metro stops apart, or about an hour's walk.

Most intercity trains stop at Roma Termini (sometimes called Stazione Termini). *Urbano* (city) buses leave from just in front, in the Piazza dei Cinquecento, and Metro Linea A and B trains depart from under the train station. Several trains and most *extraurbano* (intercity) buses depart from Stazione Tiburtina, out of the *centro storico* but accessible by Metro Linea B.

If your time is limited, it helps to plan an itinerary. Most of the major museums and galleries are open all day until 7pm or 8pm, however, some museums are closed on Monday or around lunchtime, and the Vatican museums are closed on all but the last Sunday of the month, so check ahead.

INFORMATION

Bookshops

Feltrinelli International (Map p724; Via Orlando 84; 🕒 9am-8pm Mon-Sat, 10.30am-1.30pm & 4-8pm Sun) An extensive selection of maps, travel books and titles in many different languages.

ITALY

Discount Cards

Roma Archeologia Card (☎ 06 39 96 77 00; €20, valid 7 days) Gets you into nine important attractions, including the Colosseum, Palatine and some of the Museo Nazionale Romano locations.

Emergency

Foreigners' Bureau (Map pp726-7; ☎ 06 468 62 977; Via Genova 2) Report thefts here.

Police station (Questura; Map pp726-7; ☎ 06 468 61; Via San Vitale 11; 24hr)

Internet Access

Internet cafés are plentiful and most hostels and many hotels offer access (listed under Sleeping); the area near Roma Termini offers the highest concentration.

Easy Internet Café (Map pp722-3; Via Barberini 2; per hr €2; 8am-1am) Over 100 terminals on two floors.

Telephone Center International (Map p724; Via Volturno 52; per hr €2) Good rates on international calls.

Medical Services

Each *farmacia* (pharmacy) window has a list of all-night pharmacies, or call ☎ 06 22 89 41. Pharmacists sometimes assist with minor diagnoses.

24-hour Pharmacy (Map p724; ☎ 06 488 00 19; Piazza del Cinquecento 49/50/51) Opposite Roma Termini.

Ospedale Bambino Gesù (Map pp718-19; ☎ 06 685 92 351; Piazza di Sant'Onofrio 4) Rome's paediatric hospital.

Ospedale San Gallicano (Map pp726-7; ☎ 06 588 23 90; Via di San Gallicano 25a, Trastevere)

Ospedale Santo Spirito (Map pp722-3; ☎ 06 68 35 22 41; Lungotevere in Sassia 1) Near the Vatican; multilingual staff.

Money

American Express (Map pp722-3; ☎ 06 676 41; Piazza di Spagna 38)

Thomas Cook (Map pp722-3; ☎ 06 482 81 82; Piazza Barberini 21)

Post

For general post information, call ☎ 800 160 100.

Main post office (Map pp722-3; Piazza San Silvestro 19) Near the Spanish Steps.

Vatican post office (Map pp722-3; ☎ 06 69 88 34 06; Piazza di San Pietro) Said to offer faster and more reliable service.

Tourist Information

Enjoy Rome (Map p724; ☎ 06 445 18 43; www.enjoyrome.com; Via Marghera 8a; 8.30am-7pm Mon-Sat, to 2pm Sun) Five minutes' walk northeast of Roma Termini. A well-run private tourist office with a free hotel-reservation service and travel agency; books tickets to operas, shows and offers info on nightlife as well as walking tours of Rome and visits to nearby destinations such as Ostia Antica (p738).

Rome Online (www.romaturismo.com) Everything you need to know about Rome.

Tourist information line (☎ 06 8205 9127; 9am-7pm daily)

Tourist offices Roma Termini (Map p724; ☎ 06 48 90 63 00; 8am-9pm); Via Parigi 5 (Main Tourist Office; Map p724; 9am-7pm Mon-Sat) Good information on hotels and sights. Both offices provide maps and printed information about bus services.

Vatican tourist office (Map pp722-3; ☎ 06 69 88 16 62; Piazza di San Pietro; 8.30am-7pm Mon-Sat) Next to the basilica.

SIGHTS & ACTIVITIES

When it comes to seeing the sights, that old adage *Roma, non basta una vita* (Rome, a lifetime is not enough), couldn't be more true. Possibly the only European capital with more ruins than dog poop, Rome boasts thousands of years of visible history. Although most tourists stick to the classic itinerary – the Colosseum, Forum, Pantheon and Vatican – we urge you to branch out and spend a day bicycling along the Appia Antica or wandering the Protestant Cemetery.

Colosseum

It takes a bit of imagination, but when visiting Rome's greatest known monument, the **Colosseum** (Map pp726-7; ☎ 06 399 67 700; admission with Palatine Hill €10; 9am-1hr before sunset), try to close your eyes and picture how the ancient arena would have appeared in its heyday – the marble-covered building crammed with 50,000 spectators, complete with boxed seats (some with benefactors' carved names still visible), toilet facilities, refreshment stands and a giant retractable sail to act as a roof. Instead of football, however, they would have been watching gladiators fight panthers, hippopotami and crocodiles, and occasionally, one another.

The Colosseum was built by Emperor Vespasian in AD 72 and finished by his son Titus in AD 80. During the Middle Ages, the Colosseum became a fortress, then later a quarry for travertine and marble to build Palazzo Venezia and other buildings.

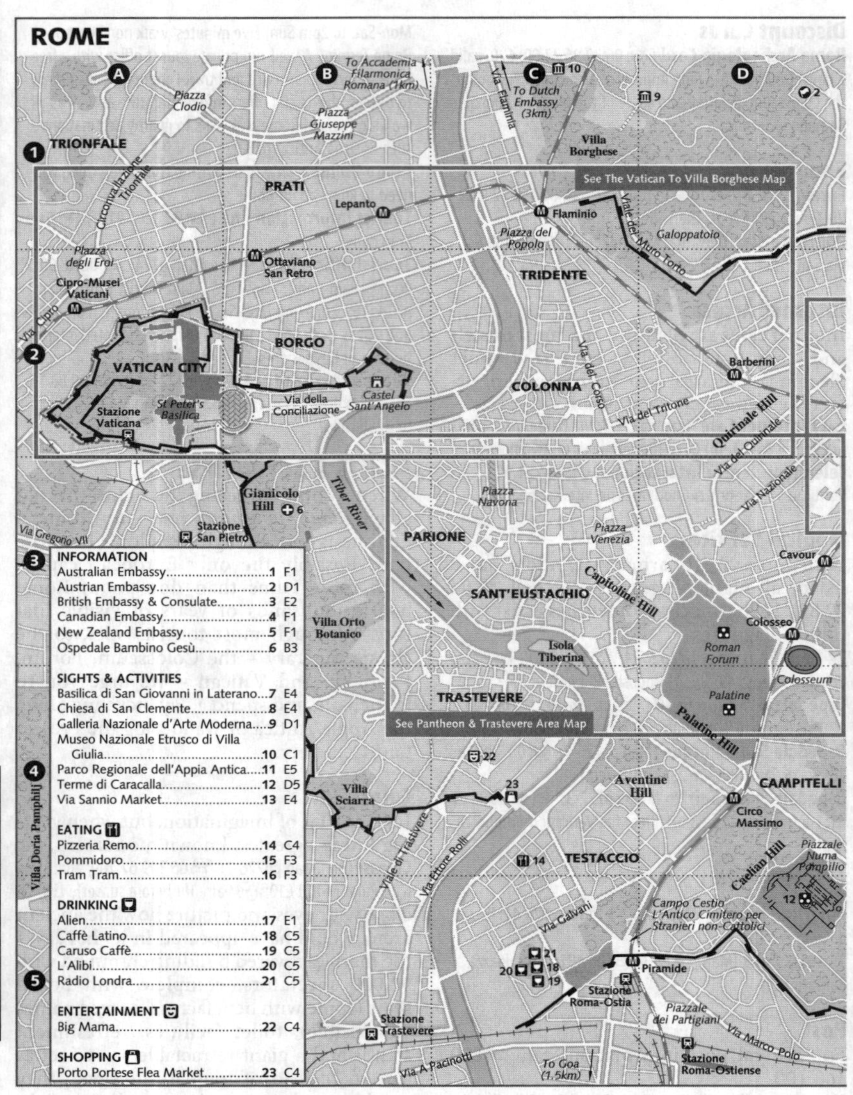

On the west side is the triumphal arch built to honour Constantine following his victory over his rival Maxentius at the battle of Milvian Bridge in AD 312. Its decorative reliefs were taken from earlier structures.

It pays to join one of the impromptu walking tours inside for an extra €8, as you get to jump the line for a guided tour of both the Colosseum and Palatine Hill.

Roman Forum & Palatine Hill

Visit the dawn of Western civilisation at the **Roman Forum** (Map pp726-7; ☎ 06 399 67 700; admission free; 9am-1hr before sunset Mon-Sat), set in a valley between the Capitoline and Palatine

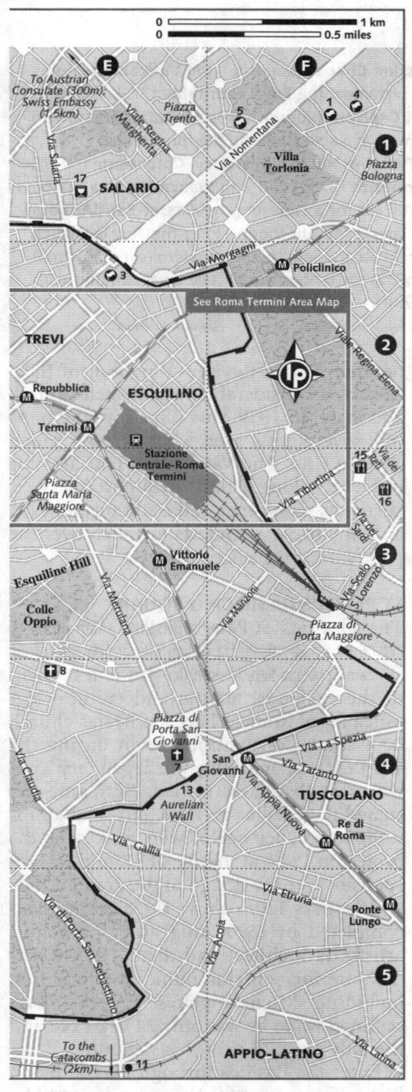

Hills. Throughout the era of the kings, the Republic and the Empire, the Forum was the political, religious and social centre of the Roman world.

In the 4th century AD, after the fall of the Roman Empire, the area fell into disuse, eventually being used as pasture land. By the medieval days, the buildings were plundered for their precious marble. Many temples and buildings were converted to other uses, while some monuments lay half-revealed. The area was systematically excavated in the 18th and 19th centuries, and excavations are continuing.

As you enter at Largo Romolo e Remo, to your left is the **Tempio di Antonino e Faustina**, built by the senate in AD 141 and transformed into a church in the 8th century. To your right are the remains of the **Basilica Aemilia**, built in 179 BC. The **Via Sacra**, which traverses the Forum from northwest to southeast, runs in front of the basilica. Towards the Campidoglio is the **Curia**, once the meeting place of the Roman senate and converted into a church. In front of the Curia is the **Lapis Niger**, a large piece of black marble that purportedly covered Romulus' grave.

The **Arco di Settimo Severo** was erected in AD 203 in honour of this emperor and his sons, and is considered one of Italy's major triumphal arches. A circular base stone beside the arch marks the *umbilicus urbis*, the symbolic centre of ancient Rome.

Southwest of the arch is the **Tempio di Saturno**, one of the most important ancient Roman temples. Dedicated to the god of chaos and disorder in 497 BC, it was later used as the state treasury. The **Basilica Giulia**, in front of the temple, was the seat of justice, and nearby is the **Tempio di Giulio Cesare**, erected by Augustus in 29 BC on the site where Caesar's body was burned.

Back towards the Palatine Hill is the **Tempio dei Castori**, built in 489 BC in honour of the Heavenly Twins, or Dioscuri. It is easily recognisable by its three remaining columns.

In the area southeast of the temple is the **Chiesa di Santa Maria Antiqua**, the oldest Christian church in the Forum, now closed to the public. Back on Via Sacra is the **Casa delle Vestali**, home of the virgins who tended the eternal flame of Rome in the adjoining **Tempio di Vesta**. The vestal virgins were chosen at the age of 10 for their beauty and virtue. They were required to stay chaste and committed to keeping the flame for 30 years.

The next major monument is the vast **Basilica di Costantino**. Its impressive design inspired Renaissance architects. The **Arco di Tito**, at the Colosseum end of the Forum, was built in AD 81 in honour of the victories

ROME IN TWO DAYS

Set your alarm early to beat the crowds for the **Sistine Chapel** (opposite), the **Vatican Museums** (opposite) and **St Peter's Basilica** (below). Stop for pizza near the **Trevi Fountain** (p725) or **Campo de'Fiori** (p723). Spend the afternoon at the **Musei Capitolini** (opposite) and head to **Trastevere** (p725) for dinner at **Le Mani in Pasta** (p733), then on to **Sette Oche** (p733) for a drink.

On day two, start at the **Roman Forum** (p718), **Palatine Hill** (p718) and the **Colosseum** (p717). Head to the Jewish Ghetto for lunch at **Sora Margherita** (p732) and into **Piazza Navona** (p722) for some *gelato* and people-watching. If you're still up for a museum, try **Castel Sant'Angelo** (p722) or **Museo e Galleria Borghese** (p725), or spend the afternoon along the **Appia Antica** (p728) or in the **Protestant Cemetery** (p729). Grab pizza and join the *passeggiata* (evening stroll) around Campo de'Fiori and splurge at **Roscioli** (p732) for dinner or deli takeaway, ending with a toast to your Roman holiday at **Bar del Fico** (p734).

of the emperors Titus and Vespasian against Jerusalem.

From here, climb the **Palatine** (admission €10; entrances are along Via di San Gregorio and Piazza dei Santa Maria Nova), where wealthy Romans built their homes and legend says that Romulus founded the city. Archaeological evidence shows that the earliest settlements in the area were in fact on the Palatine and date back to near 753 BC. Like the Forum, the buildings of the Palatine fell into ruin and in the Middle Ages the hill became the site of convents and churches. During the Renaissance, it was quite fashionable to establish a family garden here.

Again, you'll have to use your power of imagination at the **Domus Augustana** and **Domus Flavia**. Although they don't look like much now, the latter was the residence of the Emperor Domitian, who used the large rectangular room (now ruins) as the very first home entertainment system. Satellite TV having not yet been invented, Domitian instead set up his very own home athletic stadium so he could watch sports matches in splendid privacy. Also of note on the Palatine Hill are the **Tempio della Magna Mater**, built in 204 BC, and the fresco-adorned **Casa di Livia**, thought to belong to the wife of Emperor Augustus.

Vatican City

The smallest sovereign nation in the world with a population of 900, Vatican City comprises just 1 sq km west of the Tiber but houses the most important collections of artefacts, art, relics and archaeology in the Catholic world. After Italian unification in 1861, the Papal States of central Italy became part of the new Kingdom of Italy, causing a considerable rift between Church and State. In 1929 Mussolini gave the pope full sovereignty over what is now called Vatican City. The Vatican has considerable influence, along with its own postal service, currency, newspaper, radio station and even an army of Swiss Guards to watch over the pope's personal safety.

ST PETER'S BASILICA & SQUARE

The glorious **St Peter's Basilica** (Map pp722-3; ☎ 06 69 88 20 19; Piazza di San Pietro; admission free; 🕒 7am-7pm Apr-Sep, to 6pm Oct-Mar) is testament to the religious, artistic and cultural significance of Rome. There has been a church here since Constantine's reign during the 4th century, marking the legendary spot where St Peter was buried. Bramante designed the basilica in 1503, but final kudos went to Michelangelo, who took over the project in 1547, at the age of 72, and was responsible for the design of the grand dome, which soars 120m above the altar and was completed in 1590, long after the genius artist and architect had died. The cavernous interior contains numerous treasures, including Michelangelo's superb *Pietà,* sculpted when he was only 24 years old and the only work to carry his signature.

Enter the Basilica through Piazza di San Pietro, four rows of colonnades designed by Bernini. Pilgrims, nuns and tourists congregate here in long lines. Entrance to the dome is to the right as you climb the stairs to the basilica's atrium. Make the climb on foot (€4) or by lift (€7). Dress rules and security are stringently enforced – no shorts, miniskirts or sleeveless tops, and be prepared to have your bags searched.

Equally impressive is Bernini's masterpiece **Piazza di San Pietro** (St Peter's Square), laid out in the 17th century. The vast piazza is bound by two semicircular colonnades, each comprised of four rows of Doric columns, and in its centre stands an obelisk brought to Rome by Caligula from Heliopolis (in ancient Egypt). The pope usually gives a **public audience** at 10am every Wednesday in the Papal Audience Hall or St Peter's Square. You must make a booking, in person or by fax to the **Prefettura della Casa Pontificia** (Map pp722-3; ☎ 06 69 88 46 31; fax 06 69 88 38 65) on the Monday or Tuesday beforehand, between 9am and 1pm. To go in person, enter via the bronze doors under the colonnade to the right of St Peter's (facing the church). Catholics are requested to bring a letter from their parish priest.

VATICAN MUSEUMS

The buildings that house the **Vatican Museums** (Map pp722-3; adult/concession €12/8, free last Sun of month; 🕑 hours vary), known collectively as the Palazzo Apostolico Vaticano, cover an area of 5½ hectares.

The museums contain an astonishing collection of art and treasures collected by the popes, and you'll need several hours to see the most important areas. Make sure you pick up a floor-plan leaflet. There are four very helpful 'one-way' itineraries, lasting from 1½ to five hours, mapped out with the aim of simplifying visits and containing the huge number of visitors. The Sistine Chapel comes towards the very end of a full visit; otherwise, you can walk straight there, but if you'd like to visit the Stanze di Raffaello, do so first as you can't backtrack once in the chapel.

Museo Pio-Clementino contains Greek and Roman antiquities, and is on the ground floor near the entrance. Through the superb **Galleria delle Carte Geografiche** (Map Gallery) and **Galleria degli Arazzi** (Tapestry Gallery) are the magnificent **Stanze di Raffaello**, which were once the private apartments of Pope Julius II and are decorated with frescoes by Raphael. Of particular interest to Raphael fans is the magnificent **Stanza della Segnatura**, which features the artist's masterpieces *The School of Athens* and *Disputation on the Sacrament*.

From Raphael's rooms, go down the stairs to the sumptuous **Appartamento Borgia**, decorated with frescoes by Pinturicchio, and then down another flight of stairs to the **Sistine Chapel**, the private papal chapel built in 1473 for Pope Sixtus IV. Michelangelo's wonderful frescoes, *Creation* and *Last Judgment,* have been superbly restored to their original brilliance. It took Michelangelo four years, at the height of the Renaissance, to paint *Creation;* 24 years later he painted the extraordinary *Last Judgment*. The other walls of the chapel were painted by artists including Botticelli, Ghirlandaio, Pinturicchio and Signorelli.

Opening hours are very confusing but are listed on signposts all around the Vatican.

Piazza del Campidoglio & Musei Capitolini

The lowest of Rome's seven hills is **Capitoline Hill**, which had been a centre of Jupiter worship in ancient Rome (Brutus hid here in a temple – now destroyed – after assassinating Caesar) and then housed the medieval city government. None other than Michelangelo was commissioned to redesign the interior square of the **Piazza del Campidoglio** (Map pp726-7), which he had face St Peter's rather than the Forum. The grand stairs, known as the **Cordonata**, lead to the two palaces that make up the buildings of the Musei Capitolini as well as the Palazzo Senatorio, the seat of city government since 1143. A modern copy of the bronze equestrian statue of Emperor Marcus Aurelius is at the piazza's centre; the original is on display in the ground-floor portico of the **Palazzo Nuovo** (Palazzo del Museo Capitolino; Map pp726-7).

Impressing visitors since 1471, the **Musei Capitolini** (Map pp726-7; ☎ 06 96 74 00; adult/concession €6.50/4.50; 🕑 9am-8pm Tue-Sun) is the oldest antiquities museum in the world. Of its hundreds of ancient Roman sculptures and paintings, perhaps the most photographed is what's left of the colossal statue Constantine had commissioned of himself – a giant

> **MUSEUM ENTRY**
>
> Entry to various attractions is free for EU citizens aged under 18 and over 65, and reduced (usually half-price) for EU citizens aged between 18 and 25, plus those from countries with reciprocal arrangements and many university students.

ITALY

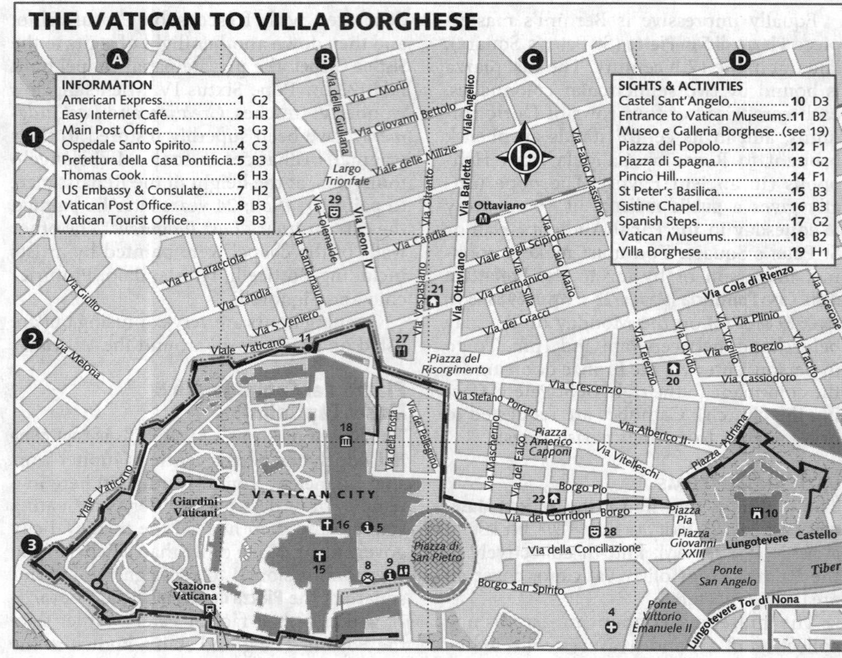

head, hand and foot, themselves larger than most adults.

Walk to the right of the Palazzo Senatorio for a lovely panorama of the Roman Forum. Walk to the left of the same building to reach the ancient Roman **Carcere Mamertino** (Mamertine Prison; Map pp726-7; ⌚ 9am-noon & 2-5pm), where it's believed St Peter was imprisoned.

The **Chiesa di Santa Maria d'Aracoeli** (Map pp726-7) is between Piazza del Campidoglio and the Monumento Vittorio Emanuele II, at the highest point of the Capitoline Hill. It is built on the site where legend says the Tiburtine Sybil told the Emperor Augustus of the coming birth of Christ.

Castel Sant'Angelo

The huge fortress in front of the Vatican is **Castel Sant'Angelo** (Map pp722-3; ☎ 06 68 19 111; Lungotevere Castello 50; adult/concession €6.50/2.50; ⌚ 9am-8pm), built in the 2nd century AD by the Emperor Hadrian for his mausoleum. It's now a museum displaying its 1900 years of history as the papal residence, fortress and prison. As the second-largest building in Rome (next to the Colosseum) it boasts dramatic views from the top.

Pantheon

Nowhere is the splendour of ancient Rome more evident than at the **Pantheon** (Map pp726-7; Piazza della Rotonda; admission free; ⌚ 8.30am-7.30pm Mon-Sat, 9am-6pm Sun, holidays 9am-1pm), the best-preserved building of its time. The original temple was built in 27 BC by Marcus Agrippa, son-in-law of Emperor Augustus, and dedicated to the planetary gods. Agrippa's name remains inscribed over the entrance. The temple's dome is an architectural marvel, even by today's standards – the oculus in the middle allows in light and was built with concrete that becomes lighter in colour the closer it gets to the oculus, dispersing weight. Many Italian kings are buried here, as is Raphael.

Piazza Navona

A few blocks west of the Pantheon, this vast and beautiful **square** (Map pp726-7), lined with baroque palaces, was laid out on the ruins of Domitian's stadium and features three

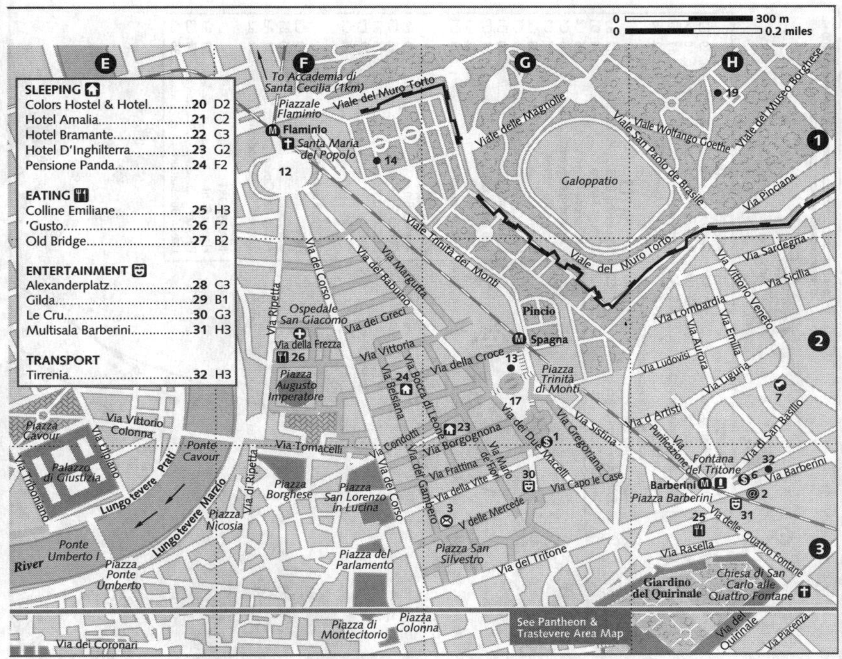

fountains. In its centre is Bernini's masterpiece **Fontana dei Quattro Fiumi** (Fountain of the Four Rivers; Map pp726-7). Visit at different times of the day, and be sure to grab a *gelato* and relax on one of the stone benches in the sun, or enjoy a cappuccino at one of the many cafés. The expense is worth it to watch the various artists mingling in the piazza and to absorb the ever-vibrant hum.

Piazza Campo de'Fiori

The **Piazza Campo de'Fiori** (Map pp726-7), affectionately called 'Il Campo', was a place of execution during the Inquisition. The artist Caravaggio went on the run after killing a man who had the gall to beat him in tennis on this piazza. Nowadays a **flower and vegetable market** is held here Monday to Saturday, artists congregate to sell their wares on Sunday, and revellers fill the many bars nightly.

The **Palazzo Farnese** (Map pp726-7), in the piazza of the same name, is just off the Campo. This magnificent Renaissance building was started in 1514 by Antonio da Sangallo, carried on by Michelangelo and completed by Giacomo della Porta. Built for Cardinal Alessandro Farnese (later Pope Paul III), the palace is now the French embassy. The piazza has two fountains, which are enormous granite baths taken from the **Terme di Caracalla** (Baths of Caracalla; see p728).

Torre Argentina

You'll walk by the **Torre Argentina sacred ruins** (where Caesar was stabbed to death by Brutus on the Ides of March in 44 BC) on your way to practically anywhere in Rome. If you miss Fluffy back home or need a respite from humans, venture downstairs to the **Torre Argentina cat sanctuary** (Map pp726-7; ☎ 06 45 42 52 40; www.romancats.com; Largo di Torre Argentina; noon-6pm, to 8pm Jun-Sep), the cutest place in the whole city. Volunteers at the sanctuary vaccinate and spay or neuter hundreds of cats, some of which are adopted out internationally. Donate money, buy adorable kitty accessories or just lower your blood pressure with an hour of petting.

Villa Borghese

This gorgeous **park** (Map pp722-3) was once the estate of Cardinal Scipione Borghese. His

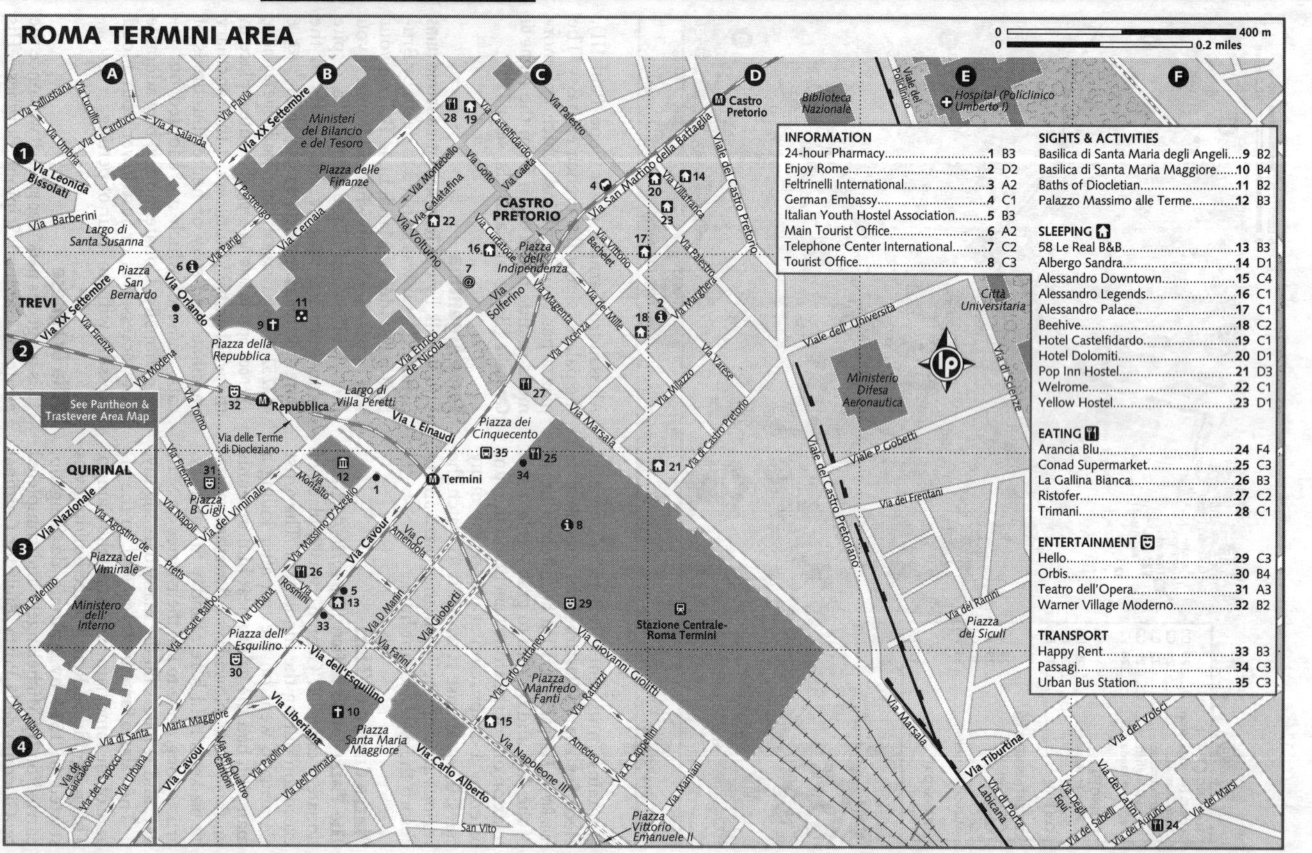
ROMA TERMINI AREA
0 400 m
0 0.2 miles
INFORMATION
24-hour Pharmacy 1 B3
Enjoy Rome 2 D2
Feltrinelli International 3 A2
German Embassy 4 C1
Italian Youth Hostel Association 5 B3
Main Tourist Office 6 A2
Telephone Center International 7 C2
Tourist Office 8 C3
SIGHTS & ACTIVITIES
Basilica di Santa Maria degli Angeli 9 B2
Basilica di Santa Maria Maggiore 10 B4
Baths of Diocletian 11 B2
Palazzo Massimo alle Terme 12 B3
SLEEPING
58 Le Real B&B 13 B3
Albergo Sandra 14 D1
Alessandro Downtown 15 C4
Alessandro Legends 16 C1
Alessandro Palace 17 C1
Beehive 18 C2
Hotel Castelfidardo 19 C1
Hotel Dolomiti 20 D1
Pop Inn Hostel 21 D3
Welrome 22 C1
Yellow Hostel 23 D1
EATING
Arancia Blu 24 F4
Conad Supermarket 25 C3
La Gallina Bianca 26 B3
Ristofer 27 C2
Trimani 28 C1
ENTERTAINMENT
Hello 29 C3
Orbis 30 B4
Teatro dell'Opera 31 A3
Warner Village Moderno 32 B2
TRANSPORT
Happy Rent 33 B3
Passagi 34 C3
Urban Bus Station 35 C3
See Pantheon & Trastevere Area Map
TREVI
QUIRINAL
CASTRO PRETORIO
Stazione Centrale-Roma Termini
Termini
Repubblica
Castro Pretorio
Piazza della Repubblica
Piazza dei Cinquecento
Piazza dell' Indipendenza
Piazza Santa Maria Maggiore
Piazza Vittorio Emanuele II
Piazza Manfredo Fanti
Piazza del Viminale
Ministero dell' Interno
Ministeri del Bilancio e del Tesoro
Ministero Difesa Aeronautica
Biblioteca Nazionale
Città Universitaria
Hospital (Policlinico Umberto I)
Via XX Settembre
Via Nazionale
Via Cavour
Via Marsala
Via Giovanni Giolitti
Viale del Castro Pretorio
Via Tiburtina

17th-century villa houses the **Museo e Galleria Borghese** (Map pp722-3; ☎ 06 3 28 10; www.galleriaborghese.it; adult/concession €8.50/5.50; 🕒 9am-7pm Tue-Sun), which has held an impressive art collection for over 300 years and includes the largest collection of Caravaggio paintings in the world. Take a walk through the leafy park, which has a zoo and a lake full of ducks, swans and turtles. You can hire boats at the lake and bicycles near the Porta Pinciana entrance. Just north of the park is the **Galleria Nazionale d'Arte Moderna** (Map pp718-19; ☎ 06 32 34 000; Viale delle Belle Arti 131; admission €6.50; 🕒 8.30am-7.30pm Tue-Sun), a *belle époque* palace housing 19th- and 20th-century paintings. The Etruscan museum, **Museo Nazionale Etrusco di Villa Giulia** (Map pp718-19; ☎ 06 32 26 571; admission €4; 🕒 8.30am-7.30pm Tue-Sun), is on the same street in Piazzale di Villa Giulia, in the former villa of Pope Julius III.

Trevi Fountain

The high-baroque **Fontana di Trevi** (Map pp726-7; Piazza di Crociferi), six blocks northeast of the Pantheon, was designed by Nicola Salvi in 1732 and immortalised in Fellini's *La Dolce Vita*. It sprawls over almost the entire piazza and depicts Neptune's chariot being led by Tritons, with sea horses representing the moods of the sea. Its water was supplied by one of Rome's earliest aqueducts, and the name refers to the three roads *(tre vie)* that converged here. The custom is to throw a coin into the fountain (over your shoulder while facing away) to ensure your return to Rome; a second coin grants a wish.

Piazza di Spagna & Spanish Steps

The exquisite **Piazza di Spagna** (Map pp722-3), church and famous **Spanish Steps** (Scalinata della Trinità dei Monti; Map pp722-3) have long provided a major gathering place for foreigners and locals alike. Built with a legacy from the French in 1725, but named after the Spanish embassy to the Holy See, the steps lead to the church; the steps were constructed to link the piazza with the well-heeled folks living above it.

In the 18th century, beautiful Italians gathered here, hoping to be chosen as artists' models. Today, beauties of both sexes still abound. To the right as you face the steps is the house where Keats spent the last three months of his life, in 1821. In the piazza is the boat-shaped fountain of the **Barcaccia**, believed to be by Pietro Bernini, father of the famous Gian Lorenzo. One of Rome's most elegant and expensive shopping streets, **Via Condotti** (Map pp722-3), runs off the piazza towards Via del Corso.

Piazza del Popolo

The vast and impressive **Piazza del Popolo** (Map pp722-3) was laid out in the 16th century at the point of convergence of three roads – Via Ripetta, Via del Corso and Via del Babuino – which form a trident at what was the city's main entrance from the north. Giuseppe Valadier redesigned it three centuries later, and today this neighbourhood is called 'the trident'. Rainaldi designed the seemingly twin baroque churches in the 17th century, and Bernini worked on the gate around the same time. **Santa Maria del Popolo** (Map pp722-3; Piazza del Popolo 12; 🕒 7am-12pm, 4-7pm) houses two magnificent Caravaggio paintings (of St Peter and St Paul). The piazza is at the foot of the **Pincio Hill** (Map pp722-3), which affords a *bella vista* of the city, especially in the early hours; Keats, Strauss, Ghandi and Mussolini liked strolling here.

Trastevere

Tras tevere literally means across the Tevere (Tiber) River. Once an Etruscan encampment, Trastevere still retains the feel of a medieval village, complete with narrow winding streets and crackly old buildings. For over a thousand years, it's been a haunt for artists, visitors and thieves, who appreciate its bohemian attitude. The neighbourhood lights up at night as all ages take to the street on the evening *passeggiata* and its cadre of bars and restaurants spill out onto the streets.

Don't miss the **Basilica di Santa Maria in Trastevere** (Map pp726-7; ☎ 06 581 48 02; Piazza di

SPQR

You see it on ancient buildings and modern manhole covers, but what does it mean? The city motto on the coat of arms of Rome, the origins are so ancient even the Romans weren't sure exactly what it stood for. *Senatus Populusque* (or *Populus Que*) *Romanus* roughly translated to 'Senate and the People of Rome'. Or, in today's terms: your tax dollars at work.

PANTHEON & TRASTEVERE AREA

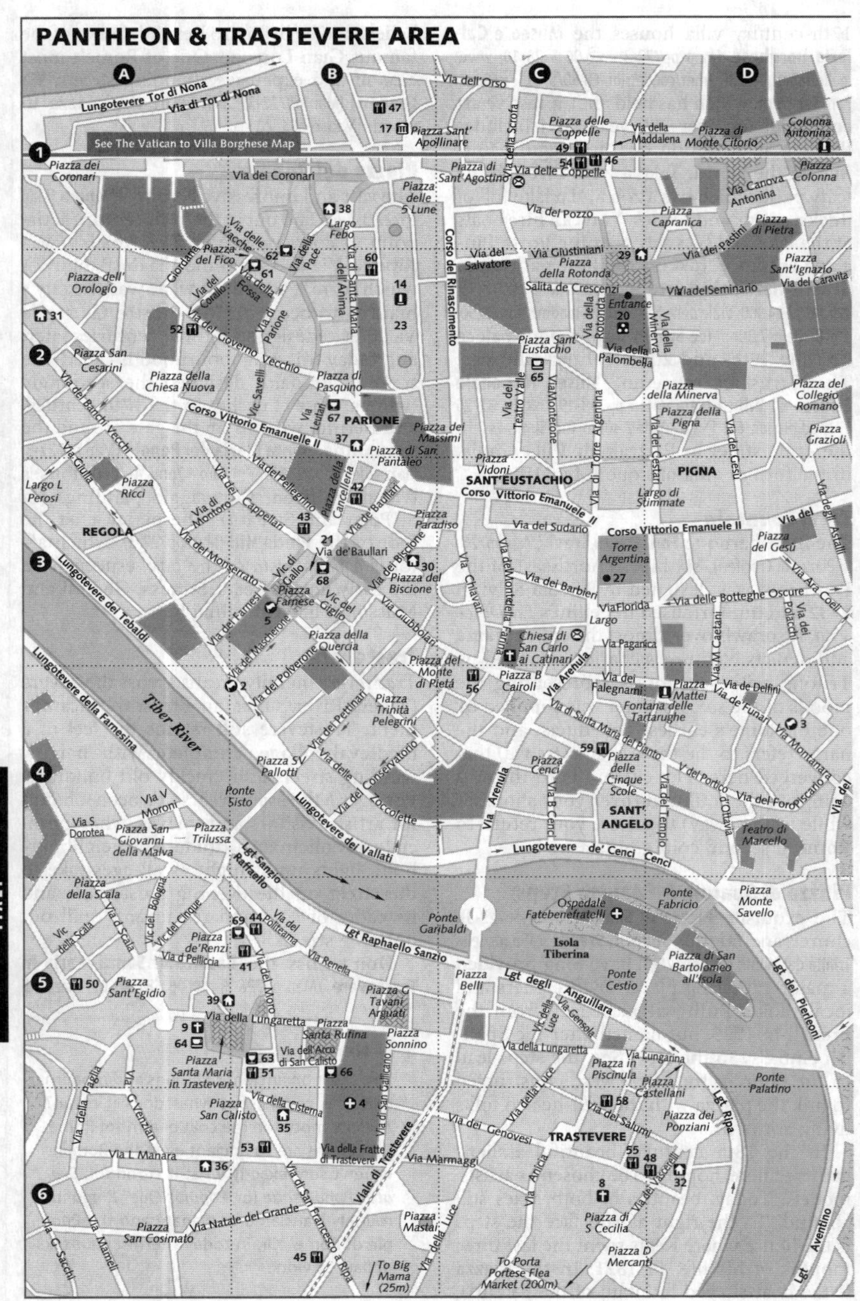

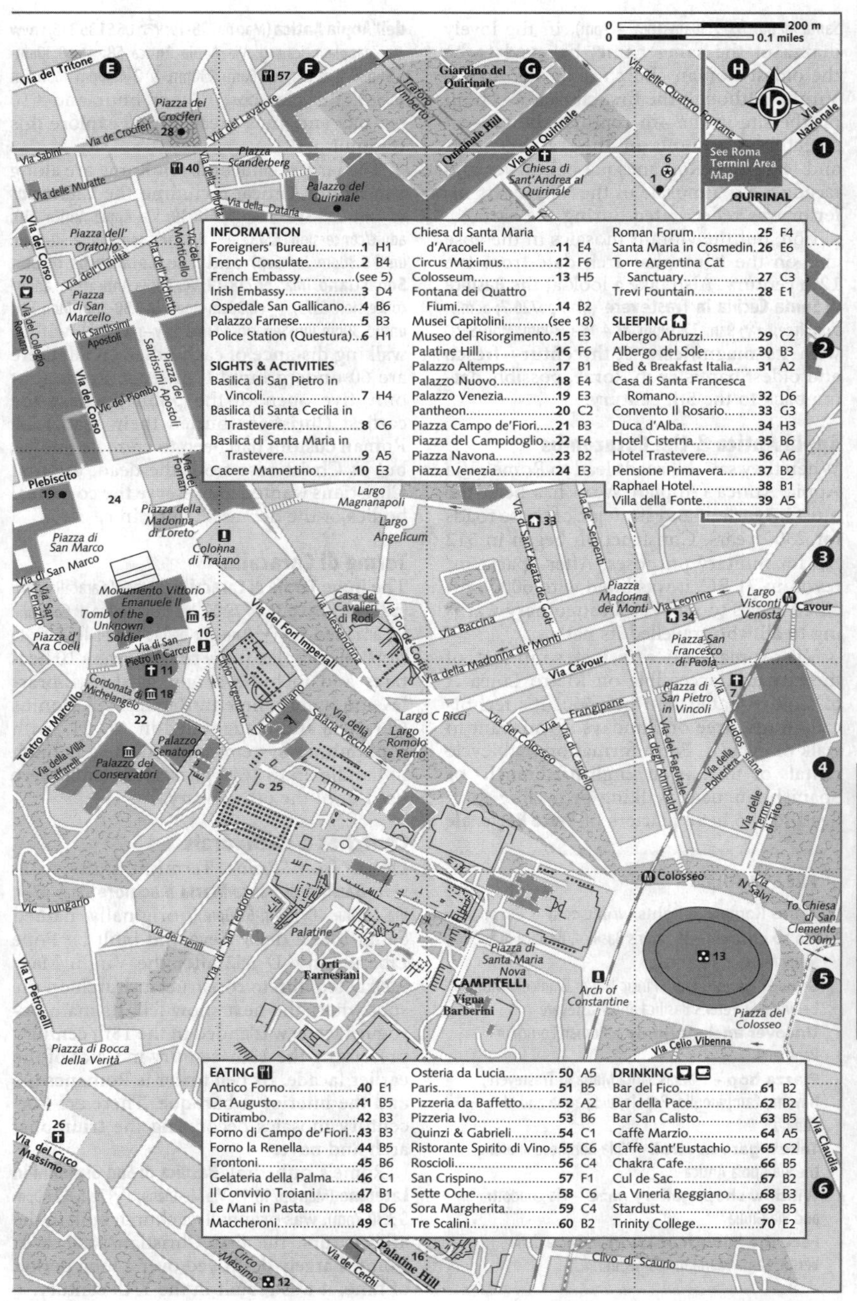
0 200 m
0 0.1 miles
INFORMATION
Foreigners' Bureau....1 H1
French Consulate....2 B4
French Embassy....(see 5)
Irish Embassy....3 D4
Ospedale San Gallicano....4 B6
Palazzo Farnese....5 B3
Police Station (Questura)....6 H1
SIGHTS & ACTIVITIES
Basilica di San Pietro in Vincoli....7 H4
Basilica di Santa Cecilia in Trastevere....8 C6
Basilica di Santa Maria in Trastevere....9 A5
Cacere Mamertino....10 E3
Chiesa di Santa Maria d'Aracoeli....11 E4
Circus Maximus....12 F6
Colosseum....13 H5
Fontana dei Quattro Fiumi....14 B2
Musei Capitolini....(see 18)
Museo del Risorgimento....15 E3
Palatine Hill....16 F6
Palazzo Altemps....17 B1
Palazzo Nuovo....18 E4
Palazzo Venezia....19 E3
Pantheon....20 C2
Piazza Campo de'Fiori....21 B3
Piazza del Campidoglio....22 E4
Piazza Navona....23 B2
Piazza Venezia....24 E3
Roman Forum....25 F4
Santa Maria in Cosmedin....26 E6
Torre Argentina Cat Sanctuary....27 C3
Trevi Fountain....28 E1
SLEEPING
Albergo Abruzzi....29 C2
Albergo del Sole....30 B3
Bed & Breakfast Italia....31 A2
Casa di Santa Francesca Romano....32 D6
Convento Il Rosario....33 G3
Duca d'Alba....34 H3
Hotel Cisterna....35 B6
Hotel Trastevere....36 A6
Pensione Primavera....37 B2
Raphael Hotel....38 B1
Villa della Fonte....39 A5
EATING
Antico Forno....40 E1
Da Augusto....41 B5
Ditirambo....42 B3
Forno di Campo de'Fiori....43 B3
Forno la Renella....44 B5
Frontoni....45 B6
Gelateria della Palma....46 C1
Il Convivio Troiani....47 B1
Le Mani in Pasta....48 D6
Maccheroni....49 C1
Osteria da Lucia....50 A5
Paris....51 B5
Pizzeria da Baffetto....52 A2
Pizzeria Ivo....53 B6
Quinzi & Gabrieli....54 C1
Ristorante Spirito di Vino....55 C6
Roscioli....56 C4
San Crispino....57 F1
Sette Oche....58 C6
Sora Margherita....59 C4
Tre Scalini....60 B2
DRINKING
Bar del Fico....61 B2
Bar della Pace....62 B2
Bar San Calisto....63 B5
Caffè Marzio....64 A5
Caffè Sant'Eustachio....65 C2
Chakra Cafe....66 B5
Cul de Sac....67 B2
La Vineria Reggiano....68 B3
Stardust....69 B5
Trinity College....70 E2
See Roma Termini Area Map
QUIRINAL
CAMPITELLI
Giardino del Quirinale
Quirinale Hill
Palazzo del Quirinale
Chiesa di Sant'Andrea al Quirinale
Via del Tritone
Via Nazionale
Via delle Quattro Fontane
Via del Quirinale
Piazza dei Crociferi
Piazza Scanderberg
Via del Corso
Piazza dell' Oratorio
Piazza di San Marcello
Piazza dei Santissimi Apostoli
Plebiscito
Piazza di San Marco
Piazza della Madonna di Loreto
Colonna di Traiano
Largo Magnanapoli
Monumento Vittorio Emanuele II
Tomb of the Unknown Soldier
Piazza d'Ara Coeli
Via dei Fori Imperiali
Casa dei Cavalieri di Rodi
Via Cavour
Via Baccina
Via della Madonna de' Monti
Piazza Madonna dei Monti
Via Leonina
Largo Visconti Venosta
Cavour
Piazza San Francesco di Paola
Piazza di San Pietro in Vincoli
Via del Colosseo
Largo C Ricci
Largo Romolo e Remo
Palazzo Senatorio
Palazzo dei Conservatori
Teatro di Marcello
Colosseo
To Chiesa di San Clemente (200m)
Piazza del Colosseo
Arch of Constantine
Piazza di Santa Maria Nova
Vigna Barberini
Orti Farnesiani
Palatine
Via di San Teodoro
Via dei Fienili
Via L Petroselli
Piazza di Bocca della Verità
Via del Circo Massimo
Circo Massimo
Via dei Cerchi
Palatine Hill
Clivo di Scaurio
Via Celio Vibenna
Via Claudia
ITALY

Santa Maria; ☎ 7.30am-1pm, 4-7pm), in the lovely piazza of the same name, believed to be the oldest Roman church dedicated to the Virgin. Although the first church was built on the site in the 4th century, the present structure was built in the 12th century and features a Romanesque bell tower and façade, with a mosaic of the Virgin. Its interior was redecorated during the baroque period, but the vibrant mosaics in the apse and on the triumphal arch date from the 12th century. Also take a look at the **Basilica di Santa Cecilia in Trastevere** (Map pp726-7; admission free; 9am-12.30pm & 4.15-6.30pm Mon-Sat), with its magnificent 13th-century fresco and oldest baptistry in Rome, possibly dating back to the 5th century.

Appia Antica & the Catacombs

When they say 'All roads lead to Rome', Via Appia Antica (Appian Way) has been the most important and strategic of those roads for 2300 years. Construction began in 312 BC for military purposes. After Spartacus' revolt in 71 BC, it was lined with 6000 crucified slaves to serve as a sanguinary warning to all who travelled its path.

Via Appia Antica is just southeast of the city and accessible on Metro Linea A to Colli Albani, then bus 660. It's technically traffic-free on Sundays if you want to walk or cycle it. For information on bicycle rentals or to join an English-, French- or Spanish-language walking or cycling tour, head to the headquarters of **Parco Regionale dell'Appia Antica** (Map pp718-19; ☎ 06 51 35 316; www.parcoappiaantica.org; Via Appia Antica 58; 9.30am-5.30pm summer, 9.30am-1.30pm & 2-4.30pm Mon-Sat winter). Bicycles cost €3 per hour and €10 per day and are a great way to explore this tranquil park.

The largest catacombs in Rome are along Via Appia Antica, including the **Catacombs of San Callisto** (Map pp718-19; Via Appia Antica 110; adult/concession €5/3; 8.30am-noon & 2.30-5pm, until 5.30pm Jun-Sep) and the **Catacombs of San Sebastiano** (Map pp718-19; Via Appia Antica 136; adult/concession €5/3; 8.30am-noon & 2.30-5pm Mon-Sat, until 5.30pm Jun-Sep, closed mid-Nov–mid-Dec), within walking distance of each other. In all, there are 60 underground tunnels in Rome (but only five open to the public) where the earliest Christians buried their dead. The Roman custom had been to cremate bodies, but as Christ rose from the dead, the first Christians wanted to preserve the corporeal bodies of the deceased…just in case.

FREE THRILLS

These Roman delights won't cost a euro:

Go to church – St Peter's Basilica, Basilica di Santa Maria in Trastevere

Sunset gaze – From Pincio Hill or Gianicolo Hill, between St Peter's Basilica and Trastevere

Uncover ancient Rome – Roman Forum or Pantheon

Piazza hop – Piazzas Santa Maria in Trastevere, Navona, Campidoglio, Popolo, di Spagna and 'Il Campo'

Take a garden stroll – Villa Borghese or along the Via Appia Antica

Window shop, gallery gaze – Via Condotti and Via Giulia

Face the 'Mouth of Truth' – Bocca della Verità, Santa Maria in Cosmedin

Terme di Caracalla

The huge **Terme di Caracalla** (Baths of Caracalla; Map pp718-19; ☎ 06 39 96 77 00; Via delle Terme di Caracalla 52; admission €6; 9am-1hr before sunset Tue-Sun, to 2pm Mon) complex (now ruins) covers 10 hectares and includes shops, gardens, libraries and entertainment. Begun by Antonius Caracalla and inaugurated in AD 217 with a plumbing system sophisticated enough to handle up to 1600 guests, the baths were used until the 6th century.

Churches & Cathedrals

Down from Roma Termini is the massive **Basilica di Santa Maria Maggiore** (Map p724; Via Cavour; 7am-6.30pm), originally named Santa Maria della Neve and built by Pope Liberius in AD 352 after the Virgin Mary instructed him to construct a church on the spot where the next snow fell. Its main baroque façade was added in the 18th century, preserving the 13th-century mosaics of the earlier façade. Its bell tower is Romanesque and the interior is baroque. There are 5th-century mosaics decorating the triumphal arch and nave.

Rome's cathedral, **Basilica di San Giovanni in Laterano** (Map pp718-19; Via Merulana; 7am-12.30pm & 3.30-7pm), was originally a church built in the 4th century, the first Christian basilica in Rome. Largely destroyed over a long period of time, it was rebuilt in the 17th century.

Basilica di San Pietro in Vincoli (Map pp726-7; Piazza San Pietro in Vincoli; 7am-12pm & 3.30-7pm), just off Via Cavour, shows off Michelangelo's magnificent statue *Moses* and his unfinished statues of Leah and Rachel, as well as the chains worn by St Peter during his imprisonment before being crucified; hence the church's name (St Peter in Chains).

Chiesa di San Clemente (Map pp718-19; Via San Giovanni in Laterano; 9am-12.30pm & 3-6pm), east from the Colosseum, defines how history in Rome exists on many levels. The 12th-century church at street level was built over a 4th-century church that was, in turn, built over a 1st-century Roman house with a temple dedicated to the pagan god Mithras.

Santa Maria in Cosmedin (Map pp726-7; Via del Circo Massimo; 10am-1pm & 2.30-6pm), northwest of the huge ruins **Circus Maximus** (Map pp726-7; Via del Circo Massimo), is regarded as one of the finest medieval churches in Rome. It has a seven-storey bell tower and its interior is heavily decorated with Cosmatesque inlaid marble, including the beautiful floor. The main attraction for masses of tourists is, however, its **Bocca della Verità** (Mouth of Truth), in front of the entrance. Legend has it that if you put your right hand into the ceramic mouth and tell a lie, it will snap shut.

Piazza Venezia

A neoclassical monument dedicated to Vittorio Emanuele II overshadows the **Piazza Venezia** (Map pp726-7). Built to commemorate Italian unification, the piazza incorporates the **tomb of the unknown soldier**, as well as the **Museo del Risorgimento** (admission free; 10am-6pm). Also in the piazza is the 15th-century **Palazzo Venezia** (9am-2pm Tue-Sat, to 1pm Sun), partially built with material quarried from the Colosseum; it was once Mussolini's official residence and is now a museum housing medieval and Renaissance art.

Baths of Diocletian & Basilica di Santa Maria degli Angeli

The **Baths of Diocletian** (Map p724; 06 488 05 30; Via Enrico de Nicola 79; admission €5; 9am-7.45pm Tue-Sun) were built at the turn of the 3rd century. Rome's largest baths could accommodate 3000 people; the complex also included libraries, concert halls and gardens and covered about 13 hectares. In AD 536, invaders destroyed the aqueduct that fed the baths and the complex fell into decay.

Parts of the ruins are incorporated into the **Basilica di Santa Maria degli Angeli** (Map p724; Piazza della Repubblica; 7.30am-6.30pm). Designed by Michelangelo, the basilica incorporates what was the great central hall and *tepidarium* (lukewarm room) of the original baths. Over the centuries his original work was drastically changed and little evidence of his design, apart from the great vaulted ceiling of the church, remains. An interesting feature of the church is a double meridian in the transept, one tracing the polar star and the other telling the precise time of the sun's zenith (visible at noon).

National Roman Museums

The important collection of five Roman museums is spread all over the city and comprises ancient art, including Greek and Roman sculpture. The two most important of its collection are housed in the 15th-century **Palazzo Altemps** (Map pp726-7; 06 683 37 59; Piazza Sant'Apollinare 44; admission €5; 9am-7.45pm Tue-Sun), near Piazza Navona. This is home to the majority of the artworks, with numerous important pieces from the Ludovisi collection. **Palazzo Massimo alle Terme** (Map p724; 06 39 96 77 00; Largo di Villa Peretti 1; admission €6; 9am-7.45pm Tue-Sun) features an equally impressive collection of frescoes and mosaics from the Villa of Livia, excavated at Prima Porta, and a knockout numismatic collection.

Villa Doria Pamphilj

Rome's largest park, **Villa Doria Pamphilj** (Map pp718-19; Via di San Pancrazio; sunrise-sunset), west of Trastevere, was laid out by Algardi in the 16th century, and offers a rejuvenating reprieve from the heady city pace. Relax by a baroque fountain, nap under a parasol pine or enjoy a stroll along the lovely walkways. To get there, you can take a bus to Via di San Pancrazio.

Protestant Cemetery

Peaceful enough to sleep for eternity is the **Campo Cestio L'Antico Cimitero per Stranieri non-Cattolici** (Map pp718-19; 06 57 41 900; www.protestantcemetery.com; Via Caio Cestio 6; donation €2; 9am-5pm, closed Sun & holidays), also known as the Protestant (non-Catholic) Cemetery. With the likes of Goethe, Keats and Shelley buried here, the tombstones read like a literary who's who.

SLEEPING

Rome has plenty of fantastic hotels in beautiful settings…if you don't mind spending €250 a night. If not, you will have to compromise on location, noise or charm, or book weeks in advance. The city tourism website (www.romaturismo.it) has an excellent listing. For B&Bs or longer-term accommodation, try www.cross-polinate.com.

The head office of the **Italian Youth Hostel Association** (Map p724; ☎ 06 487 11 52; www.ostellionline.org; Via Cavour 44; 9am-5pm Mon-Fri) has information about Hostelling International (HI) members in Italy and will assist with bookings to stay at universities during summer.

Budget

There are dozens of hostels in Rome, most near Roma Termini, and no less than 100 lower- to midrange hotels in the same area. The north side around Castel Pretorio holds the best quality low-priced places.

Pop Inn Hostel (Map p724; ☎ 06 495 98 87; www.popinnhostel.com; Via Marsala 80; dm €16-25, s €41-86, d €42-98;) Look for the hippie sticker next to the door and you'll know you've arrived at this chill locale filled with *irie;* other simpatico features include no curfew, free breakfast, free luggage storage, and laundry.

Alessandro Palace (Map p724; ☎ 06 44 61 958; www.hostelalessandropalace.com; Via Vicenza 42; dm €18-20, s/d €90/105;) This is the first and most popular of the three Alessandro hostels. Four floors (no lift) offer over 100 beds in incredibly clean four- to eight-bed dorms, all with en suite bathroom equipped with hairdryer, shower and space to spread out. The hostel's bar and pizza nights ensure parties into the wee hours.

Alessandro Legends (☎ 06 446 19 58; www.hostelalessandrolegends.com; Via Curatone 12; dm €21-26, d with shared bathroom €66;) The second of the three Alessandro hostels, with seven rooms that are good for families and quieter travellers

Yellow Hostel (Map p724; ☎ 06 49 38 26 82; www.yellowhostel.com; Via Palestro 44; dm €24-34, s/d €25/50, all incl breakfast;) Fun, young and hip, this place is well-run and immensely popular with backpackers. All amenities are included: hot showers, fully equipped kitchen, festive common room with DVD, and washer and dryers. Some dorm rooms have clean en suite bathrooms. If a single or double is available in one of the partner hotels, it's a chance to practically steal a private room.

Alessandro Downtown (Map p724; ☎ 06 443 40 147; www.hostelalessandrodowntown.com; Via Cattaneo 23; dm/d €30/90, dm/d with shared bath €25/70, incl breakfast;) The last of the three Alessandro hostels (left). Book by phone or online.

Welrome (Map p724; ☎ 06 47 82 43 43; www.welrome.it; Via Calatafina 15/19; s €40-100, d €50-110) Chatty Mary loves her job telling visitors about Roman history and where to visit, in fluent English, French or Italian. Each room is a respite from Rome – double-paned windows block out street noise and strong showers wash away the grit. There is a hairdryer, phone and refrigerator in every room.

Convento Il Rosario (Map pp726-7; ☎ 06 679 23 46; irodopre@tin.it; Via di Sant'Agata dei Goti 10; s/d/tr incl breakfast €48/82/112) Advertising itself as a 'house of welcome for pilgrims and tourists', this convent-run guesthouse is a meditative spot for those who don't mind the 11pm closing and sparse furnishings.

Pensione Panda (Map pp722-3; ☎ 06 678 01 79; www.pensionepanda.com; Via della Croce 35; s/d/tr €65/98/130, s/d with shared bathroom €48/68) Close to the Spanish Steps, this 2nd-floor *pensione* has comfortable rooms with arched ceilings and helpful, English-speaking staff.

Albergo Sandra (Map p724; ☎ 06 445 26 12; www.geocities.com/hotelsandra; Via Villafranca 10; s/d/tr incl breakfast €70/96/120, without bathroom s/d/tr €50/80/90) A mere 10-minute walk from Roma Termini, this medium-sized *pensione* has clean and pleasant rooms.

AUTHOR'S CHOICE

Beehive (Map p724; ☎ 06 447 04 553; www.the-beehive.com; Via Marghera 8; dm/d/tr with shared bathroom €22/75/100;) This is a guesthouse and hostel for those who thought they were done with hostelling. If the idea of carefully enforced 11pm quiet hours, an on-site organic café (see p733) and hanging out petting the resident cat Ingmar sounds far, far more appealing than jello shots and pub crawls, then this is probably the place for you. Seven rooms are artfully decorated and the eight-bed dorm is comfortable enough for all ages. The shared bathrooms are spotless. Reserve dorm beds way in advance.

ITALY

58 Le Real B&B (Map p724; ☎ 06 48 23 566; www.58viacavour.it; Via Cavour 58; s/d/tr incl breakfast €75/95/115;) Close to the Colosseum, this is a clean and pretty apartment, with airy rooms and a sun-drenched terrace. The friendly owners treat guests like friends, offering free access to a fridge loaded with juice, yogurt and water.

Midrange

Hotel Dolomiti (Map p724; ☎ 06 49 10 58; www.hotel-dolomiti.it; Via San Martino della Battaglia 11; s €65-90, d/tr/q €135/170/205, all incl breakfast;) A fabulous deal in the low season, ask for a *camera interna* (internal room) to get away from street noise. Fluffy towels and minibars are a welcome addition.

Casa di Santa Francesca Romano (Map pp726-7; ☎ 06 581 21 21; istituto@sfromana.it; Via dei Vascerelli 61; s/d/tr incl breakfast €70/100/123;) This former noble home is now an inn run by the Catholic church with pretty rooms and a cloistered garden around a babbling waterfall. It's open to all travellers and there are airport pick-ups for €50.

Duca d'Alba (Map pp726-7; ☎ 06 48 44 71; www.hotelducadalba.it; Via Leonina 14; s €70-210, d €80-260, tr €100-290, all incl breakfast;) In the quieter neighbourhood of Suburra, this place is just steps from the Cavour metro stop. Filled with amenities like towel warmers and large baths, the bathrooms alone are worth a stay. And then there's the buffet breakfast, with prosciutto, bacon, eggs and fruit (plus room service from 7am to 10pm).

Colors Hostel & Hotel (Map pp722-3; ☎ 06 687 40 30; www.colorshotel.com; Via Boezio 31; s/d €75/120, dm/s/d with shared bathroom €25/65/100;) Brightly painted walls and an effusively helpful staff make this residential choice near the Vatican a great bet. After cooking dinner in the kitchen with herbs plucked from the garden, dine alfresco on the terrace.

Hotel Trastevere (Map pp726-7; ☎ 06 581 47 13; www.hoteltrastevere.it; Via L Manara 24a-25; s/d/tr/q incl breakfast €80/103/130/155, apt 2-/3-person €150/180) An extremely good value place with friendly service and proximity to restaurants and nightlife, many of the spotless, spacious rooms here look out over Piazza San Cosimato in Trastevere.

Pensione Primavera (Map pp726-7; ☎ 06 68 80 31 09; Piazza di San Pantaleo 3; s/d incl breakfast €95/115, with shared bathroom €70/95;) Inexpensive places don't get much closer to the action, but street-side rooms here sound as if the action is inside. Marble staircases and 19th-century antiques make for a charming Roman holiday. Air-con rooms are available for an extra €6.

Hotel Cisterna (Map pp726-7; ☎ 06 58 17 212; www.cisternahotel.it; Via della Cisterna 7/8/9; s/d incl breakfast €98/130; closed part of Aug;) Location, location, location. In the centre of Trastevere but along a quiet street (pick a room out the back), the downside here is putting up with cramped, dark rooms. There's satellite TV and breakfast served in the courtyard.

Villa della Fonte (Map pp726-7; ☎ 06 580 37 97; www.villafonte.com; Via della Fonte d'Olio 8; s/d incl breakfast €110/160;) Here you'll find five pretty and pristine rooms, a hop from Piazza Santa Maria, and a lovely, sunny garden terrace.

Albergo del Sole (Map pp726-7; ☎ 06 687 94 46; www.solealbiscione.it; Via dei Biscione 76; s/d €120/150, with shared bathroom €65/95;) A short walk from Campo de'Fiori, this sunny spot dates from 1462. Don't mind the grumpy reception staff or the street noise, as there is lots of communal space, a pretty patio and a rooftop terrace making this hotel, one of Rome's oldest and best located, a standout.

Albergo Abruzzi (Map pp726-7; ☎ 06 679 20 21; www.hotelabruzzi.it; Piazza della Rotonda 69; s/d incl breakfast €155/195;) There's nothing special about the rooms, but the position – overlooking the Pantheon – is hard to beat, even if the piazza can be noisy and the management rests on its geographic laurels.

Other recommendations:

Hotel Amalia (Map pp722-3; ☎ 06 397 23 356; www.hotelamalia.com; Via Germanico 66; s/d incl breakfast €130/196;) Good leisure or business hotel.

Hotel Castelfidardo (Map p724; ☎ 06 446 46 38; www.hotelcastelfidardo.com; Via Castelfidardo 31; s/d €90/120, with shared bathroom €60/100) Good midrange option near Roma Termini.

Top End

Hotel Bramante (Map pp722-3; ☎ 06 688 06 426; www.hotelbramante.com; Via delle Palline 24; s/d/tr incl breakfast €160/220/235;) Marble bathrooms, fresh flowers and antique furnishings add to the small inn feel here, plus a great location and filling breakfast (with eggs and homemade pastries) doesn't hurt.

Hotel D'Inghilterra (Map pp722-3; ☎ 06 699 81 204; http://hoteldinghilterra.warwickhotels.com/; Via Bocca di Leone 14; s/d incl breakfast €287/385;) In the fashionable district near the Spanish

Steps and housed in a 16th-century *palazzo* is this resplendent hotel with one foot steeped in history and the other safely connected to plasma TVs, DSL connections and 24-hour room service.

Raphael Hotel (Map pp726-7; ☎ 06 68 28 31; www.raphaelhotel.com; Largo Febo 2; s/d incl breakfast €300/450; ☒ ❄ 💻) Renaissance art lovers with impeccable taste will appreciate the incredible beauty of this luxurious hotel. The lobby displays ceramic works by Picasso and the rooms are filled with works by Florentine masters. No amenity is forgotten, and don't miss a sunset drink at the terrace restaurant.

EATING

Romans take visible pride in their *cucina* and traditional recipes. The roots of the local cuisine are the diet of the poor, hence a preponderance of *trippa* (tripe), and the Roman-Jewish tradition, with legacies such as stuffed *fiori di zucca* (zucchini/courgette flowers) and *carciofi alla romana* (artichokes with garlic, mint and parsley). Antipasto is a standout, particularly bruschetta, and classic Roman pastas include *cacio e pepe* (with pecorino, black pepper and olive oil) and the snappy *all'amatriciana* (with tomato, pancetta and chilli). The most beloved *secondo* is *saltimbocca alla romana* (escalopes of veal sautéed with white wine, sage and prosciutto).

Restaurants, Trattorias & Pizzerias

Rome is filled with tourists, and tourists eating at restaurants set up for tourists. In general, the area around Roma Termini is filled with terrible restaurants, but has many decent foreign takeaways. Trastevere has the best options per square metre and Piazza Navona and Campo de'Fiori can offer charming alfresco or piazza-front dining.

CITY CENTRE

'Gusto (Map pp722-3; ☎ 06 322 62 73; Piazza Augusto Imperatore 9; pasta from €6) Slick and savvy, this place is a melange of pizzeria, *osteria*, wine bar and kitchen shop. It's a worthy stop any time, with an excellent wine list, an enormous cheese selection and good people-watching.

Pizzeria da Baffetto (Map pp726-7; ☎ 06 686 16 17; Via del Governo Vecchio 114; 🕑 dinner only; pizza €8) Any self-respecting pizza fan will make a stop at this Roman institution, always packed to the beams. Come very early or very late if you don't want to queue or share a table.

Ditirambo (Map pp726-7; ☎ 06 687 16 26; Piazza della Cancelleria 72; 1st/2nd courses €8/11; 🕑 closed Mon lunch) With wood-beamed ceilings, this cosy trattoria serves largely organic fare with a funky twist on Italian vegetarian, including leek pudding with marjoram sauce and red chicory (€8) and *porcini* flan with a *taleggio* (pungent soft cheese) sauce (€10).

Maccheroni (Map pp726-7; ☎ 06 683 07 895; Piazza delle Coppelle 44; 1st/2nd courses €8/13) Although the food isn't bad, come here more for the boisterous atmosphere. Diners line up for outside tables on warm summer nights and cheeky waiters entertain guests. *Trippa* is a speciality here.

Colline Emiliane (Map pp722-3; ☎ 06 481 75 38; Via degli' Avignonesi 22; 1st/2nd courses €9/14) This small trattoria tucked into a cheerless street off Piazza Barberini serves superb Emilia-Romagnan food such as homemade pasta stuffed with pumpkin.

Roscioli (Map pp726-7; ☎ 06 687 52 87; Via dei Giubbonari 21; 1st/2nd courses €14/22) Not only is the gourmet food store in the front one of the best places in town for wine, meat, cheese and hard-to-find Italian delicacies, the 10-table restaurant in the back is good enough to impress food critics off the clock.

Quinzi & Gabrieli (Map pp726-7; ☎ 06 68 79 389; Via delle Coppelle 5; 1st/2nd courses €16/28; 🕑 dinner only, closed Sun & often in August) Dine in a 15th-century palace on seafood amid a romantic setting, complete with paintings done by students of the Academy of Art. Try the spaghetti scampi flambé.

Il Convivio Troiani (Map pp726-7; ☎ 06 68 69 432; www.ilconviviotroiani.com; Vicolo dei Soldati 31; 1st/2nd courses €19/36) Known as one of the best restaurants in Rome, the three Troiani brothers' convivium has won awards for its modern take on ancient dishes, superb wine list (over 2000 strong) and impeccable decór and service. Menu items include pastry-wrapped duck foie gras with figs, and pigeon in blood-orange sauce.

WEST OF THE TIBER: TRASTEVERE, JEWISH GHETTO & THE VATICAN

Pizzeria Remo (Map pp718-19; ☎ 06 574 62 70; Piazza Santa Maria Liberatice 44; pizza from €4.50) This place is loud and rowdy – filling with party types on weekend nights – but the cheap prices, pizza and *bruschette al pomodoro* (bruschettas with tomato) make the chaos and obligatory queues worth it.

Pizzeria Ivo (Map pp726-7; ☎ 06 581 70 82; Via di San Francesco a Ripa 158; pizza €5; closed Tue) The pizzeria of choice in Trastevere for Trastevereans themselves, this place is also quite popular for grilled meats and *scamorza* (smoked cheese).

Sora Margherita (Map pp726-7; ☎ 06 68 74 216; Piazza delle Cinque Scole 30; 1st/2nd courses €5/11; lunch Tue-Sun, dinner Fri & Sat only). The most popular restaurant in the Jewish Ghetto area, this speck of a place is fronted by an even smaller speck of a door. The menu is typical Roman-Jewish – fried artichokes and zucchini blossoms, homemade pasta, chickpea soup. Don't even think about showing up on a Friday or Saturday night without a reservation.

Da Augusto (Map pp726-7; ☎ 06 580 37 98; Piazza de'Renzi 15; 1st/2nd courses €6/11) This bare-bones-but-beloved mamma's kitchen serves Roman classics – occasionally accompanied by a surly attitude.

Sette Oche (Map pp726-7; ☎ 06 58 09 753; Via dei Salumi 36; lunch & drink €6.50-7.50, 1st/2nd courses €6/13; lunch Sat-Mon, dinner 7.30pm-midnight Tue-Sun, open to 2am) Chill at the 'Seven Ducks' restaurant, pizzeria and wine bar, where the owner often plays Italian folk music in the evenings. Downstairs flaunts a Middle Eastern flair with wall tapestries, low tables and floor cushions.

Osteria da Lucia (Map pp726-7; ☎ 06 580 36 01; Via del Mattinato 2; 1st/2nd courses €8/14) Dine under the stars, laundry flittering on the line, at this terrific neighbourhood trattoria serving *trippa alla romano* (Roman tripe) that may well make you a convert.

Le Mani in Pasta (Map pp726-7; ☎ 06 58 16 017; Via dei Genovesi 7; 1st/2nd courses €8/14; closed Mon) A great value *osteria* in Trastevere, the name translates roughly as 'to have one's fingers in the pie'. Grilled fish and calamari are popular, but the reason to come here is – of course – for the pasta dishes. Try the pasta with ricotta, pancetta and nutmeg.

Paris (Map pp726-7; ☎ 06 581 53 78; Piazza San Calisto 7; 1st/2nd courses €12/18) This elegant, old-world restaurant serves excellent Roman-Jewish cuisine such as *fritto misto con baccalà* (fried vegetables with salted cod).

Ristorante Spirito di Vino (Map pp726-7; ☎ 06 58 96 689; Via dei Genovesi 31a/b; 1st/2nd courses €13/21; dinner only, closed Sun) The vaulted ceiling here tops terracotta walls and hanging dried flowers. Maître d'Romeo will show off the wine cellar, an ancient synagogue and purportedly containing some of the oldest bricks in Rome, while his wife, a scientist by training, cooks and his sommelier son suggests the perfect meal complement. Julius Caesar himself was a fan of a dish they've reinvented, *maiale mazio* (pork marinated in red wine and apple slices).

AROUND ROMA TERMINI & SAN LORENZO

Trimani (Map p724; ☎ 06 446 96 630; Via Cernaia 37; dishes from €5; closed Sun) Rome's biggest *enoteca* has a vast selection of regional wines along with excellent soups, pasta, canapés and *torta rustica* (quiche).

Ristofer (Map p724; Via Marsala 15; 2 courses €6.50-7) Where Via Vicenza hits Via Marsala, walk three steps up through a large wooden doorway and you'll reach the Termini area's best-value eatery. Granted, it happens to be the railway workers' caféteria, but everyone is welcome. Its huge portions for hungry workers and convenient location make it a great place for travellers on the run.

La Gallina Bianca (Map p724; ☎ 06 474 37 77; Via Rosmini 9; starters/pizza/dishes €3.50/6.50/7) A welcome respite for those who want to eat near Termini without suffering. Grilled vegetables and *scamorza* (smoked cheese), strawberry tiramisu and overstuffed salads are all winners.

Beehive (Map p724; ☎ 06 447 04 553; Via Marghera 8; set menu €10, takeaway lunch €5; breakfast & lunch) The downstairs organic café at the Beehive guesthouse/hostel (p730) is a quiet subterranean oasis from the Termini area jungle. Guests sup either at four tables or in the 'living room' area on delicious organic fare. Set menus might include a Greek or Sicilian salad and creamy chocolate brownies.

Arancia Blu (Map p724; ☎ 06 44 54 105; Via dei Latini 65; 1st/2nd courses €7/11; dinner, Sunday lunch) Find international vegetarian cuisine less than a 10-minute walk behind Termini. All pasta is made in-house, and the ravioli with potato and mint is especially popular.

Pommidoro (Map pp718-19; ☎ 06 445 26 92; Piazza dei Sanniti 44; mains from €11) This San Lorenzo trattoria, 500m east of the Termini, is popular with artists and intellectuals; the grilled meats are particularly good.

Tram Tram (Map pp718-19; ☎ 064 470 25 85; Via dei Reti 44; 1st/2nd courses €8/12) In the heart of funky San Lorenzo, this small trattoria, also 500m east of Roma Termini, is worth the trek: it's friendly and *molta carina* (very sweet/charming), with high ceilings, big windows, a cosy bar and loyal local clientele. The menu changes daily, but seafood dishes from southern Italy are the speciality – the swordfish is sublime – and the excellent wine list highlights small producers.

Gelati

San Crispino (Map pp726-7; Via della Panetteria 42) This *gelateria* (ice-cream shop) near Trevi Fountain, is considered to sell the best *gelato* in Rome, and for good reason. The delicious fruit sorbets change with the season – try *fichi* (fig) – but it's the divine cream-based flavours, such as ginger, honey, whisky and cinnamon, that will make you an addict.

Old Bridge (Map pp722-3; Via Bastioni di Michelangelo 5) Serving XXL scoops just across from the Vatican, this place is perfect for those who need a mid-museum pick-me-up deserving of a small religious experience.

Tre Scalini (Map pp726-7; Piazza Navona 30) While ogling in Piazza Navona, swing by Tre Scalini for good *gelato* and a memorable *tartufo nero* (black truffle) concoction.

Also recommended (though not for the indecisive), **Gelateria della Palma** (Map pp726-7; Via della Maddalena 20) has 100 flavours – the creamy mousses are a sure bet.

Snacks & Self-Catering

For quick and cheap eats, head to a bar, where you can wolf a *panini* for under €3, or a *pizza al taglio,* where a slab of oven-hot pizza, sold by weight, can cost as little as €1.50.

Antico Forno (Map pp726-7; Via delle Muratte 8) Head here for delicious oven-hot pizza slices and hearty sandwiches.

Frontoni (Map pp726-7; Viale di Trastevere) Good sandwiches made from local delicacies and sold by weight are on offer here.

Forno la Renella (Map pp726-7; Via del Moro 15-16) This tiny spot spins some of Trastevere's best pizza, plus bakes delectable cakes and macaroons.

Forno di Campo de'Fiori (Map pp726-7; Campo de'Fiori 22) This is Rome's best spot for metres of *pizza bianca* (white pizza; that is without tomato sauce).

Foragers will be orgasmic in the lively food markets, held off Viale delle Milizie, just north of the Vatican, and in Piazza Vittorio Emanuele, near Roma Termini. There's also a well-stocked **Conad Supermarket** (Map p724; Roma Termini) underneath the main concourse of the station, which is a handy stop for self-caterers.

DRINKING

The days of Roman orgies are long gone. Rome's nightlife focuses more on late-night chats over drinks and a lengthy meal with friends – much of which happens over an intimate bottle of red at an *enoteca* – than dancing 'til 4am (although both options are amply available). Much of the activity is in the centre, where Campo de'Fiori fills with young revellers, and there are atmospheric late-night spots nestled in the alleyways fringing Piazza Navona. Trastevere is packed with friendly bars and co-mingling tourists and locals.

With cafés and bars, you pay for the privilege of atmosphere. A cappuccino taken standing at the bar will cost less than sitting at an outdoor table. However, once you've nabbed that table, you can sit and watch the world go by for an hour...sometimes even two hours, depending on whether you can ever get your waiter's attention for the bill.

Cafés

Caffè Sant'Eustachio (Map pp726-7; ☎ 06 686 13 09; Piazza Sant'Eustachio 82) Open since the 1940s and near the Pantheon, this place has been wowing visitors and Romans alike with practically perfect cappuccinos and espresso drinks for over 60 years.

Caffè Marzio (Map pp726-7; Piazza Santa Maria in Trastevere) This place has terrific coffee and views onto one of Rome's prettiest piazzas; perfection comes at a price, though.

Bars & Pubs

Bar San Calisto (Map pp726-7; ☎ 06 583 58 69; Piazza San Calisto; closed Sun) Filled with drunks, bums, tourists and artists, all flock here for the groovy atmosphere that spills out onto the piazza during summer. The chocolate *gelato* is legendary.

Bar del Fico (Map pp726-7; ☎ 06 687 55 68; Piazza del Fico 24; 8-2am Mon-Sat, from 6pm Sun) Popular with local actors and artists, this pretty bar has tables beneath its namesake fig tree – providing shade on sunny days and a hit of romance at night – and a snug interior with tasteful music and local art.

Cul de Sac (Map pp726-7; Piazza di Pasquino; small dishes €5-11; noon-4pm & 6pm-12.30am Tue-Sat) Tucked into a nook off Piazza Navona, this *carina* wine bar has communal wood benches out front, a chattery interior, simple but good *enoteca* fare, such as cheeses and salads, and a robust wine list.

Chakra Cafe (06 581 66 49; Piazza San Rufino 13; snacks €6-11) A funky modern wine bar in Trastevere is a hang-out joint for locals looking to check out chill-out live music.

La Vineria (Map pp726-7; 06 688 03 268; Campo de'Fiori 15; 9.30am-2pm & 6pm-1am Mon-Sat, to 2am Sun) Hit the cosy Vineria on the Campo, once the gathering place of the Roman literati.

Trinity College (Map pp726-7; 06 678 64 72; Via del Collegio Romano 6; 11-3am) If you're hankering for a pub night, try Trinity College; it has a good selection of imported brews, great food and an easy-going ambience; it also gets packed on weekends.

Bar della Pace (Map pp726-7; 06 686 12 16; Via della Pace 3-7) With its elegant ambience and dashing in-crowd, this is an atmospheric drinking spot.

ENTERTAINMENT

Rome is one of the quieter large cities as far as nightlife goes. Romans often spend hours over dinner and at a wine bar, but there is a lively clubbing scene, especially around Testaccio.

The best entertainment guide is *Roma C'è* (www.romace.it, in Italian), with an English-language section, published on Wednesday (€1.20). *La Repubblica* and *Il Messagero*, daily newspapers, have cinema, theatre and concert listings. All are available at newsstands. Rome's entertainment schedule is particularly heady in summer, with numerous alfresco performances; be sure to catch one if possible.

For theatre, opera and sporting events, book ahead through **Hello** (Map p724; Roma Termini), **Enjoy Rome** (see Tourist Information p717) or **Orbis** (Map p724; 06 48 27 403; Piazza dell'Esquilino 37).

Nightclubs & Live Music

Rome's nightlife usually centres around private parties, restaurants and bars rather than dancing or clubbing. However, there are a few places to get your groove on. Head over to Via di Monte Testaccio, where over a dozen clubs in just a few blocks cater to locals and international students. Expect to pay upwards of €20 just to get in, which may or may not include one drink.

Goa (Map pp718-19; 06 574 82 77; Via Libetta 13; 11pm-3am Tue-Sun) With its groovy ethnic décor, Goa is where the Roman and international 'in crowd' (including, once, Leonardo DiCaprio) come to groove to DJs and house while admiring their fellow beautiful people.

Caffè Latino (Map pp718-19; Via di Monte Testaccio 96) Come here for live Latin music and a disco of Latin and funk.

Stardust (Map pp726-7; 06 583 20 875; Viccolo dei Renzi 4; 7.30pm-2am Mon-Sat, from noon Sun) A tiny Trastevere pub-meets-jazz bar, this funky haunt purrs with sultry jazz and impromptu jam sessions, and doesn't close until the last customers tumble out the door. Head here for the grooviest Sunday brunch in Rome.

Radio Londra (Map pp718-19; 06 575 00 44; Via di Monte Testaccio 65b) Popular and decked out like an air-raid shelter, this club has live music four nights a week (usually Wednesday to Saturday).

Gilda (Map pp722-3; 06 679 73 96; Via Mario de'Fiori 97) With its plush décor and vast dance floor, Gilda attracts a slightly older, jackets-required crowd.

L'Alibi (Map pp718-19; 06 574 34 48; Via di Monte Testaccio 44) This is regarded as Rome's premier gay venue.

Also recommended:

Alien (Map pp718-19; 06 841 22 12; Via Velletri 13; 10.30pm-4am Tue & Thu-Sun) For sci-fi décor, dancers on raised platforms and hip-hop rhythms.

Big Mama (Map pp718-19; 06 581 24 51; www.bigmama.it; Via San Francesco a Ripa 18; 9pm-1.30am) Just south of Piazza Mastai in Trastevere.

Cinema

Several cinemas show films in English, including **Multisala Barberini** (Map pp722-3; 06 48 21 082; www.multisalabarberini.it; Piazza Barberini 24/25/26) and **Warner Village Moderno** (Map p724; 47 77 92 01; Piazza della Repubblica 45/46), a megaplex showing Hollywood blockbusters and Italian films. Expect to pay €7, with discounts on Wednesday.

Opera & Classical Music

Teatro dell'Opera (Map p724; 06 481 60 28 706; www.operaroma.it, in Italian; Piazza Beniamino Gigli) This theatre offers Rome's finest opera from December to June; ticket prices are steep.

For a full season of orchestral, international and pop music concerts, be sure to check out the 400-year-old **Accademia di Santa Cecilia** (Map pp722-3; ☎ ticket sales 199 10 97 83; www.santacecilia.it; Parco della Musica, Largo Luciano Berio 3), held in three buildings and an outdoor venue collectively known as the Auditorium of Rome. For classical music, visit the **Accademia Filarmonica Romana** (☎ 06 323 48 90; www.teatroolimpico.it; Teatro Olimpico, Piazza Gentile da Fabriano 17), about 2km north of the city – take the bus from Piazza Giuseppe Mazzini.

SHOPPING

Shopping in Rome is undeniably fun and will no doubt lure your attention from ancient ruins. This being Italy, traffic is banned on Saturdays to accommodate the thousands of window shoppers traipsing down the three ancient Roman roads radiating from Piazza del Popolo, the main shopping district.

Fashionistas will be happiest on Via Condotti and the narrow streets fanning from Piazza di Spagna to Via del Corso, lined with expensive boutiques full of clothing, footwear and accessories from the likes of Gucci, Valentino and Armani. Via del Corso, with a nice mix of shops featuring designer knock-offs, is easier on the wallet, as is Via Nazionale. Via del Governo Vecchio is home to second-hand shops and up-and-coming designers.

If you're after art and antiques, wander the streets around Via Margutta, Via Ripetta, Via del Babuino, and Via dei Coronari, near Piazza Navona. For jewellery, the area between Ponte Sisto and Campo de'Fiori shines.

Across the Tiber, head to Via Cola di Rienzo, near the Vatican, for a good selection of clothing, shoes and food shops; the twisty streets of Trastevere harbour lots of little boutiques and design shops.

For funky finds and great bargains, head to Trastevere's **Porta Portese flea market** (Map pp718-19; 🕑 6.30am-2pm Sun), Rome's biggest and best known. It's just 400m southwest of Basilica di Santa Cecilia in Trastevere – even if you don't want to buy an antique vase or doll parts, go for the scene (but be aware of pickpockets). The excellent **Via Sannio market** (Map pp718-19; Via Sannio; 🕑 Mon-Sat morning) near Porta San Giovanni sells new and second-hand clothes.

GETTING THERE & AWAY

Air

Rome's main airport is **Leonardo da Vinci** (FCO; ☎ 06 65 95 55 71; www.adr.it), often simply called Fiumicino (after the town where it's located). Low-cost carriers, including **Ryanair** (www.ryanair.com) and **easyJet** (www.easyjet.com), are increasingly flying into **Ciampino** (CIA; ☎ 06 79 49 42 25; www.adr.it), which is closer to town. You'll find the main airline offices just north of Roma Termini, in the area around Via Bissolati and Via Barberini.

Boat

Rome's main port is in Civitavecchia, about 80km from Rome's city centre and accessible by train. Tirrenia and the Ferrovie dello Stato (FS) ferries leave for various points in Sardinia (see p809) from Civitavecchia.

A Tirrenia fast ferry leaves from Fiumicino and Civitavecchia to Arbatax and Golfo Aranci, in summer only. Bookings can be made at the Termini-based agency **Passagi** (Map p724; 🕑 7.15am-9pm), at any travel agency displaying the Tirrenia or FS sign, or online at www.traghettionline.net. You can also book directly with **Tirrenia** (Map pp722-3; ☎ 06 42 00 98 03; Via San Nicola da Tolentino 5) or at the Stazione Marittima (ferry terminal at Civitavecchia) at the ports. Take the train from Roma Termini to Civitavecchia (€4 to €8, one hour, every 30 minutes); it's about a 15-minute walk to the port (to your right) as you exit the station.

See p821 for more information on transport options.

Bus

The main terminal for intercity buses is in Piazzale Tiburtina, in front of the Stazione Tiburtina. Catch Metro Linea B from Termini to Tiburtina.

Numerous bus lines run services to cities throughout Italy; all depart from the same area and the relevant ticket offices or agents are next to the bus terminus. For general information about which company services what area, go to the tourist office or Enjoy Rome (p717); for information and to make bookings, it's best and easiest to go through a travel agent, as most can book tickets on all long-distance buses.

Cotral (☎ 800 15 00 08; www.cotralspa.it, in Italian) For the Lazio region.

Interbus (☎ 0935 56 51 11; www.interbus.it) Heads to Sicily, including Messina, Catania and Palermo.
Lazzi (☎ 06 884 08 40; www.lazzi.it, in Italian) For northern Italian cities and Tuscany.
Marozzi (☎ 06 44 24 95 19; www.marozzivt.it, in Italian) Covers Sorrento, Brindisi, Matera and Lecce.
SAIS (☎ 091 616 60 28; www.saistrasporti.it) Long-haul trips to Sicily.
SENA (☎ 800 93 09 60; www.senabus.it) Services to Siena.
Sulga (☎ 075 575 96 41; www.sulga.it) For Perugia, Assisi and Romagna.

Car & Motorcycle

It's no holiday trying to motor yourself into Rome's centre, which has many traffic restrictions and can be exceedingly nerve fraying to navigate. If you insist, the main road connecting Rome to the north and south is the Autostrada del Sole (A1), which extends from Milan to Reggio di Calabria. On the outskirts of the city it connects with the Grande Raccordo Anulare (GRA), the ring road encircling Rome. It's best to enter or leave Rome via the GRA and the major feeder roads that connect it to the city. If approaching from the north, take the Via Salaria (SS4) or Via Flaminia (SS3) exits. From the south, take Via Appia Nuova (SS7) or Via del Mare (SS8), which connects Rome to the Lido di Ostia. All provide reasonably direct routes into the city. The A12 connects the city to both Civitavecchia and Fiumicino airport.

Car-rental offices at Roma Termini include **Avis** (☎ 06 481 43 73; www.avis.com), **Europcar** (☎ 06 488 28 54; www.europcar.com), **Hertz** (☎ 06 474 03 89; www.hertz.com) and **Maggiore National** (☎ 06 488 00 49; www.maggiore.it, in Italian). All have offices at both airports as well. **Happy Rent** (Map p724; ☎ 06 481 81 85; www.happyrent.com; Via Farini 3) hires scooters (from €31 per day), motorcycles (around €104 and up) and bicycles (from €62 per week). To see Rome in an unforgettable way, they even hire out Vespas with English-speaking drivers.

Train

Almost all trains arrive at and depart from Roma Termini, though some depart from Tiburtina. From Termini, there are regular connections to all major cities in Italy and throughout Europe. You can check the timetables at the train information desks at Roma Termini (Map p724), or by calling the **reservation line** (☎ 89 20 21; 🕑 24hr) or checking the Trenitalia website (www.trenitalia.com, in Italian and English). Trains start operating at around 5.45am and end at around 11pm; the side gates close after midnight, when it's nowhere you'd want to be.

Services at Termini include telephones, money exchange, tourist information, post office, first aid (from 7am to 9pm), an underground mall and **luggage storage** (per piece for 5hr €3.80, per piece per hr 5-12hr €0.60, per piece per hr thereafter €0.20; 🕑 6am-midnight).

GETTING AROUND

To/From the Airport

There are several options for getting to and from Rome's main airport, Leonardo da Vinci, about 30km southwest of the city centre. Even though Ciampino is just 15km southeast of the city centre, it is less accessible.

The convenient Leonardo Express train service (follow the signs to the station from the airport arrivals hall), which costs €9.50, arrives at and leaves from platforms 25 to 29 at Termini and takes 35 minutes (if you have luggage, give yourself five to 10 minutes to walk to the far-end platforms). The first direct train leaves the airport at 6.37am and takes 32 minutes. Thereafter, trains run half-hourly until the last one at 11.37pm. From Termini to the airport, trains start at 5.51am and run half-hourly until the last train at 10.51pm. Another train (€5) from Fiumicino stops at Trastevere, Ostiense and Tiburtina stations, but not at Termini, with a service from the airport every 20 minutes from 5.57am to 11.27pm, and from Tiburtina from 5.06am until 10.36pm. From midnight to 5am, an hourly bus runs from Stazione Tiburtina to the airport. Taxis from the airport to the city centre run to about €50.

The **airport shuttle** (☎ 06 420 14 507; www.airportshuttle.it) offers transfers to/from Fiumicino for €26 for one passenger and €6 for each additional passenger (add 30% between 10pm and 7am) and €42 to Ciampino for one or two passengers, €6 for each additional passenger.

The **Terravision** (☎ 06 659 58 646; www.terravision.it) bus departs for Ciampino outside Termini on Via Marsala 22. The single/return journey costs €8.50/13.50 and takes about 40 minutes, depending on traffic.

To get to Ciampino using public transport, take a Blue Cotral bus (running from 6.50am to 11.40pm) from the Anagnina metro stop (line A). The airport is connected to Rome by Via Appia Nuova.

Car & Motorcycle

Negotiating Roman traffic by car is difficult enough, but you are in for enormous life-risking stress if you ride a motorcycle or Vespa. The rule in Rome is to look straight ahead to watch the vehicles in front and pray those behind are watching you. Pedestrians should always watch out for motorcycles, which often skip red lights.

Most of the historic centre is closed to normal traffic, and you are not permitted to drive into the centre from 6.30am to 6pm Monday to Friday and from 2pm to 6pm Saturday without residency or special permission.

If your car goes missing after being parked illegally, check with the **traffic police** (☎ 06 6 76 91). It will cost about €95 to get it back, plus a hefty fine.

The most major parking area closest to the centre is at the Villa Borghese; entrance is from Piazzale Brasile at the top of Via Vittorio Veneto. There is also a supervised car park at Roma Termini. Other car parks are at Piazza dei Partigiani, just outside Stazione Ostiense, and at Stazione Tiburtina, from where you can also catch the metro into the centre.

See p737 for information about car and scooter rental.

Public Transport

Rome has an integrated public transport system, so the same **Metrebus** ticket is valid for all modes of transport: bus, tram and metro. You can buy tickets at all *tabacchi* (tobacconists' shops), newsstands and from vending machines at main bus stops. Single tickets cost €1 for 75 minutes, €4 for one day, €11 for three days and €16 per week. Tickets must be purchased before you get on and validated in the orange machine as you board. Ticketless riders risk a hefty €51 fine, demanded on the spot in cash. Don't even try the 'But I'm a tourist! I didn't know!' line; it hasn't worked in a decade.

ATAC (☎ 800 43 17 84; www.atac.roma.it) is the city's public transport company. Free transport maps and details on bus routes are available at the ATAC information booth, at the **Urban Bus Station** (Map p724; Piazza dei Cinquecento) in front of Roma Termini, where many of the main bus routes terminate. Largo di Torre Argentina, Piazza Venezia and Piazza San Silvestro are other hubs. Buses generally run from about 6am to midnight, while late-night buses are marked with an owl on top of the bus sign. A fast tram service, the No 8, connects Largo Argentina with Trastevere, Porta Portese and Monteverde Nuovo.

The Metropolitana has two lines: A (the red line) and B (the blue line). Both pass through Roma Termini. Take Linea A for Piazza di Spagna, the Vatican (Ottaviano) and Villa Borghese (Flaminio), and Linea B for the Colosseum and Circus Maximus. Trains run approximately every five minutes between 5.30am and 11.30pm (12.30am on Saturday) for Line B and to 9pm for Line A.

Taxi

Roman taxi drivers can be at the top of the fleecing-foreigners game, so understand the rules before you and your bags get in the car. Make sure your taxi is licensed and metered, and always go with the metered fare, never an arranged price.

Cooperativa Radio Taxi Romana (☎ 06 35 70) oversees many operators. You can't hail a taxi as in most cities, but there are major taxi ranks at the airports, Roma Termini and Largo Argentina in the historical centre (look for the orange-and-black taxi signs). There are surcharges from €1 to €3 for luggage, night service, Sunday and public holidays. Most taxi fares within Rome's historic centre will cost from €7 to €20. Taxis are on radio call 24 hours a day.

AROUND ROME

Ostia Antica

While the ruins of Pompeii show off how the upper classes lived, Ostia's ruins display a once-thriving port city, where 100,000 Roman citizens lived and worked as far back as the 4th century BC. As Rome's port linking the Tiber River and the Mediterranean, Ostia became strategically important as both a merchant and defence centre. Barbarian invasions and the outbreak of malaria led to Ostia Antica's eventual abandonment, but Pope Gregory IV re-established the city in the 9th century AD.

Information about the town and ruins is available from the Rome tourist office or Enjoy Rome (p717).

Of particular note in the **ruins** (☎ 06 563 58 099; adult/concession €4/2; 8.30am-6pm summer, to 4pm winter) of the excavated city are the mosaics of the **Terme di Nettuno** (Baths of Neptune); a **Roman theatre** built by Agrippa; the **forum** and **Capitolium temple**, dedicated to Jupiter, Juno and Minerva; and the **Piazzale delle Corporazioni**, the offices of Ostia's 70 merchant guilds, distinguished by mosaics depicting their different trades.

To get to Ostia Antica from Rome, take the Metro Linea B to Piramide, then the Ostia Lido train (getting off at Ostia Antica). By car, take the Via del Mare or the parallel-running Via Ostiense.

Tivoli

pop 49,254

Set on a hill by the Aniene River, Tivoli was a resort town of the ancient Romans and became popular as a summer playground for the wealthy during the Renaissance. To see evidence of the latter, head to the ornate gardens of Villa d'Este, or to the ruins of Villa Adriana, to see what the Roman emperor Hadrian (as in Hadrian's Wall) thought a little summer villa should look like.

The **tourist office** (☎ 0774 31 12 49; Largo Garibaldi; 8.30am-2.30pm Tue-Sat & 3-6pm Tue-Thu) is near the Cotral bus stop.

SIGHTS

Hadrian's spectacular summer villa, **Villa Adriana** (☎ 0774 53 02 03; admission €6.50; 9am-1hr before sunset), built in the 2nd century AD, was one of the largest and most sumptuous in the Roman Empire. Although successively plundered by barbarians and Romans for building materials (many of its original decorations were used to embellish the Villa d'Este), enough resplendence remains to convey the villa's magnificence.

The Renaissance **Villa d'Este** (☎ 0774 31 20 70; Piazza Trento; admission €9; 9am-6.30pm Tue-Sun summer, to 4.30pm winter) was built in the 16th century for Cardinal Ippolito d'Este. Situated on the site of a Franciscan monastery, the villa's wonderful gardens are decorated with numerous fountains, which are its main attraction.

GETTING THERE & AWAY

Tivoli is 30km east of Rome and accessible by Cotral bus from outside the Ponte Mammolo station on Metro Linea B. Buses depart every 20 minutes (€1.60). The fastest route by car is on the Rome–L'Aquila autostrada (A24).

Tarquinia

pop 15,472

Without a Tarquinia, there would never have been a Rome as we know it. The Etruscan capital Tarquinia was founded as far back as the 12th century BC and rivalled Athens in its grand scale. Many Tarquin kings ruled Rome just after the mythic founding by Romulus after killing his twin Remus in 753 BC. Although the Etruscans were the greatest Italic rulers before the Romans, not much of their culture remains. Most of what scholars know comes from the very walls of Tarquinia's necropolis, which, along with the necropolis at Cerveteri, was recently added to the list of Unesco's World Heritage sites.

Tarquinia is about 90km northwest of Rome, between Civitavecchia and Fiumicino, and there's a **tourist information office** (☎ 0766 85 63 84; Piazza Cavour 1; 8am-2pm Mon-Sat) just past the medieval ramparts.

SIGHTS

The entire town of Tarquinia is a historical monument, but of great note is the **Museo Nazionale Tarquiniense** (☎ 0766 85 60 36; Piazza Cavour; admission incl necropolis €6.50; 9am-7pm Tue-Sun), a significant collection of Etruscan treasures housed in the 15th-century Palazzo Vitelleschi. In addition to sarcophagi laden with everyday tools, you can also admire frescoes from the tombs. Keep an eye out for a few red-and-black plates featuring acrobatic sex acts, which the Etruscans were famous for; the words 'Etruscan' and 'prostitute' were even used interchangeably.

The **necropolis** (☎ 0766 85 63 08; Via Ripagretta; admission €4 or €6.50 with museum; 8.30am-6.30pm Tue-Sun), also known as Monterozzi, dates to the 7th century BC. Of its 6000 excavated graves, 200 are painted with various scenes of Etruscan life. It's a 15-minute walk from the town centre.

SLEEPING & EATING

Tarquinia has limited accommodation, so it's best to book ahead; it makes a very fine day trip from Rome.

Hotel San Marco (☎ 0766 84 22 34; www.san-marco.com; Piazza Cavour 18; s/d €50/65) In the medieval centre, just across from the museums, is this convenient (if not exactly calming) little hotel, above a lively bar.

Trattoria Arcadia (☎ 0766 85 55 01; Via Mazzini 6; 1st/2nd courses €6.50/8.50) On a small side street in the medieval centre is this small and affordable local trattoria.

GETTING THERE & AWAY

Cotral buses leave every hour for Tarquinia from outside the Lepanto stop on Metro Linea A, arriving at Barriera San Giusto, a short distance from the tourist office.

Cerveteri

The most ancient Etruscan settlement, known as Caere, was the most important commercial centre on the Mediterranean going back to the founding of Rome, around the 7th century BC. The present-day lures are the atmospheric tombs, known as *tumoli,* great mounds of earth with carved stone bases. Treasures taken from these tombs can be seen in the Vatican Museums and the Louvre. There is a **tourist office** (☎ 06 994 06 72; Piazza Aldo Moro; 10.30am-12.30pm & 4.30-6.30pm).

Once inside the main necropolis area, **Banditaccia** (☎ 06 994 00 01; Via del Necropoli; admission €4; 9am-7pm summer, to 4pm winter, closed Mon), the *tumoli* are laid out in the form of a town. The best-preserved example is the 4th-century-BC **Tomba dei Rilievi**, adorned with painted reliefs depicting household items and cooking implements.

Antica Locanda Le Ginestre (☎ 06 994 06 72; Piazza Santa Maria 5; 1st/2nd courses €10/18; closed Mon) is well-known and brings Romans out to Cerveteri just for a meal on its outdoor terrace; the pastas are especially good.

Cerveteri is accessible from Rome by Cotral bus (1¼ hours, every 30 minutes) from outside the Lepanto stop on Metro Linea A.

NORTHERN ITALY

Italy's well-heeled north is a fascinating area of historical wealth and natural diversity. Bordered by the northern Alps and boasting some of the country's most spectacular coastline (the Cinque Terre), it also encompasses Italy's largest lowland area, the decidedly unpicturesque Po valley plain. Of the cities it's Venice that hogs the limelight, but in their own way Turin, Genoa and Bologna offer plenty to the open-minded traveller. Verona is justifiably considered one of Italy's most beautiful cities, while the medieval centres of Padua, Ferrara and Ravenna all reward a visit.

> **ETRUSCAN INFLUENCE**
>
> The Etruscans were well-known for their spicy exploits (see p739). The Roman historian Livy writes that it was the Tarquin rape of the virtuous lady Lucretia that led to the expulsion of the Tarquin kings from Rome, turning Rome from a monarchy to a Republic in 510 BC.

GENOA

pop 601,340

A city of aristocratic *palazzi* (mansions, palaces) and malodorous alleyways, of Gothic architecture and industrial sprawl, Genoa is a compelling place. You need only walk the labyrinthine, sometimes seedy streets of the *centro storico* to feel its raw energy. Birthplace of Christopher Columbus (1451–1506) and home to Europe's largest aquarium, it was once a powerful maritime republic known as *La Superba;* nowadays it's a fascinating port city well worth a stopover.

Orientation & Information

Central Genoa is concentrated between the two main train stations: Stazione Brignole and Stazione Principe. The central shopping strip, Via XX Settembre, starts a short walk southwest of Stazione Brignole and leads up to Piazza de Ferrari. From adjacent Piazza Giacomo Matteotti, Via San Lorenzo leads to the waterfront and historic centre.

For information head to one of the four **tourist offices** (airport ☎ 010 601 52 47; 9.30am-1.30pm & 2.30-5.30pm Mon-Sat, 10am-1.30pm & 2.30-5pm Sun; city centre ☎ 010 868 74 52; www.apt.genova.it; Piazza Giacomo Matteotti; 9am-1pm & 3-6pm; ferry terminal ☎ 010 246 36 86; 9.30am-12.30pm & 1.30-5.30pm; Stazione Principe ☎ 010 246 26 33; www.apt.genova.it; 9.30am-1pm & 2.30-6pm Mon-Sat).

Sights

Genoa's central square, Piazza de Ferrari, is a good place to start exploring the city.

ITALY

Grandiose and impressive, it's flanked by imposing *palazzi* – **Palazzo della Borsa** (closed to the public), **Teatro Carlo Felice** (see p742) and the huge **Palazzo Ducale** (☎ 010 557 40 04; www.palazzoducale.genova.it, in Italian; entrance Piazza Giacomo Matteotti 9; admission around €8; 🕑 9am-6.30pm Tue-Sun), once the seat of the city government, now Liguria's main exhibition space.

A short walk to the west, the 12th-century **Cattedrale di San Lorenzo** (Piazza San Lorenzo; 🕑 8-11.45am & 3-6.45pm) is a beautiful example of Italian Gothic architecture.

Located on the waterfront, the **Porto Antico** (☎ information 010 248 57 10; www.portoantico.it; 🕑 10am-6pm), Genoa's old port, was given a makeover before the city's stint as European City of Culture in 2004. Interest centres on the **Acquario di Genova** (☎ 010 234 56 78; www.acquariodigenova.it; Ponte Spinola; adult/child €14/8.50; 🕑 9.30am-7.30pm Mon- Fri, to 8.30pm Sat & Sun), Europe's largest aquarium. Designed by architect Renzo Piano, it houses 5000 animals in six million litres of water.

The city facelift didn't, however, extend to the city's dark *centro storico*. While usually crowded by day, the area to the north of Via San Lorenzo can be intimidating at night (particularly Via San Luca). Keep your eyes open and, if possible, your nose closed.

Genoa's main museums are in a series of *palazzi* on Via Garibaldi. The three most important, known collectively as the **Musei di Strada Nuova** (☎ 010 247 63 51; adult/child €7/5; 🕑 9am-7pm Tue-Fri, from 10am Sat & Sun), are housed in **Palazzo Bianco** (Via Garibaldi 11), **Palazzo Rosso** (Via Garibaldi 18) and **Palazzo Doria-Tursi** (Via Garibaldi 9). The first two feature works by Flemish, Dutch, Spanish and Italian old masters, while the third displays the personal effects of Niccolò Paganini, Genoa's legendary violinist. Tickets, valid for all three museums, are available from the bookshop in Palazzo Doria-Tursi.

Nearby, the **Galleria Nazionale di Palazzo Spinola** (☎ 010 247 70 61; Piazza Pellicceria 1; admission €4; 🕑 8.30am-7.30pm Tue-Sat, 1-8pm Sun) displays major Italian and Flemish Renaissance works.

Sleeping

Ostello Genova (☎ 010 242 24 57; hostelge@iol.it; Via Costanzi 120; per person dm/s/d incl breakfast €15/22/20; 🕑 closed Jan) Genoa's HI hostel is a functional, modern affair that makes little lasting impression, apart from its panoramic city views. Take bus 40 from Brignole; 35 or 40 from Principe.

Carola (☎ 010 839 13 40; www.albergocarola.it; Via Gropallo 4; d €70, s/d with shared bathroom €40/60) Conveniently close to Stazione Brignole, this is a classic old-school *pensione*. Guests are welcomed as if friends, and the 3rd-floor rooms are simple, small and spotless. The shared bathrooms are similarly pristine.

Hotel Bel Soggiorno (☎ 010 54 28 80; www.belsoggiornohotel.com; Via XX Settembre 19; s/d incl breakfast €82/107; ❄) An endearing mix of the modern and the antique, rooms here are full of character. The colonial-style breakfast room adds to the chintzy, yesteryear atmosphere. It's in an excellent location and has a friendly owner.

Locanda di Palazzo Cicala (☎ 010 251 88 24; www.palazzocicala.it; Piazza San Lorenzo 16; s/d €160/210; P ❄ 💻) A dash of contemporary style awaits guests at this boutique hotel. Hidden in a 16th-century *palazzo* opposite the cathedral, it has sexy high-ceilinged rooms with designer furniture and loos by Philippe Starck.

Eating

Ligurian specialities include *pesto* (a sauce of basil, garlic, pine nuts and Parmesan), *pansoti* (ravioli in ground walnut sauce) and focaccia.

Threegaio (☎ 010 246 57 93; Piazza delle Erbe 17/19r; salads €4.50, snacks €5-10) On one of Genoa's 'in' squares, this fashionable spot is ideal for a midday salad or a lingering *aperitivo* (apéritif). The bright yellow interior gets very busy at lunchtime, but the pace relaxes in the evening as the cocktails start to flow.

Il Barbarossa (☎ 010 246 50 97; Piano di Sant'Andrea 21/23r; 1st/2nd courses €7/10) Salute the model of Elvis as you enter the warm, woody atmosphere of this small, brick-vaulted *enoteca*-cum-café. There's wine by the glass (from €3.50), a daily menu of local specialities, *panini* and beer.

Il Panson (☎ 010 246 89 03; Piazza delle Erbe 5; 1st/2nd courses €9/13; 🕑 dinner Mon-Sat) A historic restaurant, in business since 1790, Il Panson is the place to sample great seafood. Everything's good, but two dishes stand out – the handmade basil ravioli in prawn sauce and the *fritto misto* (mixed fry).

Cantine Squarciafico (☎ 010 247 08 23; Piazza Invrea 3r; 1st/2nd courses €10/12; 🕑 closed Aug) Housed in a 16th-century *palazzo*, this trendy wine bar, complete with vaulted ceilings and stone columns, is an elegant place to eat. The menu of modern regional dishes changes daily but house specialities include pesto and *stoccafisso* (stockfish). There's also a 120-strong wine list to choose from.

Antica Cantina i Tre Merli (☎ 010 247 40 95; Vico dietro il Coro Maddalena 26r; 1st/2nd courses €10/15; closed Sat lunch & Sun) A smart option just off Via Garibaldi, 'The Three Crows' serves excellent Ligurian cuisine with an emphasis on fish. The house speciality *Il Ciuppin* is a superb, taste-charged seafood soup.

Drinking & Entertainment

Action centres on the *centro storico* with a number of good bars clustered around Piazza delle Erbe.

Mentelocale Café (☎ 010 595 96 48; Piazza Giacomo Matteotti 9) This is a swish ultramodern café by the entrance to the Palazzo Ducale. Sit on the Dali-inspired red sofas and sip on something cool as you eye up fellow drinkers.

Cosa Zapata (Via Sampierdarena 36; 9pm-3am Fri & Sat) Live music fans should seek this *centro sociale* (organised squat), where a younger crowd moshes to modern music within medieval walls.

Teatro Carlo Felice (☎ 010 5398 12 24; www.carlofelice.it, in Italian; Passo Eugenio Montale 4) Treat your partner to a performance at Genoa's neoclassical opera house.

Getting There & Around

AIR

Genoa's **Cristoforo Colombo airport** (GOA; ☎ 010 601 54 10; www.airport.genova.it; Sestri Ponente) is 6km west of the city.

The **Volabus** (☎ 010 558 24 14; 5.30am-10.30pm) airport shuttle leaves from Piazza Verdi (€3, 25 minutes, half hourly) outside Stazione Brignole, also stopping at Stazione Principe.

BUS

The main bus terminal is on Piazza della Vittoria, south of Stazione Brignole. Book tickets at **Geotravels** (☎ 010 58 71 81; Piazza della Vittoria 57; 9am-12.30pm & 3-7pm Mon-Fri & 9am-12.30pm Sat).

FERRIES

Ferries sail from the **ferry terminal** (☎ 166 152 39 393; www.porto.genova.it; Via Milano 51), west of the city centre. Ferry companies include:

Grandi Navi Veloci (☎ 800 46 65 10; www2.gnv.it) To/from Sardinia (Porto Torres €49, 11 hours; Olbia €38, 10 hours), Sicily (Palermo €75, 20 hours), Barcelona (€56, 18 hours) and Tunis (€104, 24 hours).

Moby Lines (☎ 010 254 15 13; www.mobylines.it) To/from Corsica (Bastia €15, four hours) and Sardinia (Olbia €42, seven hours).

Tirrenia (☎ 800 82 40 79; www.tirrenia.it) To/from Sardinia (Porto Torres €55, 10 hours; Olbia €40, 13½ hours).

TRAIN

There are direct trains to La Spezia (€8, 1½ hours, half hourly), Milan (€13.90, 1¾ hours, up to 25 daily), Pisa (€13.90, two hours, half hourly), Rome (€33.65, 5¼ hours, eight daily) and Turin (€12.90, two hours, up to 20 daily).

It generally makes little difference whether you leave from Brignole or Principe station.

RIVIERA DI LEVANTE

Curving southeast from Genoa to La Spezia, Liguria's eastern Riviera boasts some of Italy's most dramatic coastline. The highlight is the Parco Nazionale delle Cinque Terre, just north of La Spezia. Summer gets very crowded so try to visit in spring or autumn; viable bases include Santa Margherita in the north and La Spezia in the south.

There are tourist offices at **Santa Margherita** (☎ 0185 28 74 85; www.apttigullio.liguria.it; Via XXV Aprile 4; 9.30am-12.30pm & 3-7.30pm Mon-Sat, 9.30am-12.30pm & 4.30-7.30pm Sun Jun-Sep, 9.30am-12.30pm & 2.30-5.30pm Mon-Sat Oct-May) and **La Spezia** (☎ 0187 77 09 00; www.aptcinqueterre.sp.it; Viale Mazzini 45; 9am-1pm & 2-5pm Mon-Sat, 9.30am-12.30pm Sun). For information on activities in the Cinque Terre ask at the **park office** (☎ 0187 76 00 00; www.parconazionale5terre.it; Via Signorini 118; 8am-6pm) in Riomaggiore.

Sights & Activities

After you've explored elegant Santa Margherita (which won't take you long) head to **Camogli**, a gorgeous fishing village turned resort, and exclusive **Portofino**. From Portofino, you can walk to the medieval Benedictine **Abbazia di San Fruttuoso** (☎ 0185 77 27 03; Camogli; admission €4; 10am-6pm May-Sep, to 4pm Tue-Sun Mar, Apr & Oct, to 4pm Sun Dec-Feb).

For the coast's best scenery head south to the **Parco Nazionale delle Cinque Terre**. Named after its five tiny villages (Riomaggiore, Manorola, Corniglia, Vernazza and Monterosso) this Unesco-listed park encompasses some of Italy's most picturesque and environmentally sensitive coastline. The villages, all accessible by train, are linked by the 12km **Via dell'Amore** (Lovers' Lane; toll €3), a magnificent, mildly challenging day's walk.

Via dell'Amore is just one of a network of footpaths and cycle trails that crisscross the park; details are available from the park office (see opposite). If water sports are more your thing, you can hire snorkelling gear, kayaks and diving kit at the **Diving Center 5 Terre** (☎ 0187 92 00 11; www.5terrediving.com; Via San Giacomo) in Riomaggiore.

Sleeping

Ostello 5 Terre (☎ 0187 92 02 15; www.cinqueterre.net/ostello; Via B Riccobaldi 21; dm €22; 💻) In Manorola, this private hostel is justifiably popular. Beds are in six-person single-sex dorms, most of which have sea-views and all of which are clean and bright. Extras include bike/snorkel hire and laundry facilities. Book ahead.

Nuova Riviera (☎ 0185 28 74 03; info@nuovariviera.com; Via Belvedere 10/2, Santa Margherita; s/d €90/100, with shared bathroom €60/70; ☒) Housed in a lovely old villa full of antiques, chandeliers and mosaic floors, the Nuova Riviera exudes a genteel charm. Rooms, divided between the hotel proper and a nearby annex, are inviting and airy. Payment is cash only for rooms with shared bathrooms.

Hotel Astoria (☎ 0187 71 46 55; www.albergoastoria.com; Via Roma 139; s/d incl breakfast €80/130; Ⓟ) The Astoria makes a good base for exploring the Cinque Terre. Not five minutes from La Spezia train station, it offers bright rooms and big, firm beds – something you'll appreciate after a day's walking.

Other recommendations:

La Dolce Vita (☎ 0187 760044; Via Colombo 120; beds from €20) *Affittacamere* (private house renting rooms) in Riomaggiore with a range of simple holiday rooms.

Edi (☎ 0187 92 03 25; Via Colombo 111; d €55-70) Sunny rooms and apartments in Riomaggiore.

Eating & Drinking

A Pie De Ma (☎ 338 222 00 88; Via dell'Amore; snacks €5-8) An ideal pit stop for walkers tackling Via dell'Amore, this café can seriously damage your willpower. It's not the food, which is fine, but the temptation to while away the day gazing over Riomaggiore's bay.

Osteria No 7 (☎ 0185 28 17 03; Via J Ruffini 36; 1st/2nd courses €7/8) In Santa Margherita, Osteria No 7 is a real find. Boisterous and down-to-earth, it serves fantastic regional fare in great, steaming portions. Try the tasty *seppie in umido* (cuttlefish stew).

Bar Centrale (☎ 0187 92 02 08; Via Colombo 144; 💻) Hub of Riomaggiore hijinks, the Bar Centrale bar is, in the off-season, your only real carousing option; in summer it's certainly the most raucous. The Internet costs €6 per hour.

Getting There & Away

From Genoa, trains run to Santa Margherita (€2.10, 35 minutes, half hourly) and La Spezia (€8, 1½ hours, half hourly). From La Spezia, regional trains to/from the Cinque Terre villages run twice hourly between 6am and 9.15pm; unlimited travel between Levanto and La Spezia is covered by the *biglietto giornaliero Cinque Terre* (24-hour Cinque Terre rail pass; €5.40).

In summer, various ferry companies ply the coastal waters: **Servizio Marittimo del Tigullio** (☎ 0185 28 46 70; www.traghettiportofino.it) operates between Santa Margherita, Portofino, the Cinque Terre and Genoa; **Trasporti Marittimi Turistici Golfo Paradiso** (☎ 0185 77 20 91; www.golfoparadiso.it, in Italian) runs between Genoa, Camogli and the Cinque Terre; and **Navigazione Golfo dei Poeti** (☎ 0187 96 76 76; www.navigazionegolfodeipoeti.it) connects La Spezia and the Cinque Terre.

TURIN

pop 867,855

First-time visitors to Turin are often surprised. Expecting a bleak, industrial sprawl they are shocked to discover a dynamic city of royal palaces (Turin was home to Italy's royal Savoy family) and historic cafés, baroque piazzas and world-class museums. Traditionally associated with Fiat, football (Juventus) and the Holy Shroud, Piedmont's capital has rarely looked as good as it does today, its centre gleaming in the aftermath of the 2006 Winter Olympics.

Orientation & Information

Stazione Porta Nuova train station is the main point of arrival, although most trains will be using the revamped Stazione Porta Susa from 2007. From Porta Nuova cross Piazza Carlo Felice and follow Via Roma for Turin's two focal piazzas: San Carlo and Castello.

City information is available from the three **tourist offices** (Atrium Torino ☎ 011 53 51 81; www.turismotorino.org; Piazza Solferino; 🕑 9.30am-7pm; Porta Nuova train station ☎ 011 53 51 81; 🕑 9.30am-7pm Mon-Sat, to 3pm Sun; ☎ airport 011 53 51 81; 🕑 8.30am-10.30pm).

Sights

Serious sightseers should consider the **Torino Card** (48/72hr card €16/18), available at tourist offices and valid for all public transport and discounts/entry to 120 museums, monuments and castles.

Turin's grandest square is **Piazza Castello**, bordered by porticoed promenades and regal palaces. Dominating the piazza, Palazzo Madama is home to the **Museo Civico d'Arte Antica** (☎ 011 442 99 12; Piazza Castello; 🕑 closed at time of research). To the north, statues of Castor and Pollux guard the entrance to the enormous **Palazzo Reale** (Royal Palace; ☎ 011 436 14 55; Piazza Castello; adult/child €6.50/free; 🕑 9am-7.30pm Tue-Sun), built for Carlo Emanuele II in the mid-17th century. The palace's **Giardino Reale** (Royal Garden; admission free; 🕑 9am-1hr before sunset) was designed in 1697 by Louis le Nôtre, noted for his work at Versailles.

A short walk away, elegant **Piazza San Carlo**, known as Turin's drawing room, is famous for its cafés and twin baroque churches **San Carlo** and **Santa Cristina**.

Turin's main cathedral, the **Cattedrale di San Giovanni Battista** (☎ 011 436 15 40; Piazza San Giovanni; 🕑 7am-12.30pm & 3-7pm Mon-Sat, from 8am-Sun), houses the *Sindone* (Turin Shroud), a copy of which is on permanent display in front of the altar (the real thing is kept in a vacuum-sealed box and rarely revealed). Believers claim the linen cloth was used to wrap the crucified Christ; carbon dating, however, dates the cloth to the 13th century. All this, and more, is explained in the **Museo della Sindone** (Museum of the Shroud; ☎ 011 436 58 32; Via San Domenico 28; adult/child €5.50/2.50; 🕑 9am-noon & 3-7pm).

But if Turin's famous for one museum it's the **Museo Egizio** (Egyptian Museum; ☎ 011 561 77 76; www.museoegizio.org; Via Accademia delle Scienze 6; adult/child €6.50/free; 🕑 8.30am-7.30pm Tue-Sun), which houses an engrossing collection of ancient Egyptian art that is considered the world's most important outside of Cairo and London.

Towering 167m over the city centre, the **Mole Antonelliana** (Via Montebello 20) is Turin's most recognisable building. Worth a look in its own right, it nowadays houses the **Museo Nazionale del Cinema** (☎ 011 813 85 60; www.museonazionaledelcinema.org; adult/concession €5.50/4.50; 🕑 9am-8pm Tue-Fri & Sun, to 11pm Sat) and its comprehensive collection of cinematic memorabilia. Modern, interactive and fun, the museum makes a refreshing change from Turin's more traditional attractions. Don't

BLACK MAGIC CITY

Turin is a magic city. Situated on the 45th parallel, it is, according to occult lore, one of the three apexes of the white magic triangle with Lyon and Prague and of its black magic counterpart with London and San Francisco.

Mysterious and ancient lines of energy are said to converge on Turin, as do two rivers, the Po and the Dora. The Po represents the sun and the masculine, while the Dora symbolises the moon and the feminine; together they form a protective ring of water around the city.

The city's black heart is Piazza Statuto. Located in the west of the city, the Romans believed it to be cursed as its position was unfavourable for the setting of the sun. This, they claimed, was a source of negative energy, as sunset symbolised the convergence of good and evil. More prosaically, Piazza Statuto was the site of the city scaffold where thousands met their fate before passing directly through the Gates of Hell, said to lie under the piazza's central flower bed.

To combat these sinister forces, head for Piazza Castello, the centre of the city's white magic map. Bisecting the square, the line dividing the black and white halves of the city passes between the statues of Castor and Pollux outside Palazzo Reale.

Believers cite the vicinity of the Holy Shroud in the Cattedrale di San Giovanni Battista as a source of positive energy, along with the benign forces emanating from the Museo Egizio and the golden auspices of a cave under Palazzo Madama, where the Savoys used to have the master alchemists of the day practise their mysterious arts.

miss the glass **Panoramic Lift** (adult/child €4/3), which whisks you up 85m in 59 seconds – unless you suffer from vertigo.

Sleeping

Campeggio Villa Rey (☎ 011 819 01 17; Strada Superiore Val San Martino 27; per person/tent/car €7/6/1.50; ⏲ Mar-Oct) Set amid the greenery of Turin's hills, this camping ground, the closest to the city centre, is east of the Po River– take bus 61 from Porta Nuova to the end of the line, then bus 54.

Ostello Torino (☎ 011 660 29 39; ostello.torino@libero.it; Via Alby 1; per person dm/s/d incl breakfast €14.50/20/19; ⏲ closed mid-Dec–mid-Jan; P ⊠ 🖳) Turin's HI hostel is quiet, comfortable and clean with three- or eight-person dorms and family rooms. Wi-fi is a further plus. Catch bus 52 from Porta Nuova (64 on Sunday), otherwise it's a steep 1.8km walk.

Bologna (☎ 011 562 01 91; www.hotelbolognasrl.it, in Italian; Corso Vittorio Emanuele II 60; s/d incl breakfast €75/95; ❄) The Bologna's ageing corridors and innocuous public spaces lead through to rooms that are surprisingly spic, spacious and modern. To grab one you'll need to book ahead as the hotel is deservedly popular.

Dogana Vecchia (☎ 011 436 67 52; Via Corte D'Appello 4; s/d €88/105; ⊠ ❄ 🖳) Once a 17th-century inn, the Dogana Vecchia has accommodated the likes of Verdi and Mozart. Parquet, chandeliers and pot plants provide olde-world ambience, while mod cons ensure contemporary comfort.

Art Hotel Boston (☎ 011 50 03 59; www.hotelbostontorino.it; Via Massena 70; s €105-200, d €150-280; ❄ 🖳) The Boston's austere façade gives no clues as to the colourful, modern interior. Individually decorated rooms sport everything from pop art to hanging crocodiles, from floral chintz to white minimalism. The jazzy public spaces are filled with modern art including original works by, among others, Andy Warhol.

Eating & Drinking

Early evening is the time to make for one of the city's cafés and enjoy an aperitif accompanied by a sumptuous buffet of hors d'oeuvres. Two good spots are **Caffè Elena** (☎ 011 812 33 41; Piazza Vittorio Veneto 5) and **Lobelix** (☎ 011 436 72 06; Via Corte d'Appello 15f).

Il Granaio (☎ 011 562 10 03; Via San Francesco d'Assisi; mains €6; ⏲ lunch Mon-Sat) Walk through the pasta shop to this cheap, hugely popular self-service canteen. Locals flock here for great pasta and *castagnaccio* (chestnut-flour cake topped with pine kernels and rosemary).

Pizzeria Stars & Stripes (☎ 011 516 20 52; Piazza Paleocapa 2D; pizzas/1st/2nd courses €7/7/12; ⏲ closed Mon lunch & Sun) Although offering a full menu of pastas and main courses, it's the pizzas that stand out at this colourful pizzeria. Toppings range from the trad to the rad – think tandoori chicken, marinated tuna, caviar and vodka (fortunately, not all on the same pizza).

Ristorante Perbacco (☎ 011 882110; Via Giuseppe Mazzini 31; set menu €30; ⏲ 7.45pm-1am Tue-Sun) With its dim lighting and deep-red furnishings, the Perbacco provides a refined setting for first-rate Piedmontese cuisine. Connoisseurs will appreciate the wine list that's longer than the Po.

San Tommaso 10 (☎ 011 53 42 01; Via San Tommaso 10) Come here for Turin's best, and most unusual, coffee. Anyone for a tiramisu espresso or an orange cappuccino? They might offend traditionalists, but believe me, these coffees are good.

Getting There & Around

In Caselle, 16km northwest of the city centre, **Turin airport** (TRN; ☎ 011 567 63 61; www.turin-airport.com) operates flights to/from European and national destinations. **Sadem** (☎ 011 300 01 66; www.sadem.it, in Italian) runs an airport shuttle (€5.50, 40 minutes, every 45 minutes) from the corner of Via Camerana and Corso Vittorio Emanuele II.

Direct trains connect with Milan (€15.60, 1¾ hours, up to 30 daily), Venice (€32.70, five hours, five daily), Genoa (€12.90, two hours, up to 20 daily) and Rome (€43.45, seven hours, seven daily).

MILAN

pop 1.27 million

Italy's financial and fashion capital is strictly for city lovers. To enjoy its vibrant cultural scene and wicked nightlife you'll have to put up with its traffic-ridden streets and charmless city centre. There are surprisingly few must-see sights and unless you're here to shop – for which you'll require the salary of a top model – you'll not want to linger long.

Originally founded by Celtic tribes in the 7th century BC, Milan was conquered by the Romans in 222 BC and developed into a major trading and transport centre. From the 13th century it flourished under the rule of two powerful families, the Visconti and the Sforza.

Orientation

From Stazione Centrale, take the yellow MM3 underground (Metropolitana Milanese) train line to Piazza del Duomo. The city's main attractions are concentrated in the area between the piazza and Castello Sforzesco.

Information

Grazia Internet (☎ 02 6700543; Piazza Duca d'Aosta 40; per hr €4; 8am-midnight) Next to Stazione Centrale. Also wi-fi.
Main post office (Via Cordusio 4; M Duomo)
Pharmacy (☎ 02 669 09 35; Stazione Centrale; 24hr)
Police station (Questura; ☎ 02 622 61; Via Fatebenefratelli 11; M Turati)
Tourist offices Piazza del Duomo (☎ 02 725 24 300; www.milanoinfotourist.com; Via Marconi 1; 8.45am-1pm & 2-6pm Mon-Fri, 9am-1pm & 2-5pm Sat & Sun; M Duomo); Stazione Centrale (☎ 02 725 24 360; 9am-6.30pm Mon-Sat, 9am-12.30pm & 1.30-5pm Sun); Malpensa airport (☎ 02 748 67 213; 9am-5pm Mon-Fri) Pick up free guides *Hello Milano* and *Milano Mese*.

Sights

With a capacity of 40,000, Milan's landmark **Duomo** (Piazza del Duomo; admission free; 7am-7pm; M Duomo) is the world's largest Gothic cathedral. Commissioned in 1386 to a florid French-Gothic design and finished nearly 600 years later, it's a fairy-tale ensemble of 3400 statues, 135 spires and 155 gargoyles. Climb to the **roof** (admission stairs/elevator €3.50/5; 9am-5.45pm) for memorable city views.

Nearby, on the northern flank of Piazza del Duomo, the elegant iron and glass **Galleria Vittorio Emanuele II** shopping arcade leads towards **Teatro alla Scala** (see p748), the world's most famous opera house.

To the west, the dramatic 15th-century **Castello Sforzesco** (☎ 02 884 63 700; www.milanocastello.it; Piazza Castello 3; admission free; 9am-5.30pm Tue-Sun; M Cairoli) was the Renaissance residence of the Sforza dynasty. It now shelters the **Musei del Castello** (☎ 02 884 63 703; adult/child €3/free; 9am-5.30pm), a group of museums dedicated to art, sculpture, furniture, archaeology and music.

Art addicts shouldn't miss the **Pinacoteca di Brera** (☎ 02 72 26 31; www.brera.beniculturali.it; Via Brera 28; admission €5; 8.30am-7.15pm Tue-Sun; M Monte Napoleone), whose heavyweight collection includes Andrea Mantegna's masterpiece, the *Dead Christ*.

Milan's single most famous painting – Leonardo da Vinci's *Last Supper* – is in the **Cenacolo Vinciano** (☎ 02 894 21 146; www.cenacolovinciano.org; Piazza Santa Maria delle Grazie 2; booking compulsory, admission €8; 8.15am-6.45pm Tue-Sun; M Cadorna Triennale), just west of the city centre. Book a ticket and decide for yourself whether the apostle to Christ's left is really Mary Magdalene, as author Dan Brown implies in his bestseller *The Da Vinci Code*.

Tours

Autostradale (☎ 02 339 10 794; www.autostradale.it) runs three-hour bus tours that take in the Duomo, Galleria Vittorio Emanuele II, Castello Sforzesco and the Cenacolo Vinciano. The €50 ticket includes entry to see da Vinci's *Last Supper*. Tickets are available from the tourist office at Piazza Duomo. The multilingual tours depart from outside the office at 9.30am every morning except Monday.

Sleeping

Make sure you book ahead as Milan's hotels fill quickly during frequent trade fairs. And always check the rates as prices often drop by as much as a third when there's no fair on.

Hotel Nuovo (☎/fax 02 864 60 542; Piazza Beccaria 6; d/tr €100/135, s/d with shared bathroom €30/50; M San Babila) In a city where 'cheap' is an ugly word, the Nuovo is a bastion of budget accommodation. Rooms vary – some sport modern furniture, others are more spartan – but all are basic and clean. The location, just off Corso Vittorio Emanuele II, is a winner too.

Hotel Due Giardini (☎ 02 295 21 093; www.hotelduegiardini.it; Via Benedetto Marcello 47; s €25-75, d €30-130; ; M Lima) This is a laid-back family *pensione* with modest, mid-sized rooms and gnomes in the back garden. The décor leaves less of an impression than the attractive rates.

Hotel Nettuno (☎ 02 294 04 481; www.nettunomilano.it; Via Tadino 27; s €35-90, d €50-150; ; M Lima) Fresh from a new paint job, the pastel-shaded rooms here are a far cry from

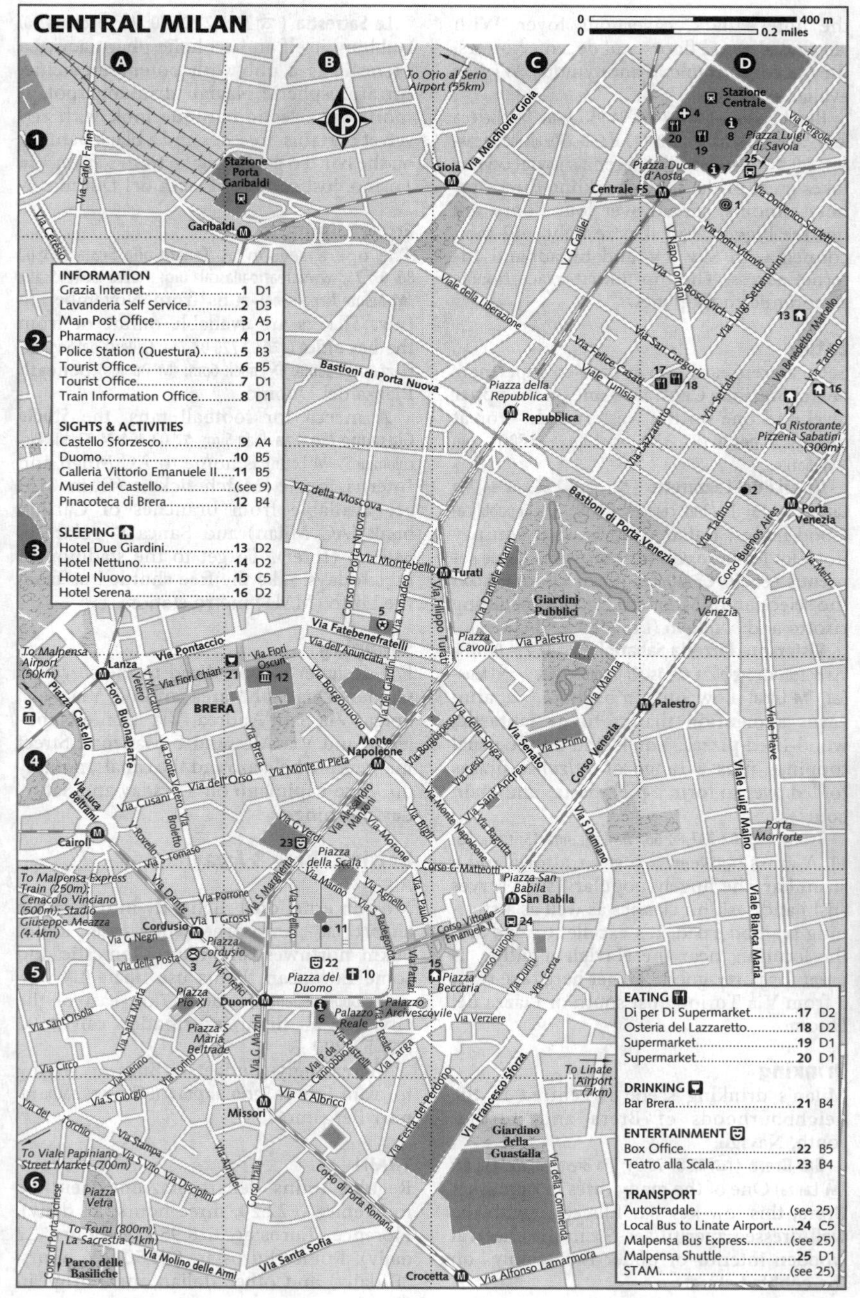
CENTRAL MILAN
0 400 m
0 0.2 miles
A
B
C
D
1
2
3
4
5
6
INFORMATION
Grazia Internet....................1 D1
Lavanderia Self Service....................2 D3
Main Post Office....................3 A5
Pharmacy....................4 D1
Police Station (Questura)....................5 B3
Tourist Office....................6 B5
Tourist Office....................7 D1
Train Information Office....................8 D1
SIGHTS & ACTIVITIES
Castello Sforzesco....................9 A4
Duomo....................10 B5
Galleria Vittorio Emanuele II....................11 B5
Musei del Castello....................(see 9)
Pinacoteca di Brera....................12 B4
SLEEPING
Hotel Due Giardini....................13 D2
Hotel Nettuno....................14 D2
Hotel Nuovo....................15 C5
Hotel Serena....................16 D2
EATING
Di per Di Supermarket....................17 D2
Osteria del Lazzaretto....................18 D2
Supermarket....................19 D1
Supermarket....................20 D1
DRINKING
Bar Brera....................21 B4
ENTERTAINMENT
Box Office....................22 B5
Teatro alla Scala....................23 B4
TRANSPORT
Autostradale....................(see 25)
Local Bus to Linate Airport....................24 C5
Malpensa Bus Express....................(see 25)
Malpensa Shuttle....................25 D1
STAM....................(see 25)
To Orio al Serio Airport (55km)
Stazione Porta Garibaldi
Garibaldi
Via Carlo Farini
Via Cenisio
Gioia
Via Melchiorre Gioia
Stazione Centrale
Piazza Luigi di Savoia
Piazza Duca d'Aosta
Centrale FS
Via Pergolesi
Via Domenico Scarlatti
Via Dom Vitruvio
V G Galilei
V Napo Torriani
Via Boscovich
Via Luigi Settembrini
Via Benedetto Marcello
Via Tadino
Viale della Liberazione
Via San Gregorio
Via Felice Casati
Viale Tunisia
Via Settala
Via Lazzaretto
To Ristorante Pizzeria Sabatini (300m)
Bastioni di Porta Nuova
Piazza della Repubblica
Repubblica
Bastioni di Porta Venezia
Porta Venezia
Corso Buenos Aires
Via Melzo
Via della Moscova
Corso di Porta Nuova
Via Montebello
Turati
Via Filippo Turati
Via Daniele Manin
Giardini Pubblici
Via Amadeo
Via Fatebenefratelli
Via dell'Anunciata
Piazza Cavour
Via Palestro
Via Marina
Palestro
To Malpensa Airport (50km)
Lanza
Via Pontaccio
Via Fiori Chiari
Via Fiori Oscuri
V Mercato
Vetero
BRERA
Piazza Castello
Foro Buonaparte
Via Borgonuovo
Via dei Giardini
Via Borgospesso
Via della Spiga
Via Senato
Via S Primo
Corso Venezia
Viale Piave
Via Brera
Monte Napoleone
Via Monte di Pietà
Via Ponte Vetero
Via dell'Orso
Via Cusani
Via Luca Beltrami
Broletto
V Rovello
Cairoli
Via S Tomaso
Via Gesù
Via Sant'Andrea
Via Bagutta
Via Monte Napoleone
Via Bigli
Via Morone
Via Alessandro Manzoni
Via G Verdi
Piazza della Scala
Via S Damiano
Viale Luigi Majno
Porta Monforte
Corso G Matteotti
Piazza San Babila
San Babila
Viale Bianca Maria
To Malpensa Express Train (250m); Cenacolo Vinciano (500m); Stadio Giuseppe Meazza (4.4km)
Via Dante
Via Porrone
Via S Margherita
Via S Pellico
Via Marino
Via Agnello
Via S Radegonda
Via S Paolo
Corso Vittorio Emanuele II
Cordusio
Via T Grossi
Via G Negri
Piazza Cordusio
Via della Posta
Via Orefici
Piazza del Duomo
Via Pattari
Piazza Beccaria
Corso Europa
Via Durini
Via Cerva
Piazza Pio XI
Duomo
Palazzo Reale
Palazzo Arcivescovile
Via Verziere
Via Sant'Orsola
Via Santa Marta
Piazza S Maria Beltrade
Via G Mazzini
Via P Reale
Via Rastrelli
Via P da Cannobbio
Via Larga
Via Circo
Via Nerino
Via Torino
Via S Giorgio
Via A Albricci
Missori
Via Festa del Perdono
Via Francesco Sforza
To Linate Airport (7km)
Via del Torchio
Via Stampa
Via S Vito
Via Disciplini
Via Armorari
Corso Italia
Corso di Porta Romana
Giardino della Guastalla
Via della Commenda
To Viale Papiniano Street Market (700m)
Piazza Vetra
Corso di Porta Ticinese
To Tsuru (800m); La Sacrestia (1km)
Parco delle Basiliche
Via Molino delle Armi
Via Santa Sofia
Crocetta
Via Alfonso Lamarmora

ITALY

the hotel's dark, cavernous foyer. With laminated wood floors and decent showers, they're comfortable, if anonymous. Wi-fi is available.

Hotel Serena (☎ 02 294 04 958; www.hotelserena.com; Via Boscovich 59; s €50-140, d €60-230, all incl breakfast; ⊠ ❄; Ⓜ Lima) The Serena's jovial owner takes great pride in his sparkling three-star hotel. Rooms, spread over four floors, are not the biggest, but they're light and mod conned with Sky TV and broadband Internet access. The top floor terrace boasts panoramic rooftop views.

Eating

Self-caterers can shop at the two supermarkets at Stazione Centrale – one on the upper level and one on the western side – or at nearby **Di per Di** (Via Felice Casati 30; 🕑 8.30am-8pm Mon-Sat).

Osteria del Lazzaretto (☎/fax 02 669 62 34; Via Lazzaretto 15; 1st/2nd courses €7/10; Ⓜ Repubblica) Good honest Italian food is what you pay not a lot for here. Go for one of the three set menus (€5.50/€7.50/€9.50) or choose from the selection of Milanese classics including risotto and *cotolleto* (breaded veal cutlet).

Ristorante Pizzeria Sabatini (☎ 02 294 02 814; Via Boscovich 54; pizza €8, 1st/2nd courses €8/9; 🕑 Mon-Sat; Ⓜ Lima) Low on atmosphere, Sabatini earns a mention thanks to its fantastic, wood-fired pizzas. You'll find all the usual toppings plus a range of *calzone* (pizzas folded over to form a pie), pastas and main courses.

Tsuru (☎ 02 837 83 66; Via Lagrange 13; sushi €6-20) A cross between a rustic trattoria and a sushi bar, the hugely popular Tsuru serves sushi and sashimi classics as well as a stunning seafood salad. It's excellent value and the location, near the Navigli nightlife, is great for party-goers. To get here take tram 3 from Via Torino, just south of Piazza del Duomo.

Drinking

Milan's drinking scene is centred in the neighbourhoods of Brera and, further south, Navigli.

Bar Brera (☎ 02 87 70 91; Via Brera 23; cocktail €6; Ⓜ Lanza) One of the many cafés in upmarket Brera, this low-key bar fills early with the well-dressed aperitif set. Sit in the cheerful wooden interior or under the awnings on the cobbled street.

La Sacrestia (☎ 333 321 07 50; Via Conchetta 20) Dubbing itself an 'alcoholic pharmacy', La Sacrestia is a pub with potent medicine. An atmospheric Navigli drinking spot, it sports an eclectic baroque look with red velvet curtains, frescoes and a black panther on the bar. To get here take tram 3 from Via Torino, just south of Piazza del Duomo.

Entertainment

The opera season at **Teatro alla Scala** (☎ 02 86 07 75; www.teatroallascala.org; Piazza delle Scala; Ⓜ Monte Napoleone) runs from November to July. Tickets are available online or from the **box office** (☎ 02 720 03 744; Galleria del Sagrato, Piazza del Duomo; 🕑 noon-6pm; Ⓜ Duomo) beneath Piazza del Duomo.

A mecca for football fans, the **Stadio Giuseppe Meazza** (San Siro; ☎ 02 404 24 32; Via Piccolomini 5; Ⓜ Lotto) is home to AC Milan and Internazionale. Match tickets (from €15) are available from branches of Cariplo bank (AC Milan) and Banca Popolare di Milano (Inter). To get to the stadium on match days, take the free shuttle bus from the Lotto (MM1) metro station.

Shopping

For designer clobber head to the so-called Golden Quad, the area around Via della Spiga, Via Sant'Andrea, Via Monte Napoleone and Via Alessandro Manzoni. Street markets are held around the canals, notably on Viale Papiniano on Tuesday and Saturday mornings.

Getting There & Away

AIR

Most international flights fly into **Malpensa airport** (MXP; www.sea-aeroportomilano.it), about 50km northwest of Milan. Domestic and some European flights use **Linate** (LIN; www.sea-aeroportomilano.it), about 7km east of the city. For all flight information call ☎ 02 748 52 200.

Increasingly, budget airlines are flying to/from **Orio al Serio airport** (BGY; www.sacbo.it), near Bergamo.

TRAIN

Regular trains depart Stazione Centrale for Venice (€22.20, three hours, 23 daily), Florence (Eurostar, €28.95, 2¾ hours, 22 daily), Rome (Eurostar, €46.50, 4½ hours, 20 daily) and other Italian and European cities. Check timetables at the station **information office** (⌚ 7am-9pm). Regional trains stop at Stazione Porta Garibaldi and Stazione Nord in Piazzale Cadorna.

Getting Around

TO/FROM THE AIRPORT

Malpensa Shuttle (☎ 02 585 98 31 85; www.airpullman.com) coaches run to/from Piazza Luigi di Savoia every 20 minutes between 5am and 11pm. Tickets for the 50-minute journey cost €5. **Malpensa Bus Express** (☎ 0331 51 90 00) buses depart from the same piazza half hourly between 5.15am and 10.35pm; tickets cost €5.50 and the trip takes 50 minutes.

By train, take the **Malpensa Express** from Cadorna underground station – there are half-hourly departures between 5.50am and 8.20pm (buses take over from 8.20pm to 11.10pm). The 40-minute journey costs €9.30, or €11.50 if you buy the ticket on board.

For Linate, **Starfly** (☎ 02 585 87 237) buses depart from Piazza Luigi di Savoia every 30 minutes between 5.40am and 9.35pm; tickets cost €3, journey time is 25 minutes. Alternatively, use local bus 73 from Piazza San Babila (€1, 20 minutes).

Autostradale (☎ 035 31 84 72; www.autostradale.it) run half-hourly buses from Piazza Luigi di Savoia to Orio al Serio between 4am and 11.30pm; the journey lasts one hour and tickets are €6.70.

BUS & METRO

Milan's public transport is excellent, with metro (MM), tram and bus services. Buy tickets (€1), valid for one underground ride or up to 75 minutes travel on city buses and trams, at metro stations, tobacconists and newsstands.

MANTUA

pop 47,820

Nestled between three lakes (Superiore, Inferiore and Mezzo), placid Mantua is a popular day trip. Best known for its immaculate medieval centre and grandiose palaces, it was for centuries (1328 to 1707) the stronghold of the Gonzaga family, one of Italy's most powerful Renaissance dynasties.

The **tourist office** (☎ 0376 43 24 32; www.turismo.mantova.it; Piazza Andrea Mantegna 6; ⌚ 9am-7pm) is helpful and efficient.

Sights & Activities

Mantua's attractions are concentrated around Piazza Sordello. Chief among them is the enormous **Palazzo Ducale** (☎ 0376 22 48 32; Piazza Sordello; adult/concession €6.50/3.50; ⌚ 8.45am-7.15pm Tue-Sun), the former seat of the Gonzaga family. The highlight of the 500 rooms and 15 courtyards is the **Camera degli Sposi** (Bridal Chamber), with 15th-century frescoes by Mantegna. To visit the *Camera* between 15 March and 15 June and 1 September and 15 October you need to book – call ☎ 041 241 18 97.

Nearby, the 15th-century **Basilica di Sant'Andrea** (☎ 0376 32 85 04; Piazza Andrea Mantegna; ⌚ 8am-noon & 3-7pm) safeguards several golden vessels said to contain earth soaked by the blood of Christ.

The weekend **market** sprawls across four piazzas, and is more diverse than similar shows in cities twice Mantua's size.

Sleeping & Eating

Albergo Bianchi Stazione (☎ 0376 32 64 65; www.hotelbianchi.mantova.com; Piazza Don Leoni 24; s/d incl breakfast €71/108) Opposite the train station, the Bianchi is more personal than many station hotels, offering a friendly welcome, smart rooms and labyrinthine corridors. Most rooms overlook a quiet internal courtyard.

Hotel ABC (☎ 0376 32 23 29; www.hotelabcmantova.it; Piazza Don Leoni 25; s/d incl breakfast €88/121; ❄) Next door to the Bianchi Stazione, this convenient hotel has big, clinically white rooms, furnished with function more than fun in mind. Prices drop considerably in the off-season.

Ristorante Masseria (☎ 0376 36 53 03; Piazza Broletto 8; pizza €7, 1st/2nd courses €7/10; ⌚ closed Thu) If not for the food, good though it is, it's worth eating here to see the 15th-century frescoes on the walls – they're the oldest existing depictions of Mantua. For a filling local dish, the *stracotta con polenta* (beef stew with polenta) is rich and tender.

Osteria Vecchia Mantova (☎ 0376 32 97 20; Piazza Sordello 26; 1st/2nd courses €7/10; ⌚ closed Mon) A warm, woody tavern, this atmospheric spot is great for local staples such as sweet *tortelli di zucca* (ring-shaped pasta stuffed with pumpkin).

Getting There & Away

The easiest way to get to Mantua is by train from Verona (€2.30, 40 minutes, hourly).

VERONA

pop 258,115

Wander Verona's atmospheric streets and you'll understand why Shakespeare set *Romeo and Juliet* here. An evocative and vibrant city, it's justly considered one of Italy's most beautiful. Known as *piccola Roma* (little Rome) for its importance in imperial days, its heyday came in the 13th and 14th centuries under the Della Scala (aka the Scaligeri) family, a period noted for the savage family feuding on which Shakespeare based his tragedy.

Information is available at the three **tourist offices** (city centre ☎ 045 806 86 80; www.tourism.verona.it; Via degli Alpini 9; 9am-7pm Mon-Sat, to 3pm Sun; train station ☎ 045 800 08 61; 9am-6pm Mon-Sat, to 3pm Sun; airport ☎ 045 861 91 63; 11am-5pm Mon-Sat). Alternatively, do your own online research at **Veron@web** (☎ 045 801 33 94; Via Roma 17; per hr €3.50; 11am-10pm Mon-Fri, 2-8pm Sat & Sun).

Sights

If you're planning to blitz the city's sights, the **Verona Card** (1/3 days €8/12) covers city transport and the main monuments.

In the corner of Piazza Brà, the 1st-century pink-and-white **amphitheatre** (☎ 045 800 32 04; Piazza Brà; adult/concession €4/3; 8.30am-7.15pm Tue-Sun, 1.30-7.15pm Mon), known as the Arena, is the third largest Roman amphitheatre in existence. With a capacity of 20,000, it's Verona's opera house (see opposite).

Walk along Via Mazzini, Verona's premier shopping strip, to Via Cappello and **Casa di Giulietta** (☎ 045 803 43 03; Via Capello 23; courtyard free, museum adult/concession €4/3; 8.30am-7.30pm Tue-Sun, 1.30-7.30pm Mon), home of the fictional Juliet. Go through the graffiti-strewn gate to look up at literature's most feted balcony. Romantic superstition suggests that rubbing the right breast of Juliet's statue (in the courtyard below the balcony) brings you a new lover. Further along the street is **Porta Leoni**, one of the city's Roman gates; the other, **Porta Borsari**, is north of the Arena.

Set over the city's Roman forum, **Piazza delle Erbe** is lined with sumptuous palaces and filled with touristy market stalls. Through the **Arco della Costa**, the quieter **Piazza dei Signori** is flanked by the **Loggia del Consiglio**, the medieval town hall regarded as Verona's finest Renaissance structure, and **Palazzo degli Scaligeri**, the former residence of the Della Scala family.

Sleeping

Ostello Villa Francescatti (☎ 045 59 03 60; fax 045 800 91 27; Salita Fontana del Ferro 15; dm incl breakfast €15.50, meal €9) Verona's beautiful HI hostel is housed in a 16th-century villa set in its own gorgeous grounds. To save yourself a steep uphill walk, take bus 73 from the train station (90 on Sundays). There's a strict 11.30pm curfew.

L'Ospite (☎ 045 803 69 94; www.lospite.com; Via XX Settembre 3; apt for 1/2/4 people €45/80/120;) Over the river from the *centro storico*, L'Ospite has six self-contained flats for up to four people. Simple and bright with wood beamed-ceilings and colourful furniture, they're ideal for families.

Hotel Torcolo (☎ 045 800 75 12; www.hoteltorcolo.it; Vicolo Listone 3; s/d €78/112;) Not 50m from Piazza Brà, the homely Torcolo is ideally located. Its mid-sized rooms range from the prim (floral bedspreads and oil paintings) to the eye-catching (wrought-iron bedsteads and timber ceilings).

Hotel Aurora (☎ 045 59 78 34; www.hotelaurora.biz; Piazza delle Erbe; s/d incl breakfast €120/135, s with shared bathroom €68;) A top of the range two-star, the Aurora has understated rooms with elegant wooden bedsteads and the occasional antique. The terrace overlooking Piazza delle Erbe is a top spot for a drink.

Hotel All'Antica Porta Leona (☎ 045 59 54 99; www.anticaportaleona.com; Corticella Leoni 3; s/d incl breakfast €95/150; P) Near Porta Leone, this dependable three-star was being spruced up when we passed through. Its good-sized, tasteful, cream-coloured rooms will be looking better than ever when you land on the doorstep.

Eating

Boiled meats are a Veronese speciality, as is crisp Soave white wine.

Trattoria All'Isolo (☎ 045 59 42 91; Piazza dell'Isolo 5a; 1st/2nd courses €6/9; closed Wed) Although not entirely tourist-free, All'Isolo's over-the-river location keeps the foreign hordes to a minimum. A small old-school trattoria, it serves homemade *bigoli* (thick wholemeal spaghetti) and challenging meat dishes such as *coniglio in umido* (rabbit stew).

Hosteria All'Orso (☎ 045 597214; Via Sottoriva 3/c; 1st/2nd courses €7/10; closed Mon lunch & Sun) This is a charming spot to start an evening in Verona's trendy riverside district. Grab a table under the timber-beamed porticoes or in the rustic-chic interior and order from the menu of tempting north Italian staples.

Al Pompiere (☎ 045 59 42 91; Vicolo Regina d'Ungheria 5; 1st/2nd courses €8/12; ⌚ Tue-Sat & dinner Mon) There's no secret to the success of this much-loved trattoria – top notch food and lovely surroundings. A must for cheese fans – there are some 120 on the menu – it also serves time-honoured Veneto classics.

Drinking & Entertainment

The opera season at the Roman **Arena** (☎ 045 800 51 51; www.arena.it; tickets €10-157) runs from July to September. There's also a winter season of classical and modern music, ballet and opera at the 18th-century **Teatro Filarmonico** (☎ 045 800 51 51; www.arena.it; Via dei Mutilati 4).

Nightlife is centred on the bars/*trattorie* of Via Sottoriva. Two goodies are **square** (☎ 045 597 120; Via Sottoriva 15; ⌚ 6.30pm-2am Tue-Sat, 5pm-1am Sun), where you can have a shiatsu massage, surf the net, drink cocktails and buy branded homewares; and the more traditional **Sottoriva 23** (☎ 045 800 99 04; Via Sottoriva 23; ⌚ 10am-2am), a low-lit cavern bar.

Getting There & Around

Verona-Villafranca airport (VRN; ☎ 045 809 56 66; www.aeroportidelgarda.it) is 12km outside the city and accessible by bus from the train station (€4.50, 15 minutes, every 20 minutes between 5.40am and 11.10pm). Ryanair flies to **Brescia airport** (VBS; ☎ 030 965 65 99), from where shuttle buses (€11, 45 minutes, one daily) connect to Verona's main train station. Departures depend on flight times – for up-to-date details click on www.cgabrescia.it.

From the main bus terminal in front of the train station, buses 11, 12, 13 and 14 (91 and 92 on Sunday) go to Piazza Brà.

Verona is directly linked by rail to Milan (€14.05, two hours, half hourly), Venice (€12.40, 1½ hours, half hourly) and Bologna (€13.90, 1¾ hours, 20 daily).

PADUA

pop 208,940

A lively university city, Padua is a fun place to hang out. But what really makes a visit worthwhile is the Cappella degli Scrovegni and its stunning Giotto frescoes. Thousands of pilgrims also come to pay their respects to St Anthony, who is buried in the city's cathedral.

From the train station, follow Corso del Popolo and its continuation Corso Garibaldi for 1.5km to the city centre. Alternatively, take buses 3 or 8.

Information is available at the two **tourist offices** (train station ☎ 049 875 20 77; www.turismopadova.it; ⌚ 9.15am-7pm Mon-Sat, 9am-noon Sun; Galleria Pedrocchi ☎ 049 876 79 27; ⌚ 9am-1.30pm & 3-7pm Mon-Sat).

Sights

The **PadovaCard** (☎ 049 876 79 27; 1 adult & 1 child €13), available from tourist offices and participating sights, provides free public transport and entry to many sights, including the Cappella degli Scrovegni (plus €1 booking fee).

Many people visit Padua just to see Giotto's extraordinary frescoes in the **Cappella degli Scrovegni** (☎ 049 201 00 20; www.cappelladegliscrovegni.it; Piazza Eremitani 8; admission €12; ⌚ 9am-7pm). The 38 colourful panels (c 1304–1306) depicting Christ's life cover Enrico Scrovegni's chapel from floor to ceiling. Visits, for which you'll need to book at least 24 hours in advance, are limited to 15 minutes.

Tickets also cover the adjacent **Musei Civici agli Eremitani** (☎ 049 820 45 51; Piazza Eremitani 8; ⌚ 9am-7pm Tue-Sun) and its collection of Veneto art.

On the other side of the *centro storico,* the **Basilica di Sant'Antonio** (☎ 049 824 28 11; Piazza del Santo; admission free; ⌚ 6.30am-7.45pm daily) is an important place of pilgrimage. Each year thousands of visitors come to file past the surprisingly gaudy **tomb** of St Anthony, Padua's patron saint.

In the square outside the basilica, the bronze equestrian statue, the *Gattamelata* (Honeyed Cat), is by the Renaissance sculptor Donatello.

Sleeping

Ostello della Città di Padova (☎ 049 875 22 19; www.ctgveneto.it/ostello2; Via A Aleardi 30; dm incl breakfast €15.50) Functional and friendly, Padua's HI hostel has beds in large single-sex dorms and four-person family rooms. Take buses 3, 8 or 12 to Prato della Valle and then ask for directions.

Hotel Sant'Antonio (☎ 049 875 13 93; www.hotelsantantonio.it; Via Santo Fermo 118; s/d €63/84, s with shared bathroom €42; ❄) On the edge of the historic centre, the three-star Sant'Antonio is a safe, if rather staid option. Rooms, sporting parquet, rugs and fading '70s-style bedspreads, are agreeable if unassuming.

Albergo Verdi (☎ 049 836 41 63; www.albergoverdidipadova.it; Via Dondi dall'Orologio 7; s/d incl breakfast €70/90; ❄) This is a brand new hotel with groovy multicoloured rooms and glaring modern art. It's not a big place and rooms are small, but the sharp contemporary look and excellent location just off Piazza del Capitaniato more than compensate.

Eating & Drinking

Dalla Zita (Via Gorizia 16; panini from €2.50) Join the hungry lunchtime hordes and order a *panino* at this well-known sandwich bar. With descriptions of more than 100 fillings on the walls you're bound to find something you like.

L'Anfora (☎ 049 65 66 29; Via dei Sconcin 13; 1st/2nd courses €5/10; ⌚ Mon-Sat) A typical old-school *osteria* – bare wooden tables and racked wine bottles – L'Anfora is a lovely place for a bowl of *pasta e fagioli* (pasta and beans) or *fegato alla veneziana* (liver and onions).

Godenda (☎ 049 877 41 92; Via Squarcione 4/6; 1st/2nd courses €8/10; ⌚ Mon-Sat) All blanched wood and minimalist lines, this is a slick contemporary *enoteca* with a list of more than 300 wines and a delicious deli menu. There are hams and cheeses, salads, smoked fish and dozens of takeaway dishes.

Getting There & Away

SITA buses (☎ 049 820 68 44; www.sitabus.it) arrive from Venice (€3.05, 45 minutes, hourly) at Piazzale Boschetti, 200m south of the train station.

There are also regional trains to/from Venice (€2.50, 40 minutes, every 20 minutes) and direct services to Verona (€9.95, 1¼ hours, every 20 minutes) and Bologna (€10.20, 1½ hours, half hourly).

VENICE

pop 271,665

Venice is a hauntingly beautiful city. At every turn you're assailed by unforgettable images – tiny bridges crossing limpid canals, delivery barges jostling chintzy gondolas, tourists posing under flocks of pigeons. But to reduce Venice to a set of pictures is as impossible as describing it in soundbites. To discover its romantic and melancholic nature you really need to walk its hidden back lanes. Parts of the Cannaregio, Dorsoduro and Castello *sestieri* (districts) rarely see many tourists, and you can lose yourself for hours in the streets between the Accademia and the train station. Stroll late at night to feel an eerie atmosphere, redolent of dark passions and dangerous secrets.

The reality of modern Venice is, however, a city besieged by rising tides and up to 20 million visitors a year. This and the sky-high property prices mean that most Venetians live over the lagoon in Mestre.

History

Venice's origins date to the 5th and 6th centuries when barbarian invasions forced the Veneto's inhabitants to seek refuge on the lagoon's islands. The city was initially ruled by the Byzantines from Ravenna, but in AD 726 the Venetians elected their first *doge* (duke).

Over successive centuries, the Venetian Republic grew into a great merchant power, dominating half the Mediterranean, the Adriatic and the trade routes to the Levant – it was from Venice that Marco Polo set out for China in 1271. Decline began in the 16th century and in 1797 the city authorities opened the gates to Napoleon who, in turn, handed the city over to the Austrians. In 1866, Venice was incorporated into the Kingdom of Italy.

Orientation

Everybody gets lost in Venice. How can you not in a city built on 117 islands with 150-odd canals and 400 bridges, only three of which cross the Grand Canal: the Rialto, the Accademia and, at the train station, the Scalzi.

It gets worse: Venetian addresses are almost meaningless to all but local posties. Instead of a street and civic number they often consist of no more than the *sestiere* (Venice is divided into six districts – Cannaregio, Castello, San Marco, Dorsoduro, San Polo and Santa Croce) followed by a long number. Some, however, do have street names and where possible we've provided them. You'll still need to know that a street can be a *calle, ruga* or *salizzada;*

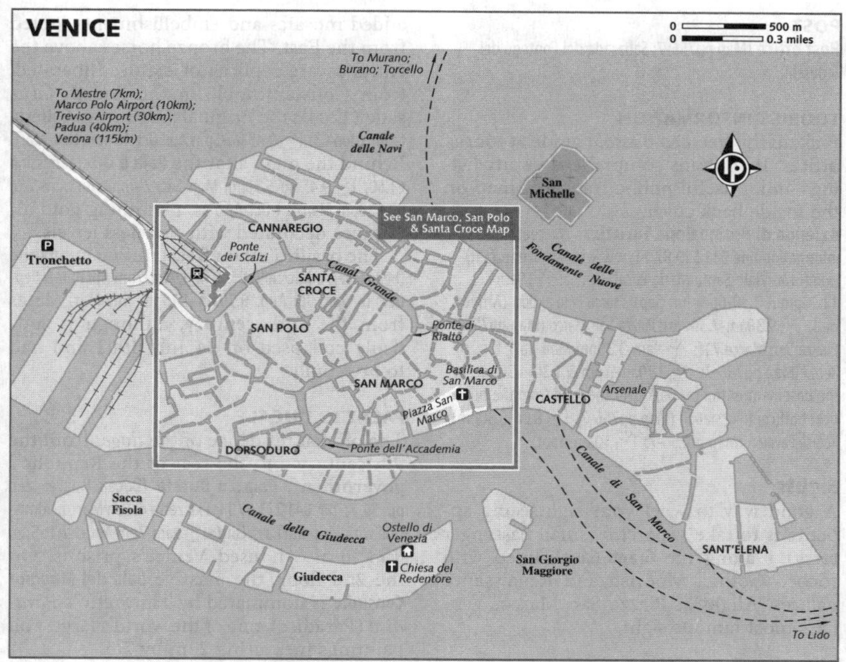

beside a canal it's a *fondamenta*. A canal is a *rio*, a filled canal-turned-street a *rio terrà*, and a square a *campo* (Piazza San Marco is Venice's only piazza).

The most helpful points of reference are the train station and Piazzale Roma in the northwest and Piazza San Marco (St Mark's Square) in the south. The signposted path from the train station to Piazza San Marco (the nearest Venice has to a main drag) is a good half-hour walk.

Information

EMERGENCY

Police station (Questura; Map pp756-7; ☎ 041 271 55 11; Fondamenta di San Lorenzo, Castello 5053)

INTERNET ACCESS

There are tons of Internet cafés in Venice, none cheap. The airport is a wi-fi hotspot.

e copie d@ Toni (Map pp756-7; ☎ 041 522 51 00; Calle delle Bande, Castello 5268; per hr €7; 🕑 9am-1pm & 3-7pm)

Internet Point San Pantalon (Map pp756-7; ☎ 041 71 46 66; Calle dei Preti Crosera, Dorsoduro 3812a; per hr €9; 🕑 9.15am-8pm Mon-Fri, 9.15am-1pm & 3.30-7pm Sat)

Internet Point Santo Stefano (Map pp756-7; ☎ 041 894 61 22; Campo Santo Stefano 2958; per hr €9; 🕑 10.15am-8pm)

Planet Internet (Map pp756-7; ☎ 041 524 41 88; Rio Terrà San Leonardo, Cannaregio 1520; per hr €8; 🕑 9am-11pm)

LAUNDRY

Speedy Wash (Map pp756-7; Rio Terrà San Leonardo, Cannaregio 1520; 8kg wash/dry €5/3; 🕑 9am-10pm)

MEDICAL SERVICES

Twenty-four-hour pharmacies are listed in *Un Ospite a Venezia* (A Guest in Venice), a free guide available in many hotels.

Ospedale Civile (Hospital; Map pp756-7; ☎ 041 529 41 11; Campo SS Giovanni e Paolo 6777)

MONEY

Most major banks have branches in the area around the Ponte di Rialto and San Marco.

American Express (Map pp756-7; ☎ 041 520 08 44; Salizzada San Moisè 1471; 🕑 9am-5.30pm Mon-Fri)

Travelex (Map pp756-7; ☎ 041 528 73 58; Piazza San Marco 142; 🕑 8.50am-7pm Mon-Sat, 9.30am-5pm Sun)

POST

Post office (Map pp756-7; Salizzada del Fontego dei Tedeschi)

TOURIST INFORMATION

Pick up the free *Leo Bussola* guide at tourist offices. It contains comprehensive city listings and a useful public transport map on the inside back cover.

Azienda di Promozione Turistica (☎ central information line 041 529 87 11; www.turismovenezia.it) Lido (Gran Viale Santa Maria Elisabetta 6a; 9am-12.30pm & 3.30-6pm Jun-Sep); Marco Polo airport (Arrivals Hall; 9.30am-7.30pm); Piazza San Marco (Map pp756-7; Piazza San Marco 71f; 9am-3.30pm Mon-Sat); Piazzale Roma (Map pp756-7; 9.30am-1pm & 1.30-4.30pm) In the basement of the car park over the road from the bus ticket office; train station (Map pp756-7; 8am-6.30pm); Venice Pavilion (Map pp756-7; 10am-6pm)

Sights

A good way to whet your sightseeing appetite is to take *vaporetto* (small passenger ferry) 1 along the **Grand Canal**, lined with rococo Gothic, Moorish and Renaissance palaces. Alight at Piazza San Marco, Venice's most famous sight.

PIAZZA SAN MARCO

Piazza San Marco beautifully encapsulates the splendour of Venice's past and its tourist-fuelled present. Flanked by the arcaded **Procuratie Vecchie** and **Procuratie Nuove**, it's filled for much of the day with tourists, pigeons, balloon-vendors and policemen. While you're taking it all in, you might see the bronze *mori* (Moors) strike the bell of the 15th-century **Torre dell'Orologio** (clock tower).

But, it's to the remarkable **Basilica di San Marco** (St Mark's Basilica; Map pp756-7; ☎ 041 522 52 05; Piazza San Marco; admission free; 9.45am-5.30pm Mon-Sat, 2-4pm Sun) that all eyes are drawn. An architectural salad of spangled spires, Byzantine domes, mosaics and marble, it was originally built to house the remains of St Mark. According to legend, the Evangelist's body was stolen from Alexandria in Egypt and smuggled to Venice in a barrel of pork. He's since been buried several times, his body now resting under the high altar. The original chapel was destroyed by fire in AD 932 and a new basilica was consecrated in its place in 1094. For the next 500 years it was a work in progress as successive *doges* added mosaics and embellishments looted from the East. The bronze horses above the entrance are replicas of statues 'liberated' from Constantinople in the Fourth Crusade (1204); the originals are in the **Galleria** (admission €3; 9.45am-5pm Apr-Oct, to 4pm Nov-Mar). Behind the main altar the **Pala d'Oro** (admission €1.50; 9.45am-5.30pm Mon-Sat, 2-4pm Sun May-Sep, to 4.30pm Mon-Sat Oct-Apr) is a stunning gold altarpiece decorated with priceless jewels.

The basilica's 99m freestanding **campanile** (bell tower; adult/child €6/3; 9am-7pm Apr-Jun & Sep-Oct, to 9pm Jul-Aug, 9.30am-4.15pm Nov-Mar) dates from the 10th century, although it suddenly collapsed on 14 July 1902 and had to be rebuilt.

PALAZZO DUCALE

The official residence of the *doges* from the 9th century and the seat of the Republic's government, **Palazzo Ducale** (Doge's Palace; Map pp756-7; ☎ 041 271 59 11; Piazzetta di San Marco; admission with Museum Pass/Card; 9am-7pm Apr-Oct, to 5pm Nov-Mar) also housed Venice's prisons. On the 2nd floor, the massive **Sala del Maggior Consiglio** is dominated by Tintoretto's *Paradiso* (Paradise), one of the world's largest oil paintings measuring 22m by 7m.

The **Ponte dei Sospiri** (Bridge of Sighs) connects the palace to an additional wing of the city dungeons. Named after the sighs the prisoners emitted en route, it owes its romantic image to Giacomo Casanova who, for a brief period, languished in the cells.

GALLERIA DELL'ACCADEMIA

One of Venice's top galleries, the **Galleria dell'Accademia** (Map pp756-7; ☎ 041 522 22 47; Dorsoduro 1050; adult €6.50, EU citizens 18-25 yr €3.50, child under 12 & EU citizens under 18 & over 65 free; 8.15am-2pm Mon, to 7.15pm Tue-Sun) traces the development of Venetian art from the 14th to the 18th century. You'll find works by Bellini, Titian, Carpaccio, Tintoretto, Giorgione and Veronese.

COLLEZIONE PEGGY GUGGENHEIM

For something more contemporary, visit the **Collezione Peggy Guggenheim** (Map pp756-7; ☎ 041 240 54 11; www.guggenheim-venice.it; Palazzo Venier dei Leoni, Dorsoduro 701; adult/student/child €10/5/free; 10am-6pm Wed-Mon). Housed in the American heiress' former home, the spellbinding collection runs the gamut of modern art with works by, among others, Bacon, Pollock, Picasso and Dali. In the sculpture garden you'll find the graves of Peggy and her dogs.

CHURCHES

As in much of Italy, Venice's churches harbour innumerable treasures; unusually, though, you have to pay to get into many of them. See the Admission Discounts boxed text (below) for details.

Scene of the annual Festa del Redentore (see right), the **Chiesa del Redentore** (Church of the Redeemer; Map p753; Campo del SS Redentore 194; admission €2.50; 10am-5pm Mon-Sat, 1-5pm Sun) was built by Palladio to commemorate the end of the great plague in 1577.

Guarding the entrance to the Grand Canal, the 17th-century **Chiesa di Santa Maria della Salute** (Map pp756-7; ☎ 041 522 55 58; Campo della Salute 1/b; sacristy admission €1.50; 9am-noon & 3.30-6pm) contains works by Tintoretto and Titian. Arguably the greatest of Venice's artists, Titian's celebrated masterpiece the *Assunta* (Assumption; 1518) hangs above the high altar in the **Chiesa di Santa Maria Glorioso dei Frari** (Map pp756-7; Campo dei Frari, San Polo 3004; admission €2.50; 9am-6pm Mon-Sat, 1-6pm Sun), the same church in which he's buried.

Some way to the east, the vast Gothic **Chiesa dei SS Giovanni e Paolo** (Map pp756-7; ☎ 041 523 59 13; Campo SS Giovanni e Paolo; admission €2.50; 9.30am-7pm Mon-Sat, 1-7pm Sun) is famous for its glorious 15th-century stained-glass window, the largest in Venice.

THE LIDO

Unless you're on the Lido for the Venice Film Festival, the main reason to visit is for the beach. Be warned, though, that it's almost impossible to find space on the sand in summer. The Lido's accessible by *vaporetto* 1, LN, 51, 52, 61 and 62.

ISLANDS

Murano is the home of Venetian glass. Tour a factory for a behind-the-scenes look at production or visit the **Glassworks Museum** (☎ 041 73 95 86; Fondamenta Giustinian 8; admission €4; 10am-4pm Thu-Tue). **Burano**, with its cheery pastel-coloured houses, is renowned for its lace. **Torcello**, the republic's original island settlement, was largely abandoned due to malaria and now counts no more than 80 residents. Its not-to-be-missed Byzantine cathedral, **Santa Maria Assunta** (☎ 041 270 24 64; Piazza Torcello; admission €3; 10.30am-6pm Mar-Oct, 10am-5pm Nov-Feb), is Venice's oldest.

Vaporetto LN services the islands from the *vaporetto* station at Fondamente Nuove in the northeast of the city.

Activities

Be prepared to pay for that most quintessential of Venetian experiences, a **gondola** ride. Official rates, for a maximum of six people, start at €73 (€91 from 8pm to 8am) per gondola for a 50-minute ride. Haggling may or may not get you a reduction.

Festivals & Events

Carnevale Masked ribaldry in Venice's ritzy knees-up in the 10 days before Ash Wednesday.
Palio delle Quattro Repubbliche Marinare Venice, Amalfi, Genoa and Pisa take turns to host this historic regatta. It's in Venice in June 2007.
Festa del Redentore Held on the third weekend in July, celebrations climax with a spectacular fireworks display.
Regata Storica Costumed parades precede gondola races on the Grand Canal; held on the first Sunday in September.

ADMISSION DISCOUNTS

The **Rolling Venice Card** (€3) is for visitors aged 14 to 29; it offers discounts on food, accommodation, shopping, transport and museums. You can get it at tourist offices, public transport ticket offices and Vela information/ticket stands. You'll need your passport and a colour photograph.

The **Venice Card** (☎ 041 24 24; www.venicecard.it; under 29 1/3/7 days €18/35/61, over 29 €28/47/68) entitles holders to discounts on museums, public transport, car parks and restrooms. It doesn't always represent a saving, so check before buying.

To visit the museums on Piazza San Marco you'll need to buy either a **Museum Pass** (☎ 041 240 52 11; www.museicivicivenezianі.it; adult/student aged 15-29 €15.50/10), which grants admission to 11 museums, or a **Museum Card** (€11/5.50), which covers fewer sights. Both are available at participating museums.

The **Chorus Pass** (☎ 041 275 04 62; www.chorusvenezia.org; adult/student €9/6) covers admission to 15 of Venice's major churches. Otherwise entry to each church is €2.50.

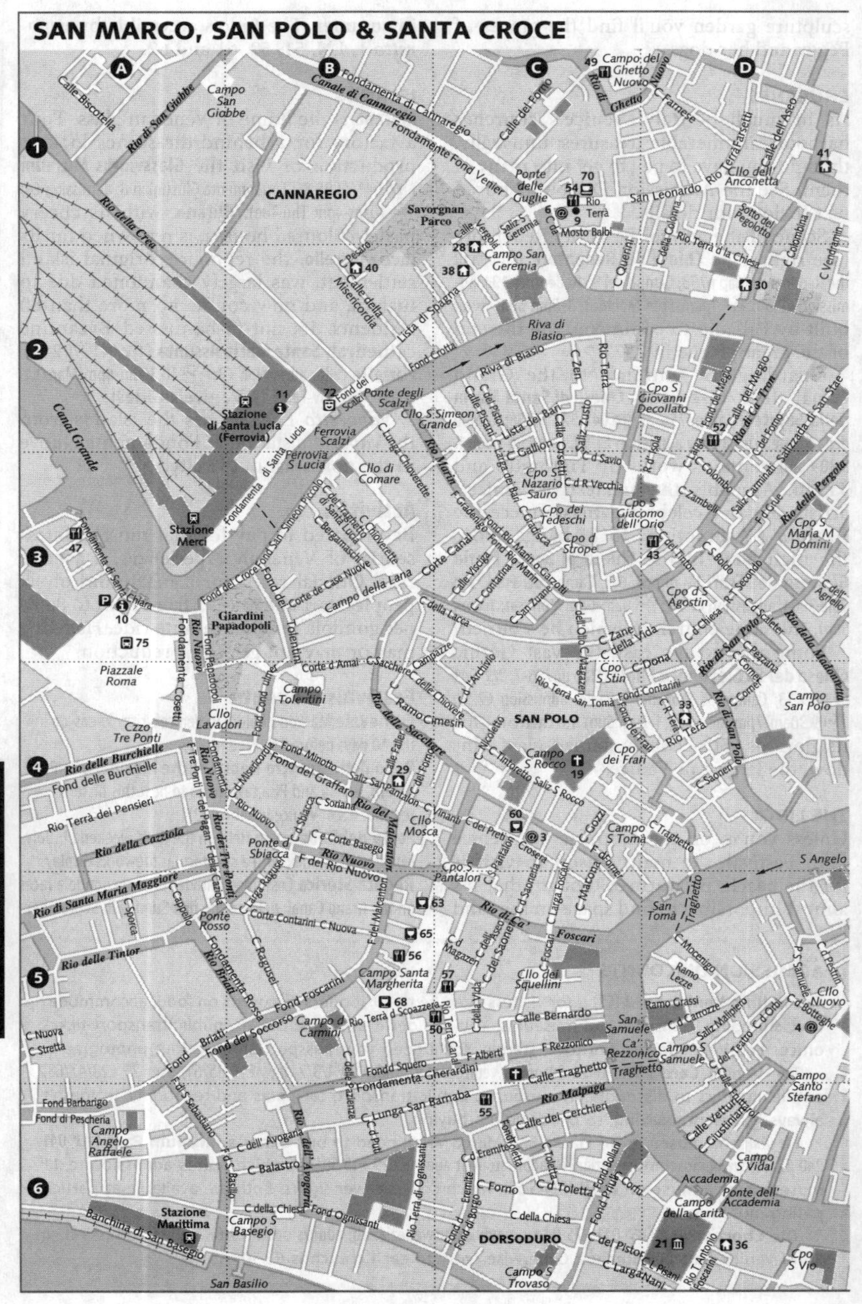
SAN MARCO, SAN POLO & SANTA CROCE
A
B
C
D
1
2
3
4
5
6
CANNAREGIO
SAN POLO
DORSODURO
Canal Grande
Canale di Cannaregio
Fondamenta di Cannaregio
Fondamente Fond Venier
Campo San Giobbe
Rio di San Giobbe
Calle Biscotella
Rio della Crea
Campo del Ghetto Nuovo
Rio di Ghetto Nuovo
C Farnese
Calle del Forno
Ponte delle Guglie
Savorgnan Parco
San Leonardo
Rio Terrà Farsetti
Calle dell'Aseo
Cllo dell' Anconetta
Sotto del Pegolotto
Rio Terà d'la Chiesa
C Colombina
C Vendramin
C Querini
C della Colonna
Mosto Balbi
Campo San Geremia
Calle Vergola
Saliz S Geremia
C Pesaro
Calle della Misericordia
Lista di Spagna
Riva di Biasio
Fond Crotta
Stazione di Santa Lucia (Ferrovia)
Stazione Merci
Fond dei Scalzi
Ponte degli Scalzi
Ferrovia Scalzi
Ferrovia S Lucia
Fondamenta di Santa Lucia
Cllo S Simeon Grande
Cllo di Comare
C Lunga Chioverette
C Chioverette
C Bergamaschi
Rio Marin
F Gradenigo
Calle Pisani
C del Pistor
C Larga dei Bari
Lista dei Bari
C Gallion
Calle Orsetti
Saliz Zusto
C d Savio
C Zen
Rio Terrà
Cpo S Nazario Sauro
C d R Vecchia
Cpo dei Tedeschi
Cpo d Strope
Cpo S Giovanni Decollato
Fond del Megio
Calle del Megio
Rio di Ca' Tron
C del Forno
Salizzada di San Stae
C Larga
C Colombo
C Zambelli
Saliz Carminati
Rio della Pergola
F d Grue
Cpo S Maria M Domini
Cpo S Giacomo dell'Orio
C del Tintor
C S Boldo
Cpo d S Agostin
R T Secondo
C d Chiesa
C d Scaleter
Rio della Madonnetta
Rio di San Polo
C Pezzana
C Cornet
C Comer
Campo San Polo
Fond Contarini
Rio Terà San Tomà
C Zane
C della Vida
Cpo S Stin
C Dona
Fond dei Frari
Cpo dei Frari
C R Terà
Rio Terà
C Saoneri
Campo S Rocco
Saliz S Rocco
C Tintoretto
C Nicoletto
Ramo Cimesin
Rio delle Sacchere
C d l'Archivio
C delle Chiovere
Campazze
C Sacchere
Corte d'Amai
Campo Tolentini
Fond dei Tolentini
Corte de Case Nuove
Campo della Lana
Corte Canal
Calle Viscigi
C Contarina
Fond Rio Marin o Garzotti
Fond Rio Marin
C S Zuane
C della Lacca
C dell'Olio
C Magazen
Fond del Croce
Fond San Simeon Piccolo
Fondamenta di Santa Chiara
Giardini Papadopoli
Fond Papadopoli
Rio Nuovo
Fondamenta Cosetti
Piazzale Roma
Czzo Tre Ponti
Cllo Lavadori
Fond Cond ulmer
Rio delle Burchielle
Fond delle Burchielle
Rio Terrà dei Pensieri
Rio della Cazziola
Rio di Santa Maria Maggiore
Rio dei Tre Ponti
F Tre Ponti
F dei Pagan
F della Croce
C d Misericordia
Fond Minotto
Fond del Graffaro
Saliz San Pantalon
Calle Faller
C del Forno
Rio del Malcanton
C Soriana
C d Sbiacca
C e Corte Basego
Ponte d Sbiacca
Rio Nuovo
F del Rio Nuovo
Larga Ragusei
Corte Contarini
C Nuova
F del Malcanton
C Ragusei
Cllo Mosca
C Vinanti
C dei Preti
Crosera
C Pantalon
Cpo S Pantalon
Campo S Tomà
C Traghetto
F drome
C Gozzi
C Saonera
C Larga Foscari
C Macona
Rio di Ca' Foscari
C Foscari
Cllo dei Squellini
C d Magazen
C dell'Aseo
C dei Saoner
S Angelo
San Tomà
Traghetto
C Mocenigo
Ramo Lezze
Ramo Grassi
C d Carrozze
Saliz Malipiero
C del Teatro
C d Orbi
C d Botteghe
Cllo Nuovo
P S Samuele
C d Pestrin
San Samuele
Campo S Samuele
Ca' Rezzonico
Campo Santo Stefano
C Frutarol
Calle Vetturi
C Giustinian
Campo S Vidal
Accademia
Ponte dell' Accademia
Campo della Carità
Cpo S Vio
C C Pisani
C Larga Nani
Rio T Antonio Foscarini
C del Pistor
Fond Priuli
C Corfu
Fond Bollani
C Toletta
C d Toletta
C d Eremite
Fond Toletta
C Forno
C della Chiesa
Fond d Eremite
Fond di Borgo
Campo S Trovaso
Rio Terrà di Ognissanti
Fond Ognissanti
C della Chiesa
Campo S Basegio
Calle dei Cerchieri
Rio Malpaga
C Lunga San Barnaba
C d Pu
Rio dell' Avogaria
C dell' Avogaria
C Balastro
F d S Basilio
Fondamenta Gherardini
Fondd Squero
F Alberti
F Rezzonico
Calle Traghetto
Traghetto
Calle Bernardo
Rio Terrà Canal
Rio Terrà d Scoazzera
Campo Santa Margherita
Campo d Carmini
C della Pazienze
Fond Foscarini
Fond del Soccorso
Fond Briati
Rio Briati
Fondamenta Rossa
Ponte Rosso
C Cappello
C Sporca
Rio delle Tintor
C Nuova
C Stretta
Fond Barbarigo
Fond di Pescheria
Campo Angelo Raffaele
F d S Sebastiano
Stazione Marittima
Banchina di San Basegio
San Basilio
Fondamenta Rossa
11
72
47
10
75
49
70
54
6
9
28
38
40
41
30
52
43
33
19
29
60
3
63
65
56
57
68
50
55
21
36
4

ITALY

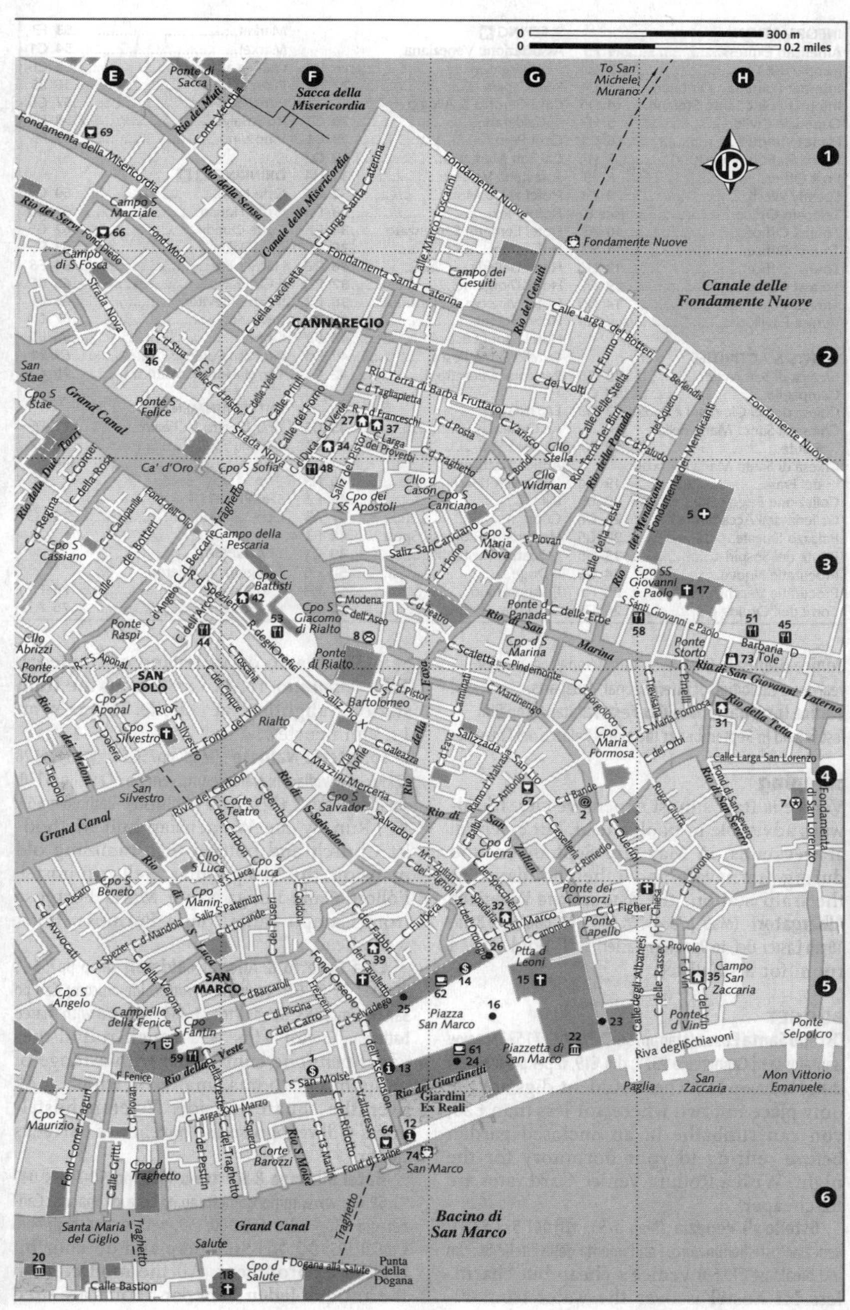
0 300 m
0 0.2 miles
E
F
G
H
1
2
3
4
5
6
Ponte di Sacca
Sacca della Misericordia
To San Michele, Murano
Rio dei Muti
Corte Vecchia
Fondamenta della Misericordia
69
Rio della Sensa
Canale della Misericordia
C Lunga Santa Caterina
Fondamente Nuove
Calle Marco Foscarini
Campo S Marziale
Rio dei Servi
Fond Diedo
66
Fond Moro
Campo di S Fosca
Strada Nova
C della Racchetta
Fondamenta Santa Caterina
Campo dei Gesuiti
Rio dei Gesuiti
Canale delle Fondamente Nuove
CANNAREGIO
Calle Larga dei Botteri
C d Stua
46
San Stae
Cpo S Stae
Grand Canal
C S Felice
C d Pistor
C delle Vele
Calle Priuli
Calle del Forno
Rio Terrà di Barba Fruttarol
C d Tagliapietta
C d Franceschi
R T d Franceschi
27
37
C d Verde
C Larga dei Proverbi
C d Posta
C Varisco
C dei Volti
C d Fumo
Calle delle Stella
C L Berlendis
C del Squero
Fondamenta dei Mendicanti
Ponte S Felice
Strada Nova
34
C d Duca
C d Traghetto
Cllo Stella
Rio Terrà dei Birri
Rio della Panada
C d Paludo
Rio delle Due Torri
C Corner
C della Rosa
Ca' d'Oro
Cpo S Sofia
48
Saliz del Pistor
C Bondi
Cllo Widman
Cllo d Cason
Cpo S Canciano
Cpo dei SS Apostoli
C d Regina
C d Campanile
Fond dell'Olio
Traghetto
Campo della Pescaria
Calle del Botteri
Cpo S Cassiano
Saliz SanCanciano
C d Forno
Cpo S Maria Nova
F Piovan
Calle della Testa
Rio dei Mendicanti
5
C d Beccarie
R d Spezieri
Cpo C Battisti
42
Calle
C d Angelo
C dell'Arco
44
R degli Orefici
53
Cpo S Giacomo di Rialto
C Modena
C dell'Aseo
8
C d Teatro
Ponte d Panada
C delle Erbe
Rio di San Marina
Cpo SS Giovanni e Paolo
17
S Santi Giovanni e Paolo
58
51
45
Barbaria D Tole
73
Ponte Storto
Ponte Raspi
Cllo Abrizzi
R T S Aponal
Ponte Storto
SAN POLO
Cpo S Aponal
C Toscana
C del Cinque
Ponte di Rialto
C S Bartolomeo
C d Pistor
C Scaletta
C Pindemonte
Cpo d S Marina
C Martinengo
C d Borgoloco
C Trevisana
C Pinelli
Rio di San Giovanni Laterno
Rio della Tetta
C Carminati
Rio della Fava
C S Maria Formosa
31
Cpo S Maria Formosa
C del Orbi
Rio dei Meloni
C Dolera
Cpo S Silvestro
Rio S Silvestro
Fond del Vin
Rialto
Saliz Pio X
Salizzada San Lio
C d Fava
Via 2 Aprile
C Galeazza
C L Mazzini Merceria
Rio
C Tiepolo
San Silvestro
Riva del Carbon
Corte d Teatro
C Bembo
Rio di S Salvador
Cpo S Salvador
Ramo d Malvasia
C S Antonio
67
C d Bande
2
Ruga Giuffa
Calle Larga San Lorenzo
Fond di San Severo
Rio di San Severo
7
Fondamenta di San Lorenzo
Grand Canal
C del Carbon
Salvador
Rio di San Zulian
C Cassellaria
C Querini
C Balbi
Cpo d Guerra
C d Rimedio
Cllo S Luca
Cpo S Luca
M S Zulian
C dei Pignoli
C dei Specchieri
Rio
Cpo S Beneto
C Pesaro
C d Avvocati
Cpo Manin
S S Luca
Saliz S Paternian
C d Locande
C dei Fuseri
C Goldoni
C dei Fabbri
C Fiubera
C Spadaria
M dell'Orologio
32
C L San Marco
Ponte dei Consorzi
C d Figher
C Canonica
Ponte Capello
C d Corona
C d Chiesa
C d Spezier
C d Mandola
C della Verona
Rio di S Luca
39
C dei Cavalletto
26
Ptta d Leoni
Calle degli Albanesi
C delle Rasse
S S Provolo
F d Vin
Campo San Zaccaria
35
14
SAN MARCO
C d Barcaroll
Frezzeria
Fond Orseolo
62
15
Cpo S Angelo
Campiello della Fenice
Cpo S Fantin
C di Piscina
C del Carro
C d Selvadego
25
Piazza San Marco
16
C del Vin
Ponte d Vin
23
22
Ponte Selpolcro
71
59
Rio della Veste
C dell'Ascension
61
24
Piazzetta di San Marco
Riva degli Schiavoni
F Fenice
C della Veste
1
S San Moisè
C Vallaresso
13
Rio dei Giardinetti
Giardini Ex Reali
Paglia
San Zaccaria
Mon Vittorio Emanuele
Cpo S Maurizio
C d Piovan
C Zaguri
C Larga XXII Marzo
C del Traghetto
C Squero
C del Ridotto
C d 13 Martin
Rio S Moisè
12
64
Corte Barozzi
74
San Marco
Fond di Farine
Fond Corner Zaguri
Calle Gritti
Cpo d Traghetto
C del Pestrin
Traghetto
Bacino di San Marco
Santa Maria del Giglio
Traghetto
Grand Canal
Salute
20
Cpo d Salute
F Dogana alla Salute
Punta della Dogana
18
Calle Bastion

ITALY

INFORMATION
American Express ... 1 F5
e copie d@ Toni ... 2 G4
Internet Point San Pantalon ... 3 C4
Internet Point Santo Stefano ... 4 D5
Ospedale Civile ... 5 H3
Planet Internet ... 6 C1
Police Station (Questura) ... 7 H4
Post Office ... 8 F3
Speedy Wash ... 9 C1
Telecom Office ... (see 8)
Tourist Office ... 10 A3
Tourist Office ... 11 B2
Tourist Office ... 12 F6
Tourist Office ... 13 F5
Travelex ... 14 G5
Venice Pavilion ... (see 12)

SIGHTS & ACTIVITIES
Basilica di San Marco ... 15 G5
Campanile ... 16 G5
Chiesa dei SS Giovanni e Paolo .. 17 H3
Chiesa di Santa Maria della Salute ... 18 F6
Chiesa di Santa Maria Glorioso dei Frari ... 19 C4
Collezione Peggy Guggenheim .. 20 E6
Galleria dell'Accademia ... 21 D6
Palazzo Ducale ... 22 G5
Ponte dei Sospiri ... 23 G5
Procuratie Nuove ... 24 G5
Procuratie Vecchie ... 25 F5
Torre dell'Orologio ... 26 G5

SLEEPING
Associazione Veneziana Albergatori ... (see 11)
B&B Capier ... 27 F2
Casa Gerotto & Alloggi Calderan ... 28 C2
Casa Peron ... 29 B4
Ca' San Marcuola ... 30 D2
Foresteria Valdese ... 31 H4
Hotel ai Do Mori ... 32 G5
Hotel Alex ... 33 D4
Hotel Bernardi Semenzato ... 34 F2
Hotel Doni ... 35 H5
Hotel Galleria ... 36 D6
Hotel Giorgione ... 37 F2
Hotel Minerva & Nettuno ... 38 C2
Hotel Noemi ... 39 F5
Hotel Santa Lucia ... 40 B2
Ostello Santa Fosca ... 41 D1
Pensione Guerrato ... 42 F3

EATING
Ae Oche ... 43 D3
All'Arco ... 44 E3
Antica Trattoria Bandierette ... 45 H3
Billa ... 46 E2
Coop ... 47 A3
Hosteria Ai Promessi Sposi ... 48 F3
I Quattro Rusteghi ... 49 C1
Il Doge ... 50 C5
Il Laboratorio ... 51 H3
La Zucca ... 52 D2
Market ... 53 F3
Market ... 54 C1
Osteria ai 4 Ferri ... 55 C6
Pizza al Volo ... 56 B5
Punto SMA ... 57 C5
Rosa Salva ... 58 H3
Vino Vino ... 59 E5

DRINKING
Café Noir ... 60 C4
Caffè Florian ... 61 G5
Caffè Quadri ... 62 G5
Chet Baker ... 63 B5
Harry's Bar ... 64 F6
Il Caffè ... 65 B5
Il Santo Bevitore ... 66 E1
Inishark ... 67 G4
Orange ... 68 B5
Paradiso Perduto ... 69 E1
Torrefazione Costarica ... 70 C1

ENTERTAINMENT
Gran Teatro La Fenice ... 71 E5
Vela ... 72 B2
Vela ... (see 75)

SHOPPING
Utz ... 73 H3

TRANSPORT
Alilaguna Fast Ferry to Airport ... 74 F6
Bus Station ... 75 A3

Venice Biennale Every even-numbered year, a major, year-long exhibition of international visual arts.
Venice International Film Festival Italy's top film fest is held in September at the Lido's Palazzo del Cinema.

Sleeping

Venice is Italy's most expensive city. It's always advisable to book ahead, but essential at weekends, in May and September, and during Carnevale and other holidays. At the train station, the **Associazione Veneziana Albergatori** (Map p753; ☎ 800 843 006; 8am-10pm Easter-Oct, to 9pm Nov-Easter) will book you a room for a small fee.

BUDGET

Ostello Santa Fosca (Map pp756-7; ☎ 041 715 775; www.santafosca.it; Cannaregio 2372; dm €19, d per person with shared bathroom €22) These student digs are the only place in town where, for less than €20, you can sunbathe in an enclosed garden before retiring to your dormitory for the night. With a Rolling Venice Card rates are €2 cheaper.

Ostello di Venezia (Map p753; ☎ 041 523 82 11; venezia@ostellionline.org; Fondamenta delle Zitelle 86; dm incl breakfast €19.50) Venice's cheap but charmless HI hostel is over the water from Piazza San Marco on the island of Giudecca. Take *vaporetto* 41, 42 or 82 from the train station, alighting at Zitelle. There's an 11.30pm curfew.

Foresteria Valdese (Map pp756-7; ☎ 041 528 67 97; www.diaconiavaldese.org/venezia; Castello 5170; dm incl breakfast €22, d €78, with shared bathroom €62;) Run by the Waldensian and Methodist Church and housed in a rambling old mansion, this is a popular, well-run hostel. Follow Calle Lunga Santa Maria Formosa from Campo Santa Maria Formosa. Book well ahead.

Casa Gerotto & Alloggi Calderan (Map pp756-7; ☎ 041 71 55 62; www.casagerottocalderan.com; Campo San Geremia 283; dm/s/d/tr €21/46/88/90, s/d with shared bathroom €36/65) This is a rough-round-the-edges *pensione*-cum-hostel with a range of anonymous rooms, many of which look over the square outside. Veteran hostel-goers will recognise the barebones barracks décor.

Hotel Minerva & Nettuno (Map pp756-7; ☎ 041 71 59 68; www.minervaenettuno.it; Lista di Spagna, Cannaregio 230; s/d/tr €50/100/150, with shared bathroom €40/70/105;) Stay here and do your bit for the environment. All the mod cons in the antique-laden Venetian rooms are fired by electricity produced from renewable sources. The owners also run the charming **B&B Capier** (www.capier.com) in a nearby Gothic building.

Casa Peron (Map pp756-7; ☎ 041 71 10 21; www.casaperon.com; Salizzada San Pantalon, San Polo 84; s/d €85/95, with shared bathroom €48/78) If all you're after is a crash pad near Venice's drinking centre, Campo Santa Margherita, Casa Peron will do. Rooms are spartan and outside noise can be a pain – unless you like being woken up at 5am by shouting workmen.

MIDRANGE

Hotel Alex (Map pp756-7; ☎ 041 523 13 41; www.hotelalexinvenice.com; Rio Terá, San Polo 2606; d incl breakfast €100, s/d with shared bathroom €48/74) The welcoming Alex provides modest, unfussy rooms in a quiet spot near Campo dei Frari. Spread over three floors (no lift), the rooms are mostly a good size and all are decorated with simple efficiency.

Hotel Santa Lucia (Map pp756-7; ☎ 041 71 51 80; www.hotelslucia.com; Calle della Misericordia, Cannaregio 358; s/d incl breakfast €80/110, with shared bathroom €60/85;) About 200m from the train station, the Santa Lucia is a dependable option, with a helpful English-speaking staff, an attractive gravelled garden and airy rooms.

Hotel Bernardi Semenzato (Map pp756-7; ☎ 041 522 72 57; www.hotelbernardi.com; SS Apostoli Calle dell'Oca, Cannaregio 4366; s €62-112, d €65-115, with shared bathroom s €38-72, d €44-72) A top choice boasting a great location, just off the main station–to–San Marco thoroughfare, you'll find refined rooms and hospitable owners here. There are further rooms available at a nearby annex.

Hotel Galleria (Map pp756-7; ☎ 041 523 24 89; www.hotelgalleria.it; Dorsoduro 878/a; d incl breakfast €120, s/d with shared bathroom €80/105;) In a 17th-century *palazzo* near the Ponte dell' Accademia, the Galleria offers old-fashioned, small rooms with wood-panelling, parquet and antiques. And with the Grand Canal lapping at your window, who cares if there are no mod cons?

Pensione Guerrato (Map pp756-7; ☎ 041 522 71 31; www.pensioneguerrato.it; Calle della Scimia 240/a, San Polo; s/d €100/125, d with shared bathroom €95) Escape the hurly-burly of the Rialto markets in this charming bolthole. Housed in a 13th-century convent, it has spacious colourful rooms with chandeliers and double-glazed windows. On the top floor there's an apartment, plus kitchen, for up to six people.

Hotel ai Do Mori (Map pp756-7; ☎ 041 520 48 17; www.hotelaidomori.com; Calle Larga San Marco 658; s €45-100, d €60-140;) Up some alarmingly steep stairs (three floors, no lift), rooms here are simple, cosy and carpeted. The pick of the bunch is room 11, with a private terrace and views of San Marco. Further beds are available in a nearby 1st-floor annex. Discounts are available for cash payment.

Ca' San Marcuola (Map pp756-7; ☎ 041 71 60 48; www.casanmarcuola.com; Cannaregio 1763; s/d incl breakfast €120/180;) From its low-key exterior you get no idea of the rococo Venetian décor within – chandeliers, gilt-framed mirrors, antiques and statuettes abound. The bright, spacious rooms are more sober but remain in theme.

Other recommendations:

Hotel Doni (Map pp756-7; ☎ /fax 041 522 42 67; www.albergodoni.it; Calle del Vin, Castello 4656; d incl breakfast €120, s/d with shared bathroom €65/95) Characterful family *pensione* near Piazza San Marco.

Hotel Noemi (Map pp756-7; ☎ 041 523 81 44; www.hotelnoemi.com; Calle dei Fabbri, San Marco 909; s €51-110, d €60-200, with shared bathroom s €30-80, d €40-120;) Decent three-star with small, elegantly appointed rooms.

TOP END

Hotel Giorgione (Map pp756-7; ☎ 041 522 58 10; www.hotelgiorgione.com; calla Larga dei Proverbi, Campo SS Apostoli 4587; s/d €173/265;) This is a refined but unpretentious four-star hotel. Rooms are decorated in time-honoured Venetian style, while downstairs you will find a billiard table, an enormous candy-like Murano chandelier in the tearoom and free umbrellas for guests.

Eating

Venetian specialities include *risi e bisi* (pea soup thickened with rice), *sarde di saor* (fried sardines marinated in vinegar and onions), and *fragolino*, a fragrant strawberry wine.

RESTAURANTS

Ae Oche (Map pp756-7; ☎ 041 524 11 61; Calle del Tintor, Santa Croce 1552a/b; pizza €5, 1st/2nd courses from €6/8) A hybrid of Tex-Mex décor and Italian food, this is one of Venice's busiest *pizzerie*. You'll find all the usual toppings, plus a range of pastas and meaty mains. Finish up with *sgroppino,* a cool, creamy, alcoholic lemon sorbet.

Vino Vino (Map pp756-7; ☎ 041 523 70 27; Calle della Veste, San Marco 2007; 1st/2nd courses €6/10; ⏰ 10.30am-midnight Wed-Mon) This is a atmospheric old-school *osteria* near Teatro La Fenice with a daily menu of local fare and a 350-label wine list. Seafood is a regular on the blackboard and is usually very good.

Antica Trattoria Bandierette (Map pp756-7; ☎ 041 522 06 19; Castello 6671; 1st/2nd courses €7/9; ⏰ closed Mon dinner & Tue) An unassuming neighbourhood trattoria, this place is known for its authentic atmosphere and excellent seafood. What exactly is on the menu depends on the day's catch, but for nonfish eaters there's a selection of fail-safe pastas and meats.

I Quattro Rusteghi (Map pp756-7; ☎ 041 71 51 60; Campo del Ghetto Nuovo, Cannaregio 2888; 1st/2nd courses €8/12) On a lovely square in the heart of Venice's former Jewish ghetto, this bustling restaurant specialises in Venetian cuisine (the *sarde di saor* is a house favourite) and local, organically produced wines. Sit inside or, in summer, on the square.

La Zucca (Map pp756-7; ☎ 041 524 15 70; Calle del Tentor, Santa Croce 1762; 1st/2nd courses from €7/12.50; ⏰ closed Sun) A wonderful, unpretentious little restaurant in an out-of-the-way spot, 'The Pumpkin' serves a range of innovative dishes prepared with fresh, seasonal ingredients. Examples? Lamb chops with artichokes and pecorino cheese; lentil soup with Swiss chard. Reservations are strongly recommended.

Osteria ai 4 Ferri (Map pp756-7; ☎ 041 520 69 78; Calle Lunga San Barnaba, Dorsoduro 2754/a; 1st/2nd courses €9/15; ⏰ closed Sun) Run by a young crew, the much-vaunted 4 Ferri (4 Irons) enjoys a deserved reputation for top-notch seafood. There's spaghetti *con il nero di seppia* (with cuttlefish ink) and grilled tuna, baccalà and bream – all of it fresh, all of it swimming in flavour. Reservations required.

Hosteria Ai Promessi Sposi (Map pp756-7; ☎ 041 522 86 09; Calle dell'Oca 4367; 1st/2nd courses €10/15; ⏰ closed Mon) Like most *trattorie* in the centre of Venice, the Promessi Sposi now makes most of its money from tourists. This shouldn't put you off though, as the food, particularly the seafood, is spot-on and the atmosphere warm and inviting.

QUICK EATS

Il Laboratorio (Map pp756-7; ☎ 340 600 79 74; Castello 6672; snacks from €2) This characterless neon-lit takeaway serves some of the best fried nibbles in Venice. Try the *arancini* (fried rice balls stuffed with meat sauce) and you'll get the idea.

Il Doge (Map pp756-7; ☎ 041 523 46 07; Campo Santa Margherita, Dorsoduro 3058/a; ice cream €2; ⏰ 10-2am Feb-Nov) This is a sweet *gelataria* on Campo Santa Margherita.

All'Arco (Map pp756-7; ☎ 041 520 56 66; Calle dell'Arco, San Polo 436; panini €3.50; ⏰ 7.30am-9pm Mon-Sat) Popular with locals, this tiny *osteria* serves wonderful, fresh *panini,* a range of *cicheti* (bar snacks) and smooth wine by the glass.

Pizza al Volo (Map pp756-7; ☎ 041 522 54 30; Campo Santa Margherita, Dorsoduro 2944; pizza from €4; ⏰ 11.30am-4pm & 5pm-1.30am) A popular takeaway, ideal for a pizza pitstop, slices here are sail-size and the family pizzas are just that – enough for three or four.

Rosa Salva (Map pp756-7; ☎ 041 522 79 49; Campo SS Giovanni e Paolo, Castello 6779; ⏰ closed Wed) Stop by this historic café for sensational *fritalle* (fried pastry puffs filled with zabaglione or cream). Then pop next door to the Gelateria Rosa Salva for an ice cream.

SELF-CATERING

For fruit and veg, as well as deli items, head for the markets near the Rialto bridge, or on the Rio Terrà San Leonardo. There are also supermarkets: **Punto Sma** (Map pp756-7; Campo Santa Margherita), **Billa** (Map pp756-7; Strada Nova, Cannaregio 3660) and **Coop** (Map pp756-7; Fondamenta di Santa Chiara, Piazzale Roma 506a).

Drinking

BARS

Café Noir (Map pp756-7; ☎ 041 71 09 25; Calle San Pantalon 3805) A mixed crowd of tourists, trendies and bohemians hang out at Café Noir. During the day you can grab a coffee and read the paper at one of the wooden tables; at night the funk goes on the stereo, the volume rises and the windows steam up.

Chet Baker (Map pp756-7; ☎ 041 523 87 27; Campo Santa Margherita, Dorsoduro 3684) A small den of a bar, Chet Baker would be the archetypal smoky jazz joint if smoking were not banned in public places. It still manages to catch the mood with a cool jazz soundtrack and a welcoming vibe. There are DJs on Wednesday, Friday and Saturday nights.

Harry's Bar (Map pp756-7; ☎ 041 528 57 77; Calle Vallaresso, San Marco 1323; ⏲ 10.30am-11.15pm) To drink a Bellini (white-peach pulp and *prosecco* – Venetian sparkling white) at the bar that invented them is an experience to tick off the list rather than a holiday highlight. Bar to the stars, Harry's is refined and hugely expensive (cocktails from €10).

Il Caffè (Map pp756-7; ☎ 041 528 79 98; Campo Santa Margherita, Dorsoduro 2963) Popular with foreign and Italian students, this is one of Venice's historic drinking spots. Known to locals as Café Rosso because of its red frontage, it's got outdoor seating and great *sprizze* (a type of apéritif).

Orange (Map pp756-7; ☎ 041 523 47 40; Campo Santa Margherita, Dorsoduro 3054) The latest addition to Campo Santa Margherita's buzzing bar scene, Orange sports a contemporary look – bright orange walls, surrealist Miró prints, MTV – and a young, multinational crowd.

Paradiso Perduto (Map pp756-7; ☎ 041 72 05 81; Fondamenta della Misericordia, Cannaregio 2540; ⏲ closed Mon) Queer-friendly and flamboyant, this restaurant-cum-club heats up late, but when the DJs pump up the decibels it jives. There's live music most weekends, often jazz, and a full food menu (1st/2nd courses €10/15).

Il Santo Bevitore (Map pp756-7; ☎ 041 71 75 60; Campo di S Fosca, Cannareguio 2393/A) A snag little pub by the bridge in Campo di S Fosca, the 'Holy Drinker' is laid-back and friendly. It's also quieter than many better-known bars, making it ideal for a relaxing drink or a light lunch.

CAFÉS

Caffè Florian (Map pp756-7; ☎ 041 520 56 41; Piazza San Marco 56/59; coffee €5-10) If you think it's worth paying €5 for an espresso, pull up a seat at Piazza San Marco's most famous café. Watch life on the square as you're serenaded by the in-house musicians. Byron, apparently, used to breakfast here.

Caffè Quadri (Map pp756-7; ☎ 041 528 92 99; Piazza San Marco 120; coffee €7-10; ⏲ late) Over the square from Florian, the historic Quadri offers more of the same – location, music and comically expensive drinks.

Torrefazione Costarica (Map pp756-7; ☎ 041 71 63 71; Rio Terrá San Leonardo, Cannaregio 1337) Connoisseurs come here for Venice's best, and cheapest, coffee (espresso €0.70, cappuccino €1.10). Espressos are smooth yet charged with flavour, cappuccinos exactly as they should be, warm and creamy.

Entertainment

Tickets for the majority of events in Venice are available from **Vela** (Map pp756-7; ☎ 041 24 24; www.hellovenezia.it) kiosks in front of the train station, at Piazzale Roma, and at the Venice Pavilion tourist office (see p754).

Gran Teatro La Fenice (Map pp756-7; ☎ 041 78 65 11; www.teatrolafenice.it; Campo San Fantin, San Marco 1977; tickets from €20) One of Italy's most important opera houses, the Fenice is back to its sumptuous best. Destroyed by fire in 1996, it was reopened in 2003 and is now in full swing.

Shopping

Classic Venetian gift options include Murano glass, lace from Burano, Carnevale masks and *carta marmorizzata* (marbled paper). There are any number of shops selling these items, but if you want the best deal go to the source. Be warned, though, genuine Burano lace is expensive; also, much of the cheaper stuff is imported from the Far East.

The main shopping area is between San Marco and the Rialto, although if you're after designer clobber head to the area west of Piazza San Marco.

Utz (Map pp756-7; ☎ 360 32 53 33; Castello 6400) Named after a Bruce Chatwin book, Utz is an Aladdin's cave of antique Venetian jewellery, glass, furniture, mirrors and assorted odds and ends. Prices are accessible if not cheap.

Getting There & Away

AIR

Most European and domestic flights land at **Marco Polo airport** (VCE; ☎ 041 260 92 60; www.veniceairport.it), 12km outside Venice. Ryanair, however, flies to **Treviso airport** (TSF; ☎ 0422 31 51 11; www.trevisoairport.it), about 30km from Venice.

BOAT

Minoan Lines (☎ 041 240 71 01; www.minoan.gr) run ferries to Corfu (€83, 22 hours), Igoumenitsa (€83, 23½ hours) and Patras (€83, 29½ hours) daily in summer and four times a week in winter.

BUS

ACTV (☎ 041 24 24; www.actv.it) buses service surrounding areas, including Mestre, Padua and Treviso. Tickets and information are available at the **bus station** (Map pp756-7) in Piazzale Roma.

TRAIN

Venice's Stazione di Santa Lucia is directly linked to Padua (€2.50, 40 minutes, three or four hourly), Verona (€12.40, 1½ hours, half hourly) and Bologna (€15.10, two hours, half hourly), and is easily accessible from Rome and Florence. You can also reach points in France, Germany, Austria, Switzerland, Slovenia and Croatia.

Getting Around

TO/FROM THE AIRPORT

To get to Marco Polo there are various options: **Alilaguna** (Map pp756-7; www.alilaguna.com) operates a fast ferry service (€10 from near Piazza San Marco, 70 minutes, hourly between 8.20am and 10.20pm); alternatively, from Piazzale Roma take either an **ATVO** (☎ 041 520 55 30; www.atvo.it, in Italian) bus (€3, 20 minutes, hourly) or ACTV bus 5d (€2, more than 50 daily).

For Treviso airport, take the ATVO **Eurobus** (€5, one hour, 16 daily) from Piazzale Roma two hours and 10 minutes before your flight departure.

BOAT

The city's main mode of public transport is *vaporetti*. The most useful routes are:

LN From Fondamenta Nuove for Murano, Burano and the Lido.
T Runs between Burano and Torcelli.
1 From Piazzale Roma to the train station and down the Grand Canal to San Marco and the Lido.
17 Car ferry between Tronchetto and the Lido.
82 All stops on the Grand Canal plus Piazzale Roma, Tronchetto and Giudecca.

Tickets, available from ticket booths at landing stations and Vela outlets, are expensive: €3.50 for a single trip (not valid on the Grand Canal); €5 for 90 minutes unlimited travel; €10.50 for 24 hours; €22 for 72 hours.

The poor man's gondola, *traghetti* (€0.50 per crossing) are used by Venetians to cross the Grand Canal where there's no nearby bridge.

CAR & MOTORCYCLE

Vehicles must be parked on Tronchetto or at Piazzale Roma (cars are allowed on the Lido – take car ferry 17 from Tronchetto). The car parks are not cheap – €20 every 24 hours – so you're better off leaving your car in Mestre and getting a train over to Venice.

FERRARA

pop 131,135

Ferrara retains much of the austere splendour of its Renaissance heyday, when, as seat of the Este family (1260–1598), it was a force to be reckoned with. Overshadowed by the menacing Castello Estense, the compact medieval centre is atmospheric and lively.

Information is available from the main **tourist office** (☎ 0532 29 93 03; www.ferrarainfo.com; 🕑 9am-1pm & 2-6pm Mon-Sat, 9.30am-1pm & 2-5pm Sun) inside Castello Estense, or a second **office** (☎ 0532 41 94 74; Piazza Municipale 11; 🕑 9am-1pm Mon-Sat) nearby.

Sights

Easily explored on foot, Ferrara's *centro storico* lies to the south of **Castello Estense** (☎ 0532 29 92 33; Viale Cavour; adult/child under 11 €6/free, plus €1 for Lion's Tower; 🕑 9.30am-5.30pm). Complete with moat and drawbridges, the castle was begun by Nicolò II d'Este in 1385 and became the Este family's residence. Highlights include the **Sala dei Giganti** (Giant's Room) and **Salone dei Giochi** (Games Salon) with frescoes by Camillo and Sebastiano Filippi.

Nearby, the pink-and-white 12th-century **Duomo** (☎ 0532 20 74 49; Piazza Cattedrale; 🕑 7.30am-noon & 3-6.30pm Mon-Sat, 7.30am-12.30pm & 3.30-7.30pm Sun) is more interesting outside than in. Take a moment to stare up at the superb three-tiered marble façade with its Gothic depiction of the Last Judgement. The cathedral **museum** (☎ 0532 24 49 49; Via San Romano 1-9; adult/under 18 €5/free; 🕑 9.30am-1pm & 3-8pm Tue-Sun) exhibits some attractive Renaissance sculptures and paintings.

Fresco fans won't want to miss **Palazzo Schifanoia** (☎ 0532 24 49 49; Via Scandiana 23; adult/under 18 €5/free; 🕑 9am-6pm Tue-Sun), one of Ferrara's earliest Renaissance buildings and another of the Este palaces. In the **Sala dei Mesi** (Room of the Months), the 15th-century frescoes are considered among the best examples of their type in Italy. Sadly, though, they're not in great nick.

ITALY

Sleeping

You won't need to overnight to see Ferrara's sights, but it's a cheap alternative to Bologna, and a viable base for Venice.

Pensione Artisti (☎ 0532 76 10 38; Via Vittoria 66; d €60, s/d with shared bathroom €25/43) Put simply, this is the best budget option in town. Its scrubbed white rooms sparkle, the central location is convenient for everything, there are kitchen facilities for guests, and the owners are super-friendly.

Hotel de Prati (☎ 0532 24 19 05; www.hoteldeprati.com; Via Padiglioni 5; s/d €75/110; ❄) A model of exquisite taste, the Prati has got it exactly right. Not an antique desk or a contemporary print looks out of place in the big, beautifully decorated rooms. Downstairs, the yellow and orange walls stage entertaining art exhibitions.

Hotel Europa (☎ 0532 20 54 56; www.hoteleuropaferrara.com; Corso Giovecca 49; s/d €74/115; P ❄) Bombed in WWII – history doesn't record if Mussolini was in his room at the time – the Europa retains a period charm despite successive renovations. Some rooms still even have their original 16th-century frescoed ceilings. Extras include wi-fi and bike hire.

Eating & Drinking

Trattoria Il Mandolino (☎ 0532 76 00 80; Via Carlo Mayr 83; 1st/2nd courses €8/10) Taking its name from the mandolin on the wall, this charmingly cluttered trattoria is a memorable place to dine on Ferrarese food. Menu staples include the house speciality, *salama da sugo con purè* (salty braised salami on a bed of mashed potato).

Fusion (☎ 0532 20 14 73; Via Delle Scienze 8/a) Unless you want to be outsmarted by the furniture, you'll need to dress up here. Red leather stools, cream sofas and industrial piping provide the setting for Fusion's sexy self-conscious drinkers. Great fun.

Messisbugo (☎ 0532 76 40 60; Via Carlo Mayr 79; 🕑 closed Mon) Despite a name that suggests Tex Mex tack, Messisbugo is actually a cool, brick-vaulted bar favoured by bohemians and students, with friendly staff, great wines and a laid-back vibe.

Getting There & Around

Ferrara is easy to get to by train. There are regular trains to Bologna (€7.85, 40 minutes, half hourly), Venice (€12.95, 1½ hours, every 45 minutes or so) and nearby Ravenna (€4.30, 1½ hours, 17 daily).

From the station take bus 1 or 9 for the historic centre.

BOLOGNA

pop 373,540

Boasting a boisterous bonhomie rare in Italy's reserved north, Bologna is worth a few days of anyone's itinerary, not so much for its specific attractions, of which there are few, but for the sheer fun of strolling its animated, arcaded streets. A university town since 1088 (Europe's oldest), it's riddled with bars, cafés and *trattorie*.

Traditionally a bastion of socialism – it's often joked that its politics are reflected in its red buildings – Bologna is famous for its food, which, in a country as food conscious as Italy, is good news indeed. Besides the eponymous bolognese sauce (*ragù*), Bologna also gave the world tortellini, lasagne and mortadella.

Information

Liong@te Internet Point (☎ 051 407 01 61; www.liongate.it; 1st fl, Via Rizzoli 9, cnr Galleria del Leone; per hr €2; 🕑 10am-midnight)
Ospedale Maggiore (Hospital; ☎ 051 647 81 11)
Police station (Questura; ☎ 051 640 11 11; Piazza Galileo 7)
Post office (Piazza Minghetti 1)
Tourist information (☎ 051 24 65 41; www.bolognaturismo.info) Piazza Maggiore 1 (🕑 9am-8pm); train station (🕑 8.30am-7pm Mon-Sat); airport (🕑 8am-8pm Mon-Sat, 9am-3pm Sun)

Sights & Activities

Bologna's porticoed *centro storico* is a vibrant and atmospheric place to wander. The place to start is pedestrianised **Piazza Maggiore** and adjoining **Piazza del Nettuno**. Here you'll find the **Fontana del Nettuno** (Neptune's Fountain), sculpted by Giambologna in 1566 and featuring an impressively muscled Neptune. On the western flank of Piazza Maggiore is the **Palazzo Comunale** (Town Hall; ☎ 051 20 31 11; admission free), home to the city's art collection and a museum dedicated to artist Giorgio Morandi. Note the immense central staircase, attributed to Bramante, which was built wide enough to allow horse-drawn carriages up to the 1st floor. Up above the main entrance, a bronze statue depicts the

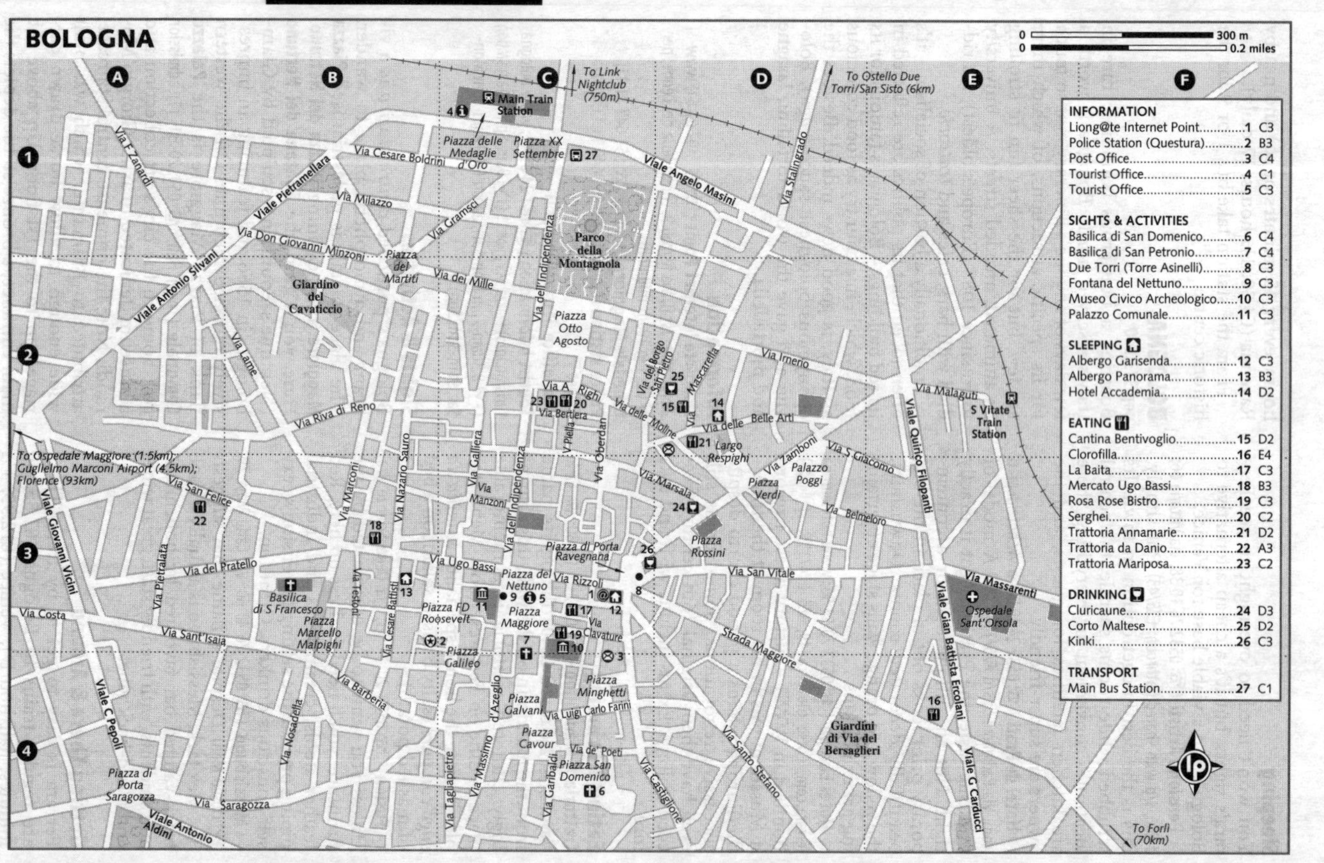
ITALY
BOLOGNA
0 300 m
0 0.2 miles
INFORMATION
Liong@te Internet Point 1 C3
Police Station (Questura) 2 B3
Post Office 3 C4
Tourist Office 4 C1
Tourist Office 5 C3
SIGHTS & ACTIVITIES
Basilica di San Domenico 6 C4
Basilica di San Petronio 7 C4
Due Torri (Torre Asinelli) 8 C3
Fontana del Nettuno 9 C3
Museo Civico Archeologico 10 C3
Palazzo Comunale 11 C3
SLEEPING
Albergo Garisenda 12 C3
Albergo Panorama 13 B3
Hotel Accademia 14 D2
EATING
Cantina Bentivoglio 15 D2
Clorofilla 16 E4
La Baita 17 C3
Mercato Ugo Bassi 18 B3
Rosa Rose Bistro 19 C3
Serghei 20 C2
Trattoria Annamarie 21 D2
Trattoria da Danio 22 A3
Trattoria Mariposa 23 C2
DRINKING
Cluricaune 24 D3
Corto Maltese 25 D2
Kinki 26 C3
TRANSPORT
Main Bus Station 27 C1
To Link Nightclub (750m)
To Ostello Due Torri/San Sisto (6km)
To Ospedale Maggiore (1.5km); Guglielmo Marconi Airport (4.5km); Florence (93km)
To Forlì (70km)
Main Train Station
S Vitate Train Station
Parco della Montagnola
Giardino del Cavaticcio
Giardini di Via del Bersaglieri
Ospedale Sant'Orsola
Basilica di S Francesco
Piazza delle Medaglie d'Oro
Piazza XX Settembre
Piazza dei Martiti
Piazza Otto Agosto
Piazza del Nettuno
Piazza Maggiore
Piazza FD Roosevelt
Piazza Galileo
Piazza Galvani
Piazza Minghetti
Piazza Cavour
Piazza San Domenico
Piazza di Porta Ravegnana
Piazza Rossini
Piazza Verdi
Palazzo Poggi
Largo Respighi
Piazza Marcello Malpighi
Piazza di Porta Saragozza
Via F Zanardi
Viale Pietramellara
Via Cesare Boldrini
Viale Angelo Masini
Via Stalingrado
Via Milazzo
Via Gramsci
Via Don Giovanni Minzoni
Via dei Mille
Viale Antonio Silvani
Via dell'Indipendenza
Via Lame
Via Irnerio
Via Malaguti
Via A Righi
Via Bertiera
Via del Borgo San Pietro
Via Mascarella
Via delle Moline
Via delle Belle Arti
Via Riva di Reno
V Piella
Via Oberdan
Via Zamboni
Via S Giacomo
Viale Quirico Filopanti
Via Galliera
Via Nazario Sauro
Via Marconi
Via Manzoni
Via Marsala
Via Belmeloro
Via San Felice
Viale Giovanni Vicini
Via Pietralata
Via del Pratello
Via Ugo Bassi
Via Rizzoli
Via San Vitale
Via Massarenti
Viale Gian Battista Ercolani
Via Costa
Via Testoni
Via Cesare Battisti
Via Sant'Isaia
Via Clavature
Strada Maggiore
Via Barberia
Viale C Pepoli
Via Nosadella
Via d'Azeglio
Via Luigi Carlo Farini
Via Santo Stefano
Via de' Poeti
Via Tagliapietre
Via Massimo
Via Garibaldi
Via Castiglione
Viale G Carducci
Via Saragozza
Viale Antonio Aldini

Bolognese Pope Gregory XIII, creator of the Gregorian calendar.

To the south, the Gothic **Basilica di San Petronio** (☎ 051 22 54 22; Piazza Maggiore; 7.30am-1pm & 2.30-6pm) is dedicated to the city's patron saint, Petronius. Its partially complete façade doesn't diminish its status as the world's fifth-largest basilica. Inside, a giant 17th-century brass sundial stretches along the floor of the eastern aisle.

It's a short walk to **Piazza di Porta Ravegnana** and Bologna's two leaning towers, the **Due Torri**. The taller of the two, the 97m **Torre Asinelli** (admission €3; 9am-6pm), was built between 1109 and 1119 and is now open to the public. Climb the 498 steps for some superb city views.

Of the city's other churches, the **Basilica di San Domenico** (☎ 051 640 04 11; Piazza San Domenico; 7.30am-1pm & 3.30-7.30pm) is noteworthy for the elaborate sarcophagus of San Domenico, founder of the Dominican order. The tomb stands in the late 12th-century Capella di San Domenico, which was designed by Nicolò Pisano and later added to by, among others, Michelangelo. Mozart, it's said, once played the church's organ.

For tombs of an altogether more sober style, head for the **Museo Civico Archeologico** (☎ 051 23 38 49; Via dell'Archiginnasio 2; adult/concession €4/2; 9am-3pm Tue-Fri & 10am-6.30pm Sun), which houses one of Italy's best Etruscan collections.

Sleeping

Accommodation is largely geared to the business market. It's expensive and can be difficult to find unless you book ahead.

Ostello Due Torri/San Sisto (☎ 051 50 18 10; hostelbologna@hotmail.com; Via Viadagola 5; dm €15.50) It's quite a hike to these two functional HI hostels, barely 100m apart, but 6km north of the city centre. Take bus 93 (Monday to Saturday daytime), 301 (Sunday) or 21b (daily after 8.30pm) from Via Irnerio or Via Marconi. Mind the 11pm curfew.

Albergo Panorama (☎ 051 22 1802; www.hotelpanoramabologna.it; 4th fl, Via Livraghi 1; s/d/tr/q with shared bathroom €60/75/85/95) Make it up to the 4th floor (there is a lift) and you'll find a lovely, family-run *pensione*. Jolly corridors with paintings and flowers lead to bright, spacious rooms, some of which have distant views of Bologna's medieval towers.

Albergo Garisenda (☎ 051 22 43 69; www.albergogarisenda.com; Galleria del Leone 1, Via Rizzoli 9; d incl breakfast €110, s/d with shared bathroom €60/85) In the shadow of Bologna's towers, the 3rd-floor Garisenda offers seven unfussy rooms and a prime location (look for the McDonalds sign near the towers). Don't expect frills or even décor, but the beds are comfy and the shared bathrooms are clean.

Hotel Accademia (☎ 051 23 23 18; www.hotelaccademia.it; Via delle Belle Arti 6; s/d €95/130, with shared bathroom €70/100; P) A good option in the thick of the orange-coloured university quarter, the three-star Accademia has fresh, tasteful rooms, modern bathrooms and satellite TV.

Eating

It's not impossible to eat badly in Bologna, but you'd have to be pretty unlucky. The university area around Via Rizzoli harbours hundreds of *trattorie* and restaurants catering to hard-up students and gourmet diners.

Trattoria da Danio (☎ 051 55 52 02; Via San Felice 50a; 1st/2nd courses €8/9, set menu €11.50) With the television on in the corner and the jovial owner chatting to friends at the bar, this is the quintessential Italian trattoria. The no-nonsense pastas and filling meat dishes are very much appreciated by the discerning locals and curious foreigners who frequent here.

Serghei (☎ 051 23 3533; Via Piella 12; 1st/2nd courses €8/11; Mon-Fri) This popular eatery owes its name to a mispronunciation – founder Sergio Pasoti was dubbed Serghei by the Teatro Comunale's Russian dancers who used to drink here. Forty years on and the visitors are still arriving, tempted by regional classics such as *tortelloni di zucca* and *tagliatelle al ragù*. Reserve.

Trattoria Annamarie (☎ 051 26 68 94; Via delle Belle Arti 17; 1st/2nd courses €10/15; closed Tue dinner & Wed) Trattoria Annamarie looks every inch the classic Bolognese restaurant that it is. Diners sit down to superb homemade pastas and delicious grilled meats under a brick-vaulted ceiling, surrounded by walls covered in photos, paintings and celebrity testimonials.

Also recommended:

Rosa Rose Bistro (☎ 051 22 50 71; Via Clavature 18; salad/pasta €7/7.50) Swish café with eccentric décor, outdoor seating and great salads.

AUTHOR'S CHOICE

Trattoria Mariposa (☎ 051 22 56 56; Via Bertiera 12; 1st/2nd courses €6/7; ⏰ closed Mon, Thu dinner & Sun) is a great example of what Bologna does so well. A small, convivial trattoria, it draws a young local crowd thanks to its down-to-earth cooking and great prices. The menu varies, but if it's on, the *garganelli con pancetta e rucola* (short pasta with pancetta and rocket) is well worth trying. Service, needless to say, is friendly, and although it's always crowded there's never any pressure to move on.

Cantina Bentivoglio (☎ 051 26 54 16; Via Mascarella 4b; 1st/2nd courses €8/10; ⏰ 8pm-2am) Nightly jazz, mega wine list, regional food.

Clorofilla (☎ 051 235 53 43; Strada Maggiore 64/c; main courses €6.50; ⏰ closed Sun) Laid-back vegetarian eatery good for salads, couscous and tofu.

Self-caterers can stock up at the covered **Mercato Ugo Bassi** (Via Ugo Bassi 27; ⏰ closed Sun) or the deli **La Baita** (☎ 051 22 39 40; Via Pescheria Vecchie 3; ⏰ 7am-8pm Mon-Sat).

Drinking

Cluricaune (☎ 051 26 34 19; Via Zamboni 18/b) A big Irish pub with all the predictable Guinness paraphernalia and premiership football on the TV, this place is very popular with local and foreign students.

Corto Maltese (☎ 051 22 97 46; Via del Borgo San Pietro 9/A) Tank up during happy hour (between 9pm and 10.30pm) to set yourself up for the commercial tunes the DJs spin on Friday and Saturday nights. There's dancing, pasta and even a pool table.

Kinki (☎ 051 587 51 78; www.kinkidisco.com, in Italian; Via Zamboni 1) It's hot! It's vinyl! Gays, lesbians and über-cool straights are welcome to work it until all hours at Bologna's most famous disco. Themed nights, top DJs, wicked sounds.

Getting There & Around

European and domestic flights arrive at Bologna's **Guglielmo Marconi airport** (BLQ; ☎ 051 647 96 15; www.bologna-airport.it), 6km northwest of the city. An Aerobus shuttle (€4.50, 30 minutes, three times hourly) departs from the main train station. Ryanair now flies to **Forlì** (FRL; ☎ 0543 47 49 21; www.forli-airport.it), 70km southeast of Bologna. **Ebus** (☎ 199 11 55 77) buses run between Forlí and the main train station to coincide with flights.

Bologna is a major rail hub. From the **main train station** (Piazza elle Medaglie d'Oro), trains run to Venice (€15.10, two hours, half hourly), Florence (€10.75, one hour, every 20 minutes) and Rome (Eurostar, €37.20, 2¾ hours, hourly). National and international coaches depart from the main **bus station** (Piazza XX Settembre).

The city is linked to Milan, Florence and Rome by the A1 (Autostrada del Sole). The A13 services Venice and Padua, and the A14 Ravenna. Traffic is restricted in Bologna's centre.

To get to the centre from the train station take bus 21 or 30.

RAVENNA

pop 139,000

Most people visit Ravenna for its remarkable Unesco-protected mosaics. Relics of the city's golden age as capital of the Western Roman and Byzantine Empires, they are described by Dante in his *Divine Comedy,* much of which was written here. Easily accessible from Bologna, this refined and polished town is worth a day trip at the very least.

The **tourist office** (☎ 0544 354 04; www.turismo.ravenna.it; Via Salara 8; ⏰ 8.30am-6pm Mon-Sat, 10am-4pm Sun) is in the *centro storico*.

Sights

Ravenna's five main monuments are covered by a single ticket (€7.50). Available at any one of the five monuments and valid for seven days, it gives entry to the Basilica di San Vitale, the Mausoleo di Galla Placida, the Basilica di Sant'Appollinare Nuovo, the Museo Arcivescovile and Battistero Neoniano. There's no individual admission prices for these monuments.

On the northern edge of the *centro storico*, the sombre exterior of the 6th-century **Basilica di San Vitale** (☎ 0544 21 51 93; Via Fiandrini; ⏰ 9.30am-7pm Apr-Sep, to 5.30pm Mar & Oct, to 5pm Nov-Feb) hides a dazzling interior with mosaics depicting Old Testament scenes. Nearby, the **Mausoleo di Galla Placidia** (☎ 0544 21 51 93; Via Fiandrini; ⏰ 9.30am-7pm Apr-Sep, to 5.30pm Mar & Oct, to 5pm Nov-Feb) contains the city's oldest mosaics. Adjoining Ravenna's unremarkable cathedral, the **Museo Arcivescovile** (☎ 0544 21 52 91; Piazza Arcivescovado; ⏰ 9am-7pm Apr-Sep, 9.30am-5.30pm

Mar & Oct, 10am-5pm Nov-Feb) boasts an exquisite 6th-century ivory throne, while next door in the **Battistero Neoniano** (Via Battistero; 9am-7pm Apr-Sep, 9.30am-5.30pm Mar & Oct, 10am-5pm Nov-Feb) the baptism of Christ and the apostles is represented in the domed roof mosaics. To the east the **Basilica di Sant'Apollinare Nuovo** (0544 21 95 18; Via di Roma; 9am-7pm Apr-Sep, 9.30am-5.30pm Mar & Oct, 10am-5pm Nov-Feb) boasts, among other things, a superb mosaic depicting a procession of martyrs headed towards Christ and his apostles.

Five kilometres southeast of the city, the apse mosaic of the **Basilica di Sant'Apollinare in Classe** (0544 47 35 69; Via Romea Sud, Classe; admission €2; 8.30am-7.30pm Mon-Sat, 1-7.30pm Sun) is a must-see. Take bus 4 from Piazza Caduti per la Libertà.

Dante spent the last 19 years of his life in Ravenna after Florence expelled him in 1302. As a perpetual act of penance, Florence supplies the oil for the lamp that burns in his **tomb** (Via Dante Alighieri 9; admission free; 9am-7pm).

Sleeping & Eating

Albergo Al Giaciglio (0544 394 03; www.albergoalgiaciglio.com; Via Rocca Brancaleone 42; s/d €43/65, with shared bathroom €38/50) Near the station, this is a welcoming family-run hotel with modest rooms and a good restaurant (set menu €13). There's fresh fish on Friday and a special vegetarian menu (€15).

Albergo Cappello (0544 21 98 13; www.albergocappello.it; Via IV Novembre 41; s/d incl breakfast €93/110;) Stylishly marrying the old with the new, the Cappello has seven ample rooms on the 1st floor of a 15th-century townhouse. Modern metallic walls and lamps with sprouting bulbs combine with coffered ceilings and frescoes.

Cá de Vén (0544 301 63; Via Corrado Ricci 24; 1st/2nd courses €8/13; closed Mon) This cavernous, high-ceilinged *enoteca*-cum-restaurant attracts visitors in droves. But that shouldn't distract you from its fine regional food (the menu changes weekly) and infinite collection of local wine.

Getting There & Around

Trains connect the city with Bologna (€7 to €15, 1½ hours, hourly) and Ferrara (€4.30, 1¼ hours, 15 daily).

In town, cycling is popular. Rent bikes from **Cooperative Sociale la Formica** (0544 370 31; Piazza Farini; per hr/day €1/7.75; 7am-8pm Mon-Sat) outside the train station, or from the **tourist office** (free; spring & summer only).

THE DOLOMITES

Stretching across Trentino-Alto Adige and into the Veneto, the stabbing sawtooth peaks of the Dolomites provide some of Italy's most thrilling scenery. With their jagged silhouettes and colourful tints (blue-grey turning to red, then purple as the sun sets), they are popular year-round – in winter for the skiing, in summer for the superb hiking.

Resorts range from exclusive Cortina d'Ampezzo (see p768) to family-oriented resorts in the Val Gardena (p768). Ski passes cover either single resorts or a combination of slopes; the most comprehensive is the **Superski Dolomiti pass** (www.dolomitisuperski.com; high season 3/6 days €110/194), which accesses 464 lifts and 1220km of runs in 12 valleys.

Hiking opportunities run the gamut from kid-friendly strolls to hardcore mountain treks. Trails are well marked with numbers on red-and-white bands on trees and rocks, or by numbers inside coloured triangles for the four *Alte Vie* (High Routes). Recommended areas include the Alpe di Siusi, a vast plateau above the Val Gardena; the area around Cortina; and Pale di San Martino, accessible from San Martino di Castrozza.

For more information on skiing and cycling, see the Activities section in the Italy Directory, p815.

Information

Information on Trentino Alto-Adige can be obtained in Trent at the **tourist office** (0461 98 38 80; www.apt.trento.it; Via Manci 2; 9am-7pm). Bolzano's **tourist office** (0471 30 70 00; www.bolzano-bozen.it; Piazza Walther 8; 9am-6.30pm Mon-Fri, to 12.30pm Sat) can also help.

For activities and accommodation in the Veneto, ask at the tourist office in Cortina – see p768.

The best online resource option is www.dolomiti.org, which has a great deal of useful information.

Getting There & Around

In Trentino-Alto Adige, **Bolzano airport** (BZO; 0471 25 52 55; www.abd-airport.it) is served by ski charter flights from the UK in the

WARNING

Even in summer the weather is extremely changeable in the Alps; though it may be sweltering when you set off, be prepared for very cold, wet weather on even the shortest walks. Essentials include good-quality, worn-in walking boots, a waterproof jacket, warm hat and gloves, light food, plenty of water and a decent map. The best maps are the Tabacco 1:25,000 series, widely available throughout the area.

winter and daily year-round flights from Rome and Milan. Otherwise the nearest airports are in Verona (see p751) or Bergamo (see p748).

On terra firma, the area's excellent bus network is run by **Trentino Trasporti** (☎ 0461 82 10 00; www.ttspa.it, in Italian) in Trentino; **SAD** (☎ 800 84 60 47; www.sii.bz.it) in Alto Adige; and **Dolomiti Bus** (www.dolomitibus.it, in Italian) in the Veneto. During winter, most resorts offer 'ski bus' services.

The main towns and the many ski resorts can be reached directly from cities such as Rome, Florence, Venice, Bologna, Milan and Genoa. Information is available from tourist offices and regional bus stations.

CORTINA D'AMPEZZO

pop 6085

Surrounded by some of the Dolomites most dramatic scenery, Cortina is one of Italy's most famous, fashionable and expensive ski resorts. Predictably it boasts first-class facilities (skiing, skating, sledding, climbing) and superb hiking; less obviously, it has some reasonably priced accommodation. Ask at the **tourist office** (☎ 0436 32 31; www.infodolomiti.it; Piazzetta San Francesco 8; 🕒 9am-12.30pm & 3.30-6.30pm) for listings.

International Camping Olympia (☎ 0436 50 57; www.campingolympiacortina.it; per person/tent & car €7.50/9; 🕒 year-round) This is a large, well-set-up camping ground 3.5km north of Cortina at Fiames. Self-sufficient with shops, a bar and pizzeria, it's accessible by bus from Cortina.

Casa Tua (☎ 0436 22 78; www.casatuacortina.com; Via Zuel 100; per person €34-60; 💻) This friendly B&B is in a picturesque mountain-chalet 2.5km from Cortina. Rooms are monastic, but the down duvets will ensure a warm night. To get here from Cortina take the bus for Zuel.

SAD buses connect Cortina with Dobbiaco (€1, 45 minutes, three times daily), where you can change for Bolzano. ATVO runs a daily service to/from Venice (€10.60, 3½ hours, one daily).

CANAZEI

pop 1855

One of the best known resorts in the Val di Fassa, Canazei is a great spot for serious skiers. It has got 120km of downhill and cross-country runs and is linked to the challenging Sella Ronda ski network. There's even summer skiing on the Marmolada glacier, whose stunning 3342m-summit marks the highest point in the Dolomites.

Spend a cheap night at the Marmolada **camping ground** (☎ 0462 60 16 60; per person/tent €9.50/9.50; 🕒 year-round), or contact the **tourist office** (☎ 0462 60 11 13; www.fassa.com; Piazza Marconi 5; 🕒 8.30am-12.15pm & 3-6pm Mon-Sat, 10am-12.30pm Sun) for accommodation lists. The resort is accessible by Trentino Trasporti bus from Trent (€5.30, 2½ hours, three daily).

VAL GARDENA

Branching northeast off the Val di Fassa, the Val Gardena is a popular skiing area with great facilities and accessible prices. In summer, hikers head to the valley in throngs – to the Sella Group and the Alpe di Siusi for rugged, high altitude walks; to the Vallunga for more accessible family strolls.

The valley's main towns are Ortisei, Santa Cristina and Selva, all offering plenty of accommodation and easy access to runs. Further information is available online at www.gardena.org, or from the towns' tourist offices:

Ortisei (☎ 0471 79 63 28; Via Rezia 1; 🕒 8.30am-12.30pm & 2.30-6.30pm Mon-Sat, 10am-noon & 5-6.30pm Sun)
Santa Cristina (☎ 0471 79 30 46; Via Chemun 9; 🕒 8am-noon & 2.30-6.30pm Mon-Sat, 9.30am-noon Sun)
Selva (☎ 0471 79 51 22; Via Mé'isules 213; 🕒 8am-noon & 3-6.30pm Mon-Sat, 9am-noon & 5-6.30pm Sun)

The Val Gardena is accessible from Bolzano by SAD bus and from Canazei in summer.

SAN MARTINO DI CASTROZZA

pop 700

At the foot of the imposing Pale di San Martino range, San Martino di Castrozza acts as a gateway to the Parco Naturale Paneveggio-Pale di San Martino. The **tourist office** (☎ 0439 76 88 67; www.sanmartino.com; Via Passo Rolle 165; 🕑 9am-noon & 3-7pm Mon-Sat, 9.30am-12.30pm Sun) can provide skiing information and help with accommodation.

Hotel GarnìMadonna (☎ 0439 681 37; www.hotelmadonna.it; Via Passo Rolle 72; per person B&B €35-60) Housed in San Martino's former post house, this inviting three-star offers 25 comfortable rooms and some picturesque views of the surrounding summits.

Trentino Trasporti buses run to/from Trent (€5.60, 2½ hours, four daily).

TUSCANY

Blessed with beauty, wine and an unparalleled artistic legacy, Tuscany's a region that largely lives up to its press. Its fabled rolling landscape has long been considered the embodiment of rural chic, a favourite of holidaying PMs and retired advertising executives, while its cities harbour a significant slice of the world's Renaissance art. Florence, in itself, boasts more world-class art than many countries. Some people never venture beyond the region's crowded capital, but with some of Italy's most striking Gothic architecture (Siena) and the Leaning Tower of Pisa both an easy trip away, to do so would be a waste.

FLORENCE

pop 367,260

Of all Italy's cities few excite foreign visitors as much as Florence. Just as 18th- and 19th-century poets swooned at its beauty, so today planeloads of tourists pour in to admire its Renaissance riches. An essential stop on everyone's Italian itinerary, it's busy year-round and can be disheartening. Much of the city centre has been surrendered to tourism and in summer the heat, pollution and crowds can be stifling. That said, it remains a charismatic city you'd be sorry to miss. The list of its famous sons reads like a Renaissance Who's Who – under 'M' alone you'll find Medici, Machiavelli and Michelangelo – and its celebrated cityscape lingers in the memory long after you've left town.

History

Many hold that Florentia was founded by Julius Caesar around 59 BC, but archaeological evidence suggests an earlier village, possibly founded by the Etruscans around 200 BC. A rich merchant city by the 12th century, its golden age arrived in the 15th century. Under the Medici Lorenzo il Magnifico (1469–92), the city's cultural, artistic and political fecundity culminated in the Renaissance.

The Medici were succeeded in the 18th century by the French House of Lorraine, which ruled until 1860 when the city was incorporated into the kingdom of Italy. From 1865 to 1870, Florence was, in fact, capital of the fledgling kingdom.

During WWII, parts of the city were destroyed by bombing, including all of its bridges except for Ponte Vecchio. In 1966 a devastating flood destroyed or severely damaged many important works of art. More recently, in 1993, the Mafia exploded a massive car bomb, killing five people and destroying part of the Uffizi Gallery.

Orientation

From the main train station, Santa Maria Novella, it's a 550m walk along Via de' Panzani and Via de' Cerretani to the Duomo. From Piazza di San Giovanni, next to the Duomo, Via Roma leads down to Piazza

TOP FIVE TUSCAN TREASURES

- Visit **David**, Michelangelo's version of Goliath's nemesis, in the Galleria dell'Accademia, Florence (p774).
- Admire Botticelli's Renaissance masterpiece **La Nascita di Venere (Birth of Venus)** in the Galleria degli Uffizi, Florence (p772).
- See that it's no misnomer: the **Leaning Tower of Pisa** is way off vertical (p777).
- **Marvel at Siena's Duomo**, one of Italy's most beautiful Gothic cathedrals (p779).
- Take in the memorable panoramic view from San Gimignano's highest tower, **Torre Grossa** (p781).

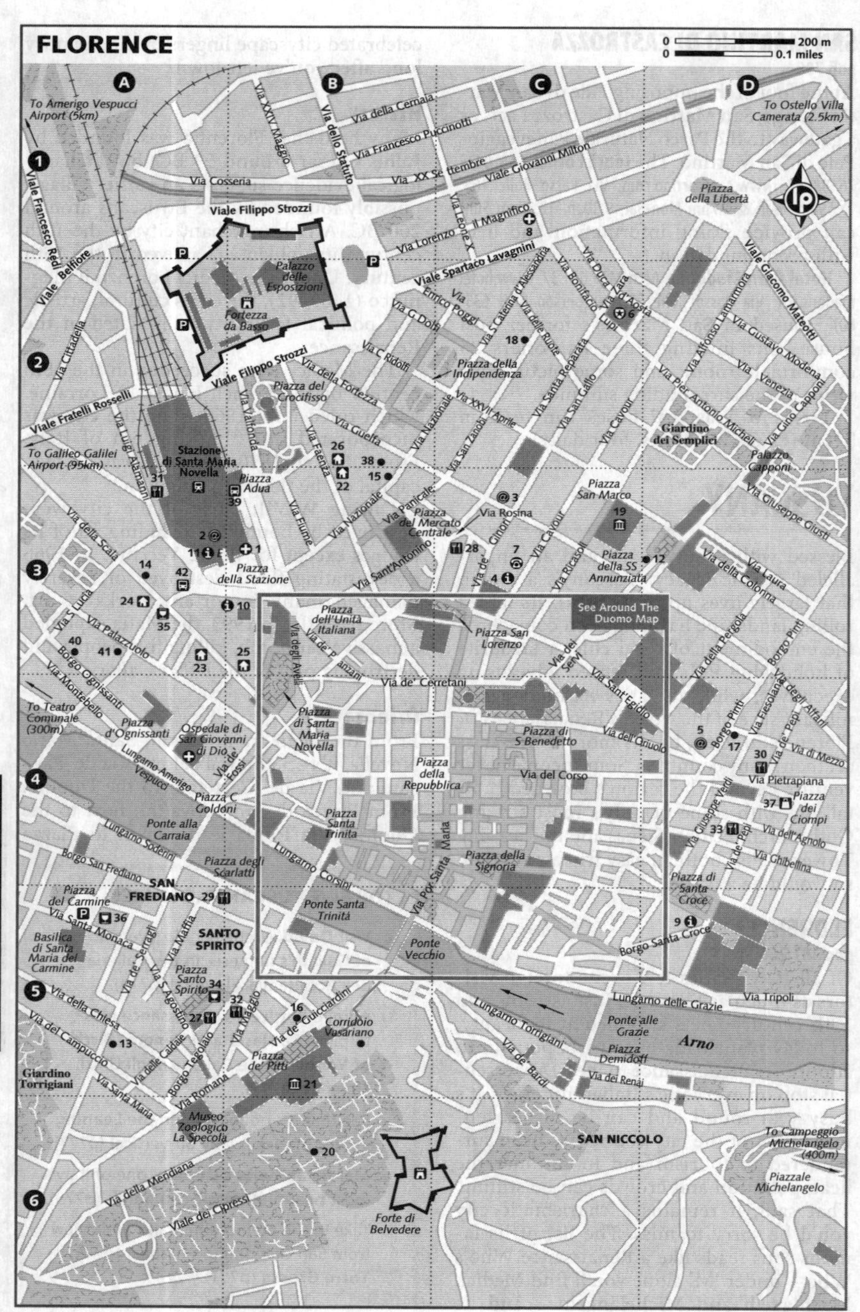
FLORENCE
0 200 m
0 0.1 miles
A
B
C
D
1
2
3
4
5
6
To Amerigo Vespucci Airport (5km)
To Ostello Villa Camerata (2.5km)
To Galileo Galilei Airport (95km)
To Teatro Comunale (300m)
To Campeggio Michelangelo (400m)
See Around The Duomo Map
Viale Francesco Redi
Viale Belfiore
Via XXIV Maggio
Via dello Statuto
Via della Cernaia
Via Francesco Puccinotti
Via Cosseria
Via XX Settembre
Viale Giovanni Milton
Viale Filippo Strozzi
Via Lorenzo il Magnifico
Via Leone X
Viale Spartaco Lavagnini
Palazzo delle Esposizioni
Fortezza da Basso
Piazza della Libertà
Viale Giacomo Matteotti
Via Cittadella
Viale Fratelli Rosselli
Via Luigi Alamanni
Via Valfonda
Piazza del Crocifisso
Via della Fortezza
Via C Ridolfi
Via G Dolfi
Via Enrico Poggi
Via S Caterina d'Alessandria
Via delle Ruote
Via Bonifacio Lupi
Via Duca d'Aosta
Via Santa Reparata
Via San Gallo
Piazza della Indipendenza
Via XXVII Aprile
Via Nazionale
Via San Zanobi
Via Cavour
Via Alfonso Lamarmora
Via Gustavo Modena
Via Venezia
Via Pier Antonio Micheli
Via Gino Capponi
Giardino dei Semplici
Palazzo Capponi
Via Giuseppe Giusti
Stazione di Santa Maria Novella
Piazza Adua
Via Faenza
Via Guelfa
Via Fiume
Via Panicale
Piazza del Mercato Centrale
Via Rosina
Via de' Ginori
Piazza San Marco
Via Ricasoli
Piazza della SS Annunziata
Via della Colonna
Via Laura
Via della Scala
Piazza della Stazione
Via Sant'Antonino
Piazza dell'Unità Italiana
Via degli Avelli
Via de' Panzani
Piazza San Lorenzo
Via de' Cerretani
Via dei Servi
Via Sant'Egidio
Via della Pergola
Borgo Pinti
Via degli Alfani
Via Fiesolana
Via S Lucia
Via Palazzuolo
Borgo Ognissanti
Via Montebello
Piazza d'Ognissanti
Ospedale di San Giovanni di Dio
Piazza di Santa Maria Novella
Piazza di S Benedetto
Via dell'Oriuolo
Piazza della Repubblica
Via del Corso
Via de' Pepi
Via di Mezzo
Via Pietrapiana
Piazza dei Ciompi
Lungarno Amerigo Vespucci
Via de' Fossi
Piazza C Goldoni
Piazza Santa Trinita
Via Giuseppe Verdi
Via dell'Agnolo
Via Ghibellina
Ponte alla Carraia
Lungarno Soderini
Borgo San Frediano
Piazza degli Scarlatti
Lungarno Corsini
Piazza della Signoria
Via Por Santa Maria
Piazza di Santa Croce
Piazza del Carmine
SAN FREDIANO
Via Santa Monaca
Basilica di Santa Maria del Carmine
Via Maffia
SANTO SPIRITO
Ponte Santa Trinità
Ponte Vecchio
Borgo Santa Croce
Via de' Serragli
Via S Agostino
Piazza Santo Spirito
Via Maggio
Via de' Guicciardini
Corridoio Vasariano
Lungarno delle Grazie
Via Tripoli
Via della Chiesa
Via del Campuccio
Via delle Caldaie
Borgo Tegolaio
Lungarno Torrigiani
Ponte alle Grazie
Arno
Piazza Demidoff
Via de' Bardi
Via dei Renai
Giardino Torrigiani
Via Santa Maria
Via Romana
Piazza de' Pitti
Museo Zoologico La Specola
SAN NICCOLO
Piazzale Michelangelo
Via della Meridiana
Viale dei Cipressi
Forte di Belvedere
ITALY

INFORMATION	Florence by Bike....18 C2	Ristorante Beccofino....29 A5
Farmacia Comunale....1 B3	Galleria d'Arte Moderna....(see 21)	Standa....30 D4
Internet Train....2 A3	Galleria del Costume....(see 21)	Supermarket....31 A3
Internet Train....3 C3	Galleria dell'Accademia....19 C3	Trattoria Casalinga....32 B5
Main Tourist Office....4 C3	Galleria Palatina....(see 21)	Trattoria Pane e Vino....33 D4
Netgate....5 D4	Giardino di Boboli....20 B6	
Police Station (Questura)....6 C2	Museo degli Argenti....(see 21)	**DRINKING**
Telecom Office....7 C3	Palazzo Pitti....21 B5	Cabiria....34 A5
Tourist Medical Service....8 C1		Joshua Tree Pub....35 A3
Tourist Office....9 D5	**SLEEPING**	La Dolce Vita....36 A5
Tourist Office....10 B3	Albergo Azzi....22 B3	
Train Information Office....11 A3	Albergo Margaret....23 A3	**SHOPPING**
Wash & Dry....12 D3	Albergo Montreal....24 A3	Flea Market....37 D4
Wash & Dry....13 A5	Hotel Aprile....25 B3	
Wash & Dry....14 A3	Hotel Marine....(see 22)	**TRANSPORT**
Wash & Dry....15 B3	Ostello Archi Rossi....26 B2	Alinari....38 B2
		ATAF Local Bus Station....39 B3
SIGHTS & ACTIVITIES	**EATING**	Avis....40 A3
Accademia Italiana....16 B5	Borgo Antico....27 A5	Hertz....41 A3
Cordon Bleu....17 D4	Mario's....28 C3	SITA Bus Station....42 A3

della Repubblica and continues as Via Calimala and Via Por Santa Maria to Ponte Vecchio.

Information

BOOKSHOPS

Feltrinelli International (Map p773; ☎ 055 21 95 24; Via Cavour 12r) Great selection of fiction and nonfiction in English.

Paperback Exchange (Map p773; ☎ 055 29 34 60; Via delle Oche 4r) New and second-hand books in English.

EMERGENCY

Police station (Questura; Map p770; ☎ 055 497 71; Via Zara 2)

INTERNET ACCESS

Internet Train (per hr about €4; 10am-8pm Mon-Fri, 11am-8pm Sat & Sun) Via dell'Oriuolo 40r (Map p773; ☎ 055 263 89 68); Via Guelfa 24a (Map p770; ☎ 055 21 47 94); Borgo San Jacopo 30r (Map p773; ☎ 055 265 79 35); beneath Stazione Santa Maria Novella (Map p770; ☎ 055 239 97 20) Opening times vary but are approximately as above.

Netgate (Map p770; ☎ 055 658 02 07; Via Sant' Egidio 12r; per hr €2; 9am-11.30pm)

LAUNDRY

Wash & Dry (☎ 800 23 11 72; 8kg wash/dry €3.50/3.50; 8am-10pm) Via Nazionale 129r (Map p770); Via del Sole 29r (Map p773); Via della Scala 52-54r (Map p770); Via dei Servi 105r (Map p770); Via de' Serragli 87r (Map p770)

MEDICAL SERVICES

Farmacia Comunale (Map p770; ☎ 055 28 94 35; Stazione di Santa Maria Novella; 24hr) Inside the train station.

Misericordia di Firenze (Map p773; ☎ 055 21 22 22; Vicolo degli Adimari 1, Piazza del Duomo; 2-6pm Mon-Fri Mar-Oct) Fee-paying medical service.

Tourist Medical Service (Map p770; ☎ 055 47 54 11; Via Lorenzo il Magnifico 59; 24hr)

MONEY

American Express (Map p773; ☎ 055 509 81; Via Dante Alighieri 22r; 9am-5.30pm Mon-Fri)

Travelex (Map p773; ☎ 055 28 97 81; Lungarno degli Acciaiuoli 6r; 9am-5.50pm Mon-Sat, 9.30am-4.50pm Sun)

POST

Post office (Map p773; Via Pellicceria 3)

TELEPHONE

Telecom office (Map p770; Via Cavour 21r; h7am-11pm) Public payphones.

TOURIST INFORMATION

Tourist offices Main office (Map p770; ☎ 055 29 08 32; www.firenzeturismo.it; Via Cavour 1r; 8.30am-6.30pm Mon-Sat, to 1.30pm Sun); Piazza della Stazione 4 (Map p770; ☎ 055 21 22 45; 8.30am-7pm Mon-Sat, to 2pm Sun); Borgo Santa Croce 29r (Map p770; ☎ 055 234 04 44; 9am-7pm Mon-Sat, to 2pm Sun); airport (☎ 055 31 58 74; 7.30am-11.30pm)

Sights & Activities

Sightseeing in Florence inevitably means time spent in queues. You'll never avoid them altogether, but by pre-booking museum tickets you'll save time. For €3 extra per museum you can book tickets for the Uffizi, Palazzo Pitti, Galleria dell'Accademia and Cappelle Medicee through **Firenze Musei** (☎ 055 29 48 83; www.firenzemusei.it; booking service 8.30am-6.30pm Mon-Fri, to 12.30pm Sat). Collect

ITALY

your ticket from the information desks at the Uffizi or Palazzo Pitti.

Entry to all state museums is free for EU citizens under 18 and over 65, and half-price for those between 18 and 25. To claim the discount you'll need your passport.

PIAZZA DEL DUOMO & AROUND

Pictures don't do justice to Florence's Gothic **Duomo** (Map p773; ☎ 055 230 28 85; 10am-5pm Mon-Wed & Fri, 10am-3.30pm Thu, 10am-4.45pm Sat, 1.30-4.45pm Sun) – while they reproduce the startling colours of the tiered red, green and white marble façade and the beautiful symmetry of the dome, they fail to give any sense of its size. One of the world's largest cathedrals – officially known as the Cattedrale di Santa Maria del Fiore – it was begun in 1294 by Sienese architect Arnolfo di Cambio and consecrated in 1436. Its most famous feature, the enormous octagonal **cupola** (dome; admission €6; 8.30am-7pm Mon-Fri, to 5.40pm Sat) was built by Brunelleschi after his design won a public competition in 1420. The interior is decorated with frescoes by Vasari and Zuccari, and the stained-glass windows are by Donatello, Paolo Uccello and Lorenzo Ghiberti. The façade is a 19th-century replacement of the unfinished original, pulled down in the 16th century.

Beside the cathedral, the 82m **campanile** (Map p773; admission €6; 8.30am-6.50pm) was begun by Giotto in 1334 and completed after his death by Andrea Pisano and Francesco Talenti. The views from the top make the 414-step climb worthwhile.

To the west, the Romanesque **battistero** (baptistry; Map p773; Piazza di San Giovanni; admission €3; noon-7pm Mon-Sat, 8.30am-2pm Sun) is one of the oldest buildings in Florence and it was here that Dante was baptised. Built on the site of a Roman temple between the 5th and 11th centuries, it's famous for its gilded-bronze doors, particularly Lorenzo Ghiberti's *Gate of Paradise*. Andrea Pisano's south door (1336) is the oldest.

GALLERIA DEGLI UFFIZI (UFFIZI GALLERY)

Home to the world's greatest collection of Italian Renaissance art, the **Galleria degli Uffizi** (Map p773; ☎ 055 238 86 51; www.uffizi.firenze.it; Piazza degli Uffizi 6; admission €6.50, audio guide €5; 8.15am-6.50pm Tue-Sun) attracts some 1.5 million visitors annually. They won't all be there when you visit, but unless you've booked a ticket (see Firenze Musei, p771), expect to queue.

The gallery houses the Medici family collection, bequeathed to the city in 1743 on the condition that it never leave the city. Highlights include *La Nascita di Venere* (Birth of Venus) and *Allegoria della Primavera* (Allegory of Spring) in the Botticelli Rooms (10 to 14); Leonardo da Vinci's *Annunciazione* (Annunciation; room 15); Michelangelo's *Tondo Doni* (Holy Family; room 25); and Titian's *Venere d'Urbino* (Venus of Urbino; room 28). Elsewhere you'll find works by Giotto and Cimabue, Filippo Lippi, Fra Angelico and Paolo Uccello, Raphael, Andrea del Sarto, Tintoretto and Caravaggio.

PIAZZA DELLA SIGNORIA

Traditional hub of Florence's political life, Piazza della Signoria is dominated by **Palazzo Vecchio** (Map p773; ☎ 055 276 82 24; admission €6; 9am-7pm Fri-Wed, to 2pm Thu), the historical seat of the Florentine government. Characterised by the 94m **Torre d'Arnolfo**, it was designed by Arnolfo di Cambio and built between 1298 and 1340. Visit the Michelozzo courtyard and the lavish upstairs apartments.

To the south, the famous **Loggia della Signoria** (Map p773) is a 14th-century sculpture showcase. The statue of *David* is a copy of Michelangelo's original, which stood here until 1873 but is now in the Galleria dell'Accademia (p774).

PONTE VECCHIO

Lined with jewellery shops, the 14th-century **Ponte Vecchio** (Map p773) was originally flanked by butchers' shops. But when the Medici built a corridor through the bridge to link Palazzo Pitti with Palazzo Vecchio, they ordered that the smelly butchers be replaced with goldsmiths.

PALAZZO PITTI

Built for the Pitti family, great rivals of the Medici, the vast 15th-century **Palazzo Pitti** (Map p770; ☎ 055 238 86 14; Piazza de' Pitti) was bought by the Medici in 1549 and became their family residence. Today it houses four museums, of which the **Galleria Palatina** (Palatine Gallery; Map p770; ☎ 055 238 86 14; admission incl Royal Apartments €6.50; 8.15am-6.50pm Tue-Sun) is the most important. Works

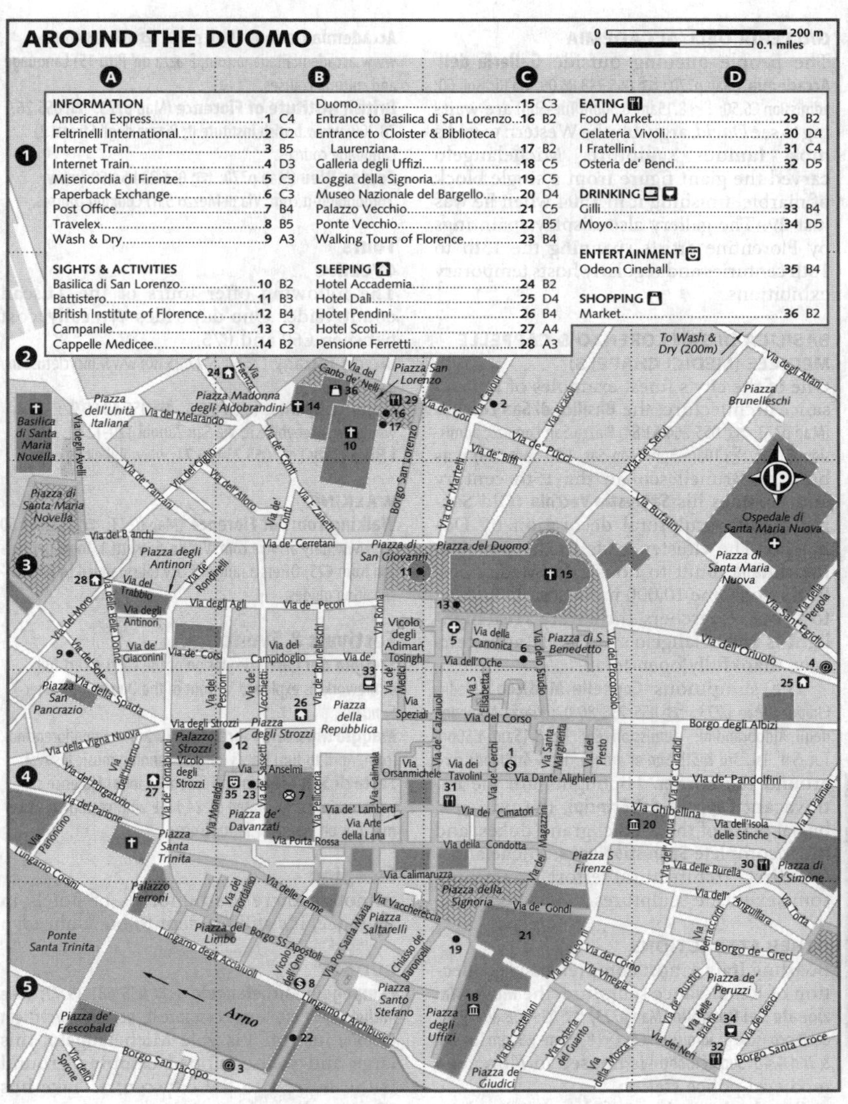

by Raphael, Filippo Lippi, Titian and Rubens adorn lavishly decorated rooms, culminating in the royal apartments. The other museums are the **Museo degli Argenti** (Silver Museum; Map p770; ☎ 055 238 87 09; admission €4; 🕑 8.15am-4.30pm Tue-Sun, 2nd & 3rd Mon each month); the **Galleria d'Arte Moderna** (Modern Art Gallery; Map p770; ☎ 055 238 86 16; admission €5; 🕑 8.15am-6.50pm Tue-Sat); and the **Galleria del Costume** (Costume Gallery; Map p770; ☎ 055 238 87 13; admission €5; 🕑 8.15am-1.50pm Tue-Sat).

Rising above the palace, the Renaissance **Giardino di Boboli** (Boboli Gardens; Map p770; admission €4; 🕑 8.15am-7.30pm Jun-Aug, to 6.30pm Apr, May, Sep & Oct, to 5.30pm Mar, to 4.30pm Nov-Feb) is well worth a wander.

GALLERIA DELL'ACCADEMIA

The people queuing outside **Galleria dell' Accademia** (Map p770; ☎ 055 238 86 09; Via Ricasoli 60; admission €6.50; 8.15am-6.50pm Tue-Sun) are waiting to see *David*, arguably the Western world's most famous sculpture. Michelangelo carved the giant figure from a single block of marble, finishing it in 1504 when he was just 29. The gallery also displays paintings by Florentine artists spanning the 13th to 16th centuries and regularly hosts temporary exhibitions.

BASILICA DI SAN LORENZO & CAPPELLE MEDICEE (MEDICI CHAPELS)

One of the city's finest examples of Renaissance architecture, the **Basilica di San Lorenzo** (Map p773; ☎ 055 264 51 84; Piazza San Lorenzo; admission €2.50; 10am-5pm Mon-Sat, 1.30-5pm Sun) was built by Brunelleschi in the 15th century and includes his **Sagrestia Vecchia** (Old Sacristy), with sculptural decoration by Donatello. The cloister leads to the **Biblioteca Laurenziana**, built to house the Medici collection of some 10,000 manuscripts. Closed to all but researchers, the library's real highlight is Michelangelo's vestibule and stairway, thankfully open to all.

The sumptuous **Cappelle Medicee** (Medici Chapels; Map p773; ☎ 055 238 86 02; Piazza Madonna degli Aldobrandini; admission €6; 8.15am-4.50pm Tue-Sat, 1st, 3rd & 5th Sun of month, 1st & 4th Mon) are around the corner. Highlights are the extravagant **Cappella dei Principi**, the principal burial place of the Medici grand dukes, and the incomplete **Sagrestia Nuova**, Michelangelo's first architectural effort containing some exquisite sculptures.

OTHER ATTRACTIONS

Boasting Italy's most comprehensive collection of Renaissance sculpture, the **Museo Nazionale del Bargello** (Map p773; ☎ 055 238 86 06; Via del Proconsolo 4; admission €4; 8.15am-1.50pm Tue-Sat & 2nd & 4th Sun of month) is housed in Florence's medieval police station.

For the best views of the city, head up to **Piazzale Michelangelo**, a steep 600m walk from the southern bank of the Arno.

Courses

Florence is well set up with schools offering courses in language, cooking, art and history. The following are well-established institutions:

Accademia Italiana (Map p770; ☎ 055 28 46 16; www.accademiaitaliana.com; Piazza de' Pitti 15) Language and cultural courses.

British Institute of Florence (Map p773; ☎ 055 267 78 200; www.british institute.it; Piazza degli Strozzi 2) Language courses.

Cordon Bleu (Map p770; ☎ 055 234 54 68; www.cordonbleu-it.com; Via di Mezzo 55r) Cooking courses.

Tours

CYCLING

The following offer tours of the Tuscan countryside. One-day rides typically cost between €60 and €75.

Bicycle Tuscany (☎ 055 22 25 80; www.bicycletuscany.com)

Florence by Bike (Map p770; ☎ 055 48 89 92; www.florencebybike.it; Via San Zanobi 120-122r)

I Bike Italy (☎ 055 234 23 71; www.ibikeitaly.com)

WALKING

Walking Tours of Florence (Map p773; ☎ 055 264 50 33; www.italy.artviva.com; Via de' Sassetti 1; tours per person from €25) Offers a range of city tours, all led by English-speaking guides.

Festivals & Events

Scoppio del Carro (Explosion of the Cart) A cart full of fireworks is exploded in front of the Duomo on Easter Sunday.

Maggio Musicale Fiorentino (www.maggiofiorentino.com; April to Jun) Italy's longest-running music festival.

Festa di San Giovanni (Feast of St John) Florence's patron saint is celebrated on 24 June with costumed soccer matches on Piazza di Santa Croce.

Sleeping

Although there are hundreds of hotels in Florence, it's still prudent to book ahead.

BUDGET

Campeggio Michelangelo (☎ 055 681 19 77; Viale Michelangelo 80; www.ecvacanze.it; per person/car/tent €10/6/6) Just off Piazzale Michelangelo, this large and well-equipped camping ground is the nearest to the city centre. Take bus 13 from the train station.

Ostello Villa Camerata (☎ 055 60 14 51; firenze@ostellionline.org; Viale Augusto Righi 2-4; dm incl breakfast €17.50; P) Housed in a 17th-century villa 4km northeast of the train station and set in its own park, Florence's HI hostel has 322 beds in various room combinations. Take bus 17, 17B or 17C from the train station. Reservations are essential in summer.

Ostello Archi Rossi (Map p770; ☎ 055 29 08 04; ostelloarchirossi@hotmail.com; Via Faenza 94r; dm incl breakfast €18-26; ⊠ 🖳) A faux-frescoed private hostel, the Archi is a busy, boisterous backpacker pad. Near the train station, it's well equipped with washing machines, microwaves and snack dispensers.

Hotel Dalì (Map p773; ☎ 055 234 07 06; www.hoteldali.com; Via dell'Oriuolo 17; d €80, s/d with shared bathroom €40/60; P) Escape the crowds at Florence's best budget hotel. Owners Marco and Samanta go out of their way to ensure a pleasant stay, while the spotless, sunny rooms provide a homely retreat from the ever-present masses down the road at the Duomo.

Albergo Margaret (Map p770; ☎ 055 21 01 38; www.dormireintoscana.it/margaret; Via della Scala 25; d €90, s/d with shared bathroom €60/70; ⊠ ❄) A warm welcome and pristine, peach-coloured rooms await guests here. One of the best budget choices on Via della Scala, it offers comfort and muted style, for which you could easily pay more.

MIDRANGE

Albergo Montreal (Map p770; ☎ 055 238 23 31; www.hotelmontreal.com; Via della Scala 43; d €130, s/d with shared bathroom €60/80; ❄) This is a slick, modern one-star with smart, if soulless, rooms and a range of mod cons (satellite TV, air-con) exceptional for the category. A further plus is the sound-proofing that ensures a good night's sleep.

Hotel Scoti (Map p773; ☎ 055 29 21 28; www.hotelscoti.com; Via de' Tornabuoni 7; s/d €70/105) On Florence's smartest shopping strip, the friendly Scoti is a gem. After a sing-along around the piano in the communal sitting room, adjourn to your airy room, decorated with simple rustic furniture.

Albergo Azzi (Map p770; ☎ 055 21 38 06; www.hotelazzi.it; Via Faenza 56; s/d incl breakfast €70/140, with shared bathroom €60/90) Heavy wood furniture, books and assorted antiques lend the Azzi an air of bohemian charm. Rooms are clean and comfortable; those facing away from Via Faenza are quieter. On the 2nd floor, the **Hotel Marine** (☎ 055 26 42 51; d €70-110; ❄) is run by the same people.

Hotel Accademia (Map p773; ☎ 055 29 34 51; www.hotelaccademiafirenze.com; Via Faenza 7; s/d incl breakfast €85/150; ⊠ ❄) The Accademia's grand staircase, magnificent stained-glass doors and carved wooden ceilings are a throwback to a more elegant age. Rooms, decked out in parquet and tasteful fabrics, are more modest, if no less appealing.

Other recommendations:

Pensione Ferretti (Map p773; ☎ 055 238 13 28; www.emmeti.it/hferretti/index.uk.html; Via delle Belle Donne; s/d incl breakfast €65/102, with shared bathroom €52/82; 🖳) Family-run *pensione* with basic, clean rooms.

Hotel Pendini (Map p773; ☎ 055 21 11 70; www.florenceitaly.net; Via degli Strozzi 2; s/d incl breakfast €110/150; ❄ 🖳) Antique-clad three-star overlooking Piazza della Repubblica.

TOP END

Hotel Aprile (Map p770; ☎ 055 21 62 37; www.hotelaprile.it; Via della Scala 6; s/d incl breakfast €150/250; P ⊠ ❄ 🖳) Housed in a Medici palace, complete with brick-vaulted corridors, this stylish hotel is a worthwhile indulgence. Rooms vary – some have four-poster beds, others frescoes – but all are attractive. There's also a gorgeous courtyard garden.

Eating

Classic Tuscan dishes include *ribollita*, a heavy vegetable soup, *cannellini* (white beans) and *bistecca alla Fiorentina* (Florentine steak). Chianti is the local tipple.

RESTAURANTS

Trattoria Pane e Vino (Map p770; ☎ 055 24 38 03; Via dell'Agnolo 105; 1st/2nd courses €4/7; 🕑 closed Sun dinner) For filling home-style food, this earthy trattoria does the job. The food – steaming bowls of *ribollita* and slabs of grilled meat – is as authentic as the dusty wine bottle décor.

Mario's (Map p770; Via Rosina 2r; 1st/2nd courses €4/8; 🕑 lunch Mon-Sat) Lunch at Mario's is fun, filling and frenetic. A noisy, cheerful place full of market workers and tourists, it serves hearty pastas and meaty main courses at prices rare for such a central spot.

Trattoria Casalinga (Map p770; ☎ 055 21 86 24; Via dei Michelozzi 9r; 1st/2nd courses €5/7; 🕑 Mon-Sat) The Casalinga is a brash, no-frills trat that offers a workaday menu of pasta staples and simple meat dishes. It's always full so is better suited to a swift fill-up than a long, lingering lunch.

Borgo Antico (Map p770; ☎ 055 21 04 37; Piazza Santo Spirito 6r; pizza/salad/2nd courses €7/7/12) On a vibrant piazza, this trendy eatery is great for whiling away a summer evening over a pizza and glass of something cool. Select from the menu of leafy salads, wood-fired pizzas and Tuscan specialities.

Osteria de' Benci (Map p773; ☎ 055 234 49 23; Via de' Benci 13r; 1st/2nd courses €9/13; 🕑 Mon-Sat) In-the-know diners flock to this modish *osteria* – raspberry-coloured walls and a wood-vaulted ceiling – for its convivial atmosphere and consistently good food. If it's on, the *carpaccio* (thinly shredded raw meat) is excellent.

Ristorante Beccofino (Map p770; ☎ 055 29 00 76; Piazza degli Scarlatti 1r; 1st/2nd courses €10/20; 🕑 closed Mon) The metropolitan décor of this innovative restaurant-cum-wine bar wouldn't look out of place in London or New York. Serving *nouvelle* takes on Tuscan cuisine, it boasts an impressive wine list and snazzy lavs.

QUICK EATS

Gelateria Vivoli (Map p773; ☎ 055 29 23 34; Via dell'Isola delle Stinche 7) Ice-cream aficionados rate the *gelati* here the city's best. Flavours range from orange chocolate to fig and walnut.

I Fratellini (Map p773; ☎ 055 239 60 96; Via dei Cimatori 38r; panini €2-3) Although no more than a hole-in-the-wall *panino* bar, I Fratellini is a city institution. Locals horde to the tiny counter for fresh-filled *panini* ready in the twinkle of an eye.

SELF-CATERING

Fresh produce is available at the central **food market** (Map p770; Piazza San Lorenzo; 🕑 7am-2pm Mon-Sat). Alternatively, there's a **supermarket** (Map p770; Stazione di Santa Maria Novella) at the train station, and a **Standa** (Map p770; Via Pietrapiana 94) east of Piazza del Duomo.

Drinking

Cabiria (Map p770; ☎ 055 21 53 72; Piazza Santo Spirito 4/r; 🕑 closed Tue) By day a pleasant enough café, Cabiria morphs into a cool bar at night. Its understated vibe lends itself perfectly to hours of languid people watching.

Gilli (Map p773; ☎ 055 21 38 96; Piazza della Repubblica 39r; 🕑 Wed-Sun) The city's grandest café, Gilli has been serving tourists with overpriced coffee since 1733.

Joshua Tree Pub (Map p770; Via della Scala 37r; happy-hr pint €3; 🕑 4pm-1am, happy hour 4-9pm) This thumping pub rocks, more often to the Beta Band than the Pogues, but the Guinness is still great. It's smoky, rowdy and totally addictive.

La Dolce Vita (Map p770; ☎ 055 28 45 95; Piazza del Carmine 6/r; 🕑 5pm-2am Tue-Sun) A swish hipster magnet favoured by cocktail-sipping fashionistas, La Dolce Vita gets very crowded at weekends.

Moyo (Map p773; ☎ 055 247 97 38; Via de' Benci 23r) A mixed crowd of sharp locals and foreign students drink at this funky modern bar. It's good for an aperitif to a background of upbeat jazz.

Entertainment

Florence's definitive monthly listings guide *Firenze Spettacolo* is sold at newsstands (€1.75). *Florence Concierge Information,* a bi-monthly city guide, runs a good what's-on website: www.florence-concierge.it.

Concerts, opera and dance are performed year-round at the **Teatro Comunale** (☎ 800 11 22 11; Corso Italia 16), which is also the venue for events organised by the Maggio Musicale Fiorentino (see Festivals & Events, p774).

English-language films are screened at the **Odeon Cinehall** (Map p773; ☎ 055 21 40 68; www.cinehall.it, in Italian; Piazza Strozzi; tickets €7.50) on Monday, Tuesday and Thursday.

Shopping

Shopping is concentrated between the Duomo and the Arno, with boutiques along Via Roma, Via de' Calzaiuoli and Via Por Santa Maria. For the big fashion guns, head to Via de' Tornabuoni and Via della Vigna Nuova.

Just north of the Duomo, the **market** (Map p773; Piazza San Lorenzo; 🕑 Mon-Sat) is the place for leather goods, clothing and jewellery, although quality and prices vary. For bric-a-brac and the occasional antique, head for the **flea market** (Map p770; Piazza dei Ciompi; 🕑 daily) north of Piazza di Santa Croce.

Getting There & Away

AIR

The main airport serving Florence is Pisa's **Galileo Galilei airport** (PSA; ☎ 050 50 07 07; www.pisa-airport.com). There's also a small city airport 5km north of Florence, **Amerigo Vespucci** (FLR; ☎ 055 37 34 98; www.aeroporto.firenze.it).

BUS

The **SITA bus station** (Map p770; ☎ 800 37 37 60; www.sita-on-line-it, in Italian; Via Santa Caterina da Siena 17) is just south of the train station. SITA buses leave for Siena (€6.50, 1¼ hours, hourly) and, via Poggibonsi, San Gimignano (€5.90, 1¼ hours, 14 daily).

CAR & MOTORCYCLE
Florence is connected by the A1 autostrada to Bologna and Milan in the north and Rome and Naples to the south. The A11 links Florence with Pisa and the coast, and a *superstrada* (expressway) joins the city to Siena.

TRAIN
Florence is well connected by train. There are regular services to/from Pisa (Regional, €5.10, 1¼ hours, every 20 minutes), Rome (€24.95, 2½ hours, half hourly), Bologna (€10.75, one hour, every 20 minutes) and Milan (Eurostar, €28.95, 2¾ hours, 22 daily). For Venice, change at Bologna. Check times at the **train information office** (Map p770; ☎ 7am-9pm) in the station's main foyer.

Getting Around
TO/FROM THE AIRPORT
Terravision (☎ 06 321 20 011; www.terravision.it) runs a bus service between the train station and Galileo Galilei airport (€7.50, one hour 10 minutes, 12 daily). Otherwise there are regular trains (€5.10, 1½ hours, hourly between 6.37am and 8.37pm).

A **Vola in Bus** (☎ 800 42 45 00; www.ataf.net) shuttle (€4, 25 minutes, half-hourly 5.30am to 11pm) connects Amerigo Vespucci airport with the SITA bus station.

BICYCLE
Alinari (Map p770; ☎ 055 28 05 00; www.alinarirental.com; Via Guelfa 85r; 🕑 9.30am-1pm & 2.45-6pm Mon-Sat, 10am-1pm Sun) rent out bikes from €7/12/24 for five hours/day/weekend.

BUS
ATAF (Map p770; ☎ 800 42 45 00; www.ataf.net) buses service the city centre and Fiesole, a small town in the hills 8km northeast of Florence. The most useful terminal is just outside the train station's eastern exit. Take bus 7 for Fiesole and 13 for Piazzale Michelangelo. Tickets (one/three/24 hours €1/1.80/4.50) are sold at tobacconists and newsstands.

CAR & MOTORCYCLE
Much of the city centre is restricted to traffic so the best advice is to leave your car in a car park and use public transport. Details of car parks are available from **Firenze Parcheggi** (☎ 055 500 19 94; www.firenzeparcheggi.it, in Italian). If your car is towed away, call ☎ 055 78 38 82.

To rent, try **Hertz** (Map p770; ☎ 199 11 22 11; Via M Finiguerra 33r) or **Avis** (☎ 199 10 01 33; Borgo Ognissanti 128r).

PISA
pop 88,990

One of Italy's most recognisable monuments, the Leaning Tower of Pisa (Torre Pendente) is a genuinely shocking sight. Veering upwards at an alarming angle, it stands in permanent defiance of the laws of gravity. Tower aside, Pisa is an unassuming university town that while pleasant enough, won't hinder you long.

Pisa's golden age came in the 12th and 13th centuries when it was a maritime power rivalling Genoa and Venice. It was eventually defeated by the Genoese in 1284 and, in 1406, fell to Florence. Under the Medici, the arts and sciences flourished and Galileo Galilei (1564–1642) taught at the university.

Orientation & Information
From Piazza Vittorio Emanuele II, just north of the train station, the Leaning Tower is a straightforward 1.5km walk – follow Corso Italia to the Arno, cross the river and continue down Borgo Stretto. At the end of Via G Carducci, bear left down Via Cardinale Pietro Maffi. You could also take bus 1 from the train station.

For city information ask at one of the three **tourist offices**: city centre (☎ 050 4 22 91; Piazza Vittorio Emanuele II 16; 🕑 9am-7pm Mon-Fri, to 1pm Sun); Leaning Tower (☎ 050 56 04 64; Piazza del Duomo 1; 🕑 9am-6pm Mon-Sat, 10.30am-4.30pm Sun); airport (☎ 050 50 37 00; 🕑 10.30am-4.30pm & 6-10pm daily).

Go online at **Internet Planet** (☎ 050 83 07 02; Piazza Cavallotti 3-4; per hr €3.10; 🕑 10am-midnight Mon-Fri, to 8pm Sat, 2.30pm-midnight Sun).

Sights
The entry times listed here are those in force at the time of research, but they change frequently – call ☎ 050 387 22 10 or log onto www.opapisa.it for confirmation.

Pisans claim that the **Campo dei Miracoli** (Field of Miracles) is among the most beautiful squares in the world. Certainly, the immaculate walled lawns provide a

ITALY

gorgeous setting for the cathedral, baptistry and tower; on the other hand, few places boast so many tat-waving hawkers.

Forming the centrepiece of the Campo's Romanesque trio, the candy-striped **cathedral** (admission €2; 10am-1pm & 2-5pm Mon-Sat, 2-5pm Sun), begun in 1063, has a graceful tiered façade and cavernous interior. The transept's bronze doors are by Bonanno Pisano, but the 16th-century entrance doors are by Giambologna.

To the west, the cupcake-like **battistero** (baptistry; admission €5; 10am-5pm) was started in 1153 and completed by Nicola and Giovanni Pisano in 1260. Inside, note Nicola Pisano's beautiful pulpit.

But it's to the campanile, better known as the **Leaning Tower** (Torre Pendente; www.opapisa.it; admission €15; 9.30am-5pm), that all eyes are drawn. Bonanno Pisano began building in 1173, but almost immediately his plans came a cropper in a layer of shifting soil. Only three of the tower's seven tiers were completed before it started tilting – continuing at a rate of about 1mm per year. By 1990 the lean had reached 5.5 degrees – a tenth of a degree beyond the critical point established by computer models. Stability was finally ensured in 1998 when a combination of biased weighting and soil drilling forced the tower into a safer position. Today it's almost 4.1m off the perpendicular.

Visits are limited to groups of 30; entry times are staggered and queuing is predictably inevitable.

Flanking the Campo, the beautiful **Camposanto cemetery** (admission €5; 10am-5pm) is said to contain soil shipped from Calvary during the crusades – soil that's reputed to reduce cadavers to skeletons within days.

Sleeping

Ostello della Gioventù (☎/fax 050 89 06 22; Via Pietrasantina 15; dm €15) In open country about 1km north of the Leaning Tower, this no-frills private hostel offers Pisa's cheapest beds. Take bus 1 from the train station and make sure you've got some insect repellent – mosquitoes are a nuisance in summer.

Hotel Francesco (☎ 050 55 54 53; www.hotelfrancesco.com; Via Santa Maria 129; s/d €90/100;) The best of the hotels lining busy Via Santa Maria (just off Campo dei Miracoli), the small family-run Francesco offers a warm welcome and bright, mod-conned rooms. It also hires out bikes (€3 per hour).

Hotel di Stefano (☎ 050 55 35 59; www.hoteldistefano.pisa.it; Via Sant'Apollonia 35-37; s/d €100/120, with shared bathroom €65/80;) There are three reasons to stay at this friendly three-star: its location – a quiet backstreet in the medieval quarter; its smart, simple rooms; and its terrace with views of the tower's top half.

Eating

Fried Fish (☎ 050 58 10 11; Via Cavalca 11; snacks €3-5) This is a great little takeaway specialising in delicious fried nibbles. The mixed platter (€5) includes fried onions, mozzarella, potatoes, octopus, prawns and bread. Perfect for eating on the hoof.

Antica Trattoria il Campano (☎ 050 58 05 85; Via Cavalca 19; 1st/2nd courses from €6/11; closed Wed) An atmospheric trattoria serving outstanding regional fare in a medieval setting, the house speciality here is the meal-in-itself *Tagliere del Re* ('cut of the king') starter – a combo of 12 antipasti.

Trattoria La Buca (☎ 050 56 06 60; Via Gallit Tussi 6; pizza/lst/2nd courses €6/7/11; closed Fri) Homestyle Tuscan grub is what they do best at this laid-back trattoria. Portions are filling, prices are reasonable and the atmosphere is unhurried.

Getting There & Away

The city's **Galileo Galilei airport** (PSA; ☎ 050 50 07 07; www.pisa-airport.com) is linked to the centre by train (€1.10, five minutes, 15 daily), or by bus 1.

Lazzi (☎ 050 462 88; www.lazzi.it, in Italian) buses depart from the airport to Florence (€11.40, two hours, hourly) via Lucca.

Regular trains run to Florence (Regional, €5.10, 1¼ hours, every 20 minutes), Rome (€26, three to four hours, 15 daily) and Genoa (€13.90, two hours, half-hourly).

SIENA

pop 54,370

Famous for its annual horse race (Il Palio), Siena is one of Italy's most enchanting medieval towns. Its walled centre, a beautifully preserved warren of dark lanes punctuated by Gothic *palazzi*, piazzas and eye-catching churches, is a lovely place to get lost. The action centres on Piazza del Campo (known as Il Campo), the sloping square that serves

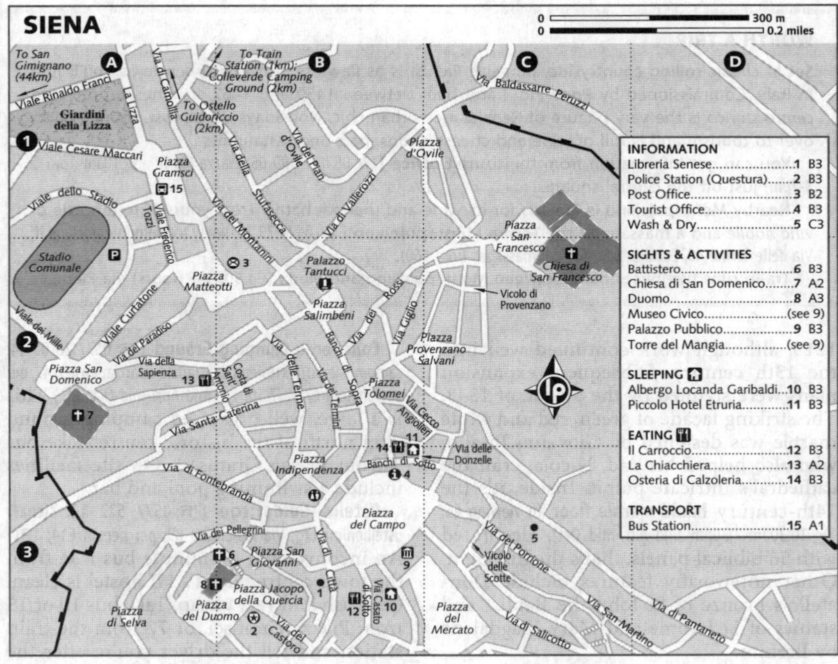

as a communal sunbed to scores of day-trippers.

According to legend, Siena was founded by the sons of Remus. In the Middle Ages its dramatic rise caused political and cultural friction with Florence. Painters of the Sienese School (most notably the 13th to 15th centuries) produced significant works of art, and the city was home to saints Catherine and Benedict.

Orientation

From the train station take bus 8, 9 or 10 to Piazza Gramsci, from where Il Campo is a short, signposted walk away. The centre's main streets – the Banchi di Sopra, Via di Città and Banchi di Sotto – curve around Il Campo.

Visitors' cars aren't permitted in the centre.

Information

Libreria Senese (☎ 0577 28 08 45; Via di Città 62-66) Bookshop with selection of English books and newspapers.

Police station (Questura; ☎ 0577 20 11 11; Via del Castoro 23)

Post office (Piazza Matteotti 1)

Tourist office (☎ 0577 28 05 51; www.terresiena.it; Piazza del Campo 56; 9am-7pm)

Wash & Dry (Via di Pantaneto 38; wash/dry €3.50/3.50; 8am-10pm)

Sights

Ever since the 14th century, the slanting, shell-shaped **Piazza del Campo** has been the city's civic centre. Forming the base of the piazza, the **Palazzo Pubblico** (Palazzo Comunale) is a magnificent example of Sienese Gothic architecture. Soaring above it, the 102m **Torre del Mangia** (admission €6; 10am-7pm mid-Mar–end Oct, to 4pm Nov–mid-Mar) was completed in 1297. On the ground floor, the **Museo Civico** (☎ 0577 22 62 30; admission €7; 10am-7pm mid-Mar–end Oct, to 5.30pm Nov–mid-Feb, to 6.30pm mid-Feb–mid-Mar) houses a rich collection of Sienese art.

The spectacular **Duomo** (☎ 0577 473 21; admission €3; 10.30am-7.30pm Mon-Sat, 1.30-5.30pm Sun Mar-May, 10.30am-8pm Mon-Sat, 1.30-6.30pm Sun Jun-Aug, 10.30am-7.30pm daily Sep-Oct, 10.30am-6pm Mon-Sat Nov-Feb) is another Gothic masterpiece. Begun in 1196 it was completed in

ITALY

WORTH A TRIP

Set in classic rolling countryside, pint-size Pienza is as flawless a medieval centre as you'll find in Italy. Commissioned by Pope Pio II and built between 1459 and 1462, its Unesco-protected *centro storico* is the very picture of Renaissance urban-chic. Nowadays it's almost entirely given over to tourism and is full of wine and cheese shops, bars and restaurants.

You can get information from the **tourist office** (☎ 0578 74 99 05; Piazza Pio II; 10am-1pm & 3-7pm) just off the central square.

Nearby Montepulciano is famous for its wine and thermal baths. Treat yourself to a bottle of *vino nobile* and a massage at the **Terme Montepulciano** (☎ 0578 79 11; www.termemontepulciano.it; Via delle Terme 46, Localita Sant'Albino; massages from €60).

Tra-in runs five buses daily between Montepulciano and Siena (€4.50, 1¾ hours) via Pienza.

1215, although work continued well into the 13th century. Subsequent expansion plans were stymied by the plague of 1348. The striking façade of green, red and white marble was designed by Giovanni Pisano, who also helped his dad, Nicola, craft the cathedral's intricate pulpit. Inside, it's the 14th-century **inlaid-marble floor** (fl viewing €6; 10.30am-7.30pm mid-Jun–mid Oct), decorated with 56 biblical panels, that's the highlight. Other noteworthy features include Donatello's bronze of St John the Baptist and statues of St Jerome and Mary Magdalene by Bernini.

North of the cathedral and down a flight of stairs, the **battistero** (baptistry; Piazza San Giovanni; admission €3; 9am-8pm Jun-Aug, to 7pm Sep-May) has a Gothic façade and a rich interior of 15th-century frescoes.

On the western edge of the walled city, the **Chiesa di San Domenico** (Piazza San Domenico 1; admission free; 7.30am-1pm & 3-6.30pm) is the last resting place of St Catherine's head. You'll find it above the altar in the Cappella di Santa Caterina. Her thumb, incidentally, is in a small window box to the right of the chapel.

Festivals & Events

Siena's great annual event is the **Palio** (2 July & 16 August), a pageant culminating in a bareback horse race round Il Campo. The city is divided into 17 *contrade* (districts), of which 10 are chosen annually to compete for the *palio* (silk banner). The only rule in the three-lap race is that jockeys can't tug the reins of other horses.

Sleeping

It's always advisable to book in advance, but for August and the Palio, it's essential.

Colleverde Camping Ground (☎ 0577 28 00 44; campingsiena@terresiena.it; Strada di Scacciapensieri 47; per person/tent €7.50/7.50; mid-Apr–mid-Oct;) This is a large, well-organised camping ground 2km north of the historic centre (take bus 3 from Piazza Gramsci). On-site facilities include a swimming pool and bar.

Ostello Guidoriccio (☎ 0577 522 12; siena@ostellionline.org; Via Fiorentina 89; per person €14; P) An inconvenient 20-minute bus ride from the town centre, Siena's HI hostel is clean, quiet-ish and very cheap. Take bus 10 or 15 from Piazza Gramsci, or 77 from the train station and tell the driver you're after the *ostello* (hostel).

Piccolo Hotel Etruria (☎ 0577 28 80 88; www.hoteletruria.com; Via delle Donzelle 3; s/d €53/83, s with shared bathroom €48;) A friendly family-run *pensione* not yards from Il Campo, the Etruria offers nine bright, basic rooms. There's a 1am curfew, but it shouldn't be a problem as Siena rarely kicks on that long.

Albergo Locanda Garibaldi (☎ 0577 28 42 04; Via Giovanni Dupré 18; d/tr/q €75/95/110, set menu €20) Smarter inside than out, this hotel is full of character and exceptional value for money. Above the trattoria of the same name, there are seven charming rooms with parquet, low wood-beamed ceilings and wrought iron bedsteads.

Eating

La Chiacchiera (☎ 0577 28 06 31; Costa di Sant'Antonio 4; 1st/2nd courses €4/6) With its rustic wooden tables and stone walls, this is an atmospheric spot. The food is seasonal, earthy and filling – try the *pici boscaiola* (thick spaghetti with mushrooms) for some deep autumnal flavours. In summer, there is outdoor seating on a quiet pedestrian street.

Osteria di Calzoleria (☎ 0577 28 90 10; Via di Calzoleria 12; 1st/2nd courses €7/11; ⌚ dinner) On a winding street meandering off the Campo, this is a lively place to sit down to a steaming bowl of *ribollita* and other regional classics; it also serves excellent *contorni* (side dishes), ideal for vegetarians.

Il Carroccio (☎ 0577 411 65; Via Casato di Sotto 32; 1st/2nd courses from €7/12; ⌚ closed Tue dinner & Wed) Recommended by the prestigious Slow Food movement (always a good sign), Il Carroccio specialises in traditional Sienese cooking. Staples include *pici* (thick spaghetti) and succulent *bistecca di chianina alla brace* (grilled steak).

Getting There & Away

Siena is not on a main train line so it's easier to take a bus. From the bus station on Piazza Gramsci, **Tra-in** (☎ 0577 20 42 46) and SITA buses run to/from Florence (€6.50, 1¼ hours, hourly) and San Gimignano (€5.20, 1¼ hours, 14 daily), either direct or via Poggibonsi.

Sena (☎ 0577 28 32 03; www.sena.it) operates services to/from Rome (€17.50, three hours, 11 daily).

Both Tra-in and Sena have ticket offices underneath the piazza.

SAN GIMIGNANO

pop 7100

Dubbed the medieval Manhattan, San Gimignano is a tiny hilltop town deep in the Tuscan countryside. A mecca for day-trippers, it owes its nickname to the 11th-century towers that soar above its pristine *centro storico*. Originally 72 were built as monuments to the town's wealth but only 13 remain. To avoid the worst of the crowds try to visit midweek, preferably in deep winter.

The **tourist office** (☎ 0577 94 00 08; Piazza del Duomo 1; ⌚ 9am-1pm & 3-7pm Mar-Oct, 9am-1pm & 2-6pm Nov-Feb) is a short walk from Piazza dei Martiri di Montemaggio, the nearest San Gimignano has to a bus terminal.

On the southern edge of Piazza del Duomo, the **Palazzo Comunale** (☎ 0577 99 03 12; Piazza del Duomo; adult/child €5/4; ⌚ 9.30am-7pm Mar-Oct, 10am-5.30pm Nov-Feb) houses San Gimignano's art gallery (the **Pinacoteca**) and tallest tower, the **Torre Grossa**. Climb to the top for some unforgettable views.

Nearby, the Romanesque **Duomo** (☎ 0577 94 03 16; Piazza del Duomo; adult/child €3.50/1.50; ⌚ 9.30am-7.10pm Mon-Fri, to 5.10pm Sat & Sun Apr-Oct, 9.30am-4.40pm Mon-Sat, 12.30-4.40pm Sun Feb, Mar & Nov-Jan), known also as the Collegiata, boasts frescoes by Ghirlandaio and a gruesome *Last Judgment* by Taddeo di Bartolo.

Hotels are expensive in San Gimignano, but there are plenty of cheaper *affittacamere* and *agriturismi* (accommodation on working farms). The tourist office has a list.

Hotel La Cisterna (☎ 0577 94 03 28; www.hotelcisterna.it; Piazza della Cisterna 23; s/d €76/98, d with view €115; ❄ 💻) In a 14th-century *palazzo* overlooking San Gimignano's central square, this historic hotel is perfectly placed. Rooms, some of which have panoramic valley views, are bright, airy and comfortable.

Enoteca Gustavo (☎ 0577 94 00 57; Via San Matteo 29; snacks from €3.50) This is an atmospheric brick-vaulted *enoteca* serving a range of delicious *bruschette, panini* and smooth local Chianti.

Gelateria di Piazza (☎ 0577 94 22 44; Piazza della Cisterna 4; ⌚ Mar–mid-Nov) Tony Blair thought the ice cream here was 'delicious'. Praise indeed!

Regular buses link San Gimignano with Florence (€5.90, 1¼ hours, 14 daily) and Siena (€5.20, 1¼ hours, 11 daily). Most require a change at Poggibonsi.

UMBRIA & LE MARCHE

Dubbed the 'green heart of Italy', Umbria is a beautiful and predominantly rural region. It harbours some of Italy's best-preserved historic *borghi* (villages) and a wealth of artistic and architectural bounty. The regional capital Perugia provides a convenient base, with Assisi an easy day trip away.

To the east, mountainous Le Marche offers more of the same, its appeal encapsulated in the medieval centre of Urbino. On the coast, charmless Ancona is an important Adriatic ferry port.

PERUGIA

pop 153,850

With its hilltop medieval centre and international student population, Perugia is Umbria's largest and most cosmopolitan city. There's not a huge amount to see, but the presence of the University for Foreigners ensures a buzz that's not always apparent in the region's sleepy hinterland. In

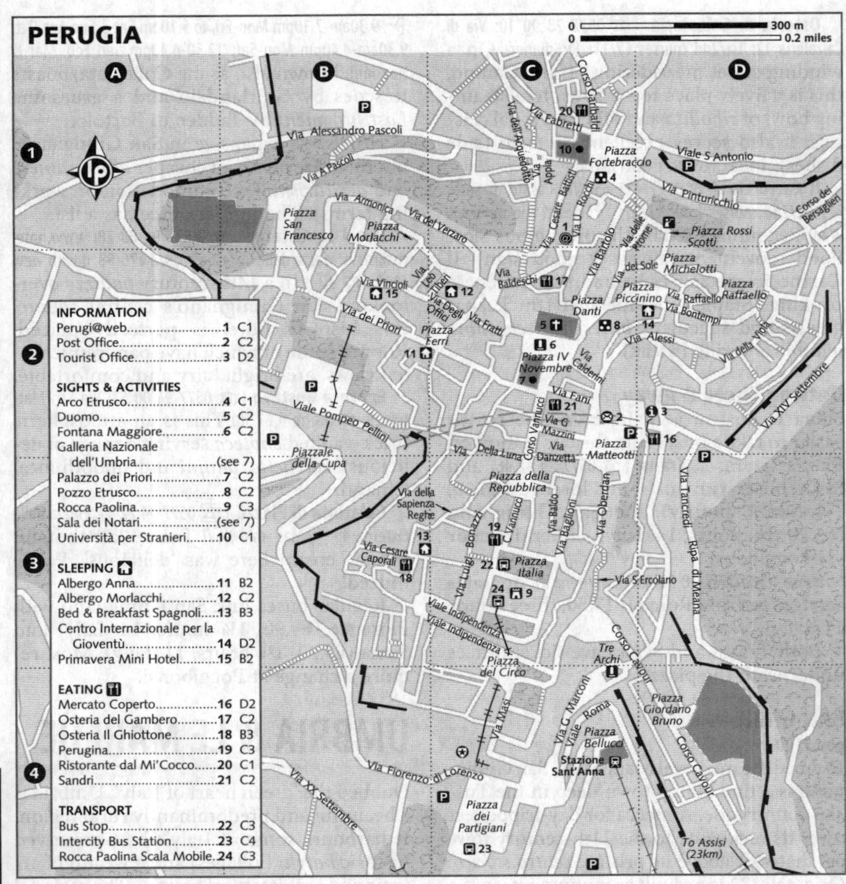

July, music fans inundate the city for the prestigious Umbria Jazz festival.

Perugia has a bloody and lively past. In the Middle Ages, the Baglioni and Oddi families fought for control of the city, while later, as a papal satellite, the city fought with its neighbours. All the while art and culture thrived: painter Perugino and Raphael, his student, both worked here.

Orientation & Information

Up the hill, Perugia's main strip, Corso Vannucci, runs north–south from Piazza Italia, where buses terminate, down to Piazza IV Novembre, the city's focal point. City maps are available at the **tourist office** (☎ 075 573 64 58; Piazza Matteotti 18; 8.30am-1.30pm & 3.30-6.30pm Mon-Sat, 9am-1pm Sun) opposite the **post office** (☎ 075 573 69 77; Piazza Matteotti).

To check your email try **Perugi@web** (☎ 075 572 01 05; Via Ulisse Rocchi 30; per hr €2.50; 10am-11pm Mon-Fri, noon-11pm Sat, 4-11pm Sun) in the historic centre.

Sights

Flanking Piazza IV Novembre, the austere 14th-century **Duomo** (☎ 075 572 38 32; Piazza IV Novembre; 7am-12.30pm & 4-6.45pm Mon-Sat, 8am-12.45pm & 4-6.45pm Sun) has an unfinished two-tone façade and, inside, an altarpiece by Signorelli and sculptures by Duccio. It's more famous, however, as being home to the Virgin Mary's wedding ring, unveiled every 30 July.

In the centre of the piazza, the **Fontana Maggiore** was designed by Fra Bevignate and carved by Nicola and Giovanni Pisano between 1275 and 1278.

The 13th-century **Palazzo dei Priori** houses Perugia's best museums, including the **Galleria Nazionale dell'Umbria** (☎ 075 572 10 09; Corso Vannucci 19; adult/concession €6.50/3.50; 🕑 8.30am-7.30pm), whose collection contains works by local heroes Perugino and Pinturicchio. Still in the *palazzo*, the impressively frescoed **Sala dei Notari** (Notaries' Hall; ☎ 075 577 23 39; Piazza IV Novembre; admission free; 🕑 9am-1pm & 3-7pm Tue-Sun) is where Perugia's nobles used to meet.

At the southern end of Corso Vannucci, the **Rocca Paolina** (Paolina Fortress) is the remnant of a massive 16th-century citadel. Exhibitions are sometimes held in the underground ruins.

Etruscan remains include the **Arco Etrusco** (Etruscan Arch; Piazza Fortebraccio) and the 36m-deep **Pozzo Etrusco** (Etruscan Well; ☎ 075 573 36 69; Piazza Danti 18; 🕑 10am-1.30pm & 2.30-6.30pm Apr-Oct, to 5pm Nov-Mar).

Courses

The **Università per Stranieri** (University for Foreigners; ☎ 075 574 61; www.unistrapg.it; Piazza Fortebraccio 4) runs hundreds of courses in language, art, history, music and architecture.

Sleeping

Centro Internazionale per la Gioventù (☎ 075 572 28 80; www.ostello.perugia.it; Via Bontempi 13; dm €14.50, sheets €2; 🕑 closed mid-Dec–mid-Jan) This is a private hostel with decent four- to six-bed dorms, a frescoed TV room and great views from the terrace. The lockout (9.30am to 4pm) and midnight curfew are strictly enforced.

Bed & Breakfast Spagnoli (☎ 075 573 51 27; www.perugiaonline.com/bbspagnoli; Via Cesare Caporali 17; s/d/tr incl breakfast €38/58/75) If a homestyle B&B is what you're after, look no further. The convivial English-speaking Spagnoli family offers guests three spacious rooms in their home near Piazza Italia.

Primavera Mini Hotel (☎ 075 572 16 57; www.primaveraminihotel.com; Via Vincioli 8; s/d €48/70; ❄ 💻) On the top floor of a 16th-century *palazzo* – hence some memorable views – this intimate two-star has spruce modern rooms decorated with understated style. Warmly recommended.

Also available:

Albergo Anna (☎ 075 573 63 04; www.albergoanna.it; Via dei Priori 48; s/d €40/62, with shared bathroom €30/48) Fourth-floor *pensione* with character to sell.

Albergo Morlacchi (☎ 075 572 03 19; Via Leo Tiberi 2; s/d €56/70, s with shared bathroom €44) Lovely art-filled place with frescoes, fireplaces and antiques.

Eating

Ristorante dal Mi'Cocco (☎ 075 573 25 11; Corso Giuseppe Garibaldi 12; set menu €13; 🕑 closed Mon) This is a fun restaurant with long communal tables and an ebullient taverna-vibe. Meals are dished up at set times – lunch 1pm, dinner 8.15pm – according to the weekly menu, written in local dialect. Meat eaters will enjoy the *polenta 'nc la salsiccia* (polenta with sausage).

Osteria Il Ghiottone (☎ 075 573 62 84; Via Cesare Caporali 12; 1st/2nd courses €7.50/10; 🕑 closed Wed) Earthy Umbrian cooking is what draws locals to this small family-run *osteria*. The homemade pasta is delicious, the lamb chops tender and the Billy Idol on the stereo kinda sweet.

Sandri (☎ 075 44 9 41; Corso Vannucci 32; 🕑 8am-11pm Tue-Sun) Perugia's premier café, Sandri has the best cakes in town, as well as free chocolates on the bar.

Don't leave town without trying Perugia's famous chocolate. There's a wide selection at **Perugina** (☎ 0755 573 66 77; Corso Vannucci 101; 🕑 9.30am-7.45pm, closed Mon morning) near Piazza Italia.

Mercato Coperto (Covered markets; Piazza Matteoti; 🕑 7am-1.30pm Mon-Sat & 4.30-7.30pm Sat) Stock up here on fresh fruit, bread, cheese and meat.

Getting There & Away

From the intercity bus station on Piazza dei Partigiani, **Sulga** (☎ 800 09 96 61; www.sulga.it, in Italian) buses depart for Florence (€9.80, two hours, one daily) and Rome (€15, three hours, five daily), continuing onto Fiumicino airport (€20, four hours). **Sena** (☎ 800 93 09 60; www.sena.it, in Italian) serves Siena (€11, 1½ hours, three daily), while **APM** (☎ 075 50 67 81; www.apmperugia.it, in Italian) and **SSIT** (☎ 0742 67 07 46; www.spoletina.com) buses head up to Assisi (€3, one hour, 13 daily).

Regional trains connect with Rome (€10.15, 2¾ hours, seven daily), Florence (€7.90, two hours, five daily) and Assisi (€1.65, 20 minutes, hourly).

Getting Around

The train station is downhill from the historic centre; take bus 6, 7 or 15A to Piazza Italia. From the intercity bus station on Piazza dei Partigiani, jump on the free **Rocca Paolina scala mobila** (public escalator; 6.15-1.45am) for the centre.

The centre is mostly closed to traffic so park in one of the supervised car parks and take the escalator up. There's a **car park** (Piazza dei Partigiani; 1st hr €0.80, per hr thereafter €1.05; 24hr) near the bus station.

ASSISI

pop 26, 030

Seen from afar the only clue to Assisi's importance is the imposing form of the Basilica di San Francesco jutting over the hillside. Thanks to St Francis, born here in 1182, this quaint medieval town is a major destination for millions of pilgrims.

The **tourist office** (075 81 25 34; www.umbria2000.it; Piazza del Comune 22; 8am-6.30pm Mon-Sat, 10am-1pm & 2-5pm Sun Apr-Oct, 8am-2pm & 3-6pm Mon-Fri, 9am-1pm & 3-6pm Sat, 9am-1pm Sun Nov-Mar) can provide practical information.

Sights

Dress rules are applied rigidly at the main religious sights, so no shorts, miniskirts, low-cut dresses or tops.

The **Basilica di San Francesco** (075 81 90 01; Piazza di San Francesco) comprises two churches. The **upper church** (8.30am-6.50pm Mon-Sat, to 7.15pm Sun Easter-Nov, to 6pm daily Nov-Easter) was damaged during a severe earthquake in 1997, but has since been restored to its former state. Built between 1230 and 1253 in the Italian Gothic style, it features superb frescoes by Giotto and works by Cimabue and Pietro Cavallini.

Downstairs in the dimly lit **lower church** (6.30am-6.50pm Mon-Sat, to 7.15pm Sun Easter-Nov, to 6pm daily Nov-Easter), constructed between 1228 and 1230, you'll find a series of colourful frescoes by Simone Martini, Cimabue and Pietro Lorenzetti and, beneath the floor, the crypt where St Francis is buried.

The 13th-century **Basilica di Santa Chiara** (075 81 22 82; Piazza Santa Chiara; 6.30am-noon & 2-7pm Apr-Oct, to 6pm Nov-Mar) contains the remains of St Clare, friend of St Francis and founder of the Order of Poor Clares.

Looming over Assisi, the massive 14th-century fortress **Rocca Maggiore** (075 81 30 53; Via della Rocca; admission €3; 10am-sunset) commands great views of the valley below.

Sleeping & Eating

You'll need to book ahead during peak times: Easter, August and September, and the Feast of St Francis (3 and 4 October).

Grotta Antica (075 81 34 67; Via Macelli Vecchi 1; s/d/tr €30/40/50) Just off central Piazza del Comune, this hospitable *pensione* offers seven clean, spartan rooms at bargain basement prices. Downstairs in the trattoria (1st/2nd courses €7/8) the food is similarly modest and well priced.

Pensione La Rocca (075 81 22 84; www.hotelarocca.it; Via Porta Perlici 27; s/d €40/48;) Near Piazza Matteotti in the upper reaches of town, La Rocca has 27 bright rooms spread over three floors. Décor is limited to functional furniture, but the spectacular views more than compensate. Noise from the downstairs restaurant (set menu €12) can be a nuisance.

Camere Santa Chiara (075 81 25 99; Vicolo Sant'Antonio; d €50) Run by the same family as the Grotta Antica, this is slightly smarter.

Trattoria Pallotta (075 81 26 49; Vicolo della Volta Pinta 2; 1st/2nd courses €7/12; closed Tue) Duck under the frescoed Volta Pinta (Painted Vault) off Piazza del Comune to this brick-vaulted, wood-beamed trattoria. The menu is unapologetically local, featuring homemade *strangozzi* (like tagliatelle), roast pigeon and rabbit stew.

Getting There & Away

APM and SSIT buses connect Assisi with Perugia (€3, one hour, 13 daily), departing from Piazzas Matteotti and Unità d'Italia. Sulga operates buses to Rome (€16.50, three hours, two daily) and Florence (€11, 2½ hours, one daily).

Assisi's train station is 4km from Assisi proper in Santa Maria degli Angeli. A bus (Linea C, €0.90, half hourly) runs between Piazza Matteotti and the station. Hourly trains run to Perugia (€1.65, 20 minutes).

ANCONA

pop 101,540

Unless you're picking up a ferry here, you won't want to hang around in Ancona. Regional capital of Le Marche and Italy's largest Adriatic port, it's an industrial workaday city with little of interest.

ITALY

Buses 1 and 4 connect the train station to the port and centre of town. The most convenient **tourist office** (☎ 071 20 11 83; ⏲ 8am-8pm Tue-Sat & 2-8pm Sun & Mon Jun-15 Sep) is at the ferry terminal. Otherwise it's a 2km slog to the **main office** (☎ 071 35 89 91; www.turismo.marche.it; Via Thaon de Revel 4; ⏲ 9am-1pm & 3.30-6.30pm Mon-Sat, 9am-1pm Sun Jun-Aug, 9am-1pm & 3-6pm Mon-Fri, 9am-1pm Sun Sep-May).

Sleeping

Ostello della Gioventú (☎/fax 071 422 57; Via Lamaticci 7; dm €16) Ancona's HI hostel is about 400m from the main train station. Divided into male and female floors, it's got beds in four- and six-person dorms. Unspectacular, but it does the job.

Hotel Fortuna (☎ 071 426 63; www.hotelfortuna.it; Piazza Rosselli 15; s/d/tr incl breakfast €55/88/98; ❄ 🖳) The pick of the station hotels, the Fortuna has spotless pale yellow rooms enlivened by tartan bedspreads and pay TV. Breakfast is abundant and there's wi-fi.

Getting There & Away

Falconara airport (AOI; ☎ 071 282 71; www.ancona-airport.it) handles daily national and European flights. **Conero** (☎ 071 280 20 92; www.conerobus.it) bus service J runs between the airport and the city centre (€1.10, 45 minutes, hourly).

Ferry operators have booths at the terminal, off Piazza Kennedy.

Adriatica (☎ 199 123 199; www.adriatica.it) To Split in Croatia (€46, 7½ hr).

Marmara Lines (☎ 071 207 61 65; www.marmaralines.com) To Cesme (€92, 55½ hr) in Turkey.

Minoan Lines (☎ 071 201 708; www.minoan.gr) To Greece's Igoumenitsa (€80, 16hr) and Patras (€72, 22hr).

Superfast Ferries (☎ 071 207 02 40; www.superfast.com) Also have services to Igoumenitsa (€74, 15hr) and Patras (€74, 21hr).

Regular trains connect Ancona with Bologna (€19.35, 2¼ hours, hourly) and Rome (Eurostar, €21.50, 3¼ hours, nine daily).

URBINO

pop 15,490

If you visit only one town in Le Marche, make it Urbino. It's a pain to get to, but as you wander its steep, Unesco-protected streets you'll appreciate the effort. Birthplace of Raphael and Bramante and a university town since 1564, it's still today a bustling centre of culture and learning.

To get to the centre from the bus terminal on Borgo Mercatale, head up Via Mazzini or take the *ascensore* (lift) to Teatro Sanzio.

Information and accommodation listings are available at the **tourist office** (☎ 0722 26 13; Via Puccinoti 3; ⏲ 9am-1pm Mon-Sat, 9am-1pm & 3-6pm Sun May-Sep).

Urbino's centrepiece is the Renaissance **Palazzo Ducale** (☎ 0722 32 90 57; Piazza Duca Federico; admission €4; ⏲ 8.30am-7.15pm Tue-Sun, to 2pm Mon), designed by Laurana and completed in 1482. Inside, the **Galleria Nazionale delle Marche** features works by Raphael, Paolo Uccello and Verrocchio.

To the north, the 15th-century **Casa di Raffaello** (☎ 0722 32 01 05; Via Rafaello 57; admission €3; ⏲ 9am-1pm & 3-7pm Mon-Sat, 10am-1pm Sun) is the house where Raphael lived until he was 16.

Albergo Italia (☎ 0722 27 01; www.albergo-italia-urbino.it; Corso Garibaldi 32; s €45-65, d €65-115 both incl breakfast; ❄) Right in the heart of the walled town, the white walls and modern fittings in the Italia's rooms contrast with the historic everything else around them.

La Balestra (☎ 0722 29 42; Via Valerio Lorenzo 16; 1st/2nd courses €7/10) Popular with local students, this cheery eatery specialises in meaty game dishes and autumnal pastas with truffles and *porcini*. If that doesn't appeal, there are also pizzas.

Trains don't run to Urbino. **Soget** (☎ 0721 54 96 20) buses link with Pesaro (€2.20, one hour, 16 daily), where you can pick up a train for Ancona. **Bucci** (☎ 0721 324 01; www.autolineebucci.com) runs two buses per day to Rome (€19, 4½ hours).

SOUTHERN ITALY

You'll hardly believe you're in the same country as Milan or Venice here, and for most Southern Italians, this is a source of pride. Long regarded by the North as the poor stepchild, the literal and figurative heel of Italy, the South is actually a treasure trove of all that is good about Italy, and the best place to experience the languid sweet life, *la dolce vita*.

Often referred to as the *Mezzogiorno* (the midday sun), the southern half of the boot is inextricably linked to its former Mediterranean invaders: Greeks, Arabs and Spanish Aragonese. The Amalfi Coast and

Capri host some of the finest scenery in the country, Matera will captivate anyone who makes the long trek and Naples is as unforgettable as your first love.

NAPLES

pop 1.04 million

As the birthplace of Sophia Loren, pizza and chaos, Naples is filled with a palpable frenetic energy, most noticeable among the hordes of young people on Vespas who congregate outside bars, cigarettes dangling just so. You're never quite sure whether they're planning a party, a revolution or a heist, but you know whichever it is, it'll be a rollicking good time.

You'll never feel more alive than when you're in Naples – though that might be partly because you'll never be more aware of your own mortality, as Vespas careen past while shady figures hover around your pockets. The ancient city was once queen of the Mediterranean and is pockmarked with a history worthy of the most cultured traveller. Naples' Museo Archeologico Nazionale is a microcosm of the city; it's got one of the best antiquities collections in the world (including an X-rated section), but the jumbled layout and lacklustre curating causes those visitors who don't look below the surface to miss its inimitable charms.

Orientation

Naples lazes along the waterfront and is divided into *quartieri* (districts). Both the Stazione Centrale and the main bus terminal are off Piazza Garibaldi, east of Spaccanapoli, the city's ancient heart. Corso Umberto I, the main shopping thoroughfare, heads southwest from Piazza Garibaldi to Piazza Bovio, skirting Spaccanapoli. The newest fashionable district is Chiaia, starting at the Galleria Umberto I and Via Toledo. Santa Lucia, to the southwest of the city, along the bay, is a serene contrast with the chaotic historical centre. In the hills above is the serene and affluent Vomero district, a natural balcony with grand Vesuvian views.

Information

DISCOUNT CARDS

Campania ArteCard (☎ 800 600 601; www.campaniaartecard.it; 3 days Naples/3 days Campania/7 days Campania €13/25/28) Free or discounted admission to dozens of museums, plus free public transportation. Pick up the card and accompanying brochure and map at the train stations, port, airport, hotels, museums or newsagents.

EMERGENCY

Police station (Questura; ☎ 081 794 11 11, to report a stolen car 081 794 14 35; Via Medina 75) Just off Via Armando Diaz.

INTERNET ACCESS/LAUNDRY

Onda Blu (☎ 081 563 49 96; Via Zannotti 11; wash & dry €4.50; 🕑 8am-8pm) Internet access *and* laundry.

LEFT LUGGAGE

Stazione Centrale (per piece for hr €3.80, per piece for 6-12hr €0.60, per piece after 12hr €0.20; 🕑 7am-11pm)

MEDICAL SERVICES

Guardia Medica After-hours medical service; phone numbers are listed in *Qui Napoli* (Here Naples; see below).

Ospedale Loreto-Mare (Hospital; ☎ 081 254 27 01; Via Amerigo Vespucci) On the waterfront, near the train station.

Pharmacy (☎ 081 268 881; Stazione Centrale; 🕑 8am-8pm)

MONEY

There are plenty of ATMs throughout the city, as well as foreign-exchange booths.

Every Tour (☎ 081 551 85 64; Piazza Municipio 5-6) Represents American Express, changes money and is a Western Union agent.

POST

Main post office (Piazza Matteotti) Off Via Armando Diaz.

TOURIST INFORMATION

Ask for *Qui Napoli* at tourist offices, published monthly in English and Italian. It lists events in the city, as well as information about transport and other services. Be aware that the tourist offices may randomly close off-season if budgets are tight.

Tourist offices Stazione Centrale (☎ 081 20 66 66; 🕑 9am-7.30pm Mon-Sat, to 1.30pm Sun); Piazza del Gesù Nuovo (☎ 081 552 33 28; 🕑 9am-8pm Mon-Sat, to 3pm Sun) Buy an ArteCard at any office.

Dangers & Annoyances

Naples' image has improved dramatically over the last decade or so and the overall crime rate, although undeniably the highest of all Italian cities, has dropped. The local Mafia – the Camorra – is more pervasive

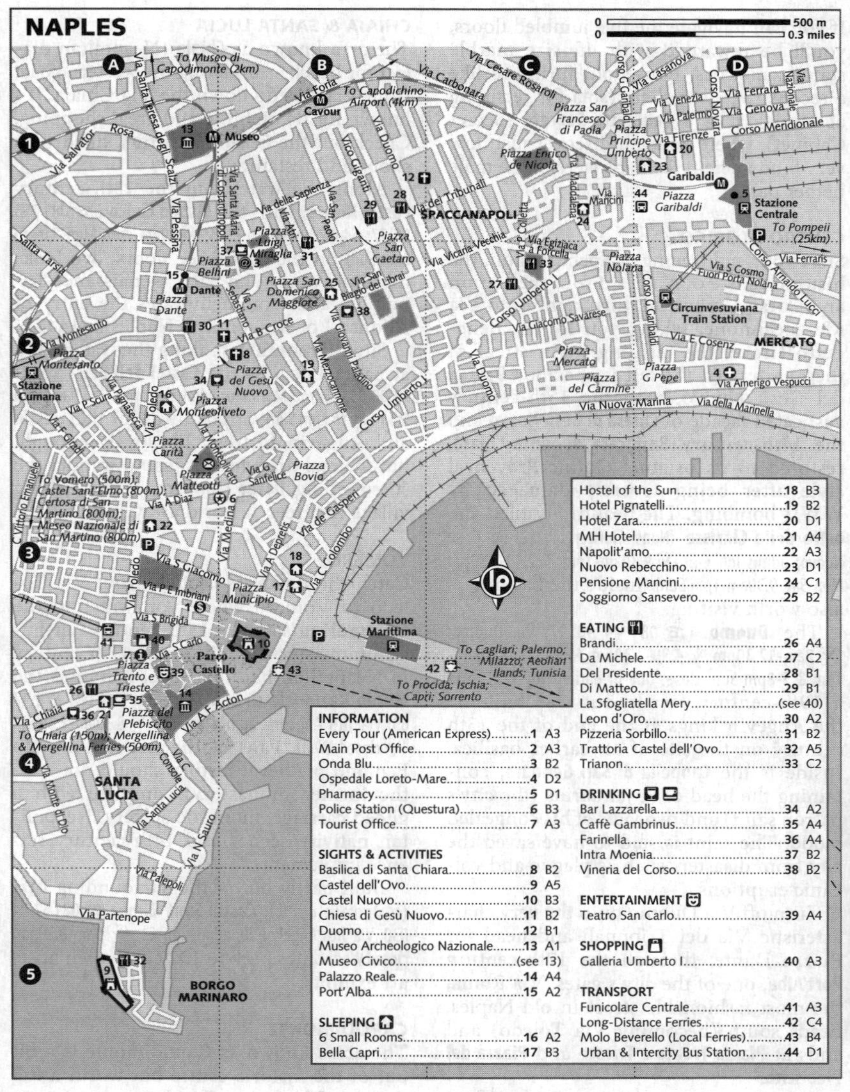

than most Neapolitans would like to admit; recent years have shown murder rates into the triple digits. However, tourists need not worry too much about being the target of a mob hit. Still, petty theft and pickpockets are rampant. Keep an eye on any bags, mobile phones, wallets or even loose necklaces, especially in crowds or as mopeds speed by.

Sights

If you visit one museum in Southern Italy, make sure it's the **Museo Archeologico Nazionale** (☎ 081 44 01 66; Piazza Museo Nazionale; adult/concession €6.50/3.50, up to €9 if special exhibit; 9am-7.30pm Wed-Mon), which houses the collection of the noble Farnese family and treasures from Pompeii and Herculaneum.

If you can navigate the five jumbled floors, you'll be rewarded with life-size marble statues, mosaics, household furniture like a reconstructed *triclinia* (sofa for reclining at meals), plus a **Gabinetto Segreto** (Secret Cabinet), where you can discover just how very fond ancient Romans were of the male nether parts.

CENTRO STORICO

Start your sightseeing at Spaccanapoli, the historic centre of Naples. From the station and Corso Umberto I, turn right onto Via Mezzocannone, taking you to Via Benedetto Croce, the bustling main street of the quarter. To the left is spacious Piazza del Gesù Nuovo, with the 15th-century rusticated façade of **Chiesa di Gesù Nuovo** and the 14th-century **Basilicata di Santa Chiara**, restored to its original Gothic-Provençal style after being severely damaged by WWII bombing. The beautifully tiled **Chiostro delle Clarisse** (Nuns' Cloisters; Piazza del Gesù Nuovo; admission €4; 9.30am-1pm & 2.30-5.30pm Mon-Sat, 9.30am-1pm Sun), inside the basilica, is also worth visiting.

The **Duomo** (081 44 90 97; Via Duomo; 8am-12.30pm & 4.30-7.30pm Mon-Sat, 8.30am-1pm & 5-8pm Sun, closes one hr earlier Nov-Feb) has a 19th-century façade but was built by the Angevin kings at the end of the 13th century on the site of an earlier basilica. Inside is the **Cappella di San Gennaro**, containing the head of St Januarius (the city's patron saint) and two vials of his congealed blood. The saint is said to have saved the city from disasters such as plague and volcanic eruptions.

Turn off Via Duomo onto the very characteristic Via dei Tribunali and head for Piazza Dante, through the 17th-century **Port'Alba**, one of the city's gates. Via Roma, the most fashionable street in old Naples, heads south (becoming Via Toledo) and ends at **Piazza Trento e Trieste** and **Piazza del Plebiscito**.

Near the piazzas is **Palazzo Reale** (081 794 40 21; admission €4.50; 9am-8pm Thu-Tue), the former official residence of the Bourbon and Savoy kings, now a museum. Just off Piazza Trento e Trieste is the world-renowned **Teatro San Carlo** (081 797 21 11; Via San Carlo 98; tours €5), famed for its perfect acoustics. Visit its lavish interior or go for a show (see p791).

CHIAIA & SANTA LUCIA

The area known as **Chiaia** (Neapolitan dialect for beach) runs along the western coast from Via Toledo down the Via Chiaia. It's known for its nightlife and great shopping. Check out the **Galleria Umberto I**, filled with shops and restaurants.

Along the waterfront the 13th-century **Castel Nuovo**, with the **Museo Civico** (081 795 58 77; adult/concession €5/4; 9am-7pm Mon-Sat, to 2pm Sun) on the first three floors, overlooks the ferry port. The early Renaissance triumphal arch commemorates the entry of Alfonso I of Aragon into Naples in 1443.

Situated southwest along the waterfront, at Santa Lucia, is the **Castel dell'Ovo** (081 24 00 055; Borgo Marinaro; admission free; 9am-6pm Mon-Sat, to 2pm Sun), originally a Norman castle and Angevin fortress. It's lovely enough, but the real draw here is just to wander the surrounding **Borgo Marinaro**, a tiny fishing village that feels a world away.

VOMERO

Catch the **Funicolare Centrale** from Via Toledo to Vomero where you will find the **Certosa di San Martino**, a 14th-century Carthusian monastery, rebuilt in the 17th century in Neapolitan-baroque style. It houses the **Museo Nazionale di San Martino** (081 578 17 69; Via Tito Angelini; admission €6; 8.30am-7.30pm; closed Wed). Fans of the writer Umberto Eco and medieval history should not miss the former monastery, complete with a gilded carriage, monastic spicery, Neapolitan nativity scenes and 14th-century science implements.

Built partly out of the surrounding tufa (volcanic rock), **Castel Sant' Elmo** (081 57 84 030; Via Tito Angelini 20; admission €3; 9am-6.30pm, closed Wed) dates back to 1329 and often hosts art exhibits.

CAPODIMONTE

The areas known as Capodimonte is a bit out of the historic centre but worth a full day visit. The former Bourbon palace is now a top-notch museum surrounded by a park, where you'll often find Neapolitan families enjoying a picnic amid the forested setting of this former noble hunting ground.

One of the better fine art museums in Southern Italy, **Museo di Capodimonte** (848 800 288; Via Miano 1; adult/concession €7.50/4, audio guide €4; 8.30am-6.30pm, closed Wed) houses the collection from the Farnese family whose patriarch became the first king of Naples in 1734. Master painters on display include El Greco, Titian and Bruegel.

Take bus 24 to reach the park and the museum.

Festivals & Events

The **Festa di San Gennaro** honours the city's patron saint and is held three times a year (first Sunday in May, 19 September and 16 December). Thousands swarm the Duomo to witness the saint's blood, held in two vials, liquefy, a miracle said to save the city from potential disasters.

Sleeping

Location is everything in Naples. Those who value convenience or have wee-hour train departures might want to stay near the train station, although it is loud and lacks the historic ambience of Spaccanapoli. Several hotels require €0.05 for the lift, including Bella Capri and Hostel of the Sun.

BUDGET

6 Small Rooms (☎ 081 790 13 78; www.at6smallrooms.com; Via Diodato Lioy 18; dm/d incl breakfast €18/45) The young or young-at-heart might not mind hauling up six flights of treacherous stairs to enjoy the Australian-run casual atmosphere, laid-back common room and lax regard for antismoking rules here. There's a full kitchen and several private rooms.

Hostel of the Sun (☎/fax 081 420 63 93; www.hostelnapoli.com; Via Melisurgo 15; dm/s/d/tr/q with shared bathroom €20/45/55/80/90, d/t/q €70/90/100, all incl breakfast; 💻) Constantly winning awards and accolades for what is practically hostel perfection, HOTS has achieved an enviable balance between social and relaxing, well-run but casual. Guests quickly become friends over a shared DVD or night out on the town at a local pizzeria. Hotel-quality private rooms on a separate floor mean softies can get in a good eight hours of sleep.

Pensione Mancini (☎ 081 553 67 31; www.hostelpensionemancini.com; Via Mancini 33; dm/s/d with shared bathroom €20/35/45, s/d/tr/q €45/60/80/100, all incl breakfast) Your parents will rest easy knowing you're being well cared for at this clean and safe hostel/hotel. A machine for free coffee and hot chocolate 24/7, in-room lockers and free luggage storage make this a great train station bet.

Bella Capri (☎ 081 55 29 265; www.bellacapri.it; Via Melisurgo 4; dm/s/d/tr with shared bathroom €22/50/60/84, s/d/tr/q incl breakfast €70/80/100/110; ❄ 💻) It's tough to hold a candle to neighbour Hostel of the Sun, but Bella Capri more than delivers. Hotel rooms are comfortably simple and safe, all with TVs and a few with terraces. The hostel was under construction when we visited, but expect brightly painted rooms, full wheelchair access, en suite co-ed dorm rooms (with hairdryers!), a festive common room with wide-screen TV and DVD player, and laundry facilities.

Hotel Zara (☎ 081 28 71 25; www.hotelzara.it; Via Firenze 81; s/d €45/65; ❄ 💻) This is one of the nicer train station hotels; it's a bit smoky but safe, with a good-size collection of English-language books.

MIDRANGE

Hotel Pignatelli (☎ 081 658 49 50; www.hotelpignatellinapoli.com; Via S Giovanni Pignatelli 16; s/d/tr incl breakfast €50/90/130) The owner here, previously a bodyguard, takes good care of guests, even cooking homemade pasta on occasion. The building is bathed in layers of history and rooms have ancient vaulted ceilings and are large enough for an echo. Email ahead for an airport (€15) or train station (€10) pick-up.

Napolit'amo (☎ 081 552 36 26; www.napolitamo.it; Via Toledo 148; s/d/tr/q incl breakfast €75/115/135/165; ❄ 💻) Feel like royalty in this 16th-century palace, packed with faded glory and stylish décor. In the heart of the Chiaia shopping district, it's walking distance to many restaurants and bars. Good off-season discounts.

WORTH A TRIP

Hapsburgs, Schmapsburgs: the Italians also knew how to make themselves one impressive palace. The lovely **Palazzo Reale** (☎ 0823 44 80 84; Via Douhet 22, Caserta; adult/concession €6/3; 🕑 8.30am-7pm, closed Tue) is easily reached on the main Naples to Rome train line in the town of Caserta; it's just a five-minute walk from the station. Never ones for subdued style, these Italians knew how to build a seriously garish palace, including gilded 7m-high doors and giant marble statues. The gardens are as marvellous as the palace apartments.

Soggiorno Sansevero (☎ 081 79 01 000; www.albergosansevero.it; Piazza San Domenico Maggiore 9; s/d €90/100, with shared bathroom €70/90; ❄) One of a three-property chain, this tasteful hotel is housed in a historic building and offers excellent value.

Nuovo Rebecchino (☎ 081 553 53 27; www.nuovorebecchino.it; Corso G Garibaldi 356; s/d incl breakfast €105/160; ❄ 💻) The best higher-end hotel near the train station, the Rebecchino is equipped with absolutely every amenity you could want: TV, direct-dial telephone, hairdryer, minibar, in-room wi-fi, large buffet breakfast, even a billiards table downstairs.

TOP END

MH Hotel (☎ 081 19 57 15 76; www.mhhotel.it; Via Chiaia 245; s €140-180, d €170-230, incl breakfast; ❄ 💻) Known as a 'design hotel' for its innumerable aesthetic touches, the MH Hotel is also perfectly located in the heart of pedestrianised Chiaia, but with much-appreciated soundproof windows. Jacuzzis and sleek furnishings give rooms a Prada-does-feng shui feel.

Eating

You might hear a passing reference or two to the fact that pizza was created here. True Neapolitan pizza is all about the purity of ingredients, time-tested leavening methods and a wood-fired brick oven. The pizzas themselves are usually nothing more than the classic *margherita* – olive oil, tomato sauce, basil and mozzarella cheese – or the *marinara* – tomatoes, garlic, oregano and olive oil. We're still not quite sure how something so simple can taste so good, but we're pretty sure it has something to do with an alchemical transformation.

Breaded mozzarella sticks and *misto di frittura* (deep-fried vegetables), such as fried zucchini flowers, are available at takeaways called *friggatorie* all over town.

PIZZA

Da Michele (☎ 081 55 39 204; Via Cesare Sersale 1/3; pizza €3.50-4.50; 🕑 10am-11pm, closed Sun) In the heart of pizza country is this, the apogee of pizza, which calls itself 'Il Tempio della Pizza'. Open since 1870, you're practically guaranteed a raucously sacred experience. Choices are *margherita* or *marinara* and water, soda or beer.

Di Matteo (☎ 081 45 52 62; Via dei Tribunali 94; pizza & calzone around €4-5; 🕑 9am-midnight, closed Sun) Careful you don't miss the tiny tiled entrance here. The owner didn't want to ruin the pizza essence with anything fancy, so expect paper plates, plastic cups…and really, really good pizza.

Del Presidente (☎ 081 21 09 03; Via dei Tribunali 120/121; pizza €4) Bill Clinton probably has no clue that one visit to Di Matteo started a shrine, but a former *pizzaiolo* (pizza maker) took the ex-pres's visit as inspiration and opened this nearby contender. Downstairs is filled with Clintonian memorabilia.

Brandi (☎ 081 41 69 28; Salita S Anna di Palazzo 1/2; pizza €5) Once a restaurant has its website translated into six languages, you might guess – correctly – that quality has lost some of its importance. Still, pizza *margherita* was invented here in 1889 (the restaurant has been open since 1780).

Pizzeria Sorbillo (☎ 081 44 66 43; Via dei Tribunali; pizza from €5) This always-packed place is a shoe-in contender for one of Naples' top pizza parlours – a long lineage of talented *pizzaioli* has ensured this.

Trianon (☎ 081 553 94 26; Via P Colletta 46; pizza €5-10) With marble-topped tables and a warm welcome, this place has been tossing very good pizzas since 1923.

NOT PIZZA

Trattoria Castel dell'Ovo (☎ 081 76 46 352; Via Luculliana 28; mains from €8) This unpretentious spot, south of Santa Lucia, serves well-priced, delicious seafood at harbour-side tables with lovely views of Borgo Marinaro.

Leon d'Oro (☎ 081 54 99 404; Piazza Dante 48; pizza €6, 1st/2nd courses €8.50/14; 🕑 closed Mon & one week in August) This is a homey old-school restaurant with good service and an intimate atmosphere. They do serve pizza, of course, but the gnocchi and steak are a welcome distraction.

La Sfogliatella Mery (☎ 081 40 22 18; Galleria Umberto I) In the heart of the Chiaia shopping district is this famed pastry shop in the elegant Galleria Umberto I shopping arcade. A must is the *Babà al Rum* pastry.

Drinking

BARS

Farinella (☎ 081 423 84 55; Via Alabadieri 10; dishes €3.50-12; 🕑 restaurant to midnight, bar to 2am, closed Sun) Absolutely oozing with atmosphere, the young and hip make their way to this Chiaia lounge and chill spot. There's live music on Tuesday.

Bar Lazzarella (☎ 081 55 10 005; Calata Trinita Maggiore 7-8) Grab a drink and sit back with the students, international travellers and young Neapolitans who flock here for a beer or a coffee with Baileys and to enjoy primo people-watching off the Piazza del Gesu Nuovo.

Vineria del Corso (Via Giovanni Paladino 8a) This is a snug wine bar featuring a good wine list, welcoming lighting, charming décor and low-key electronica played at a polite volume.

CAFÉS

Caffè Gambrinus (☎ 081 41 75 82; Via Chiaia 12) Naples' oldest and most posh café, in the heart of the city's most fashionable street, remains a beloved haunt for artists, intellectuals and musicians.

Intra Moenia (☎ 081 29 07 20; Piazza Bellini 70; salads & light meals from €8) Tucked onto a beautiful piazza, this café/bookshop/publishing house hosts the city's intellectual elite; it's arty, literary and left leaning – with excellent salads to boot.

Entertainment

The monthly *Qui Napoli* and local newspapers are the best guides to what's on when. In May, the city organises **Maggio dei Monumenti**, a month of mostly free concerts and cultural events. Ask at the tourist offices for details. **Teatro San Carlo** (☎ box office 081 797 23 31; www.teatrosancarlo.it, in Italian; Via San Carlo 98; tickets €25-120) has year-round concerts and performances of opera and ballet. There are discounts for under-30s one hour before the curtain, and 10% discount with the Campania ArteCard.

Getting There & Away

AIR

Capodichino airport (NAP; ☎ 848 88 87 77; www.gesac.it) is about 6km northeast of the city centre. In addition to Alitalia and Lufthansa, several low-cost carriers arrive in Naples, including easyJet and Meridiana. Take the Alibus airport bus (€3, 20 minutes, at least hourly) from Piazza Municipio or the port. Taxi fares are set at €21.60 with additional charges for luggage and night calls.

BOAT

Naples is above all a water city, and *traghetti* (ferries), *aliscafi* (hydrofoils) and *navi veloci* (fast ships) leave for Sorrento and the islands of Capri, Ischia and Procida from Molo Beverello, in front of Castel Nuovo. Some hydrofoils leave for the bay islands from Mergellina. Hydrofoils cost around double the price of ferries but take half the time.

Check the website www.traghettionline.net for information on all ferries in or out of Italy. The major companies out of Naples are **Tirrenia** (☎ 199 12 31 99; www.tirrenia.com), which operates ferries to Palermo (€55, 10½ hours, daily) and Cagliari (€44, 13½ hours, weekly), while its sister company **Siremar** (☎ 081 580 03 40) services the Aeolian Islands and Milazzo. **SNAV** (☎ 081 428 55 55) runs hydrofoils to the islands of Capri (€12, 30 minutes, five daily) and Palermo (€16-68, 10½ hours). **Caremar** (☎ 081 551 38 82) services Capri (hydrofoil €12, 30 minutes; ferry €6, 1½ hours), Procida and Ischia by ferry and hydrofoil. The most convenient (and cheapest) way to buy tickets is online, however, you can also purchase them at a travel agent or at the port of embarkation.

BUS

Buses leave from Piazza Garibaldi, in front of the train station, for nearby destinations, including Salerno, the Amalfi Coast and Caserta, as well as far-flung Bari (€20, three hours), Lecce (€25, 5½ hours) and Brindisi (€23, five hours). Signage is sparse, so check destinations carefully or ask at the information kiosk.

CAR & MOTORCYCLE

If you value your sanity and life, skip driving in Naples. The traffic is constant and chaotic, theft is rife and the street plan does not lend itself to easy navigation. But if you want to tempt fate, the city is easily accessible from Rome on the A1. The Naples–Pompeii–Salerno road (A3) connects with the coastal road to Sorrento and the Amalfi Coast.

TRAIN

The main Naples train station is known as Stazione Centrale (sometimes called Stazione Garibaldi). Naples is the rail hub for the south, and regular trains for most major Italian cities arrive and depart from Stazione Centrale. There are up to 30 fast trains daily to/from Rome (€10 to €20, two to three hours).

The Ferrovia Circumvesuviana operates trains for Herculaneum, Pompeii (€2.30, 35 minutes, hourly) and Sorrento (€3.20, one hour, hourly). The station is about 400m southwest of Stazione Centrale, on Corso G Garibaldi (take the underpass from Stazione Centrale). The Ferrovia Cumana and the Circumflegrea, based at Stazione Cumana in Piazza Montesanto, operate services to Pozzuoli, Baia and Cumae every 20 minutes.

Getting Around

You can make your way around Naples by bus, tram, metro and funicular. City **Unico Campania** (☎ 081 551 31 09; www.unicocampania.it) buses leave from Piazza Garibaldi for the centre of Naples and Mergellina. You can buy 'Giranapoli' tickets at bus stations and tobacconists. A ticket costs €1 and is valid for 1½ hours of unlimited public transport. A daily ticket is good value at €3. Campania ArteCards (p786) are also valid on all forms of public transport.

The main funicular connecting the city centre with Vomero is in Piazza Duca d'Aosta, next to Galleria Umberto I, on Via Toledo.

AROUND NAPLES

Pompeii

Although former residents might not think so, the Mt Vesuvius explosion in AD 79 was one of the best things that ever happened to Roman archaeology. On 24 August, the world's most famous volcano erupted, leaving behind fascinating **ruins** (☎ 081 857 53 47; www.pompeiisites.org; adult/concession €10/5, no credit cards; 8.30am-7.30pm Apr-Oct, 8.30am-5pm Nov-Mar) that provide insight into the daily life of ancient Romans, perfectly preserved under 6m of volcanic ash. Pompeii was a resort town for the wealthy, and you can still walk its roads filled with impressive temples, a forum, an amphitheatre, apartments and a shopping district. The coolest/creepiest thing to see is the casts of the volcano's victims, created in 1863 by the director of excavations pouring plaster of Paris on top of incinerated bodies. The casts are so lifelike, you can see clothing folds, hair, even the expressions of terror on faces.

THE FIRST GRAFFITI

To learn the true history of Pompeii, it's best to hear it straight from Pompeians themselves. The eruption left behind walls and walls filled with graffiti, political inscriptions and for-sale signs. Here's a taste:

- The finances officer of the Emperor Nero says this food is poison.
- Celadus the Thracian gladiator is the delight of all the girls.
- Chie, I hope your haemorrhoids rub together so much that they hurt worse than they ever have before!
- Phileros is a eunuch!

There is a **tourist office** (☎ 081 85 75 347; info pompei@tin.it; Piazza Porta Marina Inferiore 12; 8am-3.30pm Mon-Sat) just outside the excavations at Porta Marina.

Catch the Ferrovia Circumvesuviana train from Naples (€2.30, 35 minutes, hourly) and get off at the Pompeii Scavi–Villa dei Misteri stop; the Porta Marina entrance is nearby.

CAPRI

pop 7270

The Emperor Tiberius recognised the innate beauty of this Bay of Naples island. After his stepfather, the Emperor Augustus, visited on holiday, Tiberius set up permanent residence on Capri in AD 27 and built 12 summer villas where he could engage in equal parts decadence, cruelty and debauchery. It's been an upscale summer holiday destination ever since, although shopping has replaced young boys as the object of visitors' orgiastic attention.

The island is easily reached via Naples and Sorrento on ferry or hydrofoil. Although hordes and hordes of tourists visit the island's two main towns – Capri and Anacapri – it's still a stunningly beautiful island with fantastic walking, a world-famous sea grotto and high-end holiday resorts and shopping.

Ferries stop at Marina Grande and buses head up to Capri and then Anacapri. Online information can be found at www.capri.it and www.capritourism.com. There are also numerous **tourist offices** (⌚ 8.30am-8.30pm summer, 9am-3pm Mon-Sat winter; Marina Grande ☎ 081 837 06 34; ☎ Capri 081 837 06 86; Piazza Umberto I; Anacapri ☎ 081 837 15 24; Piazza Vittoria 4) around the island. Contact **Rent an Electric Scooter** (☎ 081 83 75 863; Via Roma 68; per hr €10) if you want to…well, you know.

Sights & Activities

Although it's one of the world's biggest tourist attractions, Capri's **Blue Grotto** (admission €4; ⌚ 9am-1hr before sunset, closed during rough seas) is actually a sparklingly magical sea cave that really shouldn't be missed. Try to visit early or late in the day to avoid the hordes of bus tourists. Boats leave to visit the cave from the Marina Grande and a return trip will cost €17, including the return motor boat to the grotto, rowing boat in, admission fee and singing captains; allow an hour for the trip. You'll save little money and spend more time if you catch a bus from either town, as you still have to pay for the rowing boat and admission.

The most interesting points on the island require visitors to leave their cars or tourist buses, ensuring a bit of quiet. From Marina Grande, take a walk along the architectural engineering feat of **Via Krupp**, built by a German industrialist as a series of hairpin turns hewn from the rock that wind their way (past the nudist spot Grotta dell'Arsenale) to the best viewpoint in all of Capri, the **Giardini d'Augusto**.

One hour up a walking trail, along Via Tiberio, is **Villa Jovis** (admission €2; ⌚ 9am-1hr before sunset), the ruins of one of Tiberius' villas. It's a gorgeous walk along Via Matrimonia to the **Arco Naturale** – follow the spur trail, marked by splashes of paint, winding up the piney hillside. Near Anacapri, the resplendent **Villa San Michele** (☎ 081 837 14 01; Viale Axel Munthe; admission €5; ⌚ 9am-6pm May-Sep, closes 3.30pm Nov-Feb, 4.30pm Mar, 5pm Apr & Oct) is now a Swedish cultural foundation with a small museum of antiquities.

Sleeping

High-season prices can come into effect any time between 1 May and 30 September; most places stay open from March or April until October or November. Don't even think about arriving in mid-August unless you have a reservation and a wheelbarrow full of cash, as prices shoot up on everything, even groceries.

Bussola di Hermes (☎ 081 838 2010; www.bussolahermes.com; Trav La Vigna 14, Anacapri; dm €26-28, d €70-115, tr €80-140, q €100-170, all incl breakfast; 💻) This place is a thousand times more than just a hotel. English-speaking Rita and her brother turned their father's farmhouse into 18 perfectly decorated inn rooms, plus eight dorm rooms, with touches such as hand-built Roman columns, local tile work and a dreamy rooftop terrace. A few 2nd-floor rooms have terraces and beautiful views and some of the tiny doubles are veritable steals, charging dorm prices. It's just outside Anacapri.

Albergo Stella Maris (☎ 081 837 04 52; Via Roma 27; s/d/tr €50/110/150) One of the least expensive places on Capri and a stone's throw from the centre of Capri town, it's as plain as could be, but it's central and open all year. All rooms have sea views.

Hotel La Minerva (☎ 081 837 03 74; www.laminervacapri.com; Via Occhio Marino; s €100, d €150-270, both incl breakfast; ❄) The more you pay here, the better your view gets, up to the superior double, which has sea views from the Jacuzzi. Crisp white rooms, majolica tile floors and individual bougainvillea-shaded terraces are just part of what make this a great deal. It's just off Via Camerelle, the main shopping strip in Capri.

Also available:

Hotel Loreley (☎ 081 837 14 40; www.loreley.it; Via G Orlandi 16, Anacapri; s/d/tr incl breakfast €85/125/150; ⌚ Apr-Nov) A family-owned small hotel.

Eating

Pulalli Wine Bar (☎ 081 837 4108; Piazza Umberto I; dishes from €4; ⌚ closed Tue & winter) Perched in the clock tower overlooking Capri's main piazza, this is the place in town to sip local wine and nosh on tapas, especially on the terrace during summer.

Barbarossa (☎ 081 837 1483; Porta 5, Anacapri; pizza €7, 1st/2nd courses €8/12) This is where the locals go when they want good pizza or simple pasta dishes.

La Capannina (☎ 081 83 78 899; Via Le Botteghe 12/14; pasta from €8) Metres away from Piazzetta di Capri (the main centre of Capri town) is this family-owned restaurant, Capri's most beloved for over 70 years. The island's fishermen supply the seafood daily, and the *ravioli alla caprese* (ravioli with basil, tomatoes and mozzarella) is a standout.

Capri's (☎ 081 837 71 08; Via Roma 38; pizza €7, 1st/2nd courses €10/16) Don't let the photo of Keanu Reeves scare you away. Sure, Giovanni will hit on the girls and charge you an astounding 12% service charge, but he makes up for it by serving home-grown herbs and *pomodorini* (baby tomatoes) from his garden. Take a peek out to sea from any table in the restaurant to watch as tomorrow's fish and to-die-for lobster gets reeled in.

Il Cucciolo (☎ 081 83 71 917; Trav Veterino 8; 1st/2nd courses €10/18; Mar-Oct) It's worth the hike (head towards the Blue Grotto from Anacapri) for the views of Naples and Mt Vesuvius, but the gastronomic views aren't half bad: including gorgeous *caprese* salads and seafood.

Getting There & Around

There are hydrofoils and ferries virtually every hour from Naples' Molo Beverello and Mergellina, especially in summer. In Naples, pick up the daily *Il Mattino* for sailing times. Several companies make the trip; see p791. Hydrofoils cost about €12 each way and take about 30 minutes; ferries cost €6 each way and take about 1½ hours. From Sorrento, ferries leave hourly in summer and cost about €5 (up to €11 for a hydrofoil or for the last ferry of the day). During summer, **Metro del Mare** (☎ 199 60 07 00; www.metrodelmare.com) runs ferries along the coast from Naples' Mergellina to Pompeii (€3.50, 45 minutes, three daily) and Sorrento (€4.50, one hour 35 minutes, five daily), and from Naples' Molo Beverello to Positano (€9, one hour 25 minutes, five daily) and on to Amalfi (€10, one hour 55 minutes, five daily).

Local buses connect the Marina Grande port with Capri, Anacapri and other points around the island, and run between the two main towns until just past midnight. The funicular takes passengers straight up the hill from Marina Grande to Capri town (but closes for the month of February). Tickets for the funicular and buses cost €1.30 each trip or €6.70 per daily ticket.

SORRENTO

pop 17,429

Perched on a cliff in the Bay of Naples and the jumping off point for the Amalfi Coast, Capri and Pompeii, Sorrento has been a busy seaside resort town for two millennia. Sometimes, it feels like not one of these tourists has since left, especially in August. Despite its overcrowding, Sorrento remains a beautiful city with just enough elbow room to allow visitors to soak up its beauty.

Orientation

The centre of town is Piazza Tasso, a short walk from the train station along Corso Italia. If you arrive by boat at Marina Piccola, walk south along Via Marina Piccola then climb the 200 steps to reach the piazza. From the Circumvesuviana bus and train station, walk straight ahead to Corso Italia then head left 100m.

Information

Ospedale Civile (Hospital; ☎ 081 533 11 11; Corso Italia 1)

Police station (Questura; ☎ 081 807 44 33; Corso Italia 236)

Post office (Corso Italia 210)

Sorrento Service (☎ 081 807 55 70; Via S Paolo 5/7; Internet for 30min/1hr €3/5; 10am-10pm or later in summer, until 7pm or 8pm in winter, closed Mon) For Internet access. Also offers low international phone rates.

Tourist information office (☎ /fax 081 807 40 33; www.infosorrento.it; Via Luigi de Maio 35; 8.45am-6.15pm Mon-Sat, closes 4pm Jan-Feb) An excellent office inside the Circolo dei Forestieri complex. See also www.sorrentotourism.com.

Sleeping

Many places in Sorrento close during at least part of the low season, between November and March. All the places listed below are open year-round.

Nube d'Argento (☎ 081 878 13 44; www.nubedargento.com; Via del Capo 21; per person/car €10/6, per tent €6-10) This camping ground is tucked into a sea of olive trees 1km from Piazza Tasso and 200m from the beach. You'll feel as luxurious as those at the grand hotels as you admire the sea view from the pool or dine on brick-oven-baked pizza. There are also bungalows available (from €50 for two people in the low season to €150 for six people in August).

Ostello delle Sirene (☎ 081 877 13 91; Via degli Aranci 160; dm/s/d €16/40/60) This hostel (the only one) seems like a business afterthought to the popular smoky bar next door. Rickety metal beds, no common room to speak of, and a rumbling train right outside your window make this a good option for the price only. The Internet here costs €2.60 for 30 minutes.

Hotel Pensione Linda (☎ 081 878 29 16; Via degli Aranci 125; s/d/tr €35/60/80) Hosting Hostel Sirene refugees for over a decade now, Linda's is a clean and comfortable one-star alternative with a helpful owner. Ask for a back room.

La Magnolia (☎ 081 877 35 60; www.magnoliasorrento.it; Via Caruso 14; s €50-90, d €70-120, tr €80-140; ⊠ ❄) Slip through an ancient locked gateway and pass the private citrus garden to enjoy your oasis, just steps from the excitement of Piazza Tasso. Rooms have inlaid Sorrentine wood furniture, satellite TV and a refrigerator. No breakfast salon means breakfast (€6) will be delivered to your room. Pity.

Bellevue Syrene 1820 (☎ 081 878 10 24; www.bellevue.it; Piazza della Vittoria 5; r incl breakfast €220-420; ❄ 💻 🅿) Built on top of the ruins of a Roman villa, the Bellevue was transformed into a hotel in, you guessed it, 1820, when Empress Eugenia of France stayed for three months, probably admiring the expansive view the entire time. All sorts of extras – private beach access, live outdoor concerts, excellent concierge services, terrace restaurant, bicycle rentals, even a cigar bar – make this a standout location.

Eating

Fauno Bar (☎ 081 87 81 135; Piazza Tasso 13/14/15; small dishes from €4) The central meeting point of Sorrentines for generations, this place serves good-value small meals, mouthwateringly gorgeous pastries and *gelato*, right on the main square for ample people-watching.

La Fenice (☎ 081 878 16 52; Via degli Aranci 11; pizza €5, 1st/2nd courses €7/14) Rightfully popular, this pretty spot serves delicious fresh seafood and good pizzas.

La Basilica Ristorante Pizzeria (☎ 081 877 47 90; Via Sant' Antonino; pizza €6, 1st/2nd courses €8/13; 🕑 11am-11pm) An absolutely enormous dining room by Italian standards, this pizzeria is busy and boisterous, and packed with locals who flock for the seafood dishes.

Sisa Supermercato (☎ 081 807 44 65; Via degli Arancia 157) Located just past the hostel and Pensione Linda, this is Sorrento's largest supermarket.

Getting There & Away

Circumvesuviana trains run every 30 minutes between Sorrento and Naples via Pompeii and Ercolano. At least 12 SITA buses a day leave from outside the train station for the Amalfi Coast, first stopping in Positano (€1.30, one hour) and then Amalfi (€2.40, 1½ hours). Hydrofoils and ferries leave from the port at Marina Piccola for Capri (€5.80, one hour 20 minutes, at least five daily, double in summer).

AMALFI COAST

'Dramatic scenery' doesn't do justice to the 50km of sheer rock cliff that is the Amalfi Coast. Villages are impossibly perched in-between crags, and ancient terraced farming shows off the area's abundant citrus groves and flowers. As one of the most popular tourist destinations in Italy, you won't have this scenery to yourself, not even in the dead of winter, but the magical landscape is worth it.

There are tourist offices in the individual towns. For itinerary planning, www.amalficoast.com is useful.

Getting There & Away

SITA buses head from Sorrento to Positano (€1.30) and Amalfi (€2.40). For Amalfi, the bus stops at the intersection of Via C Colombo and the SS163; you can walk into town from there. The buses run every other hour during winter and about hourly in summer.

The narrow, spectacular and tortuous coastal road is clogged with traffic in summer; be prepared for delays and incredibly tight squeezes around tour buses. Things are a little quieter at other times. **Sorrento Rentacar** (☎ 081 878 13 86; Corso Italia 210a, Sorrento) rents scooters and cars.

Hydrofoils and ferries leave Naples and Sorrento for the Amalfi Coast.

Positano

pop 3900

With its Moorish flair and colourful houses, Positano is the most photographed, fashionable and expensive town on the coast. The town centre – more steps than streets – is filled with boutiques selling 'wearable art', perfect for that quirky ceramics teacher aunt of yours. The hills behind the town are full of wonderful walks; pick up a hiking map at the **tourist office** (☎ 089 87 50 67; Via del Saracino 4; 3.30-8pm in front of the Santa Maria della Assunta church.

Hostel Brikette (☎ 089 87 58 57; www.brikette.com; Via Marconi 358; dm/d with shared bathroom from €22/65, d/tr from €75/120, all incl breakfast;) After you have your breakfast of homemade pastries and freshly brewed coffee on the seaview terrace, it's just a quick stroll to the beach, town or coastal bus from here. At night you can hang out in the brand-new Mediterranean rock-hewn bar.

Villa Maria Antonietta (☎ 089 87 50 71; Via C Colombo 41; r incl breakfast €80-100) Started as the first rental accommodation in Positano 50 years ago by the current owner's grandmother, all seven of the recently remodelled rooms here are situated alongside a flower-filled terrace and have sea views.

Villa Rosa (☎ 089 81 19 55; www.villarosapositano.it; Via C Colombo 127; d incl breakfast €160) Each room in this small, family-run villa has impeccable sea views from the terrace, where you can enjoy breakfast (or room service) from their Caffè Positano restaurant.

Il Saraceno d'Oro (☎ 089 81 20 50; Viale Pasitea 254; pizza €6, 1st/2nd courses €8/13; Mar-Oct) This is a popular eatery with decent pizzas and exceptional profiteroles, with the added bonus of homemade *limoncello* (lemon liqueur) after your meal.

Caffè Positano (☎ 089 87 50 82; Viale Pasitea 168/170; 1/2 courses €11/18) Artists, tourists and romantics head here to drink, talk and dine in the sumptuous indoor rooms or under the stars on the terrace. For a truly romantic evening, make a reservation for one of the semi-private terraces.

AROUND POSITANO

Hikers will love the classic **Sentiero degli Dei** (Path of the Gods; five to 5½ hours) – ask at the tourist office for more information. For a shorter option, head to **Nocelle**, a tiny village above Positano, accessible by walking track from the stairs near Bar Internazionale. Have lunch at **Trattoria Santa Croce** (☎ 089 81 12 60; pastas from €6; lunch & dinner spring-autumn), with panoramic views. Nocelle is also accessible by local bus from Positano via Montepertuso.

Just south of Positano is the town of **Praiano**, less scenic but with the only camping ground on the Amalfi Coast. **La Tranquillità** (☎ 089 87 40 84; www.continental.praiano.it; Via Roma 21; 2 people & tent €39, bungalow €90) has many sleeping options, and the SITA bus stops outside.

Amalfi

pop 5528

A maritime superpower during the 11th century, Amalfi is now a legendary tourist resort. Despite being packed to the gills in summer, the town retains an appealing vibe. In the centre is an impressive **Duomo** (☎ 089 87 10 59; Piazza del Duomo; admission free; 9am-7pm Apr-Jun, 9am-9pm Jul-Sep, 9.30am-5.15pm Oct & Mar, 10am-1pm & 2.30-4.30pm Nov-Feb) and nearby is **Grotta dello Smeraldo** (admission €5; 9am-4pm), a rival to Capri's Blue Grotto. This is excellent walking terrain. The **tourist office** (☎ 089 87 11 07; Corso Roma 19; 8.30am-1.30pm & 3-5.30pm Mon-Fri, to 12.30pm Sat) can provide details.

SLEEPING & EATING

A'Scalinatella Hostel (☎ 089 87 14 92; www.hostelscalinatella.com; Piazza Umberto I 5, Atrani; dm/d with shared bathroom €21/60, d €83, all incl breakfast) Just 1km west of Amalfi proper is this comfortable and quiet hostel with kitchen and laundry facilities, and a small breakfast included.

Albergo Lidomare (☎ 089 87 13 32; www.lidomare.it; Largo Duchi Piccolomini 9; s €45-60, d €70-120, tr €80-130, q €90-140, all incl breakfast;) A great deal, this well-outfitted 15-room hotel offers modern conveniences – satellite TV, minibar, jet showers or Jacuzzis, towel warmers – plus seaside resort atmosphere, including terraces, a 14th-century building and antique furnishings.

Residence del Duca (☎ 089 87 36 365; www.residencedelduca.it; Via Mastalo II Duca 3; d incl breakfast €70-180 depending on season;) Once you've made it up the tricky staircase here, you'll be rewarded with the best deal in Amalfi: petite palatial rooms, romantic terraces and a few rooms with private balconies. The original building dates back to the 900s and the rooms are styled after a 16th-century duke's palace.

Pizzeria al Teatro (Via E Marini 19; pizza €5, 1st/2nd courses €8/13; closed Nov-Mar) You'll find good local dishes and a welcoming ambience here. Follow the signs to the left from Via Pietro Capuana, the main shopping street.

Trattoria San Giuseppe (Salita Ruggerio II 4; pizza €5, 1st/2nd courses €9/14) This is a tasty, family-run joint hidden away in Amalfi's maze-

ITALY

like alleyways; follow the signs from Via Lorenzo d'Amalfi.

MATERA

pop 57,315

At first glance, Matera doesn't seem real. It is one of the oldest continuously inhabited places on earth. Prehistoric caves are just across the river from the 'newer' town, where residents and their farm animals shared caves without running water or electricity up until a few years before humans landed on the moon. The caves – known as *sassi* – are a Unesco World Heritage site and, more recently, provided the setting for Mel Gibson's bloodbath *The Passion of the Christ*, being the closest thing to ancient Jerusalem.

The **tourist office** (☎ 0835 33 18 17; www.materaturismo.it; Via Spine Bianche 22; ⌚ 9am-1pm & 4-6.30pm Mon-Sat, open Tue-Thu afternoon only in winter) has plenty of *sassi* maps.

Even people who've never considered hiring a guide might want to pool resources with a few other travellers and hire a local guide through **Sassi Tourism** (☎ 0835 31 94 58; half & full-day from €35), as many of the prehistoric caves and churches are extremely difficult to reach without a car and knowledgeable local guide (some of whose parents grew up in the *sassi*).

Sights & Activities

Within Matera proper there are two *sassi* areas to discover, **Barisano** and **Caveoso**. Soon after Carlo Levi wrote his famous book *Christ Stopped at Eboli* (1945), about poor living conditions in southern Italy, the Italian government considered the malaria-ridden area a national embarrassment and began to move citizens to the modern part of town. Now, tourists and artists are flocking to the area, and even a hi-tech firm has moved in.

In the Caveoso area, the churches of **Santa Maria d'Idris** (⌚ 10am-1.30pm & 2.30pm-6.30pm) and **Santa Lucia alle Malve** (⌚ 10am-1.30pm & 2.30pm-6.30pm) have a plethora of history, with well-preserved Byzantine frescoes dating from the 1250s. In this complex is the **Casa-Grotta di Vico Solitario** (Sasso Caveoso; admission €1.50; ⌚ 9am-8.30pm May-Sep, 10am-5pm Nov-Feb), set up to show family life 40 years ago, when a family of 10 might have shared one cave with a donkey and several pigs, but with no running water or electricity (which might have contributed to the infant mortality rate of over 50%). Contact **Sassi Tourism** (☎ 0835 31 94 58; admission adult/child 1 church €2.50/1, 3 churches €5/2, 5 churches €6/3) to purchase tickets or, alternatively, pick them up at any one of the five churches on the Circuito Urbano di Chiese Rupestri.

The **Murgia Plateau**, which you can see from the *sassi*, is filled with dozens of Palaeolithic caves and monastic developments; it needs to be explored with a guide.

Sleeping

All hotels listed are in the *sassi*.

Le Monacelle (☎ 0835 34 40 97; www.lemonacelle.it; Via Riscatto 9/10; dm/s/d/tr/q incl breakfast €16/55/86/95/135; 💻) This former monastery is also a cultural centre, and guests are invited to take part in the outdoor concerts during summer. Rooms are decorated in monastic-chic style: simple, quiet and comfortable. The building is centrally located and has wi-fi.

Sassi Hotel (☎ 0835 33 10 09; www.hotelsassi.it; Via san Giovanni Vecchio 89; dm/s/d/tr/q incl breakfast €16/60/87/120/140; ❄). Hotel rooms here are set within the Barisano caves; each one has a view of the *sassi*, and some have a private terrace. The two dorm rooms have been recently refurbished.

Sant'Angelo (☎ 0835 31 40 10; www.hotelsantangelosassi.it; Rione Pianelle, Piazza di San Pietro Caveoso; s/d incl breakfast €90/120; ⊠ ❄) Who has not wondered what it would be like to sleep in a cave? Undeniably unique for a four-star hotel, each room here was once a *sassi* home. Guest rooms have nicks in the wall that used to hold the donkey pen gates or cooking implements. Satellite TVs, grand furnishings and spa-like bathrooms allow for a bit of time travel, but without requiring the proper vaccinations.

Also available:

Torre B&B (☎ 349 162 14 01; Via Ospedale Vecchio; s/d/tr/q incl breakfast €45/65/80/95, apt for up to 6 people €180) Rooms tucked inside a fascinating private *sassi* home.

Residence San Pietro Barisano (☎ 0835 34 61 91; www.residencesanpietrobarisano.it; Rione San Biagio 52; s/d incl breakfast €75/110; ❄) Also a restaurant, blends modern with ancient.

Eating & Drinking

Ginger Caffè (☎ 0835 33 53 07; Via Lucana 54) With a great neighbourhood atmosphere, the draw here is the *apertivo* – buy a €5 drink and

ITALY

snack on a full meal's worth of delicious homemade savouries.

Il Terrazzino (☎ 0835 33 25 03; Vico San Giuseppe 7, off Piazza V Veneto; set menu €14) For a visual and gastronomic treat during summer, eat on the terrace here overlooking the *sassi*. Try their invention: *orecchiette al tegamino* (homemade ear-shaped pasta bubbling in a tomato- and cheese-filled dish; €6).

Fresh-produce market (Via A Persio) This is a daily market, just south of Piazza Vittoria Veneto.

Getting There & Away

Matera is most easily reached by long-distance bus or the private train Ferrovie Appulo Lucane, which runs hourly from Bari (€4, one hour 20 minutes). From Bari Centrale station, turn left out of the main entrance and enter the bright yellow building on the corner to catch the train to Matera. Catch a Marozzi bus between Rome's Stazione Tiburtina and Matera (€30, five hours, one daily). Buy tickets at **Biglietteria Manicone** (☎ 0835 332 86 21; Piazza Matteotti 3; 6-9am, 11am-12.15pm & 3.30-7pm Mon-Fri, 5-7pm Sat).

BRINDISI

pop 90,020

Let's face it: no one is coming to Brindisi except to catch a ferry. Despite its shady reputation, there are worse places you could find yourself for the day. There's a hostel, several Internet cafés and decent restaurants, and even a fascinating history, as Brindisi was the final port for Crusaders on the Appian Way.

From the train station, walk straight out onto Corso Umberto I towards the fountain to reach the historic centre. For the free shuttle bus to Costa Morena port (from where the Greece- and Turkey-bound ferries leave), the tourist office or the restaurants listed following, veer slightly left from the fountain facing the sea on Corso Garibaldi until you reach Piazza Vittorio Emanuele. For the ferries to Albania, continue from there and veer right onto Via del Mare.

While in town, check your email, grab a snack or play video games at **Tetris** (☎ 0831 59 09 54; Via Bastioni S Giorgio 20/22; per 20 min €1; 10.30-12am Mon-Sat, 4pm-12am Sun in Nov-Feb), or stop by the **tourist office** (☎ 0831 52 30 72; www.brindisiweb.com or www.pugliaturismo.com; Viale Regina Margherita 44; 8am-10pm Jun-Sep, 8am-1.30pm & 2.30-8pm Mon-Sat Nov-Feb), which is an attraction in itself, housed in an old Crusader palace from the 11th century.

Carpe Diem (☎ 0831 418 418, 338 323 5545; www.hostelcarpediem.it; Via Nicola Brandi 2; camping per person €5, dm/s/d incl breakfast €15/25/40, day use €6;) For day use or to overnight, stop into this well-serviced hostel. You can forgive the less-than-spotless bathrooms for all the extras, including free pick-up and drop off at the port, airport, train station or downtown (or take bus 3 from downtown), and laundry facilities (wash and dry €6). There's no kitchen to use, but Maurizio serves big plates of communal pasta for lunch and dinner (€6). Internet costs €1.50 for 15 minutes.

Albergo Venezia (☎ 0831 527 511; Via Pisanell 4, off Piazza Mercato; s/d/tr/q with shared bathroom €16/26/48/60) With prices like these and located just 200m from the free shuttle bus, keep your expectations low and you'll do fine here.

For a good and filling lunch, visit Amalia's kitchen at **Trattoria Pizzeria Regina** (☎ 0831 568 693; Largo Guglielmo da Brindisi 28; pizza from €3, set menu €10), where Amalia cooks up delicious four-course meals and pizzas single-handedly.

Getting There & Away

Appia Travel (☎ 0831 52 16 84; Viale Regina Margherita 8-9) sells bus tickets for Rome (€36, nine hours). There are rail connections to major cities in northern Italy, as well as to Bari, Lecce, Ancona, Naples and Rome, and you can fly to/from Rome, Naples, Milan, Bologna and Pisa from Brindisi's small airport, **Papola Casale** (BDS; ☎ 0831 41 21 41).

BOAT

Ferries, all of which take vehicles and have snack bars and sleeping cabins or berths, leave Brindisi for Greek destinations, including Corfu (10 to 15 hours), Igoumenitsa (nine to 12 hours) and Patra (15 to 20 hours). Boats also service Albania (daily) and Turkey (seasonal).

Most ferry companies operate only in summer. All have offices at Costa Morena, and the major ones also have offices in town along Corso Garibaldi.

Hellenic Mediterranean Lines (HML; ☎ 0831 52 85 31; www.hml.gr; Corso Garibaldi 8)

ITALY

Blue Star Ferries (☎ 0831 56 22 00; www.bluestarferries.com; Corso Garibaldi 65)
Italian Ferries (☎ 0831 59 08 40; www.italianferries.it; Corso Garibaldi 96)
Agoudimos (☎ 0831 52 14 08; www.agoudimos-lines.com; Via Anime 23)

The largest, most expensive and most reliable of the lines, HML also officially accepts Eurail and Inter-Rail passes, entitling you to travel free in deck class (paying a €15 supplement in July and August). If you intend to use your pass, it is best to reserve in advance in summer.

The port tax is €6, payable when you buy your ticket. Check in at least two hours before departure or risk losing your reservation. To get to the port of Costa Morena from the train station, take the free Portabagagli bus, a large white minibus that runs between town and the port every hour when ferries are running.

Check prices and availability at www.traghettionline.net or www.ferries.gr for destinations in Greece.

LECCE

pop 97,462

This sparkling little city hosts an astonishing array of baroque architecture; the effect is of a crazy but delightful architect gone a bit mad. Unabashedly opulent, the local style is known to Italians as *barocco leccese* (Lecce baroque), and Lecce is oft referred to as the 'Florence of the South'. The university town exudes a sassy charm and supports a vibrant bar scene at weekends. It's also home to a high population of lawyers, but don't let that discourage you from visiting this elegant surprise.

The **tourist office** (☎ 0832 24 80 92; Corso Vittorio Emanuele 24; 9am-1pm & 4-8pm Mon-Sat Jul-Sep, 9am-1pm Mon-Fri & 4-7pm Tue & Thu Oct-Jun) is near Piazza Duomo. The historic centre is a five-minute walk from the train station, or take bus 1, 2 or 4 from the station to Viale Marconi.

Sights

Lecce's baroque style is most famously on display at the **Basilica della Santa Croce** (☎ 0832 24 19 57; Via Umberto I; admission free; 8am-1pm & 4-7.30pm). A team of artists worked throughout the 16th and 17th centuries to decorate the building and its extraordinarily ornate façade. In the **Piazza del Duomo** are the 12th-century **cathedral** (admission free; 6.30am-noon & 4-6.30pm), completely restored in baroque style by Giuseppe Zimbalo, and its 70m-high **bell tower**; the 15th-century **Palazzo Vescovile** (Bishop's Palace); and the **Seminario**, with its elegant façade and baroque well in the courtyard. The piazza is particularly beautiful at night, illuminated by floodlights. In **Piazza Sant'Oronzo** you can stroll across a bridge spanning the remains of a 2nd-century-AD **Roman amphitheatre**.

Sleeping

Hotel Cappello (☎ 0832 30 88 81; Via Montegrappa 4; s/d €35/50;) The only nonbusiness hotel option in Lecce, the Cappello is plain but centrally located.

Centro Storico (☎ 0832 24 28 28; www.bedandbreakfast.lecce.it; Via Vignes 2/b; s/d with shared bathroom incl breakfast €35/57, ste €80;) This hotel has a lovely solarium and library. It's run by the same family and in the same building as **Azzurretta B&B** (☎ 338 258 59 58; www.bblecce.it, in Italian; Via Vignes 2; s/d incl breakfast €35/63), where the rooms have kitchenettes.

Sweet Place (☎ 338 87 10 295; sweet.place@fisicaonline.net; Via Frante d'Aragone 17b; s/d €35/60) An aptly named B&B run by a sweet family, you get an entire apartment to yourself here, complete with TV, hydro-massage shower and fully equipped kitchen.

B&B Prestige (☎ 0832 24 33 53; www.bbprestige-lecce.it; Via S Maria del Paradiso; s/d/tr incl breakfast €70/80/110; closed mid-Feb) On the 3rd floor of a 16th-century *palazzo*, this gem has elegantly furnished and balconied rooms, a roof garden and a hip owner.

Eating and Drinking

Il Giardino dei Mocenigo (☎ 0832 30 11 08; Via dei Mocenigo 15; 1st/2nd courses €5.50/13) A covered terrace and pasta starting at €4 make this busy restaurant a good choice.

Trattoria Casereccia (☎ 0832 24 51 78; Via Colonello Costadura 19; pasta from €6; closed Mon) This family-run favourite serves home cooking at good value prices.

Picton (☎ 0832 33 23 83; Via Idomeneo 14; 1st/2nd courses €9/16; closed Mon) Bathed in local tradition, this is the place to try local Lecce cuisine. A cosy stone fireplace and subterranean cantina add to the atmosphere, while fresh pasta and fish dishes deliver good quality.

Torre di Merlino (☎ 0832 24 18 74; Vico del Tufo; ⏰ from 8pm) The historic centre hosts a plethora of picturesque little bars; this is one of the better ones. It serves over 400 wines and dozens of meats and cheeses, which you can sample on a mixed plate (€14 to €20).

Getting There & Away

Lecce is the end of the main southeastern train line and there are trains to Brindisi (€2.30, 35 minutes, hourly), Bari (€8.60 to €12.20, two hours, hourly), Rome (€44.20, seven hours, six daily), Naples (€35.90, six hours) and Bologna (€53, 8½ hours), as well as to points throughout Puglia.

SICILY

Sicily is at once wholeheartedly Italian, but universally distinct. It witnessed cultural diversity 2000 years before the term became fashionable, and continues to see an influx of immigrants from all around the Mediterranean and beyond. The island the Italian boot seems poised to drop-kick into the Mediterranean has been occupied by dozens of invading forces for the past three millennia, all of whom left their architectural, cultural and gastronomic mark. Go one step in any direction on the largest island in the Mediterranean, and find the scars of domination: Greek temples, Arab domes, Byzantine mosaics, Norman castles, Angevin churches and baroque architecture.

Sicily's landscape is dominated by Mt Etna (3350m) on the east coast, laced with fertile citrus groves, fringed with dazzling coastline, and has a vast plateau at its heart. Although cacti cover the southern ridges, snow is not uncommon at higher elevations and can linger on Mt Etna until June. The winters are quite mild but the summers relentlessly hot. Spring and autumn are the best seasons to visit, to avoid crowds, rain and oppressive humidity.

Most ferries from Italy arrive at Sicily's capital, Palermo. If you're short on time, spend an awestruck day in Palermo looking at the sites and museums while dodging lawless drivers, and then hit Taormina to wander its chic streets and fab beaches, Syracuse for the ancient island-cum-tourist-resort of Ortygia, or Agrigento's marvellously kept Greek ruins and museum.

Getting There & Away

AIR

Flights from all over mainland Italy and from major European cities land at **Palermo** (PMO; ☎ 091 70 20 111; www.gesap.it) and **Catania** (CTA), including the main Italian airline **Alitalia** (☎ 00 39 06 22 22; www.alitalia.com). Low-cost carriers **Meridiana** (☎ 199 111 333; www.meridiana.it) and **Air One** (☎ 199 20 70 80; www.flyairone.it) both fly into Palermo and Catania.

BOAT

Sicily is accessible by ferry from Genoa, Livorno, Naples, Reggio di Calabria and Cagliari, and also from Malta and Tunisia. The main companies servicing the Mediterranean are **Tirrenia** (☎ 199 12 31 99; www.tirrenia.it), **Grimaldi** (☎ 091 58 74 04; www.grimaldi.it) and **Grandi Navi Veloci** (☎ 091 58 79 39; www.gnv.it). **SNAV** (☎ in Palermo 091 58 60 66, in Naples 081 761 23 48; www.snav.com) runs a summer ferry between Naples and Palermo. Prices vary by season and are highest from July to September. Timetables vary, so check with any Italian travel agency or on the Web at www.traghettionline.net. Book well in advance during summer, particularly if you have a car.

For information on ferries going from the mainland directly to the Aeolian Islands, see p805.

BUS

Direct bus services between Rome and Sicily are operated by **SAIS** (☎ 091 616 60 28; www.saistrasporti.it, in Italian) and **Interbus** (☎ 0935 56 51 11; www.interbus.it, in Italian), departing from Rome's Piazza Tiburtina. Buses service Messina (€27, 9¼ hours), Catania (€30, 11 hours), Palermo (€35, 12 hours) and Syracuse (€32.50, 11½ hours).

TRAIN

Taking a train to Sicily takes a bit of extra time because of the strait crossing to Messina, but you don't pay extra for the ferry. For train information, call **Trenitalia** (☎ 89 20 21; ⏰ 7am-9pm).

Getting Around

The island has good bus and train services. Buses are quite regular and reliable between larger towns. All of the towns listed in this chapter have good train connections as well. The coastal train services between Messina and Palermo and from Messina to Syracuse vary from efficient and reliable to delayed and unpredictable, as does the run between Palermo and Agrigento.

The roads can vary dramatically, from winding single lanes to vast *autostrade* (highway).

PALERMO

pop 680,000

Palermo is chaotic, traffic-laden and densely packed, but makes up for it with some of the most unique restaurants in Italy, dozens of once-grand palaces and a frenetic pace that will enliven even the most ho-hum of visitor.

It might not be the most tranquil place, but the striations of history make it a fascinating destination. Palermo has been conquered countless times by countless forces – Carthaginians, Greeks, Romans, Spaniards, Arabs, Normans, Byzantines, Savoy, Austrians et al – making the city feel like it's been shaken in a cultural, gastronomic and architectural snow globe for 2800 years and spewed out willy-nilly along a harbour. As a result it seems many residents are too exhausted to pay attention to stop signs or traffic rules, but it also means that visitors brave enough to navigate the congested streets will be rewarded with a living history lesson.

Orientation

Palermo's historic core is large but easily manageable on foot, which is lucky, as driving here equates with a death wish. You can walk from the ferry terminal or train station to any hotel listed here within 20 minutes. The main historic sights radiate out from the 'four corners' intersection (Quattro Canti).

Information

Citysightseeing Palermo (☎ 091 58 94 29; www.palermo.city-sightseeing.it; adult/child €15/7.50) One ticket buys 24 hours, enabling two separate days of sightseeing. Begins in front of Teatro Politeamo.

Lo Cascio Night Pharmacy (☎ 091 616 21 17; Via Roma 1; 🕑 all night, closed 1-4pm Mon-Fri, 9am-7pm Sat & Sun) Just in front of the train station.

Ospedale Civico (Hospital; ☎ 091 666 11 11; Via Carmelo Lazzaro)

Palazzo del Poste (Post Office; ☎ 091 753 11 11; Via Roma 322)

Police station (Questura; ☎ theft & lost documents 091 21 01 11, foreigners' office 091 651 43 30; Piazza della Vittoria; 🕑 24hr)

Pronto Soccorso (☎ 091 655 37 29) First aid.

Sun Fone Center (☎ 091 617 23 12; Via Maqueda 125; Internet per hr €2; 🕑 9am-11pm) For Internet and cheap international phone rates.

Tourist offices (www.palermotourism.com); Piazza Castelnuovo 34 (☎ 091 60 58 351; 🕑 8.30am-2pm & 3-6pm Mon-Fri); Stazione Centrale (☎ 091 616 59 14; 🕑 8.30am-2pm & 3-6pm Mon-Fri); airport (☎ 091 59 16 98; 🕑 8am-midnight Mon-Fri, 8am-8pm Sat) All are exceedingly helpful. Pick up a copy of *Agenda*, which lists everything you could possibly need: bus times and prices, museum hours and prices, local trips.

Sights

The intersection of Corso Vittorio Emanuele and Via Maqueda marks the **Quattro Canti**, the historic centre of Palermo where the four city districts converge. On each corner stands a building decorated with baroque sculptures commissioned by the Spanish viceroy when Palermo was under Spain's control. Nearby, Piazza Pretoria houses the beautifully ornate **Fontana Pretoria**, one of the only examples of Renaissance art in the entire city, brought from Florence in the 16th century. For a striking example of baroque domes, check out the **Chiesa di Santa Caterina**, and the **Palazzo del Municipio** (town hall).

Around the corner, in Piazza Bellini, you'll find Palermo's top wedding spot, the famous church **La Martorana** (Chiesa di Santa Maria dell'Ammiraglio; ☎ 091 616 1692; admission free; 🕑 8am-1pm & 3.30-5.30pm Mon-Sat, 8.30am-1pm Sun), with a striking Arab-Norman bell tower and stunning Byzantine mosaic interior. Next door is the red-domed **Chiesa di San Cataldo**, which meshes Arab and Norman styles.

Perhaps the creepiest place in…oh, just about the entire world, is the **Capuchin Catacombs** (☎ 091 21 21 17; Piazza Cappuccini 1; admission €2; 🕑 9am-12pm & 3-5pm), where there's an entire underground catacomb filled with skeletal remains and mummified bodies of Palermitans. The first underground, ahem, residents were Capuchin monks in 1599. Bodies are preserved so well here – some with arsenic or lime, others by 'straining' the body dry and then preserving it in

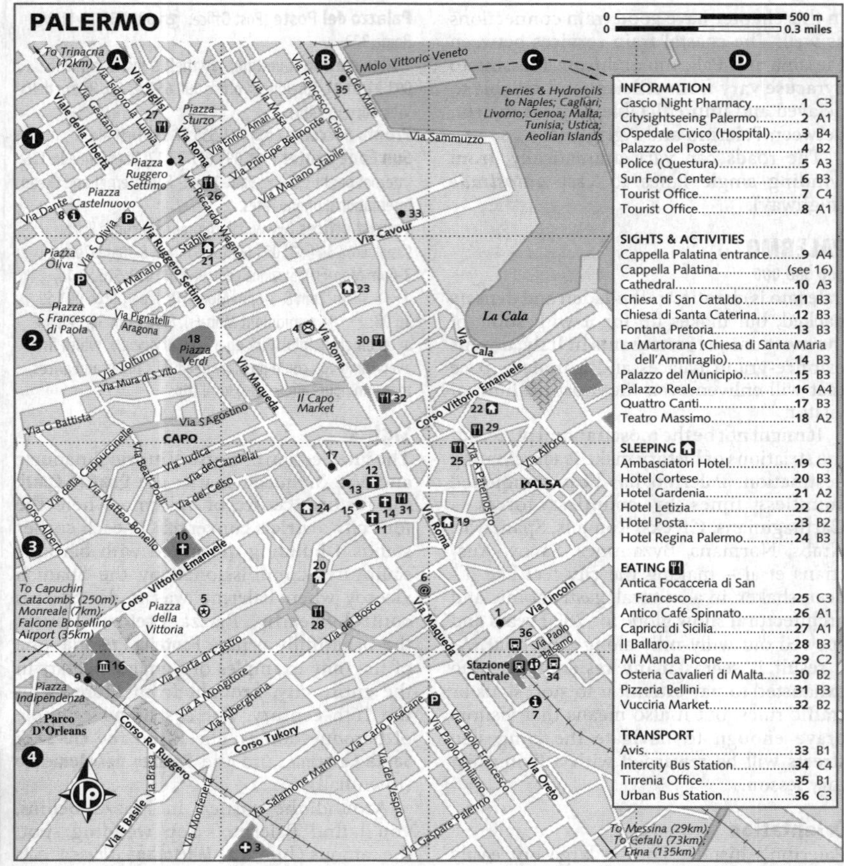

vinegar – that you can still see hair, skin and eyeballs. Just to make it more macabre, some mummies hang along the wall fully dressed and there's a 'virgin' room dedicated to unmarried young girls.

In Piazza Verdi is the grand neoclassical **Teatro Massimo** (☎ 800 655 858; www.teatromassimo.it, in Italian; guided tours adult/concession €3/2; 🕑 10am-3.30pm Tue-Sun except on rehearsal days). It took over 20 years to complete and, in 1897, opened to celebrate the unification of Italy. The theatre has become a symbol of the triumph and tragedy of Palermo itself; appropriately, the closing scene of *The Godfather III* was filmed here.

The huge **cathedral** (☎ 091 33 43 73; Corso Vittorio Emanuele; admission free; 🕑 9.30am-5.30pm), modified many times over the centuries, is a good example of Sicily's unique Arab-Norman style. At Piazza Indipendenza is **Palazzo Reale**, also known as the Palazzo dei Normanni, now the seat of the Sicilian parliament. Step inside and downstairs to see the **Cappella Palatina** (☎ 091 705 48 79; admission free; 🕑 8.30am-noon & 2-4.30pm Mon-Sat, 8.30am-2pm & 3-4.45pm Sun & holidays), a truly jaw-dropping example of Arab-Norman architecture, designed by Roger II in 1130 and lavishly decorated with exquisite mosaics. King Roger's former bedroom, **Sala di Ruggero** (☎ 091 705 43 17; admission free; 🕑 9am-noon Mon, Fri & Sat), is adorned with 12th-century mosaics; you can only visit the room with a guide (free).

Sleeping

Trinacria (☎/fax 091 53 05 90; www.campingtrinacria.it; Via Barcarello 25; per person/camp site €4.50/7.50) The area's best camping is 12 km northwest of Palermo, at Sferracavallo, by the sea. Catch bus 628 from Piazzale Alcide de Gasperi, reached by bus 101 or 107 from the station.

Hotel Regina Palermo (☎ 091 611 42 16; www.hotelreginapalermo.com; Corso Vittorio Emanuele 316; s/d with shared bathroom €23/42, d/tr incl breakfast €52/72) Just past Quattro Canti on the main street is this great value hotel. All rooms come with heating, fan and TV. Street noise can be an issue, so bring earplugs.

Hotel Cortese (☎ 091 33 17 22; www.hotelcortese.net; Via Scarparelli; s/d/tr €35/60/80, s/d with shared bathroom €30/50;) Near the chaotic open markets of Balları is this adorable hotel, housed in a 1700s villa. Enjoy the great towels, clean shared bathrooms, small shared terrace and large buffet breakfast (€4).

Hotel Gardenia (☎ 091 32 27 61; www.hotelgardeniapalermo.it; Via Mariano Stabile 136; s/d/tr €65/90/130;) All rooms at this two-star hotel are soundproofed and have DSL lines and modest private terraces.

Ambasciatori Hotel (☎ 091 610 66 881; www.ambasciatorihotelpalermo.com; 5th fl, Via Roma 111; s/d/tr/q €60/100/110/125;) This hotel's main charm is its 6th-floor rooftop terrace, where you can have breakfast or just admire the bird's-eye view. The young English-speaking staff is helpful and the shower's strong water pressure is a welcome respite after a day in Palermo. Internet costs €3 per 15 minutes.

Hotel Posta (☎ 091 58 73 38; www.hotelpostapalermo.it; Via Gagini 77; s/d/tr incl breakfast €85/112/145;) Clean bathrooms and large sleeping quarters make this a good choice. Near the post office it's been a mainstay for artists for several decades. You can get on the Net for €0.10 per minute.

Hotel Letizia (☎ 091 58 91 10; www.hotelletizia.com; Via dei Bottai 30; s/d/tr incl breakfast €85/134/155;) One of Palermo's sweetest inns, this place also seamlessly doubles as a business hotel. Thirteen pretty rooms come with wood floors and an airy ambience; there's also a cheery reading nook and a breakfast terrace (but no lift).

Eating

Palermo became a crossroads of cuisine 3000 years ago, when it was a market city dedicated to trading spices between East and West, and has been perfecting its cooking ever since. Even Homer sang the praises of the island's vegetable produce back in *The Odyssey*, and many classic Sicilian dishes come from the Saracen/Arab influence from the 800s, including pasta and ice cream.

Locals dine late and restaurants rarely open for dinner before 8.30pm.

Antico Café Spinnato (☎ 091 58 32 31; Via Principe Belmonte 107-15) This elegant pastry shop has been serving its loyal clientele since 1860. The cakes are works of art, the *gelato* heavenly and the shaded outdoor tables ideal for a coffee *granita* (slushy iced dessert).

Capricci di Sicilia (☎ 091 32 77 77; Via Instituto Pignatelli 6; 2nd courses from €7) Once a puppet theatre, this cosy restaurant serves typical Sicilian fare, with an excellent selection of antipasto; it's always whirring with locals, so make a reservation in summer.

Osteria Cavalieri di Malta (☎ 091 58 65 95; Vicolo Pantelleria 30; 1st/2nd courses €7/10; closed Wed) Posh red brocade walls, ancient beams and chandeliers somehow fit seamlessly into this casual neighbourhood restaurant. Specialities include *pasta con sardi* (fettuccine with sardines), walnut ravioli and risotto with walnuts and lemon. The classic Sicilian *cassata* (sponge cake with candied fruits and nuts) is fantastic.

Pizzeria Bellini (☎ 091 616 56 91; Piazza Bellini 6; pizza €5, 1st/2nd courses €7/10) The oldest pizzeria in town has a coveted spot, nestled in the shadow of La Martorana; come to eat at night, when the churches glow with floodlights.

Antica Focacceria di San Francesco (☎ 091 32 02 64; Via Paternostro 58; mains €8, self-service €2-7) A local institution with workers since 1834, there are three levels here including takeaway, self-service and a restaurant. Downstairs offers a bustling atmosphere and serves delicious *calzone*, pizza slices and some Palermitan speciality snacks, such as *panini* stuffed with ricotta and steaming calf innards.

Mi Manda Picone (☎ 091 616 06 60; Via A Paternostro 59; mains from €10) Nestled in a 13th-century building on Piazza San Francesco, this terrific restaurant serves top-notch contemporary cuisine in an airy arched interior. It doubles as an *enoteca*, where you can opt for generous platters of cheese and salami while sipping Sicilian *vino*.

WORTH A TRIP

In the town of **Monreale**, just 8km southwest of Palermo, is the world-famous 12th-century **Duomo** (☎ 091 640 44 13; admission free; ⌚ 8am-6pm), where the entire ceiling is covered in 6400 sq m of mosaics telling the stories of Adam and Eve, Noah, and God creating the universe in seven days. It's also worth checking out its **cloisters** (admission €4.50; ⌚ 9am-7pm Mon-Sat, 9am- 1.30pm Sun). To get there, take bus 389 from Palermo's Piazza Indipendenza.

Palermo's best open-air markets are the **Vucciria** (⌚ Mon-Sat), in the narrow streets around Piazza San Domenico, and **Il Ballaro** (⌚ daily), held in the Albergheria quarter off Via Maqueda; both have excellent offerings and unbeatable local colour.

Getting There & Away

Falcone-Borsellino airport (PMO; ☎ 091 70 20 111; www.gesap.it) is 30km west of Palermo along the A29. **Alitalia** (☎ 06 22 22; www.alitalia.it) flies in, as do some of the low-cost airlines such as **Air One** (☎ 199 20 70 80; www.flyairone.it) and **Meridiana** (☎ 199 111 333; www.meridiana.it).

The main intercity bus station is around Via Paolo Balsamo, to the right as you leave the train station. Main companies include **SAIS Autolinee** (☎ 091 616 60 28; www.saisautolinee.it, in Italian) and **Interbus** (☎ 0935 56 51 11; www.interbus.it, in Italian). They head to the mainland through Messina.

Regular trains leave from the Stazione Centrale for Milazzo, Messina, Catania, Trapani, Syracuse and Agrigento, as well as for nearby towns such as Cefalù. Direct trains go to Reggio di Calabria, Naples and Rome.

Boats leave from the port (Molo Vittorio Veneto) for Sardinia and the mainland (see p800). The **Tirrenia office** (☎ 091 602 11 11) is at the port.

Getting Around

Taxis to the airport cost about €40, but the blue **Prestia e Comandé** (☎ 091 58 04 57) buses are extremely convenient. One way costs €5 and they leave every 30 minutes, between 5am and 11pm from the city and from 6.30am to midnight from the airport. In town, they leave from near the train station (in front of Hotel Elena) and in front of Hotel Politeama. There's also an hourly train service from the airport to Stazione Centrale (€4.50) between 5.40am and 10.40pm.

Most of Palermo's city buses stop outside or near the train station. You must buy tickets before you get on the bus; they cost €0.80 and are valid for two hours, or €2.60 for a day pass.

For car rentals, there's an **Avis** (☎ 091 586 940; 113 Via Francesco Crispi; ⌚ 8.30am-1pm & 3.30-7pm Mon-Fri, 8.30am-12.30pm Sat) office near the ferry terminal.

AEOLIAN ISLANDS

The entire *Isole Eolie* (Aeolian Islands) chain is so stunning it's been declared a Unesco World Heritage site. They've been impressing visitors since Homer's hero Odysseus blew through in *The Odyssey*. Formed by a volcanic eruption, the seven islands have a landscape distinct from both Sicily and the mainland. Residents emigrated 100 years ago because of difficult living conditions, but the tourists who descend upon its beaches don't seem to mind the lack of arable farmland.

The islands have distinct personalities – from bustling Lipari to elite Panarea to the rugged beauty of Salina, Vulcano or Stromboli and the rustic, undeveloped Alicudi and Filicudi – but they all have overcrowded summers in common. Best visit in spring or autumn.

There is a **tourist information office** (☎ 090 988 00 95; www.estateolie.it, in Italian; Via Vittorio Emanuele 202; ⌚ 8am-2pm Mon-Sat & 4.30-7.30pm Mon-Fri) in Lipari. Offices on Vulcano, Salina and Stromboli are open during summer only.

Sights & Activities

On **Lipari** visit the Spanish Aragon–built **citadel** (⌚ 9am-7pm), with its fabulous **Museo Archeologico Eoliano** (☎ 090 988 01 74; admission €4.50; ⌚ 9am-1.30pm & 3-7pm Mon-Sat). There are excellent walks on the island, as well as good snorkelling and scuba diving. The tourist office has information on trails, beaches and excursions.

With its pungent sulphurous odour, **Vulcano** is a short boat trip from Lipari. The main volcano, **Vulcano Fossa**, is still active, although the last recorded period of eruption was 1888–90. You can take the one-hour hike to the crater, or a bath in the therapeutic hot mud.

On the most spectacular of the islands, **Stromboli**, you can climb the volcano. While recent activity has made it too dangerous to hike to the volcano's 841m summit, you can still hike 365m up the craters with a guide (or 270m without) and view the impressive Sciara del Fuoco (Trail of Fire) – lava streaming down the side of the volcano. Contact **Magmatrek** (☎ 090 986 57 68; www.magmatrek.it) for guided treks to the crater (they only depart if groups are large enough).

Sleeping & Eating

Camping facilities are available on Lipari, Salina and Vulcano. Most accommodation in summer is booked out well in advance on the smaller islands, particularly on Stromboli, and many places close during winter. Prices skyrocket during summer, but you can find good deals outside the high season.

LIPARI

Lipari has the most options and greatest range of accommodation, and from here the other islands are easily accessible by regular hydrofoil. Don't dismiss outright offers for *affittacamere* by touts when you arrive at the port – they're often genuine.

Diana Brown (☎ 090 981 25 84; dbrown@netnet.it; Vico Himera 3; s/d/tr €70/80/100, apt in high season up to €100; ❄) has 12 comfortable rooms that are centrally located. The self-catering apartments have small kitchenettes. Diana is a fountain of local knowledge; she and her husband also run **Gruppo di Navigazione** (www.navigazioniregina.com), featuring boat tours of all the islands.

Lazing over half the piazza, Lipari's classiest joint **Filippino** (☎ 090 981 10 02; Piazza Municipo; mains from €16) has superb seafood and top-notch service; dress to show off your tan and make a reservation. For pizza, hit the rightfully popular **La Piazzetta** (☎ 090 981 25 22; pizza from €5), off Corso Vittorio with piazza-side tables. Also recommended is tiny **La Cambusa** (☎ 349 476 60 61; Via Garibaldi 72; mains from €12), serving delicious pastas and fish.

STROMBOLI

La Sirenetta (☎ 090 98 60 25; www.lasirenetta.it; Via Marina 33; s €115, d €180-240; ❄ 💻 🏊) is a serene pad perfectly located in front of Stròmbolicchio, a towering promontory rising out of the sea at San Vincenzo. The panoramic terrace with a great restaurant encourages lingering, and the ocean-view rooms are honeymoon-worthy.

VULCANO

You'll find good value at **Hotel Torre** (☎/fax 090 985 23 42; www.hoteltorrevulcano.it; Via Favaloro 1; per person low/high season €39/78; ❄), a modest affair with large rooms, kitchens, terraces and beach access just 150m away.

ALICUDI & FILICUDI

If you want seclusion and still-wild beauty, head for Alicudi or Filicudi. The former offers the simple but nice **Ericusa** (☎ 090 988 99 02; fax 090 988 96 71; Via Regina Elena; d €62, half-board per person €60), while Filicudi has the truly delightful **La Canna** (☎ 090 988 99 56; vianast@tin.it; Via Rosa 43; s/d €40/80). There are good restaurants at both.

Getting There & Away

Ferries and hydrofoils leave for the islands from Milazzo (easily reached by train from Palermo and Messina) and all ticket offices are along Corso dei Mille at the port. If arriving at Milazzo by train, catch a Giunta bus to the port. **SNAV** (☎ 081 428 51 11) and **Siremar** (☎ 081 580 03 40) run hydrofoils (€11.30), and the latter also has ferries (€7.50).

The ferry journey takes about two hours to Lipari and five to seven hours to Stromboli (two to four daily, July to September). Hydrofoils make the journey to Vulcano (40 minutes), Lipari (55 minutes) and Stromboli (two hours and 50 minutes, seven daily), running up to seven times daily in July through September. Prices range from €5.30 to €12.50. Tickets for hydrofoils are slightly more, ranging from €9.40 to €21.30. SNAV also runs hydrofoils between the islands and Palermo (summer only).

You can also travel directly to the islands from the mainland. Siremar runs regular ferries from Naples, and SNAV runs hydrofoils from Naples, Messina and Reggio di Calabria. Occasionally, rough seas cancel sailings.

Getting Around

Regular hydrofoil and ferry services operate between the islands. Both Siremar and SNAV have booths at Lipari's port, where you can get full timetable information.

TAORMINA

pop 10,700

Perched impossibly along a rocky cliff-top promontory, Taormina is both a tiny, cobblestone village and Sicily's glitziest resort. In summer, hordes of visitors come for the chic shops and to wander the streets made famous by Goethe and DH Lawrence, two of Taormina's most famed former residents. Outside of July and August, the crowds thin enough to enjoy the Greek theatre, English gardens, island beach and labyrinthine streets that make this a popular locale.

Taormina is horribly complicated to navigate, and many hotels will gather you at the car park or train station rather than try to explain directions.

The **tourist office** (☎ 0942 2 32 43; www.gate2taormina.com; Palazzo Corvaja 1 at Lungo Santa Caterina; 8.30am-2pm & 4-7pm, closed Sun) has local maps, excursion information, and lists of *affittacamere* and B&Bs. Head to **Net Point** (☎ 0943 626 080; Via Jallia Bassia 34; per min €0.10, minimum 20 min) to check your email.

Sights & Activities

You'll recognise the famous Sicilian postcard image of **Teatro Greco** (☎ 0942 2 32 20; Via Teatro Greco; adult/concession €6/3; 9am-4pm winter, 9am to sunset summer), the Graeco-Roman theatre in the half-round looking out over the Ionian Sea. Although the Greeks built it in the 3rd century BC, the Romans did some remodelling. During summer, ask at the tourist office about open-air concerts.

From the colourful, well-tended English gardens of **Giardino Trevelyan** (9am-7pm), you'll have a panoramic view of the sea. Along the pedestrianised Corso Umberto I is **Piazza del Duomo**, which has a baroque fountain and Norman-Gothic cathedral. During summer, throw in an adventurous ride to Taormina's unique island beach, **Isola Bella**, which is accessible by **cable car** (one way/return €1.70/3; 8am-8pm, until 1am in summer, every 15 min).

Mt Etna trips (€27) can be organised through **CST** (☎ 0942 62 60 88; Corso Umberto I 101).

Sleeping & Eating

Taormina's Odyssey (☎ 0942 2 45 33; www.taorminaodyssey.com; Trav A - Via G Martino 2; dm/d incl breakfast €17/45) Just three dorm rooms and two doubles share a small kitchen and convivial common room off Fontana Vecchia and Via Cappuccini. Taormina's is a 10-minute walk from town; follow the signs for Hotel Andromaco.

Pensione Svizzera (☎ 0942 2 37 90; www.pensionesvizzera.com; Via Pirandello 26; s €95, d €100-125, all incl breakfast; Feb-Nov;) Owned by the same family since 1925, the staff here will arrange just about anything, and a shuttle runs to the beach in high season. Room prices go up as the view gets better.

Hotel Belvedere (☎ 0942 2 37 91; www.villabelvedere.it; Via Bagnoli Croce 79; s €70-134, d €118-212, all incl breakfast; Mar-Nov, Christmas; P) One of the first hotels in town (opened in 1902), this family-run spot has an enviable location, and the pretty citrus gardens and pool-side lunch service make it a holiday idyll.

Ritrovo Trocadero (☎ 0943 2 43 30; Via Pirandello 1; 8am-midnight) Trocadero is good, cheap and keeps all-day traveller-friendly hours. Try the *maccheroni trocadero*: homemade pasta with fish, tomatoes, basil and cream (€7.50). Omelettes are served all day (around €5.50).

Ristorante Luraleo (☎ 0942 62 01 64; Via Bagnoli Croci 27/31) A cross between '60s kitsch and old-world farmhouse, Luraleo features hanging copper pots, a tiled wood-burning stove and vine-draped outdoor terrace alongside tacky stained glass. Ask for the house special, an enormous plate of fresh fish and vegetables (€20 per person).

Granduca (☎ 0942 2 49 83; Corso Umberto 172; pizza from €5) Excellent pizza and a spectacular terrace make this a consistently good choice.

Getting There & Away

Taormina is easily reached on the main rail line from Messina (€3.15, 50 minutes, hourly except from 9.30am to 12.10pm) and Catania (€3.15, 45 minutes, hourly). You can also take the intercity bus **Etna Trasporti** (☎ 095 53 27 16) to Catania (€3, 1½ hours, hourly), leaving from Via Pirandello.

MT ETNA

Dominating the landscape in eastern Sicily between Taormina and Catania, Mt Etna (3350m) is Europe's largest live volcano, and is also one of the world's most active. Eruptions occur frequently, both from the four live craters at the summit and on the volcano's slopes, which are littered with fissures and extinct cones.

ITALY

Volcanic activity picks up pace from time to time, so be aware that trekking excursions are at the mercy of steam plumes and lava flows. Due to the volcano's unpredictability, you can no longer climb to the craters, although it is still possible to climb one of the peaks in front of the Rifugio Sapienza to get a small taste of the real thing. **Gruppo Guide Alpine Etna Sud** (☎ 095 791 47 55) or **Natura e Turismo** (☎ 095 33 35 43; day trips approximately €55) organise excursions involving trekking and 4WD vehicles, led by a vulcanologist or alpine guide.

Mt Etna is best approached from Catania by **AST bus** (☎ 095 746 10 96), which departs from the car park in front of the main train station at 8.30am, and leaves from Rifugio Sapienza at about 4.45pm (€5.15 return). The private **Ferrovia Circumetnea train line** (☎ 095 54 12 50; www.circumetnea.it) circles Mt Etna from Catania to Riposto, a 3½-hour trip. You can reach Riposta from Taormina by train or bus if you want to make the trip from that direction.

The youthful **Agora Hostel** (☎ 095 723 30 10; www.agorahostel.com; Piazza Curro 6; dm/d €18/45; 💻) in Catania is known for its live music, cheap eats and good bar. It's the stopping-off point for Mt Etna, which is just a 30-minute bus ride away.

SYRACUSE

pop 126,000

Few places on the planet rival the historical importance of Syracuse (Siracusa, sigh-ra-*coo*-sa). Founded in 734 BC by Corinthian settlers, it became the dominant Greek city-state on the Mediterranean, battling Carthaginians and Etruscans before falling to the Romans in 212 BC. Nowadays, the largest battles you'll find here are for parking spots in the packed historical centre, but the stunning archaeological park and position on the eastern coast make this Sicily's top destination.

Orientation

Most of Syracuse is a sprawling suburb. Everything listed in this section, except for the archaeological park, is on the island of Ortygia, linked to the mainland by the Umbertine bridge about 200m east of the train station along Corso Umberto I. The **tourist office** (☎ 0931 46 42 55; Via Maestranza 33; 🕑 8.30am-1.45pm & 3-5.30pm Mon-Fri, 8.30am-1.45pm Sat) is just east of Piazza Archimede in the centre of Ortygia.

Sights

ORTYGIA

The **cathedral** (Piazza del Duomo; admission free; 🕑 8am-noon & 4-7pm) was built in the 7th century on top of the Temple of Athena, incorporating most of the temple's original columns in its three-aisled structure. The splendid **Piazza del Duomo** is lined with baroque palaces. Just down the winding street from the cathedral is **Fontana Aretusa**, a natural freshwater spring. Greek legend has it that the goddess Artemis transformed her handmaiden Aretusa into the spring to protect her from the unwelcome attention of the river-god Alpheus. Undeterred, Alpheus turned himself into the river that feeds the spring.

NEAPOLIS-PARCO ARCHEOLOGICO

To get to the **Neapolis-Parco Archeologico** (☎ 0931 6 50 68; Viale Paradisa; adult/concession €6/3; 🕑 8am-7pm), catch bus 1 or 2 from Riva della Posta on Ortygia. The main attraction here is the sparkling-white 5th-century-BC **Greek theatre**, entirely hewn out of solid rock and facing seaward over the city. Nearby is the **Orecchio di Dionisio**, an ear-shaped artificial grotto used by Syracuse's resident tyrant Dionysius to eavesdrop on his prisoners. The impressive 2nd-century **Roman amphitheatre** is well preserved.

The excellent **Museo Archeologico Paolo Orsi** (☎ 0931 46 40 22; Viale Teocrito 66/a; adult/concession €6/3; 🕑 9am-7pm Tue-Sat, 9am-1pm Sun), about 500m east of the archaeological zone, shows off the region's history going back to prehistoric times, and includes a dizzying array of Greek and Roman artefacts.

Sleeping & Eating

Fontane Bianche (☎ 0931 79 03 33; Via dei Lidi 476; per person/tent €6/4.50; 🕑 May-Sep) About 15km southwest of town, this camping ground is near a beach that teems with active bars come summer; catch bus 21 or 22 from Corso Umberto I.

B&B Casa Mia (☎ 0931 46 33 49; www.bbcasamia.it; Corso Umberto 112; s/d incl breakfast €45/75; ❄ 💻) Many readers have written in with high marks for this B&B, even though it's across the river from Ortygia. The seven rooms all contain grand antiques, but the main draw here is the breakfast of homemade pastries and jam served on the pleasant terrace.

Sogno Sondesto (☎ 0931 21 775; www.sognosondesto.net; Via Logoteta 18; s/d/tr/q €50/70/95/120; ☒) This place comprises two comfortable rooms in a private home perfectly located on a quiet side street near the centre of Ortygia. Be sure to ask Sergio (in Italian, English, French, Spanish or Portuguese) all about Syracuse. He'll set you up right for a day of sightseeing with an enormous Sicilian breakfast.

Hotel Gutkowski (☎ 0931 46 58 61; www.guthotel.it; Lungomare Vittorini 26; s/d incl breakfast €70/100; ☒ 💻) This lovely pastel-blue, seafront hotel has an appealing minimalist décor in its 25 small rooms. Breakfast is mostly organic and health-conscious.

Castello Fiorentino (☎ 0931 21 097; Via del Crocifisso 6, trav Via Roma; pizza from €3.50) Who knew combining caviar and smoked salmon on a pizza could taste so good? This restaurant is enormous, with a few quieter side rooms, and filled with happy Syracusans, always a good sign.

Don Camillo (☎ 0931 6 71 33; Via Maestranza 96; 1st/2nd courses €11/19) Don't let the waiters in penguin suits scare you away from this upscale trattoria, long regarded as one of the best restaurants in Syracuse. The wine list runs for days and you could make a tapas meal out of a few starters.

For scrumptious Sicilian sweets, head to **Pasticceria Tipica Catanese** (Corso Umberto 46); for good local wines, accompanied by hearty cheese and ham platters, try **Fermento** (Via Crocifisso 44/46), a terrific vaulted wine bar located in the heart of *passeggiata* territory.

Getting There & Away

Services with **Interbus** (☎ 0931 6 67 10) leave from Via Trieste for Catania (€4.60, one hour, hourly Monday to Saturday) and onto Palermo (€14.20, four hours or less with direct service, about hourly). The service for Rome (€38, 12 hours) also leaves from here, connecting with the Rome bus at Catania. **AST** (☎ 0931 46 48 20) buses service the town and the surrounding area from Riva della Posta.

Trains head from the Piazza della Stazione to Taormina (€6.60, one hour, nine per day), Messina (€8.75, three hours, nine daily) and Catania (€8.15, one to 1½ hours, hourly except between 8.50am and 12.45pm). Change in Catania or Messina for Palermo (€14.80, six hours, seven per day), and in Catania for Agrigento (€12.70, 5½ hours, 6am and 10.45am).

AGRIGENTO

pop 55,900

Agrigento would hardly be on the tourist map if not for the absolutely stunning Greek temples strewn along a ridge below town. Founded around 582 BC, this was one of ancient Greece's great cities. The city proper is rather sprawling, but the medieval centre isn't bad and the ruins are a quick bus ride away.

There's a so-so **tourist office** (☎ 0922 2 04 54; Via Cesare Battisti 15; ⏰ 8.30am-1.30pm Mon-Fri). Buses 1 and 3 (€0.85) head between town, the Piazza Stazione (train station), the archaeological museum and Valley of the Temples, and bus 2 continues on to the beach of San Leone and the camping ground (see opposite).

Sights

Agrigento's **Valley of the Temples** (☎ 0922 2 61 91; admission €6, with museum €10; ⏰ 8.30am-1hr before sunset in winter, until 7pm spring & autumn, until 10.30pm Jul & Aug) is one of the major Greek archaeological sights in the world. The ancient Greek town of Agrakas was founded here in 581 BC, during the 50th Olympiad. Some of the grandest temples of the ancient Greek world are in various states of ruin, but are still a stunning sight, worth an entire day. The only temple to survive relatively intact was **Tempio della Concordia**, transformed into a church. **Tempio di Giunone**, a short walk uphill to the east, has an impressive sacrificial altar. **Tempio di Ercole** is the oldest of the structures and is equivalent in size to the Parthenon. Nearby is the **Tempio di Castore e Polluce**, partly reconstructed in the 19th century.

Cross the road to visit the imposing **Tempio di Giove**, mostly in ruins now but one of its *telamoni* (giant male statues) is perfectly preserved and on display in the museum. Giove/Jupiter was the Roman equivalent of the Greek god Zeus, and the temple you see now – one of the largest ever built in ancient Greece – was rebuilt after a 480 BC Carthaginian attack.

To better understand the ruins, head first to the **Museo Archeologico** (☎ 0922 40 15 65; admission see above; ⏰ 9am-7pm Tue-Sat, to 1pm Sun &

Mon, to 10.30pm Tue-Sat Jul-Sep), just north of the temples on Via dei Templi. Museums all around the world strive to create the kind of symbiosis attained here. All of the signage is in English, and there is a colossal example of a *telamoni*.

Sleeping & Eating

Camping Valle dei Templi (☎ 0922 41 11 15; www.campingvalledeitempli.com; Viale Emporium 192, San Leone; per person/tent/car €7/5.50/3; P) This camping ground is past the Valley of the Temples, towards the beach town of San Leone. A pool, bocce court, games, babysitting service and pizzeria make this a good location for those with kids. Bungalows are also available.

Bella Napoli (☎ 0922 2 04 35; www.hotelbellanapoli.com; Piazza Lena 6; s/d €35/65) The only low-priced hotel in the city centre, this place has good prices and rooms that are comfortable, but could use a good cleaning.

B&B Atenea 191 (☎ 0922 59 55 94; www.atenea191.com; Via Atenea 191; s/d/tr/q incl breakfast €50/80/120/160;) This place is near the vivacious shopping street Via Ataneo, with an ocean view to end all views. Take breakfast (freshly baked pastries) on the patio of the 17th-century building for a holiday treat.

Cappriccio del Mare (☎ 0922 411 761; Via Crispi; pizza €5, 1st/2nd courses €9/14) Come to this local hang-out to get your fill of Sicilian fish specialities, like spaghetti with clams and the *antipasto della casa* – smoked fish and *caponata* (Sicilian stew with eggplant and tomatoes). Near the train station, there are a few outdoor tables on a busy piazza, and inside is welcoming with peach-coloured walls.

Café Girasole (Via Atenea 68-70) This is a great little wine bar in the heart of the medieval town.

Getting There & Away

Intercity buses leave from Piazza Rosselli, just off Piazza Vittorio Emanuele, for Palermo (€11.50, two hours, four daily).

SARDINIA

Sardinia (Sardegna in Italian) is as geographically distinct from mainland Italy as it is culturally. Its ancient history goes back a millennia before Rome. Paleolithic inhabitants built settlements still evident today in the form of circular stone fortresses called *nuraghe*, about 7000 of which remain scattered on the island. Despite constant domination by Phoenicians, Romans, Pisans, Genovese and Spaniards (among others), the proud locals, known as Sardi, have retained a strong sense of identity.

Although a few towns are easy to reach by public transport, Sardinia's main draws – its beaches and *nuraghe* – really require your own wheels. The striking landscape ranges from a wild interior carved with gorges and valleys, to stunning stretches of unspoiled coastline. The island gets overwhelmed by weekenders and sun-seekers during the summer months, especially August, so spring and autumn are the best times to visit.

Getting There & Away

AIR

There are international and national flights into Sardinia's two main airports: **Cagliari Elmas** (CAG; ☎ 070 2 10 51; www.cagliariairport.it) in Cagliari, and **Fertilia** (AHO; ☎ 079 93 52 82; www.algheroairport.it) in Alghero. Weekenders are discovering Sardinia because of low-cost airlines such as Air One and Ryanair.

BOAT

Sardinia is accessible by ferry from Civitavecchia, Livorno, Genoa, Piombino, Naples and Fiumicino on mainland Italy, and Bonifacio on Corsica. Departure points in Sardinia are Olbia, Golfo Aranci, Palau, Santa Teresa di Gallura and Porto Torres in the north, Arbatax on the east coast and Cagliari in the south. To check all ferry services in the Mediterranean, go to www.traghettionline.net.

The main company, **Tirrenia** (www.tirrenia.com, in Italian), runs a service between Cagliari and Trapani, Palermo, Civitavecchia and Naples; between Olbia and Genoa or Civitavecchia; between Arbatax and Fiumicino, Civitavecchia or Genoa; from Golfo Aranci to Fiumicino; and from Porto Torres to Genoa. **Linea dei Golfi** (www.lineadeigolfi.it) runs ferries between Cagliari and Livorno, and Olbia and Piombino or Livorno. The national railway, Ferrovie dello Stato (FS), also runs a service between Civitavecchia and Golfo Aranci. **Moby Lines** (www.mobylines.it) operates services between Olbia and Civitavecchia, Livorno or Genoa, and between

Santa Teresa di Gallura and Bonifacio on Corsica. **Corsica Ferries** (www.corsicaferries.com) operates services from Golfo Aranci to Civitavecchia or Livorno. **Grandi Navi Veloci** (www.gnv.it) runs a service between Porto Torres or Olbia and Genoa.

Getting Around

Getting around Sardinia without a car can be quite a trek, although both Cagliari and Alghero are accessible by train, ferry or bus. The easiest way to get between Cagliari and Alghero is on the Logudoro bus (see p812). The main bus company is **ARST** (☎ 0800 86 50 42; www.arst.sardegna.it, in Italian), which operates extensive services throughout the island.

The main **Trenitalia** (www.trenitalia.it) train lines link Cagliari with Oristano, Sassari and Olbia, and are generally reliable but can be very slow. The private railways that link smaller towns throughout the island can be even slower. However, the **Trenino Verde** (Little Green Train; ☎ 800 46 02 20; 8am-2pm Mon-Fri), which runs a route from Cagliari to Arbatax through the scenic Barbagia region, is a relaxing way to see part of the interior.

CAGLIARI

pop 175,200

The capital and largest city on Sardinia, Cagliari (*cal*-yar-ee) offers several sightseeing days' worth of history within its medieval centre, as well as a few day trips to neighbouring beaches and even to a salt lake filled with bathing pink flamingos.

Orientation

The main bus and train stations and port are near Piazza Matteotti, where the useful city tourist office is as well. The main street along the harbour is Via Roma, and the old city stretches up the hill behind it to the castle. There are several hotels and restaurants near the port, normally not a great place in most cities, but perfectly safe and pleasant here.

Information

Guardia Medica (☎ 070 50 29 31; Via Talete 6) For after-hour medical emergencies.

Main post office (☎ 070 6 03 11; Piazza del Carmine 27)

Ospedale San Giovanni di Dio (Hospital; ☎ 070 60 92 215; Via Ospedale)

Police station (Questura; ☎ 070 60 2 71; Via Amat 9) Tucked behind the imposing law courts.

Tourist office (☎ 070 66 92 55; Piazza Matteotti 9; 9am-2pm & 3-6pm Mon-Sat) Call ahead, as it might be moving in 2007 or 2008. There are additional information offices at the airport.

World Link Center (☎ 070 67 39 42; Via Cavour 47; 9am-10.30pm) For Internet needs.

Sights & Activities

In the Citadella dei Musei, the **Museo Archeologico Nazionale** (☎ 070 68 40 00; Piazza dell'Arsenale; admission €4; 9am-8pm Tue-Sun) has a fascinating collection of Nuraghic bronzes. These bronzes are objects found in *nuraghe* all over Sardinia, and are an excellent legacy of the island's native culture.

It's enjoyable to wander through the medieval quarter. The Pisan–Romanesque **Duomo** (Piazza Palazzo) was built in the 13th century and has an interesting Romanesque pulpit.

There are good sea and city views from **Bastione San Remy** (Piazza Costituzione), above the piazza in the town's centre, which once formed part of the fortifications of the old city. Now, it's a great hang-out spot, with ice skating in winter and outdoor cafés in summer.

The **Torre di San Pancrazio** (Piazza Indipendenza; 9am-5pm Tue-Sun) is also worth a look. The **Roman amphitheatre** (Viale Buon Cammino; admission free; 9am-5pm Tue-Sun) is considered the most important Roman monument in Sardinia. During summer, opera is performed here.

A day on the **Spiaggia di Poetto**, east of the centre, is a day well spent, and you can wander across to the salt lakes to view the flamingos.

Festivals & Events

The **Festival of Sant'Efisio**, a colourful celebration mixing the secular and the religious, is held annually for four days from 1 May.

Sleeping

Bed & Breakfast La Marina (☎ 070 67 00 65, 349 17 67 368; www.la-marina.it; Via Porcile 23; s €35, d €60-70;) You'll have your own mini-apartment here. All four rooms come with use of the shared kitchen and eating area. The charming owners run the market downstairs and are a wealth of information about the area.

Albergo Aurora (☎ 070 65 86 25; www.hotelcagliariaurora.it; Salita Santa Chiara 19 at Piazza Yenne; s/d €45/65, with shared bathroom €35/48;) The brightly coloured interiors here offer a cheery holiday

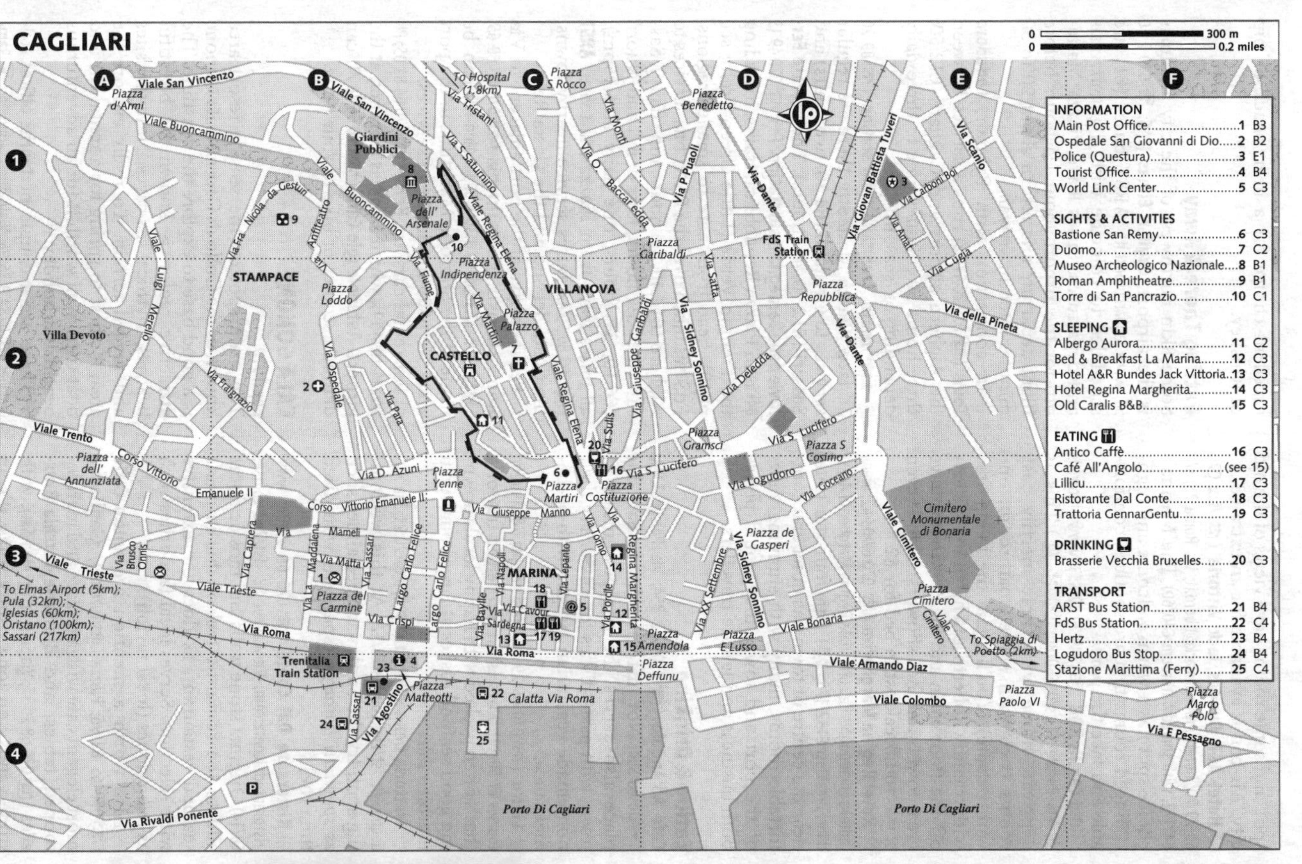
CAGLIARI
0 300 m
0 0.2 miles
A B C D E F
1 2 3 4
INFORMATION
Main Post Office....................1 B3
Ospedale San Giovanni di Dio....2 B2
Police (Questura)....................3 E1
Tourist Office....................4 B4
World Link Center....................5 C3
SIGHTS & ACTIVITIES
Bastione San Remy....................6 C3
Duomo....................7 C2
Museo Archeologico Nazionale....8 B1
Roman Amphitheatre....................9 B1
Torre di San Pancrazio....................10 C1
SLEEPING
Albergo Aurora....................11 C2
Bed & Breakfast La Marina....................12 C3
Hotel A&R Bundes Jack Vittoria..13 C3
Hotel Regina Margherita....................14 C3
Old Caralis B&B....................15 C3
EATING
Antico Caffè....................16 C3
Café All'Angolo....................(see 15)
Lillicu....................17 C3
Ristorante Dal Conte....................18 C3
Trattoria GennarGentu....................19 C3
DRINKING
Brasserie Vecchia Bruxelles....................20 C3
TRANSPORT
ARST Bus Station....................21 B4
FdS Bus Station....................22 C4
Hertz....................23 B4
Logudoro Bus Stop....................24 B4
Stazione Marittima (Ferry)....................25 C4
Viale San Vincenzo
Piazza d'Armi
Viale Buoncammino
Giardini Pubblici
To Hospital (1.8km)
Via Tristani
Piazza S Rocco
Piazza Benedetto
Via Monti
Via O. Baccaredda
Via P Puaoli
Via Dante
FdS Train Station
Via Giovan Battista Tuveri
Via Scanio
Via Carboni Boi
Via Amat
Via Cugia
Via della Pineta
Piazza Repubblica
Piazza Garibaldi
Via Satta
Via Sidney Sonnino
Via Giuseppe Garibaldi
Via Deledda
VILLANOVA
STAMPACE
CASTELLO
MARINA
Via S Saturnino
Viale Regina Elena
Piazza dell' Arsenale
Piazza Indipendenza
Via Fiume
Via Martini
Piazza Palazzo
Via Fra Nicola da Gesturi
Via Anfiteatro
Viale Luigi Merello
Piazza Loddo
Via Ospedale
Villa Devoto
Via Fra Fraignazio
Via Para
Viale Trento
Piazza dell' Annunziata
Corso Vittorio Emanuele II
Via D. Azuni
Piazza Yenne
Via Sulis
Piazza Gramsci
Via S. Lucifero
Piazza S Cosimo
Via Logudoro
Via Goceano
Piazza Martiri
Piazza Costituzione
Via Giuseppe Manno
Via Caprera
Via Maddalena
Mameli
Via Sassari
Largo Carlo Felice
Via Matta
Piazza del Carmine
Via Crispi
Viale Trieste
Via Brusco Onnis
To Elmas Airport (5km); Pula (32km); Iglesias (60km); Oristano (100km); Sassari (217km)
Via Roma
Via Bayle
Via Napoli
Via Cavour
Via Sardegna
Via Lepanto
Via Torino
Via Porcile
Via Regina Margherita
Piazza de Gasperi
Via XX Settembre
Piazza Amendola
Piazza E Lusso
Viale Bonaria
Cimitero Monumentale di Bonaria
Viale Cimitero
Piazza Cimitero
To Spiaggia di Poetto (2km)
Viale Armando Diaz
Piazza Deffunu
Trenitalia Train Station
Piazza Matteotti
Via Agostino
Calatta Via Roma
Viale Colombo
Piazza Paolo VI
Piazza Marco Polo
Via E Pessagno
Via Rivaldi Ponente
Porto Di Cagliari
Porto Di Cagliari

ITALY

spot, and some rooms have views of the old city. Air-con is available for an extra €8.

Hotel A&R Bundes Jack Vittoria (☎/fax 070 66 79 70; hotel.aerbundesjack@libero.it; Via Roma 75; s/d €47/72, with shared bathroom €40/60) The Marina's choice spot has a warm welcome and high-ceilinged rooms that are spotless, comfortable and face the port.

Old Caralis B&B (☎ 349 29 12 853; www.oldcaralis.it; Via Porcile 11; s/d €50/80; ⊠ ✻ 💻) This is a private home with three merrily cosy rooms (two with shared bathroom, one with private). You'll share the living area with friendly Roberto and his mum. It's eat-off-the-floor clean and the bathrooms have great towels and hot showers. They'll even serve you breakfast in bed for €2.

Hotel Regina Margherita (☎ 070 67 03 42; www.hotelreginamargherita.com; Viale Regina Margherita 44; s/d incl breakfast €132/175; ✻) This four-star hotel near the centre of town has quiet and comfortable rooms, many with stunning views of the port and town, that would please both business and leisure travellers.

Eating & Drinking

Café All'Angolo (☎ 070 652 354; Via Porcile 13/A; 🕑 closed Sun) Not just an ordinary bar, this place also serves the cheapest meals in town, with pasta dishes for €4.50. Try their homemade vegetarian lasagne with bechamel sauce.

Lillicu (☎ 070 65 29 70; Via Sardegna 78; 1st/2nd courses €7.50/11) This is an authentic trattoria that's often packed with happy locals downing good seafood dishes at large communal marble tables.

Trattoria GennarGentu (☎ 070 67 20 21; Via Sardegna 60; 1st/2nd courses €8/12) At this welcoming spot, try the Sardinian specialities such as *spaghetti bottarga* (spaghetti with dried tuna roe).

Ristorante Dal Conte (☎ 070 66 33 36; www.ristorantedalconte.com; Via Cavour 83; 1st/2nd courses €8/14) Original stone walls and mosaic floors add to the romantic feel of this intimate seafood restaurant, as does the extensive wine selection. Serves local favourites such as *culurgiones* (local ravioli).

Also worth a mention are **Antico Caffè** (☎ 070 65 82 96; Piazza Costituzione), Cagliari's most elegant café with a terrace and marble-topped tables, and **Brasserie Vecchia Bruxelles** (☎ 070 68 20 37; Via Sulis 4; 🕑 Mon-Sat), with stone vaults and long comfy sofas; it's an excellent choice for a beer, snack or nip of whiskey.

Getting There & Away

Some 8km northwest of the city at Elmas is the airport, **Cagliari Elmas** (CAG; ☎ 070 2 10 51; www.cagliariairport.it). ARST buses (€1) are scheduled to coincide with flight arrivals and departures. Buses leave Piazza Matteotti for the airport about 1½ hours before flight departure and return about 20 to 30 minutes after an arrival.

In connection with Ryanair, **Logudoro Tours** (☎ 079 28 17 28) runs a service between the Alghero airport and Cagliari (€12.50, three hours 50 minutes, one to three daily depending on season).

The main **Trenitalia train station** (☎ 89 20 21) faces Piazza Matteotti; there are regular services to Oristano (€4.80, two hours) and Sassari (€12.70, 4¼ hours). The private **Ferrovie della Sardegna train station** (FdS; ☎ 070 49 13 04) is in Piazza Repubblica; trains, including the Trenino Verde (Little Green Train; see p810), head from here to smaller regions. FdS has taken over the PANI bus services to Alghero (€14.40, 4½ hours, nine daily), Sassari (€15, 3¼ hours, four daily) and Nuoro (€6.10, 3½ hours, one daily at 6.15pm); all buses leave from Piazza Matteotti. **ARST** (☎ 800 86 50 42) buses service nearby towns, the Costa del Sud and the Costa Rei.

Ferries arrive at the port adjacent to Via Roma. Bookings for **Tirrenia** (☎ 070 66 60 65; 🕑 8.30am-12.30pm & 3.30-6.50pm Mon-Fri) can be made at the Stazione Marittima in the port area. See p809 for details of services.

For rental cars, try **Hertz** (☎ 070 66 81 05; Piazza Matteotti 1), which also has a branch at the airport. **Autonoleggio Cara** (☎ 070 66 34 71) can deliver a scooter or bike to your hotel.

CALA GONONE

pop 1010

The main spot on the seaside resort area known as the Golfo di Orosei, Cala Gonone is a good base to explore the coastline. The attractive region is known for beautiful beaches, mythical sea caves, Nuraghic sites and rugged terrain. To really explore the area, it's best to spring for a rental car and boat trips, well worth it for an adventurous beachfront holiday.

There are a couple of **tourist offices** (Cala Gonone; ☎ 0784 9 36 96; Viale Bue Marino 1a; 🕑 9am-

6pm Apr-Oct, to 11pm Jul & Aug; Dorgali; ☎ 0784 9 62 43; Via Lamarmora 181; 🕑 9am-1pm & 3.30-7pm Mon-Fri); the Cala Gonone office has maps, a list of hotels and plenty of local information. **Coop Ghivine** (☎ 0784 9 67 21; www.ghivine.com; Via Montebello 5, Dorgali) organises excellent guided treks and farm stays in the region from €30 per person.

Sights & Activities

From Cala Gonone's tiny port, catch a boat to the **Grotta del Bue Marino** (admission €5.50), where a guide will take you on a 1km walk to see vast caves with stalagmites and stalactites. Sardinia's last colony of monk seals once lived here, but has not been seen for quite some time. Boats also leave for **Cala Luna**, an isolated beach where you can walk along **Codula di Luna**, a fabulous gorge. The beach is packed with day-tripping tourists in summer. The boat trip to visit the grotto and beach costs around €20.

A **walking track** along the coast links Cala Fuili, about 3.5km south of Cala Gonone, and Cala Luna (about 1½ hours one way). There's also some good mountain biking and diving in the area. The tourist offices have information on local outfitters.

There is a wide range of activities for those who have time or money or both: scuba diving, PADI certification courses, sea cruises, caving, farm stays and more. The tourist office has brochures and information on dozens of operators, or check www.calagonone.com.

Sleeping & Eating

Camping Cala Gonone (☎ 0784 9 31 65; www.campingcalagonone.it; per person incl car & tent €11.50-17, 2-bed/4-bed bungalow up to €57/135; 🕑 Apr-Oct;) Along the main road from Dorgali, this camping ground has good quality, shady sites, plus a pool and restaurant, but gets overrun in August.

Pop Hotel (☎ 0784 9 31 85; www.hotelpop.com; per person incl breakfast €27-53;) Just 100m from the sea, this terracotta-hued hotel near the port has clean and pleasant rooms – all with balconies – and a decent restaurant.

Hotel Costa Dorada (☎ 0784 9 33 32; www.hotelcostadorada.it; Via Lungomare Palmasera 45; s €68-113, d €100-180, incl breakfast; 🕑 Apr-Oct) This is a romantic hotel with a swatch of beach across the street, flower-laced terraces and lovely rooms.

Hotel Su Gologone (☎ 0784 28 75 12; www.sugologone.it; s/d €95/135;) If you have your own transport, don't miss the opportunity to stay here, at the base of Sardinia's second-highest peak, about 20 minutes west of town, near Dorgali. This gorgeous white-washed hacienda has pretty rooms decorated with locally crafted furnishings, walking trails, a pool, spa and fitness centre, and a fabulous restaurant serving classic Sardinian mountain cuisine.

Getting There & Away

There are seven ARST buses a day from Nuoro through Dorgali to Cala Gonone (€4.50, 1¼ hours). If you are travelling by car, you will need a proper road map of the area.

ALGHERO

pop 43,387

Although the narrow lanes and stone defence ramparts make for a charming coastal holiday spot, Alghero is a fairly new town in comparison to other Mediterranean lands. The Genovese founded it in the 11th century and it was Catalan-controlled for hundreds of years. Hearing the Catalan dialect amid tourists arriving on new low-cost airlines, you'd swear you were in a resort on the Spanish Costa Brava, just with more pasta and *gelato*.

Orientation

Alghero's historic centre is on a small promontory jutting into the sea, with the new town stretching out behind and north along the coast.

Information

Main post office (☎ 079 97 20 252; Via Carducci 35)
Ospedale Civile (Hospital; ☎ 079 98 71 61; Via Don Minzoni)
Tourist office (☎ 079 97 90 54; www.infoalghero.it, in Italian; Piazza Porta Terra 9; 🕑 8am-8pm Mon-Sat) Near the port and just across the gardens from the bus station, this is an exceedingly helpful office.

Sights & Activities

The narrow streets of the old city and around the port are lovely. The most interesting church is the **Chiesa di San Francesco** (Via Carlo Alberto; 🕑 7.30am-noon & 5-8.30pm). Although constant remodelling has ruined the cathedral, the **bell tower** (admission €1.50;

7am-9.30pm Easter-Sep) remains a fine example of Gothic–Catalan architecture.

OUT OF TOWN

If you're up for the 654 steps down, head out towards **Capo Caccia** to witness the **Grotte di Nettuno** (079 94 65 40; adult/concession €10/5; 9am-7pm Apr-Sep, 10am-5pm Oct, 9am-4pm Nov-Mar), an underground fairyland. Outside of the low season, it's accessible with the ferry company **Navisarda** (079 97 89 61; www.navisarda.it) from the port (adult/concession €12/6, 2½ hour round-trip, hourly 9am to 5pm June to September, 10am to 3pm April, May and October), or by the FdS bus from the Via Catalogna bus stop (€4 return, 50 minutes, three daily June to September).

If you have a car, don't miss the **Nuraghe di Palmavera** (079 95 32 00; admission €2.10; 9am-7pm), 3500-year-old stone ruins 10km out of Alghero on the road to Porto Conte.

Rugged cliffs stretch down to solitary beaches out towards **Bosa**, which is one of the last habitats of the griffon vulture. The best way to see the coast is by car or motorcycle. If you want to rent a bicycle (from €7 a day) or motorcycle (from €70) to explore the coast, try **Cicloexpress** (079 98 69 50; Via Garibaldi) at the port.

Festivals & Events

In summer Alghero stages a music festival in the cloisters of the church of San Francesco. Another festival, complete with fireworks display, is held on 15 August for the Feast of the Assumption.

Sleeping & Eating

It is virtually impossible to find a room in August unless you book in advance, and you'd do best to book ahead in June or July, just in case. There is only one hotel in the historic centre.

Camping La Mariposa (079 95 03 60; Via Lido 22; per person/tent €10.50/5, bungalow up to €72; Apr-Oct) About 2km north of the centre, this low-key camping ground is on the beach.

Hotel San Francesco (/fax 079 98 03 30; www.sanfrancescohotel.com; Via Ambrogio Machin 2; s/d/tr incl breakfast €58/92/120;) The only hotel in the ambient town centre, this place has passable levels of charm in simple rooms housed in what used to be a convent.

Villa Las Tronas (079 98 18 18; www.hotelvillalastronas.it; Lungomare Valencia 1; s/d €215/280;) On its own private promontory, this former summer residence of the Italian royalty has a pool and very pretty rooms, but an overly formal feel elsewhere. Still, the views are stupendous, the breakfasts enough to cover lunch, and there are mountain bikes for pedalling the coast.

Trattoria Maristella (079 97 81 72; Via Fratelli Kennedy 9; 1st/2nd courses €7.50/11; closed Sun dinner) The most popular spot with locals, with Mediterranean-splashed décor and chatting families, this restaurant offers good value, reliable grub and alfresco dining.

Osteria Machiavello (079 98 06 28; Via Cavour 7; 1st/2nd courses €9/13; closed Tue) Quirky meat dishes and seafood is the draw here, including *cinghiale* (wild boar) and even horse. In the historic centre with a sea view and serving regional wine and seasonal cooking, it's a good bet for admiring Sardinia.

Focacce Sarde Ripiene (Via Garibaldi 11; to 1.30am) Serving delicious sandwiches, this place fronts the sea and is always packed with locals.

Caffè Costantino (Piazza Civica 30) This is a classy coffee stop in the historic centre that also serves good wine and tantalising cakes.

Getting There & Away

Alghero's airport **Fertilia** (AHO; 079 93 60 51; www.algheroairport.it) is extremely popular with low-cost airlines Ryanair and Air One, as well as Alitalia and British Airways. To reach Alghero, take the Logudoro bus from Cagliari (€12.50, four hours, one to three daily depending on season) or connect in Sassari by bus or train. There are hourly buses to Sassari (€3 to €3.50, 50 minutes, about hourly between 5.35am and 7.50pm) and a train service (€1.85, 35 minutes, 11 daily). The bus stop is next to the public gardens in the old town on Via Catalogna. To get to the train station 1km to the south-east, take the yellow city buses (€0.80).

ITALY DIRECTORY

ACCOMMODATION

In this chapter accommodation is divided into budget (under €100 for a double room), midrange (€100 to €190) and top end (€190 and up). Unless otherwise stated, prices are high-season rates for rooms with private bathrooms.

The bulk of Italy's accommodation is made up of *alberghi* (hotels) and *pensioni* – often housed in converted apartments. Prices vary enormously, but expect to pay high-season rates at Easter, in summer and over the Christmas–New Year period. Note, however, that many city centre hotels offer discounts in August to lure guests away from the crowded coasts. Northern Italy is generally more expensive than the south.

As a rough guide, reckon on paying from €40 to €120 for a double room in a one-star hotel; €50 to €150 in a two-star; and €80 to €300 in a three-star.

Italian *ostelli per la gioventù* (youth hostels) are run by the **Associazione Italiana Alberghi per la Gioventù** (AIG; Italian Youth Hostel Association; Map p724; ☎ 06 487 11 52; www.ostellionline.org; Via Cavour 44, Rome), affiliated with **Hostelling International** (HI; www.iyhf.org). A valid HI card is required, which you can get in your home country or at many hostels. Dorm rates are typically between €15 and €25, with breakfast often included. Many places also offer dinner for around €10.

Camping is well catered for in Italy, with grounds scattered throughout the country. Lists are available from local tourist offices or online at www.campeggi.com or www.camping.it. The **Touring Club Italiano** (TCI; www.touringclub.it) also publishes an annual guide called *Campeggi in Italia*. Expect to pay from €5 to €12 per person and €5 to €12 for a site. Independent camping is not permitted in many places.

To stay in the countryside consider an *agriturismo* (farm stay). Accommodation varies from spartan billets on working farms to palatial suites at luxurious rural retreats. For information check out **Agriturist** (www.agriturist.it).

Bed and breakfast (B&B) is also popular. Prices are typically between €70 and €150 for a room. Contact **Bed & Breakfast Italia** (Map pp726-7; ☎ 06 688 01 513; www.bbitalia.it; Corso Vittorio Emanuele II 282, 00186 Rome) for further information.

Religious accommodation is a reliable money-saver – about €75 for a modest double room. The **Chiesa di Santa Susanna** (www.santasusanna.org/comingToRome/convents.html) has a list of convents and monasteries throughout the country.

Italy boasts an extensive network of mountain *rifugi* (refuges). Open from July to September, they offer basic dorm-style accommodation, although some larger ones have double rooms. Reckon on €16 to €30 per person, per night (with breakfast usually included). The best source of information is the **Club Alpino Italiano** (CAI; www.cai.it, in Italian), which owns and runs many of the refuges.

Rental Accommodation

Finding rental accommodation in the major cities can be difficult. A studio flat will typically cost around €1000 per month, with a month's rent payable in advance as a deposit. An online agency with apartments on its books is **Guest in Italy** (www.guestinitaly.com).

There are dozens of agencies specialising in villa rentals. An established operator is **Cuendet** (www.cuendet.com).

ACTIVITIES

Cycling

Tuscany and Umbria are popular cycling areas. **Bicycle Tuscany** (☎ 055 22 25 80; www.bicycletuscany.com), **Florence by Bike** (055 48 89 92; www.florencebybike.it) and **I Bike Italy** (☎ 055 234 23 71; www.ibikeitaly.com) all offer guided rides – see p774. Elsewhere, there's excellent mountain-biking in the northern Alps, Sardinia and Sicily.

Lonely Planet's *Cycling in Italy* offers practical tips and several detailed itineraries.

Hiking & Walking

Thousands of kilometres of *sentieri* (marked trails) crisscross Italy, ranging from hardcore mountain treks to gentle lakeside ambles. In season (the end of June to September), the Dolomites (p767) are a favourite hiking destination. Other popular areas include the Cinque Terre (p742), Amalfi Coast (p795) and Mt Etna in Sicily (p806).

Useful websites include www.cai.it (in Italian) and www.parks.it. Lonely Planet's *Walking in Italy* has descriptions of more than 50 walks.

Skiing

Most of the country's top ski resorts are in the northern Alps, although there are excellent facilities throughout the Apennines. Skiing isn't cheap, and high season (Christmas to early January, early February to April) costs will hit your pocket hard. The best way to save money is to buy a *settimana bianca* (literally 'white week') package deal, covering seven days' accommodation, food and ski passes.

See The Dolomites section, p767, for further details.

BOOKS

To get in the mood for Italy, dip into:

- *Italy* (Lonely Planet) Where to go, why and how.
- *The World from Italy: Football, Food & Politics* (George Negus) Aussie journalist's wry take on a year in Italy.
- *Heel to Toe: Encounter in the South of Italy* (Charles Lister) Follow Lister on a moped journey through southern Italy.
- *The Dark Heart of Italy* (Tobias Jones) A no-holds exposé of Berlusconi's many shenanigans.

BUSINESS HOURS

For the purposes of this chapter, opening hours have only been provided in the Information, Eating, Drinking, Entertainment and Shopping sections when they differ from the following standards:

Banks (8.30am-1.30pm & 2.45-4.30pm Mon-Fri)
Bars & Cafés (7.30am-8pm) Many open earlier and some stay open until the small hours. Pubs often open noon-2am.
Discos & Clubs (10pm-4am) The action rarely starts much before midnight.
Pharmacies (8.30am-1pm & 4-7.30pm Mon-Fri, to 1pm Sat) Outside of these times, pharmacies open on a rotation basis, although all are legally required to post a list of places open in the vicinity.
Post Offices Major offices (8.30am-6pm Mon-Fri, to 1pm Sat) branch offices (8.30am-1.50pm Mon-Fri, to 11.50am Sat)
Restaurants (noon-3pm & 7.30-11pm, later in summer) By law, restaurants close one day a week; many also close for a couple of weeks in August.
Shops (9am-1pm & 3.30-7.30pm, or 4-8pm Mon-Sat) Increasingly, chain stores and supermarkets open from 9am to 7.30pm Monday to Saturday; some also open from 11am to 1pm and 4pm to 7pm Sunday. Food shops often close on Thursday afternoons; some other shops remain closed on Monday mornings.
Tourist Offices (8.30am-12.30pm & 3-7pm Mon-Fri) In major cities, offices generally open all day; in smaller towns opening times can vary according to the season.

DANGERS & ANNOYANCES

Petty theft is the main problem for travellers in Italy. See the Regional Directory, p1101, for more on this. An insidious form of theft to watch out for is short-changing. One popular dodge goes as follows: you pay for a €4 *panino* with a €20 note. The cashier then distractedly gives you a €1 coin and a €5 note before turning away. The trick here is to wait and chances are that the €10 note you're waiting for will appear without a word being said.

Road rules in Italy are obeyed with discretion, so don't take it for granted that cars will stop at red lights. To cross the road you'll need to step confidently into the traffic and walk calmly across. Tread carefully though – there's a lot of dog mess about. Heavy traffic also means nasty air pollution, particularly in Rome, Milan, Florence and Naples.

EMBASSIES & CONSULATES

Italian Embassies & Consulates

Australia Canberra (☎ 02-6273 3333; www.ambitalia.org.au; 12 Grey St, Deakin ACT 2600); Melbourne (☎ 03-9867 5744; consolatogenerale.melbourne@esteri.it; 509 St Kilda Rd VIC 3004); Sydney (☎ 02-9392 7900; itconsyd@itconsyd.org; Level 45, The Gateway, 1 Macquarie Pl NSW 2000)
Austria (☎ 01-712 51 21; www.ambvienna.esteri.it; Metternichgasse 13, Vienna, 1030)
Canada Ottawa (☎ 613-232 2401; www.italyincanada.com; 21st fl, 275 Slater St, Ontario, K1P 5H9); Montreal (☎ 514-849 8351; www.italconsul.montreal.qc.ca; 3489 Drummond St, Quebec H3G 1X6); Vancouver (☎ 604-684 7288; www.italianconsulate.bc.ca; Standard Bldg 1100-510 West Hastings St, BC V6B IL8)
France (☎ 01 49 54 03 00; www.ambparigi.esteri.it; 7 rue de Varenne, Paris, 75343)
Germany (☎ 030-254 40 0; www.ambberlino.esteri.it; Hiroshima Strasse 1, Berlin, 10785)
Ireland (☎ 01-660 1744; www.italianembassy.ie; 63-65 Northumberland Rd, Dublin 4)
Netherlands (☎ 070-302 10 30; www.amblaja.esteri.it; Alexanderstraat 12, The Hague, 2514 JL)
New Zealand (☎ 04-494 7170; www.ambwellington.esteri.it; 34 Grant Rd, Thorndon, Wellington)
Switzerland (☎ 031 350 07 77; www.ambberna.esteri.it; Elfenstrasse 14, Bern, 3006)
UK London (☎ 020-7312 2200; www.amblondra.esteri.it; 14 Three Kings Yard, W1K 4EH); Edinburgh (☎ 0131-220 36 95; 32 Melville St, EH3 7HA)
USA Washington (☎ 202-612 4400; www.italyemb.org; 3000 Whitehaven St, NW Washington, DC 20008); Los Angeles (☎ 310-826 62 07; la.italcons@itwash.org; Suite 300, 12400 Wilshire Blvd, 90025); New York (☎ 212-737 9100; www.italconsulnyc.org; 690 Park Ave, 10021)

Embassies & Consulates in Italy

Australia (Map pp718-19; ☎ 06 85 27 21, emergencies 800 87 77 90; www.italy.embassy.gov.au; Via Antonio Bosio 5, 00161; 8.30am-5pm Mon-Fri)

Austria Embassy (Map pp718-19; ☎ 06 844 01 41; www.austria.it; Via Pergolesi 3, 00198); Consulate (off Map pp718-19; ☎ 06 855 28 80; Via Liegi 32; 9am-4pm Mon-Fri

Canada (Map pp718-19; ☎ 06 44 59 81; www.canada.it; Via G B de Rossi 27, 00161; 8.30am-4.30pm Mon-Fri)

France Embassy (Map pp726-7; ☎ 06 68 60 11; www.france-italia.it; Piazza Farnese 67, 00168) Consulate (Map pp726-7; ☎ 06 68 60 11; Via Giulia 251; 9am-12.30pm Mon-Fri)

Germany (Map p724; ☎ 06 49 21 31; www.rom.diplo.de; Via San Martino della Battaglia 4, 00185; 8.30-11.30am Mon-Fri)

Ireland (Map pp726-7; ☎ 06 697 91 21; www.ambasciata-irlanda.it; Piazza Campitelli 3, 00186; 10am-1pm Mon-Fri)

Netherlands (off Map pp718–19; ☎ 06 36 76 71; www.olanda.it; Via della Camiluccia 701, 00135; 9am-noon Mon, Tue, Thu & Fri)

New Zealand (Map pp718-19; ☎ 06 441 71 71; www.nzembassy.com; Via Zara 28, 00198; 8.30am-12.45pm & 1.45-5pm Mon-Fri)

Switzerland (off Map pp718–19; ☎ 06 80 95 71; www.eda.admin.ch/roma; Via Barnarba Oriani 61, 00197; 9am-noon Mon-Fri)

UK (Map pp718-19; ☎ 06 422 00 001; www.britishembassy.gov.uk; Via XX Settembre 80a, 00187; 9.15am-1.30pm Mon-Fri)

USA (Map pp722-3; ☎ 06 4 67 41; www.usis.it; Via Vittorio Veneto 119a, 00187; 8.30am-12.30pm & 2-5.30pm Mon-Fri)

FESTIVALS & EVENTS

The following is a brief list of some of Italy's most famous celebrations:

February, March & April

Carnevale In the period before Ash Wednesday, many towns stage carnivals. The best known is in Venice (see p755).

Settimana Santa Italy celebrates Holy Week with processions and Passion plays. On the evening of Good Friday, the pope leads a candlelit procession to the Colosseum in Rome and on Easter Sunday he gives his traditional blessing.

Scoppio del Carro A cart full of fireworks is exploded in Florence's Piazza del Duomo on Easter Saturday (see p774).

May–September

Palio delle Quattro Antiche Repubbliche Marinare (Regatta of the Four Ancient Maritime Republics) Boat races between the four historical maritime republics – Pisa, Venice, Amalfi and Genoa. The event rotates between the towns and is usually held in June.

Il Palio On 2 July and 16 August, Siena stages its extraordinary bareback horse race (see p780).

Mostra del Cinema di Venezia (Venice International Film Festival) The international film glitterati disembark at Venice Lido for the annual film fest (see p755).

December

Natale During the weeks preceding Christmas, there are numerous processions and religious events. Many churches set up elaborate cribs or nativity scenes known as *presepi* – Naples is famous for these.

HOLIDAYS

Most Italians take their annual holiday in August. This means that many businesses and shops close down for at least a part of the month, particularly around *Ferragosto* (Feast of the Assumption; 15 August).

Italian schools close for three months in summer, for three weeks over Christmas, and for a week at Easter.

Public holidays include:

Epifania (Epiphany) 6 January
Pasquetta (Easter Monday) March/April
Giorno della Liberazione (Liberation Day) 25 April
Festa del Lavoro (Labour Day) 1 May
Festa della Repubblica (Republic Day) 2 June
Ferragosto (Feast of the Assumption) 15 August
Ognisanti (All Saints' Day) 1 November
Immacolata Concezione (Feast of the Immaculate Conception) 8 December
Natale (Christmas Day) 25 December
Festa di Santo Stefano (Boxing Day) 26 December

Individual towns also have holidays to celebrate their patron saints.

Festa di San Marco (Feast of St Mark; Venice) 25 April
Festa di San Giovanni (Feast of St John the Baptist; Florence, Genoa and Turin) 24 June
Festa di San Pietro e San Paolo (Feast of St Peter and St Paul; Rome) 29 June
Festa di Santa Rosalia (Feast of St Rosalia; Palermo) 15 July
Festa di San Gennaro (Feast of St Januarius; Naples) first Sunday in May, 19 September & 16 December
Festa di Sant'Ambrogio (Feast of St Ambrose; Milan) 7 December

INTERNET RESOURCES

Delicious Italy (www.deliciousitaly.com) Get your tastebuds in the mood.

Italian Government Tourist Board (www.enit.it) Comprehensive site of the Italian tourist board.

Lonely Planet (www.lonelyplanet.com) Comprehensive travel website.
Parks. it (www.parks.it) Information on Italy's national parks.
Trenitalia (www.trenitalia.it) Plan, book and check on Italy's railway site.
Vatican (www.vatican.va) The Vatican's official website.
What's On (www.whatsoninrome.com) A good website resource for events in Rome.

MONEY

Italy's currency since 2002 has been the euro. The best way to manage your money is to use your debit/credit cards, while keeping a fistful of travellers cheques as backup. Visa and MasterCard are widely recognised, as are Cirrus and Maestro; American Express is accepted but is less common. Credit and debit cards can be used in *bancomat* (ATMs) displaying the appropriate sign. If you don't have a PIN, some, but not all banks will advance cash over the counter.

If your credit card is lost, stolen or swallowed by an ATM, telephone toll free to have an immediate stop put on its use. For MasterCard call ☎ 800 87 08 66; for Visa ☎ 800 81 90 14; and for American Express ☎ 800 864 046.

Visa, Travelex and Amex are the most widely accepted travellers cheques, although changing even these in smaller cities can be difficult. You'll find exchange offices at major airports and train stations. For lost or stolen cheques call: Amex ☎ 800 72 000; MasterCard ☎ 800 870 866; Travelex ☎ 800 335 511; Visa ☎ 800 874 155.

You're not expected to tip on top of restaurant service charges, but if you think the service warrants it feel free to leave a little extra – 10% is fine. In bars, Italians often leave small change (€0.10/€0.20).

POST

Italy's much maligned postal system, **Poste** (☎ 803 160; www.poste.it, in Italian), has improved a lot in recent years, but is still hardly a model of efficiency.

The best service to use is *posta prioritaria* (priority mail), which guarantees delivery of letters to European destinations in three days and to the rest of the world in four to eight days. Registered mail is known as *raccomandato*, insured mail as *assicurato*.

Stamps *(francobolli)* are available at post offices and tobacconists (*tabacchi*) – look for the official sign, a big white 'T' against a black background.

TELEPHONE

Local and long-distance calls can be made from Telecom offices or public phones. Rates, particularly for long-distance calls, are among the highest in Europe. The cheapest time to call is from midnight to 8am and all of Sunday; peak rates apply from 8am to 6.30pm Monday to Friday and until 1pm on Saturday.

To make a reverse-charge (collect) international call, dial ☎ 170. All operators speak English. For international directory inquiries, call ☎ 176.

To call Italy from abroad, dial ☎ 0039 and then the area code, including the first zero.

Mobile Phones

Italy is one of the most mobile saturated countries in the world and was one of the first places to introduce video phones. Phones operate on the GSM 900/1800 network, which is compatible with the rest of Europe and Australia, but not with the North American GSM 1900 or the Japanese system (although some GSM 1900/900 phones do work here).

If you have a GSM dual- or tri-band cellular phone that you can unlock (check with your service provider), you need only buy a *prepagato* (prepaid) SIM card to use it in Italy. Companies offering SIM cards include TIM (Telecom Italia Mobile), Wind and Vodafone-Omnitel. You'll need your passport to open an account.

Phone Codes

The country code for Italy is 39. Mobile phone numbers begin with a three-digit prefix such as 330 or 339; toll-free (freephone) numbers are known as *numeri verdi* and usually start with 800; national call rate numbers start with 848 or 199.

Area codes are an integral part of all Italian phone numbers, meaning that you must always use them, even when calling locally.

Phonecards

To phone from a public pay phone you'll need a *scheda telefonica* (telephone card), although you'll still find some that accept

EMERGENCY NUMBERS

- Ambulance ☎ 118
- Carabinieri/police ☎ 112/113
- Fire Brigade ☎ 115
- Road Rescue ☎ 116

credit cards and coins. You can buy phonecards (€5, €10, €20) at post offices, tobacconists and newsstands.

TRAVELLERS WITH DISABILITIES

Italy is not an easy country for disabled travellers. Cobbled streets, blocked pavements and tiny lifts all make life difficult. Rome-based **Consorzio Cooperative Integrate** (COIN; ☎ 06 232 69 231; www.coinsociale.it) is the best point of reference for disabled travellers.

For those travelling by train, www.trenitalia.com has details of services at stations.

VISAS

EU citizens don't need a visa to enter Italy and, with a *permesso di soggiorno* (permit to stay, see below), can stay as long as they like. Nationals of Australia, Canada, Israel, Japan, New Zealand, Switzerland and the USA don't need a visa for stays of up to 90 days.

South African citizens require a visa for Italy. The standard tourist visa for a Schengen country (Italy is one of the 15 signatories of the Schengen Convention – for further details see the Regional Directory, p1109) is valid for 90 days. You must apply for it in your country of residence and you can not apply for more than two in any 12-month period. They are not renewable inside Italy.

Technically, all foreign visitors to Italy are supposed to register with the local police within eight days of arrival. However, if you're staying in a hotel you don't need to bother as the hotel does this for you.

Permesso di Soggiorno

A *permesso di soggiorno* is required by all EU citizens who stay in Italy longer than three months and by all non-EU nationals. In theory, non-EU citizens should apply for one within eight days of arriving in Italy. To get one you'll need a valid passport, containing a stamp with your date of entry into Italy (ask for this as it's not automatic); a study visa if relevant; four passport-style photographs; and proof of your ability to support yourself financially (ideally a letter from an employer or school/university). These requirements change periodically, so always check before you join the inevitable queue.

Non-EU citizens who want to study in Italy must obtain a study visa from their nearest Italian embassy or consulate.

TRANSPORT IN ITALY

GETTING THERE & AWAY

Air

The increasing number of low-cost carriers means you should be able to find a decent airfare into Italy. High season is June to September; two months either side of this is the shoulder season, with low season officially November to March. Christmas and Easter also cause fares to spike. For details of discounted fares see Tickets in the Transport in Western Europe chapter, p1112.

Italy's main intercontinental gateway is **Leonardo da Vinci airport** (FCO; www.adr.it) in Rome, but regular intercontinental flights also serve Milan's **Malpensa** (MXP; www.sea-aeroportomilano.it). Low-cost carriers generally fly into Italy's regional airports, including **Ciampino** (CIA; www.adr.it) in Rome, Pisa's **Galileo Galilei** (☎ 050 50 07 07; www.pisa-airport.com) and **Marco Polo** (VCE; www.veniceairport.it) in Venice.

The country's national carrier is Alitalia. At the time of research, the company was beset by industrial strife as management tried to impose cost-cutting measures on an increasingly insecure workforce.

International airlines flying to/from Italy include:

Air Berlin (code AB; ☎ 848 39 00 54; www.airberlin.com)
Air Canada (code AC; ☎ 06 55 112; www.aircanada.ca)
Air Dolomiti (code EN; ☎ 045 860 52 11; www.airdolomiti.it)
Air France (code AF; ☎ 848 88 44 66; www.airfrance.com)
Air New Zealand (code NZ; ☎ 06 488 07 61; www.airnz.co.nz)
Alitalia (code AZ; ☎ 06 22 22; www.alitalia.it)
American Airlines (code AA; ☎ 06 660 53 169; www.aa.com)
British Airways (code BA; ☎ 199 712 266; www.britishairways.com)

Delta Air Lines (code DL; ☎ 800-477-999; www.delta.com)
easyJet (code U2; ☎ 848 88 77 66; www.easyjet.com)
Hapag-Lloyd Express (code X3; ☎ 199 192 692; www.hlx.com)
Jet2 (code LS; ☎ in UK 44-207 170 07 37; www.jet2.com)
KLM (code KL; ☎ 199 414 199; www.klm.com)
Lufthansa (code LH; ☎ 199 400 044; www.lufthansa.com)
Qantas (code QF; ☎ 06 524 82 725; www.qantas.com)
Ryanair (code FR; ☎ 889 67 89 10; www.ryanair.com)
Singapore Airlines (code SQ; ☎ 06 478 55 360; www.singaporeair.com)
Thai Airways International (code TG; ☎ 06 47 81 31; www.thaiair.com)
Virgin Express (code TV; ☎ 800 097 097; www.virgin-express.com)

Land

BUS

A consortium of European coach companies, **Eurolines** (www.eurolines.com), operates across Europe with offices in all major European cities. Italy-bound buses head to Turin, Milan, Rome and Florence. Its multilanguage website gives details of prices, passes and travel agencies where you can book tickets.

Busabout (☎ 020 7950 1661; www.busabout.com) runs to Rome, Florence, Siena, Pisa, Ancona, Venice and La Spezia as well as 60 other European cities. It offers passes of varying duration, allowing you to use its hop-on hop-off service.

CAR & MOTORCYCLE

Traversing the Alps into Italy, the main, year-round road routes are: the Mont Blanc tunnel from France; the Grand St Bernard tunnel from Switzerland; and the Brenner Pass from Austria. All three connect with major *autostrade* (motorways).

When driving into Italy always carry proof of ownership of a private vehicle. You'll also need third-party motor insurance. For more on driving in Italy see opposite.

TRAIN

International trains depart from Rome, Milan, Naples, Turin and Venice for a number of destinations including Nice, Paris, Munich, Barcelona, Zurich and Vienna. It's always advisable, and sometimes necessary, to book seats on international trains.

For the latest fare information on journeys to Italy, contact the **Rail Europe Travel Centre** (☎ 0870 848 848; www.raileurope.co.uk).

For details of Eurail and Inter-Rail passes, both valid in Italy, see the Transport in Western Europe chapter, p1121.

Sea

Numerous ferry services connect Italy with other Mediterranean countries; for a comprehensive list log onto **Traghettionline** (www.traghettionline.net).

Unless otherwise stated, quoted prices are for a one-way deck ticket in high season. Note that Eurail and Inter-Rail pass holders pay only a supplement on the Italy to Greece routes from Ancona and Bari. See also p822 for details of the Greece 'n' Italy pass.

Major ferry companies include:

Adriatica (☎ 199 12 31 99; www.adriatica.it) Ancona to Split in Croatia (€46, 7½hr).
Agoudimos (☎ 0831 52 90 91; www.agoudimos-lines.com) Brindisi to Corfu (€54, 6½hr) and Igoumenitsa (€54, 7½hr).
Fragline Ferries (☎ 0831 54 85 40; www.fragline.gr) Brindisi to Igoumenitsa (€53, 10hr) and/or Corfu (€53, 8¼hr).
Grandi Navi Veloci (☎ 800 46 65 10; www2.gnv.it) Genoa to Sardinia (Porto Torres €49, 11hr; Olbia €38, 10hr), Sicily (Palermo €75, 20hr), Barcelona (€56, 18hr) and Tunis (€104, 24hr).
Hellenic Mediterranean Lines (☎ 0831 52 85 31; www.hml.it) Brindisi to Igoumenitsa (€44, 8hr), Patras (€54, 14hr), Corfu (€44, 11½ hr) and Kefallonia (€54, 12½hr). **Marmara Lines** (☎ 071 207 61 65; www.marmaralines.com) Ancona to Cesme in Turkey (€92, 55½ hr).
Minoan Lines (☎ 071 20 17 08; www.minoan.gr) Ancona to Igoumenitsa (€80, 16hr) and Patras (€80, 22hr); Venice to Corfu (€83, 22hr), Igoumenitsa (€83, 23½ hr) and Patras (€83, 29½ hr).
Moby Lines (☎ 010 254 15 13; www.mobylines.it) Genoa to Corsica (Bastia €15, 4hr) and Sardinia (Olbia €42, 7hr)
SNAV (☎ 0831 52 54 92; www.snav.it) Naples to Palermo (€31, 10½hr) and Lipari (€85, 5½hr); Brindisi to Corfu (€80, 3¾hr).
Superfast Ferries (☎ 071 207 02 40; www.superfast.com) Ancona to Igoumenitsa (€74, 15hr) & Patras (€74, 21hr).
Tirrenia (☎ 800 82 40 79; www.tirrenia.it) Genoa to Sardinia (Porto Torres €55, 10hr; Olbia €40, 13½ hr).

For further details on sea transport see individual town entries.

GETTING AROUND

You can get pretty much anywhere in Italy by train, bus or ferry – services are generally efficient and cheap. Domestic airlines connect major cities, but flights are relatively expensive. If driving, weigh up the pros (often considerable) against the cons of expensive petrol, motorway tolls and the difficulty of city parking.

Air

Italy's domestic airlines are **Air One** (☎ 199 20 70 80; www.flyairone.it); **Alitalia** (☎ 06 22 22; www.alitalia.it); **Meridiana** (☎ 199 11 13 33; www.meridiana.it) and **Volareweb** (☎ 199 41 45 00; www.buyvolareweb.com).

The main airports are in Rome, Pisa, Milan, Bologna, Genoa, Turin, Naples, Venice, Catania, Palermo and Cagliari, but there are other, smaller airports throughout the country.

Bicycle

Cycling is a popular pastime in Italy, particularly in the north. Tourist offices can provide details of designated bike trails and bike hire (rental costs are about €10 per day).

There are no particular road rules for cyclists, although you'd do well to equip yourself with a helmet and lights.

Bikes can be taken on any train carrying the bike logo, but you'll need to pay a bike supplement (€3.50, or €5 for Eurostars). They travel free on ferries.

Boat

Navi (large ferries) service Sicily and Sardinia; *traghetti* (smaller ferries) and *aliscafi* (hydrofoils) cover the smaller island routes, including Elba, the Aeolian Islands, Capri and Ischia. The main embarkation points for Sardinia are Genoa, Livorno, Civitavecchia and Naples; for Sicily, Naples and Villa San Giovanni in Calabria. Most long-distance ferries travel overnight.

For details of the major ferry companies see the list on opposite; otherwise, refer to individual town entries.

Bus

Italy boasts an extensive and largely reliable bus network. Buses are not necessarily cheaper than trains, but in mountainous areas such as Umbria, Sicily and Sardinia they are often the only choice. Reservations are usually only necessary for longer trips.

Major companies include **Marozzi** (www.marozzivt.it, in Italian) and **Interbus** (☎ 0935 56 51 11; www.interbus.it, in Italian).

Car & Motorcycle

Roads are generally good throughout the country and there's an excellent system of *autostrade*. There's a toll to use most *autostrade,* payable in cash or by credit cards at exit barriers. Motorways are indicated by an A on a green background, main roads *(strade statali)* by an S or SS against a blue background.

Italy's motoring organisation **Automobile Club d'Italia** (ACI; ☎ 800 116 80; www.aci.it; 24hr) is an excellent source of information and offers 24-hour emergency assistance (dial ☎ 116 from a landline or ☎ 800 11 68 00 from a mobile).

Petrol prices are high in Italy – around €1.30 for a litre of *benzina senza piombo* (unleaded petrol); *gasolio* (diesel) is cheaper at €1.20.

DRIVING LICENCE

All EU driving licences are recognised in Italy. Holders of non-EU licences must get an International Driving Permit (IDP) to accompany their national licence.

HIRE

To hire a car you must be 21 or over (23 or above for some companies), possess a valid driving licence and have a credit card (without one you will have to leave a large cash deposit). Make sure you understand what is included in the price (unlimited kilometres, tax, insurance, collision damage waiver etc) and what your liabilities are. For the best rental rates, book your car before leaving home.

The most competitive multinational car-rental agencies are:

Avis (☎ 199 10 01 33; www.avis.com)
Budget (☎ 800 472 33 25; www.budget-italy.com)
Europcar (☎ 800 01 44 10; www.europcar.com)
Hertz (☎ 199 21 31 12; www.hertz.com)
Maggiore (☎ 848 86 70 67; www.maggiore.com)

You'll have no trouble hiring a scooter or motorcycle (provided you're over 18); there are rental agencies in all Italian cities. Rates average about €20 a day for a 50cc scooter.

INSURANCE

If you're driving your own car, you'll need an international insurance certificate, known as a *Carta Verde* (Green Card), available from your insurance company.

ROAD RULES

In Italy drive on the right, overtake on the left and give way to cars coming from the right. It's obligatory to wear seat belts (including rear seat belts if fitted), to drive with your headlights on outside built-up areas and to carry a warning triangle and fluorescent waistcoat in case of breakdown. Wearing a helmet is compulsory on all two-wheeled vehicles. The blood alcohol limit is 0.05%.

Speed limits, unless otherwise indicated by local signs, are: 130km/h (in rain 110km/h) on *autostrade*; 110km/h (in rain 90km/h) on all main, nonurban roads; 90km/h on secondary, nonurban roads; and 50km/h in built-up areas. Speeding fines range from a minimum of €35 to a maximum of €1433.

Many Italian cities, including Rome, Bologna, Florence, Milan and Turin, have introduced restricted access to their historical centres. The restrictions apply to both private and rental cars, but not vehicles with foreign registrations. *Motorini* (mopeds and scooters) can enter the zones.

Train

The partially privatised **Trenitalia** (☎ 89 20 21; www.trenitalia.com) runs most train services in Italy. There are several types of trains: local *regionale* or *interregionale* trains; faster InterCity (IC) services; and quickest of all, the Eurostar (ES) trains.

Ticket prices depend on the type of train and class (first class costs almost double second class). Regional trains are cheaper than InterCity and Eurostar services, both of which require a supplement determined by the distance to travel. Eurostar ticket prices include a compulsory reservation fee. Generally, it's cheaper to buy all local train tickets in Italy – check for yourself on the Trenitalia website.

Unless otherwise stated, train prices quoted in this chapter are for an InterCity, one-way 2nd-class ticket.

Tickets must be validated – in the yellow machines at the entrance to platforms – before boarding trains.

TRAIN PASSES

Available at all major train stations, the Trenitalia Pass allows for four to 10 days of travel within a two-month period. At the time of writing, four-/six-/10-day passes cost €158/194/266.

The Greece 'n' Italy Pass (4-day adult/youth pass €199/167, 10-day adult/youth pass €319/269) entitles holders to travel on trains in Italy and Greece for four to 10 days within a two-month period, as well as a return ticket on any Superfast or Blue Star ferry between Ancona/Brindisi and Greece.

Liechtenstein

It's true, Liechtenstein makes a fabulous wine-and-cheese-hour trivia subject – *Did you know it was the sixth smallest country?... It's still governed by an iron-willed monarch who lives in a Gothic castle on a hill... Yes, it really is the world's largest producer of dentures...* But if you're visiting this pocket-sized principality solely for the cocktail-party bragging rights, keep the operation covert. This theme-park micronation takes its independence seriously and would shudder at the thought of being considered for novelty value alone. Liechtenstein would rather be remembered for its stunning natural beauty. Measuring just 25km in length and 6km in width, the country is barely larger than Manhattan. And though it might not look like much on a map, up close it's filled with numerous hiking and cycling trails offering spectacular views of craggy cliffs, quaint villages, friendly locals and lush green forests.

FAST FACTS

- **Area** 150 sq km
- **Capital** Vaduz
- **Currency** Swiss franc (Sfr); A$1 = Sfr0.95; €1 = Sfr1.58; ¥100 = Sfr1.07; NZ$1 = Sfr0.75; UK£1 = Sfr2.34; US$1 = Sfr1.23
- **Famous for** sending postcards stamped by the country's postal service, dentures
- **Official Language** German
- **Phrases** *gruezi* (hello, good day), *merci vielmal* (thank you very much), *adieu* (goodbye), *sprechen sie Englisch?* (do you speak English?)
- **Population** 32,860
- **Telephone Codes** country code ☎ 423; international access code ☎ 00

HIGHLIGHTS

- Snap a picture of the royal castle with its stunning mountain backdrop in **Vaduz** (opposite).
- Get a souvenir **passport stamp** (opposite) and send a postcard home.
- Hit the slopes at **Malbun** (p827) to brag you've skied the Liechtenstein Alps.
- Test yourself with extreme hiking along the legendary **Fürstensteig trail** (p827).

CLIMATE & WHEN TO GO

Visit Liechtenstein from December to April for skiing, and May to October for sightseeing and hiking. Alpine resorts all but close down in late April, May and November.

HISTORY

A merger of the domain of Schellenberg and the county of Vaduz in 1712 by the powerful Liechtenstein family created the country. A principality under the Holy Roman Empire from the period 1719 to 1806, Liechtenstein finally achieved its full sovereign independence in 1866. A modern constitution was drawn up back in 1921, but even today the prince retains the power to dissolve parliament and must approve every act before it becomes law. Prince Franz Josef II was the first ruler to live in the castle above the capital city of Vaduz. He died in 1989 and was succeeded by his son, Prince Hans-Adam II.

HOW MUCH?

- **Hotel bed** Sfr40-60
- **Postage stamp** Sfr1.80
- **Souvenir passport stamp** Sfr2
- **Local phone call** Sfr0.60
- **Cup of coffee** Sfr3.60

LONELY PLANET INDEX

- **1L petrol** Sfr1.75
- **1L water** Sfr2
- **500mL beer** Sfr4
- **Souvenir T-shirt** Sfr20
- **Kebab** Sfr8

Liechtenstein has no military service and its minuscule army (80 men!) was disbanded in 1868. It is best known for wine production, postage stamps, dentures (an important export) and its status as a tax haven. In 2000, Liechtenstein's financial and political institutions were rocked by allegations that money laundering was rife in the country. In response to international outrage, banks agreed to stop allowing customers to bank money anonymously. However, it remains under pressure to introduce more reforms.

In 2003 Hans-Adam demanded sweeping powers to dismiss the elected government, appoint judges and reject proposed laws. Opponents warned of dictatorship, but the prince threatened to stomp off back to Austria if he did not get his way, and the population – possibly worried what an empty Schloss Vaduz would do to tourism – backed him in a referendum. The following year Hans-Adam handed the day-to-day running of the country to his son Alois, although he remains head of state.

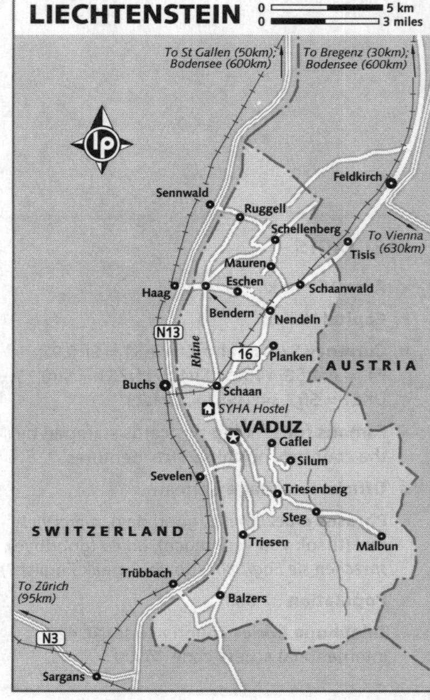

LIECHTENSTEIN

IT'S LIECHTENSTEIN TRIVIA TIME

- If you ever meet the prince in the pub, make sure he buys a round. The royal family is estimated to be worth UK£3.3 billion.
- There are 8000 companies registered in the principality – that's nearly double the population of Vaduz.
- Liechtenstein bites into a large chunk of the false teeth market – it's the world's largest exporter of the product.
- Liechtenstein is the only country in the world named after the people who purchased it.
- In its last military engagement in 1866, none of its 80 soldiers was killed. In fact, 81 returned, including a new Italian 'friend'. The army was disbanded soon afterwards.
- Until 2005, when worries came to a head about the drug TCH, Liechtenstein's cows were fed hemp to keep them chilled and producing 'better' milk.

FOOD & DRINK

Liechtenstein's cuisine borrows from its larger neighbours, and it is generally good quality but expensive. Basic restaurants provide simple but well-cooked food, although budget travellers may want to live out of the supermarket fridge. Soups are popular and usually very filling, and cheeses form an important part of the diet, as do *Rösti* (fried shredded potatoes) and Wurst.

VADUZ

pop 4930

Vaduz is the kind of capital city where the butcher knows the baker – with tidy, quiet streets, lively patio cafés and a big Gothic-looking castle on a hill, it feels more like a village than anything else. It's also all most visitors to Liechtenstein see and at times it can feel like its soul has been sold to cater to the whims of tourist hordes alighting for 17 minutes on guided bus tours. Souvenir shops, tax-free luxury goods stores and cube-shaped concrete buildings dominate the small, somewhat bland town centre enclosed by Äulestrasse and the pedestrian-only Städtle.

INFORMATION

Liechtenstein Tourism (☎ 239 63 00; www.tourismus.li; Städtle 37; 🕑 9am-noon & 1.30-5pm daily May-Oct, 9am-noon & 1.30-5pm Mon-Fri Nov-Apr) Offers souvenir passport stamps for Sfr2, plus all the usual assistance.

Main post office (Äulestrasse 38; 🕑 7.45am-6pm Mon-Fri, 8am-11am Sat)

Telecom FL Shop (☎ 237 74 00; Austrasse 77; 🕑 9am-noon & 1.30-6.30pm Mon-Fri, 9am-1pm Sat) Free Internet access.

SIGHTS & ACTIVITIES

Although the **Schloss Vaduz** (Vaduz Castle) is not open to the public, the exterior graces many a photograph and it is worth climbing up the hill for a closer look. At the top, there's a magnificent vista of Vaduz with a spectacular backdrop of the mountains. There's also a network of marked walking trails along the ridge. For a peek inside the castle grounds, arrive on 15 August (Liechtenstein's national day), when there are magnificent fireworks and the prince invites all 32,860 Liechtensteiners over to his place for a glass of wine or beer.

In the centre, the well-designed **Liechtensteinisches Landesmuseum** (National Museum; ☎ 239 68 20; www.landesmuseum.li; Städtle 43; adult/concession Sfr8/5; 🕑 10am-5pm Tue-Sun, to 8pm Wed) provides a surprisingly interesting romp through the principality's history, from medieval witch-trials and burnings to the manufacture of false teeth.

Keen philatelists will lick their lips in anticipation of the **Briefmarkenmuseum** (Postage Stamp Museum; ☎ 236 61 05; Städtle 37; admission free; 🕑 10am-noon & 1-5pm), where national stamps issued since 1912 are on display.

The national art collection is housed in a sleek modern building at the **Kunstmuseum Liechtenstein** (☎ 235 030 00; Städtle 32; www.kunstmuseum.li; adult/student & child Sfr8/5; 🕑 10am-5pm Tue-Sun, to 8pm Thu). Sixteenth- to 18th-century works from the prince's private collection are among the highlights.

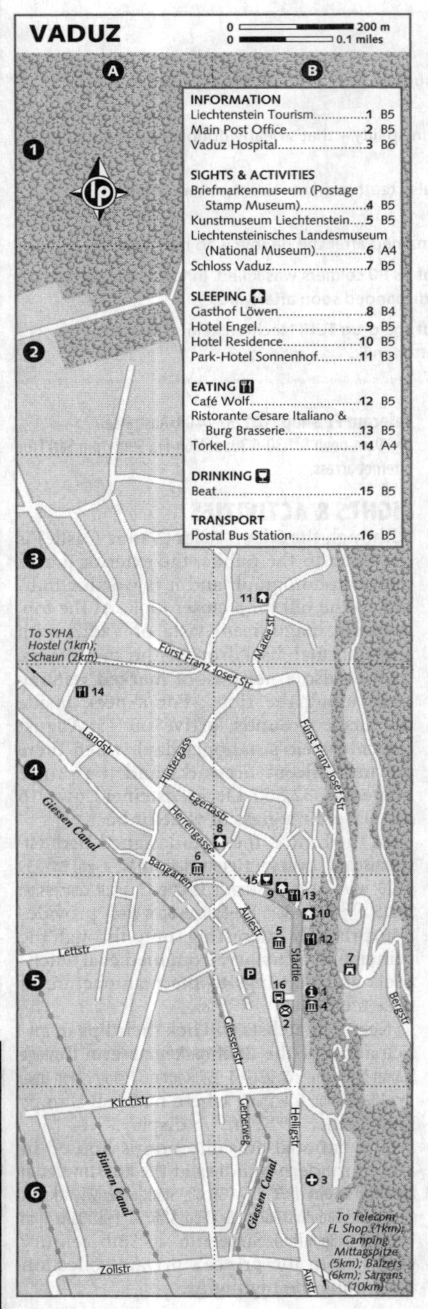

SLEEPING

Ask the tourist office for a list of private rooms and chalets outside Vaduz.

Camping Mittagspitze (☎ 392 36 77, 392 23 11; camp sites per adult/child/car Sfr8.50/4.50/4, tent Sfr8;) A well-equipped camping ground in a leafy spot with a restaurant, TV lounge, playground and kiosk. It's outside Vaduz, just south of Triesen.

SYHA hostel (☎ 232 50 22; www.youthhostel.ch/schaan; Untere Rütigasse 6; dm/d Sfr30.50/82; mid-Mar–Oct, reception closed 10am-5pm) Renovated a few years ago, this hostel caters particularly to cyclists and families. Halfway between Schaan and Vaduz, it's within easy walking distance of either.

Hotel Engel (☎ 236 17 17; www.hotelengel.li; Städtle 13; s/d from Sfr110/165; P) Rooms are modern but feel soulless at this remodelled hotel. There's an Asian restaurant (Thai and Chinese) wafting tempting aromas through the hallways, and the bonus for laptop owners is free Internet in all the rooms.

Hotel Residence (☎ 239 20 20; www.residence.li; Städtle 23; s/d from Sfr195/260; P) It's cool to see a four-star hotel doubling as a local art gallery, which is exactly what Vaduz's newest hotel does (everything on the walls is for sale). Rooms are modern, made up with lots of seagrass and muted colour schemes.

Gasthof Löwen (☎ 232 00 66; www.hotel-loewen.li; Herrengasse 35; s/d from Sfr210/265; P) Antique furniture lends added appeal to the eight elegant and spacious rooms inside this 600-year-old guesthouse. A cosy bar, fine-dining restaurant and rear outdoor terrace, overlooking grapevines and up at the castle, are extra perks.

Park-Hotel Sonnenhof (☎ 239 02 02; www.sonnenhof.li; Mareestrasse 29; s/d from Sfr250/320; closed Christmas-New Year; P) The rooms at this small luxury hotel are tip top, while the hillside views, solarium, ornate restaurant, cobbled courtyards, tinkling fountains and manicured gardens all create a privileged atmosphere.

EATING & DRINKING

Pedestrian-only Städtle street has a clutch of footpath restaurants and cafés.

Beat (☎ 236 84 84; Städtle 3; mains Sfr10-35) This spot has linen tablecloths, with a candle-lit restaurant in front and a slick bar with a lounge feel and flat-screen TVs in the

AUTHOR'S CHOICE

Café Wolf (☎ 232 43 21; Städtle 29; takeaway Sfr4-8, 2-course meal Sfr20) Locals flock here for the set two-course dinners. The menu changes daily, but always includes a veggie option. The horseshoe bar, with orchids and low lighting, is a perfect place to unwind. There is live music some evenings. Shoestring travellers will appreciate the cheap takeaway, including pasta and bratwursts.

back. DJs spin at night. The menu is loaded with soups, salads, pasta and plenty of Swiss-German fare.

Ristorante Cesare Italiano & Burg Brasserie (☎ 232 23 83; Städtle 15; mains Sfr15-30) Chow on pizza, burgers and salads at the downstairs café with a Parisian vibe, complete with red walls and brass fixtures. Upstairs there's a fancier Italian menu. With loads of ice-cream sundaes it's a good spot for the kids.

Torkel (☎ 232 44 10; Hintergasse 9; mains Sfr40-60) Just above the prince's vineyards is his majesty's ivy-clad restaurant. The garden terrace enjoys a wonderful perspective of the castle above, while the ancient, wood-lined interior is cosy in winter. The chef mixes classic with modern and has a couple of unusual veggie options.

AROUND VADUZ

Outside Vaduz the air is crisp and clear with a pungent, sweet aroma of cow dung and flowers. The countryside, dotted with tranquil villages and enticing churches set to a craggy Alps backdrop, is about as idyllic and relaxing as it gets.

Triesenberg, on a terrace above Vaduz, commands excellent views over the Rhine valley. It has a pretty onion-domed church and the **Heimatmuseum** (☎ 262 19 26; adult/student Sfr2/1; 1.30-5.30pm Tue-Sat) devoted to the Walser community, whose members came from Switzerland's Valais to settle in the 13th century.

There are 400km of **hiking trails** through Liechtenstein, along with loads of well-marked **cycling routes** (look for signs with a biking symbol; distances and directions will also be included). The most famous hiking trail is the **Fürstensteig**, a rite of passage for nearly every Liechtensteiner. You must be fit and not suffer from vertigo, as in places the path is narrow, reinforced with rope handholds and/or falls away to a sheer drop. The hike, which takes up to four hours, begins at the **Berggasthaus Gaflei** (bus 30 from Triesenberg). Travel light and wear good shoes.

MALBUN

pop 100

Nestled amid the mountains in the southeast is tiny Malbun, Liechtenstein's one and only ski resort.

The road from Vaduz terminates at Malbun. There is an ATM by the lower bus stop. The **tourist office** (☎ 263 65 77; www.malbun.li; 9am-noon & 1.30-5pm Mon-Sat, closed mid-Apr–May & Nov–mid-Dec) is on the main street, not far from Hotel Walserhof.

Although rather limited in scope – the runs are mostly novice and intermediate – the skiing is inexpensive for this part of the world and it does offer some bragging rights.

The resort has ski and snowboard schools. A one-day/-week ski pass costs Sfr37/165 for adults and Sfr31/137 for students under 28. Skis, shoes and poles cost Sfr44 for a day, and can be hired from the **sports shop** (☎ 263 37 55) in town. A chairlift at the resort operates in the summer (one way/return Sfr8/12), so you can ride up and hike down.

Hotel Gorfion-Malbun (☎ 264 18 83; www.s-hotels.com; s/d from Sfr100/160; P ⊠ 💻) is Malbun's most spacious and upmarket hotel. It caters brilliantly to children.

LIECHTENSTEIN DIRECTORY

Liechtenstein and Switzerland share almost everything, so for more information about Liechtenstein basics check out p1088.

EMERGENCY NUMBERS

The same emergency numbers apply as in Switzerland:

- Ambulance ☎ 144
- Fire ☎ 118
- Police ☎ 117

TRANSPORT IN LIECHTENSTEIN

GETTING THERE & AWAY

The nearest airports are Friedrichshafen (Germany) and Zürich, with train connections to the Swiss border towns of Buchs (via Romanshorn) and Sargans. From each of these towns, there are usually three buses to Vaduz (Sfr2.40/3.60 from Buchs/Sargans, Swiss Pass valid). Buses run every 30 minutes from the Austrian border town of Feldkirch; you might have to change at Schaan to reach Vaduz.

A few local Buchs–Feldkirch trains stop at Schaan (bus tickets are valid).

By road, Rte 16 from Switzerland passes through Liechtenstein via Schaan; it terminates at Feldkirch. The N13 follows the Rhine along the Swiss–Liechtenstein border.

GETTING AROUND

Postbus travel within Liechtenstein is cheap and reliable; all fares cost Sfr2.40 or Sfr3.60, with the higher rate for journeys exceeding 13km (such as Vaduz to Malbun). Grab a timetable from the Vaduz tourist office.

Luxembourg

A minikingdom with mighty wealth, the Grand Duchy of Luxembourg (Luxemburg, Lëtzebuerg) is the stuff of fairy tales. Let your imagination loose from the lofty heights of feudal castles, in the misty world of enchanted forests or amongst the friendly folk of wine-making villages. Listen to the story of this land's tumultuous history and be drawn into a seemingly endless tale of counts and dynasties, wars and victories, fortresses and promontories – only the dragon is missing. But a word of warning – keep imagination and stories firmly at bay until you're here. Drift off to sleep en route and chances are you'll miss Europe's third-smallest country all together (and then it really will take on fairy-tale status).

FAST FACTS

- **Area** 2586 sq km
- **Capital** Luxembourg City
- **Currency** euro (€); A$1 = €0.60; ¥100 = €0.67; NZ$1 = €0.50; UK£1 = €1.48; US$1 = €0.78
- **Famous for** banking
- **Official Languages** Lëtzebuergesch, French, German
- **Population** 440,000
- **Phrases** *moien* (hello); *äddi* (goodbye); *merci* (thanks)
- **Telephone Codes** country code ☎ 352; international access code ☎ 00; reverse-charge code ☎ 80 02 00

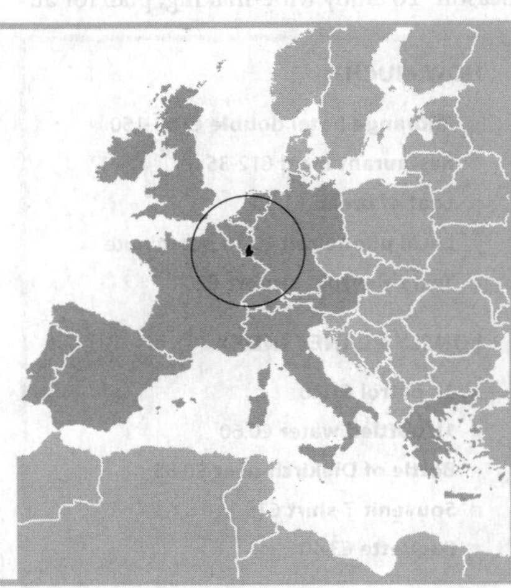

HIGHLIGHTS

- Dine on 'Europe's most beautiful balcony' at **Breedewee** (p835), one of Luxembourg City's most charming restaurants.
- Kick back in the delightful little town of **Echternach** (p838), before exploring the region's fascinating forests.
- Let your imagination reign from the towers of **Château de Bourscheid** (p838), your quintessential castle.

ITINERARIES

- **Two days** Discover the ancient heart of Luxembourg City with the beautiful Chemin de la Corniche, dark Bock Casemates where history unfolds, and a gleaming art gallery.
- **One week** The whole country is at your feet. Don't miss Echternach, a town steeped in Christian history, and the gateway to the mysterious Müllerthal. Vianden is another must. Depending on your tastes, move onto Remich for local wines or Diekirch for WWII history and cycling.

CLIMATE & WHEN TO GO

Luxembourg's climate is temperate – warm summers and cold winters. The sunniest months are from May to August, although April and September can be fine also. If you're into flowers, go in spring. For festivals and outdoor dining, join the throngs who come in summer, Luxembourg's peak season. To enjoy wine-making, plan for autumn when the Moselle villages move into harvest celebrations.

Check out Luxembourg in 2007 when, together with neighbouring regions, it shares the title of European Cultural Capital. For more see www.luxembourg2007.org.

HOW MUCH?

- **Midrange hotel double** €100-150
- **Restaurant meal** €12-35
- **Loaf of bread** €1.30
- **Local phone call** €0.30 per minute
- **Taxi ride from airport** €20

LONELY PLANET INDEX

- **1L petrol** €1.20
- **1L bottled water** €0.60
- **Bottle of Diekirch beer** €0.85
- **Souvenir T-shirt** €15
- **Baguette** €3.40

HISTORY

Once upon a time (963 to be precise), a count called Sigefroi (or Siegfried, Count of Ardennes) built a castle high on a promontory, laying the foundations of the present-day capital and beginning a dynasty that spawned rulers throughout Europe.

By the end of the Middle Ages the strategically placed, fortified city was much sought after – the Burgundians, Spanish, French, Austrians and Prussians all waged bloody battles to secure it. Besieged, devastated and rebuilt more than 20 times in 400 years, it became the strongest fortress in Europe after Gibraltar, hence its nickname, 'Gibraltar of the North'.

In 1814, it was included in the newly formed United Kingdom of the Netherlands, along with Belgium, and 25 years later present-day Luxembourg was born. But its potentially perilous position between France and Germany led to the major European powers declaring the country neutral in 1867. As a result much of its historic fortifications were dismantled, though you can still visit the damp galleries known as the Bock Casemates (p833).

Luxembourg's neutrality was quashed in 1914 when Germany invaded. It was occupied for the whole of WWI and again during WWII – for insight into the 1944 Battle of the Ardennes, visit the Musée National d'Histoire Militaire in Diekirch (p839).

After the war, Luxembourg dumped its neutral status and joined NATO and the EU. The government diversified the economy, enabling the little country to ride out the depression in the iron and steel industries during the 1970s and to become a noted financial centre and tax haven. Now home to some key EU institutions, it entered the 21st century with one of Europe's healthiest economies and continues to ride high.

The Grand Duchy's royal family is experiencing a similar high. Grand Duke Henri and Grand Duchess Maria Teresa, a Cuban-born commoner whom Henri met

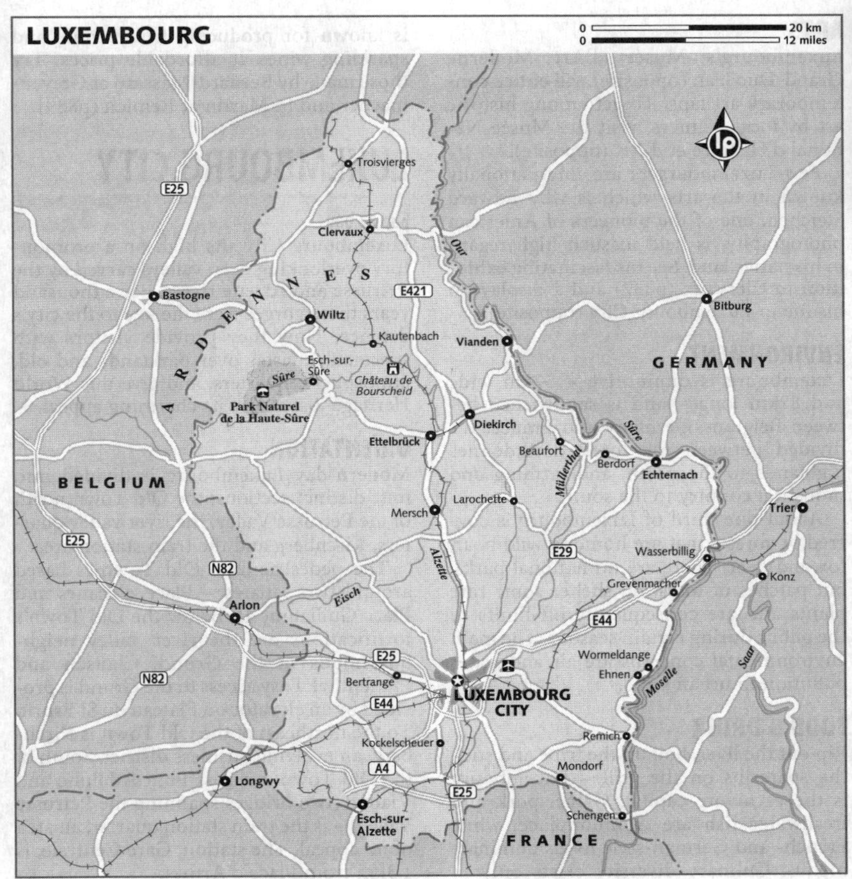

at university, came to the throne in 2000 and have brought new life to the role of the ducal family.

Culturally, things are also rosy. A gleaming new concert hall and neighbouring modern art gallery recently opened in Luxembourg City, in time to celebrate the country's 2007 stint as Cultural Capital of Europe. And the country's continued lack of higher education facilities is finally being tackled with the current construction of the University of Luxembourg.

PEOPLE

Luxembourg's 440,000 inhabitants are a confident and proud people who enjoy a high quality of life. They also have no problem with the fact that they live in a seriously small country. A motto that's occasionally seen carved in stone walls sums up the people's character: *Mir wëlle bleiwe wat mir sin* (We want to remain what we are).

More than a third of Luxembourg's population are immigrants, predominantly Portuguese and Italian.

RELIGION

Christianity was established early and today Catholicism reigns supreme. More than 95% of the population is Roman Catholic, with the church influencing many facets of life including politics, the media and education. About 3% of the population is Protestant or Jewish.

ARTS

Luxembourg's Musée d'Art Moderne Grand-Duc Jean (opposite) will entice contemporary art fans. To get among historic art by local painters, visit the Musée National d'Histoire et d'Art (opposite).

Few Luxembourgers are internationally known in the arts which is why Edward Steichen, one of the pioneers of American photography, is held in such high regard in his native land. See his fascinating exhibition in Clervaux (p837) and a display on his life in Luxembourg City (opposite).

ENVIRONMENT

Luxembourg is diminutive – 57km wide and 82km long – and is sandwiched between Belgium, Germany and France. It's divided between the forested Ardennes highlands to the north, and farming and industrial country to the south.

About one third of Luxembourg is covered by forests that are home to wild boar, fox and deer. There are no national parks, but patches of forest do shelter some rare plants and are consequently off-limits to the public during certain seasons. The main environmental concerns are air and water pollution in urban areas.

FOOD & DRINK

Rip out the liver, boil up the tripe and stick the spareribs on the grill – Luxembourg is the carnivore capital. Game, pork and freshwater fish are commonplace, while French- and German-style foods dominate menus. Culinary diversity exists only in Luxembourg City, thanks largely to the Italian and Portuguese migrant communities, as well as the broad palate of the EU.

Vegetarians are rare beasts in this part of the world. Pizza, pasta, omelettes and salads are about it in many restaurants, the notable exception being Mesa Verde (p835) in Luxembourg City.

Luxembourg's national dish is *judd mat gaardebounen* (smoked pork in a cream-based sauce with chunks of potato and broad beans). Other specialities include *ferkelsrippchen* (grilled spareribs), *liewekniddelen mat sauerkraut* (liver meatballs with sauerkraut), *traipen* (black pudding), *kuddelfleck* (boiled tripe) and *kachkeis* (cooked cheese).

Luxembourg's wine industry, based along the west bank of the Moselle River, is known for producing fruity white and sparkling wines at affordable prices. Try those made by Bernard-Massard at Grevenmacher and St Martin at Remich (p839).

LUXEMBOURG CITY

pop 82,000

Luxembourg City sits high on a promontory overlooking deep valleys carved by the Pétrusse and Alzette rivers. For a thousand years these gorges were the key to the city's defence. Now they provide visitors with spectacular vistas over parklands and old, atmospheric quarters, and give this World Heritage–listed city its charming appeal.

ORIENTATION

Modern-day Luxembourg is divided into four distinct sections: the Old Town north of the Pétrusse Valley, the river valley quarters, Kirchberg and the train station area.

The pedestrianised Old Town is based around two squares – Place d'Armes and Place Guillaume II. Below the Old Town's fortifications are the river valley neighbourhoods of the Grund, Clausen and Pfaffenthal. Easy access to the Grund is provided by an elevator on Plateau du St Esprit. To the northeast of the Old Town is Kirchberg, an evolving business district. South of the Old Town – across Pont Adolphe and Viaduc (two bridges spanning the Pétrusse Valley) – is the train station quarter, an area of no appeal. The station, Gare Centrale, is 1.3km from Place d'Armes.

INFORMATION

Discount Cards

Luxembourg Card (1/2/3 days adult €9/16/22, family of 2 adults & up to 5 kids €18/32/44) Includes admission to many attractions throughout the country plus unlimited use of public transport. It's valid from Easter to 31 October, and is available from tourist offices, train stations and hotels.

Internet Access

Cyber Beach (☎ 26 47 80 70; 3 Rue du Curé; per hr €4; 🕑 10am-8pm Mon-Fri, 1-8pm Sat & Sun) Relaxed surfing space.

Medical Services

Clinique Ste Thérèse (☎ 49 77 61; 36 Rue Zithe) Central hospital providing emergency services.

Money

ATMs can be found inside Gare Centrale, outside the main post office and inside Luxembourg Airport terminal.

Post

Main post office (25 Rue Aldringen; 🕑 7am-7pm Mon-Fri, 7am-5pm Sat)

Tourist Information

Mutli-lingual, interactive touch screens dispensing free tourist information are located on Rue du Curé in the Old Town, at Gare Centrale and at Luxembourg Airport.

Luxembourg City Tourist Office (☎ 22 28 09; www.lcto.lu; Place Guillaume II; 🕑 9am-7pm Mon-Sat & 10am-6pm Sun Apr-Sep, 9am-6pm Mon-Sat & 10am-6pm Sun Oct-Mar) Free city maps, walking tour pamphlets and events guides.

Luxembourg National Tourist Office (☎ 42 82 82 20; www.ont.lu; Place de la Gare; 🕑 8.30am-6.30pm Mon-Sat, 9am-12.30pm & 2-6pm Sun Jun-Sep, 9.15am-12.30pm & 1.45-6pm Oct-May) City and national information.

SIGHTS

Start at **Place d'Armes**, Luxembourg's central pedestrianised square, from where it's an easy walk to the **Musée National d'Histoire et d'Art** (☎ 47 93 30 1; www.mnha.lu, in French; Marché-aux-Poissons; adult/family €5/10; 🕑 10am-5pm Tue-Sun). This is the country's principal museum and houses permanent collections of Roman and medieval relics, fortification models and art dating from the 13th century.

The nearby **Bock Casemates** (☎ 22 28 09; Montée de Clausen; adult/child €1.75/1; 🕑 10am-5pm Mar-Oct) offer a view into Luxembourg's past. The honeycomb of rock galleries was carved out under the Bock by the Spaniards in 1744. Over the years the casemates have housed everything from bakeries to slaughter-houses; during WWI and WWII they were used as a bomb shelter for 35,000 locals.

Chemin de la Corniche is a beautiful promenade that offers fab views over the Grund quarter and eventually leads up to Rue du St Esprit, home to Luxembourg's other main museum, the **Musée d'Histoire de la Ville de Luxembourg** (☎ 47 96 30 61; www.musee-hist.lu, in French; 14 Rue du St Esprit; adult/student/child €5/3.70/free; 🕑 10am-6pm Tue-Sun, 10am-8pm Thu). Explore the history of the city using a glass elevator that beautifully reveals the Old Town's rocky geology.

> **LUXEMBOURG CITY IN TWO DAYS**
>
> **Place d'Armes** (left), the pedestrianised core, is the essential start, followed by the **Musée d'Histoire de la Ville de Luxembourg** (left) or the new **Musée d'Art Moderne Grand-Duc Jean** (below). Head to **Café Am Musee** (p835) for an alfresco lunch then stroll along the **Chemin de la Corniche**.
>
> On day two, explore the **Bock Casemates** (left) and take the elevator to the **Grund** (p836) for an evening drink.

The Moorish-style **Palais Grand-Ducal** (☎ 22 28 09; 17 Rue du Marché-aux-Herbes; adult/child €6/3; 🕑 mid-Jul–early-Sep, guided tours in English 4.30pm Mon-Fri & 1.30pm Sat) was built in the 1570s during Spanish rule. The royals no longer reside here; instead it's used as the Grand Duke's office.

Cathédrale Notre Dame (Blvd Roosevelt; 🕑 10am-noon & 2-5.30pm) is worth a peak to see the nation's most revered idol, the *Lady Comforter of the Afflicted*, a small, elaborately dressed statue of the Virgin and child.

Am Tunnel (☎ 40 15 24 50; 16 Rue Zithe; admission free; 🕑 9am-5.30pm Mon-Fri, 2-6pm Sun) is in the depths of the BCEE, one of Luxembourg's 180 banks. This underground art gallery devotes itself to temporary exhibitions but also has an interesting permanent display on Edward Steichen (see opposite).

Pont Grand-Duchesse Charlotte connects the Old Town with the **Kirchberg Plateau** to the northeast. This plateau is home to wide boulevards, big office blocks and EU institutions, and also accommodates the Philharmonie Luxembourg Grande-Duchesse Joséphine-Charlotte (p836) and the **Musée d'Art Moderne Grand-Duc Jean** (☎ 45 37 85 22; www.mudam.lu). Bus 18 from Gare Centrale or Place Hamilius stops at both.

SLEEPING

Budget

Camping Kockelscheuer (☎ 47 18 15; www.camp-kockelscheuer.lu; 22 Route de Bettembourg; adult/child/campsites €3.75/2/4.50; 🕑 Easter-Oct) Pleasantly situated between a forest and a sports centre, this campground is 4km southwest of the city. To get there, take bus 5 from Gare Centrale or Place Hamilius.

Auberge de Jeunesse (☎ 22 68 89; luxembourg@youthhostels.lu; 2 Rue du Fort Olizy; dm/s €17.60/29.60;

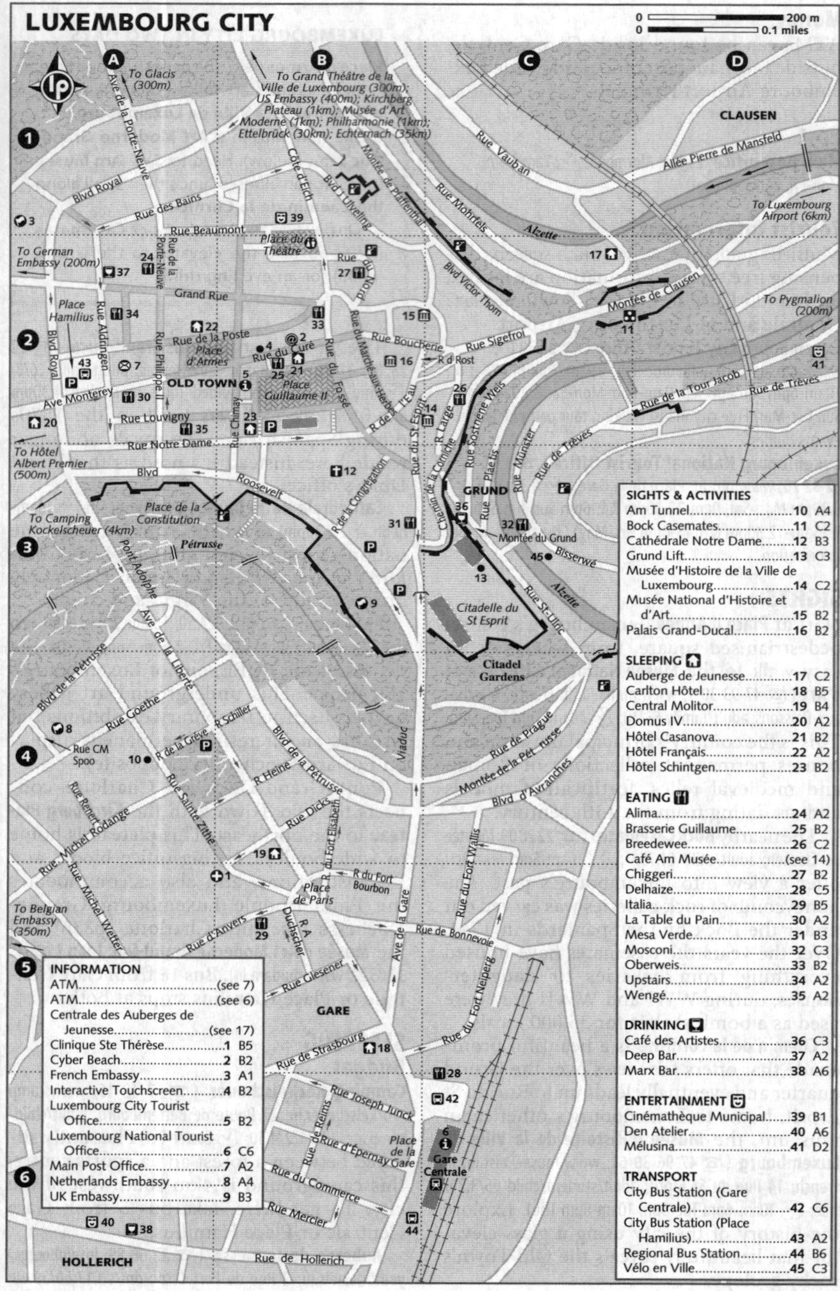
LUXEMBOURG CITY
0 200 m
0 0.1 miles
A
B
C
D
1
2
3
4
5
6
To Glacis (300m)
To Grand Théâtre de la Ville de Luxembourg (300m); US Embassy (400m); Kirchberg Plateau (1km); Musée d'Art Moderne (1km); Philharmonie (1km); Ettelbrück (30km); Echternach (35km)
CLAUSEN
Allée Pierre de Mansfeld
To Luxembourg Airport (6km)
To Pygmalion (200m)
To German Embassy (200m)
To Hôtel Albert Premier (500m)
To Camping Kockelscheuer (4km)
To Belgian Embassy (350m)
Rue Vauban
Rue Mohrfels
Alzette
Blvd Victor Thom
Montée de Pfaffenthal
Montée de Clausen
Rue Sigefroi
Rue de la Tour Jacob
Rue de Trèves
Blvd Royal
Ave de la Porte-Neuve
Rue des Bains
Rue Beaumont
Côte d'Eich
Blvd F D Roosevelt
Place du Théâtre
Rue du Nord
Rue de la Porte-Neuve
Grand Rue
Place Hamilius
Rue Aldringen
Rue de la Poste
Place d'Armes
Rue du Curé
Rue du Fossé
Rue du Marché-aux-Herbes
Rue Boucherie
R d Rost
OLD TOWN
Place Guillaume II
Ave Monterey
Rue Philippe II
Rue Louvigny
Rue Chimay
Rue Notre Dame
R de l'Eau
Rue du St Esprit
R Large
Chemin de la Corniche
Rue Sosthene Weis
Rue Plaetis
Rue Münster
Rue de Trèves
GRUND
Montée du Grund
Bisserwe
Rue St-Ulric
Blvd Roosevelt
Place de la Constitution
Pétrusse
Pont Adolphe
R de la Congrégation
Citadelle du St Esprit
Citadel Gardens
Blvd de la Pétrusse
Ave de la Liberté
Rue Goethe
R Schiller
R de la Grève
Rue CM Spoo
R Heine
Rue Sainte Zithe
Rue Dicks
Viaduc
Rue de Prague
Montée de la Pétrusse
Blvd d'Avranches
Rue Renert
Rue Michel Rodange
Rue Michel Welter
R du Fort Elisabeth
R du Fort Bourbon
Place de Paris
Rue du Fort Wallis
Rue d'Anvers
R A Duchscher
Ave de la Gare
Rue de Bonnevoie
Rue du Fort Neipperg
Rue Glesener
GARE
Rue de Strasbourg
Rue Joseph Junck
Rue de Reims
Rue d'Épernay
Place de la Gare
Gare Centrale
Rue du Commerce
Rue Mercier
HOLLERICH
Rue de Hollerich
INFORMATION
ATM (see 7)
ATM (see 6)
Centrale des Auberges de Jeunesse (see 17)
Clinique Ste Thérèse 1 B5
Cyber Beach 2 B2
French Embassy 3 A1
Interactive Touchscreen 4 B2
Luxembourg City Tourist Office 5 B2
Luxembourg National Tourist Office 6 C6
Main Post Office 7 A2
Netherlands Embassy 8 A4
UK Embassy 9 B3
SIGHTS & ACTIVITIES
Am Tunnel 10 A4
Bock Casemates 11 C2
Cathédrale Notre Dame 12 B3
Grund Lift 13 C3
Musée d'Histoire de la Ville de Luxembourg 14 C2
Musée National d'Histoire et d'Art 15 B2
Palais Grand-Ducal 16 B2
SLEEPING
Auberge de Jeunesse 17 C2
Carlton Hôtel 18 B5
Central Molitor 19 B4
Domus IV 20 A2
Hôtel Casanova 21 B2
Hôtel Français 22 A2
Hôtel Schintgen 23 B2
EATING
Alima 24 A2
Brasserie Guillaume 25 B2
Breedewee 26 C2
Café Am Musée (see 14)
Chiggeri 27 B2
Delhaize 28 C5
Italia 29 B5
La Table du Pain 30 A2
Mesa Verde 31 B3
Mosconi 32 C3
Oberweis 33 B2
Upstairs 34 A2
Wengé 35 A2
DRINKING
Café des Artistes 36 C3
Deep Bar 37 A2
Marx Bar 38 A6
ENTERTAINMENT
Cinémathèque Municipal 39 B1
Den Atelier 40 A6
Mélusina 41 D2
TRANSPORT
City Bus Station (Gare Centrale) 42 C6
City Bus Station (Place Hamilius) 43 A2
Regional Bus Station 44 B6
Vélo en Ville 45 C3

(P ⊠) The capital's only real budget option is newly renovated and fabulously located at the base of the Old Town near the foot of the forbidding casemates. Bus 16 from the airport or Gare Centrale stops nearby. Alternatively it's a 40-minute walk from Gare Centrale.

Hôtel Schintgen (☎ 22 28 44; schintgn@pt.lu; 6 Rue Notre Dame; s/d/tr €70/85/90) This hotel's handy location in the Old Town compensates for ordinary rooms.

Midrange & Top End

Carlton Hôtel (☎ 29 96 60; www.carlton.lu; 9 Rue de Strasbourg; s/d/tr from €85/98/125; 💻) This atmospheric old gem, c 1920, is tucked away on a backstreet in the train station quarter. Among its attributes are stained-glass windows, modern rooms and incredibly welcoming staff (they even love kids!). It's a pinch in July and August when prices drop by about a third.

Hôtel Français (☎ 47 45 34; www.hotelfrancais.lu; 14 Place d'Armes; s/d Mon-Fri €97/125, Sat & Sun €90/118) This intimate hotel dotted with *objets d'art* has a prized location overlooking the Old Town's busy main square.

Central Molitor (☎ 48 99 11; www.hotelmolitor.lu; 28 Ave de la Liberté; s/d/tr Mon-Fri €135/160/170, Sat & Sun €95/120/130; P ⊠ 💻) Located half way between the train station and the Old Town, this century-old hotel bills itself as a place with 'international standards, local flavours'. The distinguished domed building is more grand than the rooms (expect '80s-style décor) but, all in all, it's highly presentable.

Domus IV (☎ 46 78 78 1; www.domus.lu; 37 Ave Monterey; d with/without kitchenette €175/160; P ⊠ ✲ 💻) Zany decorations and innovative rooms (some with handy cooking facilities) are the salient features of this centrally located hotel. Breakfast is €15 extra. Inquire about weekend discounts.

Hôtel Albert Premier (☎ 44 24 42 1; www.albert1er.lu; 2a Rue Albert 1er; ste Mon-Thu from €225, continental breakfast €15, ste Fri-Sun incl breakfast from €155; P 💻) The city's most charming hotel is located 750m west of Place d'Armes on an unassuming backstreet. The swanky rooms burst with Gothic excesses. Parking costs €12 per day.

EATING

The Old Town, Grund and Clausen are the go for dining. In summer they turn into open-air terraces with tables spilling out onto pavements and tree-lined squares.

> **AUTHOR'S CHOICE**
>
> **Breedewee** (☎ 22 26 96; 9 Rue Large; mains €20-32, 3-course menu €20, 6-course dégustation menu €55; 🕑 lunch & dinner) Wooed by a view? No restaurant in Luxembourg can match it – in warm, fine weather. This modern but elegant little place has a separate terrace perched high on the Corniche in a setting that's quite unique. A dozen tables are serviced by penguin-style waiters who shuttle back and forth to the main building carrying steaming plates of French cuisine. Reservations essential.

Cafés

La Table du Pain (☎ 24 16 08; 19 Ave Monterey; baguettes €4.60-7.20; 🕑 7am-7pm; ⊠) This convivial, completely nonsmoking café does filled baguettes and big salads (€12).

Café Am Musée (☎ 26 20 25 95; 14 Rue du St Ésprit; mains €10-12; 🕑 10am-6pm Tue-Sun, 10am-8pm Thu) This well-hidden local favourite, attached to the Musée d'Histoire de la Ville de Luxembourg, is easily overlooked. At its best for a casual outdoor lunch (reservations required) on a warm day.

Oberweis (☎ 47 07 03; 19 Grand Rue; 🕑 10am-6pm Mon, 7.30am-6pm Tue-Fri, 8am-6pm Sat) Moreish cakes, chocolates and ice cream are found at this classy patisserie-cum-tearoom.

Restaurants

Brasserie Guillaume (☎ 26 20 20 20; 12 Place Guillaume II; mains €14-22; 🕑 10am-1am) The best brasserie in the Old Town is great for a late-night bite or a leisurely lunch. Modern, big and slightly brash, it caters eclectically.

Mesa Verde (☎ 46 41 26; 11 Rue du St Esprit; mains vegetarian €18.80, fish €22.75-25; 🕑 lunch Wed-Fri Sep-Jul, dinner Tue-Sat year-round; ⊠) Imaginative vegetarian and seafood dishes are the mainstay of this exotic restaurant. It's often full, and deservedly so.

Upstairs (☎ 26 27 01 12; 21 Rue Aldringen; mains €19-23; 🕑 lunch Tue-Sat, dinner Tue-Fri) This well-hidden, 1st-floor local eatery (entry is at the back of the L'Interview pub) does great Vietnamese and Japanese dishes in no-fuss surroundings. The lunch-time *plat du jour* (€10) is superb value.

Italia (☎ 48 66 26 1; 15 Rue d'Anvers; mains €19-26, homemade pastas €14; 🕑 lunch & dinner) Polished and well-run, this Italian restaurant is known for its homemade pasta. It's close to Gare Centrale.

Chiggeri (☎ 22 82 36; 15 Rue du Nord; mains €20-34; lunch & dinner) Chiggeri is a hip 1st-floor café/restaurant with French cuisine and an extraordinary wine list.

Wengé (☎ 26 20 10 58; 15 Rue Louvigny; mains €25-30; 8am-6.30pm Mon-Sat, dinner Wed & Fri) A classy food-store-cum-restaurant offering delicious French cuisine.

Mosconi (☎ 54 69 94; 13 Rue Münster, Grund; mains €26-32; lunch & dinner Tue-Sat) This was the first Italian restaurant in the Benelux (that's Belgium, the Netherlands and Luxembourg locally abbreviated) to be starred by Michelin, and it was awarded its second twinkle in 2006. Reservations are essential.

Self-Catering

There are several supermarkets around town including **Alima** (Rue de la Porte-Neuve), in the Old Town, and **Delhaize** (Place de la Gare; 7am-8pm Mon-Fri, 7am-6pm Sat, 7am-noon Sun), at the train station.

DRINKING

The Old Town, Grund, Clausen and Hollerich are the most popular spots for a drink.

Marx Bar (☎ 48 84 26; 42 Rue de Hollerich; from 5pm) A lively bar in the nightlife hub at Hollerich and an absolute humdinger – Marx Bar is *the* place to hang out.

Café des Artistes (☎ 46 13 27; 22 Montée du Grund; evenings Tue-Sun) This nostalgic Grund café has been around since 1968 and has candles that prove its age. Don't miss the piano soiree nights (Wednesday to Saturday).

Pygmalion (☎ 42 08 60; 19 Rue de la Tour Jacob; 4pm-1am Sun-Thu, 4pm-3am Fri & Sat) This moody little Irish haunt is one of several good pubs in Clausen, an area favoured by late-night revellers. Take bus 9 or night bus CN1 to get there.

Deep Bar (☎ 26 20 04 23; 11 Rue Aldringen; Wed-Mon) This Old Town bar is where you end up when all else is closed.

ENTERTAINMENT

The free entertainment guide, *Luxembourg Weekly*, is available from the tourist office.

Philharmonie Luxembourg Grande-Duchesse Joséphine-Charlotte (☎ 26 32 26 32; www.philharmonie.lu; 1 Place de l'Europe) Luxembourg's new concert venue is a stunning oval job that brings life to the boring office blocks of Kirchberg. From jazz to classical and opera, all are on offer.

Cinémathèque Municipal (☎ 47 96 26 44; 17 Place du Théâtre; adult/concession €4/2.80) This is the closest thing in Luxembourg to an art-house cinema and is cheap to boot.

Den Atelier (☎ 49 54 66; www.atelier.lu; 56 Rue de Hollerich) The main venue for contemporary live music is located about 500m west of Gare Centrale in Hollerich, an off-the-beaten-track nightlife area.

Mélusina (☎ 43 59 22; 145 Rue de la Tour Jacob; Fri & Sat) This restaurant-cum-club in Clausen and one of the city's most popular dance spots. It's big on house and even entices guest DJs.

Grand Théâtre de la Ville de Luxembourg (☎ 47 96 39 00; www.theater-vdl.lu, in French; 1 Rond-point Schuman) This performing arts complex is the nation's biggest.

GETTING THERE & AWAY

See p841 for information on international flights, trains and buses.

GETTING AROUND

To/From the Airport

Bus 16 (€1.50, 20 minutes, every 15 minutes) connects Luxembourg airport with Place Hamilius and Gare Centrale. Buses run from 5.40am to 9.40pm. A taxi costs €20.

Bicycle

The topography's not flat, but those with decent muscles will find Luxembourg City good for biking. **Vélo en Ville** (☎ 47 96 23 83; 8 Bisserwée; hire half-/full-day €12.50/20; 10am-noon & 1-8pm Apr-Oct) offers a 20% discount on full-day bicycle rentals to people under 26.

Bus

Buses are a good way to get between city quarters. The main bus stations are Place Hamilius in the Old Town and Gare Centrale. For all ticket information see p842. Most buses run from 5.30am to 10pm when a limited **late night bus service** (☎ 24 89 24 89; Fri & Sat) takes over.

Car & Motorcycle

Much of the Old Town centre is pedestrianised. The cheapest open-air car park is Glacis, located a handy 800m northwest of Place d'Armes. For details on car rental agencies, see p842.

AROUND LUXEMBOURG

Hop, skip or jump into Luxembourg – everywhere is fabulously accessible from the capital.

The Ardennes, the northern region, is spectacular country. Verdant forests hide beguiling towns nestled in deep river valleys and crowned by castles. Vianden is the prime example.

Relive fairy tales in the Müllerthal, an enchanting pocket of forested land northeast of Luxembourg City. This region is distinguished by an almost primeval landscape of gorges scoured through sandstone plateaux by ancient streams. It's fantastic for hikers, and there's no better base than Echternach.

The Gutland, a heavily farmed area immediately north of Luxembourg City, is home to Diekirch and its famous war museum. Alternatively, take time out for a tipple in the tiny wine-producing Moselle Valley to the east.

VIANDEN

pop 1600

This is Luxembourg at its most touristy, and understandably so. Round a bend in the road and before you rises the impeccably restored medieval castle of Vianden, shrouded in mist and framed by forest. If this doesn't bring back childhood tales of princes and princesses, baddies and beasts, nothing will.

Vianden's **tourist office** (☎ 83 42 57 1; www.tourist-info-vianden.lu, in French; 1a Rue du Vieux Marché; 🕑 8am-6pm Mon-Fri, 10am-2pm Sat Apr-Aug, 9am-noon & 1-5pm Mon-Fri Sep-Mar) is by the Our River.

Looming over the town is the **château** (☎ 83 41 08 1; www.castle-vianden.lu; Grand Rue; adult/child €5.50/2; 🕑 10am-4pm Nov-Feb, 10am-5pm Mar & Oct, 10am-6pm Apr-Sep). The oldest part of the castle dates to the 11th century, although a much older Roman fort is thought to have occupied the craggy outcrop in the 4th century.

Vianden's picturesque position can be photographed from the **télésiège** (chairlift; ☎ 83 43 23; 39 Rue du Sanatorium; adult/child €4.50/2.25; 🕑 10am-6pm Tue-Sun Easter-May & Oct, 10am-6pm daily Jun-Sep), which takes off from the lower bank of the river at the end of Rue Victor Hugo.

Directly opposite the tourist office is **Maison de Victor Hugo** (☎ 26 87 40 88; www.victor-hugo.lu, in French; 37 Rue de la Gare; adult/child €4/2.50; 🕑 11am-5pm Easter & Jul-Aug, 11am-5pm Sat & Sun May-Jun & Sep-Oct). Vianden was briefly home to author Victor Hugo during his 19-year exile from France and the town makes much ado about the three months he stayed here in 1871.

Sleeping & Eating

Camping de l'Our (☎ 83 45 05; 3 Route de Bettel; adult/child/campsites €4.50/2/5; 🕑 Easter-Oct) One of several campgrounds draped along the riverbank, this one is well-run and located south of town.

Auberge de Jeunesse (☎ 83 41 77; vianden@youthhostels.lu; 3 Montée du Château; dm/s/d €14.50/26.50/39; 🕑 early Jan-late Dec; ⊠) This pleasant hostel is located in the shadow of the château (and a long 1km uphill walk from the bus station). Recently refreshed décor makes it even better than before.

Hôtel Heintz (☎ 83 41 55; www.hotel-heintz.lu; 55 Grand Rue; s/d from €45/66; mains €15-25; 🕑 Easter-Oct; Ⓟ) One of the most characterful hotels in the Grand Duchy, this place started life in the Middle Ages as the inn and brewery of Trinitarian monks. The public rooms and restaurant still exude subtle charm, though the rooms are less atmospheric.

Hôtel Petry (☎ 83 41 22; www.hotel-petry.com; 15 Rue de la Gare; s/d from €50/68; mains €15-30; 🕑 mid-Feb–mid-Nov; Ⓟ) The modern rooms in this rambling riverside hotel offer either castle or river views. The restaurant serves good French cuisine, and they also dish up cheap pizzas.

Getting There & Away

To reach Vianden from Luxembourg City, take the train to Ettelbrück (30 minutes, half-hourly) and then a bus (30 minutes, 10 buses daily).

CLERVAUX

pop 1800

Hidden deep in the valley of the Clierf River, Clervaux is best associated with a permanent photographic exhibition that draws visitors from far a field.

The **tourist office** (☎ 92 00 72; www.tourisme-clervaux.lu; 🕑 2-5pm Mon-Fri Easter-Jun, 9.45-11.45am

& 2-6pm Jul-Aug, 9.45-11.45am & 1-5pm Sep-Oct) is housed in a side turret of Clervaux's castle.

The castle, razed in 1944, is visited mostly for the exhibition, **Family of Man** (☎ 92 96 57; adult/child €4.50/2.50; 10am-6pm Apr-Sep, Tue-Sun Mar & Oct-Dec), collated by Luxembourg-born Edward Steichen (1879–1973). Steichen compiled the 500 black-and-white photos in 1955 at the age of 76 and the exhibition travelled the world for years before coming to rest in Clervaux.

Clervaux's turreted **Benedictine Abbey of St Maurice** pokes out of the forest high above the town and is accessible by a 1km track from the castle. Time your visit to hear one of their **Gregorian Masses** (10.30am & 6pm Sat, 5pm Sun).

Sleeping & Eating

Camping Clervaux (☎ 92 00 42; www.camping-clervaux.lu; 33 Klatzewee; adult/child/campsites €5.30/2.50/5.50) This campground is located just 200m from the town centre.

Hôtel/Restaurant du Parc (☎ 92 06 50; www.hotelduparc.lu; 2 Rue du Parc; s/d €44/70; Feb-Dec; P) Full of character and perhaps the odd ghost, this old whitewashed mansion clings to a forested hillside overlooking town. There are just seven rooms, each fitted with a mix of modern and old. The restaurant serves well-priced French/Luxembourg cuisine.

Café/Restaurant du Vieux Château (☎ 92 00 12; 4 Montée du Château; mains €13-16; Wed-Sun) Take a break on the delightful terrace located between the two gates of the castle.

Getting There & Away

Clervaux is easily reached from Luxembourg City by train (one hour, every two hours).

ESCH-SUR-SÛRE

pop 240

Dubbed one of Europe's prettiest villages, Esch-sur-Sûre is a delight. This tiny village is built on a rocky loop in the Sûre River and is surrounded by soft distant hills that drop to steep cliffs as they reach the river. Cushioned in among all this is a true 'crumbly' – a ruined **castle** dating from 927 – around which visitors are free to wander. Stay overnight to really appreciate the village atmosphere. **Hotel Beau-Site** (☎ 83 91 34; www.beau-site.lu; 2 Rue de Kaundorf; s/d from €55/75; Mar-Dec) is down by the river and has a good restaurant.

To get to Esch-sur-Sûre, take a train from Luxembourg City to Ettelbrück (30 minutes, half-hourly) then bus it (40 minutes, five daily).

WILTZ

pop 4600

Wiltz captivates crowds throughout July for the Grand Duchy's biggest open-air theatre and musical event, the **Festival de Théâtre et de Musique** (www.festivalwiltz.lu, in French).

To get there by train from Luxembourg City (1½ hours, hourly), take the train (direction Clervaux) to Kautenbach, and catch another train from there.

ECHTERNACH

pop 5100

The ancient town of Echternach flanks the western bank of the Sûre River and makes a superb base for hiking the evocative forests of the Müllerthal.

The **tourist office** (☎ 72 02 30; Parvis de la Basilique; 10am-12.30pm & 2-5pm Mon-Fri Sep-Easter, 10am-5.30pm Easter-Aug) is in a courtyard next to the town's huge basilica.

If you happen to be in Echternach on the Tuesday after Whit Sunday, look out for the handkerchief pageant in honour of St Willibrord, an Anglo-Saxon monk who founded Echternach's abbey in the 7th century. If not, you can still visit the **basilica** (9.30am-6.30pm), the country's most important religious building, where St Willibrord's remains lie in a primitive stone coffin covered by a marble canopy.

Hikers can start with any of the marked **hiking trails** that begin near the town's bus

WORTH A TRIP

Roughly halfway between Esch-sur-Sûre and Ettelbrück, a road winds up to the magnificent **Château de Bourscheid** (☎ 99 05 70; 1 Schlasswee; adult/child €3/1.50; 9am-6pm daily Apr-Sep, 10am-5pm daily Oct, 10am-5pm Sat & Sun Nov-Mar). This 1000-year-old castle, superbly situated on a rocky bluff overlooking farmland and the Sûre River, affords some of the best views in Luxembourg. Perch like a princess on one of the cold stone ledges, and let the evocative setting conjure up images of horses, knights and invading armies across the distant windswept hills.

station. The best is path 'B' (6km; 2½ hours), which winds up via Troosknеppchen and Wolfschlucht to the **Gorge du Loup**, a sheer-sided canyon flanked by dramatic sandstone formations. Walk noiselessly through here to witness fox or deer, or wander deeper into this dreamlike world and wait for Snow White or the like to emerge. It's almost possible.

Sleeping & Eating

Camping Officiel (☎ 72 02 72; 5 Route de Diekirch; adult/child/campsites €4.80/2.80/5; Easter-Oct;) This OK campground is draped along the hillside about 200m from the bus station.

Auberge de Jeunesse (☎ 72 01 58; www.youthhostels.lu; Rue Grégoire Schouppe; dm/s/d €16.60/28.60/43.20;) This spanking new hostel is located 2km from the bus station next to a lake. From Luxembourg City take the Echternach bus to the Nonnemillen/Lac stop, from where it's a 1km walk (direction Rodenhof).

Hostellerie de la Basilique (☎ 72 94 83; www.hotel-basilique.lu; 7 Place du Marché; s/d/tr €91/108/135; Easter–mid-Nov) The best address in town offers 14 tidy rooms that don't suffer from decoration overkill.

Giorgio (☎ 72 99 34; 4 Rue André Duchscher; mains €10-30; lunch & dinner daily Apr-Oct, Wed-Mon Nov-Mar) A casual Italian restaurant, Giorgio serves crusty pizzas and al-dente pasta. Above or below ground, it's always full.

Café de Philo'soff (☎ 72 00 19; 31 Rue de la Gare; Wed-Mon) An art-nouveau showpiece with laid-back music, Café de Philo'soff has a good range of Belgian beers.

Getting There & Away

Only buses connect Echternach with Luxembourg City (45 minutes, hourly). From Echternach, buses head out to other regional towns.

DIEKIRCH

pop 6000

This pleasant little town on the banks of the gushing Sûre River definitely merits an overnight stay. Besides a sprinkling of sights, including the country's main wartime museum, it's a good base for cycling.

The **tourist office** (☎ 80 30 23; www.diekirch.lu; 3 Place de la Libération; 9am-noon & 2-5pm Mon-Fri, 2-4pm Sat Sep-Jun, 9am-5pm Mon-Fri, 10am-4pm Sat & Sun Jul-Aug) is a 10-minute walk from the train station.

An excellent collection of wartime memorabilia detailing the WWII Battle of the Bulge and the liberation of Luxembourg by US troops is presented at Diekirch's **Musée National d'Histoire Militaire** (☎ 80 89 08; 10 Rue Barnertal; adult/child €5/3; 10am-6pm Apr-Nov, 2-6pm Dec-Mar).

Diekirch has one of Luxembourg's few bicycle rental outfits, **Rent-a-Bike** (☎ 26 80 33 76; nordstad@cig.lu; 27 Rue Jean l'Aveugle; hire half-/full-day €10/15; 10am-5pm Apr-Oct). Good cycling paths follow the river all the way from Diekirch to Echternach (27km).

Sleeping & Eating

Camping de la Sûre (☎ 80 94 25; fax 80 27 86; 34 Route de Gilsdorf; adult/child/campsites €4.50/2.50/4.50; Apr-Sep) Situated on leafy grounds by the river, this campground is only a few minutes' walk from the town centre.

Hotel/Restaurant de la Gare (☎ 80 33 05; jamper@sl.lu; 73 Ave de la Gare; s/d €42/73, 3-course menu €15-35;) This family-run establishment opposite the train station offers five renovated rooms and a restaurant favoured by the locals. Take to the terrace and try the local ham – delicious.

Getting There & Away

There are trains from Luxembourg City to Diekirch (40 minutes, half-hourly).

MOSELLE VALLEY

Less than half an hour's drive east of the capital, the Luxembourg section of the Moselle Valley is one of Europe's smallest wine regions. More than a dozen towns and hamlets are draped along the **Route du Vin** (Wine Rd), which meanders from the southern border town of Schengen, past the waterfront playground of Remich, through the region's capital at Grevenmacher.

There are only two tourist offices en route from Luxembourg City: the **Grevenmacher tourist office** (☎ 75 82 75; 10 Route du Vin; 8am-noon & 1-5pm Mon-Fri, 10am-1pm Sat Jul-Aug) and the **Remich tourist office** (☎ 23 69 84 88; Esplanade; 10am-12.30pm & 1.30-6pm 15 Jun-15 Sep).

Wine tasting is the premier attraction and several *caves* (cellars) give tours. The tour at **St Martin** (☎ 23 69 97 74; 53 Route de Stadtbredimus; adult/child €2.75/1.75; 10am-noon & 1.30-6pm Apr-Oct), 1.5km north of Remich, winds through damp tunnels hewn in the rock.

Bus 450 from Remich to Grevenmacher stops there.

Caves Bernard-Massard (☎ 75 05 45 1; 8 Rue du Pont; adult/child €3/2; 9.30am-6pm Apr-Oct) in the heart of Grevenmacher is one of the region's largest producers of sparkling wine (four million bottles per year). Tours take in the slick, fully-mechanised cellar.

Sleeping & Eating

Camping Route du Vin (☎ 75 02 34; www.grevenmacher.lu; Route du Vin, Grevenmacher; adult/child/campsites €3.80/2/4; Apr-Sep) This campground is well located right on the river bank.

Auberge-Restaurant des Cygnes (☎ 23 69 88 52; hpcygnes@pt.lu; 11 Esplanade, Remich; s/d/tr €48/65/83; mid-Feb–mid-Jan; P) One of several waterfront hotels in Remich, Auberge-Restaurant des Cygnes does excellent wood-fire-baked pizzas.

Bamberg's (☎ 76 00 22; bamberg@pt.lu; 131 Route du Vin, Ehnen; s/d €65/90; mains €20-26; Wed-Mon) This hotel/restaurant in the village of Ehnen is *the* place to dine on blue European lobster.

Getting There & Away

The Moselle Valley region is difficult to explore without your own transport. Trains from Luxembourg City stop at the northern town of Wasserbillig (35 minutes, half-hourly) only. Buses run from Grevenmacher to Remich (30 minutes, four daily) and Echternach (40 minutes, hourly).

LUXEMBOURG DIRECTORY

ACCOMMODATION

The national tourist office (see p833) provides free hotel, B&B, camping and farm-stay brochures, and staff will book accommodation.

Campgrounds are abundant, although mainly in the central and northern regions. Grounds are graded: Category 3 grounds have basic facilities only and are quite scarce; Category 2 are midrange in price and facilities; Category 1 grounds are the most expensive and profuse.

Nine hostels are operated by **Centrale des Auberges de Jeunesse** (☎ 26 27 66 40; www.youthhostels.lu; 2 Rue du Fort Olisy, L-2261 Luxembourg), which is affiliated with Hostelling International (HI). Most hostels close irregularly throughout the year, so ring ahead. The nightly dorm rate, including breakfast and sheets, ranges from €14.50 to €17.60. Single/double rooms start at €26.50/39. NonHI–members pay €3 per night extra.

B&Bs are very light on the ground but there are plenty of hotels, most in the midrange (€100 to €150) or top-end (€150 to €250) brackets. Some hotels in Luxembourg City offer discounted accommodation on weekends, and/or in July and August, to make up for the Eurocrat shortfall. Discounts are noted in the relevant reviews. All tariffs provided in reviews are for rooms with attached bathrooms, unless otherwise noted.

ACTIVITIES

With a 5000km network of marked walking paths, the Grand Duchy is a hiking haven. The Müllerthal region offers fab hiking tracks (see p838), with the Ardennes a close second. Local tourist offices always stock regional walking maps. Tracks marked by white triangles connect the HI hostels. For more general information, check www.walking.lu.

Cycling is also a popular pastime – see p842 for details.

BUSINESS HOURS

The standard opening hours for banks in Luxembourg City are 8.30am to 4.30pm Monday to Friday and Saturday mornings. Post offices are generally open from 9am to 5pm weekdays and from 9am to noon on Saturday. Shops are open from 9am to 6pm Monday to Saturday, though, some shops will close for two hours at lunch.

Restaurants are open for lunch from noon to 2pm or 3pm, then for dinner from 7pm to 11pm. Pubs and bars tend to open from 11am to 1am, while club hours start at 10pm and close around 3am.

Tourist information offices hours can vary – see the individual city/town sections for specific hours.

EMBASSIES & CONSULATES

Luxembourg Embassies & Consulates

In countries where there is no representative, contact the nearest Belgian diplomatic missions (see p139).

Diplomatic missions abroad include:

France (☎ 01 45 55 13 37; fax 01 45 51 72 29; 33 Ave Rapp, F-75007 Paris)

Germany (☎ 030-263 9570; fax 030-2639 5727; Klingelhöferstrasse 7, D-10785 Berlin)
Netherlands (☎ 0703-60 75 16; fax 0703 46 2000; Nassaulaan 8, NL-2514 JS Den Haag)
UK (☎ 020-7235 6961; fax 020-7235 9734; 27 Wilton Crescent, London SW1X 8SD)
USA (☎ 202-265 4171; fax 202-328 8270; 2200 Massachusetts Ave NW, Washington DC 20008)

Embassies & Consulates in Luxembourg

The nearest Australian, Canadian and New Zealand embassies are in Belgium (see p139). The following foreign embassies are in Luxembourg City:

Belgium (☎ 44 27 46 1; 4 Rue des Girondins, L-1626)
France (☎ 45 72 71 1; 8 Blvd Joseph II, L-1840)
Germany (☎ 45 34 45 1; 20-22 Ave Émile Reuter, L-2420)
Ireland (☎ 45 06 10; 28 Route d'Arlon, L-1140)
Netherlands (☎ 22 75 70; 6 Rue Zithe, L-2763)
UK (☎ 22 98 64; 14 Blvd Joseph II, L-1840)
USA (☎ 46 01 23; 22 Blvd Emmanuel Servais, L-2535)

FESTIVALS & EVENTS

The **Luxembourg National Tourist Office** (www.ont.lu/manif-en.html) lists most annual events, such as those below, on its website.

Carnival One of the nation's biggest festivals, Carnival is held six weeks before Easter.
Buergsonndeg Bonfire Day started in pagan times and now takes place during the first weekend after Carnival.
Octave This pilgrimage dates back to the 17th century and occurs from the 3rd to 5th Sunday after Easter.
Luxembourg National Day Held on 23 June, festivities start in Luxembourg City the previous evening.
Schueberfouer (www.schueberfouer.lu, in French) One of Europe's biggest annual fun fairs, Schueberfouer takes over a parking lot in Luxembourg City for a fortnight from the last week in August.

HOLIDAYS

School holidays are from mid-July to September, the first week of November, two weeks at Christmas, a week at Carnival, two weeks at Easter and a week at Ascension.

Public holidays:

New Year's Day 1 January
Easter Monday March/April
May Day 1 May
Ascension Day Fortieth day after Easter
Whit Monday Seventh Monday after Easter
National Day 23 June
Assumption 15 August
All Saints' Day 1 November
Christmas Day 25 December

> **EMERGENCY NUMBERS**
> - Ambulance ☎ 112
> - Fire ☎ 112
> - Police ☎ 113
> - Roadside assistance (Club Automobile de Luxembourg) ☎ 26 000

MONEY

Famous for its financial sector, you'll have absolutely no trouble finding a bank to change money in Luxembourg City. ATMs are common in the capital, but few and far between outside major towns.

Tipping is not obligatory as service and VAT (value-added tax) are included in hotel and restaurant prices.

POST

Letters (under 20g) cost €0.70 to send to EU countries and €0.90 to nonEU countries.

The most useful poste restante address is: Poste Restante, Luxembourg-Centre Bureau de Post, L-1118 Luxembourg 2.

TELEPHONE

Luxembourg's international country code is ☎ 352. To telephone abroad, the international access code is ☎ 00. Call ☎ 12410 for an international operator. Numbers prefixed with ☎ 0800 are toll-free. Collect calls can be made by dialling ☎ 80 02 00.

VISAS

Citizens of Australia, Canada, Israel, Japan, New Zealand and the USA don't need a visa to visit for up to three months. There are no restrictions on EU nationals.

Visa information can be obtained online from www.mae.lu.

TRANSPORT IN LUXEMBOURG

GETTING THERE & AWAY

Air

Luxembourg's only international gateway is **Luxembourg airport** (code LUX; ☎ 24 64 1; www.lux-airport.lu), 6km east of the capital.

The national carrier, Luxair, flies to European destinations including London, Paris and Frankfurt. The airline's four decades of accident-free flying came to an end in 2002 when one of its planes crashed while landing at Luxembourg airport, killing 15 people.

Some airlines flying into Luxembourg include:

Air France (code AF; ☎ 27 30 20 06; www.airfrance.lu)
British Airways (code BA; ☎ 43 86 47; www.britishairways.com)
Czech Airlines (code OK; ☎ Belgium 32 221 71 792; www.czechairlines.com)
KLM City Hopper (code KL; ☎ Netherlands 3120 474 77 47; www.klm.com)
Lufthansa (code LH; ☎ 47 98 50 50; www.lufthansa.com)
Luxair (code LG; ☎ 24 56 42 42, arrival & departure info 24 56 50 50; www.luxair.lu)
SAS Scandinavian Airlines (code SK; ☎ Belgium 32 264 36 900; www.flysas.com)
Swiss International Air Lines (code LX; ☎ Switzerland 41 615 82 36 56)
TAP Portugal (code TP; ☎ 47 98 21 33; www.flytap.be)
VLM Airlines (code VG; ☎ 49 33 95; www.flyvlm.com)

Budget airline Ryanair flies to Frankfurt/Hahn in Germany from where there's a bus connection to Luxembourg (one-way €17, 1¾ hours, 10 daily); check www.easybycoach.com.

Land

Into Luxembourg, the main roads are the E411 from Brussels, the A4 from Paris, the E25 from Metz and the E44 from Trier in Germany. When travelling from any of these countries, fill up in Luxembourg – fuel prices here are among the lowest in Western Europe. For details about driving, see Getting Around (right).

Eurolines (☎ 26 29 80; 26 Ave de la Liberté) operates international bus services to and from Luxembourg City. Tickets can be bought from its office in the capital. Services include Amsterdam (€22, 8½ hours, one daily), Brussels (€15, 3¾ hours, one or two daily), London (€50, 11½ hours, five weekly) and Paris (€24, 5½ hours, five weekly).

Train

International train services include to Brussels (one-way 2nd-class ticket €29, 2¾ hours, hourly), Amsterdam (one-way 2nd-class ticket €50, 5½ hours, hourly), Paris (one-way 2nd-class ticket €47, four hours, six daily) and Trier, Germany (one-way 2nd-class ticket €8.40, 40 minutes, hourly). For details on the Benelux Tourrail pass, see p142. For all international enquiries, contact the Luxembourg City **station office** (☎ 49 90 49 90; 24hr).

GETTING AROUND

Bicycle

Flat paths or hilly terrain, Luxembourg has both cycling genres covered. Separate cyclist lanes wind along the Sûre River between Echternach and Diekirch, and along much of the Moselle River. For details on bike rental, see Vélo en Ville (p836) or Rent-a-Bike (p839). Bikes can be taken onboard trains for €1.10.

Bus & Train

Luxembourg does not have an extensive rail system. The main north–south train line covers some popular destinations, but for others you'll need to bus it. Both trains and buses are comfortable enough and are operated by **Société Nationale des Chemins de Fer Luxembourgeois** (CFL; ☎ 24 89 24 89; www.cfl.lu). They use the same simple fare system: a 1st/2nd-class 'short' trip (of about 10km or less) ticket is €2.25/1.50 and is valid for one hour, while a 1st/2nd-class unlimited day ticket (known as a *Billet Réseau*) is €7.50/5. The latter is good for travelling on buses and trains anywhere in the country and is valid from the first time you use it until 8am the next day.

Many visitors opt for the Luxembourg Card – for details see p832.

Car & Motorcycle

Road rules are easy to understand and standard international signs are in use. Driving is on the right. The blood-alcohol limit for drivers is 0.08%. The speed limit on motorways is 120km. An international driving licence is not necessary – your home licence will suffice. Fuel prices are among the lowest in Western Europe: lead-free costs around €1.20 per litre and diesel is €0.90.

For car rentals try the following:

Autolux (☎ 22 11 81; 33 Blvd Prince Henri)
Avis (☎ 48 95 95; Gare Centrale)
Budget (☎ 44 19 38; 300 Route de Longwy)
Hertz (☎ 43 46 45; Luxembourg airport)

The Netherlands

Everyone thinks they've got the Netherlands sussed, but it's not all about Amsterdam – is it? Sure, the Dutch capital is among the most distinctive of all European cities; it's certainly one of the most beautiful. It may very well be the most eccentric. But it's not the Netherlands' only claim to fame. Not by a long shot.

Den Haag (The Hague), Leiden, Haarlem and Delft are beguiling, sumptuous, historical cities. Maastricht is a hybrid of European influences, hemmed in by Belgium and Germany near the southernmost border. Rotterdam rivals Amsterdam for the title of the Netherlands' 'first city'; destroyed during WWII, it rebuilt itself with inimitable architecture and an earthy attitude. In the north, Friesland boasts an exclusive language and lifestyle.

How's that for starters? Best of all, the Netherlands is small and served by an efficient rail network – from north to south takes just three hours. It's a day-tripper's paradise.

FAST FACTS

- **Area** 41,526 sq km
- **Capital** Amsterdam
- **Currency** euro (€); A$1 = €.60; ¥100 = €.67; NZ$1 = €.50; UK£1 = €1.48; US$1 = €.78
- **Famous for** doing a lot with a little, extraordinary paintings, unearthly footballers, cheese, liberal attitudes
- **Official Languages** Dutch, Frisian
- **Phrases** *hallo* (hello); *dag* (goodbye); *ja* (yes); *nee* (no); *alsjeblieft* (please); *bedankt* (thanks)
- **Population** 16.4 million
- **Telephone Codes** country code ☎ 31; international access code ☎ 00

HIGHLIGHTS

- Soak up one of Europe's most beautiful and eccentric cities, **Amsterdam** (p850).
- Immerse yourself in the exhilarating urban vibe of **Rotterdam** (p867).
- Lose yourself in heady, cosmopolitan **Maastricht** (p877).
- Day trip to sumptuous **Delft** (p866) or classy **Den Haag** (p863).
- Take time out on **Texel** (p875) and **Ameland** (p875) in the windswept Frisian island chain.

ITINERARIES

- **One week** Spend three days bike riding, museum-hopping, and café-swooping in Amsterdam. Rotterdam's gritty appeal will easily occupy two days, and Maastricht's grandeur deserves at least equal time.
- **Two weeks** Allow four days for Amsterdam's many delights, then add a day trip each to beautiful Delft and the regal Hague, three days in Rotterdam, a few days on a couple of Frisian islands of your choice, and three days in Maastricht.

CLIMATE & WHEN TO GO

The warmest months are June to September. July and August are the wettest months. See p1100 for Amsterdam's climate chart. Daffodils bloom in April and tulips from late April to mid-May. High season is June to August and shoulder seasons mid-March to May and September to mid-October. Easter is busy, and tourists swarm throughout the country in summer; if driving, be wary of traffic in the last weekend of July, when seasonal crowds are heaviest. School holidays fall around mid-February, early May, most of July and August, and the second half of October.

HOW MUCH?

- **Midrange hotel double bed** €50-125
- **Canal boat tour** €10
- **Joint from an Amsterdam coffee shop** €2.50
- **Cup of coffee** €2.50
- **Bicycle hire** €8 per day

LONELY PLANET INDEX

- **1L petrol** €2.50
- **1L bottled water** €2
- **Can of beer** €0.50
- **Souvenir clogs** €22.50
- **Vlaamse frites (Flemish fries)** €2.50

HISTORY

Although the Netherlands is geographically tiny, it has been a major player in world affairs throughout the ages – often unwittingly. While the nation's borders have been repeatedly sliced and diced, the Dutch themselves have blitzed distant lands. Away from conflict, the Netherlands has made a stellar contribution to the visual arts and has initiated many world firsts in 'social engineering'.

The Netherlands' early history is bound with that of Belgium and Luxembourg – the three were known as the Low Countries until the 16th century. In 1579 provinces in the northern Low Countries formed the United Provinces, which was the basis for the Netherlands today. They were opposed to the Spanish rule that was in place, while the southern regions, which eventually became Belgium, were open to compromise. The United Provinces fought the Spanish in the 80-year-long Revolt of the Netherlands, which ended in 1648 with a treaty that recognised them as an independent republic.

The Netherlands' Golden Age lasted from about 1580 to 1740. The era's wealth was generated by the Dutch East India Company, which sent ships to the Far East for spices and other exotic goods, while colonising the Cape of Good Hope and Indonesia and establishing trading posts throughout Asia. Later the West Indies Company sailed to West Africa and the Americas. A number of Caribbean islands were also captured in a bid to thwart the Spanish. One unfortunate by-product of Dutch colonisation was the extinction of the dodo in Mauritius, largely due to introduced species.

The wealthy merchant class supported scores of artists including Vermeer, Steen, Hals and Rembrandt. The sciences thrived: Christiaan Huygens, for example, discovered Saturn's rings and invented the pendulum clock.

In 1795 the French invaded. When occupation ended in 1815, the United Kingdom of the Netherlands – incorporating Belgium and Luxembourg – was born. Earlier that year prostitution was legalised in the Netherlands by Napoleon (who wanted to control STDs), though it took until 1988 for the Dutch to define it as a legal profession and to allow prostitutes to join trade unions.

In 1830 the Belgians rebelled and became independent, and Luxembourg was split between Belgium and the Netherlands. Nine years later the Dutch part gained independence and officially became Luxembourg.

The Netherlands stayed neutral in WWI and tried to repeat the feat in WWII, only to be invaded by the Germans. Rotterdam was levelled, Dutch industry was commandeered for war purposes, and thousands of Dutch men were sent to work in Nazi factories in Germany. Most of the country's Jews were murdered.

Indonesia won independence from the Netherlands in 1949, despite Dutch military opposition. Surinam followed, peacefully, in 1975. The Antilles has close ties with the Netherlands but is self-ruled.

In 1953 a high spring tide and severe storm breached Zeeland's dikes, drowning 2000 people. Under the Delta Plan (p873) a massive engineering project was built to prevent the tragedy from repeating.

In the 1960s Amsterdam became Europe's radical heart, giving rise to the riotous squatters' movement and the promiscuity that lingers today.

Although cannabis was decriminalised in the Netherlands in 1976, it took 27 years for this ruling to be taken to its logical conclusion; in 2003 the Netherlands became the first country to legalise prescriptions of medicinal cannabis, intended as a pain reliever for cancer and multiple sclerosis sufferers, among others.

Perhaps because of the devastating Nazi occupation, the Dutch have largely embraced European integration. In 1992 European Community members met in Maastricht to sign the treaty that created the EU.

In 1993 the Netherlands became the first country to regulate doctor-assisted euthanasia, and in 2000 the practice was legalised under stringent guidelines. That year the Netherlands also became the first nation in the world to legalise same-sex marriages.

As the Netherlands has become ever more crowded, immigration has become a political hot potato. Admission is now subject to rigid guidelines, and a bill has been passed to deport 26,000 immigrants (including long-term residents) from the country.

In 2002 right-wing politician Pim Fortuyn, an advocate of zero immigration, was shot dead a few days before the Dutch general election. Fortuyn became a posthumous candidate and his party, Lijst Pim Fortuyn, went on to win 17% of the seats in the lower house of parliament.

Unbelievably, in 2004 there was another high-profile assassination. On 2 November in Amsterdam the inflammatory filmmaker and columnist Theo van Gogh was shot repeatedly before being stabbed several times; a note was impaled to his body with the knife, threatening the government, Dutch politician Ayaan Hirsi Ali, and Jewish groups. The murderer was an Islamic Moroccan; when he died, Van Gogh was finishing off a film about Pim Fortuyn.

Van Gogh was known for his controversial statements about Muslims, and he had received death threats after he made a short film, *Submission* (written by ex-Muslim Hirsi Ali), detailing the abuse of Muslim women. He dismissed the warnings, saying, 'Who would kill the village idiot?'

Ethnic tensions have been simmering in Amsterdam ever since, with a series of arson and bomb attacks from both sides – on Islamic schools and Christian churches.

In October 2005, 11 detainees died in a fire at an Amsterdam centre housing illegal immigrants and soon-to-be-deported drug runners.

PEOPLE

Nine-tenths of the population are of Dutch stock, and around half live in the western loop around Amsterdam, Den Haag and Rotterdam. Ethnic communities are concentrated in the Randstad cities (p860). Hindus and Muslims began arriving in the mid-20th century from former Dutch colonies Indonesia and Surinam, and a second wave of immigrants since the 1960s included people from Morocco and Turkey.

Around 400,000 people in Friesland speak their own language, Frisian.

RELIGION

Nearly 40% of Dutch people over 18 years of age claim they have no religious affiliation. Of the remainder, 31% are Catholic, 21% are Protestant, 5.5% are Muslim and the remaining 2.5% are split among other denominations.

The Islamic community has almost doubled in size in the last decade to 920,000. There are more than 300 mosques.

ARTS

Literature

Dutch literature flourished in the 17th century with writers such as Vondel (the Dutch Shakespeare), Bredero and Hooft. Postwar literature was dominated by Willem Frederik Hermans, Harry Mulisch and Gerard Reve and, later, Jan Wolkers, Maarten 't Hart and Frederik van der Heijden.

Tim Krabbé writes dark, complex novels about love, suffering and utter futility. *The Golden Egg* was made into a frightening Dutch film, *Spoorloos,* and later a limp Hollywood remake.

Amsterdam: A Traveller's Literary Companion, edited by Manfred Wolf, features 17 stories set in Amsterdam by leading Dutch writers.

Cinema & TV

The Netherlands' film industry is humble, producing around 20 feature films a year. Yet the Dutch have won four Best Foreign

BIG BROTHER

Many people are surprised to learn that the reality-TV franchise *Big Brother* is a Dutch invention, when it seems quintessentially American. But if you delve into the undercurrents of the Dutch social order, the concept of peering into the lives of a group of strangers makes sense. The Netherlands is Europe's most densely populated country, and while this adds immeasurably to its vibrancy, it can often seem that your neighbour is looking right over your shoulder. Maybe that's why many Dutch leave their curtains open at night so all can see inside: with space at such a premium, there's nowhere to hide, really. No doubt the admirable Dutch trait of tolerance stems from this fact, too: when you're standing cheek-by-jowl, 'love thy neighbour' is a very sensible motto.

Language Film Academy Awards – the third-best tally in Oscars history.

Joris Ivens won an international peace prize for *Song of the Rivers* (1954), a global comparison of workers' conditions.

In the 1970s Paul Verhoeven made earthy films including *Turks Fruit,* the Netherlands' most popular film. He later moved to Hollywood, serving up the sardonic, ultraviolent satires *Robocop* and *Starship Troopers,* and the ultimate revenge thriller, *Basic Instinct*.

The murder mysteries of Dick Maas, a former cartoonist, have been compared to Dario Argenti's – fascinating to look at, but riddled with plot flaws. *Amsterdammed* (1988) features a murderer who uses Amsterdam's canals to escape.

The films of Theo van Gogh (see opposite) are slick, stylish and confrontational.

The Rotterdam International Film Festival is held in February, the Amsterdam Fantastic Film Festival in April, Utrecht's Netherlands Film Festival in September and Amsterdam's International Documentary Film Festival in December.

Dutch TV is saturated with foreign programming, but one notable local product is the reality series *Big Brother,* now a worldwide franchise (see the boxed text, above).

Music

The North Sea Jazz Festival, the world's largest jazz fest, is held each summer; it recently moved from Den Haag to Rotterdam.

Rotterdam, Maastricht and Den Haag have a full calendar of performances by local orchestras and groups, and Amsterdam's Royal Concertgebouw Orchestra frequently performs abroad.

Herman Brood burst onto the pop scene in the '70s, morphing into a professional junkie/rock-and-roll star and later killing himself.

The Nits formed in 1974 and have since released a varied body of work, flirting with '60s pop, '80s New Wave, and electronica stylings.

In the early '90s gabber was unleashed, an extreme mutation of techno originating in Rotterdam. Gabber raised beats per minute to heart-attack levels, giving the finger to purists with its sheer fetishisation of sensation.

The Dutch have a major presence in the populist world DJ rankings with the likes of Tiësto.

Pop festivals flourish in the warmer months, including Pinkpop in Landgraaf, Parkpop in Den Haag and Dynamo Open Air at Neunen. Dance Valley near Haarlem pulls more than 100 bands and even more DJs to one of Europe's biggest open-air dance fests. Lowlands is a three-day alternative-music fest held at Six Flags in Flevoland.

Arling & Cameron, a duo from Amsterdam, have thrilled hipsters in recent years with downtempo lounge tunes, uptempo techno-pop and squelchy 'music for imaginary soundtracks'.

Architecture

Few countries have exerted more influence on architecture than the Netherlands.

Thick walls, small windows and round arches are some of the major characteristics of the Romanesque style (900–1250).

Pointed arches, ribbed vaulting and dizzying heights were trademarks of the Gothic era (c 1250–1600).

The Netherlands excelled in Mannerism (1520–1600), a sort of toned-down baroque.

From the mid-17th century onwards Dutch architecture began to influence France and England, but during the 1700s Dutch architects deferred to all things French, except during the Napoleonic Wars in the late 18th century when designers, influenced by Greek and Roman blueprints, came up with neoclassicism, known for its order, symmetry and simplicity.

Many big projects from the 1850s onward were neo-Gothic, harking back to the grand Gothic cathedrals. One of the leading architects of this period was Pierre Cuypers, who built Amsterdam Centraal Station and the Rijksmuseum.

As the 20th century approached Hendrik Petrus Berlage, the father of modern Dutch architecture, unleashed on the nation spartan, utilitarian designs that did away with frivolous ornamentation.

Functionalism (1927–70) drew influence from Germany's Bauhaus School, the American Frank Lloyd Wright and France's Le Corbusier.

Since the 1980s numerous 'isms' such as structuralism, neorationalism, postmodernism and supermodernism have taken root, especially in Rotterdam, where city planners have encouraged bold designs that range from Piet Blom's startling cube-shaped apartments to Ben van Berkel's graceful Erasmus Bridge. Rotterdam is also home to Rem Koolhaas, perhaps the best-known contemporary Dutch architect.

Visual Arts

The Netherlands claims a superb artistic heritage: many non-Dutch would be able to name at least one famous Dutch painter.

From the 15th century, Hieronymus Bosch's nightmarish works can be seen as an antecedent of surrealism.

During the Golden Age, Rembrandt emerged with the brightest glow of all, creating shimmering religious scenes, in-demand portraits and contemplative landscapes; Frans Hals (1582–1666) captured his subjects in unguarded moments; and Jan Vermeer (1632–75) concentrated on everyday occurrences in middle-class homes, giving a proto-cinematographic quality to his compositions.

Vincent van Gogh's (1853–90) revolutionary use of colour, coarse brushwork and layered contours established him on a higher plane than his contemporaries, yet he only sold one work while alive.

Piet Mondrian (1872–1944), along with Theo van Doesburg, founded the De Stijl movement; his style of abstract rectangular compositions came to be known as neoplasticism.

MC Escher's (1902–72) graphic art still has uncanny power: a waterfall simultaneously flows up and down; a building folds in on itself. It's popular with mathematicians and stoners alike.

WWII gave birth to the CoBrA group (Copenhagen, Brussels and Amsterdam), who saw the conflict as pitching civilised society into severe moral decline. Their antidote was to embrace the mindset of children and the mentally ill in their art.

Documentary is a speciality of contemporary Dutch photographers. Ed van der Elksen's most famous work is *Love on the Left Bank* from 1954, a photographic novel featuring a cast of Paris bohemians. Anton Corbijn is famous for his portraits of top-shelf artists and celebrities.

Theatre & Dance

The Dogtroep theatre company tours abroad and stages fancy and unpredictable 'happenings' in quirky venues such as Amsterdam's ship passenger terminal.

Robodock, featuring robots and choreographed pyrotechnics, has moved back to Amsterdam after a stint in Rotterdam.

The Dutch are world leaders in modern dance. Den Haag's Nederlands Dans Theater troupe was established in 1959, melding modern dance with classical ballet. In Rotterdam, Dansacadamie is the nation's largest dance school. Amsterdam's National Ballet performs mainly classical ballets, as well as 20th-century Dutch works.

ENVIRONMENT

The Land

The Netherlands' land mass now encompasses 41,526 sq km, roughly half the size of Scotland, and half of it lies at or below sea level in the form of polders (stretches of land reclaimed from the sea). If the Netherlands lost its 2400km of dikes and dunes the large cities would be inundated, so pumping stations run around the clock to drain off excess water. The danger of floods is most acute in Zeeland, a sprawling estuary for the Schelde, Maas, Lek and Waal Rivers.

The Netherlands' highest point, the Vaalserberg, is in the province of Limburg, at a grand elevation of 321m.

Wildlife

Human encroachment has meant few wildlife habitats are left intact. Birds offer the greatest breadth of species, now heavily protected in sanctuaries and nature reserves. The Netherlands is a paradise for bird-watchers and the wetlands are a major migration stop for European birds, particularly in the Frisian Islands, Flevoland and the Delta.

National Parks

Some 1065 sq km (nearly 3%) of the Netherlands is protected in the form of national parks. The first publicly funded national park was established in 1984 and most average 5000 hectares. Little of the Netherlands is left untouched, so the Dutch cherish what's left.

Environmental Issues

Private car ownership has risen to about 50% over late-1980s levels. Do your bit to ease congestion by riding bikes and taking the efficient trains – there's no compelling reason for travellers to hire a car in the Netherlands.

Winters have become shorter and milder; three of the warmest years on record occurred in the past decade. If sea levels rise, the Netherlands could suffer annual flooding. Dikes and storm barriers will be extended if necessary.

Pressure from the government and Greenpeace has forced Shell and the like to invest heavily in developing clean energy. Wind parks in Flevoland and Noord Holland generate a significant amount of electricity.

FOOD & DRINK

Staples & Specialities

Dutch food is hearty and designed to line the stomach; dishes include *stamppot* (mashed pot) – potatoes mashed with kale, endive or sauerkraut and served with smoked sausage or pork strips. *Hutspot* (hotchpotch) is similar, but with potatoes, carrots, onions and braised meat.

The Dutch consume 16.5kg of cheese per person per year (nearly two-thirds of it is Gouda).

Vlaamse frites (Flemish fries) are french fries made from whole potatoes. They're typically smothered in mayonnaise.

Seafood is found at street stalls, including raw, slightly salted herring cut into bite-sized pieces and served with onion and pickles. Smoked eel and *kibbeling* (deep-fried cod parings) are also popular.

International Food

Lebanese and Turkish snack bars specialise in shwarma, pitta bread filled with sliced lamb from a spit, and falafel.

The Netherlands' colonial legacy has introduced Indonesian and Surinamese cooking to the Dutch palate, and the cuisines of many other nations are also well represented, notably Japanese and Greek.

A popular Indonesian dish is *rijsttafel* (rice table), an array of savoury dishes such as braised beef, pork satay and ribs served with white rice.

Surinamese dishes blend African and Indian flavours with Indonesian; chicken, lamb and beef curries are common.

Where to Eat & Drink

As well as restaurants, there are *eetcafés,* which are affordable, small and popular publike eateries.

'Café' means a pub, also known as a *kroeg*. They generally serve food, and many have outdoor terraces. The most famous type is the cosy *bruin café* (brown café) – the name comes from smoke stains on the walls, although pretenders make do with brown paint.

Grand cafés are more spacious, have comfortable furniture and are very popular.

Theatre cafés are also popular and there are also a few *proeflokalen* (tasting houses), where you can sample dozens of *jenevers* (gins) and liqueurs.

Broodjeszaken (sandwich shops) and snack bars are everywhere.

Vegetarians & Vegans

Many restaurant menus may have one or two veggie dishes, but they might not be 100% meat- or fish-free (meat stock is a common culprit). Vegetarian restaurants often rely on organic ingredients and generally make everything from bread to cakes in-house.

Habits & Customs

The Dutch eat dinner early – popular places fill up by 7pm. You could aim for the 'second sitting', around 8.30pm to 9.30pm, although many kitchens close by 10pm.

Lunch tends to be more of a snack, and just a half-hour break is common. Coffee breaks are frequent.

Service is included in the bill and tipping is at your discretion, though most people round up 5% to 10%. In cafés and pubs it's common to put drinks on a tab and pay when you leave.

Many restaurants don't accept credit cards.

AMSTERDAM

☎ 020 / pop 743,000

Amsterdam's always been a liberal place, ever since the Golden Age, when it led European art and trade. Centuries later, in the 1960s, it again led the pack – this time in the principles of tolerance, with broad-minded views on drugs and same-sex relationships taking centre stage. Today the cannabis coffee shops and the Red Light District are still the city's top drawcards, even if that can sometimes wear thin for the locals. Quite simply, Amsterdam's more than just an X-rated theme park for Weekend Warriors and Hooray Henrys – it's also one of Europe's most breathtakingly scenic cities, with beautiful, heritage-protected 17th-century housing and some of the Continent's best museums and galleries. It has enough sensory delights to keep the shortest attention spans occupied, and it's compact and user-friendly, too. Walk or ride a bike around the canal grid, down the historic lanes of the Jordaan district, or through the Plantage and bask in the many worlds-within-worlds that make the 'Dam so thoroughly addictive.

ORIENTATION

Centraal Station is the hub. From the station the streets radiate outward across the network of canals. Dam Square is the heart, a 10-minute walk from Centraal Station. Leidseplein is the centre of (mainstream) Amsterdam nightlife, and Nieuwmarkt is a vast cobblestone square with open-air markets and popular pubs. The Red Light District is bound by Zeedijk, Nieuwmarkt and Kloveniersburgwal in the east; Damstraat, Oude Doelenstraat and Oude Hoogstraat in the south; and Warmoesstraat in the west.

INFORMATION

Discount Card

I Amsterdam Card (per 24/36/72hr €33/43/53) Available at VVV offices and some hotels. It gives admission to most museums, canal boat trips, and discounts and freebies at shops, attractions and restaurants. Also includes a GVB (Gemeentevervoerbedrijf; Municipality Transport Company of Amsterdam) Transit Pass.

Internet Access

Centrale Bibliotheek (Main Library; ☎ 523 09 00; Prinsengracht 587; 🕑 1-9pm Mon, 10am-9pm Tue-Thu, to 5pm Fri & Sat, 1-5pm Sun) Free Internet.

Internet City (☎ 620 12 92; Nieuwendijk 76; per hr €3; 🕑 10am-midnight)

Medical Services

Centrale Doktersdienst (Central Doctors Service; ☎ 592 33 33; 🕑 24hr) Doctor, dentist or pharmacy referrals.

Onze Lieve Vrouwe Gasthuis (☎ 599 91 11; Oosterpark 9) A 24-hour public hospital.

Money

American Express (Amex; ☎ 504 87 77; Damrak 66; 🕑 9am-5pm Mon-Fri, to noon Sat)

GWK (Grenswisselkantoor; ☎ 0900 0566; Centraal Station; 🕑 8am-10pm Mon-Sat, 9am-10pm Sun) Converts travellers cheques and makes hotel reservations; also at Schiphol.

Thomas Cook Dam (☎ 625 09 22; Dam 23-25; 🕑 9am-7pm); Damrak (☎ 620 32 36; Damrak 1-5, opposite Centraal Station; 🕑 8am-8pm); Leidseplein (☎ 626 70 00; Leidseplein 31A; 🕑 9am-7.30pm Mon-Sat, 10am-7.30pm Sun)

Post

Main post office (☎ 330 0555; Singel 250; 🕑 9am-6pm Mon-Wed & Fri, to 8pm Thu, 10am-1.30pm Sat)

Tourist Information

Tourist office (VVV; ☎ 0900-400 40 40; www.vvvamsterdam.nl) Stationsplein 10 (🕑 9am-5pm Mon-Fri); Centraal Track 2 (Centraal Station; 🕑 8am-8pm Mon-Sat, 9am-5pm Sun); Leidseplein 1 (🕑 9.15am-5pm Sun-Thu, to 7pm Fri & Sat)

SIGHTS & ACTIVITIES

Medieval Centre

The **Stedelijk Museum** (☎ 573 29 11; www.stedelijk.nl; 2nd & 3rd fl, Post CS Bldg, Oosterdokskade 5; adult/7-16 yr/senior/under 7 €9/5/5/free; ⌚ 10am-6pm) features around 100,000 pieces including impressionist works from Monet, Picasso and Chagall; sculptures from Rodin and Moore; De Stijl landmarks by Mondrian; and pop art from Warhol and Lichtenstein. This is a temporary home – the original is undergoing renovation until 2008.

Just north of the Royal Palace, the late-Gothic basilica **Nieuwe Kerk** (New Church; ☎ 638 69 09; www.nieuwekerk.nl; Dam; admission adult/6-15 yr/under 6 €5/4/free; ⌚ 10am-6pm Fri-Wed, to 10pm Thu) is the coronation church of Dutch royalty, with a carved oak chancel, a bronze choir screen, a massive, gilded organ and stained-glass windows. It's now used for exhibitions and organ concerts.

Amsterdam's oldest building, the **Oude Kerk** (Old Church; ☎ 625 82 84; www.oudekerk.nl; Oudekerksplein 23; adult/child €4/3.50; ⌚ 11am-5pm Mon-Sat, 1-5pm Sun) was built to honour the city's patron saint, St Nicholas. Inside there's a dramatic Müller organ, gilded oak vaults and impressive stained-glass windows. In one of Europe's great moral contradictions, the tower commands a magnificent view – of the Red Light District. Oooh, vicar…

The **Red Light District** (see the boxed text, p854) retains the power to bewilder, even if near-naked prostitutes propositioning passers-by from black-lit windows is the oldest Amsterdam cliché. If you feel a prick of desire, it's around €50 for 20 minutes.

There are some mildly interesting artefacts at the **Sexmuseum Amsterdam** (☎ 622 83 76; Damrak 18; admission €2.50; ⌚ 10am-11.30pm) – 14th-century Viennese erotica, for example. But with sensor-fitted plastic derrières farting at passers-by and an animatronic flasher accosting all-comers, it's more like a tribute to Benny Hill. A sign warns, 'You could be shocked'. Pull the other one.

The **Guan Yin Shrine** (Fo Guang Shan He Hua Temple; ☎ 420 23 57; www.ibps.nl; Zeedijk 106-118; admission free; ⌚ noon-5pm Tue-Sat, 10am-5pm Sun) is Europe's first Chinese Imperial–style Buddhist temple (completed in 2000). It's dedicated to Guan Yin, the Buddhist goddess of mercy. Images on the many-armed, long-eared statue include a prayer bell and a lotus flower.

AMSTERDAM IN TWO DAYS

Begin at the **Anne Frank Huis** (below), then scoot across town to the **Rijksmueum** (below) and the **Van Gogh Museum** (p853). Dive into the **Albert Cuypmarkt** (p858), before coming up for air (and lunch) at **Bazar** (p855). In the afternoon, stop off for a smoke at **Siberië** (p856), then follow the conga line to the **Red Light District** (p854). When the dope's worn off, order a *mojito* (rum-based cocktail) at **Café Cuba** (p856), before dining at the sumptuous **Blauw aan de Wal** (p855). On the second day, hire a **bike** (p859) and see where you end up – it's all good, and well you know it.

Nieuwmarkt

The wonderfully restored **Museum Het Rembrandthuis** (Rembrandt House Museum; ☎ 520 04 00; www.rembrandthuis.nl; Jodenbreestraat 4; adult/student/6-15 yr/under 6 €7.50/6/1.50/free; ⌚ 10am-5pm Mon-Sat, 11am-5pm Sun) is where Rembrandt van Rijn ran the Netherlands' largest painting studio, only to lose the lot when profligacy set in, enemies swooped, and bankruptcy came knocking. The museum has almost every etching he made (around 250) and holds daily etching demonstrations.

Canal Belt

The **Anne Frank Huis** (Anne Frank House; ☎ 556 71 00; www.annefrank.org; Prinsengracht 267; adult/child/under 10 €7.50/3.50/free; ⌚ 9am-9pm Apr-Aug, to 7pm Sep-Mar), where Anne wrote her famous diary, lures almost a million visitors annually with its secret annexe, reconstruction of Anne's melancholy bedroom, and her actual diary, with its sunnily optimistic writing tempered by quiet despair. Consider going in the early morning or evening when crowds are lightest.

FOAM (Fotografie Museum Amsterdam; ☎ 551 65 00; www.foam.nl; Keizersgracht 609; adult/student/senior/under 12 €6/5/5/free; ⌚ 10am-5pm Sat-Wed, to 9pm Thu & Fri) is an impressive museum devoted to painting with light. Two storeys of changing exhibitions feature world-renowned photographers such as Sir Cecil Beaton, Annie Leibovitz and Henri Cartier-Bresson.

Museumplein

To paraphrase Scharwzenegger, 'Get your ass to Rijks'. **Rijksmuseum** (☎ 674 70 47; www.rijksmuseum.nl; Stadhouderskade 42; adult/under 19 €9/free;

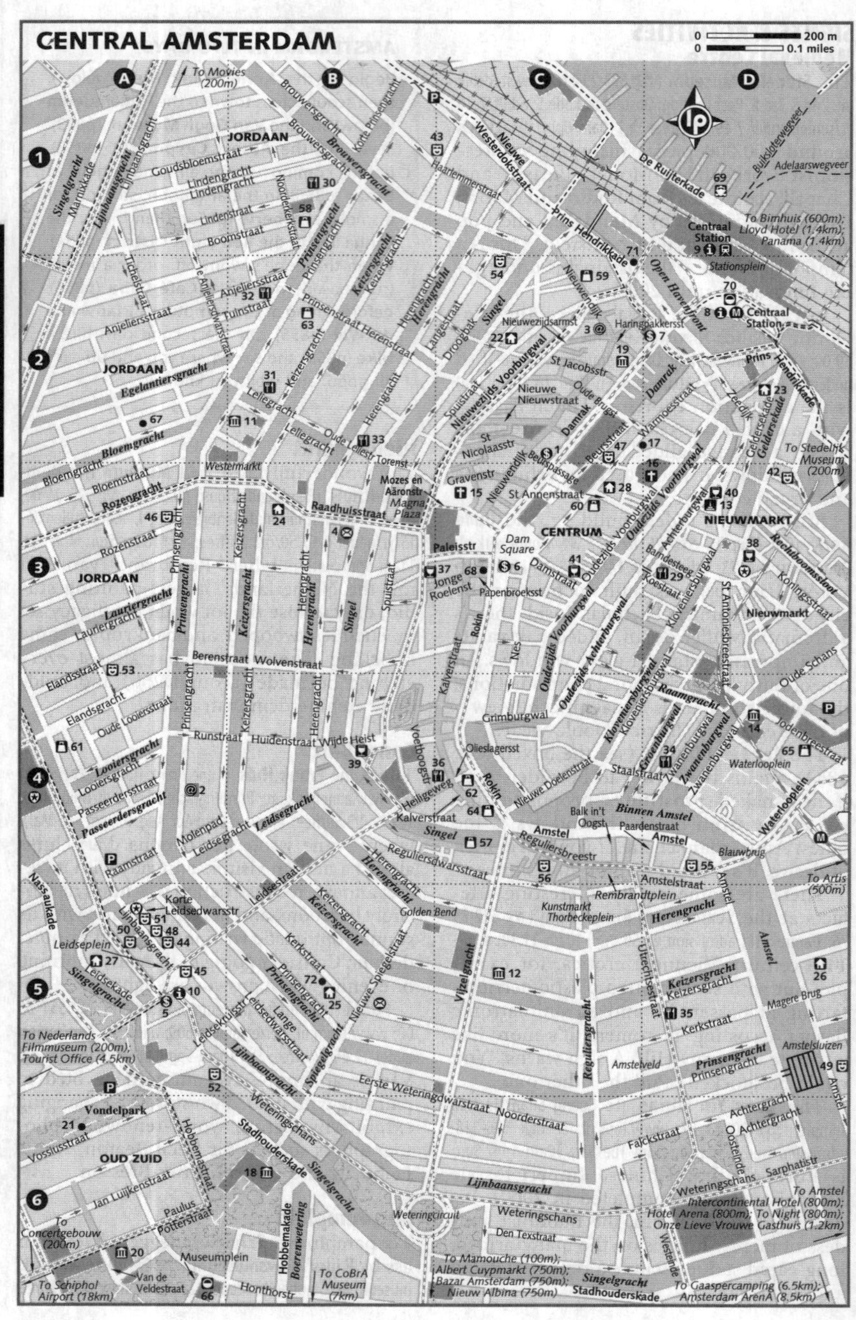
CENTRAL AMSTERDAM
0 200 m
0 0.1 miles
JORDAAN
CENTRUM
NIEUWMARKT
OUD ZUID
Vondelpark
Centraal Station
Dam Square
Leidseplein
Rembrandtplein
Museumplein
Golden Bend
Prinsengracht
Keizersgracht
Herengracht
Singel
Amstel
Damrak
Rokin
Singelgracht
Lijnbaansgracht
To Movies (200m)
To Bimhuis (600m); Lloyd Hotel (1.4km); Panama (1.4km)
To Stedelijk Museum (200m)
To Artis (500m)
To Nederlands Filmmuseum (200m); Tourist Office (4.5km)
To Concertgebouw (200m)
To Schiphol Airport (18km)
To CoBrA Museum (7km)
To Mamouche (100m); Albert Cuypmarkt (750m); Bazar Amsterdam (750m); Nieuw Albina (750m)
To Gaaspercamping (6.5km); Amsterdam ArenA (8.5km)
To Amstel Intercontinental Hotel (800m); Hotel Arena (800m); To Night (800m); Onze Lieve Vrouwe Gasthuis (1.2km)

INFORMATION	Hotel Fantasia......26 D5	Koninklijk Theater Carré......49 D5
American Express......1 C2	Hotel Quentin......27 A5	Melkweg......50 A5
Centrale Bibliotheek......2 A4	Hotel Winston......28 C3	Nachttheater Sugar Factory......51 A5
Internet City......3 C2		Paradiso......52 A5
Main Post Office......4 B3	**EATING**	Saarein......53 A3
Thomas Cook......5 A5	Blauw aan de Wal......29 D3	Siberië......54 C2
Thomas Cook......6 C3	Bordewijk......30 B1	Sinners in Heaven......55 D4
Thomas Cook......7 D2	Christophe......31 B2	Tuschinskitheater......56 C4
Tourist Office......8 D2	De Bolhoed......32 B2	Winston International......(see 28)
Tourist Office......9 D1	Foodism......33 B2	
Tourist Office......10 A5	Puccini......34 D4	**SHOPPING**
	Tempo Doeloe......35 D5	Bloemenmarkt......57 C4
SIGHTS & ACTIVITIES	Vlaams Friteshuis......36 C4	Boerenmarkt......58 B1
Anne Frank Huis......11 B2		Chills & Thrills......59 C2
FOAM......12 C5	**DRINKING**	Condomerie Het Gulden Vlies......60 C3
Guan Yin Shrine......13 D3	Absinthe......37 B3	De Looier Antiques Market......61 A4
Museum Het Rembrandthuis......14 D4	Café Cuba......38 D3	Maison de Bonneterie......62 C4
Nieuwe Kerk......15 C3	Hoppe......39 B4	Santa Jet......63 B2
Oude Kerk......16 D3	Lime......40 D3	Vroom & Dreesmann......64 C4
Prostitution Information Centre......17 C2	Proeflokaal Wijnand Fockinck......41 C3	Waterlooplein Flea Market......65 D4
Rijksmuseum......18 B6		
Sexmuseum Amsterdam......19 C2	**ENTERTAINMENT**	**TRANSPORT**
Van Gogh Museum......20 A6	Amsterdams Marionetten	ANWB......66 A6
Vondelpark......21 A6	Theater......42 D3	Bike City......67 A2
	Barney's......43 C1	Eurolines......68 C3
SLEEPING	Boom Chicago......44 A5	Fast Flying Ferries......69 D1
Aivengo Youth Hostel......22 C2	Bulldog......45 A5	GVB......70 D2
Black Tulip Hotel......23 D2	COC Amsterdam......46 A3	Lovers Museum Boat......71 C2
Budget Hotel Clemens......24 B3	Cockring......47 C2	Mike's Bike Tours......72 B5
Hans Brinker Budget Hotel......25 B5	Jimmy Woo......48 A5	St Nicholaas Boat Club......(see 44)

10am-5pm) boasts a collection valued in the billions, but until renovations finish in 2009 there'll only be 200 masterpieces displayed, including a few choice Vermeers and the crowning glory, Rembrandt's *Nightwatch* (1650). Warning: *Nightwatch* will likely be 20 deep with flashbulb-popping, focus beam-directing rubberneckers. Rather than being returned to storage, many other gems will be put on display in grateful venues around the country. Check the schedules for Amsterdam's Nieuwe Kerk (p851), Maastricht's Bonnefantenmuseum (p877), and the Dordrechts Museum in Dordrecht. There's also an annexe at Schiphol airport.

The outstanding **Van Gogh Museum** (570 52 00; www.vangoghmuseum.nl; Paulus Potterstraat 7; adult/12-21 yr/under 12 €10/2.50/free; 10am-6pm Sun-Thu, to 10pm Fri) houses the world's largest Van Gogh collection, arranged chronologically. Trace the artist's life from his tentative start though to his Japanese phase, and on to depression and the black cloud that descended over the him and his work. There's also a fantastic selection of art by contemporaries Gauguin, Toulouse-Lautrec, Monet and Bernard.

Vondelpark (www.vondelpark.nl in Dutch) is an English-style park with free concerts, ponds, lawns, thickets, winding footpaths and three outdoor cafés. It was named after the poet and playwright Joost van den Vondel, the 'Dutch Shakespeare', and is popular with joggers, skaters, buskers and lovers.

Jordaan

Originally a stronghold of the working class, the Jordaan is now one of the most desirable areas to live in Amsterdam. It's a pastiche of modest old homes and a few modern carbuncles, squashed in a grid of tiny lanes peppered with bite-sized cafés and shops. Its intimacy is contagious, and now the average Jordaan-dweller is more likely to be a gallery owner than a labourer.

Plantage & Oosterpark

Besides the well-rounded animal population, **Artis** (523 34 00; www.artis.nl; Plantage Kerklaan 38-40; adult/senior/3-9 yr/under 3 €16/15/12.50/free; 9am-6pm Jun-Sep, to 5pm Oct-May) is also home to a planetarium, a petting zoo and themed habitats. The aquarium complex has coral reefs, shark tanks and an Amsterdam canal displayed from a fish-eye view.

SLEEPING

Budget

Aivengo Youth Hostel (620 11 55; Spuistraat 6; dm from €18, d/tr €80/100;) With friendly management, an inviting, respectful vibe and a

WINDOW SHOPPING

You're not fooling anyone; you know you'll end up here. Everyone does at some stage, even if they think they're too hip, too prudish, too old…the curiosity value is just too strong. But it's not just rubberneckers and pleasure seekers who flock to the Red Light District: Amsterdam's approach to prostitution has generated reams of socioeconomic analysis, along with a raft of facts and figures – and some contradictions.

Prostitution was legalised in the Netherlands in 1815 (although brothels were only legalised in 2000). Unsurprisingly, less than 5% of Dutch prostitutes work illegally in the Netherlands. Dutch 'working girls' pay taxes and they have their own union. Pimping is against the law, but the girls are not on their own: their quarters are fitted with panic buttons in case of trouble. Should they press the button, it won't be the cops who come running.

An estimated 5% of Amsterdam prostitutes are born in the Netherlands, and there's around 1000 to 1200 working approximately 380 windows daily, in day, evening and night shifts. The girls must rent their window at a cost of between €40 and €100 per day, depending on location. Do the maths: the typical base cost for 'oral favours' or a 'quickie' is €30; the average base cost for both is €50. 'Encounters' typically last 20 minutes.

Dutch customers are most likely to visit on a Monday morning – that's when many businesses and most shops are closed. Of the international clientele, almost half are British – we don't dare speculate why.

What about the men? A few years back, three chaps installed themselves behind windows as prostitutes, a sociological experiment that generated feverish media coverage. In the end, the guys were warned not to give up their day job: no women took the bait. Rubbing salt into the wound, one of the female prostitutes even dismissed the whole incident as 'filthy'. Now, that's harsh.

funky, Middle Eastern–style décor, Aivengo is a winner. Party animals take very careful note: there's a 4am curfew.

Hans Brinker Budget Hotel (☎ 622 06 87; www.hans-brinker.com; Kerkstraat 136; dm from €21; 💻) There's a jacked-up 'Animal House' feel to the Brinker, with its bouncy bar and disco. Its website takes the art of self-mockery to uniquely Dutch extremes, offering Brinker wallpaper: 'Your home will soon have the unmistakable feeling of the Hans Brinker Budget Hotel,' it says, 'without the tangy smell, strange gargling noises, and the moaning'. Or is that the Black Tulip (opposite)?

Hotel Winston (☎ 623 13 80; www.winston.nl; Warmoesstraat 129; dm/s/d from €22/45/56) How to make a lot out of a little: take some functional rooms and get local artists to theme them with motifs including Arabian typography, jigsaw puzzles, and, fittingly for the Red Light location, bizarre sex. There's a jolly 24-hour bar and the Winston's own club (p856) next door.

Midrange

Hotel Quentin (☎ 626 21 87; www.quentinhotels.com; Leidsekade 89; s/d from €45/60) This 19th-century mansion has a nice lobby and rooms done up in bright murals and handmade furniture, although singles tend to be small and functional. If you're lucky you might get a balcony and a canal view.

Budget Hotel Clemens (☎ 624 60 89; www.clemenshotel.com; Raadhuisstraat 39; s €55, d €70-110, tr €125-150; 💻) The Clemens is a friendly place with eight warm, cosy rooms, some done up in creams and yellows, some in gold and red. Deluxe rooms have antique furniture and marble fireplaces, and all have minifridges. Rooms at the front, though on a noisy street, make up for it with balconies that overlook the Westermarkt.

Hotel Fantasia (☎ 623 82 59; www.fantasia-hotel.com; Nieuwe Keizersgracht 16; s/d €67/86; 💻) This one's perfect for moo-ching around. Pull the udder one. No, really – the owner grew up on a farm and has parlayed that into a workable obsession: this bovine-themed 18th-century house. Prints and cow motifs decorate the rooms and breakfast area, complementing the canalside location.

Lloyd Hotel (☎ 561 36 36; www.lloydhotel.com; Oostelijke Handelskade 34; d €80-300; 💻) The fabulous Lloyd is an enigma. It used to be a hotel for migrants back in the '20s, and it retains many of the original fixtures in among the contemporary flourishes. Rooms range from basic to plush.

Hotel Arena (☎ 850 24 00; www.hotelarena.nl; 's Gravesandestraat 51; d/tr from €100/165; 💻) The Arena, bordering lush Oosterpark, was once a chapel, an orphanage and a backpackers hostel. Now it's a chic 121-room hotel with a stylish restaurant, café and a well-regarded nightclub. Rooms are an ode to minimalism, while the large, split-level doubles are sun-drenched. Tip: sections A, B, E and F tend to be quieter.

Black Tulip Hotel (☎ 427 09 33; www.blacktulip.nl; Geldersekade 16; s €115, d from €145; 💻) Exclusively for gay chaps, the Black Tulip's nine rooms feature a full range of bondage equipment: slings, cages, hooks, chairs, black leather and latex. It's a professional and clean operation. All rooms have private facilities, fridge and minibar.

Top End

Amstel Intercontinental Hotel (☎ 622 60 60; www.amsterdam.intercontinental.com; Professor Tulpplein 1; r from €575; ❄ 💻 🏊) Everything about this five-star monument is simply spectacular, from its magnificent colonnaded lobby to its hefty room prices and its royal and rock-star clientele. It's a favourite of the Strolling Bones, and the lavishly decorated rooms overlook the Amstel, the river that (according to legend) Mick Jagger nearly fell into when Charlie Watts punched him out perilously close to a window.

EATING

Restaurants

Nieuw Albina (☎ 379 02 23; Albert Cuypstraat 49; mains €4.50-11.50; 🕑 lunch & dinner Wed-Mon) If you're curious about Surinamese food, try Nieuw Albina's bold and brassy flavours. The *moksi meti* (roast mixed meats over rice) is an undisputed highlight.

Bazar Amsterdam (☎ 675 05 44; www.bazaramsterdam.nl; Albert Cuypstraat 182; mains €8-14; 🕑 breakfast, lunch & dinner) Like its Rotterdam counterpart, Bazar Amsterdam is a genuine high flyer. In a glorious former Dutch Reformed church, the light-filled, Middle Eastern–style décor and tangy, tantalising North African cuisine – mixed grills, kebabs, falafels, pitta bread, tabbouleh, Turkish pizza – sees to that.

De Bolhoed (☎ 626 18 03; Prinsengracht 60-62; mains €10-15) Amsterdam's best-known vegetarian restaurant has a prime canalside location. The food is fresh, organic, and often Mexican- and Italian-inspired: pancakes, salads, burritos, homemade breads, biological wines, organic beers and cakes.

Mamouche (☎ 673 63 61; Quellijnstraat 104; mains €14.50-22; 🕑 dinner Tue-Sun) 'Sexy' is a word that tends to get bandied about when people talk about Mamouche. The case for: the seriously good modern Moroccan food – think couscous, lamb and fish – and the serious minimalism of the décor, all exposed flooring, mottled walls and beamed ceilings. Reservations are essential.

Tempo Doeloe (☎ 625 67 18; www.tempodoeloerestaurant.nl; Utrechtsestraat 75; mains €18-22; 🕑 dinner) The name means 'The Old Days' (ring a bell to gain entry) and the spice levels range from mild to *very* hot. Yet all the subtle flavours remain intact. Extraordinary. It does a top-notch version of the classic rice table (see p849). Reservations are essential.

Blauw aan de Wal (☎ 330 22 57; Oudezijds Achterburgwal 99; mains €24-27; 🕑 dinner) Tucked away in a little alley in the Red Light District, this charming 17th-century herb warehouse (complete with exposed brick and steel weights) is the setting for a French-Italian–inspired menu and a sumptuous wine list. The leafy courtyard backs onto a monastery.

Bordewijk (☎ 624 38 99; Noordermarkt 7; mains €24-29, set menus €37-52; 🕑 dinner Tue-Sun) Locals love Bordewijk: they don't come for the sparse interior, but for the super French-Italian cooking. Apparently lamb's testicles were once on the menu, but sheepish customers needn't worry – vegetarians are willingly catered to.

Christophe (☎ 625 08 07; www.christophe.nl; Leliegracht 46; mains €31-53; 🕑 dinner Tue-Sat) Jean Christophe's subtly swanky French restaurant lives up to its two Michelin stars with its lobster dishes, duck-liver terrine and an unusual elegance. The attentive service is also a cut above.

Cafés

Puccini (☎ 626 54 74; www.puccini.nl in Dutch; Staalstraat 21; mains €5.50-12.50; 🕑 lunch & dinner Tue-Sun) Refuel on Italian *panini* rolls and salads with sun-dried ingredients; Puccini's handmade chocolate and cake shop next door induces rapture.

Foodism (☎ 427 51 03; www.foodism.nl; Oude Leliestraat 8; mains €6-10) A groovy little lounge. All-day breakfasts, healthy filled sandwiches and salads, wild and wicked pasta dishes.

Quick Eats

Vlaams Friteshuis (Voetboogstraat 31) The city's best-loved fries joint since 1887. Heed the words of Vincent Vega (*Pulp Fiction*): 'You know what they put on french fries in Holland? Mayonnaise. And I don't mean a little bit on the side – they fuckin' drown 'em in it.' True, but Vlaams offers an arsenal of alternatives, including green peppercorns.

DRINKING

Café Cuba (☎ 627 4919; Nieuwmarkt 3) This place maintains fidelity to Fidel, Che and '50s Cuba, with low lighting, indoor palms, faux faded elegance, rum posters, and cane chairs and tables. Try Papa Hemingway's favourite cocktail, the *caipirinha* (a Brazilian cocktail made with a rumlike liquor), and the ubiquitous *mojito* (a rum- and lime-based cocktail). The outdoor seating is perched right on Nieuwmarkt.

Hoppe (☎ 420 44 20; Spuistraat 18) This gritty *bruin café* has been luring drinkers for more than 300 years. It has one of Amsterdam's highest beer turnovers – some achievement in a city of hops freaks. In summer the energetic crowd spews out from the dark interior and onto the Spui.

Lime (☎ 639 30 20; Zeedjik 104) Lime is cool and hip but friendly and laid-back; you won't get the stink-eye in here. The décor comes on like a Stereolab album cover – all dots and loops and browns and oranges – and the cocktails are superb.

Absinthe (☎ 320 6780; www.absinthe.nl; Nieuwe zijds Voorburgwal 171) This place is devoted to the brain-lesioning liquor reputed to be the cause of Van Gogh's self-mutilation. There is multiethnic décor with rather awkward seating arrangements, and the staff can teach you all about the signature drink. You will leave with ears intact – it's not as potent as it was in the old days.

Proeflokaal Wijnand Fockinck (☎ 639 26 95; www.wynand-fockink.nl in Dutch; Pijlsteeg 31) This fantastic little tasting house, dating from 1679, serves scores of *jenevers* and liqueurs made on-site. There's an appealing courtyard for lunch and snacks.

ENTERTAINMENT

Coffee Shops

'Café' means 'pub' throughout the Netherlands; 'coffee shops' are where one procures cannabis.

Siberië (☎ 623 59 09; Brouwersgracht 111) With a lounge-room feel, canal views and ultra-casual atmosphere, this is an addictive place that draws smokers of all ages for the friendly staff, the wicked weed, and the chance to play stoner chess with total strangers. 'Queen takes Bish…that castle thing. Ah, forget it. I resign.'

Barney's (☎ 625 97 61; www.barneys.biz; Haarlemmerstraat 98 & 102) The very popular Barney's, with its trippy biomechanical décor, has beloved all-day breakfasts as well as quality smoke (100% organic).

Nightclubs

Jimmy Woo (☎ 626 31 50; www.jimmywoo.nl; Korte Leidsedwarsstraat 18) With its uberstylish, black-lacquered, Oriental décor, Jimmy Woo is as hip as the bony projection of a femur. Plus it has a big focus on hip-hop and extracting cash from hip pockets. It's exclusive (no hippies allowed) so good luck getting in; try going with some Dutchies for best results.

Sinners in Heaven (☎ 620 13 75; www.sinners.nl; Wagenstraat 3-7) Along with Jimmy Woo, jet-set, celebrity-riddled Sinners heads the A-list of Amsterdam clubs. It serves up hip-hop, funk, beats and breaks and it's possibly harder than Woo to get into: there's always a 'guest list', and by all accounts the door bitch has quite the acid tongue. Try sleeping with a famous footballer for best results.

Winston International (☎ 623 13 80; www.winston.nl; Warmoesstraat 125) Next to the Hotel Winston (p854), it has everything from electronica to spoken word to punk to graffiti art. On Sundays there's Club Vegas, where the dress code is 'jet set' (sequins, suits, stilettos, bow ties, tiaras) and the music is lounge. Kooky fun.

To Night (☎ 694 74 44; www.hotelarena.nl; 's-Gravesandestraat 51) Each night here is different – everything from dance classics to salsa. It's worth a visit just for the magnificent interior; the chapel of this one-time orphanage has been given a solid redo, including the toilets. It's at the Hotel Arena.

Gay & Lesbian Venues

COC Amsterdam (☎ 623 40 79; www.cocamsterdam.nl; Rozenstraat 14) The Amsterdam branch of the national gay and lesbian organisation holds a variety of gay, lesbian and mixed club nights every weekend and supplies information on gay health, local support groups, special events and programmes. It's pronounced 'say-oh-say', by the way, not…

Cockring (☎ 623 96 04; www.clubcockring.com; Warmoesstraat 96) No mistaking the pronunciation, here. The 'Ring plays techno and trance downstairs, while upstairs is for cruising leather boys. Live strip shows and 'shoes only' nude parties sometimes get an airing, as does a lot of flesh.

Saarein (☎ 623 49 01; Elandsstraat 119) During the late '70s Saarein was the focal point of the Dutch feminist movement, and today it's a favoured meeting place for lesbians. There's a small menu with tapas and soups and bar staff can advise on Sapphic nightlife.

Live Music

CLASSICAL & CONTEMPORARY

Concertgebouw (Concert Bldg; ☎ for tickets 10am-5pm 671 83 45; www.concertgebouw.nl; Concertgebouwplein 2-6) Each year, this neo-Renaissance centre presents around 650 concerts attracting 840,000 visitors, making it the world's busiest concert hall (with reputedly the best acoustics). Classical musos consider the Concertgebouw a very prestigious gig indeed, as do some rock bands with classical pretensions (like King Crimson). Holds free 'lunch concerts' at 12.30pm Wednesdays, between September and June.

JAZZ

Bimhuis (☎ 788 21 50; www.bimhuis.nl; Piet Heinkade 3) The Bimhuis is Amsterdam's number-one jazz joint, attracting local and international jazz greats and holding workshops to boot. It is now in the high-profile Muziekgebouw aan 't IJ complex, and the new space has a great bar and huge windows overlooking the city.

ROCK & POP

Paradiso (☎ 626 45 21; www.paradiso.nl in Dutch; Weteringschans 6) This converted church has long been a premier rock venue since the '60s, hosting big names such as Sonic Youth, David Bowie and the Rolling Stones. Also holds dance evenings like Paradisco; there's indie and hip-hop, too.

Melkweg (Milky Way; ☎ 531 81 81; www.melkweg.nl; Lijnbaansgracht 234A) This former milk factory off Leidseplein has been a top cultural venue since the 1970s. It's an all-in-one entertainment complex with a café, a multimedia centre and top live music almost every night (everything from Afro-Celtic to thrash), plus a nightclub, a cinema, lounges, art galleries…

Theatre

Amsterdams Marionetten Theater (☎ 620 80 27; www.marionet.demon.nl; Nieuwe Jonkerstraat 8; adult/child from €12/6) In a former blacksmith's shop, this charming, intimate theatre features marionettes performing elaborate productions such as *The Magic Flute*. The skill of the puppeteers is something to see. Call or check the website for show times.

Nachttheater Sugar Factory (☎ 626 50 06; www.sugarfactory.nl; Lijnbaansgracht 238) This 'night theatre' showcases theatre, spoken word, exhibitions, poetry readings and live music, after which the space clears and it becomes a bangin' nightclub.

Koninklijk Theater Carré (☎ 0900-252 52 55, backstage tours 524 94 52; www.theatercarre.nl in Dutch; Amstel 115-125) The largest theatre in town offers mainstream international shows, musicals, cabaret, opera, operetta, ballet and circuses. Backstage tours (adult/child €8/4, 11am Saturday) are also available by reservation.

Boom Chicago (☎ 423 01 01; www.boomchicago.nl; Leidseplein 12) Performing English-language stand-up and improvised comedy year-round. See it over dinner and a few drinks – the food here's decent.

Sport

Four-times European champion Ajax is the Netherlands' most famous football team. Ajax plays in the **Amsterdam ArenA** (☎ 311 13 33; www.amsterdamarena.nl; Arena Blvd 11, Bijlmermeer), usually on Saturday evenings and Sunday afternoons August to May. Stadium tours are available.

Cinemas

Find out what's on in Thursday's papers or Wednesday's *Amsterdam Weekly*.

Movies (☎ 638 60 16; www.themovies.nl; Haarlemmerdijk 161) Art-house and indie films in Art Deco surrounds.

Tuschinskitheater (☎ 623 15 00; www.pathe.nl/tuschinski; Reguliersbreestraat 26) Blockbusters in a sumptuous Art Deco interior.

Filmmuseum (☎ 589 14 00; www.filmmuseum.nl; Vondelpark 3) Priceless archive of films; summer screenings on the outdoor terrace.

SHOPPING

Department Stores

Maison de Bonneterie (☎ 531 34 00; www.maisondebonneterie.nl in Dutch; Rokin 140) Exclusive, classic garments.

Vroom & Dreesmann (☎ 622 01 71; www.vroomendreesmann.nl in Dutch; Kalverstraat 201) Popular clothing and cosmetics.

Markets

Albert Cuypmarkt (www.decuyp.nl; Albert Cuypstraat; 10am-5pm, closed Sun) Amsterdam's largest, busiest market – it's 100 years old. Food of every description, flowers, souvenirs, clothing, hardware and household goods.

Bloemenmarkt (Singel; 9am-5pm, closed Sun Dec-Feb) 'Floating' flower market that's actually on pilings. Traders can advise on import regulations. Notorious for pickpockets.

Boerenmarkt (Farmers Market; www.boerenmarktamsterdam.nl in Dutch; Noordermarkt & Nieuwmarkt; 10am-3pm Sat) Home-grown produce, organic foods and picnic provisions.

De Looier Antiques Market (www.looier.nl in Dutch; Elandsgracht 109; 11am-5pm Sat-Thu) Jewellery, furniture, art and collectibles.

Waterlooplein Flea Market (Waterlooplein; 9am-5pm Mon-Fri, 8.30am-5.30pm Sat) Amsterdam's most famous fleas market: curios, second-hand clothing, music, used footwear, ageing electronic gear, New Age gifts, cheap bicycle parts.

Smart Drugs

Remember that importing drugs is illegal.

Chills & Thrills (☎ 638 00 15; Nieuwendijk 17; noon-8pm Mon-Wed, 11am-9pm Thu, to 10pm Fri-Sun) Herbal trips, mushrooms, psychoactive cacti, novelty bongs and life-sized alien sculptures.

Speciality Shops

Condomerie Het Gulden Vlies (☎ 627 41 74; www.condomerie.nl; Warmoesstraat 141) Hundreds of novelty condoms, lubricants and saucy gifts. So, three cheers for your willy or John Thomas; hooray for your one-eyed trouser snake.

Santa Jet (☎ 427 20 70; Prinsenstraat 7) Mexican shrines, religious icons, lanterns, candles, love potions.

GETTING THERE & AWAY

Air

Most major airlines fly directly to **Schiphol** (AMS; ☎ 0900-0141; www.schiphol.nl), 18km southwest of the city centre. For more information about getting to and from the Netherlands, including Amsterdam airline offices, see p882.

Bus

For details of regional buses in the Netherlands, call the **transport information service** (☎ 0900-9292); it costs €0.50 per minute. Fares and travel durations are covered under towns in the regional sections.

Amsterdam has good long-distance bus links with the rest of Europe and North Africa.

Eurolines (☎ 560 87 87; www.eurolines.nl; Rokin 10) tickets can be bought at their office near the Dam, and at most travel agencies and NS Reisburo (Netherlands Railways Travel Bureau) in Centraal Station. Fares are consistently lower than the train, and departures are from the **bus station** (☎ 694 56 31) next to Amstelstation.

Busabout tickets can bought through its **London office** (☎ in UK 020-7950 1661; www.busabout.com) or on the coaches themselves. Coaches stop at Hotel Hans Brinker on Kerkstraat, smack in the middle of the city.

For further details on Busabout, Eurolines and other coach services, see p1117.

Car & Motorcycle

Motorways link Amsterdam to Den Haag and Rotterdam in the south, and to Utrecht and Amersfoort in the southeast. Amsterdam is about 480km from Paris, 840km from Munich, 680km from Berlin and 730km from Copenhagen. The Hoek van Holland ferry port is 80km away; IJmuiden is just up the road along the Noordzeekanaal.

The Dutch automobile association, **ANWB** (☎ 673 08 44; Museumplein 5), provides information and services if you prove membership of your own association.

Train

Amsterdam's main train station is Centraal Station (CS). See p882 for general information about international trains.

GETTING AROUND

To/From the Airport

A taxi into Amsterdam from Schiphol airport takes 20 to 45 minutes and costs about €40. Trains to Centraal Station leave every 15 minutes, take 15 to 20 minutes, and cost €3.60/6.20 per single/return.

Bicycle

Amsterdam is cycling nirvana: flat, beautiful, with dedicated bike paths. About 150,000 bicycles are stolen each year in Amsterdam alone, so always lock up. The Dutch automobile association, **ANWB** (☎ 673 08 44; Museumplein 5), provides cycling maps and information.

For bicycle rental, try **Bike City** (☎ 626 37 21; www.bikecity.nl; Bloemgracht 68-70; per day/week €8.50/41) where there's no advertising on the bikes – you might pass for a local – or **Mike's Bike Tours** (☎ 622 79 70; www.mikesbiketours.com; Kerkstraat 134; per half-/full/additional day €5/7/5). Both companies require a passport/ID and a credit-card imprint or cash deposit.

Boat

CANAL BOAT, BUS & BIKE

Canal Bus (☎ 623 98 86; www.canalbus.nl; day pass per adult/under 13 €17/11) does several circuits between Centraal Station and the Rijksmuseum between 9.50am and 8pm. The day pass is valid until noon the next day. The same company rents canal bikes (pedal boats) for €9 per person per hour (€7 if there are more than two people per canal bike). Docks are by Leidseplein and near the Anne Frank Huis.

Lovers Museum Boat (☎ 622 21 81; www.lovers.nl; day pass from €8.50) leaves every 30 or 45 minutes from the Lovers terminal in front of Centraal Station. Discounts after 1pm.

If you blanch at the thought of the foggy windows and stale commentary of the big glassed-in canal boats, do yourself a favour and try the not-for-profit **St Nicolaas Boat Club** (☎ 423 01 01; www.petermoskos.com/boat; Boom Chicago, Leidseplein 12; donation €10), which takes small, old barges out onto the canals. Patrons are allowed to smoke dope and drink beer on board, while the captains amuse with stories about alternative Amsterdam. Departure times are according to numbers. They'll definitely show you a different side of the city, everything from the famous Mohawk Duck to the thinnest house in town.

FERRIES

There are free ferries from behind Centraal Station to destinations around the IJ, notably Amsterdam Noord. Ferries to the Eastern Docklands cost €1.

Car & Motorcycle

Amsterdam is horrendous for parking. Try the **Transferium parking garage** (☎ 400 17 21) at Amsterdam ArenA stadium. It's €5.50 per day including two return metro tickets to the city centre.

Public Transport

The best ticketing deal is the *Strippenkaart*, a multifare 'strip ticket' valid on all buses, trams and metros (p883). The GVB office also sells a one-week pass valid in all zones for €17. If you board without a ticket, the driver sells one-/two-/three-zone tickets. Ticketing is based on zones.

Night buses take over shortly after midnight when the trams and regular buses stop running. Drivers sell single tickets for €3.20. Day passes are valid on night buses but the surcharge still applies.

Taxi

Amsterdam taxis are expensive, even over short journeys. Try **Taxicentrale Amsterdam** (☎ 677 77 77).

AROUND AMSTERDAM

Aalsmeer

☎ **0297**

Here, at the world's biggest **flower auction** (☎ 39 21 85; www.aalsmeer.com; Legmeerdijk 313; adult/child €4.50/2.50; 7-11am Mon-Fri), 21 million flowers and plants worth around €6 million change hands daily; the rose is the biggest seller, outselling the tulip three to one. At one million square metres in size, the auction arena is the world's largest commercial building. Bidding usually takes place between 7am and 9.30am.

Take Connexxion bus No 172 from Amsterdam Centraal Station to the Aalsmeer VBA stop (50 minutes, five times hourly).

Alkmaar

☎ **072 / pop 94,111**

This picturesque town stages its famous **cheese market** (Waagplein; 10am-noon Fri Apr-Sep) in the main square. The market dates from the 17th century. Dealers in officious white smocks insert a hollow rod to extract cheese samples, sniffing and crumbling for fat and moisture content. Then the porters, wearing colourful hats to signify their cheese guild, heft the cheeses on wooden sledges to a large scale. An average 30,000kg of cheese is on display at the Alkmaar market at any one time.

Arrive early for more than fleeting glimpses. There are two trains per hour from Amsterdam Centraal (€6.30, 40 minutes, four hourly).

THE RANDSTAD

The Randstad (literally 'Rim City') is the Netherlands' most densely populated region (and among the world's densest), containing almost half the country's population. It stretches from Amsterdam to Rotterdam and also includes Den Haag, Utrecht, Haarlem, Leiden, Delft, Gouda and Dordrecht.

HAARLEM

☎ 023 / pop 148,000

Everybody loves Haarlem, an achingly pretty, refined city of cobblestone streets, historic buildings, grand churches and museums, cosy bars, superb restaurants and antique shops. It's only 15 minutes by train from Amsterdam, but if you tire of the capital it's well worth a stopover in its own right.

The **library** (☎ 515 76 00; Doelenplein 1; 🕑 11am-8pm Mon, Tue & Thu, 10am-4pm Sat) offers free Internet and the **tourist office** (☎ 0900-616 16 00; www.vvvzk.nl; Stationsplein 1; 🕑 9.30am-5.30pm Mon-Fri, 10am-4pm Sat Apr-Oct, 9.30am-5pm Mon-Fri, 10am-2pm Sat Nov-Mar) is helpful.

Sights

Kept in an almshouse where Frans Hals spent his final, impoverished years, the superb collection at the **Frans Hals Museum** (☎ 511 57 75; www.franshalsmuseum.nl; Groot Heiligland 62; adult/child €7/free; 🕑 11am-5pm Mon-Sat, noon-5pm Sun) features Hals' two paintings known collectively as the *Regents & the Regentesses of the Old Men's Alms House* (1664). Among other treasures are ceiling-high illustrations of the human anatomy with Biblical and mythological allusions. There's an annexe featuring modern art, including works by the CoBrA movement.

Teylers Museum (☎ 531 90 10; Spaarne 16; adult/child €4.50/1; 🕑 10am-5pm Tue-Sat, noon-5pm Sun) is the Netherland's oldest museum (1778) and houses an array of kooky inventions such as the 18th-century electrostatic machine that ran on batteries the size of a milk wagon. This eclectic collection also features paintings from the Dutch and French schools and numerous temporary exhibitions, in addition to fossils, ancient relics and mineral crystals.

The **Grote Kerk van St Bavo** (☎ 553 20 40; www.grotekerk.nl; Oude Groenmarkt 23; adult/child €2/1.50; 🕑 10am-4pm Mon-Sat) is a Gothic cathedral with a 50m-high steeple that can be seen from almost anywhere in Haarlem. It has a striking Müller organ, 30m high with around 5000 pipes.

Sleeping

Haarlem Stayokay Hostel (☎ 537 37 93; haarlem@stayokay.com; Jan Gijzenpad 3; dm €27; 💻) This lakeside youth hostel has a 10pm silence rule but no curfew. The superclean rooms are basic, but the bar-café is full of character. Take bus No 2 (direction Haarlem Noord) from the train station (10 minutes).

Hotel Carillon (☎ 531 05 91; www.hotelcarillon.com; Grote Markt 27; s/d from €38/63) The single beds may be the thinnest in all the Netherlands, but the atmosphere is fine, friendly and fun. There's a bar–sidewalk café downstairs in the Grote Kerk's shadow.

Joops Hotel (☎ 532 20 08; www.joopshotel.com; Oude Groenmarkt 20; r/studio from €85/85; 💻) More than 100 very individual rooms spread over an entire block near the Grote Kerk; studios have kitchenettes. Reception is on the ground floor of the Belly & Bolly antique shop, run by a couple of friendly chaps.

Eating & Drinking

Eko Eetkafé (☎ 532 65 68; Ziljstraat 39; mains €8-18) This organic restaurant attracts a diverse crowd: singletons, suits, grannies, groovers. The menu is also eclectic (and tasty): fish and vegetarian dishes with a clear conscience. It's a short walk from the town centre but worth it.

Specktakel (☎ 532 38 41; Spekstraat 4; mains €18; 🕑 dinner) This long and thin diner is vying for UN membership, judging by its global menu that includes Australian emu fillet and Indian lamb masala. There's streetside seating for sunny days.

Try Jopen Koyt, the local beer, in one of Haarlem's many atmospheric drinking dens. First brewed in 1401, this dark, richly flavoured drop has an alcohol content of 8.5%.

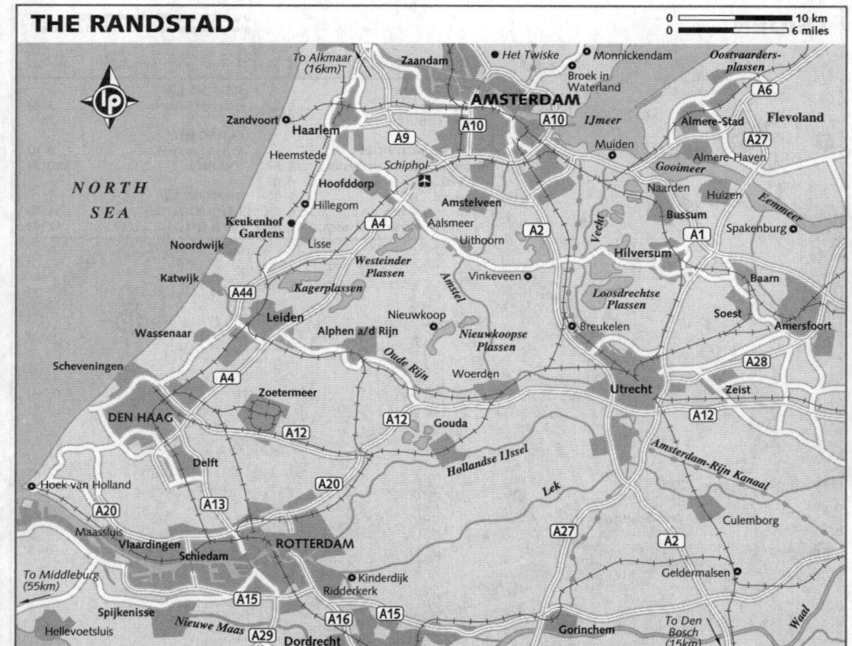

Entertainment

Patronaat (☎ 517 58 58; www.patronaat.nl in Dutch; Zijlsingel 2) This cavernous music and dance club attracts bands with banging tunes. Events start around 7pm or 9pm unless it's a midnight rave.

Getting There & Away

Sample train fares: Alkmaar (€5.70, 30 minutes, four per hour), Amsterdam (€3.60, 15 minutes, eight per hour), Den Haag (€7, 35 minutes, six per hour) and Rotterdam (€10.10, 50 minutes, four per hour).

KEUKENHOF GARDENS

Near Lisse, between Haarlem and Leiden, a beautiful enigma unfurls for just two months each year: the blooming of millions of multicoloured tulip, daffodil and hyacinth bulbs at the **Keukenhof Gardens** (www.keukenhof.nl; adult/under 11 €12.50/5.50; ⏲ 8am-7.30pm late Mar-May, cashier to 6pm).

Netherlands Railways sells a ticket (adult/under 11 €17/9) that combines entrance to the gardens and travel by express bus from Leiden CS (20 minutes).

Bus No 54 travels from Leiden through Lisse to Keukenhof. Bus No 50 travels from Haarlem to Lisse, from where you can meet bus No 54.

LEIDEN

☎ 071 / pop 118,500

Lovely Leiden is a refreshing, vibrant town, patterned with canals and attractive old buildings. It also has a few claims to fame: it's Rembrandt's birthplace, and it's home to the Netherlands' oldest university (and 20,000 students), the alma mater of Rene Descartes.

Get online at **Ortes Telecom** (Internet per hr €3). The **tourist office** (☎ 0900-222 23 33; www.leidenpromotie.nl; Stationsweg 2D; ⏲ 11am-5.30pm Mon, 9.30am-5.30pm Tue-Fri, 10am-4.30pm Sat) will help you.

Sights & Activities

The 17th-century **Lakenhal** (Cloth Hall; ☎ 516 53 60; www.lakenhal.nl; Oude Singel 28-32; adult/under 18 €4/free; ⏲ 10am-5pm Tue-Sun) houses the Municipal Museum, with an assortment of works by old masters (including a smattering of

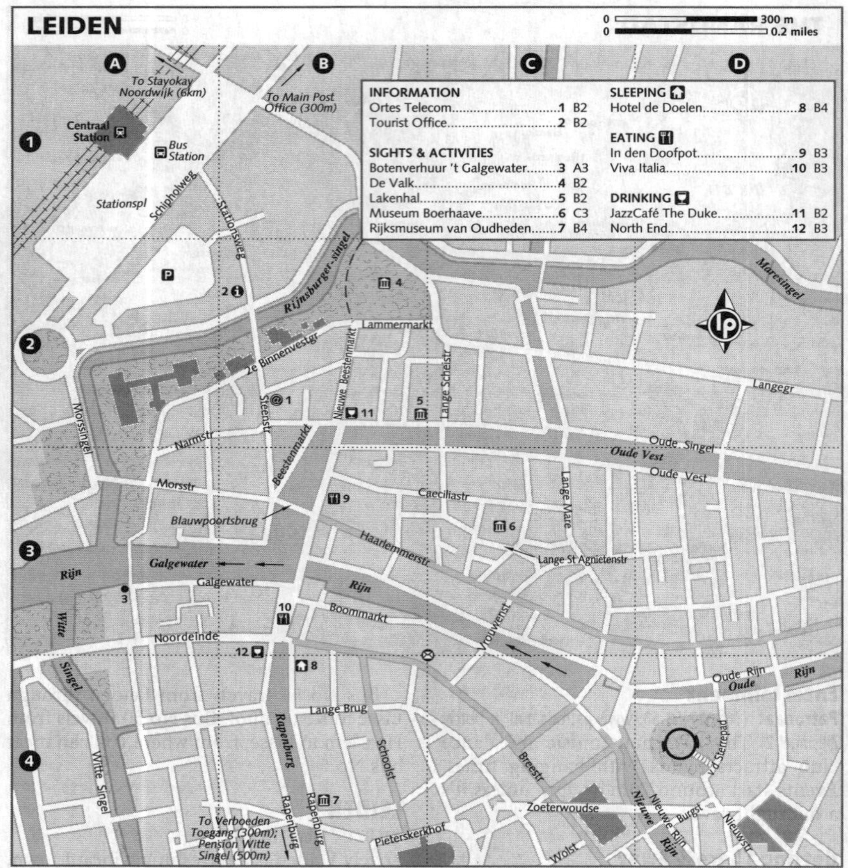

Rembrandts) as well as period rooms and temporary exhibits.

The **Rijksmuseum van Oudheden** (National Museum of Antiquities; ☎ 516 31 63; www.rmo.nl; Rapenburg 28; adult/under 18 €7.50/5.50; 10am-5pm Tue-Fri, noon-5pm Sat & Sun) has a classy collection of hieroglyphs – and 94 human and animal mummies. The entrance hall contains the actual Temple of Taffeh, a gift from Egypt for Dutch help in saving ancient monuments when the Aswan High Dam was built.

Leiden's carefully restored windmill, **De Valk** (Falcon; ☎ 516 53 53; http://home.wanadoo.nl/molenmuseum; 2e Binnenvestgracht 1; adult/under 15 €3/2; 10am-5pm Tue-Sat, 1-5pm Sun), features many presentations, including one that laments the fact that local boy Rembrandt, as a miller's son, didn't paint many windmills. The upper levels afford an inspired view of the old town.

Leiden University was an early centre for Dutch medical research, and the **Museum Boerhaave** (National Museum of the History of Science & Medicine; ☎ 521 42 24; www.museumboerhaave.nl; Lange St Agnietenstraat 10; adult/under 19 €6/3; 10am-5pm Tue-Sat, noon-5pm Sun) gathers together five centuries of pickled organs, surgical tools and skeletons in its Anatomy Theatre (it's morbid, but just try to look away).

Rent a canoe or kayak from **Botenverhuur 't Galgewater** (☎ 514 97 90; www.galgewater.nl; per hr €5; 11am-6pm Oct-May, to 10pm Jun-Sep) and explore the canals.

Sleeping

Stayokay Noordwijk (☎ 0252-37 29 20; www.stayokay.com/noordwijk; Langevelderlaan 45; dm from €20) The hostel is 45 minutes away, next to a popular beach. Take bus No 57 or 90 (last bus at 11pm) to Sancta Maria hospital and walk for 10 minutes.

Pension Witte Singel (☎ 512 45 92; www.pension-ws.demon.nl; Witte Singel 80; d €76, s/d with shared bathroom €41/62) Fresh, spacious rooms with large windows overlooking most agreeable scenery: the perfectly peaceful Singel canal in front and a typically Dutch garden out back.

Hotel de Doelen (☎ 512 05 27; www.dedoelen.com; Rapenburg 2; s/d from €75/95) Some of the Doelen's canalside rooms border on palatial opulence with all the trimmings, and even the more basic options have bath, phone and TV. Rooms come in three flavours: basic, standard and suite.

Eating & Drinking

In Den Doofpot (☎ 512 24 34; www.indendoofpot.nl in Dutch; Turfmarkt 9; mains €12-45; dinner) The interior is regal and airy, a sensuous setting for the menu's filling, French-tinged twists on Dutch cooking.

Verboden Toegang (☎ 514 33 88; www.verbodentoegang.nl in Dutch; Kaiserstraat 7; mains €13-20; dinner) This casual, elegant, wood-panelled restaurant doesn't take itself too seriously (the name means 'access forbidden'). The grub's top-notch with an emphasis on seafood, as the butterfish in white wine attests.

Viva Italia (☎ 514 88 18; Kort Rapenburg 17; mains €16-20) This classy and fine Italian joint, with its luxurious décor (including white-leather couches, no less) and fine service, dishes up upmarket victuals such as veal with rolled-in Parma ham and basil pesto.

Jazzcafé the Duke (☎ 566 15 85; www.jazzcafetheduke.nl in Dutch; Oude Singel 2) No windows, but loads of yellowing, vintage jazz posters on the walls. The motto is, 'If we don't have it, you don't need it'. It's true: you don't need windows to enjoy this atmospheric den, with its fine live jazz every night and suitably appreciative crowds.

North End (☎ 512 1541; www.north-end.nl; Noordeinde 55) This superb English-style pub is full of warmth, cosy nooks and character. It comes complete with its very own 'bourbon alley' (not very English, granted, but a welcome selection of booze all the same) and patented 'beer *strippenkaart*'.

Getting There & Away

Sample train fares: Amsterdam (€7.50, 34 minutes, six per hour) and Den Haag (€2.80, 10 minutes, six per hour). Regional and local buses leave from the bus station directly in front of Centraal Station.

DEN HAAG

☎ 070 / pop 472,100

Den Haag (The Hague), officially known as 's-Gravenhage (Count's Hedge), is the Dutch seat of government (although Amsterdam's the capital). Also home to the royal family, it's a stately, regal place that's filled with palatial embassies and mansions, green boulevards and parks, prestigious art galleries, a mouth-watering culinary scene, a clutch of tasty museums, and some throbbing nightlife. Plus it's attached to the seaside suburb of Scheveningen, worth a visit for its lively kitsch and long stretch of beach.

Surf the Web at **Kado Internet** (Spui 165; per hr €2.75). Ask the **tourist office** (☎ 0900-340 35 05; www.denhaag.com; Hofweg 1; 10am-6pm Mon-Fri, to 5pm Sat, noon-5pm Sun) for advice.

Sights & Activities

The **Mauritshuis** (☎ 302 34 56; www.mauritshuis.nl; Korte Vijverberg 8; adult/under 18 incl audio tour €11.50/free; 10am-5pm Tue-Sat, 11am-5pm Sun) is a small but grand museum, housing Dutch and Flemish works (and Andy Warhol's *Queen Beatrix*). Highlights include Vermeer's *Girl with a Pearl Earring* and Rembrandt self-portraits at ages 20 and 63. Even if you're just passing Den Haag on the train, it's well worth hopping off to visit.

The Lange Voorhout Palace was once Queen Emma's residence. Now it's home to the work of Dutch graphic artist MC Escher. **Escher in Het Paleis Museum** (☎ 338 11 20; www.escherinhetpaleis.nl; Lange Voorhout; adult/under 15 €7.50/5; 11am-5pm Tue-Sun) features notes, letters, drafts, photos and fully mature works covering Escher's entire career, from early realism to later phantasmagoria. There are some imaginative displays, including a virtual reconstruction of Escher's impossible buildings and 4D spatial dynamics, and an optical illusion photo booth, where you can take a picture of yourself that will look as if you're inside an Escher drawing.

Admirers of De Stijl and Piet Mondrian mustn't miss the Berlage-designed **Gemeentemuseum** (Municipal Museum; ☎ 338 11 20; Stadhouderslaan 41; www.gemeentemuseum.nl; adult/under 18 €8/free; 🕑 11am-5pm Tue-Sat). It also houses extensive exhibits of applied arts, costumes and musical instruments. Mondrian's unfinished *Victory Boogie Woogie* takes pride of place (so it should; the museum paid €30 million for it). There are also a few Picassos and some Eschers.

The **Panorama Mesdag** (☎ 364 45 44; www.panorama-mesdag.nl; Zeestraat 65; adult/under 13 €5/2.50; 🕑 10am-5pm Mon-Sat, noon-5pm Sun & holidays) contains the *Panorama* (1881), a gigantic 360-degree painting of Scheveningen, painted by Hendrik Willem Mesdag. The panorama is viewed from a constructed dune, with real sand and beach chairs; birdsong and wave sounds are piped through. Mesdag's command of perspective and minute detail was masterly: it's a fully immersive experience.

Madurodam (☎ 355 39 00; www.madurodam.nl; George Maduroplein 1; adult/under 11 €12.50/9; 🕑 9am-8pm) is a miniaturised Netherlands, complete with 1:25 scale versions of Schiphol, Amsterdam, windmills and tulips, Rotterdam harbour, the Delta dikes, and so on. It's an enlightening example of the Dutch tendency to put their world under a microscope (see the boxed text, p847).

The long beach at **Scheveningen** (www.scheveningen.nl) attracts nine million visitors per year. Crowds can get up close and personal when the weather gets warm and the shopping strip gets crassly commercial, but the attraction of sea and sand keeps the peace. A palpable frisson of frivolity sweetens the air.

Walk northwest along the beach and you'll come across a series of WWII bunkers, part of the Nazi Atlantic Wall defence system and an eerie reminder of the Netherlands' place in European history.

Sleeping

Stayokay Den Haag (☎ 315 78 88; www.stayokay.com/denhaag; Scheepmakerstraat 27; dm from €21) This branch of the Stayokay hostel chain has all the usual facilities including a bar, a restaurant, Internet and games. It's around 15 minutes' walk from Hollands Spoor station.

Corona Hotel (☎ 363 79 30; www.corona.nl; Buitenhof 39-42; r from €74) This pleasant hotel is across the way from the Binnenhof and has all the usual facilities and amenities, plus super comfy rooms that come in a range of un-Dutchlike styles including 'Colonial English'.

Paleis Hotel (☎ 362 46 21; www.paleishotel.nl; Molenstraat 26; s/d €135/175; ☒) The Paleis has an austere style, a fine, central location near Noordeinde, and a solarium. The rooms are well equipped and very comfortable.

Eating & Drinking

Topkapi Sense Restaurant (☎ 358 53 50; www.topkapi-scheveningen.nl; Gevers Deynootplein 36, Scheveningen; mains €11-22) An 'Ottoman' restaurant with cuisine from Greece, Turkey, Egypt, Syria, Algeria, Morocco… The couscous with sea bass is a winner, as is the baked, stuffed zucchini. Ruby red drapes and beads combine with low lighting to create a suitable atmosphere, although the guy in the corner playing cheesy tunes on his synthetic organ tempers it.

It Rains Fishes (☎ 365 25 98; www.itrainsfishes.nl in Dutch; Noordeinde 123; mains €13-24) It's the 'restaurant on the sunny side of the street', a multiaward-winning seafood concern serving grilled, fried and poached fish, mussels and scallops.

OKA (☎ 392 01 33; Herengracht 2-6; mains €15-30; 🕑 lunch & dinner Tue-Sat) This swish, authentic Japanese restaurant serves up delectable sushi and *teppanyaki* (Japanese meat and vegetable dish cooked in an iron griddle). The hostess, Ms JoJo Phang, is a bit of a personality – she says she can arrange on-site bachelor parties, ironing out all the details in a 'private talk tailored to that evening's party boy'.

Boterwaag (☎ 365 96 86; www.september.nl in Dutch; Grote Markt 8a) This old weighhouse serves as a café-restaurant and provides a distinctive drinking and eating experience with its high ceilings, large windows, candle fetish, nooks and crannies to hide out in, and great beer list. When we were here, a kooky Dutch kid was riding around inside on a unicycle and no-one batted an eyelid.

Kurzaal Bar (☎ 416 26 36; Kurhaus Hotel, Gevers Deynootplein 30) Even if you're not staying at the plush, 19th-century Kurhaus Hotel, it's worth popping in for a drink at its bar (but wear your best shoes). The Kurzaal's on the edge of a stunning dancehall-restaurant with period trimmings, painted ceiling, frescoes, chandeliers, huge potted plants, portholes, artworks, photos of Jacques Brel, Bing Crosby, etc. The Rolling Stones played their shortest ever concert here (just three minutes) before rioting teenage girls ended it.

Fiddler (☎ 365 19 55; Riviervismarkt 1; www.fiddler.nl) This large, split-level, wood-panelled English microbrewery always has a decent crowd snacking on the OK pub food and the Fiddler's own beers: an ale, a pale ale and a stout. In the end, it's probably a bit too cavernous – intimacy's hard to come by. Good location: in the eye of the Grote Kerk.

Entertainment

Nederlands Dans Theater (☎ 880 01 00; www.ndt.nl; Schedeldoekshaven 60) This world-famous dance company has three components: NDT1, the main troupe of 32 dancers; NDT2, a small group of 12 dancers under 21; and NDT3, a group of dancers over 40 who perform more dramatic works.

Paard van Troje (☎ 750 34 34; www.paard.nl; Prinsegracht 12) This emporium has club nights and live music, as well as a café. The programming's eclectic: everything from booty-shaking drum'n'bass DJs to bowel-destroying sonic terrorists the Hafler Trio.

Getting There & Around

Sample train fares: Amsterdam (€9.50, 50 minutes, four per hour), Leiden (€2.80, 13 minutes, four per hour), Rotterdam (€4.10, 22 minutes, four per hour) and Utrecht

(€9.10, 40 minutes). Tram Nos 1, 8 and 9 link Scheveningen with Den Haag; the fare is three strips. The last tram at night runs in either direction at about 1.30am. There's a tram to Delft.

DELFT

☎ 015 / pop 96,100

Ah, lovely Delft: compact, charming, relaxed. Founded around 1100, it's a very popular tourist destination. Day-trippers – and lovers of beauty and refinement – clamour to stroll Delft's narrow, canal-lined streets, gazing at the remarkable old buildings and meditating on the life and career of Golden Age painter Jan Vermeer, who was born and lived here. (*View of Delft*, one of Vermeer's best-loved works, is an enigmatic, nonrealist vision of the town.) Delft is also famous for its 'delftware', the distinctive blue-and-white pottery originally duplicated from Chinese porcelain by 17th-century artisans.

The **tourist office** (☎ 0900-515 15 55; www.delft.nl; Hippolytusbuurt 4; 🕐 11am-4pm Mon, 10am-4pm Tue-Fri, to 5pm Sat, to 4pm Sun) has free Internet.

Sights & Activities

The 14th-century **Nieuwe Kerk** (☎ 212 30 25; www.nieuwekerk-delft.nl; Markt; adult/child €3/1.50; 🕐 9am-6pm Apr-Oct, 11am-4pm Nov-Apr, closed Sun) houses the crypt of the Dutch royal family and the mausoleum of Willem the Silent. The fee includes entrance to the **Oude Kerk** (☎ 212 30 15; www.oudekerk-delft.nl; Heilige Geestkerkhof; 🕐 9am-6pm Apr-Oct, 11am-4pm Nov-Mar, closed Sun) – and vice versa. The latter, 800 years old, is a surreal sight: its tower leans 2m from the vertical. Among the tombs inside is Vermeer's.

Municipal Museum Het Prinsenhof (☎ 260 23 58; www.prinsenhof-delft.nl in Dutch; St Agathaplein 1; adult/under 16 €5/4; 🕐 10am-5pm Tue-Sat, 1-5pm Sun), a former convent, is where Willem the Silent was assassinated in 1584 (the bullet hole in the wall is covered in Perspex to protect it against inquisitive visitors). The museum displays various objects telling the story of the 80-year war with Spain, as well as 17th-century paintings.

The **Museum Nusantara** (☎ 260 23 58; www.nusantara-delft.nl in Dutch; St Agathaplein 4; adult/under 16 €3.50/3; 🕐 10am-5pm Tue-Sat, 1-5pm Sun) shines a light on the Netherlands' colonial past. There's a collection of furniture and other lifestyle artefacts from 17th-century Batavia (now Jakarta), as well as a 'colonial department' detailing the beginnings of Dutch rule in the region.

The **Vermeercentrum** (☎ 213 85 88; www.vermeerdelft.nl; Voldersgracht 21; 🕐 10am-5pm Mon-Sat, noon-5pm Sun), set to open in September 2006, promises to offer 'a fascinating voyage of discovery through the life and work of Johannes Vermeer.' The museum says it will enable visitors to 'Experience life in 17th-century Delft, experience his studio, and get to know his work'.

See Delft on a **canal boat tour** (☎ 212 63 85; adult/under 12 €5.50/3; 🕐 9.30am-6pm mid-Mar–Oct) departing from Koornmarkt 113.

Sleeping & Eating

Hotel De Emauspoort (☎ 219 02 19; www.emauspoort.nl; Vrouwenregt 9-11; s/d €80/90, caravan s/d €75/85) Comfy, old-style rooms, plus two attentively restored gypsy caravans out back. Delightful. Big fat bonus: the bakery-confectionery store right next door provides the big fat breakfast.

Hotel de Plataan (☎ 212 60 46; www.hoteldeplataan.nl; Doelenplein 10; s/d €88/99) Delft's finest accommodation is on a delightful square, and features an ace café and a downright dignified breakfast room. Standard rooms are small but elegant. Then there are the wonderfully opulent theme rooms, which come on like a Japanese love hotel: there's the Garden of Eden; the Amber, based on Eastern stylings; or the jaw-dropping Tamarinde, themed after a desert island.

Stadys Koffyhuis (☎ 212 46 25; Oude Delft 133; www.stads-koffyhuis.nl; pancakes €7-10) This warm and friendly café has a real ace in the hole: a terrace barge moored out front, where you can take your coffee and eat your delicious sandwiches and pancakes while admiring possibly the best view in Delft – the Oude Kerk, just ahead at the end of the canal.

Eetcafé De Ruif (☎ 214 22 06; www.ruif.nl in Dutch; Kerkstraat 22; mains €12-16) Wonderfully rustic, with a low ceiling, canal views and yummo lunches such as goat-cheese salads and Stellendam shrimps (seafood that's apparently very highly prised round these here parts). At night it's busier, morphing into an exceedingly popular carousing option.

Artusi (☎ 212 03 54; www.restaurant-artusi.nl; Voorstraat 20A; mains €18-22; 🕐 dinner Mon-Sat) This place is a bar as well as a restaurant, and

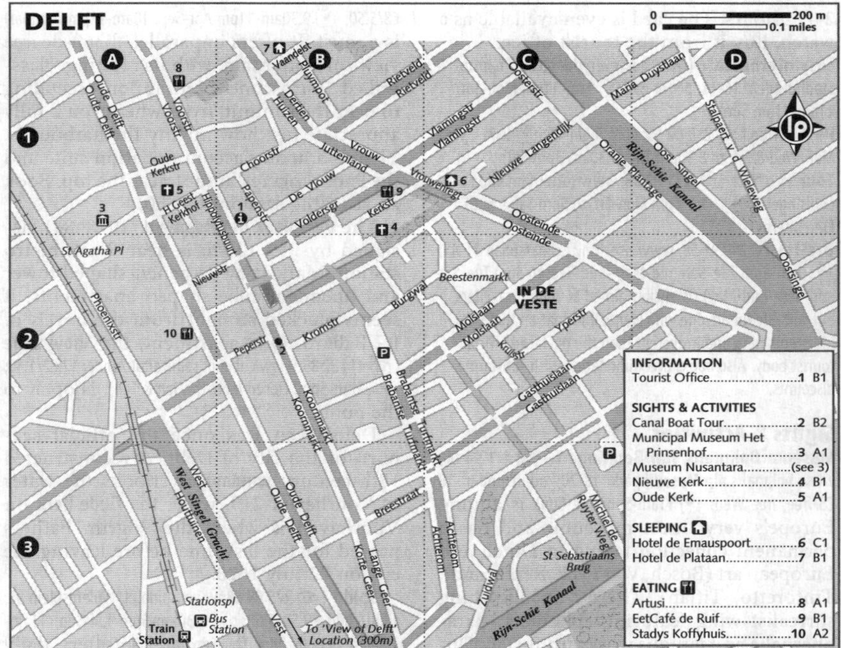

Italian dishes are the name of the game. It's stylish, but not too snobby. All the usual Italian faves are here, plus ramped up, out-of-left-field goodies such as tame duck udder with olives and balsamic sauce.

Getting There & Away

Sample train fares: Den Haag (€2.20, eight minutes), Rotterdam (€2.90, 13 minutes) and Amsterdam (€10.80, 50 minutes). Tram No 1 makes the run to Den Haag.

ROTTERDAM

☎ 010 / pop 605,000

Rotterdam, Europe's largest port and the second-largest Dutch city, was bombed flat during WWII and spent the following decades rebuilding the harbour and the centre. The result is an architectural aesthetic that's unique in Europe. Today, Rotterdam has a crackling energy, with superb nightlife, a diverse, multiethnic community, an intensely interesting maritime tradition and a wealth of top-class museums. It also has a long-standing rivalry with Amsterdam, reflected in most aspects of culture. When local football team Feyenoord meets Ajax of Amsterdam, the fur *always* flies. And when Rotterdam unleashed its extreme form of techno, gabber, on the world in the early '90s, one of its most enduring targets was Amsterdam: an early gabber single was memorably titled 'Amsterdam, Waar Lech Dat Dan?' ('Amsterdam, Where the F*** is That?').

Orientation

Rotterdam, split by the vast Nieuwe Maas shipping channel, is crossed by a series of tunnels and bridges, notably the fabulously postmodern Erasmusbrug. The centre is on the north side of the water. Huge new neighbourhoods are rising to the south. From Centraal Station (CS), a 15-minute walk along the canal-like ponds leads to the waterfront. The commercial centre is to the east and most of the museums are to the west. The historic neighbourhood of Delfshaven is a further 3km west.

Information

The Rotterdam Card offers discounts in hotels and restaurants; it's €22.50/43.50 for

24/72 hours. The card is even available as a watch. Buy it from the tourist office.

EasyInternetCafé (www.easyeverything.com/map/rot; Stadhuisplein 16-18; per hr €3; 9am-11pm Mon-Sat, 11am-11pm Sun)

Post office (233 02 55; Coolsingel 42; 9am-6pm Mon-Wed & Fri, to 8.30pm Thu, 9.30am-3pm Sat)

Tourist office (271 01 28; www.rotterdam.info; Coolsingel 5; 9am-6pm Mon-Fri, to 5pm Sat & Sun) Free Internet.

Use-It (240 91 58; www.use-it.nl; Schaatsbaan 41-45; 9am-6pm Tue-Sun mid-May–mid-Sep, to 5pm Tue-Sat mid-Sep–mid-May) Ostensibly aimed at young travellers, but suitable for anyone who wants information that's more engaging and irreverent than the po-faced official tourist body. Also books accommodation with substantial discounts.

Sights & Activities

Museum Boijmans van Beuningen (441 94 00; www.boijmans.nl; Museumpark 18-20; adult/under 18 €8/free, free Wed; 11am-5pm Tue-Sun) is among Europe's very finest museums and has a permanent collection taking in Dutch and European art (Bosch, Van Eyck, Rembrandt, Tintoretto, Titian). There's an absorbing surrealist wing featuring ephemera, paraphernalia and famous works from Dalí, Duchamp, Magritte, Man Ray and more.

The **Nederlands Architectuur Instituut** (NAI; 440 12 00; www.nai.nl; Museumpark 25; 10am-5pm Tue-Sat, 11am-5pm Sun & holidays) offers an amazingly thorough overview of Dutch architecture. Exhibitions are revelatory, and a recent multimedia presentation devoted to the utopian genius Hendrik Wijdeveld was quite honestly mind-expanding. The NAI is a worthy monument in a city that celebrates built space like no other.

The **Historisch Museum Het Schielandhuis** (217 67 67; www.hmr.rotterdam.nl; Korte Hoogstraat 31; adult/child €3/1.50; 10am-5pm Tue-Fri, 11am-5pm Sat & Sun) is in one of the city's few surviving 17th-century buildings. Exhibits focus on everyday life through the ages, such as the (purportedly) oldest surviving wooden shoe. Clogs ahoy!

The **Kunsthal** (440 03 00; www.kunsthal.nl; Westzeedijk 341; adult/under 18 €8.50/3; 10am-5pm Tue-Sat, 11am-5pm Sun & holidays) hosts around 20 temporary exhibitions (including art and design) each year. As the publicity says, everything from 'elitist to popular' gets an airing.

At 185m, a shimmy up the **Euromast** (436 48 11; www.euromast.com; Parkhaven 20; adult/under 11 €8/5.50; 9.30am-11pm Apr-Sep, 10am-11pm Oct-Mar) is a must. It offers unparalleled 360-degree views of Rotterdam, with its rotating, glass-walled 'Euroscope' contraption ascending to near the summit, from where you'll fully appreciate just how mighty the harbour is. There's a luxury accommodation suite and the Panorama restaurant near the top. Book an abseiling session (€39.50).

The **Overblaak development** (1978–84), designed by Piet Blom, is near Blaak metro station. Marked by its pencil-shaped tower and upended, cube-shaped apartments, it seems plucked straight from the novels of JG Ballard. One apartment, the **Show Cube** (414 22 85; www.cubehouse.nl; adult/under 12 €2/1.50; 11am-5pm, closed Mon-Thu Jan & Feb), is open to the public.

Delfshaven was once the official seaport for the city of Delft. A reconstructed 18th-century **windmill** overlooks the water at Voorhaven 210, while the **Oude Kerk** on Voorhaven is where the Pilgrim Fathers prayed for the last time before leaving the city on 22 July 1620.

Spido (275 99 88; www.spido.nl; Willemsplein 85; adult/child €8.50/5.50; 9.30am-5pm Jun-Sep, 11am-3.30pm Oct, to 2pm Thu-Sun Nov-Mar) offers daily harbour tours.

Sleeping

Stayokay Rotterdam (436 57 63; www.stayokay.com/rotterdam; Rochussenstraat 107-109; dm from €20.50;) A typically well-run link in the Stayokay chain, the Rotterdam version is well placed for the museums and has a low-key bar. Reception is open until 1am.

Hotel Boat de Clipper (331 42 44; Scheepmakershaven; B&B from €30;) This 'botel', docked in Rotterdam's old harbour, is perfect for soaking up the city's maritime atmosphere, even if the quarters are, inevitably, a little cramped.

Hotel Amar (425 57 95; www.amarhotel.nl; Mathenesserlaan 316; s/d €30/50;) This friendly, small place is in a leafy neighbourhood close to the Museumplein and good shopping and nightlife. Rooms are simple but comfy, and the ones at the back overlook a large and peaceful garden.

Hotel Bazar (206 51 51; www.hotelbazar.nl; Witte de Withstraat 16; s/d from €60/75) Bazar is deservedly popular for its Middle Eastern–, African- and South American–themed rooms: lush, brocaded curtains, exotically

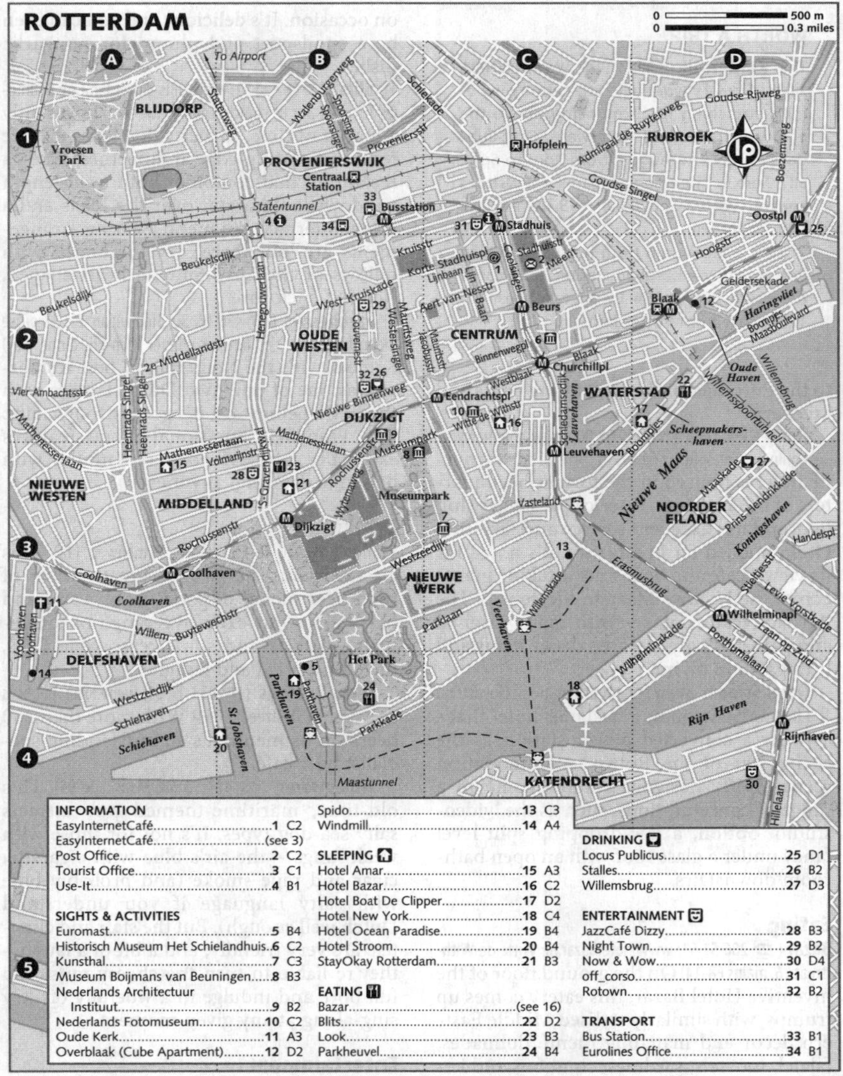

tiled bathrooms, comfy beds, and copies of *Tales from the Arabian Nights* scattered about. Breakfast is spectacular: Turkish breads, international cheeses, yogurt, fruit, cold cuts and coffee. An exceptional place to wind down, particularly as its ground-floor bar and restaurant (p855) is among the city's best.

Hotel Ocean Paradise (☎ 436 17 02; www.oceanparadise.nl; Parkhaven 21; s/d €68/88, with shared bathroom €58/68) Ocean Paradise is actually a floating hotel–Chinese restaurant–Asian supermarket pavilion; it looks like an aquatic temple. The rooms are naturally Eastern-themed and not too bad, although they get a little hot in summer. It's a nice part of town, next

WORTH A TRIP

The **Kinderdijk** (Child's Dike; www.kinderdijk.nl) features 19 working, 18th-century windmills stretching for 3km, rising above the empty marshes and waterways. On Saturdays in July and August from 2pm to 5pm, all 19 are in operation. One mill is a **visitors centre** (☎ 078-613 28 00; 9.30am-5.30pm Mon-Sat Apr-Sep).

Take a local train from Rotterdam CS to Rotterdam Lombardijen station, then catch the hourly bus No 154. By car, take the N210 12km east from Rotterdam.

to the Euromast and surrounding parks and greenery.

Hotel New York (☎ 439 05 00; www.hotelnewyork.nl; Koninginnenhoofd 1; r €98-220) The city's favourite hotel is housed in the former headquarters of the Holland-America passenger ship line, and has excellent service and facilities. Often booked far in advance, it's noted for its views, café and boat shuttle taking guests across the Nieuwe Maas to the centre. The Art Nouveau rooms – with many original and painstakingly restored décor items and fittings – are divine.

Hotel Stroom (www.stroomrotterdam.nl; Lloydstraat 1; d from €135) Stroom, a designer hotel that's actually a converted power station, is the rising star of the Rotto accommodation scene. Spiffy designer studios come in a range of configurations, such as the 'videostudio' option, a jaw-dropping split-level fancy under a glass roof with an open bathroom downstairs.

Eating

Bazar (☎ 206 51 51; www.hotelbazar.nl; Witte de Withstraat 16; mains €8-14) On the ground floor of the inventive Hotel Bazar, this eatery comes up trumps, with similarly stylised Middle Eastern décor and matching menu: dolmades, falafel, mussels, sardines, couscous and kebabs served up in tangy, attention-grabbing combinations.

Look (☎ 436 70 00; www.restaurantlook.nl; 's Gravendijkwal; mains €13-20; dinner Wed-Sun) This one's especially recommended for single people, Buffy and Francophiles. Look is a cosy little restaurant that specialises in garlic-based dishes: steamed garlic, fried garlic, garlic soup, garlic vegetables…even garlic dessert on occasion. It's delicious and you can even be a spoilsport and plump for nongarlic dishes.

Blits (☎ 282 90 51; www.blits-rotterdamt.nl; Boompjes 701; €18-30; lunch & dinner Tue-Sun) It was only a matter of time. In a city that loves diverse food and cutting-edge architecture, here's a restaurant that combines both: wall-length windows looking out over the Maas and a classy international menu. Seating arrangements are 'out there': try the bench with pillows or the Love Suite, a heart-shaped, rich red enclosure.

Parkheuvel (☎ 436 05 30; Heuvelaan 21; 3-course menu from €50; lunch & dinner Mon-Fri, dinner Sat) Some say it's the Netherlands' best restaurant; as one of only two Dutch fancies with three Michelin stars, it's got a strong claim. The French/International menu features especially fab seafood – red mullet with balsamic dressing, anyone?

Drinking

Stalles (☎ 436 16 55; Nieuwe Binnenweg 11a) This classic *bruin café* is on a great stretch of road near plenty of good shops, cafés and bars. It has an extensive range of single-malt whiskies and some reasonable food, including pizza and lasagne.

Locus Publicus (☎ 433 17 61; www.locus-publicus.com in Dutch; Oostzeedijk 364) With more than 200 beers on its menu, it's an outstanding specialist beer café.

Willemsbrug (☎ 413 58 68; Maaskade 95) This old-time, maritime-themed pub attracts salty sea-dog types. It's not for those with weak lungs – the air's blue with cigarette, cigar and pipe smoke (and probably blue with salty language if you understand Dutch well enough). But the staff and clientele are very friendly, and a bit of a laugh – they're liable to turn the cheesy music up full bore and indulge in a woefully off-key sing-along at any given moment.

Entertainment

Jazzcafé Dizzy (☎ 477 30 14; www.dizzy.nl in Dutch; 's-Gravendijkwal 129) Live music Tuesday nights and Sunday afternoons. The evening performances are scorching: everything from hot jazz to fast and funky Brazilian and salsa, with a very lively, sweaty crowd jumping out of their skins.

Now & Wow (☎ 477 10 74; www.now-wow.com; Maashaven 1) Many believe this to be Rotto's best club. It's a relaxed place, divided into two: Now for mainstream house, and Wow for funky beats. Theme nights with titles like Superbimbo say it all.

Rotown (☎ 436 26 69; www.rotown.nl in Dutch; Nieuwe Binnenweg 19) A smooth bar, a dependable live rock venue, an agreeable restaurant, a popular meeting place. The musical programme features new local talent, established international acts and crossover experiments.

off_corso (☎ 411 38 97; www.off-corso.nl in Dutch; Kruiskade 22) This is where it's at: bleeding-edge local and international DJs mashing up a high-fibre electronic diet of bleeps 'n' beats.

Night Town (☎ 436 12 10; www.nighttown.nl; West Kruiskade 26-28) This place is recommended for its fun kung-fu-sion mash-up: jazz, Latin, funk, and house.

Getting There & Away

Sample train fares: Amsterdam (€12.60, 62 minutes, four every hour), Den Haag (€4.10, 15 minutes, four every hour), and Utrecht (€8.60, 40 minutes, two every hour).

UTRECHT CITY

☎ 030 / pop 282,000

Utrecht is one of the Netherlands' oldest cities – not that you'd know it when you step off the train and find yourself lost in the maze that is the Hoog Catharijne shopping centre. The Hoog is huge…and it's attached to the station…and it seemingly goes on forever…and ever. But fight your way through and you'll emerge starry-eyed into a beautiful, vibrant, old-world city centre, ringed by striking 13th-century canal wharves. The wharves, well below street level, are unique to Utrecht and the streets alongside brim with chic shops, restaurants and cafés. The city's student community of 40,000 is the largest in the country – this is one very infectious place (in all senses of the term).

Information

Municipal library (☎ 286 18 00; Oudegracht 167; per hr €3; 🕒 10am-9pm Mon, 11am-6pm Tue-Fri, 10am-5pm Sat) Internet access.

Post office (Neude 11)

Tourist office (☎ 0900-128 87 32; www.utrecht-city.com; Vinkenburgstraat 19; 🕒 9.30am-6.30pm Mon-Wed & Fri, to 9pm Thu, to 5pm Sat) Get the free map with street index.

Sights

One of Utrecht's favourite sons, Dick Bruna, is honoured at the **Dick Bruna Huis** (☎ 236 23 61; www.dickbrunahuis.nl; Agnietenstraat 2; adult/under 17 €8/5; 🕒 11am-5pm Tue-Sun). Bruna is the creator of beloved cartoon rabbit Miffy and she naturally takes pride of place, along with an extensive overview of Bruna's career: the museum has everything from the book covers he designed for the family publishing company to a multimedia demonstration of his technique and philosophy. Obviously children will get a huge kick out of it all, but so will adults who simply appreciate superlative graphic design.

The **Museum Catharijneconvent** (☎ 231 72 96; www.catharijneconvent.nl; Nieuwegracht 63; adult/under 17 €7/5; 🕒 10am-5pm Tue-Fri, 11am-5pm Sat & Sun) has the finest collection of medieval religious art in the Netherlands, housed in a Gothic former convent and an 18th-century canal-side house.

The **Centraal Museum** (☎ 236 23 62; www.centraalmuseum.nl; Nicolaaskerkhof 10; adult/under 17 €8/5; 🕒 10am-5pm Tue-Sun) has a wide-ranging collection: applied arts dating back to the 17th century as well as paintings by some of the Utrecht School artists. There's even a 12th-century boat that was dug out of the local mud.

The **Domtoren** (Cathedral Tower; ☎ 233 30 36; www.domtoren.nl in Dutch; Domplein; adult/child €7.50/4; 🕒 10am-5pm Mon-Sat, noon-5pm Sun) is 112m high, with 465 steps. It's a tough haul to the top but well worth the exertion: the tower gives unbeatable city views. The guided tour in Dutch and English is detailed and gives privileged insight into this beautiful structure.

The tourist office can help with canal boat hire and tours.

Sleeping

Strowis Budget Hostel (☎ 238 02 80; Boothstraat 8; www.strowis.nl; dm from €14, r €55; 💻) This 17th-century building, run by a cluey group of ex-squatters, is near the town centre and has been lovingly restored and converted into a hostel. It's open 24 hours a day and has a cosy bar.

Park Hotel (☎ 251 67 12; Tolsteegsingel 34; s/d €52/65; 🅿) You'll sleep well in this comfy eight-room guesthouse occupying a canal house. It's not far from Utrecht's buzzing nightlife, and breakfast can be taken in the pretty garden out back.

NH Centre Utrecht Hotel (☎ 231 31 69; www.nh-hotels.com; Janskerkhof 10; r €120; P ⊠) This gorgeous hotel is housed in an atmospheric old building (1870). The rooms are very comfortable, with all the conveniences a business traveller would expect, and the views of the old church square are delectable. The suitably elegant Broers restaurant downstairs is an added bonus.

Eating & Drinking

Opium (☎ 231 55 15; www.restaurant-opium.nl; Voorstraat 80; mains €15-30; ⏰ dinner) This place will rock your socks off with Asian-fusion cooking that matches the gorgeous, Asian-fusion–minimalist interior – all fans, clean angles and plays of light. Softshell-crab tempura in sweet chilli sauce with spring onion and paprika gives you an idea of what's on offer.

Blauw (☎ 234 24 63; Springweg 64; set menu from €19; ⏰ dinner) Blauw has worked hard to make Indonesian food trendy in Utrecht – or at least popular. Quality's the key and the rice table, comprising 14 dishes, is a winner: young and old alike flock to scarf it down. The décor, a mix of nostalgia and uberhip minimalism, packs 'em in, too.

Goesting (☎ 273 33 46; www.restaurantgoesting.nl; Veeartsenijpad 150; mains €22-35; ⏰ dinner) Celebrities and wannabes flock to Goesting for fancies such as spit roast, Dutch asparagus, poached tournedos and 'tame duck' in a minimalist, high-society atmosphere.

Café Ledig Erf (☎ 231 75 77; Tolsteegbrug 3) This classy pub overlooks a confluence of canals at the southern tip of town. Patrons gather on tables around the oversized chessboards on the terrace, and it's always packed in warm weather.

Café Springhaver (☎ 231 37 89; www.springhaver.nl in Dutch; Springweg 50-52) This incredibly cosy bar next to the Springhaver Theater is a perfect spot to order a drink before the main feature, or just to pore over the daily news.

't Oude Pothuys (☎ 231 89 70; Oudegracht 279) Small and dark, this basement pub has nightly music – jam sessions with locals trying their hand at rock and jazz, but also touring pro bands.

Getting There & Away

Sample train fares: Amsterdam (€6.30, 35 minutes), Maastricht (€26, two hours) and Rotterdam (€8.60, 40 minutes).

THE DELTA REGION

The province of Zeeland (Sea Land) is three slivers of land nestling in the middle of a vast delta through which many of Europe's rivers drain; it dominates this peaceful corner of the Netherlands. As you survey the calm, flat landscape, consider that the region was home to two massive waterborne tragedies. In 1421 the St Elizabeth's Day flood killed more than 100,000 people; and in 1953, yet another flood laid waste to 2000 lives and 800km of dikes, leaving 500,000 homeless and leading to the Delta Project, among the world's greatest engineering feats (see the boxed text, opposite).

MIDDELBURG

☎ 0118 / pop 47,000

Middelburg, Zeeland's sleepy capital, is a friendly, low-key settlement: not exactly flush with nightlife, but perfect for exploring the region. There's no VVV but there is a **tourist shop** (☎ 67 43 00; www.touristshop.nl in Dutch; Markt 65c; ⏰ 9.30am-5pm Mon-Sat), and the **Zeeland Regional Library** (☎ 65 40 00; Kousteensedijk 7; Internet per hr €3; ⏰ 5.30-9pm Mon, 10am-9pm Tue-Fri, to 1pm Sat) has Internet access.

Sights

This pretty, airy little town is eminently suitable for walking, with cobblestones and snaking alleyways leading in and away from the town square, which hosts a famous market on Thursdays.

The sizable **Abdij** (☎ 61 35 96) complex dates from the 12th century and houses the regional government as well as three churches and two museums. Climb **Lange Jan** (€2.50), a 91m-high tower dating from the 14th century; the **Zeeuws Museum**, in the former monks dormitories, is closed until 2007 for refurbishment.

The **Stadhuis** (☎ 67 54 52; admission €2.50; ⏰ 11am-5pm Mon-Sat year-round, noon-5pm Sun Apr-Oct) grabs the eye: it's staggeringly beautiful. The Gothic side facing the Markt is from the 1400s, while the classical Noordstraat segment dates from the 1600s.

Sleeping & Eating

De Kaepstander (☎ 64 28 48; www.kaepstander.nl; Koorkerkhof 10; s/d with shared bathroom €38.50/65) It's got four rooms featuring B&B-style accom-

WORTH A TRIP

The disastrous 1953 flood was the impetus for the stupendous Delta Project, which began shortly after and was finished decades later – in 1986. The southwest river deltas were blocked using a network of dams, dikes and a remarkable 3.2km storm-surge barrier, which is lowered in rough conditions.

The **Waterland Neeltje Jans** (☎ 111 655 655; www.neeltjejans.nl; admission Nov-Mar €11, April-Oct €16; ⏲ 10am-5pm), located by the main surge barrier, is a terrific complex that explains the project in minute detail, with working models, hilarious public-service films from the '70s (complete with bad hair and funky soundtracks), and an exhilarating boat trip that takes you out onto the Oosterschelde for a panoramic view of the barriers and beyond. It's also possible to walk inside and around the barrier's pylons and see how the whole shebang works.

Bus No 104 stops at the Expo on its run between Rotterdam's Spijkenisse metro station (25 minutes from Rotterdam CS) and Vlissingen. The buses take about an hour from Rotterdam and 30 minutes from Middelburg and run every 30 minutes.

modation and a downstairs lounge and TV room for all guests. It's cosy and peaceful but best of all, it's next door to Jazz Eetcafé Desafinado.

Nieuwe Doelen (☎ 61 21 21; Loskade 3-7; r from €75) Simple rooms, pleasingly decorated. There's an enclosed garden, perfect for breakfast in fine weather.

Peper & Zout (Pepper & Salt; ☎ 62 70 58; www.peperenzout.com; Lange Noordstaat 8; mains €12-19) Peper & Zout has a casual yet elegant interior. The menu concentrates on fresh seafood, mainly various kinds of local fish. It's a popular place with a great wine list.

Jazz Eetcafé Desafinado (☎ 64 07 67; www.desafinado.nl; Koorkerkstraat 1; mains €13-20) It does exactly what it says on the tin: serves up hot jazz in steaming portions in wood-bound surroundings, with authentic jazz and blues on the stereo, old-time vinyl adorning the walls, and live jazz on Wednesday nights. The food's not too bad, although watch out for those little snail thingies they serve up as nibbles.

De Mug (Mosquito; ☎ 61 48 51; www.demug.nl in Dutch; Vlasmarkt 54-56; mains €16-21; ⏲ dinner Tue-Sat) Don't be fooled by the Heineken signs; the beer list is long and boasts many rare Trappist varieties. Also try the Mug Bitter, heavy on the hops. In the kitchen, De Mug has got quite the reputation for its trademark dishes prepared with unusual beers. The accommodation is clean and comforting.

Getting There & Away

Sample train fares: Amsterdam (€26.30, 2½ hours), Roosendaal (€10.40, 45 minutes) and Rotterdam (€17.50, 1½ hours).

THE NORTH & EAST

This region includes Friesland, which, once upon a time, incorporated regions of the Netherlands, northern Germany and Denmark until it became part of the united Netherlands. Frisians are determined to preserve their fiercely independent heritage – their anthem cheekily proclaims Friesland to be 'the best land on earth'. And though the Frisian language is similar to Dutch, pronunciation is entirely different. Apparently Frisian is the closest language to English, although English speakers will not understand it. As the Frisians themselves say: 'As milk is to cheese, are English and Frise.'

GRONINGEN CITY

☎ 050 / pop 177,300

It may be a long way from Amsterdam, but Groningen's a vibrant, youthful city, boasting all you'd expect of a progressive Dutch metropolis – it's 20,000-strong student population (which has been around since 1614 when the university opened) sees to that. There's also the requisite art museums, theatre and classical concerts, as well as gabled houses reflected in silent canals.

See the **tourist office** (☎ 0900-202 30 50; www.vvvgroningen.nl; Grote Markt 25; ⏲ 9am-6pm Mon-Fri, 10am-5pm Sat year-round, 11am-3pm Sun Jul & Aug) for more information. The **library** (☎ 368 36 83; Oude Boteringestraat 18; Internet per hr €2; ⏲ 1-8pm Mon, 10am-6pm Wed & Fri, to 8pm Thu, 11am-4pm Sat, 1-4pm Sun) has Net access.

Sights & Activities

The colourful, oddly shaped **Groninger Museum** (☎ 366 65 55; www.groninger-museum.nl; Museumeiland 1; adult/child €8/4; 🕑 10am-5pm Tue-Sun year-round, noon-5pm Mon Jul-Aug), occupying three islands in the middle of the canal in front of the station, hosts contemporary design and photography exhibitions alongside classic Golden Age Dutch paintings.

The **Noordelijk Scheepvaartmuseum** (Northern Shipping Museum; ☎ 312 22 02; www.noordelijkscheepvaartmuseum.nl; Brugstraat 24-26; adult/child €3/2; 🕑 10am-5pm Tue-Sat, 1-5pm Sun) is laid out over several floors of buildings that once comprised a 16th-century distillery. Highlights include an intricately carved replica of the church at Paramaribo – the capital of former Dutch colony Surinam – in a bottle (room three).

The 16th-century **Martinikerk** (☎ 311 12 77; Grote Markt; 🕑 11am-5pm Apr-Nov, noon-4pm Dec-Mar), at the northern corner of the Grote Markt, is eye catching. Its tower, the Martinitoren, is 96m tall and is considered to have one of the most finely balanced profiles in the country. A climb (€3; purchase ticket at tourist office) to the top yields awesome views.

When the tide retreats across the mudflats off the north coast of Groningen, locals and visitors alike attack it with abandon, marching, and inevitably sinking, into the sloppy mess, a pastime known as *wadlopen* (mud-walking).

The centre for *wadlopen* is the tiny village of **Pieterburen**, 22km north of Groningen, where several groups of trained guides are based. In Groningen, the following organisations can help: **Wadloopcentrum** (☎ 0595-52 83 00; www.wadlopen.org in Dutch; Hoofdstraat 105) and **Dijkstra's Wadlooptochten** (☎ 0595-52 83 45; www.wadloop-dijkstra.nl in Dutch; Hoofdstraat 118).

Sleeping

Hotel Garni Friesland (☎ 312 13 07; www.hotelfriesland.nl in Dutch; Kleine Pelsterstraat; s/d €35/50) The rooms here are just about as sparse as they come, but the price can't be beat and the location is central.

City Hotel (☎ 588 65 65; www.edenhotelgroup.com; Gedempte Kattendiep 25; r from €75; ⊠ 💻) These standard business rooms are a good bet for those requiring a few more creature comforts. There's a rooftop deck, free coffee and tea on every floor, free Internet, and a fine location.

Schimmelpenninck Huys (☎ 318 95 02; www.schimmelpenninckhuys.nl; Oosterstraat 53; d from €130; ⊠) The ground floor is occupied by a silver-service restaurant, pristine café and beautician. The rest of the building is filled with rooms ranging from simple, stylish standard doubles to suites with antique pieces and chandeliers.

Eating & Drinking

Goudkantoor (Gold Office; ☎ 589 18 88; Waagplein 1; mains €12-20) The architecture of this recently restored historical haunt is amazing. Dating from 1635, the 'Gold Office' features a gold-tinted exterior and graceful interior, complete with striking paintings. Oh, by the way, the food is quite good, too.

De 7e Hemel (Seventh Heaven; ☎ 314 51 41; Zuiderkerkstraat 7; mains €15-18; 🕑 dinner Tue-Sat) This is quality: De 7e Hemmel even imports Scottish mineral water direct from the Glens because of its purity. The ever-changing menu, a medley of vegan, vegetarian, fish and meat dishes, is a delight, and the cherubs, chandeliers and calming yellow shades all help to create a cosy, romantic air.

Brussels Lof (☎ 312 76 03; A-Kerkstraat 24; mains €17-22; 🕑 dinner Thu-Mon) This upmarket joint concentrates on seafood and vegetarian options, and leaves the fancy décor to the Gold Office. Mussels are a speciality and the service is top-notch.

Roezemoes (☎ 314 03 82; Gedempte Zuiderdiep 15) You can tell this gem of a *bruin café* has been around: the bullet holes from the 1672 invasion attempt are a dead giveaway. There's the occasional blues band.

Entertainment

Vera (☎ 313 46 81; www.vera-groningen.nl; Oosterstraat 44; 🕑 concerts Thu-Sat) Witness the future at this rock venue: Vera hosted a precorporate U2 before a crowd of 30-odd people in the early 1980s, while Nirvana played to a Vera audience of around 60 in the days before heroin chic.

Jazz Café de Spieghel (☎ 312 63 00; Peperstraat 11) This one's a perennial favourite, with regular live jazz music, a smooth, sultry atmosphere, and a great bar.

Getting There & Away

Sample train schedules: Amsterdam (€26.70, 140 minutes, two per hour), Leeuwarden (€8.30, 50 minutes, two per hour),

Rotterdam (€29.60, 160 minutes, two per hour) and Utrecht (€24.50, two hours, two per hour).

TEXEL

☎ 0222 / pop 13,500

Texel (*tes*-sel) is about 3km north off the coast of Noord Holland. It's remarkably diverse, with broad white beaches, lush nature reserves, forests and picture-book villages. Now 25km long and 9km wide, it consisted of two islands until 1835, when a spit of land to Eyerland Island was pumped dry. The island makes a superb getaway from the mainland rush, with beauty and isolation in abundance – except in mid-June, when spectators line the beaches for the largest catamaran race in the world, the Zwitserleven Round Texel Race (www.roundtexel.com).

Information

Get online at the **library** (Drijverstraat 7, Den Burg; per hr €3; ⏰ 2-5pm Tue-Fri, 10.30am-12.30pm Sat & Mon) and for free at the **tourist office** (☎ 31 47 41; www.texel.net; Emmalaan 66, Den Burg; ⏰ 9am-5.30pm Mon-Fri, to 5pm Sat).

Sights & Activities

Ecomare (☎ 31 77 41; www.ecomare.nl; Ruyslaan 92, De Koog; adult/child €8/5; ⏰ 9am-5pm) is chiefly a refuge for sick seals retrieved from the Waddenzee; rescued birds are the other main tenants. At the aquariums you can sidle up to sharks and even pat a sea skate, and there are seal feedings at 11am and 3pm.

Duinen van Texel National Park is a patchwork of varied dunescape running along the entire western coast of the island. Salt fens and heath alternate with velvety, grass-covered dunes. Much of the area is bird sanctuary and accessible only on foot.

Just near the windswept beach is **De Dennen**, a dark and leafy forest. Originally planted as a source of lumber, today it has an enchanting network of walking and cycling paths. In springtime the forest floor is carpeted with snowdrops first planted in the 1930s.

There are six museums on the island, covered by the **Texel Museum Combination Card** (adult/child €15/8.50) available from the tourist office.

The **Maritime & Beachcombers Museum** (☎ 31 49 56; Barentszstraat 21, Oudeschild; adult/child €4.50/3.50; ⏰ 10am-5pm Tue-Sat, noon-5pm Sun) has an extraordinary variety of junk recovered from sunken ships.

Texel's wonderful **beaches** are pristinely white and clean and include two nudist areas.

Contact the tourist office for information on cycling routes, hiking trails, boat trips, catamaran hire, pleasure flights and more.

Sleeping & Eating

Although Texel has an astounding 46,000 beds, book ahead, especially in July and August.

Hotel De 14 Sterren (☎ 32 26 81; www.14sterren.nl; Smitsweg 4, Den Burg; s/d €55/110; ⊠) On the edge of De Dennen forest, it has 14 rooms decorated in warm Mediterranean hues, most with a terrace or balcony with garden views. Its barn-house restaurant De Worsteltent is a great choice for lunch and/or dinner, with an extensive wine list alongside steak, fish and vegetarian dishes (mains €15 to €20).

Bij Jef (☎ 31 96 23; www.bijjef.nl; Herenstraat 34, Den Hoorn; s/d €72.50/90) Bij Jef is mainly known for sumptuous French-influenced cuisine (mains around €20), but also offers simple yet stylish rooms with bath, well-stocked minibar, countryside views and balconies.

Freya (☎ 32 16 86; Gravenstraat 4, Den Burg; set menu €23.50; ⏰ dinner Tue-Sat) This petite restaurant has a reputation for outstanding French and Dutch cuisine, so it's no surprise that reservations are highly recommended. The hosts are warm and welcoming, and while the place bubbles with energy, it has a decidedly romantic feel.

Getting There & Away

Trains from Amsterdam to Den Helder (€10.90, one hour) are met by a bus that connects with the **car ferry** (☎ 36 96 00; adult/child/car return €4/2/38; ⏰ 6.35am-9.35pm), which then makes the crossing in 20 minutes.

The ferry **De Vriendschap** (☎ 31 64 51; www.waddenveer.nl in Dutch; De Cocksdorp; adult/child return €20/13.50) makes the half-hour crossing from De Cocksdorp to car-free Vlieland, the nearest of the Wadden Islands.

AMELAND

☎ 0519 / pop 3600

Ameland, just 85 sq km, has four peaceful villages that are less developed than Texel's, but still provide enough social structure for travellers' needs. Large swaths of untouched natural splendour offer serenity and great cycling, but Mother Nature doesn't rule as she does on other Frisian islands.

Nes hosts Ameland's **tourist office** (☎ 54 65 46; www.ameland.nl in Dutch; Rixt van Doniastraat, Nes; 🕑 9am-12.30pm & 1.30-6pm Mon-Fri, 10am-3pm Sat), which has Internet access.

Sleeping

Stayokay Waddencentrum Ameland (☎ 55 53 53; ameland@stayokay.com; Oranjeweg 59; dm/s/d €25/45/66) Two hundred metres west of the lighthouse, with sand dunes on your doorstep. Meals, pack lunches and bicycles can be ordered.

Zeewinde (☎ 54 65 00; www.zeewinde.nl; Torenstraat 22, Nes; r from €75) Its rooms are neither large nor small, but do include a kitchenette and bathtub, a welcome relief after a day on a bike (which can be rented from reception).

Getting There & Around

Wagenborg (☎ 54 61 11; www.wpd.nl; adult/child return €11.50/6, bicycle/car €7.45/75.85) operates ferries between Nes and the port at Holwerd. Ferries (45 minutes) run almost every two hours year-round from 7.30am to 7.30pm.

From Leeuwarden, take bus No 66 (40 minutes, hourly) to Holwerd; a ticket covering this bus, the ferry and a bus ride on the island can be purchased at the Leeuwarden train station for €23.10.

HOGE VELUWE NATIONAL PARK

The **Hoge Veluwe** (☎ 0318-59 16 27; www.hogeveluwe.nl; adult/child €6/3, park & museum €12/6, car €6; 🕑 8am-8pm Apr, to 9pm May & Aug, to 10pm Jun & Jul, 9am-8pm Sep, to 7pm Oct, to 5.30pm Nov-Mar) is the Netherlands' largest national park, a mix of forests and woods, shifting sands and heathery moors, along with red deer, wild boar and mouflon (wild sheep). It also features the world-class **Kröller-Müller Museum** (☎ 0318-59 12 41; www.kmm.nl; Houtkampweg 6; adult/under 12 €5/2.50; 🕑 10am-5pm Tue-Sun & public holidays), with a Van Gogh collection and works by Picasso, Renoir and Manet.

From Arnhem, take bus No 2 (direction: Deelevy OC) to the Schaarsbergen entrance and on to the Kröller-Müller Museum. The first bus leaves at 10.10am (April to October) and there are three more through the day (one per hour in July and August). From Apeldoorn, bus No 110 leaves the station every hour from 8.42am to 4.42pm.

THE SOUTHEAST

The Dutch Southeast includes Noord Brabant, the country's largest province, primarily a land of agriculture and industry peppered with a few pleasant towns including Den Bosch. The long and narrow Limburg province is home to Maastricht, contender for the title of Finest Dutch City, as well as – wait for it – hills.

DEN BOSCH

☎ 073 / pop 134,000

This sweet old town has a top-notch church, a good museum, outstanding cafés and restaurants, and atmospheric streets. The official name is 's-Hertogenbosch (Duke's Forest), but everyone calls it Den Bosch (den *boss*). It's also the birthplace of 15th-century painter Hieronymous Bosch, and the protosurrealist is honoured with a statue in front of the town hall. The **tourist office** (☎ 0900-112 23 34; www.regio-vvv.nl; Markt 77; 🕑 1-6pm Mon, 9.30am-6pm Tue-Fri, 9am-5pm Sat) can tell you all this and more.

Sights

St Janskathedraal (☎ 613 03 14; www.sint-jan.nl in Dutch; Choorstraat 1; admission €3.50; 🕑 10am-4.30pm Mon-Sat, 1-4.30pm Sun), one of the finest Gothic churches in the Netherlands, took from 1336 to 1550 to complete.

The **Noordbrabants Museum** (☎ 687 78 77; www.noordbrabantsmuseum.nl in Dutch; Verwersstraat 41; adult/child €6.50/3.50; 🕑 10am-5pm Tue-Fri, noon-5pm Sat), in the former governor's residence, features exhibits about Brabant life and art, as well as some works by Bosch.

The tourist office can arrange boat trips around Den Bosch's canals.

Sleeping

Hotel Terminus (☎ 613 06 66; fax 613 07 26; Boschveldweg 15; s/d €31/60) These simple, brightly coloured rooms are decent enough, plus there's an appealing bar (well, they call it a 'folk pub') and regular live folk music.

Hotel Euro (☎ 613 77 77; www.eurohotel-denbosch.com; Hinthamerstraat 63; s/d from €65/85) This business hotel is part of a chain but it's still got a certain degree of warmth, even if the rooms are draped in chintzy corporate pastels. The location is central and next to a warren of great cafés and eating houses.

Eating & Drinking

Restaurant Nescio (☎ 6100900; www.nescio-restaurant.nl; Hinthammerstraat 80; dishes from €4; ⏰ dinner) Nescio only serves appetisers, the idea being that taste is emphasised via concentrated, small portions, and to sample several experiences is preferable to having just one main one. Try fancies such as 'preserved Oriental duck bolts' or ask the chef for a 'wild card': tell him your boundaries (no bull's penises, for example) and let him surprise you.

De Truffel (☎ 614 27 42; www.detruffel.com; Kruisstraat 37; mains €10-25; ⏰ dinner) In a restored warehouse, De Truffel serves top-notch Mediterranean food in a relaxed atmosphere. Get a load of this: roasted complete trout with browned almonds and a stuffed potato. Now that's attention to detail you just don't see everywhere.

Café 't Bonte Palet (☎ 613 25 32; Hinthamerstraat 97) Talk about quirky: the front window of this little hole-in-the-wall bar is stuffed with all kinds of trinkets including miniature carillons, toy cars, tiny theatrical sets, and, the crowning glory, an Asterix triptych. There's sometimes live music.

Getting There & Away

Sample train fares: Amsterdam (€12.70, one hour), Maastricht (€18, 1½ hours) and Utrecht (€7.50, 30 minutes).

MAASTRICHT

☎ 043 / pop 122,000

Make no bones about it: Maastricht is utterly beautiful. A stunner. The crown jewel of the south – of maybe the entire country. About as far from windmills, clogs and tulips as you'd want. Much of the Netherlands has a 'samey' feel to it, but here there are Spanish and Roman ruins, cosmopolitan food, French and Belgian twists in the architecture and a shrugging off of the shackles of Dutch restraint. Even the landscape's different: there are actually hilly streets and what passes for mountains ringing the centre.

Information

Centre Ceramique Library (☎ 350 56 00; Ave Céramique 50; Internet access free; ⏰ 10.30am-8.30pm Tue & Thu, 10.30am-5pm Wed & Fri, 10am-5pm Sat, 1-5pm Sun)

Grand Net Internet Café (81 Boschstraat; per hr €3)

Tourist office (☎ 325 21 21; www.vvvmaastricht.nl; Kleine Straat 1; ⏰ 9am-6pm Mon-Fri, to 5pm Sat, 11am-3pm Sun)

Sights & Activities

The **Bonnefantenmuseum** (☎ 3290190; www.bonnefantenmuseum.nl; Ave Céramique 250; adult/under 12 €7/3.50; ⏰ 11am-5pm Tue-Sun) features a 28m tower that houses various exhibits, always fun and provocative. Old masters and medieval sculpture are on one floor, contemporary art by Limburg artists are on the next, and temporary exhibitions are revelatory, such as the recent 'Travellin' Light' focus on Dada lineages. From 2006 until 2008, while Amsterdam's Rijksmuseum is undergoing renovation, the Bonnefantenmuseum will display Rijksmuseum classics from the southern Netherlands, Antwerp and Bruges.

The 16th-century **Spanish Government Museum** (☎ 321 13 27; www.museumspaansgouvernement.nl in Dutch; Vrijthof 18; admission €2.50; ⏰ 1-5pm Wed-Sun) is where Philip II outlawed his former lieutenant Willem the Silent at the start of the Eighty Years' War. The exhibits feature statues and 17th-century paintings.

Much of Maastricht is riddled with defensive tunnels dug into the soft sandstone over the centuries. The best place to see the tunnels is **Sint Pietersberg**, a Roman fort 2km south of Helpoort. This is a beautiful area, pastoral and peaceful; the fort is an arresting sight peeking over the hillside.

The Romans built tunnels throughout the hills over a period of 2000 years; at one stage, they even extended under the Netherlands–Belgium border. The tourist office leads spooky, thrilling and highly educational **cave tours** (☎ 321 78 78; per person €3; ⏰ tours 3.30pm Jul, Aug & school holidays) – this experience is highly recommended. Although tours are supposed to be in Dutch, ask for Kitty, an extremely knowledgeable, English-speaking guide.

The tourist office can arrange all manner of walking tours, cycling expeditions, and boat cruises on the Maas.

Sleeping

Botel Maastricht (☎ 321 90 23; Maasboulevard 95; s/d €37/58; 💻) Two barges lashed together make up the Botel; the smaller vessel acts as an exemplary deck for beer drinking when the sun's out. Inside, rooms are narrow and portholed for that sea-dog feel, but comfy

enough (assuming you like to suck on your knees at night). There's a beaut little ship-shape bar inside.

Maison Du Chêne (☎ 321 35 23; www.maastrichthotel.com; Boschstraat 104; s/d from €40/58) In an elegant 1855 building, the rooms here are very clean and the brasserie on the ground floor is classy. Beware: it's right on the Markt, which can make for a noisy Friday or Saturday night. Ask for rooms at the back.

Matuchi (☎ 354 06 92; Kleine Gracht 34; s/d €50/65) These rooms, above the hip bar of the same name (opposite), are elegant, minimalist and stylish, and surprisingly large for the price. All include flat-screen TVs.

Hotel la Colombe (☎ 321 57 74; www.hotellacolombe.nl; Markt 30; s/d €61/80) Also on the Markt, Hotel la Colombe is housed in a simple, white building.

Kruisherenhotel Maastricht (☎ 329 20 20, www.chateauhotels.nl; Kruisherengang 19-23; s/d from €85/145; 💻) This stunning option is housed inside the former Crutched Friar monastery complex dating from 1483. They call it a 'designer hotel', but the past hasn't been overwhelmed. Where there are modern touches like moulded furniture and padded walls, they accent the historical surrounds. The rooms feature flat-screen TVs and wall-length paintings. Sumptuous.

Eating

Take Five (☎ 321 09 71; Bredestraat 14; lunch €6, dinner from €12) Situated on a quiet street parallel to the cramped terraces of heaving Platielstraat, Take Five combines fusion cooking with a stark interior, chill-out music and engaging staff. On many nights there's live jazz.

Ginger (☎ 326 00 22; Tongersestraat 7; mains €10-20) Supersmooth and healthy Asian noodle soups come to Maastricht. And Ginger's the place to get them. Fabulous fresh ingredients in a serene and wonderful contemporary setting.

Mestizo (☎ 327 08 74; www.mestizo.nl; Bredestraat 18; mains €12-19) Need a break from French and Dutch cuisine? Try Mestizo, a very inspired Latin restaurant serving up terrific Spanish and Mexican food. Now, exactly who among us can resist marinated lamb steaks roasted with garlic and chilli? Well, vegetarians, obviously – but there's a reasonable selection for them, too.

Restaurant O (☎ 325 97 47; www.restaurant-o.nl; Rechtstraat 76; mains €18-21) Mmmm…this (mainly) seafood restaurant wins us over with striking, stylish décor, and ever-present, ever-tasty aquatic meals. Lobster soup with mussels and shrimps, anyone? Pan-roasted moonfish? There's even a separate *fruits de mer* (seafood) menu – grand! Fresh and delightful.

Beluga (☎ 321 33 64; www.rest-beluga.com; Plein 1992; 3-course meals from €45; lunch Tue-Fri, dinner Tue-Sat) With two Michelin stars, Beluga leads the pack. This sleek, angular, elegant designer restaurant on the Maas features excellent service and Frenchified cuisine that never fails to impress with its attention to detail. Picture lightly steamed sole with pan-fried langoustines and pommes à la tsarine filled with caviar, butter asparagus and a sour cream and black pepper sauce.

Drinking

Take One (☎ 321 64 23; www.takeonebiercafe.nl in Dutch; Rechtstraat 28) Cramped and narrow from the outside, this 1930s tavern is like Dr Who's Tardis: inside there's well over 100 beers from the most obscure parts of the Benelux. It's run by a husband-and-wife team who organise beer tastings and refer to their customers as 'victims'. Relax: they'll willingly help you select the beer most appropriate to your tastes.

Matuchi (☎ 354 06 92; Kleine Gracht 34) It bills itself as an 'Orient Style Lab', but it's a bit more than that: there's a dash of *A Clockwork Orange* in the interior design, mixed with *de rigueur* Arabian themes. All in all, a hot joint in which to have a cool drink.

Getting There & Away

Sample train fares: Amsterdam (€26.70, 155 minutes, hourly), Rotterdam (€25.70, 140 minutes, two per hour) and Utrecht (€23.10, two hours, hourly).

THE NETHERLANDS DIRECTORY

ACCOMMODATION

Always book accommodation ahead, especially during high season; note that many visitors choose to stay in Amsterdam even if travelling elsewhere. The tourist offices operate booking services; when booking for two, make it clear whether you want two single (twin) beds or a double bed.

In cities you should expect to pay under €50 for a double room in a budget hotel, up to €125 in a midrange hotel and from €125 for the top end. Prices are higher in Amsterdam.

Many Dutch hotels have steep stairs but no lifts, although most top-end and some midrange hotels are exceptions.

Accommodation in B&Bs is mostly found in the country – local tourist offices keep a list of B&Bs on file.

In this chapter, breakfast is included in rates unless otherwise specified, as are private bathrooms.

Lists of camping grounds are available from the tourist offices. Expect to pay roughly €8 to €20 for two people and a tent overnight, plus €3 to €6 for a car. The camping grounds have plenty of caravan hook-ups.

Stayokay (☎ 020-501 31 33; www.stayokay.com) is the Dutch hostelling association. A youth hostel card costs €15 at the hostels; non-members pay an extra €2.50 per night and after six nights you're a member. The usual HI discounts apply.

ACTIVITIES

Cycling, skating, windsurfing, sailing, boating and hanging out at the beach are popular Dutch pastimes. Check the tourist offices for further information.

BUSINESS HOURS

The working week starts around lunch time on Monday. For the rest of the week most shops open at 8.30am or 9am and close at 5.30pm or 6pm, except Thursday when many close at 9pm, and on Saturday when they close at 5pm. In Amsterdam and tourist centres you will find many shops open on Sunday. In major centres, supermarkets often have extended trading hours.

Banks are generally open 9am to 4pm or 5pm weekdays. Many museums close on Monday. Post offices open 9am to 5pm weekdays and 10am to 1pm Saturday.

Restaurants are usually open from 11am to 2.30pm or 3pm for lunch, and 5.30pm to 10pm or 11pm for dinner. Most bars open by 11am and close between midnight and 2am. Nightclubs tend to open at 9pm or 10pm and close at 3am or 4am.

In this chapter we have listed opening hours only when they deviate from these standard opening times.

DANGERS & ANNOYANCES

The Netherlands is a safe country, but be sensible all the same: watch for pickpockets in crowded areas, don't leave valuables in cars and *always* lock your bike. Never buy drugs on the street: you'll get ripped off or mugged. And don't light up joints just anywhere – stick to coffee shops.

DISCOUNT CARDS

Available from the museums themselves, a *Museumkaart* gives access to 400 museums across the country for €30 (€17 for under twenty-fives).

The **Cultureel Jongeren Paspoort** (Cultural Youth Passport, CJP; www.cjp.nl; €12.50), available from tourist offices, gives people aged under 27 discounts to museums and cultural events around the country.

EMBASSIES & CONSULATES

Dutch Embassies & Consulates

Australia (☎ 02-6220 9400; www.netherlands.org.au/index.html; 120 Empire Circuit, Canberra, ACT 2600)
Belgium (☎ 02-679 17 11; www.nederlandseambassade.be in Dutch & French; ave Herrmann-Debroux 48, Brussels 1160)
Canada (☎ 613-237 50 30; www.netherlandsembassy.ca; Suite 2020, 350 Albert St, Ottawa, Ont K1R 1A4)
Germany (☎ 030-20 95 60; www.dutchembassy.de in Dutch & German; Friedrichstrasse 95, Berlin, 10117)
New Zealand (☎ 04-471 6390; www.netherlandsembassy.co.nz; Investment House, cnr Ballance & Featherston Sts, Wellington)
UK (☎ 020-7590 3200; www.netherlands-embassy.org.uk; 38 Hyde Park Gate, London SW7 5DP)
USA (☎ 202-244 5300; www.netherlands-embassy.org; 4200 Linnean Ave NW, Washington, DC 20008)

Embassies & Consulates in the Netherlands

In Amsterdam:
France (☎ 530 69 69; www.ambafrance.nl; Vijzelgracht 2)
Germany (☎ 574 77 00; Honthorststraat 36-8)
Italy (☎ 550 20 50; www.italy.nl; Vijzelstraat 79)
Spain (☎ 620 38 11; Frederiksplein 34)
UK (☎ 676 43 43; www.britain.nl; Koningslaan 44)
USA (☎ 575 53 09; http://netherlands.usembassy.gov; Museumplein 19)

In Den Haag:
Australia (☎ 070-310 82 00; Carnegielaan 4)
Belgium (Map p864; ☎ 312 34 56; www.diplomatie.be/thehague; Alexanderveld 97)
Canada (☎ 070-311 16 00; Sophialaan 7)
Denmark (☎ 070-302 59 59; Koninginnegracht 30)
France (Map p864; ☎ 312 58 00; www.ambafrance.nl; Smidsplein 1)
India (☎ 070-346 97 71; Buitenrustweg 2)
Ireland (☎ 070-363 09 93; Dr Kuyperstraat 9)
Israel (☎ 070-376 05 00; Buitenhof 47)
Japan (☎ 070-346 95 44; Tobias Asserlaan 2)
New Zealand (☎ 070-346 93 24; Carnegielaan10-IV)
Norway (☎ 070-311 76 11; Lange Vijverberg 11)
UK (Map p864; ☎ 070-427 04 27; www.britain.nl; Lange Voorhout 10)
USA (Map p864; ☎ 070-310 22 09; http://thehague.usembassy.gov; Lange Voorhout 102)

FESTIVALS & EVENTS

February/March

Carnaval Celebrated with greater vigour in Maastricht than anywhere else in Europe, save Venice (Italy) and Sitges (Spain). The orgy of partying and carousing begins the Friday before Shrove Tuesday and lasts until the last person collapses some time on the following Wednesday.
TEFAF Maastricht Art & Antiques Show (www.tefaf.com) Held annually in mid-March.

April

Amsterdam Fantastic Film Festival (www.afff.nl) European and international fantasy, horror and science fiction movies held in late April.
Koninginnedag (Queen's Day) On 30 April it's celebrated countrywide, but especially so in Amsterdam, which becomes awash in orange costumes and fake afros, beer,

balloon animals, beer, dope, Red Bull, beer, leather boys, skater dikes, temporary roller coasters, clogs, clothes horses, fashion victims, grannies and grandpas…

May

Herdenkingsdag & Bevrijdingsdag (Remembrance Day and Liberation Day) Held 4–5 May.

Nationale Molendag (National Windmill Day) On the second Saturday in May, nearly every working windmill in the country opens its doors to visitors.

June

Holland Festival (www.hollandfestival.nl) For all of June the country's biggest music, drama and dance extravaganza centres on Amsterdam. Highbrow and pretentious meet lowbrow and silly.

July

North Sea Jazz Festival (www.northseajazz.nl) The world's largest jazz festival, now held in Rotterdam in mid-July.

August

Gay Pride Canal Parade First Saturday.

FFWD Heineken Dance Parade (www.ffwdheinekendanceparade.nl in Dutch) Rotterdam goes sick, mate, inna urban funky techno stylee in mid-August.

Uitmarkt (www.uitmarkt.nl in Dutch) The reopening of Amsterdam's cultural season for three days in late August.

September

Robodock (www.robodock.org) A full-on, extraordinary festival held in late September that blends technology and art. Humans and robots enact mixed-media performance art and theatre events with pyrotechnics, explosions, live music and projections.

November

Sinterklaas Intocht The Dutch Santa Claus arrives 'from Spain' with his staff in mid-November.

December

Sinterklaas On 5 December, families exchange small gifts ahead of Christmas religious celebrations.

HOLIDAYS

Public Holidays

Nieuwjaarsdag New Year's Day.
Goede Vrijdag Good Friday.
Eerste Paasdag Easter Sunday.
Tweede Paasdag Easter Monday.
Koninginnedag (Queen's Day) 30 April.
Bevrijdingsdag (Liberation Day) 5 May.
Hemelvaartsdag Ascension Day.
Eerste Pinksterdag Whit Sunday (Pentecost).
Tweede Pinksterdag Whit Monday.
Eerste Kerstdag (Christmas Day) 25 December.
Tweede Kerstdag (Boxing Day) 26 December.

School Holidays

Spring Holiday Two weeks in mid-February.
May Holiday First week of the month.
Summer Holiday July, August and sometimes the first few days of September.
Autumn Holiday Second half of October.
Christmas Holiday Two weeks through the first full week of January.

LEGAL MATTERS

The Dutch fuzz are helpful, with a sense of humour. One of their leaflets urges foreigners to seek help if they find themselves in trouble, like falling into a canal stoned: 'Don't be embarrassed,' they say, 'we've seen it all before.' They can hold you for six hours for questioning if you break the law.

Drugs are actually illegal in the Netherlands. Possession of soft drugs up to 5g is tolerated but larger amounts can get you jailed. Hard drugs are treated as a serious crime.

MONEY

ATMs

Automatic teller machines can be found outside most banks, at airports and at most train stations. Credit cards such as Visa and MasterCard/Eurocard are widely accepted, as are cash cards that access the Cirrus network.

Credit Cards

Report lost or stolen cards to the following 24-hour numbers:

Amex (☎ 020-504 80 00, 020-504 86 66)
Diners Club (☎ 020-654 55 11)
Eurocard & MasterCard (☎ 030-283 55 55)
Visa (☎ 020-660 06 11)

Moneychangers

Avoid the private exchange booths dotted around tourist areas. Banks and the Postbank (at post offices) stick to official exchange rates and charge a sensible commission, as does the **GWK** (☎ 0900-05 66; www.gwk.nl).

Travellers Cheques

Banks charge a commission to cash travellers cheques (with ID such as a passport).

THE NETHERLANDS

Thomas Cook and Amex don't charge commission on their own cheques but their rates might be less favourable. Shops, restaurants and hotels always prefer cash; a few might accept travellers cheques but their rates will be anybody's guess.

POST

Post offices are generally open 9am to 5pm weekdays and 10am to 1pm Saturday. Poste restante is best handled in Amsterdam.

TELEPHONE

Most public phones will accept credit cards as well as various phonecards. The official KPN-Telecom public phone boxes charge €0.10 per 20 seconds for national calls. The cost of international calls varies depending on the destination, and will change frequently as a result of competition. Ringing a mobile number costs about €0.55 per minute from a public phone. Many public phones accept credit cards, although cards issued outside of the Netherlands or Europe may require extra steps during dialling or may not work at all.

Mobile Phones

The Netherlands uses GSM 900/1800, compatible with the rest of Europe and Australia but not with the North American GSM 1900 (some convertible phones work in both places). Prepaid mobile phones are available at mobile-phone shops starting from around €40 on special.

Phone Codes

To ring abroad, dial ☎ 00 followed by the country code for your target country, the area code (you usually drop the leading 0 if there is one) and the subscriber number. The country code for calling the Netherlands is ☎ 31 and the area code for Amsterdam is ☎ 020; again, drop the leading 0 if you're calling from outside the Netherlands. Do not dial the city code if you are in the area covered by it.

Phonecards

For public telephones, cards are available at post offices, train station counters, VVV and GWK offices and tobacco shops for €5, €10 and €20. The KPN Hi card is the most common but other brands are muscling in – T-Mobile, Orange, Vodafone, Belnet etc – with superior rates. Train stations have Telfort phone booths that require a Telfort card (available at GWK offices or ticket counters), although there should be KPN booths nearby.

> **EMERGENCY NUMBERS**
>
> - Ambulance ☎ 112
> - Fire ☎ 112
> - Police ☎ 112

VISAS

Travellers from Australia, Canada, Israel, Japan, New Zealand, the USA and many other countries need only a valid passport (no visa) for a stay of up to three months. European Union nationals can enter for three months with just their national identity card or a passport expired for no more than five years. Nationals of most other countries need a so-called Schengen visa, valid for 90 days within a six-month period. Visa extensions are handled by the **Immigratie en Naturalisatiedienst** (Immigration & Naturalisation Service; ☎ 0900-123 45 61; www.ind.nl; Postbus 30125,2500 GC Den Haag).

TRANSPORT IN THE NETHERLANDS

GETTING THERE & AWAY

Air

Schiphol airport (AMS; ☎ 0900-01 41; www.schiphol.nl) is the Netherlands' main international airport. **Rotterdam airport** (RTM; ☎ 010 446 34 44; www.rotterdam-airport.nl) is much smaller.

The following airlines have offices in Amsterdam:

Air France (code AF; ☎ 654 57 20; www.airfrance.nl)
British Airways (code BA; ☎ 346 95 59; www.britishairways.com)
British Midland (code BD; ☎ 1332 854 321; www.flybmi.com)
Cathay Pacific (code CX; ☎ 653 20 10; www.cathaypacific.com)
easyJet (code EZY; ☎ 023-568 48 80; www.easyjet.com)
KLM (code WA; ☎ 474 77 47; www.klm.nl)
Lufthansa (code IH; ☎ 582 94 56; www.lufthansa.com)
Northwest Airlines (code WH; ☎ 474 77 47; www.nwa.com)

Qantas (code QF; ☎ 569 82 83; www.qantas.com.au)
Ryanair (code FR; ☎ 0900-2022184; www.ryanair.com)
Transavia (code HV; ☎ 406 04 06; www.transavia.nl)
United Airlines (code UA; ☎ 201 37 08; www.unitedairlines.nl)

Land

BUS

The most extensive European bus network is maintained by **Eurolines** (UK ☎ 08705 143219; www.eurolines.com). It offers a variety of passes with prices that vary by time of year.

Busabout (UK ☎ 020-7950 1661; www.busabout.com) is a UK-based budget alternative. It runs coaches on circuits in Continental Europe including one through Amsterdam; passes are available for two weeks, and for three weeks to three months. Services to/from Amsterdam run from April to October.

Gullivers Reisen (Berlin ☎ 030-3110 2110; www.gullivers.de in German) links Berlin to Amsterdam.

CAR & MOTORCYCLE

You'll need the vehicle's registration papers, third party insurance and an international drivers permit in addition to your domestic licence. The **ANWB** (☎ 673 08 44; Museumplein 5; Amsterdam) provides a range of information and services if you show a letter of introduction from your automobile association.

TRAIN

The Netherlands has good train links to Germany, Belgium and France. All Eurail, Inter-Rail, Europass and Flexipass tickets are valid on the Dutch national train service, **Nederlandse Spoorwegen** (Netherlands Railway, NS; international inquiries ☎ 0900-9296; www.ns.nl).

Major Dutch train stations have international ticket offices and, in peak periods, it's wise to reserve seats in advance. You can buy tickets on local trains to Belgium and Germany at normal ticket counters.

GETTING AROUND

Air

Domestic commercial flights link Schiphol to Eindhoven and Maastricht airports, chiefly used by business passengers transferring to international flights at Schiphol; flights are relatively expensive.

Bicycle

The Netherlands has 20,000km of cycling paths. The **ANWB** (☎ 673 08 44; Museumplein 5) publishes cycling maps for each province, and tourist offices have numerous routes and suggestions. Major roads have separate bike lanes, and, except for motorways, there's virtually nowhere bicycles can't go. You'll often need legs like tree trunks to combat the North Sea headwinds.

More than 100 stations throughout the country have bicycle facilities for rental, protected parking, repair and sales. To hire, in most cases you'll need to show your passport and leave an imprint of your credit card or a deposit. Private operators charge €6 to €8 per day, and €30 to €35 per week. Train station hire shops may be slightly cheaper.

Boat

Ferries connect the mainland with the five Frisian Islands. Other ferries span the Westerschelde in the south of Zeeland, providing road links to the bit of the Netherlands south of here as well as to Belgium. These are popular with people using the Zeebrugge ferry terminal and run frequently year-round. There is also a frequent ferry service on the IJsselmeer linking Enkhuizen with Stavoren and Urk. You'll also find a few small river ferries providing crossings for remote stretches of the IJssel and other rivers.

Renting a boat is a popular way to tour the many rivers, lakes and inland seas. Boats come in all shapes and sizes, from canoes to motorboats to small sailing boats to large and historic former cargo sloops. Prices vary widely, and there are hundreds of rental firms throughout the country.

Bus & Tram

Buses are used for regional transport rather than for long distances. The national *Strippenkaart* (strip card) is used on most regional buses and trams. The fares are zone-based – in most towns you punch two strips (one for the journey and one for the zone), with an additional strip for each additional zone. In the central areas of cities and towns, you usually will only need to stamp two strips – the minimum fee. A 15-strip card costs €6.70 and is available at tobacco shops, post offices, train-station counters, bookshops and newsagencies.

Plans are afoot to phase out the *Strippenkaart* by the end of 2007 and replace it with chip cards. At the time of research information was thin on the ground, but the cards will work like debit cards: money can be loaded onto them, then used to validate travel on buses, trams and metro. For more information, consult a tourist office or train station ticketing office. The authorities were also working on phasing out coin-operated ticket machines and luggage lockers at train stations, but apparently you will still be able to ask a human for service.

Car & Motorcycle

DRIVING LICENCE

You'll need to show a valid driving licence when hiring a car in the Netherlands. Visitors from outside the EU will also need an international driving permit (IDP). Car-rental firms will rarely ask for one, but the police might do so if they pull you up.

HIRE

Outside Amsterdam, the car-hire companies can be in inconvenient locations if you're arriving by train. You must be at least 23 years of age to hire a car in the Netherlands. Some car-hire firms levy a small surcharge for drivers under 25. Most will ask either for a deposit or a credit-card imprint as a guarantee of payment.

INSURANCE

When hiring a car we strongly recommend you take out collision damage waiver (CDW), an insurance policy that limits your financial liability for damage. Note that at most car-rental firms, CDW does not cover the first €500 to €1000 of damages incurred, so you're liable for this amount.

ROAD RULES

Traffic travels on the right and the minimum driving age is 18 for vehicles and 16 for motorcycles. Seat belts are required and children under 12 must ride in the back if there's room. Trams always have the right of way and if turning right, bikes have priority. At roundabouts approaching vehicles have right of way, but in practice they yield to vehicles already travelling on the roundabout.

Speed limits are 50km/h in built-up areas, 80km/h in the country, 100km/h on major through-roads, and 120km/h on freeways (sometimes 100km/h, clearly indicated). The blood-alcohol limit when driving is 0.05%.

Train

The train network is run by **Nederlandse Spoorwegen** (☎ national inquiries 0900-9296; www.ns.nl). Trains have 1st-class sections but they're hardly different from the 2nd-class areas.

Tickets can be bought at the window (for an extra €0.50 for one ticket, €1 for two or more) or from ticket machines. At the machine, check your destination and enter its code. Choose 1st/2nd class, then *zonder/met korting* (without/with discount), and finally *vandaag geldig/zonder datum* (valid today/without date). 'Without date' is for travel on another day; stamp the ticket in a yellow gadget near the platforms.

Consider a one-year Voordeel-Urenkaart (€55) for a 40% discount on travel weekdays after 9am, on weekends and public holidays, and all of July and August. The discount applies to up to three people on the same trip, as well as up to 65% cheaper evening returns from 6pm.

Portugal

Portugal is a quieter, calmer place than its exuberant neighbour, Spain. But it's far from dull. Thanks to the country's relative geographic isolation, Portugal has retained a strong and fascinating sense of identity and culture. In rural areas you still see women carrying shopping on their heads and, despite the increase in tourism, there are relatively few Tinseltown-style attractions and anonymous hotel chains. More importantly, the coffee is still some of the best in Europe and it's not served in Styrofoam with cinnamon on top.

The economic base is still very traditional, relying largely on fishing, wine and textiles. The flip side is that although EU funding has vastly improved the infrastructure, Portugal is still a relatively poor country. At least Portugal's brand new president is good at arithmetic; ex-economist Cavaco Silva has vowed to work with PM Sócrates in making sweeping social, economic and educational reforms. Gulp. Let's hope he leaves the architecture and landscape well alone; this country is pure holiday-brochure cliché, with ancient stone villages, proud historic cities, and coastal resorts that still look more like seafaring towns than glitzville-by-the-sea. Portugal is a bargain for travellers as well. You will find your euro goes a lot further here than elsewhere in Western Europe.

FAST FACTS

- **Area** 92,389 sq km
- **Capital** Lisbon
- **Currency** euro (€);A$1 = €0.60; ¥100 = €0.67; NZ$1 = €0.50; UK£1 = €1.48; US$1 = €0.78
- **Famous for** *fado*(songs), football, port, *azulejos* (tiles), salted cod
- **Official language** Portuguese
- **Phrases** *bom dia* (hello), *obrigado/a* (thank you), *desculpe* (excuse me), *adeus* (goodbye), *faz favor* (please)
- **Population** 10.4 million
- **Telephone codes** international access code ☎ 00; country code ☎ 34; reverse-charge code ☎ 120

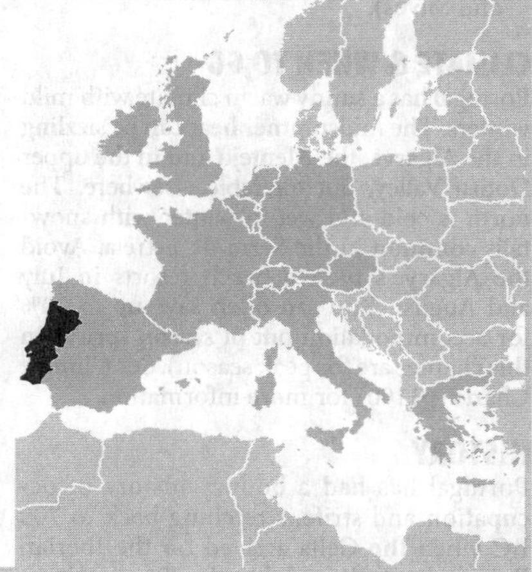

PORTUGAL

HIGHLIGHTS

- Stroll around elegant and evocative **Sintra** (p900), the traditional summer resort of Portuguese kings, studded with fabulous palaces, villas and gardens.
- Step into a medieval film set and explore the tangle of narrow alleys and steep streets of Lisbon's **Alfama district** (p893).
- Don your colour-coordinated lycra wetsuit and pick up the pace by **windsurfing** (p907) in the rugged southwestern tip of the country.
- Browse through the Moorish-inspired backstreets of **Coimbra** (p911) university town, ducking into a *tasca* (small neighbourhood tavern) for a beer and student-priced snack.
- Conquer the trails of the wild and beautiful **Parque Nacional da Peneda-Gerês** (p920).

HOW MUCH?

- **Short black coffee** €0.60
- **Underground parking** €1 per hour
- **Herald Tribune newspaper** €2.50
- **Custard tart** €0.70
- **Budget hotel room** €35

LONELY PLANET INDEX

- **1L unleaded petrol** €1.27
- **1L bottled water** €0.45
- **Beer** €1
- **Souvenir T-shirt** €6-10
- **Sandwich** €1.75

ITINERARIES

- **One week** Devote three days to Lisbon, including a night of *fado* (songs) in the Alfama and a trip to Belém. Then sidestep for a day in sumptuous Sintra. Carry on to Porto for two days, enjoying the tipple at the port lodges across the river. Wind up your week with a day in Óbidos, so pretty it was a royal wedding gift.
- **Two weeks** The same as for one week, plus two days in Unesco-listed Évora followed by a day in magical hilltop Monsaraz. Next, hit the road south to the Algarve (including a day each in Tavira, Lagos and Silves).

CLIMATE & WHEN TO GO

Portugal has a sunny warm climate with mild winters. The midsummer heat can be sizzling in the Algarve, the Alentejo and in the upper Douro Valley, but tolerable elsewhere. The north is cold and wet in winter with snowfalls common in the Serra da Estrela. Avoid the Algarve's packed beach resorts in July and August. You can often save up to 50% for accommodation out of season (prices in this chapter are for peak season). See Climate Charts (p1100) for more information.

HISTORY

Portugal has had a bouncy history of occupation and strife, stretching back to 700 BC when the Celts arrived on the Iberian Peninsula, followed by the Phoenicians, Greeks, Romans and Visigoths.

In the 8th century the Moors conquered Portugal. Arabic words filtered into the language and, today, their influence is evident in the culture, architecture and dark features of the people, particularly in the Algarve where the Moors established their capital in Silves. After the Christian conquest, new trade routes were discovered in the 15th century, creating an empire that extended to four continents and launched Lisbon as the wealthiest city in Europe. Portugal's Gothic-style Manueline architecture dates from this time. This period of opulence was short-lived; in 1580 Spain occupied the Portuguese throne for 90 years, and their imperial momentum was lost forever.

In 1755 a massive earthquake tragically destroyed most of Lisbon, followed around 50 years later by Napoleon's thwarted invasion, which further weakened the country. A period of civil war and political mayhem ensued, culminating in the abolition of the monarchy in 1910 and the founding of a democratic republic.

A 1926 military coup set the stage for the dictatorship of António de Oliveira Salazar until his death in 1970. Discontent with his regime and a ruinous war in Africa led to a peaceful military coup on 25 April 1974.

The subsequent granting of independence to Portugal's African colonies produced a flood of nearly a million refugees into the country. Their influence is reflected in the music and food, especially in Lisbon and Porto.

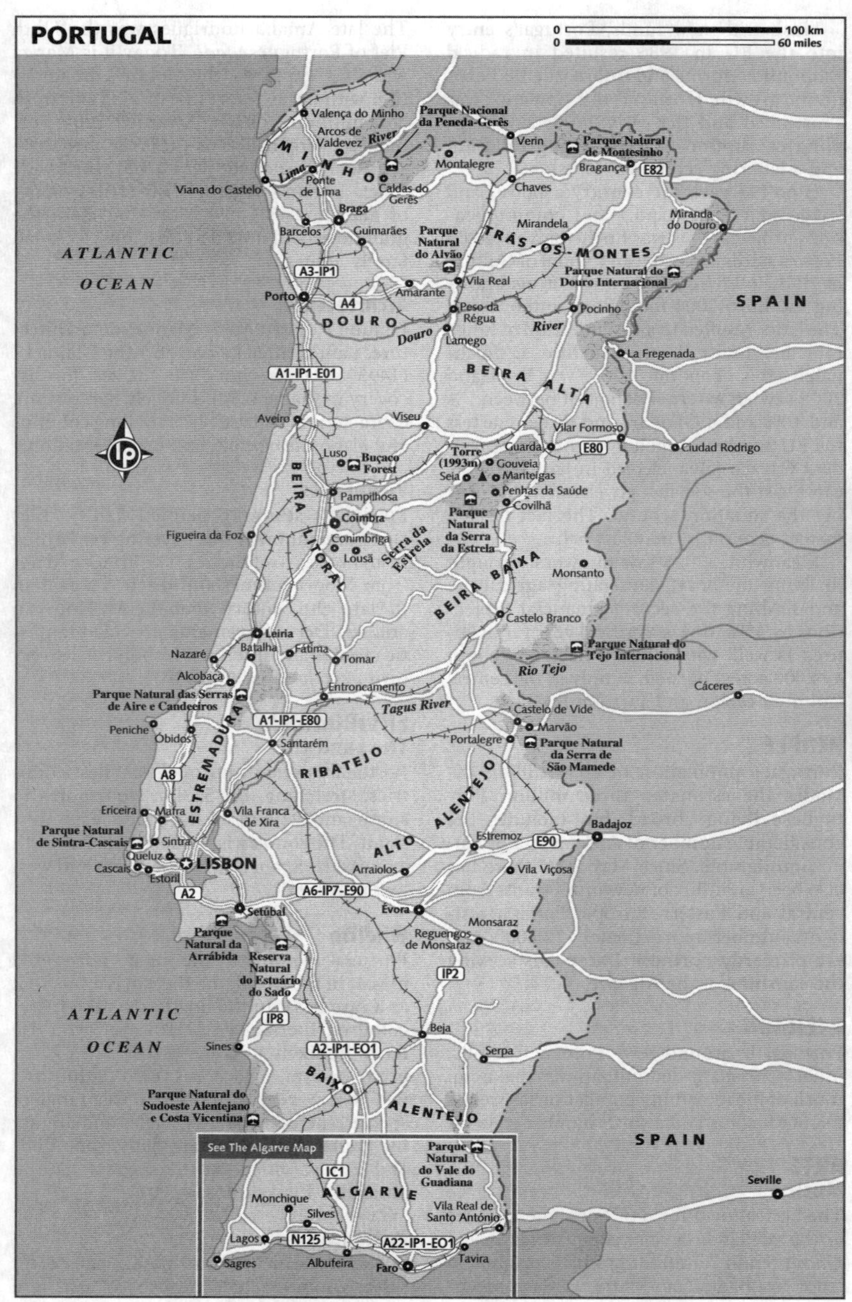
PORTUGAL
0 100 km
0 60 miles
ATLANTIC OCEAN
SPAIN
Valença do Minho
Parque Nacional da Peneda-Gerês
Arcos de Valdevez
River
Lima
MINHO
Verin
Parque Natural de Montesinho
Montalegre
Bragança
E82
Viana do Castelo
Ponte de Lima
Caldas do Gerês
Chaves
Braga
Barcelos
Guimarães
Parque Natural do Alvão
Mirandela
Miranda do Douro
TRÁS-OS-MONTES
A3-IP1
Parque Natural do Douro Internacional
Vila Real
Amarante
Porto
A4
Peso da Régua
Pocinho
DOURO
Douro
River
Lamego
La Fregenada
A1-IP1-E01
BEIRA ALTA
Aveiro
Viseu
Vilar Formoso
Guarda
E80
Ciudad Rodrigo
Luso
Buçaco Forest
Torre (1993m)
Gouveia
Seia
Manteigas
BEIRA LITORAL
Penhas da Saúde
Pampilhosa
Covilhã
Parque Natural da Serra da Estrela
Coimbra
Figueira da Foz
Conimbriga
Lousã
Serra da Estrela
BEIRA BAIXA
Monsanto
Castelo Branco
Leiria
Batalha
Nazaré
Fátima
Tomar
Parque Natural do Tejo Internacional
Alcobaça
Rio Tejo
Parque Natural das Serras de Aire e Candeeiros
Entroncamento
Cáceres
Tagus River
Castelo de Vide
A1-IP1-E80
Marvão
Peniche
Óbidos
Santarém
Portalegre
Parque Natural da Serra de São Mamede
RIBATEJO
ESTREMADURA
A8
ALENTEJO
Ericeira
Mafra
Vila Franca de Xira
Badajoz
Parque Natural de Sintra-Cascais
Sintra
ALTO
Estremoz
E90
Queluz
LISBON
Cascais
Estoril
Arraiolos
Vila Viçosa
A2
A6-IP7-E90
Setúbal
Évora
Parque Natural da Arrábida
Monsaraz
Reguengos de Monsaraz
Reserva Natural do Estuário do Sado
IP2
IP8
Beja
Sines
A2-IP1-EO1
Serpa
BAIXO ALENTEJO
Parque Natural do Sudoeste Alentejano e Costa Vicentina
See The Algarve Map
Parque Natural do Vale do Guadiana
IC1
ALGARVE
Seville
Monchique
Silves
Vila Real de Santo António
Lagos
N125
A22-IP1-EO1
Tavira
Sagres
Albufeira
Faro

Flush with new funds, Portugal's entry into the EU in 1986 resulted in radical economic reforms and unprecedented economic growth. However, this opulence was short-lived and the early 1990s saw crippling corruption charges, rising inflation and a faltering economy recession.

Expo '98 gave the country a boost, and triggered vast transport and communications projects. This was further advanced by Porto's status as European Capital of Culture in 2001, followed in 2004 by Portugal hosting the Euro 2004 football championships. The latter resulted in a vast injection of funds into the country's infrastructure. Unfortunately, this economic surge was brief and 2005 saw an external deficit of between 7% and 10% and a GDP around three-quarters the EU average. Hopefully right-wing president Cavaco Silva, elected in January 2006, can assist the socialist government in turning the situation around. The fact he is a former economist may just help.

Meanwhile, 2005 saw the worst drought in living memory, devastating agriculture and slashing the sector's financial projections by 35%. It was a critical year for bushfires as well, with 200,000 hectares (about 494,000 acres) burned, mainly in the central Coimbra region and surrounds.

PEOPLE

Portugal's population of 10.4 million excludes the estimated three million Portuguese living abroad, but includes the considerable number of African and Brazilian immigrants. Since May 2004 there has also been an influx of new immigrants from central and Eastern Europe. Foreign residents number approximately 225,000, and are primarily northern Europeans seeking the sunshine of the Algarve.

RELIGION

Portugal is around 95% Roman Catholic; other Christian denominations make up much of the remaining population, as well as many Muslims and a small number of Jews.

ARTS

Music

The best-known form of Portuguese music is the melancholy, nostalgic songs called *fado* (literally 'fate') said to have originated from troubadour and African slave songs. The late Amália Rodrigues was the Edith Piaf of Portuguese *fado*. Today it is Mariza who has captured the public's imagination with her extraordinary voice and fresh contemporary image. Awarded 2004 Portuguese Personality of the Year, her 2005 release *Transparente* was a big worldwide seller. Lisbon's Alfama district has plenty of *fado* houses (p898), ranging from the grandiose and tourist-conscious to small family affairs.

Architecture

Unique to Portugal is Manueline architecture, named after its patron King Manuel I (1495–1521). It symbolises the zest for discovery of that era and is hugely flamboyant, characterised by fantastic spiralling columns and elaborate carving and ornamentation.

Visual Arts

Portugal's stunning painted *azulejo* tiles coat contemporary life, covering everything from houses to churches. The art form dates from Moorish times and reached a peak in the late 19th century when the Art Nouveau and Art Deco movements provided fantastic façades and interiors. Lisbon has its very own *azulejo* museum (p893).

ENVIRONMENT

The Land

Portugal is one of Europe's smallest countries, stretching just 563km from north to south and 220km at its widest east–west point. The country is bordered on the north and east by Spain and on the south and west by the Atlantic.

Wildlife

Portugal is home to the most endangered big cat in the world, the Iberian lynx, as well as a rare beast in the dog family, the rusty-coloured Iberian wolf. However, you are far more likely to come across foxes, deer, otters or even wild boars. Bird enthusiasts will be kept very happy with a vast range of species, including storks, eagles and among the wetland species, flamingos, spoonbills and egrets, which can be seen in natural parks like Ria Formosa (p903).

National Parks

Portugal has 25 natural parks, nature reserves and protected landscape areas. These areas total approximately 6500 sq km – just over 7% of Portugal's land area. There are 13 World Heritage Sites in Portugal. Check them out on the Web at http://whc.unesco.org.

Environmental Issues

Portugal has been suffering from its worst drought in decades with devastating losses to livestock and agriculture. In many parts of the country, January 2005 was the driest January in more than 100 years. Travellers are urged to be prudent in hotels: don't send your towels for a daily wash and take showers, never a bath. Continuing on a watery theme, the criticism concerning the 2002 Alqueva dam near Beja continues. To create the dam, Europe's largest artificial lake, over a million oak and olive trees were cut down and some 160 rocks covered with Stone Age drawings were submerged. On a more positive note, Portugal has fast come up to speed in the recycling department with colour-coded receptacles in every town and city.

FOOD & DRINK

In the larger towns and cities in this chapter, restaurants are divided into budget (€2 to €7), midrange (€8 to €12) and top end (€13 to €20) for the average price of a main dish.

Staples & Specialities

Portuguese cuisine is home-style cooking rather than *haute cuisine*. Seafood is the national favourite, especially *caldeirada* (seafood stew), *sardinhas assadas* (grilled sardines) and the omnipresent *bacalhau* (dried cod), reputedly prepared in some 365 ways.

Meat dishes can be a letdown; consider going for the splurge with *leitão* (roast suckling pig). Chicken is best when barbecued and *piri-piri* (chilli) sauce livens up the simplest dish.

Diet-defying cafés and *pastelarias* (pastry shops) are everywhere in Portugal and offer splendid desserts and cakes.

Portuguese coffee is excellent in even the grungiest bar. A small black espresso is known as a *bica* in the south and elsewhere simply as a *café*. Half coffee, half milk is *café com leite*. Local *cerveja* (beer) includes Sagres in the south and Super Bock in the north.

Portuguese *vinho* (wine) offers excellent value in all its varieties: *tinto* (red), *branco* (white) and *vinho verde* (semi-sparkling young), which is usually white. Restaurants often serve drinkable *vino da casa* (house wine) for as little as €2.50 per 350ml jug. Port, synonymous with Portugal, is produced in the Douro Valley to the east of Porto.

Where to Eat & Drink

The line between snacks and meals is blurred. For full meals try a *tasca*, a *restaurante cervejaria* (bar-restaurant) or a *marisqueira* (seafood restaurant). Lunch time typically lasts from noon to 3pm, and evening meals from 7pm to 10.30pm.

The *prato do dia* (dish of the day) is often a bargain, as is the *ementa turistica* (tourist menu). Be very wary of the *couvert* (the bread, cheese, butter, olives and other titbits at the start of a meal): they cost extra. You can send them back without causing offence. All restaurants in this chapter are open daily for lunch (noon to 3pm) and dinner (7pm to 10pm) unless otherwise noted.

Vegetarians & Vegans

The typical Portuguese menu is tough on vegetarians, although the ubiquitous *sopa de legumes* (vegetable soup) is often included as a starter, together with the inevitable *salada* (salad). In general, the only other option (for vegetarians) is an *omeleta simple* (plain omelette) or the marginally more exciting *omeleta com queijo* (cheese omelette). Vegans have an even tougher time, although Chinese restaurants are fairly common and always have plenty of meat- and dairy-free options.

LISBON

pop 720,000

Lisbon has a seductive melancholy charm and is more like a large town than a capital city. It's small enough to walk or, if you're all blistered out, you can always hop on one of the vintage street trams that shudder up and down the hills. The city is a heady mix of crumbling pastel-coloured houses, grand squares and a maze of narrow lanes and alleys. Spread over seven hills on the Rio Tejo

LISBON

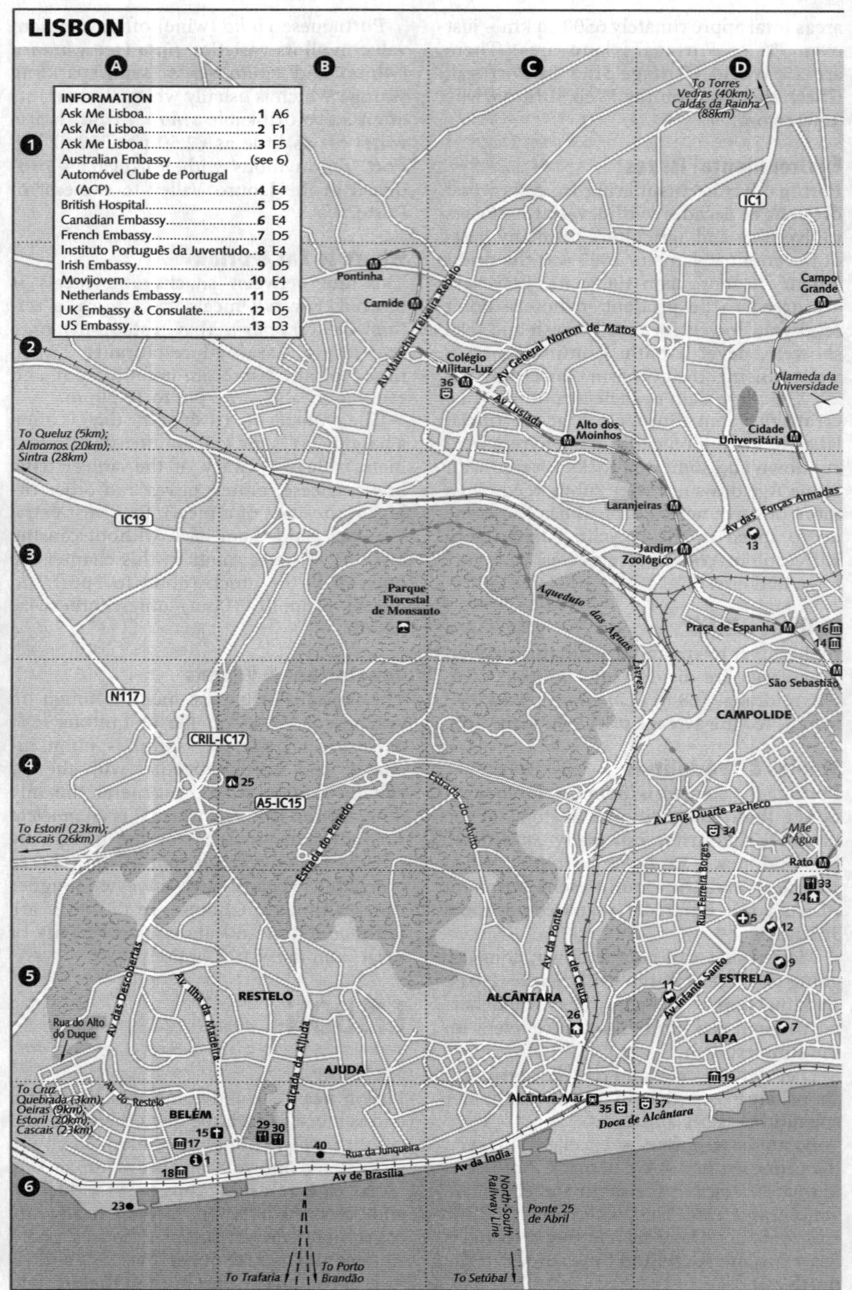

PORTUGAL

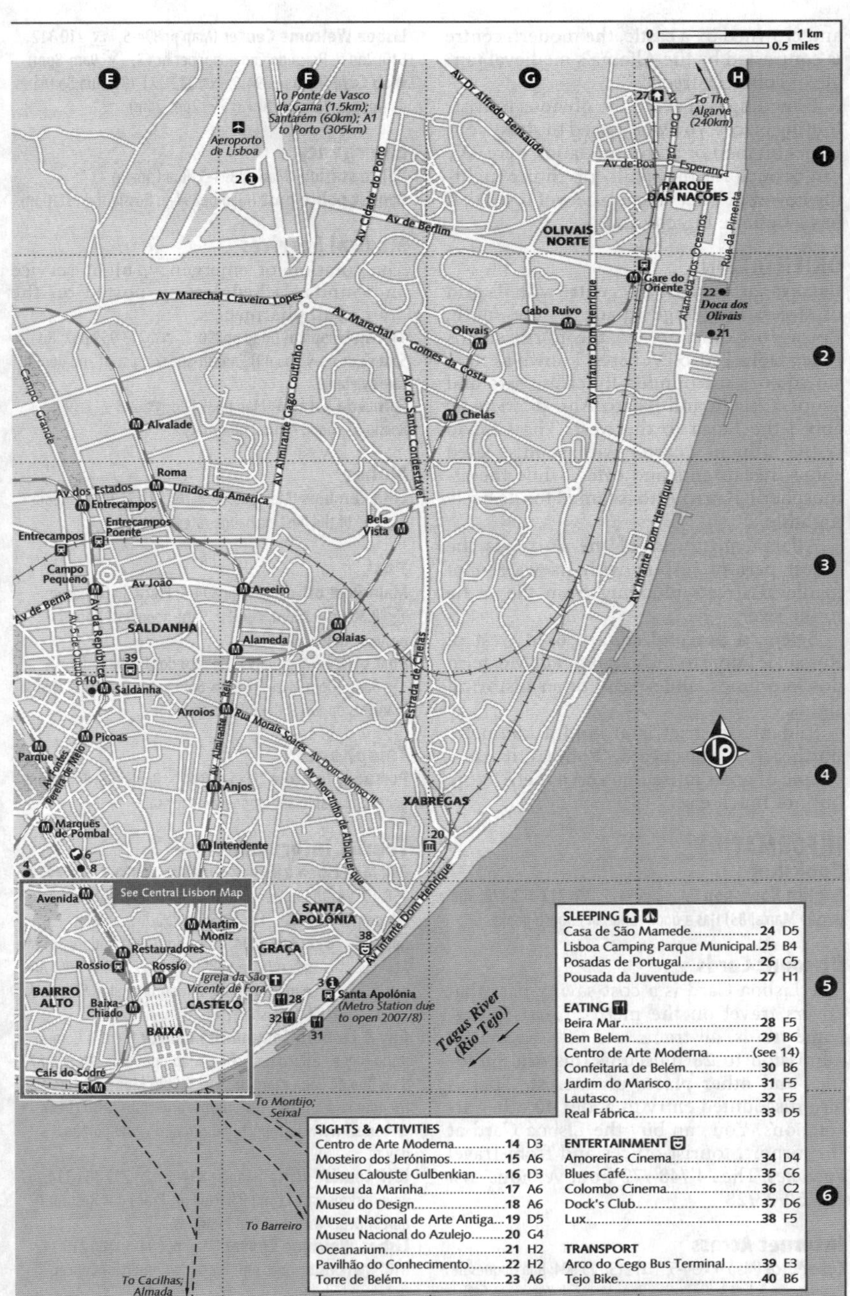
0 1 km
0 0.5 miles
E
F
G
H
1
2
3
4
5
6
To Ponte de Vasco da Gama (1.5km); Santarém (60km); A1 to Porto (305km)
Aeroporto de Lisboa
2
Av Dr Alfredo Bensaúde
27
To The Algarve (240km)
Av Dom João
Av de Boa Esperança
PARQUE DAS NAÇÕES
Rua da Pimenta
Alameda dos Oceanos
Av Cidade do Porto
Av de Berlim
OLIVAIS NORTE
Gare do Oriente
22
Doca dos Olivais
21
Av Marechal Craveiro Lopes
Av Marechal Gomes da Costa
Cabo Ruivo
Olivais
Av Infante Dom Henrique
Campo Grande
Av Almirante Gago Coutinho
Av do Santo Condestável
Chelas
Alvalade
Roma
Av dos Estados Unidos da América
Entrecampos
Entrecampos Poente
Bela Vista
Campo Pequeno
Av João
Areeiro
Av de Berna
Av da República
Av 5 de Outubro
SALDANHA
Alameda
Olaias
39
10
Saldanha
Arroios
Rua Morais Soares
Av Almirante Reis
Estrada de Chelas
Picoas
Parque
Av Fontes Pereira de Melo
Av Dom Afonso III
Av Mouzinho de Albuquerque
Anjos
XABREGAS
Marquês de Pombal
6
8
4
Intendente
20
See Central Lisbon Map
Avenida
Martim Moniz
Restauradores
Rossio
BAIRRO ALTO
Baixa-Chiado
BAIXA
CASTELO
Cais do Sodré
SANTA APOLÓNIA
GRAÇA
38
Igreja da São Vicente de Fora
3
Santa Apolónia
(Metro Station due to open 2007/8)
28
32
31
Tagus River (Rio Tejo)
To Montijo; Seixal
To Barreiro
To Cacilhas; Almada
SIGHTS & ACTIVITIES
Centro de Arte Moderna.......14 D3
Mosteiro dos Jerónimos.......15 A6
Museu Calouste Gulbenkian.......16 D3
Museu da Marinha.......17 A6
Museu do Design.......18 A6
Museu Nacional de Arte Antiga.......19 D5
Museu Nacional do Azulejo.......20 G4
Oceanarium.......21 H2
Pavilhão do Conhecimento.......22 H2
Torre de Belém.......23 A6
SLEEPING
Casa de São Mamede.......24 D5
Lisboa Camping Parque Municipal.......25 B4
Posadas de Portugal.......26 C5
Pousada da Juventude.......27 H1
EATING
Beira Mar.......28 F5
Bem Belem.......29 B6
Centro de Arte Moderna.......(see 14)
Confeitaria de Belém.......30 B6
Jardim do Marisco.......31 F5
Lautasco.......32 F5
Real Fábrica.......33 D5
ENTERTAINMENT
Amoreiras Cinema.......34 D4
Blues Café.......35 C6
Colombo Cinema.......36 C2
Dock's Club.......37 D6
Lux.......38 F5
TRANSPORT
Arco do Cego Bus Terminal.......39 E3
Tejo Bike.......40 B6

and crowned by a castle, the modern centre is contrasted by the Alfama's medieval tangle of cobbled streets.

Providing you avoid the obvious tourist-touting places, you won't need to stress your wallet on food or accommodation here. We can't vouch for the spoilt-for-choice nightlife however. That is one aspect of town that has a definite big-city buzz.

ORIENTATION

Baixa is the modern city centre with its grid of streets and huge square to the south, Praça do Comércio. To the north stands Praça Dom Pedro IV, better known as Rossio square, surrounded by cafés, bars and shops. Chiado and Bairro Alto districts lie above the Baixa to the west. The Chiado is the affluent quarter with sophisticated shops, restaurants and cafés, while the atmospheric Bairro Alto is famed for its lively nightlife.

Alfama, northeast of the Baixa, is the oldest part of Lisbon with its warren of medieval streets plunging from the castle to the river.

Belém, a peaceful suburb 6km west of Rossio, is home to the magnificent Mosteiro dos Jerónimos, and several other historical sights.

Saldanha district is around a kilometre northeast of Marquês de Pombal; it has a couple of great museums and a metro stop, but not much else.

INFORMATION

Bookshops

English Bookshop (Map pp894-5; ☎ 213 428 472; Rua de São Marçal 83) Has a good range of English books.

Discount Cards

The Lisboa Card is a cost-saving pass that covers travel on the metro, Carris buses, some trains, all trams and lifts, as well as admission to 28 museums, historic buildings and other places of interest. There's also discounted entry to about 40 other attractions. You can buy the Lisboa Card at the airport, tourist offices and from travel agencies. The 24-/48-/72-hour versions cost €13.50/23/28.

Internet Access

Cyber Bica (Map pp894-5; ☎ 213 225 004; Rua Duques de Bragança; per hr €3; 🕑 noon-2am Mon-Fri, 7pm-2am Sat)

Lisboa Welcome Center (Map pp894-5; ☎ 210 312 810; 2nd fl, Praça do Comércio; per hr €3; 🕑 9am-8pm)

Web Café (Map pp894-5; ☎ 213 421 181; Rua do Diário de Notícias 126; per hr €3; 🕑 2pm-2am)

Emergency

Police station (Map pp894-5; Rua Capelo)

Tourist police post (Map pp894-5; Rossia train station)

Medical Services

The rotation of emergency, night service and Sunday schedules are posted on the door of all pharmacies.

British Hospital (Map pp890-1; ☎ 213 955 067; Rua Saraiva de Carvalho 49) English-speaking staff and dental care available.

Farmácia Estácio (Map pp894-5; ☎ 213 211 390; Rossio 62) Good central pharmacy.

Money

Cota Câmbios (Map pp894-5; ☎ 213 220 470; Rossio 41) One of the best exchange rates in town.

Post

Main Post office (Map pp894-5; Praça do Comércio; 🕑 8.30am-6.30pm Mon-Fri, 9am-noon Sat) Handles poste restante collection.

Post office (Map pp894-5; Praça dos Restauradores; 🕑 8am-10pm Mon-Fri, 9am-6pm Sat & Sun) This second branch is opposite the ICEP tourist office.

Telephone

Portugal Telecom (Map pp894-5; Rossio 68) Telephone booths available and phonecards for sale.

Tourist Information

Ask Me Lisboa kiosks Belém (Map pp890-1; ☎ 213 658 435) At the entrance to the monastery; Lisbon airport (Map pp890-1; ☎ 218 450 660); Palácio Foz (Map pp894-5; ☎ 213 463 314; Praça dos Restauradores); Santa Apolónia train station (Map pp890-1; ☎ 218 821 606) All kiosks have free maps and the bimonthly guide *Follow Me Lisboa,* and sell the Lisboa Card.

Gay & Lesbian Community Center (Centro Comunitário Gay e Lésbico de Lisboa; Map pp894-5; ☎ 218 873 918; Rua de São Lazaro 88; 🕑 5-9pm Mon-Sat) Has gay-friendly info on bars, restaurants and clubs. Also check websites: www.ilga-portugal.org and www.portugal gay.pt.

ICEP tourist office (Map pp894-5; ☎ 213 463 314; www.askmelisboa.com; Palácio Foz, Praça dos Restauradores) Deals with national inquiries.

Lisboa Welcome Center (Map pp894-5; ☎ 210 312 810; www.visitlisboa.com; Praça do Comércio) Concentrates on Lisbon.

SIGHTS

Lisbon has an enviable roll call of sights that can be explored by foot. Alternatively, hop on the funicular, tram or metro. Admission is usually half-price for children, students and seniors, and free for everyone on Sundays.

Alfama

This ancient district resembles a medieval blockbuster set with its moody maze of twisted alleys and steeply slanted streets. The terrace at **Largo das Portas do Sol** provides *the* souvenir snapshot of the city.

Casa do Fado (Map pp894-5; ☎ 218 823 470; Largo do Chafariz de Dentro 1; adult/child €2.50/1.25; 🕑 10am-1pm & 2-5.30pm) provides vibrant audiovisual coverage of the history of *fado* from its working-class roots to a recreated *fado* house.

Dating from Visigothic times, **Castelo de São Jorge** (Map pp894-5; ☎ 218 800 620; adult/child €3/1.50; 🕑 9am-9pm Mar-Oct, to 6pm Nov-Feb) sits high above the city with spine-tingling views. If you can't hack the hike, take bus 37 from Rossio or tram 28 from Largo Martim Moniz.

Belém

This quarter 6km west of the Rossio is a grand canvas reflecting Portugal's Golden Age and is home to Lisbon's most emblematic religious building. It has a mellow vibe with chairs on squares and reputedly the best *pastéis de nata* (custard tarts) in the country (see p898).

To reach Belém take the train, bus 28 from Praça do Comércio, or tram 15 from Praça da Figueira.

Mosteiro dos Jerónimos (Map pp890-1; ☎ 213 620 034; Praça do Império; adult/child €3/1.50; 🕑 10am-5pm Tue-Sun) dates from 1496 and is a soaring extravaganza of Manueline architecture with stunning carvings and ceramic tiles.

The **Museu do Design** (Map pp890-1; ☎ 213 612 934; Praça do Império; adult/child €3/1.75; 🕑 11am-8pm Mon-Fri, 10am-7pm Sat & Sun) has a cutting-edge collection dating from the 1930s, covering Art Deco and Frank Gehry recycled pieces from the '70s.

The **Torre de Belém** (Map pp890-1; ☎ 213 620 034; admission €3; 🕑 10am-5pm Tue-Sun) symbolises the voyages that made Portugal powerful and is *the* tourist icon of Portugal. Brave the tiny steps to the turret peak for the natural high of panoramic views.

LISBON IN TWO DAYS

Kick-start your day with a coffee at **Café a Brasileira** (p898) in Baixa. Next, explore Alfama and the **Castelo de São Jorge** (left). Grab a bite, then tram it to Belém and the **Mosteiro dos Jerónimos** (left). Return to Bairro Alto for dinner at **Cervejaria da Trindade** (p897). Check out the bars here before boogying down to super-cool nightclub **Lux** (p898). The next day, catch a train to **Sintra** (p900), returning in time to watch a **fado show** (p898).

A must for old salts is the **Museu da Marinha** (Maritime Museum; Map pp890-1; ☎ 213 620 019; adult/child €3/1.50; 🕑 10am-6pm Tue-Sun, to 5pm Oct-Mar), with all kinds of seafaring paraphernalia including model ships.

Saldanha

The celebrated **Museu Calouste Gulbenkian** (Map pp890-1; ☎ 217 823 461; Ave de Berna 45; adult/child €3/free; 🕑 10am-6pm Tue-Sun; Ⓜ Praça de Espanha) has a superb collection donated by a wealthy Armenian philanthropist. There are Egyptian, Asian, Greek and Islamic artefacts and contemplative paintings by such beret-and-smock masters as Renoir, Rembrandt and Monet.

Lisbon's **Centro de Arte Moderna** (Modern Art Centre; Map pp890-1; ☎ 217 823 474; Rua Dr Nicaulau de Bettencourt; adult/child €3/free; 🕑 10am-6pm Tue-Sun; Ⓜ Praça de Espanha) is prettily approached via the gardens. Enjoy most of the biggies from Portugal's modern-art scene, including London-based Paula Rego whose childhood in Portugal is strongly reflected in her haunting and theatrical themes. Check out the excellent restaurant (see p897).

Santa Apolónia & Lapa

The following two museums are a sidestep away from the city centre, but well worth the extra shoe leather.

The **Museu Nacional do Azulejo** (Map pp890-1; ☎ 218 100 340; Rua Madre de Deus 4; adult/child €3/1.50; 🕑 10am-6pm Wed-Sun, 2-6pm Tue) languishes in a sumptuous 17th-century convent. Exhibits include a fascinating 36m tile panel of pre-earthquake Lisbon.

The **Museu Nacional de Arte Antiga** (Ancient Art Museum; Map pp890-1; ☎ 213 962 825; Rua das Janelas Verdes; admission €3; 🕑 10am-5pm Wed-Sun, 2-6pm Tue)

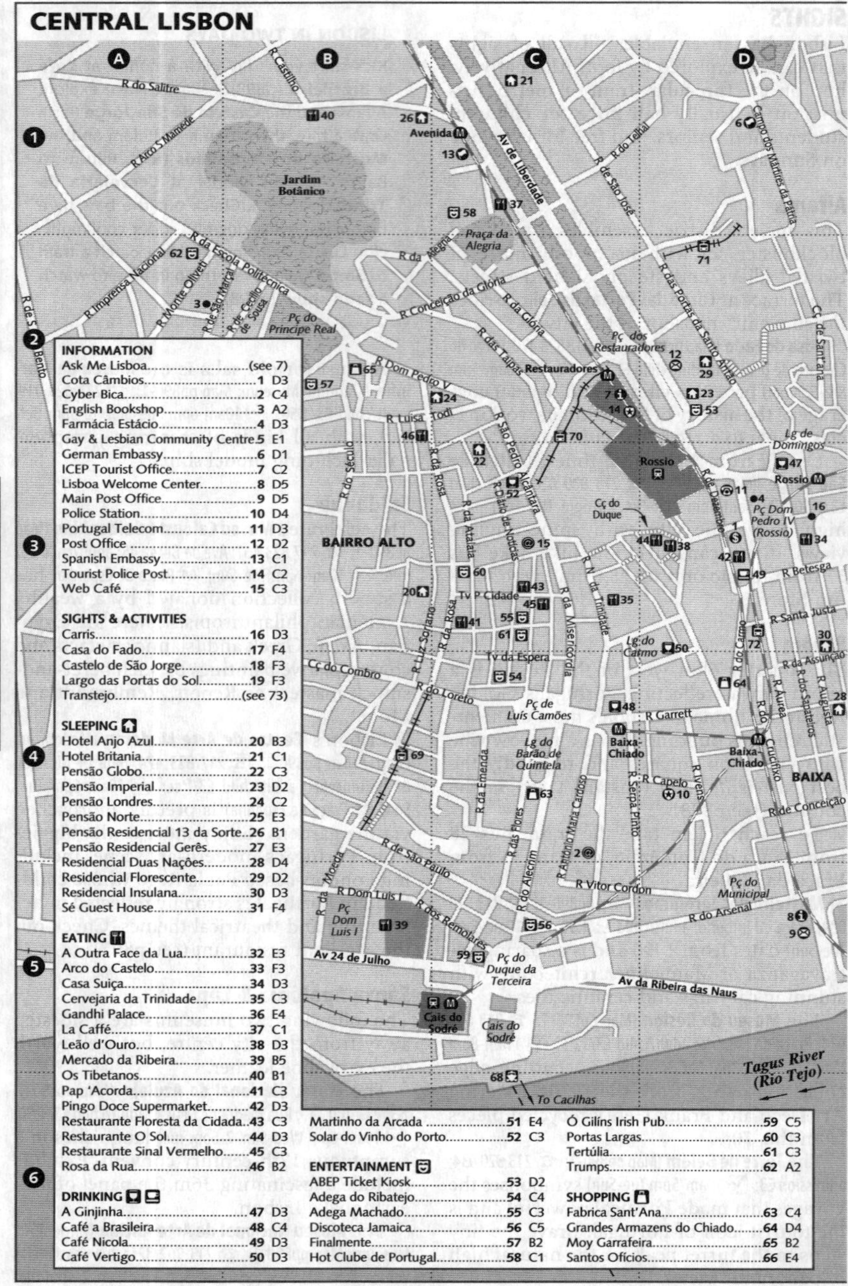
CENTRAL LISBON
INFORMATION
Ask Me Lisboa (see 7)
Cota Câmbios 1 D3
Cyber Bica 2 C4
English Bookshop 3 A2
Farmácia Estácio 4 D3
Gay & Lesbian Community Centre 5 E1
German Embassy 6 D1
ICEP Tourist Office 7 C2
Lisboa Welcome Center 8 D5
Main Post Office 9 D5
Police Station 10 D4
Portugal Telecom 11 D3
Post Office 12 D2
Spanish Embassy 13 C1
Tourist Police Post 14 C2
Web Café 15 C3
SIGHTS & ACTIVITIES
Carris 16 D3
Casa do Fado 17 F4
Castelo de São Jorge 18 F3
Largo das Portas do Sol 19 F3
Transtejo (see 73)
SLEEPING
Hotel Anjo Azul 20 B3
Hotel Britania 21 C1
Pensão Globo 22 C3
Pensão Imperial 23 D2
Pensão Londres 24 C2
Pensão Norte 25 E3
Pensão Residencial 13 da Sorte 26 B1
Pensão Residencial Gerês 27 E3
Residencial Duas Nações 28 D4
Residencial Florescente 29 D2
Residencial Insulana 30 D3
Sé Guest House 31 F4
EATING
A Outra Face da Lua 32 E3
Arco do Castelo 33 F3
Casa Suiça 34 D3
Cervejaria da Trinidade 35 C3
Gandhi Palace 36 E4
La Caffé 37 C1
Leão d'Ouro 38 D3
Mercado da Ribeira 39 B5
Os Tibetanos 40 B1
Pap 'Acorda 41 C3
Pingo Doce Supermarket 42 D3
Restaurante Floresta da Cidada 43 C3
Restaurante O Sol 44 D3
Restaurante Sinal Vermelho 45 C3
Rosa da Rua 46 B2
Martinho da Arcada 51 E4
Solar do Vinho do Porto 52 C3
DRINKING
A Ginjinha 47 D3
Café a Brasileira 48 C4
Café Nicola 49 D3
Café Vertigo 50 D3
ENTERTAINMENT
ABEP Ticket Kiosk 53 D2
Adega do Ribatejo 54 C4
Adega Machado 55 C3
Discoteca Jamaica 56 C5
Finalmente 57 B2
Hot Clube de Portugal 58 C1
Ó Gilíns Irish Pub 59 C5
Portas Largas 60 C3
Tertúlia 61 C3
Trumps 62 A2
SHOPPING
Fabrica Sant'Ana 63 C4
Grandes Armazens do Chiado 64 D4
Moy Garrafeira 65 B2
Santos Ofícios 66 E4

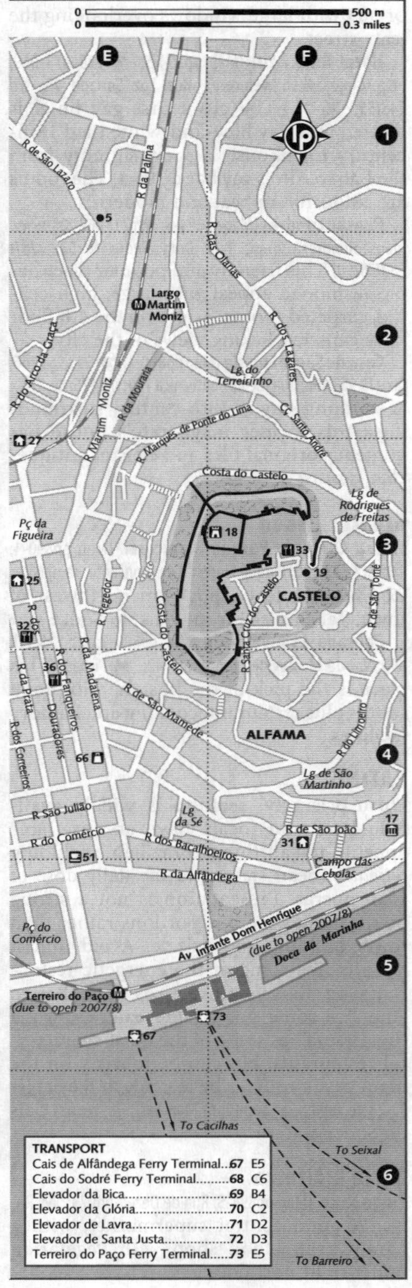

is in Lapa, Lisbon's moneyed diplomatic quarter, and houses a ripping collection of works by Portuguese painters.

Parque das Nações

The former Expo '98 site, a revitalised 2km-long waterfront area in the northeast, equals a family-fun day out. It includes a whopping **Oceanarium** (Map pp890-1; ☎ 218 917 002; www.oceanario.pt; adult/child €10/5; ⌚ 10am-7pm; Ⓜ Oriente), Europe's largest, and **Pavilhão do Conhecimento** (Living Science Centre; Map pp890-1; ☎ 218 917 100; adult/child €5/2.50; ⌚ 10am-6pm Tue-Fri, 11am-7pm Sat & Sun; Ⓜ Oriente) with over 300 interactive exhibits for kids of all ages. Take the metro to Oriente station – an equally impressive Expo project.

Alcântara

The old wharves have been slickly revamped into a gilded strip of bars and restaurants with tables sprawling out onto the promenade. After your blow-out brunch, enjoy a waterfront stroll to Belém.

TOURS

Carris (Map pp894-5; ☎ 966 298 558; www.carris.pt; Praça da Figueira; adult/child from €14/8) Offers various bus, tram and walking tours.

Transtejo (Map pp894-5; ☎ 218 820 348; www.transtejo.pt; Terreiro do Paço ferry terminal; adult/child €20/8; ⌚ Mar-Oct) Runs cruises on the Tagus. There are great views of the city from this watery perspective.

FESTIVALS & EVENTS

The **Festa do Santo António** (Festival of Saint Anthony), from 12 June to 13 June, culminates the three-week **Festas de Lisboa,** with processions and dozens of street parties.

SLEEPING

Prices listed are high season (July to mid-September) when it is advisable to reserve ahead.

Baixa & Alfama

Beira Mar (Map pp894-5; ☎ 218 871 528; Largo Terreiro do Trigo 16; s/d with shared bathroom €25/35) The river location and views create an ambience of luxury accommodation for bargain-basement prices.

Pensão Imperial (Map pp894-5; ☎ 213 420 166; 4th fl, Praça dos Restauradores 78; s/d with shared bathroom €25/35; Ⓜ Restauradores) Located a short suitcase trundle from the main square, readers have raved about this cheery place with its charismatic owner and spotless comfortably-worn rooms.

Residencial Insulana (Map pp894-5; ☎ 213 423 131; www.insulana.cjb.net; Rua da Assunção 32; s/d €45/50; ; Ⓜ Baixa) Ignore the shabby entrance, this is a real value-for-money place with good-sized carpeted rooms, satellite TV and a buzzy location in the heart of Baixa.

Residencial Florescente (Map pp894-5; ☎ 213 463 517; www.residencialflorescente.com; Rua das Portas de Santo Antão 99; s/d/t €45/55/70; P; Ⓜ Restauradores) A popular hotel on pedestrian cobbles surrounded by bars, restaurants and streetlife. Rooms are light and bright with satellite TV and wi-fi coverage.

Pensão Residencial Gerês (Map pp894-5; ☎ 218 810 497; www.pensaogeres.com; Calçada do Garcia 6; s/d with shared bathroom €50/60; ; Ⓜ Rossio) A family-run place with some English, plus religious pics, traditional tiles and fussy comfortable rooms. Go for corner room 105 with its five-star views.

Sé Guest House (Map pp894-5; ☎ 218 864 400; 2nd fl, Rua São João da Praça 97; d €70) Owner Luis is a keen traveller and cultural buff, hence the intriguing clutter of global artefacts. There are neck-craning cathedral views from several of the romantic rooms.

Also recommended are:

Pensão Norte (Map pp894-5; ☎ 218 878 941; 2nd fl, Rua dos Douradores 159; d €45, with shared bathroom €35)

Residencial Duas Nações (Map pp894-5; ☎ 213 460 710; Rua da Vitória 41; s/d €35/45, with shared bathroom €25/30)

Avenida de Liberdade

Pensão Residencial 13 da Sorte (Map pp894-5; ☎ 213 539 746; www.trezedasorte.no.sapo.pt; Rua do Salitre 13; s/d/t €40/50/60; ; Ⓜ Avenida) A popular place on a slumbering side street, with shiny tiled floors and pretty blue-and-white rooms with fridges.

Hotel Britania (Map pp894-5; ☎ 213 155 016; www.heritage.pt; Rua Rodrigues Sampaio 17; s/d €215/235; P; Ⓜ Avenida) Classic Art Deco touches and massive luxury rooms in this go-for-the-splurge hotel, a short walk from the centre.

Bairro Alto & Saldanha

Pensão Globo (Map pp894-5; ☎ 213 462 279; www.pglobo.com; Rua do Teixeira 37; s/d €20/30;) Run by friendly English-speaking folk, Globo is a no-frills cheapie. Go for rooms 301, 302 or 303 with large windows overlooking the leafy street.

Hotel Anjo Azul (Map pp894-5; ☎ 213 478 069; http://anjoazul.cb2web.com; Rua Luz Soriano 75; s/d €45/55;) The city's first gay hotel is located in a tidy blue-and-white tiled 18th-century townhouse, a short shimmy from the Bairro Alto's gay bar district. The rooms are colourful, upbeat and modern.

Pensão Londres (Map pp894-5; ☎ 213 462 203; www.pensaolondres.com.pt; Rua Dom Pedro V 53; s/d/t €50/75/90) This friendly and popular place has old-fashioned appeal with large, high-ceiling, carpeted rooms. Those on the 4th floor have camera-clicking views of the city.

Casa de São Mamede (Map pp890-1; ☎ 213 963 166; fax 213 951 896; Rua Escola Politécnica 159; s/d €75/80;) A soothing stay in 18th-century surroundings; this former magistrate's house has gorgeous original tiles and elegant antique-clad rooms.

Greater Lisbon

Lisboa Camping Parque Municipal (Map pp890-1; ☎ 217 623 100; Parque Florestal de Monsanto; camp sites €5) This is a leafy spot 6km northwest of town. Take bus 43 from Cais do Sodré.

Pousada da Juventude (Map pp890-1; ☎ 218 920 890; Via de Moscavide; dm/d €15/42; Ⓜ Picoas) This place is the pick of the hostels, with good rooms plus restaurant, cooking and laundry facilities.

EATING

Unsurprisingly, seafood is widely available here and locals have an insatiable appetite for all things Brazilian, including *feijoada* (bean stew) and the daily dose of soap operas. Presentation is not a strong point, think generous portions rather than tower building and drizzle. Avoid tourist rip-offs like some of the energetic restaurants on Baixa's Correeiros. The Bairro Alto has some good-value eateries, while the Alfama has some of the most characterful restaurants, but can be touristy on the main castle route. The **Mercado da Ribeira** (Av da 24 de Julho; 5am-2pm Mon-Sat), is near Cais do Sodré station.

Baixa & Alfama

Pingo Doce (Map pp894-5; Rua de Dezembro 73; Ⓜ Rossio) A good central supermarket, with a handy health-food shop with vegetarian buffet right next door.

A Outra Face da Lua (Map pp894-5; ☎ 218 863 430; Rua da Assunção 22; snacks €3; 9am-9pm Mon-Sat; M Rossio) Shop for vintage threads then check out the natty café with its salad range, sandwiches and healthy snacks.

Casa Suiça (Map pp894-5; ☎ 213 214 090; Praça Dom Pedro IV 96-104; snacks from €3; closed Mon; M Rossio) A wood-panelled classic with adorably-named cream cakes like susanas and kisses, plus savoury rolls.

Restaurante O Sol (Map pp894-5; ☎ 213 471 944; Calçada do Duque 23; mains €2.50-5; M Rossio) A macrobiotic and vegetarian restaurant up steep steps, with heady castle views and healthy soy-burger-style bites.

Arco do Castelo (Map pp894-5; ☎ 218 876 598; Rua do Chão da Feira 25; mains €7) Surprisingly reasonable considering the ace position across from the castle, the curries at this Indo-Portuguese restaurant tick all the right succulent/spicy boxes.

Lautasco (Map pp890-1; Beco do Azinhal 7-7A; mains €9;) Full points for atmosphere with seating on a secluded square in the shade of a magnificent rubber tree. The usual suspects are on the menu, including cod fritters and *bacalhau*.

Gandhi Palace (Map pp894-5; ☎ 218 873 839; Rua dos Douradores 214-216; mains €8; M Baixa-Chiado) Good central choice for those suffering from curry-house withdrawal; the mango milk shake is a must. If you like it hot, ask – local tastes are mild.

Jardim do Marisco (Map pp890-1; ☎ 218 824 242; Av Infante Dom Henrique, Doca Jardim do Tobaco; mains €10;) In an ideal river-side setting for a spot of refuelling, this large airy warehouse conversion has a diverse menu of grilled meats, seafood and pasta, plus cut-price kiddie choices.

Leão d'Ouro (Map pp894-5; ☎ 213 426 195; Rua 1 de Dezembro 105; mains €18; ; M Rossio) With a gracious interior of arches and tiles, classic dishes include *feijoada*. Be warned, there are several aquariums here so your dinner may just be watching you.

Avenida de Liberdade

Os Tibetanos (Map pp894-5; ☎ 213 142 038; Rua do Salitre 117; mains from €6; closed Sat & Sun; ; M Avenida) Doubles as a Tibetan Buddhist school with Zen-style surroundings, a leafy patio and a diverse meatless menu; try the Japanese mushrooms with seaweed and tofu.

Centro de Arte Moderna (Map pp894-5; ☎ 213 256 736; Rua Dr Nicaulau de Bettencourt; mains €8; lunch Tue-Sun; M Praça de Espanha) The restaurant at this museum has a tasty lunchtime buffet with more salad choice than you can shake a carrot stick at, plus good value meat and fish mains.

Real Fábrica (Map pp890-1; ☎ 213 852 090; Rua da Escola Politécnica 275; mains from €8; M Rato) This cool, if self-conscious, converted silk factory produces elegant, interesting food with an emphasis on seafood.

La Caffé (Map pp894-5; ☎ 213 256 736; Av de Liberdade 129B; mains €10; 12.30-3.30pm & 8pm-11pm Tue-Sun; ; M Restauradores) Upbeat minimalist décor plus free Internet, giant fashion-TV screens and a creative twist on Med cuisine, like chicken curry risotto and ricotta mousse with honey, spices and *ruccula* (rocket).

Bairro Alto & Saldanha

Cervejaria da Trindade (Map pp894-5; ☎ 213 423 506; Rua Nova da Trindade 20C; mains €7; M Baixa-Chiado) This vaulted restaurant has fairly pedestrian food, but the setting, in a former convent with dazzling tile work, provides serious food for thought.

Rosa da Rua (Map pp894-5; ☎ 213 432 195; Rua da Rosa 265; mains €8-10; closed Mon) A stylish eatery with minimalist metal-and-stone interior, this restaurant has an innovative menu of dishes, including fried pork with chestnuts and steak with peanut butter sauce.

Restaurante Sinal Vermelho (Map pp894-5; ☎ 213 461 252; Rua das Gáveas 89; mains €8.50-11.50; closed Sat lunch & Sun;) This elegant restaurant on a cobbled corner is decorated with breezy-blue *azulejos* and shelves of dusty bottles. The menu is reassuringly traditional with eight varieties of grilled fish and the like.

Pap 'Acorda (Map pp894-5; ☎ 213 464 811; Rua da Atalaia 57-59; mains €12-15; closed Sun & Mon;) Lisbon luvvies lord it up in this former bakery now hung with thick curtains and chandeliers. The house speciality is various takes on *acorda*, a type of purée with lashings of coriander and garlic.

Restaurante Floresta da Cidada (Map pp894-5; ☎ 213 460 621; Travessa Poço da Cidade 10-12; mains from €15) Eat in the tiled and palm-fringed terrace, choosing from a reassuringly brief menu, including meat and fish dishes topped off with creamy mango mousse.

Belém

Confeitaria de Belém (Map pp890-1; ☎ 213 637 423; Rua de Belém 86-88) A classically tiled and elegant café with reputedly the best *pastéis de nata* in Portugal. Delicious!

Bem Belém (Map pp890-1; ☎ 213 648 768; Rua Vieira Portuense 72; mains €8; closed Sun) This popular meet-and-greet place serves simple calorie-stoking food including mixed kebabs and squid with shrimps. Eat al fresco overlooking the park.

DRINKING

Lisbon delivers the goods for caffeine and calorie junkies with sumptuous Art Deco cafés, particularly around Bairro Alto and Rossio. The bars in Alcântara and Oriente areas attract a well-heeled set while Alfama has plenty of gluggable choices, including moody low-lit places for cocktail hour.

Café Nicola (Map pp894-5; ☎ 213 460 579; Rossio 24; 8am-10pm Mon-Fri, 9am-10pm Sat, 10am-7pm Sun; M Rossio) A world apart from the cookie-cutter homogeneity of the international chains, this Art Deco café is a past winner of the Café of the Year award and has a sumptuous interior – and cakes.

Martinho da Arcada (Map pp894-5; ☎ 218 866 213; Praça do Comércio 3; 8am-11pm Mon-Sat; M Baixa-Chiado) Grab a coffee at the former haunt of Pessoa and sit at a table under the arches.

Café a Brasileira (Map pp894-5; ☎ 213 469 547; Rua Garrett 120; 8am-2pm; M Baixa-Chiado) Another historic watering hole for Lisbon's 19th-century greats, with warm wooden innards and a busy counter serving daytime coffees and pints at night.

A Ginjinha (Map pp894-5; Largo de Domingos; M Rossio) A quirky gem of a place specialising in powerful *ginjinha* (cherry brandy); buy a mini tumbler for just €0.70.

Solar do Vinho do Porto (Map pp894-5; ☎ 213 475 707; Rua São Pedro de Alcântara 45; 11am-midnight Mon-Sat) Expect red carpet treatment with squishy chairs and a lengthy list of quaffing port.

Café Vertigo (Map pp894-5; ☎ 213 423 112; Travessa do Carmo 4; 10am-late) A favourite of the young literary set, this place has a bohemian buzz with a fabulous stained glass ceiling, plus newspapers and chess for kick-back time.

ENTERTAINMENT

Pick up the free monthly *Follow me Lisboa*, the *Agenda Cultural Lisboa* or quarterly *Lisboa Step By Step* from the tourist office for what's on. Check out www.visitlisboa.com (Lisbon tourist office website) and www.lisboacultural.pt (for cultural events).

Live Music

Adega Machado (Map pp894-5; ☎ 213 224 640; Rua do Norte 91; 8.30pm-3am Tue-Sun) Earthy and authentic, run by Rita, goddaughter of the legendary Amalia Rodrigues; the walls are papered with signed photos of *fado* enthusiasts – including Kirk Douglas.

Adega do Ribatejo (Map pp894-5; ☎ 213 468 343; Rua Diário de Notícias 23; 8.30pm-12.30am Mon-Sat) A dark atmospheric place with high-standard nightly *fado*.

Hot Clube de Portugal (Map pp894-5; ☎ 213 467 369; Praça da Alegria 39; 10pm-2am Tue-Sat; M Avenida) Hot, sweaty and packed with nightly gigs and raw new jazz sounds.

Ó Gilíns Irish Pub (Map pp894-5; ☎ 213 421 899; Rua dos Remolares 8-10; 10am-2am; M Cais do Sodré) Predictable blarney atmosphere with live music on Friday and Saturday evenings.

Tertúlia (Map pp894-5; ☎ 213 462 704; Rua do Diário de Notícias 60; 7pm-late Mon-Sat) Low-lit bar with newspapers, live jazz, exhibitions and a piano for the occasional tinkling of the ivories.

Nightclubs

Cover charge for nightclubs vary from €12 to €180 depending on whether there is a DJ or other attractions.

Lux (Map pp890-1; ☎ 218 820 890; Armazém A, Cais da Pedra; 6pm-6am Tue-Sat, 4-8pm Sun) Hollywood actor John Malkovich helped bankroll this super-cool club with its peacocking crowd of beautiful people.

Dock's Club (Map pp890-1; ☎ 213 950 856; Rua da Cintura do Porto; 11pm-6am Tue-Sat) Another riverside dance temple attracting a voguish clientele.

Blues Café (Map pp890-1; ☎ 213 957 085; Rua da Cintura do Porto; 11pm-6am Tue-Sat) Jazz, blues and club nights, plus dockside drinking in a cool former warehouse with chilled lighting and a chic clientele.

Discoteca Jamaica (Map pp894-5; Rua Nova do Carvalho; 11pm-4am) Enjoy reggae and '60s and '70s sounds at this pulsating night spot on an otherwise seedy street.

Gay & Lesbian Venues

Lisbon has a relaxed yet flourishing gay scene, with an annual Gay Pride Festival at the end of June.

PORTUGAL

TAKING THE BULL OUT OF BULLFIGHTING

Like it or loathe it, bullfighting is still a testosterone-fuelled important part of the Portuguese culture. However, unlike neighbouring Spain it's not standard TV viewing in every workingman's bar and, more famously, the bull is not killed in the ring.

Bullfighting here dates back 2000 years when it was recorded by a Roman historian. In the 12th century, the *tourada* (bullfight) became a way to maintain military fitness and prepare nobles for horseback battle. When one poor (albeit noble) fellow was gored to death, the bulls' horns became leather padded, as they are to this day.

The fight begins with a regal display of cavaliers dressed in 17th-century costumes and mounted on equally magnificently-harnessed horses. After complex exhibitions of *haute icole,* a single cavalier gallops within inches of the bull's horns and plants several barbed spears into the animal's neck. The stars of the next act are eight elaborately-garbed men with a death wish. The leader taunts the bull with a toddler tantrum of noisy knee-slapping and yelling before throwing himself onto the animal's head, grabbing the horns while his mates pile in to try and grab the beast. The final act features the bull being led away to be killed. Only rarely will the bull be spared and usually it is to be subjected to another fight rather than retirement in green pastures.

Portas Largas (Map pp894-5; ☎ 218 461 379; Rua da Atalaia 105; 🕑 7pm-late Tue-Sat) An institution in these parts with barn-size doors, a fun-loving vibe and giant carafes of sangria.

Trumps (Map pp894-5; Rua da Imprensa Nacional 104B; 🕑 11pm-6am Tue-Sat) Not much elbow space in these two bars; one has a dance floor for the bump and grinders.

Finalmente (Map pp894-5; Rua da Palmeira 38; 🕑 10pm-6am Mon-Sat) Expect a teeny heaving dance floor and nightly drag shows.

Cinemas

Lisbon has dozens of cinemas, including the multiscreen **Amoreiras** (Map pp890-1; ☎ 213 878 752) and **Colombo** (Map pp890-1; ☎ 217 113 222; Ⓜ Colégio Militar-Luz), both located within shopping centres.

Sport

Lisbon's football teams are Benfica, Belenenses and Sporting. Euro 2004 led to the upgrading of the 65,000-seat Estádio da Luz and the construction of a new 54,000-seat Estádio Nacional. Bullfights are staged at Campo Pequeno, recently reopened after extensive reforms, between April and October. Tickets for both sports are available at **ABEP ticket kiosk** (Map pp894-5; Praça dos Restauradores; Ⓜ Restauradores).

SHOPPING

Shopping is fun here, with plenty of idiosyncratic small shops along with glossy boutiques and shopping malls. Antique shops are mainly in the Bairro Alto district. Hand-painted ceramics can be found around Baixa and Chiado. Largo do Chiado, across Rua da Misericórdia, is home to some of Lisbon's oldest and fanciest shops. For designer boutiques take a high-heeled strut down swanky Rua Garrett. For more pedestrian fashion Rua Augusta in the Baixa is good for the international chains like Hennes, Intimisso and Zara.

Grandes Armazens do Chiado (Map pp894-5; Rua do Carmo; Ⓜ Baixa-Chiado) This shopping complex is artfully concealed behind the restored façade of the historic main department store. The FNAC here is good for books, music and booking concert tickets.

Moy Garrafeira (Map pp894-5; Rua Dom Pedro V 111) The oldest Portuguese gourmet shop has local cheeses and port, plus fabulously expensive imported wares including green tea from Japan for an eye-watering €30 for 50g.

Fabrica Sant'Ana (Map pp894-5; Rua do Alecrim 95; Ⓜ Baixa-Chiado) and **Santos Ofícios** (Map pp894-5; Rua da Madalena 87) are touristy but have an eclectic range of Portuguese folk art.

GETTING THERE & AWAY

Air

Portugália and TAP have frequent daily flights to/from Lisbon to Porto, Faro and many European cities, see p923

Bus

A dozen different companies, including **Renex** (☎ 218 940 285), operate from Gare do Oriente. The Arco do Cego terminal (Map pp890–1)

PORTUGAL

is the base for **Rede Expressos** (☎ 707 223 344; www.rede-expressos.pt) and **EVA** (☎ 213 147 710; www.eva-bus.com), which cover the whole country.

Train

Santa Apolónia station (☎ 218 816 121) is the terminus for northern and central Portugal, and for all international services. Cais do Sodré station is for Belém, Cascais and Estoril. Note that Rossio station will be closed until sometime in 2007 due to the construction of a tunnel. For Sintra, Óbidos or Nazaré you must now depart from the Sete Rios train station.

Barreiro station is the terminus for *suburbano* services to Setúbal and for some southern Portugal destinations, others depart from the better connected Gare do Oriente; connecting ferries leave frequently from the Terréiro do Paço ferry terminal (Map pp894–5). The north–south railway line, over the Ponte de 25 Abril, goes to suburban areas and will eventually carry on further to southern Portugal.

For more detailed information on all the above modes of transport see p923.

PORTUGAL

GETTING AROUND

To/From the Airport

The AeroBus runs every 20 minutes from 7.45am to 8.45pm, taking 30 to 45 minutes between the airport and Cais do Sodré; buy your ticket (€3) on the bus. A taxi into town is about €10, plus €1.50 for luggage.

Bicycle

Tejo Bike (Map pp890-1; ☎ 218 871 976; Doca Sto Amaro; per hr from €6), 300m east of Belém, provides pedal power for rides along the waterfront.

Car & Motorcycle

On the outskirts of the city there are cheap (or free) car parks near Parque das Nações or Belém. The most central underground car park is at Praça dos Restauradores, costing around €1 an hour. On Saturday afternoons and Sundays parking is normally free in the pay-and-display areas in the centre.

Public Transport

A €3.70/6.90/13.40 ticket known as the *7 Colinas* is good for one/three/five days on all buses, trams, metros and funiculars. Pick it up from Carris kiosks and metro stations. The Lisboa Card is good for unlimited travel on nearly all city transport (see p892).

BUS, TRAM & FUNICULAR

Buses and trams run from 6am to 1am, with a few all-night services. Pick up a transport map from tourist offices or Carris kiosks. A single ticket costs €1.20. There are three funiculars: Elevador da Bica (Map pp894–5), Elevador da Glória (Map pp894–5) and Elevador do Lavra (Map pp894–5), plus a wonderful 19th-century wrought-iron lift in the Baixa, Elevador de Santa Justa (Map pp894–5), which takes you nowhere but has charming views.

FERRY

Car, bicycle and passenger ferries leave frequently from the Cais do Sodre ferry terminal (Map pp894–5) to Cacilhas (€0.60, 10 minutes), a transfer point for some buses to Setúbal. From Terreiro do Paço terminal catamarans zip across to Monijo (€1.65, every 30 minutes) and Seixal (€1.35, every 30 minutes).

METRO

The metro is useful for hops across town and to the Parque das Nações. Individual tickets cost €0.70; a *caderneta* of 10 tickets is €6.15. A return ticket *(allé et retour)* is €1.25. The metro operates from 6.30am to 1am.

Taxi

Lisbon's taxis are metered and best hired from taxi ranks. Beware of rip-offs from the airport. From the Rossio to Belém is around €7 and to the castle about €5.50.

AROUND LISBON

Sintra

pop 20,000

Lord Byron called this hilltop town a 'glorious Eden' and, although best appreciated at dusk when the coach tours have left, it *is* a magnificent place. Less than an hour west of Lisbon, Sintra is a twinkling tiara of stunning palaces and manors surrounded by lush green countryside. The traditional summer retreat of Portugal's kings, Sintra is hilly, so ladies leave your high heels at home.

The **tourist office** (219 231 157; www.cm-sintra.pt; Praça da República 23) has a list of accommodation. Check your emails at the **Casa Viola** (Rua Dr Alfredo da Costa 4; per hr €2.50) near the centre.

SIGHTS & ACTIVITIES

Although the whole town resembles an historical theme park there are several compulsory eye-catching sights. Most are free or discounted with the *Lisboa Card* (see p892).

The **Palácio Nacional de Sintra** (219 106 840; adult/child €4/2; 10am-5.30pm Thu-Tue) is a dizzy mix of Moorish and Gothic architecture with twin chimneys that dominate the town.

The **Museu do Brinquedo** (219 242 171; Rua Visconde de Monserrate; adult/child €3/1.50; 10am-6pm Tue-Sun) offers serious playtime potential with 20,000 toys from all over the world.

An energetic 3km greenery-flanked hike from the centre, the 8th-century ruined ramparts of **Castelo dos Mouros** (219 237 300; adult/child €3.50/2; 9am-7pm, to 8pm Jun-Sep) provide fine views. The entrance fee includes the Monserrate Gardens (see below).

Trudge on a further 20 minutes to the exuberantly kitsch **Palácio da Pena** (219 105 340; adult/child €6/4; 10am-5.30pm Tue-Sun), where every room is crammed with fascinating treasures. Alternatively, take bus 434 (€3.20) from the station.

Monserrate Gardens (219 237 116; 9am-7pm, to 8pm Jun-Sep) are fabulously lush botanical gardens 4km from town.

En route to the gardens is **Quinta da Regaleira** (219 106 650; adult/child €10/5, guided tours €20/10; to 4pm Mar-May, Oct & Nov, to 3.30pm Dec-Feb), a magnificent World Heritage site and, as an early 20th-century neo-Manueline extravaganza, one of Sintra's highlights. Guided tours must be pre-arranged.

Cabra Montêz (917 446 668; Rua D Mafalda, Belas; www.cabramontez.com) organises canoeing excursions (from €35).

SLEEPING

Villa Marques (219 230 027; Rua Sotto Mayor 1; s/d €50/60, with shared bathroom €35/45) Fabulous tiled pictures adorn this traditional manor house with its grand staircase, grandmotherly rooms and an outside terrace that has views of the duck pond and countryside beyond.

Estrada Velha (219 234 355; Consiglieri Pedroso 16; s/d €50/60;) There are just five meticulously decorated rooms here with wood-panelling and wrought-iron beds; the downstairs bar-restaurant is excellent for light tasty fare like sweet and savoury crepes.

Lawrence's Hotel (219 105 500; www.lawrenceshotel.com; Rua Consiglieri Pedroso 38-40; s/d €188/245;) Shift your credit card into overdrive to stay at one of Iberia's oldest hotels, certainly vintage enough to have bedded both Lord Byron and William Beckford.

EATING

Xentra (219 240 759; Rua Consiglieri Pedroso 2-A; mains €6) A cavernous bar with canteen-style meals, rock music on Sunday nights and karaoke on Mondays.

Tulhas (219 232 378; Rua Gil Vicente 4-6; mains €7; closed Wed) This friendly establishment is typically full of happily chomping locals. The Tulhas menu features comfort food favourites such as *bacalhau* topped with mashed potatoes and cream, and a vegetarian dish that's *not* based on eggs or lettuce.

Café de Paris (219 232 375; Praça da República 40; mains €15) Enjoy such lush grub as rucula salad with cheese, figs and nuts in this sublime 18th-century setting, complete with nymphette ceiling mural and outside terrace overlooking the main square.

GETTING THERE & AWAY

The Lisbon–Sintra railway terminates in Estefânia, 1.5km northeast of the town's historic centre. Sintra's bus station, and another train station, are a further 1km east in the new-town Portela de Sintra. Frequent shuttle buses link the historic centre with the bus station.

Until Lisbon's Rossio station re-opens, trains run from the Sete Rios station (€1.40, 45 minutes). Buses run hourly from Sintra to Estoril (€3.10, 40 minutes) and Cascais (€3.10, 45 minutes).

GETTING AROUND

A taxi to Pena or Monserrate costs around €15 return. Horse-drawn carriages cost €60 return to Monserrate. Old trams run from Ribeira de Sintra (1.5km from the centre) to Praia das Maçãs, 12km to the west, for €1.20.

THE SPANISH-PORTUGUESE DIVIDE

Years ago, this author taught English at a Seville-based private academy to Spanish teenagers and adults. Despite being just two hours drive from Portugal, not one student had crossed the border. They seemed to view the typical Portuguese like some sort of poor relation with a speech impediment; a xenophobic view that seemed worryingly widespread. In turn, the Portuguese viewed the Spanish as being insufferably arrogant.

The roots of Portuguese-Spanish animosity dates from 1385 when Portuguese forces successfully defeated the Spanish-led invading forces. The two countries have also colonially clashed over Latin America.

More recently and more positively, EU membership has led to vastly increased trade between the two countries and the investment of Spain in Portugal and vice versa. On the ground though, travellers may well find that most Portuguese still prefer speaking French or English to Spanish and you still can't buy a bottle of Spanish rioja in the local supermarket here. Or, equally tragically, a *pastéis de nata* (custard tart) in Spain!

Cascais

pop 33,255

Cascais is a handsome seaside resort with elegant buildings, an atmospheric old town and a happy abundance of bars and restaurants. The **tourist office** (☎ 214 868 204; www.visiteestoril.com; Rua Visconde de Luz 14) has accommodation lists and bus timetables; there's also a **tourist police post** (☎ 214 863 929; Rua Visconde da Luz). You can slurp a soft drink while checking your emails at **Navegue Aqui** (☎ 214 840 150; Sebastião Carvalho e Melo 17; per hr €3; 10am-midnight Mon-Sat May-Sep, 10am-8pm Mon-Sat Oct-Apr).

PORTUGAL

SIGHTS & ACTIVITIES

Estoril is a classy palm-fringed resort 2km east of Cascais with a superb sandy beach and Europe's largest **casino** (☎ 214 667 700; www.casino-estoril.pt, in Portuguese; 3pm-3am, fl show 11pm).

Praia Tamariz has an ocean swimming pool. The sea roars into the coast at **Boca do Inferno** (Hell's Mouth), 2km west of Cascais. Spectacular **Cabo da Roca**, Europe's westernmost point, is 16km from Cascais and Sintra and is served by buses from both towns.

Wild **Guincho** beach, 3km from Cascais, is a popular surfing venue.

SLEEPING & EATING

Residencial Solar Dom Carlos (☎ 214 828 115; www.solardomcarlos.com; Rua Latino Coelho 8; s/d with breakfast €50/65;) Sparkling clean, well-placed accommodation efficiently run by English-speaking owners.

Casa da Pergola (☎ 214 840 040; www.portugalvirtual.pt/pergola.house; Av Valbom 13; d €104;) Well worth the splurge, this elegant 19th-century home is tastefully done up with expensive art and antiques. Enjoy breakfast and birdsong in the pretty garden.

Tanya's Palace (☎ 214 846 332; Sebastião Carvalho e Melo 15; mains €7) If you're suffering from hot-and-spicy withdrawal this place has decent Indian and Thai dishes to eat in or take away.

GETTING THERE & AROUND

Trains run frequently to Cascais via Estoril (€1.50, 30 minutes) from Cais do Sodré station in Lisbon. **Transrent** (☎ 214 864 566; www.transrent.pt; Centro Commercial Cisne, Av Marginal) rents cars, bicycles and motorcycles.

Setúbal

pop 114,500

Unsurprisingly, Portugal's third-largest port is famous for its excellent seafood restaurants. Aside from the catch of the day, other draws are a stunning Manueline church, a castle with views and an easy-going pedestrianised centre packed with shops and cafés. Pity about the in-your-face piped music over the city sound system.

INFORMATION

Instituto Português da Juventude (IPJ; ☎ 265 534 431; Largo José Afonso; 9am-5pm Mon-Fri) Has free Internet access for a maximum of 30 minutes.

Municipal tourist office (☎/fax 265 534 402; Praça do Quebedo) Is a five-minute walk east from the bus station (Av 5 de Outubro).

Regional tourist office (☎ 265 539 130; www.mun-setubal.pt; Travessa Frei Gaspar 10) With the oddity of a Roman fish-preserving factory under its glass floor.

SIGHTS & ACTIVITIES

Portugal's first Manueline building, the stunning **Igreja de Jesus** (Praça Miguel Bombarda; admission free; ⌚ 9am-1pm & 2-5pm Tue-Sat), has maritime motifs and twisted pillars that resemble coiled ropes. The **Galeria da Pintura Quinhentista** (Rua do Balneă Rio Paula Borba; admission free; ⌚ 9am-noon & 2-5pm Tue-Sat), just around the corner, has a renowned collection of 16th-century paintings.

Good **beaches** west of town include Praia da Figuerinha (accessible by bus in summer). Across the estuary at Tróia is a more developed beach, plus the ruins of a Roman settlement. On the ferry trip across you may see some of the estuary's 30 or so bottlenosed dolphins.

SAL (☎ 265 227 685; www.sal.pt, in Portuguese) organises walks from €5 per person. For jeep safaris, hiking and biking in the Serra da Arrábida, or canoe trips through the Reserva Natural do Estuário do Sado, contact **Planeta Terra** (☎ 265 080 176; www.planetaterra.pt; Praça General Luís Domingues 9). **Vertigem Azul** (☎ 265 238 000; www.vertigemazul.com; Av Luísa Todi 375) offers canoe and dolphin-spotting excursions. There are free wine-cellar tours of **José Maria da Fonseca Succs** (☎ 212 198 940; www.jmf.pt; Rua José Augusto Coelho 11; ⌚ 10am-12.30pm & 2-5pm Mon-Fri), the oldest Portuguese producer of table wine.

SLEEPING

Pousada da Juventude (☎ 265 534 431; setubal@movijovem.pt; Largo José Afonso; dm/d €10/23) Adequate tidy hostel with a buzzy vibe.

Pensão Bom Regresso (☎ 265 229 812; Praça de Bocage 48; d €45) Overlooks the main square; about as close to church as you can get without attending confession. Rooms are clean but monastically basic.

Residencial Bocage (☎ 265 543 080; fax 265 543 089; Rua São Cristovão 14; s/d €35/46; Ⓟ ⊠) Fairly forgettable rooms in a newish building; satellite TV and nearby parking are the major perks for the price.

Albergaria Solaris (☎ 265 541 770; Praça Marquês de Pombal 12; s/d €45/50; ⊠) Rooms have all the standard hotel clobber at this pretty tiled hotel. Go for a room with a balcony overlooking the action-packed square.

EATING

Peregrina (☎ 265 230 602; Rua dos Almocreves 74; mains €8) One of three vegetarian restaurants with a good choice of healthy grub, including quiche, tofu, nut rissoles and salads.

O Beco (☎ 265 524 617; Largo da Misericordia 24; mains €10) Locals rate this restaurant as one of the city's best. Enjoy a special seafood moment and choose one of the lobster dishes.

Xica Bia (☎ 265 522 559; Av Luisa Todi 131; mains from €10) Xica Bia has an elegant dinner-for-two setting with barrel-vault ceiling, exposed bricks and chandeliers. The menu includes plenty of thrills, including an exemplary *arroz de marisco* (shellfish rice).

GETTING THERE & AWAY

Buses leave at least hourly from Lisbon's Praça de Espanha (€3.25, one hour). Ferries shuttle across the estuary to Tróia approximately every 45 minutes (€1.30, 15 minutes).

THE ALGARVE

The Algarve is holiday-brochure heaven with superb beaches, sweeping golf courses and year-round sunshine. Although overdevelopment has blighted parts of the coast-hugging strip venture inland and you'll land solidly in Portugal again. Algarve highlights include the forested slopes of Monchique, the fortified village of Silves and windswept, historic Sagres. Faro is the regional capital.

FARO

pop 58,000

Faro is an attractive seaside town and makes a good place from which to explore the rest of this coastal strip. The centre is a picturesque jumble of pedestrian shopping streets, interspersed with pretty plazas and churches. To avoid the crowds visit out of season, especially since Brits can fly here for a no-frills fare. *The Resident* is an expat-oriented, English-language newspaper with entertainment information. Go online at **Planet Cyber Center** (☎ 289 391 974; Ferreira Neto 5; per hr €2.50; ⌚ 10am-10pm Mon-Sat). The central **tourist office** (☎ 289 803 604; www.rtalgarve.pt; Rua da Misericórdia) has informative leaflets and maps.

Sights & Activities

The palm-clad **waterfront** around Praça de Dom Francisco Gomes has pleasant kick-back cafés. Faro's beach, **Praia de Faro** (Ilha

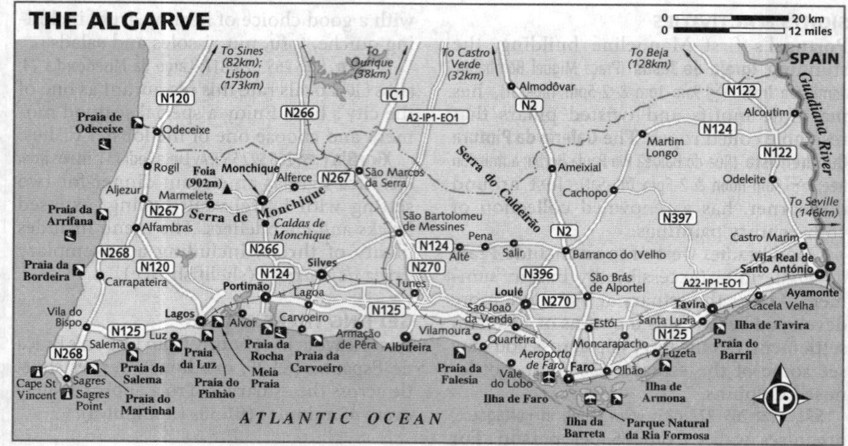

de Faro), is 6km southwest of the city; take bus 16 from opposite the bus station. Less crowded is the unspoilt Ilha Desserta in the nature park **Parque Natural da Ria Formosa** (☎ 917 811 856; www.ilha-deserta.com), where you can also take a three-hour **lagoon tour** (€20; 11am & 3pm year-round).

Sleeping & Eating

Avoid midsummer when many of the hotels are block-booked by tour groups.

Pensão Residencial Central (☎ 289 807 291; Largo Terreiro do Bispo 10; s/d €35/45;) This has large bland rooms with floral-and-white décor. The main draw is the location, with balconies overlooking the jacaranda-fringed square.

Residencial Adelaide (☎ 289 802 383; fax 289 826 870; Rua Cruz dos Mestres 7; d €50;) White and turquoise is the colour backdrop here, together with the owner's art work. Several rooms have vast terraces; all have fridges.

Residencial Algarve (☎ 289 895 700; www.residencialalgarve.com; Rua Infante Dom Henrique 52; s/d €50/60;) Cheerful, bright rooms with all the necessities, including satellite TV. Breakfast is served in a pretty internal patio.

Sol e Jardim (☎ 289 820 030; Praça Ferreira de Almeida 22; mains €9) This cavernous restaurant is a jumble of nets, jolly murals and a parrot or two. Couscous is a speciality.

O Aldeão (☎ 289 823 339; Largo de S. Pedro; mains €12) Dishes from the Alentejo and Algarve are prepared with culinary panache at this elegant restaurant overlooking lovely Igreja de São Pedro.

Getting There & Away

Faro airport has both domestic and international flights (see p923).

From the bus station, just west of the centre, there are at least six daily express coaches to Lisbon (€15, four hours), plus several slower services, and frequent buses to other coastal towns.

The train station is a few minutes' walk west of the bus station. Five trains run daily to Lisbon (€18.50, five hours).

Getting Around

The airport is 6km from the centre. Buses 14 and 16 run into town until 9pm, costing €1.35 for a single ticket. A taxi costs about €12 from the airport to the town centre.

TAVIRA

pop 12,500

Traditionally-tiled façades and a web of cobbled streets add to the charm of this laid-back town. Tavira is famed for its ecclesiastical history and seafood. The **tourist office** (☎ 281 322 511; Rua da Galeria 9) can help with accommodation and the **town hall** (Praça da Republica; 9.30am-2pm Mon-Fri) provides free Internet access.

Sights & Activities

One of the town's 30-plus churches, the **Igreja da Misericórdia**'s Renaissance façade is the most striking in the Algarve. Tavira's ruined **castle** (Rua da Liberdade; admission free; 9am-5pm Mon-Fri, 10am-5pm Sat & Sun) dominates the town. Nearby, the 16th-century **Palácio da Galeria** (☎ 281 320 540; Calçada da Galeria; admission €2; 🕒 10am-12pm & 4-7.30pm Tue-Sat) is an informative cultural centre with a rooftop contemporary art gallery and views.

Ilha da Tavira is an island beach connected to the mainland by a ferry at Quatro Águas. Walk the 2km or take the (summer only) bus from the bus station.

Enjoy pedal power with a rented bike from **Casa Abilio** (☎ 281 323 467; Rua Goao Vaz C Real 23a). For walking or biking trips call **Exploratio** (☎ 281 321 973). Kitesurfers can bounce the waves with **Escola de Kitesurf** (☎ 962 337 285; www.kitesurfeolis.com; Av Da Ria Formosa).

Sleeping & Eating

Residencial Imperial (☎ 281 322 234; José Pires Padinha 24; s/d €40/60) A lick of paint has improved this no-nonsense *pensão* with balconies and a downstairs restaurant overlooking the river.

Marés (☎ 281 325 815; José Pires Padinha 134; s/d €45/70; ❄) Enjoy well-dusted, bright rooms with terracotta tiles, satellite TV and balconies with river views.

Vila Galé Albacora (☎ 281 380 800; www.vilagale.pt; Quatro Águas; d €115) A former tuna-fishing village metamorphosed into a luxury hotel complex with health club, Turkish bath and games room. Prices plummet out of season.

Patio (☎ 281 323 008; António Cabreira 30; mains €10-15; ❄) Fatten your credit card at the town's swankiest restaurant dishing up traditional cuisine like octopus and bean stew.

Aquasul (☎ 281 325 166; Dr Augusto da Silva Carvalho 11; mains €10-14; ❄) Arty Gaudi-inspired décor and organic ingredients. The Italian-inspired dishes here include beetroot carpaccio with goat's cheese, and pizza.

Getting There & Away

Some 15 trains and six express buses run daily between Faro and Tavira (€2.45, one hour).

LAGOS

pop 25,400

In summer the pretty fishing port of Lagos has a beach party vibe; out of season it's pretty laid back as restaurants and hotels take a siesta until spring. The municipal **tourist office** (☎ 282 764 111; www.lagosdigital.com, in Portuguese; Largo Marquês de Pombal) is in the centre of town. Surf a frothy coffee while emailing at cool **Bora Café** (☎ 282 083 438; Conselheiro Joaquim Machado 17; per hr €3; 🕒 9.30am-10pm Mon-Sat).

Sights & Activities

The **Museu Municipal** (☎ 282 762 301; Rua General Alberto da Silveira; admission €2; 🕒 9.30am-12.30pm & 2-5pm Tue-Sun) houses an eclectic mix of archaeological and ecclesiastical treasures (and oddities). Admission includes the adjacent **Igreja de Santo António** (🕒 9.30am-12.30pm & 2-5pm Tue-Sun), one of the best Baroque churches in Portugal.

The beach scene includes **Meia Praia**, a vast strip to the east; **Praia da Luz** to the west; and the smaller **Praia do Pinhão**.

Blue Ocean (☎ 282 782 718; www.blue-ocean-divers.de) organises diving, kayaking and snorkelling safaris. On the promenade, fishermen offer motorboat jaunts to nearby grottoes. For horse riding contact **Quinta Paraiso Alto** (☎ 282 687 596; www.qpahorseriding.com). Rent windsurfing gear from **Windsurf Point** (☎ 282 792 315, www.windsurfpoint.com).

Sleeping

Pousada da Juventude (☎ 282 761 970; Rua Lançarote de Freitas 50; dm/d €16/45; 💻) Up there with the best. Rooms are airy and light, plus there's Internet access and a garden with hammocks.

Rubi Mar (☎ 282 180 678; www.rubi-mar.com; 2nd fl, Rua de Barroca 70; s/d €45/50, with shared bathroom €30/45) English-American run with pleasant homey rooms and breezy harbour views. Owners can also book excursions, car hire and golf.

Casa de São Gonçalo (☎ 282 762 171; Rua Candido dos Reis 73; s/d €70/90) This fine 18th-century house endearingly shows its age with plush rooms and a picturesque garden.

Eating

Restaurante Piri-Piri (☎ 282 763 803; Rua Lima Leitão 15; mains €8) A good choice serving a tasty *cataplana* (fish stew) and *piri-piri* chicken or clams. If you're a fan, pick up a bottle of the red-chilli wonder from one of the grans at the market.

Taberna de Lagos (☎ 282 084 250; 25 de Abril; mains €8) This atmospheric former warehouse has a menu of pizzas, pastas, salads and vegetarian dishes. Live music accompanies Sunday lunch.

No Patio (☎ 282 76 37 77; Rua Lançarote de Freitas 46; mains €9; ⏰ closed Sun & Mon) Owner Martin has a serious foodie background in the UK. This is British nosh at its best: steak-and-kidney pie, sticky toffee pudding and lots more home-sweet-home dishes for poor deprived Brits.

Getting There & Away

Bus and train services depart frequently for other Algarve towns and around eight times daily to Lisbon (€14.50, four hours).

Getting Around

Rent bicycles, mopeds and motorcycles from **Motor Ride** (☎ 289 761 720; Rua José Afonso 23; per day from €8.50).

MONCHIQUE

pop 6975

The pine-clad flip side to the seagulls and sand, pretty Monchique is surrounded by the forested Serra de Monchique. The **tourist office** (☎ 282 911 189; Largo dos Chorões) overlooks the park.

Sights & Activities

Igreja Matriz (Rua da Igreja) features a stunning Manueline portal, with its stone seemingly tied in knots. Follow the brown pedestrian signs around the old town's narrow streets.

Caldas de Monchique, 6km south, is a mildly heritaged yet quaint hot-spring hamlet. Some 8km west is the Algarve's 'rooftop', the 902m **Fóia** peak atop the Serra de Monchique, with heady views through a forest of radio masts.

Omega Parque Monchique (☎ 282 911 327; Caldas de Monchiqe; adult/child €8/5; ⏰ 10am-6pm) is a small ecofriendly zoo with animals kept in as near a natural environment as possible.

Alternativtour (☎ 282 420 800; from €30) organises bike and walking tours.

Sleeping & Eating

Residencial Miradouro Da Serra (☎ 282 912 163; Rua Combatentes do Ultramar; s/d €35/45) Nothing-special rooms but location is on a high with several rooms enjoying stunning views. Grab number 205 if you can.

Casa Da Nora (☎ 282 91 2 532; Largo 5 de Outubro; mains €9) The bow-tied waiters at this classy restaurant in the square dish up delicious homemade soups, fish and meat dishes.

Getting There & Away

There are eight buses daily from Portimão (€2.75, 45 minutes) to Monchique.

SILVES

pop 10,768

There is nothing self-important about this pretty town, despite it being the one-time capital of Moorish Algarve. Take the puff-you-out climb up to the fairy-tale castle crowning the hill. The **tourist office** (☎ 289 442 255; Rua 25 de Abril) can help with accommodation. Check your inbox at **It-Connect** (☎ 282 083 915; Rua Francisco Pablos 13; per hr €1.50).

Sleeping & Eating

Residencial Ponte Romana (☎ 282 443 275; Horta da Cruz; s/d €15/30) Floral-themed rooms beside the Roman bridge, with castle views and a cavernous bar-restaurant full of old-timers in flat caps and Portuguese families.

Hotel Colina Dos Mouros (☎ 282 440 420; Sitio do Pocinho; s/d €70/80; ❄ 💻) Avoid July and August and the price here seriously plummets. Sip a sundowner from your balcony overlooking the round pool with a castle backdrop.

Café Ingles (☎ 282 442 585; mains €8.50) Situated at the castle entrance, this English-owned funky place has vegetarian dishes, homemade soups, pasta and wood-fired pizza. In summer there's live music at weekends.

Restaurante Rui (☎ 282 442 682; Rua C Vilarinho 27; mains from €12) Push the boat out and select your seafood straight from the tank. The intrepid can enjoy wild boar chops.

Getting There & Away

Silves train station is 2km from town; trains from Lagos (€1.50, 35 minutes) stop nine times daily (from Faro, change at Tunes), to be met by local buses. Eight buses run daily to Silves from Albufeira (€3.30, 40 minutes).

SAGRES

pop 1940

End-of-the-road Sagres was thought to be the end of the world in pre-Columbus days. Still today, the town exudes a bleak sort of drama, the fort perched high above the thundering surf. There is a central **tourist office** (☎ 282 624 873; Rua Comandante Matoso), plus **Turinfo** (☎ 282 620 003; Praça da República), which rents cars and bikes, books hotels, arranges jeep and fishing trips and even provides Internet access, bless 'em.

Sights & Activities

The **fort** (adult/child €3/1.50; 10am-8.30pm May-Sep, 10am-6.30pm Oct-Apr) has a 12-minute slide show on the history; Henry the Navigator established his navigation school here and primed the explorers who later founded the Portuguese empire.

Visit Europe's southwestern-most point, the **Cabo de São Vicente** (Cape St Vincent), 6km to the west. A solitary lighthouse stands on this barren cape.

This coast is ideal for the surfing set; hire windsurfers at sand-dune fringed **Praia do Martinhal**.

The **Scubado Diving Centre** (282 624 594; www.scubado-algarve.com; Porto da Baleeira) organises diving trips daily at 10am and 3pm.

Sleeping & Eating

Hotel Baleeira (282 624 212; www.sagres.net/baleeira; Rua Comandante Matoso; s/d €91/121; P) A good looking low-rise hotel with direct beach access, harbour views, tennis courts and spacious smart rooms.

Mar à Vista (282 624 247; Praia da Mareta; mains €8) Bask in the sea-and-surf views from the terrace; the Med cuisine here includes pasta with lobster and eight different salads.

Getting There & Away

Frequent buses run daily to Sagres from Lagos (€2.50, 50 minutes), with fewer on Sunday. Three continue out to Cabo de São Vicente on weekdays.

CENTRAL PORTUGAL

One of Portugal's poorest regions, this central slice of the country has an outback-meets-the-Med feel with its vast plains of cattle and groves of olive trees and cork oaks. Richly historic, it is scattered with prehistoric remains and contains one of the country's most architecturally rich towns, Évora, as well as several spectacular walled villages. There are fine local wines and, for the more energetic, plenty of hiking and skiing in the dramatic Beiras region.

ÉVORA

pop 53,755

Évora has a lot going for it. Aesthetically, this city is easy on the eye with its medieval narrow alleys, juxtaposed with opulent mansions and palaces. These old-fashioned good looks are the backdrop to a lively student town surrounded by wineries and dramatic countryside. The **tourist office** (266 702 671; www.cm-evora.pt, in Portuguese; Praça do Giraldo 73) has an excellent city map. Log on at the **Cyber Centre** (266 746 923; Rua dos Mercadores 42; per hr €2.50; 9am-midnight Mon-Fri, 2pm-midnight Sat & Sun).

Sights & Activities

Évora's cathedral, **Sé** (Largo do Marquês de Marialva; adult/child €3/free; 9am-noon & 2-5pm), has fabulous cloisters and a museum jam-packed with ecclesiastical treasures.

The **Temple of Diana** (Largo do Conde de Vila Flor) was once part of the Roman Forum and is a heady slice of drama right in town.

Capela dos Ossos (266 744 307; Largo Conde de Vila Flor; admission €1; 9am-1pm & 2.30-6pm) was discovered in 1958 during restoration work. Providing a real Addams family day out, this ghoulish Chapel of Bones is constructed from the bones and skulls of several thousand people.

Turaventur (266 743 134; www.turaventur.com; Plaça 1 de Maio) offers a whole range of adrenaline-fuelled activities, including canoeing (half-day €60), mountain biking (four hours €35) and 4WD safari tours (full day €60).

Sleeping

Residencial O Alentejo (266 702 903; Rua Serpa Pinto 74; s/d €30/45;) A deeply traditional house, complete with original mosaic-tiled floors and gran on reception; the rooms here are well-sized and everything works. This is a good street for bars.

Residencial Diana (266 702 008; www.residencialdiana.com; Rua Diogo Cão 2-3; s/d €35/50; P)

AUTHOR'S CHOICE

Pensão Policarpo (266 702 424; www.pensaopolicarpo.com; Rua da Freiria de Baixo 16; s/d €50/55;) A palatial place for a paltry price; this historic manor is complete with Roman columns and part of the original city wall in the foyer. Located bang in the centre of town, the rooms are furnished with rustic Alentejan furniture and are all different; a couple have traditional tiles, others elaborate bed heads. All are cushy and bright. In short, a winner.

PORTUGAL

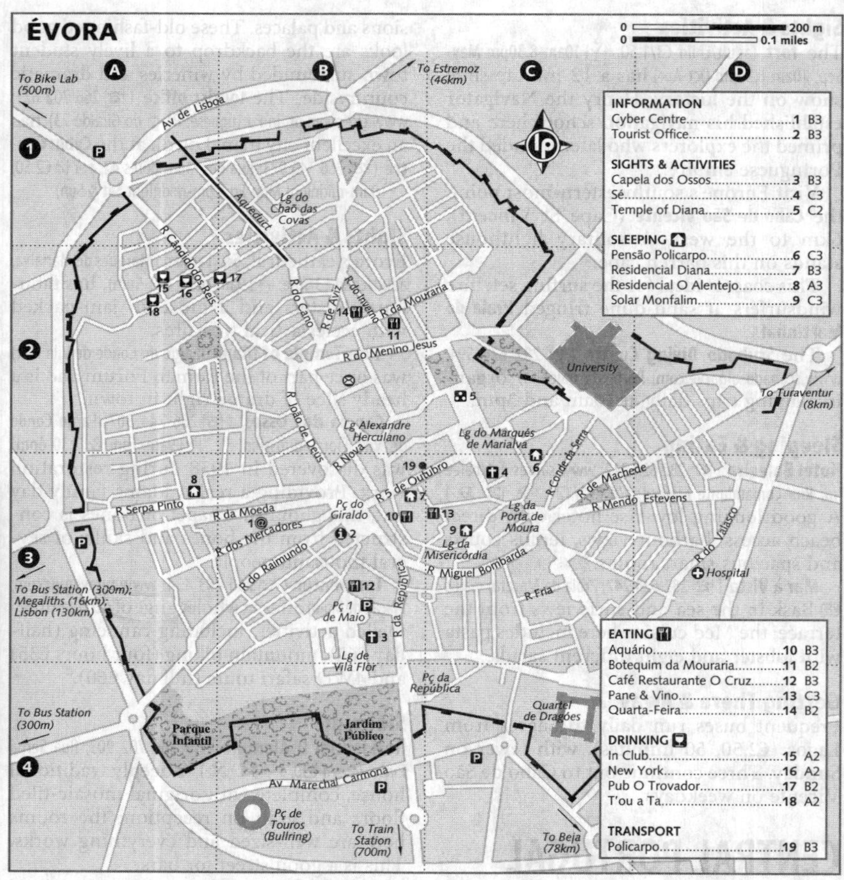

Located on a souvenir-shopping street attracting deep-pocketed tourists, this shiny comfortable hotel has high-ceilinged rooms with homely furnishings. Service can be gruff.

Solar Monfalim (☎ 266 750 000; www.monfalimtur.pt; Largo da Misericórdia 1; s/d €75/90; P ⛝ 💻) This is an exquisitely renovated 16th-century nobleman's house with an arched gallery overlooking the cobbles. Rooms are elegant, stylish and have wi-fi coverage.

Eating

Aquário (☎ 266 785 055; Rua de Valdevinos 7; mains €6) Vibrant little vegetarian restaurant with just a few daily choices, including a vegan option.

Café Restaurant O Cruz (☎ 266 747 228; Praça 1 de Maio 20; mains €6) Earthy and inexpensive for scoffing plain, filling fare like pork with clams. Outside tables overlook the magnificent San Francisco church.

Pane & Vino (☎ 266 746 960; Páteo do Salema 22; mains €7) Sunny colours, cheery staff and a vast menu including thin-crust pizzas, generous salad bar and creamy tiramisu.

Botequim da Mouraria (☎ 266 746 775; Rua da Mouraria 16a; mains €8; 🕒 closed Sun) A real insider's place; there are just a dozen bar stools and a nightly set menu of creations by master chef-cum-barman-cum-owner. Get here early to grab a pew.

Quarta-Feira (☎ 266 707 530; Rua do Inverno 16; mains €12; 🕒 closed Sun) Arm yourself with a compass; this place is well hidden. Run by friendly Ze Dias and family, enjoy sublime home cooking here with an emphasis on game and *bacalhau*.

Drinking

In Club (☎ 266 706 559; Rua do Escrivão da Cámara 16; ⌚ 8pm-1am Mon-Thu, 8pm-3am Fri & Sat) Hits its stride post-dinner, attracting a mix of suits and scruffs.

New York (☎ 266 705 675; Rua do Apóstolo 4; ⌚ 8pm-2am Mon-Fri, 9pm-3am Sat) An after-hours hang-out to perfect your morning hang-over. Live music.

Pub O Trovador (☎ 266 707 370; Rua da Mostardeira 4) A chilled-out setting attracting a voguish clientele.

T'ou a Ta (Rua do Calvário 12-14) Packing them in at weekends, this backstreet club has a frazzled bar staff and fun-loving vibe.

Getting There & Away

Évora has six buses to Lisbon (€9.80, 1½ hours) Monday to Friday and two to Faro (€11.80, four hours), departing from the station off Av Túlio Espanca (700m south-west of the centre). Three daily trains run from Lisbon (€8.15, 2½ hours).

Getting Around

Bike Lab (☎ 266 735 500; Centro Comercial da Vista Alegre, Lote 14; ⌚ summer only) rents out bicycles. **Policarpo** (☎ 266 746 970; www.policarpo-viagens.pt, in Portuguese; Rua 5 de Outubro 63) organises city tours and jaunts to megaliths and other nearby attractions.

MONSARAZ

pop 977

In a dizzy setting, high above the plain, this walled village has a moody medieval feel and magnificent views. The **tourist office** (☎ 266 557 136; Praça Dom Nuno Álvares) can advise on accommodation. Eat before 8pm as the town tucks up early to bed.

Museu de Arte Sacra (Plaça Dom Nuno Álvares; admission €1; ⌚ 10am-1pm & 2-6pm) has a good display of religious artefacts; the 15th-century fresco is quite superb. Three kilometres north of town is **Menhir of Outeiro**, one of the tallest megalithic monuments ever discovered.

Up to four daily buses run to/from Reguengos de Monsaraz (€2.15, 35 minutes), with connections to Évora.

ESTREMOZ

pop 15,400

One of three marble towns in these parts, Estremoz is like an aging *grande dame* with a face-lift: cosmetically shiny and bright but underneath slightly fading and out of touch with the times. In its prime, the town was one of the most strongly fortified in Portugal with its very own palace (now a luxurious *pousada;* upmarket inn). The **tourist office** (☎ 268 333 541; www.cm-estremoz.pt, in Portuguese; Largo da República 26) is just south of Rossio.

Sights

Museu Municipal (☎ 268 339 200; Largo D Dinis; adult/child €1.10/free; ⌚ 9am-12.30pm & 2-5.30pm Tue-Sun), in a beautiful 17th-century almshouse, specialises in fascinating pottery figurines, including an entire Easter parade.

Vila Viçosa, another marble town 17km from Estremoz, is centred around the **Palácio Ducal** (☎ 268 980 659; Terreiro do Paça; adult/child €5/free, armoury museum extra €2.50; ⌚ 9am-1pm & 3-5.30pm Tue-Sun), the magnificent ancestral home of the dukes of Bragança. It's rich with *azulejos,* frescoed ceilings and elaborate tapestries.

Sleeping & Eating

Residencial Carvalho (☎ 268 339 370; Largo da República 27; s/d €20/40) Next to the tourist office, rooms are well-dusted and spacious with newly-tiled bedrooms. Larger rooms cost more.

Café Alentejano (☎ 268 337 300; Rossio 13-15; s/d €25/40) Just a few rooms next to the restaurant, so expect culinary wafts. The space is tight but smart with front views overlooking the town's main square.

Adega do Isaías (☎ 268 322 318; Rua Almeida 21; mains €6.50-8) Huge wooden vats of wine cosy-in on the dining room. Expect a good grilling; this place specialises in steaks.

Getting There & Away

Estremoz is linked to Évora by four local buses (€3.50, 1¼ hours) and two *expressos* (€6.75, 45 minutes), Monday to Saturday.

CASTELO DE VIDE & MARVÃO

pop 4145

A worthy detour north of Estremoz, is the hilltop spa town **Castelo de Vide**, noted for its picturesque houses with Gothic doorways. Highlights are the **Judiaria** (Old Jewish Quarter), the medieval backstreets and (yet another) castle-top view. Try to spend a night here heading skywards to **Marvão**, a fabulous mountain-top walled village (population 190) 12km from Castelo de Vide. The **tourist offices** (Castelo de Vide ☎ 245 901 361; Rua de Bartolomeu Álvares da Santa 81; Marvão ☎ 245 993 886; Largo de Santa Maria) can help with beds.

On weekdays three buses run from Portalegre to Castelo de Vide (€4.80, 20 minutes) and two to Marvão (€2.65, 45 minutes).

ÓBIDOS

pop 10,809

This exquisite walled village was a wedding gift from Dom Dinis to his wife Dona Isabel (beats a fondue set) and is over-heritaged, but still well worth a visit. Highlights include the **Igreja de Santa Maria** (Rua Direita), with fine *azulejos,* and views from the town walls. The **tourist office** (☎ 262 959 231; www.cm-obidos.pt, in Portuguese; Rua Direita) has a brochure of walks in the area and can advise on accommodation. Check your email for free at **Net** (☎ 262 955 561; Rua Direita 107; 🕑 10am-10pm May-Sep, 10am-9pm Mon-Fri & 11.30am-6.30pm Sat-Sun Oct-Apr).

Sleeping & Eating

Casa dos Castros (☎ 262 959 328; Direita 83-85; d €35) Bargain price for these homey large rooms right on the main street.

Casa do Poço (☎ 262 959 358; Travessa da Mouraria; d €60; ❄) Pin-drop quiet with flagstone floors, blue tiles and courtyard setting, this hotel has a fabulous location down a wiggly flower-flanked side street.

O Pátio do Lidador (Rua Direita 15; mains €8) There's a good varied menu at his rustic-styled restaurant with a pasta and salad choice, as well as the fish and meat stalwarts.

Restaurante Alcaide (☎ 262 959 220; Rua Direita 60; mains €11) A classy place with countryside views and a menu of masterfully combined dishes like codfish with cheese, chestnuts and apple.

Getting There & Away

There's a direct bus Monday to Friday from Lisbon (€6, one hour, every 10 minutes) or via Caldas da Rainha, 10 minutes away.

NAZARÉ

pop 16,000

Nazaré is a seagulls-and-sand resort with excellent seafood and a sweeping sandy beach. The locals wear national dress to lure the tourists into buying their wares – handy for impressive pics to wow the folks back home. The **tourist office** (☎ 262 561 194) is at the end of Av da República.

Sights & Activities

The **beaches** are superb, although swimmers should be aware of dangerous currents. Climb or take the funicular to the cliff-top **Sítio**, with its cluster of fisherman's cottages and great view.

Two of Portugal's big-time architectural masterpieces are close by. Follow the signs to **Alcobaça** where, right in the centre of town, is the immense **Mosteiro de Santa Maria de Alcobaça** (☎ 262 505 120; adult/child €4.50/2.25, church admission free; 🕑 9am-7pm, to 5pm winter) dating from 1178; don't miss the colossal former kitchen.

Batalha's massive Gothic **Mosteiro de Santa Maria de Vitória** (☎ 244 765 497; admission to cloisters & unfinished chapels adult/child €3.50/2; 🕑 9am-6pm, to 5pm winter), dating from 1388, is home to the tomb of Henry the Navigator.

Sleeping & Eating

Many townspeople rent out rooms; doubles start from €35. Check at the tourist office.

Ribamar (☎ 262 551 158; fax 262 562 224; Rua Gomes Freire 9; s/d €30/45; ❄) Sporting a sunny yellow-and-white frontage a frisbee throw from the beach, this 25-room hotel has sea-view balconies and spacious bijou rooms.

Mar Bravo (☎ 262 569 169; www.marbravo.com; Praça Sousa Oliveira 71; s/d €80/100; ❄) A deluxe stay with tastefully furnished, carpeted rooms, sea views and a classy seafood restaurant complete with a 'select your lobster from the tank' option.

Casa Marques (☎ 262 551 680; Rua Gil Vicente 37; mains €5) Stout fishermen's wives dish up tasty seafood dishes. There are also kebab and pizza takeaways on the same street – fussy families take note.

Ala-Riba (☎ 262 553 516; Rua Adrião Batalha 45; mains €9) Owner José's spell in Canada equals surf-and-turf on the menu, plus lobster, *cataplana* in a breezy blue-and-white interior.

Getting There & Away

The nearest train station, 6km away at Valado, is connected to Nazaré by frequent buses. Nazaré has numerous bus connections to Lisbon (€7.50, two hours).

PORTUGAL

TOMAR

pop 17,000

A charming town straddling a river, Tomar has the storybook notoriety of being home to the Knights Templar; check out their headquarters, the outstanding **Convento de Cristo** (☎ 249 313 481; adult/child €4.50/2; 9am-6.30pm Jun-Sep, 9am-5.30pm Oct-May) monastery. Other rarities include a magnificent 17th-century **Aqueduto de Pegões** (aqueduct) and a vegetarian restaurant. The town is backed by the dense greenery of the **Mata Nacional dos Sete Montes** (Seven Hills National Forest). Tomar's **tourist office** (☎ 249 329 000; www.rttemplarios.pt, in Portuguese; Serpa Pinto) can provide town and forest maps.

Sleeping & Eating

Residencial União (☎ 249 323 161; Rua Serpa Pinto 94; s/d €25/40) Situated within a reasonable baggage-lug from the main car park, this gracious older home has dark wood furnishings, creaky floorboards and old-fashioned bathrooms.

Estalagem de Santa Iria (☎ 249 313 326; Mouchão Parque; s/d €65/85; P) Boutique hotel with just 13 large sunny rooms with balconies overlooking the park and river beyond. The restaurant is elegant and good.

Gaia (☎ 249 311 109; Rua dos Moínhos 75; mains €6; 9am-8pm Mon-Fri, to 2pm Sat) A vegetarian restaurant with just a few tables and daily dishes that can include *seitan* (wheat gluten) stew, tofu lasagne or meatless *feijada* (Brazilian bean stew).

Bela Vista (☎ 249 312 870; Rua Fonte do Choupo 6; mains €8) The town's best-known restaurant, in a riverside setting, serving dishes like roast kid (baby goat, that is) with real gastro-flair.

Getting There & Away

There are at least four express buses daily to Lisbon (€6.50, two hours) and even more frequent trains (€6.80, two hours).

COIMBRA

pop 150,000

Coimbra is a dynamic, fashionable, yet comfortably lived-in city, with a student life centred on the magnificent 13th-century university. Aesthetically eclectic, there are elegant shopping streets, ancient stone walls and backstreet alleys with hidden *tascas* and *fado* bars. Coimbra was the birth and burial place of Portugal's first king; and the country's most important city when the Moors captured Lisbon.

Information

Esp@ço Internet (Praça 8 de Maio; 10am-8pm Mon-Fri, to 10pm Sat & Sun) Free wi-fi and Internet access for 30 minutes.
Municipal tourist office (☎ 239 832 591; Praça Dom Dinis)
Regional tourist office (☎ 239 488 120; www.turismo-centro.pt; Largo da Portagem) Has pamphlets and cultural events information.
Tourist office (☎ 239 833 202; Praça da República)

Sights & Activities

Igreja de Santa Cruz (☎ 239 822 941; Praça 8 de Maio; adult/child €2.50/1.50; 9am-noon & 2-5pm) has a fabulous ornate pulpit and medieval royal tombs. Located at the bottom of the hill in the old town, you can reach the monastery via the elevator (one way €1.60) by the market.

University Velha (☎ 239 822 941; www.uc.pt/sri; admission €4; 10am-noon & 2-5pm) is unmissable in its grandeur. You can visit the library with its gorgeous book-lined hallways and the Manueline chapel dating back to 1517.

Conimbriga, 16km south of Coimbra, is the site of the well-preserved ruins of a **Roman town** (9am-8pm mid-Mar–mid-Sep, 10am-6pm mid-Sep–mid-Mar), including mosaic floors, baths and fountains. There's a good **museum** (adult/child €3/free; 9am-8pm summer, 10am-6pm winter) here with restaurant. Frequent buses run to Condeixa, 2km from the site; direct buses depart at 9.05am and 9.35am (only 9.35am at weekends) from the **AVIC terminal** (Rua João de Ruão 18, Coimbra) returning at 1pm and 6pm (only 6pm at weekends).

Odabarca (☎ 239 912 444; Parque Dr Manuel Braga; trips €8) run river trips on the Rio Mondego. Several companies rent canoes and kayaks, including **Down Stream** (☎ 966 087 358; www.down-stream.net; Quintais de Cima; from €18), the tourist office can provide you with a list. A free minibus takes you to Penacova for the 25km river journey.

Festivals & Events

Coimbra's annual highlight is **Queima das Fitas**, a boozy week of *fado* and revelry that begins on the first Thursday in May when students celebrate the end of the academic year.

THE FÁTIMA FAITHFULS

If you want to channel Dylan and buy one of the souvenir 'flesh-coloured Christs that glow in the dark' then check out Fátima, located in between Leiria and Tomar, and one of the largest religious shrines in Western Europe. Aside from gawping at the super-kitsch religious souvenirs, the place itself is pretty extraordinary with its dazzling white basilica fronted by a vast concrete forecourt. Suspiciously reminiscent of an airport runway, this was built to hold more than a million devotees and is essential during the annual pilgrimages on 12–13 May and 12–13 October when pilgrims arrive from all over the country, some walking barefoot or on padded knees in penance.

The story behind Fátima dates back to 13 May 1917, when the Virgin appeared to three children on top of a tree. The Virgin promised to return on the 13th of each month for the next five months, and amid much scepticism (yet each time accompanied by increasingly larger crowds) the three children reported successive apparitions. The word spread and by the final appearance on 13 October some 70,000 devotees had gathered and witnessed the so-called Miracle of the Sun. According to eyewitnesses, there were shooting beams of multicoloured light, and the sun intensified to a blinding swirling ball of fire. Disabilities and illnesses were miraculously cured: the blind could see, the dumb could talk and the crippled could walk (get the picture…?).

Three secrets of Fátima were also revealed to the children. The first foretold WWII and the spread of atheism. The second message was more prophetic concerning Russia and the spread of communism. The third secret was revealed in May 2000 by the Vatican, apparently predicting the attempt on the life of Pope John Paul II in 1981.

The exact site where the Virgin appeared is now a small chapel, always packed with devotees offering flowers and lighting candles. Seven masses are held here daily, including two in English; check the information booth for details. The basilica is surrounded by hotels, souvenir shops and a park with picnic tables – for those coach-loads of Portuguese families.

Whatever your religious convictions, Fátima is an extraordinary place and well worth the detour if you have a couple of hours to spare.

PORTUGAL

Sleeping

Pensão Santa Cruz (☎ 239 826 197; Praça 8 de Maio; s/d €25/32) Think threadbare large rooms in an old building in a great position overlooking one of the city's most dynamic squares.

Pensão Residencial Larbelo (☎ 239 829 092; fax 239 829 094; Largo da Portagem 33; s/d/t €25/40/55;) Well-polished, if dated, rooms with lacy curtains and views of chairs on the square; perfect for that *bica* break.

Residência Coimbra (☎ 239 837 996; www.residencia coimbra.com; Rua das Azeiteiras 55; s/d/t €25/40/55;) Glossy stylish rooms with satellite TV and fridges. There's wi-fi in the breakfast room and lobby.

Pensão Flôr de Coimbra (☎ 239 823 865; fax 239 821 545; Rua do Poço 5; s/d from €40/45) Enjoy lashings of white linen and *fin de siècle* atmosphere at this renovated family home. The rooms are large and atmospheric with high ceilings and antiques. There is a small restaurant attached with a menu that includes a daily vegetarian dish.

Casa Pombal Guesthouse (☎ 239 835 175; www .casapombal.com, in Portuguese; Rua das Flores 18; d €48, with shared bathroom €40) This place is a gem with pretty rooms painted in pastel colours and roof-top views. Dutch owner Elsa's breakfast is more generous than most.

Hotel Astória (☎ 239 853 020; www.almeida hotels.com; Av Emídio Navarro 21; s/d €84/101;) A slightly-scuffed older hotel with an air of all-round poshness, especially in the grand sitting room with its chandeliers and burgundy sofas. There's wi-fi in the lobby.

Eating & Drinking

Head to the lanes west of Praça do Comércio, especially Rua das Azeiteiras, for cheap eats.

Café Santa Cruz (☎ 239 833 617; Praçca Maio) Former chapel that has been resurrected into one of Portugal's most atmospheric cafés.

Restaurante Jardim da Manga (☎ 239 829 156; Rua Olímpio Nicolau Rui Fernanda; mains €7; closed Sat) A better breed of self-service restaurant at the back of the dramatic cupula and fountain of the Mosteiro de Santa Cruz. Vegetarian dishes available.

O Estudante (☎ 239 832 699; Rua da Sota 44-48; mains €7.50) Black-and-white photos of historic Coimbra line the walls at this no-nonsense eatery with its tasty specials including a memorable *arroz de pato* (duck with rice).

Zé Manel (☎ 239 823 790; Beco do Forno 12; mains €7-10) Great food, huge servings and a zany atmosphere with walls papered with diners' comments, cartoons and poems. Vegetarian choices.

Italia (☎ 239 838 863; Parque Dr Manuel Braga; mains €8-10) Expand your midriff at this excellent Italian restaurant on the riverfront with laden dishes of excellent pizza and pasta.

Entertainment

Coimbra-style *fado* is more cerebral than the Lisbon variety, and its adherents staunchly protective. **Bar Diligência** (☎ 239 827 667; Rua Nova 30; 6pm-2am) and **Boémia Bar** (☎ 239 834 547; Rua do Cabido 6; 8pm-2am) are popular *casas de fado*.

Á Capella (☎ 239 833 985; Capela de Nossa Senhora de Victoría, Rua Corpo de Deus, Largo da Victoría) Housed in a fabulous 14th-century former chapel with a nightly *fado* show at 9.30pm (€5).

Quebra Club (☎ 239 836 038; Parque Verde do Mondego) Has live jazz at weekends.

Via Latina (☎ 239 833 034; Rua Almeida Garrett 1) Fires up to a steamy dance pit late at night.

Getting There & Away

At least a dozen buses and as many trains run daily from Lisbon (€9.60, 2½ hours) and Porto (€9, 1½ hours), plus frequent express buses from Faro and Évora, via Lisbon. The main long-distance train stations are Coimbra B, 2km northwest of the centre, and central Coimbra A. Most long-distance trains call at both. Other useful connections include eight daily buses to Luso/Buçaco (from Coimbra A; €2.55, 45 minutes).

LUSO & THE BUÇACO FOREST

pop 2000

This region is oh-so-pretty with its dense forest of century-old trees surrounded by countryside dappled with heather, wildflowers and leafy ferns. There's even a palace here; a wedding-cake affair, which somehow works. Buçaco was chosen as a retreat by 16th-century monks and surrounds the lovely spa town of Luso.

The **tourist office** (☎/fax 231 939 133; Av Emídio Navarro) has maps and leaflets about the forest and trails, as well as free Internet access. The **Termas** (thermal baths; ☎ 231 937 910; Av Emídio Navarro; admission free; May-Oct) offers a range of treatments.

Sleeping & Eating

The Luso tourist office has a list of beds.

Astória (☎ 231 939 182; Av Emídio Navarro; s/d €30/35) Like that favourite woolly, this place is well worn but snug. There's dark wood and beams, and the location is ace if you're taking a dip in the baths.

Palace Hotel do Buçaco (☎ 231 930 101; www.almeidahotels.com; s/d from €145/185; P) Live a real-life fairy tale and stay at this truly sumptuous pile complete with gargoyles, ornamental garden and turrets. The equally elegant restaurant offers set menus for around €40.

Restaurante O Cesteiro (☎ 231 939 360; EN 234; mains €7) A large dining room with extensive menu of confident traditional dishes. The grilled chicken is a winner.

Getting There & Away

There are three buses daily Monday to Friday, two on Saturday and one on Sunday from Coimbra (€2.50, 50 minutes). There is just one train that departs around 10.30am from Coimbra B (€1.30, 30 minutes).

SERRA DA ESTRELA

The forested Serra da Estrela has a raw natural beauty and offers some of the country's best hiking. This is Portugal's highest mainland mountain range (1993m), and the source of its two great rivers: Mondego River and Zêzere River. The **main park office** (☎ 275 980 060; www.rt-serradaestrela.pt; Manteigas) has plenty of information on the Parque Natural da Serra da Estrela; additional offices are at Seia, Gouveia and Guarda.

The park publishes *Discover the Region of the Serra da Estrela,* a walking guide in English with maps and narratives (€4.25), plus a topographic map of the park (€6.60).

Sleeping

Pousada da Juventude (☎/fax 275 335 375; penhas@movijem.pt; Penhas da Saúde; dm/d from €10/25) Located 10km above Covilhã, this is an excellent hostel and good excursion base, providing meals or kitchen facilities. Buses come from Covilhã (€1.25, twice daily, July to September only), or a taxi costs €12.

Residencial Santos (☎ 271 205 400, Rua Tenente 14, Guarda; d/€45; ❄) This place is a pleasing midrange choice with gleaming rooms and an ultramodern interior with interconnecting walkways and glass lifts.

Getting There & Away

Several buses run daily from Coimbra along the park's perimeter to Seia, Gouveia, Guarda or Covilhã. Others go via Covilhã (€4, 45 minutes) to Castel Branco (€7.50, 1¾ hours) and Lisbon, and several times daily to Viseu (€6.20, 1½ hours), Porto and Coimbra.

The twice-daily IC Line 110 train links Lisbon and Coimbra to Guarda (€12.80, 4¼ hours).

Getting Around

No buses cross the park, although you can go around it. At least two buses link Seia, Gouveia and Guarda daily, and considerably more run between Guarda and Covilhã.

PORTUGAL

THE NORTH

The country's northern region is country-bumpkin heaven with its rolling landscape interspersed with dense forests and dramatic mountains. This region is also gluttony for wine-lovers: it's the home of the sprightly *vinho verde* wine, while its capital Porto is named after another tipple and is a beguiling combo of the medieval and modern. Smaller towns similarly have a real now-and-then feel including magnificent Braga, the country's religious heart, and the folkloric capital of Viana do Castelo.

PORTO

pop 300,000

Portugal's second-largest city, Porto has a real foreign feel with a gritty old quarter and steep streets lined with lofty, strung-with-washing houses. A lively city with chatter in the air and a tangible sense of history, Porto's old-world river-frontage district is a World Heritage Site. Across the water twinkle the neon signs of Vila Nova de Gaia, the headquarters of the major port manufacturers. Tipple aside, Porto is home to medieval churches, a clutch of museums and countless eateries and cafés. The city has recently taken a giant stride into the 21st century with the construction of a metro system.

Orientation

Porto centre is small enough to cover mainly by foot. The city clings to the north bank of the Douro River, spanned by five bridges across from Vila Nova de Gaia, home to the port-wine lodges. Central Porto's axis is Av dos Aliados. The picturesque Ribeira district lies along the waterfront, in the shadow of the great Ponte de Dom Luís I bridge.

Information

INTERNET ACCESS

Portweb (☎ 222 005 922; Praça General Humberto Delgado 291; per hr €2.50; 🕑 10-2am Mon-Sat, 3pm-2am Sun) Great ambience at this basement cyber café.

MEDICAL SERVICES

Santo António Hospital (☎ 222 077 500; Largo Prof Abel Salazar) Has English-speaking staff.

MONEY

Portocâmbios (Rua Rodrigues Sampaio 193)

Top Atlântico (☎ 222 074 020; trinidade@topatlantico.com; Rua Alferes Malheiro 96) Doubles as an Amex representative.

POST

Main post office (Praça General Humberto Delgado) Across from the main tourist office.

TELEPHONE

Telephone office (Praça da Liberdade 62) Where faxes can be sent.

TOURIST INFORMATION

ICEP tourist office (☎ 222 057 514; fax 222 053 212; Praça Dom João I 43) The national tourist office.

Municipal tourist office (☎ 223 393 472; www.portoturismo.pt; Rua Clube dos Fenianos 25) Next door to the tourist police office.

Tourist office (☎ 222 009 770; Rua Infante DomHenrique 63) Smaller city tourist office.

TRAVEL AGENCIES

Montes d'Aventura (☎ 228 305 157; Alameda Dr Antonio Macedo 19; 🕑 9am-6pm Mon-Fri, 10am-1pm Sat) Organises walking, cycling and canoeing trips.

Trilhos (☎ /fax 225 020 740; www.trilhos.pt, in Portuguese; Rua de Belém 94; 🕑 9.30am-6pm Mon-Fri, 10am-1pm Sat) Another option for canoe and hydrospeed excursions.

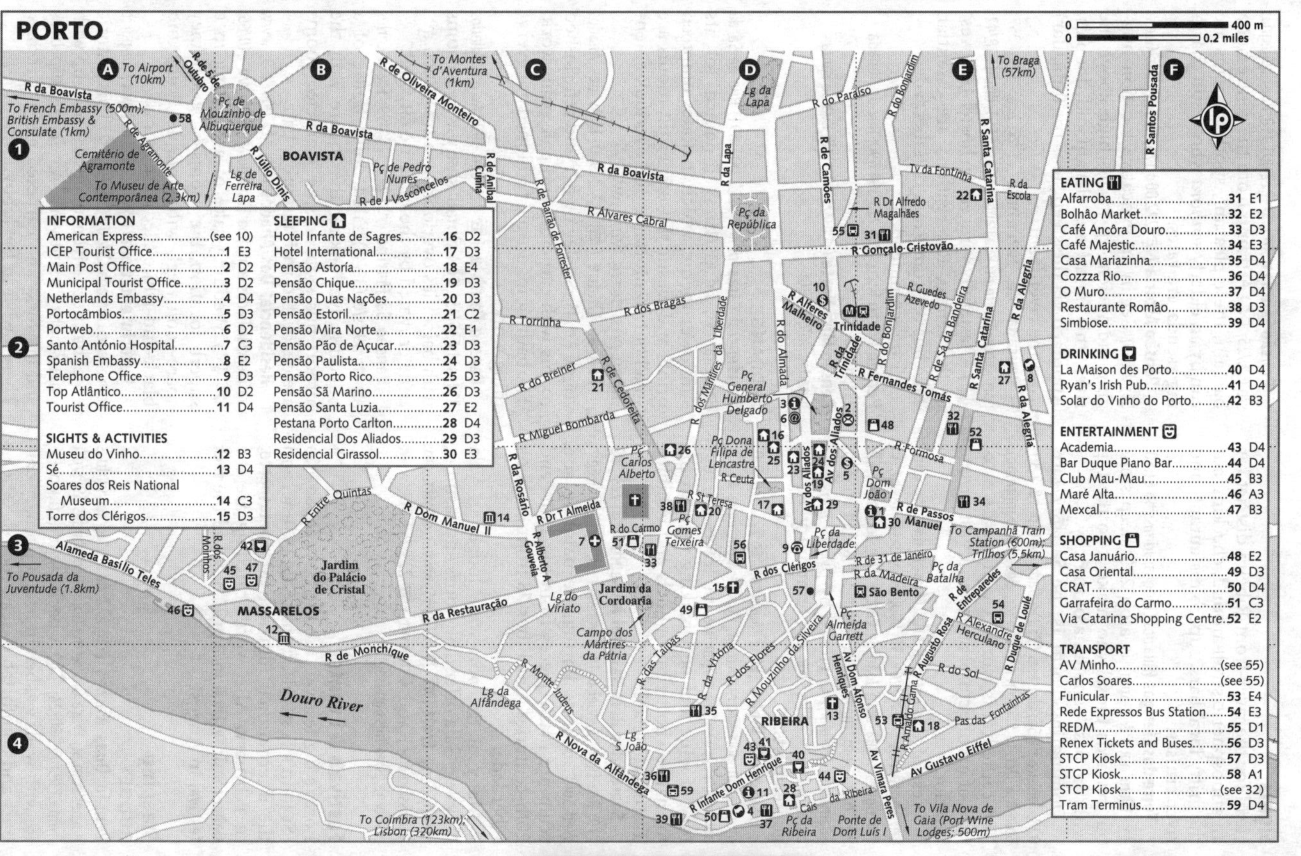
PORTO
0 400 m
0 0.2 miles
INFORMATION
American Express (see 10)
ICEP Tourist Office 1 E3
Main Post Office 2 D2
Municipal Tourist Office 3 D2
Netherlands Embassy 4 D4
Portocâmbios 5 D3
Portweb 6 D2
Santo António Hospital 7 C3
Spanish Embassy 8 E2
Telephone Office 9 D3
Top Atlântico 10 D2
Tourist Office 11 D4
SIGHTS & ACTIVITIES
Museu do Vinho 12 B3
Sé 13 D4
Soares dos Reis National Museum 14 C3
Torre dos Clérigos 15 D3
SLEEPING
Hotel Infante de Sagres 16 D2
Hotel International 17 D3
Pensão Astoria 18 E4
Pensão Chique 19 D3
Pensão Duas Nações 20 D3
Pensão Estoril 21 C2
Pensão Mira Norte 22 E1
Pensão Pão de Açucar 23 D3
Pensão Paulista 24 D3
Pensão Porto Rico 25 D3
Pensão Sã Marino 26 D3
Pensão Santa Luzia 27 E2
Pestana Porto Carlton 28 D4
Residencial Dos Aliados 29 D3
Residencial Girassol 30 E3
EATING
Alfarroba 31 E1
Bolhão Market 32 E2
Café Ancôra Douro 33 D3
Café Majestic 34 E3
Casa Mariazinha 35 D4
Cozzza Rio 36 D4
O Muro 37 D4
Restaurante Romão 38 D3
Simbiose 39 D4
DRINKING
La Maison des Porto 40 D4
Ryan's Irish Pub 41 D4
Solar do Vinho do Porto 42 B3
ENTERTAINMENT
Academia 43 D4
Bar Duque Piano Bar 44 D4
Club Mau-Mau 45 B3
Maré Alta 46 A3
Mexcal 47 B3
SHOPPING
Casa Januário 48 E2
Casa Oriental 49 D3
CRAT 50 D4
Garrafeira do Carmo 51 C3
Via Catarina Shopping Centre 52 E2
TRANSPORT
AV Minho (see 55)
Carlos Soares (see 55)
Funicular 53 E4
Rede Expressos Bus Station 54 E3
REDM 55 D1
Renex Tickets and Buses 56 D3
STCP Kiosk 57 D3
STCP Kiosk 58 A1
STCP Kiosk (see 32)
Tram Terminus 59 D4
To Airport (10km)
To French Embassy (500m); British Embassy & Consulate (1km)
To Montes d'Aventura (1km)
To Braga (57km)
To Museu de Arte Contemporânea (2.3km)
To Pousada da Juventude (1.8km)
To Coimbra (123km); Lisbon (320km)
To Vila Nova de Gaia (Port Wine Lodges; 500m)
To Campanhã Train Station (600m); Trilhos (5.5km)
BOAVISTA
MASSARELOS
RIBEIRA
Trinidade
São Bento
Douro River
Jardim do Palácio de Cristal
Jardim da Cordoaria
Cemitério de Agramonte
Pç de Mouzinho de Albuquerque
Pç da República
Pç General Humberto Delgado
Pç da Liberdade
Pç da Ribeira
Ponte de Dom Luís I
R da Boavista
R de Oliveira Monteiro
R Santa Catarina
R da Alegria
R de Cedofeita
R dos Clérigos
R de Passos Manuel
Av dos Aliados
R Nova da Alfândega
Av Gustavo Eiffel
Av Vimara Peres
R de Monchique
R da Restauração
Alameda Basílio Teles

Sights

Head for the river-front Ribeira district for an atmospheric stroll around, checking out the gritty local bars, superb restaurants and river cruises.

Torre dos Clérigos (Rua dos Clérigos; admission €1.50; 10am-noon & 2-5pm) is atop 225 steep steps but rewards those who make it to the top with the best panorama of the city.

Dominating Porto is the **Sé** (222 059 028; Terreiro da Sé; cloisters €2; 9am-12.15pm & 2.30-6pm Apr-Oct, to 5.15pm rest of year, closed Sun morning). The cathedral is worth a visit for its mixture of architectural styles and vast ornate interior.

West of the city is the **Museu de Arte Contemporânea** (226 156 500; www.serralves.pt, in Portuguese; Rua Dom João de Castro 210; admission €5; 10am-7pm Tue-Fri, 10am-8pm Sat & Sun Apr-Sep, 10am-7pm Oct-Mar), enclosed by pretty gardens and with works by contemporary Portuguese artists.

Museu do Vinho (Wine Museum; 222 076 300; museuvinhoporto@cm-porto.pt; Rua de Monchique 45-52; admission €2; 11am-7pm Tue-Sun) traces the history of wine and port making with an informative short film, models and exhibits. Tastings available.

Soares dos Reis National Museum (223 393 770; Rua Dom Manuel II 44; admission €3; 10am-6pm Wed-Sun) exhibits Portuguese painting and sculpture masterpieces from the 19th- and 20th-centuries. Catch bus 78 from Praça da Liberdade.

Many of the port-wine lodges in Vila Nova de Gaia offer daily tours and tastings, including **Croft** (223 772 965; www.croftport.com; admission free) and **Osborne** (223 757 517; www.osborne.es; admission free).

Festivals & Events

Porto's big festivals are the **Festa de São João** (St John's Festival), from 16 to 24 June, and the international film festival, **Fantasporto**, in February. Also worth catching are the **Celtic music festival** in April/May and the **rock festival** in August.

Sleeping

BUDGET

Pensão Duas Nações (222 081 616; www.duasnacoes.com.pt; Praça Guilherme Gomes Fernandes 59; s/d/t from €13.50/21.50/24;) A backpackers favourite with walls washed in bright primary colours and comfortable clean rooms.

Pensão Santa Luzia (222 001 119; Rua da Alegria; s/d €20/25;) A tramp from the centre but a bargain, these pleasant, spotless rooms are run by an elderly *senhora* who is still charging escuda-era rates.

Pensão Astória (222 008 175; Rua Arnaldo Gama 56; d €35) Set in an evocative location hugging the ancient city walls high above the river, this *hostal* has elegant old doubles. Approach via the steep steps (or funicular) from the river front.

Pousada da Juventude (226 177 257; porto@movijovem.pt; Rua Paulo da Gama 551; dm/d €18/42;) A tastefully spruced-up hostel 4km west of the centre. Reservations are essential. Take bus 35 from Praça da Liberdade.

Also recommended:

Pensão Porto Rico (223 394 690; Rua do Almada 237; d €30;)

Pensão Mira Norte (222 001 118; Rua de Santa Catarina 969; d €30)

MIDRANGE

Residencial Girassol (222 001 891; Rua de Sá da Bandeira 133; s/d €35/45) Well-named for its sunflower theme, which includes umpteen prints and plastic flowers. Front rooms are small but comfortable and overlook an enticing *pastelaria* window.

Pensão Chique (222 009 011; Av dos Aliados 206; s/d €35/45) Smiley owner and refurbished rooms with carpeting and pale paint work. The bathrooms are old fashioned but everything works.

Pensão Paulista (222 054 692; Av dos Aliados 214; s/d €35/45;) Small shiny-wood rooms with balconies overlooking a tree-lined avenue crowned by the majestic city hall.

Pensão Sã Marino (223 325 499; Praça Carlos Alberto 59; s/d €38/45) Tiled doll's house of a building overlooking the square with the airport bus stop outside. Carpeted rooms are decorated with feminine flair.

Residencial Dos Aliados (222 004 853; www.residencialaliados.com; Rua Elisio de Melo 27; s/d €40/65;) Wedding-cake of a building in a superb location, the rooms have a homey spare-room feel, with antiques, rugs and black-and-white tiled bathrooms.

Hotel International (222 005 032; www.hi-porto.com; Rua do Almada 131; s/d €55/70;) This historic hotel has been given an upbeat revamp with warm-ochre paintwork, modern sculptures and artwork, and carpeted elegant rooms. There's wi-fi in the lobby.

Also recommended is **Pensão Estoril** (☎ 222 002 751; fax 222 082 468; Rua de Cedofeita 193; d €45; ☒).

TOP END

Pensão Pão de Açucar (☎ 222 002 425; Rua do Almada 262; www.residencialpaodeacucar.com; d/€75; P ☒) Upbeat Art Nouveau décor with Escher-inspired spiral staircase. Go for the top floor with rooms opening onto the palm-fringed terrace.

Pestana Porto Carlton (☎ 223 402 300; www.pestana.com; Praça da Ribeira 1; s/d from €131/147; P ☒ ☒ ☐) Here you'll find red-carpet service in a gorgeous 16th-century setting. Rooms have city or river views and sleek glossy furnishings with all the extras. There's wi-fi in the lobby.

Hotel Infante de Sagres (☎ 223 398 500; www.hotelinfantesagres.pt; Praça D Filipa de Lencastre 62; s/d €160/175; P ☒ ☐) A luxurious pile featuring stained glass, chandeliers, carved wood ceilings and a central patio with fountain and palms. The rooms here are all different and are decorated with impeccable taste and flair.

Eating

RESTAURANTS

O Muro (☎ 222 083 426; Muro dos Bacalhoeiros 88; mains €7; closed Mon) Top-notch, well-priced restaurant on the river with delicious, filling food, including several vegetarian choices. Delightfully wacky décor ranges from dried *bacalhau* to a Che Guevara poster.

Restaurante Romão (☎ 222 005 639; Praça Carlos Alberto 100; mains €7.50) Small check-tablecloth place serving up tasty northern specialities such as tripe and roast kid. Leave room for the *torta de noz* (walnut tart).

Simbiose (☎ 222 030 398; Rua Infante Dom Henrique 133; mains €11) Swooning-couples kind of place with a candlelit dining room overlooking the river. The cuisine is no-surprises Portuguese, with a reasonable daily buffet (€7.50).

Casa Mariazinha (☎ 222 009 137; Rua de Belomonte 2-4; meal €60) Think five tables and four courses served with a flourish – and the accompanying wines – by sommelier Antonio. The food is delicious: gourmet and good to look at, prepared by Brazilian wife Neide.

Cozzza Rio (☎ 222 000 712; Rua S Francisco 8; mains €60) There's a fashionable vibe at this small restaurant (yes, that *is* how it is spelt) with its lunchtime menu of tapas and more traditional night-time fare, including octopus-studded rice.

CAFÉS, QUICK EATS & SELF-CATERING

Café Majestic (☎ 222 003 887; Rua Santa Catarina 112) An extravagant Art Nouveau relic where powdered ladies enjoy afternoon tea.

Alfarroba (☎ 222 088 720; Rua Do Bolhão; snacks €2.50) Excellent vegetarian buffet and takeaway next to Hotel Don Henrique.

Café Ancôra Douro (☎ 222 003 749; Praça de Parada Leitão 49; snacks €3) Undergoing an overhaul at time of research, this place typically heaves with students here for the veggie burgers, hot dogs and crepes.

Bolhão market (Rua Formosa; 8am-5pm Mon-Fri, 8am-1pm Sat) Sells fruit and veggies in season, plus cheese and deli goodies.

Drinking

Solar do Vinho do Porto (☎ 226 094 749; Rua Entre Quintas 220; 2pm-midnight Mon-Sat) Sophisticated setting for tasting the port made just across the river.

La Maison des Porto (☎ 936 057 340; Rua São Joã 46; 10am-12.30pm & 3-7pm Mon, Tue, Thu & Fri, 10am-12.30pm Wed & Sun) This vinotheque gets the thumbs up from readers; taste and learn about port from the charming multilingual owner.

Ryan's Irish Pub (☎ 222 005 366; Rua Infante Dom Henrique 18; 6pm-2am) There's a suitably blarney atmosphere here for enjoying the usual range of gluggable beer.

Entertainment

Academia (☎ 222 005 737; Rua São João 80; 10pm-late Tue-Sat) Revamped and stylishly hip disco-bar.

Bar Duque Piano Bar (☎ 223 20 848; Rua da Lada 98; Mon-Sat) On a street back from the Douro, this place has a nice low-key ambience, aside from karaoke nights.

Mexcal (☎ 226 009 188; Rua da Restauração 39; 10pm-4am Tue-Sat) The Latino music here is good for a little late-night hip swinging.

Club Mau-Mau (☎ 226 076 660; Rua do Outeiro 4; 11pm-4am Wed-Sat) A dodging-elbows disco with live music on Thursday nights.

Maré Alta (☎ 226 162 540; Alameda Basilio Teles; 10pm-2am Wed & Thu, 10pm-4am Fri & Sat, 8pm-4am Sun) Nail-bitingly trendy disco with occasional live gigs.

Shopping

Major shopping areas are eastward around the Bolhão Market and Rua Santa Catarina, and westward along Rua dos Clérigos.

The best central shopping mall is **Via Catarina Shopping Centre** (Rua Santa Catarina) in a tasteful building. Port is, naturally, a popular purchase in this town. Shops with a broad selection include knowledgeable **Garrafeira do Carmo** (Rua do Carmo 17), the deli **Casa Januário** (Rua do Bonjardim 352) and **Casa Oriental** (Campo dos Mártires da Pátria 111), which also specialises in *bacalhau*. Other good buys are shoes and gold-filigree jewellery. For handicrafts visit **CRAT** (Rua da Reboleira 37) in the Ribeira.

Getting There & Away

AIR

Porto is connected by daily flights from Lisbon and London, and almost-daily direct links from other European cities (see p923).

BUS

Porto has a baffling number of private bus companies; the main tourist office has a separate desk for transport queries and timetables. In general, for Lisbon and the Algarve the choice is **Renex** (☎ 222 003 395; Rua das Carmelitas 32) or **Rede Expressos** (☎ 222 052 459).

Three companies operate from or near Praceto Régulo Magauanha, off Rua Dr Alfredo Magalhães: **REDM** (☎ 222 003 152) goes to Braga; **AV Minho** (☎ 222 006 121) to Viana do Castelo; and **Carlos Soares** (☎ 222 051 383) to Guimarães.

TRAIN

Porto is a northern Portugal rail hub with three stations. Most international trains, and all intercity links, start at Campanhã, 2km east of the centre. Inter-regional and regional services depart from Campanhã or the central **São Bento station** (☎ 225 364 141); buses 34 and 35 run frequently between these two.

At São Bento station you can book tickets to any destination from any other Porto station.

Getting Around

TO/FROM THE AIRPORT

The **AeroBus** (☎ 808 200 166; www.stcp.pt; €4; 6.45am-6.15pm) runs every half hour between Aliados and the airport. TAP Air passengers get a free ride. A taxi costs around €18.

ANDANTE FARES

The Andante is a euro-economising ticket covering metro, funicular, tram and some bus routes. The initial card costs €0.50, and it may then be recharged with more credit at vending machines at metro, train and bus stations. The savings are substantial. For a detailed breakdown on the multitrip deals and season tickets pick up the *Transport Guide* pamphlet (in English) available at the city tourist offices.

BUS

Central hubs of Porto's extensive bus system include Jardim da Cordoaria, Praça da Liberdade and São Bento station (Praça Almeida Garrett). Tickets are cheapest from STCP kiosks or newsagents and tobacconists: €1.55 for a return within Porto and from €1.95 for outlying areas. Tickets bought on the bus are €1.30 for a single. There's also a €4 day pass available.

FUNICULAR

Save your puff and hop on the funicular that shuttles up and down a steep incline from Av Gustavo Eiffel to Rua Augusto Rosa (€1.35, from 8am to 8pm).

METRO

Porto's metro currently comprises four metropolitan lines that all converge at the Trinidade stop. An additional line running from the airport to the centre is scheduled to open in 2007. For an update and metro map check the website www.metrodoporto.pt. Tickets cost €1.30 for a single ride, but you can save money by investing in an Andante card (see above).

TAXI

To cross town, expect to pay about €5. An additional charge is made to leave the city limits, including across the Ponte de Dom Luís I to Vila Nova de Gaia.

TRAM

Porto has three antique trams that trundle daily along and around the Douro to the Foz district.

ALONG THE DOURO

Portugal's best-known river flows through the country's rural heartland. In the upper reaches, port-wine grapes are grown on steep terraced hills, punctuated by remote stone villages and, in spring, splashes of dazzling white almond blossom.

The Douro River is navigable right across Portugal. Highly recommended is the train journey from Porto to Peso da Régua (€6.75, 2½ hours, about a dozen trains daily), the last 50km clinging to the river's edge; four trains continue daily to Pocinho (4½ hours). **Douro Azul** (☎ 223 393 950; www.douroazul.com) and other companies run one- and two-day river cruises, mostly from March to October. Cyclists and drivers can choose river-hugging roads along either bank, although they're crowded at weekends. A detailed colour map *Rio Douro* (€3) is available from Porto bookshops.

VIANA DO CASTELO

pop 36,545

Portugal's folkloric capital specialises in making (and selling) the traditional embroidered costumes but is far from twee. This elegant port town has grandiose 16th-century buildings, superb restaurants and beaches. The **tourist office** (☎ 258 822 620; www.rtam.pt; Rua Hospital Velho) has information on festivals and the region. In August Viana hosts the **Festas de Nossa Senhora da Agonia** (see p923).

Sights

The stately heart of town is Praça da República, with its delicate fountain and grandiose buildings, including the 16th-century **Misericórdia**, a striking Renaissance building, its upper storeys supported by ornate caryatids.

Atop Santa Luzia Hill, the **Templo do Sagrado Coração de Jesus** (Temple of the Sacred Heart of Jesus; ☎ 258 823 173; admission free; 🕑 8am-7pm Apr-Sep, 8am-5pm Oct-Mar) offers a grand panorama across the river. The funicular railway is not operating, so if your ankles and knees can cope, take the steps, or a taxi, roughly 2km to the top.

Sleeping

Pousada da Juventude Gil Eannes (☎ 258 821 582; naviogileannes@movijovem.pt; Gil Eannes; dm €11) This *hostal* is located in the bowels of a grand ship. QE2 it ain't, but it's comfortable and the novelty factor is high.

Pensão Verde Minho (☎ 258 822 386; Rua do Anjinho 34-36; s/d €25/35) Ace location for foodies on a cobbled restaurant-flanked side street; the spotless rooms are pretty slick for the price.

Residencial Viana Mar (☎ 258 828 962; Av Combatentes da G Guerra 215; s/d €35/45) Well-positioned with comfortable chintzy rooms and a sunken bar that dates from the sixties when it was Viana's first nightclub.

Margarida da Praça (☎ 258 809 630; Largo 5 de Outubro 58; s/d €55/70; ❄ 💻) There's a boutique feel to this port-side place with its modern art, classy restaurant and shiny, comfortable rooms.

Eating

A Gruta (☎ 258 820 214; Rua Grande 87; mains €7) This is a snug place with half-tiled walls and a reasonable daily menu of solid local dishes. Nip across to the *pasteleria* for dessert.

Dolce Vita (☎ 258 820 214; Rua do Poço 44; mains €7) Wood-fired pizza and innovative pasta sauces make this *the* obligatory refuelling spot in town.

Zip (☎ 258 826 594; Rua Luis Jácome 17; mains €7) Well-named, this buzzy new restaurant with its red-and-wicker décor has an excellent international menu if you're suffering from *bacalhau* burn out, including crepes, pasta dishes and salads.

O Garfo (☎ 258 829 415; Largo 5 de Outubro 58; mains €8) Mixed grill, salmon and cod cakes are just some of the goodies available at this warm inviting restaurant opposite the docks.

Getting There & Away

Half a dozen express coaches daily go to Porto (€5, one hour) and Lisbon (€14, 5½ hours) Monday to Friday, with fewer at weekends.

BRAGA

pop 110,000

The religious capital of Portugal, lovely Braga is monolithic in its ecclesiastical architecture with a contemporary contrast of pedestrian streets flanked with classy cafés, shops and boutiques. The only downside is the Big Mac eyesore in the middle of the town's most beautiful square. The **tourist office** (☎ 253 262 550; www.cm-braga.pt; Praça da

República 1) can help with accommodation and maps.

Sights

In the centre of Braga is the **Sé** (museum & chapels adult/child €2/free; 8.30am-5.30pm), an elegant cathedral complex.

At Bom Jesus do Monte, a hilltop pilgrimage site 5km from Braga, is an extraordinary stairway, the **Escadaria do Bom Jesus**, with allegorical fountains, chapels and a superb view. Buses run frequently from Braga to the site, where you can climb the steps (pilgrims sometimes do this on their knees) or ascend by funicular railway (€1).

It's an easy day trip to **Guimarães** with its medieval town centre and a palace of the dukes of Bragança.

Sleeping

Pousada da Juventude (253 616 163; braga@movijovem.pt; Rua de Santa Margarida 6; dm/d €10/27) This bland but lively hostel is a 10-minute walk from the centre.

Hotel Residencial CC Avenida (253 275 722; Bragashopping; s/d €35/45) Shopoholic heaven, in the centre of a commercial centre, this modern place has pink-and-white rooms, satellite TV and friendly front-desk folk.

Albergaria da Sé (253 214 502; fax 253 214 501; Rua Gonçalo Pereira 39-45; s/d €45/50; P) A swallow's swoop from the cathedral with appropriate heady views, the rooms have hard-wood floors, sophisticated artwork and a subtle colour scheme.

Eating & Drinking

Adega Pregão (253 277 249; Praça Velha 18; mains €7) Earthy local with outdoor tables on a scenic side street. Dishes include a recommended roast lamb with chestnuts.

Taberna do Felix (253 617 701; Praça Velha 17; mains €9) Perfect for a smoochy dinner, this intimate restaurant has dim lighting, stone walls and an innovative menu, including tapas and fish fritters.

D Diogo (253 262 297; Diogo de Sousa 81-83; mains €15) Go for the splurge at this classy candlelit restaurant with its limited menu of refined fish, meat and rice dishes.

Café Vianna (253 262 336; Praça da República) A classic 19th-century café under the arches.

A Brazileira (253 262 104; Largo do Barã de S Martinho) Mildly decadent corner bar attracting effortlessly scruffy students.

Getting There & Away

Intercidade trains arrive twice daily from Lisbon (€15, five hours), Coimbra (€10, 2¼ hours) and Porto (€2, 1¾ hours), and there are daily connections north to Viana do Castelo. Daily bus services link Braga to Porto (€4.50, 1½ hours) and Lisbon (€14.50, five hours).

PARQUE NACIONAL DA PENEDA-GERÊS

Boasting some of the most stunning scenery in the country, this superb park is a popular holiday spot for Portugal's happy campers. Hikers are also keen, especially on the wilder northern region around Serra de Peneda. The area has an ancient history with dolmens, stone circles and standing stones; most are marked on local tourist maps. The park's main centre is at Caldas do Gerês, a sleepy, hot-spring village.

Information

Gerês' **tourist office** (253 391 133; fax 253 391 282) can provide information on activities and accommodation.

Other park offices are at Arcos de Valdevez and Montalegre. All have a map and an English-language booklet on the park (€3). A more detailed topographical map can be bought in Lisbon or Porto or ordered online (www.igeoe.pt, in Portuguese).

Activities

HIKING

There are trails and footpaths through the park, some between villages with accommodation. Leaflets detailing these are available from the park offices.

Day hikes around Gerês are popular. An adventurous option is the old Roman road from Mata do Albergaria (10km up-valley from Gerês by taxi or hitching), past the **Vilarinho das Furnas** reservoir to Campo do Gerês. More distant destinations include **Ermida** and **Cabril**, both with simple cafés and accommodation. Guided walks are organised by several outfits including **Incentivos Outdoors** (914 863 353) at Gerês and **Trote-Gerês** (/fax 253 659 860) at Cabril.

CYCLING

Mountain bikes can be hired from **Incentivos Outdoors** (914 863 353) or the German-run **Pensão Carvalho Araújo** (253 391 185; May-Sep).

HORSE RIDING

The national park operates **horse riding facilities** (☎ 253 390 110) from beside its Vidoeiro camping ground, near Gerês. **Equi Desafios** (☎ 253 352 803; www.equidesafios.com; Rua Dr Francisco Xavier de Araújo) in Gerês also organises treks.

WATER SPORTS

Rio Caldo, 8km south of Gerês, is the base for water sports on the Caniçada reservoir. Equi Desafios (see |) rents out canoes and other boats. For paddling the Salamonde reservoir, Trote-Gerês rents out canoes from its camp site at Cabril.

Gerês' **Parque das Termas** (admission €1; Sat & Sun Apr, daily May-Oct) has a **swimming pool** (Mon-Fri €3.50, Sat & Sun €5).

Sleeping

Although Gerês has plenty of *pensões*, you may find vacancies are limited as many are block-booked by spa patients in summer.

Cerdeira Camping Ground (Campo do Gerês; ☎ 253 351 005; fax 253 353 315; camp sites €4) Cerdeira has shady camp sites, a laundry and a mini-supermarket.

Pensão Adelaide (☎ 253 390 020; fax 253 390 029; d €40;) Bit of a hike from the centre but the views are a suitable reward. Rooms are clean and bright.

Águas do Gerês (☎ 253 390 190; Av Manuel Francisco da Costa 136; www.aguasdogeres.pt; s/d €45/55; P)A grand old building houses the town's latest hotel with its stylish and tasteful rooms, tennis and spa facilities.

Hotel Universal (☎ 253 390 020; Av Manuel Francisco da Costa; www.ehgeres.com; s/d €58/70;) A leafy patio lends an air of elegance to this main-street hotel with comfortable rooms. Shares a tennis court with the Águas hotel.

Eating

Most of Gerês *pensões* serve hearty meals to guests and nonguests. There are several restaurants, plus shops in the main street for stocking up on picnic provisions. The Cerdeira Camping Ground has a cheap restaurant of a reasonable standard.

Getting There & Away

From Braga, at least six coaches daily run to Rio Caldo and Gerês, and seven to Campo do Gerês (fewer at weekends). If you are coming from Lisbon or Porto, change at Braga.

PORTUGAL DIRECTORY

ACCOMMODATION

Most tourist offices have lists of accommodation to suit a range of budgets. In this chapter the budget category for a double room is up to €45, midrange is between €46 and €75 and top end is over €76.

Note that most accommodation options, excluding camping grounds and youth hostels, include a continental breakfast in the price.

Camping

Camping is always the cheapest option, although some camping grounds close out of season. The multilingual, annually-updated *Roteiro Campista* (€5), sold in larger bookshops or via the www.roteiro-campista.pt website, lists Portugal's camping grounds.

Ecotourism and Farmstays

Private counterparts are operated under a scheme called **Turismo de Habitação** (www.turihab.pt) and a number of smaller schemes (collectively called 'Turihab'). They allow you to stay in a farmhouse, some with self-catering cottages. Check the website or ask at tourist offices about local Turihab properties. **Turismo da Natureza Portugal** (www.icat.fc.ul.pt, in Portuguese) offers lodging throughout Portugal's national protected areas.

Guesthouses

The most common types of guesthouse are the *residencial* and the *pensão*, which are usual family owned and comfortable. Many have cheaper rooms with shared bath.

Hotels

The government grades hotels with one to five stars. For a high-season double expect to pay €60 up to as much as €250. Prices drop considerably in low season.

Pousadas

Pousadas are government-run former castles, monasteries or palaces, often in spectacular locations. For details contact tourist offices, or **Pousadas de Portugal** (☎ 218 442 001;

www.pousadasjuventude.pt; Rua Soares de Passos, 1749 Lisbon).

Youth Hostels

Portugal has 46 *pousadas da juventude* (youth hostels) within the Hostelling International (HI) system. Reserve in advance for a €1.50 fee by contacting **Movijovem** (Map pp890-1; ☎ 213 524 072; www.pousadasjuventude.pt; Av Duque d'Ávila 137, Lisbon).

If you don't already have a card from your national hostel association, you can pay a €2 supplement per night (and have a one-night, six-night or year-long 'guest card').

ACTIVITIES

Off-road cycling and bike trips are booming in Portugal; see Tavira (p904), Setúbal (p903), Évora (p907) and Parque Nacional da Peneda-Gerês (p920).

Despite some fine rambling country, walking is not a Portuguese passion. Some parks are establishing trails though, and some adventure travel agencies offer walking tours.

Popular water sports include surfing, windsurfing, canoeing, white-water rafting and water skiing. For local specialists, see Lagos (p905), Sagres (p907), Évora (p907), Tavira (p904), Coimbra (p911) and Parque Nacional da Peneda-Gerês (p921).

Alpine skiing is possible at Torre in the Serra da Estrela usually from January through to March.

The **Instituto Português da Juventude** (☎ 213 522 694; www.sej.pt, in Portuguese; Av da Liberdade 194, Lisbon) offers holiday programmes for 16 to 30 year olds (visitors too), including cycling, canoeing and rock climbing.

BUSINESS HOURS

Banks are open 8.30am to 3pm weekdays. Museums and tourist attractions are open between 10am and 5pm Tuesday to Friday, but are often closed at lunch. Shopping hours are generally 9am to 7pm weekdays, and 9am to 1pm Saturday. Restaurants are open for lunch and dinner, unless noted. Tourist offices in larger towns are generally open Monday to Saturday 9am to 7pm, in smaller towns they close for lunch from between 1.30 and 3pm. Portuguese post offices *(correios)* are open Monday to Friday 8.30am to 6pm. In Lisbon and Porto they are also open on Saturday mornings.

EMBASSIES & CONSULATES

Portuguese Embassies & Consulates

Countries hosting Portuguese embassies or consulates abroad include the following listings:

Australia (☎ 02-6290 1733; 23 Culgoa Circuit, O'Malley, Canberra ACT 2606)

Canada (☎ 613-7290 883; 645 Island Park Dr, Ottawa Ont K1Y OB8)

France (☎ 01 47 27 35 29; 3 Rue de Noisiel, 75116 Paris)

Germany (☎ 030-590 063 500; Zimmerstrasse 56, Berlin 10117)

Ireland (☎ 012-894 46; Knocksinna House, Foxrock, Dublin 18)

Netherlands (☎ 070-363 02 17; Bazarstraat 21, The Hague 2518)

New Zealand (☎ 09-309 1454; PO Box 305, 33 Garfield St, Parnell, Auckland)

Spain (☎ 915 617 800; Calle Castello 128, 28006 Madrid)

UK (☎ 0207-235 5331; 11 Belgrave Square, London SW1X 8PP)

USA (☎ 202-328 8610; 2125 Kalorama Rd NW, Washington DC 20008)

Embassies & Consulates in Portugal

Nations with embassies or consulates in Portugal include the following:

Australia (Map pp890-1; ☎ 213 101 500; Av da Liberdade 200, Lisbon)

Canada Lisbon (Map pp890-1; ☎ 213 164 600; Av da Liberdade 196); Faro (☎ 289 521 120; Rua Frei Lourenço de Santa Maria 1)

France Lisbon (Map pp890-1; ☎ 226 939 292; Calćada a Marques de Abrantes 123); Porto (☎ 226 094 805; Rua Eugénio de Castro 352)

Germany (Map pp894-5; ☎ 213 810 210; Campo dos Mártires da Pátria 38, Lisbon)

Ireland (Map pp890-1; ☎ 213 929 440; Rua da Imprensa à Estrela 1, Lisbon)

Netherlands Lisbon (Map pp890-1; ☎ 213 914 900; Av Infante Santo 43); Porto (☎ Consulate 222 080 061; Rua da Reboleira 7)

New Zealand (see the UK Embassy)

Spain Lisbon consulate (Map pp894-5; ☎ 213 472 792; Rua do Salitre 1); Porto (Map p915; ☎ 225 101 685; Rua de Dom João IV 341); Vila Real de Santo António (☎ 281 544 888; Avenida Ministro Duarte Pacheco)

UK Lisbon (Map pp890-1; ☎ 213 924 000; Rua de São Bernardo 33); Porto (☎ 226 184 789; Av da Boavista 3072); Portimão (☎ 282 417 800; Largo Francisco a Maurício 7) The UK consulate also oversees consular matters for New Zealand.

USA (Map pp890-1; ☎ 217 273 300; Av das Forças Armadas, Lisbon)

FESTIVALS & EVENTS

April

Holy Week Festival Easter week in Braga features colourful processions, including Ecce Homo, with barefoot penitents carrying torches.

May

Festas das Cruzes Held in Barcelos in May, the Festival of the Crosses is known for processions, folk music and dance, plus regional handicrafts.

June

Feira Nacional da Agricultura In June Santarém hosts the National Agricultural Fair, with bullfighting, folk singing and dancing.

Festa do Santo António The Festival of Saint Anthony fills the streets of Lisbon on 13 June.

Festa de São João Porto's big street bash is the St John's Festival, from 16 to 24 June.

August

Festas de Nossa Senhora da Agonia Viana do Castelo's Our Lady of Suffering Festival runs for three days, including the weekend nearest to 20 August, and is famed for its folk arts, parades and fireworks.

HOLIDAYS

New Year's Day 1 January
Carnival February/March (Shrove Tuesday)
Good Friday and the following Saturday March/April
Liberty Day 25 April (commemorating the 1975 Revolution)
Labour Day 1 May
Corpus Christi May/June (the ninth Thursday after Easter)
National Day 10 June
Feast of the Assumption 15 August
Republic Day 5 October
All Saints' Day 1 November
Independence Day 1 December (celebrating independence from Spain in 1640)
Immaculate Conception 8 December
Christmas Day 25 December

MONEY

There are numerous banks with ATMs located throughout Portugal. Credit cards are increasingly being accepted in hotels, restaurants and shops, however, you will normally be asked to provide photo identification. Exchange bureaux are common throughout Portugal; often located near to or even within the same building as the tourist offices.

EMERGENCY NUMBERS

- Ambulance ☎ 112
- Fire ☎ 117
- Police ☎ 112

POST

Stamps can be bought over the counter from the post office or from an automatic dispensing machine *(Correio de Portugal – Selos)*.

TELEPHONE

Mobile Phones

Mobile phone numbers within Portugal have nine digits and begin with ☎ 9.

Phone Codes

All Portuguese phone numbers have nine digits. These include area codes, which always need to be dialled. For general information dial ☎ 118, for international inquiries dial ☎ 179, and for reverse-charge (collect) calls dial ☎ 120.

Phonecards

Phonecards are the most reliable and cheap way of making a phone call from a telephone booth. They are sold at post offices, newsagents and tobacconists in denominations of €5 and €10.

VISAS

EU nationals need only a valid passport or identity card for entry to Portugal, and may stay indefinitely. Citizens of Australia, Canada, New Zealand and the United States can stay for up to 90 days in any half-year without a visa. Others, including nationals of South Africa, need a visa unless they're the spouse or child of a EU citizen.

TRANSPORT IN PORTUGAL

GETTING THERE & AWAY

Air

Portugal's main gateway is the **Aeroporto Portela** (LIS; ☎ 218 413 700) in Lisbon, approximately 8km north of the city centre. Porto's Aeroporto **Francisco Sá Carneiro** (OPO; ☎ 229 432 400) also handles international flights, as does the **Aeroporto de Faro** (FAO; ☎ 229 800 801) in the Algarve, which has the largest number of charter flights. The website for all three airports is www.ana-aeroportos.pt, in Portuguese.

Air Portugal (TAP; ☎ 289 800 218; www.tap.pt, in Portuguese) is the main international airline. **Portugália Airlines** (PGA; ☎ 218 425 559; www.pga.pt, in Portuguese) is primarily a domestic airline, but is increasingly opening up international routes including to/from Manchester, Brussels, Nice and Lyon. **Hi Fly** (☎ 210 062 480; www.hifly.aero), formerly Air Luxor, flies to major European capitals and to former Portuguese colonies in Africa, Guinea-Bissau and Sao Tome.

Following is a list of the major carriers serving Portugal with the airports they use: Lisbon, Porto or Faro. For details of carriers to/from outside Western Europe see the Transport chapter (p1112).

Air France (code AF; ☎ 218 482 177; www.airfrance.com) Lisbon, Porto.
Air Portugal (code TAP; ☎ 289 800 218; www.tap.pt) Lisbon, Porto, Faro.
British Airways (code BA; ☎ 214 154 151; www.ba.com) Lisbon, Porto, Faro.
British Midlands/Bmibaby (code WW; ☎ UK 0870 264 2229; www.bmibaby.com) Lisbon, Porto, Faro.
easyJet (code EZY; ☎ 218 413 700; www.easyjet.com) Lisbon, Faro.
Iberia (code IB; ☎ 808 261 261; www.iberia.com, in Spanish) Lisbon, Porto.
KLM (code KL; ☎ 204 747 747; www.klm.nl, in German)
Lufthansa (code IH; ☎ London 020-8750 3460; www.lufthansa.com, in German) Lisbon, Porto, Faro.
Monarch Airlines (code ZB; ☎ 289 889 475; www.fly-monarch.com) Faro.
Portugália Airlines (code PGA; ☎ 218 425 559; www.pga.pt, in Portuguese) Lisbon, Porto, Faro.
Ryanair (code FR; ☎ 229 432 400; www.ryanair.com) Porto.
Spanair (code JK; ☎ 218 4998 578; www.spanair.com) Lisbon.

There are year-round flights from the UK to Lisbon, Porto and Faro with BA, PGA and TAP. No-frills carriers include easyJet with flights from London Luton to Lisbon and from several UK airports to Faro. Ryanair flies from London Stanstead to Porto. British Midland's Bmibaby also has inexpensive flights from the East Midlands to Faro.

TAP and Continental Airlines both have a daily flight from New York to Lisbon with connections to Faro and Porto. Air France has multiple daily non-stop Paris–Lisbon and Paris–Porto connections, while PGA has a daily flight from Paris to Porto. From neighbouring Spain, TAP, Iberia and Spanair have daily Madrid–Lisbon flights. Elsewhere in Europe, KLM and TAP fly to Lisbon and Porto daily from Amsterdam, while PGA has regular direct flights to Lisbon from Berlin, Stuttgart, Cologne and Hamburg.

Land

BUS

From UK

Eurolines (☎ UK 08705-143 219; www.eurolines.co.uk) offers departures for Portugal twice weekly with several stops that include Lisbon (42 hours) and Porto (40 hours). Buses depart from Victoria coach station, travelling via the Channel ferry and stopping over in Buniel, Spain and Lille in France. The current return fare London–Lisbon is UK£179.

From Spain

Eurolines (☎ Madrid 915 063 360; www.eurolines.es, in Spanish) operates several services from Spain to Portugal, including Madrid–Lisbon (€40, eight hours), Seville–Lisbon (€36, four hours) and Barcelona–Lisbon (€80, 16 hours), all going at least three times weekly.

ALSA (☎ Madrid 902 422 242; www.alsa.es) has twice-daily Madrid–Lisbon services, while **Damas** (☎ Huelva 959 256 900; www.damas-sa.es) runs twice daily Monday to Saturday from Seville to Faro and Lagos via Huelva, jointly with the Algarve line EVA.

CAR & MOTORCYCLE

There is no border control in Portugal and there are plenty of self-service stations; some have garages that can replace batteries, repair punctures and do minor mechanical repairs, as well as carry some spare parts. Alternatively, they can direct you to the nearest car workshop. For more information about driving in Portugal see opposite.

TRAIN

The fastest and most convenient route to Portugal from the UK is with Eurostar from London Waterloo to Paris via the Channel Tunnel, and then onward to Lisbon via Irún. Contact **Rail Europe** (☎ UK 08705-848 848; www.raileurope.co.uk; return ticket around €300). From Paris, contact **SNCF** (www.sncf.com; return ticket around €210).

Renfe (☎ Spain 902 240 202; www.renfe.es; return ticket €126) has a nightly sleeper service between Madrid and Lisbon. Badajoz–Elvas–Lisbon is slow and there is only one regional service daily, but the scenery is stunning.

GETTING AROUND

Air

Air Portugal (TAP; ☎ 707 205 700; www.tap.pt) has daily Lisbon–Faro flights (under an hour) year-round. Overall, however, flights within Portugal are poor value unless you have a youth/student card; it is a lot cheaper to hop on the bus or train.

Bicycle

Mountain biking is popular in Portugal and a great way to explore the country, although given the Portuguese penchant for overtaking on blind corners, it can be dangerous on lesser roads. Bicycle lanes are rare, aside from in the natural parks: veteran pedallers recommend the Parque Nacional da Peneda-Gerês (p920). A growing number of towns have bike-rental outfits (around €10 a day). If you're bringing your own, pack plenty of spares. Bicycles can't be taken with you on trains, although most bus lines will accept them as accompanied baggage, subject to space and sometimes for an extra fee.

Boat

Portugal is not big on waterborne transport as a rule, however, there are river cruises along the Douro River from Porto (p919), Lisbon's river trips (p895) and commuter ferries.

Bus

Portugal's buses are generally modern and comfortable. However, there is a baffling number of privatised bus companies operating across the country. In Porto alone there are at least 18 bus companies, most based at different terminals.

The only company really worth worrying about is the national network, **Rede Expressos** (☎ 969 502 050; www.rede-expressos.pt, in Portuguese), which has a fleet of 100 buses, a comprehensive website and provides connections to 300 locations throughout the country. Most bus-station ticket desks will give you a computer print-out of fares, and all services and schedules will be clearly posted at each major station.

CLASSES

There are three classes of bus service: *expressos* are comfortable, fast, direct buses between major cities; *rápidas* are fast regional buses; and *carreiras* stop at every crossroad. *Expressos* are generally the best cheap way to get around (particularly for long trips, where per-kilometre costs are lowest). An under-26 card should get you a discount of around 20%, at least on the long-distance services.

COSTS

Travelling by bus in Portugal is fairly inexpensive. Refer to the Getting There & Away section of the respective city or town you are travelling to or from for distance times and fares.

RESERVATIONS

Advance reservations are only really necessary on the longer routes of the *expresso* service.

Car & Motorcycle

AUTOMOBILE ASSOCIATIONS

ACP (Automóvel Clube de Portugal; Map pp890-1; ☎ 213 180 100; www.acp.pt, in Portuguese; Rua Rosa Araújo 24, Lisbon) has a reciprocal arrangement with many of the better-known foreign automobile clubs, including AA and RAC. ACP provides medical, legal and breakdown assistance. Emergency help is available in the north (☎ 228 340 001) and the south (☎ 219 429 103).

HIRE

To hire a car in Portugal you must be at least 25 and have held your home licence for over a year (some companies allow younger drivers at higher rates). To hire a scooter of up to 50cc you must be over 18 years old and have a valid driving licence. For more powerful scooters and motorbikes you must have a valid driving licence covering these vehicles from your home country.

INSURANCE

Although most car insurance companies within the EU will cover taking your car to Portugal, it is prudent to consider extra cover for assistance in case your car breaks down. The minimum insurance required is third party.

ROAD RULES

Driving is on the right side of the road. Speed limits for cars and motorcycles are 50km/h in cities and public centres, 90km/h on normal roads and 120km/h on motorways (but 50km/h, 70km/h and 100km/h for motorcycles with sidecars). Drivers and front passengers in cars must wear seat belts. Motorcyclists and passengers must wear helmets, and motorcycles must have headlights on day and night. Using a mobile phone while driving could result in a fine.

Drink-driving laws are strict here with a maximum legal blood-alcohol level of 0.05%.

Train

Caminhos de Ferro Portugueses (CP; ☎ 808 208 208; www.cp.pt) is the statewide train network and is generally efficient, although can be slower than long-distance buses. Most trains are *regionais* (R) or *suburbanos*, stopping at stations en route. The more costly *intercidades* (IC) trains are faster, while the most luxurious and pricey are the *alfa pendulares* (AP) trains. Both the IC and AP lines require seat reservations in advance.

Spain

Just say the word 'Spain', and chances are that images of dark-haired flamenco dancers, proud bullfighters, and golden beaches bathed in sunlight immediately come to mind. Yet those clichéd images only scratch the surface of the country's character. The real Spain, captivating and complex, is a combination of the traditional and the modern. It's the passionate festivals, the historic sites and the quirky customs, but it's also the forward-thinking artists, the cutting-edge designers and the innovative chefs that are earning the country a reputation as one of Europe's most creative. No doubt, there's a lot more to today's Spain than its tourist-brochure image lets on.

The landscape is every bit as diverse and multifaceted as the culture. Spain is both the rocky shores of the Costa Brava and the desertscapes of Almería. It's the flat plains of Castilla and the peaks of the Pyrenees. It's the wet hills of Galicia and the sun-drenched beaches of Mallorca.

This landscape was the picturesque backdrop for a long and turbulent history that saw Spain rise to the height of world power, and fall into the deepest poverty. That history is visible at every turn, from the abundant Roman ruins to the Moorish-influenced *Mudéjar* architecture and the splendorous medieval cathedrals.

FAST FACTS

- **Area** 505,000 sq km
- **Capital** Madrid
- **Currency** euro (€); A$1 = €0.60; ¥100 = €0.67; NZ$1 = €0.50; UK£1 = €1.48; US$1 = €0.78
- **Famous for** sunshine, late nights, bullfighting, *gazpacho* (cold tomato soup), *Don Quijote,* Pedro Almodóvar films
- **Official Languages** Spanish (Castilian or *castellano*), Catalan, Basque, Galician *(gallego)*
- **Phrases** *hola* (hello); *gracias* (thanks); *adios* (goodbye)
- **Population** 43 million
- **Telephone Codes** country code ☎ 34; international access code ☎ 00

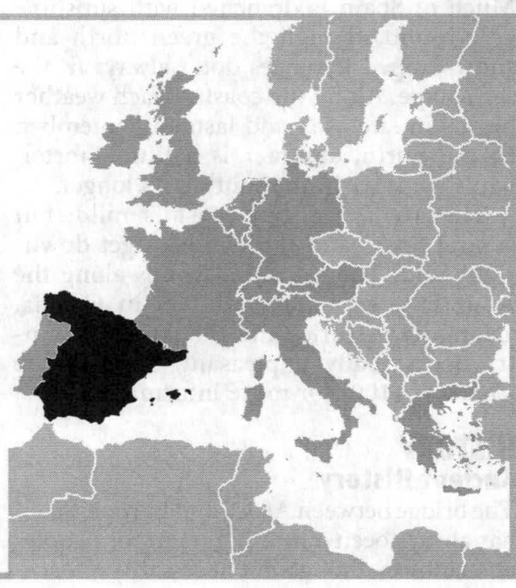

HIGHLIGHTS

- Visit one of the country's most interesting creations, Gaudí's **La Sagrada Familia** (p968) in Barcelona, fanciful yet packed with serious symbolism.
- Eat your way through **San Sebastián** (p982), a gourmand's paradise with an idyllic seaside setting.
- Join the pilgrims making their way along medieval laneways to the magnificent **Catedral del Apóstol** (p990) in Santiago de Compostela.
- Soak up the scent of orange blossom and surrender to the party atmosphere in sunny **Seville** (p1008).
- Amble under the aqueduct and around the Alcázar in magical **Segovia** (p954).

HOW MUCH?

A Real Madrid ticket €95

Bottle of Sangre de Toro wine €3.95

Bullfighter's suit €2500

Camper shoes €120

Valencia orange juice €2

LONELY PLANET INDEX

1L petrol €1.10

1L bottled water €1.50

Glass of Spanish beer €1.50

Souvenir T-shirt €18

Plate of churros €2

ITINERARIES

- **One week** Marvel at Barcelona's modernist architecture and seaside style before taking the train to San Sebastián, with a stop in Zaragoza on the way. Fit in a side trip to the Guggenheim Museum in Bilbao, and end the trip living it up on Madrid's legendary night scene.
- **One month** Make your way from Madrid to Andalucía, where you can take your time exploring picture-perfect Córdoba, Seville, Granada and Ronda. From here, spend some time on the coast, indulging in Malaga's renowned tapas scene and enjoying the pristine beaches.

CLIMATE & WHEN TO GO

Much of Spain is drenched with sunshine year-round, though the green north and snow-capped Pyrenees don't always fit the stereotype. Along the coasts, beach weather begins in late May and lasts to September. In the north, summer is a little shorter, while summer in the south lasts longer.

The Mediterranean coast is mild, but central Spain and the Pyrenees get downright cold. The rains and winds along the Atlantic coasts make winters in Galicia, Cantabria, Asturias and the Basque Country occasionally unpleasant. See Climate Charts (p1100) for more information.

HISTORY

Ancient History

The bridge between Africa and Europe, Spain has always been a meeting point for peoples and cultures, though not necessarily a peaceful one. North African pioneers first began to settle the peninsula around 8000 BC, and in the millennia that followed, Celtic tribes, Phoenician merchants, Greeks and Carthaginians trickled in. The Romans arrived in the 3rd century BC but took 200 years to subdue the peninsula. Peace was short-lived; by AD 419 the Christian Visigoths had established a kingdom that lasted until 711.

Muslim Spain & the Reconquista

By 714 Muslim armies occupied nearly the entire peninsula. Muslim dominion was to last almost 800 years in parts of Spain. In Islamic Spain (known as al-Andalus) arts and sciences prospered, new crops and agricultural techniques were introduced, and palaces, mosques, schools, public baths and gardens were built.

In 1085 Alfonso VI, king of Castilla y León, took Toledo, the first definitive victory of the Reconquista (the struggle to wrestle Spain into Christian hands). By the mid-13th century, the Christians had taken most of the peninsula, except for the state of Granada.

In the process, the kingdoms of Castilla and Aragón emerged as Christian Spain's two main powers, and in 1469 they were united by the marriage of Isabel, princess of Castilla, and Fernando, heir to Aragón's throne. Known as the Catholic Monarchs, they laid the foundations for the Spanish golden age, but they were also responsible for one of the darkest hours in Spain's history – the Inquisition, a witch-hunt to expel

or execute Jews and other non-Christians. In 1492 the last Muslim ruler of Granada surrendered to them, marking the end of the Reconquista.

The Golden Age

Christopher Columbus' so-called discovery of the Americas in 1492 kicked off Spain's golden age. Befuddled Columbus (Colón in Castilian), trying to find a new route to India, stumbled upon the Bahamas, though he never guessed he'd discovered new continents and changed the course of history. His voyages sparked a period of exploration and exploitation that was to yield Spain enormous wealth, while destroying the ancient American empires. For three centuries, gold and silver from the New World were used to finance the rapid expansion and slow decline of the Spanish empire. By the 18th century, the mighty Spanish empire was on its way out, the life sucked out of it by a series of unwise kings, self-seeking noblemen and unsuccessful wars that left the empire in shambles.

The 18th & 19th Centuries

The 18th century dawned with a war over the succession to the throne when Carlos II died heirless, but all was soon put right when Felipe V, the first Bourbon king, took control and ushered in a period of stability. Peace would last until the end of the century, when Spain declared war on France and then on Britain and Portugal. The wars proved disastrous, and Spain ultimately lost several colonies and nearly all its sea power.

In 1807–08 Napoleon's forces occupied a weakened Spain, and King Carlos IV abdicated without a fight. In his place Napoleon installed his own brother, Joseph Bonaparte. The Spaniards retaliated with a five-year war of independence, and in 1815 Napoleon was defeated by the Duke of Wellington, who had united with the Portuguese and Spanish troops. A Bourbon, Fernando VII, was restored to the Spanish throne.

Fernando's reign was a disastrous advertisement for monarchy: the Inquisition was re-established, liberals were persecuted, Spain entered a severe recession and the American colonies officially won their independence in 1824. After Fernando's death in 1833 came the First Carlist War (1834–39), which ended with Isabel II, Fernando's daughter, taking the throne. In 1868 the monarchy was overthrown during the Septembrina Revolution and Isabel II was forced to flee from Madrid. The First Republic was declared in 1873, but within 18 months the army had restored the monarchy, with Isabel's son Alfonso XII on the throne. Despite political turmoil, Spain's economy prospered in the second half of the 19th century, fuelled by industrialisation.

The disastrous Spanish-American War of 1898 marked the end of the Spanish empire. Spain was defeated by the USA and lost its last overseas possessions – Cuba, Puerto Rico, Guam and the Philippines.

The 20th Century

The early 20th century was characterised by growing instability, as anarchists and radicals struggled to overthrow the established order. In 1923, with Spain on the brink of civil war, Miguel Primo de Rivera made himself military dictator, ruling until 1930. In 1931 King Alfonso XIII fled the country and the Second Republic was declared.

Like its predecessor, the Second Republic fell victim to internal conflict. The 1936 elections split the nation in two, with the Popular Front (an uneasy alliance of leftist parties) on one side and the right-wing Nationalists (an alliance of the army, Church and the Fascist-style Falange Party) on the other.

Nationalist plotters in the army rose against the Republican government in July 1936, launching a civil war (1936–39) that would further sink the country in poverty and create bitter wounds that are still healing today. The Nationalists, led by General Francisco Franco, received military support from Nazi Germany and Fascist Italy, while the elected Republican government received support from the Soviet Union and other foreign leftists.

The war ended in 1939, with Franco the victor. Some 350,000 Spaniards died in the war, most of them on the battlefield but many others in executions, prison camps or simply from starvation. After the war, thousands of Republicans were executed, jailed or forced into exile, and Franco's 36-year dictatorship began with Spain isolated internationally and crippled by recession. It wasn't until the 1950s and '60s, when the rise in tourism and a treaty with the USA combined to provide much-needed funds, that the country began to recover.

Franco died in 1975, having named Juan Carlos, the grandson of Alfonso XIII, as his successor. Instead of accepting power, King Juan Carlos handed it over to a newly created democratic government, earning the lasting respect of the country. The first elections were held in 1977 and a new constitution was drafted in 1978. Spain joined the European Community (EC) in 1986 and celebrated its return to the world stage in style in 1992, with Expo '92 in Seville and the Olympic Games in Barcelona.

Spain Today

The modern, forward-thinking Spain of today has long since thrown off the dark cloud of Franco's dictatorship. In the late 1990s, the centre-right Partido Popular (Popular Party; PP), led by José María Aznar, took control of the nation after the long-ruling Partido Socialista Obrero Español (Spanish Socialist Party; PSOE) was voted out under accusations of corruption. The PP went on to establish programmes of economic decentralisation and liberalisation, paving the way for economic success.

In the elections of 2003, just days after the 11 March terrorist attacks in Madrid, the PP lost the presidential election to the PSOE. Newly elected President José Luís Rodríguez Zapatero made waves immediately; some of his first actions as president were to withdraw Spanish troops from Iraq and to establish parity in his cabinet, appointing eight female ministers and eight male ministers.

These days an important issue in Spain is the changing rights of the country's autonomous regions. Catalonia's revised *Estatut*, a constitution of sorts that lays out a plan for a new division of fiscal and social responsibilities, is at the forefront of this debate. The document has caused deep division among Spaniards. Supporters say it's a necessary step for Spain to deepen its democracy, while critics claim it erodes Spain's unity.

Aside from the constant and tedious back-and-forth bickering between Spain's political parties, important issues include domestic violence, drought and chronic water shortages, traffic control and an effort to decrease traffic-related deaths, and the Basque terrorist group ETA (see p987), who, at the time of writing, had recently signed a cease-fire.

PEOPLE

Spain has a population of approximately 43 million, descended from all the many peoples who have settled here over the millennia, among them Iberians, Celts, Romans, Jews, Visigoths, Berbers, Arabs and 20th-century immigrants from across the globe. The biggest cities are Madrid (3.15 million), Barcelona (1.59 million), Valencia (760,000) and Seville (700,000). Each region proudly preserves its own unique culture, and some – Catalonia and the Basque Country in particular – display a fiercely independent spirit.

RELIGION

Only about 20% of Spaniards are regular churchgoers, but Catholicism is deeply ingrained in the culture. As the writer Unamuno said, 'Here in Spain we are all Catholics, even the atheists'.

However, many Spaniards have a deep-seated scepticism about the Church. During the civil war, anarchists burned churches and shot clerics because they represented repression and corruption. Later, during Franco's rule, church-going was practically obligatory and those who shunned the Church were often treated as outcasts or targeted as delinquents by Franco's police. Some people began to see the Church as a haven for hypocrites, and the image still hasn't completely worn off.

ARTS

Literature

One of the earliest works of Spanish literature is the *Cantar de Mío Cid* (Song of My Cid), an anonymous epic poem describing the life of El Cid, an 11th-century Christian knight buried in the Burgos cathedral. Miguel de Cervantes' novel *Don Quijote* is the masterpiece of the literary flowering of the 16th and 17th centuries, as well as one of the world's great works of fiction.

The next high point, in the early 20th century, grew out of the crisis of the Spanish-American War that spawned the intellectual Generation of '98. The towering figure was poet and playwright Federico García Lorca, who won international acclaim before he was murdered in the civil war for his Republican sympathies.

Popular contemporary authors include Arturo Pérez Reverte, whose *Capitán Alatriste* books are international best-sellers; Eduardo Mendoza, whose books, including the *City of Marvels,* have been widely translated into English; and Carlos Ruíz Zafon, whose 2002 *Shadow of the Wind* was a runaway bestseller worldwide.

Cinema

Modern Spanish cinema's best-known director is Pedro Almodóvar, whose humorous, cutting-edge films are largely set amid the Movida. His *Todo Sobre Mi Madre* (All About My Mother; 1999) and *Habla Con Ella* (Talk to Her; 2002) are both Oscar winners.

Alejandro Amenábar, the young Chilean-born director of *Abre los Ojos* (Open Your Eyes; 1997), *The Others* (2001) and the Oscar-winning *Mar Adentro* (The Sea Inside; 2004), is Almodóvar's only competition for Spain's 'best director' title.

Architecture

Spain's earliest architectural relics are the prehistoric monuments on Menorca. Reminders of Roman times include the ruins of Mérida, Zaragoza, and Tarragona, and Segovia's amazing aqueduct. The Muslims left behind some of the most splendid buildings in the entire Islamic world, including Granada's Alhambra, Córdoba's awe-inspiring Mezquita and Seville's Alcázar – the latter an example of *Mudéjar* architecture, the name given to Islamic work done throughout Christian-held territory.

The first main Christian architectural movement was Romanesque. Later came the great Gothic cathedrals (such as Toledo, Barcelona, León, Salamanca and Seville) of the 13th to 16th centuries; Renaissance styles such as the plateresque work so prominent in Salamanca; and the austere work of Juan de Herrera, responsible for El Escorial (see p951). Spain then followed the usual path to baroque (17th and 18th centuries) and neoclassicism (19th century), before Catalonia produced its startling modernist (roughly Art Nouveau) movement around the turn of the 20th century, of which Antoni Gaudí's Sagrada Familia is the most stunning example.

Painting

The giants of Spain's golden age (1550–1650) were Toledo-based El Greco (originally from Crete) and Diego Velázquez, considered Spain's best painter by greats including Picasso and Dalí. Both El Greco and Velázquez were known for their insightful portraits. The genius of both the 18th and 19th centuries was Francisco Goya, whose versatility ranged from unflattering royal portraits and anguished war scenes to bullfight etchings and tapestry designs.

Catalonia was the powerhouse of early-20th-century Spanish art, claiming the hugely prolific Pablo Picasso (although he was born in Andalucía), the colourful symbolist Joan Miró and surrealist Salvador Dalí. Important artists of the late 20th century include Catalan abstract artist Antoni Tàpies and Basque sculptor Eduardo Chillida. Works by these and other major Spanish artists can be found in galleries throughout the country.

Flamenco

Getting to see real, deeply emotional flamenco can be hard, as it tends to happen semispontaneously in little bars and not on big touristy stages. Andalucía is its traditional home and your best chance of catching the real thing is probably at one of the flamenco festivals in the south, usually held in summer. You'll also find quality *tablaos* (flamenco stages) in Madrid and throughout Andalucía.

ENVIRONMENT

Spain is a geographically diverse country, with landscapes ranging from the near-deserts of Almería to the green countryside and deep coastal inlets of Galicia, and from the sunbaked plains of Castilla-La Mancha to the rugged mountains of the Pyrenees.

The country covers 84% of the Iberian Peninsula and spreads over some 505,000 sq km, more than half of which is high *meseta* (tableland). Spain is divided by several mountain chains, making it Europe's second-hilliest country after Switzerland.

The brown bear, wolf, lynx and wild boar all survive in Spain, although only the boar exists in abundance; farmers delight in shooting and roasting the tasty pest. Spain's high mountains harbour the goatlike chamois and Spanish ibex (the latter is rare) and big birds of prey such as eagles, vultures and the lammergeier. The marshy Ebro delta and Guadalquivir estuary are important for water birds, among them the spectacular greater flamingo. Many of Spain's 5500 seed-bearing plants grow nowhere else in Europe, due to the barrier of the Pyrenees. Spring wildflowers are magnificent in many country and hilly areas.

The conservation picture has improved by leaps and bounds in the past 25 years and Spain now has 25,000 sq km of protected areas, including 10 national parks. However, overgrazing, reservoir creation, tourism, housing developments, agricultural and industrial effluent, fires and hunting all still threaten plant and animal life.

FOOD & DRINK

Reset your stomach's clock in Spain unless you want to eat alone or with other tourists. Most Spaniards start the day with a light *desayuno* (breakfast), perhaps coffee with a *tostada* (piece of toast) or *pastel* (pastry), though they might stop in a bar later for a mid-morning *bocadillo* (baguette).

La comida (lunch) is usually the main meal of the day, eaten between about 1.30pm and 3.30pm. The *cena* (evening meal) is usually lighter and may be eaten as late as 10pm or 11pm; meals out with friends may well last until 1am or later. It's common to go to a bar or café for tapas around 1pm and again around 7pm or 8pm.

Specialities

Each region has its own style of cuisine and its own specialities. One of the most characteristic dishes, from the Valencia region, is paella – rice, seafood, the odd vegetable and often chicken or meat, all simmered together and traditionally coloured yellow with saffron. Another dish, of Andalucian origin, is *gazpacho,* a cold soup made from tomatoes, breadcrumbs, cucumber and green peppers. Tortillas (like omelettes) are an inexpensive stand-by snack and come in many varieties. *Jamón serrano* (cured ham) is a delicacy available in many different qualities.

Drinks

Start the day with a strong coffee, either as a *café con leche* (half-coffee, half-milk), *café solo* (short black, espresso-like) or *café cortado* (short black with a little milk).

The most common way to order a *cerveza* (beer) is to ask for a *caña,* which is a small draught beer. In the Basque Country this is called a *zurrito.* A larger beer (about 300mL) is often called a *tubo,* or (in Catalonia) a *jarra.* All these words apply to *cerveza de barril* (draught beer) – if you just ask for a *cerveza* you're likely to get bottled beer, which is more expensive.

Vino (wine) comes in *blanco* (white), *tinto* (red) or *rosado* (rosé). Exciting wine regions include Penedès, Priorat and Ribera del Duero. *Tinto de verano,* a kind of wine shandy, is good in summer. There are also many regional grape specialities, such as *jerez* (sherry) in Jerez de la Frontera and *cava* (a sparkling wine) in Catalonia. Sangría, a sweet punch made of red wine, fruit and spirits, is refreshing and very popular with tourists and in summer.

Agua del grifo (tap water) is usually safe to drink but it may not be very tasty in cities or near the coast. *Agua mineral con gas* (sparkling mineral water) and *agua mineral sin gas* (still mineral water) cost about €1.50 for a small bottle.

Where to Eat & Drink

Bars and cafés are open all day, serving coffees, pastries, *bocadillos* and usually tapas, which cost from €1 to €4 each. In the evenings these same bars fill with regulars looking for a quick beer or glass of house wine. Groups can order *raciónes,* a large-sized serving of these snacks; a *media ración* is half a *ración.* You can often save by ordering and eating food at the bar rather than at a table.

Self-caterers will no doubt be delighted with Spain's fresh-produce markets, which they will find near the centre of just about every city and town. Load yourself up on colourful veggies, fresh bread and Spanish cheeses.

Spaniards like to eat out, and restaurants abound even in small towns. At lunch time, most places offer a *menú del día* – a fixed-price lunch menu and the budget traveller's best friend. For €7 to €12 you typically get three courses, bread and a drink. The *plato combinado* (combined plate) is a cousin of the *menú* and usually includes a meat dish and a couple of side dishes. Check out the crowd before sitting down; if it's full of locals, that's a good sign.

After dinner, head to a *bar de copas* (pub), where hard drinks are pretty much the only thing on offer.

Vegetarians

Vegetarians may have to be creative in Spain. Though in larger cities and important student centres there's a growing awareness of vegetarianism, traditional restaurants often offer salads and egg tortillas, but little else for noncarnivores. Even salads may come laden with sausages or tuna. Pasta and pizza are readily available, as is seafood.

MADRID

pop 3.15 million

Spain's capital is a vibrant place, the hub of the country's government and commerce, and an exciting city bubbling over with creativity. Madrid may not have the effortless elegance of European capitals like Paris or Rome, but it has a raw energy that is infectious. Explore the old streets of the centre, relax in the plazas, soak up the culture in its excellent art museums, and take at least one night to experience the city's legendary nightlife scene.

HISTORY

Through the years city leaders have tried hard to come up with noble, capital-worthy histories for Madrid (saying, for example, that it had Roman origins), but the truth is that Madrid was little more than a muddy, mediocre village when King Felipe II declared it Spain's capital in 1561. Though established as a Moorish garrison in 854, by the 16th century the population was only 12,000. That changed fast when it became the epicentre of the Spanish court, and Felipe and crew began the long process of building a capital.

Despite being home to generations of nobles, the city was a squalid grid of unpaved alleys and dirty buildings until the 18th century, when King Carlos III turned his attention to public works. By the early 20th century Madrid finally began to take on the look of a proper capital.

The post–civil war 1940s and '50s were trying times for the capital, with rampant poverty. Nowhere was Franco's thumb as firmly pressed down as on Madrid, and the city lived under a blanket of fear and forced austerity for nearly four decades. When the dictator died in 1975 the city exploded with creativity and life, giving Madrileños the party-hard reputation they still cherish.

ORIENTATION

Spain's largest city by far, Madrid is a sprawling metropolis that can look daunting on a map. Luckily, its easy-to-navigate metro system and relatively compact city centre give travellers a fairly easy time.

The ebullient Puerta del Sol is the city's physical and emotional heart. Literally kilometre zero (all distances in Spain are measured from this point), the plaza is a hotbed of activity. Radiating away from it are the major arteries of Calle Mayor, Calle del Arenal, Calle de Preciados, Calle de la Montera and Calle de Alcalá.

South of Puerta del Sol is the oldest part of the city, with the Plaza Mayor to the southwest and the busy streets of the Huertas district to the southeast. North of the plaza is a modern shopping district and, beyond that, the east–west thoroughfare Gran Vía and the bohemian barrio (district/neighbourhood) of Chueca. To the west is the stately Palacio Real, while to the east lies the city's green lung, Parque del Buen Retiro. An upscale shopping quarter, Salamanca, lies north of the park.

INFORMATION

Bookshops

La Casa del Libro (Map p940; ☎ 90 202 64 02; www.casadellibro.com; Gran Vía 29; 9.30am-9.30pm Mon-Fri, 11am-1pm Sun; M Gran Vía) This mega bookshop has tons of English and foreign-language titles.

Petra's International Bookshop (Map p940; ☎ 91 541 72 91; Calle de Campomanes 13; 11am-9pm Mon-Sat; M Ópera or Santo Domingo) A treasure trove of used books, mainly in English.

Emergency

Ambulance (☎ 91 479 93 61)
General Emergencies (☎ 112)
Municipal Police (☎ 092)
Red Cross Emergencies(☎ 91 522 22 22)

Internet Access

Now that so many Madrileños surf the Web at home, Internet cafés have been closing left, right and centre. You can still find access in many small *locutorios* (call centres) and inside casinos and gaming houses. Also, many hostels and some hotels offer free Internet access.

Work Center (Map p940; ☎ 90 211 50 11; www.workcenter.es; Calle de Príncipe 1; per hr €2; 24hr; M Sevilla) Internet, photocopies and more. Also other branches throughout the city.

Laundry

Lavandería Cervantes (Map p940; ☎ 91 429 92 16; Calle Cervantes 6; per load wash/dry €2/1; 9am-9pm; M Sol or Antón Martín)

Left Luggage

Spain Storage (Map p940; ☎ 24hr 91 521 79 34; www.spainstorage.com; Calle del Correo 4; per week €10; 9-11am & 5-8pm Mon-Fri; M Sol) For cheap long-term storage.

Medical Services

Anglo-American Medical Unit (Map pp936-7; ☎ 91 435 18 23; 3rd fl, Calle Conde de Aranda 1; 9am-8pm Mon-Fri, 10am-1pm Sat; M Retiro) For medical help in English. Visits by appointment only.

Farmacia Globo (Map p940; ☎ 91 369 20 00; Plaza Antón Martín 46; M Antón Martín) For help with minor medical problems. This is one of several 24-hour pharmacies; others are located at Calle Mayor 13, Calle de Toledo 46 and Calle de Preciados 14. Call ☎ 010 for additional locations.

Post

Main post office (Map pp936-7; ☎ 91 396 27 33; Plaza Cibeles; Ⓜ Banco de España) It's almost fun to wait in line (which you'll surely have to do) at the beautiful Palacio de Comunicaciones.

Tourist Information

Lost Objects (☎ 91 588 43 48) **Municipal tourist office** (Map p940; ☎ 91 588 16 36; www.munimadrid.es; Plaza Mayor 27; 9.30am-8.30pm; Ⓜ Sol)
Regional tourist office (Map p940; ☎ 90 210 00 07; www.madrid.org/turismo; Calle del Duque de Medinaceli 2; 9am-8pm Mon-Sat, to 2pm Sun; Ⓜ Sevilla) Go to the calmer, less-frequented regional office for more one-on-one attention.

MADRID IN TWO DAYS

Start with breakfast in the **Plaza de Santa Ana** (left) then visit the **Museo del Prado** (left). Afterwards, walk around **El Retiro** (p939), but save energy for the **Palacio Real** (p938) and evening shopping and tapas in **Chueca** (p949). At night, catch a **flamenco show** (p948).

On day two, sign up for the tourist office's **walking tour** (p941) of historic Madrid, and then visit either the **Thyssen-Bornemisza** (p938) or the **Reina Sofía** (p938) art museums. Make time for a siesta, then hit **Viva Madrid** (p946) for drinks and dancing.

DANGERS & ANNOYANCES

Compared with most major cities, Madrid is not particularly dangerous. That said, be smart and aware, especially in touristy areas like Plaza Mayor, Puerta del Sol and Gran Vía. Pickpockets and petty thieves can be astonishingly brash – and quick.

Prostitution (and the slimy clients it attracts) along Calle de la Montera and in the Casa del Campo park means that you need to exercise extra caution in these areas. On a brighter note, increased police presence has made these areas safer.

For details about common scams, see the Spain Directory (p1031).

SIGHTS & ACTIVITIES

The best way to get under the city's skin is simply to walk its streets, sip coffees in its plazas and relax in its parks. Madrid de los Austrios, the maze of mostly 15th- and 16th-century streets surrounding the Plaza Mayor, is the oldest quarter of the city and makes for a nice stroll. You'll also enjoy exploring the cafés and interesting shops around Plaza de Santa Ana.

Don't leave without getting a glimpse of the amazing art and culture on offer here. Three of Europe's top art collections are on display at the outstanding Prado, Reina Sofía and Thyssen-Bornemisza museums.

Museo Nacional del Prado

Spain's premier museum, and one of the finest art collections in the world, the **Museo Nacional del Prado** (Map pp936-7; ☎ 91 330 29 00; http://museoprado.mcu.es; Paseo del Prado s/n; adult/child €6/3, EU students under 25 free, free Sun; 9am-8pm Tue-Sun; Ⓜ Banco de España) is a seemingly endless parade of priceless works from Spain and beyond. At the time of research, only about 1000 of the museum's total collection of 8500 paintings was on display. That will change when the Prado's expansion project, begun in 2001 and scheduled for completion in 2007, finishes and increases exhibition space by 50%.

The collection is divided into eight major collections: Spanish paintings (1100–1850), Flemish paintings (1430–1700), Italian paintings (1300–1800), French paintings (1600–1800), German paintings (1450–1800), sculptures, decorative arts, and drawings and prints. There is generous coverage of Spanish greats including Goya, Velázquez and El Greco. Prized works include Velázquez' masterpiece *Las Meninas* – depicting maids of honour attending the daughter of King Felipe IV and Velázquez himself painting portraits of the queen and king (through whose eyes the scene is witnessed) – and the Flemish El Bosco's *El Jardin de las Delicias,* a three-panelled painting of the creation of man, the pleasures of the world, and hell. Also look for works by El Greco, including *La Adoración de los Pastores* and *La Trinidad,* both with religious themes.

The museum is laid out in a loosely chronological order. Medieval and Renaissance works are found on the *planta baja* (lower floor), as are the paintings of Velázquez and the Siglo de Oro (Golden Century). Also on this floor are some of Goya's works, which continue on the 2nd floor. Look out for Goya's famous *Maja Desnuda* and *Maja Vestida;* legend has it

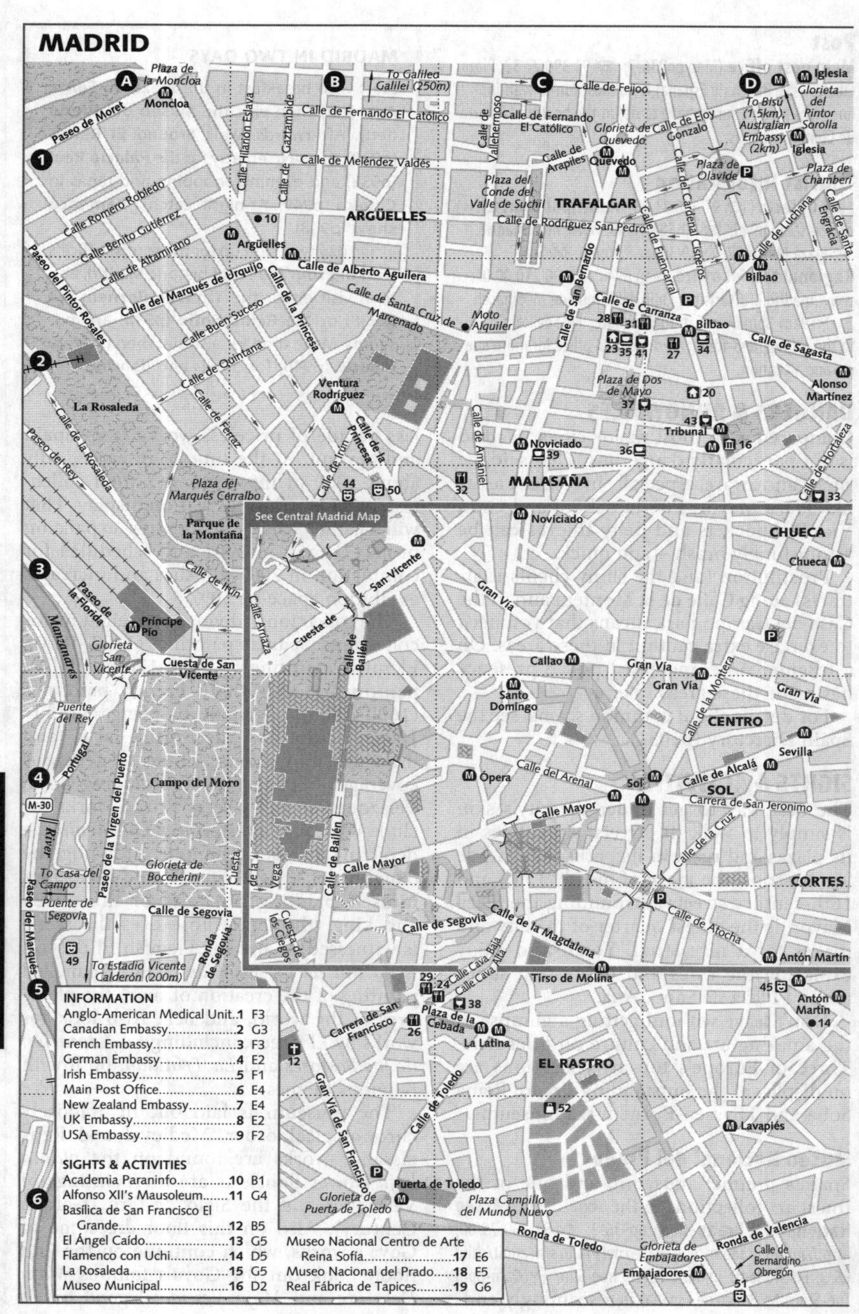
MADRID
A
B
C
D
1
2
3
4
5
6
Plaza de la Moncloa
Moncloa
To Galileo Galilei (250m)
Calle de Feijoo
Iglesia
Glorieta del Pintor Sorolla
To Bisú (1.5km); Australian Embassy (2km)
Iglesia
Paseo de Moret
Calle de Fernando El Católico
Calle de Vallehermoso
Calle de Fernando El Católico
Glorieta de Quevedo
Calle de Eloy Gonzalo
Calle de Arapiles
Quevedo
Plaza de Olavide
Plaza de Chamberí
Calle Hilarión Eslava
Calle de Gaztambide
Calle de Meléndez Valdés
Plaza del Conde del Valle de Suchil
TRAFALGAR
Calle del Cardenal Cisneros
Calle de Luchana
Calle de Santa Engracia
Calle Romero Robledo
Calle Benito Gutiérrez
10
ARGÜELLES
Calle de Rodríguez San Pedro
Calle de Fuencarral
Argüelles
Calle de Altamirano
Paseo del Pintor Rosales
Calle del Marqués de Urquijo
Calle de la Princesa
Calle de Alberto Aguilera
Calle de San Bernardo
Bilbao
Calle de Santa Cruz de Marcenado
Calle de Carranza
Calle Buen Suceso
Moto Alquiler
28
31
Bilbao
Calle de Sagasta
23
35
41
27
34
Calle de Quintana
La Rosaleda
Ventura Rodríguez
Plaza de Dos de Mayo
37
20
Alonso Martínez
Calle de Ferraz
Calle de la Rosaleda
Paseo del Rey
Calle de la Princesa
Calle de Amaniel
43
Tribunal
16
Noviciado
39
36
Calle de Hortaleza
Calle de Irún
44
50
32
MALASAÑA
33
Plaza del Marqués Cerralbo
See Central Madrid Map
Noviciado
Parque de la Montaña
CHUECA
Chueca
Calle de Irún
San Vicente
Gran Vía
Paseo de la Florida
Calle Arriaza
Cuesta de
Manzanares
Príncipe Pío
Calle de Bailén
Glorieta San Vicente
Cuesta de San Vicente
Callao
Gran Vía
Gran Vía
Gran Vía
Santo Domingo
Calle de la Montera
Puente del Rey
CENTRO
Portugal
Sevilla
Campo del Moro
Ópera
Calle del Arenal
Sol
Calle de Alcalá
SOL
M-30
Carrera de San Jeronimo
Calle Mayor
River
Paseo de la Virgen del Puerto
Calle de Bailén
Calle de la Cruz
Calle Mayor
Glorieta de Boccherini
To Casa del Campo
Cuesta de la Vega
CORTES
Puente de Segovia
Paseo del Marqués
Calle de Segovia
Calle de Segovia
Calle de la Magdalena
Calle de Atocha
49
Ronda de Segovia
Cuesta de los Ciegos
Antón Martín
To Estadio Vicente Calderón (200m)
Tirso de Molina
29
24
Calle Cava Baja
Calle Cava Alta
45
38
Antón Martín
Carrera de San Francisco
Plaza de la Cebada
26
La Latina
14
12
EL RASTRO
Gran Vía de San Francisco
Calle de Toledo
52
Lavapiés
Puerta de Toledo
Glorieta de Puerta de Toledo
Plaza Campillo del Mundo Nuevo
Ronda de Toledo
Ronda de Valencia
Glorieta de Embajadores
Calle de Bernardino Obregón
Embajadores
51
INFORMATION
Anglo-American Medical Unit.1 F3
Canadian Embassy...2 G3
French Embassy...3 F3
German Embassy...4 E2
Irish Embassy...5 F1
Main Post Office...6 E4
New Zealand Embassy...7 E4
UK Embassy...8 E2
USA Embassy...9 F2
SIGHTS & ACTIVITIES
Academia Paraninfo...10 B1
Alfonso XII's Mausoleum...11 G4
Basílica de San Francisco El Grande...12 B5
El Ángel Caído...13 G5
Flamenco con Uchi...14 D5
La Rosaleda...15 G5
Museo Municipal...16 D2
Museo Nacional Centro de Arte Reina Sofía...17 E6
Museo Nacional del Prado...18 E5
Real Fábrica de Tapices...19 G6

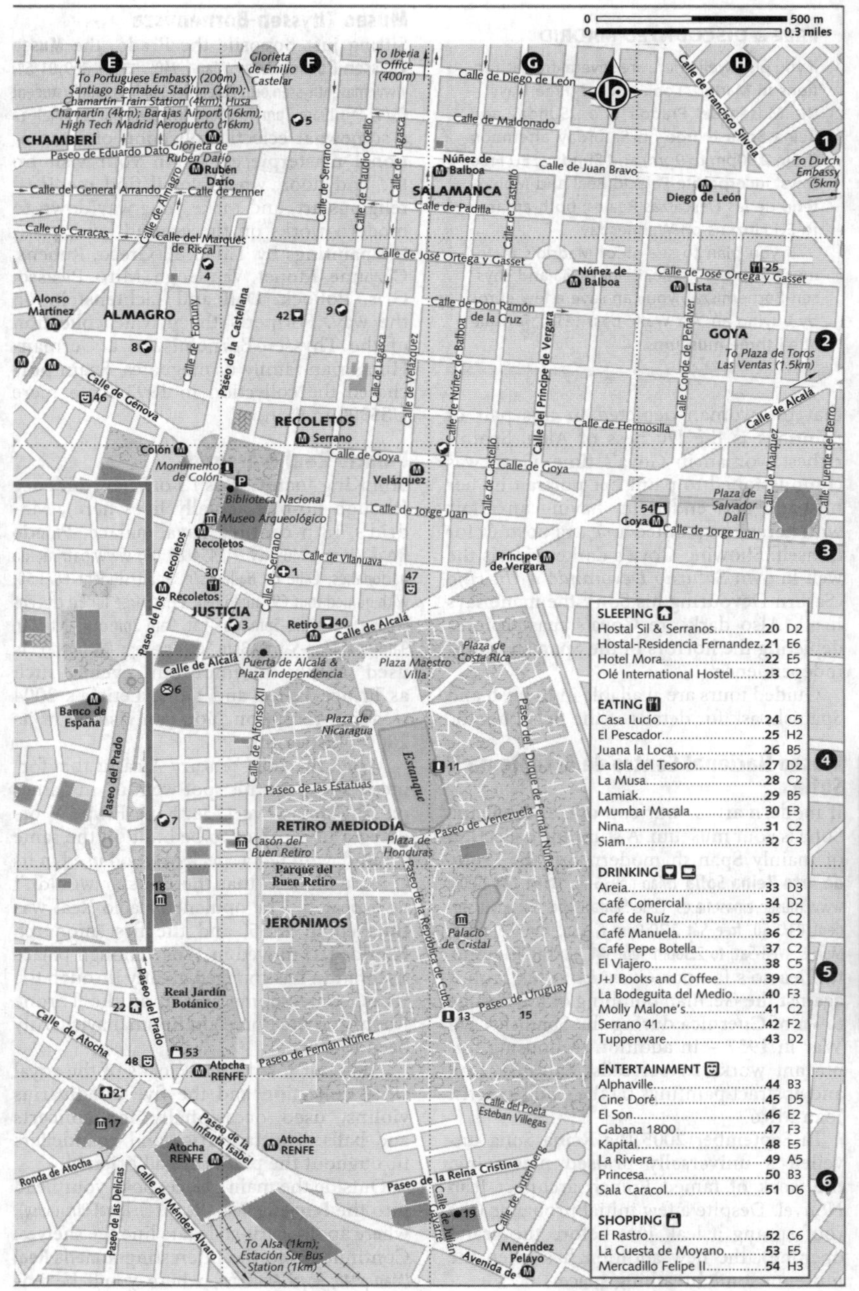
0 500 m
0 0.3 miles
To Portuguese Embassy (200m); Santiago Bernabéu Stadium (2km); Chamartín Train Station (4km); Husa Chamartín (4km); Barajas Airport (16km); High Tech Madrid Aeropuerto (16km)
Glorieta de Emilio Castelar
To Iberia Office (400m)
Calle de Diego de León
Calle de Francisco Silvela
Calle de Maldonado
CHAMBERÍ
Paseo de Eduardo Dato
Glorieta de Rubén Darío
Rubén Darío
Núñez de Balboa
Calle de Juan Bravo
To Dutch Embassy (5km)
Calle del General Arrando
Calle de Jenner
SALAMANCA
Diego de León
Calle de Padilla
Calle de Caracas
Calle del Marqués de Riscal
Calle de Almagro
Calle de Serrano
Calle de Claudio Coello
Calle de Lagasca
Calle de Castelló
Calle de José Ortega y Gasset
Lista
Calle de Don Ramón de la Cruz
Alonso Martínez
ALMAGRO
Calle de Fortuny
Paseo de la Castellana
GOYA
Calle Conde de Peñalver
Calle del Príncipe de Vergara
Calle de Núñez de Balboa
Calle de Velázquez
To Plaza de Toros Las Ventas (1.5km)
Calle de Génova
RECOLETOS
Serrano
Calle de Hermosilla
Calle de Alcalá
Colón
Calle de Goya
Velázquez
Monumento de Colón
Biblioteca Nacional
Museo Arqueológico
Calle de Jorge Juan
Plaza de Salvador Dalí
Calle de Maiquez
Calle Fuente del Berro
Goya
Recoletos
Calle de Vilanuava
Príncipe de Vergara
Paseo de los Recoletos
JUSTICIA
Retiro
Puerta de Alcalá & Plaza Independencia
Plaza Maestro Villa
Plaza de Costa Rica
Banco de España
Calle de Alfonso XII
Plaza de Nicaragua
Estanque
Paseo del Duque de Fernán Núñez
Paseo del Prado
Paseo de las Estatuas
RETIRO MEDIODÍA
Casón del Buen Retiro
Plaza de Honduras
Paseo de Venezuela
Parque del Buen Retiro
Paseo de la República de Cuba
JERÓNIMOS
Palacio de Cristal
Real Jardín Botánico
Paseo de Uruguay
Calle de Atocha
Paseo de Fernán Núñez
Atocha RENFE
Calle del Poeta Esteban Villegas
Paseo de la Infanta Isabel
Ronda de Atocha
Paseo de las Delicias
Calle de Méndez Álvaro
Paseo de la Reina Cristina
Calle de Gutenberg
Calle de Julián Gayarre
To Alsa (1km); Estación Sur Bus Station (1km)
Avenida de
Menéndez Pelayo
SLEEPING
Hostal Sil & Serranos....20 D2
Hostal-Residencia Fernandez.21 E6
Hotel Mora....22 E5
Olé International Hostel....23 C2
EATING
Casa Lucío....24 C5
El Pescador....25 H2
Juana la Loca....26 B5
La Isla del Tesoro....27 D2
La Musa....28 C2
Lamiak....29 B5
Mumbai Masala....30 E3
Nina....31 C2
Siam....32 C3
DRINKING
Areia....33 D3
Café Comercial....34 D2
Café de Ruíz....35 C2
Café Manuela....36 C2
Café Pepe Botella....37 C2
El Viajero....38 C5
J+J Books and Coffee....39 C2
La Bodeguita del Medio....40 F3
Molly Malone's....41 C2
Serrano 41....42 F2
Tupperware....43 D2
ENTERTAINMENT
Alphaville....44 B3
Cine Doré....45 D5
El Son....46 E2
Gabana 1800....47 F3
Kapital....48 E5
La Riviera....49 A5
Princesa....50 B3
Sala Caracol....51 D6
SHOPPING
El Rastro....52 C6
La Cuesta de Moyano....53 E5
Mercadillo Felipe II....54 H3

FREE & DISCOUNTED MADRID

If you plan well, there are several free attractions in Madrid. Look out for 'Free Days' – the Museo del Prado's is on Sunday and Reina Sofía is free on Saturday afternoon (from 2.30pm to 9pm) and Sunday. 'EU Free Days' incorporate Palacio Real and Monasterio de las Descalzas Reales; both are free to EU citizens on Wednesday.

If you plan to see all of Madrid's major museums (the Prado, Reina Sofía and Thyssen-Bornemisza), you can save a few euros by buying an 'Art Walk' pass (€12), for sale at all three museums.

that the woman depicted in this pair of paintings is the Duchess of Alba, Spain's richest woman in Goya's time. Goya was commissioned to paint her portrait by her husband and ended up having an affair with her, so he painted an extra portrait for himself. Showing Goya's darker side is the well-known *Saturno Devorando a Un Hijo* (Saturn Devouring his Son); the name says it all. Also dark are Goya's masterpieces depicting the horrors of the Spanish war of independence.

Guided tours are available in English and Spanish; ask for details at the ticket booth.

Museo Nacional Centro de Arte Reina Sofía

If modern art is your cup of tea, the Reina Sofía is your museum. A stunning collection of mainly Spanish modern art, the **Centro de Arte Reina Sofía** (Map pp936-7; ☎ 91 774 10 00; www.museoreinasofia.es; Calle Santa Isabel 52; adult/student €3/1.50, free Sat 2.30-9pm & Sun; 🕑 10am-9pm Mon & Wed-Sat, to 2.30pm Sun; Ⓜ Atocha) is home to Picasso's famous *Guernica* – his protest against the German bombing of the Basque town of Guernica during the Spanish Civil War in 1937 – in addition to housing important works by surrealist Salvador Dalí and abstract paintings by the Catalan artist Joan Miró.

In September 2005 the Reina Sofía unveiled a universally praised new wing, the work of famed French architect Jean Nouvel. Despite a few initial problems (the roof sprang a leak just before the grand opening), the new addition has given the museum some breathing space.

Museo Thyssen-Bornemisza

Sitting just opposite the Prado, the **Museo Thyssen-Bornemisza** (Map p940; ☎ 91 369 01 51; www.museothyssen.org; Paseo del Prado 8; adult/student €6/4; 🕑 10am-7pm Tue-Sun; Ⓜ Banco de España) is a somewhat eclectic collection of international masterpieces. Begin your visit on the 2nd floor, where you'll find medieval religious art, and make your way down to modern works on the ground level, passing paintings by Titian, El Greco, Rubens, Cézanne, Monet, Van Gogh, Miró, Picasso, Gris, Pollock, Dalí and Lichtenstein on the way. Formerly the private collection of the Thyssen-Bornemiszas, a German-Hungarian family of magnates, Spain purchased the collection in 1993 for a mere US$300 million.

Palacio Real & Around

Still King Juan Carlos I's official residence (though no-one actually lives here), Madrid's 18th-century royal palace, **Palacio Real** (Map p940; ☎ 91 454 88 00; www.patrimonionacional.es; Calle de Bailén s/n; adult/student €8/3.50, with guided tour €9, audio tour €2.50, free for EU citizens Wed; 🕑 9.30am-5pm Mon-Sat, 9am-2pm Sun Oct-Mar, 9am-6pm Mon-Sat, to 3pm Sun Apr-Sep; Ⓜ Ópera), is used mainly for important events, such as Prince Felipe and Doña Letizia's 2004 wedding reception. You can visit 50 of its 2800-plus rooms.

When the 16th-century Alcázar that formerly stood on this spot went up in flames on Christmas Eve 1734, King Felipe V ordered a new palace to be built on the same ground, with not a speck of wood used in its construction so that the disaster wouldn't be repeated. The opulent Palacio Real was finished in 1755, and the first monarch (Carlos III) moved in 1764. Though palace decoration has changed greatly through the years, some rooms, including the Throne Room and the Porcelain Room, have hardly been touched.

Look out for the 215 clocks of the royal clock collection and the five Stradivarius violins, used occasionally for concerts and balls. The tapestries and chandeliers throughout the palace are all original.

Outside the main palace, poke your head into the **Farmacia Real** (Map p940; Royal Pharmacy), where apothecary-style jars line the shelves. Continue on to the interesting **Armería Real** (Map p940; Royal Armoury), where you'll be impressed by the shiny (and surprisingly tiny!) royal suits of armour, most of them from the 16th and 17th centuries.

Plaza Mayor

Ringed with numerous cafés and restaurants and packed with people day and night, the arcaded **Plaza Mayor** (Map p940) is an atmospheric place. Built in the 17th century, the plaza was traditionally used as a market. On Sunday morning a stamp market still sets up shop.

The colourful frescoes on one side of the plaza decorate the **Real Casa de la Panaderia** (Royal Bakery), which predates the plaza and was restored after a 1790 fire. The equestrian statue dominating the plaza's centre depicts Felipe III and was placed here in 1848.

Churches

The **Catedral de Nuestra Señora de la Almudena** (Map p940; ☎ 91 522 22 00; Calle de Bailén 10; 9am-9pm; Ⓜ Ópera) is just across the plaza from the Palacio Real. Finished in 1992 after a century of work, the cathedral has never really won a place in the hearts of Madrileños. It's worth a quick peek, but this massive bulk of stone has nothing on the city's older churches, such as the largely 15th-century **Iglesia de San Nicolás** (Map p940; ☎ 91 559 40 64; Plaza San Nicolás 1; 6:30am-1.30pm & 5.30-9pm; Ⓜ Ópera), and the imposing 18th-century **Basilica de San Francisco El Grande** (Map pp936-7; ☎ 91 365 38 00; Plaza San Francisco 1; museum admission adult/student €3/2; 11am-12.30pm & 4-6.30pm Tue-Fri, 11am-1.30pm Sat Sep-Jul, 11am-12.30pm & 5-7.30pm Tue-Sun Aug; Ⓜ Puerta de Toledo).

Monasterio de las Descalzas Reales

Opulent inside though with a rather plain Plateresque exterior, the **Monasterio de las Descalzas Reales** (Convent of the Barefoot Royals; Map p940; ☎ 91 454 88 00; www.patrimonionacional.es; Plaza de las Descalzas Reales 3; adult/student €5/4, EU citizens Wed free; 10.30am-12.45pm & 4-5.45pm Tue-Thu & Sat, 10.30am-12.45pm Fri, 11am-1.45pm Sun; Ⓜ Sol or Callao) was founded in 1559 by Juana of Austria. Daughter of Spain's King Carlos I and Isabel of Portugal, Juana transformed one of her mother's palaces into the noblewomen's convent of choice. A wealthy religious house thanks to the nobles' gifts of art and other treasures, this convent is still home to a small group of nuns.

On the obligatory guided tour you'll see the celebrated Renaissance stairway, several chapels, a number of fabulous tapestries based on works by Rubens, and Juana's burial place.

Parque del Buen Retiro

Popular with joggers, families out for a stroll, lovey-dovey couples and anyone else looking for a break from the chaos of the city, **Parque del Buen Retiro** (Map pp936-7; 7am-midnight May-Sep, 7am-10pm Oct-Apr; Ⓜ Retiro), locally called simply El Retiro, is as much a Madrid tradition as tapas and *terrazas* (terrace cafés). Come on a weekend for street performers, clowns, puppet shows and the occasional theatre performance.

Start your visit along the **Paseo de las Estatuas**, a path lined with statues originally from the Palacio Real. It ends at the pretty **Estanque** (Lake) overlooked by **Alfonso XII's Mausoleum** (Map pp936-7). Rent a row boat at the northern end. Dotted about the park are a few interesting statues, such as the **El Ángel Caído** (Fallen Angel; Map pp936-7), the first-ever statue dedicated to the devil. Also interesting are gardens such as **La Rosaleda** (Rose Garden; Map pp936-7) and the sadly poetic **Bosque de los Ausentes** (Forest of the Missing), a tribute to the victims of the 11 March terrorist attack, which you'll find between the Puerta del Ángel Caído and Alfonso XII's Mausoleum.

Just outside the park is the **Real Jardín Botánico** (Map pp936-7; adult/student €2/1; 10am-dusk), which is less crowded and also lovely for strolling.

Other Sights

Brush up on the city's history and development at the well-organised **Museo Municipal** (Map pp936-7; ☎ 91 701 1863; www.munimadrid.es/museo municipal; Calle Fuencarral 78; admission free; 9.30am-8pm Tue-Fri, 10am-2pm Sat & Sun; Ⓜ Tribunal), which contains paintings and other memorabilia charting the evolution of Madrid.

Founded in 1721, **Real Fábrica de Tapices** (Map pp936-7; ☎ 91 434 05 50; www.realfatapices.com; Calle Fuenterrabia 2; admission €3; 10am-2pm Mon-Fri, closed Easter week & Aug; Ⓜ Menéndez Pelayo) still makes ornate tapestries and carpets by hand. Take one home for a mere €10,000 per sq metre.

A gift from Egypt, the authentically ancient **Templo de Debod** (Map p940; ☎ 91 366 74 15; Calle de Ferraz 1; admission free; 10am-2pm & 6-8pm Tue-Fri, 10am-2pm Sat & Sun Apr-Sep, 9.45am-1.45pm

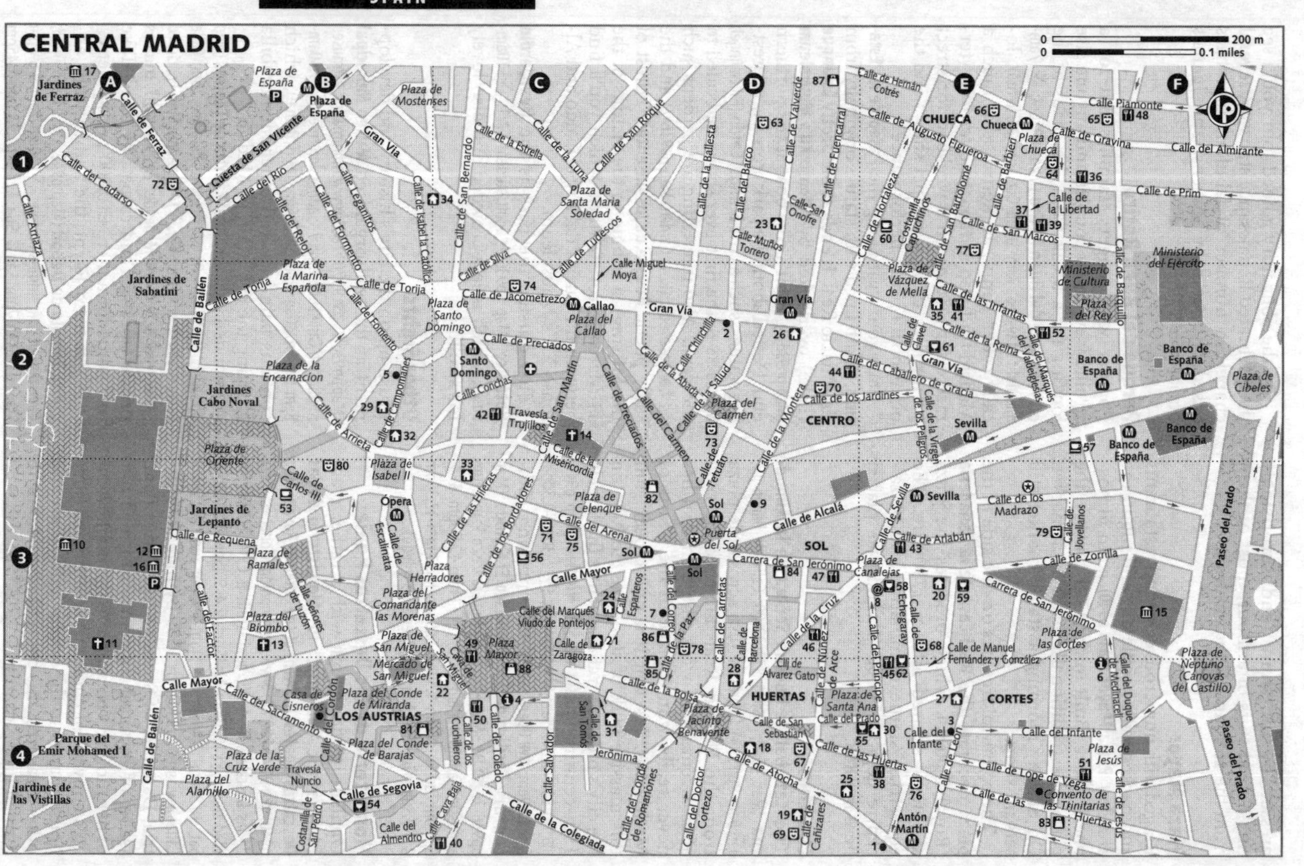
SPAIN
CENTRAL MADRID
0 200 m
0 0.1 miles
Jardines de Ferraz
Calle de Ferraz
Calle del Cadarso
Calle Arriaza
Plaza de España
Cuesta de San Vicente
Calle del Río
Calle del Reloj
Plaza de Mostenses
Gran Vía
Calle Leganitos
Calle del Fomento
Calle de Isabel la Católica
Calle de San Bernardo
Calle de la Estrella
Calle de la Luna
Calle de San Roque
Plaza de Santa María Soledad
Calle de Tudescos
Calle Miguel Moya
Calle de Silva
Jardines de Sabatini
Calle de Bailén
Plaza de la Marina Española
Calle de Torija
Calle de Jacometrezo
Callao
Plaza del Callao
Plaza de Santo Domingo
Calle de Preciados
Santo Domingo
Plaza de la Encarnación
Jardines Cabo Noval
Calle de Campomanes
Calle Conchas
Travesía Trujillos
Calle de San Martín
Calle de Arrieta
Plaza de Oriente
Plaza de Isabel II
Calle de Carlos III
Calle de la Misericordia
Calle de las Hileras
Calle de los Bordadores
Plaza de Celenque
Calle del Arenal
Ópera
Calle de Escalinata
Jardines de Lepanto
Calle de Requena
Plaza de Ramales
Calle Señores de Luzón
Plaza del Biombo
Calle del Factor
Plaza Herradores
Plaza del Comandante las Morenas
Calle Mayor
Plaza de San Miguel
Mercado de San Miguel
Cava de San Miguel
Plaza Mayor
Calle del Marqués Viudo de Pontejos
Calle de Zaragoza
Calle Esparteros
Calle del Correo
Calle de la Paz
Calle de Carretas
Calle de Barcelona
Calle de la Bolsa
Casa de Cisneros
Calle del Cordón
Plaza del Conde de Miranda
LOS AUSTRIAS
Calle del Sacramento
Plaza del Conde de Barajas
Calle de los Cuchilleros
Calle de Toledo
Calle Salvador
Calle de San Tomás
Jerónima
Plaza de Jacinto Benavente
Parque del Emir Mohamed I
Plaza de la Cruz Verde
Travesía Nuncio
Plaza del Alamillo
Calle de Segovia
Jardines de las Vistillas
Costanilla de San Pedro
Calle del Almendro
Calle Cava Baja
Calle de la Colegiata
Calle del Conde de Romanones
Calle del Doctor Cortezo
Calle de Cañizares
Calle de Atocha
Calle de la Ballesta
Calle del Barco
Calle de Valverde
Calle San Onofre
Calle Muñoz Torrero
Calle de Fuencarral
Calle de Hernán Cortés
Calle de Hortaleza
Costanilla Capuchinos
Calle de San Bartolomé
Calle de Barbieri
CHUECA
Chueca
Calle de Augusto Figueroa
Plaza de Chueca
Calle Piamonte
Calle de Gravina
Calle del Almirante
Calle de Prim
Calle de la Libertad
Calle de San Marcos
Plaza de Vázquez de Mella
Calle de las Infantas
Calle de Clavel
Calle de la Reina
Calle del Marqués del Valdeiglesias
Ministerio de Cultura
Plaza del Rey
Calle de Barquillo
Ministerio del Ejército
Banco de España
Plaza de Cibeles
Calle de la Chinchilla
Calle de la Abada
Calle de la Salud
Plaza del Carmen
Calle del Carmen
Calle de Tetuán
Calle de la Montera
Calle de los Jardines
Calle del Caballero de Gracia
Calle de la Virgen de los Peligros
CENTRO
Sevilla
Calle de Sevilla
Sol
Puerta del Sol
Calle de Alcalá
SOL
Calle de Arlabán
Calle de los Madrazo
Calle de Jovellanos
Paseo del Prado
Carrera de San Jerónimo
Plaza de Canalejas
Calle de Zorrilla
Calle de Echegaray
Calle de la Cruz
Calle de Núñez de Arce
Cllj de Álvarez Gato
Calle del Príncipe
Calle de Manuel Fernández y González
Plaza de las Cortes
Calle del Duque de Medinaceli
Plaza de Neptuno (Cánovas del Castillo)
HUERTAS
Plaza de Santa Ana
Calle del Prado
Calle de San Sebastián
Calle de las Huertas
Calle del Infante
Calle de León
CORTES
Plaza de Jesús
Calle de Lope de Vega
Convento de las Trinitarias
Calle de las Huertas
Calle de Jesús
Antón Martín

INFORMATION		
Farmacia Globo	1	E4
La Casa del Libro	2	D2
Lavandería Cervantes	3	E4
Municipal Tourist Office	4	C4
Petra's International Bookshop	5	B2
Regional Tourist Office	6	F4
Spain Storage	7	D3
Work Center	8	E3
SIGHTS & ACTIVITIES		
Academia InHispania	9	D3
Armería Real	10	A3
Catedral de Nuestra Señora de la Almudena	11	A3
Farmacia Real	12	A3
Iglesia de San Nicolás	13	B3
Monasterio de las Descalzas Reales	14	C2
Museo Thyssen-Bornemisza	15	F3
Palacio Real	16	A3
Templo de Debod	17	A1
SLEEPING		
Catalonia Moratín	18	D4
Cats	19	D4
Hostal Adriano	(see 28)	
Hostal Aguilar	20	E3
Hostal Cruz Sol	21	C3
Hostal La Macarena	22	C4
Hostal La Zona	23	D1
Hostal Madrid	24	C3
Hostal Martín	25	D4
Hostal Orly	26	D2
Hostal Santa Cruz	(see 21)	
Hostal Sardinero	27	E4
Hostal Tijcal II	28	D4
Hotel Meninas Madrid	29	B2
Hotel Miau	30	E4
Hotel Plaza Mayor	31	C4
Los Amigos Backpackers' Hostel	32	B2
Los Amigos Backpackers' Hostel	33	C3
Mucho Madrid	34	C1
Room Mate Mario	(see 32)	
San Lorenzo	35	E2
EATING		
Bar Bardemcilla	36	F1
Bazaar	37	E1
Casa Alberto	38	E4
Diurno	39	E1
El Schotis	40	C4
El Tigre	41	E2
El Zagal	42	C2
La Finca de Susana	43	E3
La Gloria de Montera	44	D2
La Trucha	45	E4
La Trucha	46	D3
Lhardy	47	D3
Maison Blanche	48	F1
Museo del Jamon	49	C3
Sobrino de Botín	50	C4
Taberna de Dolores	51	F4
Wokcafé	52	E2
DRINKING		
Café de Oriente	53	B3
Café del Nuncio	54	B4
Cervecería Alemana	55	E4
Chocolatería de San Ginés	56	C3
Círculo de Bellas Artes	57	F2
Ducados Café	58	E3
Glass Bar	59	E3
Mamá Inés	60	E1
Museo Chicote	61	E2
Viva Madrid	62	E4
ENTERTAINMENT		
Bar & Co	63	D1
Black & White	64	E1
Bogui Jazz	65	F1
Café Acuarela	66	E1
Café Central	67	D4
Cardamomo	68	E3
Casa Patas	69	D4
El Sol	70	D2
Joy Eslava	71	C3
Las Tablas	72	A1
Localidades Galicia	73	D2
Oba-Oba	74	C2
Palacio Gaviria	75	C3
Populart	76	E4
Queen Madrid	77	E1
Teatro Albéniz	78	D3
Teatro de la Zarzuela	79	E3
Teatro Real	80	B3
SHOPPING		
Art Market	81	B4
El Corte Inglés	82	D3
Flamenco World	83	E4
Gil	84	D3
José Ramírez	85	D4
Justo Algaba	86	D3
Mercado de Fuencarral	87	D1
Stamp and Coin Market	88	C4

& 4.15-6.15pm Tue-Fri, 10am-2pm Sat & Sun Oct-Mar; Ⓜ Plaza de España) was transferred here stone by stone in 1972 as a gesture of thanks to the Spanish archaeologists that helped save Egyptian monuments from the rising waters of the Aswan Dam.

COURSES

Flamenco

Uchi of **Flamenco con Uchi** (Flamenco with Uchi; Map pp936-7; ☎ 91 527 32 18; Calle Santa Isabel 9; beginners 7pm, advanced 8pm; Ⓜ Antón Martín) is one of several teachers in Madrid. Check out Flamenco World (p949) for up-to-date info on Uchi's and others' classes.

Language

The language schools below offer short-term classes and have been given the stamp of approval by the Instituto de Cervantes, the official institution created to promote Spanish language and culture.

Academia InHispania (Map p940; ☎ 91 521 22 31; www.inhispania.com; Calle de la Montera 10-12; Ⓜ Gran Vía)

Academia Paraninfo (Map pp936-7; ☎ 91 543 31 39; www. paraninfo.com; 1st fl, Calle de la Princesa 70; Ⓜ Sol)

TOURS

For an interesting themed tour, check out **Discover Madrid walking tours** (☎ 91 588 29 06; adult €4-6.50, child €2.50-5), offered in English and Spanish by the municipal tourist office (p935). The open-topped tourist bus **Madrid Visión** (☎ 91 765 10 16; www.madridvision.es; adult €14.50-19, child €8-10) is also recommended; see its website for operating times.

FESTIVALS & EVENTS

Madrid's social calendar is packed with festivals and special events. Art, music and cultural fairs are happening almost constantly; check with the tourist office or in publications such as the *Guía del Ocio* to see what's on. Major holidays and festivals include the following:

Día de los Reyes (Three Kings' Day) The three kings bring gifts to children and a mammoth parade takes over the city centre on 6 January.

Fiesta de San Isidro Street parties, parades, bullfights and other fun events honour Madrid's patron saint on 15 May.
Fiesta de Otoño The year's cultural highlight, the Autumn Festival, running from mid-October through to mid-November, is a time for music, dance and theatre.

SLEEPING

A bundle of new hotels has opened recently in Madrid, meaning that travellers are spoiled for choice when it comes to accommodation. From chic to cheap, there's a little something for everyone, but you'll need to book ahead, especially in peak season.

Prices here are subject to change. During a major holiday or trade fair, they can be pushed up by 15% or 20%, but during slower periods you might find deep discounts, especially at the top-end hotels. Check hotel websites for deals.

Los Austrias & Centro

BUDGET

Los Amigos Backpackers' Hostel (Map p940; ☎ 91 547 17 07; www.losamigoshostel.com; 4th fl, Calle de Campomanes 6; dm €16-17; 💻; Ⓜ Ópera) Owned by an experienced backpacker who wanted to create her ideal hostel, this cheerful spot boasts free wi-fi, laundry service, a community kitchen, extra-big free lockers and some of the cleanest showers we've seen. Los Amigos has another hostel on Calle del Arenal 26.

Mucho Madrid (Map p940; ☎ 91 559 23 50; www.muchomadrid.com; Gran Vía 59; dm €20; Ⓜ Gran Vía) Named the safest hostel in the world by hostelworld.com, this tidy place opened in July 2004 and was a quick hit thanks to its small rooms, colourful décor and quiet atmosphere.

Hostal Orly (Map p940; ☎ 91 531 30 12; 7th fl, Calle de la Montera 47; s/d/tr €35/46/58; Ⓜ Gran Vía) Looking out from the top floor of a grand 19th-century building, this quiet *hostal* (cheap hotel) boasts tall ceilings and wooden floors. It is also promising air-con for 2007.

Other recommendations:

Cats (Map p940; ☎ 91 369 28 07; www.catshostel.com; Calle de Cañizares 6; dm €16-18; ⊠ ❄ 💻; Ⓜ Sol) Always a party waiting to happen. On-site bar.
Hostal Santa Cruz (Map p940; ☎ 91 522 24 41; www.hostalsantacruz.com; 2nd fl, Plaza Santa Cruz 6; s/d €35/48; ❄; Ⓜ Sol) Fabulous value, with flowered bedspreads and sparkling bathrooms.
Hostal Cruz Sol (Map p940; ☎ 91 532 71 97; www.hostalcruzsol.com; 3rd fl, Plaza Santa Cruz 6; s/d/tr €40/52/70; ❄; Ⓜ Sol) Cheery. Great location.

MIDRANGE

Hostal La Macarena (Map p940; ☎ 91 365 92 21; www.silserranos.com; Cava de San Miguel 8; s €51-57, d €64-70, tr €72-84, q €84-96; Ⓜ Sol) Rooms are snug but charming at this friendly family-run place by the Plaza Mayor. The management here also runs the Hostal Sil & Serranos (opposite).

Hostal Madrid (Map p940; ☎ 91 522 00 60; www.hostal-madrid.info; 2nd fl, Calle Esparteros 6; s €50-58, d/tr €70/90; ❄; Ⓜ Sol) A great location, impeccable bathrooms and stylish rooms bathed in light make this a popular choice. There's also free wi-fi. Ask about the owner's rental apartments, ideal for families or groups.

Hotel Plaza Mayor (Map p940; ☎ 91 360 06 06; www.h-plazamayor.com; Calle Atocha 2; s €59-79, d €89-99; ❄; Ⓜ Sol or Tirso de Molina) This hotel has spacious, stylish rooms just 50m from Plaza Mayor. Original elements of this 150-year-old building (a former church) lend it a special charm.

Room Mate Mario (Map p940; ☎ 91 548 85 48; www.room-matehoteles.com; Calle de Campomanes 4; s €80-105, d €92-118; ⊠ ❄ 💻; Ⓜ Ópera) The first of a new chain of ultramod hotels, Mario's offers sleek décor and futuristic touches like purple fluorescent lights above the bed.

TOP END

Hotel Meninas Madrid (Map p940; ☎ 91 541 28 05; www.hotelmeninas.com; Calle de Campomanes 7; s €93-160, d €93-185; ⊠ ❄; Ⓜ Ópera) A refurbished 19th-century mansion, the Meninas combines old-world comfort with modern, clean-lined style.

Sol, Huertas & Atocha

BUDGET

Hostal-Residencia Fernandez (Map pp936-7; ☎/fax 91 530 81 11; Calle Sánchez Bustillo 3; s/d/tr €35/45/60; ❄; Ⓜ Atocha) Sitting on a sunny plaza across from the Reina Sofía, this quiet place offers a great deal. Rooms are bright, with wrought-iron beds, colourful décor and decent-sized bathrooms.

Hostal Martín (Map p940; ☎ 91 429 95 79; www.hostalmartin.com; Calle de Atocha 43; s €35-39, d €44-49, tr €57-64; ❄ 💻; Ⓜ Antón Martín) The decoration is a tad old-fashioned, but this is a bright and clean place to lay your head. Free wi-fi and nice bathrooms.

SPAIN

Hostal Aguilar (Map p940; ☎ 91 429 59 26; www.hostalaguilar.com; 2nd fl, Carrera de San Jerónimo 32; s/d/tr/q €37/49/66/80; ⊠ ❄; Ⓜ Sol) Kitschy but cute, Aguilar offers spacious, cheerful rooms. Ask for one that's been recently refurbished, such as large room 101.

Hostal Sardinero (Map p940; ☎ 91 429 57 56; fax 91 429 41 12; 3rd fl, Calle del Prado 16; s/d €47/59; ❄; Ⓜ Sol) A dignified sort of place, the Sardinero boasts small balconies, high ceilings, wood floors and well-equipped bathrooms.

MIDRANGE

Hostal Tijcal II (Map p940; ☎ 91 360 46 28; www.hostaltijcal.com; Calle de la Cruz 26; s/d/tr €50/66/77; ❄; Ⓜ Sol) Totally re-done a few years back, this sleek *hostal* feels like a three-star hotel, with cool blonde-wood furnishings, key cards and attractive coordinating décor.

Hotel Mora (Map pp936-7; ☎ 91 420 15 69; www.hotelmora.com; Paseo del Prado 32; s/d €57/75; ❄; Ⓜ Atocha) Near the Prado, this simple hotel is good value, with unfussy but tidy rooms, some with a view of the botanical gardens.

Hotel Miau (Map p940; ☎ 91 369 71 20; www.hotelmiau.com; Calle de Príncipe 26; s/d incl breakfast €75/85; ❄; Ⓜ Sol) For style, this boutique hotel overlooking the Plaza de Santa Ana can't be beaten, but light sleepers beware the noise from revellers below.

TOP END

Catalonia Moratín (Map p940; ☎ 91 369 71 71; www.hoteles-catalonia.es; Calle de Atocha 23; r €126-204; ❄ 💻; Ⓜ Antón Martín) The spacious, comfortable rooms here are pretty standard, but the 18th-century entryway, interior patio and lobby, which has a gorgeous spiral staircase, provide an extra dose of charm.

Malasaña & Chueca

BUDGET

Olé International Hostel (Map pp936-7; ☎ 91 446 51 65; www.olehostel.com; 1st fl, Calle Manuela Malasaña 23; dm €16; 💻; Ⓜ Tribunal or Bilbao) Bright, friendly and with several hang-out areas, this is a good place to meet people. Rooms are a squeeze though, and bathrooms leave something to be desired. Free lockers with your own lock are provided.

MIDRANGE

Hostal Sil & Serranos (Map pp936-7; ☎ 91 448 89 72; www.silserranos.com; Calle Fuencarral 95; s €45-57, d €57-70, tr €72-84, q €84-96; Ⓜ Tribunal) Squeaky clean and oozing with charm, this family-owned *hostal* is great value. For extra space and a pretty view, ask for room 318.

> **AUTHOR'S CHOICE**
>
> **Hostal Adriano** (Map p940; ☎ 91 521 13 39; www.hostaladriano.com; 4th fl, Calle de la Cruz 26; s €45-49, d €58-65; ❄; Ⓜ Sol) Absolutely fabulous. The flat-screen TV and purple walls at the entrance set the tone for Madrid's most stylish *hostal*. Rooms couldn't be lovelier: each one is individually decorated with fluffy duvets, quirky furnishings, fun colour schemes and great bathrooms.

Hostal La Zona (Map p940; ☎ 91 521 99 04; www.hostallazona.com; 1st fl, Calle de Valverde 7; incl breakfast s €50, d €55-65; Ⓜ Gran Vía) Here you'll find small, stylish rooms, lots of light and a primarily gay clientele. There's a good breakfast buffet and free Internet access for those who bring their own laptop.

Hotel San Lorenzo (Map p940; ☎ 91 521 30 57; www.hotel-sanlorenzo.com; Calle de Clavel 8; s/d/tr €52/65/99; ❄; Ⓜ Gran Vía) A quaint spot in a great location, rooms at San Lorenzo are small but charming; some include original decorative elements from this 19th-century building. There's free Internet access, if you provide the laptop.

Beyond the Centre

Husa Chamartín (☎ 91 334 49 00; www.hotelchamartin.com; Calle Augustín de Foxá; r €73-203; ❄ 💻; Ⓜ Chamartín) There's not much personality here, but this comfortable business-style hotel is a great choice if you get in to Chamartín on a late train.

High Tech Madrid Aeropuerto (☎ 91 564 59 06; www.hthoteles.com; Calle Galeón 25; r €80-150; ⊠ ❄ 💻 🏊; Ⓜ Aeropuerto) With a free shuttle service to and from the airport, this stylish place can be a lifesaver for those with an early or late flight. The outdoor pool is a nice perk.

EATING

Trendy fusion restaurants, ethnic eateries serving fare from the four corners of the globe, delicious regional specialities from all over Spain… In Madrid these days, it's possible to find just about any kind of cuisine. The city's biggest claim to fame foodwise is its traditional eateries: the chaotic

SPAIN

tapas bars of La Latina, the cavelike taverns around Plaza Mayor, and the countless neighbourhood favourites serving up local specialities such as *cochinillo asado* (roast suckling pig) or *cocido madrileño* (a hearty stew made of beans and various animals' innards).

Expect a meal in a budget restaurant to cost €20 or less, while a meal in a midrange restaurant will run from €20 to €40, and a meal in a top-end restaurant will cost more than €40.

Los Austrias & Centro

Museo del Jamón (Map p940; ☎ 91 542 26 32; Plaza Mayor 18; mains €3-15; Ⓜ Sol) Of the many bars on Plaza Mayor, this Spanish cured ham chain is one where you can eat pretty well without paying too dearly. It's good for breakfast sandwiches, and there are other outlets throughout the city.

El Zagal (Map p940; ☎ 91 542 05 57; Calle Trujillos 7; mains €6-14, menú €12; Ⓜ Callao) This family-run good-value restaurant, with its varied options of tasty Castilian fare, is popular with local office workers.

La Gloria de Montera (Map p940; ☎ 91 523 44 07; Calle del Caballero de Gracia 10; mains €7-12; Ⓜ Gran Vía) Minimalist style, tasty Mediterranean dishes and great prices mean that you'll probably have to wait in line to eat here. But it's worth it.

Siam (Map pp936-7; ☎ 91 559 83 15; Calle San Bernardino 6; mains €7.50-12; Ⓜ Plaza de España) Though owned by an American, Siam has a popular following among lovers of authentic Thai cuisine. Great for vegetarians.

Sobrino de Botín (Map p940; ☎ 91 366 42 17; Calle de los Cuchilleros 17; mains €10-27; ⊠; Ⓜ Sol) Reputedly opened in 1725, this is the oldest restaurant in Madrid and has all the old-world charm to prove it. The place is famous for its roast suckling pig.

Sol, Huertas & Atocha

La Finca de Susana (Map p940; ☎ 91 369 35 57; Calle de Arlabán 4; mains €6-12; Ⓜ Sevilla) A well-priced mix of Spanish and international fare has made this an extremely popular choice with locals and tourists alike. You'll probably have to wait a while to eat.

La Trucha Calle de Manuel Fernández y González (Map p940; ☎ 91 429 58 33; Calle de Manuel Fernández y González 3; mains €6-15, menú €12; Ⓜ Sevilla); Calle Núñez de Arce (Map p940; ☎ 91 532 08 82; Calle Núñez de Arce 6; mains €6-15; ⏲ Tue-Sun; Ⓜ Sevilla) An old standard, 'The Trout' serves a broad range of tapas and affordable meat and fish plates.

Casa Alberto (Map p940; ☎ 91 429 93 56; www.casaalberto.es; Calle de las Huertas 18; mains €12-15;

TOP TAPAS

The very best place for tapas is the area around Calle Cava Alta and Calle Cava Baja, near the La Latina metro. Other good areas include the streets around the Plaza de Dos de Mayo and the Plaza de Chueca. Expect tapas to cost €1 to €2 for something simple, €4 to €6 for an elaborate tapas, or €12 and up for something really exquisite, like a plate of Bellota ham.

El Tigre (Map p940; Calle de las Infantas 30; Ⓜ Sevilla) Chueca is full of trendy tapas bars, but it's at off-the-beaten-track spots like this one that you'll find the real deal – cheap drinks that come with generous free tapas. No wonder it's always filled to the brim with a student crowd.

El Schotis (Map p940; ☎ 91 365 3239; Calle Cava Baja 11; Ⓜ La Latina) This old-fashioned bar gives you a free tapa when you order a glass of beer or wine (€1.50).

Taberna de Dolores (Map p940; ☎ 91 433 29 43; Plaza de Jesús 4; Ⓜ Sevilla) Here since 1908, this delightful little bar smothered in tiles has beer and wine flowing freely at just €1.50 a glass.

Lamiak (Map pp936-7; ☎ 91 365 52 12; Calle Cava Baja 42; Ⓜ La Latina) A favourite with students, this is an inexpensive spot for typical-style tapas and drinks.

Juana la Loca (Map pp936-7; ☎ 91 364 05 25; Plaza Puerta de Moros 4; Ⓜ La Latina) If you can, nab a table or a bar spot at this trendy restaurant and tapas bar in La Latina, where elaborate and creative tapas are served to a mixed crowd.

Bar Bardemcilla (Map p940; ☎ 91 521 42 56; Calle de Augusto Figueroa 47; ⏲ lunch & dinner Mon-Fri, lunch Sat; Ⓜ Chueca) Owned by the renowned Bardem family of actors (Javier is famed for his roles in *Mar Adentro* and *Before Night Falls*), this upscale tapas bar is prime celebrity-spotting ground. Full meals are served too.

(M Antón Martín) Old-timey Casa Alberto has been serving traditional fare and *vermut* (vermouth) since 1827, and stepping through the doors is like stepping back in time.

Lhardy (Map p940; ☎ 91 522 22 07; Carrera de San Jerónimo 8; mains €15-25; M Sevilla) In business since 1839, this elegant spot is as beloved as La Trucha, but more upscale.

La Latina & Lavapiés

This area is best known for its tapas bars. See opposite for more.

Casa Lucio (Map pp936-7; ☎ 91 365 32 52; Calle Cava Baja 35; mains €11-21; M La Latina) Traditional and dignified, Casa Lucio is famous for its *huevos rotos,* fried eggs served runny over potatoes.

Malasaña & Chueca

These are the areas to come to for international food and creative, contemporary cuisine. Some of the city's best (and best-priced) eateries can be found along the side streets of the trendy Chueca district.

Diurno (Map p940; ☎ 91 522 00 09; Calle de San Marcos 37; mains €4-8; M Chueca) Great for a quick bite, Diurno's takeaway options include several different salads and tasty sandwiches. This all-in-one spot is also a popular café and a place to rent movies.

Bazaar (Map p940; ☎ 91 523 39 05; Calle de la Libertad 21; mains €6-9; M Chueca) An airy, Zen-inspired dining room sets the tone at Bazaar, a restaurant known for its salads and international flair.

Maison Blanche (Map p940; ☎ 91 521 53 08; Calle Piamonte 10; mains €7-11; M Chueca) A gourmet boutique and small café-style restaurant, the 'White House' has a French-inspired menu and all-white décor.

La Musa (Map pp936-7; ☎ 91 448 75 58; Calle Manuela Malasaña 18; mains €8-12; M Bilbao) Creative tapas, salads and inventive Mediterranean-style cuisine are the staples at this trendy restaurant and bar. It's very popular with the student crowd.

La Isla del Tesoro (Map pp936-7; ☎ 91 593 14 40; Calle Manuela Malasaña 3; mains €8-12; M Bilbao) Don't let the kitschy *Treasure Island* décor put you off; La Isla's internationally inspired vegetarian menu is a joy for veggie lovers. Great wine list.

Wokcafé (Map p940; ☎ 91 522 90 69; Calle de las Infantas 44; mains €8-15; closed Sun; M Sevilla) Noodle bowls, 'woks' and other Western-styled Chinese fare is served up with style at this trendy place.

Nina (Map pp936-7; ☎ 91 591 0046; Calle Manuela Malasaña 10; mains €9-13; M Bilbao) A New York–loft style restaurant owned by an expat named Nina, this eatery runs the gamut from salads to pasta and burgers, and does a mean weekend brunch.

Salamanca & Ventas

El Pescador (Map pp936-7; ☎ 91 402 12 90; Calle de José Ortega y Gasset 75; mains €12-18; closed Sun; M Lista) One of the city's best places for fresh Galician shellfish and seafood, the classy 'Fisherman' is worth a splurge.

Mumbai Masala (Map pp936-7; ☎ 91 435 71 94; Calle Recoletos 14; mains €18-30; M Recoletos) The delicious Indian fare served here has made the refined Mumbai Masala a trendy place. Come midweek for the set-price lunch menu; it's great value and far cheaper than the dinner prices.

DRINKING

Bars, whether they be quaint cafés, artsy coffee houses or late-night drinking holes, abound in Madrid. This is a city that lives life outside on the streets and plazas, and bar hopping is a pastime enjoyed by young and old alike. Locals rarely stay in one bar for long, preferring to skip from bar to bar, ordering just a drink or two then moving on.

If you're looking for a traditional bar, head to the Huertas district or to the bars around Calles Cava Alta and Cava Baja in La Latina. For an edgier feel and a gay-friendly crowd, hit Chueca. Malasaña is the place for alternative and grunge locales. In summer, the terrace bars that pop up all over the city are unbeatable.

The night-time crowd starts showing up by 8pm for predinner drinks. The mood really gets rolling around midnight, and the bars all close by about 3am on weekends, 2am on weekdays.

Bars

LOS AUSTRIAS & CENTRO

Café del Nuncio (Map p940; ☎ 91 366 09 06; Calle Segovia 9; M La Latina) Lace curtains and red-wood panelling set the tone at this bustling bar. In summer, the outdoor terrace is divine.

Museo Chicote (Map p940; ☎ 91 532 67 37; Gran Vía 12; closed Sun; M Gran Vía) A city classic popular with socialites and film stars, the Museo Chicote has a lounge atmosphere late at night and a stream of famous faces all day.

LA LATINA & LAVAPIÉS

La Bodeguita del Medio (Map pp936-7; ☎ 91 578 47 46; Calle de Alcalá 77; Ⓜ Retiro) Offering great *mojitos* (lime, mint and rum cocktail) and groovable salsa, this is a little taste of Cuba in Spain.

El Viajero (Map pp936-7; ☎ 91 366 90 64; Plaza de la Cebada 11; Ⓜ La Latina) A neighbourhood favourite drawing a mixed crowd, El Viajero has a downstairs restaurant, a cosy upstairs bar and best of all, a rooftop terrace with fantastic city views.

SOL, HUERTAS & ATOCHA

Ducados Café (Map p940; ☎ 91 360 00 89; www.ducados-café.com; Plaza de Canalejas 3; Ⓜ Sevilla) At night the otherwise drab basement of this *cafetería* (café) is transformed into a popular bar and dance spot. It draws lots of students and travellers, and is a good place to start the night.

Cervecería Alemana (Map p940; ☎ 91 429 70 33; Plaza de Santa Ana 6; 🕒 closed Tue & Aug; Ⓜ Sevilla) A classic and classy watering hole, this place is famous for its cold, frothy beers and delicious tapas. It was one of Hemingway's haunts.

Viva Madrid (Map p940; ☎ 91 429 36 40; www.barvivamadrid.com; Calle de Manuel Fernández y González 7; Ⓜ Sevilla or Sol) A landmark smothered in beautiful coloured tiles, Viva Madrid does tapas earlier in the evening and drinks late into the night.

Glass Bar (Map p940; ☎ 91 787 77 70; Carrera de San Jerónimo 34; Ⓜ Sevilla) Madrid's trendiest nightspot (at least for now), the Hotel Urban's Glass Bar is a place to see and be seen, so dress the part. On summer nights, head up to the terrace for cocktails overlooking the city.

MALASAÑA & CHUECA

Areia (Map pp936-7; ☎ 91 310 03 07; www.areiachillout.com; Calle de Hortaleza 92; Ⓜ Alonso Martínez) With its wide, bedlike couches and an Arabian-themed décor, at Areia you'll want to simply chill out and stay awhile.

Café Pepe Botella (Map pp936-7; ☎ 91 522 43 09; Calle San Andrés 12; Ⓜ Bilbao or Tribunal) The cosy velvet benches and marble-topped tables give 'Joe Bottle' a retro feel. It's best known for its sherry.

Molly Malone's (Map pp936-7; ☎ 91 594 12 01; Calle Manuela Malasaña 11; Ⓜ Bilbao) Dark wood panelling, Guinness on tap, low lights, friendly regulars…yep, it's everything you'd expect from an Irish pub.

Tupperware (Map pp936-7; Corredera Alta de San Pablo 26; Ⓜ Tribunal) Unbelievably kitschy, with plastic dolls and pictures of old TV stars as décor, this fun bar plays danceable pop and '80s music every night of the week.

SALAMANCA & VENTAS

Bisú (☎ 91 447 52 08; Calle José Abascal 8; Ⓜ Gregorio Marañón) Bisú's minimal style and its variety of techno and pop music draws a mixed crowd.

Serrano 41 (Map pp936-7; ☎ 91 578 1865; Calle de Serrano 41; Ⓜ Serrano) A stylish, upscale crowd frequents this bar near the Serrano metro station. Come in summer to hang out on the fabulous terrace bar.

Cafés

By day these cafés are great spots to grab a coffee or get recharged for more sightseeing. By night, most serve cocktails and adopt a more sophisticated attitude.

Café de Oriente (Map p940; ☎ 91 547 15 64; Plaza Oriente 2; Ⓜ Ópera) Sip coffee inside this lush modernist-styled café, or sit outside to nibble on ice cream or tapas as you admire the view of the Palacio Real. Light lunch fare is served too (mains from €7.50 to €11).

Círculo de Bellas Artes (Map p940; ☎ 91 360 54 00; Calle Marqués de Casa Riera 2; admission €1; Ⓜ Banco de España) You're charged €1 for the privilege of sipping your tea in this gorgeous *belle époque* café, but it's worth it.

J+J Books & Coffee (Map pp936-7; ☎ 91 521 85 76; Calle Espiritu Santo 47; Ⓜ Noviciado) An English bookshop and friendly café, J+J hosts events all week long and is popular with students and expats. It's a great place to meet people.

Chocolatería de San Ginés (Map p940; ☎ 91 365 65 46; Pasadizo San Ginés 5; Ⓜ Sol or Ópera) Join the sugar-searching throngs who end the night at this mythic bar (it doesn't close until 7am), famous for its freshly fried *churros* (fried sticks of dough) and syrupy hot chocolate.

Also recommended:

Mamá Inés (Map p940; ☎ 91 523 23 33; www.mamaines.com; Calle de Hortaleza 22; Ⓜ Chueca)

SPAIN

Popular with gay men, this is a meeting point and a great spot for coffee.

Café Manuela (Map pp936-7; ☎ 91 531 70 37; Calle San Vicente Ferrer 29; Ⓜ Noviciado) This cosy, old-timey café offers board games and great cocktails.

Café Comercial (Map pp936-7; ☎ 91 521 56 55; Glorieta de Bilbao 7; Ⓜ Bilbao) The faded elegance of this classic café appeals to intellectuals and the artsy crowd.

Café de Ruíz (Map pp936-7; ☎ 91 446 12 32; Calle Ruíz 11; Ⓜ Bilbao) Marble tables and velvet-covered seats give this romantic spot the air of a 1930s movie.

ENTERTAINMENT

The entertainment bible is the *Guía del Ocio,* a weekly magazine sold at newsstands for €1. Highlights are given in English at the back. The best gay guide is *Shanguide,* which you can pick up free in bars around town.

Nightclubs

Madrid is a great city for dancing; clubs and discos are found in just about every corner of the city. The big-name clubs are concentrated along and around Gran Vía, though Chueca, Malasaña and Huertas are good bets too.

Club prices vary wildly, but most charge between €8 and €15. At most places, dancing starts at around 1am and lasts until daybreak. Come Thursday through Saturday for the best atmosphere.

El Sol (Map p940; ☎ 91 532 64 90; Calle de los Jardines 3; closed Sun & Mon; Ⓜ Gran Vía) If you want more than just techno music, this funky club is a great bet. Sometimes there's a live show.

Palacio Gaviria (Map p940; ☎ 91 526 60 69; Calle del Arenal 9; Ⓜ Sol) Special international student nights and other theme nights bring the big crowds to this club near the Puerta del Sol. The entry can be a bit pricey, but the atmosphere is a notch up too.

Joy Eslava (Map p940; ☎ 91 366 37 33; www.joy-eslava.com; Calle del Arenal 11; Ⓜ Sol or Ópera) Housed in a 19th-century neoclassical theatre, Joy hosts lots of theme parties and student nights. It's a megaclub, but can still be a good place to meet people.

El Son (Map pp936-7; ☎ 91 532 32 83; Calle Victoria 6; Ⓜ Sol) You can salsa all week long at this lively Latin club. Midweek, check out the live Cuban music concerts.

Kapital (Map pp936-7; ☎ 91 420 29 06; Calle de Atocha 125; Ⓜ Atocha) A macro club boasting up to seven different dance floors (though they're rarely all open), this is the spot for the indecisive crowd.

Gabana 1800 (Map pp936-7; ☎ 91 576 06 86; Calle de Velázquez 6; Ⓜ Retiro) Catering to a slightly older crowd, the sophisticated Gabana 1800 is more a place for hanging out than really grooving.

Cinemas

Several movie theatres are huddled around Gran Vía and Calle de la Princesa.

Cine Doré (Map pp936-7; ☎ 91 549 00 11; Calle Santa Isabel 3; Ⓜ Antón Martín) The National Film Library offers fantastic classic and vanguard films for €1.50 a show at Cine Doré. Buy tickets in advance.

For a selection of original-version (international films shown with subtitles) flicks in this area, head to **Princesa** (Map pp936-7; ☎ 91 541 41 00; Calle de la Princesa 3; Ⓜ Plaza de España) or **Alphaville** (Map pp936-7; ☎ 91 559 38 36; Calle Martín de los Heros 14; Ⓜ Plaza de España).

Gay & Lesbian Venues

Chueca is Madrid's lively, gay-friendly neighbourhood, and you'll find lots of gay and lesbian bars and clubs in the area.

Black & White (Map p940; ☎ 91 531 11 41; Calle de la Libertad 34; Ⓜ Chueca) A staple of Chueca's gay scene, this popular bar has a dance floor downstairs and a room for shows or private parties upstairs.

Queen Madrid (Map p940; ☎ 91 522 09 49; Calle de Barbieri 7; Ⓜ Chueca) While not the trendiest spot in the neighbourhood, you'll always have a good time at this classic gay dance club.

Café Acuarela (Map p940; ☎ 91 522 21 43; Calle de Gravina 10; Ⓜ Chueca) For something low-key, head to this quiet bar.

Theatre

Madrid has a lively cultural scene, with concerts and shows taking place throughout the city.

Teatro Albéniz (Map p940; ☎ 91 531 83 11; Calle de la Paz 11; Ⓜ Sol) Staging both commercial and vanguard drama, this is just one of Madrid's quality theatres. For more listings, check out *Guía del Ocio* or local newspapers.

Teatro Real (Map p940; ☎ 91 516 06 06; www.teatro-real.com; Plaza de Isabel II; Ⓜ Ópera) This is Madrid's opulent opera house, and the city's grandest stage. Here you can see opera, dance or theatre, depending on the offerings.

It's also open for tours (adult/student €4/2) between 10.30am and 1pm Monday and Wednesday to Friday and 11am to 1.30pm Saturday and Sunday.

Teatro de la Zarzuela (Map p940; ☎ 91 524 54 10; Calle de Jovellanos 4; Ⓜ Banco de España) Come here for zarzuela, a very Spanish mixture of dance, music and theatre.

Sport

Get tickets to football matches and bullfights from box offices or through agents such as **Localidades Galicia** (Map p940; ☎ 91 531 91 31; www.eol.es/lgalicia; Plaza del Carmen 1; 9.30am-1pm & 4.30-7pm Mon-Sat, 9.30am-1pm Sun; Ⓜ Sol).

FOOTBALL

Madrid's three major football clubs and accompanying delirious fans are a guarantee that football fever runs high in the city.

Santiago Bernabéu Stadium (☎ 91 398 43 00; www.realmadrid.com; Calle Concha Espina 1; museum 10.30am-6.30pm, except day after game; Ⓜ Santiago Bernabéu) The mythic Real Madrid plays at this stadium. Fans can visit the stadium and take an interesting tour through the presidential box, dressing room and field.

Estadio Vicente Calderón (☎ 91 366 47 07; www.at-madrid.com; Calle Virgen del Puerto; Ⓜ Pirámides) The also celebrated Atlético de Madrid, whose fans are famed as being some of the country's most devoted, plays at the Estadio Vicente Calderón.

Though it's no match for these first-division teams, the Rayo Vallecano also plays in the city.

BULLFIGHTING

Plaza de Toros Las Ventas (☎ 90 215 00 25; www.las-ventas.com; Calle de Alcalá 237; Ⓜ Ventas) Some of Spain's top matadors (bullfighters) swing their capes in Plaza de Toros Las Ventas, the largest ring in the bullfighting world. You can see them every Sunday afternoon from mid-May through October, when fights are held in the plaza. Get tickets (from €4 in the sun, from €7 in the shade) at the plaza box office, Localidades Galicia (above) or from official ticket agents along Calle Victoria, leading up to the plaza.

Live Music

FLAMENCO

Many of flamenco's top names perform in Madrid, making it an excellent place to see interpretations of this Andalucian art. The more 'serious' shows are usually set up in a dinner/theatre style and are aimed at tourists. But many smaller bars also host once-weekly flamenco concerts or shows.

Casa Patas (Map p940; ☎ 91 369 04 96; www.casapatas.com; Calle de Cañizares 10; admission about €35; shows 10.30pm Mon-Thu, 9pm & midnight Fri & Sat, closed Sun; Ⓜ Antón Martín) One of the best *tablaos* in the city, this is a great place to see passionate dancing, though it's one of the pricier options.

Las Tablas (Map p940; ☎ 91 542 05 20; Plaza de España 9; admission €18; show 10.30pm; Ⓜ Plaza de España) Less established (but cheaper) than other *tablaos*, this intimate spot is nevertheless a great place to see a variety of flamenco styles.

Also recommended:

Bar & Co (Map p940; ☎ 91 521 24 47; Calle del Barco 34; admission €7; 9.45pm Thu; Ⓜ Tribunal) Thursday nights only, catch authentic flamenco at this intimate bar. Jazz, rock and other styles are played other nights.

Cardamomo (Map p940; ☎ 91 369 07 57; Calle de Echegaray 15; Ⓜ Sevilla) Wednesday night is the best night for live flamenco at this tiny and very authentic bar.

JAZZ

Café Central (Map p940; ☎ 91 369 41 43; www.cafecentralmadrid.com; Plaza del Angel 10; admission from €12; show 10pm; Ⓜ Antón Martín) This Art Deco bar is worth a visit on its own, but the live shows, which range from classic jazz to Latin, fusion or tango-style, are what has made it one of the most popular bars in the city.

Populart (Map p940; ☎ 91 429 84 07; www.populart.es; Calle de las Huertas 22; admission free; show 11pm; Ⓜ Antón Martín or Sol) Get here early if you want a seat because this smoky, atmospheric jazz bar is always packed with fans yearning for some soothing live jazz.

Bogui Jazz (Map p940; ☎ 91 521 15 68; www.boguijazz.com; Calle de Barquillo 29; shows 10.30pm & midnight; Ⓜ Chueca) With concert prices at just €6, this is a good bet for a low-key night of jazz.

ROCK & OTHER

Sala Caracol (Map pp936-7; ☎ 91 527 35 94; www.salacaracol.com; Calle de Bernardino Obregón 18; Ⓜ Embajadores) Though mainly rock bands (Spanish and international) take the stage here, the line-up at the 'Snail Room' is never predictable.

Galileo Galilei (☎ 91 534 75 57; www.salagalileogalilei.com; Calle Galileo 100; ; Ⓜ Islas Filipinas) A

SPAIN

classic stage just north of Argüelles, this place stages everything from comedy acts to magic shows, though its strength is up-and-coming bands.

Oba-Oba (Map p940; Calle de Jacometrezo 4; Ⓜ Santo Domingo or Callao) Right off the Plaza de Santo Domingo, this Brazilian hot spot stages great dance music and is packed with Brazilians.

La Riviera (Map pp936-7; ☎ 91 365 24 15; Paseo Bajo de la Virgen del Puerto; Ⓜ Puerta del Ángel) A club and concert venue all in one, La Riviera has a pretty Art Deco interior and open-air concerts in summer.

SHOPPING

It would be impossible to list all the great shops in Madrid in this limited space. Whether you're in search of designer labels, cheap knock-offs, fabulous shoes, tempting gourmet fare or traditional Spanish items like guitars and bullfighting gear, you'll find it somewhere in the city.

For artisan goods and typically Spanish items, explore the maze of streets in Huertas and Los Austrias. Calle de las Huertas and the surrounding streets are home to lots of small, old-fashioned shops. Closer to Plaza Mayor, seek out Calle de Toledo, Calle Esparteros or Calle de la Paz for unusual Madrileño-flavoured boutiques.

Alternative, offbeat fashion is found in Chueca; this lively barrio is also a magnet for shoe shops – there is a dozen of them along and around Calle de Augusto Figueroa. Roam Calle de Fuencarral and Calle de Hortaleza for funky clothing stores.

The glitziest shopping district is Salamanca, where all the designer labels show off for drooling window shoppers. This is also the district to find top art, antique and furniture galleries. Good places to go window shopping include Calle de Serrano, Calle de José Ortega y Gasset, Calle de Lagasca, Calle de Jorge Juan and the surrounding streets.

Keep an eye out for the following unique or interesting stores.

Flamenco World (Map p940; ☎ 91 360 08 65; www.flamenco-world.com; Calle de las Huertas 62; Ⓜ Retiro) The name says it all – flamenco dresses, shoes, CDs, how-to DVDs, books and more.

José Ramírez (Map p940; ☎ 91 531 42 29; Calle de la Paz 8; Ⓜ Sol) Find handmade guitars at this family-run shop. There's a small museum of old guitars out the back.

Justo Algaba (Map p940; ☎ 91 523 35 95; Calle de la Paz 4; Ⓜ Sol) This is the place to buy authentic bullfighters' suits; it's got everything from capes to those sexy pink tights.

Gil (Map p940; ☎ 91 521 25 49; Carrera de San Jerónimo 2; Ⓜ Sevilla) Spanish shawls and veils are the speciality at this historic shop.

Mercado de Fuencarral (Map p940; ☎ 91 521 59 85; Calle de Fuencarral 45; Ⓜ Chueca) Clubbers should head to this small mall, where at least half the clothes on sale have silver studs or leather accents.

El Corte Inglés (Map p940; ☎ 90 222 44 11; Calle de Preciados 1, 2, 3 & 9; Ⓜ Sol) Spain's enormous department store has branches all over the city and sells everything from food and furniture to clothes, appliances and toiletries. It's truly one-stop shopping.

GETTING THERE & AWAY

Air

Madrid's international **Barajas Airport** (MAD; ☎ 90 235 35 70; www.aena.es), 16km northeast of the city, is a busy place, with flights coming in from all over Europe and beyond. Airlines operating here include Spain's major national airline **Iberia** (☎ 90 240 05 00; www.iberia.com; Calle de Velázquez 130) and all the usual big names, as well as low-cost options easyJet, Air Europa, Air Madrid, Germanwings and Vueling. See Transport (p1035) for more information.

Bus

Though there are several bus stations dotted around the city, most out-of-town buses use **Estación Sur** (☎ 91 468 42 00; www.estaciondeautobuses.com; Calle de Méndez Álvaro; Ⓜ Méndez Álvaro). The largest bus company here is **Alsa** (☎ 90 242 22 42; www.alsa.es). Its many destinations include Barcelona (€25 to €34, eight hours, 21 daily), Valencia (€17, four hours, three daily) and Zaragoza (€13 to €18, four hours, 23 daily).

Other important bus companies include **Auto Res** (☎ 90 202 09 99, 91 551 72 00; www.auto-res.net) and **Continental Auto** (☎ 91 745 63 00; www.continental-auto.net).

Car & Motorcycle

If you arrive by car, be prepared to face gridlocked traffic. The city is surrounded by three ring roads, the M-30, M-40 and

SPAIN

M-50. You'll likely be herded onto one of these, which in turn will give you access to the city centre.

Car rental companies abound in Madrid; most have offices both at the airport and in town.

Train

Renfe (☎ 90 224 02 02; www.renfe.es) train services connect Madrid with just about every other place throughout Spain. There are two main train stations: Atocha, southeast of the city centre, and Chamartín, to the north. Both long-distance and *cercanías* (regional trains) trains pass through these two stations. For ticket information, visit the Renfe offices inside the stations or check out the website.

Major destinations include Barcelona (€63, five hours, seven daily), Valencia (€40, 3½ hours, 13 daily) and Zaragoza (€40, two hours, 18 daily).

GETTING AROUND

To/From the Airport

Normally, the metro (line No 8) zips you into the city from the airport's terminal two. The 12-minute trip to the Nuevos Ministerios station costs €1; from there, you can easily connect to all other stations. At the time of writing, however, the line was closed due to construction work and the final leg of the airport run was made by bus.

A taxi ride to the centre should cost about €25 and the trip takes around 20 minutes.

Car & Motorcycle

Public transport in Madrid is excellent, so having a car or motorcycle is not necessary (and is usually a big headache!). If you do have a car, be prepared to face plenty of traffic and high parking prices. Public parking is available in the city centre; a big white 'P' on a blue sign denotes a car park.

Driving around Plaza Mayor and the centre is especially challenging, as several roads dive underground and following them can be tricky.

Public Transport

Madrid's 227km of **metro** (☎ 90 244 44 03; www.metromadrid.es) lines handle nearly 700 million trips per year, or nearly two million per day. A single-ride costs €1 and a 10-ride ticket is €6.15. If you'll be using the metro often, you can get a one-, two-, three-, five- or seven-day travel pass. The metro is quick, clean, relatively safe and runs from 6am until 2am.

The bus system is also good, but working out the maze of bus lines can be a challenge. Contact **EMT** (www.emtmadrid.es) for more information.

Find out more about public transport by calling ☎ 012 or looking at www.ctm-madrid.es.

Taxi

Madrid's taxis are inexpensive by European standards. They're handy late at night, although in peak hour it's quicker to walk or get the metro. The flag fall is €1.75, after

MARKET WATCH

Madrid's street markets are great places to browse and, sometimes, to find a bargain. The most famous market is El Rastro, but others specialising in books, stamps or art are fun too.

El Rastro (Map pp936-7; Calle Ribera Curtidores; 🕒 8am-2pm Sun; Ⓜ La Latina) A bustling flea market, the chaotic El Rastro sells a bit of everything. The madness begins at Plaza Cascorro and worms its way downhill. Watch your wallet.

La Cuesta de Moyano (Map pp936-7; Paseo del Prado or Cuesta de Moyano; 🕒 9.30am-dusk Mon-Fri, 9.30am-2pm Sat & Sun; Ⓜ Atocha) Temporarily located along Paseo del Prado, this used-book market is a treasure trove of titles in Spanish and other languages.

Mercadillo Felipe II (Map pp936-7; Av Felipe II; 🕒 10am-9.30pm Mon-Fri, to 2pm Sat & Sun; Ⓜ Goya) Set among the high-priced shops of the Salamanca district, this is a popular place for cheap clothes and accessories.

Mercadillo de Filatelia y Numismática (Stamp & Coin Market; Map p940; Plaza Mayor; 🕒 8am-2pm Sun; Ⓜ Sol) This classic stamp and coin market draws hobbyists from all over the city.

Mercado de Pintura (Art Market; Map p940; Plaza del Conde de Barajas; 🕒 Sun 8am-2pm; Ⓜ Sol) Browse the original works at this small art market near Plaza Mayor.

which you are charged by the kilometre (€0.85 to €1.05). You'll be charged a supplement for airport runs or trips originating at bus or train stations.

To call a taxi from anywhere in the city, contact **Tele-Taxi** (☎ 91 371 21 31; www.tele-taxi.es).

AROUND MADRID

Get out of the city buzz and explore Comunidad de Madrid, the province surrounding the capital. Home to some of Spain's finest royal palaces and gardens, the Comunidad offers several easy day trips from the capital.

Good day trips include the royal palace complexes at **San Lorenzo de El Escorial** (☎ 91 890 59 03; www.sanlorenzoturismo.org; admission €4, EU citizens Wed free; 10am-6pm Tue-Sun Oct-Mar, 10am-7pm Tue-Sun Apr-Sep) and **Aranjuez** (☎ 91 892 43 32; www.aranjuez.com; admission €5; 10am-5.15pm Tue-Sat Oct-Mar, 10am-6.15pm Tue-Sat Apr-Sep), the traditional village of **Chinchón** (www.ciudadchinchon.com), and the university town (and birthplace of Miguel de Cervantes) **Alcalá de Henares** (www.turismoalcala.com). Also interesting is the **Valle de los Caídos** (91 890 13 98; www.patrimonionacional.es; Carretera de Guadarrama/El Escorial M-600; adult/child €5/2.50; 10am-6pm Apr-Oct, to 5pm Nov-Mar), Franco's ostentatious civil war memorial. The basilica and monument are just 9km north of San Lorenzo de El Escorial.

CASTILLA Y LEÓN

The true heart of Spain, Castilla y León is littered with hilltop towns sporting magnificent Gothic cathedrals, monumental city walls and mouth-watering restaurants.

ÁVILA

pop 53,496

Its pretty old town huddled behind intact medieval walls, Ávila has a picture-postcard look and an open-museum feel. It's a perfect place to spend a day strolling narrow laneways and soaking up history. The city is known as the birthplace of Santa Teresa, a mystical writer and reformer of the Carmelite order.

There's a **tourist office** (☎ 92 021 13 87; www.turismocastillayleon.com; Plaza Pedro Dávila 4; 9am-2pm & 5-8pm mid-Sep–Jun, 9am-8pm Sun-Thu, to 9pm Fri & Sat Jul–mid-Sep) near the Puerta del Rastro. For Internet access, try the **locutorio** (27 Av de Madrid; per hr €2; 11.30am-3pm & 5-10pm).

Sights

Don't even *think* of leaving town without enjoying the walk along the top of Ávila's wonderfully preserved 12th-century **murallas** (walls; ☎ 92 025 50 88; adult/student & child €3.50/2; 11am-6pm Tue-Sun Sep-Jun, 10am-8pm Jul & Aug), with their 2500 turrets and 88 towers. More than 1km of wall-top is open to the public, though it's divided into two sections broken up by the cathedral.

Embedded into the eastern city walls, the splendid **cathedral** (☎ 92 021 16 41; Plaza de la Catedral; admission €4; 10am-5pm Mon-Fri, to 6pm Sat, noon-5pm Sun Nov-Mar, 10am-6pm Mon-Fri, to 7pm Sat, noon-6pm Sun Apr-Jun & Oct, 10am-7pm Mon-Fri, to 8pm Sat, noon-7pm Sun Jul-Sep) was the first Gothic-style church built in Spain. It boasts rich walnut choir stalls and a long, narrow central nave that makes the soaring ceilings seem all the more majestic.

Even more beloved by locals than the cathedral is the **Convento de Santa Teresa** (☎ 92 021 10 30; Plaza de la Santa; museum admission €2; museum 10am-1.30pm & 3.30-5.30pm Tue-Sun, relic room 9.30am-1.30pm & 3.30-5.30pm daily, church 8.30am-1.30pm & 3.30-8.30pm daily), built in 1636 at the birthplace of 16th-century mystic and ascetic, Santa Teresa. It's home to relics, including a piece of the saint's ring finger, as well as a small museum about her life.

Sleeping

Pensión Santa Ana (☎ 92 022 00 63; 2nd fl, Calle Alfonso de Montalvo 2; s/d with shared bathroom €20/30) This decent budget choice is located in a quiet spot near the train station. Though basic, the eight large rooms on offer are light and comfortable and the bathrooms are extremely clean.

Hostal Arco San Vicente (☎ 92 022 24 98; www.arcosanvicente.com; Calle López Núñez 6; s €32-43, d €54-64; P) This hotel near the Puerta de San Vicente offers good value. Rooms are clean and well appointed, but feature uncomfortable beds.

Hospedería La Sinagoga (☎ 92 035 23 21; www.lasinagoga.net; Calle Reyes Católicos 22; s €50-58, d €70-82;) Occupying a 15th-century synagogue, this excellent midrange choice features quiet, comfortable and stylish rooms.

Eating & Drinking

Cafetería Hergós (☎ 92 021 33 70; Calle Don Geroni-mo 1) This bustling *cafetería* near the cathedral

SPAIN

serves up enormous *bocadillos* (€3 to €4.50) as well as delicious pastries made onsite at its *pastelería* (cake shop) in Paseo de San Roque.

Restaurante Casa Patas (☎ 92 021 31 94; Calle San Millán 4; menú €10) Locals are fond of the cheap and tasty *raciónes* served in the tiny downstairs bar in this eatery off Plaza de Santa Teresa, and they're always keen to sample the excellent lunchtime *menú* served in the old-fashioned upstairs *comedor* (dining room).

Reyes Católicos Restaurant (☎ 92 025 56 27; Calle Reyes Católicos 6; menú €17, mains €15-17) The sleek interior and sophisticated menu here are a cut above the local competition. Local specialities such as *chuletón de Ávila* (T-bone steak) are served with style.

There are several good bars just outside the Puerta de los Leales, the best of which is undoubtedly the noisy, smoky and welcoming **Bodeguito de San Segundo** (☎ 92 025 73 09; Calle San Segundo 19). It serves tasty *raciónes* (€6.50 to €17.50) and top-quality house wine by the glass (€3).

Getting There & Away

The **bus station** (☎ 92 025 65 05; Av de Madrid) is a five-minute walk northeast from the cathedral. **Larrea** (☎ 90 222 22 82) operates at least five bus services per day to Madrid's Estación Sur (€6.85, 1½ hours). There are four or more services per day to Salamanca (€5.15, 1½ hours) on **AutoRes** (☎ 91 559 89 55; www.auto-res.net) and at least two services per day to Segovia (€4, one hour) on **La Sepulvedana** (☎ 91 559 89 55; www.lasepulvedana.es).

From the **train station** (Paseo de la Estación), services go to Madrid-Chamartín (€7.75, up to two hours, 24 daily), León (€19, about three hours, three daily) and Salamanca (€7.75, 1½ hours, seven daily).

SALAMANCA

pop 163,815

Like university towns the world over, Salamanca has always known how to throw a party. Scholars caroused amid its ornate and often whimsical architecture way back during the Renaissance, and these days it's known throughout the country for its vibrant café and bar scene and rich cultural life.

King Alfonso XI founded what was to become Spain's greatest university in 1218. These days the university isn't considered to be one of Spain's most elite, but it still draws scholars from throughout Spain and beyond.

Information

Cyber Anvario (Calle la Latina 8; Internet per hr €1.50; 10am-midnight Mon-Sat, 1-10pm Sun)

Cyberplace (Plaza Mayor 10; Internet per hr €1; 11am-midnight Mon-Fri, noon-midnight Sat & Sun)

Municipal tourist office (☎ 90 230 20 02; informacion@turismodesalamanca.com; Plaza Mayor 32; 9am-2pm & 4-6.30pm Mon-Fri, 10am-6.30pm Sat, 10am-2pm Sun Sep-Jun, 9am-2pm & 4.30-8pm Mon-Fri, 10am-8pm Sat, 10am-2pm Sun Jul & Aug)

Regional tourist office (Casa de las Conchas; ☎ 92 326 85 71; www.turismocastillayleon.com; Rúa Mayor; 9am-2pm & 5-8pm daily Sep-Jun, 9am-8pm Sun-Thu, to 9pm Fri & Sat Jul & Aug)

Sights & Activities

The harmonious **Plaza Mayor** was designed in 1755 by José Churriguera, founder of the architectural style that carries his name. Equally impressive is the exterior of the glorious **Casa de las Conchas** (House of Shells), a city symbol since it was built in the 15th century and now home to a tourist office and the library.

The **university** (☎ 92 329 44 00, ext 1150; Calle de los Libreros; adult/student & child €4/2, Mon morning free; 9.30am-1pm & 4-7pm Mon-Fri, 9.30am-1pm & 4-6.30pm Sat, 10am-1pm Sun), with its ubiquitous presence, is worth a visit. You can visit the old classrooms, chapel, library and small museum.

Curiously, Salamanca is home to two cathedrals: the newer and larger cathedral was built beside the old Romanesque one instead of on top of it, as was the norm. The **Catedral Nueva** (New Cathedral; ☎ 92 321 74 76; Plaza Anaya; admission free; 9am-1pm & 4-6pm Oct-Mar, 9am-2pm & 4-8pm Apr-Sep), completed in

FIND THE FROG

The university's façade is an ornate mass of sculptures and carvings, and hidden among this 16th-century plateresque creation is a tiny stone frog. Legend says that those who find the frog will have good luck in studies, life and love. A hint: it's sitting on a skull on the pillar that runs up the right-hand side of the façade.

1733, is a Gothic masterpiece that took 220 years to build. When inside, you can make your way to the **Catedral Vieja** (Old Cathedral; admission €3.50; ⏲ 10am-12.30pm & 4-5.30pm Oct-Mar, 10am-1.30pm & 4-7.30pm Apr-Sep), a 12th-century temple with a stunning altar and several noteworthy chapels.

Sleeping

Pensión Barez (☎ 92 321 74 95; 1st fl, Calle Meléndez 19; per person with shared bathroom €12) Near to being the cheapest beds in town, they're complemented by shared bathrooms so clean that they gleam. Rooms vary in size and some are musty, so ask to see a few before deciding. Be warned that the ones at the front can be very noisy.

Hostal Catedral (☎ 92 327 06 14; 1st fl, Rúa Mayor 46; s/d €30/45) Light and attractive rooms here feature impeccable white linen, comfortable beds, sparkling bathrooms and thick windows; some have cathedral views. Recommended.

Hostal Sara (☎ 92 328 11 40; www.hostalsara.org; Calle Meléndez 11; s €35-45, d €38-50; ❄ 💻) Two-star *hostales* rarely come with the level of comfort offered here. Light and airy rooms feature satellite TV, minibars and lovely bathrooms; some even have small, fully equipped kitchenettes. Front rooms are sensibly double-glazed.

Hotel Rector (☎ 92 321 84 82; www.hotelrector.com; Paseo del Rector Esperabé 10; s/d €89/112; P ⊠ ❄ 💻) Housed in a grand Art Nouveau building, the Rector offers 13 supremely comfortable and quiet rooms, exemplary service and the best breakfast in Spain (€10).

Eating & Drinking

Café La Luna (Calle de los Libreros 4) Starting your day here with hot chocolate and *churros* will set you back only €2.

Samaniego Restauración (☎ 92 321 41 52; Calle de los Libreros 18; menú €10) This bright, cheerful place has lots of meat and fish choices, as well as daily *platos combinados* (€6.50).

Café El Ave (☎ 92 326 45 11; Calle de los Libreros 24) A few doors away from Samaniego Restauración, this cafe offers similar-priced *menús* and *platos combinados*.

Delicatessen (☎ 92 328 03 09; Calle Meléndez 25; menú €10) The fitout of this popular place is nearly (but not quite) as glamorous as its bar staff. The youngish patrons tend to start out striking poses while lolling on the sleek furniture, but become less self-conscious after downing a few drinks and grazing on a wide range of tapas.

Meson Las Conchas (☎ 92 321 21 67; Rúa Mayor 16) A total contrast to Delicatessen, here you can tuck into the hearty tapas on offer while sampling the cheap house wine and beer, chatting with the gents propping up the bar or watching music videos.

Alcacil (☎ 92 328 05 90; Calle San Pablo 49; mains €6.50-9, menú €10.50; ⏰ lunch Tue-Sun, dinner Fri & Sat) A small and extremely attractive vegetarian restaurant, Alcacil serves up simple meals made with quality ingredients. The *berenjanas al gratin* (eggplant gratin) and cream-based soups are particularly delicious.

El Bardo (☎ 92 326 90 26; Calle de la Compañia 8; mains €9-13, menú €24) Offering rustic surrounds, a good wine list and a daily *menú* with meat and vegetarian options, it's no wonder El Bardo is perennially popular.

Getting There & Away

Salamanca's **bus station** (☎ 92 323 22 66) is about 1km northwest of Plaza Mayor (bus 4 from Plaza del Mercado near Plaza Mayor will take you there). **AutoRes** (☎ 91 559 89 55; www.auto-res.net) has services to Madrid (€16, 2½ to three hours, 13 daily), Segovia (€9.15, three hours, two daily) and Ávila (€5.15, 1½ hours, seven daily). **Dainco** (☎ 90 242 22 42; www.dainco.es) travels to Santiago de Compostela (€17.65 to €22.05, 6¼ hours, one daily) and **Alsa** (☎ 90 242 22 42; www.alsa.es) goes to Bilbao (€17.65 to €22.05, six hours, one daily).

Trains travel between Salamanca and Madrid-Chamartín (€15.30, 2½ hours, seven daily) via Ávila (€7.75, one hour). There are also services to Bilbao (€27.10, 5½ hours, one daily). Bus 1 from the stop near the main post office on Gran Vía will take you to the station.

SEGOVIA

pop 55,766

The most enchanting city in Castilla, Segovia is the type of place that challenges travel writers to come up with enough superlatives to do it justice. Yes, the Roman aqueduct is majestic, the old town is atmospheric and the Alcázar is the stuff of which fairytales are made, but the sheer charm of the city's setting and the fabulous unexpectedness of its gourmet achievements are hard to put into words. You'll just have to experience it for yourself.

Information

Locutorio/Internet access (Calle de San Francisco; per hr €2; ⏰ 10am-10pm)

Municipal tourist office (☎ 92 146 67 20; www.segoviaturismo.es; Plaza del Azoguejo 1; ⏰ 10am-8pm)

Regional tourist office (☎ 92 146 03 34; www.turismocastillayleon.com; Plaza Mayor 6; ⏰ 9am-2pm & 5-8pm, closed btwn Christmas & New Year)

Sights

Start your visit at the **aqueduct**, an 894m-long engineering wonder that looks like an enormous comb plunged into the centre of Segovia. It's 28m high and was built without a drop of mortar – just good old Roman know-how.

From here, the lively commercial streets Calle de Cervantes and Calle de Juan Bravo (together referred to as Calle Real) climb into the innards of Segovia. In the heart of town is the resplendent **cathedral** (☎ 92 146 22 05; Plaza de la Catedral; adult/child €2/free, free Sun morning; ⏰ 9am-5.30pm Nov-Mar, to 6.30pm Apr-Oct), completed in 1577.

The fortified **Alcázar** (☎ 92 146 07 59; www.alcazarsegovia.com; Plaza Reina Victoria Eugenia; adult/student & child €3.50/2.50; ⏰ 10am-6pm Oct-Mar, to 7pm Apr-Sep) is perched dramatically on the edge of Segovia. Roman foundations are buried somewhere underneath this splendour, but what we see today is a 13th-century

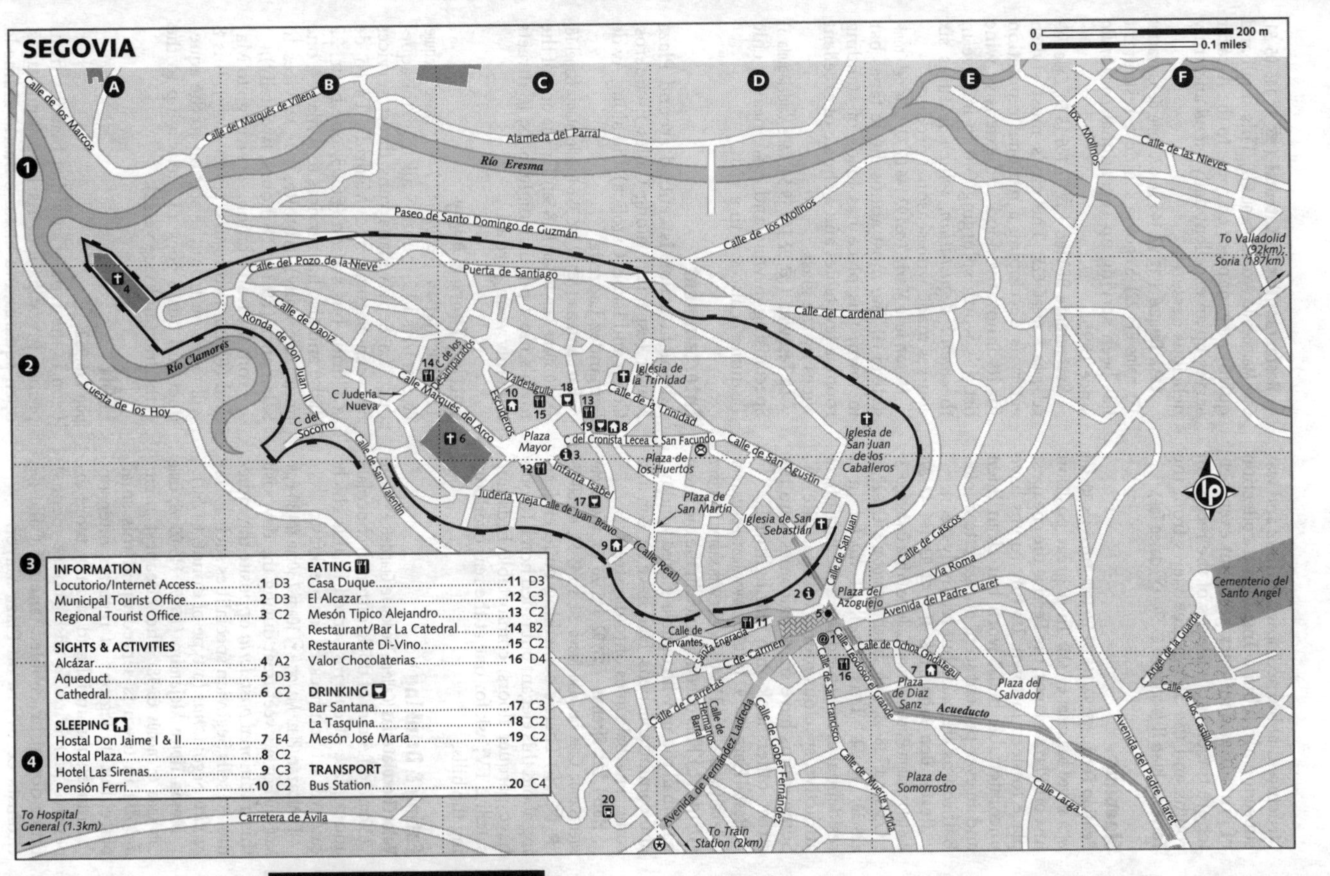
SEGOVIA
0 200 m
0 0.1 miles
To Valladolid (92km); Soria (187km)
To Hospital General (1.3km)
To Train Station (2km)
Río Eresma
Río Clamores
Cementerio del Santo Angel
Calle de los Marcos
Calle del Marqués de Villena
Alameda del Parral
Paseo de Santo Domingo de Guzmán
Calle del Pozo de la Nieve
Puerta de Santiago
Calle de los Molinos
los Molinos
Calle del Cardenal
Calle de las Nieves
Cuesta de los Hoy
Ronda de Don Juan II
Calle de Daoiz
C del Socorro
C Judería Nueva
C de los Desamparados
Calle de San Valentín
Calle Marqués del Arco
Judería Vieja
Calle de Juan Bravo
(Calle Real)
Infanta Isabel
Plaza Mayor
Escuderos
Valdeáguila
Iglesia de la Trinidad
Calle de la Trinidad
C del Cronista Lecea
C San Facundo
Plaza de los Huertos
Plaza de San Martín
Calle de San Agustín
Iglesia de San Sebastián
Iglesia de San Juan de los Caballeros
Calle de San Juan
Plaza del Azoguejo
Avenida del Padre Claret
Vía Roma
Calle de Cascos
Acueducto
Calle de Ochoa Ondategui
Plaza de Díaz Sanz
Calle Teodosio el Grande
Calle de San Francisco
Plaza del Salvador
Plaza de Somorrostro
Calle Larga
Calle de Muerte y Vida
Calle de Gober Fernández
Avenida de Fernández Ladreda
Calle de Hermanos Barral
Calle de Cervantes
C Santa Engracia
C de Carmen
Calle de Carretas
C Ángel de la Guarda
Calle de los Castillos
Carretera de Ávila
INFORMATION
Locutorio/Internet Access....1 D3
Municipal Tourist Office....2 D3
Regional Tourist Office....3 C2
SIGHTS & ACTIVITIES
Alcázar....4 A2
Aqueduct....5 D3
Cathedral....6 C2
SLEEPING
Hostal Don Jaime I & II....7 E4
Hostal Plaza....8 C2
Hotel Las Sirenas....9 C3
Pensión Ferri....10 C2
EATING
Casa Duque....11 D3
El Alcazar....12 C3
Mesón Tipico Alejandro....13 C2
Restaurant/Bar La Catedral....14 B2
Restaurante Di-Vino....15 C2
Valor Chocolaterias....16 D4
DRINKING
Bar Santana....17 C3
La Tasquina....18 C2
Mesón José María....19 C2
TRANSPORT
Bus Station....20 C4
SPAIN

structure that burned down in 1862 and was subsequently rebuilt. Inside is a collection of armour and military gear, but even better are the ornate interiors of the reception rooms and the 360-degree views from the **Torre de Juan II** (admission €1.50; closed Tue).

Sleeping

Pensión Ferri (92 146 09 57; Calle Escuderos 10; s/d with shared bathroom €17/26) In a great position just off Plaza Mayor, the Ferri is the cheapest place to sleep in town. Its tiny rooms have uncomfortable beds, worn but clean linen and an ever-present scent of cigarette smoke. Bathrooms are basic but relatively clean.

Hostal Don Jaime I & II (92 144 47 87; hostaldonjaime@hotmail.com; Calle de Ochoa Ondátegui 8; s €25-32, d €38-43, with shared bathroom s €20-22, d €25-30; P) This excellent *hostal* in a residential area behind the aqueduct offers attractive, spacious rooms with satellite TV. Some rooms have small balconies onto the street, others look onto rear lightwells.

Hostal Plaza (92 146 03 03; www.hostal-plaza.com; Calle del Cronista Lecea 11; s/d €35/45, r with shared bathroom €32; P) This decent choice in the old town has small rooms with double-glazed windows and comfortable beds. Half have air-con and some have balconies onto the street.

Hotel Las Sirenas (92 146 26 63; www.hotelsirenas.com; Calle de Juan Bravo 30; s €45-53, d €60-70; P) There's something quite endearing about this elegant but faded hotel. Rooms have parquet floors, comfortable beds and satellite TV; ask for one at the rear overlooking the hills.

Eating & Drinking

Valor Chocolaterias (Calle de Teodosio el Grande 8; 8am-12.30am;) A cup of thick, ultrarich chocolate and a plate of *churros* served in this chichi café will set you back €2 for breakfast.

El Alcazar (Plaza Mayor; 10am-2.30pm & 4.30-8pm Mon-Fri) For a sweet treat during the day, visit this traditional *pastelería* opposite the cathedral. It sells Segovian specialities such as *rosquillas Segovianas* (a type of donut, €1.50).

Meson Tipico Alejandro (92 146 00 09; Calle Cabriteria 6; menús €6-18) The cheapest *menú del día* in town is served up at this small place, but its legions of regulars often opt for more substantial and slightly more expensive *menús de la casa* (house menus). Enter down the cobbled lane off Calle del Cronista Lecea just off Plaza Mayor.

Restaurant/Bar La Catedral (92 146 05 51; Calle Marqués del Arco 32; menú €12) This small and quietly elegant place en route to the Alcázar serves up an excellent daily *menú* and truly delicious desserts.

Casa Duque (92 146 24 87; Calle de Cervantes 12; mains €14-22) Segovia's oldest restaurant has been serving up sensational *cochinillo* since 1895.

Restaurante Di-Vino (92 146 16 50; Calle Valdeláguila 7; menú €25) The city's most stylish eatery is developing a national reputation for its innovative food and extensive wine list. It's worth splurging €40 to indulge in the *menú degustatión*, which features six courses made with seasonal produce.

Méson José Maria (92 146 02 72; Calle del Cronista Lecea 11) The most atmospheric tapas bar in town, this place has loads of standing room, a few tables and a choice of excellent wines by the glass.

La Tasquina (92 146 19 54; Calle Valdeláguila 3) Specialising in wine and *cava*, nearby chic Tasquina is also worth a visit.

Entertainment

Late-night action is centred around Plaza Mayor (especially along Calles Escuderos, Colón and Isabel Católica) and along Av de Fernández Ladreda.

Bar Santana (92 146 35 64; Calle Infanta Isabel 18; 10.30am-3am, to 4am Fri & Sat) This is one of the town's most popular nightspots; it attracts a mainly young crowd.

Getting There & Away

The **bus station** (92 142 77 07; Paseo Ezequiel González 12) is a 15-minute walk from the aqueduct. La Sepulvedana runs direct services between Segovia and Madrid's Paseo de la Florida bus station (€6.05, one hour, 22 daily) and also has services to Ávila (€4, one hour, five daily). AutoRes has services to Salamanca (€9.15, 2¾ hours, two daily).

From the train station, services go to Madrid (€5.20, two hours, seven daily). Bus 8 will take you from the station to the aqueduct and bus 6 goes all the way up to the cathedral (and vice versa).

LEÓN

pop 136,952

León is the type of city that benefits from proper investigation. Its long boulevards, open squares and historic Barrio Húmedo

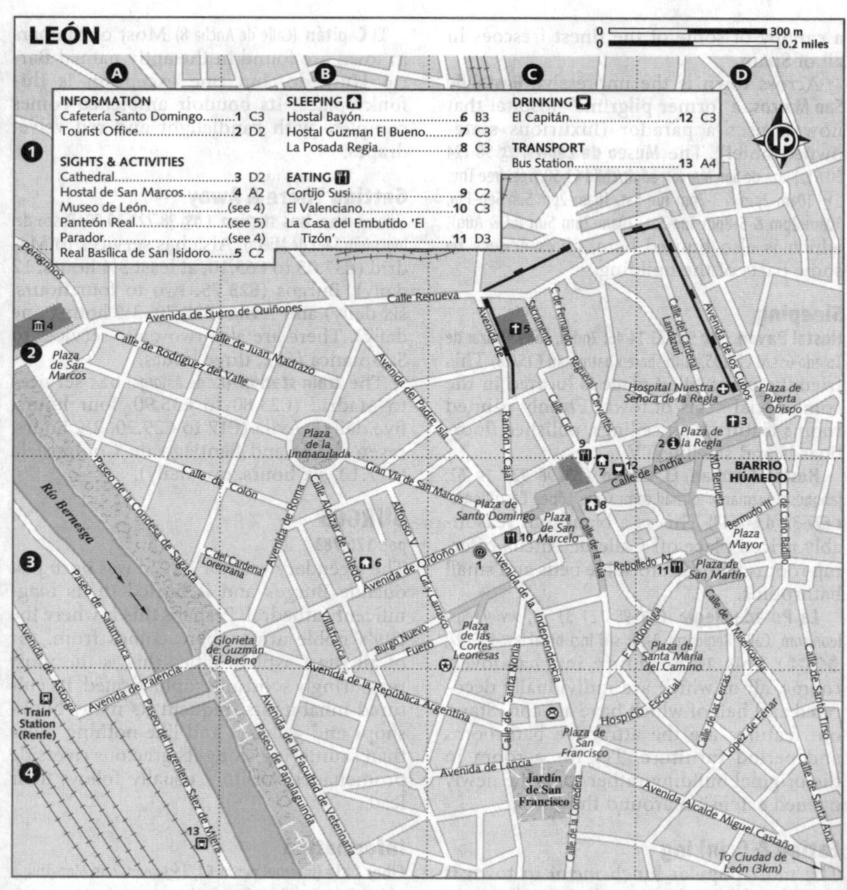

(Damp District) demand exploration, and its cathedral is one of the most magnificent in the whole of Europe.

The **tourist office** (☎ 98 723 70 82; www.aytoleon.com; Plaza de la Regla 3; 🕒 9am-2pm & 5-7pm Mon-Fri, 10am-2pm & 6-8pm Sat & Sun) is opposite the cathedral. For Internet access, try the rear of **Cafetería Santo Domingo** (Av de Ordoño II 3; per 45min €1; 🕒 8am-11pm Mon-Fri, 9am-11pm Sun).

Sights

León's best and best-known monument is its breathtaking 13th-century **cathedral** (☎ 98 787 57 70; www.catedraldeleon.org; 🕒 8.30am-1.30pm & 4-7pm Mon-Sat, 8.30am-2.30pm & 5-7pm Sun Oct-May, 8.30am-1.30pm & 4-8pm Mon-Sat, 8.30am-2.30pm & 5-8pm Sun Jun-Sep). A marvel of Gothic architecture, it has an extraordinarily intricate façade with a rose window, three richly sculptured doorways and stained-glass windows (with a surface of 1800 sq metres) that give the place an ethereal quality. Inside, there's a **museum** (admission €3.50; 🕒 9.30am-1.30pm & 4-6.30pm Mon-Fri, 9.30am-1.30pm Sat Oct-Jun, 9.30am-1.30pm & 4-7.30pm Mon-Fri, 9.30am-2pm & 4-7pm Sat Jul-Sep) entered through the church's **cloister** (admission €1).

Nearby is the **Real Basílica de San Isidoro**, a simple Romanesque church that houses the **Panteón Real** (☎ 98 787 61 61; www.sanisidorodeleon.org; Plaza de San Isidoro 4; admission €3, free Thu afternoon; 🕒 10am-1.30pm & 4-6.30pm Mon-Sat, 10am-1.30pm Sun Sep-Jun, 9am-8pm Mon-Sat, to 2pm Sun Jul & Aug), where Léonese royalty lie buried beneath

SPAIN

a canopy of some of the finest frescoes in all of Spain.

Across town is the impressive **Hostal de San Marcos**, a former pilgrims' hospital that now houses a parador (luxurious state-owned hotel). The **Museo de León** (☎ 98 724 50 61; Plaza de San Marcos; adult/child €1.50/free, free Thu; 🕑 10am-2pm & 3-7pm Tue-Sat, 10am-2pm Sun Sep-Jun, 10am-2pm & 5-8pm Tue-Sat, 10am-2pm Sun Jul & Aug), which is also housed here, gives access to some parts of the building.

Sleeping

Hostal Bayón (☎ 98 723 14 46; 2nd fl, Calle Alcázar de Toledo 6; s/d €25/35, with shared bathroom €15/28) This friendly, plant-filled place is located in the commercial heart of town. Freshly painted rooms feature high ceilings, polished floorboards and satellite TV.

Hostal Guzman El Bueno (☎ 98 723 14 62; jabghostaguzman@hotmail.com; Calle López Castrillón 6; s €27-32, d €40-48) This is a bland but reasonably priced place off Calle de Ancha offering rooms with comfortable beds and small bathrooms.

La Posada Regia (☎ 98 721 31 73; www.regialeon.com; Calle Regidores 9-11; s/d incl breakfast €59/97; ☒ ❄) This 14th-century inn has lovely rooms, all of which are individually decorated and half of which have air-con. Stand out features are the attractive bathrooms and period furniture. Try for a room in the original building rather than the newly opened extension around the corner.

Eating & Drinking

The most popular lunch *menú* in town is served – bizarrely enough – at the train station's enormous *cafetería*. It costs €10.

El Valenciano (Plaza de Santo Domingo) Check out this place for utterly delicious *bocadillos grandes* (€3) and pastries (€1.50).

La Casa del Embutido 'El Tizón' (☎ 98 726 00 94; Calle Platerías 4; mains €11-18, menús €11.50-25.50; 🕑 closed Sun dinner & Mon) This perennially jam-packed place has been serving drinks and tapas to satisfied customers since 1973 and shows no signs of its popularity wavering. It also serves *menús* in its restaurant.

Cortijo Susi (☎ 98 727 39 96; Calle López Castrillón 1; mains €12.50-16.50, menú €15) Forget stodgy and badly cooked meals featuring pig, pig and more pig, this mega-stylish addition to León's dining scene serves up a fabulous *menú* with a light and modern Mediterranean slant.

El Capitán (Calle de Ancha 8) Most of the bars in town are found in the aptly named Barrio Húmedo, but one exception is this funky place. Its boudoir ambience comes complete with candlelight and red velvet drapes.

Getting There & Away

From the **bus station** (☎ 98 721 10 00; Paseo del Ingeniero Sáez de Miera), Alsa has services to Madrid (€37.05 to €65.10, at least 3½ hours, 12 daily), Burgos (€23.75, two to four hours, six daily) and Ávila (€28.70, 3½ hours, one daily). There are also two daily services to Salamanca (€12, three hours).

The **train station** (Av de Astorga) has services to Madrid (€23.80 to €35.90, four hours, five daily), Ávila (€17 to €29.20, 2½ hours, seven daily) and Santiago de Compostela (€27.10, six hours, one daily).

BURGOS

pop 170,783

The legendary warrior El Cid was born just outside Burgos and is buried in its magnificent cathedral. Perhaps this is where the city's noble atmosphere comes from, for of all the Castilian cities this is the most reassuringly solid and sophisticated. Its cultured inhabitants frequent its many bookshops and galleries and like nothing more than sauntering along its gracious riverside promenades. Visitors usually follow their lead.

Information

Ciber Café (Internet per hr €4; 🕑 noon-2am Mon-Thu, to 4am Fri & Sat, 5pm-1am Sun)

Municipal tourist office (☎ 94 728 88 74; festejos@aytoburgos.es; Teatro Principal, Paseo Espolón 1; 🕑 10am-2pm & 4.30-7.30pm Mon-Sat, 10am-2pm Sun Oct-Jun, 10am-2pm & 5-8pm Mon-Sat, 10am-2pm Sun Jul-Sep)

Olivetti (☎ 94 726 42 28; Plaza Alonso Martínez 3; per hr €2; 🕑 9am-2pm & 4-8pm Mon-Fri) This computer shop next to the regional tourist office has three terminals offering the cheapest Internet access in town.

Regional tourist office (☎ 94 720 31 25; Plaza Alonso Martinez 7; 🕑 9am-2pm & 5-8pm)

Sights

The **cathedral** (☎ 94 720 47 12; www.catedraldeburgos.es; Plaza de Santa Maria; adult/student/child €4/2.50/1, audio guide €3.50; 🕑 ticket office 10am-1.15pm & 4-6.45pm Sep-Jun, 9.30am-1.15pm & 4-7.15pm Jul & Aug) is the Gothic jewel in Burgos' crown. On this site, a modest Romanesque church once stood, but today we see ornate spires piercing the skyline, each representing 84m of richly decorated fantasy. El Cid lies buried beneath the central dome.

The **Monasterio de las Huelgas** (☎ 94 720 16 30; adult/student & child €5/2.50; 🕒 10am-1pm & 3.45-5.30pm Tue-Sat, 10.30am-2pm Sun), an elegant Cistercian order founded in 1187 by Eleanor of Aquitaine, is still home to Cistercian nuns. Guided tours (in Spanish) are compulsory and leave the ticket office every 50 minutes or so. From the cathedral, it's a pleasant 25-minute walk west along the southern bank of the Arlanzón River.

Sleeping

Pensión Peña (☎ 94 720 63 23; 2nd fl, Calle La Puebla 18; s €17-19, d €24-26, all with shared bathroom) You'll pay bargain prices for the impeccably clean and very comfortable rooms on offer in this secure, family-occupied building.

Hotel Norte y Londres (☎ 94 726 41 25; www.hotelnorteylondres.com; Plaza Alonso Martínez 10; s €45-64, d €50-95; ⊠) Its attractive old-fashioned décor, excellent location, comfortable rooms and high standards of service mean that the Norte y Londres is often full, so book ahead.

Eating

If you're after fast food, there are plenty of cheap eateries in the streets around Calle de la Paloma, including a number of kebab joints. The main entertainment strip is Calle Sombrereria off Plaza Mayor.

Café Espana (☎ 94 720 53 37; Calle de Lain Calvo 12) Locals have been eating their breakfast here since 1921 and it's easy to see why. The surrounds are charming, the coffee (€1.50) is excellent and the *bocadillos con jamon y queso* (rolls with ham and cheese, €1.50) are delicious.

Restaurante La Riojana (☎ 94 720 61 32; Calle Avellanos 10; menú or plato del día €7.50) The cheapest lunch *menú* in town is served at this unpretentious eatery.

Prego (☎ 94 726 04 47; Calle Huerto del Rey 4; salads & pasta €5-8, pizza from €12, menú €13; 🕒 closed Jan) One of the city's few good options for vegetarians, Prego serves good pizzas and a wide range of classic Italian dishes.

Tapelia (☎ 94 727 80 00; Plaza Rey San Fernando; menú €15) Specialising in Alicantan rice dishes, this classy restaurant opposite the cathedral's ticket office serves absolutely delicious food in 'Iberian chic' surrounds. It's rare to see a *menú* of this quality for such a reasonable price and we highly recommend it.

Getting There & Away

The **bus station** (☎ 94 728 88 55; Calle Miranda) is just across the river from the cathedral. **Continental-Auto** (☎ 90 233 04 00; www.continental-auto.es) travels to Madrid (€14.55 to €22, 2¾ to 3½ hours, 16 daily) and Bilbao (€10.95, two to four hours, 14 daily). Alsa travels between Burgos and León (€23.75, two to four hours, six daily).

The **train station** (Av Conde de Guadalhorce) is southwest of the bus station, a 15-minute walk from the cathedral. Trains travel to Madrid-Chamartín (€20 to €25, five hours, six daily) and Salamanca (€19 to €20, three hours, five daily).

CASTILLA-LA MANCHA

Best known as the home of Don Quijote and Sancho Panza, Castilla-La Mancha conjures up images of lonely windmills, medieval castles and bleak, treeless plains. The characters of Miguel de Cervantes provide the literary context, but the richly historic cities of Toledo and Cuenca are the most compelling reasons to visit.

TOLEDO

pop 75,973

Toledo is a corker of a city. Commanding a hill rising above the Tajo River, it's crammed with monuments that attest to the waves of conquerors and communities – Roman, Visigoth, Jewish, Muslim and Christian – who have called it home during its turbulent history. There's no wonder it's one of the country's major tourist attractions.

Information

Locutorio/Internet (Plaza de Santiago del Arrabal; per hr €2; 🕒 12.30pm-2am)

Municipal tourist office (☎ 92 525 40 30; Plaza del Ayuntamiento; 🕒 10.30am-2.30pm & 4.30-7pm Tue-Sun, 10.30am-2.30pm Mon)

Regional tourist office (☎ 92 522 08 43; www.jccm.es; Puerta de Bisagra; 🕒 9am-6pm Mon-Sat, to 3pm Sun)

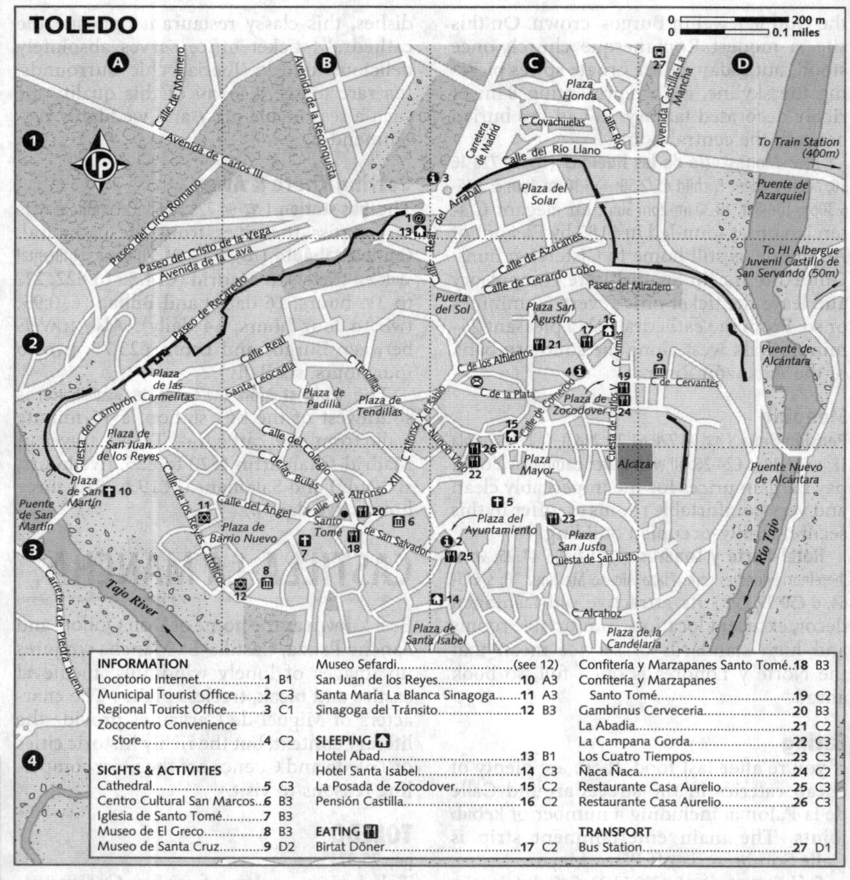

Zococentro Convenience Store (☎ 92 522 03 00; Calle de la Sillería 14; Internet per 20min €1; 🕑 10.30am-6pm) This store just off Plaza de Zocodover has a tourist information desk that is semifunded by the municipality, as well as one Internet terminal.

Sights & Activities

The **cathedral** (☎ 92 522 22 41; Calle Cardenal Cisneros; 🕑 10.30am-6.30pm Mon-Sat, 2-6.30pm Sun) is Toledo's major landmark. There's loads to see within its hefty stone walls, including stained-glass windows, tombs of kings and art by the likes of El Greco, Velázquez, Caravaggio, Raphael and Goya. You have to buy a ticket (€5.50) from the ticket office on Calle Cardenal Cisneros to enter four areas – the **Coro**, **Sacristía**, **Capilla de la Torre** and **Sala Capitular** – which contain some of the finest art and artisanship.

The **Museo de Santa Cruz** (☎ 92 522 10 36; Calle de Cervantes 3; admission free; 🕑 10am-6pm Mon-Sat, to 2pm Sun) contains a large collection of furniture, faded tapestries and paintings. Upstairs is an impressive collection of El Greco's works, including the masterpiece *La Asunción* (Assumption of the Virgin).

In the southwestern part of the old city, the queues outside an otherwise unremarkable church, the **Iglesia de Santo Tomé** (☎ 92 525 60 98; Plaza del Conde; adult/student €2/1.50; 🕑 10am-5.45pm Oct-Jun, to 6.45pm Jul-Sep), betray the presence of El Greco's masterpiece *El Entierro del Conde de Orgaz* (The Burial of the Count of Orgaz).

The **Museo de El Greco** (☎ 92 522 44 05; Calle Samuel Leví; admission €2.50; ⏲ 10am-2pm & 4-6pm Tue-Sat, 10am-2pm Sun Oct-Jun, 10am-2pm & 4-9pm Tue-Sat, 10am-2pm Sun Jul-Sep), in Toledo's former Jewish quarter, contains the artist's famous *Vista y Plano de Toledo* (View and Map of Toledo), plus about 20 of his minor works.

The **Museo Sefardi** (☎ 92 522 36 65; Calle Samuel Leví; admission €2.50; ⏲ 10am-2pm & 4-6pm Tue-Sun Dec-Feb, 10am-2pm & 4-9pm Tue-Sun Mar-Nov) is housed in the beautiful 14th-century **Sinagoga del Tránsito**. Toledo's other synagogue, the nearby **Santa María La Blanca** (☎ 92 522 72 57; Calle de los Reyes Católicos 4; adult/student & child €2/1.50; ⏲ 10am-5.45pm Oct-Mar, to 6.45pm Apr-Sep), dates back to the beginning of the 13th century.

A little further northwest is **San Juan de los Reyes** (☎ 92 522 38 02; Calle San Juan de los Reyes 2; admission €2; ⏲ 10am-6pm Oct-Jun, to 7pm Jul-Sep), a Franciscan monastery and church founded by Fernando and Isabel.

The **Centro Cultural San Marcos** (☎ 92 522 16 16; www.clavesdetoledo.com; Calle Trinidad 7; admission €4; ⏲ 10am-8pm Tue-Sat, 10.30am-2.30pm Sun), housed in the Iglesia de San Marco, is an excellent interpretative centre with 30 audiovisual displays exploring Toledo's fascinating history.

The **Alcázar** is closed for renovation and isn't expected to re-open until 2008.

Sleeping

Accommodation is often full, especially from Easter to September.

HI Albergue Juvenil Castillo de San Servando (☎ 92 522 16 76; alberguesclm@jccm.es; dm under/over 30yr €9.50/12; P 💻 🏊) Toledo's youth hostel is housed in an Arabic fortress that started life as a Visigothic monastery. Large two- or four-person rooms have comfortable beds and their own bathroom. There's a *cafetería*, laundry facilities, a swimming pool and free Internet access between 5pm and 7pm. It's a 10-minute walk down stairs and over the river from Plaza de Zocodover, or you can catch bus 11.

Pensión Castilla (☎ 92 525 63 18; Calle Recoletos 6; d €27, s/d with shared bathroom €17/24; ⊠) The seven small but charming rooms here feature polished floorboards and ceiling fans; some at the front have exposed beams and their own bathrooms. It's a clean, safe choice that is an absolute bargain at these rates.

La Posada de Zocodover (☎/fax 92 525 58 14; Calle Cordonerias 6; d €39; ❄) Seven rooms are on offer in this old, narrow building. They feature timbered ceilings, pretty brass beds, satellite TV and clean bathrooms.

Hotel Santa Isabel (☎ 92 525 31 20; www.santa-isabel.com; Calle Santa Isabel 24; s €32-35, d €49-60; P ❄) Well located in a quiet street near the cathedral, this hotel occupies an attractive 14th-century building and offers stylish, recently renovated rooms with wooden panelling, comfortable beds and smallish bathrooms.

Hotel Abad (☎ 92 528 35 00; www.hotelabadtoledo.com; Calle Real del Arrabal 1; s €86-88, d €106-109, ste €175-179; P ⊠ ❄) As hip as Toledo gets, this new hotel near the Puerta del Sol at the entrance to the old town has 22 glam rooms with wonderfully comfortable beds, stylish linen, double-glazed windows and super-swish bathrooms; most have good views.

Eating & Drinking

Ñaca Ñaca (Plaza de Zocodover 7; bocadillos €2-3.50) The takeaway *bocadillos* served up here are good for late-night munchies or midday snacks.

Birtat Döner (Calle de la Sillería) Also open late, this Turkish takeaway joint off Plaza de Zocodover sells falafel and doner kebab sandwiches for €3.

Gambrinus Cerveceria (☎ 92 521 44 40; Calle de Santo Tomé 10) This is a friendly place where you can join the locals for a quick breakfast (€2 for coffee, *tostada* and fresh orange juice) or linger at the bar over a drink and a *ración* of tasty *patatas bravas* (potatoes with garlic and tomato sauce, €6.50).

La Abadia (☎ 92 525 11 40; Plaza San Nicolás 3; mains €6-13, menú €10; ⏲ 8am-midnight Mon-Fri, noon-1am Sat, noon-midnight Sun) There are plenty of reasons why this place is so popular, but we'll single out the attractive African-influenced décor and the good coffee – and, for non-smokers, the excellent exhaust system. The upstairs bar is a great spot for breakfast or tapas and the downstairs *comedor* serves up a popular *menú*.

La Campana Gorda (☎ 92 521 01 46; Calle Hombre de Palo 13; menú €10) You'll need to get here at the very start of service if you want to score a table and sample the *menú* served in the rear *comedor* of this extremely popular tavern.

Los Cuatro Tiempos (☎ 92 522 37 82; Calle Sixto Ramón Parro 5; mains €16-20; ⏲ closed Sun dinner) You'll find this modern and extremely attractive restaurant just behind the cathedral. Inevitably full of cashed-up 30-something couples from Madrid visiting Toledo for the day, it has a sophisticated menu specialising in light servings using top-quality ingredients.

Restaurantes Casa Aurelio (mains €18-21, menú €28.50; closed Wed); Plaza del Ayuntamiento (☎ 92 522 77 16; Plaza del Ayuntamiento 8); Sinagoga (☎ 92 522 13 92; Sinagoga 1); Sinagoga (☎ 92 522 20 97; Sinagoga 6) This Toledan institution is the eatery of choice for those wanting to sample top-quality examples of rustic local specialities. The *menú* of *sopa Castillano* (soup with ham, egg and bread), *perdiz roja estifada a la Toledana* (stewed partridge in the Toledan style) and *sorbete de crema de limón al cava* (lemon and sparkling-wine sorbet) is a knockout. It ain't cheap, but it's worth every céntimo. There are three restaurants around town, two of which are in the same building.

Confitería y Mazapanes Santo Tomé (☎ 92 522 37 63; cnr Plaza de Zocodover 7 & Calle Santo Tomé 3; 10am-9pm) Toledo is known for its delicious rich *mazapán* (marzipan) – this is the best shop to buy it from.

Getting There & Away

Toledo's **bus station** (☎ 92 521 58 50; Av Castilla-La Mancha) is northeast of the old town. Continental-Auto runs services between Toledo and Madrid's Estación Sur (€4.25, 1½ hours, every 20 minutes). **Alsina** (☎ 93 265 65 92; www.alsinagraells.es) has services to Valencia (€22.50, 5½ hours, one daily) and **AISA** (☎ 92 525 62 93; www.aisa-grupo.com) travels between Toledo and Cuenca (€9.85, three hours, three daily). Bus 5 stops at the bus station every 20 minutes from 7am to 10pm (€0.85) on its route between the train station and Plaza de Zocodover.

From the **train station** (Calle Paseo Rosa), 400m east of the Puente de Azarquiel, express AV trains run to Madrid-Atocha (€8.30, 35 minutes, 10 daily). The first train from Madrid departs at 6.50am, the last from Toledo at 9.20pm. Bus 6 runs between here and Plaza de Zocodover every 10 to 15 minutes between 6.45am and 11.30pm (€0.85).

CUENCA

pop 48,937

Teetering right on the edge of the Júcar and Huécar gorges, Cuenca's *alta ciudad* (high town) is full of crumbling ancient buildings known as *casas colgadas* (hanging houses), which cling for dear life to the steep sides of the gorges. It's worth a stopover when travelling between Madrid and Valencia.

Information

Main tourist office (☎ 96 923 21 19; Plaza Hispanidad) Near the train and bus stations.

Next Level (Calle Colon 36; per hr €2; 10am-2pm & 4-10pm Mon-Fri, 11am-2pm & 4-10pm Sat & Sun) Internet access near the train station.

Old town tourist office (☎ 96 923 21 17; www.cuenca.es; Plaza Mayor 1; 9am-2pm & 4-7pm Mon-Sat, 9am-2pm Sun)

Sights & Activities

Cuenca's 15th-century **casas colgadas** are precariously positioned on a clifftop, their balconies projecting out over the gorge. To view them properly, walk over the **Puente San Pablo** (1902), an iron footbridge that crosses the ravine. Within one is the **Museo de Arte Abstracto Español** (☎ 96 921 29 83; www.march.es; adult/student €3/1.50; 11am-2pm & 4-6pm Tue-Fri, to 8pm Sat, 11am-2.30pm Sun), an exciting collection with works by Zobel, Sempere, Millares and Chillida.

Among the religious art and artefacts inside the **Museo Diocesano** (☎ 96 922 42 10; Calle Obispo Valero 2; adult/child €2/free; 10am-2pm & 4-7pm Tue-Sat, 10am-2pm Sun) are a couple of El Grecos and a stunning 14th-century Byzantine diptych. Opposite, the **Museo de Cuenca** (☎ 96 921 30 69; Calle Obispo Valero 12; adult/student €1.50/1, free Sat & Sun; 10am-2pm & 4-7pm Tue-Sat, 11am-2pm Sun) has a minor collection, in which Roman artefacts from classical Hispania are the highlight.

On the Plaza Mayor you'll find Cuenca's strange **cathedral** (☎ 96 922 46 26; admission €2; 10am-2pm & 4-6pm Mon-Fri, 10am-7pm Sat, 10am-6.30pm Sun). The lines of the unfinished façade are Norman-Gothic and are somewhat reminiscent of French cathedrals, but the stained-glass windows look like they would be more at home in the abstract-art museum.

Sleeping & Eating

Pensión Central (☎ 96 921 15 11; 2nd fl, Calle Alonso Chirino 7; s €13-15, d €22-26, all with shared bathroom) Just off the busy shopping street in the new town, this friendly place has rooms spanning the length of a long dark corridor. All

SPAIN

are in need of a coat of paint, but they're clean and offer excellent value for money.

Pensión Tabanqueta (☎ 96 921 12 90; Calle Trabuco 13; s/d with shared bathroom €15/30) Towards the top of the old town and with views of the Júcar gorge, this simple place is as clean as it is comfortable. There's a lively bar downstairs.

Posada de San José (☎ 96 921 13 00; www.posadasanjose.com; Calle Julián Romero 4; s €50, d €73-128, s/d with shared bathroom €25/38) This would have to be one of the most charming midrange hotels in Spain. Perched on the edge of Júcar gorge, the Canadian/Spanish owners have converted a 17th-century palace into a boutique hotel with a large variety of room types and prices. It's well worth paying extra for a room with a view and balcony.

Bar La Tinaja (Calle Obispo Valero 4) Just off Plaza Mayor, this very friendly bar serves up enormous *bocadillos* for €2 to €3.

Cafetería Ruiz (Calle Carretería 14) This *pastelería* on the main street of the new town serves up fabulous calorie-laden pastries and cakes in a time-warp 1970s interior. The sit-down area is closed on Sunday but the aformentioned pastries are still available for takeaway.

Meson Casas Colgadas (☎ 96 922 35 09; Calle Canónigos 3; mains €12-22, menús €27-33; closed Mon) Cuenca's most famous eatery has marvellous views of the Huécar gorge and an excellent Castilian menu. The same knockout views can be enjoyed at the downstairs bar (raciónes €6 to €12).

Getting There & Away

From the **bus station** (☎ 96 922 70 87; Calle Fermin Caballero) AutoRes travels to its Madrid bus station near Conde de Casal (€12.60, two hours, nine daily). AISA travels between Cuenca and Toledo (€9.85, up to three hours, two daily), **Samar** (www.samar.es) travels to Barcelona (€28.35, nine hours, one daily) and Alsina travels to/from Valencia (€13, 2½ to 4½ hours, three daily).

Trains travel between Cuenca's **train station** (Paseo Ferrocarril) and Madrid-Atocha (€9.90, 2½ hours, six daily). There's also a service between Cuenca and Valencia (€10.90, three hours, four daily).

Bus 1 from outside the bus station (opposite side of the road) will take you up to Plaza Mayor in the old town for €0.80.

CATALONIA

Home to stylish Barcelona, ancient Tarragona, romantic Girona, and countless alluring destinations along the coast, in the Pyrenees and in the rural interior, Catalonia (Catalunya in the local language, Catalan, and Cataluña in Castilian) is a treasure box waiting to be opened. A smallish triangle in the northeastern corner of the peninsula, this proud region was once an independent kingdom, and it still sees itself as distinctive.

BARCELONA

pop 1.59 million

Perhaps Spain's most un-Spanish city, stylish Barcelona is a forward-thinking place, always on the cutting edge of art, design and cuisine. Whether you explore its medieval palaces and plazas, gawk at the modernist masterpieces, shop for designer duds along its stylish boulevards, sample its exciting nightlife, or just soak up the sun on the city beaches, you'll be hard-pressed not to fall in love with this vibrant city.

Barcelona is a master at reinventing itself. The city has morphed from a wannabe Roman town into a prosperous medieval centre, to a rebellious city during the Spanish Civil War, and finally to its modern cosmopolitan self. The effects of so many changes can be seen on the streets. Important splashes of Gothic, Romanesque, modernist and contemporary works pop up in even the most unexpected corners of the city, haphazardly mixed together like the paella eaten for Sunday lunch.

Orientation

Plaça de Catalunya is the heart of the city and marks the divide between historic and modern Barcelona. From here, the long pedestrian boulevard Las Ramblas shoots southeast to the sea, with the busy Barri Gotic (Gothic Quarter) and El Raval (Raval district) hugging it on either side. To the northwest of the plaza is L'Eixample, the vast gridlike district where you'll find shopping areas and the bulk of the city's offices and residences.

Information

BOOKSHOPS

Altaïr (Map p970; ☎ 93 342 71 71; Gran Vía de les Corts Catalanes 616; Ⓜ Universitat) All travel books.

> **BARCELONA IN TWO DAYS**
>
> Be sure to see Gaudí's masterpieces, **La Sagrada Familia** (p968) and **La Pedrera** (p968), in L'Eixample. Next, stroll down **Passeig de Gràcia** (p974) to reach Plaça de Catalunya and the old quarter. Head down **Las Ramblas** (right) and duck into the **Barri Gòtic** (right) for a glimpse of the cathedral.
>
> On day two, visit the **Museu Picasso** (opposite) and the **Basílica de Santa Maria del Mar** (opposite) in El Born. Stop off for tapas and wine at **La Vinya del Senyor** (p974) before making your way to the **waterfront** (opposite). End the day with a meal in **La Barceloneta** (p973).

Casa del Llibre (Map pp966-7; ☎ 93 272 34 80; Passeig de Gràcia 62; Ⓜ Passeig de Gràcia) Great English section.

EMERGENCY

Guardia Urbana (City Police; Map p970; ☎ 092; Las Ramblas 43; Ⓜ Liceu)

INTERNET ACCESS

The price per hour for navigating online hovers around €3, but you can get a better rate if you buy multihour time cards.

Easy Internet Café (Map p970; Las Ramblas 29; ⏲ 8am-2.30am)

Electric Internet Company (Map p970; Carrer Misser Ferrer 1; ⏲ 9am-midnight)

WTN Internet (Map p970; Carrer Unió 16)

LAUNDRY

Wash n' Dry (Map pp966-7; ☎ 93 412 19 53; Carrer Nou de la Rambla 19; ⏲ 7am-11pm; Ⓜ Liceu)

MEDICAL SERVICES

24-hour Pharmacy (Map p970; Las Ramblas 98; Ⓜ Liceu) There's another pharmacy at Passeig de Gràcia 90. These are two of many 24-hour pharmacies in the city. See www.farmaciesdeguardia.com (in Spanish) for a full listing.

Hospital Clínic (Map pp966-7; ☎ 93 227 54 00; www.hospitalclinic.org; Carrer Villarroel 170; Ⓜ Hospital Clínic) Modern hospital with good services for travellers.

MONEY

The main tourist office (see right) has a good money-changing service. You can also head to banks such as La Caixa or **Caixa Catalunya** (branches throughout city; ⏲ 8.30am-2pm Mon-Fri & 4-8pm Thu), which offer fair rates. Avoid the *casas de cambio* (exchange houses) on Las Ramblas; the rates are exorbitant.

POST

Main post office (Map p970; ☎ 93 486 80 50; Plaça Antoni López; Ⓜ Barceloneta)

TOURIST INFORMATION

Main tourist office (Map p970; ☎ 93 285 38 34; www.barcelonaturisme.com; Plaça de Catalunya 17; ⏲ 9am-9pm; Ⓜ Plaça Catalunya)

Dangers & Annoyances

Purse snatching and pickpocketing are major problems, especially around Plaça de Catalunya, Las Ramblas and Plaça Reial. See p1031 for common scams.

Sights & Activities

LAS RAMBLAS

Spain's most famous street, the pedestrian boulevard of **Las Ramblas**, is exploding with life. Stretching from **Plaça de Catalunya** to the waterfront, it's lined with street artists, news kiosks and vendors selling everything from live chickens to blue roses.

The colourful **Mercat de la Boquería** (Map p970; ☎ 93 318 25 84; Las Ramblas 91; ⏲ 8am-8.30pm Mon-Sat; Ⓜ Liceu), a fresh food market with a modernist entryway, is one of Las Ramblas' highlights. Nearby, stop for a tour of the **Liceu** (☎ 93 485 99 14; Las Ramblas 51-59; adult/student €6/4; ⏲ 10am-1pm; Ⓜ Liceu), the city's fabulous opera house.

Also stop at the **Plaça Reial**, a grand 19th-century square surrounded by arcades and a few good restaurants. The square is known as a meeting point for drug users, so be aware. At the end of Las Ramblas stands the **Monument a Colom** (Map pp966-7; adult/child €2.50/1.50; ⏲ 10am-6.30pm Oct-May, 9am-8.30pm Jun-Sep; Ⓜ Drassanes), a statue of Columbus atop a tall pedestal. A small lift will take you to the top for panoramic views.

Just west of Las Ramblas is the **Museu Marítim** (Map pp966-7; ☎ 93 342 99 20; Av Drassanes; admission €6; ⏲ 10am-7pm; Ⓜ Drassanes). Housed in the city's medieval shipyard, a gorgeous Gothic creation, the museum takes an in-depth look at Catalonia's seafaring past.

BARRI GÒTIC

Though essentially a Gothic creation, Barcelona's looming **Cathedral** (Map p970; ☎ 93 315

15 54; Plaça de la Seu; admission museum €1, combined ticket museum, choir, rooftop & crypt €4; 🕒 church & cloister 8am-1.15pm & 4.30-7.30pm, museum 10am-1pm; Ⓜ Jaume I) was built on top of the ruins of an 11th-century Romanesque church. The façade, covered up for cleaning at the time of writing, is a neo-Gothic addition tacked on in the 19th century. Highlights include the verdant cloister, the tomb of martyr Santa Eulàlia (Barcelona's patron) and the lift to the rooftop (€2).

Not far from the cathedral is pretty **Plaça del Rei** and the fascinating **Museu d'Història de la Ciutat** (Map p970; ☎ 93 315 11 11; Plaça del Rei; adult/student €4/2.50; 🕒 10am-2pm & 4-8pm Tue-Sat, 10am-3pm Sun Oct-May, 10am-8pm Tue-Sat, 10am-3pm Sun Jun-Sep; Ⓜ Jaume I), where you can visit a 4000-sq-metre excavated site of Roman Barcelona under the plaza. The museum also encompasses several historic buildings including the **Palau Reial Major** (Main Royal Palace), once a residence of the kings of Catalonia and Aragón, and its **Saló del Tinell** (Great Hall). Entry to these buildings is included in the admission to the museum.

In summer, outdoor concerts are often held in the plaza.

EL RAVAL

To the west of Las Ramblas is El Raval district, a once-seedy, now-funky area overflowing with cool bars and shops. Visit the **Museu d'Art Contemporani de Barcelona** (Macba; Map p970; ☎ 93 412 08 10; Plaça dels Àngels 1; adult/student €7.50/6; 🕒 11am-7.30pm Mon-Fri, 10am-8pm Sat, 10am-3pm Sun Oct-Jun, 11am-8pm Mon-Fri, 10am-8pm Sat, 11am-3pm Sun Jul-Sep, closed Tue; Ⓜ Plaça Catalunya), which has an impressive collection of international contemporary art.

LA RIBERA

Translated as 'the waterfront', La Ribera is a good 10-minutes' walk from the beach, but in medieval days this was indeed a stone's throw from the Mediterranean; through the years, land was filled in, and the city expanded out into the sea. Home to Barcelona's bustling textile industry and to its wealthy merchants, La Ribera was the city's most prosperous quarter. Now it's a trendy district exploding with boutiques, restaurants and bars.

The palaces where some of those wealthy merchants once lived have been converted into the **Museu Picasso** (Map p970; ☎ 93 319 63 10; Carrer de Montcada 15-23; admission €6; 🕒 10am-8pm Tue-Sun; Ⓜ Jaume I), home to more than 3000 Picassos, most from early in the artist's career.

The heart of the neighbourhood is the elegant **Basílica de Santa María del Mar** (Map p970; Plaça Santa Maria; 🕒 9.30am-1.30pm & 4.30-8pm; Ⓜ Jaume I), a stunning example of Catalan Gothic.

The opulent **Palau de la Música Catalana** (Map p970; ☎ 90 244 28 82; www.palaumusica.org; Carrer Sant Francesc de Paula 2; tour €8; 🕒 10am-3.30pm; Ⓜ Urquinaona) is one of the city's most delightful modernist works. Designed by Lluis Domènech i Montaner in 1905, it hosts concerts daily.

La Ribera is bordered to the northeast by the sprawling **Parc de la Ciutadella** (Map pp966-7; 🕒 10am-dusk; Ⓜ Barceloneta), a park ideal for strolling or picnics. It's home to a small, kid-friendly **zoo** (Map pp966-7; ☎ 93 225 67 80; www.zoobarcelona.com; adult/child €14.50/9; 🕒 10am-7pm Jun-Sep, to 6pm Mar-May & Oct, to 5pm Nov-Feb).

WATERFRONT

Barcelona has two major ports, **Port Vell** (Old Port) at the base of Las Ramblas, and **Port Olímpic** (Olympic Port) 1.5km up the coast. Shops, seafood restaurants and nightlife options are plentiful around both marinas, particularly the Port Olímpic. Between the two ports sits the triangular-shaped fishermen's quarter, **La Barceloneta**. It's scruffy and a bit worn around the edges, but it's also a great place to escape the tourist crowds and find tasty, affordable seafood.

Barcelona boasts 4km of city *platjas* (beaches), beginning with the pebbly **Platja de la Barceloneta**, and continuing northeast to the busy **Passeig Marítim**, the sports-oriented **Nova Icària**, the long **Bogatell**, the nudist **Mar Bella** and the relatively clean **Nova Mar Bella**. On all beaches, keep a close eye on your belongings.

L'EIXAMPLE & MODERNISME

Modernisme, an architectural and cultural movement loosely defined as the Catalan version of Art Nouveau, transformed Barcelona's cityscape in the early 20th century. Most modernist works were built in L'Eixample, the district being developed at the time.

Modernisme's most famous architect was the eccentric Antoni Gaudí (1852–1926), a

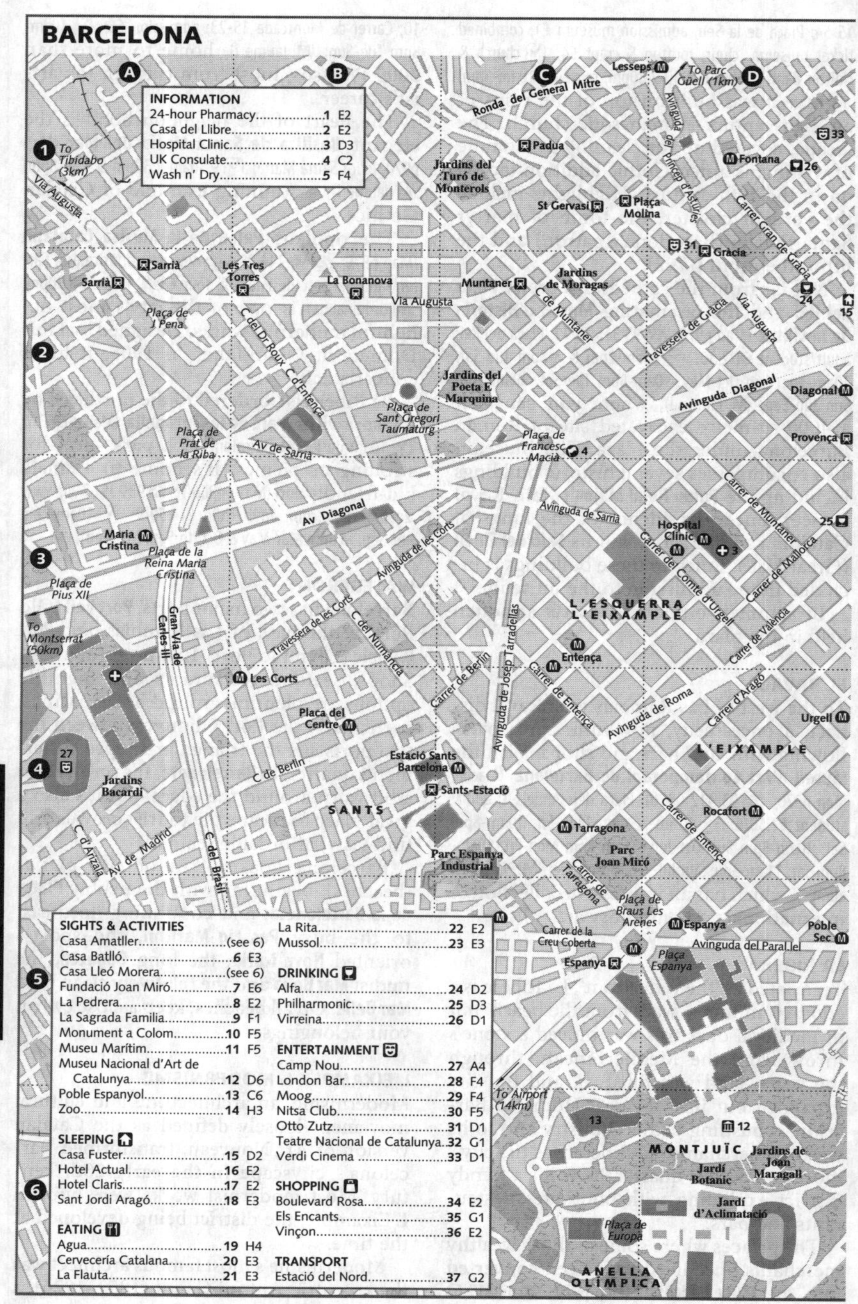
BARCELONA
A
B
C
D
1
2
3
4
5
6
INFORMATION
24-hour Pharmacy.....1 E2
Casa del Llibre.....2 E2
Hospital Clinic.....3 D3
UK Consulate.....4 C2
Wash n' Dry.....5 F4
SIGHTS & ACTIVITIES
Casa Amatller.....(see 6)
Casa Batlló.....6 E3
Casa Lleó Morera.....(see 6)
Fundació Joan Miró.....7 E6
La Pedrera.....8 E2
La Sagrada Família.....9 F1
Monument a Colom.....10 F5
Museu Marítim.....11 F5
Museu Nacional d'Art de Catalunya.....12 D6
Poble Espanyol.....13 C6
Zoo.....14 H3
SLEEPING
Casa Fuster.....15 D2
Hotel Actual.....16 E2
Hotel Claris.....17 E2
Sant Jordi Aragó.....18 E3
EATING
Agua.....19 H4
Cervecería Catalana.....20 E3
La Flauta.....21 E3
La Rita.....22 E2
Mussol.....23 E3
DRINKING
Alfa.....24 D2
Philharmonic.....25 D3
Virreina.....26 D1
ENTERTAINMENT
Camp Nou.....27 A4
London Bar.....28 F4
Moog.....29 F4
Nitsa Club.....30 F5
Otto Zutz.....31 D1
Teatre Nacional de Catalunya.....32 G1
Verdi Cinema.....33 D1
SHOPPING
Boulevard Rosa.....34 E2
Els Encants.....35 G1
Vinçon.....36 E2
TRANSPORT
Estació del Nord.....37 G2
To Tibidabo (3km)
Via Augusta
Lesseps
To Parc Güell (1km)
Ronda del General Mitre
Avinguda del Príncep d'Astúries
Padua
Fontana
Jardins del Turó de Monterols
St Gervasi
Plaça Molina
Carrer Gran de Gràcia
Gràcia
Sarrià
Les Tres Torres
La Bonanova
Muntaner
Jardins de Moragas
C de Muntaner
Travessera de Gràcia
Via Augusta
Plaça de J Pena
C del Dr Roux
C d'Entença
Jardins del Poeta E Marquina
Plaça de Sant Gregori Taumaturg
Avinguda Diagonal
Diagonal
Plaça de Prat de la Riba
Av de Sarrià
Plaça de Francesc Macià
Provença
Av Diagonal
Avinguda de Sarrià
Carrer de Muntaner
Maria Cristina
Plaça de la Reina Maria Cristina
Avinguda de les Corts
Hospital Clínic
Carrer de Mallorca
Carrer del Comte d'Urgell
Plaça de Pius XII
To Montserrat (50km)
Gran Via de Carles III
Travessera de les Corts
C del Numancia
L'ESQUERRA L'EIXAMPLE
Carrer de València
Entença
Avinguda de Josep Tarradellas
Carrer de Berlin
Les Corts
Carrer d'Aragó
Carrer de Entença
Avinguda de Roma
Urgell
Plaça del Centre
L'EIXAMPLE
Estació Sants Barcelona
Jardins Bacardi
C de Berlin
Sants-Estació
SANTS
Rocafort
Tarragona
Carrer de Entença
C d'Anzala
Av de Madrid
C del Brasil
Parc Espanya Industrial
Parc Joan Miró
Carrer de Tarragona
Plaça de Braus Les Arenes
Espanya
Poble Sec
Carrer de la Creu Coberta
Avinguda del Paral.lel
Plaça Espanya
To Airport (14km)
MONTJUÏC
Jardins de Joan Maragall
Jardí Botanic
Jardí d'Aclimatació
Plaça de Europa
ANELLA OLÍMPICA
SPAIN

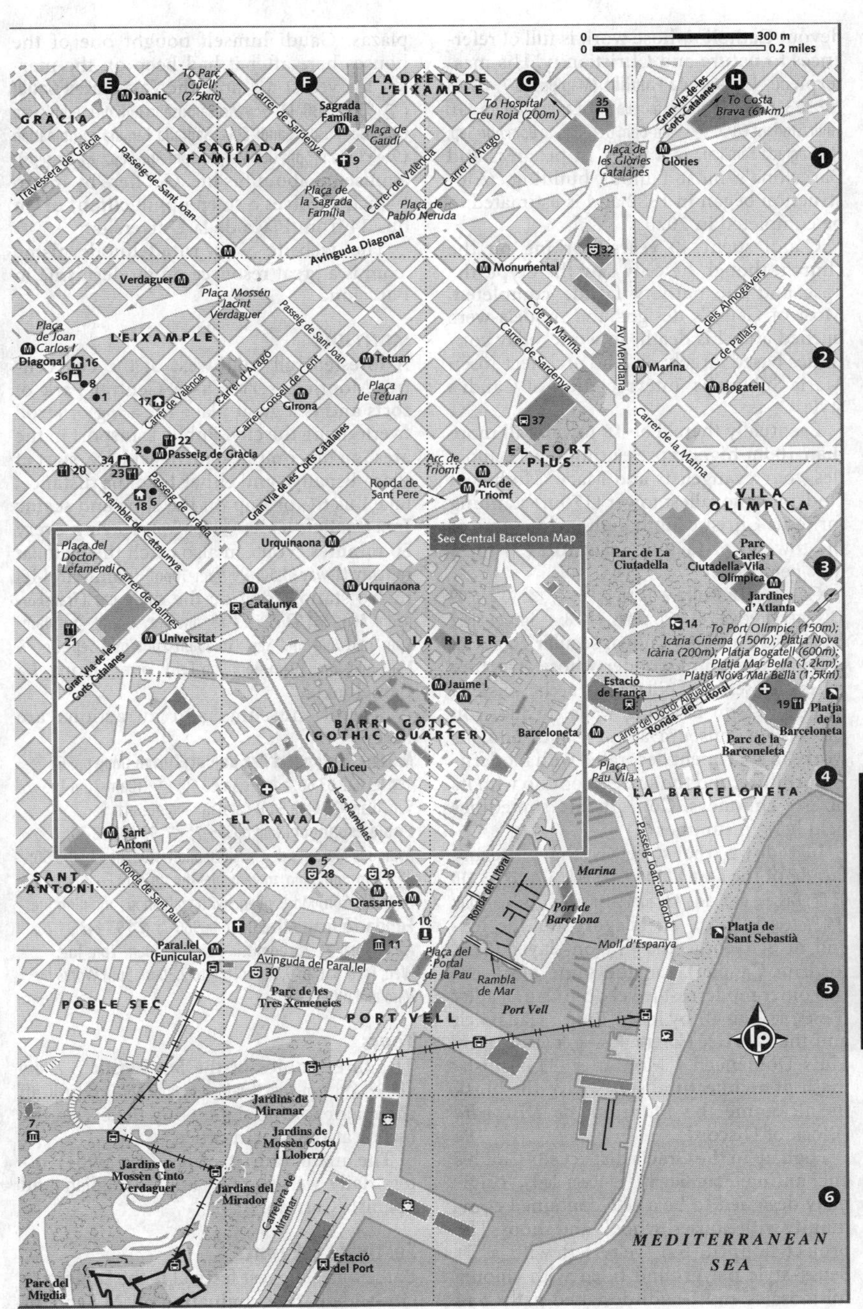

0 300 m
0 0.2 miles
GRÀCIA
LA SAGRADA FAMÍLIA
LA DRETA DE L'EIXAMPLE
L'EIXAMPLE
EL FORT PIUS
VILA OLÍMPICA
LA RIBERA
BARRI GÒTIC (GOTHIC QUARTER)
EL RAVAL
SANT ANTONI
POBLE SEC
PORT VELL
LA BARCELONETA
MEDITERRANEAN SEA
To Parc Güell (2.5km)
To Hospital Creu Roja (200m)
To Costa Brava (61km)
To Port Olímpic (150m); Icària Cinema (150m); Platja Nova Icària (200m); Platja Bogatell (600m); Platja Mar Bella (1.2km); Platja Nova Mar Bella (1.5km)
See Central Barcelona Map
Joanic
Sagrada Família
Plaça de Gaudí
Plaça de la Sagrada Família
Plaça de Pablo Neruda
Plaça de les Glòries Catalanes
Glòries
Travessera de Gràcia
Passeig de Sant Joan
Carrer de Sardenya
Carrer de València
Carrer d'Aragó
Gran Via de les Corts Catalanes
Avinguda Diagonal
Verdaguer
Plaça Mossèn Jacint Verdaguer
Monumental
C de la Marina
C dels Almogavers
C de Pallars
Av Meridiana
Plaça de Joan Carles I
Diagonal
Tetuan
Plaça de Tetuan
Marina
Bogatell
Girona
Carrer Consell de Cent
Passeig de Gràcia
Rambla de Catalunya
Carrer de la Marina
Arc de Triomf
Ronda de Sant Pere
Urquinaona
Plaça del Doctor Lefamendi
Carrer de Balmes
Catalunya
Universitat
Parc de La Ciutadella
Parc Carles I
Ciutadella-Vila Olímpica
Jardines d'Atlanta
Jaume I
Estació de França
Carrer del Doctor Aiguader
Ronda del Litoral
Platja de la Barceloneta
Parc de la Barconeleta
Barceloneta
Plaça Pau Vila
Liceu
Las Ramblas
Sant Antoni
Ronda de Sant Pau
Drassanes
Marina
Port de Barcelona
Moll d'Espanya
Passeig Joan de Borbó
Platja de Sant Sebastià
Paral.lel (Funicular)
Avinguda del Paral.lel
Parc de les Tres Xemeneies
Plaça del Portal de la Pau
Rambla de Mar
Port Vell
Jardins de Miramar
Jardins de Mossèn Costa i Llobera
Jardins de Mossèn Cinto Verdaguer
Jardins del Mirador
Carretera de Miramar
Estació del Port
Parc del Migdia
1 2 3 4 5 6
E F G H

SPAIN

devout Catholic whose work is full of references to nature and Christianity. His masterpiece, **La Sagrada Familia** (Map pp966-7; ☎ 93 207 30 31; www.lasagradafamilia.org; Carrer Mallorca 401; adult/student €8/5; 9am-6pm Oct-Mar, to 8pm Apr-Sep; M Sagrada Familia), is a work in progress and Barcelona's most famous building. Construction began in 1882 and is estimated to be completed in 2020.

Gaudí spent 40 years working on the church, though he only saw the crypt, the apse and the nativity façade completed. Most of Gaudí's designs and models were burned after his death, so work today continues based largely on lead architect Josep Maria Subirachs' interpretation of Gaudí's style.

Eventually there'll be 18 towers, all more than 100m high, representing the 12 apostles, four evangelists and Mary, Mother of God, plus the tallest tower (170m) standing for Jesus Christ. Climb high inside some of the towers (or take the elevator, €2) for a new perspective.

Gaudí's **La Pedrera** (Map pp966-7; ☎ 90 240 09 73; Carrer Provença 261-265; admission €8; 10am-8pm; M Diagonal), his best-known secular creation, is an architectural wonder whose structure relies on a series of pillars and arches instead of heavy, light-blocking walls. Inside, you can visit a museum about Gaudí and his work, an apartment decorated with modernist furniture, and the surreal rooftop with its bizarre chimneys. Concerts are sometimes held here in summer.

Just down the street is the glittering façade of the **Casa Batlló** (Map pp966-7; ☎ 93 216 03 06; Passeig de Gràcia 43; admission €16; 9am-8pm; M Passeig de Gràcia), an allegory for the legend of St George the dragon-slayer (Sant Jordi in Catalan). On the same block are two other modernist jewels, the **Casa Amatller** (Passeig de Gràcia 41) by Josep Puig i Cadafalch and the **Casa Lleó Morera** (Passeig de Gràcia 35) by Lluís Domènech i Montaner. This mishmash of architectural styles gave the block its nickname the *Manzana de Discordia* (Block of Discord).

High up in the Gràcia district sits Gaudí's enchanting **Parc Güell** (10am-dusk), originally designed to be a self-contained community with houses, schools and shops. The project flopped, but we're left with a Dr Seuss–style playground filled with colourful mosaics and Gaudí-designed paths and plazas. Gaudí himself bought one of the houses here after it had been on the market for years; it's now the **Casa-Museu Gaudí** (☎ 93 219 38 11; www.casamuseugaudi.org; admission €4, Casa-Museu Gaudí & La Sagrada Familia combination €9; 10am-6pm Oct-Mar, to 8pm Apr-Sep; M Lesseps), a museum about his life. Get here by metro (which involves a steep uphill climb) or on bus 24 from Plaça de la Universitat.

The website www.rutadelmodernisme.com is a great resource on modernisme in Barcelona.

MONTJUÏC

A forested hill southwest of the city centre, Montjuïc serves as a Central Park of sorts and is a great place for a jog or stroll overlooking the city. Public transport in the area is a bit complicated; to get here, start at Plaça Espanya and either hike the distance, take bus 61, or hop on the slow and scenic **Tren Montjuïc** (€3.50; Apr-Sep), leaving every 30 minutes. You can also catch the **funicular railway** (1-way €1.50; 9am-10pm) from Paral·lel metro station, or ride the **cable car** (Transbordador Aeri; ☎ 93 225 27 18; one-way €7.50; 11am-8pm mid-Jun–mid-Sep, 10.45am-7pm mid-Sep–Dec & Mar–mid-Jun, 10am-6pm Jan-Feb) over from La Barceloneta.

Several museums and attractions are here:

Museu Nacional d'Art de Catalunya (Map pp966-7; ☎ 93 622 03 60; admission €8.50; 10am-7pm Tue-Sat, 10am-2.30pm Sun) Catalan religious art.

Poble Espanyol (Map pp966-7; ☎ 93 508 63 30; Avinguda Marquès de Comillas; adult/student €7.50/5.50; 9am-8pm Mon, to 2am Tue-Thu, to 4am Fri & Sat, to midnight Sun) Mock village with craft shops and nightlife.

Fundació Joan Miró (Map pp966-7; ☎ 93 443 94 70; Av Miramar 71-75; admission €8; 10am-7pm Tue, Wed, Fri & Sat, to 9.30pm Thu, to 2.30pm Sun) Works by Miró and others.

Tours

The three routes of the **Bus Turístic** (1-/2-day €18/22; 9am-7pm Nov-Mar, to 8pm Apr-Oct) link all the major tourist sights. Buy tickets on the bus or at the tourist office.

The main tourist office (see p964) offers daily **walking tours** (€9) in English and Spanish/Catalan.

Festivals & Events

Barcelona's biggest festival is the **La Mercè**, a city-wide party culminating on 24 September. Another red-letter day is **Sant Joan** (St John's Day, 23 July), when days of endless firecrackers welcome summer. In June and July the **El Grec** arts festival fills Barcelona with theatre, dance and music.

Sleeping

Barcelona seems to get another four- or five-star hotel every week, and if you're looking for luxury there is no shortage of it here. You'll also find a solid selection of budget *hostales* and *pensiones* (guesthouses), mostly in the Barri Gòtic and around Plaça de Catalunya. Unfortunately, good-value midrange hotels are harder to come by. Your best bet is looking online for deals.

Numerous private apartment-rental companies operate in Barcelona. These can often be a better deal than staying in a hotel, especially if you're travelling in a group. Check out www.intobarcelona.com or www.selfcateringhols.com.

CIUTAT VELLA: LAS RAMBLAS, BARRI GÒTIC & LA RIBERA

The *Ciutat Vella* (Old City) is packed with budget *hostales* and *pensiones*. This selection of especially charming and good-value-for-money options merely scratches the surface.

Budget

Hostal Parisien (Map p970; ☎ 93 301 62 83; Las Ramblas 114; d €40-54, s with shared bathroom €20; ❄ ; Ⓜ Liceu) Popular with students, the Parisien is clean and friendly, if noisy. If you have earplugs, book one of the brighter exterior rooms.

Hostal Avinyò (Map p970; ☎ 93 318 79 45; www.hostalavinyo.com; Carrer d'Avinyò 42; d/tr €54/72, s/d with shared bathroom €24/40; 🖳 ; Ⓜ Liceu) Too bad the service here isn't as welcoming as the comfy rooms, which all boast ceiling fans, and some, balconies. Very centrally located.

Hostal Benidorm (Map p970; ☎ 93 302 20 54; www.hostalbenidorm.com; Las Ramblas 37; s/d/tr/q €35/55/75/90; ❄ ; Ⓜ Drassanes) Flowered bedspreads, sparkling tile floors and balconies overlooking Las Ramblas make this a pleasant place to stay. Perks include satellite TV and hotel-style bathrooms with marble countertops.

Hostal Lausanne (Map p970; ☎ 93 302 11 39; www.hostalresidencialausanne.com; Avinguda del Portal de l'Angel 24; s/d €50/60, with shared bathroom €30/49; Ⓜ Plaça de Catalunya) Housed in a pretty, old modernist-style building, rooms here boast soaring ceilings and attractive tile floors.

> **AUTHOR'S CHOICE**
>
> **Hotel Banys Orientals** (Map p970; ☎ 93 268 84 60; www.hotelbanysorientals.com; Carrer de l'Argenteria 37; s/d €80/95; Ⓜ Jaume I) If you want cool Barcelona style at an equally cool price, look no further than this fabulous hotel in the Born. An all white and black décor lends a distinct Mediterranean air to this chic boutique hotel.

Midrange & Top End

Hostal Boquería (Map p970; ☎ 93 302 72 60; Las Ramblas 100; s/d/tr/q €55/85/100/120; ⊠ ❄ 🖳 ; Ⓜ Liceu) Surprisingly quiet, the spic-'n'-span Boquería is great value, with bright rooms, marble counters in the bathrooms and attractive décor.

Hostal Jardí (Map p970; ☎ 93 301 59 00; www.hoteljardi-barcelona.com; Plaça de Sant Josep Oriol 1; r €70-96; ❄ ; Ⓜ Liceu) Long a city favourite, the Jardí overlooks a pretty plaza (paying extra for a room with a view is worth it!) and boasts tidy rooms, some with balconies.

Park Hotel (Map p970; ☎ 93 319 60 00; www.parkhotelbarcelona.com; Avinguda del Marquès de l'Argentera 11; s/d incl breakfast €101/124; Ⓜ Barceloneta) Head to this three-star for breezy, Mediterranean style near the waterfront. Smallish rooms are done in pale wood and a black-and-white colour scheme. If traffic noise bothers you, book an interior room.

EL RAVAL

Budget

Barcelona Ramblas (Map p970; ☎ 93 442 36 69; www.barcelonaramblas.com; Carrer Nou de la Rambla 50; per person €30, with shared bathroom €28; Ⓜ Drassanes) Right off Las Ramblas, this modern *hostal* offers good value. Spotless rooms have plaid bedspreads and prints on the walls, though bathrooms are tiny.

Also recommended:

Gat Raval (Map p970; ☎ 93 481 66 70; www.gataccommodation.com; Carrer Joaquim Costa 44; d €60, s/d with shared bathroom €38/54; ❄ 🖳 ; Ⓜ Sant Antoni) Neon-green walls, stylish décor and a laid-back attitude.

Gat Xino (Map p970; ☎ 93 324 88 33; www.gataccommodation.com; Carrer de l'Hospital 149-55; s/d incl breakfast €60/80; ❄ 🖳 ; Ⓜ Paral·lel) An upgraded version of Gat Raval.

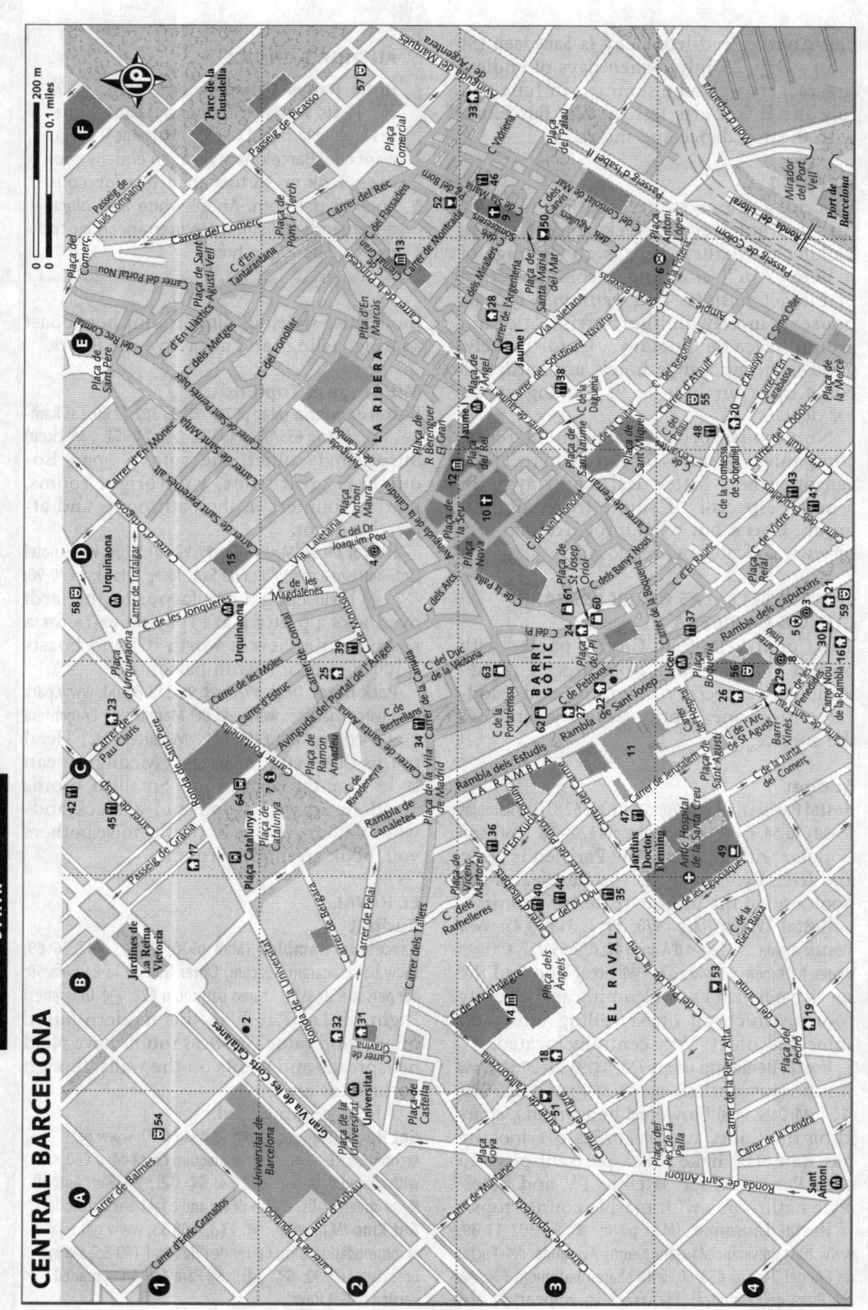
CENTRAL BARCELONA
0 200 m
0 0.1 miles
LA RIBERA
BARRI GÒTIC
EL RAVAL
LA RAMBLA
Parc de la Ciutadella
Universitat de Barcelona
Jardines de La Reina Victoria
Jardins Doctor Fleming
Antic Hospital de la Santa Creu
Port de Barcelona
Mirador del Port Vell
Moll d'Espanya
Plaça Catalunya
Plaça de Catalunya
Plaça d'Urquinaona
Urquinaona
Universitat
Plaça de la Universitat
Liceu
Jaume I
Sant Antoni
Gran Via de les Corts Catalanes
Passeig de Gràcia
Ronda de Sant Pere
Ronda de la Universitat
Ronda de Sant Antoni
Via Laietana
Avinguda del Portal de l'Àngel
Avinguda de la Catedral
Avinguda del Marquès de l'Argentera
Passeig de Picasso
Passeig de Lluís Companys
Passeig d'Isabel II
Passeig de Colom
Ronda del Litoral
Rambla de Canaletes
Rambla dels Estudis
Rambla de Sant Josep
Rambla dels Caputxins
Carrer de Balmes
Carrer d'Enric Granados
Carrer d'Aribau
Carrer de Muntaner
Carrer de Sepúlveda
Carrer de Pelai
Carrer dels Tallers
Carrer del Carme
Carrer de l'Hospital
Carrer de Ferran
Carrer de Montcada
Carrer de la Princesa
Carrer del Rec
Carrer del Comerç
Plaça Reial
Plaça Nova
Plaça de la Seu
Plaça del Rei
Plaça de Sant Jaume
Plaça de Santa Maria del Mar
Plaça Comercial
Plaça del Palau
Plaça de la Mercè
Plaça dels Àngels
Plaça de Castella
Plaça Goya
Plaça del Pedró
Plaça Antoni Maura
Plaça de Sant Pere
Plaça del Pi
Plaça de Sant Josep Oriol
Plaça de la Boqueria
A B C D E F
1 2 3 4

INFORMATION
24-hour Pharmacy........1 C3
Altaïr........2 B1
Easy Internet Café........3 D4
Electric Internet Company........4 D2
Guardia Urbana........5 D4
Main Post Office........6 E4
Main Tourist Office........7 C2
WTN Internet........8 D4

SIGHTS & ACTIVITIES
Basílica de Santa María del Mar..9 F3
Cathedral........10 D3
Mercat de la Boquería........11 C3
Museo d'Història de la Ciutat..12 D2
Museo Picasso........13 E2
Museu d'Art Contemporani de Barcelona........14 B3
Palau de la Música Catalana........15 D1
Palau Reial Major........(see 12)
Saló del Tinell........(see 12)

SLEEPING
Barcelona Ramblas........16 D4
Centric Point........17 C1
Gat Raval........18 B3
Gat Xino........19 B4
Hostal Avinyò........20 E4
Hostal Benidorm........21 D4
Hostal Boquería........22 C3
Hostal Goya........23 C1
Hostal Jardí........24 D3
Hostal Lausanne........25 C2
Hostal Opera........26 C4
Hostal Parisien........27 C3
Hotel Banys Orientals........28 E3
Hotel España........29 C4
Hotel Gaudí........30 D4
Hotel Inglaterra........31 B2
Hotel Pelayo........32 B2
Park Hotel........33 F3

EATING
Bagel Shop........34 C2
Bar-Bodega Fortuny........35 B3
Buenas Migas........36 C3
Café de l'Òpera........37 D4
El Café de l'Acadèmia........38 E3
Els Quatre Gats........39 D2
Foodball........40 B3
La Fonda........41 D4
Laie Librería Café........42 C1
Los Caracoles........43 D4
Mamacafé........44 B3
Mussol........45 C1
Organic........(see 11)
Origins 99.9%........46 F3
Ra........47 C3
Venus........48 E4

DRINKING
Bar El Jardi........49 C4
La Vinya del Senyor........50 F3
Lletraferit........51 A3
Miramelindo........52 F2
Muebles Navarro........53 B4

ENTERTAINMENT
Arena Madre........54 A1
Harlem Jazz Club........55 E4
Liceu........56 C4
Magic........57 F2
Salvation........58 D1
Tablao Cordobés........59 D4

SHOPPING
Art Market........60 D3
Caelum........61 D3
Casa Colomina........62 C3
El Mercadillo........63 C3

TRANSPORT
Aerobus Bus Stop........64 C1
Bus Turístic Bus Stop........(see 64)

Midrange & Top End

Hostal Opera (Map p970; ☎ 93 318 82 01; info@hostalopera.com; Carrer de Sant Pau 20; s/d €43/63; M Liceu) Don't expect frills, but this homy *hostal* is a friendly place with clean rooms, decent-sized en-suite bathrooms and a great location just off Las Ramblas. Cons include thin walls and no in-room TVs.

Hotel España (Map p970; ☎ 93 318 17 58; www.hotelespanya.com; Carrer de Sant Pau 9-11; s/d incl breakfast €75/105; ; M Liceu) The España boasts beautiful modernist décor, the work of famed architect Lluís Doménech i Montaner, and breezy rooms with cool tiled floors, a mustard colour scheme and simple furnishings.

Hotel Gaudí (Map p970; ☎ 93 317 90 32; www.hotelgaudi.es; Carrer Nou de la Rambla 12; s €90-130, d €120-180; M Drassanes) Gaudí-inspired mosaics decorate the lobby at this comfortable three-star near Las Ramblas.

L'EIXAMPLE

Budget

Centric Point (Map p970; ☎ 93 231 20 45; www.centricpointhostel.com; Passeig de Gràcia 33; dm €17-22, d with shared bathroom €40-55; ; M Passeig de Gràcia) This huge (400 beds!) youth hostel offers clean but spartan rooms, a kitchen and a night-time bar. Sheets cost extra, and there's a €1 surcharge for credit card payments. The owners run several other hostels in the city; see www.equity-point.com for details.

Sant Jordi Aragó (Map pp966-7; Carrer d'Aragó 268; dm €22-24; ; M Passeig de Gràcia) This friendly hostel is a great place to meet people and is a huge hit with travellers, though some complain of small rooms and bathrooms. The price includes linen and access to the Internet and kitchen, but lockers and laundry are extra.

Midrange

Hotel Pelayo (Map p970; ☎ 93 302 37 27; www.hotelpelayo.com; Carrer de Pelai 9; s/d €55/75; ; M Universitat) An unbeatable location and decent, if slightly time-worn, rooms make this spot near Plaça Catalunya a good bet.

Hostal Goya (Map p970; ☎ 93 302 25 65; www.hostalgoya.com; Carrer de Pau Claris 74; s €68, d €75-85; ; M Urquinaona) Decorated in soothing neutral tones, the cool Ikea-style Goya is one of the best deals in L'Eixample, with friendly staff, comfy rooms and a good location near the metro.

Top End

Hotel Inglaterra (Map p970; ☎ 93 505 11 00; www.hotel-inglaterra.com; Carrer de Pelai 14; s €99-160, d €119-200; M Universitat) Little brother of the famed five-star Hotel Majestic, this well-equipped hotel boasts a superb location and quiet, spacious rooms.

Hotel Actual (Map pp966-7; ☎ 93 552 05 50; www.hotelactual.com; Carrer Roselló 238; r €111-146; ; M Diagonal) Minimalist style and the tasteful use of cream and chocolate tones throughout make this stylish business hotel a comfortable spot. Good location near La Pedrera.

Casa Fuster (Map pp966-7; ☎ 93 255 30 30; www.hotelescenter.es; Passeig de Gràcia 132; r €185-485; ; M Diagonal) A modernist mansion totally refurbished to house this luscious five-star hotel, the Casa Fuster is the ultimate splurge. Even if you don't stay in one of the opulent rooms, come by for a coffee in the beautiful Café Vienés.

Hotel Claris (Map pp966-7; ☎ 93 487 62 62; www.derbyhotels.es; Carrer Pau Claris 150; r €200-475; ; M Passeig de Gràcia) One of the best all-round hotels in Barcelona, the sleek Claris is decorated with the owner's private collection of Egyptian artefacts. Rooms are lush though small. In summer, head to the rooftop restaurant and bar for great food and sometimes live music.

Eating

Barcelona is foodie heaven. The city has firmly established itself as one of Europe's gourmet capitals, and innovative, push-the-envelope restaurants abound. Many of the most creative chefs are one-time students of Ferran Adrià (see p978), whose influence on the city's cuisine is strong.

Though Barcelona has a reputation for being the 'new Spanish cuisine' hot spot, typical dishes such as rice and shellfish paella, pigs' trotters, rabbit with snails, and *butifarra* (a tasty local sausage) still form the backbone of many eateries.

Lunch is served from 2pm to 3.30pm, and dinner begins at 9pm. In between, you could snack at bars or resign yourself to eating at the touristy (and often overpriced) restaurants on Las Ramblas.

LAS RAMBLAS & BARRI GÒTIC

This part of town is loaded with restaurants, including the over-priced touristy places on Las Ramblas and the fast-food chains along Carrer de Ferran. The best places are the intimate eateries hidden among the Barri's back streets; below we've mentioned just a few of the best options. Self-caterers should make a beeline for the wildly colourful Mercat de la Boquería (p964) for fresh food.

Bagel Shop (Map p970; ☎ 93 302 41 61; Carrer de la Canuda 25; mains €3.50-8; M Liceu) Top your bagel with anything from turkey and cheese to Mallorcan *sobrassada* (soft, tangy sausage) or *butifarra* at this informal café.

Café de l'Òpera (Map p970; ☎ 93 317 75 85; Las Ramblas 74; mains €4-6; M Liceu) With a touch of faded modernist glory, this classic café is popular for breakfast, coffee or a light lunch.

Organic (Map p970; ☎ 93 342 81 03; Mercat de la Boquería stand 972; mains up to €8; M Liceu) At the far back of La Boquería market is this organic, vegan-friendly stall selling tasty food to go. The same folks have a full restaurant at Carrer de la Junta del Comerç 11.

La Fonda (Map p970; ☎ 93 301 75 15; Carrer dels Escudellers 10; mains €5.50-10, menú €8; M Drassanes) Airy and stylish, La Fonda serves Mediterranean fare ranging from pastas and rice dishes to stews and grilled meats. It's great value, so expect to wait for a table. The same owner runs La Rita (see opposite) and a host of other city restaurants, all known for their cheap lunch *menús*.

Venus (Map p970; ☎ 93 301 15 85; Carrer d'Avinyò 25; mains €7-12; closed Sun; M Liceu) Vegetarians will love the salad selection at this grungy-chic café. Takeaway food is also available.

Los Caracoles (Map p970; ☎ 93 302 31 85; Carrer dels Escudellers 14; mains €11-20; M Liceu) A city institution, 'The Snails' is a maze of tile-laden dining rooms, all decorated with photos of the famous faces who've eaten here. Specialities include snails, roasted chicken, and *suquet*, a Catalan seafood stew.

El Café de l'Acadèmia (Map p970; ☎ 93 319 82 53; Carrer Lledó 1; mains €12-20, menu €11.50; closed Sat, Sun & mid-Aug; M Jaume I) This fine restaurant serves strictly Catalan dishes in a romantic atmosphere. If you're with a group, ask to sit in the downstairs *bodega* (cellar).

Els Quatre Gats (Map p970; ☎ 93 302 41 40; Carrer de Montsió 3; mains €15-22, menu €11; M Urquinaona) The legendary modernist café where Picasso had his first exhibition, 'The Four Cats' now serves excellent (though pricey) Catalan dishes.

EL RAVAL

Foodball (Map p970; ☎ 93 270 13 63; Carrer d'Elisabets 9; foodballs €2-3; M Liceu) Brought to you by the folks at Camper shoes, the concept behind Foodball is innovative (if a little weird). All food is served in compact balls, for example, seafood paella balls, seaweed and tofu balls or chickpea balls. Try a muffin ball for dessert.

Buenas Migas (Map p970; ☎ 93 412 16 86; Plaça Bonsuccés 6; mains €4-5; ⏰ 10am-11pm Sun-Wed, to midnight Thu-Sat; Ⓜ Liceu) Quiche, focaccias and awesome desserts are served alfresco at this small café.

Mamacafé (Map p970; ☎ 93 301 29 40; Carrer del Dr Dou 10; menús €7.50-9.50; Ⓜ Liceu) The slogan here is 'healthy and creative', and it lives up to its claim with a refreshing variety of vegetarian-friendly food including soups, salads and couscous with veggies.

Bar-Bodega Fortuny (Map p970; ☎ 93 317 98 92; Carrer del Pintor Fortuny 31; mains from €6; Ⓜ Liceu) This quirky bar serves salads, couscous and hummus to a largely bohemian group of regulars. At night it's a popular lesbian hangout.

Bar Ra (Map p970; ☎ 93 301 41 63; Plaça Gardunya; menú €11; Ⓜ Liceu) Just behind La Boquería, Bar Ra is a funky bar, café and restaurant known for its big terrace (ideal in fine weather) and light, international dishes.

LA RIBERA & WATERFRONT

La Barceloneta is the place to go for seafood; Passeig Joan de Borbó is lined with excellent eateries. You can also try the many classy (and pricey) restaurants around the Plaça de Pau Vila, or head to the Port Olímpic for more pickings.

Origins 99.9% (Map p970; ☎ 93 310 75 31; Carrer Vidriera 6-8; menú €10; ⏰ 12.30pm-1.30am; Ⓜ Jaume I) A shop-restaurant combo, Origins boasts that 99.9% of everything it sells is from Catalonia. The ever-changing daily *menú* features local specialities such as *escalivada* (roasted veggies on bread) and Catalan sausages.

Agua (Map pp966-7; ☎ 93 225 12 72; Passeig Marítim 30; mains €14-22; Ⓜ Ciutadella-Vila Olímpica) One of the most stylish seafood restaurants in town, the breezy Agua specialises in rice dishes, though the menu includes a wide range of Mediterranean fare.

L'EIXAMPLE

Mussol (Map p970; ☎ 93 301 76 10; Carrer de Casp 19; mains €5.50-15; Ⓜ Plaça de Catalunya) Specialising in grilled meats and vegetables, this sprawling informal restaurant offers filling portions and excellent value. It's great for families. There's another branch at Carrer d'Aragó 261.

La Rita (Map pp966-7; ☎ 93 487 23 76; Carrer Aragó 279; mains €6-10, menú €8; Ⓜ Passeig de Gràcia) For a bit of style, this popular restaurant does the trick. Be prepared to wait in line for its pasta, seafood and traditional dishes.

Laie Librería Café (Map p970; ☎ 93 302 73 10; Carrer de Pau Claris 85; mains €6-12; ⏰ closed Sun; Ⓜ Passeig de Gràcia) This delightful, sunny café offers a delicious buffet and lunch *menú* packed with healthy food, local specialities and vegetarian options.

Cervecería Catalana (Map pp966-7; ☎ 93 216 03 68; Carrer Mallorca 236; mains €6-15; Ⓜ Passieg de Gràcia) Arrive early to try the delicious tapas and *flautas* (long skinny sandwiches) at this classic tavern off Rambla de Catalunya.

La Flauta (Map pp966-7; ☎ 93 323 70 38; Carrer Aribau 23; mains €6-15; ⏰ closed Sun; Ⓜ Universitat) Run by the same owners as Cervecería Catalana, La Flauta has the same classic *flautas* and tavern atmosphere.

Drinking

Don't worry, you won't go thirsty in Barcelona. The city abounds with day-time cafés, laid-back lounges and lively night-time bars. On weekends, bars stay hopping until 2am and most of the places listed here are open for quiet drinks as early as 8pm.

CAFÉS

Bar El Jardí (Map p970; Jardins de Rubió i Lluch; ⏰ 10am-dusk; Ⓜ Liceu) Enjoy tea, coffee, pastries or light lunch fare at this terrace café in the patio garden of the old Antic Hospital de la Santa Creu.

Caelum (Map p970; ☎ 93 302 69 93; Carrer Palla 8; ⏰ closed Mon; Ⓜ Liceu) All the delectable pastries and sweets sold in this café and shop are made in convents or monasteries. Head downstairs to the romantic vaulted basement, open evenings only.

Lletraferit (Map p970; ☎ 93 301 19 61; Carrer Joaquim Costa 43; Ⓜ Sant Antoni) With a chilled but sophisticated vibe, this is a book-lovers' café by day and a cocktail bar by night.

BARS

Muebles Navarro (Map p970; ☎ 60 718 80 96; Carrer de la Riera Alta 4; Ⓜ Liceu) Funky and decorated like a furniture flea market, this is a great place to kick back with a cold one and a tapa or two.

SPAIN

Philharmonic (Map pp966-7; ☎ 93 451 11 53; Carrer Mallorca 204; Ⓜ Provença) Call in at this popular pub for televised football matches, some English conversation, great English breakfasts and, at night, occasional live music.

Miramelindo (Map p970; ☎ 93 310 37 27; Passeig del Born 15; Ⓜ Jaume I) One of many popular bars along the Passeig del Born, Miramelindo is a long-time favourite known for its varied music and good drink selection.

La Vinya del Senyor (Map p970; ☎ 93 310 33 97; Plaça de Santa Maria del Mar 5; Ⓜ Jaume I) This is a romantic wine bar sitting under the shadow of the Basilica.

Virreina (Map pp966-7; ☎ 93 237 98 80; Plaça Virreina 1; Ⓜ Fontana) The Gràcia district, with its intimate plazas and narrow streets, is the perfect spot for a quiet drink. Virreina has a great outdoor terrace and is open day and night.

Alfa (Map pp966-7; ☎ 93 415 18 24; Carrer Gran de Gràcia 36; Ⓜ Fontana) This fun bar and dance spot is a long-time favourite. Come for great '80s and '90s music and a laid-back feel.

Entertainment

NIGHTCLUBS

For discos of every shape, size and variety, head to the Port Olímpic; in summer it's a nonstop party, and winter weekends are fun too. Expect club entry to cost from €10 to €15. The party gets going around 2am and stays strong until 5am or so.

Nitsa Club (Map pp966-7; ☎ 93 301 00 90; Nou de la Rambla 113; 🕑 Fri & Sat; Ⓜ Paral·lel) Three clubs in one: you can head for the pop zone, the techno pop zone or the house and breakbeat zone downstairs. It attracts a young, stylish crowd.

Moog (Map pp966-7; ☎ 93 301 72 82; Arc del Teatre 3; 🕑 Fri & Sat; Ⓜ Drassanes) Cool design, groovable music, a mixed crowd out to have a good time…no wonder Moog is such a hit.

Magic (Map p970; ☎ 93 310 72 67; Passeig de Picasso 40; 🕑 Thu-Sun; Ⓜ Arc de Triomf) This is one of the city's top clubs, with fantastic live music running the gamut between techno and classic rock.

Otto Zutz (Map pp966-7; ☎ 93 238 07 22; Carrer Lincoln 15; 🕑 Tue-Sat; Ⓜ Fontana) Playing a mixture of house and hip-hop, this swanky club has one of the city's top VIP sections.

CINEMAS

The best cinema for subtitled foreign films is **Verdi** (Map pp966-7; ☎ 93 238 79 90; Carrer Verdi 32; Ⓜ Fontana), in Gràcia. Big-budget Hollywood flicks are shown in English at **Icària** (Yelmo Cineplex Icària; ☎ 93 221 75 85; Carrer Salvador Espiritu 61; Ⓜ Vila Olímpica).

GAY & LESBIAN VENUES

The gay and lesbian scene is concentrated in the blocks around Carrers de Muntaner and Consell de Cent (dubbed Gayxample by the locals). Here you'll find ambience every night of the week in the bars, discos and drag clubs.

Party hard at classic gay discos such as **Arena Madre** (Map p970; ☎ 93 487 83 42; Carrer de Balmes 32; 🕑 closed Mon; Ⓜ Universitat) and **Salvation** (Map p970; ☎ 93 318 06 86; Ronda de Sant Pere 19-21; 🕑 Fri-Sun; Ⓜ Universitat).

The low-key Bar-Bodega Fortuny is a popular lesbian hangout.

THEATRE

Most theatre in the city is in Catalan. There are quite a few venues that stage vanguard drama, including the well-regarded **Teatre Nacional de Catalunya** (Map pp966-7; ☎ 93 306 57 00; Plaça de les Arts 1; Ⓜ Glòries).

SPORT

Football fans can see FC Barcelona play at **Camp Nou** (Map pp966-7; ☎ 93 496 36 00; www.fcbarcelona.com; Carrer Arístides Maillol; Ⓜ Collblanc). Even if you can't score tickets, stop by for a peek at the **museum** (gates 7 & 9; adult/student €6.50/5, tour €10.50/8; 🕑 10am-6.30pm Mon-Sat, to 2pm Sun).

LIVE MUSIC

London Bar (Map pp966-7; ☎ 93 318 52 61; Carrer Nou de la Rambla 34; Ⓜ Drassanes) This bar hosts concerts almost every night. Groups range from jazz to rock to flamenco.

Harlem Jazz Club (Map p970; ☎ 93 310 07 55; Carrer Comtessa de Sobradiel 8; Ⓜ Liceu) Here you'll find a guaranteed dose of quality jazz and enough smoke to cook a sausage.

Tablao Cordobés (Map p970; ☎ 93 317 57 11; Las Ramblas 35; Ⓜ Liceu) Though Barcelona is not the best place to see flamenco, you can catch a reasonably authentic show here.

Shopping

The queen of Barcelona's shopping districts is the Passeig de Gràcia, where high-end fashion struts its stuff. For unique clothing and shoes, browse the intimate shops in the mall-like **Boulevard Rosa** (Map pp966-7; Passeig de

Gràcia 53-57; Ⓜ Passeig de Gràcia). If you like design, you'll love gadget-happy **Vinçon** (Map pp966-7; ☎ 93 215 60 50; Passeig de Gràcia 96; Ⓜ Diagonal).

El Born, the city's original textile centre, is now a hot spot for up-and-coming designers. Check out Carrer del Rec and surrounds. Trendy, cheaper labels are found in abundance on Carrer de la Portaferrissa. Here you can also check out the punk fashions at **El Mercadillo** (Map p970; Carrer de la Portaferrissa 17; Ⓜ Plaça Catalunya) and the tasty Spanish *turrón* candy at **Casa Colomina** (Map p970; ☎ 93 317 46 81; Carrer de la Portaferrissa 8; Ⓜ Plaça Catalunya). Nearby, there's a Saturday **art market** (Map p970; Plaça de Sant Josep Oriol; Ⓜ Liceu) where you'll find prints and originals from local artists, while the connecting Plaça del Pi hosts an artisan food fair on Thursdays.

Bargain hunters love **Els Encants** (Map pp966-7; ☎ 93 246 30 30; Carrer Dos de Maig 186; 🕓 8.30am-6pm Mon, Wed, Fri & Sat; Ⓜ Glòries), a free-for-all flea market.

Getting There & Away

AIR

Barcelona's airport, **El Prat de Llobregat** (BCN; ☎ 90 240 47 04; www.aena.es), is 14km southwest of the city centre. It caters to international as well as domestic flights. Budget flights abound with easyJet, Vueling and Air Europa; even Iberia sometimes has good rates. See p1035 for contact details.

BUS

The terminal for virtually all domestic and international buses is the **Estació del Nord** (Map pp966-7; ☎ 90 226 06 06; www.barcelonanord.com; Carrer Alí Bei 80; Ⓜ Arc de Triomf). **Alsa** (☎ 90 242 22 42; www.alsa.es) goes to Madrid (€25, eight hours, 21 daily), Valencia (€23, five hours, 15 daily), Zaragoza (€12, 3½ hours, 18 daily) and many other destinations.

CAR & MOTORCYCLE

The A-7 motorway comes in from the French border, and the A-2 motorway heads towards Zaragoza. Both are toll roads. The N-II is a nontoll alternative, but it's slower and more dangerous. In general, highways near Barcelona are good, but crowded, especially in the evening and on Friday and Sunday.

TRAIN

Virtually all trains travelling to and from destinations within Spain stop at **Estació Sants** (Map pp966-7; ☎ 90 224 34 02; www.renfe.es; Ⓜ Sants-Estació). Daily trains run to most major cities in Spain, including Madrid (€63, five hours, seven daily), Zaragoza (€25, four hours, 14 daily), Valencia (€32, 3½ hours, 12 daily) and San Sebastián (€36, eight hours, two daily).

Getting Around

Information about Barcelona's public transport is available online at www.tmb.net. You can also call ☎ 010 from any city telephone and get detailed transport information.

TO/FROM THE AIRPORT

Normally, trains link the airport to the Sants and Plaça de Catalunya train stations every half-hour (€2.40, 25 to 40 minutes), but construction work on the line has made this an oftentimes slow and complicated route. You're better off taking the **Aerobus** (Map p970; ☎ 93 415 56 18) to the city centre (€3.75, 30 minutes, every 12 minutes). A taxi from the airport to Plaça de Catalunya costs about €20.

CAR & MOTORCYCLE

Parking a car is difficult and, if you choose a parking garage, quite expensive (€2.20 per hour). It's better to ditch your car and rely on public transport.

PUBLIC TRANSPORT

Barcelona's metro system spreads its tentacles around the city in such a way that most places of interest are within a 10-minute walk of a station. Buses and suburban trains are needed only for a few destinations. A single metro, bus or suburban train ride costs €1.20, but a T-1 ticket, valid for 10 rides, costs only €6.65.

TAXI

Barcelona's black-and-yellow taxis are plentiful, very reasonably priced and handy for late-night transport. The flag fall is €1.45 weekdays, and €1.55 for nights and weekends. If you can't find a street taxi, call ☎ 93 303 30 33.

MONESTIR DE MONTSERRAT

The prime attraction of Monestir de Montserrat, 50km northwest of Barcelona, is its incredible setting. The Benedictine **monastery** sits on the side of a 1236m-high

HUMAN CASTLES

An element in nearly every Catalan festival is *castellers,* or human castle builders. The tradition is simple: competing teams try to build the biggest human pyramid possible, and whoever collapses first loses. It's serious competition between *colles* (*casteller* teams).

You can see *castellers* at most major festivals throughout Catalonia. The best teams are usually from the towns of Vilafranca del Penedès and Valls, both southwest of Barcelona. Every two years a huge *casteller* competition is held in early October in Tarragona's bullring. If you're visiting then, it's definitely worth a day trip.

mountain of weird, bulbous peaks. The monastery was founded in 1025 after a statue of the Virgin Mary was found here, and pilgrims still come from all over Christendom to kiss the Black Virgin (La Moreneta), the 12th-century wooden sculpture of Mary that's regarded as Catalonia's patron.

Mass is held several times daily; at the 1pm Monday to Saturday mass the monastery's boys' choir sings.

The monastery's **information centre** (☎ 93 877 77 77; www.montserratvisita.com, www.abadiamontserrat.net; ⏲ 10am-5.45pm) has a couple of good free leaflets and maps on the mountain and monastery, as well as information about the **Museu de Montserrat** (☎ 93 877 77 77; adult/student €5.50/4.50; ⏲ 10am-5.45pm).

Eating & Sleeping

There are two accommodation options at the monastery itself.

Abat Marcet Cells (☎ 93 877 77 77; d €40) Self-catering apartments for up to four people. There's a two night minimum stay.

Hotel Abat Cisneros (☎ 93 877 77 77; s/d €46/80) For comfort and excellent value, try three-star Hotel Abat Cisneros. The restaurant (*menú* €25) here is miles better than the self-serve cafetería (mains €4 to €10) down the mountain.

Getting There & Away

The FGC R5 train runs from Barcelona's Plaça Espanya to the Aeri de Montserrat (one hour, 19 daily), from where you can catch a cable car up the mountain. Or, stop at Monistrol-Vila, where you can hop on a rack railway to head up (15 minutes, every 20 minutes). The combined return ticket costs €12.60. Find out more at www.cremallerademontserrat.com.

GIRONA

Lovely Girona, a medieval city built along the banks of the Onyar River, makes an ideal day trip or base for exploring the region. The old city sits along the river's eastern bank and is home to what was once one of Catalonia's most important Jewish communities. Get information at the **tourist office** (☎ 97 222 65 75; www.costabrava.org; Rambla de la Llibertat 1).

Sights & Activities

Wander the narrow streets of the **Call** (Jewish Quarter) and visit the former synagogue, now the **Bonastruc ça Porta Jewish Museum** (☎ 97 221 27 61; Carrer La Força 8; admission €2; ⏲ 10am-8pm Mon-Sat May-Oct, to 6pm Nov-Apr, 10am-3pm Sun year-round).

Also interesting is the **wall** (⏲ dawn-dusk) that runs around the edge of the old quarter. Walk along the top for great views. Don't leave without peeking into the looming **Gothic Cathedral** (☎ 97 221 44 26; Plaça Catedral; admission museum €4, free Sun; ⏲ 10am-7pm Mon-Fri, to 4.30pm Sat, 2-7pm Sun Nov-Mar, 10am-8pm Mon-Fri, to 4.30pm Sat, 2-8pm Sun Apr-Oct), which boasts the world's widest Gothic-style vault (23m).

Sleeping & Eating

Pensió Margarit (☎ 97 220 10 66; www.hotelmargarit.com; Carrer Ultònia 1; s €26-31, d €36-68, all incl breakfast) Across the river from the old town, the family-run Margarit is a friendly, 30-room *pensión* with no-frills furnishings. It's decorated with framed puzzles completed by the owners. They say the huge one in the dining room took 750 hours to finish!

Hotel Historic (☎ 97 222 35 83; www.hotelhistoric.com; Carrer Bellmirall 4; s/d €102/114) Housed in a historic building beside the cathedral, this is a romantic place offering small but fashionable rooms. There are apartments for rent too (€90 to €150).

Restaurant Boira (☎ 97 221 96 05; Plaça Independència 17; mains €10-19) Overlooking the river and specialising in rice and seafood dishes, Boira is a great choice for a nice meal.

Cheap eats (sandwiches, tapas and café fare) are widely available along the Ram-

SPAIN

bla de la Llibertat, running parallel to the river.

Getting There & Away

Girona's **train station** (www.renfe.es), connects with the rest of Catalonia and France. Catch the hourly trains from Barcelona (€6.25, 75 minutes) to get here.

THE COSTA BRAVA

The Costa Brava (Rugged Coast) was Catalonia's first tourist centre, and after you visit its rocky coastline, romantic cove beaches and white-washed fishing villages, you'll see why. Though overdevelopment threatens the coast's charm, this is still one of Catalonia's most beautiful areas. Save time to explore the medieval villages and important historic and cultural sites inland, including the Dalí museum in Figueres (right).

Ask for information at the **tourist offices** (🕑 10am-1pm & 4-7pm Mon-Sat, 10am-1pm Sun Sep-Jun, 9am-9pm daily Jul-Aug; Figueres ☎ 97 250 31 55; www.figueresciutat.com; Plaça del Sol; Palafrugell ☎ 97 261 18 20; www.palafrugell.net; Plaça de l'Església) in the towns around the area.

Sights & Activities

COASTAL RESORTS & ISLANDS

The Costa Brava is all about picturesque inlets and coves. Beaches tend to be small and scattered. Some longer beaches at places such as L'Estartit and Empúries are worth visiting, especially in the off season.

Cadaqués, at the end of an agonising series of hairpin bends one hour from Figueres, is postcard perfect. Beaches are of the pebbly variety, so people spend a lot of time sitting at waterfront cafés or strolling. A 15-minute walk from town is Dalí's house (see right). Some 10km northeast of Cadaqués is **Cap de Creus**, a rocky mountain park where you can hike and visit a **monastery**.

For an interesting stroll through antiquity, check out the ruins of the Greek and Roman town of **Empúries** (☎ 97 277 02 08; www.lescala-empuries.com; admission €2.50; 🕑 10am-dusk), down the coast, 2km outside L'Escala.

Past L'Escala and L'Estartit are three gorgeous beach towns near Palafrugell: **Tamariu** (the smallest, least crowded and most exclusive), **Llafranc** (the biggest and busiest), and **Calella de Palafrugell** (never overcrowded and always relaxed).

> **DIVING IN THE COSTA BRAVA**
>
> The Costa Brava is one of the best places to dive in the Mediterranean, thanks to its interesting underwater rock formations and healthy marine environment. One of the most exciting places to dive is around the **Illes Medes** (www.enestartit.es), seven small islets a kilometre off the coast from L'Estartit. These islets and their surrounding coral reefs have been declared a natural park to protect their diverse flora and fauna. Many local companies lead dives, charging around €30 per dive, including equipment. If you choose to dive on your own, you'll need permission from the park office (☎ 97 275 11 03).

DALÍLAND

This area of Catalonia, Salvador Dalí's birthplace, is home to several museums dedicated to the surrealist. **Teatre-Museu Dalí** (☎ 97 267 75 00; www.salvador-dali.org; Plaça Gala i Salvador Dalí 5, Figueres; admission €10; 🕑 10.30am-5.45pm Tue-Sun Oct-Jun, 9am-7.45pm daily Jul-Sep), housed in a 19th-century theatre converted by Dalí himself, has a huge and fascinating collection of his strange creations. The **Salvador Dalí Museum-House** (☎ 97 225 10 15; www.salvador-dali.org; Portlligat; adult/student €8/6; 🕑 10.30am-6pm Tue-Sun mid-Mar–mid-Jun & mid-Sep–Jan, 10.30am-9pm daily mid-Jun–mid-Sep), near Cadaqués, was his home and workshop. Completing the Dalí triangle is the **Casa-Museu Castell Gala-Dalí** (☎ 97 248 86 55; www.salvador-dali.org; Púbol; adult/student/child €6/4/free; 🕑 10.30am-6pm Tue-Sun mid-Mar–mid-Jun & mid-Sep–Jan, 10.30am-9pm daily mid-Jun–mid-Sep), a castle Dalí decorated for his beloved Gala.

PALS & PERATALLADA

Of the many historic towns inland from the Costa Brava, Pals and Peratallada are the most charming. **Pals** (www.pals.es), 6km inland, is an impeccably restored medieval town. Peek into the **church**, stand at the base of the 15m **Torre de les Hores** (Clocktower) and enjoy the views from the **Mirador del Pedró**.

Nearby, **Peratallada** (www.peratallada.info) is another medieval jewel. Walled and surrounded by a moat dug out of the rock (hence the name, which translates to 'cut stone'), this impossibly romantic hamlet makes a great sightseeing base.

EL BULLI

Just outside the town of Roses, in the far northern tip of the Costa Brava, sits an unassuming looking farmhouse restaurant. Step inside, however, and you'll discover the wildly unusual creations of chef Ferran Adrià, widely considered the most creative food mind working today. A reservation at the three-Michelin-starred **El Bulli** (www.elbulli.com) is all but impossible to get (of the 300,000 requests they get a year, they can only seat about 8000!), but if you do score a table be prepared for a veritable symphony of flavours and smells as you're presented with the 30 or 40 tiny dishes that make up his tasting menu. 'Liquid Ravioli', 'Deconstructed Tortilla' and 'Air' are some of his past creations.

Sleeping & Eating

Many visitors to the Costa Brava rent apartments. If you are interested in renting your own pad for a week or so, contact local tourist offices or check property-rental sites such as www.homelidays.com.

FIGUERES

With so many beautiful towns around, it really doesn't make much sense to stay in the comparatively unattractive Figueres.

Hotel Emporda (☎ 97 250 05 62; www.hotelemporda.com; Antigua Carretera de Fraça; s €58-70, d €92-110) If you must find a place to lay your head, try this friendly and stylish place with a popular restaurant (mains €10 to €15).

Lizarran (☎ 97 250 66 67; Calle Monturiol 3; tapas €1.50) Near the Dalí museum, you can get a fast, inexpensive lunch at this popular Basque-style tapas chain.

CADAQUÉS

Hotel Playa Sol (☎ 97 225 81 00; www.playasol.com; Carrer Pianc 3; r €62-160; ❄ 🅿) Right on the beach, Playa Sol offers simple rooms, most with balconies and fabulous views. The cheaper rooms have no view.

AROUND PALAFRUGELL

Hotel Port Bo (☎ 97 261 49 62; www.hotelportbo.net; Carrer August Pi i Sunyer 6, Calella de Palafrugell; per person €20-58, 2-4 person apt €60-180, 4-6 person apt €79-228, all incl breakfast) A fabulous deal in the off season, though pricey in summer, the Port Bo is a family-style hotel with comfy rooms and a fantastic breakfast.

PALS & PERATALLADA

Camping options abound on the coast near Pals.

Interpals (☎ 97 263 61 79; www.interpals.com; Av Mediterrània Km 4.5, Platja de Pals; adult €4-5.50, child €3-3.50, tent & car €40-18.50; 🕒 Ap-Oct; 🅿) A self-sufficient resort 300m from the beach, this is a well-run, clean camping ground popular with families.

Ca l'Aliu (☎ 97 263 40 61; www.calaliu.com; Carrer Roca 6, Peratallada; r incl breakfast €54-66) For real charm, head to this homy guesthouse built right in to the medieval walls of Peratallada.

Getting There & Away

Renfe (www.renfe.es) trains zip up hourly to Girona and Figueres from Barcelona. Few small towns have train stations, but you can reach any little hamlet with **SARFA** (☎ 90 230 20 25; www.sarfa.com) bus services from Girona.

TARRAGONA

pop 128,000

The 'Rome of Spain', Tarragona was founded in 218 BC and was an important Roman centre. The city's highlights are its Roman ruins, but don't neglect the bustling shopping district or its fabulous city beaches.

Get more information at the **tourist office** (☎ 97 725 07 95; www.tarragonaturisme.es; Carrer Major 39; 🕒 10am-2pm & 4-7pm Mon-Sat, 10am-2pm Sun Oct-May, 9am-9pm Mon-Sat, 10am-3pm Sun Jun-Sep).

Sights & Activities

Start at the fascinating **Museu Arqueològic** (☎ 97 723 62 09; Plaça del Rei 5; admission €2.50; 🕒 10am-1.30pm & 3.30-7pm Tue-Sat, 10am-2pm Sun Oct-May, 10am-8pm Tue-Sat, 10am-2pm Sun Jun-Sep), where you'll get an excellent understanding of Roman Spain.

Several Roman sites are scattered around town. All have the same admission price and opening hours unless stated. The **Castell del Rei** (☎ 97 724 19 52; Plaça del Rei; admission €2.50; 🕒 9am-7pm Mon-Sat, 10am-3pm Sun Oct-May, 9am-9pm Mon-Sat, 9am-3pm Sun Jun-Sep) was once part of the city walls, and from here you can reach the ruins of the **Roman Circus**, where chariot races were held.

Close to the beach sits the well-preserved **Roman amphitheatre** and on Carrer de Lleida are the remains of a **Roman forum**. The **Passeig Arqueològic** (to midnight) is a peaceful walk along a stretch of the old city walls.

The **cathedral** (Pla de Palau; 10am-1pm & 4-7pm mid-Mar–May, 10am-7pm Jun–mid-Oct, 10am-5pm mid-Oct–mid-Nov, 10am-2pm mid-Nov–mid-Mar) sits at the highest point of Tarragona. Some parts of the building date back to the 12th century.

Clean **Platja del Miracle** is the main city beach, south of the Roman amphitheatre. Other beaches are further on.

PORT AVENTURA

Near Salou, 7km west of Tarragona, is **Universal Studios Port Aventura** (97 777 90 90; www.universalmediterranea.com; adult/child €37/30; 10am-7pm Apr-Oct, Jul & Aug hrs longer, holidays & weekends only Nov-Mar), a US-style theme park, fun for the family or the young at heart. Get there by **Renfe** (www.renfe.es) train.

Sleeping & Eating

Look for tapas bars and inexpensive cafés on the Plaça de la Font. The Moll de Pescadors (Fishermens' Wharf) is the place to go for seafood restaurants.

Hotel Lauria (97 723 67 12; www.hlauria.es; Rambla Nova 20; r around €58;) This three-star hotel is worn around the corners but it's still good value, with a wonderful location and airy rooms. Apartments are also available.

SPAIN

Les Voltes (☎ 97 723 06 51; Carrer Trinquet Vell 12; mains €6.50-12) Nestled under the arches of an ancient edifice, Les Voltes boasts atmosphere and delicious regional specialities.

Getting There & Away

The **train station** (www.renfe.es; Plaça Espanya) is southwest of the old town, on the coast. More than 20 regional trains a day run from Barcelona to Tarragona (€5.40, 1½ hours), making this a great option for a day trip from Barcelona. There are about 12 trains daily to Madrid (€60.40, four hours) and Valencia (€31.30, two hours).

The **bus station** (Avinguda Roma), just off Plaça Imperial Tarraco, has services to regional cities such as Barcelona, and beyond.

ARAGÓN, BASQUE COUNTRY & NAVARRA

The arid hills and proud history of Aragón; the lush coastline and gourmet delights of the Basque Country (País Vasco); the wine country and famous festivals of Navarra: this northeastern area of Spain is brimming with fascinating destinations.

Zaragoza is the capital of the expansive Aragón region, though by no means is the city its only attraction. The parks and pretty towns of the Pyrenees are well worth exploring too.

The Basques, whose language has no known origins and is believed to be among the world's oldest, claim two of Spain's most interesting cities – San Sebastián and Bilbao – as their own. Head to stately San Sebastián for an upscale resort experience and some of the best food Spain has to offer. Visit Bilbao for a look at the majestic Guggenheim Bilbao museum.

Navarra, historically and culturally linked to the Basque Country, is well-known for its fine wines and for hosting the legendary San Fermines festival in Pamplona.

ZARAGOZA

pop 647,300

Sitting on the banks of the once-mighty Ebro River, Zaragoza is a fast growing city that's managed to hold on to its small-town feel. The centre is crowned with the fairytale Basílica del Pilar, and surrounding this place of pilgrimage are the Casco Histórico (Historic Quarter) and El Tubo (literally, The Tube), a maze of streets that hides countless tapas bars and cafés.

Founded by the all-too-modest Caesar Augustus as the Roman city Caesaraugusta, Zaragoza later became a Muslim stronghold, and that culture's influence can be seen in the widespread use of brick as a building material and in the abundance of *Mudéjar*-style architecture. There are many fascinating Roman ruins to visit here as well.

Information

Conecta-T (☎ 97 620 59 79; Calle Murallas Romanas 4; per hr €2; ⏲ 10am-11pm Mon-Fri, 11am-11pm Sat & Sun) Internet access.
Police (☎ 97 672 41 00)
Post office (☎ 97 623 68 68; Paseo de la Independencia 33)
Torreón de la Zuda tourist office (☎ 90 220 12 12; Glorieta Pio 12; ⏲ 10am-2pm & 4.30-8pm) Climb to the top for a small exhibition about Zaragoza and a view of the river bank.
Tourist office (☎ 90 220 12 12; www.turismozaragoza.com; Plaza del Pilar; ⏲ 10am-8pm) Housed in a futuristic glass cube.

Sights

Follow the Roman route through the city, visit the many *Mudéjar* styled buildings and churches, or simply soak up Zaragoza's easy-going atmosphere.

The baroque **Basílica de Nuestra Señora del Pilar** (☎ 97 629 95 64; Plaza del Pilar; admission free; ⏲ 5.45am-8.30pm Sep-Jun, to 9.30pm Jul & Aug) towers over Zaragoza both literally and figuratively. The spiritual heart of Aragón, this has long been a place of pilgrimage. The faithful flock to the **Capilla Santa** to kiss a piece of marble pillar believed to have been left by the Virgin Mary when she visited St James here in AD 40. A beloved statue of the Virgin sits atop the pillar, and her ornate skirt is changed every single day. Inside the Basilica, visit the **Museo Pilarista** (admission €1.50; ⏲ 9am-2pm & 4-6pm), where the skirts are on display.

At Plaza del Pilar's southeastern end is Zaragoza's brooding 12th- to 16th-century cathedral, **La Seo** (☎ 97 629 12 38; Plaza de la Seo; adult/child €2/1; ⏲ 10am-2pm & 4-6pm Tue-Fri, 10am-1pm & 4-6pm Sat, 10am-noon & 4-6pm Sun, 1hr later Jun-Aug). Its northwestern façade is a *Mudéjar*

masterpiece, and inside is an impressive 15th-century main altarpiece in coloured alabaster.

Begin the Roman tour of Zaragoza with a stop at the **Museo del Foro de Caesaraugusta** (☎ 97 639 97 52; Plaza de la Seo; adult/student €2/1.50; ⏲ 10am-2pm & 5-8pm Tue-Sat, 10am-2pm Sun), an interesting museum about Roman life. Some 70m below lie the remains of the Roman town, brought to life by a fantastic audiovisual show. The historically curious can also visit the **Caesaraugusta Theatre** (☎ 97 620 50 88; Calle de San Jorge 12; adult/student €3/2; ⏲ 10am-9pm Tue-Sat, to 2pm Sun), the **Caesaraugusta Public Baths** (☎ 97 629 72 79; Calle San Juan y San Pedro 3-7) and the **Caesaraugusta River Port** (☎ 97 639 31 57; Plaza de San Bruno 8). The Public Baths and River Port have the same admission fee and opening hours as the Foro. If you plan to visit all four museums, buy the Ruta Caesaraugusta (pass per adult/student €6/4.50), available at the sites themselves.

Also well worth visiting is the **Palacio de la Aljafería** (☎ 97 628 96 83; Calle Diputados s/n; admission €3, free Sun; ⏲ 10am-2pm & 4.30-8pm Sat-Wed, 10am-2pm Fri mid-Mar–mid-Oct, 10am-2pm & 4.30-6.30pm Mon-Wed & Sat, 10am-2pm Fri & Sun mid-Oct–mid-Mar), Spain's most outstanding Muslim building outside Andalucía. Built as the palace of the Muslim rulers who held the city from 714 to 1118, it is now home to Aragón's parliament. Guided tours are available.

Tours

The tourist office offers daily **walking tours** (€2) in Spanish from Easter week through to 15 October. Themed **walking tours** (€4) in English are offered Wednesday and Saturday at 10.30am year-round. Call to reserve on ☎90 220 12 12.

Sleeping

On and around the Plaza del Pilar and Av César Augusto you'll find most of the sleeping options.

Hostal Santiago (☎97 639 45 50; Calle Santiago 3-5; s €28, d €40-45;) Neon-green walls add an original touch to this otherwise standard *hostal*. The 26 rooms are cheerful and comparatively spacious, though there's a lingering smoky smell.

Hostal Plaza (☎97 629 48 30; www.hostalplaza-santiago.com; Plaza del Pilar 14; s/d €35/45;) This *hostal*, housed in a distinguished old building on the plaza, offers a great deal. Rooms have pretty décor, small but clean bathrooms and tiled floors.

Hotel Sauce (☎97 620 50 50; www.hotelsauce.com; Calle de Espoz y Mina 33; s €45-64, d €55-91;) Charming and immaculately cared for, the Hotel Sauce is one of the best options in town. Rooms are all different; those in the older section have plush carpet and a Provençal style, while newer rooms have rich dark-wood floors and elegant furnishings.

Eating & Drinking

Good tapas bars are scattered around El Tubo, especially around Plaza Santa Marta, and in La Zona, a trendy area south of the centre.

Mercado Central (Plaza de Lanuza; 8am-2pm) Get your fresh fruit and veggies at Central, the main city market.

La Retama (☎97 639 79 10; Calle Reconquista 4; mains €6.50-10.50; lunch only Mon-Thu, closed Sun) One of the few vegetarian spots around, the all-organic La Retama serves simple soups and salads, as well as more elaborate dishes such as veggie lasagne and quiche.

Casa Juanico (☎97 639 72 52; Calle Santa Cruz 21; mains €7-12; closed Tue) For cheap tapas and a friendly atmosphere, this place can't be beat, and the summer terrace is ideal.

La Sidrería (Calle Cadena 15; mains €7-15) Get self-serve cider at this authentic Asturian cider house. The house speciality is *ternasco* (lamb), served in huge portions.

Casa Portolés (☎97 639 06 65; Calle Santa Cruz 21; mains €10-18; closed Sun dinner & Mon) Next to Casa Juanico, Casa Portolés boasts a traditional air and a refined menu full of local specialities.

Getting There & Away

Zaragoza's modern new train station, Las Delicias (still under construction), offers connections throughout Spain. The high-speed AVE train connects Zaragoza with Madrid (€40, 10 daily, eight non-AVE daily) in under two hours, and with the pre-Pyrenean city of Lleida (€20 to €26, one hour, six daily, 16 non-AVE daily). Other trains head to Barcelona (€24 to €35, three hours, 14 daily), Valencia via Teruel (€21, five hours, three daily) and San Sebastián (€29, four hours, three daily) via Pamplona.

Though construction is underway on the Las Delicias bus terminal, which will one day be the city's one-stop bus stop, at the time of research stations were scattered all over town. The bus company **Agreda** (☎97 622 93 43; www.agredasa.com) runs to most major Spanish cities, including Madrid, from Paseo de María Agustín 7.

ARAGÓN

Once-mighty Aragón is now often overlooked by travellers, but the countryside north of Zaragoza offers some wonderful destinations for nature lovers (especially those with their own transport). Head to the **Parque Nacional de Ordesa** (www.ordesa.net), on Aragón's French border, for excellent hiking. **Torla** (☎tourist office 97 448 61 52; Av Ordsa 4) is the park's gateway town. The **Parque Natural de los Cañones y La Sierra de Guara** (☎97 429 32 01; www.aragob.es in Spanish), outside Huesca, is a paradise for canyoners and climbers. Most of the hotels and restaurants are found in and around the historic town of **Alquézar** (☎tourist office 97 431 82 65; www.somontano.org; Plaza Ramón y Cajal).

You can also visit **Teruel** (☎tourist office 97 860 22 79; Calle Tomás Nogués 1), sitting just between Zaragoza and Valencia, to see beautiful *Mudéjar* architecture.

SAN SEBASTIÁN

The Basque Country's most stylish city, San Sebastián (Donostia in Basque) has the air of an upscale resort, complete with an idyllic location on the shell-shaped Bahía de la

SPAIN

Concha. The natural setting – crystalline waters, a flawless beach, green hills on all sides – is captivating, but the city itself has plenty to offer as well. Head to the buzzing Parte Vieja (Old Quarter) for tempting tapas bars and restaurants showing off the best of Basque cuisine, or stroll the stately boulevards of the newer districts to soak up San Sebastián's refined air.

Information

Donosti-Net (☎ 94 342 58 70; Calle Narrica 3; Internet per hr €3.50; ⏰ 9am-11pm) This is a one-stop travellers' service, with email, office services, travel info and even a spot to leave your luggage (per day €9). English spoken.

Lavomatique (☎ 93 442 38 71; Calle de Iñigo 14; 4kg wash €4; ⏰ 9.30am-1pm & 4-7.30pm Mon-Fri, 10am-2pm Sat) Self-serve laundrette.

Post office (☎ 94 344 68 26; Calle de Urdaneta 7)

Tourist office (☎ 94 348 11 66; www.sansebastianturismo.com; Calle Reina Regente 3; ⏰ 8am-8pm Jun-Sep, 9am-1.30pm & 3.30-7pm Mon-Sat, 10am-2pm Sun Oct-May)

Sights & Activities

San Sebastián's beautiful city beaches, **Playa de la Concha** and **Playa de Ondarreta**, are popular spots year-round. The *paseo* (promenade) stretching along the waterfront is perfect for strolling, and at the far western end of it you'll find Eduardo Chillida's renowned sculpture **Los Peines del Viento** (Combs of the Wind), well worth the longish walk. East of the Urumea River is the somewhat less crowded **Playa de la Zurriola**, popular with surfers. To escape the crowds, take the small **boat** (⏰ 10am-8pm Jun-Sep) to the **Isla de Santa Clara**, an island in the middle of the bay. From here you can enjoy pretty views of the seafront.

For more good views, take the 30-minute walk up to **Monte Urgull**, a hill topped by low castle walls and a statue of Christ. The walk begins at a stairway in Plaza de Zuloaga.

The best vista in San Sebastián is from **Monte Igueldo**. Drive up or catch the **funicular** (☎ 94 321 05 64; return €1.90; ⏰ 11am-6pm Mon, Tue, Thu & Fri, to 8pm Sat & Sun Feb, Mar, Nov & Dec, to 8pm daily Apr-Jun & mid-Sep–Oct, 10am-10pm Jul-Aug) from the western end of the seafront *paseo*. At the top, visit the **Parque de Atracciones** (☎ 94 321 05 64; admission €1.50; ⏰ weekends & Jun-Aug), an old-time funfair.

San Sebastián's best museum (by far) is the **Chillida-Leku** (☎ 94 333 60 06; www.eduardochillida.com; Bº Jauregui 66 Hernani; adult/student €8/6; ⏰ 10.30am-8pm Mon-Sat, to 3pm Sun Jun-Sep, 10.30am-3pm Oct-May), located 10km outside the city centre. An outdoor sculpture garden featuring 40 large-scale works by the famed Basque artist Eduardo Chillida, this is a peaceful place ideal for picnics. To get there, take bus G2, run by **Garayar** (☎ 94 355 66 58), from Calle Okendo.

Kids and adults alike will have fun at San Sebastián's **aquarium** (☎ 94 344 00 99; www.aquariumss.com; Plaza Carlos Blasco de Imaz 1; adult/student/child €10/8/6; ⏰ 10am-8pm Mon-Fri, to 9pm Sat & Sun Easter-Jun & Sep, 10am-7pm Mon-Fri, to 8pm Sat & Sun Oct-Easter, 10am-9pm daily Jul & Aug), which is home to more than 5000 tropical fish, morays, sharks and a variety of other finned creatures.

Tours

The tourist office offers self-guided **audio tours** (☎ 68 742 06 74; www.euskatrip.com) for €10. You can also hop on the **Tourist Train** (☎ 94 342 29 73; Alameda del Blvd 25; adult/child €4.50/2.50; ⏰ 11am-9pm Jul–mid-Sep, 11am-1pm & 4-7pm mid-Sep–Jun) or the **Donosti Tour Tourist Bus** (☎ 69 642 98 47; Calle Reina Regente; adult/child €10/5; ⏰ 11am-8pm Jul & Aug, times vary Sep-Jun).

Sleeping

Countless cheap *pensiones* and *hostales* huddle in the Parte Vieja. This is a great place if you like being in the thick of things, but for more peace and quiet choose a spot south of the Old Quarter.

BUDGET

Pensión San Lorenzo (☎ 94 342 55 16; www.pensionsanlorenzo.com; Calle San Lorenzo 2; r €25-48; 💻) A cheerful place run by friendly folk, the well-located San Lorenzo offers perks such as in-room fridge, toaster, tea/coffee and free wi-fi.

AUTHOR'S CHOICE

Pensión Edorta (☎ 94 342 37 73; www.pensionedorta.com; Calle del Puerto 15; s €30-50, d €60-80, d with shared bathroom €30-60; 💻) The original stone walls and wood-beam ceilings of this 1830s building give Edorta a special charm. Stylish décor, sparkling bathrooms and extras including in-room Internet access make it super comfortable.

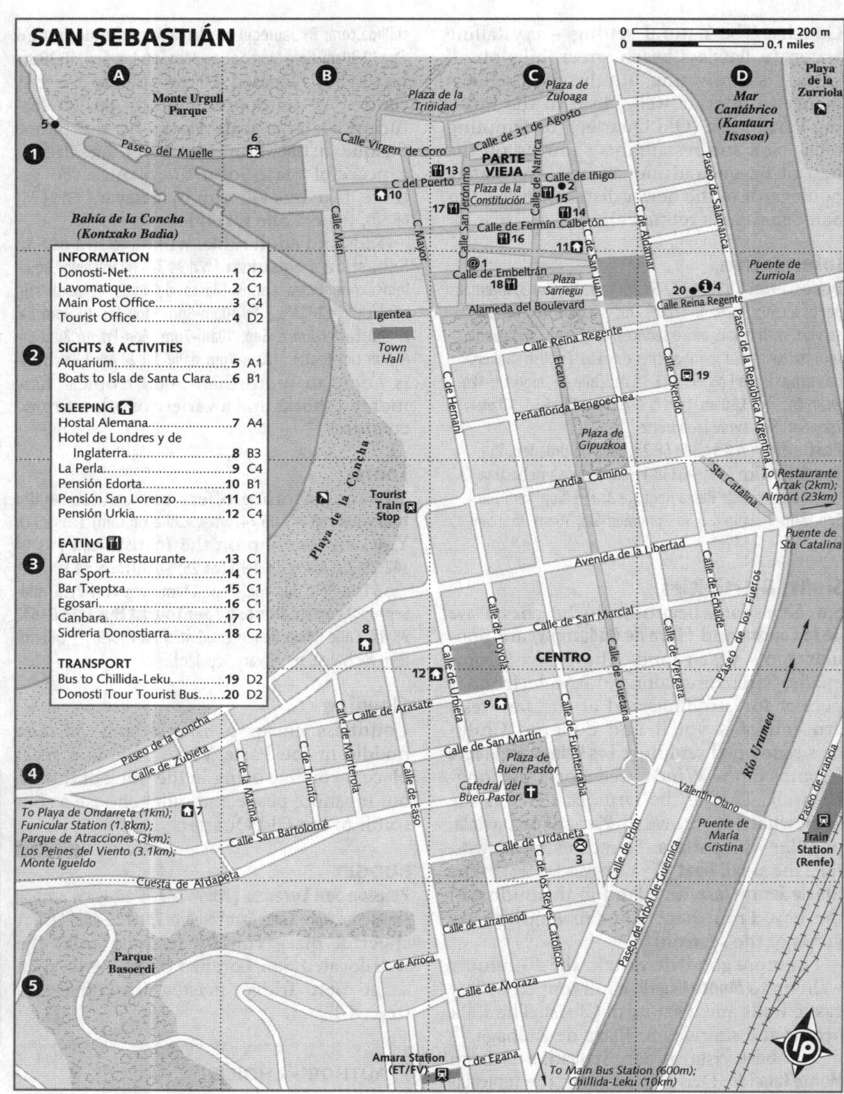

Also recommended:

La Perla (☎ 94 342 81 23; www.pensionlaperla.com; Calle de Loyola 10; s €24-35, d €35-50) Simple furnishings, high ceilings, old-fashioned feel, quiet.

Pensión Urkia (☎ 94 342 44 36; www.pensionurkia.com; Calle de Urbieta 12; s €27-32, d €32-50) Spic 'n' span. Check out big room number four– it has a cute closed-in balcony.

MIDRANGE & TOP END

Hostal Alemana (☎ 94 346 25 44; www.hostalalemana.com; Calle de San Martín 53; s €51-71, d €63-90; 💻) The Alemana is a quiet place with comfortable beds (the all-white linen and duvets are heavenly), spacious rooms, elegant bathrooms and hotel-like perks including key cards, minibars, hair dryers and in-room Internet access. Highly recommended.

Hotel de Londres y de Inglaterra (☎ 94 344 07 70; www.hlondres.com; Calle de Zubieta 2; €100-220; ⊠ ⊠ ⊟) Hands down the best hotel in town, this is a classy place offering breathtaking views of the bay.

Eating

San Sebastián is absolute paradise for food lovers. Considered the birthplace of *nouvelle cuisine* in Spain, this area is home to some of the country's top chefs and is practically a galaxy of Michelin stars. Yet not all the good food is pricey. Head to the Parte Vieja to experience San Sebastián's famed *pintxos*, Basque-style tapas.

PINTXOS

The idea with *pintxo* bars is so wonderfully simple that you'll wonder why it hasn't caught on in the rest of the world. Step one: walk in to a bar that looks appealing. Step two: graze for as long as you like, picking up whatever tiny tapas take your fancy and devour them on the spot. Step three: order glasses of *txakoli* (local fizzy wine) when you get parched. Step four: when you've finished, tell the bartender how many you ate and pay up. Step five: move on to the next bar and begin the process all over again.

Expect *pintxos* to cost between €1 (for simple creations) and €4 (for something more elaborate). Prices aren't often posted, so you may have to ask.

Bar Sport (☎ 94 342 68 88; Calle de Fermín Calbetón 10) You can't go wrong at this informal and ever-crowded bar, where seafood *pintxos* are prepared on the spot.

Bar Txeptxa (☎ 94 342 22 27; Calle Pescadería 5) Famous for its anchovies (they're served countless ways), this tiny bar near Plaza de la Constitución boasts a wall full of prizes and press clippings.

Ganbara (☎ 94 342 25 75; Calle San Jerónimo 21; ⏲ closed Mon) This intimate spot is a great place to be baptized into the world of *pintxos;* the service is friendly and the offerings mix standard ingredients with more daring items, such as spider crab and octopus.

Egosari (☎ 94 342 82 10; Calle de Fermín Calbetón 15; mains €10.50-16.50; ⏲ closed Mon & Thu) Another good choice, here you'll find a wide variety of standard and creative *pintxos*. There's also a formal dining room serving local Basque specialities.

RESTAURANTS

Aralar Bar Restaurante (☎ 94 342 63 78; Calle del Puerto 10; mains €5-14) Offering a wide range of tapas as well as good-value fish and meat dishes, this rustic spot is ideal for a leisurely lunch.

Sidreria Donostiarra (☎ 94 342 04 21; Calle de Embeltrán 5; mains €11-16.50; ⏲ closed dinner Sun & lunch Mon & Tue) Expect a memorable meal at this raucous tavern, where traditional cider is served from the barrel. The typical ciderhouse *menú* includes codfish followed by quince for dessert.

Restaurante Arzak (☎ 94 327 84 65; Av Alcalde Jose Elosegui 273; meal €80-100 without wine; ⏲ closed dinner Sun & Mon, also Tue Jan-Jun) Juan Maria Arzak, the 'father of modern Spanish cuisine', is the chef and owner of this fabulous, three-Michelin-star temple to food. More than a restaurant, it's an experience.

Drinking

The Parte Vieja is a fun place to be any night of the week. Around 8pm the tapas bars start hopping as people enjoy a predinner round of *pintxos*, and the revelry lasts until midnight midweek, and till the cock crows on weekends. Another hot spot is the area around Calle de los Reyes Católicos, behind the Catedral del Buen Pastor.

Getting There & Away

From **San Sebastián airport** (EAS; ☎ 90 240 47 04; www.aena.es), catch the **Interbus** (☎ 94 364 13 02) that runs regularly to the Plaza de Gipuzkoa in town (€3, times vary).

Trains leave the **Renfe station** (www.renfe.es; Paseo de Francia) daily, headed to Madrid (€35, eight hours, four daily), Barcelona (€36 to €46, eight to 10 hours, two daily) and Pamplona (€14 to €17, two hours, three daily), among other destinations. **Eusko Tren** (☎ 90 254 32 10; www.euskotren.es; Calle de Easo) is a private company (international passes not valid) running trains around the region.

The **bus station** (Plaza Pío XII) is a 20-minute walk south of Parte Vieja. City bus 28 makes the run to and from the centre. Get more city bus information from **CTSS** (☎ 94 300 02 00; www.ctss.es). From the station, buses leave for destinations all over Spain. **PESA** (☎ 90

210 12 10; www.pesa.net) has services to Bilbao (€8.30, one hour, up to 27 daily), while **La Roncalesa** (☎ 97 522 44 01) goes to Pamplona (€6, 1¼ hours, up to 12 daily).

BILBAO

pop 350,000

The commercial hub of the Basque Country, Bilbao (Bilbo in Basque) is best-known for the magnificent Guggenheim Museum. An architectural masterpiece by Frank Gehry, the museum was the catalyst of a turn-around that saw Bilbao transformed from an industrial port city into a vibrant cultural centre. After visiting this must-see temple to modern art, spend time exploring Bilbao's Casco Viejo (Old Quarter), a grid of elegant streets dotted with shops, cafés, *pintxos* bars and several small but worthy museums.

Information

Left Luggage (🕒 7am-10pm Mon-Fri, 8am-9pm Sat & Sun; lockers per day €1) At Termibus bus station.

Police (☎ 092, 94 420 50 00; Calle Luis Briñas 14)

Postal Transfer (☎ 94 415 30 42; Calle Santa Maria 5; Internet per hr €1.50; 🕒 9am-10pm Mon-Sat, noon-11pm Sun) Run by the state post office, this is the place to come to send packages, receive faxes or connect cheaply to the Internet.

Teatro Arriaga tourist office (☎ 94 479 57 60; www.bilbao.net; Teatro Arriaga, Paseo del Arenal; 🕒 9.30am-2pm & 4-7.30pm Mon-Sat, 9.30am-2pm Sun Jun-Sep, 11am-2pm & 5-7.30pm Mon-Fri, 9.30am-2pm & 5-7.30pm Sat, 9.30am-2pm Sun Oct-May) There's also an information kiosk beside the Guggenheim.

Sights

Designed by Frank Gehry, the spectacular **Guggenheim Museum** (☎ 94 435 90 80; www.guggenheim-bilbao.es; Abandoibarra Et 2; adult/student €10.50/6.50, child under 12 free; 🕒 10am-8pm Tue-Sun year-round, 10am-8pm Mon Jul & Aug) is an experience to remember. The building itself, undulating forms covered in titanium scales, was inspired by the shapes of ships and fish, two of Bilbao's traditional industries. Inside, the guts of the building are exposed, with few columns, support beams or, for that matter, floors and walls obstructing the view. Many credit this creation with revitalising modern architecture and creating a new standard in vanguard design.

To dig further into the local culture, head to the **Euskal Museoa** (Basque Museum; ☎ 94 415 54 23; www.euskal-museoa.org; Plaza Miguel Unamuno 4; adult/student €3/1.50; 🕒 11am-5pm Tue-Sat, to 2pm Sun), a museum documenting the history and lifestyle of the Basque people.

Take the metro to the **Puente Colgante** (Hanging Bridge; ☎ 94 463 88 54; www.puente-colgante.com; Calle Barria 3, Las Arenas Getxo; 🕒 10am-sunset) to walk or, better yet, ride across on the gondola (€0.50 to €1) that hangs from the world's oldest 'transporter bridge'. The walkers' view from the top is great.

Sleeping

Pensión La Estrella (☎ 94 416 40 66; Calle María Muñoz 6; s/d/tr €30/48/65) With the style of a boutique hotel, this fabulous 1st-floor walk-up boasts spotless rooms and a beautifully renovated façade and entryway.

Hostal Begoña (☎ 94 423 01 34; www.hostalbegona.com; Calle Amistad 2; s €38-48, d €48-61; 💻) This place has a hotel feel with a *pensión* price. It has great bathrooms and tasteful décor.

Bilbao Jardines (☎ 94 479 42 10; www.hotelbilbaojardines.com; Calle Jardines 9; s €40-60, d €60-80, tr €75-95; 💻) Opened in March 2005, this stylish two-star hotel offers tidy rooms and friendly service in the heart of the Casco Viejo. No wonder it's a hit with travellers.

Iturrienea Ostatua (☎ 94 416 15 00; Calle Santa María 14; s €50-60, d €60-66, tr €80; 💻) Pretty décor, balconies and original architectural elements such as stone walls and wood-beam ceilings give this B&B unbeatable charm.

Eating

Rio-Oja (☎ 94 415 08 71; Calle Perro 4; mains €6-12; 🕒 closed Mon) *Pintxos,* stews, local fish dishes and typical Basque cuisine are on offer at this wallet-friendly spot near the Catedral de Santiago.

Restaurante Victor (☎ 94 415 16 78; Plaza Nueva 2; mains €8-15) This very popular rustic spot has checked green tablecloths and hardy Basque fare.

Victor Montes (☎ 94 415 70 67; www.victormontesbilbao.com; Plaza Nueva 8; mains €9-16) Downstairs this is an informal *pintxos* bar packed with locals. Head upstairs for the intimate dining room, where Basque specialities such as *bacalao pil-pil* (cod in olive oil sauce) are served with style.

Drinking

Las Siete Calles, the seven parallel streets on the southern end of the Casco Viejo,

ETA

The Basque terrorist group ETA, which stands for Euskadi Ta Askatasuna or 'Basque Homeland and Freedom', has killed more than 800 people since its bloody campaign for independence began in 1961, during the Franco dictatorship. In 2006 the group announced a cease-fire and claimed to be willing to pursue peace. Only time will tell if they mean it this time.

are transformed into one big street party at night. Bars and discos line the streets, especially rowdy Calle Barrenkale. For something a bit more low-key, take your pick of the cafés on Plaza Nueva.

Getting There & Away

Bilbao airport (BIO; ☎ 90 240 47 04; www.aena.es) is the international gateway to the Basque Country and is well-served by budget airlines, including easyJet and Vueling. From the airport, bus 3247 (€1.15, 25 minutes) leaves every half-hour from 6.15am until midnight and drops you off at the Termibus bus station, where there is a tram stop and a metro station.

Bilbao has two train stations, both located beside the river. **Renfe** (www.renfe.es) offers services to Madrid (€32 to €42, six to eight hours, three daily) and Barcelona (€38 to €49, nine hours, two daily).

The national narrow-gauge railway line, **Feve** (www.feve.es), has train services heading westward to Cantabria and beyond. Often enough these bumpy rides take considerably longer than the bus trip to the same destinations.

Bilbao's main bus station (Termibus) is west of town, but sits just next to the San Mamés metro/tram stop, a five-minute ride from the city centre. **PESA** (☎ 90 210 12 10; www.pesa.net) operates services to San Sebastián (€8.30, one hour, up to 27 daily). **Alsa** (☎ 90 242 22 42; www.alsa.es) operates buses to Santander (€4.65 to €10.65, 90 minutes, up to 27 daily) while **La Unión** (☎ 94 439 50 77) heads to Pamplona (€11.20, two hours, up to six daily).

Bilbao has an outstanding public transport system, with an easy-to-follow web of trains, trams and buses crisscrossing the city and heading into the countryside.

PAMPLONA

Immortalized by Ernest Hemingway in *The Sun Also Rises,* the busy pre-Pyrenean city of Pamplona (Iruña in Basque) is, of course, the home of the wild Sanfermines (aka Encierro or Running of the Bulls) festival, but it's also an extremely walkable city that's managed to mix the charm of old plazas and buildings with modern shops and a lively nightlife.

This is the capital of Navarra, but there are few noteworthy sights in town, which means you can party all night and not feel guilty for whiling the day away in the street cafés. Make an exception for the **cathedral** (☎ 94 821 08 27; 🕒 10am-1.30pm & 4-7pm Mon-Fri, 10am-1.30pm Sat), a 14th-century Gothic creation with a neoclassical façade.

Information

Kuria.net (☎ 94 822 30 77; Calle Curia 15; per hr €3; 🕒 10am-10pm) Internet access.

Left Luggage (🕒 6.15am-9.30pm Mon-Sat, 6.30am-1.30pm & 2-9.30pm Sun) Leave bags at the bus station for €3 per day.

Police (☎ 092)

Tourist office (☎ 84 842 04 20; www.navarra.es; Calle Eslava 1; 🕒 10am-2pm & 4-7pm Mon-Sat, 10am-2pm Sun) Don't expect this otherwise helpful office to provide much guidance during ultracrowded Sanfermines (it's open 8am to 8pm daily during the festival).

Sleeping

Accommodation is expensive and hard to come by during Sanfermines; you'll need to book months in advance. Prices below don't reflect the huge (up to 300%) markup you'll find in mid-July.

Pensión Escaray (☎ 94 822 78 25; jescaray@pnte.cfnavarra.es; Calle Nueva 25; s/d with shared bathroom €18/36) This is a friendly, family-run spot with some antique furniture and old-fashioned style. Rooms boast wide wooden floorboards and high ceilings.

Hotel Castillo de Javier (☎ 94 820 30 40; www.hotelcastillodejavier.com; Calle San Nicolás 50-52; s €40, d €55-61) Rooms are on the small side here, but with the modern furnishings, new bathrooms and a superb location, we're not complaining.

Hostal Navarra (☎ 94 822 51 64; www.hostalnavarra.com; Calle Tudela 9; s/d €45/60; ⊠ 💻) With all the extras you'd expect from a hotel, the great-value Navarra is a stylish family-run place near the bus station. A fabulous choice.

SURVIVING SANFERMINES

The madcap Sanfermines festival is held 6–14 July, when the city is overrun with thrill-seekers, curious onlookers and, oh yeah, bulls. The Encierro (Running of the Bulls) begins at 8am daily, when bulls are let loose from the Coralillos Santo Domingo. The 825m race lasts just three minutes, so don't be late. The safest place to watch the Encierro is on TV. If that's too tame for you, try to sweet-talk your way onto a balcony or book a room in a hotel with views.

Eating & Drinking

Central streets such as Calle San Nicolás and Calle Estafeta are lined with tapas bars, many of which morph into nightspots on weekends.

Sagardotega Iruñazarra (☎ 94 822 51 67; Calle Mercaderes 15; mains €7.50-18) Most cider houses are out in the countryside, but this one delivers real rustic flavour in the heart of the city. Locals come especially for the €25 cider menu (with all the cider you can catch in your cup).

Bar Otano (☎ 94 822 50 95; Calle Nicolás 5; mains €8-19) Though it's known for its varied *pintxos*, Otano is also a great spot for roasted and grilled meats.

Mesón Pirineo (☎ 94 820 77 02; Calle Estafeta 41; mains €9-18) This rustic tavern offers a solid selection of Basque- and Navarran-style dishes, such as hake in green sauce with clams.

Restaurant Saraste (☎ 94 822 57 27; Calle San Nicolás 21; menú €10-15) Salads, couscous, quiche, pasta…this is one of the few restaurants in Pamplona that caters to vegetarians.

Café Iruña (☎ 94 822 20 64; Plaza Castillo 44; menú €12) This old Hemingway haunt was mentioned 14 times in *The Sun Also Rises*. It's a popular spot for breakfast, coffee or a light meal.

Bar Baserri (☎ 94 822 20 21; www.restaurantebaserri.com; Calle San Nicolás 32; pintxos €2-5, menú €12.50-22) One of the better-known *pintxos* bars, Baserri uses seasonal, local ingredients to create innovative tapas.

Getting There & Away

Renfe (www.renfe.es) trains arrive daily from Madrid (€48.50, four hours). Bus 9 connects the station with the centre.

Several companies operate out of Pamplona's central bus station near Plaza Castilla. **Burundesa** (☎ 94 822 17 66; www.laburundesa.com) heads to Bilbao (€11.60, two hours, five daily) and Vitoria (€6.80, 90 minutes, up to 11 daily). It also offers occasional services to Santander, Irun and the surfing town Zarautz. Find more information at www.autobusesdenavarra.com (in Spanish).

CANTABRIA, ASTURIAS & GALICIA

With a landscape reminiscent of parts of the British Isles, 'Green Spain' offers great walks in national parks, seafood feasts in sophisticated towns and oodles of opportunities to plunge into the ice-cold waters of the Bay of Biscay. Oh, and there's loads of rain, too.

SANTANDER

pop 183,184

Staid Santander has a relatively pretty centre, but its main drawcard is **El Sardinero**, a beach that is wildly popular with locals during summer. The town is as quiet as a graveyard for the rest of the year.

Information

Ciberlope (Calle Lope de Vega 14; Internet per hr €2; 10.30am-midnight Mon-Fri, 11.30am-midnight Sat, 5pm-midnight Sun)

Municipal tourist office (☎ 94 220 30 00; www.ayto-santander.es; Jardines de Pereda; 9.30am-1.30pm & 4-7pm Mon-Fri, 10am-2pm Sat)

Regional tourism office (☎ 94 231 07 08; http://turismodecantabria.com; Calle de Hernán Cortés 4; 9.30am-1.30pm & 4-7pm) In the Mercado del Este.

Sleeping

Hospedaje La Porticada (☎ 94 222 78 17; www.hlaporticada.com; 1st fl, Calle Méndez Núnez 6; s €28-48, d €34-48, with shared bathroom s €21-39, d €27-39) The closest thing Santander has to a backpacker hostel, this place near the bus and train stations is run by a friendly guy who makes a real effort to make it as welcoming, clean and comfortable as possible. Five of the rooms have balconies overlooking the water.

Pensión La Corza (☎ 94 221 29 50; 3rd fl, Calle de Hernán Cortés 25; d €33-50, with shared bathroom €27-40) It can be disconcerting to encounter the

SPAIN

resident pyjama-clad grandma and granddad watching TV in the lounge, but this sprawling family-run apartment is in a great position and offers clean and comfortable rooms for reasonable prices.

Eating & Drinking

Café de Pombo (☎ 94 222 32 24; Calle de Hernán Cortés 21) This elegant place occupies a prime spot on the main square and has been serving locals breakfast (coffee €1, croissant €1.30) for decades. The *picoteo* (small breakfast rolls) are delicious and the terrace is a great spot for people watching.

Arrabal 11 (☎ 94 207 43 62; Calle Arrabal 11; pintxos from €1.50; 🕒 9am-midnight Mon-Sat) Forget the rustic and often barely edible food dished out in Santander's traditional *bodegas* – the tapas choices on offer at this stylish and friendly bar are a far more attractive proposition. You'll find it halfway between Plaza Porticada and the Plaza de Pombo.

Old Santander is full of traditional-style *mesónes* (inns) and *bodegas* where you can drink, eat or do both. Two of the best are **Bodega Cigaleña** (☎ 94 221 30 62; Calle de Daoiz y Velarde 19; mains €15; 🕒 closed Sun) and **Cañadío** (☎ 94 231 41 49; Calle Gómez Oreña 15; mains €21).

The main entertainment precincts are the Puerto Chico area in the centre and the Vargas area near the train station.

Getting There & Away

Santander's ferry port is one of Spain's largest, and regular **Brittany ferries** (☎ 94 236 06 11; www.brittanyferries.co.uk) arrive here from the UK between April and November.

From the **bus station** (☎ 94 221 19 95; www.santandereabus.com; Plaza Estaciones), you can travel to Madrid on Continental-Auto (€25.60, 5½ hours, six daily) via Burgos (€10, three hours). Alsa has regular services to Bilbao (€6.05 to €11.10, 1½ hours).

Renfe trains travel to Madrid (€24.45 to €47.90, 5½ to 8½ hours, four daily) via Ávila (€18.85 to €40.60). **Feve** (☎ 94 221 16 87; www.feve.es) trains are usually slower than the bus, but are a scenic way to get to and from Bilbao (€6.75, 2½ hours, three daily).

AROUND SANTANDER

Thirty kilometres southwest of Santander is the fascinating **Cueva de Altamira**, a 270m-long cave of prehistoric paintings that's been dubbed the Sistine Chapel of the prehistoric world. The waiting list to get into the cave is years long, but you can visit an excellent on-site **museum** (☎ 94 281 80 05; http://museodealtamira.mcu.es; adult/child €2.50/free, free after 2.30pm Sat & all day Sun; 🕒 9.30am-5pm Tue-Sat, to 3pm Sun Oct-May, 9.30am-7.30pm Tue-Sat, to 3pm Sun Jun-Sep), which features good replicas of the cave art.

Getting There & Away

Catch a morning bus (€3.90 return) from Santander's bus station to Santilla del Mar, from where you can pick up a taxi to take you the 2km to Altamira.

LA CORUÑA

pop 243,088

A lively port city adorned with 19th-century houses with distinctive *galerías* (glassed-in balconies), La Coruña (A Coruña in Gallego) has an insouciant and welcoming air. It is also a fabulous place to sample the seafood dishes that Galicia is so famous for.

Information

Municipal tourist office (☎ 98 118 43 44; www.turismocoruna.com; Plaza María Pita; 🕒 9am-2.30pm & 4-8.30pm Mon-Fri, 10am-2pm & 4-8pm Sat, 10am-3pm Sun)

Regional tourist office (☎ 98 122 18 22; Dársena de la Marina; 🕒 10am-2pm & 4-7pm Mon-Fri, 11am-2pm & 5-7pm Sat, 11am-2pm Sun)

Videoclub/Marina 21 (Av de la Marina 21; Internet per hr €1.50; 🕒 10am-2pm & 5-9.30pm Mon-Sat)

Sights

With so much ocean around, beaches are naturally a major part of La Coruña's attraction. The main beach, **Playa del Orzán**, runs along the western border of the town centre.

The city's best-known and best-loved monument is the **Torre de Hércules** (☎ 98 122 37 30; Av Navarra; adult/child €2/free, free 3rd Sat of month Oct-Jun; 🕒 10am-5.45pm Oct-Mar, to 6.45pm Apr-Jun & Sep, to 8.45pm Jul & Aug), which locals claim is the oldest functioning lighthouse in the world. The 18th-century tower that stands today was built over Roman foundations. The climb is steep (232 steps) and the view from the top is wonderful. The tower is a one-hour walk from town; alternatively buses 3 and 3A (€0.96) will take you there from the Dársena de la Marina.

Sleeping & Eating

Pensión Residencia Alboráan (☎ 98 122 65 79; r.alboran@gmail.com; Calle Riego de Agua 14; s €23-26, d €33-46) The four floors of this *pensión* off Plaza María Pita are filled with freshly painted, attractively decorated rooms complete with small bathrooms. Good-sized but noisy front rooms have lovely French doors and balconies; the tiny singles are dark and claustrophobic.

Hostal Residencia La Provinciana (☎ 98 122 04 00; www.laprovinciana.net; 2nd fl, Rúa Nueva 9; s €27-35, d €36-47; P) Extremely comfortable rooms with spotless bathrooms are on offer in this large 1970s apartment. Recommended.

La Barra El Huerto (☎ 98 192 33 32; Calle Riego de Agua 33-35; tapas €3-6.50) This sleek and modern bar serves a large selection of wines by the glass (€2.50 to €3) and tapas to glammed-up locals. It's also a good spot for breakfast (toast, coffee and fresh orange juice €3).

Pizzería da Alberto (☎ 98 121 40 82; Calle de la Franja 23; pizza €4-7; 11am-1am) This tiny, fluorescent-lit place serves up pizza good enough to stand up and be counted in Naples. You can order by the slice or by the pie, and draft beer is available for €1.50. *Delizioso!*

Mesón do Pulpo (☎ 98 120 24 44; Calle Franja 9-11; mains €8-10) This is the best place in town to try the local speciality, *pulpo gallego* (spicy boiled octopus dressed with paprika, rock salt, garlic and olive oil).

Bodega Priorato (☎ 98 122 70 51; Calle de la Franja 16A) This is the real thing: an unassuming and phenomenally popular *bodega* where wine is served in a *porrón* (glass jug with a long thin spout through which wine is poured into the mouth) and where locals throw peanut shells onto the sawdust-covered floor with aplomb. Go.

SPAIN

Getting There & Away

From the **bus station** (☎ 98 118 43 35; Calle Caballeros 21), **Castromil** (☎ 90 229 29 00) travels to Santiago de Compostela (€6.15, one hour, at least 10 daily). Alsa travels to Madrid (€36.40 to €51.60, six to eight hours, 11 daily) via Burgos (€37.60).

From the **train station** (Av de Alfonso Molina), there are regular services to Santiago de Compostela (€3.40 to €4.60, 50 minutes to one hour, hourly). There are also two trains per day between La Coruña and Madrid (€44.80 to €58.90, 8¾ hours to 10¼ hours), stopping en route in Ávila (€40.60 to €53.70).

Local buses 1 and 1A (€0.96) follow a route between the train and bus stations and Av de la Marina in the centre of town.

SANTIAGO DE COMPOSTELA

pop 92,703

The supposed burial place of Saint James, Santiago (as it is commonly known) is the most beautiful city in Spain. Christian pilgrims journeying along the Camino de Santiago often end up mute with wonder on entering its medieval centre and encountering the utterly magnificent Catedral del Apóstol. Fortunately, they usually regain their verbal capacities over a celebratory late-night foray into the city's lively bar scene.

Information

Camino de Santiago information (Xacobeo; ☎ 90 233 20 10; www.xacobeo.es; Rúa do Vilar 30; 10am-8pm Mon-Fri)

CyberNova 50 (Rúa Nova 50; Internet per hr €1.50; 9am-midnight)

Municipal tourist office (☎ 98 155 51 29; www.santiagoturismo.com; Rúa do Vilar 63; 9am-2pm & 4-7pm Oct-May, 9am-9pm Jun-Sep)

Sights

The **Catedral del Apóstol** (☎ 98 156 05 27; Plaza do Obradoiro; 7am-9pm), a superb Romanesque creation of the 11th to 13th centuries, is the heart and soul of Santiago. It's said that St James' remains were buried here in the 1st century AD and rediscovered in 813. Today, visitors line up to kiss his statue, which sits behind the main altar. Mass is held at noon and 6pm daily. The **Museo da Catedral** (admission €5; 10am-1.30pm & 4-6.30pm Mon-Sat, 10am-1.30pm Sun) includes the cathedral's cloisters, treasury and crypt, as well as the Pazo de Xelmírez, a bishop's palace built in 1120. Note that the museum sells its last tickets one hour before official closing times.

To get a grasp on local culture, visit the **Museo do Pobo Galego** (☎ 98 158 36 20; www.museodopobo.es; Rúa San Domingos de Bonaval; admission free; 10am-2pm & 4-8pm Mon-Sat, 11am-2pm Sun), housed in the attractive former Convento de San Domingos de Bonaval.

The **Museo das Peregrinacións** (☎ 98 158 15 58; www.mdperegrinacions.com; Rúa de San Miguel 4; admis-

sion free; 10am-8pm Tue-Fri, 10.30am-1.30pm & 5-8pm Sat, 10.30am-1.30pm Sun) explores the pilgrim culture that has so shaped Santiago. Look out for the fascinating illuminated map showing pilgrimage destinations across the world.

Sleeping

Meiga Backpackers Hostel (☎ 98 157 08 46; www.meiga-backpackers.es; 3rd fl, Fonte de San Antonio 25; dm €14-15; ⊠) A newcomer to the Santiago sleeping scene, Meiga is sure to become a permanent fixture if it maintains its excellent standards. It offers four-, six- and eight-bed dorms with bunk beds and two squeaky-clean shared bathrooms. There's a well-equipped communal kitchen, a small but comfortable lounge, and a muffin-and-coffee breakfast is included in the rate.

Hostal Suso (☎ 98 158 66 11; Rúa do Vilar 65; s €19-20, d €35-39) This place is a real bargain! Its recently renovated rooms feature marble bathrooms and comfortable beds.

Hotel Virxe da Cerca (☎ Madrid 90 240 58 58; www.pousadasdecompostela.com; Rúa da Virxe da Cerca 27; s €70-113, d €81-123; Ⓟ) Housed in a converted Jesuit monastery, this hotel is notable for its tranquil rear garden, exemplary service and extremely comfortable rooms.

Hotelería & Restauración Sino (☎ 98 155 44 36; www.sino-compostela.com; Praciña de Arriba 5; s €75, d €75-120, all incl breakfast; ⊠) This very stylish boutique hotel is an alluring and well-priced addition to the town's midrange accommodation scene. Fifteen quiet rooms have parquet floors and well-equipped bathrooms. There's a lovely communal lounge with leather couches, a large-screen satellite TV and an Internet terminal, as well as a top-notch restaurant and bar (mains €13 to €21, menú €15).

Eating

O Dezaseis (☎ 98 156 48 80; Rúa de San Pedro 16; raciónes €3-9.50, mains €10.50-12) Near the Museo do Pobo Galego, this small eatery serves an extremely popular *menú* for €11.

Istanbul Döner Kebap (Av Rosalía de Castro 5; kebabs €3.50) The town's student population swears by the huge takeaway kebabs served up here.

Gato Negro Taberna (☎ 98 158 31 05; Rúa da Raiña; raciónes €4-8.50) This rough-as-guts

SPAIN

place serves up hefty slabs of potato-and-sardine-packed *empanada* (savoury pie) for €2.50. Served with a glass of Estrella Galicia (€1.50), they make a super-cheap and satisfying meal.

Pizza Polo (☎ 98 158 72 72; Rúa das Casas Reais 27; pizza €6) Another tasty and cheap takeaway option, Polo offers pizza of the day.

Casa Camilo (☎ 98 158 45 93; Calle Raiña 24; menú €13.50) Seafood is the local speciality, and this long-running restaurant is a good place to sample it. The fish-laden *menú* is very good value.

Casa Marcelo (☎ 98 155 85 80; Rua Hortas 1; meals €40; closed Sun-Tue) Santiago's best restaurant is nestled in the shadow of the cathedral. Its 'rustic chic' interior is only marginally less impressive than its delectable Michelin-rated set menu, which features Galician produce and changes every day.

Drinking

The old quarter is home to atmospheric bars and pubs popular with the city's large student population. Some of the best spots are around the Rúa da Conga, the Rúa San Paio de Antealtares and the Plaza Cervantes.

Casa de Xantar (☎ 98 158 19 09; Calle da Troia 10) Here you'll find a laid-back student vibe and cheap drinks accompanied by complimentary tapas.

A Taberna do Bispo (☎ 98 157 75 03; Rúa Villar 35) At this perennially packed place you'll encounter the most impressive array of tapas in town.

Getting There & Around

From the **airport** (SCQ; ☎ 98 154 75 01; www.aena.es), **Empresa Freire** (☎ 98 158 81 11) buses travel to the bus station and to Rúa do Doutor Teixeiro close to Plaza de Galicia. The service operates between 7.15am and 11.30pm on Monday to Friday and 8.30am and 10pm on Saturday and Sunday. A ticket costs €1.70. A taxi costs around €16.

From the **bus station** (☎ 98 154 24 16; Calle San Caetano) you can hop on bus 5 to get to Plaza de Galicia. Alsa buses travel to León (€23.95 to €24.65, 6½ hours, one daily) and Madrid (€37.70 to €52.70, 6¾ to 9½ hours, at least three daily). Both Castromil and Alsa have regular services to La Coruña (€5.95 to €6.15, one hour).

From the **train station** (Av de Lugo), trains go to La Coruña (€3.30 to €11.50, one hour, hourly) and Madrid (€40.50, eight hours, two daily). It's a 15-minute walk from the station to central Plaza de Galicia.

VALENCIA & MURCIA

A warm climate, an abundance of seaside resorts, and interesting cities make this area of Spain a popular destination. The beaches of the Costa Blanca (White Coast) draw most of the visitors, but venture beyond the shore to get a real feel for the region.

VALENCIA

pop 796,550

The birthplace of paella, the home of the Holy Grail and the host of the 2007America's Cup, Valencia is a friendly, if slightly chaotic city. Hugging the now dry Turia River (whose riverbed has been transformed into a wonderfully verdant park), Valencia may be Spain's third-largest city, but it's an extremely walkable place that combines old and new with effortless charm.

Head to the Barrio del Carmen, Valencia's oldest quarter, for quirky shops and the best nightlife. Other key areas are the Plaza del Ayuntamiento, the Plaza de la Reina and the Plaza Virgen.

Information

America's Cup information office (☎ 96 346 2007; www.americascup.com; Edificio Varadero, Port America's Cup)

Ono Centro de Internet (☎ 96 328 19 02; Calle San Vicente 22; per hr €2-3; 9am-1am)

Post office (☎ 96 351 23 70; Plaza del Ayuntamiento 24)

Tourist office (www.turisvalencia.es); Main office (☎ 96 398 64 22; Calle Paz 48; 9am-2.30pm & 4.30-8pm Mon-Fri); Estación del Norte (☎ 96 352 85 73; Calle Jativa; 9am-7pm Mon-Sat, 10am-2pm Sun); Plaza de la Reina (☎ 96 315 39 31; Plaza de la Reina 19; 9am-7pm Mon-Sat, 10am-2pm Sun)

Sights & Activities

You'll see Valencia's best face by simply wandering around the **Barrio del Carmen**, strolling the **Jardínes del Turia** or people watching in one of the city's many plazas.

But don't leave without a visit to the Romanesque-Gothic-baroque-Renaissance **cathedral** (☎ 96 391 81 27; Plaza Reina; 7.30am-8pm). Most interesting is the Holy Grail Chapel, which houses the chalice Christ

SPAIN

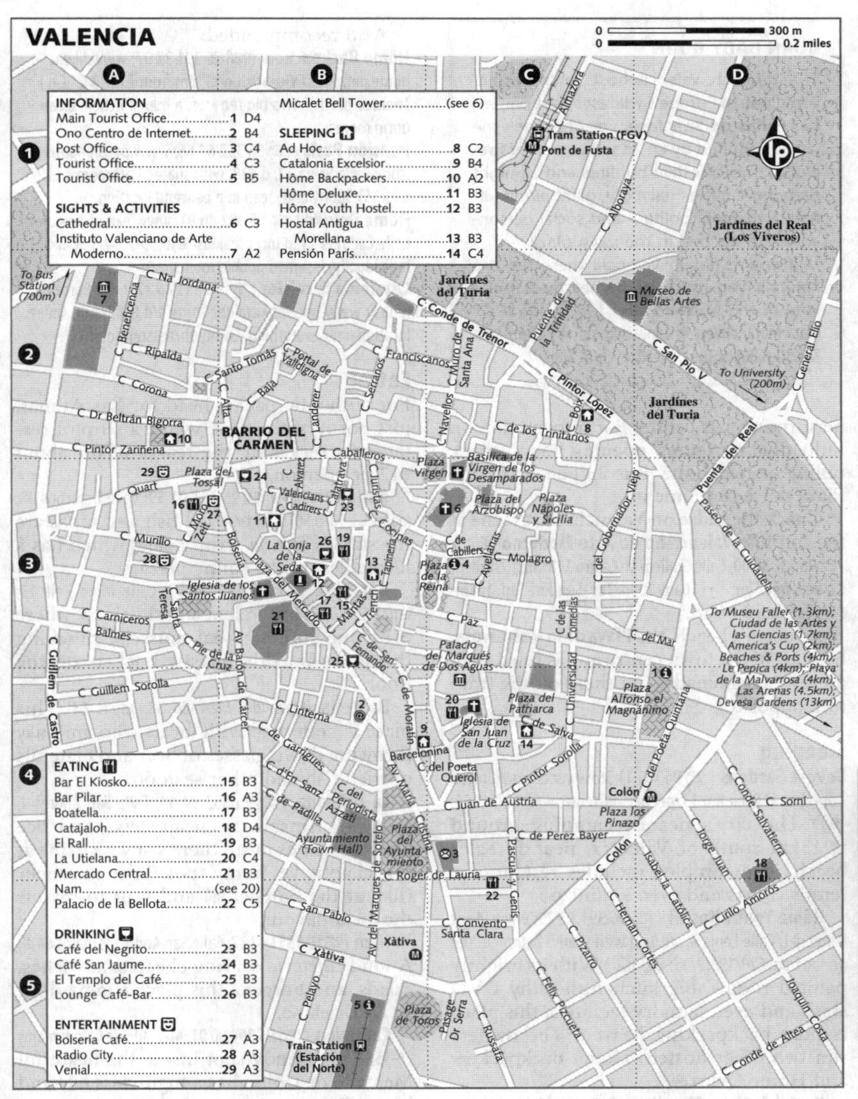

supposedly used in the last supper. It's the only Holy Grail recognised by the Vatican. Also interesting is the withered left arm of St Vincent and the **Micalet bell tower** (admission €2; 🕓 10.30am-6.30pm). Climb up for sweeping views of the city. Obligatory guided tours of the cathedral (€3) are conducted between 10am and 6.30pm.

Valencia's architectural pride and joy, the stunning **Ciudad de las Artes y las Ciencias** (☎ 90 210 00 31; www.cac.es; adult €7.50-29, student €6-22; 🕓 10am-9pm) is a large complex of museums including the L'Oceanográfic aquarium, the Príncipe Felipe science museum, L'Hemisféric IMAX theatre, L'Umbracle covered garden, and the Palau Reina Sofía

BURN BABY BURN

In mid-March, Valencia hosts what has become one of Europe's wildest street parties: **Las Fallas de San José.** For one week the city is engulfed by an anarchic swirl of fireworks, music, festive bonfires and all-night partying. On the final night, giant *niñots* (effigies), many of political and social personages, are torched in the main plaza.

If you're not in Valencia then, see the *niñots* saved from the flames by popular vote at the **Museu Faller** (☎ 96 352 54 78; Plaza Monteolivete 4; admission €2; ⏰ 10am-2pm & 4.30-8.30pm Tue-Sat, 10am-3pm Sun).

performing arts centre. For information on individual museums' opening hours, check online or telephone. Bus 35 goes from the Plaza del Ayuntamiento.

Check the pulse on Valencia's art scene at the **Instituto Valenciano de Arte Moderno** (IVAM; ☎ 96 386 30 00; Calle Guillem de Castro 118; adult/student €2/free, free Sun; ⏰ 10am-10pm Tue-Sun Jun-Sep, 10am-8pm Tue-Sun Oct-May).

Valencia's beach, the **Playa de la Malvarrosa,** lies east of the town centre and is lined with a pretty promenade. Get there on the tram (see opposite).

Sleeping

Devesa Gardens (☎ 96 161 11 36; www.devesagardens.com; Ctra El Saler Km 13; per person/tent/car €5.50/5/5.50; 🅿) The city's nearest camping ground is 13km south of Valencia, near El Saler beach. The complex includes restaurants, tennis courts and even a minizoo.

Hôme Youth Hostel (☎ 96 391 62 29; www.likeathome.net; Calle Lonja 4; s/d/tr/q with shared bathroom per person from €20/19/17/15; ⊠ 💻) With its brightly painted rooms, big kitchen, healthy DVD stash and even laundry facilities, this place is pure backpacking heaven. The owners run two other hostels, Hôme Backpackers and Hôme Deluxe.

Hostal Antigua Morellana (☎ 96 391 57 73; www.hostalam.com; Calle En Bou 2; s €38-48, d €48-58; ⊠ ❄) In an elegant renovated 18th-century building, this helpful hotel has cosy, good-sized rooms with satellite TV and balconies.

Ad Hoc (☎ 96 391 91 40; www.adhochoteles.com; Calle Boix 4; r €80-180; ❄) This charming boutique hotel has stencilled ceilings, pretty balconies and fabulous colour schemes.

Also recommended:

Hôme Backpackers (☎ 96 391 37 97; www.likeathome.net; Plaza Vicente Iborra; dm from €12; ⊠ 💻) Themed parties, two big terraces, a huge kitchen, clean dorm rooms.

Pensión Paris (☎ 96 352 67 66; www.pensionparis.com; Calle Salvá 12; d €38, with shared bathroom s €20, d €30-35) Sunny and clean in a peaceful location.

Hôme Deluxe (☎ 96 392 46 91; www.likeathome.net; Calle Cadirers 11; d incl breakfast €40; ⊠ 💻) Stylish, individually designed double rooms.

Catalonia Excelsior (☎ 96 351 46 12; Calle Barcelonina 5; www.hoteles-catalonia.com; s/d €103/128) Quiet location near everything. Comfy three-star hotel.

Eating

For authentic paella, head for Las Arenas, just north of the port, where a strip of restaurants serves up the real stuff for about €12 per person.

Bar El Kiosko (☎ 96 391 01 59; Calle Derechos 38; mains €1.50-6.50) Tasty fried fish and tapas are the staples at this scruffy café, which has a few tables on the sunny plaza.

Bar Pilar (☎ 96 391 04 97; Calle Moro Zeit 13; tapas €2-10) This Valencian classic is where everyone comes to eat mussels, chucking the shells into the plastic buckets on the floor.

Boatella (Plaza del Mercado 33; tapas €3) This place is crammed with locals who are busy throwing down glasses of beer and platefuls of fried fish and other seafood.

La Utielana (☎ 96 352 94 14; Calle San Andrés 4; mains €4-7) Amazingly cheap stews, and rice and fish dishes mean there's always a line at this chaotic yet homy spot. Take a number (like at the butcher's!) and wait to savour the local flavour.

Nam (☎ 96 351 48 37; Calle San Andrés 4; mains €4-8) A loud *cafetería* serving cheap sandwiches, salads, and burgers, this place is next door to La Utielana.

Catajaloh (☎ 96 394 00 01; Mercado de Colón; mains €6-15) This trendy spot inside the beautiful Mercado de Colón has a high-class feel and lots of light soup-and-salad options.

La Pepica (☎ 96 371 03 66; Playa de Levante 6; mains €8-20) Of the many beachside restaurants serving fish and rice dishes, this sprawling restaurant is the locals' favourite.

El Rall (☎ 96 392 20 90; Calle Tundidores 2; mains €10-15) A firm favourite, El Rall serves up paellas, meat dishes and great desserts in a funky setting and has a good outside terrace.

Palacio de la Bellota (☎ 96 351 49 94; Calle Mosén Femades 7; mains €10-22) The cured ham that hangs from the ceilings here is absolutely divine, but this place is also famous for its Valencian *all i pebre* (eel stew).

Mercado Central (Plaza del Mercado; 8am-2.30pm) One of Spain's prettiest markets, Valencia's Mercado Central is a feast of colours and smells, with nearly 1000 stallholders crammed under the market's modernist glass domes.

Drinking

Much of the action centres on Barrio del Carmen, which caters for every taste from grunge to glam.

Café San Jaume (☎ 96 391 24 01; Calle Caballeros 51) This is a stalwart of Carmen's bar scene, with lots of room upstairs and a particularly fine terrace for eyeing off the characters on Calle Caballeros.

Lounge Café-Bar (☎ 96 391 80 94; Calle Estamiñería Vieja 2) This popular international hang-out has comfy sofas and free Internet. Good snacks too.

Café del Negrito (☎ 96 391 42 33; Plaza Negrito) On a kicking little plaza, this bar is generally packed with lots of liberal, arty 30-somethings.

El Templo del Café (☎ 96 315 20 80; Av María Cristina 12) A roomy café and tea house, this is just the thing for your caffeine fix. It serves good sandwiches too.

Entertainment

Head to these bars and clubs after midnight for drinks and dancing.

Radio City (☎ 96 391 41 51; Calle Santa Teresa 19) Dance to salsa, house and cheesy pop at this popular hall. There's also occasionally live flamenco.

Bolsería Café (☎ 96 391 89 03; Calle Bolsería 41) This is a fashionable place that plays house music upstairs.

Venial (☎ 96 391 73 56; Calle Quart 26) Valencia's oldest gay club hosts theme parties throughout the year. There's a big open-plan dance floor and chill-out zone.

Getting There & Away

Valencia's airport, **Aeropuerto de Manises** (VLC; ☎ 90 240 47 04; www.aena.es), is 10km west of the centre.

From the **bus station** (☎ 96 349 72 22; Av Menéndez Pidal), daily services go to/from Madrid (€40.60, three hours), Barcelona (€37, three hours) and Alicante (€24.50, 1½ hours). From Valencia's **Estación del Norte** (Calle Jativa), trains also go to/from Madrid, Barcelona and Alicante, among other destinations.

Regular car and passenger ferries go to the Balearic Islands (see p999).

Getting Around

At the time of research, the No 5 metro line was being extended; when completed it will connect the airport, downtown and port. Aero-Bus (€2.50, 20 minutes, every 20 minutes) leaves from a stop outside the airport's upper departures area and terminates beside metro Bailén, just south of the main train station.

EMT (☎ 96 352 83 99) buses run until about 10pm, with night services until around 1am. Bus 8 connects the bus station with Plaza Ayuntamiento.

The high-speed tram leaves from the FGV tram station, 500m north of the cathedral, at the Pont de Fusta. This is a pleasant way to get to the beach, the paella restaurants of Las Arenas and the port. Metro lines primarily serve the outer suburbs.

ALICANTE

pop 312,391

With its elegant, palm-lined boulevards, lively nightlife scene, and easy-to-access beaches, Alicante is the kind of all-in-one Spanish city that makes a great one- or two-day stopover. The city is at its most charming at night, when tapas bars and taverns in El Barrio (Old Quarter) come alive. The atmosphere kicks up a big notch during the Fiesta de Sant Joan (24 June), when Alicante stages its own version of Las Fallas (see opposite).

Information

CBR Internet (☎ 96 514 14 25; Calle Teniente Álvarez Soto 8; per hr €2-3; 10am-2am)

Main Tourist Office (☎ 96 592 98 02; www.alicanteturismo.com; Calle del Portugal 17; 10am-7.30pm Mon-Fri, to 2pm Sat)

Sights & Activities

A multilevel fortress dating to the 12th century, the imposing **Castillo de Santa Bárbara** (Saint Barbara Castle; ☎ 96 526 31 31; Monte Benacantil; admission free; 10am-7pm, exhibits 10.30am-2.30pm & 4-6.30pm) affords magnificent views over the city and sea. To get here, cross the footbridge beside the Playa del Postiguet. Down the steps and a few metres back towards the centre is a long tunnel that digs deep into the mountain, leading to an elevator that climbs through the bowels of Monte Benacantil. Zoom to the top to begin the visit, then wind your way down.

In summer, head to the beach. At the base of Castillo de Santa Bárbara is the often-crowded **Playa del Postiguet**. Further on are the quieter **Playa de la Albufereta**, in an area with important archaeological ruins, and the **Playa de San Juan**. All are on bus lines 21 and 22.

For a real treat, zip over to **Isla de Tabarca**, 11km offshore (€16 return, four trips daily in summer). An old pirates' lair, the island boasts a quaint historic town, loads of restaurants and excellent scuba diving. Ferries are run by **Kon Tiki** (☎ 96 521 63 96).

To learn about Alicante's ancient history, visit **Museo Arqueológico** (MARQ; ☎ 96 514 90 00; www.marqalicante.com; Plaza Dr Gómez Ulls s/n; adult/student €3/1.50; 10am-7pm Tue-Sat); **Museu de Fogueres** (☎ 96 514 6828; Rambla de Méndez Núñez 29; admission free; 10am-2pm & 6-9pm Tue-Sun Oct-May, 10am-2pm & 5-8pm Tue-Sun Jun-Sep) focuses on the Fiesta de Sant Joan.

Sleeping

Camping Costa Blanca (☎ 96 563 06 70; www.campingcostablanca.com; Calle Convento 143, El Campello; per person €3.50-5, per tent €3.50-7.50, per car €3.50-5) Considered the best camping ground in the area, this place is 10km north of Alicante and only 200m from the beach.

Hostal-Pensión La Milagrosa (☎ 96 521 69 18; www.hostallamilagrosa.com; Calle de Villavieja 8; r per person €20, with shared bathroom €15) All rooms are smallish here, but they're clean and some have views of the Santa María church. There's free access to the kitchen, a lovely rooftop terrace and a washing machine available.

Mediterránea Plaza (☎ 96 521 01 88; www.hotelmediterraneaplaza.com; Plaza del Ayuntamiento 6; s €87-127, d €99-140) The spacious, sparkling rooms here boast wood floors and stylish décor; some overlook the plaza and have castle views.

AUTHOR'S CHOICE

Hostal Les Monges Palace (☎ 96 521 50 46; www.lesmonges.net; Calle San Agustín 4; s €27-39, d €41-52) Each room has been lovingly decorated in this renovated 1912 building. Options include canopy bed, balcony, original stone walls, antique furniture or an ultramodern design. The common areas are decorated with the owner's extensive art collection.

Eating & Drinking

Biomenú Restaurante Vegetariano (☎ 96 521 31 44; Calle Navas 17; mains €3-5) Come here for the excellent pay-by-weight salad bar, available for takeaway. There's a small organic food shop too.

Casa Ibarra (☎ 96 514 56 25; Calle Mayor 33; mains €5-10, menú €9) Popular with locals for its filling fixed-price lunch, Ibarra boasts picturesque plaza-side tables.

El Buen Comer (☎ 96 521 31 03; Calle Mayor 8; mains €7-13.50) Cheese and Iberian sausage plates, local rice dishes and seafood tapas are the specialities at this touristy but tasty spot.

Dársena (☎ 96 520 75 89; www.darsena.com; Muelle de Levante 6; mains €10-28) Of the many, many, many eating options by the port, this is the best (though not the cheapest!). Enjoy harbour views as you savour local rice and seafood specialities.

Mercado Central (Covered Market; ☎ 96 514 07 63; Av Alfonso X El Sabio) The Art Nouveau–styled covered market is ideal for self-caterers. Try local specialities such as dried tuna or octopus.

El Barrio, a web of streets around the cathedral, is packed with bars. The port is another buzzing area. Nearby coastal resorts have mega-*discotecas* (discos) that are popular in summer.

Getting There & Away

Around 12km southwest of the centre, Alicante's **El Altet airport** (ALC; ☎ 96 691 91 00; www.aena.es), gateway to the Costa Blanca, is served by charters and scheduled flights from all over Europe. Bus C-6 runs every 40 minutes between Plaza Puerta del Mar and the airport, passing by the north side of the bus station.

At the **bus station** (☎ 96 513 07 00; Calle Portugal 17), look to **Alsa** (☎ 90 242 22 42; www.alsa.es) for a ride to major destinations including Madrid (€24.60, nine hours, five daily) and Valencia (€16.30, 2½ hours, 12 daily). Alsa

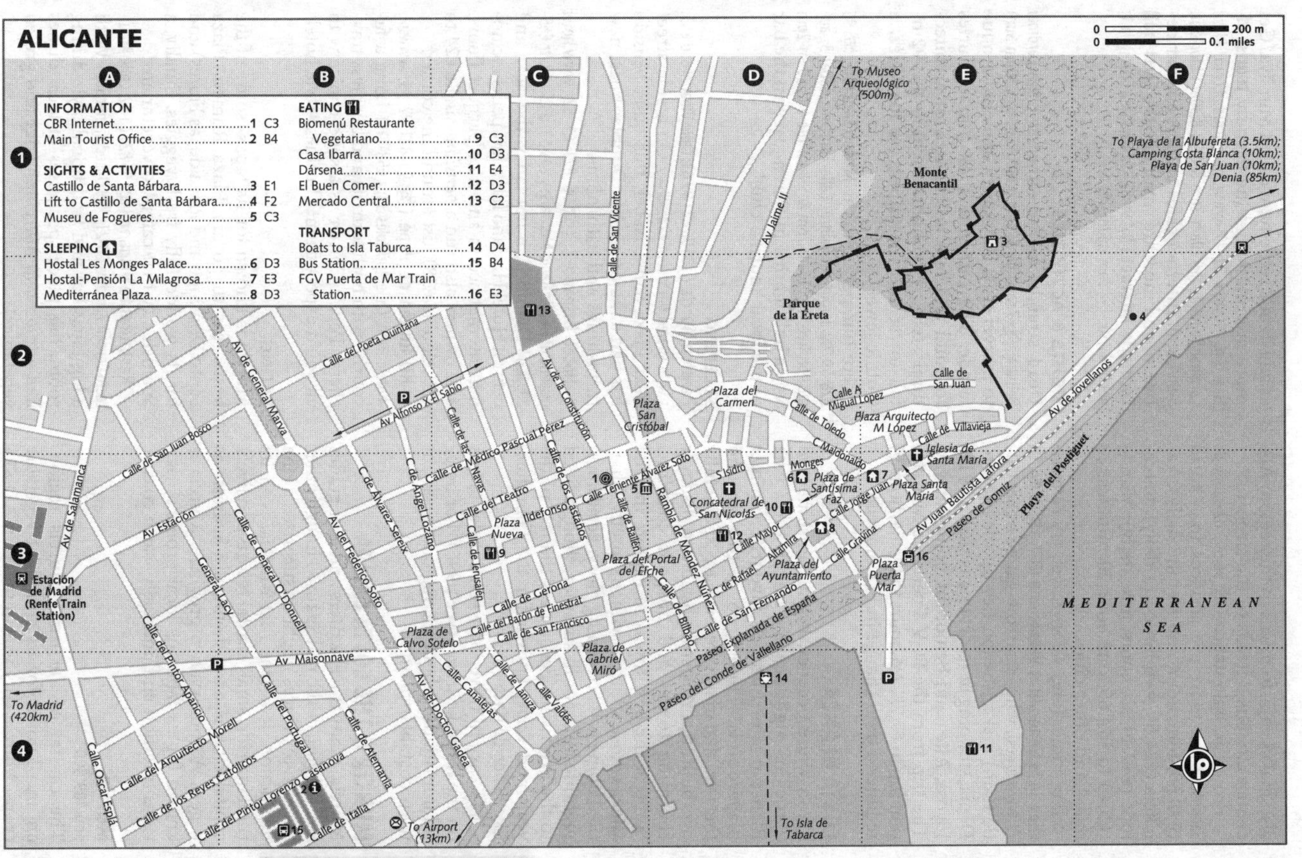
ALICANTE
INFORMATION
CBR Internet.....1 C3
Main Tourist Office.....2 B4
SIGHTS & ACTIVITIES
Castillo de Santa Bárbara.....3 E1
Lift to Castillo de Santa Bárbara.....4 F2
Museu de Fogueres.....5 C3
SLEEPING
Hostal Les Monges Palace.....6 D3
Hostal-Pensión La Milagrosa.....7 E3
Mediterránea Plaza.....8 D3
EATING
Biomenú Restaurante Vegetariano.....9 C3
Casa Ibarra.....10 D3
Dársena.....11 E4
El Buen Comer.....12 D3
Mercado Central.....13 C2
TRANSPORT
Boats to Isla Taburca.....14 D4
Bus Station.....15 B4
FGV Puerta de Mar Train Station.....16 E3
200 m
0.1 miles
To Museo Arqueológico (500m)
To Playa de la Albufereta (3.5km); Camping Costa Blanca (10km); Playa de San Juan (10km); Denia (85km)
Monte Benacantil
Parque de la Ereta
MEDITERRANEAN SEA
Playa del Postiguet
To Isla de Tabarca
To Airport (13km)
To Madrid (420km)
Estación de Madrid (Renfe Train Station)
Concatedral de San Nicolás
Iglesia de Santa María
Plaza del Ayuntamiento
Plaza Puerta Mar
Plaza de Gabriel Miró
Plaza de Calvo Sotelo
Plaza Nueva
Plaza San Cristóbal
Plaza del Carmen
Plaza del Portal del Elche
Plaza Arquitecto M López
Plaza de Santísima Faz
Plaza Santa María
Rambla de Méndez Núñez
Paseo Explanada de España
Paseo del Conde de Vallellano
Av de Jovellanos
Av Juan Bautista Lafora
Paseo de Gomiz
Av Alfonso X El Sabio
Av de la Constitución
Av del Doctor Gadea
Av de General Marva
Av del Federico Soto
Av de Salamanca
Av Jaime II
Av Maisonnave
Av Estación
Calle de San Vicente
Calle de General O'Donnell
Calle del Portugal
Calle de Italia
Calle Oscar Esplá
Calle de Alemania
Calle Canalejas
Calle de Bailén
Calle de Bilbao
Calle de Jerusalén
Calle de Gerona
Calle de los Castaños
Calle de San Fernando
Calle Mayor
Calle Valdés
Calle de Lanuza
Calle del Teatro
Calle de San Juan Bosco
Calle del Poeta Quintana
Calle de Médico Pascual Pérez
Calle Teniente Álvarez Soto
Calle de San Juan
Calle de Toledo
Calle de Villavieja
Calle Gravina
SPAIN

also makes runs to towns in the region. Alicante's city bus 6 heads to the airport.

From the **train station** (☎ 96 592 02 02; Av de Salamanca s/n), there are services to Madrid (€38.60, four hours, up to nine daily), Valencia (€24.50, two hours, 11 daily), Barcelona (€47.40, six hours, nine daily), Murcia (€5.40 to €14.60, one hour 20 minutes, 23 daily) and other cities.

For scenic (and slow) travel, try **Ferrocarriles de la Generalitat Valenciana** (FGV; ☎ 90 072 04 72; www.fgv.es), whose narrow-gauge *trenet* (little train) makes the journey up the coast to Dénia, stopping in resort towns such as Villa Joyosa, Altea and Benidorm along the way. The trip from the FGV Puerta de Mar station (up to €7.75, 2½ hours to Dénia, hourly) requires a train change in El Campello.

COSTA BLANCA

Clean white beaches, bright sunshine and a rockin' nightlife have made the Costa Blanca one of Europe's favourite summer playgrounds. There's no getting around the fact that many resorts are shamefully overbuilt, but it is still possible to discover charming towns and unspoilt coastline. Some of the best towns to explore include **Altea**, whose church with its pretty blue-tiled dome is its crowning glory; **Benidorm**, a nightlife hot spot in summer, though filled to the brim with pensioners the rest of the year; and **Calpe**, known for the Gibraltar-like **Peñon de Ifach** (332m).

It's easy to travel between coastal towns on the tramlike *trenet* (see p996). For helpful information about the region, check out www.costablanca.org.

SPAIN

MURCIA & THE COSTA CALÍDA

Murcia, many travel writers and tour guides will tell you, is 'the real Spain'. Though other Spanish provinces might be surprised at the distinction, it is true that Murcia, with its rural interior, small coastal resorts and lively capital city, is as authentically Spanish as it gets. A conservative province, Murcia is known for its fabulous local produce, rich tapas tradition and unusually warm coast.

Murcia

pop 409,800

The capital of the rural Murcia region, an area known for its abundant vegetable crops, Murcia City was founded in AD 825 as an Islamic settlement called Mursiya. Get more information at the friendly **tourist office** (☎ 96 835 87 49; www.murciaciudad.com; Plaza Cardinal Belluga; 10am-2pm & 6.30-8.30pm Mon-Sat, 5-9pm Sun). Internet cafés are few and far between, and most are small like the **Civer Troll Locutorio-Internet** (☎ 96 821 52 82; Plaza Cruz Roja 1; per hr €1.50; 9am-midnight).

SIGHTS & ACTIVITIES

Head straight to the **cathedral** (Plaza Cardinal Belluga; 7am-1pm & 5-8pm Mon-Sat, to 1.30pm Sun) to marvel at its fabulously opulent baroque façade. The cathedral took four centuries to build and is a hotchpotch of architectural styles. Highlights include the 92m-tall tower and the Capilla de los Veléz, a Gothic jewel.

For fun, peek into the **Museo Taurino** (☎ 96 828 59 76; Jardin del Salitre, Calle Francisco Rabal 3; admission free; 10am-2pm & 5-8pm Tue-Sat, 10am-2pm Sun), a bullfighting museum just past the bar of the local 'taurino club'.

SLEEPING

Pensión Murcia (☎ 96 821 99 63; Calle Vinadel 6; d €53, s with shared bathroom €23;) On a side street near Plaza Santa Isabel, this quiet *pensión* has had a major facelift. Doubles boast new furnishings and bathrooms.

Hotel Hispano-2 (☎ 96 821 61 52; www.hotelhispano.net; Calle Radio Murcia 3; s €45-52, d €50-68, tr €65-80;) Dignified, if not fancy, the clean and central Hotel Hispano has a few perks including Internet access and nice parquet floors. The owners also run a *pensión* (single €24 to €27, double €38) just around the corner.

NH Rincón de Pepe (☎ 96 821 22 39; www.nh-hoteles.com; Calle Apóstoles 34; r €58-119) Long a favourite with both tourists and business travellers, 'Pepe's Corner' is a solid choice with all you'd expect from a business-style hotel.

EATING

Murcia is known for its tapas (some of the best areas to go are Plaza Romeo, Plaza Santo Domingo and Plaza de las Flores) and for its wonderfully fresh veggies. Finally, a Spanish city that caters to vegetarians!

Restaurante Hispano (☎ 96 821 61 52; Calle Arquitecto Cerdán 7; mains €8-21; closed dinner Sun) With a big tapas bar and traditional-style dining room, this place specialises in local dishes like *dorada a la Murciana* (rice and grilled vegetables).

AUTHOR'S CHOICE

Los Zagales (☎ 96 821 55 79; Calle Polo Medina 4; tapas €1-4.50, meals from €10) Just off the Plaza Cardinal Belluga is this local favourite, an old-fashioned tapas bar where you can feast on concoctions like fried blood with onions (they say it's tasty!).

El Rincón de Pepe (☎ 96 821 22 39; Calle Apóstoles 34; mains €9-22) Set inside the Gran Casino Murcia, this is a city fixture known for innovative takes on local specialities. The owners also run an informal tapas bar just around the corner.

DRINKING

The streets around the university, in particular Calle Enrique Villar, are packed with bars that get popular Thursday through Saturday nights. The Plaza de Toros is another good option. Several bars are set up inside the plaza itself, making for a uniquely Spanish alternative to the regular bar scene.

GETTING THERE & AWAY

Renfe (☎ 90 224 02 02) trains connect Murcia with Madrid (€38.60, four hours, five daily), Alicante (€5.40 to €14.60, one hour 20 minutes, 23 daily), Cartagena (€3.60, 50 minutes, 12 daily) and other Spanish cities. From the train station, take bus 9 or 39 to Gran Vía in the city centre.

Buses serve Almería (one hour 20 minutes, 23 daily) and coastal towns such as La Manga (1½ hours, three daily).

Costa Calída

You'll find plenty of attractive spots on Murcia's Costa Calída (Warm Coast). Most popular is the **Mar Menor**, a vast saltwater lagoon separated from the sea by a 22km sliver of land known as **La Manga**. The water here is so warm you can swim year-round.

BALEARIC ISLANDS

pop 916,968

The Balearic Islands (Illes Belears in Catalan) adorn the glittering Mediterranean waters off Spain's eastern coastline. Beach tourism destinations *par excellence*, they are also home to simple fishing and farming villages and a wealth of natural, historical and archaeological treasures. Travellers who make it here will benefit from heading out of the major cities and exploring the rural hearts of each distinctly individual island.

Getting There & Away

AIR

Scheduled flights from the major cities on the Spanish mainland are operated by several airlines, including Iberia, Air Europa and Spanair.

One-way fares from Barcelona to Palma de Mallorca (45 minutes) can cost anywhere between €45 and €157. From Madrid to Palma de Mallorca (1¼ hours), you'll be looking at somewhere between €45 and €208. It's worth shopping around and booking ahead.

Flights between the islands are usually more expensive than the equivalent ferry trips, with Palma to Maó or Ibiza (both 40 minutes) costing up to €85 one way.

BOAT

The major ferry company for the islands is **Trasmediterránea** (☎ 90 245 46 45; www.trasmediterranea.es), with offices in Barcelona (☎ 93 295 90 00), Valencia (☎ 96 367 65 12), Palma de Mallorca (☎ 97 140 50 14), Maó (☎ 97 136 60 50) and Ibiza city (☎ 97 131 51 00). The frequency and duration of the services it offers varies dramatically, according to the time of year and type of ferry.

Buques convencionales (slow ferries) service the routes all year. Services on these are between: Barcelona and Palma (€198 to €228, seven hours, one daily); Palma and Maó (€40, 5½ hours, one weekly); Valencia and Palma (€198 to €228, 7½ hours, six weekly); and Palma and Ibiza (€40, four hours, one weekly). The frequencies cited here are from the low-season timetable; in the mid- and high seasons there are more-frequent services.

In the mid- and high seasons the *buques convencionales* are joined by a marginally faster 'fast ferry' and the much faster *buques rápidos* (catamarans). Services on the catamarans are between Barcelona and Palma (€80 to €173, 3¾ hours, one daily) and between Palma and Ibiza (€54, two hours, daily). Services on the fast ferry are between

Palma and Valencia (€80 to €173, 6½ hours, six or seven weekly) via Ibiza (€54).

Taking a small car from the mainland to the islands costs €146 on a *buques convencionales* and €171 on a catamaran or fast ferry. Between the islands it costs €105 on all services.

Another company, **Balearia** (☎ 90 216 01 80; www.balearia.com), operates two classes of ferry (fast and slow) from Dénia (on the coast between Valencia and Alicante) to Palma (€57 to €81, five or 9½ hours, two daily) via Ibiza (€39 to €54, two or four hours) in the mid- and high seasons. It also has year-round services between Ibiza and Palma (€39 to €54, four hours, two daily) and between Port d'Alcúdia on Mallorca and Ciutadella on Menorca (€51.30, one hour, two daily). **Iscomar** (☎ 90 211 91 28; www.iscomarferrys.com) runs a service between Ciutadella and Port d'Alcúdia (adult €27, small car €58, 2½ hours, one or two daily), as well as between Dénia and Ibiza (adult €30, small car €90, 4½ hours, six days per week). **Cape Balear** (☎ 90 210 04 44; www.capebalear.es) operates fast ferries to Ciutadella from Cala Ratjada in Mallorca (€64, 55 minutes, two services six days per week).

MALLORCA

pop 741,000

It's hardly surprising that over the decades so many great artists and writers have chosen to make this beguiling Mediterranean island their home. The capital city of Palma, with its attractive buildings and rich cultural and culinary scene, is a joy to explore. Inland, visitors can happily lose themselves trekking in the mountains before stumbling across a hilltop village seemingly unchanged for centuries. And then there are the beaches…

SPAIN

Information

Azul (Carrer Apuntadores 6, Palma; Internet per hr €3; 9.30am-3pm & 6-8pm Mon, 9.30am-3pm & 5-8pm Tue, Wed & Fri, 9.30am-3pm Sat)

Consell de Mallorca tourist office Main office (☎ 97 117 39 90; www.infomallorca.net; Plaça de la Reina 2, Palma; 9am-8pm Mon-Fri, to 2pm Sat); airport (☎ 97 178 95 56; 8.30am-8.30pm Mon-Sat, to 1.30pm Sun)

Main post office (Carrer de la Constitució 6, Palma; Internet per hr €1.50; 10am-11pm Mon-Fri, 11am-midnight Sat, noon-11pm Sun) Internet terminals in the telephone office attached to the post office.

Municipal tourist office (9am-8pm) Main branch (☎ 90 210 23 65; www.a-palma.es; Plaça d'Espanya, Palma); Passeig des Born (☎ 90 210 23 65; Palma)

Sights & Activities

An awesome mass of sandstone walls and flying buttresses, Palma's landmark **cathedral** (La Seu; ☎ 97 172 31 30; Carrer del Palau Reial 29, Palma; adult/student/child under 10 €3.50/3/free; 10am-3.15pm Mon-Fri Nov-Mar, 10am-5.15pm Mon-Fri Apr, May & Oct, 10am-6.15pm Mon-Fri Jun-Sep, 10am-2.15pm Sat year-round) overlooks the city and its port.

Opposite the cathedral is the **Palacio Real Almudaina** (☎ 97 121 41 34; Carrer del Palau Reial, Palma; adult/student €3.50/2.30; 10am-1.15pm & 4-5.15pm Oct-Mar, 10am-5.45pm Apr-Sep, closed Sat afternoon & Sun), the one-time residence of the Mallorcan monarchs. Inside is a collection of tapestries and artworks.

The **Museo de Arte Moderno y Contemporáneo** (Es Baluard; ☎ 97 190 82 00; www.esbaluard.org; Plaça Porta de Santa Catalina, Palma; adult/student €6/4.50; 10am-8pm Tue-Sun Oct–mid-Jun, 10am-midnight daily mid-Jun–Sep) is Palma's striking museum dedicated to modern and contemporary works of art. Its collection includes works from 20th-century artists including Miró and Picasso.

Those wanting to see even more of Miró's work should visit the **Fundació Pilar I Joan Miró** (☎ 97 170 14 20; Carrer Joan de Saridakis 29; adult/student/child €5/3/free, camera or video €5; 10am-6pm Tue-Sat Oct-Mar, to 7pm Tue-Sat Apr-Sep, to 3pm Sun year-round), west of the city. To get here catch bus 3 from Plaça d'Espanya or bus 6 from Plaça de la Reina.

The **Museo de Mallorca** (☎ 97 171 75 40; Carrer de la Portella 5, Palma; admission €2.50; 10am-6.30pm Tue-Sat, 10.30am-1.30pm Sun) houses archaeological finds, as well as paintings and furniture from the 19th and 20th centuries. Nearby, are the atmospheric **Banys Árabs** (Arab Baths; ☎ 97 172 15 49; Carrer de Ca'n Serra 7; admission €1.50; 9am-7.30pm Apr-Nov, to 6pm Dec-Mar), the only remaining monument to the Muslim domination of the island.

Mallorca's northwestern coast is a world away from the high-rise tourism on the other side of the island. Dominated by the Serra de Tramuntana, it's a beautiful region of olive groves, pine forests and small villages with shuttered stone buildings; it also has a rugged and rocky coastline. There are a couple of highlights for drivers: the

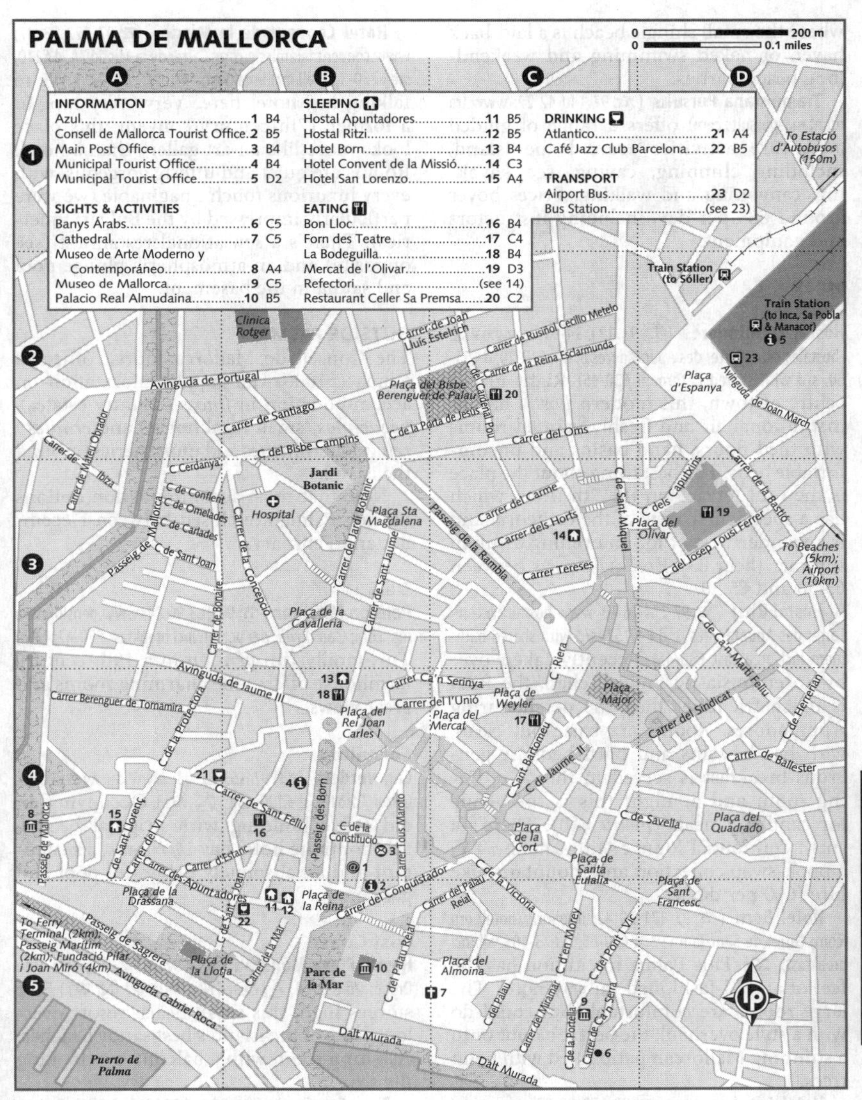

hair-raising road down to the small port of **Sa Calobra**, and the amazing trip along the peninsula leading to the island's northern tip, **Cap Formentor**.

If you don't have wheels, take the **Palma-Sóller train** (see p1003). It's one of the most popular and spectacular excursions on the island. Sóller is also the best place to base yourself for trekking, and the nearby village of **Fornalutx** is said to be the prettiest on Mallorca.

From Sóller, it is a 10km walk to the beautiful hilltop village of **Deiá**, where Robert Graves, poet and author of *I Claudius*, lived for most of his life. From the village, you can scramble down to the **Cala de Deiá**, where the small shingle beach is a laid-back haven of naked swimming and weekend-long beach parties.

Tramuntana Pursuits (☎ 97 140 42 22; www.tramuntana-pursuits.com) offers a range of guided adventure activities around the island, including climbing, caving, sea kayaking, canyoning and walking. Prices hover around €85 per day, including instructors and equipment.

Sleeping

PALMA

Hostal Apuntadores (☎ 97 171 34 91; www.palma-hostales.com; Carrer des Apuntadores 8; dm €19-20, d €55-60, s/d with shared bathroom €30/45) Right in the centre of town, this modern *hostal* has an institutional air and freshly painted rooms with tiled floors, hand basins and uncomfortable beds. The best thing about the place is the roof terrace on the 7th floor, which has a spectacular view of the cathedral and is a wonderful spot for an evening drink in summer (beer €3). Breakfast costs between €3.50 and €5.50.

Hostal Ritzi (☎ 97 171 46 10; www.hostalritzi.com; Carrer des Apuntadores 6; d €47-57, s/d with shared bathroom incl breakfast €30/45) Recently taken over by an enthusiastic English chap, the Ritzi is much friendlier than the neighbouring Apuntadores. Rooms are basic but clean, with hand basins and hard beds. A generous breakfast is served in the cute dining room and at night this is the venue for candlelit meals (*menú* €10). There's a small communal lounge with satellite TV, a book-swap collection and mountain-bike hire (€10 per day).

Hotel Born (☎ 97 171 29 42; infoborn@hotelborn.com; Carrer de Sant Jaume 3; s €50-65, d €73-105, all incl breakfast; ❄) This Palma institution has the feel of an old-fashioned railway hotel. The large rooms are comfortable but could do with a style overhaul; the best look out onto a stunning Mallorcan patio filled with palm trees.

Hotel San Lorenzo (☎ 97 172 82 00; www.hotelsanlorenzo.com; Calle de San Llorenç 14; s €118-204, d €139-246; ❄ 🏊) The charming rooms in this converted 17th-century manor house have beamed ceilings, extremely comfortable beds and luxurious tiled bathrooms; most rooms have large windows or terraces overlooking a bougainvillea-adorned pool area.

Hotel Convent de la Missió (☎ 97 122 73 47; www.conventdelamissio.com; Carrer de la Missió 7A; d €210, ste €260-320, all incl breakfast; Ⓟ ❄ 💻 🏊) We're talking hip hotel here. Very, very hip. In a former 17th-century convent, this place looks more like an art gallery than a hotel. Rooms are quiet and utterly gorgeous, with every luxurious touch imaginable (we were particularly impressed by the Bulgari toiletries). There's a sensational restaurant (see opposite) and an atmospheric plunge pool and sauna in the basement.

OUTSIDE PALMA

The Consell de Mallorca tourist office in Palma (p1000) can supply information on accommodation in *fincas* (country estates), *pequeñnos* (small rural hotels) and *ermites i refugis* (hermitages and monasteries) around the island.

Note that most accommodation options outside Palma are closed between December and February.

Deiá

Pensión Miramar (☎ 97 163 90 84; www.pensionmiramar.com; C'an Oliver; per person incl breakfast €30-42; Ⓟ) This family-run *pensión* in a 19th-century farmhouse offers nine charming rooms and great views.

Fornalutx

Cán Verdera (☎ 97 163 82 03; www.canverdera.com; Carrer Toros 1; d €190-480; ❄ 🏊) Occupying an old stone building with original beams, this boutique hotel has 11 rooms, a restaurant and an absolutely delightful pool and garden.

East Coast

Hostal Playa Mondragó (☎ 97 165 77 52; Cala Mon Dragó; s/d €32/64; 🕒 closed Nov-Apr; Ⓟ ❄ 🏊) Five storeys high, this small beach resort overlooks one of the island's best sandy beaches. Ask for a room with a balcony overlooking the sea.

Finca Son Gener (☎ 97 118 36 12; Apartat de Correus 136, Son Servera; d incl breakfast €255; 🕒 closed Dec-Feb; Ⓟ ❄ 🏊) Between the villages of Son Servera and Art'a, this idyllic retreat is set in a cluster of beautifully converted 18th-century farmhouses. Its 10 junior suites have every imaginable mod con; added extras include sea views, two pools, a restaurant and a well-stocked wine cellar.

Eating & Drinking

PALMA

La Bodeguilla (☎ 97 171 82 74; Carrer de Sant Jaume 3; tapas €5-15.50, mains €13-21; ⏰ closed Sun) A sleek and very attractive wine bar serving modern takes on traditional tapas, La Bodeguilla serves tasty morsels such as *croquetas de espinaca y taco de jamón* (spinach croquettes wrapped in Iberian ham, €6.50).

Bon Lloc (☎ 97 171 86 17; Carrer de Sant Feliu 7; menú €15; ⏰ lunch Mon-Sat; ⊠) This popular place serves a hearty four-course vegetarian *menú*.

Restaurant Cellar Sa Premsa (☎ 97 172 35 29; Plaça del Bisbe Berenguer de Palau 8; menú €20-24; ⏰ daily Sep-Jun, Mon-Fri Jul-Aug) Sitting at one of this tavern's long benches and sampling the excellent traditional Mallorcan cuisine on offer is an obligatory exercise when in Palma.

Refectori (☎ 97 122 73 47; Carrer de la Missió 7A; mains €25-26, menú €38; ⏰ closed Sat & Sun lunch) This exquisite restaurant in the modern and elegant surrounds of the Convent de la Missió hotel (see opposite) serves the best food in Palma. The chef uses top-notch local produce in his seasonal menus, concocting perfectly balanced dishes, such as Magret duck basted in spices with a red sweet-potato cream (€25).

Atlantico (Carrer de Sant Feliu 12; ⏰ 8pm-4am) With its unique combination of knockout cocktails and grunge, this is a good late-night drinking den.

Café Jazz Club Barcelona (Carrer des Apuntadores 5; admission €4; ⏰ 8.30pm-1am Mon-Thu, to 3am Fri & Sat) Another good drinking spot, this is a cramped but enjoyable live-music venue.

If you're putting together a picnic, go to the **Mercat de l'Olivar** (Plaça del Olivar; ⏰ 7am-2pm Mon-Sat), the city's central produce market, and then stop in at **Forn des Teatre** (☎ 97 171 52 54; Plaça de Weyler 9; ⏰ 8am-8pm Mon-Sat) for some of the island's signature *ensaimadas* (yeast-based pastries).

The island's nightclubs are in the port area around Passeig Marítim, Avinguda de Joan Miró and Plaça de Gomila.

Getting Around

Sant Joan airport (PMI; ☎ 97 178 90 99; www.aena.es) is approximately 10km east of Palma. Bus 1 runs from Plaça d'Espanya to the airport (€1.80) and then back to the centre via the ferry terminal (€1.10) every 20 minutes. A taxi from the airport to the centre of town will cost around €14; from the ferry terminal to the centre costs around €7.

> **LATE LAMENTED LUGGAGE**
>
> Backpackers visiting Palma will encounter problems if they need to find a safe spot to leave their luggage while waiting for flights/ferries or when on an overnight camping trip. There are no left-luggage facilities on the island and the *hostales* in Palma are loath to look after bags due to a spate of thefts in recent times. If you do leave luggage at a *hostal,* be warned that you do so at your own (considerable) risk.

Most parts of the island are accessible by bus from Palma. These generally depart from or near the **bus station** (☎ 97 117 77 77; http://tib.caib.es; Plaça d'Espanya). Mallorca's two train lines leave from the nearby **train station** (☎ 97 175 22 45). There are regular services to the inland towns of Inca (€1.80), Sa Pobla (€2.85) and Manacor (€3.70) on one line; five trains per day make the trip to Sóller (one-way/return €9/14, one hour) on the other. Both journeys are highly picturesque.

IBIZA

pop 103,000

Love it or hate it, Ibiza (Eivissa in Catalan) has a unique spirit and a formidable party reputation. It's extreme in both its landscape, which is harsh and rocky, and in the people that it attracts, many of whom fly in solely for the island's world-famous and decidedly louche clubbing scene. If poseurs give you the irrits, you should definitely give Ibiza a miss, as during the clubbing season (the only time when it's worth visiting) they're here in force.

Information

Surf@Net (Carrer de Riambau 8, Ibiza City; Internet per 30min €2; ⏰ 10am-2am)

Tourist office (☎ 97 130 19 00; www.illesbalears.es; Carrer Antoni Riquer 2, Ibiza City; ⏰ 8.30am-3pm Mon-Fri, 10.30am-1pm Sat Nov-Mar, 9am-1.30pm & 5-7pm Mon-Fri, 10.30am-1pm Sat 16-31 Oct, 9am-9pm Mon-Fri, 9.30am-7.30pm Sat Apr-15 Oct)

Wash and Dry.Com (Avinguda Espanya 53, Ibiza City; Internet per hr €2, wash & dry per load €10; ⏰ 10am-1.30pm & 5-8.30pm Mon-Fri, 10am-2pm Sat) Go online while doing a load of washing.

Sights & Activities

Ibiza City's port area of **Sa Penya** is crammed with funky and trashy clothing boutiques and arty-crafty market stalls. From here, you can wander up into **D'Alt Vila**, the atmospheric old walled town that's home to the **Museu d'Art Contemporani** (☎ 97 130 27 23; Ronda Narcís Puget; admission free; 10am-1pm & 4-6pm Tue-Fri, 10am-1.30pm Sat & Sun Oct-Apr, 10am-1.30pm & 5-8pm Tue-Fri, 10am-1.30pm Sat & Sun May-Sep); the **Cathedral** (Plaça de la Catedral; 9.30am-1.30pm & 4-7pm Tue-Sat, mass 10.30am Sun); and the **Museu Arqueològic** (☎ 97 130 12 31; Plaça de la Catedral 3; admission €2.50; 10am-2pm & 6-8pm Mon-Sat, 10am-2pm Sun mid-Mar–mid-Oct, 9am-3pm Mon-Sat, 10am-2pm Sun mid-Oct–mid-Mar).

The heavily developed **Platja de ses Figueretes** beach is a 20-minute walk south of Sa Penya, but you're better off heading south to the beaches at **Ses Salines**, a half-hour ride on bus 11 (€1.20).

Ibiza has numerous unspoiled and relatively undeveloped beaches. **Cala de Boix**, on the northeastern coast, is the only black-sand beach on the island, while further north are the lovely beaches of **S'Aigua Blanca**. On the northern coast near Portinatx, **Cala Xarraca** is in a picturesque, secluded bay, and near Port de Sant Miquel is the attractive **Cala Benirras**. On the southwestern coast, **Cala d'Hort** has a spectacular setting overlooking two rugged rock islets, Es Verda and Es Verdranell. These can all be accessed via local **bus** (www.ibizabus.com) between May and October.

The tourist office can supply information on popular hiking and mountain-bike routes.

Sleeping

IBIZA CITY

Many of Ibiza City's hotels and *hostales* are closed in the low season and heavily booked between April and October. Make sure you book ahead.

Hostal Sol y Brisa (☎ 97 131 08 18; fax 97 130 30 32; Avinguda de Bartolomé Vicent Ramón 15; s/d with shared bathroom €18/30; closed Jan & Feb) Occupying the 2nd and 3rd floors of an apartment building near the water, Ibiza City's cheapest accommodation option offers faded rooms with washbasins and saggy beds.

Casa de Huéspedes Navarro (☎ 97 131 07 71; Carrer de sa Creu 20; d/tr with shared bathroom €38/50; closed Nov-Mar) This place is in a good central location. It has 10 rooms at the top of a long flight of stairs, as well as a sunny rooftop terrace.

Hostal Parque (☎ 97 130 13 58; www.hostalparque.com; Plaça des Parc 4; s/d €70/100, with shared bathroom €50/80;) This is an excellent midrange option. Its small but airy rooms have been recently redecorated and come complete with satellite TV. Try for one with a balcony (or at least a window) overlooking the attractive *plaça* (plaza), but be prepared for lots of late-night noise. The friendly staff and downstairs *cafetería* are definite pluses. Recommended.

Hostal-Restaurante La Marina (☎ 97 131 01 72; www.hostal-lamarina.com; Carrer de Barcelona 7; s €62, d €77-150;) On the waterfront, La Marina has brightly painted rooms with wrought-iron furniture, satellite TV and tiny bathrooms; some have balconies overlooking the harbour and a couple have private terraces.

Hotel La Ventana (☎ 97 139 08 57; www.laventanaibiza.com; Carrer de Sa Carossa 13; d €177-257, ste €423; P) One of the few options in the D'Alt Vila, this charming 15th-century house is set on a leafy square. Some of the 13 rooms have their own terraces and all are beautifully decorated. Worth the splurge.

OUTSIDE IBIZA CITY

Most accommodation options outside Ibiza City are closed between November and April.

Camping Cala Nova (☎ 97 133 17 74; www.campingcalanova.com; Santa Eulária des Riu; per person/tent/electricity €6.30/6.30/3) Close to a good beach and 12km from Ibiza City, this is one of Ibiza's best camping grounds. There are 125 sites and there's plenty of shade.

Pensión Sa Plana (☎ 97 133 50 73; d with shared bathroom incl breakfast €58;) Near the S'Aigua Blanca beaches, this place has a poolside bar and barbecue.

C'an Curreu (☎ 97 133 52 80; www.cancurreu.com; Ctra Sant Carles Km 12; d €257, ste €353-396, all incl breakfast; P) This beautifully restored Eivissan farmhouse has a sauna, gymnasium, stables and a fabulous pool terrace. The rooms have exposed beams and open fireplaces.

Eating & Drinking

IBIZA CITY

Croissant Show (☎ 97 131 76 65; Plaça de la Constitució; 7am-3pm) All we can say is *ooh la la*! This is where the beautiful people come for a

SPAIN

postclubbing refuel. The croissants (€1) are as good as any baked in France, but the painting of Paris Hilton and Nicole Richie is a bit much to take.

Cerveceria Scenicus (☎ 97 131 60 74; Passeig de Vara de Rey 4) This unassuming place serves up a good-value and very tasty *plato del día* (plate of the day, €4).

Comidas-Bar San Juan (☎ 97 131 16 03; Carrer de Guillem de Montgri 8; mains €6-12; closed Sun) This is a popular, family-run tavern where diners share tables. The food is hearty and extremely good value for money.

Restaurant Car'Alfredo (☎ 97 131 12 74; Passeig de Vara de Rey 16; mains €10-25) This classy eatery has been serving up local specialities since 1934. Though Restaurant Car'Alfredo claims the paella as its house speciality, you would be much better off opting for more traditional Eivissan plates such as the flavour-packed *surtido de canapés de pan payés con anchoas y sobrasada* (assorted canapés of farmhouse bread with anchovies and spicy sausage, €6), or the simple but beautifully prepared fish dishes such as *ragut de mero y rape al Pedro Ximénez* (grouper and anglerfish stew with Pedro Ximénez wine, €25).

We recommend starting your evening with a drink and some people watching at one of the bars lining the lively Plaça des Parc. The most popular is probably the laidback **Bliss** (11.30am-midnight), which is also one of the few open during winter. Nearby

Viper (☎ 97 130 45 69; Vía Púnica 12; ⏲ 9am-3am) has an in-house DJ after 4pm.

OUTSIDE IBIZA CITY

KM5 (☎ 97 139 63 49; www.km5-lounge.com; Carretera San José 5; ⏲ 8pm-1.30am) Named after its highway location, this is where the glam set comes to dance and drink in the gardens before moving onto the superclubs. It's on the road to San Josep, 5km from Ibiza city.

Entertainment

Ibiza's summer nightlife is renowned. At night, designer-chic couples and seriously studded swingers wander the fashion catwalk of cobbled streets, dodging the outrageous PR performers hired by the superclubs to lure dusk-to-dawn clubbers. After a few drinks at the bars around the port, they head to the superclubs, all of which charge a hefty €50 or more for entry. To get to the clubs, there's a handy Discobus service that operates in summer from midnight until 6am.

The big-name clubs are **Pacha** (☎ 97 131 36 00; www.pacha.com; Av 8 d'Agost), on the northern side of Ibiza City's port; **Privilege** (☎ 97 119 80 86; www.privilege.es; Urb San Rafael), **Amnesia** (☎ 97 119 80 41; www.amnesia-ibiza.com; Cntra San Antonio), **Eden** (☎ 97 134 25 51; www.edenibiza.com; Av Dr Fleming) and **Es Paradis Terrenal** (☎ 97 134 66 00; www.esparadis.com; Av Dr Fleming) in San Antonio; **El Divino** (☎ 97 131 83 38; www.eldivino-ibiza.com; Puerto Ibiza Nueva), across the water from the town centre (hop on one of its boats); and **Space** (☎ 97 139 67 93; www.space-ibiza.es) and **Kiss** (☎ 97 130 64 17; www.kiss-ibiza.com; Carrer de les Alzines) in Platja d'En Bossa.

Between October and April only El Divino and Pacha are open, and then only on Friday and Saturday nights.

Getting Around

Buses run between the airport, **Es Codola** (IBZ; ☎ 97 180 90 00; www.aena.es), and Ibiza City every 30 minutes from 7.20am to 11.50pm in summer (€1.20, 15 minutes); a taxi costs around €12 to €15. Buses to other parts of the island leave from the series of bus stops along Avinguda d'Isidoro Macabich. Pick up a timetable from the tourist office.

Plenty of ferries make the short trip between Ibiza City and the neighbouring island of Formentera each day. Tickets cost around €20 return on a *buque convencionale* (slow ferry) and €33.50 on a *líneaJET* (fast ferry).

MENORCA

pop 77,000

Renowned for its pristine beaches, archaeological sites and environmental areas, tranquil Menorca is the least developed of the Balearics. It was declared a Biosphere Reserve by Unesco in 1993. The capital, Maó, is known as Mahón in Castilian.

Information

Ciber Principal (☎ 97 136 26 89; Carrer Nou 25, Maó; Internet per hr €3.50; ⏲ 9.30am-10pm Mon-Fri, 11am-2pm & 6-10pm Sat & Sun)
Municipal tourist office Main office (☎ 97 136 37 90; infomenorcamao@cime.es; Carrer de sa Rovellada de Dalt 24, Maó; ⏲ 9am-1.30pm & 5-7pm Mon-Fri, 9am-1pm Sat); Ciutadella (☎ 97 138 26 93; Plaça la Catedral 5; ⏲ 9.30am-1.30pm & 5-7pm Mon-Fri, 9am-1pm Sat)

Sights & Activities

Maó and Ciutadella are both harbour towns, and from either place you'll have to commute to the beaches. Maó absorbs most of the tourist traffic. While you're here, you can take a boat cruise around the impressive harbour.

Ciutadella, with its smaller harbour and historic buildings, has a more distinctly Spanish feel to it. Follow the shopping baskets to the colourful **market** (Plaça Llibertat), which is surrounded by lively tapas bars.

In the centre of the island, the 357m-high **Monte Toro** has great views of the island; on a clear day you can see Mallorca.

With your own transport and a bit of footwork, you'll be able to discover some of Menorca's off-the-beaten-track beaches. North of Maó, a drive across a lunar landscape leads to the lighthouse at **Faváritx Cape**. If you park just before the gate to the lighthouse and climb up the rocks behind you, you'll see a couple of the eight beaches that are just waiting for scramblers such as yourself to explore.

On the northern coast, the picturesque town of **Fornells** is on a large bay popular with windsurfers.

Sleeping

Many accommodation options on the island are closed between November and April.

MAÓ

Posada Orsi (☎ 97 136 47 51; posadaorsi@hotmail.com; Carrer de la Infanta 19; s/d with shared bathroom €23/38, d with shower €45-47) A riot of acid colours and stripy sofas, Orsi is (very) bright, clean and well located.

Hotel del Almirante (☎ 97 136 27 00; www.hoteldelalmirante.com; Carreterra de Maó-Es Castel; s €48-72, d €65-96; P) A magnificent Georgian-style mansion and a former residence of Nelson's second-in-command at Trafalgar, this place offers simple rooms (ask for one in the main building) and features lovely gardens, a pool, tennis court and crowds of British tourists.

CIUTADELLA

Hostal-Residencia Oasis (☎ 97 138 21 97; Carrer de Sant Isidre 33; d €46-50) In the old quarter, this old-fashioned place offers rooms set around a large garden courtyard.

OTHER AREAS

Camping S'atalaia (☎ 97 137 42 32; www.campingsatalaia.com; per person/tent/electricity €6.30/4.50/4; closed Nov-Mar) One of Menorca's two camping grounds. Camping S'atalaia is near the resorts of Santa Galdana, about 4km south of Ferreries.

Camping Son Bou (☎ 97 137 27 27; www.campingsonbou.com; per person/tent/electricity €7.50/4/4; closed Nov-Mar) This camping ground is near Son Bou, south of Alaior.

Hotel Rural Morvedrá Nou (☎ 97 135 95 21; www.morvedranou.es; Camí Sant Joan de Misa; d €100-126, ste €127-134, all incl breakfast; P) A perfect place to get away from it all, this converted 17th-century farmhouse 7km outside Ciutadella has sea views, a bar-restaurant and 16 rooms with private terraces.

Eating & Drinking

The ports in both Maó and Ciutadella are lined with bars and restaurants.

MAÓ

Casanova (☎ 97 135 41 69; Andén Poniente 15; pizza €7) This popular pizzeria makes good use of its wood-fired oven.

Es Fosquet (☎ 97 135 00 58; Moll Llevant 256; mains €10-14; 1-4pm & 8-11.30pm Thu-Sun) A tiny but chic hole-in-the-wall place, Es Fosquet serves up freshly caught fish and shellfish.

El Muelle (Moll de Llevant 33; meals €15; lunch Mon-Fri, lunch & dinner Sat) Locals swear by the down-to-earth tapas, fish dishes and *bocadillos* offered at this eatery.

Mirador Café (☎ 97 135 21 07; Plaça d'Espanya 9; 10am-2am Mon-Sat) You'll find this small and atmospheric music bar in a laneway between the top of Casta de ses Voltes and the Mercat Claustre del Carme.

CIUTADELLA

Café Balear (☎ 97 138 00 05; Plaça de Sant Joan 15; meals €25-30; lunch only Tue-Sun, lunch & dinner Sun Dec-Oct) This long-standing favourite offers attractive outdoor seating and an excellent seafood-dominated menu.

Martin's Pub (Costa d'es Moll 20) Join the crowds spilling out of this tiny bar onto the lane and you'll soon be soaking up the beer and loud Spanish techno on offer.

FORNELLS

Es Pla (☎ 97 137 66 55; Pasaje des Pla; winter menú €15, summer menú €21) The Spanish royals are said to love the lavish seafood dishes served up at this Menorcan restaurant. Its speciality is *caldereta de langosta* (spiny lobster stew).

Getting Around

Buses run from the **Mahon airport** (MAH; ☎ 97 115 70 00; www.aena.es) into Maó every half-hour from 5.45am to 10.15pm; tickets cost €1.50. A taxi costs around €10.

TMSA (☎ 97 136 04 75; www.e-torres.net) runs buses between Maó and Ciutadella (€3.75), with occasional connections to the major resorts on the southern coast. In summer there are also daily bus services to most of the coastal towns from both Maó and Ciutadella.

ANDALUCÍA

The tapping feet and clapping hands of a passionate flamenco performance is an Andalucian signature that's as distinctive as the sweet aroma of orange blossom or the voluptuous flavour offered by a glass of chilled summer *gazpacho*.

In years past, armies of Christians and Muslims fought over this sun-drenched part of Spain; these days, tourists are the only visitors to arrive in battalions, lured here by Andalucía's beaches, incomparable Islamic monuments and full-blooded culture.

SEVILLE

pop 702,516

It's obligatory to use superlatives when describing Seville, and we're happy to oblige. A sexy, sophisticated and gorgeous-looking city, it's home to two of Spain's most colourful festivals, an amazing tapas culture, fascinating and distinctive barrios and a local population that lives life to the fullest. Nothing beats a few days spent within its seductive embrace.

Information

Internetia (☎ 95 450 25 43; Calle Av Menendez Palayo; Internet per hr €2.50; 🕑 10am-1am Mon-Fri, 11am-1am Sat & Sun) The scene here is hopping, with more than 50 terminals, a lounge area for laptops and a popular café.

Municipal tourist office (☎ 95 450 56 00; Calle de Arjona 28; 🕑 8.15am-8.45pm Mon-Fri, 8.30am-2.30pm Sat & Sun)

Regional tourist office (www.andalucia.org) Constitución (☎ 95 422 14 04; Av de la Constitución 21; 🕑 9am-7pm Mon-Fri, 10am-2pm & 3-7pm Sat, 10am-2pm Sun); Santa Justa (☎ 95 453 76 26; Estación de Santa Justa; 🕑 9am-8pm Mon-Fri, 10am-2pm Sat & Sun); Airport (☎ 95 444 91 28; 🕑 9am-8.30pm Mon-Fri, 10am-6pm Sat, 10am-2pm Sun)

Turismo Seville (☎ 95 423 44 65; Plaza del Triunfo 5; 🕑 10.30am-2.30pm Mon-Fri, 10am-2pm Sat)

Sights & Activities

CATHEDRAL & LA GIRALDA

Seville's **cathedral** (☎ 95 421 49 71; Calle Alemanes; adult/student €7.50/2, free Sun; 🕑 11am-5pm Mon-Sat Sep-Jun, 9.30am-3pm Mon-Sat Jul & Aug, 2.30-6pm Sun year-round) was built on the site of Muslim Seville's main mosque between 1401 and 1507. The structure is primarily Gothic, though most internal decoration is in later styles. The adjoining tower, **La Giralda**, was the mosque's minaret and dates from the 12th century. The climb to the top is worth it for the stunning city views. One highlight of the cathedral's lavish interior is Christopher Columbus' supposed tomb, though recent research indicates he was probably laid to rest in the Caribbean and that the remains here are those of his lesser-known son Diego. The four sepulchre-bearers represent the four kingdoms of Spain at the time Columbus sailed to the Americas.

ALCÁZAR

Seville's **Alcázar** (☎ 95 450 23 23; adult/child €7/free; 🕑 9.30am-5pm Tue-Sat, to 1.30pm Sun Oct-Mar, 9.30am-7pm Tue-Sat, to 5pm Sun Apr-Sep), a residence of Muslim and Christian royalty for many centuries, was founded in 913 as a Muslim fortress. It has been adapted by Seville's rulers in almost every century since, which makes it a mishmash of styles but adds to its fascination. Make sure you book into one of the tours of the exquisite **Upper Palace** (admission €4, maximum tickets per tour 15), which are scheduled every half-hour from 10.30am to 1pm.

WALKS & PARKS

The best way to appreciate **Barrio de Santa Cruz**, the old Jewish quarter immediately east of the cathedral, is to head for the tangle of narrow streets and plazas east of the main Calle Mateos Gago artery. There's no better place to get lost.

A more straightforward walk is along the **river bank** and past Seville's famous bullring, the **Plaza de Toros de la Real Maestranza** (☎ 95 422 45 77; www.maestranza.com; Paseo de Cristóbal Colón 12; guided tours €4; 🕑 9.30am-7pm, 9.30am-3pm bullfight days), one of the oldest in Spain. The (compulsory) tour here is in English and Spanish.

South of the centre is **Parque de María Luisa**, with its maze of paths, tall trees, flowers, fountains and shaded lawns. Be sure to seek out the magnificent **Plaza de España** with its fountains, canal and a simply dazzling semicircle of *azulejo-* (ceramic tile) clad buildings.

MUSEUMS

The **Museo de Bellas Artes** (☎ 95 422 07 90; Plaza Museo 9; admission non-EU/EU citizens €1.50/free; 🕑 2.30-8.30pm Tue, 9am-8.30pm Wed-Sat, 9am-2.30pm Sun) has an outstanding, beautifully housed collection of Spanish art, focusing on local artists such as Bartolemé Esteban Murillo and Francisco Zurbarán.

Festivals & Events

The first of Seville's two great festivals is **Semana Santa**, the week leading up to Easter Sunday. Throughout the week, long processions of members of religious brotherhoods dressed in strange penitents' garb with tall, pointed hoods accompany sacred images through the city, while huge crowds look on.

The **Feria de Abril**, a week in late April, is a welcome release after this solemnity: the

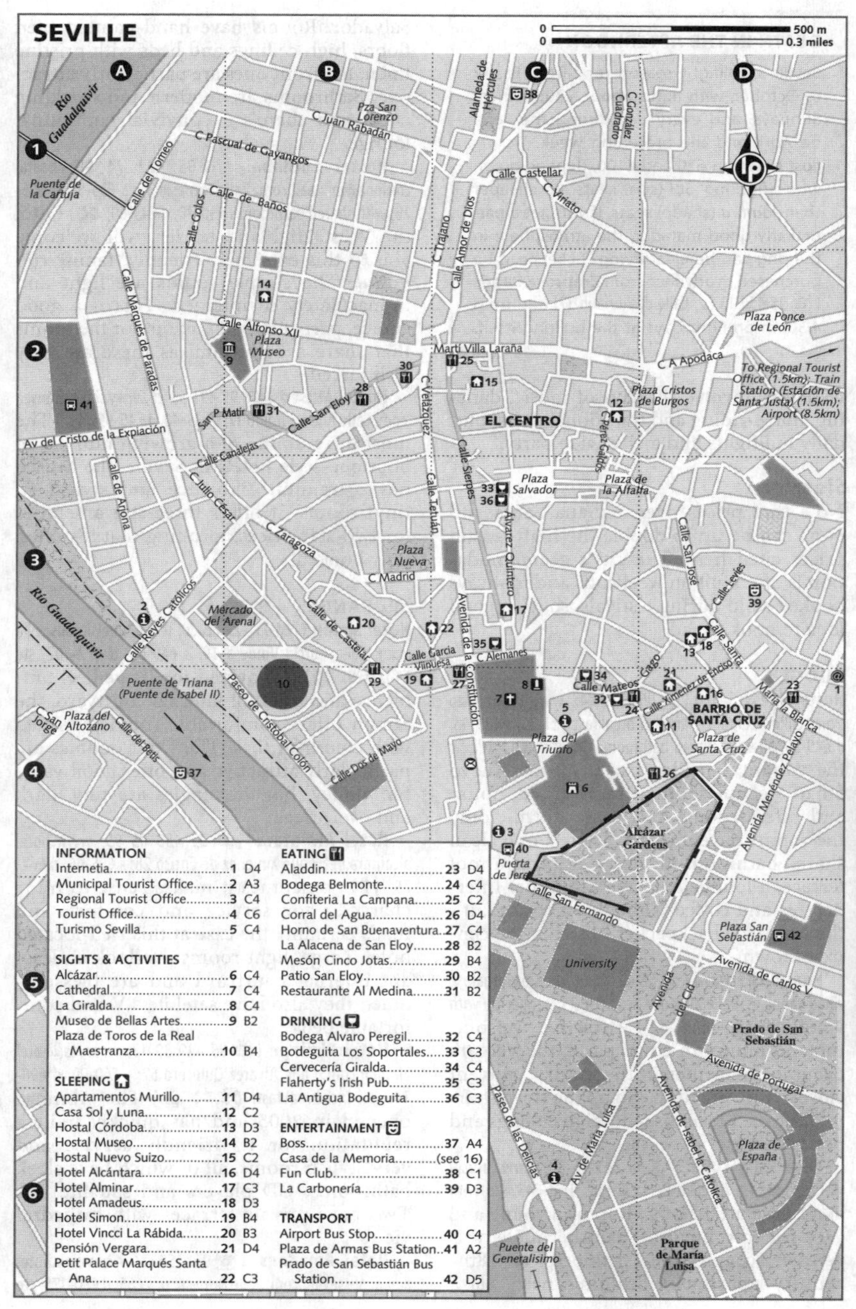
SEVILLE
0 500 m
0 0.3 miles
A
B
C
D
1
2
3
4
5
6
Río Guadalquivir
Puente de la Cartuja
Calle del Torneo
C Pascual de Gayangos
C Juan Rabadán
Pza San Lorenzo
Alameda de Hércules
C González Cuadrado
Calle Castellar
C Viriato
Calle de Baños
Calle Goles
C Trajano
Calle Amor de Dios
Calle Marqués de Paradas
Calle Alfonso XII
Plaza Museo
Martí Villa Laraña
C A Apodaca
Plaza Ponce de León
To Regional Tourist Office (1.5km); Train Station (Estación de Santa Justa) (1.5km); Airport (8.5km)
Plaza Cristos de Burgos
EL CENTRO
C Pérez Galdós
San P Matir
Calle San Eloy
C Velázquez
Av del Cristo de la Expiación
Calle Canalejas
C Julio César
Calle de Arjona
Calle Sierpes
Plaza Salvador
Plaza de la Alfalfa
Calle Tetuán
C Zaragoza
Plaza Nueva
C Madrid
Álvarez Quintero
Calle San José
Calle Levíes
Mercado del Arenal
Calle Reyes Católicos
Calle de Castelar
Avenida de la Constitución
C Alemanes
Calle García Vinuesa
Puente de Triana (Puente de Isabel II)
Paseo de Cristóbal Colón
C San Jorge
Plaza del Altozano
Calle del Betis
Calle Mateos Gago
Calle Ximénez de Enciso
Calle Santa María la Blanca
BARRIO DE SANTA CRUZ
Plaza de Santa Cruz
Plaza del Triunfo
Calle Dos de Mayo
Avenida Menéndez Pelayo
Alcázar Gardens
Puerta de Jerez
Calle San Fernando
University
Plaza San Sebastián
Avenida de Carlos V
Avenida del Cid
Prado de San Sebastián
Avenida de Portugal
Paseo de las Delicias
Av de María Luisa
Avenida de Isabel la Católica
Plaza de España
Puente del Generalísimo
Parque de María Luisa
INFORMATION
Internetia 1 D4
Municipal Tourist Office 2 A3
Regional Tourist Office 3 C4
Tourist Office 4 C6
Turismo Sevilla 5 C4
SIGHTS & ACTIVITIES
Alcázar 6 C4
Cathedral 7 C4
La Giralda 8 C4
Museo de Bellas Artes 9 B2
Plaza de Toros de la Real Maestranza 10 B4
SLEEPING
Apartamentos Murillo 11 D4
Casa Sol y Luna 12 C2
Hostal Córdoba 13 D3
Hostal Museo 14 B2
Hostal Nuevo Suizo 15 C2
Hotel Alcántara 16 D4
Hotel Alminar 17 C3
Hotel Amadeus 18 D3
Hotel Simon 19 B4
Hotel Vincci La Rábida 20 B3
Pensión Vergara 21 D4
Petit Palace Marqués Santa Ana 22 C3
EATING
Aladdin 23 D4
Bodega Belmonte 24 C4
Confitería La Campana 25 C2
Corral del Agua 26 D4
Horno de San Buenaventura 27 C4
La Alacena de San Eloy 28 B2
Mesón Cinco Jotas 29 B4
Patio San Eloy 30 B2
Restaurante Al Medina 31 B2
DRINKING
Bodega Alvaro Peregil 32 C4
Bodeguita Los Soportales 33 C3
Cervecería Giralda 34 C4
Flaherty's Irish Pub 35 C3
La Antigua Bodeguita 36 C3
ENTERTAINMENT
Boss 37 A4
Casa de la Memoria (see 16)
Fun Club 38 C1
La Carbonería 39 D3
TRANSPORT
Airport Bus Stop 40 C4
Plaza de Armas Bus Station 41 A2
Prado de San Sebastián Bus Station 42 D5

DEATH IN THE AFTERNOON

Seville's bullfight season runs from Easter to October, with fights about 6.30pm most Sundays, and every day during the Feria de Abril and the preceding week. Tickets cost between €20 and €100, depending on who's fighting. *Sol* (sun) seats are cheaper than *sombra* (shade) seats. If you get a particularly good matador, the atmosphere in the ring can be electrifying. Tickets can be purchased in advance from **Empresa Pagés** (☎ 95 450 13 82; Calle de Adriano 37) and from 4.30pm on fight days at the bullring itself.

festivities involve six days of music, dancing, horse-riding and traditional dress, plus daily bullfights and a city-wide party.

Sleeping

Note that prices over Semana Santa and Feria can be up to double the high-season prices cited here. The city's accommodation is often full on weekends and is always booked solid during festivals, so it's a good idea to book ahead.

BUDGET

Hostal Nuevo Suizo (☎ 95 422 91 47; www.nuevosuizo.com; Calle Azofaifo 7; dm incl breakfast €21-25, s €39-43, d €49-69, all with shared bathroom; ⊠ ❄ 💻) Near the vibrant San Eloy bar strip, the Nuevo Suizo occupies an attractive old house and offers rooms and some dorms; only the rooms have air-con. There's one clean shared bathroom for every 10 beds, a roof terrace, a lounge and free (24-hour) Internet, tea and coffee. Though overpriced, it's the only true backpacker hostel in the centre of town.

Pensión Vergara (☎ 95 421 56 68; pensionvergarasevilla@yahoo.es; Calle Ximenez de Enciso 11; per person with shared bathroom €20-25; 💻) Attractive, welcoming and quirky in equal parts, the Vergara occupies a former 15th-century convent close to the cathedral. Go up the steep stairs to discover 12 rooms with high ceilings and pretty décor.

Casa Sol y Luna (☎ 95 421 06 82; www.casasolyluna1.com; 1st fl, Calle Pérez Galdós 1; d €45, s/d with shared bathroom €22/38; ⊠) Run by a young and very friendly English/Spanish couple, this *pensión* occupies the 1st floor of an 18th-century apartment building near Plaza Salvador. Rooms have hand-painted tiled floors, high ceilings and beds with pristine linen; the front ones are particularly attractive. Bathrooms are modern and sparkling clean and there's a convivial communal lounge.

Hostal Córdoba (☎ 95 422 74 98; hostalcordoba@mixmail.com; Calle Farnesio 12; s €35-50, d €55-70, with shared bathroom s €30-40, d €45-60; ❄) Otto, the West Highland terrier, will welcome you to this extremely friendly, family-run *hostal*. The simple rooms are light and immaculately maintained. This is a good choice, particularly if you opt for the rooms that share a bathroom, as these are very well priced.

Hostal Museo (☎ 95 491 55 26; www.hostalmuseo.com; Calle Abad Gordillo 17; s €35-40, d €45-55; ❄) The most unassuming of a growing number of boutique-style hotels in Seville, the Museo has a tranquil ambience and stylish (if tiny) rooms. It offers three-star amenities for two-star prices, meaning that it's often fully booked.

MIDRANGE

Hotel Simon (☎ 95 422 66 60; www.hotelsimonsevilla.com; Calle Garcia Vinuesa 19; s €49-65, d €72-102, ste €107-129; ❄) Renowned for its genteel ambience and tranquil internal courtyard, the Simon offers comfortable rooms adorned with colourful tiles. The front doubles are particularly attractive and offer good value for money, but the singles are tiny, dark and overpriced.

Hotel Alcántara (☎ 95 450 05 95; www.hotelalcantara.net; Calle Ximenez de Enciso 28; s €55-66, d €62-75; ❄) Sometimes it makes sense to trade character for service and comfort, and that's certainly the case at this well-located hotel. Large, light rooms overlook a pleasant internal courtyard and are blessedly quiet; they also have satellite TV and comfortable beds.

Hotel Alminar (☎ 95 429 39 13; reservas@hotelalminar.com; Calle Álvarez Quintero 52; s €60-90, d €90-145, all incl breakfast; ⊠ ❄ 💻) The Alminar opened in 2005 and has quickly built a reputation for its friendly service and very stylish rooms, all of which have sleek bathrooms, CD players and satellite TV. Two have private terraces with cathedral views.

Hotel Amadeus (☎ 95 450 14 43; www.hotelamadeussevilla.com; Calle Farnesio 6; s €65, d €80-175, ste

€130-210; ⊠ ❄ 💻) What a gorgeous looking hotel this is! Occupying a handsome 18th-century house and filled with fresh flowers, musical instruments and antique furniture, it's a perfect base from which to explore the city. Rooms are well set up, though soundproofing is a problem in a few.

Apartamentos Murillo (☎ 95 421 09 59; apartamentos@hotelmurillo.com; Calle Reinoso 6; 1-bedroom apt €77-94, 2-bedroom apt €99-156; ❄) Families will adore these fabulously located apartments. Recently outfitted, they come complete with comfortable beds, fully-equipped kitchens, swish bathrooms and work desks. Terrific value.

TOP END

Hotel Vincci La Rábida (☎ 95 450 12 80; www.vinccihoteles.com; Calle de Castelar 24; r €84-164, ste €236-327; P ❄ 💻) Seville has a surfeit of top-class hotels, and though this centrally located option doesn't have the fame of some of its competitors, it compensates with its impressive levels of service, comfort and value for money. Rooms are large and have every amenity; suites are absolute knockouts. There are a number of sunny patios, and there's a library and rooftop bar-restaurant with cathedral views.

Petit Palace Marqués Santa Ana (☎ 95 422 18 12; msa@hthoteles.com; Calle Jimios 9-11; r €97-174; P ❄ 💻) This new hotel has the wow factor in spades. If the sleek foyer doesn't immediately bowl you over, the hi-tech rooms with their massage showers, enormous beds, clothes press, laptop computer and exercise bike certainly will. A top location and stunning décor complete an ultraglam package.

Eating

Horno de San Buenaventura (cnr Av de la Constitución & Calle García Vinuesa) A perfect stop for breakfast or a light lunch, and even better for a midafternoon cake intake, this cavernous place serves everything from early morning coffees (€1.50) and *tostadas* (€1) to lunchtime *platos combinados* (€9 including bread and wine). Tables at the downstairs window are highly prized; those not fortunate enough to score one are relegated to the upstairs area.

Confiteria La Campana (Calle Sierpes 1) The bar at the rear of this popular *pastelería* is a perfect spot to enjoy a morning coffee and croissant. For a slightly greater outlay you can even commandeer a table on the sunny front terrace.

Patio San Eloy (☎ 95 422 11 48; Calle San Eloy 9; tapas €1.50) This bar has been high on Seville's popularity meter for years. Locals of all ages flock here to perch on the tiled rear steps and catch up over *burguillos* (small filled rolls, €1.50 to €2) and cheap drinks.

La Alacena de San Eloy (☎ 95 421 55 80; Calle San Eloy 31; tapas €2-2.50, raciónes €5-18) Most of Seville's tapas bars serve rustic plates and subscribe to the 'there's nothing more atmospheric than a stuffed bull's head' school of interior decoration, but this modern place bucks the trend. Full of chattering locals sampling the excellent list of wines by the glass and ordering up big from the fabulous tapas menu, it's as stylish as it is satisfying.

Bodega Belmonte (☎ 95 421 40 14; Calle Mateos Gago 24; tapas €2-4) In the shadow of the cathedral, this ever-busy place has an impressive selection of wines and good-quality tapas.

Aladdin (Calle Santa Maria la Blanca 15; falafel sandwich €4, chicken shwarma €5) For a fresh and tasty snack, take a seat in the luridly decorated *comedor* of this friendly café. If the pumping Arabic music videos don't make you feel like dancing, the quality and price of the food on offer certainly will.

Corral del Agua (☎ 95 422 07 14; Callejón del Agua 6; mains €12-16; 🕐 closed Jan & Feb & Sun year-round) The cool courtyard and attentive service make this a great spot to enjoy an indulgent lunch or dinner. Opt for local specialities such as the *solomillo de tenera a la sevillana* (veal sirloin in the Sevillian style).

AUTHOR'S CHOICE

Restaurante Al Medina (☎ 95 421 54 51; Calle San Roque 13; mains €10.50-14.50, menú degustación €20; 🕐 closed Mon & dinner Sun) For the best Moroccan food this side of Marrakesh, make your way to this enchanting restaurant near the Museo de Bellas Artes. The décor is wonderfully evocative of the medina (as soon as we saw the fresh rose petals scattered on the tabletops we became customers for life) and the food is quite wonderful – try the *couscous de pollo* (chicken couscous) and you too will become a devotee. It's tiny (11 tables only), so make sure you book ahead.

Mesón Cinco Jotas (☎ 95 421 07 63; Calle de Castelar 1; raciónes €7-21.50, mains €14-23) It's mandatory to sample *jamón* when in Spain, and this is one of the best places in the country to do so. Its succulent '*Jamón* 5' comes from pigs that have snuffled out the finest acorns and is utterly delicious.

Drinking

Bodega Alvaro Peregil (Calle Mateos Gago) The crowd spills out onto the footpath in front of this tiny place from early morning till late at night.

Cervecería Giralda (☎ 95 422 74 35; Calle Mateos Gago 1) On the other side of the street from Alvaro Peregil, you'll find this popular bar occupying a former Muslim *hammam* (bathhouse).

Flaherty's Irish Pub (☎ 95 421 04 17; Calle Alemanes 7; 🕑 11am-late) Sports fans tend to gravitate towards Flaherty's, which occupies a premium position opposite the cathedral.

Plaza Salvador is full of drinkers every evening until around 1am, as well as on weekend afternoons. Grab a beer at La Antigua Bodeguita or Bodeguita Los Soportales and either prop up at one of the barrel tables or sit on the steps of the Parroquia del Salvador, a large baroque church. It's great fun.

Entertainment

Seville is arguably Spain's flamenco capital and you're most likely to catch a spontaneous atmosphere (of unpredictable quality) in one of the bars staging regular nights of flamenco with no admission fee.

La Carbonería (☎ 95 421 44 60; Calle Levíes 18; 🕑 9pm-4am) The sprawling La Carbonería throngs every night of the week with tourists and locals who come to mingle and enjoy the live flamenco on offer.

Casa de la Memoria Al-Andalus (☎ 95 456 06 70; Calle Ximenez de Enciso 28; adult/student/child €12/8/6) For a very different experience, book a ticket at this well-priced place, which puts on excellent nightly flamenco performances in a wonderful patio setting.

The Alameda de Hércules area, a former red-light district north of the city centre, is a buzzing place with lots of offbeat bars. Some have live music, including the **Fun Club** (☎ 95 438 93 29; Alameda de Hércules 86; live music about €5; 🕑 10pm-6am Thu-Sat).

In summer there's a lively scene along the eastern bank of the Guadalquivir River, which is dotted with temporary bars. On Calle del Betis, on the far bank, you'll find some good dance bars/discos, including **Boss** (☎ 95 499 01 04; Calle del Betis 57; admission free; 🕑 11pm-7am Wed-Sat, closed Jun-Aug), Seville's biggest nightclub.

Getting There & Away

AIR

There's a range of domestic and international flights in and out of Seville's **San Pablo airport** (SVQ; ☎ 95 444 90 00; www.aena.es), which is 8.5km from the city centre.

BUS

There are regular services from the **Plaza de Armas bus station** (☎ 95 490 80 40; Av del Cristo de la Expiración) to destinations outside Andalucía. **Socibus** (☎ 90 222 92 92; www.socibus.es) travels to Madrid (€17.50, six hours, 14 daily), and Alsa goes to Mérida (€11.55, three hours, nine daily), Cáceres (€15.55, four hours, seven daily), Barcelona (€69.40, 14½ to 16½ hours, three daily), Valencia (€45, 10 to 10½ hours, four daily) and Lisbon (€36, 7½ hours, two daily).

Buses to other parts of Andalucía use **Prado de San Sebastián bus station** (☎ 95 441 71 11; Plaza San Sebastián). **Alsina Graells** (☎ 95 740 40 40) services Córdoba (€9.45, 1¾ hours to 2¼ hours, nine daily), Granada (€17.60, three hours, 10 daily) and Málaga (€14.40, 2½ hours, 10 daily). **Los Amarillos** (www.losamarillos.com) serves Ronda (€9.90, 2½ hours, five daily). **Comes** (☎ 90 219 92 08; www.tgcomes.es) runs to Tarifa (€14.80, 3½ hours, four daily) and Cádiz (€10.30, 1¾ hours, 10 daily).

TRAIN

From Seville's **Estación de Santa Justa** (Av Kansas City), 1.5km northeast of the centre, there are super-fast AVE trains as well as regular trains to Madrid (€54.70 to €127.10, 2½ to 3¼ hours, hourly) and Córdoba (€7.55 to €38.60, 45 minutes to 1¼ hours, hourly).

Other trains serve Cádiz (€9.10 to €29.70, 1½ to two hours, 12 daily), Granada (€20.05, 3¼ hours, four daily), Málaga (€16.05, 2½ hours, six daily) and Barcelona (€72.90 to €191.20, 10½ to 13 hours, two daily).

Getting Around

Amarillos Tours (☎ 90 221 03 17) runs a bus service between the airport and Puerta de Jerez in the city every half-hour between 6.15am and 11pm daily (€2.30). A taxi will cost between €20 and €30 depending on traffic and the number of bags you have.

Bus C1, in front of Santa Justa train station, follows a clockwise circuit via Av de Carlos V, close to Prado de San Sebastián bus station and the city centre; bus C2 does the same route anticlockwise. Bus C4, south down Calle de Arjona from Plaza de Armas bus station, goes to Puerta de Jerez in the centre; returning, take C3. Tickets for these routes cost €0.95.

CÓRDOBA

pop 323,613

Modern-day Córdoba pays graceful testament to its Moorish past. Its magnificent Mezquita (Mosque) has been described as the greatest visual representation of homesickness ever constructed, and is one of the highlights of any visit to Spain.

Information

Hostal el Pilar Del Potro (Calle de Lucano; Internet per 30min €1) You'll find three coin-operated Internet terminals in the small public reception area next to the *cafetería*.

Municipal tourist office kiosks (☎ 90 220 17 74; www.turismodecordoba.org; 🕑 10am-2pm & 4.30-7pm) Helpful info at Plaza de las Tendillas, Campo Santos Mártires, Plaza Posada del Potro and the train station.

Regional tourist office (☎ 95 747 12 35; Calle de Torrijos 10; 🕑 9.30am-6pm Mon-Fri, 10am-6pm Sat, 10am-2pm Sun Nov-Feb, to 7pm Mon-Fri Mar-Oct)

Sights & Activities

The inside of the famous **Mezquita** (☎ 95 747 05 12; adult/child 10 & over/child under 10 €8/4/free, audio guide €3; 🕑 10am-7.30pm Mon-Sat Apr-Jun, to 7pm Mon-Sat Mar & Jul-Oct, to 6pm Mon-Sat Feb & Nov, to 5.30pm Mon-Sat Dec & Jan, 8.30-10.15am & 2-6pm Sun year-round), which was begun by emir Abd ar-Rahman I in 785 and enlarged by subsequent generations, is a mesmerising sequence of two-tier arches amid a thicket of columns. From 1236, the mosque was used as a church and in the 16th century a cathedral was built right in its centre – somewhat wrecking the effect of the original Muslim building. Entrance is free if you visit between 8.30am and 10am Monday to Saturday and observe strict silence.

The **Judería**, Córdoba's medieval Jewish quarter northwest of the Mezquita, is an intriguing maze of narrow streets, small plazas and traditional houses with flower-filled patios. Don't miss the beautiful little **Sinagoga** (☎ 95 720 29 28; Calle de los Judíos; admission non-EU/EU citizens €0.30/free; 🕑 9.30am-2pm & 3.30-5.30pm Tue-Sat, 9.30am-1.30pm Sun).

Southwest of the Mezquita stands the **Alcázar de los Reyes Cristianos** (Fortress of the Christian Monarchs; ☎ 95 742 01 51; adult/student €4/2, free Fri; 🕑 10am-2pm & 4.30-6.30pm Tue-Sat mid-Oct–Apr, 10am-2pm & 5.30-7.30pm Tue-Sat May, Jun & Sep–mid-Oct, 8.30am-2.30pm Tue-Sat Jul & Aug, 9.30am-2.30pm Sun year-round), with its large and lovely gardens.

On the southern side of the river, across the Puente Romano, is the **Torre de la Calahorra** (☎ 95 729 39 29; Puente Romano; adult/child €4.50/3; 🕑 10am-6pm) with a museum highlighting the intellectual achievements of Islamic Córdoba.

It's well worth the 8km trip west of Córdoba to the intriguing **Madinat Al-Zahra** (☎ 95 732 91 30; Carretera Palma del Río, Km 5.5; admission non-EU/EU citizens €1.50/free; 🕑 10am-6.30pm Tue-Sat, to 2pm Sun), a mighty Muslim city-palace from the 10th century. If you don't have a car, catch the tourist bus (€5), which leaves from Av del Alcázar at 11am and returns

SPAIN

FLAMENCO FUSION

Flamenco has become much more than the traditional signature music of southern Spain. Once exclusively the music of the Gitanos (Roma people), in recent years flamenco has also morphed into a modern fusion of different rhythms and styles. Since the 1970s, bands have experimented with blues, rock, Latin, jazz and even punk to create cool new sounds as well as a new fan base of young Spaniards. So much so that these days you are as likely to hear flamenco hip-hop blasting out of a souped-up car on a Friday night as to catch it at a tourist show.

Bands that first broke the ground in this new wave of flamenco include the bluesy-style Pata Negra, Ketama (African, Cuban and Brazilian rhythms) and Radio Tarifa (North African and medieval mix). In recent years Chambao has hit the mark with its flamenco chill and Mala Rodriguez has put flamenco hip into hip-hop.

2½ hours later. Tickets can be purchased from municipal tourist booths.

Sleeping

Instalación Juvenil Córdoba (☎ 95 729 01 66; Plaza de Judá Leví; dm under 25/25 & over €14.50/19; ⊠ ❄) What an excellent youth hostel this is! Located on a pretty plaza, it occupies two buildings (one new, one old) around attractive, palm-filled courtyards. The two-bed rooms are fabulous, with private bathroom, vaulted ceilings and comfortable single beds; the four-bed rooms have bunks and private bathroom.

Hotel Maestre (☎ 95 747 24 10; www.hotelmaestre.com; Calle Romero Barros 4 & 6; s €25-35, d €42-49; P ❄) This well-run modern hotel has a comfortable indoor/outdoor foyer sitting area and well-appointed rooms. Those at the rear are quieter and slightly larger.

Hotel González (☎ 95 747 98 19; www.hotelgonzalez.com; Calle Manríquez 3; s €27-37, d €44-71; ❄) The González may not be the most stylish of the midrange choices on offer, but it's certainly one of the cheapest and most comfortable. Large rooms have comfortable beds, satellite TV and stained pine furniture. There's also a charming patio.

Hostal Lineros 38 (☎ 95 748 25 17; www.hostallineros38.com; Calle de Lineros 38; s €32-52, d €52-58, ste €97-110; P ⊠ ❄) Rooms in this boutique hotel are individually decorated, featuring brightly painted walls, exposed beams and four-poster beds. Service can be a bit unfriendly.

Hotel Lola (☎ 95 720 03 05; www.hotelconencantolola.com; Calle Romero 3; d incl breakfast €85-122; ❄) The Lola's eight rooms feature typical Córdoban décor, with original tiled floors, beamed ceilings and antique furniture; mod cons come in the form of satellite TV and minibar. The rooms aren't quite as well maintained as they should be at these prices, but the service is exemplary.

Eating & Drinking

Taberna San Miguel (Plaza San Miguel 1; tapas €1.50, media raciónes €3-7; 🕒 closed Sun & Aug) Known locally as *El Pisto* (Barrel), this busy place has been serving rustic food and cheap jugs of Moriles wine since 1880.

Comedor Arabe-Andalusí (☎ 95 747 51 62; Plaza Abades 4; mains €4-6; 🕒 closed Mon) Set on a pretty plaza, this Arabian-style eatery has dim lighting, Persian carpets and low tables. The meat kebabs are succulent and the salads and falafel are fresh and delicious.

Bodegas Mezquita (☎ 95 749 00 04; www.bodegamezquita.com; Calle Céspedes 12; raciónes €4-6) This new addition to Cordóba's food and drink scene has a shop selling local gourmet produce and an attached and very popular *bodega* that serves more than 40 different tapas and 60 wines. There's another branch (produce store only) at Calle Corregidor Luis de la Cerda 73.

Casa Pepe de la Judería (☎ 95 720 07 44; Calle Romero 1; media raciónes €2.50-6, mains €11-18) This local classic is always busy; you can eat hearty Córdoban specialities such as *cabo de toro a la Córdobesa* (bull's tail Córdoba style, €11) in the rooms set around the patio or graze on tapas at the bar.

Bodega Campos (☎ 95 749 75 00; Calle de Lineros 32; mains €14-20; 🕒 closed Sun dinner) The restaurant of choice for wealthy Córdobeses since 1908, this swish place is where you should come to try well-cooked local specialities such as *bacalao con salsa de garbanzos y espinacas* (bacalao with a sauce of chickpeas and spinach, €18.90), served with complimentary glasses of Fino and Amontillado.

Entertainment

Jazz Café (Calle Espartería; 🕒 5pm-4am) This is a laid-back bar hosting jam sessions on Tuesday and live jazz on Wednesday.

Soul (☎ 95 749 15 80; Calle de Alfonso XIII 3; 🕒 10am-3am Mon-Fri, 5pm-4am Sat & Sun) Attracting student/arty types, this venue hosts regular live music.

Getting There & Away

From the **bus station** (☎ 95 740 40 40; Plaza de las Tres Culturas), about 1km northwest of Plaza de las Tendillas, Alsina Graells runs services to Seville (€9.45, 1¾ hours to 2¼ hours, nine daily), Granada (€11.40, 2¾ hours to four hours, 10 daily) and Málaga (€11.55, 2¾ hours to 3¼ hours, five daily). **Secorbus** (☎ 90 222 92 92; www.secorbus.es) travels to Madrid (€13.50, 4¾ hours, six daily).

From the **train station** (Av América), services go to Seville (€7.55 to €21.90, 45 minutes to 1¼ hours, 27 daily) and Madrid (€38.60 to €64.60, 1¾ hours to 2¼ hours, six daily). There are also trains to Málaga (€15.60 to €16.60, 2¼ hours, six daily) and Barcelona (€76.10 to €139.50, eight to 11 hours, four daily).

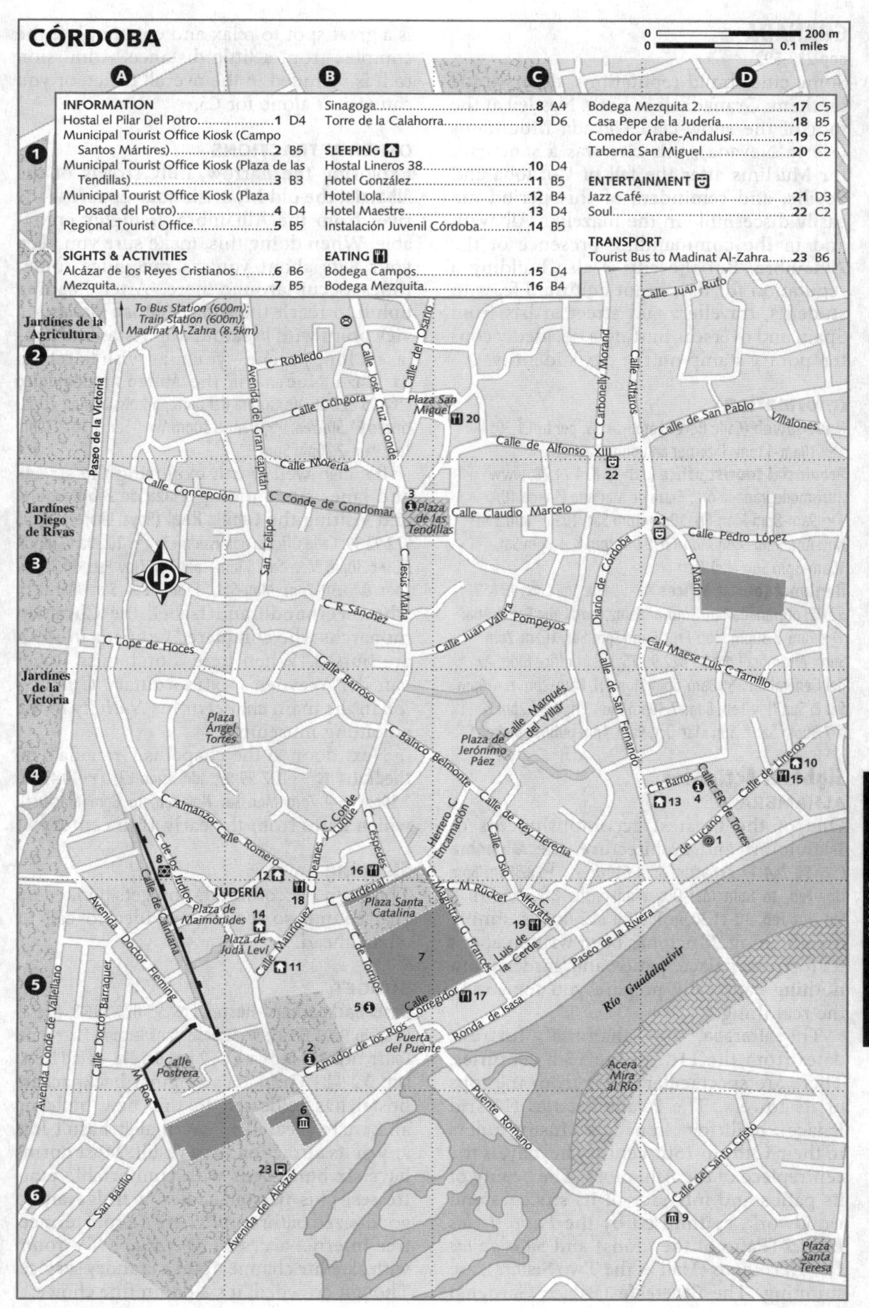
CÓRDOBA
0 200 m
0 0.1 miles
INFORMATION
Hostal el Pilar Del Potro 1 D4
Municipal Tourist Office Kiosk (Campo Santos Mártires) 2 B5
Municipal Tourist Office Kiosk (Plaza de las Tendillas) 3 B3
Municipal Tourist Office Kiosk (Plaza Posada del Potro) 4 D4
Regional Tourist Office 5 B5
SIGHTS & ACTIVITIES
Alcázar de los Reyes Cristianos 6 B6
Mezquita 7 B5
Sinagoga 8 A4
Torre de la Calahorra 9 D6
SLEEPING
Hostal Lineros 38 10 D4
Hotel González 11 B5
Hotel Lola 12 B4
Hotel Maestre 13 D4
Instalación Juvenil Córdoba 14 B5
EATING
Bodega Campos 15 D4
Bodega Mezquita 16 B4
Bodega Mezquita 2 17 C5
Casa Pepe de la Judería 18 B5
Comedor Árabe-Andalusí 19 C5
Taberna San Miguel 20 C2
ENTERTAINMENT
Jazz Café 21 D3
Soul 22 C2
TRANSPORT
Tourist Bus to Madinat Al-Zahra 23 B6
To Bus Station (600m); Train Station (600m); Madinat Al-Zahra (8.5km)
Jardínes de la Agricultura
Jardínes Diego de Rivas
Jardínes de la Victoria
Paseo de la Victoria
Avenida del Gran Capitán
San Felipe
C Robledo
Calle Góngora
Calle José Cruz Conde
Calle del Osario
Plaza San Miguel
Calle Morería
Calle Concepción
C Conde de Gondomar
Plaza de las Tendillas
Calle Claudio Marcelo
Calle de Alfonso XIII
Calle de San Pablo
Villalones
Calle Juan Rufo
C Carbonelly Morand
Calle Alfaros
Calle Pedro López
R Marín
Diario de Córdoba
C Jesús María
C R Sánchez
Calle Juan Valera
Pompeyos
C Lope de Hoces
Calle Barroso
Call Maese Luis C Tarnillo
Calle de San Fernando
Plaza Ángel Torres
Calle Marqués del Villar
Plaza de Jerónimo Páez
C Balnco Belmonte
Calle de Rey Heredia
C Almanzor
Calle Romero
C Deanes
C Conde y Luque
C Céspedes
Herrero C Encarnación
Calle Osío
C R Barros
Caller ER de Torres
Calle de Lineros
C de Lucano
C de los Judíos
Calle de Cairuana
JUDERÍA
Plaza de Maimónides
Plaza de Judá Leví
Calle Manríquez
C Cardenal
Plaza Santa Catalina
C de Torrijos
C Magistral G Francés
C M Rücker
Alfayatas
Luis de la Cerda
Paseo de la Rivera
Río Guadalquivir
Avenida Doctor Fleming
Calle Corregidor
Ronda de Isasa
Puerta del Puente
C Amador de los Ríos
Avenida Conde de Vallellano
Calle Doctor Barraquer
Calle Postrera
M Roa
Puente Romano
Acera Mira al Río
Calle del Santo Cristo
Plaza Santa Teresa
C San Basilio
Avenida del Alcázar
SPAIN

GRANADA

pop 237,592

Some cities build reputations, others trade on them. Granada does both. Nestled at the foot of the snow-clad Nevada Mountains (Sierra Nevada), this city was a sanctuary for Muslims after the fall of Córdoba and Seville, and reminders of this period are easily discernible in the mazelike Albayzín and in the commanding presence of the Alhambra. But the city is also building a reputation for its vibrant cultural life, with students, travellers and street artists from Spain and overseas putting a decidedly contemporary stamp on the city's identity.

Information

Navegaweb (Calle Reyes Católicos 55; per hr €1.50; 10am-11pm) Internet and phone access.

Provincial tourist office (95 824 71 28; www.turismodegranada.org; Plaza de Mariana Pineda 10; 9am-8pm Mon-Fri, 10am-1pm Sat, 10am-3pm Sun Nov-Apr, 9am-9pm Mon-Fri, 9am-2pm & 4-7pm Sat, 10am-3pm Sun May-Oct)

Regional tourist offices Plaza Santa Ana (95 857 52 02; otgranada@turismo-andaluz.com; Calle Santa Ana; 9am-7.30pm Mon-Fri, 10am-7pm Sat, 10am-2pm Sun); Alhambra (95 822 95 75; ticket office Bldg, Av del Generalife; 8am-6pm Mon-Fri, 8am-2pm & 4-6pm Sat & Sun Nov-Feb, 8am-7.30pm Mon-Fri, 8am-2pm & 4-7.30pm Sat & Sun Mar-Oct, 9am-1pm public holidays)

Sights & Activities

ALHAMBRA

One of the greatest accomplishments of Islamic art and architecture, the **Alhambra** (90 244 12 21; adult/child €10/free; 8.30am-6pm Nov-Feb, to 8pm Mar-Oct, night visits 8-9.30pm Fri & Sat Nov-Feb, 10-11.30pm Tue-Sat Mar-Oct) is simply breathtaking. Much has been written about its fortress, palace, patios and gardens, but nothing can really prepare you for seeing the real thing.

The **Alcazaba**, the Alhambra's fortress, dates from the 11th to the 13th centuries. There are spectacular views from the tops of its towers. The **Palacio Nazaries** (Nasrid Palace), built for Granada's Muslim rulers in their 13th- to 15th-century heyday, is the centrepiece of the Alhambra. The beauty of its patios and intricacy of its stuccoes and woodwork, epitomised by the *Patio de los Leones* (Patio of the Lions) and *Sala de las Dos Hermanas* (Hall of the Two Sisters), are stunning. The **Generalife** (Palace Gardens) is a great spot to relax and contemplate the complex from a little distance. Admission to it is included in the overall ticket, or you can visit it alone for €5.

OTHER ATTRACTIONS

Exploring the narrow, hilly streets of the **Albayzín**, the old Moorish quarter across the river from the Alhambra, is highly enjoyable. When doing this, make sure you keep your wits about you, as muggings sometimes occur around here. After heading uphill to reach the **Mirador de San Nicolas** – a viewpoint with breathtaking vistas and a relaxed, hippy scene – you may wish to return to Plaza Nueva via the **Museo Arqueológico** (95 822 56 40; Carrera del Darro; admission non-EU/EU citizen €1.50/free; 9am-8.30pm Wed-Sat, 2.30-8.30pm Tue, 9am-2.30pm Sun).

It's also well worth exploring the streets and lanes surrounding **Plaza de Bib-Rambla**, and visiting the **Capilla Real** (Royal Chapel; 95 822 92 39; Calle Oficios; admission €3; 10.30am-1pm & 3.30-6.30pm Mon-Sat, 11am-1pm Sun Nov-Feb, 10.30am-1pm & 4.30-7pm Mon-Sat, 11am-1pm Sun Mar-Oct), where Fernando and Isabel, the Christian monarchs who conquered Granada in 1492, are buried. When here, don't miss Roger van der Weyden's extraordinary *Crucifixion* in the main chapel or his *Nativity* in the adjoining museum.

Next door to the chapel is Granada's **cathedral** (95 822 29 59; admission €3; 10.45am-1.30pm & 4-7pm Mon-Sat Nov-Feb, to 8pm Mar-Oct), which dates from the early 16th century.

Sleeping

The town's accommodation gets booked up year-round, so it's a good idea to call or email ahead.

BUDGET

Oasis Backpackers' Hostel (95 821 58 48, freecall in Spain 9001 OASIS; www.oasisgranada.com; Placeta del Correo Viejo 3; 6-bed dm €15, 2-bed dm €18, all incl breakfast;) Granada's original backpackers hostel has relocated to this new building and we're pleased to say that it hasn't lost any of its attractions as a result. Most dorms have six bunk-beds with comfortable mattresses, plus personal safes, a fridge and a good-sized bathroom. There's a roof terrace, free Internet access, a *cafetería,* a TV room with satellite channels and a laundry service. Though crowded, it's a damn fine choice.

SPAIN

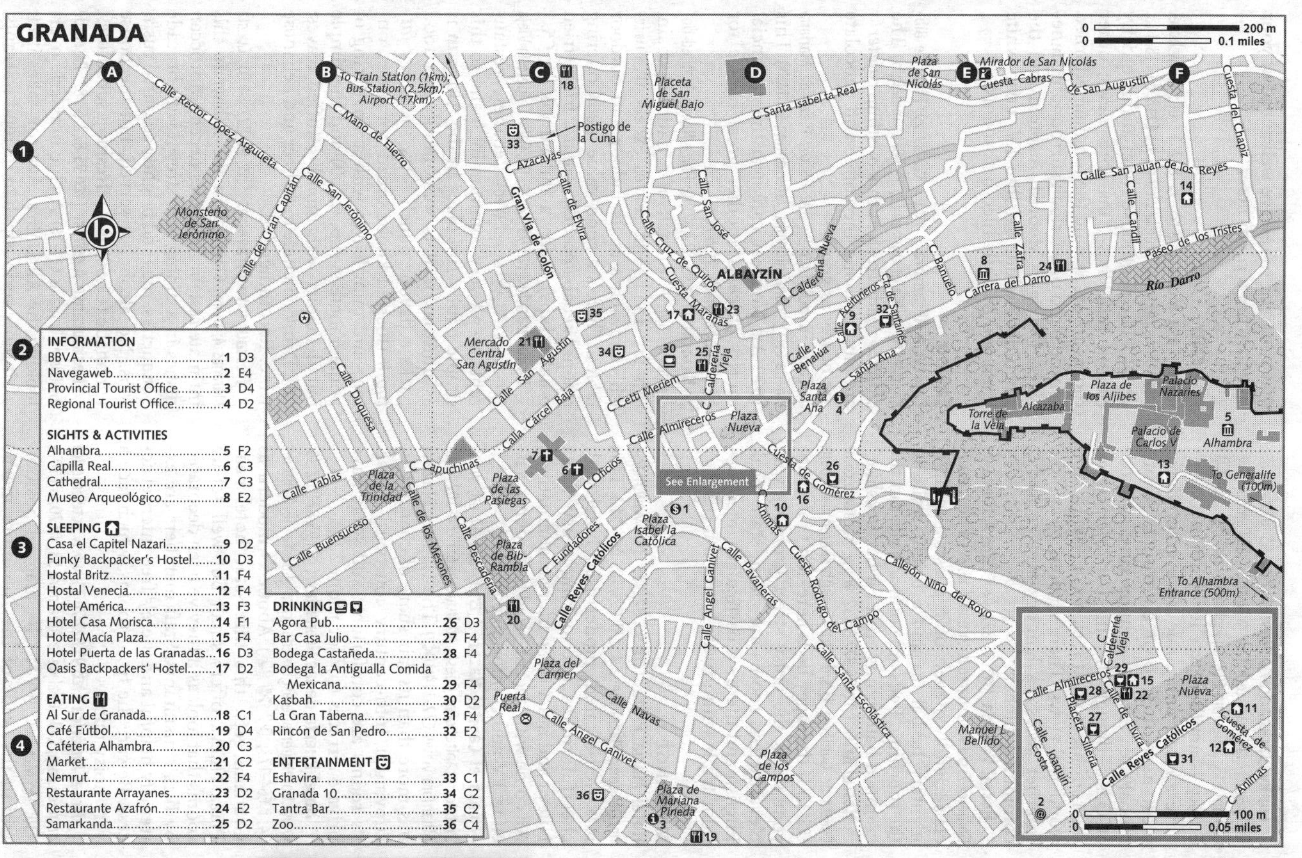
GRANADA
INFORMATION
BBVA 1 D3
Navegaweb 2 E4
Provincial Tourist Office 3 D4
Regional Tourist Office 4 D2
SIGHTS & ACTIVITIES
Alhambra 5 F2
Capilla Real 6 C3
Cathedral 7 C3
Museo Arqueológico 8 E2
SLEEPING
Casa el Capitel Nazarí 9 D2
Funky Backpacker's Hostel 10 D3
Hostal Britz 11 F4
Hostal Venecia 12 F4
Hotel América 13 F3
Hotel Casa Morisca 14 F1
Hotel Macía Plaza 15 F4
Hotel Puerta de las Granadas 16 D3
Oasis Backpackers' Hostel 17 D2
EATING
Al Sur de Granada 18 C1
Café Fútbol 19 D4
Caféteria Alhambra 20 C3
Market 21 C2
Nemrut 22 F4
Restaurante Arrayanes 23 D2
Restaurante Azafrón 24 E2
Samarkanda 25 D2
DRINKING
Agora Pub 26 D3
Bar Casa Julio 27 F4
Bodega Castañeda 28 F4
Bodega la Antigualla Comida Mexicana 29 F4
Kasbah 30 D2
La Gran Taberna 31 F4
Rincón de San Pedro 32 E2
ENTERTAINMENT
Eshavira 33 C1
Granada 10 34 C2
Tantra Bar 35 C2
Zoo 36 C4
To Train Station (1km); Bus Station (2.5km); Airport (17km)
Gran Vía de Colón
Calle Reyes Católicos
ALBAYZÍN
Alhambra
Palacio Nazaríes
Palacio de Carlos V
Alcazaba
Plaza Nueva
Río Darro
To Generalife (100m)
To Alhambra Entrance (500m)
See Enlargement
200 m
0.1 miles

SPAIN

Funky Backpacker's Hostel (☎ 95 822 14 62; funky@alternativeacc.com; Cuesta Rodrigo del Campo 13; 6-bed dm €15, 2-bed dm €18, all incl breakfast; ⊠ ❄ 💻) Funky is another excellent choice. Dorms have air-con and some have great views; most have their own bathrooms. Communal areas aren't as impressive as those at Oasis, though the tiny bar-*cafetería* on the roof has a great feel, a satellite TV and wonderful views. There's a book swap, free Internet access, a laundry service and a communal kitchen.

Hostal Venecia (☎ 95 822 39 87; 2nd fl, Cuesta de Gomérez 2; s/d with shared bathroom €15/32) The Venecia's friendly owners offer guests a complimentary herbal tea and a bright smile in the morning. Beds are comfortable, but the cramped bathrooms are a bit barrackslike.

Hostal Britz (☎ 95 822 36 52; www.lisboaweb.com; Cuesta de Gomérez 1; s/d €30/45, with shared bathroom €25/32) If the saggy beds here don't interrupt your sleep, the noisy street probably will. Nevertheless, rooms are clean, staff speak English and there's a particularly nice top-floor triple with private bathroom (€54).

MIDRANGE

Hotel Macía Plaza (☎ 95 822 75 36; www.maciahoteles.com; Plaza Nueva 4; s/d €53/78; ⊠ ❄) This is a well-located, modernised hotel with cheerful rooms overlooking noisy Plaza Nueva and quiet but dark rear alternatives. All come with decent-sized bathrooms, satellite TV and comfortable beds.

Casa el Capitel Nazari (☎ 95 821 52 60; www.hotelcasacapitel.com; Cuesta Aceituneros 6; r €60-102, with Alhambra views €72-114; ❄) The Capitel Nazari has more than its fair share of charm. Occupying a 16th-century courtyard house, its rooms are comfortable and some have private terraces (try for room 22).

Hotel Puerta de las Granadas (☎ 95 821 62 30; www.hotelpuertadelasgranadas.com; Cuesta de Gomérez 14; r €64-173; ⊠ ❄ 💻) About as modern as Granada gets, this three-star hotel near Plaza Nueva offers small but well set-up rooms that look as if they've been decorated by Ikea consultants. Staff members are extremely helpful and there's free Internet access. Beware the front rooms, which face a very noisy pub.

Hotel América (☎ 95 822 74 71; www.hotelamericagranada.com; Calle Real de la Alhambra 53; s €70, d €107-130; 🕑 Mar-Nov; Ⓟ ❄) Its magical position within the walls of the Alhambra means that you need to reserve well ahead of your stay to score a room here.

TOP END

Hotel Casa Morisca (☎ 95 822 11 00; www.hotelcasamorisca.com; Cuesta de la Victoria 9; s €118, d €118-148; Ⓟ ❄) The penthouse room at this quietly elegant hotel has Alhambra views; other rooms are set around the fountain-adorned central patio or overlook surrounding laneways. Décor is Moorish-inspired and the amenities include satellite TV, crisp white linen and brightly tiled bathrooms.

Eating

Caféteria Alhambra (☎ 95 852 39 29; Plaza de Bib-Rambla 27; ración of churros €2; 🕑 8am-midnight) The *churros* made fresh at this bustling *cafetería* are fabulous, and the coffee and chocolate are nearly as good.

Café Fútbol (☎ 95 822 66 62; Plaza de Mariana Pineda 6; 🕑 6am-midnight, later during festivals) This 1922 Art Nouveau café near the provincial tourist office is another great choice for chocolate and *churros*.

Nemrut (☎ 95 822 67 30; Plaza Nueva 1; filled bocadillos €3.50) A branch of a national chain, this fast-food joint serves excellent Turkish sandwiches at its indoor and outdoor tables. There's a good-value *menú* offering a doner kebab *bocadillo, patatas fritas* (fried potato chips), baklava and a drink for €6.

Samarkanda (☎ 95 821 00 04; Calle Calderería Vieja 5; mains €7-9; 🕑 closed Wed) Lebanese restaurants aren't very common in Spain, so this simple family-run place in the Albayzín is as unusual as it is welcoming. The food packs a flavour punch – try the tangy *fattoosh* (toasted khobz bread, tomatoes, onions and mint leaves with a smattering of pomegranate syrup; €5.50) and the simple but delicious *wara ainab* (stuffed leaves; €6). Drinks include local beer and Lebanese wine. Recommended.

Restaurante Arrayanes (☎ 95 822 84 01; Cuesta Marañas 4; mains €11-12.50) In the Albayzín, this intimate restaurant serves decent Moroccan dishes in a dining area strewn with brocade banquettes, rugs and brightly coloured cushions. No alcohol is served, but the house lemonade (€1.50) is a refreshing substitute.

Restaurante Azafrón (☎ 95 822 68 82; Paseo de los Tristes 1; mains €11-16) A chic brasserie overlooking the Alhambra, Azafrón takes itself a bit more seriously than its food warrants, but it's still an enjoyable place for a lunch or dinner, particularly if you can score a window table.

For fresh fruit and veggies, visit the large covered **market** (Calle San Agustín) near the cathedral. Quality local cheese, meats and wine can be picked up at **Al Sur de Granada** (☎ 95 827 02 45; Calle de Elvira 150).

Drinking

Bar Casa Julio (Calle Hermosa) This traditional bar is renowned for its tapas, especially the *boquerones fritos* (fried fresh anchovies).

La Gran Taberna (☎ 95 822 88 46; Plaza Nueva 12; tablas €5-9) Everyone feels welcome at this traditional-style *bodega,* where drinks are accompanied by complimentary tapas.

Kasbah (☎ 95 822 79 36; Calle Caldereria Nueva 4; tea €2; 12.30pm-12.30am) Granada's Moorish legacy lives on in the Albayzín's fabulous Arabian-style *teterías* (teahouses). One of the best is Kasbah, a candle-lit den filled with Persian rugs and secret alcoves. It also has live flamenco and belly dancing.

Other good choices for a drink or two are **Rincón de San Pedro** (Carrera del Darro 12), **Agora Pub** (Cuesta de Gomérez; closed Sun), **Bodega Castañeda** (Calle Almireceros) and **Bodega la Antigualla Comida Mexicana** (Calle de Elvira). All are near Plaza Nueva and stay open late.

Entertainment

Eshavira (☎ 95 829 08 29; www.eshavira.com; Postigo de la Cuna 2; 8.30pm-3am) Come here for live jazz and flamenco. The prices of drinks rise when the live music starts.

Granada 10 (Calle Cárcel Baja; admission €6; midnight-dawn) This place holds its 'Soul Kitchen' on Wednesday nights. It also runs the hip Tantra Bar off Calle de Elvira, which has an in-house DJ.

Zoo (Plaza Campillo; 2am-8am Thu-Sun) Slightly seedy Zoo is one of the city's longest functioning gay dance clubs.

Getting There & Away

Autocares J Gonzalez (☎ 95 849 01 64; www.autocaresjosegonzalez.com) runs a bus service between Granada's new **airport** (GRX; ☎ 95 824 52 00; www.aena.es) and the city centre. The service runs between 9.10am and 11pm (10pm on Saturday), takes 35 minutes and costs €3. A taxi costs €20 to €25.

The **bus station** (☎ 95 818 54 80; Carretera de Jaén) is 3km northwest of the centre. Buses 3 and 33 (€1) travel between the two. Alsina Graells has services to Madrid's Estación Sur (€14.70, five hours, 12 daily), Málaga (€8.90, 1¾ hours, 18 daily), Seville (€17.60, three to four hours, 10 daily) and Córdoba (€11.40, 2¾ hours, 11 daily). Alsa travels to Barcelona (€61.90 to €73.05, seven to 10 hours, six daily).

The **train station** (Av de Andaluces) is about 1.5km southwest of the centre. Catch bus 4, 6, 7, 9 or 11 (€1) going east (right) from Av de la Consitutión to get to the centre. There are trains to Madrid-Chamartín (€31.30 to €35.40, six hours, two daily), Seville (€20.05, three hours, four daily) and Algeciras (€17, 4¾ hours, three daily) via Ronda (€11.35, 2¾ hours). Two services travel to Barcelona (€52.10 to €188.60, 12 hours) via Valencia (€42.70 to €174, 7½ hours) each day.

COSTA DE ALMERÍA

The coast east of Almería in eastern Andalucía is perhaps the last section of Spain's Mediterranean coast where you can have a beach to yourself. This is Spain's sunniest region – even in late March it can be warm enough to strip off and take in the rays. For information, visit Almería City's **tourist office** (☎ 95 027 43 55; Parque Nicolás Salmerón).

Sights & Activities

The **Alcazaba** (☎ 95 027 16 17; Calle Almanzor; admission non-EU/EU citizens €1.50/free; 9.30am-1.30pm & 3.30-7pm Oct-Apr, 10am-2pm & 5-8pm May-Sep), an enormous 10th-century Muslim fortress, is the highlight of Almería City.

The best thing about the region is the wonderful coastline and semidesert scenery of the **Cabo de Gata** promontory. All along the 50km coast from El Cabo de Gata village to Agua Amarga, some of the most beautiful and empty beaches on the Mediterranean alternate with precipitous cliffs and scattered villages. Roads or paths run along or close to this whole coastline, which is a protected area. The main village is laidback **San José**, with excellent beaches nearby, such as **Playa de los Genoveses** and **Playa de Mónsul**.

North of Almería, the landscape of canyons and rocky wastelands looks like something straight out of America's Wild West. In the 1960s and '70s, Western movie makers shot dozens of films here, including parts of *The Magnificent Seven* and *A*

SPAIN

ALHAMBRA TICKETS

It is a good idea to book tickets to the Alhambra in advance. You can reserve via any branch of the Banco Bilbao Viscaya (BBVA), including the Granada branch on Plaza Isabel la Católica, or by calling ☎ 90 222 44 60 from within Spain (☎ 00 34 91 537 91 78 from abroad) or paying by credit card on the website www.alhambratickets.com. An extra €0.88 is charged for the online service.

Note that Alhambra tickets are only valid for half a day, so you'll need to specify whether you wish to visit in the morning or afternoon. To book night visits, call ☎ 95 857 51 26/7.

Fistful of Dollars. The industry left behind three Wild West town sets that can be visited; the most popular of these is **Mini Hollywood** (☎ 95 036 52 36; Carretera Nacional 340, Km 464; adult/child 4 & over/child under 4 €17/9/free; ⏲ 10am-7pm Tue-Sun Nov-Mar, to 9pm Tue-Sun Apr-Oct, closed 1 Nov-14 Dec).

Sleeping & Eating

ALMERÍA

Hostal Americano (☎ 95 028 10 15; Av de la Estación 6; s/d with shared bathroom from €18.50/32) Popular with backpackers, this basic, 50-room place is well located between the city centre and the bus station.

La Perla (☎ 95 023 88 77; fax 95 027 58 16; Plaza del Carmen 7; d €48-61; ❄ 💻) The oldest hotel in town, this recently renovated option has comfortable rooms with satellite TV.

Taberna Torreluz (☎ 95 023 43 99; Plaza Flores 3; raciónes €8; ⏲ noon-4pm & 7.30pm-12.30am) This wood-panelled bar is famed for its fabulous *raciónes*.

CABO DE GATA

Casa Emilio (☎ 95 038 97 61; r €40-50) In the quiet village of Los Escullos, a few kilometres up the coast, Casa Emilio offers clean, simple rooms with balconies, as well as a downstairs bar-restaurant.

In San José there is **Camping Tau** (☎ 95 038 01 66; www.parquenatural.com/tau; per person/tent €4.50/4.50, electricity €3-5; ⏲ closed Oct-Mar) and the friendly non-HI hostel **Albergue Juvenil de San José** (☎ 95 038 03 53; www.alberguesanjose.com; Calle Montemar; dm €12; ⏲ closed Nov-Mar).

MOJÁCAR

Hostal La Esquinica (☎ 95 047 50 09; Calle Cano 1; s/d with shared bathroom €20/25) Tiny and covered in climbing plants, this *hostal* has sweet but simple rooms with wooden beds.

Hostal Mamabel's (☎ 95 047 24 48; www.mamabels.com; Calle Embajadores 5; d/ste €65/87; ❄) The nine large rooms here have sea views, and four even have private terraces. There's also an excellent restaurant (mains €11 to €18).

Mesón Casa Egea (Paseo Mediterráneo 127, Playa Mojácar; mains €15; ⏲ closed Nov & Mon Sep-Jun) Local fishermen supply fresh fish here each day, and visitors flock to eat it in the air-conditioned dining room or on the sea-facing terrace.

Getting There & Away

From Almería's **bus station** (☎ 95 026 20 98; Plaza de Barcelona), Alsina Graells travels to Granada (€10.10 to €12.25, 2½ to four hours, five daily), Málaga (€14.55, 3¼ hours, nine daily) and Seville (€27.70 to €28.60, 7½ to nine hours, three daily).

From the **train station** (Plaza de la Estación) there are services to Madrid (€33.90 to €38, seven hours, one daily), Granada (€13.40, 2¼ hours, four daily) and Seville (€32.10, 5½ hours, four daily).

MÁLAGA

pop 553,916

Seeking *andaluz* charm? You need look no further than Málaga. This exuberant port city suffers unfairly from its proximity to the overdeveloped and unenticing Costa del Sol; in reality, it's an enticing mix of pedestrianised streets, rollicking nightlife, great tapas and world-class galleries and museums.

Information

Internet Meeting Point (Plaza de la Merced 20; per hr €1-2; ⏲ 10-12.30am) The price of Internet usage fluctuates according to time of day.

Municipal tourist office (☎ 95 213 47 30; www.malagaturismo.com; Av de Cervantes 1; ⏲ 8am-2.30pm & 4-7pm Mon-Fri, 9.30am-1.30pm Sat)

Regional tourist office (☎ 95 221 34 45; www.andalucia.org; Pasaje de Chinitas 4; ⏲ 9am-7.30pm Mon-Fri, 10am-7pm Sat, 10am-2pm Sun)

Sights & Activities

The **Alcazaba** (☎ 95 222 72 30; Calle Alcazabilla; admission €2, free after 2pm Sun; ⏲ 8.30am-7pm Tue-Sun

Nov-Mar, 9.30am-8pm Tue-Sun Apr-Oct) fortress and palace dates from the 8th century. Nearby is the recently restored **Teatro Romanano** (Roman Amphitheatre; admission free; 10am-2.30pm & 4-7pm Wed-Sat, 10am-2.30pm Sun Nov-Mar, 10am-2.30pm & 5-8pm Wed-Sat, 10am-2.30pm Sun Apr-Oct).

The hilltop **Castillo de Gibralfaro** (admission €2; 9am-5.45pm Nov-Mar, to 7.45pm Apr-Oct), a Moorish castle, commands spectacular views across the city and sea.

Málaga's **cathedral** (95 221 59 17; Calle Molina Lario; admission €3.50; 10am-6pm Mon-Fri, to 5pm Sat Nov-Mar, 10am-6.45pm Mon-Fri, to 5.45pm Sat Apr-Oct) has a peculiar lopsided look (the south tower was never completed) and a magnificent 18th-century baroque façade.

Whatever you do, don't leave without visiting the fabulous **Museo Picasso Málaga** (95 212 76 99; www.museopicassomalaga.org; Calle San Augustín 8; permanent exhibition adult/student €6/3, temporary exhibition €4.50/2.50, both €8/4; 10am-8pm Tue-Thu & Sun, to 9pm Fri & Sat). Set in the contemplative setting of the lovely 16th-century Palacio de Buenavista, the museum is stacked with more than 200 works covering the length and breadth of Picasso's astonishing career.

Sleeping

Málaga is short on accommodation, so book ahead. Prices shoot up in August and during Easter week.

Hostal La Palma (95 222 67 72; 1st fl, Calle Martinez 7; d €38-43, with shared bathroom s €23, d €30-38) Run by the genial Antonio, this excellent *hostal* has a reception area on the 1st floor and rooms on upper floors. Those on the 4th floor have washbasins and tiled floors but are a tad dark. The slightly more expensive rooms are on the floor below; these have air-con and some have private bathrooms and balconies onto the street.

Hostal Derby (95 222 13 01; fax 95 222 13 02; 4th fl, Pasaje San Juan de Dios 1; s/d €36/45, with shared bathroom €30/40;) The *senora* here is extremely friendly, and keeps her *hostal* impeccably clean. Large front rooms have views of the port.

Hotel Venecia (95 221 36 36; www.hotelvenecia malaga.com; Alameda Principal 9; s/d €58/72;) An old-fashioned place with large rooms featuring comfortable beds, satellite TV and enormous bathrooms, the Venecía is an acceptable midrange choice. There's a very good *cafetería* downstairs.

Hotel Don Curro (95 222 72 07; www.hotel doncurro.com; Calle Sancha de Lara 7; s/d €79/116; P) With 118 rooms and a loyal business clientele, this central choice deserves its three-star rating. Singles are small, but the recently renovated double rooms are a good size. Ask for an exterior room with balcony.

Hotel Larios (95 222 22 00; www.hotel-larios .com; Calle Marqués de Larios 2; r €117-193, ste 172-246;) From the Hoffman couch in the foyer to the Steinway grand in the bar, this hotel oozes style and quality. Its location couldn't be better, and its rooms are extremely comfortable. The Málagueñan owners have a commitment to fostering the city's cultural life, and host regular film festivals, poetry readings, gourmet evenings and live music in the luxe restaurant-bar. In summer the action moves to the 5th-floor terrace bar, which has spectacular views. Highly recommended.

Eating

Cortijo de Pepe (Plaza de la Merced; tapas €2-2.50, montados €2) Overlooking busy Plaza de la Merced, this long-standing favourite offers an array of well-priced tapas, tasty *montados* (small filled rolls), beer and wine.

Bar Lo Güeno (95 222 30 48; Calle Marín García 9; tapas €2-4.50; 1-4.30pm & 8pm-midnight) Cramming into this famous tapas bar is a mandatory activity while in Málaga. There are over 50 varieties of freshly prepared snacks on offer, including delicious *coquerones en vinagre* (pickled fresh anchovies, €2.50).

El Chinitas (95 221 09 72; Calle Moreno Monroy 4-6; tapas €1.50-3.50, montados €2-3) The tapas here are hit and miss, but when the chefs get it right they really shine. Opt for in-season delicacies such as *esparragos plancha* (grilled asparagus €3.50).

El Vegetariano de la Alcazabilla (95 221 48 58; Calle Pozo del Rey 5; mains €6-8; closed Sun) Honest and fresh dishes are served in unpretentious surrounds in the city's most popular vegetarian restaurant.

Al-Yamal Restaurante Árabe (95 221 20 46; Calle Blasco de Garay 7; mains €11-16; closed Sun) For a simple Moroccan meal cooked with love, make your way to this intimate eatery near the port. The aromatic *harira* (lamb and vegetable soup, €5.50) is delicious, as is the hummus served with home-baked pita bread (€2).

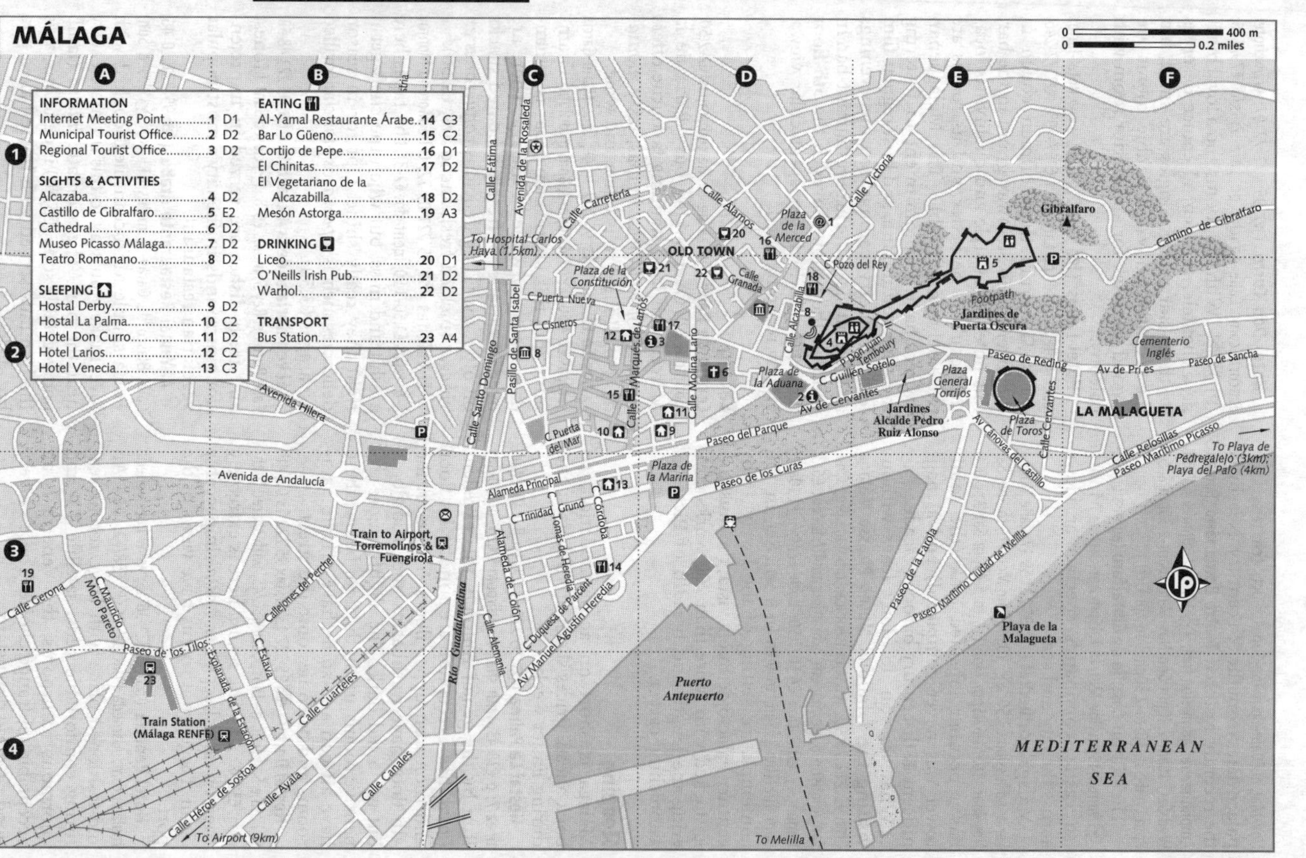
MÁLAGA
0 400 m
0 0.2 miles
INFORMATION
Internet Meeting Point....1 D1
Municipal Tourist Office....2 D2
Regional Tourist Office....3 D2
SIGHTS & ACTIVITIES
Alcazaba....4 D2
Castillo de Gibralfaro....5 E2
Cathedral....6 D2
Museo Picasso Málaga....7 D2
Teatro Romanano....8 D2
SLEEPING
Hostal Derby....9 D2
Hostal La Palma....10 C2
Hotel Don Curro....11 D2
Hotel Larios....12 C2
Hotel Venecia....13 C3
EATING
Al-Yamal Restaurante Árabe....14 C3
Bar Lo Güeno....15 C2
Cortijo de Pepe....16 D1
El Chinitas....17 D2
El Vegetariano de la Alcazabilla....18 D2
Mesón Astorga....19 A3
DRINKING
Liceo....20 D1
O'Neills Irish Pub....21 D2
Warhol....22 D2
TRANSPORT
Bus Station....23 A4
OLD TOWN
LA MALAGUETA
Gibralfaro
Jardines de Puerta Oscura
Jardines Alcalde Pedro Ruiz Alonso
Cementerio Inglés
Plaza de la Merced
Plaza de la Constitución
Plaza de la Aduana
Plaza General Torrijos
Plaza de Toros
Plaza de la Marina
Playa de la Malagueta
Puerto Antepuerto
MEDITERRANEAN SEA
Río Guadalmedina
Train to Airport, Torremolinos & Fuengirola
Train Station (Málaga RENFE)
To Hospital Carlos Haya (1.5km)
To Playa de Pedregalejo (3km); Playa del Palo (4km)
To Airport (9km)
To Melilla
Calle Victoria
Camino de Gibralfaro
Paseo de Reding
Paseo de Sancha
Av de Príes
Calle Álamos
Calle Carretería
Calle Fátima
Avenida de la Rosaleda
Calle Santo Domingo
Pasillo de Santa Isabel
Avenida Hilera
Avenida de Andalucía
Alameda Principal
Alameda de Colón
Paseo del Parque
Paseo de los Curas
Av de Cervantes
C Guillén Sotelo
P Don Juan Temboury
C Pozo del Rey
Calle Alcazabilla
Calle Granada
Calle Molina Lario
Calle Marqués de Larios
C Puerta Nueva
C Cisneros
C Puerta del Mar
C Trinidad Grund
Tomás de Heredia
C Córdoba
C Duquesa de Parcent
Av Manuel Agustín Heredia
Calle Alemania
Av Cánovas del Castillo
Calle Cervantes
Paseo de la Farola
Paseo Marítimo Ciudad de Melilla
Calle Reloisillas
Paseo Marítimo Picasso
Footpath
Calle Gerona
C Mauricio Moro Pareto
Callejones del Perchel
C Eslava
Paseo de los Tilos
Explanada de la Estación
Calle Cuarteles
Calle Héroe de Sostoa
Calle Ayala
Calle Canales

Mesón Astorga (☎ 95 234 68 32; Calle Gerona 11; meals €15-22; 🕑 closed Sun) Using the very best local produce, the chefs at this highly regarded restaurant prepare meat and fish dishes with a modern slant.

At lunch, locals tend to gravitate towards the excellent fish restaurants at Playas de Pedregalejo and del Palo, a few kilometres east of the centre, which specialise in *fritura malagueña* (fried fish, anchovies and squid).

Drinking

Serious party time kicks off at about midnight around Calle Granada and Plaza de la Merced.

O'Neills Irish Pub (Calle Luis de Velázquez 3) This place appeals enormously to young Malagueños, who can't seem to get enough Guinness and U2. Go figure.

Liceo (Calle Beatas 21) In a grand old mansion, the two levels of this bar are often full of students. The music is mainly electronic and pop.

Warhol (Calle Niño de Guevara; 🕑 Thu-Sat) This stylish haunt is frequented by a predominantly gay clientele.

Getting There & Away

The **Pablo Ruiz Picasso Airport** (AGP; ☎ 95 204 88 38; www.aena.es) handles a wide range of domestic and international flights. Buses run between it and platform 30 at Málaga's bus station between 6.35am and 11.35pm daily (€1, tickets available on bus).

Another way of travelling between the town centre and the airport is on the **Málaga-Fuengirola train**, which leaves from the city centre and stops at the bus station and airport (€1.10 Monday to Friday, €1.20 Saturday and Sunday, 15 minutes), before travelling on to Torremolinos (€1.10 Monday to Friday, €1.20 Saturday and Sunday) and Fuengirola (€1.75 Monday to Friday, €1.85 Saturday and Sunday) and then returning via the same stops.

From the **bus station** (☎ 95 235 00 61; www.estabus.emtsam.es; Paseo de los Tilos), **Daibus** (☎ 90 227 79 99; www.daibus.es) travels to Madrid (€19.65, six hours, nine daily). Alsina Graells services Granada (€8.90, 1¾ hours, 18 daily), Seville (€14.40, 2½ hours, 10 daily) and Almeria (€14.55, 3¼ hours, nine daily). **Portillo** (☎ 90 214 31 44; www.ctsa-portillo.com) travels between Málaga and Ronda (€9.40, two hours, four daily), Algeciras (€9.95 to €10.40, 1¾ to three hours, 11 daily), Cadíz (€19.70 to €20.15, four to 5½ hours, three daily), Tarifa (€12.10, two hours, two daily) and La Linéa (€10.05, three hours, four daily). Alsa travels to and from Barcelona (€70.50 to €83.50) via Valencia (€46.40 to €53.10) six times per day.

From the **train station** (Explanada de la Estación), there are services to Madrid (€52.10 to €87.50, 4¼ hours, six daily) via Córdoba (€15.60 to €25, 2¼ hours). There's also a service to Seville (€16.05, 2½ hours, eight daily).

RONDA

pop 34,832

Picturesque Ronda is split in two by the savagely deep El Tajo gorge and is at the heart of some lovely hill country.

The **Municipal tourist office** (☎ 95 218 71 19; www.turismoderonda.es; Paseo de Blas Infante s/n; 🕑 9.30am-6.30pm Mon-Fri, 10am-2pm & 3.30-6.30pm Sat & Sun) is helpful but can get crowded.

Sights & Activities

The **Plaza de Toros** (1785), considered the national home of bullfighting, is a mecca for aficionados; inside is the small but fascinating **Museo Taurino** (Bullfighting Museum; ☎ 95 287 41 32; adult/student €5/3; 🕑 10am-8pm).

The amazing 18th-century **Puente Nuevo** (New Bridge) is an incredible engineering feat crossing the 100m-deep gorge to the originally Muslim old town (La Ciudad). Those interested in learning more about the bridge's construction can visit the **interpretation centre** (☎ 64 996 53 38; adult/student €2/1; 🕑 10am-7pm Mon-Fri, to 3pm Sat & Sun) next to the bridge. At the **Casa del Rey Moro** (House of the Moorish King; ☎ 95 218 72 00; Calle Santo Domingo 17; adult/child €4/2; 🕑 10am-8pm), you can climb down La Mina, a Muslim-era stairway cut inside the rock, right to the bottom of the gorge. Also well worth a visit are the beautiful 13th-century **Baños Arabes** (Arab Baths; ☎ 65 695 09 37; Barrio Padre Jesus; adult/child €2/free, free Sun; 🕑 10am-7pm Mon-Fri, to 3pm Sat & Sun) and **Santa Maria la Mayor** (☎ 95 287 22 46; Plaza Duquesa de Parcent; admission €1.50; 🕑 10am-7pm), a 13th-century mosque that was converted into a church by Ferdinand the Catholic.

Sleeping & Eating

Hotel Morales (☎ 95 287 15 38; reserves@hotelmorales.com; Calle Sevilla 51; s €20-23, d €36-42) This friendly place offers basic but clean rooms.

Alavera de los Baños (☎ 95 287 91 43; www.andalucia.com/alavera; Hoyo San Miguel; s €60, d €80-95, all incl breakfast; closed Dec & Jan; P) A blissfully quiet hotel next to the Arab baths, the Alavera is rustic and romantic in equal measure. There are only nine rooms; try for one with a private terrace. Be warned that the climb up to town is very steep – most guests end up eating at the hotel's small restaurant (meals €25 to €30) rather than attempting it at night.

Hotel Jardin de la Muralla (☎ 95 287 27 64; www.jardindelamuralla.com; Calle Espiritu Santo 13; d/ste incl breakfast €86/107) Set in a lush garden, this charming place makes a perfect base for exploring the town. Its pool terrace, comfortable rooms and handsome common areas might mean that you're loathe to set foot outside, though!

Relax Vegetariano Café-Bar (☎ 95 287 72 07; Calle Los Remedios 27; pasta €6) This British-owned café has bright red walls, rustic wooden tables and tasty vegetarian food (something unusual in this bull-obsessed town).

Restaurante Pedro Romano (☎ 95 287 11 10; Calle Virgen de la Paz 18; mains €10-16; 10am-10pm) Ronda's most famous eatery is opposite the bullring and is an excellent and atmospheric place to sample local dishes such as braised bull's tail.

Getting There & Away

From the **bus station** (☎ 95 287 26 57; Plaza Concepción García Redondo), Portillo has services to Málaga (€9.40, two to 2¾ hours, four daily) and Los Amarillos travels to Seville (€9.90, 2½ hours, five daily).

From the **train station** (Av Andalucía), trains run to Granada (€11.35, 2¾ hours, three daily), Córdoba (€17.20 to €21.90, 2½ hours, two daily), Málaga (€8.15, two hours, one daily), Algeciras (€6.25 to €25, 1¾ to two hours, six daily) and Madrid (€34.90 to €52.60, 9¼ hours, two daily).

ALGECIRAS

pop 112,857

An unattractive industrial and fishing town between Tarifa and Gibraltar, Algeciras is the major port linking Spain with Morocco. Keep your wits about you, and ignore offers from the legions of moneychangers, drug-pushers and ticket-hawkers who hang out here. The **tourist office** (☎ 95 657 26 36; Calle Juan Cierva; 9am-2pm Mon-Fri) is near the port.

Sleeping

Hotel Reina Cristina (☎ 95 660 26 22; www.reinacristina.com; Paseo de la Conferencia; s/d €85/126; P) If you're in need of a rest after getting off the ferry, head to this gracious colonial-style hotel with its large and comfortable rooms, swimming pools and lush gardens.

Getting There & Away

BOAT

Frequent ferries to/from Tangier, in Morocco, and Ceuta, the Spanish enclave on the Moroccan coast, are operated by **Trasmediterránea** (☎ 90 245 46 45; www.trasmediterranea.es), **EuroFerrys** (☎ 95 665 11 78; www.euroferrys.com), **Buquebus** (☎ 90 241 42 42; www.buquebus.es) and other companies. There are regular services to Tangier (adult/child/car €32.90/20.30/91.80, one hour) and even more to Ceuta (adult €30.10 to €34.60, child €10.75 to €17.30, car €62.75 to €75.95, 35 minutes). Buy your ticket in the port or at agencies on Av Marina – prices are the same.

BUS

About 400m inland from the port, **Comes** (☎ 95 665 34 56; Calle San Bernardo) runs services to Tarifa (€1.70, 25 to 45 minutes, 21 daily), Cádiz (€9.75, two hours, 10 daily) and Seville (€14.80, 3¾ to 4½ hours, four daily). **Portillo** (Av Virgen del Carmen 15), 200m north of the port, goes to Málaga (€9.95 to €10.40, 1¾ to three hours, 11 daily).

TRAIN

From the **train station** (Calle Agustín Bálsamo 12), services run to Madrid (€38 to €56.30, six to 11 hours, two daily), Córdoba (€22.40 to €43.80, four to 4½ hours, two daily), Ronda (€6.25 to €25, 1¾ to two hours, six daily) and Granada (€17, 4¾ hours, three daily).

CÁDIZ

pop 130,968

Cádiz is crammed onto the head of a promontory like some huge and overcrowded ocean-going ship. Columbus sailed from here on his second and fourth voyages, and after his success in the Americas Cádiz grew into Spain's richest and most cosmopolitan city in the 18th century. The best time to visit is during the February *carnaval* (carnival), which rivals Rio in terms of outrageous exuberance.

SPAIN

For Internet access, try **EnRed@2** (Calle Isabel La Católica 3; per hr €2; 11am-3pm & 6-11pm). The **Municipal tourist office** (95 624 10 01; Plaza San Juan de Dios 11; 9.30am-1.30pm & 4-7pm Mon-Fri) has helpful staff.

Sights & Activities

The yellow-domed 18th-century **cathedral** (95 625 98 12; Plaza de la Catedral; adult/child €4/2.50; 10am-1.30pm & 4.30-7pm Tue-Fri, 10am-12.30pm Sat) is the city's most striking landmark.

Get your bearings by climbing up the baroque **Torre Tavira** (95 621 29 10; www.torretavira.com; Calle Marqués del Real Tesoro; adult/student €3.50/3; 10am-6pm mid-Sep–mid-Jun, to 8pm mid-Jun–mid-Sep), the highest of Cádiz' old watchtowers, which features sweeping views of the city.

The **Museo de Cádiz** (95 621 22 81; Plaza de Mina; non-EU/EU citizens €1.50/free; 2.30-8.30pm Tue, 9am-8.30pm Wed-Sat, 9am-2.30pm Sun) has a magnificent collection of archaeological remains, as well as a fine-art collection. The city's lively **central market** (Plaza de las Flores) is on the site of a former Phoenician temple.

Sleeping & Eating

Quo Qádis (/fax 95 622 19 39; www.quoqadis.com; Calle Diego Arias 1; dm incl breakfast €6-12, d €30, with shared bathroom €24;) Housed in an older mansion, this independent youth hostel has somewhat crowded but cheerful accommodation on offer.

Hostal Bahía (95 625 90 61; Calle Plocia 5; d €52-69;) Just off the bustling main square (but with double-glazed windows), this well-maintained *hostal* is a safe choice.

Hospedería Las Cortes de Cádiz (95 621 26 68; www.hotellascortes.com; Calle San Francisco 9; s €70-97, d €102-134, all incl breakfast; P) Housed in an elegant 19th-century mansion, this charming hotel has comfortable rooms and facilities including a café, roof terrace and gym.

Freiduría Las Flores (95 622 61 12; Plaza de Topete 4; seafood per 250g €2.50-8) Cadíz' *freidurías de pescado* (fried-fish bars) are wonderful spots to grab a cheap but delicious meal; Las Flores sells the catch of the day and local specialities such as *puntillitas* (tiny legs of baby squid).

El Faro (95 622 19 59; Calle San Félix 15; mains €15-20) The city's most famous restaurant specialises in fresh *pescados de la bahía* (fish from the bay). Happily, its national reputation doesn't mean that the atmosphere is intimidating or the prices outrageous. Its attached tapas bar is excellent.

Getting There & Away

From the Cádiz **bus station** (95 680 70 59; Plaza de la Hispanidad), Sociobus goes to Madrid (€21.55, eight hours, three daily). Portillo and Comes service Algeciras (€9.75, two hours, 10 daily), Seville (€10.30, 1¾ hours, 10 daily), Málaga (€19.70 to €20.15, four to 5½ hours, two daily) and Tarifa (€7.70, two hours, five daily).

From the **train station** (Plaza Sevilla), services go to Seville (€9.10 to €29.70, 1½ to two hours, 12 daily), Madrid (€59.90 to €92.70, 5¼ hours, two daily) and Córdoba (€32.80 to €51.10, three to 3½ hours, three daily).

TARIFA

pop 17,418

Windy, laid-back Tarifa is so close to Africa that you can almost hear the call to prayer issuing from Morocco's minarets. The town is a bohemian haven of cafés and crumbling Moorish ruins. There's also a lively windsurfing and kite-surfing scene.

Stretching west are the long, sandy (and largely deserted) beaches of the Costa de la Luz (Coast of Light), backed by cool pine forests and green hills.

The town's **tourist office** (95 668 09 93; www.aytotarifa.com; Paseo de la Alameda; 9am-9pm Jun-Sep, to 3pm Oct-May) has lots of information on the area, as has the independently run website www.tarifainfo.com. For Internet access, try **Planet** (Calle Santísima Trinidad; per hr €3; 10.30am-2.30pm & 6-10pm).

Sights & Activities

When here, explore Tarifa's winding old streets and visit the **Castillo de Guzmán** (95 668 46 89; Calle Guzmán El Bueno; adult/child €2/1; 11am-2pm Tue-Sat year-round & 6-8pm Tue-Sat Jul-Sep, 5-7pm Apr-Jun, 4-6pm Oct-Mar), which dates from the 10th century.

The waters of Algeciras Bay are prime whale- and dolphin-watching territory. **Whale Watch España** (95 662 70 13; www.whalewatchtarifa.net; Av Constitución 6; adult/child from €30/20) is one of a number of companies running daily boat excursions.

The tiny, protected **Playa Chica**, just southeast of the centre, is best for swimming. **Playa de los Lances**, the 10km-long beach beloved of wind- and kite-surfers, stretches northwest from Tarifa. For windsurf and kite-surf rental and classes, try places along Calle Batalla de Salado. Board, sail and wetsuit rental costs around €70 per day; windsurfing courses for beginners start at around €150.

Sleeping & Eating

Hostal Alameda (☎ 95 668 11 81; www.hostalalameda.com; Paseo de la Alameda 4; s/d €30/50; ❄) Good value, smallish rooms are on offer here. Some have sea views.

La Casa Amarilla (☎ 95 668 19 93; www.lacasaamarilla.net; Calle Sancho IV El Bravo 9; r €36-60, 2-person studio €47-70, 3-person studio €63-94) Right in the thick of things, this place has exquisite (and slightly quirky) studios and rooms.

Café Central (☎ 95 668 05 90; Calle Sancho IV El Bravo; 🕑 9am-1am) This legendary café posts a daily wind report on its walls and serves the best breakfast in town.

Mesón Perulero (☎ 95 668 19 97; Plaza San Hiscio; tapas €1.50) In a gorgeous building with an airy patio, this place does excellent fishy tapas; try the *ortigas de mar* (anemones). There's live flamenco here in summer.

Souk (☎ 95 668 07 08; Huerta del Rey 11; mains €10-14; 🕑 closed Tue) For the aromas and tastes of nearby Morocco, nothing beats this atmospheric eatery.

Getting There & Away

Comes (☎ 95 668 40 38; Batalla del Salado) runs buses to Algeciras (€1.70, 25 to 45 minutes, 21 daily), La Línea (€3.50, one hour, seven daily), Cádiz (€7.70, two hours, five daily) and Seville (€14, three hours, four daily). Portillo travels to/from Málaga (€12.10, two hours, two daily).

FRS (☎ 95 668 18 30; www.frs.es; Estación Marítima) runs fast ferries between Tarifa and Tangier (adult/child/car €27/16/73, 35 minutes, five daily).

GIBRALTAR

pop 26,404

The British colony of Gibraltar is like 1960s Britain on a sunny day. It's both safe and old-fashioned, attracting coachloads of day-trippers from the Costa del Sol who come here to be reassured by the helmet-wearing policemen, the double-decker buses and the fried-egg-and-chip–style eateries.

Occupying a huge lump of limestone almost 5km long and over 1km wide near the mouth of the Mediterranean, the colony of Gibraltar has certainly had a rocky history. It was the bridgehead for the Muslim invasion of Spain in AD 711. Castilla finally wrested it from the Muslims in 1462, but in 1704 an Anglo-Dutch fleet captured it. Spain gave up military attempts to regain it from Britain after the failure of the Great Siege of 1779–83, but after 300 years of concentrated Britishness, both Britain and Spain are now talking about joint Anglo-Spanish sovereignty.

Information

To enter Gibraltar you must have a passport or EU national identity card. Gibraltar is outside the Schengen area, and visitors who intend to enter from Spain should ensure that they have a double-entry visa if they wish to return to Spain. Nationals from certain countries require a visa to enter; contact the Immigration Department on rgpimm@gibgibtelecom.net for more details.

The currency is the Gibraltar pound. Change any unspent Gibraltar pounds before you leave. You can also use euros or pounds sterling while here.

There's Internet access at **General Internet Business Centre** (☎ 44227; 36 Governor's St; per hr £3; 10am-10pm Tue-Sat, noon-9pm Sun & Mon).

To call Gibraltar from Spain, the telephone code is ☎ 9567; from other countries dial the international access code, then ☎ 350 and the local number. To call Spain from Gibraltar, just dial the nine-digit Spanish number. There are a couple of **tourist offices** (www.gibraltar.gov.gi; Main office ☎ 74950; Duke of Kent House, Cathedral Sq; 🕑 9am-5.30pm Mon-Fri; Casemates Sq ☎ 74982; 🕑 9am-5.30pm Mon-Fri, 10am-3pm Sat, 10am-1pm Sun).

Sights & Activities

Central Gibraltar can get crowded and claustrophobic, but the **Gibraltar Museum** (☎ 74289; Bomb House Lane; adult/child £2/1; 🕑 10am-6pm Mon-Fri, to 2pm Sat), with its interesting historical collection and Muslim-era bathhouse, is worth a peek. Wander into the **Alameda Botanical Gardens** (Red Sands Rd; 🕑 8am-sunset) for some chill-out time.

The large **Upper Rock Nature Reserve** (☎ 74950; adult/child/vehicle £8/4/1.50; 🕑 9.30am-

7pm), covering most of the upper rock, has spectacular views. The rock's most famous inhabitants are its colony of Barbary macaques, the only wild primates in Europe. Some of these hang around the **Apes' Den** near the middle cable-car station; others can often be seen at the top station or Great Siege Tunnels. Other attractions include **St Michael's Cave**, a large natural grotto renowned for its stalagmites and stalactites, and the **Great Siege Tunnels**, a series of galleries hewn from the rock by the British during the Great Siege to provide new gun emplacements.

A **cable car** (adult/child return £8/4.50; 9.30am-5.15pm Mon-Sat year-round, 9.30am-5.15pm Sun Apr-Oct) leaves its lower station on Red Sands Rd every few minutes. For the Apes' Den, disembark at the middle station.

Sleeping & Eating

Compared with Spain, expect to pay through the nose for accommodation and food.

Emile Youth Hostel (☎ 51106; www.emilehostel.com; Montagu Bastion, Line Wall Rd; dm incl breakfast £15-20, s £20-30, d £30-50) The Emile is extremely basic and has a slightly sleazy atmosphere – it's not recommended for women travelling solo.

Cannon Hotel (☎ 51711; www.cannonhotel.gi; 9 Cannon Lane; d incl breakfast £45, s/d with shared bathroom & breakfast £24.50/36.50) This friendly and recently refurbished hotel is in the heart of town. It has a bar, charming patio and airy rooms.

Lord Nelson (☎ 50009; 10 Casemates Sq; mains £5-8; 10am-2am) Landlubbers and sailors alike gravitate towards this brasserie, which is decked out as Nelson's ship. Fish and chips (£6.50) are popular, but the mussels in white wine, garlic and cream (£7) are tastier. There's live music at weekends.

House of Sacarello (☎ 70625; 57 Irish Town; mains £5-11; 9am-7.30pm Mon-Fri, to 3pm Sat) This attractive eatery is known for its cream teas (£3) and vegetarian menu options.

For basic pub grub and plentiful drinks try **Star Bar** (☎ 75924; Parliament Lane; 7am-11pm), Gibraltar's oldest pub; or the **Clipper** (☎ 79791; Irish Town; Sunday roasts £6; 9.30am-11pm), which offers sport on TV and friendly bar staff. Rousing renditions of 'Rule Britannia' can usually be had at both places for no charge.

Getting There & Away

GB Airways (code GT; ☎ 79300, in UK 0845-77 333 77; www.gbairways.com) has flights daily to/from London's Heathrow and Gatwick airports. One-way fares start at £41. **Monarch Airlines** (code ZB; ☎ 47477, in UK 08700-405040; www.flymonarch.com) flies from London's Luton and from Manchester; return fares start at about £96.

There are no regular buses to Gibraltar, but La Línea bus station is only a five-minute walk from the border.

To take a car into Gibraltar, you need an insurance certificate, registration document, nationality plate and driving licence. You do *not* have to pay any fee, despite what con artists might try to tell you. The border is open 24 hours and there is plentiful parking outside the city walls, though very little within them.

EXTREMADURA

A sparsely populated stretch of vast skies and open plains, Extremadura is far enough from most beaten tourist trails to give you a genuine sense of exploration, something for which Extremeños themselves have always had a flair.

TRUJILLO

pop 9283

Trujillo is a delightful little town that can't be much bigger now than it was in 1529, when its most famous son, Francisco Pizarro, set off with his three brothers and a few local buddies for an expedition that culminated in the bloody conquest of the Incan empire.

There's a **tourist office** (☎ 92 732 26 77; ofitur@ayto-trujillo.com; Plaza Mayor; 10am-2pm & 4-7pm) on Plaza Mayor. For Internet, try **Ciber Recio** (Calle de la Encarnación; per hr €2; 9am-midnight), opposite the Museo del Queso.

Sights

A **statue of Pizarro** dominates the splendid Plaza Mayor. On the plaza's southern side, the **Palacio de la Conquista** (closed to visitors) sports the carved images of Francisco Pizarro and the Inca princess Inés Yupanqui.

Up the hill, the **Iglesia de Santa María la Mayor** (admission €1.50; 10am-2pm & 4.30-7pm) is an interesting hotchpotch of 13th- to 16th-century styles, with some fine paintings by Fernando Gallego of the Flemish school. At the top of the hill, Trujillo's Moorish **castillo** (admission €1.50; 10am-2pm & 4-6.45pm) is an impressive structure commanding great views.

The **Museo del Queso** (Museum of Cheese; 92 729 00 81; www.museodelqueso.org; Calle Barrionuevo 7; admission €2; 10am-2pm & 5-7pm Mon-Fri, 10am-2pm Sat) is a new addition to the town's cultural attractions. The admission price includes a tasting of *Torta del Casar*, the local favourite.

Sleeping & Eating

Pensión Plaza Mayor (92 732 23 13; www.aloja2.com; 2nd fl, Plaza Mayor 6; s/d €21/36;) In the thick of the action (if there can be said to be such a thing in Trujillo), this recently opened *pensión* offers large rooms with satellite TV and comfortable beds.

Posada Dos Orillas (92 765 90 79; www.dosorillas.com; Calle Cambrones 6; r €70-107;) Who would have thought that a simple town like Trujillo would be home to one of the country's most exquisite boutique hotels? The 13 rooms here are individually decorated and have wooden ceilings, satellite TV, brass beds and swish bathrooms. Its courtyard restaurant (mains €15 to €19), which features lots of vegetarian choices, is perfect on summer nights.

Restaurante Pizarro (92 732 02 55; Plaza Mayor 13; mains €8.50-15.50) The Pizarro offers a stellar position on the main square and a simple but tasty *menú* for €13.

Restaurante La Troya (92 723 13 64; Plaza Mayor 10; menú €15) The *menú* here is absolutely enormous – perfect for patrons who've just spent eight hours labouring in the fields; overwhelming for anyone else. The quality of the dishes is only average, but the surrounds are attractive and it's very family friendly.

Getting There & Away

From the **bus station** (92 732 12 02; Calle San Juan Bautista de la Salle 1), 500m south of Plaza Mayor, AutoRes and **Mirat** (92 732 03 14; www.mirat.net) travel to Cáceres (€2.85, 45 minutes, eight daily). AutoRes also travels to Mérida (€6.95, 1¼ hours, three daily) and Madrid (€14.90 to €19, three to four hours, five daily).

CÁCERES

pop 91,010

Cáceres' *ciudad monumental* (old town), built in the 15th and 16th centuries, is so perfectly preserved it can seem lifeless at times. The town's action centres on Plaza Mayor, at the foot of the old town, and busy Av de España, a short distance south.

The **regional tourist office** (92 701 08 34; otcaceres@bme.es; 9am-2pm & 4-6pm Mon-Fri Oct-May, 9am-2pm & 5-7pm Mon-Fri Jun-Sep, 9.45am-2pm Sat & Sun year-round) is on Plaza Mayor and the **municipal tourist office** (92 724 71 72; Calle Ancha 7; 10am-2pm & 4.30-7.30pm Mon-Fri Oct-May, 10am-2pm & 5.30-8.30pm Mon-Fri Jun-Sep) is in the old town. For Internet access, try **Ciberjust** (Calle Diego Maria Crehuet 7; per hr €2; 10.30am-11.30pm Mon-Fri, 5-11.30pm Sat & Sun).

Sights & Activities

The *ciudad monumental* is still surrounded by walls and towers raised by the Almohads in the 12th century. Entering it from Plaza Mayor, you'll see ahead the fine 15th-century **Concatedral de Santa María** (admission to museum €1.50; 10am-1pm & 4-6pm Oct-Jun, 10.30am-1.30pm & 5-7pm Jul-Sep).

Many of the old city's churches and imposing medieval mansions can be admired only from the outside, but you can visit the impressive **Museo de Cáceres** (92 701 08 77; www.museosextremadura.com; Plaza de la Veletas 1; admission non-EU/EU citizens €1.50/free; 10am-1pm & 5-6.15pm Tue-Sat, 10.45-11.45am & 5-6.15pm Sun Oct–mid-April, 10am-1pm & 6-7.15pm Tue-Sat, 10.45-11.45am & 6-7.15pm Sun mid-April–Sep), which is housed in a 16th-century mansion built over a 12th-century Moorish *aljibe* (cistern).

Sleeping

Hotel Iberia (92 724 76 34; www.iberiahotel.com; Calle Pintores 2; s/d €43/54;) Enter this elegant former palace, and you'll be immediately won over. The rooms are extremely comfortable and the best ones (at the front) have the added extra of double-glazing. Amazing value for money.

Alameda Palacete (92 721 12 62; www.alamedapalacete.com; Calle General Margallo 45; s/d incl breakfast €44/60;) Another conversion of a grand old building, this quiet place near Plaza Mayor has a boutique feel. Its eight rooms have been lovingly decorated by the proud owner and feature gorgeous linen and spacious bathrooms.

Eating & Drinking

El Corral de las Cigüeñas (Calle Cuesta de Aldana 6; 8am-1pm & from 8pm Wed-Sat, from 6pm Sun) In the heart of the *cuidad monumental,* the fabulous ivy-clad courtyard of this café-bar is a wonderful spot for breakfast. On summer nights it hosts live music and discos.

Casa Mijhaeli (92 724 32 60; Calle Barrio Nuevo 6; mains €9-15; closed dinner Sun;) With a stylish and modern fitout, this brasserie in a street behind Plaza Mayor is a great place to enjoy a bowl of pasta (€6 to €7.50) or a vegetarian main.

Mesón Los Arcos (92 724 51 45; Plaza Mayor 22; menú €15, mains €12-26) To sample well-priced meals featuring Extremeño pork and cheese products, you need look no further than this bustling tavern just off the plaza.

Getting There & Away

From the **bus station** (92 723 25 50; Carretera Gijón-Sevilla), 1.5km southwest of Plaza Mayor, AutoRes and Mirat travel to Trujillo (€2.85, 45 minutes, eight daily) and **Leda SA** (92 723 43 56; www.leda.es) goes to Mérida (€4.50, 1¼ hours, four daily).

From the **train station** (92 723 50 61; Av de Alemania), services go to Madrid (€16.80 to €37, three to 4¼ hours, seven daily) and Mérida (€3.60 to €13, one hour, seven daily). There's also a daily train to Lisbon, Portugal (€37 to €163.50, 5¼ hours).

MÉRIDA

pop 52,763

Once the biggest city in Roman Spain, Mérida is home to more ruins of that age than anywhere else in the country and is a wonderful spot to spend a few archaeologically-inclined days. The **tourist office** (92 400 97 30; otmerida@eco.juntaex.es; Av José Álvarez Saenz de Buruaga; 9am-1.45pm & 4-6pm Mon-Fri Oct-May, 9am-1.45pm & 5-7pm Mon-Fri Jun-Sep, 9.30am-2pm Sat & Sun year-round) is by the gates to the Roman theatre. For Internet access, try **Cibersala** (Calle Camilo Cela 28; per hr €2; 11am-2pm & 4.30pm-midnight).

Sights

The awesome ruins of Mérida's **Teatro Romano & Anfiteatro** (92 431 25 30; admission €6.50) shouldn't be missed. The theatre was built in 15 BC and the gladiators' ring, or Anfiteatro, seven years later. Combined, they could hold 20,000 spectators. Other monuments of interest are the **Casa del Anfiteatro** (92 431 85 09; admission €3.50), the **Casa Romana del Mitreo** (92 430 15 04; admission €4), the **Alcazaba** (92 431 73 09; admission €3.50), the **Basílica de Santa Eulalia** (92 430 34 07; admission €3.50; 10am-1.45pm & 4-6.15pm) and the **Museo Nacional de Arte Romano** (92 431 16 90; adult/student & child €2.50/1.50, free Sat afternoon & Sun morning; 10am-2pm & 4-6pm Tue-Sat Dec-Feb, 10am-2pm & 4-9pm Tue-Sat Mar-Nov, 10am-2pm Sun year-round).

The opening hours for all sites except the basilica and the museum are 9.30am to 1.45pm and 4pm to 6.15pm October to May, and 9.30am to 1.45pm and 5pm to 7.15pm June to September. It's definitely worth buying an **entrada conjunta** (combined entry ticket; adult/student & child €9/5), which gives you entrance to all sites within a 24-hour period. You can purchase it from a ticket booth outside the Teatro Romano and Anfiteatro.

Various other reminders of imperial days are scattered about town, including the **Puente Romano**. At 792m, it's one of the longest bridges the Romans ever built and it's still possible to walk its length.

Sleeping & Eating

Hostal Nueva España (92 431 33 56; fax 92 431 32 11; Av de Extremadura 6; s €22-25, d €35-38;) The owners of this *hostal* on the main road near the train station have gone to some trouble to make the common areas here attractive. Rooms are freshly painted and very clean, if a bit worn.

Hostal El Alfarero (92 430 31 83; www.hostalelalfarero.com; Calle Sagasta 40; s €30-40, d €40-45;) This friendly place has simple but very clean rooms with hi-tech showers and hand-painted washbasins. There's a lovely downstairs patio and a small lounge.

Café-Bar Bocados (92 431 67 66; Calle Suárez Somonte 96; tostada & coffee €2) Stop at this bright café for breakfast before visiting the Roman ruins, which are directly opposite.

El Yantar (92 431 63 54; Av de José Álvarez Seaz de Buruaga) A few doors down from Bocados, this is a fabulous shop-tavern specialising in quality Extremeño produce.

Casa Benito (92 433 07 69; Calle San Francisco 3; tapas €2-3, boccadillos €2.50) Established in 1870, this atmospheric tapas bar celebrates the art of bullfighting, with photographs, posters and bulls' heads adorning every wall.

Café Galileo (92 431 55 05; Calle John Lennon 28; pizza €4-6.50, pasta €5.50-6.50) There can't be too many places in the world where you dine while sitting over glass-covered Roman ruins, but that's what happens at the Galileo. If that's a tad too archaeological for you, the roof terrace overlooking the Alcazaba is an equally impressive alternative. The food's adequate rather than inspired.

Getting There & Away

The **bus station** (☎ 92 437 14 04; Av Libertad) is across the river. You can walk across the Puente Lusitania or catch bus 4 to get to the centre of town (€0.70). Leda SA travels to Seville (€11.55, three hours, one daily) and Cáceres (€4.50, 1¼ hours, four daily). Auto Res services Madrid (€20.20 to €25, four to five hours, eight daily) and Trujillo (€7 to €14, one to 1¼ hours, four daily).

From the **train station** (Calle Cardero), services run to/from Cáceres (€3.60 to €13, one hour, seven daily), Seville (€12, 4¾ hours, one daily Monday to Friday) and Madrid (€20.75 to €31, 5½ to seven hours, five daily).

SPAIN DIRECTORY

ACCOMMODATION

In this chapter, budget options (doubles €60 and under) include everything from dorm-style youth hostels to family-style *pensiones* and slightly better heeled *hostales*. At the upper end of this category you'll find rooms with air-conditioning and private bathrooms. Midrange *hostales* and hotels (€61 to €120) are more comfortable and most offer standard hotel services. Business hotels, trendy boutique hotels, and luxury hotels are in the top-end category (€121 and up). All prices quoted are for rooms with attached bathroom unless otherwise specified.

Always check room charges before putting down your bags and remember that prices can and do change with time. The price of any type of accommodation varies with the season and accommodation prices listed in this book are a guide only. In most cases, we've given either high-season prices or the full range of prices.

Virtually all accommodation prices are subject to IVA *(impuesto sobre el valor añadido)*, the Spanish version of value-added tax, which is 7%. This may or may not be included in the price. To check, ask: *Está incluido el IVA?* (Is IVA included?). In some cases you will be charged the IVA only if you ask for a receipt.

Camping

Spain's camping grounds vary greatly in service, cleanliness and style. They're rated from first to third class and priced accordingly. Expect to pay €5 and up per person, tent and/or car/camper. There are lots of helpful online guides, including www.vayacamping.net.

Some camping grounds close from around October to Easter. With very few exceptions, camping outside camping grounds is illegal, as is building fires. You'll need permission to camp on private land.

Hotels, Hostales & Pensiones

Most other options fall into the categories of hotels (one to five stars, full amenities), *hostales* (high-end guesthouses with private bathroom; one to three stars) or *pensiones* (guesthouses, usually with shared bathroom; one to three stars). Expect a double room at a *pensión* to cost €35 and up per night. At a *hostal* the price will raise slightly to around €45 and up, and a three-star hotel will cost at least €70. Often, you can get great hotel deals online.

Youth Hostels

Albergues juveniles (youth hostels) are cheap places to stay, especially for lone travellers. Expect to pay €15 and up per night. Spain's official Hostelling International (HI) organisation **Red Española de Albergues Juveniles** (REAJ; ☎ 91 522 70 07; www.reaj.com) has 200 youth hostels spread throughout Spain, and though they're often heavily booked by school groups, the official hostels are almost never as good value as the privately run ones. These official hostels require HI membership (buy a membership card for €3.50 at virtually all hostels), most have curfews, and some only admit young (ie under 30) travellers, especially in peak season. At private hostels, you'll get none of this bother, and far more charm to boot.

ACTIVITIES

Cycling

Bike touring isn't as common as in other parts of Europe because of deterrents such as the often-mountainous terrain and summer heat. It's a more viable option on the Balearic Islands than on much of the mainland, although plenty of people get on their bikes in spring and autumn in the south. Mountain biking is popular; areas such as Andalucía and Catalonia have many good tracks.

Skiing

Skiing is cheap compared with the rest of Europe, and facilities and conditions are good, but queuing at lifts can be a mad scramble. The season runs from December to May. The most accessible resorts are in the Nevada Mountains, close to Granada, and the Pyrenees, north of Barcelona. Contact tourist offices in these cities for information. Affordable day trips can be booked through travel agents.

Surfing, Windsurfing & Kite Surfing

The Basque Country has good surf spots, including San Sebastián, Zarauz and the legendary left at Mundaca. Tarifa, with its long, deserted beaches and ceaseless wind, is generally considered to be the windsurfing capital of Europe. It has also recently seen a rise in the sport of kite surfing.

Walking

Spain is a trekker's paradise. Read about some of the best treks in the country in Lonely Planet's *Walking in Spain*. Useful for hiking and exploring some areas are maps by Editorial Alpina, some with information in English. The series combines information booklets with detailed maps. Buy them at bookshops, sports shops and sometimes at petrol stations.

Some of Spain's best walking areas are in its natural and national parks. Throughout Spain, you'll find GR (*Grandes Recorridos*, or Great Treks) trails. These are indicated with a red-and-white marker and are usually easy to navigate. The Camino de Santiago (St James Way) is perhaps Spain's best-known trek.

BUSINESS HOURS

Generally, people work Monday to Friday from 9am to 2pm and then again from 4.30pm or 5pm to about 8pm. Some people still follow the tradition of heading home for lunch and a siesta. Shops and travel agencies are usually open regular business hours on Saturday too, though some may skip the evening session. Large supermarkets open from 9am until 9pm, but many smaller grocers close for lunch from 2pm until 5pm.

Museums all have their own unique opening hours; major ones tend to open for something like normal business hours (with or without the afternoon break), but often have their weekly closing day on Monday.

Banks are open from 8.30am until 2pm, Monday to Friday.

Main post offices in provincial capitals are usually open from either 8.30am to 2pm or 8.30am to 8.30pm Monday to Friday, and from about 9am to 1.30pm Saturday.

Restaurants open 1.30pm until 3.30pm and 8.30pm until 11pm; bars open in the early evening and serve until around 2am.

COURSES

There are hundreds of private language colleges throughout the country; the **Instituto Cervantes** (www.cervantes.es; Spain ☎ 91 436 76 00; Palacio de la Trinidad, Calle Francisco Silvela 82, 28028 Madrid; UK ☎ 020-7235 0353; 102 Eaton Sq, London SW1 W9AN) can send you lists of these and of universities that run courses. Also have a look at the excellent website www.spanish-in-spain.biz.

DANGERS & ANNOYANCES

Stay alert, and you can avoid most of these thievery techniques. Common scams include the following:

- Kids crowding around you asking for directions or help. They may be helping themselves to your wallet.
- A man pointing out bird droppings on your shoulder; it's chocolate (or some other brown substance his friend has sprinkled on you), and if he tries to help clean it off he'll probably take off with your belongings.
- Kids playing football. You get involved in the game. They have easy access to your pockets and/or bags.
- Girls 'reading' maps or newspapers as they walk. The paper just covers their arm, which is then free to reach into purses or backpacks.
- The guys who tell you that you have a flat tyre. Beware, this may be a ruse to steal your car once you pull over and get out to check.

- The classic snatch-and-run. Never leave your purse, bag, wallet, mobile phone etc unattended or alone on a table.

EMBASSIES & CONSULATES

Spanish Embassies & Consulates

Following is a list of Spanish diplomatic missions abroad. For more information see www.mae.es.

Australia Canberra (☎ 02-6273 3555; embespau@mail.mae.es; 15 Arkana St, Yarralumla, Canberra ACT 2600); Melbourne (☎ 03-9347 1966); Sydney (☎ 02-9261 2433)
Canada (www.embaspain.ca) Ottawa (☎ 613-747 2252; embespca@mail.mae.es; 74 Stanley Ave, Ottawa, Ontario K1M 1P4); Montreal (☎ 514-935 5235; conspmontreal@mail.mae.es); Toronto (☎ 416-977 1661; www.cgspaintoronto.com)
France (☎ 01 44 43 18 00; www.amb-espagne.fr; 22 Ave Marceau, 75381 Paris, Cédex 08)
Germany (☎ 030-254 0070; www.spanischebotschaft.de; Lichtensteinallee 1, 10787 Berlin)
Ireland (☎ 269 16 40; embespie@mail.mae.es; 17A Merlyn Park, Ballsbridge, Dublin 4)
Portugal (☎ 21-347 2381; embesppt@mail.mae.es; Rua do Salitre 1 Lisbon)
UK London (☎ 020-7235 5555; embespuk@mail.mae.es; 39 Chesham Pl, London SW1X 8SB); Edinburgh (☎ 0131 220 1843); Manchester (☎ 0161 236 1262)
USA (www.spainemb.org) Boston (☎ 617-536 2506); Chicago (☎ 312-782 4588); Houston (☎ 713-783 6200); Los Angeles (☎ 323-938 0158); Miami (☎ 305-446 5511); New Orleans (☎ 504-525 4951); New York (☎ 212-355 4080); San Francisco (☎ 415-922 2995); Washington DC (☎ 202-452 0100; cog.washington@mae.es; 2375 Pennsylvania Ave NW, Washington DC 20037)

Embassies & Consulates in Spain

Some 70 countries have their embassies in Madrid. Most embassies' office hours are 9am to 2pm.

Australia (☎ 91 441 93 00; www.spain.embassy.gov.au; Plaza del Descubridor Diego de Ordás 3, Edificio Santa Engracia 120)
Canada (Map pp936-7; ☎ 91 423 32 50; www.canada-es.org; Calle de Núñez de Balboa 35)
France (☎ 91 435 55 60; Calle Salustiano Olózaga 9)
Germany (☎ 91 557 90 00; zreg@madri.auswaertiges-amt.de; Calle Fortuny 8)
Ireland (Map pp936-7; ☎ 91 576 35 00; Calle de Claudio Coello 73)
Netherlands (☎ 91 353 75 00; nogovmad@ctv.es; Av Comandante Franco 32)
New Zealand (Map pp936-7; ☎ 91 523 02 26; www.nzembassy.com; Plaza Lealtad 2)
Portugal (☎ 91 782 49 60; Calle Pinar 1)
UK Madrid (Map pp936-7; ☎ 91 319 02 00; Calle Fernando el Santo 16); Barcelona (Map pp966-7; ☎ 93 366 62 00; www.ukinspain.com; Avinguda Diagonal 477)
USA Madrid (Map pp936-7; ☎ 91 577 40 00; www.embusa.es; Calle de Serrano 75); Barcelona (☎ 93 280 22 27; http://barcelona.usconsulate.gov; Paseo Reina Elisenda de Montcada 23)

FESTIVALS & EVENTS

Spaniards indulge their love of colour, noise, crowds and partying at innumerable local festivals, fiestas and *ferias* (fairs). Many are based on religion. Most local tourist offices can supply detailed information. Following is a partial list of important festivals.

January

Festividad de San Sebastián Held in San Sebastián on 20 January; the whole town dresses up and goes berserk.

February & March

Carnaval A time of fancy-dress parades and merrymaking celebrated around the country on the eve of the Christian Lent season (40 days before Easter). The wildest parties are in Tenerife, Cádiz and Sitges.
Las Fallas de San José Valencia's week-long mid-March party, with all-night dancing and drinking, mammoth bonfires, first-class fireworks and processions.

April

Semana Santa Parades of holy images and huge crowds, notably in Seville, during Easter week.
Feria de Abril A week-long party held in Seville in late April, a kind of counterbalance to the religious peak of Easter.

July

Sanfermines The highlight of this originally religious festival is the running of the bulls, in Pamplona. It's held in early July.

August

Semana Grande A week of heavy drinking and hangovers all along the northern coast during the first half of August.

September

Festes de la Mercè Barcelona's week-long party, held around 24 September. It honours the patroness of Barcelona, La Mercè.

HOLIDAYS

Spain has at least 14 official holidays a year, some observed nationwide, some very local. When a holiday falls close to a weekend,

SPAIN

Spaniards like to make a *puente* (bridge), taking the intervening day off, too. The holidays listed following are observed virtually everywhere.

New Year's Day 1 January
Three Kings' Day (when children receive presents) 6 January
Good Friday before Easter Sunday
Labour Day 1 May
Feast of the Assumption 15 August
National Day 12 October
All Saints' Day 1 November
Feast of the Immaculate Conception 8 December
Christmas 25 December

The two main periods when Spaniards go on holiday are Semana Santa (the week leading up to Easter Sunday) and the month of August. At these times accommodation in beachside resorts can be scarce and transport heavily booked.

LANGUAGE

Spanish, or Castilian *(Castellano)* as it is more precisely called, is spoken throughout Spain, but there are also three other important regional languages: Catalan *(Català)* – another Romance language with close ties to French – is spoken in Catalonia, and dialects of it are spoken in the Balearic Islands and in Valencia; Galician (*Gallego*), similar to Portuguese, is spoken in Galicia; and Basque (*Euskara;* of obscure, non-Latin origin) is spoken in the Basque Country and in Navarra.

LEGAL MATTERS

Spaniards no longer enjoy liberal drug laws. No matter what anyone tells you, it is not legal to smoke dope in public bars. There is a reasonable degree of tolerance when it comes to people having a smoke in their own home, but not in hotel rooms or guesthouses.

If you are arrested in Spain, you have the right to an attorney and to know the reason you are being held. You are also entitled to make a phone call.

MAPS

If you're driving around Spain, consider investing in a road atlas with detailed road maps as well as maps of all the main towns and cities. Most travel shops and petrol stations stock them.

Good city and road maps are widely available in bookshops and petrol stations. Michelin maps, which come in many scales and formats, are among the most reliable.

MEDIA

Magazines

International current-affairs magazines (or their international editions) can be found in major cities and resort areas. Among Spain's numerous magazine titles, the most popular is the glossy and gossipy *¡Hola!*.

Newspapers

The major daily newspapers in Spain are the solidly liberal *El País,* the very conservative *ABC*, the more populist *El Mundo,* and the Catalonia-focused *La Vanguardia.* There's also a welter of regional news and sports dailies, many of them with a regional slant.

International press, such as the *International Herald Tribune,* and daily papers from Western European countries reach major cities and tourist areas on the day of or day after publication.

Radio

You'll hear a lot of talk radio and a substantial proportion of music in English. The national pop/rock station, RNE 3, has well-varied programming.

Television

Spanish TV is nothing to get excited about. Gossip shows, talent shows and Big Brother–style reality shows make up the bulk of programming. Most TVs receive six channels: two state-run (TVE1 and La2), three privately run (Antena 3, Tele 5 and Canal Plus) and one regional channel.

MONEY

Spain's currency is the euro (€). Banks tend to give better exchange rates than do the currency-exchange offices. Travellers cheques attract a slightly better rate than cash. It's easy to withdraw money – Spain has one of the world's highest ATM-to-person ratios, probably because most small shops still prefer cash over credit cards.

In Spain, VAT (value-added tax) is known as *impuesto sobre el valor añadido* (IVA). On accommodation and restaurant prices, there's a flat IVA of 7%, which is usually, but not always, included in quoted prices. On such items as retail goods, alcohol and electrical appliances, IVA is 16%. Non-EU visitors, however, don't always have to pay the tax. If you spend €90.15 or more in one store (services don't count), you're eligible for a tax refund. First, request a Spain Refund Cheque, then fill it out and present it to a customs officer at the airport or border crossing. They will stamp it and you can then cash it in. Find more information at www.spainrefund.com.

In restaurants, prices include a service charge, and tipping is a matter of personal choice – most people leave some small change; 5% is plenty, 10% is generous. It's common to leave small change in bars and cafés. Bargaining in Spain is not common, though you could ask for a discount for long-term room rental and the like.

POST

Stamps are sold at post offices and *estancos* (tobacco shops with the Tabacos sign in yellow letters on a maroon background). A standard airmail letter or card costs €0.29 to send within Spain, €0.57 to the rest of Europe and €0.78 to the rest of the world.

Mail to/from Europe normally takes up to a week, and to North America, Australia or New Zealand around 10 days, but there could well be some long, unaccountable delays.

Poste-restante mail can be addressed to you at either poste restante or *lista de correos,* the Spanish name for it, at the city in question. It's a fairly reliable system, although mail may well arrive late.

TELEPHONE

Blue public payphones are common and fairly easy to use. They accept coins, phonecards and, in some cases, credit cards.

A three-minute call from a payphone costs about €0.15 within a local area, €0.35 to other places in the same province, €0.45 to other provinces, or €1 to another EU country or the USA. Telephone service in Spain is not cheap, but there are discounts at night (between 8pm and 8am) and on weekends.

International reverse-charge (collect) calls are simple to make: dial ☎ 900 99 00 followed by the country code. For example: ☎ 61 for Australia, ☎ 44 for the UK, ☎ 64 for New Zealand, ☎ 15 for Canada, and ☎ 11 (AT&T) for the USA.

EMERGENCY NUMBERS

Ambulance ☎ 061

Fire ☎ 080

General Emergencies ☎ 112

Police ☎ 091

Fax

Most main post offices have a fax service, but you'll often find cheaper rates at Internet cafés or copy shops.

Mobile Phones

Mobile phone numbers in Spain start with the number 6. Calls to mobiles vary, but a three-minute call should cost about €1.20.

Phone Codes

Telephone codes in Spain are an integral part of the phone number. All numbers are nine digits and you just dial that nine-digit number, wherever in the country you are calling from. All numbers prefixed with ☎ 900 are toll-free numbers.

Phonecards

A wide variety of *tarjetas telefónicas* (phonecards) are available at post offices, newspaper kiosks and *estancos.*

TIME

Spain is one hour ahead of GMT/UTC during winter, and two hours ahead of GMT/UTC from the last Sunday in March to the last Sunday in September.

TOURIST INFORMATION

Most towns and large villages of any interest have a helpful *oficina de turismo* (tourist office) where you can get maps and brochures. A **nationwide phone line** (☎ 90 130 06 00; 8am-10pm) offers basic information in English. See www.spain.info for more.

Tourist Offices Abroad

Spain has about 30-odd international tourist offices:

Canada (☎ 416-961 3131; www.tourspain.toronto.on.ca; 2 Bloor St W, Toronto)

SPAIN

France (☎ 01-45 03 82 50; www.espagne.infotourisme.com; 43 Rue Decamps, Paris)
Germany (☎ 030-882 6543; berlin@tourspain.es; Kurfürstendamm 63, Berlin)
Portugal (☎ 01-21 354 1992; lisboa@tourspain.es; Ave Sidónio Pais 28, Lisbon)
UK (☎ 020-7486 8077, brochure request 0084 59 400 180; www.tourspain.co.uk; PO Box 4009, London, W1A 6NB)
USA (☎ 212-265 8822; www.okspain.org; 35th fl, 666 Fifth Ave, New York, NY)

VISAS

Citizens of EU countries can enter Spain with their national identity card or passport. Citizens of the UK must have a full passport, not just a British visitor passport. Non-EU nationals must take their passport.

Norway, Iceland and EU citizens do not need a visa. Nationals of Australia, Canada, Israel, Japan, New Zealand, Switzerland and the USA need no visa for stays of up to 90 days, but must have a passport valid for the whole visit. This 90-day limit applies throughout the EU. South Africans are among the nationalities that do need a visa.

It's best to obtain the visa in your country of residence. Single-entry visas are available in 30-day and 90-day flavours, and there's a 90-day multiple-entry visa, too, though if you apply in a country where you're not resident, the 90-day option may not be available. Multiple-entry visas will save you a lot of time and trouble if you plan to leave Spain (to go to, say, Gibraltar or Morocco), then re-enter it.

Spain is one of the Schengen countries; see p1109 for details of the other countries. A visa for one Schengen country is valid for the others. Compare validity, prices and permitted entries before applying.

Norway, Iceland and EU nationals planning to stay in Spain more than 90 days are supposed to apply for a residence card during their first month in the country. This can be a complicated procedure; if you intend to subject yourself to it, consult a Spanish consulate before you go to Spain, as you'll need to take certain documents with you.

WORK

Norway, Iceland and EU nationals are allowed to work in Spain without a visa, but if they plan to stay more than three months they are supposed to apply within the first month for a residence card. Virtually everyone else is supposed to obtain (from a Spanish consulate in their country of residence) a work permit and, if they plan to stay more than 90 days, a residence visa. These procedures can be difficult and time-consuming.

Having said that, quite a few people do manage to work in Spain one way or another – although with Spain's unemployment rate running at around 15%, don't rely on it. Teaching English is an obvious option; a TEFL (Teaching English as a Foreign Language) certificate will be a big help. Another possibility to consider is gaining summer work in a bar or restaurant in a tourist resort, many of which are run by foreigners.

TRANSPORT IN SPAIN

GETTING THERE & AWAY

Air

Spain has many international airports, including the following:

Alicante (ALC; ☎ 96 691 94 10)
Almería (LEI; ☎ 95 021 37 00)
Barcelona (BCN; ☎ 93 298 38 38)
Bilbao (BIO; ☎ 94 486 96 63)
Girona (GRO; ☎ 97 218 60 00)
Ibiza (IBZ; ☎ 97 180 90 00)
Madrid (MAD; ☎ 90 235 35 70)
Málaga (AGP; ☎ 95 204 88 04)
Menorca (MAH; ☎ 97 115 70 00)
Palma de Mallorca (PMI; ☎ 97 178 92 08)
Reus (REU; ☎ 97 777 98 32)
Santiago de Compostela (SCQ; ☎ 98 154 75 00)
Seville (SVQ; ☎ 95 444 90 00)
Valencia (VLC; ☎ 96 159 85 00)
Zaragoza (ZAZ; ☎ 97 671 23 00)

Detailed information about these and other airports can be found through **AENA** (☎ 90 240 47 04; www.aena.es).

Budget airlines have completely changed travel to, and within, Spain, making short breaks much easier and more wallet-friendly.

The informative website www.flycheapo.com tells you which budget airlines fly where. Some of the major budget airlines flying to Spain include easyJet, Ryanair, Vueling and Air Europa.

SPAIN

Airlines operating in Spain include the following:

Aer Lingus (code EI; ☎ 90 250 27 37; www.aerlingus.com)
Air Europa (code UX; ☎ 90 240 15 01; www.aireuropa.com)
Air France (code AF; ☎ 90 220 70 90; www.airfrance.com)
Air Madrid (code NM; ☎ 90 251 52 51; www.airmadrid.com)
Alitalia (code AZ; ☎ 90 210 03 23; www.alitalia.com)
BMI Baby (code WW; ☎ 90 210 07 37; www.bmibaby.com)
British Airways (code BA; ☎ 90 211 13 33; www.ba.com)
British Midland (code BD; ☎ 91 393 72 53; www.flybmi.com)
Delta (code DL; ☎ 90 111 69 46; www.delta.com)
easyJet (code EZY; ☎ 90 229 99 92; www.easyjet.com)
Germanwings (code 4U; ☎ 93 297 11 55; www.germanwings.com)
Iberia (code IB; ☎ 90 240 05 00; www.iberia.com)
Jet2 (code LS; ☎ 44 207 170 07 37; www.jet2.com)
KLM (code KL; ☎ 90 222 27 47; www.klm.com)
Lufthansa (code LH; ☎ 90 222 01 01; www.lufthansa.com)
Monarch Airlines (code ZB; ☎ 90 250 27 37; www.flymonarch.com)
Ryanair (code FR; ☎ 80 722 02 20; www.ryanair.com)
SAS (code SK; ☎ 07 707 27 727; www.sas.se)
Spanair (code JK; ☎ 90 213 14 15; www.spanair.com)
Swiss Air (code LX; ☎ 90 111 67 12; www.swiss.com)
US Airways (code UA; ☎ 90 111 70 73; www.usairways.com)
Virgin Express (code TV; ☎ 90 288 84 59; www.virgin-express.com)
Vueling (code VY; ☎ 90 233 39 33; www.vueling.com)

Land

BUS

There are regular bus services to Spain from European cities such as Lisbon, London and Paris. From London, the popular mega-company **Eurolines** (☎ 08705-808 080; www.eurolines.com) offers regular services to Barcelona (26 hours), Madrid (25 to 28 hours) and other cities. Advance bookings and student ID cards can get you deep discounts. The Eurolines Pass (€115 and up) allows travel throughout Europe, though only to major destinations.

CAR & MOTORCYCLE

If you're driving or riding to Spain from England, you'll have to choose between going through France or taking a direct ferry from England to Spain (see below).

TRAIN

Unless you're simply hopping over the border from France or you already have a rail pass, travelling to Spain by train doesn't make much sense. The cost of a Eurostar train from London to Barcelona (via Paris) can be €200 or more, which is more expensive than many budget airline tickets.

For details on long-distance rail travel, contact the **Rail Europe Travel Centre** (☎ 08705-848848; www.raileurope.co.uk) in London. See p1120 for more on rail passes and train travel through Europe.

Sea

MOROCCO

Several companies offer regular ferry services between Spain and Morocco. **Trasmediterránea** (☎ 90 245 46 45; www.trasmediterranea.es) offers routes including Algeciras–Tangier (€45 to €60, up to 1½ hours) and Almería–Nador (€71.60, six hours). Other possible routes include Algeciras–Ceuta, Gibraltar–Tangier, Tarifa–Tangier, Málaga–Melilla and Almería–Melilla. Fast jetfoil service (at nearly double the price) is available for most of these routes. Taking a car will cost €100 and up.

Don't buy Moroccan currency until you reach Morocco, as you will get ripped off in Algeciras.

UK

If you want use your own car, a ferry is your best bet. **Brittany Ferries** (☎ in UK 08705-360360; www.brittany-ferries.com) runs Plymouth–Santander ferries (24 hours) twice-weekly April through mid-November and once-weekly in March. A one-way ticket with a car starts at about £240.

P&O European Ferries (☎ in UK 08705-980 333; www.poferries.com) runs Portsmouth–Bilbao ferries (35 hours) two or three times weekly year-round. A one-way ticket with a car starts at £270.

GETTING AROUND

Students and seniors are eligible for discounts of 30% to 50% on almost all types of transport within Spain. The travel agency **TIVE** (☎ 91 543 74 12; tive.juventud@madrid.org; Calle Fernando el Católico 88, Madrid; 9am-2pm Mon-Fri) specialises in discounted travel for students and young people.

Air

As Spain's major domestic airline **Iberia** (☎ 90 240 05 00; www.iberia.com) gets more competition from smaller companies, domestic travel prices have fallen. A ticket to Madrid from Barcelona starts at €50, but can reach €350 or more for last-minute travel. Book online for the best fares. For airline contact information see p1035.

Bicycle

Finding bikes to rent in Spain is a hit-and-miss affair, so it's best to bring your own. However, the Spanish do enjoy recreational cycling, so getting hold of spare parts shouldn't be a problem. Cyclists should be aware that quiet roads may suddenly merge into frenetic *autopistas* (freeways) without much warning.

Spain's high-speed AVE and Talgo trains will not allow bicycles on board unless boxed, but slower regional trains will. Provided there's room, buses will take bikes in their lower luggage hold (you'll probably have to remove the front wheel).

Boat

Regular ferries connect the Spanish mainland with the Balearic Islands. In bad weather or rough seas, services will be restricted. For more details see p999. The main companies:

Balearia (☎ 90 216 01 80; www.balearia.com)
Iscomar (☎ 90 211 91 28; www.iscomarferrys.com)
Trasmediterránea (☎ 90 245 46 45; www.trasmediterranea.es)

Bus

Spain's bus network is operated by countless independent companies and reaches into the most remote towns and villages. Many towns and cities have one main bus station where most buses arrive and depart, and these usually have an information desk giving information on all services. Tourist offices can also help with information. The best-known national service is run by **Alsa** (☎ 90 242 22 42; www.alsa.es).

Bus tickets vary greatly in cost, depending on the popularity of the route. For example, a ticket from Madrid to Santiago de Compostela costs about €53, while a ticket from Madrid to Málaga, a comparable distance, costs just €20.

It is not necessary, and often not possible, to make advance reservations for local bus journeys. It is, however, a good idea to turn up at least 30 minutes before the bus leaves to guarantee a seat. For longer trips, try to buy your ticket in advance.

Car & Motorcycle

Spain's roads vary enormously but are generally quite good. Fastest are the *autopistas;* on some, you have to pay hefty tolls (from Zaragoza to Barcelona, for example, it's about €17). Minor routes can be slow going but are usually more scenic. Trying to find a parking spot in larger towns and cities can be a nightmare. Spanish drivers will seemingly park anywhere, but *grúas* (tow trucks) can and will tow your car. The cost of bailing out a car can be €200 or more.

Spanish cities do not have US-style parking meters at every spot. Instead, if you park in a blue zone from 8am to 2pm or from 4pm to 8pm, you have to obtain a ticket from a street-side meter, which may be a block away. Display the ticket on the dash. If you bring your own vehicle into Spain, remember to always carry the vehicle registration document.

Petrol stations are easy to find along highways and *autopistas*. They sell the more-expensive *gasolina* (unleaded) petrol as well as *gasóleo* (diesel).

AUTOMOBILE ASSOCIATIONS

The Spanish automobile club **Real Automovil Club de España** (RACE; ☎ 90 240 45 45; www.race.es) offers a 24-hour, nationwide, on-road emergency service.

DRIVING LICENCE

All EU member states' driving licences (pink or pink and green) are recognised. Other foreign licences should be accompanied by an International Driving Permit. These are available from automobile clubs in your country and valid for 12 months.

HIRE

Rates vary widely from place to place. The best deals tend to be in major tourist areas, including airports. Expect a compact car to cost €30 and up per day. See p1118 for information on major car-hire companies.

INSURANCE

Third party motor insurance is a minimum requirement, and it is compulsory to have a Green Card, an internationally recognised proof of insurance, which can be obtained from your insurer.

ROAD RULES

Driving in Spain is not too bad. Locals respect road rules but do have a tendency to tailgate. Speed limits are 120km/h on the *autopistas,* 90km/h or 100km/h on other country roads and 50km/h in built-up areas. The blood-alcohol limit is 0.04%, though some politicians are pushing for a zero-tolerance law. Seat belts must be worn, and motorcyclists must always wear a helmet and keep headlights on day and night.

Train

Trains are mostly modern and comfortable, and late arrivals are the exception rather than the rule.

Renfe (☎ 90 224 02 02; www.renfe.es), the national railway company, runs numerous types of trains, and travel times can vary a lot on the same route. So can fares, which may depend not just on the type of train but also the day of the week and time of day. Renfe's website is a great resource for schedule and fare information.

Regionales are all-stops trains (think cheap and slow). *Cercanías* provide regular services from major cities to the surrounding suburbs and hinterland, sometimes even crossing regional boundaries. Long-distance trains go by several names (eg Altaria, Diurno, Estrella), depending on the exact services they offer. Talgo is faster than the rest, and the most expensive.

The high-speed AVE train runs from Seville to Madrid, and from Madrid to Zaragoza and Llerida (and soon on to Barcelona). It's the most comfortable way to travel, though it's not cheap – a Seville–Madrid ticket costs €70 one way.

On overnight trains, you have the comfortable option of staying in a cabin with a bed for only slightly more than the price of a regular ticket. Most cabins are divided by sexes, though if you're travelling with friends, your entire group can stay together.

You can buy tickets and make reservations online, at stations, at travel agencies displaying the Renfe logo and in Renfe offices in many city centres.

TRAIN PASSES

Rail passes are valid for all long-distance Renfe trains, but Inter-Rail users have to pay supplements on Talgo, InterCity and AVE trains. All passholders making reservations pay a small fee.

Renfe's Flexipass is a rail pass valid for three to 10 days' travel in a two-month period. In tourist class, three days costs €170, and 10 days is €380. The pass can be purchased from agents outside Europe, or at main train stations in Spain. Spanish residents are not eligible for this pass.

SPAIN

Switzerland

Switzerland is an easy country to swallow; it melts in your mouth as smoothly as the rich chocolates and creamy cheeses it is famous for. With a kind of slap-you-in-the-face natural beauty Hollywood filmmakers salivate over and a reputation as a summer and winter sports paradise, it's pretty hard to not get hooked. Switzerland is where people first skied for fun, and along with heavenly powder pistes and ultraglam resorts (think St Moritz), the country dishes up enough adrenalin-pumping fuel to keep your inner junkie satiated for weeks (think out-of-this-world hiking or flying through the sky on a pair of manmade wings).

Okay, so all the clichés you've heard about Switzerland are likely true. It's pretty damn easy to envision rosy-faced goat herders yodelling to a clinking cowbell melody amid sky-scraping peaks. But even though they've perfected the whole G-rated Matterhorn look, don't mistake the Swiss for a bunch of Goody Two-Shoes. This is the country, after all, that invented absinthe and LSD. It's as well known for secret bank accounts and shady business deals as for fondue and droopy-roofed chalets. Small, fiercely independent and culturally complex (there are four official languages, Swiss German, French, Italian and Romansch), the Swiss have expensive tastes. Cities like Geneva (the most cosmopolitan), Zürich (the most outrageous), Bern (the most charming) and Lucerne (the most beautiful) heave with heady artistic activity, legendary nightlife and some of the planet's highest living standards.

FAST FACTS

- **Area** 41,285 sq km
- **Capital** Bern
- **Currency** Swiss franc (Sfr); A$1 = Sfr0.91; €1 = Sfr1.56; ¥100 = Sfr1.07; NZ$1 = Sfr0.75; UK£1 = Sfr2.26; US$1 = Sfr1.22
- **Famous for** cheese, the Matterhorn, banking
- **Official Languages** French, German, Italian, Romansch
- **Phrases** *gruezi* (hello, good day), *merci vielmal* (thank you very much), *adieu* (goodbye), *sprechen sie Englisch?* (do you speak English?)
- **Population** 7.4 million
- **Telephone Codes** country code ☎ 41; international access code ☎ 00

HIGHLIGHTS

- Gasp at gargantuan mountain vistas, partake in white-knuckle adrenalin adventures or spend a night in the hay in the gorgeous **Jungfrau region** (p1081).
- Play in the mighty Matterhorn's shadow in everyone's favourite Swiss ski town, **Zermatt** (p1062).
- Immerse yourself in **Bern**'s (p1045) elegant medieval charm and pulsating party scene.
- Soak up seriously sexy ambience sipping wine at a lakeside café in Switzerland's sultry Italian canton, **Ticino** (p1064).
- Eat lunch in the revolving restaurant at the top of the **Schilthorn** (p1083), dominated by mammoth Eiger, Mönch and Jungfrau (Ogre, Monk and Virgin) mountain views.

ITINERARIES

- **One week** Start in vibrant Zürich. Shop famous Bahnhofstrasse or hit a hip new martini bar. Head to the Jungfrau region next, and explore some kick-ass (think James Bond racing an avalanche down a sheer snowy rock face) Alpine scenery. Take a pit stop in beautiful Lucerne before finishing up in fabulously medieval Bern.
- **Two weeks** As above, then head west for French immersion lessons in international Geneva or cosmopolitan Lausanne. Spend a few nights in Neuchâtel and Freiburg cantons, stopping to taste *the* cheese in Gruyères. Zip down to Zermatt or across to St Moritz to partake in a little skiing. Loop east to experience Switzerland's Italian side.

HOW MUCH?

- **Hostel dorm bed** Sfr28
- **Bottle of absinthe** Sfr50
- **100km by train** Sfr30
- **City bus ride** Sfr2-3
- **Local telephone call** Sfr0.60

LONELY PLANET INDEX

- **1L petrol** Sfr1.74
- **1L bottled water** Sfr2
- **Half-pint of beer** Sfr4
- **Souvenir T-shirt** Sfr20
- **Kebab** Sfr9

CLIMATE & WHEN TO GO

Although there are plenty of crystal clear, sunny days, winters in Switzerland can be cold, snowy and sometimes (especially around Zürich) rather grey, with temperatures between 2°C and 6°C. Summers mix sunshine with rain. Temperatures range from 20°C to 25°C, except in Ticino, which has a hotter, Mediterranean climate. You will need to be prepared for a range of temperatures, depending on your altitude.

Visit Switzerland from December to April for winter sports, and May to October for general sightseeing and hiking. Alpine resorts all but close down in late April, May and November. See also Climate Charts (p1100).

HISTORY

The first inhabitants of the region were a Celtic tribe, the Helvetii. The Romans arrived in 107 BC via the Great St Bernard Pass, but were gradually driven back by the Germanic Alemanni tribe, which settled in the region in the 5th century AD. Burgundians and Franks also came to the area, and Christianity was gradually introduced.

The territory was united under the Holy Roman Empire in 1032, but central control was never tight, and neighbouring nobles fought each other for local influence. Rudolph I spearheaded the Germanic Habsburg expansion and gradually brought the squabbling nobles to heel.

The Swiss Confederation

Upon Rudolph's death in 1291, local leaders saw a chance to gain independence. The forest communities of Uri, Schwyz and Nidwalden formed an alliance on 1 August 1291, which is seen as the origin of the Swiss Confederation (their struggles against the Habsburgs are idealised in the legend of William Tell). This union's success prompted other communities to join: Lucerne (1332), followed by Zürich (1351), Glarus and Zug (1352), and Bern (1353).

Encouraged by successes against the Habsburgs, the Swiss acquired a taste for

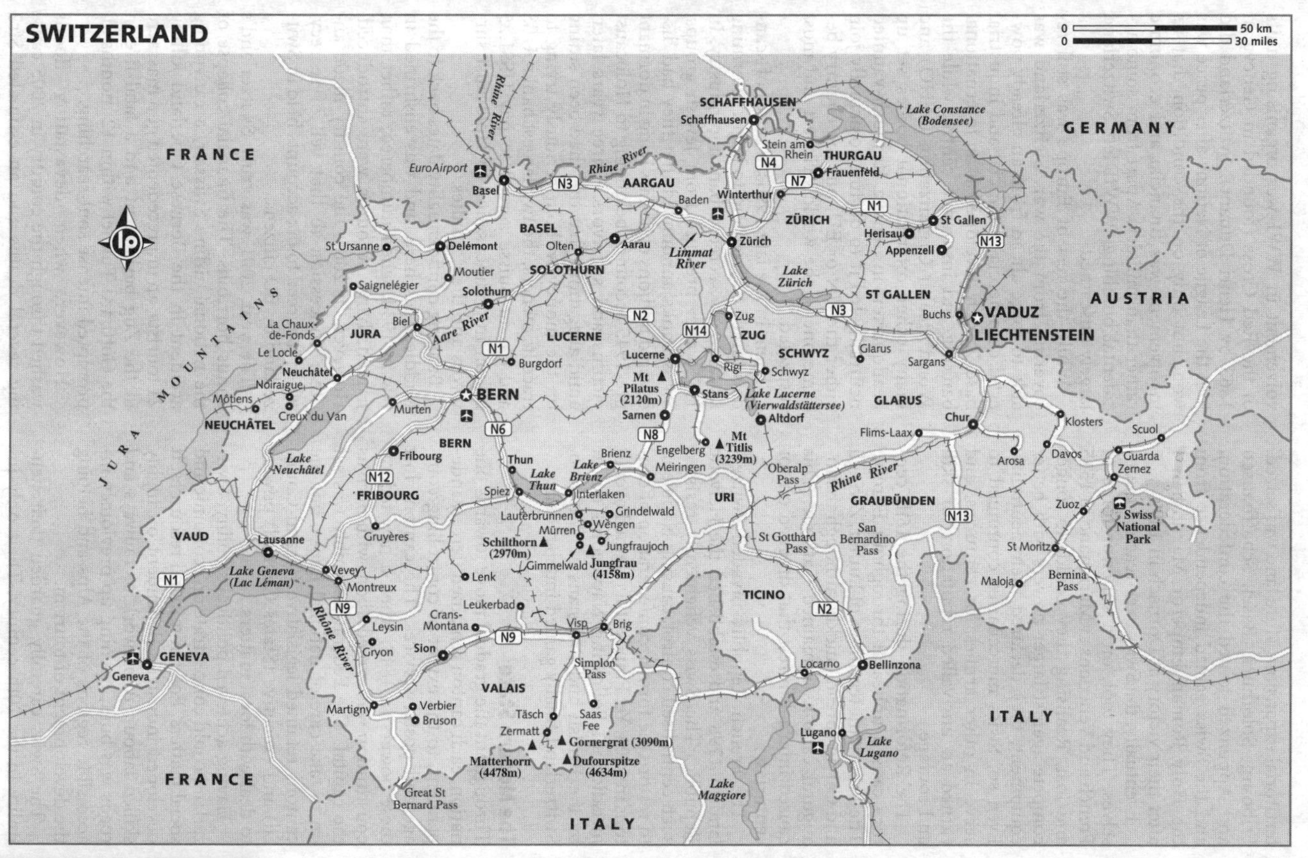
SWITZERLAND
0 50 km
0 30 miles
FRANCE
GERMANY
AUSTRIA
ITALY
JURA MOUNTAINS
Rhine River
EuroAirport
Basel
N3
Rhine River
AARGAU
SCHAFFHAUSEN
Schaffhausen
Lake Constance (Bodensee)
Stein am Rhein
N4
THURGAU
N7
Frauenfeld
Winterthur
Baden
N1
St Gallen
BASEL
ZÜRICH
Herisau
N13
St Ursanne
Delémont
Olten
Aarau
Limmat River
Zürich
Appenzell
Moutier
SOLOTHURN
Lake Zürich
Saignelégier
Solothurn
ST GALLEN
N3
Buchs
VADUZ
N2
Zug
La Chaux-de-Fonds
Biel
Aare River
LUCERNE
N14
ZUG
LIECHTENSTEIN
JURA
SCHWYZ
Glarus
Le Locle
N1
Burgdorf
Lucerne
Rigi
Sargans
Schwyz
Neuchâtel
Mt Pilatus (2120m)
Noiraigue
Stans
Lake Lucerne (Vierwaldstättersee)
Môtiens
BERN
GLARUS
Murten
Creux du Van
Sarnen
Altdorf
Chur
NEUCHÂTEL
Klosters
N6
Scuol
N8
Flims-Laax
BERN
Mt Titlis (3239m)
Engelberg
Lake Neuchâtel
Fribourg
Brienz
Arosa
Davos
Guarda
Thun
Lake Thun
Lake Brienz
Meiringen
Oberalp Pass
Rhine River
Zernez
N12
FRIBOURG
Spiez
Interlaken
URI
GRAUBÜNDEN
Zuoz
Grindelwald
Swiss National Park
Lauterbrunnen
Wengen
N13
Gruyères
VAUD
Mürren
St Gotthard Pass
San Bernardino Pass
Schilthorn (2970m)
Lausanne
Jungfraujoch
St Moritz
Gimmelwald
Jungfrau (4158m)
Lake Geneva (Lac Léman)
Vevey
N1
Lenk
Maloja
Bernina Pass
Montreux
TICINO
N9
Leukerbad
Rhône River
N2
Crans-Montana
Leysin
Visp
Brig
N9
Gryon
Sion
GENEVA
Geneva
Simplon Pass
Locarno
Bellinzona
VALAIS
Verbier
Martigny
Bruson
Täsch
Saas Fee
ITALY
Zermatt
Lugano
Gornergrat (3090m)
Lake Lugano
Matterhorn (4478m)
Dufourspitze (4634m)
FRANCE
Great St Bernard Pass
Lake Maggiore
ITALY

territorial expansion. More land was seized. Fribourg, Solothurn, Basel, Schaffhausen and Appenzell joined the confederation, and the Swiss gained independence from the Holy Roman Emperor Maximilian I after their victory at Dornach in 1499.

Eventually, the Swiss over-reached themselves. They took on a superior force of French and Venetians at Marignano in 1515 and lost. Realising they could no longer compete against larger powers with better equipment, they declared their neutrality. Even so, Swiss mercenaries continued to serve in other armies for centuries, and earned an unrivalled reputation for skill and courage.

The Reformation during the 16th century caused upheaval throughout Europe. The Protestant teachings of Luther, Zwingli and Calvin spread quickly, although the inaugural cantons remained Catholic. This caused internal unrest that dragged on for centuries.

The French Republic invaded Switzerland in 1798 and established the Helvetic Republic. The Swiss vehemently resisted such centralised control, causing Napoleon to restore the former confederation of cantons in 1803. Yet France still retained overall jurisdiction. Following Napoleon's defeat by the British and Prussians at Waterloo, Switzerland finally gained independence.

The Modern State

Throughout the gradual move towards one nation, each canton remained fiercely independent, to the extent of controlling coinage and postal services. The cantons lost these powers in 1848, when a new federal constitution was agreed upon, with Bern as the capital. The Federal Assembly was set up to take care of national issues, but the cantons retained legislative (Grand Council) and executive (States Council) powers to deal with local matters.

Having achieved political stability, Switzerland could concentrate on economic and social matters. Poor in mineral resources, it developed industries dependent on highly skilled labour. A network of railways and roads was built, opening up previously inaccessible regions of the Alps and helping the development of tourism.

The Swiss carefully guarded their neutrality in the 20th century. Their only involvement in WWI was organising units of the Red Cross (founded in Geneva in 1863 by Henri Dunant). Switzerland did join the League of Nations after peace was won, but only on the condition that its involvement was financial and economic rather than military. Apart from some accidental bombing, WWII left Switzerland largely unscathed.

While the rest of Europe was still recovering from the war, Switzerland was able to forge ahead from an already powerful commercial, financial and industrial base. Zürich developed as an international banking and insurance centre, while the World Health Organization (WHO) and many other international bodies set up headquarters in Geneva. Its much-vaunted neutrality led it to decline to actually join either the UN or EU, but the country became one of the world's richest and most respected.

Then, in the late 1990s, a series of scandals forced Switzerland to begin reforming its famously secretive banking industry. In 1995, after pressure from Jewish groups, Swiss banks announced that they had discovered millions of dollars lying in dormant pre-1945 accounts, belonging to Holocaust victims and survivors. Three years later, amid allegations that they had been sitting on the money without seriously trying to trace its owners, the two largest banks, UBS and Credit Suisse agreed to pay US$1.25 billion in compensation to Holocaust survivors and their families.

Banking confidentiality dates back to the Middle Ages here, and was enshrined in law in 1934, when numbered, rather than named, bank accounts were introduced. However, in 2004, the country made another concession to that veil of secrecy, when it agreed to tax accounts held in Switzerland by EU citizens.

The year 2001 was truly Switzerland's annus horribilis. The financial collapse of the national airline Swissair, a canyoning accident in the Bernese Oberland killing 21 tourists, an unprecedented gun massacre in the Zug parliament and a fatal fire in the Gotthard Tunnel within 12 months all prompted intense soul-searching.

However, when devastating floods washed through the country in 2005 causing several deaths and an estimated Sfr2

IT ALL HAPPENED IN SWITZERLAND

- Albert Einstein came up with his theories of relativity and the famous formula 'E=MC²' in Bern in 1905.
- Switzerland gave birth to the World Wide Web at the acclaimed CERN (European Centre for Nuclear Research) institute outside Geneva.
- Val de Travers, near Neuchâtel, claims to be the birthplace of the mythical green alcohol absinthe.
- The first acid trip took place in Switzerland. In 1943, chemist Albert Hofmann was conducting tests for a migraine cure in Basel when he accidentally absorbed the lysergic acid diethylamide, or LSD, compound through his fingertips.
- Of the 800-or-so films a year produced by India's huge movie-making industry, more are shot in Switzerland than in any other foreign country. 'For the Indian public, Switzerland is the land of their dreams', film star Raj Mukherjee has said. Favourite destination shoots include the Berner Oberland, Central Switzerland and Geneva.
- Switzerland's central Alpine region possesses one of Europe's richest traditions of myth and legend. Pontius Pilate is said to rise out of the lake on Mt Pilatus, near Lucerne, every good Friday (the day he condemned Jesus Christ) to wash blood from his hands – and anybody who witnesses this event will allegedly die within the year. Tiny 'wild folk' with supernatural powers, called Chlyni Lüüt, were once reputed to inhabit Mt Rigi, also near Lucerne. Their children's spleens were removed at birth, giving them the ability to leap around mountain slopes.

billion damage, there were fewer anguished cries about what was going wrong with Switzerland and more pragmatic debate on what should be done.

Switzerland swung to the conservative right in its parliamentary government in 2003, and today recognises that it's facing universal challenges; it has begun to reach out more to the world. In 2002 it finally became the 190th member of the UN. In 2005 it joined Europe's 'Schengen' passport-free travel zone (effective 2007) and, in theory, opened its borders to workers from the 10 new EU members.

It still isn't a member of the EU itself and, although the French-speaking regions would like it, doesn't look like becoming one anytime soon. However, in many ways Switzerland no longer views isolation as quite so splendid.

PEOPLE

Switzerland's name may stand for everything from knives to watches, but don't expect this nation to take a stand for anyone other than itself. Militarily neutral for centuries, and armed to the teeth to make sure it stays that way, in Switzerland it's the Swiss Way or the highway.

With a population of 7.4 million, Switzerland averages 174 people per square kilometre. Zürich is the largest city (population 338,794) followed by Geneva (179,426), Basel (161,800) and Bern (120,596). Most people are of Germanic origin, as reflected in the breakdown of the four national languages. Around 20% of the population are residents but not Swiss citizens.

The Swiss are polite, law-abiding people who usually see no good reason to break the rules. Living quietly with your neighbours is a national obsession. Good manners infuse the national psyche, and politeness is the cornerstone of all social intercourse. Always shake hands when being introduced to a Swiss, and kiss on both cheeks to greet and say goodbye to friends. Don't forget to greet shopkeepers when entering shops. When drinking with the Swiss, always wait until everyone has their drink and toast each of your companions, looking them in the eye and clinking glasses. Drinking before the toast is unforgivable, and will lead to seven years of bad sex…or so the superstition goes. Don't say you weren't warned.

In a few mountain regions such as Valais, people still wear traditional rural costumes, but dressing up is usually reserved for festivals. Yodelling, playing the alp horn and Swiss wrestling are also part of the Alpine tradition.

RELIGION

The country is split pretty evenly between Protestantism (40%) and Roman Catholicism (46%). Most of the rest of the population are recorded as 'unaffiliated'. The dominant faith varies between cantons. Strong Protestant areas are Bern, Vaud and Zürich, whereas Valais, Ticino and Uri are mostly Catholic. Most Swiss pay a *kirchensteur* (church tax) – a percentage of their income tax that the government distributes to the churches through state subsidies.

ARTS

Many foreign writers and artists, such as Voltaire, Byron, Shelley and Turner have visited and settled in Switzerland. Local and international artists pouring into Zürich during WWI spawned the dadaist movement there.

Paul Klee (1879–1940) is the best-known native painter. He created bold, hard-lined abstract works. The writings of philosopher Jean-Jacques Rousseau (1712–78), in Geneva, played an important part in the development of democracy. Critically acclaimed postwar dramatists and novelists, Max Frisch (1911–91) and Friedrich Dürrenmatt (1921–90), entertained readers with their dark satire, tragi-comedies and morality plays. On the musical front, Arthur Honegger (1892–1955) is Switzerland's most recognised composer.

The Swiss have made important contributions to graphic design and commercial art. Anyone who's ever used a computer will have interacted with their fonts, from Helvetica to Fruitiger to Univers. The father of modern architecture, Le Corbusier (1887–1965), who designed Notre Dame du Haut chapel at Ronchamps in France, Chandigarh in India and the UN headquarters in New York, was Swiss. One of the most-acclaimed contemporary architectural teams on earth, Jacques Herzog and Pierre de Meuron, live and work in Basel. Winners of the prestigious Pritzker Prize in 2001, this pair created London's acclaimed Tate Modern museum building.

Gothic and Renaissance architecture are prevalent in urban areas, especially Bern. Rural Swiss houses vary according to region, but are generally characterised by ridged roofs with wide, overhanging eaves, and balconies and verandas enlivened by colourful floral displays, especially geraniums.

To the chagrin of many, Switzerland also sports some pretty artistic graffiti. Giant intricately spray-painted patterns (along with less savoury pieces) grace buildings scattered along railway tracks near train stations.

ENVIRONMENT

Mountains make up 70% of Switzerland's 41,285 sq km. Farming of cultivated land is intensive and cows graze on the upper slopes as soon as the retreating snow line permits.

The Alps occupy the central and southern regions of the country. The Dufourspitze (4634m), a peak on the Monte Rosa Mountains, is the highest point, although the Matterhorn (4478m) is more famous.

Glaciers account for a 2000-sq-km area. The Aletsch Glacier is Europe's largest valley glacier at 169 sq km.

The St Gotthard Mountains, in the centre of Switzerland, is the source of many lakes and rivers, including the Rhine and the Rhône. The Jura Mountains straddle the border with France, and peak at around 1700m. Between the two systems is the Mittelland, also known as the Swiss Plateau, a region of hills crisscrossed by rivers, ravines and winding valleys.

The most distinctive Alpine animal in Switzerland is the ibex, a mountain goat that has huge curved and ridged horns. There are about 12,000 of them left in the country.

Switzerland has just one national park, the Swiss National Park. At just 169 sq km it is quite small but offers opportunities for walking and ibex viewing.

Switzerland has long been an environmentally aware nation. Its citizens diligently recycle household waste and cities encourage the use of public transport. The policy in the mountains is to contain rather than expand existing resorts.

Global warming could have a serious impact on Switzerland because of the effect on

Alpine glaciers. Since the 1950s the federal government has introduced various measures to protect forests, lakes and marshland from environmental damage and, in 1991, it signed the Alpine Convention, which seeks to reduce damage caused by motor traffic and tourism.

FOOD & DRINK

Lactose intolerants will struggle in this dairy-obsessed country, where cheese is a way of life. The best-known Swiss dish is fondue, in which melted Emmental and gruyère are combined with white wine, served in a large pot and eaten with bread cubes. Another popular artery-hardener is *raclette,* melted cheese served with potatoes. *Rösti* (fried, buttery, shredded potatoes) is German Switzerland's national dish, and is served with everything.

Many dishes are meaty, and veal is highly rated throughout the country. In Zürich it is thinly sliced and served in a cream sauce *(Gschnetzeltes Kalbsfleisch)*. *Bündnerfleisch* is dried beef, smoked and thinly sliced. Like their northern neighbours, the Swiss also munch on a wide variety of Wurst (sausage).

Wine is considered an essential accompaniment to lunch and dinner. Local vintages are generally good quality, but you might never have heard of them, as they are rarely exported. The main growing regions are Italian- and French-speaking areas, particularly in Valais and by Lakes Neuchâtel and Geneva.

Buffet-style restaurant chains, such as Manora, have a huge selection of freshly cooked food at low prices. Migros and Coop are the main supermarket chains. Street stalls are a good place to pick up cheap eats – you'll find kebabs and sandwiches everywhere. If you're fond of kebabs (as we are), the stalls on Zürich's Niederdorfstrasse (p1073) are some of our favourites in the country. Bratwurst and pretzel stands (sometimes the pretzels are even stuffed with meats and cheeses) also abound in German cantons.

Restaurants sometimes close between meals (generally from 3pm to 5pm), although this is becoming rare in large cities, and tend to have a closing day, often Monday. Cafés usually stay open all day. Bars are open from lunch time until at least midnight. Clubs get going after 10pm and close around 4am.

In cities and larger towns there are dedicated vegetarian restaurants. Most eateries also will offer a small selection of nonmeat options, including large salad plates.

Finally, Switzerland makes some of the most delectable chocolate in the world – don't miss it!

BERN

pop 120,596

One of the planet's most underrated capitals, Bern is a fabulous find. With the genteel, old soul of a Renaissance man and the heart of a high-flying 21st-century gal, the city is at once medieval and modern. The 15th-century old town is gorgeous enough to sweep you off your feet and make you forget the century (it's definitely worthy of its 1983 Unesco World Heritage site protection order). But edgy vintage boutiques, artsy-intellectual bars and raging nightlife will slam you back into the present.

Bern was founded in 1191 by Berchtold V and named for the unfortunate bear (*bärn* in local dialect) that was his first hunting victim. The bear remains the heraldic mascot of the city today. Attractions include checking out Paul Klee's, visiting Einstein's home and taking a swift float down the Aare River's blue-green waters.

ORIENTATION

The compact centre of old town is contained within a sharp U-bend of the Aare River. The train station is on the western edge within easy reach of all the main sights, and offers bike rental and airline check-in.

INFORMATION

Bookshops

Stauffacher (☎ 031 311 24 11; Neuengasse 25; 🕑 8am-6.30pm Mon-Fri, to 4pm Sat) English-language bookshop.

Discount Card

BernCard (per 24/48/72hr Sfr17/27/33) Admission to the permanent collections of all museums, plus free public transport and discounts on city tours.

Emergency

Police station (☎ 031 321 21 21; train station)

SWITZERLAND

Internet Access

Inside Internet Bar (☎ 031 313 81 91; Aarbergergasse 46; per hr Sfr7-9; 🕑 11am-12.30am Mon-Sat, noon-10pm Sun) Fully stocked bar and groovy atmosphere.

Medical Services

Emergency doctor, dentist, pharmacist (☎ 090 057 67 47; 🕑 24hr)
University hospital (☎ 031 632 21 11; Fribourgstrasse; 🕑 24hr) West of the centre, has a casualty department.

Post

Main post office (Schanzenstrasse; 🕑 7.30am-6.30pm Mon-Fri, 8am-noon Sat)

Tourist Information

Bern tourist office (☎ 031 328 12 28; www.berne tourism.ch; train station; 🕑 9am-8.30pm daily Jun-Sep, 9.30am-6.30pm Mon-Sat & 10am-5pm Sun Oct-May) Offers two-hour city tours by coach (Sfr25, daily April to October, Saturday November to March) and foot (Sfr14, daily June to September) in summer. Its free booklet, *Bern aktuell,* has plenty of useful information. There's another tourist office by the bear pits.
Bern Youth Guide (www.youthguide.ch) This online service has some excellent tips and links.

Travel Agencies

STA Travel (☎ 031 302 03 12; Falkenplatz 9; 🕑 9.30am-6pm Mon-Fri, 10am-1pm Sat) Budget and student travel agency.

SIGHTS

Old Town

Pick up a city map from the tourist office (Sfr1) and start exploring. Don't pay too much attention to the map though. The best places are often found on detours down skinny side alleys. Stumble into a funky retro cellar shop, selling penis-shaped peppermint candies alongside chunky silver rings. Keep an eye out for a gallery selling all sorts of shells and bright beaded necklaces or a hideaway bar of the trendiest proportions.

Classic not-to-be-missed stops on your conventional map include the **ogre fountain**, in Kornhausplatz, depicting a giant enjoying a meal of wriggling children. The **Zeitglockenturm**, dividing Marktgasse and Kramgasse, is a colourful clock tower with revolving figures that herald the chiming hour.

The unmistakably Gothic, 15th-century cathedral **Münster** (🕑 10am-5pm Tue-Sat, 11.30am-5pm Sun) is worth stepping into. It features imposing, 12m-high, stained-glass windows and an elaborate main portal.

Just across the Aare River are the **bear pits** (Bärengraben). Though bears have been the entertainment at this site since 1857, it's really depressing to see such majestic beasts doing tricks for treats in such a cramped, concrete environment – this author had to turn away pretty quickly.

> **BERN IN TWO DAYS**
>
> Stroll around **old town** (above). Check out the clock tower and ogre fountain, duck into the myriad cellar shops. Lunch at the popular **Altes Tramdepot** (p1049), then visit the **Einstein museum** (right). At night bar-hop around town.
>
> Spend morning number two looking at paintings; try the **Paul Klee Centre** (right) and the **Kunstmuseum** (p1048). If it's warm, go swimming in the **Marzili pools** (p1048) or float down the swift **Aare River** (p1048).

Einstein Museum

The world's most famous scientist developed his theory of relativity in Bern in 1905, and the small **Einstein Haus** (☎ 031 312 00 91; www.einstein-bern.ch; Kramgasse 49; adult/student & senior Sfr6/4.50; 🕑 10am-7pm Apr-Oct, 1-5pm Tue-Fri, noon-4pm Sat Feb, Mar & Nov–mid-Dec, closed mid-Dec–Jan) has been given a facelift recently to celebrate the centenary of that discovery.

The humble apartment where Einstein lived with his young family while working as a low-paid clerk in the Bern patent office has been redecorated in the style of the time. Numerous multimedia displays now flesh out the story of the subsequent general equation – $E=MC^2$, or energy equals mass multiplied by the speed of light squared – which fundamentally changed humankind's understanding of space, time and the universe.

Paul Klee Centre

Renzo Piano's remarkable building, the **Zentrum Paul Klee** (☎ 031 359 01 01; www.zpk.org; adult/concession/child Sfr14/12/6, extra Sfr2 for special exhibitions; 🕑 10am-5pm Tue, Wed & Fri-Sun, to 9pm Thu) is Bern's Guggenheim. Curving up and down

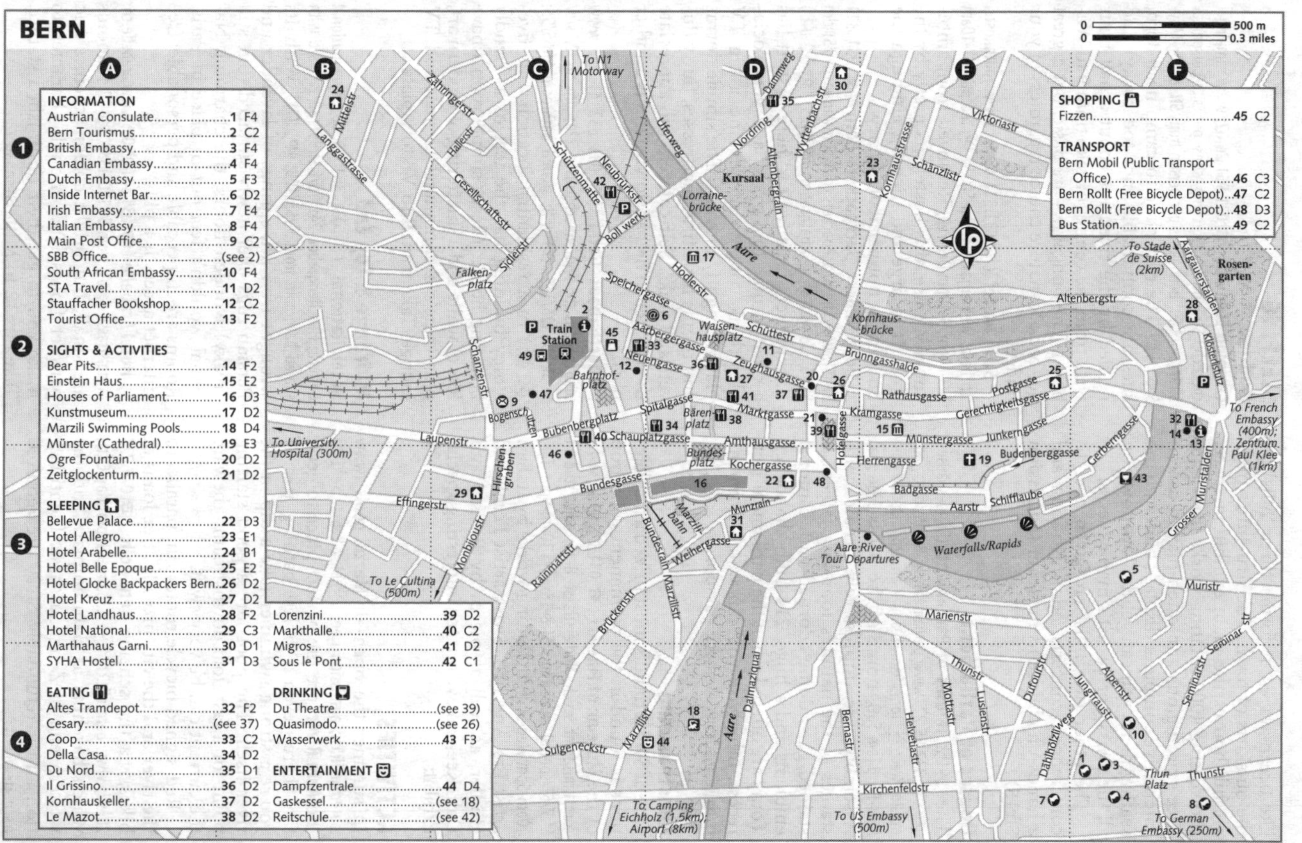
BERN
0 500 m
0 0.3 miles
INFORMATION
Austrian Consulate 1 F4
Bern Tourismus 2 C2
British Embassy 3 F4
Canadian Embassy 4 F4
Dutch Embassy 5 F3
Inside Internet Bar 6 D2
Irish Embassy 7 E4
Italian Embassy 8 F4
Main Post Office 9 C2
SBB Office (see 2)
South African Embassy 10 F4
STA Travel 11 D2
Stauffacher Bookshop 12 C2
Tourist Office 13 F2
SIGHTS & ACTIVITIES
Bear Pits 14 F2
Einstein Haus 15 E2
Houses of Parliament 16 D3
Kunstmuseum 17 D2
Marzili Swimming Pools 18 D4
Münster (Cathedral) 19 E3
Ogre Fountain 20 D2
Zeitglockenturm 21 D2
SLEEPING
Bellevue Palace 22 D3
Hotel Allegro 23 E1
Hotel Arabelle 24 B1
Hotel Belle Epoque 25 E2
Hotel Glocke Backpackers Bern 26 D2
Hotel Kreuz 27 D2
Hotel Landhaus 28 F2
Hotel National 29 C3
Marthahaus Garni 30 D1
SYHA Hostel 31 D3
EATING
Altes Tramdepot 32 F2
Cesary (see 37)
Coop 33 C2
Della Casa 34 D2
Du Nord 35 D1
Il Grissino 36 D2
Kornhauskeller 37 D2
Le Mazot 38 D2
Lorenzini 39 D2
Markthalle 40 C2
Migros 41 D2
Sous le Pont 42 C1
DRINKING
Du Theatre (see 39)
Quasimodo (see 26)
Wasserwerk 43 F3
ENTERTAINMENT
Dampfzentrale 44 D4
Gaskessel (see 18)
Reitschule (see 42)
SHOPPING
Fizzen 45 C2
TRANSPORT
Bern Mobil (Public Transport Office) 46 C3
Bern Rollt (Free Bicycle Depot) 47 C2
Bern Rollt (Free Bicycle Depot) 48 D3
Bus Station 49 C2
To N1 Motorway
To Stade de Suisse (2km)
To French Embassy (400m); Zentrum Paul Klee (1km)
To University Hospital (300m)
To Le Cultina (500m)
To Camping Eichholz (1.5km); Airport (8km)
To US Embassy (500m)
To German Embassy (250m)
Train Station
Kursaal
Rosengarten
Aare
Lorrainebrücke
Kornhausbrücke
Waterfalls/Rapids
Aare River Tour Departures
Bahnhofplatz
Bärenplatz
Bundesplatz
Waisenhausplatz
Falkenplatz
Thun Platz
Marzilibahn
Mittelstr
Langgastrasse
Zähringerstr
Hallerstr
Gesellschaftsstr
Sidlerstr
Schützenmatte
Neubrückstr
Bollwerk
Uferweg
Nordring
Dammweg
Altenbergrain
Wyttenbachstr
Kornhausstrasse
Schänzlistr
Viktoriastr
Aargauerstalden
Altenbergstr
Klösterlistutz
Hodlerstr
Speichergasse
Schüttestr
Aarbergergasse
Neuengasse
Zeughausgasse
Brunngasshalde
Rathausgasse
Postgasse
Gerechtigkeitsgasse
Kramgasse
Junkerngasse
Münstergasse
Budenberggasse
Gerberngasse
Marktgasse
Spitalgasse
Bubenbergplatz
Schauplatzgasse
Amthausgasse
Kochergasse
Herrengasse
Hotelgasse
Badgasse
Aarstr
Schifflaube
Grosser Muristalden
Muristr
Schanzenstr
Bogenschützen
Laupenstr
Hirschengraben
Bundesgasse
Effingerstr
Monbijoustr
Munzrain
Weihergasse
Bundesrain
Marzilistr
Rainmattstr
Brückenstr
Sulgeneckstr
Dalmaziquai
Bernastr
Helvetiastr
Mottastr
Lusienstr
Thunstr
Dufourstr
Dählhölzliweg
Jungfraustr
Alpenstr
Marienstr
Seminarstr
Kirchenfeldstr
A B C D E F
1 2 3 4

like ocean waves, it forms three 'hills' on the outskirts of town. The structure's middle hill houses the main exhibition space, showcasing 4000 rotating works from Paul Klee's prodigious and often-playful career. Interactive computer displays built into the seating mean you can get the low-down on all the Swiss-born artist's major pieces.

The other two 'hills' are given over to conferences, concerts, administration and a hands-on children's museum (admission Sfr15).

Houses of Parliament

The 1902 **Houses of Parliament** (Bundeshäuser; ☎ 031 332 85 22; www.parliament.ch; Bundesplatz; admission free; tours 9am, 10am, 11am, 2pm, 3pm & 4pm Mon-Fri, 11am Sat), home of the Swiss Federal Assembly, are impressively ornate, with statues of the nation's founding fathers, a stained-glass dome adorned with cantonal emblems and a huge, 214-bulb chandelier. Tours are offered when the parliament is in recess, otherwise you can watch from the public gallery. Bring a passport.

Kunstmuseum

One of Switzerland's most prized art collections is found in the permanent collection of the **Museum of Fine Art** (☎ 031 328 09 44; www.kunstmuseumbern.ch; Hodlerstrasse 8-12; adult/student Sfr7/5, special exhibitions Sfr8-18; 10am-9pm Tue, 10am-5pm Wed-Sun), including works by Italian artist Fra Angelico, Swiss artist Ferninand Hodler, as well as pieces by Picasso and Dalí. Keep an eye out for interesting special exhibits.

ACTIVITIES

In summer the open-air **Marzili pools** (www.aaremarzili.ch; admission free; May-Sep), beside the **Aare River**, are the perfect place to get a tan; there's even a topless bathing area. If you're a strong swimmer take a dip in the river itself. The pools are a good starting point for a fast float downstream – beware the current can be very swift.

Red-signed bicycle routes run parallel to the river and the city provides free loans of bikes, via the scheme **Bern Rollt** (☎ 079 277 28 57; www.bernrollt.ch; 7.30am-9.30pm May-Oct), which has huts at Bahnhofplatz and the western end of Zeughausgasse. Identification and a refundable Sfr20 are required as a deposit.

SLEEPING

Budget

Camping Eichholz (☎ 031 961 26 02; www.campingeicholz.ch; Strandweg 49; camp sites per site/person/car Sfr9/7.50/3.50, bungalows per person from Sfr18; May-Sep;) The best place to camp near Bern, sites are comfortable (not too rocky) and nestled by the river. It's about a half-hour walk from the centre (or take tram 9 to Wabern). The bungalows are basic, but a great get-back-to-nature choice regardless of your budget.

SYHA hostel (☎ 031 311 63 16; www.youthhostel.ch/bern; Weihergasse 4; dm Sfr35; reception 7-10am & 3-10pm, 5-10pm Dec-Feb) Removed from ambient city noise, this hostel sits pretty by the river. It is large and friendly, although the building is not particularly new.

Hotel Glocke Backpackers Bern (☎ 031 311 37 71; www.bernbackpackers.com; Rathausgasse 75; dm Sfr36, s/d with shared bathroom Sfr70/125; P) Backpackers usually head here first. It has a great lounge that's cosy and very sociable (think comfy couches and a big TV playing nightly movies). The simple dorms and rooms have firm mattresses, fluffy duvets and sinks. Self-caterers will appreciate the kitchen. The bar downstairs is another plus.

Marthahaus Garni (☎ 031 332 41 35; www.marthahaus.ch; Wyttenbachstrasse 22a; dm Sfr39, s/d/tr Sfr110/125/155, s/d with shared bathroom Sfr65/95;) In a residential location, this five-storey building has the feel of a friendly boarding house. Clean, simple rooms have lots of white and a smattering of modern art, plus there's a communal kitchen and TV lounge. Take tram 9 to Viktoriaplatz.

Midrange & Top End

Hotel National (☎ 031 381 19 88; www.nationalbern.ch; Hirschengraben 24; s/d/f Sfr85/130/180, s/d with shared bathroom from Sfr55/100; P) With its wrought-iron lift, springs of lavender and Persian rugs over newly surfaced (but still creaky) wooden floors, the charming National wouldn't feel out of place in Paris. Rooms are impeccable and personable; free Internet access is a plus.

Hotel Arabelle (☎ 031 301 03 05; www.arabelle.ch; Mittelstrasse 6; s/d from Sfr120/135;) Rooms are small, but bright colour schemes and parquet floors lend enough character to make you forget their diminished stature. Take bus 12 to Mittelstrasse.

Hotel Kreuz (☎ 031 329 95 95; www.hotelkreuz-bern.ch in German; Zeughausgasse 26; s/d from Sfr120/170) This very modern hotel has smart rooms with all the creature comforts, a tiny bar with unique metal and stained-glass light fixtures and a restaurant serving Swiss-German fare (mains Sfr15 to Sfr30).

Hotel Belle Epoque (☎ 031 311 43 36; www.belle-epoque.ch; Gerechtigkeitsgasse 18; s/d from Sfr195/280; ⊠ 💻) Standards are very high at this lovely and romantic old-town hotel with opulent Art Deco furnishings. Check out the TV tucked into steamer-trunk–style cupboard.

Hotel Allegro (☎ 031 339 55 00; www.allegro-hotel.ch; Kornhausstrasse 3; s/d from Sfr220/260; ⊠ ❄ 💻) Décor ranges from sleek 'Asiatic' to brassy 'Broadway' and there's even a Paul Klee–themed suite at this unpretentious hotel. It's in a great location, just above old town, with fabulous views from its front rooms.

Bellevue Palace (☎ 031 320 45 45; www.bellevue-palace.ch; Kochergasse 3-5; s/d Sat & Sun from Sfr260/350, Mon-Fri Sfr350/460; P ⊠ ❄ 💻) Bern's only five-star hotel is the first choice address for Bern's power brokers and international statesmen such as Nelson Mandela.

AUTHOR'S CHOICE

Hotel Landhaus (☎ 031 331 41 66; www.landhausbern.ch; Altenbergstrasse 4; dm Sfr30, d/f from Sfr140/180, with shared bathroom from Sfr110; P ⊠ 💻) The dorms are stall-like and rather unappealing, but if you'd like the perks of staying in a classy hotel without the price, they're bearable. If you've got more dough, this historic hotel is fantastic. It has a stripped-back modern interior, with spiral wooden stairs and spacious individually renovated rooms. There's a relaxed, friendly atmosphere and a guest kitchen. The slick downstairs restaurant/bar (live jazz on Thursday evenings) adds lively ambience.

EATING

Wall-to-wall cafés and restaurants line the popular meeting places of Bärenplatz and Theaterplatz, as well as the more upmarket Gerechtigskeitsgasse. The restaurants listed here do not close between meals.

Restaurants

Le Mazot (☎ 031 311 70 88; Bärenplatz 5; mains Sfr11-30) Very cosy with dark wood panels, this place is a well-known specialist in Swiss food. There is a massive *rösti, raclette* and fondue menu. For those with small stomachs, half-portions are available. Sit outside in the glassed-in patio on warm days.

Il Grissino (☎ 031 311 00 59; Waisenhausplatz 28; mains Sfr12-25) With 'bump knees with your neighbour'–style seating (claustrophobics beware), this oft-packed pizza and pasta joint emits a boisterous vibe. Choose from more than 30 different pizzas; the large is big enough for two (unless you're super hungry).

Altes Tramdepot (☎ 031 368 14 15; Am Bärengraben; mains Sfr15-25) Locals don't let the touristy bear pit location keep them away and neither should you. This cavernous brewery is a Bern favourite, serving Swiss specialities along with a variety of international dishes. The atmosphere is as inviting as the cuisine.

Cesary (☎ 031 318 93 83; Kornhausplatz 11; mains Sfr15-30) New and trendy, this super-swank Italian restaurant and lounge attracts a well-dressed crowd. After work it's all about the suits and ties, but when dark descends so do the little black dresses and Gucci purses. Stop by for an aperitif and people watching from the comfort of a suave white leather stool.

Du Nord (☎ 031 332 23 38; Lorrainestrasse 2; mains Sfr17-35) A trendy and alternative crowd flocks to this laid-back, gay-friendly restaurant in the Lorraine quarter for well-prepared, modern international cuisine, drinks at the bar and occasional gigs.

Lorenzini (☎ 031 310 50 67; Hotelgasse 10; mains Sfr20-55) A bit of a Bern institution, the Lorenzini complex of wine bars and an Italian restaurant is popular with young professionals looking for coffee and salad or a full meal of homemade pasta. The patio is perfect for people watching.

Della Casa (☎ 031 311 21 42; Schauplatzgasse 16; mains Sfr28-40; 🕒 8am-11.30pm Mon-Fri, to 3pm Sat) One of the best, albeit meat-obsessed, places in town, it is an old, cosy eatery with floral curtains, leadlight lamps and traditional Swiss specialities.

Kornhauskeller (☎ 031 327 72 72; Kornhausplatz 18; mains from Sfr32) Dine under tall vaulted arches covered in frescos in the stunning subterranean restaurant or sip cocktails with Bern's beautiful people in the bar on the mezzanine level – make sure to check out the historic stained-glass windows.

Quick Eats & Self-Catering

Markthalle (Bubenbergplatz 9; mains Sfr5-8) Slurp down pizza, kebabs and spaghetti standing at a Formica table or perched on bar stools in this buzzing central arcade filled with all sorts of cheap eateries.

Sous le Pont (☎ 031 306 69 55; Schützenmatte; snacks & light meals Sfr5-15; 🕑 11.30am-2pm & 6pm-midnight Tue-Fri; 6pm-2am Sat) Organic meat and lots of vegetarian options are offered in the semichaotic surrounds of Reitschule. Every Wednesday, there's a speciality evening showcasing a different cuisine.

Self-caterers can buy up big at **Coop** (Neuengasse; 🕑 8am-8pm Mon-Sat) and **Migros** (Marktgasse 46; 🕑 8am-8pm Mon-Sat), which also have cheap self-service restaurants (Sfr3 to Sfr7).

DRINKING

See the *Bern Guide* available from the tourist office, for details on Bern nightlife.

Du Theatre (☎ 031 311 17 71; Hotelgasse 10) Part of the upmarket Lorenzini complex, this chic lounge bar has a cool 30-something crowd parked on its plump 1970s leather sofas.

Quasimodo (☎ 031 311 13 81; Rathausgasse 75) Backpackers staying at the Hotel Glocke will like the convenience of this techno bar-club downstairs. Arrive after 10pm and you'll find the small dance floor packed with swaying, sweaty revellers from all parts of the globe, including Switzerland.

Wasserwerk (☎ 031 312 12 31; www.wasserwerkclub.ch; Wasserwerkgasse 5) The main techno venue in town, this has a bar, club and sometimes live music. It boasts that both Moby and the Prodigy played here in their heyday.

ENTERTAINMENT

Gaskessel (☎ 031 372 49 00; www.gaskessel.ch; Sandrainstrasse 25) Inside this graffiti-covered domed building in Marzili is a countercultural centre, with lots of trance, rap and some popular gay evenings.

Dampfzentrale (☎ 031 311 63 37; www.dampfzentrale.ch; Marzilistrasse 47) This refined performing arts centre combines jazz, funk and soul music gigs with avant-garde art exhibitions and dance. It's in a pleasant riverside spot and serves a brilliant Sunday brunch.

Reitschule (☎ 031 306 69 52; www.reitschule.ch; Schützenmatte) While determinedly cleaning up its act and trying to keep the drugs out, this infamous – and ramshackle – centre for alternative arts, music and theatre still retains a bit of its old charisma, attracting local slackers, students and curious tourists.

Sports

Bern's new 32,000-seat **Stade de Suisse** (www.stadedesuisse.ch) was built over the demolished former Wankdorf Stadium. It will be one of the four Swiss venues when Austria and Switzerland co-host football's Euro 2008 championship.

SHOPPING

From luxury boutiques to family-run tobacco stores selling Cuban cigars and creative flasks, Bern has its shopping bases covered. There are loads of stores in old town – check out the area around Kornhausplatz as well as Marktgasse and Spietgasse. Some of the most unique boutiques (for men and women) are hidden in underground cellars, so be sure to wander down at least a few flights of stairs.

Fizzen (☎ 031 311 1116; Bollwerk 17) For decent second-hand garb (along with loads of crazy coloured condoms) visit this locally recommended place.

There is an open-air market on Bärenplatz each Tuesday and Saturday (daily in summer). On the first Saturday of the month there is a craft market in front of the cathedral.

If truly local souvenirs interest you, grab a Toblerone chocolate – it's made in Bern.

GETTING THERE & AWAY

There are daily flights to Lugano, London, Paris, Amsterdam and other European destinations from Bern-Belp airport. Postbuses depart from the western side of the train station.

Three motorways intersect in the northern part of the city. The N1 runs from Neuchâtel in the west and Basel and Zürich in the northeast. The N6 connects Bern with Thun and the Interlaken region in the southeast. The N12 is the route from Geneva and Lausanne in the southwest.

Trains connect to most Swiss towns, including Basel (Sfr36, 70 minutes, hourly),

Geneva (Sfr49, 1¾ hours, hourly), Interlaken (Sfr25, 50 minutes, hourly) and Zürich (Sfr47, 70 minutes, hourly).

GETTING AROUND

Bern-Belp airport (BRN; ☎ 031 960 21 11; www.alpar.ch) is 9km southeast of the city centre. A frequent bus links the airport to the train station (Sfr15, 20 minutes).

Bus and tram tickets cost Sfr1.90 (maximum six stops) or Sfr2.80. A city day pass and regional network is Sfr12. If you're planning on clubbing, **Moonliner** (www.moonliner.ch) night buses depart Friday and Saturday nights from Bahnhofplatz at 12.45am, 2am and 3.15am; passes aren't valid and fares start at Sfr5. Tickets can be purchased at all bus tops.

Many taxis wait by the train station. They charge Sfr6.50 plus Sfr3.10 per kilometre (Sfr4 after 8pm and on Sunday).

From May to October there are free loans of city bikes outside the train station. Bring ID and a Sfr20 deposit.

FRIBOURG, NEUCHÂTEL & THE JURA

From the evocative medieval cantonal capitals of Fribourg and Neuchâtel to the mysterious green hills and deep dark forests of the Jura, the country's northwest corner proffers a wealth of sights and escapes well off the beaten track, yet is still an easy day trip from Bern. Be it marvelling at majestic ice creations or following the call of the devilish green fairy into the wayward Val de Travers, travelling here promises a brilliant sensory experience.

NEUCHÂTEL

pop 31,004

Spend an afternoon cruising Neuchâtel's open-air cafés, walking along its glittering lake and feasting your eyes on the charming sandstone elegance of its old town and your stress will melt away. The canton's compact capital is really just a laid-back French-style resort surrounded by vineyards. If you're looking to do a little shopping, the central pedestrian zone is packed with all sorts of souvenir shops and funky, reasonably priced boutiques. The pedestrian zone and Place Pury (the local bus hub) are about 1km from the train station; walk down the hill along Ave de la Gare.

The **tourist office** (☎ 032 889 68 90; www.ne.ch/tourism; Place du Port; 🕑 9am-noon & 1.30-5.30pm Mon-Fri, to noon Sat Sep-Jun, to 7pm Mon-Sat, 4-7pm Sun Jul & Aug) is in the main post office by the lake.

Sights & Activities

The 12th-century **Chateau de Neuchâtel** (☎ 032 889 60 00; 45min tours free; 🕑 10am-4pm Apr-Sep) and the adjoining **Collegiate Churches** are the centrepieces of old town. The striking cenotaph of 15 statues dates from 1372. Nearby, the **prison tower** (☎ 032 717 76 02; Rue J de Hochberg 5; admission Sfr1; 🕑 8am-6pm Apr-Aug) offers broad views of the town and lake.

Visit the **Musée d'Art et d'Histoire** (Museum of Art & History; ☎ 032 717 79 20; Esplanade Léopold-Robert 1; adult/student Sfr9/6, free Wed; 🕑 10am-6pm Tue-Sun), on the waterfront, to see 18th-century beloved clockwork figures.

Sleeping

Oasis Neuchâtel (☎ 032 731 31 90; auberge.oasis@bluewin.ch; Rue du Suchiez 35; dm/d Sfr24/60; 🕑 Apr-Oct) Glorious views and friendly accommodation are this independent hostel's trademarks. It's about 2km from the centre; take bus 1 (Cormondréche) to Vauseyon and follow the signs towards Centre Sportive.

Hôtel de l'Ecluse (☎ 032 729 93 10; www.hoteldelecluse.ch; Rue de l'Ecluse 24; s/d from Sfr100/150; P 💻) Elegant rooms in this fine house sport brass beds and kitchenettes. Breakfast is served in the bar and there are a couple of terraces for guests to lounge on.

Hôtel Alpes et Lac (☎ 032 723 19 19; www.alpesetlac.ch; Place de la Gare 2; s/d from Sfr125/180; P ❄ 💻) A stately 19th-century hotel across from the train station. Digs are comfortable enough to chill in and offer mod cons such as wi-fi (Sfr5/11 per 30 minutes/24 hours). There are two restaurants (one Swiss, one Chinese).

Eating

Local specialities include fresh trout, tripe and *tome neuchâteloise chaude*, a baked cheese starter.

La Creperie (☎ 032 725 17 71; Rue de Hôpital 7; crepes from Sfr6.50) Tables are practically piled on top of each other at this cluttered little spot in the heart of town. It's nearly always

THE GREEN FAIRY

It was in the deepest darkest depths of Couvet in the Val de Travers – otherwise dubbed the Pays des Fées (Fairyland) – that absinthe was first distilled in 1740 and produced commercially in 1797. (However, it was a Frenchman called Pernod who made the bitter green liqueur known with the distillery he opened just a few kilometres across the French–Swiss border in Pontarlier.)

From 1910, following Switzerland's prohibition of the wickedly alcoholic and ruthlessly bitter aniseed drink, distillers of the so-called 'devil in the bottle' in the Val de Travers moved underground. In 1990 the great grandson of a preprohibition distiller in Môtiers came up with Switzerland's first legal aniseed liqueur since 1910 – albeit one which was only 45% proof alcohol (instead of 50% to 75%) and which scarcely contained *thujone* (the offensive chemical found in wormwood, said to be root of absinthe's devilish nature). But in March 2005, Switzerland lifted its absinthe ban and the **Blackmint – Distillerie Kübler & Wyss** (☎ 032 861 14 69; www.blackmint.ch; Rue du Château 7, Môtiers) distilled its first true and authentic batch of the mythical *fée verte* (green fairy) from valley-grown wormwood. Mix one part crystal-clear liqueur with five parts water to make it green. When we got a group of friends together back home to sample the stuff, reports of trails and light and floaty feelings started coming in after the first glass.

full. There are dozens upon dozens of sweet and savoury crepes, including one with absinthe. The coffee is strong and as French as the ambience.

Le Brasserie Jura (☎ 032 725 14 10; Rue de la Treille 7; lunch menu Sfr16.50, mains Sfr15-35) With a name like Jura Brasserie, this hot spot couldn't be more local. Food is cooked to fill. *Tripes à la Neuchâteloise* (tripe) is the menu star and vegetarians are well catered for with vegetable *rösti*, veg-stuffed ravioli or six-cereal ravioli doused in goat-cheese sauce.

Appareils de Chauffage (☎ 032 721 43 96; Rue des Moulins 37; mains from Sfr15) Grab a board game from the bar and settle in for a few hours at this funky café serving quality coffee and a range of spirits and beer. There are Swiss and international dishes on the menu.

Cafe des Halles (☎ 032 724 31 41; Rue du Trésor 4; pizzas Sfr 20, mains Sfr35) In an impressive historic house dating back to 1569, this place is the gourmet's central choice. The cooking is mainly French, but also includes scrumptious pizzas and pastas. Dine outside on the large shaded terrace overlooking the main square. The set three-course dinners for Sfr45 are good value.

Coop (Rue de la Treille 4) Self-caterers can stock up on local wine, cheeses and absinthe at this branch of the Coop chain.

Entertainment

La Case à Chocs (☎ 032 721 20 56; www.case-a-chocs.ch; Quai Philippe Godet 16; concerts Sfr10-15; Thu-Sun) An alternative venue in a converted brewery with live music, occasional cinema and art shows. Check the website for details.

Getting There & Around

There are fast trains to Geneva (Sfr42, 70 minutes, hourly) and Bern (Sfr19, 35 minutes, hourly). Postbuses heading to the Jura leave from the station.

Local buses cost Sfr1.80 to Sfr2.80 per trip.

VAL DE TRAVERS

Hikers come to Val de Travers to marvel at the enormous **Creux du Van** abyss. This spectacular crescent-moon wall, a product of glacial erosion, interrupts the habitually green rolling countryside in startling fashion – it is just 1km long, but plunges 440m to the bottom (the first 200m is a sheer stony drop). The Creux is most easily reached on foot from Noiraigue, which can be reached by hourly train from Neuchâtel (Sfr6.60, 20 minutes). The round-trip hike can take up to five hours depending on the route.

If you're in search of the truth about absinthe, visit the distillery in **Môtiers** (see the boxed text, above). Trains run from Neuchâtel (Sfr10.40, 35 minutes).

FRIBOURG

pop 32,553

Medieval Fribourg (dating back to the 12th century) boasts the usual cathedrals and art museums, but for something different focus on the beer.

With two great breweries in town you can't go wrong. Head to **Brasserie du Cardinal** (☎ 058 123 16; www.cardinal.ch; Passage du Cardinal; tours Sfr10; 🕑 8.30-10am & 1.30-3pm Mon-Thu) to sample one of Switzerland's best-known lagers, brewed here since 1788. Tours demonstrate how water, malt and hops are turned into nine different types of Cardinal beer.

Small-time microbrewery **Brasserie Artisanale de Fribourg** (☎ 026 322 80 88; Rue de la Samaritaine 19; 🕑 8am-5pm Sat) is run by a couple of mates who began the enterprise as an amusing pastime (and now run it as a Saturday hobby!). The one-room brewery produces just 50 hectolitres a year. Pay Sfr4 for a bottle of its golden German-style Barbeblanche or Barberousse with subtle caramel and honey aromas.

Imaginative and luxurious **Auberge aux 4 Vents** (☎ 026 347 36 00; www.aux4vents.ch; Res Balzli Grandfrey 124; s/d Sfr120/170, s/d/tr/q with shared bathroom from Sfr50/100/140/160; P), just outside the city limits, is our sleeping pick. The eight rooms are individually designed. We especially liked room 'bleue', featuring dreamy blue flowery period furnishings and a tub on rails that rolls out through the window for a bath beneath stars. The highly recommended conservatory-style restaurant overlooks a stunning medieval Fribourg panorama. To get to the '4 Winds', 2km north in Grandfrey, drive north along Rue de Morat and turn right immediately before the train bridge.

Fribourg is easily accessible by train from Bern (Sfr14, 30 minutes, hourly).

GRUYÈRES

Known above all for the cheese by the same name, beautiful **Gruyères** attracts busloads of tourists who gawk at the fine 15th- to 17th-century homes and the 13th-century fairytale castle on the hill. We'd suggest you follow their example.

The secret behind gruyère cheese is revealed at the **Maison du Gruyère** (☎ 026 921 84 00; www.lamaisondugruyere.ch; adult/student/child Sfr5/4/2; 🕑 9am-7pm Apr-Sep, to 6pm Oct-Mar) in Pringy, 1.5km from Gruyères. Cheesemaking takes place four times daily between 9am and 3pm and can be watched through glass windows.

Cheese is produced in a couple of traditional mountain chalets along the **Sentier des Fromageries**, a trail leading through green Gruyère pastures. Ask at the Maison du Gruyère for the brochure outlining the two-hour walk (about 8km).

The **Musée HR Giger** (☎ 026 921 22 00; adult/child Sfr10/5; 🕑 10am-6pm Apr-Oct, 10am-5pm Tue-Sun Nov-Mar), housed in a 16th-century mansion, is a shrine to HR Giger's expansive imagination – fans of the *Alien* movies will especially relish the place – along with all things occult and bizarre. Be sure to check out the very Giger-style bar across the road afterwards.

A restored 19th-century manor, **Le Pâquier** (☎ 026 912 20 25; www.lepatchi.ch; Rue de la Gare 10, Le Pâquier; s/d/tr Sfr60/90/120; P), 3.5km northwest of Gruyères, is a good sleeping bet.

The cosy, cowbell-strewn **Chalet de Gruyères** (☎ 026 921 21 54; www.chalet-gruyeres.ch; Rue du Château 53; fondues & raclettes Sfr28) serves a great *croûte en fromage* (hot, open-faced cheese sandwich); meringues come with the thickest gruyère double cream ever.

There are trains from Fribourg (Sfr16.80, 40 minutes, hourly). The town is a 10-minute walk uphill from its station.

JURA CANTON

Its grandest towns are little more than enchanting villages and this northwestern corner of the country remains undiscovered. Deep, mysterious forests and impossible green clearings succeed one another across the low mountains of the Jura and some 1200km of marked paths across the canton give hikers plenty of scope.

The capital is Delémont, but there is little reason to linger. Instead, head west to the delightful medieval village of **St Ursanne** instead. Along with a 12th-century Gothic church, there are clusters of ancient houses, a 16th-century town gate and lovely stone bridge. The town is on the Doubs River's banks and kayaking is popular in summer. **Le Clip** (☎ 032 461 37 22; Place du Mai 1, St Ursanne; trips Sfr45) runs exciting half-day trips.

Hôtel Demi-Lune (☎ 032 461 35 31; www.hotels-suisse.ch/demi-lune in French; Rue Basse 2, St Ursanne; s/d from Sfr75/125) has classy rooms overlooking the river.

Trout is the local speciality and you can get a good version at **La Cicogne** (☎ 032 461 35 45; St Ursanne; mains from Sfr20), an unpretentious spot opposite the church.

From Delémont there are trains to St Ursanne (Sfr6.60, 17 minutes, hourly).

GENEVA

pop 179,426

If one city on the planet could truly say it fits the whole world on its hand, surely it would be Geneva (Genève in French, Genf in German). Strung along the sparkling shores of Europe's largest Alpine lake, this is about as international as it gets. Its people chatter in every language under the sun (in fact almost 40% of them are not Swiss) and this cosmopolitan city of bankers, diplomats and transients likes to boast that 'it belongs not so much to Switzerland as to the world'. This rings pretty true: the UN, WHO, International Red Cross, International Labour Organisation…you name them, they're in Geneva. In fact, the place is home to some 200-odd top-dog governmental and nongovernmental international organisations.

ORIENTATION

The Rhône River runs through Geneva, dividing it into *rive droite* (right bank) and *rive gauche* (left bank). On the northern side is the main train station, Gare de Cornavin; south of the river lies the old town. In summer, Geneva's most visible landmark is the Jet d'Eau, a giant fountain on the southern shore.

INFORMATION

Emergency

Police Station (☎ 117; Rue de Berne 6)

Internet Access

For a list of free-access public wi-fi terminals in Geneva, see www.espritdegeneve.ch.

Internet Café de la Gare (☎ 022 731 51 87; per 10/30mins Sfr2/4, per hr Sfr6; 8.30am-10pm Mon-Thu, 9.30am-11pm Fri & Sat, 9.30am-10pm Sun) In the train station, on the Place de Montbrillant side.

Internet Resources

City of Geneva (www.ville-ge.ch)

International Geneva Welcome Centre (www.cagi.ch)

Medical Services

Cantonal hospital (☎ 022 372 33 11; Rue Micheli-du-Crest 24)

Permanence Médico Chirurgicale (☎ 022 731 21 20; Rue de Chantepoulet 1-3) A private 24-hour clinic.

Servette Clinique (☎ 022 733 98 00; Ave Wendt 60) Emergency dental treatment.

Telephone advice service (☎ 111) For medical information.

Post

Main post office (Rue du Mont-Blanc 18; 7.30am-6pm Mon-Fri, 8.30am-noon Sat)

Tourist Information

Genève tourist office (☎ 022 909 70 00; www.geneve-tourisme.ch; Rue du Mont-Blanc 18; 10am-6pm Mon, 9am-6pm Tue-Sat)

Travel Agencies

American Express (Amex; ☎ 022 731 76 00; Rue du Mont-Blanc 7; 8.30am-5.45pm Mon-Fri, 9am-noon Sat)

STA Travel (☎ 022 329 97 33; Rue Vignier Leschol 3; 9.15am-6pm Mon-Fri, 9am-noon Sat)

SIGHTS & ACTIVITIES

City Centre

The city centre is so compact it's easy to see many of the main sights on foot. Start a scenic walk through the old town at the **Île Rousseau**, home to a statue in honour of the celebrated freethinker. Head west along the southern side of the Rhône until you reach the 13th-century **Tour de L'Île**, once part of the medieval city fortifications. Then walk south down the narrow, cobbled Rue de la Cité until it becomes Grand-Rue. **Rousseau's birthplace** is at No 40.

A short detour off Grand-Rue leads you to the part-Romanesque, part-Gothic **Cathédrale St Pierre**, where John Calvin preached from 1536 to 1564. The cathedral rests on a significant **archaeological site** (☎ 022 311 75 74; Cour de St Pierre 6; adult/student Sfr5/3; 10-11.30am & 2-4.30pm Mon-Fri, 10am-5pm Sat, noon-5pm Sun). A visit reveals some fine 4th-century mosaics and a 5th-century baptismal font.

You'll find the **Jet d'Eau** on the lake's southern shore. Calling this a fountain is an understatement. The water shoots up with incredible force (200km/h, 1360HP), to create a 140m-high plume. At any one time there are seven tonnes of water in the air, and much of it falls on spectators who venture out on the pier.

United Nations

The Art Deco **Palais des Nations** (☎ 022 907 48 96; Ave de la Paix 9-14; tours adult/student Sfr8.50/6.50;

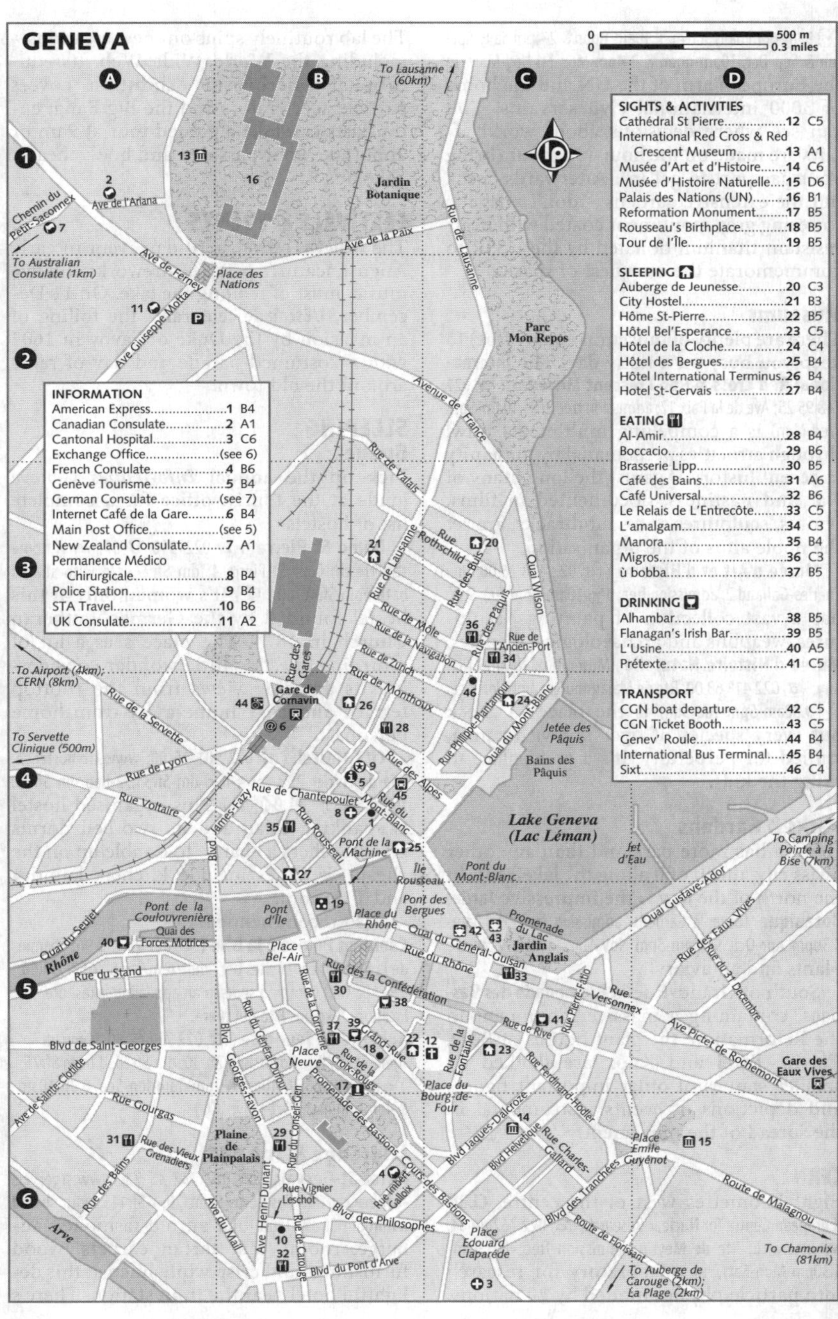

GENEVA
0 500 m
0 0.3 miles
SIGHTS & ACTIVITIES
Cathédral St Pierre....12 C5
International Red Cross & Red Crescent Museum....13 A1
Musée d'Art et d'Histoire....14 C6
Musée d'Histoire Naturelle....15 D6
Palais des Nations (UN)....16 B1
Reformation Monument....17 B5
Rousseau's Birthplace....18 B5
Tour de l'Île....19 B5
SLEEPING
Auberge de Jeunesse....20 C3
City Hostel....21 B3
Hôme St-Pierre....22 B5
Hôtel Bel'Esperance....23 C5
Hôtel de la Cloche....24 C4
Hôtel des Bergues....25 B4
Hôtel International Terminus....26 B4
Hotel St-Gervais....27 B4
EATING
Al-Amir....28 B4
Boccacio....29 B6
Brasserie Lipp....30 B5
Café des Bains....31 A6
Café Universal....32 B6
Le Relais de L'Entrecôte....33 C5
L'amalgam....34 C3
Manora....35 B4
Migros....36 C3
ù bobba....37 B5
DRINKING
Alhambar....38 B5
Flanagan's Irish Bar....39 B5
L'Usine....40 A5
Prétexte....41 C5
TRANSPORT
CGN boat departure....42 C5
CGN Ticket Booth....43 C5
Genev' Roule....44 B4
International Bus Terminal....45 B4
Sixt....46 C4
INFORMATION
American Express....1 B4
Canadian Consulate....2 A1
Cantonal Hospital....3 C6
Exchange Office....(see 6)
French Consulate....4 B6
Genève Tourisme....5 B4
German Consulate....(see 7)
Internet Café de la Gare....6 B4
Main Post Office....(see 5)
New Zealand Consulate....7 A1
Permanence Médico Chirurgicale....8 B4
Police Station....9 B4
STA Travel....10 B6
UK Consulate....11 A2
To Lausanne (60km)
Jardin Botanique
Parc Mon Repos
Chemin du Petit-Saconnex
Ave de l'Ariana
To Australian Consulate (1km)
Ave de la Paix
Rue de Lausanne
Ave de Ferney
Place des Nations
Ave Giuseppe Motta
Avenue de France
Rue de Valais
Rue Rothschild
Rue des Buis
Quai Wilson
Rue de Môle
Rue de la Navigation
Rue des Pâquis
Rue de l'Ancien-Port
Rue de Zurich
Rue des Gares
Gare de Cornavin
Rue de Monthoux
To Airport (4km); CERN (8km)
Rue de la Servette
Rue Philippe-Plantamour
Quai du Mont-Blanc
Jetée des Pâquis
Bains des Pâquis
To Servette Clinique (500m)
Rue de Lyon
Rue des Alpes
Rue Voltaire
Rue de Chantepoulet
Rue du Mont-Blanc
Blvd James-Fazy
Rue Rousseau
Lake Geneva (Lac Léman)
Pont de la Machine
Île Rousseau
Pont du Mont-Blanc
Jet d'Eau
To Camping Pointe à la Bise (7km)
Pont des Bergues
Pont de la Coulouvrenière
Quai des Forces Motrices
Pont d'Île
Place du Rhône
Promenade du Lac
Quai Gustave-Ador
Quai du Seujet
Rhône
Place Bel-Air
Quai du Général-Guisan
Jardin Anglais
Rue des Eaux Vives
Rue du Stand
Rue du Rhône
Rue du 31 Décembre
Rue des la Confédération
Rue Versonnex
Rue Pierre-Fatio
Rue de Rive
Ave Pictet de Rochemont
Rue du Général-Dufour
Rue de la Corraterie
Grand-Rue
Rue de la Fontaine
Blvd de Saint-Georges
Blvd Georges-Favon
Place Neuve
Rue de la Croix-Rouge
Gare des Eaux Vives
Place du Bourg-de-Four
Rue Ferdinand-Hodler
Ave de Sainte-Clotilde
Promenade des Bastions
Rue Gourgas
Blvd Jaques-Dalcroze
Plaine de Plainpalais
Rue du Conseil-Gen
Blvd Helvétique
Rue Charles-Gallard
Place Emile Guyénot
Rue des Vieux Grenadiers
Cours des Bastions
Route de Malagnou
Rue des Bains
Rue Vignier
Leschot
Rue Imbert Galloix
Blvd des Tranchées
Arve
Ave du Mail
Ave Henri-Dunant
Blvd des Philosophes
Place Edouard Claparède
Route de Florissant
To Chamonix (81km)
Rue de Carouge
Blvd du Pont d'Arve
To Auberge de Carouge (2km); La Plage (2km)

9am-6pm daily Jul-Aug, 10am-noon & 2-4pm daily Apr-Jun & Sep-Oct, 10am-noon & 2-4pm Mon-Fri Nov-Mar) is the European arm of the UN and the home of 3000 international civil servants. You can see where decisions about world affairs are made on the hour-long tour (bring your passport to get in). Afterwards check out the extensive gardens – don't miss the towering grey monument coated with heat-resistant titanium donated by the USSR to commemorate the conquest of space.

Museums

There are plenty of museums (many free) to keep you busy on a rainy day. The **International Red Cross & Red Crescent Museum** (☎ 022 748 95 25; Ave de la Paix 17; admission free; 10am-5pm Wed-Mon) is a compelling multimedia trawl through atrocities perpetuated by humanity in recent history. Against the long litany of war and nastiness, documented in films, photos, sculptures and soundtracks, are set the noble aims of the organisation.

Musée d'Art et d'Histoire (☎ 022 418 26 00; Rue Charles-Galland 2; admission free; 10am-5pm Tue-Sun) has a vast collection of paintings, sculptures, weapons and archaeological displays. **Musée d'Histoire Naturelle** (Museum of Natural History; ☎ 022 418 63 00; Rte de Malagnou 1; admission free; 9.30am-5pm Tue-Sun) is the place to check out every species of tiger known to man, stuffed for perpetuity. It's a good place to bring the kids.

Parks & Gardens

Geneva has more parkland than any other Swiss city, much of it along the lakefront. In the north of the city is the impressive **Jardin Botanique** (Botanic Gardens; admission free; 8am-7.30pm Apr-Oct, 9.30am-5pm Nov-Mar) with exotic plants and an aviary.

South of Grand-Rue is **Promenade des Bastions**, containing a massive monument to the Reformation: the giant figures of Bèze, Calvin, Farel and Knox are flanked by smaller statues of other important figures and depictions of events instrumental in the spread of the movement.

CERN

Eight kilometres west of the centre, **CERN** (European Centre for Nuclear Research; ☎ 022 767 84 84; www.cern.ch; Rte de Meyrin; admission free; 9am-5.30pm Mon-Sat), is a laboratory for research into particle physics funded by 20 nations. The lab routinely spins out new creations – including the World Wide Web. Its educational Microcosm exhibition covers particle accelerators and the Big Bang; enthusiasts can take a guided tour at 9am or 2pm (take your passport and book ahead). Take bus 9.

FESTIVALS & EVENTS

The **Geneva Festival**, a 10-day event in early August, features parades, fireworks and live music, most of it along the lake. On 11 December, **L'Escalade** celebrates the foiling of an invasion by the Duke of Savoy in 1602 with a costumed parade and day of races around the old town.

SLEEPING

Budget

Pick up the annual *Info-Jeunes Genève* guide at the tourist office for a complete list of hostels.

Hôme St-Pierre (☎ 022 310 37 07; www.homestpierre.ch; Cour St-Pierre 4; dm Sfr27, s/d with shared bathroom Sfr40/60;) It's women only at this hostel founded by the German Lutheran Church in 1874. The place sees a lot of returning guests – little wonder considering its amazing views from the rooftop terrace and cosy home-away-from-home persona.

City Hostel (☎ 022 901 15 00; www.cityhostel.ch; Rue de Ferrier 2; 3- or 4-bed dm Sfr31, 2-bed dm Sfr35, s/d Sfr58/85; P) This organised hostel is spanking clean and its two-bed dorms give travellers a chance to double up on the cheap. Facilities include kitchen, laundry and TV room.

Also recommended:

Camping Pointe á la Bise (☎ 022 752 12 96; Chemin de la Bise 19; camp sites per adult/tent/car Sfr7.50/7/6.50; Apr-Oct) Camping spots in an appealing lakeshore location. Take bus E to get there.

Auberge de Jeunesse (☎ 022 732 62 60; www.yh-geneva.ch; Rue Rothschild 28-30; dm Sfr26, d from Sfr75; reception 6.30-10am & 2pm-1am Jun-Sep, 6.30-10am & 4pm-midnight Oct-May;)

Midrange & Top End

Hotel St-Gervais (☎ 022 732 45 72; www.stgervais-geneva.ch; Rue des Corps-Saint 20; r Sfr115, with shared bathroom Sfr85) Just like an old-fashioned auberge, rooms tout tartan carpets, wood furnishings and crisp white linen at this delightful hotel near the train station. There's

> **AUTHOR'S CHOICE**
>
> **Hôtel de la Cloche** (☎ 022 732 94 81; hotelcloche@freesurf.ch; Rue de la Cloche 6; s/d from Sfr50/85; ⊠) Hôtel de la Cloche – an old-fashioned hotel in a bourgeois home – is a dying breed. And more is the pity. Monsieur Chabbey runs this small, one-star hotel with grace and panache, opening the door as a butler welcoming one home. Likewise, it is Monsieur Chabbey who delivers breakfast to each room from 8am every morning (each of the eight rooms have a table and chairs), sorts out the bill and so on. Elegant fireplaces, period furnishings, wooden floors and the odd chandelier add a touch of grandeur. Some rooms with wrought-iron balconies face the Jet d'Eau.

wi-fi available and it's stumbling distance from the train station.

Hôtel International Terminus (☎ 022 906 97 77; www.international-terminus.ch; Rue des Alpes 20; s/d/tr from Sfr120/160/180; P ⊠ 💻) This three-star hotel has absurdly low rates for Geneva, making it one of the best-value places near the train station (in winter a double room can go for even less). Rooms are well appointed, some come with swanky red carpets, and all come with cable TV.

Hôtel Bel'Esperance (☎ 022 818 37 37; www.hotel-bel-esperance.ch; Rue de la Vallée 1; s/d from Sfr120/160; ⊠) This hotel is small, simple and slightly worn, but rooms are quiet and clean, there's a shared kitchen and the place is just a few minutes' walk from the old town. The flower-filled rooftop terrace, with table and chairs for lounging, is a delight when it's warm and sunny.

Auberge de Carouge (☎ 022 342 22 88; Rue Ancienne 39; s/d/tr/q Sfr130/180/210/250; P) With its tree-shaded garden and the artsy scene of Théâtre de Carouge around the corner, this hotel oozes old-world appeal. Its room count is just a couple over a dozen, so get in quick.

Hôtel des Bergues (☎ 022 908 70 00; www.hoteldesbergues.com; Quai des Bergues 33; s/d from Sfr600/730; P ⊠) Even the most basic rooms at this national monument drip marble and are decorated with copies of works by Claude Monet. The Suite Royal (a serious steal at just Sfr6600 per night!) is a sight to behold – a 134-sq-metre apartment with Jacuzzi, DVD, private terraces, dressing room, dining room and, just in case, bullet-proof windows.

EATING

Geneva is the cuisine capital of Switzerland, with a wide range of choices.

Restaurants

In the old town, terrace cafés and restaurants crowd along the medieval Place du Bourg-de-Four.

Boccaccio (☎ 022 329 45 22; blvd Georges-Favon 45; mains Sfr14-25) This popular Geneva restaurant is done up like an Italian village with murals on the walls. A business crowd packs the place at lunch. The menu focuses on pizza, pasta and salads. Sit outside during summer.

L'amalgam (Rue de L'Ancien-Port 13; mains Sfr15-20) Locals flock to this locals'-favourite café for its rotating menu of simple food; decorations include African art, palms and ochre tones. The mood is decidedly mellow. It's a tiny joint with no phone.

Café Universal (☎ 022 781 18 81; blvd du Pont d'Arve 26; mains Sfr15-30) With heavy chandeliers, monster mirrors and 1920s posters, this place is chic and French. It draws an arty crowd into its tightly packed interior.

ù bobba (☎ 022 310 53 40; Rue de la Corraterie 21; mains Sfr15-42) A cultured crowd gathers at this dining spot, decked in red and gold and oozing attitude. Particularly hot is its u jardinù bobba, one of Geneva's best roof terraces. Inventive mains range from veal medallions with pistachio nuts (Sfr42) to Gorgonzola-dunked gnocchi (Sfr25).

Café des Bains (☎ 022 321 57 98; www.cafedesbains.com; Rue des Bains 26; mains Sfr20-40) Beautiful objects and an eye for design are trademarks of this fusion restaurant where Genevan beauties flock. The king prawns pan-fried with green pepper, sweet Thai basil and mango and served with a mint and apricot mousse certainly won our hearts. Veggie options are plentiful and excellent.

Le Relais de L'Entrecôte (☎ 022 310 60 04; Rue du Rhône 49; starters/mains Sfr10/25) If entrecôte and fries (some say the best steak and chips in Geneva) are your cup of tea then this busy bistro wedged between designer shops is for you. Try to snag the table with lake view.

Brasserie Lipp (☎ 022 311 10 11; Rue des la Confédération 8; plat du jour Sfr20-28, mains Sfr35) Eternal favourite with the Genevois; come for a drink and snack or full meal – everything from oysters to a perch fillet. There's an outdoor terrace in summer. It's on the 2nd floor of the shopping arcade.

Quick Eats & Self-Catering

Rue de Fribourg, Rue de Neuchâtel, Rue de Berne and the northern end of Rue des Alpes are loaded with kebab, falafel and quick-eat joints. Eat in or take away at the following places:

Migros (Rue des Pâquis; 8am-7pm Mon-Fri, 8am-6pm Sat) Head to this supermarket to stock up on supplies. You'll also find baguettes (Sfr2) and sandwiches (Sfr4) in its self-service restaurant.

Manora (Rue de Cornavin 4; mains Sfr5-15) Rather tasty buffet food, including extensive salad and dessert bars, are served at this quick-eat Swiss chain.

Al-Amir (Rue de Berne 22; kebabs Sfr8) This hole-in-the wall Lebanese takeaway serves the best kebab in town.

DRINKING & ENTERTAINMENT

The latest nightclubs, live-music venues and theatre events are well covered in the weekly *Genéve Agenda* (free from the tourist office). Try strolling around the Quartier des Pâquis (between the train station and the lake); it's packed with pubs and bars.

La Plage (☎ 022 342 20 98; Rue Vautier 19) The Beach in Carouge is a timeless watering hole with bare wood tables, checked lino floor, green wood shutters and tables outside.

Alhambar (☎ 022 312 13 13; www.alhambar.com; Rue de la Rôtisserie 10; noon-2pm Mon, noon-2pm & 5pm-1am or 2am Tue-Fri, 5pm-2am Sat, 11am-midnight Sun) With a buzzing atmosphere, an eclectic music programme and the best Sunday brunch in town, Alhambar provides an oasis of theatricality in an otherwise staid shopping district.

Flanagan's Irish Bar (☎ 022 310 13 14; Rue du Cheval-Blanc 4) Popular with the city's English-speakers and expats, this pub keeps Guinness flowing into the wee hours.

L'Usine (☎ 022 328 08 18; Place des Volontaires 4) In a converted factory, it's something of a city party-base. The drinking is fairly cheap and the entertainment ranges from dance nights and concerts to cabaret, theatre and other nocturnal diversions.

Prétexte (☎ 022 310 14 28; Rue du Prince 9; admission Sfr10; 11pm-5am Thu-Sat) With a healthily kitsch décor, two bars and a dance floor, this opulent place is the main gay club.

GETTING THERE & AWAY

Geneva airport (GVA; ☎ 022 717 71 11; www.gva.ch) is an important transport hub and has frequent connections to every major European city. **EasyJet** (code EZ; ☎ 084 888 82 22; www.easyjet.com) is a popular budget carrier with flights to many European destinations.

Next to Jardin Anglais is a ticket booth for **Compagnie Générale de Navigation** (CGN; ☎ 022 312 52 23; www.cgn.ch), which operates a May to September steamer service to all towns and major villages bordering Lake Geneva (Lac Léman), including those in France. Destinations include Lausanne (Sfr30, 3½ hours, hourly) and Montreux (Sfr42, 4½ hours, hourly). Eurail and Swiss Pass holders are valid on CGN boats or there are CGN boat day passes for Sfr55.

International buses depart from **Place Dorcière** (☎ 022 732 02 30; Place Dorciére), off Rue des Alpes. There are buses to London (Sfr145, 17 hours, twice weekly) and Barcelona (Sfr100, 10 hours, twice weekly).

An autoroute bypass skirts Geneva, with major routes intersecting southwest of the city: the N1 from Lausanne joins with the E62 to Lyon (130km) and the E25 heading southeast towards Chamonix.

Sixt (☎ 022 732 90 90; Place de la Navigation 1) generally has the best daily rates for last-minute car hire.

Trains run to most Swiss towns including Zürich (Sfr78, three hours, hourly) and Interlaken (Sfr65, three hours, hourly).

There are regular international trains to Paris (Sfr105 by TGV, 3½ hours, eight times daily), Hamburg (Sfr285, 10 hours, daily), Milan (Sfr84, four hours, daily) and Barcelona (Sfr105, nine hours, daily).

GETTING AROUND

Getting from the airport is easy with regular trains into Gare de Cornavin (Sfr2.60, six minutes). Bus No 10 (Sfr2.20) does the same 5km trip. A taxi costs Sfr25 to Sfr35.

There are free bikes available from **Genève Roule** (☎ 022 740 13 43; www.geneveroule.ch; Place de Montbrillant 17; 7.30am-9.30pm May-Oct). Bring your ID and Sfr20 for a deposit.

Buses, trams, trains and boats service the city, and ticket dispensers are found at all stops. Tickets cost Sfr1.80 (within one zone, 30 minutes) and Sfr2.20 (two zones, one hour). A day pass costs Sfr6 for the city or Sfr12 for the whole canton. Tickets and passes are also valid for CGN boats that travel along the city shoreline.

LAKE GENEVA REGION

Switzerland's Riviera lines the shores of Europe's largest lake – known to many as Lake Geneva, to Francophones as Lac Léman – and rivals its French counterpart as a magnet for the rich and famous. Amid a climate mild enough for palm trees to grow, are swanky yet charming little resort towns such as Vevey and Montreux. There's also the marvellous emerald spectacle of tightly ranked vineyards spreading in terraces up the steep hillsides.

LAUSANNE

pop 115,916

In a fabulous location overlooking Lake Geneva, Lausanne is an enchanting beauty with several distinct personalities: the former fishing village, Ouchy, with its summer beach-resort feel; Place St-François, with stylish, cobblestone shopping streets; and Flon, a warehouse district of bars, galleries and boutiques. It's also got a few amazing sights. One of the country's grandest Gothic cathedrals dominates its medieval centre.

The **tourist office** (☎ 021 613 73 21; www.lausanne-tourisme.ch; Place de la Navigation 4; ⌚ 9am-6pm) is next door to the Ouchy metro station. You can buy the Lausanne Card here (Sfr15, valid two days), which allows unlimited travel anywhere in the city by bus and train.

Sights & Activities

MUSÉE DE L'ART BRUT

Perhaps the most alluring **museum** (☎ 021 647 54 35; www.artbrut.ch in French; Ave de Bergiéres 11; adult/student Sfr8/5; ⌚ 11am-1pm & 2-6pm Tue-Fri, 11am-6pm Sat & Sun) in the country, the collection here is a fascinating amalgam of 15,000 works of art created by untrained artists – psychiatric patients, eccentrics and incarcerated criminals. The works offer a striking variety, at times a surprising technical capacity and in some cases an inspirational world-view. Biographies and explanations are in English. The museum is about 600m northwest of the Place St Francois.

CATHEDRALE DE LAUSANNE

This glorious Gothic **cathedral** (⌚ 7am-7pm Mon-Fri, 8am-7pm Sat & Sun Apr-Sep, to 5.30pm Oct-Mar) is arguably the finest in Switzerland. Built in the 12th and 13th centuries, highlights include the stunningly detailed carved portal, vaulted ceilings and archways, and carefully restored stained-glass windows.

MUSÉE OLYMPIQUE

Lausanne is home to the International Olympic Committee, and sports aficionados can immerse themselves in archival footage, interactive computers and memorabilia at the information-packed **Musée Olympique** (☎ 021 621 65 11; www.olympic.org; Quai d'Ouchy 1; adult/student/child Sfr14/9/7; ⌚ 9am-6pm Mon-Wed & Fri-Sun, 9am-8pm Thu May-Sep, closed Mon Oct-Apr).

Sleeping

Camping de Vidy (☎ 021 622 50 00; www.campinglausannevidy.ch; Chemin du Camping 3; camp sites per site/tent/car Sfr8/12/3.50) This camping ground is on the lake just to the west of the Vidy sports complex. Sites are well maintained and it's popular with families in summer. Get off bus 2 at Bois de Vaux.

Jeunotel SA (☎ 021 626 02 22; www.jeunotel.ch; Chemin du Bois-de-Vaux 36; dm Sfr30, s/d with shared bathroom Sfr60/80; P 💻; bus 2) The cheaper rooms feel rather dismal with exposed block walls, but the place caters to young Swiss staying for weeks at a time and the bar can become lively at night, making it a good spot to practice another language.

Lausanne Guesthouse & Backpacker (☎ 021 601 80 00; www.lausanne-guesthouse.ch; Chemin des Epinettes 4; dm Sfr35, s/d with shared bathroom Sfr81/88; ⊠ 💻) This tastefully renovated 1894 townhouse perched high on a hill has stunning views. The garden terrace is great for summertime chilling and meeting other backpackers. The entire place is nonsmoking. Parking costs Sfr10.

Le Château d'Ouchy (☎ 021 616 74 51; www.chateaudouchy.com; Place du Port 2; s/d from Sfr125/240; P ✖ 💻) A whimsical castle (mostly built in the 19th century around the original medieval tower, complete with dungeon) with

rooms furnished in Louis XIII style but, sadly, showing signs of age.

Eating

Le Mix Snack Bar (☎ 078 808 79 68; Rue Central 29; mains from Sfr4.50) Small and smoky with cheery orange walls, this low-key place fills up at lunch when locals flock in for a sandwich, kebab, burger or coffee.

Café de l'Hôtel de Ville (☎ 021 312 10 12; Place de la Palud 10; mains from Sfr10) This café tempts you to linger over steamy cups of coffee and trashy French tabloids for hours on end. It's a favourite with students and travellers chowing on organic dishes surrounded by the buzz of animated conversation. At night come for drinks.

L'Éléphant Blanc (☎ 021 312 71 77; Rue Cité-Devant 4; mains Sfr18-25; Mon-Fri) On warm days tables spill out of the restaurant and onto the footpath in front of this tiny and popular student haunt. It's a good place to fill your stomach before boozing.

Café du Vieil Ouchy (☎ 021 616 21 94; Place du Port 3, Ouchy; mains Sfr18-37; Thu-Mon) The sunny terrace is the perfect spot for a summer meal of *rösti* and other Swiss classics. In winter linger over a creamy fondue inside cosy timber environs.

Café-Restaurant du Vieux Lausanne (☎ 021 323 53 90; Rue Pierre Viret 6; mains from Sfr20; lunch & dinner Tue-Fri, dinner only Sat) The French and Swiss cooking comes in generous portions at this old stalwart, although meat is the central theme. In summer you can sit beneath the narrow pergola out the back.

Drinking & Entertainment

Lausanne is one of the country's busier cities for nightlife. Look for the free listings booklet *What's Up* in many bars.

Le Bleu Lézard (☎ 021 321 38 35; Rue Enning 10) World-music jam sessions and film nights make this cavelike basement bar a happening spot. Cure your Sunday hangover with the all-day brunch.

Pinte Besson (☎ 021 312 59 69; Rue de l'Ale 4) The city's oldest tavern has been serving local wines to Lausannois punters since 1780. The place oozes the atmosphere of another age and makes no concessions to modern modishness.

Giraf Bar (☎ 021 323 53 90; Escaliers du Marché; closed Sun & Mon) This tiny smoke-filled bar fills up on a Friday or Saturday night. The giraffe-skin motif is repeated inside on lampshades and the music can reach back to the 1980s.

Mad – Moulin a Danse (☎ 021 312 11 22; www.mad.ch in French; Rue de Genéve 23; admission Thu-Sun Sfr20; Wed-Sun) A typical large club that's generally packed on weekends, it relies on music theme nights to keep things interesting. The downstairs cellar bar has free admission on Wednesday. On Sunday's the club hosts Trixx Club for gays and lesbians.

Getting There & Around

Buses service most destinations (Sfr1.80 for up to three stops, or Sfr2.80 one-hour unlimited stops in central Lausanne). The metro connects Ouchy with the train station and costs the same as the buses.

There are trains to/from Geneva (Sfr20, 50 minutes, three hourly), Bern (Sfr30, 70 minutes, one or two hourly) and Interlaken Ost (Sfr55, two hours, two hourly). For boat services see p1058.

VEVEY

pop 15,400

It's easy to see why Charlie Chaplin chose to spend the last 25 years of his life in Vevey. The swanky little place (one of Switzerland's two main Riviera resorts), with a colourful old square bumped up against the lake, is located in beautiful country. It also has a number of unique shops and lazy-day cafés. On summer Saturdays the sprawling square turns into a bustling marketplace with traditionally dressed merchants selling local handicrafts and wines.

For sleeping try the **Riviera Lodge** (☎ 021 923 80 40; www.rivieralodge.ch; Place du Marché; dm Sfr26, d with shared bathroom Sfr80; P) in a hip 19th-century townhouse near the waterfront. The hostel's rooftop terrace has great views. The futuristic lounge makes a good reading nook. At the time of research guests received free bus tickets to the Château de Chillon and 50% off admission.

Le National (☎ 021 923 76 25; Rue du Torrent 9; mains Sfr10-20) is a great place to eat and drink. Chill at the cool bar with leaning glass-topped tables and stools or, for the more lounge-inclined, spots by the window. The restaurant serves a mix of international dishes.

MONTREUX

pop 22,800

In 1971 Frank Zappa was doing his thing in the Montreux casino when the building caught fire, casting a pall of smoke over Lake Geneva and inspiring the members of Deep Purple to pen their classic rock number *Smoke on the Water*.

The showpiece of the Swiss Riviera has been an inspiration to writers, artists and musicians for centuries. Famous one-time residents include Lord Byron, Ernest Hemingway and the Shelleys. It's easy to see why – Montreux not only boasts stunning Alps views and tidy rows of pastel buildings, it's also home to Switzerland's most extraordinary castle, the ever-popular Château de Chillon.

Each year the town hosts the **Montreux Jazz Festival** (☎ 021 963 82 82; www.montreuxjazz.com) in early July. It runs for two weeks. Free concerts take place every day, but count on Sfr40 to Sfr100 for one of the big gigs.

Sights

Switzerland's most popular fortress, **Château de Chillon** (☎ 021 966 89 10; www.chillon.ch; adult/student/child Sfr8.50/6.50/4; 9am-7pm Apr-Sep, 9.30am-5pm Mar & Oct, 10am-4pm Nov-Feb) was originally constructed on the shores of Lake Geneva in the 11th century. It caught the public imagination when Lord Byron wrote *The Prisoner of Chillon* about Bonivard, a prior chained in the dungeons for almost four years in the 16th century.

You can easily spend a couple of hours touring the tower, courtyards, dungeons and staterooms containing weapons, frescoes and furniture.

The castle is a pleasant 45-minute walk along the lakefront from Montreux. Otherwise take trolley bus 1 (Sfr2.60, Veytaux stop), which passes by every 10 minutes.

Sleeping & Eating

Auberge de Jeunesse (☎ 021 963 49 34; Passage de l'Auberge 8, Territet; dm from Sfr32; ⏲ mid-Feb–mid-Nov) This waterfront hostel has a cheery atmosphere and simple rooms. Dorms come with as few as two beds. Catch bus No 1 from the train station.

Hôtel Masson (☎ 021 966 00 44; www.hotelmasson.ch; Rue Bonivard 5; s/d Sfr150/230; P) In the hills just west of Montreux, this one-time vintner's mansion is on the Swiss Heritage list of the country's most beautiful hotels. The grounds are luxurious, and the place reeks of old-world European charm. A small sauna and Jacuzzi are extra perks.

La Rose des Sables (☎ 021 961 15 46; Ave des Alps; mains from Sfr3; ⏲ lunch) Inexpensive sandwiches, croissants, quiches and a mouthwatering chocolate selection make this charming patisserie a lovely lunch option.

Café du Grütli (☎ 021 963 42 65; Rue du Grand Chêne 8; mains Sfr20-30; ⏲ Tue-Sat) Head to this eatery, hidden away in the old part of town, for good home cooking – ranging from *rösti* with ham to hearty meat dishes and the inevitable fondue.

Getting There & Away

There are trains to Geneva (Sfr26, 70 minutes, hourly) and Lausanne (Sfr9.80, 25 minutes, three hourly). Make the scenic journey to Interlaken via the GoldenPass Panoramic, with changes at Zweisimmen and Spiez (Sfr60, three hours, daily; rail passes valid).

GRYON & LEYSIN

Leave the beaten track and soak up the Swiss Alpine experience in untouristy **Gryon** (1130m), southeast of Montreux. It's close to the ski fields of Villars, some great meadow hiking trials and home to the fantastic **Swiss Alp Retreat** (☎ 024 498 33 21; Chalet Martin; www.gryon.com; dm/d from Sfr18/52; P 💻). The hostel, run by a Swiss-Australian couple, has a laid-back vibe and gets rave reviews from travellers. It runs a number of popular excursions, including summer glacier skiing trips (Sfr125). Ask about ski-and-stay packages in winter.

To reach Gryon you will need to take a train from Lausanne to Bex (Sfr18, 40 minutes, hourly) and then the cogwheel train to the village (Sfr5.80, 30 minutes, hourly). The hostel is a five-minute walk from the train stop. Follow the signs.

Another tranquil Alpine spot, **Leysin** attracts skiers, snowboarders, hikers and meditators. In a 19th-century guesthouse the **Hiking Sheep** (☎ 024 494 35 35; www.hikingsheep.com; dm/d with shared bathroom from Sfr27/74; P ⊠ 💻) is another longtime favourite with backpackers. It has breathtaking views from its balconies, a pine-forested backyard and great vibes. Don't miss the hammocks. All sorts of activities can be arranged.

Leysin is accessible by a cogwheel train from Aigle (Sfr8.40, 30 minutes, hourly); there are trains to Aigle from Lausanne (Sfr29, 30 minutes, hourly).

VALAIS

It's pretty hard not to be seduced in Matterhorn country, where endless panoramic vistas and breathtaking views win over even the toughest critics. An area of extraordinary natural beauty, the Valais boasts the 10 highest mountains in Switzerland – all over 4000m. It's also home to one of the most popular, and best, skiing and boarding destinations in Europe, Zermatt. When the snow melts and the valleys turn lush and green the opportunities for hiking are boundless.

ZERMATT

pop 5500

One word says it all: Matterhorn. Synonymous with Switzerland, the Alps' most famous peak (4478m) keeps solitary vigil over this skiing, mountaineering and hiking hotspot.

On 13 July 1865 Edward Whymper led the first successful ascent of the mountain. The climb took 32 hours but the descent was marred by tragedy when four team members crashed to their deaths in a 1200m fall down the North Wall.

Skiers and snowboarders prefer going down to climbing up. The town doubled in size during the ski boom of the 1960s and '70s. For the rich and stylish, Zermatt is a place to see (as well as ski) and be seen (skiing or otherwise).

Orientation & Information

Zermatt is small, easy to navigate and car-free. The main street is Bahnhofstrasse, but street names are rarely used.

You can go online for free (or bring your laptop for a wi-fi moment) at **Papperla Pub** (right). The **tourist office** (☎ 027 966 81 00; www.zermatt.ch; Bahnhofplatz 5; 🕒 8.30am-noon & 1.30-6pm Mon-Fri, 9.30am-noon & 4-6pm Sat & Sun late Sep–mid-Jun, 8.30am-6pm Mon-Sat, 8.30am-noon & 1.30-6pm Sun mid-Jun–Sep) has all the local info.

Sights & Activities

Views from the cable cars and gondolas are pretty much uniformly breathtaking. The cogwheel train to **Gornergrat** (3090m) is one of the highlights. The mountain railway (Sfr36 one way) takes 25 to 43 minutes and there are two to three departures an hour. For the best views of the Matterhorn sit on the right-hand side. Alternatively, it takes around five hours to walk up from Zermatt to Gornergrat.

A walk in the **cemetery** is a sobering experience for any would-be mountaineer, as numerous monuments tell of untimely deaths on Monte Rosa and the Matterhorn.

Alpin Center (☎ 027 966 24 60; www.zermatt.ch/alpincenter; Bahnhofstrasse 58; 🕒 8am-noon & 2-6pm mid-Nov–Apr & Jul-Sep) contains the ski and snowboard school and the mountain-guides office *(Bergführerbüro)*. For climbing the Matterhorn guides recommend previous experience, one week's preparation, and the small matter of Sfr1130 per person. Also ask here about Haute Route ski touring and heli-skiing. In the off-season you can reach them by phone only (between 9am and 11am and 2pm and 5pm Monday to Friday).

SKIING & SNOWBOARDING

Zermatt has numerous demanding slopes to test the experienced and intermediate skier in three main skiing areas: **Rothorn**, **Stockhorn** and **Matterhorn Glacier Paradise** (formerly Klein Matterhorn). In all, there are 245km of ski runs and free ski buses simplify transferring between areas. February to April is peak time but in early summer the snow is still good and the lifts are less busy. Beginners have fewer options on the slopes.

The Klein Matterhorn is topped by the highest cable car station in Europe (3820m), providing access to the highest skiing on the Continent. It also has the most extensive summer skiing in Switzerland (up to 21km of runs) and is the starting point for skiing at the Italian resort of Cervinia. The No 7 run down from the border is an exhilarating, broad avenue, great for intermediates and above. Be aware bad weather can close the lifts leading up to the Klein Matterhorn on either side. Runs can be icier on the Italian side too (the skiing in Cervinia is best in March), but there are plenty of options. Don't leave it too late to get the lifts back up, or you could find yourself staying overnight!

A day pass for all ski lifts in Zermatt (excluding Cervinia) costs Sfr67/57/34 for adults/seniors & students/children and Sfr75/64/38 including Cervinia.

Sleeping & Eating

Be warned, many hotels and restaurants close between seasons.

Hotel Bahnhof (☎ 027 967 24 06; www.hotelbahnhof.com; dm Sfr33, s/d with shared bathroom from Sfr67/88; 🕒 closed around mid-Oct–mid-Dec) A long-time mountaineers' mecca, the hotel has an impressive industrial-size kitchen, large dorms, and doubles with balconies facing the Matterhorn. It is directly opposite the station and gets good marks for cleanliness and service.

Hotel Blauherd (☎ 027 967 22 91; www.hotels-suisse.ch/blauherd; Wiestistrasse; s/d Sfr95/190; 🅿) Rooms are clean and cosy at this friendly chalet-style hotel. The buffet breakfast is generous and you can use the pool in the nearby Hotel Cristiania. Staff will pick you up at the train station – it's a bit of a walk from the centre of town.

Restaurant Weisshorn (☎ 027 967 57 52; Am Bach 6; fondue Sfr25-28; meal Sfr40-50; 🕒 mid-Jun–Sep & mid-Nov–Apr) The garish mural of Chichenitza, the Mexican temple, contrasts with the glowing orange Matterhorn table lamps. The food range is just as odd, from nachos and *quesadillas* (flour tortillas with savoury fillings) to fondue.

Drinking & Entertainment

Papperla Pub (☎ 027 967 40 40; Steinmattstrasse 34; ⌚ 2.30pm-2am year-round) This is *the* après-ski pub in Zermatt, especially during the slow season (like January). Around the circular bar arranged on a couple of levels are high tables with stools or, if you prefer, low lounges. A DJ is usually in action and there's no shortage of ski resort drinking hijinks.

Broken Bar Disco (☎ 027 967 19 31; Bahnhofstrasse 41; ⌚ 10pm-4am year-round) Down in a vaulted cellar of the Hotel Post, this is a popular dance dive where you can jive on a keg and expend any energy leftover after the day on the slopes. The Hotel Post is home to various other bars and eateries.

Getting There & Around

Zermatt is car-free. Dinky little electric vehicles are used to transport goods and serve as taxis and so on around town. Leave your vehicles in the huge open parking area in Täsch (Sfr7.50 per day), or one of the several covered garages there and take the train (Sfr7.80, 12 minutes) into Zermatt.

Trains depart from Brig, stopping at Visp en route. It's a steep, scenic journey (one way/return Sfr37/65, 80 minutes, hourly). Swiss Passes are valid. There is no discount for Eurail Pass holders. The only way out is to backtrack, but if you're going to Saas Fee you can divert there from Stalden-Saas. The popular and scenic *Glacier Express* travels between St Moritz and Zermatt (see p1069).

LEUKERBAD

If you're looking for a little thermal rest and relaxation, this is the place to get it. Leukerbad, west of Brig, is home to Europe's largest thermal centre. The majestic mountain walls encasing the village like an amphitheatre grander than anything the Romans could have conceived make an awe-inspiring backdrop for outdoor bathing meditations.

There are no less than 10 different places to take to the waters, but the biggest and best is **Burgerbad** (☎ 027 472 20 20; www.burgerbad.ch; Rathausstrasse; admission Sfr21; ⌚ 8am-8pm Sun-Thu, to 9pm Fri & Sat) with indoor and outdoor pools, whirlpools and water massage jets. If you tire of soaking, ride the cable car up the sheer side of the northern ridge of mountains to Gemmi Pass (2350m; one way/return Sfr15.50/24). It's a good area for hiking. To walk to the top of the pass takes two hours.

Weisses Rössli (☎ 027 470 33 77; off Dorfplatz; s/d with shared bathroom Sfr50/100) is an attractive place with a helpful friendly host. There is a restaurant serving Valais specialities on the ground floor.

Leukerbad is 16km north of Leuk, which is on the main rail route from Lausanne to Brig. A blue postbus goes from outside the Leuk train station to Leukerbad (Sfrf10.40, 30 minutes, hourly) usually at 42 minutes past the hour; last departure is 7.42pm.

TICINO

Sip chardonnay in a colourful piazza café in the late afternoon and shiver as the Mediterranean air whips hot and spicy across your sun-speckled head. Check out the peacock-proud posers, clad in a style that is so *this* season, propelling their scooters in and out of frenetic village traffic. Melodic notes and lots of hand gestures, steaming plates of pasta, creamy gelatos. Did you cross the border into Italy? No, this is just the Switzerland Heidi failed to mention.

South of the Alps, Ticino (Tessin in German) has a distinct look. The canton manages to perfectly fuse Swiss cool with Italian passion, as evidenced by a lusty love for Italian comfort food and full-bodied wines that's balanced by a healthy respect for rules and regulations.

BELLINZONA

pop 17,100

Ticino's capital is a quiet stunner. Strategically placed at the conversion point of several valleys leading down from the Alps, Bellinzona is visually unique. Inhabited since Neolithic times, it is dominated by three grey-stone, fairy-tale medieval castles that have attracted everyone from Swiss invaders to painters such as JMW Turner. Turner may have liked the place, but Bellinzona has a surprisingly low tourist profile, in spite of its castles together forming one of only six Unesco World Heritage sites in Switzerland.

The **tourist office** (☎ 091 825 21 31; fax 091 825 38 17; www.bellinzonaturismo.ch; Viale Stazione 18; ⌚ 9am-

6.30pm Mon-Fri, 9am-noon Sat), in the post office, can provide information on Bellinzona and the whole canton.

You can roam the ramparts of the two larger castles, **Castelgrande** or **Castello di Montebello**, both of which are still in great condition and offer panoramic views of the town and countryside.

The rooms at the **Hotel San Giovanni** (☎ 091 825 19 19; www.hotelzimmer.ch; Via San Giovanni 7; s/d with shared bathroom Sfr50/90) feel cluttered and bland, but it's the cheapest decent option around town.

The only place to sleep just inside the old town (part of the city wall stands menacingly behind it) is the pleasant **Albergo Croce Federale** (☎ 091 825 16 67; fax 091 826 25 50; Viale Stazione 12; s/d Sfr100/150). Rooms are straightforward but light, and the restaurant downstairs is cheerful.

Osteria Ticinese (☎ 091 825 16 73; Via Orico 3; pasta Sfr11-15, mains Sfr13-16) dishes up hearty portions of standard Italian fare in cheerful environs. It gets really crowded around lunch.

Bellinzona is on the train route connecting Locarno (Sfr7.20, 25 minutes, twice hourly) and Lugano (Sfr11.40, 30 minutes, twice hourly).

LOCARNO

pop 14,400

The rambling red enclave of Italianate townhouses, piazzas and arcades ending at the northern end of Lake Maggiore, coupled with more hours of sunshine than anywhere else in Switzerland, give this laid-back town a summer resort atmosphere. Locarno gained notoriety when it hosted the 1925 Peace Conference intended to bring stability to Europe after WWI.

Piazza Grande is the centre of town. You can gulp down shots and smoke Cuban cigars while checking your email at the Latino-style **Pardo Bar** (☎ 091 752 21 23; Via della Motta 3; per hr Sfr20; 🕑 11am-1am). In the nearby casino complex is the **tourist office** (☎ 091 751 03 33; locarno@ticino.com; 🕑 9am-6pm Mon-Fri, 10am-5pm Sat, 10am-2pm Sun).

Sights & Activities

Don't miss the formidable **Madonna del Sasso**, up on the hill with panoramic views of the lake and town. The sanctuary was built after the Virgin Mary allegedly appeared in a vision in 1480. It features a church with 15th-century paintings, a small museum and several distinctive statues. There is a funicular from the town centre, but the 20-minute climb is not demanding (take Via al Sasso off Via Cappuccini) and you pass some shrines on the way.

In August more than 150,000 film buffs hit town for the two-week **Festival Internazionale di Film** (International Film Festival; ☎ 091 756 21 21; www.pardo.ch; Via Luini 3). Cinemas are used during the day but at night films are shown in the open-air on a giant screen in the Piazza Grande.

Sleeping & Eating

Vecchia Locarno (☎ 091 751 65 02; www.hotel-vecchia-locarno.ch; Via della Motta 10; s/d with shared bathroom Sfr50/95) Rooms are gathered around a sunny internal courtyard, evoking Mediterranean flavours. The simply furnished digs are comfortable. Ask for one with views over the old town and hills.

Grand Hotel Locarno (☎ 091 743 02 82; ww.grand-hotel-locarno.ch; Via Sempione 17; s/d Sfr160/340; P ✗ 💻) Grand in name and looks, this is an old-style relic of *belle époque* proportions. Rooms in this historic building are a trifle faded but the best of them still retain the elegance of a bygone era.

Lake Maggiore has a great variety of fresh and tasty fish. Look out for *persico* (perch) and *corigone* (whitefish).

Osteria Chiara (☎ 091 743 32 96; Vicolo della Chiara 1; mains Sfr15-30) Tucked away on a cobbled lane, this has all the cosy feel of a grotto. Sit at tables beneath the pergola or by the fireplace for chunky dishes of, say, *malfatti con zucca al timo* (big gnocchi-style pasta with pumpkin and thyme). From the lake follow the signs up Vicolo dei Nessi.

For self-caterers on Piazza Grande there's a Coop supermarket and a Migros De Gustibus snack bar.

Drinking

Sport Bar (Via della Posta 4) A fairly run-of-the-mill place by day, this rough-and-tumble bar with a red-walled dance space out the back and beer garden on the side is an extremely popular hangout with Locarno's young and restless.

Getting There & Away

The St Gotthard Pass provides the road link (N2) to central Switzerland. There are trains from Brig (Sfr50, 2½ hours, hourly) that pass through Italy en route. You change trains at Domodóssola across the border, so take your passport.

LUGANO

pop 26,100

Switzerland's southernmost tourist town is a sophisticated slice of Italian life, with colourful markets, upmarket shops, pedestrian-only piazzas and lakeside parks. Resting on the shore of Lake Lugano, with Mounts San Salvatore and Bré rising on either side, it's also a great base for lake trips, water sports and hillside hikes.

The old town is a 10-minute walk down the hill to the east. On the lake side of the Municipio building is the **tourist office** (☎ 091 913 32 32; info@lugano-tourism.ch; Riva Albertolli; 9am-6.30pm Mon-Fri, to 12.30pm & 1.30-5pm Sat, 10am-3pm Sun, closed Sat & Sun Dec-Feb).

Sights & Activities

Wander through the mostly porticoed lanes woven around the busy main square, Piazza della Riforma (which is even more lively when the Tuesday and Friday morning markets are held). Via Nassa is the main shopping street and indicates there is no shortage of cash in this town.

The simple Romanesque **Chiesa di Santa Maria degli Angioli** (St Mary of the Angels; Piazza Luini; 8am-5pm), against which a now-crumbling former hotel was built, contains two frescoes by Bernardino Luini dating from 1529. Covering the entire wall that divides the church in two is a grand didactic illustration of the Crucifixion. The closer you look, the more scenes of Christ's Passion are revealed, along with others of him being taken down from the cross and the Resurrection. The power and vivacity of the colours are astounding.

Chomp into some cocoa culture at the **Museo del Cioccolato Alprose** (☎ 091 611 88 56; www.alprose.ch; Via Rompada 36, Casalano; adult/child Sfr4/1; 9am-6pm Mon-Fri, to 5pm Sat & Sun). As well as getting a chocolate-coated history lesson, you can watch the sugary substance being made. Get there by the Ferrovia Ponte Tresa train (Sfr6).

Alternatively, take a **boat trip** to one of the many photogenic villages hugging the shoreline of Lake Lugano. One of the most popular is car-free **Gandria**, a tiny hillside village with historic homes and shops, and narrow winding alleyways right down to the water. If you hit town at meal times you can tuck into a traditional Ticinese dish in one of the many **grotti**.

Sleeping

Many hotels close for at least part of the winter.

Hotel & Hostel Montarina (☎ 091 966 72 72; www.montarina.ch; Via Montarina 1; dm Sfr25, s/d Sfr80/120; mid-Mar–Oct; P) Behind the train station is this charming hotel, whose best rooms are airy, with timber floors and antiques. The nearby hostel has rooms with four to 16 bunk beds. A buffet breakfast is available for Sfr12.

Hotel Pestalozzi (☎ 091 921 46 46; www.attuale.com/pestalozzi.html; Piazza Independenza 9; s/d from Sfr85/160;) A renovated Art Nouveau building, this is a good central deal. Rooms have a fresh feel, with crisp whites and blues dominating the decoration. The cheapest share bathrooms and don't have air-con.

Hotel Federale (☎ 091 910 08 08; www.hotel-federale.ch; Via Regazzoni 8; s Sfr160, d Sfr190-260; P) If you can afford the grand top-floor doubles with lake views, this place beats many multi-stellar places hands-down. A short luggage-laden stumble from the train station, it is in a quiet spot with immaculately kept rooms and friendly staff. There is wi-fi in the lobby.

Eating & Drinking

Head to the pedestrian-only piazzas to tempt the tastebuds, with *panini* (bread rolls; Sfr5) and gelati (Sfr3) from street stalls, or larger meals in the pizzerias and cafés spilling onto the streets.

L'Antica Osteria del Porto (☎ 091 971 42 00; Via Foce 9; mains Sfr25-35) Savour local fish and Ticinese dishes such as *brasato di manzo al Merlot con polenta gratinata e legume* (grilled beef with polenta and vegetables). The terrace overlooking the Cassarate stream is pleasant, and you also have lake views.

Soho Café (☎ 091 922 60 80; Corso Pestalozzi 3; 10am-1am Mon-Fri, 4pm-1am Sat) This place is buzzing and chill at the same time. Filled with Lugano's beautiful people, stop by the orange-lit bar for a drink before slipping into a chair for catch-up chat with friends. DJs keep the music loud enough to groove too, but quiet enough to have a conversation.

Entertainment

Desperados (☎ 091 921 11 97; Via al Forte 4; 🕑 10pm-5am) This late-night disco bar is hot, cramped and sweaty – in other words the perfect nightclub. The entrance is on a tiny square off Vicolo Orfanotrofio.

Getting There & Around

Lugano is on the same road and rail route as Bellinzona. Two postbuses run to St Moritz (Sfr74, four hours, daily in summer but only Friday, Saturday and Sunday in winter). Swiss Pass holders will still pay Sfr11 and everyone needs to reserve their seats the day before at the bus station, the train information office or by calling ☎ 091 807 85 20. Buses leave from the bus station on Via Serafino Balestra, though the St Moritz bus also calls at the train station.

GRAUBÜNDEN

Rural charm, untamed beauty and some of the world's most haute couture skiing are on the menu in Graubünden (Grisons, Grigioni, Grishun). It's easy to get off the trodden path here. The roads are mostly narrow, winding and often pocked. Great carpets of deep green felt seem to have been draped over the valleys and lower hills of this, the country's biggest canton. An outdoor adventurer's paradise, the region features more than 11,000km of walking trails, more than 600 lakes and 1500km of downhill ski slopes – including super swanky St Moritz and backpacker mecca Flims-Laax.

CHUR

pop 31,900

Chur, the canton's capital and largest town, is one of the oldest settlements in Switzerland, tracing its history back some 3000 years. Today it serves as a gateway for the region, although it's not a very obvious tourist attraction – buildings are stark and grey. For a town map see the **tourist office** (☎ 081 252 18 18; Grabenstrasse 5; 🕑 1.30-6pm Mon, 8.30am-noon & 1.30-6pm Tue-Fri, 9am-noon Sat).

The **Kunstmuseum** (☎ 081 257 28 68; Postplatz; admission Sfr12; 🕑 10am-noon & 2-5pm Tue, Wed & Fri-Sun, 10am-noon & 2-8pm Thu) has a collection of artwork by the three Giacomettis (Alberto, Augusto and Giovanni), and exhibits by local sci-fi artist HR Giger (of *Alien* fame).

The **Hotel Franziskaner** (☎ 081 252 12 61; fax 081 252 12 79; Kupfergasse 18; s/d from Sfr65/110) is located right on the old town square and can get a little rowdy on weekends but we think that just adds to its charm. Rooms are clean and plenty comfortable with simple pine furniture. The cheapest share bathrooms.

Easily Chur's most atmospheric old-time eatery, **Speiserestaurant Zum Alten Zollhaus** (☎ 081 252 33 98; Malixerstrasse 1; mains Sfr30) is the kind of place where black-and-white–clad waitresses bustle beneath centuries-old timber beams and serve up local and Swiss German dishes, including lots of fresh game meat in autumn.

A restless student population has led to high-density bar activity in the old town. The scene is on Untere Gasse, basically a row of bars. **Street Café** (☎ 081 253 714; Grabenstrasse 47) is one of the trendier hangouts for the earlier part of the evening.

Chur is connected to Zürich (Sfr40, 85 minutes, hourly) and St Moritz (Sfr38, two hours, hourly).

FLIMS-LAAX

They say if the snow ain't falling anywhere else, you'll surely find some around Flims-Laax. These towns, along with tiny Falera, 20km west of Chur, form a single ski area known as the Weisses Arena (White Arena), with 220km of slopes catering for all levels. Laax in particular is known as a mecca for snowboarders, who spice up the local nightlife too. The resort is barely two hours by train and bus (less by car) from Zürich airport.

There main **tourist office** (☎ 081 920 92 00; www.alpenarena.ch; Via Nova; 🕑 8am-6pm Mon-Fri, to 4pm Sat May-Oct, to 5pm Mon-Sat Nov-Apr) is in Flims-Dorf.

The ski slopes range as high as 3000m and are mostly intermediate or easy, although there are some 45km of more challenging runs. A one-day ski pass includes ski buses and costs Sfr62 (plus Sfr5 for the KeyCard that you use to access the lifts).

Laax was the first Swiss resort to allow snowboarders to use the lifts back in 1985, and remains a mecca for snowsurfers, with two huge half-pipes (one said to be the biggest in the world) and a freestyle park huddled around the unfortunately named Crap Sogn Gion peak. The season starts in late October on the glacier and, depending on snowfalls, in mid-December elsewhere.

In summer try your hand at **river rafting** on a turbulent 17km stretch of the Vorderrhein between Ilanz and Reichenau. It will take you through the **Rheinschlucht** (Rhine Gorge), somewhat optimistically dubbed Switzerland's Grand Canyon, but impressive enough for all that. **Swissraft** (☎ 081 911 52 50; www.swissraft.ch) offers half-/full-day rafting for Sfr109/160.

It may resemble an awful 1970s housing estate, but **Riders Palace** (☎ 081 927 97 00; www.riderspalace.ch; Laax Murschetg; dm Sfr30-60; d to Sfr200 per person; 💻) is actually a curious bit of designer cool for the snow party animal (hotel motto: sleeping is for dreamers). You can go for basic but comfortable bunk-bed accommodation or stylish rooms (with baths by Philippe Starck). The pricing system is a trifle complicated, and can include your ski pass. The so-called Multimedia rooms are doubles/triples with Playstation, DVD player and Dolby surround sound. The whole place is wi-fi wired and located 200m from the Laax lifts. Its lobby bar is open to the general public and picks up après-ski traffic that continues until well into the night, occasionally with live acts.

Postbuses run to Flims and the other villages in the White Arena area hourly from Chur (Sfr12.40 to Flims-Dorf, 30 minutes). A local free shuttle bus connects the three villages.

ST MORITZ

pop 4900

Just like rolled jeans and big sunglasses, ski resorts are constantly going into and out of style. A few years ago it was all about Aspen, but this season the name on everyone's lips in the rich-famous-royal (or maybe just young and super fabulous) clique is St Moritz. The place is definitely hot. And with its smugly perfect lake and aloof mountains, the town also looks a million dollars.

Orientation & Information

Hilly St Moritz Dorf is above the train station, with luxury hotels, restaurants and shops. To the southwest, 2km around the lake is the more downmarket St Moritz Bad; buses run between the two. St Moritz is seasonal and becomes a ghost town during November and from late April to early June.

The train station near the lake rents out bikes in summer and changes money from 6.50am to 8.10pm daily. The **St Moritz tourist office** (☎ 081 837 33 33; stmoritz.ch; Via Maistra 12; 🕑 9am-5pm Mon-Fri) has all the usual traveller info.

Activities

Skiers and snowboarders will revel in the 350km of runs on the slopes of **Corviglia-Marguns** (☎ 081 830 00 00; www.bergbahnenengadin.ch; day lift ticket Sfr63, ski & boot rental Sfr45). The choice for beginners is limited. There are also 160km of **cross-country trails** (equipment rental Sfr20) and 120km of marked **hiking paths**.

You can also try golf (including on the frozen lake in winter), tennis, in-line skating, fishing, horse riding, sailing, windsurfing and river rafting, to mention just a few. The tourist office has a list of prices and contacts.

Sleeping & Eating

Youth Hostel St Moritz Bad (☎ 081 833 39 69; www.youthhostel.ch/st.moritz; Via Surpunt 60; dm with half-board Sfr46; 💻) Backing on to the forest and cross-country ski course, this large, modern hostel has excellent facilities. There's mountain bike rental, compulsory half-board and a TV lounge. From the train station take the bus towards Maloja and get off at the Hotel Sonne. From here it is a six-minute walk.

Chesa Chantarella (☎ 081 833 33 55; www.chesa-chantarella.ch; Via Salastrains; s/d Sfr95/190; 🕑 Jun-Sep & Dec-Apr; Ⓟ) High up over town, this is a charming, knock-about sort of place that also happens to house one of the town's better-value eateries for local cooking and fondue.

Hotel Waldhaus am See (☎ 081 836 60 00; www.waldhaus-am-se.ch; s/d Sfr170/320; Ⓟ 💻) Brilliantly located in grounds overlooking the lake and a short walk from the train station, this place has pleasant rooms, many with enticing views. It has its own sizzling restaurant too, with grilled meat specialities.

Jöhri's Talvo (☎ 081 833 44 55; Via Gunels 15; mains Sfr10-20) This place, beyond Bad in nearby Champfér, is the best valley restaurant, serving up fish and local dishes in rustic surroundings.

Engiadina (☎ 081 833 32 65; Plazza da Scuola 2; fondue from Sfr32 per person) This comfortable, cosy spot is famous for fondue, and that's the best thing to eat here (it's Sfr38.50 per person with champagne). It's open year-round.

Drinking

Around 20 bars and clubs have dancing and/or music. While you bop to the beat your wallet might also be waltzing itself wafer-thin, because nights out in St Moritz can be nasty on the banknotes.

Bobby's Pub (☎ 081 834 42 83; Via dal Bagn) This vaguely pub-type place with undulating bar and a wide selection of beers attracts young snowboarding types in season, and just about everyone in town out of season, being one of the few places open year-round.

Getting There & Away

Two postbuses run to Lugano (Sfr74, four hours, daily summer; Friday, Saturday and Sunday winter). You must reserve a seat the day before. Call ☎ 081 837 67 64. The bus costs Sfr10 for those holding Swiss Travel passes.

The *Glacier Express* plies one of Switzerland's most famous scenic train routes, connecting St Moritz to Zermatt (Sfr138, 7½ hours, daily) via the 2033m Oberalp Pass. It covers 290km and crosses 291 bridges. Novelty drink glasses in the dining car have sloping bases to compensate for the hills – remember to keep turning them around!

SWISS NATIONAL PARK

The road west from Müstair stretches 34km over the Ofenpass (Pass dal Fuorn, 2149m), through the thick woods of Switzerland's only **national park** (www.nationalpark.ch; Jun-Oct) and on to **Zernez**, which is home to the **Chasa dal Parc Naziunal Svizzer** (National Park House; ☎ 081 856 13 78; www.nationalpark.ch; 8.30am-6pm, to 10pm Tue Jun-Oct). It is on the main road just as it leaves the east end of town and is open the same months as the park. It provides hiking details with locations to see particular animals.

There's no charge to enter the park and parking is free. Walkers can enter by trails from Zernez, S-chanf and Scuol. Deviating from the paths is not permitted. Regulations prohibit camping, littering, lighting fires, cycling, picking flowers, bringing dogs into the park, or disturbing the animals in any way. Fines of up to Sfr500 may be imposed for violations.

Sleeping & Eating

There are several hotel and restaurant options in Zernez and a couple in the park itself.

Il Fuorn (☎ 081 856 12 26; www.ilfuorn.ch; dm Sfr19, s/d from Sfr75/140, half-board extra Sfr30; Jun-Oct) In the middle of the national park by the

A LITTLE ANIMAL MAGIC *Sarah Johnstone*

If you'd like a break from people and their playthings, the Swiss National Park provides an ideal spot far from the madding crowd. It's a place to enjoy the vast, untrammelled countryside.

The park was established in 1914, the first such park to be created in Europe. At 172.4 sq km, it is smaller than most American and Canadian national parks, but the command of conservation is more rigorously adhered to. The key principle is to keep things natural. This even means holding down the number of paths to a minimum, to lessen the impact of human curiosity.

Such care has led to a flourishing of flora and fauna. You can view a number of animals that are not usually seen – ibex, marmot, chamois and deer roam through the park at will.

A three-hour walk from S-chanf to Trupchun is especially popular in October, when you can get close to large deer. The Naturlehrpfad circuit near Il Fuorn gives an opportunity to see bearded vultures, released into the wild since 1991.

In summer 2005, one of the descendants of the handful of Slovenian brown bears released into the wild in northern Italy since the 1990s caused a storm by, er, wandering over the border into the Val Müstair near the Ofenpass (Pass dal Fuorn). He came to join the small number of wolves that have again been roaming the east of the canton since 2002. The appearance of the bear attracted floods of animal-spotters, but the hullabaloo was short-lived, as the bear wandered back into Italy. In September he was back and upsetting locals by killing a dozen or more sheep to keep hunger at bay.

main road, it is a handy hulk of a place with surprisingly pleasant rooms (unless you want to opt for the very basic dorm with huddled-together mattresses). Trout is big on the menu.

Hotel Bär & Post (☎ 081 851 55 00; www.baer-post.ch; s/d Sfr90/160) In business since 1905, this is one of the town's choicest options. The best rooms are really spacious, local stone pine predominates and there is also a sauna on the premises. The restaurant, decked out in typical timber style for the region, is a good place to sample local cooking (mains Sfr20 to Sfr40).

Getting There & Away

Train services regularly run from Zernez to St Moritz (Sfr16.80, 50 minutes), with stops at S-chanf, Zuoz and Celerina. Change trains at Samedan for the latter and for St Moritz.

ZÜRICH

pop 338,794

If you haven't actually visited Switzerland's most populous city, you are more likely to associate its name with being a boring banking capital than an up-and-coming urban hot-spot. That is a real shame, because contemporary Zürich has a kind of pulsating energy not readily found elsewhere in Switzerland. Now that its Street Parade has overtaken London's Notting Hill Carnival, Zürich is host to Europe's largest yearly street party. In addition to this its former industrial quarter has been transformed into a hip nightlife venue catering to a youngish crowd, and this happening 'Züri-West' district has the same buzz as Berlin's Prenzlauerberg or Mitte. The infamous 'gnomes', as the British like to call Zürich's bankers, are still in evidence, but sometimes they can astonish you by whizzing by on a Segway scooter.

ORIENTATION

Zürich is at the northern end of Lake Zürich (Zürichsee), with the city centre split by the Limmat River. Like most Swiss cities it is compact and easy to navigate. The main train station (Hauptbahnhof) is on the western bank of the river, close to the old centre.

INFORMATION

Bookshops

Orell Füssli Bookshop (☎ 044 211 04 44; Bahnhofstrasse 70) Great source of fiction and travel books in English.

Travel Book Shop (☎ 044 252 38 83; Rindermarkt 20) Sells English-language travel books and maps.

Discount Card

ZürichCard (per 24/72hr Sfr15/30) Available from the tourist office and the airport train station, this provides free public transport, free museum admission and more.

Internet Access

Quanta (☎ 01 260 72 66; cnr Niederdorfstrasse & Mühlegasse; per hr Sfr10; 🕑 9am-midnight)

Medical Services

Bellevue Apotheke (☎ 044 252 56 00; Theaterstrasse 14) A 24-hour chemist.

Cantonal University Hospital (☎ 044 255 11 11; Rämistrasse 100) Casualty department.

Post

Main post office (☎ 044 296 21 11; Kasernenstrasse 95-97; 🕑 7.30am-8pm Mon-Fri, 8am-4pm Sat) There's a more convenient location at the main train station.

Tourist Information

Zürich tourist office (☎ 044 215 30 00; www.zurichtourism.ch; train station; 🕑 8.30am-8.30pm Mon-Fri, to 6.30pm Sat & Sun) Arranges hotels, car rentals and excursions.

SIGHTS

Many things to see and do in Zürich don't cost a cent. In addition to the sights listed here there are numerous art galleries.

Old Town

Allocate at least a couple of hours to explore the cobbled streets of the pedestrian-only old town lining both sides of the river. You never know what a turn down an intimate alleyway might reveal – perhaps a 16th-century guildhall, a tiny boutique, cosy café or maybe courtyards and fountains.

Elegant **Bahnhofstrasse** is simply perfect for window-shopping and affluent Züricher-watching. The bank vaults beneath the street are said to be crammed with gold and silver. Above ground, you'll find luxury shops selling the best Switzerland can offer – from watches and clocks to chocolates, furs, porcelain and fashion labels galore.

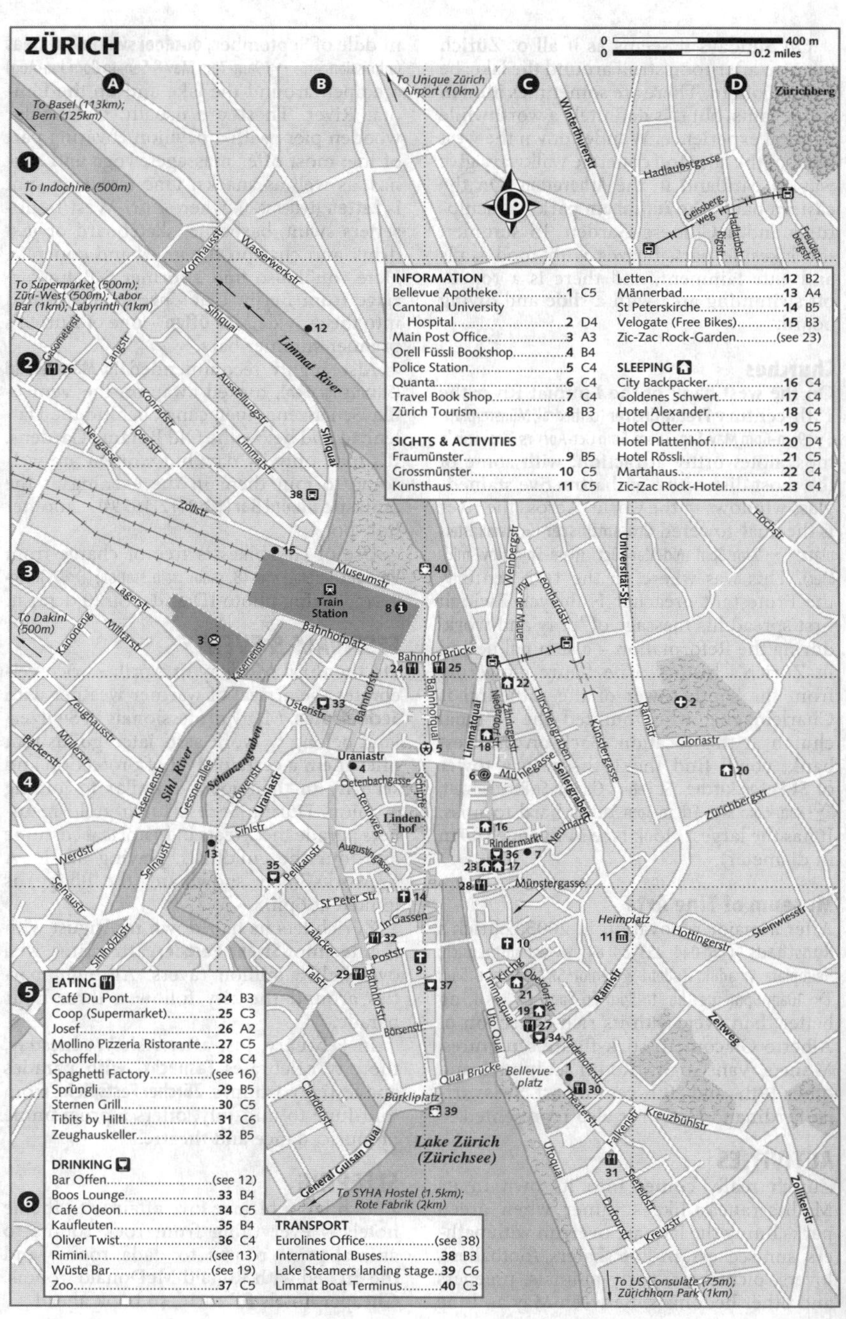

ZÜRICH
0 400 m
0 0.2 miles
A
B
C
D
1
2
3
4
5
6
To Basel (113km); Bern (125km)
To Indochine (500m)
To Unique Zürich Airport (10km)
To Supermarket (500m); Züri-West (500m); Labor Bar (1km); Labyrinth (1km)
To Dakini (500m)
To SYHA Hostel (1.5km); Rote Fabrik (2km)
To US Consulate (75m); Zürichhorn Park (1km)
Zürichberg
Limmat River
Sihl River
Lake Zürich (Zürichsee)
Train Station
Lindenhof
Bellevue-platz
Bürkliplatz
Heimplatz
Winterthurerstr
Hadlaubstgasse
Geissberg-weg
Hadlaubstr
Rigistr
Freudenbergstr
Wasserwerkstr
Kornhausstr
Sihlquai
Gasometerstr
Langstr
Konradstr
Josefstr
Neugasse
Ausstellungstr
Limmatstr
Zollstr
Museumstr
Lagerstr
Militärstr
Kanonengasse
Bahnhofplatz
Kasernenstr
Zeughausstr
Müllerstr
Bäckerstr
Usteristr
Bahnhofstr
Bahnhof Brücke
Bahnhofquai
Limmatquai
Niederdorfstr
Zähringerstr
Hirschengraben
Künstlergasse
Weinbergstr
Auf der Mauer
Leonhardstr
Universität-Str
Rämistr
Gloriastr
Zürichbergstr
Hochstr
Uraniastr
Oetenbachgasse
Rennweg
Schipfe
Mühlegasse
Seilergraben
Neumarkt
Rindermarkt
Münstergasse
Gessnerallee
Schanzengraben
Löwenstr
Sihlstr
Werdstr
Selnaustr
Sihlhölzlistr
Augustinergasse
Pelikanstr
St Peter Str
In Gassen
Talacker
Poststr
Talstr
Kirchg
Oberdorf str
Börsenstr
Utoquai
Quai Brücke
Stadelhoferstr
Theaterstr
Claridenstr
General Guisan Quai
Kreuzbühlstr
Falkenstr
Seefeldstr
Dufourstr
Kreuzstr
Zollikerstr
Hottingerstr
Steinwiesstr
Zeltweg
INFORMATION
Bellevue Apotheke 1 C5
Cantonal University Hospital 2 D4
Main Post Office 3 A3
Orell Füssli Bookshop 4 B4
Police Station 5 C4
Quanta 6 C4
Travel Book Shop 7 C4
Zürich Tourism 8 B3
SIGHTS & ACTIVITIES
Fraumünster 9 B5
Grossmünster 10 C5
Kunsthaus 11 C5
Letten 12 B2
Männerbad 13 A4
St Peterskirche 14 B5
Velogate (Free Bikes) 15 B3
Zic-Zac Rock-Garden (see 23)
SLEEPING
City Backpacker 16 C4
Goldenes Schwert 17 C4
Hotel Alexander 18 C4
Hotel Otter 19 C5
Hotel Plattenhof 20 D4
Hotel Rössli 21 C5
Martahaus 22 C4
Zic-Zac Rock-Hotel 23 C4
EATING
Café Du Pont 24 B3
Coop (Supermarket) 25 C3
Josef 26 A2
Mollino Pizzeria Ristorante 27 C5
Schoffel 28 C4
Spaghetti Factory (see 16)
Sprüngli 29 B5
Sternen Grill 30 C5
Tibits by Hiltl 31 C6
Zeughauskeller 32 B5
DRINKING
Bar Offen (see 12)
Boos Lounge 33 B4
Café Odeon 34 C5
Kaufleuten 35 B4
Oliver Twist 36 C4
Rimini (see 13)
Wüste Bar (see 19)
Zoo 37 C5
TRANSPORT
Eurolines Office (see 38)
International Buses 38 B3
Lake Steamers landing stage 39 C6
Limmat Boat Terminus 40 C3

On Sundays it seems as if all of Zürich takes an afternoon stroll around the lake; be sure to join in. There are sometimes human traffic jams, but it is definitely a worthwhile cultural experience. Wander down the west bank of the lake and concrete walkways give way to parkland in the **Arboretum**. On the eastern bank, the **Zürichhorn** park has sculptures and a Chinese Garden. In summer, the lakeside park buzzes with food stalls and entertainment, and there is a roped-off swimming area with a slide and diving board.

Churches

On the west bank of the Limmat River the 13th-century **Fraumünster** (cathedral; Münsterplatz; 9am-6pm May-Sep, 10am-5pm Oct-Apr) is Zürich's most noteworthy attraction, with some of the most distinctive and attractive stained-glass windows in the world. Across the river is the dual-towered **Grossmünster** (Grossmünsterplatz; 9am-6pm mid-Mar–Oct, 10am-5pm Nov–mid-Mar). This was where, in the 16th century, the Protestant preacher Huldrych Zwingli first spread his message of 'pray and work' during the Reformation – a seminal period in Zürich's history. The figure glowering from the south tower of the cathedral is Charlemagne, who founded the original church at this location. Back on the west bank, you'll find the 13th-century tower of **St Peterskirche** (St Peter's Church; St-Peterhofstatt; 8am-6pm Mon-Fri, to 3pm Sat) is hard to miss. It has the largest clock face in Europe (8.7m in diameter).

Museum of Fine Arts

After a major renovation in 2005, Zürich's **Kunsthaus** (044 253 84 84; www.kunsthaus.ch; Heimplatz 1; adult/student & senior Sfr12/7, free Sun; 10am-9pm Tue-Thu, to 5pm Fri-Sun) is looking better than ever, with its rich collection of Alberto Giacometti stick-figure sculptures, Monets, Van Goghs, Rodin sculptures and other 19th- and 20th-century art. Swiss artist Ferdinand Hodler is also represented.

ACTIVITIES

Zürich really comes into its own in its Mediterranean-like summer when green parks lining the lake are overrun with bathers, sun seekers, in-line skaters, footballers, lovers, picnickers, party animals, preeners and other hedonists. Between May and the middle of September, **outdoor swimming areas** (admission Sfr6; 9am-7pm May & Sep, to 8pm Jun-Aug) are open around the lake and up the Limmat River. These are usually rectangular wooden piers with a pavilion covering part of the; most offer massages, yoga and saunas, as well as snacks. One favourite spot is **Letten** (Lettensteg), where Züri-West trendsetters swim, barbecue, skateboard or just drink and chat on the grass and concrete. Here you'll also find a former S-Bahn carriage from Berlin that's been transformed into the crowded **Bar Offen** – one of Zürich's premier summer bars.

Also highly recommended is **Männerbad** (Schanzengraben), tucked away on the Venice-like Schanzengraben canal, behind the Hallenbad and below the Old Botanic Gardens. It's men-only by day; but women are welcome to join them in the evening at the fantastic **Rimini Bar** (044 211 95 94) – another hot spot.

Use of city bikes is free of charge from **Velogate** (platform 18, main train station; 7.30am-9.30pm). Bring photo ID and a Sfr20 deposit.

FESTIVALS & EVENTS

On the third Monday in April, Zürich celebrates the arrival of warmer weather with **Sechseläuten**. Many professionals in Switzerland belong to work-associated guilds that offer them a certain level of protection and security in their jobs – similar to joining a union. During Sechseläuten guild members parade the streets in historical costume and tour the guildhalls, playing music. A fireworks-filled 'snowman' (the Böögg) is ignited at 6pm.

Zürich lets its hair down in August with the techno **Street Parade**, attracting well over half a million ravers. All-night parties around the city follow a three-hour parade.

In February, just after Ash Wednesday, the city celebrates **Fasnacht**, with parades and festive costumes. **Zürcher Festspiele**, from mid-June to mid-July, offers a programme of music, dance and theatre.

SLEEPING

Zürich has a bizarre love affair with theme hotels – everything from rock rooms to animal-print rooms to dada rooms and the 'in bed with Ronald McDonald' rooms. Cheaper hotels fill early, so book ahead.

Budget

City Backpacker (☎ 044 251 90 15; www.city-backpacker.ch; Niederdorfstrasse 5; dm Sfr31, s/d Sfr66/92) You climb a hell of a lot of stairs to reach reception in this bustling favourite, but it's worth the trek. Smack in the middle of old town, the hostel offers sparkling dorms and doubles, self-catering kitchen and coin laundry. With lounge chairs and sky-scraping city views, the summer rooftop terrace is the best spot in Zürich to wind down at sunset with a few cold beers.

SYHA Hostel (☎ 043 399 78 00; www.youthhostel.ch; Mütschellenstrasse 114, Wollishofen; dm Sfr38, s/d Sfr99/116; 💻) Expensively overhauled in 2005, this huge hostel now features a swish reception/dining hall and sparkling modern bathrooms. Dorms remain quite small, though. Take tram 7 to Morgental or S-Bahn to Wollishofen.

Martahaus (☎ 044 251 45 50; www.martahaus.ch; Zähringerstrasse 36; dm Sfr 38, s/d Sfr115/150, with shared bathroom Sfr85/100) With 1970s black leather lounges in the spacious breakfast room–cum-lounge and a roof terrace, this is a fun, friendly place to stay. Other features include a bar, laundry and gym. Negatives include street noise and tiny, shared bathrooms.

Dakini (☎ 044 291 42 20; www.dakini.ch; Brauerstrasse 87; s/d from Sfr65/90; 💻) This relaxed B&B attracts a bohemian crowd of artists and performers, academics and trendy tourists who don't bat an eyelid at its location near the red-light district. Five bedrooms in two apartments share kitchen and bathroom. Take tram 8 to Bäckeranlange.

Midrange & Top End

Hotel Alexander (☎ 044 251 82 03; www.hotel-alexander.ch; Niederdorfstrasse 40; s/d from Sfr95/140; P ⛝) It's smack in the centre of old town, and the rooms are sparkling clean with polished floorboards, white walls and nice touches like chocolates on the pillows. The bathrooms stand out with huge showers and a Mediterranean tile motif. Breakfast is included, there's wi-fi and an attached takeaway spot to quell late night munchies.

Hotel Otter (☎ 044 251 22 07; www.wueste.ch; Oberdorfstrasse 7; s/d Sfr100/130) This flamboyantly quirky hotel is by far our favourite place to stay in town. The 17 rooms are each fantastically unique – one's a safari lodge, another a religious grotto, and then there's the Arabian-themed room. Not to be missed. The location, on fashionable Oberdorfstrasse, is very central, too.

Hotel Plattenhof (☎ 044 251 19 10; www.plattenhof.ch; Plattenstrasse 26; s/d from Sfr165/205; P) This place manages to be cool without looking pretentious. It features a youthful, vaguely Japanese style, with low beds and mood lighting in its newest rooms. Even the older rooms are stylishly minimalist. Take tram 6 to Platte.

Hotel Rössli (☎ 044 256 70 50; www.hotelroessli.ch; Rössligasse 7; s/d from Sfr180/210) There's a calming, ascetic quality to this boutique hotel with its white walls and furnishings only occasionally disrupted by greys, mint greens or pale blues. It also has an elegant bar.

Also recommended:

Goldenes Schwert (☎ 044 250 70 80; www.gayhotel.ch; Marktgasse 14; s/d from Sfr130/165) Gay hotel with some elaborately themed rooms; the top floor gets the least noise from the downstairs disco.

Zic-Zac Rock-Hotel & Zic-Zac Rock-Garden (☎ 044 261 21 81; www.ziczac.ch in German; Marktgasse 17; d Sfr160, with shared bathroom Sfr75/120; 💻) Novelty place featuring rock-star rooms in bold colours and an attached restaurant that is a slice of Americana in Switzerland (mains Sfr15 to Sfr25).

EATING

Zürich has a thriving café culture and hundreds of restaurants serving all types of local and international cuisine. A good place to start exploring is Niederdorfstrasse and the backstreets nearby, which are filled with wall-to-wall cafés, restaurants and bars of every description. Most restaurants stay open from early morning to late evening.

Restaurants

Spaghetti Factory (☎ 044 251 94 00; Niederdorfstrasse 5; pasta Sfr15-22) With a fun, buzzing atmosphere, this restaurant serves delicious bowls of its namesake dish (22 choices). The spaghetti with pesto sauce is delicious. The place often has long lines. Portions are just right.

Zeughauskeller (☎ 044 211 26 90; Bahnhofstrasse 28a; mains Sfr15-30) The menu at this huge, atmospheric beer hall offers 20 different kinds of sausages in eight languages, as well as numerous other Swiss specialities of carnivorous and vegetarian varieties.

Mollino Pizzeria Ristorante (☎ 044 261 01 17; Limmatquai 16; mains Sfr18-25) Head to this lively restaurant for mouth-watering pizzas, delicious cappuccino and exquisite lake views. Sit outside when it's warm, inside amid the cheery frescos when it's blustery.

Sprüngli (☎ 044 244 47 11; Bahnhofstrasse 21; chocolates from Sfr2, mains Sfr19-28) The mother of all chocolate shops, it's a Zürich legacy and must for chocoholics. Choose from a huge range of truffles and cakes from downstairs display cases, or mingle with the well-heeled crowd in the elegant 1st-floor tearooms for a rather special experience.

Café Du Pont (☎ 044 211 66 77; Beatenplatz 4; mains Sfr20-30) There's no question this is a kitschy spot that takes the movie scene a little overboard – all the entrées are named for classic films and TV screens periodically play previews. Still the cavernous place (think industrial) has a feisty vibe. The mostly American menu serves lots of Tex-Mex, pasta, burger and seafood dishes with better than average results. A favourite with the expat community, it's also a good (and noisy) spot to bring the family.

Josef (☎ 044 271 65 95; Gasometerstrasse 24; mains Sfr20-48) A Züri-West stalwart, Josef frequently changes it décor and Swiss-Italian menu, but always has a good wine list and remains constantly popular with the 'in' set, even if just for a drink.

Quick Eats

Cheap eats abound around the train station, especially in the underground Shopville. Niederdorfstrasse has a string of snack bars offering pizza, kebabs and Asian food for about Sfr9.

Sternen Grill (Bellevueplatz/Theatrestrasse 22; snacks Sfr5-8) This is the city's most famous – and busiest – sausage stand; just follow the crowds streaming in for a tasty grease fest.

Tibits by Hiltl (☎ 044 260 32 22; Seefeldstrasse 2; dishes per 100g Sfr3.70) Tibits is where with-it, health-conscious Zürchers head for a light bite when meeting friends. There's a tasty vegetarian buffet, as well as fresh fruit juices, coffees and cake.

Schoffel (☎ 044 261 20 70; Schoffelgasse 7; mains Sfr8-16) On weekend mornings, locals flock to this café for a leisurely coffee and newspaper read within the cheery yellow modern-art–filled walls. Soups, salads and big bowls of yogurt and fruit are on the menu.

DRINKING

Late-night pubs, clubs and discos clutter Niederdorfstrasse and adjoining streets. Zürich's former industrial area has become one of its hippest neighbourhoods: the much-vaunted 'Züri-West' quarter starts roughly west of the train station. Langstrasse, directly behind the station, is a minor red light district with loads of popular bars clustered along its side streets. Its safe to wander through, although you may be offered drugs or sex.

Wüste Bar (☎ 044 251 22 07; Oberdorfstrasse 7) One of our top choices, this small and groovy spot underneath the Otter Hotel has plush red seats and a cowhide bar. There's sometimes live music.

Oliver Twist (☎ 044 252 47 10; Rindermarkt 6) English-speakers gravitate towards this pub, which serves Irish, British, Australian and South African beers. It's a smoky, noisy place, often standing-room-only and somewhat of a meat market.

Café Odeon (☎ 044 251 16 50; Am Bellevue) Lenin and James Joyce once downed drinks at this swish, smoky bar with marble walls and chandeliers. Come for the Art Nouveau interior, but ignore the quite ordinary food.

Boos Lounge (Schweizergasse 6) This place was packed when we stopped by, and it was early on a Monday afternoon. Slick and modern, it's a top choice for an after-work cocktail amid mod red walls, multihued lighting and a disco ball.

ENTERTAINMENT

Züritipp is the city's events magazine, available around town and from the tourist office. Generally dress well and expect to pay Sfr15 to Sfr30 admission to enter Zürich's clubs.

Supermarket (☎ 044 440 20 05; www.supermarket.li; Geroldstrasse 17; admission from Sfr15) Zürich's number one club is smaller than the name suggests, but boasts three cosy lounge bars around the dance floor, a covered back courtyard and an interesting roster of DJs playing house music.

Indochine (☎ 044 448 11 11; www.club-indochine.ch; Limmatstrasse 275; from 10pm Thu-Sat) Models and rich kids mingle between the dimly lit fat Buddhas of this faux opium den. Zürich's equivalent to London's Chinawhite or Paris' Buddha Bar.

Labyrinth (☎ 044 440 59 80; Pfingstweidstrasse 70) Zürich's top gay club features half-naked pole-dancing narcissists flaunting their six packs and lots of eye-candy at the bar. Take tram 4 to Förrlibuckstrasse.

Kaufleuten (☎ 044 225 33 22; www.kaufleuten.com in German; Pelikanstrasse 18) A club with a long history and hot reputation at the top end of the market. Dress to impress, as everyone in here looks like they walked out of a model shoot or film set. The place boasts that Prince and Madonna were once guests. Tram 2 or 9 to Sihlstrasse will get you there.

Labor Bar (☎ 044 272 44 02; www.laborbar.ch; Schiffbaustrasse 3; from 10pm Fri & Sat, from 9pm Sun) The set for local celebrity Kurt Aeschbacher's TV show, this is the epitome of retro chic, with lots of Plexiglas and diffused coloured light. It's always filled with beautiful people; Friday is Celebreighties and Sunday 'for gays and friends'.

Rote Fabrik (☎ 044 481 91 43; www.rotefabrik.ch in German; Seestrasse 395) A long-standing Zürich institution, this club has managed to hold its own throughout the years. It stages everything from rock concerts to original-language films, theatre and dances, and has a bar and restaurant. Take bus 161 or 165 from Bürkliplatz.

GETTING THERE & AWAY

Unique Zürich airport (ZRH; ☎ 043 816 22 11; www.zurich-airport.com) is 10km north of the city centre. It's a small international hub with two terminals.

The N3 approaches Zürich from the south along the shore of Lake Zürich. The N1 is the fastest route from Bern and Basel and is the main entry point from the west.

There are direct trains to Stuttgart (Sfr61, three hours, daily), Munich (Sfr86, 4½ hours, daily), Innsbruck (Sfr66, four hours) and Milan (Sfr72, four hours, daily), as well as many other international destinations. There also are departures to most of the Swiss towns, including Lucerne (Sfr22, 50 minutes, hourly), Bern (Sfr48, 70 minutes, hourly) and Basel (Sfr32, 65 minutes, hourly).

GETTING AROUND

Trains make the 10-minute trip from the airport to the main train station (Sfr5.40) around every 10 minutes. Taxis cost around Sfr50.

There is a comprehensive, unified bus, tram and S-Bahn service in the city, which includes boats plying the Limmat River. Short trips under five stops are Sfr2.30. A 24-hour pass, including travel to and from the airport, is Sfr10.80. For unlimited travel within the canton, including extended tours of the lake, a day pass costs Sfr28.40, or Sfr20 after 9am (9-Uhr-Pass).

Lake steamers depart from Bürkliplatz from early April to late October (Swiss Pass and Eurail valid, Inter-Rail 50% discount). Taxis in Zürich are expensive, even by Swiss standards, at Sfr6 plus Sfr3.50 per kilometre.

CENTRAL SWITZERLAND & BERNER OBERLAND

Welcome to the fairy-tale Alpine creation they call the Berner Oberland, a region so silver-screen perfect that you'll think you have conjured it up. Pretending that you are James Bond in *On her Majesty's Secret Service* pursuing villains down the sheer face of the Schilthorn, kicking plumes of white fluffy powder up into a deep-water blue sky – that can't be real! Well, Mark Twain *did* once write that no opiate compared with walking through the Berner Oberland...but super-hero fantasies aside, it *is* real. Travelling through the Berner Oberland is a lot like having your cake and eating it too. Not only are you able to spend endless mesmerizing hours staring at the sheer, outrageous beauty of those snow-white, jagged, craggy, so-big-they're-going-to-swallow-you-whole mountains that are found everywhere, but you can also play in them.

In summer the region turns into a recreation of Heidi's turf – all sparkling mountain lakes and tinkling cowbells. Sleep in the hay in tiny Gimmelwald or go hiking around eye-catching Mürren. Thrill-seekers and backpackers congregate around Interlaken (although it's also got loads for all types of travellers), with a reputation for offering every adventure sport under the sun. When you have had your fill of outdoor adventures, spend some time in soul soothing Lucerne.

LUCERNE

pop 58,600

Lapped by a scenic lake and surrounded by mountains of myth, a picture of this once small fishing village and its wooden Kapellbrücke (Chapel Bridge) is enough to connote the very essence of Switzerland. One of Switzerland's major draw cards Lucerne is a collage of medieval bridges, old squares and watery vistas. Legend has it that an angel with a light showed Lucerne's first settlers where to build a chapel, and in good weather even an atheist might describe the city's location as heaven-sent.

Orientation & Information

The mostly pedestrian-only old town is on the northern bank of the Reuss River. The train station is centrally located on the southern bank. The **Internet Shop** (☎ 041 211 21 31; cnr Pilatustrasse & Seebrücke; per hr Sfr10; 🕑 9am-10pm Mon-Sat, to 8pm Sun) is across from the train station. Beside platform three is **Luzern tourist office** (☎ 041 227 17 17; www.luzern.org; Zentralstrasse 5; 🕑 8.30am-7.30pm Mon-Fri, 9am-7.30pm Sat & Sun Apr-Oct, to 6pm Nov-Mar).

Sights

If you plan to visit several of Lucerne's many museums, consider purchasing the Sfr29 Museum Pass, valid for one month. It lets you into all museums as often as you want.

OLD TOWN

Your first port of call should be the medieval old town with ancient rampart walls and towers, 15th-century buildings with painted façades and the two much-photographed covered bridges. **Kapellbrücke**, dating from 1333, is Lucerne's best-known landmark. It's famous for its distinctive water tower and the spectacular 1993 fire that nearly destroyed it. Though it has been rebuilt, fire damage is still obvious on the 17th-century pictorial panels under the roof. In better condition, but rather dark and dour, are the *Dance of Death* panels under the roofline of **Spreuerbrücke** (Spreuer Bridge).

PICASSO MUSEUM

You'll find yourself face-to-face with the artist at this **museum** (☎ 041 410 35 33; Furrengasse 21; adult/student Sfr8/6; 🕑 10am-6pm Apr-Oct, 11am-1pm & 2-4pm Nov-Mar). The main attraction is nearly 200 photographs by David Douglas Duncan that show an impish Picasso at work and play in his Cannes home during the last 17 years of his life. The intimate black-and-white photos also portray his muse, Jacqueline, and his children. Don't expect to find much of Picasso's own work, other than a few ceramics and sketches, however.

ROSENGART COLLECTION

By contrast, the **Sammlung Rosengart** (☎ 041 220 16 60; www.rosengart.ch; Pilatusstrasse 10; adult/student Sfr15/9, combined with Picasso Museum Sfr18/16; 🕑 10am-6m Apr-Oct, 11am-5pm Nov-Mar) *does* contain a significant amount of Picasso's art. Showcasing the works retained by Angela Rosengart, a Swiss art dealer and friend of Picasso's, its ground floor is entirely devoted to the Spanish master. In the basement, there's a selection of sketches and small paintings by Paul Klee; upstairs you'll find works by Cezanne, Kandinsky, Miró, Modigliani, and a fine handful of works by Marc Chagall.

VERKEHRSHAUS

Planes, trains and automobiles are the name of the game in the huge, family-oriented **Transport Museum** (☎ 041 370 44 44; Lidostrasse 5; adult/student/child Sfr24/22/10; 🕑 10am-6pm Apr-Oct, to 5pm Nov-Mar), east of the city centre, that's devoted to Switzerland's proud transport history. Space rockets, a communications display, simulators, a planetarium and an **IMAX theatre** (Sfr16 extra) all help make this Switzerland's most popular museum. For unrivalled views of the town and lake, take off 140m above the complex in the Hi-Flyer, a captive balloon you can ride for an extra Sfr20 (15 minutes' duration). Take bus 6, 8 or 24 from Bahnhofplatz.

Activities

If you're ready to face your fear factor contact **Outventure** (☎ 041 611 14 41; www.outventure.ch; Hansmatt 5, CH-6362, Stansstad), which has the usual adrenalin-junkie fixes on offer, including bungy jumping (Sfr160), tandem paragliding (Sfr150), canyoning (Sfr170) and glacier trekking (Sfr170). There's a daily shuttle from tourist office.

In addition there are options for scenic cruises on the lake, including aboard old-fashioned paddle steamers. Check out

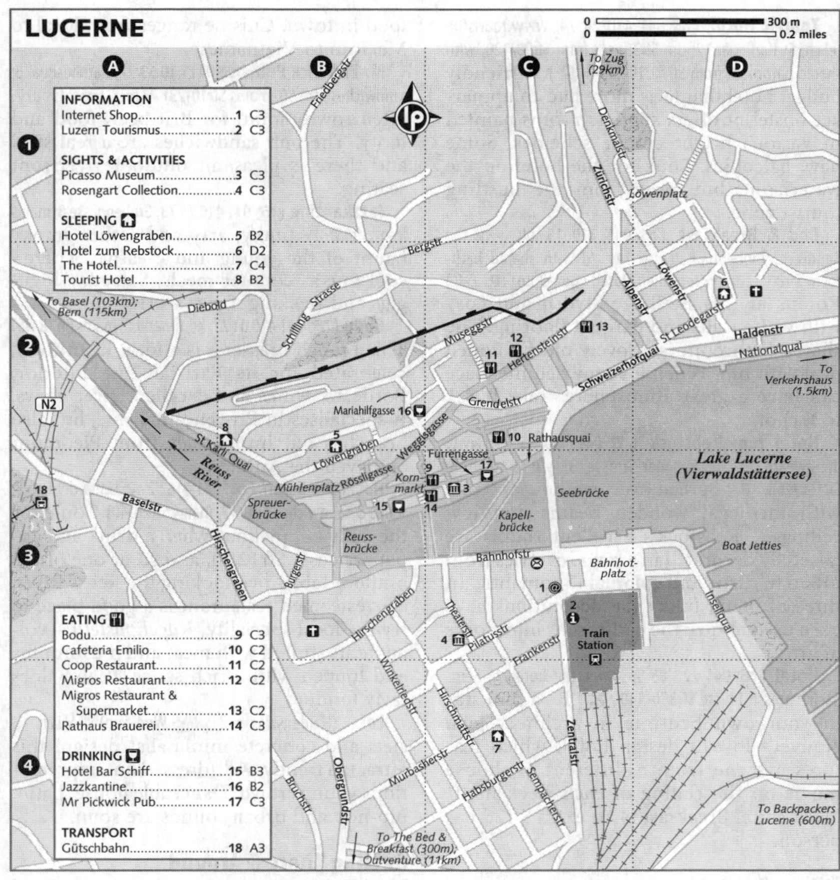

www.lakelucerne.ch (in German) for more information or stop by the tourist office.

Festivals & Events

Lucerne's six-day **Fasnacht** celebrations are more boisterous and fun than Basel's carnival. The party kicks off on 'Dirty Thursday' with the emergence of the character 'Fritschi' from a window in the town hall, when bands of musicians and revellers take to the streets. The carnival moves through raucous celebrations climaxing on Mardi Gras (Fat Tuesday), and is over on Ash Wednesday.

Sleeping

Lucerne has some great budget options, most of which are nicer than midrange places.

Backpackers Lucerne (☎ 041 360 04 20; www.backpackerslucerne.ch; Alpenquai 42; dm Sfr28, d Sfr66; reception 7-10am & 4-11pm) Backpackers love this lively, longtime favourite, with balconies overlooking the lake in a leafy spot. Clean and friendly, its facilities include kitchen and laundry. It's a 15-minute walk southeast of the train station.

Hotel Löwengraben (☎ 041 417 12 12; www.loewengraben.ch; Löwengraben 18; dm Sfr30, s/d from Sfr120/165; ⊠) In a converted prison with basic, whitewashed, 'cell-like' rooms and some fancier suites (albeit with bars on the windows), the hotel is good for novelty value. There's also a trendy bar and nightclub. In the winter, prices drop by about Sfr20.

Tourist Hotel (☎ 041 410 24 74; www.touristhotel.ch; St Karliquai 12; dm Sfr35, s/d from Sfr90/120, with shared bathroom from Sfr70/100; ⊠ 💻) A friendly budget hotel that feels more like an upmarket hostel, it offers spotless rooms painted in various bright colour schemes. Some have balconies. Look for the hotel on the waterfront, but away from the bustling tourist zone.

Bed & Breakfast (☎ 041 310 15 14; www.theBandB.ch; Taubenhausstrasse 34; s/d with shared bathroom Sfr80/120; ⏲ reception closed noon-3pm; P ⊠) Rooms at this B&B are stylish and cosy with white walls and parquet flooring. The shared bathroom is a lovely old-fashioned deal with tub. When it's crowded the place can have a great atmosphere. Take bus 1 to Eichof.

Hotel zum Rebstock (☎ 041 410 35 81; www.hereweare.ch; St Leodegar-Strasse 3; s/d & tr from Sfr160/260; P) Spread over two houses – one with medieval wooden beams and low ceilings – Rebstock's excellent rooms are tastefully decorated in a range of styles from urban to rustic and colonial to romantic. In three of them, funky tile decorations have been used to turn the bathrooms into works of art.

Hotel (☎ 041 226 86 86; www.the-hotel.ch; Sempacherstrasse 14; ste Sfr350-540; ❄) Be a film star in your own bedtime in architect Jean Nouvel's low-lit design hotel, which features a scene from a different art-house movie on the ceiling of each sleek matt-black suite. Breakfast is an extra Sfr25 per person.

Eating & Drinking

Many places in Lucerne double as bars and restaurants. Places open for breakfast and stay open until late in the evening. Self-caterers should head to Hertensteinstrasse, where cheap eats are plentiful. There's a Coop restaurant, two Migros restaurants and a supermarket.

Cafeteria Emilio (☎ 041 410 28 10; Ledergasse 8; mains Sfr6-14) You'll be rubbing shoulders with other diners at this tiny place, but it has a certain charm and you won't find cheaper pizzas, pastas and salads.

Rathaus Bräuerei (☎ 041 410 52 57; Unter der Egg 2; mains Sfr8-30) Sit outside by the water or inside amid the shiny copper beer tanks. This atmospheric restaurant serves big glasses of home brews and some of the most delicious food in town. Cuisine ranges from local to Mexican to Vietnamese.

Mr Pickwick Pub (☎ 041 410 59 27; Rathausquai 6; sandwiches Sfr6.50, mains Sfr10-23) Visit this lively, often rowdy joint, for Brit beer, food and footy. The pub sandwiches are a real steal and there is pleasamt outdoor riverfront seating.

Jazzkantine (☎ 041 410 73 73; Grabengasse 8; mains from Sfr15) A funky, arty and rather smoky haunt of the young and creative. There's cool music, counter meals, Saturday-night gigs and weeknight jazz workshops.

Bodu (☎ 041 410 01 77; Kornmarkt 5; mains Sfr18-45) This French brasserie is a local institution, celebrated for its Parisian-café interior, Bordeaux wines and excellent river views. It specialises in Provençal cuisine, but also branches out into dishes from Piedmont and even the Antilles.

Hotel Bar Schiff (☎ 041 418 52 52; Unter der Egg 8; soups & sandwiches Sfr8-12, mains Sfr20-40) Come for the daily happy hour when a drink and appetizer costs Sfr12.50, and sit at one of the outdoor tables overlooking the Reuss River. The esteemed restaurant is a good place to try the local speciality, *Kügelipastetli* – vol-au-vents stuffed with meat and mushrooms and topped with a rich sauce. It also does tasty fondue.

Loft (Haldenstrasse 21; ⏲ Wed-Sun) With a steel-and-concrete minimalist design, this attracts a trendy, well-dressed but unpretentious young crowd. Danceable house, Latin, hip-hop and urban sounds are spun.

Getting There & Around

The N2/E9 motorway, which connects Basel and Lugano, passes by Lucerne. The N14 is the road link to Zürich. Trains connect Lucerne to Bern (Sfr30, 1½ hours, hourly), Geneva (Sfr70, 3¼ hours, hourly), Interlaken (Sfr26, two hours, hourly), Lugano (Sfr56, 2½ hours) and Zürich (Sfr19, 50 minutes, hourly).

INTERLAKEN

pop 15,000

Flanked by the stunning Lakes Thun and Brienz, and within yodelling distance of the mighty peaks of the Jungfrau, Mönch and Eiger, is ever-popular Interlaken. It's a great base for exploring the delights of the Jungfrau region. As it caters to backpackers like nowhere else in Switzerland, many budget travellers make this their main stop in the country. Solo travellers looking to meet like-minded individuals will have a field day here. Interlaken also is a mecca for thrill seekers. Many a traveller leaves with a much lighter wallet after blowing mind-boggling amounts of cash on a range of white-knuckle, high-adrenalin sports. Most are not disappointed. If you're not into the backpacker scene, don't fear, the town is also home to a range of charming guesthouses and modern hotels.

Orientation & Information

Most of Interlaken lies between its two train stations, Interlaken Ost and West, which both offer bike rental and daily money-exchange facilities. The main shopping street, Höheweg, runs between the stations, and you can walk from one to the other in 20 minutes.

Near Interlaken West is the **main post office** (cnr Marktgasse & Höheweg) and **Interlaken tourist office** (☎ 033 826 53 00; www.interlakentourism.ch in German; Höheweg 37; 🕑 8am-6.30pm Mon-Fri, to 5pm Sat, 10am-noon & 4-6pm Sun Jul & Aug, 8am-noon & 1.30-6pm Mon-Fri, to noon Sat Sep-May).

Sights & Activities

EXTREME SPORTS

Interlaken is the world's second-biggest adventure sports destination, just behind New Zealand, and everything you can think of in this regard is offered from here (although the activities take place in the greater Jungfrau region). Options include skydiving (Sfr380); paragliding (Sfr150); night sledding past frozen waterfalls followed by a fondue dinner (Sfr95); skiing or snowboarding including transport, lift ticket and appropriate clothing and gear rental (Sfr165); and fly-in, drink a glass of champagne then hit the virgin powder glacier skiing (Sfr250). In summer there's canyoning, where you jump, slide and rappel down rocks and waterfalls (from Sfr125) and rafting on the class III–IV Lütschine River (Sfr95).

The vast majority of excursions occur without incident, but there's always a small risk of injury. Two tragically fatal accidents (canyoning in the Saxetet Gorge and bungee jumping off the Stechelberg-Mürren cable car) about five years ago fortunately have not been repeated, but it is always a good idea to ask about safety records and procedures.

Those without lots of cash should check out the hiking trails, all with signposts giving average walking times, that dot the area.

The major operators, each able to arrange most sports, include the following:

Alpin Center (☎ 033 823 55 23; www.alpincenter.ch; Hauptstrasse 16)

Alpin Raft (☎ 033 823 41 00; www.alpinraft.ch; Hauptstrasse 7)

Outdoor Interlaken (☎ 033 826 77 19; www.outdoor-interlaken.ch; Hauptstrasse 15)

Swissraft (☎ 033 823 02 10; www.swissraft.ch; Obere Jungfraustrasse 72)

MYSTERY PARK

For something a little less extreme (especially if you have the kids along) head to **Mystery Park** (☎ 033 827 57 57; Hauptstrasse 43; adult/child Sfr48/28; 🕑 10am-6pm). The latest brainchild of Erich von Däniken, the out-there author of the 1970s best-seller *Chariots of the Gods*, this theme park features replicas of Aztec pyramids and more space-aged buildings, where virtual reality/computer technology will invite you to consider Mr Däniken's theory that human beings descended from aliens.

Sleeping

Balmer's Herberge (☎ 033 822 19 61; www.balmers.ch; Hauptstrasse 23; dm Sfr27, s/d/q with shared bathroom Sfr33/76/132; 💻) Young Americans have flocked to this cosy Swiss chalet with a raucous summer-camp feel for more than 50 years – it's a great place to meet people and party. On the negative side you're locked out of your room (even the doubles) during the day, you'll be constantly harassed to partake in the adventure sports and the staff even charges you to use the kitchen. If you can resist the temptation to buy, however, it's a good deal.

River Lodge (☎ 033 822 44 34; www.riverlodge.ch; Brienzstrasse 24; dm from Sfr28, s/d Sfr62/84; 💻) Originally a camping area, this place was destroyed in the 2005 floods and rebuilt as a more upmarket joint, although a few dorms bed are available. River views are featured from each of the bungalows lining the waterfront, which house between one and four people in bunks. In summer the hosts encourage you to bring the feather

AUTHOR'S CHOICE

Hotel Lötschberg/Susi's B&B (☎ 033 822 25 45; www.lotschberg.ch; General Guisan Strasse 31; B&B s/d Sfr105/135, hotel s/d from Sfr120/165; P ☒) This place has received consistently positive reviews over its 100 years of continuous operation, for its personal service and friendly hosts. Rooms here are spotless, and each is individually and thoughtfully decorated with homemade art on the walls. The attached B&B offers the cheapest digs, although these are still quite comfortable. In the main house, rooms come in a variety of sizes. A few are quite small, so ask when booking if you're claustrophobic. If you can nab it, grab the attic 'honeymoon' room. It has a huge slanted window that boasts in-you-face mountain views. In summer the place gets really full, and the outdoor patio with sturdy wooden benches and tables is a great place to chill out and meet other travellers.

The hotel arranges quite a few activities for guests. 'Cooking with Fritz' (Sfr 30) is its latest endeavour. Well worth the price, the host teaches you how to make traditional Swiss fondue and *rösti* from scratch. Fritz also takes guests paragliding (Sfr130) and for night sledding and fondue (Sfr75). Both cost less than going through the in-town companies, but are only open to guests.

duvet outside and sleep under the stars by the water. A communal kitchen and bikes and kayaks for guests are extra perks.

Backpackers Villa Sonnenhof (☎ 033 826 71 71; www.villa.ch; Alpenstrasse 16; dm/d from Sfr33/98; reception 7.30-11am & 4-9pm, to 10pm Jun-Aug;) Widely regarded as the cleanest and most genteel of Interlaken's hostels, this place still has plenty going on – in the corner somewhere you're likely to find at least a few folks reliving their last skydive over pints of beer. Spacious, renovated rooms have nice touches such as steamer trunks and balconies, some with Jungfrau views. There's a small kitchen, a lounge and table tennis in the garden.

Funny Farm (☎ 079 652 61 27; www.funny-farm.ch; Hauptstrasse; dm Sfr35;) Another budget powerhouse, Funny Farm has a raucous feel and draws in hordes of Australians. It revels in its anarchic, ramshackle premises – somewhere halfway between a squat and an island shipwreck. There's a ramshackle house surrounded by makeshift bars and a swimming pool, but guests don't care; they're here for the party.

Hotel-Gasthof Hirschen (☎ 033 822 15 45; www.hirschen-interlaken.ch; Hauptstrasse 11; s/d from Sfr90/180) Following a Sfr400,000 renovation in 2004, this 16th-century heritage-listed Swiss chalet is enjoying a new lease of life. Rooms are now 'rustic modern', with parquet floors, bathroom pods and wireless LAN (local area network).

Victoria-Jungfrau Grand Hotel & Spa (☎ 033 828 28 28; www.victoria-jungfrau.ch; Höheweg 41; s/d Sfr510/620) The granddaddy of Interlaken hotels, the Victoria easily outclasses everything else in town. From its swanky lobby and pampering spa to its old-world rooms, this 1865 landmark is the last word in Swiss style.

Eating & Drinking

Balmer's has the town's hottest after-dark scene (especially when its club is open), with Funny Farm a close second, and guests rarely leave at night. Self-caterers can stock up on beer (and food) at the **Coop Pronto** (Höheweg 11).

Balmer's Café & Grill (☎ 033 822 1961; www.balmers.ch; Hauptstrasse 23; mains Sfr10-12) The American-style food (think big juicy burgers and greasy fries) served here is quite good and fairly priced, making it an option even if you're not staying at the hostel. The lounge-like atmosphere with wooden tables and a roaring fire is appealing. There's local beer on tap and fondue for Sfr16 per person. The downstairs club, Metro Bar, rocks the house Sunday through Wednesday nights. It gets going after 11pm.

Per Bacco (☎ 033 822 97 92; Rugenparkstrasse 2; mains Sfr12-15; 9am-1am Mon-Sat) With a quaint wine-cellar feel, this sophisticated place has a sophisticated wine list to match. It tends to attract a well-dressed older crowd, but anyone looking for cosy atmosphere, good wine and hearty bowls of yummy pasta won't be disappointed.

Des Alpes (☎ 033 822 2323; Höeweg 115; mains Sfr12-25) With priceless Jungfrau sunset views, this restaurant is deservedly popular. If the weather is clear at least pop in for a coffee or cocktail. The food is good too, with a variety of Swiss dishes and meat fondue.

Top o'Met (☎ 033 828 66 66; 18th fl, Metropole Hotel, Höheweg 37; buffet from Sfr10.50, mains from Sfr18) Sip on a cocktail and enjoy the sweeping mountain views. Or stop by for an ice-cream sundae, meal or coffee during the day.

Bären (☎ 033 822 7676; Marktgasse 19; mains from Sfr20) *Rösti* and Bratwurst are the house specialities at this locally recommended restaurant. It also does very good fondue, salads with homemade dressing and other delicious Swiss dishes. Sit outside when it's warm.

Golder Anker (☎ 033 822 16; Marktgasse 57; mains Sfr20-40) The junkie, the banker, the tourist and the hotel proprietor – meet them all at the Golder Anker. Rebuilt after the 2005 floods, this well-respected establishment serves interesting dishes, ranging from chicken fajitas and red snapper to ostrich steaks. It also has a roster of live bands and international artists.

Getting There & Away

Main roads go east to Lucerne and west to Bern, but the only way south for vehicles, without a detour around the mountains, is the car-carrying train from Kandersteg, south of Spiez. Trains to Grindelwald (Sfr9.80, 40 minutes, hourly), Lauterbrunen (Sfr8, 20 minutes, hourly) and Lucerne (Sfr30, two hours, hourly) depart from Interlaken Ost. Trains to Brig (Sfr40, 1½ hours, hourly) and Montreux via Bern (Sfr92, two hours, hourly) leave from either Interlaken West or Ost.

JUNGFRAU REGION

Dominated by the famous Eiger, Mönch and Jungfrau (Ogre, Monk and Virgin) mountains, the Jungrfrau Region boasts the country's highest density of dramatic scenery. In winter, the Jungfrau is a magnet for skiers and snowboarders, with 200km of pistes. A one-day ski pass for Kleine Scheidegg-Männlichen, Grindelwald-First, or Mürren-Schilthorn costs Sfr56.

The Lauterbrunnen Valley branches out from Interlaken with sheer rock faces and towering mountains on either side, attracting an army of hikers and mountain bikers. Cowbells echo in the valley and every house and hostel has a postcard-worthy view. Many visitors choose to visit this valley on a day trip from Interlaken.

Grindelwald

Picturesque Grindelwald was once a simple farming village. Today it's the largest ski resort in the Jungfrau, nestled in a valley under the north face of the Eiger.

Grindelwald tourist office (☎ 033 854 12 12; www.grindelwald.ch in German; 🕑 8am-7pm Mon-Fri, to 6pm Sat, 9am-noon & 2-5pm Sun Jul-Sep, shorter hr & closed Sun btwn seasons) is located in the centre at the Sportzentrum, 200m from the train station.

The First is the main **skiing** area in winter, with runs stretching from **Oberjoch** at 2486m to the village at 1050m. In the summer it caters to **hikers** with 90km of trails about 1200m, 48km of which are open year-round. You can catch the longest **cable car** in Europe from Grindelwald-Grund to Männlichen, where there are more extraordinary views and hikes (one way/return Sfr29/46).

The cosy wooden chalet housing the excellent **SYHA hostel** (☎ 033 853 10 09; www.youthhostel.ch/grindelwald; Terrassenweg; dm from Sfr31, d from Sfr76; 🕑 reception from 3.30pm Mon-Sat, from 5pm Sun) is perched high on a ridge with magnificent views. Avoid the 20-minute slog from the train station by taking the Terrassenweg-bound bus to the Gaggi Säge stop. The hostel closes between seasons.

Near the Männlichen cable-car station, the modern **Mountain Hostel** (☎ 033 854 3838; www.mountainhostel.ch; dm/d with shared bathroom from Sfr35/88; Ⓟ) is a good base for sports junkies. Cyclists are especially welcomed. Rates include free ice-skating and swimming at a nearby facility.

The **Residence** (☎ 033 854 55 55; www.residence-grindelwald.ch; s/d from Sfr90/150; Ⓟ ⊠) is in quiet location on the eastern side of the village. Family-run, cosy and modern it has a terrace restaurant and allows you free access to a nearby hotel's swimming pool. There's a terrace restaurant overlooking the Wetterhorn.

On the way out of town, **Onkel Tom's Hütte** (☎ 033 853 52 39; Im Graben 4; pizzas Sfr13-30; 🕑 4-10.30pm Tue, noon-2pm & 4pm-midnight Wed-Sun) is an atmospheric place serving good pizzas in three sizes (to suit any appetite). It's very popular and usually requires a wait.

For steaks, sandwiches and burgers along with good views, try **Memory** (☎ 033 854 31 31; mains Sfr15-25) inside the Eiger Hotel. It also does tasty *rösti* and fondue.

Self-caterers can stock up at Coop supermarket opposite the tourist office.

The village is easily reached by road. There is a train to Interlaken Ost (Sfr9.40, 40 minutes, hourly).

Lauterbrunnen

Tiny Lauterbrunnen, with its attractive main street cluttered with Swiss chalet architecture, is friendly and down-to-earth. It's known largely for the impressive **Trümmelbach Falls** (admission Sfr10; 9am-5pm Apr-Nov), 4km out of town, where, inside the mountain, up to 20,000L of water per second corkscrews through a series of ravines and potholes shaped by the swirling waters. A bus from the train station (Sfr3) takes you to the falls.

Camping Jungfrau (☎ 033 856 20 10; adult/tent Sfr9/6, cabins per person Sfr25), at the end of Main St, has excellent facilities and awesome views of towering peaks and sheer cliffs.

Just a two-minute walk from the train station, the **Valley Hostel** (☎ 033 855 20 08; www.valleyhostel.ch; dm/d from Sfr18/44; P) offers up comfy rooms (many of them have balconies), a communal kitchen and a mellow environment.

When it comes to culinary matters, Lauterbrunnen has few options. Stock up at the Coop near the tourist office, or try the restaurant at the **Hotel Oberland** (☎ 033 855 12 41; Main St; mains from Sfr17). It has a big menu of *rösti*, pasta and salads.

Gimmelwald

Decades ago an anonymous backpacker scribbled these words in the Mountain Hostel's guest book: 'If heaven isn't what it's cracked up to be, send me back to Gimmelwald.' Enough said. When the sun is out in Gimmelwald, the place will take your breath away. Once a secret bolthole for hikers and adventurers looking to escape the region's worst tourist excesses, tiny Gimmelwald is seeing a lot more foot traffic these days. But even increasing crowds can't diminish its scintillating, textbook Swiss scenery and charm.

The hamlet is particularly enchanting in winter, when weathered wooden chalets peep out from a thick blanket of snow and the mountains feel close enough to touch.

After a long summer hike, bed down in the barn at **Esther's Guesthouse** (☎ 033 855 54 88; www.esthersguesthouse.ch; barn accommodation Sfr22, s/d with shared bathroom Sfr40/80). Offered June to October, sleeping in the straw is surprisingly comfortable. A generous breakfast of organic food and a shower are included. If you'd rather not roll in the hay, there are lovely rooms in the main house (the place was expanding when we stopped by). If you can't stay, stop in to pick up homemade beef jerky (some of the best we've ever tasted), cheeses and other organic products.

The **Mountain Hostel** (☎ 033 855 17 04; www.mountainhostel.com; dm Sfr23;) recently added an outdoor hot tub, so now you can *literally* soak up their jaw-dropping mountain views. The simple, rustic place does snacks and sells beer, and the super-friendly owners have loads of area tips.

Restaurant-Pension Gimmelwald (☎ 033 855 17 30; mains Sfr18) has hearty cooking, including fondue and farmers' barley soup. Don't miss the 'Gimmelwalder Horse-Shit Balls' for Sfr4. You'll have to visit to find out what they're made from.

To reach Gimmelwald hike up a steep trail (it's sometimes closed in winter due to avalanche danger) for about an hour and a half from Stechelberg or get a lift on the cable car (one way Sfr8). A great way to get to Stechelberg from Lauterbrunnen is to hike along a flat path for about 1½ hours. The trail passes through dramatic scenery. From Mürren, Gimmelwald is a pleasant 40-minute walk downhill, or catch the cable car (one way Sfr8).

Mürren

Arrive in Mürren on a clear evening, when the sun hangs low on the horizon, and you'll think you've died and gone to heaven. The peaks feel so close you're sure you can touch them, and staring slack-jawed at the towering masses of rock (some of the best views in the region) could be considered an activity in itself.

In summer, the **Allmendhubel funicular** (one way/return Sfr12/7.40) takes you above Mürren to a panoramic restaurant. From here, you can set out on many hikes, including

SWITZERLAND

the famous **Northface Trail** (2½ hours), via Schiltalp to the west, which offers outstanding views across the Lauterbrunnen valley. There's also an easier **Children's Adventure Trail** (one hour).

Sleeping options within Mürren include **Eiger Guesthouse** (☎ 033 856 54 60; eigerguesthouse@muerren.ch; dm from Sfr50, d with shared bathroom Sfr120), by the train station, which has a bar, restaurant and games room. There's also **Hotel Edelweiss** (☎ 033 855 13 12; edelweiss@muerren.ch; s/d Sfr95/190), which is perched right on the edge of a cliff and has vertiginous views, particularly through the large windows of its lounge and indoor restaurant. Try for a room with a balcony.

Tham's Snacks & Drinks (☎ 033 856 01 10; mains Sfr15-28; noon-9pm Jul & Aug) serves Thai, Singaporean, Malaysian and other Asian dishes cooked by a former five-star chef who's literally taken to the hills to escape the rat race. Tham's keeps irregular hours during the low season, so call ahead. Try the Hotel Blumental's rustic **Restaurant La Grotte** (☎ 033 855 18 26; mains Sfr16.50-35) for highly regarded fondues and flambés, although it's becoming slightly touristy in summer. Both it and Tham's are along the lower main thoroughfare.

One of the best parts about Mürren is getting there. From Lauterbrunnen take a cable car to Grütschalp, then switch to the train (Sfr9.40 total). The ride yields tremendous unfolding views across the valley to the Jungfrau, Mönch and Eiger peaks.

Schilthorn

There's a fantastic 360-degree panorama from the 2970m **Schilthorn** (www.schilthorn.ch) one that's possibly even better than from Jungfraujoch. On a good day, you can see from Titlis around to Mont Blanc, and across to the German Black Forest. Yet, some visitors seem more preoccupied with practising their delivery of the line, 'The name's Bond, James Bond', than taking in the 200 or so mountains. That's because a few scenes from *On Her Majesty's Secret Service* were shot here in late 1968/early 1969. You can watch them on a 180-degree panoramic screen at the free **Touristorama** in the cable car building.

The revolving **Piz Gloria Restaurant** (mains Sfr15-35) is really quite amazing. The food (pasta, burgers, etc) is reasonably priced; and the views come with million-dollar smiles.

In winter there is a gnarly but heavenly **ski run** down to Mürren. You will need to be a pretty advanced rider to try it – it's long and steep and the moguls can be massive. If you know what you are doing, however, you will have a blast – think deep powder and places to catch lots of air. A day pass to Schilthorn-Mürren costs Sfr65 (you won't have to pay again for the cable cars).

If you are not skiing, you will need a Sfr115 excursion trip (Half-Fare Card and Swiss Pass, 50% off, Eurail Pass 25%) going to Lauterbrunnen, Grütschalp, Mürren, Schilthorn and returning through Stechelberg to Interlaken. A return from Lauterbrunnen (via Grütschalp), and Mürren costs about Sfr100, as does the journey up and back via the Stechelberg cable car.

Jungfraujoch

The train trip to Jungfraujoch (3454m) is touristy and expensive, but you do it anyway because (a) it's generally an once-in-a-lifetime experience and (b) you have to see it for yourself. Plus, there is a reason why about two million people a year visit this, the highest train station in Europe. On a clear day the outlook is indisputably spectacular. Good weather is essential so call ☎ 033 855 10 22 for taped forecasts in multiple languages before leaving.

From Interlaken Ost the journey is 2½ hours each way (Sfr169 return). Trains go via Grindelwald or Lauterbrunnen to Kleine Scheidegg. From here the line is less than 10km long but took 16 years to build. Opened in 1912, the track powers through both the Eiger and the Mönch, pausing briefly for travellers to take happy snaps of views from two windows blasted in the mountainside, before terminating at Jungfraujoch.

There's a cheaper 'good morning ticket' of Sfr145 if you can drag yourself out of bed for the early train (6.35am from Interlaken) and leave the summit by noon. From 1 November to 30 April the discount applies to the 6.35am and 7.35am trains, and there's no noon restriction. Eurail pass-holders get 25% off, Swiss Pass holders slightly more.

NORTHERN SWITZERLAND

This region is left off most people's Switzerland itineraries, which is why you should visit. Sure, it is known for industry and commerce, but it also has some great attractions. Breathe in the sweet (okay slightly stinky) odours of black-and-white cows as you roll through the bucolic countryside. Take time to explore the tiny rural towns set among green rolling hills and on Lake Constance (Bodensee) and the Rhine River on the German border.

BASEL

pop 161,800

Visit Basel in the summer. Strangely, given its northerly location, the city has some of the hottest weather in the country. When the mercury starts rising the city sheds its notorious reserve and just cuts loose. As locals bob along in the fast-moving Rhine (Rhein) River, cool off in the city's numerous fountains, whiz by on motor scooters and dine and drink on overcrowded pavements, you could almost be in Italy, rather than on the dual border with France and Germany.

Basel's (Bâle in French) idyllic old town and many enticing galleries and museums are top draws at any time of year. The famous Renaissance humanist, Erasmus of Rotterdam, was associated with the city and his tomb rests in the cathedral.

Orientation & Information

The pedestrian-only old town and most popular sights are all on the south bank in Grossbasel (Greater Basel). **Internet Pub** (☎ 084 489 19 91; Steinentorstrasse 11; per hr Sfr8; 🕑 9am-10pm Mon-Thu, to 8pm Fri, to 5pm Sat) is a smoky joint where you can down a beer and surf the Web. The **main post office** (Rudengasse 1; 🕑 7.30am-6.30pm Mon-Fri, 8am-noon Sat) is in the city centre. The **main tourist office** (☎ 061 268 68 68; www.baseltourismus.ch; Stadtcasino, Barfüsserplatz; 🕑 8.30am-6pm Mon-Fri, 10am-5pm Sat, 10am-4pm Sun) is at this address until 2007; afterwards check the website for new office location. There is another branch of the **tourist office** (☎ 061 268 68 68; 🕑 8.30am-6.30pm Mon-Fri, 9am-2pm Sat & Sun) at the train station.

Sights & Activities

With its cobbled streets, colourful fountains, medieval churches and stately buildings, the old town is a wonderful place to wander. In Marktplatz check out the impressive rust-coloured **Rathaus** (town hall), with frescoed courtyard. The 12th-century **Münster** (cathedral), southeast from Marktplatz, is another highlight, with Gothic spires and Romanesque St Gallus doorway.

Theaterplatz is a crowd-pleaser, with a curious **fountain**, designed by Swiss sculptor Jean Tinguely. His madcap scrap-metal machines perform a peculiar water dance, delighting children and weary travellers alike. Also check out the 700-year-old **Spalentor** gate tower, a remnant of the town's old city walls, with a massive portal and grotesque gargoyles.

Art lovers should head to the **Kunstmuseum** (☎ 061 206 62 62; www.kunstmuseumbasel.ch; St Albangraben 16; adult/student Sfr10/5, free 1st Sun of month; 🕑 10am-5pm Tue-Sun). It holds the largest art collection in Switzerland, including works by Klee and Picasso.

Of the private Swiss art collections made public, Hildy and Ernst Beyeler's is probably the most astounding. In the **Beyeler Collection** (☎ 061 645 97 00; www.beyeler.com; Baselstrasse 101; adult/student/child under 10 Sfr21/12/free; 🕑 10am-6pm Thu-Tue, to 8pm Wed) the quality of the 19th- and 20th-century paintings is matched only by the way Miró and Max Ernst sculptures are juxtaposed with similar tribal figures. All are fabulously displayed in Italian architect Renzo Piano's open-plan building. Take tram 6 to Riehen.

Festivals & Events

Basel makes much of its huge **Fasnacht** spring carnival, even though many people prefer Lucerne's exuberant celebrations. The festival kicks off at 4am exactly on the Monday after Ash Wednesday with the **Morgestraich**. The streetlights are suddenly extinguished and the large procession starts to wend its way through the central district. Participants wear elaborate costumes and masks, restaurants and bars stay open all night and the streets are packed with revellers. The main parades are on the Monday and Wednesday afternoons, with Tuesday afternoon reserved for the children's parade.

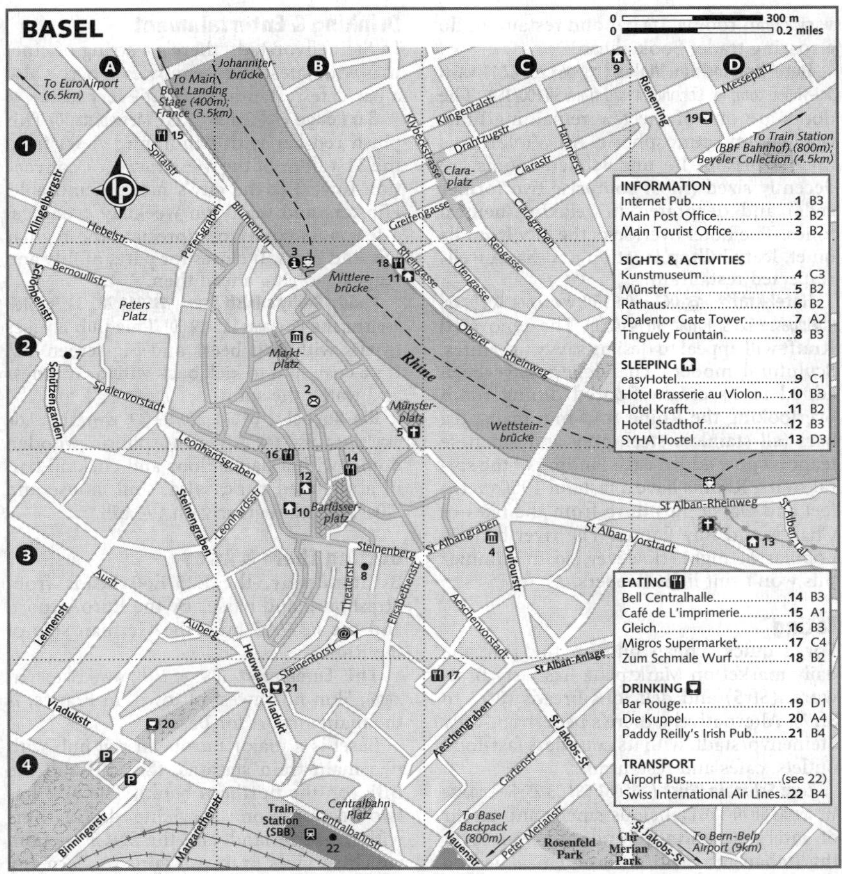

Sleeping

Hotels are often full during Basel's numerous trade fairs and conventions, so book ahead.

easyHotel (www.easyhotel.com; Riehenring 109; r from Sfr30; ⊠) What's plastic and orange and cheap all over? Yep, after the no-frills airline easyJet, here's the second instalment in Stelios Haji-Ioannou's hotel empire. Rooms are functional, clean, modern and, if not especially aesthetically appealing, slightly better than in the London outlet. Variable pricing sees costs rise at busy times (up to Sfr140 when we looked, but could go above that). Book well ahead, and if possible get a room with air-conditioning so you won't have to open a window on to the noisy street.

Basel Backpack (☎ 061 333 00 37; www.baselback pack.ch; Dornacherstrasse 192; dm Sfr31, s/d/f Sfr80/96/144; ⊠ 💻) This friendly independent hostel in a converted factory building has cheerful, colour-coded eight-bed dorms and more sedate doubles and family rooms. Breakfast is extra.

SYHA hostel (☎ 061 278 97 39; www.youthhos tel.ch/basel; St Alban Kirchrain 10; dm Sfr35, s/d from Sfr80/82; Ⓟ 💻) This is the older of the two official hostels in town, less conveniently but more attractively located in a quiet, leafy spot.

Hotel Stadthof (☎ 061 261 87 11; www.stadthof .ch; Gerbergasse 84; s/d with shared bathroom Sfr80/120; ⊠) Tucked into a corner of buzzing Barfüsserplatz, this hotel has rudimentary but very clean rooms. Its bar and restaurant do a roaring trade. Book ahead.

Hotel Brasserie au Violon (☎ 061 269 87 11; www.au-violon.com; Im Lohnhof 4; s/d from Sfr100/150) The doors are one of the few remaining hints that quaint, atmospheric Au Violon was once a prison. Its understated rooms are decently sized (most comprise two former cells) and decorated in relaxing neutral tones. The hotel overlooks the city from its quiet, leafy hilltop location and has a well-respected restaurant.

Hotel Krafft (☎ 061 690 91 30; www.hotelkrafft.ch; Rheingasse 12; s/d from Sfr145/230) The renovated Krafft will appeal to design-savvy urbanites. Sculptural modern chandeliers have been added to its creaky-floored dining room overlooking the Rhine, and minimalist tea bars (all stainless steel, grey and Japanese teapots) now adorn each landing of the spiral stairs. Rooms have a tasteful 1950s retro feel and classic furniture from the likes of Charles and Ray Eames. The river bank is popular at night, however, so in summer this won't suit light sleepers.

Eating

For a quick, cheap bite on the run, the daily market on Marktplatz has tasty Bratwurst (Sfr5) and delicious breads (Sfr3 to Sfr7). Alternatively, there's pedestrian-only Steinenvorstadt, with its countless fast-food outlets, cafés and restaurants.

Zum Schmale Wurf (☎ 061 683 33 25; Rheingasse 10; mains Sfr10-30) Delicious smells and an air of intergenerational bonhomie waft over this Italian antipasto, pasta and meat heaven on the river. Lunch menus (Sfr18.50) occasionally branch out into global cuisine, with *merguez* (French spicy beef) sausages or jambalaya.

Café de L'imprimerie (☎ 061 262 36 06; St Johanns Vorstadt 19; 2-course menu Sfr14.50-16.50) An unpretentious bistro offering filling meals at affordable prices; locals like to lounge over pints at the sturdy wood tables.

Gleich (☎ 061 261 48 83; Leonhardsberg 1; mains Sfr18) Anticarnivores cherish the large vegetarian menu and minimalist décor at this longtime favourite haunt.

For self-caterers, there's the local **Migros** (Sternengasse 17). Or for a huge selection of organic local produce (including 200 different cheeses) try the **Bell Centralhalle** (cnr Streitgasse & Weisse Gasse).

Drinking & Entertainment

In Steinenvorstadt, there's a string of cinemas with latest-release movies. There's also a bar/café/restaurant to suit every taste.

Bar Rouge (☎ 061 361 30 31; Messeplatz 10) This plush red bar with panoramic views from the 31st floor of the *Messeturm* (or convention tower) is the city's most memorable. Hipsters and (early on weekday evenings) a few suits come to appreciate the regular DJs and films. It closes for parts of July and August, so ring ahead then.

Paddy Reilly's Irish Pub (☎ 061 281 33 36; Steinentorstrasse 45; mains Sfr5-12.50) This pub entices expats with Brit beers and big-screen TV. It's a cosy spot to kick back with a Guinness and watch the sport.

Die Kuppel (☎ 061 270 99 39; www.kuppel.ch; Binningerstrasse 14) An atmospheric wooden dome, with a dance floor and cocktail bar, in a secluded park; salsa, soul, house and '70s/'80s are regularly on the bill.

Getting There & Away

By motorway, the E25/E60 heads from Strasbourg and passes by the EuroAirport, and the E35/A5 hugs the German side of the Rhine.

The **EuroAirport** (BSL or MLH; www.euroairport.com), 5km northwest of town, in France, is the main airport for Basel.

Basel is a major European rail hub with two main train stations, the SBB and the BBF (on the northern bank). The SBB has two sections, one servicing destinations within Switzerland, and the SNCF section, which services France. Trains to Germany leave from the BBF station.

Destinations include Paris (Sfr69, five hours, seven times daily). Local trains to the Black Forest stop only at BBF, though fast EC services stop at SBB, too. Main destinations along this route are Amsterdam (Sfr180, eight hours, daily), Frankfurt (Sfr80, three hours, daily) and Hamburg (Sfr198, 6½ hours, daily). Services within Switzerland leave from SBB. There are fast trains to Geneva (Sfr71, three hours, twice hourly) and Zürich (Sfr30, 70 minutes, twice hourly).

Getting Around

For the EuroAirport catch bus No 50 from in front of the SBB Station (Sfr6.60). City buses and trams run every six to 10 minutes

(Sfr1.80 for four or fewer stops, Sfr2.80 for central zone, or Sfr8 for a day pass). By the SBB station is a hut offering free bike loans in summer.

SCHAFFHAUSEN

pop 32,900

On the northern bank of the Rhine, Schaffhausen has a quaint medieval old town, filled with beautiful oriel windows, painted façades and ornamental fountains. It's a pleasant day trip from Zürich.

Schaffhausen tourist office (☎ 052 625 51 41; tourist@swissworld.com; Fronwagturm; 9am-5pm Mon-Fri, 10am-noon Sat, to 4pm Sat & 10am-1pm Sun Jun-Aug) is in the heart of the old town.

The best views around are found at the 16th-century hilltop **Munot fortress** (admission free; 8am-10pm May-Sep, 9am-5pm Oct-Apr). The summit is a 15-minute walk from the centre of town. **Rheinfall** (Rhine Falls) is a 40-minute stroll westward along the river, or take bus 1 to Neuhausen. Though the drop is only 23m, the waterfall is considered the largest in Europe, with an extraordinary amount of water thundering over it. The 45km of the Rhine from Schaffhausen to Constance is one of the river's most stunning stretches. It passes by meadows, castles and ancient villages, including **Stein am Rhein**, 20km to the east, where you could easily wear out your camera snapping pictures of the buildings in the picture-perfect Rathausplatz.

The **SYHA hostel** (☎ 052 625 88 00; fax 052 624 59 54; Randenstrasse 65; dm Sfr24; Mar-Oct) is in an impressive 16th-century former manor house (although the place does smell a bit musty). Take bus No 3 to Breite. The **Fischerzunft** (☎ 052 632 05 05; www.fischerzunft.ch; Bahnhofstrasse 46; s/d from Sfr142/215), one of Switzerland's most opulent hotels away from the big city, has a subtle Oriental theme, with printed silks in the bedrooms and a sinfully expensive restaurant (menus up to Sfr265!).

Check out **Fass-Beiz** (☎ 052 625 46 10; Webergasse 13; dishes Sfr7.50-25) for food and drinks. An alternative bar-café, it has a laid-back atmosphere and serves tasty sit-down dishes with an excellent vegetarian selection. There are music gigs and theatre performances in the cellar below.

Schaffhausen has good roads in all directions. Trains run to Zürich (Sfr17.20, 50 minutes, hourly).

APPENZELLERLAND

Just as Tasmania is to Australians and Appalachia to Americans, Appenzellerland is the butt of many a Swiss joke – its people the country's bumpkins, reputedly slow on the uptake. The roots of this backward reputation are fairly easy to divine. To use just one example, Innerhoden, one of the two semicantons that make up Appenzellerland, unusually still holds a yearly open-air parliament and it didn't permit women to vote until 1991. Even then, the Supreme Court had to intervene.

In a general sense, however, many foreigner visitors find the Appenzellers' devotion to rural tradition immensely charming and just what they expected from Switzerland. Appenzellerland has beautiful villages, mostly untouched by modern times. Life moves along at an enviably relaxed pace – the contented locals may know more than they are credited with.

The pastel hued village of **Appenzell** is a feast both for the eyes and the stomach. Behind the highly decorative façades of its traditional Swiss buildings lie numerous cafés, confiseries, cheese shops, delicatessens, butchers and restaurants all offering local specialities. (Inevitably, given Appenzell's popularity with guided bus tours, there are plenty of shops selling tacky trinkets, too.)

It's suitable for lunch and a wander on a Sunday afternoon, or you could come for longer and explore the surrounding hills. Whichever you choose, remember to come hungry and with enough space in your luggage for chocolate, cheese and alcoholic souvenirs.

The train station is 400m from the town centre. The **tourist office** (☎ 071 788 96 41; www.appenzellerland.ch in German; Hauptgasse; 8am-noon & 2-5pm Mon-Fri, 9am-noon & 2-4pm Sat) is in the centre.

Gasthaus Traube (☎ 071 787 14 07; www.hotel-traube.ch; s Sfr85-110, d Sfr150-180; closed Feb) is the most charming place to sleep in town (look for it just off Landsgemeindeplatz behind Hotel Santis). The rooms are small, but feature wooden beds and new bathrooms with sliding frosted glass doors. The on-site restaurant feels like a traditional tavern and serves good fondue.

There is a train to St Gallen (Sfr12, 30 minutes, twice hourly).

SWITZERLAND DIRECTORY

ACCOMMODATION

Switzerland caters to all budgets – you can camp, sleep in a barn, stay in a hostel or live it up in a five-star hotel. However, prices may seem steep at even the most inexpensive places compared with other parts of Europe. Tourist offices always have brochures listing prices and facilities of local accommodation.

Hostels, hotels and pensions most often include breakfast in their price, and while many rooms are tiny, most are of quite high standard and almost all include wonderful feather duvets. In budget places breakfast is basic: generally just a beverage with bread rolls, cheese spread, butter and jam.

Most hostels and budget hotels have two classes of rooms – cheaper rooms with shared bathroom and shower facilities and more expensive rooms with private bathroom. For budget rooms expect to pay under Sfr100, while midrange places will set you back anywhere from Sfr100 to Sfr200. Top-end places will cost anything from Sfr200.

Barns

When their cows are out to pasture in the summer, Swiss farmers have habitually put their empty barns to good use, allowing travellers to sleep in them for a very small fee of about Sfr20. It's a unique experience that disappoints few. **Aventure sur la paille** (☎ 041 678 1286; www.aventure-sur-la-paille.ch) produces a booklet listing participating farmers.

Hostels

Switzerland has two types of hostels: official Swiss Youth Hostels (SYHA), affiliated with Hostelling International (HI), where nonmembers pay an additional 'guest fee' of Sfr6, and the independent hostels. Independent hostels tend to be more charismatic and better bets for solo travellers or anyone looking to meet other backpackers. Prices listed in this book for SYHA hostels do not include the guest fee. On average a dorm bed in either type of hostel costs between Sfr20 and Sfr30.

ACTIVITIES

There are dozens of ski resorts throughout the Alps, the pre-Alps and the Jura, and some 200 different ski schools. Equipment hire is available at resorts and ski passes allow unlimited use of mountain transport.

There is simply no better way to enjoy Switzerland's spectacular scenery than to walk through it. There are 50,000km of designated paths, often with a convenient inn or café located en route. Yellow signs marking the trail make it difficult to get lost, and each provides an average walking time to the next destination. Slightly more strenuous mountain paths have white-red-white markers. The **Schweizer Alpen-Club** (SAC; ☎ 031 370 1818; www.sac-cas.ch in German; Monbijoustrasse 61, Bern) maintains huts for overnight stays at altitude and can also help with extra information.

Lonely Planet's *Walking in Switzerland* contains track notes for walking in the Swiss countryside.

You can water-ski, sail and windsurf on most lakes. And there are more than 350 lake beaches. Rafting is possible on many Alpine rivers, including the Rhine and the Rhône.

Bungy jumping, paragliding, canyoning and other high-adrenalin sports are widely available throughout Switzerland, especially in the Interlaken area.

BUSINESS HOURS

Most shops are open from 8am to 6.30pm Monday to Friday, with a 90-minute or two-hour break for lunch at noon. In towns there's often a late shopping day till 9pm, typically on Thursday or Friday. Closing times on Saturday are usually 4pm or 5pm. At some places, such as large train stations, you may find shops are open daily. Banks are open 8.30am to 4.30pm Monday to Friday, with some local variations. Eating and drinking establishments are open for lunch and dinner unless otherwise noted in our reviews.

EMBASSIES & CONSULATES

Swiss Embassies & Consulates

For a comprehensive list of Swiss embassies overseas, visit www.eda.admin.ch.

Australia (☎ 02-6162 8400; www.eda.admin.ch/australia; 7 Melbourne Ave, Forrest, Canberra, ACT 2603)

Canada (☎ 613-235 1837; www.eda.admin.ch/canada; 5 Marlborough Ave, Ottawa, Ontario K1N 8E6)
Ireland (☎ 01-218 6382; www.eda.admin.ch/dublin; 6 Ailesbury Rd, Ballsbridge, Dublin 4)
New Zealand (☎ 04-472 1593; vertretung@wel.rep.admin.ch; 22 Panama St, Wellington)
South Africa (☎ 012-452 06 60; www.eda.admin.ch/pretoria; 225 Veale St, Parc Nouveau, New Muckleneuk 0181, Pretoria)
UK (☎ 020-7616 6000; www.eda.admin.ch/london; 16-18 Montague Pl, London W1H 2BQ)
USA (☎ 202-745 7900; www.eda.admin.ch/washington; 2900 Cathedral Ave NW, Washington DC 20008-3499)

Embassies & Consulates in Switzerland

All embassies are found in Bern. Consulates can be found in several other cities, particularly in Zürich and Geneva. Australia and New Zealand have no embassy in Switzerland, but each has a consulate in Geneva. Most of Bern's embassies are located southeast of the Kirchenfeldbrücke. For a comprehensive list, go to www.eda.admin.ch.

Australia (☎ 022 799 91 00; www.australia.ch; Chemin des Fins 2, Grand-Saconnex, Geneva)
Austria (☎ 031 356 52 52; bern-ob@bmaa.gv.at; Kirchenfeldstrasse 77-79, Bern)
Canada (Bern ☎ 031 357 32 00; www.canada-ambassade.ch; Kirchenfeldstrasse 88; Geneva ☎ 022 919 92 00; 5 Ave de l'Ariana)
France (Bern ☎ 031 359 21 11; www.ambafranch-ch.org; Schosshaldenstrasse 46; Geneva ☎ 022 319 00 00; www.consulfrance-geneve.org; 11 Rue J Imbert Galloix)
Germany (Bern ☎ 031 359 41 11; www.deutsche-botschaft.ch; Willadingweg 83; Basel ☎ 061 693 33 03; Schwarzwaldallee 200)
Ireland (☎ 031 352 14 42; Kirchenfeldstrasse 68, Bern)
Italy (☎ 031 350 07 77; Elfenstrasse 14, Bern)
Netherlands (☎ 031 350 87 00; www.nlembassy.ch; Kollerweg 11, Bern)
New Zealand (☎ 022 929 03 50; Chemin des Fins 2, Grand-Saconnex, Geneva)
UK (Bern ☎ 031 359 77 00; www.britain-in-switzerland.ch; Thunstrasse 50; Geneva ☎ 022 918 24 00; Rue de Vermont 37-39; Zürich ☎ 01 383 65 60; Hegibachstrasse 47)
USA (Bern ☎ 031 357 70 11; http://bern.usembassy.gov; Jubiläumsstrasse 93; Geneva ☎ 022 840 51 60; Rue Versonnex 7; Zürich ☎ 043 499 29 60; Dufourstrasse 101)

FESTIVALS & EVENTS

Many events take place at a local level throughout the year (check with the local tourist offices as dates often vary from year to year). Following is just a brief selection.

February

Fasnacht A lively spring carnival of wild parties and parades is celebrated countrywide, but with particular enthusiasm in Basel and Lucerne.

March

Combats de Reines From March to October, the lower Valais stages traditional cow fights known as the Combats de Reines.

April

Landsgemeinde On the last Sunday in April, the people of Appenzell gather in the main square to take part in a unique open-air parliament.

July

Montreux Jazz Festival Big-name rock/jazz acts hit town for this famous festival (www.montreuxjazz.com) held during the first two weeks of July.

August

National Day On 1 August, celebrations and fireworks mark the country's National Day.
Street Parade Zürich lets its hair down in the second week of August with an enormous techno parade with 30 lovemobiles and more than half a million excited ravers.

October

Vintage Festivals Down a couple in wine-growing regions such as Neuchâtel and Lugano in early October.

November

Onion Market Bern takes on a carnival atmosphere for a unique market day held on the fourth Monday of November.

December

L'Escalade This historical festival held in Geneva on 11 December celebrates deliverance from would-be conquerors.

GAY & LESBIAN TRAVELLERS

Attitudes toward homosexuality are reasonably tolerant in Switzerland and the age of consent is 16. Zürich has a lively gay scene and hosts the Christopher Street Day march in late June. It is also home to **Cruiser magazine** (www.cruiser.ch in German), which lists significant gay and lesbian organisations, and has extensive listings of bars and events in Switzerland (Sfr4.50).

Take a look at **Pink Cross** (www.pinkcross.ch in German) for more insights into gay life in Switzerland.

HOLIDAYS

New Year's Day 1 January
Easter March/April – Good Friday, Easter Sunday and Monday
Ascension Day 40th day after Easter
Whit Sunday & Pentecost 7th week after Easter
National Day 1 August
Christmas Day 25 December
St Stephen's Day 26 December

INTERNET RESOURCES

Switzerland has a strong presence on the Internet, with most tourist-related businesses having their own website; a good place to start is **Switzerland Tourism** (www.myswitzerland.com), with many useful links.

LANGUAGE

Located in the corner of Europe where Germany, France and Italy meet, Switzerland is a linguistic melting pot with three official federal languages: German (spoken by 64% of the population), French (19%) and Italian (8%). A fourth language, Rhaeto-Romanic, or Romansch, is spoken by less than 1% of the population, mainly in the canton of Graubünden. Derived from Latin, it's a linguistic relic that has survived in the isolation of mountain valleys. Romansch was recognised as a national language by referendum in 1938 and given federal protection in 1996.

English-speakers will have few problems being understood in the German-speaking parts. However, it is simple courtesy to greet people with the Swiss-German *grüezi* and to inquire *Sprechen Sie Englisch?* (Do you speak English?) before launching into English.

In French Switzerland you shouldn't have too many problems either, though the locals' grasp of English probably will not be as good as the German-speakers'. Italian Switzerland is where you will have the greatest difficulty. Most locals speak some French and/or German in addition to Italian. English has a lower priority, but you'll still find that the majority of hotels and restaurants have at least one English-speaking staff member.

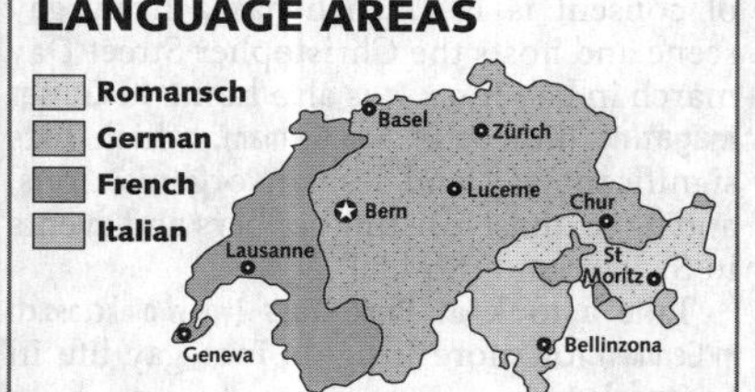

MONEY

Swiss francs (Sfr, written CHF locally) are divided into 100 centimes (called *rappen* in German-speaking Switzerland). There are notes for 10, 20, 50, 100, 200, 500 and 1000 francs, and coins for five, 10, 20 and 50 centimes, and one, two and five francs.

All major travellers cheques and credit cards are accepted. Nearly all train stations have currency-exchange facilities open daily. Commission is not usually charged for changing cash or cheques but it's gradually creeping in. Shop around for the best exchange rates. Hotels usually have the worst rates.

There are no restrictions on the amount of currency that can be brought in or taken out of Switzerland.

There's no need to tip in Switzerland, unless you feel the service was really superlative. Tips are included in meal prices.

ATMs are widespread throughout the country.

POST

Postcards and letters to Europe cost Sfr1.30/1.20 priority/economy; to elsewhere they cost Sfr1.80/1.40. The term poste restante is used nationwide or you could use the German term, *Postlagernde Briefe*. Mail can be sent to any town with a post office and is held for 30 days; show your passport to collect mail. Amex also holds mail for one month for people who use its cheques or cards.

Post office opening times vary but typically they are open from 7.30am to noon and from 2pm to 6.30pm Monday to Friday and until 11am Saturday.

TELEPHONE

The privatised Swisscom is the main telecommunications provider. The minimum charge in Swisscom payphones is Sfr0.60, though per-minute rates are low. Swisscom charges the same rate for national or local calls. During the day it's Sfr0.08 per minute, and during evenings and weekends it drops

EMERGENCY NUMBERS

- **Ambulance** ☎ 144
- **Fire** ☎ 118
- **Motoring breakdown assistance** ☎ 140
- **Police** ☎ 117
- **REGA air rescue** ☎ 1414

to Sfr0.04. Regional codes no longer exist in Switzerland. Although the numbers for a particular city or town all start with the same two or three digits (for example Zürich ☎ 01, Geneva ☎ 022), numbers must always be dialled in full (ie always include telephone codes), even when you're calling from within the same town.

International call prices have dropped substantially in recent years. A standard-rate call to the USA/Australia/UK costs Sfr0.12/0.25/0.12 per minute. Standard rates apply on weekdays (day or night), and there are reduced rates on weekends and public holidays. Many telephone boxes no longer take coins; the prepaid *taxcard* comes in values of Sfr5, Sfr10 and Sfr20, and is sold in post offices, kiosks and train stations.

You can purchase a SIM card from Swisscom for your mobile phone as well as prepaid cards. Calls are not cheap, however. The SIM card costs about Sfr40 and then calls are almost Sfr1 per minute, although they're cheaper at nights and weekends. Mobile service in Switzerland is generally excellent – even in the mountains.

Hotels can charge as much as they like for telephone calls, and they usually charge a lot, even for direct-dial calls.

TOURIST INFORMATION

Local tourist offices are extremely helpful. They have reams of literature to give out, including maps (nearly always free). Offices can be found everywhere tourists are likely to go and will often book hotel rooms and organise excursions. If you are staying in resorts, ask the local tourist office whether there's a Visitor's Card, which is excellent for discounts.

Switzerland Tourism also sells the **Swiss Museum Passport** (www.museumspass.ch; adult/student Sfr30/25), which will save you big bucks if you plan to visit more than a handful of museums. Note that if you've purchased a Swiss Pass, entrance to all Swiss museums is free.

VISAS

Visas are not required for passport holders from Australia, Canada, New Zealand, South Africa, the UK or the USA. A maximum three-month stay applies, although passports are rarely stamped.

TRANSPORT IN SWITZERLAND

GETTING THERE & AWAY

Air

The busiest international airports are **Unique Zürich** (ZUR; ☎ 043 816 22 11; www.uniqueairport.com) and **Geneva International Airport** (GEN; ☎ 022 717 71 11; www.gva.ch/en), each with several nonstop flights a day to major transport hubs such as London, Paris and Frankfurt. Most international airlines fly into Switzerland, as do a few budget operators. EasyJet offers regular services from London to/from Basel and Geneva, while bmibaby flies from East Midlands, in the UK, to Geneva. Switzerland's international carrier is Swiss International Airlines (known as Swiss).

Airport departure taxes are always included in the ticket price.

Air Berlin (code AB; ☎ 084 873 78 00; www.airberlin.com)
Air France (code AF; ☎ 01 439 18 18; www.airfrance.com)
American Airlines (code AA; ☎ 01 654 52 57; www.americanairlines.com)
bmibaby (code BD; ☎ 041 900 00 13 00; www.bmibaby.com)
British Airways (code BA; ☎ 0848 845 845; www.britishairways.com)
Delta Airlines (code DL; ☎ 0800 55 20 36; www.delta.com)
easyJet (code EZ; ☎ 0848 888 222; www.easyjet.com)
flybe (code BEE; ☎ 1392 268 500; www.flybe.com)
Helvetic (code OAW; ☎ 043 557 90 99; www.helvetic.com)
Lufthansa (code LH; ☎ 01 447 99 66; www.lufthansa.com)
SkyEurope (code NE; ☎ 043 557 90 99; www.skyeurope.com)

Swiss International Airlines (code LX; ☎ 0848 853 00 00; www.swiss.com)
United Airlines (code UA; ☎ 01 212 47 17; www.united.com)

Lake

Lake steamers from Germany and Austria traverse Lake Constance (Bodensee) to Switzerland. For boat information contact the operators based in Switzerland (☎ 071 463 34 35), Austria (☎ 055 744 28 68) or Germany (☎ 075-3128 1398).

From Italy you can catch a steamer across Lake Maggiore into Locarno. Contact **Navigazione Lago Maggiore** (NLM; ☎ 084 881 11 22, 091 751 18 65) for more information.

France can be reached from Geneva via Lake Geneva (Lac Léman); contact **Compagnie Générale de Navigation** (CGN; ☎ 022 08 48 81 18 48) for more information.

Land

BUS

With such cheap flights available, there are few people who travel to Switzerland by bus these days. **Eurolines** (☎ 090 057 37 47; www.eurolines.com) has services to Eastern Europe, Austria, Spain, Germany and Portugal, but distances are long.

If you want to visit several countries by bus, the UK-based **Busabout** (☎ in UK 020 7950 1661; www.busabout.com) operates summer services from Bern to Paris, and from Lauterbrunnen (for Interlaken) to Paris and Venice. See the Busabout website for details. Prices start at UK£219 for a two-week consecutive pass.

CAR & MOTORCYCLE

Roads into Switzerland are good despite the difficulty of the terrain, but special care is needed to negotiate mountain passes. Some, such as the N5 route from Morez (France) to Geneva, are not recommended if you have not had previous mountain-driving experience.

Upon entering Switzerland you will need to decide whether you wish to use the motorways (there is a one-off charge of Sfr40). Arrange to have some Swiss francs ready, as you might not always be able to change money at the border. Better still, pay for the tax in advance through Switzerland Tourism or a motoring organisation. The sticker (called a *vignette*) you receive is valid for a year and must be displayed on the windscreen. A separate fee must be paid for trailers and caravans (motorcyclists must pay too). Some Alpine tunnels incur additional tolls.

TRAIN

Located in the heart of Europe, Switzerland is a hub of train connections to the rest of the Continent. Zürich is the busiest international terminus. It has two direct day trains and one night train to Vienna (nine hours). There are several trains daily to both Geneva and Lausanne from Paris (three to four hours by superfast TGV). Travelling from Paris to Bern takes 4½ hours by TGV. Most connections from Germany pass though Zürich or Basel. Nearly all connections from Italy pass through Milan before branching off to Zürich, Lucerne, Bern or Lausanne. Reservations on international trains are subject to a surcharge of Sfr5 to Sfr30, which depends upon the date and the service.

GETTING AROUND

Air

Internal flights are not of great interest to most visitors, owing to the short distances and excellent ground transport. **Swiss International Air Lines** (www.swiss.com) is the local carrier, linking major towns and cities several times daily, including Zürich, Geneva, Basel, Bern and Lugano.

Bicycle

Despite the hilly countryside, many Swiss choose to get around on two wheels. You can hire bikes from most train stations (adult/child Sfr30/25 per day) and return to any station with a rental office, though this incurs a Sfr6 surcharge. Bikes can be transported on most trains; SBB (the Swiss rail company) rentals travel free (maximum five bikes per train). If you have your own wheels you'll need a bike pass (one day Sfr15, with Swiss travel pass Sfr10). Local tourist offices often have good cycling information. Bern, Basel, Geneva and Zürich offer free bike loans from their train stations.

Bus

Yellow postbuses are a supplement to the rail network, following postal routes and

PASSES & DISCOUNTS

Swiss public transport is an efficient, fully integrated and comprehensive system, which incorporates trains, buses, boats and funiculars. Convenient discount passes make the system even more appealing.

The **Swiss Pass** (www.swisstravelsystem.ch) is the best deal for people planning to travel extensively, offering unlimited travel on Swiss Federal Railways, boats, most Alpine postbuses, and trams and buses in 35 towns. Reductions of 25% apply to funiculars and mountain railways. These passes are available for four days (Sfr262), eight days (Sfr362), 15 days (Sfr430), 22 days (Sfr495) and one month (Sfr545); prices are for 2nd-class tickets. The **Swiss Flexi Pass** allows free, unlimited trips for three to eight days within a month and costs Sfr270 to Sfr460 (2nd class). With either pass, two people travelling together get 15% off. Both passes now allow you free admission to all Swiss museums, making them an even better bargain.

The **Swiss Card** allows a free return journey from your arrival point to any destination in Switzerland, 50% off rail, boat and bus excursions, and reductions on mountain railways. It costs Sfr165 (2nd class) or Sfr240 (1st class) and it is valid for a month. The **Half-Fare Card** is a similar deal minus the free return trip. It costs Sfr99 for one month.

Except for the Half-Fare Card, these passes are best purchased before arrival in Switzerland from **Switzerland Tourism** (www.myswitzerland.com) or a travel agent. The **Family Card** gives free travel for children aged under 16 if they're accompanied by a parent and is available free to pass purchasers.

There are also passes valid for any four days of unlimited travel in Switzerland and either Austria or France (Sfr391) within two months.

linking towns to the more inaccessible regions in the mountains. In all, routes cover some 8000km of terrain. Services are regular, and departures tie in with train arrivals. Postbus stations are next to train stations, and offer destination and timetable information.

Car

The **Swiss Touring Club** (Touring Club der Schweiz; ☎ 022 417 27 27; www.tcs.ch; Chemin de Blandonnet, Case postale 820, CH-1214, Venier/Geneva) is the largest motoring organisation in Switzerland. It is affiliated with the AA in Britain and has reciprocal agreements with motoring organisations worldwide.

You do not need an International Driving Licence to operate a vehicle in Switzerland. A licence from your home country is sufficient. There are numerous petrol stations and garages throughout Switzerland if you break down.

For the best deals on car hire you have to prebook. Some of the lowest rates are found through **Auto Europe** (www.autoeurope.com). One-way drop-offs are usually free of charge within Switzerland, although a collision-damage waiver costs extra.

Be prepared for winding roads, high passes and long tunnels. Normal speed limits are 50km/h in towns, 120km/h on motorways, 100km/h on semimotorways (designated by roadside rectangular pictograms showing a white car on a green background) and 80km/h on other roads. Mountain roads are well-maintained but you should stay in low gear whenever possible and remember that ascending traffic has the right of way over descending traffic, and postbuses always have right of way. Snow chains are recommended during winter. Use dipped lights in *all* road tunnels. Some minor Alpine passes are closed from November to May – check with the local tourist offices.

Switzerland is tough on drink-driving; if your blood alcohol level is over 0.05% you face a large fine or imprisonment.

Train

The Swiss rail network covers 5000km and is a combination of state-run and private lines. Trains are clean, reliable, frequent and as fast as the terrain will allow. Prices are high, and if you plan on taking more than one or two train trips it's best to purchase a travel pass (above). All fares quoted in this chapter are for 2nd class; 1st-class fares are about 65% higher. All major stations are connected by hourly departures, but services stop from around midnight to 6am.

Most train stations offer luggage storage, either at a counter (usually Sfr5 per piece) or in 24-hour lockers (Sfr2 to Sfr7). They also have excellent information counters that give out free timetable booklets and advise on connections. Train schedules are revised yearly, so double-check details before travelling. For train information, consult the excellent website for the **Schweizerische Bundesbahnen** (SBB; www.sbb.ch) or call ☎ 090 030 03 00 (Sfr1.19 per minute).

Regional Directory

CONTENTS

Accommodation	1095
Activities	1098
Children	1099
Climate Charts	1100
Courses	1100
Customs	1100
Dangers & Annoyances	1101
Discount Cards	1102
Electricity	1103
Embassies & Consulates	1103
Gay & Lesbian Travellers	1103
Insurance	1104
Internet Access	1104
Legal Matters	1104
Maps	1105
Media	1105
Money	1105
Photography, Video & DVD	1108
Post	1108
Solo Travellers	1108
Telephone	1108
Time	1109
Tourist Information	1109
Travellers With Disabilities	1109
Visas	1109
Volunteering	1110
Weights & Measures	1110
Women Travellers	1110
Work	1110

Readers should note there are two types of directories in this book: the Regional Directory and individual country directories. The Regional Directory serves as a comprehensive resource for the whole of Western Europe. The country directories appear at the end of each country chapter and are a roundup of specific details pertaining to that country. Some subjects will be covered in both directories (eg general accommodation options are outlined in this Regional Directory, but prices are covered in the country directories). Though you should look at both directories for information, they cross-reference each other, making it easier to find what you're looking for.

ACCOMMODATION

The cheapest places to stay in Europe are camping grounds, followed by hostels and accommodation in student dormitories. Cheap chain hotels are popping up in the northern half of Europe, but guesthouses, *pensions,* private rooms and B&Bs have much more character and are often good value. Self-catering flats and cottages are worth considering with a group, especially if you plan to stay somewhere for a while. During peak holiday periods accommodation can be hard to find, and unless you're camping it's advisable to book ahead. Even camping grounds can fill up, especially in or around big cities.

Accommodation listings in this guide have been ordered by price, from cheapest to most expensive (ie budget to top end), and all prices quoted include private bathroom facilities unless otherwise stated (the exceptions to this are the France and Austria chapters). See the country directories for more details about local accommodation.

B&Bs & Guesthouses

There's a huge range of accommodation above the hostel level. In the UK and Ireland myriad B&Bs are the real bargains in this field, where you get bed and breakfast in a private home. In some areas every second house will have a B&B sign out the front. In other countries similar private accommodation – though often without breakfast – may go under the name of *pension,* guesthouse, *gasthaus, zimmer frei, chambre d'hôte* and so on. Although the majority of guesthouses are simple affairs, there are more expensive ones where you'll find bathrooms and other luxuries.

With B&Bs especially, make certain that they are centrally located and not in some dull and distant suburb.

Camping

Camping is immensely popular in Western Europe (especially among Germans and the Dutch) and provides the cheapest accommodation. There's usually a charge per tent

RESERVATIONS

Cheap hotels in popular destinations (eg Paris, London, Rome) – especially the well-run ones smack in the middle of desirable or central neighbourhoods – fill up quickly. It's a good idea to make reservations as many weeks ahead as possible, at least for the first night or two. An email or a three-minute international phone call to reserve a room (followed, if necessary, by written confirmation and/or deposit) is a lot cheaper and less frustrating than wasting your first day in a city looking for a place to stay.

If you arrive in a country by air and without a reservation, there is often an airport accommodation booking desk, although it rarely covers the lower strata of hotels. Tourist offices often have extensive accommodation lists, and some will go out of their way to find you something suitable. In most countries the fee for this service is very low and, if accommodation is tight, it can save you a lot of running around. This is also an easy way to get around any language problems. Agencies offering private rooms can be good value; staying with a local family doesn't always mean that you'll lack privacy, but you'll probably have less freedom than in a hotel.

Sometimes people will come up to you on the street offering a private room or a hostel bed. This can be good or bad – there's no hard-and-fast rule – but just ensure that before you commit you negotiate a clear price and make sure that it's not way out in a dingy suburb somewhere. As always, be careful when someone offers to carry your luggage; they might relieve you of more than the load off your back.

or site, per person and per vehicle. The national tourist offices often provide booklets or brochures listing camping grounds all over their country. See p1102 for information on the Camping Card International.

In large cities, most camping grounds will be some distance from the centre. For this reason camping is most popular with people who have their own transport. If you're on foot, the money you save by camping can quickly be eaten up by the cost of commuting to/from a town centre. You may also need a tent, sleeping bag and cooking equipment, though not always. Many camping grounds rent bungalows or cottages accommodating two to eight people.

Camping other than at designated camping grounds is difficult; there are not many places in Western Europe where you can pitch a tent away from prying eyes, and you usually need permission from the local authorities (the police or local council office) or from the owner of the land (don't be shy about asking – you may be pleasantly surprised by the response).

In some countries, such as Austria, the UK, France and Germany, free camping is illegal on all but private land; in Greece it's illegal altogether. This doesn't prevent hikers from occasionally pitching their tent for the night, and they'll usually get away with it if they have only a small tent, are discreet, stay only one or two nights, take the tent down during the day and do not light a campfire or leave rubbish. At worst, they'll be woken up by the police and asked to move on.

Hostels

Hostels offer the cheapest (secure) roof over your head in Western Europe, and you don't have to be a youngster to use them. Most hostels are part of the national Youth Hostel Association (YHA), which is affiliated with **Hostelling International** (HI; www.hihostels.com) – formerly called the IYHF (International Youth Hostel Federation). The name change was done, in part, to de-emphasize the youth aspect.

Technically, you're supposed to be a YHA or HI member to use affiliated hostels, but you can often stay by paying an extra charge that will usually be set against future membership. Stay enough nights as a nonmember and you automatically become a member.

In Bavaria, Germany, the strict maximum age for anyone staying in a hostel, except group leaders or parents accompanying a child, is 26. However, most countries don't adhere to an age limit despite the 'youth' in their name – although at times there might be a €3 surcharge for geezers over 26.

To join the HI you can ask at any hostel or contact your local or national hostelling office. The HI website has links to all national hostel organisations.

At a hostel, you get a bed for the night plus use of communal facilities, which often includes a kitchen where you can prepare your own meals. You are usually required to have a sleeping sheet; simply using your sleeping bag is not permitted. If you don't have your own approved sleeping sheet, you can usually hire or buy one. Hostels vary widely in character, but the growing number of travellers and increased competition from other forms of accommodation, particularly the emergence of private 'backpacker hostels', have prompted many places to improve their facilities and cut back on rules and regulations. Increasingly, hostels are open all day, strict curfews are disappearing and 'wardens' with sergeant-major mentalities are becoming an endangered species. In some places you'll even find hostels with single and double rooms. Everywhere the trend is moving toward smaller dormitories with just four to six beds.

If you have a credit or debit card you now can book HI hostel rooms up to six months in advance through the website.

PRIVATE HOSTELS

There are many private hostelling organisations in Europe and hundreds of unaffiliated backpacker hostels. Private hostels have fewer rules (eg no curfew, no daytime lockout), more self-catering kitchens and a much lower number of large, noisy school groups. They often also have a much more party-friendly attitude.

However, whereas HI hostels must meet minimum safety and cleanliness standards, facilities vary greatly in private hostels. Dorms in some private hostels, especially in Germanic countries, can be co-ed.

The following websites are recommended as resources for hostellers; all of them have booking engines, helpful advice from fellow travellers and excellent tips for novice hostellers.

Hostel Planet (www.hostelplanet.com)
Hostels.com (www.hostels.com)
Hostelz (www.hostelz.com)

Hotels

Above the B&B and guesthouse level are hotels, which at the bottom of the bracket may be no more expensive than the B&Bs or guesthouses, while at the other extreme are luxury five-star properties. You'll often find inexpensive hotels clustered around the bus and train station areas, which are always good places to start hunting, however, these areas can be charmless and scruffy. Look for moderately priced places closer to the interesting parts of town.

Check your hotel room and the bathroom before you agree to take it, and make sure you know what it's going to cost – discounts are often available for groups or for longer stays. Ask about breakfast; sometimes it's included, but other times it may be obligatory and you'll have to pay extra for it. If the sheets don't look clean ask to have them changed right away. Check where the fire exits are.

If you think a hotel room is too expensive ask if there's anything cheaper; often hotel owners may have tried to steer you into more expensive rooms. In fact you can sometimes find affordable rooms in some of Europe's famous old hotels simply by asking. They may be in the attic or have a weird shape but can be great value. In southern Europe in particular, hotel owners may be open to a little bargaining if times are slack. It is common practice for business hotels (usually more than two stars) to slash their rates by up to 50% on Friday and Saturday nights when business is dead. Save your big hotel splurge for the weekend.

Rental Accommodation

Rentals can be advantageous for families travelling together or those staying in one place for at least one week. You have the freedom of coming and going when you like without worrying about curfews and strict checkout times, plus a feeling of coming 'home' after a hard day of sightseeing. All rentals should be equipped with kitchens (or at least a kitchenette), which can save on the grocery bill and allow you to peruse the neighbourhood markets and shops, eating like the locals do. Some are a little more upmarket with laundry facilities, parking pads, daily maid services and even a concierge.

Check with local tourist offices in individual country chapters for a list of rental properties or try the following websites, just a few of scores: www.holiday-rentals.com, www.vacations-abroad.com, www.homelidays.com and www.holidayhavens.co.uk.

BOOK ACCOMMODATION ONLINE

For more accommodation reviews and recommendations by Lonely Planet authors, check out the online booking service at www.lonelyplanet.com. You'll find the true, insider lowdown on the best places to stay. Reviews are thorough and independent. Best of all, you can book online.

Resorts

From foreboding Irish mansions to grand Swiss hotels, Western Europe has its fair share of luxury resorts, where travellers can enjoy memorable experiences. As noted above, ask about deals and rooms cheaper then the average. Travellers might find ski resorts in mountainous towns in Germany, France and Switzerland somewhat 'less' expensive, as they are as common as hotels in major cities.

University Accommodation

Some university towns rent out student accommodation during holiday periods. This is very popular in France and the UK as universities become more accountable financially.

Accommodation will sometimes be in single rooms (more commonly in doubles or triples) and may have cooking facilities. Inquire at the college or university, at student information services or at local tourist offices.

ACTIVITIES

Europe offers countless opportunities to indulge in more active pursuits than sightseeing. The varied geography and climate supports the full range of outdoor pursuits: windsurfing, skiing, fishing, hiking, cycling and mountaineering. For local information see the individual country chapters.

Boating

Europe's many lakes, rivers and diverse coastlines offer a variety of boating options unmatched anywhere in the world. You can houseboat in France, kayak in Switzerland, charter a yacht in Greece, hire a catamaran in the Netherlands, row on a peaceful Alpine lake, join a Danube River cruise from Amsterdam to Vienna, rent a sailing boat on the Côte d'Azur or dream away on a canal boat along the extraordinary canal network of Britain (or Ireland, or France) – the possibilities are endless. See individual country chapters for more details.

Cycling

Along with hiking, cycling is the best way to really get close to the scenery and the people, keeping yourself fit in the process. It's also a good way to get around many cities and towns.

Much of Western Europe is ideally suited to cycling. In the northwest, the flat terrain ensures that bicycles are a popular form of everyday transport, though rampant headwinds often spoil the fun. In the rest of the region, hills and mountains can make for heavy going, but this is offset by the dense concentration of things to see. Cycling is a great way to explore many of the Mediterranean islands, though the heat can get to you after a while.

Popular cycling areas among holidaymakers include the Belgian Ardennes, the west of Ireland, much of the Netherlands, the coasts of Sardinia and Puglia, anywhere in the Alps (for those fit enough), and the south of France.

If you are arriving from outside Europe, you can often bring your own bicycle along on the plane. Alternatively, this guide lists many places where you can hire one.

See p1116 for more information on bicycle touring, and the Getting Around sections in individual country chapters for rental agencies and tips on places to go.

Hiking

Keen hikers can spend a lifetime exploring Western Europe's many exciting trails. Probably the most spectacular are to be found in the Alps and the Italian Dolomites, which are crisscrossed with well-marked trails; food and accommodation are available along the way in season. The equally sensational Pyrenees are less developed, which can add to the experience as you often rely on remote mountain villages for rest and sustenance. Hiking areas that are less well known but nothing short of stunning are Corsica, Sardinia and northern Portugal. The Picos de Europa range in Spain is also rewarding and Scotland's West Highland Way is world renowned.

The **Ramblers' Association** (☎ 020-7339 8500; www.ramblers.org.uk) is a charity that promotes long-distance walking in the UK and can help you with maps and information. The British-based **Ramblers Holidays** (☎ 01707-331133; www.ramblersholidays.co.uk) in Hertfordshire offers hiking-oriented trips in Europe and elsewhere.

For shorter day-hikes, local tourist offices are usually excellent resources. Just ask. Examples of questions that yielded directions for excellent walks include 'Where can I walk and see windmills?' in the Netherlands, and 'Where can I get deep into the forest?' in the Black Forest in Germany.

Every country in Western Europe has national parks and other interesting areas or attractions that may qualify as a hiker's paradise, depending on your preferences. Guided hikes are often available for those who aren't sure about their physical abilities or who simply don't know what to look for. Read the Hiking information in the individual country chapters in this book and take your pick of the alternatives presented.

Skiing

In winter, Europeans flock to the hundreds of resorts located in the Alps and Pyrenees for downhill skiing and snowboarding, though cross-country skiing is very popular in some areas.

A skiing holiday can be expensive once you've added up the costs of ski lifts, accommodation and the inevitable après-ski drinking sessions. Equipment hire (or even purchase), on the other hand, can be relatively cheap if you follow the tips in this guide, and the hassle of bringing your own skis may not be worth it. As a rule, a skiing holiday in Europe will work out about twice as expensive as a summer holiday of the same length. Cross-country skiing costs less than downhill since you don't rely as much on ski lifts.

The skiing season generally lasts from early December to late March, though at higher altitudes it may extend an extra month either side. Snow conditions can vary greatly from one year to the next and from region to region, but January and February tend to be the best (and busiest) months.

Ski resorts in the French and Swiss Alps offer great skiing and facilities, but are also the most expensive. Expect high prices, too, in the German Alps, though Germany has cheaper (but far less spectacular) options in the Black Forest and Harz Mountains. Austria is generally slightly cheaper than France and Switzerland (especially in Carinthia). Prices in the Italian Alps are similar to Austria (with some upmarket exceptions like Cortina d'Ampezzo), and can be relatively cheap given the right package.

Possibly the cheapest skiing in Western Europe is to be found in the Pyrenees in Spain and Andorra, and in the Sierra Nevada range in the south of Spain. Both Greece and Scotland also boast growing ski industries – Greece is particularly good value. See the individual country chapters for more detailed information.

For comprehensive reports on ski conditions, try www.onthesnow.com.

Windsurfing & Surfing

After swimming and fishing, windsurfing could well be the most popular of the many water sports on offer in Europe. It's easy to rent sailboards in many tourist centres, and courses are usually available for beginners.

Believe it or not, you can also go surfing in Europe. Forget the shallow North Sea and Mediterranean, and the calm Baltic, but there can be excellent surf, and an accompanying surfer scene, in southwest England and west Scotland (wetsuit advisable!), along Ireland's west coast, the Atlantic coast of France and Portugal, and the north and southwest coasts of Spain. See the individual country chapters for more detailed information.

CHILDREN

Successful travel with young children requires some careful planning and effort. Don't try to overdo things; even for adults, packing too much sightseeing into the time available can cause problems. And make sure the activities include the kids as well – balance that day at the Louvre with a day at Disneyland Paris. Include children in the trip planning; if they've helped to work out where you will be going they will be much more interested when they get there. Europe is the home of *Little Red Riding Hood, Cinderella, King Arthur* and *Tintin,* and is a great place to travel with kids. Lonely Planet's *Travel with Children,* by

Cathy Lanigan (with a foreword by Maureen Wheeler), is an excellent source of information.

Most car-rental firms in Europe have children's safety seats for hire at a nominal cost, but it's essential that you book them in advance. The same goes for highchairs and cots (cribs); they're standard in most restaurants and hotels but numbers are limited. The choice of baby food, formulas, soy and cow's milk, disposable nappies (diapers) and the like is good in most Western European supermarkets.

CLIMATE CHARTS

For general advice on when to travel in Western Europe, see p27. Our climate charts (right) provide a snapshot of Western Europe's weather patterns.

COURSES

If your interests are more cerebral, you can enrol in courses in Western Europe on anything from language to alternative medicine to organic farming. Language courses are available to foreigners through universities or private schools, and are justifiably popular since the best way to learn a language is in the country where it's spoken. The individual country chapters in this book give pointers on where to start looking for courses. In general, the best sources of detailed information are the cultural institutes maintained by many European countries around the world; failing that, try the national tourist offices or embassies. Student exchange organisations, student travel agencies and organisations such as the YMCA/YWCA and HI can also put you on the right track. Ask about special holiday packages that include a course.

CUSTOMS

Duty-free goods are no longer sold to those travelling from one EU country to another. For goods purchased at airports or on ferries *outside* the EU, the usual allowances apply for tobacco (200 cigarettes, 50 cigars or 250g of loose tobacco), alcohol (1L of spirits or 2L of liquor with less than 22% alcohol by volume; 2L of wine) and perfume (50g of perfume and 0.25L of *eau de toilette*).

Do not confuse these with duty-paid items (including alcohol and tobacco)

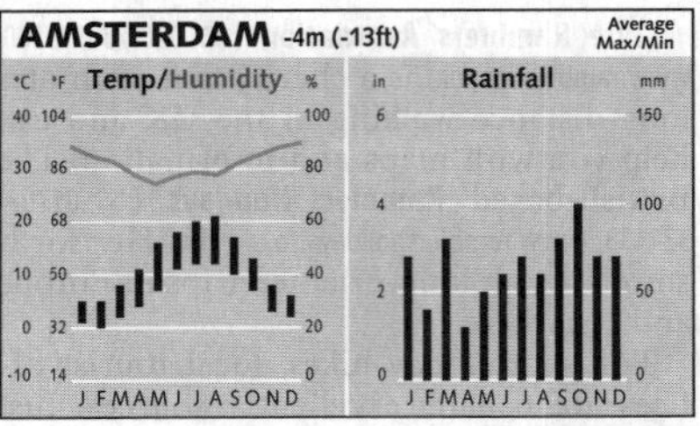

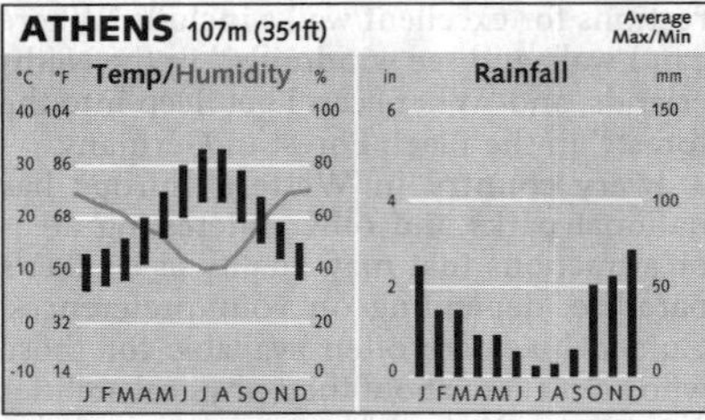

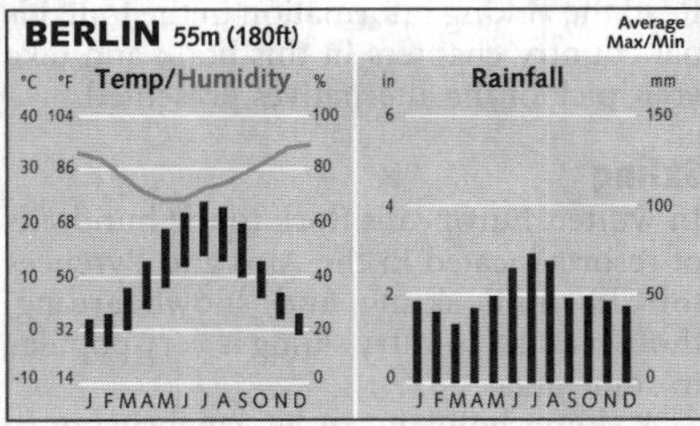

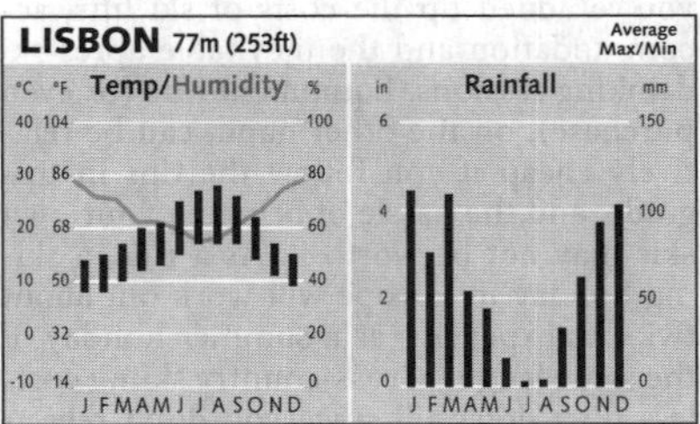

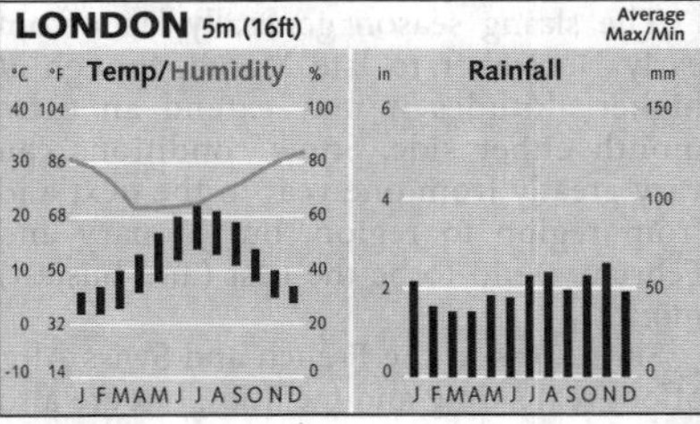

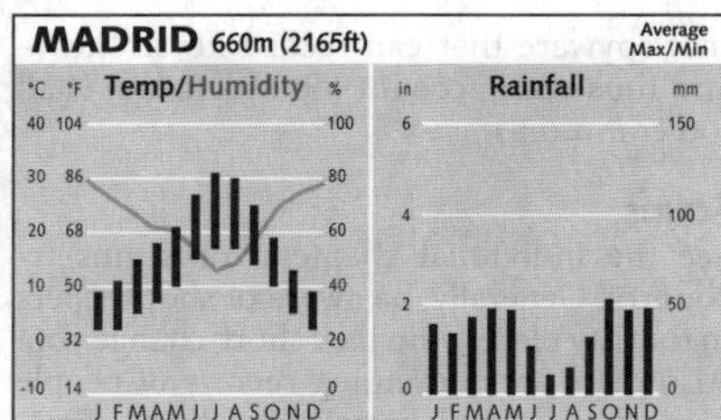

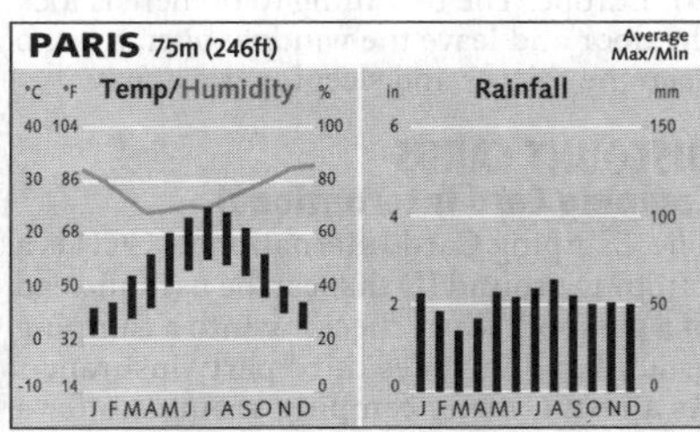

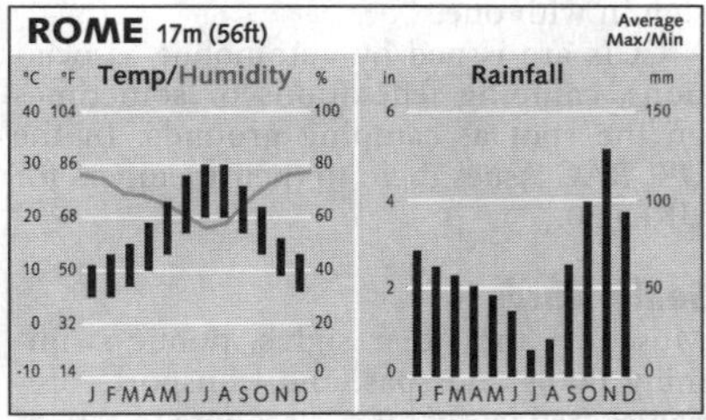

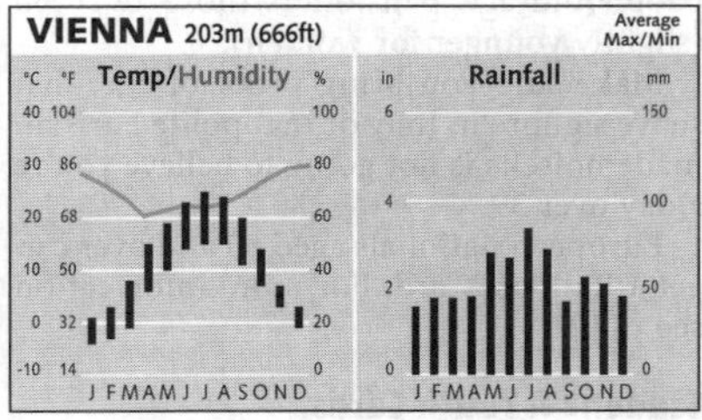

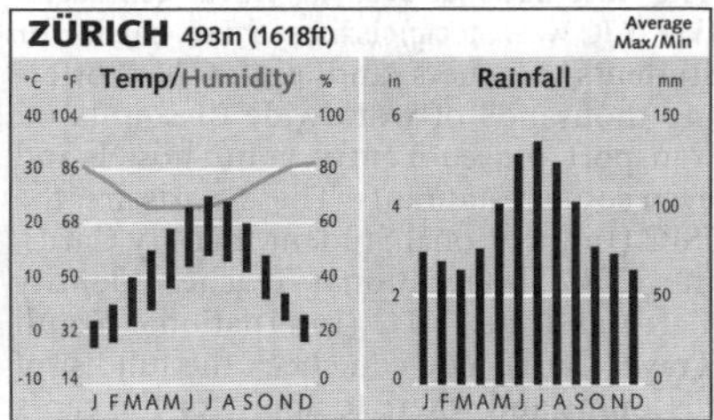

bought at normal shops and supermarkets in another EU country, where certain goods might be more expensive. (Cigarettes in France, for example, are cheaper than in the UK.) In this case the allowances are more than generous: 800 cigarettes, 200 cigars or 1kg of loose tobacco; 10L of spirits (more than 22% alcohol by volume), 20L of fortified wine or apéritif, 90L of wine or 110L of beer; and unlimited quantities of perfume.

DANGERS & ANNOYANCES

On the whole, you should experience few problems travelling in Western Europe – even alone – as the region is well developed and relatively safe. But do exercise common sense. Whatever you do, don't leave friends and relatives back home worrying about how to get in touch with you in case of an emergency. Work out a list of places where they can contact you or, best of all, phone home now and then or email.

Also, leave a record (ie a photocopy) of your passport, credit and ATM cards and other important documents someplace safe. If things are stolen, replacement is much easier with the vital details available.

Drugs

Always treat drugs with caution. There are a lot of drugs available in Western Europe, sometimes quite openly (eg in the Netherlands), but that doesn't mean they're legal. Even a little harmless hashish can cause a great deal of trouble in some places. See p1104 for details.

Don't even think about bringing drugs home with you either: if you have what energetic customs officials may think are 'suspect' stamps in your passport (eg Amsterdam's Schiphol airport), they may well decide to take a closer look. And drugs sent through the mail can result in arrest for the recipient.

Theft

Theft is definitely a problem in Europe, and nowadays you also have to be wary of other travellers. The most important things to guard are your passport, papers, tickets and money – in that order. It's always best to carry these next to your skin or in a sturdy leather pouch on your belt. Train-station lockers or luggage-storage counters are useful places to store your bags (but *never* valuables) while you get your bearings in a new town. Be very suspicious about people who offer to help you operate your locker. Carry your own padlock for hostel lockers.

You can lessen the risks further by being careful of snatch thieves. Cameras or shoulder bags are an open invitation for these people, who sometimes operate from motorcycles or scooters and expertly slash the strap before you have a chance to react. A small daypack is better, but watch your rear. Be very careful at cafés and bars; loop the strap around your leg while seated.

Pickpockets are most active in dense crowds, especially in busy train stations and on public transport during peak hours. A common ploy is for one person to distract you while another zips through your pockets. Beware of gangs of kids – either dishevelled-looking or well dressed – madly waving newspapers and demanding attention. In the blink of an eye, a wallet or camera can go missing.

Be careful even in hotels; don't leave valuables lying around in your room.

Parked cars containing luggage and other bags are prime targets for petty criminals in most cities, particularly cars with foreign number plates and/or rental-agency stickers. While driving in cities, beware of snatch thieves when you pull up at the lights – keep doors locked and windows rolled up high.

In case of theft or loss, always report the incident to the police and ask for a statement. Otherwise your travel-insurance company won't pay up.

A word of warning – fraudulent shopkeepers have been known to quickly make several charge slip imprints with your credit card when you're not looking, and then simply copy your signature from the one that you authorise. Try not to let your card out of sight and always check your statements upon your return.

If you will be travelling for a while, you might consider having a trusted person at home who can go online to check your bank account from time to time. Identity thieves can steal your details and loot your account. Prompt action can stop this and get you restitution. (One main reason not to do this yourself from Internet cafés is that spyware that can record keystrokes – and thus your account login details – is all too common.)

Scams

See the individual chapters for scams by country. Generally, be aware of shopkeepers in touristy places who may short-change you. Also there are continuing reports of people being gassed on night trains heading to Eastern Europe. The best thing to do here is lock the door and leave the window open a bit to keep the thieves and sleeping gas at bay.

DISCOUNT CARDS

Camping Card International

The Camping Card International (CCI) is a camping ground ID that can be used instead of a passport when checking into a camping ground and includes third party insurance. As a result, many camping grounds offer a small discount (usually 5% to 10%) if you sign in with one.

CCIs are issued by automobile associations, camping federations or sometimes on the spot at camping grounds. In the UK, RAC issues them to their members for UK£6.50.

Senior Cards

Museums and other sights, public swimming pools and spas, and transport companies frequently offer discounts to retired people/old-age pensioners/those over 60 (slightly younger for women).

Make sure you bring proof of age; that suave signore in Italy or that polite Parisian mademoiselle is not going to believe you're a day over 39.

European nationals aged 60 and over can get a Railplus Card. For more information see p1121.

Student & Youth Cards

The **International Student Travel Confederation** (ISTC; www.istc.org) issues three cards for students, teachers and under-26s, offering thousands of worldwide discounts on transport, museum entry, youth hostels and even some restaurants. These cards are: the ISIC (International Student Identity Card), the ITIC (International Teacher Identity Card) and the IYTC (International Youth Travel Card). You can check the full list of discounts and where to apply for the cards on the ISTC website. Issuing offices include **STA Travel** (www.statravel.com).

For under-26s there's also a specific European card, the Euro<26. For information check out www.euro26.org.

ELECTRICITY

Voltages & Cycles

Most of Europe runs on 220V, 50Hz AC. The exceptions are the UK, which has 240V, and Spain, which usually has 220V but sometimes still has the old 110V or 125V, depending on the network (some houses can have both). Some old buildings and hotels in Italy (including Rome) might also have 125V. All EU countries were supposed to have been standardised at 230V by now, but like many things in the EU this is taking longer than anticipated.

Check the voltage and cycle (usually 50Hz) used in your home country. Most appliances that are set up for 220V will handle 240V without modifications (and vice versa); the same goes for 110V and 125V combinations. It's always preferable to adjust your appliance to the exact voltage if you can (some modern battery chargers and radios will do this automatically). Just don't mix 110/125V with 220/240V without a transformer (which will be built into an adjustable appliance).

Several countries outside Europe (such as the USA and Canada) have 60Hz AC, which will affect the speed of electric motors even after the voltage has been adjusted to European values. CD and tape players (where motor speed is important) will be useless, but things like electric razors, hairdryers, irons and radios will be fine.

Plugs & Sockets

The UK and Ireland use chunky, three-pin square plugs. Most of the Continent uses the 'europlug' with two round pins. Greece, Italy and Switzerland use a third round pin in a way that the two-pin plug usually (but not always in Italy and Switzerland) fits. If your plugs are of a different design, you'll need an adaptor. Get one before you leave since the adaptors available in Europe usually go the other way. If you find yourself without one, however, a specialist electrical-supply shop should be able to help.

EMBASSIES & CONSULATES

See the individual country directories for the addresses of embassies and consulates.

As a tourist, it is vitally important that you understand what your own embassy (the embassy of the country of which you are a citizen) can and cannot do. Generally speaking, it won't be much help in emergencies if the trouble you're in is remotely your fault.

Remember that you are bound by the laws of the country that you are in. Your embassy will show little sympathy towards you if you end up in jail after committing a crime locally, even if such actions are legal in your own country.

In genuine emergencies you might get some assistance, but only if other channels have been exhausted. For example, if you need to get home urgently, a free ticket home is exceedingly unlikely as the embassy would expect you to have insurance. If you have all your money and documents stolen, it might assist with getting a new passport, but a loan for onward travel is almost always out of the question.

GAY & LESBIAN TRAVELLERS

In cosmopolitan centres in Western Europe you'll find very liberal attitudes toward homosexuality. Belgium, the Netherlands, and (believe it or not) Spain have legalised full same-sex marriages. The UK offers civil partnerships granting all or most of the rights of marriage, while France, Germany, Luxembourg and Switzerland offer limited-rights partnerships.

London, Paris, Berlin, Amsterdam, Madrid and Lisbon have thriving gay communities and pride events. The Greek islands of Mykonos and Lesvos are popular gay beach destinations.

The following websites are useful:

Damron (www.damron.com) The USA's leading gay publisher offers guides for lesbians and gays to world cities.

Gay Journey (www.gayjourney.com) A mish-mash of gay travel-related information, including lists of gay-friendly hotels in Europe.

International Lesbian and Gay Association (www.ilga.org) Campaigning group with some country-specific information on homosexual issues (not always up-to-date) and a conference calendar.

Spartacus International Gay Guide (www.spartacusworld.com) A good male-only directory of gay entertainment venues in Europe and the rest of the world.

See individual country chapters for more organisations, as well as gay and lesbian venues. For ages of consent, see right.

INSURANCE

It's foolhardy to travel without insurance to cover theft, loss and medical problems. Start by seeing what your own insurance covers, be it medical, homeowners or renters. You may find that many aspects of travel in Western Europe are covered. You may also find gaping holes. If you need to purchase coverage, there's a wide variety of policies, so check the small print. Some policies specifically exclude 'dangerous activities', which can include scuba diving, motorcycling, winter sports, adventure sports or even hiking. Some pay doctors or hospitals directly, but most require you to pay upfront, save the documentation and then claim later. Some policies also ask you to call back (reverse charges) to a centre in your home country, where an immediate assessment of your problem is made. Check that the policy covers ambulances or an emergency flight home.

The policies handled by **STA Travel** (www.statravel.com) and other student travel agencies are usually good value. In the UK, the website **Money Supermarket** (www.moneysupermarket.com) does an automated comparison of 450 partner policies and comes up with the best for your needs.

For health insurance see p1123; see p1118 for details on car insurance.

Worldwide cover to travellers from over 44 countries is available online at www.lonelyplanet.com/travel_services.

INTERNET ACCESS

As broadband access in homes becomes common in Western Europe, the number of Internet cafés is shrinking. You'll still usually find them in tourist areas and around big train stations. Otherwise you may end up at online gaming parlours where you can compose an email asking for money from home or bragging about the incredible deal you got on a new frock while boys blast aliens all around you. Costs average about €3 per hour. When in doubt ask at a tourist office, it's a top question after 'where are the toilets?'

Hostels, hotels and other accommodation usually have some sort of access. This can range from a computer in the corner to wireless (wi-fi) access in every room. Note that the latter can sometimes cost €30 or more.

In general wi-fi (WLAN in Germany) access is best the further north in Western Europe you go. But it can be found in all countries, from cute cafés to train stations to libraries. If you have your own laptop with a wi-fi card, just open it up and see what signals are out there. Often you'll find access is through large providers such as **t-mobile** (hotspot.t-mobile.com), which charge €6 or more per hour.

To find wi-fi hot spots, try sites such as www.jiwire.com.

LEGAL MATTERS

Most Western European police are friendly and helpful, especially if you have been a victim of a crime. You are required by law to prove your identity if asked by police, so always carry your passport, or an identity card if you're an EU citizen.

Ages of Consent

The age of consent for heterosexual and homosexual intercourse is generally between 14 and 16 across Europe, although some countries such as Ireland and Northern Ireland have a higher age limit of 17 for certain types of sex. You can generally purchase alcohol (beer and wine) between 16 and 18 (usually 18 for spirits), but if in doubt, ask. Although you can drive at 17 or 18, you might not be able to hire a car until you reach 25 years of age.

Illegal Drugs

Narcotics are sometimes openly available in Europe, but that doesn't mean they're legal. The Netherlands is most famed for its liberal attitudes, with 'coffee shops' openly selling cannabis. However, even here, it's a case of the police turning a blind eye. Possession of cannabis is only decriminalised not legalised (apart from medicinal use). Don't take this relaxed attitude as an invitation to buy harder drugs; if you get caught, you'll be punished.

Equally, in Belgium, the possession of up to 5g of cannabis is legal but selling the drug isn't, so if you get caught at the point of sale you could be in trouble. In Portugal, the possession of *all* drugs has been decriminalised. Once again, however, selling is illegal.

Britain downgraded cannabis from a Class B to a Class C drug several years back. If you are caught, you will probably just be given an informal, on-the-spot warning and have your drugs confiscated. However, police can still arrest users, especially if they are caught smoking in public, in front of children or get aggressive when confronted.

Switzerland has gone the other way. It was moving towards decriminalisation but then had a last-minute legal about-face. Some people still smoke pot openly, but if police decide to enforce the law you'll face up to a Sfr400 fine just for possession of cannabis. Spain and Italy have also tightened their cannabis laws recently.

If in any doubt, err on the side of caution. For your own safety, don't even think about taking drugs across international borders.

Smoking

Cigarette smoking bans have been progressively introduced across Europe since 2004. Countries that now prohibit smoking in bars and restaurants include Ireland, Italy, Northern Ireland and Scotland. Smoking at railway stations or on public transport is banned in the Netherlands, Switzerland and Spain. Further bans are expected in England and Germany in 2006 and 2007, while the Netherlands is creating nonsmoking areas in restaurants and bars (possibly including 'coffee shops' selling cannabis!). So with such change afoot, ask before lighting up.

MAPS

Good maps are easy to find in Europe and in bookshops beforehand. Lonely Planet publishes plastic-coated, full-colour maps to Western European cities including Amsterdam, Barcelona, Berlin, Brussels, Dublin, London, Paris, and Rome.

Road atlases are essential if you are driving or cycling. Leading brands are **Freytag & Berndt** (www.freytagberndt.com), **Hallwag, Kümmerly + Frey** (www.kuemmerly-frey.ch) and **Michelin** (www.michelin.com).

Maps published by European automobile associations such as Britain's **AA** (www.theaa.com) and Germany's **ADAC** (www.adac.de) are usually excellent and sometimes free if membership of your local association gives you reciprocal rights.

Tourist offices are another good source for (usually free and fairly basic) maps.

MEDIA

Newspapers & Magazines

Keeping up with the news in English is obviously no problem in the UK or Ireland. In larger towns in the rest of Western Europe you can buy the excellent *International Herald Tribune*, as well as the colourful but superficial *USA Today*. Among other English-language newspapers widely available are the *Guardian*, the *Financial Times* and the *Times*. Also readily available are *Newsweek*, *Time* and the *Economist*.

Radio & TV

Close to the Channel you can pick up British radio stations, particularly BBC's Radio 4. There are also numerous English-language broadcasts – or even BBC World Service and Voice of America (VOA) rebroadcasts on local AM and FM radio stations. Otherwise, you can pick up a mixture of the BBC World Service and BBC for Europe on medium wave at 648kHz AM and on short wave at 1296kHz, 6195kHz, 9410kHz, 12095kHz (a good daytime frequency), 15485kHz and 17640kHz, depending on the time of day. BBC Radio 4 broadcasts on long wave at 198kHz. VOA can usually be found at various times of the day on 7170kHz, 9530kHz, 9690kHz, 9760kHz, 11825kHz, 15165kHz, 15205kHz, 15335kHz and 15580kHz.

Cable and satellite TV are common in hotels. CNN International and Eurosport can be found throughout Western Europe, as can BBC World and other networks.

MONEY

For security and flexibility, diversify your source of funds. Carry an ATM card, credit card, cash and possibly travellers cheques. See p1101 on carrying money safely.

ATMs

Every country in this book has international ATMs allowing you to withdraw cash directly from your home account, and this is the most common way European travellers now access their money. However, you should always have a back-up option, as

THE EURO

A common currency, the euro is used in 12 EU states: Austria, Belgium, Luxembourg, France, Finland, Germany, Greece, Ireland, Italy, the Netherlands, Portugal and Spain. New EU member states in Eastern Europe might join the so-called 'euro zone' in 2007 or 2008. Denmark, Britain and Sweden have held out against adopting the euro for political reasons.

The euro has the same value in all EU member countries. The euro is divided into 100 cents. There are seven euro notes (five, 10, 20, 50, 100, 200 and 500 euros) and eight euro coins (one and two euros, then one, two, five, 10, 20 and 50 cents). One side is standard for all euro coins and the other side bears a national emblem of participating countries.

some readers have reported glitches with ATMs in individual countries, even when their card worked elsewhere across Europe. In some remote villages, ATMs might be scarce, too.

You will have problems if you don't have a four-digit PIN number – check with your bank. If your card is rejected, try again in a few hours' time. Make sure you bring your bank's phone number, and if your card fails again, call them.

When you withdraw money from an ATM the amounts are converted and dispensed in local currency. However, there will be fees (see opposite). If you're uncertain, ask your bank to explain.

Finally, always cover the keypad when entering your PIN and make sure there are no unusual devices attached to the machine, they can copy your card's details or cause it to stick in the machine. If your card disappears and the screen goes blank before you've even entered your PIN, don't enter it – especially if a 'helpful' bystander tells you to do so. If you can't retrieve your card, call your bank's emergency number as soon as possible.

Cash

Nothing beats cash for convenience…or risk. If you lose it, it's gone forever and very few travel insurers will come to your rescue. Those that do will limit the amount to somewhere around €300 or £200.

If flying into Western Europe from elsewhere you'll find ATMs and currency exchanges in the arrivals area of the airport.

Credit Cards

Credit cards are handy for major purchases such as air or rail tickets, and offer a lifeline in certain emergencies.

Visa and MasterCard/Eurocard are more widely accepted in Europe than Amex and Diners Club; Visa (sometimes called Carte Bleue) is particularly strong in France and Spain. There are, however, regional differences in the general acceptability of credit cards. In the UK, for example, you can usually flash your plastic in the most humble of budget restaurants; in Germany some restaurants don't take credit cards. Cards are not widely accepted off the beaten track.

To reduce the risk of fraud always keep your card in view when making transactions; for example, in restaurants that do accept cards, pay as you leave, following your card to the till. Keep transaction records and either check your statements when you return home, or set up an online login to manage your account while still on the road.

Like ATM cards, banks have loaded up credit cards with hidden charges for foreign purchases. Cash withdrawals on a credit card almost always are a much worse idea than using an ATM card due to the fees and high interest rates. And purchases in currencies different from home are likely to draw various currency conversion surcharges that are simply there to add to the bank's profit. These can run up to 5% or more. Your best bet is to check these things before leaving and try to use a card that offers the best deal. The website www.flyertalk.com has a forum called 'Best Card for Foreign Exchange', which has many useful tips.

International Transfers

International bank transfers are good for secure one-off movements of large amounts of money, but they might take three to five days and there will be a fee (about £25 in the UK, for example). Be sure to specify the name of the bank, plus the sort code and address of the branch where you'd like to pick up your money.

In an emergency, it's quicker and easier to have money wired via **Western Union** (www.westernunion.com) or **MoneyGram** (www.moneygram.com). All are quite costly.

Moneychangers

In general, US dollars and UK pounds are the easiest currencies to exchange in Western Europe. Get rid of Scottish and Welsh pounds before leaving the UK; nobody outside Britain will touch them.

Most airports, central train stations, big hotels and many border posts have banking facilities outside regular business hours, at times on a 24-hour basis. Post offices in Europe often perform banking tasks, tend to be open longer hours, and outnumber banks in remote places. While they always exchange cash, they might balk at handling travellers cheques that are not in the local currency.

The best exchange rates are usually at banks. *Bureaux de change* usually – but not always – offer worse rates or charge higher commissions. Hotels are almost always the worst places to change money.

Taxes & Refunds

Sales tax applies to many goods and services in Western Europe (although the amount – 10% to 20% – is already built into the price of the item). Luckily, when non-EU residents spend more than a certain amount (around €75) they can usually reclaim that tax when leaving the country.

Making a tax-back claim is straightforward. First, make sure the shop offers duty-free sales. (Often a sign will be displayed reading 'Tax-Free Shopping'.) When making your purchase ask the shop attendant for a tax-refund voucher, filled in with the correct amount and the date. This can be used to claim a refund directly at international airports, or be stamped at ferry ports or border crossings and mailed back for a refund.

None of this applies to EU residents. Even an American citizen living in London is not entitled to rebate on items bought in Paris. Conversely, an EU passport holder living in New York is.

Tipping

Tipping has become more complicated, with 'service charges' increasingly being added to bills. In theory, this means you're not obliged to tip. In practice, that money often doesn't go to the server and they might make it clear they still expect a gratuity.

Don't pay twice. If the service charge is optional remove it from the bill and pay a tip. If the service charge is not optional, don't tip.

Generally waiters in Western Europe tend to be paid decent wages. For more details about tipping see the individual country chapters.

Travellers Cheques

As travellers cheques have been overtaken in popularity by international ATMs it's become more difficult to find places that cash them.

That said, having a few travellers cheques can be a good back-up. If they are stolen you can claim a refund, provided you have a record of cheque numbers, but it is vital to store these numbers away from the cheques themselves. Amex and Thomas Cook travellers cheques are reliable brands, while cheques in US dollars, British pounds or euros are the easiest to cash. When changing them, ask about fees and commissions as well as the exchange rate.

MINIMISING ATM CHARGES

When you withdraw cash from an ATM overseas there are several ways you can get hit. Firstly, most banks add a hidden 2.75% loading to what's called the 'Visa/Mastercard wholesale' or 'interbank' exchange rate. In short, they're giving you a worse exchange rate than strictly necessary. Additionally, some banks charge their customers a cash withdrawal fee (usually 2% with a minimum €2 or more). If you're really unlucky, the bank at the foreign end might charge you as well. Triple whammy. If you use a credit card in ATMs you'll also pay interest – usually quite high interest – on the cash withdrawn.

Most experts agree that having the right bankcard is still cheaper than exchanging cash directly. If your bank levies fees, larger, less frequent withdrawals are better.

PHOTOGRAPHY, VIDEO & DVD

Photography

Those of you using a digital camera should check that you have enough memory to store your snaps – a 256MB card will probably be enough. If you do run out of memory space your best bet is to burn your photos onto a CD. Increasing numbers of processing labs and Internet cafés now offer this service (it helps to have your own USB cable as some cameras use oddball connections and the place may not have a card reader). Some places provide a USB on request, but be warned that many of the bigger chain cafés don't let you plug your gear into their computers, meaning that it's back to plan A – the CD.

If you are travelling with a laptop you can download your own pictures and with a wi-fi connection be quickly posting your images online or emailing them to jealous friends and loved ones. There you are, topless on the Mediterranean for the world to see – almost in real time. You can also often send your photos out via Internet cafés.

If you're using film, your destination will dictate what film to take or buy locally. In places like Ireland and Britain, where the sky is often overcast, photographers should bring higher-speed film (eg 200 ISO). For southern Europe (or northern Europe under a blanket of snow and sunny skies) slower film is the answer (100 ISO or lower).

Film and camera equipment are available everywhere in Western Europe, but shops in larger cities and towns have a wider selection.

Lonely Planet's *Travel Photography*, by Richard I'Anson, is a helpful guide to taking the pictures you've always wanted.

Video

Properly used, a video camera can give a fascinating (or often mind-numbing) record of your holiday. Unlike still photography, video means you can record scenes like countryside rolling past the train window. Make sure you keep the batteries charged and have the necessary charger, plugs and transformer for the country you are visiting. In most countries it is possible to obtain video cassettes easily in large towns and cities. And do us just one favour – stop taping long enough to view your scene outside of the tiny monitor.

DVD

European DVD discs and players are formatted for the PAL (Secam in France) TV system as opposed to the NTSC system used in the USA and Japan.

DVDs are encoded with a regional code (for America and Canada this is 1, for Europe and South Africa 2 and for Australia and New Zealand 3). If you buy a disc in Europe check that its code corresponds with that of your DVD player at home as a player coded 1 or 3 will not play a disc that is coded 2. A way round this is to look for universally compatible players and discs carrying a 0 code.

POST

From major European centres, airmail typically takes about five days to North America and about a week to Australasian destinations, although mail from such countries as Greece is much slower. See the individual country chapter for local costs.

Poste restante services, where friends and family can write to you care of the main post office, are still offered, but email has rendered these largely obsolete. Express services such as **DHL** (www.dhl.com) are best for essential deliveries.

SOLO TRAVELLERS

There are few dangers travelling solo throughout Western Europe, but women should take extra precautions (see p1110). Be aware that accommodation places can charge higher single supplement fees, and you might find you're not at the best table in restaurants as a lone diner. Hitchhiking is risky and not recommended at all, particularly for single travellers.

TELEPHONE

You can ring abroad from almost any phone box in Europe. Public telephones accepting stored-value phonecards (available from post offices, telephone centres, newsstands and retail outlets, see opposite) are virtually the norm now; in some countries (eg France) coin-operated phones are almost impossible to find. Many people also use Internet cafés or places aimed at immigrants to make cheap calls home. Treat your hotel phone and its often hidden and outrageous rates the same way you'd treat a thief.

Mobile Phones

Travellers can rent (or purchase) phones with international capabilities. GSM cellular phones are compatible throughout all the countries in Western Europe, but prices vary according to hiring companies.

Phone Codes

For individual country and city area codes see the Fast Facts box at the start of each country chapter.

Toll-free numbers throughout Western Europe generally have an ☎0800 prefix (also ☎0500 in Britain). You'll find toll-free emergency numbers (ambulance, fire brigade, police) under Telephone in the country directories.

Phonecards

For most calls from public phones you're usually better off with a local phonecard. Reverse-charge (collect) calls are often possible, but not always. From many countries, however, the Country Direct system lets you phone home by billing the long-distance carrier you use at home (at rates usually higher than a local phonecard). The numbers can often be dialled from public phones without even inserting a phonecard. Calls made using a credit card are almost always very expensive.

TIME

Most of the countries covered in this book are on Central European Time (GMT/UTC plus one hour), the same time used from Spain to Poland. Britain and Ireland are also on GMT/UTC and Greece is on East European Time (GMT plus two hours).

Clocks are advanced on the last Sunday in March one hour for daylight-saving time, and set back on the last Sunday in October. During daylight-saving time Britain and Ireland are GMT/UTC plus one hour, Central European Time is GMT/UTC plus two hours and Greece is GMT/UTC plus three hours.

TOURIST INFORMATION

Tourist offices in Western Europe are common and almost universally helpful. They can find accommodation, issue maps, advise on sights and activities and help with more obscure queries such as 'Where can I wash my clothes?'

Country chapters in this book list national and regional tourist offices. You'll also find the details for the local office in almost every city and town.

TRAVELLERS WITH DISABILITIES

Cobbled medieval streets, 'classic' hotels, congested inner cities and underground metro systems make Western Europe a tricky destination for people with mobility impairments. However, the train facilities can be okay, and some destinations boast new tram services or lifts to platforms. The following websites can help with specific details.

Accessible Europe (www.accessibleeurope.com) Specialist European tours with van transport. Prices start at about €500 for four days.

Lonely Planet message board (thorntree.lonelyplanet.com) Share experiences on the Travellers With Disabilities branch.

Mobility International Schweiz (www.mis-ch.ch) Good site listing 'barrier-free' destinations in Switzerland and abroad, plus wheelchair-accessible hotels in Switzerland. Sadly, only partly in English. Address English emails to info@mis-ch.ch.

Mobility International USA (www.miusa.org) Publishes guides and advises travellers with disabilities on mobility issues.

Rolliday (www.rolliday.net) This house-exchange programme also includes lists of accessible (to varying degrees) camp sites, youth hostels and hotels in Europe – some properly tested and given a stamp of approval.

Royal Association for Disability & Rehabilitation (www.radar.org.uk) Publishes a comprehensive annual guide, *Holidays in Britain & Ireland – A Guide for Disabled People.*

Society for the Advancement of Travelers with Handicaps (www.sath.org) Reams of information for travellers with disabilities.

VISAS

A visa is a stamp in your passport or on a separate piece of paper permitting you to enter the country in question and stay for a specified period of time.

Most readers of this book, however, will have very little to do with visas. With a valid passport you should be able to visit Western European countries for up to three months, provided you have some sort of onward or return ticket and/or 'sufficient means of support' (money).

In line with the Schengen Agreement there are no passport controls at borders between Austria, Belgium, Denmark, Finland, France, Germany, Greece, Iceland, Italy, Luxembourg, the Netherlands, Norway, Portugal, Spain, Sweden, and most recently, Switzerland. Think of this zone as one country in terms of your three-month stay. It won't work to try to stay in each of the countries for three months. So if you are planning to stay in Western Europe for longer than three months, make certain that you leave the Schengen zone before your 90 days are up (say by a jaunt to the UK or the Czech Republic) and then return, getting a new entrance stamp in your passport.

Border procedures between EU and non-EU countries can still be thorough, though citizens of Australia, Canada, New Zealand and the USA don't need visas for tourist visits to any Schengen country or the UK. For additional details, see the Visa section of the directories in the country chapters.

For those who do require visas, it's important to remember that these will have a 'use-by' date, and you'll be refused entry after that period has elapsed. It may not be checked when entering these countries overland, but major problems can arise if it is requested during your stay or on departure and you can't produce it.

VOLUNTEERING

If you want to gain greater European insight, a short-term volunteer project might seem a good idea. However, most voluntary organisations levy high charges for airfares, food, lodging and recruitment (from about US$300 to US$1000 per week) making such work costly. Let's face it, Western Europe is fairly well off so the need for volunteers from abroad is low.

One exception is **WWOOF International** (www.wwoof.org), which helps link volunteers with organic farms in Germany, Slovenia, Czech Republic, Denmark, the UK, Austria and Switzerland. A small membership fee (€10 to €30) is required to join the national chapter and occasionally an extra administration fee is charged to send you a list of farms looking for additional hands. In exchange for your labour, you'll receive free lodging and food.

WEIGHTS & MEASURES

The metric system is in use throughout Western Europe. However, in Britain non-metric equivalents are common (distances continue to be given in miles and beer is sold in pints not litres).

Continental Europe shows decimals with commas and thousands with full stops (for numbers with four or more digits the French use full stops or spaces).

There's a metric conversion chart on the inside front cover of this book.

WOMEN TRAVELLERS

Women travellers, in general, will find Western Europe relatively enlightened and shouldn't often have to invent husbands that will be joining them soon or boyfriends that will be back any minute. If you do find yourself in an uncomfortable situation or area, leave, or pipe up and make a racket. In parts of Spain, Italy and Greece you may find men more aggressive in their stares or comments.

WORK

Working in Europe is not always straightforward. Officially, an EU citizen is allowed to work in any other EU country, but the paperwork can be complicated for long-term employment. Other nationalities require special work permits that can be almost impossible to arrange, especially for temporary work.

However, that doesn't prevent enterprising travellers from topping up their funds by working in the hotel or restaurant trades at beach or ski resorts or teaching a little English – and they don't always have to do this illegally.

The UK, for example, issues special 'working holiday' visas to Commonwealth citizens who are aged between 17 and 30, valid for 12 months' work during two years (see www.ukvisas.gov.uk). Your national student exchange organisation might be able to arrange temporary work permits to several countries.

Seasonal Work in Western Europe

Work Your Way Around the World, by Susan Griffith, gives practical advice, as does *Summer Jobs Abroad,* edited by David Woodworth.

Remember, if you find a temporary job, the pay might be less than that offered to locals. Typical tourist jobs (picking grapes in France, washing dishes in Alpine resorts, working at a bar in Greece) often come with board and lodging. The pay is essentially pocket money, but you'll have a good time partying with other travellers.

Starting points include:

Jobs in Europe (www.jobs-in-europe.net) Contains links to hundreds of organisations looking to employ Europeans and non-Europeans (with the correct work permits, of course).

Jobs in the Alps (www.jobs-in-the-alps.com) Mainly service jobs like chambermaids, bar staff and porters. Some linguistic skills required.

Natives (www.natives.co.uk) Summer and winter resort jobs and various tips.

Picking Jobs (www.jobs-in-the-alps.com) Includes some tourism jobs, too.

Season Workers (www.seasonworkers.com) Ski resort work and summer jobs; also has English teaching jobs.

Transport in Western Europe

CONTENTS

Getting There & Away	**1112**
Air	1112
Land	1114
Sea	1115
Getting Around	**1115**
Air	1115
Bicycle	1116
Boat	1117
Bus	1117
Car & Motorcycle	1117
Hitching	1120
Public Transport	1120
Tours	1120
Train	1120

GETTING THERE & AWAY

Part of the adventure is figuring out how to get to Western Europe, and in these days of severe competition among airlines there are plenty of opportunities to find cheap tickets to a variety of gateway cities.

Options for reaching Western Europe by land or sea are pretty limited. International strife has lead to the closure of most land routes from Asia, while watery options are limited to the luxury *Queen Mary 2* from the USA and freighters from various ports worldwide.

AIR

Major gateways to Western Europe include airports in London, Paris, Amsterdam, Frankfurt, Munich and Rome. However, with connections you can reach dozens of airports across the continent. Once in Europe you can take advantage of discount carriers to get around (see p1115).

For details on airports, see the relevant sections of the country chapters.

International Airlines

Almost every international airline serves Europe. The following are the main international airlines based in Europe and key carriers elsewhere that serve Europe.

Aer Lingus (EI; www.aerlingus.com)
Air Canada (AC; www.aircanada.ca)
Air France (AF; www.airfrance.nl)
Air New Zealand (NZ; www.airnz.com)
Alitalia (AZ; www.alitalia.com)
American Airlines (AA; www.aa.com)
Austrian Airlines (OS; www.aua.com)
BMI (BD; www.flybmi.com)
British Airways (BA; www.britishairways.com)
Cathay Pacific (CX; www.cathaypacific.nl)
China Airlines (CI; www.china-airlines.com)
Continental Airlines (CO; www.continental.com)
Delta Air Lines (DL; www.delta.com)
Iberia (IB; www.iberia.com)
Japan Airlines (JL; www.jal-europe.com)
KLM Royal Dutch Airlines (KL; www.klm.nl)
Lufthansa (LH; www.lufthansa.com)
Malaysia Airlines (MH; www.malaysiaairlines.com.my)
Northwest Airlines (NW; www.nwa.com)
Qantas (QF; www.qantas.com.au)
Singapore Airlines (SQ; www.singaporeair.com)
South African Airways (SA; www.flysaa.com)
Swiss International Air Lines (LX; www.swiss.com)
TAP Air Portugal (TP; www.tap-airportugal.pt)
Thai Airways International (TG; www.thaiairways.com)
United Airlines (UA; www.unitedairlines.nl)
Virgin Atlantic (VS; www.virgin-atlantic.com)

Tickets

An air ticket alone can gouge a great slice out of anyone's budget, but you can reduce the cost by digging for discounted fares. Stiff competition has resulted in widespread discounting.

THINGS CHANGE...

The information in this chapter is particularly vulnerable to change. Check directly with the airline or a travel agent to make sure you understand how a fare (and ticket you may buy) works and be aware of the security requirements for international travel. Shop carefully. The details given in this chapter should be regarded as pointers and are not a substitute for your own careful, up-to-date research.

For long-term travel there are plenty of discount tickets that are valid for 12 months, allowing multiple stopovers with open dates. For short-term travel, cheaper fares are available by travelling midweek, staying away at least one Saturday night or taking advantage of short-lived promotional offers.

You may choose to use a travel agent for your tickets to Western Europe but you will often have to pay a surcharge for this service. But if you have complicated plans, lots of questions or just need some handholding you may find an agent very worthwhile. Some travel agencies charge rock-bottom prices, but beware of back-alley operators. You may decide to pay more by opting for the safety of a better-known travel agent. Companies such as STA Travel, which has offices worldwide, are not going to disappear overnight and they offer good prices to most destinations.

Consider your eventual itinerary when looking for tickets. Some cheap fares may be on airlines that require one or more connections. For the same money or just a bit more you may be able to fly nonstop, saving yourself hours of travel time. It also pays to watch for ads for tickets to Europe – chances are if one airline is offering cheap fares, they all are. And beware of hidden fees that can add hundreds to the cost of your ticket. British carriers in particular are adept at advertising bargain fares with huge and hidden fuel and other surcharges.

COURIER FLIGHTS

Courier tickets are a great bargain if you're lucky enough to find one. You get cheap passage in return for accompanying packages or documents through customs and delivering them to a representative at the destination airport. You are permitted to bring along a carry-on bag, but that's often all. Be aware that this type of ticket is usually very restricted, so check carefully before purchasing.

Most courier flights only cover the major air routes. They are occasionally advertised in newspapers, or you could contact air-freight companies listed in the phone book.

The **International Association of Air Travel Couriers** (IAATC; www.courier.org) offers access to its website and booking service for US$45.

INTERNET

Buying tickets to Western Europe is easily done via the web, which allows seemingly

CLIMATE CHANGE & TRAVEL

Climate change is a serious threat to the ecosystems that humans rely upon, and air travel is the fastest-growing contributor to the problem. Lonely Planet regards travel, overall, as a global benefit, but believes we all have a responsibility to limit our personal impact on global warming.

Flying & climate change

Pretty much every form of motorized travel generates CO² (the main cause of human-induced climate change) but planes are far and away the worst offenders, not just because of the sheer distances they allow us to travel, but because they release greenhouse gases high into the atmosphere. The statistics are frightening: two people taking a return flight between Europe and the USA will contribute as much to climate change as an average household's gas and electricity consumption over a whole year.

Carbon offset schemes

Climatecare.org and other websites use 'carbon calculators' that allow travellers to offset the level of greenhouse gases they are responsible for with financial contributions to sustainable travel schemes that reduce global warming – including projects in India, Honduras, Kazakhstan and Uganda.

Lonely Planet, together with Rough Guides and other concerned partners in the travel industry, support the carbon offset scheme run by climatecare.org. Lonely Planet offsets all of its staff and author travel.

For more information check out our website: www.lonelyplanet.com/climatecare.

endless price and schedule comparisons. Individual airlines sites often have fares you won't find elsewhere. In particular look for web-only discounts. If you have the luxury of time, start your search many months before you plan to go and once you have a sense of the going rates you'll know when you see a really good deal.

Of course, checking a variety of airline websites can soon become tedious. That's where the convenience of travel websites can be unmatched.

Websites that can be useful include the following (many have branches specific to countries, eg for Australia add .au to the address). For other useful sites, see the geographic-specific listings below.

Expedia (www.expedia.com) Full service.
Hotwire (www.hotwire.com) Full service.
Kayak (www.kayak.com) Excellent site that checks both airline and discount websites.
Orbitz (www.orbitz.com) Full service with the widest range of fares.
Priceline (www.priceline.com) Full service.
Travelocity (www.travelocity.com) Full service.

SECOND-HAND TICKETS

You'll occasionally see advertisements on youth-hostel bulletin boards and in newspapers for second-hand tickets. That is, somebody purchased a return ticket or a ticket with multiple stopovers and now wants to sell the unused portion of the ticket. Unfortunately, these tickets are worthless as the name on the ticket must match the name on the passport of the person flying.

STUDENT & YOUTH FARES

Full-time students and people under 26 sometimes have access to better deals than other travellers. The better deals may not always be cheaper fares but can include more flexibility to change flights and/or routes. You have to show a document proving your date of birth, a valid International Student Identity Card (ISIC) or an International Youth Travel Card (IYTC) when buying your ticket and boarding the plane. See www.istc.org for more information.

From Africa

Rennies Travel (www.renniestravel.com) and **STA Travel** (www.statravel.co.za) have offices throughout Southern Africa. Check their websites for branch locations.

From Asia

STA Travel proliferates in Asia:

Bangkok (☎ 02-236 0262; www.statravel.co.th)
Hong Kong (☎ 2736 1618; www.statravel.com.hk)
Japan (☎ 03 5391 2922; www.statravel.co.jp)
Singapore (☎ 6737 7188; www.statravel.com.sg)

Another resource in Japan is **No 1 Travel** (☎ 03 3205 6073; www.no1-travel.com); in Hong Kong try **Four Seas Tours** (☎ 2200 7760; www.fourseastravel.com/english).

From Australia

For the location of STA Travel branches call ☎ 1300 733 035 or visit www.statravel.com.au. **Flight Centre** (☎ 133 133; www.flightcentre.com.au) also has offices throughout Australia. For online bookings, try www.travel.com.au.

From Canada

Travel Cuts (☎ 800-667-2887; www.travelcuts.com) is Canada's national student travel agency. For online bookings see p1113 with a .ca in place of .com.

From New Zealand

Both **Flight Centre** (☎ 0800 243 544; www.flightcentre.co.nz) and **STA Travel** (☎ 0508 782 872; www.statravel.co.nz) have branches throughout the country. The site www.travel.co.nz is recommended for online bookings.

From USA

STA Travel (☎ 800-781-4040; www.statravel.com) is found across the USA. Many discount travel agents are known as consolidators (although you won't see a sign on the door saying 'consolidator'). San Francisco is the ticket consolidator capital of America, although good deals can be found in Los Angeles, New York and other big cities. Consolidator tickets are good for unsold seats unloaded by the airlines. They are usually heavily restricted: no changes permitted of any kind.

For online booking, see p1113.

LAND

You can easily get to Western Europe from the rest of Europe by road, bus or train. Things become more complicated as you get further away, however.

It *is* possible to get to Western Europe by rail from Central and eastern Asia, but count on spending at least eight days doing it. Four different routes wind their way to Moscow: the Trans-Siberian (9297km from Vladivostok), the Trans-Mongolian (7860km from Beijing) and the Trans-Manchurian (9001km from Beijing) all use the same tracks across Siberia but have different routes east of Lake Baikal; the Trans-Kazakhstan (another Trans-Siberian line) runs between Moscow and Urumqi in northwestern China. Prices vary enormously depending on where you buy the ticket and what is included – advertised 2nd-class fares cost around UK£600 from Beijing to Moscow.

There are countless travel options between Moscow and Western Europe. Most people will opt for the train, usually to Berlin or Vienna. Lonely Planet's *Trans-Siberian Railway* is a comprehensive guide to the route with details of costs, highlights and travel agencies that specialise in the trip.

SEA

Mediterranean Ferries

There are many ferries crossing the Mediterranean between Africa and Western Europe. The ferry you take will depend on your travels in Africa, but the options include: Spain–Morocco, France–Morocco, France–Tunisia, Italy–Tunisia. There are also ferries between Greece and Israel via Cyprus.

Ferries are often filled to capacity in summer, especially to/from Tunisia, so it's advisable to book well in advance if you're taking a vehicle across. See the Transport section in the relevant country chapters for more information.

Passenger Ships & Freighters

Cunard's **Queen Mary 2** (www.cunard.com) sails between New York and Southampton 20 times a year; the trip takes six nights each way and costs under US$3000 for two people in a standard double cabin. Deals abound.

A more adventurous alternative is as a paying passenger on a freighter. Freighters are far more numerous than cruise ships and there are routes to Western Europe from all continents. Passenger freighters typically carry six to 12 passengers (more than 12 would require a doctor on board) and, though less luxurious than dedicated cruise ships, give you a real taste of life at sea.

Schedules tend to be flexible and costs are around US$100 a day. **Strand Travel** (www.strandtravel.co.uk) is a good source of info.

GETTING AROUND

Travel within most of the EU, whether by air, rail or car, is made easier owing to the Schengen Agreement, which abolished border controls between member states. All travellers must still carry a passport; there are two passport-control lines – EU and non-EU nationals. This was designed to speed up entries for EU nationals. Britain, Ireland, Switzerland and Liechtenstein are the only EU countries currently outside the agreement.

Budget airlines are revolutionising the way people cover long distances in Europe. However, hopping a plane deprives you of the fun of travelling by train and the cultural experiences of navigating train stations.

AIR

Getting around Western Europe by air has exploded in popularity during the past few years thanks to the proliferation of discount carriers and cheap fares. It is possible to go from London to Berlin at times for under €30. These sorts of fares are common, and more interestingly, dozens of tiny airports across Europe now boast airline service, so that a trip to Italy doesn't mean choosing between Milan and Rome, but rather scores of airports up and down the boot.

It is now possible to put together a practical itinerary that might bounce from London to the south of Spain to Florence to Amsterdam in a two-week period; all at an affordable price and avoiding endless train rides.

But with cheap fares come many caveats. First, some of the barebones carriers are just that. Discount leader Ryanair prides itself on nonreclining seats, nonexistent legroom and nonexistent window shades. At some of its far-flung airports any customer service will also be nonexistent. Scores of other discount airlines are following this model.

A second caveat involves the airports. If you really want to go to Carcassonne in the south of France, then getting a €20 ticket from London will be a dream come true. But if you want to go to Frankfurt in Germany and end up buying a ticket to 'Frankfurt-Hahn', you find yourself at a small airport 70km west of Frankfurt and two hours away by bus.

In this book you will find dozens of airports with air service. Check their websites for information on the latest service details to the airport.

Airlines in Western Europe

Although many people first think of budget carriers when they consider a cheap ticket in Western Europe, the older established airlines such as British Airways and Lufthansa are also worth considering. They often have competitive airfares and serve major airports close to main destinations. See p1112 for a list that includes these carriers.

Major budget carriers in Western Europe are listed below. All have excellent websites showing maps with their ever-changing web of services. See the country chapters for scores of smaller airlines with more limited service.

Air Berlin (www.airberlin.com)
Easyjet (www.easyjet.com)
Ryanair (www.ryanair.com)
Virgin Express (www.virgin-express.com)

The best place to buy cheap airline tickets is over the internet. In fact many airlines only sell their cheapest tickets over the net. Various websites compare fares across a range of airlines within Europe. One of the best is www.skyscanner.net, which gets results from mainstream and discount carriers.

Air Passes

The three major airline alliances (listed below) each offer various schemes where you can purchase flights within Europe if you fly to Europe with one of the member carriers. Typically these cost about US$65 to US$100 per flight.

OneWorld (www.oneworld.com)
Sky Team (www.skyteam.com)
Star Alliance (www.staralliance.com)

BICYCLE

A tour of Western Europe by bike may seem like a daunting prospect but help is at hand. The **Cyclists' Touring Club** (CTC; ☎ 0870 873 0060; www.ctc.org.uk) is based in the UK and offers its members an information service on all matters associated with cycling (including cycling conditions, detailed routes, itineraries and maps).

The key to a successful trip is to travel light. What you carry should be largely determined by your destination and the type of trip you're taking. Even for the shortest and most basic trip it's worth carrying the tools necessary for repairing a puncture. Other things you might want to consider packing are spare brake and gear cables, spanners, Allen keys, spare spokes of the correct length and strong adhesive tape.

Wearing helmets is not compulsory but is advised. A seasoned cyclist can average about 80km a day, but this depends on the terrain and how much you are carrying.

For more information on cycling, see p1098 and the Activities section of individual country chapters.

Purchase

For major cycling tours it's best to have a bike you're familiar with, so consider bringing your own rather than buying on arrival. If you can't be bothered with the hassle, there are plenty of places to buy in Western Europe (shops sell new and second-hand bicycles or you can check local papers for private vendors).

Rental

It is easy to rent bicycles in Western Europe and you can often negotiate good deals. Rental periods vary. Local tourist offices will carry information on rental outlets. Occasionally you can drop the bicycle off at a different location so you don't have to double back on your route.

Transporting a Bicycle

If you want to bring your own bicycle to Western Europe, you should be able to take it with you on the plane relatively easily. Check with the airlines for details before you buy your ticket as each one has different policies.

Within Western Europe, bikes can sometimes be brought with you onto a train, subject to a small supplementary fee. See the Transport section in the individual country chapters.

Fast trains can rarely accommodate bikes: they might need to be sent as registered luggage and may end up on a different train from the one you take. This is often the case in France and Spain. Eurostar charges UK£20 to send a bike as registered luggage on its routes. You can transport your bicycle with you on Eurotunnel through the Channel Tunnel.

The UK-based **Bike Express** (☎ 01642-251 440; www.bike-express.co.uk) is a coach service where cyclists can travel with their bicycles. It runs in the summer in the UK, France, Italy and Spain, with pick-up/drop-off points en route.

BOAT

Several ferry companies compete on all the main ferry routes, and the resulting service is comprehensive but complicated. The same ferry company can have a host of different prices for the same route, depending upon the time of day or year, the validity of the ticket or the length of your vehicle. It is worth planning (and booking) ahead where possible as there may be special reductions on off-peak crossings and advance-purchase tickets. Most ferry companies adjust prices according to the level of demand (so-called 'fluid' or 'dynamic' pricing), so it may pay to offer alternative travel dates. Vehicle tickets usually include the driver and a full complement of passengers.

Major ferry routes for users of this book include the thicket of services between Britain and France as well as routes between Italy and Greece. See the relevant chapters for details.

Rail-pass holders are entitled to discounts or free travel on some lines. Food on ferries is often expensive (and lousy), so bring your own when possible. It is also worth knowing that if you take your vehicle on board, you are usually denied access to it during the voyage.

BUS

Buses sometimes have the edge in terms of costs, but are generally slower and less comfortable than trains and at times not as cheap or quick as airlines. Europe's biggest network of international buses is provided by a group of bus companies that operates under the name of **Eurolines** (www.eurolines.com). There are a lot of services and it is possible to travel very far for under €100.

See the Transport section in the individual country chapters for more information about long-distance buses.

Bus Passes

Eurolines' various affiliates offer scores of national and regional bus passes. See the country chapters for details as well as the Eurolines website.

Busabout (☎ UK 020-7950 1661; www.busabout.com) operates buses that complete set circuits around Europe, stopping at major cities. You get unlimited travel per sector and can 'hop-on, hop-off' at any scheduled stop, then resume with a later bus. Buses are often oversubscribed, so prebook each sector to avoid being stranded.

Departures are every two days from April to October, or May to September for Spain and Portugal. The circuits cover all countries in continental Western Europe, and you can pay to add on Greece, Scandinavia and/or a London–Paris link.

Passes allowing you to cover a lot of territory start at under US$500.

CAR & MOTORCYCLE

Travelling with your own vehicle allows increased flexibility and the option to get off the beaten track. Unfortunately, cars can be inconvenient in city centres when you have to negotiate one-way streets or find somewhere to park amid a confusing concrete jungle. Eurotunnel (see p414) transports cars through the Channel Tunnel.

Automobile Associations

Perish the thought of ever breaking down in some remote rural village in the Pyrenees or the isolated Irish countryside. But it happens. Should you find yourself in a predicament, you can contact the local automobile association for emergency assistance. It can provide a variety of road-side services such as petrol refills, flat-tyre repair and towing, plus predeparture information such as maps, itineraries and even accommodation reservations. Check with the main motoring association in your home country for coverage options.

Campervan

A popular way to tour Europe is for three or four people to band together to buy or rent a camper van. London is the usual embarkation point. Some good British publications and websites to check out for camper van purchases are **Loot** (www.loot.com), **TNT magazine** (www.tntmag.co.uk/uk) and **AutoTrader** (www.autotrader.co.uk).

Some second-hand dealers offer a buy-back scheme when you return from Europe, but we've received warnings that some dealers don't fully honour the refund commitments. Buying and reselling privately is more advantageous if you have the time.

Camper vans usually feature a fixed high-top or elevating roof and two to five bunk beds. Apart from the essential gas cooker, professional conversions may include a sink, fridge and built-in cupboards. Prices and facilities vary considerably and it's certainly worth getting advice from a mechanic to see if you are being offered a fair price. Getting a mechanical check (from UK£40) is also a good idea. Once on the road you should be able to keep budgets lower than backpackers using trains, but don't forget to set some money aside for emergency repairs.

The main advantage of going by camper van is flexibility. Transport, accommodation and storage are all taken care of. Unfortunately, the self-contained factor can also prove to be one of the downsides. Conditions can get very cramped, tempers can become frayed and your romantic, hippy-style trail may dissolve into the camper van trip from hell.

Driving Licence

Proof of ownership of a private vehicle should always be carried (a Vehicle Registration Document for British-registered cars) when touring Europe. An EU driving licence is acceptable for driving throughout Europe.

Many non-European driving licences are valid in Europe. Some advise carrying an International Driving Permit (IDP), but this costly multilingual document sold by national auto clubs is rarely necessary – especially to rent a car.

Fuel

Fuel prices can vary enormously from country to country (though it's always more expensive than in North America or Australia) and may bear little relation to the general cost of living. Ireland's Automobile Association maintains a good web page of European fuel prices at www.aaroadwatch.ie/eupetrolprices.

Unleaded petrol and diesel is available across Western Europe.

Hire

The big international rental firms will give you reliable service and a good standard of vehicle. Usually you will have the option of returning the car to a different outlet at the end of the rental period. Rates vary widely but expect to pay somewhere between €25 and €70 per day. Prebook for the lowest rates – if you walk into an office and ask for a car on the spot, you will pay more. For really good deals, pre-pay for your rental. Fly/drive combinations and other programmes are worth looking into. Major companies include:

Avis (www.avis.com)
Budget (www.budget.com)
Europcar (www.europcar.com)
Hertz (www.hertz.com)

Brokers can cut hire costs. The UK's **Holiday Autos** (☎ 0870 400 0010; www.holidayautos.com) has low rates and offices or representatives in over 20 countries, or try **Autos Abroad** (☎ 0870 066 7788; www.autosabroad.co.uk). In the USA, **Kemwel Holiday Autos** (☎ 877-820-0668; www.kemwel.com) has many deals.

No matter where you rent, it is imperative to understand exactly what is included in your rental agreement (collision waiver, unlimited mileage etc). Make sure you are covered with an adequate insurance policy. And Americans should take note: less than 4% of European cars have automatic transmissions, so if you need this, you'll pay more than double for your car.

The minimum rental age is usually 21 or even 23, and you'll need a credit card.

Motorcycle and moped rental is common in such countries as Italy, Spain, Greece and the south of France.

Insurance

Third party motor insurance is compulsory in Europe if you are driving your own car (rental cars usually come with insurance). Most UK motor insurance policies automatically provide this for EU countries. Get your insurer to issue a Green Card (which may cost extra), an internationally recognised proof of insurance, and check that it lists all the countries you intend to visit. You'll need this in the event of an accident outside the country where the vehicle is insured. Also ask your insurer for a European Accident Statement form, which can simplify things if the worst happens. Never sign statements you can't read or understand – insist on a translation and sign only if it's acceptable.

It's a good investment to take out a European motoring-assistance policy, such as the AA Five Star Service or the RAC European Motoring Assistance. Expect to pay about UK£50 for 14 days' cover, with a 10% discount for association members. Non-Europeans might find it cheaper to arrange international coverage with their national motoring organisation before leaving home. Ask your motoring organisation for details about free services offered by affiliated organisations around Western Europe.

Every vehicle travelling across an international border should display a sticker showing its country of registration. There's also a variety of rules for mandated equipment. In the UK, contact **RAC** (☎ 0870 5533 533; www.rac.co.uk) or **AA** (☎ 0800 085 7240; www.theaa.com) for more information.

Motorcycle Touring

Western Europe is made for motorcycle touring, with good-quality winding roads, stunning scenery and an active motorcycling scene. The weather is not always reliable though, so make sure your wet-weather gear is up to scratch. The wearing of helmets for rider and passenger is compulsory everywhere in Western Europe. See country chapters for additional rules.

On ferries, motorcyclists can sometimes be squeezed in without a reservation, although booking ahead is certainly advisable during peak travelling periods.

Take note of local customs about parking motorcycles on footpaths (sidewalks). Though this is illegal in some countries, the police usually turn a blind eye as long as the vehicle doesn't obstruct pedestrians. Don't try this in Britain – your feeble excuses to traffic wardens will fall on deaf ears.

If you are thinking of touring Europe on a motorcycle, try contacting the **British Motorcyclists Federation** (☎ 0116-284 5380; www.bmf.co.uk) for help and advice. An excellent source of information for travellers interested in more adventurous biking activities can be found at **Horizons Unlimited** (www.horizonsunlimited.com).

Purchase

Britain is probably the best place to buy as second-hand prices are good and, whether buying privately or from a dealer, the absence of language difficulties will help you establish exactly what you are getting and what guarantees you can expect in the event of a breakdown.

Some good British papers to check out for vehicle purchases are **Loot** (www.loot.com), **TNT magazine** (www.tntmag.co.uk/uk) and **AutoTrader** (www.autotrader.co.uk).

Bear in mind that you will be getting a car with the steering wheel on the right-hand side in Britain. If you want left-hand drive and can afford to buy new, prices are usually reasonable in Greece, France, Germany, Belgium, Luxembourg and the Netherlands. Paperwork can be tricky wherever you buy, and many countries have compulsory roadworthiness checks on older vehicles.

Road Conditions

Conditions and types of roads vary across Western Europe, but it is possible to make some generalisations. The fastest routes are four- or six-lane dual carriageways/highways, ie two or three lanes either side (motorway, autobahn, autoroute, autostrada etc). These roads are great for speed and comfort but driving can be dull, with little or no interesting scenery. Some of these roads incur expensive tolls (eg in Italy, France and Spain) or have a general tax for usage (Switzerland and Austria), but there will usually be an alternative route you can take. Motorways and other primary routes are almost always in good condition.

Road surfaces on minor routes are not perfect in some countries (eg Greece), although normally they will be more than adequate. These roads are narrower and progress is generally much slower. To compensate, you can expect much better scenery and plenty of interesting villages along the way.

Road Rules

Motoring organisations can supply members with country-by-country information about motoring regulations, or they may produce motoring guidebooks for general sale.

With the exception of Britain and Ireland, driving is on the right.

Take care with speed limits, as they vary from country to country. You may be surprised at the apparent disregard of traffic regulations in some places (particularly in Italy and Greece), but as a visitor it is always best to be cautious. In many countries, driving infringements are subject to an on-the-spot fine. Always ask for a receipt.

European drink-driving laws are particularly strict. The blood-alcohol concentration (BAC) limit when driving is between 0.05% and 0.08%, but in certain areas it can be *zero* percent. See the individual country chapters for more details on traffic laws.

HITCHING

Hitching is never entirely safe in any country in the world, and we don't recommend it. Travellers who decide to hitch should understand that they are taking a small but potentially serious risk. People who do choose to hitch will be safer if they travel in pairs and let someone know where they plan to go. Single women should never hitch.

Don't hitch from city centres; take public transport to suburban exit routes. Hitching is usually illegal on motorways – stand on the slip roads or approach drivers at petrol stations and truck stops. Look presentable and cheerful and make a cardboard sign indicating your intended destination in the local language. Never hitch where drivers can't stop in good time or without causing an obstruction. At dusk, give up and think about finding somewhere to stay. If your itinerary includes a ferry crossing (for instance, across the Channel), it might be worth trying to score a ride before the ferry rather than after, since vehicle tickets sometimes include all passengers free of charge.

It is sometimes possible to arrange a lift in advance: scan student notice boards in colleges, or contact car-sharing agencies. Such agencies are particularly popular in Germany (*Mitfahrzentrale;* see p481).

PUBLIC TRANSPORT

Bus & Metro

Most Western European cities have excellent public transport systems with some combination of subways, trains, trams and buses. Service is usually comprehensive. Major airports generally have fast train or subway links to the city centre. See the country chapters for more information.

Taxi

Taxis in Western Europe are metered and rates are high. There might also be supplements (depending on the country) for things such as luggage, the time of day, the location from which you boarded and for extra passengers. Good public transport networks make the use of taxis all but unnecessary, but if you need one in a hurry they can usually be found idling near train stations or outside big hotels.

Lower fares make taxis more viable in such countries as Spain, Greece and Portugal. Don't underestimate the local knowledge that can be gleaned from taxi drivers. They can often tell you about the liveliest places in town and know all about events happening during your stay.

TOURS

Package tours, whether tailor-made or bog-standard, cater for all tastes, interests and ages. See your travel agent or look in the small ads in newspaper travel pages. The internet is also an excellent resource to find unusual tours that might not receive media or trade attention.

Specialists include **Ramblers Holidays** (☎ 017 07-331133; www.ramblersholidays.co.uk) in Britain for hiking trips and **CBT Tours** (☎ 800-736-2453; www .cbttours.com) in the USA for bicycle trips.

Young revellers can party on Europe-wide bus tours. **Contiki** (www.contiki.com) and **Top Deck** (www.topdecktravel.co.uk) offer camping or hotel-based bus tours for the 18 to 35 age group. Both companies sell tours to customers worldwide.

For people aged over 50, **Saga Holidays** (www .sagaholidays.com) offers holidays ranging from cheap coach tours to luxury cruises and has cheap travel insurance.

TRAIN

Trains are a popular way of getting around: they are comfortable, frequent and generally on time. The Channel Tunnel makes it possible to get from Britain to continental Europe using the **Eurostar** (www.eurostar.com). See country chapters for more details.

For many people, travel in Europe would not be travel in Europe without trains. But note that the traditional image of compartments with little wine bottle holders and various characters roaming the corridor is being replaced by fast and modern trains that are more like especially comfortable versions of airliners. Diners have mostly been replaced by snack bars or trolleys, although most people buy their food before boarding.

In the south, train fares are quite cheap. In the north, fares can be more expensive but there are many deals. See the country chapters for details.

Every national rail company has a website with a vast amount of schedule and fare information. For international details, the German national railroad **Deutsche Bahn** (www.bahn.de) has excellent schedule and fare information in English for trains across Europe. The website **The Man in Seat 61** (www.seat61.com) has good train descriptions and details.

If you plan to travel extensively by train, you might enjoy the *Thomas Cook European Timetable,* which gives a cleverly condensed listing of train schedules and indicates where supplements apply or where reservations are necessary. The timetable is updated monthly and is available from **Thomas Cook** (www.thomascookpublishing.com) outlets and bookshops in the UK (online elsewhere in the world).

Paris, Brussels, Frankfurt, Munich, Milan and Vienna are important hubs for international rail connections. See the relevant city sections for details and budget ticket agents.

Note that European trains sometimes split en route in order to service two destinations, so even if you know you're on the right train, make sure you're in the correct carriage too.

Tickets

When weighing up ticket options consider the many cheap ticket deals offered by the railways. These include advance-purchase reductions, one-off promotions or special circular-route tickets. Normal international tickets are valid for two months, and you can make as many stops as you like en route; make your intentions known when purchasing and inform train conductors how far you're going before they punch your ticket.

Fast Trains

Western European trains (outside of Greece and Portugal) are fast, frequent and often comfortable. High-speed networks (300km per hour or more) continue to expand and have given the airlines major competition on many routes. The internal TGV and ICE networks in France and Germany respectively are comprehensive and are excellent ways to get around. The AVE network in Spain and Italy's own high-speed network are growing fast. **Eurostar** (www.eurostar.com) links London to Brussels and Paris in about two hours. **Thalys** (www.thalys.com) links Paris with Brussels, Amsterdam and Cologne. In 2009 a new line will open linking Paris to Frankfurt via Strasbourg.

Slower but still reasonably fast trains that cross borders are called EuroCity (EC). It is a good idea (sometimes obligatory) to make seat reservations at peak times and on certain lines.

Overnight Trains

The romantic image of the European night train is becoming a lot less common with the popularity of budget airlines. However, you can still find a good network of routes from the north to Italy.

Couchette bunks are comfortable enough, if lacking a bit in privacy. There are four per compartment in 1st class or six in 2nd class. A bunk costs around UK£15 for most international trains, irrespective of the length of the journey.

Sleepers are the most comfortable option, offering beds for one or two passengers in 1st class, and two or three passengers in 2nd class. Charges vary depending on the journey, but they are significantly more expensive than couchettes.

Rail Passes

Shop around, as pass prices can vary between different outlets. Once purchased, take care of your pass as it cannot be replaced or refunded if lost or stolen. European passes get reductions on Eurostar through the Channel Tunnel and on certain ferry routes (eg between France and Ireland). In the USA, **Rail Europe** (☎ 877-257-2887; www.raileurope.com) sells all sorts of rail passes.

EURAIL

There are so many different passes to choose from and such a wide variety of areas and time periods covered that you should have a good idea of your itinerary before purchasing one. These passes can only be bought by residents of non-European countries, and are supposed to be purchased before arriving in Europe.

Eurail passes are valid for unlimited travel on national railways and some private lines in the Western European countries of Austria, Belgium, France, Germany, Greece, Ireland, Italy, Luxembourg, the Netherlands, Portugal, Spain and Switzerland (including Liechtenstein), plus several more neighbouring ones.

Eurail is also valid on some ferries between Italy and Greece. Reductions are given on some other ferry routes and on river/lake steamer services in various countries.

The Eurailpass is the standard pass for travellers 26 years and over. It provides unlimited 1st-class travel only: 15 days to three months costs US$605 to US$1703. This is the best pass for those who want to spend most of their time on trains.

The Eurailpass Flexi is also for travellers 26 and over. It offers 1st-class travel for any chosen days within a two-month period: 10/15 days US$715/940. This is a better option for most people.

The Eurailpass Youth pass offers the same options as the standard Eurailpass, but for those aged under 26 years, and for 2nd-class travel only. Passes cover periods from 15 days to three months for US$394 to US$1108. This is the classic backpacker's pass.

The Eurailpass Youth Flexi offers the same options as the standard Eurailpass Flexi, but for those aged under 26, and for 2nd-class travel only: 10/15 days for US$465/611.

Two to five people travelling together can get a 'saver' version of all passes mentioned above, saving about 15%.

Also for non-Europeans is the Eurail Selectpass, which gives buyers the option of choosing which countries it covers and for how long. Options are myriad and can offer significant savings over the above passes if, for example, you are only going to three or four countries.

EURODOMINO

There is a Eurodomino pass for some of the countries covered in the Inter-Rail pass (see right), and it's worth considering if you're homing in on a particular region (however in a major blow to budget travellers, France, Italy and Spain have left the scheme). These passes are sold in Europe to European residents. Adults (travelling 1st or 2nd class) and those under 26 can opt for three to eight days valid travel within one month. An example is unlimited 2nd-class travel in Germany for three days for UK£140.

INTER-RAIL

These passes are available to European residents of more than six months standing (passport identification is required). Terms and conditions vary slightly from country to country, but in the country of origin there is a discount of around 50% on the normal fares.

The **Inter-Rail pass** (www.interrailnet.com) is split into eight zones. In Western Europe, Zone A is Ireland; C is Austria, Denmark, Germany and Switzerland; E is Belgium, France, Luxembourg and the Netherlands; F is Portugal and Spain; and G is Greece, Italy and Italy–Greece ferries. The other zones cover Scandinavia and parts of Eastern Europe. This pass is not valid on some high-speed services.

The Inter-Rail pass is available in two classes: adult and youth (under 26). Prices for any one zone for 16 days are UK£215/145; two zones for 22 days UK£295/205; and the all-zone global pass for one month UK£405/285. This is the classic European backpacker's pass.

NATIONAL RAIL PASSES

If you're intending to travel extensively within one country, check what national rail passes are available as these can sometimes save you a lot of money; details can be found in the individual country chapters.

Security

You should be quite safe travelling on most trains in Western Europe, but it pays to be security conscious nonetheless. Keep an eye on your luggage at all times (especially when stopping at stations) and lock compartment doors at night.

Health

CONTENTS

Before You Go	**1123**
Insurance	1123
Recommended Vaccinations	1123
Further Reading	1123
In Transit	**1123**
Deep Vein Thrombosis (DVT)	1123
In Western Europe	**1123**
Availability of Health Care	1123
Environmental Hazards	1124
Sexual Health	1124

BEFORE YOU GO

We recommend you carry a spare pair of contact lenses and glasses, and take your optical prescription with you. Bring medications in their original, clearly labelled containers. A signed and dated letter from your physician describing your medical conditions and medications, including generic names, is also a good idea. If carrying syringes or needles, be sure to have a physician's letter documenting their medical necessity.

INSURANCE

If you're an EU citizen, the European Health Insurance Card (EHIC; available from most health centres or, in the UK, from post offices or online at www.ehic.org.uk) covers you for most medical care. EHIC will not cover you for nonemergencies or emergency repatriation. Citizens of other countries should find out if there is a reciprocal arrangement for free medical care between their country and the country visited. If you do need health insurance, strongly consider a policy that covers you for the worst possible scenario, such as an accident requiring an emergency flight home. Find out in advance if your insurance plan will make payments directly to providers or reimburse you later for overseas health expenditures. The former option is generally preferable, as it doesn't require you to pay out-of-pocket costs in a foreign country.

RECOMMENDED VACCINATIONS

No jabs are necessary for Western Europe. However, the WHO recommends that all travellers should be covered for diphtheria, tetanus, measles, mumps, rubella and polio, regardless of their destination.

FURTHER READING

Health Advice for Travellers is an annually updated leaflet by the Department of Health in the UK, available free at post offices and online at www.dh.gov.uk. It contains some general information, legally required and recommended vaccines for different countries, and reciprocal health agreements. Lonely Planet's *Travel with Children* includes advice on travel health for younger children.

IN TRANSIT

DEEP VEIN THROMBOSIS (DVT)

Blood clots may form in the legs during plane flights, chiefly because of prolonged immobility. The main symptom of DVT is swelling or pain in the foot, ankle, or calf, usually but not always on just one side. When a blood clot travels to the lungs it may cause chest pain and breathing difficulties. Travellers with any of these symptoms should immediately seek medical attention.

To prevent the development of DVT on long flights you should walk about the cabin, contract and relax the leg muscles while sitting, drink plenty of fluids, and avoid alcohol and tobacco.

IN WESTERN EUROPE

AVAILABILITY OF HEALTH CARE

Good health care is readily available and for minor illnesses pharmacists can give valuable advice and sell over-the-counter medication. They can also advise when more specialised help is required and point you in the right direction. The standard of dental care is usually good; however, it is sensible to have a dental check-up before a long trip.

ENVIRONMENTAL HAZARDS

Altitude Sickness

Most people are affected to some extent by lack of oxygen at high altitudes (over 2500m). Symptoms of Acute Mountain Sickness (AMS) usually develop during the first 24 hours at altitude but may be delayed up to three weeks. Mild symptoms include headache, lethargy, dizziness, difficulty sleeping and loss of appetite. AMS may become more severe without warning and can be fatal. Severe symptoms include breathlessness, a dry, irritative cough (which may progress to the production of pink, frothy sputum), severe headache, lack of coordination and balance, confusion, irrational behaviour, vomiting, drowsiness, and unconsciousness. There is no hard-and-fast rule as to what is too high: AMS has been fatal at 3000m, although 3500m to 4500m is the usual range.

Treat mild symptoms by resting at the same altitude until recovery, usually a day or two. Paracetamol or aspirin can be taken for headaches. If symptoms persist or become worse, however, *immediate descent is necessary;* even 500m can help. Drug treatments should never be used to avoid descent or to enable further ascent.

Diamox (acetazolamide) reduces the headache of AMS and helps the body acclimatise to the lack of oxygen. It is available only on prescription. Those who are allergic to sulfonamide antibiotics may also be allergic to Diamox.

In the UK fact sheets are available from the **British Mountaineering Council** (www.thebmc.co.uk; 177-179 Burton Rd, Manchester, M20 2BB).

Heatstroke

Heatstroke occurs after excessive fluid loss and inadequate replacement of fluids and salt. Symptoms include headache, dizziness and tiredness. Dehydration is already happening by the time you feel thirsty – aim to drink sufficient water to produce pale, diluted urine. Replace lost fluids by drinking water and/or fruit juice, and cool the body with cold water and fans. Treat salt loss with salty fluids such as soup or Bovril, or add a little more table salt than usual to foods.

Hypothermia

The weather in Europe's mountains can be extremely changeable at any time of year. Proper preparation will reduce the risk of getting hypothermia. Even on a hot day the weather can change rapidly; carry waterproof garments and warm layers, and inform others of your route.

Hypothermia starts with shivering, loss of judgment and clumsiness. Unless rewarming occurs, the sufferer deteriorates into apathy, confusion and coma. Prevent further heat loss by seeking shelter, warm dry clothing, hot sweet drinks and shared bodily warmth.

Insect Bites & Stings

Mosquitoes are found in most parts of Western Europe. They may not carry malaria but can cause irritation and infected bites. Use a DEET-based insect repellent.

Sand flies are found around Mediterranean beaches. They usually cause only a nasty itchy bite but can carry a rare skin disorder called cutaneous leishmaniasis.

SEXUAL HEALTH

Contraception, including condoms, is widely available in Western Europe; however, emergency contraception may not be. The **International Planned Parent Federation** (www.ippf.org) can advise about the availability of contraception in different countries. When buying condoms, look for a European CE mark, which means they have been rigorously tested.

Language

CONTENTS

Dutch	1125
French	1126
German	1128
Greek	1129
Italian	1131
Portuguese	1133
Spanish	1135

This language guide offers basic vocabulary to help you get around Western Europe. For more extensive coverage of the languages included in this guide, pick up a copy of Lonely Planet's *Western Europe Phrasebook.*

DUTCH

PRONUNCIATION

Vowels

a short, like the 'u' in 'cut'
a, aa long, like the 'a' in 'father'
au, ou pronounced somewhere between the 'ow' in 'how' and the 'ow' in 'glow'
e short, as in 'bet', or like the 'er' in 'fern' (with no 'r' sound)
e, ee long, like the 'ay' in 'day'
ei as in 'vein'
eu like the 'u' in 'fur', with no 'r' sound
i short, as in 'it'
i, ie long, like the 'ee' in 'meet'
ij like the 'ey' in 'they'
o short, as in 'pot'
o, oo long, as in 'note'
oe like the 'oo' in 'zoo'
u short, similar to the 'u' in 'urn'
u, uu long, like the 'u' in 'flute'
ui similar to the sound of 'er-y' in 'her year' (with no 'r' sound) or, if you're familiar with it, like the 'eui' in the French *fauteuil*

Consonants

ch, g like the 'ch' in the Scottish *loch*; it's like a hiss produced by tightening the tongue against top of the throat
j like the 'y' in 'yes'

ACCOMMODATION

hotel *hotel*
guesthouse *pension*
youth hostel *jeugdherberg*
camping ground *camping*

Do you have any rooms available? *Heeft U kamers vrij?*
How much is it per night/per person? *Hoeveel is het per nacht/ per persoon?*
Is breakfast included? *Zit er ontbijt bij inbegrepen?*

single room *eenpersoons kamer*
double room *tweepersoons kamer*
one night *één nacht*
two nights *twee nachten*

CONVERSATION & ESSENTIALS

Hello. *Dag/Hallo.*
Goodbye. *Dag.*
Yes. *Ja.*
No. *Nee.*
Please. *Alstublieft/Alsjeblieft.*
Thank you. *Dank U/je (wel).*
You're welcome. *Geen dank.*
Excuse me. *Pardon.*
Sorry. *Sorry.*
Do you speak English? *Spreekt U/Spreek je Engels?*
How much is it? *Hoeveel kost het?*
What's your name? *Hoe heet U/je?*
My name is ... *Ik heet ...*

EMERGENCIES – DUTCH

Help! *Help!*
Call a doctor! *Haal een dokter!*
Call the police! *Haal de politie!*
Go away! *Ga weg!*
I'm lost. *Ik ben de weg kwijt.*

SHOPPING & SERVICES

a bank *een bank*
the market *de markt*
the newsagents *de krantenwinkel*
the pharmacy *de drogist*
the post office *het postkantoor*
the stationers *de kantoorboekhandel*
the tourist office *de VVV/het toeristenbureau*
What time does it open/close? *Hoe laat opent/sluit het?*

SIGNS – DUTCH

Ingang	Entrance
Uitgang	Exit
Informatie/ Inlichtingen	Information
Open	Open
Gesloten	Closed
Kamers Vrij	Rooms Available
Vol	Full/No Vacancies
Politiebureau	Police Station
Verboden	Prohibited
WC/Toiletten	Toilets
Heren	Men
Dames	Women

TIME, DAYS & NUMBERS

What time is it?	*Hoe laat is het?*
today	*vandaag*
tomorrow	*morgen*
yesterday	*gisteren*
in the morning	*'s morgens*
in the afternoon	*'s middags*

Monday	*maandag*
Tuesday	*dinsdag*
Wednesday	*woensdag*
Thursday	*donderdag*
Friday	*vrijdag*
Saturday	*zaterdag*
Sunday	*zondag*

0	*nul*
1	*één*
2	*twee*
3	*drie*
4	*vier*
5	*vijf*
6	*zes*
7	*zeven*
8	*acht*
9	*negen*
10	*tien*
11	*elf*
100	*honderd*
1000	*duizend*

TRANSPORT

What time does the ... leave/arrive?	*Hoe laat vertrekt/arriveert de ...?*
(next)	*(volgende)*
boat	*boot*
bus	*bus*
tram	*tram*
train	*trein*

I'd like to hire a car/ bicycle.	*Ik wil graag een auto/fiets huren.*
I'd like a one-way/ return ticket.	*Ik wil graag een enkele reis/ een retour.*

1st class	*eerste klas*
2nd class	*tweede klas*
left luggage locker	*bagagekluis*
bus stop	*bushalte*
tram stop	*tramhalte*
train station	*treinstation*
ferry terminal	*veerhaven*

Directions

Where is the ...?	*Waar is de ...?*
Go straight ahead.	*Ga rechtdoor.*
Turn left.	*Ga linksaf.*
Turn right.	*Ga rechtsaf.*
near/far	*dichtbij/ver*

FRENCH

PRONUNCIATION

Most letters in French are pronounced more or less the same as their English counterparts. Here are a few that may cause some confusion:

- **j** like the 's' in 'leisure', eg *jour* (day)
- **c** before **e** and **i**, like the 's' in 'sit'; before **a**, **o** and **u** it's pronounced as English 'k'. When undescored with a 'cedilla' (**ç**) it's like the 's' in 'sit'.
- **r** pronounced from the back of the throat while constricting the muscles to restrict the flow of air
- **n, m** where a syllable ends in a single **n** or **m**, these letters are not pronounced, but the vowel is given a nasal pronunciation

ACCOMMODATION

the hotel	*l'hôtel*
the guesthouse	*la pension (de famille)*
the youth hostel	*l'auberge de jeunesse*
the camping ground	*le camping*

Do you have any rooms available?	*Est-ce que vous avez des chambres libres?*
How much is it per night/per person?	*Quel est le prix par nuit/par personne?*
Is breakfast included?	*Est-ce que le petit déjeuner est compris?*

EMERGENCIES – FRENCH

Help!	*Au secours!*
Call a doctor!	*Appelez un médecin!*
Call the police!	*Appelez la police!*
Leave me alone!	*Fichez-moi la paix!*
I'm lost.	*Je me suis égaré/e.*

for one person	*pour une personne*
for two people	*pour deux personnes*
for one night	*pour une nuit*
for two nights	*pour deux nuits*

CONVERSATION & ESSENTIALS

Hello.	*Bonjour.*
Goodbye.	*Au revoir.*
Yes.	*Oui.*
No.	*Non.*
Please.	*S'il vous plaît.*
Thank you.	*Merci.*
You're welcome.	*Je vous en prie.*
Excuse me. (to get someone's attention)	*Excusez-moi.*
Sorry. (forgive me)	*Pardon.*
Do you speak English?	*Parlez-vous anglais?*
How much is it?	*C'est combien?*
What's your name?	*Comment vous appelez-vous?*
My name is ...	*Je m'appelle ...*

SHOPPING & SERVICES

a bank	*une banque*
chemist/pharmacy	*la pharmacie*
the ... embassy	*l'ambassade de ...*
market	*le marché*
newsagents	*l'agence de presse*
post office	*le bureau de poste*
a public telephone	*une cabine téléphonique*
stationers	*la papeterie*
the tourist office	*l'office de tourisme/le syndicat d'initiative*
What time does it open/close?	*Quelle est l' heure de ouverture/fermeture?*

TIME, DAYS & NUMBERS

What time is it?	*Quelle heure est-il?*
today	*aujourd'hui*
tomorrow	*demain*
yesterday	*hier*
morning	*matin*
afternoon	*après-midi*

Monday	*lundi*
Tuesday	*mardi*

SIGNS – FRENCH

Entrée	Entrance
Sortie	Exit
Renseignements	Information
Ouvert	Open
Fermée	Closed
Chambres Libres	Rooms Available
Complet	Full/No Vacancies
(Commissariat de) Police	Police Station
Interdit	Prohibited
Toilettes, WC	Toilets
Hommes	Men
Femmes	Women

Wednesday	*mercredi*
Thursday	*jeudi*
Friday	*vendredi*
Saturday	*samedi*
Sunday	*dimanche*

1	*un*
2	*deux*
3	*trois*
4	*quatre*
5	*cinq*
6	*six*
7	*sept*
8	*huit*
9	*neuf*
10	*dix*
100	*cent*
1000	*mille*

TRANSPORT

When does the (next) ... leave/arrive?	*À quelle heure part/ arrive le (prochain) ...?*
boat	*bateau*
bus (city/intercity)	*bus/car*
tram	*tramway*
train	*train*

left luggage (office)	*consigne*
timetable	*horaire*
bus stop	*arrêt d'autobus*
train station	*gare*
ferry terminal	*gare maritime*

I'd like a ... ticket.	*Je voudrais un billet ...*
one-way	*aller simple*
return	*aller retour*
1st-class	*de première classe*
2nd-class	*de deuxième classe*

I'd like to hire a car/ bicycle. *Je voudrais louer une voiture/ un vélo.*

Directions

Where is ...? *Où est ...?*
Go straight ahead. *Continuez tout droit.*
Turn left. *Tournez à gauche.*
Turn right. *Tournez à droite.*
near/far *proche/loin*

GERMAN

PRONUNCIATION

Unlike English or French, German has no real silent letters: you pronounce the **k** at the start of the word *Knie* (knee), the **p** at the start of *Psychologie* (psychology), and the **e** at the end of *ich habe* (I have).

Vowels

As in English, vowels can be pronounced long, like the 'o' in 'pope', or short, as in 'pop'. As a rule, German vowels are long before one consonant and short before two consonants, eg the **o** is long in *Dom* (cathedral), but short in *doch* (after all).

a short, like the 'u' in 'cut' or long, as in 'father'
au like the 'ow' in 'vow'
ä short, as in 'cat' or long, as in 'care'
äu like the 'oy' in 'boy'
e short, as in 'bet' or long, as in 'obey'
ei like the 'ai' in 'aisle'
eu like the 'oy' in 'boy'
i short, as in 'it' or long, as in 'marine'
ie as in the 'brief'
o short, as in 'not' or long, as in 'note'
ö like the 'er' in 'fern'
u as in 'pull'
ü similar to the 'u' in 'pull' but with lips stretched back

LANGUAGE

Consonants

Most German consonants sound similar to their English counterparts. One important difference is that **b**, **d** and **g** sound like 'p', 't' and 'k', respectively when word-final.

b as in 'be'; as 'p' when word-final
ch as in Scottish *loch*
d as in 'do'; as 't' when word-final
g as in 'go'; as 'k' when word-final
j like the 'y' in 'yet'
qu as 'k' plus 'v'
r can be trilled or guttural, depending on the region
s as in 'sun'; like the 'z' in 'zoo' when followed by a vowel
sch like the 'sh' in 'ship'
sp, st as 'shp' and 'sht' when word-initial
tion the 't' is pronounced as the 'ts' in 'its'
v like the 'f' in 'fan'
w like the 'v' in 'van'
z like the 'ts' in 'its'

EMERGENCIES – GERMAN

Help! *Hilfe!*
Call a doctor! *Holen Sie einen Arzt!*
Call the police! *Rufen Sie die Polizei!*
Go away! *Gehen Sie weg!*
I'm lost. *Ich habe mich verirrt.*

ACCOMMODATION

hotel *Hotel*
guesthouse *Pension, Gästehaus*
youth hostel *Jugendherberge*
camping ground *Campingplatz*

Do you have any rooms available? *Haben Sie noch freie Zimmer?*
How much is it per night/person? *Wieviel kostet es pro Nacht/Person?*
Is breakfast included? *Ist Frühstück inbegriffen?*

a single room *ein Einzelzimmer*
a double room *ein Doppelzimmer*
one night *eine Nacht*
two nights *zwei Nächte*

CONVERSATION & ESSENTIALS

Good day. *Guten Tag.*
Hello. *Grüss Gott.* (in Bavaria and Austria)
Goodbye. *Auf Wiedersehen.*
Bye. *Tschüss.* (informal)
Yes. *Ja.*
No. *Nein.*
Please. *Bitte.*
Thank you. *Danke.*
You're welcome. *Bitte sehr.*
Sorry/Excuse me. *Entschuldigung.*
Do you speak English? *Sprechen Sie Englisch?*
How much is it? *Wieviel kostet es?*
What's your name? *Wie heissen Sie?*
My name is ... *Ich heisse ...*

SHOPPING & SERVICES

a bank	*eine Bank*
the chemist/ pharmacy	*die Apotheke*
the ... embassy	*die ... Botschaft*
the market	*der Markt*
the newsagents	*der Zeitungshändler*
the post office	*das Postamt*
the stationers	*der Schreibwarengeschäft*
the tourist office	*das Verkehrsamt*
What time does it open/close?	*Um wieviel Uhr macht es auf/zu?*

TIME, DAYS & NUMBERS

What time is it?	*Wie spät ist es?*
today	*heute*
tomorrow	*morgen*
yesterday	*gestern*
in the morning	*morgens*
in the afternoon	*nachmittags*
Monday	*Montag*
Tuesday	*Dienstag*
Wednesday	*Mittwoch*
Thursday	*Donnerstag*
Friday	*Freitag*
Saturday	*Samstag, Sonnabend*
Sunday	*Sonntag*
0	*null*
1	*eins*
2	*zwei/zwo*
3	*drei*
4	*vier*
5	*fünf*
6	*sechs*
7	*sieben*
8	*acht*
9	*neun*
10	*zehn*
11	*elf*
12	*zwölf*
13	*dreizehn*
100	*hundert*
1000	*tausend*

TRANSPORT

What time does ... (leave/arrive)?	*Wann (fährt ... ab/ kommt ... an)?*
the boat	*das Boot*
the bus (intercity)	*der (überland) Bus*
the tram	*die Strassenbahn*
the train	*der Zug*

SIGNS – GERMAN

Eingang	Entrance
Ausgang	Exit
Auskunft	Information
Offen	Open
Geschlossen	Closed
Zimmer Frei	Rooms Available
Voll/Besetzt	Full/No Vacancies
Polizeiwache	Police Station
Verboten	Prohibited
Toiletten (WC)	Toilets
Herren	Men
Damen	Women

What time is the next boat?	*Wann fährt das nächste Boot?*
I'd like to hire a car/ bicycle.	*Ich möchte ein Auto/Fahrrad mieten.*
I'd like a one-way/ return ticket.	*Ich möchte eine Einzelkarte/ Rückfahrkarte.*
1st class	*erste Klasse*
2nd class	*zweite Klasse*
left luggage locker	*Schliessfächer*
timetable	*Fahrplan*
bus stop	*Bushaltestelle*
tram stop	*Strassenbahnhaltestelle*
train station	*Bahnhof (Bf)*
ferry terminal	*Fährhafen*

Directions

Where is the ...?	*Wo ist die ...?*
Go straight ahead.	*Gehen Sie geradeaus.*
Turn left.	*Biegen Sie links ab.*
Turn right.	*Biegen Sie rechts ab.*
near/far	*nahe/weit*

GREEK

ALPHABET & PRONUNCIATION

Pronunciation of Greek letters is shown in the table on p1130 using the closest similar-sounding letter in English.

Letter Combinations

Some pairs of vowels are pronounced separately if the first has an acute accent (eg **ά**), or the second has a dieresis (eg **ϊ**). All Greek words of two or more syllables have an acute accent indicating where the stress falls.

ει, οι	**i**	like the 'ee' in 'feet'
αι	**e**	as in 'bet'

EMERGENCIES – GREEK

Help!	*voithia!*
Call a doctor!	*fonakste ena yatro!*
Call the police!	*tilefoniste tin astinomia!*
Go away!	*fighe/dhromo!*
I'm lost.	*eho hathi*

ου	**u**	like the 'oo' in 'mood'
μπ	**b**	as in 'be'
	mb	as in 'amber' (or like the 'mp' in 'ample')
ντ	**d**	as in 'do'
	nd	as in 'bend' (or like the 'nt' in 'sent')
γκ	**g**	as in 'go'
γγ	**ng**	like the 'ng' in 'angle'
γξ	**ks**	as in 'yaks'
τζ	**dz**	like the 'ds' in 'suds'

The suffix of some Greek words depends on the gender of the speaker, eg *asthmatikos* (masculine) and *asthmatikya* (feminine), or *epileptikos* (m) and *epileptikya* (f).

ACCOMMODATION

a hotel	*ena xenothohio*
a youth hostel	*enas xenonas neoitos*
a camping ground	*ena kamping*
I'd like a ... room.	*thelo ena dhomatio ...*
single	*ya ena atomo*
double	*ya dhio atoma*
How much is it per person/night?	*poso kostizi ya ena atomo/vradhi?*
for one night	*ya mia nichta*
for two nights	*ya dhio nichtes*
Is breakfast included?	*simberilamvanete to proiono?*

CONVERSATION & ESSENTIALS

Hello.	*yasu* (informal) *yasas* (polite/plural)
Goodbye.	*andio*
Yes.	*ne*
No.	*okhi*
Please.	*sas parakalo*
Thank you.	*sas efharisto*
That's fine/You're welcome.	*ine endaksi/parakalo*
Sorry/Excuse me.	*signomi*
Do you speak English?	*milate anglika?*

THE GREEK ALPHABET

Greek	English	Pronunciation
Α α	**a**	as in 'father'
Β β	**v**	like the 'v' in 'vine'
Γ γ	**gh/y**	like a rough 'g', or like the 'y' in 'yes'
Δ δ	**dh**	like the 'th' in 'then'
Ε ε	**e**	as in 'egg'
Ζ ζ	**z**	as in 'zoo'
Η η	**i**	like the 'ee' in 'feet'
Θ θ	**th**	like the 'th' in 'throw'
Ι ι	**i**	like the 'ee' in 'feet'
Κ κ	**k**	as in 'kite'
Λ λ	**l**	as in 'leg'
Μ μ	**m**	as in 'man'
Ν ν	**n**	as in 'net'
Ξ ξ	**x**	as in 'taxi'
Ο ο	**o**	as in 'hot'
Π π	**p**	as in 'pup'
Ρ ρ	**r**	slightly trilled 'r'
Σ σ/ς	**s**	as in 'sand' (ς at the end of a word)
Τ τ	**t**	as in 'to'
Υ υ	**i**	like the 'ee' in 'feet'
Φ φ	**f**	as in 'fee'
Χ χ	**kh/h**	like the 'ch' in Scottish *loch*, or as a rough 'h'
Ψ ψ	**ps**	like the 'ps' in 'lapse'
Ω ω	**o**	as in 'lot'

How much is it?	*poso kani?*
What's your name?	*pos sas lene/pos legeste?*
My name is ...	*me lene ...*

SHOPPING & SERVICES

Where is a /the ...?	*pu ine ...?*
bank	*mia trapeza*
... embassy	*i ... presvia*
market	*i aghora*
newsagents	*to efimeridhon*
pharmacy	*to farmakio*
post office	*to takhidhromio*
tourist office	*to ghrafio turistikon pliroforion*
What time does it open/close?	*ti ora aniyi/klini?*

TIME, DAYS & NUMBERS

What time is it?	*ti ora ine?*
today	*simera*
tomorrow	*avrio*
yesterday	*hthes*
in the morning	*to proi*
in the afternoon	*to apoyevma*

SIGNS – GREEK

Εισοδος	Entrance
Εξοδος	Exit
Πληροφοριες	Information
Ανοικτο	Open
Κλειστο	Closed
Αστυνομικος Τμημα	Police Station
Απαγορευεται	Prohibited
Τουαλετες	Toilets
Ανδρων	Men
Γυναικων	Women

Monday	*dheftera*
Tuesday	*triti*
Wednesday	*tetarti*
Thursday	*pempti*
Friday	*paraskevi*
Saturday	*savato*
Sunday	*kiryaki*

1	*ena*
2	*dhio*
3	*tria*
4	*tesera*
5	*pende*
6	*eksi*
7	*epta*
8	*okhto*
9	*enea*
10	*dheka*
11	*edeka*
100	*ekato*
200	*dhiakhosia*
1000	*khilya*

TRANSPORT

What time does the ... leave/arrive?	*ti ora fevyi/ftani ...?*
boat	*to plio*
bus (city)	*to leoforio (ya tin poli)*
bus (intercity)	*to leoforio (ya ta proastia)*
tram	*to tram*
train	*to treno*

I'd like a ... ticket.	*tha ithela isitirio ...*
one-way	*horis epistrofi*
return	*me epistrofi*
1st-class	*proti thesi*
2nd-class	*dhefteri thesi*

left luggage	*horos aposkevon*
timetable	*dhromologhio*
bus stop	*i stasi tu leoforiu*

Directions

Go straight ahead.	*pighenete efthia*
Turn left.	*stripste aristera*
Turn right.	*stripste dheksya*
near/far	*konda/makria*

ITALIAN

PRONUNCIATION

Vowels

Vowels sounds are generally shorter than English equivalents:

- **a** as in 'art', eg *caro* (dear); sometimes short, eg *amico/a* (friend)
- **e** short, as in 'let', eg *mettere* (to put); long, as in 'there', eg *vero* (true)
- **i** short, as in 'it', eg *inizio* (start); long, as in 'marine', eg *vino* (wine)
- **o** short, as in 'dot', eg *donna* (woman); long, as in 'port', eg *ora* (hour)
- **u** like the 'oo' in 'book', eg *puro* (pure)

Consonants

The pronunciation of many Italian consonants is similar to that of their English counterparts. Pronunciation of some consonants depends on certain rules:

- **c** like the 'k' in 'kit' before **a, o** and **u**; or the 'ch' in 'choose' before **e** and **i**
- **ch** like the 'k' in 'kit'
- **g** like the 'g' in 'get' before **a, o, u** and **h**; or the 'j' in 'jet' before **e** and **i**
- **gli** like the 'lli' in 'million'
- **gn** like the 'ny' in 'canyon'
- **h** always silent
- **r** a rolled 'rr' sound
- **sc** like the 'sh' in 'sheep' before **e** and **i**; or 'sk' before **a, o, u** and **h**
- **z** like the 'ts' in 'lights', except at the start of a word, when it's pronounced as the 'ds' in 'suds'

Word Stress

Word stress generally falls on the second-last syllable, as in spa-*ghet*-ti, but when a word has an accent, the stress falls on that syllable, as in cit-*tà* (city).

ACCOMMODATION

hotel	*albergo*
guesthouse	*pensione*
youth hostel	*ostello per la gioventù*
camping ground	*campeggio*

LANGUAGE

EMERGENCIES – ITALIAN

Help!	*Aiuto!*
Call a doctor!	*Chiama un dottore/medico!*
Call the police!	*Chiama la polizia!*
Go away!	*Vai via!*
I'm lost.	*Mi sono perso/a* (m/f)

Do you have any rooms available? *Ha delle camere libere/C'è una camera libera?*
How much is it per night/per person? *Quanto costa per la notte/per ciascuno?*
Is breakfast included? *È compresa la colazione?*

a single room *una camera singola*
a twin room *una camera doppia*
a double room *una camera matrimoniale*
for one night *per una notte*
for two nights *per due notti*

CONVERSATION & ESSENTIALS

Hello. *Buongiorno.* (pol)/*Ciao.* (inf)
Goodbye. *Arrivederci.* (pol)/*Ciao.* (inf)
Yes. *Sì.*
No. *No.*
Please. *Per favore/Per piacere.*
Thank you. *Grazie.*
You're welcome. *Prego.*
Excuse me. *Mi scusi.*
Sorry. (excuse me/forgive me) *Mi scusi/Mi perdoni.*
Do you speak English? *Parla inglese?*
How much is it? *Quanto costa?*
What's your name? *Come si chiama?*
My name is ... *Mi chiamo ...*

SHOPPING & SERVICES

a bank *una banca*
chemist/pharmacy *la farmacia*
the ... embassy *l'ambasciata di ...*
market *il mercato*
newsagents *l'edicola*
post office *la posta*
stationers *il cartolaio*
tourist office *l'ufficio di turismo*

What time does it open/close? *A che ora (si) apre/chiude?*

TIME, DAYS & NUMBERS

What time is it? *Che ora è?/Che ore sono?*
today *oggi*
tomorrow *domani*
yesterday *ieri*
morning *mattina*
afternoon *pomeriggio*

Monday *lunedì*
Tuesday *martedì*
Wednesday *mercoledì*
Thursday *giovedì*
Friday *venerdì*
Saturday *sabato*
Sunday *domenica*

1 *uno*
2 *due*
3 *tre*
4 *quattro*
5 *cinque*
6 *sei*
7 *sette*
8 *otto*
9 *nove*
10 *dieci*
11 *undici*
100 *cento*
1000 *mille*

TRANSPORT

When does the ... leave/arrive? *A che ora parte/arriva ...?*
boat *la barca*
ferry *il traghetto*
bus *l'autobus*
tram *il tram*
train *il treno*

bus stop *fermata dell'autobus*
train station *stazione*
ferry terminal *stazione marittima*
1st class *prima classe*
2nd class *seconda classe*
left luggage *deposito bagagli*
timetable *orario*
I'd like a one-way/return ticket. *Vorrei un biglietto di solo andata/di andata e ritorno.*
I'd like to hire a car/bicycle. *Vorrei noleggiare una macchina/bicicletta.*

Directions

Where is ...? *Dov'è ...?*
Go straight ahead. *Si va sempre diritto.*
Turn left. *Giri a sinistra.*
Turn right. *Giri a destra.*
near/far *vicino/lontano*

SIGNS – ITALIAN

Ingresso/Entrata	Entrance
Uscita	Exit
Informazione	Information
Aperto	Open
Chiuso	Closed
Camere Libere	Rooms Available
Completo	Full/No Vacancies
Polizia/Carabinieri	Police
Questura	Police Station
Proibito/Vietato	Prohibited
Gabinetti/Bagni	Toilets
Uomini	Men
Donne	Women

PORTUGUESE

PRONUNCIATION

Portuguese uses masculine and feminine word endings, usually '-o/-a' respectively – to say 'thank you', a man will therefore use *obrigado*, a woman, *obrigada*.

Vowels

a short, like the 'u' in 'cut'; long, like the 'ur' in 'hurt'
e short, as in 'bet'; long, as in 'there'
é short, as in 'bet'
ê long, like the 'a' in 'gate'
i short, as in 'it'; long, as in 'see'
o short, as in 'pot'; long as in 'note' or like the 'oo' in 'good'
ô long, as in 'note'
u like the 'oo' in 'good'

Nasal Vowels

Nasalisation is represented by an 'n' or an 'm' after the vowel, or by a tilde over it, eg **ã**. The nasal 'i' exists in English as the 'ing' in 'sing'. You can practise by trying to pronounce vowels while holding your nose, as if you had a cold.

Diphthongs

au like the 'ow' in 'now'
ai like the 'ie' in 'pie'
ei like the 'ay' in 'day'
eu like 'e' followed by 'w'

Nasal Diphthongs

Try the same technique as for nasal vowels. To say *não*, see if you can pronounce 'now' through your nose.

ão nasal 'ow' (owng)
ãe nasal 'ay' (eing)
õe nasal 'oy' (oing)
ui similar to the 'uing' in 'ensuing'

Consonants

c as in 'cat' before **a**, **o** or **u**; like the 's' in 'sin' before **e** or **i**
ç like the 'c' in 'celery'
g as in 'go' before **a**, **o** or **u**; like the 's' in 'treasure' before **e** or **i**
gu as in 'guest' before **e** or **i**
h not pronounced when word-initial
nh like the 'ni' in 'onion'
lh like the 'lli' in 'million'
j like the 's' in 'treasure'
m not pronounced when word-final – it simply nasalises the previous vowel, eg *um* (oong), *bom* (bõ)
qu as 'k' before **e** or **i**; elsewhere as in 'queen'
r when word-initial, or when doubled (**rr**) within a word it's a harsh, guttural sound similar to the 'ch' in Scottish *loch*; in the middle or at the end of a word it's a rolled 'r' sound. In some areas of Portugal it's always strongly rolled.
s as in 'so' when word-initial and when doubled (**ss**) within a word; like the 'z' in 'zeal' when between vowels; as 'sh' when it precedes a consonant, or at the end of a word
x like the 'sh' in 'ship', the 'z' in 'zeal', or the 'x' in 'taxi'
z like the 's' in 'treasure' before a consonant or at the end of a word

Word Stress

Word stress is important in Portuguese, as it can affect meaning. It generally occurs on the second-to-last syllable of a word, though there are exceptions. In words with a written accent, the stress always falls on that syllable.

ACCOMMODATION

hotel	*hotel*
guesthouse	*pensão*
youth hostel	*pousada da juventude*
camping ground	*parque de campismo*

Do you have any rooms available?	*Tem quartos livres?*

EMERGENCIES – PORTUGUESE

Help!	*Socorro!*
Call a doctor!	*Chame um médico!*
Call the police!	*Chame a polícia!*
Go away!	*Deixe-me em paz!* (pol)/ *Vai-te embora!* (inf)
I'm lost.	*Estou perdido/a.* (m/f)

How much is it per night/per person?	*Quanto é por noite/por pessoa?*
Is breakfast included?	*O pequeno almoço está incluído?*
a single room	*um quarto individual*
a twin room	*um quarto duplo*
a double room	*um quarto de casal*
for one night	*para uma noite*
for two nights	*para duas noites*

CONVERSATION & ESSENTIALS

Hello.	*Bom dia.*
Goodbye.	*Adeus.*
Yes.	*Sim.*
No.	*Não.*
Please.	*Se faz favor.*
Thank you.	*Obrigado/a.* (m/f)
You're welcome.	*De nada.*
Excuse me.	*Com licença.*
Sorry. (forgive me)	*Desculpe.*
Do you speak English?	*Fala Inglês?*
How much is it?	*Quanto custa?*
What's your name?	*Como se chama?*
My name is ...	*Chamo-me ...*

SHOPPING & SERVICES

a bank	*um banco*
a chemist/pharmacy	*uma farmácia*
the ... embassy	*a embaixada de ...*
the market	*o mercado*
the newsagents	*a papelaria*
the post office	*os correios*
the stationers	*a tabacaria*
the tourist office	*o (posto de) turismo*
What time does it open/close?	*A que horas abre/fecha?*

TIME, DAYS & NUMBERS

What time is it?	*Que horas são?*
today	*hoje*
tomorrow	*amanhã*
yesterday	*ontem*
morning	*manhã*
afternoon	*tarde*

Monday	*segunda-feira*
Tuesday	*terça-feira*
Wednesday	*quarta-feira*
Thursday	*quinta-feira*
Friday	*sexta-feira*
Saturday	*sábado*
Sunday	*domingo*

1	*um/uma* (m/f)
2	*dois/duas* (m/f)
3	*três*
4	*quatro*
5	*cinco*
6	*seis*
7	*sete*
8	*oito*
9	*nove*
10	*dez*
11	*onze*
100	*cem*
200	*duzentos*
1000	*mil*

TRANSPORT

What time does the ... leave/arrive?	*A que horas parte/ chega ...?*
boat	*o barco*
bus (city/intercity)	*o autocarro/a camioneta*
tram	*o eléctrico*
train	*o combóio*

bus stop	*paragem de autocarro*
train station	*estação ferroviária*
timetable	*horário*

I'd like a ... ticket.	*Queria um bilhete ...*
one-way	*simples/de ida*
return	*de ida e volta*
1st-class	*de primeira classe*
2nd-class	*de segunda classe*

I'd like to hire ...	*Queria alugar ...*
a car/bicycle	*um carro/uma bicicleta*

Directions

Where is ...?	*Onde é ...?*
Go straight ahead.	*Siga sempre a direito/ Siga sempre em frente.*
Turn left.	*Vire à esquerda.*
Turn right.	*Vire à direita.*
near/far	*perto/longe*

LANGUAGE

SIGNS – PORTUGUESE

Entrada	Entrance
Saída	Exit
Informações	Information
Aberto	Open
Fechado	Closed
Quartos Livres	Rooms Available
Posto Da Polícia	Police Station
Proíbido	Prohibited
Empurre/Puxe	Push/Pull
Lavabos/WC	Toilets
Homens (h)	Men
Senhoras (s)	Women

SPANISH

PRONUNCIATION

Vowels

An acute accent (as in *días*) generally indicates a stressed syllable and doesn't change the sound of the vowel.

- **e** as in 'met'
- **i** as in 'marine'
- **o** as in 'or' (without the 'r' sound)
- **u** as in 'rule'; the 'u' is not pronounced after **q** and in the letter combinations **gue** and **gui**, unless it's marked with a diaeresis (eg *argüir*), in which case it's pronounced as English 'w'
- **y** (see Consonants below)

Consonants

- **b** a cross between English 'b' and 'v'
- **c** a hard 'c' as in 'cat' when followed by **a**, **o**, **u** or a consonant; like the 'th' in 'thin' before **e** and **i**
- **ch** as in 'church'
- **d** as in 'do' when word-initial; elsewhere like the 'th' in 'then'
- **g** as in 'get' when word-initial and before **a**, **o** and **u**; elsewhere much softer. Before **e** or **i** it's a harsh, breathy sound, similar to the 'h' in 'hit'
- **h** silent
- **j** a harsh, guttural sound similar to the 'ch' in Scottish *loch*
- **ll** like the 'lli' in 'million'; some pronounce it rather like the 'y' in 'yellow'
- **ñ** a nasal sound, as in 'ni' in 'onion'
- **q** like the 'k' in 'kick'; **q** is always followed by a silent **u** and is combined only with the vowels **e** (as in *que*) and **i** (as in *qui*)
- **r** a rolled 'r' sound; longer and stronger when initial or doubled
- **s** as in 'see'
- **v** the same sound as **b**
- **x** like the 'ks' sound in 'taxi' when between vowels; like the 's' in 'see' when it precedes a consonant
- **y** at the end of a word or when standing alone (meaning 'and') it's pronounced as the Spanish **i**. As a consonant, it's somewhere between the 'y' in 'yonder' and the 'g' in 'beige', depending on the region.
- **z** like the 'th' in 'thin'

EMERGENCIES – SPANISH

Help!	*¡Socorro!/¡Auxilio!*
Call a doctor!	*¡Llame a un doctor!*
Call the police!	*¡Llame a la policía!*
Go away!	*¡Váyase!*
I'm lost.	*Estoy perdido/a.* (m/f)

ACCOMMODATION

hotel	*hotel*
guesthouse	*pensión/casa de huéspedes*
youth hostel	*albergue juvenil*
camping ground	*camping*
Do you have any rooms available?	*¿Tiene habitaciones libres?*
How much is it per night/per person?	*¿Cuánto cuesta por noche/por persona?*
Is breakfast included?	*¿Incluye el desayuno?*
a single room	*una habitación individual*
a double room	*una habitación doble*
a room with a double bed	*una habitación con cama de matrimonio*
for one night	*para una noche*
for two nights	*para dos noches*

CONVERSATION & ESSENTIALS

Hello.	*¡Hola!*
Goodbye.	*¡Adiós!*
Yes.	*Sí.*
No.	*No.*
Please.	*Por favor.*
Thank you.	*Gracias.*

SIGNS – SPANISH

Entrada	Entrance
Salida	Exit
Información	Information
Abierto	Open
Cerrado	Closed
Habtaciones Libres	Rooms Available
Completo	Full/No Vacancies
Comisaría	Police Station
Prohibido	Prohibited
Servicios/Aseos	Toilets
Hombres	Men
Mujeres	Women

You're welcome. *De nada.*
I'm sorry. *Lo siento/Discúlpeme.*
Excuse me. *Perdón/Perdóneme.*
Do you speak English? *¿Habla inglés?*
How much is it? *¿Cuánto cuesta?/¿Cuánto vale?*
What's your name? *¿Cómo se llama?*
My name is ... *Me llamo ...*

SHOPPING & SERVICES

a bank *un banco*
chemist/pharmacy *la farmacia*
the ... embassy *la embajada ...*
the market *el mercado*
newsagents *el quiosco*
stationers *la papelería*
the post office *los correos*
the tourist office *la oficina de turismo*
What time does it open/close? *¿A qué hora abren/cierran?*

TIME, DAYS & NUMBERS

What time is it? *¿Qué hora es?*
today *hoy*
tomorrow *mañana*
yesterday *ayer*
morning *mañana*
afternoon *tarde*

Monday *lunes*
Tuesday *martes*
Wednesday *miércoles*
Thursday *jueves*
Friday *viernes*
Saturday *sábado*
Sunday *domingo*

1 *uno, una*
2 *dos*
3 *tres*
4 *cuatro*
5 *cinco*
6 *seis*
7 *siete*
8 *ocho*
9 *nueve*
10 *diez*
11 *once*
100 *cien/ciento*
100 *cien/ciento*
1000 *mil*

TRANSPORT

What time does the next ... leave/arrive? *¿A qué hora sale/llega el próximo ...?*
boat *barco*
bus (city/intercity) *autobús, bus/autocar*
train *tranvía*

I'd like a ... ticket. *Quisiera un billete ...*
one-way *sencillo/de sólo ida*
return *de ida y vuelta*
1st-class *de primera clase*
2nd-class *de segunda clase*

left luggage *consigna*
timetable *horario*
bus stop *parada de autobus*
train station *estación de ferrocarril*

I'd like to hire ... *Quisiera alquilar ...*
a car *un coche*
a bicycle *una bicicleta*

Directions

Where is ...? *¿Dónde está ...?*
Go straight ahead. *Siga/Vaya todo derecho.*
Turn left. *Gire a la izquierda.*
Turn right. *Gire a la derecha/recto.*
near/far *cerca/lejos*

Behind the Scenes

THIS BOOK

Western Europe is part of Lonely Planet's Europe series, which includes *Eastern Europe*, *Mediterranean Europe*, *Central Europe*, *Scandinavian Europe* and *Europe on a Shoestring*. Lonely Planet also publishes phrasebooks to these regions.

This book was commissioned in Lonely Planet's London office, and produced by the following:

Commissioning Editors Judith Bamber, Tashi Wheeler, Meg Worby
Coordinating Editors Kim Noble, Lauren Rollheiser
Coordinating Cartographer Malisa Plesa
Coordinating Layout Designers Steven Cann, Carlos Solarte
Managing Editors Imogen Bannister, Melanie Dankel
Managing Cartographer Mark Griffiths
Assisting Editors Elisa Arduca, Michelle Bennett, Jackey Coyle, Kate Evans, Chris Girdler, Anne Mulvaney, Sally O'Brien, Kristen Odijk, Dianne Schallmeiner, Laura Stansfeld, Helen Yeates
Assisting Cartographers Barbara Benson, Csanad Csutoros, Matt Kelly, Valentina Kremenchutskaya, Erin McManus, Anthony Phelan, Jolyon Philcox, Helen Rowley, Simon Tillema
Cover Designer Marika Kozak
Colour Designer Yvonne Bischofberger
Project Manager Ray Thomson, Glenn van der Knijff
Language Content Coordinator Quentin Frayne

Thanks to Elizabeth Anglin, Fiona Buchan, David Burnett, Helen Christinis, Sally Darmody, Jennifer Garrett, Mark Germanchis, Will Gourlay, Laura Jane, Katie Lynch, Kate McDonald, Clara Monitto, Trent Paton, Wibowo Rusli, Gina Tsarouhas, Jeanette Wall, Celia Wood

THANKS

RYAN VER BERKMOES

Thanks to my old friend Claudia Stehle who helped immeasurably – and found takeaway coffee when my life depended on it. One day you're cooking in Thailand, the next you're lost in the Witch's Hole. Thanks also to my long-ago colleague Angela Cullen who taught me many language skills. I'd call Carsten Ivers tow-headed, but he might weep. Rather I'll thank him on behalf of the thousands of German dowagers whose feet are as soft and smooth as a virgin's. And thanks to Stefi Graf whose mythical smelly tennis shoes launched my career. At Lonely Planet, the indefatigable Mark Griffiths, delightful Tashi Wheeler and patient Kim Noble made this yet another fun project. My fellow authors made it a delight too, especially Sarah, who cracked me up. Finally kudos to my Munich shopper and partner Erin Corrigan for, well, everything. Oh, and Cake for Nugget. Says it all.

AARON ANDERSON

Thanks to Becca, the love of my life, my motivator, and sometimes devil's advocate. Thanks to my mum (Joyce); grandma (Pauline); Uncle Joe; John (my Austrian Dad) plus family – Liz, Tommy and Sebastian; and Becca's parents – David and Patricia Blond. All my friends who listen to my stories about weird places they may never give a crap to see. My Peeps from Memphis: Jered, Bramlett, Jerry, Jeff Green, Brian @ Outdoors, Sydney and the Cannons. *Mi amigo*, Juan Carlos. My neighbours Russell, Brett, Nan and kids. Big thanks to Major Freedom who always keeps me pumped up about life…and finally to H.S.T. aka Dr Gonzo (1937-2005), I hope the cannon shot got you far enough along.

SARAH ANDREWS

Many, many, many thanks to the friends who made my travels so much more fun and enlightening. An especially big *gracias* to gourmand queen Genevieve, meatball master Des, Atlético fans Nuria and Fede, and Zaragoza experts Theresa, Dani and Tomás. A nod to all the helpful tourist offices along the way and to the gang at Lonely Planet for making this mammoth project go so smoothly. Lastly, a huge hug of thanks to my patient husband, Miquel.

OLIVER BERRY

As always, far too many names and far too little space. Firstly to Jenks for those late nights on The Ark, and for keeping the boat afloat in my absence; to Susie Berry for doing the same back at the ranch. Over on the other side of the Channel, thanks to Jean-Claude Lamartine, Melanie Duchamp, Claude Fourcade, Robert Martin, Sophie Lambert and all the other people I met along the way; to John Huston and Stephen Ambrose; to all the boys of Bayeux and Colleville-Sur-Mer; and to the staff at Normandy's War Cemeteries. Over at the Planet, to Nicola for steering the ship; to Meg Worby, Tashi Wheeler and all the people in the map-room for making sense of my scrawl. Lastly, thanks to the Hobo, as always, for being there when all other lights went out.

BECCA BLOND

Thanks to my sister Jessica for making research in Zurich and Liechtenstein heaps more fun. Big thanks to Bernd Fasching at City Backpacker in Zurich for the hospitality and all the helpful tips. In Interlaken, thanks to Susi and Fritz for the skiing, fondue and hospitality. On the home front, thanks to my fabulous boyfriend Aaron and my dog Duke, I love you both. As always thanks to my family and friends – you know who you are by now.

TERRY CARTER & LARA DUNSTON

Lara and Terry would like to thank all the friendly folk across Greece who put up with our endlessly nosy questions about their towns, hotels, restaurants and bars with good humour.

GEERT COLE & LEANNE LOGAN

To start, a big thank you to family and friends at home for their conviction that we could do life on the road with two kids in tow. And an extra big *bedankt* to Roos and Bert Cole in Belgium for making it happen; to our daughters Eleonor and Gwynevere, for loving the traveller's life; and to our best buddies, Sixy and Bluey. Thanks too for the enthusiastic support of Jean-Claude Conter at the Luxembourg National Tourist Office, Els Maes and Tama d'Haen at Toerisme Vlaanderen, Catherine Langue at the Office de Promotion du Tourisme Wallonie-Bruxelles and Anousjka Schmidt at Brussels International. To the readers and travellers who offered advice, insights and criticisms, thanks again. Lastly, *merci* to all those at Lonely Planet who were involved in the book's production.

DUNCAN GARWOOD

I owe a lot of thanks for this job. In no particular order, thanks to Meg Worby for commissioning me, and to Alex Leviton for her tips on Umbria and Le Marche. On the road, *grazie* to Lorenzo in Bologna, Viviana in Milan, Antonella, Dora and Nanni in Genoa, and Paola Galasso in Turin. Tourist office staff were generally helpful, especially Luca in Verona and Sandra Mattarello in Padua. On a personal note I owe a huge debt to my in-laws Nicla and Aniello Salvati, and, as always to Lidia and the boys, Ben and Nick.

SARAH JOHNSTONE

Thanks to all the usual suspects, plus Nicole Röbel at Berlin Tourismus Marketing, Doris Annette Schütz of Lübeck und Travemünde Tourist-Service, Christine Lambrecht, Dr Annette Zehnter, Paul Gronert and Nadine in Dessau and everyone else who helped out. I'm grateful to fellow author Ryan for covering, ahem, the bird-flu zone, and indebted to the night-porter in my Cologne hotel for saving me from the *amokläufer* incanting loud death threats in the wee hours…who turned out to be merely an inconsiderate gangsta rapper. Finally, thanks to Richard Priest for being the only one to truly appreciate the ridiculous humour of that story!

JOHN LEE

Hearty thanks are due to Val Shore in Visit Britain's Toronto office for her initial assistance and deluge of information. In the UK, thanks to my brother Michael for coming down to check out the Brighton pubs in the January snow. Ongoing thanks to my old mate David for always providing a comfy near-London base to crash for the small price of a few imported Tim Hortons doughnuts. And to my friends in Canada, thanks for staying in contact during the long write-up period: the beers at the end tasted especially good. Finally, thanks to my mum.

ALEX LEVITON

Thanks to bestest friend and Lonely Planet five-timer Len 'Il Muffino' Amaral, my travelling companion and driver extraordinaire, for getting us out of Palermo alive. *Mille grazie* to Zach Nowak and Ivana diBiase in Perugia for some much-needed midterm relaxation and Naples information. Thanks to all the fabulous tourist office employees: Pilar Visconti and Emilio Damiata in Palermo, Luisa Besalduch in Cagliari, Tania Clericuzio in Rome, Silvana in Alghero and Cosimo Meca in Brindisi. Also to local friends: Giulio and Vibeke Castelli, Tegan Schioler, Friar John Kapenda, Isaac Driver and fellow author Duncan Garwood in Rome, Sergio in Syracuse, Maurizio in Brindisi, Maria DiOvia in Matera, and, most importantly, the incomparable Luca Coda, from the back of whose Vespa Naples was reported. Back home, my appreciation goes out to David Liu for fabulous Rome recommendations, Emanuela Boni at ENIT LA, and Rah Bickley for keeping me on track.

VIRGINIA MAXWELL

My greatest thanks go to my travelling companion, Max Handsaker, who accompanied me to innumerable tapas bars, kept me amused and awake over late-night dinners and sang along with Franz Ferdinand in the car. You are a total joy Maxie. Thanks also to Meg Worby for giving me the job, Tashi Wheeler and Csanad Csutoros for answering my queries during write-up and Sarah Andrews and Ryan Ver Berkmoes for putting it all together.

CRAIG MCLACHLAN

A hearty thanks to all those who helped me out on the road, but most of all to my exceptionally beautiful wife Yuriko and our boys Riki and Ben.

JOESPHINE QUINTERO

A very special *obrigada* to the especially helpful tourist offices in Lisbon, Coimbra, Porto and Braga, as well as the many readers who wrote in with useful suggestions and comments. I would also like to thank Robin Chapman for sharing observations, ideas – and a regular bottle of wine at the end of a long day on the road. Thanks also to Ryan Ver Berkmoes for his support, and the Lonely Planet commissioning editors who were involved with this title.

MILES RODDIS

As always, a packful of thanks to Ingrid, who regaled me daily with tales of her skiing exploits as I explored the inner recesses of Andorra's hotels and restaurant kitchens. Thanks too to tourist office staff Lourdes, Meritxell and Eva (Andorra la Vella), Nelson (Pas de la Casa), Paula (Ordino) and Ana (Canillo).

STUART SCHUFFMAN

Major love goes out to Alex Leviton who acted as mentor and voice of reason throughout my entire Lonely Planet experience thus far. Big thanks also goes out to Kristen Holden who saved my behind. I also want to thank the friendly and helpful tourist and transit officials who helped me find all the weird and crazy info I needed to get. Thanks to my family and friends who still like me even though I locked myself in a room and ignored them for a month so I could write about Ireland. I also wanna give a big shout out to all the beautiful people I met on the road who enriched my travel experience, especially the Talbot St kids and all my folks from Abbey Court. Oh, I almost forgot, thanks to anyone who ever bought me a beer or let me stay at their house.

SIMON SELLARS

Thank you to Justine for everything and more. Special thanks to the Buglet and to Fripp & Eno. At Lonely Planet, many thanks to Neal Bedford, Csanad Csutoros, Mark Griffiths, Meg Worby, Judith Bamber, Kim Noble and Ryan Ver Berkmoes. It's been real.

ANDREW STONE

I have my brother David to thank above all others not just for the use of his bases in the Highlands and Dundee on this research trip (and all the other trips over the years) but for introducing me to Scotland in the first place – starting with a low-budget, two-week, very wet camping trip to Loch Lomond and the Western Isles back in the late 1980s. My gratitude also goes to Hege Tollerud from the Liverpool and Merseyside tourist information centre, Glenda Davies from Visit Wales, Caroline Gray from See Glasgow and Jude Henderson from Visit Scotland, all of whom went out of their way to make useful suggestions for new places to check out.

OUR READERS

Many thanks to the travellers who used the last edition and wrote to us with helpful hints, useful advice and interesting anecdotes:

A Chloe Adams, Lisa Adams, Phil, Hilary & Pippa Andre, Ben Andrew, Trevor Angel, Hugh Annand, Sarah Armstrong, Larry Arthur, Silvia Ascarelli, Amy Atzell, Michael Avila **B** Don Bacon, Leyla Bagloul, Bianca Barbaro, Denise Bardan, Carolina Barreira, Alessandro Bavila, Alicia Berger, Emily Berquist, Ivana Bezecna, Mary Bickmore, Roger Bielec, Burke Bindbeutel, Sven Birkemeier, Kate Black, Harry Blackley, Kerry & Jim Bloodworth, Brian Boag, Sanne Bogers, Juerg Boss, Kate Botkin, Pamela & George Bours, Robert Braiden, Julie Branaghan, Michael Brant, Anne Brasier, Valerie Bridgeman, Joan Brown, Caryl Burgess, John Burke, Deborah Burnett, Linde Butterhoff, Christian Byhahn **C** Michelle

Cahalone, Norman Cain, Juan Campo-Cossio, James Carr, Dave Carter, Romelle Castle, Amy Cavagna, Cherie Chasling, George Chatziargyris, Florence Choo, William Christ, Shelia Christos, J M Cimelli, Angela Cirelli, Mona Clark, Carmen Clarke, Simon & Lis Clarke, Martin Clohessy, Beryl Coe, Loyola Colebeck, Krista Coleman, Ans Compaijen, Ron & Sheila Corbett, Andrew Cosgrave, Robert Cotter, Carlos Coupland, Daniel Cox, Kate Crane, Bev Crawford, Mike Crook, Chris Crowther, Bruce Cullen, Oliver Cumming, Rebecca Cutri-Kohart **D** Alan Dangerfield, Bob & Pat Davis, Lynn Dawson, David de Kleine, Vittorio del Duca, Annemie Deruytter, Anke Dijkstra, Gina Doubleday, Mirka Doubravova, Peter Doyle, Linda Drath, Rachel Drew, My Le Ducharme, Jenni Duncan, Caroline Dussault **E** Pippa Ellwood, Laura Elvin, Aaron Epstein, Jim Espie **F** Rachel Faggetter, Emmanuel Fankhauser, Ole Fosse Fardal, Enzo & Maria Fassinelli, Capodici Fatima, Karen Feigh, Laura Fielding, Lynette Filips, Rosalee Firth, Max Francis, Catarina Frazão, Daniel Friedrich, Mr & Mrs Fyvie **G** Bernadette Gabris, Abraham Garcia, Stratos Giannikos, Megan Gibbs, Douglas & Isolde Gibson, Diana Gill, Planet Glassberg, Christian Glockner, Malby Goodman, Brad Goodsell, Lewis Goulding, Helen Graham, Maggie & Hugh Gravelle, Sarah Graybeal, Jim Green, Charles Greenless, Romualdo Grillo, Susil Gupta, Anna Guttman **H** Ronald Hakenberg, Bas Halmans, Eric Halvorson, Alex Hammond, Erja Hänninen, Lucy Hardwick, Marc Harkness, Alison Harris, Chris Hartman, Patricia Havekost, Sandi Heimlich, Dane Henderson, Susan Herman, John Hesketh, Georgina Hewes, N Hill, Adam Hobill, Urska Hocevar, Martine Hofstede, Liz Holman, Holly Hooper, Tina Hough, Sandra Hribar, Bernard Hudson, Margaret Huggett, Geoff Hutcheison **I** John Iaquinto, Vigdis Isachsen **J** Henry Jackson, Neil Jackson, Paul Jackson, Magnus Jansson, Ann Jarjoura, Hanne Johnson, Barry Johnston, Chris Jones, M D Jones, Ronaele Jones, Muijel Juittio, Alex Julyan **K** Russell Kallen, Kosta Karapas, Lisa Keeley, Simon Kerby, M J Kinrade, Andy Kirk, Mary Kitler, Dave Klassen, Roni & Ayala Klaus, Regina Klumpe, Claudine Knobel, Floris Kortie, Ivana Kotalova, Ann Kramer, Nicolas Kucera, Maja Kunzelmann, Maxene Kupperman-Guinals, Anatoliy Kurmanaev **L** Andrea la Fratta, E Lambert, Colin Lamont, M Langham, Donald & Nancy Lareau, Ame Latine, Mick Lauson Jr, Carol Lawless, Sarah Lawson, Tram Anh Le, Tony Lees, Frances & Andrea Lench, Michael Leonard, Stephen Leong, Mauro Leoni, Rebecca Letven, Jamie Leveille, Anthony Liem, Sharon Lim, Simon Lock, Ute Loeffelsend, Cassie Lovel **M** Chris MacCarthy, Evan Macauley, Dawn MacDonald, Kristina Macku, David Marchant, Angel Marcos, Joanne Marshall, Debra McBride, Jamie McBride, Alastair McCall, Chandra McCann, Ray McClure, J S McLintock, Gabi Mcnicol, Simon Mcsorley, Tim Meddings, Martin Meder, John Meredith, John & Lynn Midgley, Jacqueline Miedema, Sanna Miettunen, Tiziana Milizia, Langdon Miller, Mike Mimirinis, Seda Minas, Brenda Miskie, Fergus Mitchell, Paul Mitchell, Tina Mizgalski, Heather Monell, Ana Montenegro, Seung Hyun Moon, Kay Mould **N** Stephen Nau, Gretchen Newberry, Boonsin Ng, Mikael Nojd, Larry North **O** Keith O'Brien, Torlach O'Connor, F M Oddy, Anthony Oldfield, Catherine O'Neill, Jerry Ostradicky, Tim Ottevanger, Marc Ozimec **P** Shalom Paul, Tomaz Pintar, Amy Polaczyk, Pascal Portelli, David Price, Alexandra Prichard, Christopher Prusaski **Q** Scott Quellhorst **R** Wolfgang Rabl, Karlmarx Rajangam, Emanuele Ramella, Ute Ramseger, William Reeves, Maria Ressel, Thomas Reydon, Peter & Yumiko Riley, Christiane Rochon, David Rogers, Michaela Ronzoni, Andrew Roper, Jan Roscoe, Sue Royal S Gabbriela Sabados, Karen Sarah, Seumas Sargent, Lone Scherfig, Alan Schneider, Deborah Schubert, Nichola Scott, Richard Scotton, Anne Sear, Alice Seet, Linda Shaw, Nicole Sheldon, John Sheppard, Cindy Shurtleff, Andrea Sita, Fiona Skewes, Max Sommers, Ian Southwell, Claudia Spener, Bonnie Spoales, Graham Stagg, Clare Staines, Marianne Stam, Alistair Staton, Ivan Stockley, Karin Sturzenegger, Anna Swindells, Thor & Mary Swope **T** Lynette Taylor, Sandra Tegtmeier, Nienke Ten, Malla Tennila, Laura Theng, Michael Thompson, Panom Thongprayoon, Fab Tomlin, Nicole Trombley **U** Susanne Ueberhuber, Iggy Urquhart, Reg Urquhart **V** Koert van den Beukel, Cari van Rood, Camille van Wessem, Wim Vandenbussche, Shay Vella, Mathias Viaene, Mário Vilar **W** Raoul Wainwright, Catherine Waldby, Alan & Liz Walter, Andy Ward, Sabine Wehinger, Eva-Lena Weinstock, Angela Wendling, B Weston, Karen Weston, John & Deborah Wheaton, Ada Whitaker, Ian Williams, Kathleen Williams, Norman Williams, Maggie Willsher, Dale Wilson, Lennart Wingelaar, Edwin Wolff, Ken Wong, Sharon Wood, Caroline Woodgate, David Woodhouse, D S Wyber **Y** Andrew Yale

ACKNOWLEDGMENTS

Many thanks to the following for the use of their content:

Map data contained in colour highlights map © Mountain High Maps 1993 Digital Wisdom, Inc.

SEND US YOUR FEEDBACK

We love to hear from travellers – your comments keep us on our toes and help make our books better. Our well-travelled team reads every word on what you loved or loathed about this book. Although we cannot reply individually to postal submissions, we always guarantee that your feedback goes straight to the appropriate authors, in time for the next edition. Each person who sends us information is thanked in the next edition – and the most useful submissions are rewarded with a free book.

To send us your updates – and find out about Lonely Planet events, newsletters and travel news – visit our award-winning website: **www.lonelyplanet.com/contact**.

Note: We may edit, reproduce and incorporate your comments in Lonely Planet products such as guidebooks, websites and digital products, so let us know if you don't want your comments reproduced or your name acknowledged. For a copy of our privacy policy visit www.lonelyplanet.com/privacy.

Index

ABBREVIATIONS

L Luxembourg
G Germany
F France

A

Aachen 525-7
abbeys, *see* churches
Aberdeen 258-9
absinthe 1052
accommodation 1095-8
Acropolis 564-5, 8
activities 1098-9, *see also* cycling, diving & snorkelling, hiking, kayaking, mountain biking, skiing & snowboarding
  birdwatching 231, 263
  boating 1098
  canyoning 371, 1079
  golfing 257, 263, 1068
  horseback riding 680, 921
  rock climbing 258
  skydiving 1079
  surfing 266, 689-90, 1031, 1099
  white-water rafting 240, 371, 1079
  windsurfing 542, 635, 1099
  yatching 635
Aegina 587
Aeolian Islands 804-5
Agios Nikolaos 614
Agrigento 808-9
air travel 1112-16
Aix-en-Provence 384-5
Ajaccio 406-8, **407**
Alcázar 1008
Algarve, the 903-7
Algeciras 1024
Alghero 813-14
Alhambra 1016
Alicante 995-8, **997**
Alonnisos 628-9
Alsace 317-23
Amalfi Coast 795-7
Amboise 344-5
Ameland 875-6
Amsterdam 850-60, **852**, **7**
  accommodation 853-5
  attractions 851-3
  drinking 856
  emergency services 850
  entertainment 856-7
  food 855-6
  gay & lesbian travellers 856-7
  Internet access 850
  itineraries 851
  postal services 850
  Red Light District 854
  shopping 858
  tourist information 850
  travel to/from 858
  travel within 858-9
ancient Agora 565
ancient Corinth 576
Andalucía 1007-26
Andorra 45-54, **45**, **47**
  accomodation 52
  activities 52
  business hours 52
  costs 46
  embassies 52
  emergencies 53
  history 46
  Internet resources 52
  population 46
  travel to/from 53
Andorra la Vella 46-50, **48-9**
Anne Frank Huis 851
Annecy 372-5, **373**
Antwerp 121-5
Appenzellerland 1087
Aragón 980-8
Aran Islands 686-7
Arcachon 353
archaeological sites
  Acropolis of Lindos 618
  ancient Corinth 576
  ancient Delphi 580-1
  ancient Mycenae 577
  Caesaraugusta Theatre 981
  Castell del Rei 978-9
  Kamiros 618
  Knossos 609
  Neapolis-Parco Archeologico 807
  Ostia Antica 738-9
  Phaestos 609
  Pompeii 792
  Teatro Romano & Anfiteatro 1029
architecture
  Art Nouveau 112, 291, 932
  baroque 425-6
  Bauhaus movement 460, 463-4, 644-5, 848
  Gallo-Roman 289
  Gothic 425, 932
  Mannerism 847
  Manueline 888
  medieval architecture 360
  Modernisme 965-8
  neo-Gothic 848
  Renaissance architecture 360, 714
  Romanesque 847
area codes, *see inside front cover*
Arles 388
art galleries, *see* museums & galleries
arts 38-40, *see also individual countries*
Assisi 784
Asturias 988-92
Athens 561-74, **562**, **570**
  accommodation 566-7
  attractions 564-6
  dangers 564
  drinking 568-9
  emergency services 563
  entertainment 569-70
  festivals & events 566
  food 567-8
  gay & lesbian travellers 570
  Internet access 563-4
  itineraries 561
  postal services 564
  shopping 570
  telephone services 564
  tourist information 564
  travel to/from 571
  travel within 572
ATMs 1105-6
Augsburg 488
Austen, Jane 199
Austria 55-108, **55**, **57**, 12
  accommodation 101-2
  activities 102-3
  books 103
  business hours 103

000 Map pages
000 Photograph pages

climate 56
costs 56, 104
festivals & events 103-4
food 59
gay & lesbian travellers 104
geography 59
history 56-8
holidays 104
itineraries 56
language 104
literature 58
music 58-9
planning 56
politics 58
population 58
postal services 105
religion 58
telephone services 105
tourist information 105
tours 67
travel to/from 106-7
travel within 107-8
visas 105
Austro-Hungarian Empire 56
Avebury 192
Avignon 385-8, **386**
Ávila 951-2

B

Bach, Johann Sebastian 454, 459
Bad Doberan 468
Bad Ischl 89-91
Baden-Baden 498-9
Baden-Württemberg 492-9
Balearic Islands 999-1007
Bamberg 484-5
Barcelona 963-75, **966-7**, **970**
accommodation 969-72
attractions 964-8
dangers 964
drinking 973-4
eating 972-3
emergency services 964
entertainment 974
festivals & events 968-9
Internet access 964
itineraries 964
postal services 964
shopping 974-5
tourist information 964
tours 968
travel to/from 975
travel within 975
Basel 1084-7, **1085**
basilicas, *see* cathedrals & basilicas
Basilique du Sacré Cœur 301, **590**
Basque Country 980-8
Bastia 403-5
Bath 199-202, **200**
Bauhaus Building 464-5
Bavaria 472-89
Bavarian Alps 489-91
Bayeux 329-31, **330**
Bayonne 354-5
Beaune 364-5
beer
Austria 59
Belgium 113, 114
Brasserie Artisanale de Fribourg 1053
Brasserie du Cardinal 1053
Germany 428, 482
Guinness Brewery 658
Oktoberfest 477, **11**
Beethoven, Ludwig van 522
Belfast 691-7, **693**
Belgium 109-42, **109**, **110**
accommodation 138-9
activities 139
arts 112-13
beer 113, 114
Benelux Tourrail 142
business hours 139
climate 110-11
costs 111
embassies 139
emergency services 141
environment 113
festivals & events 139-40
food 113-14
history 111
holidays 140
itineraries 110
literature 112 planning 110-11
population 112
postal services 140
religion 112
sport 113
telephone services 140
travel to/from 140-1
travel within 142
vegetarians & vegans 114
visas 140
Bellinzona 1064-5
Berchtesgaden 489-90
Berlin 428-46, **431**, **432-3**, **434-5**, **438**, **439**
accommodation 438-41
attractions 431-8
dangers 431
drinking 442-3
emergency services 431
entertainment 443
festivals 438
food 441-2
gay & lesbian travellers 445
history 429-30
Internet access 430
itineraries 430
maps 430
postal services 431
shopping 444
tourist information 431
tours 437-8
travel to/from 444-5
travel within 445-6
Berlin Wall 429, 437
Bern 1045-51, **1047**, **594**
Besançon 378-80
Biarritz 355-6
Bilbao 986-7
birdwatching 231, 263
Birmingham 213
Black Forest 499-504, **500**, **594**
Blackmint-Distillerie Kübler & Wyss 1052
Blarney Stone 673
Blois 338-40, **339**
boat travel 1115, 1117
boating 1098
Bologna 763-6, **764**
Bonaparte, Napoleon 286, 406-8, 930
Bonifacio 408-9
Bonn 522
books 28-9
Austria 103
Britain 274
Germany 545
Hay-on-Wye 270
health 1123
Ireland 702 Italy 816
novels 39
Bordeaux 350-3, **351**
Braga 919-20
Brandenburg 446-8
Brandenburg Gate 431-5
Brecon 269
Bregenz 100-1
Bremen 531-3, **532**
Brighton 183-6, **185**
Bristol 203-5
Britain 143-282, **143**, **145**
accommodation 272-3
activities 272-3
arts 146-7
books 274

Britain *continued*
- business hours 274
- climate 144
- disabilities, travellers with 277
- embassies 274
- employment 277
- environmental issues 148
- festivals & events 274-5
- food & drink 148
- gay & lesbian travellers 275
- geography 147
- itineraries 144
- literature 146
- media 275-6
- money 276
- planning 144
- population 144
- postal services 276
- public holidays 275
- religion 144-6
- telephone services 276-7
- tourist information 277
- travel to/from 277-9
- travel within 279-82
- visas 277
- wildlife 147

British Museum 159
Brittany 333-8
Bronte sisters 225
Brú na Bóinne 663
Bruges 129-32, **130**, **591**
Brunelleschi, Filippo 714
Brussels 114-20, **116**
Buçaco Forest 913
Buckingham Palace 161
bullfighting 899, 948, 1023
Burgos 958-9
Burgundy 360-9
Burren 682-3
bus travel 1117
business hours 816, *see also individual countries*
Byzantine Empire 555

C

Cáceres 1028-9
Cádiz 1024-5
Cagliari 810-12, **811**
Cahors 359-60
Cala Gonone 812-13
Calais 325-6
Calvi 405-6
Cambridge 216-19, **217**
Cannes 394-7, **396**
Cantabria 988-92
Canterbury 180-2
canyoning 371, 1079
Capri 792-4
car travel 1117-20
- hire 1118
- insurance 1118-19

Caravaggio, Michelangelo Merisi da 714, 729
Carcassonne 401-2
Cardiff 268-70
Carnac 334-5
Cascais 902
Castelo de Vide 909-10
Castilla y León 951-9
Castilla-La Mancha 959-63
castles & palaces
- Albertina 66
- Alcázar 1008
- Bamburgh Castle 230
- Blarney Castle 673
- Blenheim Palace 209-10
- Buckingham Palace 161
- Burg Rheinfels 510
- Carrickfergus Castle 697
- Castle Howard 224
- Château Azay-le-Rideau 343
- Château d'If 381
- Château de Chambord 340
- Château de Chaumont-sur-Loire 340-1
- Château de Chenonceau 343
- Château de Cheverny 340
- Château de Chillon 1061-2
- Chateau de Langeais 343
- Chateau de Neuchâtel 1051
- Château de Versailles 312
- Dunluce Castle 698
- Durham Castle 227
- Edinburgh Castle 246
- Hampton Court Palace 165
- Heidelberg Schloss 495
- Hever Castle 183
- Hofburg 63, **7**
- Hohenschwangau 488-9
- Kilkenny Castle 667
- Leeds Castle 183
- Lincoln Castle 220
- Malahide Castle 663
- Neues Palais 446
- Neuschwanstein 488-9
- Palace of Holyroodhouse 246
- Palacio de la Aljafería 981
- Palacio Real 938-9
- Palacio Real Almudaina 1000
- Palais des Papes 387
- Palazzo Reale 789
- Schloss Belvedere 65
- Schloss Nymphenburg 476
- Schloss Sanssouci 446
- Schloss Schönbrunn 66
- Schloss Schwerin 466
- Schloss Vaduz 825
- Tower of London 162
- Wartburg 459
- Windsor Castle 179

Catacombes 295
Catacombs of San Callisto 728
Catacombs of San Sebastiano 728
Catalonia 963-80
cathedrals & basilicas, *see also* churches & abbeys
- Aachen Dom 526
- Ávila cathedral 951
- Basílica de Nuestra Señora del Pilar 980
- Basilica di San Francesco 784
- Basilica di San Lorenzo 774
- Basilica di San Marco 754
- Basilica di Santa Maria Maggiore 728
- Basilique du Sacré Cœur 301, **590**
- Basilique Notre Dame de la Garde 381
- Canterbury Cathedral 180
- Catedral del Apóstol 990
- Catedral Nueva 952-3
- Cathedrale de Lausanne 1059
- Cathédrale de Notre Dame de Paris 298-9
- Cathédrale Notre Dame (Reims) 314-15
- Cathédrale Notre Dame (Rouen) 328
- Cathédrale Notre Dame (Strasbourg) 320
- Cathédrale Orthodoxe Russe St-Nicolas 389-90
- Cathédrale St-André 350
- Cattedrale di San Giovanni Battista 744
- Christ Church Catherdral 656
- Dom St Marien 457
- Duomo (Florence) 772, **6**
- Duomo (Milan) 746
- Duomo (Siena) 779
- Durham Cathedral 227

000 Map pages
000 Photograph pages

Exeter Cathedral 192
Freiburg Münster 502
Glasgow Cathedral 252
Kölner Dom 517
Lincoln Cathedral 220
Liverpool Cathedral 236
Mezquita 1013
St Patrick's cathedral 656
St Paul's Cathedral 162
St Peter's Basilica 720-1
Salisbury Cathedral 190
Seville Cathedral 1008
Stephensdom 63
Winchester Cathedral 188
York Minster 221
cell phones 1109
Cézanne, Paul 384
Chagall, Marc 389
Chamonix 369-72, **370**
Champagne 314-17, **314**
Champs-Élysées 300
Chartres 313
Chester 234-5
children, travel with 1099-100
Chios 623-4
Chur 1067
churches & abbeys,
see also cathedrals & basilicas
Bath Abbey 199
Capela dos Ossos 907
Église St-Michel 398
Frauenkirche 449
Fraumünster 1072
King's College Chapel 216-17
Marienkirche 469
Panagia Ekatontapyliani 599
Panthéon 295
Ste-Chapelle 299
Tintern Abbey 268
Westminster Abbey 159-61
Whitby Abbey 226
Wieskirche 482
cinema 29-30, 83, 85, 146, 147, 288
Clear Island 674
Clervaux 837-8
Cliffs of Moher 682-3
climate 27, 1100-1
coffee 62
Coimbra 911-13, **592**
Collins, Michael 648
Cologne 517-22, **518**, **520**
Colosseum 717-18
Columbus, Christopher 929
Connemara 687-8
Constance 505-6
consulates 1103, *see also embassies under individual countries*
Córdoba 1013-15, **1015**
Corfu 629-31, **630**
Corinth 575-6
Cork 668-73, **670-1**
Corsica 403-9
Costa Blanca 998
Costa Brava 977-8
Costa Calída 998-1000
Costa de Almería 1019-20
costs 27-8, *see also individual countries*
Côte d'Azur 388-98
Cotswolds 212-13
County Wicklow 664-5
courses 1100
credit cards 1106 Crete 606-15, **606**
Cuenca 962-3
current events 36
customs 1100-1
Cyclades 588-606
cycling 1098, 1116-17
Belgium 139
Britain 212, 255-6, 266, 273
France 322, 373-4, 410
Germany 505, 544-5
Italy 815
Portugal 920, 922
Spain 1030-1

D

da Vinci, Leonardo 344, 746
Dalí, Salvador 977
dangers 1101-2,
see also individual cities
Danube Valley 75-8
Deep vein thrombosis 1123
Delft 866-7, **867**
Delos 598
Delphi 580-1
Den Bosch 876-7
Den Haag 863-6, **864**
Derry 698-9
Dessau 463-6
Diekirch 839
Dijon 360-3, **361**
Dinard 337-8
Dingle Peninsula 679-81
disabilities, travellers with 1109
Britian 277
Greece 639
Ireland 705
Italy 819
discount cards 1102-3
Disneyland Paris 312
diving & snorkelling
Britain 241, 274
Greece 634
insurance 1104
Ireland 674, 702
Italy 743, 804, 813
Portugal 907
Spain 977
Dodecanese 615-21
Dolomites 767-9
Donegal 689-91
Dordogne region 357-9
Douro River 919
Dover 182-3
Dresden 448-52, **450**
drinks 42-4, *see also* beer, wine, wineries
absinthe 1052
coffee 62
driving licences 1118
drugs 1101, 1104-5
Dublin 652-63, **654-5**, **657**, **589**
accommodation 658-9
attractions 653-8
drinking 660-1
eating 659-60
emergency services 652
entertainment 661-2
gay & lesbian travellers 661
Internet access 652
itineraries 653
postal services 653
tourist information 653
tours 658
travel to/from 662
travel within 662-3
Dunkirk 326-7
Duomo (Florence) 772, **6**
Durham 227-8
Düsseldorf 522-5, **523**

E

Echternach 838-9
Edinburgh 244-50, **245**
accommodation 247-8
attractions 246-7
drinking 248-9
eating 248
emergency services 244
entertainment 249
festivals & events 247
Internet access 244
postal services 246
tourist information 246
travel to/from 249
travel within 249-50

INDEX

Edinburgh Castle 246
Eiffel Tower 294, **5**
Einstein, Albert 1046
electricity 1103
embassies 1103,
  see also individual countries
emergencies, *see inside front cover*
employment 1110-11
England 148-240, **149**, **589**
  history 148-51
  population 151
  travel to/from 176-7
environment 41-2, 1124
Épernay 315-16
Epidavros 577
Erfurt 457-8, **458**
Esch-Sur-Sûre 838
Estremoz 909
etiquette 30-1
Étoile 300
Etruscans 739-40
Eurodomino 1122
Évora 907-9, **908**
exchange rates, *see inside front cover*
Exeter 192-3
Extremadura 1027-30

F

Falls Rd 692
Faro 903-4
Fátima 912
Ferrara 762-3
ferries 1115
festivals 30, *see also individual countries and citites*
films 29-30, 83, 85, 146, 147, 288
Flanders 121-33, **123**
Flims-Laax 1067-8
Florence 769-77, **770**, **773**
  accommodation 774-5
  attractions 771-4
  courses 774
  eating 775-6
  emergency services 771
  entertainment 776
  festivals & events 774
  history 769-77
  Internet access 771
  postal services 771
  shopping 776
  telephone services 771
  tourist information 771
  tours 774
  travel to/from 776-7
  travel within 777
food 42-4
football
  museums 233
  World Cup 2006 426
France 283-418, **283**, **285**
  accommodation 409-10
  activities 410-11
  architecture 289
  arts 288-9
  business hours 411
  climate 284
  costs 284
  embassies 411-12
  festivals & events 412
  food 290-1
  gay & lesbian travellers 412
  geography 289
  history 284-7
  itineraries 284
  legal matters 412
  literature 288
  money 412-13
  planning 284
  population 287
  postal services 413
  prehistoric sites 359
  public holidays 412
  religion 287-8
  telephone services 413
  travel to/from 414-16
  travel within 416-18
  unemployment 287
  vegetarian & vegan travellers 291
  visas 413-14
  wildlife 289
  wine 290
Franco, General Francisco 930
Frankfurt-am-Main 511-17, **512-13**
Freiburg 502-5, **503**
French Alps 369-78
French Revolution 286, 300
Fribourg 1051-3
Friedrichshain 438
Füssen 488-9

G

Galicia 988-92
galleries, *see* museums & galleries
Galway 683-6, **684**
gardens, *see* parks & gardens
Garmisch-Partenkirchen 490-1
Gaudí, Antoni 965-8
gay travellers 1103-4, *see also individual cities and countries*
Geneva 1054-9, **1055**
Genoa 740-2
geography 41, 932
Germany 419-552, **419**, **421**
  accommodation 544
  activities 544-5
  architecture 425-6
  arts 424-6
  beer 428
  books 545
  business hours 545
  climate 420
  costs 420
  dangers 545
  disabilites, travellers with 548
  discount cards 545
  embassies 545
  employment 548
  environmental issues 427
  ettiquette 428-9
  festivals & events 546
  folklore 525
  food 427-9
  gay & lesbian travellers 546
  geography 427
  history 420-3
  literature 424
  media 546-7
  money 547
  music 425
  planning 420
  population 423-4
  postal services 547
  public holidays 546
  religion 424
  reunification 423
  sport 426
  telephone services 547
  travel to/from 548-9
  travel within 549-52
  vegetarian & vegan travellers 428
  visas 548
  wildlife 427
Ghent 125-9, **127**
Giant's Causeway 697-8
Gibraltar 1026-7
Gimmelwald 1082
Girona 976-7
Glasgow 250-5, **251**
Glastonbury 202-3
Glendalough 664-5
Goethe, Johann Wolfgang von 459

000 Map pages
000 Photograph pages

golfing 257, 263, 1068
Goslar 464
Granada 1016-19, **1017**
Graubünden 1067-70
Graz 78-81, **78**
Greece 553-644, **553, 556-57**
  accommodation 634
  activities 634-5
  arts 558-9
  business hours 635
  children, travel with 635
  climate 554
  costs 554
  customs 635
  dangers 635
  disabilities, travellers with 639
  drinks 561
  embassies 635-6
  environmental issues 560
  festivals & events 636-7
  food 560-1
  gay & lesbian travellers 637
  geography 559
  history 554-8
  Internet access 637
  Internet resources 637
  itineraries 554
  language 637
  literature 558-9
  money 637-8
  planning 554
  population 558
  postal services 638
  public holidays 637-44
  religion 558
  sport 558
  telephone services 638
  tourist information 638-9
  travel to/from 639-41
  travel within 641-4
  visas 639
  wildlife 559-60
Greek Islands 586-634
Grenoble 375-8, **376**
Grindelwald 1081-4
Groningen City 873-5
Gruyères 1053
Guggenheim Museum 986
Guinness Brewery 658

H
Haarlem 860-1
Hadrian's Wall 231-2
Hague, the 863-6, **864**
Hallstatt 91-2
Hamburg 533-40, **534-5**
Hamelin 528-9
Hania 610-12, **611**
Hanover 527-8
Han-Sur-Lesse 136-7
Harz Mountains 464-5
Hay-on-Wye 270
health 1104, 1123-4
Heidelberg 495-8, **496-7**
Hesse 511-7
Hexenloch 502
hiking 1098-9
  altitude sickness 1124
  Andorra 50
  Austria 98
  Britain 225, 226, 231, 273
  France 371, 375, 410
  Germany 491, 501, 510-11, 544-5
  Greece 583, 585, 612, 635
  hypothermia 1124
  Italy 767-9, 815
  Luxembourg 838-9, 840
  Scotland 237-8, 240, 255, 258, 259
  Spain 920, 1031
  Switzerland 1052, 1062, 1081, 1082-3
  Wales 266, 271
history 36-8
Hitler, Adolf 422, 473
holidays 27, *see also individual countries*
Holy Grail 992-3
horse racing 213
horseback riding 73, 680, 921
Hugo, Victor 837
Hydra 587

I
Ibiza 1003-6, **1005**
impressionists 289
Innsbruck 93-7, **94, 594**
insurance 1123
  health 1104
  vehicle 1118-19
Interlaken 1078-81
Internet access 1104
Internet resources 29
  airfares 1113-14
  Andorra 51
  car hire 1118
  disabilities, travellers with 1109
  Edinburgh 244
  employment 1111
  flights 1116
  Greece 637
  Ireland 703
  Italy 817
  London 158
  Paris 294
  sport 41
  Switzerland 1090
  volunteering 1110
Inter-Rail 1122
Inverness 261-2
Ioannina 582-3
Ionian Islands 629-34
Ios 602-3, **603**
IRA 648, 649-50
Iraklio 607-9, **608**
Ireland 645-708, **645, 647**
  accommodation 701-2
  activities 702
  arts 650-1
  books 702
  business hours 702
  climate 646-50
  costs 646
  disabilities, travellers with 705
  diving 675
  embassies 702-3
  festivals & events 703
  food & drink 651-2
  gay & lesbian travellers 703
  geography 651
  history 646-50
  Internet resources 703
  itineraries 646
  kayaking 675
  literature 650
  maps 703
  money 703-4
  planning 646-50
  population 650
  postal services 704
  public holidays 703
  religion 650
  telephone services 704
  tourist information 704-5
  travel to/from 705-6
  travel within 706-8
  Troubles, the 649
  visas 705
Irish Republican Army (IRA) 648, 649-50
Isle of Mull 260
Isle of Skye 264
Italy 709-822, **709, 711**
  accommodation 814-15
  activities 815-16
  arts 712-14

Italy *continued*
- books 816
- climate 710
- costs 710
- dangers 816
- disabilities, travellers with 819
- embassies 816-17
- etiquette 715-16
- festivals & events 817
- food & drink 715-16
- geography 714
- history 710-12
- Internet resources 817-18
- itineraries 710
- literature 712-13
- money 818
- planning 710
- population 712
- postal services 818
- public holidays 817
- religion 712
- telephone services 818-19
- travel to/from 819-20
- travel within 821-2
- visas 819

Ithaki 632
itineraries 32-5, *see also individual countries and cities*

J

Joan of Arc 314-15, 327-9
Jungfrau region 1081-4
Jungfraujoch 1083
Jura region 378-80, 1051-3

K

Karpathos 618-19
kayaking 1098
- Belgium 137, 139
- France 411
- Greece 631
- Ireland 689
- Portugal 907
- Scotland 240, 241
- Switzerland 1053
- Wales 266

Kefallonia 632-3
Kilkenny 667-8
Killarney 675-8, **677**
Kilmainham Goal 656-7
Kitzbühel 98
Klagenfurt 81-2
Knossos 609
Kos 619-20
Kreuzberg 434-5

L

La Coruña 989-90
La Rochelle 348-9
La Sagrada Familia 968
Lagos 905-6
Lake Constance 504-6
Lake District 237-40
Lake Geneva 1059-62
language 1125
Languedoc-Roussillon 401-3
Lascaux Caves 359
Lasithi Plateau 613
Lausanne 1059-61, **1060**
Lauterbrunnen 1082
Le Marche 781-5
Leaning Tower of Pisa 778
Lecce 799-800
Lefkada 631
legal matters 1104-5
Leiden 861-3, **862**
Leipzig 453-6, **455**
León 956-8, **957**
Les Calanques 406
Les Eyzies de Tayac 358
lesbian travellers 625, 1103-4, *see also individual countries and cities*
Lesvos 624-6
Leukerbad 1064
Liechtenstein 823-8, **823**, **824**
- business hours 816
- climate 824
- costs 824
- food & drink 825
- history 824
- planning 824
- travel to/from 828
- travel within 828

Lienz 98-100
Lille 323-5
Limerick 681-2
Lindau 506
Linz 76-8
Lisbon 889-903, **890-1**, **894-5**, **592**
- accommodation 895-6
- attractions 893-5
- drinking 898
- eating 896-8
- emergency services 892
- entertainment 898-9
- festivals & events 895
- gay & lesbian travellers 898-9
- Internet access 892
- itineraries 893
- postal services 892
- telephone services 892
- tourist information 892
- tours 895
- travel to/from 899-900

Liszt, Franz 460
literature 40-1, *see also individual countries*
Locarno 1065-6
Loch Ness 261
Loire region 338-45, **590**
London 151-79, **152-3**, **156-7**, **160**, **5**, **10**
- accommodation 165-8
- attractions 158-65
- dangers 158
- drinking 172
- eating 168-72
- emergency services 158
- entertainment 173-5
- festivals & events 165
- gay & lesbian travellers 174-5
- history 154-5
- Internet access 158
- Internet resources 158
- itineraries 158
- markets 176
- postal services 158
- shopping 175-6
- tourist information 158
- tours 165
- travel to/from 176-7
- travel within 177

Londonderry 698-9
Lorraine 317-23
Louis XIV 286
Lourdes 356-7
Louvre, Musée du 299, **8**
Lower Saxony 527-31
Lübeck 540-2
Lucerne 1076-8, **1077**
Lugano 1066-7
Lüneburg 529
Luther, Martin 459
Luxembourg 829-42, **829**, **831**, **9**
- accommodation 840
- activities 840
- arts 832
- Benelux Tourrail 142
- business hours 840
- climate 830
- costs 830

000 Map pages
000 Photograph pages

embassies 840-1
festivals & events 841
food & drink 832
geography 832
history 830-31
itineraries 830
money 841
planning 830
population 831
postal services 841
public holidays 841
religion 831
telephone services 841
travel to/from 841-2
travel within 842
visas 841
Luxembourg City 832-7, **834**, **591**
Lyon 365-9, **367**

M

Maastricht 877-9, **878**
Madrid 933-51, **936-7**, **940-1**
accomodation 942-3
attractions 935-41
courses 941
dangers 935
drinking 945-7
eating 943-5
emergency services 934
entertainment 947-9
festivals & events 941-2
gay travellers 947
history 934
itineraries 935
lesbian travellers 947
markets 950
postal services 935
shopping 949
tapas 944
tourist information 935
tours 941
travel to/from 949
travel within 950-1
mafia 713
Magdeburg 462-3
Magna Carta 190
Maison Carrée 402
Málaga 1020-3, **1022**
Malbun 827
Mallorca 1000-3, **1001**
Manchester 232-4
Mani 579-80
Mantua 749
maps 1105
Marseille 380-4, **383**
Marvão 909-10
Matera 797-8
Matisse, Henri 389
Matterhorn 1062-3
measures 1110,
see also inside front cover
Mecklenburg-Western Pomerania 466-72
media 1105
Meissen 452-3
Melk 76
Menorca 1006-7
Menton 398
Mérida 1029-30
Merkel, Angela 423
Meteora 581-2, **581**
metric conversions,
see inside front cover
Michelangelo 714, 729
Middelburg 872-3
Milan 745-9, **747**
mobile phones 1109
Monaco 398-401, **399**
accommodation 400
attractions 400
festivals 400
food 400-1
postal services 400
tourist information 400
travel to/from 401
Monchique 906
Monestir de Montserrat 975-6
money 27-8, 1105-7,
see also inside front cover
moneychangers 1107
Monsaraz 909
Mont St-Michel 332-3, **590**
Montignac 358-9
Montmartre 298
Montreux 1061-2
Moselle Valley (G) 507-8, **594**
Moselle Valley (L) 839-40
motorcycle travel 1117-20
insurance 1119
road rules 1119-20
Mt Athos 586-8
Mt Etna 806-7
Mt Olympus 585-6
mountain biking
Andorra 51
Britain 258
France 380
Greece 661
Italy 815
Portugal 907, 914
Scotland 240
Spain 1031
Mozart, Amadeus 83-4
Munich 473-81, **474-5**
accommodation 477-8
attractions 475-7
drinking 480
festivals & events 477
food 478-80
gay & lesbian travellers 480
history 473
Internet access 474
postal services 474-5
shopping 480
tourist information 475
tours 477, 479
travel to/from 480-1
travel within 481
Murcia 992-9, **998-9**
Mürren 1082-3
museums & galleries 159
Alte Pinakothek 476
Ashmolean 206
Autostadt 530
Baltic 228
Benaki Museum 566
BMW Museum 477
British Museum 159
Castel Sant'Angelo 722
Centre National d'Art et de Culture Georges Pompidou 299-300
Deutches Museum 476
Dokumentation Obersalzberg Museum 489
Einstein Museum 1046
Fitzwilliam Museum 217
Galleria degli Uffizi 772
Germanisches Nationalmuseum 486
Guggenheim Museum 986
Hamburger Bahnhof 436
International Red Cross & Red Crescent Museum 1056
Iraklio archaeological museum 607
Jewish Museum 437
Jüdisches Museum 476
Kelvingrove Art Gallery & Museum 250
Leopold Museum 65
Liechtensteinisches Landesmuseum 825
Mauritshuis 863
Mercedes-Benz Museum 492-3
Musée d'Art Moderne et d'Art Contemporain 389
Musée d'Orsay 294-5

INDEX

Musée des Beaux-Arts 345
Musée du Louvre 299, **8**
Musée du Petit Palais 387
Musée National d'Histoire et d'Art 833
Musée National du Moyen Âge 295
Musée Olympique 1059
Musée Picasso 300
Musée Rodin 295
Musei Capitolini 721-2
Museo Archeologico Nazionale 787-8
Museo Nacional Centro de Arte Reina Sofía 938
Museo Nacional del Prado 935, 938
Museo Picasso Málaga 1021
Museu Picasso 965
Museum Boijmans van Beuningen 868
Museum Het Rembrandthuis 851
Museum of Byzantine Culture 583
Museum of Science & Industry 232
National Archaeological Museum 565-6
National Gallery 656
National Gallery of Scotland 246
National Museum (Dublin) 653
National Portrait Gallery 159
National Roman Museums 729
Natural History Museum 162
Palais des Beaux-Arts 324
Pergamonmuseum 435
Picasso Museum 1076
Porsche Museum 493
Residenzmuseum 475-6
Sammlung Rosengart 1076
Staatliches Museum 466
Städelsches Kunstinstitut 514
Stasi Museum 437
Stedelijk Museum 851
Tate Britain 161
Tate Modern 163
Ulster Folk & Transport Museums 692
Van Gogh Museum 853
Vatican Museums 721
Victoria & Albert Museum 161
music 58, 115
Mussolini, Benito 712

000 Map pages
000 Photograph pages

Mycenae 577
Mykonos 588, 597-8, **597**, **596**

N

Nafplio 576-7
Nancy 322-3
Nantes 345-7
Naples 786-92, **787**
national parks & reserves
Brecon Beacons National Park 269
Dartmoor National Park 194-5
Exmoor National Park 195-6
Hoge Veluwe National Park 876
Hohe Tauern National Park 99-100, **594**
Killarney National Park 676
North York Moors National Park 225-7
Parc Naturel Régional du Haut-Jura 380
Parco Nazionale delle Cinque Terre 742
Parque Nacional Da Peneda-Gerês 920-1
Parque Natural de los Cañones y La Sierra de Guara 982
Peak District National Park 215-16
Pembrokeshire Coast National Park 270
Saxon Switzerland 453
Snowdonia National Park 271-2
Swiss National Park 1069-70
national rail passes 1122
Navarra 980-8
Naxos 600-2, **601**
Nazaré 910
Nazis 58, 422
Netherlands 843-84, **843**, **845**, **591**
accommodation 879
activities 879
architecture 847-8
arts 846-8
Benelux Tourrail 142
business hours 880
cannabis 846
climate 844
costs 844
dangers 880
discount cards 880
embassies 880
environmental issues 849
etiquette 850
festivals & events 880-1
food 849-50
geography 848-9
history 844-6
itineraries 844
legal matters 881
literature 846
money 881-2
planning 844
population 846
postal services 882
public holidays 881
religion 846
telephone services 882
travel to/from 882-3
travel within 883-4
vegetarian/vegan travellers 849-50
visas 882
wildlife 849
Neuchâtel 1051-2
Newcastle-Upon-Tyne 228-30
Nice 389-94, **392-3**, **12**
Nîmes 402-3
Normandy 327-33
North Frisian Islands 542-4
North Rhine-Westphalia 517-27
Northeastern Aegean Islands 621-6
Northern Ireland 690-701
Northumberland 230-2
Nuremberg 485-7

O

Oban 260
Oberstdorf 491
Óbidos 910
Oktoberfest 477, **11**
Olympia 580
Olympics 580
Orkney Islands 262-3
Ottoman Empire 555
Oxford 205-9, **207**

P

Padua 751-2
painting 39-40
palaces, *see* castles & palaces
Paleohora 612-13
Palermo 801-4, **802**
Pamplona 987-8
Pantheon 722
Paris 291-312, **292-3**, **296-7**, **298**
accommodation 301-5
attractions 294-301
dangers 294
drinking 307
emergency services 294
entertainment 307-8
food 305-7

history 291
Internet access 291-4
Internet resources 294
postal services 294
shopping 308-9
tourist information 294
tours 301
travel to/from 309
travel within 309-12
parks & gardens
Englischer Garten 477
Hyde Park 162
Keukenhof Gardens 861
Parque del Buen Retiro 939
Paros 598-600, **599**
Parthenon 565
Patmos 620-1
Patra 574-5
Peloponnese, the 574-80
Penzance 196-7
Perugia 781-4, **782**
Phaestos 609
phonecards 1109-10
photography 74, 1108
Picasso, Pablo 300, 965, 1021, 1076
Pienza 780
Piraeus 572-4, **573**
Pisa 777-8
Pizarro, Francisco 1027
Plaka 570
planning 27-31
climate 27, 1040
Plymouth 193-4
Poitiers 347-8
Pompeii 792
Pont du Gard 403
population 38
Porto 914-18, **915**
Portsmouth 186-8
Portugal 885-926, **885, 887**
accommodation 921-2
activities 922
arts 888
bullfighting 899
business hours 922
climate 886
costs 886
embassies 922
festival & events 923
food & drink 889
geography 888
history 886-8
money 923
planning 886
population 888
postal services 923
public holidays 923
religion 888
telephone services 923
travel to/from 923-5
travel within 900, 925-6
vegetarian & vegan travellers 889
visas 923
wildlife 888
Positano 795-6
postal services 1108
Potsdam 446-8, **447**
Provence 380-8
public transport 1120
Pythagoras 621, 622

Q

Quedlinburg 465
Quercy 359-60
Quimper 333-4, **334**

R

Randstad 860-72, **861**
Ravenna 766-7
Red Cross 1042
Regensburg 487-8
Reims 314-15
religion 38, *see also individual countries*
Renaissance 712
reservations 1096
responsible travel 30-1, 1113
Rethymno 609-10
Rhine Valley 510-11
Rhineland-Palatinate 507-11
Rhodes 615-18, **616, 617**
Rhône region 360-9
Ring of Kerry 678-9
Riviera di Levante 742-3
road rules 1119-20
Rochefort 136-7
rock climbing 258
Romantic Rd 482-3
Rome 716-40, **718-9**, **722-3**, **724**, **726-7**
accommodation 730-2
attractions 717-30
drinking 734-5
eating 732-4
emergency services 717
entertainment 735-6
history 716
Internet access 717
itineraries 720
postal services 717
shopping 736
tourist information 717
travel to/from 736-7
travel within 737-8
Ronda 1023-4
Rostock 469-70
Rothenburg Ob Der Tauber 485
Rotterdam 867-71, **869**
Rouen 327-9, **328**
Rubens, Pieter Paul 122
Rügen Island 472
running of the bulls 987

S

Sagres 906-7
St Andrews 257
St David's 270
St Francis 784
St James 990
St John 621
St Moritz 1068-9
St Patrick 688
Salamanca 952-4, **953**
Salisbury 190-1
Salzburg 82-8, **84**
Salzkammergut 89-93, **90**
Samaria Gorge 612
Samos 621-3, **623**
San Gimignano 781
San Sebastián 982-6, **984**, **593**
Sanfermines 987
Santander 988-9
Santiago de Compostela 990-2, **991**, **592**
Santorini 604-6, **605**, **596**
Sappho 625
Sardinia 809-14
Sarlat-la-Canéda 358
Saronic Gulf Islands 586-8
Saxony 448-56
Saxony-Anhalt 462-6
scenic train journeys
Diakofto-Kalavryta Railway 575
Jungfraujoch 1083
northwest England 240
Schaffhausen 1087
Schiller, Friedrich von 460
Schiltach 499-501
Schilthorn 1083
Schleswig-Holstein 540-2
Schwerin 466-7, **467**
Scotland 240-64, **242**, **589**
activities 240
environmental issues 243-4
geology 243
history 240-3

Scotland *continued*
language 244
national parks 243
nationalism 241-3
population 244
wildlife 243
Segovia 954-6, **955**, **593**
senior travellers 1102
Serra da Estrela 913-14
Setúbal 902-3
Seville 1008-13, **1009**
Shakespeare, William 210
Shankill Rd 692
Sherkin Islands 674
Shetland Islands 263
Shrewsbury 213-15
Sicily 800-9
Siena 778-81, **779**
Silves 906
Sinn Fein 648
Sintra 900-1
Sitia 614-15
Skiathos 627-28
skiing & snowboarding 1099
Andorra 50, 51
Austria 98
France 369-78, 410-11
Germany 490-1, 544-5
Greece 635
hypothermia 1124
Italy 767-9, 815-16
Scotland 258
Spain 1031
Switzerland 1062, 1063, 1067-8, 1079, 1081-2, 1083
Skopelos 628
skydiving 1079
Sligo 689
smoking 1105
snorkelling, *see* diving & snokelling
snowboarding, *see* skiing & snowboarding
soccer, *see* football
solo travellers 1108
Sorrento 794-5
Spain 927-1038, **927**, **929**
accommodation 1030
activities 1030-1
architecture 931-2
arts 931-2
bullfighting 1010
business hours 1031
climate 928
costs 928
courses 1031
dangers 1031-2
embassies 1032
employment 1035
environmental issues 932
festivals & events 976, 988, 994, 1032
food & drink 932-3
history 928-31
Internet access 934
itineraries 928
language 1033
legal matters 1033
literature 931
maps 1033
media 1033
money 1033-4
planning 928
population 931
postal services 1034
public holidays 1032-3
religion 931
telephone services 1034
tourist information 1034-5
travel to/from 1035-6
travel within 1036-8
vegetarian travellers 933
visas 1035
whale watching 1025
wildlife 932
Sparta 577-8
Spetses 587-8
Sporades 626-9
sports 40-1, *see also* football, horse racing
Stirling 256-7
St-Malo 335-7, **337**
Stonehenge 191-2
Stralsund 470-2, **471**
Strasbourg 317-22, **318-9**
Stratford-Upon-Avon 210-11
St-Tropez 397-8
students 1102-3, 1114
Stuttgart 492-4, **493**
surfing 1099
Bundoran 689-90
Spain 1031
Wales 266
sustainable travel 30-1
carbon offset schemes 1113
Centre for Alternative Technology 268, **589**
Switzerland 1039-94, **1039**, **1041**, **12**
accommodation 1088
activities 1088
arts 1044
business hours 1088
climate 1040
costs 1040
embassies 1088
environmental issues 1044-5
festivals & events 1089
food & drink 1045
gay & lesbian travellers 1089
geography 1044
history 1040-3
Internet resources 1090
itineraries 1040
language 1090
money 1090
population 1043-4
postal services 1090
public holidays 1090
religion 1044
skiing 1088
telephone services 1090-1
tourist information 1091
travel to/from 1091-2
travel within 1092-4
trekking 1088
visas 1091
wildlife 1044, 1069
Sylt 542-3
Symi 619
Syracuse 807-8

T
Taormina 806
Tarifa 1025-7, **1025**
Tarquinia 739-40
Tarragona 978-80, **979**
Tavira 904-5
taxes 1107
telephone services 1108-9, *see also individual countries*
Texel 875
Thale 465
theft 1101-2
Thessaloniki 583-5, **584**
Thuringa 456-62
Tiberius 792
Ticino 1064-7
time 1109, 1154-5
tipping 1107
Tirol 93
Titisee 501-2
Toledo 959-62, **960**

000 Map pages
000 Photograph pages

Tomar 911
tourist information 1109
Tours (city) 341-3, **342**
tours 1120
train travel 1114-15, 1120-2
travellers cheques 1107
Treaty of Versailles 422
Triberg 501
Trier 508-10, **509**
Trinity College 653
Trojan War 578
Troyes 316-17
Trujillo 1027-8
Tübingen 494-5
Turin 743-5
Tuscany 769-81
Tyrol 93

U

Umbria 781-5
United Nations 1054-6
Urbino 785
Utrecht City 871-2

V

vaccinations 1123
Vaduz 825-7, **826**
Val de Travers 1052
Valais 1062-4
Valencia 992-9, **993**
van Gogh, Vincent 388, 848, 853
Vatican City 720-1
Venice 752-62, **753**, **756-7**
  accommodation 758-9
  activities 755
  attractions 754-5
  drinking 760-1
  eating 759-60
  emergency services 753
  festivals & events 755-8
  history 752
  Internet access 753
  postal services 754
  shopping 761
  tourist information 754
  travel to/from 761-2
  travel within 762
Vermeer, Jan 848
Verona 750-1
Versailles 312-13
Vevey 1061
Viana do Castelo 919
Vianden 837
Vienna 59-75, **60**, **64**
  accommodation 67-9
  activities 67
  attractions 62-7
  drinking 70-2
  eating 69-70
  emergency services 62
  entertainment 72-3
  festivals & events 67
  Internet access 62
  itineraries 63
  postal services 62
  shopping 73
  tourist information 62
  travel around 74-5
  travel to/from 73-4
vikings 221, 231, 646
visas 1109-10
volunteering 1110
Vorarlberg 100-1

W

Wales 264-72, **265**
  activities 266
  environmental issues 267
  geography 267
  language 267
  literature 266
  nationalism 266-7
  population 267
  travel to/from 267
  travel within 267-8
  wildlife 267
Wallonia 133-8
Warnemünde 469-70
Waterford 666-7
Waterland Neeltje Jans 873
weather 27, 1100-1
weights & measures 1110, *see also inside front cover*
Weimar 459-61, **461**
Wells 202
Wernigerode 464-5
Westminster Abbey 159-61
Westport 688
Wexford 665-6
Whitby 226-7
white-water rafting 240, 371, 1079
Winchester 188-9
windsurfing 542, 635, 1099
wine
  apple-wine taverns 515
  France 290
  Germany 428
  Heurigen 71-2
  Museu do Vinho 916
wineries
  Bordeaux 352
  Côte d'Or 363
  Moselle Valley 507-8
  Rhine Valley 510-11
  Route du Vin 839-40
  Vienna 67
Wismar 467-70
Wolfgangsee Lake 92-3
Wolfsburg 529-31
women travellers 1110
World Cup 2006 426
Würzburg 483-4
WWI 286, 420-2
  Battle of the Somme Memorials 327
  Ferdinand, Archduke Franz 56-8
  museums 133
  sites 132-3, **9**
WWII 155, 286-7, 422, 429
  Bastogne 138
  Bayeaux War Cemetery 331
  Buchenwald Concentration Camp 462
  Dachau 481
  D-Day Beaches 331-2
  Dunkirk 326-7
  Hitler's bunker 490
  Merseyside Maritime Museum 235
  Mittelbau Dora 463
  Musée Mémorial 1944 Bataille de Normandie 330-1
  Musée National d'Histoire Militaire 839
  Obersalzberg 489
  Reichstaggebäude 434, **7**
  Sachsenhausen Concentration Camp 448
  Vienna Holocaust memorial 62-3

Y

yachting 635
York 221-4, **223**
Yorkshire Dales 224-5
Ypres 132-3

Z

Zakynthos 633-4
Zaragoza 980-2, **981**
Zermatt 1062-4, **595**
Zürich 1070-5, **1071**

12am
1am
2am
3am
4am
5am
6am
7am
8am
9am
10am
11am
12pm
Mon
Sun
International Date Line
ARCTIC OCEAN
Queen Elizabeth Is (Can)
Ellesmere Is (Can)
9am
Greenland (Denmark)
GREENLAND SEA
CHUKCHI SEA
BEAUFORT SEA
Banks Is (Can)
Victoria Is (Can)
BAFFIN BAY
11am
NORWEGIAN SEA
Russia
Alaska (US)
5am
Baffin Is (Can)
Iceland
NORTH SEA
3am
4am
HUDSON BAY
BERING SEA
United Kingdom
Canada
LABRADOR SEA
GULF OF ALASKA
8am
Ireland
2am
6am
NORTH ATLANTIC OCEAN
7am
8.30am
Azores (Port)
United States
Spain
Portugal
Bermuda (UK)
1am
Midway Is (US)
NORTH PACIFIC OCEAN
Morocco
Canary Is (Sp)
Mexico
GULF OF MEXICO
The Bahamas
Cuba
Haiti
Hawaii (US)
Eastern Caribbean Islands
Mauritania
Mali
12pm
Cape Verde
CARIBBEAN SEA
Guatemala
Nicaragua
Senegal
Guinea
Burkina Faso
Panama
Venezuela
Guyana
Colombia
Suriname
Liberia
Ghana
Galapagos Is (Ecuador)
GULF OF GUINEA
EQUATOR
Kiribati
Ecuador
8am
Samoa
2.30am
Ascension (UK)
Peru
Brazil
9am
7am
Tahiti
French Polynesia (Fr)
Tonga
Cook Is (NZ)
Bolivia
12am
2am
SOUTH ATLANTIC OCEAN
Pitcairn Is (UK)
3.30am
Easter Is (Chile)
1am
Paraguay
Uruguay
Chile
Argentina
New Zealand
Tristan da Cunha (UK)
12.45am
Chatham Is (NZ)
SOUTH PACIFIC OCEAN
Gough Is (UK)
Falkland Is (UK)
South Georgia & South Sandwich Is (UK)
Bouvet Is (Norway)

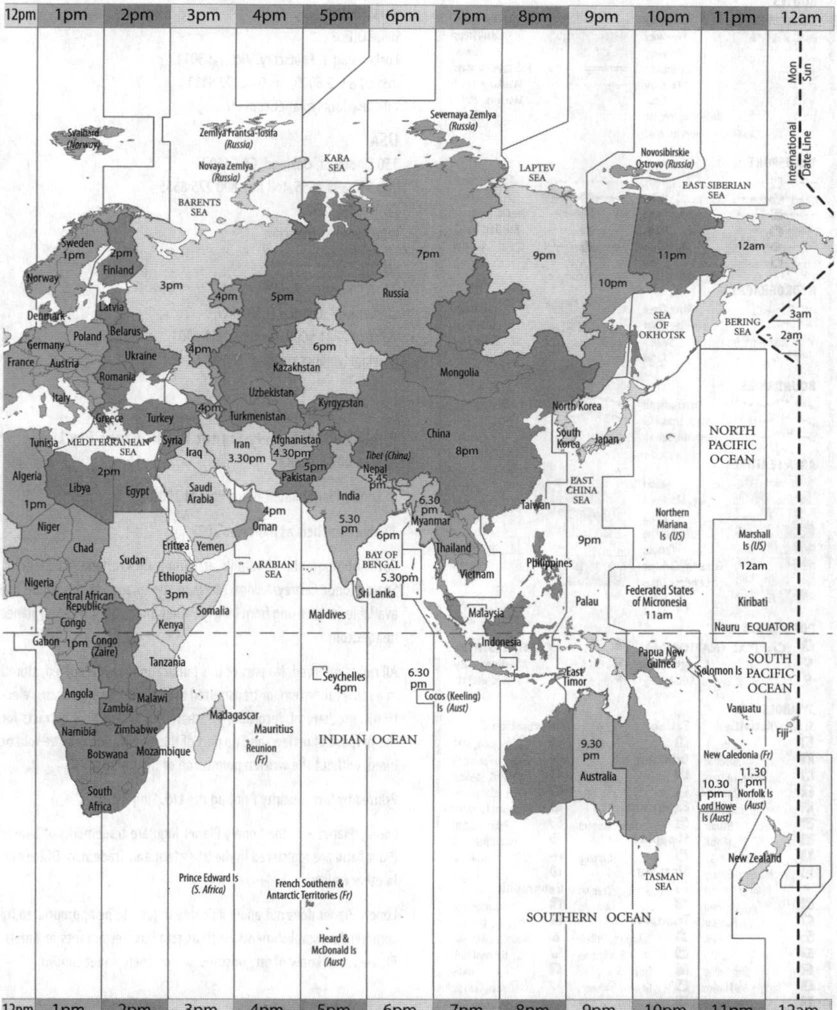

12pm	1pm	2pm	3pm	4pm	5pm	6pm	7pm	8pm	9pm	10pm	11pm	12am

Mon
Sun
International Date Line
Svalbard (Norway)
Zemlya Frantsa-Iosifa (Russia)
Severnaya Zemlya (Russia)
Novaya Zemlya (Russia)
KARA SEA
LAPTEV SEA
Novosibirskie Ostrovo (Russia)
EAST SIBERIAN SEA
BARENTS SEA
Sweden 1pm
2pm
Finland
Norway
3pm
4pm
5pm
7pm
Russia
9pm
10pm
11pm
12am
Denmark
Latvia
Poland
Belarus
Germany
Ukraine
France
Austria
Romania
4pm
6pm
Kazakhstan
Mongolia
SEA OF OKHOTSK
BERING SEA
3am
2am
Italy
Uzbekistan
Kyrgyzstan
Greece
Turkey
4pm
Turkmenistan
North Korea
Tunisia
MEDITERRANEAN SEA
Syria
Iraq
Iran 3.30pm
Afghanistan 4.30pm
China
8pm
South Korea
Japan
NORTH PACIFIC OCEAN
Algeria
2pm
Libya
Egypt
Saudi Arabia
5pm
Pakistan
Tibet (China)
Nepal 5.45 pm
1pm
India
6.30 pm
EAST CHINA SEA
Taiwan
Northern Mariana Is (US)
4pm
Oman
5.30 pm
Myanmar
Niger
Chad
Eritrea
Yemen
6pm
9pm
Marshall Is (US)
Sudan
ARABIAN SEA
BAY OF BENGAL
5.30pm
Thailand
Philippines
12am
Ethiopia
Nigeria
3pm
Vietnam
Central African Republic
Sri Lanka
Palau
Federated States of Micronesia 11am
Kiribati
Somalia
Congo
Kenya
Maldives
Malaysia
Nauru EQUATOR
Gabon
1pm
Congo (Zaire)
Indonesia
Tanzania
Papua New Guinea
SOUTH PACIFIC OCEAN
Solomon Is
6.30 pm
Seychelles 4pm
East Timor
Angola
Malawi
Cocos (Keeling) Is (Aust)
Zambia
Vanuatu
Madagascar
Mauritius
Fiji
Namibia
Zimbabwe
INDIAN OCEAN
9.30 pm
Botswana
Mozambique
Reunion (Fr)
New Caledonia (Fr)
Australia
11.30 pm
10.30 pm
Norfolk Is (Aust)
South Africa
Lord Howe Is (Aust)
New Zealand
Prince Edward Is (S. Africa)
French Southern & Antarctic Territories (Fr)
TASMAN SEA
SOUTHERN OCEAN
Heard & McDonald Is (Aust)

12pm	1pm	2pm	3pm	4pm	5pm	6pm	7pm	8pm	9pm	10pm	11pm	12am

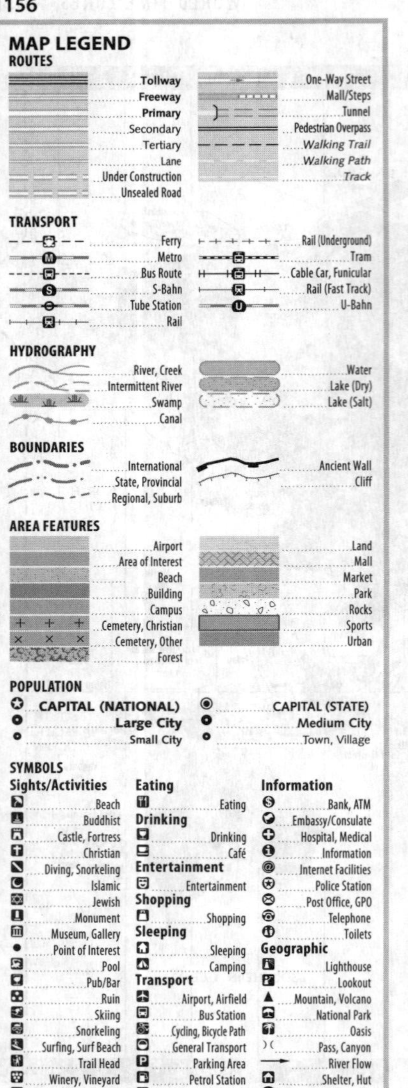

LONELY PLANET OFFICES

Australia
Head Office
Locked Bag 1, Footscray, Victoria 3011
☎ 03 8379 8000, fax 03 8379 8111
talk2us@lonelyplanet.com.au

USA
150 Linden St, Oakland, CA 94607
☎ 510 893 8555, toll free 800 275 8555
fax 510 893 8572
info@lonelyplanet.com

UK
72–82 Rosebery Ave,
Clerkenwell, London EC1R 4RW
☎ 020 7841 9000, fax 020 7841 9001
go@lonelyplanet.co.uk

Published by Lonely Planet Publications Pty Ltd
ABN 36 005 607 983

Cover photograph: Windmills at Campo de Criptana, La Mancha, Spain, Conor Caffrey/Axiom. Many of the images in this guide are available for licensing from Lonely Planet Images: www.lonelyplanetimages.com.

Printed by SNP Security Printing Pte Ltd, Singapore